THE SPENSER ENCYCLOPAEDIA

THE SPENSER ENCYCLOPAEDIA

A. KENT HIEATT
Editorial Consultant

DIANE DROSTE
Copy Editor

NADINE GRIMM
Technical Co-ordinator

THE SPENSER ENCYCLOPAEDIA

A.C. HAMILTON General Editor
DONALD CHENEY Senior Co-Editor W.F. BLISSETT Co-Editor
DAVID A. RICHARDSON Managing Editor
WILLIAM W. BARKER Research Editor

LONDON AND NEW YORK

First published by University of Toronto Press

This edition published 1996
by Routledge, 2 Park Square, Milton Park, Abingdon, Oxfordshire OX14 4RN
Simultaneously published in the USA and Canada by Routledge
711 Third Avenue, New York, NY 10017

First issued in paperback 2014

Routledge is an imprint of the Taylor & Francis Group, an informa business

Canadian Cataloguing in Publication Data
Main entry under title:

The Spenser Encyclopaedia

Includes bibliographical references.
ISBN 0-8020-2676-1

1. Spenser, Edmund, 1552?–1599 – Dictionaries, indexes, etc.
I. Hamilton, A.C. (Albert Charles), 1921–

PR2362.S7 1990 821'.3 C90-095007-2

British Library Cataloguing in Publication Data

The Spenser Encyclopaedia

1. Poetry in English. Spenser, Edmund, 1552?–1599
I. Hamilton, A.C. (Albert Charles), 1921– . 821.3

ISBN 13: 978-0-415-05637-3 (hbk)
ISBN 13: 978-0-415-75561-0 (pbk)

Publication of this book was made possible by grants from the Canadian Federation for the Humanities, using funds provided by the Social Sciences and Humanities Research Council of Canada, and from the National Endowment for the Humanities.

Contents

Directions for Use

1. Articles are arranged **alphabetically** within the text of the encyclopaedia itself.
2. Related articles have been identified within general categories in the **classification of articles**.
3. More specific topics may be located through the **general index**.
4. A parenthetical **asterisk** in the text of an article refers to another article which treats the subject at hand.
5. **Citations** within articles are given parenthetically in a short form, typically:

   (*author + date:page*)
   (*author + date, volume:page*)
   (*author + book.chapter or section*)
   (*title + book.chapter or section*)

6. The **reading list** at the end of an article tells the reader where to turn for further information. If an item is cited in only one article, a full description is given. If an item is cited in more than one article, a short form is used at the end of the articles and full bibliographic information is provided in the **bibliography**.
7. Unless indicated otherwise, **quotations** of classical sources are taken from the Loeb Classical Library. Spenser's poetry is quoted from the *Poetical Works* ed 1912, and his prose is from the *Variorum Prose* volume (i/j and u/v normalized).

Classification of Articles

Articles in the encyclopaedia are in alphabetical order. Relations among the articles are indicated in the classification system below. General categories are shown in the first section; all the articles related to each general category are listed in the second section. For example, a reader interested in genre would look under 'genres and forms' to find a complete listing of relevant encyclopaedia articles. (See also the Index.)

Arts: Dramatic, musical, visual
Alciati, Andrea
Apelles
architecture
buildings
dance
drama, medieval
emblematics
emblems
games, Renaissance
illustrators
masque
masque of Cupid
miniatures
music
pageants
pictorialism
song
tapestries
triumphs
visual arts

Biography
Boyle family
Cambridge
Kilcolman Castle
London
Merchant Taylors' School
Noot, Jan van der
patronage
Ponsonby, William
Singleton, Hugh
Spenser, Edmund

Characters (in *FQ* unless otherwise indicated)
Abessa, Corceca, Kirkrapine
Acrasia
Adicia, Souldan
Aemylia
Aesculapius
Aladine, Priscilla
Amavia, Mortdant, Ruddymane
Amoret
Amyntas (*CCCHA*)
angel, Guyon's
Archimago
Argante, Ollyphant
Artegall
Arthur in *FQ*
Astrophel (*Astrophel*)
Ate
Awe
Bead-men
Belge
Bellamour
Belphoebe
Blandamour
Blandina, Turpine
Blatant Beast
Bonfont, Malfont
Bracidas, Amidas
Braggadocchio
Bregog, Mulla (*CCCHA*)
Briana
Brigands
Britomart
Bruin, Matilde
Burbon
Busirane
Caelia
Calepine
Calidore
Cambell, Canacee, Cambina
cannibals
Care
Chrysogone
Claribell
Clarinda
Colin Clout
Contemplation
Corflambo, Poeana
Coridon
Crudor
Cymoent, Cymodoce
Daunger
Despair
Despetto, Decetto, Defetto
Disdain
Dolon
dragon, Cupid's
Duessa
dwarfs
Error
Fanchin, Molanna
faunus, fauns
Ferryman
Fisher
Florimell
Foster
Fradubio
Genius
Geryoneo
Giant with the scales
Glauce
Gloriana
Grantorto
Grill
Guyon
Hellenore
hermits
Hobbinol (*SC*)
Ignaro
Life and Death
Lucifera
Lust
Malbecco
Maleger
Malengin
Mammon
Marinell
Medina, Elissa, Perissa
Meliboe
Mercilla
Merlin
Mirabella
Munera, Pollente
Nature
Night
Occasion
Orgoglio
Palmer
Paridell
Pastorella
Patience
Paynims
Phaedria
Philotime
Pleasure
Proteus
Pyrochles, Cymochles
Radigund
Red Cross Knight
Rosalind (*SC*)
Salvage Man
Sanglier
Sansfoy, Sansjoy, Sansloy
Satyrane
satyrs
Sclaunder, slander
Scudamour
Serena
Shamefastnesse
Squire of Dames
Tantalus, Pilate
Terpine
Timias
Triamond
Tristram
Trompart
Una
Venus

Verdant
villeins
Womanhood

Chivalric and courtly matter
armor
baffling and degradation
Castiglione, Baldesar
chivalry
court
courtesy as a social code
courtesy books
heraldry
Nennio
tournaments
warfare

Contemporaries, historical
Alençon
Burghley, William Cecil, Lord
Essex, Earl of
Grey, Arthur
James I of England
Leicester, Earl of
Oxford, Earl of
Scudamore family

Contemporaries, literary
Alabaster, William
'Areopagus'
Aylett, Robert
Barnfield, Richard
Breton, Nicholas
Bruno, Giordano
Bryskett, Lodowick
Camden, William
Campion, Thomas
Chapman, George
Churchyard, Thomas
Constable, Henry
Daniel, Samuel
Davies, John
Dekker, Thomas
Digby, Everard
Donne, John
Dyer, Edward
E.K.
Fraunce, Abraham
Gascoigne, George
Golding, Arthur
Googe, Barnabe
Gosson, Stephen
Greene, Robert
Greville, Fulke
Harington, John
Harvey, Gabriel
Herbert family
Jonson, Ben
Lodge, Thomas
Lyly, John
Marlowe, Christopher
Nashe, Thomas
Peele, George
Pembroke, Countess of
Raleigh, Walter
Rich, Barnaby
Shakespeare, William
Sidney, Philip
Sidney, Robert
Sidney circle
Turbervile, George
Watson, Thomas
Wilson, Thomas

Genres and forms
allegory
allegory, historical
anacreontics
[*Complaints*]
elegy, pastoral
epigram
epithalamium
fables
fabliau
fantasy literature
genres
georgic
heroic poem before Spenser
heroic poem since Spenser
hymn
letter as genre
Ovidian epic
paradox
pastoral
romance
romance since Spenser
satire
science fiction
sonnet, sonnet sequence
tragedy

History
antique world
Britain, Britons
Burgundy
chronicles
Elizabeth, images of
Elizabeth and Spenser
Elizabethan age
history
Ireland, the cultural context
Ireland, the historical context
Lear
Mary, Queen of Scots
The Mirror for Magistrates
monarchy
New World
radicalism in Spenser
Renaissance
Rome
Troy
Wales

Imitations and adaptations
Arthur ... since Spenser
FQ, children's versions
imitations ... 1579–1660
imitations ... 1660–1800

Influence and reputation
1579-1800
Browne, William
Bunyan, John
Burton, Robert
Butler, Samuel
Chatterton, Thomas
Collins, William
Cowley, Abraham
Crabbe, George
Digby, Kenelme
Drayton, Michael
Drummond, William
Dryden, John
Fanshawe, Richard
Fletcher, Phineas and Giles
Gray, Thomas
Hall, Joseph
Herbert, George
Hurd, Richard
Johnson, Samuel
Marvell, Andrew
Milton, John
Oldham, John
Peacham, Henry
Pope, Alexander
Prior, Matthew
Reynolds, Henry
Thomson, James
Tourneur, Cyril
Waller, Edmund
1800–1900
Victorian age
Blake, William
Browning, Elizabeth Barrett
Browning, Robert
Byron, George Gordon, Lord
Coleridge, Samuel Taylor
Hawthorne, Nathaniel
Hazlitt, William
Hopkins, Gerard Manley
Hunt, Leigh
Keats, John
Lamb, Charles
MacDonald, George
Marx & Spenser
Melville, Herman
Ruskin, John
Scott, Walter
Shelley, Percy Bysshe
Tennyson, Alfred, Lord
Wordsworth, William
1900–present
Doughty, Charles M.
Joyce, James
Woolf, Virginia
Yeats, William Butler
Countries
America to 1900
Canada
China
France
Germany
Italy
Japan

Language and language arts
archaism
Ciceronianism
copia
dialect
dialogue, poetic
dialogue, prose
epideictic
etymology
hieroglyphics
language, general
logic
morphology and syntax
names, naming
neologism
pronunciation
proverbs
punctuation
puns
rhetoric
rhetoric in Spenser's poetry
rhetorical criticism
speech
style
style, prose

Latin literature
Lucretius
Ovid
Pindar
Platonism
Pythagoras
Socrates
Statius
Theocritus
Virgil

Medieval to mid-16th century

Agrippa
Alanus de Insulis
Amadis of Gaul
Ariosto, Lodovico
Arthur, legend of
Arthur in ME romances
Boccaccio, Giovanni
Boiardo, Matteo Maria
Chaucer, Geoffrey
Chrétien de Troyes
Christine de Pisan
Dante Alighieri
Deguileville, Guillaume de
Douglas, Gavin
Erasmus, Desiderius
Ficino, Marsilio
Geoffrey of Monmouth
Gower, John
Hawes, Stephen
Henryson, Robert
Hypnerotomachia Poliphili
Langland, William
Lindsay, David
Lydgate, John
Machiavelli, Niccolò
Malory, Thomas
Mantuan
Nicholas of Cusa
Petrarch, Petrarchism
The Plowman's Tale
Rabelais, François
Romance of the Rose
Skelton, John
Trissino, Giangiorgio

Renaissance

du Bartas, Guillaume de Salluste
du Bellay, Joachim
Camoens, Luis Vaz de
French Renaissance literature
Guarini, Giovanni Battista
humanism
Leland, John
Montemayor, Jorge de
Neo-Latin poetry
Palingenius
Scottish antecedents
Tasso, Torquato
Tasso in England
Tudor poetry

Themes and topoi

appearance
apples
Arcadia
beauty
body
fire
Fortune
foundlings
garlands
hair
hero
hunt
identity
light
lineage
mirrors
mutability
primitivism
psychomachia
quest
ship imagery
time
topos
veils

Virtues and vices

chastity
courtesy
envy
holiness
justice and equity
magnanimity, magnificence
pride
shame
sins, seven deadly
temperance
virtues

Women, marriage, sexuality

androgyne
gender
Hermaphrodite
heroine
marriage
sex
women, defense of

Works, Spenser's

Amoretti, Epithalamion
Astrophel
Axiochus
Brief Note of Ireland, A
Colin Clouts Come Home Againe
commendatory sonnets
Complaints
- *Ruines of Time, The*
- *Teares of the Muses, The*
- *Virgils Gnat*
- *Prosopopoia, or Mother Hubberds Tale*
- *Ruines of Rome*
- *Muiopotmos*
- *Visions*

Daphnaïda
Faerie Queene, The
- *FQ* I
- *FQ* II
- *FQ* III
- *FQ* IV
- *FQ* V
- *FQ* VI
- *FQ* VII
- *FQ*, commendatory verses and dedicatory sonnets
- *FQ*, proems

Fowre Hymnes
letters, Spenser's and Harvey's
Prothalamion
Raleigh, Letter to
Shepheardes Calender, The
- *Shepheardes Calender*, mottos
- *Shepheardes Calender*, printing and illustration

Theatre for Worldlings, A
Vewe of Ireland, A
works, lost

Introduction

From its inception, *The Spenser Encyclopaedia* has been an entirely cooperative enterprise. When David A. Richardson first conceived the project and proposed it to me at a conference in 1977, the moment seemed to us opportune for two reasons.

First, there had been a Renaissance of sorts in Spenser criticism following an earlier period that had been monumentalized by the Johns Hopkins *Variorum Edition* of Spenser (1932–49). With pardonable exaggeration, John Erskine Hankins wrote in 1971 (he was addressing Spenser critics; others may recall that decade differently) that 'the 1960s will be remembered as a great period of Spenser scholarship, for then were published a record number of books about *The Faerie Queen*.' With the new critical orthodoxies emerging in the 1970s, which would generate their own scholarship, the time had come to assess both what had been done and left undone in Spenser studies by gathering into one volume the best that the present generation of critics had to say about Spenser.

Second, *A Milton Encyclopaedia* was about to appear, and it seemed appropriate that a similar work be compiled for the poet whom Milton had acknowledged to be his 'Original,' especially since readers of Spenser lacked any companion or reference guide, and H.S.V. Jones' *Spenser Handbook* was half a century out of date.

Four prerequisites seemed to me essential to the successful completion of a Spenser encyclopaedia. First, an editorial team responsible for the extended labors that would be involved in its planning and execution. That prerequisite was satisfied when David Richardson agreed to be Managing Editor if I would be the General Editor, and Donald Cheney and A. Kent Hieatt agreed to be the two Co-editors.

The second prerequisite was the assurance of full cooperation by the community of Spenser scholars. At the International Conference on Cooperation in the Study of Edmund Spenser (Duquesne University, October 1978, funded in part by a grant from the National Endowment for the Humanities), a panel discussion was held on questions that exercised us: for example, is there any present need to alphabetize our knowledge of Spenser? would readers of his poetry be best served by an encyclopaedia? and (most important to us) if we undertook some such project, could we expect contributors to write articles?

Encouraged by a generally positive response to these three questions, especially to the last, we held another panel discussion at the Modern Language Association conference in New York in December 1978. At a number of subsequent meetings (notably the annual Spenser meetings at Kalamazoo and the MLA conferences), a debate was initiated about what topics should be included in an encyclopaedia to provide the kind of knowledge readers need to understand and appreciate Spenser's poetry.

By this time in our deliberations there seemed to be a consensus that an encyclopaedia was needed for several reasons: to compile essential scholarship for critics writing on Spenser, to provide an authoritative source of information for teachers in English studies, and to give students and general readers a comprehensive reference book about Spenser.

Being assured of cooperation, we turned to our third prerequisite: a publisher. We were greatly encouraged in December 1980 when the University of Toronto Press offered a contract to publish the projected work if it was approved by a review committee. Now we could assure potential contributors that they could expect their entries to be published by a major academic press.

The final prerequisite, funding, was essential for several reasons. It would allow the editors scattered at four universities to meet regularly during the early stages of planning in order to draw up a list of topics, decide on contributors, establish editorial standards for the many kinds of articles, and compose a style sheet. Also, it would allow us to employ a research assistant, graduate assistants, and a staff to copyedit and keyboard the articles. Finally it would pay for such essential expenses as copying, mailing, and telephoning. Most important, funding would allow us to use computers for all stages of editing to ensure accuracy and consistency for a work of about a million words.

My initial expenses were generously met by the School of Graduate Studies of Queen's University, and I wish to thank particularly Dr John Beal who served then as Dean of Research Services. In addition, beginning in July 1985, the University allowed me to teach half-time (at half-pay) in order to keep up with the editing. Cleveland State University supported David Richardson by setting up editorial offices in the university library.

Major funding for the Canadian and American teams was provided by the Social Sciences and Humanities Research Council of Canada (SSHRCC) and the Research Tools Program of the National Endowment for the Humanities (NEH), respectively, from 1980 through 1988. We are deeply grateful to both funding bodies for their willingness to share support for an international project over most of a decade. Our editorial procedures, planning, and schedules profited much by the need to satisfy their stringent requirements, and also by the reports of their anonymous reviewers.

The decade of this project brought some changes among the editors. While the Editorial Board remained essentially the same, the Canadian Co-editor, A. Kent Hieatt, who had been most heavily involved in the onerous initial planning, accepted a less-demanding position as Editorial Consultant in order to devote his time to Shakespeare studies. William Blissett agreed to take his place. William W. Barker, who had been engaged as a research assistant to check the scholarship of entries and suggest revision, proved so valuable that in 1981 he became Research Editor.

Entries in the Encyclopaedia

Topics were selected chiefly on one basis: would the information in an entry help our implied reader – projected as an intelligent senior undergraduate – to understand and appreciate Spenser's poetry in the context of his age and our own? (This question has proven most difficult to answer, for just why and when would anyone turn from reading the poetry to reading the encyclopaedia?) An initial list prompted by our own reading of the poetry was supplemented by topics treated in critical studies of Spenser, and by suggestions from those who responded to invitations given at conferences and in notices and letters. The list was continuously amended: an entry would be added if a contributor made a reasonable case for its inclusion, absorbed if treated better elsewhere, and cancelled if there was no contributor who could meet the high standards set by the other entries.

The entries are designed to 'cover' Spenser's poetry, insofar as we could anticipate a reader's demands. Accordingly, there are separate entries on each of his minor poems and their genres, and on each book, major episode, and major character in *The Faerie Queene.* As the Classification of Articles indicates, there are entries on Spenser's life, education, friends, fellow poets, and the various influences on him. Topics that treat the 'backgrounds' of the poetry are quite selective, in part because we were not compiling a general Renaissance encyclopaedia. Often the choice depended on the competition for space and – perhaps regrettably – on contemporary interests. Thus, there is an entry on John Dee, who is referred to only three times in the *Variorum* Spenser, but none on Lazare de Baïf, who is referred to eleven times; there are two entries on number symbolism but none directly on the moral and spiritual allegory of *FQ* 1.

A special effort has been made to relate Spenser to earlier writers and especially to minor Elizabethan poets. Since he has long been known as the 'poet's poet' – though for hardly more than that title – a number of entries are included to place him in the English literary tradition through his influence on separate writers and his reputation in various literary periods. Most major writers and most literary periods are included. This kind of entry has been extended to include Spenser's reputation in other countries such as France and Japan, though there are surprising omissions which many dozens of inquiries could not rectify, for example, Spain. The final list of almost 700 entries represents a reasonable compromise among competing demands. While each entry aspires to include the best that is known on any topic, admittedly the best may not be good enough. But enough has been given to challenge the reader to 'make it new' by using the knowledge given in an article, supplementing or correcting or supplanting it. One must allow, though, that contributors faced an almost impossible challenge because of lack of space: in effect, they were asked to express clearly, comprehensively, and persuasively what should be known about any topic in one-tenth the space they regarded as the absolute minimum.

Contributors

The first two years of the project were largely taken up by the effort to match each entry with the most suitable contributor, that is, one who could write most knowledgeably and authoritatively on the topic, whether a senior scholar or recent Ph.D. But first we needed to learn what to expect of them, for none of us had ever read an article for a Spenser Encyclopedia. Accordingly, we asked a dozen Spenser critics to write on assigned topics so that we could learn what to ask for and what to expect. On the basis of this experiment, including our own efforts to produce a paradigm (which we immediately dismissed), I drew up guidelines for contributors.

To decide whom to ask, we first read the publications or doctoral dissertation of a potential contributor. After extensive correspondence, and with full agreement among the editors, I began to invite scholars to contribute. We were greatly heartened by their willingness to give generously of their time without remuneration, not even Costard's three farthings. Surely there are few professions or occupations in our society in which so many individuals are willing freely to contribute so much of their time and special knowledge. At final count, there are more than 400 contributors from some 20 countries.

Editorial Procedure

The articles have been as thoroughly edited as time and our ability have allowed. The first draft of each article was carefully researched by William Barker at the Robarts Library of the University of Toronto, and then edited by myself and one co-editor before being returned to the contributor with our suggestions. (While it may often have seemed so to contributors, there was no deliberate effort to make our commentary on an article longer than the article itself.) Until the pressure of time demanded a change in our editorial procedures, the revised draft was read by myself and a Co-editor before being sent to our editorial office for keyboarding at Cleveland State University. There, David Richardson, aided by Diane Droste, reviewed it most scrupulously for accuracy, clarity of exposition, and consistency with our editorial norms. The keyboarded version with its commentary was then returned either to Donald Cheney or myself before being submitted to the contributor with further suggestions. The amended article as approved by the contributor was then returned for a final review before being sent to Cleveland for final corrections and storage. At this stage – and for considerably less than half of the total number of articles because of Cheney's willingness ever to do more than anyone could expect of him – I was aided by William Blissett.

Despite this elaborate editorial procedure, however, the contributor alone is finally responsible for what is said, as the name below each entry is meant to testify. Kent Hieatt persuaded us early in our editing that our own views had no place at all in the encyclopaedia; and if we deserve any praise at all for our labors, it is for our constantly and painfully exercised forbearance. The usual rubric applies without exception: the opinions expressed in the articles are those of the contributors alone – and so are any errors or omissions, for which the editors bear no responsibility. Three of us even decided not to contribute any articles ourselves, not because we endorse the Groucho Marx principle that we would never contribute articles to a work that had us as editors but because editing itself has taken most of our time for most of a decade.

A.C. Hamilton

Acknowledgments

We are grateful to these scholars for their generous help in reviewing draft articles and advising both authors and editors:

Percy G. Adams
Elizabeth F. Alkaaoud
Ward Allen
Hermione de Almeida
R.C. Alston
Jay P. Anglin
Sydney Anglo
Jack Armistead
Heather Asals
Jane Ashelford
Leonard R.N. Ashley
William Ashworth
Richard Axton
P.J. Ayres

John D. Baird
Carlos Baker
Anthony A. Barrett
W.J. Bate
John C. Bean
Theodore S. Beardsley, Jr
Munro Beattie
Lester A. Beaurline
John Bell
Dan Ben-Amos
Larry Benson
Carl T. Berkhout
Ruth Berman
Dinah Birch
Edward T. Bishop
Rhonda L. Blair
Florence S. Boos
Jackson C. Boswell
Jennifer Brady
A.R. Braunmuller
Philip Brockbank
Timothy Brownlow
Dorothy H. Brown
H. David Brumble, III
Sargent Bush, Jr

Thomas O. Calhoun
Hilbert H. Campbell
Marion Campbell
David Carlson
Sheila T. Cavanagh
Terence Cave
Fausto Cercignani
Tessa R. Chester
Mary Ann Cincotta
Albert R. Cirillo
Lorna Close
Nicholas H. Clulee
Gordon Coggins
Fred Cogswell
Thomas J. Collins
Patrick Collinson
Ann Jennalie Cook
Margaret A. Cooper
D.H. Craig
Brian Crossley
Rebecca W. Crump
Charles Crupi
Patrick Cullen
Eugene R. Cunnar
Jared Curtis

Peter M. Daly
Reed Way Dasenbrock
Gwendolyn Davies
Neville Davies
Robertson Davies
Rowena Davies
C. Roger Davis
Roger Deakins
Diana de Marly
Richard L. DeMolen
Robert W. Dent
A.H. de Quehen
Mario A. Di Cesare
H.C. Dillow
Sandra Djwa
E.J. Dobson
Bettie Anne Doebler
Cay Dollerup
Ian Donaldson
E.S. Donno
Edward Doughtie

Mary Jane Edwards
Robert L. Entzminger
Andrew V. Ettin
William Eversole

B. Feinstein
Craig Ferguson
Andrew Fichter
John Finlayson
Stanley Fish
Alan Fisher
John H. Fisher
Robert F. Fleissner
James W. Flosdorf
R.A. Fowkes
Alastair Fowler
William E. Fredeman
Albert B. Friedman
D.L. Frost

Carmel Gaffney
Helen Gardner
Lee Gibbs
O.N.V. Glendinning
Jonathan Goldberg
K.L. Goodwin
John E. Grant
John Webster Grant
Judith Skelton Grant
Douglas Gray
J.M. Gray
Francis G. Greco
Donald Greene
E.R. Gregory
Dustin H. Griffin
Jeremy Griffiths
Margaret W. Grimes
Joan Grundy
Ralph Gustafson

Susan K. Hagen
David G. Hale
John Hale
Bert Hansen
Duncan S. Harris
Clive Hart
Michael Hattaway
William S. Heckscher
Kurt Heinzelman
Avril Henry
Jack W. Herring
Philip Herzbrun
M. Thomas Hester
W. Speed Hill
Robert B. Hinman
Susan D. Hodges
Robert Hoehn
Arthur W. Hoffman
Joan Ozark Holmer
Cyrus Hoy
Suzanne W. Hull
Robert D. Hume
William B. Hunter, Jr
Frank L. Huntley

Ian Jack
A.N. Jeffares
David L. Jeffrey
William C. Johnson
Gordon Johnston
D.G. Jones
Constance Jordan
Elise Bickford Jorgens

Coppélia Kahn
Walter Kaiser
Frank S. Kastor
W.J. Keith
W.H. Kelliher
Walter Kendrick
Hugh Kenner
Nicolas K. Kiessling
G. Douglas Killam
Bruce A. King
E.R. Knauer
K.G. Knight
W. Nicholas Knight
Jan Karel Kouwenhoven
Doris Kretschmer

Albert C. Labriola
Kenneth Larsen
K.M. Lea
Guy Lee
Judith Lee
Alexander Leggatt
Roger C. Lewis
Sandra S. Lewis
Leanore Lieblein
Stanton J. Linden
John Loftis
George Logan
Roger Lonsdale
Bryan F. Loughrey

T. McAlindon
Wallace T. MacCaffrey
Michael McCanles
Patrick A. McCarthy
William A. McClung
Alan MacColl
James McConica
Margaret MacCurtain
Donald J. McGinn
Jean McIntyre
D.F. McKenzie
T.D. MacLulich
Millar MacLure
Juliet McMaster
Douglas J. McMillan
M.B. McNamee, SJ
John MacQueen
John R. Maier
Nicholas Mann
W.C. Margolin
Natalie Maynor
Peter E. Medine
Giorgio Melchiori
Edmund Miller
James Miller
Lewis H. Miller, Jr
Jane Millgate
Earl Miner
Robert S. Miola
Leslie G. Monkman
Robert L. Montgomery
Louis Adrian Montrose
Patricia A. Morley
Jean Dietz Moss
John Moss
R. Gordon Moyles
Przemyslaw Mroczkowski
James J. Murphy
John M. Murphy

W.H. New
Karen Newman
Charles Nicholl
David Nolan
Yukinobu Nomura
David Norbrook
Douglas A. Northrop

Robert O'Driscoll
Mary Oates O'Reilly

Richard J. Panofsky
Brian Parker
Lee T. Pearcy
Derek Pearsall
Russell A. Peck
T. Anthony Perry
Enid Rhodes Peschel
William S. Peterson
J.D. Pheifer
Maria R. Philmus
G.W. Pigman III
G.M. Pinciss
Zailig Pollock
Elizabeth Pomeroy
Lois Potter
Allan Pritchard
Foster Provost
M.R. Pryor

Kenneth Quinn
Ricardo J. Quinones
Randolph Quirk

Wesley D. Rae
M.V. Rama Sarma
Dale B.J. Randall
Carl J. Rasmussen
Anthony Raspa
J.C.A. Rathmell
Ronald A. Rebholz
Karen Reeds

Edmund Reiss
Eleanor Relle
Anne Renier
Brenda E. Richardson
Christopher Ricks
James A. Riddell
John M. Riddle
Isabel Rivers
Kenneth E. Robinson
Lillian S. Robinson
Alan Roper
Elliott Rose
Eleanor Rosenberg
Malcolm Ross
Joan Rossi
Murray Roston
Beryl Rowland
Michael Rudick
Alan Rudrum
Gordon Rupp
Lawrence V. Ryan

Phillips Salman
Lawrence A. Sasek
John Scarborough
V.J. Scattergood
C. Schaar
Richard Schell
Winfried Schleiner
Charles B. Schmitt
R.J. Schoeck
M.A. Screech
Jean-Charles Seigneuret
Raman Selden
B. Sellin
Naseeb Shaheen
I.A. Shapiro
John T. Shawcross
Jane Shen
Helena M. Shire
Edward Sichi
James H. Sims
Patrick Sims-Williams
William L. Sipple
D.J. Skipper
Victor Skretkowicz
Meredith Skura
Malcolm South
Ian Sowton
David Staines
E.G. Stanley
William T. Stearn
Donald G. Stephens
Stanley Stewart
Jack Stillinger
G.M. Story
Thomas B. Stroup
Joseph H. Summers
Andrea Sununu
Robert H. Super
Mihoko Suzuki
Roger G. Swearingen

Marcelle Thiébaux
Joan Thirsk
Claud A. Thompson
Craig R. Thompson
J.B. Trapp
F.B. Tromly
W.M. Tydeman

Jan Veltman
Brian Vickers

Frederick O. Waage
Eugene M. Waith
Kathryn Walls
C.H. Wang
J.P. Ward
John Warden
Richard Waswo
Elizabeth Waterston
D. Douglas Waters
Andrew D. Weiner
Seth Weiner
Edward R. Weismiller
Richard H. Wendorf
Lydia Wevers
Karen Widdicombe
Karina Williamson
G.A. Wilkes
Gregory Wilkin
Thomas Willard
Robert F. Willson, Jr
Jean Wilson
Timothy Wilson
Leigh Winser
Chauncey Wood
Susan Wolfson
Warren W. Wooden
Frank Woodhouse
David Woodward
Andrew P. Woolley
Leslie J. Workman
Deborah K. Wright
Douglas J. Wurtele
Marion Wynne-Davies

Laetitia Yeandle

Editorial work was assisted by the dedicated efforts of staff at our home universities:
QUEEN'S UNIVERSITY, KINGSTON
Elizabeth Campbell *research, bibliography*
Jane Farnsworth *research, bibliography*
UNIVERSITY OF MASSACHUSETTS
Patricia Sweetser *research, bibliography*
UNIVERSITY OF TORONTO
Patricia Cavanagh *research, bibliography*
Stephen G. Phillips *systems analysis*
Fred Unwalla *research, bibliography, illustrations*
CLEVELAND STATE UNIVERSITY
Elizabeth J. Bryan *records*
Marilyn Bukvic *keyboarding, office management*
Eunice Manders *bibliography*
Jane E. and William D. Vasu *computer support*
Thanks also to volunteers and assistants in Cleveland who helped with proof-reading, indexing, and other activities:
James Connolly
Susan Motsch
Karen Schmidt
John Schoenbeck
Theodore Schoenbeck
Donald Stewart

We are especially grateful to two federal agencies in the United States and Canada:
THE NATIONAL ENDOWMENT FOR THE HUMANITIES (NEH: Research Materials, Division of Research Programs), and
THE SOCIAL SCIENCES AND HUMANITIES RESEARCH COUNCIL OF CANADA (SSHRCC).
The encyclopaedia has benefited from their rigorous scrutiny and generous funding. We take special note of the good counsel and collegiality of program directors and officers Dorothy Wartenberg, Gail Halkias, and Helen Agüera of the NEH.

In addition to many contributions from others, the Cleveland editorial office is particularly grateful to the following for substantial financial support:
THE CLEVELAND FOUNDATION
STATE OF OHIO BOARD OF REGENTS
Barnes & Noble at CSU
Sid Waldman, Manager
English-Speaking Union
Donald Cairns, Pres
Thomas and Patricia Frutig
Huntington National Bank
W. Powell Jones
David N. and Inez Myers
Leland and Helen Dwan Schubert
Mrs. William C. Treuhaft

and to these colleagues for long-standing help at Cleveland State University:
Chairs of the Department of English
Louis T. Milic
Barton R. Friedman
Glending Olson
Deans of the College of Arts & Sciences
Bruce F. Turnbull
J. Eric Nordlander
A. Harry Andrist
Georgia E. Lesh-Laurie
Deans of the College of Graduate Studies
Ronald G. Schultz
Georgia E. Lesh-Laurie
A. Harry Andrist
Directors of the Office of Research Services
Morton Cooper
Charles Urbancic
Provost and Vice-President for Academic Affairs
John A. Flower
Directors of the Library
H. Duncan Wall
Janet Mongan
Bruce Langdon
Richard Swain
Hannelore B. Rader
Director of Publications and Printing
Susann P. Bowers
President of the University
John A. Flower

Contributors

ADAMS, SIMON
University of Strathclyde
court
ALLEN, MARILLENE
Toronto
trees
ALLEN, MICHAEL J.B.
University of California, Los Angeles
Ficino, Marsilio
ALLOTT, MIRIAM
University of Liverpool
Keats, John
ALPERS, PAUL
University of California, Berkeley
Bower of Bliss
poet's poet, the
style
ALTMAN, JOEL B.
University of California, Berkeley
justice and equity
ANDERSON, JUDITH H.
Indiana University
Artegall
Belphoebe
Britomart
Cambell, Canacee, Cambina
Langland, William
ANDREW, MALCOLM
Queen's University, Belfast
birds
ATTRIDGE, DEREK
Rutgers University
quantitative verse
AUKSI, PETER
University of Western Ontario
Calvin, Calvinism
BAKER-SMITH, DOMINIC
University of Amsterdam
Parnassus
winds
BAMBOROUGH, J.B.
Linacre College, Oxford
Burton, Robert
BARKER, WILLIAM W.
Memorial University of Newfoundland
Erasmus, Desiderius
fairies
Merchant Taylors' School
reference works, modern
tournaments
BARNEY, STEPHEN A.
University of California, Irvine
reference works, Spenser's
Troy
BARTON, ANNE
Trinity College, Cambridge
Jonson, Ben
BAWCUTT, PRISCILLA
University of Liverpool
Douglas, Gavin
BAYLEY, PETER
University of St Andrews
Braggadocchio
BEDNARZ, JAMES P.
Long Island University
Alençon
Geryoneo
Golding, Arthur
Grindal, Edmund
Young, John
BELLAMY, ELIZABETH J.
University of Alabama, Birmingham
Trompart
BENDER, JOHN
Stanford University
narrative
pictorialism
BENSON, PAMELA JOSEPH
Rhode Island College
Bellamour
Fisher
women, defense of
BENTLEY, D.M.R.
University of Western Ontario
Canada, influence and reputation in
BERGERON, DAVID M.
University of Kansas
pageants
BERNARD, JOHN D.
University of Houston
Blandina, Turpine
Claribell
Contemplation
hermits
Sanglier
BERRY, REGINALD
University of Canterbury
Dryden, John
BIEMAN, ELIZABETH
University of Western Ontario
Fowre Hymnes
BIES, WERNER
University of Trier
Germany, influence and reputation in
BJORVAND, EINAR
University of Oslo
Complaints: Prosopopoia
Prothalamion
BLACK, L.G.
Oriel College, Oxford
Dyer, Edward
The Faerie Queene, commendatory verses and dedicatory sonnets
BLACKBURN, WILLIAM
University of Calgary
Merlin
BLISSETT, WILLIAM
University of Toronto
Calepine
caves
Doughty, Charles M.
labyrinths, mazes
stanza, Spenserian
BLYTHE, JOAN HEIGES
University of Kentucky
Ate
Deguileville, Guillaume de
sins, seven deadly
BOND, RONALD B.
University of Calgary
Blatant Beast
Despetto, Decetto, Defetto
envy
homilies
BONO, BARBARA J.
State University of New York, Buffalo
Dido
BOOTH, MARK W.
University of Wyoming
song
BORNSTEIN, GEORGE
University of Michigan
Yeats, William Butler
BORRIS, KENNETH
McGill University
courtesy
Salvage Man
BRADEN, GORDON
University of Virginia
Catullus
Complaints: Virgils Gnat
Latin literature
BRADY, CIARAN
Trinity College, Dublin
A Brief Note of Ireland
Grey, Arthur
BREGMAN, ALVAN
University of Toronto
Constable, Henry
BRENNAN, MICHAEL G.
University of Leeds
Herbert family
Ponsonby, William
Singleton, Hugh
BRILL, LESLEY
Wayne State University
Blandamour
The Faerie Queene, proems
Hellenore
Paridell
Scudamour
BRINK, JEANIE R.
Arizona State University
Davies, John
BRINKLEY, ROBERT A.
University of Maine, Orono
Ariadne
Bracidas, Amidas
BRISSENDEN, ALAN
University of Adelaide
dance
BROMWICH, DAVID
Princeton University
Hazlitt, William
BROOKS, NIGEL
University of Victoria
triumphs
BROOKS-DAVIES, DOUGLAS
University of Manchester
Archimago
Bruno, Giordano
Egypt
The Faerie Queene I
Lucifera
Mercury
monarchy
mysteries
Una
BROWN, JAMES NEIL
Orpheus
BROWN, JANE W.
Earlham College
villeins
BRUTEN, AVRIL
St Hugh's College, Oxford
morphology and syntax
pronunciation
BURCHMORE, DAVID W.
Cleveland
Occasion

BURCHMORE, SUSAN C.
Baldwin-Wallace College
Occasion

BURROW, JOHN A.
University of Bristol
Chaucer, Geoffrey

BUXTON, JOHN
New College, Oxford
visual arts
Wales

CAIN, THOMAS H.
McMaster University
Elizabeth, images of
New World

CALLAHAN, VIRGINIA W.
Howard University
Alciati, Andrea

CAMPBELL, GORDON
University of Leicester
catalogues

CANNY, NICHOLAS
University College, Galway
Ireland, the historical context

CARLEY, JAMES P.
York University
Leland, John

CARSCALLEN, J.
University of Toronto
temperance

CARTMELL, DEBORAH
University of Leicester
buildings

CHANEY, EDWARD
Lincoln College, Oxford
Machiavelli, Niccolò

CHAUDHURI, SUKANTA
Presidency College
Amyntas
Browne, William
Coridon

CHAUDHURI, SUPRIYA
Jadavpur University
Grill
metamorphosis
Proteus

CHENEY, PATRICK
Pennsylvania State University
Triamond

CHERNAIK, WARREN L.
Queen Mary College, London
Waller, Edmund

CLARK, SANDRA S.
Birkbeck College, London
Clarinda
Dekker, Thomas
Glauce
Greene, Robert

COIRO, ANNE
Rutgers University
fables

COMITO, TERRY
George Mason University
bowers
fountains
wells

COOKE, MICHAEL G.
Yale University
Byron, George Gordon, Lord

COOPER, HELEN
University College, Oxford
Mantuan
pastoral
satire

COYLE, MARTIN
University of Wales College of Cardiff
Lear

CRAMPTON, GEORGIA RONAN
Portland State University
topos

CREWE, JONATHAN V.
University of Tulsa
Nashe, Thomas

CRINÒ, ANNA MARIA
University of Pisa
Italy, influence and reputation in

CROFT, P.J. (dec)
Sidney, Robert

CURRAN, STUART
University of Pennsylvania
Shelley, Percy Bysshe

DANIELSON, DENNIS
University of British Columbia
God

DATTA, KITTY SCOULAR
Jadavpur University
demons
Hecate

DAUBER, ANTOINETTE B.
Hebrew University
veils

DAVIDSON, CLIFFORD
Western Michigan University
drama, medieval
Isis Church

DAVIDSON, PETER
University of St Andrews
Fanshawe, Richard

DAVIES, STEVIE
University of Manchester
monarchy

DAVIS, WALTER R.
Brown University
Alma, castle of
Fraunce, Abraham

DAY, JOHN T.
St Olaf College
dialogue, prose

DEAN, CHRISTOPHER
University of Saskatchewan
Arthur in Middle English Romances

DEES, JEROME S.
Kansas State University
homiletics
narrator of *The Faerie Queene*
ship imagery

DEMPSEY, JOANNE T.
University of San Diego
angel, Guyon's

DeNEEF, A. LEIGH
Duke University
Bonfont, Malfont
Complaints: Ruines of Time
poetics, Elizabethan
Raleigh, Letter to
Serena
Timias

DICK, SUSAN
Queen's University, Kingston
Woolf, Virginia

DIXON, MICHAEL F.N.
University of Toronto
Bruin, Matilde
copia
rhetoric in Spenser's poetry

DOERKSEN, DANIEL W.
University of New Brunswick
Medina, Elissa, Perissa
predestination

DONNELLY, MICHAEL L.
Kansas State University
ecphrasis
tapestries

VAN DORSTEN, JAN (dec)
Complaints: Visions
Noot, Jan van der
A Theatre for Worldlings

DOYLE, CHARLES CLAY
University of Georgia
folklore

DUBROW, HEATHER
Carleton College
epithalamium

DUNCAN-JONES, KATHERINE
Somerville College, Oxford
Astrophel
Astrophel
Barnfield, Richard

DUNDAS, JUDITH
University of Illinois
Apelles
Complaints: Muiopotmos
ut pictura poesis

DUNLOP, ALEXANDER
Auburn University
number symbolism, modern studies in

DUNN, R.D.
Vancouver
Camden, William

EADE, J.C.
Australian National University
astronomy, astrology
chronographia
constellations

EAVES, MORRIS
University of Rochester
Lamb, Charles

ECCLES, MARK
University of Wisconsin
Burghley, William Cecil, Lord
James I of England
Rich, Barnaby
Watson, Thomas

EDWARDS, A.S.G.
University of Victoria
Hawes, Stephen
Lydgate, John

EDWARDS, CALVIN R.
Hunter College
Arachne
Cyparissus
Daphne
Europa
Hyacinthus
Myrrha
Narcissus
Peleus, Thetis
Phaethon

ERICKSON, WAYNE
Georgia State University
The Faerie Queene, geography of

ERIKSEN, ROY TOMMY
University of Tromsø
Gascoigne, George

ERSKINE-HILL, HOWARD
Pembroke College, Cambridge
Pope, Alexander

ESTRIN, BARBARA L.
Stonehill College
foundlings

EVANS, MAURICE (dec)
Guyon
hero
memory
Palmer

EVETT, DAVID
Cleveland State University
architecture
scholarship, 1579–1932

FAIRER, DAVID
University of Leeds
Warton, Thomas, the younger

FAIRLEY, BARKER (dec)
Doughty, Charles M.

FARMER, NORMAN K., JR
University of Texas
illustrators

FERGUSON, MARGARET W.
University of Colorado
du Bellay, Joachim
Complaints: Ruines of Rome

FLINKER, NOAM
Ben Gurion University
Aylett, Robert

FOX, DENTON (dec)
Henryson, Robert

FRANTZ, DAVID O.
Ohio State University
Argante, Ollyphant
Foster

FREER, COBURN
University of Georgia
Herbert, George

FRENCH, MARILYN
New York City
gender

FRIEDMAN, DONALD M.
University of California, Berkeley
Marvell, Andrew

FRUSHELL, RICHARD C.
Pennsylvania State University, McKeesport
imitations and adaptations, 1660–1800

FÜGER, WILHELM
Free University
Ignaro
Joyce, James

FUJII, HARUHIKO
Osaka University
Japan, influence and reputation in

FUKUDA, SHOHACHI
Kumamoto University
Bregog, Mulla
Fanchin, Molanna
Tourneur, Cyril

FUMERTON, PATRICIA
University of California, Santa Barbara
miniatures

GAIR, REAVLEY
University of New Brunswick
Areopagus

GALLAGHER, PHILIP J. (dec)
Pandora
Prometheus

GALYON, LINDA R.
Iowa State University
dragon, Cupid's
Scudamore family
Squire of Dames

GARSON, MARJORIE
University of Toronto
Scott, Walter

GENT, LUCY
Polytechnic of North London
Hypnerotomachia Poliphili

DE GERENDAY, LYNN ANTONIA
University of Pittsburgh
thresholds

GIAMATTI, A. BARTLETT (dec)
Elizabeth and Spenser

GILL, ROMA
University of Sheffield
Marlowe, Christopher

GLECKNER, ROBERT F.
Duke University
Blake, William

GLESS, DARRYL J.
University of North Carolina
Abessa, Corceca, Kirkrapine
armor of God
law, natural and divine
nature and grace

GLOBE, ALEXANDER
University of British Columbia
Eden

GOLD, EVA
Southeastern Louisiana University
Cymoent, Cymodoce

GRABES, HERBERT
Justus-Liebig University
mirrors

GRANT, PATRICK
University of Victoria
elements
triplex vita

GRAZIANI, RENÉ
University of Toronto
The Faerie Queene II

GREEN, RICHARD FIRTH
University of Western Ontario
games, Renaissance

GREENBLATT, STEPHEN
University of California, Berkeley
identity

GREENE, THOMAS M.
Yale University
antique world
Renaissance

GRISSOM, MARGARET
Saint Mary's College, Raleigh
stones, precious

GROSS, KENNETH
University of Rochester
books in *The Faerie Queene*
myth, mythmaking
names, naming

GUILLORY, JOHN D.
Johns Hopkins University
Milton, John

HAMMOND, PAUL
University of Leeds
Oldham, John

HANKINS, JOHN E.
University of Maine
Acrasia
chaos
psychomachia

HANNA, RALPH, III
University of California, Riverside
Patience

HANNING, R.W.
Columbia University
Chrétien de Troyes
fabliau

HANSEN, ABBY
Wellesley
stones, precious

HARDIN, RICHARD F.
University of Kansas
Adicia, Souldan
Dolon
Drayton, Michael
Fletcher, Phineas and Giles
Mercilla

HARDISON, O.B., JR (dec)
humanism

HARMON, WILLIAM
University of North Carolina
rhyme

HARVEY, E. RUTH
University of Toronto
psychology
Sapience

HARVEY, ELIZABETH D.
University of Western Ontario
heroine

HATCH, RONALD B.
University of British Columbia
Crabbe, George

HAWKINS, PETER S.
Yale University, Divinity School
Cybele
Jerusalem, New
Rome

HAYMAN, JOHN
University of Victoria
Ruskin, John

HEALE, ELIZABETH
University of Reading
Grantorto
Munera, Pollente

HEDLEY, JANE
Bryn Mawr College
lineage

HELGERSON, RICHARD
University of California, Santa Barbara
poet, role of the

HELLER, W. TAMAR
Williams College
Christine de Pisan

HENDERSON, JUDITH RICE
University of Saskatchewan
letter as genre
rhetorical criticism

HENINGER, S.K., JR
University of North Carolina
cosmogony, cosmology
hieroglyphics
Pythagoras
The Shepheardes Calender

HERENDEEN, W.H.
University of Windsor
Aemylia
bridges
Gloriana
Nereids
rivers
sea

HIEATT, A. KENT
University of Western Ontario
Shakespeare, William
tetrads

HIEATT, CONSTANCE B.
University of Western Ontario
falconry

HILL, CHRISTOPHER
Balliol College, Oxford
radicalism in Spenser

HILL, EUGENE D.
Mount Holyoke College
Digby, Everard

HILLER, GEOFFREY G.
Monash University
apples
fire
light
Night
HIRSCH, PENNY LOZOFF
Northwestern University
Melville, Herman
HOENIGER, CATHLEEN
Queen's University, Kingston
natural history
HOENIGER, F. DAVID
University of Toronto
Aesculapius
medicine
HOLAHAN, MICHAEL
Southern Methodist University
Ovid
HOLLANDER, JOHN
Yale University
alexandrine
Donne, John
music
HORTON, RONALD A.
Bob Jones University
Aristotle and his commentators
dwarfs
Satyrane
virtues
HOSINGTON, BRENDA M.
University of Montreal
The Faerie Queene, children's versions
Ferryman
Idle Lake
HUGHES, FELICITY A.
Flinders University
imagination
HULSE, CLARK
University of Illinois, Chicago
Ovidian epic
HUME, ANTHEA
University of Reading
Duessa
HUMFREY, BELINDA
Saint David's University College
dragons
HUNT, JOHN DIXON
University of East Anglia
gardens
HUNTER, G.K.
Yale University
Lyly, John
HUTCHINSON, MARY ANNE
Utica College
Boyle family
HYDE, THOMAS
Hamden, Conn
Busirane
Cupid
vision
INGHAM, PATRICIA
St Anne's College, Oxford
dialect
ISOMAKI, RICHARD
West Virginia University
Pyrochles, Cymochles
JACK, R.D.S.
University of Edinburgh
Drummond, William, of Hawthornden
Scottish antecedents
JARDINE, LISA
Jesus College, Cambridge
Cambridge
JAVITCH, DANIEL
New York University
courtesy books
JOHNSON, BARBARA A.
Indiana University
Bunyan, John
JOHNSON, CLAUDIA L.
Marquette University
Johnson, Samuel
JOHNSON, D. NEWMAN
Office of Public Works, Dublin
Kilcolman Castle
JOHNSON, DEBORAH
University of Bristol
garlands
JOHNSTON, ARTHUR
University College of Wales
Collins, William
Gray, Thomas
JORDAN, RICHARD D.
University of Melbourne
Faunus, fauns
Joyce, James
satyrs
KANE, SEAN
Trent University
Fathers, Latin
idols, idolatry
Phaedria
KASKE, CAROL V.
Cornell University
Amavia, Mortdant, Ruddymane
Bible
chastity
hair
KAWANISHI, SUSUMU
University of Tokyo
Lust
KEACH, WILLIAM
Brown University
Arlo Hill
primitivism
KEEFER, MICHAEL H.
University of Guelph
Agrippa
KELLOGG, ROBERT
University of Virginia
Red Cross Knight
KENNEDY, JUDITH M.
St Thomas University, Fredericton
Googe, Barnabe
Mirabella
Montemayor, Jorge de
The Shepheardes Calender, mottos in
KENNEDY, WILLIAM J.
Cornell University
Fradubio
heroic poem before Spenser
Paynims
Petrarch, Petrarchism
Sansfoy, Sansjoy, Sansloy
Virgil
KIEFER, FREDERICK
University of Arizona
Fortune
KING, JOHN N.
Ohio State University
Reformation
sacraments
KINNEY, ARTHUR F.
University of Massachusetts
Gosson, Stephen
poetics, humanist
Reynolds, Henry
KINSMAN, ROBERT STARR
University of California, Los Angeles
proverbs
Skelton, John
KIRKPATRICK, ROBIN
Robinson College, Cambridge
Dante Alighieri
KLEIN, JOAN LARSEN
University of Illinois
Bacchus
Fates
KLEMP, PAUL J.
University of Wisconsin, Oshkosh
imitations and adaptations, 1579–1660
KNOTT, JOHN R., JR
University of Michigan
heaven
KOSTIĆ, VESELIN
University of Belgrade
Trissino, Giangiorgio
KRIEG, JOANN PECK
Hofstra University
America to 1900, influence and reputation in
KRIER, THERESA M.
University of Notre Dame
shame
KRUEGER, CHRISTINE
Marquette University
Victorian age
KUCICH, GREG
University of Notre Dame
Hunt, Leigh
LAMB, MARY ELLEN
Southern Illinois University
Pembroke, Countess of
LAMBERT, ELLEN Z.
Boston University
elegy, pastoral
LAMBERT, MARK
Bard College
Malory, Thomas
LEPAGE, JOHN LOUIS
University of British Columbia
mutability
LERNER, LAURENCE
Vanderbilt University
marriage
LESLIE, MICHAEL
University of Sheffield
armor
baffling and degradation
gardens
heraldry
LEVAO, RONALD L.
Rutgers University
Nicholas of Cusa
LEVY, F.J.
University of Washington
history
LEWALSKI, BARBARA KIEFER
Harvard University
patronage
LOEWENSTEIN, JOSEPH
Washington University
echo, resonance
masque
LOGAN, MARIE-ROSE
Rice University
androgyne
LUBORSKY, RUTH SAMSON
Philadelphia
The Shepheardes Calender, printing and illustration of

LYONS, BRIDGET GELLERT
Rutgers University
melancholy
McCABE, RICHARD A.
Trinity College, Dublin
Hall, Joseph
providence
McCLURE, PETER
University of Hull
Virgin Mary, imagery of
McCOY, RICHARD C.
Queen's College, City University of New York
chivalry
McFARLAND, THOMAS
Princeton University
Coleridge, Samuel Taylor
McFARLANE, IAN D.
Wadham College, Oxford
Neo-Latin poetry
MacINNES, DEBORAH
University of North Carolina
Boethius
MacKENZIE, NORMAN H.
Queen's University, Kingston
Hopkins, Gerard Manley
MacLACHLAN, HUGH (dec)
Arthur, legend of
Britain, Britons
George, St
magnanimity, magnificence
Philotime
MACLEAN, HUGH
State University of New York, Albany
Complaints
Complaints: The Teares of the Muses
Orgoglio
McNEIR, WALDO F.
University of Oregon
Churchyard, Thomas
MACPHERSON, JAY
University of Toronto
romance since Spenser
MALLETTE, RICHARD
Millsaps College
Aladine, Priscilla
Meliboe
Rosalind
MANLEY, LAWRENCE
Yale University
conventions
London
MANNING, JOHN
Queen's University, Belfast
emblems
gods and goddesses
Venus
MARESCA, THOMAS E.
State University of New York, Stony Brook
hell
MARINELLI, PETER V.
University of Toronto
Ariosto, Lodovico
Harington, John
MARKS, HERBERT
Indiana University
names, naming
MARRE, LOUIS A.
University of Dayton
Corflambo, Poeana
MARSHALL, DONALD G.
University of Iowa
Hurd, Richard

MAY, STEVEN W.
Georgetown College
Oxford, Earl of
MERIVALE, PATRICIA
University of British Columbia
Pan
MILLER, DAVID LEE
University of Alabama
Calidore
MILLER, JACQUELINE T.
Rutgers University
Cynthia
Jove
Juno
MILLS, JERRY LEATH
University of North Carolina
chronicles
Geoffrey of Monmouth
The Mirror for Magistrates
Raleigh, Walter
MILWARD, PETER, SJ
Sofia University
religious controversies
MOHL, RUTH
Brooklyn College, City College of New York
Spenser, Edmund
MORGAN, GERALD
Trinity College, Dublin
Aquinas, Thomas
MOSER, KAY R.
Baylor University
Browning, Elizabeth Barrett
MULRYAN, JOHN
Saint Bonaventure University
Boccaccio, Giovanni
mythographers
MURRIN, MICHAEL J.
University of Chicago
Cleopolis
fairyland
Panthea
NEUSE, RICHARD T.
University of Rhode Island
Adonis, gardens of
masque of Cupid
Pastorella
NEWMAN, KAREN
Brown University
Guarini, Giovanni Battista
NICHOLS, FRED J.
Graduate Center, City College of New York
punctuation
NÍ CHUILLEANÁIN, EILÉAN
Trinity College, Dublin
Ireland, the cultural context
NOHRNBERG, JAMES
University of Virginia
Acidale
The Faerie Queene IV
O'CONNELL, MICHAEL
University of California, Santa Barbara
Alabaster, William
allegory, historical
Dixon, John
The Faerie Queene V
Giant with the scales
Mary, Queen of Scots
O'CONNOR, JOHN J.
Rutgers University
Amadis of Gaul

ORAM, WILLIAM A.
Smith College
Brigands
Daphnaïda
Pleasure
ORMEROD, DAVID
University of Western Australia
body
ORUCH, JACK B.
University of Kansas
Nature
topographical description
works, lost
OSSELTON, NOEL
University of Newcastle upon Tyne
archaism
OTTEN, CHARLOTTE F.
Calvin College
plants, herbs
OWEN, W.J.B.
McMaster University
Wordsworth, William
PAGLIA, CAMILLE
University of the Arts, Philadelphia
sex
PARKER, PATRICIA
Stanford University
romance
PARKINSON, DAVID
University of Saskatchewan
Lindsay, David
PASTER, GAIL KERN
George Washington University
cities
PATRIDES, C.A. (dec)
angels
Fall and Restoration of Man
PATTERSON, ANNABEL
Duke University
fables
DE PAUL, STEPHEN
University of Ottawa
God
PEARSON, D'ORSAY W.
University of Akron
Theseus, Hippolytus
witches
PETERS, HELEN
Memorial University of Newfoundland
paradox
PETTI, ANTHONY G. (dec)
handwriting, Spenser's
PIEHLER, PAUL
McGill University
Daunger
Disdain
places, allegorical
Romance of the Rose
woods
PITCHER, JOHN
St John's College, Oxford
Essex, Earl of
PITT, ROBERT D.
Memorial University of Newfoundland
quest
PLETT, HEINRICH F.
University of Essen
Ciceronianism
epideictic
POPHAM, ELIZABETH A.
Memorial University of Newfoundland
Arcadia

PRESCOTT, ANNE LAKE
Barnard College
Belge
Burbon
Burgundy
French Renaissance literature
giants
Mammon
Rabelais, François
Sclaunder, slander
Tantalus, Pilate
Titans
QUILLIGAN, MAUREEN
University of Pennsylvania
Alanus de Insulis
puns
reader in *The Faerie Queene*
QUINN, DAVID B.
University of Liverpool
A Vewe of ... Ireland
QUINT, DAVID
Princeton University
Tasso, Torquato
QUITSLUND, JON A.
George Washington University
beauty
Platonism
RADCLIFFE, JOHN G.
Winnipeg
Upton, John
RADZINOWICZ, MARY ANN
Cornell University
heroic poem since Spenser
RAJAN, BALACHANDRA
University of Western Ontario
closure
REES, CHRISTINE
King's College, London
Cowley, Abraham
REES, JOAN
University of Birmingham
Daniel, Samuel
Greville, Fulke
REID, ROBERT L.
Emory and Henry College
Holiness, house of
psychology, Platonic
soul
REVARD, STELLA P.
Southern Illinois University, Edwardsville
Graces
Hesiod
Muses
Pindar
RICHARDSON, J.M.
Lakehead University
Palingenius
zodiac
RILEY, ANTHONY W.
Queen's University, Kingston
Marx & Spenser
RINGLER, WILLIAM A., JR (dec)
Tudor poetry
ROBERTS, GARETH
University of Exeter
Circe
magic
magic, amatory
ROBERTSON, JEAN
University of Southampton
Sidney, Philip

ROCHE, THOMAS P., JR
Princeton University
Amoret
The Faerie Queene III
Florimell
Marinell
ROLLINSON, PHILIP B.
University of South Carolina
Cicero
genres
hymn
magnanimity, magnificence
Maleger
ROSE, MARK
University of California, Santa Barbara
Castle Joyous
science fiction
ROSS, CHARLES
Purdue University
Boiardo, Matteo Maria
RØSTVIG, MAREN-SOFIE
University of Oslo
number symbolism, tradition of
topomorphical approach
ROTHSTEIN, ERIC
University of Wisconsin
Butler, Samuel
ROWSE, A.L.
All Souls College, Oxford
Elizabethan age
RUPPRECHT, CAROL SCHREIER
Hamilton College
dreams
Radigund
RUTHVEN, K.K.
University of Melbourne
conceit
etiological tales
etymology
metaphor, simile
senses, five
RYDÉN, MATS
University of Uppsala
flowers
SALE, ROGER
University of Washington
canto
SAMBROOK, JAMES
University of Southampton
Thomson, James
SANDLER, FLORENCE R.
University of Puget Sound
Awe
Foxe, John
SCHIRMEISTER, PAMELA
Middlebury College
Hawthorne, Nathaniel
SCHNEIDER, DEBRA BROWN
Sonoma State University
holiness
SCHULER, ROBERT M.
University of Victoria
alchemy
science
SESSIONS, WILLIAM A.
Georgia State University
georgic
Lucretius
SHAPIRO, MARIANNE
New York University
sestina
SHAVER, ANNE
Denison University
Diana
The Faerie Queene, children's versions

SHAW, W. DAVID
University of Toronto
Tennyson, Alfred, Lord
SHEIDLEY, WILLIAM E.
University of Connecticut
Breton, Nicholas
Turbervile, George
SHERRY, BEVERLEY
University of Sydney
dialogue, poetic
speech
SHORE, DAVID R.
University of Ottawa
Colin Clout
Colin Clouts Come Home Againe
E.K.
Hobbinol
Verdant
SHUMAKER, WAYNE
University of California, Berkeley
occult sciences
SILBERMAN, LAUREN
Baruch College
Hermaphrodite
SINFIELD, ALAN
University of Sussex
Bead-men
Caelia
puritanism
SKULSKY, HAROLD
Smith College
Despair
Malbecco
Malengin
SLOANE, THOMAS O.
University of California, Berkeley
Wilson, Thomas
SMARR, JANET LEVARIE
University of Illinois
anacreontics
SNARE, GERALD
Tulane University
glossing
SNYDER, SUSAN
Swarthmore College
du Bartas, Guillaume de Salluste
SPEAR, JEFFREY L.
New York University
Victorian age
SPIVACK, CHARLOTTE
University of Massachusetts
fantasy literature
STANWOOD, PAUL G.
University of British Columbia
Hooker, Richard
STEADMAN, JOHN M.
The Huntington Library
Care
Error
imitation
imitation of authors
reading, Spenser's
STERN, VIRGINIA F.
New York City
Harvey, Gabriel
STIEBEL, ARLENE M.
California State University, Northridge
Digby, Kenelme
STILLMAN, CAROL A.
University of Notre Dame
Isis, Osiris
Nennio

STOCKER, MARGARITA C.
University of Liverpool
Astraea
eschatology
STRANG, BARBARA M.H. (dec)
language, general
STUMP, DONALD V.
Virginia Polytechnic Institute and State University
pride
tragedy
SVENSSON, LARS-HÅKAN
Lund University
Actaeon
hunt
Morpheus
Statius
SZŐNYI, GYÖRGY E.
Attila József University
Dee, John
Hermeticism
TANNIER, BERNARD
University of Paris XIII
animals, fabulous
France, influence and reputation in
TAY, WILLIAM A.
University of California, San Diego
China, influence and reputation in
TAYLER, EDWARD W.
Columbia University
nature and art
TAYLOR, BEVERLY
University of North Carolina
Arthur, legend of, since Spenser
TAYLOR, DONALD S.
University of Oregon
Chatterton, Thomas
TESKEY, GORDON
Cornell University
allegory
Arthur in *The Faerie Queene*
Homer
THORPE, DOUGLAS
University of Saskatchewan
MacDonald, George
TOBIN, J.J.M
University of Massachusetts, Harbor Campus
Apuleius
TOLIVER, HAROLD
University of California, Irvine
Briana
cannibals
Crudor
TONKIN, HUMPHREY
University of Hartford
The Faerie Queene VI
TOURNEY, LEONARD
University of California, Santa Barbara
style, prose
TRISTRAM, PHILIPPA M.
University of York
Life and Death
TUCKER, HERBERT F.
University of Virginia
Browning, Robert
TUNG, MASON
University of Idaho
emblematics
ULREICH, JOHN C., JR
University of Arizona
Genius
UMUNC, HIMMET
Hacettepe University
Chrysogone
VAN DYKE, CAROLYNN
Lafayette College
personification in *The Faerie Queene*
WADDINGTON, RAYMOND B.
University of California, Davis
Chapman, George
Socrates
WALKER, DENIS
University of Canterbury
appearance
WALKER, JULIA M.
State University of New York, Geneseo
Terpine
WALKER, STEVEN F.
Rutgers University
Theocritus
WALL, JOHN N.
North Carolina State University
Book of Common Prayer
Church of England
Church of Rome
WALLER, GARY
Carnegie Mellon University
Sidney circle
WARD, ALAN
Wadham College, Oxford
neologism
WARKENTIN, GERMAINE
University of Toronto
Amoretti, Epithalamion
sonnet, sonnet sequence
WARNKE, FRANK J. (dec)
baroque
WATSON, ELIZABETH PORGES
University of Nottingham
Camoens, Luis Vaz de
WAWN, ANDREW
University of Leeds
The Plowman's Tale
WEATHERBY, HAROLD L.
Vanderbilt University
Axiochus
Fathers, Greek
WEBSTER, JOHN
University of Washington
logic
Pyrochles, Cymochles
rhetoric
WELLS, ROBIN HEADLAM
University of Hull
Campion, Thomas
Virgin Mary, imagery of
WEST, MICHAEL
University of Pittsburgh
warfare
WHIGHAM, FRANK
University of Texas
courtesy as a social code
WHITE, ROBERT A.
The Citadel
Shamefastnesse
WHITWORTH, CHARLES WALTERS, JR
University of Birmingham
Lodge, Thomas
Peele, George
Tristram
WILLIAMS, FRANKLIN B., JR
Georgetown University
commendatory sonnets
Una's lamb
WILLIAMS, WILLIAM PROCTOR
Northern Illinois University
bibliography, critical
The Faerie Queene (text)
WILSON, R. RAWDON
University of Alberta
character
game
space
time
WITTREICH, JOSEPH
Graduate Center, City University of New York
Apocalypse
oracles
prophecies
visions
WOFFORD, SUSANNE L.
Yale University
Rich Strond
WOLK, ANTHONY
Portland State University
Hercules
WOOD, D.N.C.
St. Francis Xavier University
Tasso in England
WOODBRIDGE, LINDA
University of Alberta
Womanhood
WOODHOUSE, J.R.
Pembroke College, Oxford
Castiglione, Baldesar
WOODMAN, THOMAS M.
University of Reading
Prior, Matthew
WOODS, SUSANNE
Brown University
versification
WOUDHUYSEN, H.R.
University College, London
Leicester, Earl of
letters, Spenser's and Harvey's
WRIGHT, THOMAS E.
California State University, Northridge
Bryskett, Lodowick
YEAGER, R.F.
University of North Carolina, Asheville
Gower, John
YOUNG, ALAN R.
Acadia University
Peacham, Henry
YOUNG, R.V.
North Carolina State University
epigram
ZITNER, SHELDON P.
University of Toronto
The Faerie Queene VII

THE SPENSER ENCYCLOPAEDIA

Abbreviations

ab abridged
app appendix
b born
BCP Book of Common Prayer
BL British Library
BMC British Museum Catalogue
c circa; century
cf compare
ch(s) chapter(s)
comm ver commendatory verses
comp compiled by
d died
ded dedication
diss dissertation
DNB Dictionary of National Biography
ed(s) edited by; edition(s); edition of
EETS Early English Text Society
eg for example
emb(s) emblem(s)
Eng English
enl enlarged
ep(p) epistle(s)
esp especially
facs facsimile
ff following
fol(s) folio(s)
fig(s) figure(s)
fl flourished
Fr French
Ger German
Gr Greek
ie that is
IE Indo-European
illus illustrated, illustrator
Ir Irish
Ital Italian
KJV King James Version (Bible)
L, LL Latin, Late Latin
Library CC Library of Christian Classics
ME Middle English
ms(s) manuscript(s)
no(s) number(s)
ns new series
OE Old English
OED Oxford English Dictionary
OF Old French
OI Old Irish
ON Old Norse
op opus
os old/original series
PGr Patrologia grecae
p(p) page(s)
pl(s) plate(s)
PLat Patrologia latina
PRO Public Record Office
pts parts
r recto
ref(s) reference(s)
Ren Renaissance
rev revised
rpt reprint(ed)
RSV Revised Standard Version (Bible)
Rus Russian
ser series
sig(s) signature(s)
sonn sonnet
Span Spanish
SP State Papers
STC Short Title Catalogue (rev ed)
STS Scottish Text Society
sv(v) sub verbo(verbi)
tr translated by; translation
univ university
v verso
Var Variorum edition
vol volume

Spenser's Works
(page refs to ed 1912 except as marked)

Am Amoretti (pp 561–77)
  epistle
  comm ver commendatory verses
anac anacreontics 1–4 (pp 577–8)
As Astrophel (pp 546–60)
  epigraph
  'As' 'Astrophel'
  'Clorinda' 'Lay of Clorinda'
  'Thestylis' 'Muse of Thestylis'
  'Aeglogue' 'Aeglogue upon Sidney'
  'Elegie' 'Elegie for Astrophill'
  'Epitaph' 1 'Epitaph upon Sidney'
  'Epitaph' 2 'Another Epitaph'
Ax Axiochus (*Var Prose* pp 21–38)
  epistle
  'To the Reader'
Brief Note Brief Note of Ireland (*Var Prose* pp 235–45)
Colin Clout Colin Clouts Come Home Againe (pp 535–45)
  epistle
comm sonn commendatory sonnets (pp 603–4)
Com Complaints (pp 469–526)
  'Printer to Reader'
  Time Ruines of Time (pp 471–8)
    dedication
  Teares Teares of the Muses (pp 479–86)
    epistle
  Gnat Virgils Gnat (pp 486–93)
    dedication
  Mother Hubberd Prosopopoia: Mother Hubberds Tale (pp 494–508)
    epistle
  Rome Ruines of Rome (pp 509–14)
  Muiopotmos Muiopotmos, or The Fate of the Butterflie (pp 515–20)
    epistle
  Vanitie Visions of the Worlds Vanitie (pp 521–2)
  Bellay Visions of Bellay (pp 523–5)
  Petrarch Visions of Petrarch (pp 525–6)
Daph Daphnaïda (pp 527–34)
  epistle
Epith Epithalamion (pp 579–84)
FQ The Faerie Queene Books I–VII (pp 1–406)
  FQ ded dedication (p 2)
  FQ proem(s) proems(s)
  FQ arg(s) argument(s)
  FQ VII *Cantos of Mutabilitie*
  FQ comm ver commendatory verses (pp 409–10)
    CV 1 'Vision'
    CV 2 W.R.
    CV 3 Hobynoll
    CV 4 R.S.
    CV 5 H.B.
    CV 6 W.L.
    CV 7 Ignoto
  FQ ded sonn dedicatory sonnets (pp 410–13)
    DS 1 To ... Hatton
    DS 2 To ... Burghley
    DS 3 To ... Oxford
    DS 4 To ... Northumberland
    DS 5 To ... Cumberland
    DS 6 To ... Essex
    DS 7 To ... Ormond and Ossory
    DS 8 To ... Howard
    DS 9 To ... Hunsdon
    DS 10 To ... Grey of Wilton
    DS 11 To ... Buckhurst
    DS 12 To ... Walsingham
    DS 13 To ... Norris
    DS 14 To ... Raleigh
    DS 15 To ... Pembroke
    DS 16 To ... Carey
    DS 17 To ... Ladies in the Court
  FQ Letter Letter to Raleigh (pp 407–8)
FH Fowre Hymnes (pp 585–99)
  epistle
  HL Hymne of Love
  HB Hymne of Beauty
  HHL Hymne of Heavenly Love
  HHB Hymne of Heavenly Beautie
Harvey Sonn commendatory sonnet to Harvey (p 603)
Nennio Sonn commendatory sonnet on *Nennio* (p 603)
Proth Prothalamion (pp 600–2)
Scanderbeg Sonn commendatory sonnet on Scanderbeg (p 603)
SC Shepheardes Calender (pp 415–68)
  'To His Booke'
  Epistle Epistle to Harvey
  Gen Arg General Argument
  Jan Januarye
    Arg Argument
    emb(s) emblem(s)
    gloss
  Feb Februarie
  March
  Apr Aprill
  Maye
  June
  Julye
  Aug August
  Sept September
  Oct October
  Nov November
  Dec December
  envoy
Theatre A Theatre for Worldlings (pp 605–8)
  epigrams 1–6 with epilogue
  sonn I–II sonnets I–II
  sonn 12–15 *Visions from Revelation*
Three Letters Three Proper Letters (pp 609–32; *Var Prose* pp 13–18, 449–77)
Two Letters Two Commendable Letters (pp 633–43; *Var Prose* pp 3–12, 441–7)
  'Iam' 'Iambicum Trimetrum'
  'Orn' 'Ad Ornatissimum virum'
Vewe Vewe of Ireland (*Var Prose* pp 39–231)

A

Abessa, Corceca, Kirkrapine These figures appear among the representatives of evil whom Una confronts after Redcrosse has deserted her and allied himself with Duessa. In merely sixteen stanzas (*FQ* 1 iii 10–25), they illustrate the richness Spenser achieves through superimposed allusions to scripture and to contemporary religious issues, through deft placing of episodes, and through patterns of imagery that forcefully express themes central to *FQ* 1.

By having Una wander in 'wildernesse and wastfull deserts' (iii 3), Spenser reinforces earlier suggestions that she represents the true church (i 4–5, 12–13; iii argument) and links her with the woman of Revelation 12, 'clothed with the sunne.' Protestant readers usually identified this luminous figure with the church fleeing from Antichrist to find safety in a place that symbolized her first habitation among gentiles (cf the Geneva gloss for Rev 12.6: 'The Church was removed from among the Jewes to the Gentiles, which were as a baren wildernes, and so it is persecuted to and fro'). In her meeting with Abessa and Corceca, Una's identity is clarified by contrast, not with outright irreligion, but with vices that parody true religion.

The full significance of this parody becomes evident through scriptural associations. When Abessa first appears, she is following a heavily traveled path at the foot of an ancient mountain. She carries a 'pot of water,' cannot 'heare, nor speake, nor understand,' and dwells in an eternally dark 'cotage small' with her mother, Corceca (iii 10–14). The road she follows and her dwelling in the wilderness identify Abessa as a literary descendant of those Israelites who, having proved faithless, failed to reach the Promised Land (Num 14.20–35). The water pot recalls a similar vessel carried by the Samaritan woman who confronts Christ in John 4.7–30; this woman's sexual promiscuity, unorthodox religion, and initial blindness to Christ's identity reveal a fleshly mind. Like her and like the erring Israelites, Abessa clings to the flesh, defined both as pleasures of the material world (iii 18) and as a religion that retains superficial features of true worship but pollutes it with idolatry and reduces it to a system of arid forms.

Abessa's deafness, muteness, and intellectual blindness also associate her with various New Testament figures whose sensory deficiencies declare their need for the grace that roots out sin and enables perception of spiritual truth. Yet Christ heals these biblical figures, and the Samaritan woman of John 4 gradually recognizes that she has met the Messiah. In contrast, Abessa flees in terror of Una, whose beauty manifests Christ's alluring grace, and her lion, here a symbol of Christ's awesome justice manifested in earthly executors of his will.

Abessa's biblical progenitors imply that she embodies reprobation, the condition of men to whom divine truth presents itself but who lack the grace to comprehend it. Interpreted most broadly, her name suggests Latin *abesse* 'absence or deficiency of being' – the long-established theological definition of evil. Appropriately, this representative of evil deficiency is the offspring of Corceca, a coinage derived from Paul's references to the 'foolish heart ... ful of darkenes' (Rom 1.21), to the veiled 'hearts' of Jewish readers of the Law (2 Cor 3.15), and to the gentiles who have 'their cogitation darkened ... because of the hardenes of their heart' (Eph 4.18).

These allusions indicate that both mother and daughter share the spiritual ignorance which is a major characteristic of evil figures throughout Book 1. Their affinity with darkness recalls that of the monster Error (i 14, 16), foreshadows the mental vacuity of Ignaro (viii 30–4), and allows us to foresee the emphasis Spenser will give to education in faith in the house of Holiness (x, esp 18–20).

Corceca dramatizes the state of spiritual blindness by confining herself in 'eternall night,' fasting incessantly, and engaging in perpetual prayer (iii 12–14). Her blindness of heart, suggested by her name (L *cor* heart + *caecum* blind), engenders a religion of obsessive ritual acts devoid of the essential elements of faith and love. Corceca's devotions present an exaggerated instance of a recurring evil in Judeo-Christian religion, an evil manifest in the Pharisees and, according to contemporary Protestant polemics, in the religious orders of Roman Catholicism.

Hence, Abessa's name also suggests 'abbess.' As head of the parodic religious house that harbors Corceca and Kirkrapine, she reflects the major charges such as licentiousness and ignorance that Protestants brought against monks. More important, because of their isolation within imprisoning walls, monks and nuns were also said to neglect the charity God's law demands while seeking salvation through obedience to rules that needlessly elaborate that law. Their legalism was thought to foster spiritual arrogance by implying that salvation could be achieved through human merit rather than through faith alone.

This monastic presumption is expressed by the magical cast of Corceca's worship, obsessed with the mystically potent numbers three and nine. Monasticism was also thought to instill an excessive and irreligious dread because trust in merit and the resulting failure to trust in grace breed fear of divine justice. Accordingly, fear is the dominant emotion Abessa and Corceca display in the presence of God's emissaries.

These spiritual defects appear not only in Corceca and Abessa, but in the Red Cross Knight as well. Because Una meets Corceca and Abessa in his absence, their deficiencies serve most directly to emphasize her strengths. Faithfully seeking the knight who has become her enemy (iii 15, 21, 30), Una embodies fidelity – issuing in the charity that 'suffreth long,' 'seketh not her owne things,' and 'doeth never fall away' (1 Cor 13.4–8). By placing this episode shortly after Redcrosse becomes companion to Duessa (ii 26–7), who is another, more dangerous figure of Pharisaic and Roman Catholic errors, Spenser hints that Corceca's and Abessa's faults are the ones into which Redcrosse has himself fallen. As Redcrosse descends toward his collapse in canto vii and his relapse in canto ix, their characteristics become increasingly dominant features of his own spiritual condition: fear of divine justice, forgetfulness of God's grace, and vain self-reliance.

Spenser endows even Kirkrapine, who is present for only five stanzas (iii 16–20), with meanings relevant to *FQ* 1 as a whole. Appearing under Aldeboran because this star 'causeth the destruction and hindrances of buildings ... and begetteth discord' (Agrippa *Occult Philosophy*, cited in Brooks-Davies 1977:39), he embodies various active consequences of Abessa's and Corceca's legalistic superstition. His chief features are turbulent violence, lechery, greed, and cunning.

Kirkrapine's violence makes him a symbol of the political force that often supports false religion and benefits from the superficial legitimacy it confers. His greater relatives in Book 1 include Sansfoy, the giant Orgoglio, and the Dragon which is symbolic epitome and metaphysical source of all the rest. Each of these evil figures owes something of its nature to the 'Kings of the earth' who indulge and abuse the Babylonian whore (Rev 17). Kirkrapine is like those scriptural ancestors in being Abessa's violent lover. He feeds 'her fat with feast of offerings' gained through sacrilegious thefts which deprive churches of means to aid the poor and of ornaments that dignify worship; his name, appropriately, denotes 'church robber.'

Because he gives his plunder to Abessa, acquires it by cunning as well as force, and operates 'when all men carelesse slept,' Kirkrapine represents, primarily, the pre-Reformation plundering of the church in England by Rome. More specifically, he diverts revenue from 'Churches' to Abessa; that is, from the (ideally) preaching, socially active secular clergy, to the cloistered and (according to Protestants and reforming Catholics) invariably corrupt and self-indulgent regular clergy who dominated the spiritually somnolent past.

Using 'cunning sleights' Kirkrapine enters churches through the window and so associates himself with another scriptural ancestor, the 'thief and robber' of John 10, who is contrasted with Christ himself, the true shepherd and the true door. Protestant authors often attacked monasteries for establishing themselves as markets of merits earned by the labors of the inmates and available for purchase by donors. Kirkrapine acts as agent of such an institution, 'blind Devotions mart' (iii argument).

Such diversions of church funds represent particular instances of a timeless evil, for Kirkrapine's scriptural lineage also includes the sons of Eli (1 Sam 2.22, 29) who grew fat on offerings of first fruits. This timelessness suggests that the corruptions he embodies may also refer to Henry VIII's wholesale plundering of churches, abbeys, and monasteries, and to thefts committed by Elizabethan bishops and lay magnates. Although such implications are secondary, a number of scholars argue for their primacy on the grounds that Tudor laymen and bishops were often criticized for holding plural benefices, allowing sees and smaller cures to remain vacant, and by various other 'sleights' diverting church revenue to private uses (see Falls 1953, Kermode 1964–5, Nohrnberg 1976). DARRYL J. GLESS

Brooks-Davies 1977:37–9, on Kirkrapine; Mother Mary Robert Falls 1953 'Spenser's Kirkrapine and the Elizabethans' *SP* 50: 457–75; Darryl J. Gless 1979 *'Measure for Measure', the Law, and the Covenant* (Princeton) ch 2; Hamilton in *FQ* ed 1977 (notes to I iii 10–25); Horton 1978:146; Kermode 1964–5; Nohrnberg 1976:208, 218 n 293, on Kirkrapine; O'Connell 1977:50–1.

Acidale A fountain in Greece, reported by Renaissance mythographers to be the haunt of the Graces (Boccaccio *Genealogia* 1.16, Giraldi *De deis gentium* 13). The name appears in *Epithalamion* 310 as 'the Acidalian brooke' where Spenser reports (on his own authority) that Maia bathed before Jove lay with her: the brook suggests the vernal and virginal freshness of the June bride (Maia = May). The poet's beloved is again presented as Acidalian in *FQ* VI x, where silver waves tumble at the foot of Mount Acidale (7). This stream, where nymphs bathe, may derive from the nameless brook in *SC, Aprill* 35–7, since it too is the site of Colin's poetic inspiration to celebrate a fourth Grace; in both instances, song is tuned 'to the waters fall.' Earlier, in *FQ* IV v 5, Venus is said to have left her cestus 'On *Acidalian* mount, where many an howre / She with the pleasant *Graces* wont to play.' Venus herself can be 'the Acidalian.'

The Acidale of *FQ* VI x is a culminating example of several related *topoi* of site, scene, scenario, and sanctuary found throughout the poem. (1) The *locus amoenus* or 'pleasant place' is a sensuously embellished refuge, resort, grove, glade, oasis, theater, island, or bower. The undertone is escapist, as the name suggests: *a + kēdos* 'without care' ('Ne ought there wanted ... to banish bale ... Therefore it rightly cleeped was mount *Acidale*' x 8; see Giraldi 1548:552). (2) A park or garden created by nature or an art of nature, preternaturally endowed with a full complement of representative species, and with an atemporal efflorescence or fruitfulness. Acidale includes 'a wood ... In which all trees of honour stately stood, / And did all winter as in sommer bud' (6). (3) The scene of surprised or surreptitiously observed beauty or delectation: Cymochles in the Bower of Bliss (II v 28–34), Serena among the cannibals (VI viii 36–44), and Diana spied on by Faunus (VII vi 45–7). (4) The daemonologically charged and liminally fixed topography: a site whose shape is, as it were, cast by a spell, such as the circle made by Fradubio's tree, or the 'fairy ring' implied by the circular dance of Acidale's revelers. (5) The place of divine alignment: an earthly site oriented on an astronomically specific point or portal overhead, through which heavenly influence might pass, or on which the heavens turn, or a cynosure to be contemplated by an attuned mind. Examples are the New Jerusalem beyond the Mount of Contemplation, Venus' heavenly house overseeing the Garden of Adonis, the cell of the gods and heaven's gate over Arlo Hill in the *Cantos of Mutabilitie* (VII vi 37–9, vii 3–5, 45, 48), and Ariadne's stellar crown over the dance on Acidale.

The pleasance and park topoi link Acidale with the Garden of Adonis, pleasance and skeptophilic topoi with the Bower of Bliss. Skeptophilic, daemonological, and cosmographic topoi make for (6), the site of a hierophantic manifestation of the noumenon veiled by phenomena, such as Nature on Arlo Hill. Finally, Acidale is (7) the scene of a knight's instruction in (or initiation into) the mystery of his virtue. Because of its visionary disclosure, the Mount of Contemplation is a suggestive analogue. And because of the presentation and exposition of the symbols for Calidore's virtue – namely the Graces – Acidale stands for the educational or disciplinary institution (house, seminary, or shrine) where one typically finds the hero's official recognition, matriculation, or adoption by an alma mater. The general recognizability of Acidale in terms of topoi from the rest of the long poem is not irrelevant: the place is haunted not only by the fays, but also by the project of *The Faerie Queene* itself.

Various classical allusions, which enrich the Acidalian scenario mythographically, also analogize it to other parts of the poem. The allusions are polarized by two motifs: an epiphany or cynosure of divine beauty (for courtesy is an *aesthetic* of conduct), and a disturbance of divine harmony or agreement (courtesy is an art of making one's conduct agreeable to others). First is the analogy between the disruption of the Graces' dance by Calidore and the disruption of Theseus' wedding by the Lapiths and Centaurs. With this we may compare the threatened nuptials of Florimell and Marinell, where the hundred knights stand in place of the *Cent*aurs, and Artegall like Hercules saves the day. Next there is the analogy between the exaltation of Colin's mistress and the stellification of Ariadne's wedding crown after her abandonment by Theseus to the satyrs. With this we may compare the revelation to the satyrs of the truth of the forsaken Una's beauty. Finally, there is the analogy between Calidore's immersion in the shepherds' world and the rustication of Paris on Mount Ida, where he sees the three goddesses (III ix 36; cf VI ix 36). With this we may compare Calidore seeing the three Graces on Mount Acidale (II vii 55; cf viii 6 for the Idaean goddesses and Graces). According to Colin (VI x 22), Jove begot the three Graces on the way home from the wedding of Thetis. That otherwise happy occasion was disrupted by the strife between the three goddesses; on his holiday Jove may have been reconceiving the three quarreling goddesses as the three harmonious Graces.

The Acidale-Ida analogy also invites us to compare the 104 Graces dancing on the Mount with the 104 authentic beauties competing for the prize at Satyrane's beauty contest in IV v – the belt Florimell acquired on Acidale (5). In Lucian's *Dialogues of the Gods* 20, Pallas insists that Paris judge Aphrodite without this prize's original, a love charm. Despite this handicap, the goddess of love prevails with 'partiall *Paris*' (*FQ* II vii 55), just as the false Florimell wins the chastity token, despite her inability to keep it on, and despite its being thought that Amoret 'should surely beare the bell away,' as Florimell once brought the belt away from Acidale (IV v 13, 5). On Acidale, the chastity of Colin's mistress is preeminent among her charms, and she 'above all other lasses beare[s] the bell' (VI x 26). If the belt is the bell, the bell may be the *ball*, the prize Venus bore away from Ida. As an acquired iconographical property, such a ball appears in the possession of Britomart. As an armed Venus who 'bore / The prayse of prowesse from them all away,' the martial maid is awarded the spoils of war, namely the prize beauty who wins 'beauties prize' in the subsequent contest (IV iv 48). Thus, in making his own belle one of the Graces from whom Venus herself borrows her vaunted gifts (VI x 15), Spenser returns the rhetoric in question to something like its original Acidalian-Idaean provenance.

The story of the rusticated Calidore also implies Idaean originals. His wrestling feats, his winning and awarding of crowns, his love affair with the local beauty and its timely fruit, and his defense of his pastoral hosts from marauders all conform to late-classical and medieval versions of Paris' sequestration in the countryside of Ida, before repatriation to Troy. Moreover, the traditional scene presented by the three goddesses is sometimes treated as a dream-vision. In Jean Lemaire de Belges' account of Paris' pastoral days, the sleeping subject also has a vision of many beautiful nymphs and fays who turn in flight upon his awakening; he chases and catches one of them, and begs to know their identity (*Les Illustrations de Gaule et singularites de Troye* 1.24). In Thomas Heywood's *Oenone and Paris*, Paris also views the fairies' merry round: Spenser has Heywood's rhyme on *groom* and *broom*, the bagpipes' shrillness, shepherds dancing to fairy measures, local swains tuning their odes, and a Venus who is 'Acidalia' (52, 60, 66–8, 95).

Analogies between the gifts of the Idaean goddesses and of the Acidalian Graces also are pertinent here, especially gifts of fortune, body, and mind (*FQ* VI x 23; cf *Amoretti*

74). Jean Lemaire (1.35) cites the *Clementine Recognitions* (10.40) to the effect that Paris chose among the Venus of lust, the Pallas of courage, and the Juno of chastity. The identification of one of the Graces' aspects with virginity facilitates an interpretation of one triad into the other; Pallas herself was virginal. The three Graces of Juvenescence, Splendor, and Enjoyment thereby become the three virtues of Chastity, Beauty, and Love. In *Colin Clout* 464–71, Spenser praises his mistress as the union of all three, and adds a fourth Grace of 'peerlesse grace.' The celebration is restaged on Acidale, with the same modulation of the *dea certe* of *Aprill* ('surely a goddess') into the *dea quarta* (a 'fourth goddess,' eg, the new Diana of Peele's *Araignment of Paris*).

An Idaean original for the matter of Troy compares instructively with a putative Acidalian source for the matter of Spenserian romance. With antecedents like the disappearing dance of the fairy-like ladies in Chaucer's *Wife of Bath's Tale* ('Vanysshed was this daunce, he nyste where' 991–6; cf 'vanisht ... which way he never knew' *FQ* VI x 18), Calidore's vision reinvents Arthur's dream, thus realizing the foreconceit of Spenser's poem. Reappearing as the pastoralist of his original debut, the poet pipes in an Arcadia that his pastourelle fiction posits only to destroy. A potentially immodest self-introduction and querulous apologia turns out to be a self-effacing valedictory.

Besides Ida, two other source scenes from established poetic tradition inform the Acidalian scenario. Boiardo and Petrarch, resources already adopted and adapted by Spenser's more immediate predecessors, suggest Acidale's foreconceit in scenes that point us towards these poets' own great inventions. The knight who stumbles on his own allegorical situation at a daemonological site is a convention of chivalric romance and a favorite device of Boiardo's *Orlando innamorato*. At the time Calidore sees the Graces, he has fallen under the spell of love and beauty. Boiardo formalizes the enchantment satirically when he has the knight Ranaldo drink of the fount of disdain, while having the beautiful Angelica drink of the fount of love; spying Ranaldo asleep, the bewitched lady showers the knight with flower petals, but he is unmoved by this pass and flees her advances (1.3.32–50). At great remove from this occasion, Ranaldo is brought to his senses. Sleeping where he once rejected the lady, the kill-courtesy is now tormented by Cupid and the revengeful Graces. Flower-pelted by these unkindly ones, he thinks better of his former offense to love, drinks of its fount, and goes off in search of Angelica's grace and favor (2.15.43–63). Acidale also shows the Graces throwing flowers where an expression of love is meant, a knight who has offended the Graces, a lover confronting occasion in allegorical form, and the romance motors of attraction or infatuation and repulsion or disenchantment. Spenser's scene shares with Boiardo the cross-cultural encounter of mortal and goddess, knight and nymph, human and fairy, champion and damozel, Celtic and classical, Hobgoblin and Apollo.

In his first commendatory sonnet ('Vision'), Raleigh announced that the Graces had deserted Petrarch's tomb for the train of Spenser's Fairy Queen. If so, they should be found on Acidale. In Petrarch's *Bucolicum carmen* 3 and 10, the poet is allegorically depicted as surprising the scene of his own inspiration. His shepherd persona discovers maidens dancing around a laurel deep in the forest; catching sight of the intruder, they invite him to gaze at their immortal faces. Then they bestow on him a laurel branch and send him back to his Daphne to tell her that he has seen the Muses – never beheld by the vulgar – dancing on the sacred hill where the Pegasan fountain gushes, singing chorally as each moved in her circle. With such a story he can hope to supplant Apollo as Daphne's lover. Spenser's reinvocation of this scene of vocation makes a point of his service to Petrarchism, or its service to the Fairy Queen. He rescues the Petrarchan métier from Elizabethan poetasters while maintaining their mythological conceits (see Watson *Hekatompathia* 33, Barnabe Barnes *Parthenophil and Parthenophe* 13; cf VI x 13, 26). Spenser no less than Petrarch implies the poet's authority to confer his laurels on himself. The inaugural scene for Petrarch's calling provides the valedictory for Spenser's: the poet who wins his laurels from others at the outset must nonetheless award them to himself in the dénouement.

Celebrating the poet's own poetry, Acidale's Colin also celebrates his mistress-muse in place of Venus, and so implies the Renaissance celebration of beauty itself. There are two related Acidalian topoi with which a poet praised the beauty of the mistress: the incomparability topos and the syncretic topos. The mistress would have won the judgment of Paris over the three original rivals; and being more or less beyond compare, she exhibits the goddesses' gifts as her graces. She is a pantheon, a Pandora ('all-gifts'), or Pasithea (the fourth 'all-divine' Grace, whom Giraldi says combines the other three; 1548:577). Thus when Ariosto comes to the topic of a beauty who would have shamed the three contesting goddesses, he follows it with the topic of a picture painted by Zeuxis, who chose five girls out of many as models for a single picture of Helen or Venus (*Orlando furioso* 11.70–1). Paris, confronted with a vision of three beauties, chooses among them, taking the part of the one representing the sensual part. Zeuxis, conversely, chose several models and combined their best parts to form the unified ideal of beauty – and to give back to Venus what various beauties had borrowed from her. Spenser cites the Zeuxian procedure (attributing it to Apelles) both at Satyrane's beauty contest (IV v 12) and in the final dedicatory sonnet 'To all the gratious and beautifull Ladies in the Court.' Thus the Acidalian Calidore is an unwitting Paris, surprised by beauty and a choice of lives; Colin is an unwitting Zeuxis, composing a beautiful unity from a multeity. The poet combines what the cannibals in this legend mentally divide: their fantasies each turn on the naked Serena's separate parts. Where the cannibal fetishistically honors one part of one woman, Calidore honors one woman of exceptional parts. But Colin honors one ideal embodiment in whom the beauties of many women are collected, as the true lover of beauty is bound to do, according to the culminating speech of Castiglione's *Courtier* (ed 1928:317–18).

Castiglione's spokesman is referring to this conceptualization of beauty when he says that 'Beautie is the true monument and spoile of the victory of the soule' (p 311). In the Bower, Cymochles fed his eye on 'spoyle of beautie' (II v 34). Regarding Pastorella, Calidore does the same thing (VI ix 12, 26). The cannibals, 'which did live / Of stealth and spoile,' come upon their sleeping beauty while they 'seeke for booty,' and the brigands are likewise 'fed on spoile and booty' (viii 35–6, x 39). Acidale is the true form of what all these lovers of beauty are seeking to possess.

If we could see virtue we would love it, according to Sidney's *Defence*, whose poet may hope to 'steal to see the form of goodness (which seen [men] cannot but love) ere themselves be aware' (ed 1973b:93). Plato taught that every human soul has contemplated true being, but not every soul recalls this very clearly. Earthly likenesses of justice and temperance lack luster; with beauty the case is different. Wisdom one cannot see by the sense of sight – our desire for her had been passionate if we could. But for beauty alone is it ordained to be manifest to sense – the loveliest form of them all (*Phaedrus* 249D–50D after Hackforth tr). Acidale symbolizes the ultimate realization of the poet's will to give visible form to the ideate, and to disclose its beauty and attraction.

The form in question is a double circle about a central 'one,' the form of the Plotinian and Ficinian metaphysical universe, which sets the mental cosmos of soul in rotation about mind centered on the true and beautiful One at their center and as their source. Neoplatonic images of such a cosmic encirclement of a wellspring as a dance are found in Synesius' first hymn and Boethius' *Consolation of Philosophy* (3 metrum 9). Hence the importance of Ariadne's heavenly crown for Acidale. The use of this crown image to exemplify an encircling dance of nymphs footing it featly on the grassy ground occurs in Thomas Lodge's *Scyllaes Metamorphosis* 11. But the figure of a choric round dance for the heavenly motions goes back to the choruses of the Athenian drama (eg, Euripides *Ion* 1074–86) and Plato's *Timaeus* 40C and *Epinomis* 982E. Spenser's figure is particularly anticipated in the triple zodiacal ring in Dante's heaven of the sun, where Dante says that we must reposition Ariadne's crown on the celestial pole to conceive his vision (*Paradiso* 13.1–27). The need to make Spenser's figure the focus of the same rotation suggests a similar transcending of the actualities of the physical universe in favor of the poetic or idealist heterocosm 'deepe within the mynd' (VI proem 5).

The link between Ariadne and the dance is originally from Homer (*Iliad* 15.590–2): the notable thing Daedalus built was not a labyrinth, but a dance floor for Ariadne. Later tradition (eg, Plutarch *Life of Theseus* 21) reports that when the hero led the youths out of the labyrinth he taught them a dance. Something like this happens to Spenser's reader, who enters *The Faerie Queene* by way of the labyrinthine Wood of Error, and leaves it by way of the circular configuration of the dance on Acidale: Spenser's poem is a mighty maze, but not without a choreographic plan. At the outset, his legends may suggest the difficulty of undertaking something new, of comprehending something we have not read. Near the beginning of his quest, the quester will be confronted with some sort of riddle; near the end, conversely, he will break some sort of spell. Calidore begins, he says, 'to tread an endlesse trace, withouten guyde, / Or good direction, how to enter in' (VI i 6), and his ending of the revels on Acidale signals the corresponding closure – the breaking of the dance (X II). *The Faerie Queene* also breaks off, but its Acidalian beauty is incapable of being forgotten. Because of this beauty, we may penetrate the poem's darkest riddles, and yet its spell remains unbroken. JAMES NOHRNBERG

Acrasia Her destructive passion first revealed in *FQ* II i, her Bower and damsels described in canto v, her wantonness anticipated by her servant Phaedria in canto vi, and finally encountered in canto xii, Acrasia is the enchantress who is the great enemy of temperance. She has caused the death of Mortdant, the consequent death of Amavia, and the blood-stained hands of Ruddymane; Guyon therefore sets out on his quest to deprive her of her powers. After he and the Palmer travel through her Bower of Bliss, resisting its enchantments, they find her languishing on a bed of roses, with her lover Verdant sleeping with his head in her lap. Guyon entraps her in the Palmer's 'subtile net' (as Vulcan entraps Venus and Mars; see Ovid *Metamorphoses* 4.171–84), then binds her in 'chaines of adamant' (xii 81–2). He destroys her Bower completely and restores her lovers to their human forms from the bestial forms they had assumed under her enchantment (except for Grill, who chooses to remain a beast).

Her name derives from the medieval Latin *acrasia*, which combines Greek *acrāsiā* 'badly mixed quality' and *acrasia* 'incontinence' (*OED* – the latter sense analyzed in some detail in Aristotle *Nicomachean Ethics* 7). She is the antithesis of the temperate body revealed in the castle of Alma (ix), and, as Joseph Wybarne noted in 1609, 'each part of the body hath some disease sent from the Witch *Acrasia*, which is intemperance' (*Sp All* p 119). Her garden and the Bower of Bliss are patterned after Tasso's paradisal garden of the enchantress Armida (*Gerusalemme liberata* 15–16), who is identified as the concupiscible faculty of the soul, an emblem of libido, and (as with Guyon and the Palmer) successfully resisted by the two knights who come to rescue Rinaldo. Her fountain has a prototype in the fountain of Acratia (concupiscence) in Trissino's *Italia liberata*. The description of Acrasia herself owes much to *Gerusalemme liberata* 16.18 except for the translucent veil that covers her lower body. This detail was probably recalled from Chaucer's description of Venus in the garden of love (*Parliament of Fowls* 267–73); Chaucer in turn echoes Boccaccio's *Teseida*. Acrasia first appears as a seductress in the early tablet of Cebes (Steadman 1960). The classical model for her and many of the witches named above is Homer's Circe (*Odyssey* 10), whose poisoned cup changes men into beasts. In Homer, Odysseus receives from Hermes the herb moly (identified by early commentators as reason or wisdom) as an antidote; rather than succumb to her charms, he forces Circe to obey him and restore his transformed men to human shape.

Guyon first hears of Acrasia's mischief from the dying Amavia, who warns that 'Her blisse is all in pleasure and delight, / Wherewith she makes her lovers drunken mad' (i 52); in this state they become victims of her witchcraft. Mortdant had been poisoned by 'drugs of foule intemperance' (54); he is finally killed after escaping from her when he drinks from her enchanted cup (cf Duessa's cup at I viii 14, and its biblical source, the cup of the Whore of Babylon which contains 'the wine of the wrath of her fornication' in Rev 18.3, 6). The words on her cup say that death must follow if its contents are mixed with pure water from the fountain of the chaste nymph. When Mortdant drinks deeply, he falls dead.

This seems to mean that the internal shock of so much cold water causes hypothermia and death. But in terms of *psychomachia*, both Mortdant (death-giving) and Amavia (love of life) are internal impulses of the soul. Long indulgence of unrestrained appetites finally disillusions a person and destroys any wish to live, leading to suicide unless evil passions are subjected to the restraining hand of temperance. Guyon (temperance) and the Palmer (reason) provide such restraint. They do not kill Acrasia (the concupiscible faculty) but subject her to the bonds of moderation. She loses her power to destroy the soul when controlled by these bonds. Of those lovers who have tasted her charms, only Verdant seems to recover, and then only after Guyon applies 'counsell sage'; the others are not happy to be saved, some because of their shame for having been discovered, others because they are angry to see Acrasia bound. The implication is that temperance is hard to attain partly because few want it. Spenser's test is to convey a sense of the artificiality, passiveness, and obsessiveness of the intemperate spirit, while at the same time recognizing and depicting its considerable charms.

Unlike other enchantresses in *The Faerie Queene*, Acrasia never speaks. Her wiles are exercised through her physical beauty and her artfully sensuous environment. The song of the rose (xii 74–5), so exquisite an image of her charms, is not sung by her but by a distant 'some one,' apparently one of the 'lascivious boyes' who with 'Many faire Ladies' make up her court. Wrapped in chains and deprived of her environment by Guyon, she loses her power. At III i 2, she is sent to Gloriana's court 'With a strong gard'; yet this retinue is not to prevent her escaping so much as 'all reskew to prevent,' that is, to prevent others from freeing her in order to be bound by her. Her sensuality is marked by passivity rather than any strong passion, in contrast with the energy and action required of the temperate spirit.

JOHN E. HANKINS

Actaeon Spenser's use of the Actaeon myth in *The Faerie Queene*, though not extensive, aptly illustrates the subtle relation between a learned Renaissance poem and its literary context. His chief model is Ovid, whose account provides the narrative and descriptive details which he transforms, adapts, and reinterprets: Diana's grotto in Gargaphie, her bathing with her maids, Actaeon's coming upon her naked, her wrath, his transformation into a stag, and his death by his own hounds (*Metamorphoses* 3.138–252).

(See **Actaeon** Fig 1.)

Spenser's most extended treatment of the myth occurs in *FQ* VII vi, where Faunus' spying on the naked Diana and his subsequent punishment recall Ovid's story. His avowed purpose here is to explain the presence of wolves and thieves in Ireland, but the episode is more than an oblique comment on the political conditions there. Faunus' intrusion on Diana and her abandonment of Arlo Hill are treated with deft irony and contrasted to Mutabilitie's assault on Cynthia, which carries overtones of Satan's rebellion and the Fall. Faunus' crime is similarly perpetrated against Diana, but being only an act of voyeurism, it appears harmless and ludicrous by comparison. Yet Faunus resembles Mutabilitie: like her he overreaches, and he corrupts the nymph Molanna with 'Queene-apples' and 'red Cherries' emblematic of the Fall (43). While her presumption is on a cosmic scale and is associated with the introduction of sin and death into the world, his is set in a pastoral milieu and related to the degeneration of the natural instincts into concupiscence.

In addition to parodying Mutabilitie's revolt, the Faunus episode also parodies Ovid, partly because Faunus is a much cruder character than Ovid's Actaeon; half man and half goat, he is clearly related to Pan. He is a 'lover of fleeing nymphs' according to Horace (*Odes* 3.18), and he is first mentioned in *The Faerie Queene* as chasing a nymph who is rescued and metamorphosed by Diana (II ii 7). In the *Cantos of Mutabilitie*, his animal lusts again get the better of him; his reaction on seeing Diana naked is an indiscreet guffaw 'for great joy of somewhat he did spy' (VII vi 46). Such wantonness distinguishes him from Ovid's Actaeon, who stumbles upon Diana by accident and is explicitly acquitted of any designs on her;

Faunus by contrast is a deliberate voyeur. Spenser's deviation from Ovid on this point, though contributing to the parodic effect, is not unprecedented, since most medieval and Renaissance commentators claimed that Actaeon actively obtruded himself on Diana.

These commentators interpreted the myth in economic terms as unrewarded liberality (the dogs fed by Actaeon are ungrateful servants), in political terms as excessive curiosity (Actaeon tries to pry into the secrets of his superiors), and in moral terms as emblematic of sensual passion (Actaeon's dogs are his emotions which destroy him). The last of these interpretations is especially relevant to Faunus, for the 'conceit' which this foolish faun 'profest' to his sorrow links him to other literary texts where the figure of Actaeon is hounded by impulses ranging from simple concupiscence to spiritualized amatory suffering of the kind described by sonneteers from Petrarch to Daniel. Moreover, there are important differences between the conclusions of Spenser's tale and Ovid's: unlike Actaeon who, as a stag, is killed by his own hounds, Faunus is clad in a deerskin (cf Conti *Mythologiae* 6.24) and then only pursued by Diana's hounds, for 'The Woodgods breed ... must for ever live.' The Faunus-Diana episode is a playful conflation of three tales from the *Metamorphoses* (those of Actaeon, the brook Alpheus' union with the nymph Arethusa in 5.577–641, and Diana's banishment of her maid Callisto in 2.463–5) with *Fasti* 2.267–58, where Faunus tries to rape Omphale, fails, and is ridiculed. Spenser creates something new; yet the relevance of the Actaeon myth is central and indisputable (it is mentioned at VII vi 45), and there is no need to look for a source in *Daphnis and Chloe*.

Similarly, Calidore's vision of the Graces on Mount Acidale borrows and transforms motifs from the Actaeon myth: the paradisal character of the two places (one the haunt of Diana, the other of Venus), Calidore's spying and imprudent intrusion, and the Graces' abandonment of Mount Acidale (which parallels Diana's leaving Arlo Hill). There is no explicit verbal connection with Ovid, however, and the relevance of the myth to the Mount Acidale episode is indirect at best. In contrast, Spenser's account of Venus' intrusion upon Diana (III vi 17–19) borrows directly from Ovid to describe Diana's grotto and her attendant nymphs. The whole scene is rich in irony, as the goddess of love looks for her fugitive son among Diana's chaste attendants. Again Spenser transforms his classical source, for the outcome of Venus' intrusion, unlike that of Actaeon's, is propitious: Venus and Diana are reconciled, and there is no actual or figurative death.

In addition to narrative and descriptive motifs, Spenser borrows an important theme from Ovid's description of Diana's grotto: 'Nature by her own cunning had imitated art' (*Met* 3.158–9). This theme is integral to Renaissance treatments of the *locus amoenus* and is often associated with the contest between nature and art, as in II v 29, xii 59, and III vi 44. Sometimes the connection with Ovid is striking; sometimes it seems that associations derived from the Actaeon passage have begun to lead a life of their own. In II iii 20–42, where Belphoebe and Braggadocchio meet, there are similarities to Ovid's text: a beautiful lady, described in sonneteer's language and accoutred as a huntress, is spied on by a rash beholder. Belphoebe is an embodiment of Diana's chastity; the poet does not know 'whether art it were, or heedlesse hap' that flowers entwine with her hair; finally, Braggadocchio's assault (like Faunus') results in flight, though this time it is Belphoebe who flees and not the male intruder. Like Spenser's other allusions to the Actaeon myth, the scene's transformation of earlier texts contributes to the poem's analysis of love and temperance, nature and art.

LARS-HÅKAN SVENSSON

Barkan 1980; Walter R. Davis 1962 'Actaeon in Arcadia' *SEL* 2:95–110; Doyle 1973; Friedmann 1966; Hawkins 1961; Holahan 1976; R.N. Ringler 1965–6; Svensson 1980:68–91.

Adicia, Souldan In *FQ* v viii, Arthur and Artegall rescue Samient from pagan knights, then mistakenly fight each other. Samient's name may derive from ME *sam* (together) because she is the occasion for the two knights' meeting and because she seeks 'finall peace and faire attonement' (21). She says that her queen, Mercilla, has sent her on an embassy to the hostile Adicia (Gr *adikia* injustice), who with her husband, the Souldan (a variant of *sultan*), has tried to subvert the 'Crowne and dignity' of Mercilla's reign. Artegall dons the armor of one of Adicia's slain knights and gains entrance to her castle by pretending to bring Samient as a captive. Arthur challenges the Souldan, defeats him, and with Artegall's help takes the castle. Adicia flees to the woods, where she is transformed into a 'Tygre.'

This canto expands the scope of Book v as the two knights join to attack injustice on an international scale. Their mistaken battle ends in a standoff because they are equal; like Arthur, Artegall (*Arth* + Fr *égal* equal) incorporates all the virtues (a comprehensiveness attributed to justice since Aristotle). The Souldan suggests the purported despotism of Muslim rulers, and in the 'great wrongs' (viii 24) he inflicts through Adicia, he anticipates Grantorto, the 'great wrong' of canto xii. His man-eating horses and raging wife represent qualities of an irrationally violent tyrant.

Adicia seems in part the idea of injustice and the Souldan its practical consequences. (A similar symbiotic pairing is that of Pollente and his daughter Munera in v ii.) Mercilla's negotiating with Adicia and not with her husband indicates the antithetical relation between justice and injustice. Adicia's animal savagery suggests a fundamental principle of injustice in fallen nature, in contrast to the merciful justice of redeemed humanity; images of pagan and Christian monarchy are similarly contrasted in v viii and ix. After Arthur overthrows her lord, the animal imagery associated with Adicia intensifies: she is likened to 'an enraged cow' and 'a mad bytch' before her metamorphosis into a tigress. She appears as a political variant of the 'Terrible Mother,' not unlike Shakespeare's savage Queen Margaret (a 'tiger's heart wrapp'd in a woman's hide' *3 Henry VI* I iv 137; see Cirlot 1962 sv 'Mother,' Jung 1956:179–82). Her survival after defeat does not mean that Arthur and Artegall have failed, only that the principle she represents cannot be driven from this world.

Upton first noted in Arthur's fight with the Souldan an allusion to England's victory over Philip II and the Spanish Armada (*Var* 5:226–8). The Souldan's 'Swearing, and banning most blasphemously' (28) refers to Catholic cursing and excommunication of English Protestants. More specific attributes of the Souldan's chariot suggest the Armada: the height of the chariot reminds the reader of the high turrets, and the unwieldiness of his machine recalls the oversized Spanish ships so easily outmaneuvered 'with incredible Celerity and Nimbleness' by English ships (Camden, in the *Annals* for 1588, ed 1970:320), just as Arthur moves about and evades the Souldan. The 'yron wheeles and hookes' are common attributes of ancient chariots of war (see Upton's note to stanza 41 in *Var* 5:230, and cf the invaders' 'thre hundreth charets set with hookes' in 2 Macc 13.2); they enforce the image of the Souldan's cruelty while recalling images of Spanish instruments of torture or perhaps even the hooks on the sides of the landing craft prepared by the Duke of Parma (see Camden *Annals* for 1588, ed 1970:311). The light from Arthur's shield suggests the blinding action of grace by alluding to the English fire ships and the providential intervention that finally defeated the Armada.

(See **Adicia** Fig 1.)

A further historical reference is found in the simile comparing the Souldan's horses to Phaethon's (40). Philip II's well-known impresa was a picture of Apollo with the words *Iam illustrabit omnia* (now he will illuminate all things); Spenser has turned Philip's Apollo into Phaethon, unable to control his horses (Graziani 1964b). Like Phaethon, who attempted to usurp the position of Apollo, god of justice, and was destroyed, the Souldan (whose name suggest a pun on *sol* 'sun' + *dan* 'master') is felled by Arthur, the true sun of justice he thought to control.

Furthermore, the image of Phaethon suggests the pagan aspect of the Souldan, who is compared to Diomedes (31) and to Hippolytus (43). Like the Phaethon image, each of these comparisons has a special force. For instance, in the comparison of the Souldan to Diomedes, Arthur is implicitly likened to Hercules who overcame Diomedes and thereby achieved a 'victory over the tyrants of this world' (Dunseath 1968:193, following Bersuire 1509: fol 69v 'diomedes significat mundi tyrannos'). Arthur's rage at the Souldan (35) may be the noble madness or wrath expected of the Herculean hero.

In his Herculean victory over the Souldan, Arthur reenacts his victory over Orgoglio in Book I viii. Other correspondences between the eighth cantos of *FQ* I and V bear noting: in both battles, the special hero of the book is inside the castle; a virgin (Una, Samient) and her female nemesis (Duessa, Adicia) witness the battle; Arthur empties the castle; the villainess flees into the wilderness. Such parallels indicate a symmetry between the private and public virtues of the two books. The Souldan extends Orgoglio's pride into the body politic, his elevation in the chariot indicating overreaching pride. He embodies the lust for power that can tempt any prince, a lust that Spenser calls idolatry (19), recalling the idolatry of Orgoglio's castle (I viii 35).

RICHARD F. HARDIN

Aptekar 1969; Cirlot 1962; Fletcher 1971; Jung 1956 *Symbols of Transformation* vol 5 in ed 1953–79; *FQ* ed 1977.

Adonis, gardens of In the ancient cult of Adonis, the death of the young vegetation god was ritually mourned in late summer at the so-called Adonia; urns of rapidly blossoming and wilting flowers or herbs, known as gardens of Adonis, were placed on his shrine. These became a proverbial expression for any rapid growth (and decay). Plato uses them as a symbol of the frivolity of those who write down their ideas and opposes them to the serious cultivation of philosophy by those who engage in spoken dialogue (*Phaedrus* 276–7). Pliny the Elder's remark that the gardens of kings Adonis and Alcinous were celebrated in antiquity led to the idea that there was an actual Garden of Adonis (*Natural History* 19.19).

In the Renaissance, the gardens of Adonis flourished anew, sometimes in guises that left their classical prototypes obscured. Pliny's Garden of Adonis was often regarded as a version of the earthly paradise (Adon and Eden were thought to be etymologically connected) and at times fused with the ephemeral gardens of the ancient religious festivals. Justus Lipsius, for example, advises the reader of his *De constantia* (1584; Eng tr 1594), 'Looke into the holie Scripture, and you shall see that gardens had their beginning with the world, God himself appointing the first man his habitation therein, as the seate of a blessed and happie life. In prophane writers the gardens of Adonis, of Alcinous, Tantalus, and the Hesperides are grown into fables and common proverbes' (ed 1939:13). The sixteenth-century reader would have found the nonscriptural gardens treated in a number of mythological handbooks; for example, Conti's entry on Adonis typically covers a wide range of topics from literature and history to proverb lore (*Mythologiae* 5.16). In the *Adages* (1.1.4), Erasmus cites many classical sources of the gardens of Adonis, and describes them as denoting brief and trivial pleasures. In *The Praise of Folly*, he likens the Fortunate Isles where Folly was born to gardens of Adonis. In his commentary on Plato's *Phaedrus*, Ficino treats the gardens as mere metaphor, an example of frivolous and fruitless play, though he adds that writing is the most beautiful of games (M.J.B. Allen in Ficino ed 1981:213). Shakespeare gives the proverbial gardens a positive and seemingly untraditional twist in the Dauphin's words to Joan of Arc, 'Thy promises are like Adonis' garden, / That one day bloom'd and fruitful were the next' (*1 Henry VI* I vi 6–7). For Jonson, the gardens are similarly ideal places of the poetic imagination and function as hyperbolic courtly compliment (eg, *Every Man Out of His Humor* 4.8).

The gardens of Adonis are also referred to in Greek pastoral elegy, particularly Theocritus' Idyll 15, 'The Women at the Adonis-Festival' (cited in Conti 5.16), where the Adonia is a living ritual celebrating the sacred drama of love, death, and anticipated resurrection enacted by Adonis and his consort Aphrodite. With its mythic-elegiac pattern and feminine ambience, the idyll seems a remarkable foreshadowing of some of the central motifs of *FQ* III.

Spenser refers three times to gardens of Adonis: at *FQ* II x 71, *Colin Clout* 804, and in the argument to *FQ* III vi. The elaborate account that follows this last reference, however, describes a single Garden of Adonis. In using both the plural and singular, Spenser clearly means to call up the idea of the cultic and proverbial gardens and to fuse these with the idea of an earthly paradise. All of Spenser's gardens of Adonis have at least this much in common: they are places of origin. In the first, the lone Elf finds his ideal female or Fay, 'Of whom all *Faeryes* spring, and fetch their lignage right.' In the second, Cupid 'his owne perfection wrought' so that shortly he 'was of all the Gods the first.' In the third, most comprehensively, 'there is the first seminarie / Of all things, that are borne to live and die' where Amoret is 'trained up in true feminitee' until, like Cupid, she 'to perfect ripenesse grew' (III vi 30, 51–2).

In *Colin Clout*, Colin refers to the gardens of Adonis when he tells his fellow shepherds the philosophic myth of the origin and power of love: 'For him the greatest of the Gods we deeme, / Borne without Syre or couples, of one kynd, / For *Venus* selfe doth soly couples seeme, / Both male and female, through commixture joynd, / So pure and spotlesse *Cupid* forth she brought, / And in the gardens of *Adonis* nurst: / Where growing, he his owne perfection wrought' (799–805). Cupid's 'virgin birth' from the hermaphroditic Venus apparently signifies the spontaneous growth of a cosmic eros, love in its widest, most impersonal definition as the mutual attraction of things animate and inanimate. In the gardens of Adonis, this eros becomes more than unconscious attraction: it becomes personified. As memorials to the dead or dying god, the gardens at the same time anticipate his rebirth: naturalistically and ritualistically they affirm the repetition that is manifest in the annual cycle of vegetation and the succession of generations of living things. In the terms of Colin's Platonic myth-making, it is right that Eros should reach his perfection in these gardens, because there he learns to *remember* and 'see' the lineaments of divine beauty even when its outward manifestation decays.

The Cupid of the gardens of Adonis, Colin insists, is the love god of the shepherds, not of the court. One reason could be that the gardens represent a kind of elegiac epitome of a shepherds' calendar, so that the love that is nursed and ripens there shares in the pastoral idea of care for persons, animals, and things, because of their physical and metaphysical frailty. As a philosophical counterpoise to the idea of the court, therefore, the gardens of Adonis bear on the central question of *Colin Clout*, the possibility of establishing 'home' in a place of exile, one comparable to the 'paradise within' with which the angel Michael seeks to console another about to be exiled at the end of *Paradise Lost*.

At *FQ* II x 70–3, the gardens of Adonis appear as part of a myth of poetic creation; they seem to be a prototype of what Spenser calls Fairyland, the imaginary space created and peopled by the poet's imagination. According to the book Guyon reads in the castle of Alma, Prometheus created a man he called Elf, 'the first authour of all Elfin kind: / Who wandring through the world with wearie feet, / Did in the gardins of *Adonis* find / A goodly creature, whom he deemd in mind / To be no earthly wight, but either Spright, / Or Angell, th'authour of all woman kind; / Therefore a *Fay* he her according hight, / Of whom all *Faeryes* spring.' The Spenserian poet, then, is part Prometheus and part Elf – both a heaven-defying secondary creator punished for his insolence and an otherworldly displaced person wandering through the world until he unexpectedly arrives at a privileged place or moment (in the gardens of Adonis the two are the same) where he 'finds' his ideal creature who becomes the source of the Fairy lineage, that is, of his invention. His serendipity recalls Chaucer's ironic self-portrait, Sir Thopas, who rides off to find his own 'elf-queene' in the 'contree of Fairye' but gets no further than a fight with the three-headed giant Olifaunt (*Sir Thopas* in *CT* VII 788, 802, 808, 842). Spenser's luckier or more ambitious Elf has an Elfant among his descendants, as well as '*Elfar*, who two brethren gyants kild, / The one of which had two heads, th'other three' (II x 73). By such indirections, Spenser acknowledges his 'elvyssh' poetic father (prologue to *Sir Thopas*).

The Fairy lineage that Guyon's book details is based largely on a series of puns, jokes, and rhetorical variations on the name Elf. At least in one of its dimensions, Spenser seems to hint, his fiction results from verbal exuberance or free play that will disconcert readers looking only for a serious mimesis of the worlds of history and nature. His gardens of Adonis may thus be regarded as a defense of the frivolous verbal play that Socrates, using the same image, condemns in the *Phaedrus*.

In *FQ* III vi, the way to the Garden of Adonis consists of another allegory of the genesis of the Fairy fiction, but this time in terms of a contrast between an original, harmonious state of nature and contrasting tendencies that threaten to disrupt this harmony. The canto begins with the story of twins conceived through spontaneous generation by Chrysogone ('golden birth'), herself daughter of the fairy Amphisa ('both natures'). For these Venus figures, reproduction is an untroubled, automatic affair without need of men; but this paradisal state of affairs is contradicted by Chrysogone's shame and bewilderment at her unplanned pregnancy and by Venus' anxious pursuit of her son Cupid. By running away from his mother's 'blisfull bowre of joy above,' Cupid shows that in the very bosom of a happy, self-sufficient nature there is the urge toward fission, individuation, and a separate destiny.

In her search for Cupid, Venus is joined by Diana; when they find the newborn twins in the wilderness, each takes one of the babes and names her. The goddesses here become representatives of Renaissance or Spenserian didacticism. Diana has her babe 'upbrought in perfect Maydenhed, / And of her selfe her name *Belphoebe* red'; Venus takes hers to the Garden of Adonis 'To be upbrought in goodly womanhed, / And in her litle loves stead, which was strayd, / Her *Amoretta* cald, to comfort her dismayd' (28). Without knowing it, Venus and Diana act out the educational project that is *The Faerie Queene*: the attempt to fashion a 'noble person.' Chrysogone's babes are the raw material to be so fashioned.

Venus' 'joyous Paradize, / Where most she wonnes, when she on earth does dwel,' has none of the features we might expect for the nursery and education of Amoret. The image is complex, heterogeneous, and difficult if not impossible to visualize as a single entity. The description alternates disconcertingly between the vividly concrete and the highly generalized or abstract. Just when the garden seems to be a definite place with a distinct topography, it fades into the no-place of a conceptual scheme, only to reappear later as an actual location. This alternation looks like Spenser's way of dramatizing the ever-problematic relationship between image and idea that his allegorical epic has undertaken to explore.

It is the Garden of Adonis as philosophical idea, 'the first seminarie / Of all things, that are borne to live and die' (30), that has received most attention in twentieth-century criticism. The principal concern has been to determine which conceptual system – Aristotelian, Platonic, Neoplatonic, Augustinian, to mention the chief ones – best accounts for the view of nature projected in the Garden. Discussion of this question has by no means ended, but in recent decades other questions have moved to the forefront. What kind of image or myth is the Garden of Adonis? What is its relation to other settings in *The Faerie Queene*, like the Bower of Bliss (II xii) or Mount Acidale (VI x)? How is it related to the narrative fiction and the main themes of Book III?

Despite the often illuminating responses to such questions, the enigma of Spenser's Garden remains largely intact. Perhaps it is one of those complex images, like Keats' Grecian urn, that is meant to tease us out of thought. Alternatively, it may be that our understanding of the Garden will advance again once its 'philosophy' and its symbolism are analyzed together. For example, the 'thousand thousand naked babes' waiting to be clothed before they leave the Garden may be 'seminal reasons' or 'vegetal souls' (Milne 1973); but one must also consider their bearing on the Garden's narrative-dramatic functions in Book III.

C.S. Lewis' idea of an 'allegorical core' in each book of *The Faerie Queene*, proposed half a century ago, still seems eminently useful for the Garden of Adonis. His suggestion – that the allegorical core 'shows us the Form of the virtue ... not only in its transcendental unity ... but also "becoming Many in the world of phenomena"' (1936:334) – ascribes an excessively Platonist poetics to *The Faerie Queene*, but is valuable for its insistence on the connection between the core and the surrounding narrative. For the Garden of Adonis, we could invert Lewis' formula so that the Garden becomes a symbol of the Many, and the narrative (in the traditional sense of the story-line) becomes the realm of the One, that is, the path on which the type moves towards the achievement of individual identity.

In such a view, the philosophical and strictly mythic elements of the Garden would accordingly emphasize its collective nature, the way it encompasses ever-larger classes of beings and areas of experience. Contrariwise, at those points where the Garden picks up a narrative thread or even hints at a known narrative, individuality is implied, or at any rate the beginnings of individuation. Examples of narrative thread are the story of Venus and Adonis, continued from the tapestry in Malecasta's castle (III i 34–8), and the story of Amoret's infancy. Stories alluded to but not continued from elsewhere in the poem include that of Cupid and Psyche, which is brought to a happy ending in the Garden (vi 49–50). The reference to the flower Narcissus 'that likes the watry shore' (45) hints at a familiar story. In each case, but with varying degrees of ambiguity, we sense a striving towards an individual destiny separate from the collective.

In simplest terms, there is Amoret, one babe among thousands in the Garden. She is distinct from the others, though just how distinct is a question that only her narrative will answer. Then there is Adonis. As vegetation god, he is part of the great seasonal cycle of which the gardens dedicated to him are a miniature epitome. But as a beautiful boy beloved of Venus and resistant to her blandishments, he suggests the beginnings of chastity that in Book III is the way of individuation, because it means not doing what comes naturally and having a strong sense of one's separateness from others. Adonis' story suggests the largely negative aspects of chastity; for him, as for Shakespeare's Adonis, love is 'a life in death' (*Venus and Adonis* 413). Only from the perspective of his mysterious resurrection in the Garden (46–9) does this 'life in death' take on positive meaning, becoming part of the paradox of human love, where the self loses itself to the other only to be miraculously restored to itself. The Garden, finally, is that landscape of the soul – it might just as well be named the Garden of Psyche – from which the soul thought itself an exile or fugitive, but which it rediscovers once it understands that world and soul are not mutually antagonistic but aspects of one reality.

RICHARD T. NEUSE

Bennett 1932; Berger 1960–1; Cheney 1966; Comito 1978; Ellrodt 1960; Ficino ed 1981; Giamatti 1966; Hankins 1971; Justus Lipsius 1939 *Two Bookes of Constancie* (tr John Stradling 1594) ed Rudolf Kirk and Clayton M. Hall (New Brunswick, NJ); I.G. MacCaffrey 1976; Milne 1973.

Aemylia The young woman whom Amoret meets in Lust's cave (*FQ* IV vii). When Amoret escapes, she remains behind with the old hag until released when Belphoebe slays Lust. Aemylia then accompanies the wounded Amoret until the two, 'in full sad and sorrowfull estate,' are aided by Arthur. They stay overnight with the railing Sclaunder, and the next day encounter Placidas pursued by the giant Corflambo, whom Arthur defeats. Placidas is the look-alike friend of Amyas, a 'Squire of low degree' who was to have eloped with the high-born Aemylia, but was captured at their trysting spot by Corflambo and imprisoned in his castle where Poeana, the giant's daughter, fell in love with him. (It is at this same trysting spot that Aemylia was captured by Lust.) Placidas had managed to join Amyas in prison and had then offered to go in his place to Poeana, at which point he escaped. Now he leads Arthur and the ladies to Amyas. Aemylia and Amyas are reunited and perhaps married (the text is unclear on this point) as are the 'reformd' Poeana and the 'trusty Squire' Placidas (ix 15–16).

Aemylia's story of love and a thwarted elopement – the self-sacrifice of friendship which, in turn, leads to a tetrad combining love, friendship, concord, and forgiveness – is the stuff of medieval romance. It consists of two distinct narrative prototypes: the tale of friendship (as in the Middle English *Amys and Amiloun*) is turned to the theme of love, that of love ('the squire of low degree') is adapted to a narrative of friendship. While the two commonly appear together, with one or the other accorded a 'privileged' status, in the Aemylia episode Spenser's strategy of narrative indirection avoids any hierarchy. Instead, he gives his narrative a dual focus, so that they assume equal weight. The last-minute union between Placidas and Poeana introduces a relationship which may be identified as concord rather than as love or friendship, and thus assimilates the episode into the larger themes of Book IV.

Spenser achieves this dual focus by introducing Aemylia's story *in medias res*, through the framing narrative of Amoret, and then developing it chronologically both forward and backward. The effect is to supplant Aemylia from the center of her own story and make her an aspect of Amoret. As the narrative moves backward in time to tell us of Aemylia, it takes for granted those inner sexual desires which drove her to ignore the advice of family and friends, and stresses instead the public consequences of her decision and how it may be judged by others, including the reader. Her crime is indiscretion rather than wantonness. Spenser gives her desire but no soul or psyche to torment her, and her shallowness contrasts with Amoret's psychological complexity. The often confusing connection between appearances and inner desire in Aemylia's story unfolds as Placidas tells how the captive Amyas becomes subject to Poeana; how, out of pure friendship, he fills his friend's place in order to help him escape; and then how, when trying to free his friend, he himself escapes while Amyas remains imprisoned. Spenser intentionally multiplies the superficial parallels between the stories of Amyas and Aemylia.

In the last phase of Aemylia's story, Spenser achieves a kind of narrative *concordia discors* that reinforces his praise of friendship at the opening of canto ix. Structurally and thematically, it echoes the episode of Cambell, Triamond, Cambina, and Canacee, and the image of the interlinked relationships between erotic, kindred, and friendly love presented in canto iii. The two episodes comprise two quaternions of Book IV, illustrating the idea that love must harmonize four rather than two sets of personalities, each set comprising complementary opposites (Nohrnberg 1976:621).

But, unlike its mirror episode, all the thematic and narrative details of the Aemylia-Amyas, Placidas-Poeana quaternion are designed to stress diversity rather than affinity. Most noteworthy is the absence of all kindred ties: the two men look alike but are friends and not twins. Instead of using mistaken identity to complicate his plot (the conventional use of such twins, as in Shakespeare's *Comedy of Errors*), Spenser withholds the detail of their physical resemblance to make it the culminating recognition for the reader. But as the confusion of names in the argument of canto ix illustrates, it is a recognition that is based on circumstantial appearances and emphasizes the unknown as well as the known. The statement that the 'Squire of low degree' marries 'Paeana' (ix 9 in *FQ* 1596) makes no sense unless we accept that the chivalric name applies to Placidas as well as to Amyas; or that one of the two names, Poeana or the Squire of low degree, is an error; or that Spenser meant for us to see that this tetrad really consists of two people with dual personalities rather than four individuals. Whichever way, the 'recognition' is one that reveals similarities without denying individuation. These details, compounded by the episode's narrative circuitousness and its repeated emphasis on the problem of judging appearances and the meanings of events, stress the eventual recognition of harmony among unrelated individuals rather than point to an underlying oneness that unites people.

If we accept Camden's readings of their names (*Remains* ed 1984:58), Amyas and Aemylia are themselves almost doubles: *Amias* 'beloved' derives from Greek *amulios* 'Faire spoken' (also the root of 'Aemilius[a]'): here, lovers depend on being beloved, which is a concordant version of Corflambo's corrupt mutuality. Placidas and Amyas also suggest by their names the kinship between concord and friendship that enters the allegory of the Temple of Venus. These, however, are affinities that Spenser discovers rather than develops, although his technique of belated discovery leading to final recognition is itself part of the theme of the episode.

Unlike the Cambell and Triamond sequence, the harmony here is one which can ignore uncertainty and doubt. The episode leaves unexplored the relation between virginity (or its loss) and virtue. Each of the four characters has moral shadows that are never illumined, although the concord among them is conclusive and convincing. Amoret and the reader, however, learn a healthy suspicion of appearances. It is little wonder, then, that this episode is most often likened to Shakespeare's comic vision: characters consent to their mates in spite of some moral imperfections. Lighter than a dark comedy, it is perhaps a gray one – even to the extent that the last act, the acceptance of Poeana (punishment, expiation) as Paeana (praise, healer – the typographic change occurs at ix 9, in the 1596 edition), makes it a comedy of conversion and forgiveness.

W.H. HERENDEEN

Aesculapius The name Aesculapius is a Latin form of *Asklepios*, an early Greek physician who by the fifth century BC was worshiped as the god of medicine. He is the 'farre renowmed sonne / Of great *Apollo*,' god of the healing sun, and the mortal Coronis (see *FQ* I v 36–44). Following Boccaccio (*Genealogia* 7.36), Spenser makes him a brother of Tryphon, 'soveraine leach' and 'surgeon' of the sea gods, and father of Podalyrius (III iv 43, IV xi 6, VI vi 1). Aesculapius was reared by Chiron, a centaur, from whom he learned the art of medicine (see Pindar *Pythian Odes* 3, Ovid *Metamorphoses* 2.630). The most famous temple in his honor, surrounded by sanatoria, was at Epidaurus. While stories developed of his miraculous cures, most early accounts suggest that his medical priests' methods of therapy were chiefly scientific and natural, though with occasional recourse to music, as was customary in Greece and Rome. Statues and Roman coins usually present him as a kindly bearded figure holding a caduceus, or staff, around which is wound a sacred snake, symbol both of wisdom and of rejuvenation since it sloughs its skin. Cooper writes that he is 'honoured in the fourme of a serpent' (*Thesaurus* 1565; see also Cartari 1571:84–90). Whitney's *A Choice of Emblemes* includes his portrait (1586:212).

(See **Aesculapius** Fig 1.)

Spenser read in Virgil how Jupiter, incensed by Aesculapius' presumption in restoring Hippolytus to life, hurled him into Hades by his thunderbolt (*Aeneid* 7.761–73). The tale is retold in Renaissance works on mythography by Boccaccio (*Genealogia* 5.19) and Conti (*Mythologiae* 4.11), and in Charles Estienne's *Dictionarium*. In accord with medieval tradition, which contrasts spiritual healing by the divine with mere therapy of the body by physicians, Spenser further developed and Christianized the legend, perhaps directly influenced by commentaries on Virgil.

Chained for ever in a dark and comfortless cave in hell by the wrath of God, Spenser's Aesculapius continually and vainly strives to restore his health with salves and to slake the eternally raging fire (I v 36, 40). Having ignored the welfare of his soul, he is incapable of fulfilling the biblical injunction, 'Physicion, heale thy self' (Luke 4.23), however great his medical skill. He reluctantly agrees to attempt to cure Sansjoy's wounds (44), but we learn nothing more of Sansjoy's fortunes, since none returns from hell 'without heavenly grace' (31). Spenser contrasts Aesculapius both with Christ and Arthur as physicians of the soul, and with Phoebus the sun who 'recure[s]' himself (44); and also Aesculapius' infernal therapy with the holy therapy Redcrosse receives from Patience (x 23–8) and from the Well of Life (xi 48–50).

F. DAVID HOENIGER

Emma J. Edelstein and Ludwig Edelstein 1945 *Asclepius: A Collection and Interpretation of the Testimonies* 2 vols (Baltimore).

Agrippa (Henricus Cornelius Agrippa of Nettesheim, 1486–1535) Famous in the sixteenth century as an evangelical humanist, a bold and aggressive satirist, and a magician who reputedly came to a bad end. His life and his writings abound in paradoxes. He was an ambitious courtier who wrote vehemently against the corruption of royal courts. From 1510 until his death, he was involved in violent controversies with the preachers, inquisitors, and theologians of the Franciscan and Dominican orders, who drove him from several positions and condemned his books; yet, while his polemics earned him a reputation as a pre-Lutheran reformer, he never broke with the Catholic church. Although a lifelong student of magic and the occult, he also proclaimed that the Scriptures and a pure faith in God offered the only way to truth.

His two major works, *De occulta philosophia* (ms version 1510, expanded version pub 1533) and *De incertitudine et vanitate scientiarum et artium* (1530; Eng tr *Of the Vanitie and Uncertaintie of Artes and Sciences* 1569, rpt 1575), were known throughout Europe and were drawn upon by many Elizabethan writers, including Sidney, Greville, Harvey, Nashe, Marlowe, and, almost certainly, Spenser. *De occulta philosophia* incorporates material from many sources, most notably the texts attributed to Hermes Trismegistus, the Cabala (which Agrippa knew through the works of Giovanni Pico and Reuchlin), medieval magical texts such as the *Picatrix*, and a wide range of classical and patristic texts, especially those of a Neoplatonic bent. *De vanitate* is encyclopedic in a different sense. With a mixture of evangelical high seriousness, sly paradox, witty abusiveness, and shrill invective, it sets out to show that all human arts and sciences are false and of no use for salvation: only through faith in God can spiritual regeneration and true knowledge be obtained.

These two works may appear to contradict one another. But the magical Hermetic-Cabalistic-Neoplatonic syncretism of the former and the loosely skeptical fideism of the latter are both based upon an Hermetic doctrine of regeneration and deification which Agrippa also found in Christian, Cabalistic, and Neoplatonic texts, and which he understood as the central principle of both magic and the Christian religion. Moreover, while *De vanitate* does not spare such disciplines as logic, dicing, prostitution, and scholastic theology, it attacks only the most obviously demonic forms of magic, and actually praises others. To Spenser's generation, the attractiveness of Agrippa's two major works (and of *De vanitate* especially) seems to have lain in their unstable but persuasive fusion of apparently Protestant doctrines with occult and Neoplatonic ideas.

Spenser certainly knew of Agrippa, perhaps through Gabriel Harvey, who wrote in 'A New Yeeres Gift': 'A thousand good leaves be for ever graunted *Agrippa*. / For squibbing and declayming against many fruitlesse / *Artes*, and Craftes, devisde by the *Divls and Sprites*, for a torment, / And for a plague to the world: as both *Pandora*, *Prometheus*, / And that cursed *good bad Tree*, can testifie at all times' (*Three Letters* 3 in *Var Prose* p 465). Whether Spenser read *De vanitate* as closely as did Sidney remains in doubt (see Hamilton 1956). But his account of the Ape's court in *Mother Hubberds Tale* (659–716, 794–921) suggests indebtedness to Agrippa's chapter 68, which describes life at court as 'wholye voyde of shame, and what naughtines so ever in any place is found in cruel beasts, al this seemeth to be assembled in the route of courtiers, as in one body: there is found ... the deceit of the Foxe ... the scoffinge of the Ape.' The jests of chapter 3 (eg, 'it is saide of a Prieste ... who when he had many burnte offringes, to the ende he mighte not offende againste Grammar, he consecrated them with these woordes, *Haec sunt Corpora mea*, that is, these are my Bodies ... From whence came that Opinion of the *Waldenses* ... and of others of later time, about the *Eucharist*, but of this woorde, *is*?') are echoed in lines 385–9 of the same poem: 'Of such deep learning little had he neede, / Ne yet of Latine, ne of Greeke, that breede / Doubts mongst Divines, and difference of texts, / From whence arise diversitie of sects, / And hatefull heresies, of God abhor'd.' *De occulta philosophia* is one possible source of Spenser's knowledge of Neoplatonic doctrines, of numerology, and of the Cabala; other aspects of the work, such as Agrippa's chapters on talismanic imagery (2.35–49), may also have been of interest to him. His contemporary reputation as an arch-magician (*archimagus*) may have contributed to Spenser's portraits of the learned magicians Archimago and Busirane. MICHAEL H. KEEFER

There is a modern rpt in 2 vols (Hildesheim 1970) of a sixteenth-century ed of the Lyons *Opera* (c 1600). The standard study is Charles G. Nauert, Jr 1965 *Agrippa and the Crisis of Renaissance Thought* (Urbana). See also A.C. Hamilton 1956 'Sidney and Agrippa' *RES* ns 7:151–7; Michael H. Keefer 1988 'Agrippa's Dilemma: Hermetic "Rebirth" and the Ambivalences of *De vanitate* and *De occulta philosophia*' *RenQ* 41:614–53; Eugene Korkowski 1976 'Agrippa as Ironist' *Neophil* 60:594–607; Paola Zambelli 1976 'Magic and Radical Reformation in Agrippa of Nettesheim' *JWCI* 39:69–103.

Alabaster, William (1568–1640) In *Colin Clouts Come Home Againe* (1595), lines 400–15 are devoted to praise of Alabaster and his *Elisaeis*, which Spenser must have read in manuscript during his 1589–91 sojourn in England. Among the dozen poets mentioned by Colin, only Alabaster and Daniel appear under their own names – the rest are assigned pastoral disguises – and none is praised at greater length than Alabaster. Spenser's enthusiasm for Alabaster and his poem may have come in part from their sharing friends at Cambridge (Spenser at Pembroke, Alabaster at Trinity: matriculated 1584, BA 1587–8, fellow 1589, MA 1591). But more importantly, they shared a poetic subject: in 1590, Spenser had just brought out *FQ* I-III, which he dedicated to Queen Elizabeth and asserted was in a veiled way about her rule and her realm. The younger poet also intended to dedicate his Latin *Elisaeis* to the Queen and to celebrate her career in a more explicit way. It may be this sharing of subject matter and genre that causes Spenser to praise Alabaster by name; he does not see his young competitor in epic as a threat but warmly commends him to the Queen's notice and favor.

Spenser's remark that Alabaster, though a skilled poet, was 'knowen yet to few' would prove prophetic. Alabaster is known – yet to few – not for his anti-Catholic epic in Latin but for a small collection of English devotional sonnets. (Samuel Johnson praised also his Latin tragedy *Roxana* as the finest Latin verse written by an Englishman before Milton.) The *Elisaeis* was never completed. Alabaster had projected in his title a 12-book epic on the model of the *Aeneid*, but finished only a first book of 753 lines of hexameter verse. It treats Elizabeth's sufferings early in Mary's reign, her estrangement from Mary, her being taken to London from her sickbed at Ashridge, and her imprisonment in the Tower in spring 1554. Elizabeth is portrayed as the innocent victim of powerful evil forces who must endure what is thrust upon her with stoic fortitude. Most of the book is taken up with mapping the progress of evil through a series of fictional encounters. Satan appears before the papacy, personified as the Whore of Babylon, to stimulate her to promote the Catholic cause and to sow dissension in England. She flies to England and appears in sleep to Stephen Gardiner, Mary's Lord Chancellor, to stir him to bring Elizabeth into Mary's disfavor. When Gardiner accuses Elizabeth of complicity in Wyatt's rebellion, evil has emanated from its source to encircle the Protestant princess. Though the poem has some local descriptive successes, it does not sustain sufficient narrative interest. Alabaster's real concern was style: florid descriptions and similes, punctuated by terse epigrams, alternate with heavily rhetorical speeches.

Though Spenser alludes to events in Mary's reign in Book I, there is no very obvious influence of *FQ* I-III on the *Elisaeis*. Nor does the *Elisaeis* appear to have exerted any direct influence on *FQ* IV-VI. Alabaster's poem remained in manuscript until 1979. The young Milton, however, appears to have read it and made use of it in composing his own miniature Latin epic on the Gunpowder Plot, *In Quintum Novembris*.

In view of the virulent anti-Catholicism of the *Elisaeis*, there is some irony in the course of Alabaster's life. He went as chaplain to Essex on the Cádiz expedition in 1596, then the following year suddenly converted to Catholicism. After being detained in London, he escaped and went to Rome and Spain. The next decade of Alabaster's life is a perplexity of diplomatic intrigue, repeated imprisonment, release, escape, and a series of recantations and reconversions to Catholicism. Finally in 1618 he returned decisively to the Anglican fold, married, and became known through a number of Latin treatises as a divine learned in mystical and cabalistic lore.

Alabaster commemorated Spenser in a Latin epitaph. It has been suggested that these verses were among those Camden says were thrown into his grave by mourning poets, but since Alabaster was on the continent at the time, they were surely composed later.

In Edouardum Spencerum, Britannicae
poeseos facilè principem
Hoc qui sepulcro conditur si quis fuit
Quaeris viator, dignus es qui rescias.
SPENCERUS istic conditur, si quis fuit
Rogare pergis, dignus es qui nescias.

('On Edward Spenser, easily the prince of British poetry. If thou askest, passerby, who he was who is buried in this tomb, worthy thou art to learn: Spenser is buried here. If thou proceedst to ask who he was, worthy thou art never to learn.')

MICHAEL O'CONNELL

William Alabaster 1979 *The Elisaeis* tr and ed Michael O'Connell *SP* Texts and Studies 76; Alabaster 1959 *Sonnets* ed G.M. Story and Helen Gardner (Oxford). Verses on Spenser are contained in Oxford, Bodleian Library, Ms Rawlinson D.293. For Alabaster's life, see the introduction to the Story and Gardner edition; Louise Imogen Guiney 1939 ed *Recusant Poets* (London) 1.335–49; and Mark Eccles 1982:4–5.

Aladine, Priscilla The story of Aladine and Priscilla (*FQ* VI ii-iii) is interlaced with that of Tristram, whom Calidore discovers slaying a 'proud discourteous knight' (ii argument). The dead knight's lady narrates the first part of this story, telling Calidore that they had happened upon a pair of lovers (Aladine and Priscilla) 'in joyous jolliment / Of their franke loves' (16), and that her knight, desiring this new lady, had attacked and wounded her unarmed lover. When he could not find Priscilla, who had fled into the woods, the discourteous knight went on his way, battering his own lady in frustration until Tristram challenged him.

After an interlude in which Calidore dubs Tristram as his squire and leaves him in charge of the discourteous knight's lady (ii 24–39), Calidore finds the wounded Aladine and the grieving Priscilla in a 'covert glade.' He helps her carry her lover to his father's house, where Priscilla cures Aladine by watching over him all night and washing his wounds with her tears. Since she is overcome by fear of shame (being of higher rank than her lover), Calidore accompanies her to her father's castle, bearing the head of the discourteous knight and telling her father an equivocal version of the story: that Priscilla was 'Most perfect pure, and guiltlesse innocent / Of blame ... Since first he saw her' and rescued her from the knight whose head he is carrying (iii 18).

Elements in this episode invite comparison with other incidents in the Legend of Courtesy. The intrusion of the discourteous knight upon trysting lovers provides an early instance in Book VI of the vulnerability of the pastoral retreat or private vision; it anticipates Calidore's interruption of Calepine and Serena and of Colin's vision on Mount Acidale, as well as the hostile intrusions of the Blatant Beast, Turpine, the cannibals, and the Brigands. It recalls as well the interruption of Redcrosse and Duessa by Orgoglio (I vii) and that of Aemylia by Lust (IV vii 15–18). Book VI recurrently emphasizes practical problems of courteous behavior between persons of different social rank: Tristram must justify his combat against a knight (ii 7); Priscilla must be persuaded by Calidore to help carry her lover ('let it not you seeme disgrace, / To beare this burden on your dainty backe' 47). Some of the participants show skill in putting the best construction on their own situations. 'To cheare his guests,' the wise old Aldus tempers his grief by means of a philosophical generalization about 'the weakenesse of all mortall hope' (iii 5–6); somewhat less generously, the proud knight's lady finds words to honor Priscilla's beauty while salving her own wounded self-esteem: 'Faire was the Ladie sure, that mote content / An hart, not carried with too curious eyes' (ii 16). For a book in which 'comely guize ... And gracious speach' (i 2) will be seen as essential means to forge courteous bonds, it seems fitting that this early episode should suggest the name of Aldus Manutius, the humanist publisher of Aldine texts: 'And *Aldus* was his name, and his sonnes *Aladine*' (iii 3).

RICHARD MALLETTE

Alanus de Insulis (Alain de Lille) (c 1116–c 1202) Author of a number of theological works which gained for him the title 'doctor universalis,' Alanus was a central figure of the twelfth-century Neoplatonic revival of learning in France. He is best known for his two Latin allegories, *De planctu Naturae* (*The Complaint of Nature*) and *Anticlaudianus*. In sixteenth-century England, he was also reputed to have written commentaries on the prophecies of Merlin.

Of particular importance to Spenser is *De planctu*, which had been a major source both for Jean de Meun's continuation of the *Romance of the Rose* and for Chaucer's *Parliament of Fowls*. Referring directly to Alanus' text, Spenser calls *De planctu* by a mistranslated Middle English title, *Plaint of kindes* (*FQ* VII vii 9; Chaucer correctly titles it *Pleynt of Kynde* in *PF* 316). As a result, and because of the coyness of Spenser's final alexandrine ('Go seek he out that *Alane* where he may be sought'), readers have doubted whether Spenser actually knew *De planctu*. No printed editions of the poem were available in sixteenth-century England. However, given the striking congruity of concerns in Alanus and Spenser, it is useful to assume that Spenser was familiar with manuscripts of *De planctu* (several were available to him, of which nine are still extant; see Quilligan 1983:162).

De planctu is an allegorical debate between a poet-narrator and a personified figure of female authority, Natura, who wears an elaborately described garment representing all of physical creation. The subject of their debate has been widely assumed to be sodomy, but the strange grammatical terminology in which Natura phrases her complaint suggests an overriding concern with the impact of poetic language on human sexuality. (In the complaint, '[man] is subject and predicate: one and the same term is given a double application. Man here extends too far the laws of grammar' Alanus ed 1980:68.) This complex debate, echoed by the similar debate in *Romance of the Rose* between the dreamer and Reason, stands behind Spenser's redefinition of the language of sexuality in *FQ* III, where Genius, another character from *De planctu*, plays a prominent part in the Garden of Adonis (vi 31–2).

Of equal importance for Spenser's allegory in *FQ* VII is Natura's correction of the poet's too-literal way of reading Ovidian fable. Alanus' Natura teaches the poet to interpret allegorically a tear in her garment at the place where man had been figured. It is to this garment that Spenser refers in his description of the ineffable numinousness of his Dame Nature's veil. In Natura's lessons on interpretation, we see the shared allegorical concerns between Alanus' emphasis on the right reading of a text (*textus* a woven thing, a garment) like Ovid's, and Spenser's remythologizing of Ovid's story of Actaeon (Quilligan 1983:161–6).

MAUREEN QUILLIGAN

For the Latin text of *De planctu Naturae*, see Alanus 1978, ed Nikolaus M. Häring in *SMed* 3rd ser 19.2:797–879; also *PLat* 210:431A–82C and Thomas Wright, ed 1872 *The Anglo-Latin Satirical Poets and Epigrammatists of the Twelfth Century* vol 2, Rolls Series 59 (London). The English translation by Douglas M. Moffat (New York 1908) has been superseded by that of James J. Sheridan (Toronto 1980). See also Guillory 1983:62–6; Quilligan 1977; Quilligan 1983.

---

alchemy The literature of alchemy, with its suggestive symbolism of transmuting base metals into gold and of creating a life-preserving elixir and a magical philosophers' stone, was a rich source of allusion for Renaissance poets like Shakespeare, Donne, Henry Vaughan, and the English Spenserians. Aiming at the perfection of matter, the sincere practice of alchemy generally inspired positive metaphors of transformation, though some skeptical authors saw even the honest alchemists as misguided or foolish. The charlatans and counterfeiters who pretended success at transmuting base metals into gold were, along with their greedy or gullible victims, a common target of satire and ridicule, as in Jonson's *Alchemist*. Given the wide currency of both positive and negative uses of alchemical reference throughout Renaissance literature, Spenser's canon contains surprisingly few direct allusions to the so-called Royal Art.

While Spenser exhibits a general knowledge of cosmogony, he has little interest in theories of matter. The general notions of the universality of material substance and the changeability of material form in the Garden of Adonis (*FQ* III vi 37–8) are consonant with alchemical theories, but he ignores metals and minerals and confines himself to living bodies. This omission is odd, because the Garden is called the seminary of 'all things, that are borne to live and die,' but no reference is made to the ubiquitous belief that the 'seeds' of metals 'grow' towards perfection in the earth. Guyon's argument against mining may characterize Spenser's own attitude toward precious metals and stones (II vii 16–17): while not evil, they are no more than earth or mud, and not only inspire greed but tempt man to ally himself with formless, inert matter and so lose sight of his spiritual nature (see Kendrick 1974). Since material (exoteric) alchemy seeks to change the forms of base metals and thereby produce gold, it is even less defensible than mining metals found in nature. Predictably, then, Spenser's direct references to alchemy are either conventional in application or negative in tone.

The most common alchemical term in Renaissance literature is *distill*. Often it carries no alchemical association but merely describes the appearance of drops of moisture, as in the drops of sweat on Acrasia's breast (II xii 78). The potentially alchemical analogy here is realized in Donne's 'The Comparison' 1–6 (Thomson 1977). Spenser himself, however, does invoke a visual image of alchemical distillation in the description of Winter as an old man whose breath freezes on his hoary beard: 'And the dull drops that from his purpled bill / As from a limbeck did adown distill' (VII vii 31). The limbeck (alembic) is the cap or 'beak' of the alchemist's still, which collects the vapor from the lower vessel (the cucurbit) and conveys the condensed droplets to a receiver. As when he uses *transmewed* for *transmuted* (II iii 37), Spenser here employs alchemical terms in their conventionally figurative sense, though Winter's purple 'beak' enlivens the image with humor. More puzzling perhaps is the simile that describes the drying up of Timias' inner organs by his undisclosed passion for Belphoebe: 'As percing levin [lightning], which the inner part / Of every thing consumes, and calcineth by art' (III v 48). *To calcine* is a specifically alchemical term meaning to dry out and thus reduce (a metal) to a fine powder by heat; 'by art' suggests the art of alchemy. Yet there seems to be a contradiction between the artificial process of calcination and the natural phenomenon of lightning, which was commonly believed to consume the insides of those it struck (Heninger 1960:79). Throughout *The Faerie Queene*, formlessness of the body is emblematic of moral corruption; and here Timias' 'alchemical' consumption underscores the negative view of his self-destructive passion.

Other, more indirect, allusions to alchemy appear in *The Faerie Queene*. These are invariably negative, though there is no direct satire of alchemy itself. Mammon's forge may parody an alchemist's furnace (II vii 35–6); and if it is meant to contrast the orderly kitchen (stomach) of Alma's castle (II ix 29–32), it represents the diseased belly of the avaricious man as a horribly distorted gold-producing machine. The soot-covered Mammon himself (II vii 3) is the very caricature of the begrimed empiric common to Renaissance art and literature. Another parody, this time of alchemical transmutation, may be implied in a further portrait of avarice, Munera, who is so enamored of her 'mucky pelfe' that her hands have turned to gold and her feet to silver (V ii 9–27).

The creation of false Florimell by the Witch is also reminiscent of an alchemical process (III viii 5–8). Her body is made of 'purest snow' and 'tempred with fine Mercury, / And virgin wex'; 'golden wyre' is substituted for the true Florimell's 'yellow lockes,' and a satanic 'Spright' is inserted 'to rule the carkasse dead.' Quicksilver or mercury was one of the main alchemical ingredients; but it was also a theoretical principle of matter, accounting for a substance's volatility, fluidity, and malleability. The 'virgin wex' may be an ironic glance at the mysterious but wonder-working *lac virginis* (virgin's milk) of the alchemists. (An unpublished Elizabethan alchemical poem explains that 'Lac virgynen / [is] cauled virgins wax in our englysh tonge' [Ms Ashmole 1480, fol 72a].) Furthermore, the process of 'making' gold is commonly described as the infusion of a 'spirit' or 'seed' into the 'prime matter' (or 'chaos') to which the base metal has been reduced, thus giving it the 'form' of gold. If Spenser had these alchemical notions and terms in mind (and they were common enough that no unusual knowledge would be required), he would be playing on the alchemical *associations* of these terms (and of the 'golden wyre') in order to deepen the resonances of 'counterfeisance' and deception in the false Florimell. Moreover, all the main elements of this created figure (snow, wax, and mercury) share the property of fusibility, and the form that each takes is temporary and therefore undependable. Her fickleness is perhaps symbolized by her body's unstable constituents: she is a counterfeit 'fool's gold.'

The Faerie Queene is full of stories of transformation; but when Spenser compares physical, moral, or psychological changes to changes in matter, he turns not to alchemical transmutation for his imagery but simply to the four elements (earth, water, air, fire). Thus Redcrosse's defeat by Orgoglio can be seen as a descent from the highest element (fire) to the lowest (earth) (Hamilton 1961a:76); but this interpretation seems to depend on the pervasive notions of hierarchy and mutability rather than on alchemy. More relevant to alchemy perhaps, Medway's vesture is presented as *argentum liquidum* or mercury (IV xi 45; see Fowler 1964:173).

Some readers, however, have suspected that alchemy is more than a source of incidental metaphor or allusion in *The Faerie Queene*. For example, Northrop Frye connects Redcrosse's red and white (silver) shield 'not only with the risen body of Christ and the sacramental symbolism which accompanies it, but with the union of the red and white roses in the Tudor dynasty' and also with the 'chymical marriage' of the 'red king' and 'white queen,' allegorical figures that stand for Sol and Luna, the 'red' and 'white' stones, or the alchemist's theoretical sulphur and mercury. All this symbolism presumably culminates in the betrothal of the 'red' knight and the 'white' Una (Frye 1957:144, 195). Although Frye claims Spenser is 'clearly acquainted' with alchemical allegory, he makes no more of this pregnant suggestion. What could have motivated Spenser to invoke these alchemical associations, if indeed he does?

One answer lies in reading certain episodes of *The Faerie Queene* as esoteric alchemical allegories, accessible only to those steeped in the subject. Occultist contemporaries of Spenser such as Jacques Gohory (d 1576) and alchemists like Elias Ashmole (1617–92) interpreted medieval romances such as the *Romance of the Rose* and *Amadis of Gaul* as alchemical allegories, and the German Michael Maier and others read classical myth in the same way. The only hint of such an approach to Spenser by a near-contemporary is found in Sir Kenelm Digby's famous *Observations* on the difficult numerological stanza at *FQ* II ix 22 (c 1628, rpt in *Var* 2:472–8). Parenthetically, he asks whether the three angles of the triangle referred to in this stanza might not be 'resembled to the 3 great compounded Elements in mans bodie, to wit, Salt, Sulphur and Mercurie ... ?' These 'tria prima' are the three elements of all matter which Paracelsus (d 1541) substituted for the more traditional four. Later, Digby refers to the 'three dimensions, to wit, Longitude, Latitude and Profunditie,' of all solid bodies. These 'three dimensions' of matter, deriving ultimately from Aristotle's *De caelo*, are found in fifteenth- and sixteenth-century English alchemical poems and prose texts; they are fully expounded in Roger Bacon's version of the *Secreta secretorum*, which also celebrates the sphere as the most perfect form (see Schuler 1978:55n). Digby's other notes on Spenser (*Sp All* p 211) contain no further alchemical information, and these few comments in *Observations* hardly render *The Faerie Queene* an alchemical allegory. Another alchemist, George Starkey, wrote in 1678 a commentary in both prose and Spenserian stanzas upon Sir George Ripley's fifteenth-century poem *The Compound of Alchymy* (see *Sp All* p 270); but his use of Spenser's poetic form is as far as he goes. It is quite possible, of course, that some as-yet-unknown alchemists may have found hidden meanings in *The Faerie Queene* as others did in the medieval romances and classical myths.

Perhaps convinced that an absence of overtly expressed esoteric beliefs can itself be construed as evidence of such beliefs (see Mulryan 1972), some modern scholars have gone beyond the tentative hints of Digby and Frye, and have claimed that Spenser himself intended his poem to be an elaborate alchemical allegory. Recently, for example, C.G. Jung's influential theory, that throughout its history material alchemy was really an external manifestation of an inner quest for psychic wholeness, has led to a major revaluation of alchemical writings – and of literary works containing alchemical elements. In Jungian terms, the 'alchemical' allegory of Redcrosse shows how the process of individuation effects the 'psychological transformation of a "clownishe younge man" into a perfected Saint George of England' (Rockwood 1972: x). Here the 'alchemical wedding' cited by Frye becomes the union of the Jungian *animus* and *anima*. Moreover, *FQ* I is said to describe a 'psychotherapeutic discipline' by which the reader's own personality can be integrated.

Another attempt to find esoteric meanings in *The Faerie Queene* also relies on the alchemical interpretation of certain symbols and events, but it rests finally on a suggestive but unproven link between Spenser and the Hermetic 'mystical politics' of Bruno (Brooks-Davies 1983). Here, the alchemical wedding of Redcrosse and Una is but the most important of several 'alchemical plots' in Book I; and in Book V Elizabeth/Mercilla, the descendent of another alchemical marriage (between Britomart and Artegall), becomes the 'Mercurian monarch' par excellence. Some of the political ideas in this view (eg, the 'king's two bodies' and the 'world emperor' as applied to Elizabeth/Astraea) can be documented, but the connection with an esoteric alchemical tradition (and hence this whole reading of the poem) remains speculative.

Any alchemical interpretation of *The Faerie Queene* as a whole is beset by several major problems. Alchemy was an occult activity whose chief secrets, so the alchemists always claimed, were transmitted orally from one adept to another. Secondly, alchemical texts, usually in the form of obscure allegories that freely appropriate religious and literary symbols, are (for the non-initiate) notoriously difficult to understand; even more tentative, then, must be any identification of arcane alchemical meanings in a complex work of literature that is itself eclectic and polyvalent. Further, a comprehensive alchemical 'reading' of *The Faerie Queene* would have to examine all episodes and images which are potentially alchemical and explain their relevance: such details as the killing by Arthur (a solar figure) of the brothers Pyrochles (fire) and Cymochles (water) so that Guyon can be reborn (see *FQ* ed 1977, notes to II iv 41 and xii 78), Chrysogone's impregnation by the sun (III vi 1–9), the *ouroboros* serpent (IV x 40, discussed by Brooks-Davies, but not in terms of alchemy; cf Taylor 1949:55 and Frye 1978:129), and the caduceus (whose alchemical significance goes beyond that suggested by Brooks-Davies; eg, see Martinus Rulandus the Elder 1612:344; Burland 1967:134, 162). Finally, if one finds alchemical motifs used positively (as even Frye does in the alchemical wedding), one must also account for the apparently negative associations of alchemical allusions elsewhere in the poem (for an attempt to reconcile opposing attitudes in Milton, see Lieb 1970: 229–44).

Given the esoteric nature of the subject, it is likely that a complete understanding of Spenser's imaginative use of alchemy will remain almost as elusive as the philosophers' stone itself. ROBERT M. SCHULER

For alchemy, both generally and in relation to Donne, Paracelsus, Digby, Starkey, and Jung, see Alan Pritchard 1980 *Alchemy: A Bibliography of English-Language Writings* (London). On Gohory, see D.P. Walker 1958:96–106. On Maier, see John Read 1936 *Prelude to Chemistry: An Outline of Alchemy, its Literature and Relationships* (London) pp 228–54. On alchemical poetry, see Robert M. Schuler, comp 1979 *English Magical and Scientific Poems to 1700: An Annotated Bibliography* (New York). On esoteric alchemy, see Schuler 1980 'Some Spiritual Alchemies of Seventeenth-Century England' *JHI* 41:293–318.

Brooks-Davies 1983; C.A. Burland 1967 *The Arts of the Alchemists* (London); Northrop Frye 1978 *Northrop Frye on Culture and Literature: A Collection of Review Essays* ed Robert D. Denham (Chicago); Heninger 1960; Walter M. Kendrick 1974 'Earth of Flesh, Flesh of Earth: Mother Earth in the *Faerie Queene*' *RenQ* 27:533–48; Michael Lieb 1970 *The Dialectics of Creation: Patterns of Birth and Regeneration in 'Paradise Lost'* (Amherst); Mulryan 1972; Robert J. Rockwood 1972 'Alchemical Forms of Thought in Book I of Spenser's *Faerie Queene*' diss Univ of Florida; Martinus Rulandus the Elder 1893 *A Lexicon of Alchemy* (1612) tr A.E. Waite (London); Robert M. Schuler, ed 1978 *Three Renaissance Scientific Poems*, *SP* Texts and Studies 75; Szönyi 1984; F. Sherwood Taylor 1951 *The Alchemists: Founders of Modern Chemistry* (New York); Patricia Thomson 1977 'A Precedent for Donne's "The Comparison"' *N&Q* 222:523–4; Julia M. Walker 1985 '"Advice Discrete": The Catalyst of Unity in Book I of *The Faerie Queene*' *SpN* 16:45–6.

Alciati, Andrea (1492–1550) In 1522, this renowned Italian professor of jurisprudence produced the first and most famous Renaissance emblem book – a manuscript of Latin epigrams describing things from history or nature and symbolizing things elegant and useful for painters, goldsmiths, or sculptors. He continued to add new emblems for subsequent editions printed during his lifetime until the number reached 212. At the time of Spenser's death in 1599, more than 100 editions had appeared, including translations in French, German, Italian, and Spanish. Spenser could have known any number of editions of Alciati's emblems, including those with Claude Mignault's commentary which were published by the Plantin press from 1573 on. Also he would have known the first full-scale English emblem book, Geoffrey Whitney's *Choice of Emblemes* (1586), which contained at least 87 adaptations of emblems by Alciati.

(See **Alciati** Fig 1.)

Alciati's 212 emblems (cited here from ed 1621) were useful for many poets, including Spenser (see *Var* index, Freeman 1948, Roche 1964, Nohrnberg 1976). *The Shepheardes Calender*, with its mottoes (here called 'emblemes'), woodcuts, and longer verses, reflects in form the emblematic triad. The fable of the Oak and the Briar in *Februarie* is reminiscent not only of Aesop and Chaucer but more especially of Alciati's Emblem 124, *In momentaneam felicitatem* [on momentary happiness]. In the *Visions of the Worlds Vanitie*, the account of the Eagle and the Scarabee (4) and of the ship whose course is stopped by the Remora (9) may be from Emblem 169, *A minimis quoque timendum* [even the smallest must be feared], and Emblem 83, *In facile a virtute desciscentes* [on those who deviate easily from virtue]. Indeed, the theme of the entire cycle may have been suggested by these two emblems.

The Faerie Queene abounds in examples of the ingenious ways in which Spenser adapted the emblematic method to epic form by using a full verbal description to replace the visual image with moral elucidation. Among the most striking examples are the images of Una (the true faith) seated on a 'lowly Asse' (I i 4) and of false Duessa (the Church of Rome) atop a seven-headed beast (vii 17); these correspond to Emblems 7, *Non tibi sed religioni* [not for you but for religion], and 6, *Ficta religio* [false religion]. VIRGINIA W. CALLAHAN

Alciati ed 1581; Alciati ed 1621; Henry Green 1872 *Andrea Alciati and Books of Emblems* (London); *Index Emblematicus* 1985 ed Peter M. Daly and Virginia W. Callahan, 2 vols (Toronto); Nohrnberg 1976.

Alençon François, Duc d'Alençon, and (from 1576) d'Anjou (1554–84). Catherine de' Medici first proposed the marriage of her youngest son to Queen Elizabeth early in 1572, after the failure of the previous negotiations for a match with his brother, the Duc d'Anjou (the future Henri III). The offer was renewed regularly during the following years, but neither Elizabeth nor the English council showed much interest in it. Their attitude changed in the summer of 1578, after Alençon had offered to assist the Netherlands in their revolt against Spain. If he were serious and could obtain the backing of Henri III, then it appeared to men as diverse as Lord Burghley and William of Orange that a marriage might be the means of forging an alliance between England and France to support the Dutch Revolt. Less enthusiastic were the Earl of Leicester and Sir Francis Walsingham, who had advocated an Anglo-Protestant intervention in the Netherlands the previous autumn. By 1579, the negotiations had proceeded sufficiently for Alençon to send his confidant Jehan de Simier to England, and then to arrive there himself (15 August).

What is surprising about the courtship is the extreme ardor exhibited by the ugly, pockmarked, 25-year-old Duke and the 45-year-old Queen, who may have viewed this as her last chance to bear children and so create a dynasty. Simier was the perfect courtier and master of love-play; remarkably astute in cultivating Elizabeth's confidence, he soon became her favorite. On one occasion, he stole her nightcap from her bedchamber and with her permission sent it to Alençon, who had already obtained her handkerchief. She bestowed on both Simier and Alençon nicknames, terms of endearment such as were reserved for her closest associates. Playing on his name, she called Simier her 'ape'; and on the basis of his appearance, Alençon became her 'frog.' Simier, in return, vowed to be 'the most faithful of her beasts' (Greenlaw 1932:114).

Elizabeth's desire to marry Alençon provoked widespread discontent and protest. Preachers found scriptural precedent to denounce it; ballads and pamphlets warned of its consequences. In May 1579, the privy council objected to the 'great confusion' that would be generated by the 'coming hither of Catholics, and above all Frenchmen, who were their ancient enemies.' In particular, English hostility to the match had been fueled by the slaughter of Huguenots in the St Bartholomew's Day Massacre (24 August 1572), which was widely believed to have been plotted by Alençon's mother. His own reputation as a religious moderate was discredited by his involvement in the execution of the surrendered Huguenot garrisons of La Charité and Issoire in the spring of 1577.

Affairs had become critical by the time Alençon stealthily arrived at court in 1579. Two attempts had been made to assassinate Simier, and rumor blamed Leicester. In retaliation, Simier informed the Queen that although the Earl objected to her marriage and pretended to be her disconsolate lover, he had secretly wedded her cousin Lettice Knollys, Countess of Essex, a year earlier on 21 September 1578. The Queen was said to have placed Leicester temporarily under house arrest, after contemplating sending him to the Tower. During August, the Puritan John Stubbs published *The Discoverie of a Gaping Gulf*, a vitriolic attack on the proposed marriage, for which he and his printer, Hugh Singleton, were sentenced to have their right hands cut off at a public ceremony in November 1579. At this time, Leicester's nephew Philip Sidney, perhaps at his uncle's insistence, wrote a letter to Elizabeth strongly urging her to abandon

Alençon. Sidney's absence from court during the first half of 1580 was probably a result of the disfavor he incurred for voicing this opinion.

It has been suggested that the *Shepheardes Calender* eclogues comment extensively on the French match (McLane 1961); but E.K.'s copious annotations and commendatory letter were finished by 10 April 1579, and no clear evidence exists for the theory that the *Calender* reflects political events concerning Alençon which developed several months later.

Virgils Gnat has been interpreted by Greenlaw (1910) as Spenser's explanation to Leicester (the shepherd) that he (the gnat) had merely tried to warn of the dangers posed by Alençon (a poisonous snake), for which he was discredited and dispatched to Ireland (the underworld). By this interpretation, the poet's warning would have been *Mother Hubberds Tale*, a political allegory probably first written in 1579 as a reaction to the French match, and revised in 1591 (shortly before publication in *Complaints*) to reflect Spenser's horror at the prospect of James' succession, currently being engineered by Burghley. Both periods of crisis left traces in the poem; but topical analysis of it as a commentary on the French match is complicated by the updated allusions of 1591, as well as by Spenser's extremely fluid method of historical allegory, whereby one character can represent different people, each defined by a specific context.

The Ape in *Mother Hubberd* appears to have been initially created in response to the Queen's pet name for Simier. At the beginning of the poem, he is a ruthless schemer who seeks advancement 'Abroad where change is' (101); later, he is the perfect model of the false courtier, skilled in 'thriftles games' and 'costly riotize' (794–810), as Simier was portrayed by his enemies. Other passages, however, reflect the revisions of 1591; and Robert Cecil, Burghley's son, becomes the target of Spenser's wit. The Ape who stands 'uprearing hy / Upon his tiptoes' (663–4), wearing 'an old Scotch cap' (209), now mimics the diminutive Cecil, a supporter of the Stuart succession.

The Fox of Spenser's beast fable also represents two historical figures in different contexts. At the beginning of the poem, Alençon is parodied not as a frog but as the wily fox of the Reynard cycle; in a satire of the Duke's ambition to seize his brother's throne and become King of France, the Fox voices a long complaint concerning his exclusion from 'our fathers heritage' (124–72), before resolving with the Ape to become 'Lords of the world.' But in most of the poem, the Fox strongly alludes to Burghley. When, for instance, the poet remarks that the Fox has 'loded' his children with so many 'lordships' that 'with the weight their backs nigh broken were' (1156–8), a reference to Robert Cecil's hunchback is likely.

In *The Faerie Queene*, Belphoebe's brief encounter with Trompart and Braggadocchio may provide a second glance at the French match, as Trompart (Simier) excessively praises his cowardly master (a crude parody of Alençon), only to see him spurned by Belphoebe (Elizabeth), who disdains his 'filthy lust.' Numerous similarities between Braggadocchio and Trompart (in II iii 21–46) and the Fox and Ape (in *MHT* 951–1018) may thus stem from a common source – the perception of Alençon and Simier as frightened, ineffectual braggarts. Before Braggadocchio meets Belphoebe, Archimago has promised to steal Arthur's sword for him (iii 18), just as the Fox and Ape purloin the sleeping lion's scepter and crown – 'those royall signes' (1016) signifying British rule. Belphoebe's subsequent meeting with Timias (Raleigh, Spenser's patron) contrasts the true courtier with his false counterpart (III v 28–50).

The Alençon courtship significantly affected Spenser's professional career. His dedicatory sonnet to the deceased Leicester in *Gnat*, declaring that he had been wronged, hints that the angry Earl had mistreated him. The plot of *Gnat* suggests that as a subordinate he had presumed to offer an unsolicited warning, which Leicester deemed impudent. When Spenser embarked for Ireland in August 1580 as Lord Grey's secretary, he may have felt remorse for opportunities that vanished along with Leicester's patronage, even as he resolved to make the best of his present life 'In savadge soyle, far from Parnasso mount' (*FQ* Grey Sonn). It seems unlikely that Leicester terminated Spenser's service merely because he had indiscreetly satirized Burghley, Alençon, and Simier in the early version of *Mother Hubberd*. That theory is based in large measure on the mistaken premise that the poem was 'called-in' after creating a scandal in 1579; rather, it was suppressed in 1591, the year of its publication (see **Complaints*; *Var* 8:580–5). However, *Mother Hubberd* was presented as having been written 'long sithens ... in the raw conceipt of my youth' (*MHT* epistle); and it does epitomize the kind of outspoken support that Leicester spurned, so it may have contributed to Spenser's Irish exile. The threat to the nation that Spenser perceived in Elizabeth's marriage to Alençon gave rise to a fable of deposition, linked to an invasion by 'a warlike equipage / Of forreine beasts' (1118–19). When revising the poem for publication in 1591, he apparently saw the same danger posed by James and his retainers.

JAMES P. BEDNARZ

Doris Adler 1979 'The Riddle of the Sieve: The Siena Sieve Portrait of Queen Elizabeth' *RenP 1978* pp 1–10; Adler 1981 'Imaginary Toads in Real Gardens' *ELR* 11:235–60; Greenlaw 1910; W.T. MacCaffrey 1981; Conyers Read 1925 *Mr Secretary Walsingham and the Policy of Queen Elizabeth* 3 vols (Oxford) ch 2, 5, and 8; John Stubbs 1968 *John Stubbs's 'Gaping Gulf' with Letters and Other Relevant Documents* ed Lloyd E. Berry (Charlottesville, Va).

alexandrine The twelve-syllable line (six-stressed in English verse), as basic to French poetry as iambic pentameter to English, was named for the twelfth-century *Roman d'Alexandre*. Its use in concluding the *Faerie Queene* stanza, as well as elsewhere in his work, made it almost a Spenserian trademark, and its subsequent deployment in English poetry seems ever conscious of this. In early Tudor verse – as a pair of trimeters run together – it constituted the first line of the rhyming couplet form called by Gascoigne the 'poulter's measure.' It was first independently used by Surrey in a psalm translation and, as an occasional variation, in his important blank-verse Englishing of *Aeneid* 4 (pub 1554). The first original poem to use it is Turbervile's *Of Ladie Venus* (1567). Sidney frequently employs alexandrines in the *Old Arcadia*, as well as in the opening sonnet, and five subsequent ones, of *Astrophil and Stella*.

Spenser's first alexandrine is apparently inadvertent, in a translation from Marot in *Theatre for Worldlings*: interestingly, it embodies – as if in an over-determined slip – another Spenserian trademark. It describes nymphs 'That sweetely in accorde did tune their voice / Unto the gentle sounding of the waters fall' (epigram 4). Its first avowed use in Spenser is, characteristically, at a moment of closure, at the end of *Januarye* of *The Shepheardes Calender* (it also occurs as the first line of each stanza of the lament in *November*). Alexandrine couplets are used to close the whole of the *Calender*, in the verse envoy ('Loe I have made a Calender for every yeare') which recasts the 144 syllables of the 6 tetrameter triplets of the opening invocation ('Goe little booke') into 144 syllables in 6 alexandrine couplets, reinforcing a sense of modality of closure in the 12-syllable line. Also the 12 lines each of 12 syllables make 144, the measure of a man in the wall of the New Jerusalem (Rev 21.17).

It is this mode which is engaged in the *Faerie Queene* stanza. Here, the final alexandrine is used in such a wealth of ways as to suggest a synecdoche of the variation in structure, tone, and function of the stanza form itself, described so elegantly by Empson (1947:33). The alexandrine can be divided syntactically into 6 + 6 syllables to frame opposition, contrast, or parallels, or 4 + 4 + 4 to envelop some triad or narrational unfolding; it calls attention to its own summary and fundamental nature, as in 'The gentle warbling wind low answered to all' (II xii 71) at the end of the famous and widely imitated stanza about the music in the Bower of Bliss. It can become more or less transparent or opaque as its internal structure, like that of the whole stanza, is locally made more or less apparent.

When successive stanzas are used as strophes in an inset lyric, the alexandrine can seem more refrainlike. The great refrain of *Epithalamion* (variations on 'sing / That all the woods may answer and your eccho ring') manifests the skill with which Spenser pulls the alexandrine together (rather than allowing the disjunction between two trimeters to point up antithesis). The fourth foot has the less prominently stressed 'and' which tends to break down such a division at the same time that the paired terms 'answer' and 'eccho' might tend to enforce the binary structure.

The recognition of Spenser's imprint on the alexandrine, particularly as an instrument of closure in a pentametric context, is evident not only in the work of his immediate followers but, in the wake of Dryden's use of it in occasional triplets, well into the eighteenth century. JOHN HOLLANDER

John Hollander 1988 *Melodious Guile: Fictive Pattern in Poetic Language* (New Haven) pp 164–79.

---

allegory (Gr *allēgoria* other speaking) An allegory is a fiction told in such a way as to indicate, by 'aptly suggestive resemblance' (*OED*), a clear structure of nonfictional ideas. It is presented, therefore, as being secondary to a meaning that the reader must try to recover by engaging the text in interpretative play.

Allegory differs from the related forms, parable and fable, by including in its narrative conspicuous directions for interpretation (such as naming the serpent of *FQ* I i 18 'Errour'). Whereas in parable or fable we are offered a complete (and sometimes surprising) interpretation when the story is over, in allegory we find only the iconic rudiments of an interpretation we must build for ourselves, within certain constraints, as we proceed. This has two important consequences: it allows an allegorical narrative to develop at much greater length, and it promotes a sustained interaction between reader and text that has many of the features of a game.

Letter to Raleigh In describing *The Faerie Queene* as a 'continued Allegory, or darke conceit' (Letter to Raleigh), Spenser joins two distinct notions of allegory derived from antiquity, one having its origin in the technical analysis of figures of speech, the other in philosophical interpretations of Homer.

According to the first, or rhetorical, notion, allegory is defined as a metaphor carried on at unusual length, as when troubles in the state are described in terms of a ship in a storm. Its proper pleasure is in recognizing clearly how each thing in a narrative wittily corresponds to some other thing in its meaning. Thus Puttenham writes, in *The Arte of English Poesie* (1589), '*Allegoria* is when we do speake in sence translative and wrested from the owne signification, neverthelesse applied to another not altogether contrary [which would be *irony*], but having much conveniencie with it' (3.18). This account is closely modeled upon that of Quintilian (1st century AD), whose famous definition of allegory as 'continued metaphor' Puttenham repeats (*Institutio oratoria* 9.2.46; cf 8.6.44).

According to the second, or hermeneutic, notion (Gr *hermēneia* interpretation), allegory is seen as a code by which philosophical and spiritual ideas are hidden in mythical tales: 'there are many mysteries contained in poetry,' Sidney confides, 'which of purpose were written darkly, lest by profane wits it should be abused' (*Defence*, ed 1973b:121). Here the proper pleasure is in obscurity, sublimity, and fullness: the sense that the truth beyond the veil of narrative would not be sufficiently valued unless gotten with effort (Augustine *De doctrina christiana* 2.6.8); that this truth, at its highest, is incomprehensible except through indirect images and tales (Dante *Epistolae* 10.29, ed 1966:193); and that no interpretation can state the meaning in full because the truth of the book is, finally, the truth of the world (Boccaccio *Genealogia* 14.10, 12, 17).

Because Spenser's phrase 'continued Allegory, or darke conceit' recapitulates traditional ideas of allegory that are themselves in need of critical analysis, it should be taken not as an objective description of the poem before us but rather as an indication of how the poet would like us to respond. Spenser is not telling us how to classify his poem: he is telling us how to enjoy it.

To see allegory in the terms proposed in this article, as a game designed by the writer and played by the reader, will elucidate another remark in the Letter: that *The Faerie Queene* is intended to 'fashion' its reader in 'vertuous and gentle discipline.' The reader is to be morally changed not just by seeing examples of admirable conduct but by becoming engaged, through the play of interpretation, in the theory of virtue. Spenser's allegorical writing, like Dante's, fashions an intellectual habit.

interpretative play Traditionally, critics have set out to define what allegory *is* in isolation from how it is engaged by a reader; and they have sought, in consequence, to locate its doubleness of sense inside the text. Even Coleridge thinks of the allegorical text as controlling two carefully articulated lines of development: one set forth explicitly as narrative addressed to the eye while the other, having primary authority, is 'folded in,' or implied, by analogies addressed to the mind. Such a definition tries to be more objective than it is here possible to be. For by focusing on the work in itself, and its presumably inflexible meaning, the most salient feature of allegory is ignored: its deliberate and continuous provocation of what has been called 'the restructuring of the text by each reader' (Honig 1959:29).

Although we are expected to think of the 'darke conceit' as a presence hidden inside the text, more detached analysis will show that it is a convention or rule governing information around a circuit: the narrative is accompanied by iconic details suggesting a deeper meaning inside it, these details are used by the reader to incorporate other elements of the narrative into a comprehensive structure of meaning, and this structure is in turn modified and enriched by further reading. Thus it seems as if the reader, by reorganizing the experience of the narrative into a more coherent pattern of ideas, draws closer to truth while reading further.

The illusion that the meaning of an allegory resides somewhere inside its text is most persuasive, however, when the range of possible interpretations is narrow. For this reason, allegorical poets often will begin with a fairly obvious conceit so that we will imagine an objective meaning throughout, even when we cannot see what it is. Langland, for instance, tells a fable of rats who discuss hanging a bell on the cat, but tells it in such a way that we recognize easily his political subject ('Prologue' 146–207). Spenser likewise keys our expectations of *The Faerie Queene* as a whole by showing, in its first episode, a knight and a woman-serpent engaged in a struggle that can easily be interpreted as the conflict of holiness and spiritual error.

Episodes such as these may persuade us, by extension, that a work conceals inside itself a clear train of thought that is carried through from beginning to end. In complex allegories, notably those of Dante and Spenser, we seem to be directed, through the process of interpretation, toward a point where all mystery is dispelled in the presence of truth. But what we encounter instead is a point where all further progress is blocked by the inadequacy of language to express something that is always beyond it. It is here that the allegorical poet will stage the breakdown of language into paradox (*FQ* VII vii 13) or will insist that to get past the barrier it is necessary to resort to 'shadowy prefaces' (*Paradiso* 30.78) directing the mind of the reader beyond them. Such images are presented as the steps of a ladder that will be discarded when we have climbed it. Thus the effect of 'secondariness' which is cultivated by allegory is at once sublime (because we seem to participate in the essence of meaning) and frustrating (because we cannot express it).

The existence of an ineffable center of meaning where all interpretations seem to converge is something that the reader is encouraged to accept in order to enjoy the process of trying to get there. Even in cases where the meaning is clear, as in satirical allegories such as Swift's *Tale of a Tub*, Arbuthnot's *History of John Bull*, or Addison's allegory of true and false wit (*Spectator* 63), what gives pleasure is the opportunity of playing with the terms of the comparison, and not the prospect of discarding the narrative once we have laid bare its hidden kernel of truth. While the object of chess is to checkmate the opponent's king, the purpose of the game is rigorous, combinative play – which is a fair description also of how an allegory compels us to read. To engage in this sort of play we must enter into a *convention of secondariness* wherein it is assumed that the allegorical text exists only to reach toward something outside its reach.

three distinctions Any narrative, from the Song of Solomon to *Alice in Wonderland*, may be made to mean something other than itself by fanciful interpretation, even when its author could not possibly have intended, or understood, the new meaning. Some narratives, however, are written to encourage readers to interpret in a particular way: hence the first distinction between *allegorical reading* and *allegorical writing*.

The second distinction shows the two aspects of *allegorical writing*: *allegory as convention*, where an entire work is presented as being secondary to a meaning that is always outside it, and *allegory as trope*, a more limited, rhetorical device forming the texture of narrative in allegorical works. Allegorical tropes can appear also in works, such as the epics of Homer and Virgil, that are not allegorical throughout. Typical kinds of allegorical tropes are personified abstractions such as Furor in the *Aeneid* (1.294), extended metaphors such as the lame Prayers who come after swift-footed Atē, or Madness (*Iliad* 9.502), and significant buildings such as Spenser's house of Alma (*FQ* II ix).

The third distinction separates *allegory as convention* into *allegorical rhetoric* and *allegorical aesthesis*. *Allegorical rhetoric* includes everything a writer may do to make the reader interpret the narrative in a particular way. *Allegorical aesthesis* describes how that process of interpretation actually works in the reader, who translates the narrative into conceptual form.

1
allegory
2
a) allegorical reading b) allegorical writing
3
a) allegory as trope b) allegory as convention
a) rhetoric (sender) b) aesthesis (receiver)
allegorization of non-allegorical works (Homer; Song of Songs)
interpretation as intended effect

In practice it is hard to make *allegorical rhetoric* and *allegorical aesthesis* stand clearly apart because the distinction between them accounts only crudely for what is really an uninterrupted circuit of play between reader and text. A gap in the text – between, for instance, the image of a serpent vomiting books and the notion of theological error – is first taken out of the narrative by the reader and then reconstituted abstractly as an opposition between a sign and its meaning. In so doing, the reader is sensitized to a new gap that has been opened between this interpretative opposition and the rest of the narrative from which it has been taken. The reader therefore uses that opposition to absorb further experience of the text into a larger structure of meaning wherein no gap or inconsistency between narrative and truth will be felt. Yet while the goal of interpretation is to eradicate all signifying difference in a motionless ideal, the very work of moving toward that ideal opens more spaces than it can close. The true purpose, therefore, of that increasingly problematic structure of meaning which we accumulate as we read is not to capture the truth but to engage us in further, and more powerful, interpretative play.

This is most apparent in allegories like *The Faerie Queene* and Dante's *Divine Comedy*, which provide more scope and flexibility for the process of interaction between reader and text. By introducing traditional ideas and symbols into the narrative and leaving precise relations between them unstated, several broad contexts of meaning are offered within which the reader may construct several interpretations of the same passage; and for any or all of these responses the reader will find confirmation by reading further. It thus becomes possible to think that there are, beneath the surface of the text, discrete levels of meaning that will eventually converge on the truth.

To understand how allegory works as an imaginative system – that is, to construct a *poetics* of allegory – we must detach ourselves from this belief in a definitive meaning so that we can observe from outside how it regulates the loop of interpretative play. In short, we are concerned not with the truth of the belief but with how it works as a convention.

allegory as convention When an allegorical trope appears in a nonallegorical work, its purpose is to clarify an argument (as in the fable of the belly in Livy 2.32.9) or to intensify our perception of something described. In the *Iliad* (4.440), a personification of enmity (Eris) strides between the armies as they move to attack; and though she is small when we first see her, as the space narrows between the armies she grows larger until her head strikes the sky.

There is nothing ambiguous about this, and no reason to hold the image in mind as we read further. By intensifying our experience of the narrative at one point, it has done its job. This is not the case, however, in allegorical works where it seems as if every image or trope, however clear in itself, communicates mysteriously with all the rest in bending toward truth. In such works there seem to be two kinds of meaning: that which can be deciphered at any point in the text, and that to which all such localized meanings incline.

In Guillaume de Lorris' portion of the *Romance of the Rose*, for example, the significance of each of the arrows that the God of Love shoots at the narrator is clearly explained; yet we are told shortly after that the work as a whole is a mystery with a *senefiance* (significance) that is not to be revealed until the conclusion: 'The sothfastnesse that now is hid, / Without coverture shal be kid [shown] / Whann I undon have this dremyng, / Wherynne no word is of lesyng [falsehood]' (lines 2071–4 in ed 1965–70; tr Chaucer, lines 2171–4). In Jean de Meun's continuation we are told the same thing – that the poet will 'gloss' and 'expound' the meaning of his text at the end – even as we find allegorical tropes that are easily deciphered as the stages of seduction (15,115–23, 15,291–430 in ed 1965–70): Franchise (bold forwardness), carrying a shield escutcheoned with promises and a lance sharpened with sweet imploring, beats back all resistance from Dangier (forbidding coldness). And when we finally reach the conclusion, which is transparently bawdy, the promised revelation turns out to be not a disclosure but another sequence of images – the pilgrim trying to push his staff into a small hole in the shrine – pointing to a reality outside the text.

The specifically literary aspect of Jean de Meun's wit is lost on us if we fail to appreciate this conclusion as a parody of the circumstances in which allegories typically end (the greatest example, from our point of view, being Dante's *Divine Comedy*). For in such endings, instead of being offered a disclosure of what all the previous signs mean, we are confronted with a new collocation of symbols indicating that the truth to which they point is too sublime ever to be apprehended directly. Jean de Meun's conclusion points to an act that we recognize but that propriety rather than mystery forbids him to describe openly. Thus while preserving the formal structure of an allegorical conclusion, he reverses its affect so that the transcendental signified is no longer ineffably sublime but unspeakably carnal. In a purely structural sense, there is little difference between this and the sequence of astonishing visions with which Dante's *Paradiso* is brought to an end. In both, the promised end remains outside the work, even though it seems as if we have come through a labyrinth of signs to a point where the gap of 'secondariness' between the work and its referent is asymptotically small.

It is precisely this irreducible 'secondariness' that makes the reading of allegory more active than what we normally experience in other narrative forms, such as romance or epic. For there is an intriguing connection, as we can see in the novels of Thomas Pynchon, between allegory and paranoia: both cause us to build a network of connections behind a visible array of unconnected things. We may refer to this impulse as *hermeneutic anxiety*, the feeling that superficially independent events are wired together under the narrative surface and that it is the business of the interpreter to discover the connections between them.

Allegorical writers often will arouse this anxiety by expressing contempt for anyone who finds the enigma hard to decode (*FQ* II proem 4). But the division of the audience into those who understand and those who do not is really a division inside the experience of each reader, who feels at some moments as if the play of signifiers will never find its end in the presence of truth and at other moments as if it may be possible finally to draw back the veil and grasp what is hidden behind it.

This dialectic is kept in motion by the complementary relationship, in *allegory as convention*, between rhetorical stimulus and aesthetic response. It is not a case of the interpreter recapturing something already thought out by the poet, but of engaging the system of meaning that the poet has made.

The reader might suspect an occult correspondence, for instance, between the 'Rich strond' on which Marinell is wounded and the seashore to which Florimell is driven several cantos later, even though no specific connection between them is indicated in the text (Hamilton in *FQ* ed 1977, note on III vii 25). And when the reader has made enough connections of this kind a structure of meaning will seem to emerge from behind the narrative surface. But there is no authoritative structure, worked out in advance by the poet, against which any interpretation might be tested to see how close it comes to the truth. The poet instead uses allegorical rhetoric to suggest contexts of meaning (holiness, temperance, chastity, etc) within which the interpretative game can be played. Thus, while specific interpretations cannot represent what the poet intended to mean, they do represent what the poet intended his readers to do.

The commentaries by Kenelm Digby and Upton on the numerological stanza describing the house of Alma at *FQ* II ix 22 are good examples of how allegory as convention sets up a dynamic interaction between reader and text. It is clear from the stanza itself – a tour de force of allegorical rhetoric – that Spenser has created the conditions of meaning which are then actualized in ways he could not have foreseen. For while both commentators assume that what they find in the text has been put there beforehand, what in fact they are doing is engaging a rhetorical system in learned, readerly play.

mental space To read is to follow a sequence of words through time and to construct, as one reads, a unified idea of the whole. But because this process is largely unconscious, we tend to think of the unity we build into narratives as being inherent in them. Only when a plot is poorly organized, or extravagantly diffuse, is it necessary for the reader deliberately to subordinate inessential detail in order to follow the story.

Allegorical narrative is unusual in this respect because it intentionally violates our sense of causal relations and natural setting – our sense, that is, of the believably real – and forces us to unify what we read according to some other standard: we search for its meaning. Hence allegorical narratives are often, in Aristotelian terms, badly constructed: paratactic, digressive, episodic, and replete with iconographic details that have nothing to do with the story. Yet it is precisely this operational disorder that allows us to construct any number of meanings.

For this reason, a complex allegorical work is likely to offer some rudimentary gestalt that we can use to direct the otherwise unlimited freedom of interpretative play. The most sophisticated example of this is in the *Divine Comedy*, where the reader is prompted to construct an elaborate spatial model so that the experience of reading may be organized into a pattern that makes interpretative sense. Although this is not true to the same extent of *The Faerie Queene*, we *are* made to feel as if its action is taking place within a comprehensive, spatial design: the unfolding of twelve quests from a center at Cleopolis, to which everything refers back for its meaning.

When we examine Spenser's allegorical rhetoric more closely, we can see that it is designed to provoke the reader, at every level, to conceptualize spatially a narrative experienced in time. Redcrosse's adventures with Error and Archimago, for instance, fall out of sequence to arrange themselves laterally as opposite evils: open heresy on the one side, devious hypocrisy on the other. Orgoglio's dungeon is situated by the reader not before the Mount of Contemplation, but beneath it, thus making a contrast between purified vision and the blindness of ignorant pride.

Allegorical places, such as the house of Holiness and the house of Pride, the gardens of Adonis and Acrasia, Mount Acidale and Gloriana's court, break free of sequence and pair off in the mind as binary conceits; and the train of events through which these places are joined becomes peripheral commentary on them. Even when we come down to the level of diction, Spenser's use of orthographic signifiers, iconic names, and complicated puns encourages us to read the words semantically 'inward' (as we must, more radically, in *Finnegans Wake*), instead of attending exclusively to their syntactic purpose of advancing the narrative line (see Craig 1959 and 1967, Quilligan 1979).

These effects are processed by the mind in such a way that it seems as if every part of the work eventually can be coordinated with every other in one complex, synchronic design. Yet even at this stage, the existence of difference as a necessary component of structure gives the impression that the truth remains incomplete: the full significance of any part cannot be known without understanding the whole, which in turn is unknowable without knowing the parts.

This dilemma, known to modern critics as the 'hermeneutic circle,' causes the reader to imagine its resolution in a centered and luminous point where the mind can enter completely into what it has sought and where no further interpretation is necessary, or possible, because all signifying difference is gone. The Neoplatonists, with whom allegorical poets have much in common, call this point, simply, the One; and Dante describes it, with characteristic precision, as a point into which the scattered leaves of the universe are gathered. (In religious allegory, the image of the heavenly Jerusalem is traditionally the threshold to this point of truth.) We may call it the *singularity*.

It has been noted, however, that our response to this interpretative endgame is contained by an economy of rapture and frustration, since we cannot express the truth we think we have found. This is registered by the poets themselves, who emphasize the difference between their encounter with the presence of meaning and the 'colourd showes' with which they are compelled to express it (*FQ* III proem; Dante *Paradiso* 1.1–12, 33.121–45). When we think of the singularity as if it were behind the surface of the text, and direct all lines of interpretation toward it, its effect is not unlike that of the 'vanishing point' in linear perspective: we feel that we are not so much following a sequence of words as penetrating into the center.

from interpretation to practice It is natural to think of *allegorical reading* as a symmetrical reversal of *allegorical writing*, where the interpreter simply loosens the knot the poet has tied. In fact, allegorical interpretation, chiefly of the Homeric epics, began well in advance of any sustained allegorical works and played a significant role in their emergence.

The earliest allegorical interpretations of Homer were made in roughly the same period that literacy became pervasive in Greece. By mapping an elegantly limited system of graphic signs onto the acoustic field, writing made it possible to think of a text as containing, inside its visible letters, an invisible but infinitely more various and meaningful sound. From this distinction of sign and breath, where the breath is authentic and the sign its derived and imperfect container, it is natural to proceed to a distinction between the 'outer shell' of the story (now referred to, by analogy, as its 'literal' meaning) and the hidden truth, or 'undermeaning' (*hyponoia*), that the author really intended.

Allegorization of nonallegorical works arose when this conception of a poem as a 'text' – a collection of secondary marks referring to a presence inside it – worked together with the natural tendency of people to make earlier works of literature relevant to present concerns. And because these concerns were, broadly speaking, scientific and moral, many events in the Homeric poems were given scientific or ethical meanings. Thus the adultery of Ares and Aphrodite, which is exposed when they are caught in the net of Hephaestus, was interpreted as an allegory of the divine creator binding the forces of opposition and concord in the net of the logos.

Like the *Aeneid* for its medieval interpreters, the Homeric epics were seen, through the veil of allegory, as providing a complete education. Homer thus became all things to all readers: a physicist, a Stoic, a Pythagorean, a Neoplatonist, even an oracle to Byzantine Christians for whom Odysseus at the mast was a figure of Christ on the Cross. It is from this tradition of encyclopedic commentary on the Homeric epics (and eventually on the Scriptures and the poems of Virgil and Ovid) that allegorical works derived their claim 'to give us all knowledge' (Sidney ed 1973b:121). Early examples are Macrobius' *Commentary on the Dream of Scipio* (late 4th to early 5th c AD) and Martianus Capella's *Marriage of Mercury and Philology* (5th c AD), the latter being an allegorical treatise on the seven liberal arts that had many imitators, from Alanus de Insulis in the *Anticlaudianus* (12th c) to Hawes in the *Pastime of Pleasure*. While the greatest encyclopedic descendant of Martianus' work is the *Divine Comedy*, we can see the influence of this drive for complete mental structures in

Spenser's idea of organizing his poem according to the twelve private moral virtues.

An important factor in the birth of Christian hermeneutics, and therefore of Christian allegorical poetry, was the influence of Homeric hermeneutics on the interpretation of the Hebrew Scriptures by Philo Judaeus, who in turn influenced Origen, the first important Christian interpreter of Scripture. Origen used the methods of the interpreters of the poets to read the Old Testament, seeing the story of Eden, for instance, not as literally true but as an allegory of the original state of the soul before it is tainted by sin in the world. It is this application to the Bible of an Hellenic exegetical method that produced the Christian tradition of meaning.

Although ancient interpreters found several kinds of meaning in the Homeric poems (moral, cosmological, philosophical, and mystical), the idea that a narrative might conceal several distinct but related meanings was slow to develop. It is indicated in Servius' commentary on Virgil's *Aeneid* (late 4th or early 5th c), where the word *polysemus* ('having many significations') is used to describe how Virgil's narrative works (ed 1878–87, 1:6). But Servius does not pursue this in the commentary itself, even though he claims that the mysteries of the philosophers, the theologians, and the Egyptians are unified allegorically in *Aeneid* 6 (2:1). Although its roots are to be found in Stoic hermeneutics, Alexandrian Neoplatonism, and Hebrew prophecy, the idea of an organized structure of meaning operating through different but logically related senses would appear to be a Christian achievement. It is to be found in one of the most remarkable and influential examples of allegorical interpretation: the commentary on Genesis in Augustine's *Confessions* (late 4th c), where it is said that God has given us not only the power to express one idea in several ways but also to understand in several ways that which has been obscurely delivered in one (13.24).

The allegorical interpretation of pagan myths had been active for about a millennium before what is traditionally regarded as the first thoroughgoing allegory appeared: Prudentius' *Psychomachia* (late 4th or early 5th c). The old assumptions that were used (and would continue to be used for Virgil and Ovid) to justify fanciful interpretations of nonallegorical works eventually influenced the poets themselves to become the basis of a new kind of imaginative writing – one in which the work is presented as being secondary to a truth that is somewhere beyond it.

early allegories Although ancient authors wrote no extended, allegorical narratives, they produced many allegorical tropes that influenced medieval and Renaissance authors. There are philosophical myths in the Platonic dialogues (which Ficino and the Neoplatonists imagined to be rich in hidden significance), political allegories in the comedies of Aristophanes, personified abstractions such as Power and Madness in the Greek tragedians, and a poem by Alcaeus describing the state under the figure of a ship in rough seas. This last was imitated by Horace (*Odes* 1.14) in a version cited by Quintilian (*Institutio oratoria* 8.6.44) and has since been the standard rhetorical example of allegory.

The most notable example of an allegory from the pre-Christian era is a narrative by Prodicus of Ceos (reported in Xenophon *Memorabilia* 2.1.21), in which the young Heracles must choose between two maidens personifying Virtue and Pleasure. This is carried over into Latin literature in a close imitation by Silius Italicus (*Punica* 15.18–128), although the choice now is given to Scipio. In general, however, the main contribution of ancient writers to the later allegorical tradition was in the nature of instantiated universals such as – to choose examples from the early Christian era – Boethius' Lady Philosophy, Statius' hall of Sleep (*Thebaid* 10.84–117), and Claudian's goddess of Nature (*De consulatu Stilichonis* 2.424–48). One significant exception is the more elaborate, and in some respects strikingly medieval, allegory of life presented in the 'Tablet of Cebes' (1st c AD).

In the Hebrew Scriptures, the most notable allegorical tropes are the image of Israel as a vine in Psalm 80 (cf John 15.1–6) and the allegory of the giant of metals in Daniel 2.31–5. The latter is a complex political allegory that is transformed brilliantly by Dante into the Old Man of Crete (*Inferno* 14.94–120) and skillfully adjusted to new political circumstances by Gower in the prologue to his *Confessio Amantis*. (See also Judges 9.8, 2 Kings 14.9.)

Although the *Psychomachia* is traditionally regarded as the earliest allegory, a case could be made for the Book of Revelation (late 1st c) because it deliberately engages the reader in interpretative play by presenting itself as a mysterious text. The influence of this work on the later allegorical tradition (including Prudentius) is complex and profound, and its imagery pervades every major allegorical work up to Bunyan's *Pilgrim's Progress* in the seventeenth century.

One interesting feature of Revelation that occurs in many later allegorical visions, such as Addison's 'Vision of Mirzah' (*Spectator* 159) and Johnson's 'Vision of Theodore' (ed 1825, 9:162–75), is the presence in the work of two figures: a narrator interpreting the things that he sees and a guide (in Revelation, an angel) who helps him to decode the symbols. (The most famous guides of this kind in allegorical literature are Virgil and Beatrice in the *Divine Comedy*.) The dialogue that takes place between narrator and guide suggests to the reader a range of interpretations that is authorized (and limited) from inside the text, thus providing the reader with a model of how to respond.

The title of the *Psychomachia* means a battle of virtues and vices for the soul, an idea that is probably derived from psychological interpretations of the Homeric *theomachia*, or 'battle of the gods,' in *Iliad* 20. Set battles of this kind between figures such as Chastity and Lust become, after Prudentius, a permanent fixture of allegorical writing as late as Phineas Fletcher's *Purple Island* and Bunyan's *Holy War*. But it is the conclusion of the *Psychomachia* that shows most clearly how this work differs from the allegorical tendencies of poets such as Claudian. Having defeated the vices, the virtues build for the soul a temple that is modeled on the heavenly Jerusalem of Revelation; and the poem then moves to its close in a sequence of increasingly mystical images that suggests we are penetrating into the center of truth. This effect of mystical penetration at the conclusion characterizes later allegorical writing with remarkable consistency, and is achieved with unsurpassed force at the end of the *Divine Comedy*. In Spenser, it occurs at the end of the *Cantos of Mutabilitie* and can also be felt in moments of interpretative centering such as the house of Holiness, the Garden of Adonis, and the dance of the Graces on Mount Acidale.

Prudentius' achievement – the composition of a full-scale allegory in which all of the parts seem to refer to a single, transcendent presence – is a reflection of the larger achievement of his age. For medieval Christendom, everything in nature could be thought of as part of a book written by God, in which the smallest detail is engaged in the larger signifying movement of the whole toward the original Word. The assumptions necessary for the allegorical interpretation of Homer and Virgil had expanded to become, in effect, a complete metaphysics wherein a habit of thought previously restricted to texts became a system for reading the world.

In these circumstances, it was natural for poets to imitate the divine creator by implying that there is a logos, or originative presence, behind the literal surface, and that it may be approached only by interpreting the signs of the text. Allegorical literature flourished, therefore, in a remarkable variety of forms from celestial journeys, such as Alanus' *Anticlaudianus*, to a 'bestiary of love' by Richart de Fournival.

biblical exegesis Biblical interpretation influenced allegorical writers in two ways: it generated a rich store of traditional images carrying widely familiar interpretations (images used with extraordinary originality by Dante, Langland, and Spenser), and it reinforced those general assumptions about texts that are necessary to allegory as convention. A gigantic biblical commentary, such as the *Glossa ordinaria*, by extracting innumerable and unexpected meanings from apparently simple stories, establishes a normative conception of how serious texts are to be read.

The central idea of biblical interpretation is that history follows a symbolic plan organized by God: events recorded in the Old Testament have been made to happen so as to foreshadow incidents in the life of Christ as these are set down in the New Testament. Abraham's sacrifice of a ram instead of his son, Isaac, thus is a *type* (Gr *typos* stamp) of the crucifixion where Jesus (the *antitype*) is the victim who suffers in place of mankind. St Paul actually uses the word *allegory* ('Which things are an allegory' KJV) to describe how Isaac and Ishmael – one born to a slave-woman, the other born free – symbolize the difference between the economies of law and grace (Gal 4.24). It should be noted that *typology* is a procedure of interpretation that was devised for reasons not unlike those that gave rise to Homeric hermeneutics: to incorporate texts into a structure of meaning quite alien to what their authors could have intended. 'What is Plato,' asked Numenius the Pythagorean, 'but Moses speaking Attic Greek?' (Clement of Alexandria *Stromata* 1.22.150).

Medieval interpreters included these typological relations in a more complex structure of levels explained in the mnemonic distich cited in the prefaces to the *Glossa ordinaria*: 'Littera gesta docet, quid credas allegoria, / Moralis quid agas, quo tendas anagogia' ('The *letter* teaches the events, the *allegory* what you should believe, the *moral* [sense] what you should do, the *anagogy* where you are headed' *PLat* 113: cols 28c and 33c; Lubac 1959–64, 1:23).

All three levels beyond the literal are called *allegorical* in a general sense. But the typological relation between Old Testament events and their fulfillment in Jesus ('those things which are to be believed under the new law,' as Nicholas of Lyra puts it in the *Glossa ordinaria*), is accounted for on the *allegorical* level strictly so-called. The *moral* or *tropological* level works in the same way as ancient moralizations of Homer (the drunken Noah as the intemperate man), instructing us in the conduct of life without reference to history. Finally we have the *anagogical* ('going up') or, as it sometimes is called, the *eschatological* level ('last' or 'highest things'), which refers to what Nicholas calls 'those things that are to be hoped for in the future state of blessedness.' Here the temporal character of the system is resumed as events in the text are referred forward now not to the ministry and Passion of Jesus but to his second coming at the Apocalypse. Thus the last book of the Bible, Revelation, discloses the highest level of meaning.

A passage frequently interpreted according to the fourfold scheme is the crossing of the Red Sea by the Israelites and the destruction of Pharaoh's army when it tries to follow. Literally it is an event in the history of God's people; allegorically it prefigures the baptism of Christ in the desert; morally it is the triumph of virtue over an army of sins; and anagogically it typifies, as part of the quest for the Promised Land, the entry of the elect into Jerusalem, when the sea gives up its dead. (For Dante's application of the four levels to the exodus from Egypt, see the *Epistle to Can Grande*, *Epistolae* 10.7, ed 1966:173, here assumed to be authentic; for an important discussion of the significance of the order of levels, see Lubac 1:168–9; *Bible.)

Typology has been seen by some modern scholars not only as a handy system of interpretative contexts but as a procedure of composition actually followed by poets who 'imitate,' in a phrase adopted from Hugh of St Victor, 'God's way of writing' (Singleton 1965:112). Even for interpretative purposes, however, the medieval application of levels was haphazard and inconsistent – more so, perhaps, than in its modern adherents (Tuve 1966:3). It is one thing to say that typology influenced the poets in the two general ways mentioned (ie, by creating a store of images and by conditioning attitudes to texts); it is something else again to say that the poets followed its logic implicitly.

Such claims have been made most vigorously for Dante, who does indeed indicate, in the *Epistle to Can Grande*, that the *Divine Comedy* should be read in this way (though it is surely suspicious that to demonstrate this he cites from his poem a quotation of Scripture). What Dante intends to supply in this epistle, however, is a general framework of meaning, a gestalt for coordinating on a large scale the complex play of associations that the poem calls forth. Yet the fourfold system has sometimes been supposed to be a much more specific exegetical technique providing the key to each episode in turn (R. Hollander 1969:51). Reading the *Divine Comedy* is not so conveniently managed.

Another modern use of the term *typology*, and one that bears more directly on Spenser, is to denote any relationship where signifier and signified are held apart by time. To call Britomart a 'type' of Elizabeth, however, bears only a superficial resemblance to Joshua's role as a type of Christ. And it obscures the dynastic meaning and classical provenance of Spenser's conceit, which is Virgilian rather than Pauline. Typology is a specialized kind of allegorical reading that should not be confused with allegorical writing.

narrative structure Although allegories seem to divide into narratives of conflict (Bunyan's *Holy War*) and narratives of quest (Bunyan's *Pilgrim's Progress*), the two principles are usually found working together, with one playing the dominant role. Conflict, in which Spenser's knights are frequently engaged, provides a frame for sharply pictorial, allegorical tropes: 'God helpe the man so wrapt in *Errours* endlesse traine' (I i 18). And a quest, such as Arthur's, brings the larger conventions of allegory into play so that the narrative seems to move inward, as it moves forward, toward a center of meaning.

A typical example of how these principles organize narrative is the Old French *Tourneiment Antichrist* of Huon de Meri. At the center of the poem there is a psychomachy, in the manner of Prudentius, that is presented as an elaborate chivalric tournament: as the virtues joust against the vices, the tropological sense of each fight can be worked out from the decorated shields of the fighters. This pattern of individual and distinct conflicts is arrayed, however, along the line of a story in which the narrator moves from the city of Despair on the night before the tournament to the city of Hope on the night after. And the latter is identified, as we should expect, with the celestial Jerusalem of Revelation. Very few medieval allegories fail to conform to this pattern.

Though conflict is the most typical form of allegorical trope, the effect that it typifies can be achieved in a number of ways: by dialogue between characters with significant names (such as Bunyan's Mr Worldly-Wise or Spenser's Crudor); by iconic structures such as Spenser's house of Pride or Dante's colored stairs leading up to Purgatory's gate; and by suggestive ordering, as when Redcrosse meets Sansfoy after abandoning Una, or when Dante meets Matelda after entering Eden. What one notices first about these is their curiously episodic character: rather than being joined by any evident and necessary structure of causes, individual events are joined only by the fact of the narrator's passage through each on his journey. The connections between events must be supplied by the interpreter who brings them together in a structure of meaning: after abandoning Una, Redcrosse meets Sansfoy not purely by chance, as it seems in the text, but because loss of faith follows loss of the truth.

Allegorical tropes cause readers to think inward, or across the narrative line, by encouraging them to investigate how many things a single episode or place, such as the Garden of Adonis, may be taken to mean. But attention is realigned with the direction of the narrative by another interpretative concern: that of building a linear sequence not at the level of cause and effect, but of meaning. We cannot perceive logical development from one episode to the next – in Dante, Langland, Spenser, or Bunyan – without engaging the text thus in interpretative play.

Allegorical writers will often provide at the outset an image of the goal to which interpretation is directed so that the unity of the narrative will appear to subsist in that goal. In Canto 1 of the *Divine Comedy* Dante hears from Virgil of the celestial city he will reach at the end of the *Paradiso*. In the prologue and first passus of *Piers Plowman* we see the tower of Truth to which the dream-quest of Piers is directed; and at the beginning of *Pilgrim's Progress* we see the heavenly Jerusalem to which the pilgrim makes his way throughout the work. For the greater part of *The Faerie Queene* the goal of the quest is Cleopolis, to which Arthur is headed and the knights must return. We imagine that our understanding of the poem will be complete at the moment its narrative ends: when the twelve virtues are united in Arthur and the space separating him from Gloriana is closed.

Renaissance epic and romance Much discussion of allegory in the sixteenth century is centered on Ariosto's *Orlando furioso*. The purpose of such discussion, as with Homer before, is to make the poem morally innocuous and philosophically profound when in fact it is neither. One commentator, Simone Fornari, compares the enchantment of Ariosto's narrative to the Homeric sirens, whose pleasant singing lures men to their deaths; and he warns that the reader is safe only when bound to the mast of an allegorical truth that the narrative conceals. While it is unlikely that Spenser would have shared this notion of the *Furioso* as a 'continued Allegory,' it is likely that he found the notion attractive and intended, in precisely this way, to 'overgo' Ariosto.

Another reason for allegorizing the *Furioso* was to give it that structural unity which had become, with the recent enthusiasm for Aristotle's *Poetics*, an important criterion of value in a heroic poem. The single, unified action of the *Furioso*, it was said, is the war of the pagan king, Agramante, against Charlemagne. But since that conflict takes up only a small portion of the action, some way must be found to make all other episodes and stories conform. This could be done by regarding the adventures of the various knights as moral allegories referring to the unifying theme: the pagan knights represent vices in Agramante, the Christian knights virtues in Charlemagne.

No such comprehensive scheme troubled Ariosto, and those parts of his poem that are allegorical stand out just as clearly as those that are not. The problem of determining how much of a work is designed to elicit allegorical reading becomes more complicated with Tasso, who was himself undecided as to whether or not his *Gerusalemme liberata* is an allegory. (In one of his letters, no 76, he admits to being unable to recall having written his poem allegorically, yet feels he must have done so because he now finds so many allegories in it; ed 1853–5, I:185.)

In 1576, Tasso wrote a 'Prose Allegory' (printed in 1581) in which he justifies those elements of romance for which he had been criticized on moral and aesthetic grounds. The whole army besieging Jerusalem (that city being the traditional image, as we have seen, of the *telos* of allegory) now represents for Tasso one man in pursuit of the good; and the romance adventures that take place when the Christian paladins are separated by the enchantress Armida are to be seen as allegories of the private moral virtues. Only when the army is united and subordinated again under Goffredo (Reason) in a state of 'natural justice' can the concerted effort for 'political felicity' begin (*GL* 1581).

The influence of this piece of critical jerry-building is apparent in Spenser's initial conception of *The Faerie Queene* (see Letter and I xi 7): twelve knights representing the twelve private moral virtues refer, throughout their adventures, to Arthur. Only when their quests are accomplished can the public virtues be shown in a concerted war against the Pagan King. Although this scheme acts as a gestalt for the interpreter to organize his responses to the poem, Spenser himself was not confined by it.

the picture theory of language We have seen that allegory as convention generates commentary in its audience and at the same time regulates the play of such commentary within a clearly defined set of contexts: politics, morality, cosmology, and religion. At first this may seem to confine the reader to a procedure of mechanical decoding that will stop when the meaning is clear – an impression that accounts for the hostility of the Romantics to allegory. But because the interpreter, in seeking to close up the gaps perceived in the text, only opens up more, and because the work is designed precisely to sustain that effect, the goal of a complete interpretation always recedes beyond grasp. In the quest to stabilize meaning, the number of analogies it seems necessary to bring in actually increases with time until the allegorical work can come to seem strangely voracious, drawing all knowledge into its margins.

This may be accounted for in part by the conventions of the form. But it is also a consequence of a theory of language of which allegory is the most extreme expression, a theory in which meaning, at some ideal level of visual form, always floats free of any acoustic involvement with words. Words, therefore, are thought of as imperfect pictures of meanings that exist in their purest state, outside the linguistic requirement of sound, in icons and symbols. These may be combined, like pixels, into larger pictures of states of affairs. We may then think of language as an organized whole composing a universe of signs in a total picture that is a 'mirror of nature.'

A further property of these visual signs, according to the theory, is that they acquire, when abstracted from sound, a certain universality of reference that connects them to the underlying reason, or *logos*, of nature; and it is this universality that makes them polysemous. As Fornari, following Pico della Mirandola, explains, the universe is so organized that *fire* at one level of creation will correspond with the *sun* at the next level up and beyond that with the *angelic intellect* burning with love. Creation is ordered thus by an intricate pattern of correspondences from which all allegorical meaning is derived and on which, as a consequence, the polysemy of language is based (Fornari *Spositione* 1549–50, 2:3–4; Pico *Heptaplus* 2nd preface, ed 1572–3, I:6–8). As words depend less on their acoustic medium and more on the images they call up in the mind, they can signify more things. And instead of referring in all directions at once, the signifying traffic moves in an orderly and gradual way in one direction: up toward the One which is the source of the *logos*. When we read an allegory, we have the impression of following the same path: we identify correspondences between different parts of the text, correspondences not explicitly signaled in it but called forth by analogy, and we see the network as tending ultimately toward a presence of meaning that is the center and the source of the whole.

One critical point of strain in this theory is the scant provision it makes for things not normally pictured as objects: holiness, temperance, anger, or justice (see *personification). Allegorical imagery appears to fill in this lack, and thus to support the picture theory of language at a critical point, by confining abstract universals to visual forms. The figure of a maiden called Shamefastnesse, who is herself more intensely shamefast than what she stands for in others, makes a descriptive function curve back on itself so that we have a description of a description in which nothing is described, or what has been called a 'self-predicating universal' (Nuttall 1967:42). The absurdity is then hidden by converting the abstract universal into a physical source that is as yet uncontaminated by the actual world where it must flow into objects: 'She is the fountaine of your modestee,' Alma tells Guyon, 'You shamefast are, but *Shamefastnesse* it selfe is shee' (II ix 43).

When we think about language in this way – and it is the way allegorical poets must think about it, as Dante suggests in the *Epistle to Can Grande* – we imagine that what is really true exists only in an empyrean of visual forms transcending language and cleansed of acoustic impurity. Because these assumptions about language are bound to the process of reading, and therefore to texts, it is hardly surprising that the allegorical interpreters, from Clement of Alexandria to Natale Conti, believed the poets to have learned the secrets concealed in their poems from the Egyptian hieroglyphics. Nor is it surprising that Renaissance mythographers were so important to poets such as Chapman and Spenser.

By placing absolute meaning beyond words, the picture theory of language organizes writing into a hierarchy that may be imagined on three levels. At the top, we have the singularity to which all interpretation aspires: a point where the mind is at one with what it contemplates, as an insect turns green on its leaf. Beneath this full presence of meaning, on the second level, is the allegorical work, which we are encouraged to interpret in order to reach for that presence: a poetic text, bristling with ambiguous symbols and complicated tropes, which it is at least theoretically possible for the poet to complete. But while we can imagine *The Faerie Queene* coming to an end after twelve books, with all of its parts numbered and governed in a comprehensive design, we think of commentary about it as having no conceivable end in sight. For by entering into the margin where commentary takes place we have stepped down to the third level of the hierarchy, where language is less pictorial, because farther from truth, and where discursive syntax is more important than symbolic form.

An explanation we would read here on, say, the Garden of Adonis, is easier to follow at any particular moment than what we find in the text; but it seems forever unfinished. Thus the space of commentary suggested by the edge of the page is extended until it seems as if the world is gathered into the margins of the poem and encyclopedically organized by it.

information When we detach ourselves from the picture theory of language to consider allegorical imagery in informational rather than semiotic terms, this hierarchy can be turned on its side and seen as a continuum. And whether we move toward the ineffable at one end of the continuum or the copiously talkative at the other, what we are engaged in at every point is a trade-off between precision of statement and economy of signs. The longer a message is, the more certain we can be of its meaning because there is more redundancy in it: what the sender wishes to say is expressed in several different but mutually confirming ways, and the message gains clarity as alternative meanings are excluded. Cognition, from this point of view, is not a measure of how much is held in the mind, but of how much is excluded by means of further qualification. To say more than is necessary, however, is to waste information; and as soon as we begin to economize on information (as in a telegram), we become more ambiguous because we rely increasingly on the receiver to fill in the gaps of our message.

When we are told that a knight has been caught in the folds of a serpent, we can complete the message in several ways: by saying that the serpent is Satan and the knight humanity in general, that the serpent is the Church of Rome and the knight the Christian church in the sixteenth century, that the serpent is the Roman Empire and the knight the Christian church in the first century, that the serpent is the Passion and the knight Jesus, that the serpent is Lust and the knight Chastity, and so on. We cannot say which of any number of substitutions applies until we have more information to exclude those that do not – or until we are given enough information at least to exclude some, as when the serpent is identified as 'Errour' (I i 18). It is not a question of all possibilities being simultaneously true, but of all being equally uncertain. Yet it is characteristic of allegory to assume the former and to encourage us to think that the image somehow contains all imaginable meanings in all plausible contexts: uncertainty is conceived of as polysemy.

When we seek to unpack some of these meanings, we do so by commentary, which may seem like the work of excavating an inexhaustible store. From an informational perspective, however, we may see commentary as specifying one possibility at a time to the exclusion of others: that is, it adds redundancy to the message to achieve greater specificity on one particular point. The movement in the opposite direction – toward economy of signs and increased ambiguity – is precisely what we find in moments of allegorical 'infolding' such as the Garden of Adonis. We can understand what the commentator is saying, though we fear he will go on forever; we must interpret and complete what the poet is saying, though we sense now that there is some rational limit to how much he will say; and when we are finally drawn into the singularity where all difference is stilled in the unity of truth, we find it means too much to mean anything whatever (see *closure).

The natural response to this blockage is to draw back into the surrounding movement of images and to resort to commentary on *these* in order to explain *it*: in short, to add redundancy to the message. (We explain, for instance, the mystery of Spenser's goddess of Nature, and the enigma she speaks at VII vii 58, by referring back to the cycle of seasons and then turning again to refocus on her, and so on indefinitely.) Thus the singularity is itself inescapably a part of the movement it promises to escape; or, to put it in less autonomous terms, the idea of absolute meaning is but one of the signs we employ in the effort to get beyond signs.

What would happen if an allegorical poet were to realize this with full conviction and then seek to exploit it in a self-conscious and writerly way? Such a poem might exemplify the conception of allegory championed by Paul de Man as a 'rhetoric of temporality.' According to de Man, allegory is at all times aware of the contradictory structure of the assumptions on which it proceeds: on the one hand, the author appears to assume that everything he says emanates from, and ultimately returns to, an ideal meaning that is beyond the figurative distortions of language; and on the other hand, the author recognizes this assumption to be false because, in assuming one can return to an original point and find it unchanged, the reality of time is denied. Such writing tries to recapture temporality by dramatizing its own failure to break out of time; and it is characterized, therefore, by the stylized reiteration of a gesture that is always unfinished. In this way, it forces upon us an awareness of time because time itself is, in de Man's intriguing apothegm, 'truth's inability to coincide with itself' (1979:78). Something of this perspective on allegory, as writing that turns back on itself to dramatize the futility of its aim, emerges at the end of the *Cantos of Mutabilitie*.

But it is much more characteristic of allegorical poets to proceed under the assumption that truth can indeed coincide with itself, when the work of interpretation has been done, in a comprehensive folding together of signs. By inciting the interpreter to pursue such a moment of complete understanding, and to pursue it reiteratively through time, allegory achieves its distinctive effect, which is to regulate the scope of interpretation without coming to any definitive end. It establishes an aesthetics of temporality – an encounter with meaning as a process in time – inscribed within a rhetoric of absolute truth. By believing conventionally, that that truth can finally be reached, the interpreter keeps meaning in play.

GORDON TESKEY

John Ahern 1982 'Binding the Book: Hermeneutics and Manuscript Production in *Paradiso* 33' *PMLA* 92:800–9; Auerbach ed 1959:11–76 'Figura'; Stephen A. Barney 1979 (bibliography); Barney 1981 'Visible Allegory: The *Distinctiones Abel* of Peter the Chanter' in Bloomfield 1981:87–107; Barney 1982 'Allegory' in *Dictionary of the Middle Ages* 1982–9 ed Joseph R. Strayer, 1:178–88 (New York) (bibliography); Joel D. Black 1983 'Allegory Unveiled' *Poetics Today* 4:109–26; Morton W. Bloomfield 1972 'Allegory as Interpretation' *NLH* 3:301–17; Bloomfield, ed 1981 *Allegory, Myth, and Symbol* (Cambridge, Mass); Boccaccio ed 1930; Félix Buffière 1956 *Les Mythes d'Homère et la pensée grecque* (Paris); Cast 1981; Marie-Dominique Chenu 1955 'Involucrum: Le myth selon les théologiens médiévaux' *Archives d'histoire doctrinale et littéraire du moyen âge* 30:75–9; Chenu 1964 'La Décadence de l'allégorisation; un témoin, Garnier de Rochefort' in *L'Homme devant Dieu: Mélanges offerts au Père Henri de Lubac* in *Théologie* 57 (Paris) 2:129–35; Gay Clifford 1974 *The Transformations of Allegory* (London); Comparetti ed 1895; *Court of Sapience* ed 1984; Dante ed 1966; Paul de Man 1969 'The Rhetoric of Temporality' rpt in *Blindness and Insight: Essays in the Rhetoric of Contemporary Criticism* 2nd ed, Theory and History of Literature 7:187–228 (Minneapolis 1983); de Man 1979 *Allegories of Reading: Figural Language in Rousseau, Nietzsche, Rilke, and Proust* (New Haven); Fletcher 1964; Simone Fornari 1549–50 *La Spositione ... sopra l'Orlando furioso* 2 vols (Florence); Perceval Frutiger 1930 *Les Mythes de Platon: Etude philosophique et littéraire* (Paris); Frye 1965; Frye 1982; Johannes Geffcken 1928 'Allegory' in *Encyclopaedia of Religion and Ethics* ed James Hastings, et al (New York) 1:327–31; Stephen Greenblatt, ed 1981 *Allegory and Representation* (*EIE* 1979–80, Baltimore); Lavinia Griffiths 1985 *Personification in 'Piers Plowman'* (Cambridge); Hinks 1939; Robert Hollander 1969 *Allegory in Dante's 'Commedia'* (Princeton); Honig 1959; Bernard F. Huppé and D.W. Robertson, Jr 1963 *Fruyt and Chaf: Studies in Chaucer's Allegories* (Princeton); Jackson 1964; Hans Robert Jauss 1968 'Entstehung und Strukturwandel der allegorischen Dichtung' in *La Littérature didactique, allégorique et satirique* ed Hans Robert Jauss, in *Grundriss der romanischen Literaturen des Mittelalters* 6.1:146–244 (Heidelberg); Jauss 1970 'Genèse et structures des genres allégoriques' in *La Littérature didactique, allégorique et satirique* 6.2:203–80; Samuel Johnson 1825 *Works* 9 vols (Oxford); Marc René Jung 1971 *Études sur le poème allégorique en France au moyen âge* (Bern); Robert E. Kaske 1973–4 'Dante's *Purgatorio* XXXII and XXXIII: A Survey of Christian History' *UTQ* 43:193–214; William J. Kennedy 1972 'Irony, Allegoresis, and Allegory in Virgil, Ovid and Dante' *Arcadia* 7:115–34; Robert Lamberton 1986 *Homer the Theologian: Neoplatonist Allegorical Reading and the Growth of the Epic Tradition* (Berkeley and Los Angeles) (bibliography); Lewis 1936; Lubac 1959–64; MacQueen 1970; Joseph Mazzeo 1978 'Allegorical Interpretation and History' *CL* 30:1–21; Timothy Murray 1987 *Theatrical Legitimation: Allegories of Genius in Seventeenth-Century England and France* (New York); Murrin 1969; Murrin 1980; A.D. Nuttall 1967 *Two Concepts of Allegory: A Study of Shakespeare's 'The Tempest' and the Logic of Allegorical Expression* (London); Jean Pépin 1958; Pépin 1970 *Dante et la tradition de l'allégorie* Conférence Albert-le-Grand 1969 (Montreal); Pico ed 1572–3; Quilligan 1979; J. Stephen Russell, ed 1988 *Allegoresis: The Craft of Allegory in Medieval Literature* (New York); Charles S. Singleton 1965 '"In Exitu Israel de Aegypto"' in *Dante: A Collection of Critical Essays* ed John Freccero (Englewood Cliffs, NJ) pp 102–21; Torquato Tasso 1853–5 *Lettere* ed Cesare Guasti, 5 vols (Naples); Teskey 1986; Van Dyke 1985; Stephen L. Wailes 1987 *Medieval Allegories of Jesus' Parables* (Berkeley and Los Angeles); Jon Whitman 1987 *Allegory: The Dynamics of an Ancient and Medieval Technique* (Cambridge, Mass).

allegory, historical In his major poetry Spenser devotes significant attention to symbolic portrayal of the contemporary world and to moral comment on its political and religious issues. This dimension of his poetry has generally been called the 'historical allegory.' The term is misleading, however, especially if it suggests to readers that such concerns are frequently expressed in topical allegories that parallel the moral allegory. In fact, Spenser more often refers to the contemporary world allusively, through momentary indications of a moral relationship between the poem and its political context. At certain points, particularly in the second half of *The Faerie Queene*, this concern for contemporary events and issues does grow into full-scale allegorization. But it is more accurate to speak of the historical dimension of Spenser's poetry, a term that includes the full range of allusion, satire, symbolic characterization, historical catalogue, and topical allegory.

The historical dimension of *The Shepheardes Calender* and *The Faerie Queene* derives from Spenser's ambition to be the acknowledged laureate poet of Elizabethan England (see Helgerson 1983). He wished his voice to be heard by those in power, especially the Queen. His celebrations of Elizabeth and his concern about her policies are of a piece with his desire to create a poem of moral engagement, concerned not only with private behavior but with a larger sense of England's moral and political identity. To a nation arrived at the edge of empire, Spenser hoped to provide a vision of accomplishment and possibility.

Because of the fragmentation of Italian politics in the sixteenth century, Spenser could not find such a vision in his Italian models, Ariosto and Tasso. The model for his engagement with history he found rather in Virgil, whose *Eclogues*, *Georgics*, and *Aeneid* are vitally concerned with questions of national identity and morality. Spenser's most profound debt to Virgil remains the latter's redirection of pastoral and epic toward history. What he found most attractive was the way Virgil confronted his age – and his ruler – with a complex vision of celebration and judgment.

Spenser read the historical dimension of Virgil refracted through the late-fourth-century commentary of Servius. Though Servius sees topical allegory in the *Eclogues*, he describes the treatment of history in the *Aeneid* as purely allusive. Equally significant is his insistence that Virgil celebrates all of Roman history from the arrival of Aeneas in Latium down to his own day, but in a concealed and fragmented way. In this, he distinguishes Virgil's weaving of history into the fictional fabric of his poem from Lucan's direct representation. In describing the allusive nature of the *Aeneid*, Servius defines a relationship that can be most aptly called typological: Aeneas is both ancestor and prophetic type of Augustus; historical events are made to appear fulfillments of things caused or shadowed in the epic fiction, as Dido's tragedy stands behind the tragedy of Carthage. For Spenser the significance of such an understanding of history in the *Aeneid* lies in the model it provides of an epic typologically connecting fictional past with historical present. Virgil's example may also suggest why Spenser did not begin with topical allegory in the early books of *The Faerie Queene* but initially treated history more allusively.

In *The Shepheardes Calender* Spenser follows Virgil's precedent by directing several of the eclogues toward his own political world. Arguments have been made that the entire *Calender* is a topical allegory (most notably McLane 1961 who sees the poem as a multifaceted warning to the Queen of the dangers of marrying Alençon). But few readers have been persuaded. Certainly *Aprill*, *Maye*, *Julye*, and *September* are concerned in a primary way with contemporary issues. *Aprill* celebrates Elizabeth's rule through iconographic details that point to the peace and contentment of her reign. By placing the eclogue fourth, Spenser enforces the parallel to Virgil's celebratory Eclogue 4. The other three, however, are critical of Elizabeth's policies toward the church. In these pastoral dialogues, Spenser gives the interlocutors names that suggest contemporary churchmen; and by exploiting the gospel metaphor of shepherd, he is able to address such questions as Elizabeth's suspension of her independently minded Archbishop of Canterbury (Edmund Grindal, shadowed in *Julye* as 'Algrind') and depredations of church livings by venal courtiers (*September*). The political comment in the three eclogues grows increasingly specific until in *September* Hobbinol warns Diggon Davie to speak less plainly about the corruption from which the reader understands Diggon's prototype had suffered (102–3). Taken together, and in the context of the poetic coming-of-age represented by *The Shepheardes Calender* as a whole, the four eclogues show a poet determined to direct his work toward the public world, yet aware of the consequent dangers and difficulties. Also evident is the way Spenser moves between the poles of celebration and critical judgment in his engagement with history.

The historical dimension of *The Faerie Queene*, though more complex, remains true to this beginning. In the Letter to Raleigh, Spenser calls attention to the way Gloriana and Belphoebe are used to celebrate the Queen; Una, Britomart, and Mercilla also partake of such celebratory aims. Each book of the poem except the sixth contains a figure who mirrors Elizabeth in some fashion and ties the virtue in question to her accomplishments as Queen. The proems to the first three books in particular play suggestively with the idea that the attentive reader will discover the Queen in the fiction. *FQ* II proem 4 asserts that by following 'certaine signes' in the poem Elizabeth will find not only herself but a mirror of her 'owne realmes in lond of Faery.' But the poet also sits in judgment of his world; the poem is saved from becoming mere flattery by the moral scheme into which these celebrations of royal accomplishments are set. On occasion he will even hint at negative royal images, implying not so much satire as caveats for the Queen. One such example is the image of the proud and ambitious Lucifera, suggestively called 'A mayden Queene' and linked to images of the sun that Elizabeth also used (I iv). In *FQ* IV, he constructs an episode that advises the Queen to take the disgraced Raleigh back into her favor (vii 23–viii 18).

How exactly the poem reflects history has been a tantalizing question for readers. One consequence of Spenser's assertion that Elizabeth's England is mirrored in the poem has been the temptation to claim detailed and explicit allegorical connections. Indeed, several of the dedicatory sonnets appear to hint that prominent noblemen or their ancestors are to be found in the poem. In his *Discourse on Satire* (1693) Dryden claims that 'the original of every knight was then living in the court of Queen Elizabeth; and [Spenser] attributed to each of them that virtue which he thought most conspicuous in them.' In his edition of 1758 Upton makes specific identifications, though he generally considers them as more allusive than allegorical. In the late nineteenth and early twentieth centuries, this tendency led critics to discover detailed historical allegories which were frequently more indebted to the learning and imagination of the writer than to the poem. (For Book I, for example, Lilian Winstanley constructed a detailed allegory of the Reformation under Henry VIII; see also *Dixon.) Later arguments for detailed historical allegories include Kermode 1962 and 1964, and Hankins 1971.

But it is important to consider whether the narrative surface of the poem does in fact gesture toward an historical reality beyond it, and how the narrative makes such gestures. What we discover in answering these questions is that the poem points toward history intermittently and then by means of particular devices. Sometimes the narrative will suggest a reference, particularly when a character is meant to allude to the Queen. At other times, an allusive name or an iconographic element will indicate the reference. Occasionally the reader is alerted by a curious narrative detail, as when the mention of 'divine *Tobacco*' suggests Raleigh (III v 32). Through such moments, the reader comes to understand that the historical world does not impinge constantly upon the poem but is rather an impending presence that in a general way pervades its moral reality.

Although Spenser did come to write historical allegory in the second half of *The Faerie Queene*, in the first three books the historical dimension is conveyed by allusions that point to a typological relationship between poem and history. Book I most consistently and successfully creates this Virgilian sense of a fictional world set in an undefined past which finds its fulfillment in the present. The Book of Revelation is the principal medium through which Spenser defines the relationship. He depends on the historical reinterpretation of Revelation by the Reformers, in which the symbols of the

Roman Empire were redefined as the Roman church; in this way, he points to a specifically English fulfillment of the spiritual mythos of Revelation. Typically, when the pressure of the moral allegory is somewhat lessened, the poem will gesture allusively toward the contemporary progress of the Reformation in England as an analogous battleground of spiritual forces. Most of the allusions are concentrated in the reign of Mary, when England, like Redcrosse, strayed from the path of Protestant faith. For example, the narrative suggests that Una, separated from Redcrosse and driven out into the wilderness like the woman of Revelation 12.6, may be seen as a version of Elizabeth in her sufferings under Mary (I iii 2). Indeed, the name Una was used as a cult title of Elizabeth, alluding to her virginity. The effect of this relationship between Una and Elizabeth is to indicate the Queen's role in guiding England back from apostasy and despair to spiritual strength. The reader is thus to understand that the sacred archetype of Revelation is relevant both to the individual and to history.

In Books II and III, the historical dimension is more intermittent. Belphoebe is used in both books to connect temperance and chastity to Elizabeth's political character. In Book III, Britomart also bears a typological relationship to Elizabeth as her fictional ancestor; the stanzas that relate her progeny and her Trojan ancestry tie her to Elizabeth as a prophetic example of female strength (iii 21–50, ix 44–51). These historical catalogues and the one contained in the book Arthur reads in *FQ* II x are drawn from Tudor chronicles that themselves show the popular fascination with national history. In the context of the poem, the catalogues are concerned to demonstrate the tumultuous processes of history that will lead to the peace of Elizabeth's reign. Both Britomart and Elizabeth embody an historical *discordia concors*: Britomart early, fictional, prophetic; Elizabeth present, actual, fulfilling. In *FQ* II x, Spenser contrasts Arthur's *Briton moniments* with the idealized history of Guyon's Elfin chronicle; he thus indicates that the order of history the poem projects is an ideal held up to his age.

Spenser's method of treating history alters significantly in the second half of the poem. Here we find narratives specifically fashioned to reflect historical situations, narratives which can be properly described as historical allegory. The first of these portrays Raleigh's disgrace over his marriage and the deception he practiced on the Queen (IV vii 23–viii 18). In the earlier allusive reference to Raleigh, Spenser had portrayed the love of Timias and Belphoebe as a general and idealized image of the relationship of courtier and queen (III v 13–55). But in Book IV, the episode is clearly designed to comment on a specific situation, and its purpose is to plead the cause of Raleigh's return to favor. Such historical allegories come to dominate the poem in Book V, especially in its second half. There are many references to contemporary political issues in the early cantos (eg, the issue of monopolies in the episode of the tollbridge, ii 5–19, or the threat of insurrection in the Giant with the scales, ii 29–54); but in the second half, the primary purpose of such episodes (eg, the trial of Duessa in canto ix, the rescue of Belge in x, and Burbon's recovery of Flourdelis in xi 43–65) is to portray and justify particular events.

One consequence of this historical allegory is a blurring of moral focus in the poem. Since the fictional episodes are designed to reflect historical events, they tend to assume their morality from history. At its best *The Faerie Queene* moves on a moral and psychological plane in which poet and reader seem imaginative collaborators in interpreting experience. The allusive approach to history in the early books contributes to this collaboration, since contemporary events are admitted more as an illustrative adjunct to the moral dimension. But historical allegory appears to reverse the order and make history primary; as a consequence, the moral vision of the poem must wait upon the ambiguities of the actual world. Some readers have felt that the historical allegory, besides giving Book V a more apologetic character, diminishes the poem's imaginative vitality.

In its final completed book, the poem draws back from history. Unlike the previous books, Book VI contains no figure who represents the Queen. Though it begins by finding the etymology of *courtesy* in the word *court*, its narrative never comes close to portraying the Elizabethan court. It has been suggested that Calidore shadows Sidney or the Earl of Essex but in fact no heraldic or narrative details support such an identification. The allegorical core of the book, Colin's vision of the Graces, substitutes personal for political sources of inspiration as Colin begs Gloriana's pardon for singing the praises of a fourth Grace, his own love, instead of hers (in *SC, Aprill*, the fourth Grace had been Eliza). The historical dimension of *The Faerie Queene* essentially ends with Book V; in the final completed book, Spenser turns inward, away from history.

Among Spenser's minor poems, only *Mother Hubberd's Tale* can be said to have a significant historical dimension. Though scarcely his most polished or consistent work of political comment, it may well be his most daring. In its first two-thirds, the poem is a traditional estates satire and appears to share with *The Shepheardes Calender* certain political concerns, especially over the church. Some commentators have also seen in it a covert warning about the Alençon marriage, which would place it close to 1579. Yet the heartfelt lament about the trials of a suitor at court (892–914) appears to derive from Spenser's own experience in 1589–90; and in its final third, the poem turns into a beast fable which oddly redoubles the earlier court satire. Here the political cunning of the Fox is portrayed in terms that refer to Burghley, the powerful Lord Treasurer, with surprising boldness (1137–1204). The supposition that the Fox satirizes Burghley is strengthened by the contemporary belief that *Complaints*, in which *Mother Hubberd* was published in 1591, was 'called in,' that is, suppressed by the government; and it is true that the poem was not reprinted until after the death of Robert Cecil, Burghley's son. If the poem is Spenser's most daring piece of historical comment, it may also be the one he had most cause to regret: in the last stanza of *FQ* VI, he complains feelingly that some unspecified verses had brought him 'into a mighty Peres displeasure.' No peer's displeasure was less to be invited than Burghley's. MICHAEL O'CONNELL

Cain 1978; Fichter 1982; Greenlaw 1932; Hankins 1971; Frank Kermode 1962 'Spenser and the Allegorists' *PBA* 48:261–79, and Kermode 1964–5 (both essays rpt in Kermode 1971); McLane 1961; O'Connell 1977. See also the summaries of earlier criticism in the *Variorum* 'Historical Allegory' appendices.

Alma, castle of Alma represents the immortal, God-given, rational soul that 'doth rule the earthly masse, / And all the service of the bodie frame' (IV ix 2). Spenser refers to her as 'the soule' and to her castle, the temperate body, as 'the fort of reason' (II xi 1). The immediate source of the name may have been current Italian usage: John Florio defines *Alma* as 'the soule of man.' It is both a poetical contraction of the original Latin and Italian *anima*, whose meanings evolved from 'breath' to 'the vital principle' to 'the soul,' and the feminine form of Latin *almus*, 'that [which] norisheth: fayre: beautifull,' as in the common phrase *alma mater* (T. Cooper 1565; cf *FQ* II ix 18–19; and see Florio ed 1611 and others from 1578 on).

The soul has been figured as a woman in Christian culture since the early Middle Ages, and so appears in Dante's *Divine Comedy* (Beatrice), the Middle English *Pearl*, Francesco Colonna's *Hypnerotomachia Poliphili* (1499), and, more recently, in Jung's concept of the image of the male soul as female 'anima.' Spenser's characterization of Alma as the much-sought-after virgin in whom heaven rejoices (ix 18–19), identifies the human soul as bride of Christ. His description beginning with her 'robe of lilly white' and ending with her head crowned with roses, suggests that virginity (the lily; cf Una in I xii 22 and Belphoebe in II iii 26) can develop its potential for both human and divine love (the rose, sacred to Venus; cf Belphoebe, III v 51).

The castle of Alma belongs to a long tradition of allegorical castles, such as the Castle of Anima in Passus 9 of *Piers Plowman* B-text (c 1377), and the castle in du Bartas' *Divine Weeks* 1.6 (1578). Spenser describes it enigmatically in *FQ* II ix 22. In the earliest extended commentary on a single stanza of *The Faerie Queene* (1644), Kenelm Digby interprets the circle, perfect and without beginning or end, as the mind or soul; the triangle, imperfect and the first of the geometrical figures, as the body. The quadrate he interprets as the four humors uniting body and soul (choler, blood, phlegm, and melancholy). The proportions, seven and nine, refer to the created world (the seven days of Creation, the seven known planets) and to the immortal world beyond (the nine hierarchies of angels). It has been pointed out that these lines may be read 'either as an architectural description of Alma's Castle or as a geometrical description of the human body, or as generally allusive arithmology, or as step-by-step instructions for a specific geometrical construction or arithmetical operation' (Fowler 1964:260). The stanza may also convey an image of the universe – the lower regions, the earth with its four elements, and 'the circle set in heavens place' – as well as of the music of that 'worke divine' with its three parts created as *discordia concors* ending in the great diapason.

Literally it is a castle; the primary allegorical reference is to the human body with its basic parts of legs (triangle), chest (quadrate), and head (circle), as the introductory stanza suggests in its celebration of the temperate human body (ix 1; cf xi 1–2). As the subsequent description implies, however, the castle of Alma is not merely the body inhabited by the soul but also the house that is the soul, traditionally divided into three parts: the vegetable soul of nourishment and growth (the triangle of the lower functions), the sensitive soul (the quadrate of the breast), and the intellectual soul (the circle of memory, judgment, and imagination). Bartholomaeus Anglicus had earlier used triangle, quadrate, and circle to image the three functions of the soul in his *De proprietatibus rerum* (see ed 1582:14r).

The functions of the vegetable soul are presented in a simple tour of the castle (ix 24–32). The terms of the description are concrete details that indicate their referents immediately: the lips appear as a porch, the mustache as a vine over it, the teeth as 'Twise sixteen warders,' the throat as a hallway, the stomach as a kitchen, and so on. The rather startling metaphorical juxtapositions create indirect humor which finally becomes direct, in puns on the 'Port Esquiline' through which waste matter 'was avoided quite, and throwne out privily' (32).

The functions of the sensitive soul are presented differently, in a single scene set in the parlor of the heart (33–44), where implications are conveyed by the characters' actions and reactions rather than by static images. In a sophisticated courtly scene out of medieval romance, Spenser describes the diverse passions of the heart as dames and courtiers. Arthur and Guyon pay court to ladies and discover things about themselves. In an ironic contretemps, Arthur discovers that the lady he courts is Prays-desire, an image of the desire for glory that motivates him; in a similarly comic encounter, Guyon finds that his lady is Shamefastnesse, an image of the fear of shame that is at the center of his character.

Returning to description again for a presentation of the functions of the intellectual soul in the castle's 'Turret' (45–60), Spenser stresses not simple images or a scene but rather a set of generalized and abstract characterizations that call upon the heroes' abilities to understand and make distinctions. The focus is on Alma's three counselors: the young Phantastes (imagination) who foresees the future (both true visions and lies), the mature unnamed counselor who comprehends present events, and old Eumnestes (memory) who records the past. Taken together, they suggest prudence, the practical wisdom needed to govern the body so as to preserve the whole in temperance by learning from the past, considering the consequences of action in the future, and judging and acting accordingly in the present (see Panofsky 1955:149–51).

The progress of Arthur and Guyon through the three regions of the castle of Alma suggests an education whereby they come to know their own souls, as they move from sensation to feeling to understanding, from youth to maturity to age. The three regions may also suggest the four traditional levels of exegesis of the Bible. The journey itself is the literal level. The vegetative region may represent the allegorical or historical reflection of things we know; the sensitive region, the moral sense of what choices we must make; and the intellectual region, the anagogical sense of what things mean in the fullness of time.

The castle of Alma may be contrasted detail-by-detail with the vision of intemperance in the house of Mammon in II vii (Nohrnberg 1976:327–31, 343–51). It should also be compared with the vision of temperance in the house of Medina in canto ii, where Medina frantically tries to keep the perilous mean between excess and defect. Alma's castle is the image of achieved temperance figured as the fitting together of parts (L *temperare* to mix equally): harmony among parts of the body, among parts of the soul, between body and soul, and between human and divine. WALTER R. DAVIS

Barkan 1975; Hopper 1940; Jordan 1980; Panofsky 1955.

Amadis of Gaul A composite romance that describes the life and adventures of Amadis of Gaul and his descendants. Deriving ultimately from French prose stories about Arthur, a romance of Amadis of Gaul existed in the fourteenth century, but the redaction by Garci Rodriguez de Montalvo (4 vols, 1508) introduced the hero to Spanish readers. When a fifth book, an original addition also by Montalvo, was published in 1510, a pattern was established. Other Spanish writers added further books. The romance grew in both size and popularity first in Spain and then, after 1540, in France and other countries until it finally reached 24 volumes and was known in most major European languages. Since the process of translation into English did not start until 1590, most Englishmen knew it in the French version which, because it added language and episodes from the *Orlando furioso* and other romances, is often quite different from the Spanish. Sidney, who borrowed the main plot of his *Arcadia* from episodes in Books 8 and 11, praised *Amadis* for its ability to move readers 'to the exercise of courtesy, liberality, and especially courage' – even though it 'wanteth much of a perfect poesy' (ed 1973b:92).

Spenser's debt is much harder to establish in detail. The general features of *Amadis* and *The Faerie Queene* are common to many romance narratives, and both works draw upon a similar chivalric tradition. In addition both incorporate, in different degrees, elements of pastoralism and allegory. Many set scenes in both works are also standard in romance: the bed in Dolon's chamber (*FQ* V vi 27) has a counterpart in *Amadis* (3.6, 15.23), as does the seven-headed beast of Revelation (*FQ* I vii 18, *Amadis* 14.31). Since these and other parallels are common to romance narrative, they are probably best regarded as analogues.

Yet at least one part of *The Faerie Queene* suggests that Spenser read *Amadis*. The house of Busirane contains motifs of the wall of flame (III xi 21), the exposed heart (xii 21), and the procession of Cupid (xii 3ff). All three occur separately in *Amadis* but are found together in the episode of Amadis and Zahara (8.85ff). Despite a major difference in the outcome – the romance counterpart of Amoret dies when her enchanter is killed by Amadis of Greece – Spenser seems to have derived the idea and many of the details from *Amadis*.

JOHN J. O'CONNOR

Citations given above are to the books of the French *Amadis*, published as 21 separate volumes in Antwerp, Paris, or Lyon from 1548 to 1581. Book I has an edition by Hughes Vaganay (Paris 1918). See O'Connor 1970:287–9.

The Ancient, Famous, and Honourable History of Amadis de Gaule 1619 (Books 1–4; Book 1 first pub 1590, Book 2 in 1595) tr Anthony Munday (London); Al. Cioranescu 1963 *L'Arioste en France* (Paris); John J. O'Connor 1970 *'Amadis de Gaule' and Its Influence on Elizabethan Literature* (New Brunswick, NJ).

Amavia, Mortdant, Ruddymane At *FQ* II i 35, Guyon and the Palmer come upon the dying Amavia and her recently dead husband Mortdant beside a well or spring, with their child Ruddymane, who sits in her lap playing in the blood flowing from her self-inflicted wound. She accuses fortune and the heavens of injustice, commends her child to fortune, and bids him live and testify by his bloody hands that she died guiltless of any crime. When she was pregnant with this child, she informs Guyon, her good and beloved husband left on a knightly quest, in the course of which he was drugged by Acrasia and seduced into an adulterous liaison. Taking the guise of a palmer, and undergoing en route a painful childbirth in a wood, Amavia found a Mortdant who had ceased to reason and reformed him. Then Acrasia slyly gave him a drink designed to kill him when 'Bacchus with the Nymphe does lincke.' The pair departed in apparent safety; but on their way home, Mortdant happened to drink of this well, thus catalyzing instead of tempering the delayed-action poison within him, and fell dead, whereupon Amavia stabbed herself – from which she now dies. Guyon and the Palmer reflect sadly on this overthrow of reason by passion, they give the couple a pagan funeral (see *hair), and Guyon vows vengeance. According to the otherwise erroneous synopsis in the Letter to Raleigh, this vow is 'the beginning of the second booke and the whole subject thereof.' In canto ii, Guyon tries unsuccessfully to wash Ruddymane's 'guiltie' hands in the nymph's well. His explanations of why he cannot are 'corrected' by the Palmer: the indelibility arises not from any fault, either in the well, whose feminine shape and soil-resistant property originated in its nymph's resistance to the lustful Faunus, or in the blood, valuable as a 'sacred Symbole' of vengeance and of Amavia's innocence and chastity. Satisfied, Guyon gives Ruddymane to the Palmer and takes up Mortdant's bloody armor; they leave for the castle of Medina.

In part, Amavia's story exemplifies passion with such pathos as to enlist the passions of the reader. The reader then participates in Guyon's quest for its control by temperance. The reader is irresistibly reminded of original sin: the love triangle of Mortdant, Acrasia, and Amavia somehow refers psychologically to that inner conflict between concupiscence and moral law described in Romans 7, and typologically to Adam's fall (eg, Acrasia as conflation of both tempters, Eve and the Satan-serpent) – the original cause of this concupiscence as well as of the inherited guilt manifested in Ruddymane. These two biblical subtexts are connected both in their own exegesis and in the poem, particularly in the situation of Mortdant recounted in canto i. The four alternating evil and good forces that impinge upon him – Acrasia, Amavia, the cup, and the well (especially the first three as described by Guyon in stanza 57) – correspond to the four 'laws' in Paul's summary of his story (Rom 7.22–5). In terms of self-knowledge, Paul says he progressed (as does Mortdant) from happily oblivious intemperance to rational continence to realization of the sinfulness of his continuing concupiscence.

Of Mortdant (original spelling at 49) the etymology 'him that death does give' (55) was doubtless intended honorifically and chivalrically (as in 'your dead-doing hand' iii 8) but turns out to identify him as the 'one man' by whom 'sinne entred into the world, and death by sinne, and so death went over all men' (Rom 5.12; see also 1 Cor 15.21–2; and for Spenser's and E.K.'s paraphrase of both, see *SC, Nov* emblem and gloss). In addition, beneath Amavia's exculpation of him 'For he was flesh' (i 52), there may be a Pauline diagnosis of his inherent weaknesses (Fowler 1960–1). Since he does not literally give death to anyone (except proleptically to Ruddymane, ii 2, and allegedly to Acrasia, according to her heartbroken pose), it is Adam's fall which explains both his name and the charm, which resembles the curse of death on the forbidden fruit (Gen 2.17).

Psychologically, the cup has been identified as concupiscence, or involuntary evil desires, both because Mortdant's volition is played down by Spenser's saying Acrasia deceived him with a cup and because only in trying to be good does one become aware of involuntary evil. Mortdant's two sins thus reflect Augustine's reputed tracing of concupiscence to the Fall: 'because man would not abstain from evil when he could, it was inflicted on him, that he could not abstain, though he would' (quoted by Hugh of St Cher ed 1645, 7: fol 42 col 4 on Rom 7.9).

Mortdant is executed by the pure well either for an undeliberate and victimless sin or for a mortal one of which he has repented. Yet neither of these sins exceeds in gravity those of Acrasia's other lovers, whose punishment is to be metamorphosed into beasts (xii). As if to accentuate his fate by theirs, Mortdant too was temporarily 'transformed' by his initial adultery 'from his former skill' (i 54) – an Elizabethan synonym for man's specific faculty. His failure to recognize Amavia, dramatizing the drug's blockage of his reason, thus confirms that Amavia allegorizes reason. His impure death from contact with purity bears a physical parallel to Guyon's faint and apparent death upon emerging from Mammon's realm to the pure air (vii 66, viii 7, 13) – but one which does not tell us much. Only Paul's portrayal of law in Romans 7 as announcing spiritual or eternal death – not baptism, or a too-sudden reformation, or the virtue attainable by pagans, or the opposite extreme of insensibility to the erotic, or the female generative principle – can explain the death of Mortdant.

Amavia is at once an actor like Mortdant and a narrator. Her name can mean 'I have loved,' 'she loves in order to live,' or '[she] that loves to live' (i 55), or '[she] who loves life,' all of which point to the literal story or to her serving as an example of intemperate grief. Her initial speeches and her general role as a suicide for love imitate Virgil's Dido (Nelson 1963:179, 181), or the chaste Dido. Her painful childbirth in a wood while seeking her philandering husband imitates the similar plight of the mother of Tristram in Malory (*Morte Darthur* 8.1). But this is only part of her complicated and controversial symbolism. Her loss and reclamation of Mortdant recalls the Palmer's previous loss and recovery of Guyon, as Amavia herself points out, 'As wont ye knights to seeke adventures wilde' (50). In that Amavia literally acted as the voice of reason in reclaiming Mortdant and emblematically 'wrapt [herself] in Palmers weed' (52), she may exemplify the rational person and somehow reflect not only the Palmer but also such female personifications as Reason in *Romance of the Rose*, who offers herself to the hero, and Logistilla in *Orlando furioso* (6.43–6), who opposes Alcina, a prototype of Acrasia. She tries to redress the Fall reenacted by Mortdant and Acrasia; so reason remained more or less untainted by the Fall (Peter Martyr Vermigli 1583, 2: fol 223 col 2), constituting in its historical role as natural law the sole guide of mankind until the advent of Mosaic law (Rom 5.13–14; Geneva gloss; Luther ed 1883–1987, 56: 315).

Although Amavia is doing everything for her charge that the Palmer did for Guyon, she cannot control him, for just at this point Acrasia deceives Mortdant with the poisoned cup – a reversal the Palmer never experiences. That Mortdant's reform under Amavia's tutelage actually causes this backlash of feeling illustrates the paradox of negative suggestibility noted even by secular authors such as Ovid (*Amores* 3.4.11; see also *Metamorphoses* 15.138) and Montaigne ('That Our Desire Is Increased by Difficulty'), but treated extensively in Romans 7, where the law's 'Thou shalt not lust' actually revives lust. Besides this law, Amavia also corresponds to 'the law of my minde' and 'inner man,' which approves Mosaic law's prohibitions but is balked by 'the law of sinne, which is in my membres' (7.22–3, especially in Origenistic and Catholic exegesis of Romans, which stress reason and natural law). Her character as thus revealed vitiates her reliability as teller inasmuch as she is undisturbed by, and seemingly ignorant of, concupiscence or frailty, even endearingly but insufficiently excusing Mortdant's first sin on the grounds that 'all flesh doth frailtie breed' (52); so reason and pagan ethics condone concupiscence. Her complacent tolerance is shattered by his death: even frailty is declared sinful by Mosaic law as embodied in the well, which in this regard 'goes beyond' classical ethics (Calvin ed 1960a:143, on Rom 7.7). In reaction, she accuses the heavens of injustice (i 36–7, 49–51).

In one way or another, Amavia's suicide fulfills Acrasia's curse on her (55). 'Losse of love' could mean either loss of the beloved, which goes with the 'loves-in-order-to-live' etymology of her name, or loss of the emotion, which goes with 'she who loves life.' Amavia's terminal mood, 'hating life and light' (45; cf 36), reverses her characterization as '[she] who loves life.' One of Spenser's motives for giving his reason-figure this name is that its reversal might dramatize the confession of inadequacy which Augustine sees in the rationalistic ethics of the Stoics: although it pins its hopes on this life alone ('loves to live'), it concedes that this life may frequently become so intolerable as to warrant suicide (*City of God* 19.4). Consequently, although Amavia first resists, she later shares and augments Mortdant's 'Tragedie' (ii 1). While we admire her, the way in which she wishes her child luck and abandons him to the mercies of the forest (i 37; she does not know that Guyon and the Palmer are there) seems unfeeling. (Similarly, the protagonist of *Daphnaïda*, in despair over the death of his spouse, ignores the welfare of their child by irresponsibly contemplating suicide, 77–91, 442–8.) Such irrationality under pain identifies Amavia as mere reason, not the right or divinely illuminated reason embodied in the Palmer. Her grief is caused by Mosaic law without grace (here symbolized by the well), which leads to despair, to cursing God as the cause of one's own damnation (cf i 49), and sometimes to suicide (Luther ed 1883–1987, 42:133, on Gen 3.12). Thus Guyon's summary is faithful (omitting the well) to the end if not the beginning of Amavia's story: 'passion ... Robs reason of her due regalitie, / And makes it servant to her basest part' (57).

Yet even Ruddymane is not so unqualifiedly innocent as Amavia (ii 1, 3; cf i 37, ii

10). That she imbibes the poison of the cup, albeit innocently, is indicated not only by the curse but by Guyon's otherwise curious remark that she also drank the cup (ii 4). Because he goes on to refer to her and Mortdant as a single 'senselesse truncke' (4), presumably she did so through intercourse, suggested again by the converse metaphor of drinking as linking (i 55). This defilement by association, as by a venereal disease, seems to explain away her sins. The Palmer – reasoning from the well's acceptance of her blood when it falls directly into it (40) and her claim to innocence (37) – virtually equates her with the Virgin Mary insofar as her blood symbolizes another and typologically significant part of human nature, the 'seed of the woman' (Gen 3.15) which did not carry 'blemish criminall' (37), that is, original sin (transmitted by the seed of the man), and hence was able to produce in the Virgin Mary an Adamically innocent 'seed,' the avenger Christ. The link between this final typological and genetic role and her psychological one seems to lie in her association with nature (Fowler 1960–1:148) – more exactly, mankind's generative nature and natural law – whose corruption is frequently qualified as adventitious and imaged as a wound.

Ruddymane's name means 'red hand.' His literal birth was incommodious but acceptable to the nymphs (i 53); his recapitulatory second birth at the well with Guyon as midwife is condemned by the nymph as unclean. As a foundling washed, whether successfully or not, by a superior male figure and a nymph, Ruddymane recalls both Jerusalem in Ezekiel 16 and Bacchus in the Greek epigram also echoed in the lines 'So soone as Bacchus with the Nymphe does lincke' and 'in dead parents balefull ashes bred' (i 55, ii 2; Kaske 1976). The last two of Guyon's three conjectures about the stain's indelibility (ii 4) constitute two standard definitions of original sin (Fowler 1960–1:144). This child of Mortdant and Amavia represents mankind (see ii 2) tainted at birth by original sin (Rom 5.12–21, 39 Articles 9, Hamilton 1958b:157–8, Fowler 1960–1:144), as the well allegorizing Mosaic law declares. Since the well does nothing for Ruddymane but diagnose his state, baptism is conspicuous by its absence (cf Fowler 1960a:145, 147, Fowler 1960–1, and others). Just as the well's nymph, allegorizing man's original righteousness, rejects both Ruddymane and the lustful Faunus, who allegorizes both the Tempter and concupiscence (ii 7–9; Fowler 1960–1:146), so Mosaic law holds up this righteousness as an impossibly high standard and thereby serves only to condemn for having original sin both the concupiscent adult and the innocent child. In ii 10, there is nevertheless a note of hope based on Ruddymane's role as mankind. In a final reversal, amplifying Amavia's 'testament' (i 37), he is also declared to represent, to borrow Milton's phrase, 'that greater man' who escaped inheriting original sin by being born of an altogether chaste woman, but whose vicarious assumption of it (allegorized not only by Ruddymane's present stain on his hands but by his future donning of his father's bloody arms; see *Piers Plowman* B, 18, where Christ's joust 'in Piers armes ... humana natura') expiates it for all the others (Kaske 1976:207–8; cf Evans 1970:119, Hamilton 1958b:158). CAROL V. KASKE

The religious works cited in this article and some other relevant medieval and Renaissance commentaries on Romans include Augustine ed 1957–72 *The City of God against the Pagans* tr George E. McCracken, et al 7 vols (Loeb Library); Augustine *Sermones in scripturis* 153–4 (*PLat* 38:824–41); John Calvin 1960a *Calvin's Commentaries: The Epistles of Paul the Apostle to the Romans and to the Thessalonians* tr Ross Mackenzie (Grand Rapids, Mich); Hugh of St Cher 1645 *In epistolas Pauli* in *Opera* (many eds through 1598) 7 (Lyon); Lapide 1627 *In epistolas Pauli* in Lapide 1614–45; Luther *Genesisvorlesung* and *Der Briefe an die Römer* in ed 1883–1987, 42, 56, Eng tr in ed 1958–75, 1–8 (Genesis), 25 (Romans); Origen *Commentaria in ... Romanos* tr Rufinus (*PGr* 14); Peter Martyr Vermigli 1568 *Commentaries [on] Romanes* tr H. B[illingsly] (London); Vermigli 1583.

For Spenser, see Brooks-Davies 1977; Evans 1970; Fowler 1960a; Fowler 1960–1; Hamilton 1958b; Hankins 1971; Hoopes 1954; Kaske 1976; Kaske 1979; Lemmi 1929; L.H. Miller 1966; Nelson 1963; Spenser *FQ* ed 1965a; *FQ* ed 1977; *FQ* ed 1978; A. Williams 1948; K. Williams 1966.

America to 1900, influence and reputation in The first direct reference to Spenser in American literature appears in Anne Bradstreet's poem 'In Honour of Queen Elizabeth' (1643), where her glory is said to be so great that not even Spenser's poetry can do it justice. A second reference, to 'Phoenix Spenser' in her elegy for Sidney in *The Tenth Muse* (1650), was dropped from the 1678 edition, an indication that Bradstreet had been made aware that Spenser was not the author of the unsigned elegy for Sidney in the 1593 anthology *The Phoenix Nest* (Crowder 1944).

Evidence exists that seventeenth-century Harvard students copied portions of Spenser's poems, and eighteenth-century Yale students were familiar enough with them for John Trumbull to have made *Epithalamion* the basis for a ribald parody in 1769. Late in the century, the influence of James Thomson led young American poets to experiment with the Spenserian stanza. One such attempt by Elihu Hubbard Smith, called 'In Imitation of Spenser: A Fragment' (1791), might better have been named 'In Imitation of Thomson,' for it combined the landscape detail of *The Seasons* with the Gothicism of *The Castle of Indolence* (Franklin 1970:923–5). Smith was the close friend of Charles Brockden Brown, America's earliest creator of romance fiction, whose enthusiasm for William Sotheby's translation of C.M. Wieland's *Oberon*, fashioned into Spenserian stanzas, caused him to call for a similar translation of *The Faerie Queene* to overcome the obstacle of Spenser's language (Brown 1805).

No such effort was forthcoming, however, and in 1817 the *North American Review* reiterated Brown's call by pointing to the need for a critical edition to elucidate the allegory (Gilman 1817). The significance of the article lies in its year of publication, 1817, a crucial one for the *Review* when its conservative founder, William Tudor, gave over leadership to the more liberal Willard Phillips who encouraged contributions from such romantics as Dana, Bryant, and W.E. Channing. Though willing to admit of the fatigue induced by a 'steady perusal from beginning to end' of *The Faerie Queene*, Bryant nonetheless proclaimed it the repository of a poetic language so perfect that it remained unparalleled (Bryant ed 1884, 1:152). His comments were part of a series of four lectures on English poetry delivered in New York in 1826, the first important study done in America on the subject. Later they formed the introduction to his anthology *A Library of Poetry and Song* (1871) which included five selections from Spenser. William Cullen Bryant was the only nineteenth-century American poet of note to use the Spenserian stanza (James Gates Percival's *Prometheus* [1820–2] has not survived) and did so in just one poem, his paean of praise to his native land, 'The Ages' (1821).

Spenser fared well in the 1820s and 1830s when American writers and painters sought ways to romanticize their country's natural landscape. The epithalamium pronounced by Samuel L. Mitchill at the 1823 opening of the Albany lock of the Erie Canal echoed Spenser's *Prothalamion* in its rapture at the wedding of the waters of the Hudson River with those of the Great Lakes (Colden 1825:60–1). Samuel F.B. Morse had studied with Benjamin West in England, and, influenced by West's Spenserian canvasses, 'Una and the Lion' and 'Fidelia and Speranza' as well as by Copley's 'Red Cross Knight with Fidelia and Speranza,' had produced 'Una and the Dwarf' for the art gallery that graced the Hudson River steamboat *The Albany*. James Fenimore Cooper's pictorial descriptions of landscape draw on the same kind of forest quality seen in West's 'Una and the Lion' and Allston's romanticized landscape in 'Flight of Florimel.' The strongest of these influences on Cooper can be found in *The Pioneers* and *The Prairie* (Krieg 1985).

From the best American critic of the 1830s and 1840s, Edgar Allan Poe, we have only the speculation that Milton's famed 'darkness visible' may have been suggested by Spenser's 'A litle glooming light, much like a shade' in *FQ* I i 14 (Poe 1836), and a left-handed compliment that excepted only *The Pilgrim's Progress* and *The Faerie Queene* from his general opinion of all allegories: 'contemptible' (Poe 1845a). At another point, he seems deliberately to misunderstand Spenser's meaning in *Mother Hubberd* 895–6 and 905–6 in order to justify revising the text by omitting the final comma in line 906 (Poe 1845b).

Before the first American edition in 1839, the unavailability of texts seems to have been as much a factor in Spenser's lack of popularity as were the perceived obstacles of his language and mode. The Transcendentalist educator Amos Bronson Alcott valued Spenser as a moralist, but was forced to send to England for copies of *The Faerie Queene* to use at his Temple School in Boston. About this time began the practice of publishing prose redactions of *The Faerie Queene* designed for children. The first and best of these was a retelling of Book I, *Holiness, or The Legend of St. George: A Tale from Spencer's Faerie Queene* (1836), by Nathaniel Hawthorne's future mother-in-law, Elizabeth (Palmer) Peabody, though published anonymously. In 1842, two such redactions appeared: Caroline Kirkland's *Spenser and the Faery Queen*, and John S. Hart's *Essay on the Life and Writings of Edmund Spenser with a Special Exposition of 'The Fairy Queen'* (see also *FQ, children's versions).

Through works such as these, the practice followed by the more privileged families in nineteenth-century America of reading *The Faerie Queene* in the nursery moved into the public classroom. There is little evidence that either public or private study did much to increase Spenser's reputation, though critic Samuel Gilman had argued ardently in 1817 that Americans – especially American children – should read *The Faerie Queene* as a form of mental discipline as well as for the pleasure it would yield. Gilman blamed his countrymen's inability to read the allegory on an impatience for immediate understanding bred by such things as childhood riddle books that present riddle and answer side by side on adjoining pages, and storytellers too eager to point out their moral. While his argument is well made, the relegation of *The Faerie Queene* to the nursery and classroom had the effect of placing Spenser beyond the pale of serious poetic consideration for many Americans.

When Little, Brown published *The Poetical Works of Edmund Spenser* in 1839, the *North American Review* claimed that with this first American edition 'Spenser is now universally acknowledged, both in England and in this country, to belong to the first class of poets' (Cleveland 1840:175). In 1841, the *New York Review* prophesied that the edition 'would elevate the literary taste of our country' (8[Jan]:50). The editor of the five-volume edition was George S. Hillard, attorney and literary critic. His preface makes quite clear his intention, to eliminate the 'learned rubbish' of the Todd edition published in London in 1805 by paring the notes to a minimum. One democratic principle thus served was the reduction in price which had kept the Todd edition 'quite out of the reach of a large majority of readers.' A second democratic principle was served in the editor's 'Observations on *The Faerie Queene*,' in which he dismisses both the historical and spiritual levels of meaning, and directs his readers to the narrative and its characters, the true object of Spenser's interest, 'a warm flesh-and-blood interest, not in the delineation of a virtue, but in the adventures of a knight or lady.' Such feelings can be shared by all readers, Hillard claims, and need no interpretation.

The attempt at democratization was successful enough to warrant reprints of the 1839 edition in 1848 and 1853 before Little, Brown issued a new edition in 1855 featuring extensive scholarly notes by Francis J. Child of Harvard, who was just beginning his great work of collecting old English and Scottish ballads. This edition became the one favored by the more highly educated in America, while the Hillard edition was taken over by the Philadelphia firm of W.P. Hazard in 1855 and appeared only once more, in 1857, outstripped by the Child work which persisted through editions in 1860, 1864, 1866, and 1875. As the publication history suggests, Spenser seems to have been claimed not by the masses of Americans in the second half of the nineteenth century, but by the intellectual class. Except for Shakespeare, he was the most popular dissertation subject in Renaissance studies, with *The Faerie Queene* a clear favorite. The greatest number of these dissertations were written at Yale, Harvard, and Princeton (see McNamee 1968).

George S. Hillard became a close friend of Hawthorne in the year his edition was published, 1839. The coincidence and the edition reawakened Hawthorne's early love for the poet whose allegorical mode exerted a strong influence on his own writing and provided a moral structure for his fictions. Specific Spenserian themes and characters have been discerned in his works, as they have been, though to a lesser degree, in the writings of Melville, who shared his enthusiasm for Spenser but not his sensibility. Melville's ironic use of Spenserian themes often projects his own dark vision of an indifferent universe.

Neither Spenser nor the first American edition of his works can be shown to have had an important influence on Ralph Waldo Emerson. It is possible that his interest in Spenser came about chiefly through his newly established friendship, in July 1835, with Amos Bronson Alcott, whose appreciation of Spenser as a teacher of virtues and morals seems to have influenced Emerson's judgment of the poet's worth. In the same month that the two met, Emerson borrowed two volumes of Spenser from the Harvard College Library and copied *Hymne of Beautie* 127–33 into his journal (Cameron 1941:25). These lines appear in his essay 'The Poet,' written some time between 1841 and 1843, as evidence for the Platonic belief that 'the soul makes the body, as the wise Spenser teaches' (ed 1971–, 3:14). A similar sentiment along with the same lines from Spenser was used in an 1837 lecture, 'The Eye and Ear' (ed 1959–64, 2:264), and line 133 appears yet again in *English Traits* (1856) as an example of Platonic thought in English literature.

Disagreement between Emerson and Alcott about evaluating Spenser, whether to assign 'poet' or 'moralist' as his primary title, may be inferred from a journal entry of October 1835 in which Emerson muses on the modern reader's difficulty in imputing to a dead artist the precise high thoughts or emotions inspired by his art in others. Singling out Spenser and his allegory, he claims we hesitate to credit the poet with the meaning we ourselves find in it. It is unlikely that the hesitation was Emerson's. That Alcott's estimate of Spenser as a moralist prevailed over Emerson's appreciation of his poetic genius is borne out by Emerson's categorizing Spenser as one of the 'Ethical Writers' (along with Donne, Milton, Bunyan, and More) in a January 1836 lecture. Rather than a planned lecture on Spenser (fifth in a series of ten on English literature), he substituted a second one on Shakespeare, a safe substitution, since American audiences in general shared the feelings of their more literate countrymen that there was no more universal poet than Shakespeare (Krieg 1985a).

Emerson's public references to the poet thereafter were limited to paralleling Spenser's golden mean 'Be bold, be bold ... Be not too bold' to what Emerson termed Plato's 'circumspection' in *Representative Men* (1850), and a partial reference in the late essay 'Resources' to Spenser's Wood of Error. Occasionally he entered a line of Spenser in his journal; and once, shortly after he had published a volume of poems in 1846, he indicates what may have been his true evaluation of Spenser as poet. Reflecting on the delight Spenser seems to take in his art for its own sake, Emerson turns to *Muiopotmos* as an example of the poet's artistry and compares it to that of a weaver who can confidently defy all competitors with the superiority of the art he alone can fashion on his loom (ed 1960–82, 9:453).

In an earlier journal entry that comments on the exhibition of paintings by Washington Allston in Boston during the summer of 1839, Emerson makes oblique reference to Spenser, linking his genius to that of Allston: both are 'Elysian,' lacking in emotion (7:222). This sentiment was shared by a fellow Transcendentalist, critic John Sullivan Dwight, in his review of the 1839 American edition of Spenser in the *Christian Examiner* (May 1840). Years later when Emerson edited an anthology of his favorite poems, *Parnassus* (1874), he included selections from *FQ* I, *Epithalamion*, *Hymne of Beautie*, and some lines from *Mother Hubberd* which he titled 'Spenser at Court.'

Others among the Transcendentalists who made reference to Spenser were Margaret Fuller in *Woman in the Nineteenth Century* (1845), where she extolled *The Faerie Queene* for its delineation of female character, and Henry David Thoreau, whose familiarity with Spenser is evident from his first published work, *A Week on the Concord and Merrimack Rivers* (1849) with its four Spenserian references. The first compares a New England scene to that described in *FQ* III v 39 (Thoreau ed 1968, 1:196). The second quotes the concluding couplet of *Ruines of Rome* 29 (1:264); the third occurs in a discussion of dreams that includes Spenser's description of the sleep-inducing environment in which Morpheus dwells (1:316); and the fourth, the last four lines of *FQ* II xii 29, appears as the epigraph for the final chapter of the book. *A Week*, the record of a trip made with his brother in the fall of 1839, abounds in poetic quotations, for Thoreau was widely read, especially in English poetry. The use of Spenser quotations beyond the more usual limit of *FQ* I might have some relation to the American edition published in the year of the trip. The record of the river journey was written during the two years Thoreau spent at Walden Pond, and his published account of that experience also includes some lines from *FQ* I i 35, which he claims he would be proud to own as the motto of his cabin (2:158).

While the quotations from Spenser do not indicate any real influence on Thoreau's work, they at least show evidence of an appreciative reading, and none of the ambivalence of a reader such as Walt Whitman, a self-proclaimed 'rough' of the America of the 1840s, who lacked the educational advantages of Thoreau and his fellow Concordians. In an attempt at self-education, Whitman kept notebooks in the late 1840s and early 1850s into which he inserted literary selections, articles, and his own notes. For a time he was interested in the English poets, including Spenser, and his notes betray mixed feelings of distaste for the fact that the poet had 'danced attendance like a lackey for a long time at court,' and of admiration for the way their author's 'reverence for purity and goodness is paramount to all the rest' (ed 1902, 9:77–8).

In 1888, James Russell Lowell published his book of essays on *The English Poets*, which included his 1856 lecture on Spenser. Here for the first time since Bryant's 1826 lecture was a genuine appreciation of Spenser from an American writer. Lowell's long-sustained passion for his subject pervades the essay. His delight in Spenser's poetry and his awareness of how little it was known to his countrymen led him repeatedly to break off his commentary and insert huge chunks of the work under discussion. He completely disregards the worries of earlier Americans concerning both the allegory in *The Faerie Queene* and its difficulties of language. The allegory, he claims, can be set aside, as a mere poetic 'fashion' of Spenser's time; and the language is seen as proof of what Lowell deemed Spenser's greatest glory, the fact that it was he who brought to his native tongue a melody and harmony it had not known (see Lowell 1888:59). In his youth, Lowell produced numerous poems in imitation of Spenser, the best of which was 'Callirhoe,' later revised as 'Ianthe.' His appreciation of the poet did not prevent him from parodying Spenser in his 1853 comic poem 'Our Own,' where a verse table of contents pokes fun at Spenser's headings to the books of *The Faerie Queene*.

Lowell's essay had little impact on a reading public caught up in the new enthusiasm for literary realism. William Dean Howells, the arch-realist who exerted great literary influence at the time, confessed in *My Literary Passions* (1895) that Lowell's praises made him want to read Spenser, but he found it impossible. Perhaps the deepest cut of all came from the gentle Quaker poet, John Greenleaf Whittier, who, in his preface to the 1876 anthology of favorite poems, *Songs of Three Centuries*, expressed a preference for Thomson over Spenser.

Disheartening though most of these reactions to Spenser are, it may not be assumed that little or no influence is to be found outside the works of Hawthorne and Melville. Spenser himself had located Fairyland on the frontier of knowledge when, anticipating the inquiry 'Where is that happy land of Faery?' he referred his imagined questioner to the ever-expanding limits of geographical knowledge of the New World (*FQ* II proem 1–4), thereby suggesting that the regions of Fairyland, though yet unknown, might be discovered there at any moment. The efforts of the American pre-Romantics, Bryant, Cooper, and the artists of the Hudson River School to idealize the New World natural landscape caused them to follow Spenser's suggestion and to seek in landscape not only the picturesque and sublime, but moral qualities as well. For this there was no better model than Fairyland, where there was a direct correspondence between the physical conditions of the regions of faery and the spiritual condition of the individual soul. This same moral structure, though not always fully realized in the allegories of Hawthorne, brought him to the ranks of the most powerful writers of his century, and became a link between the romance tradition of English poetry and the prose romance as it developed in America.

JOANN PECK KRIEG

Charles Brockden Brown 1805 'Spencer's *Fairy Queene* Modernized' *Literary Magazine* 3:424–5; William Cullen Bryant 1884 *Prose Writings* ed Parke Godwin, 2 vols (New York); Kenneth Walter Cameron 1941 *Ralph Waldo Emerson's Reading* (Raleigh, NC) corr ed 1962; [H.R. Cleveland] 1840 'Spenser's Poetical Works' (review of *The Poetical Works of Edmund Spenser* ed George S. Hillard) *North American Review* 50(Jan):174–206; Cadwallader D. Colden 1825 *Memoir Prepared at the Request of a Committee of the City of New York ... at the Celebration of the Completion of the New York Canals* (New York); Richard Crowder 1944 '"Phoenix Spencer": A Note on Anne Bradstreet' *NEQ* 17:310; Ralph Waldo Emerson 1959–72 *Early Lectures* ed Stephen E. Whicher, Robert E. Spiller, and Wallace E. Williams, 3 vols (Cambridge, Mass); Emerson 1960–82 *Journals and Miscellaneous Notebooks* ed William H. Gilman et al, 16 vols (Cambridge, Mass); Emerson 1971– *Collected Works* ed Robert E. Spiller and Alfred R. Ferguson (Cambridge, Mass); Benjamin Franklin, ed 1970 *The Poetry of the Minor Connecticut Wits* (Gainesville, Fla); Samuel Gilman 1817 'The Faery Queen of Spenser' *NAR* 5(Sept):301–9; Joann Peck Krieg 1985; Krieg 1985a 'Spenser and the Transcendentalists' *ATQ* 55:29–39; James Russell Lowell 1888 *The English Poets* (Boston); Lawrence F. McNamee 1968 *Dissertations in English and American Literature ... 1865–1964* Supplement 1 in 1969, Supplement 2 in 1974 (New York); Edgar Allan Poe 1836 'Pinakidia 67' *Southern Literary Messenger* (August); Poe 1845a [Review of *The Coming of the Mammoth*] *Broadway Journal* 12 July; Poe 1845b 'Fifty Suggestions 43' *Graham's Magazine* 34(June):364; Henry David Thoreau 1968 *Writings* 20 vols (New York); W. Whitman ed 1902.

Amoret Spenser's figure for the married state of love, 'goodly womanhed,' in *FQ* III and IV. She is the twin of Belphoebe, the figure for virginity; and their initial relationship and adventures spell out Spenser's allegory of these two states which are the two extremes of his virtue of chastity. Amoret's story runs from her birth and early education in the Garden of Adonis (III vi) to her final disappearance in IV ix, although we do not hear Scudamour's story of her courtship until IV x.

Rescue and separation are key motifs in her adventures. She is rescued by Venus immediately after her birth to Chrysogone and brought to the Garden of Adonis (III vi 28–9); in the 1590 version of the poem, she is rescued by Britomart from Busirane's enchantment and reunited with Scudamour (xii).

With the addition of Books IV–VI in 1596, Spenser rewrote the ending of Book III: although Amoret is rescued by Britomart, she remains separated from Scudamour for the rest of the poem. The new series of her adventures in Book IV continues the theme of rescue and separation. In the opening canto, we learn that Busirane had enchanted her at her wedding to Scudamour, a development that casts a new light on her torment by Busirane in the last two cantos of Book III, which in the 1590 version portrays merely the romance motif of the distressed maiden finally restored in happy union with her true love. The complication of this motif at the beginning of IV alters her adventures, so that we learn more about her nature and are made aware of her marriage and of Scudamour's winning her from the Temple of Venus (IV x). Both events are presented as prior to her imprisonment by Busirane, and both are crucial to understanding Busirane's power over her. Nothing in Scudamour's remarks to Britomart before she enters the house of Busirane (III xi 7–24) indicates that Amoret is anything more than 'My Lady and my love' (11), although he does suggest that she has yielded her favors to him (17). Therefore the description of the marriage celebrations as the occasion of her separation from Scudamour (IV i 3) comes as a surprise, and her abduction is now to be seen as a violation of the sacred bond of matrimony. It is significant that we learn of this violated bond at the beginning of the Legend of Friendship, and that the last we hear of either of these lovers – Scudamour's story of winning Amoret – should represent an affirmation of the virtue. Amoret's adventures in Book IV are thus contained within the frame of her wedding and her wooing, and this reversal and fragmentation of the essentially linear story fits the fragments into an allegorical mosaic of the complementary virtues of chastity and friendship.

Amoret's birth is placed at the center of Book III, and her imprisonment by Busirane occupies its last two cantos. In both episodes, she is of less significance than the circumstances that surround her. Her miraculous birth to Chrysogone through impregnation by the sun is overshadowed by the circumstances of the birth. She is paired with Belphoebe but immediately separated from her by Venus, who takes her (as a replacement for her lost son, Cupid) to the Garden of Adonis, where she is brought up as the companion of Pleasure, the child of Cupid and Psyche. This Venus is the good Venus of the Renaissance mythographers: her association with a married Cupid and the fertile domain of the Garden of Adonis confirm that she represents married love in the poem. Up to this point, there is no possibility of judging Amoret's nature.

With the two principal episodes involving Amoret, those at the house of Busirane and the Temple of Venus (III xi-xii, IV x), the problem of interpreting her does arise. Her imprisonment has been seen as resulting from a fear of sex, which puts her in the power of Busirane, the abuse of love (Roche 1964). Alternatively, her imprisonment has been attributed to Scudamour's bold mastering of her in the Temple of Venus, his practice of 'maisterie' (Hieatt 1962). Both claims are based on moral and psychological interpretations, and neglect Spenser's allegorical characterization. Why Amoret learned so little about love, in either the Garden or the Temple, remains an unanswered question. That Busirane's power is both potent and awful and that he is the enemy of chastity is undoubted. In Book III, Amoret is defined by her allegorical surroundings: her miraculous birth, her adoption by Venus, and her nurturing in the Garden of Adonis tell us about her only through the circumstances of her placement; and even in the Busirane episode, she does not speak about her predicament until the enchantment has been broken by Britomart. Only in Book IV does she begin to take on any life as a character.

Amoret's adventures in IV repeat the theme of rescue and separation, and she is twice brought to a possible reunion with Scudamour. In the first, she wanders away from Britomart – 'faire *Amoret*, of nought affeard, / Walkt through the wood, for pleasure, or for need' (vii 4) – and is 'rapt by greedie lust'; in the second, she simply drops out of the poem with no explanation why she is not recognized by Scudamour (ix). This second event has been interpreted as a maddening narrative inconsistency – perhaps a moment where Spenser nodded – yet attention to the allegorical narrative may reveal an order that is not apparent from a literal reading.

In canto i, Britomart and Amoret ride along after leaving the house of Busirane, Britomart deceiving Amoret with her warlike male appearance, until they come to a castle where no knight may stay without a lady. A young knight claims Amoret for his own, and is defeated by Britomart, who then pities him, reveals herself as a woman, and claims her right as a woman to include him as her companion. Amoret and Britomart subsequently go to bed together. The episode is both ludicrous and serious in that it recapitulates the opening canto of Book III, where Britomart, again because of her disguise, misleads the unchaste Malecasta to her bed. In the interim, Britomart has passed from an unfledged woman in love to a woman who has experienced the house of Busirane and is now sharing her bed with Amoret, a figure of married love. Later in this same canto, Scudamour (who had been left behind with Glauce when Britomart entered the house of Busirane) is abused by Duessa and Ate with the information that the knight served by Glauce has gone to bed with Amoret (47–9). Thus an enmity is created between Scudamour and Britomart, to be resolved only in canto vi, where Britomart reveals herself both to Scudamour and to her own love, Artegall. The revelation of Britomart's true gender relieves Amoret's fears in canto i and Scudamour's jealousy in canto vi. When Britomart leaves behind her nurse in Book III and takes Amoret as her companion in the first half of IV, the exchange suggests a passage from childhood to maturity. Scudamour's complementary exchange, of wife for nurse, may be equally suggestive.

Amoret's final adventure with Britomart is at Satyrane's tournament for Florimell's girdle. After the other ladies fail to secure the belt around their waists, Amoret succeeds, but to no avail because the raucous crowd wants to award the prize to the false Florimell (v 19–20): chaste love is overcome by false beauty. After this disappointing injustice, Britomart and Amoret ride off again, to a chance encounter with Scudamour and Artegall, the latter still disguised as the Salvage Knight. On Britomart's victory and revelation of self, both Artegall and Scudamour are relieved of their false opinions of Britomart (vi 28–32); and at this point, where Scudamour and Amoret might once more have been united, Amoret has disappeared.

Her solitary sojourn is interrupted by Lust, who carries her off to his den. Here again the question of Amoret's responsibility for her own capture is offset by the inclusion of the young Aemylia, whose assignation with her squire has made her susceptible to lust as Amoret's actions have not. The distinction between the two women is further developed when Timias' attempts to rescue and console Amoret are misinterpreted by Belphoebe, who asks 'Is this the faith' and flees (vii 36–7). Timias despairs at the loss of his beloved Belphoebe.

The episode has been interpreted as Spenser's depiction of Elizabeth's wrath at Raleigh's secret marriage to her lady-in-waiting, Elizabeth Throckmorton. Like the Queen, Belphoebe seems not to have made a proper judgment, as we, who know Amoret to be faultless here and a figure of married love in the poem as a whole, tend to realize. Since lust can be an external as well as an internal passion, we are free as readers to see that Aemylia must experience the internal passion and Amoret be, once more, the passive victim of an external Lust. The fact that it is her twin sister, unrecognized and unrecognizing, who destroys Lust adds an ironic nicety to Spenser's 'defense' of Raleigh's misdemeanor.

Aemylia and Amoret (for the last time) are rescued by Arthur (viii 19–22) who cures Amoret's wounds with some of the 'pretious liquour' he had presented to Redcrosse in I ix 19, where it is described as that 'liquor pure ... That any wound could heale incontinent.' Arthur's intervention in previous books as a figure of grace signals that this liquor is grace to heal the wounds inflicted on Amoret by Lust and (inadvertently) by Timias. Aemylia will be restored by time (and by marriage in the next canto); Amoret requires divine intervention as a passive victim of another's misdeeming. Spenser is playing a dangerous game in this episode: he must justify his figure of married love, exonerate the undoubted indiscretion of Raleigh and his lady, and avoid the wrath of Elizabeth. Probably for this very reason, he shows Arthur, Amoret, and Aemylia all subjected to the venom of Sclaunder. Since the reader knows that Sclaunder's vilifications are false, Arthur and his two ladies can ride off to reunite Aemylia with Amyas. Again, however, just when we might expect Spenser to reunite Scudamour and Amoret (IV vi 36 or vii 4), she is no longer present; and at the urging of Arthur and Britomart, Scudamour tells his story of winning Amoret.

Scudamour's story is crucial for Amoret's existence as a figure in the poem. Some readers will see his 'bold' venture in winning Amoret as an enactment of the legend in the house of Busirane: 'Be bold, be bold ... Be not too bold' (III xi 54); others will see it as comparable to Adam's need to draw Eve away from her watery narcissism. In any case, this is the last we hear of either one of these sad but faithful lovers; and even before we finish this story, Spenser pushes us into the even sadder story of Florimell, whom he has left languishing since III viii.

Florimell's story will end happily with Marinell finally coming to marry her (V iii). She has been imprisoned within the watery walls of Proteus' house for seven months (IV xi 4), just as Amoret has spent seven months within the fiery walls of the house of Busirane (III xi 10, IV i 4). Although we cannot know what Spenser had in mind for the reunion of Scudamour and Amoret beyond the canceled original ending of Book III, his careful elaboration of the first part of Amoret's narrative, at the moment of Scudamour's winning her, suggests a conscious juxtaposition of the stories of these two loving couples. THOMAS P. ROCHE, JR

Amoretti, Epithalamion (See ed 1912:561–84.) Spenser's sonnet sequence *Amoretti* and his marriage hymn *Epithalamion* were published in a single octavo by William Ponsonby in 1595 (Johnson 1933 no 15; *STC* 23076). The book was entered in the Stationers' Register 19 November 1594, and Ponsonby's title page describes the contents as 'Written not long since' (only sonnet 8 seems to predate the 1590s; see L. Cummings 1964). *Amoretti* is a unified sequence of 89 sonnets; *Epithalamion* is a canzone-like poem of 23 stanzas and an envoy. Intervening between them are four light 'anacreontic' poems. Except for one of the Anacreontics, each sonnet and stanza occupies a single page, and the volume is visually unified by a decorative border employed throughout, though *Epithalamion* has a separate half title. The poems are recognized as Spenser's tribute to Elizabeth Boyle, whom he married probably on the feast of St Barnabas, 11 June 1594, the day of the summer solstice according to the Julian calendar then used in England. The biographical associations of the poems were closely scrutinized early in this century (*Var* 8:631–8, 647–52) but remain unchallenged.

Amoretti belongs to the popular Renaissance genre of the sonnet sequence, most influentially employed by Petrarch. Sonnet sequences or canzonieri (song books) are composed of separate poems (Petrarch referred to his as *rime sparse* 'scattered rhymes') which make their own dispersedness an emblem of the desolation of the suffering lover who composes them. In contrast, the epithalamium is a classical genre, one public and festive in purpose rather than private and expressive of personal grief. Spenser's imagination was perhaps the least naturally equipped of all great writers of sonnet sequences for the exigencies of the genre: to Petrarch's spiritually troubled meditation on the 'scattering' of his poems, he brought to bear a vision which was fundamentally inclusive. Thus *Amoretti*, though it pays homage to the convention of the suffering lover, is paradoxically a book made up of happy leaves, and it moves steadily towards the moment in sonnet 68 when the poet announces the fulfillment of his hopes.

In the classical marriage song, Spenser encountered a genre which rejoices in an integrated vision. Thus, while *Epithalamion* is still that Spenserian poem which appeals most intimately and concretely to its readers, it is also very learned and highly conventional. Written in an antique genre, woven with consummate skill into a fabric of personal, classical, folkloric, and theological allusions, the poem deals with two themes central to Spenser's imagination: the generation of life in human and divine love, and the relation between the mortal experience of change and the heavenly attribute of constancy. Here too Spenser transforms the convention, for the marriage hymn is not sung by the public and representative voice of priest or friend, but by the bridegroom himself, whose poetic gift is thus committed to the task of singing the mortal figures of himself and his bride into the sacramental bonds of what is ideally the most enduring of human social relationships.

The pairing of two such works in one book has puzzled critics, who for practical reasons usually treat them separately. But Spenser's linking a group of short poems with a longer one has precedents in both English and continental collections of poetry. The epithalamium by Marc-Claude de Buttet which provided Spenser with a number of verbal allusions (McPeek 1939:160–84) was associated with a collection of sonnets by a repeated motto celebrating the Amalthée in whose honor (if not for whose marriage) the poems were collected. Such graceful devices were made plausible by the convention prevalent since Statius and confirmed by Scaliger (1561, 3.101), that the bridegroom has suffered love's trials but is now to be freed of them because his obdurate lady has relented (as Medway at last gives in to the wooing of Thames in *FQ* IV xi 8). Sidney's epithalamium speaks of 'justest love' having vanquished '*Cupid's* powers' (*Old Arcadia* 63.3 in ed 1962), and Puttenham begins his rules for the genre by contrasting 'honorable matrimonie' with the 'vaine cares and passions' of mutable love (*Arte of English Poesie* 1.26). The epithalamium as a form thus represents release after trial, amplitude after limitation (Forster 1969, Tufte 1970). In so doing, Spenser's chosen genre also – and by no means accidentally – fulfills the Book of Common Prayer's statement that marriage 'was ordeined for a remedie against sinne, to avoid fornication, that such persons as have not the gift of continencie, might marry, and keepe them selves undefiled members of Christs bodie' (*BCP*, eg, 1580).

Spenser extracts these possibilities from the convention, but he transforms them into a social vision by enclosing the smaller and more limited sphere of Cupid's activities represented by the 'little loves' of *Amoretti* within the amplitude of 'justest love' represented by the marriage hymn. In *FQ* III, Cupid usurps Jove's place: 'Lo now the heavens obey to me alone, / And take me for their *Jove*, whiles *Jove* to earth is gone' (xi 35). But here, as in a Renaissance triumph, the greater and more powerful form absorbs and transforms the lesser, a strategy which particularly lends itself to Renaissance theories about the relative status of men and women.

To achieve this, Spenser employs a design he uses recurrently: the moralized pageant of time. In *The Shepheardes Calender*, Colin's aimless wanderings in 'the common Labyrinth of Love' are expressed in twelve eclogues in order 'to mitigate and allay the heate of his passion' and 'to warne ... the young shepheards ... of his unfortunate folly' (Epistle to Harvey). These are 'proportioned to the state of the xii. monethes' by means of a seasonal cycle beginning in January, to show us that despite Colin's December despair the Christ-child's winter birth ensures our eventual redemption. In the *Cantos of Mutabilitie*, the pageant of the months is intended to instruct Mutabilitie in the principles of orderly change; Spenser's calendar there is the 'year of grace' beginning in March, the month of the Annunciation.

The workings of time are a subject of both *Amoretti* and *Epithalamion*. In *Amoretti*, time seems to be arrested as the lover suffers: 'How long shall this lyke dying lyfe endure, / And know no end of her owne mysery: / but wast and weare away in termes unsure, / twixt feare and hope depending doubtfully' (*Am* 25). In contrast, *Epithalamion* makes possible the lover's entry into time, as it celebrates his wedding day, that one day which is to be his alone. These counterpoised visions of time are presented with great complexity in the physical design of the two works (Hieatt 1960; Dunlop 1969, 1970). Alastair Fowler (1970b) has argued that the entire volume has a unifying design of 117 sonnets and stanzas arranged in a five-part pattern, *A B C B A*. These units are made up as follows: (*A*) sonnets 1–34; (*B*) sonnet 35; (*C*) the 47 sonnets from 36 to 82; (*B*) sonnet 83; (*A*) a unit of 34 made up of sonnets 84 to 89, the 4 Anacreontics, and the 24 stanzas of *Epithalamion*.

Even if the two works combine to form a coherent structure, each possesses its own pattern. The Lenten trials of *Amoretti* belong to the mutable world of the moon; its presiding deity is Cupid and its length is that of winter's 89 days, though the addition of the four Anacreontics yields the 93 days of spring. *Epithalamion* belongs to the sun and to the sphere ruled by Christ; it gives us the 24 hours of the solstitial day itself, on which the Cupid-poet and his untouchable Diana are transformed into an Elizabethan bride and groom. This elaborate scheme has precedents in the Augustinian-Pythagorean tradition of poetic design (see *topomorphical approach), and Spenser uses many such devices elsewhere in his poetry. Its details and significance are still being debated (eg, Kaske 1978), but its outline is firm enough to convince all but the most skeptical that Spenser's marriage book is not the miscellaneous compilation it has sometimes been thought. Once demonstrated, the design of *Epithalamion* is quite apparent; probably its secret was simply lost by later readers unsympathetic to the visual conceits of medieval and Renaissance poetry. The design of *Amoretti* is much less penetrable. Today, as possibly in Spenser's own day, it can be 'judged onely of the learned' (*SC* Epistle to Harvey), but in 1594 no more than two need have been in on the secret, for the problematic action of time is surely traced here for the edification of those most deeply concerned, the bride and groom.

For its sources, *Amoretti* draws on the standard *topoi* of the love lyric which originated in Horace, Ovid, and Propertius. Many of these had been transmitted in medieval vernacular and Latin lyric to the early Italian sonneteers. They were eventually assembled by Petrarch into a compositional repertoire which later European lyricists both drew on and enriched through their own study of the classical poets, of Petrarch, and of each other. While Spenser's debt to this tradition is evident, none of the poets on whom he draws most closely – Petrarch, Desportes, Tasso – is quite congenial to him. He rejects Petrarch's sonnet form outright, and employs – only to repudiate it implicitly – the psychic stasis of Petrarch's constantly reformulated canzoniere. Like other Elizabethans, Spenser exploits Desportes, but chiefly for his conceits. A recent reading of Torquato Tasso leaves its mark, especially on the later sonnets of *Amoretti*. Yet though Tasso's Platonism may have attracted him, Spenser's copiousness and the Italian poet's compact elegance remain in conflict. If his search for alternatives led Spenser as far as the 'conjugal lyric' of Bernardo Tasso and others, it left no evidence in *Amoretti.* The most lasting influence remains that of du Bellay, less on specific poems than in that seriousness of temperament which in the 1580s had drawn Spenser away from the paradoxes of amorous lyric towards the moral and philosophical tradition of the didactic sonnet represented in *Complaints.* Spenser's reluctant commitment to continental Petrarchism is not balanced by a significant debt to the native poets of *Tottel's Miscellany* and their heirs. Here as elsewhere, he creates his own vision of the possibilities of his chosen genre: he assimilates to the canzoniere echoes of the Psalms, the Song of Solomon, and the collects of the Book of Common Prayer, or of Renaissance Latin versions of Anacreon, and stubbornly resists conventions of the sonnet or sonnet sequence which conflict with the structure he is assembling.

Nonetheless, like all Renaissance sonneteers Spenser exploits standard topoi (fire and ice, the 'galley' sonnet, the solitude of the lover, the slanderer), and like them he shows the influence of rhetorical training, varying poems on the same subject for purposes of display (*Am* 7, 8, 9, 12, 16 on the lady's eyes), or juxtaposing variant treatments in order to effect some essential change in the pattern of the sequence (58, 59). He can take a conceit from Desportes, as he does in sonnet 22, and turn the resulting poem into a key element in his plan; and his treatment of Tasso can embrace both inventive variation and the homage of direct translation. The outstanding example of this assimilative method is sonnet 67, 'Lyke as a huntsman after weary chace,' which, at the same time as it pays tribute to Petrarch, Wyatt, Tasso, and Marguerite de Navarre (Prescott 1985), uses suppressed Christological echoes to enact the conquest of the beloved which the Petrarchan sonnet sequence otherwise so persistently defers.

The religious wonder with which Spenser contemplates the anagogic significance of his beloved (eg, *Am* 68), and the growing conviction of critics that a Lenten calendar is present in the collection, have lured some readers to interpret the sonnets as literally moral or liturgical; but in *Amoretti* as elsewhere, an essential feature of Spenser's imaginative universe is its capacity for structural irony and amused variation. Repeatedly the sonnets suggest the liturgical potential of an image, yet turn gracefully away from making it explicit. The result is a reservation of strength for the celebratory aspect of the poems, and an opening of the sequence to other kinds of association drawn from Neoplatonic love theory and cosmogonic myth. *Amoretti* is above all a smiling sequence: its opening poem announces happy leaves, lines, and rhymes, and we are allowed to suspect that certain conventions are being very lightly mocked, rather in the manner of sonnet 18, where the lady 'turnes hir selfe to laughter' before the abject spectacle of the lover's pleading (Bieman 1983). As a result, *Amoretti* is distinguished among sonnet sequences for its 'goodly temperature' (*Am* 13), that benign moderation of tone and absence of exhausting paradox which come from Spenser's modification of the sonnet sequence's characteristic lamenting stance by the celebratory purpose of his volume as a whole (Martz 1961). The title evokes the 'legions of loves with little wings' that lurk in the lady's glance (*Am* 16) or will flutter about the marriage bed in *Epithalamion* 357–9. It suggests a lightness and intimacy which is borne out by the gravely humorous wordplay in many of the poems and by the ideal of mutual love which they keep before us: 'Sweet be the bands, the which true love doth tye, / without constraynt or dread of any ill' (*Am* 65).

In the Petrarchan sonnet sequence (eg, Sidney's *Astrophil and Stella*), the lover engages in reiterated poetic lament for his lady's failure to accept a suit which he is wrong to press in the first place. But in *Amoretti*, the poet's love is virtuous; it seeks 'to knit the knot, that ever shall remaine' (*Am* 6). Instead of being tormented by an unworthy passion, the lover is afflicted by the puzzling juxtaposition in his lady of ideal beauty and obdurate cruelty. From one point of view, the poet's beloved is a sovereign presence whose light kindles heavenly fire in his frail spirit; in sonnet 7 he asks, 'Fayre eyes, the myrrour of my mazed hart, / what wondrous vertue is contaynd in you, / the which both lyfe and death forth from you dart / into the object of your mighty view?' In her radiant certitude, she descends more directly from Dante's Beatrice (Hardison 1972) than from the shifting and evanescent figure of Petrarch's Laura, though she is a *donna gentile* envisioned in terms of the systematic Neoplatonism of the late Renaissance. Yet in some sonnets, the poet attacks her with astonishing force; she is 'more cruell and more salvage wylde, / then either Lyon or the Lyonesse'; she 'shames not to be with guiltlesse bloud defylde, / but taketh glory in her cruelnesse' (*Am* 20). Here the Petrarchan heritage of *Amoretti* becomes evident: the *donna gentile* is equally a 'proud love, that doth my spirite spoyle' (33) who wages unremitting warfare on her suitor in a remarkable hypertrophy of the 'beloved warrior' conceit dear to the Petrarchists. This obduracy becomes the chief problem her lover must address in trying to comprehend her significance.

The severity of such poems as 'Trust not the treason of those smyling lookes' (47) is hard to relate to the wondering stance of other sonnets, until we realize that in *Amoretti* those extremes of amorous experience which another sonneteer would fuse in the paradoxes of a single poem are polarized in sharply differing sonnets. Here Spenser was aided by his own characteristic method of constructing sonnets. He early rejected both the Italian rhyme scheme with its dialectical structure and the English sonnet with its concluding reversal, in favor of an aggregative form devised by himself. Its pattern (*abab bcbc cdcd ee*) produces a cohesive network of interlaced rhymes culminating in a final confirmatory couplet. Employing it meant that instead of exploring the contradictions of love within single sonnets Spenser was more likely to dismantle the Petrarchan oxymoron and mingle sonnets praising the lady with others that sharply condemn her. In a Petrarchist sequence, the paradoxes of the individual sonnet have two results: a woven stylistic effect of timeless allusiveness, and an equally timeless situation of inner debate. The result is brilliant, but essentially static. By frequently deploying the Petrarchist contraries in different sonnets, indeed by giving us two conflicting views of the lady, Spenser forces us out of the stasis and narcissism of the Petrarchan sequence into a consideration of the problems of action in the situation itself. However static and fragmenting the convention of the canzoniere, he views it as a potential scene for moral action.

In *Amoretti*, both lover and lady are eventually engaged in this action, though only in ways which the convention of *rime sparse* will permit, for the sphere of *Amoretti* always remains that of frustration and mutability. Insofar as it is a Petrarchan sequence, *Amoretti* like hundreds of such collections represents the unchanneled diversity, the mutability, of the uncreative love in which poet and lady are struggling. But in the arrangement of the sonnets is hidden a paschal motif which silently points to the regenerative and integrative tasks before the lover. In Cupid's variable sphere, this redemptive scheme remains veiled, like the implicit Christological meanings of certain sonnets; but its tacit presence ensures the eventual rejoicing of the wedding day even in the conventional desolation of the concluding sonnets.

In sonnet 1, the poet attempts to please his lady by offering her a record of his own endurance, the poems of *Amoretti* itself. Three sonnets at the beginning and three at the end compose a frame which displays the poems resulting from this courtship. The sequence begins in established conventions – the lover's address to his book, the onset of his affliction, the virtues of his lady – and terminates in the equally conventional sorrow in which his love must (in this case temporarily) conclude. A number of the poems are tied to dates in the church calendar for early 1594. In sonnet 4, the poet makes a New Year's Day announcement of his passion, telling his lady that his 'fresh love ... long hath slept in cheerlesse bower.' This probably means he has loved for some time in silence, an interpretation borne out by his otherwise confusing claim later in the spring (60) that he has already been in love for a year. Now at 'Janus gate' he speaks of his love at last, inviting his 'faire flowre, in whom fresh youth doth raine,' to 'prepare your selfe new love to entertaine.' But between his first open admission of love and the Easter Day rejoicing in which God's blessing is called down upon the now mutually committed pair, lover and lady must become potential husband and wife. Thus at the same time as her lover frames the book which testifies to his trials, the lady must naturalize herself in the relationship of marriage. She must give over the 'portly pride' which her lover tries so hard to praise (5), and submit her as-yet-uncreative liberty to the 'Sweet ... bands' (65) of human and natural love. The poet in turn must accept that the lady's seeming obduracy is not mere rigor but a sign of potential constancy. The disposition of the sonnets within the larger scheme of the whole volume represents emblematically this shared process of discovery.

Perceiving the arrangement of *Amoretti*'s sonnets requires three kinds of information which writers and readers in Renaissance England would ordinarily have possessed. First is a willingness, arising in their schoolroom experience of rhetorical composition, to accept that repetition, pairing, and deliberate inversion of poetic elements may advance the reading of a work as effectively as pure narrative (which is rare in sonnet sequences in any case). Second is a knowledge of the 30-year almanac which regularly appeared in editions of the Book of Common Prayer from the 1560s on. Thus, sonnet 62, seemingly a New Year's poem like sonnet 4, refers rather to Lady Day, 25 March, which the Prayer Book informed churchgoers is 'the same day supposed to be the first day upon which the worlde was created, and the day when Christ was conceived in the wombe of the virgin Marie' (*BCP*). If consecutive dates are assigned to the sonnets preceding and following, Spenser's Easter sonnet (68) falls on 31 March, which was Easter Day in 1594, and sonnet 22, 'This holy season fit to fast and pray,' falls on 13 February, Ash Wednesday (Dunlop 1969). *Amoretti* also owes to the almanac its groupings of eighteen sonnets; as well as being the golden number for 1594, eighteen was the 'epactal' number for that year, indicating that the moon was in the eighteenth year of the cycle which every nineteen years brings its shorter circuit into congruence with that of the sun (Brown 1973). Thus the Prayer Book and its almanac offered Spenser three interlocking calendars, one beginning on 1 January, the second the lunar year beginning on 1 March, and the third the 'year of grace' beginning on 25 March.

Finally, the January-to-June calendar of *Amoretti* represents the half-year round comprising the events connected with the Lord's birth, life, resurrection, and death, from Christmas Day to Corpus Christi. In medieval times this bifurcation was emphasized by the way the liturgical calendar seemed to fall into two parts, an 'active' one concerned with the extremes of sacred and profane drama, and the more secular period (harvest time in Europe) from Trinity Sunday to Advent, which was without special symbolic coherence (Phythian-Adams 1972). The interplay between the calendars in the almanac in Spenser's Prayer Book, and this deeply rooted awareness of the ceremonial pace of the year's religious observances, offered opportunities the Spenserian imagination could hardly have resisted.

Within the larger pattern it shares with *Epithalamion*, the *Amoretti* sequence thus appears to constitute a triptych of 'scattered rhymes,' each panel of which exploits the intricate relationship of these calendars in various ways. The first panel is composed of the three introductory sonnets followed by the eighteen which precede the Lenten sonnet 22. The concluding panel opens with the eighteen rejoicing sonnets which begin on Easter Day and closes with three conventional sorrowful poems. In the central panel of 47, each poem represents, in a general way, a day in Lent of 1594, and thus a moment in the lovers' Lenten preparation of themselves for a new life. The groups of eighteen keep before us the image of the moon, symbol of the female principle in Spenser's cosmogony, which in *Epithalamion* will be replaced by that of the sun's cycle, image of the male principle. Finally, it has recently been noted that the 89 sonnets are equal in number to the 89 readings provided by the Prayer Book for the Sundays and holy days of the ecclesiastical year (Prescott 1985).

Some useful but still inconclusive work has been done to refine this pattern, which has been regarded with healthy skepticism (G.K. Hunter 1973, 1975; Kaske 1978). But the lapidary gesture with which Spenser mirrors the central 47-unit block of the *Amoretti-Epithalamion* design within *Amoretti* itself, though using a different set of poems, suggests that the sequence (and one might extend this to the book as a whole) expresses the Renaissance interest in harmonic ratios. The collection is like a fretted fingerboard or a scale: Spenser 'perceives a length to be tabulated in terms of duplicated intervals. Pause at such and such a point on this length, and the remaining length is charged with analogous proportions' (Nohrnberg 1976:71). In this sense of harmonious proportion, obscured here by the struggle of the lovers, the joy of the wedding day will in due course openly express itself.

In the eighteen sonnets which follow his January declaration, the poet works that series of variations on the contrasted themes of the lady's sovereign virtue and her obstinacy which enables him both to praise her excellence and yet create an impasse between the lovers: 'With such strange termes her eyes she doth inure, / that with one looke she doth my life dismay: / and with another doth it streight recure, / her smile me drawes, her frowne me drives away' (*Am* 21). In this, the lover's perceptions – changeable and various like those of all Petrarchan lovers – resemble Spenser's Mutabilitie, who will be instructed by Nature on the right relationship between change and steadfastness: the variability of earthly things is in fact a dilation of being which ultimately works their ordained perfection (*FQ* VII vii 58). But at this point the lover is in the situation of Cupid's victims as they are described in *Hymne of Love*, 'languishing like thrals forlorne' (136). In that hymn, Spenser outlines clearly the process which a lover must undergo to be worthy of his lady; it recapitulates in simple form much standard Renaissance love theory, as the lover is first depicted in confusion and sorrow and then, in the 'hard handling' (163) to which Cupid and the lady's obduracy subject him, learns the steadfastness which distinguishes true lovers.

'For things hard gotten, men more dearely deeme' (*HL* 168). In *Amoretti* 22 (the number signifies temperance), the poet makes an Ash Wednesday vow: he will 'builde an altar to appease her yre: / and on the same my hart will sacrifise, / burning in flames of pure and chast desyre.' This poem and this vow initiate the central panel of Spenser's triptych, an exploration of the 'lyke dying lyfe' of Lenten denial in which the lover wanders 'carefull comfortlesse, / in secret sorow and sad pensivenesse' (25, 34). In the series of 40 sonnets that includes 23-62 (one for each of the fasting days of Lent, and for each of the poet's pretended 40 years), the Petrarchan contraries are exhausted in the attempt to reconcile them. 'Sweet warriour when shall I have peace with you?' sonnet 57 asks in open homage to Petrarch's famous oxymoron; 'High time it is, this warre now ended were.' The poet's struggles in these poems are intimately linked with the incompleteness of vision which is the central problem of the repeated sonnet 35 and 83, the keystones of the design that Fowler argues unites *Amoretti* with *Epithalamion*. The two sonnets mirror each other in an emblematic representation of the fruitless self-contemplation of the Narcissus-figure who is the subject. Like Narcissus, the lover starves in the midst of plenty, and the impasse that separates the lovers is thus an insult to Creation: 'What then remaines but I to ashes burne, / and she to stones at length all frosen turne?' (*Am* 32).

Within the paschal design, however, the assurance of rebirth is implicit; we have heard its note in the confident persistence of the lover's voice (which recalls the exhortations of the Song of Solomon) and seen its plentitude in the copiousness with which pairs of sonnets transmute affliction into joy (see Nohrnberg 1976:68-71). Sonnets 58 and 59 form just such a pair, which begins the restoration of the lover's fortunes by contrasting two views of the beloved's seeming pride. In sonnet 58, she is reminded, 'Weake is th'assurance that weake flesh reposeth / In her owne powre, and scorneth others ayde': pride is seen here as an obstacle to the shared condition of a happy union. But in sonnet 59, this theme is converted rhetorically to its benign opposite: narrow pride is transmuted into a steady constancy 'that nether will for better be allured, / ne feard with worse to any chaunce to start.' This poem is a version of the conventional galley sonnet, and here as elsewhere Spenser deliberately transforms the reader's expectations by turning an accustomed motif to an unexpected purpose.

Sonnet 60 is a key poem in assessing both the design and tone of *Amoretti*. At this critical point, when struggle is giving way to knowledge, Spenser distances the experience with an amusing conceit: as a lover in servitude, he occupies the planetary sphere of Cupid, whose imaginary cycle, 'by that count, which lovers books invent,' is 40 years long. In *Epithalamion*, the fanciful sphere of the god of love will give way to the actual sphere of the Ptolemaic cosmos; and the agonizingly slowed time perceived by the suffering lover to the majestic regularity of the real time of his wedding day. But all this is deftly done; here, at this crucial moment of transformation, as later in the Anacreontics and in the 'consummation' stanza of *Epithalamion*, Spenser smiles.

The metamorphosis of cruelty into constancy clears the way for the poet's recognition in sonnet 61 that his beloved's rigor is to be explained by her anagogic function. In this poem, the woman of stone is transformed into 'The bud of joy, the blossome of the morne,' and her lover from the ashes of fruitless desire into a man who can humbly admit, 'Such heavenly formes ought rather worshipt be, / then dare be lov'd by men of meane degree.' There follows sonnet 62, with its 'shew of morning mylde ... betokening peace and plenty to ensew,' a March New Year which cancels the suffering begun in January.

The implications of this new beginning are apparent in sonnet 63, where the poet announces that 'After long stormes and tempests sad assay ... I doe at length descry the happy shore.' The galley-sonnet conceit is identical to that in sonnet 59; that it should be repeated to another purpose stresses the oneness towards which the lovers must move. Yet Spenser's design is not all duplication; part of the charm of *Amoretti* is the grace with which the upward movement of the lover's education in resolving contradictory aspects of his beloved is countered by the downward movement in which this numinous and transcendent figure is eventually naturalized in the sublunary orbit which an obedient bride must occupy. Spenser's problem here is also a concern of *FQ* III: the lady's fear to marry lest she lose her liberty (Kaske 1978). In sonnets 61–7, the lady is thus invited to share in the lover's earlier discovery of humbleness. He is both her guide and her prefiguration in this task, which culminates in sonnets 66 and 67. Coordinated with Good Friday and Holy Saturday in Spenser's calendrical scheme, these poems are triumphs of an art which can convey a liturgical subtext while at the same time preserving an elegant secular surface. In sonnet 66, the lady's incarnation of her love in the meanness of the poet's darkness is seen (in consonance with his treatment of permanence and change in *FQ* VII) as a 'dilation' of her light. In sonnet 67, a magisterial variation on the topos of the hind inherited from Petrarch and his epigones, Spenser invokes Psalm 42, 'As the hart braieth for the rivers of water,' to portray his lady entering of her own free will into the relationship which he will hymn with such joy in the ensuing Easter sonnet. There, all contradiction will be resolved in the lovers' mutual vow. And the lines with which that poem ends are those which will begin the Communion on St Barnabas' Day, the day of their marriage (Kaske 1977).

Despite the lovers' Lenten trial of endurance, *Amoretti* is thus almost devoid of the Augustinian tension that the sonnet sequence inherited from Petrarch. Though it plays freely with Petrarchan conceits, they are means to an end, and much the same is true of its Neoplatonism as well. Spenser persistently 'salvages' negative topoi – the galley sonnet, spring solitude, the hind escaped – in order to give them integrative power. This inclusiveness operates at every level, from the interwoven calendars of its springtime chronicle, to the gesture in which the lover's education is made to include that of his lady, to the letters of 'Elizabeth' he praises in sonnet 74, which unite under one name the poet's Queen, mother, and bride.

In the rejoicing sonnets which follow his Easter hymn, Spenser rewrites a series of notable topoi so as to produce this sense of integration. One of these is the Spider and the Bee poem (71), which answers more constructively to its earlier version in sonnet 23. Another is sonnet 70, 'Fresh spring the herald of loves mighty king,' where the conventional sorrows of the lover, desolate amidst verdant nature, are set aside in favor of a joyous invitation to 'pluck the day.' Yet here the beloved is bidden not to Hymen's masque, which lies before her in *Epithalamion*, but 'to wayt on love amongst his lovely crew,' which, however charmingly put, reminds us of the fearful masque of Cupid in *FQ* III and Amoret's imprisonment by Busirane. In sonnet 72, the image of the poet's 'fraile fancy fed with full delight,' which 'doth bath in blisse and mantleth most at ease,' actually disrupts the celebratory mood of the sonnets around it, for fancy or imagination is the weakest of the faculties in Renaissance psychology. A note of sensuality crops up in the two sonnets on the lady's breasts (76, 77), and in others (75, 78, 79) images of her are first suggested and then canceled in a thoughtful revision which signals the poet's awareness that a state of being beyond the 'harts astonishment' of sonnet 81 awaits him.

In many of these poems, there is an uneasy balance between the desire for sexual fulfillment and the knowledge that it cannot yet take place. Thus in sonnet 83 we meet with the Narcissus poem again, a reduplicative token of the perilous balance which must be maintained during the state of betrothal. The poet is much aware of this, as he shows in sonnet 84: 'Let not one sparke of filthy lustfull fyre / breake out, that may her sacred peace molest.' In the concluding sonnets of the sequence, even this nervous balance is disrupted. The 'Venemous toung, tipt with vile adders sting' (86) – the slanderer who figures in much courtly poetry (cf Sclaunder, Blatant Beast) – makes his appearance, that necessary serpent in the poet's Eden who symbolically unleashes the destructive force of sexuality misapprehended, as well as intruding the problematic question of society into the lovers' solipsistic world (DeNeef 1982:74–6). Three final poems, all variations on the topos of the lover's solitude, express the inevitable sense of loss which results. In completing the frame initiated by sonnets 1–3, they signal the three lunar months between 31 March and 11 June and, by their insistence on the need for a meditative space between betrothal and marriage, recall the three months Britomart and Artegall are required to wait before their nuptials (Brown 1973).

In *FQ* IV, Florimell is imprisoned in a seagirt dungeon by Proteus, who has failed to move her 'constant mind' to love; she languishes for love of Marinell, who will not have her: 'There did this lucklesse mayd seven months abide, / Ne ever evening saw, ne mornings ray, / Ne ever from the day the night descride, / But thought it all one night, that did no houres divide' (xi 2, 4). Here the psychic imprisonment of fruitless love is equated with the absence of time. In contrast, the love of Venus and Adonis is time-*full*; it endures perpetually because Adonis, father of all forms, is 'eterne in mutabilitie' (III vi 47). *Amoretti* captures both these aspects of Spenser's mythopoeia. As the 'scattered rhymes' of a never-satisfied lover, its stasis exemplifies the aimless diversity of a love which, however idealistic, is still incomplete. That completeness will come only when constancy can both contain and transcend the mutable nature of 'cruell love' in the creation of true concord (*Epith* 317; Tufte 1970), and the eternal and the temporal inform and act through each other. In *Amoretti*, this possibility is foreshadowed in the paschal calendar veiled in the diversity of 'little loves' which are the poems. But in *Epithalamion*, the concord of temporal and eternal is fully revealed in an emblematizing which takes the very form of that most 'timely' of days, when the sun seems to stand still.

An important instrument of this process is the generic transformation which moves us as readers from sonnet sequence to wedding hymn. In *Amoretti* and *Epithalamion*, two works separate in themselves yet united in purpose are made to contemplate each other in a structural chiasmus: Italianate posed against classical, moon against sun, trial against fulfillment. The central bridging term is the mischievously light, but nonetheless metamorphic Anacreontics, for all of which except the first Spenser has sources in French poetry or Anacreon himself. In the first epigram, the poet, made bold by Cupid, is stung when he searches a hive for honey; in the second, chaste Diana exchanges one of her darts for Cupid's, and the god of love wounds the poet's lady with it. In the third, Cupid mistakes the poet's beloved for his mother, Venus. In the fourth, a diminutive fable in six stanzas, cruel Cupid, despite his mother's amused advice, tries to capture a bee and is stung for his hardihood. This genuinely funny poem has a powerfully erotic conclusion: Venus heals the wound with salve and bathes the miscreant 'in a dainty well / the well of deare delight.' But Cupid, restored, succeeds in wounding the poet, who now pines in anguish awaiting the appeasement of his passion. These poems recapitulate unresolved elements in *Amoretti*, the paralysis of the lovestruck poet and the similarly inactive chastity of the lady (figured here as the lunar goddess, Diana). Typically, Spenser introduces images (honey, salve, well) which can be vested with a biblical meaning but here seem erotic because any other significance is obscured by physical frustration.

The centering of a source of erotic tension at an important structural point in the volume is not unlike the placing of the Garden of Adonis 'in the middest' of *FQ* III. The poems make clear that the lover's suffering is necessary to his eventual bliss (Miola 1980), and they also bring into the open the not-yet-explicit sexuality of the contract between the Spider and the Bee in a way appropriate to the anticipation of the betrothal period (Kaske 1978). Indeed, within the epigrams themselves a process of recapitulation and dismissal can be seen, as the immature lover and unmoved maiden of the first and second epigrams are transformed in the third and fourth into the Venus and Cupid of erotic allegory. In the Latin epithalamia of Statius and Claudian, Venus and Cupid play important roles in bringing about marriages. Catullus also mentions Venus, but he observes that without Hymen, god of marriage, she can take no pleasure 'such as honest fame may approve' (61.62). The erotic allegory of the Anacreontics, this would suggest, has a dual role: it acknowledges the incitements of the goddess of love and her errant son, but in the diminutive scale of the poems, their hilarity and postponement of closure prepare us for the necessary subordination of Venus and Cupid to Hymen. 'Anacreontics' were perceived as poems in which care is banished. By their recapitulation of the lover's woes in a deliberately objectifying tone of amusement, these little fables both admit and dismiss the sorrows of love; and their transforming laughter prepares us for the joy of the wedding day, which after this brief interlude now awaits us.

In *Amoretti*, the stasis and timelessness of the sonnet sequence is equated with uncreating love and Cupid's limited sphere. In order to have meaning, the act of generation must be framed within the concentric spheres of society, nature, the aesthetic theophany of the Muses and Graces, and finally the Christian heaven (Greene 1957). Thus, when *Epithalamion* is joined to *Amoretti*, timeless struggle gives way to 'endlesse matrimony' (*Epith* 217), and we hear and see the full diapason of Spenser's harmonic scheme, made accessible at last by the social and religious act in which erotic love is consecrated to the earthly life and spiritual destiny of the lovers. These large considerations are framed in a poem whose appeal is the instantaneous and delightful one evoked by the ordinary pleasures of a midsummer wedding in a small provincial place.

The sources of *Epithalamion* lie deep in Spenser's own development. Many of his poems constitute preliminary exercises (Hallett Smith 1961) for this masterpiece: the lost *Epithalamion Thamesis* (which may survive in the marriage of Thames and Medway in *FQ* IV xi), the *Aprill* eclogue of *The Shepheardes Calender*, the betrothal of Una and Redcrosse in *FQ* I xii. Perhaps from the confidence of long experiment, Spenser's use of his literary sources in *Epithalamion* is direct and appreciative in contrast with the reserve with which he had approached the Petrarchan canzoniere in *Amoretti*. With strength of purpose and eclectic method, he draws on the full range of classical, Neo-Latin, and French epithalamia. Like Catullus (61), he calls up the ritual of the wedding day; and the English poem catches the same combination of genial good humor and ceremonial awe as the Roman. Like Statius' Stella (*Silvae* I.2), the bridegroom is a poet. As in Statius and in Claudian's *Epithalamium* of Honorius and Maria, the supporting mythological personages give the poem a cosmogonic dimension which modifies Catullus' festal abandon. Finally, like his French near-contemporary Buttet, Spenser associates his epithalamium with a sonnet sequence.

But there are changes as well, such as the restriction of Venus and Cupid to the miniature arena of the Anacreontics. The epithalamic poet is conventionally a spokesman for society, who invokes the events and ceremonies of the day like the arranger of a masque. Spenser makes poet and bridegroom one: 'Helpe me mine owne loves prayses to resound,' he begs those Muses who had earlier aided him to lament (*Teares* I, 49–52). The bridegroom is thus at once social voice and subjective presence, organizer of Hymen's masque and one of its central participants. Classical and Renaissance epithalamia usually celebrate the union of noble houses, though Puttenham had already imagined a bourgeois setting. In Spenser, the couple is an ordinary gentleman and his lady, and the celebrations take place not in a palace but amidst the rural scenes of Spenser's Ireland, perhaps Kilcolman, Cork, or Youghal. In earlier epithalamia, the pleasures of the bedded pair are enthusiastically anticipated in fescennine allusions; and with greater propriety, the poet also looks forward to the princely child who will be born of their union. In Spenser, conjugal pleasure is never doubted, and the poet asks less for a personal heir than for 'a large posterity, / Which from the earth, which they may long possesse' may eventually 'heavenly tabernacles there inherit, / Of blessed Saints for to increase the count' (417–23).

By transforming his model in these ways, Spenser provides *Epithalamion* with the basis of a typological structure. As poet he is Orpheus, who mastered nature with his harmonies; as ordinary Elizabethan he is Adam, our earthly progenitor. As spiritual being he typifies Christ, his marriage 'signifying unto us the mistical union that is betwixt Christ and his Churche' (*BCP* and see Allman 1980), and reminding us of the ultimate spiritual significance of generation itself. This typological pattern is a self-contained one, balancing the similarly self-contained erotic concept of *Amoretti*; against Cupid's governance of the sphere of unfulfilled love, it poses the ordering of the sphere of fulfilled love on the principles of the Creator (for the pairing of the genealogies of Cupid and Christ in *Fowre Hymnes*, see Mulryan 1971).

But these separate concepts are linked in a larger structure by filiations which evoke the mythopoeia of *The Faerie Queene*: the Orphic cosmology which gives us, in the persons of Phoebus the sun and Phoebe the moon, the male and female principles which inform the world (Fowler 1964:82–3, and chs 8–9). As beseeching male and obdurate female in *Amoretti*, the lovers occupy the static and insecure world of the moon as representative of change and transience; and the yearly cycle of solemn feasts, though authentic, remains hidden. In *Epithalamion*, Phoebus Apollo governs, and male completeness absorbs to itself in marriage the imperfection of the female. In a typical Elizabethan moral paradox, this makes it possible for the female to emerge as truly constant, the law-giving figure and generative force which she becomes within the social and sacramental bonds of marriage. Just so, in the poem, when Apollo's light has given way to night, the moon reappears not as chaste Diana or heavenly Phoebe but as Cynthia, protectress of women in childbirth.

One of the most effective instruments in the process by which *Amoretti* is incorporated in and transcended by *Epithalamion* is the contrast in tone between the two works. *Amoretti* has the rarefied atmosphere of Petrarchan complaint. No one else exists in its world besides the striving lover and his obdurate lady. Spenser's temperate tone modifies the ethos of complaint but does not alter the isolation of the lovers. This is a long way from the jollity of *Epithalamion*; there the poet, though he sings alone, is not lost in complaint but joyfully exhorts the crowd of participants – both mythical and local – to join in the celebration. Spenser takes pains 'to make the poem as native, immediate, and personal as he could, within the limits of decorum' (Smith 1961:139). Thus *Epithalamion* has a concreteness and a pictorial quality which transform the conventions of the genre (Clemen 1968) and subsume the narrower beauties of the sonnets. There is some precedent for this in Puttenham's remarks on epithalamia, but more in the deliberately provincial character of the celebrations of the wedding of Thames and Medway in *FQ* IV xi. The amplitude of *Epithalamion*'s structure is thus matched by the spaciousness of a style which can give us both the graces of the nymphs of Mulla and the raucous cries of boys in the street, both the transcendent images in which the bride is portrayed before the ceremony and the wine poured out afterwards 'not by cups, but by the belly full' (251). A principal device is climax: Spenser's practice of treating an image in a simple and infectious way, and then in successive stanzas unfolding it at greater and greater levels of power. A calculated inversion of this method is his use of understatement, which we have already seen in the artful repression of the Christological elements in *Amoretti* and in the 'goodly temperature' of the sequence. It takes a social and ethical form in the praise of the bride's downcast glance in *Epithalamion* (159–61, 234–5), but it appears also as an expressive choice, in the natural modesty with which the poet refers to the marriage bed, and in his generous and self-abnegating wishes for the happiness of his posterity.

The subject of *Epithalamion*, as befits a marriage song, is harmony. The intricate musical harmonies of the stanza structure (see *echo) make us sensuously aware of this, as does the refrain – ever varying, yet ever constant – which weaves the separate stanzas together from opening invocation to concluding envoy. At every point, Spenser calls on perceivable concords – the song of birds, the caroling maidens in their circle, the 'roring Organs' (*Epith* 218) – to evoke and give voice to the unperceived concords he must bring us to understand. Harmony is made operative in human life by the creating power of time; the Hours who help to dress the bride in stanza 6 are described as 'ye fayre houres which were begot / In Joves sweet paradice, of Day and Night, / Which doe the seasons of the yeare allot, / And al that ever in this world is fayre / Doe make and still repayre.' In stanza 7, the poet begs the sun god Apollo, 'fayrest Phoebus, father of the Muse,' for a place in time on his own behalf: 'let this day let this one day be myne, / Let all the rest be thine'; and throughout his poem Spenser focuses intensely on expressing the importance of this particular point in time, this 'one day' on which he and his bride will enter creating time themselves.

Epithalamion demonstrates in the design of its song the harmony of which it sings. The invocation and envoy represent it quite literally as a artifact, an ornament wrought for his bride by a poet who has long worked to adorn others with his praise and who now seeks the aid of the Muses in a personal cause, 'mine owne loves prayses to resound' (line 14). The poem is divided into 23 stanzas and a brief envoy; the stanzas, composed of long and short lines in slightly variant combinations, resemble canzone stanzas in their amplitude and complexity but have a rhyme scheme of Spenser's own devising. This is dictated in part by deliberate irregularities in stanza length, in part by an apparent desire to make every stanza fall roughly into four sections. Each stanza is a set piece recording one of the phases of the wedding-day activity. As individual units, they recall the separateness of *Amoretti*'s sonnets; but the linking refrain binds the 24 into a design which forms an emblem of the hours of the day – indeed, its quarter-hours – on which the wedding is thought to have taken place, 11 June 1594. Thus, at stanza 17, the coming of night at the latitude of Kilcolman, Cork, and Youghal is marked by a change in the refrain: 'The woods no more shal answere, nor your echo ring.' The astronomical details of the poem's siting are worked out with some care (see Eade 1972).

The cycle of the hours represented by the 24 stanzas is set within a larger, less immediately apparent structure representing the cycle of the year. The number of long lines in the poem add up to 365, and the 68 short lines represent the sum of the 4 seasons, 12 months, and 52 weeks. Without the envoy, the long lines total 359, the number of days through which the sphere of the sun moves while the celestial sphere travels its full 360 degrees. 'Spenser wishes to communicate the relationship between the daily shortcomings of the sun and the total measure of 365 days created by this shortcoming, and between the 359 long lines of the full-size stanzas and the 365 long lines of the poem complete with envoy' (Hieatt 1960:44). The seven lines of the envoy thus function as numerical compensation for the 'incompleteness' of the cycle of 359, and the poem can claim in its final line that it is 'for short time an endlesse moniment.' This paradox reminds us of the description of Adonis as 'eterne in mutabilitie' and also of Nature's ruling that things in their mutability 'are not changed from their first estate; / But by their change their being doe dilate' (VII vii 58). In its design (one critic has called it a 'poetic orrery' Pearcy 1980–1:248), *Epithalamion* attempts to achieve that harmony between the mutable and constant which is one of Spenser's deepest preoccupations, juxtaposing the placid creating and repairing power of the Hours in their perfect celestial circuit with the urgent and specific time of the disciple of Apollo, who can beg from Phoebus in his shorter circuit only one day for his own concerns, the day of the solstice.

The poem thus must function as an instrument of transformation, a means of invoking and mastering the order of nature. This sense of transformation is present from the beginning, as the poet calls the Muses from sorrowful lament to celebratory joy, and turns from his familiar stance of solitary complaint to the firm confidence of 'So Orpheus did for his owne bride, / So I unto my selfe alone will sing' (16–17). Spenser's source here is Virgil's account of the legend of Orpheus: 'But he, solacing love's anguish with his hollow shell, sang of thee, sweet wife – of thee, to himself on the lonely shore; of thee as day drew nigh, of thee as day declined' (*Georgics* 4.464–6). In Virgil's lines, there is already a hint of the calendrical image Spenser develops so fully, and it suggests what the myth fully supports: Orpheus' connection with the order of nature. For the mythographers, Orpheus is at once the most blighted of lovers (losing Eurydice to the sudden madness which makes him look back as they journey out of Hades) and a powerful magus, whose 'mery musik and mellifluate, / Complete and full wyth nowmeris od and evyn,' as Henryson earlier described it, conveys the mathematical principles on which the cosmos is organized (*Orpheus and Eurydice* 237–8; see Fox in Henryson ed 1981: cv–cx). For Natale Conti, Orpheus brings uncivilized men together in a gentler way of life, teaching them to found cities and observe the bonds of marriage; Conti also recounts the many traditions which make Orpheus the son of Apollo (*Mythologiae* 7.14). In *Epithalamion*, the refrain persistently reminds us of the ordering power of musical numbers; in his song, this new Orpheus will bring the order of nature under his control: 'The woods shall to me answer and my Eccho ring' (line 18). And like Orpheus, the poet will call up the image of his beloved from the obscuring darkness of inchoate love (Neuse 1966).

Spenser's service to Apollo governs the division of *Epithalamion* into the seemly ceremonies leading up to the wedding, which take place under the tutelage of Apollo in his role as giver of laws, and the jollity after it, which is governed by the unbuttoned Bacchus, god of wine and celebration. The right order created by the presence of Apollo as guardian of conduct thus presides over the masque of Hymen which occupies the first half of the poem. Stanza by stanza, the poet convokes the companions of the masque: first the Muses themselves, who are bidden to sing of joy and solace to the bride as she is dressed, then nature in the figures of the nymphs of forest, river, and field who will weave her garlands, deck her bower, and bind her hair. In stanza 5, the bride is summoned to awake by the 'lovelearned' song of the birds: 'The merry Larke hir mattins sings aloft, / The thrush replyes, the Mavis descant playes ... So goodly all agree with sweet consent, / To this dayes merriment.' The images of concord which have thus been established gather in force as the bride awakes and is dressed by the Hours and Graces, 'Goddesses of al bountie and comelines' as E.K. calls them (*SC, Aprill* gloss). Her eyes are compared to stars which, once dimmed by cloud, are now brighter than Hesperus. When in stanzas 7 and 8 she emerges into the sun, these concords take a cheerful domestic form: the clamor of minstrels and the caroling of girls. Yet all is resolved in one consonance, even among the boys who 'run up and downe the street, / Crying aloud with strong confused noyce, / As if it were one voyce' (137–9).

Spenser's technique of unfolding images from simple to more complex, of moving from the immediately personal to the philosophical and mythopoeic, is exemplified both in the way the masque of Hymen moves through meadow and stream and down village street to the moment when the bride emerges, and in the successive revelations of the bride herself as she comes forth in stanzas 9–11. In stanza 9, she is first Phoebe, virginal in white like the moon for which she is named, then an angel, and finally a 'mayden Queene' with modest downcast gaze. Stanza 10 is a formal blazon of her beauties like those which praise the lady in countless medieval and Renaissance love lyrics. Yet this blazon reaches beyond its origins in merely amatory verse to recall the wording of the biblical Song of Solomon. In stanza 11, the moral meaning of these successive images of perfection is climactically revealed in the terrifying image of Medusa's shield, deliberately placed to arrest and awe the watcher (Young 1973–4). What is revealed, however, in this vision, is an entirely inward beauty: 'There dwels sweet love and constant chastity, / Unspotted fayth and comely womanhood, / Regard of honour and mild modesty, / There vertue raynes as Queene in royal throne, / And giveth lawes alone' (191–5).

Stanzas 12 and 13, in which the wedding ceremony takes place, trace closely the rites of the Book of Common Prayer (W.C. Johnson 1976). They are at once the formal and the visionary center of *Epithalamion*, as the Garden of Adonis is at the center of *FQ* III. Spenser's eyes remain on the bride before the altar, as the organ and choristers peal out the musical harmonies to which her fulfillment in harmonious matrimony will give social meaning. The interchange of earth and heaven at the crucial moment is manifest both in her role as worshiper, listening to 'the holy priest that to her speakes,' and as one who is worshiped by the very angels serving about the altar who flock to peep into her face. It is only at this point, as 'The praises of the Lord in lively notes' sound about the bride's downcast head, that the bridegroom steps forth in person to ask, 'Why blush ye love to give to me your hand, / The pledge of all our band? / Sing ye sweet Angels, Alleluya sing, / That all the woods may answere and your eccho ring' (238–41); and with the sublime pun on wedding ring and ringing echoes, their union is solemnized.

If the first half of the poem has belonged to the bride as representative of Apollonian order and to the maidens attending her, the second half belongs to Bacchus, to the 'yong men of the towne,' and to the groom. No longer the invoker of the masque and its wondering observer, the poet is now an involved participant in a happy wedding party and the larger scene of revelry that still attends the bonfires of the midsummer celebration in many places in Europe. It is here that the unresolved erotic problems of *Amoretti* are finally worked out. Spenser's foremost task in this second part is to raise and answer the challenge which the darker powers of sexuality and social disorder (hinted at in the merriment of the youths and the urgency of the groom) pose to the Apollonian clarity of the hymeneal procession and its virginal central figure. The theme of sexuality unleashed is also pressed on him by the fescennine motifs which are to be expected in an epithalamium. But here the epithalamist cannot invite the revelers to muffle with their noise the cries of the bride behind the closed chamber door, for with the poet-bridegroom we enter that chamber and the scene in which marriage begins to act out its mundane course.

Sexuality first appears in comic form, in stanza 15 where the longing groom laments, 'But for this time it ill ordained was, / To chose the longest day in all the yeare, / And shortest night, when longest fitter weare.' (Fittingly, too, this stanza, in a spatial joke, is one line shorter than any other except the envoy.) It is precisely here that Spenser points most strongly – though with sudden irony – to the day's astronomical significance: 'This day the sunne is in his chiefest hight, / With Barnaby the bright, / From whence declining daily by degrees, / He somewhat loseth of his heat and light.' In doing so, he reminds us not only of the power of Phoebus but of its limits; and in the ensuing stanzas, he evokes the darkness that comes with its waning. The refrain modulates into the negative – 'The woods no more shal answere' – and the joyful sounds of man and nature cease with the light. The bride, earlier arrayed by the Hours and Graces, now lies between perfumed sheets, but her damsels must leave her alone. The groom who before called up the masque of Hymen now must employ his Orphean gift of utterance and his mastery of number to dispel fear of 'perrill and foule horror,' of 'false treason' and 'dread disquiet.' He must send about their business 'the Pouke' and 'other evill sprights,' mischievous witches, hobgoblins, and birds of evil omen. As in the village scene of the earlier part of the poem, these homely superstitions are part of Spenser's endearing naturalization of his great images of order and truth in the intimately understood scene of his readers' own world. But at work at this moment is a strength resembling that which forces Busirane to reverse his charms (*FQ* III xii): like Jove engendering Majesty upon Night herself (*Epith* 330–1), the poet confronts and masters the evil face of darkness with the power of his own magic. In this act, suffering lover is finally transformed into Christian husband, for only when the charms of this new Orpheus have dispelled the phantoms and shriekings of fearful darkness can the 'trew night watches' of 'stil Silence' take the place of daytime sun and festive song.

It is in this mood of 'sacred peace' that in stanza 20 the marriage is consummated. Like the angels that flew about the bride's head as she approached the altar, 'an hundred little winged loves' are invited to play their sports about the bed. Yet the poet's tone is light and dismissive: 'For greedy pleasure, carelesse of your toyes, / Thinks more upon her paradise of joyes, / Then what ye do, albe it good or ill.' This is not the mythopoeic eroticism with which Spenser earlier depicted Venus' continuing conjunction with Adonis in *FQ* III vi 46, nor is it the amusing naughtiness of the Anacreontics. All the cares 'which cruell love collected' have been 'sumd in one, and cancelled for aye' (317–18). The epithalamic task of absorbing the erotic into the social order is nearly complete.

In the final stanzas of the poem, Spenser obeys the further epithalamic convention that the poet wish the union be blessed with issue. In doing so, he develops yet another of those crescendos of implication which distinguish his poem. In stanza 21, the preoccupied poet recognizes at his window the familiar face of 'Cinthia, she that never sleepes, / But walkes about high heaven al the night.' The moon goddess is not only the bringer of light in darkness ordained by the celestial order but the goddess of childbirth as well. In this and the next stanza, the poet begs all the gods of generation – Cynthia, 'great Juno' patron of the laws of wedlock, 'glad Genius,' 'fayre Hebe,' and 'Hymen free' – to 'Send us the timely fruit of this same night.'

The word *timely* chimes throughout *Epithalamion* in a variety of auspicious meanings; here it signifies that which is of time, one with time, and its effect is to make the child of epithalamic convention the focus of the cosmographical design of the whole poem. Yet in Spenser's climactic stanza 23, all this is in turn canceled and summed in one, as in the time-bound individual child is forecast a whole long posterity. Amidst the 'dreadful darknesse' inhabited by 'wretched earthly clods' like Edmund and Elizabeth is imagined the temple of high heaven, aflame not with Hymen's single tead, but with 'a thousand torches flaming bright.' The solitary poet with whom we began ceases his song in hope of begetting a race 'Of blessed Saints for to increase the count.' In thus reminding us of the spiritual world above the earthly bustle (Clemen 1968:96), Spenser completes the upward-reaching theological movement of *Epithalamion*. But he also replaces the genealogy of Cupid (child of Plenty and Poverty; see *HL* 53) with the genealogy of his own people, one founded in individual history and issuing in eschatology. The closed narcissism of *Amoretti* 35 and 83 has been reviewed and dismissed in the poet's wishes for his inheritors.

In *Epithalamion*'s seven-line envoy, Spenser returns to the image of the poem as device:

> Song made in lieu of many ornaments,
> With which my love should duly have bene dect,
> Which cutting off through hasty accidents,
> Ye would not stay your dew time to expect,
> But promist both to recompens,
> Be unto her a goodly ornament,
> And for short time an endlesse moniment.

Do these lines speak of gifts to the bride which were delayed, or adornments which were lost (*Var* 8:494, 650)? Do they refer to unwritten sonnets of *Amoretti* (Judson 1945:172)? Is the poem as a whole a form of recompense for the limitations of human time (Hieatt 1960:56–9)? Or does the poet here 'shed all poetic disguises and renew [his] history on the stage where all are merely players for the short time allotted to them' (Neuse 1966:174)? An answer is suggested by the fact that *Epithalamion* is suffused with images and figures of exchange and compensation. Some of these may originate in the allusion to lovers' counting games in Catullus 5 (Pearcy 1980–1); others certainly allude to the different circuits of the spheres (Hieatt 1960:32–41). But they are all made more intelligible by the generic convention which regards a wedding hymn as treating the lover's just reward after his trial. Seen in this way, the images of exchange and compensation express the interplay Spenser recognizes between love and law, multiplicity and unity, change and concord. The effect of the envoy is to incorporate the poem in this interchange, making it a sounding emblem of Spenser's long-held conviction that constancy 'is not, in this world at least, a power "contrayr" to Mutabilitie. It is a purpose persisting through mutability, redeeming it. It combines the energy of love with the stability of law; it is not a denial of change but a direction for work' (Hawkins 1961:101–2).

Epithalamion, writes Hallett Smith (1961: 136), 'is a poem which needs no defense.' The general affection in which Spenser's wedding hymn is held has meant that criticism, when not panegyric, has largely been divided between early efforts to identify bride and date, sources and style (*Var* 8:647–58, Greene 1957), and attempts since 1960 to correlate Hieatt's description of its numerological scheme with Spenser's known procedure in this and other poems (see modern studies in *number symbolism). Hieatt's central argument is now doubted by only the most adamant critics of numerological analysis; however, his theory that the 'compensatory' design offers a message of consolation has been rejected or seriously qualified (Neuse 1966, Welsford 1967, Kaske 1978, and others). And some of the details of his scheme still provoke debate (see W.V. Davis 1969, Eade 1972, Hieatt 1960 and 1961, Pearcy 1980–1, Welsford 1967, Wickert 1968).

Such debate is only to be expected, for numerological readings are most vulnerable in their minute details. Hostile critics tend to insist that schematic patterns must be both rigid and complete to be credible. But our expanding knowledge of spatial strategies of composition and reading suggests that schematic patterns are often deliberately varied or interrupted by their makers for expressive reasons. For example, since 11 June is 103 days after 1 March, the numerological scheme explored by Hieatt should place the poet's plea that 'this one day be myne' at the 103rd long line (line 125), yet it in fact occurs at the 105th. The conjunction is too close not to be noticed and too imperfect not to be debated, especially since Spenser could easily have revised the sentence to claim his day precisely in the 103rd long line, yet did not. If the discrepancy was intended, there are several possible reasons. Common superstition often obliges the folk craftsman to work a flaw into his design as a charm, or to signify its human origin; like the 'ribald' in a civic pageant, it is there to remind us of our mortality (Kipling 1977b). Medieval conventions of schematic ordering permit the elaboration of such designs by the deliberate addition or subtraction of elements (Hopper 1938:82). Then there is sheer wit, which Spenser himself employs in making the longing stanza 15 shorter by a line.

Epithalamion has been almost untouched by recent post-structuralist criticism, perhaps because it is so intransigently logocentric. However, Douglas Hamer once wondered with flat literalism why Irish crowds might have lined the street in a year of simmering rebellion for the marriage of a hated Englishman (1931:287). In his study of Spenser's genre, Thomas M. Greene (1957) argued a weakness in stanza 20 (the consummation), and he continues to regard the poem from a deconstructionist standpoint as in fact reversing its convention (1982:50). Taken as a whole, the volume evades such skepticism by admitting its own premises so totally. Indeed, it could be said to reverse the deconstructionist procedure by beginning in the area of doubt and misprision and out of it *reconstructing* a mode of discourse so comprehensive as to defy acceptance on any terms other than its own. Spenser uses the symbolic images and the formal conventions of his time to produce an intensity of social meaning so great that *Epithalamion* still touches deeply those who enter into a shared life, though they may share nothing with Spenser himself.

Epithalamion is arguably Spenser's greatest poem: his most fulfilled personally and spiritually, and his most complete aesthetically. In it, as at crucial points elsewhere in his work, he adopts a first-person stance or a persona closely identified with himself. But in *Epithalamion*, this figure's longing can at last be fulfilled as it can never be in Colin's pastoral laments in *The Shepheardes Calender*, in the vision of which Calidore later deprives that piping shepherd in *FQ* VI x 17–18, or even in the expectant stance of the prayer which forms the 'unperfite' eighth canto of *FQ* VII. *Epithalamion* is bound to other parts of Spenser's work as well, in particular to the mythopoeic vision of the generation of being in *FQ* III, and to the themes of social concord examined in *FQ* IV. In *Epithalamion*, these myths of generation and concord are situated in a vision of the poet's own historical and temporal existence. The result, as in all of Spenser's later works, is to sharpen and focus the question of the relation between energy and order, the existential and the eternal. As the 1590s progress, Spenser prevailingly treats this problem in the form of a diptych. Thus the paired genres of *Amoretti* and *Epithalamion* are paralleled by the pairings of *Fowre Hymnes* and the pairing of the two *Cantos of Mutabilitie*. In each case an unchanneled source of energy – the lover, Cupid, Mutabilitie – is first envisioned and comprehended with wit and compassion, and then juxtaposed to a perfected and higher version of that energy – the married man, Christ, constancy – which both contains and transcends it. In this way, we find Spenser even at the end of his career at work fashioning in one more form the great myth of spiritual liberation which earlier underlay the time-scheme of *The Shepheardes Calender*, and which was then expressed in the freeing of Amoret from her bondage to Busirane, and the prayer for liberation at the conclusion of the *Cantos of Mutabilitie*. This is the liberation he makes possible for himself and his bride when, in *Epithalamion*, he calls up Hymen's masque through his mastery of numbered song, surmounting the limitations of Cupid's sphere and the greater threat of darkness itself by devising his poem as a simulacrum of the divinely ordained round of the cosmographical day within which human action pursues its humble but transcendently important course.

GERMAINE WARKENTIN

It will be clear from the essay above how much I am indebted to the several hundred scholars and critics who have studied these poems before 1985. I have cited specific obligations where possible, and drawn much from other work which is known to all Spenserians (particularly Hieatt 1960) and is cited in the General Bibliography. The edition of the *Book of Common Prayer* cited is 1580 (*STC* 16307; like other *BCPs* of these decades, its almanac includes 1594). For special insights, I am particularly indebted to Eileen Jorge Allman 1980 '*Epithalamion*'s Bridegroom: Orpheus-Adam-Christ' *Renascence* 32:240–7; John D. Bernard 1980 'Spenserian Pastoral and the *Amoretti*' *ELH* 47:419–32; Fowler 1970b; Hawkins 1961; W. Speed Hill 1972 'Order and Joy in Spenser's *Epithalamion*' *SHR* 6:81–90; Kaske 1978; Luborsky 1980; Waldo F. McNeir 1965 'An Apology for Spenser's *Amoretti*' *NS* ns 14:1–9; Martz 1961; Richard Neuse 1966 'The Triumph over Hasty Accidents: A Note on the Symbolic Mode of the "Epithalamion"' *MLR* 61:163–74; Nohrnberg 1976; Charles Phythian-Adams 1972 'Ceremony and the Citizen: The Communal Year at Coventry, 1450–1550' in *Crisis and Order in English Towns, 1500–1700* ed Peter Clark and Paul Slack (London), pp 57–85.

Amyntas A 'shepherd,' now dead, who attended Cynthia's (ie, Elizabeth's) court (*Colin Clout* 432–43); he was both poet and patron, piping with 'passing skill' and supporting others who did so. His beloved, Amaryllis, mourns his death (564–71).

Amyntas has long been identified with Ferdinando Stanley, Lord Strange, fifth Earl of Derby (Church in Spenser ed 1758b, Morris 1963). Amaryllis is then Alice Spencer, daughter of Sir John and Lady Spencer of Althorp (to whom Spenser claimed kinship; see *Colin Clout* 536–71) and wife of Stanley. Spenser dedicated *Teares of the Muses* to her in 1591, praising her 'noble match with that most honourable Lord the verie Paterne of right Nobilitie'; and later Milton wrote *Arcades* and *Comus* for her and her family. Nashe, too, apparently refers to Stanley in *Pierce Penilesse* when he criticizes Spenser for not celebrating 'Amyntas' in the 1590 *Faerie Queene*: 'But therefore gest I he supprest thy name, / Because few words might not comprise thy fame' (ed 1904–10, 1:244).

Stanley was about 35 years old when he died on 16 April 1594; the tribute to him in *Colin Clout* must have been written or revised shortly thereafter, as the opening indicates: 'There also is (ah no, he is not now) / But since I said he is, he quite is gone' (432–3). The lines are a brief elegy for him as poet and patron; he was also praised by Chapman, Harington, and others. He was the principal supporter of a company of actors known as Strange's (later, Derby's) men. (After his death they became the Lord Chamberlain's men, Shakespeare's company.) A few of Stanley's poems may survive in *Bel-vedére, or The Garden of the Muses* (1600); others have survived in manuscript (see May 1972–3).

'Amyntas' is a stock pastoral name descending from Theocritus (Idyll 7) and Virgil (Eclogues 2, 3, 5, 10). It is common in Renaissance pastoral, including the work of Mantuan (Eclogues 2, 3, 6) and Barclay (Eclogue 5). The best-known instances are Tasso's Italian play *Aminta* and Watson's *Amintae gaudia* and *Amyntas* (the last translated into English by Fraunce as *The Lamentations of Amyntas* 1587, with three more editions shortly after). Thus, the 'Amintas' lamented at *FQ* III vi 45 is evidently not Stanley but Watson's hero, finally transformed into the amaranthus (W.A. Ringler 1954). SUKANTA CHAUDHURI

anacreontics Although Anacreon, a Greek poet of the sixth century BC, had long been known by name, the texts of 60 odes attributed to him first came to light in 1549 when the scholar Henri Estienne (Henricus Stephanus) found them appended to an eleventh-century manuscript of the *Greek Anthology*. He published these *Odae* with his own Latin translations of 31 of them (Paris 1554, rpt 1556), and again in his *Carminum poetarum novem ... fragmenta* along with a complete Latin translation and the works of eight other Greek poets (1560). The Anacreontic poems were later discovered to have been composed by a number of poets over seven centuries. However, they were attributed to Anacreon in Estienne's anthology, which was reprinted many times and was certainly known to poets such as Watson, Jonson, and Herrick.

Ronsard, one of Estienne's friends, immediately wrote imitations of the newly discovered odes; and Remy Belleau translated a number of them into French (1555), adding a few of his own anacreontics at the end. Soon other poets from France, Italy, and England were copying both Anacreon and Ronsard. Sidney tried imitating the anacreontic meter ([∪]∪-∪-∪--) in a song labeled 'Anacreon's kind of verses' in the *Old Arcadia* (ed 1973a:163), and Barnabe Barnes used the same meter for his 'carmen anacreontium' in *Parthenophil and Parthenophe* (1593; ed 1971:123–5). Usually, however, the themes rather than the meter inspired the anacreontics of European poets. Popular anacreontic themes include the rejection of worldly cares and heroic ambitions in favor of the carefree enjoyment of wine, love, and song; the celebration of small or trivial objects; and (combining both of these) brief narratives about the little Cupid who hides in a flower and stings like a bee, or appears at one's door like a little boy wet with rain and then shoots his unsuspecting host.

Spenser uses the Cupid-as-bee theme in both the first and last of the four poems placed between the *Amoretti* and *Epithalamion* (ed 1912:577–8). This theme can be traced back to both Anacreon and Theocritus; but Spenser's poems seem to be based almost entirely on Renaissance imitations, especially by Tasso and either Ronsard or Baïf (Hutton 1941). The last two stanzas of the fourth poem are Spenser's own development; their reference to the poet's own feelings has been called a 'Petrarchizing' of the anacreontic mode (Baumann 1974:40, 42). His second poem concerns an exchange of arrows between Cupid and Diana. In the third, Cupid mistakes Spenser's beloved for his own mother. These poems have been labeled 'Anacreontics,' although the original 1595 edition does not distinguish them from the rest of the *Amoretti* by any heading or separation (*Var* 8:455). Another Cupid narrative, anacreontic in character though not directly imitative of a Greek ode, occurs in *FQ* III vi 11–26, where Venus searches for her son.

The placing of the Anacreontics between the *Amoretti* and *Epithalamion* has perplexed readers. The poems have been called a 'haphazard addition' which ought to be ignored (G.K. Hunter 1973:124, Martz 1961: 152), as well as a sort of interlude or playful pause between two serious acts (Nohrnberg 1976:68–9). Sidney had similarly used his anacreontic as a song in the interlude between two acts of the *Arcadia*; and two Cupid poems appear at the end of Shakespeare's sonnets, followed by 'A Lover's Complaint.' Spenser's use of anacreontics as interlude, therefore, would be in keeping with other Renaissance treatments of their traditional theme of turning from serious to more playful and pleasurable topics.

Yet Spenser's Anacreontics have also been taken to have a serious meaning, integral to the volume in which they occur. They seem to provide a coda to the *Amoretti*, summing up its themes and preparing for the marriage poem (Cummings 1970–1, Miola 1980). Furthermore, the title *Amoretti* evokes the little cupids associated with anacreontic odes. Various organizational patterns have been proposed which integrate the Anacreontics into Spenser's sequence and thus enhance their meaningfulness in relation to the surrounding poetry (Dunlop 1980, Fowler 1970b).

Like Spenser, several other Renaissance poets end their sonnet sequences with anacreontic poems. Their model seems to have been Ronsard, whose 'Sonnets à diverses personnes' (in his *Oeuvres* 5th ed 1578) are followed by an imitation of the ode on the lodging of Cupid. In general, the brief odes provide a witty, epigrammatic ending to a sequence, functioning rather like the final couplet of an English sonnet. Although Shakespeare's final two sonnets derive ultimately from another poet in the *Greek Anthology*, they share a similar theme: Cupid's brand falls into the hands of Diana's nymphs, who plunge it into a spring that subsequently becomes a medicinal hot spring, although its waters cannot cure the poet of his love. The dipping of Cupid's brand into a 'bath' or 'well' and the well's healing virtues are close to the themes of Spenser's fourth anacreontic. Spenser uses the combinations of Diana and Cupid or Venus, both in his Anacreontics and in *FQ* III, to explore the possibilities of chaste married love.

Spenser refers to Anacreon in *Hymne of Heavenly Beautie*, published one year after the *Amoretti* volume. Describing Sapience as a beautiful queen, he contrasts his high subject and lowly skill with the lowly subject and high skill of Anacreon of Teos (218–24): 'But had those wits the wonders of their dayes / Or that sweete *Teian* Poet which did spend / His plenteous vaine in setting forth her prayse, / Seene but a glims of this, which I pretend, / How wondrously would he her face commend, / Above that Idole of his fayning thought, / That all the world shold with his rimes be fraught?' The moral status of Anacreon's poetry had been questionable from the start, so *vaine* may be a pun which, along with *Idole*, criticizes the frivolous pagan poet from a Neoplatonic and Christian point of view. Despite his own enthusiasm for the poems, Estienne had included in his preface to *Carminum poetarum novem* a warning that they might be abused by readers who sought only voluptuous pleasure from poetry. The odes themselves acknowledge (albeit with protest) the power of duties, time, and death to undermine life's pleasures; they recognize the limitations to the good they celebrate. Spenser does not take the line of Jonson and Marini in equating Anacreon's drunkenness with poetic rapture (Jonson ed 1925–52, 8:637; Michelangeli 1922:99–100). For Spenser, however serious its function within a given context, anacreontic verse seems to mean brief, light, narrative verse about Cupid, often with relation to the poet himself.

JANET LEVARIE SMARR

A modern text and translation of the *Anacreontea*, including fragments from various sources, is in J.M. Edmonds, ed 1931 *Elegy and Iambus* 2 vols, Loeb Classical Library.

Michael Baumann 1974 *Die Anakreonteen in englischen Übersetzungen* (Heidelberg); Gordon Braden 1978 *The Classics and English Renaissance Poetry* (New Haven) pp 255–8; Peter M. Cummings 1970–1 'Spenser's *Amoretti* as an Allegory of Love' *TSLL* 12:163–79; G.K. Hunter 1973; James Hutton 1941 'Cupid and the Bee' *PMLA* 56:1036–58; Janet Levarie 1973 'Renaissance Anacreontics' *CL* 25:221–39; Martz 1961; Luigi Alessandro Michelangeli 1922 *Anacreonte e la sua fortuna nei secoli* (Bologna); Miola 1980.

androgyne Venus is represented as an androgyne (a single individual uniting the traits of both sexes) in *FQ* IV x 41 and in *Colin Clout* 800–2. In both passages, the goddess is described as possessing male and female characteristics and able to procreate without the help of a consort. In the Temple of Venus passage, her attributes are remote from human gaze, for her statue is veiled. In one other passage of *The Faerie Queene*, moreover, androgyny is associated with self-sufficient procreation and with mystery: Nature, described by Mutabilitie as 'the highest him, that is behight / Father of Gods and men by equall might' (VII vi 35), is presented by the narrator as 'great dame *Nature*,' with veiled head and face, so that 'Whether she man or woman inly were, / That could not any creature well descry' (vii 5).

In most antique and Renaissance representations of bisexual deities in the visual arts, effeminate male figures were portrayed (often on the model of Hadrian's favorite, Antinous), rather than explicitly hermaphroditic individuals; examples of the latter tended to verge on the grotesque or obscene (Wind 1958). Spenser's verbal descriptions, however, resemble the Aphroditus of Cyprus and similar deities described by ancient mythographers (Delcourt 1961). That Venus and Nature are veiled may indicate his sense that explicit disclosure of the physical image would detract from their 'sacred completeness' as primal figures of fertility and make them into hermaphroditic grotesques (Fletcher 1971:95, Cheney 1972).

The term *androgyne* appears with some frequency in sixteenth-century French literature. In Ronsard, it figures the union of two bodies; in Marguerite of Navarre, the spiritual union of the soul with Christ. Whether erotic or spiritual, the concept stems from the fantastic myth of origins attributed to Aristophanes in Plato's *Symposium* 189E-92E, which Ficino translated into Latin and Italian and made the object of a Christianizing commentary. In their erotic poetry, the Pléiade occasionally used the term *Hermaphrodite* in a roughly equivalent sense, their source being Ovid's *Metamorphoses* 4.285–388, a myth not of a primal state of unity preceding sexual difference, but of the loss of that difference in sexual intercourse. Alchemical works, with their illustrations of a fused 'hermaphrodite' in the transforming 'bath,' contributed to further mingling of the two myths.

With the exception of certain episodes like the hermaphroditic embrace of Amoret and Scudamour in the stanzas which concluded the 1590 Book III, or the glimpse of the Red Cross Knight 'swimming in that sea of blisfull joy' at the end of Book I (xii 41), physical union between the sexes does not constitute a major element in Spenser's narrative dynamics. But the androgyne is a recurrent image of human completeness or containment. A lady 'full of amiable grace, / And manly terrour' (III i 46), Britomart embodies chaste love as an ideal for both women and men until she is unmasked in combat by Artegall and accepts the prospect of a marriage which will lead to the generation of Elizabeth. Britomart is an 'almost bisexual figure'; her chastity is not a rejection of sexuality but its actualization; she stands in contrast to Florimell who denies her own sexuality and that of others, and to Busirane for whom sexuality is a source of lust and oppression (Brill 1971). This interpretation, which employs Freudian theories of the libido, is complemented by one which compares Britomart and Belphoebe with Radigund and Florimell: the former have been called 'Apollonian' androgynes and the latter 'Dionysian' (Paglia 1979). This distinction establishes two categories of bisexuality within the Spenserian imagination: one is self-contained and joins psychosexual elements to morality and aesthetics; the other subjects them to primeval forces.

Queen Elizabeth herself, by destiny and choice, exhibited attributes of both sexes, as woman and ruler. Spenser's androgynes thus emerge from the work of a loyal subject concerned to fashion a good governor and a virtuous individual, and of a visionary poet whose narrative technique mingles polarities of male and female with comparable oppositions between night and day, dark and light, time and eternity. His use of androgyny brings into play mythopoetic structures which belong to both Greco-Roman and Judaic traditions (Meeks 1974).

MARIE-ROSE LOGAN

Brill 1971; Cheney 1972; Marie Delcourt 1961 *Hermaphrodite: Myths and Rites of the Bisexual Figure in Classical Antiquity* tr Jennifer Nicholson (London); Fletcher 1971; Wayne Meeks 1973–4 'The Image of the Androgyne: Some Uses of a Symbol in Earliest Christianity' *HistRel* 13:165–208; Camille A. Paglia 1979 'The Apollonian Androgyne and *The Faerie Queene*' *ELR* 9:42–63; Wind 1958.

---

angel, Guyon's The angel who watches over Guyon, after the knight's passage through Mammon's house, incarnates the love that is the subject of the narrator's marveling commentary: 'And is there care in heaven? and is there love / In heavenly spirits to these creatures bace, / That may compassion of their evils move? / There is' (*FQ* II viii 1–8). The heavenly care rendered visible in the angel's descent is manifested in Christ's redemptive journey through history. Guyon's quest imitates one episode of that journey when the solitary knight, traveling through a desert wilderness, encounters and resists the temptations of Mammon (I.G. MacCaffrey 1976:101). Paradoxically, as he emerges from his infernal ordeal, moving upward to 'living light,' the hero falls into a deathlike trance (vii 66). The faint indicates the limit of his powers: the body's need for food and rest, the soul's hunger for that which self-reliant nature cannot comprehend. At this moment of crisis, the angel appears, evoking remembrance of the ministering spirits who came to Christ after his trial in the wilderness (Matt 4.11). The mystery of the grace that touches Guyon is preserved in the angel's revelation to the Palmer that 'he that breathlesse seemes, shal corage bold respire' and in his own promise 'evermore' to 'succour, and defend' the knight against his enemies and God's.

The descent of an emissary god or angel bearing a message to earth is one of the noblest conventions of epic literature. Renaissance versions of the motif derive from Virgil's description of the flight of Mercury (*Aeneid* 4.219–78) and its models in the epics of Homer (Greene 1963:7). Spenser's representation of the angel transfigures its classical, medieval, and Neoplatonic sources in both literary and pictorial memory to direct attention to ultimate sources, ultimate ends.

Characteristically, the passage of the celestial descent describes the swift, dramatic movement of a figure through space. Guyon's guardian is first known not in the motion of flight, but in a voice calling the Palmer back to his charge. Like Tasso's Gabriele (*Gerusalemme liberata* 1.13–14), the angel submits himself to mortal sight in the form of 'a faire young man.' But the wings at his back identify him as one of the cherubim, whose special gift is knowledge of the truth of God (Bartholomaeus Anglicus *De proprietatibus rerum* 2.9). A fifteenth-century Italian sermon notes 'the painters' license to give the angels wings to signify their swift progress in all things' (Baxandall 1972:50). Spenser accommodates his vision of grace to human eyes by giving his angel wings 'like painted Jayes.' Among the visual arts in the collections of Leicester and others of the court were illustrated Books of Hours displaying angels golden-pinioned, red-, blue-, purple-, and peacock-winged (Tuve 1970:127–9). Spenser reinterprets these traditional images through visual and literary allusions that enlarge the immediate narrative context of the descent: the angel's aspect 'Like *Phoebus* face adorned with sunny rayes, / Divinely shone.' The comparison conveys the effect of dazzling light and suggests an analogy with the divine Son who entered the world to redeem it. Spenser does not explicate the simile, but, in the rhetorically defined imagery of his angelic portraiture, visual perception yields to visionary experience. The vision is presented to the Palmer and to the reader – but not to Guyon, 'slumbring fast / In senseless dreame.' The irony of the knight's unconsciousness points to the truth of the relationship of the figures in tableau and to the cosmic setting of Guyon's journey. The angel is not a figure in a dream, and it is in the climactic isolation of the knight's unconsciousness that his relationship to God becomes clearest: 'the love he cannot give, he receives for he is in God's world' (Sonn 1961:29).

The image of Phoebus dissolves immediately into a stanza-long epic simile comparing the angel to '*Cupido* on *Idaean* hill,' a deity and setting apparently alien to the knight of Maidenhead (Cheney 1966:67). But the angel-Cupid comparison is the converse of the 'angel-like' images of the god of love in the dream-visions of romance literature (Hyde 1986:156–7). The god in the comparison is the celestial Cupid invoked in *FQ* I proem 3. The point of the comparison is a point of change, in time and in the poem, a reorientation of vision (Berger 1957:42). Cupid has 'laid his cruell bow away' and is revealed in the presence of his mother, the celestial Venus, and his sisters, the Graces. The unclassical grouping of these figures on Ida (R.M. Cummings 1970:319) and their displacement in the local habitations of Spenser's fiction (cf VI x 8–9) suggest the imagination's search for the true source of beauty, love, and joy. But in the presence of the angel, in this moment of mysterious convergences, Guyon is placed within that love recognized by Ficino as 'the perpetual knot and link of the universe' ('Commentary' on Plato's *Symposium* 3.3; Wind 1958: 41). By this love, the human alliances of the poem are drawn into a new purposiveness (Berger 1957:49). The angel alerts the Palmer to the enemies at hand. The Palmer intercedes for Guyon with Arthur, the human instrument of grace. Arthur, as Guyon's 'dayes-man' (viii 28) dispatches Pyrochles and Cymochles, in fulfillment of the angel's revelation. 'By this, Sir *Guyon* from his traunce awakt' (53), and the action of the quest is renewed.

JOANNE T. DEMPSEY

Michael Baxandall 1972 *Painting and Experience in Fifteenth Century Italy* (Oxford); Berger 1957; Cheney 1966; R.M. Cummings 1970; Ficino ed 1985; Greene 1963; Hamilton 1961a;

Hamilton intro to Book II in *FQ* ed 1977; Hyde 1986; I.G. MacCaffrey 1976; Panofsky 1939; Carl Robinson Sonn 1961 'Sir Guyon in the House of Mammon' *SEL* 1:17–30; Tuve 1970: 112–38.

---

angels According to a commonplace of Renaissance thought, all things are arranged hierarchically 'from the Mushrome to the Angels' (Ward ed 1622:2). Moreover, the angels are themselves ordered according to a scheme twice specified by Spenser as 'trinall triplicities': in *The Faerie Queene*, during the betrothal of the Red Cross Knight and Una (I xii 39), and in *Heavenly Love* (64–70), where the 'Angels bright' are envisaged as congregated about the throne of God, their tasks clearly defined. Oddly, however, the nine orders of angels are reduced to eight in *Heavenly Beautie*; in ascending sequence, they are: Powers, Potentates, Seats, Dominations, Cherubim, Seraphim, Angels, and Archangels.

The immediate appeal is to the time-honored scheme first propounded by the pseudonymous fifth-century writer who, adopting the name of Dionysius the Areopagite, St Paul's convert in Athens (Acts 17.34), arranged the angels into a hierarchy (again in an ascending sequence) of Angels, Archangels, Principalities, Powers, Virtues, Dominations, Thrones, Cherubim, and Seraphim (*De coelesti hierarchia* 7–9). Although enormously popular throughout the Middle Ages, the scheme was not the only one available. In two other alternatives, the angels were rearranged into 'trinall triplicities' so different from the primary scheme that the inevitable result was galloping confusion. On the advent of the Reformation, at any rate, every scheme was promptly dismantled. The principle of order among the angels was retained because the Bible makes it 'most plaine' that there are indeed 'degrees of angels' (Perkins 1591: sig B5v), but schemes like the popular one advanced by Pseudo-Dionysius were dismissed by both Luther and Calvin.

Spenser's list of angelic orders in *Heavenly Beautie* may reflect both his desire to adhere to the traditional 'trinall triplicities' and his unease over the common confusion about their precise arrangement. All the same, the importance of angels as executors of the divine behests is given decisive prominence. In *Teares of the Muses*, Angels are seen 'waighting on th'Almighties chayre' (510); in *Heavenly Beautie*, Angels and Archangels 'attend / On Gods owne person, without rest or end' (97–8); and in *The Faerie Queene*, they sing 'before th'eternall majesty' (I xii 39). In *Amoretti* 8, they 'come to lead fraile mindes to rest / in chast desires on heavenly beauty bound.' Their creation and duties are described in *Heavenly Love* 50–70. Incidental references to angels scattered throughout Spenser's poetry (eg, they are said to wear a 'heavenly coronall ... before Gods tribunall' *FQ* III v 53) show how entirely they inhabited his imagination. In *The Faerie Queene*, the primacy of grace emphasized in Book I – 'Ne let the man ascribe it to his skill, / That thorough grace hath gained victory. / If any strength we have, it is to ill, / But all the good is Gods, both power and eke will' (x 1) – leads to an even more lucid affirmation on 'th'exceeding grace / Of Highest God' whose angelic ministers are dispatched 'to and fro, / To serve to wicked man, to serve his wicked foe' (II viii 1–2; see Guyon's *angel).

Following Revelation 12.3–4, 7–9, Spenser records the prehistoric war in heaven when 'a whole legione / Of wicked Sprights did fall from happy blis' (III ix 2; cf viii 8 and *HHL* 71–98). This vision of their fall is countered by two glorious epiphanies. On the Mount of Contemplation, Redcrosse sees the New Jerusalem: 'As he thereon stood gazing, he might see / The blessed Angels to and fro descend / From highest heaven, in gladsome companee, / And with great joy into that Citie wend, / As commonly as friend does with his frend' (I x 56). Its secular counterpart is the climactic vision of Mercilla: her cloth of state is upheld by little angels and thousands more encompass her throne (V ix 29). On the whole, then, Spenser's angelology is thoroughly traditional. C.A. PATRIDES

Robert Ellrodt 1980 'Angels and the Poetic Imagination from Donne to Traherne' in *English Renaissance Studies Presented to Dame Helen Gardner in Honour of Her Seventieth Birthday* (Oxford) pp 164–79; Lewis 1964:40–2, 71–4; William Perkins 1591 *A Golden Chaine* tr R. Hill (London); Samuel Ward 1622 *The Life of Faith* 3rd ed (London). On the rise and fall of the Pseudo-Dionysian scheme, see C.A. Patrides 1982 *Premises and Motifs in Renaissance Thought and Literature* (Princeton) ch 1.

---

animals, fabulous Both fabulous animals and animals with fabulous characteristics are images compounded within the mental faculty of the fantasy (or imagination). In the description of Phantastes' cell, all perceived reality is mixed together with things imagined, so that apes and lions, lovers and children, are found with 'Infernall Hags, *Centaurs*, feendes, *Hippodames*' (*FQ* II ix 50). Even though these images may be 'such as in the world were never yit,' they exist in the mind and are therefore subject to interpretation.

Yet by comparison with the many other beasts in Spenser's poetry, fabulous animals are rarely mentioned. Basilisk, centaur, chimera, cockatrice, dragon, griffin, hydra, minotaur, phoenix, unicorn, and various sea monsters are the only ones named directly, though others, such as Duessa's seven-headed beast (I vii 16–18) and the Blatant Beast (V xii and VI) may be termed fabulous even though Spenser has reworked them from the Bible or traditional fable. Except for these two, fabulous animals are seldom directly present in the narrative except in pageants (cf *MHT* 122–4); usually they are mentioned in similes and ecphrases.

Six are used in similes. According to classical lore as transmitted through medieval bestiaries, the cockatrice and basilisk are lizardlike creatures that can kill with their gaze; eyes have the same power, and thus the poet's beloved in *Amoretti* 49 can 'kill with looks, as Cockatrices do,' and Corflambo 'Like as the Basiliske of serpents seede, / From powrefull eyes close venim doth convay / Into the lookers hart, and killeth farre away' (IV viii 39).

The unicorn and lion are traditional enemies; the lion, being the only creature that can capture the fabulous unicorn (a beast that may not be tamed, according to Job 39.12–15), lures it to attack, then slips aside so that its horn (precious because of its special medical and near-magical powers) becomes caught in a tree. Thus, in an extended simile where Pyrochles is described as the unicorn and Guyon as the lion (II v 10), the point is not only that Guyon is more clever but also that Pyrochles is an especially difficult opponent. Since the unicorn was known for its wrath, the comparison with the fiery Pyrochles is the more apt.

Another traditional mythical struggle is that between the dragon and the griffin (a lion with eagle's wings, one of the four beasts in the vision at Dan 7.4). At *FQ* I v 8, Redcrosse is compared to the griffin and Sansjoy to the dragon – 'With hideous horrour both together smight.' The comparison of Redcrosse's enemy to a dragon is entirely apt: all his enemies may be termed dragons. To picture Redcrosse as a griffin seems less apt; yet in this battle, Redcrosse shares the bestiality, magnanimity, covetousness, and strength which are traditionally attributed to the griffin (see note on *FQ* I v 8.2 in ed 1977).

Another fabulous animal is the hydra, that many-headed serpent slain by Hercules (Ovid *Metamorphoses* 9.68–74). The comparisons of Duessa's seven-headed beast and the Blatant Beast to the hydra (I vii 17, VI xii 32) imply that they can be overcome only by the ultimate hero.

Centaurs appear in both ecphrases and pageants. They are painted on the walls of Phantastes' chamber (II ix 50); the tapestries of the house of Busirane show Saturn transforming himself into a centaur (III xi 43); 'relicks of the drunken fray' between the Lapiths, Centaurs, and Hercules are exhibited in the house of Ate (IV i 23); November rides the 'dreadfull' centaur Chiron, son of Saturn, in the pageant of the months (VII vii 40). Centaurs in these various displays recall the ancient mythological world in which the natural and the human are often mixed, sometimes with dangerous consequences.

Only a few animals appear as part of the direct experience of characters in *The Faerie Queene*, and even then their presence is shadowy. Trompart asserts that 'Dragons, and Minotaures' haunt the wilderness in which Hellenore is lost (III x 40); although Trompart is not the most reliable witness, his claim seems plausible to the reader who has already met several dragons in the narrative. Dreadful sea monsters, many of them believed to exist, delay Guyon's progress towards Acrasia's island: as the narrator comments, 'Ne wonder, if these did the knight appall' (II xii 25). Yet the Palmer tells Guyon that they are not real monsters but imaginary shapes 'disguiz'd / By that same wicked witch' Acrasia, thus instructing him to separate vain images from reality – a continuation of the theme established earlier in the visit to Phantastes' chamber.

Certainly the most important fabulous animals in Spenser's poetry are the five images of absolute evil derived from classical and Christian tradition and the Bible, chiefly Revelation: Error (I i), Lucifera's dragon (v), Duessa's seven-headed beast (vii), the Dragon killed by Redcrosse (xi), and the Blatant Beast (V x, VI).

BERNARD TANNIER

For further discussion, see Bernard Tannier 1980 'Un bestiaire maniériste: monstres et animaux fantastiques dans *La Reine des Fées* d'Edmund Spenser' in *Monstres et prodiges au temps de la Renaissance* ed Marie Thérèse Jones-Davies (Paris) pp 55–65. For medieval lore, see T.H. White 1954 and Bartholomaeus Anglicus 1582, Book 18; for the Renaissance, see Topsell 1607; for a mid-seventeenth-century critical examination of much of this lore, see Book 3 of Sir Thomas Browne 1981 *Pseudodoxia Epidemica* ed Robin Robbins, 2 vols (Oxford). See also Carroll 1954; Hamilton's notes to *FQ* ed 1977; Robin 1932; and Beryl Rowland 1973 *Animals with Human Faces: A Guide to Animal Symbolism* (Knoxville, Tenn).

antique world Spenser uses the word *antique* in many different senses, so that the meaning of the phrase *antique world* in his works is not always consistent or clear. A useful way to examine his range of meanings and their relationships is to consider the proems to the books of *The Faerie Queene*.

The word *antique* appears in four proems and in the second stanza of the *Cantos of Mutabilitie*, *antiquity* in one, and *former ages* in another. In the reference to Mutabilitie's 'antique race' (VII vi 2), the adjective means 'primeval, original.' In the phrase 'antique praises,' which refers to the celebration of Queen Elizabeth (III proem 3), the adjective means 'antic' in the sixteenth-century sense: 'fanciful,' 'formulated in an imaginative fiction.' In I proem 2 and II proem 1 and 4, *antique* means primarily 'of that past recounted in this poem.' In Book V proem 1 (see also 3 and 9), 'the antique world' means primarily the Golden Age: the period of virtue, simplicity, and harmony which, according to many classical writers, initiated human history. The myth of the Golden Age, which Spenser would have known best from Ovid's *Metamorphoses* I, was revived by frequent descriptions in Renaissance texts. It was supposedly followed by the Silver, Bronze, and Iron Ages, each harsher and more violent than its predecessor. The Iron Age was associated with the present, so that the myth expressed nostalgia for a pristine happiness opposed to fallen reality. In IV proem 3, the phrase 'former ages,' also evoking a nobler past, appears to refer primarily to classical antiquity, since an allusion to Socrates follows immediately.

Spenser's use of *antiquity* in *FQ* VI proem 4 and 6 seems to bring together somewhat elusively several of these meanings: the past of this poem, the Golden Age, the civilization of ancient Greece and Rome, all presented as superior to the shrunken present. This elision of meanings is typical of Spenser. Each of those distinguished above is present to some degree in all the uses cited. In this way, through the various nuances of the word *antique*, a medieval, chivalric world overlaps with classical antiquity, a historical period overlaps with a mythical fiction, and all are associated with the action of the poem.

Of these diverse referents accruing to a single word, one had special force in Spenser's education and in his culture: the civilization of ancient Greece and Rome. The word *antiquity* in his age was already coming to denote primarily that civilization, as it does today. Spenser's own relationship to this particularly influential era of the past was complex and remains in some aspects confused, but three questions help to organize what is known about this relationship. First, with what elements of antiquity (authors, works, genres, myths, values, ideas) did he have contact? Second, through what intermediary avenues did this contact occur? Third, how were these elements, already altered by the passage of history, further assimilated and transmuted in his poetry?

The sixteenth century witnessed a dramatic renewal of interest in classical antiquity throughout northern Europe, a renewal which had been anticipated roughly a century earlier in Italy (see *humanism, *Renaissance). This renewal heavily influenced literature written in the national vernacular languages; it produced a large body of Neo-Latin poetry and prose; it affected the ways in which men and women viewed their human dignity and their existence on earth; it directed the minds of the intellectual elite back to their pagan and Christian origins; it dominated the education of the young. Merchant Taylors' School, which Spenser attended, had as its first headmaster a devotee of the 'new learning,' Richard Mulcaster. There can be no doubt that Spenser's early schooling had a strong humanist character.

The principal subject studied at Tudor grammar schools was Latin. The acquisition of Greek was in contrast a much rarer phenomenon, reserved for a select group of students at the most advanced schools; even in these cases, few students equaled the proficiency all achieved in Latin. The best schools generally introduced boys to Latin literature in the form of the *Precepts of Cato* (a series of moralizing distichs), and then taught them to read texts by such major authors as Cicero, Terence, Virgil, Horace, and Ovid. Aesop and Lucian were sometimes taught to younger boys in Latin translation. Neo-Latin authors, generally Mantuan and Erasmus, were often included as well. Great stress was placed upon memorizing; at Winchester, for example, all boys who reached a given level were required to learn twelve lines of Ovid's *Metamorphoses* a week, thus about 500 lines a year. It is quite likely that Spenser knew long passages of Latin poetry by heart.

As students advanced, they were required to write Latin compositions imitating those of the classics under study. They were also encouraged to keep commonplace books, in which they entered notable maxims, idioms, *topoi*, epithets, images, and turns of phrase garnered from their reading. These books were then mined when the student came to write his own compositions. Thus imitation was central to the educational process, not only in the conception of an entire composition but in its smallest elements. This process did not of course ensure a grasp of the true distinction or particular spirit of a given author, and doubtless it led most schoolboys to produce a merely mechanical likeness. But it did produce a strong pressure for continuity both of genre and of semantic unit; and in this respect, its effects are traceable on virtually every page of Spenser's writing.

Spenser's instruction at grammar school was followed by seven formative years at Cambridge, where he received the degrees of BA and MA. His formal education there took the form of attendance at lectures, delivered in English, and public disputations with other students. In 1570, his second year at the university, a revised set of statutes governing its curriculum was approved by the Queen. Since these statutes are extant, they can inform us concerning the texts and subjects taught, although it would be naive to assume that they were invariably followed to the letter. For a future BA, they prescribe rhetoric (Quintilian, Hermogenes, Cicero), logic (Aristotle and Cicero), and 'philosophy' (Plato, Pliny, Aristotle's *Problems*, *Ethics*, and *Politics*). Lectures on the Greek texts in this list would probably have discussed them in Latin translation. An MA candidate studied quadrivial subjects (arithmetic, geometry, Ptolemaic astronomy), drawing, more philosophy, and Greek (both the language and such authors as Homer, Isocrates, Demosthenes, and Euripides). The fact that language training was necessary at this level suggests that readings in Greek authors consisted of selected excerpts. A Cambridge professor of Spenser's era refers to student theatricals enlivening winter evenings with Euripides, Sophocles, Aristophanes, Plautus, Terence, and Seneca (Judson 1945:26). But his nostalgic and expansive tone makes it unclear whether this list is to be taken altogether literally.

Humanism at Cambridge had received strong impetus during the middle third of the century from a group of scholars led by Sir John Cheke and Roger Ascham, a group based at St John's College but influential well beyond its walls. Spenser's student friendship with Gabriel Harvey, an erudite classical scholar, must in itself have widened and sharpened his interest in ancient literature. A passage in a published letter from Harvey to Spenser drops the names of authors Harvey clearly thought his fellow student *ought* to be reading: '*Tully* [Cicero], and *Demosthenes* nothing so much studyed, as they were wonte: *Livie*, and *Salust* possiblye rather more, than lesse: *Lucian* never so much: *Aristotle* muche named, but little read: *Xenophon* and *Plato*, reckned amongest Discoursers, and conceited Superficiall fellowes' (*Three Letters* 3, *Var Prose* p 460). This may or may not be an accurate reflection of Cambridge taste in 1580, but it evokes an atmosphere in which it is fashionable to talk about ancient writers and debate the rise and fall of reputations. The little reading of Aristotle reported by Harvey, in marked contrast with the statutes' prescriptions, suggests that the study of this author was mediated by that medieval scholastic philosophy whose survival at Cambridge would exasperate Milton two generations later.

Although we shall never know with any certainty just how widely Spenser read in classical literature, the uncertainty is particularly acute in the case of Greek. He must have learned some at university, if not at school, but it is hard to say how much. On the one hand, he knew enough to form the names of characters in *The Faerie Queene* from Greek roots. His friend Lodowick Bryskett, in his fictional dialogue *Discourse of Civill Life*, describes Spenser as 'perfect in the Greek tongue' (ed 1970:21). The Letter to Raleigh refers to Homer, Plato, and Xenophon; *SC, March* imitates an idyll by Bion and 'Astrophel' another; echoes of Plato's *Timaeus* and of Plutarch can be found in the *Fowre Hymnes*; the Pastorella story in *FQ* VI may be indebted to Greek romances; a translation of the pseudo-Platonic dialogue *Axiochus* into English may be Spenser's. The Greek emblems which conclude *Maye* form an hexameter found in Theognis. Other allusions and 'sources' could be cited.

Yet on the other hand, all of Spenser's known sources that involve a Greek text were also available to him in another language. The *Axiochus* translation, for example, is based on a Latin version of the Greek by a certain Welsdalius. At *FQ* II vii 52 and IV proem 3, two serious errors concerning the participants in two Platonic dialogues raise the question whether Spenser had read the *Phaedo* and the *Phaedrus* in any language. Although E.K. in his Argument prefacing *The Shepheardes Calender* cites Theocritus as 'the first head and welspring' of the eclogue form, there is very little of Theocritus in the work itself. The eclogue closest to his idylls, *August*, depends more immediately on Sannazaro, Baïf, and Ronsard, as well as Virgil. *March* does not derive from Bion directly but either from Latin or a French translation. Spenser may have read many Greek authors in translation or in original excerpts, but there seems to be no firm evidence other than the tribute of his friend Bryskett that he could read Greek texts of any length in the original.

The case of Latin literature is totally different. There is ample evidence that Spenser's mind was steeped in it, especially in its poetry. He translated the *Culex* (mistakenly attributed by his contemporaries to Virgil) as *Virgils Gnat*, and he drew heavily on *Ciris* (another pseudo-Virgilian poem) for an episode at *FQ* III ii 30–51. Many other passages in his poetry allude to specific passages in Latin poetry, and his entire corpus is dense with phrases, images, motifs, and details stemming originally from ancient Latin writing.

Nonetheless, it is not easy to state with precision just how widely Spenser read in Latin. He certainly knew Cicero, Terence, Virgil, Horace, and Ovid – all likely school texts. He certainly knew works by Seneca and Statius; he uses the latter's *Thebaid* in *The Faerie Queene*. He must have read some Caesar, Pliny, Sallust, Quintilian, and Livy. Lucretius was less commonly read during the Tudor period, but some readers claim that he influenced Spenser. Spenser translates the opening of *De rerum natura* in *FQ* IV x 44–7, although there is no strong evidence that he read the entire Latin poem. Elements from Diodorus Siculus appear in *The Shepheardes Calender* and elsewhere. It is doubtful that Spenser knew well the elegists Catullus, Propertius, and Tibullus. The structure of *Epithalamion* is fundamentally Catullan, but this structure had become conventional during the continental Renaissance. Of the Late Latin authors, Spenser clearly knew Macrobius and the protomedieval philosopher Boethius. The list of authors could probably be lengthened if individual motifs or phrases implied conclusive proof of Spenser's familiarity with a given ancient text. But the use of commonplace books was so heavy, the passage from imitation to topos so common, that this kind of attribution is risky.

More useful than seeking to compile a reading list is asking how Spenser 'knew' a given classical text at all. Like most readers, he apparently tasted many more books than he digested. *FQ* II x, for instance, suggests that his grasp of Roman history was weak. The discussion of ancient historical evidence in *Vewe of Ireland* has many references which have proven untraceable or simply wrong. For example, the word *mantelum* (cloak) is assigned to a passage in the *Aeneid* where it does not appear (*Var Prose* p 99). The ideal of historical precision was not high during Spenser's lifetime, and he did nothing to raise it.

More generally, it should be remembered that Elizabethans, like moderns, could read a book for many reasons: as a storehouse of usable phrases and images; as a rhetorical performance exhibiting a variety of classified tropes; as an imitation or emulation of a well-known earlier work; as a set of positive and negative moral examples; as 'matter' for instruction and as a source of ideas; as an allegorical source with implications for ethics, metaphysics, or theology, especially if the surface appeared to be unrewarding. Even so gifted a mind as Spenser's would not have approached all books, including the classics, with all these considerations at work simultaneously. On the basis of his published works, we can guess which ancient writers he read with the most sympathetic attention and active receptivity; but except for two or three dominant masters, we can only guess. We can be sure only that the assumptions and expectations guiding his reading differed both from our own and from those of the original ancient audience.

Spenser's contact with the classics was achieved through a series of screens. First was the screen of language, formidable in the case of Greek, less opaque in the case of Latin, but nonetheless interposing a foreign element between reader and text. For most Greek texts, translation was probably an additional screen. Massive historical change was also a screen between the culture or cultures of antiquity and that of Elizabethan England. No reader at any period can accurately estimate the density of this screen. Tudor England witnessed a growth in the awareness of historical change more or less coincident with the growth of native humanism, but it would remain for men and women of the seventeenth century to gauge the profundity of change with something approaching that clarity we like to call 'modern.' Spenser never reached the awareness of his younger contemporary Jonson, although this contrast should not stamp him as a correspondingly weaker poet. But it is fair to say that the screen of change was doubled for him and almost all his contemporaries by an imperfect perception of change. Further, when pagan authorities and Christian authorities were seen to differ, many Renaissance writers, including Spenser, attempted to minimize or reconcile the difference, often in the process reading with a bias the texts they were reinterpreting. Thus the very conflict of authorities could be considered a screen to understanding.

Still another, more visible screen lay in the immense corpus of glosses, commentaries, and interpretations which intermittently illuminated but also oversimplified or obscured classic texts. Many of these commentaries were published along with the texts and were impossible to avoid, just as E.K.'s glosses cannot be avoided in reading *The Shepheardes Calender*. In many sixteenth-century editions of Virgil, for example, the original text would occupy a relatively small part of the folio page, the rest of which was given over to commentators. These could include both Late Latin figures such as Servius and Donatus, and modern humanist scholars such as Badius Ascensius. Some editions would mingle many chronological layers of 'explanation' and interpretation, which could be grammatical, philological, historical, rhetorical, moral, religious, or allegorical. This screen of commentary on single works is not always easily distinguishable from original treatises which reiterate, reformulate, embroider, simplify, and wittingly or unwittingly distort the content of the classical text.

Plato's dialogues, which were subjected to many reformulations both pagan and Christian, are perhaps the clearest example of how screens are created by commentary's ramification and deformation of a text. One of the most influential philosophical treatises of the Italian Renaissance was Ficino's 'Commentary' on Plato's *Symposium*. It in turn helped to produce a new wave of Neoplatonic treatises throughout Europe which both disseminated and altered its thought. This is why it is difficult to sort out specific sources for Spenser's Neoplatonism in *Colin Clouts Come Home Againe* and *Fowre Hymnes*.

Beyond the screen of commentary stood another composed of encyclopedic gatherings, florilegia, manuals, dictionaries, and handbooks designed to make antiquity more accessible. Among the best known examples are the *Adages* and *Apothegms* of Erasmus, the *Mythologiae* of Conti and comparable mythographic compilations by Vincenzo Cartari and Cintio, and the farraginous Elizabethan compendium commonly called *Batman uppon Bartholome*. Encyclopedic collections like these brought together information and misinformation of a superficial kind enabling people to seem better educated than they were. Their net effect was to fragment what was known about antiquity into bits of knowledge or pseudo-knowledge: proverbs, anecdotes, iconographic details, debased myths, random facts, cliché descriptions. This screen also prevented such a reader as Spenser from perceiving ancient civilization as anything like a series of organic cultural configurations.

The final screen was the peculiar temperament, taste, imagination, and bent of mind of Spenser himself, who responded to the tangled values and traditions of ancient, medieval, and Renaissance Europe as a unique, discriminating agent, never receiving the imprint of the past as a *tabula rasa* but as a specific, developing, idiosyncratic artist. To enumerate these screens is not to belittle the humanism of Spenser's age but rather to describe the particular forms of mediation then at work in the perennial interplay between past and present.

Understanding this Tudor interplay is needed to understand Spenser's assimilation and transmutation of ancient culture in his poetry. It was not easy to intermingle late medieval, native English elements with what Spenser knew of the classics and with what he knew of the continental Renaissance, which was itself attempting to achieve a similar synthesis. The task of incorporating Greek and Roman culture into the contemporary world was markedly easier in France, since the leaders of the French poetic revival were much more willing to jettison almost all their native, medieval culture. This was not so in England, however, least of all with Spenser, whose first major work deliberately imposed an archaic English flavor and vocabulary on the imported literary mode of pastoral.

We can measure the tension in this imposition and, more broadly, the tension in English humanism by noting E.K.'s ambivalence in his introductions and annotations to *The Shepheardes Calender*. He is clearly anxious to point out (sometimes erroneously) all the echoes and allusions to ancient and continental sources; yet in his prefatory Epistle to Harvey, he attacks those who, finding the English language barren, have 'patched up the holes with peces and rags of other languages, borrowing here of the french, there of the Italian, every where of the Latine.' E.K.'s linguistic purism seems to fit badly with his literary eclecticism. Spenser would have avoided so awkward a straddle, but he had to cope nonetheless with the problem of assimilation.

Spenser himself seems to have written a fair amount of Latin verse as a young man. His first letter to Harvey speaks of an *Epithalamion Thamesis* and a *Stemmata Dudleiana* (*3 Lett* 1, *Var Prose* pp 17–18); and his second letter contains a poetic tribute to his correspondent in 237 Latin hexameters ('Ad ornatissimum virum' in *2 Lett* 1, *Var Prose* pp 8–12), although this 'one existing specimen of Spenser's Latin verse gives us no high idea of his skill in the scholarly art' (Renwick in *Var Prose* p 259).

A deeper concern and a far more difficult challenge to the young Spenser was to write quantitative verse. The predicaments inherent in this enterprise, disagreements over specific words and syllables, and poetic trial balloons occupy a substantial part of his published correspondence with Harvey, to whom he expostulated, 'For, why a Gods name may not we, as else the Greekes, have the kingdome of oure owne Language, and measure our Accentes, by the sounde, reserving the Quantitie to the Verse' (*3 Lett* 1, *Var Prose* p 16). Here he underestimates the difficulty of cultural assimilation, and illustrates the larger and more difficult drama of creating a vernacular humanist poetry.

The most tangible evidence of Spenser's early humanist ambitions lies in his translation from Latin of the pseudo-Virgilian *Culex* as *Virgils Gnat*, published with the *Complaints* in 1591 but probably an earlier work. This is a creditable version which no longer makes a strong appeal to modern taste. Like many Renaissance translators, he felt no compunctions about adding to his original, so that the resulting English poem is considerably longer than the Latin; but it is reasonably accurate and is especially faithful to the shifting tone of the original. Also included in the *Complaints* is a translation from French of the *Antiquitez* of Joachim du Bellay as *Ruines of Rome*, as well as a translation of du Bellay's poetic epilogue to this work, entitled *Songe*, as *Visions of Bellay*. This latter series had been part of Spenser's first published work, a group of translated visionary poems in *A Theatre for Worldlings*, which appeared in 1569 when the poet could not have been much older than seventeen. Another poem in *Complaints*, *Ruines of Time*, associates the fall of Rome with the fall of an ancient British city, Verulam; this poem's elegiac style reflects du Bellay's influence. *Teares of the Muses*, also in *Complaints*, laments the fallen state of the Muses in the present age, in contrast to the prestige and inspirational power they once enjoyed. In various ways, all of these poems express pathos, that sense of loss and privation endemic to the humanist enterprise. However *Muiopotmos* in the same collection displays a more playful humanism, opening with an echo of the *Iliad* and closing with an echo of the *Aeneid*, as though to frame with epic allusions the mingled regret and mock-heroic bravura of its narrative.

The *Complaints* as a collection reflects a more self-consciously humanistic Spenser than does *The Shepheardes Calender*, despite E.K.'s learned annotations. Of the pastorals, three exemplify diverse aspects of his relation to antiquity. *March* includes an anecdote traceable to Bion's fourth idyll, lengthened with details from Moschus' first. Translations of both poems were available to Spenser, and these, rather than the original Greek, seem to have been his immediate sources. (The attempt in *March* to assimilate a coy, decorative, slender hellenistic pastoralism to native English rusticity has not generally been admired.) *August* presents a singing match between two shepherds, a highly conventionalized pastoral sub-genre leading back through many Renaissance examples to Virgil's third and seventh eclogues, themselves indebted to the first, seventh, and eighth idylls of Theocritus. Spenser substitutes a rollicking English roundelay for the slower-paced contests of the convention and brings off poetic assimilation of undeniable appeal. *October* expresses aspirations for poetry beyond the pastoral low style and cites Servius' famous 'Virgilian progression' from eclogue to georgic to epic (lines 55–60). Although Cuddie here refuses Piers' invitation to let his 'Muse display her fluttryng wing' (43), the ambition to write a Virgilian epic in the high style is formulated vigorously, and Colin Clout is named as one who might one day fulfill it. Piers' evocation of heroic grandeur, soaring above the 'lowly dust' of pastoral, already situates *The Shepheardes Calender* as the first step in Spenser's own Virgilian progression.

The implicit promise of *October* is explicitly affirmed by the opening lines of *The Faerie Queene*: 'Lo I the man' and the lines that follow paraphrase those all sixteenth-century readers believed to open Virgil's *Aeneid* and describe Spenser's own progression from pastoral to epic. Thus they set *The Faerie Queene* in a tradition whose central figure was Virgil, preceded by Homer as the Letter to Raleigh reminds us, and followed by Ariosto and Tasso. They invite the reader to consider Spenser's poem in the Virgilian, or more broadly the classical, tradition sketched by Piers in *October*. The dissonance between this tradition and the Ariostan epic-romance was reduced for Spenser because the body of commentary associated with each tended to nudge them closer to each other, to represent them as more alike than they actually are. Spenser believed that he could be faithful at once to the classical line and to the Italian line which for him harmoniously extended the classical. He misgauged their unlikeness, thus heightening the problem of poetic assimilation but not necessarily impoverishing the substance of his greatest work.

Assimilation of ancient culture in *The Faerie Queene* takes diverse forms, many of which are liable to misunderstanding. Renwick's caveat is still useful: 'The use of quotations may be proof of study, but it is not necessarily proof of intellectual discipleship, still less of complete acceptance of a system of thought. Nor did quotations necessarily come direct from their originals, for many phrases and arguments had done duty many times, and not always the same duty or in the same connexion' (*Var* 4:235).

Similar caution is advisable when we consider Spenser's use of a given passage from an ancient narrative. It may be legitimate to examine in detail his transmutation of a story, for example, the recasting of Ovid's Diana and Actaeon myth in the Faunus episode of *FQ* VII vi. But fragments of Ovid's version of that myth can be traced in many other passages of the English poem – one scholar has pointed to ten (Friedmann 1966) – and a survey of such passages does not take into account intermediate retellings of the Ovidian story which Spenser may have known. Thus assimilation and transmutation are slippery concepts. They can operate at the smallest, almost microscopic level of the poem as well as at the very broadest global level; but it is easier to demonstrate their presence than to describe their function and effect.

In theory, various types of assimilation can be distinguished, although for practical analysis these tend to shade into each other. The kind of fragmentation just noted distributes minuscule details over the body of the poem; for example, the pumice stone, which is not found in England but in Ovid's description of Diana's grotto, is relocated in Spenser's fairy world (*Met* 3.158; *FQ* II v 30, III v 39). At the other extreme, the virtue of magnificence is incarnated by Arthur and derived from the supreme Aristotelian virtue of magnanimity, as the Letter to Raleigh makes clear. In contrast with this macrocosmic conception, there is the stereotyped narrative unit such as the descent to the house of Morpheus (I i 39–44), which derives from earlier accounts in the *Iliad*, the *Aeneid*, Statius' *Thebaid*, Chaucer's *Book of the Duchess*, and Politian's *Stanze per la Giostra*; likewise, the bleeding tree motif (I ii 30–4) derives from earlier examples in the *Aeneid*, Dante's *Inferno*, Boccaccio's *Filocolo*, and Ariosto's *Orlando furioso*. There is the imitation of a recognizable passage from a single ancient text, such as the imitations of Virgil's Hades (I v 32–5, II vii 21–3); this type allows more scope for textual analysis and thus for an understanding of the actual process of poetic transmutation. There is the general resemblance in narrative elements between two sharply different plots, such as the resemblance between Spenser's story of the true and false Florimells (III-IV) and the story of Euripides' *Helen*, a tragedy which also involves an actual woman and her magically contrived look-alike. There is the allusion to a genre of ancient literature, as when the Greek romance of Longus, Heliodorus, and Achilles Tatius is revived in the Pastorella story (VI ix-xii). There is comic burlesque, as when Aeneas' encounter with Venus (*Aeneid* I) is travestied in Trompart's meeting with Belphoebe (II iii 21–33). There is the lifting of a scene from the pseudo-Virgilian *Ciris* already mentioned; and there is the allegorization of a straightforward narrative, such as the sea-change of Homeric elements at II xii 2–38. There is Spenser's free translation of a set passage, such as the hymn to Venus (IV x 44–7) which Englishes the opening lines of Lucretius' *De rerum natura*. There is finally a type of assimilation too diffused for quotation which can be regarded only as an imaginative or spiritual kinship, 'Unseene of any, yet of all beheld' (VII vii 13).

There is indeed very little in *The Faerie Queene* which is *not* assimilative of something, whether it is ancient or whether it can be located somewhere else in Spenser's enormous cultural heritage. The basic process of the poem is parodic, if the implication of ridicule is removed from that term, for almost everything in it constitutes a revision or displacement of something else, much of which ultimately has classical roots. 'His originality has long been recognized to lie in his devotion to other poets and to myths he recombined from other sources' (Fletcher 1971:105–6). Part of this revising, displacing, and recombining can be attributed to Spenser's deliberate artistic will; another part, indefinable and immeasurable, can be attributed to the screens standing between the poet and the materials he sought to revise.

The paraphrase of Lucretius' opening lines in Book IV illustrates the interaction between subtext and Renaissance text. Spenser shares Lucretius' quasi-religious awe before the natural regeneration of the spring season, but he Englishes the Latin with a proper sense of his own independence. Part of the difference stems, of course, from the larger context of each invocation. Venus in *The Faerie Queene* is one in a series of personifications; in the Latin, she is a deified force in a work which demystifies all other traditional deities. But there are significant verbal variations as well. Spenser reduces slightly Lucretius' celebration of the goddess as *genetrix* (life-giving) and as *alma* (nourishing) in order to heighten her role as a pacifier and source of joy: 'Mother of laughter, and welspring of blisse' (IV x 47). It is she who prepares for pleasure all that is fair and glad on earth; and this 'pleasure,' in contrast to the Christian and Stoic austerities which also attracted Spenser, acquires a brave intensity which the Latin could not have achieved. In Lucretius, Venus stimulates lusty, even violent activity; in Spenser, the 'fury' of sex is absorbed in a cheerful and frisky animal gaiety. Perhaps the most characteristically Spenserian line praises Venus not only for creating the world (Conti's idea, not Lucretius') but also for maintaining it against destruction: 'And dayly yet thou doest the same repayre' (x 47). This repairing, with its implication of a perennial struggle between undoing and remaking, is Spenser's most vivid personal signature. However keen his awareness of his actual historical remoteness may or may not have been, here he distances his own poem and its metaphysics from their prestigious source.

Of all ancient writers, Virgil and Ovid dominate *The Faerie Queene*. In some respects they represent antithetical pressures on Spenser's imagination. He seems to have perceived Virgil, rightly or wrongly, as a poet of stability. Aeneas embodies, according to the Letter, 'a good governour and a vertuous man,' and this he was thought to have remained steadfastly throughout his many trials. Spenser's view of Aeneas may well have been influenced by such a commentator as the Florentine Neoplatonist Cristoforo Landino, whose allegorical reading of the *Aeneid* presents Aeneas as a kind of ideal Stoic – wise, temperate, strong, successful, resistant to all perturbations. The Virgilian principle endows each book of *The Faerie Queene* with whatever continuity, progression, and steady movement toward victory it possesses. It also endows action with dignity and nobility, and allows the reader to hope that this action will alter the state of affairs definitively, irreversibly.

In Virgil, Spenser found an authority endowed with both his own moral seriousness and his capacity for stubborn hope in temperate courage when faced with misfortune. He also found an imagination strong enough to confront an underworld and authoritative enough to provide a model for his own descents into the terrible darkness which permanently threatens his poetic universe. The descents into a demonic underworld of *FQ* I v, II vii, and IV i, more pagan than Christian, depend upon Virgil as a guide, especially the first two; yet even here Spenser finds his own note. There is nothing in the *Aeneid* comparable to 'The trembling ghosts with sad amazed mood, / Chattring their yron teeth, and staring wide / With stonie eyes' (I v 32). The presence of Virgil allowed Spenser to explore personal fantasies of horror and provided the example of a survival from horror in a universe moving toward concord.

The presence of Ovid in *The Faerie Queene* can be situated at a pole opposite to Virgil's. The Ovidian principle is that force which turns every victory into a partial failure, which distracts every narrative from proceeding directly to its end, which calls into question the stability of character, of plot, and of cosmos. The same force also invests the fluctuating physical world with the dynamism which informs the Garden of Adonis and the marriage of the rivers.

Spenser gives evidence of knowing most or all of Ovid's works, but the ancient work which nourished his epic beyond all others was the *Metamorphoses*. From that labyrinth of changes, as it was visible to him through screening intermediaries, he would have learned the possibilities of mythography for moral and metaphysical meaning; he would have learned the charm of structural distraction, postponing the promised end; and he might also have learned the deceptiveness of intended conclusions. His poem, at any rate, typically withholds a 'Virgilian' finality for an Ovidian divagation or frustration. Spenser would have found in the *Meta-*

morphoses blurred divisions between supernatural and natural, divine and human, transcendent divine and immanent divine, pantheistic world and inert world, possessed prophet and earthbound versifier. The absence of sharp divisions between metaphysical realms permitted the creation of a fairy world in which the status of creatures and places is happily ambiguous; the very term *fairy* illustrates this ambiguity. What he partly failed to see in Ovid's corpus is the witty skepticism shading into cynicism, not least toward the subject of erotic love. Part of that skepticism would have been screened out by the moralistic recuperations of the commentators. But the Faunus story of *FQ* VII vi demonstrates that not all Ovidian comedy was lost on him, as it demonstrates his pleasure in creating his own, quite explicitly Ovidian metamorphosis.

Perhaps most crucially, Spenser found in *Metamorphoses* 15 a usable philosophy of eternal mutability, there attributed to the sage Pythagoras. The transformations which occupy the fourteen preceding books are revealed now as manifesting the fundamental activity of the universe, the constant transformation of the elements, of things, of creatures, and of forms. Spenser's most memorable dramatizations of this philosophy are in the Garden of Adonis (III vi) and the *Cantos of Mutabilitie*, but in fact his poem is saturated with an intuition of the fragility and cyclicity of all things. *The Faerie Queene* is a poem of primeval alternations – of day and night, light and darkness, victory and defeat, joy and sorrow, love and strife, life and death, creation and destruction. It bears witness to these perennial alternations, sometimes in the mode of celebration, sometimes in the mode of lament. The very last line expresses lament; but that final moment cannot cancel out the joy of the union of Venus and Adonis, of matter and form, a union whose offspring are mortal but which is nonetheless suitable for celebration. Ovidian alternation, mutability, cyclicity are of course the patterns of Spenserian narrative itself, always impeding the Virgilian drive toward a conclusive repose, but yielding in the end to a provisional and partial closure.

Thus Spenser responded to Ovid with the intuitions of a great poet, even though he never freed himself from the constrictions of his own cultural and temporal provinciality. He may never have realized how radically his art and his world differed from Ovid's; he may never fully have recognized the distortions imposed by the screens of fifteen centuries of sedimented interpretation. But his work does exemplify admirably the range of artistic strategies available to the Tudor humanist poet in assimilating not only Ovid but all of the ancient world he knew. Even if he perceived that world eccentrically, fragmentarily, ethnocentrically, it gave him an alternative vocabulary, with alternate myths, structures, values, images, channels of feeling, all of which produced a polyvocality that thickens the texture of his poetry and complicates its meanings.

THOMAS M. GREENE

Ellrodt 1960; Ettin 1982; Fletcher 1971; Friedmann 1966; Hankins 1971; Hughes 1929; Judson 1945; Lotspeich 1932; Nohrnberg 1976.

Apelles of Cos (or perhaps Chios) (fourth century BC) The fame of Apelles as the greatest painter of antiquity extended into the Renaissance. Although none of his works survived, his fame was attested by many classical writers, including Pliny, Lucian, Ovid, and the poets of the Greek Anthology. According to Pliny the Elder (*Natural History* 35.79–80), what distinguished him from the other notable painters of his time was the indefinable grace of his pictures. He was praised for knowing when to take his hand from a picture before it was spoiled by too much effort. His works included the *Aphrodite anadyomene* ('Aphrodite Rising from the Sea'), to which Spenser alludes as a supreme depiction of ideal beauty (*Heavenly Beautie* 211–14).

So impressed was Spenser with the fame of Apelles that in his *FQ* Court Sonnet he ascribes to him a story associated with Zeuxis, another great artist of the ancient world: Cicero relates that when Zeuxis set out to paint Helen of Troy and was unable to find a perfect model, he assembled five maidens of Crotona, taking the best features from each (*De inventione* 2.1.3). Whether or not Spenser confused Apelles with Zeuxis, his point in the sonnet is that the artist in pursuit of the ideal cannot find models here below: 'The Chian Peincter, when he was requirde / To pourtraict *Venus* in her perfect hew, / To make his worke more absolute, desird / Of all the fairest Maides to have the vew' (cf *FQ* IV v 12). Similarly, Spenser, drawing 'the semblant trew' of Queen Elizabeth, has to see many beautiful ladies of the court. Elsewhere he refers to Zeuxis by name, linking him with the sculptor Praxiteles as exemplars of the highest skill in portraiture (III proem 2). In these stories of ancient painters and sculptors which had come down to the Renaissance through classical authors, he found ready-made symbols of his own artistic ideals.

JUDITH DUNDAS

Cast 1981; Ernst H. Gombrich 1976 *The Heritage of Apelles: Studies in the Art of the Renaissance* (Ithaca, NY).

Apocalypse The last book of the Bible, the Book of Revelation, rife with political implications and the source for much Christian theology, exerted a powerful influence upon the arts in Elizabethan England. As Harvey writes tellingly to Spenser (*Three Letters* 3, *Var Prose* p 471),

> I hearde once a Divine, preferre *Saint Johns Revelation* before al the veriest *Maetaphysicall Visions*, and jollyest conceited *Dreames* or *Extasies*, that ever were devised by one or other, howe admirable, or superexcellent soever they seemed otherwise to the worlde. And truely I am so confirmed in this opinion, that when I bethinke me of the verie notablest, and moste wonderful Propheticall, or Poeticall Vision, that ever I read, or hearde, me seemeth the proportion is so unequall, that there hardly appeareth anye semblaunce of Comparison.

For Harvey, the Apocalypse is a good pattern to set before English poets, and it had come to Spenser's attention early: for *Theatre for Worldlings*, he translated four *Visions from Revelation* which center on St John's visions of the beast with seven heads, the great whore riding that beast, the Word of God riding a white horse, and the New Jerusalem. Almost all of van der Noot's commentary that accompanies *Theatre* refers to these *Visions*. However Spenser may have regarded *Theatre*, it clearly held great sway over him, perhaps by awakening his interest in visionary literature, and almost certainly through the example it provided for cross-breeding sacred prophecy with contemporary history and for intermixing dreadful visions with irenic ones. *Theatre* turned Spenser's attention to the Apocalypse.

Paraphrases of and quotations and echoes from the Apocalypse have been observed and tabulated in *Amoretti*, *Colin Clouts Come Home Againe*, *Daphnaïda*, *Epithalamion*, *Hymne of Heavenly Beautie*, *Hymne of Heavenly Love*, *Prothalamion*, and *Complaints* (Shaheen 1976). In *The Shepheardes Calender*, Spenser first emerges as a Revelation-like poet by tuning his pastoral in an apocalyptic key; but it is *The Faerie Queene* that most fully manifests the influence of the Book of Revelation, with Spenser repeatedly echoing that book by appropriating its imagery and its themes (especially of worldly appearances versus spiritual realities, and of providence as the sovereign control of history), by employing its strategies, recasting its visions and then using them as a medium for reflecting upon current affairs and as a metaphor for English history. The largest group of scriptural echoes in *The Faerie Queene* is to Revelation, with over 40 clustering in Book I, in addition to the 13 in Book II, 9 in III, 4 in IV, 8 in V, and 5 in VI (Shaheen 1976:181). Thus the influence of the Apocalypse is felt throughout the entire poem, which presents a characteristically Protestant exposition of the salient apocalyptic themes.

So conspicuous is the apocalyptic element in *The Faerie Queene* that Thomas Warton objected in the mid-eighteenth century to the blending of sacred mysteries with secular allegories, and to the interweaving of apocalyptic with romance elements (*Var* 1:368). But that objection was countered a century later by John Wilson, who found in *The Faerie Queene* 'the sublime application by a poet of a prophet's verses' (*Var* 1:370):

> It is not too bold to say that Edmund Spenser borrows the pen of St. John – and that the two revelations coincide – or rather that there is but one revelation – at first derived from heaven, and then given again – in poetry, which, though earth-born, claims kindred with the issue of the skies. Of old – and why not now? – it was allowed – as Cowper finely says – that 'the hallowed name / Of prophet and of poet were the same.'

Spenser may not be the inaugurator of a

new prophetic vision, but he is a partaker in John's, recognizing in current history the Revelation archetype and therefore viewing that history as approaching ever nearer to the apocalyptic consummation.

Both Warton and North were preceded in their perception of Spenser's indebtedness to St John by Henry More, who proposed the Apocalypse as sourcebook and model for one episode in *FQ* I vi: 'Methinks *Spencer*'s description of *Una*'s Entertainment by Satyrs in the Desart, does lively set out the condition of Christianity since the time that the Church of a Garden became a *Wilderness*' (*Sp All* p 249). Even earlier, John Dixon, a contemporary reader of *The Faerie Queene*, correlated several episodes with passages in the Book of Revelation. In his annotations to the 1590 edition, he presents Elizabeth as the great protagonist of history, and *FQ* I as an allegory of the Reformation, in this way linking both the historical and moral allegory of the poem with the visionary drama of John's prophecy (Hough 1964).

Modern criticism, however, has extended *The Faerie Queene*'s parallels with Revelation beyond Book I to the poem as a whole, and beyond imagery and themes to such matters as strategy, structure, and genre as they involve the entire poem (see Bennett 1942, Hankins 1971, Kermode 1971, O'Connell 1977, Sandler 1984, Wittreich 1979). The whole of *The Faerie Queene*, therefore, can be seen as a revelation in itself – a series of theophanies, a Tudor Apocalypse (Williams 1975).

We now know that the Book of Revelation is an intricate prophetic structure whose features were individually isolated in the sixteenth century and then synthesized in the seventeenth century within elaborate structural analyses such as those of Joseph Mede and Henry More. Structural synchronism, typological patterning, vision enfolding itself in commentary, text enthralling its audience and becoming involved in numerical systems of threes, sixes, and sevens – these were (and continue to be regarded as) the distinctive features of a prophetic structure that presents a gathering self-awareness within the gradual unfolding of vision. With this refined conception of the structure of apocalyptic prophecy, we may now examine its bearing on *The Faerie Queene*.

The Renaissance was bent upon subordinating history to some general scheme, some keys to which were to be found by relating the Book of Revelation to the chronicles (Levy 1967:5, 89). At least up to the time of John Bale, historiography stressed the idea of six ages of history followed by a seventh or sabbath age. According to Bale's *Comedy Concernynge Thre Lawes* (c 1548), the seven ages of the world – the first six ages extending from Adam to Christ, the seventh from Christ to the end of the world – encompass another historical pattern: three periods respectively, of nature, bondage, and grace (Firth 1979:38–9). Satan's release from bondage, moreover, was expected to result in the trial of the last days which was said to correspond with the final centuries of papal domination of the church.

Spenser's Letter to Raleigh, which projects two poems, each in twelve books, is responsible for the notion that *The Faerie Queene* is composed of the free-standing walls of a much larger, uncompleted structure. A poet who follows Chaucer might be expected, almost by design, to promise more than he delivers and might even be thought to employ poetic fragments deliberately, using them to sanction the possibility that his poem is more a plan than a ruin – a calculated, coherent, but still incomplete form with its own internal structure and external abrasions.

If endings matter in poetry, each half of *The Faerie Queene* ends in the same way, with the binding and unleashing of the beast – an event, which takes its symbolic point from the whole tradition of Revelation commentary, is part of a fourfold pattern: releasing virtuous prisoners, freely binding oneself to virtuous service, binding evil, and avoiding bondage by evil (see Gray 1975, Firth 1979). Put another way, the middle and end of *The Faerie Queene* are congruent. Indeed, this single structural feature raises still other possibilities: that Bale's conceptualization is a paradigm for the total structure of *The Faerie Queene*; that the fragmentary Book VII is Spenser's way of pointing out that his age has entered a crucial phase in the seventh period of history; that, as a fragment, Book VII emblematizes the incompleteness of history itself; and that its three cantos – vi, vii, and viii – are a way of focusing a pattern of nature, bondage, and grace folded into the corresponding cantos of virtually every other book in the poem.

Merlin's prophecy (which comes near the beginning of *FQ* III and is thus foregrounded in the central books) repeats in miniature this tripartite pattern of the poem as a whole: under the rule of nature, Britain is reduced to disorder; next, under the rule of law, history is reorganized by a vengeful god; finally, after a succession of woes, the nation is returned to order and peace through an act of grace and by the agency of a Virgin Queen. Merlin's prophecy affirms the apocalyptic notion that history is a great map of providence and that prophecy itself is the chief evidence of providence in the world. It is 'the streight course of heavenly destiny, / Led with eternall providence' that guides history and brings things to pass, that moves history 'by dew degrees and long protense ... unto her [ie, Elizabeth's] Excellence.' Eventually a universal peace will confound all this civil jar: 'Then shall a royall virgin raine ... But yet the end is not' (III iii 24, 4, 49–50). In this last line, Merlin divests secular prophecy of the apocalyptic element which he is credited with having introduced to the tradition. Here he quiets millennial expectations and dampens apocalyptic fervor.

Furthermore, in the midst of his prophetic utterance, Merlin is 'stayd, / As overcomen of the spirites powre, / Or other ghastly spectacle dismayd' (50). Prophecy comes into the present but does not go beyond; history is continuous, and those who hear this prophecy are cheered with heavenly comfort and renewed with hope as they return to Fairyland. One must finish forging the godly nation, Spenser implies, and in this joins the company of certain of his contemporaries who, within the context of the Apocalypse, maintained a distinction between variable England and invariable Jerusalem, between the world of men and the angelic company, between an earthly paradise and the heavenly kingdom.

The Faerie Queene epitomizes the apocalyptic thinking, tentative and guarded, of Spenser's own time, even as it confirms in certain of its details the contention that the sabbatical numbers, six and seven, appear to be deliberately chosen so that the *Cantos of Mutabilitie* participate in the poem's numerical system as a fraction rather than as a fragment (Nohrnberg 1976:85). The poem itself moves through and then out of history into the sabbath of eternity: there are three books, then another three, and then the *Cantos* themselves form a cluster of three parts. Overlaying this pattern of threes is a structure of six books followed by a fragmentary seventh that fulfills itself only in the final lines of a final fractional canto. The theme of bondage is at the center of each book of the poem, but at the center of each of its twin halves, *FQ* II and V, emphasis shifts from bondage (Guyon in the house of Mammon) to release from the captive state (Artegall's liberation from thralldom). And at the very center of this apocalyptic poem, as a shrill trumpet sounds (III xii 1), the themes of redemption and deliverance come to the fore in the story of '*Amoret* in caytive band ... these seven monethes' being delivered by Britomart (xi 10).

Such a pattern is contained in the individual books as well. If the sixth and seventh are cantos of nature and bondage, the eighth is regularly the canto of grace – thus in Book I, 'heavenly grace doth him uphold' (viii 1); in Book II, 'th'exceeding grace / Of highest God' sends 'blessed Angels ... to and fro' (viii 1); and in Book IV, 'goodly grace she did him shew' (viii 6). However muted the threefold pattern of nature, bondage, and grace may be in certain of the books, Book VI gathers it into focus through the Hermit's place in canto vi, the bound squire in vii, and Serena in viii, who led 'by grace of God' (38) is freed by Calepine.

In *Christus triumphans* (1556), Foxe provides a probable conceptual and structural analogue for Spenser's poem, dramatizing Revelation in a way that focuses its last act upon the Reformation and thereupon narrows its allegory to England. Foxe's play is 'unfinished, as the drama of history is.' The proposed conclusion to what Foxe calls his apocalyptic comedy, 'the wedding, lies just beyond the point at which the action stops; or just so the coming of Christ lies just beyond the point which the drama of history had reached in 1556' (Bauckham 1978:79). Accordingly, 'the Red Cross Knight's story ends with a prophecy of apocalypse, and Arthur, if the poem had been completed, would have been united with the Queen whom he had previously experienced in his vision. It is a definition of apocalypse that in it vision and reality become one' (I.G. MacCaffrey 1976:92); and, we might add, it is a definition of an apocalyptic poem that until history is complete the poem cannot be complete. In Spenser's poem, Nature's concluding words are of apocalypse, though Nature's are not the poem's final words; and even in the very first book, the most apocalyptic in the entire poem, the ending is tentative, a new beginning rather than a determinate conclusion, with the movement toward revelation and apocalypse interrupted by a counterturn, a regression (P.A. Parker 1979:55, 69, 75–6, 80).

If Foxe may be said to domesticate the Apocalypse, Spenser, in turn, contributes to its secularization by tracking its reference points to the spiritual history of mankind. In the very act of postponing apocalypse, Spenser implies that the beast still rules history because it is still enthroned in man and so continues to manifest itself both there and in the world.

Harvey once chided Spenser for not recognizing that the golden age is now. Yet Spenser's objective in *The Faerie Queene* is not to further the Tudors' messianic pretensions but to scrutinize them. In the process, he resists the expectations of his own time by distancing apocalypse into the future and by making the development of the individual a prelude to the apocalypse in history. Spenser seems to be recognizing two separate aspects of the apocalyptic vision: a panoramic apocalypse set in the future near the end of time that itself may be the type of the other apocalypse, the one that really matters – the present-tense apocalypse realized first in the individual and then *perhaps* in history (see Frye 1982:136–7).

The Faerie Queene is finally not an historian's or a theologian's but a poet's Revelation. For Spenser, the cosmic struggle of the Apocalypse was a matter not for scholarly erudition but for human engagement. Here was being played out the great epic of history and the essential drama of human life; here, to appropriate words from Shakespeare's Sonnet 107, is to be found a mirror on 'the prophetic soul / Of the wide world, dreaming on things to come.' (See also *eschatology, *oracles, *prophecy, *visions.)

JOSEPH WITTREICH

John Bale 1548 *The Image of Bothe Churches* (Antwerp; rpt Amsterdam and New York 1973); John Foxe 1556 *Christus triumphans* (London); Foxe 1583 *Actes and Monuments* (London); Joseph Mede 1643 *The Key of the Revelation* tr Richard More (London); Henry More 1669 *An Exposition of the Seven Epistles to the Seven Churches* (London); More 1680 *Apocalypsis apocalypseos* (London).

Bauckham 1978; Bennett 1942:III, 114–15; Firth 1979; Frye 1982; J.C. Gray 1975 'Bondage and Deliverance in the "Faerie Queene": Varieties of a Moral Imperative' *MLR* 70:1–12; Hough 1964; Frank Kermode 1967 *The Sense of an Ending: Studies in the Theory of Fiction* (New York); Kermode 1971:39–44; Levy 1967; Sandler 1984; Shaheen 1976; Kathleen Williams 1975 'Milton, Greatest Spenserian' in Wittreich 1975:25–55; Wittreich 1979.

appearance The deceptiveness of outward appearance in Spenser's poetry must be set in the context of the biblical injunction, 'Judge not according to the appearance' (John 7.24), and Erasmus' complaint that the 'stupid generality of men often blunder into wrong judgements, because they judge everything from the evidence of the bodily senses, and they are deceived by false imitations of the good and the evil' ('Sileni Alcibiadis' *Adages* 3.3.1; tr in M.M. Phillips 1964:276). The traditional Silenus-figure illustrates his point: the box shows a small, ugly image of the foolish god Silenus but when opened reveals a god hidden within.

In *The Faerie Queene*, the full congruence of appearance and reality may be a mark of simple truth, reflecting the commonplace belief in the unity of truth found in the philosophical and homiletic literature of the period (eg, I xii 8; see Fowler 1964:5). Falsehood is double and therefore duplicitous, a want of such congruence. Outward appearances are often the means of an intentional dissembling: apparent semblance serves only to define real dissemblance. To the extent that Fidessa resembles a virtuous lady, she also resembles Una; but the apparent resemblance of the two shows their lack of resemblance, and, thus, the truth of the one and the falseness of the other. In the same way, Corceca's semblance of holiness is simultaneously her dissembling of holiness, the virtue fully manifest in Caelia. In some instances, the outward appearance of a specific character is falsely duplicated: Archimago assumes the appearance of the Red Cross Knight so totally that the reader is warned that '*Saint George* himself ye would have deemed him to be' (I ii 11), as does Una (iii 26–40). Archimago is not Redcrosse, but then the Redcrosse who is about to encounter Sansjoy and Despair is not a 'jolly knight' either. Other instances include the real Una and the dream Una created by Archimago, and the real and snowy Florimells.

This manner of moral definition is not restricted to persons: the outward appearance of the house of Pride glittering with gold foil hides the ruinous condition beneath it. The house of Holiness, by contrast, plainly manifests what it is. 'What is excellent in any way is always the least showy,' comments Erasmus (in Phillips 1964:274); a similar distrust of the showy pervades *The Faerie Queene*. (*Show* as a noun is generally negative in Spenser's usage; cf his positive use of the verb *show* meaning 'make manifest.') The real danger of the Bower of Bliss is hidden (and, for the reader, indicated) by its gorgeous but factitious beauty. As visual delights become more appealing, the possibility of deceit becomes greater. Duessa poses a subtler threat to Redcrosse than Error, Sansfoy, or Orgoglio since her danger is less easily recognized. Similarly, the Bower of Bliss is a subtler test of Guyon's virtue than the house of Mammon, the danger of which is readily perceived.

The moral imperative of the narrative is the biblical injunction to 'judge righteous judgement' (John 7.24). There is no guarantee, however, that we will not be misled by our senses: *in*sight must be added to sight. As the most rational of the senses in the Platonic hierarchy, sight is less misleading than the others – thus its great importance in *The Faerie Queene*. But, by itself, sight cannot penetrate to the hidden reality. Plato denies that we can truly know the contingent phenomena of our empirical world, which is one of becoming and seeming, and therefore imperfect, mutable, delusive; true knowledge is possible only of the perfect unchanging world of rational ideal forms, the world of being (*Phaedo* 65). In biblical terms, only God is capable of righteous judgment because '*God seeth* not as man seeth: for man loketh on the outward appearance, but the Lord beholdeth the heart' (1 Sam 16.7). Guided by reason and sight, however, we may obtain some access to the world of truth and reality beyond that of changeable phenomena.

The need to distinguish between appearance and reality is also shown in the narrative as unveiling or unmasking. Once Redcrosse has achieved his quest and restored Una to her rights, her real beauty and truth, veiled earlier, are revealed. Archimago's disguises are similarly revealed, and the nature of his duplicity declared. The most dramatic instance of unmasking occurs when Duessa is stripped: beneath the splendor of her outward appearance is revealed her real physical grotesqueness, a metaphor of her duplicity and moral repulsiveness. Here, falsehood is confronted by simple truth, in the form of Una. All is apparent; the figures are what they appear to be, seeming is being, and thus a measure of knowledge of truth and reality has been won, against all odds, from this deceptive world of appearances: 'Such then (said *Una*) as she seemeth here, / Such is the face of falshood, such the sight / Of fowle *Duessa*, when her borrowed light / Is laid away, and counterfesaunce knowne' (I viii 49).

Disguise is allowed only for virtuous ends, as when Britomart resolves to hide her sex in male armor 'and plaine apparaunce shonne' (III i 52), or Artegall disguises himself as one of the Souldan's knights in order to capture Adicia (V viii 26), or Calidore disguises himself as a shepherd to free Pastorella (VI xi 36–51). Appearance is an important motif in Spenser's 'darke conceit' praising Elizabeth whose beauty can be revealed only by being reveiled: 'O dred Soveraine / Thus farre forth pardon, sith that choicest wit / Cannot your glorious pourtraict figure plaine / That I in colourd showes may shadow it' (III proem 3).

DENIS WALKER

apples Spenser follows tradition in frequently associating apples with temptation and love. They are tempting pastoral delicacies: Colin Clout, the witch's son who dotes on Florimell, and Faunus all offer varieties of them as gifts or bribes (*SC, June* 43–4;

FQ III vii 17, VII vi 43). Their proverbially beautiful color and shape figure in several descriptions of feminine beauty which are ultimately indebted to the Song of Solomon. In *Epithalamion*, for example, the bride's cheeks are like red apples (173). Belphoebe's breasts swell beneath her thin garment like 'young fruit in May' (presumably apples yet to mature) (*FQ* II iii 29; cf *Amoretti* 76). In *Amoretti* 77, the beloved's breasts are described emblematically rather than realistically as 'twoo golden apples'; and their 'price' is measured by their superiority to apples coveted in classical mythology – those taken by Hercules from the Garden of the Hesperides and those which tempted Atalanta in the race against her suitor (cf *FQ* II vii 54; from Conti *Mythologiae* 7.7, according to Lotspeich 1932:69).

In classical mythology, apples are usually associated with temptation and moral danger. The 'glistring' but deadly fruit which Mammon offers Guyon in the Garden of Proserpina (*FQ* II vii 54–5) recalls the golden fruit with which Pluto tempts Proserpina (Claudian *Rape of Proserpina* 2.290–3). Mammon's tree is described as the source of all the fateful fruit of mythology: the Hesperidean apples, those with which Atalanta was outwitted, the apple with which Acontius tricked Cydippe into vowing marriage to him (Ovid *Heroides* 20, 21), and that which Ate used to provoke the quarrel of the goddesses which was judged by Paris (cf *FQ* IV i 22, VI ix 36).

The diversity of these myths and of their Renaissance interpretations makes their significance hard to define. Some myths are associated with avarice: Conti links the Hesperidean apples and those of Atalanta with wealth, and interprets Tantalus (who reaches for them in II vii 58) as an emblem of avarice. All the apples from Mammon's tree have been seen as emblems of blasphemous ambition of divine knowledge (Kermode 1960:161–5). They may also be emblems of fleshly lust, particularly because Hercules' theft of the apples of the Hesperides was a common sexual metaphor (see Marlowe *Hero and Leander* 2.297–300, Shakespeare *Love's Labor's Lost* IV iii 336–7). Yet one cannot identify the symbolic meanings of these apples too specifically, for they indicate generally *worldly* goals, the gaining of which may bring grief or disaster.

Elsewhere apples are associated with true beauty and healthy life. Those which grow in abundance can suggest vigor and strength, as in the image of the withered apple tree reviving to bear fresh fruit, which describes Cambell rejuvenated by his magic ring (IV iii 29). In particular, Mammon's tree parodies the biblical Tree of Life whose fruit and balm preserve Redcrosse (I xi 46–8). These have a *natural* beauty: they are 'rosie red' (their color may also suggest redemption through Christ's blood; Hankins 1971:118). Unlike the fruit of the nearby Tree of Knowledge which brought death, they give 'happie life to all.' Their connotations of beauty, vigor, fertility, and divine grace are Spenser's most comprehensive and elaborate example of the apple as an image of goodness and life. As a poet, he would have appreciated Proverbs 25.11: 'A worde spoken in his place, is like appels of golde.'

GEOFFREY G. HILLER

Apuleius Born c AD 125 in Madaura, North Africa, Apuleius was a Latin writer of considerable interest to Spenser and his contemporaries. As a Neoplatonist and rhetorician, he was approved as a rich stylist by the humanist educators Erasmus and Vives; his work was ransacked for plots, images, and motifs by dramatists, including Shakespeare.

Apuleius' masterpiece, the *Metamorphoses*, translated into English by William Adlington in 1566 as *The Golden Asse*, is a comic 'novel' involving the often bizarre adventures of Lucius, a man transformed into an ass as punishment for his curiosity about witchcraft. Adlington defends the work as 'a figure of mans life [which] toucheth the nature and manners of mortall men, egging them forward from their Asinall forme, to their humane and perfect shape' (ed 1915: xvii). Spenser may also have known *De deo Socratis*, a declamation on the *daimon* or genius of Socrates; the *Apologia*, a self-defense against the charge that he had gained his bride by magic; and the *Florida*, a miscellaneous collection of topics for declamation. One of these topics treats the supremacy of hearing over seeing as a means to truth, a latent theme in *The Faerie Queene*; another interprets Hercules' triumphs as external versions of inner spiritual victories (see Dunseath 1968:53–4). In *De deo Socratis*, Spenser would have found the Platonic view that not only is each man given a genius to guide him through life as a kind of objectified conscience (see Lewis 1964:42; cf Guyon's Palmer), but also that all men are protected by a genius whose concern is the universal 'care / Of life, and generation of all,' like Agdistes (*FQ* II xii 47; see Lotspeich 1932:62). The conclusion of *De deo Socratis* presents a moral summary of the career of Ulysses and his constant companion, Wisdom, who descend into the underworld and return without being transformed by the cup of Circe; these passages are analogous to Guyon's narrow escape from the house of Mammon with its Garden of Proserpina and his Ulysses-like triumph in the Bower of Bliss (II vii, xii). The *Apologia* provides a brief excursus on Venus as a binary deity, both vulgar (producing the common passions of love and lust in man and beast) and heavenly (leading the soul to purest love free from physical desire). Some incorporation of this double Venus may lie behind Spenser's frequent allusions to Venus and her diffraction into various female figures in *The Faerie Queene* and the *Fowre Hymnes*.

At the center of *The Golden Ass* (Books 4–6) is the story of Cupid and Psyche, a narrative of sin, suffering, and redemption, or (less religiously) of error, separation, and reunion. Psyche undergoes her trials with patience and resourcefulness, qualities which, together with the grace of divine intervention, bring about her marriage and apotheosis. From the sixth century on, this tale had been allegorized as a story of the soul and heavenly desire or, according to Boccaccio, of the soul and pure Love (*Genealogia* 5.22; see Lotspeich 1932:104). Spenser refers explicitly to the tale in *Muiopotmos* (see D.C. Allen 1968:26–31), and was fascinated by it primarily because it embodies problems of sexuality, male power and female fear, and the resolution of these tensions in the ritual of marriage. Psyche's experience is a rite of passage to a more responsible and sexually awakened level of womanhood (Katz 1976). She is thus an appropriate teacher of 'true feminitee' to Amoret, making her daughter Pleasure Amoret's companion (*FQ* III vi 50–1). The trials of separation and the tensions of sexual passion and their transcendence in marriage are the chief contributions of Apuleius' Psyche to the character of Britomart and also to the facets of her womanly development in Belphoebe, Amoret, and Florimell (Hamilton 1961a:138–69).

Since Apuleius' tale of Cupid and Psyche seems to epitomize the larger pattern of his story, Spenser may have drawn on other parts of Lucius' adventures in order to illustrate the twists and turns of passion. Socrates' mutilation by the sexual sorceress Meroe resembles the wounding of Amoret by the sorcerer Busirane (III xii 20–1). Pastorella's capture by bandits (VI x 43) finds analogies in the career of Charite, another suffering heroine (whose career interested Ariosto), to whom the tale of Cupid and Psyche is told. Most important, Spenser's account of Britomart's visit to Isis Church (V vii) may borrow details from the description of Cupid's palace in Adlington's translation of Apuleius; and his story of her relation to Isis may be modeled in part on Lucius' commitment to that goddess, whom Apuleius also associates with equity (Graziani 1964a:378). (See also *demons.)

J.J.M. TOBIN

Apuleius ed 1915 (Loeb Classical Library) is a rev ed by S. Gaselee of Adlington's translation of *The Golden Ass*. The *Apologia* and *Florida* appear together in the translations of H.E. Butler 1909 (Oxford). P.G. Walsh 1970 *The Roman Novel* (Cambridge) has the best discussion of Apuleius. He is treated as an allegorist in the iconographical tradition by E.H. Gombrich 1972 *Symbolic Images: Studies in the Art of the Renaissance* (London) pp 34–5, 46–55; and Wind 1958:19, 61–2, 236–8. The fullest discussion of the religious aspects of the conclusion of the novel is in Apuleius ed 1975. See also Phyllis B. Katz 1976 'The Myth of Psyche: A Definition of the Nature of the Feminine?' *Arethusa* 9:111–18; and Alexander A. Scobie 1978 'The Influence of Apuleius' *Metamorphoses* in Renaissance Italy and Spain' in *Aspects of Apuleius' 'Golden Ass'* ed B.L. Hijmans, Jr, and R.Th. van der Paardt (Groningen) pp 211–30. For the English tradition, see J.J.M. Tobin 1984a 'Apuleius and Milton' *RPLit* 7:181–91; and Tobin 1984b *Shakespeare's Favorite Novel: A Study of 'The Golden Asse' as Prime Source* (Lanham, Md).

Aquinas, Thomas (c 1225–74) Spenser locates the moral argument of *The Faerie Queene* within the philosophical system of 'Aristotle and the rest' (Letter to Raleigh), thereby testifying to the continuity of the tradition of scholastic Aristotelianism. Although new commentaries on the works of Aristotle appeared throughout the course of the sixteenth century, the old commentaries by Thomas Aquinas were repeatedly printed. Aquinas' continuing high reputation, unmatched by that of any other medieval commentator on Aristotle, derives from that exceptional lucidity and precision which earned for him the title 'Expositor' and gave rise to the adage that where Thomas was silent, Aristotle was mute.

Recent scholarship has shown that scholasticism and humanism are not essentially opposed. Scholasticism not only survived the impact of humanism in the 1520s and 1530s but subsequently experienced a strong revival. In England, this revival is reflected in the theology studied at Cambridge, which was at once scholastic and Protestant. One consequence was the increased authority of Aquinas' *Summa theologiae* (1265–73). It became a central part of the philosophical tradition on which Spenser draws, and it sheds light on several problems in the moral design of *The Faerie Queene*: holiness as a moral virtue, the moral range of temperance, the identity of justice and courtesy, and constancy as a culminating virtue.

Holiness or religion is the first of Spenser's moral virtues because faith is the foundation of virtue (*ST* 2a2ae 161.5 *ad* 2) and religion is a confession of faith through certain external signs (2a2ae 94.1 *ad* 1). Holiness is said by Aquinas to be essentially identical with but notionally distinct from religion, the most excellent of the moral virtues (2a2ae 81.6, 81.8). The distinction corresponds to that between the elicited and commanded acts of religion (2a2ae 81.4 *ad* 2). By the virtue of religion is strictly understood the elicited acts of religion, whereas holiness includes the acts commanded by religion as well (and, especially in the Legend of Holiness, acts of fortitude).

Spenser's notion of temperance distinguishes between a specific virtue (ie, one determined by its own special object, as temperance by the desires and pleasures of touch) and a general virtue (ie, one possessing a quality that is common to virtue in general, as the moderation that is signified by temperance is common to virtue in general; *ST* 1a2ae 61.4). Within the specific virtue of temperance, Aquinas classifies twelve distinct virtues: shamefastness, the sense of honor (both integral parts of temperance), continence, gentleness, clemency, humility, studiousness, modesty in outward bodily movements, modesty in dress (seven potential parts of temperance), abstinence, sobriety, and chastity (three species or subjective parts of temperance; 2a2ae 143). These virtues together constitute the moral subject matter of the Legend of Temperance.

At the meeting of Artegall and Calidore, Spenser writes that 'They knew them selves' (*FQ* VI i 4). The mutual recognition of his knights of Justice and Courtesy expresses the essential identity of the virtues they represent, for legal justice is virtue complete in relation to one's neighbor, and courtesy or *honestas* is virtue complete in itself (*ST* 2a2ae 58.5, 145.1).

In Book VII, Spenser proceeds to constancy, and thus to the summit of moral virtue, for constancy is included by Aquinas under the Ciceronian magnificence (*ST* 2a2ae 128 *ad* 6). By the virtue of constancy, Spenser understands that the perfection of virtue in performing great deeds lies in planning them and carrying them through with firmness of purpose to the end.

Milton said of Spenser that he was 'a better teacher then *Scotus* or *Aquinas*' (*Sp All* p 215). It is no idle comparison, for the poetic aptness of Milton's words is matched by their philosophical relevance.

GERALD MORGAN

Aquinas ed 1964–81; William T. Costello 1958 *The Scholastic Curriculum at Early Seventeenth-Century Cambridge* (Cambridge, Mass); F. Edward Cranz 1978 'The Publishing History of the Aristotle Commentaries of Thomas Aquinas' *Traditio* 34:157–92; Kristeller 1956; Kristeller 1974; Moloney 1953; Gerald Morgan 1981 'Spenser's Conception of Courtesy and the Design of the *Faerie Queene*' *RES* ns 32:17–36; Morgan 1986a 'The Idea of Temperance in the Second Book of *The Faerie Queene*' *RES* ns 37:11–39; Morgan 1986b 'Holiness as the First of Spenser's Aristotelian Moral Virtues' *MLR* 81:817–37; Charles B. Schmitt 1975 'Philosophy and Science in Sixteenth-Century Universities: Some Preliminary Comments' in *The Cultural Context of Medieval Learning* ed John Emery Murdoch and Edith Dudley Sylla (Dordrecht, Holland) pp 485–537; Schmitt 1983a; Schmitt 1983b.

Arachne (Gr 'spider') In *Muiopotmos*, Spenser rewrites Ovid's story of the tapestry-weaving contest between Arachne and Minerva (*Metamorphoses* 6.5–145) to explain the hereditary hatred that the spider Aragnoll has for the butterfly Clarion. In Ovid's version, the tapestry of Minerva (Pallas Athena) is a vision of the order, dignity, and justice of the gods. It shows her victory over Neptune in a contest to determine the name of Athens; the contest is judged by a council of gods headed by Jove, and the olive tree that signals Pallas' victory is a symbol of peace and harmony. In the corners of the tapestry she weaves four stories that exemplify divine justice, as warnings to those who, like Arachne, challenge the authority of the gods and are transformed as punishment. Arachne's tapestry, by contrast, presumes to challenge the authority of Pallas and to indict the gods for sexual riot and injustice. In her tapestry Jove, Neptune, Phoebus, and Saturn undergo a series of metamorphoses to deceive, seduce, or rape various mortals. As an artist who refuses to acknowledge her debt to the goddess Pallas, Arachne asserts a human perspective; and the spider into which she is transformed becomes an ironic symbol of the autonomous imagination spinning its works out of itself.

Spenser's Arachne is a 'presumptuous Damzel' who 'rashly dar'd' to defy Pallas (269–70). This characterization is like Ovid's and is typical of allegorizations of the story since the fourteenth-century *Ovide moralisé*. Arachne is one of the defeated proud whose likeness Dante sees in the pavement of *Purgatory* 12.43–5. Reversing Ovid's order, Spenser begins his story with a description of Arachne's tapestry. He follows Ovid closely in picturing Europa's abduction by Jove in the form of a bull (the only one of Arachne's stories he keeps), but adds details from Ovid's earlier, fuller account of Europa (*Met* 2.873–5). Although he closely translates Ovid in portraying Pallas' story of her contest with Neptune, he omits the warning stories she weaves into the corners of her tapestry. Instead, he has Pallas weave among the olive leaves a picture of a butterfly of such delicacy and verisimilitude that Arachne immediately knows she has lost the contest. This butterfly in effect replaces Pallas' stories of divine justice in Ovid's poem, but it reminds us ironically of Venus' unjust transformation of the innocent Astery into a butterfly earlier in Spenser's poem (Brinkley 1981); it also anticipates the final element in Spenser's tapestry, the view of Clarion trapped in Aragnoll's web, 'His bodie left the spectacle of care.' Perhaps not by coincidence, Astery is also the name of one of Jove's victims in Arachne's tapestry (*Met* 6.108).

Ovid's contest has no clear winner. Pallas, angry at Arachne's success in portraying the gods' misdeeds, rips Arachne's tapestry, strikes her head with a shuttle, and then in pity transforms her into a spider as she tries to hang herself. In Spenser's poem Arachne's own envy poisons her and induces her metamorphosis: 'Yet did she inly fret, and felly burne, / And all her blood to poysonous rancor turne' (343–4). Ovid describes Arachne's metamorphosis objectively; Spenser stresses the repulsive and venomous qualities of the spider: 'And her faire face to fowle and loathsome hewe, / And her fine corpes to a bag of venim grewe' (351–2).

Spenser translates Ovid's comment that neither Pallas nor Envy could find a flaw in Arachne's tapestry (6.129–30), but he adds a significant detail about Envy's venom: 'Such as Dame *Pallas*, such as Envie pale, / That al good things with venemous tooth devowres, / Could not accuse' (301–3). Although it is somewhat illogical to say that Pallas could not fault Arachne's work, this characterization of Envy anticipates the description of Arachne at the moment she is metamorphosed and echoes the account of her offspring Aragnoll, whose 'bowels so with ranckling poyson swelde, / That scarce the skin the strong contagion helde' (255–6). The poisonous envy of Arachne and Aragnoll relates them to the personification of Envy in the house of Pride, who chews 'Betweene his cankred teeth a venemous tode, / That all the poison ran about his chaw' (*FQ*

I iv 30), and to the 'venemous despite' of the Blatant Beast (VI xii 41). Envy and the Beast are both backbiters of poets; by extension, so are Arachne and Aragnoll.

Envy plays a pivotal role in *Muiopotmos* (Bond 1976). Ladies of the court envy Clarion's beautiful wings (105–6), which are themselves the result of the nymphs' envy of Astery for her skill in gathering flowers (124). The nymphs slander her by telling Venus that Cupid has secretly aided her; Venus, anxiously remembering Cupid's secret love of Psyche, transforms Astery into a butterfly whose wings have the colors of all the flowers she once gathered. The narrator comments ironically that 'none gainsaid, nor none did ... envie' Clarion's feeding on the pleasures of the fields (152). In fact, Clarion is caught in an overdetermined web of ironies, cosmic and otherwise (Anderson 1971a). He is unaware that his 'cruell fate is woven even now / Of *Joves* owne hand' (235–6), and that Aragnoll's web of envy and hatred is already waiting for him in the garden. Spenser explicitly associates fate with the spider's web in *The Faerie Queene* when Agape visits the house of the Fates and is dismayed to see her sons' 'thrids so thin, as spiders frame' (IV ii 50). Later, the personified Detraction, companion of Envy, 'faynes to weave false tales and leasings bad' (V xii 36).

Muiopotmos has been interpreted as 'an allegory of the wandering of the rational soul into error,' with Aragnoll as the satanic figure traditionally associated with the spider (D.C. Allen 1968:31). In such a reading the web is an image of the fallen human condition, thematically similar to the 'wandring wood' at the threshold of *The Faerie Queene* (I i 13). The web-net is a recurrent image in Book II, explicitly associated with Arachne in the house of Mammon and the Bower of Bliss. Early in the book Archimago plots against Guyon: 'Eftsoones untwisting his deceiptfull clew, / He gan to weave a web of wicked guile' (i 8). Archimago's 'clew' is perhaps 'an allusion to the ball of thread which led Theseus out of the labyrinth. Instead of a guide through a maze, Archimago's untwisted clew forms a web to enclose the knight' (Hamilton in *FQ* ed 1977:172). As a version of that labyrinth which is a central archetype in *The Faerie Queene* (Fletcher 1971:24–34), Arachne's web seems to have for Spenser the same ambivalence as the labyrinth: threatening and entrapping, but also artistic and beautiful.

Both allusions to Arachne in *FQ* II have ominous connotations, but they differ in tone. The web that hangs from the arches in Mammon's 'house of Richesse' is obviously sinister: '*Arachne* high did lift / Her cunning web, and spred her subtile net, / Enwrapped in fowle smoke and clouds more blacke then Jet' (vii 28). The web suggests a satanic trap ready to ensnare anyone who reaches for the house's gold; it is like the fiend who follows Guyon with claws held ready to kill him if he transgresses the Stygian laws (27). The smoky, dirty web may imply that the gold is never used, and it reminds us of the earlier description of Mammon himself, dressed in 'coate all overgrowne with rust' and 'darkned with filthy dust' (4). Personifying the spider as Arachne evokes the contest with Pallas and reminds us of her traditional association with pride and envy. Arachne is an appropriate emblem for the tempter Mammon.

The association of Acrasia's veil with Arachne's web is equally sinister in implication, but it also creates a sense of extraordinary beauty: 'More subtile web *Arachne* cannot spin, / Nor the fine nets, which oft we woven see / Of scorched deaw, do not in th'aire more lightly flee' (II xii 77). The veil in which she is 'arayd, or rather disarayd,' both conceals and reveals. A similar ambiguity appears in the texture of the tapestry in the house of Busirane, where the gold interwoven with the silk both hides and shows itself (III xi 28). The gold-snake simile at the end of the stanza is as sinister as the allusions to Arachne, but the dominant impression created by Spenser's treatment of the tapestry is his admiration of its art. He never forgets that Arachne was a superb artist, and it may have pleased his etymological fancy to note the derivation of both *text* and *textile* from the Latin *texere* (Bond 1976:149). Perhaps he saw Arachne's web as an image of his own poem.

Yet the veil-web comparison in the Bower, beautiful as it is, implies that Acrasia is 'the spider in the web' (Hamilton in *FQ* ed 1977:296). The labyrinth is often symbolized by a web with a spider at its center, and the spider is one of the images of the 'Terrible Mother' archetype (Neumann 1963:177, 233). This negative version of the Great Mother figure is often represented as a witch or enchantress with the power to fetter, emasculate, or transform men. Homer's Circe, for example, one of Spenser's models for Acrasia, first appears singing and moving to and fro before a great web (*Odyssey* 10).

The Palmer counters Acrasia's Arachnean web with his own 'subtile net' (II xii 81), analogous to the net with which Vulcan trapped Venus and Mars, and which Ovid says surpasses the art of the spider's web (*Met* 4.178–9). Spenser reverses Ovid's comparison when he says in *Muiopotmos* that not even Vulcan's net can match Aragnoll's 'curious networke' (361–74).

CALVIN R. EDWARDS

Erich Neumann 1963 *The Great Mother: An Analysis of the Archetype* 2nd ed (New York).

Arcadia Virgil mentioned the Greek province of Arcadia in only two of his *Eclogues* (7.4, 26; 10.26, 31–3), but it became identified almost immediately as the generic site of pastoral poetry (Snell ed 1953:281–309). Combining the historical Arcadia with the ideal landscape of Greek pastoral poetry (as in Theocritus' *Idylls*), Virgil created an extremely malleable fiction capable of reflecting both the negative results of contemporary political policies (Eclogues 1 and 9) and the messianic prophecy of an imperial golden age (Eclogue 4). Moreover, he extended Arcadia's political implications to other literary forms. In his *Georgics*, he suggests that social ideals can be achieved only through systematic effort analogous to farming; in the *Aeneid* (8.313–27), the Arcadian king Evander lays the symbolic foundation of the Augustan empire by establishing the citadel of Rome, and provides a model for Aeneas in the story of Saturn's Golden Age.

In the Neo-Latin eclogues and vernacular pastoral of the Middle Ages, allusion to Eden and the parable of the good shepherd reinforced Virgil's practice, turning social commentary in the direction of dream vision or satire. By the sixteenth century, pastoral's 'representative anecdote' (Alpers 1982) – the shepherd piping while his sheep graze – was a utopian image as well as a literary stance, generically defined by pastoral poetry but not limited to it in application (Frye 1970:109–34, Levin 1969). In Elizabethan England, it accommodated the contemporary political situation of a peaceful empire, agrarian economy, and female ruler while reinforcing Protestant rhetoric (Montrose 1983). Thus the relatively 'feminine' language of pastoral tended to displace the traditionally martial political idiom (Yates 1975). Pastoral infiltrated the Petrarchan lyric, epic, romance, and drama; and the political significance of the fiction of Arcadia was evident in public pageants and royal entertainments (eg, Sidney's *Lady of May*), which transformed the gardens of the nobility's great houses into models of the state.

Sidney's *New Arcadia* integrated myth, literary convention, and pageantry to define the pastoral community's potential for political anatomy; Spenser's more fragmentary use of the Arcadian fiction parallels Sidney's. *The Shepheardes Calender* and later *Colin Clouts Come Home Againe* recall different versions of the pastoral world to satirize church and state, to dramatize an ideal relationship between ruler and country, to reflect Colin Clout's psychological condition, and to comment on the ethical and social functions of poetry. In *Colin Clout* and *The Faerie Queene*, Spenser adopts the naive persona of shepherd-poet to create an illusion of external and objective observation of the epic world; the result is typically Arcadian, an ambivalent mixing of encomium and criticism (Cain 1978). There is only one explicit recreation of a shepherd society in *The Faerie Queene*, but some version of Arcadia also forms the thematic, symbolic, or narrative focus of each book of the epic: Eden (I xi-xii), the Bower of Bliss (II xii), the Garden of Adonis (III vi), the garden of true friendship at the Temple of Venus (IV x 21–8), the Golden Age (V proem 1–9), Meliboe's community of shepherds and Colin Clout's retreat at Acidale (VI ix-xi), and finally Arlo Hill (VII vii) with its pageantry of cosmic politics. These provide paradigms for the operation of the larger fiction, in which Fairyland represents – simultaneously or in sequence – contemporary or historical England, romance world, or allegorical landscape (Iser 1980). They define emblematically the goal of each separate heroic quest, and more important, they define 'by ensample' the utopian 'governement such as might best be' which is a stated goal of the poem (Letter to Raleigh). (See also **Faerie Queene*, geography of.)

ELIZABETH A. POPHAM

Paul J. Alpers 1982 'What is Pastoral?' *CritI* 8:437–60; Curtius ed 1953:183–202 'The Ideal Landscape'; Wolfgang Iser 1980 'Spenser's Arcadia: The Interrelation of Fiction and History' Center for Hermeneutical Studies, Protocol 38 (Berkeley); Montrose 1983; Panofsky 1955:295–320 '*Et in Arcadia Ego*: Poussin and the Elegiac Tradition'; Shore 1985; Bruno Snell 1953 'Arcadia: The Discovery of a Spiritual Landscape' in *Discovery of the Mind: The Greek Origins of European Thought* tr T.G. Rosenmeyer (New York) pp 281–309.

archaism Most speakers of the language even today have on call a number of words known to be 'old' and felt to have a special dignity – words such as *forsake* 'desert' or *tide* 'time' which have somehow escaped the taint of modern life and are set apart for the more solemn occasions and for the expression of elevated thoughts. The literary device of archaism draws its strength from this common feeling about language, though the forms it takes and the purposes it has been made to serve vary from writer to writer. Of all English poets, Spenser is the best known for his archaizing, and words such as *eath* and *forworn* are still to be found in dictionaries of modern English with the label 'Spenserian.' They are kept in the dictionaries because Spenser is generally (and rightly) thought to have given us much of what we recognize as the traditional diction of older English poetry. One of the pleasures of reading his works is to see how and why he weaves in the old with the new, though we need always to remember that many words which seem archaic now were not so then: *emprise, guerdon, wain* – these and many others like them may have seemed quite ordinary to the sixteenth-century reader.

The deliberate use of 'old' words is not uniform throughout Spenser's poetry. They are, for instance, common enough in *The Faerie Queene* and are especially conspicuous in parts of *The Shepheardes Calender*; but they contribute less to the distinctive style of certain other poems such as the *Amoretti*, where Spenser hardly goes further than did some of his contemporaries in drawing on the verbal effects of earlier poets. In the rural dialogues of *The Shepheardes Calender*, the obsolete language has the dramatic function of suggesting a rough, unhewn simplicity in the characters even though their speech is not devoid of learned terms. E.K. observes that 'olde and obsolete wordes are most used of country folke' (*SC* Epistle), and it is hard now to distinguish archaism and dialect on philological grounds (though some scholarly attempts have been made at doing so). In their literary effect the two things conveniently combine in the context of the pastoral poem: then, as now, the countryman's ways of speech were felt to be both pure and 'old.'

In *The Faerie Queene*, the effect of the old language is quite different: it serves not to suggest rugged honesty and earthiness but rather to evoke an ideal world of the past which is the setting of the poem. E.K. again provides evidence when he says that old and obsolete words also 'bring great grace and ... auctoritie to the verse' (*SC* Epistle). The more technical terms of chivalry belong here since inevitably these had become antiquated with the waning of courtly customs, and words such as *gage, joust*, and *ventail* are old in a quite different sense from that in which rural dialect is old. But Spenser also draws on the language of English medieval writings (especially the romances) for many words of more general meaning which had already been replaced or were at least going out of fashion in his day. Some of the commonest are *dight* 'adorn,' *eftsoons* 'at once,' *eke* 'also,' *hight* 'is called,' *list* 'desire,' *mote* 'must,' *stour* 'conflict,' *weet* 'know,' *welkin* 'sky,' *whylome* 'formerly.' Such words later came to be associated with the elevated themes of romance and poetry. They have served the imagination of generations of readers by giving an instant verbal access to an idealized past.

The question of how accurately Spenser has followed his medieval exemplars is of more than philological interest. Some later archaizing poets (Chatterton is the best-known example) indulge in pseudo-archaic forms, even creating spurious 'old words.' At times Spenser misinterpreted the language of older writers: he uses *yede* as an infinitive ('to go,' eg *FQ* II iv 2) when it was really a past tense; *dernely*, which he uses in the sense 'dismally' (at II i 35), properly meant 'secretly' in Middle English (cf III xii 34). Yet such genuine errors must seem few when we recall that there were as yet no scholarly texts of early English writers, and that reliable dictionaries or other etymological aids to them were nonexistent.

Spenser's archaism is not merely a matter of opting for an outdated vocabulary: spelling, inflection, and grammar play their part too. English orthography was in an unsettled state in the sixteenth century; and in the texts that we have, it is hard to know how much of the spelling represents his preferences, and how much is merely the printer's habit. But the variable state of English spelling meant that a writer could, if he wished, give a whole range of words an antique look: an example is the occurrence of Germanic-type spellings in the Spenser text even for words patently of French origin (*despight, quight*, etc).

In its inflections, too, the language was in a state of flux. Spenser can, for instance, equally well write 'he thinks' or 'he thinketh'; and though we can now say which one of these was to survive as the modern form, it is uncertain whether *thinketh* was felt to be archaic or specially poetic in his time. With other inflections there can be no doubt. The normal infinitive and present-tense plural form of the verb *to know* was then *know* or *knowe* (with the final *-e* not pronounced). In using the form *knowen*, Spenser restores a typical Chaucerian ending, and at the same time helps himself to an extra syllable to make his verse scan. This typical Middle English *-n* inflection is often attached (quite unhistorically) to foreign loanwords, as in *atchieven, displeasen*. The best known of all his archaizing devices, the past participle prefix *y-* (going back to an Old English *ge-*), is also found with foreign as well as native stems: *yclad, yglanced, ymet, ytold*. Outdated inflectional forms serve to help him in his rhyme scheme; for example, he uses the old uninflected plural form *brother* to rhyme with *another*, and the form *skyen* 'skies' to rhyme with *shyne*. Metrical reasons may often be found for other obsolescent forms in his text: *muchel* 'much,' *n'ould* 'would not,' *sith* and *sithens* 'since,' *withouten*, and so on.

Lines such as 'Fast did they fly, as them their feete could beare' (v viii 39) show patterns of inversion which we should now associate with an older poetic style; but they may well have seemed to be within current verse conventions to Spenser's contemporaries, and not markedly old-fashioned. There are other grammatical patterns which certainly would have looked archaic, such as *ne ... ne* 'neither ... nor,' and the use of *gan* with the infinitive (*gan look* 'began to look,' or simply 'looked'). In some phrases, such as 'one the truest knight alive' (I iii 37), there may even be a conscious embedding of Chaucerian syntax.

In following his models Lydgate and Chaucer (repeatedly identified by E.K. as a source of old words), Spenser was felt by Sidney to have gone too far in his experiments (ed 1973b:112); and the famous rebuke by Jonson, that '*Spencer*, in affecting the Ancients, writ no Language' (ed 1925–52, 8:618), expressed a distaste for Spenserian devices felt by some writers in the earlier part of the seventeenth century who (outside the pastoral at least) had come to prefer a poetic style closer to the common usage of their own day.

But Spenser's archaism is no doubt in part a deliberate tactic. The glosses to *The Shepheardes Calender* serve to advertise as well as explain the old words in it. Spenser was living at a high season of experiment in the vernacular when the English language was generally admitted to stand in need of enrichment. One way of achieving this was to draw on its past, and there was a role for the poet in thus making the language anew. Similar experiments were taking place in France (with the poets of the Pléiade) and in Italy, and justification for retaining obsolescent words was to be found in the theory of du Bellay as well as in the practice of Virgil. Yet any such conscious experimenting with language on Spenser's part comes second to an instinctive imitation of admired masters – the very popularity of Chaucer had kept near-obsolete words alive in poetry. Spenser did not distort the language by favoring the forms of the past, but his archaism served to perpetuate an already traditional vocabulary.

Poets of later generations were to make

grateful use of what was old in Spenser's language. Milton uses characteristically Spenserian items such as *areede* 'counsel,' *beldame*, *maugre*, *unweeting*, and *yclept*, especially in his early poetry, though he passes by the more extreme forms of dialectal archaism, and the older morphological and syntactical oddities which Spenser had pressed into service. The 1679 folio edition of Spenser's works appends 'A Glossary, or An Alphabetical Index of Unusual Words Explained.' From the selection of words felt to be in need of explanation in eighteenth-century editions of Spenser's poetry (*baleful*, *bevy*, *doughty*, *seare*, etc), we can know that, for the common reader at least, the comprehensibility of his language was by then on the wane. For instance, the introduction to *The Second Part of Mr. Waller's Poems* (London 1705) contrasts the language of Spenser and Edmund Waller (who wrote some 60 years after) by saying that Waller's 'Language, like the Money of that time, is as Currant now as ever; whilst the other's words are like old Coyns, one must go to an Antiquary to understand their true meaning and value' (Atkinson 1937:189). But this increasing unfamiliarity with Spenser's language provides in turn the necessary background to the deliberate and widespread revival of Spenserian (and pseudo-Spenserian) words and spellings by Keats, Coleridge, Byron, and other writers of the Romantic period. NOEL OSSELTON

John W. Draper 1919 'The Glosses to Spenser's "Shepheardes Calender"' *JEGP* 18:556–74; Gans 1979; Bernard Groom 1955 *The Diction of Poetry from Spenser to Bridges* (Toronto); Ingham 1970–1; R.F. Jones 1953; Johan Kerling 1979 *Chaucer in Early English Dictionaries* (Leiden); McElderry 1932; Partridge 1971; Pope 1926; Renwick 1922; Rubel 1941; Spenser *SC* ed 1895; Wrenn 1943; S.P. Zitner 1966 'Spenser's Diction and Classical Precedent' *PQ* 45:360–71. See also lists in Atkinson 1937:203–6 and Carpenter 1923:295–8.

Archimago This evil magician of *FQ* I and (briefly) II first appears after, and symbolically out of, the defeat of Error. Initially he is an emblem of hypocrisy, with his book, rosary beads, and the appearance of piety implied in his knocking of 'his brest' in imitation of the penitent publican of Luke 18.13 (I i argument, 29; Ripa 1603:200 *Hippocresia* 'Hypocrisy'). Part of his larger significance is explained by his name, revealed at 43: he is the arch image-maker, the fabricator of dreams, also the arch-magus or primal magician. Since Renaissance magi operated largely through their own and their subjects' imaginations, however, these two roles in fact merge: he is the magician who induces images of delusion within the imaginations of all fallen human beings, reminding us of the idolatry of the natural imagination (Nohrnberg 1976:126–7, 130; D.P. Walker 1958). Thus, as a supposed hermit, he 'lives in hidden cell' (30), where *cell* suggests the *cellula phantastica*, the front ventricle or compartment of the brain which was understood to house the imagination or fantasy (II ix 50–2).

(See **Archimago** Figs 1–4.)

The quality of Archimago's magic emerges at I i 36, where he seeks from 'His Magick bookes ... mighty charmes, to trouble sleepy mindes,' curses heaven, and invokes terrible Daemogorgon (see *Var* I:190–2). In consequence of his 'spelles,' 'Legions of Sprights ... like little flyes' emerge from the nether world. The word *Legion* is chosen advisedly, to allude to the man possessed with demons, whose 'name is Legion' (Mark 5.2–13; in 1629, Francis Quarles refers to 'accursed *Archimagoes* booke / (That cursed Legion)' *Sp All* p 179). While the simile of the flies, which harks back to Error's brood who are compared to gnats at i 23, reminds us that flies were emblems of the deceptive power of the imagination (II ix 51), it also identifies Archimago in passing with 'Beelzebub the prince of devils' (Matt 12.24) and lord or 'master of flies' ('A Brief Table of the Interpretation of the Propre Names' appended to 1560 Geneva Bible). Significantly, Archimago selects 'the falsest twoo' spirits to aid him in his intention to 'abuse [Redcrosse's] fantasy' (I i 38, 46), for the evil dyad denies Una's integrity and makes Archimago the begetter of Duessa-Fidessa, who appears in the narrative at ii 13 as an indirect consequence of Redcrosse's dreams. Archimago's books of black magic with their spells are symbolically linked with Error's 'vomit full of bookes' (i 20) as the opposite of Fidelia's Bible 'Wherein darke things were writ, hard to be understood' (x 13). With her 'larger spright,' Fidelia can move mountains (20). Spenser here touches on the difference between magic and miracle and between black magic and white magic, which was fundamental to Reformation theological polemic and led inevitably to the association of Roman Catholicism with black magic. More particularly, the fact that popes were identified as necromancers suggests that Archimago is a necromantic papal Antichrist. *Pathomachia* (1630; *STC* 19462; *Sp All* p 180) contains a passing reference to 'Archimago the Jesuite.' Hence his appearance as a fatherly 'aged Sire, in long blacke weedes yclad' (i 29) parodically anticipates that of the faithful and virtuous Palmer of II i 7, in part a white magician.

As an heretical Catholic enchanter with hints of the papal necromancer about him, Archimago is descended from the Simon Magus of Acts 8 and the miracle-working false prophet who opposes Christ, the knight 'Faithful and true' of Revelation 19.11–20. But as the arch image-maker, the grand hypocrite rejoicing in his deceptions, he is the offspring of Satan, who 'in several shapes ... goeth about to seduce us ... and is so cunning that he is able, if it were possible, to deceive the very elect' (Burton *Anatomy of Melancholy* 3.4.1.2; see Mark 13.22). It is fitting that the arch dissembler should present such a plurality of personae and possess so many literary antecedents. To the sources already named should be added the magician hermit of Ariosto's *Orlando furioso* 2.12–15 and the enchanter Ismeno from Tasso's *Gerusalemme liberata*. To the list of his personae should be added that of Una, one of whose colors, black, he appropriates as he also appropriates her sadness (I i 29; cf 4); and also that of Contemplation. It is aged Contemplation, who also lives in a hermitage (x 46; cf i 34), who finally displaces Archimago's illusions and evil spirits with a vision of angels and the heavenly Jerusalem (x 55–7). Also, Archimago's hermitage is near a crystal stream 'Which from a sacred fountaine welled forth alway' (i 34); this stream is all too seductively proleptic of the enervating fountain and 'streame, as cleare as cristall glas' of vii 6 as well as being a parody of Fidelia's 'Christall face' (x 12) and the 'river of water of life, cleare as crystal' in the heavenly Jerusalem (Rev 22.1). In the poem's overall structure, Archimago's dwelling is answered by the hermitage of VI v 34–5.

Archimago's role as deceiver is elaborated further in I ii 11 where he adopts Redcrosse's attire for his own, 'so pretending to a faith he has not' (Nelson 1963:175) and recalling the papal 'beast [from] out of the earth' disguised as the Christological lamb (Rev 13.11 and Geneva gloss). At ii 10, he also becomes Proteus, simultaneously the emblem of man's almost infinite power over his mortality through celebrating his mutability (Pico, Orphic *Conclusiones* 28: 'Whoever cannot attract Pan approaches nature and Proteus in vain' ed 1572–3, I:107) and the wily, sophistical sea god, magician of chaos. Archimago's Protean metamorphoses into bird, fish, fox, and dragon suggest his magical command over the four elements of air, water, earth, and fire. The fox and dragon are traditionally Satanic, too, though Ovid observes that Proteus can change himself into a serpent (*anguis*, *Metamorphoses* 8.734), as does Virgil (*draco*, *Georgics* 4.408). Guileful Malengin is similarly Protean at *FQ* V ix 17.

Archimago appears before Una disguised as Redcrosse at I iii. His allegorical identity as the principle of lawlessness is confirmed, however, when he succumbs in battle to lawless Sansloy (35–9). A simile identifies Archimago with 'fierce *Orions* hound' (31), the destructively scorching Dog Star, associated with Proteus by Virgil in *Georgics* 4.425–7. (Paradoxically, Orion itself is the constellation of winter storms: *Aeneid* 1.535, Geneva gloss to Job 38.31). Having established his world of delusive images – a world which has more than a passing similarity to that of the 'daedale' poet himself – Archimago officially disappears from the action of Book I, leaving his work to be done by the surrogates he has generated. When he reappears at I xii 24 as the messenger bearing Fidessa/Duessa's letter of accusation, his disguise is swiftly penetrated. At the beginning of Book I, he could successfully create an illusion of marriage (i 48). Now, at this moment of betrothal which has its source in the marriage of Revelation 21, we enter a period of apocalypse where evil itself is unmasked and comically and festively bound (xii 35–6; see also Rev 20.1–3).

Yet Archimago rebounds in Book II, for evil will finally be defeated only at the end of time, and Spenser's land of faerie is recognizably our fallen world in which 'That cunning Architect of cancred guile ... work[s] mischiefe' (I i 1–2), by deceiving temperate Guyon with an apparently violated Duessa and inducing him to fight Redcrosse. Specifically, Archimago releases wrath in Guyon just as he had induced rage in Redcrosse (I ii 5; II i 13, 25), though temperance is victorious over Archimago's mischief and the Palmer, who has been displaced temporarily by the enchanter, returns (II i 31).

Archimago's other appearances in Book II are less significant. Trompart and Braggadocchio deceive him with their boasts of prowess, and he flies away to obtain Arthur's sword for the braggart knight (iii 11–19; in 19, Archimago is compared to 'The Northerne wind' since the north is connected with evil: Isa 14.13, Jer 1.14). At vi 47–51, he again parodies the Palmer's *gravitas* and good counsel (cf Ripa 1603:85–6 *Consiglio*) as he stands by the Idle Lake of *accidie* (sloth) 'in an auncient gowne' with his 'hoarie locks [crowned with] great gravitie' and cures irascible Pyrochles' burning by the application of 'balmes and herbes': 'And him restor'd to health, that would have algates dyde.' Thus he preserves the principle of wrath and discord and mimes the infernal Aesculapius' attempt to cure Sansjoy at I v 36–44, though in fact Archimago saves Pyrochles only in order that he might be destroyed by Arthur (II viii 18–52). In this canto, Archimago actually confronts his benevolent double the Palmer and, bearing Arthur's sword, parodies the solar prince himself. His moment of glory is, however, as brief as it is illusory. After the deaths of Pyrochles and Cymochles and the consequent restoration of Guyon and Guyon's reunion with the Palmer, Archimago flees, fittingly accompanied by discordant Atin. We never meet him again, though he is mentioned at III iv 45; he is dispersed into the other evil characters, and especially evil or ambivalent magicians, part of the 'eternal invisible powers' operating throughout the poem (I.G. MacCaffrey 1976:32). This dispersal was recognized, for instance, in 1609 by Joseph Wybarne, who saw the Antichrist 'figured' in *The Faerie Queene* by '*Archimagus, Duessa, Argoglio* the Soldane and others' (*Sp All* p 120).

DOUGLAS BROOKS-DAVIES

Brooks-Davies 1977; Brooks-Davies 1983; Giamatti 1968; Giamatti 1975; Hamilton 1961a; Kermode 1964–5; Nelson 1963; Nohrnberg 1976; D.P. Walker 1958; Waters 1970.

architecture Spenser's treatment of buildings is never really pictorial; he never seems to have set out to imagine structures that are visually or even conceptually coherent or historically accurate. Hence when Scudamour and Glauce approach the house of Care, they see 'a little cottage, like some poore mans nest' (*FQ* IV v 32). Inside, however, they find a place big enough for seven giant smiths to labor at a giant forge. It would seem that Spenser first invented characters and actions, and then supplied building features to accommodate them. For his details, he calls on the tradition of architectural description that begins in Homer (especially *Odyssey* 7, describing the palace of Alkinoos), and runs through Virgil and Ovid and the romances of the Middle Ages to Boiardo, Ariosto, Marot, du Bellay, and Sidney. In this tradition, authors use architectural details – often directly imitating or alluding to earlier works – to convey social, moral, or psychological information about the characters who inhabit the buildings. Particular details in Spenser's poetry have been traced to medieval and Renaissance sources, and to the Bible (especially the Temple of Solomon, and the New Jerusalem of Rev 21), but the tradition encourages an eclectic approach, and none of his structures owes its essential character to any single source (Hard 1934).

Most of Spenser's architectural details are medieval, a fact that may express a conscious archaism (Girouard 1963), but also reflects the actual world in which he lived. For centuries the building practices passed on from master to apprentice changed little, so that the houses of ordinary people retained similar characteristics whether built in 1350 or 1550 (Mercer 1975). In any case, Spenser gives few details about such buildings as Corceca's 'cotage small' (*FQ* I iii 4) or Meliboe's 'cottage clad with lome' (VI ix 16); they have doors, roofs, and rooms – and that is all we know. Since virtually no churches were constructed in sixteenth-century England (Summerson 1953:99–100), the ecclesiastical architecture Spenser saw was overwhelmingly medieval. But he does not specify individual features of most of the churches and chapels in *The Faerie Queene*; when he does, they are usually too general to be stylistically significant. Isis Church, for instance, is 'Borne uppon stately pillours' and 'arched over hed' (V vii 5); whether the pillars are classical or Gothic, the arches round or pointed, he does not say. The chivalric character of the poem means that many of the buildings are castles, most fully represented by the house of Alma (II ix). For all the anthropomorphic symbolism which makes it an allegory of the human body, it has the main features of traditional fortified dwellings: wall, gate, porch, portcullis, barbican, hall with kitchen and storage areas ('offices' in the usage of the time) on one side and private apartments ('solar') on the other.

Change did occur in the houses of the gentry, extensively remodeled or built new in great numbers during the sixteenth century. Although Henry VII and Henry VIII commissioned important building projects, during the rest of the century royal patronage was scanty, and the important work was done for great courtiers and entrepreneurs. The transfer of patronage may be reflected in *Mother Hubberds Tale*: the upstart Fox 'lifted up his loftie towres' while 'the Princes pallaces fell fast' and the 'auncient houses' and 'olde Castles' of the traditional peerage decayed (1173–9).

The most ubiquitous development, an emphasis on façade and in particular on external symmetry, occurred as the shift from feudalism toward capitalism changed the manor house from a place for defense to a place for show, expressing economic and social rather than military power. Of this change there is no unequivocal sign in Spenser's work, unless perhaps in the account of the house of Pride, with 'goodly galleries farre over laid, / Full of faire windowes' (I iv 4). Abundant glass was a feature of most of the new Tudor houses, from Henry VII's Richmond onward; for this reason, suggestions that in Pride's palace or Panthea's 'bright towre all built of christall cleene' (I x 58) Spenser has some specific model in mind – Hampton Court, Burghley House, Wollaton – seem doubtful (Hard 1934:306, McClung 1977:103). Galleries, long well-lit rooms used for recreation and to display pictures and other possessions, were also included in many new houses and added to existing houses like Penshurst and Haddon. It may be significant that in *The Faerie Queene* these items of conspicuous consumption appear only in the homes of dangerous women such as Lucifera, Malecasta, Radigund. We cannot be sure because any particular architectural detail will take its moral tone from its context. Lucifera's 'loftie towres' (I iv 4) symbolize pride, as many other elements of the passage make clear. The 'stately Turret' of the house of Alma reaches equally high but expresses only a legitimate aspiration: it 'likest is' to the 'heavenly towre' God built for his own dwelling (II ix 47). Similarly, the most up-to-date kind of architectural décor in the poems – the Manneristic tapestries and wall-paintings like those which Tudor patrons bought or commissioned from continental artists – mostly ornament Spenser's morally dubious rooms. But the moral differences between the murals in the house of Alma (II ix 53) and the tapestries of Busirane (III xi 28–46) arise from subject matter, not style or medium.

Spenser's use of architecture is epitomized in the Temple of Venus (IV x). The ensemble (moat, bridge, fortified gate, gardens, and temple proper) derives from the *Romance of the Rose* and other medieval dream visions, and most of the terms ('Corbes,' 'pillours,' 'roofe') are stylistically neutral. The significant exception is the 'Doricke guize' of the bridge's pillars (stanza 6). This may refer to the English enthusiasm for the classical orders articulated in John Shute's *First and Chief Groundes of Architecture* (1563) and widely expressed in building of the time through the application of classical pillars and pilasters to otherwise non-classical structures. The temple itself is compared (x 30) with the Temple of Diana at Ephesus and with the Temple of Solomon (given a generally classical appearance in the illustrations of the Geneva and other sixteenth-century Bibles, but depicted as Gothic in many prints and paintings); its 'hundred marble pillors' (37) could come from Vitruvius, but also from medieval romance, the *Hypnerotomachia poliphili*, or Winchester Cathedral. Although the flavor is generally pagan, no particular style or even form can be envisaged because Spenser nowhere supplies the necessary visual pointers, does not tell us whether the pillars are columns or pilasters, fluted or smooth, skinny or fat, whether the building is round or square or rectangular. The effects are achieved more by the accumulation than by the logical interrelation of the details, and while those may be less exotic than some specified in *Orlando furioso* or *Huon of Bordeaux*, the whole does not finally give more 'sense of the actual' (Hard 1934:302) than do the medieval and classical authors on whose architectural descriptions Spenser modeled his own. DAVID EVETT

Alan T. Bradford 1981 'Drama and Architecture under Elizabeth I' *ELR* 11:3–28; Buxton 1963; Dundas 1965; Mark Girouard 1963 'Elizabethan Architecture and the Gothic Tradition' *ArchitHist* 6:23–39; Girouard ed 1983; Hard 1934; William A. McClung 1977 *The Country House in English Renaissance Poetry* (Berkeley and Los Angeles); Eric Mercer 1962; Mercer 1975 *English Vernacular Houses* (London); Summerson 1953.

Areopagus The Court of ancient Athens, the name was adopted by what seems to have been an informal Elizabethan literary coterie centered around Philip Sidney. Its members included Greville, Dyer, Harvey, Daniel Rogers, Thomas Drant, Spenser, and perhaps others. Little is known about their meetings.

In a letter to Harvey of October 1579, written from Leicester House (*Two Letters* 1 in *Var Prose* p 6), Spenser announced that

> the twoo worthy Gentlemen, Master *Sidney*, and Master *Dyer*, [who] have me ... in some use of familiarity ... have proclaimed in their *areiōi pagōi*, a generall surceasing and silence of balde Rymers, and also of the verie beste to: in steade whereof, they have by authoritie of their whole Senate, prescribed certaine Lawes and rules of Quantities of English sillables, for English Verse: having had thereof already greate practise, and drawen mee to their faction.

Harvey replied enthusiastically on October 23, 'Your new-founded *areion pagon* I honoure more, than you will or can suppose: and make greater accompte of the twoo worthy Gentlemenne, than of two hundreth *Dionisii Areopagitae*' (*2 Lett* 2 in *Var Prose* p 442). Spenser had stressed the very strong recommendation he had given to Sidney and Dyer of Harvey's abilities, and Nashe later allowed Harvey membership in the Areopagus, though suggesting he was a latecomer: 'that same *Areopage* ... a forreyner newe come over' (Nashe ed 1904–10, 3:43). On 14 January 1579, Daniel Rogers sent a poem to Sidney in which he describes Sidney's friends as 'a happy band of like-minded fellows [*iucunda caterva sodales*], from whose close friendship a pious love is generated. Among them in holy virtue Dyer excels, steward of judgment and butler of talent; next comes Fulke, dear offspring of the House of Greville. With them, when leisure hours permit these pious studies, you discuss the ultimates of the law, of God and of the good' (Latin text in van Dorsten 1962:179). Rogers seems to have been seeking admission to this clearly informal group and may well have been associated with it for a brief period.

This Areopagus was not an academy in the formal European sense, like the various French or Italian literary and scholarly academies, or even an informal though recognized group like the Pléiade (the group of French poets which included Ronsard and du Bellay). Although Sidney and Harvey knew of these institutions and their purposes, the Areopagus seems rather to have been an literary gathering of poets and patrons who met to share common ideas, probably including ideas for revitalizing English poetry. It existed, if at all, for only a short time. The group may have first come together around October 1579. Rogers, who by September 1580 was a captive in Germany, and who was in Ghent in January 1579 (van Dorsten 1962:68, 179), may have visited London in mid-1579; Greville was in Ireland by 11 May 1580 (*Calendar of the Carew Manuscripts* [1575–88] 2:254); Spenser left London for Ireland around 9 July 1580 (Judson 1945:72); and Harvey left London (in disgrace) to return to Cambridge in January 1581 (Harvey ed 1913:39–40). The members of the Areopagus, then, could have met regularly only for about nine months.

In describing the objectives of the group, Spenser implies that they had adopted Drant's rules for quantitative verse. Those rules are lost; but his scheme appears to have been based, at least in part, on principles borrowed from the rules of classical prosody, whereas Harvey advocated working out a system based upon actual English pronunciation. While these various schemes no doubt encouraged writers to look more closely at English prosody, none was successful. The Areopagus' interest in classical meter, however, suggests a wider purpose. To judge from the writings of those apparently associated with the group, they were in favor of an enhanced status for the *doctus poeta* (the learned poet), they approved of the position of the poet as 'senator' or legislator of literary taste, and they were enthusiastic about all experiments to relate the modern poet to classical antiquity. Their interests were consonant with E.K.'s elaborate commentary on *The Shepheardes Calender*, which creates an image of Spenser as the new Virgil, worthy of full-scale philological and critical annotation. REAVLEY GAIR

For a history of the notion of the Areopagus – for which extravagant claims have been made in earlier scholarship – see Howard Maynadier 1908–9 'The Areopagus of Sidney and Spenser' *MLR* 4:289–301; and *Var Prose* pp 479–80. The fullest discussion is in the unpublished PhD diss of W.R. Gair 'Literary Societies in England from Parker to Falkland (c 1572–1640)' (Cambridge Univ 1969).

Argante, Ollyphant Twin sister and brother giants, children of the incestuous relationship of Typhoeus and his mother, Earth; while still in the womb, the two 'In fleshly lust were mingled both yfere, / And in that monstrous wise did to the world appere' (*FQ* III vii 48). Typhoeus is identified by Thomas Cooper (1565) as 'a great gyaunt, the sonne of Titan ... Also a great puissant wynde: a whirlwynde,' which suggests the union of Aeolus and Earth that produced Orgoglio, another figure associated with lust (I vii 9).

Argante is the first to appear in the poem: at III vii 37, she is seen carrying the Squire of Dames, 'Whom she did meane to make the thrall of her desire.' When Satyrane attempts to rescue him, he is himself overcome and borne off by her. Later both are rescued by a knight who has been pursuing her and who is identified as the martial maid Palladine. At xi 3–6, Ollyphant is seen pursuing an unidentified young man with similar intent of 'beastly use.' Again, it is not Satyrane whom the giant fears, but the chaste Britomart, 'For he the powre of chast hands might not beare, / But alwayes did their dread encounter fly.' In pursuit of him, Britomart comes to a fountain where she finds the despairing Scudamour (xi 7).

Argante is an alternate name for the lustful Morgana of romance; it may derive from Greek *argos* 'shining' or 'swift,' with a suffix underscoring her gigantism; hence the references to her 'firie eyes,' 'sun-broad shield,' and 'lustfull fyre' (vii 39, 40, 49). Ollyphant appears as 'a greet geaunt' in Chaucer's tale of *Sir Thopas*. The 1590 *Faerie Queene* identifies him as one 'that wrought / Great wreake to many errant knights of yore, / Till him Chylde *Thopas* to confusion brought' (vii 48); in 1596 the reference to Thopas is dropped. The name, which means 'elephant' and was applied specifically to an elephant's tusk (Roland's horn was named Olifant), seems evocative of phallic grossness: Lust in IV vii has comparably elephantine features.

The two giants, representative of monstrous sexual practices, are consistent with Spenser's general depiction of giants as rebels against established order (Lotspeich 1932:63). Virtuous female knights, directing their sexual energies properly, prove the most effective deterrent against them; knights who love frivolously, like the Squire of Dames, or who possess merely natural heroism, like Satyrane, are no match for them. DAVID O. FRANTZ

Ariadne Daughter of Minos, King of Crete, Ariadne helped Theseus escape the labyrinth after he had killed the Minotaur, then sailed with him to Naxos where he deserted her. She was found by Bacchus, who married her, giving her the crown of Thetis which he later made into her constellation, the Corona Borealis (Randall 1896).

In Ovid, Theseus' desertion of Ariadne shows the indifference of heroes to the victims incidental to their careers (*Met* 8.172–82). The abandoned Una in *FQ* I iii has been seen as an abandoned Ariadne: compare her lament that the lion is less cruel to her than her knight, and the ass 'More mild in beastly kind, then that her beastly foe,' Sansloy (4, 44), and Chaucer's Ariadne: 'Meker than ye fynde I the bestes wilde!' (*Legend of Good Women* 2198; Nohrnberg 1976:271–2). Spenser directly mentions Ariadne only once, when her crown becomes a simile for a 'precious gemme,' Colin Clout's love, encircled by the garland of dancers on Mount Acidale (*FQ* VI x 13); like this vision, Ariadne's crown presents an ideal of order.

Spenser conflates the myth of Ariadne with the battle at the marriage of Hippodamia and Pirithous between the Centaurs and Lapiths, in which Theseus participated. In Spenser, the battle occurs at the wedding of Ariadne and Theseus – which he seems to have invented – and Ariadne's crown, perhaps now a gift from Theseus, becomes a token of their union.

Spenser's revision makes Theseus a true lover and the heroism which disrupts the wedding an instance of those 'fierce warres' which accompany 'faithfull loves' in the poem. An ideal, the marriage of Theseus and Ariadne occurs only in the elusive context of Colin's art as Calidore observes it. When Calidore steps forward to examine Colin's ideal more closely, the vision vanishes; presumably the fiction of a wedding between Ariadne and Theseus must vanish as well, leaving heroic strife in its place. Like Ariadne's crown, their union remains the kind of happy ending which can never be fully sustained in a narrative where the contingencies of heroic strife provide the vehicle for allegory. ROBERT A. BRINKLEY

Ariosto, Lodovico (1474–1553) In the long history of Italian chivalric literature, which developed among the populace and was finally converted in the Renaissance to courtly uses, Ariosto's *Orlando furioso* was the second poem by a Ferrarese aristocrat to glorify the Este lords. Based directly on *Orlando innamorato*, by the Count of Scandiano, Matteo Maria Boiardo, a work truncated in its sixty-ninth canto by its author's death in 1494, the *Furioso* was begun around 1505 and reached its final form as a poem of 46 cantos in 1532. In adopting but transforming Boiardo's characters and providing complexly interwoven conclusions to his aborted actions, Ariosto brought to a climax a centuries-old fascination with Carolingian and Arthurian narrative. Boiardo had cast the chaste Orlando – the stalwart Roland of the *chanson de geste* – in the role of infatuated lover of the enchantress Angelica, strikingly uniting two of the great repositories of narrative in the Middle Ages: the martial Matter of France, associated with Charlemagne's wars, and the romantic Matter of Brittany, associated with Arthurian knight-errantry and enchantments. In plunging the hero into madness resulting from sensual love, Ariosto capped his predecessor's innovation by linking the medieval hero with the Hercules *furens* of classical literature. By repeatedly evoking this third great repository of narrative, the so-called Matter of Rome, and particularly by the seriousness with which he absorbed and domesticated Virgil's *Aeneid*, Ariosto redirected the course of chivalric poetry, effecting a wedding of classical epic and medieval romance. *Orlando furioso* provided Spenser with his most proximate model for *The Faerie Queene*; the continual presence in his imagination of the older poem is readily discernible to any reader who knows both.

The *Furioso* occupies a position of pivotal importance in the transmission and development of epic, particularly Virgilian epic, from the classical period to the Renaissance. Nevertheless, since Boiardo's poem remains relatively unknown to English readers, and since it provides the very foundations upon which Ariosto built his own poetic edifice, a brief look at the *Innamorato* becomes essential. Apart from the novelty of Orlando as lover, Boiardo effects a second important innovation in chivalric romance: he provides a contrast to the undignified portrait of Orlando by inventing another more acceptable hero, the young warrior Ruggiero, son of a Christian mother and infidel father. Though the youth is brought to France as an Achilles-like talisman during the invasion of Charlemagne's realms by Agramante of Africa, he is fated to be converted to Christianity and to marry Bradamante, who is the sister of Rinaldo, Orlando's cousin and rival in love. Here the strain of dynastic praise in Virgilian epic is suddenly renewed in chivalric form, for the fated pair, providentially chosen to initiate a splendid new civilization in northern Italy, will found the Este family. As mythical archetypes of the members of that ducal house, Ruggiero and Bradamante function as romantic equivalents of Aeneas and the much more shadowy Lavinia. Before the *Innamorato* breaks off, the pair have met by chance on a battlefield, fallen in love and plighted their troth, been abruptly separated, and come to the verge of a series of chivalric adventures in a world of magic and marvels.

Boiardo is ultimately responsible for the assimilation, within a fundamentally comic-romantic-chivalric poem, of an *Aeneid*-like strain of dynastic praise that runs through Renaissance epic thereafter. He is also the immediate source of other elements characteristic of the *Furioso*, chiefly the multiplicity of its narratives and the vast array of characters. From Boiardo, Ariosto inherits not only the straggling, extensively elaborated tale of the rivalry of Orlando, Rinaldo, Sacripante, and Ferraù for the love of the perpetually elusive Angelica, and the equally long and populous tale of the pagan invasion by Agramante and Rodomonte, but also the barely initiated story of the two dynastic lovers, to which he immediately gives an independent development and a central prominence. As mythical archetypes of the Estensi, Bradamante and Ruggiero are fundamentally Ariostan creations, and they function as literary ancestors of Spenser's Britomart and Artegall, who are types of the Tudors.

Ordered multiplicity is the keynote of the *Furioso*'s beginning. In his opening stanzas, Ariosto at once synchronizes and redevelops the three main narratives that the less artful Boiardo had introduced randomly and in succession. He also gives them an epic resonance deriving from Homer and Virgil, marking a clear break from the medieval tradition in which Boiardo worked. Addressing his patron, Cardinal Ippolito d'Este, Ariosto announces his own manipulation of the triple subject: Agramante's wrath (*ire*) and his pursuit, amid wars and loves (*l'arme, gli amori*), of his war on the Emperor; the madness of Orlando, resulting from sensual fury; and the heroic acts (*gesti*) of Ruggiero, destined to be Ippolito's ancestor. The implication of the initial four stanzas is that the defeat and expulsion of the infidel and the conversion and marriage of Ruggiero are concomitant and ultimately successful labors.

Ariosto's perspective is without precedent in chivalric romance, and is indeed more proper to epic. He works at once in two distinct times, the chivalric era of Charlemagne and his own newly imperial age of the sixteenth century; his artistic purview captures in a single glance the prophetic past and the accomplished fruits of his own contemporary civilization, which he often praises by direct address, deliberately interrupting his romance narrative. The historical intrusions are part of a conscious artistic procedure, introducing a specifically Virgilian element almost entirely absent from Boiardo and characteristic, within this romance tradition, only of Ariosto.

The complexity of his handling of the interwoven narratives is reinforced by the complexity of his historical vision, in which the Carolingian myth is buttressed by contemporary reality. Past and present interact continually in the *Furioso*: the fiction provides both a matrix and a mirror of future events, and the poem, ultimately societal in its orientation and address, opens its final canto by hailing the great and learned individuals who compose the poet's audience. Ariosto's continual sense of history climaxing in a transplanted but now flourishing and splendid, if threatened, civilization is evoked repeatedly in *The Faerie Queene*.

The pressure of this background on Spenser contributes not only to the way his poem appears on the page, but to some of its innermost workings as an extended narrative in which heroic, romantic, chivalric, comic, historical, dynastic, and allegorical elements are freely combined. The very shape assumed by *The Faerie Queene* derives ultimately from these developments in Italian narrative of the late fifteenth and sixteenth centuries. As in *Orlando furioso*, which Spenser is recorded as having wanted to 'overgo' (*Three Letters* 3, *Var Prose* p 471), *The Faerie Queene*'s action is narrated in cantos and stanzas rather than in the blank verse that, since the time of Surrey's translation of Books 2 and 4 of the *Aeneid*, was the obvious equivalent to the unrhymed hexameters of the ancient epic poets. This verse form represents the survival into learned poetry of popular traditions of medieval Italian narrative, in which the tale is spoken by a minstrel to an audience of townspeople gathered in a public place, the variable length of the delivery being determined by the length of time the auditors could be expected to attend the recital of one of the *canti* or songs. Another line of continuity with change is established by the reflective, hortatory, moralizing, or lyrical proems with which Spenser opens his books. Like Ariosto's, these proems are a survival in highly artistic form of the minstrel's opening invocation of the saints or the Virgin. Significantly, Spenser uses his first proem to invoke Venus and Mars, asserting that his poem will be 'moralized' by fierce wars and faithful loves. This deliberately recalls Ariosto's opening statement which, by linking 'arms' and 'loves,' adds a romantic dimension to Virgil's 'arms and the man I sing.'

The plurality of actions announced here once again links *The Faerie Queene* to the intermediate heroic tradition of the Renaissance rather than directly to its classical ancestors. In contrast to classical epic, with its action centered largely on a single dominant figure like Achilles, Odysseus, or Aeneas, Spenser opts for the simultaneous multiplicities of romantic epic as handled by Ariosto, and (in Books III and IV, at least) for a narrative technique imitated from his Italian model. Derived from medieval French narrative, and masterfully adopted by Ariosto, who describes it (2.30, 13.81) by a metaphor of weaving, the technique of *entrelacement* or 'interlace' involves interleaving separate stories and maintaining them in a state of suspension and incompletion by constantly cutting from one to another at climactic points. Spenser's *Faerie Queene* might be considered one vast interlace, inasmuch as the six completed books are begun on successive days at Gloriana's court and are (ideally) simultaneous and concurrent. A realistic chronology based on the Letter to Raleigh would have each action beginning a day later than its predecessors but running for many days thereafter, during which the other adventures would be simultaneously proceeding. Yet by the time we finally see Guyon, Redcrosse's adventures are over and done with, and the notion of interlace posited by the Letter is modified or perhaps even canceled.

In a further complication, however, *The Faerie Queene* is arranged not only into Ariostan cantos but also into a proposed twelve books in imitation of Virgil's twelve – books, moreover, that celebrate different virtues in different narrative modes through the actions of a number of different heroes and heroines, who embody those virtues as they are being formed. Characters endowed with particular personalities (Redcrosse characteristically sad and solemn, Britomart humorously impetuous and fiery) are thus vehicles of ideas in ways both similar to and different from those of Ariosto. Here some contrasts are necessary. Ariosto keeps a whole vast world, global in extension, deliberately suspended and incomplete until two main objects have been achieved: the liberation of Paris after the final defeat of the pagans, and the celebration of the dynastic marriage, with which the *Furioso* concludes. In contrast, Spenser begins afresh with every book except the fourth, providing a fundamentally new cast of characters, as well as a new set of actions dictated by the allegory appropriate to the virtue being fashioned. In this tendency to proliferating multiplicity and open-endedness (Arthur's marriage to Gloriana is an endlessly receding objective), *The Faerie Queene* seems closer to romance and its 'sub-generation' of allegory – its tendency to create a constant supply of surrogates for the main characters – than to epic. At the root of this tendency undoubtedly lies the medieval reading of epic characters as allegorical figures, a technique that divides and subdivides a human personality into many 'characters' who represent different, warring aspects of that one personality. Hence, the pressure exerted by classical epic is towards unity of action and character, while the tendency of medieval romance and allegory is towards multiplicity and dispersion; *The Faerie Queene* maintains a perpetual tension between the two.

Renaissance epic is distinguished from its classical ancestors not only by its chivalric dress but predominantly by its tendency to overt allegory. For all their abundance of personality and richness of event, Ariosto's main narrative lines, constantly broken and indefinitely prolonged but ultimately coordinated and congruent, are fewer and more distinct than Spenser's, since they are headed by three heroes to whom the poem's episodes are attached throughout. Orlando heads one narrative line and Ruggiero another; in the third, Ariosto finds a new use for a wise fool, Orlando's cousin Astolfo, who represents the greatest of the poet's triumphs, in turning to allegorical account a simple comic stock character of Carolingian fiction. The resulting triadic plot structure corresponds to Ariosto's initial announcement of his triple subject: first, an intractably sensual lover (Orlando) whose reward at the poem's midpoint is madness; second, a more recognizably human type (Ruggiero) who gains a bride and a new territory in Italy; and finally, a converted buffoon (Astolfo), a wise lunatic of another kind than Orlando, who alone of the poem's characters looks down on the poem's various madnesses from the lunar height of canto 34, and whose leisurely but directed errancies, in counterpoint to Orlando's and Ruggiero's erratic voyages, are ultimately central to the defeat of Agramante. The underlying impulse to unity in the *Furioso* comes from this triadic organization, manifested most clearly in the poem's frequent contrasts among the three male figures. Allegorically, they function on a hierarchical scale of love, love understood in its widest sense; the various rhetorical modes in which their adventures are cast are appropriate to their places on the scale. On an essential level, the *Furioso* contrasts animal, human, and transcendent love in an art based on the Horatian ideal of laughing seriousness.

Undoubtedly, Spenser was capable of finding meaning for himself in the organization, language, and varying narrative modes of Ariosto's poem. Nevertheless, the *Furioso* came to him, through an intervening critical tradition, as a work interpreted both morally and allegorically, though in ways that failed signally to show how it established its meaning and values through laughter. Various Italian critics interpreted the poem in two ways. The first involved discrete, localized moralizations of characters and episodes; these summary interpretations, obvious and often absurd, appeared at the head of the cantos in various editions from 1542 onwards, and were of an easily dismissable type, often using events and characters as examples to imitate or avoid. The second type, represented by the work of Simone Fornari, was found in independent volumes of interpretation which provided learned and exhaustive, if tediously detailed, readings of such matters as Ruggiero's love for the enchantress Alcina or Astolfo's voyages. These more learned interpretations differ from the former in at least attempting to pursue allegory into the form and structure of the poem, and to reveal it operating on an extended level. Harington gives evidence of knowing both kinds, both in his translation of the *Furioso* and in his appended commentary. Generally speaking, the allegorists may have performed two main services: they revealed Ariosto as operating within a context of learned allegory (which Spenser knew from other sources), and they pointed to his transformation into allegorical symbols of comic and romantic paraphernalia from Boiardo, thereby providing Spenser with a model for his own further transformations of Ariosto. In fact, Ariosto ranged as freely and independently in the *Innamorato* as Spenser did in the *Furioso*; neither of them felt any compulsion to re-create his predecessor's meaning or structure, but each used and recombined elements of the model at will for his own very different artistic purposes. Ariosto's absorption and domestication of the *Innamorato*, a subject to which criticism has been curiously inattentive for centuries, provides an instructive example for the ways in which later epic poets, imbued with their source, absorb Ariosto. But until Ariosto's true relationship to Boiardo is clarified, criticism will continue to assert that Spenser allegorized the romantic epic, a statement that radically falsifies the development of the form and Ariosto's role as an artist within the tradition. Though Spenser and Ariosto wrote very different kinds of allegory, both of them were fully aware that it was in allegory that the epic was essentially rooted. PETER V. MARINELLI

Alpers 1967b:160–99; Durling 1965; Giamatti 1966; Greene 1963; Marinelli 1987.

Aristotle and his commentators The authority of Aristotle in the Western world did not end with the Middle Ages, though it became less central and comprehensive. His writings remained an important part of the body of classical learning that Renaissance humanists sought to know more accurately and completely. It is true that his treatises on logic lost some prestige with the rise of rhetorical humanism in the fifteenth century and after the reforms of Lefevre d'Etaples in 1492 and Peter Ramus in 1543, and his scientific writings were largely discredited by the attacks of Bruno and Bacon and the rise of experimental science in the seventeenth century. But his moral-philosophical writings retained much of their former importance.

Two of them, the *Politics* and the *Nicomachean Ethics*, underpinned inherited social and religious dogmas and were at least starting points for serious Renaissance thinkers. The *Ethics* held an honored place in Protestant humanistic education beginning with Philipp Melanchthon whose *Enarrationes* synthesized the *Ethics* with the Ten Commandments. In England, the Aristotelian ethical tradition culminated in Book I of Hooker's *Of the Laws of Ecclesiastical Polity* (1593), a work almost as central to the Anglican theological tradition as Thomas Aquinas' *Summa theologiae* (also founded on the *Ethics*) was to the Roman Catholic. These and other treatises of Aristotle continued to furnish a map of knowledge for Western Europe. Philosophy continued Aristotle's division between the natural sphere, treated in the *Physics* and other works, and the moral, treated in the *Ethics* and *Politics*. The latter works divided moral philosophy into the ethical and political spheres.

In literary criticism, Aristotle's influence began rather than ended or diminished with the Renaissance. The *Poetics*, available in Latin translation in 1498 and in Greek in 1508, became well known with the publication of Francesco Robortello's text, Latin translation, and commentary in 1548. Thereafter the *Poetics*, accommodated to Horace's *Ars poetica* and somewhat to Plato, came to dominate Renaissance critical discussion. Modified and systematized by the Italians, the teaching of Aristotle regained in neoclassical literary theory much of the authority it had acquired in all areas of secular knowledge, after similar adjustments, during the late Middle Ages.

In Spenser criticism, claims for Aristotelian influence on *The Faerie Queene* have undergone the same correctives as have those for Plato's influence. J.J. Jusserand, John Erskine, Viola Hulbert, Josephine Waters Bennett, and particularly Rosemond Tuve were less willing to assume Spenser's direct indebtedness to Aristotle than were William Fenn DeMoss, who read *The Faerie Queene* as a kind of versified *Ethics*, and Ernest Sirluck, who so read Book II (*Var* 2:414–26; Tuve 1966, ch 2; Sirluck 1951–2:73–100). The Aristotelian ethical tradition was not the only one in the Middle Ages. Platonic and Stoic traditions had eclipsed the Aristotelian before the Christian era, and through the writings of Cicero and the Church Fathers were well established in medieval ethical thought long before the mid-twelfth century, when Greek texts of Aristotle came to the West from Constantinople and Latin translations of Arabic texts and commentaries from Moorish Toledo reached Paris and other European intellectual centers. The patristic assimilation of Plato and the Stoics to Christian dogma began almost a millennium before the efforts of the Franciscan Alexander of Hales and the Dominicans Albertus Magnus and Thomas Aquinas to fuse church teaching with Aristotle.

The work of these syncretists was encouraged by a papal edict of 1231 allowing the use only of those works of Aristotle purged of error, thus relaxing a recent edict of the Paris Council of 1210 which had banned his natural philosophy entirely. The most important of these, Thomas Aquinas, wrote not only theological treatises but also commentaries on Aristotle's works, including the *Physics*, *Metaphysics*, *Ethics*, *De anima*, *Posterior Analytics*, and part of *De interpretatione*. Intent on purifying Aristotle textually as well as theologically, Aquinas gained the services of the young Flemish Dominican scholar William of Moerbecke, who translated almost all of Aristotle's works from the Greek into Latin. William was indebted in turn to the examples of Robert Grosseteste, Bishop of Lincoln, translator of the *Ethics*, and his student Roger Bacon. The three centuries separating Aquinas and Spenser yielded hundreds of commentaries on the *Ethics* alone.

In the commentaries, the Aristotelian tradition of the virtues blends with the Platonic-Stoic tradition of the four cardinal virtues and their branches descending from Cicero through Macrobius, Martin of Braga (Pseudo-Seneca), Alanus de Insulis, Aquinas, the anonymous *Speculum morale*, and scores of lesser medieval theorists. When Spenser in the Letter to Raleigh cites 'Aristotle and the rest' in support of his treatment of magnificence as a subsuming virtue (see *magnanimity), he is acknowledging his indebtedness to what he regarded as a coherent tradition of ethical thought deriving ultimately from Aristotle but augmented and refined by many learned successors. For Spenser, among the most important contemporary interpreters of moral philosophy were the Italian syncretists Giraldi Cintio and Alessandro Piccolomini. Cintio's *Tre dialoghi della vita civile* (prefixed to part 2 of *De gli hecatommithi* 1565) and, to a much lesser extent, Piccolomini's *Della institutione morale* (1560) were the sources of Bryskett's *A Discourse of Civill Life* (written c 1586, pub 1606), in which Spenser appears as an interlocutor and which is perhaps the most illuminating contemporary discussion of the ethical theory found in *The Faerie Queene*.

In literary criticism as in moral philosophy, the assumption that modernity had inherited from the ancient world a coherent body of knowledge led some Italian scholars to conclude that contradictions between classical thinkers were only apparent. Accordingly, they set to work reconciling Aristotle with Plato and both with Horace, whose authority in literary theory antedated that of the Greeks in medieval thought. Averroes' twelfth-century Arabic commentary on the *Poetics*, translated by Hermannus Alemanus in the thirteenth century and published in Venice in 1481, omits crucial passages and garbles others, assigning to poetry a didactic function and rhetorical method foreign to Aristotle. This function and method, however, were quite in keeping with what the Middle Ages had drawn from Horace, whose *Ars poetica* assigned to poetry rhetorical aims (pleasure and profit) and criteria (credibility and decorum).

Despite Hermannus' effort, the *Poetics* remained virtually unknown until the sixteenth century, when major commentaries appeared in Latin, by Francesco Robortello (1548), Vincenzo Maggi (1550), Pietro Vettori (1560), and Antonio Riccoboni (1584), and in Italian, by Lodovico Castelvetro (1570) and Alessandro Piccolomini (1575). This succession of commentaries shows, in general, a growing maturity of perception and, correspondingly, a willingness to differ with Aristotle on particular points. The same increasing independence of view appears in eclectic arts of poetry by Antonio Sebastiano Minturno (1559), Julius Caesar Scaliger (1561), and Francesco Patrizi (1586), as well as in polemical discourses on the implications of the *Poetics* for the modern genre of the romance by Cintio (1549), Giovanni Pigna (1554), and Torquato Tasso (1587). The discourses on the romance provided Spenser with theoretical justification for the hybrid form of *The Faerie Queene*. (See Weinberg 1961 for the *Poetics* in Renaissance Italy.)

In England, references in Ascham's *Scholemaster* and in the correspondence of Sir John Cheke indicate some acquaintance with the *Poetics* at Cambridge by the 1540s. Other references appear in the writings of continental scholars residing in England during the 1550s. Aristotle's ideas receive passing notice in critical treatises by Thomas Lodge (1579), William Webbe (1586), and George Puttenham (1589). His authority in criticism was attacked by Bruno in lectures at Oxford in 1583 and in *Eroici furori* in 1585. Sidney's *Defence of Poetry* (1583?) was the first treatise in English to make substantial use of the *Poetics*. Identifiably Aristotelian ideas in the *Defence* include the imitative function of poetry, its superiority to history, its concern with universals rather than with particulars, and the pleasure deriving from the imitation even of unpleasant subjects. Sidney's discussions of the unities and of catharsis, however, show that he did not rise above his Italian contemporaries in his understanding of Aristotle. In a letter to Spenser of 7 April 1580, Harvey remarks that at Cambridge Aristotle is 'muche named, but little read' (*Three Letters* 2, in *Var Prose* p 460). Few Elizabethan allusions to Aristotle's critical ideas prove more than a second-hand acquaintance with the *Poetics* (Herrick 1930:8–34).

Among the features of *The Faerie Queene* commonly attributed to Aristotle's influence, the most obvious occurs in the Letter to Raleigh, in Spenser's division of the extended poem into twelve books on the 'private morall vertues' and twelve more on the political, according to the standard division of moral philosophy based on Aristotle's *Ethics* and *Politics*. In the *Ethics*, however, eleven or thirteen private virtues may be found, but not twelve. This discrepancy has been accounted for in several ways: by adding Arthur's virtue of magnificence to the Spenserian total of twelve to produce an Aristotelian total of thirteen (DeMoss 1918–19); by seeing it as reflecting the strong tradition of twelve Aristotelian virtues among the successors of Aquinas, who divides justice into internal (*circa passiones*) and external (*circa operationes*) to form a total of twelve (Hulbert in *Var* 1:354–6); or by defining 'the twelve private morall vertues, as Aristotle hath devised' as simply such virtues as Aristotle would call private moral (Renwick in *Var* 1:361). The objection that Spenser's inclusion of justice in the first six books as a private moral virtue violates the private-political dichotomy announced in the Letter would have little weight to the educated Elizabethan, who would recall that Aristotle formally treats justice in the *Ethics* (Book 5!) rather than in the *Politics* and that his justice is both personal and political. Likewise, Spenser's assigning magnificence to Arthur as an inclusive virtue 'according to Aristotle and the rest' was evidently not the result of a misreading of the *Ethics* but a choice based on firm medieval precedent (Tuve 1966).

Reflections of Aristotle occur frequently in the text of *The Faerie Queene*. The Aristotelian concept of good as single and of evil as manifold (*Ethics* 2.6) is allegorized in the first episode of Book I, when Una, with Redcrosse, gazes in amazement at the multitudinous cannibalistic brood of the slain Error (i 25–6). With the exception of justice in V ix, temperance is the only virtue of Spenser's series treated in anything like an Aristotelian way as a mean between extremes. The golden mean is implicit in the episodes of Medina's castle (II ii), the castle of Alma (ix 33–44), and the voyage to the Bower of Bliss (xii 2–9), and explicit in occasional expository comment (i 58, ii argument, xii 33). Bryskett, following Cintio, attempts to reconcile the idea of the medial as morally normative with the Christian obligation to abstain from evil: 'And therfore *Aristotle* said right well that the meane of vertue betweene two extremes, was a *Geometricall* meane which hath a respect to proportion, and not an *Arithmeticall* meane which respecteth equall distance: so as you must understand that vertue is not called a meane betweene two extremes, because she participateth of either of them both, but because she is neither the one nor the other' (ed 1970:155). Still, the virtuous mean of Spenserian temperance is not, in its moral aspect, Aristotle's balance point between excess and defect but the rejection of Satanic temptation such as Christ's in Matthew 4.1–11, an incident reflected in Guyon's experience in the house of Mammon (II vii) and given epic treatment by Milton in *Paradise Regained*. In its psychological aspect, Spenserian temperance conflates the Aristotelian mean with the Thomistic counterpoising of the irascible and concupiscible passions, in which the passions form a *discordia concors* under the rule and arbitrament of reason (cf II i 58 and *Summa theologiae* Ia 81.3). Spenser's and Aquinas' concept of the harmonious personality derives less from the *Ethics* than from *De anima* (the primary source of Elizabethan faculty psychology) and Plato's *Republic* (4.441–2, 9.580–1). It is true that Aristotle, like Spenser, remarks in the *Ethics* on the greater difficulty in combatting pleasure than pain (2.3; cf *FQ* II vi 1). Also, the names Phaedria, Philotime, and Acrasia have been attributed to the Greek of the *Ethics* (*Var* 1:356; 2:241, 262). Braggadocchio is, among other things, perhaps a counterfeit of Aristotle's magnanimous man (*Ethics* 2.7, 4.3; *FQ* II iii 10). Nevertheless, Spenserian temperance is indebted not so much to the *Ethics*, which applies the mean to all the virtues, as to the tradition of the cardinal virtues, which restricts it to temperance and assimilates the classical perspective to the Christian.

The description of the Garden of Adonis is probably indebted to *De anima* (2.2) and the *Physics* (1.9) regarding the cooperation of matter and form (*Var* 3:258, 260). Spenser's treatment of the virtue of friendship parallels a long passage in Bryskett that synthesizes Cicero, Plato, and Aristotle (*Ethics* 8.1) on the subject (*Var* 4:291, 293). Spenser's placing of the Book of Friendship immediately before the Books of Justice and Courtesy perhaps reflects Aristotle's conception of friendship as the basis of society, as the principle of concord in the state (*Ethics* 8.1).

Spenser echoes Aristotle's praise of justice as the chief virtue (*FQ* V proem 10). The organization of *FQ* V reflects his division of justice into personal and political, distributive and corrective, and voluntary and involuntary modes, and his distinguishing between law and equity as kinds of justice and between force and fraud as forms of injustice (*Ethics* 5.1–2). The golden mean is reflected in the trial of Duessa at Mercilla's court, where Artegall appears excessive in zeal but deficient in pity and Arthur excessive in pity but deficient in zeal (*FQ* V 9). The *Cantos of Mutabilitie* may owe something to Aristotle's account of changeless bliss (*Ethics* 7.14). Of the minor poems, the *Julye* eclogue of *The Shepheardes Calender* has been thought to teach the mean of moderation in religion, what will later be called the *via media* of Anglicanism (DeMoss 1918–19); but the allegory can be interpreted more naturally as favoring Puritan lowliness.

Although almost all these reflections of Aristotle's moral philosophy may be attributed to medieval and Renaissance intermediaries, Spenser's direct acquaintance with the *Ethics* may be assumed. The same may not be said of the *Poetics*. A phrase such as 'Distraught twixt feare and pitie' (*Time* 579) reflects Aristotle's doctrine of catharsis, but this was a critical commonplace available from any number of contemporary sources. Incidents such as Artegall's discovery of the female identity of Britomart (IV vi) or of the spurious identity of Braggadocchio (V iii) are too common in romance narrative to prove direct indebtedness to Aristotle's discussion of recognition. Spenser's literary-critical Aristotelianism was likely secondhand and, like his Aristotelian moral philosophy, adulterated by syncretists and systematizers. Most of it derived from the practical application of Aristotle's ideas to the defense of Ariosto's *Orlando furioso*. Sixteenth-century Italian critics, interpreting the *Poetics* as a prescriptive document, had extended Aristotle's 'rules' for tragedy to comedy and epic. Enthusiasts for the new vernacular literature rose to defend *Orlando furioso*, Dante's *Divine Comedy*, and Guarini's *Il pastor fido* against the neoclassical purists, who acknowledged only those genres mentioned by the classical authorities. Ariosto's sprawling poem was vulnerable to the Aristotelian critical criteria of unity and probability, as then understood, and to the Horatian criteria of moral utility and decorum. In this stormy controversy which lasted from about 1550 to 1583, the most significant participants for Spenser were the moderates Giraldi Cintio and Giovanni Pigna, who quarreled but came to similar conclusions, and the elastic traditionalist Alessandro Piccolomini, whose vernacular translation and commentary marked a gain in accuracy over those of Castelvetro and his predecessors.

The defense of romance, though ostensibly Aristotelian, was conducted ultimately on Horatian principles. The diffuseness of romance seemed to violate the Aristotelian requirement of unity. Its use of the marvelous seemed to violate Aristotelian probability. The solution was that Horace had admitted pleasure as one of the aims of poetry. Cristoforo Landino in his edition of Horace's *Opera* (Florence 1482) had declared that variety is a means of pleasure in poetry. Consequently, Cintio could justify the episodic structure of romance narrative – its multiple plots, digressions, disjunctions – as a means of fulfilling this purpose of poetry (*Discorso intorno al comporre dei romanzi* 1549). Furthermore, episodic structure need not, said Pigna, be construed as conflicting with Aristotle's statements about plot if episodes be regarded as separate from the plot proper – as 'accidents' rather than 'essence' of the narrative (*I romanzi* 1554). Heroic poetry permits many actions of many persons (Cintio), especially if, as in the case of the epic, it focuses on the actions of one man (Pigna). Variety, in any case, is more important than unity (Castelvetro). Aristotle's comparison of the poet to the historian was also much quoted in support of the poet's freedom of narrative method (eg, by Minturno, Cintio, and Pigna), as was Horace's observation that the poet may begin his story in the middle of the chronological sequence of events for greater economy and focus.

In defending the use of the marvelous, apologists for romance contended less with Aristotle than with his misconstruction by Italian neoclassical commentators. The latter interpreted Aristotle's definition of poetry as imitation to mean that it imitates previous writers rather than nature and construed his requirement of probability as fidelity to nature (verisimilitude) rather than as internal consistency, which was subsumed under the Horatian doctrine of decorum. Pigna defended the credibility of supernatural elements that agree with the beliefs of the audience. The Christian miraculous, he argued, is acceptable in a Christian era, the pagan in a pagan. Cintio allowed the fabulous in digressions if the main action were true. But the central vindication of the marvelous, as of diffuseness, was that it is pleasurable and that, on Horatian authority, pleasure is a legitimate purpose of poetry.

In the introduction to his *Discourse*, Bryskett admits that he envies 'the happinesse of the Italians' who have popularized moral philosophy by translating and commenting upon Plato and Aristotle (ed 1970:21). Obviously, Aristotle had not been entirely displaced by Plato and Cicero in the intellectual hierarchy of Renaissance moralists but, assimilated with these and other authorities, had taken on new life.

RONALD A. HORTON

A standard modern translation is in Aristotle ed 1984. Schmitt 1983a and Schmitt 1983b give valuable background. F. Edward Cranz 1984 *A Bibliography of Aristotle Editions 1501–1600* rev ed Charles B. Schmitt (Baden-Baden) is the standard guide to the texts in all languages. For a summary of editions published in England, see *STC* (752ff). See also O.B. Hardison, Jr 1970 'The Place of Averroes' Commentary on the *Poetics* in the History of Medieval Criticism,' in *Medieval and Renaissance Studies* ed John L. Lievsay (Durham, NC) pp 57–81; Herrick 1930; E.N. Tigerstedt 1968 'Observations on the Reception of the Aristotelian *Poetics* in the Latin West' *SRen* 15:7–24; Weinberg 1961.

On Spenser, see Bennett 1942:229–30; William Fenn DeMoss 1918–19 expanded in DeMoss 1920 *The Influence of Aristotle's 'Politics' and 'Ethics' on Spenser* (Chicago); Erskine 1915; Viola Blackburn Hulbert 1931 'A Possible Christian Source for Spenser's Temperance' *SP* 28:184–210 (rejects Aristotle); H.S.V. Jones 1926 (on Melanchthon's *Enarrationes* and Aristotelianism in Spenser); Jusserand 1905–6; Jerry Leath Mills 1977 'Spenser's Letter to Raleigh and the Averroistic *Poetics*' *ELN* 14:246–9 (refers 'Aristotle and the rest' to the Averroistic *Poetics* rather than to the true *Poetics* or the *Ethics*); Sirluck 1951–2; Tuve 1966 (shows how what has been identified as 'Aristotelian' can also be found in common medieval sources).

Arlo Hill The location of the debate between Mutabilitie and the gods before 'great dame *Nature*' in the *Cantos of Mutabilitie*; the last of the major settings for moments of mythical and philosophical condensation in *The Faerie Queene*. Spenser introduces Arlo Hill as 'the best and fairest Hill / That was in all this holy-Islands hights,' and goes on to tell 'how *Arlo* through *Dianaes* spights ... Was made the most unpleasant, and most ill' (VII vi 36–55). His account subtly interweaves native Irish and pagan classical materials.

The geographical original of Arlo Hill is Galtymore, the last and highest peak in a range of mountains that begins two miles north of Kilcolman Castle in County Cork and extends eastward about thirty miles through County Limerick into County Tipperary. The western part of this range is called the Ballahoura Hills, the eastern part the Galty Mountains. Spenser refers to the entire range as 'old father *Mole*' and seems to expect his readers to recall that he had already done so in *Colin Clouts Come Home Againe* (57, 104–5). With an elevation of 3018 feet, Galtymore rises well above the surrounding Galtys and Ballyhouras; it is clearly visible from Kilcolman, some twenty miles away, which has an elevation of only 329 feet.

(See **Arlo Hill** Fig 1.)

Arlo Hill takes its name from the glen of Aherlow (commonly called 'Arlo' or 'Harlo' by English writers) immediately below Galtymore. The slopes of the mountain are now precipitous and barren, although they may once have featured that 'grove of Oakes' which Spenser tells us crowned the 'two marble Rocks' from which the river Behanna (Spenser's Molanna) is said to spring. The top of Galtymore is divided into two peaks about a quarter of a mile apart, with a relatively level space between them; it is here that Judson would locate the gathering of all 'heavenly Powers, and earthly wights, / Before great Natures presence' (Judson 1933:53). The traditional associations of Galtymore in Irish folklore conflict with its historical associations in ways which Spenser found significant. While Galtymore figures prominently in native legend and epic as a traditional haunt of old Irish gods and fairies (Joyce 1878:330–1), the glen of Aherlow was a notorious resort of outlaws in Spenser's day (see Renwick in *Var Prose* p 288). In *Vewe of Ireland* (*Var Prose* pp 56–7), Irenius names Arlo as one of the fertile lowlands controlled by English landowners but taken over during the War of the Roses by 'the Irishe whom before they had banished into the mountaines.' These negative associations are presumably behind Spenser's reference to 'fowle *Arlo*' in 'Astrophel' 96. They are implicitly transferred with the name Arlo to the otherwise noble and pleasant mountain in *FQ* VII.

Spenser superimposes an intricate Ovidian significance on the native identity of Aherlow and Galtymore in his etiological account of how the mountain came to be cursed and abandoned by Diana. The story of how Diana was spied upon by the 'Foolish God' Faunus while bathing in Molanna's 'sweet streames,' and her subsequent punishment of both the woodland god and the river nymph who had been bribed to help him, combines elements from three episodes in the *Metamorphoses*: Actaeon's accidental sight of the naked Diana (3.138–252), Diana's punishment of the nymph Callisto after Jove had seduced her (2.401–507), and the river Alpheus' union with the nymph Arethusa (5.572–641). In addition, Spenser may have been influenced by Ovid's account of Faunus' discovery and ridicule when he attempted to rape Omphale (*Fasti* 2.267–358). Each of these Ovidian episodes takes place in a pastoral setting relevant to Spenser's treatment of Arlo Hill. Jove sees Callisto as she is roaming the slopes of Mount Maenalus, and the pregnant Callisto is eventually banished by Diana from a secluded pool located in this same region. More tellingly, it is in the vale of Gargaphie, located near a mountain stained with the blood of animals killed in the hunt, that Actaeon happens to see Diana bathing in her shaded grotto. Gargaphie is typical of those secluded, deceptively idyllic settings which become locations for passion, violence, and suffering in the *Metamorphoses*.

The story of Diana's curse on Arlo Hill functions simultaneously at several levels within larger patterns of meaning in the *Cantos of Mutabilitie*. Most important, it presents an ostensibly digressive and tonally contrasting minor narrative with complicated thematic and symbolic links to the main narrative of Mutabilitie's challenge to the gods (eg, Faunus' insult to Diana parodies Mutabilitie's insult to Cynthia). In this respect, Arlo's mythical identity is central to Spenser's response to, and revision of, Ovid throughout *FQ* VII (see esp R.N. Ringler 1965–6, Holahan 1976).

The minor narrative in canto vi is also an inventive mythopoeic account of an Irish landscape that mattered deeply to Spenser: the story of Molanna and her eventual marriage to Fanchin accurately describes the river Behanna as it flows down from Galtymore and joins the river Funsheon. Although Spenser may have been influenced by myths of locality in Italian Renaissance literature, he was probably also familiar with Irish geographical legends and folk tales (see Gottfried 1937, R.M. Smith 1935a). His tale of Diana's abandoning Arlo Hill and leaving it to 'Wolves and Thieves' (55) also has historical and political implications about unrest in Ireland. If Arlo Hill represents a fallen Eden, it also represents 'an Irish paradise lost' (Holahan 1976:259).

How does the implied victory of mutability on Arlo Hill at the end of canto vi relate to Nature's judgment against Mutabilitie on Arlo Hill at the end of canto vii? Arlo may instance Spenser's way of including change, contradiction, and loss within a larger providential order (see Herendeen 1981); or the tale of Arlo's decline may be a deliberately inadequate and archaic pagan perspective on issues which can be resolved only within the medievalizing Christian perspective of canto vii. Yet the irony of Spenser's setting Mutabilitie's trial in a place which undergoes striking change, along with his complicated rhetorical relation to his reader here – the ambiguous tone of '(Who knowes not *Arlo-hill*?)' in vi 36, the extravagant *occupatio* in 37 ('A speaker emphasizes something by pointedly seeming to pass over it' Lanham 1968:68) – remain enigmatic features of the *Cantos of Mutabilitie*.

WILLIAM KEACH

armor Arms and armor figure prominently throughout *The Faerie Queene*, though most is barely identified. Despite his knowledge of Elizabethan warfare, Spenser rarely attempts detailed description of historically authentic armor except that worn in tournaments: his vocabulary suggests instead the common currency of romance. Since symbolic armor was an established convention – visual and literary, classical and modern, pagan and Christian – his sparing references have a disproportionate resonance. Spenser's age witnessed a self-conscious neo-medievalism, expressed in art, architecture, public ceremony, and literature; the chivalric paraphernalia of earlier times was resurrected, but also codified and amplified, latterly much aided by the growth of a sophisticated antiquarianism led by Camden. Much of the symbolic lore concerning armor was clustered around the two principal chivalric ceremonies, the creation of a knight and (in rare cases) his degradation. The symbolism was further developed and refined in the ceremonies of the specific orders of knighthood: the Order of the Garter, for instance, had detailed meanings attached to its insignia in the Henrician revision of its statutes and register, the *Liber niger*.

Spenser was not the only Renaissance poet to use symbolic armor. Boiardo (*Orlando innamorato*), Ariosto (*Orlando furioso*), and Tasso (*Gerusalemme liberata*) drew on the Christian, medieval, and chivalric symbolism of arms and on the epic tradition. From Homer onwards, the equipment of heroes and gods had been described and allegorized. So the reader of *The Faerie Queene* on encountering Arthur's great shield made by Merlin looks back to Arthurian legends, to the shields of Atlante (*Orlando furioso*) and Aeneas (*Aeneid*), and to Achilles' divine arms made by Hephaestos (*Iliad*). The symbolic meaning of such armor came through late classical and medieval authors such as Fulgentius and Prudentius, and was expanded and elaborated in books of hieroglyphs and emblems. The armor found in contemporary literary works was accorded the same interpretative treatment in explications by Fornari and (in English) Harington of Atlante's shield in *Orlando furioso*. Through classical and medieval mythographers, Spenser and his contemporaries were also aware of the association of armor with virtue.

Among the conditions governing the presence of arms and armor in *The Faerie Queene* is Spenser's freedom to draw eclectically upon chivalric, scriptural, and literary conventions through which the equipment of his knights constituted a symbolic language. The poet could be confident that his readers would understand his references and appreciate his refinements, modifications, and conflations of their shared inheritance, most notably in the armor of God.

Although Britomart is not obviously a *miles Christi*, when she removes her armor in Castle Joyous and is subsequently wounded (*FQ* III i 58, 65), we recognize in her lack of foresight an error akin to that of Redcrosse before Orgoglio's castle (I vii 2). She too learns the lesson: later in Dolon's castle, she remains fully armed and alert (V vi 23). Similarly, the lack of virtue in knights who have surrendered to vice is portrayed in their abandonment of their armor, for example, Cymochles and Verdant (II v 28, xii 80). In Book VI, knights are divested of their armor in dubious moral situations: Aladine enjoying his love (ii 18), Calepine with Serena (iii 20), and Calidore taking off his armor on entering the pastoral life (ix 36) but later concealing it under his 'shepheards weeds' to rescue Pastorella (xi 36).

The traditional meanings associated with armor are important for an understanding of many of the arms of Spenser's characters. The description of Arthur's 'glitterand armour' seems to gather to itself the symbolism of Ephesians 6, of virtue, and of the perfect knight and hero (I vii 29–37). The plumes of his helmet suggest the rituals of antique triumphs as well as proclaiming Christian hope in the Resurrection and his quasi-sacerdotal role. Its dragon-crest appears to allude to the traditional iconography of the legendary *King* Arthur, to the heraldic Dragon of Cadwallader and thus to Wales and the Tudor dynasty, and by the same token to the descriptions of heroes in the epic tradition. Equally potent are the internal resonances: the dragon-crest anticipates 'that old Dragon' encountered by Redcrosse in canto xi. Arthur's shield possesses a wide and rich range of allusions, despite its lack of device: it differs from Atlante's magical shield in *Orlando furioso* in being composed not of carbuncle but of diamond, which is superior in hardness and according to symbolic and hieroglyphic texts suggests divine grace. It petrifies and annihilates his enemies, corresponding to the powers of Minerva's shield. As with other arms, the shield may allude to classical mythology and literature: in disarming, Britomart is compared to Minerva leaving aside her '*Gorgonian* shield' (III ix 22). That both Arthur's and Britomart's shields are related to Minerva's suggests the richness of internal correspondence between shields within the poem; similarly, the actions involving Arthur's shield in the battle with Orgoglio recall (but also significantly differ from) those involving Redcrosse's shield.

Weapons such as the spear also relate characters to literary and legendary precursors. Britomart is again connected with Minerva (identified also by her spear) in being 'term'd Knight of the Hebene speare' (IV v 8), though the use of 'Hebene' for ebony also associates her with Hebe, goddess of spring and fertility. That her spear is 'enchaunted' (III i 7) makes it a symbolic weapon like Arthur's shield. Britomart acquires her armor from trophies hanging in her father's church, and the description of the spear as by '*Bladud* made' (iii 60) links it with the king said to be a particularly wise and potent peacemaker.

Similarly, the arms said to be 'Achilles armes, which Arthegall did win' (III ii 25) link Artegall not only with Achilles but also with other classical heroes, such as Odysseus, who wins Achilles' arms from Ajax, and Mandricardo, who gains Hector's arms in *Orlando innamorato*. In Satyrane's tournament, Artegall appears in 'armour ... With woody mosse bedight, and all his steed / With oaken leaves attrapt, that seemed fit / for salvage wight,' the poem's only instance of the 'quyent disguise' of tournament armor (IV iv 39), which in the late sixteenth century had become increasingly exotic, matching in its exuberance the elaborate neo-medieval plots and characters adopted by the participants (Nashe's superb satire in *The Unfortunate Traveller* ed 1904–10, 2:271–8 exaggerates, but not by much). Here both armor and shield contribute to the image of the Salvage Knight.

Spenser takes advantage of the tradition of decorating shields with symbolic images or devices. These include the 'shield of love' won and borne by Scudamour (IV x 3), which plays on his name and relates him both to the traditions of amatory literature and to other images of Cupid within the poem. Some devices possess several different, but related, meanings: St George's red cross is symbolic both of Christ and of England, it recalls both the Crusaders and the Order of the Garter, and it may also gesture topically to Elizabethan armies in Ireland. Some devices still elude convincing interpretation, such as that on the shield of the unnamed discourteous knight: 'A Ladie on rough waves, row'd in a sommer barge' (VI ii 44).

Some weapons are individualized, such as Arthur's sword Morddure (II viii 21) and Artegall's Chrysaor (V i 9), where the naming of the weapon and explanation of its characteristics and origins adds to our understanding of its possessor's role in the poem. Sometimes Spenser requires the reader to select from a range of possible meanings the one appropriate to a particular character or situation: Cupid, Belphoebe, Maleger, and Gardante all wield bows and arrows; and while a common theme may be detected, the particular meaning depends upon our understanding of the whole character. When Trevisan flees with his head 'unarmd' (I ix 22), the absence of the helmet, which is associated with the 'hope of salvation' (1 Thess 5.8), shows that he is almost overcome by despair. During her adventures, Britomart may remove her helmet as sanctioned by medieval and mythographic traditions concerning the association of love and armor, but when she utters her complaint at the long search for her future husband (III iv 7–11), the removal of her 'lofty creast' symbolizes both love and despair.

Arms and armor possessed further meanings associated with chivalry. Turpine's unfitness as a knight is first signaled by his forsaking 'Both speare and shield' (VI iv 7), and the Salvage Man's inherent nobility is first indicated by his taking them up as he leads Calepine and Serena to safety (iv 13). The spear and shield as tokens of knighthood are also used to describe Britomart's arming and assumption of the role of a knight (III iii 60). The shield was accorded preeminent status by writers on chivalry, because 'The shelde is gyven to the knyght to sygnefye the offyce of a knyght' (Lull ed 1926:81–2). As a result it was regarded as 'the principall part of Armes' (Favyn ed 1623:13). In *The Faerie Queene*, this significance can be seen, for example, in Artegall's seizure and Talus' subsequent defacement of Braggadocchio's shield when the false knight is revealed as such (V iii 37–9; see *baffling), and in Artegall's condemnation of Burbon for surrendering improperly his 'honours stile, that is your warlike shield' (V xi 55). Unchivalric weapons such as clubs and maces tend to be wielded by figures either evil (eg, Argante, III vii 40, and Lust, IV vii 25) or for other reasons beyond the pale of civilized, knightly conduct: Talus' 'yron flale' (V i 12) has an antecedent in the club of Hercules but becomes an instrument befitting remorseless and somewhat inhuman absolute justice. MICHAEL LESLIE

Berman 1983; Favyn ed 1623; Allan H. Gilbert 1942 'Spenserian Armor' *PMLA* 57:981–7; Leslie 1983; [*Liber niger*] 1724 *The Register of the Most Noble Order of the Garter, from Its Cover in Black Velvet, Usually Called the Black Book* tr and ed John Anstis, 2 vols (London); Ramon Lull 1926 *The Book of the Ordre of Chyvalry* tr William Caxton, ed Alfred T.P. Byles, EETS os 168 (London); Strong 1977.

armor of God A biblical symbol drawn from Ephesians 6.10–17 and related texts (esp 1 Thess 5.8 and Rom 13.12, 14), and prominent in *FQ* I. As Spenser describes the origins of the Red Cross Knight's quest in the Letter to Raleigh, the hero begins as a 'clownishe young man,' but once he puts on the armor brought by Una – 'the armour of a Christian man specified by Saint Paul v. Ephes.' – he suddenly seems 'the goodliest man in al that company.' That armor, which shows the 'cruell markes of many a bloudy fielde,' displays 'a bloudie Crosse' on breastplate and shield (I i 1–2), features which suggest that *The Faerie Queene* plans to exploit the biblical significances of the Pauline armor.

Renaissance commentators note that Ephesians begins with a summary of Paul's doctrine of salvation, which insists that, according to his eternal plan, God has 'chosen us in him, before the fundacion of the worlde, that we shulde be holie' (1.4). *In him* introduces an idea central to Ephesians, to the Reformed Protestantism dominant in Spenser's England, and to *FQ* I. To achieve holiness, Christians must be incorporated by divine grace into the body of Christ. Then they may participate in his perfect righteousness and so be justified, receiving salvation by grace alone and cooperating with grace in order to achieve good works.

The insistence that these processes can occur only 'in Christ' bears implications important for *FQ* I. Existence in Christ is expressed metaphorically in numerous scriptural references to the 'putting on' of the Saviour or of garments which symbolize him (eg, Matt 22.11–13, Rom 13.14, Gal 3.27, Eph 4.22–4, Rev 7.9). 'The armor of God' is a military version of this theologically significant metaphor of clothing. As in Paul's exhortation that the faithful 'put on the new man, which after God is created in righteousnes, and true holines' (Eph 4.24), the clothing metaphor insists on both the graciously determined and the humanly willed elements in the life of holiness. Like a garment, holiness represents God's perfect righteousness, applied from without to cover man's radical imperfection. Spenser's contemporary Henry Smith declares that the phrase 'put on Christ' (Rom 13.14) signifies that he covers us like a garment to hide 'our unrighteousness with his righteousness' (1593).

As Smith also explains, however, the exhortation to 'put on the armour of light' (Rom 13.12) stresses Christ's actions to assist the elect in their active struggle to achieve sanctification or holiness of life, an endeavor in which human will cooperates with grace. Treating Ephesians 6, Calvin and others add that 'the shield of faith' (6.16) defends Christians from diabolic assault on actual, not imputed, holiness, while 'the sworde of the Spirit, which is the worde of God' (6.17), allows them to slay the enemy (ed 1948:339). Moreover, because 'the armor of God' refers primarily to the grace which sanctifies, Reformed theologians may (without contradicting their belief that saving grace can be neither resisted nor lost) complain of man's failure to employ his armor properly. Commenting on Ephesians 6.11, 'Put on the whole armour,' Calvin remarks that men are all careless in using the graces God offers. We are commonly, he says, like soldiers who are about to meet the enemy yet foolishly remove their armor (ed 1948:339; cf *FQ* I vii 2–15).

These theological contexts suggest that Redcrosse's armor may represent or call attention to the mystical incorporation in – or putting on – of Christ which effects and signifies justification; the contrast between God's purity and power and man's total corruption and impotence; the cooperation in which human will abets yet resists the effects of sanctifying grace; and related operations of grace – afflictions, solicitations, impulsions, and even apparent absences – that oblige the elect to recognize their need for divine aid or that induce or empower them to cooperate, by means of a renewed if frail and mutable will, in their sanctification.

Redcrosse's sudden transformation, recorded in the Letter, suggests his justification, his calling to the service of God, and the imputed goodness that calling entails. His investment in the armor depicted at I i 1–2 likewise indicates his justification. His subsequent adventures therefore explore the experience of one who is numbered among the elect, to whom righteousness is imputed, and who must labor to achieve the actual holiness that results from sanctification. Within a few stanzas, his conflict with Error highlights the contrast between divine strength and human impotence, for the armor, not the knight's virtue, allows him to view the enemy plainly (i 14, contrast 12). Although he defeats Error through grace ('more then manly force' 24), 'force,' not faith, predominates in his mind (19.6–7, 24.1–5; contrast 19.3). Then Una declares, 'Well worthy be you of that Armorie, / Wherein ye have great glory wonne this day' (27). These ironic contradictions help to define holiness: the pure operations of grace are corrupted by the channel, the human will, through which they work. This implication persists even in the final battle in canto xi, where Redcrosse's repeated 'falls' carry their usual theological or moral implication: to fall before this Satanic dragon is to fall into sin. Again the knight displays his old penchant for despair and again desires to remove his armor (26–8). As with all sins of the elect, providential ordinance, experienced sometimes as fortune or chance, renders these lapses profitable (29, 45).

These moments show too that the armor sometimes inflicts torment: 'That erst him goodly arm'd, now most of all him harm'd' (27). Later, the shield does not protect Redcrosse from the Dragon's sting: 'The mortall sting his angry needle shot / Quite through his shield, and in his shoulder seasd' (38). Such details become explicable when the reader recognizes that the life of faith includes suffering and sinfulness as parts of purification and strengthening. As the Geneva commentators remark, one operation of faith is to effect 'a wounding of the heart' (gloss to Ps 51.17). This can sometimes work through the agency of Despair, whose accusing 'speach ... as a swords point through [Redcrosse's] hart did perse' (ix 48), and so functions like the 'worde of God ... sharper then anie two edged sworde ... a discerner of the thoghtes and the intentes of the heart' (Heb 4.12).

These negative functions of the armor suggest the severity that grace imposes in a regimen finally beneficent, one in which Redcrosse's weapons, rather than the knight himself, gain ultimate victory (xi 53). The overall emphasis of the armor of God in *The Faerie Queene* is therefore powerfully optimistic; the armor manifests joyous triumph over the forces of darkness and chaos. This theme appears with special buoyancy when Arthur first enters the poem, his divine armor shining 'farre away, / Like glauncing light of *Phoebus* brightest ray' (vii 29–36). (See also *armor, *nature and grace, *predestination, *Reformation.)

DARRYL J. GLESS

John Calvin 1948 *Commentaries on the Epistles of Paul to the Galatians and Ephesians* tr William Pringle (Grand Rapids, Mich); Richard Greenham 1612 *Works* (London; rpt Amsterdam and New York 1973) fols Dd5v-Ee3r; Latimer ed 1844–5, 1:26; Henry Smith ed 1593.

Cullen 1974:21; Hankins 1971:109; Leslie 1983:104–17, 128–31; Upton in *Var* 1:176.

Artegall The name of Artegall (usually spelled Arthegall in the 1590 *FQ*), knight of Justice and hero of *FQ* V, may be construed as '[thou] art equal' (Fr *égal* fair, equitable, just, impartial), and as 'equal [to] Arthur' (who is in fact identified as Artegall's maternal half-brother, III iii 27). Artegall is also related to Britomart as her prophesied spouse (26) and by the syllabification of their names (Britomartegall), a coincidence implying both concord in their eventual union and androgynous potential within each individually: Britomart in armor brandishing a phallic lance, Artegall 'in womanishe attire' 'twisting linnen twyne' (V v 22, vii 37). Variously theirs is a potential for balance and synthesis or for imbalance and antithesis.

As Arthur's destined mate, the Fairy Queen, first appears to him in a dream, so Britomart's appears first to her in a vision. In III ii 24–5, Britomart falls in love with a perfected image of Artegall, an ideal that he approaches but never fully achieves in the poem. This image features centrally the inscription 'Achilles armes, which Arthegall did win.' Like most things that bear on his figure, this syntactically ambiguous description (Artegall as possessor of arms or as possessed by them) resonates with ambivalence. It recalls at once Achilles' prowess and epic heroism but also his vulnerability, effeminacy, and wrath. Since Achilles' armor was awarded to brainy Odysseus rather than to brawny Ajax, the inscription hints further at the interior content of justice – for 'in the mind the doome of right must bee' (V ii 47) – and at the danger, in applying justice, of a strain between interior judgment and physical force, with the result that might is right. In addition to the ascription of Artegall's arms to Achilles, his heraldic device is an ermine, both a symbol of chastity (and as such, an icon used by Queen Elizabeth and applicable to Britomart here) and an animal associated with Hercules, a justicer like Artegall and like him associated with the powers and weaknesses of Achilles (Dunseath 1968:48–59, Aptekar 1969:153–71).

After Britomart's vision, Artegall first appears in IV iv 39, on the third day of Satyrane's tournament, disguised in woody moss and oak leaves and bearing on his shield the motto *Salvagesse sans finesse* (wildness, savagery, or incivility without refinement, sensitivity, or art). Here, unrecognizable as either Artegall or knight of Justice, he hews and slashes with his sword, the 'instrument of wrath.' 'No lesse then death it selfe,' he overbears others and 'tyrannize[s]' in 'his bloodie game,' until 'in middest of his pryde' he is struck by Britomart's spear and slides, in comic relief, 'Over his horses taile' to the ground, 'Whence litle lust he had to rise againe' (41–4). With the effect of the spear compared to a cooling and recomforting shower of rain (crudely put, a well-timed bucket of cold water), his encounter with it suggests the meeting of Typhonic passion with Diana's formidable yet fertile purity. More complexly, this encounter symbolizes the meeting of male force and form with female force and form – of two sets of terms, rather than of two terms simply, as is the case on other occasions of disguise by the principal couple (and principle of coupling) in *The Faerie Queene*.

Artegall, assuming that his defeat has deprived him of the false Florimell, leaves the tournament in foul temper, allies himself with Scudamour, and plots vengeance on the unwitting Britomart. Finding and attacking her, he soon again finds himself on the ground at the end of her enchanted spear; but this time, like the hound on the undisguised Artegall's helmet (III ii 25), he thrusts at her from below – as if 'an eger hound' were thrusting 'to an Hynd within some covert glade' – delivers 'her horses hinder parts' a deadly wound, and thus compels her to battle foot-to-foot with him (IV vi 12–13). The erotic nature of this second encounter in the flesh is even more obvious and violent than the first.

But the eventual outcome of the second is reconciliation or loving 'accord' – heartfelt harmony, to gloss Spenser's own word etymologically and phonologically (41). When in the course of conflict Artegall suddenly views Britomart's face, her 'divine' beauty first numbs his cruel and vengeful purpose and then evokes his wonder and reverence (21–2). She responds similarly to the sight of his face: her hand falls down, refusing longer to wield her 'wrathfull weapon' against him (27). Their mutual responses testify to the loveliness of beauty and to the power of love. Through this power, the 'salvage knight' assumes his actual name and implicitly his destined identity (28, 31). While this identity promises marriage with Britomart and royal descendants, it impels him first to Book V and the quest of justice. *FQ* IV thus suggests that Artegall's accord with Britomart enables his quest, yet *FQ* V begins as if Britomart had never existed. That his love does not accompany him and is absent even as a memory during the first third of Book V casts in a glaring light the special nature of justice and the oddities of Artegall's figure in its early cantos.

Justice, defined as a social rather than a private virtue, is distinguished by the objectivity, exteriority, and impersonality of its concerns. In theory, it deals with things external to the Justicer and to those to whom he ministers justice; it is no respecter of persons. Whether in classical or Christian theory, the Justicer himself is seen as an animation or personification of justice – as an embodied abstraction rather than as a self. By the nature of justice, then, the absence of Britomart from Artegall's quest makes sense: his personal concerns are, properly speaking, irrelevant to it (Anderson 1970c).

But Spenser's portrayal of Artegall in V i-ii strongly suggests that such theoretical irrelevance translates in practice and in human actuality into oversimplification, insensitivity, and simple inhumanity. Framed by quixotic fanfare (V i 1–2, 30, ii 1), Artegall's first exploit imitates the Old Testament judgment of Solomon but in doing so leaves unresolved what to do with the dead lady's head and her murderer. Resourcefully, Artegall determines that the murderer's penalty should be to bear with him his victim's head. As the comparison of the murderer to a 'rated Spaniell' suggests, Artegall's justice is appropriate to a barnyard, where wayward farm dogs are similarly disciplined; yet, 'Much did that Squire Sir *Artegall* adore, / For his great justice': Spenser's tone is decidedly parodic (i 29–30).

Artegall's second exploit, the dismemberment of Lady Munera, and his third, the leveling of the leveling Giant with the scales, indicate still more brutally the reductive inhumanity of his justice. At the same time and increasingly, he responds to the objects of his justice as if he were two beings. While intending the slaughter of Munera, he pities her; later, he disputes rationally and at length with the Giant before Talus summarily settles the matter by shoving the Giant over a cliff. Artegall's dual responses suggest a growing strain between romance knight and virtuous abstraction, between the private man and the animation of justice, between Artegall's personal nature and needs and those of his exteriorized and impersonal ideal. The Justicer's disguising himself in order to participate in the romance world of Marinell's spousals further dramatizes the strain between the two sides of his identity in Book V.

This strain reaches a crisis in canto v, where Artegall battles with the Amazon Radigund, who subdues men, dresses them like women, and compels them shamefully to spin. Artegall first overcomes her, but as he stoops to behead her he discovers in her face the 'miracle of natures goodly grace'; suddenly he perceives 'his senses straunge astonishment' (12), as he earlier did in his battle with Britomart. Caught all too humanly between unacceptable alternatives – insensitive cruelty, the vice corresponding to justice, and vain pity, the vice corresponding to mercy (13) – he willfully and wrongly abandons his sword, the symbol of his justice, and surrenders to her. The differences between this surrender, with its consequences, and his earlier experience with Britomart are instructive. Where earlier his senses overrode his intention and his hand dropped the 'cruell sword' of its own accord, here he makes a sudden, rash decision to fling away his sword. Where earlier Britomart's response accorded with his generosity, here Radigund swoops down on him like a bird of prey, exulting in her unearned victory and imprisoning him.

Had Artegall beheaded the beautiful Radigund, his act would have appeared maliciously cruel – personal, hence far more vicious than the extermination of Lady Munera. (Talus, not Artegall, executes justice on Munera; and Radigund conspicuously lacks the ambiguously dehumanizing details of Munera's golden hands and silver feet, of her metal or bejeweled extremities, which recall those of Langland's Lady Meed.) Yet Artegall's surrender to Radigund is hardly right, either. At this point in the poem, however, although Spenser offers insistently ironic reflections on Artegall's 'goodwill' (V 17), he offers no dramatically meaningful alternative to the 'wilfull' choice Artegall makes. Nor does history. Artegall falls here because after five cantos of dispensing impersonal justice he acts like a private and sentient human being. His choice has much in common with that of Milton's Adam.

Not surprisingly, the first references to Artegall's 'true love' (V 57; cf 38, 56) – referring both to his fidelity or 'trouthe' and to Britomart, his beloved – occur soon after this fall into a recognizably human context; and love is in time the principle that comes to his rescue. Trapped in Radigund's Radegone, the state of an exclusively self-centered woman, Artegall, fallen but paradoxically faithful, images fallen man waiting for mercy, itself an expression of love. Paradoxically too, the state into which he falls, though an unhealthy extreme, operates as a curative balance to the equally extreme impersonality and exteriority of his actions in the opening two cantos of Book v. Only in falling does he find enough awareness of self to remember Britomart, or enough interiority to be mindful of love. His female dress suggests not only his humiliation but also his acquisition of 'the softer qualities' proper to a courteous knight or to 'a civilized and well-balanced person' (K. Williams 1966:134). His rescue by Britomart suggests, moreover, the internalized transformation of justice through love – that is, the charging of justice with a significance that is fuller, deeper, and more specifically Christian.

On release from Radegone, however, Artegall separates again from Britomart and accompanied only by Talus returns to his quest for justice, which remains a social virtue committed to an exterior world. His challenge is now to realize his internally enriched virtue in a world distinct from the private and privileged concerns of the self. The Justicer himself might have improved as a human being; but the need to channel this change into Tudor history or, in the poet's case, into an objectively (hence, a justly) historical narrative collides with the intractable facts of history itself (cf O'Connell 1977:149–56).

Leaving Radegone, Artegall first encounters then allies himself with Arthur, now his equal; together they move into a landscape increasingly saturated with references to contemporary history. These include the execution of Mary, Queen of Scots (Duessa), Henri de Navarre's apostasy to gain the French throne (Burbon and Flourdelis), and the plights of the Netherlands (Belge and her seventeen sons) and Ireland (Irena's island). In reality this is a landscape of moral compromises, disappointments, and failures at least as much as one of absolute truths and achieved ideals. At the end of *FQ* v, the only sounds Artegall hears will come from Envy, Detraction, and the Blatant Beast.

For a single reason – Artegall's alliance with Arthur – his fortunes on leaving Radegone are better, but only for two cantos. The formation of this alliance in v viii and its subsequent *modus operandi* suggest why. At first and from the outside, Arthur mistakes Artegall for the pagan he has been pursuing, rectifying his misjudgment only when the Lady Samient (sameness, togetherness) intervenes to stop their fighting and each raises his ventail and exposes to view the face beneath the helmet and thus the person within the armor. Motivated by affection in this recognition scene, Artegall gives himself – more emphatically, his 'selfe' – to Arthur, best and most Christian of princes; and Arthur, apologizing that he mistook 'the living for the ded' – the redeemed for the lost – enters into an 'accordaunce,' or accord, with Artegall, each swearing faith to the other and 'either others cause to maintaine mutually' (viii 12–14). This whole encounter could hardly be designed more clearly to testify to the internalized and transformed value of Artegall's virtue after Radegone or, more specifically, to introduce his cooperation with Arthur in subsequent cantos (Anderson 1976:167–73).

So long as they remain together, the quest for justice they share runs smoothly. Together they overcome the Souldan, a powerful and ungodly tyrant, and Adicia, the principle of injustice the Souldan has wed; then they outmaneuver Malengin, a diabolically rapacious thief and the principle of Guile itself. Finally, during the trial of Duessa, they stand like the two scales of a balance on either side of Mercilla, Arthur feeling compassion for Duessa's 'dreadfull fate' and Artegall bent against her 'with constant firme intent, / For zeale of Justice' (ix 37, 46, 49). Variously but consistently, their actions complement and complete one another. Because Arthur responds with 'ruth' to Duessa, Artegall does not need to. In contrast to his earlier encounters with Munera and Radigund, Artegall is spared a contradiction between passion and abstraction or love and justice.

When Arthur and Artegall separate, however, contradiction closes in upon him with a vengeance. Finding Burbon and Flourdelis besieged by an unruly mob, Artegall swings abruptly back and forth between the responses of a courteous knight and those of an unyielding Justicer. Alternately he sees Burbon's shield as an instrument of war and as a defining moral and religious emblem, and alternately he regards Burbon himself as a fellow knight beset and as a reprehensible apostate (xi 44–57). There is no uncompromising way either to assist Burbon and Flourdelis or to abandon them. He is now caught between the conflicting demands of virtue and history.

Having made the more generous choice of aiding Burbon and thereby through further delay having further endangered Irena, Artegall resumes his primary mission barely in time to stay her execution. But once in her land, he overcomes her oppressor Grantorto (illegal possession on a grand scale), thus freeing her, and then turns his attention to a thorough, radical reform of her rebellious country. In the midst of this reform, however, he is recalled 'To Faerie Court,' and on his way there reviled by Envy, Detraction, and the Beast: 'And still among most bitter wordes they spake, / Most shamefull, most unrighteous, most untrew' (xii 27, 42). It is fitting that the last bitter words addressed to Artegall should be syntactically ambiguous, the second line here representing either the very words spoken or the poet's indignant judgment on them. In his fate at the end of Book v, Artegall is like – in fact, equal to – Arthur, Lord Grey de Wilton, to whom Spenser was secretary in Ireland and to whom Artegall's figure in v xii alludes. In bleak and deliberate contrast to the idealized reading of history afforded Arthur in Belge's land (x-xi), Artegall's ending, like Grey's, testifies loudly and personally to the frustration, disillusionment, and injustice of an objective and exterior world.

JUDITH H. ANDERSON

Anderson 1970c; Anderson 1976; Aptekar 1969; Dunseath 1968; O'Connell 1977; K. Williams 1966.

Arthur, legend of The figure of Arthur – Spenser's 'image of a brave knight, perfected in the twelve private morall vertues' and his proposed hero, both public and private, of *The Faerie Queene* – elicited a complex cultural and literary response from Elizabethan readers. For them, Prince Arthur was not only Spenser's representation of moral and theological concepts but also the ancient British 'Arthure, before he was king,' a figure highly esteemed for centuries. Thus it is important to consider the external political and literary values involved in Spenser's decision to use an ancient British hero whose history was long and complex.

Arthur was primarily an historical figure, the greatest of the British monarchs. Although his career had been extravagantly embellished by enthusiastic chroniclers and writers of romances, it was firmly established in the early histories of the nation and had been elaborately reworked in both literary and political mythology. These histories began with Nennius' *Historia Brittonum* (c 800) in which Arthur, a sixth-century *dux bellorum*, successfully led the British (Celts) against the encroaching Anglo-Saxons in twelve battles. According to the *Annales Cambriae* (c 950), his career ended in 537 when he was killed at the Battle of Camlann.

By the high Middle Ages, this tradition was well established and had been embellished with folktale and myth. The reputable historian William of Malmesbury, in his *Gesta regum anglorum* (1125), accepted an historical Arthur, one proclaimed in true histories although his tomb could not be found. While acknowledging that 'ancient dirges still fable his coming,' William was careful to separate fact from the fables that had accumulated around Arthur, especially stories of his expected return in order to revive the fortunes of his people.

Few glimpses remain, however, of this folklore Arthur. In one early story, *The Spoils of Annwfn* (c 900, collected c 1275), Arthur rides to the Celtic Otherworld in his ship Prydwen and returns with a magic cauldron (apparently a cornucopian precursor of the Grail). In another, *Culhwch and Olwen* (about 1100, included in the *Mabinogion*), he has acquired a court and has conquered lands beyond Britain; he has a resident magician, famous weapons all with names, a queen named Gwenhwyvar, a nephew Gwalchmei (Gawain), and the loyal retainers Bedwyr (Bedivere) and Kei (Kay).

By about 1139, Geoffrey of Monmouth had completed his *Historia regum Britanniae*, an account of the history of the Britons on which many later histories are based. Arthur figures as a glorious British monarch and, at the height of his career, Emperor of the West. According to Geoffrey, he was conceived when his father Uther Pendragon, with the aid of Merlin's magic, tricked his mother Igerne ('the Lady Igrayne' in the Letter to Raleigh) by taking the form of her husband. Raised in secrecy away from his father's court, Arthur succeeded to Uther's throne at the age of fifteen; he then subdued the Saxons, expanded his control over Scotland, Ireland, Iceland, Gothland, and the Orkneys, and established peace for a period of twelve years. When Roman ambassadors arrived demanding tribute, he rejected them and set sail for Europe to confront the Roman forces, leaving his nephew Mordred as vicegerent. Having conquered them, Arthur was about to cross the Alps when word arrived that Mordred had usurped the throne. The king returned to Britain and finally killed his nephew in Cornwall; but during this final battle he was seriously wounded, whereupon he was taken to the Isle of Avalon to be healed.

Later historians such as the Norman poet Wace (*Roman de Brut* 1155) and his English translator and adaptor, Layamon (*Brut* c 1200), accepted Geoffrey's history though other historians were skeptical. Reputable clerics such as William of Newburgh in his *Historia rerum anglicarum* (c 1196–8) condemned Geoffrey for passing off fabulous tales as history, for pretending that the ravings of an unknown magician (Merlin) were actually prophecy, and for writing in Latin to make everything look honest.

In Geoffrey's hands, however, Arthur is both an 'historical' imperialist and a potential hero of romance. He fights giants, distinguishes himself in single combat, and dispenses aid and honor from his court – a fusion of 'history' and romance that became fertile ground for the development of Arthurian legend in the Middle Ages.

Late in the twelfth century, Chrétien de Troyes produced five Arthurian romances. Influenced chiefly by Geoffrey and Chrétien, later writers created an intricate Arthurian empire, filled with chivalry, courtly love, and the remnants of primitive myth, in which Arthur's knights undertake numerous quests to defeat those hostile to the Round Table and its values. While for Chrétien Arthur is at times a figure of some scorn (*Erec et Enide*, *Lancelot*), in later romances such as the *Didot Perceval* (c 1200) he is portrayed as an established king of renown and the paragon of chivalry, from whose court individual knights emerge on adventures, the most important of which is the quest for the Grail. This mysterious vessel, first described by Chrétien in *Perceval*, rapidly became identified (following Celtic myths) as the chalice of the Last Supper, guarded by a Grail King who traced his descent from Joseph of Arimathea.

In this continental tradition, Arthur had varying degrees of political significance; hence the geography of these romances, much like Spenser's Fairyland, tends to be ambiguous, with the action placed in a dreamlike landscape in which moral, spiritual, and cultural questions can be explored and, at times, resolved. In some romances, like Wolfram von Eschenbach's *Parzival* (c 1205), the quest for the Grail spiritualizes the Arthurian world; in others, like the Vulgate *La Queste del saint graal* (c 1215–35), the Grail calls into question the values of the Round Table as its Arthurian knights are forced to confront the secular codes by which they live, and often to reject them if they are to achieve salvation.

Malory's *Morte Darthur* (pub 1485), the version of Arthurian romance most readily available to Spenser's readers, can be (and was) read either as endorsing or as condemning the Arthurian world. It is often considered a nostalgic romance of peace written during the Wars of the Roses, depicting the evolution of moral, social, and eventually spiritual order (symbolized by the Round Table) in a politically chaotic world. Yet it may be argued that the romance reveals a world controlled by a revenge code based on an inordinate sense of personal honor, a world that collapses because of an act of incest committed by Arthur himself, an adulterous affair between his Queen Guinevere and Lancelot, and the helplessness of the knights in the face of sin and guilt. In its later episodes, as in the Vulgate *Queste*, the quest for the Grail confronts certain knights, particularly Lancelot and his son Galahad, with the need to reject secular values and engage in spiritual battle against sin.

Sixteenth-century readers disagreed about the value of Arthurian romances like Malory's. Ascham denounced them in his *Scholemaster* (1570) as tales of 'open mans slaughter, and bold bawdrye' (ed 1904:231). Erasmus thought them nonsense. Nashe considered them 'fantasticall dreames of those exiled Abbie-lubbers' (ed 1904–10, 1:11). Even E.K., in his gloss to *SC, Aprill* 120, attacked 'certain fine fablers and lowd lyers, such as were the Authors of King Arthure the great and such like.' By contrast, in his epilogue to *The Book of the Ordre of Chyvalry* (1484?), Caxton laments, 'O ye knyghtes of Englond where is the custome and usage of noble chyvalry that was used in the dayes [of King Arthur] ... Ther shalle ye see manhode curtosye and gentylnesse' (ed 1928:82–3). Sidney maintains that 'honest King Arthur will never displease a soldier' (*Defence of Poetry* ed 1973b:105–6). Yet, however variously interpreted, Malory's romance and others continued to be read. Although it would seem arguable that the Matter of Britain should have run its course in England by the sixteenth century, and that the Reformation must have raised antagonism to the old Roman religion of the romances, there were five editions of the *Morte Darthur* between 1485 and the end of the sixteenth century when Spenser chose Arthur as hero of his own romance.

The sixteenth century produced considerable debate about the historical Arthur as well. In his preface to Malory, Caxton summons up an impressive list of 'Arthuriana' to rebut disbelievers, including Arthur's sepulchre at Glastonbury (where the monks claimed to have discovered his bones in 1191), a royal wax seal at Westminster Abbey, Gawain's skull at Dover, and the Round Table at Winchester Castle, where it is still found today. Chroniclers and antiquarians traveled the country to examine the evidence. Some, like John Rastell, were skeptical; others, like John Leland, were impressed. The latter journeyed to Glastonbury to handle the lead cross, inscribed 'Hic jacet sepultus inclitus rex Arturius in insula Avalonia' ('Here lies buried the renowned King Arthur in the Isle of Avalon'), claimed to have been found with Arthur's bones. Camden offered an engraving of the cross in the 1607 edition of his *Britannia* (p 166).

Yet some Elizabethans believed, and some believe today, that Arthur's bones still rested at Glastonbury, or were irretrievably lost at its dissolution in 1539. Not only Avalon but Camelot itself had been identified, again by Leland. Having traveled to Cadbury Hill just south of Glastonbury, he wrote, 'At the very south ende of the church of South-Cadbyri standith Camallate, sumtyme a famose toun or castelle, apon a very torre or hille ... The people can telle nothing ther but that they have hard say that Arture much resortid to Camalat' (ed 1907–10, 1:151).

The debate over the historical Arthur had been initiated by Henry VII's Italian-born historian, Polydore Vergil, who directly questioned the existence of Arthur and the Round Table (*Anglica historia*). In response, Leland's influential *Assertio inclytissimi Arturii regis Britanniae* (1544, tr 1582) was followed by works by such Welsh writers or writers on Wales as Arthur Kelton (1546, 1547), Sir John Price (1573), and Thomas Churchyard (1587). Richard Harvey, brother of Gabriel Harvey, also wrote on the subject in 1593.

The major English chroniclers of the fifteenth and sixteenth centuries, such as Hardyng, Grafton, Fabyan, and Holinshed, were more cautious in using familiar Arthurian material from Geoffrey of Monmouth. They record Arthur's battles against the Saxons, the names of his weapons, and Geoffrey's vision of a king who unites Britain under a monarchy. They allow him some glory on the continent, record his final battle with Mordred, and accept in detail the discovery of his bones at Glastonbury. This historical conservatism continued into the next century in writers such as the historian John Speed and the poet William Warner.

Yet the Arthur of history and romance was much less important in the sixteenth century than the political Arthur. Geoffrey's *Historia* had included a set of cryptic prophecies by Merlin, predicting a time when British (ie, Welsh and Cornish) fortunes, which had collapsed after the Saxon invasions, would once again arise, led by Arthur, the once and future king (*rex quondam rexque futurus*) who would bring peace to the land.

Such prophecies were considered, especially in Wales, to be fulfilled when the Welsh Henry Tudor gained the throne in 1485. Henry made astute political use of the myth as part of a conscious and continued effort to consolidate his authority: he not only sponsored genealogists to establish his claim to Arthurian descent through his grandfather, Owen Tudor, but also chose the name Arthur for his first son, who was born at Winchester and later proclaimed the first Prince of Wales (see Anglo 1961–2 for a different view of Henry VII's Arthurian propaganda).

Arthur Tudor died, however, shortly after his marriage to Katherine of Aragon in 1501. His brother succeeded as Henry VIII and, inspired by his father, had the Round Table (already painted in the Tudor colors, white and green) repaired in 1517. As Arthur *redivivus*, Henry consciously played out the romance role of Arthur's illustrious descendant. By the 1530s, however, his notion of British empire had come to involve more than self-flattery. As he escalated his struggle with Rome over an annulment of his marriage to his dead brother's wife, he threatened to move England toward ecclesiastical independence, for which he needed historical justification.

This he found in the ancient British monarchy, alluded to in the prologue of the Act in Restraint of Appeals (1533) which began, 'Where by divers sundry old authentic histories and chronicles it is manifestly declared and expressed that this realm of England is an empire, and so hath been accepted in the world' (Elton 1982:353). The *Anglica historia* was finally published in 1534 when Henry VIII apparently decided that Polydore Vergil's willingness to endorse Henry's imperial position was more important than his reluctance to follow Tudor desires in endorsing the more fanciful Arthurian legends. Polydore confirmed that the imperial crown was the inheritance of all British monarchs from the time of Constantine the Great, so that, although he discredited Arthur's fabulous empire, he saw Arthur and Henry as the inheritors of a British empire already in existence.

After the Act in Restraint of Appeals, the term 'Imperial Crown' became customary in sixteenth-century government documents. Even Mary retained the title of Empress when she relinquished the title of Supreme Head of the Church; and Elizabeth's Act of Supremacy of 1559 affirmed that her crown was the 'Imperial Crown' once again. By the time of John Dee, Elizabeth's astrologer, the attractiveness of the theory of British empire lay not in its patriotic justification of a precarious throne or of the separation of the British church from the papacy but in its confirmation of England's right to the New World. Dee argued in *General and Rare Memorials Pertayning to the Perfect Arte of Navigation* (1577) that Britain possessed a colonial empire because of Arthurian conquests, using materials from Geoffrey to give Elizabeth title to much of Europe and even the New World. (The *OED*, in fact, credits Dee with having been the first to use the phrase 'Britysh Empire.')

Few patriotic English writers were prepared to question any aspect of British Arthurianism. To be sure, in the fifteenth century Lydgate included Arthur in his *Fall of Princes*, but he carefully ascribes the collapse of Arthur's power not to pride but to Mordred's treason. More daring is *The Misfortunes of Arthur* (1587), a Senecan revenge tragedy performed before the Queen, in which Thomas Hughes presents Arthur as destroyed by fortune because of his ambition and incest. Richard Lloyd, in *A Briefe Discourse of ... the Nine Worthies* (1584), has Arthur summarize his career and then condemn himself for incest with his married sister; Mordred is shown as the agent of divine retribution in murdering him.

For readers of *The Faerie Queene*, Arthur was already a complex figure. In spite of Ascham's denunciation, Arthurian romances remained popular throughout the sixteenth century. Moreover, Arthur was a favorite figure in public spectacles and popular mythology: he appeared in pageants, and a society of archers was named after him (see Millican 1932). It was left to Spenser, while echoing all these aspects of sixteenth-century Arthurianism, to recreate Arthurian romance as a vehicle of spiritual and ethical instruction, one which would embody his age's concerns, aspirations, beliefs, and vision of its own perfected self.

Hugh MacLachlan

William Caxton 1928 *The Prologues and Epilogues* ed W.J.B. Crotch, EETS os 176 (London); Elton 1982; Leland ed 1907–10.

Sydney Anglo 1961–2 'The *British History* in Early Tudor Propaganda' *BJRL* 44:17–48; Anglo 1969; Geoffrey Ashe, et al, eds 1968 *The Quest for Arthur's Britain* (London); Richard W. Barber 1986 *King Arthur: Hero and Legend* (Woodbridge, Suffolk; first pub 1961 as *Arthur of Albion*); Diane Bornstein 1976 'William Caxton's Chivalric Romances and the Burgundian Renaissance in England' *ES* 57:1–10; James P. Carley 1984 'Polydore Vergil and John Leland on King Arthur: The Battle of the Books' *Interpretations* (Memphis) 15.2:86–100; Richard Cavendish 1978 *King Arthur and the Grail: The Arthurian Legends and Their Meaning* (London); E.K. Chambers 1927 *Arthur of Britain* (London); John Darrah 1981 *The Real Camelot: Paganism and the Arthurian Romances* (London); Christopher Dean 1987 *Arthur of England: English Attitudes to King Arthur and the Knights of the Round Table in the Middle Ages and the Renaissance* (Toronto); Robert Huntington Fletcher 1966 *The Arthurian Material in the Chronicles, Especially Those of Great Britain and France* 2nd ed, expanded by a bibliography and critical essay for the period 1905–65 by Roger Sherman Loomis (New York); Greenlaw 1932; Denys Hay 1952 *Polydore Vergil: Renaissance Historian and Man of Letters* (Oxford); Stephen Knight 1983 *Arthurian Literature and Society* (London); Norris J. Lacy, ed 1986 *The Arthurian Encyclopedia* (New York); Loomis 1959; Loomis 1963; Merriman 1973; Millican 1932; Rosemary Morris 1982 *The Character of King Arthur in Medieval Literature* (Cambridge); D.D.R. Owen 1983 'Arthurian Legend' in *European Writers: The Middle Ages and the Renaissance* ed William T.H. Jackson and George Stade (New York) 1:137–60; Reiss, et al (forthcoming); R.F. Treharne 1967 *The Glastonbury Legends: Joseph of Arimathea, the Holy Grail and King Arthur* (London); Jessie L. Weston 1920 *From Ritual to Romance* (Cambridge).

Arthur, legend of, since Spenser Despite its relatively slight use of traditional Arthurian lore, *The Faerie Queene* may be regarded as scarcely less important than Malory's *Morte Darthur* in transmitting the figure of Arthur to later English writers. It was Spenser's work that kept Arthur before poets and readers between 1634 and 1816, a time when Malory was unprinted and little known. Perhaps more important, Spenser by enhancing the image of Arthur provided later writers with an idealized hero unrelated to the dissolution of civilization represented by Malory, a character totally unlike the bold but morally flawed and frequently unwise king of medieval verse and prose romances. Spenser created a figure that, while recalling the old nationalistic spirit and mythic appeal of the early pseudo-histories and oral legends, accrued new political, moral, and religious dimensions.

Although most post-medieval English writers have drawn on stories found in Malory but ignored by Spenser – the formation of the Round Table, Guinevere and Lancelot's illicit love, Mordred's rebellion – their depiction of Arthur has borne the imprint of Spenser's noble prince. This kingly ideal continues to be a potent, though increasingly humanized, force for good in a world where moral evil, whether represented as a dragon or a malignant political ideology, must be opposed.

Spenser's radical revision of Arthur and his combination of romance with epic expanded the already wide range of tones and themes of medieval Arthurian works, helping to engender remarkably varied new treatments of the legend from the seventeenth century to the present. Ranging from episodic romance to tightly unified novel, from sentimentalism to satire, from allegory and mysticism to realism and surrealism, Arthurian literature in its abundance (more than 400 works written since 1800) and diversity represents perhaps the most vibrant and variegated legend found in English letters.

Few of Spenser's contemporaries or immediate successors followed his lead in featuring Arthur as a significant and noble character. Two romances, Christopher Middleton's *Chinon of England* (1597) and Richard Johnson's *Tom a Lincolne* (c 1599–1607) imitate the medieval pattern of making Arthur's court the center of chivalry from which quests originate. Neither writer emulates Spenser's practice of introducing an idealized Arthur at strategic moments to assist the lesser heroes and exemplify virtues they are striving to attain. Although in both works the eponymous hero meets a fairy monarch, neither the Fairy King who tests Chinon nor the Fairy Queen who bears Tom a Lincolne's son derives anything from Spenser's Gloriana.

Ralph Knevet's seventeenth-century imitation and continuation of *The Faerie*

Queene employs Spenser's concept of Arthur as a model and a unifying device (see also Renaissance *imitations and adaptations). The preface announces that Knevet's *Supplement of the Faery Queene* (c 1633) will fulfill Spenser's intention, expressed in the Letter to Raleigh, of illustrating 'the other part of polliticke vertues' in the person of Arthur, 'after that hee came to be king.' As in *The Faerie Queene*, each of Knevet's books, written in Spenserian stanzas and numbered 7 through 9, features a knight of Gloriana's court who embodies a separate virtue, whereas Arthur, linking the three books, epitomizes all the virtues perfectly achieved and combined. Arthur in Book 7 knights the hero, later rescues him, and vanquishes a giant. In Book 8, he fights a tournament to save a damsel who has petitioned Gloriana for help. Book 9 relates the story of his court. These incidents, like Spenser's Arthurian episodes, while having no specific parallel or source in Arthurian tradition, derive from a fund of familiar romance materials.

The Arthurian strain is less pronounced in another seventeenth-century continuation of *The Faerie Queene*, Samuel Sheppard's *The Faerie King* (c 1650). The work imitates Spenser's manner by depicting allegorically the principal political events of the present, with the intention of glorifying Charles I. The fact that Arthur never actually appears in the work, though his sword is mentioned, suggests how poorly Sheppard grasped Spenser's use of Arthur as a structuring device and thematic tool, and also how substantially literary interest in the king was waning.

The associations with the Tudor monarchy, which Spenser had stressed, recommended Arthurian legend to partisans of the Stuart dynasty. Conversely, seventeenth-century supporters of Parliament and Protestant reform dismissed it as mere fiction, tracing the origins of English government not through Arthur to Brutus, but through the laws of Arthur's Saxon enemies. Partly because of these political implications, three major poets of the century abandoned their plans to write epics on the Matter of Britain. Although Jonson projected an Arthurian work, he rejected both Spenser's stanza form and 'matter' (see 'Conversations with Drummond' in Jonson ed 1925–52, 1:132). Milton, in *Mansus* 80–4 (c 1639) and *Epitaphium Damonis* 161–8 (1639), spoke of treating Arthurian story in epic fashion. After serving in the Commonwealth government, however, he mentioned Arthur only briefly and skeptically in his *History of Britain* (c 1644–9) and memorialized his early interest in him merely through allusions in *Paradise Lost* and *Paradise Regained*. Dryden's unrealized plans for an Arthurian epic were influenced by *The Faerie Queene*. He announced that 'after *Virgil* and *Spencer*' he would allegorically depict 'living Friends and Patrons of the Noblest Families' and suggest 'the Events of future Ages, in the Succession of our Imperial Line' (*Discourse concerning Satire* 1693, in ed 1956–, 4:23). His 'Dramatick Opera' *King Arthur* (1691), which represents Arthur's efforts to win his betrothed, blind Emmeline, from a wicked Saxon magician, though essentially depicting the King of the pseudohistories and oral legend, shares with *The Faerie Queene* the purpose of celebrating the ruling monarch by association with Arthur, and possibly echoes the Bower of Bliss (*FQ* II xii 63–8) when Arthur resists the temptation represented by bathing damsels.

Two epic poems by Richard Blackmore at the end of the seventeenth century reveal substantial indebtedness to Spenser. Their titles, *Prince Arthur* (1695) and *King Arthur* (1697), reflect his adherence to Spenser's plan of treating Arthur's career before and after he became king. His epics, like *The Faerie Queene*, allegorize characters and contemporary events, especially Catholic and Protestant controversies, and praise the ruling William of Orange in the character of Arthur. According to his preface, *Prince Arthur*, which recounts the young hero's rout of the Saxons and conquest of England, Ireland, and Scotland, follows the rules of epic literature broken by Ariosto and Spenser, who became 'lost in a Wood of Allegories ... wild, unnatural, and extravagant.' Although Blackmore abandons Spenser's practice of using a separate figure to embody each of the virtues represented by Arthur, *Prince Arthur* like *The Faerie Queene* examines holiness as the first virtue. The work may show more particular indebtedness to its Spenserian model by including a review of English history before Arthur's reign and 'forecasting' the future kings of Britain, culminating in the present monarch. *King Arthur* follows Spenser's plan to illustrate the political virtues by testing Arthur's use of reason to achieve self-control. Some of the narrative and descriptive details closely echo Spenser's: Arthur defeats a dragon in an episode recalling the Red Cross Knight's adventure, and like Guyon (*FQ* II xii 42–87), he resists the temptations of sensuality in the garden of an enchantress who turns men into beasts.

Not until the early nineteenth century do English writers again treat Arthurian story in a lofty epic manner. Reginald Heber's fragment *Morte D'Arthur* (begun c 1810, pub 1830) reshapes and inventively expands material from the first part of Malory in Spenserian stanzas and archaic language. Less successful is Edward Bulwer-Lytton's *King Arthur* (1848), an attempt 'to construct from the elements of national romance, something approaching to the completeness of epic narrative' (preface). Bulwer transports Arthurian characters to improbable settings and adventures (Arthur battles walruses at the North Pole among Innuit pygmies), emphasizing by unintentional ludicrousness the contrasting greatness of Tennyson's achievement in raising 'national romance' to the stature of epic.

Although Tennyson's *Idylls of the King* (1842–85) stresses by its title the work's nature as a series of separate pieces, its account of the rise and fall of Arthurian civilization in twelve unified books invites comparison with the epic proportions of *The Faerie Queene*; and it was greeted in its first issue of four idylls as promising a full epic that would be national, Christian, and universal. The stories come from Malory and *The Mabinogion* and center on the Round Table, featuring the coming and passing of Arthur, notable love affairs, and the Grail quest. Despite a story line entirely different from *The Faerie Queene*, the parallels are clear in Tennyson's final overall scheme of a dozen separate tales, usually focusing on various protagonists but with Arthur, representing the ideals of the perfect society, central to each. Verbal echoes and striking details also suggest Tennyson's mindfulness of Spenser. Like *The Faerie Queene*, the idylls celebrate the ruling monarch through the figure of Arthur and allude to contemporary concerns. Tennyson like Spenser associates his king with Christ and provides in the example of Arthur, along with the negative example of imperfect knights, a pattern for virtuous gentlemen. He allies his king with Spenser's noble prince by insisting that his Arthur is 'Ideal manhood closed in real man' rather than the wanton, warring figure found in Geoffrey of Monmouth and Malory ('To the Queen' 38–44). The *Idylls* demonstrate in both the inadequate courtiers and the exemplary king the interconnection of private and public virtues which Spenser indicated would be his complete theme.

Despite Tennyson's concentration on society's failure to implement the King's ideals, the conception of Arthur which he shared with Spenser posits the possibility that individuals may achieve otherworldly perfection. But much as Spenser accentuates the contrast between ideals and human actualities by juxtaposing the chronicles of Fairyland and Britain, Tennyson shows the perfect man, Galahad, leaving Camelot for the celestial city. This theme, which underlies the movement of Spenser's hero from Britain to Gloriana's court, is perhaps reiterated in Tennyson's concluding suggestion, only tentatively expressed in a simile, that the King may pass from a desolate Britain to a fair city where he is welcomed like a returning hero ('The Passing of Arthur' 457–61).

Tennyson's resurrection of Arthur as the subject of grand poetry was resourceful and daring, for since Spenser no work of comparable stature had made serious use of Arthurian material. After Blackmore's ponderous epics, the legends had primarily been exploited for comic and satiric purposes. During the Age of Reason, a pervasive hostility to tales of chivalry and romance caused writers to ignore Arthurian legend, which they equated with superstition, passion, and barbarity (see Addison's criticism of Spenser in *An Account of the Greatest English Poets* 1694, written, as he later admitted, before he had actually read Spenser). A striking and representative depiction of Arthur at this time is the king in Fielding's burlesque, *Tragedy of Tragedies, or The Life and Death of Tom Thumb the Great* (3 eds 1730–1).

Father of Tom's beloved Huncamunca, Arthur is here a drunken, absurd figure, reminiscent of chapbook representations, who serves Fielding's overriding purpose of mocking extravagant contemporary tragedies.

Scott's romance *The Bridal of Triermain* (1813), which depicts a lover's quest in Plantagenet England based on the Sleeping Beauty story, features an Arthurian episode with comic nuances. Like Spenser's work, it employs the device derived from Chaucer's *Sir Thopas* of a quest for a lady encountered in a dream. The allegorical temptations overcome by the hero in the narrative which frames the Arthurian episode resemble Guyon's temptations in the Bower of Bliss (*FQ* II xii 55–68). Wordsworth in *The Egyptian Maid* (1835) similarly fashions a wry, original episode using familiar Arthurian characters. A number of works by less significant writers draw on Arthurian legend to satirize literary styles and social and political practices, two of the most engaging being John Hookham Frere's ottava rima burlesque *The Monks and the Giants* (1817–18) and Thomas Love Peacock's prose romance *The Misfortunes of Elphin* (1829), which derives material from medieval Welsh lore. Most durable of the nineteenth-century satires is Mark Twain's *Connecticut Yankee in King Arthur's Court* (1889). Through the device of time-travel, the novel exposes the barbarity of the Middle Ages and the flawed political and social conditions of Twain's own day, while also suggesting the genuine nobility of Arthur which is obscured by his society's pomposity and cruelty.

Similar satire, comedy, and burlesque continue in twentieth-century fiction. James Branch Cabell's romance novel *Jurgen* (1919) traces the adventures of a thirteenth-century pawnbroker who, traveling to other eras, enjoys love affairs with Guenevere, Helen of Troy, and a Persian goddess. This eccentric work sarcastically exposes discrepancies between the chivalric code and human behavior, but emphasizes that myths have value precisely because they depict ideals not yet practiced by society. T.H. White's *Once and Future King* (1938–58), which like *The Faerie Queene* takes up Arthur's story before he becomes king, and Thomas Berger's *Arthur Rex* (1978) resemble virtually all the comic versions of the legend in depicting an Arthur totally different from Spenser's. They return to Malory's flawed figure but present his imperfections not as sin so much as inescapable human infirmity. And like most humorous treatments of the legend, they also demonstrate the grandeur of Arthur's vision and the pathos of human inability to enact it.

Whereas for Malory, Spenser, and Tennyson a central theme of Arthurian material is the need for individuals to espouse the social and moral ideals embodied in the Round Table or Gloriana's court, many nineteenth- and twentieth-century writers probe the plight of the individual at odds with society. Among Tennyson's contemporaries, Pre-Raphaelite painters and poets such as William Morris, Dante Gabriel Rossetti, and A.C. Swinburne adapt Arthurian legend to imply that personal liberty must be won in part by flouting the religious and social values of the chivalric world. This theme is taken up by a number of poetic dramatizations of Arthurian love stories written from the 1890s to the 1920s. While some, such as J. Comyns Carr's *King Arthur* (1895), depict the Lancelot-Guinevere tale, most, including Thomas Hardy's *Famous Tragedy of the Queen of Cornwall* (1923) and John Masefield's *Tristan and Isolt* (1927), focus on the related love story of Tristram and Isolde. The most ambitious in conception are four plays, collectively entitled *Launcelot and Guenevere: A Poem in Dramas* (1891–1907), completed by Richard Hovey, who projected a cycle of three trilogies recording the history of the Round Table.

The psychological turmoil investigated in these dramas has throughout the twentieth century become the focus of more artful poetry and fiction. Edwin Arlington Robinson in three substantial narrative poems (*Merlin* 1917, *Lancelot* 1920, *Tristram* 1927) examines the psychological intricacies of the characters against the backdrop of a civilization verging on disaster. This view of a world at war, which dominates Arthurian fiction of the 1930s and 40s, also marks many of the narratives written in the 1970s and 80s. Endeavoring to recast traditional materials in the light of modern understanding of history and psychology, some of these recent novels have debased Arthur's character while emphasizing the primitive setting, the mud, stench, and carnage of Dark-Age England, as well as the complex psychological ingredients of incest, Oedipal conflicts, and adultery in the stories of Mordred's rebellion and Guinevere's infidelity. Arthur has been depicted as a sadistic fool and a crippled megalomaniac. Most often, he is simply a good man struggling to preserve some stability and nobility in a gravely imperfect world.

The supernatural and symbolic facets of Arthurian legend are accentuated in such novels as Charles Williams' *War in Heaven* (1930), John Cowper Powys' *Glastonbury Romance* (1932), and C.S. Lewis' *That Hideous Strength* (1945), and in such poems as Williams' *Taliessin through Logres* (1938) and *The Region of the Summer Stars* (1944). These works emphasize the mystical Grail lore and depict the eternal conflict between forces of light and darkness. Whereas the magical ingredients and the struggle of good against evil often reappear in comparatively trivial science fiction, important poets such as T.S. Eliot (*The Waste Land* 1922) and David Jones (*In Parenthesis* 1937, *The Anathemata* 1952, *The Sleeping Lord* 1974) have used the mystic elements of Arthurian legend in powerful evocations of modern desolation. Like these poets, novelists James Joyce (*Finnegans Wake* 1939) and Walker Percy (*Lancelot* 1977) have demonstrated the pervasiveness of Arthurian myth in modern literary consciousness by employing traditional material as important leitmotifs (see *fantasy literature).

Whether Arthur's story is placed in elegant settings of romance or in repugnant naturalistic scenes, whether it is treated as allegory, psychological realism, or science-fiction fantasy, continuing interest in the legend suggests the appeal of its mythic dimension, transmitted to subsequent generations not by the early chroniclers or modern historians and psychiatrists, but by the romances of Malory, Spenser, and Tennyson. As an embodiment of the endeavor to order experience, to civilize the brutal, worship the good, and add grace to life, Arthur has survived Enlightenment neglect and reincarnations in vastly inept writing. Despite persistent debunkings, he cannot be invoked in modern literature without bearing vestiges of both the tragic figure of Malory and the stainless hero of Spenser and Tennyson.

BEVERLY TAYLOR

Comprehensive lists and discussions of Arthurian works written in English after Spenser may be found in Roberta Florence Brinkley 1932 *Arthurian Legend in the Seventeenth Century* (Baltimore); Howard Maynadier 1907 *The Arthur of the English Poets* (Boston); Merriman 1973; Millican 1932; Reiss, et al (forthcoming); Beverly Taylor and Elisabeth Brewer 1983 *The Return of King Arthur: British and American Arthurian Literature since 1900* (Cambridge); Raymond H. Thompson 1985 *The Return from Avalon: A Study of the Arthurian Legend in Modern Fiction* (Westport, Conn); Elise van der Ven-Ten Bensel 1925 *The Character of King Arthur in English Literature* (Amsterdam).

Arthur in Middle English romances King Arthur appears as a character in twenty Middle English romances written between the latter half of the thirteenth century and the beginning of the sixteenth, and representing all the ME dialectal regions. They are *Alliterative Morte Arthure*, *Arthur*, *The Avowing of King Arthur*, *The Awntyrs off Arthure at the Terne Wathelyne*, *Golagros and Gawane*, *The Grene Knight*, *Lancelot of the Laik*, *Lybeaus Desconus*, *Merlin* by Herry Lovelich, *Merlin: A Prose Romance*, *Le Morte Arthur*, *Of Arthour and of Merlin*, *Sir Gawain and the Carl of Carlisle*, *Sir Gawain and the Green Knight*, *Sir Landeval*, *Sir Launfal*, *Sir Perceval of Galles*, *The Turke and Gowin*, *The Weddynge of Sir Gawen and Dame Ragnell*, and *Ywain and Gawain*.

Arthur in the ME romances reflects three main traditions. The first comes from his representation in Geoffrey of Monmouth's *Historia regum Britanniae* and the many chronicles derived from it, the second from the *Roman de Brut* (Wace's French adaptation of Geoffrey), and the third from the French romances of the twelfth and thirteenth centuries. These traditions were, respectively, of Arthur as a military leader and a genuine historical king of Britain whose exploits included defeating the Roman Empire and who died in battle against the traitor Mordred; of Arthur, in a kingdom that is essentially fictitious, as the head of the Round Table, a society dedicated to the highest chivalric ideals, coming to his destruction because of the adulterous love between his wife, Guinevere, and his finest knight, Lancelot; and of Arthur, treated respectfully, comically, or satirically, as the head of a court which acts as the starting point for adventures by individual knights.

The first tradition, that of Arthur as military leader and historical figure, appears in *Of Arthour and of Merlin*, Lovelich's *Merlin*, the *Prose Merlin* (all of which are partial translations of the Vulgate *Merlin*), and in the fragmentary chronicle poem *Arthur*. Concerned almost exclusively with battles and fighting, these works do not create developed characters; in them, Arthur is only a successful soldier who wins great victories, frequently no more important to the narrative than many of his knights. The *Alliterative Morte Arthure* is the only poem of literary merit written in this tradition. It tells of Arthur's deeds from the time he was challenged by the Emperor Lucius of Rome: his fight with the giant of Michael's Mount, his wars with the Romans, his further conquests in Italy, his return to Britain to quell Mordred's rebellion, and his death there. One way to interpret this narrative is to see that Arthur's fortunes rise so long as the wars he fights are just and fall when they are unjust. His fate, therefore, is a punishment for his sin of aggression. A very different way of reading claims that the poet greatly admires Arthur and always presents him as heroic and splendid. Fortune pulls him down, as is her nature, but his reputation will live on after his death. A third reading argues that Arthur's career reflects contemporary events of the fourteenth century, and thus the *Alliterative Morte Arthure* is specifically political as well as generally didactic.

Le Morte Arthur illustrates the second medieval tradition about Arthur. Here, the king, although a weaker character than Lancelot, the poem's hero, is not a tragic figure. Throughout the romance, he reacts to others rather than exerting his own leadership. At the end, pushed by Gawain's hatred, he engages in a war which he does not want and which leads indirectly to his death. Only in the battle against Mordred, where the moral issues are clear, does he pursue an independent course resolutely.

In the third tradition, Arthur is the head of a renowned court from which knights, who may not even be traditional knights of the Round Table, set out on adventures. Straightforward examples include *Lybeaus Desconus*, *Sir Perceval of Galles*, and *Ywain and Gawain*, which are translations and modifications of earlier Old French romances; and *Sir Gawain and the Carl of Carlisle*, *The Grene Knight*, and *The Turke and Gowin*, which derive in part from Celtic folk tales. In *Sir Gawain and the Green Knight*, another tale based in part on Celtic material, the nature of the court and the king is deliberately made more ambiguous than in the other romances. The court is in its 'first age' and Arthur is 'child gered,' keen to hear or do an adventure before dinner, ready to exchange blows with the Green Knight, and then willing to pretend that the whole affair was only a Christmas game once Gawain's fate seems to have been sealed when the Green Knight survives the blow from the axe.

Some romances openly diminish or criticize Arthur. In the first part of the *Avowing*, for example, the king is no more than an adventurous knight prepared to risk his life like any other in a daring adventure. In the second half, unlike Gawain who remains aloof, he joins Kay in a practical joke of dubious taste and so descends to the level of a fabliau character. In *Sir Landeval* and *Sir Launfal*, where an opponent is needed for the good fairy to overcome, Arthur, and to a greater extent Guinevere, simply fill this role, and in their intemperate pursuit of the hero act unjustly and maliciously. Arthur also behaves badly in *The Weddynge of Sir Gawen*, where he is so desperate to save his life that he forces Gawain into a distasteful marriage with a foul hag. Here he serves only as a foil for the hero. A similar contrast between Arthur and Gawain appears in *Golagros and Gawane*, but here Arthur serves another purpose, too. In speaking out against foreign domination, Golagros seems to be speaking for Scottish independence from English rule. By opposing him, Arthur becomes a symbol for English tyranny and intolerance.

Although it is possible that Spenser knew ME Arthurian romances other than Malory's *Morte Darthur*, since many of these works could still be found at the end of the sixteenth century in either manuscript or printed form, there is little likelihood that he actually borrowed from any of them. The importance of the ME Arthurian romances to him is not what they contributed to his knowledge of King Arthur and his knights but that they were one ingredient, possibly a major one, in shaping the knowledge and expectations of the audience to whom his poem was addressed.

CHRISTOPHER DEAN

The principal modern editions of the ME romances are *The Alliterative Morte Arthure* 1976 ed Valerie Krishna (New York); *Arthur: A Short Sketch of His Life and History in English Verse of the First Half of the Fifteenth Century* 1864 ed Frederick J. Furnivall, 2nd ed, EETS os 2 (London); 'The Avowing of King Arthur, Sir Gawain, Sir Kay, and Baldwin of Britain' in Walter Hoyt French and Charles Brockway Hale, eds 1930 *Middle English Metrical Romances* (New York) pp 607–46; *The Awntyrs off Arthure at the Terne Wathelyne* 1969 ed Robert J. Gates (Philadelphia); 'Golagros and Gawane' in F.J. Amours, ed 1897 *Scottish Alliterative Poems in Riming Stanzas* STS 27, ser 1 (Edinburgh); 'The Grene Knight' in Frederic Madden, ed 1839 *Syr Gawayne* (London) pp 224–42; *Lancelot of the Laik* 1870 ed W.W. Skeat, 2nd ed, EETS os 6 (London); *Lybeaus Desconus* 1969 ed M. Mills, EETS os 261 (London); Herry Lovelich 1904–32 *Merlin* ed Ernst A. Kock, EETS es 93, 112, os 185 (London); *Merlin: A Prose Romance* 1865–99 ed H.B. Wheatley, EETS os 10, 21, 36, 112 (London); *Le Morte Arthur* 1903, ed J. Douglas Bruce, EETS es 88 (London); *Of Arthour and of Merlin* 1973–9 ed O.D. Macrae-Gibson, EETS 268, 279 (London); *Sir Gawain and the Carl of Carlisle in Two Versions* 1951 ed Auvo Kurvinen (Helsinki); *Sir Gawain and the Green Knight* 1925 ed J.R.R. Tolkien and E.V. Gordon, 2nd ed rev Norman Davis 1967 (Oxford); 'Sir Landevale' in Thomas Chestre 1960 *Sir Launfal* ed A.J. Bliss (London); 'Sir Perceval of Galles' in French and Hale 1930:529–603; 'The Turke and Gowin' in Madden 1839:243–55; 'The Weddynge of Sir Gawen and Dame Ragnell' ed Laura Sumner, rpt in W.F. Bryan and Germaine Dempster eds 1941 *Sources and Analogues of Chaucer's 'Canterbury Tales'* (Chicago) pp 242–64; *Ywain and Gawain* 1964 ed Albert B. Friedman and Norman T. Harrington, EETS os 254 (London).

Arthur in *The Faerie Queene* Spenser says in the Letter to Raleigh that he has chosen 'king Arthure' as his hero not only because of his personal excellence but also because he is 'furthest from the daunger of envy, and suspition of present time.' Nevertheless, many incidents in Arthur's story, such as the fight with Geryoneo (v xi), are presented as reflections of recent political events; and Arthur was seen in Spenser's time as a remote ancestor of Elizabeth I, to whom *The Faerie Queene* is dedicated. In this, Spenser is typical of Renaissance poets who follow Virgil's example by raising the popular material of legend to the dignity of classical form. Consequently, he has made Arthur's role in *The Faerie Queene* similar to that of Aeneas in Virgil's epic: both heroes are ancestors of the person to whom the poet has dedicated his poem (but see *Britomart). Spenser's most striking departure from tradition may be seen in his plan to describe Arthur's adventures before he is king (see *Arthur, legend of). Whereas in *Morte Darthur* and *Sir Gawain* Arthur is necessarily confined, as the center of authority, to a small part in the action, in Spenser's narrative he is free to wander through Fairyland, performing exemplary feats. As further background to his entry into Fairyland, we are told that when Arthur's education was completed by Timon ('to whom he was by Merlin delivered to be brought up'), he saw the Fairy Queen in a dream and resolved upon waking to find her. Spenser's allegorical intention is indicated by the Queen's name, Gloriana, and by the suggestion that Arthur will encounter each of the twelve patrons of the twelve moral virtues. In his pursuit of glory, Arthur is 'perfected in the twelve private morall vertues' as each of those virtues is perfected by him: 'So in the person of Prince Arthure I sette forth magnificence in particular, which vertue ... is the perfection of all the rest, and conteineth in it them all' (Letter; see *magnanimity). Thus, according to the plan set forth in the Letter, the narrative of *The Faerie Queene* is to be seen as contributing at every point to Arthur's moral formation before his reappearance in history as king of the Britons.

In the *Iliad*, the god Hephaestus is persuaded to make for Achilles a magnificent suit of armor which, as we learn in *FQ* III ii 25, is later won by Artegall, the 'equal of Arthur.' Like Homer's hero, Arthur is equipped with magnificent armor and weapons, which are described when he first enters the poem (I vii 29–36). We find later that his charger is named Spumador (golden froth) and that his sword, Morddure (hard-biter), which Merlin forged in Mount Aetna and tempered in the river Styx, cannot be turned on its owner (II viii 20–1). Spenser describes Arthur's helmet as 'over ... spred' by an heraldic dragon representing Arthur's father, Uther Pendragon (dragon-head). This image recalls the dragon of Cadwallader, which Henry Tudor – later Henry VII and Elizabeth's grandfather – displayed on his standard when he marched from Milford Haven to claim England's crown (Millican 1932:39).

A baldric, stretching across the breastplate from shoulder to hip and supporting the sword, is decorated with precious stones likened to stars. The central stone, lying over the heart, is 'Shapt like a Ladies head' (I vii 30), presumably representing Gloriana. Arthur's diamond shield (see Alpers 1967b:166–79 for discussion of sources) cannot be broken or pierced, is brighter than the sun, renders powerless all magic spells and illusions, and transforms enemies to stone, stone to dust, and dust to nothing. These powers are held in check by a cover that is removed only twice – accidentally in the fight with Orgoglio (viii 19) and deliberately in the fight with the Souldan (V viii 37–8; yet cf xi 21). Finally, we are told that Arthur's armor was brought to Fairyland after his death, where it may be seen to this day.

The character of Arthur may be described as reconciling heroic action and love, just as *The Faerie Queene* unites romance and epic. Entering the poem after Una has learned of the knight of Holiness' imprisonment by Orgoglio (pride), Arthur defers his quest for the Fairy Queen in order to come to the rescue. He slays Orgoglio (I viii 24), wounds the apocalyptic dragon (16), seizes the keys to the dungeon from Ignaro (34), tears down the iron door (39), and redeems Redcrosse 'After long paines and labours manifold' (40). Finally he strips and exposes Duessa, who represents craftiness and hypocrisy (46–9). Even as he performs these vigorous actions, Arthur suffers from an amorous 'wound' (ix 7) caused by his dream of the Fairy Queen. While literally this 'restlesse anguish' (III iv 61) is an erotic symptom, Spenser gives it an ethical meaning: Arthur's love-wound represents the disproportion he feels between his immediate desire for fame and the long struggle toward its accomplishment in deeds. This desire is presented as the foundation of virtue. Arthur's magnificence is therefore not a static ideal but an energy that gathers into itself the force of all other virtues, directing the whole toward heroic achievement.

When Arthur is persuaded to tell of his nocturnal vision of the Fairy Queen (I ix 12–16), he reveals his uncertainty as to whether his quest for Gloriana has come by chance or by that 'fatall deepe foresight' (7) which we are to recognize in his destiny as king of the Britons. Allegorically, he is being led by providence to seek out the fame he will achieve as king. His quest is mentioned in the invocation to *The Faerie Queene* ('fairest *Tanaquill*, / Whom that most noble Briton Prince so long / Sought through the world, and suffered so much ill' I proem 2), and its structural function in the epic is suggested when Arthur and Redcrosse part: '*Arthur* on his way / To seeke his love, and th'other for to fight / With *Unaes* foe, that all her realme did pray' (ix 20). While Arthur moves toward the center of Fairyland, Redcrosse (and, by implication, the other knights Arthur will encounter) moves outward on a quest assigned to him at the court to which Arthur is headed.

In Book II, Arthur's role, though larger, confirms this general pattern. He enters in canto viii to rescue Guyon from two pagans who intend to despoil the knight of Temperance of his armor. Pyrochles insists on using Arthur's own sword against him, despite Archimago's warning that it will not hurt its master. After killing Cymochles, Arthur shows his 'Princely bounty and great mind' (viii 51) by offering to spare Pyrochles on certain conditions; and when these are refused he kills Pyrochles too. Allegorically, the episode demonstrates Arthur's mastery of the passions of concupiscence and rage.

The structure of the poem is implied when Guyon and Arthur travel together to the house of Alma: Guyon tells Arthur that he is serving the Fairy Queen on his present quest; and when Arthur expresses his desire also to serve her, Guyon says that he would conduct him to Fairy court were he not outward bound. The allegorical significance of Arthur's quest is then made explicit at the house of Temperance when he meets Praysdesire, who mirrors what is essential in him: she is inclined to 'pensive thought' because of her 'great desire of glory and of fame' (ix 36, 38). In the house's chamber of memory, Guyon reads a history of Fairyland while Arthur reads the history of his own people in *Briton moniments*, a chronicle that leads up to Uther Pendragon before breaking off suddenly at the moment when Arthur himself would have entered the story (x 68).

After Guyon has left on his voyage to Acrasia's bower, Arthur undertakes to defend the allegorical house of the body against a siege directed by Maleger who, because he represents sickness, is 'most strong in most infirmitee' (xi 40). The battle is modeled on Hercules' struggle with Antaeus: because Maleger regains his strength whenever he touches the ground, Arthur must finally drown him in a 'standing lake' (46). Book II concludes with Guyon's voyage to the Bower of Bliss, leaving Arthur to recover in the house of Temperance.

Up to this point, Arthur's structural role in the poem conforms with what we are led to expect in the Letter. But in Book III, with the entry of Britomart in quest of Artegall, complications develop, for this new couple takes on many of the symbolic values previously associated with Gloriana and Arthur (Roche 1964:48). While Artegall is Arthur's half-brother (iii 26–8) and, as his name implies, in some sense his 'equal,' Britomart is like Arthur in several ways: she is a 'royall Infant' (ii 49) with a concealed identity and a magic weapon; she is seeking a lover seen in a vision, she is frequently drawn off course to help others, and she performs Arthur's role in Book III by aiding Scudamour (in a quest he had been assigned, according to the Letter, at Cleopolis). In the opening stanzas of the book, a parallel between Arthur and Britomart is suggested by parallel naming – she 'the famous *Britomart*,' he 'The famous Briton Prince' (i 1, 8); and Britomart's adventure at Castle Joyous, in which Malecasta lies down by her side as she sleeps (58–62), seems to parody Arthur's dream. The similarity between Artegall and Arthur is maintained by the prophecy of Merlin, who foretells, in words that recall the treason of Mordred, Artegall's death by treachery (iii 28).

The most important similarity between Arthur and Britomart has its basis in the political myth that the Tudors were Arthur's descendants. Adjusting this myth to follow more closely the pattern of a dynastic epic in the Virgilian tradition, Spenser derives Queen Elizabeth's lineage from an ancestor of her own sex: the Briton princess from whom will descend the line of Briton kings. Thus, Arthur's authority in popular tradition as the ideal British monarch is communicated to Britomart in Spenser's poem, and through her to Elizabeth.

Following the pattern established in Book II, wherein the knight of one book encounters the patron of the virtue to be treated in the next, Guyon and Britomart joust in III i and are reconciled by Arthur, an event indicating his role as that virtue which unifies all other virtues. Arthur is then separated from Timias and Guyon by the appearance of Florimell, whom he pursues until overcome by darkness – she flying in terror from him because, as Spenser mentions in a significant detail, his arms are unknown in Fairyland (iv 51).

Although Arthur's thoughts at this point seem remote from his function in Spenser's plan, the passions he suffers during this night indicate his desire for glory: 'And thousand fancies bet his idle braine / With their light wings, the sights of semblants vaine: / Oft did he wish, that Lady faire mote bee / His Faery Queene, for whom he did complaine: / Or that his Faery Queene were such, as shee' (54). The significance of Arthur's passion is set forth in the opening stanzas of the following canto: his apparently digressive pursuit of Florimell calls him forward on his 'first poursuit' (v 2). And his tendency to admire ladies other than the one he is seeking (eg, Poeana at IV ix 6) is intended not to suggest waywardness but a nobility of character with which Arthur is more generously endowed than any other knight in the poem, with the exception of Britomart: 'in brave sprite [love] kindles goodly fire, / That to all high desert and honour doth aspire' (III v 1). In Arthur, ethos and eros are one and the same.

In Book IV, Arthur's sense of purpose seems less intense: he is described 'Seeking adventures, where he mote heare tell' and searching for Timias, whom he once meets without recognizing (vii 42–7). In canto viii, he encounters Amoret and Aemylia, who have recently escaped from the cave of Lust; and he cures Amoret's wound with the medicinal liquor he had once given Redcrosse (20, I ix 19). After killing Corflambo in a fight where his skill at wisely evading blows is noted (IV viii 44), Arthur frees Amyas from Corflambo's castle by a clever stratagem, arranges 'through his well wonted grace' (ix 14) the marriage of Poeana and Placidas, and departs with Amoret under his care. While Amoret, characteristically, fears him, his thoughts have returned to his quest: 'Him selfe, whose minde did travell as with chylde, / Of his old love, conceav'd in secret brest, / Resolved to pursue his former quest' (17). This image of gestation (like the reference, when he first tells his story, to 'time in her just terme' I ix 5), reminds us of his similarity to Britomart, whose quest for Artegall will result in her bringing forth the line of Briton kings.

After leaving Poeana and Placidas, Arthur discovers four knights representing four aspects of masculine passion attacking Scudamour and Britomart (IV ix 20–31). Although his heart swells with indignation at the sight of 'so unequall match' (32), he shows characteristic restraint and diplomacy when enforcing a truce. As the seven knights ride together, 'accorded all anew' (40), Scudamour is asked how he won Amoret at the Temple of Venus. This would seem the appropriate moment for Arthur to present Amoret, who has been traveling under his protection, thus reuniting the lovers who had been reunited earlier by Britomart in the canceled stanzas concluding the 1590 edition of Book III. But Spenser seems to have forgotten her.

In his first appearance in Book V, Arthur encounters Artegall in an episode similar to the encounter of Britomart and Guyon at the beginning of III and of Guyon and Redcrosse at the beginning of II. Mistaking Artegall for a Paynim knight, Arthur attacks and they collide with an equal and opposite force (viii 9). The suggestion here that Arthur and Artegall are in some sense identical is underlined when they are reconciled by Samient.

The knights then learn of the Souldan and his wife Adicia (injustice), whom they set out to punish in an episode culminating in one of Arthur's most dangerous battles (viii 28–45). When he is unable to wound the Souldan decisively, Arthur is compelled to unveil the terrible light of his shield. This probably signifies what was officially regarded as England's miraculous deliverance from the Spanish Armada.

Having defeated this symbol of military force, Arthur and Artegall defeat political fraud by destroying Malengin (ix 8–19). They then proceed to the court of Mercilla, who represents that ideal exercise of law by which justice is tempered with mercy – as is indicated when she places Artegall on one side of her throne, Arthur on the other (37). Arthur pities the defendant, Duessa, for her nobility of birth but withdraws his support when her viciousness is revealed.

Arthur's final adventure in Book V is to free Belge and her sons from the tyranny of Geryoneo (x 15–xi 35) – a complex political allegory concerning English support of the Protestant Low Countries against Spanish-Catholic aggression. Arthur defeats Geryoneo's Seneschall and three of his knights; and in the battle against Geryoneo, Spenser emphasizes Arthur's readiness to give ground while 'watching advauntage' to seize opportunities offered by fortune. It is with this in mind that we should read Arthur's words to Belge after he has defeated, largely by a strategy of watchful restraint, the enemy of justice: 'Deare Lady, deedes ought not be scand / By th'authors manhood, nor the doers might, / But by their trueth and by the causes right' (xi 17). After restoring Belge and her sons by destroying the monster Echidna (suggesting the Spanish Inquisition), Arthur resumes his pursuit of Gloriana: 'thenceforth he went / And to his former journey him addrest, / On which long way he rode, ne ever day did rest' (35).

In Book VI, Arthur leaves Timias and Serena to be cured by the Hermit so that he may attend to the chastisement of Turpine (vi 17). Why this contemptible opponent, who stalks the prince through the middle cantos, should occupy such a prominent place in Arthur's deeds may be understood if we recall Arthur's role in the moral allegory, which is to combat whatever force offers an insuperable threat to the virtue represented in any one book.

Turpine in the book of courtesy offers just such a threat. Calidore can do nothing with him because for courtesy to have a positive effect it must work upon a rudimentary desire for community, however perverted the desire may be (as with Briana and Crudor in canto i). Although Arthur fights a terrific battle against that most obvious affront to courtesy, Disdain (viii 12–18), his main opponent in this book must be seen as violating more fundamental principles of trust. And Turpine, by his cruelty, cowardice, inhospitality, treachery, and deceit, fills this role admirably. Furthermore, Arthur's actions against Turpine indicate the foundation of signs on which all courtesy is based. Arthur first forbids Turpine to wear the 'brave badges' of knighthood (vi 36); and he later takes the more extreme step of hanging him upside-down from a tree, thus converting him into a sign of the negation of courtesy: 'that all which passed by, / The picture of his punishment might see' (vii 27; see *baffling).

Arthur is less impersonal in the book of courtesy: we see his joy at finding Timias, and his compassion and care for the suffering of his squire and Serena (v 23, 32–41). But when we last see him he has, as we should expect, resumed his 'first quest' for the Fairy Queen 'in which did him betide / A great adventure' (viii 30). What this is we never learn. The effect of Arthur's grandeur as a character is achieved largely by this continual reminder that his dealings with other characters, however friendly, are deviations, even distractions, from his central concern, which always lies beyond our horizon – and beyond his.

Early readers of *The Faerie Queene* were concerned principally with identifying which of Elizabeth's courtiers Spenser intended to figure in Arthur. Greenlaw first established that any identification is misleading in principle because historical references cannot be sustained: a character like Arthur may in different episodes suggest different courtiers (Leicester early in the poem, Essex later), but in most he will suggest no one at all (*Var* 1:494). Much attention has been given to the meaning of Spenser's term *magnificence* and to specifying in what sense Arthur may be taken as symbolizing grace. According to Spenser's stated intentions in the Letter, Arthur is to represent not divine grace but that perfection of human nature which unites all virtues in itself. Left on its own, this ideal would suggest a Pelagian self-sufficiency, to which grace would be unnecessary. That is why the angel watches over Guyon before Arthur arrives: not to identify Arthur with grace but to qualify his moral perfection as still being in need of divine aid.

More recent views of Arthur have been influenced by the statement that Spenser's knights 'metaphorically make up the body and mind of Prince Arthur,' thus forming out of Spenser's uncompleted plan 'a unity, like a torso in sculpture' (Frye 1963:69, 76; for the coinage of the term 'Arthurian torso,' see Lewis 1948; for its application to Spenser, see Nohrnberg 1976:33–58). A single image, however, cannot be expected to accomplish all things; and this 'Arthurian torso' clearly works better when referring to Spenser's creative project than it does when referring to Arthur. Indeed, even when the image refers exclusively to the creative project, and is used simply to elucidate the developing pattern of Arthur's quest within the plan of the whole, it is limited because it is static. The knights are not incorporated into the torso of Arthur but are assisted by him to become more fully what each represents, even as he is perfected through them. The relation of the virtues to him therefore is not assimilative but interactive. Recognizing this difference, we may entertain a new idea of Arthur.

Such an idea must do more than the 'torso,' which allows us to see Spenser's hero as controlling the relationship between *The Faerie Queene* as we have it and the larger whole Spenser imagined. It must also preserve the distinctness of the virtues without losing sight of their relation to Arthur's quest. These conditions are fulfilled if we think of Arthur as a cybernetic governor regulating the imaginative system so that a steady state is maintained by periodic adjustment. Entering the story at critical points in its action, when the energies of narrative are either paralyzed or in danger of becoming entirely random, Arthur regulates the growth of the poem by periodically refocusing its energies on Gloriana. Thus the principle of control represented by Spenser's hero gives to the knights, collectively and individually, an ethos – just as it gives Arthur the character of 'a good governour and a vertuous man' (Letter).

GORDON TESKEY

Bennett 1942:53–60; Frye 1963:69–87; Giamatti 1975:53–63; Greenlaw 1932; C.S. Lewis 1948 *Arthurian Torso: Containing the Posthumous Fragment of 'The Figure of Arthur' by Charles Williams and a Commentary on the Arthurian Poems of Charles Williams* (London); Nohrnberg 1976:35–58.

Astraea The goddess of justice in classical mythology. According to Hesiod (*Works and Days*) and Ovid (*Metamorphoses* I.149–50), this virgin goddess, the last of the immortals, abandoned the blood-soaked earth when it entered its sinful Iron Age, taking the faculty of justice with her; in the heavens she became the constellation Virgo, the astrological virgin (cf *FQ* v i 11, *Daphnaïda* 218–19). In Virgil's fourth eclogue, the return of the Golden Age is heralded by the return of Astraea (Virgo) to earth, for justice is a fundamental condition of the earthly harmony that distinguishes the Golden Age. Since this eclogue was understood by patristic commentators to prophesy the coming of the Messiah, the Astraean figure who is his harbinger was also Christianized as the 'righteousnes [or justice] and peace' which characterize the New Jerusalem, the Christian counterpart of the Golden Age (Ps 85). When Astraea returns, earth will regain the order of justice and may anticipate the reign of Christ, the sun of righteousness (Mal 4.2) and 'Prince of Peace.'

The theme of the classical Golden Age provided a political mythology in which Elizabeth was regarded as the 'Astraea' of the Protestant Reformation: the Protestant 'Christian Emperor' described by Foxe as the restorer of true religion. Thus, under Elizabeth/Astraea, the reformed England represented a golden age that prefigured the new order to be established by Christ's coming.

In Elizabethan pastoral, the portrayal of Elizabeth as an Astraean figure often assumes Messianic overtones. Spenser's own fourth eclogue is 'purposely intended to the honor and prayse of our most gracious sovereigne, Queene Elizabeth,' who is portrayed as a pastoral shepherdess on the Astraean model (*SC, Aprill* Argument). Since Astraea/Virgo was associated with the *ver aeternum* (perpetual spring) of the Golden Age and its natural fecundity, the celebration of 'Eliza' as Astraea is aptly placed in the month of 'April shoure' (7), when spring renews the earth. The flowers of spring and the magical virtue of Astraea as a virgin are compounded in a compliment to the Virgin Queen, 'that blessed wight: / The flowre of Virgins ... In princely plight' (47–9). (Here, as often, the Astraean figure can refer also to the Virgin Mary). Like Astraea, Eliza is a 'goddesse' (97), 'Of heavenly race' (53). Her deification is placed in the seventh line of the seventh stanza of Colin's song since that number could signify her immaculate and virginal qualities: 'No mortall blemishe may her blotte' (54). It is mainly in the purity of her justice that the sovereign virtue of a monarch resides: as Spenser insists, justice is 'Most sacred vertue she of all the rest, / Resembling God in his imperiall might ... That powre he also doth to Princes lend, / And makes them like himselfe in glorious sight' (*FQ* v proem 10).

Since by justice peace is established, Eliza is offered as well a crown of olives 'for peace ... Such for a Princesse bene principall' (*Aprill* 123–6). The pun on *principle*, *primary*, and *princely* evokes the establishment of peace as the monarch's first responsibility. Just as Virgil's Astraea brought peace to a Rome wracked by civil war, so Elizabeth, as the daughter of the houses of both York and Lancaster, in herself represents the harmonious resolution of the Wars of the Roses in England. As 'The Redde rose medled with the White yfere' (68), she is the Astraean 'flowre' of golden-age peace.

The significance of Astraea for the national destiny is articulated for *The Faerie Queene* by Merlin's prophecy that in the new golden age of peace a royal virgin shall dispense justice: 'Thenceforth eternall union shall be made / Betweene the nations different afore, / And sacred Peace shall lovingly perswade / The warlike minds, to learne her goodly lore, / And civile armes to exercise no more: / Then shall a royall virgin raine' (III iii 49). In *FQ* v, the Book of Justice, Spenser most evidently counterpoints (as he had implicitly in *Mother Hubberd* 1–8) the current decay and degeneration of the world – its present 'stonie age,' which is a further descent from Hesiod's Iron Age – with the restorative capacity of Astraean justice as represented by Elizabeth. While the decay of the world intimates the approach of the Last Day, it also preludes the coming of the Messiah. Spenser's *contemptus mundi* in the proem to Book v is thus an appropriate introduction to the potential restoration of the world by the power of justice. He finds the model for hope in Saturn's Golden-Age reign (proem 9–10), when, as the handmaiden of God's justice, Astraea provides an exemplum for his earthly lieutenants, or 'Princes' (10). Especially she provides an epiphanic model for Elizabeth as 'Dread Soverayne Goddesse, that doest highest sit / In seate of judgement, in th'Almighties stead ... with magnificke might and wondrous wit' (11). She remains only a model, though, because Spenser does not imply that she returns to the earth as Elizabeth. For the earthly – and therefore necessarily fearsome – implementation of her 'great justice' in a world in which the Golden Age has not returned, Artegall is 'instrument' (11), just as Astraea, who trains him, is source and symbol for the proper exercise of justice on earth. At one level of the allegory, then, the restoration of 'Irena' is the restoration of peace (Gr *eirēnē*) by the implementation of justice (through Artegall).

Since Astraea stands in contrast to earthly degeneration and disorder, it is appropriate that she should bring to *FQ* VII apprehensions of harmony to balance the claims of Mutabilitie. As Virgo, she is 'the righteous Virgin' led by August in the procession of the Months (vii 37), and she bears the corn symbolic of the fact that she 'plenty made abound' in the Golden Age. In the other half-month shared with Virgo, September, Libra's scales (38) provide a retrospective linkage to the Astraean attributes evoked in the previous stanza, since Astraea was classically portrayed as bearing the scales of justice. This final appearance of Astraea in her purest form reminds us that she represents more than Elizabeth, even though some consonance between Elizabeth and the providential order is expressed by Spenser in Astraean figures.

MARGARITA C. STOCKER

Cheney 1966; Fowler 1964; Levin 1969; Stocker 1986; Wells 1983; Yates 1975.

astronomy, astrology Today we associate astronomy with light years, quasars, and color photography from Saturn, but Spenser and his contemporaries would have associated it with a complex geometry, the practice of medicine, or astronomy's close cousins, astrology and alchemy. The subject would have called to mind Psalm 19: 'the heavens declare the glorie of God, and the firmament sheweth the worke of his hands.'

Two years after the publication of *FQ* I–III in 1590, William Molyneux completed the first celestial globe produced in England, which may be seen today in the Middle Temple Library, London. This handsome and practical, if elementary, astronomical model relied upon contemporary continental counterparts for its information, but it testifies to increasing English interest in astronomical inquiry. It also indicates the essentially Ptolemaic base on which that inquiry was still being conducted.

Just over a thousand stars were plotted on the globe, each of them, of course, equidistant from the center of the sphere. But the equidistance was not solely determined by the design of the model; it also indicated the Ptolemaic notion that all stars lay on the surface of the same sphere, their brightness being a function of their size. These stars were thought to be limited in number and 'fixed' (a label that distinguishes them from the planets, revolving each in its own sphere). Dozens of English Renaissance handbooks repeat Ptolemy's figures: there are 1022 stars in the heavens, each one with its specific magnitude, ranging from 107 times to 18 times greater than the earth.

The main analytical tools of this naked-eye astronomy were mathematics and quantification. Thomas Hood, for instance, appointed lecturer in mathematics to the citizens of London, thought it worthwhile to expound to them what was 'the whole soliditie of the Globe' (ie, the volume of the earth). For one estimate, he adopted Ptolemy's measure of 62 1/2 miles per degree at the equator and concluded, by a mathematically correct calculation, that the earth's volume must be 192,197,184,917 and 473/1331 cubic miles (1590: fol 20).

More useful for the poet were the data attributed to heavenly bodies by the literary tradition which associated the stars with myth: the constellation Leo was the Nemean lion slain by Hercules; Virgo was Astraea, the goddess of justice who fled from the earth – and so with all the groups of stars. In the second century AD, Ptolemy's catalogue named 48 constellations (shown on Molyneux's globe), and described each star in terms of its position within its constellation: the second star in Hercules, for instance, is 'the one on the right shoulder beside the armpit.' This inheritance was powerfully realized in the planispheres of 1515 for which Albrecht Dürer did drawings and which had a profound influence on later representations of the heavens.

Several contemporary works give a general impression of how Spenser and his lay contemporaries regarded the universe: William Cuningham's *Cosmographical Glasse* (1559), Thomas Blundeville's *M. Blundeville His Exercises* (1594), and Thomas Hood's *Use of Both the Globes* (1592). Gabriel Harvey thought it a shame that Spenser did not know more of such writings and make more use of them. But given the subtlety of some of Spenser's astronomical allusions (see *constellations), Harvey's perhaps crusty remark may reflect a difference in intellectual temperament and sensibility rather than knowledge.

Spenser's technical knowledge of astronomy is shown in the proem of *FQ* v, which describes the progressive degeneration of the world. In his day, the church taught (as it always had) that God created and controls a geocentric universe, and that change and decay in its operation were the result of human sinfulness. Astronomers, however, increasingly maintained the view that cosmic change was cyclic, and even contemplated the possibility of a heliocentric universe.

Spenser seems to reflect this view in the *Cantos of Mutabilitie*; but in the proem to Book v, he claims that 'Long continuance' has caused the (sinful) world to deviate, and it 'growes daily wourse and wourse.' Not just the earth's but 'the heavens revolution / Is wandred.' The Ram has 'shouldred' the Bull, and the Bull has 'butted' the Twins so fiercely that they have crushed the Crab and borne it 'Into the great *Nemoean* lions grove.' At this point, Spenser breaks off his enumeration, knowing that his readers could continue it for themselves. By implication, the Fish have finally encroached upon the Ram's terrain, where the zodiacal circle completes itself; thus, the cycle has been left intact with each constellation moved one place forward.

This passage, where the zodiacal constellations are shunted like a freight train, has been taken to refer simply to the precession of the equinoxes (see Knobel 1:449); but it probably also refers to the phenomenon of trepidation. Precession is now well understood as a function of the fact that the pole of the celestial equator describes a circle around the pole of the ecliptic (the sun's path around the heavens on a geocentric projection) once every 25,800 years. Spenser's age, however, inherited a different version which is exemplified by Thomas Hood (1592: sig B4v).

In Hood's account, if we observe the motion of the heavens over the long term, various bodies appear to rotate around the earth on different paths and at different rates. The most spectacular revolution is that of the moon, which completes a cycle in slightly less than a calendar month. The outermost planet, Saturn, revolves through the heavens once every thirty years or so. The 'fixed' stars, however, move at the rate of only one degree every 72 years (or 100 years in Ptolemy's estimate); recognizing their motion requires attention to historical record and confidence in its accuracy. Once these motions are recognized as periodic and circular, however, their variations can be accounted for in a single coherent (and ultimately regular) system.

To account for these appearances of motion, Hood posits as a model a nest of concentric and translucent spheres which were able to rotate against each other in certain prescribed ways, with the planets free to change position within the boundary layers of their respective spheres. Eight spheres accounted for the seven planets (including the sun and moon) and the fixed stars. The working model, however, required the invention of two more spheres. An outermost tenth sphere (the *primum mobile*, or 'prime mover') provided the main driving force for the other nine; its function was to impart the daily east-west motion to the heavens at large. A ninth, 'crystalline' sphere accounted for the much slower and apparently west-east motion of the fixed stars. This apparent west-east motion is analogous to a rapidly rotating spoked wheel which appears to be rolling slowly in reverse. In the case of the fixed stars, the contrary motion – precession – is extremely slow: on Ptolemy's reckoning, one west-east rotation corresponds to over 13 million east-west rotations.

In the proem to *FQ* v, Spenser dramatically alludes to one effect of this precession: the constellations of the zodiac gradually move to the east, out of those compartments of the zodiac to which they originally gave their names. Another supposed effect involves the 'obliquity of the ecliptic.' In the course of the year, the sun appears to travel through the zodiac in a circle called the 'ecliptic,' since eclipses can occur only when the moon also lies on it. The sphere of the heavens, which rotates daily on an axis through the celestial poles, has an equator which lies in a different plane from the sun's ecliptic, at an angle to it which was known as the 'obliquity of the ecliptic.' Spenser's age inherited a theory that this angle was subject to variation, over a cycle of 7000 years. This supposed phenomenon was known as 'trepidation.' (To extend the previous analogy, the spinning spoked wheel also has a slight wobble on its axle; and its rim, seen end on, represents the band of the zodiac.)

In the proem to *FQ* v, therefore, Spenser probably had in mind trepidation rather than precession. This explanation reduces the degree of exaggeration that otherwise appears in his saying that the heavens 'range, and doe at randon rove / Out of their proper places farre away.' The motion of precession is relatively simple, and not in the least random; but random roving is a much more plausible description for the observed dislocation of the heavens produced by different components working at varying rates in different directions.

Spenser amplifies his picture of decay: the sun is 'miscaried with the other Spheres. / For since the terme of fourteene hundred yeres, / That learned *Ptolomaee* his hight did take, / He is declyned ... Nigh thirtie minutes to the Southerne lake; / That makes me feare in time he will us quite forsake' (*FQ* v proem 7). A dislocation reckoned to have a rate of only half a degree in fourteen centuries is hardly cataclysmic by any explanation, and the church would have prepared mankind to expect the Second Coming well in advance of the imagined catastrophe. Thus, his gloomy apprehension may not be entirely genuine, especially since dislocations of this kind were commonly regarded as cyclic. The point of the poet's first-person intervention may therefore be quite complex – certainly suiting a mood of eschatological pessimism, but also perhaps trading on his audience's awareness of how he has redeployed conventional astronomical wisdom to suit that mood.

Another subtle instance of trading on common knowledge (and possibly on more advanced knowledge) may lie in *Amoretti* 60, where he asserts that 'Mars in three score yeares doth run his spheare.' Anyone moderately versed in astronomy would have understood immediately that he could not be talking about that planet's sidereal revolution (the time it takes to circle the heavens once), since that revolution period was commonly given as two years (a rather imprecise rounding-off of 687 days). Clearly, then, some other period is intended if Spenser knew anything at all of his subject.

One explanation may be derived from the complex astrological calculations used to determine a person's supposed life expectancy. One value assigned to Mars in this system was 66, for which 'three score' might be a reasonable approximation. This figure of 66, however, was arrived at by totaling the number of 'terms' (degrees on the zodiac) which were astrologically assigned to Mars; they were not, in any direct sense, related to the 'circles voyage' mentioned in the poem.

Another explanation is suggested by Ptolemy, the chief authority in classical astronomy, who assigned 79 years as the time it took Mars and the sun to return to their same relative positions in the heavens. 'Three score' may well be someone's slip for 'four score' (see Dodge in *Var* 8:440); and the rest of the sonnet lends plausibility to this inherently likely emendation. The lover complains that he has been tormented for a 'yeare' that has seemed longer than the forty previous years of his life. He now looks to the 'yeare ensuing' (his forty-second) to resolve his case. It happens, though, that when the 79-year 'restitution cycle' of Mars and the sun has been completed, Mars will itself have passed through 42 revolutions ($42 \times 687 = 28{,}854$ days; $79 \times 365.25 = 28{,}854.75$ days). The completion of Mars' cycle thus matches the hoped-for end of the lover's 'long languishment.' Although the double relevance of 42 to this sonnet may be coincidental, there is no doubt that the whole *Amoretti* sequence and its companion *Epithalamion* are structured on principles that give importance to calendrical calculations (see Hieatt 1960, 1973a).

Finally, it would be misleading to make a strong distinction between astronomy and astrology in Spenser's day, since naked-eye astronomy was then hardly more than the servant of cosmographical theory on one side, and of the practice of astrology on the other. Poets tended to use astrology not as a self-contained set of practices (or superstitions) but for its poetic resonances, which derived primarily from its close association with classical mythology.

By comparison with Chaucer, Spenser makes little overt use of astrology; but when he does use its language, it is in a manner that also implies a confidence in his audience's ability to understand him. For example, he presents Phantastes as one who might be thought 'borne with ill disposed skyes, / When oblique *Saturne* sate in the house of agonyes' (*FQ* II ix 52). 'Obliqueness' is not a property of Saturn or of any other planet; it is, instead, jointly a function of a planet's being at a particular position in the zodiac, and of the terrestrial latitude at which its temporary motion is observed. But Spenser can nonetheless properly refer to Saturn as being 'oblique.' Just as *opposition* has a purely technical sense and also a strong metaphoric overlay, so the semantic range of *oblique* can call up notions of perversity; and Saturn, even if only incidentally 'oblique' at Phantastes' birth, cannot have meant him well.

The meaning of 'the house of agonyes' here is less apparent, since none of the twelve astrological houses is conventionally so labeled. Three of them, however, bode ill: the sixth is concerned with sickness, the eighth with death, and the twelfth is commonly labeled 'prison.' Technically, the extent of a celestial body's obliqueness is related to the horizon (logically the eastern horizon where it rises, not the western where it will eventually set); and since the twelfth house, the worst, borders immediately upon that eastern horizon, it is a fair assumption that the twelfth house is Spenser's 'house of agonyes'. Such aptness and economy in his astronomical and astrological language argue an impressive degree of knowledge in at least some part of his original audience. (See *cosmogony, cosmology) J.C. Eade

Thomas Blundeville 1594 *M. Blundevile His Exercises, Containing Sixe Treatises* (London; rpt Amsterdam 1971); William Cuningham 1559 *The Cosmographical Glasse* (London; rpt Amsterdam 1968); J.C. Eade 1984 *The Forgotten Sky: A Guide to Astrology in English Literature* (Oxford); Heninger 1977; Thomas Hood 1590 *The Use of the Celestial Globe in Plano* (London; rpt Amsterdam and New York 1973); Hood 1592 *The Use of Both the Globes, Celestiall, and Terrestriall* (London; rpt Amsterdam and New York 1971); Johnson 1937; E.B. Knobel 1916 'Astronomy and Astrology' in *Shakespeare's England* 1:444–61.

Astrophel The name used by Sidney in *Astrophil and Stella*; it means 'lover of a star' and refers to the poet's love for his Stella, or 'star.' Elegists, including Spenser, commonly referred to Sidney as 'Astrophel' or (more rarely) the etymologically preferable 'Astrophil' (Sidney ed 1962:458). In *Colin Clouts Come Home Againe*, Colin lists his favorite poets at the court 'Now after *Astrofell* is dead and gone' (449), and later refers to '*Urania*, sister unto *Astrofell*' (Mary Herbert, Countess of Pembroke). Spenser's 'Pastorall Elegie' on Sidney is entitled 'Astrophel,' the name used in prologue 10, lines 6–8, 30, 150, and 186, and in the immediately following 'Lay of Clorinda,' lines 30 and 99.

In 'Astrophel' 196, Spenser bestows the name on a flower into which Stella and Astrophel are jointly metamorphosed. Stella here refers not so much to the mistress in Sidney's poems as to his wife and his poetic inspiration. He says the flower was formerly called 'Starlight,' or 'Of others *Penthia*, though not so well' (193–4); the latter may have been the source for 'Penthea' in John Ford's play *The Broken Heart* (1633). The flower has been identified both with *aster tripolium*, 'the Sea Starwort or Michaelmas Daisy' (*OED*), and with a putative flower called *astrophyllum*, or 'star-leaf,' although neither of these matches Spenser's description. His flower is red and then fades to blue, 'standeth full of deow' all day long, and has a star ('Resembling *Stella*') in its 'midst' (184–96). The flower 'borage' (Marquand in *Var* 7:498) is not a convincing identification, nor do Spenser's alternative names correspond to any known actual flowers. Like the elegy as a whole, the name is probably a deliberate fiction.

In *Daphnaïda* 346, Alcyon in his fourth lay of complaint commands his flock to 'Feede ye hencefoorth on bitter *Astrofell*.' Here there is no definite allusion to Sidney, though the name would resonate with appropriate associations of sudden death and shattered hopes. This Astrofell may be the plant asphodel (Collier and Renwick in *Var* 7:443); but it is clearly an unpleasant plant, linked in the line following with 'stinking Smallage, and unsaverie Rew' – quite unlike asphodel, which is associated from Homer onwards with immortality and the Elysian fields. There is probably no specific botanical reference but rather a remote association with the dead Sidney.

Katherine Duncan-Jones

Astrophel (See ed 1912:546–60.) A collection entitled *Astrophel: A Pastorall Elegie upon the Death of the Most Noble and Valorous Knight, Sir Philip Sidney* was suffixed to *Colin Clouts Come Home Againe* (1595). It bears a separate title page and a dedication 'To the most beautifull and vertuous Ladie, the Countesse of *Essex*,' Sidney's widow, Frances Walsingham, who had married Robert Devereux, second Earl of Essex, in the summer of 1590. There are seven elegies in the collection.

(1) 'Astrophel,' Spenser's pastoral elegy (sigs E4r-F4v), discussed in detail below. It consists of 3 prefatory stanzas, 33 stanzas of elegy, and 3 describing the grief of Astrophel's fellow shepherds, in sixains rhyming *ababcc*. The concluding lines prepare us for:

(2) A 'dolefull lay' imagined as sung by 'his sister that *Clorinda* hight' – that is, Sidney's sister, Mary Herbert, Countess of Pembroke (sigs G1r-G3r). It has often been suggested that this was written by the Countess herself, but stylistic evidence and the close links between the two poems make it virtually certain that Spenser is the author (O'Connell 1971; see also Long 1916, Osgood 1920; cf Herbert ed 1977:56). It has eighteen six-line stanzas (half the number in the previous elegy) for a total of 108 lines: Sidney's *Astrophil and Stella*, in the authoritative 1598 edition, totals 108 sonnets (Fowler 1970b:174–80). Whatever the more abstruse significance of Spenser's number, undoubtedly it conceals a tribute to Sidney's achievement as a love poet. The two final stanzas introduce 'dolefull layes' written by 'many other moe,' headed by:

(3) 'The Mourning *Muse* of *Thestylis*' (sigs G3r-H2r), an elegy by Lodowick Bryskett, 195 lines of iambic hexameters whose intricate but irregular rhyme scheme influenced that of Milton's *Lycidas*. Of the elegies in the collection, this may have been written earliest, for it was entered in the Stationers' Register to John Wolfe on 22 August 1587 as 'the mourninge muses of *Lod Bryskett* upon the Deathe of the moste noble Sir *Phillip Sydney* knight.' A manuscript version in Lambeth Palace Library (Bacon Papers, Ms Tenison 841, item 3), though possibly autograph, is impossible to date. It has some interesting variants, such as 'his loving Lady' for 'his lovely *Stella*' (93; see Bryskett ed 1972:297–311). Bryskett must have known Sidney quite well, for he was one of his companions during three years of continental travel, 1572–5. Spenser and Bryskett are drawn together in:

(4) 'A Pastorall Aeglogue upon the Death of Sir *Phillip Sidney Knight*' (sigs H2r-H4v), a verse dialogue between Lycon and Colin (ie, Bryskett and Spenser; no doubt we should notice that the names are anagrams of each other). As well as dramatizing their shared loss, the poem may well be a collaboration between the two poets, for it has some very Spenserian touches. In his *Discourse of Civill Life* (1606), Bryskett portrays Spenser and himself working in close conjunction on their literary projects. Both (3) and (4) are closely modeled on Italian poems by Bernardo Tasso (see Mustard 1914).

On a fresh gathering begin three further elegies, reprinted (with errors) from *The Phoenix Nest* (1593; for discussion and a collation of the variants, see ed 1931:115–32):

(5) 'An Elegie, or Friends Passion, for His *Astrophill*' (sigs I1r-K2r), a *faux-naïf*, semi-allegorical account of Sidney's death by Matthew Roydon, in 39 stanzas of iambic

tetrameters rhyming *ababcc*. This poem is the same length as the opening 'Astrophel,' so, in spite of its previous appearance in *The Phoenix Nest*, it may have been written for the Spenser-Bryskett collection. Roydon's elegy has often been quoted by Sidney's biographers because it evokes his personal charm, 'A sweet attractive kinde of grace' (103); yet of the five elegists, Roydon is the only one not known to have been personally acquainted with Sidney. Though praised by Nashe as a comic poet (preface to Greene's *Menaphon* 1589, sig A2v), Roydon and his works remain extremely elusive (see Bang 1913, Moore Smith 1914). The 'friend' of the title, a melancholy man who describes Sidney and his death, is unlikely to be Roydon himself but may be some loftier figure such as Essex or Robert Sidney.

(6) 'An Epitaph upon the Right Honourable Sir *Phillip Sidney* Knight: Lord Governor of Flushing' (sigs K2r-K3r) by Raleigh, fifteen quatrains in pentameters rhyming *abba*, which give an unusually close account of Sidney's birth, education, and career. The half-envious tone with which Raleigh celebrates Sidney's early and glorious death – he 'past with praise, from of this worldly stage' (36) – is particularly poignant in view of his own later career and death on the scaffold in 1618. The elegy is also found in the Arundel Harington Manuscript (see ed 1960, 1:255–7, 2:356–8; see also Raleigh ed 1951:5–7, 97–8).

(7) 'Another of the Same' (sigs K3v-K4r), a forty-line, ten-stanza elegy in poulter's measure, almost certainly by Sidney's friend Sir Edward Dyer, though it has been attributed on internal evidence to Greville (see *Phoenix Nest* ed 1931:130–1). It was first attributed to Dyer by Edmond Malone in 1821, and stylistic and verbal links with his other poems provide confirmation. Line 25 ('Harts ease and onely I, like parables [corrected to 'parallels' in 1611] run on') seems to refer to Dyer's 'Amarillis,' in which Charamell is metamorphosed into 'harts ease' and Choridon into an owl (Sargent 1935:192–5, 198–9, 211–13). The allusion seems to be to Sidney's two closest friends, Dyer and Greville, who live on divided. Dyer and Greville jointly had inherited Sidney's books (see Sidney ed 1973b:149, 218).

Spenser seems to have experienced considerable difficulty in composing an elegy for Sidney (who died 17 October 1586). In his epistle to the Countess of Pembroke which prefaces *Ruines of Time* in *Complaints* (1591), he speaks of the deaths of Sidney and his two uncles, saying that since his arrival in England his friends have upbraided him 'for that I have not shewed anie thankefull remembrance towards him or any of them; but suffer their names to sleep in silence and forgetfulnesse.' Though *Time* commemorates Sidney in nine stanzas (281–343) which follow briefer laments for Leicester, Warwick, the Earl of Bedford, and Sidney's mother, these are not so much an elegy as a short outcry at the loss of Sidney as poet and patron. The two-stanza envoy addressed to the 'Immortall spirite of *Philisides*' refers appropriately to 'this broken verse' as his only funeral offering. An 'Eglogue: Made Long since upon the Death of Sir Philip Sidney' (published in Francis Davison's *Poetical Rhapsody* 1602), a highly Spenserian dialogue between 'Thenot' and 'Perin,' has Thenot inquiring: 'Ah, where is *Collin*, and his passing skill? / For him it fits our sorrow to fulfill'. This poem (by 'A.W.,' who may be simply 'Anonymous Writer') cannot be dated precisely, but may belong to the early 1590s (see Davison ed 1931–2, 1:36–44, 2:106–11). As late as 1594, *The Lamentation of Troy, for the Death of Hector* by 'I.O.,' a crude and inconsistent mythologizing of the death of Hector/Sidney, dedicated to Sidney's friend Lord Willoughby, commends its subject to 'good *Spencer* the only *Homer* living': 'Write then O *Spencer* in thy Muse so trim, / That he in thee and thou maiest live in him' (sig B2r; cf A3v).

Though we cannot date 'Astrophel' and its succeeding 'Lay of Clorinda' precisely, we are probably safe in approaching it as one of the latest formal elegies on Sidney, composed some time between 1591 (*Complaints*) and late 1595 (*Colin Clout*). Whereas Bryskett's elegies appear to be located in Ireland, the first referring to '*Liffies* tumbling streames' ('Thestylis' 4) and the second to the Irish-sounding but as-yet-unidentified river '*Orown*' ('Aeglogue' 4; Bernardo Tasso had simply *rio*), nothing in Spenser's 'Astrophel' or 'Clorinda' indicates where they were written. However, given the close links between Spenser's elegies and Bryskett's, especially in the 'Aeglogue' between Lycon and Colin, it seems likeliest that 'Astrophel,' too, was written in Ireland, some time between 1591 and Spenser's return to London in the winter of 1595–6. According to *Amoretti* 33, Bryskett spurred Spenser on to continue *The Faerie Queene*; he may also have stimulated him to produce his long-awaited elegy.

The lateness of 'Astrophel' explains several features to which earlier commentators have objected, chiefly its presentation of Stella as Astrophel's sole love, who dies with him (175–80). This has often been regarded as a gaffe, since Penelope Devereux, Lady Rich, was alive and flourishing; and it was she, not Sidney's wife Frances, on whom Sidney's 'Stella' was modeled (see Hudson 1935, Duncan-Jones 1986). It has been suggested that Spenser's absences in Ireland meant that he was ignorant of *Astrophil and Stella*: 'who Stella actually was may well have escaped his memory' (M.W. Wallace 1915:256). For a poet so concerned with social relationships, this would seem lamentable carelessness.

Spenser's fictionalizing of Sidney's love story probably sprang from close knowledge of the relevant facts, which he would surely have known as an intimate of such a leading courtier as Raleigh. If Spenser wished to show Sidney as a lover, he had to make Stella die. Frances Sidney, widow and dedicatee of the poem, was now the Countess of Essex, and could not be depicted as still mourning her previous husband. Still less could Penelope Rich, who from 1590 onwards openly transferred her favors from her husband, Lord Rich, to her lover, Lord Mountjoy, be shown as Astrophel's chaste star. Of the women in Sidney's life, only his sister could be presented as still mourning him in 1591 or later. Spenser's portrayal of Stella as Astrophel's sole love, combined with his dramatization of the Countess of Pembroke as 'Clorinda,' was a creative way of dealing with a very awkward situation. A 'Stella' who is clearly a poetic ideal rather than a particular woman enabled Spenser to show Sidney as a love poet without implying either that he had written poems to a married woman or that the Countess of Essex's life was at an end. He deftly removes Sidney/Astrophel from real life entanglements. In 'Clorinda,' the presentation of Sidney's spirit in Paradise, enjoying 'Sweet love still joyous, never feeling paine. / For what so goodly forme he there doth see, / He may enjoy from jealous rancor free' (82–4), is a delicate way of reassuring the women close to Sidney that they need now feel no guilt or anxiety about the man who had written so much about the anguish of earthly love.

A broader criticism of 'Astrophel' has been that it is cold and conventional, that 'the quality of inspiration could not be summoned at the moment, and perhaps it was from a lack of material with which to round out an adequate poem that Spenser had recourse to borrowings more strikingly inappropriate then than now' (Shafer in *Var* 7:486). The poem's classical analogues are Bion's first idyll and Ovid's account of Venus and Adonis (*Metamorphoses* 10.519–739). Its immediate source has been identified as Ronsard's *Adonis* (1563; see Harrison 1934), itself a paraphrase of Bion. More recently, Ronsard's poem has been compared with Spenser's to show how Spenser celebrates *amor umano* (human love) at its highest, rather than *amor ferino* (bestial love; Bondanella and Conaway 1971). Though the extreme sensuousness of Ronsard's poem may have made it an inappropriate model for celebrating the heroic Sidney, Spenser's transformation of it is thorough.

The actual events leading up to Sidney's death comprise the other source of the poem, and their absorption into the Venus and Adonis myth gives an heroic dimension lacking in Ovid (O'Connell 1971). The Netherlands are transformed into 'a forest wide and waste,' the Spaniards into 'the brutish nation,' and the Dutch among whom he died into 'A sort of shepheards' (93, 98, 139). The period between Sidney's wounding and death (22 September-17 October) is imaged in the ten stanzas between Astrophel's wounding and death (115–74).

Many earlier elegies on Sidney also sought to edify readers with some literal details of his last days: for example, George Whetstone's *Sir Phillip Sidney, His Honourable Life, His Valiant Death, and True Vertues* (1587), John Philip's *Life and Death of Sir Phillip Sidney* (1587), and Angel Day's *Upon the Life and Death of Sir Phillip Sidney* (1586?). But 'Astrophel' is a poet's poem, analogous to Shelley's *Adonais*. Spenser explicitly addresses his fellow poets and presents his elegy for their judgment alone (1–12). The intricate numerical structure and fine poetic texture of 'Astrophel' and 'Clorinda,' which have yet to be fully analyzed, may help to explain why Spenser took so long to elegize Sidney. He was not recording events but, as so often, transforming them into art for the benefit of a highly sophisticated audience. He is celebrating Sidney as a love poet, not a soldier. In 'Astrophel,' Sidney is immortalized as a poetic 'flowre' (184), while 'Clorinda' offers reassurance about his 'immortall spirit' in Paradise, 'Where like a new-borne babe it soft doth lie' (61, 69). We should admire Spenser's achievement in assimilating the horrors of Sidney's actual death from septicemia into a carefully organized and aesthetically satisfying 'double elegy.' (Contrast Greville's account of Sidney's death, ed 1986:77–83). The remoteness of Spenser's elegies from biographical reality is their glory, not their weakness.

KATHERINE DUNCAN-JONES

The Arundel Harington Manuscript of Tudor Poetry 1960 ed Ruth Hughey, 2 vols (Columbus, Ohio); W. Bang 1913 'Elizabethanische Miscellen: I. Roydoniana' *Bulletins de la classe des lettres* (Académie Royale de Belgique) pp 115–20; Peter E. Bondanella and Julia Conaway 1971 'Two Kinds of Renaissance Love: Spenser's "Astrophel" and Ronsard's "Adonis"' *ES* 52:311–18; Bryskett ed 1972; Francis Davison 1931–2 *A Poetical Rhapsody, 1602–1621* ed Hyder Edward Rollins, 2 vols (Cambridge, Mass); Katherine Duncan-Jones 1986 'Sidney, Stella and Lady Rich' in Jan van Dorsten, et al, eds *Sir Philip Sidney: 1586 and the Creation of a Legend* (Leiden) pp 170–92; Greville ed 1986; Thomas Perrin Harrison, Jr 1934 'Spenser, Ronsard, and Bion' *MLN* 49:139–45; Hudson 1935; Percy W. Long 1916 'Spenseriana: *The Lay of Clorinda*' *MLN* 31:79–82; G.C. Moore Smith 1914 'Matthew Roydon' *MLR* 9:97–8; Mustard 1914; Charles Grosvenor Osgood 1920 'The "Doleful Lay of Clorinda"' *MLN* 35:90–6; *Phoenix Nest* ed 1931; Sargent 1935.

Ate The antithesis of friendship and of the concord intended at the creation of the world, Ate, who is 'raised' by Duessa from 'the dwellings of the damned sprights' (*FQ* IV i 19), plays an important role in *FQ* IV. (She is first mentioned in II vii 55 as having plucked the golden apple from the Garden of Proserpina and thus caused the dispute among Venus, Juno, and Minerva which led to the Trojan War.) The account given of her at IV i 19–31 is largely a depiction of her 'dwelling,' 'Hard by the gates of hell,' its walls hung with monuments of her ruinous effect on history (Babylon, Thebes, Rome, Salem, Troy), as well as on persons (Nimrod, Alexander, the Argonauts). The landscape of thorns and 'barren brakes' parallels the desolation near Despair's cave (I ix 33–4). That Ate is 'borne of hellish brood' and had until 'of late' a monstrous shape links her also to Error. Her grotesque appearance with forked tongue and twisted mouth, and the contrary actions of her hands, ears, and feet (recalling the seven deadly sins riding 'unequall beasts' I iv 18), signify her double-dealing nature. It is fitting that being 'glad of spoyle and ruinous decay,' she testifies against Duessa in the trial at Mercilla's court (V ix 47).

While most frequently called 'hag,' Ate, like Duessa, can appear beautiful (IV i 31) in accordance with the 'fair is foul and foul is fair' motif of *FQ* IV-V, most evident in the existence of both true Florimell and false Florimell.

Ate enters *FQ* IV with Blandamour, Duessa, and Paridell, the four representing false friendship in contrast to the tetrad of true friendship: Cambina and Cambell, Canacee and Triamond. She provokes discord between Scudamour and Britomart, Scudamour and Glauce (i 47–54), Blandamour and Paridell (ii 11–19), the knights at the tournament for Florimell's girdle (leading to their dispersal, v 22–7), and Druon, Claribell, Blandamour, and Paridell, whose climactic battle involving Britomart and Scudamour only Arthur may resolve (ix 20–35). Ate may be said to generate all the negative characters and scenes in the second half of *The Faerie Queene*, including Care who forges 'yron wedges' (v 35), Lust who destroys the concord of love (vii 12), Sclaunder, that filthy hag whose spiteful words 'pricke, and wound' Arthur, Amoret, and Aemylia (viii 26), Corflambo (38–9), Radigund (V iv 37–44), Malengin (ix 5), Malfont (25–6), Envy and Detraction (xii 28–43), and the Blatant Beast (37–41).

Ate also relates to the wrathful figures in Book II, such as Furor, Pyrochles, Cymochles, Occasion, and Strife. Most striking is Atin (a male Ate), whose name suggests the Old French *atine* 'incitement to battle' (Hieatt 1957). As Pyrochles' 'varlet' (iv 37), he berates Guyon, pricks Cymochles, chides Pyrochles, widely stirs up 'Coles of contention and whot vengeance,' and finally flees with Archimago (viii 11, 56).

Ate (Gr *atē* reckless impulse; *aaō* hurt [mentally], mislead, infatuate), the goddess of discord, is related to the classical Furies conceived as revengers of earthly crimes, as in Shakespeare's *Julius Caesar*: Antony speaks of 'Caesar's spirit, ranging for revenge, / With Ate by his side come hot from hell' (III i 270–1). In Spenser, the Furies appear as a multitude ('And thousand furies wait on wrathful sword' II ii 30; cf IV ii 1) and as single figures (Tisiphone and Persephone in *Gnat* 342, 422; Megera in *Teares* 164). They are glossed by E.K. as 'the Authours of all evill and mischiefe' (*SC, Nov* 164 gloss). Like Ate, they are portrayed as forces which confuse the good and enflame the wicked to more evil.

In Homer, Agamemnon blames Ate (equated with Erinys) for his disastrous feud with Achilles, and recounts how Zeus hurled her from Mount Olympus for causing the strife between himself and Hera which altered the circumstances of Herakles' birth (*Iliad* 19.91–131). According to Hesiod, Chaos begat Night who begat Eris (Strife) who begat Ate (*Theogony* 116–230). Aspects of the interior of Ate's house in *The Faerie Queene* parallel those in the Temple of Mars in Statius' *Thebaid* 7.34–63, in Boccaccio's *Teseida* 7.29–37, and in Chaucer's *Knight's Tale* (*CT* I [A] 1967–2050). Spenser's Ate also resembles Virgil's Rumour (*Aeneid* 4.173–97) and his Allecto who, by firing Amata's fury, indirectly destroys the Latin-us-Aeneas concord and causes the battles in the last six books (*Aeneid* 7.323–58).

While classical in origin, Spenser's Ate also is clearly influenced by Christian treatments of wrath as one of the seven deadly sins. In French allegorical pilgrimages, such as Rutebeuf's *Voie de paradis* (c 1265) and Jean de la Mote's *Voie d'enfer* (c 1340), each sin has a house like Ate's. In *Voie d'enfer*, Wrath eats a man whose death she has caused and drinks his blood (as in *FQ* IV i 26). Also, Ate's dwelling (or self), like Wrath's, is typically surrounded by thorns which allow an easy entrance but prevent departure (see i 20 and the Lydgatean version of Deguileville's *Pèlerinage de la vie humaine* 15,593–605). Generally speaking, Ate, like Milton's Satan, represents a mad self-concern working contrary to creativity, imagination, community, love, concord, and proper relation to God.

JOAN HEIGES BLYTHE

Joan Heiges Blythe 1973 'Spenser's *The Faerie Queene*, IV, i, 20' *Expl* 32, item 29; A. Kent Hieatt 1957 'Spenser's Atin from *Atine*?' *MLN* 72:249–51.

Awe A 'gyantlike' guard who stands at the porch of Mercilla's palace, warding off 'guyle, and malice, and despight' (*FQ* V ix 22). Arthur and Artegall are led past him by Order, in a traditionally formal approach to the sovereign, through the great hall into the presence chamber, to Mercilla herself sitting in state, surrounded by her attributes, which include Dice, Eunomie, Eirene, Temperance, and 'sacred *Reverence*, yborne of heavenly strene' (32). In welcoming them, she abates 'somewhat of that Majestie and awe, / That whylome wont to doe so many quake' (35). Yet for all her 'piteous ruth' (50), she will soon allow judgment to proceed in the condemnation and execution of Duessa, the chief offender because she has opposed the royal authority.

Throughout *The Faerie Queene*, *awe*, with its adjective *awful*, is associated with royalty. Although Artegall and Arthur in the present episode are not formally Mercilla's subjects, their behavior is proper for a subject, approaching the sovereign with initial awe at her magnificence, and then with appreciation of the order of the realm (which proceeds from the maintenance of peace through the punishment of malefactors such as Bonfont) and finally with admiration and reverence in the presence of majesty itself. In its extended meaning, awe is a dread mingled with reverence in the presence of supreme authority or sacredness (see *OED* sv 1, 2) either of God or of God's majesty reflected in monarchy. Such awe informs Spenser's invocation of Elizabeth at the outset of his poem as 'Goddesse heavenly bright, / Mirrour of grace and Majestie divine' (I proem 4).

Awe was appropriate only for the public office of the Tudor Queen, not for her private person, a legal distinction inherited from the Middle Ages (see Axton 1977, Kantorowicz 1957). The reverence accorded to Elizabeth indicated a general recognition that, among all the dangers of disintegration and faction, the survival and prosperity of the Tudor state depended upon the maintenance of her sovereignty in Parliament, and upon her personal capability as the active head of government in all its branches.

An informative Elizabethan source is the 'Exhortation to Obedience,' one of the official homilies read frequently in the churches. Its argument runs from the appreciation of order in nature to order in society divinely supported, and maintained by an active magistracy and the free rational consent of the governed who are its beneficiaries. To support this notion of consent, the homily cites Romans 13.5: 'We must needs obey, not only for fear of vengeance, but also because of conscience, and even for this cause pay ye tribute, for they [rulers] are God's ministers' (translation in homily). In this ecclesiastical context, obedience to the Queen is supported by biblical examples (Elizabeth like David is 'God's anointed').

While the Queen commands awe from her subjects, she is herself constrained by her awe of God from whom her being and power are derived. This aspect of Tudor orthodoxy is expressed in Erasmus' 'Praier for the Peace of the Church,' published in the authorized *Primer* of 1545: 'Geve unto Princes and rulers the grace to stand in awe of the, that thei so maye guyde the common weale as thei shuld shortly rendre accomptes unto the that art king of kynges.' FLORENCE R. SANDLER

Marie Axton 1977 *The Queen's Two Bodies: Drama and the Elizabethan Succession* (London); 'An Exhortation concerning Good Order, and Obedience to Rulers and Magistrates' in *Homilies* ed 1623; *The Primer Set Furth by the Kinges Majestie and His Clergie* 1545 (London; rpt Delmar, NY 1974).

Axiochus (See *Var Prose* pp 19–38.) A short dialogue in Greek between Socrates and Axiochus, an old man, concerning the fear of death; an English version (pub 1592) has been attributed to Spenser. From the first century AD, the original author was believed to be Plato, for despite its unusual style, its characters and scenes are typical of the Platonic corpus. From an early date, the work was also attributed to Aeschines; in the fifteenth century, Neoplatonic philosophers thought it was by Xenophon. It was very popular in the Renaissance, being translated into Latin (by Ficino, Rudolph Agricola, and others), French (by Etienne Dolet and Philippe Duplessis-Mornay), and Italian. There were also reports of a translation into English by one 'Edw. Spenser,' and by the late eighteenth century this was thought to be one of the lost works of Edmund Spenser (see Osborne 1744 and Upton 1758 in *Var Prose* p 487).

The English *Axiochus* was rediscovered in this century by Frederick Padelford who in 1934 published a facsimile, with introduction and facsimiles of a Greek version and a Latin translation (1568, by Rayanus Welsdalius) upon which the English appears to be based. Padelford strongly favored Spenser as the translator, claiming that the work was done before the poet left England in 1580. He based his assertion on four main points. The first name 'Edw.' could simply be a mistaken expansion by the printer, Cuthbert Burbie, of the abbreviation of Edmund as 'Ed.' on title pages of other works. The note 'To the Reader' at the head of the translation refers to 'the delightfull pleasures his verses yeeldeth,' suggesting the translator was a well-known published poet. Spenser could have known *Axiochus* through his connection with Sidney, who knew Duplessis-Mornay. Finally, there are many parallels between this translation of *Axiochus* and Spenser's poetry.

Padelford's claim provoked controversy. Some suggested that he did not have enough evidence to make any positive identification of the translator, or claimed that the translator was really Anthony Munday (who may indeed have written the euphuistic 'sweet speech or Oration' discovered later in a more complete copy of *Axiochus*). Others, including Douglas Bush (1935), supported Padelford's claim.

There the matter stood until Rudolf Gottfried included *Axiochus* (but not the 'sweet speech') in the *Variorum Prose* – not because he found the external evidence compelling but because of Padelford's verbal parallels, to which he added many others. The authority of the *Variorum* seems to have silenced the debate (summarized by Gottfried in *Var Prose* pp 487–96). Three articles published subsequently build upon earlier arguments and constitute a strong case (though almost exclusively on external evidence) for Munday's authorship (Wright 1959, 1961, 1963).

Considered singly, the verbal echoes can be written off as coincidental; but, as Gottfried argued, numbers count, and the cumulative effect is impressive. Still more noteworthy, though not noticed by Padelford or Gottfried, is an echo in *FQ* II xii 51, not of a word or short phrase, but of an entire clause from *Axiochus*, extending to five lines in the 1592 text, where Socrates is describing the Elysian Fields (*Var Prose* p 37). Such verbal correspondences do not prove that Spenser translated *Axiochus*. He could have adapted the passage for *The Faerie Queene* directly from the Latin and known nothing of an English prose version, for the dialogue was popular in the sixteenth century. Given the association of Spenser's name with the translation, however, the discovery of a sustained paraphrase in the poetry weighs in favor of his authorship.

HAROLD L. WEATHERBY

There is no extended treatment of the possible influence or relationship of the thought or imagery of *Axiochus* to Spenser's poetry.

On *Axiochus*, see Plato 1930 *Dialogues apocryphes* ed Joseph Souilhé in *Oeuvres complètes* (edition Budé) 13.3 (Paris) pp 117–36. On the English translation, see *The 'Axiochus' of Plato Translated by Edmund Spenser* ed Frederick Morgan Padelford (Baltimore 1934; reviewed by Douglas Bush in *MLN* 50[1935]:191–2); *Var Prose* pp 269–77, 487–96; see also David V. Erdman and Ephim G. Fogel 1966 *Evidence for Authorship: Essays on Problems of Attribution* (Ithaca, NY) pp 423–7; Harold L. Weatherby 1985 '*Axiochus* and the Bower of Bliss: Some Fresh Light on Sources and Authorship' *SSt* 6:95–113; Celeste Turner Wright 1959 'Young Anthony Mundy Again' *SP* 56:150–68; Wright 1961 'Anthony Mundy, "Edward" Spenser, and E.K.' *PMLA* 76:34–9; Wright 1963 '"Lazarus Pyott" and Other Inventions of Anthony Mundy' *PQ* 42:532–41.

Aylett, Robert (1583–1655?) This minor seventeenth-century poet was most clearly influenced by Spenser in his six books of poetic meditations (*The Brides Ornaments* 1621–5, *Peace with Her Foure Garders* 1622, *Thrifts Equipage* 1622) on themes such as heavenly love, justice, mercy, prayer, peace, and death. Each book consists of five meditations composed in Spenserian stanzas. *The Brides Ornaments* is prefaced by a verse translation of the Song of Solomon.

The proem to *The Brides Ornaments* I provides a thin narrative framework for the meditations. The narrator sets up a Protestant pattern of spiritual regeneration based on Spenser's house of Holiness (Padelford 1936:5). A bevy of allegorical ladies cures and educates the speaker much as Caelia and her daughters tend Redcrosse in *FQ* I x. They make him spiritually fit to enter the Court of Heavenly Love and redirect his sexual energies in accord with the doctrines expressed in Spenser's *Hymne of Heavenly Love*. The narrator ignores Spenser's *Hymne* in the first stanzas of the proem, suggesting that 'Homer, Virgil, Spencer' never 'waited on the glorious Court / Of Heavenly Love'; but most of the narrative is more closely related to this hymn than to *The Faerie Queene*. Aylett's argument to the Song of Solomon ('My Muse, that whilome, swaid by lust ... Now viewes her vanity') echoes Spenser's 'Lo I the man, whose Muse whilome did maske' (*FQ* I proem 1), but it is closer to the retraction of 'lewd layes' in *Heavenly Love* (8–14). Much of what follows in the meditations of *The Brides Ornaments* is likewise paralleled in *Heavenly Love*.

Other specific examples of Aylett's use of Spenser include *Thrifts Equipage* 57–8, which quotes passages from stanzas 40–6 of the Despair episode in *FQ* I ix in a meditation on 'Death' (see also *Sp All* pp 158–9, 163–6, 169–71). His poetic achievement is thin and mediocre at best. Spenserian in its form and ideas but Miltonic in its Protestant ethos, his verse provides undistinguished examples of seventeenth-century imitation.

NOAM FLINKER

Lewalski 1979:67, 231–2, 427; Frederick Morgan Padelford 1936 'Robert Aylett' *HLB* 10:1–48; Padelford 1938–9 'Robert Aylett: A Supplement' *HLQ* 2:471–8.

B

Bacchus The wine god. He and his feminine votaries, the bacchantes, were associated in classical mythology with drunken and erotic frenzies. Because he was fabled to be the first to cultivate the grape, he was also considered a fertility god. He had many names (eg, Dionysus, Liber Pater) and was identified with the Egyptian fertility god Osiris, with whom he shares many attributes (Klein 1986:101–2). Spenser knew the forms, attributes, and myths of Bacchus as they appeared in Renaissance and classical texts, and he alludes to the traditional attributes of Bacchus in his minor poems (eg, *SC, Oct* 105–8, *Epithalamion* 250–5).

In *The Faerie Queene*, Spenser both integrates and transforms Bacchic figures and myths. When Una encounters the fauns and satyrs, for example, the pagan pastoral world with which Bacchus was always associated is made an instrument of 'Eternall providence,' although Bacchus himself appears only allusively as '*Bacchus* merry fruit' (*FQ* I vi 7, 15). But when Bacchus is dissociated from the natural world, he is associated with evil, for example, in the Bacchic figure of Gluttony in the parade of deadly sins (iv 22).

In *FQ* II, Amavia ascribes to Bacchus the poisoned cup of Acrasia which drives her lovers 'drunken mad' and then to their deaths (i 52, 55). Her cup signifies the wine of concupiscence and is opposed to the water that signifies abstinence and virginity, as the metamorphosis of Diana's nymph suggests (ii 6–10; cf Kaske 1976). The false Genius at the gate of the Bower of Bliss resembles Comus, god of revelry, as well as the young Bacchus (see Cartari 1571:414–16). Like Bacchus, he offers 'A mighty Mazer bowle of wine ... Wherewith all new-come guests he gratifide' (xii 49). Bacchus' grapes hang on the next porch and 'themselves ... incline' into the hands of 'passers by'; they are also squeezed into wine by a bacchante-like figure, Excesse. Spenser gives the 'embracing vine' and inclining grapes the seductive attributes of Acrasia in a conflation reminiscent of the traditional pairing of Bacchus and Venus (see Cartari 1571:442–3, and the emblems of Sambucus 1564:172, La Perrière 1539 no 2, Junius 1565 no 52, and Whitney 1586:42). Perhaps to confirm this union, further on in the Bower is a phallic fountain decorated with the ivy sacred to Bacchus (Boccaccio *Genealogia* 5.25, Cartari 1571:428–30) and the shapes of Venus' 'naked boyes.' Thus Spenser's false Genius recalls traditional descriptions of Bacchus and Comus as voluptuaries; he is linked to the eroticism of the bacchantes, now rendered passive; and he points to the presence deep in the Bower of a libidinous but sterile Venus. Spenser also links Bacchic elements in the Bower with the lifelessness of art – as opposed to the fecundity of nature – when he says that some of Excesse's grapes and the ivy on the fountain are made of gold by hidden 'art.' This art may be that which wrought the Garden of Proserpina, where Tantalus reaches eternally for golden apples placed beyond his grasp (vii 53–66). 'Greedie *Tantalus*,' therefore, may represent the source and end of the Bacchic gluttony which permeates the Bower (see Alciati ed 1581 no 84 *Avaritia* 'Greed,' and Holloway 1952), a fitting prefiguration because Bacchus, the son of Proserpina in some legends, was also a god in hell (Giraldi 1548:384; Conti 1567: fols 147, 150, 155v; Cartari 1571:426).

After Guyon destroys the Bower, Bacchus is relegated to his Renaissance form as a fabulous mythological figure found in stories and in figures of speech like metonymy. Although he still signifies wine and lust, he is no longer demonic. In Castle Joyeous, for instance, Spenser conflates Bacchus' male and female attributes into the shadowy allegorical figure of 'Bacchante' (III i 45). In the castle of Malbecco, Bacchus as wine plays a part in the game of courtly love (ix 30–1). In the castle of Busirane, however, when we see the tapestry on which the classical Bacchus 'to compasse *Philliras* hard love' has 'turnd himselfe into a fruitfull vine, / And into her faire bosome made his grapes decline' (xi 43), it appears in retrospect that the false Genius and Excesse were meant to represent mirror images of the same sins (cf II xii 54). By depicting Bacchus here on a tapestry, Spenser may indicate that the Bacchic and venerean temptations which were nearly passive in the Bower have become wholly inanimate by the time Britomart reaches the castle, possessing only the apparent movement of art.

Much later, in Book V, Spenser introduces us to Bacchus in his beneficent Egyptian role as Osiris, husband of Isis, and associates him with the crocodile. Although he dissociates this figure from Bacchus' vinous attributes by denying to the priests of Isis Church the use of wine – a use which Spenser and others linked to chthonic, unruly forces (vii 10–11; Plutarch *Moralia* 353 B-C in ed 1970 ch 6) – he does show the crocodile ingesting flames and tempests and thus reassociates him with forces of unrule (vii 15).

By moving from names and places traditionally associated with the western Bacchus to those associated with the Egyptian Bacchus, Spenser may have wished to emphasize the movement from the destruction of Bacchus' negative attributes to the consequent release of his positive attributes.

JOAN LARSEN KLEIN

Alciati ed 1581; Boccaccio ed 1951; Cartari 1571; Conti 1567; Giraldi 1548; Hieatt 1975a; J[ohn] Holloway 1952 'The Seven Deadly Sins in *The Faerie Queene*, Book II' *RES* ns 3:13–18; Junius 1565; Kaske 1976; Joan Larsen Klein 1986 'The Demonic Bacchus in Spenser and Milton' *MiltonS* 21:93–118; de La Perrière 1539; Plutarch ed 1970; Sambucus 1564; Whitney 1586.

baffling and degradation From time immemorial many professions and social distinctions have been signified by the possession of special garments or accoutrements; and correspondingly the loss of such status has been signaled by their formal, often forcible, removal. Commonly, a disgraced cleric is still said to be 'unfrocked'; and the Elizabethans looked back (especially in Shakespeare's play) to such unique events as Richard II's formal abdication, for which he arrived 'apareled in vesture and robe royall the diademe on his head, and the scepter in his hand,' and which ended when he 'delyvered his scepter and croune to the duke of Lancastre' (Hall 1550: fol viiiv-ixr). The creation of a knight originally involved the giving of ritual clothing; similarly, his degradation was signaled by the removal of his characterizing costume and accountrements, even – though rarely – in Spenser's lifetime. The term *baffling* was sometimes applied generally to such chivalric degradation but usually referred more specifically to a particular action indicating dishonor.

Two characters in *The Faerie Queene* are degraded by being 'baffuld': Braggadocchio and Turpine (V iii 37, VI vii 27). Both are publicly humiliated for dishonorable crimes (especially lying or perjury) and for their consequent chivalric unworthiness. The 'traytour *Turpin*' is punished for his attempted murder of Arthur; such high treason was usually the only crime that resulted in degradation in Spenser's day. The ceremony was rare but must have been spectacular: for example, when in 1569 the Earl of Northumberland was expelled from the highest English form of knighthood, the Order of the Garter, the ceremony took place at the home of the Order, St George's Chapel in Windsor Castle, and included the hacking to pieces of his arms, armor, and banner. Surviving accounts confirm the sense of ritual and the frightening violence of Spenser's descriptions (see J. Nichols 1823, 1:263; BL, Harley Ms 304, fol 84v; see also Leslie 1983).

Turpine is 'despoyle[d] of knightly banerall' (VI vii 26), but Braggadocchio's punishment is given in more detail: Talus 'from him reft his shield, and it renverst, / And blotted out his armes with falshood blent, / And himselfe baffuld, and his armes unherst, / And broke his sword in twaine, and all his armour sperst' (V iii 37). The destruction of Braggadocchio's arms and armor, the symbols of his fraudulent claim to knightly status, closely resembles such ceremonies of degradation as that to which the Earl of Northumberland was subject.

When *baffuld* is used in *The Faerie Queene*, it means more than general degradation. The origins of the term are far from clear, but it is used by Edward Hall in his *Union of the Two Noble Families of Lancaster and York* (1550). Hall explains that to be baffled is considered 'a great reproche amonge the Scottes, and is used when a man is openly perjured, and then they make of hym an Image paynted reversed, with hys heles upwarde' (sig G4r; ed 1809:559). Turpine, like Braggadocchio, is a liar; and Arthur 'by the heeles him hung upon a tree, / And baffuld so.' Although this action is similar to that reported by Hall, there is one important difference: whereas baffling is usually performed on a man's picture, or metaphorically on his good name (see the examples cited in *OED*), Spenser stresses that the actual person, Braggadocchio, is 'himselfe baffuld.' Yet he shows his awareness that baffling is normally connected with a representation when he describes the punishment of Turpine, who is 'baffuld so, that all which passed by, / The picture of his punishment might see.' The reference here to 'picture' may allude to the manner in which characters and events in *The Faerie Queene* operate as moral exempla: the baffling of Braggadocchio and Turpine acts as an emblem embedded in the poem for the education of 'all which passed by,' particularly those who are on a quest.

MICHAEL LESLIE

Barnfield, Richard (1574–1627) In *Palladis Tamia* (1598), Francis Meres included Barnfield in a list of English poets, headed by Sidney, whom he considered 'best for Pastorall' (G.G. Smith 1904, 2:231). Thomas Warton regarded him as perhaps occupying the first place among the 'minor poets of Elizabeth's reign,' and concluded his *History of English Poetry* (1781) with a plea for a collected edition, which did not appear until over a century later. Barnfield's link with Spenser is signaled in the subtitle of the only book about him, Harry Morris' *Richard Barnfield, Colin's Child* (1963). According to Morris, 'No poet of merit was ever so closely allied to another as Barnfield was to Spenser' (p 18).

His first published work, *The Affectionate Shepheard* (1594), is a strange but vivid two-part complaint documenting the love of the shepherd Daphnis for the 'sweet-fac'd Boy' Ganimede, who is courted also by 'faire Queene *Guendolen*.' It is dedicated to Lady Penelope Rich, and has been thought to reflect her personal life (Hudson 1935). The poem abounds in details of country sports, animals, food, and clothes, and includes a six-stanza digression suggesting with much ingenuity that young Ganimede should have his hair cut: 'Faire-long-haire-wearing *Absolon* was kild' (sig C2v). Little though Spenser might have liked association with so uncompromising a celebration of 'disorderly love, which the learned call paederastice,' it was probably the *Januarye* eclogue of *The Shepheardes Calender*, and E.K.'s notes on lines 57 and 59, which sent Barnfield to Virgil's second eclogue (Morris 1963:17). Barnfield's *Cynthia, with Certaine Sonnets* (1595, dedicated to William Stanley, Earl of Derby) is prefaced with a justification of the earlier poem as 'nothing else, but an imitation of *Virgill*, in the second Eglogue of *Alexis*.' Here he also declared his indebtedness to Spenser, craving indulgence for *Cynthia* 'if for no other cause, yet, for that it is the first imitation of the verse of that excellent Poet, Maister *Spencer*, in his *Fayrie Queene*' (sig A3r-v; *Sp All* p 39).

Cynthia consists of an account, in nineteen Spenserian stanzas, of a vision of the judgment of Paris in which Jove awards the golden apple to Queen Elizabeth. Blending royal panegyric and Spenserian verse form, the poem is a highly miniaturized echo of *The Faerie Queene*, as a specimen stanza may show (sig B4v):

In Westerne world amids the Ocean maine,
In compleat Vertue shining like the Sunne,
In great Renowne a maiden Queene doth raigne,
Whose royall Race, in Ruine first begun,
Till Heavens bright Lamps dissolve shall nere be done:
In whose faire eies Love linckt with vertues been,
In everlasting Peace and Union.
Which sweet Consort in her full well beseeme
Of Bounty, and of Beauty fairest Fayrie Queene.

Cynthia is followed by twenty sonnets exploring further the love of Daphnis for Ganimede, an ode describing Daphnis transferring his affections from Ganimede to a fair 'Lasse' who turns out to be 'Eliza' (ie, Queen Elizabeth), and an epyllion in sixains on the tragedy of Cassandra.

Barnfield's other poems reflect the influence of his friends Abraham Fraunce and Thomas Watson as much as that of Spenser, though in his *Poems, in Divers Humors* (published as the final section of *The Encomion of Lady Pecunia* 1598), he declares his devotion to Spenser, 'whose deepe Conceit is such, / As passing all Conceit, needs no defence' (in sonnet 'To His Friend Master R.L.'), and opens 'A Remembrance of some English Poets' with this tribute: 'Live *Spenser* ever, in thy *Fairy Queene*: / Whose like (for deepe Conceit) was never seene. / Crownd mayst thou bee, unto thy more renowne, / (As King of Poets) with a Lawrell crowne' (*Sp All* p 56). This latter poem celebrates Spenser, Daniel, Drayton, and Shakespeare as living poets whereas the immediately previous poem, 'Against the Dispraysers of Poetrie,' commemorates dead ones such as Sidney and Gascoigne.

Barnfield acquired an association with Shakespeare through the inclusion in *The Passionate Pilgrim* of his 'As it fell upon a day' (from *Poems, in Divers Humors*); the same poem, shortened by 30 lines, was also included in *Englands Helicon* (1600). It is unlikely that Barnfield had any part in either publication, for by 1598 or even earlier he had retired to his native Staffordshire, living there for the next 30 years without publishing any more poetry.

KATHERINE DUNCAN-JONES

There are editions of Barnfield's poems by A.B. Grosart (1876), Edward Arber (1882), and Montague Summers (1936a). An edition by E.J.N. Bramall (1936b) was printed but not published (a proof copy is in the Bodleian Library, Oxford); *The Encomion of Lady Pecunia, or The Praise of Money* 1598 (London) is rpt 1974 (Amsterdam and Norwood, NJ). See also Hudson 1935; Waldo F. McNeir 1955 'Barnfield's Borrowings from Spenser' *N&Q* 200:510–11, which shows how *Cynthia* adopts the phrasing of *FQ* I-III; Morris 1963.

baroque The term *baroque* is notorious for the controversy that has attended its meaning and its appropriate use as a concept in literary history. Its application as a literary term was first suggested in passing in 1888 by the art historian Heinrich Wölfflin, who proposed that the difference between the poetic styles of Ariosto and Tasso might have a parallel in the difference between the styles of Renaissance and Baroque visual artists. Wölfflin characterizes Tasso's style with the formula 'weniger Anschauung, mehr Stimmung' ('less visualization, more mood'), and finds in the poet of the *Gerusalemme liberata* a kind of imagistic chiaroscuro and a degree of emotional saturation which contrast markedly with the clear and linear visual imagination and ironic aesthetic distance typical of Ariosto.

In Wölfflin's terms, a case might be made for *baroque* as a term descriptive of some aspects of Spenser's work, the texture of which (particularly in *The Faerie Queene*) frequently recalls Tasso in its languorous beauty of sound and its overt demand for the reader's emotional involvement with the fiction. In the century since Wölfflin, however, literary studies of the baroque have undergone considerable complication, and the term is now most frequently applied to authors whose extravagance of wit, eccentricity of form, purposeful violation of decorum, and lack of concern for sensuous beauty in diction and imagery are deeply alien to Spenser and Tasso alike. In most recent studies, Tasso is viewed as a transitional figure between Renaissance and baroque.

In English literature, *baroque* has come to be employed to describe such seventeenth-century phenomena as metaphysical poetry (especially Crashaw's), Jacobean drama, and the anti-Ciceronian prose of Bacon, Burton, and Browne. Critics have concentrated on such devices as conceit and paradox, and such stylistic traits as irony, ambiguity, and verbal complexity; intricate manipulations of time-schemes and a predominantly dramatic orientation perceptible even in nondramatic genres have also received attention (eg, from Lowry Nelson, Jr 1961). Although this use of the term *baroque* remains the most common, the relatively recent emergence of the term and concept of *mannerism* as a designation for some writing found in the last decade of the sixteenth century has, for some authorities, displaced the term *baroque* forward chronologically so that it evokes Milton, Otway, and the early Dryden (eg, see Sypher 1955).

The use of *baroque* to designate any major aspect of Spenser's work would seem unwise. His firm sense of genre and poetic form, his observance of decorum, and, most of all, his use of imagery to create a plausible mimesis of the natural world rather than a frank artifact either intellectualized

(Donne) or phantasmagoric (Crashaw) – all these things mark him as a Renaissance author. It may be noted, however, that the late occurrence of the English Renaissance and the consequent presence of early baroque Italian stimuli in Spenser's milieu make inevitable an occasional proto-baroque coloration in his essentially Renaissance work. FRANK J. WARNKE

Bender 1972; Roy Daniells 1963 *Milton, Mannerism and Baroque* (Toronto); *Milton Enc* sv 'Baroque, Milton and'; James V. Mirollo 1984 *Mannerism and Renaissance Poetry: Concept, Mode, Inner Design* (New Haven); Lowry Nelson, Jr 1961 *Baroque Lyric Poetry* (New Haven); Wylie Sypher 1955 *Four Stages of Renaissance Style* (Garden City, NY); René Wellek 1946–7 'The Concept of Baroque in Literary Scholarship' *JAAC* 5:77–109, rpt with 'Postscript 1962' in his *Concepts of Criticism* ed Stephen G. Nichols, Jr (New Haven 1963) pp 69–127; Heinrich Wölfflin 1964 *Renaissance and Baroque* tr Kathrin Simon (London), first pub 1888.

du Bartas, Guillaume de Salluste (1544–90) A Gascon Huguenot in the service of Henri de Navarre, du Bartas was widely admired in Spenser's England for his sacred poetry. His first publication, *La Muse chrestiene* (1574), included a brief epic based on the biblical story of Judith and Holofernes, an allegorical dream-vision of the triumph of faith, and the poem that gave the volume its title: 'L'Uranie,' which recounts how a Christian muse, adapted from the classical Muse of astronomy, appeared to the young poet and exhorted him to turn from secular themes to the words and works of God. Devotion to Urania bore fruit in an ambitious poem of Creation and sacred history: *La Sepmaine ou création du monde* (1578), based on the first two chapters of Genesis but vastly expanded with theological speculation, contemporary science, and moral reflection. This hexaemeral poem, filling in the biblical account of creation in six days, was followed by *La Seconde Sepmaine* (1584), which presented only the first two 'days' of a planned 'week' that was to take in all of human history beginning with Adam's fall and culminating in the eternal Sabbath. In his later years, du Bartas continued his Second Week from the calling of Abraham to the Babylonian Captivity; these sections, the Third and Fourth Days, were published piecemeal after his death. Elaborated not only with more learning and theological disputation but with extended battle descriptions, allegorical interludes, ecphrases, and passionate speeches of love and war, *La Seconde Sepmaine* even in its unfinished state more than doubled the length of its predecessor; the two Weeks together constitute a poem of over 20,000 lines.

Fervently admired in France for a short period, the works of du Bartas gained longer popularity in Renaissance England, especially through the translations of Joshua Sylvester (1563–1618), which appeared between 1590 and 1614. But the English vogue of du Bartas began well before these translations and involved some of Spenser's associates from the period before he left for Ireland in 1580. Sidney may have translated *La Sepmaine* (for evidence about this lost work, see Sidney ed 1962:339). Harvey lauded du Bartas frequently and extravagantly, placing him with or even above Homer, Euripides, Virgil, and Dante, and only a degree below the Bible itself (eg, Harvey ed 1913:115, 137, 168; Relle 1972:403, 411; Harvey 1593: sig G4r-v).

Spenser seems to have shared the general esteem for du Bartas; but although he took pleasure in the Fourth Day of the First Week, according to Harvey (ed 1913:161), he was influenced very little by the epic Weeks and only in limited ways by Urania and her message. In the envoy to *Ruines of Rome*, he adds to the praise of his source, du Bellay: 'And after thee, gins *Bartas* hie to rayse / His heavenly Muse, th'Almightie to adore' (459–60). Thus, du Bartas comes 'after' du Bellay not only in chronology but also in his move beyond secular poetry to immutable divine truths (Prescott 1978:51). Very likely, 'L'Uranie' underlies the Muses' lament in *Teares of the Muses* about poets who debase their high calling in flatteries and lewd loves, and especially Urania's plea for poetry that is heavenly in both matter and treatment: 'contemplation of things heavenlie wrought' (526).

To what degree did Spenser himself heed Urania's call? Ponsonby's preface to *Complaints* attributes to him several works, none of them now extant, of a scriptural or divine nature: translations of Ecclesiastes and the Song of Solomon, *The Dying Pellican*, *The Howers of the Lord*, *The Sacrifice of a Sinner*, and *The Seven Psalmes* (Printer to Reader). A Uranian redirection may inform the scheme of *Fowre Hymnes*, with the latter two presented as a 'retractation' of the first two, 'making in stead of those two Hymnes of earthly or naturall love and beautie, two others of heavenly and celestiall' (*FH* epistle). Though the heavenly hymns complement rather than contradict the thoroughly Platonic earthly hymns, they do represent a reorientation in their explicit Christianity.

In general, however, within the shared province of Christian epic, Spenser and du Bartas remain fairly far apart. The one recognizable echo of the *Sepmaines* in *The Faerie Queene* that has been noted is local: the description of the house of Alma (*FQ* II ix) parallels in conception and in several details du Bartas' paean to the human body in the First Week, Sixth Day (477–708; see Upham 1908 App B:506–18). *The Faerie Queene*, for all its moral seriousness, is not a divine poem; rather than reaching for scriptural truth, it approaches a complex reality through shadows and fictions. Whereas du Bartas embroiders and embellishes biblical narrative, Spenser creates his own framework, choosing in his subject of 'Arthure, before he was king' to be free even of the constraints that received Arthurian legend might place on his inventive scope. Stylistically, *The Faerie Queene* owes nothing to the *Sepmaines*; and, although both epics work by accumulation, du Bartas' paratactic mode differs fundamentally from the hypotaxis favored by Spenser.

It was probably the comprehensive magnitude of their major works that led contemporaries to link Spenser and du Bartas and to measure the greatness of one by his outdoing of the other (Hall *Virgidemiarum* 1597, Fitzgeffrey *Affaniae* 1601, and R.R. in verses to *Devine Weekes* 1605, all in *Sp All* pp 54–5, 84–5, 99–100; even Sylvester, the translator, refers to Spenser as 'our mysterious EL-FINE oracle' in the first section of the Second Week, see du Bartas ed 1979, 1:317). The two appealed to the same audience; and followers of Spenser like Drayton, William Browne, and Giles and Phineas Fletcher often show as well the influence of du Bartas' style and matter. SUSAN SNYDER

Guillaume de Salluste du Bartas 1935–40 *Works* ed Urban T. Holmes, et al, 3 vols (Chapel Hill) (French texts with English apparatus); du Bartas ed 1979 (Sylvester's tr); L.B. Campbell 1959; E.R. Gregory, Jr 1970 'Du Bartas, Sidney, and Spenser' *CLS* 7:437–49; Prescott 1978; Kurt Reichenberger 1963 *Themen und Quellen der Sepmaine* (Tübingen); Eleanor Relle 1972 'Some New Marginalia and Poems of Gabriel Harvey' *RES* ns 23:401–16; Alfred Horatio Upham 1908 *The French Influence in English Literature from the Accession of Elizabeth to the Restoration* (New York).

Bead-men The Red Cross Knight must encounter the 'seven Bead-men' and learn works of mercy in their hospice before he can visit the Mount of Contemplation (*FQ* I x 36–45); this episode contrasts with Lucifera and her six wizards, who comprise the seven deadly sins (iv 12–35). The seven good works are entertaining strangers, giving food and drink to the hungry and thirsty, clothing the naked, relieving prisoners, comforting the sick and dying, burying the dead, and caring for widows and orphans. The list originates in the Sermon on the Mount (Matt 25:34–46); it was developed by Lactantius in the fourth century, and codified by Thomas Aquinas as the seven corporal works of mercy. The topic did not receive much attention at the Reformation, but it was treated by Heinrich Bullinger in his influential *Decades*. Like Bullinger, Spenser follows Lactantius rather than Aquinas, who separates food and drink and leaves out the widows and orphans (Mounts 1939).

The insistence on good works in this episode, in which Redcrosse learns how to frame his life 'In holy righteousnesse, without rebuke or blame' (x 45), does not necessarily represent a Roman Catholic tendency (cf Whitaker 1950:54–6). Protestants also emphasized that Christians should work in the world (Redcrosse is not permitted to remain on the Mount of Contemplation at x 63). Their point was that the works which people perform out of their own resources cannot ensure salvation, and this seems to be acknowledged by Spenser in the prior attention to Fidelia and the state of Redcrosse's soul (18–29), and in the opening stanza of the canto.

What does raise questions about the religious basis of *The Faerie Queene* is the recurring use of Roman Catholic figures like beadsmen, palmers, and hermits (see Oetgen 1971). Beadsmen were paid to pray for benefactors or for the souls of the dead, using a string of beads to keep count of the number of times they repeated set phrases. They would seem to epitomize all that the reformed churches found mechanical and deluded as a way of relating to God; in the homily 'Of Good Workes,' the telling of beads comes first in a list of 'papisticall superstitions and abuses.' The issue is specially strange and complicated in the episode of the Bead-men, because they do not in fact spend their days in prayer, mechanical or otherwise, but 'in doing godly thing' (36): they represent the active life, not the contemplative. Such figures derive from Spenser's Italian models. In Ariosto's *Orlando furioso*, a hermit able to work miracles teaches Ruggiero, baptizes him and Sobrino, and heals Oliver (41.52–60, 43.187–96). In Tasso's *Gerusalemme liberata*, the hermit Peter counsels the Christians and encourages them by foretelling their success and arranging public prayers (opening stanzas of Book II). Spenser's use of such conventional figures may indicate a disjunction between Protestantism and these literary models, rather than a respect for Roman Catholic religious practices.

ALAN SINFIELD

Chew 1962:131–3; Charles E. Mounts 1939 'Spenser's Seven Bead-men and the Corporal Works of Mercy' *PMLA* 54:974–80; Jerome Oetgen 1971 'Spenser's Treatment of Monasticism in Book I of *The Faerie Queene*' *ABR* 22:109–20.

beauty When Spenser began writing, beauty in style and as a topic (eg, a lady's beauty) were more problematic than praiseworthy. Poetry which pleased through its verbal music and brilliance was either beyond the reach of mid-Tudor poets or contrary to their moral aims. A lady's beauty was apt to seem at odds with either her virtue or her lover's. The author of *SC Aprill*, *Muiopotmos*, *The Faerie Queene*, and the later shorter poems was one of the first English writers for whom beauty was central among the qualities to be praised and cultivated poetically. When Shakespeare referred in sonnet 106 to 'beauty making beautiful old rhyme,' he may have had Spenser's poetry in mind. Words such as *fair* (found in ten columns of Osgood's *Concordance*) pervade Spenser's vocabulary of praise along with *gentle*, *noble*, *glorious*, and *true*, the hallmarks of virtue.

Like Sidney, but more abundantly and consistently, Spenser transmitted to his contemporaries and posterity several convictions: that true beauty is, like the soul, heavenly in origin, and physical beauty is ordinarily emblematic of virtue; that once beauty has been understood as essentially spiritual, love in response can be distinguished from vulgar desire; that beauty and the pleasure derived from it are among the defining traits of art; and that poetry may best inculcate virtues through beautiful images. Like Sidney's, Spenser's poetics depends on 'the saying of Plato and Tully ... that who could see virtue would be wonderfully ravished with the love of her beauty.' Also, 'Poesy ... should be *eikastike* (which some learned have defined: figuring forth good things) ... [not] *phantastike* (which doth, contrariwise, infect the fancy with unworthy objects)' (*Defence* ed 1973b:98, 104). Spenser was more schematic than Sidney in distinguishing eikastic from fantastic phenomena, but the difficulty of separating essentials (truth) from appearances (often false) is a central theme for him as for Sidney, with beauty serving as a source of both confusion and clarity.

Spenser's aesthetic principles serve a moral vision in which virtue is understood primarily as love, and Venus, 'Queene of beautie and of grace' (*FQ* IV x 44), stands for order and civility rather than lawless passion. A beautiful lady provides the motive in several heroic quests, and union with beauty rewards virtue. The paradigm is Arthur, inspired by his dream of Gloriana: 'From that day forth I lov'd that face divine; / From that day forth I cast in carefull mind, / To seeke her out with labour, and long tyne' (I ix 15). Gloriana's power over the hero's imagination lies in her beauty, which is insubstantial and remote. Several other lovers' quests involve variations on Arthur's predicament: separation haunted by a memorable vision of someone perceived as 'divine.'

Virtue is fully rewarded by union with beauty only at the end of the Red Cross Knight's quest, when Una is presented as his intended bride in several stanzas emphasizing 'The blazing brightnesse of her beauties beame' (I xii 21–3). This union seals the knight's destiny as a saint, but the bliss of his heaven on earth is only a foretaste, interrupted by obligations to Gloriana. Similarly, but without theological overtones, the unions of Britomart and Artegall and of Calidore with Pastorella are enjoyed briefly and marriage is postponed (IV vi 19–46, V vii 37–45, VI x 32–40 and xii 12–13).

Despite his reasons for linking beauty with virtue and truth, Spenser continued to see even true beauty as problematic. Virtuous love and personal satisfaction may conflict with duty; true beauty is difficult to distinguish from false, and both are usually remote. Beauty can tempt, distract, and degrade. Colin in *The Shepheardes Calender* is desolate and has renounced poetry, all for the love of 'fayre *Rosalind*' (*Aprill* 27), whom he associates with withered flowers (*Dec* 103–14). In *Colin Clout*, a post-1590 revision of the poet's persona as lover and poet, 'Faire *Rosalind*' is represented as 'of divine regard and heavenly hew,' not cruel; her superiority leads the poet's thoughts heavenward (907–51), yet loving her is still a splendid misery. The virtuous admirers of Gloriana, Florimell, Belphoebe, and Artegall all see beauty from a distance and then even the glimpse is gone, leaving frustration as a spur to virtue.

Separation of the lover from a distant beauty motivates poetic as well as heroic activity: see any of the invocations and blazons of Elizabeth in *The Faerie Queene*, or the lover's hymn to 'Great *Venus*, Queene of beautie and of grace' (IV x 44–7; cf *Hymne of Beautie* 1–28). Even in *Epithalamion*, which celebrates a personal triumph of love in possession of beauty, the poet's strategies involve distancing the objects of praise and delight.

Love involves movement, either aspiring or descending; Spenser's distancing strategies serve to motivate more than to promote disinterested contemplation. Beauty may be found in mortal forms inferior to the lover, but beauty itself is an immortal quality, as Ficino and other philosophers had taught. In nature, 'formes are variable and decay ... And that faire flowre of beautie fades away' (*FQ* III vi 38). Such beauty is nevertheless praiseworthy, reminding us of both mortality and regeneration. Furthermore, the sexual desire to beget one's likeness is an appetite for beauty, 'For beautie is the bayt which with delight / Doth man allure, for to enlarge his kynd' (*Colin Clout* 871–2; cf *Hymne of Love* 99–119). Desire for prolonged delight in a union with beauty may be immature and escapist (Spenser's catalogue of unworthy lovers and love objects would be a long one), or it may be ennobling.

Noble lovers aspire to unite with an immortal beauty, heavenly in origin and destiny. Beauty in human form is akin to the transcendental beauty associated with God and heaven, the source of that light which Spenser finds in all forms of beauty. In *Amoretti* 79, he distinguishes between physical beauty that is commonly praised and 'the trew fayre, that is the gentle wit, / and vertuous mind.' The body's beauty will 'lyke flowres untymely fade,' but 'true beautie ... doth argue you / to be divine and borne of heavenly seed.' The soul's fruition in union with such a beauty is often in prospect, though seldom accomplished; love properly tempered remains steadfast in a devotion reaching beyond desire to an ideal not to be possessed on earth.

In Spenser's most discursive treatment of these themes, *Fowre Hymnes*, the enjoyment of beauty available through love of another human being is disciplined by distinctions drawn from Plato's *Symposium*, and described in the language of religious devotion. The lover in the first hymn, feeling that he has been blessed by heaven, admires 'His harts enshrined saint, his heavens queene, / Fairer then fairest, in his fayning eye' (*HL* 215–6). The first two hymns describe the imaginative activity through which 'a fairer forme,' 'A more refyned forme,' the soul's beauty, is separated from the body in which beauty is imperfectly manifested (*HL* 190–6, *HB* 211–31). By this account, when lovers choose the partners they were destined for before their souls' descent to earth, the 'heavenly beautie' which the lover 'fashions in his higher skill' gives him access to his 'forms first sourse'; he admires in his beloved 'The mirrour of his owne thought' (*HB* 190–224).

As reassuring as Spenser is here about the 'sweete sympathie' available to 'likely harts' combined 'in loves gentle band,' narcissism rationalized remains narcissism, and the problems inherent in love and beauty on the human plane are not so much solved in the first pair of hymns as they are transcended in the second, where beauty is found in an ascending series of cosmic entities which inspire religious love, culminating in Sapience, 'The soveraine dearling of the *Deity*,' and leading 'at last up to that soveraine light, / From whose pure beams al perfect beauty springs' (*HHB* 184, 295–6). This passage makes explicit an all-pervading assumption in Spenser's poetry, and one of the reasons for aligning it with Platonism: love may call us to the things of this world, which are good because they participate in the beauty of their heavenly source, but we will be fully satisfied only by a return to the source.

Spenser's art serves both to orient us toward the sources of beauty, truth, and goodness in several spheres of experience – natural, human, and divine – and to anatomize the falsehoods and confusion that arise in response to all that we need but fail to find in experience. It is a commonplace of Renaissance culture that art perfects nature; but the beauty of art may arise, like eroticism, from a desire to escape mutable nature and the burdens of a virtuous life. Spenser's poetry shows repeatedly that he understood this desire but countered it by insisting that beauty not conducive to virtue must be illusory.

Moral virtue exists only in an energetic response to 'the chaungefull world' (*FQ* III vi 33), so any art is suspect which repudiates nature and offers a respite from change in an earthly paradise (as does the Bower of Bliss, II xii 50–1). False beauty, produced by vicious artistry (usually witchcraft), is an enticing appearance cloaking ugliness, sinister purpose, or mere worldliness. Such beauties must be known for what they are and rejected; like money, with which it is paired as an object of appetite, physical beauty occasions intemperance rather than love (see II xi 9, Nelson 1963:227–8).

Both in its true and its false forms, beauty is as problematic as love. The eikastic beauty of ideal figures in *The Faerie Queene* (Una, Gloriana, Florimell, Belphoebe, Artegall) sometimes occasions fantasies even in the more virtuous (Redcrosse, Arthur, Timias, Britomart); conversely, Spenser often surprises us by endowing fantastic beauty with a fair degree of goodness. Many readers of Book II are disturbed when Guyon, 'with rigour pittilesse,' destroys the 'goodly workmanship' of Acrasia's palace and gardens, 'And of the fairest late, now made the fowlest place' (xii 83) when he might have abandoned it to gradual decay. Is Spenser unconsciously revealing his ambivalence, artfully dramatizing a defect in Guyon's supposedly well-developed virtue, or exposing our less-than-temperate investment in worldly goods and pleasures? All of these possibilities make sense.

Guyon's temperance is challenged again by the fleeting appearance of Florimell, 'the fairest Dame alive' (III i 18), whom he and Arthur pursue. Losing track of her at nightfall, Arthur is troubled by 'thousand fancies' reminiscent of his dream of Gloriana: 'Oft did he wish, that Lady faire mote bee / His Faery Queene ... Or that his Faery Queene were such, as shee' (iv 53–4; cf I ix 13–14). As she passes through the central books, Florimell picks up as many kinds of significance as she has admirers, all of them concentrically related to her allegorical identity as 'beautie excellent' (III iv 45) and her character as a lady of the court, virtuous but fugitive.

The uncertain status of the aesthetic and moral values represented by Florimell is evident when a 'snowy' simulacrum – an amalgam of witchcraft, chemical cosmetics, sonnet conventions, and courtly affectation – is created (III viii 5–9); she is generally accepted as true beauty and a proper object of chivalric contention while the real Florimell suffers imprisonment by Proteus (30–43). The episodic disruptions caused by the false Florimell (ending only in V iii 13–28, when she vanishes in the presence of her original) illustrate the appeal of beauty imitated in unnatural art. The true Florimell (another work of art, richly allusive to poetry and mythology, but given soul by an Idea) conveys a metaphysical lesson concerning beauty and virtue: traversing the mutable world of forest, shore, and sea, she suffers but remains inviolate, enacting the relation of immaterial form to elemental matter, and of the soul to the mutable world into which it has fallen. (On the Platonic allegory suggested by Florimell's flight and imprisonment, see Roche 1964:159–62; K. Williams 1966:138–50; Nohrnberg 1976:568–86; Kane 1983:466–74.) This aspect of the narrative's significance is present early in Book III but never emphasized; Florimell gains status as another Psyche, another Proserpina, only at the end of her sufferings in the cave of Proteus (IV xi 1–4, xii 25–35).

Some beauties vanish because, like the false Florimell, they are no more substantial than a rainbow, a 'glorious picture' on the air (V iii 25), but beauties of greater value also disappear. Queen of them all is Dame Nature in the *Cantos*, who vanishes 'whither no man wist' (VII vii 59) as soon as she has shown why Mutabilitie is more beautiful than terrible. Another vanishing occurs in *FQ* VI on Mount Acidale. Calidore witnesses the Graces dancing to Colin Clout's piping, ringed by 'An hundred naked maidens lilly white' and with 'Another Damzell, as a precious gemme' at the center (x 11–20). The narrator remarks upon 'the beauty of this goodly band,' stressing that the central figure 'Seem'd all the rest in beauty to excell,' although the others are 'Handmaides of *Venus*' and she is only 'that jolly Shepheards lasse.' Calidore is unable to enjoy beauty as beauty, and afraid of being deluded; 'Therefore resolving, what it was, to know,' he intrudes; the dancers all vanish, including Colin's beloved, 'which way he [Calidore] never knew.' Although Colin breaks his pipe in anger over this loss and explains that 'none can them bring in place, / But whom they of them selves list so to grace,' he proceeds to explain who the dancers were and what the dance had meant. This episode illustrates that 'beauty soveraine rare' (27) is essential to all that Spenser valued most, but 'the truth of all' (18) survives loss of the beauty that revealed it. In fact, the whole truth with which Spenser was concerned seems to have been constituted as much by disruption and loss as by delight in his access, through experience and imagination, to ideal beauty.

Jon A. Quitslund

Dundas 1985; Kane 1983; Nohrnberg 1976:461–70. The first context for Spenser's conception of beauty should be courtly experience and ideology. See Castiglione's *Courtier*, and José Guidi 1980 'De l'amour courtois à l'amour sacré: la condition de la femme dans l'oeuvre de B. Castiglione' in *Images de la femme dans la littérature italienne de la Renaissance* ed André Rochon (Paris) pp 9–80. Garin 1965:114–35 interprets a variety of discourses on love and beauty; for Ficino and the Platonic tradition, see 'The Idea of Beauty' in M.J.B. Allen 1984:185–203. Major texts are collected in *Philosophies of Art and Beauty: Selected Readings in Aesthetics from Plato to Heidegger* ed Albert Hofstadter and Richard Kuhns (New York 1964); for interpretation see Moshe Barasch 1985 *Theories of Art from Plato to Winckelmann* (New York). James L. Jarrett 1957 *The Quest for Beauty* (Englewood Cliffs, NJ) is an important study of pertinent issues in aesthetics.

Belge The widowed mother of seventeen sons, twelve devoured by the tyrant Geryoneo; Mercilla sends Arthur as her champion (*FQ* V x-xi). The general outline of the historical allegory is plain: as her name suggests, Belge represents the Low Countries as a whole; her sons are the provinces that today make up Benelux and northeastern France. Twelve are lost to Spain, and five still resist in the marshy north. The two 'Springals' sent to beg help from Mercilla are Holland and Zeeland, with whose representatives Elizabeth signed the Treaty of Nonsuch in 1585. Geryoneo represents the might of Catholic Spain, and his Seneschall a governor appointed by Philip II, such as Alva or Parma. Belge's devastated city recalls fallen Antwerp, and her husband represents either Charles the Rash, Duke of Burgundy, whose death in 1477 transferred the Netherlands first to the Hapsburg empire and then to Philip, or more likely, the recently assassinated Dutch leader William the Silent. More important than precise identification, however, is that Belge needs a protector until her sons are safe. The prince himself plays the role adopted by Leicester when he left for the Netherlands in late 1585 accompanied by a crowd of enthusiastic gentlemen including Sidney. The year-long campaign was largely a failure. Spenser would have read glowing reports about it in Holinshed's *Chronicles* (1587), however, and in the early 1590s the Spanish were partly pushed back; so Arthur's accomplishments, though exaggerated and romanticized, are not wholly untrue to what was known when *FQ* V was published in 1596.

The episode is one of several at the end of Book V that consider the virtue of justice in relation to rebellion, sovereignty, and international affairs. Like the Burbon episode, it defends a militantly anti-Spanish and anti-Catholic foreign policy. True, Spenser detested rebellion on principle, but for Mercilla to oppose a tyrant is just; like Philip, Geryonco has betrayed his subjects and hence sacrificed his legitimacy. To oppose him befits a charitable queen whose royal condescension to an oppressed people is symbolized by Arthur's 'low dismounting' when he greets Belge. Like Elizabeth, Arthur rightly declines the lady's offer of sovereignty, although Leicester himself (to the Queen's fury) accepted the 'governorship.'

Spenser cared deeply about the Low Countries. Not only were they of strategic and economic importance to England, he knew at first- or secondhand many statesmen and writers who formed a network of Anglo-Netherlander friendships through which political, religious, and literary influence traveled from the Continent (van Dorsten 1962, 1970). Indeed, Spenser's first published verses were made for a refugee from Antwerp, van der Noot. The persecutions and massacres tormenting Belge were vividly painful to many Englishmen, and for them – if not for some modern readers – Arthur's victory would be emotionally resonant. Spenser, furthermore, did not invent the basis of his allegory. Leicester was met in the Netherlands by pageants treating his mission as a chivalric quest and 'Belgia' as a weeping widow, an image deepened by its echo of the widowed Jerusalem, 'princesse among the provinces' (Lam 1.1–2). He himself appeared as a new Arthur or Hercules come to expel monsters and idol worshipers, and Elizabeth as both Justice and Clemency (Schulze 1931, Strong and van Dorsten 1964).

Spenser associates Arthur with Hercules and hence with Book v's deeper mythological patterns. Arthur's victory, moreover, is religious as well as political: having eliminated the Seneschall, a figure of merely delegated power, and next the tyrant himself, Arthur turns to the idol created by superstition's 'vaine fancies' and then summons and slays the idol's defender, a Sphinx-like dragon. In the historical allegory, this dragon signifies the Inquisition (like the Sphinx, a poser of questions to which a wrong answer means death); but it also bodies forth hellish spiritual error that eats away at mankind in its 'hidden shade.' Arthur is thus not only a rescuer but a revealer, who – like Hercules dragging up the hellhound Cerberus – can force monstrosity into the light. Book v, however, allows few unmodified triumphs. Belge is 'restor'd to life' and her Springals 'replanted'; but the rebirth is incomplete, for many sons remain lost. In a fallen world, there is a limit to what even Arthur can do.

Anne Lake Prescott

Viola Blackburn Hulbert 1939 'The Belge Episode in *The Faerie Queene*' *SP* 36:124–46; Knight 1970; W.T. MacCaffrey 1981; Northrop 1968–9; Phillips 1969–70; Schulze 1931; Strong and van Dorsten 1964; R.B. Wernham 1980 *The Making of Elizabethan Foreign Policy 1558–1603* (Berkeley and Los Angeles); Charles Wilson 1970 *Queen Elizabeth and the Revolt of the Netherlands* (London).

Bellamour In *FQ* VI xii 3–22, Bellamour and Claribell are the happy noble couple, resident at Castle Belgard, to whom Calidore brings Pastorella after rescuing her from the Brigands and with whom he leaves her when he returns to hunting the Blatant Beast. The brief episode recounts the history of the forbidden love and eventual marriage of Claribell and Bellamour, the exposure of their child, and their recognition that Pastorella is their lost daughter because of a rose-shaped birthmark on her breast. The narrative of the lost child rediscovered by noble parents has been retold many times in romance. Perhaps the best-known version is the story of Perdita in Shakespeare's *Winter's Tale*, based on Robert Greene's *Pandosto*, which in turn looks back to earlier Greek romance and myth.

The names Claribell, Bellamour, and Castle Belgard are all related through their root in the Italian *bella* 'beautiful.' Claribell (the 'fayrest Ladie then of all that living were' xii 3) is famous for her beauty; her name suggests the powers of light through the Latin *clarus* (illustrious, shining), and she makes 'clear' or 'evident' (a third sense of *clarus*) Pastorella's relationship to her. Bellamour (Fr *amour* love) loves Claribell's beauty and 'in his youthes freshest flowre' was 'A lustie knight, as ever wielded speare'; the language here plays on a white flower, the bellamour (see *Amoretti* 64), and conflates Italian *bella* with Latin *bellum* (war). The possible conjunction of their names into 'Claribellamour' is one of many reconciliations of male and female in *The Faerie Queene* (Nohrnberg 1976:607). Castle Belgard plays on *bella* and *guardare*, either 'to look at' or 'to guard, protect': the castle may have a good view, but more importantly it now protects Pastorella's beauty as it had imprisoned her mother. Claribell's handmaid Melissa (Gr *melissa* bee, honey) appropriately becomes maid to the flower-bearing Pastorella: in Greek myth (and the Eleusinian mysteries), the *Melissae* were the attendants of Proserpina's mother.

Pamela Joseph Benson

du Bellay, Joachim (1522–60) In Spenser's words, du Bellay was the 'first garland of free Poësie / That *France* brought forth, though fruitfull of brave wits' (*Rome* Envoy). Born in Anjou to noble but impoverished parents, orphaned early and raised by a brother he despised, du Bellay found, at the Collège de Coqueret in Paris, a second home among the group of young humanist poets, including Ronsard, who were to call themselves the Pléiade. Many of his best works seem marked by his early experience of being dispossessed of his heritage; but the melancholy poet of exile and ruin (his own and Rome's) was also an eager architect of the French Renaissance and envisioned an era in which the glories of ancient literature would be rebuilt in France. Although other Renaissance poets had preceded him in time (notably Scève and Marot), du Bellay saw himself as an innovator, with considerable justification. His *Deffence et illustration de la langue françoyse* (1549) articulated with polemical fervor the new theories of the Pléiade. As the early spokesman for those theories, which Spenser associated with qualities of freshness and freedom, as the author of the first sequence of Petrarchan love sonnets in French (*L'Olive* 1549), and above all as the author of three highly original sonnet sequences about modern and ancient Rome (*Les Regrets*, *Les Antiquitez de Rome*, and *Songe*, all 1558), du Bellay merited Spenser's epithet 'first.' He merited it also as the earliest and most important French influence on Spenser's imagination.

His first demonstrable encounter with du Bellay came when he was asked to translate poems by Petrarch and du Bellay for the English edition of van der Noot's *Theatre for Worldlings* (1569). This commission may have been arranged by Richard Mulcaster, Spenser's teacher at Merchant Taylors' School. An innovative educator who shared with continental theorists like du Bellay a strong desire to 'defend and illustrate' the vernacular language, Mulcaster's linguistic nationalism led him to advocate translation as an important means of enriching English culture. In his *Elementarie* (1582), he invokes the example of Cicero, who 'transported' Greek learning to Rome. Mulcaster also urges English writers to 'enlarge' their vocabulary by borrowing words 'from our neighbours speches, and the old learned tungs' (ed 1925:282–3, 173). Some of his statements about the means and ends of cultivating one's native language are so close to passages in du Bellay's *Deffence* that we may infer direct influence; other passages, however, show Mulcaster shaping his arguments in original ways for his English audience, thereby practicing his own cardinal precept that 'all our foren learning' should be 'applyed unto use through the mean of our own [tongue]' (p 274). He opposes those English humanists whose reverence for Latin prompts 'contempt' for vernacular translation; he also opposes those who maintain that English should be kept pure – 'unmixt and unmangeled with borowing of other tonges,' as Sir John Cheke had declared in a letter printed in Hoby's translation of Castiglione's *Courtier* (1561). Mulcaster stresses both the necessity and the value of such borrowing; at the same time, he advocates a critical attitude toward translated foreign texts (some of which may 'seme verie miserable' without their foreign masks) and elaborates orthographic rules for controlling foreign terms, binding them 'to the rules of our writing ... as the stranger denisons be to the lawes of our cuntrie' (p 174). His witty name for this process is *enfranchisement*: the foreign term or phrase is to be freed from its original context in order to obey the 'custom, reason and sound' of English. It seems likely that Mulcaster's admiration for foreign languages and literary achievements, as well as his theory of 'enfranchisement' and his sturdy faith in the inherent strengths of English, influenced Spenser in his formative years at Merchant Taylors' School. The talented student who would later be chided for his use of archaic and 'invented' words evidently shared Mulcaster's and du Bellay's conviction that the writer who aspires to greatness needs to appropriate words and ideas freely from whatever sources are available: 'For whenever the minde is fraught with matter to deliver,' as Mulcaster observes, 'it seketh both home helps, where theie be sufficient ... and where the own home yeildeth nothing at all, or not pithie enough, it craveth help of that tung, from whence it received the matter of deliverie' (p 173).

Spenser's work of translation for *Theatre* (a strikingly international and generically heterogeneous publication comprising poetry, prose commentary, and emblematic woodcuts) allowed him to extend his skills in English by working with French poetry and possibly with Flemish and Italian texts as well. Van der Noot, a Dutch exile living in London, evidently asked Spenser to do English versions of three parts of *Theatre*: eleven sonnets from du Bellay's *Songe*, a series of fifteen allegorical dream-visions about Rome's fall; four sonnets by van der Noot himself which were based on Revelation and which replaced four of du Bellay's poems; and six 'epigrams,' some in sonnet form, others in *douzains*, derived from Marot's French translation of Petrarch's canzone 'Standomi un giorno.' That canzone was also a major source for du Bellay's *Songe*, so Spenser encountered its powerful meditations on mutability in two different French versions, and perhaps in the original Italian, too, as he worked on *Theatre*.

The parallels between du Bellay's visions of Rome and Petrarch's visions of Laura, object of an idolatrous passion and symbol of the poet's desire for secular immortality (the laurel wreath of fame), made a profound impression on the young poet. His blank verse renditions of du Bellay's intricately rhyming sonnets are – by Elizabethan standards – remarkably faithful to the originals, despite a few lapses caused by haste or by misunderstanding of the French; and his very decision to use blank verse may signify more than simply an awareness of the fact that it is more difficult to rhyme in English than in French. Blank verse, which Surrey had used in his translation of the *Aeneid*, connoted an epic grandeur appropriate for the didactic aims of van der Noot's book. Moreover, Spenser's choice of blank verse may show his appreciation of the most original feature of du Bellay's sonnets: their use of a genre conventionally associated with private erotic themes for visionary meditations on a topic of grave public significance.

In his three sonnet sequences about Rome, du Bellay created a kind of poetry new in European literature. It blended characteristic themes of humanist writing – reflections on mutability and on desire for a fame that outlasts monuments – with the themes of amatory poetry: the beloved's beauty and coldness, the lover's despair, anger, and hope. In the sonnets of *Songe*, which are more dreamily repetitive and less syntactically dense than those of *Antiquitez*, Spenser found qualities of style and mood that would have been especially congenial to him. The speaker of these poems is again and again arrested by a vision: 'je vy,' writes du Bellay, 'I saw,' writes Spenser; and the sonnets typically go on to provide, in their octaves, verbal equivalents of the visual emblems – a triumphal arc, a proud tree, an eagle – that accompany the text on the page. The sestets then describe the disastrous fall of the visionary object and often, very briefly, the speaker's response to it ('O grevous chaunge!' sonnet 9, or 'I was with so dreadfull sight afrayde,' sonnet 11). These melancholy poems, with their stress on visual spectacle, foreshadow the mature Spenser's tendency to interrupt narrative progress, in *The Faerie Queene*, with descriptions of fixed objects or places poised on the brink of change.

The importance of Spenser's *Theatre* translations for his later development is suggested by his return to them sometime in the late 1570s or 1580s; revised English versions of *Songe* and Marot's Petrarch canzone were published in *Complaints* (1591) as *Visions of Bellay* and *Visions of Petrarch*. Spenser made more substantial changes on the former sequence than on the latter, perhaps because he was working at about the same time on translating du Bellay's *Antiquitez* as *Ruines of Rome*. Although other English poets (notably Sir Arthur Gorges and John Soowthern) were also turning to du Bellay for inspiration in the 1580s, Spenser was clearly more imaginatively engaged with this foreign source than any of his contemporaries were. The revised translation of *Songe*, which uses a Surreyan rhyme scheme and smooths some of the awkward rhythms of the early blank verse sonnets, is occasionally less close to the French than the 1569 version. *Bellay*, however, is a more faithful rendering of the sonnet sequence as a whole because it includes the four poems omitted in *Theatre*. By translating them instead of van der Noot's sonnets based on Revelation, Spenser restores to *Songe* its formal integrity and also some of its theological ambiguity. Each of the poems omitted from *Theatre* alludes to Rome's destruction by forces from the North in a way that may have seemed overly topical to the temperate Protestant van der Noot; moreover, one of the omitted sonnets (*Bellay* 13) might have offended Protestant sensibilities because it shows the dreamer not only admiring Rome with idolatrous Petrarchan fervor but also seeing her rise again after a shipwreck. In making a new and complete version of *Songe*, Spenser gave his English readers a poetic landscape no less morally dangerous, although considerably less clearly signposted, than that through which Redcrosse wanders in *FQ* I. Du Bellay's dreamer, who seems temporarily to forget his Christian duty after the opening sonnet, may indeed be a model for Redcrosse, who first meets Duessa, symbol of the Roman church, in a dream, and then forgets his faith as he pursues her.

Although du Bellay was no admirer of papal Rome (in *Regrets* 89, for instance, he compares her to a duplicitous witch), in *Songe* he is meditating on ancient Rome, and only intermittently criticizes her pride and greed; he is far from sharing van der Noot's vision of her as Whore of Babylon. Through the process of retranslating *Songe* and following du Bellay closely on the metaphorical journey to the pagan underworld depicted in *Antiquitez*, Spenser evidently came to feel a need to distinguish his theological perspective from that of his Catholic humanist guide.

In the envoy to *Rome*, Spenser hints at doubts about du Bellay's spiritual credentials. After praising him as France's 'first garland,' and then, somewhat more equivocally, as the poet who earned immortality by giving 'a second life to dead decayes,' he mentions the Protestant poet du Bartas: 'And after thee, gins *Bartas* hie to rayse / His heavenly Muse, th'Almightie to adore.' Du Bartas, du Bellay's successor in point of time, is also by implication his spiritual superior, serving a heavenly Muse very different from the spirits of the pagan dead invoked reverently by du Bellay in *Antiquitez* I.

This envoy, possibly written later than *Rome* itself, inaugurated a new stage in Spenser's relation to du Bellay: henceforth he was less a translator than an imitator seeking a degree of independence from his source. His quest was marked, however, by his pessimistic sense that neither his own career nor English culture was flourishing. In *Teares of the Muses*, which laments the victory of Ignorance over the English muses, England's literary poverty is ironically contrasted with France's riches through Spenser's echoes of such Pléiade poems as du Bellay's 'La Musagnoeomachie' (1550), which celebrates the defeat of Ignorance by French muses.

Spenser's bitter perception of England's cultural backwardness also emerges in *Visions of the Worlds Vanitie*, a series of ruin visions modeled on *Songe*. By deviating from their source in both form and content, however, these sonnets show Spenser strengthening his country's muses even as he broods on the vanity of human achievement. Unlike *Bellay*, *Vanitie* uses a Spenserian rhyme scheme; and its visions are moralized in a characteristically Spenserian way. The penultimate sonnet, moreover, builds up to a final warning against pride by symbolically humiliating France, England's old military rival, with a reference to the Gauls' failure to take Rome's capitol after the Battle of Allia (390 BC). Du Bellay had cited this story in the concluding chapter of the *Deffence* to spur his compatriots to avenge old wrongs by 'pillaging' Rome's literary treasures. Spenser's version of the story, in contrast, obliquely urges the English to compete with the French; for both poets, literary imitation serves patriotic aims.

Ruines of Time, probably written like *Teares* and *Vanitie* around 1590, is Spenser's boldest appropriation of du Bellay and also his most sustained meditation on the dangers of being too closely tied to foreign powers, as a translator may be and as Queen Elizabeth had risked becoming by planning to marry a French Catholic duke. The poem's major character, Verlame, clearly recalls the nymph of the Tiber depicted in

Songe 10. Spenser's lady, however, is related to du Bellay's Rome not only by textual allusion but also by her status as the *genius loci* of a British city founded by Rome. A small 'Princesse' dependent for her fame and very existence on the great 'Empresse' who once ruled Britain, Verlame fell when Rome did; in the first part of the poem she laments their joint ruin. As if to highlight his desire to break free of du Bellay's influence as England had broken free from both imperial and Catholic Rome, Spenser has Verlame suddenly change her subject matter. In the long middle section of the poem (183–343), she devotes her considerable powers of rhetoric to lamenting the recent deaths of Sidney, Leicester, and other English patrons of Spenser. She thus prepares for a conclusion in which du Bellay is symbolically supplanted by an English Protestant muse, Sidney, whose ashes are carried in a biblical 'Arke' to heaven. There they receive 'a second life' (669) that pointedly contrasts with the purely secular second life du Bellay gave the 'dead decayes' of Rome.

Ruines of Time introduces a volume permeated by du Bellay's influence; the very title may recall his autobiographical 'Complainte du desesperé' (1552) and, more distantly, his *Regrets* – the sonnet sequence Spenser did not translate, but which he almost certainly read and may have remembered when he wrote *The Faerie Queene* and *SC, October*. Although echoes of du Bellay appear in *Amoretti* and *Epithalamion*, only in *Complaints* does his influence dominate. In *The Faerie Queene*, his is one of the many foreign voices Spenser recreates for his own purposes, sometimes in descriptions of 'antique ruines' which symbolize pride and the force of mutability, and once in a passage that brilliantly completes the work of interpretive translation begun in *Complaints*. Spenser takes the crown that du Bellay, following Virgil and Lucretius, had given to Rome in a famous simile of *Antiquitez*, and places it on the head of the personified Thames (*Aeneid* 6.784–7, *De rerum natura* 2.606–9, *Rome* 6.1–4, *FQ* IV xi 27–8). In so doing, he illustrates the Renaissance concept of imitation as a process of translation whereby not only words but entire cultures are transported across time and space to new homes. The crown 'embattild wide / With hundred turrets' was originally worn by the Trojan mother goddess Cybele; it is thus an apt emblem for the historical myth of *translatio studii* (transfer of culture) which du Bellay had invoked throughout his career to support his hope that Rome's glories could be brought to France as Troy's, according to Virgil, had been brought to Rome. Du Bellay believed that such translation required transformation; Spenser implied that it required reformation as well.

MARGARET W. FERGUSON

Mulcaster citations are from Mulcaster 1925 *Elementarie* ed E.T. Campagnac (Oxford). On du Bellay, see ed 1948 and *'Les Regrets' et autres oeuvres poëtiques* 1966 ed J. Jolliffe and M.A. Screech (Geneva); Henri Chamard 1900 *Joachim du Bellay 1522–1560* (Lille); Greene 1982; Pigman 1982; Rebhorn 1980; Margaret Brady Wells 1972 'Du Bellay's Sonnet Sequence *Songe*' *FS* 26:1–8. On du Bellay and Spenser, see M.W. Ferguson 1984; Manley 1982; Prescott 1978; Rasmussen 1981; Renwick 1925; Satterthwaite 1960; Stein 1934. For further bibliography, see Prescott 1978 and Satterthwaite 1960.

Belphoebe (L *bella* 'lovely' + Phoebe, a moon goddess identified with Diana) The best gloss on Belphoebe occurs in Spenser's Letter to Raleigh: he explains that Belphoebe's figure shadows forth the virtue and beauty of Queen Elizabeth's private (as distinct from her royal or imperial) person, and that Belphoebe's name (like Raleigh's own name for Elizabeth, 'Cynthia') refers to the goddess of chastity. In *FQ* III proem 5, Spenser explicitly invites Raleigh's Cynthia/Elizabeth to recognize in Belphoebe the reflection of her own 'rare chastitee'; and in *The Ocean to Cynthia* (1592?), Raleigh also uses the name Belphoebe to designate the private person of an idealized Elizabeth.

Seen first in *FQ* II, Belphoebe is both radically idealized and complexly full of human promise; if she is also full of unresolved tensions between mythic and mortal realities, she is the richer and more nearly perfect or complete for their presence. When she reappears in *FQ* III and IV, she is less credibly mythic and less fully ideal, compromised by her involvement with humanity and historical reality. In this subsequent diminution, it is possible to see the poet's growing disappointment – even his disillusionment – with the English Queen.

Belphoebe's advent in *The Faerie Queene* occasions both lyric reverence and dramatic comedy, each heightening the other. For eleven stanzas (II iii 21–31), the longest sustained portrait in *The Faerie Queene*, the poet himself conceives and reverently depicts her in terms variously Petrarchan, mystical, courtly, mythic, biblical, classical, and legendary. His reverence is framed by the farcically boorish behavior of Braggadocchio and Trompart, with whom the exalted but unwitting Belphoebe soon finds herself locked in comic encounter (32–44).

The complexity of the traditions surrounding the goddess Phoebe/Diana doubtless contributed to Spenser's richly ambiguous portrait of her namesake Belphoebe in *FQ* II. Traditionally, the moonlike Diana is both unapproachable virgin and mammary mother-goddess; and her double nature is etymologically embedded in the relation of *moon* to the Latin *mensis* (plural *menses*). Similarly complex, Belphoebe is both Venus and Virgo; and like the twin comparisons of her to Diana and to the Amazon Queen Penthesilea that cap her portrait in Book II, she is also both mythic and human.

In the first stage of this portrait, she seems more angelic than human and more conventionally rhetorical than real, a poetic perception rather than a person. As the description proceeds, however, she becomes relatively more natural: she is pictured in space and time, actively engaged in landscape and legend. Petrarchan hyperboles characterize the first five stanzas, or first stage (cheeks 'Like roses in a bed of lillies shed,' faire eyes darting 'fyrie beames,' 'ivorie forhead,' honeyed words, eyelids adorned with 'many Graces'); yet their traditional erotic charge is balanced here, if not quite defused, by her mystical and majestic powers (Berger 1957:137).

Descriptions of Belphoebe's raiment, weapons, and hair in stanzas 26, 29, and 30 associate her especially with the Amazons; but stanzas 29–30 also associate her with Venus disguised as a follower of Diana (cf *Aeneid* I.314–28), and her buskins and hunting in stanzas 27–8 further associate her with Diana (Tuve 1970:124–7). These last two stanzas, however, are devoted to Belphoebe's legs, which 'Like two faire marble pillours ... doe the temple of the Gods support, / Whom all the people decke with girlands greene, / And honour in their festivall resort.' While essentially pagan in reference, and perhaps suggesting the folk festivals of May, this comparison evokes associations as radically diverse as 1 Corinthians 6.19, Song of Solomon 5.15, and the *Romance of the Rose* 20,785–816. The last three lines of stanza 30 may suggest to modern readers Botticelli's *Primavera* (*Spring*), a painting in which Zephyrus, the west wind, touches the nymph Chloris with the result that 'flowers issue from her breath, and she is transformed into Flora, the resplendent herald of spring' (Wind 1958, quoted from rev ed 1967:115). As Belphoebe flees through the forest, and as flowers, leaves, and blossoms enwrap themselves in her flying hair, her figure suggests a seasonal revival rather different from the heavenly revival of stanza 22.

While Belphoebe's beauty and virtue securely transcend the laughter that Braggadocchio's lust invites, the poet's description enables us to make sense of the braggart's outrageous sexual advances and to see what he responds to so inappropriately. Although Braggadocchio misapprehends Belphoebe's nature, his claim that 'The wood is fit for beasts, the court is fit for thee' (39) ensures that we notice her extravagance, her limitation as well as her ideality in human terms – for from a fully human perspective, Belphoebe's speech on honor ('In woods, in waves, in warres she wonts to dwell' II iii 41) is as extreme as Hotspur's 'easy leap, / To pluck bright honor from the pale-fac'd moon' (*1 Henry IV* I iii 201–2). The encounter of Belphoebe and Braggadocchio juxtaposes honor and cowardice, ennobling desire and lustful appetite, solitary purity and social degeneracy; and like Ruddymane's soiled hands and the pure fountain in II ii, these contraries cannot mix. They fly apart as untouched by one another at the end as they were at the outset. Like Diana and Faunus in *FQ* VII, both Belphoebe and Braggadocchio shadow forth extremes of human reality, one ideal and the other instinctual, one angelic and the other animal; and as long as they must remain so absurdly separate, they mock human dreams of unity, completion, or fulfillment.

Having learned of Belphoebe's association with Elizabeth in the proem to Book

III, we read later in canto vi of Amoret, her twin sister. Chrysogone and the generative power of the sun are the parents of these complementary twins, who are separated at birth, Amoret to be fostered by Venus and Belphoebe by Diana. Once sundered, the twins are never successfully reunited, and neither by herself fulfills her seeming potential for wholeness in *The Faerie Queene*. Their *separation* – indeed, their *a-partness* – becomes for each tantamount to the dividing of such twinned psychic and cosmic forces as desire and chastity, inclusion and exclusion, amorphous attraction and formal repulsion – pairs which together make possible unified experience.

Aside from the poet's glossing of Belphoebe's symbolism in the proem and canto vi, her entrance into the action of Book III occurs in canto v 34. Her experiences here recall incidents in Book II, specifically the Bower of Bliss and her own earlier encounter with Braggadocchio. This time, however, the honorable-but-vulnerable Timias has replaced that one-sided extreme, the dishonorable braggart. This substitution signals a shift in Belphoebe's involvement in humanity, as do her admission of her own mortality (v 36) and the allusive connection of Timias' experience with the historical Raleigh's (eg, the reference to tobacco at v 32). Like other characters from earlier books who reappear in *FQ* III (Arthur, Guyon, Redcrosse), Belphoebe now operates in a different context of meaning, one less simply allegorical and more romantic and symbolic. As a result, we have an increased sense of both her *kindness* (naturalness and generosity) and its limitations.

Reinforcing the poet's (and Trompart's) perception of Belphoebe in *FQ* II, Timias awakens from the swoon induced by his wound and perceives Belphoebe both as heavenly and as arousing a pure – but purely human – desire. Belphoebe is initially disconcerted to find Timias rather than a wild beast at the end of the bloody track she has been pursuing; but she pities his imperiled plight and binds up his wounded thigh; with her damsels, she places him on his horse and leads him to her forest dwelling. There she cures his wound, which symbolizes the lust of the Foster who inflicted it; but she herself wounds the squire's heart. This psychic wound is at once deeper and, because hopeless of remedy, more desperate.

The poet repeatedly laments and criticizes this figurative wounding, but he tries to stop short of blaming Belphoebe directly (v 41–3). He could hardly do otherwise, for she fails utterly to comprehend the nature of Timias' malady, namely, human love. While her lovely nature invites Timias' response, her inviolate insularity makes her radically insensitive to the cause of his emotion. But finally the poet's language seems, almost despite himself, to suggest that she is deliberately unsympathetic to the lovestruck Timias: 'But that sweet Cordiall, which can restore / A love-sick hart, she did to him envy [refuse to give]' (v 50).

Quickly the poet turns from this suggestion of unkindness to mythologize Belphoebe, or rather her 'Rose,' the daughter of her morn, dearer to her than life, the flower adorning her honor: he shifts our attention from the failures of her relation with Timias to a timeless realm of virtue. The mythologized rose originates in a heavenly paradise, where it was planted by God and then transplanted to 'gentle Ladies brest,' where it 'beareth fruit of honour and all chast desire' (v 52). Offering inspiration to all beautiful women, the rose provides a virtuous model worthy of their emulation. Unfortunately, however, the model has little immediate relevance to Belphoebe's effect on Timias, whose desire, though as honorable and chaste as humanly he can make it, is hardly virginal.

Belphoebe's rose quintessentially symbolizes virginal chastity, which the poet recommends to his living audience: 'That Ladies all may follow her ensample dead' (v 54). Irreducibly ambiguous, this last phrase means either 'her example when dead' or 'her dead or lifeless example' (Anderson 1982:54–7). The phrase affords a fitting epitaph for the unresolved and unresolvable relation of Timias and Belphoebe in *FQ* III and a further, sadder comment on the tensions implicit in Belphoebe's figure. It implies once again both her otherworldliness and her human limitation and foreshadows her inability to fulfill the perfection that her figure seemed to promise in *FQ* II iii. It anticipates the poet's similar view in the proem to Book IV, when he urges '*Venus* dearling dove' to 'chase imperious feare' from his Queen's high spirit, 'That she may hearke to love, and reade this lesson often' (5).

Belphoebe last appears in *FQ* IV vii-viii, where her story becomes openly and inextricably intertwined with Amoret's. In canto vii, for the first time since their birth, Belphoebe finds herself in the presence of her twin sister. Perhaps more accurately, she fails to find herself, for she never gives any sign of recognizing her twin; and the promising possibility of reunion or reconciliation between the sisters is aborted. Wounded accidentally by Timias in his battle to save her from Lust, Amoret is simply abandoned by Belphoebe when she most needs her help. Timias is similarly abandoned by Belphoebe, and in consequence, he too abandons Amoret; disconsolate, he razes his identity by breaking his weapons, forbearing human converse, and assuming a brutish appearance. He becomes a fitting commentary on the aborted reunion of Belphoebe with Amoret as he similarly abandons himself.

Belphoebe's rejection of Timias and Amoret, like so much in her final appearance, is both suggestive and elusive. For many readers, it alludes to Raleigh's secret marriage to Elizabeth Throckmorton (one of Queen Elizabeth's maids of honor) and their consequent imprisonment in 1592 by the outraged Queen. When Belphoebe comes upon the embattled Timias and Amoret in *FQ* IV vii, she puts Lust to flight, pursues him to his lair, and kills him; in the meantime she leaves the wounded Amoret to Timias. As she had cured Timias' wounded thigh in Book III, so she now conquers Lust, only to find Timias wiping the tears from Amoret's fair eyes 'and kissing them atweene, / And handling soft the hurts, which she did get' (35). Again, as before in Book III, Timias' recovery from an assault of lust is followed by his succumbing to amorousness of another sort, less simply animal but no less troublesome in its social consequences.

No more than before does Belphoebe understand this human love. She operates in terms of absolute virtues and unearthly ideals – virginal chastity, not chaste love; the beatific rose, not the rose of romance. In the Legend of Chastity, Spenser mythologizes her rose in order to transcend (or sublimate) the impasse of her relation with Timias. But in the Legend of Friendship, their impasse affords no such escape: this time, the *presence* of Amoret is undeniable even to Belphoebe, even if she cannot recognize who she really is. When she finds Timias and Amoret together, her first impulse is to slay them with the very arrow she used on Lust, for she cannot distinguish between lust and love. Curbing her wrath, she accuses Timias of betrayal, turns her face from them both, and flees.

At the beginning of *FQ* IV viii, the poet describes Belphoebe's wrath against Timias as 'the displeasure of the mighty,' a description more appropriate to the English Queen than to a beautiful huntress dwelling in wild woods. As Belphoebe flees, the poet thus strengthens her association with Elizabeth and Timias' with Raleigh. Both here and at the end of canto vii, he also stresses that time alone – a power external to his own influence or imagination – can provide a remedy for Belphoebe's haughty scorn of Timias. Spenser's story now reflects its Elizabethan context and is therefore tied more closely to the historical world outside the control of his fiction.

In contrast to these realistic references to time, Belphoebe's reconciliation with Timias in *FQ* IV viii is artificial in the extreme. Spenser reunites them through a sympathetic turtledove and a lapidary's heart. Day after day, as Timias laments his loss, a similarly bereft dove joins and comforts him, until one day he ties round her neck a ruby 'Shap'd like a heart, yet bleeding of the wound, / And with a litle golden chaine about it bound' (6). The ruby was Belphoebe's gift to Timias prior to their estrangement; ironically, it is a jeweler's replica – a simulacrum – of Amoret's real heart in the masque of Cupid (see also Brink 1972). Since the dove is a bird sacred to Venus, both squire and poet are perhaps turning to yet another substitute to try to circumvent the amatory impasse in their story.

Wearing the heart, Timias' dove flies to Belphoebe and lures her to him. Once there, she fails to recognize the disfigured squire but nonetheless pities him, asking whether heavenly disgrace, human wrath, or self-induced despair has made him so wretched. Timias, frustrated by Belphoebe's inability to understand his disfigurement, at length informs her that she herself, as agent and object, is its sole cause. She then abates 'her inburning wrath' and receives him again to favor. By the end of this episode, however, they have not progressed beyond their much earlier situation, except, perhaps, that both are now less vitally exemplary, the one diminished by the needs of human flesh and the other by insensibility toward them.

Brevity, understatement, and anticlimax signal the irony of Timias' reconciliation with Belphoebe. Ramifications of this irony are not far to seek, whether in Elizabethan history or within the poem itself. Although ostensibly happy, Timias' reinstatement foreshadows the self-enclosed vulnerability of Meliboe: 'Fearlesse of fortunes chaunge or envies dread, / And eke all mindlesse of his owne deare Lord' (IV viii 18; cf VI ix). Moreover, when *FQ* IV was published in 1596, Raleigh, though long since released from prison, remained in disfavor, the real state of his relation to his Queen thus at odds with Timias' return from exile. Writing presumably from the Tower in 1592, while still imprisoned on account of his marriage, Raleigh complained of Elizabeth: 'A Queen shee was to mee, no more Belphebe,' and again, 'Bellphebes course is now observde no more, / That faire resemblance weareth out of date' (Raleigh ed 1951:34–5, 37). As if paralleling these complaints, Spenser's Belphoebe disappears from *The Faerie Queene* after IV viii 18.

JUDITH H. ANDERSON

Anderson 1971b; Anderson 1982; Bednarz 1983; Berger 1957; Berleth 1973; Brink 1972; Cain 1978; Cheney 1966; Goldberg 1981; Miller 1988:224–35; O'Connell 1977; K. Williams 1966.

Bible In an intensely Christian culture such as that of the Renaissance, the Bible was the book of books. In Protestant England in Spenser's time, its privileged status was expressed by the first of the official Homilies: 'Unto a Christian man, there can be nothing either more necessary or profitable, than the knowledge of Holy Scripture; forasmuch as in it is contained God's true word, setting forth his glory, and also man's duty ('A Fruitful Exhortation to the Reading and Knowledge of Holy Scripture' in *Certain Sermons or Homilies* 1547). Households rich enough to afford books would normally have owned a Geneva Bible and used it daily for private and family devotions. The literate poor could find a Great or a Bishops' Bible displayed for private reading in every parish church. Elizabethans also had the Bible read to them with documentable frequency. Everyone was expected to attend church on Sunday; moreover, the universities compelled daily attendance at their own chapels. In the Book of Common Prayer, the services of Morning and Evening Prayer required the recitation of the whole Psalter each month and a yearly lectionary of both Old and New Testament readings. In addition, the service of Holy Communion always involved public reading of the Lesson (usually a passage from an Epistle) and the Gospel prescribed for the Sunday or feast day (see *Church of England). In England, as in all nations exempt from Counter-Reformation censorship, it was only natural that a serious poet should make some use of the Bible.

versions The history of versions of the Bible, even of sixteenth-century versions, is too complicated to be presented in detail here. The student of Spenser's use of the Bible will occasionally need to check a supposed borrowing in a sixteenth-century edition of the original Greek or Hebrew and in the subsequent English and Latin versions together with their occasional revisions. These are usually synonymous in sense but may differ widely, even within a single language, in the nuances of wording which are sometimes most important to a poet (see comparisons in Landrum 1926, Shaheen 1976).

Since the original Greek and Hebrew texts were part of the curriculum at Merchant Taylors' School, Spenser may have studied them, though one cannot confidently say how well he remembered them. (His main use of Hebrew, the pun on *Sabbaoth* and *Sabaoth* in *FQ* VII viii 2, could have been derived from translations alone; see Allen 1949; Shaheen 1976:171–2). The Latin versions most relevant to his poetry include the Vulgate, Erasmus' annotated parallel-text translation of the New Testament (first ed 1516 without annotations, many later rev eds), Calvin's translation in his commentaries on the New Testament, and the Junius-Tremellius-Beza Bible (the favorite Latin Bible of Protestants, consisting of the annotated Old Testament and Apocrypha of Tremellius and Junius [first ed 1575–9], and the annotated New Testament of Beza [first ed 1557], later revised by Junius and sometimes accompanied by the New Testament of Tremellius). The Old Testaments of Münster and Pagninus and the Bible by Castellio are less important.

In English, Spenser could have known the Great Bible (1539, rev 1540), the Bishops' Bible (1568, rev 1569 and 1572), the Rheims New Testament (1582), and the Geneva (1560, rev 1576). His use of the Vulgate, the Great, the Bishops', and the Geneva has been distinguished in *The Faerie Queene* (Shaheen 1976), indicating that Spenser used no one version to the exclusion of others. Of the various English versions, the most popular by the last quarter of the sixteenth century was the Geneva, and it is the one most often cited by Spenser critics. The educated Englishman of his day might also have seen rare copies of the pioneering English translations of Tyndale, Coverdale, 'Matthew,' and Taverner; but Spenser is unlikely to have borrowed from them directly (Landrum 1926:518–19, Shaheen 1976:13–14).

Spenser lived in a translational interregnum when no single English version enjoyed such overriding verbal authority as Jerome's Vulgate had for Roman Catholics and the King James version for later centuries of English-speaking readers. Only by checking these many versions can one assess his verbal departures from a biblical subtext. A departure may be merely stylistic, since 'the diction of English Bibles in the Tyndale tradition, which heavily favors words of Anglo-Saxon origin, hardly blends with the highly poetic diction and rhythms of the Spenserian stanza' (Shaheen 1976:54). Any study of the changes is further complicated by the status of the Bible as a heard or spoken text. Furthermore, the educated knew their Bible in both Latin and English, and were likely to translate from the one to the other extemporaneously.

commentaries We can infer that Spenser knew and used biblical commentaries from their prevalence in the library of his alma mater, Pembroke College, Cambridge (see James 1905), and from his professional association with the commentary on Revelation in van der Noot's *Theatre for Worldlings*. The fundamental fact for understanding Spenser's Duessa, for example, is the product of exegesis – that her biblical model, the Whore of Babylon, represents the Roman Catholic Church. When he writes that Mortdant with Acrasia 'knew not ... his owne ill' (*FQ* II i 54), his wording parallels verbatim Augustine's paraphrase of the condition of Paul's persona in Romans 7. The paradox that Redcrosse's armor 'now burnt, that earst him arm'd, / That erst him goodly arm'd, now most of all him harm'd' (I xi 27) parallels almost as closely Augustine's paraphrase of Paul's subsequent condition, 'with your own arms, the enemy conquered you, with your own arms, he slew you' (Kaske 1984:94–5).

Proper study of the Bible in the sixteenth century included the reading of commentaries. Although one watchword of the Reformation was *sola Scriptura* (Scripture alone), this could be taken not radically, to mean that the Bible alone is its own interpreter to the eye of faith, but conservatively, to mean that no doctrine or practice may stand unless based on Scripture. Even the Geneva Bible (on most issues more Protestant than the Church of England) contains glosses, which doubled in number in the Tomson revision of 1576. Many of its editions begin with a hermeneutical preface that recommends reading 'interpreters' – so long, of course, as they do not contradict the Creed and Ten Commandments. English Protestants did not eschew even Catholic commentaries (see A. Williams 1948; Donne ed 1953–62, 10:364–401); and they widely consulted not only the Reformers, but Erasmus, the *Glossa ordinaria*, Nicholas of Lyra, and the Greek and Latin Fathers, especially Augustine. Such Catholic and medieval exegesis provides, then, a repository of traditions which had not yet been called into question. The commentaries help us to read the Bible in the light of older meanings, to unearth religious commonplaces available to Spenser in forms now lost to us, and to document the possibility that a given idea could have occurred to a writer of his place and time.

Spenser and the Bible On the whole, Spenser uses the Bible more than does Shakespeare because he is a learned and a thematic poet, but less than does Milton because he is often more secular and retains more of the Catholic heritage. Unlike either

Shakespeare or Milton, he wavers between biblicism, syncretism, and secularism in different works or even different sections of the same work. The Bible disappears from his secular poems such as *Prothalamion* and *Muiopotmos* (note their absence from Landrum's tabulation, 1926:538–44). Syncretism is exemplified in *An Hymne of Heavenly Beautie*, especially by Spenser's insertion of 'those *Idees* ... which *Plato* so admyred' into the biblical heaven of blessed souls (82–3); his reliance on the Bible diminishes in his syncretic and more medieval moments. What follows will illustrate how even when he is at his most biblical, his Bible is still encrusted with traditions derived from commentaries, devotions, homilies, idealistic literature, the liturgy, and religious art.

Spenser often mentions the Bible explicitly. Many of his translations are biblical: four of the sonnets in *Theatre for Worldlings* versify subjects taken from Revelation; and among his lost works are translations of *The Seven Psalms*, Ecclesiastes, and *Canticum canticorum* (Song of Solomon). In the Letter to Raleigh, he cites Ephesians (6.11–17) to explain the symbolism of Redcrosse's armor as 'the armour of a Christian man.' In *FQ* I, Redcrosse gives Arthur as a parting gift 'his Saveours testament' (ix 19). In the House of Holiness, Fidelia holds a book 'signd and seald with blood,' out of which she teaches 'Of God, of grace, of justice, of free will' (x 13, 19). The Bible may harm its readers unless it is interpreted by the church. Fidelia's 'sacred Booke, with bloud ywrit' contains 'darke things ... hard to be understood' (x 13, 19; cf 2 Pet 3.16); and when Redcrosse hears them, he is filled with despair at his unworthiness and once again wishes to die (21–9, cf ix 50–1). In x 53, the Law given to Moses on Mount Sinai is characterized as the Pauline letter which killeth, as 'bitter doome of death and balefull mone' which is 'writ in stone / With bloudy letters by the hand of God.' Since for Spenser the Old Testament too is written with blood, and since Fidelia's syllabus is comprehensive, her book seems to be the whole Bible.

Spenser alludes to Revelation more than any other book of the Bible (Landrum 1926:517) and most often in Book I (42 out of 60 citations in *FQ*, according to Shaheen 1976:181–2). Many references are associated with Duessa in her role as biblical Whore of Babylon. Though Luther, Calvin, and the lectionary of the Book of Common Prayer did not stress Revelation among the books of the Bible, later Protestants did, and saw the Whore of Babylon (Rev 17–18) as the Roman Catholic Church. The contrast between her and the Woman Clothed with the Sun (Rev 12, interpreted as the true church) provided them with a scriptural defense against the charge of having split the church. They would have recognized Duessa's gold cup, seven-headed beast, and scarlet robe as attributes of the biblical Whore and hence as signs of Roman Catholicism. This Protestant politico-religious reading was stressed by many commentaries on Revelation, of which an exceptional number existed in English, including the long commentary by van der Noot in *Theatre for Worldlings* (1569), where Spenser's first work was published.

After Revelation in number of borrowings come the Psalms (Landrum 1926:517, Shaheen 1976:181). Some borrowings are straightforward allusions: for instance, 'And eke with fatnesse swollen were his eyne' (*FQ* I iv 21) from 'Their eyes swell with fatnesse' (Psalter of BCP, Ps 73.7); others are stylistic borrowings of rhetorical devices such as that syntactic parallelism characteristic of *The Faerie Queene* as a whole and elegantly exemplified in Una's lament (I vii 22–5). The Psalms were arguably the best-known book of the Bible; they also existed in the most versions. During Spenser's literary career, three versions of the Psalms were authorized for use in churches: the Bishops'; a metrical version; and one which was originally Coverdale's, then incorporated (with a few changes) first into the Great Bible and then into the Book of Common Prayer. The last two were often included in a copy of the Geneva Bible along with its own version. In the metrical version by Sternhold and Hopkins there is no 'shepherd' in Psalm 23, so great was the latitude of the variations. These occurred partly because the Psalms were often sung to a tune, which they had to be made to fit. One consequence of the different translations must have been that the Psalms were remembered not in precise quotations like 'The Lord is my shepherd' but in typical sentiments, in imagery, in sub-genres, or perhaps, like a secular book, in mere form and style. Hence verbal borrowings may not be an adequate measure of psalmic influence.

The Psalms were also translated into meter in whole or in part by many qualified poets: Wyatt, Surrey, Gascoigne, Sidney (in collaboration with his sister Mary), Campion, Bacon, Crashaw, Carew, Milton – and Spenser (the Seven [Penitential] Psalms – 6, 32, 38, 51, 102, 130, 143 – are among his lost works). These translators would often experiment with verse forms, apparently motivated by aesthetics as well as religion; the Sidneys employ different stanza forms for almost every Psalm. Sidney admires the rhetoric of the Psalms and finds in the psalmist a model for the inspired poet (*Defence of Poetry* ed 1973b:77). So much establishes the a priori likelihood that the Psalms influenced poets generally and that they more than any other book of the Bible fathered a biblical poetics. The frequency as well as the range of Spenser's use thus reflects the status of the Psalms, which exemplifies in the extreme both the omnipresence and the verbal confusion of the Bible as a whole. Another book of predictable importance to Spenser was Genesis, quoted in the description of the Garden of Adonis (III vi 34; Gen 1.22, 28).

The section of the Bible labeled Apocrypha by Protestants held a fascination for Spenser which seems unusual in view of its subsequent eclipse. In his time, it is not so remarkable in that all Bibles contained these books; English Protestant Bibles inserted them between the Old Testament and the New, and the popular 'Prayer of Manasses, Apocryphe,' between 2 Chronicles and Ezra. Though the Geneva Bible cautions that they be 'not received by a commune consent to be red and expounded publikely in the Church' (Geneva Bible 1560:386r), the Church of England – anti-Genevan on this issue – recommended these books for morality, though not for establishing doctrine (Article 6 of the 39 Articles), and ordered some of them to be read in church. Judith, Tobit, Wisdom of Solomon, Ecclesiasticus, and Baruch formed most of the Old Testament lessons for Morning and Evening Prayer in October and November of the liturgical year. Landrum finds 33 uses of the Apocrypha in Spenser's works (1926:518). 2 Esdras 14 inspired the theme of the degeneration of the world in *FQ* IV viii 31 and V proem; 2 Esdras 4 and 2 Maccabees 9.8 inform the image of the Giant with the scales (V ii). A long-recognized, striking, and pervasive use of the Apocrypha is the portrayal of Sapience in *An Hymne of Heavenly Beautie* (183–288). This evocative figure harmonizes Neoplatonism with the Bible – with Proverbs 9 but also with the Apocryphal Wisdom 7–9 and Ecclesiasticus 51, both of which were then read in church. Spenser's preferences for and uses of Revelation, the Psalms, and the Apocrypha reflect their peculiar status in his particular time and place.

Another section of the Bible of predictable importance to Spenser was the Gospels, which are particularly pervasive in *Heavenly Love*. In *The Faerie Queene*, three apparently secular contexts include Gospel material: the associations of Nature with the transfigured Christ (VII vii 7), of the cock that providentially awakens Britomart with 'The bird, that warned *Peter* of his fall' (V vi 27), and of the parthenogenesis of Amoret and Belphoebe with that of Christ (III vi 3, 27). There has been much critical discussion of the similarities between Christ and Guyon at Mammon's cave, best described as neither religious nor secular but syncretic. The Gospel may be evoked to portray Guyon and Britomart as types of Christ and of Peter, or as antitypes, focusing on their differences, or as analogues to them on a natural level. Or there may be no religious reason for these associations beyond their familiarity which makes them like classical myths – archetypes, or at least subjects familiar enough for allusion.

The ways in which Spenser used the Bible are many and diverse. Shaheen has made a beginning by collecting hundreds of verbal borrowings, and by qualifying some with the word *Compare* and others as perhaps only chance similarities. Such statistics, however, can go only so far in assessing which works are the most biblical in quality. For one thing, the difficult distinction remains to be drawn in each case between a mere inconspicuous borrowing and an allusion which demands recognition. Spenser's frequent references to biblical characters clearly constitute allusion (though a few, such as Augustus Caesar, belong more to secular history). Some idea of their frequency can be gathered from skimming the entries in Whitman's *Subject-Index*. The fully drawn biblical characters discussed above – the Whore of Babylon and Sapience – contribute more than mere numbers of borrowings to the biblical element in *FQ* I and *Heavenly Beautie*. In the latter, God himself is also felt as a biblical character, not just as a theological concept. Other things being equal, a tone of religious earnestness adds to biblical quality. On all counts, a third work that ranks with these is *Heavenly Love*. Christ's life is recounted twice, chiefly from the Gospels (133–68, 234–45). Events of which the Bible contains only hints are the preincarnate generation of God the Son (cf John 1.1–18) and the Fall of the Angels (cf Isa 14.12). As in *FQ* I and *Heavenly Beautie*, some doctrinal points, such as the mystical union at the end, are only remotely biblical, for Spenser's portrayal even of Christ is colored by tradition. *SC, Julye* is also very biblical, not only in its allusions and its meter, which is that of the Psalms as translated by Sternhold and Hopkins, but also in its plain style – a biblical feature shared by his other moral eclogues and *Mother Hubberds Tale*.

Some allusions are undoubtedly oblique though nonetheless conspicuous. Sophistry is displayed when Phaedria misapplies 'consider the lilies of the field' (*FQ* II vi 15–16; cf Matt 6.28–9), and when the formal priest, advising the Fox and the Ape of the easy life of Protestant clergy, says 'Ne is the paines so great, but beare ye may' (*Mother Hubberd* 446), playing on 'There hath no tentation taken you, but ... ye may be able to beare it' (1 Cor 10.13). Some religious imagery is parodic: the unarmed Red Cross Knight meets the giant Orgoglio as David meets Goliath (*FQ* I vii 7–8; cf 1 Sam 17.37–40); and the Giant with the scales (V ii) not only echoes Apocryphal villains but parodies God's leveling of mountains and weighing of unquantifiable things (Isa 40.4, 12; Wisd of Sol 11.21; Job 28.25). Enjoyment of these ironies depends on the reader's recognition of the scriptural echo.

Since the Bible was central in Elizabethan culture and in the training of poets, it is likely to have influenced not only Spenser's vocabulary, characters, and rhetoric but also the more theoretical aspects of his poetics. The entire *Faerie Queene* is structured around the repetition of images in good and bad senses (*in bono* and *in malo*) – a biblical structure explored by medieval exegesis. In *FQ* I, the alternation of good and bad cups, women, beads, wells, castles, and processions gives the feeling of a progressive self-correction, yielding the conclusion that vice is to virtue as abuse is to the proper use of the same thing. The strategy is versatile and adaptable to secular literature because tied not to dogma but to categories of good and evil, better and worse. Because of this biblical structure, the reader of *The Faerie Queene* should follow the instruction sometimes prefixed to the Geneva Bible, 'Consider the ... agreement that one place of Scripture hath with another, whereby that which seemeth darke in one is made easie in another.'

The four senses of allegory which medieval exegesis found in the Bible are defined in the mnemonic jingle, 'Littera gesta docet, quid credas allegoria, / Moralis quid agas, quo tendas anagogia' ('The *letter* teaches the events, the *allegory* [or typology] what you should believe, the *moral* [sense, or tropology] what you should do, the *anagogy* where you are headed' *PLat* 113: cols 28c and 33c; Lubac 1959–64, 1:23). Although ostensibly rejected by most Protestant exegesis, their applicability to secular literature was affirmed by Dante (*Epistle to Can Grande*) and Boccaccio (*Genealogia* 1.3), and was vaguely reaffirmed by Spenser's contemporary Sir John Harington, in both his preface and notes to his translation of *Orlando furioso*. They are useful chiefly as pigeonholes for the different kinds of subject matter an allegorical text can simultaneously contain, though rarely are all four of them found in a single passage either in the Bible or in secular literature.

The anagogical sense is rare; in *The Faerie Queene*, only the 'New Jerusalem' which Redcrosse glimpses from the Mount of Contemplation is pure anagogy, 'where you are headed' (*FQ* I x 55–7). Tropology, in contrast, is practically ubiquitous in sacred and secular texts, as even Protestants admit; the character Despair (I ix) is pure tropology, 'what you should – or should not – do,' especially since he functions as Redcrosse's inner voice. This moral sense was usually conveyed in one of two modes: either in personifications such as Despair (alien to the canonical Scriptures but frequently imposed upon them), or in concrete examples, which Protestants generally preferred (eg, Luther's exegesis of Leah and Rachel [1543], in ed 1883–1987, 43:666–8). Spenser abounds in personifications as well as examples; hence we infer that his poetics, while biblical, is still medieval, not yet as Protestant as that of seventeenth-century authors like Herbert.

Among the four senses, 'allegory' in its limited sense of 'what you should believe' is better known by the medieval term *figura* or the modern *typology*. Even the usually literalistic Reformers recognized a typological sense in the Bible, though some refused to see it in secular literature. In terms of mode, typology means simply the paralleling of one person, group, or event in salvation history by another. As *quid credas* emphasizes, typology also denotes a subject matter, the Christian shaping of history around salvation into mutually reflecting parts: Creation, Fall, vicissitudes of Israel, Redemption, Second Coming, and Last Things. Typology defined in terms of subject matter is exemplified in Spenser's Duessa and her biblical prototype, the Whore of Babylon, fitting the Reformation into salvation history as one of the Last Things. Typological exegesis had been employed within the Bible by Paul himself in order to read prophecies of Christ into seemingly irrelevant Old Testament history. Indeed, typology is so structural to the Bible that Northrop Frye can say, 'the two testaments form a double mirror, each reflecting the other but neither the world outside' (1982:78).

Claims as sweeping have been made for the admittedly looser literary uses of typology: since Auerbach's essay 'Figura' (1959), it has been traced in even the most secular literature, and extended so broadly as to coincide with symbolism, historicism, or intertextuality. True, if only the mode remains, as in more secular literature, typology does fade out into history repeating itself. But if the credal subject matter remains, literature exhibits a still distinctly biblical 'applied typology' – recapitulating an event in salvation history on the smaller stage of a private life (Charity 1966:160–1; see also Charity's Index under 'typology, applied'). To apply typology is to combine it with morality, as in the imperative to imitate Christ (eg, *FQ* I x 40).

The Faerie Queene contains six clear and widely recognized typological episodes: Arthur's rescue of Redcrosse from Orgoglio's dungeon (I viii) reenacts the credal Harrowing of Hell (with suggestions from 2 Thess 2.8 and Rev 12, 17, and 19); Redcrosse's rescue of the King and Queen of Eden from their prison by killing the Dragon (xi-xii) recalls Christ's death, Harrowing of Hell, and Resurrection; his betrothal to Una (xii) prefigures the Marriage of the Lamb to the New Jerusalem in Revelation 19–20; and Guyon lying apparently dead at the mouth of a cave guarded by an angel recapitulates a moment both in Christ's Temptation in the Wilderness and in the Resurrection (II viii). Two striking reenactments of the Fall (exemplifying retrospective typology) are the initial exile of the King and Queen from Eden (recounted in the Letter to Raleigh and in I vii 44), and Mortdant's drinking Acrasia's wine in a garden and magically bequeathing it as a bloodstain to his infant son Ruddymane (II i 39–ii 10; see *Amavia). While Spenser's mostly fictional literal level vitiates the historical element in his typology, the very presence of typology undergirds his minutely topical political allegories with a philosophy of world history.

In Spenser's age, the Bible wielded an authority perhaps greater than in any other period, although verbal echoes were less prevalent partly because of the many translations then in use. Spenser's favorite books of the Bible were Revelation, Psalms, and Genesis; his favorite section of the Bible was the Gospels; and he had an unusual fondness for the Apocrypha. Some of the many ways in which he used the Bible are as a source of various borrowings, as a model for style and structure, and as a repository of material for allusions – whether straightforward or ironic, whether to words, images, characters, plots, or themes – that would elevate his human book into a means of grace. CAROL V. KASKE

EDITIONS OF THE BIBLE Modern editions of

the Vulgate reflect the Clementine revisions of 1590–2; references to it should ideally be checked in a pre-Clementine Vulgate such as can be found, with minor variations, in the 1527 ed of Erasmus' New Testament, in the many editions by Estienne, and in the two sixteenth-century polyglots (in which last can also be found important versions in Greek, Hebrew, and other languages): the first or Complutensian Polyglot (Alcalá de Henares, first released 1522); the second, Antwerp, or Royal Polyglot published by Plantin (ed A. Montanus, Antwerp 1569–72). Erasmus' New Testament in L and Gr is legibly reprinted along with its annotations in Erasmus ed 1703–6 vol 6. The first ed of the Geneva Bible (1560) has been reprinted with an introduction by Lloyd E. Berry (Madison, Wis 1969); its glosses are insufficient for Spenser studies, however, because they do not include many (mostly translations of glosses in the Beza-Junius New Testament) added by Tomson in his revision of 1576, published separately and thereafter frequently substituted for the New Testament in complete Geneva Bibles, eg, London 1587, 1594, etc. The King James (or Authorized) Version of 1611 and the Douai Old Testament are too late for Spenser – although the King James sometimes brings out a sense latent in earlier versions, and the Douai is helpful as an aid to understanding the Vulgate. English versions can be compared in parallel in *The Genesis Octapla* ed Luther A. Weigle (New York 1965; includes Tyndale, Great, Douai, Geneva, rev Bishops') and *The New Testament Octapla* ed Luther A. Weigle (New York 1962; as preceding).

HISTORIES OF THE BIBLE The fullest history, covering Hebrew, Greek, and Latin, is *The Cambridge History of the Bible* vol 3 *The West from the Reformation to the Present Day* ed S.L. Greenslade (Cambridge 1963). The basic bibliographical work is T.H. Darlow and H.F. Moule 1903–11 *Historical Catalogue of Printed Editions of the Bible* 2 vols (London), vol 1 *Historical Catalogue of Printed Editions of the English Bible, 1525–1961* rev A.S. Herbert (London 1968), with excellent notes. See also Naseeb Shaheen 1984 'Misconceptions about the Geneva Bible' *SB* 37:156–8.

BIBLICAL COMMENTARIES, MOSTLY IN ENGLISH Most exegesis available to Spenser was in Latin; for the student who knows no Latin, some Elizabethan commentaries and compendia either written in or immediately translated into English are listed briefly below. For commentaries on Revelation, see works listed in *STC* by John Bale (*The Image of Both Churches*), Heinrich Bullinger (*A Hundred Sermons upon the Apocalips*), François du Jon (or Franciscus Junius) the Elder (*Apocalypsis*), Augustine Marlorat, John Napier, and Jan van der Noot (*Theatre*). Commentaries on other books of the Bible are listed in *STC* under Gervase Babington, Calvin (many of his commentaries and exegetical sermons were translated in Spenser's time), Erasmus (*Paraphrases*; the Annotations in his New Testament were not translated), Luther (only some of whose commentaries were translated), and Peter Martyr Vermigli (esp *Common Places*). See also the glosses on the Geneva Bible, esp in the Tomson rev NT of 1576 and frequently in subsequent eds. The Parker Society reprints the English works of most of the English reformers (55 vols); its editions can be used as a commentary through the cumulative index of Scripture and as a theological compendium through their indexes of subjects both individual and cumulative. There are modern annotated translations of almost all the works of Calvin (Calvin Translation Society) and of Luther (ed 1958–75). See also the definitive annotated ed of Luther ed 1883–1987, in Latin and German. Fully annotated editions such as Hooker ed 1888 give a good idea what commentaries English clergymen of the late sixteenth century were using. Three helpful studies of commentaries in Renaissance England are Richard L. Greaves 1976 'Traditionalism and the Seeds of Revolution in the Social Principles of the Geneva Bible' *SCJ* 7:94–109; Craig R. Thompson 1971 'Erasmus and Tudor England' in *Actes du congrès Erasme* (Amsterdam) pp 29–68; and A. Williams 1948.

SPENSER AND THE BIBLE The principal work for *FQ* is Shaheen 1976; on what it covers, it is perhaps as definitive as one can be in an area so blurry as allusion; but it excludes from its collation Rheims, Greek, Hebrew, and Renaissance Latin versions. Grace Warren Landrum 1926 'Spenser's Use of the Bible and His Alleged Puritanism' *PMLA* 41:517–44 contains faulty reasoning and data (on which see Shaheen) but provides the most comprehensive statistics on the shorter poems and the prose. For specific treatment of allusions or background, see D.C. Allen 1949 'On the Closing Lines of *The Faerie Queene*' *MLN* 64:93–4; 'Figura' in Auerbach ed 1959; Israel Baroway 1934 'The Imagery of Spenser and the *Song of Songs*' *JEGP* 33:23–45; Brooks-Davies 1977; A.C. Charity 1966 *Events and Their Afterlife: The Dialectics of Christian Typology in the Bible and Dante* (Cambridge); Cullen 1974; Dunseath 1968; Fletcher 1971; Hankins 1945; Hume 1984; Carol V. Kaske 1969; Kaske 1976; Kaske 1984 'Augustinian Psychology in *The Faerie Queene* Book II' in *Literature and Religion* ed William L. Stull *HSL* 15.3(1983)–16.1(1984):93–8; James L. Kugel 1981 *The Idea of Biblical Poetry: Parallelism and Its History* (New Haven); Lewalski 1979; Joshua McClennen 1947 *On the Meaning and Function of Allegory in the English Renaissance* (Ann Arbor); Nohrnberg 1976; Osgood 1917; Patrides and Wittreich 1984 (esp Sandler 1984); Ted-Larry Pebworth 1971 'The Net for the Soul: A Renaissance Conceit and the Song of Songs' *RomN* 13:159–64; Sinfield 1983; Tuve 1966; Waters 1970; Weatherby 1982. Accurate biblical parallels are also provided in some eds of Spenser, esp *FQ* ed 1965a, ed 1977, and *Var.*

---

bibliography, critical The works of most sixteenth-century authors, including Spenser, are usually transmitted to us through the medium of print. Thus, an understanding of how this transmission has occurred and its effect on the text is important in assessing both the nature of the text and, wherever possible, the nature of the copy on which it was based. The process of finding the principal exemplar of a text, or coming as close as evidence and judicious inference will allow, is the core of modern textual criticism. Modern textual critics, following procedures worked out by W.W. Greg and others, choose as their copy-text (base text) the earliest printed version unless there is a surviving authorial manuscript or evidence that the author substantially revised the work. As Greg (1950–1) argues, an author who may intervene in the words and phrases (the 'substantives') of subsequent editions of a work will seldom intervene in the punctuation, spelling, and capitalization (the 'accidentals') unless undertaking a new version. For English Renaissance literature, this theory of copy-text is still the basis for an acceptable working method.

Modern textual criticism is very much assisted by analytical bibliography, that is, the accurate and meticulous examination of multiple examples of a text's physical embodiment as printed book. Such examination attempts to identify one edition as distinct from another, and to trace the individual pages of a book through the entire printing process from typesetting through printing and binding. It uses our growing knowledge of the operation of printing houses and the history of the book trade. One major branch of this field of study is descriptive bibliography, the close technical description of existing copies of a particular edition or set of works. Another is enumerative bibliography, the recording of the basic facts of publication and identification for a complete range of primary or secondary works.

No known autograph copy of any of Spenser's poems survives, although a copy of *Amoretti* 1 was once believed to be in his hand (Beal 1980, 1.2:526, item SpE 1; see *handwriting). We do know, however, that behind each printed first edition lay a manuscript copy, most likely a fair copy, of the poem, probably in Spenser's own hand but based on any number of working drafts. For instance, various versions of *The Faerie Queene* must have circulated in manuscript: Harvey in 1580 writes as though he had read some of it (*3 Lett* 2; *Var Prose* p 472), and *FQ* II iv 35 was published in Fraunce's *Arcadian Rhetorike* in 1588. Until the Copyright Act of 1709, copyright in a printed work belonged to the publisher-printer, not the author. Once the publisher had paid the agreed sum and received the manuscript, legal ownership passed from author to publisher. The publisher would have the manuscript duly licensed by appropriate state or church authorities, entered in the Stationers' Register and would pay the fee. Then the stationer was free to print and distribute the work. A manuscript set in type by compositors would be subject to any number of alterations over which the author had little control. That whole category of 'house style,' that is, alternative spellings, minor marks of punctuation, italics, and capitals (especially in prose), and the like, were almost entirely within the compositors' prerogative. Often they had distinct preferences for spellings of common words (eg, *do* or *doe*) as well as for punctuation; and in justifying copy, they would alter spelling, spacing, and punctuation to make the copy fit the measure. All such changes in what the author had actually written were entirely permissible methods of compositorial intervention during Spenser's lifetime and for over a century afterward.

One other form of intervention, though not permissible, was often practiced. If a compositor could not read the copy, or if he believed there was an error, he would often supply what seemed to him the proper reading, usually without consulting any authority. Compositors were also subject to the usual human failings: they misread, transposed letters, and lost their place in the copy.

It was not the practice at this time for the printer-publisher to supply the author with proofs; indeed, within the print shop, they were not pulled before the printing began. In many cases, however, authors were allowed to join the printer's proofreader in reading the sheets as they came from the press. If errors were found, and if the printer agreed that they should be corrected, the press would be stopped and normally corrections would be made on the spot before printing resumed. The previously printed sheets would not be discarded but would remain as part of the final set of sheets produced, folded, and bound. As a consequence, it is fairly common to find no two identical copies of the same edition of the same book. Of the 1590 quarto *Faerie Queene*, for example, 'it is quite possible that there are no two copies whose readings agree throughout' (Johnson 1933:13).

Spenser seems to have attended the print shop very faithfully when he was in London, as is attested by the number of his works printed during his London visits. The *Variorum* editors and de Sélincourt (in Spenser ed 1910) note that the regularity of the printed spellings and other qualities of his poems seem to indicate an unusually close relationship between an original manuscript and the printer's text. This may indicate that Spenser supervised the poem through the press, or that Singleton and John Harrison, the publishers of *The Shepheardes Calender*, and Ponsonby, the publisher of the other poems, took special care to ensure textual accuracy. The normal working methods of the book trade mean that individual copies give readings that may represent the final authorized version but others that may be quite incorrect. For example, in two extant copies of *Complaints*, line 414 of *Teares of the Muses* reads 'And they them heare, and they them highly prayse.' Other copies read (correctly) 'they him ... they him' – a significant difference that affects interpretation of the line. Lines 445–50 of the two variant copies read 'What bootes it then to come from glorious / Forefathers, or to have been nobly bred? / What oddes twixt *Irus* and old *Inachus*? / Twixt best and worst, when both alike are ded; / If none of neither mention should make, / Nor out of dust their memories awake?' All other copies read (correctly) 'bredd ... *Inachus*, ... dedd ... memorias' – small but telling differences.

Three points need to be remembered: (1) no single variant or small collection of variants can have the same effect as a texture created by the cumulative effect of many variants in their poetic context; (2) if one is unaware of the existence of one or more variants, one may unwittingly follow an uncorrected text; and (3) surviving copies may retain only a fraction of the variants which once existed. Only now are we beginning to recognize how the complexity of printing had complex effects on the text which we read (see Evans 1965).

One other point concerning the early printings of Spenser's works deserves comment: we do not and cannot know how many copies of a given work were printed and, therefore, what percentage of all copies printed has survived. After 1587, the Stationers' Company decreed that only 1500 copies of any sheet could be printed without type being reset, a make-work rule for compositors. Of the possible 1500 copies of the second edition of *The Faerie Queene* (1596), about 110 survive, less than one in fifteen. The low survival rate means that many textual variations may be lost.

Most of Spenser's works were not reprinted in his lifetime, and only *The Faerie Queene* appears to have been revised by Spenser during its reprinting. *The Shepheardes Calender* appeared in five editions, but each is a reprint of its predecessor. *Daphnaïda* appeared in a second edition (1596), but this is also a reprint of the first (1591). Except for the first three books of *The Faerie Queene*, revised for a second printing, then, only first editions have authority; all subsequent editions, being reprints, are subject to the errors which occur in any act of replication.

The folio editions (1609, 1611–17, 1679) are derivative reprintings from previous editions, except for the first publication of Book VII in the 1609 folio of *The Faerie Queene*. These later folios show in their spelling an editorializing that brings them into conformity with current practices. Although the folios have no new authority – except for *FQ* VII – and show further decay of the text through copying, for a century they served as the basis for Spenser's text.

In 1715, John Hughes edited a six-volume duodecimo edition of the works in which he relied almost entirely on the folios of 1609–17 and felt free to modernize the text in spelling and capitalization. While he did offer some corrections of obvious errors (eg, the substitution of Calepine for Calidore in *FQ* VI vi 17), these were probably based on good sense rather than textual criticism, for at I i 12.5, he miscorrects *and hardy* by dropping *and* instead of *hardy*. Since this is actually corrected in the 'Faults Escaped' of the 1590 quarto, it would seem that he did not consult, or did not carefully consult, early editions.

John Jortin, in his *Remarks on Spenser's Poems* (1734), was the first to indicate how Spenserian textual criticism must proceed. He believed that the text could be improved by a full collation of all the editions from first through the last folio, and although he was either unwilling or unable to perform this task, the anonymous reviser of the Hughes edition in 1750 appears to have done so. This reviser consulted the 1590 *Faerie Queene* extensively, and regularly preferred its readings to those of Hughes and the folio editions on which he relied. So thorough is his use of the 1590 quarto that it caused the editor, almost certainly because of the considerable haste which we know was involved in preparing and printing the second edition of Hughes, to print the original ending of Book III rather than the 1596 ending.

In 1751, Thomas Birch produced a three-volume edition of Spenser. Although he too knew the importance of collating early editions and relied heavily on both the 1590 quarto and the 'Faults Escaped' printed at the end of that edition, his method and the choices he made in variant readings were not sufficiently methodical. He did not always follow the authority of either quarto, and often adopted readings from later folio editions, some from as late as 1679. For all its faults, however, the Birch edition is significant for further establishing the textual authority, in theory if not in practice, of the earliest editions. This recognition came much earlier to *The Faerie Queene* than to the minor poems and, indeed, to the first three books in the 1590 quarto than to the last three in the 1596 quarto.

In 1758, an anonymously edited *Faerie Queene* was issued by Tonson in a cheap two-volume octavo edition. Although ostensibly a reprint of the 1750 second edition of Hughes' text, it relies even more heavily on the 1590 quarto, especially the 'Faults Escaped.'

The same year saw the greatest advance, or restoration, of the text of *The Faerie Queene* since 1596: Upton's two-volume quarto edition published by J. and R. Tonson. Upton returned to the early editions, both the 1590 and 1596 quartos, as well as to the folios. He made the first quarto the basis for Books I-III, also collating this portion of the text against the second quarto, and he made the 1596 quarto the basis for Books IV-VI. In addition, he used two copies of each quarto edition, only one of which had the Welsh words at II x 24, as he records in his apparatus. While his general approach to the text is sound and remarkably in line with modern ideas of textual criticism, in carrying it out he fell prey to the eighteenth-century habit of emending an author's text freely to suit his own ideas about the poem, justifying his need for these conjectural emendations on the 'foulness' of the papers which Spenser gave to the printer and the inattention of the printers of the quartos. Yet his practice of placing most of these emendations in notes so that readers might decide for themselves did avoid contamination of the text itself.

In 1758 also appeared the edition of *The Faerie Queene* by Ralph Church, the first editor to attempt a complete survey of editions. He was the first to recognize and significantly comment upon the variant dedications, the number of prefatory poems, the presence or absence of the Letter to Raleigh, the variations between the first and second quartos (which he mistakenly identified as octavos instead of quartos gathered in eights) of Books I-III. His views on the editions from the first folio onwards are much in line with present-day assumptions. His base text for the first three books was the first quarto; for the last three books, the second quarto; and for Book VII, the first folio of 1609. He also objected to the tendency toward modernization which had begun with the first folio and which, by the middle of the eighteenth century, had a disastrous effect on the text of the poem. Church still introduced emendations from the 1679 folio and later editions, and emended in ways which make sense but which are totally without the authority of earlier texts. In addition, since he had adopted the view (which he does not document) that Spenser did not oversee the printing of either quarto edition, he felt free to repunctuate heavily. Although his text is better than any earlier one, it is still not wholly satisfactory. By 1758, then, the text of Spenser's works had become established, for good or ill, with Hughes (1715) a standard for the minor poems and Upton (1758) a standard for *The Faerie Queene*.

In 1805, Henry John Todd produced an eight-volume 'variorum' edition of all of Spenser's works. He used the early editions of all the works published in Spenser's lifetime, and except for his erroneous choice of the third quarto with reliance also on the second and fifth quartos as the base text for *The Shepheardes Calender*, his work is generally sound and finally remedied the difficulties Hughes had introduced into the texts of the minor poems. His editing of *The Faerie Queene* is much more conservative than either Upton's or Church's, though he too fell prey to confusion over the mixed binding formats of the folios. His editing of *Vewe* is extremely good, for he used two manuscripts as well as the first printed edition. His was the first edition since 1679 to print E.K.'s glosses and the Arguments in *The Shepheardes Calender*, and his text is generally an advance over all previous editions, especially of the minor poems. Only the Spenser-Harvey correspondence suffers, for he did not edit it as a unit but provided only extracts at the end of his edition and quoted other parts in the prefatory material. Todd also brought together a number of poems associated with Spenser, did not attribute *Brittain's Ida* to him, and collected and edited the Spenser material from *Theatre for Worldlings*. His edition is not only the culmination of nearly a century's editorial work on Spenser, but also became the standard against which future editions were measured until the work of J.C. Smith in 1909 and Ernest de Sélincourt in 1910.

However, three further important editions appeared in the nineteenth century. F.J. Child's edition of the poetic works appeared in Boston in 1855. Although not the first American edition (see *America to 1900), it was the first in half a century to reedit the texts on either side of the Atlantic. But it would appear that, rather than going back to the originals and starting fresh, Child used a copy of Todd and compared it with various copies of the sixteenth- and seventeenth-century editions. Thus, he provides very few variant readings in his apparatus and repeats several misprints in Todd.

The most interesting later-nineteenth-century edition is the five-volume poetic works prepared in 1862 by John Payne Collier, at the time an important scholar but now notorious as a forger of various Renaissance documents. His edition is a very direct assault on Todd's. Although Collier's work on Spenser's text is basically sound in conception, his violence in attacking Todd, his very scanty recording of textual variants, and his reliance on what is now known to be a forgery (the 'Drayton Folio' of Spenser) have given him a bad reputation. Since he did not, as he claimed, consult and collate every text from 1579 to 1679, his edition is unreliable. Yet he was the first editor to rely on the first quarto for the text of *The Shepheardes Calender*, although without noting that he occasionally adopted a reading from a later quarto or folio. Furthermore, although he charged Todd with gross inaccuracy, he occasionally asserted a reading to be an error in Todd although it comes from one of the later folio texts which he professed to have consulted. As with so much of Collier's other work, whatever might have been good about his edition is tainted by his duplicity and violent temper.

During 1895–7, T.J. Wise brought out a six-volume edition of *The Faerie Queene* which was based on the 1590 quarto for Books I-III, the 1596 quarto for Books IV-VI, and the 1609 folio for Book VII. It is not a particularly good or new edition, but neither is it particularly bad. But the subsequent scandal surrounding Wise – for he too was a forger and sophisticator of rare books and pamphlets – has caused it to do a 'disappearing act' in later editions of the poem. It is interesting to note that the catalogue of the Ashley Library, the magnificent collection formed by Wise and later acquired by the British Museum, records a 1590 quarto of *The Faerie Queene* and only the second volume (Books IV-VI) of the 1596 quarto. We see here a relationship between book collecting and textual criticism.

In 1869, the Globe edition of Spenser's *Complete Works* edited by Richard Morris appeared, with a biography of Spenser by J.W. Hales. This quickly became the standard reading edition and was very frequently reprinted. Morris was a very conservative editor and much of his textual work is merely the faithful reproduction of the earliest edition. This in itself was a useful policy, but too often he emends unnecessarily, and often without notation. He would have better served Spenser's text had he offered simply a faithful reprint of the early editions.

The final work in the older fashion of textual criticism is the Reverend Alexander B. Grosart's edition of 1882–4, in nine volumes (originally intended to be in ten, but an index and apparatus volume was never completed). Grosart very carefully collated all the editions published in Spenser's lifetime, and his critical apparatus lists a full range of the textual variants between these editions, though not all of them. Perhaps the edition's greatest weakness stems from his firm conviction that Spenser oversaw all the quarto editions of *The Shepheardes Calender* and his consequent acceptance of the fifth quarto as of the greatest authority when actually it has the least.

The modern era of textual studies, what has been called 'the new bibliography,' began at the close of the nineteenth century. It placed great emphasis on a careful and analytical study of the entire physical means which brought a work from the poet's mind and hands through the manuscripts to the print shop into type and eventually into a printed book. These various aspects of book production were known to the earlier editors, who nevertheless considered them to be primarily antiquarian and bookish concerns; now they became the prime substance of all textual work. A better understanding developed of how material reached print in the English Renaissance and of exactly how printers carried out their work. It was no longer possible to blame stupid compositors for a reading which the editor disliked for aesthetic reasons; there was an increasing understanding of the importance of physical evidence and accurate description of that evidence; and there was an unwillingness to emend a text without proper evidence brought forward and explained by the editor.

First to benefit from this new attitude was the Oxford edition of *The Faerie Queene*, edited in two volumes by J.C. Smith in 1909, followed by the *Minor Poems* edited by Ernest de Sélincourt in 1910. Smith's preface (p vii) indicates the change in attitude: 'Aiming not at a reprint but a true text, I have not hesitated to depart from 1596 wherever I believed it to be in error and the error the printer's. But it is not part of an editor's duty to correct, though he may indicate, mistakes made by the author himself. There are many such in the *Faerie Queene*.' He then goes on to cite examples of six such errors. He also reversed the course of previous editing of *The Faerie Queene* by coming down forcefully for the view that Spenser had corrected the 1590 quarto and thus had invested authority in the 1596 quarto for all six books. This has remained standard editorial opinion.

De Sélincourt's edition of the *Minor Poems* is even more magisterial. He demonstrates beyond conjecture (by tracing a series of misprints from quarto to quarto and eventually to the folio) that each successive edition of *The Shepheardes Calender* was merely a reprint of its immediate predecessor and that Spenser exercised authority over none but the first. He compared texts more carefully than any previous editor, and his textual procedures are the same as Smith's.

In a significant new departure for the Oxford edition, both editors acknowledge the necessity of collating multiple copies of various editions, particularly those printings which serve as base texts for their editions.

However, although both Smith and de Sélincourt indicate that they have collated multiple copies, they do not always clearly record the results of this work and are relatively unclear about what copies they did collate. For a work where only a handful of copies survives – only three of *Daphnaïda*, for example – one may assume that all, or nearly all, were collated. Smith was faced with a more difficult problem because of the nearly 110 copies of the 1596 quarto of *The Faerie Queene*, but his list of copies consulted is very meager. Only two were fully collated for Books I-VI, and no multiple copies of the 1609 folio were fully collated for Book VII. However, the conservative nature of the editing, the selection of 1596 as the base text for all of *The Faerie Queene* and of the first quarto for *The Shepheardes Calender*, the reversal of the tendency to modernize the orthography, and the very conservative emendations of punctuation are all features of the Oxford edition which established it as the standard authoritative text for the twentieth century, a position which at least de Sélincourt's *Minor Poems* still holds.

The last major effort with Spenser's text was part of the monumental Variorum project which began issuing from Johns Hopkins University in 1932 and, textually at least, concluded in 1949, and of which Johnson's descriptive bibliography of editions before 1700 forms a part. For all of the *Variorum*'s virtues, textually it marks no advance. It does more to record the history of the text from 1579 to 1949 than any previous edition, both in listing variants and in printing statements of previous editors. Yet its text is virtually the same for all the works as that presented by Smith and de Sélincourt. Since it was intended to present a reference text to which the commentary and other matters are appended, and since its size and expense were such that it was never used as a reading edition, it has never replaced the Oxford edition. For *The Faerie Queene*, it offers collations of multiple copies of the base text, yet many of the copies listed were only 'spot collated' for known variants, a practice that will never reveal any variants except known ones.

Despite the many editions of Spenser, only two works have ever been examined in the detail we have come to expect as the usual standard for a critical edition: the first printing of *Prothalamion* was thoroughly examined in Horton 1944, and *Complaints* was carefully studied and edited for the *Variorum*. Although *The Faerie Queene* has received some detailed treatment in Evans 1965 and Shaheen 1980, nothing approaches the kind of work done on the text of Shakespeare. A few studies point in that direction: Meyer 1962, R.M. Smith 1958, and Stillinger 1961. Recent editions of *The Faerie Queene* by Hamilton (1977) and Roche (1978) do little to improve the textual situation: the former is a reprint of Smith's, and the latter a reprint of the 1596 quarto with additions of the canceled ending of Book III and of Book VII from the 1609 folio.

As for the physical description of Spenser's early editions, a thorough description was begun in Johnson 1933. Before Johnson, some editors had described early editions (eg, Jortin), but many were confused by the physical makeup of the early volumes. Even Todd was thrown when he tried to describe volumes that bound up 1611–12 and 1613 copies of *The Faerie Queene* with the 1617 minor poems. Although Johnson's work goes some way toward accurately describing the early editions, he was too early to make full use of the advances in analytical bibliography. Today, one would like facsimile reproductions of all of the various editions described, full notes on collational variants, and an up-to-date list of locations of copies. Johnson's notes are nevertheless very full and accurate and provide a substantial amount of information about the printing history of the works. A thorough revision of his work will lay the basis for a fresh assessment of Spenser's text.

Although much work has been devoted to the text of Spenser, much remains to be done. For those works which survive in a very small number of copies (*Three Letters*, *SC*, *Daphnaïda*, *Amoretti*, *Epithalamion*, and *Prothalamion*), we may safely assume that de Sélincourt and the *Variorum* editors have extracted most of the surviving textual evidence. Therefore, pending the discovery of new variant copies (or of errors in the work of these editors), it is likely that the texts are as accurate and faithful as they will ever be. But for those which exist in large numbers of surviving copies (*FQ*, *Complaints*, *Colin Clout*, and *Fowre Hymnes*), much more should be done in collating the earlier editions. For example, since both the 1590 and 1596 editions of the first three books of *The Faerie Queene* can be argued to have authority, and since Spenser may have seen them both through the press, both editions must be fully collated.

The Shepheardes Calender is a particularly difficult and complex textual problem because of its mixing of woodcuts, glosses, and different stanzaic forms; further analytical investigation of its bibliography may yield valuable data for fresh critical examination. Three other works also present unusual texts in need of careful study: *FQ* VII, *Complaints*, and *Vewe* were printed without Spenser's seeing them through the press. Our knowledge of the fate of other early English texts which passed through the press without authorial supervision urges us to determine the nature of their composition, proofing, and printing.

William Proctor Williams

The best survey of the early editions is still Johnson 1933, though see also the textual notes throughout the *Variorum*. For early editions of *FQ*, see Frank B. Evans 1965 'The Printing of Spenser's *Faerie Queene* in 1596' *SB* 18:49–67; and Naseeb Shaheen 1980 'The 1590 and 1596 Texts of *The Faerie Queene*' *PBSA* 74:57–63. For *SC*, Jack Stillinger 1961 'A Note on the Printing of E.K.'s Glosses' *SB* 14:203–5 is useful; see also **SC*, illustrations. Also useful are Dan S. Horton 1944 'The Bibliography of Spenser's *Prothalamion*' *JEGP* 43:349–53, and Sam Meyer 1962 'Spenser's *Colin Clout*: The Poem and the Book' *PBSA* 56:397–413. *Var* 8 has a fine commentary on *Complaints*, and *Var Prose* gives a thorough analysis of the prose works, especially *Vewe* (the Harvey-Spenser letters are incorrectly broken up as main text and appendix). For manuscripts, see *handwriting. The best introduction to eighteenth-century editions is still Wurtsbaugh 1936. For standard introductions to the bibliography of the early printed book, see McKerrow 1927; and Gaskell 1972. See also Edward Arber, ed 1875–94 *A Transcript of the Registers of the Company of Stationers of London 1554–1640* 5 vols (London); Beal 1980; W.W. Greg 1950–1 'The Rationale of Copy-Text' *SB* 3:19–36.

birds The works of Spenser contain nearly 200 references to birds. He mentions between 40 and 50 different species, including many garden and woodland birds, a range of predators and game birds, and a few exotic and mythological birds (see list below). A poet writing in the late sixteenth century had access to a substantial tradition of comment on and interpretation of the characteristics of numerous species. This tradition, derived from classical and medieval encyclopedias and bestiaries, manifested itself in various other forms, especially the fable and beast epic, popular and ecclesiastical art, the emblem book, and the proverb. Such forms have a common approach, in that they are more concerned with moral comment than with precise observation, and the information they embody ranges from the accurate to the absurd. Though the sixteenth and early seventeenth centuries constitute a period in which a more scientific ornithology developed, the references to birds by the poets of the period mainly reflect traditional associations.

The two species mentioned most frequently by Spenser are the eagle and the dove (or turtledove, or culver). In each case, a minority of the allusions are broadly naturalistic, while a clear majority function by reference to traditional stories and associations. Thus the eagle is portrayed as a supremely formidable predator on a few occasions (eg, *FQ* V iv 42, V xii 5), but is more often used in one of its symbolic roles – as Jove's bird (eg, II xi 43, *Vanitie* 4), the torturer of Prometheus (*FQ* II x 70), the symbol of Roman imperial power (*Rome* 17–18), or the bird which can gaze at the sun (eg, *FQ* I x 47, *Bellay* 7) and renew its failing vigor by immersing itself in water (*FQ* I xi 34). The two last-named qualities are based on well-known traditions, elaborated from biblical and classical texts, and specified in the bestiaries (eg, T.H. White 1954:105–8).

A similar pattern may be discerned in Spenser's treatment of the dove. It is portrayed literally, as the hunted game bird, in a number of places (eg, *FQ* III iv 49 and Howard Sonn), but it occurs more frequently in a symbolic manner – as the bird of Venus (eg, *FQ* IV proem 5, *Teares* 402), as a less specific symbol of love (eg, *FQ* IV viii 11, *Epithalamion* 358), and in its principal symbolic role, as exemplar of fidelity. In this role, it is seen as representing both general faithfulness between lovers (eg, *Epith* 24,

Colin Clout 340) and, more particularly, the constancy of a widow to her dead husband (eg, *FQ* IV viii 3, 'Astrophel' 178). The idea behind these associations is specified by Maplet, who says of the turtledove that 'hir best praise is in keeping undefiled wedlock and (lesing hir Mate) for hir constant Widowhoode' (1567:176). Though Spenser acknowledges no literal distinction between *dove*, *culver*, and *turtle dove*, he almost invariably uses the term *turtle (dove)* when alluding to the idea of faithfulness – partly, no doubt, for the sake of the alliteration with the almost inevitable epithet 'trew.'

As a consequence of the substantial inherited tradition of bird lore, most of Spenser's references to birds may be readily explained. Only two have presented significant problems of identification. 'The Whistler shrill' (*FQ* II xii 36) is plausibly identified as the curlew (Harrison 1950:39–41), while the problematic case of the unspecified bird 'which shonneth vew' (II ix 40) is still debated (Hough 1961). In contrast, the significance of most of Spenser's bird references could hardly be clearer. A good example is provided by his treatment of the owl – often termed 'ghastly' (ie, terrible, terrifying) – which regularly appears as a bird of ill omen, sometimes specifically associated with death (as in I v 30), at other times, more generally with the negation of positive values and life-giving forces (as in I ix 33, *Time* 130). The familiarity of such associations made it possible for the medieval poet to produce extended catalogues of birds, each linked with its typifying trait, as in Chaucer's *Parliament of Fowls* (337–64). Spenser alludes to the same ideas, but does not use the catalogue method – though it is perhaps implicit in his groups of threatening and of celebrating birds (*FQ* II xii 36, *Epith* 74–91). Familiarity also facilitates passing reference to notions like the greed of the ostrich (*FQ* II xi 12) and the rapacity of the cormorant (VI iv 29). Elsewhere, Spenser uses such ideas more allusively, as in two passages describing Braggadocchio – the comparisons with the kestrel and the capon suggesting (respectively) his knavishness and his cowardice (II iii 4, III viii 15).

Traditional bird lore is not, however, a monolithic system. While some birds were emphatically connected with one particular value, others were associated with a range of values (and an equivalent range of illustrative stories and moral applications); in such cases, the poet was free to select whatever was most appropriate to his purposes. Thus, the cuckoo is treated neutrally as a messenger of spring in *Amoretti* 19, though elsewhere it is often the subject of moral censure on account of its nesting habits. Similarly, while sometimes regarded as threatening cuckoldom, the cuckoo's voice can also be criticized on purely aesthetic grounds, as in *Amoretti* 85. Topsell observes: 'The voice of this birde is "Coco," without alteration, and the often reiteration thereof breedeth no delight in the hearer' (ed 1972:239). This view of the cuckoo's song has also been regarded as proverbial (Tilley 1950, C 894; Whiting 1934, C 600; F.P. Wilson 1970:160; it is, however, omitted from C.G. Smith's [1970] list of Spenserian proverbs).

Spenser's allusions to birds are most precise when he is dealing with falconry, but even on this subject, they often tend toward the figurative. Thus, the word *tower*, while used in its technical sense, of the hawk's upward and circling flight (*FQ* VI ii 32), is also handled in a metaphorical manner (VI x 6, *Time* 128). Indeed, Spenser's bird references, particularly those concerned with predators, often occur in figures of speech. The most common of these are similes for moments of human conflict, and they conform to a discernible pattern: a scene is briefly described in which a predator threatens, pursues, or seizes a game bird, or puts to flight a flock of such birds; the moral and emotional sympathies of the reader are usually identified with the victim (eg, in *FQ* III iv 49, III vii 39, V xii 5), but occasionally with the aggressor (eg, in II viii 50, V ii 54). It is hardly coincidental that Spenser's bird references should occur so frequently in figures of speech, for while they may provide valuable insight into his methods of composition and his habits of mind, their primary function remains that of embellishment.

bird species mentioned by Spenser bittern, chicken (*also* capon, cock), cormorant, crane, crow, cuckoo, daw, dove (*also* culver, turtledove), duck, eagle, falcon, goose, goshawk, hawk (*also* eyas hawk, tercel), heron (*also* hernshaw), jay, kestrel, kite (*also* puttock), lapwing, lark, mavis (*ie* song thrush), mew (*ie* seagull), night raven, nightingale, ostrich, ouzel, owl (*also* screech owl, strich), partridge, peacock (*also* pavone), phoenix, plover, raven, ruddock, sparrow, stork, swallow, swan, tedula, thrush, titmouse, vulture, whistler (*ie* curlew?). There are also various instances both of unspecified birds, and of birds referred to by brief typifying descriptions (eg, 'the bird that can the sun endure' *Bellay* 85) rather than by name.

MALCOLM ANDREW

Thomas P. Harrison 1950 'The Whistler, Bird of Omen' *MLN* 65:539–41; Harrison 1956 *They Tell of Birds: Chaucer, Spenser, Milton, Drayton* (Austin, Tex); Graham Hough 1961 'Spenser and Renaissance Iconography' *EIC* 11:233–5; Florence McCulloch 1960 *Mediaeval Latin and French Bestiaries* (Chapel Hill; rev ed 1962); Maplet 1567; Beryl Rowland 1978 *Birds with Human Souls: A Guide to Bird Symbolism* (Knoxville, Tenn); Kitty W. Scoular 1965 *Natural Magic: Studies in the Presentation of Nature in English Poetry from Spenser to Marvell* (Oxford); C.G. Smith 1970; Tilley 1950; Edward Topsell 1972 *The Fowles of Heaven or History of Birdes* ed Thomas P. Harrison and F. David Hoeniger (Austin, Tex); William Turner 1903 *Turner on Birds* (1544) ed A.H. Evans (Cambridge); T.H. White 1954; Whiting 1968; F.P. Wilson 1970.

Blake, William (1757–1827) Blake's tempera painting, 'The Characters in Spenser's *Faerie Queene*' (executed c 1825) is his only major commentary on Spenser. When he was about twenty, he wrote 'An Imitation of Spencer' (in *Poetical Sketches* 1783), which indicates an early interest in his Renaissance predecessor, but he employed Spenser's name only three more times in his poetic and graphic works. The earliest of these, in his Notebook, comes at the end of a pencilled quatrain from the Amavia-Ruddymane episode (*FQ* II ii 2.1–4), the spelling and text following Hughes' 1715 edition. The sketched emblem above the lines, one of a series of 64 he projected in 1787–92 as 'Ideas of Good and Evil,' pictures a boy about to capture a flying cherub in his hat, a second tiny figure outstretched dead at his feet – Blake's interpretation, perhaps, of Ruddymane's future. The preceding emblem is of a mounted, armored knight, castle in the background, deserting a kneeling, supplicating woman – perhaps Mortdant abandoning Amavia for Acrasia. No inscription accompanies this emblem. When he engraved some of these emblems for the 17 plates of *For Children: The Gates of Paradise* (1793), the cherub-catching boy becomes plate 7 but without the Spenser quotation, and the knight-and-lady emblem does not appear.

(See **Blake** Fig 1.)

The two other appearances of Spenser are in Blake's graphic work: one a labeled portrait (based on an earlier portrait by George Vertue) as part of a projected series of 18 or more 'Heads of the Poets' (c 1800–3), commissioned by William Hayley for a frieze in his library. The other is in one of Blake's 116 illustrations (1794–1805) to the poems of Thomas Gray. Ostensibly pictorializing Gray's homage to Spenser in *The Bard* ('The verse adorn again / Fierce War, and faithful Love, / And Truth severe, by fairy Fiction drest' 125–7), the illustration is of a gargantuan, youthful, curly-haired, and heavily robed figure whose face is more that of the 'Pindaric Genius' of Blake's illustration to Gray's title page than it is of the 'real' Spenser. Above and to his left are, apparently, 'Truth severe' (with quasi-clerical robe, holding an open book toward which his demurely downcast eyes are directed) and 'fairy Fiction' (with curly hair and short beard, dressed in a bodysuit with harlequinized pointed collar, holding an open scroll down to his left but gazing rather blankly into space). To Spenser's right are vignettes of the cave of Despair (with Despair himself offering a knife to a naked figure, face in hands) and the house of Mammon. In Spenser's outstretched hand is another tiny figure, standing with hunched shoulders and half-backward look toward his creator. The diagonal axis of the design makes it clear that, however creative Spenser (or his essential 'poetic genius') was, his creations are born under the auspices of 'Truth severe,' dressed in 'fairy Fiction,' but are fated to leap into the 'dangerous world' (the phrase is from Blake's *Song of Experience* 'Infant Sorrow') of Mammon and Despair. At best Spenser the Poet seems to emerge here as the 'Poor Moralist' of the final stanza of Gray's 'Ode on the Spring,' a personification of imagination gone sour in the service of a specious morality.

In contrast to this paucity of specific references to Spenser, allusions to the entire range of his poetry appear in Blake's work from *Poetical Sketches* through his three epic prophecies, *The Four Zoas*, *Milton*, and *Jerusalem*, the last of these roughly contemporary with his drafting of *The Faerie Queene* tempera. The poems most strikingly present one way or another, in addition to *The Faerie Queene*, include *Ruines of Time*, *Teares of the Muses*, the *Visions* from *Complaints*, *Amoretti*, and *Epithalamion*. Rarely are the verbal allusions to these poems complimentary; rather, in the spirit of his ideas that 'Opposition is True Friendship' and 'Imitation is Criticism,' Blake subjects many of Spenser's basic ideas, as he understood them, to severe criticism. These ideas include conventional conceptions of good and evil (the classical virtues and vices); reliance on the validity of the cycle of nature and the world of time (see esp Blake's four season poems, 'To Morning,' and 'To the Evening Star' in *Poetical Sketches*); belief in and poetic use of the courtly love tradition (see *The Book of Thel* and *The Four Zoas*); self-demeaning subservience to and praise of a worldly monarch; allegiance to the traditional Muses of memory rather than Blake's 'muse' of imagination (see 'To the Muses' and his prose treatise, *A Vision of the Last Judgment*); exploitation of warfare, glory, and other worldly values of chivalry (see, eg, *King Edward the Third*); conventional religious and social ideas inherited from Homer, Virgil, Ariosto, and Tasso; approval of the doctrine of *concordia discors*, for Blake the 'peace' that only 'mutual fear' effects (see *The Marriage of Heaven and Hell*, 'The Human Abstract'); elevation, even deification, of chastity, virginity, prudence, temperance, self-righteous holiness, and Talus-like justice into principles of model human conduct (see *Marriage*, *The Book of Thel*, *Visions of the Daughters of Albion*) – and, finally, Spenser's embodiment of these, and other like ideas equally pernicious to Blake, in the allegorical structure of *The Faerie Queene* in his effort to 'fashion a gentleman or noble person in vertuous and gentle discipline' (Letter to Raleigh).

For Blake, 'allegory' is a product of reason and memory, a diseased imagination; it is the opposite of 'vision' or 'sublime allegory,' of which the Bible is his best exemplar, for the Bible is literally inspired by the Word, Jesus Christ, whom he equates with the Human Imagination. Thus Blake's painting of the characters in *The Faerie Queene* is both a searing criticism of Spenser as well as an heroic attempt to redeem the 'true' imaginative Spenser from his 'spectrous' self laboring benightedly under the burden of the errors detailed above.

(See **Blake** Fig 2.)

Organized as a procession patterned on Blake's earlier critical pictorialization of Chaucer's Canterbury pilgrims (1808–10), the Spenser painting (a long rectangle 18 × 53 1/2 inches) divides into six main segments. From left to right, Redcrosse, Una (sidesaddle on an ass), lion, dwarf, and Dragon; the Palmer (with Ruddymane cradled in his right forearm and hand), Guyon, and Grill; Britomart with Grill ominously holding her horse's head and reins; Artegall and Talus; Arthur with Talus holding his horse's reins; Calidore and the Blatant Beast. Leading the procession is the dwarf, whom Blake transforms by way of a halo and swaddling bands into the Christ-child (the 'childe' who is the true Christian warrior). Bringing up the rear are the captured Duessa and Archimago, neither of whom, nor the Beast at their feet, Blake regards Spenser as having eliminated from his 'world.' In the upper half of the painting are, left to right, the New Jerusalem (toward which, as a version of Blake's prophecy *Jerusalem*, the procession should be moving but isn't); Cynthia-Diana soaring from a crescent moon; the dome of St Paul's Cathedral (Blake's epitome of historical institutionalized religion in England); a sceptered, magnificently haloed and starry-nimbused Jove-Jehovah (Blake's arch-tyrant Urizen or 'The God of This World') whose spread arms 'embrace' the whole procession below; Astraea on a cloud with her scales (the constellations Virgo and Libra); and to the far right the 'sun' of Spenser's fallen world, an archer-Mars in a spiky blood-red cloud above assorted Greek temples, the earthly historical Jerusalem (Babylon), and the tower of Babel – all situated in a rocky, only dimly illuminated wasteland landscape.

Although relying on the various symmetries of the painting for interpretive purposes is risky, the supernal-terrestrial vertical associations are indicative of part of Blake's commentary. The New Jerusalem hovers shiningly above the foremost group of figures (Book I), but its soaring Gothic spires tend to mock Redcrosse's upright spear, oddly peaked helmet, and the large red cross on his shield. The crescent moon, with its implications of Elizabeth as well as Cynthia, shines directly above the Palmer and Guyon, whose spear, in turn, points diagonally upward toward St Paul's. The cathedral itself is above Grill, who is afoot but leans toward and leers upward at Guyon. The God of This World hangs his right hand rather limply above Britomart's head while his left, holding a scepter, rests above Artegall, who points upward with his left forefinger at Astraea's scales. Talus is directly beneath the scales, paradoxically naked with spiked iron hair. Arthur, next in line after Talus, extends his right hand toward Artegall and thereby directly under Astraea's down-turned gaze, while with his left hand he gestures toward Calidore's spearhead and Mars in his blood-red cloud. Finally, Calidore rides beneath the Grecian temples and, in extending his right arm backward as if to keep Duessa and Archimago out of the 'pilgrimage,' he places it below the tower of Babel.

As in the poem, the identities of the main characters tend to merge into others the more one studies the painting and Spenser's text. For example, Britomart is clearly also Belphoebe, Amoret, and Queen Elizabeth, as well as the Whore of Babylon and, remarkably, Chaucer's Wife of Bath (as Blake presents her in his Chaucer painting). Artegall is also to be seen as Arthur (with royal cape and crown) just as Arthur, in the fifth position, is Artegall, Talus standing naked between the two with gigantic flail and spear. Calidore is most heavily armored of all, precisely as Spenser describes Arthur, and reveals nothing of his shepherd's garb – Blake's acerbic comment on the illusoriness and folly of Book VI's return to a pastoral 'Eden.' In addition, his gentle finger-wagging, no-no gesture back at the bound and head-bent Duessa and Archimago is clearly Blake's comic parody of Spenser's ultimate futility in his battle against the two arch-deceivers as well as of Calidore's ineffectuality with respect to the Blatant Beast. Una, haloed and minus her veil, is the Virgin Mary riding the ass of Christ's triumphal entry into Jerusalem, her testament 'with bloud ywrit' (transferred to her by Blake from Fidelia) open on her knees; thus even as she is Elizabeth accompanied by her royal lion and guarded by Redcrosse, perhaps even a fallen Eve, she 'becomes' the pregnant Mary who gives birth to the Christ-child (childe) who leads as in the Bible, but whom no one in the entire tableau, except Una, notices or follows. Guyon wears shepherd's weeds over his armor, an emblem of Calidorean hypocrisy intensified by the rigid self-restraint imaged in the cowled, bald, monklike Palmer's firm grasp of the reins of Guyon's horse. Guyon, in turn, stares back sternly (yet, one must surely imagine, with lust in his heart) at Britomart and therefore away from the Palmer, Una/Mary, and the dwarf/Christ-child. Redcrosse thrusts his shield between himself and Una while holding his spear uselessly upright, the Dragon/Error writhing beneath his horse's hooves as puissantly alive as Duessa, Archimago, and the Blatant Beast are at the other end of the 'poem.' As Blake wrote once, 'The Beast and the Whore rule without controls,' and to him that is sadly the case in *The Faerie Queene* regardless of what Spenser says to the contrary.

These are but a few of Blake's extraordinary manipulations of Spenser's intentions and 'truths.' Others abound the more one studies the intricate patternings and details of the painting with the poem open beside it. Clearly Spenser is, to Blake, entrapped in the depths of Error's den and 'cannot find [the] path' (*FQ* I i 13, 10). In *Milton* (c 1800–4), Blake presents his eponymous character as equally beset by errors of a similar sort, but in the course of that poem the Milton who is a 'true poet' beneath his benighted religious and moral trappings is enabled to redeem himself from those errors to become, in a sense, one with Blake and the biblical prophet-poets, and with Blake's 'image' of the Human Imagination, Jesus Christ. In the Spenser painting, however, Milton's precedessor is so beset that he needs a Blake to 'redeem' him – by 'translating' the characters of *The Faerie Queene* into the manifold embodiments of Spenserian error from which the imaginative Spenser as 'true poet' may be extricated. Thus the dwarf/Christ-child strides purposefully out of the left border of the painting toward what will be his crucifixion (in the 'world' of Spenser's poem) and subsequently toward his building of 'Jerusalem / In Englands green and pleasant Land,' as Blake wrote in his famous, stirring hymn prefatory to *Milton*. The shining city to the upper left, then, is at once the embodiment of Spenser's Cleopolis (the palace of the Fairy Queen herself and thus a measure of Spenser's imaginative blindness), the New Jerusalem Redcrosse sees but postpones his travel toward, and Blake's Jerusalem figured as the eternal Sun/Son. As Blake wrote of Christ in his poem, *The Everlasting Gospel*, 'God's Mercy and Long Suffering / Is but the Sinner to Judgment to bring,' so Blake brings Spenser to the bar in this extraordinary painting. It is therefore his 'poem' on Spenser to match his poem *Milton*, his poem *Jerusalem*, and his painted masterpiece, *A Vision of the Last Judgment*.

ROBERT F. GLECKNER

For further discussion, see Robert F. Gleckner 1985 *Blake and Spenser* (Baltimore). The *Faerie Queene* painting (with other works) is reproduced in Gleckner, but see also John E. Grant and Robert E. Brown 1974–5 'Blake's Vision of Spenser's *Faerie Queene*: A Report and an Anatomy' *Blake Newsletter* 31, 8:56–85 for a color printing with commentary.

Blandamour With Paridell and Duessa, Blandamour and Ate make up a group of quarrelsome and inconstant lovers in *FQ* IV i who parody the friendship-in-love of Cambell and Cambina, Triamond and Canacee. As Book III anatomized the forms of love between two people, Book IV explores the broader context of love within social groups. Blandamour, of 'fickle mind full of inconstancie' (i 32), is an inconstant lover and a disloyal friend; his actions are disruptive and his words slanderous. The first part of his name may suggest insincerity (the 'fayned blandishment' absent from the Temple of Venus, x 26), lightness (L *blandus* 'merry' + a fickle 'blending' of loves), or perhaps blindness (by a near pun on the traditional iconography of Cupid). Indiscriminately, he pairs himself at various times with Ate, the most hideous figure in Book IV, and with the false Florimell, the most beautiful. The narrator explains Blandamour's promiscuity as the result of the 'sting of lust, that reasons eye did blind ... So blind is lust, false colours to descry' (ii 5, 11). One source for his name may be the reference in Chaucer's *Sir Thopas* (*CT* VII 900) to 'Pleyndamour' (spelled Blayndamour in Thynne's 1532 edition).

Blandamour appears throughout Book IV (in cantos i, ii, iv, v, and ix) as an example of the human discord that opposes the concord of friendship. Though he is described as a 'man of mickle might' (i 32), the narrator consistently refers to him with an irony that diminishes and disarms him. He quarrels continually with Paridell, his fitting companion in lust, envy, and fickleness. 'This gallant' is defeated by Britomart in an encounter that is treated as a comically unsuccessful courtship (35–7); he wins the false Florimell from Ferraugh but only by attacking him from behind without first challenging him (ii 6); and in Satyrane's tournament, he is defeated first by Ferramont and then by Britomart (iv 19, 45). His only 'victory' comes when he exposes Braggadocchio as a coward (iv 9–11). He last appears in the melee of shifting alliances at ix 20–34. This second unstable group of four (Blandamour, Paridell, Druon, and Claribell) recalls his first appearance in canto i but has a broader symbolic design, as the contest takes on overtones of the four elements, the four winds, the four humors, and chaos itself. Thus we last see him as an image of human and cosmic discord. He will be mentioned once more, as Duessa's paramour, conspiring with her to deprive Mercilla of royal power (V ix 41).

LESLEY BRILL

Blandina, Turpine The story of Turpine and Blandina, enemies of courtesy, is strategically placed in two episodes near the center of *FQ* VI. Although Calidore will eventually capture the Blatant Beast, his surrogate Calepine is first defeated by Turpine, who is subsequently conquered by Arthur. These two discrete narratives (iii 27–iv 8 and vi 18–vii 27) together illustrate a major obstacle to civility and the difficulty of overcoming it.

Calepine and Serena encounter Turpine after the lady has been bitten by the Beast. Turpine first scornfully refuses to take Calepine (who has put Serena on his horse) across a raging river, and then orders the door of his Castle of the Ford shut against him, as against all knights-errant, unless he fights him first. After the couple has passed a cold night outdoors, Turpine attacks the defenseless knight and, when the latter fails to elude him by hiding behind Serena's back, wounds him sorely. Only the sudden appearance of the Salvage Man saves Calepine's life. Later Arthur, accompanied by the Salvage Man, seeks to avenge Turpine's discourtesies but spares his life when his wife Blandina covers him with her 'garment' and begs for mercy. Arthur pardons him on condition that he forswear chivalry forever, is entertained by Blandina all night, and in the morning departs. Unregenerate, Turpine suborns two credulous young knights to avenge upon Arthur a suppositious wrong. In the ensuing fight one knight is killed; the other, Enias (named only later, at viii 4), is spared on condition that he bring Turpine to Arthur. Enias does so, and this time Arthur leaves the villain 'baffuld' (ie, disgraced), hanging by his heels from a tree as an 'ensample' to others of the fate of treasonous discourtesy (see *baffling).

Turpine, whose name connotes shame (L *turpis* disgraceful, shameless), is perhaps Spenser's most egregiously discourteous knight. He is a coward, bullying the weak and cringing from the strong. His character derives from Ariosto's Pinabello (*Orlando furioso* 22.47–98), the first syllable of whose name is a common element in the names of Turpine and Calepine. (Ariosto's villain is no coward, however. Moreover, he and his *meretrice* [whore] – an even less kindred precursor of Blandina – have established a custom of disarming knights and disrobing ladies that links them perhaps more closely to the hair-and-beard-collecting Maleffort and Briana in VI i.) In his impeachment of Turpine (vi 34), Arthur names Turpine's use of 'guile,' his 'wicked custome' at the castle door, and his cowardice. He might also have mentioned his lack of compassion and charity toward the weak or needy.

His wife Blandina is in some ways the opposite of her lord, for she displays an excess of courtesy to offset his defect. As her name implies, she is outwardly as bland as he is haughty, and her blandishments to Arthur save her husband's life. But her compliant cheer is 'false and fayned,' and she habitually uses sweet talk to 'allure' to their peril those who are susceptible to external displays of courtesy. Her deception of Arthur may imply that false, attractive women represent a greater threat to noble manhood than do even the most treacherous men.

Enias, the knight who is gulled into being the unwitting instrument of Turpine's treachery, is basically noble. His only real offence to chivalry is his accepting the promise of 'a goodly mead' from Turpine (vii 4). Enias' intentions are good, he quickly recognizes Arthur's true virtue when he meets him, and unlike Turpine he is corrigible. When he and Turpine approach the sleeping Arthur, Enias refuses to be tempted into spilling his new 'lieges blood.' His name may derive from Greek *hēnia* 'bridle or reins,' signifying perhaps that excess of courteous valor can be checked by reason or example.

Several motifs connect these characters to the dominant themes of Book VI. One is deception. Unlike the guileless Calepine, Arthur invents a sleight to gain entry into Turpine's hall (cf Calidore with the Brigands in canto xi), and even Enias seeks to convince Turpine that Arthur is dead. That true and false appearances of courtesy are hard to distinguish is emphasized by the motif of seeking protection from one's lady. The unarmed Calepine's hiding behind Serena resembles Turpine's finding concealment with Blandina; the reader is challenged to perceive the difference. Another linking motif is the 'shame' of bearing another's body. In canto ii, Calidore readily supports Aladine, whereas Turpine finds a similar suggestion from Calepine shameful. Finally, Turpine's cruelty also likens him to Crudor; but unlike baseness, cruelty can be corrected. That Turpine, though nobly born, is repeatedly described as 'base' involves him in the book's argument about the roots of courtesy in nature or nurture. He is the only knight in Book VI (and one of only two in the whole poem) to be baffled and the only one to suffer the foot-on-neck humiliation of base subjection.

JOHN D. BERNARD

Blatant Beast Epitome and culmination of intractable evil in *The Faerie Queene*, the Blatant Beast is a 'hellish Dog' (VI vi 12) encountered first by Artegall as he returns from Irena's kingdom to Gloriana's court, and subsequently sought by Calidore during his travails, the 'endlesse trace' of Courtesy (i 6). Eventually tracked down, captured, and subdued by Calidore after it has wounded Serena and Timias, it finally breaks loose to range again at liberty, a more pernicious evil than before (iii 24–8, v 12–24, xii 38–41). Its nature is defined principally by the figures with whom it consorts: Envy and Detraction, who 'combynd in one, / And linckt together' have an appropriate ally in the Beast (v xii 37), and Despetto, Decetto, and Defetto, who 'in one compound ... conjoynd' discover in the Beast a monstrous incarnation of their combined subhuman powers (VI v 14). The Beast is analogous to the 'ravenous wolfe' on which Envy rides (I iv 30); its 'cruell clawes' and 'ravenous pawes' recall the descriptions of other invidious characters, such as Malbecco, Care, and Sclaunder (VI xii 29; cf III x 57; IV v 35, viii 23).

Spenser's descriptions of the Beast focus on its mouth, which contains perhaps a hundred, perhaps a thousand, tongues, all of which 'bray' with the cacophonous sound of dogs, cats, bears, tigers, serpents, and reproachful mortals (V xii 41–2, VI xii 27–33). As a principle of discord, the Beast represents the abuse and perversion of language, the distinctively human gift on which 'civill conversation' and 'gracious speach' rely (VI i 1–2), since ideally 'the tongue by instructing, conferring, disputing, and discoursing, doth gather, assemble, and joyne men together with a certaine naturall bonde' (Guazzo ed 1925, 1:122). The Beast is also endowed with rusty iron teeth, which cause the rankling, incurable wounds that fester within those it bites (VI vi 1–2, 9, xii 26); this detail links it with the Dragon of Redcrosse (I xi 13) and with the apocalyptic beast of Daniel 7.7, to which Thomas Lodge alludes as a type of detraction (ed 1883, 4:19).

Noisy and hurtful, the Beast is properly *blătant*. Not to be confused with present-day English *blātant*, the adjective derives from the verb *blatter* 'to speak or prate volubly,' which Spenser connects with envy in *Vewe of Ireland* (*Var Prose* p 63; cf L *blatero* 'to babble' and Scots *blate* 'to bleat'). Joseph Wybarne suggests another etymology in discussing that virtue 'transcendent and heroycall,' which the Bible ascribes to Samson, poets to Hercules, and 'our writers to Prince Arthur': this 'vertue hath beene three wayes assaulted, First, by calumniation, for actions done by divine instinct, have ever found some *Zoylus*, *Momus*, *Mastix*, or tongue of blattant beast, so called of *blaptō*, to hurt' (1609:72). The rabid Beast's actions, and perhaps its name, are reminiscent of the proverbial Ovidian phrase *livor edax* 'biting envy' (*Amores* 1.15.1).

Two genealogies trace the 'hellishe race' of the monster. Calidore tells Artegall that the Beast is the offspring of Cerberus and Chimaera (VI i 7–8); the Hermit who ministers to the wounded Timias and Serena says it comes from the 'commixtion' of Echidna and Typhaon (vi 9–12). Hesiod's Echidna, half fair nymph and half horrible serpent, couples with the wind god Typhaon to produce a savage generation: the vicious dogs Orthus and Cerberus, and the Lernaean Hydra, whose might defeated even Hercules and whose daughter was Chimaera, a three-headed, fire-snorting prodigy (*Theogony* 295–324). Spenser's hellhound was bred in this demonic nursery 'Till he to perfect ripenesse grew,' just as virtue lay hidden in its own 'sacred noursery ... Till it to ripenesse grew' (VI proem 3, i 8).

These pedigrees, which enlarge the Beast's awesome significance, imply more than a simple relation between nurture and nature, and account for more than its canine attributes. The Beast's dam, Echidna, helps to explain the peculiar union of Blandina and Turpine, for she is at once both fair and foul and thus a fit symbol for the union of flattery and detraction, both sins of the mouth. Fanciful distortions of slander underlie the Beast's connection with Chimaera, whom mythographers known to Spenser gloss as 'the arts of rhetoric' (Conti *Mythologiae* 9.4; see also Nohrnberg 1976:692 n 78). As son of Typhaon, the Beast is a blustering wind monster, a windbag like Orgoglio (Nohrnberg 1976:694). It is in the tradition of Virgil's winged Fama, Chaucer's Dame Fame whose messenger is Aeolus, and Shakespeare's Rumor who makes the wind his post-horse. The Beast races through the poem and is deflated, humorously, only for a time when Calidore 'forst him gape and gaspe, with dread aghast, / As if his lungs and lites were nigh a sunder brast' (VI iii 24–6).

When Calidore informs Artegall that courtesy's task is to overtake or otherwise subdue the Beast, he concedes that the monster is particularly elusive: 'Yet know I not or how, or in what place / To find him out, yet still I forward trace' (i 7). As Book VI progresses, Spenser stresses the elusiveness of the Beast in two ways. First, he keeps it out of Calidore's reach: the more avidly pursued, the more rapidly it recedes to the circumference of the poem. It draws Calidore away on a centrifugal search and distracts him from the centripetal movement to the seat of virtue and courtesy located 'deepe within the mynd' (proem 5). Spenser intimates that the source of defamation is not easy to isolate, and that the spread of rumor is hard to contain, as the Beast leads Calidore 'Through hils, through dales, throgh forests, and throgh plaines' and further, from court to cities, to towns, to country, to farms, and to open fields (ix 2–3). Envy and detraction are pandemic; coursing 'Through every place' and 'Through all estates,' even the church, the Beast 'rageth sore in each degree and state' (xii 22–5, 40).

The second method Spenser uses to stress the elusive ubiquity of the Beast is to introduce it into the narrative when the reader and its victims least expect it: when Artegall is triumphant, when Timias is heedless and unaware, when Serena is blithely oblivious to danger. Spenser thus emphasizes the fragility of carelessness and security in a fickle, perilous world and underscores the futility of resting on one's laurels when good name and reputation can so quickly be damaged. This conceptual antithesis between serenity and the forces represented by the Beast is a Renaissance *topos*; Alberti, for example, describes Calumny as the enemy of *alypia*, or Security of Mind (Cast 1981:35, 38). The innocent repose and calm of mind so earnestly sought in Book VI elude characters who are charged with fending off the inscrutable opponent of concord. Because the Beast attacks the guiltless especially, rending 'without regard of person or of time' (xii 40), the Hermit's stoic counsel (vi 7, 14) is an inadequate shield against its savagery.

Spenser magnifies the Beast's insidiousness by tainting others in Book VI with its attributes, just as he allows Error, the original monster, to insinuate itself as error throughout Book I. Through poison-mouth imagery, for instance, he associates the Beast with the bear that abducts the baby rescued by Calepine, and with the tiger that attacks Pastorella (iv 17–22, x 34). Through canine imagery, he affiliates the Beast with Despetto and his crew, with the cannibals who threaten Pastorella, and with the Brigands who 'Like as a sort of hungry dogs ... Doe ... snatch, and byte, and rend' (xi 17). Whenever Spenser rhymes *name* or *fame* with *blame* or *shame*, the dis-gracing Beast is implicit. Turpine, the fierce Lapiths (x 13), and the discourteous knight who injures Aladine's reputation (ii 16–21) are all aspects of the shadows cast by the Beast's presence in the book. Even Calidore comes under its sway as he infects the pastoral landscape with his envy of Meliboe's kingdom, awakens the envy of Coridon, and intrudes invidiously on the charmed circle of the Graces.

For all his vulnerability to Envy, throughout much of Book VI Calidore is associated with the 'Gallic' Hercules, whose strength and virtue consist, like Orpheus', in his eloquence. French Renaissance writers in particular had been quick to seize on Lucian's description of a picture he had seen in Gaul, in which the hero drew his followers by chains extending from his tongue to their ears (*Herakles* 4.6 cited by Galinsky 1972:222–3; cf Cain 1978:169–72, MacIntyre 1966). Insofar as Calidore is comparable to Hercules in general (eg, xii 32, 35), Spenser rationalizes the Beast's escape from the iron chain in which it had been leashed, for Horace had remarked that even Hercules, 'who crushed the fell Hydra and laid low with fated toil the monsters of story found that Envy is quelled only by death that comes at last' (*Epistles* 2.1.10–12). This same Horatian passage links the initial victory of Redcrosse over Error to Calidore's final problematic confrontation with the Beast. This tradition is compatible with the biblical admonition that 'the tongue can no man tame. It is an unrulie evil, ful of deadelie poyson' (James 3.8), and with the prophecy that the old serpent, bound for a thousand years, 'must be losed for a litle season' (Rev 20.3). Insofar as Calidore is comparable to Orpheus, who from the beginning of Spenser's career was his prime exemplar of the poet's civilizing power, the triumph of the Blatant

Beast at the end reverses the pattern of *SC, October*, where Orpheus' music charms and tames permanently the 'hellish hound' (28–30; see Cain 1978:178–80). This reversal symbolizes the poet's shaken confidence in the poet's heroic role: the Beast's persistence attests to a disillusionment with 'Sidneyan notions of the end of literature as inculcating ethical action' and a 'growing pessimism over the effectiveness of poetry to initiate societal reform' (DeNeef 1979:16).

In the last three stanzas of Book VI, the Beast leaves the remote and golden world of fiction to become a brazen reality confronting Spenser directly. It roams through the contemporary Elizabethan world unchallenged and finally turns its 'venemous despite' on the poet himself (xii 40–1). Spenser had always recognized that poetry was a favorite target for envious detractors and for willful misreaders such as Lord Burghley, if he is the 'mighty Pere' who had reproved the first installment of the poem (IV proem, VI xii 41); but in the conclusion to the book, he is especially embittered about the extent to which both his 'former writs' and 'this homely verse' have been and will be blotted by what he calls the 'gealous opinions and misconstructions' of his critics (Letter to Raleigh). The last three stanzas emphasize the disjunction between Fairyland and the actual world; they suggest that Calidore's pursuit and capturing of the Beast is 'wish-fulfillment,' and that his temporary victory over it is the most 'ridiculous of all Elfin homecomings' (Berger 1961b:43). In the final two lines, the idealism, which from the beginning had animated Spenser's heroic labors as epic poet, gives way to cynical expediency, as Spenser contorts the maxim 'measure is a treasure' into a dispirited recommendation that poets should merely placate their audiences if they wish to succeed. At this point, the Beast's tongues overwhelm the poet's voice: the uncreating word of the Antilogos reigns supreme, brooding over the end of the poem.

Of all the fiends, monsters, and dragons in *The Faerie Queene*, the Blatant Beast alone terrorizes the poet. It alone attacks those close to him: Lord Grey and Raleigh, figured as Artegall and Timias, respectively. All the more inadequate, then, is Jonson's comment, recorded by William Drummond: 'That in that paper S. W Raughly had of the Allegories of his Fayrie Queen by the Blating beast the Puritans were understood' (Jonson ed 1925–52, 1:137). Although Cavalier poets were content to appropriate the Beast as a symbol of Puritanism (Hughes 1918), modern readers have found Spenser's Beast an arresting image of the gracelessness that can poison the gentle and artful use of language. RONALD B. BOND

Aptekar 1969; Berger 1961b; Cain 1978; Cast 1981; A. Leigh DeNeef 1979 '"Who now does follow the foule Blatant Beast": Spenser's Self-Effacing Fictions' *RenP 1978* pp 11–21; Leslie Hotson 1958 'The Blatant Beast' in D.C. Allen 1958:34–7; Merritt Y. Hughes 1918 'Spenser's "Blatant Beast"' *MLR* 13:267–75; Nohrnberg 1976; Joseph Wybarne 1609 *The New Age of Old Names* (London).

Boccaccio, Giovanni (1313–75) Though Boccaccio is remembered today for his *Decameron*, a cycle of short prose narratives in Italian, his other vernacular works were just as well known in the Renaissance: his prose *Il filocolo*, *L'ameto*, *Fiammetta* and verse *Filostrato*, *Teseida*, and *Il ninfale fiesolano*. Likewise his Latin works: the *Buccolicum carmen*, a cycle of sixteen eclogues; two series of biographical narratives, *De casibus virorum illustrium* (*On the Fall of Illustrious Men*) and *De claris mulieribus* (*Concerning Famous Women*); and the *Genealogiae deorum gentilium libri* (*Books of the Genealogy of the Pagan Gods*, often referred to simply as the *Genealogia*), a handbook of classical mythology to which was often appended a guide to geographical names.

Most of these works were available to Elizabethan readers in their original languages or in French and (for the Latin works) Italian translations (Mulryan 1974). Some were also translated into English: *De casibus* (in Lydgate's version 1494, etc), *Filocolo* (1567), *Fiammetta* (1587), *Ninfale fiesolano* (1597; not in *STC*; see Wright 1957:108–12). The *Decameron* did not appear in a complete English translation until 1620, though imitations and translations of individual stories had appeared well before then. Boccaccio appealed to Elizabethan readers as an entertaining storyteller, as a writer on the theme of love, but also as a Latin moralist, one who was 'at once learned, correct, and romantic in his attitude toward history, story material, the pastoral, and the pagan gods' (Tuve 1936:148).

Spenser read Boccaccio and incorporated many elements of his work into his own poetry, but the evidence for this influence is sketchy. The *Genealogia* is cited as a principal source for his myth (see Burchmore 1981, Lotspeich 1932), though he does not seem to have followed it as closely as he did Conti's *Mythologiae*. There are many instances where he could have received his classical mythology direct from the ancients or from an intermediate source, such as another poet or mythographer, or a dictionary (Starnes and Talbert 1955). Yet he seems to have followed Boccaccio in his portrayal of Daemogorgon, and it seems likely that he consulted the *Genealogia* regularly (see, eg, the discussions of Cyparissus and the girdle of Venus in Lotspeich 1932:51, 115). Perhaps more important than the details from Boccaccio is the notion of a Christianized paganism (that is, paganism Christianized through interpretation) that Spenser and his contemporaries found in the *Genealogia*.

Another work usually cited as important for Spenser is the *De claris mulieribus*. Here, however, the link is based on a single significant 'mistake' in Spenser's text, where he portrays Hercules subdued and weakened by Iole rather than Omphale (*FQ* V v 24–5). This follows Boccaccio's chapter on Iole, whom he presents as having overcome Hercules by subtle blandishments in revenge for her father's murder. The figure of the woman successfully feminizing the man has a clear parallel in Spenser's text to Radigund weakening Artegall, and it has been argued that the introduction of Boccaccio's Iole gives force and direction to the portrayal of Radigund (Tuve 1936).

Other parallels may be found in Spenser's reference to the *Decameron* at *FQ* IV x 27 ('Myld *Titus* and *Gesippus* without pryde' – two friends in *Decameron* 10.8 commonly referred to in Elizabethan literature) or in a possible hint of the revolt of the Amazons from *Teseida* 1 in *FQ* V. (For many such parallels, see *Var* index.) Scholarly inquiry into Boccaccio's influence on specific passages in Spenser has been nearly exhaustive. Yet his importance in the traditions of eclogue, historical and mythological narrative, epic, theory of love, and Christianizing of pagan mythology suggests that the intertextual relationships of the two authors have yet to be properly explored.

JOHN MULRYAN

The best life and general study is Vittore Branca 1976 *Boccaccio: The Man and His Works* tr Richard Monges and Dennis J. McAuliffe (New York). The major works in Italian are found in Boccaccio 1964– *Tutte le opere* ed Vittore Branca (Verona). The standard English translation of *Decameron* is by John Payne, rev Charles S. Singleton, 3 vols (Berkeley and Los Angeles 1982). See also *Amorous Fiammetta* tr Bartholomew Yong (London 1587), rev Edward Hutton (London 1952); Boccaccio ed 1930; *Concerning Famous Women* tr Guido A. Guarino (New Brunswick, NJ 1963); *The Fates of Illustrious Men* (abr) tr and abr Louis Brewer Hall (New York 1965); and *Il Filocolo* tr Donald Cheney (New York 1985). For editions of the *Genealogia*, see Ernest Hatch Wilkins 1919–20 'The Genealogy of the Editions of the *Genealogia deorum*' *MP* 17:425–38. Translations of the 16th and early 17th centuries are listed in *STC* 3172–84. A general study is Herbert G. Wright 1957 *Boccaccio in England from Chaucer to Tennyson* (London). See also Rosemond Tuve 1936 'Spenser's Reading: The *De claris mulieribus*' *SP* 33:147–65.

body The human body recurs throughout *The Faerie Queene* as an isolated poetic image, as part of the narrative, or as an allegorical landscape setting. Its manifold associations as a thematic device provide a sequence of self-replicating poetic nodes, reminiscent of the attempts of early Modernist novelists to compose in the leitmotif manner. Yet the human body is more than an insistent structural device: it is central to the poem's whole meaning – in an important sense, it is what the poem is 'about.'

The human body functions most obviously as the external depiction of an internal moral state. Sin may be commonly recognized as a moral disease by its literal occurrence as a diseased human body, the body of the sin's perpetrator grown monstrous, infected, and disordered. The serpent-woman Error is described in the context of vomit and filth (I i 20); the unmasked Duessa reveals the hideousness of her *nuda veritas* (naked truth) by the scurf, scabs, and dung of her physical corruption (viii 46–8); and the true natures of the seven deadly sins personified in the house of Pride are manifest by their bodies. 'Full of diseases' is the 'carcas blew' of Gluttony, 'And a dry dropsie through his flesh did flow.' Lechery is 'clothed ... full faire' in a green gown 'Which underneath did hide his filthinesse,' and is venereally tormented with 'that fowle evill ... That rots the marrow, and consumes the braine.' Avarice's craving is (punningly) 'A vile disease' and 'in foote and hand / A grievous gout tormented him full sore' (IV 21–9). The Red Cross Knight's sin, which he must expiate in the house of Holiness, is disease, too: 'festring sore ... twixt the marrow and the skin,' so that Repentance must 'embay / His bodie in salt water smarting sore, / The filthy blots of sinne to wash away' (X 25–7).

Chaucer, following such heirs to Cicero's *Rhetorica ad Herennium* as Geoffrey of Vinsauf and John of Garland, commonly characterizes sin as disease: for instance, the Pardoner is a eunuch and the Cook has a mormal. Another medieval example is the well-known description of gluttony in the pageant of the deadly sins in *Piers Plowman* (B-Text, 5.296–362): the foul corrupt body of Gloton becomes the site of a grotesque Black Mass. This use of the human body as a parodic sacrament – an outward sign of inward disgrace – parallels the commonplace treatment of the body as a building. 'The body may be represented as a microcosm, as an island, as a state, as a city, as a castle, or as a house' (Cornelius 1930:14), and also as a garden.

Allusions to the human body as God's temple derive from the Bible. In 2 Corinthians 5.1, the body is 'our earthlie house of this tabernacle'; if destroyed, it will be succeeded by 'a buylding given of God ... eternal in the heavens.' In Wisdom 9.15, it is 'the earthlie mansion' which 'kepeth downe the minde.' Most important are the admonitions in 1 Corinthians 3.16 – 'Knowe ye not that ye are the Temple of God, and that the Spirit of God dwelleth in you?' – and in 1 Corinthians 6.19 – 'Know ye not, that your bodie is the temple of the holie Gost, which is in you, whome ye have of God? and ye are not your owne.' These are conventionally linked to traditional exegesis of Solomon's Temple whose contents and construction, with their attendant symbolism, are described in detail in Exodus 25–31 and 1 Kings 6–8. The Geneva Bible illustrates 1 Kings with woodcuts of the Temple, and the tripartite structure of the actual edifice was interpreted symbolically in four modes, architectural, cosmological, temporal, and corporeal. The ultimate, typologically revivified and fulfilled temple is therefore the individual body of the warfaring and wayfaring Christian, the microcosm of Solomon's Temple, where the *ulam* (vestibule) is the legs, the *hekhal* (holy place) is the thorax and heart, and the *devir* (holy of holies) is the head. Such explication, based on Josephus' *Jewish Antiquities* (5–8) and Philo's *De vita Mosis* (2.15–22), had wide currency through the symbolic interpretations of Puritan and millenarian writers.

A building which conveys the proportions of the individual human body is a constant motif in *The Faerie Queene*. Best known is the house of Alma (II ix), where Guyon tours the body as it should exist in a state of physical, and hence moral health. Its antithesis is the Bower of Bliss (II xii), which shows the corrupted body abandoned to physical pleasure. Here Guyon's tour centers on the pulsations of the nodal fountain (60), from which flows the 'silver flood' percolating through 'every channell' even as the heart controls the tidal ebb and flow of the blood in Galenic physiology (see Brooke 1949).

A less obvious version of the microcosm, compared to the explicit anthropomorphism of the castle of Alma, is the house of Pride in Book I, an episode which strongly recalls 1 Corinthians 6.18 – 'Flee fornication: everie sinne that a man doeth, is without the bodie: but he that committeth fornication, sinneth against his owne bodie.' Entering this edifice, Redcrosse fails to recognize in it the debased person he has become after deserting Una and sinning with Duessa. The clay of the building's fabric is described in the 'squared bricke' of its construction, which, significantly, is mentioned in the fourth stanza of the fourth canto, to signify the four elements and the four seasons which typify the fallen world of corrupt matter. The knight enters the castle of his own corrupt body through the 'gates ... open wide' of its mouth (6), is ingested into its microcosmic postlapsarian Adamic digestive system, and eventually finds his way out through the anus (the 'privie Posterne'), the Esquiline gate of the castle posterior, stumbling through the 'fowle way' of his own sin and the 'donghill of dead carkases' of his own moral death (V 52–3).

The house of the body has a long and complex history which Spenser employs with thoroughness and complexity. A contemporary would have encountered it, at both first and second hand, in Italian architectural theorists like Alberti and their anthropometric interpretations of the classical canons of Vitruvius, where the modulus of the proportions of the human body is an index for the design and construction of the ideal building – a concept surviving in our own century in Le Corbusier's Modulor (see Panofsky 1955:55–107). A *locus classicus* is Augustine's account of Noah's ark in *The City of God* (15.26), where the measurements given by God for its construction (Gen 6.13–18) are construed as the proportions of the ideal human body in its supine position, and hence typologically predictive of the body of the crucified Christ. The ark is therefore a blueprint for a physical as well as a moral architecture; and medieval church architecture, following the rules of Honorius of Autun, plans the ecclesiastical edifice of nave, transept, and chancel as a depiction of the cruciform image of Christ's suffering and human redemption. To enter a church building is to enter a large-scale reproduction of one's idealized self; the door through which one enters, originally in the south aisle before being transferred in later design to the west end, is the image of the wound in Christ's side caused by the spear of Longinus. Metaphorically, the blood and water which gush from this wound are the sacraments through which one enters the church and the life of redemption.

The characters which the errant knights encounter in their quests may be seen as aspects or projections of their own psychic selves (eg, Redcrosse abandons Una and therefore encounters Sansfoy), but they may often be seen too as images of their own bodies as fallen sinners or imperfect moral states, or as images of their own purified bodies as they might become through the intercession of the tortured body of Christ suffering on the Cross, or of his mystical body, which is the communion of all Christians in the church itself. 'It is body allegory that articulates St Paul's teaching on mutual interdependence (1 Cor. 12). A series of vivid metaphors about the feet, ears, eyes, and other "members" of the body supports the Apostle's analogy on the harmonious work of Christ's mystical body, the Church' (Wurtele 1980:63).

In the context of Renaissance educational theory as we encounter it in the courtesy books, Spenser's desire 'to fashion a gentleman or noble person in vertuous and gentle discipline' (Letter to Raleigh) is, in part, the goal of producing a perfected physical body. The 72 cantos of the six completed books may correspond to the 72 years of the completed human life span as given in sixteenth-century manuals such as *The Kalender of Shepherdes* (ed 1892:10). In such a system of calendrical number symbolism, each adventure or quest would take a year to enact via the twelve cantos/months of each book. Hence *The Faerie Queene* may represent a version of the traditional scheme of the ages of man.

The visual landscape which each knight encounters is varied and complex, but at one level, the accomplishment of each quest represents a completed tour of one human body. In Book III, the central episode has a specific locale – the *mons veneris* of the eternal embrace of Venus and Adonis, in stanza 340 of the 679 stanzas in the 1590 edition. In Books I and II, the center is occupied by the parodic *locus amoenus* (or *locus amoris*) of the primal temptations which Redcrosse and Guyon are called upon to resist at I vii 12 and II vii 53–5. That the earth is itself a human body, with its own veins, arteries, and organs, is a belief at least as old as Seneca's *Natural Questions* (3.15.1); and the parallels between the signs of the individual planets and houses of the zodiac and particular parts of the body were established in the earliest Hermetic fragments, and enthusiastically proclaimed by such Renaissance magi as Robert Fludd. When Redcrosse plucks a bough 'out of whose rift there came / Small drops of gory bloud, that trickled downe the same,' and hears the 'piteous yelling voyce' of the wretched Fradubio, he is inhabiting just such an essentially animistic world (I ii 30–1).

If the ultimate human body is the mystical body of Christ, which is synonymous with the unity of Christendom, it is imaged in the New Jerusalem, as found in Revelation and as seen in a vision by Redcrosse after the purgation he has endured in the house of Holiness. The story of *The Faerie Queene* is therefore the story of how an individual may transcend the earthly city, imaged en route in the bodies, gardens, temples, castles, and cities encountered in an anthropomorphic and geomorphic landscape. In their quests through the labyrinths of the fallen world, the knights encounter, and must recognize, all the flawed, debased, proleptic versions of the goal which is their obsessive pursuit, the resurrected body of the heavenly city, 'The new *Hierusalem*, that God has built' (I x 57; cf *City of God* 22).

DAVID ORMEROD

For more background, see Barkan 1975, esp pp 201–76; Baybak, et al 1969; N.S. Brooke 1949 'C.S. Lewis and Spenser: Nature, Art and the Bower of Bliss' *CamJ* 2:420–34; Brooks-Davies 1977:161; Chew 1962; Cornelius 1930; Curtius ed 1953:136–8; Fowler 1964, app 1; John Harvey 1972 *The Mediaeval Architect* (London) pp 225–7; Heninger 1977:145–58; G.L. Hersey 1976 *Pythagorean Palaces* (Ithaca, NY) on numerological and other patterns in Renaissance architecture; *Kalender* ed 1892; Nohrnberg 1976:326–51; Panofsky 1955; Robert van Pelt 1981 'Man and Cosmos in Huygens' Hofwijck' *ArtHist* 4:150–74; Strong 1979 on Renaissance gardens and corporeal form; 'Temple' in *Encyclopaedia Judaica* 15:942–88 (New York 1971); Rudolf Wittkower 1962 *Architectural Principles in the Age of Humanism* 3rd rev ed (London) pp 112–26; Douglas Wurtele 1980 'Spenser's Allegory of the Mind' *HAB* 31:53–66 on the allegory of Alma's castle.

Boethius Anicius Manlius Severinus Boethius (c 480–524) was a late Roman statesman, philosopher, and theologian, who served as consul under the Ostrogothic king Theodoric. His brilliant career as statesman ended with his being accused of treason, a charge he vigorously denied in his most famous work, *De consolatione Philosophiae*. He was exiled by Theodoric and put to death one year later.

Boethius planned to translate and reconcile the works of Plato and Aristotle. Although he did not finish the project, he translated and wrote commentaries on most of Aristotle's logical works, which were all the Middle Ages possessed of Aristotle until the late twelfth century. He also wrote several theological treatises, most notably *De trinitate*.

While in exile, Boethius wrote *The Consolation of Philosophy*, which reflects his interest in philosophy and demonstrates his method of examining seemingly inscrutable matters through deductive reasoning. The work is a prosimetrum (sections of prose alternating with verse passages); its framework is a dream-vision. The narrator, deep in grief and resentment over his unjust imprisonment, is visited by Lady Philosophy who comes to lead him to an understanding of the relationship of fortune and fate to providence, of his own worth as a man, of his free will, and of the ultimate good.

The *Consolation* was popular in the Middle Ages and the Renaissance, as attested by the more than 400 extant manuscripts and by some 30 editions in almost 60 printings published between 1471 and 1500 (Reiss 1982:155). It was a favorite of commentators and translators, the latter including King Alfred, Jean de Meun, Chaucer, and Queen Elizabeth. There were three English translators in the sixteenth century besides Elizabeth: J. Walton (1525), George Colvile (1556), and Thomas Chaloner. Sixteenth-century writers interested in the *Consolation* include More, Lyly, Wyatt, Sidney, and Hooker. Although there is no evidence at all that Spenser was directly influenced by the *Consolation*, it is likely that he read it: printed editions were available, and Pembroke College possessed a manuscript copy when he was there.

The narrator's chief illusion needing to be remedied by Lady Philosophy is the assumption that fortune rules human affairs and is responsible for bad things happening to good people and good things happening to bad people. The themes developed are *ubi sunt*, human vanity, and the vicissitudes of time and fortune. Spenser's *Ruines of Time*, *Daphnaïda*, and *Teares of the Muses* present similar themes. Philosophy demonstrates logically that it is the nature of fortune to be capricious. Boethius' goddess Fortuna became commonplace in the Middle Ages and was a popular subject in Renaissance emblem books. Spenser's Mutabilitie reflects a more complex view of change than does Fortuna. She manifests the effects of original sin and titanic pride and challenges the Boethian notion of providence. In the end, however, she submits to Nature's verdict even as Fortuna accepts her place in the order of things.

Lady Philosophy demonstrates that man errs in valuing worldly gifts bestowed by Fortuna – riches, honor, and fame – instead of valuing his own natural gift of reason, and that he further errs in seeking these false goods as the supreme good. This part of her lesson (Book 2 of the *Consolation*) offers the most striking parallels to Spenser. Philosophy argues that the necessities of life are bestowed by nature and that human beings would be able to live contentedly with these were it not for greed. Her argument is summed up in the image of the Golden Age (2 metrum 5). In his lecture to Mammon, Guyon uses similar arguments (*FQ* II vii 15–17). If there is anything approaching a direct parallel between Boethius and Spenser, it occurs here. Both passages describe men loading themselves down with superfluity, gold being torn from the womb of the earth, and avarice erupting into fire. Both Lady Philosophy and Guyon see nature as a moral guide. Her castigation of man's self-ignorance bears comparison with *Teares*, especially with Urania's complaint and with Melpomene's observation that 'Man without understanding' is a 'Most miserable creature' (127–8). More striking is Philosophy's argument that the difference between man and beast is one of self-knowledge, of knowing oneself to be a rational creature and God to be the supreme good. In this lesson, she links human vices to specific beasts to emphasize her point that the wicked forsake nature and cease to be human even though they retain the shape of human beings (4 prose 3). One may compare Spenser's pageant of the seven deadly sins and the hog Grill who 'hath so soone forgot the excellence / Of his creation' and chooses 'To be a beast, and lacke intelligence' (*FQ* I iv 18–35, II xii 87).

Philosophy's ultimate goal is to teach the narrator that the world is ruled by providence, with fate, nature, and fortune as administrators. Her view of the world is both Platonic and Aristotelian. Employing Neoplatonic imagery and the notion of cosmic love binding the disparate elements, she argues that a beneficent God directs providence. During the Middle Ages, Boethius was a major source of Platonism. Although Spenser had recourse to Plato himself and to the Italian Neoplatonists Ficino and Pico, Boethius' utterances on cosmic love would have interested him, even though there is no evidence of direct influence on the *Fowre Hymnes* or *FQ* IV x 34–5. With the possible exception of Aristotle, no one treats the theme of stability through mutability as thoroughly as Boethius; here a comparison with the *Cantos of Mutabilitie* is rich in parallels and striking in the contrast of attitudes (see esp Spenser ed 1968:38–41). Spenser's narrator in the cantos takes little comfort in Nature's revelation, while Boethius' narrator makes it his consolation.

DEBORAH MACINNES

The standard modern Latin edition is by Ludovicus Bieler *Anicii Manlii Severini Boethii Philosophiae consolatio* Corpus Christianorum series Latina 94 (Turnholt 1957); there are also translations by Richard Green (1962), V.E. Watts (Harmondsworth 1969), and S.J. Tester (Loeb ed 1973). General studies are Margaret Gibson 1981 *Boethius: His Life, Thought and Influence* (Oxford) and Edmund Reiss 1982 *Boethius* (Boston). For a discussion of the influence of the *Consolation*, see Pierre Courcelle 1967 *'La Consolation de Philosophie' dans la tradition littéraire* (Paris) and Howard Patch 1935 *The Tradition of Boethius* (New York). James 1905 identifies the *Consolation* as part of Ms 155, which was owned by Pembroke College when Spenser was a matriculant. Brents Stirling 1933 'The Concluding Stanzas of *Mutabilitie*' *SP* 30:193–204 argues that the outcome of the debate is indebted to Boethius.

Boiardo, Matteo Maria, Count of Scandiano (1441?-94) Boiardo's romantic epic, *Orlando innamorato* (*Roland in Love* 1483, first full edition 1495), is an intermediate source between medieval romances and the sixteenth-century chivalric poems of Ariosto, Tasso, and Spenser. Ariosto's *Orlando furioso* (written, like the *Innamorato*, for the Este family of Ferrara) continues Boiardo's story of Charlemagne's greatest knight, the love-stricken Orlando, and thereby passes on to Spenser the principal elements in the narrative.

Spenser and Boiardo inherit the same romance tradition and often elaborate on it in similar ways. Both poets share a nostalgic but unsentimental sympathy for the customs of chivalry, and they create marvels without mocking them. Both ransack medieval and classical texts, particularly Ovid's *Metamorphoses*. And in weaving separate story lines into an interlaced structure, Boiardo develops a pattern found later in Ariosto and Spenser.

As a chivalric epic, the *Innamorato* combines several traditions that also lie behind *The Faerie Queene*. Boiardo found an epic treatment of courtly love in Boccaccio's *Teseida* (*Book of Theseus*), which had been published in 1475 with the commentary of Pier Andrea dei Bassi; a similar blend of love and war had appeared in such romances as the *Spagna*, the *Rinaldo*, and *Huon of Bordeaux*, where the love stories and marvels of Arthurian legends had infiltrated the military tales of Charlemagne dating from Crusader times. Boiardo makes the merger of Arthurian and Carolingian romances a central theme of the *Innamorato*, but like Spenser, he eliminates most of the Round Table characters. The result in both the *Innamorato* and *The Faerie Queene* is a magical Arthurian landscape occupied by mostly non-Arthurian figures. Boiardo's Fata Morgana (the Italian Morgan le Fay) is as crucial as Spenser's Prince Arthur, and like him appears in the poem relatively infrequently.

Boiardo borrowed his Christian knights from medieval romance sources, to which he added the Saracens: the enchanting Angelica, the Tatar king Agricane, the lovelorn Sacripante, the female warrior Marfisa, and Rodamonte. Virgil's *Aeneid* supplied him with details of characterization (for example, both Agricane and Rodamonte recall Turnus), as well as numerous devices and scenes which heighten the *Innamorato*'s epic quality.

Medieval romances and mythographic encyclopedias showed Boiardo an allegorical mode that prefigured Spenser's own combination of romance themes and epic seriousness. For instance, both poets create an extended allegory of Occasion, whom Guyon and Orlando must seize by the forelock in the traditional manner; and in both cases the heroes are beaten for failing to do so (*FQ* II iv, *OI* 2.8–9). Subsequently, Guyon descends into Mammon's cave, a place like the underworld of Boiardo's Fata Morgana, who is mistress of the world's precious metals; in this respect, Guyon's counterpart in the *Innamorato* is Ranaldo, who participates in an underworld allegory of avarice when a magic wind prevents him from stealing a golden chair.

Although sixteenth-century readers interpreted Boiardo's poem allegorically, probably they did not find much serious religious purpose in it. There is religious conflict in the siege of Paris, and Saracens like Agricane and Brandimarte convert to Christianity; but Boiardo is unlike Spenser in making little use of biblical language or typology.

The question remains whether Spenser knew Boiardo's poem directly, and it is complicated by the fact that several slightly different versions of the *Innamorato* appeared during the sixteenth century. As early as 1506, Niccolò degli Agostini had written and published three additional books continuing Boiardo's story; these were included in a revision of the *Innamorato* by Lodovico Domenichi published in 1545 and often reprinted in the sixteenth century. Sidney's sister Mary, Countess of Pembroke, seems to have owned a copy, and Robert Tofte used Domenichi's text when he translated the first three cantos in 1598. Another altered version of the *Innamorato* appeared in 1541. In this, Francesco Berni turned Boiardo's Emilian grammar into standard Florentine (Ranaldo becomes Rinaldo, for example). He expanded prologues, interspersed new stanzas which he dedicated to his own acquaintances, and eliminated some of Boiardo's vigorous figures of speech. Although Milton cites Berni's version in his *Commonplace Book*, it was not really popular until the eighteenth century and was not reprinted at all between 1545 and 1725.

Evidence of Spenser's knowledge of Boiardo is further complicated by the intervening position of Ariosto, whose *Orlando furioso* expands and continues Boiardo's story in a compatible style and tone, so that it is almost impossible to prove to which poet Spenser may be referring. For example, when Spenser compares Cambina's Nepenthe to 'that same water of Ardenne, / The which *Rinaldo* drunck in happie howre, / Described by that famous Tuscane penne' (*FQ* IV iii 45), we can take the Tuscan pen to refer either to Berni's Tuscanized version of the *Innamorato* or to Ariosto's *Furioso*, whose use of Florentine rather than Emilian dialect was a signal event in the literary world of the Italian Renaissance. The reference may be either to Ranaldo's first drink from the fountain of hatred (*OI* 1.3.35), to his drink from the stream of love (*OI* 2.15.59), or to his final, curative (and therefore perhaps more 'happie') drink at the end of Ariosto's poem (*OF* 42.63). Ariosto recalls the second *Innamorato* incident in his first canto, explicitly in connection with the Forest of Arden (*OF* 1.78). Although Lewis claims that Spenser 'means Boiardo's Rinaldo' in this passage (1966:111), he is making the point that this is not Tasso's Rinaldo; Boiardo's hero is essentially indistinguishable from Ariosto's.

Charles Ross

Blanchard 1925; Matteo Maria Boiardo *Orlando innamorato* ed Aldo Scaglione, 2nd ed, 2 vols (Turin 1963) tr Charles Ross (Berkeley and Los Angeles 1989); Lewis 1936:297–310; Lewis 1966:111–20; Marinelli 1987.

Bonfont, Malfont Spenser's worries over being misinterpreted frame the whole second installment of *The Faerie Queene*. Book IV opens with a complaint that the 'rugged forhead' that wields 'kingdomes causes, and affaires of state' has accused his earlier works of sowing seeds of loose behavior; Book VI concludes pessimistically that a mighty peer will censure this last work as well. And Book V, the most blatant historical allegory of the poem, opens with Spenser asking pardon of Elizabeth for daring to discourse about her 'righteous' judgments. It is not surprising, then, that when he begins his clearest political incident – Elizabeth's dealings with Mary, Queen of Scots, in V ix – he is openly apprehensive.

As Artegall and Guyon enter Mercilla's palace, at the screen of the presence chamber – the place of justice as at *FQ* V x 37 – they pass a poet 'whose tongue was for his trespasse vyle / Nayld to a post, adjudged so by law' (ix 25). The poet's name, Bonfont (well or source of goodness; *Bon Fons* in 1596 *FQ*), has been publicly erased and rewritten as Malfont ('welhed / Of evill words'): 'the substitute name represents the poet's submission to the truth vested in the authoritative figure of the ruler, Mercilla, and it translates a social reality, that the poet's words are at the sovereign's command' (Goldberg 1983:1). This image of the blaspheming 'Poet bad' is a dramatic warning to those who slander or malign the monarch, but it is also a sign of Spenser's own self-consciousness at this moment when he is about to describe Duessa's trial. Malfont may be Spenser's attempt to ensure that he will emerge from the canto as a Bonfont in Elizabeth's eyes and remain like Chaucer a 'well of English undefyled' (IV ii 32), for it is not only Duessa who is on trial in this canto but also the poet himself. He is risking the judgment of James VI of Scotland in portraying Mary, Queen of Scots, as Duessa; and he is risking the judgment of Elizabeth in daring to interpret the highly controversial trial of her queenly rival. Through the figure of the fictional poet, Spenser accedes to sovereign authority and suffers proleptically the retribution authority might exact.

This emblem of the 'Poet bad' thus reveals the caution with which any Renaissance poet turned to contemporary politics: the fear of royal censure, the danger that his text may be misread and misinterpreted as slanderous 'evill words,' and the frequent necessity to protect his own voice by creating surrogate poets in the text itself. Spenser had ample reason to be afraid of political reprisal: James not only took offense at Spenser's depiction of his mother's trial but also demanded that the poet be punished. Spenser, however, has anticipated such reprisal and, through the figure of Bonfont-Malfont, has already placed himself on trial and suffered the punishment James would require. (See also DeNeef 1982, *Sclaunder.)

A. Leigh DeNeef

Book of Common Prayer Spenser's Prayer Book was the Book of Common Prayer of 1559, augmented by the Ordinal (rites for the ordination of bishops, priests, and deacons) of 1559 and the revised Lectionary for Morning and Evening Prayer of 1561, which restored to the English liturgical calendar a number of saints' days omitted in earlier reformed calendars, including St George on 23 April. While at Cambridge, Spenser might also have used the *Liber precum publicarum* of 1560, a Latin translation of portions of the 1559 Book of Common Prayer intended for use in college chapels. This version of the Prayer Book provided Latin translations of the daily offices and Holy

Communion among its contents, but omitted the rites of baptism and marriage, services not often used in college chapels (see *BCP* ed 1976 and Cuming 1982). Also unlike the English Prayer Book, this version explicitly provided for reservation of the consecrated elements for private Communion of the sick and for the celebration of Holy Communion at funerals.

The Elizabethan Prayer Book was a modest revision of the second Prayer Book prepared by Archbishop Thomas Cranmer during the reign of Edward VI (1552). The first English Prayer Book appeared in 1549; the 1552 revision sought to move the Church of England further from a medieval understanding of Christian worship as the activity of the priest and toward Cranmer's understanding of it as the action of all God's people. As part of the Elizabethan Settlement of Religion, the Prayer Book of 1559 reinstituted Cranmer's central aim to consolidate and simplify the many and diverse texts required for the conduct of worship after the medieval manner into a single book in the vernacular which was to be used by clergy and layfolk alike. 'Now from henceforth,' he wrote in the preface to the first Prayer Book in 1549, 'all the whole realm shall have but one use' (*BCP* 1549 preface; rpt *BCP* 1559). In his preface to the Great Bible (1540), Cranmer echoed Erasmus' plea that farmers and weavers as well as the noble and learned might 'learn all things, that they ought to believe, [and] ought to do.' Together with the Great Bible, the Books of Homilies (1547, 1563), translations of Erasmus' *Paraphrases* (1548, 1552), the Primers (1553, 1559), and the Bishops' Bible (1572), the Prayer Book made possible a reformation in Tudor England effected primarily through changing the language of public worship and reading of the Bible (see the essays in Booty, et al 1981). Worship according to the Prayer Book, conducted wholly in English, united clergy and layfolk in a common Christian life and gave the Church of England an identity based not on confessional adherence to authoritative doctrine or on adult experience of election but on daily and weekly participation in its public rites through which the community was built and significant private events such as birth, coming of age, marriage, and death were made part of a sanctified public life.

Cranmer's model was the practice of the patristic church. He retained the biblical sacraments of baptism and Holy Communion. He sought to restore baptism as a public rite done at the main service on Sundays and holy days, and he sought to restore weekly Communions by all people instead of daily Mass said privately by priests. He also retained the medieval rites of ordination, marriage, confirmation, penance (as prayers of confession and absolution within other public rites, with allowance for private confession if desired), and unction (as the services for visitation and Communion of the sick), although he denied them equal status as sacraments. In addition, he devised services for burial and for the thanksgiving of women after childbirth ('purification' or 'churching' of women), and he provided a catechism to instruct children before their confirmation by a bishop. To this collection he also added the previously composed Great Litany (1544) as well as other occasional prayers.

Cranmer's directions make the Prayer Book rites the primary context for public reading of the Bible. He retained the ancient calendar of the church year, beginning in Advent and moving to the season of Trinity by way of Christmas, Epiphany, Lent, and Easter, with its cycle of seasons made visible through changing colors for hangings and vestments. Although Cranmer drastically reduced the number of saints' days and holy days, he retained special observations of days for New Testament saints and other major events in the life of Jesus such as Ash Wednesday, the days of Holy Week, and Ascension. For each of these, as well as for the Sundays of the church year, he provided specific readings from the epistles and gospels to be used at celebrations of Holy Communion. He also conflated the seven 'hours' of the medieval breviary into two daily offices of Morning and Evening Prayer (also called 'Matins' and 'Evensong'). His office lectionary provided for the Psalter to be read once a month, the Old Testament once a year, and the New Testament three times a year at these services. All clergy were required to read the offices daily; parish clergy were required to read them publicly, ringing their church bells so that their parishioners could join them. The Primers adopted the daily offices for individual and family use, making the practice of Christian devotion outside of church an extension of the daily prayer, Bible reading, and praise taking place in the churches.

Elizabethan church leaders were more concerned that all parishes should use the Book of Common Prayer than that all should perform its rites in the same way. Enforcement of ceremonial uniformity was erratic and not consistently applied. Nevertheless, the framers of the Elizabethan Settlement had created a ceremonial standard when they reinstated the 'Ornaments Rubric' of the Edwardian period. According to this rubric, clergy while celebrating Communion were directed to wear eucharistic vestments (alb and chasuble or cope); in leading the offices, they were to wear a surplice. Communion was to be received, kneeling, in both 'kinds' (ie, bread *and* wine). In place of the medieval altar in the 'east' end of the church at which the celebrant stood with his back to the congregation, a table covered with 'a fair white linen cloth' was to be placed in the aisle between the choir stalls so that the priest could assume something more like the ancient basilican posture for celebration as he stood on the 'north' side of the chancel facing his congregation as they assembled in the choir seats on the 'south' side of the chancel. Objecting to the private Masses typical of the medieval church (in which each priest was required to celebrate Mass daily), Cranmer instructed that while the priest should always be ready to celebrate Holy Communion every Sunday and holy day, he should not do so unless 'there be a good number to communicate with the priest, according to his discretion.' His hope to have at least a weekly celebration of Holy Communion in all churches was achieved in the cathedrals, but the old noncommunicating habits of layfolk in the Middle Ages persisted. The Prayer Book of 1559 required all to receive Communion at least three times a year and always at Easter, but among a laity accustomed to the medieval pattern of an annual reception after extensive penitential preparation, this change of habit was hard to achieve.

Morning and Evening Prayer were read daily in all churches; the Great Litany was added to Morning Prayer on Wednesdays, Fridays, and Sundays. On Sundays and holy days, Holy Communion was added to Morning Prayer and the Litany, at least as far as the sermon and the 'general prayer for the whole estate of Christ's Church militant here in earth, and one or mo[re] ... Collects.' Clergy licensed by the church to preach were allowed to deliver their own sermons; those not licensed were to read a sermon from the Books of Homilies. Evening Prayer was also typically an occasion for the preaching of sermons and for instructions in the catechism (see Booty in *BCP* ed 1976:372–82). The musical settings of John Merbecke (1550) and others made possible the singing of the offices, Psalms, and eucharistic texts, a practice which flourished in cathedrals and collegiate chapels (see Beckwith and Gelineau in Jones, et al 1978:263–71, 449). The composition of rich polyphonic settings for Prayer Book texts and for special anthems and motets continued throughout the reign of Elizabeth, making it one of the great ages of English church music.

Debates about the eucharistic theology of the Prayer Book obscure its principal purpose, which was to bring all English folk together to use one rite, to hear the Bible read and sermons preached, to give voice to their concerns in prayer, and to join at one table to receive the consecrated bread and wine, 'that our sinful bodies may be made clean by his body, and our souls washed through his most precious blood, and that we may evermore dwell in him, and he in us.' Cranmer reacted strongly against the medieval theology of transubstantiation (the belief that the substance of the eucharistic bread and wine became Christ's body and blood at the recitation of the 'Words of Institution' by a priest) because he believed that Christ's resurrected body was always 'at the right hand of the Father.' He also objected to the medieval practice of making the Mass a private devotion of the priest in which the people participated only by watching. For Cranmer, Christ is present to the faithful participants in the Communion rite through the action of offering, blessing, and receiving the bread and wine through which they are 'fulfilled with thy grace, and heavenly benediction' and 'obtain remission of our sins, and all other benefits of his passion.' He thus substituted a temporal metaphor (Christ present in the bread and wine during the Communion rite through his actions with them on behalf of the participants) for a spatial or corporeal metaphor (Christ present under the accidents of bread and wine after their consecration apart from their function in the Mass). Cranmer saw the Communion elements as being for human use, not 'to be gazed upon, or to be carried about' (Article 25 of the Thirty-nine Articles) to suggest they have importance outside the eucharistic action. In time, the Church of England characteristically affirmed Christ's 'real presence' in the Holy Communion, but refused to be pinned down to a specific explanation of that presence, preferring instead to affirm the Holy Communion as a locus for asserting the mystery of Christ's ongoing presence to his church. In any case, from Cranmer forward, the Church of England understood the Christian life as created and identified by participation in the sacraments of baptism and Holy Communion and as instructed and directed by the discipline of Bible reading and prayer enabled by the daily offices.

Spenser's treatment of the sacraments in *FQ* I follows in the tradition of Cranmer's interpretation. When Redcrosse is twice overcome by the Dragon, he falls first into the Well of Life and then at the foot of the Tree of Life (xi 29, 46), each of which provides what he needs to restore his ability to fight on and ultimately succeed. Here, in allusions to the Prayer Book sacraments, Spenser makes clear that these features of the fairy landscape are essential to Redcrosse's success; their importance for the poem lies, however, in what they enable him to do, not in and of themselves apart from his actions. The Well and the Tree enter the poem only when they are needed to enable Redcrosse to fight on; although they bring with them traditional associations, they do not have significance in the poem apart from their role in furthering the effectiveness of Redcrosse's efforts in his struggle.

Spenser's poetry is rich in allusion to the language and practice of Prayer Book worship. Redcrosse has the armor of God that gives off 'A litle glooming light' (i 14), a reference to the 'armor of light' which the Collect for the First Sunday of Advent asks that God 'put upon us.' His armor displays 'a bloudie Crosse' (2), the sign of the cross bestowed in baptism (to which the Puritans objected) 'in token that hereafter he shall not be ashamed to confess the faith of Christ crucified, and manfully to fight under his banner against sin, the world, and the devil, and to continue Christ's faithful soldier and servant unto his life's end' (*BCP* ed 1976:275 'Public Baptism'). Sir Guyon's inability to wash the blood from the hands of Ruddymane (*FQ* II ii 3–12) must also be seen in relationship to the water of baptism and its ability to 'wash away ... sin' (*BCP* ed 1976:271). *Hymne of Heavenly Love* echoes the language of the Prayer Book Communion in describing Christ as 'that most blessed bodie': 'the food of life, which now we have, / Even himselfe in his deare sacrament, / To feede our hungry soules' (148, 194–6). In *Amoretti* 22, Spenser refers to Lent as 'This holy season fit to fast and pray.' (W.C. Johnson 1974 identifies extensive allusions to the eucharistic lectionary throughout the *Amoretti*.) In *Epithalamion*, the beloved proceeds 'to th'high altar, that she may / The sacred ceremonies there partake, / The which do endlesse matrimony make,' as 'the holy priest that to her speakes ... blesseth her with his two happy hands' (215–25); there, 'even th'Angels which continually, / About the sacred Altare doe remaine, / Forget their service and about her fly' (229–31; cf the Te Deum from Morning Prayer: 'To thee all angels cry aloud ... To thee Cherubin and Seraphin, continually do cry'). In *The Shepheardes Calender*, Spenser reflects the attitude toward the saints embodied in the Collect for All Saints' Day ('grant us grace so to follow thy holy saints in all virtues and godly living') when he has Thomalin say, 'The hylls, where dwelled holy saints, / I reverence and adore: / Not for themselfe, but for the sayncts [who] bene to heaven forwent, / theyr good is with them goe: / Theyr sample onely to us lent, / that als we mought doe soe' (*Julye* 113–20).

Spenser's poetry is thus constantly informed by the complex of Christian language he experienced through daily involvement in worship created and enabled through use of the Book of Common Prayer. Echoes of its texts and allusions to its rites are found throughout his works. He wrote public poetry, and the interpretation of Christianity reflected and promoted in his work is neither the private devotional religion of medieval layfolk observing the Mass nor Tudor Puritans' equally private vision of a Christianity not yet realized, but rather the public Christianity achieved through the Prayer Book's emphasis on corporate participation in public worship.

JOHN N. WALL

On the Prayer Book, see *BCP* ed 1976; Booty, et al 1981; W.K. Lowther Clarke and Charles Harris, eds 1932 *Liturgy and Worship: A Companion to the Prayer Books of the Anglican Communion* (London); G.J. Cuming 1982 *A History of Anglican Liturgy* rev ed (London); H. Davies 1961–70; Jones, et al 1978; and Francis Procter and Walter Howard Frere 1901 *A New History of 'The Book of Common Prayer'* (London). On Spenser and the Prayer Book, see W.C. Johnson 1974; Wall 1983; Wall 1988; Whitaker 1950.

books in *The Faerie Queene* Among the vast assortment of mythic forms and emblematic creatures in *The Faerie Queene*, Spenser describes a number of books. If not exactly characters or independent agents, these may yet possess a more-than-natural power, and often can help focus our sense of what is at stake in the careers of other figures. The quester may at times become a reader of books as well as a warrior or lover, while the writer of books may come to seem as dangerous an enemy or blocking agent as any more fantastic monster. The depiction of a book sometimes occasions Spenser's reflections on his own literary project; and yet his books also sometimes lose some of their discrete, familiar qualities as verbal artifacts, becoming slightly uncanny entities embedded in a larger texture of images. Thus defamiliarized, such books may make us somewhat less certain of what our own relation to the read or written word may be, what strange things a book can or cannot do, where it serves or fails as an adequate metaphor.

Three categories of books are represented within the poem: sacred, magical, and historical. The first group includes Redcrosse's 'Saveours testament ... writ with golden letters ... A worke of wondrous grace, and able soules to save,' which he presents to Arthur (I ix 19); and Fidelia's book, 'both signd and seald with blood, / Wherein darke things were writ, hard to be understood,' which instructs Redcrosse himself (I x 13). The chief magical books are Archimago's (I i 36) and Busirane's (III xii 31–2), both of which conjure demonic spirits or phantasms for the sake of deception, mastery, and torture: the one misguides Redcrosse with dreams of his own lust and false evidence of Una's infidelity; the other wounds the faithful Amoret with the literalized conceits of courtly love. The twinned accounts of Britain and Fairyland read by Arthur and Guyon in the chamber of Eumnestes (II x) represent the major examples of history or chronicle in the fiction of *The Faerie Queene*, though we should also add those 'antique rolles' and 'bookes' to whose ghostly and more or less secular authority Spenser appeals throughout his romance. The books described 'literally' in the poem seem often to be codices rather than scrolls; whether they are manuscripts or printed copies is not clear, but they do all seem singular and precious.

This taxonomy is not exhaustive; the three types can overlap, or else one can become a metaphor for another. Thus, for example, the historical books read in Alma's house, one based on actual British chronicle and the other a fantastic embroidery of the Tudor line, also compose for Spenser a nearly sacred scripture, since both shape history according to the lineaments of Spenser's imperial typology. They are history, but prophetic history. Likewise, Busirane's magic books are plainly literary as well, since they stand at one level for the secular poetic tradition of Petrarchism (being, in a sense, versions of the 'book of love' alluded to in *Amoretti* I, 10, and 21). But their enchanting power may represent the poet's sense of how Petrarchan tradition has become inscribed on his culture's erotic consciousness; that the books are merely human creations which have become perversely sacred may explain why the 'living bloud' in which they are written recalls both the holy book of Fidelia and the 'bloudy letters' which Spenser says are inscribed on the Mosaic tablets of the law (I x 53). Another example of how fluid the categories of books are is found in the 'bookes and artes' of the 'Hermite' Archimago (i 36). These recall at first the more purely 'marvelous' props of Ariosto's enchanters; and yet, within the Protestant allegory of Book I, they must be interpreted as figures for the falsely sacralized books, authorities, or 'revelations' of the Roman church which serve to mislead or enchant Redcrosse in his guise as a type of primitive Christianity. Such books could thus represent those works of the medieval exegetical tradition which, while pretending to draw their doctrinal authority or power from Scripture, functioned mainly to shroud that text with seductive and duplicitous mystery, even (as some reformers thought) supplanting its true histories entirely by means of superadded allegorical fictions which the church itself claimed as truth. Archimago's books, or the falsely divine revelations they represent, would presumably be opposed by the true book which is the Bible. Spenser's representation of this latter, however, is often in itself ambiguous, in part because of the way the poet may relate it to other magical emblems in his fiction. We may not be sure, that is to say, what the power or scope of any image of the Bible is supposed to be. What we make of Redcrosse's 'Saveours testament,' for example, may change greatly depending on what meaning we give to the diamond box of ointment which he receives from Arthur in return. And although the fact that Fidelia carries both a book and a chalice suggests some attempt to discriminate images of the textual and ceremonial aspects of faith, we may wonder whether the meaning of those images overlap, or else whether the book itself, though obviously a Bible in some sense, may not also represent some further vehicle of instruction or revelation for which the book serves as a potent metaphor.

By rendering the narrative function of the book so uncertain, and by linking it to allegorical objects drawn from other symbolic realms, Spenser manages radically to expand the conceptual and imaginative meanings of the book image. Even if it seems to be a Bible, a book is no one thing in *The Faerie Queene*, either historically or metaphorically. Indeed, even the different 'books' which compose the major units of the poem are both singular, autonomous quest-legends – whose 'cantos,' named on the model of Dante and Ariosto, stand in lieu of the episodic 'books' of classical epic – and allegorical fractions of that larger, unfinished 'book' which is *The Faerie Queene*.

Strict questions of taxonomy are probably less crucial than the book's function within the mythic narrative itself. What Spenser avoids here is as significant as what he accomplishes. For instance, no figure in *The Faerie Queene* is like the protagonist of the typical Chaucerian dream poem, who falls asleep over a volume of fables or visions which provide the substance, model, or solution to his fantasy, or who encounters in his dream the author he has been reading. Spenser's apocalyptic romance does not employ the image of a divine book or scroll unfolded in the heavens, as in Revelation. Even Mutabilitie's eschatological history is discovered much like any other chronicle among the archives of Fairyland, laid up 'mongst records permanent' (VII vi 2). Spenser was apparently unattracted by Alanus de Insulis' grand figure of Creation as the act of a god inscribing divine shapes onto the parchment of Nature's material book. Neither do we find anything like the Bible's most radical trope of reception, that of the visionary's eating a sacred scroll that is sweet in the mouth but bitter in the stomach, as in Ezekiel 3 or Revelation 10; there is only the demonic parody of this image in the monster Error's vomiting *out* the poisonous 'bookes and papers' of sectarian religious controversy (I i 20), the writings of apocalyptic enthusiasts and *false* prophets. As a counter to this grotesque, demonic image are books which are more clearly ponderable, human things. Despite a few broad references to the 'immortal booke of fame,' Spenser tends to eschew the kind of grandly metaphysical or supernatural images of the book found in biblical and medieval writing. Post-Reformation thinker that he is, Spenser usually conveys a clearer sense of the book as a vessel of individual or collective memory, a vehicle of Grace perhaps but one whose magic is more plainly a magic of the inward mind or cultural tradition, though often a text which requires a learned interpreter.

Spenser's complex treatment of the book becomes clearer in two crucial scenes of broken or interrupted reading of books. The first of these comes in *FQ* II x, when Arthur reads the history of Britain through to the account of his own father Uther, only to find that the text ends abruptly, 'Without full point, or other Cesure right' (68), just before it would have described the life of the hero who is himself reading it. As both legendary king and Spenserian character, Arthur thus occupies a curious gap in that history. And though he takes a 'secret pleasure' in the story he reads, and indeed reflects much of its glory, his absence from the history suggests that Spenser would wish to free *his* Prince Arthur from the constraints of both imperial genealogy and national history. Here it may seem as if the breaking off of the legendary history, and Arthur's breaking off of his reading, allow the author to explore the identity and power of Arthur within the more liberated, ahistorical wanderings of romance. The book of history, this episode seems to assert, cannot quite contain the book which is *The Faerie Queene*, nor can it limit the visionary career of its central hero.

The idea that there may be some danger in reading a book, or in being absorbed by or identified with the story it tells, comes through even more clearly at the end of Book III. In the inner chamber of Busirane's house, Britomart discovers Amoret chained to a pillar, while the enchanter sits before her with his books, 'Figuring straunge characters of his art, / With living bloud he those characters wrate, / Dreadfully dropping from her dying hart' (xii 31). Here Amoret is both controlled by and violated by the book. She is in a sense both its reader and its subject, just as Busirane seems to be both reading and writing (ie, 'figuring') in his book a spell composed of her own blood, love, and fear. At Britomart's entrance, Busirane immediately throws down his books, moving from slow magical murder in order to attack Amoret directly with a knife. Britomart disarms him, but that does not free his victim. The spell woven around her from the book seems to involve her mind and fate so much that simply throwing it away will not disenchant her (unlike Prospero, whose burying of his book and wand is the occasion of his renouncing magic). Hence Britomart, at Amoret's insistence, must force the magician to take up his book again, reversing the spell through a further act of reading, as if only through the book could the book's magic be dissolved.

A great distance separates the cruel and domestic scene of reading in Busirane's house from the more redemptive mode of instruction from a sacred book in the house of Holiness. The Busirane episode is indeed a kind of dark, limiting case of Spenser's use of the book image. If we take it as the effective end (if not as the ultimate *telos* or triumph) of the book's magical, communicative function in the first three books of the poem, we may sense why Spenser dropped the explicit figure of the book in Books IV-VII. The intimate relation of reader to book may, of course, have seemed an inadequate form of trial for the more public virtues treated in the second half of *The Faerie Queene*. Still, no visible book mediates the visions in Isis Church or on Mount Acidale, perhaps because too much ambivalence hedges the depiction of the book after the lessons of Busirane's house. For the time being, one may at least note the loss of the figure of the book in *FQ* IV-VII as a relatively empirical fact about the poem, and leave it as an open problem for later interpreters.

KENNETH GROSS

No special study of the iconography of books in literary romance exists, but see the discussion in Curtius ed 1953:302–47, which deals with the book as discursive metaphor in theological and philosophical writing, as well as the loosely phenomenological account of medieval and Renaissance attitudes toward the book in Donald R. Howard 1976 *The Idea of the Canterbury Tales* (Berkeley and Los Angeles) pp 56–67. See also Jesse M. Gellrich 1985 *The Idea of the Book in the Middle Ages: Language Theory, Mythology, and Fiction* (Ithaca, NY).

Bower of Bliss The domain of the enchantress Acrasia, the arch-foe of temperance in *FQ* II. There are vivid anticipatory accounts of it at the beginning of Book II (i 51) when Guyon undertakes his mission, and in the middle (v 27–34, the extraordinary representation of Cymochles' erotic self-indulgence); it becomes the main scene of action in canto xii when Guyon penetrates to its heart, destroys it, and thus enacts what is clearly intended to be the definitive victory of the virtue he represents. Guyon and the Palmer do not arrive at Acrasia's realm until the middle of the canto, but critics often refer to the whole of *FQ* II xii as 'The Bower of Bliss.' There is a certain appropriateness to this broader use. The whole canto is conceived as a set piece; some of the temptations met in the Bower are anticipated outside it; the purposeful traveling that brings Guyon and the Palmer to the Bower continues once they are in it; and, finally, the whole canto involves the experience of anticipation, which is sustained – even after Guyon reaches the place 'Whereas the Bowre of *Blisse* was situate' (42) – by a continual uncertainty about when one has actually arrived at the Bower itself.

'The Bower of Bliss' is much the longest canto in *The Faerie Queene* (87 stanzas; cf 77 and 68 stanzas in the next longest, II x and I x), and it has always been felt to have an importance commensurate with its length. Some of this prominence is due to its place in Book II, and one could explain the length of the canto simply by pointing out that other concluding episodes, as in Books I and III, occupy two cantos. But the Bower of Bliss has been felt to have a significance beyond that of other climactic episodes and 'allegorical cores.' At least from the time of the great Romantic critics, the episode has been seen as peculiarly representative of Spenser's poetry. The interpretive problems with which an account of the episode must begin lead one to fundamental questions of Spenserian poetics.

The Bower of Bliss in the strict sense – that is, the place itself – is an earthly paradise, one of many poetic representations of an idyllic locale where an ideal life is led. For Christian writers, the loss of the true earthly paradise, Eden, compromised all subsequent imaginings of it. Everything about the Bower of Bliss – the stasis, the fragility, the erotic self-dissipation – shows that it is a false paradise, the very appeal of which reveals that we are creatures who no longer dwell in innocence. Yet the fact that this appeal is not merely sinful but compelling and deeply problematic is suggested by the way Spenser uses the phrase 'bower of bliss' elsewhere. It is one of several laudatory epithets of his beloved's 'Fayre bosome' in *Amoretti* 76; and he puts it in the mouth of the wounded Timias, who imagines that Belphoebe, the maiden who rescues him, is an angel sent 'from her bowre of blis' (*FQ* III v 35). These uses of the phrase in honorable erotic contexts suggest some of what is at stake in Acrasia's 'paradice of pleasure' (another of the epithets in *Am* 76).

In both its action and its main allegory, the Bower of Bliss canto is a virtual *summa* of heroic poetry, as Spenser understood it. The action is based on two august models. The *Odyssey* (books 10 and 12) supplies models for the enchantress who turns men into beasts (see *Circe), for the voyage through perils with which the canto begins, and for some of the perils themselves – Scylla and Charybdis, which Spenser moralizes into the Gulf of Greediness and the Rock of Reproach (xii 3–9), the Wandering Rocks, which Spenser turns into more alluring Wandering Islands (11–14), and the Sirens (30–3). The second half of the canto is based on Tasso's *Gerusalemme liberata* (14–16), in which two knights voyage to the pleasure-island of the pagan princess Armida in order to rescue her lover, the Christian knight Rinaldo; Spenser closely imitates some of the enticements Tasso's knights encounter, notably the rose song (*GL* 16.14–15, *FQ* II xii 74–5) and the fountain with its two women bathing (*GL* 15.56–62, *FQ* II xii 60–8). The journey to Acrasia, both on sea and on land, consists of repeated confrontations with such moral perils and enticements. In allegorizing a heroic voyage, the canto answers to Renaissance views of Odysseus' travels as the moral testing of human virtue, and it emulates similar episodes in Spenser's Italian predecessors. The conflict between reason and the senses is at the heart of Tasso's episode, which itself imitates Ariosto's allegory of the enchantress Alcina and her realm (*Orlando furioso* 6–7) – an episode upon which Spenser drew at several points in *The Faerie Queene*. The moral point and coloring of Spenser's episode would thus not have seemed strange to his contemporaries, and we may take as our initial guide to its meaning Milton's praise in *Areopagitica*:

> That virtue therefore which is but a youngling in the contemplation of evil, and knows not the utmost that vice promises to her followers, and rejects it, is but a blank virtue, not a pure; her whiteness is but an excremental [ie, external] whiteness; which was the reason why our sage and serious poet Spenser, whom I dare be known to think a better teacher than Scotus or Aquinas, describing true temperance under the person of Guyon, brings him in with his palmer through the cave of Mammon and the bower of earthly bliss, that he might see and know, and yet abstain.

Milton speaks to the first difficulty the modern reader is likely to have with the Bower of Bliss – the fact that most of the enticements held out to Guyon, the attractions that are intended to divert him from his mission, are more alluring than they should appear to the knight of Temperance. The terms in which Milton praises the episode suggest, on the contrary, that felt attraction is unavoidable, since we are human, and that overcoming such attractions is of the essence of what is a human virtue and not, say, an angelic endowment. Hence Spenser characteristically gives a full representation of the pleasures and (less frequently) the terrors which test Guyon's resolution. Even when the temptation is anticipated and known in advance (one of the Palmer's functions), Guyon and the reader are made to experience it fully. This poetic tactic can claim to have not only the moral validity of which Milton speaks, but also the aesthetic validity attributed to heroic poetry in Sidney's *Defence of Poetry*. Sidney attributes the didactic efficacy of poetry to the fact that it embodies moral instruction in moving images and actions, and he prefers it to the bare precepts of philosophy precisely because it engages the reader's feelings.

Yet all the authority of Spenser's predecessors and contemporaries will not silence the voice that says of Acrasia's rose song, 'it is not only Guyon but the reader whose moral alertness is lulled by stanzas such as these, and their tone is that which predominates in one's memory of *The Faerie Queene*.' The words are H.J.C. Grierson's (1929:54), but he is expressing the dominant nineteenth-century view of the poem. Hazlitt said that the long passage that includes the rose song 'has all that voluptuous pathos, and languid brilliancy of fancy, in which this writer excelled.' Almost a century later Yeats said, 'He is a poet of the delighted senses, and his song becomes most beautiful when he writes of those islands of Phaedria and Acrasia, which gave to Keats his *Belle Dame sans merci* and his "perilous seas in faery lands forlorn."' Even Edward Dowden, the Victorian critic who wrote of Spenser as 'poet and teacher,' said, 'The enchantress Acrasia in her rosy bower is so bewitchingly fair and soft that it goes hard with us to see her garden defaced and herself rudely taken captive.' The heart of all these remarks is a felt disparity or conflict between moral purpose in *The Faerie Queene* and whatever most fills and pleases the imagination – between, as Grierson put it, the Puritan and the Poet in Spenser. The readiness of nineteenth-century writers to detach Spenser's visions and representations from the moral realm, where they are problematically erotic, to the imaginative, where they fulfill special sensual and visionary needs, shows that we are dealing with a profound difference between Renaissance and Romantic poetics.

It would be easy enough to say, then, that we must correct our impulses as modern readers by our historical awareness of Spenser's intentions (not to mention a more adequate understanding of Puritanism and Renaissance ideas of poetic didacticism). Indeed it has often been argued, in effect, that if the reader is a vulnerable Guyon, he should take Milton as the Palmer who will steer him past the hazardous stanzas of the Bower of Bliss. But the 'pure' sensory and imaginative delights of the Bower are not a Romantic invention. Early imitations and citations show that for Spenser's contemporaries, too, details of the Bower could provide aesthetic pleasure unqualified by moral reservation. Furthermore, it is by no means unusual for a great poem to contain more than its writer consciously knew and to release new meanings and arouse new interests in writers and readers of later epochs. Even confining ourselves to poetic intentions, it seems clear that Spenser meant the Bower to be more attractive and problematic, for both hero and reader, the further one penetrates it. The hero, who at first disdainfully rejects the bowl and cup of wine offered by Genius and Excess (49, 57), halts at the sight of the bathing maidens, for 'His stubborne brest gan secret pleasaunce to embrace' (65). Similarly, the clear pattern earlier in the canto of anticipating and then experiencing a trial is blurred and complicated as the Palmer and Guyon approach Acrasia herself: the music of the Bower and the seductive enchantress herself are presented not once but twice (music in 70–1, 74–5; Acrasia in 72–3, 76–9), in a passage that is at once the longest, richest, most pleasurable, and most diffuse of the episode. One should therefore beware of too readily denying – whether in the name of historical or moral awareness – the pleasures of the Bower and the moral and aesthetic problems they present. To do so is to deny our own prerogatives as readers – we might recall that Milton's tribute to this canto occurs in his tract against prior restraint on publication – and to give over any possibility of thinking of Spenser as a living poet, one who matters for us, as he most assuredly mattered for those Romantics who are sometimes the whipping boys of modern Spenserians.

The essay that reawoke modern interest in Spenser, the final chapter of C.S. Lewis' *Allegory of Love* (1936), owes its power to the fact that it treats Spenser as a living poet, and it is no mistake that the center of Lewis' argument is a revised account of the Bower of Bliss. Resisting the Romantic view of the Bower as a privileged locale of poetry and the imagination, Lewis argued that it is an erotic realm as dangerous as the poet claims, for 'it is a picture, one of the most powerful ever painted, of the whole sexual nature in disease.' Lewis drew particular attention to the voyeurism of the Bower: he showed that erotic gratification is displaced onto visual experience and argued that there is no normal sexual pleasure or fulfillment in the Bower, as there is in Spenser's good earthly paradise, the Gardens of Adonis (III vi). He made his case by appealing to specific lines and stanzas, one of which (61) will show the strengths and limitations of his account:

And over all, of purest gold was spred,
A trayle of yvie in his native hew:
For the rich mettall was so coloured,
That wight, who did not well avis'd it vew,
Would surely deeme it to be yvie trew:
Low his lascivious armes adown did creepe,
That themselves dipping in the silver dew,
Their fleecy flowres they tenderly did steepe,
Which drops of Christall seemd for wantones to weepe.

In this stanza describing the fountain in which the naked damsels bathe and display themselves, the final lines show that Lewis was right to oppose a merely aesthetic account of what Hazlitt called Spenser's 'voluptuous pathos'; they bear out what Lewis said of another stanza: 'Any moralist may disapprove luxury and artifice; but Spenser alone can turn the platitude into imagery of such sinister suggestion.' Lewis taught us that words like *lascivious* and *wantones* are not mere moral labels but reveal the dangers of self-indulgence and self-dissipation by being embedded in verse of deep sensuous appeal. (Note, for example, the way *lascivious* is given sensory presence by the alliteration with *low*, and the way the very length of the word is made sinister by *adown did creepe*.) Yet Lewis did not fully reveal the poetry he knew was there, because his interests were those of a moralist (which is one thing) and a proselytizer (which is another). He therefore tended to treat morally revealing words as what he called 'danger signals,' and he was all too ready to impose moral labels of his own on the temptations of the Bower of Bliss. One of his main hostile labels was 'artificial.' In the case of the stanza just quoted, he omitted the powerful closing lines and simply dismissed the first five by professing not to know, 'whether those who think that Spenser is secretly on Acrasia's side, themselves approve of metal vegetation as a garden ornament, or whether they regard this passage as a proof of Spenser's abominable bad taste.'

Lewis thus left a mixed heritage to Spenser criticism. Despite all he revealed about the vision and the verse of *The Faerie Queene*, he put readers and critics in the position of having to choose moral sides in rather too simple a way. In the case of the Bower, he perhaps encouraged too easy a profession of immunity from its appeal, and he turned an important topos, the relation between art and nature, into a critical red herring. His argument that in *The Faerie Queene* art is unequivocally bad and nature is good threw down a critical gauntlet which later critics felt obliged to pick up again and again, and it also revealed what is most limiting in his account of the Bower of Bliss. Persuaded as he was of 'the exquisite health' of Spenser's imagination, he was unable to inquire into the disturbing fascination of the Bower of Bliss or into the nature of the problems it engages.

In particular, Lewis completely ignored the one passage that has persistently bothered readers and critics – Guyon's destruction of the Bower (83):

But all those pleasant bowres and Pallace brave,
Guyon broke downe, with rigour pittilesse;
Ne ought their goodly workmanship might save
Them from the tempest of his wrathfulnesse,
But that their blisse he turn'd to balefulnesse:
Their groves he feld, their gardins did deface,
Their arbers spoyle, their Cabinets suppresse,
Their banket houses burne, their buildings race,
And of the fairest late, now made the fowlest place.

Where Tasso's Armida dissolves her palace by her own magic after her lover rejects her, Acrasia's realm is eradicated by the hero in an act of moral vengeance. No reader can ignore the vehemence with which Spenser represents Guyon's action; the question is how we interpret it. Among Spenserians, there has been a strong tendency to view it as morally, psychologically, or spiritually justified. It is argued that the action answers to the radical evil in Acrasia's bower, or that Guyon (as *microchristus*) is harrowing hell, or that he becomes an elemental, cleansing force of Nature, or that his action bears witness to the recovery of the will or the restoring of the senses to their proper place. Against such views, other critics argue that the knight of Temperance's act here is notably intemperate, and students and the common reader continue to find the stanza disturbing.

There is good reason to feel uneasy with this stanza. There is a relentlessness in the syntax and rhetorical schemes and a vehemence of diction that make it impossible to read and pass by as we do with the sights and temptations encountered on the way to Acrasia. After the climactic sight – Acrasia displayed on a bed of roses (77–8, two stanzas of entrancing but self-dissipating sensuousness), followed by the poet's contemplation of her lover's poignant youthfulness and loss of manhood (79–80) – the pattern of seeing and knowing ends, and the canto concludes with represented actions. The last of these actions, we should note, is not Guyon's destruction of the Bower but the restoration of Acrasia's beasts to their human form and the resentment of one of those beasts, the hog Grill, at this retransformation. Grill has his own history in post-Homeric commentary and mythology, and Spenser's use of him has prompted a good deal of commentary – as if the wry finality of the Palmer's parting words, 'Let *Grill* be *Grill*, and have his hoggish mind,' does not contain, even if it acknowledges, the tensions underlying the heroic choices here. But for all Grill's prominence – it is as if Sancho Panza got his chance to speak up in *The Faerie Queene* – it is Guyon's destruction of the Bower that presents the fullest and most significant interpretive challenge.

Just as the Bower of Bliss, with its exquisite artifice, expresses and tests human aesthetic powers, so critics' accounts of the Bower's destruction express and test their views of Spenser's poetry and of poetry itself. Grierson says, 'There is no virtue in the mere destruction of the beautiful. The moralist must convince us that the sacrifice is required in the interest of what is a higher and more enduring good, that the sensuous yields place to the spiritual. It is this Spenser fails to do imaginatively, whatever doctrine one may extract intellectually from the allegory.' Words like these seem quite unspecialized, the voice of the common reader. But Grierson's objection clearly derives from a specific poetic which takes spiritual and sensual as equally fundamental, and which (as in Coleridge's preferring symbolism to allegory) distrusts what appears to be their separation. For such a poetic, 'imaginative failure' is a fundamental flaw, but this is not the only way to express what is problematic about the destruction of the Bower. When a more recent critic, Stephen Greenblatt (1980), refers to Guyon's 'supreme act of destructive excess,' he too seems to be speaking in no unusual way. But when he expands this phrase to say, in part, that 'the violence directed against Acrasia's sensual paradise is in itself an equivalent of erotic desire,' it is clear that he views the relation between the moral and the sensual differently from Grierson, or from Yeats, who regarded the destruction of the Bower as the imposition of an official morality in which the poet had no imaginative investment.

The Bower of Bliss is a touchstone for its interpreters' poetics, because pleasure, fantasy, artifice, and the relation of art and nature are central matters in the canto. Spenser imitates Tasso in some of the verses about art and nature, but one revision of his sources shows that he meant to emphasize the problem of poetry and its powers. Unlike Ariosto and Tasso, he does not attribute his false paradise to the magic of its reigning sorceress. When he calls Acrasia's realm 'the most daintie Paradise on ground' and says, 'And that, which all faire workes doth most aggrace, / The art, which all that wrought, appeared in no place' (58), he directly invokes a topos of aesthetic praise; nor can he evade his own complicity in this paradise since 'the art which all that wrought' is in some sense his own. In opening his representation of the Bower to such questions, Spenser engages important problems of Elizabethan poetics. The poet, Sidney says, 'doth not only show the way [to virtue], but giveth so sweet a prospect into the way, as will entice any man to enter into it. Nay, he doth, as if your journey should lie through a fair vineyard, at the first give you a cluster of grapes, that full of that taste, you may long to pass further' (ed 1973b:92). If the reader accepts this invitation to the Bower of Bliss, he will not only find Sidney's metaphors made literal – pleasing prospects, a journey through a vineyard, an enticing bunch of grapes at the entrance – but will find them represented in a way that brings out both their pleasures and their dangers. These very metaphors often appear in Elizabethan writings as ways of representing the allurements and treacheries of the senses, of love, and of poetry.

The destruction of the Bower is a touchstone for larger issues of poetics, because a serious account of it should derive from a view of the preceding moral and psychological encounters. When MacCaffrey says, 'the violence of the hero's destructiveness ... is the rage of the artist who sees his gift of imagination abused' (1976:251-2), she is drawing on her analysis of the Bower's false appeal to an innocence we have lost: 'abuse of edenic blessings,' in her view, necessarily produces 'defacement of Eden.' Similarly for Greenblatt, the violence of Guyon's self-assertion reveals the threat of dissolution in Acrasia's pleasures, just as the historical situations he invokes to explain the tensions of the episode – service to the Queen and colonial domination – are homologous to its chief danger (submission to a female) and its main exemplary action (invading and subduing an exotic realm). So far as underlying poetics goes, perhaps the most important point at issue is the coherence of the poet's sensibility. Nineteenth-century accounts of the Bower of Bliss viewed Spenser as at war with himself because it was assumed that the components of the canto, morality and imagination, were inherently opposed. Lewis' argument that Spenser knew the Bower for what it was drew these two elements together and defended the integrity of both the canto and its author. Subsequent interpretations, particularly those which appeal to Spenser's culture and take its claims at face value, have viewed the poet, like the hero he represents, as in command of himself and his materials. MacCaffrey, for example, rewords her observation that 'Guyon's act is partly a self-protective gesture by the poet,' so as to make the gesture conscious and intentional: 'a self-critical corrosiveness must be an element in valid human art.' In general, Spenserians have been uneasy about separating the imaginative power of the Bower of Bliss from the poet's and reader's conscious awareness. But there is surely nothing – except perhaps this very notion of absolute moral integrity – to make us deny literary power and value to works which are immersed in deep psychological, social, and cultural tensions. The extraordinary 'after-life' of the Bower of Bliss, its fascination for poets and readers over the centuries, may be due not to Spenser's having solved all the problems he raised, but to his dwelling so fully within them.

PAUL ALPERS

Durling 1954; Greenblatt 1980; H.J.C. Grierson 1929 *Cross Currents in English Literature of the Seventeenth Century* (London); Lewis 1936; I.G. MacCaffrey 1976; Nellist 1963.

---

bowers For Spenser, a bower is primarily a bedroom or other private chamber (hence the opposition to public rooms, as in 'Astrophel' 28: 'bowre and hall'); it may also be a cottage, a rural or sylvan retreat, a haunt for hermits and other recluses. In either case, it is a place of intimate habitation.

Gardens, covert dales, shady and often murmurous glens are also seen as 'bowers' in a related sense when the natural world, rightly or wrongly, is perceived as a safe dwelling place. The sense of being at home in the world is implicit in the different sources on which Spenser draws in imagining his natural bowers: myths of paradise or the Golden Age (see Giamatti 1966), images of pastoral ease, rhetorical traditions like those of the *locus amoenus* (the 'lovely place' or pleasance that is a setting for love; see Curtius ed 1953:183–202) or of Venus' elaborate garden precincts (developed from late classical epithalamia, philosophized by 'Dan Geffrey' and 'Alane' [*FQ* VII vii 9] as the pristine realm of Nature, and transmitted – with a renewal of their fairy glamour – by Italian romance). Yet the notion of bowering in the landscape, or of being embowered by it, is particularly Spenserian. Thus what are simply *dulcis requies* (sweet repose) and *pura voluptas* (pure or simple pleasure) in the pseudo-Virgilian *Culex* (89) become in Spenser's rendering a location where 'Sweete quiet harbours in his harmeles head, / And perfect pleasure buildes her joyous bowre' (*Gnat* 134–5; cf *SC, March* 17): Spenser takes the classical image and expands it into a place that surrounds and holds. Likewise, the 'litle nest' in the midst of Phaedria's Idle Lake offers the weary traveler a flowery bedchamber barely hinted at in the garden of Armida that Spenser found in Tasso's *Gerusalemme liberata* (*FQ* II vi 12, 16; cf *GL* 15–16).

As these examples suggest, the invitation to make oneself at home in a fallen world must always be problematic; every dimension of the bower's enticement demands continuous scrutiny from Spenser's characters and from his readers. The enclosure the bower offers may nurture true worth, as in the heavenly 'bowre' or 'noursery' of virtue (*FQ* VI proem 3–4) or in the well-girt Garden of Adonis, the bower of Spenser's version of Venus Genetrix (III vi 31; Nohrnberg 1976:519–20 cites a relevant classical precedent from Columella's *De re rustica* 10.192–214). The landscapes where Una and Pastorella are 'environ'd' by awestruck satyrs or respectful shepherds (I vi 9–14, VI ix 8) may suggest the possibility of a similar benevolence in more ordinary worldly circumstances. The concentric harmonies of these scenes, however base the participants may appear, prefigure the 'girlond' of Graces Calidore observes on Mount Acidale (VI x 12). But Serena's encounter with the cannibals, and Hellenore's with a more libertine band of satyrs, offer disturbing parodies of such earthy environings (VI viii 39, III x 44). Too often the world's 'clasping armes' (II xii 53) are more ambush than embrace, and bowers become prisons where worth is entombed. Victims of Acrasia's stifling charms soon find themselves in 'darksom dens' (II v 27), and Pastorella's triumphs give way to a pirate cave where she wakes up under a heap of corpses (VI xi 20–1).

The bower's shade and the drowsiness it inspires are equally ambiguous. Sometimes an angelic light shines in a 'shadie delve' like the one outside Mammon's dwelling where Guyon is watched over, or in the woods where Una compels unexpected homage (II viii 2, 4–5; I iii 4). Both Arthur (I ix 13; contrast the false dream at i 48) and Calidore (VI x 3–4) find in visionary slumber or pastoral idleness illuminations that no conscious striving could win them. More often, however, the shade proves resistant to heaven's light; and the result of premature relaxation and disarming is violent betrayal (eg, II i 39–41; III v 28–9; IV vii 17–18; VI ii 16–20, 40–3, iii 20–7). The bloody bower, with its 'soiled gras' or blasted blossoms (II i 41), is a frequent emblem of such abruptly terminated Edenic daydreams.

The shadow and enclosure of bowers are psychological as well as physical. Bowers are places of intensified inwardness, where distinctions between inner feeling and its outward site disappear – as in the word *pleasance* itself (I ii 30, vii 4; VI x 5; cf *joyous/joyance*, IV x 23). Sometimes an irresponsible or self-defeating solipsism is signified, as in Phaedria's 'sweet solace to her selfe alone' (II vi 2–3), or Timias' melancholy in a 'gloomy glade' that is a sort of parody (with discarded weapons and names carved on trees) of the lover's bower (IV vii 38–9, 46). At best, the bower's privacy often encourages a dangerous obliviousness to incursions from without. In *FQ* VI, Spenser is especially concerned with the vulnerability of the 'contemplative cynosure' offered by such bowers (Nohrnberg 1976:659). But at the same time, he is seeking a true inwardness in which 'civill conversation' might be grounded: the hidden bower from which, in a world of trackless wandering and false tokens, both noble behavior and authentic language may flourish (VI proem 1–7, i 1–2, 6).

Both psychologically and structurally, bowers in *The Faerie Queene* are contrasted with sea and forest: bounded places with open space, homecoming (real or imagined) with quest and errancy. The determinacy of the bower explains its frequent use as a numerical and thematic 'center,' a privileged encapsulation of the poem's meaning (see Baybak, et al 1969; Fletcher 1971:11–37). But the relation of bowers to the elements around them is dialectical, not a simple opposition. The sea is the site of tempests that make one long for an island refuge; but it has its own embowering depths that are, at least potentially, an image of heavenly dwellings (III iv 43). Sometimes, as for the unhappy Florimell, the sea's Protean embrace seems like 'Eternall thraldome,' beauty's prison (III viii 37, 42); but it is also capable of illuminations whose figure is the seaborn Venus (IV xii 1–3). The vision of floods 'fertile ... in generation' (IV xii 1) calls to mind the Garden of Adonis, but the problematic nature of Marinell's watery bower also reminds us that a mutable realm of time and matter will always remain perilous to navigate. Florimell, having been fostered by the Graces on Mount Acidale, may in fact be kin to Amoret (IV v 5), but she is more elusive and, until her story's climactic moment, continually exiled in the woody or watery landscapes through which she flees.

The woods are as mixed in their implications as the sea. To mistake forest for bower, wilderness for paradise, the way for the goal, is to fall into a dangerous trap, as the preoccupation with Error in Book I makes abundantly clear (i 7–10, 34–5, ii 28–30, vii 2–8). Yet in Books III and IV, the kinship of Amoret and Belphoebe indicates that Venus and Diana – dwellers in bower and 'wanton wildernesse,' respectively (III vi 22) – are not irreconcilable. From *Muiopotmos* and *Virgils Gnat* to the Bower of Bliss, earthly gardens always suggest to Spenser the danger of another Fall if one yields to their seductions. Yet the task he sets his characters is not to abjure the world but to learn how to inhabit it properly. They must discover true bowers in the midst of the wilderness they dare not forget they inhabit (see Williams 1962:10–64).

The most satisfactory bowers, though most difficult of access, are landscapes where earth becomes a habitation fit for the gods (the temporal for the timeless, the sensuous for the spiritual): the Garden of Adonis (III vi 29–50), Mount Acidale (VI x 5–31), and Arlo Hill (VII vi 36–55, vii 8–12). Here enclosure is not darkness or limit but the clarity of perfect order, which Spenser's own *copia* renders seamless and complete. The Garden of Adonis, as well as being an allegory of generation, is an image of perfected temporality, its destructive potential safely locked away by blissfully embracing lovers (III vi 48–50). It is, however, a perfection of which we only hear; for the poem's characters, it belongs irrevocably to the past and is defined precisely by its difference from the world outside its walls. In contrast, the emphasis at Acidale and Arlo is on the glimpses of Edenic perfection, however fleeting, that may be vouchsafed even in a fallen world.

The rigor that may be required if mortals are to prolong such vision is suggested by Belphoebe's bower, an 'earthly Paradize' hidden away in the very midst of the threatening woods (III v 39–40). To the squire 'of meeke and lowly place,' it seems as if a creature 'heavenly borne, and of celestiall hew' has descended to minister to him (47). Yet he lives without hope of possessing the virgin beauty to whose service he is pledged, and the virtues of Belphoebe's nurturing environment are sustained only by an unremitting moral discipline.

To a degree, the relation between Amoret's nurture in the Garden of Adonis and Belphoebe's strenuous regimen in the woods (Spenser suggests that hers is the true 'bowre of blis,' of which the easy charms of Acrasia's garden are but 'guilefull semblaunts' III v 35, II xii 48) is recapitulated in the relation between Mount Acidale and Arlo Hill. The first bower in each pair is a vision of Edenic harmony; the second intimates how one might come to terms with a fallen world. Deity is manifested on Acidale in 'pleasaunce' (VI x 9), on Arlo for the sake of legal proceedings. Like Amoret, Acidale is under the protection of Venus; like Belphoebe, Arlo is associated with Diana. The Garden of Adonis and Mount Acidale are images of an effortless and 'safe felicity' (III vi 49), of spontaneous self-fulfillment. But they seem approachable only in moments of visionary intensity. To suppose that they represent the world in which we ordinarily dwell would be to commit the error of Acrasia's victims.

In contrast, Belphoebe's wilderness is stained with blood, and Arlo is a real place in Ireland that has become a wilderness. (Belphoebe is herself no goddess but 'daughter of a woody Nymphe' v 36, which may serve to reinforce her implication in the world of time and matter; for the punning conflation of *silva* and *hyle*, woods and matter, see Nelson 1963:159–60.) Nevertheless, both sites have with 'busie paine' been made ready for a divine transplant (III v 52–3, VII vii 3–5): the flower of chastity blooms in Belphoebe's woods, and in the splendid order with which Arlo is adorned the constancy of Nature herself is manifested .

The two sorts of bower exemplify the contrast between what has been called 'hard' and 'soft' primitivism (see Lovejoy and Boas 1935): between an accord with the world achieved through an easy fulfillment of desire and an accord based on abstention and self-control. Book VI takes up this duality with particular insistence. Bowers where lovers foolishly disarm themselves in order to enjoy the moment's pleasure alternate with the glades where Tristram and the Salvage Man practice an ascetic discipline (ii 31–2, iv 13–14). One way of making a place in the world is neatly summed up by the Hermit – his cottage 'like a little cage' of green (v 38) – who rhymes *containe* with *restraine* (vi 7), which is Meliboe's advice, too, from his lowly pastoral bower (ix 16–25). But Calidore is equally drawn to the more sensuous and spontaneous environment of Pastorella on her hillock, and to the visionary whirl of naked maidens on Mount Acidale. Finally, Spenser implies, one need not choose between the wisdom to which the ear attends and the pleasure on which the 'hungry eye' must feed (ix 26). Both 'hard' and 'soft' versions of pastoral have their legitimate claims. The symmetries of *FQ* III-IV and of *FQ* VI suggest that, for the lover and the poet alike, rigor and relaxation are complementary moments in one's embowerment in the world.

Another set of oppositions concerns the role of artifice in the attempt to find, or make, a home in the world. Amoret must proceed from the Garden of Adonis to the Temple of Venus, from a wholly natural bower to a garden where art plays 'second natures part' (IV x 21), supplying its defects: hers is a progress from nature to culture, from a place Venus has chosen for her own to the edifice men have erected to worship her, from growth and desire to the harmony of married love. In Acrasia's Bower of Bliss (II xii 42–87), however, art conceals rather than perfects nature: in contrast to Venus' garden and to Mount Acidale, her bower is a place of physical and psychic disarray. Its victims are lulled into a fatal looseness by the illusion that they can find in the pleasure of the fading rose a way back to the timeless joys of Paradise. The other varieties of false dwelling in Book II are all related to this lie.

Phaedria's careless self-absorption may seem as different from Acrasia's calculating voluptuousness as her biblical lily (Matt 6:28) is from the pagan rose celebrated in the enchantress' garden. Yet Phaedria is Acrasia's servant, and the pleasures of her bower are equally false (II vi 11–18, 24–5). Both characters refuse to acknowledge the Fall. In this perspective, the Bower of Bliss may be seen as a revelation of the inner nature of Phaedria's floating island, a manifestation of the falsity to which in her obliviousness she might have been blind.

Mammon's 'gloomy glade' is the site of an equally artificial way of life (II vii 3); but his willful violation of 'Untroubled Nature,' ripping open her 'quiet wombe' to produce molten 'Fountaines of gold and silver' (15–17), is the opposite of Phaedria's thoughtless utopianism. Guyon learns that to dwell properly in the world is neither to surrender to it nor merely to plunder it. Whether Persephone's garden (the innermost recess of Mammon's realm) represents intellectual curiosity, desire for immortality, or presumptuous pride, its sinister inversion of Edenic imagery appears to represent some form of sterile self-assertion that is the 'woomb' only of death (51–64).

The tapestries of Castle Joyous present a false simulacrum of the real Garden of Adonis, one that ends in death rather than perpetuity (III i 34–8). The problems raised by such artifice are as much epistemological as ethical. Britomart is searching for the outward manifestation of an inner state to which she cannot give a name; hence she may thematize Spenser's own anxieties about the efficacy of language. In the farcical confusion in the castle's bowers (here, bedrooms, but as in the woods, places of disarming), the dramatis personae of the traditional courts of love appear as shadows, empty images: rhetoric, as opposed to the seminal 'word' that animates the Garden of Adonis (III vi 34). In Busirane's more sinister court, fancy's images have eerily preempted living persons (III xi-xii); and in the figures of Sclaunder and the Blatant Beast, Spenser continues to worry about the power of language ungrounded in reality (IV viii 26, V xii-VI). The poet's prayer to be translated from a world of 'forgerie' and 'fayned showes' to the 'silver bowre' of true virtue indicates the similarity between his quest and the lover's (VI proem). As was earlier suggested in Britomart's encounter with Merlin, words may either veil reality or unfold it (III iii 15, 19), just as the world may imprison beauty or provide for it an authentic habitation. TERRY COMITO

Baybak, et al 1969; Lovejoy and Boas 1935; Curtius ed 1953; Giamatti 1966; Nelson 1963; George H. Williams 1962 *Wilderness and Paradise in Christian Thought* (New York).

Boyle family On 11 June 1594, Spenser married Elizabeth Boyle (d 1622), who is traditionally, though not certainly, identified as the poet's beloved in the *Amoretti* (see sonnet 74) and as his betrothed in *Epithalamion*. She was a cousin of Richard Boyle, who established the family in Ireland. Richard (1566–1643) claimed descent from the Boyle family which had lived in Herefordshire from the eleventh century. His father, Roger, was a younger son who moved to Kent in the mid-sixteenth century. His cousin Stephen, who lived in Northamptonshire, was father of the Elizabeth Boyle who married Spenser. Both Roger and Stephen Boyle died young. Roger's two surviving sons went up to Bene't (now Corpus Christi) College, Cambridge, on scholarship. The elder, John, took holy orders and later, through the influence of his brother, became Bishop of Cork. The younger son, Richard, left Bene't to study at the Middle Temple. Too poor to complete his studies in the law and much too ambitious to settle for a career as a clerk, he resolved to try his luck in Ireland. Within twenty years of arriving in Dublin in 1588, he had become the richest man in Ireland. After a succession of honors, he was created Earl of Cork in 1620.

Richard Boyle spent his first years in Ireland seeking preferment in political and literary circles. He became a favorite of the Irish Secretary, Sir Geoffrey Fenton (whose daughter became his second wife in 1603). He knew Lodowick Bryskett through whom, apparently, he met Spenser. As he had for himself, he arranged profitable marriages for his two sisters whom he brought to Ireland after 1590. He seems also to have brought his cousins Alexander and Elizabeth Boyle over from Northamptonshire. Both of his sisters lived near Youghal, and Elizabeth Boyle most likely met Spenser at one of their houses.

After Spenser's death in 1599, Richard Boyle took great interest in Elizabeth's livelihood: he arranged both of her subsequent marriages and financed the education of her son Peregrine Spenser. Just over a year and a half after Spenser's death, she married Roger Seckerstone, who was an acquaintance of Boyle; their only son, Richard, was his godson. Her third husband, Captain Robert Tynte, was another friend of Boyle; they were married in 1612 at Boyle's house. Three extant letters to Richard from Elizabeth Tynte indicate her gratitude for his generosity (one is reproduced in Judson 1945, opposite p 168). The family connection continued when Boyle arranged for his orphaned niece to marry Elizabeth Tynte's stepson. MARY ANNE HUTCHINSON

Nicholas Canny 1982 *The Upstart Earl: A Study of the Social and Mental World of Richard Boyle, First Earl of Cork, 1566–1643* (Cambridge); Judson 1945; Welply 1924.

Bracidas, Amidas Upon leaving the Castle of the Strond where the marriage of Marinell and Florimell has taken place, Artegall comes upon 'two comely Squires, / Both brethren, whom one wombe together bore,' quarreling over a coffer of treasure (*FQ* V iv 4–20). The elder, Bracidas (Gr *brachys* + *idia* few possessions), explains that each of them inherited islands (at the time, equally 'great and wide') from their father, Milesio. Originally, too, Bracidas was engaged to '*Philtera* the faire, / With whom a goodly doure I should have got,' while his younger brother Amidas (L *am* + Gr *idia* love of possessions) was engaged to the virtuous but poor Lucy (L *lux* light; hence '*Lucy* bright'). With the passage of time, however, the sea washed away most of Bracidas' land and deposited it on Amidas' island, whereupon Philtera (Gr *phil* + L *terra* love of land) left Bracidas for Amidas, who abandoned Lucy. Lucy threw herself into the sea in despair but was saved by floating on a coffer to Bracidas' island; there she bestowed on him both her self and the treasure in the coffer. Philtera now claims that the coffer was hers and that she is entitled to have it back.

For all the elements of romance in the story, with their suggestions of conflicting claims of poetic justice at stake, Artegall adjudicates the dispute on the basis of a single narrow issue, turning it into an exemplum of the validity of natural law and the importance of equity (see *justice and equity). On the one hand, we should accept as providential what time and nature provide; on the other, members of a society must learn to live by principles that all can accept. Of equity, Aristotle writes that 'in every community there is thought to be some form of justice' (*Nicomachean Ethics* 8.9). Here, Artegall starts from the basis of an essential agreement between the two brothers over what form of justice should govern their dispute. They are agreed on the question of alluvion, the natural growth of one island and the decay of the other: Amidas is unchallenged when he says that 'not for it this ods twixt us doth stand' (15). Artegall applies the same principle to cover all property lost at sea. If Amidas has a right to his brother's land because 'the sea it to my share did lay,' Bracidas has an equal right to the treasure, whether or not it formerly belonged to Philtera. Speaking the same words to each brother in parallel judgments, he declares 'That what the sea unto you sent, your own should seeme' (17–18).

In discovering the principle that should govern this dispute, Artegall provides a specific application of a theme he had enunciated on his way to the Castle of the Strond, in his debate with the Giant with the scales, who had pointed to alluvion as an instance of the natural disorder he would correct. Artegall had replied that 'whatsoever from one place doth fall, / Is with the tide unto an other brought' (ii 39), and that the sea operates according to a natural law with which one may not interfere. ROBERT A. BRINKLEY

Braggadocchio Comic characters are rare in epic, even in Italian romantic epic. Braggadocchio, vainglorious coward and boaster, is more ludicrous than the braggarts in Ariosto's *Orlando furioso*. He is also more important and memorable: although a minor figure, he plays a role in seven cantos from *FQ* II iii to V iii and is a travesty of all the qualities of the chivalric knight. By representing an extreme of weakness and folly, he effectively contributes to Spenser's analysis of temperance and intemperance, true and false gentility, and truth and deceit – of worthiness and worthlessness generally. False, mean, and lustful, base and self-regarding in all his aims and deeds, he is incapable of virtuous action. Superficially he resembles the Ape of the satirical *Mother Hubberd* – 'Souldier,' 'Magnifico,' and coward (199, 665, 1005–13) – but he is a more fully realized comic character.

Braggadocchio's general affinity to the tone and mood of Ariostan romantic epic is undeniable. Although he has been thought to derive specifically from the boastful Mandricardo, Ariosto's King of Tartary is a noble figure, not a churl or impostor, and although sometimes extravagant is not wholly ridiculous. In his cowardly aspect, Braggadocchio is more closely related to Ariosto's Martano (*Var* 2:206–11). He is not as close kin to the *miles gloriosus* of Roman comedy and the braggart captain of Italian comedy as is usually claimed, for he is only an amateur, and his baseness, pretentiousness, and meanness of spirit are stronger than his easily exposed braggartism. He is Aristotle's rash man: 'boastful and only a pretender to courage' (*Nichomachean Ethics* 3.7). Whether he ultimately descends from Menander's *alazon*, the boastful soldier of Greek New Comedy, is an unanswerable question. By Spenser's time, a wide variety of stage figures of swagger and oath was well known: Herod in the medieval mystery plays, the civilian boaster Ralph Roister Doister, bragging Vices like Ambidexter in Thomas Preston's *Cambises*. Others were shortly to appear: Shakespeare's Falstaff and Parolles, Jonson's Captain Bobadill.

Braggadocchio first appears at *FQ* II iii 4, terrorizing the even more ignoble Trompart into becoming his 'liege-man.' He is then terrified himself by the appearance of a 'real' knight, Belphoebe; subsequently, his base nature is further revealed when he makes a lustful attempt upon her. As a figure from comedy, he seems something of a sport in the allegorical world of the early cantos of Book II, but his arrival anticipates the change to the more Ariostan method and atmosphere which predominate in Books III and IV.

In III viii, Braggadocchio's dalliance with the false spirit who appears in the guise and garments of Florimell is challenged by Ferraugh. He accepts the challenge; but riding off as if to take up his station a furlong away, he simply goes on riding and escapes. In III x, he refuses in a spuriously chivalric way – as a 'doughtie Doucepere' – the humiliated Malbecco's offer of money to help redress the latter's wrong, though he and Trompart have secret designs on the money; he is soon terrified by the satyrs, however, and flees. At III viii 11–15, this counterfeit knight gains the counterfeit lady, false Florimell, from the witch's son. In IV iv, he takes his turn at the tournament as a 'masked Mock-knight' and becomes the 'sport and play' of other knights; but in IV v, he is chosen by the false Florimell over them. In V iii, he is finally exposed by Artegall and humiliated by Talus – shaved, 'baffuld' (see *baffling), his sword broken and armor dispersed. His shield, with 'the Sunne brode blazed in a golden field' (14), is a parody of Arthur's 'sunlike shield' (viii 41).

Spenser invented the name *Braggadocchio* by adding the Italian augmentative suffix to the English *brag*. With the spelling slightly altered to *braggadocio*, the word has come to mean 'empty boasting' as well as 'boaster' in present-day English.

PETER BAYLEY

John M. Hill 1970 'Braggadocchio and Spenser's Golden World Concept: The Function of Unregenerative Comedy' *ELH* 37:315–24; James V. Holleran 1962 'Spenser's Braggadochio' in *Studies in English Renaissance Literature* ed Waldo F. McNeir (Baton Rouge) pp 20–39; J. Dennis Huston 1968–9 'The Function of the Mock Hero in Spenser's *Faerie Queene*' *MP* 66:212–17; John Leon Lievsay 1941 'Braggadochio: Spenser's Legacy to the Character-Writers' *MLQ* 2:475–85.

Bregog, Mulla In his tale of the marriage of the rivers Bregog and Mulla (*Colin Clout* 104–55), which he claims to be 'No leasing new, nor Grandams fable stale, / But auncient truth confirm'd with credance old' (102–3), Spenser incorporates Irish topography, the folktale motif of escaping couple and pursuing father, and the etiological tale of Alpheus and Arethusa (*Metamorphoses* 5.572–641). He insists on his personal relationships to these rivers, referring to the Bregog as 'my river' (92) and elsewhere speaking of 'Mulla mine, whose waves I whilom taught to weep' (*FQ* IV xi 41). Repeating the song he had sung to the visiting 'shepheard of the Ocean' (66), Colin tells of Mulla, the daughter of old Mole, who has matched her with Allo and forbidden her to marry her beloved Bregog. The wily Bregog disperses his stream and flows underground to meet Mulla; Mole is furious and blocks the former watercourse of the Bregog with a violent landslide, so that the lover loses his identity in becoming one with Mulla: 'so deare his love he bought' (155).

(See **Arlo Hill** Fig 1.)

Much of this 'mery lay' is based on topography well known to Spenser. His Irish property was walled to the north by the Ballyhoura Hills and the Galty Mountains, which he calls 'Old father *Mole*' in reference to the legendary Irish giant Slieve Smól. To the west and south, it was bounded by the Awbeg (then known as 'Narrow Water'), which he names Mulla from Kilnemullach ('church on the Mulla,' an earlier name for nearby Buttevant Abbey). To the east, it was bounded by the Bregog ('deceitful') which flows south (part of the time underground) to meet the Awbeg, after which the combined streams flow into the Blackwater (or 'Broad Water'), which Spenser calls Allo (from Mayallo or Mallow, a city on its banks).

Colin's tale is a local, pastoral, and comic counterpart to the 'lamentable lay' recited by his neighboring 'shepheard,' Raleigh, who was nicknamed 'Water' by Queen Elizabeth and who presented himself as an unrequited lover in his *Ocean to Cynthia* (see Cheney 1983:16–18). Seeing himself like his neighbor, a 'wight forlore' in search of royal favor, Spenser mythologizes his landscape in a way that celebrates his homecoming to a beloved Ireland alongside a sense of exile from his other, English home.

Spenser refers to this tale in *FQ* VII vi 38–55, when he tells a similar tale of Fanchin's union with Molanna, sister of the Mulla 'Unto whose bed false *Bregog* whylome stole.'

SHOHACHI FUKUDA

Cheney 1983; Gottfried 1937; Herendeen 1981; Joyce 1878; Judson 1933.

Breton, Nicholas (1555?-1626?) A prolific and popular contemporary of Spenser, Breton wrote pastoral, allegorical, amatory, satiric, and devotional poetry, prose in many of the same kinds, and also romances, characters, dialogues, and essays.

Shortly before the 'new Poete' appeared with *The Shepheardes Calender* in 1579, Breton published several volumes resembling those by 'old' poets like his stepfather Gascoigne, his stepfather's friend George Whetstone, and early Elizabethan allegorists such as John Hall, Googe, or Richard Robinson. *A Floorish upon Fancie* (1577) contains an elaborate parody of the courts of love and sets in motion allegorical machinery similar to Spenser's, including a forest in which one wanders away from the true path, a 'beaten way' traveled by fools, and castles housing personified abstractions: the Fort of Fancy, Virtue's School, and finally the Fort of Fame, which the poet learns cannot be scaled on a ladder whose rungs are rhymes. The allegory serves as an introduction and apology for a collection of social verse entitled 'Toyes of an Idle Head,' poems strung together by commentaries detailing the occasions of composition similar to the prose links used by Gascoigne in *A Hundreth Sundrie Flowres* (1573). Among them, and among the similar poems in Breton's *Workes of a Young Wyt* (also 1577), are several dream poems that combine stereotypic amatory autobiography with thin and sometimes obscure but frequently effective visionary imagery, such as a desolate landscape containing the Hill of Hard Hap (site of a series of misfortunes), the Vale of Misery (where the victims are suffering), the skull-shaped Cave of Care (in which Care studies a book of precautions), and the Dungeon of Despair (from which no one emerges).

In *The Wil of Wit* (1597, but first published before 1582 in an edition now lost), Breton recapitulated his previous allegories and resolved to abandon fancy and seek fame through virtue. From that time until 1590, apparently having given up hope of gaining preferment through his poems, he seems to have spent his time in other pursuits, perhaps abroad. From 1590 to 1622, however, he flooded the bookstalls with his writings, and wrote verse that appeared in such collections as *The Phoenix Nest* (1593) and *Englands Helicon* (1600). This work catered to the tastes of the book-buying public but retains his recognizable stamp. Whether in allegory, dream-vision, meditation, homily, or prayer, Breton offers sincere but simple piety, conventional moralism, and an understanding of his subjects that does not transcend the ordinary.

Although he dedicated several works to the Countess of Pembroke, portraying her as a model of devotion, he does not seem to have been a member of the Sidney circle at a time or in a way that would have brought him into close contact with Spenser. 'Amoris Lachrimae,' his elegy on his 'friend' Sidney, printed in *Brittons Bowre*, though a thoroughly conventional exercise in funeral rhetoric, compares favorably with Spenser's 'Astrophel' for specificity and elaboration. Breton's 'Epitaph upon Poet Spencer' in *Melancholike Humours* (1600), by contrast, is perfunctory and unpersuasive, celebrating the fashionable passion more than the deceased poet. The epitaph mentions *The Faerie Queene*, *The Shepheardes Calender*, and *Mother Hubberds Tale*, but any traces of Spenser's influence in Breton's other poetry serve primarily to underscore the differences between the learned, philosophical, and architectonic Spenser, with his sense of vocation as a national poet, and the unpretentious Breton, whose works lack elaborate formal structure, whose themes are commonplace, and who makes no claim for the importance of his writings.

As a religious poet, Breton has been likened to the Spenser of *Fowre Hymnes*, but his devotional writings mainly explore personal contrition and pronounce standard pious admonitions. *The Pilgrimage to Paradise* (1592), which may have been precipitated by the appearance of the 1590 *Faerie Queene*, explores in Breton's earlier allegorical mode the issue of salvation. In one long central passage, the pilgrim, with help from his guide, a female personification of Virtue, defeats a seven-headed, seven-tailed monster (with a sting in each tail) – not in battle, but in debate. Overcome by arguments, the heads representing each of the deadly sins one by one implode and fall back into the devil's body.

Although Breton's religious poetry falls lamentably short of Spenser's in intellectual range and depth, and his allegory usually lacks the rich surface imagery that brings Spenser's to life, his pastorals, the works for which he has been most praised, exceed Spenser's in clarity, realism, and precision of statement. Breton can strike a pure Arcadian tone, combining simple sentiments of love and constancy with a delight in wordplay, rhyme, and rustic scenery. In the prose work *Fantasticks: Serving for a Perpetuall Prognostication* (entered in the Stationers' Register 1604, extant edition 1626), Breton turned his talent for observation of nature to the creation of a post-pastoral shepherd's calendar, characterizing months, seasons, hours, and certain holidays in a series of charming descriptive essays.

In his progress from courtly amateur to writer for the press, Breton followed a less demanding path than the Virgilian career of Spenser, but one well suited to his own moderate ambitions and talents and to the tastes and capacities of the ever-expanding reading public he addressed.

WILLIAM E. SHEIDLEY

Breton ed 1879 may be supplemented by Breton 1952 *Poems (not Hitherto Reprinted)* ed Jean Robertson (Liverpool), which also has the life and a checklist of the works.

Briana As with the other courted ladies in *FQ* VI (Priscilla, Blandina, Serena, Mirabella, and Pastorella), Briana serves Spenser as a means to explore relations between love and the protocols of courtship and hospitality (i 11–47). Although the defects portrayed in Book VI are primarily social (shame is a surprisingly prominent motif, eg, stanzas 12, 14), they are often psychological. Briana's flaw is manifested as defective hospitality but arises from the nature of her attachment to Crudor. Her forwardness has encouraged a high disdain in him, and she is forced to comply with the bizarre conditions that he lays down: with the help of her seneschal Maleffort, she cuts off the locks of ladies and beards of men who seek to traverse the narrow pass that her castle commands. This hair is to line a mantle which Crudor wants as a dowry before he will love her in return. Here Spenser adapts an Arthurian story, the Castle of Beards from *Perlesvaus* (see *Var* 6:365–7); his version retains the sense of inhospitality and perverted social games in his original, but adds a parallel disgrace to the lady and omits the grimmer display of maimed slaves and severed heads in his original.

Unlike Mirabella, Briana is not herself proudly aloof, for she does love Crudor. Unlike Blandina, she is neither sly nor hypocritical; in fact, she is open to the point of blatancy both in conversation and in nearly falling from the battlements in 'piteous mourning' when her champion is defeated. Although proud, she is not evil like Lucifera in Book I. Even so, Calidore cannot reform her merely by kindness or admonition. When she refuses his counsel the first time he offers it, he tells her that showing courtesy to strangers will gain her greater honor than obtaining Crudor's love. His response thus establishes a fuller paradigm of the virtues that civility combines, and distinguishes the ways aggressive knights and shrewish ladies should be treated. Whereas with Crudor Calidore must turn to armed combat, with Briana he practices restraint in the face of provocation and limits his defense to a general justification of force as needed. When she lectures him for slaying her men, he answers merely that 'it is no blame / To punish those, that doe deserve the same.' That maxim is upheld again when Calepine slays the cannibals (viii) and Calidore slays the Brigands (xi).

In this episode, Spenser questions just how far force may proceed against wrongdoers without destroying courtesy. Crudor must be physically punished but not killed. Without her henchmen, Briana is no threat to life, and so Calidore meets her 'womanish disdaine' with even temper: 'To take defiaunce at a Ladies word ... I hold it no indignity.' At his second attempt, Calidore's courtesy wondrously changes her once he forces Crudor to love her 'Withouten dowre or composition.' Finding a way to tame her sharp tongue (the name Brian means 'shrill voice' according to Camden ed 1984:61; cf Fr *bruyant* 'noisy') is not a severe test for Calidore, who never falters. Her case does not demand the complex judgment required in a dubious social predicament like Priscilla's as recounted in the next episode. This first of Calidore's trials of courtesy sets a pattern for the balanced application of justice, strength, and generosity to the codes of chivalry.

HAROLD TOLIVER

bridges Like other allegorical places, a bridge over a river in *The Faerie Queene* serves a generic function: to embody the idea of restricted passage either to a desired goal or (like an initiatory test) from one kind of existence to another. In the Roman world, bridges were presided over by the gods Janus and Portunus, and were associated with rituals of initiation, having significance as legal and figurative thresholds to moral and social behavior (Cicero *De natura deorum* 2.27, Livy *Ab urbe condita* 2.10). Folkloric elements, which link bridges to various kinds of violent or unsocial activity, appear in medieval romance and religious allegory (Malory *Morte Darthur* 6.10, Catharine of Siena *The Orcherd of Syon*). Bridges also figure prominently in the iconography of civic humanism; observant Renaissance travelers took note of their presence in a landscape. A well-maintained bridge was a sign of social order and stability; a large and beautiful one (such as the Rialto or London Bridge) epitomized cultural achievement. Whatever the period, bridges served as a focal point illustrating how art of one sort or another relates to nature.

The relatively small number of bridges which appear in Spenser's poetry show various aspects of these associations. London Bridge is imagined as the city's foot mastering the Thames (*FQ* III ix 45); a ruined bridge is a figure of human splendor destroyed by mutability (*Time* 547–60). The bridge to the island of Venus (*FQ* IV x 6–20) is the only path by which Scudamour can reach Amoret and the region of revealed love, friendship, and concord. It is guarded by personifications of the obstacles to courtship and furnished with architectural features which, in conjunction with the flow of water past its piers, suggest the cooperation of nature and art on the island itself. Generally, Spenser is concerned to show that the humane arts spring from nature, rather than that they transcend or tame nature.

The bridge of Pollente (V ii 4–28) appears to be a necessary path for the poor in their daily needs as well as for the rich; their passage is unjustly taxed by its master, and trapdoors in it suggest his fraudulent deceitfulness. Artegall and Talus, by restoring customs to their natural use in killing Pollente and Munera, return the bridge to its role in Book IV as an extension of society's rightful path through life. Since similar abuses of right of passage are associated with frustrated love in Malory (6.17) and Ariosto (*Orlando furioso* 29.31–49), it is not surprising that Britomart must overcome her own obstacles at this same bridge when she is on her way to rescue Artegall (V vi 36–9).

W.H. HERENDEEN

A Brief Note of Ireland (See *Var Prose* pp 233–45.) A set of three state papers (PRO, SP 63/202/4/59) known collectively after the title of the first. The group remains among the most doubtful of writings attributed to Spenser. Though known to scholars for some time, *Brief Note* became officially considered part of Spenser's works only with its publication in Grosart's complete edition (1882–4). Since then its status has been vigorously challenged by some scholars, trenchantly defended by others, and tacitly ignored by a majority unsure of its value and unwilling to enter into controversy on its behalf.

The difficulties presented by *Brief Note* are twofold. First, the collection is quite heterogeneous, each of the items being wholly distinct from its fellows in tone, style, content, and objective. Second, no original or contemporary copy has survived. The one complete copy is in an early-seventeenth-century hand (possibly Sir Dudley Carleton's), and the principal basis of its attribution is the copyist's endorsement of the group of folios which he has used as 'A briefe discourse of Ireland. by Spencer.' An even later manuscript entitled 'Spensers discours breifly of Ireland' is a copy of only the third and last item in *Brief Note* (BL Harleian Ms 3787 no 21). The first paper in the collection, the brief note proper, is a concise 250-word summary of Ireland's economic and fiscal value. It estimates that there are 5530 townlands in the island containing 38,640 plowlands which in the reign of Edward IV yielded a revenue of £14,146 to the crown. Customs and other revenues yielded over £88,000 besides the casual income of wardships and advowsons. These estimates are wildly inaccurate. Medieval Irish revenues never came close to yielding a surplus over costs and certainly not in the troubled times of Edward IV. On these points alone, Spenser's authorship may be doubted. In *Vewe of Ireland*, he displays a far more realistic sense of Ireland's revenue potential, and his own interpretation of the decline of the medieval lordship in the later fifteenth century is even more pessimistic than the historical record would seem to warrant. There is also a marked discrepancy between the estimate of 43,920 plowlands in *Vewe* and that given here. The figures, however, do correspond closely to estimates in the 'Book of Howth,' a mid-sixteenth-century compilation of earlier records, and it seems likely that the description in *Brief Note* was a copy of a similar compilation. The document bears no mark of the principal concerns of Ireland in Spenser's time, and there seems little to link it to him except the possibility that he made a copy for his own purposes.

The provenance and date of the second item in *Brief Note* are easier to determine. A petition headed 'To the Queene,' it is a desperate plea for redress on behalf of the planters of Munster ruined by the sudden overthrow of their settlement in October 1598. Though florid and often hysterical in expression, the argument expounded in its 3000 words is quite coherent. The root cause of the planter's troubles lay in the June 1595 rebellion of the Earl of Tyrone, who rose up in fear of the imminent seizure of his lands by unscrupulous government officers. Having revolted, Tyrone determined to extend the war by fomenting rebellion in each of the provinces. The arrival of his agents in Munster was the signal for all the discontented natives to rise up and destroy the new English settlement established through the confiscation of the rebel Earl of Desmond's lands in 1584. The petition offers two reasons for the plantation's collapse. First, insufficient attention had been given to developing and defending the settlement. Second, the surviving natives had been treated too leniently, and now, far from being attracted to the settlement's exemplary civility, they despised it and plotted ceaselessly for its destruction.

Both points were conventional in contemporary analysis, and both have largely been confirmed by modern research. Emigration to the plantation had fallen off sharply by the mid-1590s. The government provided only a troop of 142 men for its defense. Plans to establish a militia among the settlers themselves were never developed, and on the very eve of the uprising they could muster no more than 200 men. At the same time, the number of surviving native landholders was far greater than had originally been expected. Through pardons or proofs of innocence, many succeeded in evading confiscation or in reclaiming their land. As a result, the plantation was surrounded by large areas still in native possession: 'an archipelago of little islands of Englishness' in a hostile sea (Sheehan 1982:11).

The petition thus provides a fairly accurate description of conditions in Munster in the late 1590s, but its very orthodoxy raises specific problems in regard to its authorship. Spenser, it is true, shared the common experience of the dispossessed planters, but there is nothing in the tract that can be identified as specifically Spenserian. Moreover, certain opinions seem to conflict with those he expresses in *Vewe*. The curious depiction of Tyrone as a desperate man forced into rebellion seems closer to the views of Captain Thomas Lee and others who wished to make peace with Tyrone. Its style, too, as has often been noted, is quite unlike Spenser's; and though the point is perhaps subjective, it gains significance when the tract is compared with a number of contemporary petitions emanating from Munster, which are remarkably similar to it both in tone and argument and with which Spenser has never been associated (cf esp 'The supplication of the blood of the English' BL Add Ms 34313, fols 88–122). The petition may thus be seen as part of a moderately concerted propaganda effort on the part of the Munster planters in which Spenser may or may not have had a hand.

There can, however, be little doubt concerning Spenser's authorship of the third and final item in the collection: 'Certaine pointes to be considered of in the recovery of the Realme of Ireland.' This is not only the one piece in *Brief Note* that has been doubly attributed to him: it is also the one that is closest in emphasis and argument to *Vewe*. Tersely written in a schematic deductive form, it essays in about 800 words to prove that attempts to recover Ireland either by peaceful reform or by piecemeal conquest will inevitably fail, and to argue that 'great force must be the instrument [and] famine ... the meane' of subjugation. It then sketches briefly the number of men required and the strategy to be pursued. It allows a short respite before the pestilence is unleashed to offer some rebels a pardon 'of life onelie' (*Var Prose* pp 244–5). The later Harleian copy ends with a piece of doggerel in praise of the Earl of Essex, who is to undertake the campaign. All these points will be immediately familiar to readers of the *Vewe*, and even the few discrepancies which have been noted can be explained in terms of the exigencies of a changing military situation (eg, an alteration in the tactics proposed to deal with Tyrone). Here, shorn of pleasant antiquarian digressions, inconsistent qualifications, and a subtle evasion of logical consequences, is the essence of the brutal argument of *Vewe*. As such, though modest in itself, 'Certaine pointes' is an invaluable tool in a critical analysis of the complexities and internal contradictions of *Vewe*; and it is understandable that some scholars unwilling to confront the fundamentally ruthless thrust of the *Vewe* have chosen to ignore this piece also.

Two speculations may be offered as to the provenance of *Brief Note*. It is possible that the group formed part of a larger collection of dispatches which Spenser brought from Munster to Whitehall in December 1598. Perhaps the spokesman for the Munster planters, he may have delivered their petition at court and seized the opportunity to present his own far more rigorous proposals which had been silenced through the suppression of *Vewe*. But it is possible also that the relationship of all three items is entirely fortuitous, that they were grafted together by the seventeenth-century copyist simply as curiosities of yesteryear and given their common endorsement merely because Spenser's short tract was the most memorable.

CIARAN BRADY

The definitive edition of the text is by Rudolf Gottfried in *Var Prose* pp 233–45. In his Commentary (pp 430–40) and in Appendix IV (pp 533–7), he is inclined to claim too much. His own ingenious list of verbal and syntactical correspondences with the rest of Spenser's work, intended to support the attribution of the entire piece to Spenser, consists of similarities which are either commonplace or tendentious. The most serious attack on *Brief Note*, Hulbert 1936–7, claims too much in the opposite direction. Her criticism of the first two items is reasonably effective, but her dissociation of Spenser from 'Certaine pointes' is forced and unconvincing. Throughout she shows no familiarity with the manuscript of *Brief Note*. On the relationship of 'Certaine pointes' to the *Vewe*, see Brady 1986. See also MacCarthy-Morrogh 1986; Anthony Sheehan 1982; and Sheehan 1983 'Official Reaction to Native Land Claims in the Plantation of Munster' *IHS* 23:297–318.

Brigands In *FQ* VI x, an outlaw band destroys Meliboe's shepherd community, driving off its flocks and planning to enslave its people. When the leader attempts against the will of his men to keep Pastorella for himself, a battle erupts; he is killed, Pastorella is wounded, and most of the shepherds are slaughtered. Calidore later enters their caves, rescues Pastorella, and slays her captors.

The motif of brigands living at the edge of civilized society (Cooper 1565 defines Ital *brigante* as 'an ancient people in the north part of England') may owe something to Spenser's concern with the bands of Irish outlaw rebels mentioned in *Vewe*, though the episode has its literary roots in the melodramatic action of Greek romance. In Achilles Tatius' *Clitophon and Leucippe* 8.16, a pirate chief attempts to keep Leucippe for himself and is killed by his men who wish to sell her to slavers; in Heliodorus' *Ethiopica* 5, a pirate band destroys itself when its leaders quarrel over the captured heroine. Spenser's episode may be more deeply indebted to an incident from Longus' *Daphnis and Chloe* 2, where the unarmed pastoral community of the protagonists is attacked by warriors from a neighboring city; both episodes qualify the picture of an idealized pastoral life by stressing its vulnerability. In a fallen world the pleasant, unenvious retreat Meliboe praises to Calidore can be maintained only if armed knights exist to protect the helpless shepherds against external threats.

The Brigands are the last and worst of such threats to civil harmony in *FQ* VI; they dwell symbolically apart on a barren island, in the dark caves usually associated in the poem with the threateningly irrational or uncivilized. In the anthropology of Book VI, they resemble the cannibals of canto viii who also dwell at the borders of civilization, raiding it periodically for food and booty. But whereas the cannibals form a community of savages, the Brigands are civilized creatures gone bad. The cannibals are moved by animal impulses of hunger and lust, while the Brigands participate in a money economy and want Pastorella for trading purposes. Yet the savages possess certain minimal civilized restraints which the Brigands lack: when their priest forbids them to rape Serena before they slaughter her, the narrator comments that 'religion held even theeves in measure' (viii 43). By contrast the Brigands, who are compared to hungry dogs (xi 17), cannot restrain themselves from anarchic strife. WILLIAM A. ORAM

Britain, Britons One historical tradition in the sixteenth century claimed that the history of Britain began with the fall of Troy, with the subsequent wanderings of the Trojans, and with the discovery and renaming of Albion by the Trojan Brutus, descendant of Aeneas. In its many versions, the tradition had the authority of more than seven centuries of British chronicle history.

The story of Britain's Trojan ancestry is told first in Nennius' *Historia Brittonum* (c 800) and then most authoritatively in Geoffrey of Monmouth's *Historia regum Britanniae* (c 1139). Claiming to translate an ancient book from the original 'British' language into Latin, Geoffrey relates that after the destruction of Troy Aeneas fled to Italy where he founded a second Troy, later to become the Roman Empire. Soothsayers predicted that his great-grandson Brutus would one day kill his own father (Silvius) and wander the world in exile, but eventually would end his life with great renown. The prophecy was fulfilled: Brutus accidentally killed his father while hunting; in exile, he was told by the goddess Diana of the island which awaited him and his followers and which she prophesied would become another Troy.

This island, inhabited only by a band of giants, was called Albion. (The name has been variously explained, and three of the standard derivations are alluded to in *The Faerie Queene*: from L *albus* 'white' for the white cliffs of Dover [see the play on 'white rocks' at II x 6]; from the name *Albine*, the eldest of the 'fiftie daughters' of Dioclesian [or Danaus], II x 7–9; or from the figure of Albion, curiously descended from Noah's son Ham through Isis and Osiris yet son of Neptune and enemy of Hercules, at IV xi 15–16. A fourth derivation, not in Spenser, is from Gr *olbios* 'prosperous.') Brutus renamed the island after himself and renamed his companions Britons (from *Brut-ans*; see Geoffrey's *Historia* 1.16). From this beginning, Geoffrey traces British history through almost 2000 years to the death of Cadwallader and the end of the first British empire. What Geoffrey does for England in his legendary genealogy, Virgil does for Rome in his *Aeneid*. By the seventh century, the Franks had a similar genealogy through Francio, a son of Hector. Even Geoffrey's critics, such as Giraldus Cambrensis and William of Newburgh, accepted the Trojan origins of Britain.

The tradition continued in popular works like Higden's *Polychronicon* (c 1327), Hardyng's *Chronicle* (c 1440–64), and the *Chronicles of England* published by Caxton (1480). The Tudor chroniclers – Fabyan, Grafton, Holinshed, and Stow – tell the same story with variations. Yet there were skeptics: John Rastell prefaced his narrative of Brut in *The Pastyme of People* (1529) with a disclaimer that although 'many men suppose it to be but a feined story' (sig A2r), Geoffrey's narrative does bear retelling, if not for its historical truth then for its moral examples of God's punishment of the sinful. Skepticism becomes disbelief in writers like Polydore Vergil and other humanist historians (John Twyne, George Lily, Thomas Lanquet). By the early seventeenth century, we find a remarkable ambivalence in Selden's comment on Drayton's *Poly-Olbion* (1613): 'Touching the *Trojan Brute*, I have (but as an Advocat for the Muse) argued; disclaiming in it, if alledg'd for my own Opinion' (ed 1931–41, 4: viii). There is a conflict here between the desire to keep what was universally recognized as an ancient tale and the growing need to represent history scientifically from verifiable documents.

Perhaps the strongest encouragement to uphold the Trojan origins of Britain came from the Tudor monarchs. The notion of ancient and imperial lineage appealed to these recent descendants of dynastic compromise. Their coats of arms included Brutus and Arthur, and official genealogies traced their titles back to Brutus. Receptions and pageants in their honor repeatedly drew inspiration from the vast range of heroes and events in traditional British history. Henry VII was flattered by it in the Worcester pageants of 1486; Henry VIII used it in the London pageants for the reception of the Emperor Charles V in 1522; London welcomed Philip and Mary in 1554 with Gogmagog, giant of Albion, and Corineus, the Trojan giant-wrestler; Elizabeth received a similar welcome in the pageant of 1559. Even James I, who also claimed British blood, was flattered in a royal passage through London in 1604 with the reminder that the kingdom was 'By *Brute* divided, but by you alone, / All are againe united and made *One*' (see Bergeron 1971:85). James officially restored the ancient Welsh name of the island – Great Britain.

It is uncertain how seriously Spenser regarded the story of Britain's Trojan ancestry. In one manuscript of the *Vewe of Ireland*, Irenius remarks of 'the Tale of *Brutus*' that it is 'as impossible to proove, that there was ever any such *Brutus* of *England*, as it is, that there was any such *Gathelus* of *Spaine*' (*Var Prose* p 82 line 1152n). Yet in telling the story in the chronicle history read by Arthur (II x 9–13), in Merlin's prophetic chronicle of Britomart (III iii 22), and in Paridell's account of his Trojan ancestors (III ix 33–51), he made it central to the dynastic and imperial themes of *The Faerie Queene*. Fittingly, then, when Arthur finishes reading *Briton moniments*, he exclaims upon learning about 'The royall Ofspring of his native land': 'How brutish is it not to understand.' (See also articles on *Arthur.) HUGH MACLACHLAN

Geoffrey Ashe 1982 *Kings and Queens of Early Britain* (London); Bergeron 1971; G. Gordon 1946:35–58; Antonia Gransden 1974–82 *Historical Writing in England* 2 vols (Ithaca, NY); Hanning 1966; Kendrick 1950; Hugh A. MacDougall 1982 *Racial Myth in English History: Trojans, Teutons, and Anglo-Saxons* (Montreal); Millican 1932; Parsons 1929; Tatlock 1950; Yates 1975.

Britomart The name of Spenser's Britomart combines *Briton* with *martial*; appropriately, Merlin's prophecy links her progeny to Elizabeth I (*FQ* III iii 49). Her name also derives from *Britomartis*, a nymph who is associated with, and sometimes identified as, Diana, goddess of chastity, and whose flight from her would-be lover to the sea in Callimachus' hymn to Diana resembles Florimell's in *FQ* III. The nymph Britomartis is also the object of an apostrophe in the pseudo-Virgilian *Ciris*, which is the primary source for Glauce's conversation with Britomart in *FQ* III ii. Armed and in love, Britomart is a *Venus armata* (Wind 1958 quoted from rev ed 1967:91–6) or 'martiall Mayd' (III ii 9), who combines the purity of her namesake in *Ciris* with the passion of the same poem's Scylla, whose role she approximates in conversing with Glauce. In the same conversation, moreover, Britomart's words echo closely those of Ariosto's impassioned Fiordispina, Spenser's model for Malecasta (Alpers 1967b:180–3).

Britomart embodies the double nature of Diana and, in the terms of Book III, the combined potency of Amoret and Belphoebe and the potential for concord between them. When enclosed in her armor, she is both an infolded Venus and an unfolded Mars. Although wounded proleptically in the castle of Malecasta, she is wounded through the protective confinement and encasing integrity of her armor for the first time in the house of Busirane; and yet, along with Amoret, the principle of love (L *amor*) she liberates, she is made 'perfect hole,' at once whole and wanting (Goldberg 1981:78–9, Quilligan 1983:198–9). For Britomart – as distinct from Amoret, her more simply allegorical charge – the psychic readiness she achieves by the close of Book III is vital yet preliminary to completion.

Britomart's fortunes inform Books III through V. With Arthur, she has the most extensive career in the poem: she is titular knight of Book III, recurrent focus in IV, and savior of the hero of V. She travels through changing landscapes of meaning: from an interiorized Book III of dreams and fantasies that explores the mind's power to project its own shapes on reality, to a revisionary Book IV in which narrative and symbolic structures dissolve and reform, to a more radically exteriorized Book V focused on a social virtue and alluding insistently to a broad spectrum of Elizabethan history. Britomart's figure cannot be understood in isolation from the various contexts in which she appears. Even in Book III, she is a different sort of hero from Redcrosse and Guyon, appearing in fewer cantos than her predecessors but progressively defined through relations of sympathy and antipathy with characters and events in every canto in the book. If in Book V we should suppose we are back in III, we would mistake Britomart's last appearance for a fulfillment different from what it actually is. Her story, instead, is paradigmatic for Books III-V: progress and anguish, prophecy and incompletion.

Britomart's domination of the first third of Book III largely accounts for our enduring impression of her (Anderson 1976:98–106). Defined at the outset by comparison, she first unseats Guyon (Temperance) to indicate the superiority of her virtue – her power and more specifically her chastity – and then is reconciled to him and his companion Arthur to suggest the harmony of all their powers. She makes offense her defense in this first action, in strong contrast to the timorous Florimell who flees into canto i pursued by the lustful Foster and, while Britomart stands firm in her own quest, promptly flees out of it. Britomart's second action is to relieve the Red Cross Knight in his clash with Malecasta's champions, an act that at once suggests her virtuous affinity to him and the differences between their specific powers. Britomart's virtue is relevant to the failures of chastity Redcrosse suffered in *FQ* I, and a number of echoes between her early adventures and his enforce their likeness (eg, III i 54, I i 53, ii 45; cf III i 47, I ii 30). Unlike him, however, she is assessed sympathetically from within her own condition in these cantos rather than from a critical vantage point outside it. For example, when she tells white lies (ii 8) or when she is nearly drawn into the clutches of Malecasta, the poet invites amused sympathy rather than moral outrage. Britomart's innocence is a function of youth, purity, and inexperience; Redcrosse's is culpable ignorance.

Like all literary characters, Spenser's are constructs of language, but they are not all constructs of just the same sort: Britomart is a character in an allegorical romance, but she is less simply a metaphor and more simply herself than are the heroes of earlier books. Modeled on Ariosto's Bradamante, she has a greater degree of *human* autonomy. As recounted in III ii, Britomart falls in love with the perfected image of Artegall, whom she views in a magic globe. Emboldened by Merlin's revelation that Artegall is her destined mate, she actively seeks the embodiment of her vision throughout Book III and well into IV. Her person has a history (III ix 38–51) and, at least in these two books, a future; like Arthur, she is involved in historical time. She has a father rather than a myth of origin, a nurse rather than a Palmer, and a destiny firmly on earth; she looks and is more human than her predecessors among the poem's protagonists – much as is the virtuous human love she potentially embodies. Her conversation with Glauce about Artegall, for example, would be suitable for the stage with little alteration; and her complaint by the sea, in which she gives voice to her emotions, closely resembles a Petrarchan sonneteer's. As thus portrayed, she *makes* metaphor instead of merely being its embodiment and is not only aware of her own emotions but also consciously shaping them. Unfortunately, the particular condition she voices in III iv is frustrated desire, a mixture of love and hate ('Ah who can love the worker of her smart?' xii 31) that she will meet again in more objectified form in the house of Busirane. Immediately after her complaint, her courage kindled by 'Love and despight,' she finds Marinell a convenient object on which to vent the violence of her passion. She never knows of his hostility to love or even hears his name: only the reader appreciates his ironical relation to her quest and, in time, to Artegall (IV vi 28).

Above all, Britomart's distinction as a titular hero is her womanhood. A woman disguised as a man, she affords the poem some of the advantages Shakespeare was later to find in similarly disguised figures such as Rosalind or Portia. Britomart's disguise frees her from a woman's customary social role, and her sex frees her from a man's; through her, the poet can more freely examine the relation of the self to desire, of desire to artistic form, and of the desiring self to its historical destination, its destiny in time.

Another freedom for the poet, like the notion of disguise itself, involves playfulness. Britomart's youth, sex, and disguise feed the humor with which her figure is repeatedly touched in the early cantos. Warm rather than harshly satirical, this humor coexists easily with her human dignity, as it could not with the dignity of a character conceived in more exclusively abstract terms. It embraces colloquial touches (ii 26), Glauce's comic concoction (ii 49–51), Merlin's ancestry (from Matilda [battle maid], 'a faire Ladie Nonne,' daughter of Pubidius, conceivably suggesting L *pubes*, *pubis* 'puberty'; see Berger 1969b:248), and his unwizardly burst of wizardly laughter (iii 13, 19). Such humor is especially evident in Malecasta's castle (III i), where 'the *Lady of delight*,' Unchastity herself, mistakes the disguised Britomart's sex, falls into a passion for her, and under cover of night slips panting and trembling into her bed. But the romance seductress achieves only the upraised sword of the outraged virgin, much as will Busirane cantos later. In this brush with farce, Britomart emerges 'triumphantly innocent' (Alpers 1967b:377–80), though slightly hurt by Gardante (Looking), one of Malecasta's knights. As when she receives the love wound from the vision of Artegall, Britomart is caught 'unwares' when Malecasta sneaks upon her, and again when Busirane's knife wounds her chest (i 61, ii 26, xii 33). *Unwares* both characterizes the vulnerability of Britomart's inexperience, which is part of her innocence, and suggests how her quest is a *Bildungsroman* (*Bildung* to be taken in its senses of 'forming,' 'fashioning,' 'growth,' 'generation,' 'education,' and *Roman* in its Renaissance sense of 'romance').

Absent from the central third of Book III, Britomart reappears in canto ix to reestablish her relation to history, this time as a Trojan descendant, 'kin' to Paridell and 'partner of [his] payne' (40, 51). She is a virtuous alternative to the destructive passion of Paridell and Hellenore (an idle Paris and a whorish Helen) and thus to passion's fire as a destructive force in history. She next tracks Ollyphant to the anguished Scudamour and, learning of his beloved Amoret's imprisonment, passes through fire to rescue her from Busirane, her torturer. Busirane is an evil artist-magician; in *The Faerie Queene* such figures always perversely express and prey on the human imagination. Essentially, his house objectifies, enlarges, and thereby distorts the erotic landscape of the whole of Book III. While Britomart's fears, fancies, and aggressions feed into this house and those of others, notably Scudamour and Amoret, do as well, and while all lovers are vulnerable in varying degrees to its power, it is no single lover's projection. It is a place of love's perversion, empowered by love itself. Britomart's story – the smoky, sulphurous Etna in her breast, the 'selfe-pleasing thoughts' that feed her pain, her guidance by blind Cupid, her 'Love and despight,' her vulnerability in Castle Joyous, and even her kinship with Paridell's pain (ii 32, iv 6, 8–9, 12) – explains why she is there: Busirane is a fearful and perverted obstacle to love, but he testifies to the potency of desire.

Awareness is finally why Britomart has to see the house of Busirane: once again to look and be wounded, as before in the magic globe and Malecasta's Castle. She has to pass through the flames. Busirane is abusive and evil, but he is an authentic presence in history, in myth, in Ovid, in Petrarchan sonnets, and in Britomart's experience (Lewis 1936:341, K. Williams 1966:109–10). Like Mammon and Acrasia, he is there in the way things are, if not in the way they ought to be; and like them, he must be first acknowledged, then mastered, before he can be disempowered. He hurts, he educates, he violates psychic innocence, but if he is not tracked to his house – to the very place where he *resides* – he cannot be overpowered by chaste love, and innocence will remain arrested and incapable.

Having freed Amoret but (in the 1596 version) having also found Scudamour departed, Britomart enters Book IV with Amoret in her care. Here ambiguous pronominal referents repeatedly blur the distinction and relation between the two women, a Spenserian technique variously suggesting 'a hermaphroditic vision of static union' (Lanham 1967:445) or, in the larger context of Book IV, the oscillation of narrative and symbolic modes and of unfolded and infolded meanings (Anderson 1971b:187–92). Britomart next appears briefly at the end of IV iv, where she wins Satyrane's tournament for the Knights of Maidenhead and in the process summarily topples her nearest rival, Artegall, who is disguised as the 'Salvage' (wild, savage, uncivil) Knight and therefore unknown to her. (This canto corresponds to III iv, in which Britomart similarly topples Marinell, 'loves enimy,' and is similarly compared to a welcome shower of rain; compare III iv 13, 26 with IV iv 47.) In the laughable beauty contest that follows (and reflects on) the tournament, Britomart, herself disguised, displays 'Her lovely *Amoret*' and rejects the fraudulent glitter of False Florimell, preferring the 'vertuous government' of 'her owne *Amoret*' – that is, her own virtuously governed love (v 13, 20).

Disgruntled by defeat in the tournament and by his loss of False Florimell, its grand prize, the disguised Artegall and the now-jealous Scudamour waylay Britomart in canto vi. In the battle that ensues, Britomart at last recognizes Artegall, the object of her quest, and Artegall recovers his name, assuming his destined identity for the first time in the poem (28). The resolution of this battle is concord, but its earlier stages are hate and love. In the course of it, Artegall wounds deeply the 'hinder parts' of Britomart's horse (13), forcing her to alight, to cast away her enchanted spear, and to fight – as before in the houses of Busirane and Malecasta – with only a sword. Artegall never wounds Britomart directly, as she does him (15); but his wounding her horse (traditionally associated with the passions) and his thus disabling her virginal spear suggest the erotic power of the wounds she already bears (Hamilton 1961a:182).

On foot, Artegall has the better of Britomart until his sword shears away her ventail, exposing her 'angels face' (v 19), and thereby canceling his vengeful purpose and even his ability to hold his sword. When Britomart views his face, she responds the same way to love's overpowering force: she is unable to lift her weapon and, even against her will, speaks mildly to him. In stages recalling the progress of the *Amoretti* from wonder and worship to suit and siege and entreaty and blandishment, Artegall brings Britomart to 'bay,' and then with more vows and oaths gains her consent, when time permits, to marry (41). Soon after, they separate, he to pursue his quest in *FQ* v and she to seek Amoret with Scudamour. Except for a brief appearance in IV ix to reemphasize Amoret's loss, Britomart does not reappear until v vi – the canto in Book v which corresponds to this earlier accord with Artegall.

Doubts and fears beset Britomart's mind when she reappears in Book v, waiting impatiently for Artegall's return. When she hears from his iron man, Talus, that he has been captured by the Amazon Radigund, she flies into a jealous rage, supposing he has betrayed their love. Her response is irrational yet striking in its explosive energy and realistic directness, which resist easy allegorizing and could easily be imagined on stage: her 'unquiet fits' of jealousy issue in her question 'whether he did woo, or whether he were woo'd' (vi 15). Britomart laments the loss of a man, her lover, not the loss of the virtue of Justice; and this personalizing of Artegall's failure further strains the already troubled development of Book v.

Learning subsequently from Talus that Artegall languishes in the fetters of female tyranny, not love, the wrathful Britomart dons armor and sets out, full of inward pain, to rescue him. As before in the poem, her progress is educational; and when she frees him, she is a more reasonable person, more fully aware of principles beyond her own passions. But her route to him has a high cost, for it is pointedly and recurrently shown to be a process of suppression and transference, the replacement of an immoderate woman by a myth. Britomart herself must finally be discarded. Thus, to the extent she improves as a person, she becomes herself irrelevant as one (Anderson 1970c:71–2).

Prior to her battle with Radigund, Britomart encounters the treachery of Dolon (vi) and in Isis Church (vii) experiences a final rite of passage. Although she foils Dolon and is enlightened by Isis, both episodes are disturbing from narrative or mythopoeic points of view. Dolon tries to destroy her in order to wreak vengeance on Artegall, for whom he mistakes her. Britomart, in the meantime, has no clue as to Dolon's motives and is only concerned with the sense of betrayal and treachery she feels inwardly; that she is nearly betrayed by – in fact, in – a bed only intensifies the ironies of this episode. Twice the poet accentuates the discrepancy between Britomart's concerns and those being imposed upon her by the Legend of Justice (vi 31, 38). She is caught between an inward point of view and one concerned with an abstract principle of justice that is wholly outside her.

In Isis Church, Britomart has a richly mythopoeic 'dream of sexuality, death, and birth' that as a myth of procreative power is unmatched anywhere else in the poem (Miskimin 1978:32–3). She dreams that she is Isis and that the phallic crocodile impregnates her. Isis' Priest, whom many commentators follow, rationalizes Britomart's dream into an allegory of dynastic justice; he fails entirely to acknowledge the potencies in it that raise 'troublous passion' in her mind (vii 19, 21–3). In both the Dolon and Isis episodes, Britomart's psychic experiences are reduced to an externalized allegory of justice, even while the meanings this reduction discards are made to stand out.

Britomart proceeds from Isis Church to a battle with Radigund that is remarkable for its fury. Radigund, while she never becomes indistinguishable from Britomart (as Sansjoy, for instance, becomes indistinguishable from Redcrosse), is a parodic antitype of her and a real threat to her integrity. Although Britomart finally crushes Radigund, she is painfully wounded by her in the process. The battle between them not only indicates hatred of the other, but also a hatred and specifically a sexual wastefulness that are self-destructive (vii 29, 31). This self-hatred may externalize and purge Britomart's own passionate excesses; yet it is so extreme that it affects her self more simply and suggests her own cooperation in the replacement, then discarding, of her person.

With Radigund defeated, Britomart reforms the city of Radegone and becomes truly like the Isis of the Priest's moralistic reading of her dream. Artegall, speaking never a word when freed, leaves with Talus to resume his quest; Britomart, in anguish, simply leaves the poem. Progeny for Britomart and Artegall is prophesied in the poem (III iii 22–4); but in the closing cantos of Book v, it is hard to believe that Artegall can ever return to Britomart to realize those prophecies in time.

JUDITH H. ANDERSON

Alpers 1967b; Anderson 1970c; Anderson 1971b; Anderson 1976; Berger 1969b; Goldberg 1981; Gross 1985:145–80; Hamilton 1961a; Hughes 1929; Richard A. Lanham 1967 'The Literal Britomart' *MLQ* 28:426–45; Lewis 1936; Miskimin 1978; Quilligan 1983; K. Williams 1966.

Browne, William, of Tavistock (1591?-1643?) Spenserian poet who attended Oxford and the inns of court. The Earls of Pembroke were his patrons, and his friends included such noted Spenserians as Drayton, Wither, and John Davies of Hereford. His poems eulogize Colin Clout and his works, most extensively in *Britannia's Pastorals* 2.1.986–1004, where Colin (addressed by the narrator as 'Divinest Spenser, heav'n-bred, happy Muse') sings to the goddess Thetis of 'th'heroic knights of fairyland' until he is interrupted by angels and carried off to heaven, 'where now he sings the praise / Of him that is the first and last of days.' There follows mention of a projected monument to Spenser which was thwarted by 'All-guilty Avarice' (1011–44).

Of Browne's minor poems, the six extant sonnets of his *Visions* imitate Spenser's own emblematic visions, *Vanitie*, *Bellay*, *Petrarch*, and the 'tragicke Pageants' which conclude *Ruines of Time*. Browne's first sonnet recalls the opening of *Vanitie*, and the swan and garden images in sonnets 3 and 5 echo *Time* (589–95, 519–32); but while Spenser's visions treat time and death generally, Browne's hint at specific topical allusions. Sonnet 4 in *Caelia* (a series of 14 sonnets) directly refers to 'heavenly Spenser's wit.' Browne's translation from du Bellay's *Antiquitez* sonnet 3 is based on Janus Vitalis' Latin version rather than on Spenser's *Rome*. His masque of Circe acted at the Inner Temple (Jan 1615) suggests parallels with *FQ* II, but Circe, unlike Phaedria or Acrasia, is sympathetically and romantically portrayed.

Browne's two major works are strongly Spenserian. *The Shepheards Pipe* (1614) contains seven eclogues by Browne which imitate *The Shepheardes Calender*. Cuttie is the poet Christopher Brooke, and Philarete is Browne's friend Thomas Manwood; 'Willie' (who represents Browne as Colin represented Spenser) echoes *October* in seeking to arouse Cuttie's poetic ambitions (Eclogue 5), and the elegy on Philarete (Eclogue 4) recalls Colin's elegy on Dido in *November*.

The Shepheardes Calender is clearly the model for Browne's distinctively English rusticity and his creation of a consistent, substantial shepherd community (repeated in the framework of *Britannia's Pastorals*). His shepherds have English names (sometimes from Spenser: Piers, Thomalin, Hobbinoll, Palinode), the diction intermittently echoes Spenser's rustic archaisms, and the verse forms recall *The Shepheardes Calender* (although without precisely imitating any of Spenser's elaborate stanzas). However, nature is depicted more realistically than in Spenser's stylized, symbolic landscapes, with less mythology and pathetic fallacy; and there is no seasonal motif as a unifying formal principle. His shepherd-poets face open rivalry and animosity instead of neglect. In his eclogues, common experience and social and economic relations replace Spenser's universal themes of love, art, time, age, and death.

Britannia's Pastorals (Book 1, 1613; Book 2, 1616; ms fragment of Book 3) may be the most elaborate attempt ever made to imitate *The Faerie Queene* with respect to its atmosphere of romance, general structure, and interlacing of many subplots. Specific parallels include the 'cruel swain' who wounds Doridon and abducts Marina, somewhat as Sansloy abducts Una from Archimago (*BP* 1.2.609–47, *FQ* I iii). Marina's subsequent voyage with her abductor recalls Florimell in the Fisher's boat (*BP* 1.2.761–812, *FQ* III viii 21–8). Marina is imprisoned by Famine, as Florimell by Proteus and Amoret by Lust (*BP* 2.1.495–816; *FQ* III viii 41, IV vii 8). Like Florimell, Marina obtains release after her lament is overheard (*FQ* IV xii, *BP* 2.5.905–56).

Meanwhile, Doridon is found by his mother and cured by a hermit in a homelier parallel to Marinell's rescue and cure by Tryphon (*BP* 1.3.1–146; *FQ* III iv, IV xi 6–7). Remond and Doridon search for Fida and fear the worst on seeing her dead hind's traces, as Satyrane does on seeing Florimell's slain palfrey (*BP* 2.2.393–415, *FQ* III vii 30–1). *BP* 2.2 ends with a weeping swain, a huntress, and a savage who respectively recall the disconsolate Timias, Belphoebe, and Lust (IV vii-viii). The river-nymph Walla (*BP* 2.3.763–850) also suggests Belphoebe.

However, *Britannia's Pastorals* is basically pastoral, whereas *The Faerie Queene* uses pastoral at chosen points for special purposes. The symbolic functions of Spenser's pastoral thus grow diffuse and often disappear in Browne's poem. As in *The Faerie Queene*, there are inset myths about classical gods (Pan and his love, 2.4; Cupid and Psyche, 3.2) and objects of nature (Walla and Tavy, 2.3; cf especially the nymph in *FQ* II ii 7–9). Browne's setting is touched with the romantic and mythic lights of Spenser's imaginary landscape, but it is localized in Browne's native Devonshire and is more vividly detailed.

Although *Britannia's Pastorals* lacks a sustained allegory, it does have allegorical interludes, the most extensive being the story of Riot and his repentance (1.4–5). Riot derives from Spenser's Furor and Ate (*FQ* II iv, IV i), but his reform and transformation in the house of Repentance resemble the Red Cross Knight's sojourn in the house of Holiness (I x). With this story is woven the career of Aletheia or Truth, a figure suggesting Spenser's Una. Here Idya (England) mourning Henry, Prince of Wales, recalls Spenser's desolated Belge (V x). Both poets strongly embraced the Protestant cause, and Geryon is again Spain (*BP* 1.5.147). Moreover, Aletheia is 'chiefest consort of the Fairy Queen' (1.5.364); the praise of Elizabeth which follows recalls Spenser's political myth. Later, Spenser's skill at satirical allegory is recalled in the grotesque figures of Limos and Athliot (Famine and Wretchedness; *BP* 2.1.495–547, 2.5.311–78). But the diminutive fairies of *BP* 3 are worlds away from Spenser's noble race of Faerie.

Browne's allegorical sequences suggest the symbolic 'cores' of each book of *The Faerie Queene*; but unlike Spenser's, their themes do not inform the body of the narrative. They appear rather as departures or digressions, alongside direct, nonallegorical discussions of politics, poetry, and other topics. This digressive mode of composition contrasts with Spenser's organic sense of form, relevance, and interrelation.

Yet *Britannia's Pastorals* embodies a genuinely Spenserian tradition: intricate romance narrative in an idealized setting, passing at times into open allegory, reaching out towards moral concerns on the one hand and politics, society, literature, and culture on the other. Verbal echoes of Spenser's other works as well as *The Faerie Queene* are too pervasive to note. Browne may not imitate the deeper structural and intellectual design of *The Faerie Queene*, but he gauges and reproduces the primary impact of Spenser's imagination.

SUKANTA CHAUDHURI

William Browne 1894 *Poems* ed Gordon Goodwin, 2 vols (London); an edition of Browne's *The Masque of the Inner Temple (Ulysses and Circe)* ed R.F. Hill appears in *A Book of Masques in Honour of Allardyce Nicoll* (Cambridge 1967) pp 179–206. See also Herbert Ellsworth Cory 1911 'Browne's *Britannia's Pastorals* and Spenser's *The Faerie Queene*' *UCC* 13:189–200; Grundy 1969; Frederic W. Moorman 1897 *William Browne* (Strasbourg).

Browning, Elizabeth Barrett (1806–61) References to Spenser in Elizabeth Barrett Browning's letters and notebooks begin in her twenty-first year and continue throughout her life, indicating that her knowledge of his works, especially *The Faerie Queene*, was comprehensive, acquired early, and easily recalled. This ready knowledge, as well as her respect for his poetic craftsmanship, made quotations from his works a natural choice in 1843 when she was asked to supply mottoes for the forthcoming publication *A New Spirit of the Age*. In her poem *A Vision of Poets*, she includes Spenser in the list of honored poets (346–8). In her rhymed romance *Lady Geraldine's Courtship*, she gives her hero the task of wooing his beloved Geraldine by reading her 'the pastoral parts of Spenser' (stanza 40).

Her references to Spenser followed naturally from her high opinion of his work, stated most fully in her anonymous review of an anthology called *The Book of the Poets* (Browning 1842). Here she describes *The Faerie Queene* as 'the great allegorical poem of the world' and declares that 'Spenser's business is with the lights of the world, and the lights beyond the world.' In reviewing the English poets before Spenser, she claims that only Chaucer has a comparably lofty and kingly stature; she finds both to be 'the most cheerful-hearted of the poets,' yet notes a difference between them: 'Chaucer has a cheerful humanity: Spenser, a cheerful ideality. One rejoices walking on the sunny side of the street: the other, walking out of the street in a way of his own, kept green by a blessed vision ... One holds festival with men ... the other adopts for his playfellows, imaginary or spiritual existences.' These existences, however, were not always pleasing to her. In her diary for 1831, she describes Spenser's poetry as 'too immaterial for our sympathies to enclasp it firmly. It reverses the lot of human plants: its roots are in the air, not earth!' (ed 1969:102). In *A Vision of Poets* she describes Spenser's poetry as perhaps too visionary: 'And Spenser drooped his dreaming head / (With languid sleep-smile you had said / From his own verse engendered.) / On Ariosto's till they ran / Their curls in one.' Yet in spite of this criticism, she writes in the *Athenaeum* review that 'we miss no humanity in [*The Faerie Queene*] because we make a new humanity out of it and are satisfied in our human hearts.' Indeed, her admiration for Spenser's poetics was unbounded. In the same review she declares, 'But never issued there from lip or instrument, or the tuned causes of nature, more lovely sound than we gather from our Spenser's Art.' His rhythm she describes as 'the singing of an angel in a dream' (p 522).

As one might expect from this sustained praise, EBB assimilated many qualities of Spenser's verse. Her greatest debt to him is in diction and rhythm. A comparison of their concordances indicates how frequently she scattered Spenserian language throughout her work. Her style has even been described as 'Spenserian language combined with Byronic emotions' (Hayter 1962:24). A letter of 1826 shows most clearly the influence of his rhythm on her poetry (Kelley and Hudson 1984, 1:246). Here she defends her practice of changing the established accent of a word according to its position in a line by naming Spenser as her authority and by quoting specific examples from *The Faerie Queene* to prove her point (I xii 41; II i 42, 50; ii 19). G.K. Chesterton describes her as 'Elizabethan in her luxuriance and her audacity, and the gigantic scale of her wit' (1903:263); and no doubt her early, intensive study of Spenser shaped her general poetic style. KAY R. MOSER

Elizabeth Barrett Browning 1969 *Diary by E.B.B.* ed Philip Kelley and Ronald Hudson (Athens, Ohio); Browning 1974 *Poetical Works* intro Ruth M. Adams (Boston). G.K. Chesterton 1903 *Varied Types* (New York); Alethea Hayter 1962 *Mrs. Browning: A Poet's Work and Its Setting* (London); Philip Kelley and Ronald Hudson, eds 1984 *The Brownings' Correspondence* 6 vols (Winfield, Kans).

Browning, Robert (1812–89) The extent of Spenser's influence finds a test case in Browning's poetry, where a paucity of direct borrowings and a contrary poetic manner mask deeper connections with Spenserian material, structure, and sensibility. Even the superficial tonal contrast reveals similarities in the ways each poet approaches his craft. Whereas Keats and Tennyson are the major nineteenth-century followers of Spenser's musical lead, Browning imitates him otherwise, and perhaps more authentically, in forging a literary idiolect out of past poetry. His prosody and diction indeed derive partly from Spenser's, as in the increasingly alliterative treatment of pentameter from *The Ring and the Book* (1868–9) onwards, or in such archaisms as *all and some* (passim) and the uniquely Spenserian *grail* (for *gravel*) at *Sordello* 6.382 (1840).

Letters Browning wrote in 1837 and 1840 allude casually to *Faerie Queene* I viii 40 and V vii 31; a very late letter of 1889 misquotes line 100 of *Visions of the Worlds Vanitie* and misattributes it to *Visions of Bellay* (Browning ed 1950:12, 21; ed 1976:53). At the beginning and the close of the quest romance 'Childe Roland' (1855), Spenserian precedents have been proposed for the 'hateful cripple' (Archimago, Ignaro) and for the 'slughorn' (Arthur's and Britomart's horns; cf *FQ* I viii 3–5, V vii 27); and it has been argued that 'Love among the Ruins' (1855) owes imagistic and thematic debts to *Ruines of Time* and *Ruines of Rome* (Golder 1924:968–71, Thornton 1968:178–9). The intrusive narrator of *Sordello* is described at 3.597 as an 'archimage,' and the highly personal 'Numpholeptos' (1876) allegorizes the speaker's relations with his muse-beloved as a series of incomplete quests reminiscent of *The Faerie Queene*.

These allusions, which span the whole of Browning's career, suggest that he read all of Spenser, could recall his reading in some detail, and did so in central texts. Further, most of his Spenserian references point to a set of mutability *topoi*, stressing the epistemological ambiguity of appearances and an ethic whereby prideful works precipitate spiritual falls. Taken together, Browning's scattered textual echoes testify to affiliations with the imaginative traditions of English Protestantism (Maynard 1977:324). Spenser, whose likeness hung beside Milton's (and later Bunyan's) in his study, represented for him the first native exponent of an elaborate yet iconoclastic art scrupulously alert to its own limits.

Browning's Protestant drive and his particular brand of Victorian historicism converged upon subjects drawn from Renaissance art and Reformation thought, fields of interest he was among the first to regard with modern eyes. His knowledge of Spenser and extraordinary familiarity with Neoplatonic speculations, Renaissance magical treatises, and emblem books quickened Browning's apprehension of mutability. Even his phenomenology of the 'infinite moment' ('By the Fire-side' [1855]) or 'good minute' ('Two in the Campagna' [1855]) acknowledges, as do Spenser's epiphanies, the presence of the past and the pressure of the future – in a literary tradition no less than in a life well led. 'All good stories, fairy or otherwise,' Browning wrote in 1846, 'are *meant* for grown-up men' (ed 1933:12). He stood in relation to the Romantics much as Spenser had stood in relation to the romances; and, like Spenser, he used the conventions of romance in correctively ironic yet affirmative ways. Browning's chivalric and fairy imagery typically form part of a plot of constructive disillusionment, where naive romanticizing is repudiated to secure a basis for the worldlier romancing of fancy with fact.

'This was the place!' the questing knight Roland discovers at length, and the cabalistic musician Abt Vogler (1864) likewise comes to rest in 'The C Major of this life.' But for both of Browning's speakers, as for Redcrosse and Colin Clout, the dilation of being that transpires at such a moment of natural repose remains tempered by a thirst for grace: 'Infinite passion, and the pain / Of finite hearts that yearn' ('Two in the Campagna'). Neoplatonic, Gnostic, alchemical, Protestant (see Bieman 1970, Matthews 1965, Waters 1977), Spenser and Browning both sound a dominant chord of unfulfilled hope: the desire of the imperfect soul for the 'Sabaoths sight' and the 'Sabbaoth God' who enables it (*FQ* VII viii 2). Politically, too, both Spenser and Browning are most at ease when writing home-thoughts from abroad to an England they love best from afar. Browning's occasional jingoism and Spenser's patriotic idealizations serve each poet as a compensation for his marginality. At once exiles and voluntary expatriates, both poets find themselves 'in-dwellers' (VII vi 55) in elective homes, which lie far from their biographical beginnings yet give access to the adult sources of creativity.

Within the tradition of English Protestantism, Spenser's challenging example endorsed the preeminence of epic but raised doubts whether the genre could successfully embrace individual effort and cultural history within a Protestant perspective. The affinities between Browning's two most ambitious works and *The Faerie Queene* are instructive for students of either poet. The six-book epic *Sordello* offers a number of parallels with *The Faerie Queene*'s symmetries. Both split into mirroring halves: in each, the fourth book resumes an action that the third has left conspicuously hanging, the second and fifth submit achieved private virtues to various public tests, and the sixth constitutes a reprise of personal struggles that the first has settled more handily. In each poem, these struggles are at last resolved – if at all – only by the intervention of a figure of the poet himself, who thereby becomes implicated in his fiction in ways that highlight the difficulties of trying (in a Protestant epic) to mediate between the cultural and the personal. Spenser's answer to these difficulties is to pluralize the epic world by situating his several protagonists in each other's contexts (Redcrosse and Guyon, Britomart and Artegall). Browning is his epic successor in carrying such strategies to the extremes of *The Ring and the Book*. In this work, moreover, he seeks to limit the relativism his Protestant strategies appear to invite, by basing his own interpretation of the documentary facts upon the archetypal myth of St George. And of that myth, which informs Browning's life as well as his writings, the most memorable instance remains *Faerie Queene* I (see DeVane 1947, Langbaum 1966). HERBERT F. TUCKER

Robert Browning 1933 *Letters* ed Thurman L. Hood (London); Browning 1950 *New Letters* ed William Clyde DeVane and Kenneth Leslie Knickerbocker (New Haven); Browning 1976 'Letters from Robert Browning to the Rev J.D. Williams, 1874–1889' ed Thomas J. Collins and Walter J. Pickering *BIS* 4:1–56; Browning 1981 *Poems* ed John Pettigrew, 2 vols (New Haven).

Elizabeth Bieman 1970 'An Eros *Manqué*: Browning's *Andrea del Sarto*' *SEL* 10:651–68; William C. DeVane 1947–8 'The Virgin and the Dragon' *YR* ns 37:33–46; Harold Golder 1924 'Browning's *Childe Roland*' *PMLA* 39:963–78; Robert Langbaum 1966 'Browning and the Question of Myth' *PMLA* 81:575–84; Jack Matthews 1965 'Browning and Neoplatonism' *VN* 28:9–12; John Maynard 1977 *Browning's Youth* (Cambridge, Mass); R.K.R. Thornton 1968 'A New Source for Browning's "Love among the Ruins"' *N&Q* 213:178–9; D. Douglas Waters 1977 'Mysticism, Meaning, and Structure in Browning's "Saul"' *BIS* 5:75–86.

Bruin, Matilde The story of Sir Bruin, recounted by his wife Matilde, forms the second of two linked, parallel episodes comprising *FQ* VI iv. In the first, Calepine and his lady Serena are rescued from the villainous Turpine by the fortuitous intrusion of the Salvage Man, magically impervious to injury and never before moved by compassion, who treats their wounds and takes them deep into the forest to recuperate. In the second (17–38), Calepine, wandering alone and unarmed, encounters a 'cruell Beare' with a baby between its bloody jaws. Unhampered by armor, Calepine gives chase and, in his turn, becomes a rescuer by thrusting a stone into the bear's gorge and then strangling it. Against all expectations, the baby is uninjured; and Calepine, now lost, carries it until sunset when by good fortune he escapes the forest to discover Matilde lamenting the 'cruell fate' of childlessness. Sir Bruin has defeated the giant Cormoraunt in three battles and now rules the land in peace; but Cormoraunt bides his time, constantly threatening and increasingly bold, as Bruin grows older and lacks an heir, despite a prophecy that 'there should to him a sonne / *Be gotten, not begotten*' who would kill the fiend. Calepine's foundling would seem to fulfill the prophecy, and Matilde accepts the baby to raise as her own.

Both episodes are digressions from the story of Calidore's quest to subdue the Blatant Beast, and they display a traditional pattern of fairy tale: the hero (Calepine, Bruin) requires fortuitous aid from a magical helper (Salvage Man, stone, baby) against a villain (Turpine, bear, Cormoraunt). The progressively deeper withdrawal into the wilderness, although digressive, involves motifs basic to Calidore's quest; but these are reduced to their fundamentals in the elements of fairy tale. The Salvage Man complements the bear: courtesy and its antithesis are rooted equally in untutored instinct, but the former signifies humanity and the latter, brutishness. Calidore's 'No greater shame to man then inhumanitie' (VI i 26) proclaims the essential villainy of Book VI; but the bear's 'inhumanity' is mere instinct without volition, a fairy-tale villainy vulnerable to the most primitive of weapons. Calepine, although helpless against Turpine's inhumanity, conquers its fairy-tale equivalent with ease and finality.

Yet Bruin's defeat of Cormoraunt, like Calidore's of the Blatant Beast, is conditional and temporary; and his need for an heir marks the transcending of fairy tale and its limited ethos. He does not live happily ever after. His defeat of Cormoraunt 'in three battailes' recalls the three-day battle with the Dragon in Book I, while it contrasts sharply with Redcrosse's absolute victory. Like the Dragon, Cormoraunt is a spiritual threat whose 'daily vaunt' signals a brooding, potential menace to Bruin's quiet state; metaphorically, he is the stemmed flood embodied in the 'next brooke,' threatening an 'endlesse losse' preventable only if the promised son 'should drinke ... dry' the brook. (The cormoraunt, *corvus marinus*, is a sea-raven, etymologically linked in the sixteenth century with *corvus vorans*, devouring.) The prophecy echoes Isaiah's Messianic vision (Isa 34) that when Edom lies waste 'the pelicane [cormorant] ... shal possesse it' (Isa 34.11) but also John's prophecy that at the end 'there was no more sea' (Rev 21.1) and recalls Spenser's account of Merlin's conception: 'wondrously begotten ... On a faire Ladie Nonne, that whilome hight / *Matilda*' (*FQ* III iii 13). Such allusions from the Bible and Arthurian legend give Calepine's foundling a place in Spenser's allegory of providential order in English history and a spiritual resonance transcending the magical invulnerability of fairy tale he shares with the Salvage Man.

The baby also resembles Ruddymane, orphaned by the excesses of Amavia and Mortdant (II i-ii), whom Guyon delivers into the foster care of Medina (II iii 2), embodiment of the golden mean. This parallel suggests that Matilde and Bruin, like Medina, represent self-control, an implication fortified by the pun deriving Bruin's name from *bear*. The bear, described principally as a creature of jaws and teeth, anticipates the Blatant Beast (VI 9, XII 27–8) and serves as paradigm for destructive appetites shown by the villains throughout Book VI who, like Cormoraunt, add a will to destroy to the bear's brute instinct. The cormorant commonly symbolizes voraciousness, and the impending threat to Bruin's state comes metaphorically from the literal 'incontinence' of a brook flooding its banks. Bruin owes both his control of Cormoraunt and his appropriateness as a protector of the child rescued from his namesake to his mastery over the instinctive 'bear' within. Insofar as the baby will fulfill the prophecy to continue and complete the mastery of Cormoraunt when he drinks dry the brook and enforces 'continence,' he functions less as a traditional magical helper than as a symbol of redemptive potential in the human spirit to control the roots of inhumanity in its own destructive instincts.

Bruin and his foundling, like the bear and Cormoraunt, anticipate other figures. The helper is seen in the Hermit, whose aegis is explicitly spiritual, as well as the ring of 'Nymphes and Faeries' protecting the Graces on Mount Acidale from 'all noysome things' (X 7). The foundling's antithesis is Pastorella, who cannot save the quiet pastoral state from destruction and who precipitates the death of her protector. Meliboe is Bruin without the child; and the doomed shepherd's words, like the child, confute Matilde's lamentation on fortune in a strong echo from Boethius: 'In vaine ... doe men / The heavens of their fortunes faulte accuse, ... Sith each unto himselfe his life may fortunize' (IX 29–30), a doctrine reechoed in the Hermit's prescription of self-control as cure for the physically untreatable bite of the Blatant Beast itself (VI 14). Such parallels generalize the significance of these episodes, giving narrative digressions status as paradigms of theme and structure.

MICHAEL F.N. DIXON

Sverre Arestad 1947 'Spenser's *Faery* and *Fairy*' *MLQ* 8:37–42; Ashton 1957; Michael F.N. Dixon 1974–5 'Fairy Tale, Fortune, and Boethian Wonder: Rhetorical Structure in Book VI of *The Faerie Queene*' *UTQ* 44:141–65; Alexander Haggerty Krappe 1930 *The Science of Folklore* (London); Latham 1930.

Bruno, Giordano (1548–1600) The Italian iconoclastic humanist Giordano Bruno, irascible, vain, and flamboyant as he was, could not have been more different in temperament from Spenser. Yet temperamental difference has little to do with influence, and on the face of it the possibility of a connection between them seems strong. Bruno was in England from 1583 to 1585, published several of his works there, and dedicated two of them to Sidney (*Lo spaccio de la bestia trionfante* 1584 and *De gli eroici furori* 1585). Spenser had already been introduced into the Sidney circle by 1579, as he indicates in his letter to Harvey of 16 October (*Two Letters* 1).

Attractive though a Bruno-Sidney-Spenser connection is, however, it cannot be proved. Presumably Sidney had read some Bruno, yet he may not have; Spenser's curious mind could have led him to Bruno, yet we cannot say with certainty that it did. It is worth noting that the question even of Bruno's motives in dedicating *Lo spaccio* and the *Eroici furori* to Sidney, let alone of Bruno's influence on Sidney, remains problematic (Weiner 1980–1). One must be even more cautious in considering any relationship between Spenser and Bruno.

Bruno was one of the principal Hermetic-Cabalistic philosophers of the Renaissance. His espousal of Copernicanism, as in *La cena de le ceneri* and *De l'infinito, universo e mondi* (both 1584), is not so much 'modern' as mystical, a part of his recognition that everything is central in a universe in which nothing is eccentric because, as pantheistic Platonism recognizes, the whole is in the part and the part in the whole. Or, as Bruno writes in *Lo spaccio*, 'Natura est deus in rebus' (Nature is God in all things, ed 1964a:235). His Platonism – or, more strictly, Neoplatonism – posits that through knowledge, exertion of the will, and above all love, one can discover the divine principle within oneself as well as in the external world. This minor variant on 'Natura est deus in rebus' is the message that emerges particularly from the elaborately emblematic *Eroici furori*, where it is embodied in the concept of the possessed lover or 'heroic enthusiast' (for a contemporary parody of the Brunian lover, see Berowne in Shakespeare's *Love's Labor's Lost* IV iii). Lastly, Bruno possessed a vision of a Christian commonwealth, of a united Christendom purged of schism. This again was a corollary of his view of the universe as simultaneously infinite and one.

Unfortunately, Bruno's Christianity was found heretical and he was burned at the stake. *Lo spaccio*, where his concern with Christian union is most clearly expressed, seems remarkably close to the natural and magical religion of the pure Egypt of the Hermetic *Asclepius* dialogue (ed 1964a:241–2). For him, as for others, Christianity was completely compatible with Hermeticism and natural magic, including astrology and belief in the sympathetic power of stellar 'influence.' Hence *Lo spaccio* is an astrological fable ostensibly about reforming the heavens by replacing corrupt constellations with their pure equivalents.

What, then, can we conclude about Bruno in relation to Spenser? First, the many apparent similarities between their works are likely to be the result of coincidence or common sources. Second, although we would expect to find explicit allusions to or recognition of the *Eroici furori*, Bruno's most popular work, in the *Amoretti*, *Fowre Hymnes*, and *FQ* III and IV, we do not. (Sidney, in contrast, may acknowledge Bruno in the 'furie' of *Astrophil and Stella* 74.) More positively, however, the Fortune of Bruno's *Lo spaccio* may have influenced Spenser's Mutabilitie (see Levinson 1928, Pellegrini 1943, Nohrnberg 1976:745). Moreover, Bruno's missionary zeal in *Lo spaccio*, expressed through an astrological and 'Egyptian' outlook, may have influenced the astrological and Protestant imperial outlook of *The Faerie Queene* (Yates 1979:105). Some of the poem's Egyptian elements and *chronographiae* may be indebted to Bruno (Brooks-Davies 1983, ch 1). Yet these are perhaps only beginnings. It may be that Spenser's moving and exuberant delight in the minute particulars of the phenomenal world and his sense of its absolute unity owe something at least to Bruno's conviction that the One is present in the Many (as in *De l'infinito*). Possibly the astrological program of *Lo spaccio*, complete with constellation star totals, offers a partial explanation of Spenser's stellar numerology (Fowler 1964). The influence of Bruno on Spenser has yet to be fully mapped. DOUGLAS BROOKS-DAVIES

The principal Italian dialogues are *La Cena de le Ceneri* 1584 (*The Ash Wednesday Supper* tr Stanley L. Jaki [The Hague 1975]; tr Edward A. Gosselin and Lawrence S. Lerner [Hamden, Conn 1977]); *De la causa, principio e uno* 1584 (*Cause, Principle and Unity* tr Jack Lindsay [Castle Hedingham, Essex 1962]); *De gli eroici furori* 1585 (*The Heroic Frenzies* tr Paul Eugene Memmo, Jr [Chapel Hill 1964b]); *Lo spaccio de la bestia trionfante* 1584 (*The Expulsion of the Triumphant Beast* tr Arthur D. Imerti [New Brunswick, NJ 1964a]). These Italian texts, representing a fraction of the author's mostly Latin work, are gathered in Giordano Bruno 1972 *Dialogi Italiani* ed Giovanni Aquilecchia, 3rd ed with notes by Giovanni Gentile (Florence).

General studies include Dorothea Waley Singer 1950 *Giordano Bruno: His Life and Thought* (New York) with a translation of Bruno's *De l'infinito* (*On the Infinite Universe and Worlds*) and, of singular importance, Yates 1964; Kristeller 1964 has a chapter on Bruno. For Bruno in England, see Grant McColley 1937 'William Gilbert and the English Reputation of Giordano Bruno' *AnnSci* 2:353–4; Robert McNulty 1960 'Bruno at Oxford' *RN* 13:300–5; Andrew D. Weiner 1980–1 'Expelling the Beast: Bruno's Adventures in England' *MP* 78:1–13; and Yates 1979. See also Ronald B. Levinson 1928 'Spenser and Bruno' *PMLA* 43:675–81 and Angelo M. Pellegrini 1943 'Bruno, Sidney, and Spenser' *SP* 40:128–44. Other literary discussions include Brooks-Davies 1983, Fowler 1964, and Nohrnberg 1976.

Bryskett, Lodowick (c 1546–1612) About six years older than Spenser, Bryskett attended Trinity College, Cambridge, but not while Spenser was at Pembroke Hall. The two were friends for more than twenty years, worked closely together in the civil service in Ireland, and shared their interests in philosophy. Spenser addresses him in *Amoretti* 33, and in *Astrophel* includes two of his poems in memory of Sidney: 'The Mourning Muse of Thestylis' and 'A Pastorall Aeglogue upon the Death of Sir Phillip Sidney Knight.' He may be the 'Thestylis' in *Colin Clout* 156–62 and 651–9, and in 'Clorinda' 97–102. Spenser is one of the interlocutors in Bryskett's prose dialogue, *A Discourse of Civill Life* (1606).

Lodovico or Lodowick was the son of Antonio Bruschetto, a wealthy Anglo-Italian merchant. He first served in Ireland in 1565 under Sir Henry Sidney and later participated in Philip Sidney's European grand tour (1572–4). Spenser may have met Bryskett in London with Sidney, and in 1581 and 1582 both were serving in Dublin under the Lord Deputy, Lord Grey of Wilton. Though Bryskett was Clerk of the Council in Dublin about 1575 to 1582, he was not appointed Secretary of State for Ireland, as Lord Grey recommended, so that he withdrew, as he wrote, 'to the quietness of my intermitted studies' (ed 1970:4). Bryskett often used Spenser as his assistant and made certain sinecures possible for him. Spenser was Bryskett's deputy clerk of the Council of Munster from about 1584 to 1589.

After 1582, while he was in retirement in Ireland, Bryskett finished his translation of Cintio's *Tre dialoghi della vita civile* (the second, nonnarrative part of *De gli hecatommithi* [*Hundred Tales*] of 1565); these dialogues became the bulk of Bryskett's own *Discourse*. He also used small parts of ethical treatises by two other sixteenth-century Italians: Alessandro Piccolomini's *Della institutione morale* (1560) and Stefano Guazzo's *La civil conversatione* (1574). His translation is notably accurate in an age when paraphrase rather than literal rendering was the rule. Following the tradition of the prose dialogue, he frames his translated materials with original, fictional settings introducing Cintio's three dialogues, each of which is devoted to one day's discussion. The first day's dialogue projects the ideal education of the child; the second treats the instruction of the young man from childhood into his twenties; and the final, longest section thoroughly examines the flowering of all the active virtues in the mature man.

Bryskett produces a frame narrative of charming verisimilitude. He offers the 'first fruites' of his study to Lord Grey, reassigning Cintio's speakers to himself and a group of nine friends who visit him in his cottage outside Dublin. Early in the text, he invites Spenser to speak on moral philosophy ('knowing him to be not onely perfect in the Greek tongue, but also very well read in Philosophie, both morall and naturall'); but Spenser asks to be excused 'at this time,' for he says they all know that

> I have already undertaken a work tending to the same effect, which is in *heroical verse*, under the title of a *Faerie Queene*, to represent all the moral vertues, assigning to every vertue, a Knight to be the patron and defender of the same: in whose actions and feates of armes and chivalry, the operations of that vertue, whereof he is the protector, are to be expressed, and the vices and unruly appetites that oppose themselves against the same, to be beaten downe and overcome. Which work, as I have already well entred into, if God shall please to spare me life that I may finish it according to my mind, your wish (M. *Bryskett*) will be in some sort accomplished. (ed 1970:21–2)

Spenser suggests, instead, that Bryskett read his translation of Cintio, 'comprehending all the Ethick part of Moral Philosophy.' The company agrees to help in its revision by listening to and discussing Bryskett's manuscript, though they 'shewed an extreme longing after [Spenser's] worke of the *Faerie Queene*, whereof some parcels had bin by some of them seene' (p 23).

This mixture of truth and fiction is sustained in the opening and closing of each part of Bryskett's treatise, which 'is by way of dialogue ... to discourse upon the morall vertues, yet not omitting the intellectuall, to the end to frame a gentleman fit for civill conversation, and to set him in the direct way that leadeth him to his civill felicitie' (p 6). The *Discourse*, then, offers in a prose dialogue materials presented in Sidney's *Arcadia* and Spenser's *Faerie Queene* (Mills 1973). THOMAS E. WRIGHT

Bryskett ed 1970; Bryskett ed 1972; Henley 1928; Jenkins 1932; Deborah Jones 1933 'Lodowick Bryskett and His Family' in *Thomas Lodge and Other Elizabethans* ed Charles J. Sisson (Cambridge, Mass) pp 243–361; Judson 1945; Judson 1947; Mills 1973; Mustard 1914; Henry R. Plomer and Tom Peete Cross 1927 *The Life and Correspondence of Lodowick Bryskett* (Chicago); Quinn 1966; Spens 1934:139–44.

buildings There are two major critical approaches to Spenser's many castles, fortifications, temples, theaters, dungeons, rooms, and ruins. The first is taken by Coleridge who views the topography and, by implication, the buildings of *The Faerie Queene* as 'mental' spaces, 'truly in land of Faery' ('Spenser' 1818, in ed 1936:36), and the second by Warton (1754), who identifies some of the buildings in Fairyland as actual places in Elizabethan London and its environs.

Some of Spenser's buildings have clear literary origins. The contrasted dwellings of Lucifera and Caelia or of Alma and Acrasia originate in such allegorical structures as those of Fame and Rumor in Chaucer's *House of Fame*, the Palaces of Worldly Felicity and of Virtue in Jean Cartigny's *Wandering Knight* (Eng tr 1581), or the buildings belonging to the lustful Alcina and the rational Logistilla in Ariosto's *Orlando furioso* (6, 10). The women in Spenser's poetry are frequently described as buildings (eg, the bride in *Epithalamion* 177–80 or Serena in *FQ* VI viii 42) in the tradition of earlier allegorical narratives in which the Virgin is described as a holy building (the ultimate source being Song of Solomon and Revelation). The metaphor of building is one of the most frequently used in the Bible, and Spenser often compares his edifices to biblical prototypes. The house of Pride is equated with the house built upon sand (I iv 5, Matt 7.24–7), Alma's house is compared to Babel (II ix 21), the Temple of Venus is contrasted to the Temple of Solomon (IV x 30), and God is celebrated as universal architect in *Hymne of Heavenly Beautie* (36–42). Horace's *exigi monumentum* seems to be the motivating force behind *Ruines of Time*, Spenser's most explicit treatment of *ut architectura poesis*, in which the lasting monuments of poets are celebrated over the ephemeral achievements of worldly builders (400–13).

Buildings in *The Faerie Queene* are either places of 'instruction' (literally 'edifications') or places of destruction. Archimago's hermitage is a visual correlative to the enchanter's store of 'pleasing wordes' (I i 34–5): it functions as an image of verbal entrapment, as do Despair's cave (I ix 33ff), Ate's dwelling (IV i 20), the house of Sclaunder (IV viii 23), and the cave of Malengin (V ix 6). These dwellings seem to be made more of syntax than of stone. Similarly, Alma's house is as much a metaphor as a representation of an actual or recognizable Elizabethan edifice. Arthur and Guyon abandon their interest in architecture in favor of the books containing their genealogies; the castle is transformed into an 'alma mater,' both a place of instruction and a 'house' of descent.

Nevertheless, the house of Temperance and certain other buildings in *The Faerie Queene* seem remarkably substantial: the towers, porters' lodges, screens, great halls, kitchens, and gardens are recognizably Elizabethan. Even the fantastic design of Alma's house ('The frame thereof seemd partly circulare, / And part triangulare' II ix 22) is not untypical of some contemporary architecture, for example, Elizabethan houses with an *E*-shaped ground plan, Thomas Tresham's triangular lodge at Rushton (see Buxton 1963: plate 5), or the architect John Thorpe's designs, including a plan for a house in the form of his own initials. Spenser's descriptions of actual buildings are not far removed from his accounts of the seemingly fantastic structures in Fairyland: the impression of the Middle Temple in *Prothalamion* (132–6) is just as indistinct as Isis Church (*FQ* V vii), another temple of justice, which could even be modeled on the Middle Temple in Holborn. In his *Survey of London* (1598, 1603), Stow remembers the Knights Templars when passing the Middle Temple, as does Spenser in *Prothalamion* (134–6). He explains that the original function of the order was to safeguard pilgrims visiting the sepulchre; the Knights were dedicated to the stoic life and clothed all in white. His account recalls Spenser's description of the priests of Isis Church, 'All clad in linnen robes with silver hemd' (V vii 4). Furthermore, the Templars were formerly called the Knights of the Temple of Solomon. Their original temple in Jerusalem may have been an attempted reconstruction of Solomon's temple. Given Artegall's connection with Solomon (V i 26–8) and the association of Spenser's temple with justice, Isis Church may have reminded a contemporary audience of the Holborn temple.

In the *Complaints*, the poet vehemently attacks an overreaching builder generally thought to be Lord Burghley (*Mother Hubberd* 1172–80, *Time* 407–20). Burghley, Elizabeth's chief counselor, was renowned for his extensive building schemes; his great houses (Burghley House and Theobalds) are usually regarded as the most extravagant of the period. Both the house of Pride and the dwelling of Mammon may allude to his costly architecture, and may have provoked the 'mighty Peres [presumably Burghley's] displeasure' alluded to in *FQ* IV i 1 and VI xii 41.

These suggestions remain speculative, but they substantiate the impression that Spenser's buildings are not simply the 'mental' spaces posited by Coleridge but, as Warton suggests, may have some basis in fact. Spenser blends the imaginary with the actual, placing his buildings in both Fairyland and Britain: he plays the fantastic off against the factual. It is significant that some early readers refer to Spenser's poem itself as a 'building': for example, Thomas Edwards describes Spenser as a builder of a 'golden, Angellike, and modest Aulter' (*Cephalus and Procris* 1595), Richard Carew commemorates the poet's 'pallace architecture' (*A Herrings Tayle* 1598), and Sir John Roe refers to *The Faerie Queene* as a building 'some dozen Stories high' ('To Sir Nicholas Smyth' 1602). These early critical remarks, together with the frequent and extensive accounts of building in Spenser's poetry, invite the reader to interpret the various edifices as places from which to view the poet's allegorical structure as a whole.

references to buildings A list of Spenser's major references to buildings emphasizes the difficulties in approaching his many edifices systematically. It is sometimes difficult to know where to stop. Caves and dens have been included here because they sometimes are seen as buildings: Mammon's dwelling, although usually referred to as a cave by Spenser's readers, is only 'Like an huge cave' (II vii 28); and Merlin's dwelling is 'an hideous hollow cave (they say)' (III iii 8), but it is also a 'Bowre' which seems to have been built.

shorter poems *Theatre* sonnets 2, 3, 4, 15; *SC, Oct* 80–1; *Time*; *Teares* 580; *Gnat* 126–7, 135, 187, 562, 580; *Mother Hubberd* 1173–82, 1349–58; *Rome*; *Muiopotmos* 246, 300; *Bellay* (as *Theatre*) 2, 3, 4, 14; *Colin Clout* 285, 724–6, 776; *Amoretti* 14, 22, 54, 65; *Epithalamion* 47–53, 149, 177–80, 204–22, 299, 420–2; *HB* 126, 142, 202; *HHL* 102; *HHB* 36–42, 249; *Prothalamion* 132–9; *FQ* Ormond Sonnet.

first references in *FQ*: *Book I* Error's den (i 13); Archimago's hermitage (34); house of Morpheus (39); Corceca's cottage (iii 14); house of Pride (iv 4); Pluto's house (v 32); Lucifera's dungeon (45); secret cabin of Satyrane's father (vi 23); Orgoglio's castle and dungeon (vii 15); Despair's cave (ix 33); house of Holiness (x 3); architecture of the New Jerusalem (55); Cleopolis (58); 'brasen towre,' prison of Una's parents (xi 3); palace in Eden (xii 13).

Book II Medina's castle (ii 12); Mammon's dwelling (vii 20); Alma's castle (ix 10); Bower of Bliss (xii 42).

Book III Castle Joyous (i 31); Merlin's dwelling (iii 7); the bower of Cymoent (iv 43); Belphoebe's dwelling (v 39); arbor of Adonis (vi 44); witch's cottage (vii 6); bower of Proteus (viii 37); castle of Malbecco (51); Malbecco's 'balefull mansion' (x 58); Busirane's castle (xi 21).

Book IV castle of the tournament of Satyrane (i 9); Ate's dwelling (20); house of the Fates (ii 47); the house of Care (v 32); resting place of Britomart, Artegall, and Scudamour (vi 39); Lust's cave (vii 8); cabin of Timias (38); Sclaunder's cottage (viii 23); Corflambo's castle and dungeon (51); Poeana's bower (59); Temple of Venus (x 5); house of Proteus (xi 9).

Book V Castle of the Strond (ii 4); Pollente's castle (20); Radigund's castle and city (iv 35); Artegall's pavilion before Radigund's city gate (46); Dolon's house (vi 22); Isis Church (vii 3); castle of the Souldan (viii 45); Adicia's bower (ix 1); Malengin's cave (6); Mercilla's palace (ix 21); Belge's city and castle (x 25); Irena's palace (xii 25).

Book VI castle of Crudor (i 22); castle of Aldus (iii 2); Turpine's Castle of the Ford (37); dwelling of the Salvage Man (iv 13); hermitage and chapel (v 34); Meliboe's cottage (ix 16); dwelling of the Brigands (x 41); Castle Belgard (xii 3).

Cantos of Mutabilitie Cynthia's palace (vi 8); Jove's palace (15); Diana's bower (41); Nature's pavilion (vii 8).

DEBORAH CARTMELL

Cummings 1971; Dundas 1965 (compares the eclectic organization of *FQ* with Elizabethan architectural taste); Fowler 1964 (views Spenser's poetry alongside Neoplatonic architectural theories of proportion); Giamatti 1975 (discusses buildings in relation to patterns in the poem); Frederick Hard 1930; Hard 1931 'Spenser and Burghley' *SP* 22:219–34; Hard 1934 (Hard's pioneering but only suggestive essays are concerned with connections between Spenser's buildings and Elizabethan architecture); R.F. Hill 1970 'Spenser's Allegorical "Houses"' *MLR* 65:721–33 (the building episodes in *FQ* seen as evidence of Spenser's inconsistent allegorical method); Rathborne 1937 (includes a useful discussion of literary precursors to Spenser's episodes involving buildings).

Bunyan, John (1628–88) Spenser's *Faerie Queene* and Bunyan's *Pilgrim's Progress* belong to a long tradition of narrative allegory. The longstanding belief that *Faerie Queene* I influenced Bunyan illustrates the difficulty of isolating a work's direct indebtedness to another from their mutual involvement in a common tradition. Noting that both *Faerie Queene* I and *Pilgrim's Progress* provide a paradigm for the Christian life, Samuel Johnson proposed a connection between the two works (Boswell ed 1934–50, 2:238, for 30 April 1773); and critics up to the twentieth century have developed the case for such influence (eg, L.A.H. 1858; Kötz 1899; the fullest argument is in Bunyan ed 1859–60, 4:561–3).

The two works have four elements in common. Each includes a divine resting place where the protagonist is initiated into Christian truths (Spenser's house of Holiness and Bunyan's House Beautiful). Both Redcrosse and Christian are granted visions of a heavenly city from a mountain top. In both works the paradigm of the Christian life includes battle with a demonic monster (Spenser's Dragon and Bunyan's Apollyon). Finally, in both works the protagonist confronts despair. Despite these similar patterns, however, Bunyan's status as a mechanick preacher and his own insistence on his unlettered background make a direct connection unlikely; and parallels between the works are too general to provide a prima facie case for such indebtedness (Golder 1930, Wharey 1904). More recently, criticism has focused on their mutual familiarity with specific traditions: popular romances and religious tracts (Golder 1929, 1931), emblems (Freeman 1948), the parables which figure in sermon literature (MacNeice 1965:26–50). The two authors differ, however, in audience, construction, technique, and manipulation of sources; most importantly, Spenser knew the classics whereas Bunyan knew only the Bible.

The most fruitful discussions of their relationship have emerged among critics seeking to define allegory. As 'continuous allegories' (Frye 1957:91) or 'allegories of certainty' (Berek 1962:5), the two works portray the 'Protestant hero triumphant' and bear witness to the 'autonomy of the artist since the Reformation' (Honig 1959:79, 87). Their allegories have been contrasted in terms of two modes, 'battle' and 'progress' (Fletcher 1964:157, 160; see pp 151–61). If simplification is the basic principle of all allegory, then 'Spenser simplified as a philosopher, Bunyan as a preacher' (Freeman 1948:207). The most striking difference between them may be in their creation of characters: Spenser's characters are recognized in terms of external appearance, Bunyan's through their names and speech; the latter are more 'types' than abstractions (Freeman 1948). Alternatively, the two works may be seen as relating differently to their pre-text, which for both authors is the Bible (Quilligan 1979; see Frye 1957:194).

As Protestant writers, both Spenser and Bunyan manipulate biblical imagery and romance motifs to represent a paradigm of regeneration for the individual Christian. Both define the Christian life as solitary, full of perils, which each characterizes with stock imagery such as the prescription in Ephesians 6.11 to 'Put on the whole armor of God'; but their purposes are so different that they transform these images in diametrically opposite ways. Spenser creates a knight; Bunyan, an exile who becomes a foot soldier. Redcrosse is a 'champion of the English Protestant cause'; Christian is a 'solitary pilgrim of eternity' (Wells 1983:46). *Faerie Queene* I is a quest; *Pilgrim's Progress*, a pilgrimage. As a result, romance elements predominate in *Faerie Queene* I, whereas they are used only intermittently in *Pilgrim's Progress* (in Christian's battle with Apollyon or in his encounter with Giant Despair, for example). Bunyan does not use erotic relationships at all. The stages Christian goes through correspond clearly to the Calvinist paradigm of conversion. Redcrosse's experience, by contrast, portrays spiritual growth through a succession of failures and reflects the intrinsic difficulty of the attempt to be holy, if we conceive of that attempt as a struggle against illusion and error, lust, joylessness, and despair. Unlike Christian, Redcrosse is not Everyman: he is both more (as St George and in his relationship to England) and less (in that he is the knight of Holiness, distinct from the other classical, Christian, and aristocratic virtues celebrated in the poem). Christian is designed to encapsulate the experience of all Christians in the world, with only a few other characters such as Faithful and Hopeful to complement him; Redcrosse is more an abstraction than a type, and the development of holiness is incorporated in one chivalric adventure. Finally, Christian arrives at the heavenly city, but Redcrosse is allowed only to see it and then must return to the world. Bunyan's portrayal of the Christian life reaches closure.

Even more fundamental differences between the two works can be seen in their stated aims. Spenser's intention to 'fashion' a gentleman is far removed from Bunyan's, announced in his 'Apology,' to turn his readers into heavenly travelers. Both works begin with statements about allegory itself, and here the contrast is even more striking. Spenser emphasizes the darkness of allegory and deliberately creates a work difficult to interpret and differentiate as to its 'accidents' and 'intendments.' Events do not in themselves directly reveal meaning; meaning is discoverable only by a constant and conscious process of transposition to which the reader is invited by such signals as dislocations, riddles, and difficulties in the literal level itself, and by ornaments and allusions that invoke essential associations and ideas. The surface fiction of the knight's adventures keeps the literal and allegorical levels far apart. This distance gives the work its power, because it enlists the reader in a process which, by forcing him to explicate the poem, 'fashions' him at the same time.

Bunyan, on the other hand, acknowledges darkness as such to be indefensible and points to the Scriptures as his model for allegory, emphasizing its clarity and the impossibility of finding any more direct language to describe religious experience. He speaks metaphorically not to deflect us towards meaning but to embody directly the experiential truth about the Christian's experience; he offers the most direct mimesis possible of the way a Christian perceives his life. Differences of this kind between *The Faerie Queene* and *The Pilgrim's Progress*, more than their similarities, are essential to understanding the strategies and purposes of each. BARBARA A. JOHNSON

John Bunyan 1859–60 *Complete Works* ed Henry Stebbing, 4 vols (London; rpt Hildesheim and New York 1970). Peter Berek 1962 *The Transformation of Allegory from Spenser to Hawthorne* (Amherst, Mass); Harold Golder 1929–30 'Bunyan's Valley of the Shadow' *MP* 27:55–72; Golder 1930 'Bunyan and Spenser' *PMLA* 45:216–37; Golder 1931 'Bunyan's Giant Despair' *JEGP* 30:361–78; L.A.H. 1858 'The Poet and the Dreamer' *MethQR* 4th ser 8.40:209–27; Otto Kötz 1899 '"Faerie Queene" und "Pilgrim's Progress"' *Anglia* 22:33–80; Louis MacNeice 1965 *Varieties of Parable* (Cambridge); James Blanton Wharey 1904 *A Study of the Sources of Bunyan's Allegories* (Baltimore).

Burbon The knight whom Artegall rescues from rascals employed by the tyrant Grantorto and restores to his fickle lady Flourdelis (*FQ* v xi). He is also transparently the ex-Huguenot Henri IV, first of the Bourbon dynasty and after 1589 the lawful king; his beloved's name refers to the fleur-de-lis, royal symbol of France – much of which refused to recognize him even after his conversion to Catholicism in July 1593 (on which occasion there is no evidence he made the famous remark attributed to him, 'Paris is well worth a Mass'). The 'rude rout' includes Henri's rebellious subjects and their Spanish allies summoned by the Guise family, which headed the militantly Catholic 'League' and is represented in *FQ* v by Guizor and (implicitly) by Duessa, since Mary, Queen of Scots, was a Guise on her mother's side. Artegall's action signifies Elizabeth's aid to Henri (which Spenser exaggerates), and Artegall himself may recall either Essex or Sir John Norris. Many readers find this historical allegory irritatingly thin, but Henri had deeply stirred Spenser's England. Propaganda about him proliferated in the form of reports and poems (at first sometimes dedicated to Sidney or Leicester), creating an image for Henri not unlike that of a Spenserian knight, his victories and famous white plume noted with admiration.

(See **Burbon** Fig 1.)

Artegall's campaign shows the merciful justice of Elizabeth's foreign policy: her legitimate interference on behalf of a wronged prince. The episode is fittingly placed near the equally just interference on behalf of wronged subjects in the Belge affair. Burbon, however, has thrown away his shield (his Protestant faith; cf Eph 6.16 'the shield of faith'; see also canto xii argument). His excuses, that he acted under compulsion and that he hoped to win peace and Flourdelis, are at best inconsistent. Artegall's contempt for such weakness and ambition recalls Elizabeth's own anger and even her motto *semper eadem* (always the same); but, like Elizabeth, he nevertheless continues to help, his decision to do so emerging in stanza 57 after several *yet*s and an *albe*.

With its shabby knight and embarrassed lady, this remarkably unheroic episode demonstrates how in a fallen world even just political action unfolds through strain, confusion, and compromise. Furthermore, certain details suggest a deeper dislocation: Artegall's servant Talus, who chases Burbon's enemies, is compared to a thresher; and Burbon claims weakly that he will resume his shield when 'time doth serve.' Each in his ambiguous or parodic way points to the relationship of justice to time. As Spenser states more explicitly in the proem to Book v, our heroes, like the sun, ride a course deflected from perfection. Only during God's final threshing can we hope for full justice. ANNE LAKE PRESCOTT

On Henri IV: Maurice Andrieux 1955 *Henri IV* (Paris); Antoine, Duc de Lévis-Mirepoix 1971 *Henri IV* (Paris). On Spenser: Bennett 1942, ch 15; Greenlaw 1932; Knight 1970; Northrop 1968–9; Phillips 1969–70.

Burghley, William Cecil, Lord (1520–98) Elizabeth's Lord Treasurer and most trusted statesman did not care for poetry, and

Spenser did not care for Burghley. In *Mother Hubberds Tale*, begun probably about 1579, Spenser satirizes him as the crafty fox who increased his own treasure and built lofty towers and who 'no count made of Nobilitie' (1183) nor of soldiers, learned men, or the common people (Greenlaw in *Var* 8:571–4, Hard in *Var* 8:373–5). Spenser implies that if the Queen were to marry Alençon, Burghley would be the real ruler of England. In *Ruines of Time*, he again calls Burghley the fox and laments that learning and soldiers go unrewarded, 'For he that now welds all things at his will, / Scorns th'one and th'other in his deeper skill' (216, 440–55). Even the dedicatory sonnet to Burghley in *The Faerie Queene* (1590) declares that 'To you ... Unfitly I these ydle rimes present, / The labor of lost time, and wit unstayd: / Yet if their deeper sence be inly wayd ... Perhaps not vaine they may appeare to you.' When Spenser revised *Mother Hubberd* in 1590, he lamented 'What hell it is, in suing long to bide ... To have thy Princes grace, yet want her Peeres' (896, 901). The next year, Elizabeth rewarded him for *The Faerie Queene* by granting him a pension of £50 a year for life. Thomas Churchyard wrote rhymes to the Queen protesting that her treasurer had not paid his pension (Birch 1754, 1:131); these rhymes were wrongly attributed to Spenser in John Manningham's diary for 1602 and Thomas Fuller's *History of the Worthies of England* in 1662. But Burghley did not withhold Spenser's pension, for Exchequer accounts record regular payments of it to Spenser's agents, including his publisher, William Ponsonby (Berry and Timings 1960:254–9).

After publishing *Amoretti* in 1595, Spenser began the second part of *The Faerie Queene* by answering Burghley's sharp censure of his poems 'For praising love, as I have done of late, / And magnifying lovers deare debate; / By which fraile youth is oft to follie led, / Through false allurement of that pleasing baite, / That better were in vertues discipled, / Then with vaine poemes weeds to have their fancies fed.' 'Such ones ill judge of love, that cannot love,' he adds, 'To such therefore I do not sing at all, / But to that sacred Saint my soveraigne Queene' (IV proem). Book VI ends with the fear that Spenser's verse cannot hope to escape the Blatant Beast any more than his former work had escaped that censure 'With which some wicked tongues did it backebite, / And bring into a mighty Peres displeasure' (xii 41). The *Complaints* had been published in 1591 and then 'called in,' as both John Weever and Thomas Middleton wrote; as a result *Mother Hubberd* was omitted from the *Works* in 1611 and was not printed again until after Burghley's son Robert died in 1612.

'Burghley usually read either to improve the minds of others by his duty of censorship or to improve his own mind,' but 'he rarely read in English' (Beckingsale 1967:249–50). The books dedicated to him were often in Latin (like Camden's *Britannia*) or translated from Latin (like Golding's Caesar – but not his Ovid – and Googe's Palingenius – but not his *Eglogs, Epytaphes, and Sonettes*), or were chronicles (like Grafton's and Holinshed's) or useful books (like Ascham's *Scholemaster* and books on mathematics, gardening, and health). All the poems dedicated to him were in Latin, not English. Peele sent him a manuscript 'history of Troy in 500 Verses,' but the endorsement of Peele's letter mentions no reward (Horne 1952:105–6). The printer Richard Field apologizes for dedicating to him *The Arte of English Poesie* (1589) on 'so slender a subject, as nothing almost could be more discrepant from the gravitie of your yeeres and Honorable function.' Spenser was unfortunate in that William Cecil, a great statesman, was unable to recognize a great poet.

MARK ECCLES

B.W. Beckingsale 1967 *Burghley: Tudor Statesman, 1520–1598* (London) pp 245–60; Berry and Timings 1960; Thomas Birch 1754 *Memoirs of the Reign of Queen Elizabeth, from the Year 1581 till Her Death* 2 vols (London; rpt New York 1970); Fuller 1662, 2:220; David H. Horne 1952 *The Life and Minor Works of George Peele* in Peele ed 1952–70, vol 1; John Manningham 1976 *The Diary of John Manningham of the Middle Temple, 1602–1603* ed Robert Parker Sorlien (Hanover, NH) p 78.

Burgundy The great duchy founded in 1363 by the French king's son, Philip the Bold. Established in its full glory by Philip the Good (1419–67), it included most of what is now the French province of Burgundy, northeast France, Belgium, Luxembourg, and the Netherlands. When Charles the Rash, brother-in-law of England's Edward IV, fell at the battle of Nancy (1477), the lands that had supported Europe's most dazzling court passed to the Hapsburgs or, later, to France. Yet Burgundian culture lingered into the early sixteenth century, especially in the Low Countries (Spenser's 'Belge'), and was deliberately recalled in the 1580s by the leaders of the Netherlands' revolt against Hapsburg Spain.

Sometimes allies, sometimes enemies, England and Burgundy were tied by marriages, friendships, trade, chivalric ceremony, and the Burgundian books that Edward IV and Henry VII owned or that Caxton printed (Armstrong 1983, Green 1980, Painter 1976). Burgundy helped shape the English court's love of emblematic pageants and tournaments staged as allegorical romances, its notion of knightly honor, its taste in architecture, portraiture, and tapestry (Kipling 1977a). Even in Spenser's day, Burgundian style remained visible in older buildings and survived in court and civic entertainments. And, whether in the original French, in translation, or mediated through writers like Stephen Hawes and John Skelton, Burgundian historians and poets such as Raoul Le Fèvre, Olivier de La Marche, Guillaume Filastre, Jean Molinet, and Jean Lemaire de Belges continued to affect a culture now more impressed by Italy and France.

There is much we still do not know about Spenser and Burgundy: which texts he might have read or heard about from Flemish writers like Jan van der Noot, the possibly Burgundian element in some of the buildings, tapestries, and jousts he imagines, what fellow feeling he might have had for Burgundian court poets who served politically powerful women. In at least several areas, however, something can be said.

For example, Spenser's conception of Arthur's virtue, magnificence, includes both chivalric prowess and learning, a Burgundian emphasis (Kipling 1977a); Arthur's interest in national history (*FQ* II x) was shared by the Burgundian dukes, who were particularly enthusiastic patrons of work by historians such as Georges Chastellain and Philippe de Comines. Burgundian court pageantry, moreover, included figures found also in Spenser: hermit knights, Arthur, St George and his dragon, Hercules (popular as a purported ancestor of the dukes), and giants. Many of these also appeared in the ceremonies with which towns in the Low Countries welcomed the arrival in the 1580s of their anti-Spanish allies; when in *FQ* V x-xi Spenser allegorizes English military aid to 'Belge,' he incorporates them (Schulze 1931, Strong and van Dorsten 1964, Kipling 1977a).

It has been argued that Spenser's allegory is more Burgundian than Italian (Kipling 1977a). *The Faerie Queene* and La Marche's *Chevalier délibéré* (1483), for example, share a landscape largely disconnected from the specifics of locale and time, one in which episodes of allegorized errancy alternate with more static emblematic scenes. Such a claim, however, needs to take account of a French tradition at least as old as Bernard of Clairvaux's (12th-c) conversion of Jesus' parable of the prodigal son into an allegorical journey with personifications in the manner of Prudentius ('De fuga et reductione filii prodigi'). From Bernard's story of a youth on the horse 'Desire' who travels from error to pride to despair to vision and rapture, a line stretches through French writers like Deguileville to Lydgate in England and, in Burgundy, to La Marche and his Flemish imitator, Jean Cartigny, whose *Voyage du chevalier errant* (Antwerp 1557) probably influenced *FQ* I (Evans in Cartigny ed 1951: xxxiv ff, Cullen 1974:13–16). La Marche was translated by Stephen Bateman (*The Travayled Pylgrime* 1569) and Lewis Lewkenor (*The Resolved Gentleman* 1594); both worked from the 1553 Antwerp edition in Spanish. Cartigny's *Voyage* was translated by William Goodyear in 1581 as *The Wandering Knight*.

La Marche's urbane and nostalgic allegory gives a specifically Burgundian turn to this tradition; like Spenser, he combines an allegorical quest with dynastic homage, here an elaborate if melancholy vision of the Burgundian rulers' doomed but glorious battles with Dolor and Debility. La Marche's armed hero rides his horse 'Will' through the fields of Pleasure and Time; although accompanied by Reason or Thought, he is misled by 'that subtile stingbraine Error' (Bateman's tr of 1569: sig F3v), visits a palace of proud worldlings, and stumbles through a quaking landscape to a wasteland with (in Bateman's version) Dispaire, Dispraise, Disdaine, and Ire. After a period of recuperative instruction and further lessons in mutability from Dame Memorie, the new wise knight is ready for death. It seems likely that Spenser read La Marche, probably in Bateman's competent fourteeners with their attractive woodcuts. Militantly opposed to older Catholic customs, though, Bateman disallows La Marche's hermits and intrudes urgent doubts about the value of glory; in this regard, at least, and despite its Protestantism, *The Faerie Queene* edges back into an earlier, more Burgundian climate in which hermits and palmers are still, on occasion welcome, and knights can seek fame.

(See **Burgundy** Figs 1–2.)

Spenser may also have read the Burgundian historian and poet, Lemaire de Belges, who recounts the legendary migrations of giants and heroes into Europe and the adventures of figures such as Isis, Osiris, Hercules, and the giant Geryon (*Les Illustrations de Gaule et singularitez de Troye* 1510–13; vols 1–2 of ed 1882–91). This material was widely available, but one detail suggests that Spenser was attracted by Lemaire's association of the archaic world with Flemish matters: exactly the combination in *FQ* V. Lemaire tells of a tyrannical giant, Druon, who lived in a castle near the river Scheldt close to what is now Antwerp; he forced travelers to yield half their goods and, if anyone miscalculated, stole everything and cut off the victim's hand. At last one of Caesar's soldiers killed him, so people and property could move safely once more. The arms of Antwerp – two hands above a castle – referred to this legend, and Druon himself lived on as the city's famous giant, usually called Antigonus, the most celebrated of many Flemish ceremonial giants born in Burgundian times, often refurbished, and enlivening civic processions to this day.

Spenser must have read in Holinshed's *Chronicles* (1587) how in 1582 Druon's statue welcomed the Duke of Anjou with rueful thoughts on tyranny (other figures exhorted him to remember his Burgundian ancestry), but in any case the Antwerp giant was a celebrity. It seems likely that his story figures in *The Faerie Queene* but, as befits a criminal giant, dismembered into three textual parts. First is Artegall's beheading of the giant-like Pollente, who extorts money from those who pass his bridge (V ii 5–19). Second is Artegall's visit to the castle of Pollente's daughter Munera, whose hands (and feet) he nails 'on high, that all might them behold' (26), just like the hands above the castle in Antwerp's coat of arms. Third is the appearance of 'sterne *Druon*' in IV ix 20, who rejects 'Ladies love.' There is no known source for Druon's name (Belson 1964), but it and his hardness seem like fragments of the famous Flemish giant.

By incorporating recollections of Druon into Artegall's victory over Pollente and Munera, Spenser could remind his readers of the ruined Flemish city now subject to Spain and the Inquisition; he thus introduces early in Book V the legends and imagery he will revive when the robber giant, castle-dwelling Geryoneo of Spain, succumbs to Arthur's magnificence (X 6–xi 14). That there may also be some 'Egyptian' symbolism in the image of the mutilated Munera (Manning 1984) further indicates that in these early cantos Spenser establishes a complex of associations that recall both the primitive world and the struggles tormenting the once glorious lands where modern champions fight giants similar to those defeated long ago in Hercules' and then Caesar's time. A hero's work is never done.

ANNE LAKE PRESCOTT

For further reading, see *Belge and the following: C.A.J. Armstrong 1983 *England, France, and Burgundy in the Fifteenth Century* (London), Richard Firth Green 1980 *Poets and Princepleasers: Literature and the English Court in the Late Middle Ages* (Toronto), and Kipling 1977a, all of which cover earlier scholarship on the Burgundian court and English culture. On Burgundy, see Jean-Philippe Lecat 1982 *Quand flamboyait la Toison d'or* (Paris); and Richard Vaughan 1973 *Valois Burgundy* (London). Texts are Jean Cartigny 1951 *The Wandering Knight* tr William Goodyear (1581), ed Dorothy Atkinson Evans (Seattle), which includes the parable of Bernard of Clairvaux; Olivier de La Marche 1898 *Le Chevalier délibéré* (ed of c 1500) ed F. Lippmann (London); and Jean Lemaire de Belges 1882–91 *Oeuvres* ed J. Stecher, 2 vols (Louvain). English translations are *STC* 1585, 4700–4700.5, and 15139.

For Spenser, see Dorothy F. Atkinson 1943–4 '*The Wandering Knight*, the Red Cross Knight and "Miles Dei"' *HLQ* 7:109–34; Kipling 1977a, ch 8; Kathrine Koller 1942 '*The Travayled Pylgrime* by Stephen Batman and Book Two of *The Faerie Queene*' *MLQ* 3:535–41 (the author believed that Bateman's version was directly influenced by Cartigny, not recognizing a translation of La Marche; nor does she consider the possible influence on *FQ* I); R.J. Manning 1984 'Devicefull Sights: Spenser's Emblematic Practice in *The Faerie Queene*, V. 1–3' *SSt* 5:65–89; Anne Lake Prescott 1989 'Spenser's Chivalric Restoration: From Bateman's *Travayled Pylgrime* to the Redcrosse Knight' *SP* 86:166–97. See also George D. Painter 1976 *William Caxton* (London).

Burton, Robert (1577–1640) Oxford academic and author of *The Anatomy of Melancholy* (1621, 1624, 1628, etc), an encyclopedic treatment of morbid psychology (and much else). Although Burton's literary sources are mainly classical, he demonstrates a lively interest in contemporary English literature, and refers to or quotes from Spenser on nine occasions in the *Anatomy*. He owned copies of *Complaints* and *The Shepheardes Calender*, but does not quote either work. Although no copy of *The Faerie Queene* is listed among the books in his library, all of his seven quotations are from it, and all but one are from *FQ* III or IV. He calls Spenser 'our modern Maro' (*AM* 3.1.3), and would seem to have been attracted to the 'faithfull loves' rather than the 'Fierce warres' moralized in *The Faerie Queene*: all his quotations occur in his section on Love Melancholy, and he cites Spenser together with other 'facete [ie, elegant, graceful] modern Poets' who have written love poetry (*AM* 3.2.3.1). Since he elsewhere calls Chaucer 'our English Homer,' he may have thought of Spenser as a refined polished 'modern' poet with a relationship to Chaucer corresponding to Virgil's relation to his more primitive predecessor.

There are two quotations from *The Faerie Queene* in the first edition of the *Anatomy*: *FQ* IV ix 1–2 (*AM* 3.1.3) and *FQ* V viii 1 (*AM* 3.3.3.3). The first of these is correctly quoted but incorrectly referenced; the second appears to have been taken from a note in Robert Tofte's *The Blazon of Jealousie* (1615), as it reproduces certain variants in the text found in Tofte. When Burton was revising for his fourth edition (1632), he added five shorter quotations, all from *FQ* III and IV; they are rather inaccurate and appear to have been done from memory. (For example, lines from *FQ* III xi 44 describing Mars' sufferings from love – 'How oft for *Venus*, and how often eek / For may other Nymphes he sore did shreek, / With womanish teares, and with unwarlike smarts, / Privily moystening his horrid cheek' – appear in *AM* 3.2.3.1 as 'The mighty Mars did oft for Venus shreeke, / Privily moistening his horrid cheeke / With womanish teares.') These additions suggest that Burton was fairly familiar with at least parts of *The Faerie Queene*, or perhaps had recently reread it.

His sympathy with Spenser may well have been wider and deeper than this evidence would suggest. The two men shared certain attitudes – for example, a temperamental predisposition to favor the middle way between extremes – and Burton could easily have accepted the greater part of Spenser's moral teaching. One modern critic has gone so far as to call Burton 'the best commentator' on Spenser (Hughes 1926:562), and certainly passages in the *Anatomy* may illuminate parts of Spenser's work. (Cf Spenser's account of the cave of Despair in *FQ* I ix with Burton on 'Symptoms of Despair' in *AM* 3.4.2.4; and *Fowre Hymnes* with Burton on 'Love's Beginning, Object, Definition, Division' in *AM* 3.1.1.2.) But direct influence by Spenser on Burton is hard to prove, and the parallels between them may spring only from their shared Christian and humanistic background. Although Burton was an omnivorous reader and an indefatigable quoter of other works, he rarely seems to have been deeply affected by another writer; he tends to take from others what suits the thrust of his immediate argument, and in the case of Spenser that meant accounts of love and its powerful effects.

J.B. BAMBOROUGH

Burton ed 1893; Hughes 1926.

Busirane A brief prologue scene outside its gates introduces the perplexing episode of the house of Busirane and helps to explain its themes and its climactic role in *FQ* III. Britomart comes upon Scudamour disarmed, weeping, and questioning the providence that permits Amoret's captivity (xi 7–13). Britomart has learned from Merlin that her own love is providentially guided, and here she will both act and speak for providence. She will execute the 'heavenly justice' that Scudamour doubts, but first she counsels patience, urging him to 'submit ... to high providence.'

Busirane's fiery gate insidiously confronts her with the need to practice the submission she preaches. Taking the sulphurous fire as a divine manifestation, she hesitates: 'What monstrous enmity provoke we heare, / Foolhardy as th'Earthes children, the which made / Battell against the Gods? so we a God invade.' As Scudamour relapses into despair, Britomart reconsiders. The unquenchable fire may be only a false appearance of the supernatural, a 'shew of perill.' She proves it so by charging forward like 'a thunder bolt' – like Jove's weapon against 'th'Earthes children' and not, as she had feared, like the one of the Titans themselves. The enchanted fire stands for lustful Mulciber, the burning that Britomart had earlier despaired of controlling in herself (see III ii 37, 43, 52 and cf V vii 14–15); but, like Busirane's house as a whole, it also misrepresents the 'Most sacred fire ... which men call Love' (iii 1).

These preliminaries establish for the reader and for Britomart two ideas essential to understanding what follows: that the house of Busirane will challenge faith in the divine order and that it will involve a 'shew of perill,' an unreal but still dangerous view of love.

Britomart's adventure unfolds in three stages in the three rooms of the house. In the 'utmost rowme,' she finds tapestries depicting 'all *Cupids* warres ... And cruell battels, which he whilome fought / Gainst all the Gods,' as well as an image of Cupid on an altar with the inscription, 'Unto the Victor of the Gods this bee.' The second room proves richer still, recording in gold reliefs 'A thousand monstrous formes ... Such as false love doth oft upon him weare' and hung with relics of human heroes whom Love has conquered and disgraced. Britomart witnesses the masque of Cupid in this room; she then enters the inner sanctum, the third room where she finds Busirane alone with Amoret (xii 27–30).

The architecture of the house constitutes a sequence with a design on both Britomart and the reader. The altar with its image of Cupid follows inductively from the mythological tapestries and then leads, summarily because deductively, to the human and historical relics of the second room. Reinforcing this program, Busirane's artifices increase in verisimilitude, historical proximity, and inwardness. The tapestries depict the gods in their 'divine resemblance wondrous lyke,' though in two dimensions; the reliefs, adding the third dimension, are wrought 'as they living were.' The masque brings a dramatic mode, the most lifelike of all. Depictions of Cupid illustrate this pattern: first the figure in the mythical, archaic tapestry, then the free-standing idol of antique paganism, and finally 'the winged God himselfe' (xii 22) dominating a Renaissance masque peopled with figures from medieval love allegory. The increasing immediacy of Busirane's artifice as regards both historical moment and artistic mode suggests an increasing inwardness of its reception when Amoret enters as its individual victim. When she enters, and again when Britomart invades the inner room, the perspective of the narrative shifts to suggest that Busirane and his masque have become Amoret's internal nightmare.

Although it draws upon romance traditions (see *Var* 3:290–8, 353–66), the house of Busirane is more than a court of love. It is a temple to the Cupid who abetted Paridell's seductive arts in the previous episode (x 4–5), and its architectural-rhetorical program aims to instill belief in Cupid's omnipotent and malevolent divinity. Busirane depicts a world of 'maisterie' (i 25) in which gods and humans, women and men alike, are helpless and degraded victims, in which resistance wins only continuing torture, and in which emotional integrity cannot fail to be destroyed by compulsion (Nestrick 1975:60–70). Fidelity has no meaning in such a world – a conclusion that Busirane tempts Amoret to be bold enough to accept. The sophistication of this challenge to her chastity complements the primitive violence of the Foster's lust for Florimell in i 15–17 (and the lust which Amoret fears from Britomart in IV i, and later from Lust himself in vii 4ff), as well as Florimell's imprisonment by Proteus, likewise of seven months' duration (see III xi 10; IV i 4, xi 4).

Readers experience not only Busirane's artistic program, however, but also a counter-program that exposes his effort to master Amoret by misrepresenting the mastery of Cupid. This counter-program draws in part upon prior experience in reading Book III and in part upon interchange of engagement and detachment in the narrative. Britomart is implicated in both.

Nearly everything in Book III prepares both Britomart and the reader to reject Busirane's view of love. For example, the rebellion against the gods that Cupid achieves easily in the tapestries Britomart has judged foolhardy in the prologue scene (xi 22). Busirane's neo-pagan view of love and history as lacking order or *telos* is countered by Merlin's prophecy (iii 21–49) and by the poet, who declares that antiquity did well to deem Love a god not merely because 'over mortall minds [it has] so great might,' but because it directs mortal minds and actions 'aright' and effects 'The fatall purpose of divine foresight ... in destined descents' (2). The god who elsewhere in *FQ* III stirs 'up th'Heroes high intents, / Which the late world admyres for wondrous moniments' (2), here treads all such monuments underfoot in Busirane's gold reliefs (xi 52). Britomart's own development into a female hero counters Busirane's pictures of male heroes degenerating into 'womanish' passivity (eg, 44, or Scudamour at 27). The Gardens of Adonis answer the tapestries' version of metamorphosis as meaningless cruelty.

Spenser's narrative encourages ironic detachment while rendering fully the insidious attractions of Busirane's art. The poet feels 'Wondrous delight,' for example, in viewing the rape of Ganymede (34), a response that deepens to imaginative engagement in the next stanza when he reports a speech that a tapestry could only suggest. In the following stanzas, apostrophe and the present tense carry further the poet's, and perhaps Britomart's, loss of detachment. At the same time, Spenser subtly fosters moral as well as aesthetic judgment. The tapestries – 'all of love, and all of lusty-hed, / As seemed by their semblaunt did entreat' (29) – may not be what they seem, and they do more than treat the subject of love; they 'entreat' the observer to engagement and assent (see I.G. MacCaffrey 1976:108).

Spenser withholds Britomart's reactions to Busirane's house until the end of each descriptive sequence when they can measure the reader's. Her first reaction, like the poet's, is wonder (xi 32, 34, 40, 49, 53); but she is no whit discouraged from prosecuting her first intent (50), and her amazement includes suspicion. The inscriptions make Busirane's rooms a riddle whose 'sence' she, like the reader, cannot 'construe' (50, 54). She wants to know who owns all this and what it means.

Her wonder and puzzlement, moreover, do not bar moral judgment. The first stanza to report her reactions also concludes the description of Cupid's altar: 'And underneath his feet was written thus, / *Unto the Victor of the Gods this bee:* / And all the people in that ample hous / Did to that image bow their humble knee, / And oft committed fowle Idolatree' (49). There are no people in that ample house, however (53). This inconsistency suggests that Britomart sees in the image of Cupid the idolatry it implies. The reader who does not see this has just had an ambiguous warning: 'Ah man beware, how thou those darts behold' (48). As soon as she reappears as observer, Britomart begins to carry out the counter-program to Busirane's enchantments, dispelling the aesthetic autonomy that depicts and reinforces Love's cosmological and psychological tyranny and preparing for the final disenchantment when she enters the third room, 'Neither of idle shewes, nor of false charmes aghast' (xii 29).

The models for Busirane's art suggest further that the climactic challenge to chastity in *The Faerie Queene* is one of life enthralled and fixated by art, especially by literary and social conventions of courtship. The tapestries, for instance, depict stories routinely explained in antiquity, the Middle Ages, and the Renaissance as lies told by the poets (Hyde 1986:174). Ovid had woven these *caelestia crimina* (heavenly crimes) into Arachne's tapestry as an ironic miniature of his own anti-Olympian poem (*Metamorphoses* 6.1–145), and Spenser's many 'mistakes' (see *Var* 6:291–7) may be meant as lies about lies.

Busirane's obvious association with poetry (his books and verses at xii 31–2, 36 and the theatrical induction of his masque in 3–5) accords with this view, as does the conjectural explanation of his name as *Busy-reign*, 'the male imagination trying busily (because unsuccessfully) to dominate and possess woman's will' (Berger 1971:100). He has also been seen as a figure of *abuse*, which could mean deceit, imposture, or delusion (Gosson's *Schoole of Abuse* had recently linked the term specifically to poetry and drama); abuse associates him convincingly with Busiris, an Egyptian tyrant whose disdain for the rights of guests Ovid cites as an example for male lovers (Roche 1964:81–3). Significantly, St Augustine cites Busiris when ridiculing pagan gods for the crimes, especially adultery, that poets and theaters ascribed to them (*City of God* 18.12). Like his all-powerful deity, Busirane images the tyranny of literary and social conventions over the fulfillment they purport to serve.

This view suggests an answer to the riddle of 'Be bold, be bold ... Be not too bold' (xi 54). In part, Busirane's inscriptions seem to caution against the male aggressiveness that won Amoret for Scudamour at the Temple of Venus and may now have caused her captivity (see IV x 4, 10, 16–19, 54, 56 and Hieatt 1962:509–10). But perhaps Scudamour can never be bold enough to confront Amoret without the trappings of the courtship battle, without the shield of love that is his defense as well as his name and nature. Scorning the equivocal inscriptions, Britomart is bold throughout her adventure in the house of Busirane, bold enough to witness, to experience, even to affirm love's deity as a poetic figure – but also bold enough to enter the sanctum of fiction and expose the sordid effects of its abuse. THOMAS HYDE

Berger 1971; DeNeef 1979; Donno 1974; Fowler 1964; Hieatt 1962; Hyde 1986; I.G. MacCaffrey 1976; Nestrick 1975; Roche 1964; C.A. Thompson 1972.

Butler, Samuel (1613–80) Spenser provided the basis for the eponymous hero of Butler's most famous work, *Hudibras* (1663–78). In his quixotic Puritan zealot, Butler alludes to the Sir Huddibras of *FQ* II ii 17 and 37, who is similarly violent and unwise, foolhardy, and given to 'sterne melancholy,' selftorment, and envy (the relationship of the two was remarked by Butler's eighteenth-century editor, Zachary Grey, in his footnote to *Hudibras* 1.1.40). The context of Spenser's Legend of Temperance suits a satire on such coercive bigots, and Butler clearly expected his audience to be familiar with Spenser's poem. There are, however, only a few direct verbal echoes. *Hudibras* 1.3.1–2 ('Ay me! what perils do inviron / The man that meddles with cold Iron!') is directly indebted to *FQ* I viii 1 (see also *Var* 5:157, 159). If Butler alludes more generally to *The Faerie Queene*, he does so as to England's preeminent exemplary long poem in his time, a chivalric romance that might serve him as the romances read by Don Quixote had served Cervantes, an author Butler clearly imitated.

A loose, parodic allusion to Spenser's mode would have led Butler to use in *Hudibras* formal principles like those of a book of *The Faerie Queene*, as he did, most centrally the conception of events as illustrating a single hero's character. There is another group of six significant characteristics that Butler's poem shares with Spenser's but, as a group, with no other works that might have served as reference points for a mock-heroic of the early 1660s, such as classical and continental epics, contemporary English epics (Davenant's *Gondibert*, Cowley's *Davideis*), and popular chivalric literature (eg, Richard Johnson's *The Seaven Champions of Christendome* 1596–7). (1) The hero pursues a quest as agent or type of a governing figure who has both patriotic and spiritual authority; and therefore (2) the quest occurs within the moralized landscape of, significantly, his native country. (3) The hero moves through disconnected adventures so that stress falls on spontaneity, fortune, and purpose deferred by accident. Often readers cannot guess the sequence of events or their conclusion; providence, authorial control of plot, and historical destiny remain hidden. (4) Instead of a running allusion to a narrative pattern like the fall of Troy or the Fall of Man, *The Faerie Queene* and *Hudibras* assimilate a large number of historical and mythological fragments. They call upon the reader's learning, and they reinterpret rather than expatiate on what they borrow from the past. (5) Abstract discourse is as integral to illuminating the text as is physical action. (6) Spenser and Butler pointedly and strategically deviate – in different directions – from the poetic idiom of their day, and they do so by applying similar principles of aesthetic decorum. *The Faerie Queene*'s grave, musical, antique style contrasts with *Hudibras*' odd rhymes, doggerel, and burlesque; but Spenser also gives Butler a model for his innovative boldness.

These relationships of conception, form, method, and style allow one to consider *Hudibras* a continuation as well as a mockery of *The Faerie Queene* and its tradition. *Hudibras* displays what *FQ* II might be like if Huddibras, not Guyon, were its corporate and individual type of spiritual striving. ERIC ROTHSTEIN

Samuel Butler 1663–78 *Hudibras* (London; rpt Menston, Yorks 1970); Butler ed 1973; see also *Sp All* p 280.

Byron, George Gordon, Lord (1788–1824) Byron showed a lively, though not systematic, interest in Spenser. While making much of Pope in public statements, he found Spenser's 'the measure most after [his] own heart,' and implied that he found it easiest to wield. Without Spenser, it seems fair to say, Byron might never have been in a position to declare, 'I awoke one morning and found myself famous' (*Letters and Journals* ed 1973–, 4:13). *Childe Harold's Pilgrimage* I and II (1812), the cause of his overnight acclaim, adopted not only the blank mold of the Spenserian stanza but also a quasi-Spenserian protagonist: Byron's 'Childe' is the novice to Spenser's 'Knights,' and his 'pilgrimage' is a weakened form of the Spenserian quest.

In terms of sheer bulk, most of Byron's writing in the first half of his career, before his departure from England in 1816, took the form of the Spenserian stanza; and he had no sooner quit England under duress (and, as it turned out, for good) than he went back to that intricate shape and music in *Childe Harold* III (1816) and IV (1818).

Clearly more than a casual technical aptitude was involved in Byron's Spenserianism. *Childe Harold* IV contains some of his most compelling and best sustained poetry; the Spenserian stanza helped him first to free himself from the scattershot, ad hominem approach he took with Pope's heroic couplet, and finally to bring under manifest control some of the profoundest reaches of his mind. Yet more than external form is at issue. When Byron in his last long poem, *The Island*, again had recourse to the pentameter couplet, he infused it with a Spenserian vein of romance.

Byron went to his great Elizabethan forerunner for more than a stanza, but less than a full-fledged allegory. The only poem of Byron's that could pretend to the title of allegory is *The Dream*; and it restricts the mode to remote neurotic tableaux, without dramatic plausibility, conceptual intricacy, or amplitude in social or political relations. He did not possess Spenser's gift for graphic scene-making or for elaborate arrays of ideological elements and conditions embodied in human form. The allegorical art of fusing primal concretization and esoteric conceptualization Byron neither studied nor sought.

What Byron and Spenser had in common was nevertheless complex and powerful: a motivation born of finding themselves in unofficial exile; a power of analyzing, with stark and startling sensitivity, the history and politics of their time; and a penchant for immersing themselves in moments and scenes as revelations of value. The ways they gave expression to these attributes do not coincide, but they unmistakably apply them in the same field of history. While Spenser sees states embodied, or needing to be embodied, in history, Byron sees an all-but-kaleidoscopic series of topical conditions.

Spenser wrote when historiography was still universal and dynastic, before Clarendon and Burnet, Hume and Gibbon had introduced and consolidated an ironic, secular, circumstantial methodology. Byron in turn was an avid reader of history, from the ancients to Gibbon; but born as he was some months before the French Revolution and coming to maturity in Napoleon's heyday, he moved and breathed in an atmosphere of tumultuous transformation, when the very *making* of history contradicted the putative norm of stability that still held sway in Elizabethan times. The *Cantos of Mutabilitie* attest to Spenser's empirical grasp of the force of incertitude and disorder; but even here his aspiration to 'that Sabaoths sight' proclaims the same concept of history that we see in the castle of Alma, as Guyon sedately pores over the definitive book of history. By contrast, Childe Harold is very much on the site of history, treading where its occasions were yet warm underfoot.

Of the five factors that enter into the making of creative work – tradition, temperament, experience, the times, and native talent – only the last truly connects the 'poet's poet' and Europe's poet. Spenser was a conservative in politics, Byron a sort of impulsive, transnational liberal; Spenser was a devoted, if frustrated courtier, Byron a largely unassimilated nobleman; Spenser flourished in the era of an unexpectedly central and dominant virgin queen, Byron lived under an ineffectual king and saw his hopes of a feminine renaissance dashed by the untimely death of Princess Charlotte; and Spenser, whether in *The Shepheardes Calender* or in *The Faerie Queene*, made a schematic and systematic world, while Byron, alike in *Childe Harold* and *Don Juan*, recorded an emergent and volatile course of experience. Even the personal lyrics of *Amoretti* and *Epithalamion* embody an orderliness and stateliness vastly at odds with Byron's contact with women and with marriage, just as *Vewe of Ireland* and *FQ* v embody a politics of dominion quite contrary to Byron's.

There may be a hint of Spenser's *Fowre Hymnes* in the patches of idealism we find in Byron's *Hebrew Melodies* and the Aurora Raby episodes in *Don Juan*. That hint serves only to highlight the degree to which Byron, while so significantly associating himself with Spenser and even following him, emerges on his own, in a new world of substance and value. He offers 'Fierce loves and faithless wars' (*Don Juan* 7.7) in place of the 'Fierce warres and faithfull loves' that 'moralize' Spenser's song (*FQ* I i). The difference between Spenser and Byron may be conceived as that between romance and romanticism.

More concretely, in romance we see a structural multifariousness, a copious journey in the mind occurring as the exfoliation of concepts that show correspondences with the real world while making no concessions to it. Pageantry and principle are its hallmarks; formality is its ambience; and narrative is its inevitable medium. In romanticism, there is material rather than structural variety, and the emphasis falls on spontaneity and intensity of response to experience, on a seemingly innate pressure to accommodate plurality and discover (where romance imposes) central and radiant concepts. Detail, in romanticism, partakes of the surprise of whatever is suddenly suffused with significance. Indeed, surprise is its métier. Though romanticism would appear to use as many sudden encounters as romance, its encounters follow no order, adhere to no pattern. Childe Harold makes a journey that proves both geographically and emotionally casual, whereas the Red Cross Knight (who is after all an apprentice and ostensibly an upstart knight himself) follows the necessary pattern of his inheritance of royalty on earth and sanctity in heaven. Personality, rather than formality, gives us the stamp of romanticism. Lyric, not narrative, is its characteristic mode. Indeed, romanticism radically redefines narrative, stripping it of predictability, continuity, and extension, and leaving it as an assembly of diversified operations around an uncertain nucleus. In sum, romance orients itself toward an ultimate ideal; romanticism unveils a volatile and vulnerable idealism.

In one respect, Byron's adoption of the Spenserian stanza manifests the hardiness and the versatility of the form. In another respect, it shows his tact as an artist, his ability to honor his forerunner while also exploiting him, to reminisce while also reconstituting him. That effect of reconstitution may be the most important mark of the relationship between the two poets, because it entails the fullest manifestation not just of Byron's prowess but of Spenser's seminal *and* evolutionary status in the English mainstream. MICHAEL G. COOKE

George Gordon, Lord Byron 1973– *Letters and Journals* ed Leslie A. Marchand (Cambridge, Mass). W. Jackson Bate 1970 *The Burden of the Past and the English Poet* (Cambridge, Mass); Harold Bloom 1973 *The Anxiety of Influence: A Theory of Poetry* (New York); Robert F. Gleckner 1967 *Byron and the Ruins of Paradise* (Baltimore) ch 9; J.R. de J. Jackson 1980 *Poetry of the Romantic Period* (London) pp 138–53; Peter J. Manning 1978 *Byron and His Fictions* (Detroit) esp ch 6 'History and Allusion'; Wilkie 1965.

C

Caelia After his encounter with Despair, Redcrosse is taken by Una to the house of Holiness which is governed by Caelia (or Coelia), the heavenly one, the mother of the virtues. She lives a life balanced between prayer and good works: 'All night she spent in bidding of her bedes, / And all the day in doing good and godly deedes' (*FQ* I x 3; cf Corceca, iii 13–14). Through the ministrations of her household, Redcrosse is prepared for his ascent of the Mount of Contemplation: this is 'the way to heavenly blesse' (x argument).

Caelia's daughters are Fidelia, Speranza, and Charissa – faith, hope, and charity, as in I Corinthians 13:13: 'And now abideth faith, hope and love, even these three: but the chiefest of these is love.' Fidelia, dressed in white for purity, carries in one hand a cup with a serpent in it and in the other a book: this is how St John the Evangelist was traditionally depicted. The snake in the cup alludes to an attempt to kill him with poisoned wine, to the brazen serpent which Moses held aloft in the wilderness to cure the plague of fiery serpents (Num 21:8–9), and to the pagan physician Aesculapius: so it is a type of Christ the Physician, who was believed to have cured the world of sin (see Kellogg and Steele in *FQ* ed 1965a:41). John wrote the most theological of the Gospels, that which seeks to define faith. Spenser establishes the Protestant priority (Fidelia is the eldest): good works (the province of Charissa, the youngest) are pleasing to God only when performed within a true faith. The English church declared in its Thirty-nine Articles, 'Works done before the grace of Christ, and the Inspiration of his Spirit, are not pleasant to God.'

From 'her sacred Booke,' Fidelia teaches Redcrosse doctrines accessible only through divine revelation, 'That weaker wit of man could never reach, / Of God, of grace, of justice, of free will' (x 19). These are the issues which almost led Redcrosse to yield to Despair (ix 35–54): the justice of the Protestant doctrine of grace which held that some people are chosen by God without any relevant exercise of free will. This denial of the scope of human understanding and insistence upon scriptural revelation was the usual Protestant position. The opposite, syncretist, Neoplatonic position – that a true knowledge of God may be intuited by natural reason, for instance by classical pagan writers – is often attributed to Spenser, and, indeed, it is implied elsewhere in the canto, especially when the Mount of Contemplation is compared to the pagan Parnassus as well as to biblical mountains (x 54; see Sinfield 1983:20–30).

In *FQ* I x 20, the powers of faith are celebrated: Joshua commanding the sun to stand still, Isaiah making the sun go backwards, Gideon's spectacular destruction of the Midianites, Moses leading the Israelites through the Red Sea, Christ's statement that faith can move mountains (Josh 10:12–14, 2 Kings 20:8–11). Redcrosse is dismayed when he compares the revelations of faith and his life hitherto, but Speranza, hope, is there to comfort him (22). Her anchor recalls St Paul's statement that hope is 'an ancre of the soule' (Heb 6:18–19); her dress is blue, the color also representing hope ('which is layd up ... in heaven': Col 1:5). Caelia says that Redcrosse's 'distressed doubtfull agonie' is a 'commune plight' and the healer is Patience. The problem is deep-rooted and the solution long and painful, perhaps reflecting the anguish which might attend the Protestant insistence on the disjunction between divine goodness and human imperfection. But Redcrosse has supports which were lacking in the cave of Despair (ix) and the outcome is never in doubt.

Now Redcrosse is ready to meet Charissa,

who has brought forth a child (this suggests Redcrosse, a new child of the faith). Spenser is careful to distinguish the love of charity from '*Cupids* wanton snare' (30); Charissa is associated by her 'turtle doves' and 'yvorie chaire' with Venus (31), but we are to understand Venus Urania, the Neoplatonic symbol of heavenly beauty. This symbolism leads some commentators to a Neoplatonist reading in which Charissa transcends Fidelia and Speranza (see Brooks-Davies 1977:93, 97–8), rather than to the Protestant reading proposed here, in which she becomes significant only through them. But Charissa's 'friendly chearefull mood' (32) does not seem transcendent, and her teaching (which is taken up by Mercy and the Bead-men) is limited to the practical good works, making one's faith effective in the world. ALAN SINFIELD

Calepine A secondary knight of courtesy, Calepine appears in *FQ* VI iii, iv, and viii. As canto iii begins, Calidore has restored Priscilla to her parents without embarrassing her; resuming his quest, he suffers an embarrassment of his own in blundering upon a knight solacing a lady in a covert shade. He begs pardon for the apparent discourtesy and then sits down to relate his long adventures. The lady, Serena, wandering about the fields to make herself a garland, is set upon by the Blatant Beast and carried off. Calidore overtakes the Beast and makes him drop Serena, then departs.

The knight running to aid his wounded lady is now identified as Calepine. Readers will note the affinity of his name with that of Calidore, whose 'less gifted surrogate' (Cheney 1966:195) he is to be. Some detect in it part of a threefold bookish pleasantry in Book VI: Aldus (see *Aladine) was a leading publisher, and Calepinus and Mirabellus (cf Mirabella) were, respectively, a well known and an obscure lexicographer. (Another Callapine, son of Bajazeth, Emperor of Turkey, appears briefly as Tamburlaine's last adversary in the second part of Marlowe's play: the name is not invented.) The name may suggest 'beautiful speech' in Greek (Parker 1960:233), but in spite of his 'faire blandishment' and 'sensefull speach' to Matilda (iv 27, 37), and 'speaches kind' to Serena (viii 50), he is not so well spoken as to deserve such a name. Another derivation, from *chalepos* (sore, grievous, afflicted, difficult) points to his unhappiness, his lack of and need for the serenity that is the true name and nature of his lady (Cheney 1966:201–4, Tonkin 1972:66).

Though a courtly figure in the Legend of Courtesy, Calepine is usually dismounted and often unarmed. He sets Serena on his steed and accompanies her on foot, approaching at evening a fair palace across a river. Here he meets an armed knight and a fair lady whose names disclose their natures – the villainous Turpine, the flattering Blandina. Turpine refuses to take Calepine across the river, calls him a peasant knight, and chides him with having lost his own mount shamefully. (Since Serena is riding a knight's charger, something may have been omitted here, or some discrepancy in the narrative left uncorrected.) Blandina does not reprove Turpine but offers Calepine her palfrey, appropriate for a lady not a knight. Calepine refuses courteously and wades the river. Having laughed at his challenge, Turpine rides away. The porter shuts the gate on the couple, and Turpine sends further insults, though Blandina mildly entreats him to relent. Calepine keeps watch over Serena until daybreak, when they go forth, he on foot, she mounted. Turpine pursues, challenges, and charges the disadvantaged man, who can do no better than to hide behind Serena's back, in the hope apparently that the churlish Turpine may not have abandoned all chivalry to women. The reader must wonder at this strange inadequacy in one who is called 'this most courteous knight' (iv i).

At length Turpine strikes Calepine through the shoulder and is at the point of killing him when a Salvage Man intervenes and puts the ruffian to flight. Applying herbal remedies to Calepine's wound, he leads the couple to his dwelling and gives them simple shelter and food; there the medicine restores the knight but not the lady, his wounds being outward and physical, hers inward and moral.

In a brief moment foreshadowing the pastoral sojourn of Calidore among the shepherds, Calepine one day walks out to take the air and hear the thrushes sing. Suddenly he sees a bear with a squalling infant in its bloody jaws. Running the faster because he is not in armor, he pursues the bear and makes it drop the baby, whereupon he first thrusts a stone down the beast's throat and then strangles it. For the first time Calepine has shown alacrity and resourcefulness. The baby is mysteriously unharmed, but Calepine cannot find his way back to Serena. After much wandering with the baby crying to be fed, he hears a voice of lamentation and approaches to comfort a lady. The lady, Matilde, tells how her husband, Sir Bruin, in time past had overcome the giant Cormoraunt, but that the long ascendency of Bruin and Matilde has been overshadowed by their childlessness and the threat of the giant's return to power unless a child 'Be gotten, not begotten' (iv 32). Calepine has repeated the subjection of the giant by killing the bear, and he overcomes the sterility of the marriage and fulfills the prophecy by presenting the babe to Matilde.

Relieved of the child, Calepine is alone, unhorsed, unarmed. He declines, with thanks but without explanation, the horse and arms Matilde offers him. His grief at separation from Serena is such that he vows not to rest until he finds her. He thereupon leaves the story for three cantos, though he is not forgotten. The Salvage Man misses him, sorrows, and departs with Serena, bearing Calepine's arms, all but the sword which Calepine had hidden. Serena too in her flight through the wilderness remembers Calepine but blames him unjustly (viii 33). Falling asleep exhausted, she is found by a cannibalistic and piratical Salvage Nation and is stripped and raised on an altar for sacrilegious rites.

'By chaunce, more then by choyce' (viii 46) – again the note of the fortuitous so frequent in Book VI – Calepine comes near and is alerted by the sound of bagpipes and shrieks. By starlight and twinklings of unholy fire he sees the heathen sacrifice being prepared and steps in decisively, with sardonic irony sending swarms of devotees to hell as if in sacrifice to the very fiends they worship. He rescues and unties his lady, then comforts and questions her, but such is her shame that she remains silent and unknown all night. Daylight makes known to him his beloved Serena, but what they say or do, then or thereafter, is left undisclosed. WILLIAM BLISSETT

Cheney 1966; M. Pauline Parker 1960 *The Allegory of the 'Faerie Queene'* (Oxford); Tonkin 1972; K. Williams 1966:191, arguing that Calepine, being unencumbered by armor, exhibits a free delight in liberty that is 'part of the nature of courtesy.'

Calidore Mentioned as one of Gloriana's knights at *FQ* III viii 28, Calidore appears only in cantos i-iii and ix-xii of Book VI, 'Contayning the Legend of S. Calidore, or of Courtesie.' In cantos iv-viii, he pursues the Blatant Beast offstage while the narrative pursues the fortunes of other characters.

The title of Book VI implies that Calidore and courtesy are synonymous. His name suggests the Greek *kala dora* 'beautiful gifts' – presumably those of the Graces, who bestow 'all gracious gifts ... Which decke the body or adorne the mynde' (x 23). Spenser introduces him as the most courteous knight at the Fairy court, 'beloved over all,' and stresses the 'given' or innate quality of his virtue, 'planted naturall' rather than learned (i 2; cf ii 1–3).

Yet Calidore is an ambiguous figure. His name also echoes the Latin *calidus* 'fierce,' *callidus* 'skillful' or 'adroit,' and perhaps *callidus auro* 'skillful with gold.' Spenser's initial descriptions seem rather to unfold than to limit the possibilities of Calidore's name; like the much-debated stanzas on his pastoral 'truancy' (x 1–4; see Maxwell 1952), they support conflicting evaluations. Spenser praises Calidore's 'gentlenesse of spright,' but at the same time he stresses the fierceness, or aptitude for 'batteilous affray,' that will set him apart from his meeker equivalent, Calepine. The inventory of his beautiful gifts includes 'comely guize,' 'gracious speach,' 'faire usage and conditions sound'; but the diction hints at a certain manipulative superficiality in the skill with which he trades on this endowment. Charming enough to 'steale mens hearts away,' Calidore 'with the greatest purchast greatest grace: / Which he could wisely use, and well apply, / To please the best' (i 2–3).

Spenserian courtesy combines an inner quality (gentleness) with the judgment ('skill') needed to enact that quality and a talent for enacting it gracefully (Culp 1971). Calidore is obviously gentle and graceful, and his fierceness gives him an edge over Calepine in 'skill.' The nature of his skill, however, seems always in question. Spenser stresses the role of judgment in courteous conduct ('yet ought they well to know / Their good'), concluding that 'Great skill it is such duties timely to bestow' (ii 1). The next stanza nevertheless contrasts those 'that have greater skill in mind' with those to whom courtesy comes easily. Ostensibly the contrast flatters Calidore, 'Whose every deed and word ... Was like enchantment' (3); the less beautifully gifted work harder to achieve less. Yet the comparison honors Calidore for an unreflective 'skill,' not one based on knowledge of his good; and it measures success 'in the eyes of men' – an unsure criterion when applied to one who 'through both the eyes, / And both the eares did steale the hart away' (ii 3; cf i 2, quoted above).

Calidore's actions hardly resolve the moral ambiguity of his 'skill.' Spenser tells us he 'loathd leasing' and 'loved simple truth,' and Colin tells us the Graces dance naked to signify lack of guile (i 3, x 24). Yet Calidore swears to Priscilla's father that she is not only pure and innocent but 'Most perfect pure, and guiltlesse innocent / Of blame' – hedging the emphatic lie with a throwaway qualifier ('Since first he saw her' iii 18). Three stanzas later he stumbles in on the 'quiet loves delight' of Calepine and Serena – and instead of withdrawing, sits down to talk shop with Calepine while Serena wanders off. In canto x he plays the intruder again with Colin Clout, recapitulating a motif that associates him with the enemies of courtesy: the knight who surprises Aladine, the pair who attack Arthur, the 'Salvage Nation,' the tiger that charges Pastorella, the Brigands, and the Blatant Beast itself.

Calidore's most notorious failure may be his most excusable: falling in love with Pastorella, he abandons the quest to which he is pledged. Yet the manner in which he sets about to 'insinuate his harts desire' (ix 27) among the shepherds is questionable. Praising the uncorrupted simplicity of their lives, he proceeds to offer Meliboe gold and Pastorella courtly blandishments. Taking full, calculated advantage of his superiority to Coridon, he patronizes the shepherd only to use him as an easy foil. His apology for crashing the dance of the Graces in canto x seems 'inappropriately hearty' (Tonkin 1972:139), another instance of the 'affected serenity' or 'insensitively sanguine and self-promoting mode of address' that readers have found troublesome (Nohrnberg 1976:668, Cain 1978:172). It is unclear whether he takes Pastorella's virginity (x 38) or plans to return after leaving her with her parents. But it is quite clear that he makes the most of his other conquest, as he leads the muzzled Beast on a 'ticker-tape parade through Faerie' (Berger 1961b:43): the crowds, says Spenser, 'much admyr'd the Beast, but more admyr'd the Knight' (xii 37). The repeated verb links Calidore and his antagonist, as they have been linked throughout the Legend of Courtesy, in the ambiguity of 'outward shows' whose relation to 'inward thoughts' is never sure (proem 5).

In its contemplative purity Spenserian courtesy is the social analogue to cosmic harmony, as the celebrated stanza on Ariadne's crown suggests (x 13). This harmony finds its ceremonial emblem in the dance and its ethical basis in the union of mildness, candor, and generosity (24). Ideally, this vision of courtesy should inform the practice of the 'skill men call Civility' (23). In its practical form, however, Spenserian courtesy bears the traces of a social code popularized in courtesy books like Castiglione's *Courtier* (see also *courtesy as a social code). The destabilizing of economic and class structures in sixteenth-century England led to a social environment marked less by the harmonious order of dance than by intense competition, insecurity, and conflict among the aristocracy (Stone 1965). In this context the outward shows of courtly manner tended to be staged for their strategic value, the ethical basis of which is aggressiveness rather than mildness, discretion rather than candor, and self-interest rather than generosity.

The rivalry between Calidore and Coridon nicely illuminates the way actions 'coded' by Elizabethan culture as courteous could be deployed as competitive strategies (Nohrnberg 1976:709–10). Calidore's deference to Coridon uses the gestures of mildness, candor, and generosity to dominate a rival. The rivalry thus offers evidence both of Calidore's courtesy and, equally, of his manipulative 'skill.' Should we conclude then that through Calidore Spenser impugns the courtly code? Passages that suggest such an intention include Spenser's disparagement of the 'present age' (proem 4–5), the insistent qualifications with which the narrator equates court and courtesy at the beginning of canto i, and the narrator's anti-courtly animus in excusing Calidore's truancy (x 3–4). Yet too ironic a reading of Calidore may obscure a deeper and more consequential ambivalence in the poem. After all, Calidore's problem – how to represent true courtesy in action – is also the poet's. And while he bears the tooth marks of many critics, in the poem itself Calidore (unlike Artegall) seems invulnerable to the Beast's attack. How deep do these ironies run?

In the proem Spenser concludes that 'vertues seat is deepe within the mynd, / And not in outward shows, but inward thoughts defynd.' Yet 'goodnes,' as Hooker remarks, 'doth not moove by being, but by being apparent' (*Laws* 1.7 in ed 1977–, 1:80). Spenser's problem in 'fashioning' exploits for the patron of courtesy is precisely to define the inward thought through outward shows. The inherent difficulty of doing so is suggested by the Blandina episode (canto vi). Sheltering Turpine under her skirts, preserving him from Arthur's sword with words and tears that are only 'wynd, and ... water' (42), Blandina completes an emblematic tableau whose motto could easily be the proem's resonant couplet. Arthur spares Turpine, just as Calidore had spared Crudor; but as the names imply, the outcomes are quite different: crudity can be refined, turpitude cannot. The profoundest irony in this disturbing scene may be that the Salvage Man shares none of Arthur's misguided compunctions (40). No less innately courteous than Arthur, and at least as powerful, he is also proof against Blandina's arts, being innocent of any 'skill' in the medium shared by liars and poets.

In a world of Blandinas, courteous acts will always be hard to construe. As gambit, the 'courteous' gesture works only by appearing not to be self-interested, appealing instead to the beholder's moral idealism. Exactly the same conditions hold for the truly courteous gesture: its virtuous motive is wholly 'apparent' only when circumstances offer no grounds for the imputation of self-interest. Yet unless we cast out all skepticism, these conditions tend to become an impossible test. Motive must be inferred by 'reading' an action in its context – yet context or circumstance is precisely what no agent can control. In an age when books are published to secure patronage or advancement to public office, even the literary praise of virtue is an action qualified by self-interest. Moreover, the opening and closing stanzas of the books first published in 1596 suggest that Spenser found the 'outward shows' of the poem itself grievously misconstrued (IV proem 1–4, VI xii 40–1).

The Faerie Queene closes with a compelling image of the poet wounded by his own creature, and this might give us pause in lowering the sword of judgment on his protagonist. Book VI is the legend of 'Calidore, or of Courtesie,' and there is finally no deciding whether that enigmatic *or* balances synonyms or pivots between alternatives. Divine essences may be 'defynd' in the inwardness of contemplative vision – and only there. Calidore's task, like Spenser's, is to enact that essence in a public world. There is no 'skill' known to poets, knights, or literary critics that can carry pure inwardness into the overdetermined contexts of action without calling its definition into question.

DAVID LEE MILLER

Berger 1961b; Cain 1978; Cheney 1966; Culp 1971; J.C. Maxwell 1952 'The Truancy of Calidore' *ELH* 19:143–9; Miller 1979a; Miller 1988; Neuse 1968; Nohrnberg 1976; Tonkin 1972.

Calvin, Calvinism The difficulty of relating Spenser to Jean Calvin (1509–64) is compounded by the ambiguities, varying sympathies, and eclecticism of *The Faerie Queene*, and by the fluidity of Calvinism and its 'shifting centralities' (McDonnell 1967:5), which were espoused differently by apologists in varying national contexts, sometimes to the point of disagreeing with Calvin.

Archbishop Cranmer's early interest in Calvin – as head of the one widely influential Reformed Church in Geneva, as a force in continental politics, and as a leading commentator on Scripture – led him to incorporate some of Calvin's theological emphases in the founding doctrines of the Church of England, the Forty-Two Articles of 1553. Thomas Norton, Cranmer's son-in-law, translated Calvin's *Institutes of the Christian Religion* (1536–59) into English in 1561. At least four groups were responsible for popularizing and disseminating Calvin's theology: exiles who returned from the continent during Somerset's Protectorate (1547–52) and after Elizabeth's accession to the throne; influential individual voices such as those of the Polish Calvinist Jan Laski, who was in London in 1548, and the Scottish Reformer John Knox who returned to Edinburgh in 1559, explaining and promoting both the church government and doctrines of Calvin; congregations of French and Dutch Calvinists in London in the 1560s; and academic circles, especially in Cambridge, discussing and upholding Calvin's attractively systematic theology.

In *The Faerie Queene*, Una's comforting words to Redcrosse – 'Why shouldst thou then despeire, that chosen art?' (I ix 53) – with their possible reference to a doctrine of election whereby God's 'greater grace' rather than human merit determines justification, both encourage and frustrate students of Spenser's alleged Calvinism. Her phrasing recalls, even if the narrative's unglossed actions do not, Calvinists who see themselves as regenerate believers 'that are chosen his' (x 57).

Yet there are grounds for dissociating Spenser from professed Calvinism. Unlike Calvin, he pointedly upholds the crown's authority over the Church (cf Article 37 of the Thirty-nine) and prefers a celibate clergy (*Vewe* in *Var Prose* p 222). Moreover, championing 'the outwarde shewe' and 'the semelye forme and Comelye order of the Churche' (p 223) befits a man who spent his adult life as a conservative official serving a state whose Established Church and its ceremonies, unlike Calvinistic worship, could involve the stimulation of the 'roring Organs' and joyous choristers celebrated in *Epithalamion* (218–21). Although Spenser uses Reformation ideals and imagery in *The Shepheardes Calender* and *The Faerie Queene* and alludes tantalizingly to Calvin's heightened sense of the Augustinian doctrine of predestination, his poetry 'of the delighted senses' (Yeats ed 1961:370) utterly transcends Calvin's aesthetic austerity; and his political, Reform-minded Protestantism, even if parallel to Calvin's, may in fact not be Calvinist in doctrine or origin at all.

Commentators have long been at odds over the Calvinistic elements in Spenser. Early critics often group him among Calvinist writers, claiming that he followed Calvin to a 'very great extent' and calling *FQ* I 'essentially Calvinist' since 'Fidelia ... teaches ... the very core of Calvinistic doctrine' (Padelford 1914). Later, more cautious commentators limit that influence, terming Spenser's religion basically orthodox (Marshall 1959), or even describing him as 'a conservative Anglican' and 'certainly not a Calvinist,' since on crucial issues 'he invariably disagrees with Calvin' (Whitaker 1950:52, 8, 69). An agreeable synthesis characterizes the latest studies, in which large claims (eg, the Calvinist principles in Books I and II are 'easy, all too easy, perhaps, to discern') become more tenable examinations of the way in which doctrinal minutiae illuminate the poet's place in the Calvinist temper or sensibility generally (Boulger 1980:153, 163, 3–4), and in which contradictory textual evidence and Spenser's studied ambiguities are first confronted before being presented as evidence that such complexities 'can be understood only in the light of this dominant theology,' however much one may wish to modify or soften its influence (Sinfield 1983:14). Other studies emphasize Spenser as a Protestant and Reformation poet whose values, best understood in a broader tradition, entirely transcend dogmatic, doctrinal loyalties (King 1982, Hume 1984).

Calvin's *Institutes* treat the great, common doctrines of the syncretic theological tradition as developed and explored by the Church Fathers; but his emphases and dramatic phrasing often throw into relief certain themes magnified by subsequent expositors. These include God's absolute sovereignty and majesty and man's total dependence upon God alone; human depravity rooted in original sin; unconditional predestination ('election'); regeneration (for the elect) through the Word and Spirit rather than through baptism or perseverance (see *Fall and restoration); a process of salvation moving from consciousness of sin, through election and justification, to sanctification and glorification. Those who saw Calvinism as a dangerous theology tended to stress human dignity, reason, and free will – 'erected wit' rather than 'infected will,' to borrow Sidney's phrasing – and they drew attention to the natural and spiritual powers which make human beings capable of laudable achievement in culture, glorious in both body and soul, and able to effect much of their own regeneration in the image of God.

It is difficult to identify Calvinistic elements in Spenser's treatment of the sacraments. Even if Fidelia's cup should remind readers of Calvin's insistence that the sacrament is useful only to the faithful (I x 13), Spenser seems to give images of baptism (I ii 43, xi 30), the eucharist (I ix 19), and other sacramental images (I xi 48, II iii 22, IV iii 48–9) active power to restore, heal, and renew. Their intrinsic efficacy suggests the power of the Real Presence and seems comfortably in keeping with the catechisms and prayer books of the English church. Spenser's emphasis here clearly 'does place limits upon [Calvin's] influence' (Marshall 1959).

The key issue in the debate over Calvinistic influence has been the relationship between the orders of nature and grace, especially in *FQ* I and II. If a case for such an influence can be made, it is through this *topos*, which Article 10 repeats in a manner reminiscent of Calvin: if fallen man through 'his owne naturall strength' has 'no power to do good workes,' even if free to will them, in peril he must rely upon 'the grace of God by Christe.' The 'infected sin' of Redcrosse and man's 'strength ... to ill' (I x 25, I) underline the problematic relationship between human effort and divine power, especially in Book I (level of grace) and Book II (nature *and* grace), where the action is recognizably if loosely Calvinistic. The distinctions forcefully made by A.S.P. Woodhouse (1949) have been judged not valid by Hume (1984:65), who concludes that they have no relevance to the structure of the poem. Those who find Woodhouse's reading persuasive, however, agree that the accommodation of nature to grace, a staple of religious thought from the medieval church to the sixteenth-century English church, has in Spenser's handling become a sharper, Calvinistic antithesis. Thus, although the narrative sequence sets up some interpretive difficulties, the general movement – from corrupt and sinful will, through the temptation of despair, to sanctification by grace and then to joy and glory – is Calvinistic in emphasis: natural man is as spiritually bankrupt as his natural powers are insufficient. Hence grace must correct nature's defects and make a new start possible. Reason and Una's guidance help to counter the Calvinistic sense of man's bankruptcy, but Redcrosse's weaknesses, shown against Error, Orgoglio, and the Dragon, clearly demand spiritual powers of resistance not his own. Heavenly grace aids Guyon and Arthur equally (II viii 1, xi 30), though Arthur at times can also represent God's operative grace, working with, not forcing help on, the dispirited. The profound sense of contrast between the despair-filled depths of sinful individuals (attributable to the 'hereditary depravity and corruption of our nature' Calvin *Institutes* 2.1.8) and their subsequent, serenely joyful sense of vocation and vision of glorification (cf *FQ* I xii 39) owes a great debt to Calvin's dramatic sense of the spiritual life, even if the later books of *The Faerie Queene* attribute increasingly less to divine intervention and providential direction but center instead on human potential and achievement. PETER AUKSI

A recent translation of the *Institutes* is Calvin ed 1960, with excellent bibliography, indexes, and scholarly apparatus. For Calvin in the context of the other continental reformers, see Kilian McDonnell 1967 *John Calvin, the Church, and the Eucharist* (Princeton). Calvin's influence on English literature in general is treated in J.D. Boulger 1980 *The Calvinist Temper in English Poetry* (The Hague); King 1982 (a general survey from a much-needed historical perspective); and Sinfield 1983 (includes a detailed study of the movement away from Calvinism in *FQ* III-VI). For Spenser specifically, see also Hume 1984 (*SC* and *FQ* in the context of militant Protestantism; see esp ch 4); Marshall 1959; Frederick M. Padelford 1914 'Spenser and the Theology of Calvin' *MP* 12:1–18; Whitaker 1950 (an essential monograph on Spenser's religion, with emphasis on the source materials; perhaps overemphasizes conservatism and orthodoxy in Spenser's thought); A.S.P. Woodhouse 1949 (an influential though much debated discussion of nature and grace in *FQ*); Woodhouse 1960.

Cambell, Canacee, Cambina With Triamond (Telamond), Cambell is designated a hero of *FQ* IV by its title page, and with his spouse Cambina, who is Triamond's sister, and his own sister Canacee, who is Triamond's spouse, he belongs to the focal foursome of Book IV. This foursome is an idealized emblem of friendship – of the 'lovely,' or loving, bond at once between like and like and between like and unlike: man and man, woman and woman, man and woman. Cambell's name, like Canacee's, comes from Chaucer's *Squire's Tale*, but its second vowel has been altered from Chaucer's *a* (Camballo) to *e*, plausibly to suggest the association of Cambell's nature with Latin *bellum* (war). Cambina's name, from Italian *cambiare* (to change, exchange, transform) and by analogy suggesting English *combine*, indicates a nature both different from and complementary to Cambell's belligerence.

Spenser barely introduces Cambell, Triamond, Canacee, and Cambina in *FQ* IV ii 30–1 before interrupting his present narrative to comment for three stanzas (32–4) on its origin in Chaucer. This digression is the first in a series of three, subsequently including the journey of Agape to the Fates (ii) and the battle of Triamond with Cambell to win Canacee's hand (iii). Whether simply to reinforce antique and Chaucerian resonance or more specifically to indicate thematic congruence with Chaucer's *Knight's Tale* (Hieatt 1975a:75–9) or an endless series of regressive narrators (Goldberg 1981:31–41), this digression begins by imitating the opening of the Chaucerian tale told not by the Squire but by his father, the Knight.

Having already asserted Chaucer's authorship of the battle between Cambell and Triamond, Spenser next remarks that the story of the battle is nowhere extant and, digressing more expansively, laments that time should have devoured even the poet's 'threasure endlesse deare.' He then explains that he has dared 'revive' the fragmentary *Squire's Tale* only through the 'infusion sweete' of Chaucer's poetic spirit into his own. Spenser thereby introduces in terms of the poet's own narrative activity the theme of infusing – pouring into, becoming – that Spenser's myth of Triamond and his brothers unfolds, dilates, and embodies (Anderson 1971b:193–5). The penultimate line that Spenser addresses to Chaucer's spirit – 'I follow here the footing of thy feete' (ie, both 'tracks' and 'metrical stresses') – wittily includes likeness and difference, since it refers to both poets' dominant use of an iambic pentameter line in their major works and to the use in his own of a stanzaic form not to be duplicated exactly in Chaucer's. Spenser's wit thus points the fact that he not only imitates but everywhere transforms.

In the Renaissance editions of Chaucer that Spenser is likely to have used (as in modern ones), the *Squire's Tale* is unfinished, but it is preceded by the Epilogue to the *Man of Law's Tale* instead of the Squire's own Prologue and succeeded by the *Merchant's Tale* instead of the Franklin's. The Merchant, a less generous and tactful figure than the Franklin, speaks the observations on the Squire and his tale that immediately follow it and, at least when spoken by the Franklin, mercifully interrupt it. Since Renaissance editors attributed these lines to the Merchant and noted, immediately after the *Squire's Tale* breaks off, that 'There can be founde no more of this fore said tale, whiche hath ben sought i[n] dyvers places,' it would have been more difficult, although not impossible, for Spenser to have discerned the gently comic tone of the next speaker's interruption. But Spenser is unlikely to have missed the parody within the Squire's tale itself, which 'reads at times as if its author had swallowed a rhetorical handbook whole but had not fully digested it' (Donaldson in Chaucer ed 1975:1086–7). This tale, which threatens to be interminable unless interrupted, parodies the very form of romance, a form that inherently carries the potential for limitless extension (P.A. Parker 1979:83, 94–5).

The attraction for Spenser of Chaucer's unfinished, parodic Canterbury romances – the *Squire's Tale* and *Sir Thopas* – is remarkable. Such Chaucerian parody underlies and enriches *The Faerie Queene*, even while its meaning differs from Spenser's own. Spenser did not merely replicate Chaucer's parodies of romance, and still less did he insensitively moralize their comedy out of existence. Instead, he both assimilated and transformed them, much as Triamond's spirit revives and transforms those of his dead brothers.

The action of Chaucer's *Squire's Tale* that is relevant to Spenser's continuation(s) of it is readily summarized. A knight bears a magic mirror and ring to Canacee, a king's daughter. The mirror has the power to reveal any danger to king or kingdom, to distinguish friend from foe, and to uncover a false lover; and it surely contributed to Spenser's conception of the wondrous glass in which Britomart first sees her true love, Artegall (*FQ* III ii 17–26). The ring enables its wearer to converse with birds and to understand the healing properties of plants. Canacee's long conversation with a jilted falcon in Chaucer may anticipate the squire Timias' empathetic turtledove in *FQ* IV viii 3–12.

To Canacee's father, the knight gives a magic sword that can penetrate any armor and alone can heal the wounds inflicted with it. Though transmuted, the ring Cambell wears in his battle with Triamond that 'Had power to staunch al wounds' (IV ii 39) descends from powers combined in Canacee's ring and her father's sword. The conclusion of the second part of the *Squire's Tale* – 'And after woll I speke of Camballo / That fought in lystes with the brethern two / For Canace, er that he myght her wyn' – presumably also led to the battle of Spenser's Cambell with three brothers on his sister's behalf. Notably, however, Spenser circumvents the suggestion of incest in his source by making Cambina Cambell's spouse (cf Cheney 1983:19–21).

Cambina, looking like the fulfillment of an iconographer's wish, comes at once to rescue her brother when his life is imperiled and to rescue the narrator when his story begins to seem endless (IV iii 36–7). Her arrival is wondrous, clamorous, and violent. She rides in a chariot drawn by angry lions and holds in her hands a caduceus, symbolizing peace, and a cup of nepenthe, able to assuage pain and hatred. Aligned with blind Cupid and Cybele, goddess of fertility and civilization, both of whose chariots are drawn by lions and both of whom hypostatize powers of generative love (Roche 1964:23–30, III xii 22), Cambina first pleads and reasons with Cambell and Triamond to stop fighting; but when speech does not avail, she uses her magical (and irrational) powers, first striking the combatants with her rod to disable their warlike passions and then ministering to each a drink from her cup. Instantly the combatants kiss, and three stanzas later Cambell, Triamond, Canacee, and Cambina, are 'all alike' united in 'perfect love' (iii 52).

In *FQ* IV iv, this idealized foursome joins a variously discordant group of eight traveling to Satyrane's tournament, where Cambell and Triamond, exchanging armor, literally fight for one another and thereby realize their bond of friendship. Assimilated into the meaning of the tournament, the four ideal friends are present in little more than name when we hear the last of them in IV v.

JUDITH H. ANDERSON

Anderson 1971b; Chaucer ed 1969; Chaucer 1975 *Chaucer's Poetry: An Anthology for the Modern Reader* ed E.T. Donaldson, 2nd ed (New York); Cheney 1983; Goldberg 1981; Hieatt 1975a; P.A. Parker 1979.

Cambridge By the second half of the sixteenth century, Cambridge University, although already an ancient institution, was nonetheless something of a backwater by international standards. In the first part of the century, it had produced a series of distinguished men of letters: Ascham, Cheke, Smith, Watson, and Redman (described rhapsodically by Nashe in his preface to Greene's *Menaphon*). By Spenser's time (he matriculated in 1569), the university's reputation as a center for a humanized liberal arts training had declined, at the same time as it was undergoing a rapid numerical expansion to supply the new men for the administration of the centralized Tudor government and for the preaching of the established faith. When Elizabeth visited the university in 1564, it consisted of 1267 members (fellows, students, etc); by 1569, it was 1630 strong; and by 1575, Dr Caius counted 1813, crowded into the fourteen colleges and halls which in the 1570s were the undergraduates' residences.

The life of the university was directed by a set of statutes which from the 1530s onwards had been revised several times: in 1535 by Henry VIII, who banned scholastic teaching and the study of canon law, in 1549 by Edward VI, and in 1559 and 1570 by Elizabeth. There was a brief return to the older scholastic curriculum during the reign of Mary. Under the reformed statutes, BA students following a four-year course focused on elementary dialectic (the humanist version of logic or formal ratiocination) and advanced rhetoric (proficiency in Latin grammar was the only entrance requirement – and even that was waived for choristers); they progressed through a program of reading in the major classical authors (Virgil, Horace, and Cicero, together with Aristotle's *Nicomachean Ethics* and *Politics*) to natural philosophy (elementary science). To this was added some mathematics (bookkeeping), geometry (basic Euclid), and Greek, starting with the New Testament (providing opportunity for scriptural studies and catechism) and going on to some Greek oratory (Demosthenes and Isocrates) and possibly some drama (all studied in Greek-Latin parallel texts). When Gabriel Harvey lectured on Greek at Pembroke Hall in 1573, he gave an extremely modest course (including a survey of transliterated Greek terms found in the titles of Latin works). Studies in law, medicine, and natural science had apparently failed to keep pace with continental Europe, and the student who wished to pursue an academic career in one of these subjects customarily completed his education at one of the great European universities like Bologna or Padua. Thus, the aspiring John Dee went to Europe as a matter of course to continue his mathematical and medical studies, and later claimed that in Paris he was offered a professorship for the same learning that had earned him the name of magician in England.

Despite the attempt by the university statutes to provide a uniform curriculum, by the mid-century a boy's college (entrance to university was at about fourteen to sixteen years of age) was the center of his studies. Thus the 1560 statutes of Trinity provide for nine lectureships for teaching within the college: five in dialectic, two in Greek and Latin literature, one in Greek grammar, and one in mathematics (Mullinger 1884, app A). Each student was in the care of a tutor and followed daily academic exercises with other members of his college. His tutor supervised his studies and also his personal behavior (the letter purportedly by Harvey's tutor to Harvey's father in Nashe's *Have with You to Saffron-Walden* gives a glimpse – however fictionally embellished – into the relationship of tutor and pupil; in Nashe ed 1904–10, 3:65–9). At Corpus Christi (or Bene't) College in the 1570s, for instance, the average day began with morning prayers, followed by three lectures – on Aristotle's natural philosophy, his organon (or logic), and John Seton's *Dialectica* (a Cambridge textbook on rudimentary logic and argumentation, based on the humanist dialectician Agricola). At noon, Greek studies consisted of the construing of a text (such as some Homer or Demosthenes), followed by grammar instruction. Probably students at various stages in their degree course attended various of these classes: the Seton, for instance, is clearly designed for the first year of instruction. In the afternoon, rhetoric instruction consisted either of textbook instruction, or of a reading of Cicero (presumably either his rhetoric texts, or a speech or letter for analysis and imitation). At the end of the afternoon, the scholars of the college debated a 'sophism' (a dubious or facetious question which the student had to attack or defend). This daily program was occasionally supplemented with scriptural reading, the debating of a scriptural 'common place' or doctrinal question by one or more of the fellows of the college, or of a 'problem' by the BAs of the college, or by the sophisters (those who had completed their first two years' training). On Saturday evening, a demonstration 'declamation' (formal speech) was given by two of the BAs or two of the scholars (Norfolk County Archives).

As this account shows, members of a single college mixed frequently for instruction. It was presumably in the course of such lectures and debates at Pembroke Hall that Spenser became acquainted with Harvey, who became a fellow of Pembroke Hall in 1570, when Spenser was a sophister there. Although students were obliged to attend university lectures in addition to their college tasks, and were fined for nonattendance (eg, see the 1560 Trinity statutes), their educational center was then (as now) their college. There is no guarantee that any student would have encountered a student at another college, or even that he would have heard a prominent lecturer giving a particular university course.

Those students with an interest in particular specialist disciplines not explicitly catered for within the BA curriculum were, however, occasionally taken up by fellows with 'research' knowledge in those areas (particularly if they could afford to pay well for such tuition). Dee, a student at St John's in the 1540s, studied Greek mathematics privately with the great Greek scholar John Cheke, just as the mathematician Thomas Harriot later studied science and navigation with the distinguished geographer Richard Hakluyt at his Oxford college, Christ Church, and Sidney studied chemistry in private. Within the university, one may characterize as sources of 'influence' groups of like-minded intellectuals discussing specialist problems, corresponding, and exchanging books (see *Areopagus). LISA JARDINE

For Spenser at Cambridge, see Judson 1945, ch 5. Still important is James Bass Mullinger 1884 *The University of Cambridge* (vol 2) (Cambridge). The university statutes are reprinted in John Lamb, ed 1838 *A Collection of Letters, Statutes, and Other Documents* (London). Charles Henry Cooper and John William Cooper 1842–1908 *Annals of Cambridge* 5 vols (Cambridge) gives a year-by-year account of the university, and John Venn, ed 1910 *Grace Book Δ* (Cambridge) contains the records of the university for 1542–89, including Spenser's graduations. For religious disputation during Spenser's time at Cambridge, see Porter 1958. More general treatments of university life and educational history are Kenneth Charlton 1965 *Education in Renaissance England* (London); Mark H. Curtis 1959 *Oxford and Cambridge in Transition, 1558–1642* (Oxford); Hugh Kearney 1970 *Scholars and Gentlemen: Universities and Society in Pre-industrial Britain, 1500–1700* (London); and Joan Simon 1966 *Education and Society in Tudor England* (Cambridge). For details in curriculum, see Lisa Jardine 1974; and Jardine 1976 'Humanism and Dialectic in Sixteenth-Century Cambridge: A Preliminary Investigation' in Bolgar 1976:141–54.

Camden, William (1551–1623) Historian, antiquary, educator, and poet, Camden attended Christ's Hospital and St Paul's School, London, and Oxford (possibly with Sidney); appointed second master (1575) then headmaster (1593) of Westminster School; appointed Clarenceux King of Arms at the recommendation of Fulke Greville (1597). His great topographical history, the *Britannia*, was published in Latin in 1586. Camden added to and revised the three other editions published in Spenser's lifetime (1587, 1590, 1594).

Spenser's general indebtedness to the *Britannia* is probably more than can ever be exactly determined, but it is at least discernible in *FQ* II x and III iii in the chronicles of British kings, in *FQ* IV xi in the marriage of Thames and Medway, and in *Vewe of Ireland*.

For his account of British kings, Spenser drew on a wide variety of sources but primarily Geoffrey of Monmouth and to a much lesser extent Camden. There was no inconsistency in drawing material from two such opposed views of history, and Camden probably shared the view that 'historicall fiction' (Letter to Raleigh) was the proper substance of a national epic. It is nevertheless somewhat ironic that Camden and Geoffrey meet in Spenser since Camden's reputation was in no small part due to his daring rejection of the fabulous narrations of Geoffrey, including much of the Arthurian legend (see further Harper 1910). The Latin poem of 189 lines entitled 'De connubio Tamae et Isis,' published in fragments in the *Britannia* and usually ascribed to Camden, has been related to the *Epithalamion Thamesis*, which Spenser wrote but never published (see lost *works and Oruch 1967), and either or both may be the principal source for the river marriage in *FQ* IV. In *Vewe*, Spenser cites Camden's authority on 'the *Gallish* speache' of ancient Ireland and on the supposed habit Irishmen had of turning themselves into wolves once a year (*Var Prose* pp 93, 109) – a legend Camden recounts and discredits in his chapter on County Tipperary. Both writers were seeking to illustrate Irish credulity.

It is possible that Spenser and Camden met. In *Ruines of Time*, Spenser praises Camden as 'the nourice of antiquitie, / And lanterne unto late succeeding age' (164–75). It has been conjectured that the first 175 lines of *Time* were originally conceived as part of a separate poem in commendation of Camden's *Britannia* (Renwick in *Var* 8:527–8, Tuve 1970:148–9). Camden for his part praises Spenser as one 'who was borne to so great a favour of the Muses, that he surpassed all our Poets, even *Chawcer* himselfe' (*Sp All* p 178 and passim; see also p 20). R.D. DUNN

Levy 1967; McKisack 1971; Hugh Trevor-Roper 1971 *Queen Elizabeth's First Historian: William Camden and the Beginnings of English 'Civil History'* (London).

Camoens, Luis Vaz de (c 1524–80) Portugal's greatest poet was distantly related by marriage to Vasco da Gama, the hero of his epic, *The Lusiads* (*Os Lusíadas* 1572, 'the Sons of Lusus'; a companion of Bacchus and mythical founder of Portugal). This extraordinary epic of maritime expansion describes da Gama's voyage to India in 1497–8. Camoens wrote courtly pastorals, love poetry, and comedies before sailing to India in 1553. He returned to Lisbon in 1570, having composed his epic over years of extreme and adventurous hardship. His criticism of Portuguese imperialism appears openly in his satires and by inference in passages of warning and exhortation in his epic. He died in poverty shortly before Philip II of Spain annexed Portugal.

The frequently striking parallels between Camoens' minor works and those of Spenser probably derive from their common reading, especially in Italian poetry and the mythographers. Spenser may have read *The Lusiads*, however; its language would have presented little difficulty to any competent reader of Latin and Italian. He would have sympathized with Camoens' patriotism and his feeling for both his country's achievements and the language of their celebration (though not with his militant Catholicism). Certainly he would have admired Camoens' magnificent descriptions, his learning, and his use of allegory. Suggestive points of comparison include the account of his frescoes of the Creation in the sea-gods' palace (*Lusiads* 6.10–12; *Hymne of Love* 64–98) and Venus' search for her son Cupid, who is campaigning against perverse lovers (*Lusiads* 9.25–35; *FQ* III vi 12–15, xi 44–6, VI vii 32–7). In one episode, Camoens relates how Cupid shoots arrows into the sea at Venus' command and smites the Nereids with a desire for da Gama and his sailors which is later consummated on the isle of Love (*Lusiads* 9.47–87). In celebrating the reestablishment of elemental concord through grace and *virtus*, this episode is thematically and mythographically close to the marriage of Thames and Medway (*FQ* IV xi-xii). While Camoens emphasizes the particular, human triumph of his hero, and Spenser the universal (though related to the microcosm through historical reference), both poets handle a Renaissance commonplace with epic fullness.

ELIZABETH PORGES WATSON

Standard editions include *Obras completas* ed Hernâni Cidade, 3rd ed, 5 vols (Lisbon 1962–72); *Os Lusíadas* ed Reis Brasil (José Gomes Bras) (Lisbon 1964) and ed Frank Pierce (Oxford 1973); *Rimas* ed Alvaro J. da Costa Pimpâo (Coimbra 1953; rev ed 1973); *The Lusiads* tr Richard Fanshawe (1655), ed Geoffrey Bullough (London 1963); *The Lusiads* tr William C. Atkinson (Harmondsworth 1952); *The Lusiads* tr Leonard Bacon (New York 1950). See also Bowra 1945:86–138; William Freitas 1963 *Camoens and His Epic* (Stanford); Tillyard 1954:238–50.

Campion, Thomas (1567–1620) Best known to modern readers for his airs (ie, lute songs), Campion first made his reputation as a writer of Latin verses. These, together with a treatise on prosody (*Observations in the Art of English Poesie* 1602), reflect the humanist preoccupations of the Areopagus (see also *quantitative verse). Campion was highly regarded by his contemporaries: Camden includes him with Sidney, Spenser, Shakespeare, and 'other most pregnant witts of these our times, whom succeeding ages may justly admire' (*Remaines* 1605; *Sp All* p 99).

Campion's admiration for Spenser is best seen in the Latin *Poemata* of 1595, as in his epigram 'Ad Ed. Spencerum': 'Sive canis silvas, Spencere, vel horrida belli / Fulmina dispeream ni te amem, et intime amem' ('Whether you sing of the forests or of the horrid bolts of war, Spenser, I swear I love you and love you dearly' ed 1967:440–1). Of particular note in the *Poemata* is the celebratory poem *Ad Thamesin* in which Campion commemorates the defeat of the Armada seven years earlier. Like the catalogue of rivers in *FQ* IV xi, it belongs to a long tradition of epideictic rhetoric, in which a river or town is a symbol of both national and personal glory. In the poem's concluding apostrophe to the Queen, word placement suggests that Campion is alluding to the popular use of 'Una' as one of Elizabeth's pseudonyms: 'O diva, o miseris spes Elisabetha Britannis / Una' ('O goddess Elizabeth, sole hope of wretched Britons' 281–2, ed 1967:376–7). In *Umbra*, the central 'myth bears some resemblance to Spenser's tale of Amoret and Belphoebe' in *FQ* III (Davis in ed 1967:360). Other celebratory poems from the *Poemata* include the elegy 'Ad Dianam' (ed 1909:329) and the epigram 'Ad pacem' (2.4, ed 1909:271). In these Campion, like Spenser, praises the aging queen as a goddess of springtime and renewal, and in the latter he hails her as 'benigna servatrix' ('kind preserver') of the British nation. ROBIN HEADLAM WELLS

Thomas Campion 1909 *Works* ed Percival Vivian (Oxford); Campion 1967 *Works* ed Walter R. Davis (Garden City, NY).

Canada, influence and reputation in When the intellectual history of Canada is written, it will surely contain a chapter on the country's university English departments, institutions from which much of its high culture has emanated, including its distinguished contribution to Spenser studies. A.S.P. Woodhouse (eg, Woodhouse 1949) and A.C. Hamilton (most notably, Hamilton 1961a) have been instrumental in engendering and sustaining the Spenser renaissance of our own day, as have other eminent Spenserians such as A. Kent Hieatt. A mere roll call of some Canadian critics of Spenser gives a sense of the breadth and depth of academic interest in the poet in Canada: William Blissett, Ronald B. Bond, Thomas H. Cain, René Graziani, Patricia Parker, David R. Shore and, of course, Northrop Frye, who has paid critical and creative tribute to Spenser in influential essays and comments on *The Faerie Queene* and in the transformed Spenserian romance that is *The Secular Scripture* (1976). Some 'firsts' in Spenser scholarship further emphasize the Canadian contribution: *A Theatre for Spenserians* (Kennedy and Reither 1973) is the outcome of the first international conference on Spenser, held at the University of New Brunswick in 1969; the *Spenser Newsletter*, started at the University of Western Ontario in 1970, is the first journal devoted to Spenser; and *The Spenser Encyclopedia* is the first such compendium to be devoted to the poet.

Not fortuitously, the major instance of Spenser's presence in Canadian literature is the work of a former University of Toronto student, James Reaney, who wrote his doctoral thesis under Northrop Frye on 'The Influence of Spenser on Yeats' (1958); his *A Suit of Nettles* (1958) is a series of twelve eclogues modeled on *The Shepheardes Calender*. With its cast of geese, its satirical thrust, and its formalistic panache, *A Suit of Nettles* is at once resonantly Spenserian and idiosyncratically original: alongside a Mopsus and a Mome Fair are Yeatsian echoes, satirical attacks, and regional references that ground its poems in the modern world and in contemporary Ontario. Later Reaney works such as *One-Man Masque* (1960) also exhibit the influence of Spenser. So also does the fiction of Hugh Hood, another University of Toronto student, who attended A.S.P. Woodhouse's classes on Spenser and also heard Frye lecture on the poet. Not only does the twelve-part structure of Hood's *Around the Mountain* (1967) echo that of *The Shepheardes Calender*, but its final, wintry sketch was written with Spenser's poem specifically in mind (see Struthers 1979:41–8). Two other Toronto students whose work reveals some Spenserian influence are Margaret Avison and Jay Macpherson: Avison refers to 'Old Mutabilitie' in her 'Dispersed Titles' (in *Winter Sun* 1960), and Macpherson makes use of Spenser's Merlin in 'The Old Enchanter' (in *The Boatman* 1957) and in 'Masters and Servants' (in *Welcoming Disaster* 1974).

Various other Canadian writers who (like Reaney, Hood, Avison, Macpherson, and even Frye) can broadly be categorized as modernists, also reveal the influence of Spenser. While Malcolm Lowry alludes only casually to Spenser (in *October Ferry to Gabriola* 1970), Robertson Davies (in an unpublished 1984 letter) counts him as an influence, albeit 'chiefly in the way of extending [his] realm of fantasy.' More evident is the influence of Spenser on two other modern poets: A.M. Klein, whose 'Yehuda Ha-Levi, His Pilgrimage' (1941) uses Spenserian archaism and the Spenserian stanza to tell a tale of 'charmed minstrelsy,' and Ralph Gustafson, whose 'Golden Chalice' (1935) is a narrative in 59 Spenserian stanzas and whose 'Epithalamium in Time of War' (1944) owes a considerable debt to Spenser's *Epithalamion*. While Gustafson's enthusiasm for Spenser was generated at Oxford, both he and Klein were probably exposed to the poet at university in their home province of Quebec, as very likely was another Quebec writer, John Glassco, who records playfully that he liked to read 'Spenser to the music of Bach, opening [his] mind to all the resources of sound, rhythm and syntax, without judgement, embracing the effect of nuance, drowning [himself] in a feast of images and vowels, in a kind of sensuous verbal fog' (1970:222). While a Romantic revivalist such as Glassco availed himself of a Keatsian Spenser, the more austere sensibility of the Montreal novelist Hugh MacLennan contented itself by allowing a 'procession of swans on the Thames' to recall images from *Prothalamion* (in a letter of 1928; Cameron 1981:30). MacLennan's Eliot-like leap from Thames present to Thames past may indicate primarily a knowledge of *The Waste Land*, a possibility reminding us that, Reaney, Hood, and a very few others aside, Canadian writers of the modern period have been only slightly or indirectly influenced by Spenser.

This is also true of Canadian writers of the eighteenth, nineteenth, and early twentieth centuries. There are casual references to Spenser in the prose writings of the Colonial period. Mrs Simcoe, for example, refers to him in her *Diary* entry for 12 June 1792, and Joseph Howe quotes from *The Faerie Queene* in his *Travels* entry for 11 September 1828. In addition, there are epigraphs from *The Faerie Queene* in at least two prose works of the nineteenth century: the English writer Anna Jameson's *Winter Studies and Summer Rambles in Canada* (1838) and Agnes Maule Machar's *Roland Graeme: Knight*. 'Ever since ... I read Spenser's "Faërie Queen,"' says Machar's Graeme, 'it seemed to me the noblest task a man could devote himself to, ... "To ride abroad redressing human wrongs," or whatever corresponds to that in our prosaic age' (1892:124). In the twentieth century, Lucy Maud Montgomery expanded a serial entitled 'Una of the Garden' into *Kilmeny of the Orchard* (1910) and later created the dreamy figure of Una Meredith in *Rainbow Valley* (1919).

Among Canada's early poets, all of whom were heavily indebted to Romantic and Victorian models, the influence of Spenser was both direct and indirect. In 'The Frogs' (1888) by Archibald Lampman, there is an intertextual sense of the Bower of Bliss that probably comes through Tennyson and Keats. Lampman's later love poetry, however, may reveal the direct influence of the *Amoretti*. Similarly, the epithalamic section that concludes one of the most intriguing pre-Confederation poems, Charles Sangster's *St. Lawrence and the Saguenay* (1856), may indicate a direct debt to Spenser's spousal verses. The allegorical pretensions of Sangster's poem may also indicate a direct debt to Spenser, but the qualities of Byron and Shelley in its Spenserian stanzas suggest that his primary debt was to the Romantics. The direct influence of Spenser (as well as his indirect influence through Keats) is discernible in the work of another nineteenth-century poet, Charles Mair, who recorded that as a youth he read 'Spenser's *Fairy Queen* in Charles Knight's excellent edition for a boy, in which the finest stanzas were connected by descriptive prose, and never wearied me' (Shrive 1965:16). Unfortunately, the contrived diction of Mair's own poems, including the 'Song' of 'The Last Bison' (1890) which is in Spenserian stanzas, proves wearying to most readers. The same can be said of such early derivations of *Childe Harold* as Joseph Clinch's *The Captivity of Babylon* (1840) and Joshua Marsden's *A Farewell to Nova Scotia and New Brunswick* (1816), both of which, like *The St. Lawrence and the Saguenay*, put Spenserian stanzas at the service of religious beliefs whose frontier simplicity Spenser would have found dismaying. More intriguing to Spenser might be the later attempts of Tom MacInnes to adapt the Spenserian stanza to the landscapes and anecdotes of British Columbia in such poems as 'The Chilkoot Pass' (1898) and 'On Beacon Hill' (1901). Although many arbitrary and uncreative applications of the Spenserian stanza exist in Canadian poetry past and present, many poets who have used the form (recent ones include Earle Birney in 'For Steve' [1945] and Leonard Cohen in 'Stanzas for H[enry] M[oscovitch]' [in Moscovitch 1982]) have done so in apparent consciousness of its potential, not merely as a narrative vehicle, but also as a framing device for the picturesque scenes and human tableaux of Canada's more cultivated areas.

There are few even casual references to Spenser in contemporary Canadian writing, perhaps because many writers of the post-modern bent pride themselves on their lack of formal education, their rejection of fixed forms, and their hostility to the English tradition. Nevertheless, a prominent Canadian post-modernist, Robert Kroetsch, has admitted that he 'actually used Spenser when [he] wrote *The Sad Phoenician*' (1979) and that Spenser is a writer against whom he tests himself. For Kroetsch, the 'poet's poet' is a 'comparative mythologist,' a games player, an essayist of the unconstrained imagination (see *Labyrinths of Voice* 1982:101–3). Moreover, Spenserian resonances can be detected in *Ear Reach* (1982), by George Bowering, another prominent Canadian post-modernist who, like Kroetsch, has close ties with a university English department.

Without entirely endorsing any of the myths that have grown up around Canadian culture, one may suggest that the urge to form and the tendency towards Puritanism which many feel are the qualities of pioneering and northern cultures may account in part for the elective affinity of Canadians in the past for the structured thought and stern moralism of Milton, rather than for the emergent narratives and colorful allegories of Spenser. Mary O'Brien, a nineteenth-century Canadian pioneer, wrote in her journal, 'I ... stirred a bowl of cream into butter ... reading Milton all the time' (ed 1968:118). With the pioneer imperative and the Puritan ethos on the wane in Canada, and the country's university English departments as strong as ever or stronger, perhaps the conditions are right for an increase in Spenser's influence and reputation among Canadian writers and readers.

D.M.R. Bentley

Peter Aichinger 1979 *Earle Birney* (Boston); D.M.R. Bentley 1983–4 'Through Endless Landscapes: Notes on Charles Sangster's 'The St. Lawrence and the Saguenay' *ECW* 27(Winter):1–34; Elspeth Cameron 1981 *Hugh MacLennan: A Writer's Life* (Toronto); L.R. Early 1983–4 'Lampman's Love Poetry' *ECW* 27(Winter):116–49; Northrop Frye 1971 *The Bush Garden: Essays on the Canadian Imagination* (Toronto) on James Reaney; Mollie Gillen 1975 *The Wheel of Things: A Biography of L.M. Montgomery, Author of 'Anne of Green Gables'* (Don Mills, Ont); John Glassco 1970 *Memoirs of Montparnasse* (Toronto); Joseph Howe 1973 *Western and Eastern Rambles: Travels Sketches of Nova Scotia* ed M.G. Parks (Toronto); Wendy Keitner 1979 *Ralph Gustafson* (Boston); Carl F. Klinck, gen ed 1965 *Literary History of Canada: Canadian Literature in English* rev ed 3 vols (Toronto 1976); Robert Kroetsch 1982 *Labyrinths of Voice: Conversations with Robert Kroetsch*, ed Shirley Newman and Robert Wilson (Edmonton); Alvin A. Lee 1968 *James Reaney* (New York); Agnes Maule Machar 1892 *Roland Graeme: Knight* (New York); Henry Moscovitch 1982 *New Poems* (Oakville, Ont); Mary O'Brien 1968 *Journals ... 1828–1838* ed Audrey Saunders Miller (Toronto); Norman Shrive 1965 *Charles Mair: Literary Nationalist* (Toronto); Elizabeth Posthuma Gwillim Simcoe 1911 *The Diary of Mrs. John Graves Simcoe, Wife of the First Lieutenant-Governor of the Province of Upper Canada, 1792–6* ed J. Ross Robertson (Toronto); J.R. (Tim) Struthers, ed 1979 *Before the Flood: Hugh Hood's Work in Progress* (Downsview, Ont); Clara Thomas 1967 *Love and Work Enough: The Life of Anna Jameson* (Toronto).

cannibals Spenser's cannibals (the Salvage Nation of *FQ* VI viii 35–49) represent an extreme of collective incivility. In them, courtesy has not merely gone awry but has been turned inside out. Their victim, Serena, is both a romantic heroine and an aspect of the social and psychological 'serenity' that is at issue and at risk in all places of retreat in Book VI. Unfortunately, the remoteness that fosters ease and grace also harbors barbarity. Lacking inborn human instincts and the nurtured discipline of gentlemen, the cannibals represent an organized bestiality and communal disorder.

Unlike the Brigands who appear later, the cannibals do not trade or sell goods, nor do they produce a champion like the Brigands' captain who becomes Pastorella's protector. They are nomads who forage daily for whatever fortune leaves in their path. Like shepherds, they know the rudiments of festivity, having arrived in Fairyland by way of Greek romance and Italian pastoral (Staton 1966), though their provenance extends from the Cyclops in *Odyssey* 9, to Boiardo's Lestrigoni in *Orlando innamorato* 2.18, to accounts of the western Celts, to the starving rebels in contemporary Ireland (see McNeir 1968). Rather than piping shepherd songs, however, they howl to horns and bagpipes; rather than dancing around a garlanded figure, they engage in discordant and chaotic group movement around a sacrificial victim. The closest parallel to Spenser's episode is

Achilles Tatius' Alexandrian romance, *Clitophon and Leucippe* (3.9–22), where swarthy herdsmen capture Leucippe and, through a ruse, are made to believe they have sacrificed her. Tatius' brigands attempt to eat the entrails of their captive, however, as part of the propitiatory sacrifice of a virgin to their god. Spenser's cannibals propose to offer Serena's blood to their god and 'feed with gurmandize' on her flesh.

The incivility of the cannibals originates in their giving free rein to primitive impulses, especially lust: as with so much individual cruelty in Spenser, the roots of this collective discourtesy lie in a perverted eroticism. Once they have stripped away Serena's jewels and clothing (marks of her feminine dignity and social status), they turn from hungry butchers to courtly lovers, dismembering her with their 'lustfull fantasyes.' In this, the cannibals recall the ceremonial games of tamer rustics and parody the Petrarchan conventions of love, including an inventory of the parts of the sonnet lady. Their bagpipe cacophony travesties the merry piping of Colin among the Graces (VI x). Their deep woodland and shoreline barbarity, like the pastoral retreat of cantos ix-xi, is far from the civilized world; their savagery shows the harmonious civility of Mount Acidale to be all the more ideal, momentary, and vulnerable.

Spenser's point in the cannibal episode is not, however, that primitivism is inevitably a perversion of 'the sacred noursery / Of vertue' (proem 3). The satyrs of Book I are not similarly depraved in their treatment of Una, for instance; the instincts of the Salvage Man in Book VI are sound even if his training is deficient. But if primitive instinct is to be a source of virtue, it must be combined with the disciplines of courtesy, which the cannibals lack. The satyrs are drawn to Una because they instinctively recognize Truth. The cannibals, however, are faulty philosophers and theologians: as heathens, they misinterpret the 'straunge mischaunce' that delivers Serena to them as a grace from their god; they impose their own misreading on the wanderings and the 'wreckfull wynde' that provide their victims. The incongruities of the rites they perform reinforce that point. When the priest chastizes their desire to profane their victim, the narrator tells us that religion holds 'even theeves in measure'; but he goes on to characterize their rites as 'divelish ceremonies.' Calepine righteously sends their 'damned soules to hell' and sacrifices their priest 'to th'infernall feends.'

Thus the cannibals undo most of courtesy's alliances and functions in courtship, art, religion, and justice. They make an imposing ally of the Blatant Beast, which they surpass in going beyond defamation and backbiting to the most extreme of bad welcomes, the eating of the guest. Their damage to Serena is correspondingly severe. Although she is rescued, their barbarity leaves her in a state of shock and prepares the reader for an almost equally vicious invasion of the shepherd domain later by the Brigands who murder Meliboe and his wife. Like other barbarous characters in Book VI, the cannibals demonstrate that courtesy must go well-armed and supported by virtue nourished 'deepe within the mynd' (proem 5).

HAROLD TOLIVER

canto (Ital 'song') The term used by Dante and Ariosto for a section of a poem; first used in English by Spenser in *The Faerie Queene* (see Drayton ed 1931–41, 2:5).

Dante's cantos in the *Divine Comedy* are each approximately 130 lines. He seems attentive to the word's root meaning (from *cantare* 'to sing') and to have decided that between 40 and 50 tercets are as much as can or should be 'sung' at one time. His episodes are short, so there are often as many as two or three in a single canto; and only rarely does the end of a canto coincide with the end of an episode. Ariosto's cantos in *Orlando furioso* vary widely in length but average almost 1000 lines. Their most distinctive feature is their use as a means of creating or sustaining suspense, rather like the end of a chapter in a novel or fadeout in a soap opera which halts and suspends one strand of a multiple, intertwined story at a moment of high piquancy, excitement, or danger.

Spenser's cantos often contain two or three episodes and vary greatly in length, from 30 to 87 stanzas (V i, II xii). He may have derived much from Dante and Ariosto but not his use of the canto. He uses cantos as he uses lines and stanzas, as rhetorical and thematic units. Since he uses all these units in ways difficult for modern readers to understand easily, consideration of his cantos best begins with a consideration of his lines and stanzas.

In a typical Spenserian stanza, each line is a unit, the stanza itself is a unit, and shifts within the stanza create other units, as in *FQ* I v 46:

> A ruefull sight, as could be seene with eie;
> Of whom he learned had in secret wise
> The hidden cause of their captivitie,
> How mortgaging their lives to *Covetise*,
> Through wastfull Pride, and wanton Riotise,
> They were by law of that proud Tyrannesse
> Provokt with *Wrath*, and *Envies* false surmise,
> Condemned to that Dongeon mercilesse,
> Where they should live in woe, and die in wretchednesse.

Each line is self-contained; and the stanza, which begins with *ruefull* and ends with *wretchednesse*, is also a unit. So, too, are lines 1–3, which place the 'ruefull sight' before us, and 4–9, which describe how it came into being.

By making 'the hidden cause of their captivitie' central to our view of the 'wretched thrals' in the house of Pride, Spenser, as he often does, gives more than one reason as the 'cause' and does not adjudicate between them: they are here because they mortgaged their lives to covetousness *and* because they were mercilessly condemned by the 'proud Tyrannesse' Lucifera. They did, and they were done unto. Further, Spenser's syntax is loose enough to yield two readings for a single line: 'Provokt with *Wrath*, and *Envies* false surmise' refers both to 'They' and to the 'proud Tyrannesse' in the preceding line. 'They,' having mortgaged their lives to covetousness, were 'Provokt with *Wrath*' when condemned by Lucifera; and Lucifera, 'Provokt with *Wrath*' at seeing their 'wastfull Pride, and wanton Riotise,' condemned them. This ambiguity creates an intimate relation between accused and accuser.

The stanza holds together materials for evaluation that are at once clear and problematic. We understand the situation morally, but are not asked to make an unambivalent moral judgment; even the tyrant acts 'by law.' We see too that Spenser enacts his allegories within single stanzas. By reading '*Envies* false surmise' as happening in turn both to the condemned and to Lucifera, we see much of what Spenser means by pride, and thereby much of what he seeks for holiness. (On the Spenserian *stanza, see Empson 1930:43–5, and esp Alpers 1967b:36–69.)

This stanza is typically not difficult, and to see how Spenser makes it is to see how slowly and patiently he asks us to read. Most of what we need to know in order to understand any one stanza is given within that stanza and in the few preceding it. He seems to have been extremely careful in calculating, depending on the simplicity or intricateness of the action, how much of a retentive memory a slow, patient reader can be expected to have. In some places (as in the later cantos in Book I) the action is sufficiently linear that the reader can remember several cantos; in others (as in the early cantos of Book IV) the action is so dense, the characters so difficult to distinguish from each other, that no more than a few stanzas can be retained. Any consideration of Spenser's larger units, cantos and books, must proceed from this understanding of how he constructs his smaller units, and of his sense of the reader's memory and proper reading pace. The pace need not be so slow that we must analyze each stanza, but must be slow enough to allow almost every line and each stanza to be genuine reading units.

At the end of *FQ* IV ii, Spenser writes, 'Great matter growing of beginning small; / The which for length I will not here pursew, / But rather will reserve it for a Canto new.' As in most of his references to cantos, he seems here only to say that 54 stanzas are enough for this canto, and that he has reached a convenient place to pause. Nor is he being disingenuous here, for many canto divisions (like this one) seem to be merely conveniences – so much so that he clearly had no *idea* governing the form and structure of the canto in *The Faerie Queene*. (For different and differing views on this matter, see Fowler 1964:51–9 and Røstvig 1980.) Yet many cantos are quite clearly organized to place an emphasis or to offer a sense of a subject variously considered by juxtaposing descriptions, incidents, speeches, and emblems.

The opening canto of the poem, for instance, contains two major episodes: the defeat of Error, and the night Redcrosse and Una spend in the house of Archimago. Narratively, the episodes are related only sequentially: first one and then the other. By putting them within a single canto, Spenser asks us to see, first, how error can be defeated, as a triumph of human strength and faith, and, second, how such triumphs do not render Redcrosse (or anyone) invulnerable to errors caused by deceit and self-deception. *FQ* II iv is more complicated. Spenser begins with the emblematic capture of Furor and Occasion, and then gives us Phedon's haunting tale of terrors and susceptibilities caused by circumstance, occasion, and misfortune. As in *FQ* I i, the defeat or capture of an abstract quality (error, occasion) does not obliterate it, either from Spenser's world or our own. At the end of the canto, Spenser introduces Atin, who demonstrates that while some people (or parts of all of us) seek to avoid occasion, others (or other parts of all of us) rush toward it.

Elsewhere, especially in Book VI, Spenser uses canto form as a kind of dialectic. For example, Serena and Timias, grievously wounded by the Blatant Beast in canto vi, are told by the Hermit that the only cure for their wounds 'Is to avoide the occasion of the ill' (14). The 'thesis' thus urges the view that, since the Blatant Beast strikes everywhere, it can be avoided only by withdrawing, staying in a hermitage, and saying farewell to knightly adventure and service, as the Hermit himself has done. The 'antithesis' is the triumph of Arthur and the Salvage Man over Turpine and his rude groom, which does much to restore the possibility of heroic courtesy. Yet the end of the canto serves not as 'synthesis' so much as a means of keeping both messages or themes alive for us: Blandina flatters Arthur into granting 'her husbands peace' (43), which allows Turpine to plan revenge upon him. Yet Arthur himself leaves unscathed, neither a victim needing to withdraw nor a hero.

In none of these examples is the canto's boundary meant to be conclusive: we are not done with error after I i, with occasion after II iv, or with the appeal of withdrawal from knightly action after VI vi. At most, the canto places an emphasis, even in the large set pieces where a single episode or description occupies an entire canto. For instance, at the house of Holiness (I x), we come to understand that Redcrosse's condition after being rescued from Despair requires his going there; likewise, at the end of the canto, we know that Redcrosse is now ready to fight the Dragon. Holiness is a state apart, so it can have a house apart and a canto apart.

Though this canto is perhaps the most self-contained of all 75 in *The Faerie Queene*, we recognize that holiness cannot be embodied as if once and for all in a single canto. Holiness is pain and abiding peace; it is contempt of this world and rejoicing at spiritual recovery on earth; it is 'bitter *Penance* with an yron whip' and 'a woman in her freshest age, / Of wondrous beauty, and of bountie rare'; it juxtaposes 'For bloud can nought but sin, and wars but sorrowes yield' with 'thou Saint *George* shalt called bee, Saint *George* of mery England, the signe of victoree' (27, 30, 60–1). To contemplate holiness is to consider patience, beauty, fruitfulness, despair, human wretchedness, human heroism, glimpses of heaven, and tasks on earth – all matters we know we are not done with at the end of this canto.

So the close of a canto is mostly Spenser's way of pausing without ever giving a sign that he is out of breath. Whatever 'meaning' we may find in the construction of his cantos is best governed by remembering how much he does with the smaller units of line, stanza, and sequences of stanzas, as well as 'the unwearied variety and seamless continuity of the whole' (Lewis 1936:358). Robert Bowes, a contemporary of Spenser, referred in 1596 to 'the second p[ar]t of the Fairy Queene and ixth chapter,' seeming to indicate that he read no more into Spenser's use of cantos than one might find in separate chapters of any literary work (*Sp All* p 45). We can see more than that in the assembling of many cantos, but it is important to take only and as much as Spenser gives us.

Spenser's sequence of lines, stanzas, and cantos rolls out like a magic carpet that unfolds before us and rolls up behind us as we move across it. Nonetheless, most readers rightly pause at the ends of cantos, and many cantos can be read as isolated units. 'Now gins this goodly frame of Temperance / Fairely to rise,' Spenser writes at the beginning of II xii. The line tells us that one frame of Temperance is just now beginning to rise as we start this last canto of the book. No one will be badly mistaken about Spenser's understanding of temperance by reading the Bower of Bliss episode by itself. Someone coming to *The Faerie Queene* for the first time would do much better to read I i slowly than all of Book I quickly, as happens all too often. Most of Spenser's cantos begin with a stanza that offers a proposition or asks a question; the rest of the canto explores the matter, as if testing an hypothesis. Many of his deepest chords can be heard and felt only by considering long sequences of cantos and whole books; but since his small units are very important to him, and he seems to ask us, therefore, to read as if we were not eager to find out what happens next, most of his meanings are available to us if we read the cantos one at a time, even in isolation. That all he writes is true, but nothing is ever final, is central to Spenser's wisdom. Practically speaking, then, readers seeking to come to terms with his ways and means can do well to consider cantos as units, as important as the units of lines, stanzas, and books. Spenser need have had no defined intellectual conception of a canto for that to be true. ROGER SALE

***Cantos of Mutabilitie*.** See ***The Faerie Queene*, Book VII**

Care Personifications of care recur throughout Spenser's poetry. Wakeful dogs lie before the dwelling of Morpheus, 'Watching to banish Care their enimy, / Who oft is wont to trouble gentle Sleepe' (*FQ* I i 40). Before the house of Richesse sits 'selfe-consuming Care,' keeping watch lest Force or Fraud should break in (II vii 25). 'Unquiet *Care*' appears in the 'confused rout' of persons following Cupid in the house of Busirane (III xii 25). At Mercilla's court, a 'sage old Syre' bearing the name 'The *Kingdomes care*' pleads against Duessa (V ix 43).

More elaborate is the description of the symbolic dwelling of the blacksmith Care, who assisted by six servants forges 'unquiet thoughts, that carefull minds invade' (IV v 35). Here Spenser portrays the 'gealous dread' (45) that disturbs Scudamour's rest after Ate (Discord) has made him suspect the loyalty of Britomart and Amoret. Elsewhere (*Hymne of Love* 252–72), Spenser treats 'that monster Gelosie' as the worst of the myriad torments which 'make a lovers life a wretches hell'; and in Scudamour's ordeal, he depicts that 'melancholy solicitude,' the *solicitudo melancholica* which medieval and Renaissance physicians had identified with heroic love.

Behind the image of Care's smithy lie two traditional but antithetical concepts of the forge – as a symbol of jealousy or a figure of harmony. In Italian usage, *martello* (hammer) might signify 'jealousie or suspition in love' (Florio 1598); and both the concept of care and the metaphor of percussion occur in Renaissance etymologies of jealousy (*zelo typia*). Bruno had compared the lover's heart to Vulcan's smithy. The imagery of the lover's sighs as bellows (*FQ* IV v 38) was conventional. The red-hot tongs with which Care nips Scudamour under his side resemble the pincers with which Grief in the masque of Cupid 'pinched people to the hart' (III xii 16).

The significance of Care's six assistants, each stronger than the other, has been variously explained. The seven smiths may symbolize the seven days of the week, and the scene has several analogies with Vulcan's forge; for example, the description of the sixth groom, 'like a monstrous Gyant,' echoes Homer's description of Vulcan (Upton in *Var* 4.197). Spenser specifically compares the largest and mightiest of the six 'strong groomes' to two of Vulcan's Cyclopean assistants, Bronteus and Pyracmon. The graduated scale of the hammers, which 'Like belles in greatnesse orderly succeed,' may be reminiscent of the musical experiments traditionally attributed to Pythagoras (Nelson 1963:250). These interpretations are not mutually exclusive, and to some extent they complement one another, reinforcing the symbolism of jealousy and discord. Since Homer's *Odyssey*, Vulcan had served as a type of the jealous husband. Christian apologists, moreover, identified him with the biblical smith Tubalcain, whose name was interpreted etymologically as signifying *aemulatio* (jealousy).

According to a legend that circulated widely in late classical antiquity and during the Middle Ages and Renaissance, Pythagoras had discovered the principles of harmony by correlating the musical tones produced by certain smiths at a forge with the diverse weights of their hammers. In most versions of this legend, there are only four smiths, or at most five (the fifth being eliminated as discordant); the addition of a sixth occurs in Franchino Gafori's *Theorica Musicae*. Alternative versions of the legend credited Jubal with similar experiments, identifying the forge as the smithy of his half-brother Tubalcain. Spenser has radically altered the significance of this motif, converting a traditional symbol of concord into an image of discord and placing his primary emphasis not on harmony but on inner disharmony and 'gealous discontent': 'For by degrees they all were disagreed' (IV v 36). JOHN M. STEADMAN

Lemmi 1929; Steadman 1979.

Castiglione, Baldesar (1478–1529) '*Castilio* of no small reputation' (*Three Letters* 2). The fleeting reference in Harvey's letter, familiar and pithy, to Spenser seems the only piece of external evidence that Spenser might have had direct acquaintance with Castiglione's work. In the absence of any further reference to him or his *Book of the Courtier* (*Il cortegiano* 1528), hypotheses about Spenser's use of that particular treatise must be pure speculation. The great vogue for courtesy books during Spenser's formative years has been demonstrated (Javitch 1978), including editions of Thomas Hoby's translation of *The Courtier*; and it seems, from contemporary enthusiasm for the work, likely that he read it, certain that he knew of it. Even so, without external evidence it is impossible to say that Spenser culled ideas from Castiglione rather than from other courtesy works, or, more probably, from authors such as Ariosto, whose compositions were permeated with similar courtly ideas.

Castiglione and Spenser had many (and usually rugged) features of their diplomatic life and experience in common, and each must have seen the vacuous sycophancy of the court, while recognizing the essential need for sensitive individuals to belong to that protected environment if they were to ensure, for themselves and their families, a civilized survival. That tension unites the moods of the two men and of their creative works, and must make us review traditional opinions about so-called idealism in their writing.

That said, there are many analogous relationships in their work, from the generic statement of intent in the Letter to Raleigh 'to fashion a gentleman or noble person in vertuous and gentle discipline' to the court practices in *Mother Hubberds Tale* (643–942), though these last seem more realistic than any of Castiglione's criticisms, Spenser's bleak description there being akin rather to Pius II's satire of 1444, itself well known through Alexander Barclay's translation. Those lines may reflect the court practices of *Courtier* 1 and 2, but in their astringency they echo Castiglione's criticism of the 'frivolity and vanity' of courtly accomplishments which have no good or useful end to them (*Courtier* 4.4).

The most obvious parallel seems to be that Castiglione and Spenser express ideals of courtesy, but even here doubt must exist because of the controversy over Castiglione's idealism: is his portrait an ideal or is it a subtle illustration of practical diplomacy, working through a reconciliation within the courtier himself of sycophancy and *virtù*, when, as Tasso later noted (*Il Malpiglio* 1585), the greatest *virtù* is dissimulation? So, too, we may be begging questions in assuming analogies between Bembo's discourse on Platonic love in *Courtier* 4, and the *Fowre Hymnes* (particularly *Hymne of Love* and *Hymne of Beautie*). The Platonic doctrine of love, visible in *Amoretti*, *SC*, *October*, *Colin Clout* and in the love of Timias and Belphoebe (*FQ* III–IV) may equally show the general influence of Petrarchism or direct influence from Bembo's own *Asolani*. An ideal of a rural court is visible in germ in Castiglione's brief dramatic eclogue *Tirsi*; and this, with his descriptions of the Urbino court, also has analogous if sporadic manifestations in *The Shepheardes Calender* and *The Faerie Queene*, and in the sojourn at court in *Colin Clout*. But it is doubtful that Spenser knew the *Tirsi*. One questions, too, whether the dirge in *November* (83–92) is a reminiscence of Castiglione's lament for Falcone in the rare *Alcon*, as is sometimes alleged. The closest parallel with anything which Castiglione wrote is in *Ruines of Rome* (7) where the Italian's best sonnet, 'Superbi colli,' is visible in garbled form, probably imitated from a French translation (and probably from du Bellay).

For reference to most of the possible echoes, the *Variorum* index is sufficient; to go beyond those cross-references is simply to prolong and extend an amusing but speculative search for sources which are at present unverifiable. J.R. WOODHOUSE

The standard modern edition is Baldesar Castiglione 1964 *Il libro del cortegiano* ed Bruno Maier, 2nd ed (Turin); translations include those of Thomas Hoby (1561), often reprinted, and Charles S. Singleton (New York 1959). For a brief biography, see C. Mutini 1979 in *Dizionario biografico degli Italiani* ed Alberto M. Ghisalberti (Rome) 22:53–68. Interpretations of *The Courtier* include Robert W. Hanning and David Rosand, eds 1983 *Castiglione: The Ideal and the Real in Renaissance Culture* (New Haven); Carlo Ossola and Adriano Prosperi, eds 1980 *La corte e il 'Cortegiano'* 2 vols (Rome); Wayne A. Rebhorn 1978 *Courtly Performances: Masking and Festivity in Castiglione's 'Book of the Courtier'* (Detroit); J.R. Woodhouse 1978; and Woodhouse 1979 'Book Four of Castiglione's *Cortegiano*: A Pragmatic Approach' *MLR* 74:62–8. For discussion regarding the English reception and for Spenser, see Javitch 1978; Kelso 1929; Kostić 1959a; Mason 1935; Tonkin 1972; and Robin Headlam Wells 1977 'Spenser and the Courtesy Tradition: Form and Meaning in the Sixth Book of *The Faerie Queene*' *ES* 58:221–9.

Castle Joyous In the episode of Castle Joyous (*FQ* III i 20–67), Spenser contrasts the heroic constancy of Britomart's chaste love for Artegall with the delights of Malecasta's court of erotic self-indulgence. The Castle's name may have been suggested by the Palazzo Gioioso that Angelica creates for Ranaldo in Boiardo's *Orlando innamorato* (1.8.1–14) or by Joyous Gard, Lancelot's castle to which he brings Guinevere in Malory's *Morte Darthur*. Yet Castle Joyous is only its 'commune name' (31), suggesting that the true name of this palace of unchastity may be quite different.

The episode begins when Britomart comes upon Redcrosse battling six knights who seek to make him serve their mistress Malecasta (L *male* badly + *casta* chaste), who has decreed that any knight approaching her castle must either renounce his own lady and accept her as his mistress or defeat her six knights. Ironically, the knight who successfully defends his own lady's honor by overcoming the knights will gain Malecasta's love as his reward. One way or another, a change of love, an inconstancy, will be demanded of the adventurer.

Britomart easily defeats the knights, and she and Redcrosse enter the castle where they are struck by the sumptuous decor, which is described at length. Particularly important is a tapestry which shows Venus wooing Adonis, enticing him to leave his companions and sleep and bathe with her in secret delight, safe from the dangers of an active life of hunting; but despite her pleas that he give up hunting, Adonis is slain and his body transformed into a flower. The story was well known from Ovid's *Metamorphoses* 10.519–739 and from Conti's *Mythologiae* 5.16 (see Lotspeich 1932:32–3). As recounted in the description of the tapestry, it suggests the self-indulgent quality of the erotic life at Malecasta's court and contrasts suggestively with the later appearance of Venus and Adonis as figures of truly joyous and fruitful activity in the Garden of Adonis (III vi).

Attempting to convert her to the luxurious eroticism of the castle, 'Dauncing and reveling both day and night, / And swimming deepe in sensuall desires' (i 39), Malecasta entreats Britomart to disarm. The love comedy that follows suggests Britomart's naiveté as well as her generosity of spirit. Malecasta is mistakenly encouraged by her visitor's courteous speech; and in an incident modeled on Ariosto's description of Alcina's secret visit to Ruggiero in *Orlando furioso* 7, she visits Britomart's bed. Unlike Ruggiero, however, Britomart is in no mood for dalliance: when she finds a stranger by her side, she leaps up and seizes her sword, thereby terrifying Malecasta whose shrieks rouse the household.

Britomart emerges from Castle Joyous with her constancy demonstrated. Before she departs, however, she is struck by the arrow of Gardante, one of the six knights who challenge all travelers. The names of these knights, revealed at just the moment that Britomart raises her visor and ignites Malecasta's passion, suggest a conventional ladder of lechery (Fowler 1959, Gilbert 1941), a progression of the kind of erotic activities to which Castle Joyous is devoted: Gardante, Parlante, Jocante, Basciante, Bacchante, and Noctante, which may be translated as seeing, speaking, toying, kissing, reveling, and whiling away the night.

The wound that she receives from Gardante is a token of Britomart's initiation to love. Spenser's description of the blood staining her white smock recalls Adonis' blood staining his white skin in the tapestry and looks forward to other erotic wounds that occur in Book III, among them Amoret's in the Busirane episode and the slight wound that Britomart herself receives from the enchanter. Most notably, Spenser describes in the following canto how Britomart originally fell in love with Artegall by viewing his image in a magic mirror, whereupon Cupid, very much like Gardante, wounded her with a bolt from his bow. It is this wound of love, burning in her breast, that has driven Britomart into the world in quest of Artegall. More immediately, however, the slight wound she receives from Gardante recapitulates her experiences in Castle Joyous. She has raised her visor and allowed herself to be seen. Moreover, because of her sympathy for Malecasta as a fellow lover, she has allowed herself in the name of courtesy to engage in the activities of the castle, albeit at the elementary level of polite conversation.

Britomart's vulnerability lies in the fact that she is in love; the stain on her smock produced by Gardante's arrow suggests her own passion. Because she loves, she, like Redcrosse, finds herself in the vicinity of Castle Joyous, challenged by the six knights who present her with one option only: to take Malecasta, the 'Lady of delight,' for her mistress. Like the Venus of the tapestry who transforms Adonis in his agony into a pretty flower, Malecasta and her servants understand how to turn the pains of love to pleasurable account. But Britomart's spirit is of a different order; for her, love's wound leads not to enervated idleness but to heroic activity, to 'noble deeds and never dying fame' (iii 1). MARK ROSE

---

catalogues Sidney allows that poetry 'under the veil of fables [may] give us all knowledge, logic, rhetoric, philosophy natural and moral' (ed 1973b:121); and poetical catalogues are the repositories of encyclopedic wisdom, printed successors to the oral mnemonic lists of antiquity. They have roots in wisdom literature, rhetoric, satire, encyclopedic literature, moral and homiletic writing, and technological and scientific treatises (Barney 1982). Catalogues are believed to constitute the earliest substratum in the epics of antiquity. The catalogue of ships in Homer's *Iliad* (2.479–759) is now considered Mycenaean in origin, and its names and places are thought to derive from songs composed at the time of the Trojan War. Such lists enabled Homer's auditors to associate their own families with those who fought at Troy. William Tailleur's 'Catalog of Such Noblemen, Lords, and Gentlemen of Name, as came into this Land with William the Conquerour,' published by Holinshed, served the same purpose for Elizabethans. Although Spenser's catalogues have their ultimate origins in classical epic (see *Hesiod), they also draw on the lists which abound in Chaucer, Gower, Guillaume de Lorris, Ariosto, Boiardo, and Tasso. After Spenser, the tradition flourishes in such poets as Drayton and Milton, and continues, in verse and prose, to Walt Whitman and James Joyce.

Spenser's most important geographical catalogue is his celebration of the marriage of Thames and Medway in *FQ* IV xi 11–53. This passage enumerates sea gods and founders of nations, both drawn from Conti 2.8; famous world rivers; English and Irish rivers (in 24 stanzas, 24–47), drawn from Holinshed, Camden, and his own experience; and Nereids taken largely from Conti 8.6. The catalogue is organized on numerological principles (see Fowler 1964:182–91).

Spenser's central historical catalogue is his tripartite history of Britain from its beginning to the Tudors. This series of chronicles is modeled on Virgil: Servius writes of Virgil's treatment of Roman history in *Aeneid* 6 that 'all of Roman history from the arrival of Aeneas up to his own time is celebrated ... this plan lies hidden, because the chronological order is confused' (note on 6.752). Spenser's order is similarly 'confused': he plunges *in medias res* with an account of the 'auncient booke, hight *Briton moniments*.' This catalogue (II x) spans British history from the arrival of Brutus to the succession of Uther Pendragon, Arthur's father. The account is subsequently continued with Merlin's chronicle, which extends the story from Artegall (who takes the place of his half-brother Arthur in the chronicle) to Elizabeth, the 'royall virgin' (III iii 27–50). The third installment is Paridell's account of the period from the fall of Troy to the arrival of Brutus in Britain (ix 33–51). Although Spenser draws on Geoffrey of Monmouth, Holinshed, Hardyng, and Stow for his materials, in form he imitates Virgil's treatment of Roman history as described by Servius. Paridell's narrative derives specifically from Aeneas' speech to Dido (*Aeneid* 2–3).

Spenser's poems also contain a myriad of smaller catalogues with equally ancient roots. At their simplest level, they are rhetorical figures based on classical poetry. The third part of rhetoric, amplification, encourages the division of material into lists, and the parallel expression of such material. A compact example of the latter is the use of *articulus*, lists of nouns without articles or conjunctions: 'Infernall Hags, *Centaurs*, feendes, *Hippodames*, / Apes, Lions, Aegles, Owles, fooles, lovers, children, Dames' (II ix 50). Such amplification may be combined with anaphora, in which the same word begins a sequence of phrases: 'Of Magistrates, of courts, of tribunals, / Of commen wealthes, of states, of pollicy, / Of lawes, of judgements, and of decretals' (53).

The ancient *topos* of the catalogue (or blazon) of the female anatomy finds its fullest expression in the description of Belphoebe (II iii 22–31). Shorter examples include VI viii 42–3, *Epithalamion* 167–203, *Amoretti* 15 and 64, and *SC, Aprill* 64–72. Such catalogues derive in the first instance from medieval and Renaissance love poetry, and have classical antecedents (eg, Claudian *Epithalamium* 265–71); but Spenser is also indebted to the Song of Solomon (4–7), which he is said to have translated (*Complaints* 'Printer to Reader').

Spenser's catalogues of flowers derive from classical pastoral, and include the conventions of presenting flowers to one's beloved (Theocritus 11.45, 56–7; Virgil *Eclogues* 2.45–50; cf *SC, Aprill* 136–44), adorning the grave with flowers (presented in a fresh variation in the 'Lay of Clorinda,' where the flowers deck the body in Paradise, 67–72), and the tempting garden of *Muiopotmos* (187–200). A related botanical list is the catalogue of trees at *FQ* I i 8–9, which places Spenser in a tradition descending from Virgil and Ovid through Chaucer, Boccaccio, and Guillaume de Lorris. In addition to these formal catalogues, there are many examples of Spenser's listing characters and places, as in the procession of the seven deadly sins (I iv), the masque of Cupid (III xii), and the poets in *Colin Clout* (380–455).

Poetry has always been associated with catalogues. As Frye notes, 'primitive poetry delights in catalogues, long lists of strange names, the names which are potent in magic, which are the keys to history, which summon up the deeds and loves of heroes and gods. This love of lists and catalogues runs through English literature from *Widsith* to Tolkien' (1970:97). GORDON CAMPBELL

Stephen A. Barney 1982 'Chaucer's Lists' in *The Wisdom of Poetry* ed Larry D. Benson and Siegfried Wenzel (Kalamazoo, Mich) pp 189–223; Braden 1975; Curtius ed 1953; Lewis 1964:199; O'Connell 1977:69–98.

Catullus (Gaius Valerius Catullus, c 84–c 54 BC) Latin poet, author of a hundred-odd poems, all but eight quite short. Lost sight of during the Middle Ages, they had turned up again by the fourteenth century and were widely printed and imitated in the Renaissance; Sidney's *Certain Sonnets* 13 is the first appearance of a Catullus poem in English (Ringler in ed 1962:428). The most important for Spenser was number 61 (in modern editions), an epithalamium in which the poet talks the wedding day through, calling upon the various participants as their times come. Spenser took over this general type for his *Epithalamion*, as well as some of the specific sequence of action and occasional phrases; he varied the classical form most significantly in combining the roles of poet and bridegroom. A few other details may have come from Catullus' other epithalamia, which are slightly different in form (62, an exchange between two choruses, and 64, an epyllion). From all three descends an ample tradition of imitation in later antiquity and the Renaissance, in which Spenser was also widely read and from which he took his sense of the propriety of a decorative expansiveness generally lacking in Catullus 61. Spenser's *Prothalamion* also draws, somewhat more distantly, on this body of material.

Otherwise, Catullus seems a minor figure in Spenser's background. Echoes of what are now his most famous poems – about his fiercely sexual and tormented love for a woman he calls Lesbia – can be found in Spenser's work (McPeek 1939:64–5, 107–8; Pearcy 1980–1); but their world is not Spenser's, and the connections are for the most part hard to disentangle from the intervening tradition. The topics of the Lesbia poems had become widely absorbed into the general repertoire by Spenser's time – the Neo-Latin poet Johannes Secundus (1511–36) was a particularly assiduous and popular imitator. The level of performance that Malbecco witnesses a satyr achieve with Hellenore – 'Nine times he heard him come aloft ere day' (*FQ* III x 48) – could owe something to Catullus 32 – 'novem continuas fututiones' – but has a more likely source in Ovid (*Amores* 3.7.25–6).

GORDON BRADEN

Greene 1957; McPeek 1939; John Mulryan 1972 'The Function of Ritual in the Marriage Songs of Catullus, Spenser and Ronsard' *Ill-Quart* 35.2:50–64; Sandra R. Patterson 1979–80 'Spenser's *Prothalamion* and the Catullan Epithalamic Tradition' *Comitatus* 10:97–106; Pearcy 1980–1.

---

caves A cave combines the elements of earth and air: it is a breathing space largely enclosed by earth or rock; the presence of water or fire is incidental. A defined position fortified by nature, usually covert or secret, it serves as a base for retreat or sortie. By extension, art supplying nature's part, caves may include any hollow structure from the simplest den or bower to palaces and fortresses and underground kingdoms, provided that the verbal context demands or allows some relevant association with the elemental notion. The cave may be a place of shelter or danger (or both), a threshold to a better state or a trap that shuts forever.

The cave is a traditional setting for significant action in classical writing. To take only the example of Virgil, some germane passages may be listed briefly: *Aeneid* 1.52–63 (the cave of Aeolus), 166–8 (the freshwater cave of the nymphs in Lybia); 2.13–20, 50–3 (the hollow, cavernous Trojan horse); 3.381–3 (the 'trackless track' or pathless journey to Italy), 420–32 (the abyss of Charybdis, the cavern of Scylla, with the warning that it is best to go the long way round), 443–4 (the Sibyl to be sought deep in a rocky cave), 558 (avoiding Charybdis), 617 (Cyclops' cave); 4.165 (the cave marriage, planned by Juno, 124); 5.575–604 (the Troy game, explicitly related to the Cretan labyrinth, 588–91); 6.10, 42–3, 77–8, 98–9 (the cave of the Sibyl), 27–34 (the representation of the Cretan labyrinth on the temple doors), 126–9 (easy descent, difficult return), 200, 237, 573–9 (cavern-jaws of Avernus, Hydra, Tartarus), 268–72 (the dark descent of Aeneas and the Sibyl), 519 (the Trojan horse pregnant with soldiery); 7.10 (Circe weaving in her secret grove), 568–71 (the fury Allecto disappears into the jaws of a cavern); 8.94–101 (journey up a winding river with overarching greenery), 193–280 (the evil cave of Cacus, enemy of Hercules), 416–25 (the cavern-forge of Vulcan), 630 (the mother-wolf, foster mother of Romulus and Remus, outstretched in the green cave of Mars); 12.908–18 (Juturna leads Turnus through a maze). Other cave references in Virgil include Eclogue 4.50 (the world's massive dome); 5.5–6, 19; 6.13, 74; 9.41; Georgic 4.333–4 (a bower of the nymph Cyrene beneath the river's depths), 418–22 (the vast cavern of Proteus), 467 (the jaws of Taenarus, the portals of Dis).

The episode by which Spenser plunges the reader into *The Faerie Queene* is unique in its concentration of imagery of cave and labyrinth: when the Red Cross Knight and Una leave the plain to shelter under trees, they find 'a hollow cave, / Amid the thickest woods' (I i 11), the den of the monster Error, so that taking shelter involves an encounter with danger. The victory (in keeping with the lesson of Book I and of the whole poem) is real but not final, for the 'little lowly Hermitage' of Archimago, 'Downe in a dale' (34), proves no less than Error's den to open downwards, to the house of Morpheus 'Amid the bowels of the earth' (39). Later, the mortally injured Sansjoy is first 'hid in secret shade' and then with the aid of Night, who dwells in 'darkesome mew,' conducted down the 'yawning gulfe of deepe *Avernus* hole' (v 15, 20–1, 31), to be cured by Aesculapius in the cave where he is imprisoned 'Deepe, darke, uneasie, dolefull, comfortlesse' (36). Orgoglio, the son of Earth's 'hollow womb' by blustering Aeolus, is a 'monstrous masse of earthly slime, / Puft up with emptie wind, and fild with sinfull crime' (vii 9: the moral allegory is combined here with physical allegory; windstorms and earthquakes were thought to be engendered in caves). After Redcrosse is rescued from the cavelike dungeon of Orgoglio, he meets his most insidious enemy, Despair, who is inseparable from the cave which is his mind's place, and then encounters the open enemy, the Dragon, huge as a hill, with 'jawes ... like the griesly mouth of hell' (xi 12). Yet even in the first book, where the associations are overwhelmingly negative, the poet allows some sense of the cave as a place of spiritual restoration: in the house of Holiness, the knight is placed 'Downe in a darkesome lowly place farre in' to cure his conscience (x 25), and a sacred housling fire is lit at the nuptials of Redcrosse and Una, and kept burning within a 'secret chamber' (xii 37).

In Book II, Acrasia's victims are 'Captiv'd eternally in yron mewes, / And darksom dens,' and Cymochles similarly lies 'in Ladies lap entombed' (v 27, 36); but in keeping with its deceptiveness, against which the reader is continually warned, the Bower of Bliss itself is presented as a sunlit arbor easy of access. The most elaborate structure in the whole poem, the castle of Alma, while making the fullest use of architectural analogies, is given only the minimal cavelike character, even where one might expect it in the hollows of trunk and skull. It is rather the villainous enemies of the house who scramble out of their rocks and caves. The most fully described cave in *The Faerie Queene*, the house of Mammon, is entirely sinister. Guyon in the wilderness happens upon an old man sunning his gold in a 'gloomy glade' (vii 3). The miser, startled, furtively pours his coins into a hole in the ground and then entices the knight to descend to see his subterranean haunt, which opens out into a Plutonian realm of all imaginable riches, where a fiend dogs the knight's footsteps to tear him to pieces if once he touches anything offered him: this fiend is the danger of entrapment, animated and moralized.

The later books show an increasing equipoise between positive and negative associations of caves. The magic mirror in which Britomart first sees Artegall 'round and hollow shaped was, / Like to the world it selfe, and seem'd a world of glas' (III ii 19): here the cave element of earth has been refined and given the transparency of air. Whatever reservations we may have about Guyon following Mammon, we cannot fault Britomart for her deep attention and self-commitment, though in the ensuing description of Merlin's 'deepe delve,' his 'hideous hollow cave,' his 'balefull Bowre' (imprisonment in which has been caused by his following 'false Ladies traine'), we are sufficiently reminded of the continuing dangers lurking in caves (iii 7–11).

In the story of Florimell and Marinell, the cave is ostensibly a shelter, really a prison (ultimately, perhaps, Proteus' sublunary world of change considered as a place of confinement). The hero has been fostered in a cave but his mother's lethal solicitude is early adumbrated by a reference to the sea's 'hollow bosome' and 'greedie gulfe' (iv 22) as the sea nymph Cymoent hides her son. Concurrently, Florimell is held in the bower of Proteus, a 'hollow cave' which proves to be a 'Dongeon deepe' (viii 4, 37, 41). The sinister quality fully developed in the house of Mammon carries over through the motif of buried treasure to the story of Malbecco, who at the beginning mews Hellenore in close bower and at the end crawls into 'a cave with entrance small' beaten by roaring billows (x 57–8); it also gives a foretaste of the grimly claustrophobic house of Busirane, early described as a 'secret den' (xi 10).

But at the center of Book III lies the Garden of Adonis, the 'wombe' of all life; and in the center of that, in an 'arbour' in 'thickest covert' lie the lovers who are the parents of all things (vi 36, 44, 48). True, Time is active in the Garden, and the boar is penned beneath in a rocky cave; but the impression of replenishment is far stronger than that of destruction. Amoret is fostered here; she grows to womanhood in the Temple of Venus, a place more open, airy, and spacious: its many rooms provide delay in access to its inmost penetralia, but they are 'Delightfull bowres' (IV x 24) in sharpest contrast to Busirane's gloomy chambers and to the caves and dungeons that proliferate elsewhere in Book IV. These include Ate's 'darksome delve farre under ground' (i 20), the 'deepe *Abysse*' or 'hideous *Chaos*' (ii 47) of the underground house of the Fates, the cavelike cottage of Care where Scudamour spends a sleepless night (v 32), the cave of Lust (vii 8), the dungeon of Corflambo (viii 51), and the dungeon-cave of Proteus, 'Under the hanging of an hideous clieffe,' a 'sea-walled fort' (xii 5, 18).

Every good work of justice in Book v issues ultimately from Astraea's cave of instruction in which the goddess nurtures Artegall (i 6). Other caves are few and entirely negative: the empty rooms of Dolon's 'loathed bowre' (vi 35), a metaphoric mention of the 'dreadfull mouth of death' (iv 12), the prison of Radigund in which Artegall is held captive (vii 37), and the cave of Malengin (ix 6). To these may be added the repeated references to the monster lurking under the Idol's altar at the center of Geryoneo's power (x 29, xi 21). Here Spenser has little to say that can be organized by the metaphor of the cave; the same is largely true of Book VI and entirely true with the *Cantos of Mutabilitie*, where there are no caves at all and the one retired spot is on a hilltop. In the Legend of Courtesy, the Salvage Man dwells in the forest in a good cave of sorts (VI iv 13), but the Hermit's cell by contrast is located on the plain and is called a 'cage' (v 38). The evil cave is figured in the 'hellish dens' of the Brigands (xi 41), from which, after penetrating 'the secrets of their entrayles,' Calidore rescues Pastorella. The main action, the quest of the Blatant Beast, never takes Calidore into a cave or even under cover, but the Beast's origins are emphatically stated so as to link it with many another monster in the poem: it was begotten of Echidna by Typhaon 'In fearefull darkenesse ... Mongst rocks and caves' (VI vi 11). (See also *labyrinths.)

WILLIAM BLISSETT

Blissett 1989; Curtius ed 1953, ch 10 'The Ideal Landscape'; Heninger 1960:131; Charles Paul Segal 1969 *Landscape in Ovid's 'Metamorphoses'* (Wiesbaden) pp 20–3.

---

chaos According to the tradition inherited by Spenser, chaos or the first matter (*prima materia*) provided the material of all things in the cosmos. In the first step of Creation, God called this matter into existence out of nothing (*ex nihilo*). In the second step, he separated it into the four elements which arranged themselves in order of their specific gravity, with fire at the top and earth at the bottom. The sun, the planets, and the stars constituted the region of fire or ether, and were unchanging in their substance since they were made wholly of one element. The moon and the regions within its orbit, including the earth, retained all four elements, which were perpetually separating and recombining according to a heavenly pattern in the mind of God. In the third step, God recombined the elements in proportions suitable to each thing created, some of which remained inanimate (rocks, soil) while others were endowed with the 'breath of life' (Gen 2.7). This order of nature was perverted by Mutabilitie, who claims to be the daughter of 'great *Earth*, great *Chaos* child' (*FQ* VII vi 5–6, 26).

Since the bodies of living creatures undergo generation and corruption or birth and death, they must change into each other, a transformative process which implies a basic substance for them all, known as first matter. The initial creation of bodies used a certain amount of matter, but as earth's population increased, more was needed; hence there must be a reservoir of first matter, as yet unformed, that provides the raw material of new bodies. This reservoir is called chaos – 'huge eternall *Chaos*, which supplyes / The substances of natures fruitfull progenyes' (Garden of Adonis, III vi 36).

The relation between chaos and creation is partly explained by Augustine in his commentary on Genesis, *De Genesi ad litteram*. He holds that the World Soul or Holy Spirit brought into existence bodies formed according to the divine pattern in the mind of God. This pattern contained all forms that exist in the visible world from the beginning to the end of time, but they could be imposed only on matter capable of receiving them. Corresponding to the divine forms, there had to be in first matter various 'seeds' or 'germens' capable of developing into plants or animals. Although the first plants reproduced themselves by their seeds, there were no plants to bear seeds for them but instead certain capabilities of producing plants which Augustine called seminal reasons (*rationes seminales*). These determined the forms that created bodies would take; and though they did not initiate creation, they guided it, somewhat as the genes function in modern physiology (cf Augustine *De trinitate* 3.9: 'As the mother is pregnant with unborn offspring, so is the world itself pregnant with the causes of unborn things'). 'Great *Earth*, great *Chaos* child' (VII vi 26) is therefore viewed as the universal mother, from which all things are born and to which all must return.

Spenser follows tradition in saying that chaos lies in 'the wide wombe of the world' located in 'the deepe *Abysse*' (III vi 36, IV ii 47). His use of *abysse* suggests that he was indebted to biblical sources: the two adjectives that Virgil uses to describe chaos ('domos ... *vacuas* et *inania* regna' *Aeneid* 6.269) are also used in the Vulgate Latin translation of Genesis 1.2: 'Terra autem erat *inanis* et *vacua*, et tenebrae erant super faciem abyssi, et spiritus Dei ferebatur super aquas' (an earlier translation of the Septuagint into Latin had used the phrase 'invisibilis et incomposita,' so the Virgilian phrasing may have influenced Jerome). Later Church Fathers regularly used *abyss* as an equivalent of *chaos*.

The antithesis between form and formlessness in *The Faerie Queene* symbolizes the war between virtues and vices in the human soul (see *psychomachia). A probable source for this comparison is Francesco Piccolomini who sees virtue as form and vice as the formlessness of chaos (*Universa philosophia de moribus* 1583, 6.19). Yet chaos is also a source for the beauty of form as opposed to the ugliness of deformity.

Chaos is represented by three allegorical places: forests or woods, caves, and lakes. The 'griesly' forest through which the knights travel in *FQ* III i suggests the 'griesly shade' of chaos (vi 37), and the beautiful Florimell who bursts out of the thickest brush on her white palfrey suggests form emerging from first matter. The Greek *hyle* means both 'forest' and 'first matter,' as does its Latin derivative *silva* or *sylva*, and beauty of form could arise from first matter through the agency of Love (Venus, Cupid). When Florimell is imprisoned in caves under the palace of Proteus, she represents the beauty implicit in first matter, for Proteus was interpreted as the unformed matter of living things. 'Florimell may (at least at this point) be the *anima semplicetta* come from the sweet golden clime into the sea of matter and the power of Proteus. Her imprisonment seems very like an allegory of the descent of the soul into material embodiment' (Lewis ed 1967:126). Accordingly, her release from Proteus' dungeon may signify form emerging from matter, in the way in *Hymne of Love* that Love 'Out of great *Chaos* ugly prison crept' (57–63), the first step in the creation and ordering of the universe.

JOHN E. HANKINS

Patrides 1966, ch 2 discusses chaos with many 17th-c citations. For Spenser, see Hankins 1971:65–70 and 228–34. See also Feinstein 1968.

Chapman, George (1559?-1634) Born about seven years later than Spenser, Chapman seems to have answered his poetic vocation only in maturity, thereby widening the temporal gap between them. In consequence, although they were sufficiently contemporary to have shared many public concerns and for a time to have sought patronage from the same circles, Chapman represents a subsequent poetic generation. The obscurity of his style has caused him to be associated – mistakenly – with the Metaphysical poets, but any surface difference from Spenser cloaks a stronger affinity. Chapman is Spenser's successor in the line of visionary poets that extends to Milton and Blake.

Chapman's activities as poet, dramatist, and translator place him second only to Jonson as a man of letters. His most important original poems were the first published. *The Shadow of Night* (1594) consists of two hymns, Orphic in spirit and presented as religious mysteries, that anatomize man's fallen condition and prescribe remedies. The second weaves a complex, three-level allegory – philosophical, political, and poetic – about the triune identity of the moon goddess as Cynthia, Diana, and Hecate. *Ovids Banquet of Sence* (1595), a riposte to the then-fashionable Ovidian erotic narratives, ironically displays an Ovid who facilely misuses Platonic doctrine for the purposes of seduction. As the title-page emblem indicates, the entire poem is an illusion, a warning that we cannot trust our senses. In his continuation of Marlowe's *Hero and Leander* (1598), Chapman seeks to redirect the incomplete poem by restoring the dignity and seriousness of Ovidian epic seen from the perspective of the moralized commentaries on the *Metamorphoses*. Although his Jacobean poems exhibit a decline in quality, they are interesting experiments: *The Teares of Peace* (1609), an uneasy combination of Hermetic revelation and medieval dream-vision, presents his most sustained defense of learning; *An Epicede, or Funerall Song* (1612) mourns the death of Prince Henry in a 'speaking picture' designed in close collaboration with the engraver William Hole; and *Andromeda Liberata* (1614) offers political allegory within mythological narrative in the manner of the new court masques.

Chapman initiated his Homer translation with *Seaven Bookes of the Iliades* and *Achilles' Shield* (both 1598); in 1609, *The Teares of Peace* announced his visionary inspiration by Homer and his renewed dedication to the t^sk of translation. The *Iliads* was finished in 1611, the complete *Odysses* in 1615, and the two published together as *The Whole Works of Homer* the next year; the lesser Homerica followed later (1624?). In spite of his unfulfilled promise to publish 'my Poeme of the mysteries / Reveal'd in Homer' (*Iliads* 'To the Reader' 143–4), Chapman does not burden his translations with Platonic exegesis, although he supplies an extended gloss. In his view, the epics are totally mythic – 'naked Ulysses, clad in eternall Fiction,' as he put it (*Odysses* 'To the Earle of Somerset'). Disdaining 'word-for-word traductions' ('To the Reader' 120), he believed the translator's task was to make Homer's universal values comprehensible to his own time and culture. His English systematically renders explicit the philosophical and ethical attitudes that he perceived as implicit in the texts. His statement that the 'Proposition' of each epic is contracted in its first word (*wrath* and *man*) epitomizes his approach to translation: 'in one, the Bodie's fervour and fashion of outward Fortitude to all possible height of Heroicall Action; in the other, the Mind's inward, constant and unconquerd Empire' ('Somerset'). Even if not all modern readers have experienced the degree of enthusiasm that Keats felt for Chapman's Homer, his own description of the translations as 'The Worke that I was borne to doe' ('Epilogue' to the *Hymns*) is one to which many have given assent.

Chapman's direct indebtedness to Ficino has been long established; and as his various theoretical statements make plain, Platonism provides the key to his thought and poetics. Writing as a Platonic mystagogue, he uses meaningful obscurity to conceal the truth of his revelation from the profane many but reveal it to the worthy few. He believes that poetry is an epiphany of truth attained through divine inspiration. The vatic poet accommodates this truth to human understanding through symbolic images, fables, and myths. Few men will undertake the intellectual and spiritual discipline necessary to comprehend such poetry; however, for the 'understanders' it will 'turne blood to soule' and 'heighten [man's] transition into God' (*Teares of Peace* 559, 'Somerset' 44). Chapman's conception of form is central to his poetics. The poet announces his general intentions by choice of a conventional literary form; this acts as container for the inner form of the myth, fable, or story (usually understood through the traditions of allegorical commentary) that expresses the indwelling form or 'soul' of the truth, a conception deriving from the Platonic Idea.

This outline should suggest numerous points of resemblance between Chapman and Spenser, most particularly in Chapman's narrative poems. Both write as allegorists and Christian Platonists. Both conceive of the poet as visionary; and the persona of the Orphic singer, the poet as reformer and harmonizer, figures large in their poetic strategies. As is typical of prophetic poets, the choice of genre is important to them. Commitment to the Renaissance notion of a hierarchy of poetic kinds leads them to value most highly the supreme lyric and narrative forms, hymn and epic. (Interestingly, both tend to translate hymn into a narrative mode, treating it as epic.) The archetypes of temple and labyrinth, upon which Spenser organizes his narratives, are also structural principles in Chapman's poems. Frequently Chapman's narratives are presided over by iconic female figures – Cynthia, Ceremony, Justice, Religion – located at the center of the narrative or of the narrator's consciousness. Embodying social institutions, these figures are complemented by occasional exemplars of human perfection – Hymen, Prince Henry, Perseus – who, although nominally male, actually are androgynous, symbolizing in their union of male and female attributes wholeness and spiritual harmony. Very like Spenser's, the thrust of Chapman's vision is integrative, typically expressing itself in the theme beloved by Renaissance Platonists, *concordia discors*.

In *The Shadow of Night*, the *Hymnus in Noctem* may answer Arthur's complaint against Night in *FQ* III iv (MacLure 1966:10), and the *Hymnus in Cynthiam* seems to have absorbed not the superficies of Spenserian style and manner but the lessons of narrative construction and allegorical technique evident in the 1590 *Faerie Queene*. Glancing at such historical events as the Alençon courtship, the campaigns in the Low Countries, and the victory over the Armada, this hymn celebrates the emergence of Elizabethan imperialism and the great Queen who directed that emergence. It should be paired with *De Guiana, Carmen Epicum* (1596), another 'epic hymn' concretely extending the earlier approval of imperialist expansion with an appeal in behalf of Raleigh's colonial expedition. Spenser's Letter to Raleigh, in which he sets forth the scheme of *The Faerie Queene* and, incidentally, praises Raleigh's 'excellent conceipt of Cynthia,' indicates the community of interest between the two poets. If these early works show Chapman absorbing the substance of *The Faerie Queene*, there are recognizable Spenserian gestures in *The Teares of Peace* with the episode of Murther in his cave (1128–70), in the handling of the theme of temperance, and in the simile about 'errant Knights, that by enchantments swerve, / From their true Ladyes being; and embrace / An ougly Witch, with her phantastique face' (456–8). The form of the poem, however, would suggest that Chapman is thinking of Spenser's *Complaints* as much as *The Faerie Queene*.

Despite such affinities, most readers record a sharper sense of the differences between the two poets. Their conceptions of epic provide one bench mark: Chapman's veneration for Homer as opposed to Spenser's receptiveness to the Italian romances. Another is the unlikeness of their styles, which – at least to some degree – signifies differences in philosophic attitudes. Chapman embraces the Florentine Neoplatonism of Ficino, Pico della Mirandola, and their circle, employing its language of religious mysteries. Just as Spenser's style is less opaque, so his particular brand of Platonism has proven less susceptible to analysis. Put another way, Chapman's poems, however difficult in the working out, are designed to have a circumscribable meaning. In this respect, he is more a poet of closure than Spenser, whose epic absorbs annotation, spongelike, seeming as open-ended in meaning as it is in its fragmentariness. Finally, Chapman's interests – for instance, his fascination with optical illusion and perspective problems and his Jacobean preoccupation with self-destructive willfulness – often point to his membership in the poetic generation that followed Spenser. Perhaps that serves to define the relationship as securely as we can. More than rival, follower, or imitator – although something of these can be discerned – Chapman might best be described as Spenser's successor in the poetic tradition which claimed both their allegiances. RAYMOND B. WADDINGTON

Editions include Chapman 1874–5 *Works* ed R[ichard] H[erne] Shepherd, 3 vols (London); Chapman 1910–14 *Plays and Poems* ed Thomas Marc Parrott, 2 vols (London); Chapman 1941 *Poems* ed Phyllis Brooks Bartlett (New York); Chapman 1970 *Plays: The Comedies* ed Allan Holaday, et al (Urbana, Ill); Chapman 1987 *Plays: The Tragedies* ed Allan Holaday, et al (Woodbridge, Suffolk); and Homer ed 1967. A standard general study is Millar MacLure 1966 *George Chapman* (Toronto). Critical writings include Murrin 1969; Raymond B. Waddington 1974 *The Mind's Empire: Myth and Form in George Chapman's Narrative Poems* (Baltimore); Waddington 1983 'Visual Rhetoric: Chapman and the Extended Poem' *ELR* 13:36–57.

---

character 'Characterization' needs to be distinguished from 'character': the former is the narrative process by which the latter is created. Character, the product (and what, generally, our reading constructs and remembers), may be thought of as a narrative agent developed through the layering of distinct traits, attributes, and perspectives: that is, to the minimal notion of a narrative agent may be added a name, physical or mental traits, emblems, symbols, social roles, literary allusions, stock literary roles, mythic and archetypal figuration, rhetorical tropes, interaction and association with other characters, and direct and indirect commentary. Always verbal artifacts, literary characters may be developed through all these possible layers in characterization, but they may also be as simple as a name and a single narrative act.

Character might seem at first a minor aspect of Spenser's *Faerie Queene*, or a subject already contained within the definitions of allegory and its constitutive element, personification. On analysis, however, it turns out to be a multiform aspect of his narrative that requires a number of distinct steps in its investigation. Freed from theories based upon realistic fiction, it turns out to be a surprisingly intricate concept that may be studied on four levels, each with subordinate elements. First, character is a dimension of allegory constituted by a number of conventions. Second, major characters possess definite narrative functions while secondary characters appear and disappear according to allegorical demands. Third, major characters undergo continuous development (or unfolding) through narrative episodes such that their characterization extends over the scope of an entire book, and occasionally beyond. Fourth, they are partly defined by mental attributes and conflicts that do not belong altogether to allegory but rather to romance and the heroic poem.

Allegorical characterization is a traditional method that employs a limited set of conventions in order to establish a correlation between concepts and aspects of character. Concepts are embodied in various concrete manifestations to create what Angus Fletcher has called 'walking Ideas' (1964:28). Such characterization may be analyzed in terms of proper names and etymology, symbolism, emblems, iconography, personification, and typology. The result is a character built up out of a few explicit traits that represents an integrated network of concepts (Occasion's bald spot, her hair, her tongue, her relation to Furor, the presence of Phedon). Although such characters are reductive (that is, psychologically depthless), their characterization is multiphased. (See Fletcher 1964, Oram 1984.)

Spenser's method makes significant use of proper names. A name such as Calidore, Britomart, or the Red Cross Knight tells the reader in advance something important about the character. Certain minor characters, such as Orgoglio, Mammon, Medina, or Alma, are virtually encapsulated in their names, while others, such as Archimago, Duessa, Florimell, or Pastorella, are given an initial level of characterization by their names which is then extended. Names in Spenser's narrative are always significant to some degree, especially when the name, such as Acrasia, Paridell, Braggadocchio, or Pastorella, is literary. Their allusiveness, whether self-evident or enigmatic, is an invariable aspect of Spenserian characterization.

Symbolism occurs either in a quality of the character's physical appearance, or in some accoutrement associated with the character. Symbolic aspects are normally metonymic: Occasion's bald spot and her obscuring hair that 'Grew all afore, and loosely hong unrold' (*FQ* II iv 4) symbolize her fleeting momentariness, her embodiment of opportunity that must be both recognized and grasped immediately or be lost. Similarly, Munera's 'golden hands and silver feete' (v ii 10) associate her with wealth. Accoutrements such as Redcrosse's armor (which alludes to Eph 6 but stands for the virtues that Paul attributes to a Christian), Britomart's hebon spear, Artegall's antique armor, and Braggadocchio's plumed helmet all symbolize some aspect of the moral concept represented by the character. The major characters, preeminently Arthur, show several symbolic properties: like the allegory itself, they represent complex networks of logically interwound concepts. Often physical aspects derive from the iconographical tradition; that is, they are recognizable as belonging to a traditional character-type in literature and art. Occasion's bald spot is iconographic in this sense (but her relationship to Furor is not) as are Time's scythe and 'flaggy wings' (III vi 39).

Spenser's characters are personifications in that they represent aspects of concepts or related concepts, but it is evident that at least the major characters are not simplistic. Although they all personify concepts, there are obvious differences in complexity between secondary and major characters. These latter more fully represent interwoven networks of related concepts. A further level of complexity arises from the extended figural or typological functions of the major characters. Redcrosse incorporates the historical significance of St George and, as such, exceeds the limitations of even a complex personification both as a type of Christ and as a type of every virtuous Englishman. The major characters also typify the human possibilities of their virtues. Narratively, the figural dimension of characters indicates, by analogy or disanalogy, the moral qualities of minor characters in the same episode (as well as pointing directly towards the totality of the separate virtues represented by Arthur). Britomart's chastity, devotion, and love are projected upon the less complex characters of Belphoebe and Amoret as their type. Spenser's allegorical characterization may be said to invoke a number of specific conventions in order to achieve multiphased representations of conceptual networks, to produce figural or typological characters both on an intrinsically narrative level (the shadowing forth of partial but analogous concepts) and on an extrinsically historical level (actual persons, such as every virtuous Englishman or Queen Elizabeth). The major characters play diverse roles in the intricate structure of episodes.

Characterization is closely related to Spenser's narrative methods in general. Each character possesses definite narrative functions. Secondary characters reflect the central figure, the hero and heroine, by contrast or comparison. The function of such characters as Occasion, Orgoglio, Mammon, Despair, Impotence, or Impatience, though they are themselves reductive, even notational, is relatively complex, since each represents not merely a concept but a specific crisis in the hero's development. They engage the hero, offer a precise challenge, constitute steps in a process of development towards that which the hero must become, and must be overcome by narratively appropriate means. As narrative agents, all the characters participate in the poem's narrative and thematic intricacies. On the one hand, in either a positive or negative manner they are placed within the shadow cast by the major character (eg, in Book III, all minor characters represent nodes in the network constituted by such concepts as appetite, desire, perversion, chastity, and love). On the other hand, they form a densely allusive system of cross-reference. For example, the character of Malecasta (III i), the Lady of Delight, represents a mode of appetitive incontinence, deepened both by the etymological associations of her name and by such symbolic accoutrements as her Castle Joyous and the ecphrastic tapestries that portray the story of Venus and Adonis. Yet her narrative function is both to challenge Britomart on the level of crude sexuality and to anticipate the more serious challenge presented by Busirane in cantos xi and xii. Characters act within a book's conceptual structure (the virtue, such as chastity in Book III, the fashioning of which determines the narrative), allude to and reflect each other. The characters derive much of their significance from this intricate narrative interplay. Thus they can be said to act within the narrative world according to the assumptions (premises or axioms) of the book in which they appear (for example, in Book III, the transcendental importance of virginity, pure desire, faithful love, devotion, and married love) and according to the interrelated concepts associated with the quest: the problem of justice, for example, though always present in ordinary human life is not embodied in any character in Book III because, being distinct from the problems of chastity, no relevant narrative assumptions require its appearance. When characters do play roles in more than one book, they need not represent the concepts which govern the book in which they chiefly appear; Artegall represents Justice in Book v but not in IV.

In *The Faerie Queene*, characterization incorporates narrative involvement. Although characters are allegorical and frequently little more than personifications, they are neither self-contained nor independent of the narrative action in which they appear. In each book, the hero may be seen to develop through a series of episodes, each of which centers upon a crisis appropriate to a certain aspect of the virtue being fashioned. The crucial episodes involve allegorically appropriate secondary characterization.

The involvement of characters in the narrative actions has given rise to two primary modes of interpretation. The relations of episodes to conceptual structure may be understood synchronically as a spatial distribution of all the subordinate elements of the virtue of the book, or diachronically as a development in which the hero perfects the virtue by having passed through actions in which subordinate elements are displayed. According to the first mode, characters may be said to unfold as they reveal, in a spatially distributed but nondevelopmental display, the subordinate aspects of the concepts they represent. According to the second, the characters develop, or even mature, through a temporal sequence.

The major characters of *The Faerie Queene* have been called 'cyropaedic heroes' (Fletcher 1971:50, specifically referring to Xenophon's *Cyropaedia*, which narrates the adventures of the Persian emperor Cyrus, but generally suggesting any narrative in which the hero's education is foregrounded). In Book III, Britomart's adventures unfold from the minor crisis of Malecasta's castle to the major crisis of Busirane's: the rescue of Amoret represents, as the final point in this process, the perfection of chastity. In Book II, the narrative movement takes Guyon from the minor crisis involving Furor and Occasion, through a series of actions, such as the temptations that Mammon proffers in canto vii, representing increasingly strong challenges to the virtue of temperance, to the final crisis, an almost overpowering assault upon temperance, in the Bower of Bliss. In each book, specific narrative actions display the subordinate elements of its virtue. It is possible to interpret this as a spatial arrangement of the logical aspects of a moral concept (see *logic, *space) or as a diachronic unfolding of the steps through which the hero learns the lessons appropriate to a specific moral development. Characterization, on both the secondary and the primary levels, reflects, and is dependent upon, narrative structure.

Spenser's major characters are partly characterized by mental conflicts (psychomachia) that do not belong entirely to the tradition of allegorical characterization but primarily to the traditions of epic narrative and romance. Mental conflict arises when the hero becomes trapped in a dilemma. Although he may clearly understand the values represented by his quest and his duty towards them, he may confront a temporary attraction that emerges from the narrative action and works to undercut them. On this level, Spenser adapts a standard method of characterization which derives from medieval romances, especially those by Chrétien, in which the hero typically finds himself caught between the claims of duty and pleasure. Ultimately this method is classical and derives from the narrative practice of Homer and Virgil and in particular Ovid (primarily in the characterization of several female characters in the *Metamorphoses*, such as Myrrha, who are divided by opposing claims but who, in long interior monologues, rationalize one set of values over another). It has been called 'split awareness' and can perhaps best be seen in the labyrinthine characterization that Cervantes gives to Don Quixote, who exists in a state of irresolvable conflict between a number of opposed values (R.R. Wilson 1980–1:126–9; see also Gransden 1970, Milowicki and Wilson 1980).

Spenser's adaptation of the Ovidian split awareness is simpler than Cervantes' but both fascinating and instructive. His heroes encounter situations in which values conflict: one set of values, arising out of the narrative movement, undercuts another inherent in the quest. Redcrosse endures adventures in which his faith may seem to weaken (accepting Archimago's illusion of Una, accepting Duessa as Fidessa, experiencing pride, descending into despair, and so forth). Guyon is so tempted by anger and – upon entering the Bower of Bliss – by lust that he must be cautioned by the Palmer. In the midst of an arcadian world, Calidore confronts the pastoral values, principally *otium*, that undercut the values of knighthood. Even Arthur, in his battle with Maleger, experiences a temporary condition of split awareness when he feels 'smitten ... with great affright, / And trembling terror did his hart apall' (II xi 39). Spenser uses the conflicts created by temptation (though always a narratively appropriate temptation) to intensify his heroic characterizations. The negation of an idea clarifies it and establishes its boundaries. This interaction of the two traditions of characterization, allegorical and Ovidian, constitutes one of the most fascinating complexities of Spenser's narrative method. A similar deepening of apparent character-type can be observed in *The Shepheardes Calender*, where stock pastoral characterizations are shifted in the direction of specific conceptual conflicts.

The fusion of allegorical and Ovidian characterization becomes most striking when the simple allegorical type, whom the hero encounters as a challenge in an episode of appropriate crisis, actually embodies the temptation against which the hero must struggle. For example, the challenge represented by Orgoglio to Redcrosse is narratively important, for Orgoglio represents, in that specific narrative moment, precisely the negative side of the hero's dilemma: the self-indulgence (in pride) that 'splits' his mind from his awareness of duty. This exteriorization of the Ovidian split awareness recurs, to some degree, in each book and indicates a level of innovation that has not been sufficiently noted. Spenser's understanding of literary characterization is complex and cannot be separated either from his knowledge of previous narrative literature or from his immense narrative competence. Character is essentially a narrative, not a psychological, concept.

R. Rawdon Wilson

Chatman 1978; Thomas Docherty 1983 *Reading (Absent) Character: Towards a Theory of Characterization in Fiction* (Oxford); Fletcher 1964; Fletcher 1971; Goldberg 1981; K.W. Gransden 1970 'Allegory and Personality in Spenser's Heroes' *EIC* 20:298–310; Baruch Hochman 1985 *Character 'in' Literature* (Ithaca, NY); I.G. MacCaffrey 1976; Uri Margolin 1983 'Characterization in Narrative: Some Theoretical Prolegomena' *Neophil* 67:1–14; Margolin 1986 'The Doer and the Deed: Action as a Basis for Characterization in Narrative' *Poetics Today* 7:205–25; Edward Milowicki and Rawdon Wilson 1980 '"Character" in *Paradise Lost*: Milton's Literary Formalism' *MiltonS* 14:75–94; William A. Oram 1984 'Characterization and Spenser's Allegory' *SpKal 1984* pp 91–122; Shlomith Rimmon-Kenan 1983 *Narrative Fiction: Contemporary Poetics* (London); Robert Scholes and Robert Kellogg 1966 'Character in Narrative' in *The Nature of Narrative* (New York) pp 160–206; R. Rawdon Wilson 1979 'The Bright Chimera: Character as a Literary Term' *CritI* 5:725–49; Wilson 1980–1 'Drawing New Lessons from Old Masters: The Concept of "Character" in the *Quijote*' *MP* 78:117–38.

chastity Titular virtue of *FQ* III, whose patron is the female knight Britomart. Chastity is divided by Spenser into virginity and faithful monogamy. Their separate and equal status is embodied in the twin sisterhood of the virgin Belphoebe, namesake and foster child of Diana, and Amoret, foster grandchild of Venus and lover of Scudamour. In *The Faerie Queene*, the state of chastity is symbolized by a girdle, and the two kinds of chastity are seen in the two females who possess it: as a chaste wife, Venus possessed it; after her adultery, it devolved upon the virgin Florimell (IV v). Whether these two chastities represent two chronological stages of one life or two intrinsically different attitudes towards sex, is a matter of dispute.

Although Spenser alleges that chastity is one of Aristotle's virtues (Letter to Raleigh), it is only remotely so. Aristotle's doctrine of the mean doubtless dictated that Spenser's characteristic form of the virtue would be the positive chastity of monogamous love (exemplified in Britomart), a mean between virginal chastity, properly defined as residing in the will (exemplified in Belphoebe), and promiscuity (exemplified in Malecasta and Hellenore: III i, ix-x). Another conceptualization of chastity which hovers in the background is the medieval notion of three recommended ways of life: virginity, celibate widowhood, and marriage (in descending order of asceticism). Christianity is largely responsible for elevating virginity above the others, although no more than classical ethics did it praise frigidity or the inability to attract a mate. Erasmus in his influential *Colloquies* portrays a suitor answering his beloved's claims for abstinence by defining the two kinds of chastity: the absolute abstinence which befits a woman before marriage; and the chastity within marriage which consists in the partners having children for the state and for Christ, being married more in their minds than in their bodies, and inuring themselves to practice abstinence as they grow older ('Proci et puellae' *Colloquies* ed 1965:95).

In their treatment of chastity, Spenser's love lyrics essentially agree with *The Faerie Queene*. Erasmus' values are invoked in *Epithalamion*, except the last component of marital chastity (sexual restraint in marital relations), for Spenser celebrates the wedding night as a release from all restraint (360–7; see also *Prothalamion* 103). In *The Faerie Queene*, however, Spenser may be faulting Scudamour for, among other things, lack of restraint on the wedding night (IV i 3; see Hieatt 1975a:124). In the *Amoretti*, the protagonist for his part wages a not-always-successful struggle to keep his thoughts chaste, that is, not too physical, during the betrothal period (sonnets 67 to the end, esp 76–7, 84, 88, and the Anacreontics; see Kaske 1978:274–80). Because the lady is unmarried, the major conflict is to persuade her to move from virginal to marital chastity. The lovers never experience the Petrarchan conflict of chastity with love, as in Sidney's *Astrophil and Stella*. For them, the main issue is the interpersonal one of dominance and submission versus equality (Kaske 1978:280–5). In the *Fowre Hymnes* as elsewhere, lust is the opponent of chastity; but here it is unconventionally defined more in terms of promiscuity ('Disloiall lust' *HB* 170) than of physicality or marital status. (In *Hymne of Love*, the relationship becomes physical, but marriage is never mentioned.)

Like Shakespeare, Spenser opposes arranged marriages along with other barterings of the bride such as tournaments (IV iii, v) as precluding choice, especially on the part of the woman (ix 29). Indeed, he hails wedded love with such enthusiasm that C.S. Lewis with pardonable exaggeration (ignoring, for example, the endings of late Middle English romances) saw him as the first poet to link marriage to romantic love, a sentiment which had hitherto been thrust by arranged marriages into the outlawry of courtly love (1936 passim, esp pp 298–360).

For Spenser, not only free choice but love is a necessary adjunct or even a part of marital chastity, supplying the spontaneous element, since a willed fidelity to someone of no appeal would be unnatural. For this reason, the love-plots which begin in Book III and continue through Book IV and some even into Book V emphasize not so much the negative as the positive, and often (eg, III ii-iii) dwell on love-psychology to the exclusion of moral dos and don'ts (as the Letter says, they 'intermeddle' 'Accidents' with 'intendments'). In consequence, love aligns with chastity against lust and involves Spenser's entire sexual ethic. Extramarital sexual intercourse (except that which apparently takes place between Calidore and Pastorella, VI x 38) is condemned as lust and unchastity, though with varying severity (for the whore Duessa in *FQ* I, the tone is one of severity; for Paridell and Hellenore in III ix, it is the dismissive bawdry of the fabliau), as are the briefly mentioned homosexuality, bestiality, and incest (II v 28; III ii 40–1, vii 47–9). Nevertheless, the high-minded major characters struggle less to resist seduction and condemn the unchaste (eg, III i 63–7) than to locate, understand, and adjust to the beloved. A young woman can be sinless and still fantasize as does Britomart about the sort of man she would like to marry (ii 22–3). Spenser even portrays some women (and a man, Marinell, iv 25–6, v 9) who say no for the wrong reasons, either to lovers (Mirabella, VI vii 28–viii 2; and two of the women who resist the Squire of Dames, III vii 58–60) or to a spouse (Amoret in refusing Scudamour's advances in IV x; see Roche 1964:72–83, K. Williams 1966:103–11).

Spenser makes his main embodiment of chastity female partly because chastity was considered the chief desideratum, indeed, the 'fairest vertue, farre above the rest,' for a woman (III proem 1). He makes his exemplary female a knight in line not only with his pervasive allegory of virtue as knighthood but with his local descriptive purpose of psychologizing lovers, to indicate that some power and freedom of movement (such as an independent legal status or public vocation might provide) are necessary to allow the woman to locate and pursue her ideal man.

In a way puzzling to some modern readers, Spenser advocates virginity in Belphoebe and praises a minor female character who 'chastity [abstinence] did for it selfe embrace' (III vii 60). That such negative chastity is part of Aristotelian temperance is indicated by the introduction of Belphoebe in the Book of Temperance (II iii). Accordingly, Guyon, the knight of Temperance, also demonstrates negative chastity (xii 68–9); his conflict with and defeat by Britomart (III i) demonstrates the difference between negative and positive chastity, showing a slight preference for the latter. Spenser seems to have thought that a religious vocation, which in his church was open only to males, might well demand celibacy. He praises a man, the hermit Contemplation, for negative religious chastity (I x 48), and shows sympathy for pagan male examples of the practice, the priests of Isis (V vii 9, 19) and Hippolytus (I v 37–9). The Protestant praise of a married priesthood is comically misapplied by being put in the mouth of his 'formall Priest' in *Mother Hubberds Tale* (475–8). This stand is conservative, though by no means unique for his time. Although, like medieval Catholics, Protestants still admired a dedication so complete that it rendered sexual experience impractical, they exalted marriage above the other two states (cf the Geneva glosses on I Cor 7.1–9, 25–40 with Cornelius a Lapide's Catholic glosses, which attack various Reformers). Although they denied to its ceremony the name of a sacrament, they officially abrogated the practice of offering publicly to God a lifelong vow of celibacy (Erasmus compares it to self-castration in 'Proci et puellae' ed 1965:96). Hooker, Herbert, and Cosin, however, recommend that priests should marry only if practical exigencies demand it (George and George 1961:266–7).

Yet this does not explain Spenser's admiration for females who vow to remain virgins. Never does he assign a specifically religious motive to them (indeed, one is contrasted with a nun, III vii 58). But he uses religious language for Belphoebe (eg, vi 3; see also 27, both descriptions traditional for Mary's parthenogenesis of Christ), portrays God as pleased by this virtue among others (V 52–5), and seems in these passages to rehabilitate vowed virginity in a traditional direction at least to the level of equality with marriage (Ellrodt 1960:55–6).

Traditional Catholics advised those seeking spiritual perfection to abstain from all sexual pleasure. On the basis of proof-texts such as Matthew 19.10–12, 1 Corinthians 7.1–9 and 25–40, and Revelation 14.4, they held that such a resolution made for the sake of Christ is meritorious in and of itself, more so than is marriage. More ascetic still, Augustine and his strict followers held that the sexual act is the transmitter of original sin to the child and that in our fallen state the parents cannot perform it without concupiscence, a venial sin at best, unless (as some commentators add) it is for the sake of procreation (Noonan 1965:135, 138, 250–2). In one religious or quasi-religious passage at least, Spenser for all his commitment to love inherits some of this Pauline and Augustinian revulsion against the sexual act: he praises Chrysogone's parthenogenesis of Belphoebe as 'Pure and unspotted from all loathly crime, / That is ingenerate in fleshly slime' (vi 3, see also 27).

There are other possible justifications for virginity on the natural level. One is that grooms demanded that their brides be virgins. Such merely provisional virginal chastity is allegorized in Britomart's spear or lance, which makes her invincible so long as she fights on horseback: the weapon is finally rendered useless when her intended husband, Artegall, forces her to fight on foot (IV vi 13–14), indicating that the virtue will not characterize her relations with him. Its phallic connotations harmonize with this provisional virginity in that both are part of her aggressive pursuit of him. Alternatively, love might be reconcilable with virginal chastity, for the tradition of the *dialoghi d'amore* (eg, in Castiglione's *Courtier*) had built into courtly love the possibility of platonic love even between the sexes. The poet exhorts his seemingly dedicated virgins Belphoebe and Queen Elizabeth to love someone eventually (III v 54, IV proem 4–5). Virginal platonic love between members of the same sex is praised under the label of chastity in IV x 26–7; moreover, this chaste affection binds Britomart and her friends who are knights and, of course, males (III i 12); hence it may even be the kind of love Belphoebe would accept from Timias, though then it is illogical of her to resent his being sexually attracted to someone else (IV vii argument, 35–6).

Another earthly value served by virginal chastity, one traditionally adumbrated in the myths of Diana and of the Amazons (both invoked for Belphoebe), is the woman's extra-domestic vocation, something which Spenser advocates. Marital chastity entails the 'wombes burden,' which will eventually end Britomart's career (III iii 28). In an age before legalized birth control and abortion, virginal chastity represented the only means whereby a woman like Britomart, Belphoebe, and her real-life model Queen Elizabeth could pursue a public vocation and, in an age when (at least in theory) the husband ruled the wife, preserve her autonomy (Montrose 1980:156, Neale 1934:78). In essence, such arguments from vocational expediency (albeit a different vocation) constituted the grounds on which Protestants retained religiously vowed virginity. By a curious remystification, the vocationally expedient virginity of Elizabeth and Belphoebe was dignified by imagery drawn from the Catholic praises of the sex-transcending lives of Christ, the Virgin Mary (Yates 1975:78–9), and clerical celibates (III v 52–5, viii 42–3). Elizabeth had restored virginal chastity to its medieval position 'farre above the rest.' Thus the religious overtones surrounding Belphoebe would seem to be evoked mainly as analogy not as theme, as a sociological supernaturalism. By another paradox, the imagery for both virgins was also drawn from the Petrarchan mistress whose refusal, whether chaste, prideful, or merely sadistic, serves to keep the lover in self-gratifying frustration (Forster 1969:122–47). In this respect, Belphoebe's virginal chastity is ambivalent because, as Spenser's second Anacreontic notes, Diana trades weapons with Cupid, using his to draw the suitors she plans to reject. Even if all these traits could be justified theologically and mythically, Spenser's connivance at Belphoebe's dog-in-the-manger attitude about Timias can only be explained politically, as connivance at that expedient platonic polyandry whereby Elizabeth kept her courtiers loyal and her suitors interested (Neale 1934:73, 75–90; Williams 1966:97–102).

Sometimes, too, as in medieval poetry, the sexual realm stands for the entire moral life, in which case virginity symbolizes integrity or even a return to prelapsarian innocence. This symbolism explains why Alma, owner of the castle of the body, is both perfect and a virgin (II ix 18, xi 2): not, as a reader ignorant of the Garden of Adonis might infer and as Augustine and his followers had asserted, because fallen man would do better to abstain from sexual activity as disruptive of a well-ordered soul or body, but in order to symbolize that this body is just as God made it. Spenser's negative form of chastity, then, is outwardly more traditional and yet more problematic; he seems to have adapted imagery traditional for virginal chastity to new ideas (platonic love, feminism, and flattery of a ruler). His exaltation of the positive, marital form of chastity determines most of his ethic, plots, and characters in Books III-IV and represents his most distinctive contribution to Anglo-Saxon attitudes. CAROL V. KASKE

Some background is given in John Bugge 1975 *Virginitas: An Essay in the History of a Medieval Ideal* (The Hague), and John T. Noonan, Jr 1965 *Contraception: A History of Its Treatment by the Catholic Theologians and Canonists* enl ed 1986 (Cambridge, Mass).

Chatterton, Thomas (1752–70) Spenser's prosody, diction, and 'historical' coloring figure repeatedly in Chatterton's works, alongside such other major influences as Pope, Chaucer, Camden, Collins, Charles Churchill, and James Macpherson. Spenser was as important as any of these in shaping the impulse which led to the pretended fifteenth-century 'Rowley' poems, and to one strikingly 'modern' (and relatively unknown) mock-pastoral fragment, 'Hobbinol and Thyrsis.' The variety of these influences indicates Chatterton's eclecticism, however, and warns against overemphasizing any single one.

Spenser's archaism and sensuous imagery seem clearly to have shaped both Chatterton's idea of imitating medieval works and the particular texture of his imitations, especially in the Rowleyan poems 'Englysh Metamorphosis,' where Chatterton attempts to rival Spenser's stanza, archaic spellings, Arthurian matter, and narrative, and 'The Tournament,' with its interest in chivalry. The non-Rowleyan 'Hobbinol and Thyrsis,' a coarse political and literary satire, draws repeatedly on *The Shepheardes Calender*. Chatterton's medium in the major Rowleyan works is the Rowleyan stanza, a ten-liner with gradually evolving prosodic characteristics; it clearly owes more to the Spenserian stanza than to any other possible source. He used it to suggest an English precouplet prosody and adapted it in many ways.

Other uses of Spenser are more peripheral to Chatterton's achievement, although his scattered borrowings are bewildering both in quantity and variety: he draws from *The Faerie Queene*, *The Shepheardes Calender*, *Muiopotmos*, and *Teares of the Muses*. About one percent of the special Rowleyan vocabulary is apparently drawn from Spenser, primarily from John Hughes' 1715 or 1750 glossaries (Chatterton ed 1971:1178).

DONALD S. TAYLOR

Thomas Chatterton 1971 *Complete Works* ed Donald S. Taylor and Benjamin B. Hoover, 2 vols (Oxford); E.H.W. Meyerstein 1930 *A Life of Thomas Chatterton* (London); Donald S. Taylor 1978 *Thomas Chatterton's Art* (Princeton).

Chaucer, Geoffrey (c 1343–1400) The works of Chaucer were more widely read and more sincerely admired in Tudor England than those of any other Middle English poet (though Gower and Lydgate were mentioned almost as often). In his *Arte of English Poesie* (1.31), Puttenham names Chaucer, with Gower, at the head of that succession of 'courtly makers' whose work had redeemed English poetry from the imputation of barbarousness; and in his *Defence of Poetry*, Sidney speaks of Chaucer and Gower as the first writers to 'beautify our mother tongue' and compares them to Dante, Boccaccio, and Petrarch in Italian (ed 1973b:74). For the Elizabethans, Chaucer's dream poems, his *Canterbury Tales*, and above all the *Troilus* were vernacular classics. Shakespeare was acquainted with them (A. Thompson 1978), and references to Chaucer's wisdom and wit occur frequently in the other writings of the period (Spurgeon 1925).

No Elizabethan writer, however, displays a closer relationship to Chaucer than does Spenser. This kinship was early recognized, in the epitaph on Spenser's tomb as reported by Camden, which begins: 'Hic prope Chaucerum situs est Spenserius, illi / Proximus ingenio, proximus ut tumulo' ('Here, buried next to Chaucer, lies Spenser, close to him in wit, and as close in his tomb'). Similarly, Nashe refers to '*Chaucer*, and *Spencer*, the *Homer* and *Virgil* of England.' These judgments were endorsed a century later by Dryden in his preface to *Fables, Ancient and Modern*: '*Spencer* more than once insinuates, that the Soul of *Chaucer* was transfus'd into his Body; and that he was begotten by him Two hundred years after his Decease' (*Sp All* pp 75, 28, 311).

Spenser refers to Chaucer eight times in his poetry. In *The Faerie Queene*, he is 'Dan *Chaucer*' (IV ii 32), 'Dan Geffrey' (VII vii 9), and 'that good Poet' (VI iii 1); and in the pastoral poems always 'Tityrus' (*SC, Feb* 92, *June* 81, *Dec* 4, envoy 9; *Colin Clout* 2). 'Dan,' an archaic title of respect derived from Latin *dominus*, is otherwise used by Spenser only of classical gods and heroes; and 'Tityrus,' the name of a shepherd in Virgil's *Eclogues* traditionally identified with Virgil himself, also suggests classical status. Chaucer's authoritative standing for Spenser is implicitly compared with that of 'Romish *Tityrus*' (*SC, Oct* 55) for his Latin successors. In the envoy to *The Shepheardes Calender*, Spenser describes his relation to Chaucer in terms which recall the envoy to *Troilus and Criseyde*, where Chaucer (himself imitating Statius) had acknowledged his own latter-day inferiority to Virgil and other Latin classics (5.1786–92). In each case the later poet claims only to be following earlier masters, 'kissing' or 'adoring' their footprints. Spenser implies a similar relationship in *FQ* VII vii 9, when he avoids describing Nature's clothes by referring to Chaucer, just as Chaucer had escaped the same problem in the *Parliament of Fowls* (316–18) by referring to a yet earlier authority, Alanus de Insulis.

Yet Chaucer was more than just a link in the chain of Spenser's authorities. In the same passage where he notes Chaucer's use of Alanus, Spenser speaks of his predecessor as one in whose spirit 'The pure well head of Poesie did dwell.' He had used the same image twice before. In *FQ* IV ii 32, Chaucer is called 'well of English undefyled'; and in *SC, June* 93–4, Colin expresses the wish that 'on me some little drops would flowe, / Of that the spring was in his learned hedde.' Poetry, pure English, and good learning flow from Chaucer as from a pristine source of fresh spring water. Whatever his own sources, Chaucer was for Spenser, as for Tudor readers generally, the main fountainhead of the English poetic tradition. Three times in the pastoral poems, Colin Clout (Spenser himself in shepherd's clothing) is said to have learned his songs from Tityrus (*SC, June* 81–2, *Dec* 4; *Colin Clout* 2). In the first of these passages, Colin even speaks of Tityrus as his actual teacher: 'The God of shepheards *Tityrus* is dead, / Who taught me homely, as I can, to make.'

Three of Spenser's references to Chaucer go beyond the conventional generalities of literary eulogy and reveal something of how the Elizabethan poet read his predecessor's works. In *SC, Februarie*, two shepherds representing the contrasting attitudes of age and youth naturally fail to agree about life or love; but when old Thenot offers to tell a 'tale of truth' which he learned in his youth from Tityrus, young Cuddie enthusiastically agrees, and the two unite for once in praise of the master. Cuddie: 'To nought more *Thenot*, my mind is bent, / Then to heare novells of his devise: / They bene so well thewed, and so wise, / What ever that good old man bespake.' Thenot: 'Many meete tales of youth did he make, / And some of love, and some of chevalrie' (94–9). Thus, in Chaucer's tales or 'novells,' the wisdom of the old proves acceptable to young Cuddie, and the youthful excitement of love and war once more stirs old Thenot. Chaucer's poetry transcends the opposition between youth and age which the eclogue otherwise displays, because his combination of wisdom and story attracts both equally. What follows clinches the compliment. Old Thenot's fable of the Oak and the Briar does combine story and wisdom, but not in Chaucer's inimitable way ('cleane in another kind,' as E.K. notes), so young Cuddie impatiently rejects it: 'Here is a long tale, and little worth' (240).

The *June* eclogue shows Chaucer in a different light. Colin's lament for the death of Tityrus harmonizes with the tone of a poem 'wholly vowed to the complayning of Colins ill successe in his love' (Argument). The shepherd mentions Chaucer's 'mery tales' (presumably referring to the *Canterbury Tales*, as E.K. notes), but speaks of him chiefly as a poet of love complaint: 'Well couth he wayle hys Woes, and lightly slake / The flames, which love within his heart had bredd.' The 'little drops' which flow from the Chaucerian spring here turn into the 'trickling teares' which Colin would teach even woods and trees to shed: 'But if on me some little drops would flowe, / Of that the spring was in his learned hedde, / I soone would learne these woods, to wayle my woe, / And teache the trees, their trickling teares to shedde' (93–6). Although Chaucer speaks of himself in *Troilus* as 'the sorwful instrument, / That helpeth loveres, as I kan, to pleyne' (1.10–11), readers do not now commonly think of him as a poet of love complaint. Yet the modern Chaucer canon includes a *Complaint to His Lady* and the so-called *Complaint of Venus*; the *Complaint of Mars*, the *Complaint unto Pity*, and *Anelida and Arcite* all conclude with elaborate bills of complaint; and there are many other places where his lovers complain less formally of the unattainability, infidelity, or death of a beloved: the man in black in the *Book of the Duchess*, for instance, or Troilus in *Troilus and Criseyde*.

It is also particularly important in this connection to notice that the canon of Chaucer's works was not the same for Spenser as it is for us today. Spenser read Chaucer in one of the family of very similar editions beginning with Thynne's in 1532 and ending with the 1561 folio associated with the name of John Stow, most probably in the last of these (Hieatt 1975a:19–23, Miskimin 1975:247–50). This 1561 volume of *The Woorkes of Geffrey Chaucer* contains no fewer than 39 pieces not written by him, only a few of which are ascribed to other writers such as Lydgate and Gower. Thus Spenser would probably have credited Chaucer with most of the love complaints by other poets which he found in Stow: the *Complaint of the Black Knight*, for instance, and *La Belle Dame sans Mercy*.

Chaucer appears in yet another light in *FQ* IV ii 32–4, stanzas which form the prologue to Spenser's continuation of his *Squire's Tale*. Chaucer probably never finished writing this tale; but the 1561 folio treats its latter part as lost ('There can be founde no more of this fore said tale, whiche hathe ben sought i[n] dyvers places'), and Spenser accordingly laments its loss through the action of 'cursed Eld.' This passage imitates the opening of *Anelida and Arcite* where Chaucer had lamented the near-loss of an old story rescued from a Latin source. Here, as in *FQ* VII and the *SC* envoy, Spenser sees himself in the same relation to Chaucer as Chaucer stood to his Latin predecessors; but in this case he actually sets out, relying upon an 'infusion sweete / Of thine owne spirit, which doth in me survive,' to recreate at least the substance or 'meaning' of what Chaucer himself wrote. The Chaucer in question here is not the master of complaining lovers but rather 'that renowmed Poet' who recorded the battles of Cambell and Triamond. Chaucer was in fact far less a poet of battle than of love; but he did intend the *Squire's Tale* to deal in 'aventures and ... batailles' (V 659), and the Squire's father, the Knight, does describe a siege, a single combat, and a tournament in his tale. Spenser clearly had the *Knight's Tale* as well as the *Squire's Tale* in mind when speaking of Chaucer's 'warlike numbers and Heroicke sound,' for his story of Cambell and Triamond opens with a direct imitation of the Knight's first line, altered only to fill the metrical gap caused by the loss of syllabic final *-e* since Chaucer's time: Chaucer's 'Whilom, as olde stories tellen us' becomes 'Whylome as antique stories tellen us.' The *Knight's Tale* enjoyed considerable popularity in Tudor times; and for Spenser, as for Dryden after him, it was an English model of that heroic or epic kind whose chief subject is fighting.

Spenser's explicit references to Chaucer thus acknowledge his mastery in three particular kinds: entertaining stories with a moral meaning, complaints of love, and epic narratives of deeds of arms (see *fables, **Complaints*, *heroic poem, *romance). Turning now to those places where, without necessarily mentioning him, Spenser most plainly imitates Chaucer, we find that in *The Shepheardes Calender* and other minor poems he draws most on the first two kinds, and especially on Chaucer's love complaints, while in *The Faerie Queene* he looks most to Chaucer's warlike numbers, and also to the allegorical set pieces of poems such as the *Parliament of Fowls*. Spenser's creative mind thus turned to those of Chaucer's poems which coincided most closely with his own work in hand. He never had any occasion to draw on Chaucer's fabliaux (unless the story of Malbecco, *FQ* III ix-x, recalls the *Merchant's Tale*) or his religious narratives. Conversely, since Chaucer did not cultivate pastoral, he had little to contribute to Spenser's shepherds' world – only the delightful cameo of the 'lytel herdegromes' (*House of Fame* 1224–6), which Spenser thriftily used twice (*SC, Feb* 35–41, *FQ* VI ix 5).

love complaints Spenser's chief imitation of Chaucerian love complaint is to be found, not in the lamentations of Colin in *The Shepheardes Calender* nor even in the volume of 'sundrie small Poemes' entitled *Complaints* (1591), but in *Daphnaïda* (also 1591). Considered structurally, as a short narrative poem culminating in a formal complaint, *Daphnaïda* belongs with Chaucer's *Complaint of Mars*, *Complaint unto Pity*, and *Anelida and Arcite*; but its chief Chaucerian source is the *Book of the Duchess* (Nadal 1908). Chaucer's elegy for the dead wife of John of Gaunt provided an obvious model. In each poem, the bereaved husband is represented as a man in black, encountered by the narrator in a dream forest (Chaucer) or pastoral landscape (Spenser). Like Chaucer's man in black, Spenser's Alcyon (who derives his name, oddly, from the Ovidian heroine celebrated earlier in Chaucer's poem, 62–220) describes his loss to the narrator in enigmatic terms. The heraldic allegory of *Daphnaïda* 99–168 corresponds to the chess allegory of *Book of the Duchess* 652–709. In Chaucer's poem, however, this allegorical announcement introduces a long conversation in which the narrator continues to behave as if he does not understand the loss, and it is only at the very end that the bereaved man speaks in plain terms ('She ys ded!' 1309) which force an equally plain response from the narrator ('Be God, hyt ys routhe!' 1310). In *Daphnaïda*, on the other hand, when Alcyon's heraldic enigma proves too much for the narrator's 'dull wit' (176), it is explained almost immediately; and there follow Alcyon's long formal complaint, the narrator's unavailing efforts at comfort, and the bereaved man's desperate exit 'With staggring pace and dismall lookes dismay' (564).

C.S. Lewis observed of *Daphnaïda* that 'nothing could show more clearly how imperceptively [Spenser] read the Chaucer whom he so revered' (1954:369). Certainly Spenser does not match the subtlety with which Chaucer, through the real or assumed incomprehension of the narrator, holds off the moment of impotent consolation for inconsolable loss until the last possible moment. Unlike Chaucer's, Spenser's poem is hung with the trappings of woe, from the gloomy autumnal evening of its opening onwards; yet its more funereal approach serves only to display the extreme difficulty of saying anything helpful on such an occasion – a difficulty which the *Book of the Duchess*, with a wide detour, had managed to arrive on the other side of.

fables The tale of the Oak and the Briar, told by Thenot as an example of Tityrus' skill in combining instruction with entertainment, draws attention to Chaucer as a fabulist; but neither that tale, nor Piers' tale of the Fox and the Kid in *SC, Maye*, nor the story of the Ape and the Fox in *Mother Hubberds Tale* displays any marked dependence on Chaucer's one masterpiece in the fable genre, the *Nun's Priest's Tale*. *Mother Hubberd* has some clear Chaucerian reminiscences (eg, line 1026 echoes *CT* I 1625–6); but its picaresque satirical fable is not at all in Chaucer's manner, and the style of its long couplets anticipates Dryden much more than it recalls Chaucer. But with *Muiopotmos* the case is different. The absence of Chaucerian echoes in the long burlesque account of the arming of the butterfly (*Mui* 57–96), where Spenser might have been expected to recall the corresponding passage in *Sir Thopas* (*CT* VII 839–87), supports the impression created by *The Faerie Queene*, that Spenser chiefly thought of *Thopas* not as a merry tale at all, but as a real romance of love and chivalry (see below). But the *Nun's Priest's Tale* certainly did furnish a model for *Muiopotmos* – which may even be regarded as providing, like *Daphnaïda* but more successfully, a modern variation on a Chaucerian theme. Spenser's poem has rightly been described as mock-heroic, for it opens with echoes of the *Iliad* and ends like the *Aeneid*; but it is best considered as a mock tragedy, like the *Nun's Priest's Tale* which follows and burlesques the Monk's series of tragedies. Spenser twice invokes Melpomene, the muse of tragedy (*Mui* 9–15, 413–14); and his story, like Chaucer's tale of Chantecleer, concerns the fall of a splendid creature into a miserable death (though Chaucer's hero escapes in the end). His butterfly, like Chaucer's cock, falls victim to a hidden adversary – the malevolent spider, who lies 'lurking ... in awayte' like Chaucer's fox in the cabbage patch (*Mui* 247, *CT* VII 3225–6) – and the butterfly's fall, like Chantecleer's, is accompanied by extravagant outcries of grief (*Mui* 409–16, *CT* VII 3338–54), with much talk of Fate and Fortune (*Mui* 225–7, 235, 241, 381, 417–18; *CT* VII 3234–50, 3338). Spenser's poem, decorated with inset pseudo-Ovidian tales of metamorphosis (Astery 113–44, Arachne 257–352) and lacking the Priest's learned digressions, creates a lighter and more graceful effect than Chaucer's; but the essence of Chaucerian tragedy is there: 'evere the latter ende of joye is wo' (*CT* VII 3205).

chivalric romances *Sir Thopas* takes its rightful place along with tales of the Knight and the Squire as a prime model and source for the poetry of chivalric love and adventure in *The Faerie Queene*. Spenser's romantic epic draws on all three poems, and even attempts to supply, or at least suggest, endings for the two of them which survived as fragments: *Thopas* because of the Host's impatient interruption, the *Squire's Tale* because (as he thought) 'cursed Eld' had obliterated most of it.

Spenser's continuation of the *Squire's Tale* in *FQ* IV ii-iii takes up the Squire's promise to 'speke of Cambalo, / That faught in lystes with the bretheren two / For Canacee er that he myghte hire wynne' (*CT* V 667–9). Spenser makes what he can of this puzzling hint (Cambalo is Canacee's brother) by having Cambell challenge his sister's suitors to fight him for her in 'listes' (iii 4), thus fulfilling the heroic potential of the story; but his claim to have hit upon Chaucer's lost 'meaning' (ii 34) cannot be taken seriously. He takes liberties with the Squire's story by adding a third brother, and devises an intricate bond between this brother, Triamond, and his former adversary, Cambell, each of whom marries the other's sister. The resulting foursome, cross-linked by kinship, love, and friendship into a harmonious tetrad, has been compared to a somewhat similar foursome formed at the end of the *Knight's Tale* (Theseus, Ypolita, Emelye, and Palamon; see Hieatt 1975a:72–3). The tetrad certainly plays an important part in Spenser's Legend of Friendship in *The Faerie Queene*, but it does not fulfill any demonstrable intention of Chaucer's Squire. Yet Spenser, like Milton (*Il Penseroso* 109–15), clearly did regard the *Squire's Tale* as one of Chaucer's major achievements, and he draws on it in *The Faerie Queene*, not only for the story of Cambell and Canacee, but also for some of the marvelous properties which his romance needed: the magic ring which protects Cambell (IV ii 39, *SqT* 146–55), Merlin's magic mirror (III ii 18–21, *SqT* 132–41), and the 'pin' which Phaedria uses to guide her boat (II vi 5, *SqT* 127).

While Spenser's treatment of love and friendship in the central books of *The Faerie Queene* has been seen as owing much to the *Knight's Tale* (Hieatt 1975a, ch 3), definite parallels between the two great epic-romances are surprisingly hard to spot. Most occur in scenes of armed combat, when Spenser may recall the one great battle scene in Chaucer, the tournament between Palamon and Arcite for the hand of Emelye. Thus the Florimell tournament in *FQ* IV iv (in which Cambell and Triamond take part) contains several recollections of Chaucer's tournament: the opening lines of stanza 34 echo *Knight's Tale* 2612, for instance. Yet the evidence suggests, most unexpectedly, that Spenser turned more often to *Sir Thopas* than to the *Knight's Tale* in creating his own chivalric world. Not only do words and phrases from Chaucer's burlesque romance occur quite frequently in the text (see below), but also the two fantastic motifs which together make up Chaucer's plot, such as it is, inspired in Spenser a quite remarkable creative response: the hero's love-quest for the elf queen, and his encounter with a giant who bars his way to her.

Giant adversaries play an important part in *The Faerie Queene*, and several of them display characteristics which recall Chaucer's Olifaunt: they carry great 'maces' (I vii 10, III vii 40, IV viii 43, *Thopas* *CT* VII 813) and swear by Turmagant (VI vii 47, *Thopas* 810), and one has three heads, like Olifaunt (II x 73, *Thopas* 842). Indeed, Olifaunt himself puts in an appearance at one point as a figure of lust (III xi 3–6), greedily pursuing a young man. Spenser's Ollyphant (a spelling derived from 'Oliphaunt' in the 1561 Chaucer text) represents excessive and perverted sexuality. This was made clear earlier by the Squire of Dames (III vii 48–9), who described how Ollyphant was incestuously linked with his lustful twin sister, the giantess Argante, in the womb. In the original 1590 version of that passage, the Squire says that the giant used to play havoc with errant knights 'Till him Chylde *Thopas* to confusion brought.' J.W. Bennett saw this as evidence that Spenser began *The Faerie Queene* first as a reworking and continuation of *Sir Thopas* (1942:11–15). If this is so, Spenser took considerable pains to conceal the fact. Even the single reference to Thopas is eliminated in the 1596 edition, with the appearance of Ollyphant alive and well four cantos later.

Yet *Sir Thopas* did play an important part in the evolution of *The Faerie Queene*. Spenser's use of Chaucer's giant as a type of aberrant sexuality in the Legend of Chastity suggests that he saw in *Thopas* a moral allegory in which uncontrolled physical desire, represented by Olifaunt, stands in the way of the pure and virtuous love which draws the hero, who is 'chaast and no lechour' (*Thopas* 745), to seek out a fairy queen. Such a reading of Chaucer's burlesque would help to explain why Spenser drew upon it for perhaps the most solemn and significant episode in the whole of *The Faerie Queene*: Arthur's vision of the Fairy Queen (I ix 8–15). The derivation of this episode from Sir Thopas' vision of the 'elf-queene' (*Thopas* 772–96) has seemed so improbable that critics have looked hard, without success, for a more dignified original; but if Spenser did read *Thopas* at one level as a serious moral allegory (a notable case of combining wisdom with entertainment), then the difficulty disappears, and the parallels can be recognized without embarrassment as representing surely the most remarkable of Spenser's borrowings from Chaucer. After 'pricking' aimlessly in a forest, each hero is overcome by weariness and lies down to sleep in a glade. He dreams of the 'Queene of Faeries' or the 'elf-queene' – 'with whose excellent beauty ravished,' as Spenser put it in his Letter to Raleigh, 'he awaking resolved to seeke her out.'

Spenser evidently saw in the vision of Sir Thopas a fitting representation of the moment when a young knight's inchoate longings for love and glory fix on a definite object, foreseen but achievable only with difficulty. 'Childe' Arthur, as Spenser calls him on two occasions when he fights a giant (Geryoneo V xi 8, 13, and Disdain VI viii 15), certainly numbers among his ancestors the would-be giant killer 'child Thopas' (*Thopas* 830). No doubt Spenser did see Chaucer's joke (though it would be hard to prove this); but he also found in *Thopas* the potential for a serious, even an improving, romance of love and chivalry.

allegorical tableaux Spenser's other main debt to Chaucer in *The Faerie Queene*, along with that to romances such as the *Squire's Tale* and *Sir Thopas*, is to the dream poems. He draws upon these particularly in allegorical set pieces. Here we are concerned not with the Chaucer of 'warlike numbers and Heroicke sound' but with the Chaucer of philosophical allegory, follower of such poets as Alanus de Insulis. Four of Spenser's set pieces in *The Faerie Queene* owe a particular debt to Chaucer. The first is the description of the house of Morpheus (I i 39–44), which may be compared with Chaucer's treatment of the same subject in the *Book of the Duchess* (153–94). Here Spenser follows Chaucer mainly in following Ovid, but he characteristically responds to the opiate effect of Chaucer's description of the streams which 'Came rennynge fro the clyves adoun, / That made a dedly slepynge soun' (161–2), preserving the same sonorous rhyme in his own corresponding lines (41.2–5). More significant, though less obvious, is the affinity between the court of Philotime visited by Guyon with Mammon (*FQ* II vii) and Chaucer's house of Fame. Philotime (love of honor) represents the attractions of ambition and renown, which are among the goods of fortune with which Mammon tempts Guyon. Like Chaucer's goddess of Fame, she sits in state on a magnificent throne at the upper end of a great pillared hall, which is entered through a golden gate (*FQ* II vii 40, *House of Fame* 1306); and in both halls, the favors of the great lady are contended for, noisily and confusedly, by a mass of people from every nation under the heavens (II vii 44, *HF* 1528–32). But Spenser's treatment of the theme differs from Chaucer's in a way characteristic of both authors. If Chaucer explicitly dissociates himself from the pursuit of fame, it is only by a few muted remarks from the narrator, which suggest unambitious stoic apathy rather than moral outrage (*HF* 1873–82). In *The Faerie Queene*, on the other hand, the whole context suggests a clear moral condemnation of everything that Philotime stands for: 'unlike Chaucerian allegorical ironies, Spenser's use of *ironia* is unambiguous and explicit' (Miskimin 1975:263).

But the most important of Chaucer's dream allegories for Spenser was the *Parliament of Fowls*. Already in the first canto of *The Faerie Queene*, Spenser imitates Chaucer's catalogue of trees (I i 8–9, *PF* 176–82); and the broken bows and arrows decorating the walls of the house of Busirane (III xi 46) recall the broken bows hung 'in dispit of Dyane the chaste' on the walls of Chaucer's Temple of Venus (*PF* 281–4). More surprisingly, Spenser's own august Temple of Venus (IV x 29–58) takes some features from its morally dubious English predecessor (Bennett 1957:119–21). Like Chaucer's, Spenser's temple has a setting of 'luxurious plentie,' with every kind of tree and flower; and the figure of Dame Concord who sits in its porch (IV x 31–5) corresponds to that of Dame Peace who sits at the door of Chaucer's temple. In describing Concord, however, Spenser also recalls other passages where Chaucer, following Boethius, speaks of the ordering of the four warring elements (*Troilus* 3.1751–64, *KnT* [*CT* I (A) 2991–3]; *CCCHA* 843–52, *Hymne of Love* 78–93; Tuve 1970:49–63). Spenser's Venus, in fact, represents the power of universal harmony, as Chaucer's does not; and although she shares with Chaucer's Venus the covering of a 'slender veile' (*FQ* IV x 40, *PF* 270–3), the effect in her case is not suggestively erotic. By contrast, in that passage of the *Cantos of Mutabilitie* where Spenser mentions the 'Foules parley' and its author by name (VII vii 9), his imitation preserves faithfully the spirit of Chaucer's portrait of Nature – a portrait which, in the *Parliament*, follows and contrasts with the portrait of Venus (Bennett 1957:112–13). The 'great goddesse' Nature who hears Mutabilitie's plea against Jove on Arlo Hill, surrounded by an assembly of gods and all living creatures, is essentially the same as, though grander than, the 'noble goddesse' Nature who presides over the assembly of every kind of bird in Chaucer's poem. Both sit on a hill in a bower or pavilion made of branches growing over their heads, and both are compared to the glory of the sun (*FQ* VII vii 6–8, *PF* 299–305). Spenser of course knew other accounts of Nature besides Chaucer's, but his tribute to 'old *Dan Geffrey*' in this context is the grandest of all his acknowledgments to his great predecessor.

This survey of some of Spenser's more evident and incontrovertible debts to Chaucer in love complaint, fable, chivalric romance, and allegorical tableau falls far short of exhausting the catalogue of passages in his work which demonstrably have an origin in his reading of the 1561 folio Chaucer. Others which may be mentioned are the observations on gentilesse in *FQ* VI iii 1 (approximating to *Wife of Bath's Tale* [*CT* III (D) 1170]) and on the incompatibility between love and mastery in *FQ* III i 25 (directly adapted from *Franklin's Tale* [*CT* V (F) 764–6]) and IV i 46; an imitation in *FQ* II x 24 of the obscure and heraldically allusive high style of the Monk's stanza on Peter of Spain (*Monk's Tale* [*CT* VII 2383–90]); and the echo of *Troilus* 1.232–5 in Arthur's account of his falling in love (*FQ* I ix 12).

meter and language There remain the more general questions of Chaucer's influence on the meter and language of Spenser's poetry. Of Chaucer's metrical forms, Spenser uses four. *SC, March* employs one version of the tail-rhyme stanza (rhyming *aabccb*) found in *Sir Thopas* and no doubt understood by Spenser as a popular, ballad-like meter appropriate for shepherds. At the other, upper end of the hierarchy of stanza forms lie the heavy stanza of the Monk's tragedies (*ababbcbc*), variants of which are used by Spenser for two of his most dolorous eclogues (*SC, June* and *Nov*), and also the rhyme-royal stanza, used by Spenser as by Chaucer for dignified subjects (*Fowre Hymnes*, *Time*). In accordance with the usage of his own day, however, Spenser's hierarchy differs from Chaucer's in confining the couplet entirely to low subjects. The couplet is a low form, according to Elizabethan theorists, because it makes the smallest possible demands on the ear's educated capacity to 'carry' a rhyme sound: 'this is the most vulgar proportion of distance or situation, such as used *Chaucer* in his Canterbury tales, and *Gower* in all his workes' (Puttenham *Arte* 2.10 [ie, 2.11]). Spenser accordingly used the couplet only for the telling of fables or animal stories: *SC, Februarie*, *Maye*, and *September*, and *Mother Hubberds Tale*.

Mother Hubberd proves, if proof is necessary, that Spenser was perfectly capable of writing correct ten- or eleven-syllable lines in couplets, as in other forms such as rhyme royal or his own *Faerie Queene* stanza. The result is metrically quite like Chaucer's long couplet, as that is conventionally read today. But in *Februarie*, *Maye*, and *September*, he writes a much rougher couplet line, most often with nine syllables and four main stresses: 'There grewe an aged Tree on the greene, / A goodly Oake sometime had it bene, / With armes full strong and largely displayd, / But of their leaves they were disarayde' (*Feb* 102–5). It may be this, rather than the smoother movement of *Mother Hubberd*, that Spenser heard when he read Chaucer's long couplets, in the *Nun's Priest's Tale* or the *Knight's Tale* or the *General Prologue*. Many of Chaucer's decasyllabic lines are reduced to nine syllables if the final *-e*'s are not pronounced ('Whan Zephirus eek with his sweet[e] breeth'). Even if Spenser did pronounce these *-e*'s (which is unlikely), the badly spelled and corrupt text of the 1561 folio would still have yielded a very irregular and bumpy result. Here is Stow's text of *General Prologue* 19–22: 'It befell that season on a day / In Southewarke at the Taberde as I lay / Redie to go in my pilgrimage / To Caunterbury with devoute courage.'

In a prefatory epistle to Speght's edition of Chaucer (1598), Francis Beaumont claims that Spenser's 'much frequenting of *Chaucers* antient speeches causeth many to allow farre better of him, then otherwise they would' (*Sp All* p 54). The language of Spenser's poetry certainly owes much to his reading of Chaucer, but the task of proving that this or that word or form could only have come directly from him seems less easy the more one knows about other late-medieval and Tudor poetry. For one thing, many other Renaissance poets had already turned to their medieval English predecessors in the attempt to make their language richer and more copious by the use of archaic expressions. Thus, an undoubted archaism such as *sithe* meaning 'time' (as glossed by E.K. in *SC, Jan* 49) would appear from evidence provided by the *OED* to have been a familiar item in the Elizabethan poetic lexicon. Spenser could have discovered it in Chaucer, but there is no particular reason to think that he did. The same is true of morphological archaisms such as the *y-* prefixed to past participles and the *-en* added to verbs in the present plural. Nor can it be assumed that Tudor poets, Spenser or others, would necessarily take their Middle English out of Chaucer alone. Chaucer was undoubtedly the most frequently printed and most widely read medieval English poet in Spenser's day, but other writers such as Gower and Lydgate also have to be reckoned with. A minor instance of this principle is provided by one of the best known of Spenser's 'Chaucerisms,' the compound noun *derring do* meaning 'daring deeds' (*SC, Oct* 65, *FQ* II iv 42, etc). This certainly goes back to a line in Chaucer's *Troilus*, 'In durryng don that longeth to a knyght' (5.837); but the *OED* points out that the collocation was picked up by Lydgate in his *Troy Book* (2.4869, 3.3957, etc), and that it is only in sixteenth-century editions of this work that the verbal noun appears in Spenser's form, *derring*, with a medial *-e-*.

Yet when all allowances have been made for other Middle English sources and for the general currency of certain archaisms in Tudor poetry, the identifiably Chaucerian element in Spenser's language remains considerable. Some of the words which he uses could only have been gathered directly from a reading of Chaucer. In *The Faerie Queene*, for instance, *cordwaine* (II iii 27, etc), *checklaton* (VI vii 43), *jane* (III vii 58), and *giambeux* (II vi 29) must all have come from *Sir Thopas* (*CT* VII 732, 734, 735, 875). Again, Spenser's peculiar use of *yond* in the sense 'mad' (*FQ* II viii 40, etc) must derive from a misreading of Chaucer's phrase 'a tygre yond in Ynde' (*Clerk's Tale* [*CT* IV (E) 1199], where *yond* means 'yonder'). In addition to such indubitable instances, of course, Chaucer is much the most likely source in fact for many of those words, phrases, and forms which could in theory have come from other writers.

No edition of Chaucer's works had a glossary until Speght's in 1598, so Spenser's occasional misunderstandings of old words such as *yond* cannot fairly be blamed as negligent. Indeed, there is every reason to suppose that he read attentively as well as widely in the 1561 folio volume. Yet there is much to be said for C.S. Lewis' judgment that 'Chaucer and pseudo-Chaucer were less important to him than he himself liked to believe' (1954:356). Spenser certainly uses Chaucer a great deal, but his major borrowings such as those from the *Book of the Duchess* in *Daphnaïda*, from the *Nun's Priest's Tale* in *Muiopotmos*, and from *Sir Thopas*, the *Squire's Tale*, and the *Parliament of Fowls* in *The Faerie Queene*, all in their different ways serve to show above all just how boldly he departs from his original. He claimed that Chaucer's 'owne spirit' survived in him 'through infusion sweete'; but it is precisely, one might say, the spirit of poems such as the *Book of the Duchess* or *Sir Thopas* which does not survive in his work. The obliquity of the one, the irony of the other, and the comedy in both – these are qualities generally alien to what has been called the 'serious subtlety' of Spenser's muse (Miskimin 1975:40). The same qualities are missing also in Spenser's imitations of the *Parliament of Fowls*, perhaps for him the most congenial of Chaucer's works. He shared many of Chaucer's ideas, especially on love and on nature, but he is a very different kind of poet. For all his verbal borrowings, he does not write like Chaucer; and he has his own ways, which are not Chaucer's, of making narrative meaningful. No reader or writer in the age of Elizabeth could avoid coming to terms with Chaucer, the one dominating figure in the newly constituted English literature. In Spenser's case, this accommodation was a complex one, involving a great deal of admiration, much borrowing, a certain amount of genuine misunderstanding, and an incalculable degree of deliberate, though undeclared, independence. JOHN A. BURROW

Citations to Chaucer follow Chaucer ed 1987.

SIXTEENTH-CENTURY EDITIONS OF CHAUCER AND CHAUCER APOCRYPHA: Chaucer ed 1969; Chaucer ed 1894–7, 1:27–46 (editions), 7 passim (apocrypha); Eleanor Prescott Hammond 1908 *Chaucer: A Bibliographical Manual* (New York) pp 114–27 (editions), 406–63 (apocrypha); Miskimin 1975, ch 7; Charles Muscatine 1963 *The Book of Geoffrey Chaucer* (San Francisco).

SPENSER'S RELATION TO CHAUCER *General studies*: Crampton 1974; Hieatt 1975a; Warton 1762 (section 5 'Of Spenser's Imitations from Chaucer' still valuable).

Individual works: Anderson 1971a; Anderson 1982; Anderson 1985; J.A.W. Bennett 1957 *'The Parlement of Foules': An Interpretation* (Oxford) ch 3; J.W. Bennett 1942; Normand Berlin 1966 'Chaucer's *The Book of the Duchess* and Spenser's *Daphnaïda*: A Contrast' *SN* 38:282–9; J.A. Burrow 1983 '*Sir Thopas* in the Sixteenth Century' in Gray and Stanley, pp 69–91; Harris and Steffen 1978; Alice E. Lasater 1974 'The Chaucerian Narrator in Spenser's *Shepheardes Calender*' *SoQ* 12:189–201; Thomas William Nadal 1908 'Spenser's *Daphnaïda*, and Chaucer's *Book of the Duchess*' *PMLA* 23:646–61; Nadal 1910 'Spenser's *Muiopotmos* in Relation to Chaucer's *Sir Thopas* and *The Nun's Priest's Tale*' *PMLA* 25:640–56; Nelson 1973:87–9; Oram 1981.

Language: McElderry 1932; Rubel 1941, ch 13.

China, influence and reputation in Unlike Shakespeare, who has twice been completely translated, Spenser has never been popular with the Chinese. He is not even mentioned in most modern anthologies of Western poetry. Despite the upsurge of literary translation in mainland China since 1979, which has included work from Chaucer as well as Shakespeare, Spenser has gone unnoticed. Perhaps as a consequence, even the general guidebooks to Western English literature sometimes fail to include him. An attempt to translate *The Faerie Queene* was made in the 1950s by the distinguished poet Pien Chih-lin, a veteran translator of Shakespeare; but his manuscript was lost during the Cultural Revolution.

The situation in Taiwan is only slightly better. Since English poetry and the history of English literature are compulsory courses for nearly all university English majors, Spenser is sometimes read in collections such as the Norton Anthology. Yet translation of his poetry has been limited to brief quotations in the various histories of English literature written in Chinese. The proem to Book I, together with a plot summary of *The Faerie Queene* and a short biographical and critical introduction to Spenser, is offered by the noted translator, critic, and essayist Liang Shih-chiu in his monumental *Ying-kuo wen-hsüeh shih* (*History of English Literature* 1985). Also translated by Liang is the first sonnet of *Amoretti*, but he observes that *The Faerie Queene* is almost impossible to translate into Chinese because of the poetic form.

Ch'uan-t'ung ti yü hsien-tai ti (*The Classical and the Modern* 1974) by the Taiwanese poet and critic C.H. Wang includes two studies in comparative literature which concern Spenser. The first examines the bird as the allegorical messenger of love in *The Faerie Queene* and in the *Li sao* (*Encountering Sorrow*, traditionally ascribed to Ch'ü Yüan, fl 313–290 BC). The second looks at sartorial emblems and quest motifs in the two poems.

Of interest to English readers is H[sin-]c[h'ang] Chang's *Allegory and Courtesy in Spenser: A Chinese View* (1955), which begins with a discussion and translation of the central chapters of *Ching hua yüan* (*Romance of the Flowers in the Mirror*, written in the early nineteenth century by Li Ju-chen); it tries to distinguish between Chinese and Spenserian allegory, showing that Spenser relies more heavily on personification. The final chapter, however, shows that there are distinct similarities between Confucian and Western ideals of courtesy.

WILLIAM S. TAY

chivalry In its historical development, chivalry presents a confusing picture. Beginning as an early medieval warrior code, it originally meant military skill on horseback, as its etymology from the French *chevalerie* indicates. From the Middle Ages onwards, it had an aristocratic bias, but initially its values were simple enough: strength and plunder were primary, and, on a slightly higher plane, loyalty and a desire for glory motivated the knight. By the twelfth century, the Crusades began to contribute a religious goal and justification for chivalric aggression, and the literature and legends of Arthurian romance infused the code with ideals of courtly love and service. Chivalry thus evolved into an odd mixture of piety and belligerence, game and earnest, art and life. Although increasingly anachronistic, it endured as an imaginative force in the Renaissance. Its influence upon the literature and courtly ceremonies of Elizabethan England persisted; and, throughout *The Faerie Queene*, Spenser recalls the 'goodly usage of those antique times, / In which the sword was servant unto right' (III i 13).

Many critics still regard both Elizabethan chivalry and Spenser's poetry as exercises in romantic illusion and nostalgia, arguing, for example, that chivalry for Spenser has no contact with the 'realities of knighthood' or even with the 'human predicament,' because it had become a 'purely literary' conception (Moorman 1967:135, 122). While for others chivalry is 'still powerful as a source of inspiration for personal conduct, still the accepted vehicle for expressing the sense of glory and personal idealism that is connected with the notion of *noblesse*, it has lost any necessary connection with the life of the gentleman considered as a functioning member of the body politic.' In this view, Elizabethan chivalry represented a 'patently outdated code of values' which was 'tied to actuality only by the slenderest of threads' (A.B. Ferguson 1960:103, 125–7).

In the Elizabethan age, chivalry was in fact a powerful ideology, capable of reconciling various social contradictions. The aristocracy was still strong but its position was greatly altered. The centralization of state control had transformed 'once-formidable local potentates ... into fawning courtiers and tame state pensionaries' (Stone 1965:385). Many Elizabethan aristocrats fiercely resisted this change; and, although feudalism was dead, the image and ethos of the feudal knight still retained its appeal. The Earls of Leicester and Essex and Sir Philip Sidney rushed to the battlefields of Ireland and the continent to vindicate their country's honor, and Spenser celebrated their exploits. He accompanied Lord Grey during bitter campaigns in Ireland, later transforming him into Artegall, the knight of Justice in *FQ* v, and the Irish conflict into a holy crusade against the savage and the infidel. At the court, the Accession Day tilts provided another outlet for aristocratic belligerence as well as a safer and more satisfying means of displaying magnificence. No longer the dangerous wargame of the Middle Ages, the Elizabethan tournament allowed its contestants to reenact their glory-days as feudal warriors. Spenser draws on the elaborate pageantry of the Elizabethan court for the rites of the Order of Maidenhead and its 'yearely solemne feast' in honor of the Fairy Queen (II ii 42).

Chivalry's value as royal propaganda was no less important; and its legendary hero, Arthur, figures prominently in the *Faerie Queene*. Tudor monarchs sometimes exploited Arthurian mythology to advance their claims to the throne, and Tudor pageants and histories, drawing on Geoffrey of Monmouth, traced the dynasty's descent back to Cadwallader (see *history). Spenser patriotically incorporates this legendary history into his own account of the Queen's lineage. In *FQ* II x, he traces the ancient line founded by Brutus down to the time of Arthur's father. Merlin's prophecy (III iii 26–49) follows the line's descent to extinction with Cadwallader but also predicts its restoration by Henry VII and its dynastic triumph in the reign of a 'royall virgin.'

In his account of 'My glorious Soveraines goodly auncestrie' (III iii 4), Spenser shows his command of chivalric historiography with its peculiar blend of antiquarian knowledge and mythic creativity. His early patron, Robert Dudley, the Earl of Leicester, employed several heralds and writers to compile pedigrees showing the ancient nobility of his line. Spenser wrote the *Stemmata Dudleiana* (a genealogical work now lost) in honor of the Dudleys, and he may have reused some of this material in the *Faerie Queene*'s legendary histories.

For Spenser, chivalry's ritual function is as important as its mythological content. 'Ceremonial forms not horses are the basis of chivalry. As both the institution and the ideal assumes, chivalry is a ritualized social arrangement where custom is the predominant cohesive force ... The chivalric code is a quasi-legal social code which supplies a rudimentary jurisprudence, a customary form whose spirit is courtesy, or better, grace' (Fletcher 1971:190). The tournament, chivalry's main rite in the Renaissance, combined a sporting contest, mock combat, and social drama into a form of conflict-negotiation, enacting in its ceremonies the *discordia concors* or harmonious discord which is an informing principle of Spenser's poetry. *FQ* IV shows most clearly how chivalric custom can sustain concord through discord because it celebrates a friendship achieved through combat. The Temple of Book IV's paradoxical amity includes Concord who is flanked by two young men 'Both strongly arm'd, as fearing one another,' yet held in equilibrium by the 'amiable Dame' between them (x 31–2). Guyon, too, skilled in 'tourney and in lists debate,' can adroitly 'turne his earnest unto game, / Through goodly handling and wise temperance' (II i 6, 31); and Britomart and an unnamed knight are restored to 'goodly fellowship' with no breach of chivalric custom (IV i 15). Chivalry's blend of sporting belligerence, reckless courage, and delight in magnificence are all idealistically evoked by Guyon's praise of 'the high heroicke spright, / That joyes for crownes and kingdomes to contend; / Fair shields, gay steedes, bright armes be my delight: / Those be the riches fit for an advent'rous knight' (II vii 10).

Yet Spenser's treatment of chivalric rites and values is often as skeptical as it is idealistic. He sometimes mocks the chivalric absurdities of his heroes with an irony recalling Ariosto's. Guyon's embarrassing defeat by Britomart, his comically lame excuses, their 'reconcilement,' and the abrupt, almost farcical chase after Florimell in *FQ* III i 6–18 satirize not only the literary conventions of chivalric romance but the 'golden chaine of concord tyde' by chivalric custom. More ominously, the tournament or joust may be rendered corrupt or frivolous by its context: though 'Greatly advauncing his gay chevalree,' Redcrosse's triumph occurs in the lists of the house of Pride (I v 16), and the six lecherous champions who are 'traynd in all civilitee, / And goodly taught to tilt and turnament' are liegemen to the wicked Malecasta (III i 44).

Chivalry can also degenerate into vaunting bellicose pride as the ideal of honor lapses into the vainglory of Braggadocchio or the purely personal goal of Belphoebe, which serves no social purpose (Berger 1957:192). Moreover, instead of resolving conflict, chivalric combat often simply increases discord. Satyrane's tournament settles nothing, and hostilities keep breaking out among the contestants (IV iv, ix 25–35). Guyon fails to end the quarrel between Huddibras and Sansloy: 'He [Love] maketh warre, he maketh peace againe, / And yet his peace is but continuall jarre' (II ii 26). Chivalric combat is often irrelevant to the protagonists' central quests, and the quest itself is often inherently indeterminate, part of the 'endlesse worke' which both Spenser and his heroes undertake.

Finally, chivalry's orderly customs are useless amidst the lawlessness and brutality of real warfare. In Book V, combat is ruled out as a means of adjudication when property is threatened. Artegall refuses to settle the conflict between Sanglier and the unarmed Squire by 'blooddy fight,' and he opposes 'battailes doubtfull proofe' in the struggle between Bracidas and Amidas (i 25, iv 6). Chivalry seems to have no connection to the struggles of Book VI, and at times knights seem to fare best in this savage landscape when freed of their 'heavy armes' (iv 19). Appropriately, an important character in the book is the hermit, a traditional figure in chivalric romance and pageantry, who has abandoned his arms forever: 'weary to / Of warres delight, and worlds contentious toyle, / The name of knighthood he did disavow' (v 37).

Spenser's treatment of chivalric custom and ceremony is complex throughout *The Faerie Queene*. His conception of chivalry is both serious and playful, and he firmly grounds its ideals in a social code and function. In his later works, however, he seems increasingly estranged from chivalry's courtly context, and some readers of Book VI find a deepening disillusionment in his removal of the action from the court, once the center of chivalric rites and values. Spenser's final tribute to chivalric heroism in *Prothalamion* is certainly elegiac and melancholic. There he praises the Earl of Essex as the 'flower of Chevalrie' who will deliver his country from 'forraine harmes' through 'prowesse and victorious armes' (150–6). Yet there is a sense that, while 'some brave muse may sing / To ages following' of Essex's noble victories (159), it will not be Spenser's muse. His thoughts are fixed on the Earl of Leicester; and, in the midst of the nuptial festivities, he mourns the death of his noble patron. The adjoining Temple and its inns of court remind him of the decline of chivalry's noble heroes and the rise of a new bourgeois class in their place: 'Where now the studious Lawyers have their bowers / There whylome wont the Templer Knights to byde, / Till they decayd through pride' (134–6). Spenser remains loyal to his patrons and their values, but his awareness of chivalry's ideological and ceremonial power is balanced by his appreciation of its limitations and liabilities. RICHARD C. MCCOY

Bornstein 1975; Arthur B. Ferguson 1960; Ferguson 1986 *The Chivalric Tradition in Renaissance England* (Washington, D.C.); Huizinga ed 1924; Maurice Keen 1984 *Chivalry* (New Haven); Leslie 1983; Richard C. McCoy 1989 *The Rites of Knighthood: The Literature and Politics of Elizabethan Chivalry* (Berkeley and Los Angeles); Ivan L. Schulze 1933 'Notes on Elizabethan Chivalry and *The Faerie Queene*' *SP* 30:148–59; Schulze 1935; Stone 1965; A. Young 1987.

Chrétien de Troyes (d about 1190) The greatest vernacular narrative poet of his age,

Chrétien wrote five chivalric Arthurian romances, probably between 1170 and 1190: *Erec et Enide, Cligés, Lancelot* (or *The Knight of the Cart*), *Yvain* (or *The Knight of the Lion*), and *Perceval* (or *The Story of the Grail*). Although it is hardly possible that Spenser ever read these works, they established literary traditions of love and adventure, of Arthur, Lancelot, and Guinevere, that flourished in the thirteenth-century French 'Vulgate Cycle,' became well-known in England through Malory's adaptations, and ultimately exerted a strong influence on the form and content of *The Faerie Queene*.

Chrétien's art reflects twelfth-century humanism in its use of Virgil and Ovid, along with Neoplatonic concepts borrowed from the philosophical school of Chartres (known to Spenser through the account of the goddess Nature in Chaucer's *Parliament of Fowls*). His romances also respond to a new courtly milieu, in which a self-aware social elite of nobles and secular clerics concerned itself with moral, psychological, and emotional issues hitherto the province of (primarily monastic) intellectuals writing in Latin. A need to remake the self through a refined perception of, and dedication to, crucial ideals of behavior and feeling animates the quests of Chrétien's protagonists, who thereby anticipate the exemplary knights of *The Faerie Queene* through whom Spenser aimed 'to fashion a gentleman or noble person in vertuous and gentle discipline' (Letter to Raleigh). By presenting ironically the skewed values of the Arthurian court, from which the hero must distance himself if he is to excel and grow, Chrétien initiates a tradition of anti-court satire which Spenser inherited and revivified in *Colin Clouts Come Home Againe*.

The major values of Chrétien's imagined universe undergo critical scrutiny: courtly love in *Cligés* and *Lancelot*, prowess in *Yvain* and *Perceval*. After *Erec*, Chrétien tends to treat his characters and situations with considerable detachment, allowing the audience to enjoy his works as virtuoso fictions as well as symbolic narratives. The powers and limits of fiction-making become a central concern in *Cligés* and *Yvain*, articulated by means of artist-surrogates such as Jehan, Thessala, and Lunete, who attempt to control the unfolding action, and marvelous artifacts such as Jehan's tower (*Cligés* 5487–8), a symbol of the artist's created world that anticipates, though without overt moralization, Spenserian analogues like the Bower of Bliss (*FQ* II xii) or Busirane's house (III xi).

Chrétien's narrator – often intrusive and unreliable – stands between author and audience and allows the poet to establish ironic perspective or narrative ambiguity. In analyzing the emotions of the characters (especially love), the narrator uses an allegorical technique that is occasional rather than consistent, and psychological rather than moral or religious. Christian themes or events are evoked in *Lancelot* (where the hero has Christ-like attributes and his quest recalls the Harrowing of Hell) and *Cligés* (where the heroine's name, Fénice, and her feigned death allude to the Resurrection); but their purpose seems more parodic than allegorical.

The shifting tonality and complex strategies of Chrétien's art prompt analysis as well as enjoyment of his romances' improbable adventures. The attentive audience thus created by and for symbolic fictions persisted from Chrétien's day to Spenser's, and facilitated the latter's achievement as a poet of philosophical romance.

R.W. HANNING

Editions include *Erec et Enide* ed Mario Roques, *CFMA* 80 (Paris 1968); *Cligés* ed Alexandre Micha, *CFMA* 84 (Paris 1970); *Le Chevalier de la Charrete* (Lancelot) ed Mario Roques, *CFMA* 86 (Paris 1972); and *Le Chevalier au Lion* (*Yvain*) ed Mario Roques, *CFMA* 89 (Paris 1968).

Jean Frappier 1957 *Chrétien de Troyes* (Paris); Hanning 1977; L.T. Topsfield 1981 *Chrétien de Troyes: A Study of the Arthurian Romances* (Cambridge); Tuve 1966; Vinaver 1971; Winthrop Wetherbee 1972 *Platonism and Poetry in the Twelfth Century: The Literary Influence of the School of Chartres* (Princeton).

Christine de Pisan (c 1364–1431) A scholar and significant early feminist, Christine may have influenced Spenser's account of the Amazons in *The Faerie Queene* by the chapters on Amazons in her *Livre de la cité des dames* (c 1405). If so, Britomart's fight with Radigund in *FQ* V vii shows how Spenser responds to a feminist source on the controversial issue of female power, and specifically female rule.

A learned woman of Italian origin who can be called France's first professional woman author, Christine wrote over twenty works in many genres between 1390 and 1429. *La Cité* was one of those which grew out of her role as chief correspondent during the Querelle de la Rose, when she condemned as misogynic Jean de Meun's conclusion to the *Romance of the Rose*. This debate allowed her to analyze male attitudes toward women, including the literary conventions of courtly love (*Epistre au dieu d'amour, Le Dit de la Rose*), and also to voice her own theories about women's place in society (*La Cité* and *Le Trésor de la cité des dames*). Of these latter works, *La Cité* is the boldest. It is a dialogue in three books, in which Christine, offended by antifeminist writings, sets out to build a city of the great women of the past, aided by Reason, Righteousness, and Justice. Much of the work describes the excellence of these women, with historical justifications drawn from works such as Boccaccio's *De claris mulieribus* and Jacopo da Voragine's *Legenda aurea*.

Although her works were neglected after the seventeenth century, they were known in England as early as the 1390s and in the fifteenth and sixteenth centuries were widely available, both in French manuscripts which circulated in aristocratic circles and, by the sixteenth century, in printed translations (by Spenser's time, five works had been published). *La Cité* in Brian Anslay's translation as *The Boke of the Cyte of Ladyes* appeared in 1521.

Christine's uniquely feminist account of Amazonia (in *Cyte* I.16–19) connects her work with Spenser's Amazons in *FQ* V vii. The life of the Amazon Queen Penthesilea in Christine's *Epistre d'Othéa* may have influenced the account of Radigund, and the account of her death in the *Cyte* may have influenced the scene of Radigund's slaying (Tuve 1970:124). In Christine's version, Pyrrhus, the son of Achilles and traditionally the slayer of Penthesilea in medieval and Renaissance versions of the story, kills the Queen during the Trojan War: 'When he sawe the heed bare by whiche her yelowe heere appered [he] gave her so grete a stroke that he clefte in sondre the heed and the brayne' (*Cyte* I.19). Britomart strikes the Amazon Queen a similar blow that 'empierced to the very braine, / And her proud person low prostrated on the plaine' (V vii 33).

Although this conquest of the Amazon also recalls Clorinda's death in *Gerusalemme liberata* (12.64), in Tasso's version (which also draws on the Penthesilea story) there is no head wound. Penthesilea's death was a popular subject in medieval and Renaissance accounts of Amazons, but Christine's version differs from others, including fifteenth-century English variants (Caxton, Lydgate, *Laud Troy Book*), in specifying that Penthesilea was killed by a blow to the head (Boccaccio, Christine's main source, does not detail the death). In a typical version, such as Benoît de Sainte-Maure's, Pyrrhus cuts off Penthesilea's arm and then dismembers her; by shifting the deathblow from arm to head, Christine emblematizes the tragic defeat of a female head of state, an allegory which is repeated by Spenser in a more conservative sense. Like Christine's Penthesilea, last of the great Amazon queens, Radigund is the last autonomous female ruler of what is literally a city of ladies, 'A goodly citty and a mighty one' (*FQ* V iv 35), called Radegone after her. That she falls by a head wound is appropriate in a book of judicial dismemberments which, in her case, punish the threat posed to conventional gender hierarchies by a woman head of state. In particular, the Protestant ideology of marriage, with its emphasis on woman's subordination to man as her 'head,' determines Spenser's response to the feminist discourse represented by Christine's text and embodied in her Amazons. Although he continues to praise Elizabeth, whom contemporary propagandists often likened to an Amazon, his language in Book V is similar to that of John Knox, who characterizes the female ruler as a monstrous 'head' that deforms the body politic.

Britomart's progress from warrior-maid to promised wife similarly suggests that Spenser's most significant revision of Christine's text – the substitution of a female warrior for the man who slays the Penthesilea figure – is ideologically charged. Britomart reverses her position as an Amazonian figure to take Artegall's place as an opponent of Amazons, a reading enhanced by parallels between Christine's account of Penthesilea's death and Artegall's encounters, first with Britomart and then with Radigund, which precede the death of the Queen (*FQ* IV vi, V v). Britomart's similarity to Radigund as a Penthesilea figure is heightened by the way that the description of her 'yellow heare' in the battle with Artegall (IV vi 20) echoes the reference to Penthesilea's 'yelowe heere' in the *Cyte* (I.19). As in Christine's account, where Pyrrhus, defeated during his first battle with Penthesilea, must return to conquer her, two battles are required to subdue Radigund; Britomart's blow to the Amazon's head completes the gesture Artegall interrupted earlier when, unlacing Radigund's helmet, he raises his sword 'Thinking at once both head and helmet to have raced' (V v II). Britomart's battle with her may thus be read as a psychomachia in which she delivers the deathblow to her own power; her subsequent repeal of the 'liberty of women' in Radegone (vii 42) also symbolizes the suppression of the feminist ideal represented by Christine's city of ladies. W. TAMAR HELLER

A recent biography is Charity Cannon Willard 1984 *Christine de Pizan: Her Life and Works* (New York). *The Boke of the Cyte of Ladyes* tr Brian Anslay (1521) is reprinted in *Distaves and Dames* ed Diane Bornstein (Delmar, NY 1978). Maureen Cheney Curnow 1975 'The *Livre de la cité des dames* of Christine de Pisan: A Critical Edition' (diss Vanderbilt Univ) includes a history of the Anslay translation; Hull 1982:125 lists the Anslay translation among books circulating in the English Renaissance controversy about women. Kleinbaum 1983:65–8 shows that Christine's Amazonia differs from numerous medieval and Renaissance versions by embodying not male fantasy but a detailed argument in favor of female government. Miskimin 1978 claims that a manuscript of Christine's *Trésor* is a source for Isis and the crocodile in *FQ* V vii.

chronicles Spenser incorporates into *The Faerie Queene* a three-part chronicle of British history: in *FQ* II x, Arthur reads from *Briton moniments* the chronicle of Briton kings from Trojan Brute to Uther Pendragon, his own father (5–69); in III iii, the history continues in Merlin's prophecy of the lineage of Britomart and Artegall up to the glorious succession of Queen Elizabeth which ends 800 years of Saxon rule (27–50); and in III ix, the chronicle is completed by tracing the history of Troy from its fall to its refounding as Troynovant (27–50).

Spenser's historical survey embodies careful study and organization of materials (see Harper 1910). Following Geoffrey of Monmouth's *Historia regum Britanniae* as his basic source, he consulted at least eleven other works for particular details, often using several for a single stanza. They include Gildas' *De excidio et conquestu Britanniae* (6th century; pub 1525, 1567, 1568), Caxton's *Chronicles of England* (1480, etc), Fabyan's *New Chronicles of England and France* (1516, etc), Stow's *Summarie of Englyshe Chronicles* (1565, etc) and *Chronicles of England* (1580), the 1574 and 1578 additions to the *Mirror for Magistrates*, Holinshed's *Chronicles* (1577, rev ed 1587), and Camden's *Britannia* (1586, etc; tr 1601).

To some modern readers, Spenser's chronicles may seem tedious and intrusive, but in their Elizabethan context, they are amply justified (see II x 69). Spenser's own estimation of their relevance may be inferred from his placing the main section in canto x, a canto generally reserved for important thematic material. The Renaissance heroic poem was invariably historical in subject and setting. By aligning himself with 'all the antique Poets historicall' (Letter to Raleigh), and by linking Arthur's career to recitals of past and future events, Spenser lends a kind of documentary weight and reflected historicity to the world of his poem. Such linking of fiction with history and prophecy is conventional in epic from Homer through Milton. Further, the chronicles complement Spenser's general epideictic intent in using the topos *genus* (praise through chronicling of genealogical descent) and in providing a series of typological foreshadowings of Elizabeth in the figures of queens and heroines from Britain's past (Cain 1978). Moreover, they contribute very strongly to the political dimensions of the poem.

The early history of Britain – the murky period from the supposed founding of the nation by the Trojans to the Norman Conquest – was of interest and importance to Spenser's audience for several reasons. One was a strong nationalistic desire to piece together an heroic past like that of other European nations, most of which claimed mythic links with a civilized antiquity antedating their occupation by the Romans. Another was the patriotic contrivance by Tudor propagandists, if not by the monarchs themselves, of Tudor descent from King Arthur. A third reason, a consequence of the English Reformation, was religious as well as political: European Catholics argued for papal sovereignty over the English church partly on the historical grounds that Christianity had been brought to the island by St Augustine, an emissary and representative of the Church of Rome. Against this position, the ancient British history asserted that Christianity in Britain was instituted much earlier by Joseph of Arimathea during the reign of King Lucius (see *FQ* II x 53) and that its development was separate and independent of Rome from the start.

On these and other topics, British history filled large gaps in the available accounts of European civilization; and not to accept them was to admit that the early inhabitants of the land had been too barbarous to leave any record. When the Italian-born historian Polydore Vergil rejected the ancient chronicle history in his *Anglica historia* (1534, 1546, 1555), his work was attacked throughout the century. Though defended in 1582 by the Scot George Buchanan, tutor of the future King James, Polydore was vehemently attacked by Leland (1544), John Bale (1548), Richard Harvey (1593) and others. The accounts of Geoffrey of Monmouth were accepted in part by most Tudor chroniclers, including Holinshed, Grafton (1569), and Stow. While Spenser may not have believed their 'facts' (see *Var Prose* p 86), the chronicles were almost mandatory material for a poem on Arthur.

More fundamental than political and religious issues is artistic unity – the appropriateness of the histories in their poetic contexts and their thematic function in the poem. Spenser's second British chronicle is clearly related to the story of Book III, since Merlin's prophecy concludes with Britomart's reward for chaste and loyal devotion to Artegall and to the life of heroic virtue. His first chronicle is more problematic. It has been seen to dramatize the earthly progress of mankind, in which the communal suffering and sinfulness of the Britons demonstrate that divine grace is needed to accomplish ends denied to individual human effort (Berger 1957). Various patterns in the changing periods covered by the narrative support this view, including one involving a series of progressively changing periods. Brute's dynasty is an age of raw nature; Donwallo's is one of law. The birth of Christ at II x 50 marks a transition from human to divine law and from the earthly city symbolized by Rome to the city of God. Throughout this history, there is a disproportion between the efforts and the effectiveness of individual kings, a general lack of emphasis on moral causality, and a dramatizing of 'the intransigence of real facts to meaning' (Berger 1957:103). Spenser's pessimism about the course of human affairs is contained within the optimism of a trust in providential grace (see *providence).

The poetic context of the chronicle is the account of Alma's three counselors whose interaction constitutes an allegory of the proper method of reading histories and thus encourages Arthur and the reader to seek a definite meaning in the narrative that follows (Mills 1978). On one level the counselors represent the three parts of prudence (memory, intelligence, and foresight) which, when applied to history, lead one to remember the past and to act in the present so as to ensure the continuity of the future, a formula repeatedly stressed in the literature dealing with the education of princes and governors that proliferated in Renaissance humanism. Accordingly, one may expect Spenser's chronicle to constitute an allegory of temperance in history.

Although generally following Geoffrey of Monmouth, Spenser departs from him to construct a sequence divisible into four periods, the first three each ending with the failure of a king to produce male heirs. (In the fourth period, that failure became a triumph with the reign of Elizabeth.) The first period ends with Porrex after Lear had 'no issue male him to succeed' (II x 27, 36); the second with the death of Lucius, civil war, and Roman invasion (54); and the third with Octavian and the invasions of the Huns and

Picts (61). Within each dynasty, the process is the same: a strong new beginning with subsequent moral and political degeneration through various kinds of intemperance, ending in sterility and extinction. The end generally accords with the providential view of history in Tudor thought: God punishes men and nations on an historical scale, often deferring retribution to later generations but never ceasing to intervene in the historical process. The warning to Arthur (the chronicle breaks off just before his birth in the fourth dynasty) is clear, and clearly related to the virtue of temperance treated in Book II.

The British chronicle is followed by a much shorter account of the Elfin race, a story of uninterrupted success and fertility, in studied contrast to its dismal oscillations and setbacks. This history is a 'conscious and poetic idealization' which flatters Tudor rulers (Elficleos/Henry VII, Oberon/Henry VIII, Tanaquill/Gloriana/Elizabeth) and projects an image of political stability and continuity throughout time (O'Connell 1977; see also Rathborne 1937). Together, the chronicles present examples of two kinds, juxtaposing the admonitory history of Britain with the inspirational history of Fairyland.

When the British history continues as prophecy in *FQ* III iii, Spenser arranges his materials to indicate Elizabeth's descent from the union of Britomart and Artegall (49), thus asserting the Tudor connection to ancient British stock and specifically to the Arthurian line.

The three-part chronicle of British history in Books II and III reveals a further level of coherence and an extension of the historical allegory by its numerological arrangement, which uses Jean Bodin's parallel, described in his *Methodus ad facilem historiarum cognitionem* (1566), between important phases of history and the traditional 'climacterics' or crucial periods of human life in multiples of 7 (the bodily number) and 9 (the number associated with the soul), especially 49, 63, and 81. One example out of many is the placing of Arthur. The first part of the chronicle begins in II x 5 and ends in the second line of 68 with Uther Pendragon, for a total of 63 stanzas or 567 lines, figures which combine the middle climacterics of human life and human history, and appropriately the most perilous of the three since Arthur's mission remains uncompleted. Further, the number of rulers from Brute to Uther mentioned by name is 62, making Arthur 63, a number regarded as symbolic of the harmony between body and soul, as in the castle of Alma which is 'Proportioned equally by seven and nine' (II ix 22). Arthur's association with 63 emphasizes the harmony achieved by temperance and suggests that, at least for his reign and the golden age of his avatar Elizabeth, the fortunes of the British could approach those of the Elfin line, whose moral advancement is signaled by the numbers in their chronicle, a total of seven 9-line stanzas (II x 70–6) or 63 lines ending with the reign of Gloriana. (For a full account of the numerological arrangement in the three-part chronicle, see Mills 1976; see also Røstvig 1980 for another series of numerical patterns in the Book II chronicle that further affirms Spenser's view of the British history as providential and ultimately optimistic.)

By their elaborate patterning, Spenser's chronicles are far from dreary summaries of pseudo-history. To the chronicle materials with their inherent nationalistic and political implications, Spenser brought an array of moral, philosophical, aesthetic, and architectonic principles that makes these sections in large measure a statement of his concept of the poet's mission, especially as that mission involved investing meaning in structural form. From *The Shepheardes Calender* through *Amoretti*, *Epithalamion*, and *The Faerie Queene*, his works constantly dramatize the struggle of an imperfect individual or society to achieve the harmony and perfection embodied in the form of the work itself. His chronicles depict this struggle on the level of nations and their history on earth.

JERRY LEATH MILLS

Mills 1976; Mills 1978; Joan Warchol Rossi 1985 *'Britons moniments*: Spenser's Definition of Temperance in History' *ELR* 15:42–58.

---

chronographia 'time description' This term is taken from Puttenham's *Arte of English Poesie*, where it is applied to any sort of temporal reference: 'so if we describe the time or season of the yeare, as winter, summer, harvest, day, midnight, noone, evening, or such like: we call such description the counterfait time. *Cronographia* examples are every where to be found' (1589:200). For example, instead of saying explicitly that spring was just beginning, a Renaissance poet would normally choose to say that 'Sol was entering Aries'; the frequency of such periphrases implies that audiences were familiar with the sun's seasonal movement through the zodiac.

The 12-degree band of sky which lies 6 degrees north and 6 degrees south of the sun's apparent annual path through the heavens is divided laterally into 12 segments, the signs of the zodiac. When the astronomical year opens with spring in the northern hemisphere, the sun enters the band's first segment, which is called the sign of Aries. By midsummer, a quarter of a year later, the sun has moved 90 degrees and lies in the sign of Cancer. (The sequence is Aries, Taurus, Gemini, Cancer, and so on; each sign contains 30 degrees, the 12 of them making up the 360 degrees of a circle.)

It is this seasonal motion that the poets refer to with such confident shorthand. In *Epithalamion*, for instance, Spenser relies on presumably common knowledge when he says, 'This day the sunne is in his chiefest hight, / With Barnaby the bright' (265–6). 'In his chiefest hight' identifies the summer solstice (midsummer's day), because the sun's midday height above the southern horizon is at its maximum when it enters the sign Cancer at midsummer.

After invoking the church calendar (midsummer's day is the feast of St Barnabas), Spenser elaborates by describing the sun's future behavior: 'From whence declining daily by degrees, / He somewhat loseth of his heat and light, / When once the Crab behind his back he sees' (267–9). To understand this passage, we must recognize a number of factors: that the sun's 'chiefest [midday] hight' coincides with its entry into the sign of the Crab, Cancer; that by convention, the sun (like the moon and the planets) is imagined to face in the direction it is moving; and that the sun gradually decreases in declination (distance from the celestial equator) as it moves southwards after the summer solstice. Thus, even this fairly straightforward seasonal reference entails a wealth of implication and association.

Another type of astronomical shorthand is shown at *FQ* I ii 1: 'By this the Northerne wagoner had set / His sevenfold teme behind the stedfast starre, / That was in Ocean waves yet never wet, / But firme is fixt.' 'The Northerne wagoner' refers to Boötes, a neighbor of perhaps the best-known northern constellation, the Great Bear or Dipper. One of the Bear's common alternative names is 'Charles' Wain' (wagon), which, according to myth, is driven by the nearby Boötes (Spenser's 'wagoner'). The 'stedfast starre' is Polaris, the pole star, set close enough to the north celestial pole to mark its position. Since at the relatively high latitude where Spenser lived, neither the 'stedfast starre' nor Ursa Major ever sets, what does 'behind the stedfast starre' signify? At London's latitude (52 degrees), a disk of stars which never falls below the horizon is centered on Polaris and has a radius of 52 degrees. The disk contains the Great Bear and revolves around the Little Bear. In the course of this revolution, the Great Bear reaches one point which is its lowest below, and another which is its highest above, the Little Bear (relative to the northern horizon). To an observer facing due north, the Great Bear at its highest point will be directly *in front of* the Little one (ie, nearer the observer), and at its lowest point it will be directly *behind* it (ie, farther away).

Boötes both rises and sets every 24 hours; and even though the Great and Little Bears do not rise or set, they will be, of course, invisible if it is daylight. At what time of night, then, has Boötes just disappeared? Spenser tells us that 'chearefull Chaunticlere' has 'warned once, that *Phoebus* fiery carre / In hast was climbing up the Easterne hill' (*FQ* I ii 1). Here, at last, is a phrase whose sense we can grasp immediately: dawn is rapidly approaching. But what of the time of year? Inspection of a celestial globe shows that, to satisfy the poet's description, the sun must be lying near the border between the signs of Cancer and Leo, as it did on or about 11 July during the later sixteenth century.

Spenser uses the same system of double time reference in three other places in *The Faerie Queene*: at I iii 16, II ii 46, and III i 57. Besides the passing of night, a seasonal date is implicit in each description. In the first, Aldeboran (a first-magnitude star in Taurus) is 'mounted hie' when Una is waiting for dawn to appear; this combination places the sun near the middle of Virgo in late August. In the second, Orion the hunter is setting when night is 'far spent'; that is, the sun is close to Capricorn in midwinter. In the third, the Hyades (a minor constellation in Taurus) are setting when the stars are 'halfe yspent'; therefore, the sun must be in, or close to, Aries in spring.

Spenser uses astronomical images for several different purposes. The zodiacal procession of *FQ* VII vii 32, which is chronographic only because the twelve signs imply or embody the twelve months, derives from emblematic and iconographic tradition and is fully appropriate to the pageant described. In *Epithalamion*, on the other hand, specific allusions to the rising and setting of sun, moon, and Venus are subtly placed in the poem's time scheme and reflect the actual motions of these bodies on the day celebrated (see Eade 1972:173–8). The structure of *Prothalamion* may depend in part on a quasi-seasonal pairing of the signs of the zodiac (Fowler 1975, ch 4), but, beyond the possibility that the sun is in Virgo (an appropriate season for a betrothal), there seems to be no evidence of a cryptic seasonal date (see *constellations). J.C. EADE

Eade 1972; Fowler 1975.

Chrysogone The daughter of Amphisa, Chrysogone is mother of the twins Belphoebe and Amoret, whom she conceives by exposure to the sun's beams (*FQ* III vi 4–10, 26–8). She may recall Chrysogone, the virgin wife of Amphicles, whom Theocritus praises for her charity and motherly virtue (Epigram 13). Her name (Gr *chryseos* gold +*gonē* race) has been taken as meaning 'golden-born' (J.W. Draper 1932:100). Another sense, more pertinent to Spenser's emphasis on her beautiful children, is found in Cooper's definition (1565) of *chrysogonum* as 'that bryngeth foorth golde' or Cotgrave's (1611) of *chrysogone* as 'gold-producing.' The association with gold further reinforces an association with the myth of Danae, impregnated by Jove's golden shower (III xi 31). Also, gold was traditionally associated with the sun and therefore with Spenser's story of Chrysogone (cf Valeriano *Hieroglyphica* 21: 'Alchemists consider gold a solar metal').

The myth of Chrysogone is an allegory of generation in cosmic as well as human terms: her impregnation by Titan in a silvan setting symbolizes the process of generation in the elemental world (vi 8–9), and at the same time figures a childbirth spared Eve's penalty of bearing children in pain (27). The allegory is essentially based on the classical theory of origins, as explained by Lucretius and expanded by Ovid (*De rerum natura* 5.795–806, *Metamorphoses* 1.416–37, respectively). According to this theory, the origin of physical life was principally due to the generative effects of heat and moisture upon matter. The sun with its heat, and the moon with its moisture, were commonly regarded as the agents of such generation. In the mythological tradition, the cosmogonic agency of these heavenly bodies was attributed to their respective titular deities, Apollo and Diana, who were called by various names including Titan and Titania. That Spenser names the sun Titan in this context may reflect his use of Ovid here.

Chrysogone is herself the child of Amphisa, whose name (Gr 'double nature'), and absence of any specified consort, suggest an androgynous or self-creative nature. Like the Chaos in the Gardens of Adonis 'which supplyes / The substances of natures fruitfull progenyes' (vi 36), Amphisa provides matter in the form of Chrysogone, whose story serves as a thematic prelude to the Gardens, where the theme of generation is elaborated on a universal scale through the myth of Venus and Adonis.

HIMMET UMUNC

Berleth 1973; T. Cooper 1565; Randle Cotgrave 1611 *A Dictionarie of the French and English Tongues* (London; rpt Columbia, SC 1950); J.W. Draper 1932; Geller 1976; Goldberg 1975–6.

Church of England In Spenser's time, the Church of England was a national church by 'lawes established' (Hooker *Laws* 1.1.2) through acts of Parliament during the reigns of Henry VIII, Edward VI, and Elizabeth I. In Henry's reign, the Act in Restraint of Appeals (1533) and the Act of Supremacy (1534) rejected papal authority and asserted the authority of the King as 'Supreme Head' of the church in England, a title also conferred upon Henry's son Edward when he succeeded to the throne in 1547. This independent English church was further defined by publication of an authorized English Bible (1539) and, in Edward's reign, of authorized texts of a Book of Homilies (1547), a translation of Erasmus' *Paraphrases* of the Gospels and Acts (1548), versions of a Book of Common Prayer (1549, 1552), a set of Articles of Religion (1552), and a Primer (1553). After a brief period of return to papal allegiance in the reign of Mary (1553–8), the independence of the English church was reestablished by the Elizabethan Settlement of Religion (1559) through acts of Parliament affirming Elizabeth as 'Supreme Governor' and proclaiming a revised Book of Common Prayer (1559) as the basis for national religious uniformity. This Prayer Book was soon followed by revised versions of other authorized documents of the Edwardian church, including the Primer (1560), the Book of Homilies augmented by additional sermons (1563), the English Bible (1568), and the Articles of Religion (1563, 1571).

a national church In reasserting a 'national' identity, the English reformers understood themselves to be recovering an ancient concept of church organization. In the patristic age, the church was *ekklesia* (Gr) or *ecclesia* (L): a 'community or whole body of Christ's faithful people collectively' (*OED*). In the second and third centuries, each city had a bishop; ecumenical councils were councils of these bishops. From the fourth century, five patriarchates (Rome, Constantinople, Jerusalem, Alexandria, and Antioch) emerged with far more than local authority and helped establish the concept of regional jurisdiction within the church. In the medieval English church, the Archbishop of York, with jurisdiction over many northern dioceses, had the title 'Primate of England'; the Archbishop of Canterbury, with jurisdiction over southern dioceses and overriding authority for the whole kingdom, was 'Primate of All England.' The concept of national churches was not confined in medieval times to England: national primacies were also found in France, Scotland, Spain, Poland, Hungary, and the three Scandinavian kingdoms. Although acknowledging the supremacy of the Pope, these national churches exercised great power within their own areas, and claimed their privileges not just from historical precedent but also from the Bible, especially from the image of Israel as a people, nation, or kingdom of the elect. When the English church severed its allegiance to the papacy in the 1530s, there was, then, a long tradition of thought about the status of an 'elect nation' and a state church on which it could draw to understand its new situation.

Tudor images of the church as the nation gathered in prayer, or as the nation turned toward God in penance and praise, are very different from modern images of the church as a voluntary association of like-minded people. Yet the Tudor assertion of identity between church and nation in which religious authority operated within a framework created by act of Parliament, with the monarch as supreme authority for both church and nation, must form the context for our understanding of the course of Christian history in England in the sixteenth century. With the monarch and not the Pope as 'Supreme Head' or 'Supreme Governor' of the church, there came a sense of national, rather than either international or merely individual or local, constituency; the future of the church in England would now be tied to the destiny of an England understood to be an 'elect nation' in whose history God was at work. At the same time, the government and its citizenry would be called upon by the church to respond to the imperatives for social reform integral to the concept of church embodied by Archbishop Thomas Cranmer (1489–1556) and his followers in the official documents of the English church during Edward's reign. The abolition of the monastic system and of medieval images of priesthood and ministry would now mean that the task of Christian living was the responsibility of all and not just of a sacred elite, a transformation of the medieval church made possible by Cranmer's vernacular texts and rites.

Thus, as Elizabeth was Supreme Governor of the Church of England and Queen of all the people, the church she governed sought to bring the benefits of Christ's passion to the whole nation and not just to an elect few; her clergy said weekly that Christ's redemptive death was for 'the whole world' which was thus enabled to do 'all such good works as [God] hast prepared for us to walk in' (BCP communion rite). Toward this end, the Elizabethan Settlement of Religion sought through an imposed uniformity of rite and affirmation of belief to bring all English folk to a common Christian practice. As a result, all her subjects were required by law to be baptized in infancy and, as adults, to be confirmed and to receive Holy Communion at least three times a year (one of which had to be at Easter) in their parish churches, a major step forward from the medieval requirement of a single annual communion but still far short of Cranmer's goal of receptions every Sunday and holy day.

The Elizabethan church was named *Anglicana Ecclesia* in official Latin documents, from which the word *Anglican* emerged in the seventeenth century as a convenient adjective form of 'Church of England' (contemporaneous with emergence of the expression *Roman Catholic*). In whatever form, the title of the English church reflected a desire to be inclusive, both of all the English and of all that 'church' could mean for the English, that influenced the developing Church of England through the years of Elizabeth's reign. This was made easier because the English church, although it shared many reforming goals with continental Protestant groups, was not tied to the narrow biblicism or the new theological formulations of any of them. Having retained from the medieval church the basic structure of ordained ministry and church administration, derived its vernacular rites from the structures of medieval worship, and affirmed the importance of the ancient creeds, the English church had access to the full history of Christian discourse on matters of belief and doctrine. It could thus accept theological diversity within certain limits, so long as it could secure acceptance of its authority and reject attempts from within to modify the basic doctrinal and liturgical accords which had been adopted during the reign of Edward VI and reaffirmed as part of the Elizabethan Settlement of Religion.

These accords define the Church of England as a Christian body fundamentally corporate, liturgical, and sacramental, encompassing the whole body of baptized English folk who, through participation in word and sacrament and response in charitable action, participate in God's reconciling work and further his purposes for England. Thus church authorities valued participation in the regimen of corporate worship in parishes, chapels, and cathedrals more highly than they did uniformity of theological understanding or experience of election. Because of this, our formulations of the religious issues that divided some of the English from others during Elizabeth's reign need to be reached within a context that acknowledges the particular (and unique) character and progress of the Reformation in England.

In his first Prayer Book, Cranmer declared that although 'there hath been great diversity in saying and singing in churches within this realm ... henceforth all the whole realm shall have but one use' (*BCP* 1549 preface; rpt in *BCP* 1559). Such common use, he believed, would bring English worshipers into 'the blessed company of all faithful people' and make it possible for them to 'do all such good works as [God] hast prepared for us to walk in,' so as to continue in 'that holy fellowship' unto 'everlasting life' (*BCP* 1559 communion rite). Cranmer's church, intended to transform a people into a Christian commonwealth, was thus forged of many elements: an emerging sense of national identity and purpose, a faith in the renewing power of the Word of God through its scriptural and liturgical expressions, and a commitment to the Christian life as active love of one's neighbor rather than passive and contemplative devotion among those bound to a monastic rule, all articulated through a series of liturgical observances which used the power of the state to transform national religious life.

the evolving church (1534-1603) The English church that Spenser knew was in the third phase of its reformation. The first, from the Act of Supremacy in 1534 to the death of Henry VIII in 1547, and the second, from the accession of Edward VI to his death in 1553, were under the direction of Archbishop Cranmer. The third, from the accession of Elizabeth in 1558, was led by Archbishops Matthew Parker (1504–75), Edmund Grindal (1519?-1583), and John Whitgift (1530?-1604). In each phase, the rate of change and the areas in which it occurred were both enabled and frustrated by the behavior of the monarch. Specific reforms could take place rapidly when they met the needs of the crown; but when they did not, the 'Supreme Head' or 'Supreme Governor' of the church could be an obstacle to change. This interaction between the reformers' goals and political opportunity created by the monarch's desires persisted throughout the sixteenth century; the resulting erratic pace of reform suggests both the possibilities and the frustrations of reforming the church using the power of political authority.

Henry VIII's desire to divorce Catherine of Aragon provoked England's first step into reformation, for Cranmer and other church leaders used the opportunity to authorize an English translation of the Bible and to begin experimenting with the use of English in worship. When the English reformers' wish to correct abuses in the monastic system and to change the model of Christian living from one emphasizing contemplative devotion to one encouraging active love of one's neighbor coincided with Henry's need for monastic wealth, the result was a gradual abolition of the whole monastic system.

During the reign of Edward VI, Cranmer was able to move rapidly toward a complete transformation of the Church of England into a vernacular church. Under the influence of Erasmus, Cranmer concluded that the sacramentally enabled life of Christian charity was more important than narrow theological unanimity. As a result, he published a series of books which transformed English worship and taught the value of doing good works but chose not to publish a detailed, systematic exposition of the reformed faith. Most basic was the Book of Common Prayer (1549, 1552), which gave clergy and laity a single book in the vernacular rather than the many liturgical books in Latin required to celebrate the medieval Mass. The Book of Common Prayer gave a context for Cranmer's other books: an official Bible in English (1539) to be read during its services, an English edition of Erasmus' *Paraphrases* of the Gospels and Acts (1548) to provide a standard interpretation of the New Testament, a Book of Homilies (1547) to be preached at Holy Communion, and a Primer (1552) to shape private and family devotion in accord with the Prayer Book model. Thus, from the reign of Edward VI, the theological emphasis of the English church was on public worship as the context for reading and interpreting the Bible, for participating in (rather than reoffering, as in the medieval Mass) Christ's sacrifice, for conveying grace to enable the life of charity, and for transforming individuals into the 'blessed company of all faithful people.'

Cranmer also prepared a set of 42 Articles of Religion (1552) defining basic matters of polity and doctrine for the Church of England which were revised and consolidated into 39 Articles during the reign of Elizabeth (1563, 1571). These Articles assert that the church in England is the visible company that reads the Bible, worships according to the Book of Common Prayer, retains the three-fold ministry of bishops, priests, and deacons, and respects the authority of the ancient creeds. They affirm the use of English in worship, reject medieval ceremonial practices, and assert the importance of the divine initiative and faithful human response for achieving salvation. References to other official documents contained within the Articles ('justification,' we are told, is to be understood in relationship to the Homily of Justification) make clear that Cranmer thought of the positions articulated in the Articles as having their meaning in relationship to his entire reform program with the Book of Common Prayer at its center. Thus what was central to the intentions of the English reformers was maintenance of the ongoing life of the English church as a worshiping community in the context of which the Bible was read and expounded, prayer was offered, the sacraments were participated in, and the people were empowered 'to live a new life ... in love and charity with [their] neighbors' (BCP communion rite).

This has been called a defiance on the part of the English church of efforts 'to categorize it confessionally' (Pelikan 1984:184), for none of these positions accords with definitions of the terms *protestant*, *reformed*, or *catholic* as they were articulated among Lutherans, Zwinglians, Calvinists, or those loyal to the papacy. But the experience of those traditions as they emerged from the theological and liturgical diversity of the late medieval church was that the cost of more restrictive definition in one area of belief or practice was the abandoning of diversity in another. Thus the fullness of Calvinist definitions of predestination, for example, led to an impoverishment of liturgical life in the reformed tradition which Calvin, who with Cranmer favored weekly communions, would not have supported. Cranmer and his followers refused to abandon the breadth of these positions as defined by the Articles; they preferred to hold all aspects of their understanding of the church together and to retain access to the richness of Christian tradition even at the expense of definitional clarity and residual potential for conflict.

The Reformation in England was interrupted by Mary's submission of the church to the papacy (1553); it began its third phase in 1558 with the accession of Elizabeth, with a new Act of Supremacy (1559) declaring her 'Supreme Governor' of the church, and with an Act of Uniformity (1559) reauthorizing use of the Prayer Book and its attendant documents. In this phase, under the leadership of Parker (Archbishop from 1559–75), Grindal (1576–83), and Whitgift (1583–1604), the English church renewed Cranmer's liturgical reforms and sought to complete his agenda for social change. The Elizabethan Book of Common Prayer (1559), augmented by a revised lectionary or directory of regular readings from the Bible (1561), continued Cranmer's basic design for public worship. The Book of Homilies was reprinted (1563) with a second Book attached so that all clergy could preach at Holy Communion, as the Prayer Book specified. Cranmer's Articles were revised slightly and reissued in 1563 and 1571 as the Thirty-Nine Articles of Religion. The Primer was also reissued (1559), and Foxe's *Actes and Monuments* (1563; better known as the Book of Martyrs because it celebrates the perseverance of Cranmer and others who were executed during Mary's reign in witness to their faith in the reformed church) and Jewel's *Apologia ecclesiae anglicanae* (1562; tr as *An Apologie or Aunswer in Defence of the Church of England* 1562, 1564) joined the English Bible and Erasmus' *Paraphrases* as required texts in parish churches and cathedrals. The local parish church, the chapel of the noble house or college, and the urban cathedral thus became repositories of texts which brought the biblical narratives and a developing sense of a distinctively English religious identity (articulated in Foxe and Jewel) into conjunction with the daily lives of English folk through their participation in the Prayer Book liturgies.

worship in daily life Since Spenser was born during the reign of Edward VI, he would have been baptized according to the 1549 or 1552 Prayer Book. After spending his infancy and early childhood during Mary's reign, he was probably seven when the Elizabethan Settlement restored the reformed faith and the 1559 Prayer Book became the official liturgical text. Thus his experiences of Christianity during late childhood, years of schooling, and entry into adulthood were formed by worship according to that Prayer Book and the biblical readings it appointed for daily Morning and Evening Prayer and communion on Sundays and holy days. When he was at Cambridge, a Latin translation of the Prayer Book was used in worship in the college chapels. Although like other reformed churches the English church reduced the number of official sacraments to two (baptism and Holy Communion), Cranmer retained in the Prayer Book what Spenser calls 'sacred ceremonies' (*Epithalamion* 216) for confirmation, marriage, ordinations, penance, and ministry to the sick. Thus Spenser was probably confirmed, married, and buried according to its rites, since during the reign of Elizabeth the Prayer Book was used to recognize publicly such personal and private events.

Unlike continental reformers who emphasized Sunday worship, Cranmer retained for the English church the ancient calendar of church seasons and annual feasts and fasts, although he drastically reduced the number of saints' days. Time was marked by the seasons of the church year, beginning with Advent, moving through Christmas and Epiphany to Lent ('This holy season fit to fast and pray' *Amoretti* 22), Easter, and Whitsunday (or Pentecost), and concluding with the long Trinity season, counting Sundays after Trinity Sunday. English society organized itself around the annual liturgical calendar, using its rhythm of feasts, fasts, and saints' days to mark the beginnings of court sessions and university terms as well as to signal turning points in the agricultural year. Although the liturgical year began with Advent, the calendar year began with 25 March (the Feast of the Annunciation), and the Book of Common Prayer specifies 1 January as New Year's Day (cf E.K.'s defense of Spenser's beginning the year with January, in *SC* General Argument).

This social function of church practice is reflected in Spenser's work in a variety of other ways. National custom joined with church observance to make the twelve days of the Christmas season into a major annual festival, which Elizabeth observed at court with lavish feasting and entertainments. Her courtiers responded by presenting her with expensive gifts. Since *FQ* 1590 was licensed to William Ponsonby on 1 December 1589 and dedicated to Elizabeth, Spenser may have intended it as his present to her for the 1589–90 Christmas season. The twelve-day feast of the Fairy Queen at which Spenser claims the knights are given their quests (Letter to Raleigh) may refer to Elizabeth's observance of Christmastide.

Elizabethan clergy were required to conduct public readings of Morning and Evening Prayer daily, and to ring the church bells so their parishioners could gather to take part or recite their prayers privately at the same time. The primer provided modified prayer book rites for use in daily prayer outside the church, thus furthering the orientation of private prayer toward the public and corporate worship that defined the English church. The English shared with continental reformers a desire to make the Bible central to Christian life, but created a liturgical context for its reading: in observing the Daily Offices, clergy and layfolk recited the Psalter monthly in a translation taken from the Great Bible (1539) and read the New Testament three times yearly and the Old Testament annually. Additional readings from the Bible were assigned as Epistles and Gospels at Holy Communion on Sundays and other feast days, which included eighteen saints' days as well as other holy days such as All Saints', Ascension, the Purification of and the Annunciation to the Virgin Mary, and Ash Wednesday. Unlike the continental reformed churches, the Church of England retained the Apocrypha, those books of the Vulgate Old Testament not included in the Hebrew canon, although it restricted their authority to providing 'example of life and instruction of manners' rather than, with Rome, using them to establish doctrine (Article 6), as Spenser reflects in his allusions (Shaheen 1976:207–8). In cathedrals, the order of service on Sundays and holy days began with the reading or singing of Morning Prayer, continued through the recitation of the Great Litany and Holy Communion with sermon, and concluded with Evening Prayer, often with instruction in the catechism. In parish churches, the same order of services was followed except that at least three parishioners ready to receive communion with the priest were required for the full communion rite to be performed; otherwise, it ended after the Creed and sermon. This requirement put an end to the medieval practice of private Mass, for it took Jesus' promise to his disciples to be present when two or three are gathered together in his name (Matt 18.20) as a mandate that Holy Communion not be celebrated unless an appropriate number were present to receive.

Cranmer's intent was to make public worship the center of community life, with prayer and Bible reading in the language of the people. He also sought to have sermons every Sunday and holy day, whether or not the local priest was educated enough to write his own sermons. Yet, as Spenser suggests in *Mother Hubberds Tale*, Cranmer's vernacular rites and printed sermons could make the life of clergy seem undemanding. Not all English clerics lived up to the Erasmian model Cranmer aspired to, in which priests knew all the biblical languages. In Spenser's poem, the Ape and the Fox seek the life of a priest who needs to know neither Latin nor Greek, but who gets by quite well so long as he takes care 'his service well to saine, / And to read Homelies upon holidayes' (392–3), using the excuse that ignorance enables him to avoid 'Doubts mongst Divines, and difference of texts' (387) and to spend more time at 'playes' (394).

ecclesiastical structure The Elizabethan church retained the ancient structure of a threefold ordained ministry consisting of bishops, priests, and deacons. England, including Wales, was divided into 27 dioceses, each headed by a bishop, and into two provinces of York and Canterbury, each headed by an Archbishop who was also the bishop of that diocese. As Supreme Governor of the English church, Elizabeth appointed bishops and archbishops; parish rectorships and other jobs open to priests were often controlled by the nobility or by wealthy landowners who had authority to choose on whom to bestow the 'living' of the parish (a fixed sum of money attached to an ecclesiastical benefice; sought by the Fox, *MHT* 480–520) or the office of a chaplain. This practice sometimes led to 'pluralism' (the holding of more than one living), absenteeism, and hiring out of actual parochial work to others, since appointments were often made as rewards to favorites with no regard for their interest in or aptitude for the job. Salaries were low, so clergy from aristocratic backgrounds often accepted multiple livings and then employed as assistants or curates poor clergy who were willing to work for a portion of parish income.

Such practices often led to the actual work of pastoral care being carried out by poorly trained clergy while able priests pursued careers through currying favor with the nobility. In theory, the bishops did not approve of pluralism; efforts to correct the practice are part of the program of reform for the English church from the time of Cranmer. Spenser, in *Mother Hubberds Tale*, introduces us to a priest who advises the Fox and the Ape to apply to 'some Noble man' (489) who can help them become 'jolly Prelates' who 'arise / Daylie ... To Deanes, to Archdeacons, to Commissaries, / To Lords, to Principalls, to Prebendaries,' rather than aspiring to remain 'some honest Curate, or some Vicker' (419–23, 429). Diggon makes a similar attack on 'covetise' shepherds who 'strayen abroad' in search of wealth and thus cannot hear the call of their sheep when they are in distress (*SC, Sept* 82, 93). In practice, however, the bishops tolerated pluralism since they depended on the patronage system to support the clergy. As products of the same system, the bishops had learned to work with the nobility and the Queen, accepting as a condition of the office the periodic intervention of powerful layfolk in the conduct of church business and their use of church appointments to reward their own favorites. Advancement in the church thus depended on success in attracting the favor of the wealthy and powerful, a system which could result in the church's appearing at times to be an Erastian defender of the existing political or social order staffed by self-serving professionals more influenced by those who controlled their livings than by their superiors in the church hierarchy or their ordination vows.

Pluralism, because it deprived many English folk of the quality of pastoral care they expected, caused tension between the church and its laity throughout Elizabeth's reign. Yet it proved a difficult problem to solve. More open to solution if not less controversial was the medieval legacy of ill-educated and poorly trained clergy, the time-serving 'Mass-priests' of Reformation polemic. Spenser, who served as secretary to Bishop Young of Rochester in 1578, knew that the reformers sought to correct this problem by instituting high standards of education, training, and conduct for English clerics. During the sixteenth century, attrition of priests ordained before the Reformation and higher standards for new ordinands gradually improved this situation, so that by the seventeenth century charges of clerical incompetence were much less frequent.

During the reign of Elizabeth, however, education for clergy and the system of appointments became issues in the conflict between the Puritan party and the church hierarchy, the Puritans in effect accusing the bishops of preferring ignorant but obedient clergy. When the church held training sessions for older clergy envisioned by Cranmer and supported by then-Archbishop Grindal, the Puritans sought to use them as occasions to win converts to their cause. This provoked Elizabeth to demand in 1577 that these meetings be abolished. Grindal opposed her and was suspended from his episcopal duties, a conflict illustrative of the tensions between needs for order and demands for change that influenced the course of development taken by the English church in the sixteenth century.

controversies As the matter of educating clergy indicates, hardly any issue distinguishing the medieval church from its reformed successors proceeded without controversy as much political and social as theological or doctrinal. The several religious traditions that emerged from the medieval church during the Reformation period were shaped by their origins in controversies over belief and practice that persisted for generations. No tradition appeared fully developed; each was shaped by the nature of its opposition and by the demands of polemical interchange. Thus, Cranmer's English Prayer Book of 1549 was soon followed by a revision in 1552 because the Archbishop found the original version susceptible to interpretation according to medieval eucharistic theology; revisions in 1559 moved the eucharistic theology of the Prayer Book toward a position more inclusive than the 1552 version. In another tradition, the understanding of predestination, now seen as fundamental to Calvin's thought actually developed over nearly three decades, did not achieve its distinctive articulation until the edition of his *Institutes* published in 1559.

Thus the development of reformed traditions proceeded in the midst of contention and the taking of sides. This has influenced the way we have understood the Church of England, a tradition that resisted detailed exposition of its theological positions because it was chiefly concerned with reform of worship and national life and sought a broad consensus on matters of doctrine. Yet it continued to be challenged to define itself in relationship to controversies articulated in much narrower terms than those it chose to use, terms set by continental traditions more concerned with systematic theological exposition. When we try for the sake of neat definition to force the richness of the English position into the formularies of continental traditions, we falsify something basic about it, however tempting the desire to explain its beliefs in terms of those used by other religious movements.

To cite but one example, belief or lack of belief in the doctrine of God's predestination of the elect is often used to associate the English church with the Calvinist tradition and to distinguish it from the position taken by those loyal to the papacy. Yet identifying in the formularies of the English church or in the writings of its adherents either the desire for reform or the affirmation that God in some sense predestines the selection of those who are to be saved is not sufficient to permit such labeling. All European religious traditions, including the Church of Rome, were in the process of reforming abuses in the sixteenth century in ways that would set them apart from the medieval church, and all churches, again including the Roman, accepted some doctrine of predestination. It was part of the common inheritance of western Christendom from the New Testament and from St Augustine. What distinguishes Calvin's final position from others is the extent to which he embraces predestination as central to his understanding of God and of God's redemptive activity, including the affirmation that both the saved and the damned are predestined by God from before all time, so that all other aspects of Christian belief are shaped by this affirmation.

Concerned that the medieval church had made salvation possible on the basis of human merit, all the reformed traditions sought to reassert the importance of God's initiative and to base one's hope for salvation in God's power to save rather than in human effort. In the structure of this presentation, the eternal character of God's behavior came to be emphasized, so that one could rest one's hope in the everlastingness of divine aid in working out one's eternal destiny. In this context, therefore, one might speak meaningfully of salvation as being predestined, such a claim coming at the end of an affirmation of the ground of human hope in the divine initiative. By 1559, however, Calvin had gone far beyond such a position to make the eternal nature of God's actions central to his affirmation of the nature of God and thus to make God's pre-selection of the elect and the damned the starting point of his understanding of salvation rather than its end point. Predestination thus became the ground of hope for the possibility of salvation rather than a final reason to affirm hopefully the consequences of a life lived in thanksgiving for God's saving actions and empowered by his grace. From such a position various corollaries would flow – including a concern for finding inner assurance of election and for distinguishing the company of the elect from within the larger body of humanity – that would take the Calvinist traditions far from the emphasis on corporate worship and the promotion of charity towards one's neighbor characteristic of the Cranmerian tradition embodied in the English church.

This position thus represents a theological development which can be said to have been prepared for by Christian tradition while still representing a move beyond what had been generally accepted as the mainstream of Christian thought on the subject of the eternal nature of divine power. But the position of the English church was more cautious; from the Edwardian Articles of Religion (1552) through the reign of Elizabeth it was willing to affirm belief in predestination to life as a 'comfort to godly persons' at least as far as it 'be generally set forth in Holy Scripture,' but cautioned against affirming the Calvinist corollary of predestination to damnation as 'a most dangerous downfall' (Articles of Religion, Article 17). This official English affirmation of predestination, which would have seemed cautious to St Augustine, is clearly a pastoral statement concerned to guide clergy in interpreting a controversial term for their congregations, not an assertion of agreement with Calvin's formularies still in the process of development. Far more important to the English reformers was the creation of a worshiping community incorporating the whole nation at one altar by one liturgical 'use,' in reference to which all theological statements about individuals must be interpreted. Thus the Church of England, against much opposition, refused to remove from the Prayer Book its claim that baptized children 'have all things necessary for their salvation, and be undoubtedly saved' (BCP confirmation rite). In the English church, a degree of theological diversity could be tolerated on a matter like predestination; abandonment of the Prayer Book could not.

Whatever the specific point of polity or doctrine at issue, we also need to remember that in England such controversies were pursued in the context of a larger struggle for control of the right to use the word *church*. Because of the inclusivist aims of the English hierarchy and of the papacy, the rhetorical strategies of all participants in religious controversy attempted not to define their positions as formal codifications of belief to be compared to the formularies of other differing but inherently distinct adversaries, but instead sought to establish only one position as tenable and to deny the claim to legitimacy of any other. Thus to affirm allegiance to the papacy in Elizabeth's reign was to risk a charge of treason in part because of the ongoing conflict between papist Spain and Protestant England but also because of the rhetorical organization of a claim that national identity had both political and religious dimensions. Conversely, the papacy could not accept the English church's claim to independent religious authority. This structuring of the language of religious controversy added to the energy with which it was pursued; it can lead us to miss the fact that all parties to these controversies shared many points of doctrine and that their differences are often exaggerated by their refusal to admit the legitimacy or even the possibility of another's position. When in the seventeenth century terms like 'Anglican' and 'Roman Catholic' became available to make distinctions conveniently, a new conceptual structuring of religious identity had occurred.

controversies with Rome Edward's reign and the early years of Elizabeth's were dominated by controversies over the claims of the Church of Rome and the legal status of its English adherents. Jewel's *Apologie* was the most notable English response, while Foxe's descriptions of the martyrdoms of Cranmer and his followers (in his Book of Martyrs) helped develop the English church's identity in opposition to papal claims. Later, this conflict became institutionalized and ritualized, with the persecution of English folk loyal to the papacy rising and falling in harmony with the perceived threat of Spanish intervention in English life. Spenser's use of conventional polemical identification of Rome with the Antichrist and the Whore of Babylon in his depictions of Archimago, Duessa, and the house of Pride in *FQ* I reflects this development.

controversies with Puritans The later years of Elizabeth's reign were concerned primarily with periodic controversies arising from within the Church of England. Tracing the development of this opposition requires care because it involves the appearance of a movement which by the 1570s had become known as Puritanism. From the earliest days of the English Reformation there was disagreement about the form and direction religious change would take, a concern that surfaced in opposition to the 1549 Book of Common Prayer, which to some seemed susceptible to the same theological interpretation as the medieval Mass. Cranmer responded with the revision of 1552, the Prayer Book used in exile by those fleeing Mary's persecutions. Yet further dissent took specific programmatic direction during Mary's reign among a group of English exiles who took refuge in Calvin's Geneva and saw his version of a reformed church at first hand during the years when he was evolving the full implications of his theology of predestination. As a result, they decided that even the 1552 Book of Common Prayer was insufficiently 'pure' in its revision of medieval worship and that its promise of salvation was inadequately strong. When they returned to England upon the accession of Elizabeth, they brought a revision of the Authorized or 'Great' Bible of 1539, with a Preface by Calvin and extensive annotations expounding his interpretation of Scripture (pub in 1560, it became known as the Geneva Bible).

The Geneva exiles objected to the Elizabethan Settlement of Religion. They decided to work for the abandonment of Cranmer's reform program and the substitution of a church polity and a set of doctrinal emphases closer to the model developed by Calvin for Geneva and later adapted by John Knox for Scotland. Because they claimed they wanted to 'purify' the English church of such remaining (and, they believed, lamentable) medieval practices as ordination of bishops, priests, and deacons, wearing of vestments, use of set prayers, making the sign of the Cross at baptism, kneeling to receive communion, and giving a ring at weddings, they became knows as Puritans.

Thus, originally, the Puritan movement was concerned to establish its understanding of purity in doctrine and worship. Obviously not everyone in the English church who desired religious reform was a Puritan, only those who accepted the claim that Cranmer's reform program based on the Book of Common Prayer was an inadequate way to achieve reform and needed to be abolished. According to sixteenth-century usage, the concept of a 'moderate episcopal Puritan' (Lake 1982) is a contradiction in terms. Puritans by definition were those who attacked the office of bishop and the worship of the English church, not because they agreed with the English hierarchy theologically but disagreed with it liturgically, as some historians have claimed, but because they understood the centrality of both the episcopal office and Prayer Book worship to the theology of the English church and were opposed to that theology. Those who sought to reform English society through the means Cranmer devised were supporters of the English church, not to be numbered among its Puritan detractors.

Disagreement between the Puritan group and the established church first surfaced in the vestiarian controversy, named for protests against the use of vestments such as the cope in cathedrals and the surplice or chasuble in parish churches and college chapels. The protesters were answered by Archbishop Parker's demand that the royal supremacy be affirmed, the Articles of Religion supported, and the discipline of the Prayer Book observed (*Advertisements* 1566).

A second debate with the Puritans was instigated by the *Admonition to the Parliament* (1572), in which the Puritans sought exemption from using the Prayer Book and other practices found objectionable. This conflict widened to include larger questions of the nature of church government and the correct definition of church membership. Two of the central controversialists, Bishop Whitgift and his Puritan opponent Thomas Cartwright, exchanged a series of attacks and counterattacks in which Whitgift reaffirmed the inclusiveness of the Church of England, its government, and the Prayer Book.

Whitgift became Archbishop of Canterbury in 1583 and renewed Parker's desire to impose a minimum of conformity to the Church of England's program of reform through use of the Prayer Book. This provoked a third, more prolonged conflict, lasting into the 1590s, that produced both the delightfully scurrilous antiepiscopal tracts of Martin Marprelate and the elegantly judicious response of Richard Hooker in his *Of the Laws of Ecclesiastical Polity* (1593). In the *Laws*, Hooker defends and justifies the structure of English church government and use of the Book of Common Prayer. Seeking a common ground with Puritan opposition, he affirms an essential relationship between God's love of his people revealed in the gift of the natural order and of human reason and his love revealed in the special gift of grace mediated through the church and its sacraments. This appeal to a triple source of authority – revelation, reason, and custom – contributed to a developing Elizabethan sense of the English church as a *via media* or middle way between the Church of Rome, with its grounding of authority in tradition and the papal office, and Calvinist churches, with their locating of authority in revelation, especially biblical example. The concept of an Anglican *via media* eventually became a major element in the English church's understanding of itself, but it needs to be viewed as an historical category of thought and a term used in apologetic discourse rather than as a description of what the English church set out to be or actually became.

Thus one aspect of Puritanism to which Hooker responded was its attack on the rites of the Prayer Book and the manner in which they were conducted; another was the Puritan attack on the English church's structure of ministry and the relationship between church and state. The rites of the church seemed papist to the Puritans; they rejected, for instance, the use of traditional clerical vestments such as the cassock and surplice worn during the daily offices of Morning and Evening Prayer or the alb and chasuble or cope worn during celebration of the sacraments. They opposed the making of the sign of the Cross on the forehead at baptisms and confirmations and the giving of a ring at weddings. They also preferred worship emphasizing plain, hortatory sermons and spontaneous prayers to the use of set prayers, biblical lectionaries, liturgical preaching, and weekly celebrations of Holy Communion called for by the Book of Common Prayer. They objected to the observation of saints' days, holy days, and seasonal observances of feasts and fasts, preferring instead to treat each Sunday as a day of strict observance, prayer, and sermon-going. They especially objected to the annual twelve-day observance of Christmastide, abolishing it as soon as they came to power in the seventeenth century.

While the English church took its models for church government from the patristic age, and thus ordained bishops, priests, and deacons, the Puritans sought a church organization based on their interpretation of New Testament examples, in which each congregation would have a minister aided by elders and deacons elected from that congregation. This 'presbyterian' form of organization (named after Gk *presbyter*, the New Testament word translated by the English church as 'priest' and the Puritans as 'elder') was approved by Calvin and adopted in Scotland at the behest of his disciple John Knox. Sixteenth-century Puritans wanted to continue a national church, in which ministers were to assume a strong disciplinary role in regulating the personal conduct of its members, a prospect Elizabeth did not welcome. The development of congregational models of church organization, in which each congregation functions independently of others with little sense of identity beyond local boundaries, was to be a major development of the seventeenth century.

During Elizabeth's reign, Puritans developed the implications of their beliefs in directions that increasingly distinguished them from the official positions of the English church. Those who sought a 'purified' church extended their demands to include more fundamental matters of church belief and self-understanding. Calvin's distinctive notion of double predestination was especially important in this shift, as the Puritan emphasis on self-discipline and personal rectitude informed attempts to distinguish the elect, now understood to be the only people to whom the benefits of God's redemptive work applied. Cartwright, for example, demanded that the church baptize only the children of those who were recognized to be among the elect. Ultimately this concern led to the creation in some parishes of elite inner circles of the elect distinguished from the majority of parishioners (as in John Cotton's St Botolph's Church in Boston, England early in the 17th c). This development was intolerable to those who supported Cranmer's vision of a national church which nurtured and celebrated God's choice of England as an elect nation. Also, while Calvin recognized the importance of the sacraments, he saw them as signs of grace conveyed independently of their performance. He also believed that preaching was itself a vehicle of grace. Cranmer's followers, on the other hand, recognized the importance of proclaiming the Word of God through disciplined reading of the Bible and preaching in the context of performing the communion rite; Word and sacrament went together in one action, the hearing of the Word preparing the congregation for reception of the sacrament, which formed the proper setting for the delivery of sermons. Grace was conveyed by the sacraments, although God of course could use other vehicles if he chose. These differences led to Puritan demands for a more active preaching clergy and abandonment of the sacramental system through which the English church believed grace ('all ... benefits of his passion' BCP communion rite) was made available to all and received by the faithful.

The theologically sophisticated Puritans in Spenser's day may appropriately be called Calvinists because they found in his writing a theological justification for their characteristic desire to distinguish between the people of England and the true church of Christ, which could only be the invisible company of the elect. They also found in Calvin's Geneva and Knox's Scotland a piety and worship more congenial to their temperament. That is, they yielded authority for the interpretation of doctrine to the formulations of Calvin, developed the implications of his distinctive theological positions, and understood their necessary consequences for the life of a Christian body. While many held Puritan opinions for other reasons, those who justified them theologically did so with reference to Calvin. Some have tried to find a wider Calvinist influence in the English church, but its basic goals, structures, and texts were already in place by 1552 when Calvin was no more than one among many continental reformers. Later theologians like Jewel and Hooker either ignored him or rejected his doctrines outright. Hooker especially was concerned to show that Calvin incorrectly repudiated natural law and human reason.

theology of the Elizabethan church The concerns and vocabulary of Elizabethan theology are hardly intelligible without reference to continental theology, but they are not simply restatements of Luther, Zwingli, or Calvin. Cranmer echoed the Lutheran Augsburg Confession of Faith (1530) in Article 19 of his Articles of Religion (1552) by defining the church as 'a congregation of faithful men, in which the pure Word of God is preached, and the Sacraments be duly ministered according to Christ's ordinance.' Pope Pius IV would have agreed, and would have joined Calvin in concurring that justification is by faith and not merit, that Christ is really present in the Eucharist, and that God predestines selection of the elect; yet the leaders of various traditions could not often recognize the extent of their agreement. Their differences arose among the ways in which such basic points of doctrine were interpreted and the implications about Christian behavior and church practice those interpretations seemed to require. As a result, they were often unable to admit that they had anything in common.

What made the English church distinctive is the extent to which it based its self-understanding on the performance of its corporate life in Prayer Book worship rather than in adherence to a specific interpretation of doctrine. Cranmer and his followers agreed with the continental reformers on rejection of papal authority, on the importance of the vernacular Bible and vernacular worship, and on the importance of affirming God's free and unmerited gift of grace. But they did not follow Luther in effectively uniting justification and salvation, nor did they anticipate Calvin's emphasis on the predestination of both the elect and the damned. Instead, for Cranmer, life begins in sin and is justified by grace conveyed to the faithful by the sacraments of baptism and Holy Communion 'by the which [God] doth work invisibly in us' (Article 25), making possible good works of charity by which 'a lively Faith may be as evidently known as a tree discerned by its fruits' (Article 12), leading at the end to salvation. Repeatedly the Elizabethan church was challenged to develop this doctrinal statement in a Calvinist direction, but it always refused, in spite of the fact that many clergy found some aspects of Calvin's thought helpful in expressing their faith. The English church always emphasized the importance of the doctrine of Incarnation, God in Christ at work in the world, and the life of active charity in imitation of Christ, which is antithetical to the mature Calvin's concern with predestination to election as essential to understanding the nature of God and thus to interpreting all of Christian proclamation. In keeping with Calvin's emphasis, developed even more rigorously by his followers, Calvinists rapidly lost any sense of a need to balance preaching and sacrament. In addition, they interpreted good works as having to do primarily with demonstrating election, promoting personal rectitude, and engaging in spiritual warfare, while the emphasis of the English church, beginning with publication of the 1547 Book of Homilies, was on good works as social charity done to build the Christian commonwealth.

Implicit in Cranmer's eucharistic theology is this emphasis on the life of love and charity performed in thanksgiving for God's gift of grace first bestowed in baptism and continued through the Eucharist. Such a life Cranmer believed would lead to the transformation of England into the Christian commonwealth and become as well the path to citizenship in the New Jerusalem. Individual Christian lives took their meaning from participation in the life of the community, and found their hope for salvation in God's promises to that community. Through participation in the Eucharist, that community found itself to be the body of Christ in the world, enabled by reception of 'all ... benefits of his passion' to carry out his redemptive work.

This active and transformational understanding of the work of grace through reception of the communion bread and wine informs Cranmer's theology of real presence in the Eucharist. In preparation for the priesthood, Cranmer had learned the eucharistic theology of the medieval church, which understood the Mass as a reoffering of Christ's sacrifice on the Cross, performed by the priest for the people. As a result of the priest's recitation of the narrative of the Last Supper, the substance of the bread and wine became the body and blood of Christ. Luther adapted this interpretation of the Real Presence to claim that although the substance of bread and wine remained along with the accidents of appearance, the substance of the body and blood of Christ joined the substance of bread and wine. Both of these are spatial metaphors for presence; Christ is present to the congregation in the Eucharist as one body to another. Cranmer adopted instead a temporal metaphor in which Christ is present in his *actions* in relation to the congregation, so that he is in them and they are one in him. Through participation in the Eucharist, members of the congregation receive 'remission of sins and all other benefits of his passion' (BCP communion rite) and are made 'very members incorporate in [Christ's] mystical body.'

In his eucharistic theology, Cranmer was influenced by Zwingli, although his position is far from one in which the Eucharist is merely an effective reminder of the past act of Christ's sacrifice. His theology differed from Calvin in insisting that the Eucharist is a vehicle for grace rather than a mere sign of grace independently received. Balancing proclamation of the Word (through public reading of the Bible and preaching) with sacramental enactment of the Word, the Prayer Book affirms the two as working together to convey God's grace to humanity, enabling the life of active charity that is both the sign of a 'true and lively faith' and the way to salvation.

Cranmer also rejected medieval models of the Christian life based on monastic ideals which functioned to make the Mass the private devotion of the priest and contemplative piety (practiced by using devotional techniques such as the rosary) the 'work' of the laity. In their place, he made the Mass a community meal which could not be celebrated unless both clergy and laity received the bread and wine. He asserted Christ's summary of the law as the definition of desirable Christian behavior for all: love God and love your neighbor as your self. Participation in the sacraments enables participation in Christ, so that the recipients become 'very members incorporate in thy mystical body ... we in him and he in us,' and thus receive 'remission of our sins and all other benefits of his passion' (BCP communion rite). So enabled, the congregation would go out to 'do all such good works as thou hast prepared for us to walk in.'

Cranmer's communal emphasis is especially clear in his transforming the private rite of penance of the medieval church into a public confession during the Eucharist itself, making it corporate, substituting reception of the consecrated bread and wine for acts of penance, and having the whole movement lead to and enable the life of active charity. For similar reasons, he moved the reception of the bread and wine to a place within the prayer of consecration and shifted the location of the Gloria to the end of the rite so that it now served as a song of praise to God in thanksgiving for what had been accomplished by participation in the sacrament.

aspects of religion in Spenser's poetry When the Red Cross Knight, at the urging of 'that godly aged Sire' (*FQ* I x 48), turns from the vision of the New Jerusalem and resumes his quest for it through service to Una in the world, he replicates the English church's turn away from medieval piety toward the life of active charity. He also enacts a refusal to drain that worldly activity of significance by putting it inside a doctrine of predestination that would render the choice meaningless. An emphasis on Word and sacrament together, emblematized in the exchange of gifts between Redcrosse and Arthur of a New Testament and a box containing 'liquor pure' (ix 18–19), structures the concluding cantos of Book I. Redcrosse's preparation to defeat the Dragon is incomplete without both his instruction in the house of Holiness and his healing by the Well of Life and the Tree of Life (x-xi). This healing by grace is unmerited, for it happens without regard for his deserving, and it may even be said to occur by fortune or chance that he falls, in defeat, in or near these sources of restoration (xi 29, 45). Grace, he finds, is available in the ordinary course of events to the one who fights the right battles, who strives actively to 'cast away the works of darkness, and put [on] the armor of light, now in the time of this mortal life' (BCP collect for Advent). His victory over the Dragon then leads to his betrothal to Una and to public celebration; the result of receiving 'all ... benefits of [Christ's] passion' through the sacraments (BCP communion rite) is the building-up of Christian community through public celebration of the private and interpersonal.

Thus, Redcrosse demonstrates what it means to become 'thine owne nations frend / And Patrone' (x 61). In Cranmer's terms, the body politic of England was coterminous with the English church as the Body of Christ. One nation, gathered at one table and united in a single eucharistic rite, would be enabled by God to realize the true Christian commonwealth, a well-functioning hierarchy in which virtue was defined in social terms, as it is in *The Faerie Queene*. By avoiding contention and accepting responsibility for fulfilling the social roles in which they found themselves, the English would live in 'love and charity' with their neighbors (BCP communion rite), receiving justice in legal matters and protection against external threats in return for orderly and cooperative behavior toward their social superiors and inferiors.

In *Hymne of Heavenly Love*, Spenser echoes the Prayer Book's eucharistic language – 'most blessed bodie' (148), 'food of life' (194), 'feede our hungry soules' (196) – and uses Christ's summary of the Law to structure his presentation of the Christian life ('Him first to love ... Then next to love our brethren' 190–7). The emphasis here, as elsewhere in Spenser, is on charity as a human response to God's love: 'We should them love, and with their needs partake ... Such mercy he by his most holy reede / Unto us taught, and to approve it trew, / Ensampled it by his most righteous deede' (208–13). For Cranmer, the task of Christian love was to promote Christian community; in Spenser, marriage is the means for love to create that community. Since all the English were required by law to receive communion at Easter, Spenser would have had in mind the eucharistic feeding that communicates to the present God's love revealed in the passion and resurrection of Christ when in *Amoretti* 68 he asserts human love leading to marriage is the appropriate response to that divine love: 'So let us love, deare love, lyke as we ought, / love is the lesson which the Lord us taught.' For Spenser, the movement of time and the meaning of events are defined in relation to the official liturgical calendar of the English church, not the sabbatarian emphasis of the Puritans.

Because of its concern for corporate participation in worship and for raising the level of Christian knowledge, the English church stressed lay education in the basics of the faith and clerical in theology and pastoral skills. For the laity, a vernacular Bible and Prayer Book encouraged a rise in literacy. The Ten Commandments, the Lord's Prayer, and the Apostles' Creed replaced medieval iconography on the walls of English churches; knowing these was a requirement for admission to communion. The didactic intent of all Spenser's writings thus puts him in accord with fundamental intentions of the established church. In addition, the ease with which he alludes to the liturgical calendar, together with his celebration of 'sacred ceremonies' (216) in *Epithalamion* and his praise for bishops worthy of the title in *The Shepheardes Calender*, should make clear that among his goals was advancing the reform program set in motion by Cranmer in the reign of Edward VI and affirmed by the Elizabethan Settlement. The social context in which the virtues of holiness, temperance, and chastity are displayed in *FQ* I-III and the obviously social nature of friendship, justice, and courtesy, explored and promoted in IV-VI, echo Cranmer's own sense of the appropriate context in which to understand and pursue the Christian life. The integral relationship between Word and sacrament, at the heart of the Prayer Book's structuring of worship, underlies the way Spenser depicts the victory of Redcrosse over the Dragon in *FQ* I. The appropriate context for understanding the religious dimension of Spenser's poetry is, therefore, not found within any tradition of thought or piety that opposed the Church of England, but is to be located firmly within the practice of its corporate life, the use of the Book of Common Prayer and attendant documents toward the ends envisioned by Cranmer and pursued by his Elizabethan followers.

JOHN N. WALL

For basic texts, see the reading lists for *Bible, *Book of Common Prayer, *Calvin, *Erasmus, *homilies, *Hooker, *Puritanism, *Reformation. See also Jewel ed 1963. Printed sources are described in Milward 1977. General historical and theological background is introduced by Dickens 1964; G.R. Elton 1977 *Reform and Reformation: England 1509–1558* (Cambridge, Mass); Ozment 1980; Pelikan 1984. More detailed studies include William A. Clebsch 1964 *England's Earliest Protestants, 1520–1535* (New Haven); Collinson 1982; H. Davies 1961–70; George and George 1961; William P. Haugaard 1968 *Elizabeth and the English Reformation* (Cambridge); R.T. Kendall 1979 *Calvin and English Calvinism to 1649* (New York); McConica 1965; Rosemary O'Day and Felicity Heal, eds 1976 *Continuity and Change: Personnel and Administration of the Church of England, 1500–1642* (Leicester); Olsen 1973; Jasper Ridley 1962 *Thomas Cranmer* (Oxford); D.D. Wallace 1982.

For developments in literature in relation to the church, see King 1982, Sinfield 1983, and Norbrook 1984.

For Spenser and religion, the fullest statements are Hume 1984, Wall 1988, and Whitaker 1950. Other studies include Dunlop 1969, King 1985, Lake 1982, McLane 1961, Shaheen 1976, Wall 1983, and Peter White 1983 'The Rise of Arminianism Reconsidered' *P&P* 101:35–54.

Church of Rome In *The Faerie Queene*, the Church of Rome is richly and vividly evoked, functioning behind both Archimago and Duessa as the enemy of Christian faith and the English church (Una) and of social justice and the British crown (Mercilla). This intermingling of religion and politics and of domestic and international concerns reminds us of the complex ways in which religious controversy informed almost every interaction of life in Elizabethan England. The vividness of Spenser's language and the persistence with which he returned to the subject suggest the importance this controversy held for him. Such fervor characterized the language used by partisans of both sides. Yet the urgency of English attacks on Rome and of Rome's attacks on the English reformers should remind us of the need to understand both the Roman and the English churches from outside the language of polemic as well as from within it.

Both churches claimed continuity with the church of an earlier time; thus we need to see how both traditions continued some aspects of the medieval church and departed from others. In the case of Rome, emphasis on the continuity achieved by maintaining the papal office may obscure the extent to which implementation of the Counter-Reformation separated the sixteenth-century Roman church from its medieval predecessor. Yet for the sake of maintaining a claim to continuity, both the Roman and the English churches reinterpreted their medieval inheritance, redefining their understanding of catholicity to exclude those elements of Christian belief and practice they rejected for themselves and found in the other.

controversy Spenser's texts here participate in profound and deeply felt conflict. Defending the English church, John Jewel in 1563 illuminated the terms in which this conflict was articulated: 'if we do show it plain that God's Holy Gospel, the ancient bishops, and the primitive church do make on our side, and that we ... have returned to the apostles and old catholic fathers ... and if they themselves which fly our doctrine and would be called catholics shall manifestly see how all these titles of antiquity, whereof they boast so much, are quite shaken out of their hands ... we then hope and trust that none of them will be so negligent and careless of his own salvation but he will at length study and bethink himself to whether part he were best to join him' (*Apologie* Latin ed 1563, tr 1564; ed 1963:17). For Jewel, the conflict was not between two independent religious traditions whose relative merits and claims might be assessed, but between two parts of one community over which had authority for authentic use of Christian vocabulary. At issue was the ability to promise salvation. Only the side which could honestly do so was truly the church, worthy to call itself catholic; the other side might boastfully call itself catholic, but its claims could only be false. Since the controversialists all operated from within one tradition or the other and recognized no outside authority which might have adjudicated their differences, such argument could only lead to heightened rancor and increased bitterness.

the struggle for religious authority The harsh tone of this religious controversy points to the fact that the struggle for the religious allegiances of the English was as much over issues of control and establishing of authority, matching rival claims made on behalf of the papacy with those made for the British crown, as it was over rival interpretations of Christian belief between the Roman and the English churches. To the English reformers, those accepting the authority of the Bishop of Rome were 'Romish' or 'Romanist,' their faith 'papistic' or 'papistical,' all terms used derisively. The Pope's claims to authority over English Christians were 'usurped,' 'so-called,' 'boastful,' or 'pretended.' In the terms of Jewel's argument, differences between the two were to be accounted for in terms of Rome's departure from the church's ancient and universal practice, to which the English church had returned.

To those who accepted the Pope's authority, however, the English reformers were heretics and rebels against God and his rightful agents, divisive 'innovators' whose separation from Roman discipline sundered the 'ancient' unity of the church and relinquished any claim the English church might have to participate in the oneness, holiness, and universality characteristic of the true church. Such catholicity could be secured only by the papal office and marked by allegiance to the authority of that office. These English 'schismatics' had become 'infidels,' their queen a 'tyrant' who had 'usurped' the throne of England. By the 1570s, the Pope had declared Elizabeth excommunicate, her subjects no longer bound to obey her.

Thus, since both parties disputed each other's right to deem itself 'catholic,' to refer to the Church of Rome in the sixteenth century as 'catholic' is already (if advertently) to have taken sides. Like the term *Anglican*, the term *Roman Catholic* came into common use only in the seventeenth century. The appearance of these terms marks a new stage in the relationship between the traditions, suggesting that each after nearly a hundred years of separation had achieved an identity apart from the other no longer so dependent on the mere negation of a rival. Now each had established its own interpretation of the past and its own recognizable styles of worship, theological reflection, and piety. From the perspective of this new identity, each could acknowledge the other as a church, however difficult or problematic the terms by which that recognition was achieved. Neither full religious toleration in England nor total acceptance of the claims of the English church by the papacy was as yet in the offing; but at least the Pope seemed to give up real hope of restoring his authority in England, and the English monarchy began to seek ways of accommodating a continuing minority loyal to Rome. Against that background, the familiar names for these two bodies began to emerge, implying on both parts a widening of the meaning of the word *church* to accommodate more than one tradition.

development of separation For Spenser's time, we must get behind such terms to a period in which all of the traditions that emerged from the medieval Western church during the Reformation were sorting out the directions in which they might go, choosing some alternatives and ruling out others, in the context of their controversies with each other. In Spenser's early childhood, the Latin Mass was celebrated in cathedrals and parish churches. Henry VIII's eldest daughter, Mary, had restored the authority of the Pope in religious matters which had been severed during the reigns of her father and her half-brother Edward. The bishops who refused to submit to papal authority were burned as heretics, as were many of their followers. Others left England for exile in Protestant Europe.

After the Elizabethan Settlement of Religion in 1559 following Mary's death and Elizabeth's accession to the throne in 1558, the Book of Common Prayer was used in public worship, and religious authority was defined by act of Parliament to reside in the ordained hierarchy with the monarch as Supreme Governor of the church. As a result, those English who remained loyal to the papacy found themselves caught between their affirmation of Elizabeth's authority and their allegiance to the Pope. They also faced growing domestic hostility. In addition to Jewel's defense of the English church, John Foxe in his Book of Martyrs described vividly the deaths of English reformers burned by Mary and helped make opposition to Rome a popular cause.

Yet the division between the two churches, so clear and dramatic by the beginning of the seventeenth century, was slow to develop. Spenser in *A Theatre for Worldlings* used anti-Roman polemic at a time when conformity with the Elizabethan Settlement was at best sporadically enforced. In the 1560s, penalties for attending a clandestine Mass, for refusing to take the Oath of Supremacy, or for failing to attend services of the established church were limited to paying fines or losing one's political office. In remoter parts of England, especially in the dioceses to the north and west of London that escaped close episcopal supervision, some clergy of the English church continued to celebrate the Mass in the old ways. Even among parishes officially loyal to the English church, reports of survival of medieval ceremonial practices continued into the seventeenth century. Noble families who retained their own chaplains could with little difficulty arrange for Roman worship in their family chapels. Many of the English (called Church Papists) retained their traditional religious loyalties and avoided trouble by attending services of the English church.

In so fluid a situation, the English church authorities could never be sure how many people remained loyal to the papacy or were willing if not eager to reacknowledge papal authority. Throughout her reign, Elizabeth feared a rising against her at every sign of public unrest. Events of the late 1560s and early 1570s and of the late 1580s provoked periods of heightened tension. Opposition to the reformed English church found a rallying point in Mary, Queen of Scots, who would have succeeded Elizabeth to the throne of England had Elizabeth died. After Mary was banished from Scotland in 1568 and fled to England, Elizabeth kept her under house arrest, afraid to give her liberty to attract followers but reluctant to execute her. Mary's presence inspired the Earls' Rebellion of 1569–70 and prompted the bull *Regnans in excelsis* issued by Pope Pius V (22 February 1570) which excommunicated Elizabeth and challenged her legitimacy as Queen.

Elizabeth's government responded by intensifying its attempts to identify papal loyalists and heightening the penalties imposed on those who refused to acknowledge her authority. Parliamentary statutes of the 1570s and 1580s declared as acts of treason the denial of the Queen's authority in religious matters, obedience to the papal bull, residence in England if one were a priest ordained by authority of the Pope, or protection of such a priest from prosecution. Anyone convicted of violating these statutes was liable to punishment by death, a fate bestowed on over 250 people before the end of Elizabeth's reign.

In addition, laws mandated that all Englishfolk affirm their loyalty to the English church and participate in its worship, receiving communion at least three times a year. This increased pressure on those loyal to Rome to conform, at least outwardly, to the worship of the established church. The Roman church responded to the increased difficulty of ministering to the faithful English in a variety of ways. From their base in Louvain, English expatriates loyal to Rome produced devotional and theological works in English, eventually including an English translation of the Vulgate New Testament (1582), and smuggled them into England. With the establishment of a seminary at Douai in 1568 (later moved to Rheims) to train clergy for ministry to the English, England again became a field for missionary activity. Graduates, called 'seminary priests,' began to arrive in England in 1574 and were followed by members of the new Jesuit order in 1584, augmenting the work of aging priests ordained during Mary's reign.

The arrival of these new clergy marked the introduction of the Counter-Reformation into England. Since the text and ceremonial of the post-tridentine Mass were different from the Sarum rite or any of the other local English rites of the medieval church, some of the older priests and layfolk loyal to Rome were surprised at how the church of their memories differed from the one they now were brought from abroad. Some must have also felt renewed pressure to interpret loyalty to Rome as rejection of Elizabeth's claims to temporal as well as religious authority. Nevertheless, renewal of the ministry of the Roman church in England resulted in a rise in the numbers of people who refused to attend the services of the English church. Known as recusants, they now faced at least heavy fines and the threat of other punishments, the severity of which fluctuated with Elizabeth's sense of foreign threat to her reign.

This increase in visible loyalty to the Roman church at home coincided with a period of difficulty in England's relations with European governments supported by the papacy. In the 1580s, as the Spanish sought to undermine Elizabeth's rule from within or attack her directly (highlighted by the Armada adventure of 1588 but continuing into the 1590s with Spanish intervention in Ireland), Elizabeth protected herself domestically. She had Mary executed in 1587 and rallied popular support for defense against her enemies abroad by equating loyalty to Rome with support for Spanish conquest. Pressures for religious conformity increased along with punishment for recusancy.

Thus the period in which Spenser was writing *The Faerie Queene* was one in which anti-papal feeling ran especially high in England. Yet the actual numbers of those English who can be considered adherents to the Roman church in the sixteenth century is difficult to determine. Many traditionally minded rural people must have continued to employ folk elements of medieval religion long past the sixteenth century; many members of the gentry refused to commit themselves decisively, wary of irrevocable moves in case Elizabeth did not survive the early years of her reign and they had to accept Mary Stuart as Queen of England. On the other hand, true adherence to the Church of Rome meant especially attendance at her sacraments and participation in her disciplines, a requirement made difficult by the small number of priests. One estimate of practicing adherents to the Church of Rome at the end of Elizabeth's reign puts the number at 40,000 in a country of over 3,000,000 people (Dures 1983:55–7). Since the gentry who remained loyal to the Pope had economic and political power to protect themselves from government pressure as well as houses large enough to accommodate private chapels and to hide priests, they had both freedom and occasion to develop their religion. Thus, over time, the Roman church in England became not exclusively but largely a religion practiced in private homes by members of the gentry, not a religion practiced in public by large numbers of ordinary people.

developments in worship and theology Neither the English church nor the Church of Rome saw itself as breaking continuity with the Christian past, although both did so. For the Roman church, this break involved centralizing authority within the organization of the church, emphasizing the organizational and doctrinal authority of the Pope, codifying belief and restricting the scope of permitted discussion in theological matters, and establishing liturgical uniformity. In the medieval period, there had been substantial local variation in worship and wide-ranging debate over the location of authority and the substance of belief; after Trent, the Roman church was better organized but less diverse than its medieval predecessor. Erasmus, for example, was one of the papacy's strongest defenders against Luther, and yet the Counter-Reformation was uncomfortable with his scholarly legacy. Papal control had been much debated in the medieval church; many wanted stronger and more frequent councils to check what was seen as excessive centralization of church government. The Counter-Reformation, however, was a victory for the papacy, which won dramatic new powers of control in the Council of Trent (1545–64).

Trent also clarified doctrinal positions on

issues raised by the reformers; again, the result was narrower doctrinal definition, less room for theological exploration, and an increased papal authority to limit debate and to demand adherence to approved interpretations. Trent inaugurated a period of papal triumphalism unprecedented in the Western church; it gave renewed emphasis to the Pope's claim that to be Peter's successor and Christ's vicar meant to have the final and deciding voice in matters of doctrine, worship, and conduct of life. In time, this development of papal authority by the Council of Trent transformed the life of the whole Roman church.

By contrast, the Church of England experienced a weakening of central authority that led to more variety in expressions and diversity of interpretations of the faith at the expense of a rigorous sense of direction and a clear doctrinal identity. This came about in part because the bishops of the English church, in sharing power with Elizabeth in church matters, could find her powerfully supportive if their aims and means coincided but a serious obstacle if they did not. In either case, the close involvement of the English church with political and social matters would affect profoundly the direction of its life.

In their various reassessments of medieval theology, both churches agreed that justification is an act of God appropriated by faith. Yet they disagreed on the role of human agency before and after the bestowal of grace. To the Church of England, one was completely dependent on God's free gift of grace to make faith itself possible and to enable the doing of good works which were the signs of faith. To the Church of Rome, while human activity did not of itself earn grace, it did prepare for the gift of grace; furthermore, human effort cooperating with grace after its bestowal earned additional merit. For both churches, a life of good works enabled by grace led to salvation. Unlike some continental reformers, neither the Roman nor the English churches confused justification with salvation. To achieve justification was to begin rather than end the Christian life. Both reconciled St Paul's emphasis on justification by faith with St James' claim that faith without works is dead, but with differing emphases. The English church's emphasis on grace as a gratuitous gift led it to find divine love manifest most clearly in relation to the redemptive work of Christ, so that the sacraments conveyed 'all ... benefits of his passion' (BCP communion rite). Thus Christians were to give thanks for God's gift of himself by giving of themselves in charity to their neighbors. In this scheme, the saints were important because they led exemplary lives.

In contrast, the Roman church emphasized human cooperation with God in the work of salvation, which led to a concern for those who revealed God's special love. To devout supporters of the papacy, devotion to the Blessed Virgin Mary and to the saints was appropriate and meritorious because through them God communicated his love. Thus, to appeal to the saints to intercede with God on one's behalf was to participate in the divine love of humanity. Counter-Reformation spirituality renewed the importance of religious orders, sacramental confession, private contemplative devotion, and the cult of the saints, furthering the development of an identity distinct from the piety of the English church. To the English church, the Roman position on faith and works seemed to limit the power of grace and make it divisible; to the Roman church, the English resolution seemed to undercut the importance of human agency.

Both churches valued the sacraments of baptism and communion as vehicles of grace. Trent's codification of the understanding of the Mass as a sacrifice repeated by the priest led to a reemphasis on the Mass as a devotion of the priest, the retention of Latin for the rite, and the repetition of its central prayer by the priest in a voice inaudible to the congregation. Christ was present in the objective transformation of the substance of the bread and wine into the physical body and blood of Christ (transubstantiation). In seeking to make the Mass the center of religious life as well as the object of devotion, Trent encouraged more frequent confessions and regular receptions of the consecrated bread. The English church also sought more frequent receptions (of both bread and wine) and to that end made confession and absolution a part of corporate worship. To it, however, the idea of sacrifice in the communion rite was understood to refer to Christ's 'full, perfect, and sufficient sacrifice, oblation, and satisfaction for the sins of the whole world' (BCP prayer of consecration) and to the congregation's offering of a 'sacrifice of praise and thanksgiving' in response to its reception of 'all ... benefits of his passion' through participation in the communion rite. Through this rite, in English rather than Latin and in an audible voice instead of inaudibly after the Roman ceremonial pattern, Christ was present in the consequences of his actions, making the congregation one 'in him.'

The English church thus rejected the Roman belief, emphasized at Trent, that the earthly body of Christ was substantially present in the consecrated bread and wine. Instead, Christ was present in his redemptive, recreative, and enabling role, conveyed through the action of the rite, as he becomes present 'in us, and we in him.' For both churches, baptism was the rite of incorporation into the church; it conveyed grace to initiate the Christian life and thus in dire need could be performed by layfolk as well as clergy. The Roman church also treated marriage, penance, holy orders, confirmation, and unction of the sick as sacraments. The English church retained these rites in its Book of Common Prayer but thought of them as being, in Spenser's words, 'sacred ceremonies' (*Epithalamion* 216) which were part of the ordinary life of the church but not fully sacraments.

Differences in styles of religious life accompanied these contrasts in belief. The Counter-Reformation church eliminated as much as possible locally differing liturgical traditions that enriched the medieval church, such as the English uses of Sarum and York; in their place came the Mass of the Roman rite, fully prescribed as to text and ceremonial, to be imposed uniformly throughout the world of Roman Christianity. Trent also sought to abolish medieval traditions of personal piety which stressed rigorous abstinence on fast days and elaborate celebrations on feast days; the seminary priests and Jesuits who came to England after 1570 often remarked on the persistence of these medieval customs on the part of their English faithful. Instead, Counter-Reformation spirituality stressed frequent confession and reception at the Mass, an emphasis difficult to experience in England since often no priest was available to celebrate Mass. Rome also encouraged prayer for the intercession of the Blessed Virgin Mary and the saints and the use of private devotional aids such as the rosary and other special devotions. It retained and reemphasized the monastic model for the Christian life, including acceptance of the ideals of poverty, chastity, and obedience for secular clergy as well as for those who were members of religious orders. The Counter-Reformation was also a time of rigorous personal discipline and the pursuit of deep religious experience, as well as a time of growth in the number and variety of religious orders. St Ignatius Loyala, who developed an influential technique of meditation and founded the Jesuit Order, exemplifies the power and enduring character of both developments in the spiritual disciplines of the Roman church.

In relation to medieval models, the Church of England dramatically changed its emphasis. The monastic system was abolished under Henry VIII and Edward; briefly reestablished under Mary, it was again abandoned with the accession of Elizabeth. Along with the monasteries went the monastic ideal of Christian asceticism, to be replaced by an emphasis on charity towards one's neighbor leading to the creation of the Christian commonwealth. Private, contemplative devotions to Mary and the saints were abandoned; public worship in which the congregation took part became the new standard for the Christian life. Cranmer collapsed the seven-office *regulum* of the monastic day into the two offices of Morning and Evening Prayer. Primers in English made these offices of Bible reading, Psalm reciting, and prayer into models for personal and family devotion.

While the Roman church emphasized belief in purgatory and the value of prayers and Masses said for the dead, the English church stressed the need to resolve one's relationship with God in this life and rejected the possibility that the living could affect the eternal destiny of the dead through performing good works. The English church drastically simplified the church calendar of holy days and saints' days, restricting them to the commemoration of New Testament figures and events; the saints became examples of true Christian living rather than intercessors with God. Whereas Trent made the Latin Vulgate the official version of the Bible for the Roman church, the English church emphasized the importance of vernacular translations. Although it retained the books of the Vulgate, it placed those which were not in the official Hebrew canon into a special section called the Apocrypha, making them authoritative only in matters of morals, not doctrine.

Spenser and Rome Because those loyal to the Roman church could not worship or profess their faith openly in England after 1559, we cannot be sure of the extent to which Spenser had direct knowledge of it. He was a child during at least part of Mary's reign, and thus as an adult he may have remembered something of the pre-Reformation ceremonial revived during her reign. The Cambridge of his university years was a center of religious debate and the source of leaders for both the established church and the Puritan opposition – and of students who left to attend Roman seminaries on the continent. Thus Spenser could have known sons of recusant families whose knowledge of Roman worship was more immediate. He could also have read medieval theologians and may have seen imported books defending the Roman faith. He certainly read the Greek and Latin Fathers as well as reformed interpretations of them. His early works suggest, however, that his understanding of the Roman church was shaped primarily by reformed polemic according to which the medieval clergy were lazy and ignorant, and abused their vows of celibacy; the confidence with which Piers attacks Palinode in *SC, Maye* as a 'shepheard, that does the right way forsake' because his kind 'Passen their time ... In lustihede and wanton meryment' (41–2, 165) need not be based on personal observation. Similarly, his satire in *Mother Hubberds Tale* targets reformed clergy who persist in those traits and refuse to take the Reformation seriously. Even though they have 'laid away' 'Their penie Masses, and their Complynes meete' (452–5), they have not yet become good shepherds in the tradition of *Piers Plowman*, Chaucer's Parson, and Spenser's own Piers. Indeed, the change from Latin to English and from a celibate to a married clergy may, according to Spenser, have increased opportunity for abuse of the priestly vocation. *Mother Hubberd*'s corrupt cleric remembers the old priests' 'holie things to say, / At morne and even' (450–1); Spenser here notes that the 'small devotion' of the reformed church leaves *Mother Hubberd*'s priest free to 'follow any merrie motion' (457–8) rather than to observe the seven offices of the medieval breviary. Here the change in rite has brought about no reform of the church or society; true reform is achieved only when lives, especially those of the clergy, are changed.

Piers' reference to the clergy's desire for 'greedie governaunce' (*SC, Maye* 121) points to another complicating factor in Spenser's perception of the Roman church, the extent to which English-Roman relations were affected by political issues and shifts in power. The background for his depiction of the Church of Rome in *The Faerie Queene* is the turbulent 1580s, when the threat to Elizabeth from Spain, acting in the name of Rome, became critical. In 1570, the bull excommunicating her came at the urging of the French and over Spanish objections; but by the 1580s the chief threat to England came from Spain, although Elizabeth recognized the Roman church behind the maneuverings of Mary, Queen of Scots, and Italian contacts with Ireland. With mission priests coming into England in increasing numbers, she feared that they would rally English recusants to oppose her. Although rebellion was always unlikely, tensions were heightened by the polemics of William Allen and Robert Parsons, leaders of the mission who published works arguing the virtue of executing Elizabeth.

As a result, her subjects who retained allegiance to the papacy were forced to demonstrate their devotion to Elizabeth. Those who convinced her government of their loyalty were usually left alone; those who failed to demonstrate their trustworthiness suffered deprivations. The most severe government response, however, was directed against Roman priests. At one point over half of those who had come into England were imprisoned and tortured; many were executed publicly as a powerful reminder of the cost of opposition to Elizabeth's authority in religious affairs. Yet the presence of a community in England loyal to Rome, even if ostensibly devoted to Elizabeth's secular authority, and of those who were ready to change religious allegiance for political gain, constituted a threat to the government that could never be ignored. In this regard, specifics of difference in doctrine were not important: what mattered was the ability of the papacy to command allegiance and support unrest.

In the midst of this period of heightened religious tension, Spenser became one of Elizabeth's agents in Ireland, a country in which the English government's ability to command allegiance to the English church was far less strong than in England and in which the populace was always potentially or actually hostile to Elizabeth's authority. Here, as he worked on his major poem, Spenser must have been more conscious of the Roman church as a threat than if he had remained in England. A work overtly addressed to Elizabeth and intended to further the reforming work of the Church of England, *The Faerie Queene*, especially in Book I, again draws on the tradition of Reformation polemic to link Rome and the Pope with the images from Revelation of the Whore of Babylon and the Antichrist. While radical reformers saw in Revelation a literal prediction of Apocalypse, imminent arrival of the Kingdom of God from beyond history, Spenser uses it to describe contemporary events as revealing God's actions in and through history. In these terms, the Pope's claims divided English loyalties and offered a false image of the church; thus in Book I, evil, grounded in duplicity, is characterized by the ability to create false appearances.

For Spenser, the dual claim of the Pope as authority over religious as well as political concerns is expressed in the duality of Archimago and Duessa opposing simultaneously both the English church (Una) and the English Queen (Mercilla). Although Mary, Queen of Scots, who occasionally illuminates the role of Duessa (explicitly in Book V), was dead by 1590, the line of succession to the English throne was not certain and could have passed to a monarch with papal sympathies had Elizabeth died. Archimago's repetition of the Ave Maria (I i 35) would have identified him had Redcrosse been able to 'read' his cross correctly at the beginning of the book. English and Roman claims to authority in interpreting Christian language divided precisely over whether the Mass in Latin or the Holy Communion in English delivered Christ truly. Here Spenser presents Duessa's cup (viii 14) as promoting Redcrosse's downfall, while the Tree of Life and Well of Life episodes in canto xi revive him and link the sacraments of the English church, functioning to convey grace and enable communicants to 'continue in ... holy fellowship and do all such good works as [God] hast prepared for us to walk in' (BCP communion rite), with their fulfillment in the eschatological banquet. In the contrasts between Duessa and Una, between Archimago and Redcrosse, between the house of Pride and the house of Holiness, Spenser articulates the struggle characteristic of sixteenth-century controversy to claim for one side or the other the title of true church.

To make the claims of Elizabeth and her church against Rome, Spenser reinterprets the common medieval heritage of both churches. Una riding on her 'lowly Asse' (i 4) invokes the English church's claims to Mary's biblical role, but Archimago's Ave Maria (35) embodies the Roman church's interpretation of Mary as intercessor which was rejected by the reformers as usurping Christ's role as 'our only mediator and advocate' (BCP communion rite). Medieval Arthurian material which provides the basic landscape and plot structure for *The Faerie Queene* makes Elizabeth's case for the legitimacy and antiquity of her claims to rule (a matter of religious concern, since the Pope had declared her illegitimate and excommunicate). Such traditional generic material also asserts the authority of the English church to describe itself as in continuity with England's religious past. Yet Spenser transforms his generic models to support the concerns of the English reformers. By dropping the Grail motif and the narratives of Arthur's knights, he substitutes Elizabethan aspirations and models of virtuous behavior for their medieval predecessors. Even as St George ceases to be one whose intercessions are sought and becomes one whose life is a model for imitation, so Spenser participates in the Church of England's recreation of the Christian life as the pursuit of active charity rather than passive devotion to the Mass or to the saints.

At the same time, Spenser's depiction of the Church of Rome is far richer and more complex than conventional categories of Reformation polemic seem to permit. Duessa and Una may manifest diametrically opposed ways of being – the one displaying incongruity between appearance and reality and the other manifesting congruity. Yet in at least one way of reading the names in Book II, Spenser depicts Rome, Canterbury, and Geneva under the names Perissa, Medina, and Elissa as 'sisters ... The children of one sire by mothers three' (ii 13), a difference in degree rather than kind. Spenser's implicit condemnation of Kirkrapine in Book I, together with his depiction of the Blatant Beast's despoliation of a monastery in *FQ* VI xii 23–5, suggests that he disapproved of the iconoclastic destruction of the medieval church's artistic legacy. Rather than rejecting religious art and the institution of monasticism outright, he seems only to condemn their aggrandizement of wealth at the expense of the needy. The issues treated in Book I, although grounded in specific Elizabethan Roman-English religious conflicts, also concern broader issues such as the nature of language and the ethical implications of duplicity, regardless of the context in which such issues occur.

Clearly a supporter of the English church in its reformation, Spenser vigorously opposed efforts by the papacy to undermine Elizabeth's government. Yet, even though he could assert that in religion 'that which is trewe onelye is and the rest are not at all' (*Vewe* in *Var Prose* p 221), his support for the established church was not unqualified. Uneasy with any clergy who pursued involvement in 'greedie governaunce' for personal ends rather relieving poverty and ignorance through social reform, Spenser in *Vewe* avoids opportunities to blame Rome for England's difficulties in Ireland. Irenius holds ignorance as much as the papacy responsible for what he judges the deplorable state of religion in Ireland, since although the Irish 'are all Papistes by theire profession' they are 'in the same so blindelye and brutishly enformed for the moste parte as that ye woulde rather thinke them *Atheists* or infidles.' Their adherence to Rome is thus a matter of form rather than substance, since an Irishman can 'saie his pater noster or his *Ave marye* without anie knowledge or understandinge what one worde theareof meanethe' (p 136). The English are also at fault for their approach to mission work. Irenius objects to English clergy who have 'impressed' the 'Protestantes profession' upon the Irish 'with terrour and sharpe penalties ... rather [than] delivered and intymated with mildenes and gentlenes soe as it maie not be hated before it be understode'; thus Irish antagonism for the English church is understandable since they hate it 'thoughe unknowen even for the verye hatred which they have of the Englishe and theire government' (p 221). Irenius' solution is a tactical one – repair the fabric of Irish churches and schoolhouses, train clergy native to Ireland, and change the English clergy's attitude toward the Irish, as well as increase efforts to prevent Roman priests from getting into Ireland. A resolution of the religious dimensions of the Irish problem thus awaited a political solution not dependent on the determination of divine truth. In any case, as Spenser knew at the end, the effect of time and mutability is to 'cut down' the play of change and difference, including that which divides religious traditions, finding in slander and ignorance a greater enemy of Christian truth than diversity in its interpretation (*FQ* VII viii 1). JOHN N. WALL

On Elizabethans loyal to the Church of Rome, see John Bossy 1975 *The English Catholic Community, 1570–1850* (London); Alan Dures 1983 *English Catholicism, 1558–1642* (Harlow, Essex); Peter Holmes 1982 *Resistance and Compromise: The Political Thought of the Elizabethan Catholics* (Cambridge); Patrick McGrath 1967 *Papists and Puritans under Elizabeth I* (London); Adrian Morey 1978 *The Catholic Subjects of Elizabeth I* (London); Arnold Pritchard 1979 *Catholic Loyalism in Elizabethan England* (Chapel Hill); William Raleigh Trimble 1964 *The Catholic Laity in Elizabethan England, 1558–1603* (Cambridge, Mass).

On Counter-Reformation Catholicism and the Church of England, see A.G. Dickens 1968 *The Counter Reformation* (New York); H. Outram Evennett 1968 *The Spirit of the Counter-Reformation* ed John Bossy (Cambridge); Pierre Janelle 1949 *The Catholic Reformation* (Milwaukee); Hubert Jedin 1957–61 *A History of the Council of Trent* tr Ernest Graf, 2 vols (Edinburgh); Jones, et al 1978; Milward 1977; Marvin R. O'Connell 1974 *The Counter Reformation 1559–1610* (New York); Ozment 1980; Pelikan 1984.

On Spenser and Reformation polemic, see King 1982; Wall 1988; Waters 1970.

Churchyard, Thomas (c 1520–1604) In many volumes of miscellaneous verse most often written in fourteeners, Churchyard complained of his poverty and disappointments and moralized on fortune and God's rule. He contributed 'Shore's Wife' to the *Mirror for Magistrates* (1563) and wrote the program for the Queen's entertainment at Bristol in 1574. For eight years he served under Lord Grey in Scotland and Ireland; later he fought in Flanders and France and recounted his exciting adventures in 'A Tragicall Discourse of the Unhappy Mans Life' in *Churchyardes Chippes* (1575). Subsisting precariously as a hanger-on at court, towards the end of his life he found a patron in Sir Julius Caesar, who persuaded the Queen to give him a pension (Chester 1935). Nashe in *Four Letters Confuted* (1593, ed 1904–10, 1:309) compliments Churchyard's 'aged Muse, that may well be grand-mother to our grandeloquentest Poets at this present.'

In *Colin Clout* (396–9), Spenser refers to Churchyard as 'old *Palemon* free from spight, / Whose carefull pipe may make the hearer rew: / Yet he himselfe may rewed be more right, / That sung so long untill quite hoarse he grew.' Churchyard alludes to this notice in *A Musicall Consort* (1595) and *A Pleasant Discourse of Court and Wars* (1596; *Sp All* pp 40–1, 46). In *Churchyards Challenge* (1593), he refers to Spenser as 'now the spirit of learned speech' (*Sp All* p 29). WALDO F. MCNEIR

Cicero (Marcus Tullius Cicero, 106–43 BC) A major Renaissance poet like Spenser could hardly have avoided being influenced by Cicero, the great orator, statesman, philosopher, and letter writer of ancient Rome. He studied his writings in some detail both at school and university and continued to read and refer to them in later life. Although Harvey satirically reported that Cicero was not studied as he used to be (*Three Letters* 2, in *Var Prose* p 460), there is no external evidence for his statement. Cicero remained the major exemplar of Latinity in an educational system that was devoted to the study of Latin. Yet his influence on Spenser is not as direct as the general knowledge of him might suggest.

The numerous writings of Cicero were widely studied in the Renaissance as models of style and expression (see *Ciceronianism); he was also seen as the principal theorist of Latin rhetoric. Yet it is in the area of ethics that he would have most influenced Spenser, for he was the chief synthesizer and transmitter of Greek ethical thought to the Latin West. The *Tusculanae disputationes* (*Tusculan Disputations*) and *De officiis* (*On Duties*) were immensely influential in Renaissance humanism. His concept of temperance, for instance, is closely related to the courtesy presented in Book VI of *The Faerie Queene*; one of the four primary virtues in *De officiis*, it is there presented in terms of decorum and propriety (1.27.93–42.151) and is in this sense a virtue opposed to the impropriety and vicious behavior of the Blatant Beast.

Cicero's ethical writings also include important treatises on friendship (*De amicitia*) and old age (*De senectute*). They may be related to *FQ* IV on friendship and to the debate on old age in *SC, Februarie*. However, Thenot, the spokesman for old age in the eclogue, owes nothing to Cicero's Cato, the defender of old age in *De senectute*. Thenot's rejection of love (69–70, 85–93) presents an argument different from Cato's more sophisticated attack on the pleasures of youth (12.39–13.44). Likewise, Cicero's dialogue on friendship may not actually apply directly as one might first think to the ideas of friendship in *FQ* IV. *De amicitia* is comprehensive within its discussion of specifically male friendship, but does not look at the relational and usually competing forces of romantic, heterosexual love which are developed in *The Faerie Queene*. In the tradition of courtly romance, love is stronger than friendship; yet for Cicero, romantic love did not exist as understood in the late Middle Ages and Renaissance, and male friendship was the highest and best human relationship. The ethical discussion of *De amicitia* sheds only a partial light on the notion of friendship in Spenser.

Editors and commentators on Spenser often cite Cicero as source for many aphorisms and expressions in the poetry (about 50 are cited in the *Var Index*), for example, *De natura deorum* (*On the Nature of the Gods*) for details of Spenser's mythology. Yet the information in Cicero was also found elsewhere (sometimes in later writers who merely reported what Cicero had said), making a direct connection between them hard to establish.

We know Spenser would have read Cicero in school and even memorized passages from him. Yet when we turn to his prose writings, we find the few echoes of Cicero to be inconsistent or wrong. The only explicit reference to Cicero in Spenser's works is found in *Vewe of Ireland*, where Irenius supports an argument by reference to a Ciceronian aphorism: 'ffor all is the Conquerours as *Tully* to *Brutus* saieth' (*Var Prose* p 52); yet this is not Cicero at all, but Livy (21.13; see *Var Prose* p 285). It is interesting to see how Spenser dresses up a faultily remembered tag by a specific reference; the ring of the truth is affirmed by a reference to the greatest orator of antiquity. Another example: midway in *Vewe*, Irenius argues for more stringently repressive measures against the Irish, and enforces his argument with the 'sayinge *Quem metuunt oderunt*' (they hate the one they fear; pp 146–7). Although the Latin tag is found in *De officiis* (2.7.23, as quoted from the poet Ennius), Cicero's argument is the opposite of Irenius'. The only sound basis of government is the respectful affection of the governed; repressive rule based on fear will never work (2.7.23–6). Yet Irenius supports such repression. Unless this is a conscious and willful distortion, it seems that Spenser knew the tag but not its context; he could have picked it up in many places, for instance, in Erasmus' *Adages*. A third example: in a Latin poem to Harvey (*Two Letters* 1, in *Var Prose* p 10), while bemoaning the fate of poets who must compromise their art to please the public, Spenser observes, 'sic Stultorum omnia plena' (so everywhere [the world is] full of fools), echoing Cicero's 'stultorum plena sunt omnia' (*Ad familiares* 9.22.4). Yet Cicero uses the aphorism in an entirely different discussion of obscene and euphemistic diction in public conversation. Again this tag was widely current (see *Var Prose* p 260). The authority of the phrase, not the actual context of its original use, would be enough to impress the reader.

Spenser's indifferent use of Cicero's ethical theory and actual language suggests that he was aware of the cultural value of a knowledge of Cicero but that he was not deeply immersed in his writings beyond his initial encounter with them during his schoolboy and university years.

PHILIP B. ROLLINSON

Ciceronianism As a descriptive term, *Ciceronianism* does not apply to the reception of Cicero's writings as a whole but is restricted to the imitation of his style. The basic axiom of this style is *copiose et ornate dicere* which entails the dominance of manner (*verba*) over matter (*res*). This aim is realized by the amplification of words and ideas and their variation by means of tropes and figures. The result of such procedures is carefully balanced syntactic periods with symmetrical arrangements (parallelism, antithesis, progression) of sound and sense. The striving for regularity and musicality of diction is furthermore supported by the use of *clausulae* or rhythmical cadences at the ends of sentences. Quintilian was the first to profess himself a disciple of Cicero, and he was not to remain the only one. In the Renaissance, the rediscovery of Ciceronian orations and rhetorical treatises that had been neglected in the Middle Ages restored their author's reputation as a master of style. Henceforth Cicero's language served as the guideline for purging medieval Latin of its barbarisms and solecisms. In the course of this pursuit, an ardent controversy arose over the degree and extent of *imitatio*. The purists (Bembo, Longueil) contended that Cicero was the only possible model for imitation and therefore endeavored to convert their own works into pastiches of his rhetorical art. Their idolatry of him even went so far that they admitted only such constructions, phrases, and cadences as could be found in the Ciceronian canon. The opponents of these 'apes of Cicero,' as they were derisively termed, advocated in their turn a concept of selective imitation that was adaptable (*aptum*) to both the respective subjects and the participants in the act of communication. Erasmus' satirical dialogue, *Ciceronianus* (1528), that marked a turning point in the appreciation of Cicero, Roger Ascham's educational treatise, *The Scholemaster* (1570), and Gabriel Harvey's Cambridge oration, *Ciceronianus* (1577), maintained that only a revival of Cicero's ideal union of wisdom and eloquence could rescue Ciceronianism from degenerating into an empty aesthetic formalism. Such censures and warnings did not, however, restrain Elizabethan writers from copying Ciceronian sentence patterns in their vernacular compositions. Spenser's prose style makes no exception to this rule, displaying a predilection for long sentence periods, variety of expression, and symmetry of lexical units, as the Letter to Raleigh clearly shows. At the turn of the century, the anti-Ciceronian movement gained in strength. Bacon's *Advancement of Learning* (1605) demanded an adequate proportion of 'words' and 'matter.' Cicero was succeeded by Seneca in the role of a classical authority, and the new style which now became the fashion was characterized by brevity, parataxis, discontinuity, and sententiousness.

HEINRICH F. PLETT

Marc Fumaroli 1980 *L'Age de l'eloquence: Rhétorique et 'res literaria' de la renaissance au seuil de l'époque classique* (Geneva); Remigio Sabbadini 1885 *Storia del Ciceronianismo* (Turin); Izora Scott 1910 *Controversies over the Imitation of Cicero as a Model for Style* (New York); Alvin Vos 1979 '"Good Matter and Good Utterance": The Character of English Ciceronianism' *SEL* 19:3–18.

Circe The goddess and enchantress Circe was the daughter of the Sun and the Oceanid Perse, according to most authorities in the ancient world (Homer *Odyssey* 10.138–9; Hesiod *Theogony* 956–7, 1011; Apollonius Rhodius *Argonautica* 4.591) and the Renaissance ('who knows not Circe / The daughter of the Sun?' Milton *Comus* 50–1). Odysseus' encounter with her represents three dangers: bestial enslavement in her transformation of his companions (10.233–43), loss of masculinity in the sexual invitation against which he is warned by Hermes (296–301), and carefree indulgence in the pleasant sojourn on her island, Aeaea (466–74). It is a matter of debate whether she represents a moralized temptation in Homer, for after she has been outwitted by Odysseus she proves hospitable, helpful, and full of good advice. The episode may better be seen as expressing a fear of magical female sexuality. As such, Homer's Circe is the archetype of all women who threaten to transform and enervate men – from Apuleius' Pamphile to Shakespeare's Cleopatra and Milton's Dalila.

Circe became a monitory exemplum even in the ancient world. Xenophon's temperate Socrates uses the transformation of Odysseus' companions to warn against excessive indulgence, and his Odysseus is a model of self-restraint (*Memorabilia* 1.3.7). Gryllus teases Odysseus for believing that he has given proof of self-control in rejecting Circe's embraces (Plutarch *Beasts Are Rational* 988 in *Moralia*). Yet Apollonius' Circe is surprisingly moral: she is ordained by Zeus to purify Jason and Medea from the crime of murdering Apsyrtus (*Argonautica* 4.559–61, 691–752). Horace moralizes the story: if Ulysses, the exemplar of virtue and wisdom, had drunk from Circe's cup, 'enslaved by a whorish mistress, he would have become shamed and witless' (*Epistles* 1.2.17–26). Cicero imagines the villainous Verres as having drunk of Circe's cup (*In Q. Caecilium Oratio* 17.57). Petronius treats comically the Homeric fear of being unmanned, when mock-Odyssean Encolpius finds himself impotent with the courtesan Circe (*Satyricon* 126–8).

Circe has been described as the most typical moralized myth of the Renaissance and one of its best-known symbolic figures (Bush 1968:13–16, Tuve 1957:130). The Renaissance inherited and developed allegorizations in which she appears with vicious meanings, generally conceived as intemperance. The commentator Eustathius reads Homer's Circe as gluttony; Servius (on *Aeneid* 7.19) sees her as a famous prostitute whose alluring pleasures dehumanize men. Like the commentators on Homer, Virgil, and Ovid (*Metamorphoses* 14), the mythographers interpret Ulysses' transformed companions as men given over to drunkenness and pleasure. The Circe emblems of Alciati (1621, Emblem 76 *Cavendum a meretricibus* 'One must beware of whores') and Whitney (1586:82 *Homines voluptatibus transformantur* 'Men are transformed by pleasures') bluntly sum up her usual Renaissance meanings.

(See **Circe** Fig 1.)

Conti interprets Circe in terms of natural science: as the daughter of the Sun (heat) and a sea nymph (moisture), she signifies *commistio* (mixture) and her four handmaids the elements; accordingly, she is associated with generation, corruption, and change. He says that Ulysses (the immortal soul) is not susceptible to change, unlike his companions (the body and its faculties). In his encounter with Circe, Ulysses, with divine aid, displays admirable valor and constancy: 'So, if I may sum up, in this story the meaning the ancients wished to convey is that a wise man, whether good or ill befall him, must govern himself temperately' (*Mythologiae* 6.6). Sandys' English commentary on Ovid follows Conti closely (ed 1970:652–4).

Dante, Luther, and Ascham used allegorizations of Circe as warnings to their countrymen. Virtue having fled the valley of the Arno, men there have changed their nature as if Circe had turned them out to graze (*Purgatorio* 14.40–2). Luther castigates the Germans with an allusion to the transformation of Ulysses' companions (commentary on Genesis 23.5–6, ed 1958–75, 4:208–9). Ascham warns at length of the dangers for the young Englishman at the Circean courts of Italy (*Scholemaster* ed 1904:225–9).

Spenser's Duessa is particularly Circean in her appearance as the Whore of Babylon at *FQ* I viii 14, where she and her cup are described in details from *Metamorphoses* 14.55–8. The *Ovide moralisé* had identified Circe with the Whore, and Protestant exegetes of Apocalypse identified the Babylonian Roman church as 'that great witche *Circes*' (Roberts 1978). Apollonius' location of Aeaea, Circe's home, in Italy (*Argonautica* 3.309–13, 4.659–62), followed by numerous mythographers and dictionaries, may have established an Italianate Circe who came to represent an Italianate Catholic church. Duessa's effects on Timias are typically enervating and unmanning, and her defeat by Arthur marks him as Ulyssean.

Earlier and less obvious manifestations of a Circean Duessa are at I ii 28–45 and vii 2–6. Her association with Fradubio has weakened and unmanned him (ii 42): his transformation into a tree echoes that of Ariosto's Astolfo by the Circean Alcina. Duessa's double transformation of Fradubio and Fraelissa is an ironic Ovidian metamorphic parody: the metamorphosis of Baucis and Philemon into trees expressed their marital fidelity (Sandys calls them 'the patternes of chast and constant conjugall affections' ed 1970:391); that of Fradubio – and hence of Fraelissa – his inconstancy. Redcrosse hears their story as he dallies with Duessa in a typical earthly paradise or *locus amoenus*, unattending to its ironic warning about his companion. His own unmanning takes place subsequently in a comparable location, and again the consequence of dalliance with the Circean Duessa is enfeebling.

Circe and her allegorizations largely shape *FQ* II through episodes which anticipate Guyon's experiences in Acrasia's Bower. The Late Latin *acrasia*, as well as recalling Trissino's Acratia, derives in part from Greek *akrasia* (the quality of being badly mixed; hence intemperance). So Conti's explanation of Circe as *commistio* in turn derives from a false etymology for *Kirkē* from *kerannumi* ('mix'; see *Mythologiae* 6.6 and Appendix), and corresponds to Spenser's conception of intemperance as a faulty mixture. Circe's cup in Homer mixes pleasant ingredients with baneful drugs (*Odyssey* 10.233–8), as does that in *Metamorphoses* 14.273–6. Ovid describes how she adds baleful juices to lie hidden under the sweetness, the very opposite to the commonplace humanist metaphor for the healthful medicine of instruction under sweetened fiction: a warning to unwary readers of Acrasia's delicious garden. In Amavia's account (i 51–6), Acrasia makes her lovers 'drunken mad' with 'words and weedes of wondrous might,' thus identifying her as the Circe of *Aeneid* 7.19, 'the pitiless goddess with the powerful herbs.' Mortdant is 'transformed from his former skill' (54), the metaphoric *transformed* alluding to Circean metamorphosis. Acrasia overgoes her classical prototypes in that she exanimates as well as transforms bodies (v 27). Phaedria adumbrates Acrasia and her garden (vi 12–18): she too has her *locus amoenus* and her song, and lays Cymochles' head in the typical *grembo molle* (soft lap) of Italian Circes (Giamatti 1966:202). The Garden of Proserpina is a chthonic counterpart to the *loci amoeni* of Phaedria and Acrasia. To add to other interpretations of the silver seat or stool with which Mammon tempts Guyon (vii 53, 63), it may be noted that Circe offers Odysseus a silver-studded chair and footstool (*Odyssey* 10.314–15; Kermode 1971:74–5; *Var* 2:268–9).

After these anticipations, the Ulyssean Guyon and reader experience Acrasia and her Bower in canto xii. Their various Circean antecedents in classical and Renaissance literature have been extensively noted (see reading list). The maritime monstrosities, although they owe details to Pliny and Gesner, may have been suggested by the polymorphous prodigies of nature attending Circe in *Argonautica* 4.672–81. The actual beasts in Acrasia's garden, with their bellowing provoked by greed, lust, and pride (xii 39), accord with the interpretations of Conti and others, that Circe's various animals represent different vices (see *Grill). Guyon is fortunate in having a constantly attendant Hermes in the Palmer, armed with his caduceus.

First we encounter a series of liminary Circean allusions. The ivory gates (43–6) depict the Argo's voyage and Circe's niece Medea, who for Conti and others signified *immoderatam libidinem* (excessive lust). Next we encounter three Circean figures. Genius (46–9) has Circe's cup and magical staff 'with which he charmed semblants sly.' He is a perversion of the Genius in the Garden of Adonis (III vi) and of the good meanings of generation, a significance Conti gives Circe; and he is himself an effeminated manifestation of Circean unmanning. Excess (55–7) has the Circean cup and offers a temptation to moral drunkenness in her untempered wine. Verdant (72–80), the latest victim of Circean Acrasia, sums up the consequences of yielding to all three temptations: enslavement, loss of masculinity, and pleasant rest. The Palmer robs Homer's Circe of her benevolent retransformation; and in contrast to Odysseus' companions who emerge younger and more handsome (*Odyssey* 10.395–6), Acrasia's victims are shown as unmanly and shamed.

In *FQ* III, where heroic virtue is female, the Circe figure, Busirane, is conversely male. Appropriately, with his Ovidian tapestries, he is an Ovidian Circe, one who reverses his charms at the insistence of Britomart's Ulyssean sword (xii 36; cf *Met* 14.296–301).

Cambina (IV iii 37–50) is a surprising Circe. Like her original, she is beautiful and has a demi-goddess mother who teaches her magic (Roberts 1978:435). Good Circes are rare: those of Apollonius and William Browne (*Masque of the Inner Temple* [*Ulysses and Circe*]) are exceptions. The iconography of Cambina is complicated and eclectic in its combination of many mythological figures (Roche 1964:22–31, Fowler 1964:157–9). Spenser has in addition made his Concord a *conjunctio oppositorum* (conjunction of opposites) in that she provides good meanings for the Circe story and reconciles its opposites, Circe and Mercury. Cambina's name plays with Circe's characteristic metamorphic abilities, but she out-Circes Circe in that she effects a benevolent change on her original's suspect actions and meanings. In her hands, the Circean cup stills care and causes amity; the rod calms strife. She is a half-Mercurian peacemaker; *pacifer* is used uniquely in Ovid at *Metamorphoses* 14.291 as an epithet for Mercury. The triumphant reconcilement is that of Circe and Mercury: Cambina holds the former's cup and the latter's caduceus, opposites in Acrasia's Bower. Spenser may have been influenced by Conti's *commistio*, as *commiscere* can mean 'to unite, to bring together' as well as 'to mix.' Cambina is a figure of the way that her meaning is arrived at: she is a concordance of the Circe story. Her triumphal entry as a good Circe with her cup answers that of the bad Circean Duessa at I viii 14.

The Faerie Queene's last Circean figure is Mutabilitie. Like Circe she is beautiful, has the golden wand which Renaissance authors attribute to Circe (see Alciati, Emblem 76), magically dims the moon, and encounters her old opponent Mercury (VII vi 14–18). Her constant epithet 'Titanesse' (Spenser's coinage) echoes Ovid's favorite use in the *Metamorphoses* of Circe's patronymic: *Titania*, daughter of the Titan Sun. Mutabilitie threatens to take Circe's power of change to cosmic proportions. Cambina offered a positive aspect of Circean change: Mutabilitie has to learn that she is unaware of one of Circe's profound significances. All her witnesses, including the elements and the seasons (the interpretation of Circe's attendants in Conti and Sandys respectively) testify to the constancy of change. Nature's verdict (VII vii 58) reveals to Mutabilitie that change is also a generative process, that 'when one thing decays, something else with the same form never arises, but something very different' (Conti 6.6). Like that of the *Ballet comique de la reine* (Paris 1582), *The Faerie Queene*'s last Circe is in fact one aspect of Nature in disguise.

GARETH ROBERTS

D.C. Allen 1970; Leonora Leet Brodwin 1974 'Milton and the Renaissance Circe' *MiltonS* 6:21–83; Bush 1968; Durling 1954; Fowler 1964; Giamatti 1966; Hughes 1943; Kermode 1971:60–83; Roberts 1978; Rosemond Tuve 1957 *Images and Themes in Five Poems by Milton* (Cambridge, Mass).

cities Of the cities mentioned by Spenser, the most significant are Rome, Jerusalem, Verulam, London, and London's allegorical counterparts in *The Faerie Queene*, Troynovant and Cleopolis. References to Rome far outnumber those to any other city, while direct mention of Spenser's native London is confined to *Prothalamion* 127–9.

Set apart from the natural landscape by the geometry of its forms, the city is a symbol of human community both on earth and in heaven. It often expresses purpose and plan; as New Jerusalem, it symbolizes the goal of a Christian's earthly pilgrimage. Spenser's thinking about the city must have been shaped first by experience of his birthplace, which during his lifetime grew in size, wealth, and power to become a capital city of Europe and increasingly saw itself as heir of Western empire, succeeding Troy and Rome.

Unlike other London-born contemporaries such as Dekker or Jonson, however, Spenser does not set his work in London or make its daily life his subject. His idea of a city is more clearly influenced by literary and scriptural tradition drawn from a wide variety of texts. He pictures the city as walled and set beside a river: its walls and gates guard the city from external threats, its river sustains the life within. Yet nearness to a river also implicates the city in mutability, a threat city dwellers have traditionally sought to counter by centering their cities around monuments built to stand against change. Towers – from the prosaic bricky tower of the Temple in *Prothalamion* to the crystal tower of Cleopolis (*FQ* I x 58) and the more splendidly heavenly towers of New Jerusalem (55) – figure prominently as images of spiritual aspiration, of splendor and pride; collapsed, like the tower of Babel alluded to in II ix 21, they necessarily express poignant vulnerability to time and fortune.

Though a city might contain a court at its center, for Spenser's contemporaries 'court' and 'city' usually signified different places and contrasting ways of life. London, 'the City,' municipally independent from the royal city of Westminster, stood for an aggressive mercantilism which was often at odds with what its citizens perceived as court interests and values. We may trace this distinction in Venus' search for Cupid as she moves from courts to cities to the country (III vi 13–15), and in Calidore's similar pursuit of the Blatant Beast (VI ix 3); both suggest movement away from the center and down a hierarchical scale. Other references to the city suggest that Spenser identified courts with cities as seats of power and culture, perhaps to emphasize his culture's continuity with the urbanism of antiquity. The conventional debates between city and country (as in Horace's *Satires* and *Epistles*), or between court and country in Renaissance poetry, have little interest for him, even in *The Shepheardes Calender* where we should expect to find them. Elements of those debates appear obliquely in *Julye*, where the contrast between the goatherd's proud hill and the shepherd's lowly plain redefines the city-country debate between self-assertion and retirement; and in *October*, where two classical buildings on a hilltop evoke the ancient city-state and the secular immortality it offered to poets like Virgil who chose heroic over pastoral themes (the illustrations to the two eclogues further emphasize the contrast). The idea of a city also informs the Renaissance debate over art and nature, the city being seen as both a work of art and a center for art. Spenser treats this theme idyllically in *FQ* IV xi: the pageantry of town-bearing rivers at the marriage of Thames and Medway idealizes the interrelationship of nature, power, and culture in English life.

But Spenser is less interested in city-country or court-country oppositions than in the contrasting cities in *The Faerie Queene* which become symbolic of contrasting ethical and social possibilities. His idea of the city thus defines itself not in pastoral terms as nature's antithesis but in the terms of Renaissance civic humanism as transmitted by such early influences on him as Petrarch and du Bellay. The humanists took from the ancients a vision of civilized life as essentially urban: only a city enabled man to realize his highest earthly potential. Citizenship involved allegiance to an external order but, more important, to an ideal state of being, a city within (see Plato *Republic* 592B). From Scripture and Augustine, the humanists inherited a concept of antithetical cities, the earthly city and the city of God, and the hope of improving man's city while living as a citizen of God's. The sixteenth-century innovation of entertaining belief in an ideal earthly city led to the proliferation of ideal city-plans and the sweeping redesign of cities. Awareness of the defects of the actual city led to a revival of literary and religious utopianism as expressed in More's Utopia or Campanella's City of the Sun.

Renaissance urbanism touches Spenser most closely in the fascination he shares with the humanists in the ruins of Rome as an image of decay and loss yet also of enduring secular inspiration and cultural continuity. Cities become for him powerful representations of his own imaginative conflict between melancholy preoccupation with mutability and stronger hopes for significant endeavor. His early pessimism about urban civilization surfaces in the crude images of destruction which climax every vision in *Theatre for Worldlings*. In *Ruines of Time*, he uses a fallen ancient city, Verulam, to compare the city's monumental function – namely, to provide a physical record of accomplishment – with the similar role of poetry to commemorate heroic deeds. The doleful female who personifies Verulam emphasizes the melancholy aspect of ruins, for the city has sunk into almost complete oblivion. As a negative exemplum, she expresses the fears Spenser has for his own culture, and suggests that even a Sidney can be redeemed for memory only by strenuous poetic effort. In *The Faerie Queene*, the fate of a city seems far less important than in the poems of Homer, Virgil, and Tasso which Spenser imitates. The city is replaced as locus of action with the psychological landscape of romance tradition, or with individual, personalized social units such as courts, castles, and caves.

Yet his emphasis on fame in the Letter to Raleigh indicates the important role in Books I–III for the idea of a city: secular immortality was the supreme gift the ancient city-state had to offer its heroes. He provides two earthly cities, Cleopolis (city of fame) and Troynovant (New Troy or London). With respect to the former, he adapts the Augustinian contrast between earthly and heavenly cities to clarify the relation of faith and good works: the heavenly city that Redcrosse sees in the distance far outshines the earthly Cleopolis, but the earthly fame which Gloriana offers in reward for deeds is a good in itself. Only after achieving earthly fame by aiding Una may Redcrosse bend his 'painefull pilgrimage' to the heavenly Jerusalem (I x 55–61). This resolution allows Spenser to develop contrasts between the two earthly cities in *FQ* II x, when Guyon and Arthur read their nations' historical chronicles in the tower of Alma's castle, the repository of memory. With its golden wall, crystal tower, and bridge of brass, Cleopolis has the monuments characteristic of the ideal Renaissance city, and its history is the record of progressive achievement of the civilized arts under magnanimous rulers. The story of Troynovant implies a darker reading of history. The British chronicle is far less city-centered than the Elfin one, and far more filled with strife. Troynovant takes on a greater glory in *FQ* III ix when Britomart and Paridell celebrate the Trojan renewal. Yet Spenser sounds a warning note about the destructive strength of the forces which the city must hold in check, forces represented in nature by the river's 'roring rage' (45) and in society by Paridell's parodic reenactment of Trojan history in the seduction of Hellenore.

Classical traditions of the city inform other aspects of *The Faerie Queene*. The personification of the city as heroic woman appears in a reference to Cybele (IV xi 28), and influences Spenser's treatment of the contrasted Duessa and Una – whore and bride, Babylon and Jerusalem. Many individual buildings, particularly turreted castles, function as small cities linked to the larger structure by their common geometry and human manufacture. The working of the human body in the house of Temperance (II ix) is an allegory of the ideal body politic. The city's promise of secular immortality traditionally symbolized by honorable entombment is mirrored negatively by the dungeon in the house of Pride (I v 47–9), where proud city founders like Nimrod and Antiochus, and Roman heroes from Romulus to Antony, are thrown in heaps. These negative reminders of the earthly city suggest why Spenser presents Cleopolis, and Gloriana herself, indirectly. The ideal earthly city is less a place attained than a social ideal forever in the making.

GAIL KERN PASTER

Giulio C. Argan 1969 *The Renaissance City* tr Susan Edna Bassett (New York); Hans Baron 1968 *From Petrarch to Leonardo Bruni* (Chicago); Garin 1969; Manley 1982; Manley 1986; Gail Kern Paster 1985 *The Idea of the City in the Age of Shakespeare* (Athens, Ga).

Claribell The name of three minor characters in *The Faerie Queene*, two female and one male. The name (from L *clarus* + *bellus*) connotes fame and beauty or possibly, in one case, fame and war (L *bellum*).

Claribell (1) is the unfortunate noblewoman who is wrongly slain by her jealous lover Phedon (II iv 16–36). Famous for her beauty, she belongs to the familiar literary type of the slandered bride. Spenser probably borrowed her story from that of Ginevra and Ariodante in Ariosto (*Orlando furioso* 4–6), as mediated by Bandello, Belleforest, and possibly Turbervile. Shakespeare later borrowed Claribell's story for his Hero in *Much Ado about Nothing* (see Potts 1958:49–51), and he may have given Spenser's name for her to Ferdinand's sister in *The Tempest* (II i 245).

Claribell (2) is one of a quartet of warring knights pacified by Arthur in *FQ* IV ix 20–40. Second in an ascending scale of improper attitudes toward sexual love beginning with 'sterne *Druon*,' who eschews it altogether, 'lewd *Claribell*' loves 'out of measure'; but he is not fickle like 'Love-lavish *Blandamour*' nor promiscuous yet indifferent like 'lustfull *Paridell*.' These warriors are first encountered by the chaste Britomart and 'gentle' Scudamour, who watch them clash like the four contending winds released by Aeolus. This simile suggests other versions of the Pythagorean tetrad that governs the design of Book IV. Sometimes Claribell is allied with Druon against Blandamour and Paridell, so that two who are constant with respect to love oppose two who are not. Sometimes he joins with Blandamour against Druon and Paridell, so that those who value love oppose those who do not. Later, Arthur intervenes to aid Britomart and Scudamour, who had been attacked by the four; and he is about to punish them for their follies when Britomart and Scudamour pacify him. Since Amoret accompanies Arthur, the resolution may be viewed as the displacement of an original chaotic tetrad by a more harmonious double one.

Claribell (3) is the mother of Pastorella, with whom she is reunited in VI xii 3–22. Like Claribell (1), she is the beautiful daughter of a famous lord; she loves and is loved by a somewhat lowlier knight. But in this instance the father opposes the match, for like other tyrannical fathers in Spenser (eg, the father of Priscilla in VI iii and 'old *Mole*' in *Colin Clout* 104–55), he has higher marital aspirations for his child. Hence, he casts the lovers into prison, where they nevertheless succeed in consummating their love. The fruit of this union, born in bondage, is Pastorella, who, like Perdita in Shakespeare's *Winter's Tale*, is 'Delivered to [a] handmayd,' left exposed in a wild place, fostered by a shepherd, and later wooed by a noble youth. Meanwhile, Claribell and Bellamour are released upon the death of her father and marry. As is typical in pastoral romances about royal foundlings, during her visit with Calidore the handmaid Melissa recognizes Pastorella by her birthmark and tells Claribell the whole story, whereupon parents and child are reunited. The last of many tales in Book VI of the vicissitudes of lovers, Claribell's story seems to vindicate true love even when that love challenges parental authority.

Apart from their common fame with regard to beauty, there is little to connect these three characters who bear the same name. The name of Claribell (3)'s lover and husband, Bellamour, supplies a slight link with Claribell (2) through the latter's association with both Blandamour and Scudamour. Nevertheless, the three Claribells seem to constitute a progressively optimistic view of love. Claribell (1), abused by a friend, is killed by her lover. Claribell (2) misuses love but is corrected and assimilated to a larger pattern of concordant friendship. Through her steadfastness, Claribell (3) is eventually united with her lover, both are reunited with their child, and their love itself is reconciled with society at large.

JOHN D. BERNARD

Clarinda (L *clarus* renowned) Messenger and maidservant to the Amazon queen Radigund, who entrusts her to act as go-between in her abortive affair with the captive Artegall (*FQ* V iv-v). Her name may recall Tasso's woman warrior Clorinda; or *clarion*, in reference to her role as spokesman, and perhaps to her 'sounding loud a Trumpet from the wall' (iv 50; cf also the other Latin meanings of *clarus* 'loud, bright'). Initially Radigund's 'trusty mayd' of long standing, Clarinda becomes her mistress' confidant in love; but her role changes when she too falls in love with Artegall. (Spenser illustrates the reversal with images of the fisherman fallen into the brook and caught, and the doctor turned patient, V 43.) All three characters become involved in a network of compromise and deceit. Unable to reveal her true feelings, Clarinda misrepresents the messages that Radigund and Artegall send to each other through her, pretending that each remains obdurate. She violates the trust Radigund has placed in her by trying to win Artegall's love for herself, promising him freedom when she means only to bind him more tightly. Artegall compromises his own honor by offering to accept first Radigund's, then Clarinda's, favors in hope of being released.

Unlike Glauce, true nurse and faithful confidant to Britomart, Clarinda is like the bad nurse who steals a child's food for herself (V 53). Traditionally, nurse figures have played morally ambiguous roles in the love affairs of their mistresses: for example, Juliet's nurse, or Myrrha's in *Metamorphoses* 10.382–468, or Phaedra's in the *Hippolytus* of both Euripides and Seneca. Other analogous maidservants and confidants include Dido's sister Anna (*Aeneid* 4), the maidservant Cypassis who has an affair with her mistress' lover (Ovid *Amores* 2.7–8), and perhaps the faithful Clarice, who protects the lovers in *Floris and Blancheflour* by telling lies on their behalf (for an English version c 1250 see ed 1927). A close analogue to the triangular situation of Artegall-Radigund-Clarinda is found in the *Astrée* of Honoré d'Urfé (1568–1625), where Celadon, Astrée's lover, is rescued from a river by the nymph Galathea, who falls in love with him and sends a servant, Leonida, to plead her cause. Like Clarinda, Leonida falls in love with the object of her mistress' affection; but like Artegall, Celadon remains true to his own lady (1.40–1). In John Fletcher's play *The Sea Voyage* (1622), a similar motif is found: the Amazonian Clarinda falls in love with the captive Albert, to whom she acts as jailer; she becomes vindictive when she discovers he has another mistress.

In Renaissance literature, Amazons, unlike other warrior women, are shown as deceitful, untrustworthy, and sexually unscrupulous. Radigund and Clarinda conform to this pattern. Perhaps because they betray their natures as women in failing to submit to masculine authority, they are unable to be true and honorable, either to the man they love or to each other.

SANDRA S. CLARK

Cleopolis (Gr 'city of fame') The capital of Fairyland (*FQ* I vii 46), which Spenser describes most fully at *FQ* II x 72–3 though he makes scattered references to it throughout Books I-III. He does not mention the city in the second installment (Books IV-VI). It may be a seaport (II ii 40, x 73), probably in Asia, since the Red Cross Knight travels from Cleopolis to Mesopotamia. Elfinan, the second of the fairy monarchs, founded the city; Elfiline enclosed it with a golden wall; and Elfant built the crystal tower of Panthea. Later the magician king Elfinor constructed a sea bridge made of brass, which may have been part of the city. Each new year, Gloriana holds there a twelve-day feast, when knights come to hear of adventures and when the quests of each book originate (II ii 42–3, Letter to Raleigh). Of the court Spenser says little. For the knights, there is the Order of Maidenhead (I vii 46, II ii 42), and Florimell and Amoret once lived there (III v 10, vi 52–3).

For Cleopolis, Spenser drew upon two traditions, romance and humanist. The Huon cycle of romances, which gave him his notion of fairyland, had a fairy capital named Monmur with walls of polished marble that shone like crystal. Ariosto provided the other details. The fay Alcina, who lives in the East Indies, has a seaport and ships, and a golden wall around her park (*Orlando furioso* 6.59).

The humanist tradition gave Spenser his method. In 1514, Quintianus Stoa did a Latin encomium of Paris, which he called *Cleopolis*. In a sense, Spenser does the same for London. The logic is euhemeristic: 'In his account of the origin of the fairy nation, Spenser treats his elves and fays as contemporary historians treated the pagan gods, that is as famous men, whose immortality is the earnest of their fame' (Rathborne 1937:142). Cleopolis is then a mirror of London's glorious past, and Gloriana's twelfth-day feast corresponds to the Elizabethan twelve days of Christmas, during which the New Year came. Spenser invents wonders to convey the quality of this history. The knights of Gloriana's court do not possess special powers, but they live in a city and a land of marvels which intimate their worth and fame, a fame which Spenser also gives them by his poem.

MICHAEL J. MURRIN

closure Though *The Faerie Queene* stands as the longest unfinished poem in English, the aesthetic justification (if any) for its remaining unfinished has not been methodically explored. It is often assumed that unfinished poems would have been finished had the author been given world enough and time, or that they were left unfinished because of errors in literary planning which the subsequent execution was unable to rectify. It would be rash to say that the second proposition has never been applied to *The Faerie Queene*, but it certainly has not gathered a significant minority around it. The first proposition is widely taken for granted. When C.S. Lewis tells us that Spenser's poem is 'of a kind that loses more than most by being unfinished' and adds that 'its centre, the seat of its highest life, is missing' (1954:380), he maximizes the cost of incompleteness. When Northrop Frye tells us that its first six books 'form a unified epic structure' regardless of how much might have been added that wasn't (1963:70), he is minimizing the same cost. Both critics consider closure to be the natural end of the poem. If the end is not attained, the reasons for not attaining it are not thought of as literary reasons. Neither critic thinks of resistance to closure as a significant force in the poem, still less as a force by which the end of the poem might conceivably be dominated.

If the arguments that the poem is satisfactorily closed were summarized, a composite version of them might read as follows. *The Faerie Queene* seems to provide its own specific plan for closure in the accompanying Letter to Raleigh. It can be argued strongly that the six books of the 1596 poem implement the Letter to an extent sufficient to establish it as the poem's blueprint; deviations of the poem from the Letter are no more than are to be expected in a literary work of such dimensions and fall far short of undermining the Letter's status. The omission of the Letter from the 1596 edition indicates the author's confidence that the Letter's principles are adequately embedded in his text. The very first encounter in *The Faerie Queene* (that of the Red Cross Knight with Error) prophesies a closure to which the poem is thereafter committed to proceed.

This dominant view has been only intermittently and largely implicitly questioned. Isabel MacCaffrey finds that 'the open-endedness of Spenser's poem is expressed in a pattern of reiterated inconclusiveness.' The abrupt conclusion of Book IV is a sign that 'the poet has allowed Proteus to triumph over Procrustes' (1976:330–1). Book IV does indeed offer opportunities for a student of the poem's fluidity or even its self-subversiveness. These possibilities are traced in detail by Jonathan Goldberg (1981). Patricia Parker considers dilation and deferral as persistent elements in the poem (1979); such an examination, if extended, could lead to the conclusion that resistance to closure is part of the poem's constitution. The various contributors to Atchity 1972 recognize that the poem's inconclusiveness, manifested in the 'dangling states' of its love affairs, may be an important part of its identity. Susan Fox, for example, proceeds to the extent of suggesting that 'it is probably in its very incompleteness that the over-riding plan of the poem is most evident' (Atchity 1972:29). Angus Fletcher notes the tendency of allegory 'toward infinite extension' and suggests that it can only be overcome by 'arbitrary closure,' a device he finds strongly exhibited in *The Faerie Queene* (1964:176–7).

If the arguments for resistance to closure were mobilized, a composite version of them might read somewhat as follows. The Letter to Raleigh is not an unambiguous vantage point since it is not necessarily offered by the author. Since it does not precede but follows the poem, discrepancies between the Letter and the poem result in the poem's fluidity taking precedence over the Letter's closural undertakings. While the deviations in the three books of the 1590 edition may not seem substantial, they do involve the consideration of other than Aristotelian virtues and the very late assignment of the protagonist's mission in Book III. These deviations are compounded in the 1596 edition by the episodic organization of Book IV, by the shift to social and civic rather than individual virtues, by the accumulation of relationships left in 'dangling states,' and by the distraction from the mission in Book VI being presented as competitive with the mission itself (as at x 1–2). The omission of the Letter from the 1596 edition suggests, not that it is successfully embedded in the poem, but rather that it can no longer claim the applicability that it once possessed. The abandonment of the happy ending to the 1590 Book III is a movement away from finality. When the 'holy day' which once concluded Book III becomes the 'Sabaoths sight' longed for in the *Cantos of Mutabilitie*, the exercise of deferral is taken to its limits. The encounter with Error at the opening of Book I prophesies not closure but the delusive finality of apparent closures. The transient triumph over the Blatant Beast at the climax of Spenser's last complete book is testimony to the impossibility of true closure. The *Cantos of Mutabilitie* may be part of a whole, but they are also a fragment succeeded by a sub-fragment. The disappearance of the Graces from Mount Acidale is followed by the disappearance of Nature from Arlo Hill. The final fragments appropriately offer us the final disappearance: that of the poem itself. The vanishing of the poem is managed with extraordinary skill. A fragment of two cantos is followed by a sub-fragment of two stanzas. The last two lines effect a further diminuendo, from the double *bb* of the repeated *Sabbaoth* to the single *b* of the unrepeated *Sabaoths sight*. The poem's self-effacement enables it to remain unfinished without submitting to arbitration by its purposiveness or by the potentially endless flow of its errancy. (For a fuller discussion of the suggestions in the preceding paragraph, see Rajan 1985.)

Not every Spenser scholar will be persuaded by these arguments, but their cumulative effect is surely to suggest the strength of anticlosural forces in the poem. Moreover, these forces are not to be viewed as obstinately resisting by their proliferation the organizing reach of a grand design. They may have a status not unequal to that of the very design they disrupt. The poem can be profitably dichotomized as pattern versus flow, organization versus proliferation, epic versus romance, purposiveness versus errancy, spatial disposition versus sequential disclosure, and, more modernistically, oeuvre versus text. The typical response to such dichotomization is to assign a privileged status to one term in the dichotomy, thus authorizing it to control our reading of the poem. The second term is then reduced to minor or even marginal status. Critics have so far tended to allow the first array of terms to shape our reading of the poem, but Spenser criticism is not necessarily advanced by reversing valuations and bestowing on the second array the privileges previously given to the first one. Two of the oppositions cited – epic versus romance and purposiveness versus errancy – recognize *The Faerie Queene* as a mixed-genre poem based upon the tension between genres rather than upon their conflation or concurrence. A poem which seems equally committed to contrary stylizations of experience is making a statement about the nature of experience which should not be simplified by partisan reading policies which affiliate themselves to one of the stylizations. The difficulty, moreover, is not fully met by agreeing that an adequate reading should be in some way bipartisan. A fully adequate reading of the poem should be based, not on either array in the engagement of its contesting forces, nor even on the sum of what is discerned from both arrays, but on the shifting line and the altering tensions of the engagement itself as it proceeds through the poem.

A poem which allows as much as Spenser's does to the 'endless worke' of created plenitude cannot properly be closed, particularly if it declines to avoid responding to the destructive potential of that plenitude. At the same time, it cannot submerge itself in indiscriminate hospitality to the multifariousness of the actual. It must remain open but not helplessly open. There must be, embedded in its errancies and intricacies, an ongoing awareness of the design of things, an awareness that persists however much it may be mimetically deflected by the errancies of the fable or (to use Spenser's language) by the diversion of intendment by accident. Thus closure is foreseen but deferred, with the poem remaining receptive to and even infiltrated by the finality which it cannot fully attain. Mutabilitie is recognized but constrained, given status but denied supremacy. The dichotomies by which the poem is shaped remain in an engagement which is part of its identity and which the reader therefore is implicitly requested not to arbitrate. A reading of *The Faerie Queene* based on these understandings has yet to be fully carried out. It promises much to the Spenserian scholar.

BALACHANDRA RAJAN

Kenneth John Atchity, ed 1972 *Eterne in Mutabilitie: The Unity of 'The Faerie Queene'* (Hamden, Conn); Balachandra Rajan 1985 *The Form of the Unfinished: English Poetics from Spenser to Pound* (Princeton).

Coleridge, Samuel Taylor (1772–1834) Like all the other major English Romantic poets, Coleridge was profoundly influenced by Spenser. One of his early poems was in frank apprenticeship entitled 'Lines in the Manner of Spenser' (1795), and its six stanzas show the youthful poet to be fascinated by the language and mood of *The Faerie Queene*, though he here attempts to extrapolate those elements for a love poem:

Sleep, softly-breathing God! his downy wing
Was fluttering now, as quickly to depart;
When twang'd an arrow from Love's mystic string,
With pathless wound it pierc'd him to the heart.
Was there some magic in the Elfin dart?
Or did he strike my couch with wizard lance?
For straight so fair a Form did upwards start
(No fairer deck'd the bowers of old Romance)
That Sleep enamour'd grew, nor mov'd from his sweet trance!

This experiment utilizes the Spenserian stanza, as does a poem to Joseph Cottle published anonymously in September of the same year. Coleridge's later and major poems in the Spenserian manner, however, though they unmistakably display a Spenserian mood and archaism of language, do not employ the distinctive stanza. The matter is somewhat curious in light of the virtuoso use of that stanza by the second-generation Romantic poets, Byron, Keats, and Shelley. But Coleridge's *Rime of the Ancient Mariner* (1797, published in *Lyrical Ballads* in 1798, and without doubt the poet's most famous poem and probably his finest one as well) manages to be Spenserian in feeling, though set at sea and written in ballad quatrains: 'He holds him with his skinny hand, / "There was a ship," quoth he. / "Hold off! unhand me, grey-beard loon!" / Eftsoons his hand dropt he.' The ballad stanza points to Bishop Percy's *Reliques* (1765) as the poem's most immediate conditioning factor. Behind Percy, however, there was Hurd's *Letters on Chivalry and Romance* (1762), which were much indebted to Spenser, and that Coleridge had Spenser himself in the back of his mind is shown by the poem's repeated archaisms. Indeed, the word *Eftsoons*, which was added in the revision of 1802, is especially Spenserian, as Coleridge indicates in a notebook entry of March 1819: 'Spenser, Eftsoones' (ed 1957–73, 3: no 4501). The archaisms were particularly insistent in the first published version of the poem, and Wordsworth objected that 'it seems that The Ancyent Mariner has upon the whole been an injury to the volume, I mean that the old words and the strangeness of it have deterred readers from going on' (letter of 24 June 1799, in *Letters: Early Years* ed 1967:264). Coleridge accordingly revised and pruned the language to the version we now encounter, but its Spenserian debt remains palpable.

Even more patently Spenserian is a second of Coleridge's greatest productions, *Christabel* (1797, 1800, pub 1816), though in this poem, too, he eschews the Spenserian stanza, substituting instead experimental meters and forms of his own. Still, the poem is deeply Spenserian. Like *The Faerie Queene*, Coleridge's poem is uncompleted; like that work, it looks toward an extended continuance; like the earlier poem, this one is a story of knighthood and enchantment, of chivalry and romance: 'My sire is of a noble line, / And my name is Geraldine: / Five warriors seized me yestermorn, / Me, even me, a maid forlorn: / They choked my cries with force and fright, / And tied me to a palfrey white.' The poem maintains its chivalric mood and setting throughout:

They crossed the moat, and Christabel
Took the key that fitted well;
A little door she opened straight,
All in the middle of the gate ...
The lady sank, belike through pain,
And Christabel with might and main
Lifted her up, a weary weight,
Over the threshold of the gate;
Then the lady rose again,
And moved, as she were not in pain.

Indeed, so ineluctably Spenserian is the whole tendency of *Christabel* that Keats was directly inspired by it to compose his own wondrous *Eve of St Agnes*, a masterpiece that pays homage to the Spenserian essence of Coleridge's poem by being itself cast into superb Spenserian stanzas.

Because much of his poetry is occasional, humorous, or experimental, because, most of all, after about 1800 Coleridge virtually gave up his aspiration to write great poetry, there is not a large amount of explicit Spenserian reference in the bulk of his verse. Nevertheless, it is clear that from early to late he was saturated in Spenserian language and situation. For instance, in a late poem first published in 1834, called 'The Pang More Sharp than All: An Allegory,' he writes about the loss of love and refers to Merlin's 'crystal orb' (cf *FQ* III ii 19). A poem of about 1832 called 'Forbearance' begins with the lines 'Gently I took that which ungently came, / And without scorn forgave: – Do thou the same,' which invite comparison to *SC, Februarie* 21–2, 'Ne ever was to Fortune foeman, / But gently tooke, that ungently came.' Still again, in a letter to the *Morning Post* in March 1798, Coleridge prefaced his poem 'The Raven': 'Sir, I am not absolutely certain that the following Poem was written by EDMUND SPENSER, and found by an angler buried in a fishing-box – "Under the foot of Mole, that mountain hoar, / 'Mid the green alders, by the Mulla's shore."' These lines invite comparison with Spenser's *Colin Clouts Come Home Againe* 56–9: 'One day (quoth he) I sat, (as was my trade) / Under the foote of *Mole* that mountaine hore, / Keeping my sheepe amongst the cooly shade, / Of the greene alders by the *Mullaes* shore.'

For yet another instance, a poem called 'A Tombless Epitaph,' first published in *The Friend* in November 1809, invokes 'Idoloclastes Satyrane' in its first line; and some letters called 'Satyrane's Letters' were appended to the *Biographia Literaria* in 1817. The reference in each case is to Spenser's Satyrane who rescues Una from the satyrs.

And as a final example from his poetry, Coleridge in his 'Monody on the Death of Chatterton' asks, in 1794, 'Is this the land of song-ennobled line? / Is this the land where Genius ne'er in vain / Pour'd forth his lofty strain? / Ah me! yet Spenser, gentlest bard divine, / Beneath chill Disappointment's shade / His weary limbs in lonely anguish lay'd.'

The awareness of Spenser preoccupied Coleridge the critic no less variously than it did Coleridge the poet. In his notations on earlier writers (ed 1955:559), he writes of Spenser:

> Of Criticism we may perhaps say, that these divine Poets, Homer, Eschylus, and the two Compeers, Dante, Shakespeare, Spencer, Milton, who deserve to have Critics, *kritai*, are placed above Criticism in the vulgar sense, and move in the sphere of Religion while those who are not such, scarcely deserve Criticism, in any sense. – But speaking generally, it is far, far better to distinguish Poetry into different Classes; and instead of fault-finding to say, this belongs to such or such a class – thus noting inferiority in the *sort* rather than censure on the particular poem or poet.

In this same tone of ultimate praise, he says that

> Not only Chaucer and Spenser, but even Shakspeare and Milton have as yet received only the earnest, and scanty first gatherings of their Fame – This indeed it is, which gives it's full dignity and more than mental grandeur to Fame, that which at once distinguishes it from Reputation, and makes it's attainment a fit object of pursuit to the good, and an absolute duty to the Great; that it grows with the growth of Virtue and Intellect, and co-operates in that growth; it becomes wider and deeper, as their country, and all mankind are the countrymen of the man of true and adequately exerted Genius, becomes better and wiser. (p 545)

Coleridge maintains this tone of unalloyed praise in more specific contexts of Spenserian reference:

As characteristic of Spenser, I would call your particular attention in the first place to the indescribable sweetness and fluent projection of his verse, very clearly distinguishable from the deeper and more inwoven harmonies of Shakspeare and Milton. (p 547)

In Spenser, indeed, we trace a mind constitutionally tender, delicate, and, in comparison with his three great compeers, I had almost said *effeminate*; and this additionally saddened by the unjust persecution of Burleigh, and the severe calamities, which overwhelmed his latter days. These causes have diffused over all his compositions 'a melancholy grace,' and have drawn forth occasional strains, the more pathetic from their gentleness. But no where do we find the least trace of irritability, and still less of quarrelsome or affected contempt of his censurers. (p 548)

Arguing in the *Biographia Literaria* (ch 18) against Wordsworth's theory that the language of a good poem in no respect differs 'from that of prose,' Coleridge invokes Spenser by way of rebuttal: 'I remember no poet, whose writings would safelier stand the test of Mr. Wordsworth's theory, than SPENSER. Yet will Mr. Wordsworth say, that the style of the following stanzas [*FQ* I ii 2, v 2] is either undistinguished from prose, and the language of ordinary life? Or that it is vicious, and that the stanzas are *blots* in the Faery Queen?' (ed 1969–, 7.2:76).

In his *Table Talk*, on 24 June 1827, he says that 'Spenser's Epithalamion is truly sublime; and pray mark the swan-like movement of his exquisite Prothalamion. His attention to metre and rhythm is sometimes so extremely minute as to be painful even to my ear, and you know how highly I prize good versification.' This entry is accompanied by a revealing note by its compiler, Henry Nelson Coleridge:

How well I remember this Midsummer-day! I shall never pass such another. The sun was melting behind Caen Wood, and the calm of the evening was so exceedingly deep that it arrested Mr. Coleridge's attention. We were alone together in Mr. Gillman's drawing-room, and Mr. C. left off talking, and fell into an almost trance-like state for ten minutes whilst contemplating the beautiful prospect before us. His eyes swam in tears, his head inclined a little forward, and there was a slight uplifting of the fingers, which seemed to tell me that he was in prayer. I was awe-stricken, and remained absorbed in looking at the man, in forgetfulness of external nature, when he recovered himself, and after a word or two, fell by some secret link of association upon Spenser's poetry. Upon my telling him that I did not very well recollect the Prothalamion: 'Then I must read you a bit of it,' said he; and fetching the book from the next room, he recited the whole of it in his finest and most musical manner. I particularly bear in mind the sensible diversity of tone and rhythm with which he gave: – 'Sweet Thames! run softly till I end my song,' the concluding line of each of the ten strophes of the poem.

When I look upon the scanty memorial, which I have alone preserved of this afternoon's converse, I am tempted to burn these pages in despair. Mr. Coleridge talked a volume of criticism that day, which, printed *verbatim* as he spoke it, would have made the reputation of any other person but himself. He was, indeed, particularly brilliant and enchanting; and I left him at night so thoroughly *magnetized*, that I could not for two or three days afterwards reflect enough to put anything on paper.

As complement to his opinion on *Prothalamion*, one might turn to a letter of 19 April 1824 where he refers to *Epithalamion* as 'Spencer's delightful Ode, which needs only the omission of something less than a third to be the most perfect Lyric Poem in our language' (ed 1956–71, 5:357). Other critical comments are not so directly to the point, but are not without interest, such as: 'It is, indeed, worthy of remark that all our great poets have been good prose writers, as Chaucer, Spenser, Milton; and this probably arose from their just sense of metre' (ed 1955:416). Or again, he praises Jeremy Taylor by calling him 'this Spenser of English prose' (p 259).

In his notebooks Coleridge in 1803 referred to 'Spenser' as one of the projected sections in his vast but unrealized *magnum opus*. A variant of the projection was contained in a letter to Southey of 1 August 1803, where he says that 'I have assuredly a right to demand more than four guineas a sheet for the *Copy right* of so compleat a work as my Chaucer, Spenser, Shakespear, Milton, Taylor, etc etc will be – without boasting, a great Book of Criticism respecting Poetry and Prose' (ed 1956–71, 2:960). No such book answering precisely that description appeared. Coleridge did, however, render something of its substance, at least as far as Spenser is concerned, in his public lectures. In his notebooks for March 1819 (no 4501) appear several of his critical opinions on Spenser; these emphases are largely the same as those contained in the fragments of his 'Lectures of 1818' (see Coleridge ed 1936, where there are also printed some marginalia on *FQ* contained in a set of Anderson's *British Poets*). In the 1936 edition (pp 32–8), following an interesting and lengthy theoretical discussion of allegory, there appears in Lecture 3, under the rubric 'Spenser,' a discussion that constitutes Coleridge's most extended criticism of that poet. Perhaps a collage of quotations can render something of its character and line of observation:

There is this difference, among many others, between Shakspere and Spenser: – Shakspere is never coloured by the customs of his age ... In Spenser the spirit of chivalry is entirely predominant, although with a much greater infusion of the poet's own individual self into it than is found in any other writer ... No one can appreciate Spenser without some reflection on the nature of allegorical writing ... Narrative allegory is distinguished from mythology as reality from symbol; it is, in short, the proper intermedium between person and personification ... As characteristic of Spenser, I would call your particular attention in the first place to the indescribable sweetness and fluent projection of his verse [here follows *FQ* I iii 3]

2. Combined with this sweetness and fluency, the scientific construction of the metre of the Faery Queene is very noticeable. One of Spenser's arts is that of alliteration [three examples follow from I iii 3, v 33] ... He is particularly given to an alternate alliteration, which is, perhaps, when well used, a great secret in melody [three illustrations follow from I iii 5, 8, 4]. You cannot read a page of the Faery Queene, if you read for that purpose, without perceiving the intentional alliterativeness of the words; and yet so skilfully is this managed, that it never strikes any unwarned ear as artificial, or other than the result of the necessary movement of the verse.

3. Spenser displays great skill in harmonizing his descriptions of external nature and actual incidents with the allegorical character and epic activity of the poem [two illustrations: I ii I and v 2] ... Observe also the exceeding vividness of Spenser's descriptions. They are not, in the true sense of the word, picturesque; but are composed of a wondrous series of images, as in our dreams ... [illustration: I vii 31–2]

4. You will take especial note of the marvellous independence and true imaginative absence of all particular space or time in the Faery Queene. It is in the domains neither of history or geography; it is ignorant of all artificial boundary, all material obstacles; it is truly in land of Faery, that is, of mental space ...

5. You should note the quintessential character of Christian chivalry in all his characters, but more especially in his women ...

6. In Spenser we see the brightest and purest form of that nationality which was so common a characteristic of our elder poets. There is nothing unamiable, nothing contemptuous of others, in it. To glorify their country – to elevate England into a queen, an empress of the heart – this was their passion and object ...

The discourse concludes by describing Spenser in terms of the polarity of imagination and fancy by which Coleridge set so much theoretical store: 'Lastly, the great and prevailing character of Spenser's mind is fancy under the conditions of imagination, as an ever present but not always active power. He has an imaginative fancy, but he has not imagination, in kind or degree, as Shakspere and Milton have; the boldest effort of his powers in this way is the character of Talus.'

In addition to his formal criticism of Spenser, Coleridge in numerous places shows himself to be steeped in Spenser's writings, which he repeatedly invokes for reference or illustration, sometimes in areas far removed from poetry. In political contexts, for instance, he more than once refers to *Vewe of Ireland*. In his *Logic*, he cites *Ruines of Time* 428–9 to make a grammatical point: 'Take, for example, the two following lines from Spenser: "For not to dip the hero in the lake / Could save the son of Thetis from *to die*." Here the infinitive, "to dip", is a substantive as the nominative case of the verb, "could save"; and at the *same* time but in a different relation, it is a verb active' (ed 1969–, 13:17). Coleridge is here borrowing the lines and their use from the philosophical grammarian James Harris. He is more casual in a letter from Germany on 26 October 1798, where in describing the look of some Hanoverian women, he says 'Their Visnomies seem'd like a goodly Banner spread in defiance of all Enemies' (ed 1956–71, 1:431), which is adapted from *Amoretti* 5, and used by Coleridge in other contexts as well. Again, in a letter of 21 December 1825, he quotes three lines (145–7) from *Muiopotmos*.

Coleridge especially liked to quote a certain passage in *The Shepheardes Calender* to describe his own dormant poetic hopes. For instance, in a letter of 30 March 1820 (5:23–4), he writes:

> O! how often, when my heart has begun to swell from the genial warmth of thought as our northern Lakes from the (so called) bottom-winds when all above and around is Stillness and Sunshine – how often have I repeated in my own name the sweet Stanza of Edmund Spenser – [*Oct* 109–14] *Read this as you would a note at the bottom of a page*.
>
> But ah! Maecenas is ywrapt in clay
> And great Augustus long ago is dead -
>
> this [*Oct* 61–2] is a natural sigh, and natural too is the reflection that follows – [*Oct* 73–8 revised].

Coleridge repeatedly returned to these lines. In a letter of January 1826 he says, 'There is a noble passage in Spencer's Calendar in which the sage and learned Poet had, doubtless, inebriations of his Master, Plato, in his thoughts, the "*sober inebriation*" to wit, from the contemplation of the Good, the True, and the Beautiful in the absence of worldly anxieties' (6:541–2). In a letter of 23 May 1818 he says that 'Tomorrow is haunted by the Ghost of Yesterday. I might exclaim with Spenser,' and he then quotes *October* 109–14, adding, on this occasion, line 115, 'But ah! my courage cools ere it be warm' (4:862). The same lines are quoted again in a letter of 6 December 1818, prefaced here with the words, 'Yet sometimes, spite of myself, I cannot help bursting out into the affecting exclamation of our Spenser, (his "wine" and "ivy garland" interpreted as competence and joyous circumstances,) – ' (4:893).

As is evident from the foregoing, Spenser's immersion in Plato was especially congenial to Coleridge. As he said in Appendix E to *The Statesman's Manual* in 1816, 'The accomplished author of the Arcadia, the star of serenest brilliance in the glorious constellation of Elizabeth's court, our England's Sir Philip Sydney! He the paramount gentleman of Europe, the poet, warrior, and statesman, held high converse with Spencer on the *Idea* of Supersensual beauty; on all "earthly fair and amiable," as the *Symbol* of that Idea; and on Music and Poesy as its living *Educts*!' (ed 1969–, 6:101–2). Coleridge returned to this emphasis in 1830, in *On the Constitution of the Church and State*: 'SIR PHILIP SIDNEY, the star of serenest brilliance in the glorious constellation of Elizabeth's court, communed with SPENSER, on the IDEA of the beautiful' (10:65).

But perhaps the finest witness to the overwhelming idealism with which Spenser was associated in Coleridge's mind is a passage in his 'Answer to *Mathetes*' that appeared in *The Friend*:

> I will compare, then, an aspiring youth, leaving the schools in which he has been disciplined, and preparing to bear a part in the concerns of the world, I will compare him in this season of eager admiration, to a newly-invested knight appearing with his blank unsignalized shield, upon some day of solemn tournament, at the Court of the Fairy-queen, as that sovereignty was conceived to exist by the moral and imaginative genius of our divine Spenser. He does not himself immediately enter the lists as a combatant, but he looks round him with a beating heart: dazzled by the gorgeous pageantry, the banners, the impresses, the ladies of overcoming beauty, the persons of the knights – now first seen by him, the fame of whose actions is carried by the traveller, like merchandize, through the world; and resounded upon the harp of the minstrel. – But I am not at liberty to make this comparison. If a youth were to begin his career in such an asemblage, with such examples to guide and to animate, it will be pleaded, there would be no cause for apprehension: he could not falter, he could not be misled. But ours is, notwithstanding its manifold excellences, a degenerate age: and recreant knights are among us far outnumbering the true. A false Gloriana in these days imposes worthless services, which they who perform them, in their blindness, know not to be such; and which are recompenced by rewards as worthless – yet eagerly grasped at, as if they were the immortal guerdon of virtue. (ed 1969–, 4.1:401)

THOMAS MCFARLAND

Samuel Taylor Coleridge ed 1835–6; Coleridge 1912 *Poetical Works* ed Ernest Hartley Coleridge (London); Coleridge ed 1936; Coleridge 1955 *Coleridge on the Seventeenth Century* ed Roberta Florence Brinkley, intro Louis I. Bredwold (Durham, NC); Coleridge 1956–71 *Collected Letters* ed Earl Leslie Griggs, 6 vols (Oxford); Coleridge 1957–73 *Notebooks* ed Kathleen Coburn, 3 vols (Princeton); Coleridge 1969– *Collected Works* gen ed Kathleen Coburn (Princeton).

Colin Clout The most important character in *The Shepheardes Calender* and the central figure in *Colin Clouts Come Home Againe*, Colin Clout also plays a crucial role in *FQ* VI x.

Colin was a lower-class name, often associated with rustics (L *colonus* 'farmer'; Kinsman 1950:17–23); a clout is a rag or a clod of earth. The combination of rusticity and alliteration in Colin's name recalls Piers Plowman, a man of the people and a voice of wisdom both in Langland's poem and in much subsequent didactic verse of the fifteenth and sixteenth centuries. Spenser's use of the name was perhaps inspired in part by Marot's *Complaincte de Madame Loyse de Savoye* (1531), the source of his *November* eclogue; Marot's speakers, like Spenser's, are called Thenot and Colin.

The full name, however, was undoubtedly inspired by Skelton's *Colyn Cloute* (c 1522), a satirical (though not a pastoral) monologue whose titular speaker is dismayed by clerical abuse and the discontent it causes. Skelton's satire would have interested Spenser, and may have influenced the moral eclogues of *The Shepheardes Calender*. Of greater interest was Skelton's Colyn himself, a rustic whose moral vision is enforced by a belief in the unique and almost prophetic authority of his plain-speaking poetic voice. Skelton's portrayal of Colyn is an assertion of the value of poetry in English verse unequaled before Spenser, and perhaps helped inspire the remarkably confident self-definition of the 'new Poete' in the text and commentary of the *Calender*.

Spenser's Colin Clout is shepherd, poet, and unfortunate lover. He is also for Spenser, as for Skelton, an authorial persona: the identification is insisted upon by E.K., confirmed by Spenser's indication of autobiographical intent in the dedication of *Colin Clout* and by brief references to Colin in *Ruines of Time* 225 and *Daphnaïda* 229, and acknowledged by many writers who used the name as a pseudonym for Spenser (see *Sp All* pp 330–1, also Pope's *Pastorals, Summer* 39–40; later uses of the name stem from Spenser rather than Skelton, whose *Colyn Cloute* was largely forgotten after the sixteenth century [Edwards 1981:12]). Spenser's use of Colin is parallel to Virgil's use of Tityrus, as understood by the Renaissance identification of Virgil with the Tityrus of Eclogue 1. The *Calender* portrays Colin as the disciple of Tityrus, though it distinguishes between the 'Romish *Tityrus*' (*SC, Oct* 55), and that Tityrus who is Colin's immediate master in the art of English verse and who is identified implicitly in Spenser's text and explicitly by E.K. as Chaucer. The allusions serve both to establish Spenser's place in the English poetic tradition and to hint at his intention to do for England what Virgil had done for Rome: above all, to produce for his country a national epic, the highest goal of Renaissance poetic endeavor.

Spenser's poetic promise is suggested throughout the *Calender* by Colin's mastery of the art of pastoral song: his elaborately rhetorical lover's complaint in *Januarye*; his lay of Eliza, which creates a golden realm of song, in *Aprill*; the *August* sestina (a form prestigious by reason of its Petrarchan antecedents and its formal complexity); the transmutation of grief into Christian joy through the power of pastoral elegy in *November*; and the catalogue and demonstration of achieved wisdom (a Renaissance prerequisite for poetic greatness) in *December*. In *Colin Clout*, Colin's poetic mastery is reflected in the esteem of his fellow shepherds, in the admiration of the courtly-wise Shepherd of the Ocean (Raleigh) for his lay of Bregog and Mulla, in the favor he is accorded at court, in his poetic revelation of the ideal nature of love, and in his commitment to the continuing celebration of beauty through praise of Rosalind.

The most persuasive demonstration of the power of Colin's art is in *FQ* VI, when the magic of the dance on Mount Acidale is invoked by the music of the shepherd's pipe. Here the harmony of Colin's art is fully triumphant: his beloved (who disdained his music in the *Calender* and *Colin Clout*) is by it 'advaunst to be another Grace' (X 16). While all these demonstrations of poetic excellence reflect on Spenser himself, their more important role is to assert the value of the poetic art which he, like his persona Colin, serves in all humility.

Colin as shepherd-poet, then, represents Spenser as pastoral poet. Yet Spenser's treatment of Colin also contains specific autobiographical touches. For example, Colin's friendship with Hobbinol is, at least in the *Calender*, an allusion to Spenser's friendship with Gabriel Harvey. Colin's gratitude to Wrenock in *December* is a compliment to Richard Mulcaster, Spenser's headmaster at Merchant Taylors' School. Several incidental remarks concerning Colin in the *Calender*, particularly as clarified by E.K.'s gloss, recollect Spenser's secretaryship to John Young, Bishop of Rochester. Colin's journey from his pastoral home to Cynthia's court in *Colin Clout* recalls Spenser's 1589 journey with Raleigh from Kilcolman to London and Elizabeth's court.

Yet Colin cannot be equated systematically with Spenser. E.K. insists on an autobiographical basis for the relationship with Rosalind in the *Calender*, but we remain uncertain whether her loss to the shadowy Menalcas in *June* is prompted by historical fact or poetic expediency. Certainly it would be rash to insist that Colin's renewed lament for Rosalind in *Colin Clout* represents Spenser's continuing despair over a woman he may have loved and perhaps lost about a dozen years in the past. Further, the country lass to whom Colin pipes on Mount Acidale may be as much (and as little) the Elizabeth Boyle of *Amoretti* and *Epithalamion* as she is the Rosalind of *The Shepheardes Calender*. In the *Calender*, Colin begins as a 'Shepeheards boye' in *Januarye* (1), passes through 'yeeres more rype' in *June* (46), and enters old age in *December*. Spenser is perhaps 27 and eagerly looking forward to overgoing Ariosto by writing his *Faerie Queene* when the Colin of the *Calender* is saying farewell to all delights and is rapidly approaching death. Colin's survey of the four ages of man in *December* helps to make *The Shepheardes Calender* 'a Calender for every yeare'; at the same time, it distances the shepherd who has completed his life's career from the poet who has only begun his literary career. *Colin Clout* explores the difficulties encountered and the satisfactions to be gained by the poet who would transmute a fallen environment into a golden world of song. Spenser's concern for poetry is apparent in Colin's words, but probably we cannot assume that Colin's reactions to Cynthia's court are a direct record of Spenser's to Elizabeth's. *Colin Clout* in fact adds little to our knowledge of Spenser's life beyond the details we learn from the dedicatory epistle. And in our last encounter with Colin in *FQ* VI X, where he plays the music which summons the dance and afterwards explains its meaning, all autobiographical detail is irrelevant, save for Spenser's joyful devotion to the mysteries of his art and his continuing belief in its importance to his readers.

DAVID R. SHORE

Edwards 1981; Robert S. Kinsman 1950 'Skelton's "Colyn Cloute": The Mask of "Vox Populi"' in *Essays Critical and Historical Dedicated to Lily B. Campbell* (Berkeley) pp 17–23.

Colin Clouts Come Home Againe (See ed 1912:535–45.) An autobiographical eclogue in which Spenser reassumes the pastoral persona of Colin Clout he had used in *The Shepheardes Calender*. By having Colin tell an audience of curious shepherds about the visit paid him by the Shepherd of the Ocean, the songs they exchanged, his having yielded to the other's urging to accompany him across the sea and visit the court of Cynthia, the wonders and horrors he there encountered, and his decision to return to his pastoral home, Spenser recalls under pastoral guise the visit of Sir Walter Raleigh to Kilcolman, his urging Spenser to accompany him to England, their 1589 journey to London, Spenser's introduction to the court of Elizabeth, her favorable response to his poetry, and his eventual decision to return home to Ireland.

The date of composition is problematic. A number of lines must have been written after the 1591 dedication to Raleigh. Lines 552–5 congratulate the 'noble swaine' who is in 'sole possession' of Charillis (Anne Spencer), words almost certainly addressed to Robert Sackville, whom Anne married in December 1592. Line 543 describes Amaryllis (Alice Spencer), the youngest of the three sisters, as 'highest in degree,' a situation which did not arise until 1593, when her husband (Lord Strange, Spenser's Amyntas) became Earl of Derby. A few lines later (564–7), Amaryllis is described as having been 'freed ... from *Cupids* yoke by fate,' an allusion to the Earl's death on 16 April 1594. In the last of the undoubtedly late additions (432–4), Colin's lament for Amyntas, Spenser alludes to the process of revision made necessary by changes in historical circumstance: 'There also is (ah no, he is not now) / But since I said he is, he quite is gone, / *Amyntas* quite is gone and lies full low'.

Possibly there were other, more extensive revisions. The song that Colin describes as having been sung by the Shepherd of the Ocean may be the poem Raleigh wrote about his fall from favor after he married Elizabeth Throckmorton in 1592. Colin's avowal of devotion to 'one, whom all my dayes I serve' (464–79) may be a 1594 addition intended by Spenser to declare his love for Elizabeth Boyle. His account of 'loves perfection' (835–94) was possibly written about the same time as *Fowre Hymnes* and added to *Colin Clout*. But the evidence adduced for these arguments is far from convincing. The most likely hypothesis remains that Spenser wrote the poem in 1591, shortly after his return from England, that he presented the manuscript to Raleigh in December of that year in grateful return for his 'singular favours and sundrie good turnes shewed to me at my late being in England' (epistle), and that this manuscript was substantially the same as the poem published in 1595 when presumably he was once again in London, this time to arrange for publication of the six books of *The Faerie Queene*.

We know little of contemporary response to the poem, though we do find some traces of its popularity and influence in the pastoral verse of such early seventeenth-century Spenserians as Drayton, Browne, and Wither. But as the Spenserian mode gave way to new fashions in poetry, Spenser came increasingly to be remembered as the author of *The Faerie Queene*; and his contribution to pastoral, a genre which attracted considerable critical attention through the seventeenth and eighteenth centuries, came to be defined in terms of *The Shepheardes Calender* alone. It is entirely typical that Pope praises the achievement of the *Calender* but never mentions *Colin Clout* in his 1709 *Discourse on Pastoral Poetry*.

Recently, however, *Colin Clout* has shared in the general renewal of interest in Spenser. Since the *Variorum*, the complete poem has been edited with commentary by S.K. Heninger, Jr (1970), and by Anna Maria Crinò (1956), who provides the English text with facing Italian translation. While the poem has not generated as much critical activity as *The Shepheardes Calender* or *Amoretti* and *Epithalamion*, it has received fairly widespread recognition as one of the most attractive of Spenser's poems, both for its stylistic ease and for the glimpse it seems to provide of the author himself.

Colin Clout has quite properly been characterized as 'fluent,' 'easy-going,' 'leisurely,' and 'relaxed.' Its style is, nevertheless, the achievement of careful and discernible artistry. When Spenser tells Raleigh that he is presenting him with a 'simple pastorall, unworthie of your higher conceipt for the meanesse of the stile,' he is in part alluding to his poem's adherence to the middle or 'mean' of the three traditional levels of rhetoric; and in part (rather as he does in the prefatory poem to *SC*) he is assuming that conventional Renaissance pose which Castiglione called *sprezzatura*. Spenser is far less prone than most Elizabethans to disavow the importance of his poetic achievement – what initially appears mere self-deprecation on his part is invariably revealed to be the artist's humility before the evident greatness of his art – but he certainly shared the awareness of his age that 'that may bee saide to be a verie arte, that appeareth not to be arte, neither ought a man to put more diligence in any thing than in covering it' (Castiglione ed 1928:46).

Colin Clout avoids the archaisms that help to distance reader from text in *The Shepheardes Calender*, and adopts a language closer than most of Spenser's poetry to the norms of everyday speech. The opening lines evoke a sense of comfortable familiarity that extends both to the relationship between poet and reader – 'The shepheards boy (best knowen by that name)' – and to the relationship between poet and subject – 'Sate (as his custome was) upon a day' (1, 4). The narrative ease of the opening lines, together with the comfortable stance of Colin himself (10–11) and the freedom from care of the shepherds gathered around, 'The whiles their flocks devoyd of dangers feare, / Did round about them feed at libertie' (54–5), serves to establish a tonal background, a colloquial norm, periodically and economically reinforced by brief interchanges between Colin and his listeners. This background unobtrusively highlights and unifies the tonally, thematically, and stylistically varied passages that constitute the body of the poem.

Synopses of *Colin Clout* tend to stress its narrative elements, but its overall movement is more discursive than narrative. The remarks of Colin's fellow shepherds are sufficient to define our status as listeners to a conversation that only incidentally tells a story and to ensure that we are drawn forward by question and response rather than by a linear pattern of events. Its manner is in some ways reminiscent of Tudor poetry written in the native tradition of the plain style, a tradition from which Spenser learned more than is sometimes acknowledged. Yet the lyric flights of Colin's songs of praise would not have been possible for a poet of the 1560s and 1570s, nor would Spenser's remarkably flexible handling of the poem's quatrains. The decasyllabic cross-rhymed quatrain (*abab*) is not an uncommon form, but Spenser's artful denial of its inherent tendency to impose its form on the poet's material constitutes an innovation almost of the order of the Spenserian stanza. Whereas in Barnabe Googe's 'Epytaphe of the Death of Nicolas Grimaold' (1563), one of the better early Elizabethan poems, the quatrains are obvious formal and thematic building blocks, and in modernized punctuation each is properly closed by a period, in *Colin Clout*, the quatrains are often so unobtrusive that their presence may not even be noticed.

Spenser often distracts his reader from a persistent awareness of the quatrain by counterpointing grammatical and metrical divisions. For example, he begins a sentence in one quatrain and ends it in the first line of the next (as in 156–60), or he contains a unit of thought within the second and third lines of a single quatrain (as in 161–2). He also begins the poem with a rhyme pattern that hovers between quatrains and terza rima (*ababcbcdede*, with the first major pause coming, quite unpredictably, after the initial *d* rhyme). This pattern might be variously described as a tercet preceding two quatrains, or as two quatrains and an intervening tercet; but neither description does much to explain how we experience the lines. Its purpose, however, is not to provoke complex theoretical speculation but simply to disarm expectation and lead the reader into a linguistic realm that is clearly artful but whose precise configurations are not obviously predetermined or foreknown.

The apparently simple verse form of *Colin Clout* is, then, remarkably flexible. When the quatrains are not emphasized, the rhyme-links carry the reader easily through verse paragraphs of narrative, praise, or condemnation. By varying the extent to which quatrain divisions are stressed or elided, Spenser gives the poem a kind of musical phrasing, using the formal modulations to accentuate shifts in thematic focus. Quatrain emphasis can be used simply to mark an interval between movements (eg, 676–9), or to signal that a particular movement is drawing to a close (as in the final quatrain of the river fable, 348–51). It can give compressed, emblematic significance to a larger passage of narrative, as in Colin's portrayal of the exchange of verses between himself and the Shepherd of the Ocean (76–9), or in the fearful vision of those who boldly seek their fortunes from the sea (208–11). It can also increase lyric intensity by highlighting a particular rhetorical moment and setting it apart from its narrative and dramatic surroundings, as in the linked series of quatrains in Colin's most elevated hymn of praise (464–79).

Spenser's description of *Colin Clout* as a 'simple pastorall' masks an accomplishment more complex than a straightforward translation of personal history into pastoral metaphor, although there is no reason to question his statement that the poem agrees 'with the truth in circumstance and matter.' The eclogue is rich in allusions to actual people. The identification of Cynthia with Elizabeth is beyond question, as is the Shepherd of the Ocean with Raleigh. Daniel and Alabaster are referred to by name. In the catalogue of poets, Astrofell is Sidney, Amyntas is Lord Strange, and Alcyon is Sir Arthur Gorges (so named in *Daphnaïda*). The descriptions of Harpalus, Corydon, Palin, Alcon, Palemon, and Aetion also seem to refer to particular poets, but considerable speculation has reached no consensus about their identities. It would be pleasant to accept Malone's suggestion (*Var* 7:473) that Spenser's reference to Aetion is an early tribute to Shakespeare – 'Whose *Muse* full of high thoughts invention, / Doth like himselfe Heroically sound' (446–7) – but the evidence is tantalizingly absent.

Most of the ladies in Colin's list of Cynthia's attendant nymphs can be identified with reasonable certainty: Urania is Sidney's sister Mary, Countess of Pembroke; Theana is Anne Dudley, Countess of Warwick, Marian is her sister Margaret Clifford, Countess of Cumberland; Mansilia is the Marquess of Northampton; Galathea could be either Katherine Gifford, Lady Wallop, or Frances Howard, Countess of Kildare; Neaera is Elizabeth Sheffield, Countess of Ormond; Stella is undoubtedly Sidney's widow Frances, now Countess of Essex, and not Penelope, Lady Rich, the Stella of Sidney's sonnets; and Phyllis, Charillis, and Amaryllis are the three Spencer sisters, Elizabeth, Anne, and Alice. Flavia and Candida, not identifiable, are probably general compliments included to avoid offending those who might resent being omitted from a necessarily selective list.

The most important identification is that of Colin himself. Obviously, it is in some sense true in *Colin Clout*, as in *The Shepheardes Calender*, that 'by Colin is ever meante the Authour selfe' (*September* gloss). The autobiographical allusions are undoubtedly an accurate if stylized representation of actual events. But this does not mean we should expect a complete correspondence between Colin and Spenser, nor does it justify our demanding biographical significance from every poetic detail. Colin, like Spenser, is a poet, and he too is an exile in a land which at times is so close to the reality of Elizabethan Ireland as to threaten the repose traditional to the pastoral landscape, most notably in Colin's comparison of Cynthia's realm with his pastoral home (308–27). Yet when Colin crosses the sea, he does so for the first time, and he encounters Cynthia's land and court with an innocence that cannot be equated with Spenser's renewed encounter with England and the servants of Elizabeth – including some whom he undoubtedly met about ten years earlier when he was a member of the Sidney circle, and Raleigh, whom he knew from his early days in Ireland when they served together under Lord Grey.

For all its autobiographical detail, Spenser's purposes in *Colin Clout* cannot adequately be defined in terms of autobiography. The poem's lack of a persistent autobiographical focus becomes immediately apparent if we set *Colin Clout* against such poems as 'Gascoignes Woodmanship' (1573) or Thomas Hoccleve's early fifteenth-century *La Male Regle* and *Complaint*. In these poems, the subject (unusual in medieval or Renaissance poetry) is the poet's own thoughts and actions and his attempts to come to terms with his own nature; his source of poetic coherence is the narrative pattern provided by his own experience. In *Colin Clout*, the narrative element is sporadic and, after Colin's arrival at court, almost nonexistent.

The poem is silent, moreover, about much that must have been of central importance to Spenser. We see nothing in *Colin Clout* of his aspirations or frustrations as a civil servant, and we are told little about his expectations regarding the journey to England. We are not even informed of the heroic nature of the song which Colin presents to Cynthia; that it is *The Faerie Queene* is demonstrable only from information found outside the poem itself. When Spenser arrived in London, he had probably been absent from the city for about ten years, and he arrived at a time when the English poetic voice was beginning to find major expression on the London stage. It is impossible to imagine Spenser (author of nine lost comedies) remaining oblivious to the new strength of secular drama throughout probably more than a year's stay in London; but *Colin Clout* is as silent about its author's experience of London drama as it is about his experience of all other aspects of the city, or about his probable brief return to Ireland in 1590.

The poem's fiction casts a flickering light on biographical facts, but it expects from its reader a certain amount of tact and a willingness not to raise demands more appropriate to an historical memoir. Hobbinol, for example, to the limited extent his portrayal requires an autobiographical reference, is firmly identified for the reader of *The Shepheardes Calender* with Gabriel Harvey. So far as we know, Harvey never visited Ireland; but that should not prevent us from seeing in *Colin Clout* a kindly reaffirmation of Spenser's youthful friendship. In *Colin Clout*, as in the *Calender*, Colin is the unfortunate lover of Rosalind, but to insist that Spenser's treatment of Rosalind provide an accurate commentary on his own romantic affairs is to impose a demand the poem is neither prepared nor concerned to meet. The precise correspondences between its fiction and autobiographical fact are unknowable and were probably never entirely clear to any but Spenser's closest friends; but where we need to know, Spenser makes the correspondence sufficiently obvious (for example, the court Colin encounters on his journey is clearly rooted in historical fact).

All literary fictions are a making new of conventions, and for an understanding of *Colin Clout*, the most important conventions are pastoral. Colin is the 'shepheards boy ... That after *Tityrus* first sung his lay' (1–2), and his poem is in direct line of descent from Virgil's first eclogue, in which the shepherd-poet Tityrus recalls a voyage similar in important respects to Colin's own. Tityrus sees in Rome a city that towers far above anything in his rustic experience, and he encounters there a ruler who is for him nothing less than an earthly god ('erit ille mihi semper deus'). Pastoral is often a vehicle of praise for what lies beyond its normal bounds. In Virgil's first eclogue, as often in subsequent pastoral literature, the lowly viewpoint of the shepherd emphasizes by contrast the grandeur of what he wonderingly surveys. Colin, too, visits a land that surpasses anything known to his rustic audience: 'Both heaven and heavenly graces do much more ... abound in that same land, then this' (308–9). He, too, meets a ruler to whom the appropriate response is akin to worship: 'More fit it is t'adore with humble mind, / The image of the heavens in shape humane' (350–1). The language of Colin's praise is in part influenced by Virgil's fourth, 'messianic' eclogue, with its prophetic celebration of the return of the virgin goddess of justice and the renewal of the Golden Age ('iam redit et Virgo, redeunt Saturnia regna'). Spenser's poem draws not only on Virgil, though, but also on a long tradition of pastoral panegyric, including the pastoral praises of Elizabeth that are a common motif in Elizabethan pageantry and popular song.

Spenser's praise of the Elizabethan court in *Colin Clout* is strongly qualified. Colin sees Cynthia's realm as a place of 'happie peace and plenteous store' (310), and her presence as goodly graced by shepherd-poets who 'do their *Cynthia* immortall make' (453) and by nymphs in whom 'All heavenly gifts and riches locked are' (489). However, he sees the court also as a place of 'painted blisse' (685), 'Where each one seeks with malice and with strife, / To thrust downe other into foule disgrace, / Himselfe to raise' (690–2), a place where love's 'mightie mysteries' are profaned by men who 'of love and of his sacred lere ... all otherwise devise, / Then we poore shepheards are accustomd here' (783–8). The disparity between these two views has suggested to some that the poem is flawed by an essential lack of unity, though most readers do not seem to experience *Colin Clout* as a 'failure.' Moreover, the usual accompanying suggestion that Spenser was unable imaginatively to bridge the gap between his idealistic expectations and his disillusionment with the reality of Elizabeth's court ascribes to him a surprising degree of naiveté. He was about 37 when he made the voyage to England, and he had seen much of the ways of the world and the realities of power. There is in fact no direct evidence in *Colin Clout* that he was disappointed by a failure to obtain some hoped-for reward. Shortly before the poem was written, he was awarded a £50 annual pension, presumably an expression of Elizabeth's approval of *The Faerie Queene*; and there seems no reason to read as irony Colin's words of gratitude for Cynthia's 'everie gift and everie goodly meed' (592).

From Theocritus to the present, the idea of pastoral simplicity has always contained an element of ambiguity, embodying both contentment and penury, innocence and ignorance. This ambiguity can be exploited in various ways. A stress on the negative aspects of the pastoral life leads naturally into panegyric, setting the lowly shepherd before the lofty object of his praise; a stress on its positive aspects leads just as naturally into satire, the good shepherd serving as a measure of the shortcomings of urban society.

In exposing the corruption of the world which he rejects in favor of his native pastures, Colin follows the practice of numerous other literary shepherds, including Diggon Davie in *September*. The shepherd whose journey most closely parallels Colin's is the aged shepherd in the seventh canto of Tasso's *Gerusalemme liberata* (1581), who tells Erminia of his disillusionment with his days at court. (Meliboe echoes his story in *FQ* VI.) But like Diggon Davie and most of his predecessors, Tasso's shepherd encounters nothing truly worthy of praise; the court he describes could never contain a being like Cynthia. Usually, as in the moral eclogues of *The Shepheardes Calender*, pastoral satire is pervasive and views its object from a single perspective.

A few pastoral works, however, do combine negative with positive views of courtly power. The first act of Tasso's *Aminta* (1573, pub 1580) includes both a satirical attack on life at court and a panegyric of the court of the Duke of Ferrara. In spite of some similarities in detail to *Colin Clout*, though, Tasso simply presents a satirical generalization and a particular exception. In Spenser's eclogue, the fallen and unfallen courts are one and the same. Probably the closest analogue to *Colin Clout* in this regard is Virgil's first eclogue which the opening reference to Tityrus recalls. In it, imperial power guarantees Tityrus a life of settled tranquillity, making possible his shepherd's songs beneath the spreading beech; but this same power is also responsible for the violent upheavals which disrupt life in the surrounding fields ('undique totis / usque adeo turbatur agris' 11–12), and which force Tityrus' friend Meliboeus into exile. The ambiguity is central and unresolved. Spenser probably learned from Virgil the potential of pastoral to provide a complex image of urban society, which, though fallen, is not totally precluded from participation in the ideal. While unlike the pastures which are the usual haunt of Colin and his shepherd audience, it is the true center of interest for Spenser and his readers alike.

Any account of the thematic unity of *Colin Clout* must allow not only for the praise and condemnation of the court, but also for such diverse elements as Colin's lay of Bregog and Mulla, the Shepherd of the Ocean's song of Cynthia, the account of the sea voyage, the cosmogony which is Colin's revelation of love's perfection, and Colin's final assertion of devotion to Rosalind. Perhaps *Colin Clout* can be viewed as an exploration of love in its various aspects: the celebration of the court is largely a celebration of beauty and those who sing its praise, the attack on the court is primarily (though not entirely) an attack on its abuse of love, and, finally, both the relationship between friends and that between a subject and his queen can legitimately be defined in terms of love.

It is difficult to understand, however, why Spenser should have taken time away from *The Faerie Queene* only to do in little what he was already completing on a larger scale in the allegory of love in *FQ* III and IV. The fairly lengthy account of the sea journey remains difficult to accommodate to a reading which would place the primary stress on the treatment of love. Considered simply as an exploration of love, *Colin Clout* is disappointingly limited: the poem has little of the psychological depth of the house of Busirane, little of the emotional resonance of *Epithalamion*. Even more important, such a reading fails to provide an overall principle of unity: a recurrent concern with love does not of itself imply any more unity than belongs to any collection of verses sharing a common theme.

The dominant presence in *Colin Clout* is Colin himself, assured and confident in a poetic role the emphasis of which is no longer on future promises as in *The Shepheardes Calender*, but on present ability and achievement. Part of pastoral's attraction for Spenser was the opportunity it offered him to explore in what is essentially a landscape of the mind the idea of poetry itself. *Colin Clout* does not just explore love; it explores love as the subject of poetry. The poem's unity can be partly understood in light of its persistent concern with Colin and his role as shepherd-poet, a concern that makes Spenser's treatment of love in *Colin Clout* something quite different from his treatment in *The Faerie Queene* and *Fowre Hymnes*.

Colin's meeting with the Shepherd of the Ocean, the first stage of his story, is an opportunity for song: 'He pip'd, I sung; and when he sung, I piped, / By chaunge of turnes, each making other mery' (76–7). The meeting is also a coming together of poetic modes. Colin's river fable evokes a human world of considerable violence, a world of desire, frustration, deceit, and revenge. Yet the tale involves no Ovidian metamorphoses; it remains securely within the confines of Colin's pastoral home. The Bregog, Mulla, Mole, and Allo maintain their geographically accurate natural identities throughout a song that is less a warning of the dangers of illicit love than a demonstration of the pastoral poet's ability to transform objective setting into subjective creation: 'this was a mery lay: / Worthie of *Colin* selfe, that did it make,' comments Thestylis (157–8).

The more somber notes of the fable go unremarked, but they suggest the shepherd-poet's potential for moving beyond the limitations of the pastoral world and pastoral song. The desirability of such a move is implicit in the contrast between Colin's 'mery lay' and the Shepherd of the Ocean's 'lamentable lay, / Of great unkindnesse, and of usage hard' (164–5). Like Colin's song, this is a demonstration of poetic excellence: 'Right well he sure did plaine,' says Marin (173). But it is a courtly song and grows out of a nobler soil, a region inhabited by Cynthia herself; and, in relation to it, Colin's pastoral home appears to be nothing but a place of banishment. The Shepherd of the Ocean's injunction that Colin forsake 'that waste, where I was quite forgot' (183) is a direct consequence of Colin's mastery of the pastoral art.

Colin's is a poet's journey, which is one reason why *Colin Clout* does not present us with a more fully rounded portrait of Spenser and his personal or political activities. The sea voyage is a generic as well as a spatial passage, a transition from the known security of pastoral through the uncertain paths of the sea ('Horrible, hideous, roaring with hoarse crie' 199) into the heroic realm which is the proper home of Gloriana as well as Cynthia, the realm for which Spenser originally left pastoral behind in the opening lines of *The Faerie Queene*. But unlike the heroic poet with his 'trumpets sterne,' Colin retains the 'oaten quill' that is the sign of his pastoral calling. He comes not to celebrate heroic deeds but to transform into the golden realm of song the beauteous virtue that inspires knights and poets alike to heroic achievement. Colin's account of his journey is prefaced by the promise of a hymn of praise, an enduring creation: 'Wake then my pipe, my sleepie *Muse* awake, / Till I have told her praises lasting long' (48–9). Since the poem's focus is as much on Colin as on the song he sings, his visit to Cynthia's court also explores the potential for poetry at the court itself, assessing its ability to sustain the demands of the poet's song.

That the court provides fit matter for poetry is obvious both from Colin's own elevated praise of Cynthia and her nymphs and from the prominent role of the poets who (in Cynthia's court if not in Elizabeth's) are the only men of note in attendance on the Queen. The golden court is essentially a self-enclosed circle of poetic praise: twelve nymphs reflect and participate in the heavenly beauty of which Cynthia is the foremost earthly embodiment, twelve poets sing the praises of that beauty, and at their center is Cynthia herself and the shepherd-poet whose song ascends with its subject to 'The cradle of her owne creation: / Emongst the seats of Angels heavenly wrought' (613–14).

But the court is the center of earthly power as well as the center of earthly beauty, and those who seek power all too often pervert the devotion that is the basis of the poet's lyric celebration. It is full of men who pose as servants of Cupid: 'For all the walls and windows there are writ, / All full of love, and love, and love my deare' (776–7). Yet in fact they profane Cupid's 'mightie mysteries' when they pursue love 'with lewd speeches and licentious deeds' and 'use his ydle name to other needs, / But as a complement for courting vaine' (787–90). Love, then, becomes an empty word, an 'ydle name,' in a world that is concerned not with enduring realities but with present appearances: 'Even such is all their vaunted vanitie, / Nought else but smoke, that fumeth soone away' (719–20). Like Colin, the shepherd-poet can express his abhorrence of a world wherein 'he doth soonest rise / That best can handle his deceitfull wit' (692–3); but he is powerless to incorporate its abuses into the harmony of his song: 'For sooth to say, it is no sort of life, / For shepheard fit to lead in that same place' (688–9). Colin's only power is the creative power of language; and among those who care only for temporal advantage, language becomes merely one more instrument of deception: 'For highest lookes have not the highest mynd, / Nor haughtie words most full of highest thoughts: / But are like bladders blowen up with wynd, / That being prickt do vanish into noughts' (715–18). Words themselves become meaningless tokens.

But Colin's attack on the court's abuse of love implies no denial of the value of his own devotion to beauty. When he follows his attack with an account of the birth and power of Cupid, his words seem to Cuddie the evident product of divine inspiration: 'it seemes that some celestiall rage / Of love ... is breath'd into thy brest' (823–4). Colin agrees that 'loves perfection ... passeth reasons reach, / And needs his priest t'expresse his powre divine' (835–8), but he disavows neither the role nor the task. We are reminded that Spenser thought poetry to be 'no arte, but a divine gift and heavenly instinct ... poured into the witte by a ... celestiall inspiration' (*October* Argument). Though Colin's account of love is a poetic and not a theological revelation (it begins in the Garden of Adonis and ends in the Court of Cupid), it is a genuine revelation. '*Colin*, thou now full deeply hast divynd: / Of love and beautie,' comments Melissa (896–7). Colin's cosmogony reveals that 'love is Lord of all the world by right' (883); and though his vision owes something to Empedocles, it owes more to the Christian humanism that is at the heart of Spenser's poetry: 'So let us love, deare love, lyke as we ought, / love is the lesson which the Lord us taught' (*Amoretti* 68). The poet's 'delivering forth ... is not wholly imaginative,' remarks Sidney (ed 1973b:79). Colin's divination of love's perfection is an emphatic assertion of the transcendent value of the poet's art and of the ideals he serves and strives to reveal.

Colin's departure from court implies a recognition that the song of praise cannot accommodate the discordant notes of courtly folly; perhaps, too, it implies a recognition that the demands of poetry and the demands of public life are ultimately distinct even for a man fully committed to both. However, Colin never abandons the poetic allegiance Cynthia's presence has inspired, not even in his concluding role in the poem as unfortunate lover of Rosalind. Earlier he had said of Cynthia that 'long while after I am dead and rotten: / Amongst the shepheards daughters dancing rownd, / My layes made of her shall not be forgotten[,] / But sung by them with flowry gyrlonds crownd' (640–3). Rosalind, like Cynthia, is 'of divine regard and heavenly hew' (933). In *The Shepheardes Calender*, Colin's unhappy love serves to disrupt his art; in *Colin Clout*, it provides an inspiration and a theme: 'Yet so much grace let her vouchsafe to grant / To simple swaine, sith her I may not love: / Yet that I may her honour paravant, / And praise her worth, though far my wit above' (939–42).

Colin has discovered that his noblest function is not to confront the fallen world but to recreate the golden one in a song of praise that shall be 'a goodly ornament, / And for short time an endlesse moniment' (*Epithalamion* 432–3). It is a lesson which Spenser himself must have found attractive as he struggled to wrestle an intractable reality into the ideal form of active virtue in the concluding books of *The Faerie Queene*.

David R. Shore

Burchmore 1977; Terry Comito 1972 'The Lady in a Landscape and the Poetics of Elizabethan Pastoral' *UTQ* 41:200–18; Thomas R. Edwards 1971 *Imagination and Power: A Study of Poetry on Public Themes* (New York); Shore 1985; Spenser ed 1929:180–90.

Collins, William (1721–59) As the title of his volume of *Odes* (1746) proclaims, Collins was a descriptive and allegorical poet. His odes are addressed to such abstractions as Fear, Pity, Peace, and the Passions. Although the differences between Spenser's slow-moving epic and Collins' Horatian and Pindaric odes are great, it was to *The Faerie Queene* that many mid-eighteenth-century poets including Collins looked for true poetic creativity. The description by Hughes of Spenser's allegorical mode is almost a prescription for Collins' odes: 'Allegory ... is a kind of Picture in Poetry ... indeed the *Fairy Land* of Poetry, peopled by Imagination' (Spenser ed 1715, 1: xxx, xxxiv). Spenser was praised for being the sort of poet that Collins aimed to be, a poet of 'strong and circumstantial imagery,' of 'tender and pathetic feeling,' with 'a most melodious flow of versification and a certain pleasing melancholy in his sentiments' (J. Warton ed 1806, 2:29).

Together with Milton, Spenser influenced Collins' choice of poetic language. With the authority of Spenser's practice to justify him, he pushed his language away from the prose of his day, partly by a delight in alliteration and assonance, partly by putting 'his words out of the common order' and affecting 'the obsolete,' as Johnson objected (*Life of Collins*). His debt to Spenser is never to the archaic vocabulary used by other eighteenth-century Spenserian imitators, but is usually to particular sounding phrases, in which the Spenserian elements may not be in themselves archaic, but which are apt for Collins' own context because of alliteration: *secret Shade*, *shriller Shriek*, *warlike Weeds*, *rudely rends*, *Grief beguiled*, *read aright*, *Spear and Shield*, *bubbling Runnels*, *weak Wretch*, *Grim and Griesly*, *in Robe array'd*, *swelling source*. Collins uses a small number of Spenserian archaisms – *the whiles*, *Salvage*, *watchet*, *elder Time*, *Youthly* – but he adapts words and phrases from Spenser to create his very original vocabulary – *Grief-full*, *throbbing Heart*, *melting Eyes*, *uncouth*, *fatal Day*, *troublous*, *yelling*, *Affrights*, *regardful*, *furious Heat*, *hollow Murmurs*, *Glades and Glooms*, *heartless*, *sovreign Pow'r*, *gentle Mind* (see notes in Lonsdale 1969:365–566 passim).

Collins makes one particular use of an episode in *The Faerie Queene*. At the beginning of the 'Ode on the Poetical Character,' he retells Spenser's story of the award of Venus' cestus, which became Florimell's, to the false Florimell (IV v 1–20). In Collins' version, the girdle, which signifies chastity, could be worn only by Amoret (Collins' '*one*, unrival'd Fair') among all the ladies present, but it was awarded to the false Florimell, from whose 'loath'd, dishonour'd Side' it fell. Collins furnishes a parallel story of the making of the cest of Creative Imagination on the fourth day of creation. This cest, like the girdle of Florimell, can be worn by few; and Collins' poem implies that no poet since Milton has been worthy of it. The ethical significances of Florimell's girdle are combined with the aesthetic significances of Collins' 'Cest of amplest Pow'r' to embody a concept of the creative poet that is largely Miltonic but also Spenserian. This is the most original use of a *Faerie Queene* episode by any eighteenth-century poet. Collins deliberately aims to do something 'new' in poetry, and for him Spenser is not a model but an antique exemplar. ARTHUR JOHNSTON

The standard text is Collins 1979 *Works* ed Richard Wendorf and Charles Ryskamp (Oxford); the edition in Lonsdale 1969 has many references to Collins' echoes of earlier poets. Richard Wendorf 1981 *William Collins and Eighteenth-Century English Poetry* (Minneapolis) contains some discussion of Spenser and Collins. See also Janice Haney-Peritz 1981 '"In Quest of Mistaken Beauties": Allegorical Indeterminacy in Collins' Poetry' *ELH* 48:732–56; Joseph Warton 1806 *An Essay on the Genius and Writings of Pope* 2 vols, 5th ed (London); Earl R. Wasserman 1967 'Collins' "Ode on the Poetical Character"' *ELH* 34:92–115; A.S.P. Woodhouse 1965 'The Poetry of Collins Reconsidered' in Frederick W. Hilles and Harold Bloom, eds *From Sensibility to Romanticism* (Oxford) pp 93–137.

commendatory sonnets (See ed 1912:603–4.) Like most poets of his age except Shakespeare, Spenser wrote advertisements for his friends' books in the form of commendatory poems, a minor verse genre originating with and scarcely surviving the Renaissance. His three commendatory sonnets of the 1590s are of less literary than biographical interest, for they reveal his association with a coterie who published translations of eight continental books, who are linked by the court, Cambridge, and Lincoln's Inn, and who shared Spenser's publisher Ponsonby. In 1595, 'William Jones, Gent.' published *Nennio*; the guess in the revised *STC* that this was the Sir William Jones who later became a judge is confirmed by his statement in his 1594 translation of J. Lipsius' *Sixe Bookes of Politiques* that he was in daily attendance on the Lord Keeper, Sir John Puckering. Two of his books were published by Ponsonby. His Irish service postdates Spenser's death. Sir William was a barrister of Lincoln's Inn, as was his namesake Zachary Jones, now known to be the Z.I. who translated *The Historie of George Castriot, Surnamed Scanderbeg* (1596), also published by Ponsonby. Zachary was Spenser's contemporary at Cambridge, and he dedicated *Scanderbeg* to Spenser's kinsman by marriage, Sir George Carey. The final commendatory poem by Spenser appears before Cardinal Contarini's popular *Commonwealth and Government of Venice* (1599), translated by the Queen's Master of Ceremonies, Sir Lewis Lewkenor, another Cambridge man. It is dedicated to Anne, Countess of Warwick, one of the dedicatees of Spenser's *Fowre Hymnes*. The lines are reminiscent of the poet's two *Ruines* poems in *Complaints*. Although not concerned in the publication of *Venice*, in 1595 Ponsonby acquired but never used the copyright of another Lewkenor book, *The Estate of English Fugitives*. (The *Variorum* editors also include the poet's 1586 sonnet to Harvey in the category of commendatory verse, but this is actually a complimentary verse epistle rather than the commendation of a particular book.) FRANKLIN B. WILLIAMS, JR

Var 8:263–6, 505–9; Franklin B. Williams, Jr 1966 'Commendatory Verses: The Rise of the Art of Puffing' *SB* 19:1–14; Williams 1968 'Spenser, Shakespeare, and Zachary Jones' *SQ* 19:205–12.

Complaints (See ed 1912:469–526. See also articles below on the separate works in the order of their publication:

1 *The Ruines of Time*
2 *The Teares of the Muses*
3 *Virgils Gnat*
4 *Prosopopoia, or Mother Hubberds Tale*
5 *Ruines of Rome: By Bellay*
6 *Muiopotmos, or The Fate of the Butterflie*
7 three *Vision* poems:
 Visions of the Worlds Vanitie
 The Visions of Bellay
 The Visions of Petrarch.)

The genre of complaint (L *planctus*, Fr *compleinte* lamentation, grieving) in England is, in the largest sense, a subcategory of reprobative literature closely related to and in some measure deriving from the admonitory sermon and homiletic literature of the Middle Ages. In the Elizabethan era, it signifies a plaintive lyric or narrative poem, ordinarily in the form of a monologue, expressing grief for unrequited love, the miscarriage of a speaker's hopes or expectation, or the sorrows of the human condition in a fallen world.

Complaint had by Spenser's time somewhat diverged in character and emphasis from its medieval antecedent. Typically conceptual, impersonally corrective, and sober in tone (where satire of the period as a rule focused scornfully, with a great range of tonal variety, on particular and specific abuses), medieval complaint, rooted in the presumption of man's fallen state, emphasized the moral corruption of human nature, the decay of the world, and what Chaucer called man's 'lak of stedfastnesse' (ed 1957:537). An Elizabethan poet's interest in complaint might still be expressed, as in the immensely popular *Mirror for Magistrates*, in the morally earnest contexts of the Falls of Princes, the corruption of mankind, and the theme of *contemptus mundi*; but in the later decades of the century, traditional emphases of medieval complaint were often rendered in the pragmatic and particularized strain (formally classical in origin) of socio-political satire, as in Gascoigne's *Steele Glas* (1576) or Lodge's *Fig for Momus* (1595). Further, the elaborate development over a long period of the literary complaint in Italy and France (and, in England, by Chaucer), together with the continuing influence of classical models, notably Ovid, had demonstrated the varied potential of other approaches to the genre.

One might, for instance, employ lyric or narrative modes of the pastoral kind to lament a lost Golden Age, the consequences of the Judgment of Paris, or the effects of unrequited love on shepherd and nature, in poems like many of those collected in *Englands Helicon* (1600); or prefer sonnets and lyrics in the Petrarchan vein (with its substantively Neoplatonic and formally Ovidian overtones) on the order of Surrey's 'Complaint of the Lover Disdained,' first published in Tottel's *Songes and Sonettes* (1557), to explore the complexities of love, with particular reference to the woes of a neglected lover. Daniel's pioneering *Complaint of Rosamond* (1592) exemplifies an important sub-genre, the forsaken woman's complaint. Recalling such classical figures as Medea and Dido, and deriving immediately from Churchyard's 'tragedy' of Jane Shore (included in the 1563 ed of *Mirror for Magistrates*), it is effectively a new kind of complaint poem, by virtue of its use of romantic pathos and mythological ornament to modulate a serious elegiac tone. Spenser thought highly enough of Daniel's gift for complaint to praise his fine touch in 'Tragick plaints and passionate mischance' (*Colin Clout* 427). The work of the French poet and humanist critic du Bellay, whose early love sonnets had been imitated by Nicholas Grimald (in Tottel), provided another kind of model for thoughtful complaint. Du Bellay's sonnet sequence, *Antiquitez de Rome* (1558), a somber meditation on the proud power and subsequent fall of Rome tempered by recurrent reminders of the poet's capacity to preserve something of value in spite of time's erosive power, was of much substantive and formal interest to the young Spenser, whose first renderings of sonnets from du Bellay's *Songe* (fifteen allegorical 'visions' appended to *Antiquitez*) in the 1569 edition of van der Noot's *Theatre*, were reworked for the *Complaints* volume, where the poet's early translation of *Antiquitez* also appears.

Then, too, the combination by earlier French and English poets of plaintive materials with larger narrative in various ways and to distinctive ends bears significantly on the formal and structural variety of Elizabethan complaint. In *The Temple of Glas*, Lydgate had shown how simple dramatic complaint might be transmuted by the introduction of narrative and digressive elements into a form recalling that of Machaut's relatively sophisticated *dits amoureux*. Whether the rhyme scheme of complaints incorporated into a narrative differed from that of the larger poem (as in Chaucer's *Book of the Duchess*) or conformed to it (as in the *Romance of the Rose*), complaint might serve as decorative punctuation within a narrative considered by the poet to be of primary importance (as, generally, in Guillaume de Lorris' portion of the *Romance of the Rose*); or, conversely, decorative complaint might be of greater interest to the poet than the narrative containing it (as in Lydgate's *Flour of Curtesye* and *Complaint of the Black Knight*). The complaint might even be employed as a functional or motivating force in the narrative. Chaucer, perhaps influenced in this regard by Machaut and Jean de Meun, used plaintive materials in the *House of Fame*, and particularly in *Troilus and Criseyde*, to underscore the dramatic impact of narrative; but he also used complaint, notably in Troilus' soliloquy on predestination (4.960–1082), to emphasize the poignant bearing of encompassing natural and universal forces on the knowledge and experience of individual men and women.

From the outset of his career, Spenser was much attracted to the genre of complaint. His earliest published work, the translations for van der Noot of Petrarch's sixth canzone (from Marot's French translation) and du Bellay's *Songe*, took good note of his originals' sober reminder that in the fallen state, where 'all is nought but flying vanitie,' only grief endures (*Theatre* epigram 6, sonnet 1). The *Cantos of Mutabilitie*, posthumously published in 1609 and presumably the last of Spenser's works, were structured about what is in effect a woman's complaint raised to a higher power, reflecting the poet's dismay in a world 'woxen daily worse,' governed by 'the ever-whirling wheele / Of Change' (*FQ* VII vi 1, 6). The accents of complaint regularly sound in *The Shepheardes Calender* and *FQ* I-III, as well as in the *Complaints* volume itself, which includes plaintive materials of greater range and interest than the publisher's prefatory summary ('complaints and meditations of the worlds vanitie, verie grave and profitable') might suggest.

Entered in the Stationers' Register on 29 December 1590, *Complaints* was printed in London by Ponsonby in 1591. There has been some confusion about the date of this edition because the internal title page of *Muiopotmos* is dated 1590. A plausible explanation is that when the printer of the *Complaints* volume reached this point he reckoned that the volume would be ready for sale in 1590 Old Style, and dated the title page of *Muiopotmos* accordingly (F.R. Johnson 1933). Some of these poems may have circulated privately in earlier manuscript versions, but this was probably not true for the volume as a whole. In a somewhat disingenuous prefatory epistle, Ponsonby takes personal responsibility for collecting and publishing the poems in the volume; but it is probable that the friendly reception accorded *The Faerie Queene* encouraged poet and publisher jointly to undertake the venture. Collations of multiple copies show that the text underwent very careful proofreading during printing; many of the variants suggest that one of the proofreaders was Spenser himself. The epistle has special interest by virtue of its allusions to nine lost works by Spenser.

There is no finally definitive evidence that the volume was 'called in' (ie, officially withdrawn from sale) soon after publication by the authorities in London, on the ground that passages in *Ruines of Time* and *Mother Hubberds Tale* covertly attacked Burghley, the Lord Treasurer. But a number of contemporary allusions suggest that some such official action took place. In an epigram of 1599, John Weever observed that Spenser's '*Ruines* were cal'd in'; five years later, Thomas Middleton in two several works offhandedly referred to 'Mother *Hubburd* ... she that was calde in' (*Sp All* pp 69, 97). It is not clear whether these allusions refer to single poems or to the volume containing them (or, in Middleton's case, to an early manuscript of *Mother Hubberd*); they may even be no more than gossip. Yet in 1592 an anonymous attack on Burghley (whose nepotism was widely known) speaks of 'sufficient matter [of complaint against Burghley] which is not extracted out of *Mother Hubberds* tale, of the false fox and his crooked cubbes'; the allusion adds point to Gabriel Harvey's remark in the same year that 'Mother-Hubbard in heat of choller ... wilfully over-shott her malcontented selfe,' and to Nashe's reference a year later to 'sparkes of displeasure' kindled in high places by some 'substance of slaunder' thought to inform the poem (*Sp All* pp 24, 27). If there is matter in these hints, Burghley, notoriously contemptuous of poets, may very possibly have borne a grudge against Spenser, as Edward Phillips was to assert in 1675, although John Manningham's diary of 1602–3 and Thomas Fuller's *History of the Worthies of England* had spoken only of Spenser's distress in the face of Burghley's neglect (Stein 1934:98–9; *Sp All* pp 90, 253–4, 269). However that may be, when the first Folio of Spenser's works appeared in 1611, *Mother Hubberd* was omitted and offending passages in *Time* were revised; only after the death in 1612 of Burghley's son, Robert Cecil, was *Mother Hubberd* restored to its place in subsequent printings of the Folio. Yet the fact that at least 44 complete or partial copies of the *Complaints* volume have survived lends force to the conclusion that an official effort to suppress the volume was either ineffective or halfhearted.

The nine poems or groups of poems that make up *Complaints* are not ordered chronologically, but with a view to the initial establishment of theme and tone, the decorous allocation of groups of poems dedicated to the three daughters of Sir John Spencer of Althorp (with whose family Spenser claimed kinship), and the matching of original or substantially original pieces with translations.

The Ruines of Time, consisting of 98 seven-line stanzas, stands alone at the beginning of the volume. Mood and structure recall du Bellay's *Antiquitez*; generically the piece combines complaint with elegy and 'vision poem.' Dedicated to Sidney's sister, the Countess of Pembroke, *Time* is at once a lament for the passing of earthly glory and a celebration of the immortalizing power of poetry; a central and lyrically elegiac passage celebrates Sidney's character and poetic achievement, triumphant over death and 'rustie darknes' (349).

Each of three groups of poems that follow (dedicated respectively to Alice, Lady Strange, Anne, Lady Compton and Mountegle, and Elizabeth, Lady Carey) is equipped with its own title page, a curious circumstance possibly reflecting Spenser's desire to present each lady with her own part of the larger collection. The first group includes *The Teares of the Muses* and *Virgils Gnat*. In the former, each Muse successively laments the savage neglect of learning and poetry in a barbarous age. The poem is effectively a literary manifesto that recalls the nationalistic efforts of the Pléiade while insistently warning the reader that to neglect these Muses is to subvert the universal harmony they communicate to mankind. *Gnat*, 'long since dedicated' to the Earl of Leicester, is an artful adaptation in ottava rima of the pseudo-Virgilian pastoral *Culex*; a prefatory sonnet associates 'this Gnatts complaint' with some unidentified injustice suffered by the poet at Leicester's instance.

Prosopopoia [Gr 'a personification'] *or Mother Hubberds Tale* and *Ruines of Rome, by Bellay* make up a second group. The pentameter couplets of *Mother Hubberd*, Spenser's only full-length satire, recount the adventures of an Ape and a Fox (thought to glance at Simier, agent of the French Duc d'Alençon, and at Burghley; and more largely to figure the brutishness and craft of natural man; see *Var* 8:568–80), whose ability to outface all comers in social, ecclesiastical, and courtly realms enables them to prosper until they are brought down by 'high *Jove*' (1225). Plaintive elements are relatively muted in this combination of beast fable and *états-de-monde* literature; but the poem, at first blush something of a maverick in Spenser's gallery of complaints, points to causes of social ills as other poems in the volume grieve for their effects. *Rome*, notable primarily for its verbal and thematic influence on Shakespeare's sonnets (Hieatt 1983), is an early rendering of du Bellay's *Antiquitez*: Spenser substitutes the English form for his original's Italian sonnets, and adds an 'Envoy' celebrating the achievements of du Bellay and du Bartas.

The final section again pairs original work with translation: three groups of (chiefly) early sonnets keep company with the relatively sophisticated *Muiopotmos, or The Fate of the Butterflie*. The 55 ottava-rima stanzas of this delicate and mordant verse narrative tell of the 'faultles' (418), gifted, and pleasure-seeking Clarion, destroyed by the spider Aragnoll, whose envious malice (shared by gods and men) is explicable only in terms of fate or chance. An element of historical allegory may be present, but what matters is the microcosmic demonstration of Spenser's talent for combining genres and making new myths from old, as he draws on classical epic, Chaucer, and Ovid to make a sophisticated complaint for the complexity of the human predicament. Three groups of emblematic 'vision poems' conclude the volume: *Visions of the Worlds Vanitie*, *The Visions of Bellay*, and *The Visions of Petrarch* emphasize the ephemeral character of earthly power, beauty, and pride. Only the twelve poems of *Vanitie* are altogether original; the fifteen English sonnets comprising *Bellay* include revisions of the blank-verse quatrains translated from the *Songe* for van der Noot, together with new versions of the four poems by du Bellay omitted earlier; *Petrarch* includes six English revisions of the *Theatre* epigrams and a new concluding sonnet, of which line 12 recalls the final couplet of *Time*, hinting at the poet's concern for thematic unity in the volume.

Spenser's responsiveness to complaint in one sense may derive from his connections with Sidney and the Areopagus coterie (van Dorsten 1981:203, 205; Phillips in *Sp All* pp 271–3). The young Spenser's rather self-conscious disdain for 'balde Rymers' in his letter to Harvey of October 1579 (*Two Letters* 1) speaks through more than one poem in the *Complaints* volume, which now and again reflects something of the character and direction of the group's early poetic experiments, together with a fierce contempt for the unlearned ignorance of 'base vulgar' outsiders (*Teares* 567). More generally, the attraction of complaint for Spenser is conditioned by his obsessive fascination with mutability, his sense of the true poet's special insight and mission, and his plain delight in making poetry. While the contrast of lament for the world's decline and vanity with aspiration to the changeless felicity of heavenly bliss may indeed recur throughout his work, Spenser's emphasis often falls less on things hoped for than on things seen: the frustrating counterclaims of love and poetry, hypocrisy victorious while suitors languish, and 'inconstant mutabilitie' (*MHT* 723) everywhere pressing upon a poet and his art. In tragic, pastoral, or Petrarchan measures, complaint offered an apt vehicle for melancholy comment on the theme 'all that moveth, doth in *Change* delight' (*FQ* VII viii 2). Yet Spenser is always alert to the dramatic counterpoint, implicit in the genre, between despair and trust in the poet's power to discern enduring patterns within the flux of human existence, to guide mankind through life's dark wood, and at last, perhaps (as du Bellay would 'all eternitie survive' *Rome* Envoy), by his art to gain immortality. Certainly the influence of du Bellay is pervasive in these *Complaints*: the symbolic potential of his emblematic manner and the subtle force of his musing regard for antiquity, at once admiring and rueful, made a strong appeal to Spenser, who takes special care to underline, in the Envoy to *Rome* and elsewhere, du Bellay's (somewhat uneasily expressed) faith in the poet's power over time.

Spenser the maker, finally, is attracted to complaint in formal and structural contexts. A brief interest in complaint as distinctive entity soon gives way to the experimental combination of plaintive materials with other elements to enhance dramatic effect or heighten emotive force and immediacy. With *The Shepheardes Calender* (notably in *November*), the poet's care for such combinations deepens into a concern for structural articulation, and for the subtle delineation of Colin's character; the allusions to Chaucer that appear in close conjunction with the plaintive eclogues implicitly call up the old artificer's example in the genre of complaint to underscore the power of an art irradiated by Christian faith to triumph over time (*November* emblem). In *FQ* I–II, the lamentations of Una, Arthur, and Amavia, and of Duessa, look on to the subtly crafted formal complaints of Britomart, Cymochles, and Arthur in Book III, which match decorative figure to psychological insight and care for larger idea within an organically disciplined structure. Formal examples of complaint appear less often in the later books, as fictional complaint is transmuted to the poet's own expressions of disenchantment with the times, the customs, and his hopes. Yet the proems to Books V and VI, recording the poet's frustration and dismay in a world where all things 'range, and doe at randon rove / Out of their proper places farre away' (V proem 6), still recall the expressions of the *Complaints* volume, in some real sense their parent and original.

But the volume's importance reaches well beyond its connection with a single poetic genre. The judgment that, together with *The Shepheardes Calender*, these poems are 'the record of Spenser's growth to maturity' (Dodge in Spenser ed 1908:57) is to the point, although *Complaints* stands to the *Calender* somewhat as geological cross section to geographical panorama. The *Calender* is a carefully arranged, decorous, and aesthetically unified demonstration in the pastoral mode of 'this our new Poete['s]' promise at length 'to keepe wing with the best' (Epistle to Harvey). The poems in *Complaints*, composed for various occasions over twenty years, have been arranged, too, but rather loosely and for a variety of thematic, social, and professional ends. *Complaints* presents a profile of the ground from which the major poems spring. The volume provides clear evidence of Spenser's concern to make the literary resources of classical, continental, and native tradition speak again in his art to an age vexed by the enemies of learning and poetry; its poems record his developing capacity to manipulate and combine many genres, with particular but not in every sense primary reference to complaint. The volume is of special interest on three other counts: Spenser's attention to the puzzles and the promise of language, his exploration of a variety of allegorical modes and related structural patterns, and (chiefly) his emerging idea of the poet's character and responsibility.

The dismay that marks Spenser's response in these poems to the decay of learning is matched by his contempt for its immediate effect on the language of poetry: 'rymes of shameles ribaudrie / Without regard, or due Decorum kept,' flung 'to the vulgar sort ... at randon' (*Teares* 213–4, 319–21). The character of the diction in the collection as a whole, insofar as one can distinguish between early and late work, reflects the poet's movement toward a 'dewe observing of Decorum everye where' (*SC* Epistle to Harvey; see Rubel 1941:221–33). The translations from French and Latin, once dismissed as inexact, careless, even senseless, are of special interest in this regard. They illustrate and in effect encapsulate the poet's respect for ancient and modern literary example, his equally firm resolve to make English poetry in his own way, and his emerging recognition that grace and authority in verse depend primarily on constant attention to the delicate play of language. That he undertook these translations indicates a certain sympathy with the humanist insistence (enunciated in du Bellay's *Deffence*) on a knowledge of poetry in other tongues than one's own; yet the resolve to be his own man informs the decision to recast his originals in blank verse, English sonnets, or ottava rima. He is regularly concerned to match diction to idea, choosing language that enforces sonority and enhances rhythmic effect. In the 1569 rendition of du Bellay's *Songe*, his substitution of blank verse for the sonnets of the original may indicate sympathy with the Areopagus' experiments in quantitative verse; yet he took special care to reproduce du Bellay's integration of moral emphasis with poetic conceit (see van Dorsten 1970:83–4). The English sonnets of *Bellay* do not match the linguistic accuracy of 1569; but Spenser's changes in diction make for increased smoothness and rhythm, appropriate to the reintroduction of rhyme: thus, poetic considerations govern these very Elizabethan revisions. Even in the early and in itself unremarkable *Rome*, when Spenser stumbles or falls short in the effort to capture the tonal effects of his original, one sees the poet reaching for *le mot juste* (see Prescott 1978:49; also Hall 1974).

Gnat represents a real advance: something between translation and paraphrase, the poem effectively combines reasonable accuracy with elaborative passages that conform to the original idea yet accord with tolerant Elizabethan taste in this kind. The relaxed character of Spenser's approach to his task in *Gnat* anticipates the confident control of his adaptations and imitations of French and Italian poetry in *Amoretti* and *The Faerie Queene*. In fact, even those poems in *Complaints* particularly concerned to deplore the decline of poetry by implication affirm the capacity of true poets who look to past example and the Muses' aid to compose enduring verse; *Muiopotmos* shows that the thing can be done. Apart from the uneasy aside in *Mother Hubberd* that commoners and courtiers alike may 'the best speaches with ill meaning spill' (716), there is little in these poems to anticipate Spenser's later recognition (given special force in the account of Bonfont-Malfont in *FQ* v ix 25–6) of the ambivalence of language and the linguistic ambiguities that turn in a poet's hand (see DeNeef 1982:118–33).

No single poem in *Complaints* fully anticipates the subtly polysemous allegory of *The Faerie Queene*; but the wide range of simple and complex, historical and moral allegory represented in the volume underscores the poet's commitment to that mode in the Letter to Raleigh, and provides an instructive record of elements that are fused and combined in the superb allegorical instrument that Spenser forges as he makes the big poem. The incorporation of plaintive elements with narrative is merely one aspect of a larger movement: developing mastery of poetic structure keeps company (for allegory, as Frye observes, is a structural element in narrative; 1965:12) with the exploration of steadily more sophisticated allegorical modes. The vision pieces, *Mother Hubberd*, and *Muiopotmos* are of special interest in this connection.

Vanitie, *Bellay*, and *Petrarch* exemplify the early character of Spenser's responsiveness to the iconic and didactic art of the emblem book and the literary reflections of that art form in Marot and du Bellay. Spenser's vision poems are often loosely termed 'allegorical'; but theirs is a relatively closed and static allegory, and their emblematic images are not typified by structural coherence (Bender 1972:85–6, Cave 1982:150). If these poems testify to Spenser's early interest in emblematic modes, they scarcely hint at his immensely varied and energized combination of visual and verbal effects (looking rather to the complex genre of the impresa than to the comparatively simple methodology of emblem literature) in stanza form, image, and delineation of character in *The Faerie Queene* (Bender 1972:112–34, Leslie 1985).

Mother Hubberd finds Spenser directly engaging the problem of structure in an allegorical poem: to identify the piece simply or even primarily as a beast fable combining historical-political allegory with sharp satire of more general application has some point, yet structural 'inconsistencies' must then be ascribed to the poet's haste or carelessness, or accounted for in terms of a natural taste for compendiousness (Craig 1983). The allegory in fact extends also to the maker and his art, specifically to the problem of coordinating multiple narrative strands, even to the poet's care to preserve creative integrity within a miasmic surround (Atchity 1973, Van den Berg 1978). The roughcast character of the poem contributes to its satiric effect and also is part of a dynamically organic structure. Spenser's awakening sense of the challenge and the promise of the special task confronting the allegorical poet informs *Mother Hubberd*, which in this sense anticipates his effort in the several proems of *The Faerie Queene* to discover and define the place of the poet in his poem. Mother Hubberd's discourse, 'so bluntly tolde' (1388), artfully records Spenser's recognition that allegory is both a structural principle in fiction and an instrument of self-discovery.

Muiopotmos, finally, is structurally complex and various: it recalls the emblematic mode of the early vision poems (substituting for their solemn morality an exquisitely decorative art) in a narrative – by turns epic, mock-heroic, plaintive, and tragic – which combines revamped Ovidian mythology with myth that is all Spenser's own. The poet leaves room for 'a milde construction' (*Mui* epistle), but neither a historical nor a 'moral' reading will altogether serve. It may be thought that *Muiopotmos* is equally a celebration of art, especially of the poet's wide-ranging capacity to alter, make, and unmake myth, and an allegory of metamorphosis, dominant in an imperfect world yet everywhere informing and witnessing to the delicate power of the poet's art. Somewhat as *Gnat* overgoes the other translations in part by virtue of the relatively assured and relaxed treatment of its original, Spenser in *Muiopotmos*, confident of his grasp of allegory in these contexts, can allow the structure of his poem considerable freedom: control is matched by a certain relinquishment. That is perhaps the most intriguing sense in which *Muiopotmos* looks to the artistic strategies of *The Faerie Queene*.

The *Complaints* volume is perhaps most valuable as an extended commentary, by way of (often implied) precept and translated or original example, on the poet and his art. The eclogues and apparatus of *The Shepheardes Calender* insistently proclaim, 'See what an English poet can do'; the *Complaints* volume murmurs, 'This, then, is what it means to be a poet.' *The English Poete* is lost; but these poems show, in the light especially of the Argument to *October*, what might probably have been the *Poete*'s bones and sinews. They testify in the first instance to Spenser's strong sense of literary tradition and genre, as well as to his ability to bring something new to all he undertakes, adapting traditional forms and conventions to his several purposes. Ponsonby's epistle does not parallel E.K.'s alignment of Spenser with his predecessors in pastoral, but its allusions to lost poems witness to Spenser's conviction that a poet who expects at length to compose the best and most accomplished kind of poetry must try his wings in many genres.

The Shepheardes Calender and its apparatus had acknowledged the special place of Chaucer among Spenser's literary ancestors. In *Complaints*, this role is assigned to Sidney, now 'mongst that blessed throng / Of heavenlie Poets and Heroes strong' (*Time* 340–1), certainly 'the perfecte paterne of a Poete' for Spenser (*SC*, *Oct* Arg), whose dedication of *Time* recalls that 'hope of all learned men, and the Patron of my young *Muses*,' and whose account in *Mother Hubberd* of the ideal courtier, modeled on Sidney, notes that recurrently to withdraw the 'minde unto the Muses' (760) is to receive infusions of every kind of knowledge. Sidney's account in the *Defence of Poetry* of 'lamenting Elegiac' (ed 1973b:95) may have some bearing on the careful art that recurrently qualifies the melancholy undersong of *Complaints*; however that may be, these poems reveal Spenser's broad subscription to an idea of the poet that on several counts conforms with Sidney's as well as with the prevailing tenor of Renaissance thought. Time would erode Spenser's confidence in the practical efficacy of Sidney's ideals for poetry, but the *Complaints* volume scarcely anticipates that somber turn.

That the poet must be learned E.K. takes for granted in the Argument to *October*, emphasizing in his gloss chiefly Spenser's accomplished rhetoric. But the *Complaints* speak of learning in a larger sense: they show forth an artist well versed in classical and European literary resources; alert to astronomical and astrological lore, the mysteries of number, the interplay of poetry and history, the power of Camden's antiquarian art; and mindful of the huge scope of knowledge requisite for the composition of epic and divine poetry. The Muses in *Teares* often touch on the 'heavenly gift of wisdomes influence' (86) that in bad times no longer informs poetry: Polyhymnia in particular mourns the neglect of learning in terms that anticipate Jonson's description of the poet as one who possesses 'the exact knowledge of all vertues, and their Contraries,' and can 'apprehend the consequence of things in their truth' (ed 1925–52, 8:595, 628).

In the Letter to Raleigh (and elsewhere), Spenser notices the force of 'doctrine by ensample': the poet teaches, and moves the reader to virtuous action, by means of a persuasive fiction. Each poem in the *Complaints* volume more or less prominently illustrates his continuing commitment to that principle, and to the view that the poet by his art helps an embattled society to make right choices. So Calliope, in *Teares*, underlines the importance of rehearsing in epic measures the deeds and lineage of 'old Heroës': 'For if good were not praised more than ill, / None would choose goodnes of his owne freewill' (439–56). Equally, the poet, by virtue of his access to the knowledge of natural forms and divine truth, may safeguard a whole people (499–510). At the midpoint of *Muiopotmos*, noting the dangers that attend our lives, Spenser somberly observes that 'none, except a God, or God him guide, / May them avoyde, or remedie provide' (223–4). Traditionally, the God-guided poet-priest, in scriptural and secular contexts, stands ready to advise his monarch (and so guide the nation); so in *Mother Hubberd* Jove sends Mercury to remind a sleeping lion-king of his responsibilities, while *Teares* speaks of the 'sacred skill' by which true poets emulate their priestly ancestors (559–64, 583). Nor is Spenser content merely to reiterate received doctrine: his revisions in *Bellay* and *Petrarch* point to an early concern to distinguish visionary from secondhand experience, in order to identify the special character of his poetic (and priestly) authority (Hyde 1983). The poet-priest is a prophet, too; through the pervasively gloomy measures of *Time* runs the thematic reminder that, if virtuous deeds are subject all to 'change of time' (465), poetic vision transforms and preserves the ruins of time: 'who so will with vertuous deeds assay / To mount to heaven, on *Pegasus* must ride, / And with sweete Poets verse be glorifide' (425–6). The poet is at once seer and the instrument of a divinely ordered plan.

Finally, Spenser's continuing fascination with the tradition, character, and (especially) the idea itself of the Muses, implicit in the Argument to *October* and glancingly in evidence throughout the *Complaints* volume, is centrally on view in *Teares*, which finds him acknowledging the weight of traditional thought while reaching tentatively toward veiled truths. He was well acquainted with the wide range of commentary on the subject: the Muses in *Teares* are not merely associated with learning or actively opposed to ignorance but are themselves the means of transferring divine wisdom to mankind and (as the poem's numerical structure emphasizes) collectively representative of universal harmony (Snare 1969). Whether or not Spenser in this early poem is already delimiting the Muses' creative functions in relation to those of the poet (Berger 1968a), Polyhymnia's concluding plaint in particular may well prefigure Spenser's quest for an *ur*-Muse, the 'greater Muse' (*FQ* VII vii 1) that subsumes these several Muses and their genres too.

Merlin's glass enables King Ryence shrewdly to know what the future would bring; Britomart glimpses her destiny there. For those who would 'rede' Spenser's art, the *Complaints* volume is in some sense just such a 'looking glasse.' If the volume does not altogether 'shew in perfect sight, / What ever thing' *The Faerie Queene* contains, it is in these contexts a 'worthy worke of infinite reward' (*FQ* III ii 18–21). As an entity, *Complaints* speaks to the matter of the poet's high calling and responsibility in a world where time and change seem to bear absolute rule; while the pervasively somber tone of each poem is entirely decorous for a gathering of 'complaints,' they collectively mirror Spenser's profound belief in the poet's power, reaching through time, to recall and affirm the enduring truth of larger harmonies, higher laws. 'It is not on these *Complaints* that Spenser's poetic reputation rests' (Renwick in *Complaints* ed 1928:179); but the volume is invaluable for its anticipations of Spenser's mature art.

HUGH MACLEAN

Var 8:273–416, 521–627; *Complaints* ed 1928:179–260. Atchity 1973; Bender 1972, esp pp 149–97; Berger 1968a; Bradbrook 1960, esp pp 102–6; Terence Cave 1982 'The Mimesis of Reading in the Renaissance' in *Mimesis: From Mirror to Method, Augustine to Descartes* ed John D. Lyons and Stephen G. Nichols, Jr (Hanover, NH) pp 149–65; Joanne Craig 1983 '"Double Nature": Augmentation in Spenser's Poetry' *ESC* 9:383–91; DeNeef 1982:28–40; Jan A. van Dorsten 1970:75–85; van Dorsten 1981 'Literary Patronage in Elizabethan England: The Early Phase' in Lytle and Orgel 1981:191–206; Dundas 1985:4–6, 95–6, 194–205, passim; Frye 1957; Frye 1965; H. Gaston Hall 1974 'Castiglione's "Superbi Colli" in Relation to Raphael, Petrarch, Du Bellay, Spenser, Lope de Vega, and Scarron' *KRQ* 21:159–81; Helgerson 1983:83–5; Hieatt 1983; Hyde 1983; Johnson 1933:24; Michael Leslie 1985 'The Dialogue between Bodies and Souls: Pictures and Poesy in the English Renaissance' *Word and Image* 1:16–30; Loewenstein 1986; H. Maclean 1978; MacLure 1973; Manley 1982; Miller 1983; Nelson 1963:64–83; Nohrnberg 1976:672–80, passim; Peter 1956; Prescott 1978, esp pp 37–75; Rossell Hope Robbins 1979 'The Structure of Longer Middle English Court Poems' in *Chaucerian Problems and Perspectives* ed Edward Vasta and Zacharias P. Thundy (Notre Dame, Ind) pp 244–64; Rubel 1941:221–33; Satterthwaire 1960:66–132, passim; Hallett Smith 1952, esp pp 103–26, 212–15; Snare 1969; Stein 1934; Tung 1984; Van den Berg 1978; James Wimsatt 1968 *Chaucer and the French Love Poets: The Literary Background of the 'Book of the Duchess'* (Chapel Hill).

Complaints: The Ruines of Time (See ed 1912:471–8.) How does a Christian poet appropriately negotiate between the grief that arises from contemplating tragic images of historical decay or destruction and the joy occasioned by visions of resurrection and divine providence? How does the poet situate an individual's death in relation to the rise and fall of various civilizations? And how may human mourning be turned into consolation, or despair into hope? These are the central ethical and emotional issues that make *The Ruines of Time* a fitting introduction to Spenser's volume of *Complaints*.

Time opens conventionally with a dedication to Mary Sidney, Countess of Pembroke, in which Spenser announces his poetic purpose: in his 'small Poeme, intituled by a generall name of the *Worlds Ruines*' to memorialize the 'noble race' from which Philip Sidney and his sister have sprung. The first section of the poem proper is a dream-vision in which the poet-observer encounters Verlame, genius of the Roman-British city of Verulam, and listens to her lament the destruction of Rome, Verulam, and Troynovant (22–175), the deaths of several members of the Dudley-Sidney family (176–343), and the general decline of poetry itself (344–469). After listening to her lengthy harangue, the dreamer, 'inlie greeving' over what he has heard, is presented with a pageant of twelve emblems (491–672): the first six are images of civic and personal destruction whose 'sad spectacles' leave him 'sore agast' and much 'troubled in my heavie spright'; the second six are icons of resurrection and victory more specifically focused on Sidney himself and apparently offering the dreamer a more appropriate consolation in face of the universal ruins of time. Thus he can return, in the envoy (673–86), to his original intention of elegizing the immortal spirit of his deceased patron as a pattern of civic, familial, and poetic virtue.

The most immediate problem the poem poses for the modern reader is to identify Spenser's various personages. This is especially true of the middle section of Verlame's lament, which refers cryptically to Robert Dudley, first Earl of Leicester ('A mightie Prince' 184), Ambrose Dudley ('his brother' 239), his widow Anne ('dearest Dame' 244), and so on through Francis and Edward Dudley, Sidney, and Sidney's sister. The problem of identification is compounded by the fact that at least three different people are addressed as 'thee' in the poem – the narrator, Mary Sidney, and Philip Sidney. Even the speaker is confused: at times Verlame is the sole voice; at others (eg, 253–9) her voice merges with his; at still others (eg, 309–29) the speaker seems to be Spenser's persona, Colin Clout. Earlier critics (eg, Renwick in *Complaints* ed 1928) suggested that these confusions abound because the poem is a patchwork of previous pieces; more recent criticism, while emphasizing the work's overall coherence, has still not satisfactorily explained these rather basic difficulties.

The three sections of Verlame's lament raise additional interpretive difficulty. Her praise of Rome and Verulam would have been more than a little suspicious to a Protestant audience and may well represent a critique of Spenser's sources for this section, Petrarch's *Rime* 323 and du Bellay's *Antiquitez de Rome* (Rasmussen 1981). Verlame demonstrates, in short, the disordered passions that arise from vain and excessive attachments to fleeting earthly glories. At the same time, however, Spenser may have intended to sketch a metaphoric lineage of civic descent (Rome-Verulam-Troynovant-London) which would give both direction and purpose to social history and a providential pattern of divine intervention within which both the contemporary city and its private inhabitants can locate their earthly responsibilities and obligations. This intent seems to be corroborated in Verlame's lament over the Dudleys. Although her complaint against those poets who have failed to memorialize the family sounds suspiciously like her lament that no historians, save Camden, have properly eternalized the glories of the fallen cities, the more important feature of her history of the Dudleys is that each succeeding generation keeps alive and improves upon the virtue of its forebears. In the final section of Verlame's lament – on the failures of patronage – Spenser attempts to define the poet's obligations and responsibilities to record such civic and familial fame as will serve to incite future 'vertuous deeds.' Once again, however, the distortion of Verlame's perspective complicates the moral lesson, for the poet's task is not simply to erect immortal monuments (even poetic ones are vain, 'Devour'd of Time' 420), but to demonstrate how the past comes to affect and perpetuate 'noble acts' in the present.

The central issue of *Time*, then, is not how to memorialize past losses, whether through lamentation or complaint, but how to use the fact of historical ruin and temporal loss as a positive context for present action. As frequently happens in Spenser's verse, the poet himself becomes the fullest exemplum of that action, and for this reason he focuses on the figure of Sidney. As English hero, worthy family member, and true Protestant poet, Sidney represents a model of ethical action by which others might measure or evaluate their own virtuous behavior. To this extent, then, the poem offers in Sidney a moral incentive to the country as a whole, to the Countess of Pembroke as a surviving family member, and to Spenser himself as heir to Sidney's poetic legacy.

The twelve 'strange sights' with which the poem ends suggest the difficulties in either expressing or interpreting a valid historical and ethical model. The ostensible glories of the first six – a golden idol on an altar, a stately tower, a pleasant paradise, a mighty giant, a great bridge, and two white bears – relentlessly collapse into ashes and dust. They seem to represent images of cultural mythology, of the human will to create permanent earthly monuments. Excessive faith in them, however, leads to a sinful idolatry that tries to deny historical change. The inevitable ruin of such monuments can effect only grief and pain because they are not contextualized by any higher or broader temporal vision. Sorrow is also occasioned by the second set of six emblems, but here grief is carefully constrained by a consistent pattern of ascent and a fuller awareness of temporal progress. The swan who flies heavenward while singing his own elegy, the Orphic harp that becomes a constellation, the coffin borne aloft by angels, the virgin rising to the call of the bridegroom, the wounded knight whose steed bears him to heaven, and the ark that carries a deceased's ashes to glory – all confirm the necessity and the value of mourning. But they also situate that sorrow in each instance in relation to an equally compelling sense of happiness and joy. As in conventional *consolationes*, it is through the careful accommodation of these responses – tragic and comic, fearful and hopeful, worldly and otherworldly – that the poet finds a satisfactory answer to the universal ruins of time.

A. LEIGH DENEEF

Complaints ed 1928; DeNeef 1982; M.W. Ferguson 1984; MacLure 1973; Nelson 1963; Rasmussen 1981; R.R. Wilson 1974.

Complaints: The Teares of the Muses (See ed 1912:479–86.) *Teares* immediately follows *Ruines of Time* and is the second of nine works in the *Complaints* volume; its 100 stanzas are divided into a nine-stanza introduction and the nine Muses' several complaints, each comprising nine stanzas of lament (Euterpe is allowed ten) and a final stanza that serves as transitional refrain (see **Complaints* for a full discussion of the genre). Clio, Melpomene, Thalia, Euterpe, Terpsichore, Erato, and Calliope in turn complain of the decline of learning and poetry in a corrupt age given over to 'ugly Barbarisme / And brutish Ignorance' (187–8); as *Time* had glanced scornfully at Burghley (216–17), Clio and Calliope here castigate 'mightie Peeres' who neglect learning and the arts (79–96, 467–72). The final two complaints adopt different emphases: whether divine wrath or fatal influence accounts for the dark power of sin, Urania can 'make men heavenly wise, through humbled will' (522); Polyhymnia, deploring the profanation of poetry's 'hidden mysterie,' observes that the Queen and some few others respect and exercise an art anciently reserved to 'Princes and high Priests' (568, 560). Yet the conclusion of *Teares* recalls the first and final eclogues of *The Shepheardes Calender* (and looks on to the disappearance of the Graces at *FQ* VI x 18): glancing at his initially 'unlucky,' finally 'hoarse and weary' Muse, Colin broke his pipe, then hung it on a tree (*Jan* 67–72, *Dec* 140–2). These Muses 'all their learned instruments did breake. / The rest, untold, no living tongue can speake' (*Teares* 599–600, 1611 Folio).

Teares exemplifies Spenser's natural inclination (most fully realized in *FQ*) to draw together and synthesize a mass of discrete source materials. His clear sympathy with the Pléiade's requirement that the vernacular poet be steeped in ancient literature is seen in passages that look directly to du Bellay's verse and prose; Urania's account of her 'heavenlie discipline' indicates his admiration for du Bartas' *Sepmaine* and 'Uranie' (see *Var* 8:322–7; Prescott 1978:51–2, 209–10). Whether his knowledge of the Muses derives directly from Macrobius, Giraldi, and others, or, more probably, from Renaissance dictionaries, *Teares* confirms Spenser's familiarity with the tradition. Known only to the wise and virtuous, and forever opposed to ignorance, the Muses, who represent encyclopedic knowledge, transmit divine wisdom (in particular the conception of cosmic harmony) to the souls of mankind. In the context of Spenser's evolutionary historical vision, *Teares* records some dissatisfaction with the tradition of the Muses: culturally fixed and permanent, and in paradoxical consequence not altogether adequate for the poet who must transform and revise ancient myth, these learned ladies may have been considered by Spenser, even thus early, as elemental parts of the complex unity of that 'greater Muse' invoked in *FQ* VII vii 1. A scriptural undersong echoes also in *Teares*, notably in the complaints of Melpomene, Euterpe, and Urania, which recall the New Testament on the deceitful power of sin. Renaissance, medieval, and scriptural elements, finally, are contained within a numerical structure in which nine, traditionally associated with the soul, and with the heavens and angelic virtue (see Fowler 1964:55, 274, 280), is the ruling number, hinting at permanent rhythms within the flux of time and change.

As the Letter to Raleigh bears centrally on Spenser's 'general intention' and method in *The Faerie Queene*, *Time*, *Teares*, and the Argument to *October* together reflect his early concern with the poet's calling and with the springs (and limits) of his creative power. The importance of *Teares* in this connection is often undervalued. If the allusion in *A Midsummer Night's Dream* to 'The thrice three Muses mourning for the death / Of Learning, late deceas'd in beggary,' described by Theseus as 'some satire, keen and critical, / Not sorting with a nuptial ceremony' (V i 52–5), in fact glances at *Teares* (first suggested by Warburton 1747; see Brooks in Shakespeare ed 1979: xxxix), Theseus' quick rejection of this entertainment is decorous rather than meanly dismissive. However that may be, post-Elizabethan audiences are not much moved by the poem's 'dolefull din' (357) nor by Spenser's fervid care to preserve high poetic ideals from the common rout of men. A rage to date *Teares* (and to identify 'pleasant *Willy* ... dead of late' 208) has also distracted attention from the poem's placement in the *Complaints* volume and the range and distribution of its scriptural echoes. 'Willy' has not been identified, although ingenious (not to say tortured) cases have been advanced for Shakespeare and Sidney, and (a trifle more persuasively) for Lyly; the date of composition also remains uncertain. Given the flourishing condition of English literature in 1590, so sharply in contrast with the literary scene ten years before, it may be that an early version of these free-standing complaints was composed about 1578–80, and that some years later, with the *Complaints* volume in view, Spenser revised (at least) Thalia's lament and that of Euterpe (the Muse of lyric poetry and song), contriving that the latter should conclude at the precise midpoint of the poem, thus emphasizing, through structure, the larger harmonies represented by the Muses. The placement of *Teares* in the volume ensures that the ethical and social emphases of *Time* are directly followed by reminders of the poet's 'celestiall skill, / That wont to be the worlds chiefe ornament' (73–4), and of his privileged access to 'sacred lawes' (561). If *Time*, structurally keyed to the number seven (traditionally corporeal, and symbolic of the mutable world; see Fowler 1964:58), celebrates chiefly the poet's role in historical and secular contexts, *Teares*, structurally dependent on the ennead, symbol of soul and the high-ranging intellect (p 274), draws attention rather to the spiritual power that informs and speaks through his art.

The conclusion of the poem is somewhat ambiguous. To stress particularly the force of Urania's 'heavenlie discipline' (expressed in the art of Elizabeth and her disciples) is to emphasize Spenser's essentially hopeful responsiveness to the Renaissance tradition of a Christian muse; the poem then recalls du Bartas' 'Uranie' and anticipates especially *Heavenly Love* and *Heavenly Beautie*. Alternatively, the poem's continuing reminders of the power of sin, the absence from Polyhymnia's lament of scriptural echoes, and the final breaking of their instruments by all nine Muses, combinedly point to Spenser's uneasy sense (apparent in *SC* and steadily more prominent in *FQ*) that time-bound poetry cannot attain to Sidney's ideal of a reformative art. The poem's final line leaves room for still another reading. 'The rest, untold, no living tongue can speake' may be a first expression of the poet's longing for 'that same time when no more *Change* shall be, / But stedfast rest of all things firmely stayd / Upon the pillours of Eternity' (*FQ* VII viii). By this view, Spenser's Queen and her gifted coterie of true believers may preserve a remnant of the 'secret skill' of past ages; but his Muses grieve still, nor merely for the continuing impotence of the poet and his art in bad times: their complaints show this poet's sense of the bounds that irrevocably limit even his 'divine gift and heavenly instinct' (*Oct* Arg) in a world subject to 'wicked *Time*' (III vi 39). HUGH MACLEAN

Complaints ed 1928:181–3, 204–18; *Var* 8:310–33. Berger 1968a; L.B. Campbell 1959; Fowler 1964; Prescott 1978; Satterthwaite 1960; Shakespeare ed 1979; Snare 1969; Starnes 1942; John M. Steadman 1963 '"Meaning" and "Name": Some Renaissance Interpretations of Urania' *NM* 64:209–32; Stein 1934.

Complaints: Virgils Gnat (1579–80 or later; pub 1591. See ed 1912:486–93.) A pastoral narrative in ottava rima: a sleeping shepherd, threatened by a poisonous snake, is stung awake by a gnat, which he kills before seeing and killing the snake; the ghost of the gnat comes to him in a dream and reproaches him for his ingratitude. In the *Complaints* volume, the poem is said to be 'Long since dedicated' to Leicester (d 1588), and is prefaced by a Spenserian sonnet that casts Spenser as the gnat and Leicester as the shepherd: 'Wrong'd, yet not daring to expresse my paine, / To you (great Lord) the causer of my care, / In clowdie teares my case I thus complaine.' The most influential interpretation relates the poem to *Mother Hubberds Tale*, and thence to Elizabeth's proposed marriage (1579–80) to Alençon, who thus becomes the Catholic snake (Greenlaw 1910, in *Var* 8.543–4, 571–5); a counterproposal takes the snake to be Lettice Knollys, Leicester's mistress – 'that she-wolf' to Elizabeth – whom he married in 1578 (Mounts 1952). Spenser's sonnet itself begs any reader who deciphers the allegory ('any *Oedipus* unware') to keep it to himself ('Let him rest pleased with his owne insight'); and the biographical dimension remains obscure.

The poem's strictly literary roots are less mysterious. What follows the sonnet is a translation of *Culex*, a classical Latin hexameter poem of considerable popularity in the Renaissance. Together with the semi-Ovidian *Muiopotmos* (also in ottava rima), *Virgils Gnat* provides the antique grounding for the *Complaints* volume and its genre. (The gnat's lengthy description of Hades may specifically have reminded Spenser of the Induction to the *Mirror for Magistrates*.) Moreover, Spenser's interest in the Latin poem would have been further if not decisively enhanced by its reputed authorship by Virgil. Since Joseph Scaliger's edition (1572), it has been included in the so-called Appendix Vergiliana (which also contains *Ciris*, the model for *FQ* III ii 30–51); Scaliger himself thought it good enough to be the product of Virgil's maturity, though Spenser probably shared the more general conviction that it was a specimen of juvenilia. Some obvious anticipations of the *Aeneid* are themselves among the reasons *Culex* is now largely thought not to be Virgil's at all – perhaps a deliberate though clumsy forgery. But Renaissance judgment (including that of no less a connoisseur than Pietro Bembo) was disarmed by the prospect of viewing Virgil's talent at a specially early stage; Vida indeed recommended imitating *Culex* as training for the would-be epic poet – a start on the famous Virgilian career model, the *rota Virgilii* or 'wheel of Virgil' by which the poet moved from pastoral to georgic to epic (Vida *De arte poetica* 1527, 1.459–65 in ed 1976; Curtius ed 1953:231–2).

Spenser would naturally superimpose his own ambitions on those ascribed to Virgil: 'Hereafter, when as season more secure / Shall bring forth fruit, this Muse shall speak to thee / In bigger notes, that may thy sense allure, / And for thy worth frame some fit Poesie' (*Gn* 9–12; see William Lisle 1628, *Sp All* p 178). The opening lines of *The Faerie Queene* respond to this promise, and it is not surprising to find passages in *Virgils Gnat* reflected elsewhere in Spenser's big poem (notably *Gn* 345–52 and *FQ* I v 34, *Gn* 541–3 and *FQ* II xii 6; see further, *Var* 8:341).

As a translator, Spenser is by Renaissance standards fairly close. There are a few straightforward howlers (an epithet for Bacchus in *Culex* 111 is parleyed into an otherwise unattested 'king *Nictileus*' in *Gn* 173), but many of the apparent misconstructions disappear when checked against the Renaissance text Spenser probably used (identified in Lotspeich 1935 as Antonius Dumaeus' 1542 ed of Virgil's works [Antwerp]; rpt in *Var* 8:550–8). Spenser ventures a few additions of a detectably moralizing tone. Thus, Sisyphus' impiety is specified as a sin of pride manifested in a failure 'to the sacred Gods to pray' (*Gn* 390; cf *Culex* 243–5); and a catalogue of mythic carnage is summed up with a newly Spenserian evaluation: 'all that vaunts in worldly vanitie, / Shall fall through fortunes mutabilitie' (*Gn* 559–60, inserted between the fourth and fifth feet of *Culex* 342). The animus of the opening sonnet and the generic environment of the *Complaints* volume may be felt in the new detail with which the gnat's angry ghost is described (*Culex* 209, *Gn* 325–8). Other additions are merely explanatory in a helpful way – a line is inserted to tell us who Telamon's 'bondmaide' was (*Gn* 490: 'Ixione' = Hesione) – and most are in the mode of genial paraphrastic exfoliation that is second nature to Elizabethan translators. So 'Multa ... gaudia' (*Culex* 120) becomes 'great mirth and gladsome glee' (*Gn* 184), and 'nec Indi / Conchea bacca maris pretio est' (*Culex* 67–8) uncurls into 'Ne ought the whelky pearles esteemeth hee, / Which are from Indian seas brought far away' (*Gn* 105–6). Half a line in the original – 'Ac venit in terras coeli fragor' (*Culex* 352) – prompts a five-line description of a storm (*Gn* 580–4). The cumulative effect of this kind of amplification turns a 414-line Latin poem into a 688-line English one. What happens in the process is less a change in the poem's meaning than an elaboration of its texture.

Even that shift is in its way a form of fidelity. The predilection of Renaissance translators for decorative amplitude usually distorts the austerity of classical Latin, but in this case the original anticipates that predilection to a notable degree. Not everything that reads like expansion in *Virgils Gnat* really is. The final extravagant catalogue of flowers, for instance, has its rearrangements and replacements in Spenser; but there are just as many entries in the Latin list, and the English takes up only slightly more space (*Culex* 398–409, *Gn* 665–80). Spenser's looseness in adaptation dilates on the central mock-heroic absurdity of *Culex*: adoxographic inflation of the trivial, a minimal story line whelmed in tenuously motivated poetic display. If *Culex* is not, in fact, an inept fake, it is a cunningly parodic *jeu d'esprit* with the repertoire of the epic poet's art, loosed from its grounding; and the wisdom of recommendations such as Vida's is that that repertoire is perhaps best learned and appropriated in the spirit of play. *Muiopotmos* may testify to a similar instinct on Spenser's part (Vida also recommends a spider epic), though with somewhat sterner materials. In the case of *Virgils Gnat*, decorative playfulness was merely the most sensible response to the original.

GORDON BRADEN

Oliver Farrar Emerson 1918 'Spenser's *Virgils Gnat*' *JEGP* 17:94–118; Greenlaw 1910; Hughes 1929; Lotspeich 1935; D.L. Miller 1983; Charles E. Mounts 1952 'Spenser and the Countess of Leicester' *ELH* 19:191–202. On *Culex*, see *CHCL* 1982, 2:471, 860; a modern text and translation are in the Loeb Virgil, vol 2.

Complaints: Prosopopoia, or Mother Hubberds Tale (See ed 1912:494–508.) The fourth poem in the volume of *Complaints*, *Prosopopoia, or Mother Hubberds Tale* is a fable told by 'a good old woman' traditionally named Mother Hubberd (see Opie and Opie 1951:321) to a group of friends who, during a time of plague (as in Boccaccio's *Decameron*), have gathered around an unnamed narrator to provide him with 'gladsome solace' and distraction from his illness – even though the poem is preoccupied with moral and civil sickness. Her story so pleases him that he sets it down (in rhyming couplets) for others.

The tale is a series of four linked episodes of disguise, deceit, and discovery, each exposing the ignorance and weakness of one of the estates in sixteenth-century society. A Fox and an Ape, 'disliking ... their evill / And hard estate' in which 'a few have all and all have nought' (46, 141) set out as vagrants to improve their fortunes. In the first story (45–342), the Ape disguised as a soldier and the Fox as his servant meet a 'simple husbandman' who, fooled by their appearance, allows the Ape to become a shepherd with the Fox as his dog to guard his flock. Within half a year, they have eaten all the lambs and most of the sheep, killing the rest before they steal away. This episode establishes the greed of those in care of others and the ease with which they deceive simple folk.

The satire becomes much sharper in the second episode (353–574). Now the Fox and Ape, disguised as clerks, the one in a gown and the other in a cassock, set out to beg for alms. An officious priest who asks for the document allowing them to beg is fooled by a false document produced by the Fox, for he cannot read. In a speech advising them how to gain a benefice (483–544), he catalogues ecclesiastical abuses of the time. The Fox and the Ape follow his advice by becoming a priest and a parish clerk. After they abuse their offices, complaints by their parishioners alert the authorities. On the eve of an official visitation, they sell off their living and steal away.

In the third episode (581–942), the target of satire shifts to the court. Following a mule's advice on how to advance at court, the Ape dresses as a gentleman, the Fox as his groom. Unlike the 'rightfull' or good courtier (described at length, 717–93), the Ape is masterful at deceit, backbiting, and 'thriftles games.' When even the corrupt courtiers find their greed and falseness objectionable, they are forced to leave.

The fourth and final episode (949–1384) tells of their greatest deception, one that needs a higher intervention to be corrected. In the forest, they come across a sleeping lion, and steal his crown, scepter, and skin. After a short argument, the Fox allows the Ape to wear the royal emblems of power, provided he agrees to be ruled by him. Then begins their tyranny over the other beasts: they steal from them by keeping various offices and leases for themselves, by controlling all benefices, and by squeezing wealth from the nobility. When a sheep comes to complain that her lamb has been slain by the wolf, the Fox excuses him: 'For there was cause, els doo it he would not.' In the earlier episodes, the church, the court, and even the simple folk were able in the end to protect themselves, but now the criminals have corrupted the source of authority, the monarchy. Intervention can come only from above. Their gross abuse of rule is seen by Jove, who sends Mercury down to investigate. Mercury awakens the lion, who brings the offenders to public judgment. The Fox is 'uncased' (unclothed); the Ape has his tail cut off and ears trimmed. The narrator, who began with a brief apology for the 'Base ... style, and matter meane' of the tale, ends with another: 'weake was my remembrance it to hold, / And bad her tongue that it so bluntly tolde' (44, 1387–8).

Despite the pretensions of naiveté, *Mother Hubberds Tale* has long been seen as a subtle work of social criticism, or veiled political satire, which may date the poem. Although it was published in 1591, in the dedication to Lady Compton and Mountegle, Spenser says that it was 'long sithens composed in the raw conceipt of my youth.' Although no key to the topical allusions of the whole poem has been found, the mule's description of a court favorite whose 'late chayne his Liege unmeete esteemeth; / For so brave beasts she loveth best to see, / In the wilde forrest raunging fresh and free' (628–30) may allude to Elizabeth's anger when she learned in 1579 that Leicester had secretly married. A second topical allusion has been found in the bitter complaint of the unsuccessful suitor at the court: 'To have thy Princes grace, yet want her Peeres' (901) has been taken to refer to Spenser's treatment by the Queen's minister, Burghley. Yet 'apart from these two apparently patched-in passages, *Mother Hubberds Tale* needs no explanation in terms of personal or political reference' (Nelson 1963:82). Likewise, the fourth episode has been interpreted as an historical allegory of events in 1579: the Queen is being warned of the machinations of the French ambassador, Simier (whom she punningly called her 'ape'), in league with Burghley, her Lord Treasurer (perhaps here the Fox?), who sought to have her marry the French Duc d'Alençon.

Although such readings are incomplete and do little to respond to the poem as a whole, they attempt to answer a question that has troubled historians of this text: was the poem banned? A few contemporaries of Spenser claimed that *Mother Hubberd* offended the authorities and that it was suppressed. In his letter to the reader in *The Ant and the Nightingale, or Father Hubburds Tales* (1604), Thomas Middleton says: 'Why I call these *Father Hubburds Tales*; is not to have them cald in againe, as the Tale of *Mother Hubburd*' (*Sp All* p 97). Harvey's remark in 1592, that 'I must needs say, Mother-Hubbard in heat of choller, forgetting the pure sanguine of her sweete Faery Queene, wilfully over-shott her malcontented selfe' (*Sp All* p 24; cf p 32), brought Nashe's rejoinder: 'Who publikely accusde or of late brought *Mother Hubbard* into question, that thou shouldst by rehearsall rekindle against him the sparkes of displeasure that were quenched?' (p 27). This claim – that unsold copies of *Complaints* were gathered up by the authorities – has been disputed, for there are still 44 extant copies, a high number even compared with books of normal circulation. Perhaps the attempt to suppress was too slow. Certainly the poem was not reprinted in the collected works of 1611, though it was added in a later revised edition (after 1612, the year Burghley's son died). Whatever the exact nature of events, the poem early gathered the reputation of having offended someone in high power, and that person is usually said to be Burghley.

The debate over topical allusions may suggest that the figures and episodes of *Mother Hubberd* are original creations devised by Spenser for specific satirical purposes. They belong, however, to the genre of the beast fable. Spenser's generic title, *Prosopopoia*, is the name of a rhetorical figure explained by Puttenham (*Arte* 3.19) as 'Counterfait inpersonation,' a term which serves to characterize the procedure of the Fox and the Ape as they 'counterfeit' the figures of good shepherds, clergy, courtiers, and royalty (Van den Berg 1978).

The chief known source of *Mother Hubberd* is the medieval romance *Renard the Fox*, which existed in several French and Dutch versions and two English translations. In both stories, animal allegory is used as a vehicle for general satire. The *Renard* cycle treats many of the same incidents and disguises: the pilgrimage, the Fox as priest and the Ape at court with the eventual usurpation of the throne, and even the somewhat surprising escape of the Fox from any real punishment.

Spenser's direct satire of contemporary court life voices criticism that in many respects is as old as satire itself. Yet he is able to blend and transform traditional material into an artistic unity. He stays within the tradition of the beast fable but renews and revitalizes it.

In the introduction, the traditional Chaucerian, astrological chronographia has been framed with extreme care. Spenser points to an intimate relation between the decline of the year and the moral decline of the world by drawing a clear parallel between the fall of the year and the Fall. This 'sinfull world' has let loose evil powers of sickness and death. The sickness is not only individual but social and cosmic (Atchity 1973). In the story that follows, the Fox, inspired by a new capitalist individualism, courts change to serve him in his pursuit of fortune, but ends up the slave of change. As he pursues external, material change only, he considers an external disguise of his true nature sufficient to serve his purpose, much like his famous successor, Jonson's Volpone. Like Volpone, however, his ultimate, unavoidable downfall affects not only himself and the Ape but the whole of society. The Fox and the Ape are carriers of an infection against which society has not yet learned to defend itself.

Spenser seeks through his art to restore to order that social and moral chaos brought about by the cunning creatures of this world. Accordingly, he invests the four episodes of his simple tale with a clear structure. There are evident parallels between the first and the last and the two middle episodes, the Fox and the Ape taking unscrupulous advantage of the corrupt church and court. In the first and last episodes, however, they introduce evil into the traditional and harmonious world of the unsuspecting husbandman and that of the innocent, sleeping lion. In the first, they deceive the world of the husbandman, who represents the lowest estate of hierarchical sixteenth-century society; in the last, they usurp royal power, the highest estate. The two beasts move through a world so unprepared for crafty malice that the Fox can pass himself off as a shepherd even in the religious sense. Religion has become so debased that spiritual cleanness is confused with external appearance. The priest's worthiness is discernible from his garments ('the finest silkes' 461), the courtier's ability from his fashionable dress, and the leader's authority from the symbolic presence of the royal robe. Spenser scores his last, witty point at the expense of the world of appearance when the Ape is made to appear like a man, by trimming his tail and ears. And so, rather abruptly, Spenser ends his tale without a tail.

EINAR BJORVAND

Var 8 has full discussion of dates, sources, and topical allusions. See also Atchity 1973; Greenlaw 1932:104–24; Iona Opie and Peter Opie 1951 *The Oxford Dictionary of Nursery Rhymes* (Oxford); Padelford 1913–14; Stein 1934, esp pp 78–101; and Van den Berg 1978.

Complaints: Ruines of Rome: By Bellay (See ed 1912:509–14.) Spenser's *Ruines of Rome*, like the French sonnet sequence by du Bellay that it translates, constitutes a small but fascinating chapter in the story of Renaissance efforts to interpret the mystery of Rome's rise and fall. The awesome and melancholy spectacle of ancient Rome's ruins inspired du Bellay to write two vernacular sonnet sequences – *Les Antiquitez de Rome* and *Songe*, both published in 1558 – that were to haunt Spenser's imagination throughout his career: echoes of these two French works occur at significant moments in *The Faerie Queene* but are most pervasive in *Complaints*. More than half the works in that volume translate or imitate du Bellay. *Rome*, a reasonably faithful if not always felicitous version of *Antiquitez*, concludes with an original envoy praising the French poet as the 'first garland of free Poësie / That *France* brought forth.' The homage is handsome, but both the envoy and the preceding sonnets hint that Spenser used the discipline of translation to define himself against as well as through the voice of his French Catholic original.

Du Bellay describes *Antiquitez* in his dedicatory sonnet to the King (not translated by Spenser) as a verbal effort to 'rebuild' Rome's glory in France; like his earlier treatise *La Deffence et illustration de la langue françoyse* (1549), *Antiquitez* illustrates the humanist belief that a culture and language may be enriched by the imitation and translation of ancient texts. Du Bellay's expressions of hope in the possibility of a future rebirth of letters in France are countered, however, both in the *Deffence* and in *Antiquitez*, by his perception of the present poverty of his native language and contemporary culture, and by his often pessimistic vision of history as a fatal cycle of growth and decay. Rome's fate prompts him to despair at times about all human efforts to withstand that entropic force which Spenser called 'Mutabilitie.'

The 32 sonnets of *Antiquitez* explore metaphysical and moral questions suggested by the ancient ruins, the chief one being the cause of Rome's fall. Some of the sonnets depict her as a victim of fate, in the guise of barbarian pillagers; others blame her hubris and self-destructive civil wars. Oscillating – between and within sonnets – among attitudes of wonder, pity, and moral critique, du Bellay creates a drama of mood, perception, and interpretation that arises as much from his reading of classical and modern texts as from his observation of architectural ruins.

The experience of seeing those ruins is profoundly frustrating for the newcomer trying to grasp Rome's meaning, and du Bellay repeatedly suggests that the 'image' of her ancient grandeur is better preserved in the writings of famous authors than in the 'dead painting' of buildings (*Antiquitez* 5). Literary imitation, conceived as an act of 'reviving' those ancient Roman spirits invoked with incantatory fervor in sonnets 1 and 15, therefore becomes a major theme of the sequence as well as a pervasive technique. Even sonnets such as 3 and 7, which are virtual translations of poems by an unknown Neo-Latin author and Castiglione respectively, acquire new resonance from their placement in a sequence that emphasizes the difficulty of interpreting the historical traces of Rome's glory and that exhibits throughout the poet's almost Platonic sense of being at many removes from truth (Joseph Loewenstein, unpublished paper). The very form of the sequence, fragmentary sonnets loosely strung into a quest narrative that alludes ironically to Aeneas' descent into the underworld in *Aeneid* 6, dramatizes the poet's role as a belated imitator, a 'gleaner,' as he suggests in sonnet 30, gathering 'the reliques ... Which th'husbandman behind him chanst to scater' (Spenser's translation).

It is not known when Spenser completed his translations of *Antiquitez*; they may date from the early 1570s, soon after he had made his blank-verse translations of *Songe* for van der Noot's *Theatre for Worldlings* (1569). Alternatively, both *Rome* and the revised version of *Songe* that Spenser published as *Visions of Bellay* in *Complaints* may date from the 1580s. The envoy to *Rome* was certainly written after 1579 (it alludes to a poem by du Bartas published in that year), but the envoy uses a different rhyme scheme from the other *Rome* sonnets and may postdate them. In any case, throughout the years when he was coming of age as a poet, Spenser was evidently reading and brooding on du Bellay's Roman poems – not only the *Antiquitez* and the emblematic dream visions of *Songe* but also the longer sequence about modern Rome, *Les Regrets*.

He presents his version of du Bellay's *Antiquitez* as an achievement of cultural translation, an act that is, in a favorite Renaissance paradox, at once new and repetitive: 'Cease not to sound these olde antiquities,' he tells his lute in sonnet 32, 'For if that time doo let thy glorie live, / Well maist thou boast, how ever base thou bee, / That thou art first, which of thy Nation song / Th'olde honour of the people gowned long.' Adroitly modifying du Bellay's claim to be the first *French* writer to sing of Rome's honor – a claim that itself reformulates a boast made by Horace – Spenser symbolically places himself in a line of poets extending across time and space to Virgil, who had described the 'long-gowned' Romans in *Aeneid* 1. By echoing his predecessors and adapting their words to a new cultural context, Spenser illustrates poetry's power to reanimate the past.

Neither poet maintains unequivocally a faith in poetic immortality; indeed, Spenser follows du Bellay quite closely in exploring different metaphysical perspectives on the ultimate fate of both the world and human artifacts. In the envoy, however, he counters du Bellay's concluding doubt that writing can outlive monuments of marble: praising his achievement of giving 'a second life to [Rome's] dead decayes,' Spenser asserts that du Bellay has earned 'endles' days. The envoy goes on, however, to praise a later French (and Protestant) poet for raising high his 'heavenly Muse, th'Almightie to adore'; this mention of du Bartas suggests that du Bellay's project of reviving the pagan Roman spirits may need to be supplemented – if not directly opposed – by faith in the Christian God and his promise of immortality for believers.

Spenser hints at differences between his and du Bellay's theological perspectives on Rome not only in the envoy but also in earlier moments of the sequence where the translations depart strikingly from the French original. *Rome* 27, for instance, describes papal efforts to excavate and rebuild

Rome's monuments with phrases that transform du Bellay's admiring tone into one of moral disapproval. Spenser presents us with a scene of pride like Lucifera's palace in *FQ* I iv 4–5 as he substitutes for du Bellay's vision of restored 'divine works' an image of Rome 'Repayring her decayed fashion' with 'buildings rich and gay.' *Rome* 28 deviates so much from du Bellay's description of Rome as a ruined old oak tree still revered by young plants with 'firm roots' that one reader feels that 'Spenser has missed the point' (Renwick in *Var* 8:389). Spenser may, however, have deliberately changed the point: his tree has a moral unsoundness ('all rotten' and 'meate of wormes') absent in the French; and he suggests, as du Bellay does not, that the devotion symbolized by the young trees is an error that springs directly from the 'rinde' of the old tree of Rome and that need not taint everyone. Whereas du Bellay focuses on the continuing 'honor' of Rome, Spenser places both the original honor and its later worshipers firmly in the past. This poem shows translation blending into critical reinterpretation as du Bellay's images of both ancient Rome and her modern heirs are filtered through a Protestant lens.

Spenser not only departs from his source in interesting and arguably purposeful ways; he also finds rhymes, rhythms, and alliterative patterns that offer apt English equivalents for the French original. In sonnet 12, for example, he uses alliteration and enjambment to dramatize the image of Rome rising pridefully to a point of uneasy balance: 'So did that haughtie front which heaped was / On these seven Romane hils, it selfe upreare / Over the world.' And in sonnet 15 he creates, through plangent rhythm and superb rhyme, a description of Rome's spirits that is even richer in meaning than du Bellay's original: yoking *returning* with *mourning*, Spenser uses both adjectives to characterize the Roman spirits who are unable to cross the infernal river Styx except in the form of grieving 'images.' In the French poem, *retour* appears in a negative phrase modifying the river rather than the spirits, and the rhyme words (*tenebreuses*/ *umbreuses*) do not suggest, as Spenser's do, a link between two apparently different but in truth intimately related concepts. The English rhyme, nearly but not quite perfect, epitomizes a theme that is central to *Rome* and to Spenser's entire poetic career: acts of imaginative return to a desired place or state of being almost always entail mourning, awareness of what has been irretrievably lost or changed.

Despite moments of great eloquence, *Rome* is in general the work of a talented apprentice; *Antiquitez*, in contrast, is a masterpiece. By alternating between poems of ten- and twelve-syllable lines, and by brilliantly using the Italian sonnet form's characteristic shift of viewpoint between a regularly rhymed octave (*abba abba*) and a more variously rhyming sestet (*ccd eed* or *ede*), du Bellay creates a more subtle and contrapuntal verbal music than Spenser, at this point in his career, can achieve with the Elizabethan sonnet in its Shakespearean form of three unlinked quatrains with alternating rhyme followed by a couplet. Many of his lines sound inadvertently awkward, prolix where du Bellay's are taut. Spenser's rendering of 'mon cry' in *Antiquitez* 1 as 'my shreiking yell' has been cited as an example of his 'noisy style' (Renwick in *Var* 8:380); Spenser might well have agreed. Both in the envoy to *Rome*, where he uses an interlocking rhyme scheme that anticipates the harmonies of *Amoretti*, and in the *Ruines of Time*, he moves from translating du Bellay to imitating him freely, in skillful and obliquely critical ways.

Rome may be appreciated as a stage in Spenser's development, an arena for exploring the resources and limits of his native tongue. These translations are also, however, important in a wider context than that of Spenser's career. It has been argued convincingly that Shakespeare's *Sonnets* are indebted to *Rome* (Hieatt 1983); the two sequences share a profound concern with time, change, and modes of continuity, both literary and biological. Their striking thematic and verbal parallels suggest, moreover, that Shakespeare appreciated and exploited one of the most original aspects of du Bellay's *Antiquitez* as translated by Spenser: the transfer of traditional motifs of Petrarchan love poetry to the more public arena of humanist meditations on Rome. The psychological drama of the *Antiquitez* derives in part from du Bellay's decision to present his relation to Rome as if he were a lover pursuing an incomparable but cruel mistress who frustrates his desires and, like Petrarch's Laura, becomes in death an object of lament (Rebhorn 1980). Excavating and transforming the Petrarchan subtext of Spenser's translations, Shakespeare endows his male beloved with some of Rome's wondrous qualities – and also with her capacity to be immortalized in verse. Both in its own right, then, and as a bridge between the greater sonnet sequences of du Bellay and Shakespeare, Spenser's youthful work shows how translation may be a culturally significant and seminally creative act.

MARGARET W. FERGUSON

M.W. Ferguson 1984; Hieatt 1983; MacLure 1973; Manley 1982; Pigman 1982; Rebhorn 1980.

Complaints: Muiopotmos, or The Fate of the Butterflie (See ed 1912:515–20.) (Gr *muia* fly+*potmos* fate) Possibly written close to 1590, the date on its title page, *Muiopotmos* was published in the 1591 volume of *Complaints*. It is a little epic or epyllion (see *Ovidian epic), corresponding to the *Culex* in the Renaissance canon of Virgil's works. Its style suggests the maturity of the poet, as well as the freshness of a holiday mood. It may have been composed when Spenser had just completed the first three books of his greater epic, or perhaps in an interlude while he was working on it.

Spenser had translated the *Culex* as *Virgils Gnat* earlier in his career, although both it and *Muiopotmos* appear for the first time in the *Complaints*. Both works suggest that he was preoccupied, or at least entertained, by the theme of the insect. Poems on insects had well-known precedents in Hellenistic or Alexandrian literature, including Lucian's encomium on a fly and the pseudo-Homeric battle of frogs and mice known as the *Batrachomyomachia*. The praise of tiny creatures and the narration of their exploits and downfalls – often merely a demonstration of rhetorical skill – helped to prepare the way for *Muiopotmos* as a work of art in its own right. Genre provides an essential clue to understanding the poem. Its tone is set by Spenser's dedication to Lady Carey (or Carew), to whom he addresses a dedicatory sonnet to *The Faerie Queene*, with the offer of a more personal tribute later. In fulfillment of this promise, he asks that she 'make a milde construction' of *Muiopotmos*: that she treat it indulgently and not too seriously.

The playful aspect of the poem is most apparent in the discrepancy between insignificant insects and epic treatment. To depict a lower form of life with human characteristics is in itself enough to raise a smile, as in Chaucer's story of Chauntecleer in the *Nun's Priest's Tale*. Spenser's humor, however, is more delicate and his style more consciously elegant. Despite the epic reverberations of his name, Clarion (L *clarus* bright) is less concerned with fame than with seeking whatever pleasures his garden paradise has to offer. It is all too evident that his weapons are purely decorative; and he is pathetic rather than tragic when he falls victim to his ancient enemy, the spider. Yet his armor has been called 'No lesse than that, which *Vulcane* made to sheild / *Achilles* life from fate of *Troyan* field' (63–4); and the account of his death is modeled on that of the warrior Turnus at the end of Virgil's *Aeneid* (12.951–2).

Spenser's master in *Muiopotmos* is Ovid, whose *Metamorphoses* describe a series of encounters between gods and men, in which the latter are condemned not to death but to change, as though to illustrate the constancy of essential being within the changeableness of forms (cf the Garden of Adonis in *FQ* III vi). Metamorphosis mitigates the punishments inflicted on those who are sinners in the eyes of the gods, and saves from extinction those whom the gods love but whom even they are powerless to keep alive as mortals. It is as if the gods and fate itself were playing games that are more than games, in that they possess an inner significance which we cannot altogether comprehend. Thus Spenser invents an Ovidian type of myth to explain the origin of the butterfly (113–44). It revolves around the jealousy directed toward a skilled flower-gatherer named Astery, first by her companions and then by Venus, who is led to believe that Cupid, enamored of the girl as he once was of Psyche, is assisting her. To punish the supposed crime, Venus turns Astery into a butterfly, allowing her to continue to gather flowers and even display their colors in her wings.

Spenser derives his other myth, of the spider's origin, from Ovid, from whom he deliberately departs by making Arachne transform herself by envy into the spider, instead of making Minerva the instrument of metamorphosis (257–352). The girl who lived for pleasure becomes the butterfly; the girl who was marvelously skilled in weaving tapestries becomes the spider, who continues to weave nets of exquisite craftsmanship, while exuding the venom associated with her original envy. Finally, to explain the traditional hatred that spiders bear toward flies and butterflies, an embroidered butterfly is added to Minerva's competition tapestry as her crowning achievement and hence the final spur to Arachne's envy.

In borrowing Ovid's story of the contest between Minerva and Arachne, Spenser also reduces the many scenes on Arachne's tapestry to one, the myth of Europa, rather than describing the several loves of the gods which appear in Ovid (as they do in the tapestries of *FQ* III xi as well). His story conflates Ovid's two accounts in *Metamorphoses* 2.843–75 and 6.103–7, possibly with further borrowings from Moschus and Achilles Tatius. His restricted subject concentrates the opposition between the two tapestries, balancing them better as ecphrases (since Minerva's also has only one scene in Spenser's account) and emphasizing the disorderly, lustful theme of Arachne's tapestry in contrast to the orderly, lawful theme of Minerva's.

The poet's attitude to his story is fanciful and playful. His little myths, like his mock epic style, keep events at a distance, setting off their beauty. The reader is conscious of a storyteller who alludes constantly to literary tradition while he makes it known that he is himself creating a work of art. Moreover, all the deities are shown to be artists in their creations, and even the spider is a supreme craftsman in preparing his trap for the butterfly. The poem expresses a love of beautiful craftsmanship, and it does so through its own jewel-like surface – polished, descriptive, and based more on the antithetical nature of butterfly and spider than on individual character and plot.

Critics have puzzled over the question of the poem's meaning. Some readers find an historical allegory in the antagonists: Essex and Burghley, or Spenser himself and Burghley, or Sidney and Burghley. The possibilities of this kind of interpretation are endless but difficult to prove. If the poem does have an historical dimension, it may simply portray the hazards of court life, particularly for a butterfly-poet surrounded by the envious.

A moral interpretation may be justified on grounds that insects were viewed as mirrors of human life. The butterfly, for example, can stand for the frivolous pursuit of pleasure; it can also stand for the human soul (Gr *psyche* means both 'soul' and 'butterfly'). Similarly, the spider is traditionally associated with the devil and various forms of evil, such as deceit and envy. Given the roles of 'riotous' butterfly and wicked spider in the garden (a type of Eden), Clarion may represent the human soul succumbing to the temptations of pleasure. A Calvinist predestination may even determine his fate. Yet does he really deserve it? In the ordinary sense of the word, he cannot be guilty: as butterfly, he cannot sin, and Spenser calls him 'faultles' (418). But in his symbolic role, his downfall may warn mortals that careless pleasure-seekers will inevitably meet their doom. This is the order which the universe imposes on all beings, and Aragnoll is its instrument. Spenser's poem, however, does not present a despairing view of the universe, but rather offers us a beautiful tapestry in which spiders as well as butterflies have their place.

Whatever interpretation is adopted, the moral resolves itself into the familiar one, that in this world the life of pleasure cannot last. Spenser frequently speaks of the transitoriness of earthly bliss with such expressions as 'Nothing is sure, that growes on earthly ground' (*FQ* I ix 11). Any of these might serve as a motto to inscribe under an emblematic butterfly and spider web. Yet the poem does not have the narrowly didactic purpose of an ordinary emblem. While the moral fits the theme of the *Complaints* volume, it does not obtrude. The poem remains like a rich jewel, at once festive and symbolic, adorning the lady for whom it is intended. JUDITH DUNDAS

D.C. Allen 1968:20–41 'Edmund Spenser: "Muiopotmos, or The Fate of the Butterflie"'; Anderson 1971a; Bond 1976; Brinkley 1981; Franklin E. Court 1970 'The Theme and Structure of Spenser's *Muiopotmos*' *SEL* 10:1–15; Judith Dundas 1975 '*Muiopotmos*: A World of Art' *YES* 5:30–8; Dundas 1985.

Complaints: Visions (See ed 1912:521–6.) *Complaints* ends with three sets of 'Visions' – *Visions of the Worlds Vanitie*, *The Visions of Bellay*, *The Visions of Petrarch* – emblematic sonnets on the limitations of power and on transitoriness in general. Their importance to the volume is emphasized in the subtitle to *Complaints*: 'Containing sundrie small Poemes of the Worlds Vanitie.'

Visions of the Worlds Vanitie, twelve sonnets in the Spenserian form, opens with a sonnet in which the dreaming poet meditates on the wickedness and folly of an age that despises the mean and humble. The next ten present 'strange showes' that depict what the poet has thought: a bull is vexed by a brize (gadfly); a crocodile is forced to allow the tiny 'tedula' to feed upon his jaws; a scarab beetle destroys the offspring of the proud eagle; a small swordfish wounds the 'huge *Leviathan*' of the ocean, the whale; a spider poisons a huge dragon; 'a goodly Cedar ... Of wondrous length, and streight proportion' is destroyed by a worm that feeds upon 'her sap and vitall moysture'; an elephant, proud that he bears a 'gilden towre' on his back, is undone by an ant that creeps into his 'nosthrils'; a swiftly moving ship is suddenly retarded by 'a little fish,' the remora (sucker-fish) that attaches itself to the hull; a lion that had feasted on other beasts is defied by a wasp ('So weakest may anoy the most of might'); a goose (the traditional bird of foolishness) saves ancient Rome from an invasion of the Gauls. The final sonnet offers advice prompted by 'these sad sights': 'Learne ... to love the low degree ... For he that of himselfe is most secure, / Shall finde his state most fickle and unsure.'

These visions of the world's vanity form a series of rhetorical proofs of the initial and concluding statements. The images are conventional; their success, though limited, lies in their subtle modulation and their cumulative effect, much as in Lyly's prose style with its piled-up imagery of the animal, vegetable, mineral, and historical worlds. Thus, the story of the scarab and the eagle is the oft-reworked motif of an ancient adage given in Erasmus' *Adages* as 'Scarabeum aquilam quaerit' (the scarab annoys the eagle) and Alciati's Emblem 169 *A minimis quoque timendum* ('One must also fear the least'). The cedar and the worm is a clever adaptation of the conventional lore (found in Bartholomaeus Anglicus 17.23) that not even the tree worm can harm the cedar. The battle of the swordfish and the whale is mentioned in Pliny (32.6.6). The image of the remora and the ship comes from Alciati's Emblem 83 *In facile a virtute desciscentes* 'On those who easily withdraw from virtue'). In Pliny, the *trochilus* (not 'tedula') feeds from the crocodile's mouth; such lore, originally from Herodotus, was common knowledge among the school-educated in Spenser's time. Aesop, though not directly used, is an indirect source for the tales of the elephant and the ant, and the lion and the wasp (cf the Elephant and the Mouse, and the Lion Tormented by Flies). The very weight of the conventional lore, altered here and there by the author for delight and surprise, serves to prove the claims regarding the ease with which the least may annoy or bring down the great. Although there is little evidence that Spenser was admonishing any noble person of the time, the critique is political in the broadest sense: it reminds those in power of their slippery state and of their need to pay heed to the less well placed; it flatters the humble by reminding them (esp in sonnet 11) of their possible importance in the lives of the powerful.

The Visions of Bellay continues the theme both more specifically, for its fifteen sonnets treat the fall of ancient Rome, and more broadly, for the fall of Rome as spiritual and political capital of western Europe implies the decline of much more than individual vanity. The difference in tone is immediately apparent: the sonnets are more learned, the imagery more complex and less immediately accessible. The sudden shift is due of course to the change in author, for as the title tells us, the series is the work of du Bellay. It is a translation of his *Songe* originally appended to *Les Antiquitez de Rome*, translated elsewhere in *Complaints* as *The Ruines of Rome*. Spenser had translated all but numbers 6, 8, 13, and 14 of the *Songe* as blank-verse sonnets in *Theatre* (1569, with woodblock illustrations); his revision now gives the entire sequence in a formal rhymed pattern. As visions, the poems are more dreamlike than the preceding series of vanities, though here the proposition is emphatically the same: 'all is nought but flying vanitee.' After the introductory sonnet in which a ghost summons the poet to behold 'this worlds inconstancies,' the first three allegorical visions show the destruction by natural causes of a diamond building, a diamond spire, and a splendidly carved triumphal arch – all emblems of empire; next, a 'barbarous troupe of clownish fone' ignorantly chops down the oak of Dodona, the symbol of the greatness of Troy (from which Rome was derived); huntsmen pursue and kill the wolf (stepmother of Romulus and Remus); the young female eagle (symbol of Rome) flies too high and tumbles 'All flaming downe'; a wind blows away the horrifying apparition of 'a strange beast with seven heads' (the Church of Rome); the palm, olive, and 'faire greene Lawrell branch' embellishing the figure of a bearded giant (the river Tiber) suddenly decay; a virgin (presumably one of the Vestal Virgins) laments her declining beauty, caused by civil strife and the crimes of the seven-headed Hydra; a white bird ascends singing amidst a shining fire when suddenly a 'silver dew' falls, leaving only the stench of 'noyous sulphure' (a reference to the evils brought on Rome by the Donation of Constantine); a beautiful stream is soiled by satyrs who drive away the hundred nymphs that grace the river's bank; a richly laden ship (the ship of state) is suddenly assailed by a storm and founders, though later it is raised again; a splendid city is destroyed by a north wind that blows away its weak and sandy foundation; finally, Typhaeus' sister (actually Rhea, a patron goddess of Rome and daughter of Typhoeus, though in the sonnet with the attributes of Bellona, goddess of war) is brought down from her triumph at the water's edge by the heavens with a sudden clap of thunder. Although any close discussion of the sequence takes us away from Spenser to du Bellay, it is worth noticing that certain motifs may be found elsewhere in Spenser's work: the weeping virgin (*Time*), the Roman Hydra (Duessa's dragon is seven-headed), the building built on sand (the house of Pride), the diamond building (Panthea), the triumphant giantess (Mutabilitie). Moreover, the constant play on the imagery of water and rivers in the sequence is closely related to a similar preoccupation in Spenser's own verse, where the relation between water and time is pronounced.

The final series of seven sonnets, *The Visions of Petrarch*, offers a more personal view of 'this tickle trustles state / Of vaine worlds glorie.' The imagery is even more opaque than in the preceding series: a hind is chased to death by a white and a black dog; an ebony and ivory ship is driven by a storm to founder on a hidden rock; a lightning flash rends a 'fresh and lustie Lawrell tree'; a spring of water and its gentle environs are suddenly swallowed up the the 'gaping earth'; a phoenix, dismayed at the sight of the broken laurel and the destroyed spring, impales himself with his beak; a fair lady who refuses love is shrouded by a dark cloud, wounded in the heel by a 'stinging Serpent,' and dies, though she mounts to heavenly joy. The successive images of disappointment drive the poet to despair and force him to remind his lady – presumably his patroness, Lady Carey – that 'though ye be the fairest of Gods creatures, / Yet thinke, that death shall spoyle your goodly features.'

These lines, so direct and specific, offer an odd conclusion to the three series and to the entire *Complaints* volume. We have been carried from observations on the general condition of nature (and human existence) through the political to the erotic. These seven sonnets are reworkings (via Marot) of Petrarch's Canzone 6 (*Rime* 323) lamenting the death of Laura. In *Theatre*, they appear in an earlier form as six rhymed 'Epigrams' (see *epigrams). (The earlier four-line conclusion is replaced by a seventh sonnet based on the envoy to Petrarch's canzone; only the repeated rhyme-word *rest* still echoes Spenser's earlier ending.) The order in the three series of visions is significant, the increasing complexity and obscurity of their imagery making emphatic the increasing mystification and disturbance sensed by the poet before the destruction of the great, the powerful, and the beautiful around him.

The three series of visions bring the *Complaints* to an end by presenting the poet (as in *Time* and *Teares*) as perceptive reporter of social abuses, crimes against art, and the general decline of all things. At the beginning of the volume, the speakers are Verlame, the Muses, or Mother Hubberd; here at the end, however, the poet himself (whether in his own voice or as the voice for the visions of others) now speaks. We have moved from moral advice to eschatological meditation. Whether this order to the poems in *Complaints* is intentional (by printer or author) or accidental, it is clear from the concluding visions that the volume is unified. JAN VAN DORSTEN

---

conceit A thought is conceived in the mind, we read in *Daphnaïda* (29–35), in much the same way as a child is conceived in the womb; and what is thus conceived is called a 'conceit.' As a literary critical term, *conceit* has two distinctive features. First, it is cognate with *concept* but distinguishable from it, and signifies mental activities which differ from those which engender concepts. Secondly, it denotes an activity as well as the results of that activity – 'conceiving and its product,' in the *OED* definition. Each of these features is of interest to literary critics, because the first encourages speculation about the matrix which generates conceits, and the second reveals the shortcomings of literary investigations which ignore conceitedness as a process and focus instead on conceits as products which can be catalogued and discussed in isolation from the poems in which they occur.

The distinction between *concept* and *conceit* can be formulated clearly in terms of the late seventeenth-century distinction between judgment and wit which became popular among critics with a vested interest in purging poetry of conceits. As a rival discovery procedure to judgment (whose logical and analytic methods are designed to eliminate confusion by demarcating the differences between things), wit operates by analogy and synthesis to establish similarities, especially those hidden and unexpected similarities in dissimilars which cause surprise and delight once they are revealed. The operational procedures of judgment result in concepts; those of wit, in conceits. Judgment observes, for instance, that a girl's neck is not at all like 'a bounch of Cullambynes' (*Amoretti* 64), because necks and columbines differ from one another so radically in their forms and functions that it is ludicrous to allege similarity between them on such trivial (and indeed disputable) grounds as color (ie, whiteness). Wit, on the other hand, makes the comparison possible by centering the very feature which judgment deems marginal, expecting ingenious readers to delight in discovering that what clinches the comparison is a suppressed term (L *collum* neck) which, in the structure of the conceit, functions rather like an enthymeme in a logical proposition. What brings the absent *collum* cryptically into the company of 'Cullambynes' is the context in which it occurs, namely a list of flowers including 'Gillyflowers,' 'Roses,' 'Pincks,' and 'Jessemynes'; had the context been birds instead of flowers, the buried term would have been the Latin *columba* (dove).

It so happens that in this case the conceit is generated by wordplay, and specifically the witty construction of an argument by (pseudo)etymology on the 'evidence' of a bilingual pun – as when Spenser elsewhere wishes the Earl of Essex 'happinesse of [his] owne name / That promiseth the same' (*Prothalamion* 153–4), because the Earl of Essex is Robert Devereux and *heureux* is French for 'happy.' But conceitfulness may be manifest in something as nonverbal and purely relational as 'proportion,' as in the case of *Amoretti* 53, which compares a girl to a panther on the grounds that both play with their prey. 'A conceit is not an image ... It is a piece of wit. It is ... the discovery of a proposition referring to one field of experience in terms of an intellectual structure derived from another field' (Cunningham 1953:36). In other words, Spenser is not claiming that girls look like panthers (the imagizing fallacy) but that they act like panthers.

Among several factors which have contributed to our relative ignorance of Spenserian conceits is the absence of contemporary observations on the poetic theory which supported them. Equally puzzling is the apparent willingness of Spenser and his contemporaries to accept the low valuation placed by sixteenth-century psychologists on the only mental faculty from which conceitful thinking could be said to emanate, the *cellula phantastica* in the front ventricle of the brain. Here sits Spenser's Phantastes, who is said to indulge in 'idle fantasies' and to be the source of 'all that fained is, as leasings, tales, and lies' (*FQ* II ix 49–52) – and also, presumably, whole poems as well as their constituent conceits, seeing that Spenser himself describes *The Faerie Queene* as a 'darke [ie, enigmatic] conceit' (Letter to Raleigh). Phantastes' activities were disparaged as 'mere' fancy by Augustan critics before being downgraded further by Romantic critics as an ersatz form of imagination, the artifice and wit of its conceits condemned for artificiality and frigid ingenuity. And when metaphysical poetry was rediscovered in the wake of the imagist movement in the twentieth century, Donne's 'functional' conceits were praised to the detriment of Spenser's so-called decorative conceits.

Hence the common assumption that Renaissance English poetry contains two sorts of conceit, one good and the other bad. The 'good' kind is believed to manifest an original and mature fusion of thought and feeling ('felt thought') and to be found in poems by Donne and some other (but not all) seventeenth-century metaphysical poets; it is recognizable immediately in such lines as Donne's 'Wee dye and rise the same, and prove / Mysterious by this love' ('The Canonization'), which depend for their effect on wittily compressed analogies between sacred enigma and profane bewilderment, sex and religion, erection and Resurrection. The 'bad' kind of conceits, on the other hand, are the staple of sixteenth-century lyrists and sonneteers, Spenser included, and are conventional, decorative, naive, and tedious; they are typified by lines such as 'If Pearles, hir teeth be pearles both pure and round' in a blazon of his mistress' features (*Amoretti* 15), or 'My love is lyke to yse, and I to fyre' (*Amoretti* 30) in a familiar reworking of the Petrarchan idiolect of unrequited love. Conceits which resist being compartmentalized in this way – such as the extended comparison of love to a theatergoer (*Amoretti* 54) – tend to be ignored.

Against this bundle of prejudices, Rosemond Tuve directed her fundamentally important if somewhat obscure study *Elizabethan and Metaphysical Imagery* (1947), which stresses continuities between sixteenth- and seventeenth-century poetics by focusing on the rhetorical and logical structures of Renaissance imagery. In attempting to reconstruct the conditions in which such poems were written and read, however, she makes the understanding and appreciation of conceitful poetry more difficult than ever, and the only Spenserian to follow the implications of her analytic methods in making visible the 'invisible' subtleties of Spenserian conceits has been Alastair Fowler. Tuve and Fowler work on the assumption that the conceit is a mode of structuring subject matter and not the subject matter itself. In doing so, they break significantly with the older assumption – dauntingly displayed in the work of M.B. Ogle and to a lesser degree in Lisle Cecil John's – that a conceit is not a process but a product.

Defined as a product – that is, as the result of a comparison: hair like gold wires, roses and lilies complexion, love as a wound, and so on – each conceit becomes extractable from its context and can have its pedigree traced back to some ancient Greek or Latin poem. So when Spenser apostrophizes his own *Amoretti* in the opening sonnet ('happy lines, on which with starry light, / those lamping eyes will deigne sometimes to look'), scholars have often extracted a product (eyes = stars) and then, by unitizing it, demonstrated that the 'same' conceit is used not only by a dozen or more English writers from Chaucer to Shakespeare (as well as by continental Renaissance poets, especially Petrarch) but also in Latin poems by Propertius and Ovid, and, by inference, even in the Greek of Callimachus. Diachronic chains of this kind (often with missing links: genuine gaps or scholarly oversight?) can be appended to any Spenserian sonnet; and on the basis of contiguity of conceits, a theory of literary continuity can be constructed which sees Spenser as either a skillful manipulator or as a mindless cataloguer of wholly conventional materials. Clearly, this way of defining conceits is itself the product of a certain type of historical scholarship which needs to be supplemented, if only because it has had such a reductive and deleterious effect on the reputation of Spenser's so-called 'minor' poems, especially the *Amoretti*, many of which have been construed as mere containers for conventional conceits and of interest largely to historians of Petrarchism. K.K. RUTHVEN

J.V. Cunningham 1953 'Logic and Lyric' *MP* 51:33–41; Fowler 1975, ch 5; Jay L. Halio 1966 'The Metaphor of Conception and Elizabethan Theories of the Imagination' *Neophil* 50:454–61; Lisle Cecil John 1938 *The Elizabethan Sonnet Sequences: Studies in Conventional Conceits* (New York); M.B. Ogle 1913 'The Classical Origin and Tradition of Literary Conceits' *AJPh* 34:125–52; Rossky 1958; K.K. Ruthven 1969 *The Conceit* (London); Tuve 1947.

Constable, Henry (1562–1613) One of the earliest of the English sonneteers, Constable wrote his secular poems before his conversion to Catholicism and subsequent self-exile in 1591; the editions of *Diana* (1592, 1594?) represent partial and unauthoritative selections from these poems, the later edition 'augmented' by a number of sonnets not by him. It is now thought that the carefully ordered sequence of 'H.C. Sonets' found in the Todd manuscript provides the author's definitive collected text (Victoria and Albert Museum, Ms Dyce 44). There, 63 numbered sonnets are arranged in three groups, each with three sets of seven poems, to represent a progressive movement toward the 'climatericall' number 63 which allows the poet 'to employe the remnant of [his] wit to other calmer thoughts lesse sweete and lesse bitter' (Constable ed 1960:179). The climacteric (a word arguably used first in English by Constable) results from multiplying the numbers 7 and 9; it recognizes the supposedly crucial nature of the sixty-third event in a series.

Spenser's *Amoretti* (pub 1595) show only a few insignificant verbal echoes of Constable (far fewer than can be traced in Shakespeare, Drayton, or Daniel) and use a different sonnet form. Spenser's sequence, however, takes a major turn at the sixty-third sonnet, where the poet finally descries 'the happy shore' and finds himself rewarded with his mistress' love; he leaves behind the *dolce-amaro* or bittersweet suffering of unrequited Petrarchan love (but see **Amoretti*). Moreover, Constable's partiality for French sources, Neoplatonic motifs, and extended conceits reflects a general influence on English sonneteers, including Spenser.

Though generally unadmired by later critics, Constable's poetry shows a facility and inventiveness that raises his work above the common rank, and his reputation among his contemporaries was high. In his note on the allegory of *Orlando furioso* 34, Harington quotes the entire sonnet to King James ('Where others hooded with blind love do fly'), declaring Constable to be a 'well learned Gentleman and my very good frend.' The names of Spenser and Constable appear close together in various contemporary sources (see *Sp All* pp 4, 71, 73, 242), basically in recognition of their common reputation as writers of lyric poetry. However, their disparate social and religious backgrounds, careers, and concerns help to explain why so few points of contact are to be found in their work.

The 'Pastoral Song betweene Phillis and Amaryllis' in *Englands Helicon* (1600), sometimes mentioned as a parallel to the song in *SC, August* (*Var* 7:339, 346), is now attributed to Henry Chettle, not to Constable. ALVAN BREGMAN

Henry Constable 1960 *Poems* ed Joan Grundy (Liverpool).

constellations Spenser's allusions to the constellations allow two inferences: that they were understandable to his contemporaries without reference to chart or handbook; and that their variety, splendor, and mythological associations made them an immediate presence in his world. The advantage of gaining some familiarity with them as conventionally depicted in Spenser's day is demonstrable from *Faerie Queene* II ii 46. There, Orion the hunter, one of the best-known groups of stars, is described as setting while 'flying fast from hissing snake.' According to classical mythology, when a scorpion killed Orion, both were elevated to the sky and placed so that one rises as the other sets; and so readers have identified Spenser's 'snake' with Scorpio. But in conventional representations of the stars, more than half the interval between Scorpio and Orion is occupied by a very snaky object – a single-headed Hydra, poised to strike at Orion's back. The sense of urgency implicit in 'flying fast' is therefore much more realistic and intelligible if the snake is identified with Hydra.

For another example, in *SC, Julye* 17–24, he describes the sky in this way:

And now the Sonne hath reared up
his fyriefooted teme,
Making his way betweene the Cuppe,
and golden Diademe:
And rampant Lyon hunts he fast,
with Dogge of noysome breath,
Whose balefull barking bringes in hast
pyne, plagues, and dreery death.

Since *The Shepheardes Calender* traces an annual cycle, in this context *reared up* means 'moved upwards away from the celestial equator [in summer],' not 'driven upwards from the horizon [at noontime].' The cup is Crater, standing on the back of Hydra; the diadem is Corona Borealis (Ariadne's Crown); the lion is Leo; and the dog is Canis Major, which rises with the sun in high summer. In Spenser's time, the Dog Star was associated with the plague, and the poet depicts the panting hound spreading infection, as E.K. notes.

Astrological interpretation of certain passages in Spenser depends on a knowledge of Ptolemy's catalogue of the stars, with which Spenser was familiar (Fowler 1964). For instance, the Bower of Bliss episode may be affected by the fact that Libra is one of the mansions or houses of Venus. According to Ptolemy's numeration, Libra contains eight stars in its main configuration; perhaps that is why the Bower of Bliss episode has eight main characters. Any single match of this kind can be dismissed as coincidence; but there are a number of such correspondences, like that between the stars of Scorpio and the house of Mammon (Fowler 1964:118). Since astronomy in Spenser's day was primarily a science of number, it inevitably played a part in his numerical strategies (see *number symbolism).

This strategy may be seen perhaps most clearly in *Prothalamion*, its 180 lines being the number of degrees in a hemisphere. The astronomical reference to the grooms as Castor and Pollux, 'the twins of *Jove* [who] decke the Bauldricke of the Heavens bright' (stanza 10), insinuates the rest of the zodiac though the other constellations are hidden under cryptic astronomical allusions. Each of the other stanzas corresponds to an intervening constellation in the zodiac. For example, stanza 1 corresponds to Virgo, which lies ten signs back from Gemini. In stanza 3, Spenser alludes to the constellation Cygnus by referring to '*Jove* himselfe when he a Swan would be / For love of *Leda*.' Scorpio (the third sign in the scheme, two signs on from Virgo) and Cygnus are associated because, at Spenser's latitude, the two constellations rise together. From details like these, it becomes clear that the poem's ten stanzas correspond to ten of the Ptolemaic constellations (see Fowler 1975:59–86, though for a different pattern).

The astronomical pattern is best seen at the end of the poem, its point of rest: if the constellation Gemini is placed just above the horizon and 30 degrees east of north, then Corona Borealis (corresponding to the prospective brides) will simultaneously lie poised above the western horizon at a similar (and symmetrical) distance to the west of north. The heavenly counterparts are thus framed within the visible hemisphere of the heavens, whose 180 degrees correspond to the number of lines in the poem.

J.C. Eade

Fowler 1964; Fowler 1975; Hieatt 1960.

Contemplation The Red Cross Knight's spiritual education at the house of Holiness reaches its climax in his encounter with Contemplation on top of a steep hill (*FQ* I x 46–68). There Mercy, who has conducted the knight through the hospital or halfway house of the seven Bead-men, turns him over to an emaciated old hermit, 'heavenly *Contemplation*,' under whose tutelage he completes the discipline of the house with a vision of the New Jerusalem and a discovery of his own true identity as St George. Spenser's account of a contemplative vision as the consummation of spiritual progress, which must be followed by a return to active life, draws on the mainstream of Christian mysticism as fed, and to some degree modified, by classical philosophy and medieval literary exegesis. The episode reveals a view of contemplative activity which is repeated throughout his poetry.

In its unfolding, the encounter strongly echoes the mystical tradition of the Middle Ages. Though the aged Contemplation is nearly blind, 'Yet wondrous quick and persant was his spright, / As Eagles eye, that can behold the Sunne' (47), an allusion to St John, who was traditionally the most contemplative of the four Evangelists and whose symbol was an eagle. In asking Contemplation to show Redcrosse 'the way ... To that most glorious house' whose keys have been entrusted to him by Fidelia (50), Mercy evokes the mystical notion of a spiritual pilgrimage of life derived from Prudentius' *Psychomachia*, in which the Christian pilgrim endures the temptations of the world to earn a vision of his ultimate happiness. The three stages of this progress (purgation, illumination, and perfect union) are reflected in canto x by Redcrosse's instruction under Patience, Mercy, and now Contemplation, whose revelations constitute the climactic 'unitive way,' or contemplation of the divine attributes and concomitant perfection of the soul. The hermit shows Redcrosse the 'way' that leads, 'after labours long,' to joyous rest (52). From the highest mount, the knight can see the path to the resplendent city of Revelation 21, which in contemporary Protestant exegesis represents the church of Christ in heaven, as Caelia's house represents his church on earth.

The Aristotelian tradition, invoked by Spenser in the Letter to Raleigh, lays great stress on a return from contemplation to action. According to Aristotle's *Nicomachean Ethics*, the 'virtues' (*aretai*) are excellences or capacities of either the moral or the intellectual compartment of the soul. The moral virtues are realized in action (*praxis*), and this realization in turn makes possible that of the intellectual virtues. Of the latter, Aristotle recognizes two: practical wisdom (*phronesis*), which is the cognitive component of action, and theoretical or 'pure' wisdom (*sophia*), the highest excellence of which man is capable. The realization or 'activity' (*energeia*) of *sophia* is what Aristotle calls 'contemplation' (*theoria*), that is, the realization of our highest intellectual faculty and the source of the most complete human happiness. This activity, however, is essentially divine, being normally reserved for the gods. Therefore, Aristotle redirects the virtuous man to action as the consummation of a truly human life. In the Christianized Aristotelianism of Thomas Aquinas, Aristotle's two intellectual virtues, theoretical wisdom and practical wisdom, become as many as four. Of these, *sapientia* (wisdom) and *intellectus* (intuitive knowledge, Aristotle's *nous*) are in turn sometimes incorporated into the mystical tradition as the last gifts of the Holy Spirit, granted chiefly to contemplatives in the stages of illumination and perfection.

Paradoxically, in Spenser's episode it is Contemplation himself who gives voice to the Aristotelian bias, urging Redcrosse's return to the active life. Taken by the beauty of the New Jerusalem, which outshines even Cleopolis, Gloriana's city of fame, the hero longs to remain in contemplative ecstasy. But Contemplation, emphasizing the value of earthly fame based on active virtue, insists that Cleopolis mirrors the valid glory of its ruler, who is herself 'heavenly borne, and heaven may justly vaunt' (59). He therefore encourages Redcrosse first to pursue this earthly glory in her service, only after which he may hang up his 'suit of earthly conquest' and undertake his 'painefull pilgrimage' to the heavenly Jerusalem presaged by the present vision. There he will be named St George of England, take his place among the blessed, and share their eternal peace and contemplative repose (60–2). After Redcrosse has freed Una's parents from the Dragon, there is, in Una's unveiling (I xii 22), a contemplative moment which evokes the phase of mystical contemplation known as 'spiritual betrothal,' or marriage of the soul to God, its celestial spouse, here placed in an earthly paradise which recalls the vision of the heavenly paradise in canto x. Again Redcrosse postpones his felicity, until he has fulfilled his obligation to the active life by six years of service to Gloriana. These final cantos reflect a well-established classical and Christian view of action as the normal fulfillment of contemplation, and of contemplation as the necessary foundation of action.

Spenser's view of contemplation receives further support from medieval and Renaissance literary theory. In the Middle Ages, for example, the contemplative life was specifically identified with Virgil's *Eclogues* (the active life with the *Aeneid*, and the life of pleasure with the *Georgics*; see Comparetti ed 1895:117). This connection is echoed in the *Advancement of Learning* (1605), where Bacon cites the shepherd Abel, 'living in view of heaven,' as 'a lively image of a contemplative life' and Cain as an image of the active life (ed 1857–74, 6:138, 2:146ff). The contemplative aspects of pastoral were also assimilated to the medieval understanding of classical epic, still lively in Spenser's day. In the exegesis of the *Aeneid* as an allegory of the moral life by commentators from Bernard Sylvestris in the twelfth century to Cristoforo Landino in the fifteenth, the turning point in Aeneas' odyssey is his descent/ascent into contemplation in Book 6. Now perfect in virtue, the hero is prepared to return to his active quest for a new Trojan homeland in Italy.

Contemplation in Spenser's poetry reflects these literary, theological, and philosophical associations. Britomart's active pursuit of her dynastic destiny, for example, is founded on her vision of Artegall in Merlin's magical glass (III iii). In addition, each of the six completed books contains an 'allegorical core' which provides a visionary exposition of that book's central virtue and gives the reader, and in most cases the questing knight as well, a fresh illumination of the ensuing action. This epiphany is connected with pastoral in the Pastorella episode of *FQ* VI x. At its dramatic climax, Calidore stumbles upon Colin Clout's vision of the Graces, who embody the courtesy the knight displays in the active life to which he soon returns.

The same relationship between action and contemplation informs Spenser's more direct musings on his life as poet and man. In *Amoretti* 80, he portrays his own courtship as an interlude of 'rest' from the 'race ... Through Faery land,' now half-completed, in which the 'contemplation of [his lady's] heavenly hew' will raise his 'spirit to an higher pitch' of heroic composition. In the *Hymne of Heavenly Beautie* (127–40), contemplation of God's 'workes' gives way to that 'heavenly contemplation' in which the mind leaves behind 'this darke world' and fixes its sight 'like the native brood of Eagles kynd' on 'that bright Sunne of glorie,' Spenser's Platonized Christ. Finally, the *Cantos of Mutabilitie* point to an ultimate contemplative state, corresponding to the one that Contemplation promised to Redcrosse in *FQ* I x: on the other side of that great Pauline 'change' (VII vii 58–9) the toiling poet, and all others, will 'rest eternally' (viii 2).

JOHN D. BERNARD

Collins 1940; Alberto Grilli 1953 *Il problema della vita contemplativa nel mondo greco-romano* (Milan); Hankins 1945; Kaske 1969; John M. Steadman 1962 'Felicity and End in Renaissance Epic and Ethics' *JHI* 23:117–32; Evelyn Underhill 1911 *Mysticism* (New York); Whitaker 1952.

conventions Rules, devices, and procedures by which writers adapt matter to form, means to ends, and parts to wholes; also the means by which they relate their work to the work of others. The term usefully describes any aspect of form, genre, rhetoric, diction, or prosody in which, consciously or unconsciously, Spenser shares a practice with his predecessors or contemporaries, or initiates a practice later followed by others. No catalogue could exhaust the variety of conventions invented by Spenser, but some of his more general assumptions about conventions may be gathered from the ways he uses them and from the pervasive concern in his poetry with moral and aesthetic standards of appropriateness.

Spenser's assumptions about conventions are guided first of all by views inherited from antiquity. Classical thinkers agreed that conventions are artificial because the correlation between nature and technique is never immediate, but they debated whether conventions order human acts and products on the basis of unchanging natural principles or of changing social expectations. In the tradition of poetic theory descending from Aristotle, nature is not only the object imitated by art but also the principle which determines the fitness or decorum by which the artistic conventions and devices of a work are adapted to each other. The rhetorical tradition represented by Cicero and others, however, stresses the social character of conventions, the tacit core of consent that underlies their origin, transmission, and communicative function.

In Spenser's poetry, as elsewhere in the literary culture of the Renaissance, these two traditions fruitfully coexist. Spenser usually assumes that the proper, decorous use of conventions harmonizes nature and art, and, conversely, that poems 'which have no skill to rule them right, / Have now quite lost their naturall delight' (*Teares* 551–2). At the same time, he also acknowledges the social properties of conventions, especially their transmission by tradition and their power to affect an audience on the basis of its literary knowledge and expectations. As a poet in the midst of human history and rarely, if ever, at the ultimate source of things, he relies heavily on the secondhand resource of antique precedents to authorize his use of conventions (Letter to Raleigh, *FQ* I proem 2, III iv 1–2, IV ii 32–4, VII vi 2). As a rhetorician conscious of the expectations of his audience, he often invokes conventions conspicuously (eg, VII vi 37, VI proem 2). For Spenser, however, the social order is also a natural order, so that his reliance on precedent or a manipulation of the audience need not depart from the abiding, natural standards of fitness. By writing pastoral before epic, he observes a convention that derives from Virgil's precedent and belongs to the realm of art; but he also respects a natural correspondence between the hierarchy of conventional genres and the ordered scale of being.

Sixteenth-century terminology helped to subordinate conventions to the idea of natural order, but it also contained the potential for conflict between the two. The term *convention*, which lays such heavy stress on social agreement that it is virtually an antonym for *nature*, did not become current in its specific literary sense in English until the nineteenth century. *Custom*, *use*, and *usage*, the nearest sixteenth-century equivalents used by Spenser, refer primarily to the process of exercise and repetition through which the principled procedures of an art become acquired habits. When combined with the connotation of habit, however, the secondary reference of those terms to the actual procedures themselves could suggest that, as the habits of a society, conventions might become divorced from natural principles in the course of their transmission. Spenser occasionally voices a fear that conventions may be wholly mutable and arbitrary (V proem 4). In the absence of natural principles (which are also divine), conventions may be corrupted, becoming 'wicked customes,' 'evill fashion,' or 'ungentle usage' (VI i 26, V ii 28, VI iii 42). Conversely, the divine order, always implicit where conventions harmonize with nature, may actually supersede nature as the primary standard to which conventions are adapted, for example, where scriptural techniques predominate over the techniques of secular literature (as at points in *FQ* I), or where the conventions of literature give way to those of worship and prayer (as at *FQ* VII viii 2).

While Spenser assumes that conventions are linked to abiding, transhistorical principles, he also regards them as a record of changing human experience. In *FQ* VII, he uses a variety of literary conventions – ancient, medieval, and contemporary – to trace a history of the human response to change. The different conventions in which this response is embodied ultimately support Nature's verdict: 'all things ... are not changed from their first estate; / But by their change their being doe dilate' (VII vii 58). For Spenser, conventions are the cultural means by which nature tends toward increasing complexity and diversity. He thus anticipates the later historicist and pluralist approach toward conventions while retaining an allegiance to ancient views of natural and divine law.

LAWRENCE MANLEY

The history of the idea of convention is the subject of Lawrence Manley 1980 *Convention, 1500–1750* (Cambridge, Mass). The role of conventions in Elizabethan poetry is treated in Hallett Smith 1952. Several essays by Harry Berger, Jr, develop the view that through his self-conscious use of literary conventions Spenser constructs a reading of history as articulated into different conventionalized world views; see esp his 'Introduction' to Berger 1986c.

copia *Copia* takes the measure of a poet's resources: his learning, technical scope, and imaginative vision. Latin for 'abundance,' copia acquired specific rhetorical connotations summarized in Erasmus' definition of the term as 'plentitude of words and things' functioning to 'enrich' and 'expand' a subject 'until nothing can be added' in style or content (*De copia* in ed 1974–, 24:298). With other Renaissance humanists, he championed copia both to revitalize school Latin and to escape the formulaic limitations of the scholastic logical idiom. They also shared with the later Middle Ages, when experimenting in serious vernacular literature began, a recognition of the acute need for 'enrichment' by copia if Italian, French, and English were to emulate the achievements of admired classical models. Spenser exemplifies this humanistic focus: 'plentitude' becomes a hallmark of his art.

His range of genre, from erotic lyric through pastoral satire to romance-epic, demanded a matching abundance of appropriate lexical, metrical, and stanzaic innovations to assimilate these traditional modes into English, since each genre prescribes its own decorum of structure (*dispositio*) and style (*elocutio*). Spenser responded with prodigious inventiveness, from the modified sonnet form of *Amoretti* and unprecedented metrical variety of *The Shepheardes Calender* to the flexible grace of his complex schemes devised for *The Faerie Queene* and *Epithalamion*. Typically, he complements this formal variety with imagistic abundance. In the night prayer from *Epithalamion*

(334–52), for instance, he rings multiple changes on natural and supernatural threats lurking in darkness, from cries in the night and 'deluding dreames' to witches, ghosts, and birds of ill-omen. The very inclusiveness of this catalogue accommodates a generalized human experience and, reflecting the poem as a whole, suggests a communal ritual: common fears are evoked, then negated with the incantational rhythm of 'Let no,' 'Let not,' 'Ne let,' 'Let none.'

Abuses of copia (inappropriate elaboration or ornamentation) occur rarely in Spenser, except as deliberate devices of characterization to indicate mental or moral imbalance. The lovesick lyric voice of *Amoretti* is a frequent offender, as are voices of complaint in *Complaints* and *The Shepheardes Calender*: 'I love thilke lasse, (alas why doe I love?) / And am forlorne, (alas why am I lorne?)' (*Jan* 61–2), and figures of evil in *The Faerie Queene* who affect elaborate disguises and prolific eloquence, such as Archimago in his tortuous forty-word paraphrase of 'no' in *FQ* I i: 'Ah my deare Sonne (quoth he) how should, alas, / Silly old man, that lives in hidden cell, / Bidding his beades all day for his trespas, / Tydings of warre and worldly trouble tell? / With holy father sits not with such things to mell' (30), and Archimago's false sprite in Una's likeness with her labyrinthine plea, 'Yet thus perforce he bids me do, or die. / Die is my dew: yet rew my wretched state / You' (51).

Unlike his characters, Spenser habitually observes decorum, seeking comprehensiveness, not excess, and *The Faerie Queene* epitomizes his goal. Its exploration, with epic richness, of subjects so complex as holiness, temperance, or courtesy most nearly approaches Erasmus' ideal where 'nothing can be added.' The teeming world of Fairyland filters a multitude of commonplaces from sources as diverse as the Bible and folklore through Spenser's formative imagination (see *topos). Details of character, setting, and incident, and of rhyme, trope, and meter, function in concert to realize concretely his abstract conception of the subject (*inventio*). Each detail, therefore, is significant, and much of our initial difficulty and subsequent pleasure as readers of *The Faerie Queene* arise from copia, the sheer 'plentitude' of enrichment we must absorb in order to develop an interpretation commensurate with Spenser's original invention.

MICHAEL F.N. DIXON

The standard Renaissance textbook was Erasmus's *De duplici copia verborum ac rerum commentarii duo* (first authorized ed 1512), tr Betty I. Knott in Erasmus ed 1974–, vol 24. Doran 1954:46–51 discusses copia in relation to the exuberant language of the stage. The aesthetics of copia are analyzed in Mary E. Hazard 1976 'An Essay to Amplify "Ornament": Some Renaissance Theory and Practice' *SEL* 16:15–32.

Corflambo, Poeana When the lovers Aemylia and Amyas attempt a nocturnal rendezvous, they are intercepted by figures of lust: she is carried off by Lust to his cave, where she is imprisoned until Belphoebe rescues her, and he is imprisoned by the giant Corflambo, whose daughter Poeana falls in love with him. Amyas' friend Placidas exchanges identities with him and becomes Poeana's lover and eventual husband. Attempting to flee, Placidas is rescued by Arthur, who kills Corflambo and restores the lovers to their proper mates (*FQ* IV viii 38–ix 17).

Corflambo (L *cor* heart + Fr *flambeau* flaming torch) is characterized by his 'infectious sight' which vanquishes all his victims 'By casting secret flakes of lustfull fire / From his false eyes, into their harts and parts entire.' As a figure of the destructive power of lust, he must be struck down by Arthur, much as Orgoglio was in I viii.

Corflambo's daughter Poeana, by contrast, is treated far more gently by Arthur and by the poet. A lady who 'given is to vaine delight, / And eke too loose of life, and eke of love too light,' she is a figure not of lust but of an unseemly inversion of proper sex roles, and is akin to such figures as Malecasta, Hellenore, and Radigund. So great is her charm that on first seeing her Arthur himself, 'halfe rapt, began on her to dote,' before recollecting himself, taking her prisoner, and releasing her father's captives. Once Corflambo's tyranny has been undone, however, Arthur arranges her marriage to Placidas, with a substantial dowry. The happy ending to Poeana's story is perhaps reflected in the double etymology of her name, from Latin *poena* 'pain' (she is first seen 'Complayning of her cruell Paramoure') and from *paean* (cf the 'joyous glee' of viii 52; in the 1596 ed, her name is given as Paeana at ix 9). Our last view of her is of a happily married woman who has 'thenceforth reformd her waies, / That all men much admyrde her change, and spake her praise.'

LOUIS A. MARRE

Coridon (Corydon) The name of two shepherds in *Colin Clouts Come Home Againe* and one in *FQ* VI. In *Colin Clout*, 'Coridon' is one of Colin's fellow shepherds in Ireland, who asks him about the terrors of the sea (200). Another 'Corydon,' of 'hablest wit' though 'meanly waged,' is a 'shepheard' at Cynthia's (ie, Elizabeth's) court (382–3); he has been variously but inconclusively identified as Fraunce, Dyer, or Thomas Watson (*Var* 7:465–6, H.S.V. Jones 1930:296).

The Coridon of *FQ* VI ix-xi is a more fully developed figure. The most ardent of Pastorella's shepherd-admirers, he is scorned by the nobly born maiden in favor of Calidore, who outshines him at dancing and wrestling. Coridon proves resentful, selfish, and cowardly. He abandons Pastorella to a tiger's clutches, and Calidore must rescue her. He flees the Brigands who murder Meliboe and capture Pastorella, and reluctantly returns with Calidore to infiltrate the band. Taking no active part in Calidore's heroic mission, he seems unduly rewarded when Calidore gives him all the recovered flocks.

In *Colin Clout*, Coridon/Corydon is used simply as a stock pastoral name, found in Theocritus (Idylls 4, 5), Virgil (Eclogues 2, 7), and Calpurnius Siculus (Eclogues 1, 4, 7). It was also used by many Renaissance Neo-Latinists including Mantuan (Eclogue 9.5), and in England before Spenser by Barclay (Eclogues 1–3) and Googe (Eclogues 3, 8). It also occurs in romances such as Greene's *Ciceronis Amor* (1589), Lodge's *Rosalynde* (1590), and Sidney's *Arcadia* (1593 edition: 'Coredens' in manuscripts). The name was often, as (presumably) in *Colin Clout*, applied allegorically to real persons, from the Emperor Constantine (Petrarch, Eclogue 6.144) to the Provost of King's College, Cambridge (Giles Fletcher the elder, 'Aecloga de contemptu ministrorum'; see Berry 1961).

In *The Faerie Queene*, the name of the unattractive Coridon was perhaps suggested to Spenser by his namesake in Theocritus' earthy and satirical Idylls 4 and 5, and perhaps even by a punning recollection of the fact that Theocritus' Coridon is a 'cowherd' (cf *FQ* VI x 37). Probably the name also recalls the shepherd-lover Corydon in Virgil's Eclogue 2, self-described as a *rusticus* whose gifts, like Coridon's, are powerless to win him the love he so greatly desires (A. Williams 1967:72). Coridon's degeneration may thus indicate Spenser's final dissatisfaction with conventional pastoral, while Calidore continues his greater chivalric quest, taking the high-born Pastorella with him.

SUKANTA CHAUDHURI

cosmogony, cosmology Like most of his contemporaries, Spenser accepted a description of the universe recorded by Ptolemy late in the classical period and interpreted by a long line of Christian exegetes, most importantly by Augustine and Bede. This cosmology places the Earth at the center of the universe and surrounds it by a series of concentric spheres which carry the planets and the fixed stars. This finite system, which comprises what the deity has created, is bounded by the *primum mobile*, or 'first mover.' Outside the *primum mobile* lies the empyrean, the domicile of the Judeo-Christian God, the angels, and the saints.

(See **cosmogony** Fig 1.)

Our Earth, a perfect sphere, provides the fixed center around which this complex system revolves. It consists of four elements (earth, air, fire, water) which mix together in various combinations to produce the multifarious objects in physical nature palpable to our senses. According to Pythagoras and his followers, including Plato and Aristotle, the four elements are defined also in a theoretical way and arranged schematically in a stable yet constantly changing system of contrarieties and agreements known as the *tetraktys*, or quaternity (Heninger 1977:166). This tetrad pattern with its *concordia discors* allows for both permanence and transience, and underlies the Elizabethan concept of mutability. In the *Cantos of Mutabilitie*, Nature calls upon this theory to rule against Change. She concedes 'that all things stedfastnes doe hate / And changed be,' but counters by noting that 'being rightly wayd / They are not changed from their first estate; / But by their change their being doe dilate: / And turning to themselves at length againe, / Doe worke their owne perfection so by fate' (*FQ* VII vii 58; see Jortin in *Var* 6:300).

Surrounding the Earth is a series of seven concentric spheres, each carrying one of the planets. Closest to Earth is the Moon, followed by Mercury, Venus, the Sun, Mars, Jupiter, and Saturn. Each planet completes a regular periodic revolution within its sphere: the Moon, for instance, completes its orbit in 28 days, while Saturn requires 30 years. Spenser was at least distantly aware of this lore: 'They that in course of heavenly spheares are skild,' he says, 'To every planet point his sundry yeare: / in which her circles voyage is fulfild'; but he seems to contradict the commonly known fact that Mars' orbit took approximately two years when he states that 'Mars in three score yeares doth run his spheare' (*Amoretti* 60; see *astronomy).

The seven spheres of the planets are bounded by the sphere of fixed stars. All of the fixed stars are conceived as equidistant from the Earth, attached to the underside of an enormous sphere which requires 1000 years to complete a revolution. Because these stars are fixed relative to one another, they can be grouped into constellations, twelve of which identify the signs of the zodiac.

According to Aristotle (*De caelo* 270b17–25), the planetary spheres and the sphere of fixed stars are composed of a fifth element, a quintessence known as *ether*. The planets and fixed stars are palpable to our senses; but being composed of ether, unlike sublunary creatures, they are not subject to mutability. Spenser bases *Amoretti* 55 on the distinction between the four elements and this heavenly quintessence.

The finite universe reaches its limit with the sphere of fixed stars. Encompassing the whole, however, is a boundary sphere known as the *primum mobile*. In *Hymne of Heavenly Beautie*, Spenser casts his glance from the lowest elements to the upper reaches of the ethereal spheres, which are enclosed by 'that mightie shining christall wall, / Wherewith he hath encompassed this All' (41–2). In accordance with the providential scheme, God (usually assisted by an angel) turns the *primum mobile* so that it makes a complete revolution once every 24 hours. Energy is then transmitted by friction downward through the spheres until it reaches Earth. In this fashion our universe is kept in motion, and God's will is transformed into physical fact. In medieval Christian mythology, a female figure known as Nature acts as God's viceregent on Earth and presides over the created universe and all its creatures (cf *FQ* VII vii 5–13).

Outside the *primum mobile* lies the empyrean, an infinite region without material substance or bounds, residence of all eternal beings. In the Judeo-Christian tradition, this is the location of heaven.

As the planetary spheres turn, each hums because of the friction and produces a musical note. These seven notes comprise a musical scale, the music of the spheres, which underlies the concept of universal harmony. The symphony of the Muses which Spenser presumes in *Teares of the Muses* is a metonymy for this concept; each Muse, in fact, resides on a particular planet and plays a particular musical note.

(See **cosmogony** Fig 2.)

Several cosmogonies were common in Spenser's day. The most familiar and authoritative was the biblical hexaemeron in Genesis, a detailed report of what God created on each of the first six days. In this account, creation culminated in the appearance of mankind and led directly to the sabbath, when God rested and all his creatures sang 'hosanna.' References to this opening chapter of human history are often closely interwoven in the fabric of Spenser's poetry.

Almost equally well-known were several classical accounts of how the world began, presented most concisely and explicitly in the mythology of Hesiod. In Spenser's work, the influence of Hesiod's *Theogony* is seen most clearly in the genealogy of several characters (Night, for example: *FQ* I v 22; cf *Hymne of Love* 50–6). Pythagoras offered a more theoretical account of how cosmos arose out of chaos: the four elements under the impulse of a cosmic force called Love defined themselves as combinations of two of the four basic qualities (moist, dry, hot, cold) to form the *tetraktys*. Plato reported this Pythagorean cosmogony in his *Timaeus* and established it as a basic premise in scientific thought. In the opening lines of his *Metamorphoses*, Ovid combined these mythological and scientific views of creation, which he described as a pacific event whereby Love achieved harmony among the warring elements (see *Colin Clout* 835–52 and *Hymne of Love* 57–112; for a Christianized version, see *Heavenly Love* 22–77). In *Teares*, it is Nature herself who 'formed [all things] of a formelesse mas' (502). Spenser was fully acquainted with all these notions about Earth's origins, and some scholars have found in his writings a debt to Empedocles and Lucretius as well.

Several poems of Spenser deal with cosmological themes. *The Shepheardes Calender* advertises on its title page 'twelve Aeglogues proportionable to the twelve monethes'; it uses motifs of the zodiac and corollary systems to relate the microcosm to the macrocosm, the little world of man to the vast design of mutable nature. *Teares* calls upon the traditional motif of the Muses playing in concert to represent the universal harmony which is now threatened by ignorance and violence. *Epithalamion* demonstrates how human and personal love fits into the cosmic plan. Several passages in *The Faerie Queene* interpret man's position in time and space, perhaps most notably the episodes of the Bower of Bliss (II xii 42–87), the Garden of Adonis (III vi 30–50), the Temple of Venus (IV x 29–58), and the Giant with the scales (V ii 30–50). The *Cantos of Mutabilitie* carefully explain that although continuous change is inescapable, there is a providential order supervised by Nature which ensures the enactment of God's eternal law.

Spenser's most consistently cosmological work, however, is *Fowre Hymnes*, a poem of cosmic speculation that ranks with the greatest devotional works in English literature. In a comprehensive review of the cosmic forces that govern the human condition, Spenser looks from a Platonist perspective and points out the divinely designated path which leads inexorably from an enjoyment of love and beauty in this world to an appreciation of heavenly love and heavenly beauty. The hierarchical arrangement of the four hymns takes us from the foundations of the universe through its physical dimensions and beyond the *primum mobile*, until we are deposited before the Almighty himself. S.K. HENINGER, JR

court Neither Spenser's experience of, nor his attitude towards, the court is easy to establish. There are too many gaps in his biography, and recent scholarship has revealed the dangers of an overly literal interpretation of allusions to persons and events in his work (Oram 1983:45, Meyer 1969, ch 6). Very little, in fact, can be stated with certainty. Spenser hovered on the fringes of the court in 1579–80 when he was attached to the Earl of Leicester's household and in 1590–1 when he returned briefly from Ireland in the company, it is assumed, of Sir Walter Raleigh. Whether he ever entered its inner precincts remains a matter for speculation. The only evidence for the earlier period is provided by one comment in the not entirely reliable *Two Letters* (*Var Prose* p 7). For the later, the literary allusions are to some extent substantiated by the grant of a pension in 1591.

The apparently limited nature of his career was typical of many Elizabethan lay intellectuals. The Queen was not a generous patroness of the arts, nor was her court as open a 'point of contact' for the political nation as it has been described (Elton 1976). At its center was the small, almost static, body of Elizabeth's intimate servants, companions, and advisors who made up its permanent membership. About them was a broader penumbra of transitory figures: members of the nobility making periodic appearances, individuals with a personal entrée to the Queen (eg, her godson John Harington and Edward Dyer), younger sons seeking a career, or the followers of great court figures in the process of entering the Queen's service. They were not truly of the court; and to obtain access and advancement, they needed the assistance of someone in the inner circle – in Spenser's case, Leicester or Raleigh. Spenser's progression from Bishop Young's service to Leicester's, Lord Grey's, and then to that of the crown in Ireland followed a fairly normal pattern.

What complicates any interpretation of Spenser's comments on the court is the ambiguity surrounding his ambitions: specifically, whether he seriously aspired to become Elizabeth's resident laureate (Wells 1983:5–6). It is no longer so clear that he regarded his career in Ireland as an exile or a disgrace (Meyer 1969:158–9). Thus the three extended attacks on the court found in *Mother Hubberd* 607–925, *Colin Clout* 660–770, and *FQ* VI ix should not necessarily be read as the personal reflections of a disappointed place-seeker. The themes that run through them – the court as the center of courtesy and civility and the opposition of the court and the country life, together with the catalogue of courtly vices and virtues – were established concerns of the pastoral, and hardly novel (Renwick in *Var* 7:478, Greenlaw in *Var* 8:369). Even the apparent eulogy of Leicester as the virtuous courtier (*CCCHA* 739–40) derives its model from Castiglione, and should not be taken as a literal description of its subject.

As revealing as the difficulty of separating the personal from the conventional in the depiction of the court as an institution is the questionable accuracy of the two portraits of the court elite of the early 1590s: the *FQ* dedicatory sonnets and the encomium on the ladies who 'me graced goodly well' in *Colin Clout* (485–583). No reason for the addition of the seven later sonnets to the original ten has yet been discovered. Five of the first group and three of the latter are dedicated to men who were clearly of the court's inner circle: Lord Burghley, Sir Christopher Hatton, Charles, Lord Howard of Effingham, Lord Buckhurst, the Earl of Essex, Sir Francis Walsingham, Lord Hunsdon, and Raleigh. All were either major officeholders or privy councilors. Yet the remaining six were not. Three had Irish service in common: Lord Grey, the Earl of Ormond, and Sir John Norris (though both Ormond and Norris had a personal entrée to the Queen). The others – the Earls of Cumberland, Northumberland, and Oxford – were more peripheral figures. They were the heirs of older noble families hostile to the Reformation, who were the objects of efforts (unsuccessful in the case of Oxford) to woo them to the regime.

The encomium on the ladies, if the accepted identification of ten of the twelve is correct, presents an even more eccentric picture. Two of the ladies, the Countess of Pembroke and Lady Carew (*recte* Carey), were also the subjects of dedicatory sonnets. In *Colin Clout*, Lady Carey appears with her sisters Lady Strange and Lady Compton, the three being the daughters of Spenser's distant relative Sir John Spencer of Althorp. Four of the ladies were members of the Dudley connection: the Countess of Huntingdon (Leicester's sister), the Countess of Warwick (his sister-in-law), Lady Pembroke (his niece), and, more distantly, Lady Rich. The remaining three were two Englishwomen married to Irish peers, the Countesses of Ormond and Kildare, and the Marchioness of Northampton, a Swede who had entered the court as a girl and married an English peer.

It should not be assumed that this passage was a eulogy of the reigning court beauties. For one thing, the Countess of Huntingdon was roughly Elizabeth's age, while Lady Warwick and Lady Northampton were in their forties. But even more importantly, most of the ladies were not prominent at the court. Only Lady Warwick and Lady Northampton were members of the inner circle (as Spenser specifically states, 499–500, 509): both were gentlewomen extraordinary of the privy chamber and among Elizabeth's closest female companions. Certain of the others had experience of the court – Lady Carey was married to Hunsdon's son (himself a future lord chamberlain), while Lady Kildare was a daughter of Howard of Effingham and may have been a maid of honor – but there is no other evidence to show that they were close to the Queen.

Spenser's motives in placing them about Cynthia, so obviously an allusion to Elizabeth, can only be guessed at. Shared literary interests (as well as patronage) may have been the case with Lady Carey and Lady Pembroke, as it may also have been in the inclusion of Northumberland, Cumberland, and Oxford among the subjects of the dedicatory sonnets. For the others, personal and political loyalties were probably of most importance. It is doubtful that they were placed there out of ignorance, for however limited his direct experience of the court, Spenser was a member of the Elizabethan political elite, and knew who its leading figures were. Rather, as may be suggested of his portrait of the court as a whole, the encomium was another example of his cavalier use of allusions to contemporaries to suit his own purposes. It is as a guide to his own ideals and allegiances that Spenser's descriptions of the court and its personalities should be read, not as an account of Elizabethan political realities.

SIMON ADAMS

Simon Adams 1985 'Eliza Enthroned? The Court and Its Politics' in *The Reign of Elizabeth I* ed Christopher Haigh (London) pp 55–77 and (for bib) 251–2; G.R. Elton 1976 'Tudor Politics: The Points of Contact. III. The Court' *TRHS* 5th ser 26:211–28; Sam Meyer 1969 *An Interpretation of Edmund Spenser's 'Colin Clout'* (Cork); William A. Oram 1983 'Elizabethan Fact and Spenserian Fiction' *SSt* 4:33–47; Wells 1983; Pam Wright 1987 'A Change of Direction: The Ramifications of a Female Household, 1558–1603' in *The English Court: From the Wars of the Roses to the Civil War* ed David Starkey (London) pp 147–72.

courtesy The idea of courtesy originated in the Middle Ages. Although some classical concepts are analogous, medieval and Renaissance interpretations of the virtue most influenced Spenser. As a chivalric virtue featured in medieval romances like *Gyron le curtoys*, it was an obvious choice for the subject of a book in Spenser's romance that fashioned various virtues. Not always simply a secular code of behavior involving etiquette, affability, and humanity, medieval courtesy had theological implications, for its affinities with charitable love of one's neighbor opened it to religious treatment. Since various writers praised Christ, God, or heaven for perfect courtesy, the virtue was even used as a metaphor for the perfections of the divine order. Spenser likewise interprets courtesy theologically to some extent, so that it is a comprehensive social virtue aptly completing the sequence of virtues in *The Faerie Queene*.

Though not so common in Spenser's time as previously, religious applications of courtesy were not unusual. In the Geneva and Bishops' Bibles, for example, courtesy appears in a context that, according to Luther's commentary, identifies the distinguishing outward characteristics of Christian spirituality: 'be courteous, Not rendring evil for evil ... but contrarie wise blesse, knowing that ye are thereunto called, that ye shulde be heires of blessing' (1 Pet 3.8–9; cf Eph 4.31–2). Calidore comparably 'rewards' Coridon 'well' 'for ill' (VI ix argument). In any case, Elizabethan biblical translators assume that courtesy expresses Christian values.

Since the religious view of courtesy was primarily medieval, Spenser's recourse to it befits the rather nostalgic neo-medievalism of *The Faerie Queene*. Moreover, just as manifestations of beauty were virtual theophanies for many sixteenth-century Platonists, so courtesy, as an art of conduct involving both love and aesthetics, may well have seemed attractive to him as a universal metaphor. Accordingly, beauty is central for Book VI, as names like Calidore, Mirabella, Claribell, and Castle Belgard attest. The dance of the Graces in canto x presents gracious behavior as a reflection of heavenly love and beauty, so that 'grace' develops complex thematic resonance. Courtesy conceived as a transcendent ideal would have been attractive also as a ready, venerable alternative to the debased courtesy of mere 'outward shows' that Spenser deplores (proem 4–5), thus providing him an authoritative means to evaluate social norms.

The courtesy books further account for Spenser's approach because many depend to some extent on philosophico-theological views of virtue. Most that were written before the sixteenth century provide ethical guides to etiquette including proper religious observance. Many of these, like Geoffrey de la Tour-Landry's *Livre du Chevalier de la Tour*, link manners and courtesy with virtue and spiritual salvation; and some, like Christine de Pisan's *Epistre d'Othéa* and Jacques Legrand's popular *Livre de bonnes moeurs*, are emphatically Christian manuals of civil life. Early courtesy books tend to assume that manners and social intercourse at best express inner virtue conceived according to Christian doctrine; later ones, though far more urbane, apply such standards more subtly to social life. Despite their differences, della Casa's *Galateo*, Guazzo's *Civile Conversation*, and Castiglione's *Courtier* treat proper social conduct as a function of inner virtue. Actions, dress, and speech should suit the occasion (time, place, and persons concerned) so far as reason and virtue permit. Virtues like temperance, prudence, humility, affability, and, in a general sense, charity would thus be exercised, and the varieties of self-love disciplined. The new emphasis by these writers on the aesthetics of social behavior complements their moral standpoint because they associated beauty with good. Venus Urania presides, in effect, over Guazzo's civil code, for he assumes that heavenly love for intellectual beauty promotes civility (ed 1925, 1:234–7). Bembo's oration again gives civil life this 'holy' standard: the courtier should pursue divine beauty, and sustain that conception in all his activities (Castiglione ed 1928:303–23).

Both Guazzo and Castiglione explore the inner dimensions of civil life in ways that further elucidate Spenser's courtesy. Guazzo examines the role of action and contemplation in social intercourse, assuming that learning and 'contemplation of thinges Celestiall and divine' render it 'more easie and sure' (1:216, 48–9), and Spenser proceeds similarly in Book VI (see Tonkin 1972:300–6). Guazzo's stress on charity and humility in conduct is plainly Christian (1:100–1, 158, 192), and Pettie (Guazzo's Elizabethan translator) makes the largely implicit association of courtesy with spirituality explicit (1:228). The *Courtier*, too, applies metaphysico-theological doctrine to social considerations, but further relates social conduct to interactions of the virtues and analyzes human capacities for virtuous acts (pp 266–73). The ideal courtier's 'every deede' is 'compact and framed of all the vertues' so that his life is an aesthetically unified whole answerable to the virtues as its parts (pp 94–5; cf pp 36, 67–8, 266–73). Many further works of the period, such as the casuists' and moral philosophers' treatises, and religious social guides like John Woolton's *Christian Manual* (1576), regard conduct in even more sweepingly philosophico-religious terms.

Likewise, courtesy as Spenser's 'roote of civill conversation' or civilized intercourse (VI i 1) consists of more than 'comely carriage, entertainement kynde, / Sweete semblaunt,' and 'friendly offices that bynde' (x 23), for it involves many further considerations relating to its origin in 'vertues seat ... deepe within the mynd' (proem 5). Moral analysis is not only explicit, as at i 40–2, but also presented through situational exemplars and allegory. Fortitude, prudence, patience, mercy, temperance, and affability are parts of courtesy; fortitude especially is crucial, for example, when Pastorella's deliverance depends on Calidore's rejection of Coridon's false claim that he witnessed her death (xi 27–35; cf 18.9, 24). Probably the essential components are humility and charity: 'true curtesie' is 'lowly,' reaches out to all, and springs from 'heavenly seedes of bounty soveraine' (proem 3–5). Like the moral philosophers, Spenser further uses the current psychology to articulate ethical theory. The senses, passions, and humors explicitly account for the Blatant Beast's poisonous effects, providing a psychological rationale for the cultivation of temperance and prudence as parts of courtesy (vi 1–16). But Book VI, like many other Renaissance works, is partly an allegory about perfecting relations between the aspects of human nature, and endeavors to do so for the better practice of courtesy.

In deriving courtesy from virtue's seat within the mind, Spenser supplements psychology and moral philosophy with Christian doctrine. His invocation of a vatic *furor* assumes that courtesy has a divine origin and profound significance worthy of poetic theology (VI proem 2–4). The introductory adventure pointedly has Crudor pledge reformation upon a 'crosse' to Calidore (i 43), who is a type of Christ when he 'redeemes' Pastorella (xi argument) in a way that reflects Christ's Harrowing of Hell (xi 43–51; see Maurice Evans 1970:224). The Beast's victims are treated under explicitly Christian auspices (v 35–6), and Calidore's ultimate expulsion of it from 'the sacred Church' makes clear that courtesy's quest impinges on spiritual goals (xii 23–5). While the episode of the Graces is central for understanding this aspect of courtesy, much further insight can be gained through investigation of the other adventures for theological allegory. Spenser finds this social virtue applicable not to society conceived according to secular considerations only, but rather as it further involves the church as the society of Christians with God and each other.

Courtesy thus provides a summation of *The Faerie Queene*, which is founded on the Legend of Holiness and seeks 'to fashion a gentleman' in both 'vertuous and gentle discipline' (Letter to Raleigh). Through this divine 'poetry of conduct' (Lewis 1936:351), the virtuous life becomes an art in a sixteenth-century sense, rather as the *Courtier* recommends. By Book VI, virtues have become sufficiently manifest that they may be exercised with spontaneity and grace as harmoniously coordinated parts of courtesy. Hence the virtue is both *dulce et utile*, or capable of giving others insight into good by way of delight. The arts of conduct thus have regenerative implications and, insofar as *The Faerie Queene* is an epically transfigured courtesy book itself, Spenser's courtesy epitomizes his larger endeavor.

KENNETH BORRIS

For a further account of courtesy, see Kenneth Borris 1985 'A Commentary on Book Six of *The Faerie Queene*' diss Edinburgh University, Introduction, 'Courtesy,' and 'Survey of Criticism.' General surveys with useful bibliography include Bornstein 1975; James W. Holme 1910 'Italian Courtesy-Books of the Sixteenth Century' *MLR* 5:145–66; and Kelso 1929. On the theological potential of medieval courtesy, see D.S. Brewer 1966 'Courtesy and the *Gawain*-Poet' in Lawlor 1966:54–85; W.O. Evans 1967 '"Cortaysye" in Middle English' *MS* 29:143–57; Sister Anna Maria Reynolds 1979 '"Courtesy" and "Homeliness" in the *Revelations* of Julian of Norwich' *FCEMN* 5.2:12–20; and J. Stephen Russell 1982–3 '*Pearl*'s "Courtesy": A Critique of Eschatology' *Renascence* 35:183–95. For the often neglected importance of ethics, theology, and metaphysics to Renaissance courtesy books, see further, eg, those of Lodowick Bryskett, Lilio Gregorio Giraldi, Girolamo Muzio, Giovambattista Nenna, Matteo Palmieri, and Annibale Romei. On Neoplatonic aesthetics of conduct, see Garin 1965, chs 2, 4; Mazzeo 1965; John Charles Nelson 1958 *Renaissance Theory of Love: The Context of Giordano Bruno's 'Eroici furori'* (New York); and Edward Williamson 1947 'The Concept of Grace in the Work of Raphael and Castiglione' *Italica* 24:316–24.

Important Spenserian studies, which also discuss related matters like nobility and nurture, include Berger 1961b; Culp 1971; Nohrnberg 1976; and Tonkin 1972. On the theological aspect, see P[eter] C. Bayley 1966 'Order, Grace and Courtesy in Spenser's World' in Lawlor 1966:178–202; Evans 1970, ch 10; Judson 1932; Roche 1964:200; Gerald Snare 1975 'The Poetics of Vision: Patterns of Grace and Courtesy in *The Faerie Queene*, VI' *RenP 1974* pp 1–8; and K. Williams 1966, ch 6.

courtesy as a social code C.S. Lewis' description of courtesy as 'the poetry of conduct' (1936:351) has long been subject to a philosophical extension making courtesy a metaphor for cosmic harmonies (and rescuing it from the apparent triviality of 'good manners'). But prior to the philosophical sense, the term denoted a social code now grown largely unfamiliar, of managed relations among members of a hierarchical society. If we are to discern the changes Spenser rang on this received idea, by means of which he helped to invent the more extended sense of cosmic harmonies, we must first consider the social functions of courtesy.

The code arose in direct response to a major shift in the definition of social elevation, from a stress on birth to a stress on achievements, from parentage to deeds, as Marlowe's Tamburlaine has it. Elite identity gradually came to depend not on inherited or god-given absolute attributes, but on characteristics which could be acquired by human effort. The main cause of this shift in definition was a marked increase in upward social mobility: during the sixteenth century in England, the ruling elite (some 2–5 percent of the population) increased in size much more rapidly than the whole population. Among the immediate causes of this surge were Henry VIII's dissolution of the monastic land holdings, which distributed land, the principal sign of status, far more broadly than before, throughout the upper reaches of the social order, prodding into mobility many among the gentry and yeomanry; and the humanist educational revolution, which arrived from Italy with a call for interdependence between political eminence and the technical skills of literacy and bureaucracy. The privileges accompanying new lands and new activities drew many men from obscurity to the newly central court, now the national mart of opportunity. Both these events date from the 1530s; a generation later, when Hoby's translation of Castiglione's *Book of the Courtier* appeared (1561), the dispersion of ambition and privilege was well advanced.

This demographic shift of new men into the ruling elite aroused a storm of controversy best seen as a crisis of legitimacy. Many saw the change as a corrupting invasion; many others saw it as a well-deserved access of recognition, or at least of opportunity. Elizabethan courtesy theory arose as a corpus in this context of strife. While some texts were imported from Italy (Castiglione, Guazzo's *Civile Conversation*), others were native products (Elyot's *Boke Named the Governour*, Puttenham's *Arte of English Poe-*

sie), but all functioned to order and manage this controversy over social legitimacy.

Four managing functions of the discourse of courtesy may be discerned, keeping in mind that, given the variety of interpretations to which it was subject, the overall effect of its management of the conflict was uneven, possibly self-contradictory. Its original aim was the repression of illicit mobility. Castiglione's Sir Frederick Fregoso proposes to define the ideal courtier in order 'to disgrace therfore many untowardly Asseheades, that through malapartnesse [presumption] thinke to purchase them the name of a good Courtier' (ed 1928:29). In effect, this sentence inaugurates the project of courtesy theory, in an explicitly combative way. Hand in hand with such repression went the gesture of reascription whereby the established elite strove to reclaim the self-evident 'natural' superiority its forebears had enjoyed. The institution of the ideal courtier was designed both to cast the existing elite as approximations of the ideal and to disenfranchise the fakes.

But these strategies, because codified in print, might be learned: the skills defined by Castiglione's ideal could be acquired by those not born to them, the very men whose faking was to be measured by the ideal yardstick. The literature of exclusion thus came paradoxically to empower social mobility, its third effective function, by the very promulgation of the techniques upon which the distinctions rested. This function disrupted the program of repression at two levels. Not only were the non-legitimate enabled to enter the privileged classes, but the absolute status of those classes was drawn into question. For when the test failed to discriminate, the distinction itself was undermined: if class difference is not obvious, then who is to say that *all* aristocrats have not worked their way, more or less recently, into positions of power and privilege?

Finally, a fourth function of the courtly code must be noted. The techniques of courteous distinction consisted mainly in activities of speech and behavior which were either grounds for distinction or pathways to advancement for the ambitious. Many rose to the aristocracy by such means, or stayed there; a great many more tried to rise and failed. But these same techniques might recast failure, by asserting elite status through the sheer practice of the discourse. If elite identity becomes visible in style, then stylized behavior of the right sort can confer such identity, even without the material perquisites of rank. So we must allow for the way courteous discourse could reconstitute the *attempt* at mobility as its *achievement*.

Insofar as courteous behavior was public, it should be conceived as a kind of rhetoric, designed to persuade an audience of one's identity. Many of its techniques can then be seen as rhetorical devices, which can conveniently be grouped in three sets. One set consists of those tropes that justify stratification into the binary ranks of gentle and base, usually by representing contingent differences as absolute, or by projecting them into the remote past in a myth of sacred origins. These devices stipulate one's membership in the elite, and then claim privilege and power for the self by asserting the rightful superiority of the group. The other two sets, tropes of promotion and rivalry, stipulate the elite's entitlement as a group, and argue for including or excluding the individual. The tropes of promotion impute value to the self, superiors, or allies through praise or flattery. This set includes the famous posture of *sprezzatura*, where one puts on a guise of effortlessness, making elevation seem natural by hiding one's artful preparation and effort; and the gesture of self-deprecation, which extracts ratifying compliment and reassurance from an audience by a false humility which they feel bound to contradict. The third set, tropes of rivalry, assaults rivals with blame or slander. Here we find the operations of sumptuary regulation, a detailed system of specifications which disallowed various kinds of cloth and styles of garment to certain ranks, in order to maintain rigid distinctions between social orders and penalize the ambitious for falsifying their identity by the illegitimate use of symbolic dress. Here too we find the accusation of 'Italianate Englishman,' an insult that plays complexly on 'proper' and 'debased' practice of the techniques of Italian humanist courtesy. Many who damned others for devious Italianate falsification of image themselves practiced the skills of indirect self-display enjoined by Castiglione.

Spenser uses – and questions – the intricate assumptions of this courteous discourse in many ways, on the whole exhibiting a profound ambivalence about such courtly values. His correspondence with Harvey enacts a version of his own new man's posturing in courtly suit, while *Mother Hubberds Tale* records angry frustration at such slippery struggle. The appointment to Ireland both promoted and marooned him: far from the center of things, yet (like one of his knights in the wilderness) the center's agent, he played out all four functions of courtly performance. The Spenser of *Vewe*, colonial deputy and architect of a plan for pacification by starvation, actively identified himself with authority and its repression of presumption. And the Spenser of the poetry strove to remythologize a nobility now gone sour, decayed from past glories and purities: his knights scour the land for impostors, but are often deceived by them, both rhetors like Braggadocchio and shape-changers like Archimago. Yet the poems also served as his means of personal access to the center: offered as a ground for recognition and ratification (not only for himself but for the newly civilized realm of England), they were judged worth a pension by the Queen. Spenser may have hated courtly corruption, even thought it constitutive of the court, but he treasured his own aristocratic connections, and offered up his literate service to the Queen's court (complete with seventeen dedicatory sonnets, all addressed to notables, to introduce *FQ*). And yet in the end, the poet remained marginal; he consoled himself with his poem, grasping achievement by equating it with his poetic activity, defining the discourse itself as arrival, as the fruit of his ambitions, not their mode. His death in poverty and exile from his Irish home of a lifetime, burned out by rustic brigands, could no more displace an achievement so defined than had his twenty-year exile from England itself; his final return to the center, for burial at Westminster Abbey, was finally ratified by poets and courtiers alike.

Spenser's life and art also manifest all three sets of courtly technique. The distinction between gentle and base is a founding attribute of his imaginative universe, brought repeatedly into question and redefined, yet always reaffirmed. And of course, *The Faerie Queene* itself constitutes a gigantic myth of origins, the past as matrix and criterion for the English present. Then there are the innumerable operations of the poetry of praise, both literal (in service of Elizabeth, or Lord Grey, or himself) and ironic (as in the proem to *FQ* v, where the portrait of Elizabeth as Astraea is so obscure, or the close of ii, where that grand poetic product the Bower of Bliss is razed). Perhaps most important in direct relation to courtesy are the tropes of blame and slander that embody social rivalry. Characters such as Envy and Detraction dog the steps of those who, like Artegall, seek to impose justice in a world where so much rests on audience approval. More complex are the dark aspects of *FQ* vi, the Legend of Courtesy. The antagonist is the Blatant Beast, stuffed full of tongues, invader of privacy and soiler of reputations. The Beast is usually equated with slander, but a sense of courtesy as a social code would suggest connections with what we would now perhaps call publicity: the despotism of the audience, invasive and insatiable, and fed by the postulate of a courtesy that locates all security in audience legitimation. If for the courtier the need for witness underlies all sense of self, then the Blatant Beast appropriately attacks those in the privacy of recreation or procreation, absolutes of interiority where the inner self is forged. Even the poem itself, fruit of a similar privacy, is finally torn by the Beast; and the retiring poet settles for seeking to please, however bitterly. And what are we to make, lastly, of the subtle homology between the Beast and his knight Calidore, whose principal trope, echoed throughout his book, is the invasion of privacies – of knights and ladies making love, of the pastoral realm generally and Meliboe's humble home, and most deeply, of the hidden dance of the Graces, where he envies his own eyes? Must the knight of Courtesy bring rhetorical consciousness wherever he goes? Can his store-bought shepherd's weeds ever be anything but a costume? Are all degrees and states now ruled by the corrupting imperatives of courtesy and the Blatant Beast? Such a view may well be Spenser's final violent judgment of courtesy as a social code.

Frank Whigham

Pierre Bourdieu 1977 *Outline of a Theory of Practice* tr Richard Nice (Cambridge); Burke 1950; David Cressy 1976 'Describing the Social Order of Elizabethan and Stuart England'

L&H 3:29–44; Elias 1978; Michel Foucault 1977 'Nietzsche, Genealogy, History' in his *Language, Counter-Memory, Practice* tr Donald F. Bouchard and Sherry Simon, ed Donald F. Bouchard (Ithaca, NY) pp 139–64; Erving Goffman 1967 *Interaction Ritual: Essays on Face-to-Face Behavior* (Garden City, NY); Greenblatt 1980; Helgerson 1983; Javitch 1978; Lytle and Orgel 1981; W.T. MacCaffrey 1961; Montrose 1980; John Neale 1958 'The Elizabethan Political Scene' in his *Essays in Elizabethan History* (New York) pp 59–84; George B. Parks 1961 'The First Italianate Englishmen' *SRen* 8:197–216; Lawrence Stone 1965; Stone 1966 'Social Mobility in England, 1500–1700' *P&P* 33:16–55; Whigham 1981; Whigham 1984.

courtesy books Spenser's choice of courtesy as the virtue of *FQ* VI, as well as his prefatory claim that the purpose of his heroic poem is 'to fashion a gentleman or noble person in vertuous and gentle discipline' (Letter to Raleigh), have prompted some readers to consider *The Faerie Queene* as a courtesy book in verse (eg, Caspari 1954). To the extent that it aims to improve the morals and social manners of its readers, the poem does share some of the didactic motives of Renaissance conduct books and may be related to the history of that genre (for which, see Kelso 1929, 1956). Yet, Spenser's departures in Book VI from contemporary courtesy books are more apparent than his dependence on them (see Tonkin 1972). A survey of the most popular Elizabethan conduct books reveals that courtesy for Spenser is a more inward, less superficial virtue than the etiquette and 'outward shows' they prescribe.

English conduct books in the mid-sixteenth century, from Elyot's *Boke Named the Governour* (1531) to the *Institucion of a Gentleman* (1555), did not discuss or theorize about courtesy in much detail. For more specific treatment of its formal requisites, late Tudor Englishmen had to turn to Italian works. The eventual availability of these books in English translations discouraged the production of native courtesy books, at least until the seventeenth century. Thus, when Elizabethan writers discuss polite manners, they often defer to Italian authorities rather than set down new rules.

In the draft of a letter composed between 1575 and 1580, Spenser's friend Gabriel Harvey claims that his contemporaries at Cambridge, dissatisfied with the traditional curriculum, were reading the latest available foreign books, starting with manuals of conduct, in order to familiarize themselves with the manners of city and court, where they hoped to obtain eventual employment. He lists the following courtesy books as most popular: 'Philbertes Philosopher of the Courte, the Italian Archebysshoperies brave Galateo, Castiglioes fine Cortegiano, Bengalassoes Civil Instructions to his Nephew Seignor Princisco Ganzar: Guatzoes newe Discourses of curteous behavior' (ed 1884:78–9). These books offer a representative picture of the eclectic courtesy literature available to Elizabethan readers and provide a thematic background against which Spenser's conception of courtesy can be compared.

Of all the books in Harvey's list, Castiglione's *Il cortegiano* (1528) was the most influential and widely read Italian courtesy book in late Tudor England. Some Elizabethans apparently read it in the original Italian, using the work as a primer of Italian as well as of courtliness. But the work was made more available to them in Thomas Hoby's English translation (*The Courtier* 1561; rpt 1577, 1588, 1603), and in Bartholomew Clerke's Latin version (1571; rpt 1577, 1585, 1593, 1603), as well as in various French versions.

More than a handbook of etiquette, *The Courtier* is concerned primarily with defining the profession and attributes of a perfect courtier, and with the ways he may best fulfill his role as servant and adviser of his prince. Much of the courtier's success with his peers and sovereign depends, however, on his ingratiating manners. According to Castiglione's speakers, grace stems from *sprezzatura*, the ability to make effort appear effortless, that is, to make acquired skills seem unrehearsed and artifice seem artless. In addition to such artificial spontaneity, graceful court conduct also demands that the courtier always be ready to alter his mood and personality, or to accommodate himself and his views to the different dispositions of those he converses with. The quality that grants him such admirable elasticity is *mediocrità*, an Italian Renaissance restatement of the Aristotelian doctrine of the mean; it entails balancing or moderating any trait with its opposite. *Sprezzatura* and *mediocrità* are sources of social grace, advocated not simply because they appeal to the aesthetic tastes of a courtly elite, but because they are the necessary and effective means of maintaining a favorable relationship with one's prince.

Although the courtier's relationship to his prince is all-important and determines fundamental aspects of his conduct, it receives relatively little explicit discussion in *The Courtier*. Despite the dissembling of Castiglione's speakers, however, it becomes apparent that the pressures of autocratic rule shape their standards of politeness. For example, norms of elegance at court, not to mention the ladies' intolerance of unrelieved gravity, require the courtier to be witty and to treat serious matters playfully. A more essential (though virtually unstated) reason for possessing these abilities, however, is that they serve to enhance the courtier's relationship with his prince when the latter is more disposed to be entertained than to be burdened by weighty affairs. Similarly, because the ruler's favor or assent can often be won more easily by appealing to his pleasurable impulses, the courtier must develop artistic and recreative skills and, in general, be a dilettante. His ironic modesty and studied indirection are graceful ploys which not only aim to delight his peers but are also part of a repertory of stratagems to obtain the princely favor that is more likely to be won when the stratagem is disguised by reticence and nonchalance. The ruler's intolerance of presumptuous self-promotion is ultimately the chief reason for mastering *sprezzatura*. Moreover, the deference required of the courtier demands that he veil and underplay his talents in order not to outshine his superior.

Indirection is so prized at court and obviousness is considered so unseemly that dissimulation must characterize most aspects of the courtier's conduct. To some extent, the courtly milieu prizes deceit because it baffles or eludes individuals of baser, plainer tastes and thereby serves to assert the social superiority and refinement of the aristocrat. But to a greater extent, dissimulation is conditioned by the prudential relationship the courtier must maintain with his prince. Transactions with a despotic ruler simply demand deceitful conduct.

In effect, *The Courtier* presents an art of pleasing the prince, since nearly every courtesy the courtier is asked to cultivate can be used successfully to win or preserve the sovereign's good will. This pragmatic aspect explains the book's great success in sixteenth-century Europe. It is not merely an idealistic, nostalgic commemoration of an irretrievable high point of Renaissance civilization. Modern readers, like earlier anticourtly ones, may be dismayed by the growing sense that most of the beautiful manners Castiglione advocates are made necessary by the loss of sincerity and free expression in the sycophancy that individuals are made to bear in a despotic political system. Sixteenth-century readers, however, found *The Courtier* instructive and relevant precisely because it provided a model of polite behavior tailored to autocratic rule and the despotic courts which had become the centers of power and fashion.

Castiglione's was only one of several popular Italian books. The book that heads Harvey's list, Philibert de Vienne's *Le Philosophe de court* (1547), was translated into English by George North as *The Philosopher of the Court* (1575). It was intended as a subtle but devastating mock encomium of courtiership that pressed to extremes Castiglione's dilettantism, flattery, dissimulation, elasticity, and prudence. For example, the author urges courtly pliancy in this way (ed 1575:108–9):

> The Gentleman Courtyer is ... plyant like waxe, redie to receyve any honest or frendly impression. For if it be needefull to laughe, hee rejoyceth: If to be sad, he lowreth: If to be angry, he frowneth: If to feed, he eateth: If to faste, he pyneth. And to conclude, he is ready to doe whatsoever it be, according to the humors and complexions of his felowship and Courtly companie, althoughe his affections are cleane contrary.

Such ingratiating deceit must be performed with prudence and made to seem natural. Courtly grace consists of the scrupulous concealment of all ambition and feeling. Philibert's ironic exaggeration of Castiglione's precepts did not prevent Harvey's contemporaries from accepting this satirical philosophy of worldly success as a pragmatic mirror of court conduct. (Not surprisingly,

Harvey claims that Machiavelli's *Prince* was also avidly read by his fellow Cantabrigians.) Instead of appreciating the original satirical and anti-Italian intention of *Le Philosophe de court*, Elizabethans were prepared to read it as sensible and pragmatic advice about how to succeed at court (Javitch 1971a).

The second work in Harvey's list, Giovanni della Casa's *Galateo*, originally appeared in Venice in 1558, and was first published as a separate treatise in 1559. Along with *The Courtier*, it remains the best known of the Italian courtesy books; but it does not seem to have been as popular among Elizabethans as Castiglione's book or as Guazzo's *Civile Conversation*. Robert Peterson's translation was the only sixteenth-century English version (*Galateo: A Treatise of Maners* 1576), though it is likely that some Elizabethans read it in Italian or French. According to della Casa, the desire to please is the aim of all good manners. While his work teaches what forms of conduct are pleasing, it concentrates on displeasing behavior that must be shunned, reflecting the increasing tendency of later Renaissance moralists to regulate behavior (especially concerning bodily functions) in public. The particularities of social or antisocial conduct scrutinized in the *Galateo* are striking – for example, the proper use of the napkin or other utensils at table, offensive habits like belching, nose-picking, spitting, paring nails, wearing a toothpick about the neck. Della Casa does not dwell as extensively on physical comportment as on verbal manners which reflect an individual's lack or possession of courtesy. Again, he does not set down rules of proper conversation so much as proscribe aberrations in verbal exchange. Lying, bragging, blasphemy, backbiting, mockery, pompousness, and abject servility are to be shunned.

Galateo provides no new theory of courtesy, and its rules of etiquette do not seem very different from those in prior handbooks like Caxton's *Book of Curtesye* (1477–8) or Erasmus' much more widely read *De civilitate morum puerilium* (1530, Eng tr 1532 and later) – except in one important respect. Unlike his predecessors, della Casa does not limit attention to one aspect of polite conduct. He is not concerned just with training children, with table manners, or with the comportment of a single sex or group. He seeks instead to formulate a code of good manners, based on decorum and prevailing custom, that could apply to every civilized person. His code is clearly devised for a larger segment of society than Castiglione's courtly enclave. This enlargement of the social theater where courtesy is practiced corresponds to the increase in number and social importance of 'gentle folk' who were not highborn aristocrats or courtiers, a change also reflected in the gradual displacement of the word *courtesy* (from *court*) by the Latinate word *civility* (L *civilis* civil, civic) to denote polite conduct.

The third book cited in Harvey's list reflects by its title the Elizabethan taste for a theory of courtesy that could combine courtly and civil standards of politeness: 'Bengalassoes Civill Instructions to his Nephew Princisco Ganzar' (first pub in Eng as *A New Yeeres Gift: The Courte of Civill Courtesie* 1577; rpt 1582, 1591). Though the printer claims that it is a translation of an unprinted Italian text, it may well have been the work of its 'translator' S.R. (Simon Robson?), purporting to be of Italian origin simply to lend it more authority. Although cruder and more cumbersome than *Galateo*, like della Casa's, this manual assumes that deference and decorum lie at the heart of courtesy, that manners manifest themselves primarily in verbal conduct, and therefore that to be courteous one must master the art of conversing with one's inferiors and one's betters. It not only prescribes 'How a man shall acquite himselfe towardes noble persons,' or 'How a man shall answer to the prayse and thankes ... offred by his betters or equals' (sig A3v); it also provides practical model speeches and 'stately phrases' for these and other social situations where courtesy is displayed by proper verbal conduct. Although now virtually forgotten, this handbook continued to appeal to Elizabethans as combining Italianate cachet with Tudor utilitarianism.

The demand for a combination of courtly and civil standards of courtesy also explains why Elizabethans were reading, at the same time, two such different arts of conduct as *The Courtier* and Stefano Guazzo's *La civil conversatione* (1574), the last book cited in Harvey's list. Guazzo's treatise enjoyed a great vogue in Europe from the moment it was published in Italy until well into the seventeenth century. *The Civile Conversation*, as it was called in English, appeared in only two Elizabethan editions: George Pettie's translation of Books 1–3 in 1581, and then another edition in 1586 which included Book 4 translated by Bartholomew Yong. However, the work was quite widely owned and read by Elizabethans, more often than not in conjunction with *The Courtier* (see Javitch 1971b:180–1).

Guazzo's book is devised as a dialogue between the author's brother William and Anniball Magnocavalli, a doctor who turns out to be the author's spokesman. Magnocavalli begins by refuting the possibility that man can fulfill himself in solitary retirement, an option William wishes to take after his experience of the futility of political action at court. Magnocavalli acknowledges that moral fulfillment is not provided by service in institutions like the court or, for that matter, by political participation. The 'civil conversation' he advocates, which can allow man to fulfill himself as a social being, is 'a vertuous kinde of living in the world' that depends not so much on political institutions as on the inner self. 'To live civilly,' he maintains, 'is not sayde in respect of the citie, but of the quallities of the minde: so I understand civile conversation not having relation to the citie, but consideration to the maners and conditions which make it civile' (ed 1925, 1:56). His 'conversation' requires 'the use of two thinges ... that is, of our tongue, and of our behaviour.' Nonetheless, like della Casa, Guazzo dwells more on language than on behavior as such, and he leaves it to the reader to infer the manners which would be the extension of his directives for proper speech. He thus contributes to the modern, more restricted meaning of *conversation*, even though by it he means social intercourse in general.

Guazzo defines civil conversation both by what it is and by what it is not (a long section is devoted, at first, to such abuses of social communication as slander and flattery). His social pattern can be seen as a late-Renaissance reaction to a code of politeness heretofore determined by courtly values. In contrast to the cult of appearances and self-manipulation advocated in *The Courtier*, Guazzo's art of conduct stresses honesty and plain dealing. Despite the author's awareness that certain social situations require some dissembling, he more often insists on avoiding any discrepancy between the inner and outer self, and defies various requisites of graceful court conduct. *Sprezzatura*, for example, is criticized as an insincere affectation. The kind of dilettantism that makes a courtier appealing smacks only of shallow virtuosity. When the main speaker proposes that 'in speach wee ought not to looke so much to the grace and finesse of it, as to the gravitie and goodnesse of it' (1:136), he displays Guazzo's preference for substance rather than form, and his distaste for graceful ornamentation, in behavior as well as in speech.

Guazzo is reluctant to condemn necessary gestures of good breeding; and his sympathies for plain dealing are restricted by his desire to make man 'acceptable in companie,' to achieve which may require some discrepancy between inner feeling and outer comportment. Yet despite his compromise between the claims of sincerity and the obligations of politeness, Guazzo's art of conduct is often critical of the dissimulation, flattery, dilettantism, and ornamentation that characterize courtliness. Unlike Castiglione's code, Guazzo's is not shaped by the imperatives of pleasing the prince. Book 4 of *The Civile Conversation*, which describes in detail a banquet held in honor of Lord Vespasian Gonzaga, illustrates by the hosts' conduct the deference owed a local potentate. Yet Guazzo also seeks to make exemplary the aristocrat's politeness, and his book is more often concerned with the civility individuals owe their equals and their inferiors than with their ingratiating conduct towards superiors. More than the other conduct books of Harvey's list, it emphasizes that courtesy requires men 'to beare themselves aright / To all of each degree, as doth behove' (*FQ* VI ii 1).

By 1590, Englishmen felt a need for a code of polite behavior that could be practiced in civil society at large, one that would not defy Elizabethan court decorum altogether, and yet – unlike Castiglione's art of conduct – would not degenerate into shallowness, affectation, and fraud when put into practice. *The Civile Conversation* was popular in England because it met these needs. The influence of *The Courtier* declined partly because a growing number of Englishmen came to share Guazzo's perception that Castiglione's norms of politeness could not but be abused in the vicious struggle for favor at court. Yet *The Civile Conversation* did not displace *The Courtier* altogether in England. Despite their basic differences, both books remained simultaneously influential and were read together at the end of Elizabeth's reign. The coexisting appeal of both Italian conduct books suggests that Elizabethans found no difficulty in combining both Guazzo's and Castiglione's doctrines of politeness. Spenser probably reflects contemporary views when he intimates that courtesy ought to be a virtue which reconciles Castiglione's courtliness with Guazzo's civility (VI i 1):

Of Court it seemes, men Courtesie doe call,
For that it there most useth to abound;
And well beseemeth that in Princes hall
That vertue should be plentifully found,
Which of all goodly manners is the ground,
And roote of civill conversation.

DANIEL JAVITCH

MODERN EDITIONS Giovanni della Casa 1914 *A Renaissance Courtesy-Book: Galateo of Manners and Behaviours* tr Robert Peterson (Boston, a facs rpt of della Casa ed 1576; also rpt Amsterdam and New York 1969); della Casa 1958 *Galateo, or The Book of Manners* tr R.S. Pine-Coffin (Harmondsworth); della Casa 1975 *Galateo* ed Ruggiero Romano (Turin); della Casa 1986 *Galateo* tr Konrad Eisenbichler and Kenneth R. Bartlett (Toronto). Baldassare Castiglione ed 1928; Castiglione ed 1959; Castiglione 1973 *Il libro del cortegiano con una scelta delle opere minori* ed Bruno Maier, 3rd ed (Turin); Castiglione 1974 *Il cortegiano* ed Vittorio Cian, 4th ed (Florence; first pub 1897). William Caxton 1868 *Caxton's Book of Curtesye* ed Frederick J. Furnivall, EETS es 3 (Oxford). Guazzo ed 1925.

FURTHER READING For reading lists, see Virgil B. Heltzel 1942 *A Check List of Courtesy Books in the Newberry Library* (Chicago); Kelso 1929. Helpful introductions to Renaissance courtesy books are Mazzeo 1965; and J.R. Woodhouse 1978. See also Leonard R.N. Ashley 1965 'Spenser and the Ideal of the Gentleman' *BHR* 27:108–32; Fritz Caspari 1954 *Humanism and the Social Order in Tudor England* (Chicago); Elias 1978; Daniel Javitch 1971a '*The Philosopher of the Court*: A French Satire Misunderstood' *CL* 23:97–124; Javitch 1971b 'Rival Arts of Conduct in Elizabethan England: Guazzo's *Civile Conversation* and Castiglione's *Courtier*' *YIS* 1:178–98; Javitch 1978; Judson 1932; Kelso 1956; John L. Lievsay 1961 *Stefano Guazzo and the English Renaissance, 1575–1675* (Chapel Hill); Mason 1935; Tonkin 1972; Whigham 1984.

Cowley, Abraham (1618–67) Precocious poet and self-termed 'Muses Hannibal'; author of love lyrics, comedies, an incomplete epic, odes, elegies, essays, verse translations, and histories; buried in Poets' Corner of Westminster Abbey beside Chaucer and Spenser. In his essay 'Of My Self,' Cowley describes his initiation into poetry (ed 1906:457–8):

> I remember when I began to read, and to take some pleasure in it, there was wont to lie in my Mothers Parlour ... *Spencers* Works; this I happened to fall upon, and was infinitely delighted with the Stories of the Knights, and Giants, and Monsters, and brave Houses, which I found every where there: (Though my understanding had little to do with all this) and by degrees with the tinckling of the Rhyme and Dance of the Numbers, so that I think I had read him all over before I was twelve years old, and was thus made a Poet as immediately as a Child is made an Eunuch.

Cowley nicely captures Spenser's appeal to an imaginative child. Although the eunuch analogy is disquieting, he may have in mind chiefly the irrevocability of his commitment to poetry (cf his contemporary Marvell's witty Latin epigram 'Upon an Eunuch; a Poet'). With its emphasis on his immaturity, however, the analogy suggests that the adult Cowley may have felt ambivalent about his vocation and the poet who inspired it.

Prompted by this passage, critics have detected Spenserian influence on two of Cowley's very early works, 'Constantia and Philetus' and 'Pyramus and Thisbe' (in *Poetical Blossoms* 1633), chiefly on general grounds of romantic narrative and fluent versification (Nethercot 1931:10–11; Loiseau 1931:318, 613–14). It is in the later work, however, that the relationship between the two poets becomes significant.

Formally, Cowley seems to have learned from Spenser the expressiveness of both a well-placed alexandrine and a complex stanza form. Again, he regards such debts ambivalently. He jokes about bad imitations of Spenser, making Dogrel (his poetaster in *The Guardian*) excuse a hypermetrical line, 'The last is a little too long: but I imitate *Spencer*' (ed 1906:205). Yet his own fondness for, and justification of, the alexandrine may be a direct if not necessarily conscious outcome of his delight in the 'Dance of the Numbers' in *The Faerie Queene* (McBryde 1900–1:29–31); and the stanzas of *Prothalamion* and *Epithalamion* may provide distant precedents for Cowley's pindarics (Loiseau 1931:570).

Cowley's lyric 'Her Name' has been called a 'neo-Spenserian epithalamium,' partly because of its variation on Spenser's refrain in the lines 'Then all the fields and woods shall with it ring; / Then *Ecchoes* burden it shall be' (Cowley ed 1905:135, Trotter 1979:31). Cowley again adopts this motif in the elegiac passage on Falkland in *The Civil War* 3.541–4 (ed 1973:121). In both contexts, it is modified by self-conscious wit, signaled in the Falkland passage by the repeated 'meethoughts.' In general, Cowley's handling of pastoral hyperbole is more strained and less imaginatively assured than Spenser's.

The Civil War gave Cowley a subject on a Spenserian scale. Perhaps it is surprising that he does not make more extensive use of *The Faerie Queene* in his two unfinished works, *The Civil War* and *Davideis*; a possible explanation lies in his verse epistle 'To Sir William Davenant,' where he argues that it is time for heroic poetry to put away the childish things of 'Fairy Land' (ed 1905:42). Yet, as Dryden observes, 'he has contradicted himself by his own Example' ('Of Heroique Playes: An Essay' Dryden ed 1956–, 11:13). *The Civil War* is indebted to Spenser specifically for individual rhymes and archaisms, and generally for models of such allegorical elements as the figure of Rebellion (see Pritchard in Cowley ed 1973:43–4).

On *Davideis*, Samuel Wesley wrote in 1693 that 'it has Gondibert's Majesty without his stiffness, and something of Spencer's Sweetness and Variety, without his Irregularity' (ed 1947:23). The poem also uses intermittent allegory and has some passages in common with *The Civil War*, notably the description of hell in Book 1, which bears a generic resemblance to Spenser's underworld and cave descriptions (eg, *FQ* IV xi 4), and which has numerous classical precedents and Renaissance parallels (McBryde 1900–1:503–27). The most Spenserian figure is Envy (ed 1905:246), vividly described in terms deriving (like Spenser's) from Ovid's *Metamorphoses* and a common iconographical tradition (*FQ* I iv 30–1, V xii 29–32; *Var* 5:266; Aptekar 1969:201–5), although Cowley varies his details from Spenser's, perhaps deliberately. For example, instead of feeding on a snake, Envy is consumed by vipers 'Sucking black *bloud*' (cf Spenser's Error, I i 24–5). It is hard to prove direct influence, but it is harder to believe that Cowley does not recall *The Faerie Queene* here. Allegory apart, he owes something in spirit if not letter to *FQ* IV in choosing the theme of friendship as glorified in David and Jonathan, and in his concept of Neoplatonic love in Book 2.

In interpreting the ideological conflict of his own time, Cowley has recourse to the same biblical and legendary images as *FQ* I: the serpent or dragon of Revelation and the victorious St George. For him, Cromwell is Antichrist: even in his Restoration ode, the fear lingers 'Lest that great *Serpent*, which was all a *Tail*, / (And in his poys'nous folds whole *Nations Pris'ners* made) / Should a third time perhaps prevail' (ed 1905:422). The focus on the tail and the significant number three recall Spenser's Dragon and the final battle of *FQ* I xi. Cowley had already envisaged a royal rescue from tyranny in 'A Discourse by Way of Vision, concerning the Government of *Oliver Cromwell*,' which concludes with triumph over the evil one by an angelic youth who represents the Stuart dynasty and wears the Order of the Garter with its St George emblem: 'In his fair hand (what need was there of more?) / No Arms but th' *English* bloody Cross he bore' (ed 1906:376). The second line echoes 'But on his brest a bloudie Crosse he bore' (*FQ* I i 2), but Cowley shrinks the power and complexity of Spenser's original allegory into a piece of Stuart propaganda where the insignia are narrowly associated with the Stuart cause.

Cowley seems consciously to distance

himself from the romance epic tradition. 'It is time,' he wrote of poetry, 'to recover it out of the *Tyrants* hands, and to restore it to the *Kingdom* of *God*, who is the *Father* of it. It is time to *Baptize* it in *Jordan*, for it will never become clean by bathing in the *Water* of *Damascus*' (ed 1905:12–13). Although there are some interesting Spenserian connections in his mature work, especially when he allegorizes a subject, and although he comes closer to Spenserian myth and pageantry in his posthumously published Latin *Plantarum* (6 books, 1668), Spenser's influence is everywhere diluted by the classical sources they have in common and diminished by Cowley's own changing tastes. What had impressed him as a child about *The Faerie Queene* was never erased from his imagination, but he did not fully assimilate the Spenserian experience into his adult thought and style. CHRISTINE REES

Abraham Cowley 1905 *Poems* ed A.R. Waller (Cambridge); Cowley 1906 *Essays, Plays, Sundry Verses* ed A.R. Waller (Cambridge); Cowley 1973 *The Civil War* ed Allan Pritchard (Toronto).

Hans-Hellmut Krempien 1936 *Der Stil der 'Davideis' von Abraham Cowley* (Hamburg); Jean Loiseau 1931 *Abraham Cowley: Sa vie, son oeuvre* (Paris); John McLaren McBryde, Jr 1898–9 'A Study of Cowley's *Davideis*' *JGP* 2:454–527; McBryde 1900–1 'A Study of Cowley's *Davideis* II' *JGP* 3:24–34; Arthur H. Nethercot 1931 *Abraham Cowley: The Muse's Hannibal* (London); David Rawlinson 1963 'Cowley and the Current Status of Metaphysical Poetry' *EIC* 13:323–40; David Trotter 1979 *The Poetry of Abraham Cowley* (London); Samuel Wesley 1947 *'An Epistle to a Friend Concerning Poetry' (1700) and 'An Essay on Heroic Poetry' (1697)* Augustan Reprint Society 2.2, intro Edward N. Hooker (Los Angeles).

Crabbe, George (1754–1832) Renowned as the 'last Augustan' for his continued use of the heroic couplet at the end of the eighteenth and the beginning of the nineteenth century, Crabbe is deservedly famous for his 'real picture of the poor.' *The Village* (1783), his most famous early poem, opens with a strong attack on the pastoral tradition. He satirizes 'sleepy bards' who perpetuate the 'flattering dream' of a golden age, while they neglect the actual working conditions of rural workers. Although he makes no direct reference to Spenser's *Shepheardes Calender*, referring to Virgil and 'mechanic echoes of the Mantuan song' (ed 1905–7, 1:120), he clearly has in mind the English pastoral tradition which draws in large part on Spenser. Earlier eighteenth-century poets had frequently written pastorals which combined realistic and idealistic conventions, creating a confusing and often sentimentalized melange of the two. Interestingly, while Crabbe condemns the idea of treating rural workers as pastoral figures, throughout *The Village* he uses much of the language and some of the rhetorical figures from the pastoral tradition. As a result of this fusion of new realistic content with older poetic forms, his treatment of country life found a ready acceptance with his audience and opened the way to a new realism in poetry.

Although Crabbe repudiated the eighteenth-century pastoral tradition with its Spenserian roots, he nevertheless read and admired Spenser's poetry from an early age. Throughout his life, moreover, he continued to experiment with the Spenserian stanza. In his biography of his father, Crabbe's son notes that among his father's juvenilia is a poem entitled 'The Judgment of the Muse, in the Metre of Spenser.' In *Silford Hall* (a verse tale written shortly before his death and collected in *Posthumous Tales*), Crabbe himself points to his early reading of Spenser by including a partly autobiographical character who read Spenser (among many other authors and books) as a youth. His first published poem noticeably influenced by Spenser is 'The Birth of Flattery' (1807), which contains an address to the 'muse of my Spenser, who so well could sing / The passions all, their bearings and their ties; / Who could in view those shadowy beings bring, / And with bold hand remove each dark disguise, / Wherein love, hatred, scorn, or anger lies' (ed 1905–7, 1:224). In further tribute, Crabbe revises the couplets in which these lines appear in manuscript, providing a pair of Spenserian stanzas before continuing with his customary heroic couplets for the remainder of the poem.

In writing about disordered or 'shadowy' states of mind, Crabbe often uses a stanza form that is either wholly Spenserian or owes much to Spenser. Two unfinished poems ('Where am I now?' and 'The Insanity of Ambitious Love,' edited from ms in Crabbe ed 1960) use a number of verse forms which derive from the Spenserian stanza; Crabbe varies line and stanza length, apparently to give a sense of fevered imagination. His two published 'dream' poems ('Sir Eustace Grey' and 'The World of Dreams') are written in stanzas of eight octosyllabic lines rhyming *ababbcbc*. In the unfinished poem 'Tracy,' he follows the Spenserian model exactly in several sections while developing a dream vision. The excerpt with the provisional title 'Matilda,' written in an eight-line stanza, contains a similar visionary experience.

Crabbe does not mention Spenser often in his writing, but in the Preface to *Tales* (1810), he links him to Ariosto and speaks of their 'enchanters, spirits, and monsters.' In 'David Morris,' a posthumously published poem, he creates the melancholic figure of David Morris who resembles Spenser's figure of Despair, and who actually quotes several lines from Despair's argument with the Red Cross Knight over suicide. Crabbe has David say, 'Will Spencer sang, "When weary Mortals die, / Let none ask How, or whence, or where, or Why"' (edited from ms in Crabbe ed 1960:142; cf *FQ* I ix 42). In allowing David to refer mistakenly to 'Will Spencer,' not Edmund Spenser, he indicates to the reader that David possesses only a superficial acquaintance with Spenser's poem and theme, and therefore is not to be trusted entirely. That Crabbe should have been attracted to Spenser's portrayal of the argument between Redcrosse and Despair is easy to understand. In this scene, Spenser not only offers a superb rendering of man's inability to overcome the difficulties of the human condition through human means; he also creates a powerful backdrop to evoke melancholy. This backdrop with its descriptions of darkness, cliffs, caves, owls, and graves became part of the archetype for the eighteenth-century gothic tradition.

Since most of Crabbe's poems are naturalistic accounts of everyday life, and since specific references to Spenser of the kind found in 'David Morris' are rare, it is difficult to gauge the extent of his detailed knowledge of Spenser. Yet he was clearly attracted to Spenser, finding that Spenser's connections with the romance *typos* as well as his intricate stanza form served as powerful aids in the evocation of alternative worlds of madness, vision, and despair.

RONALD B. HATCH

George Crabbe 1834 *Life and Poems* ed George Crabbe, Jr, 8 vols (London; this edition includes the son's biography of his father); Crabbe 1905–7 *Poems* ed Adolphus William Ward, 3 vols (Cambridge); Crabbe 1960 *New Poems* ed Arthur Pollard (Liverpool); Crabbe 1985 *Selected Letters and Journals* ed Thomas C. Faulkner (Oxford); Crabbe 1988 *Complete Poetical Works* ed Norma Dalrymple-Champneys and Arthur Pollard, 3 vols (Oxford).

T[erence] Bareham 1977 *George Crabbe* (New York); Bareham and S. Gatrell 1978 *A Bibliography of George Crabbe* (Folkestone, Kent); Lilian Haddakin 1955 *The Poetry of Crabbe* (London); Ronald B. Hatch 1976 *Crabbe's Arabesque: Social Drama in the Poetry of George Crabbe* (Montreal); René Huchon 1907 *George Crabbe and His Times: 1754–1832* tr Frederick Clarke (London); Beth Nelson 1976 *George Crabbe and the Progress of Eighteenth-Century Narrative Verse* (Lewisburg, Pa); Peter New 1976 *George Crabbe's Poetry* (London).

Crudor (L *crudus* raw; cruel) Crudor is both cruel and crude. His chief offense or flaw is an arrogant breaking of the chivalric code in exercising power over Briana who loves him passionately (*FQ* VI i). He tests her love unfairly by forcing her to make him a mantle 'With beards of Knights and locks of Ladies lynd.' Yet, compared with the Salvage Man, he is not defective in breeding, and compared with Turpine he is not irredeemably base, for he hurries to the defense of Briana and fights for her staunchly. The central question about Crudor is how his faults are to be curbed or cured. In answering it, Spenser distinguishes carefully between him and Briana's steward, Maleffort, and suggests comparisons between Artegall and Calidore. Force and persuasion support one another but also have their particular applications.

Spenser distinguishes vengeance from patient, generous courtesy when Calidore decides not to slay Crudor. When he finds him defenseless and salvable, force yields to mercy. But Crudor is neither immediately reformed nor merely subdued and punished. He swears, somewhat reluctantly, on the sword, representative of disciplinary moral codes that remove the need for external policing. Henceforth an internalized spiritual and chivalric discipline must keep him in check.

To be effective, however, such private codes must be placed in an interpretive context. In defeat before Calidore, Crudor is lectured on flesh's frailty and the need for self-mastery, generosity, and mercy. That lesson in humility along with the personal oath is sufficient at least to stop his 'usage sterne' and presumably to curb his capricious pride. It teaches him that the goal of knighthood is service, not personal gratification. Together with Briana's, his change underscores the alliance between justice and courtesy that has been sketchily established in the meeting between Calidore and Artegall (VI i 4–10). More importantly, it reaffirms the charitable basis of civility.

HAROLD TOLIVER

Cupid The god of love, or more precisely, of amorous desire, appears in Spenser's poetry more often and in greater variety than any other god or goddess. He plays in Spenser nearly the entire range of his repertoire in earlier literature. The Alexandrian winged infant, for example, plies his bow in *SC, March*, *FQ* III vi, and the 'Anacreontics.' The medieval god of love, now the full-grown lord of poems like *The Romance of the Rose* and *The Court of Love*, looks like Guyon's angelic guard in *FQ* II viii 6 and figures in the Mirabella episode (VI vii-viii) and several of the *Amoretti*. Spenser's masque of Cupid in *FQ* III xii imitates Petrarch's *Trionfo d'Amore* with its neopagan, all-powerful Cupid. Both *The Faerie Queene* and *Muiopotmos* draw on Apuleius' tale of Cupid's marriage to Psyche, which produces a daughter, Pleasure. Neoplatonic speculative mythography makes its theology of love felt in *Colin Clouts Come Home Againe* and the *Fowre Hymnes*.

On these various traditions, Spenser imposes no obvious coherence or unity. Indeed, he often emphasizes diversity or contradiction, even within single works. One stanza of the *Hymne of Love* (50–6), for instance, conflates different versions of Cupid's genealogy to give him too many parents: he is born of Venus as usual in mythology, but 'Begot of Plentie and of Penurie' as in Plato (*Symposium* 178, 195, 203). Though sometimes condemned as a blunder or taken as evidence of incomplete revision, this stanza presents its impossible genealogy as a mystery beyond mortal understanding (Mulryan 1971). *Colin Clout* similarly reports two versions of Cupid's nativity (799–842). *The Faerie Queene* contradicts both poems in making Cupid the son of Jove (I proem 3). Cupid's blindness, usually his crucial iconographical attribute (Panofsky 1939:95–128), is no more consistent than his lineage. In *The Faerie Queene*, he is sometimes blind (I i 51; II iii 23; III ii 35, iv 9; IV v 29; VI ix 11), sometimes blindfolded (III xi 48, xii 22; VI vii 33), and once all-seeing (III x 4).

Similar complexities invest Cupid's other standard attributes, his weapons, and call into doubt any simple application of iconography. The *Hymne of Love* gives an unusually full interpretation of Cupid's arrows or darts as inspiring beams of true beauty derived from heaven's eternal light, which glance through mortals' eyes to their hearts and there kindle flames of desire 'To multiply the likenesse of their kynd ... Not for lusts sake, but for eternitie' (100–4). Sometimes these beams dart specifically from the eyes of the beloved, as in *FQ* II iii 23 and *Amoretti* 57. This Neoplatonic allegory of enamorment – one of the hardest-worked conceits in love poetry – appears first in the Provençal troubadours and derives from ancient and medieval speculations about the psychology, physiology, and metaphysics of love (eg, *SC, March* Arg, 97 gloss). In *The Faerie Queene*, Cupid wounds both Arthur and Britomart in this fashion (I ix 7–16, III ii 26–35); but the Neoplatonic view of Cupid's weapons conflicts with several of his other attributes and activities. It seems reversed in Cupid's malevolent scorn as he subjects the heavenly gods to degrading transformations (III xi 29–45), and it does not explain why Guyon's angel should look like an *unarmed* Cupid, why the armed Cupid should be excluded from Alma's house or the Gardens of Adonis (II ix 34, III vi 49), or why, begging the Queen to inspire him with the beams of her heavenly beauty, Spenser should also beg Cupid to lay his bow aside (I proem 3–4).

More perplexing in *The Faerie Queene* than these iconographical ambiguities is a pervasive moral ambivalence rare in Spenser's mythological figures. Cupid promotes the 'lustfull fires' at Castle Joyous (III i 39), for example; but later Love is hailed as an ally of providence itself: 'Well did Antiquitie a God thee deeme' (iii 1–3). All this contradictory variety poses the essential question about Cupid in Spenser's poetry, that is, whether Bacon's judgment in the *De sapientia veterum* applies to Spenser: 'The accounts given by the poets of Cupid, or Love, are not properly applicable to one and the same person' (ed 1857–74, 6:729). Has Spenser forged a consistent mythology of love or merely reproduced the confusions of literary tradition?

The source study that occupied the first half of this century presumed the latter answer to this question, by locating Cupid's diversity in Spenser's diverse sources. More recently, iconographical methods borrowed from art historians have joined source study with interpretation and claimed to reveal some patterns within Spenser's confusing use of Cupid, the clearest of which is a distinction between two Cupids. *FQ* III iii 1–2, for instance, distinguishes between two kinds of love: the flame of filthy lust that burns in brutish hearts, and a 'Most sacred fire ... which men call Love' and which, as a heavenly ally of providence, could appropriately be called a god. These stanzas are minimally mythological, but other passages in *The Faerie Queene* and the shorter poems seem to sustain an iconographical distinction between true and false Cupids that has been accepted by many commentators. What C.S. Lewis calls 'the False Cupid' is blindfolded, plays cruel sports with his bow and arrows, and kindles lustful fires in the hearts of random victims (1967:18–35). The true Cupid, in this view, goes unarmed in places set apart from the world of men – on Mount Ida, in Alma's house, and in the Gardens of Adonis (*FQ* II viii 6, ix 34; III vi 49) – and this Cupid Spenser asks to inspire his poem (I proem 3).

Differentiating two Cupids has a long tradition before Spenser (Mulryan 1974). It emerges in the medieval habit of reading myths and images both *in bono* and *in malo* (positively and negatively), and was later diagrammed onto the hierarchical cosmos of Neoplatonism. The Neoplatonic earthly and celestial Cupids appear explicitly in Spenser's poetry rather late (in *Colin Clout* 799–806, 839–52); but many commentators have aligned them with the iconographical distinction between the false Cupid, armed and tyrannical, and the true god of love, benevolent and gentle.

Although distinguishing two Cupids may seem to reveal some coherence in Spenser's diverse mythology, it distorts the ground of that coherence, Spenser's attempt to forge not merely a coherent mythology but a poetic theology of love. Two opposed and irreconcilable gods of love make sense only iconographically; theologically they imply an unacceptable Manichaeism. In fact, Spenser persistently relates human erotic impulses to the heavenly love that created and sustains the universe. The mysterious union of these loves is the point of the conflated genealogies of Cupid in *Colin Clout* and the *Hymne of Love*, which identify the cosmogonic love of metaphysics with the waspish Cupid of erotic poetry. Apparent distinctions in *The Faerie Queene* between two Cupids actually prove on closer inspection to affirm a single one. Rather than two opposed gods, *FQ* II viii 6, II ix 34, and III vi 49 insist upon there being one Cupid, armed and threatening at some times and places, peaceable and gracious at others.

Despite their perplexities, Spenser's works do present a coherent mythology of love. Indeed, they comprise a poetic theodicy of Cupid – that is, an attempt to justify human love by metaphorically justifying the divinity of Love. This theodicy is clearest in the shorter poems, when Colin Clout, years after denying Cupid's divinity in *The Shepheardes Calender* ('perdie God was he none' *Dec* 50), returns to preach Cupid's gospel in *Colin Clout*. Colin broke his pipe in *December*, bearing out Cuddie's view that love thwarts the poetic faculty (*Oct* 97–102); but Cuddie, too, returns in the later pastoral to recognize that love inspires Colin's poetry (823–34). This movement toward a theodicy of Cupid in Spenser's shorter poems culminates in the first pair of the *Fowre Hymnes* and is qualified rather than repudiated in the second pair.

On the whole, Spenser reverses the direction of the *Romance of the Rose*, Dante's *Vita nuova*, and Petrarch's *Trionfi*, which gradually expose the god of love as no more than personified desire. In these and other medieval poems, Cupid's divinity turns ironic, figuring lovers' self-deluding or idolatrous worship of their own passion. Spenser works instead to 'make religion,' so that for him the same self-delusion becomes blasphemy – making Cupid serve 'for sordid uses,' taking a god's name in vain (*Colin Clout* 783–97). Spenser was no pagan; but within the confines of his fiction, Cupid is one of the true gods.

Though in a different mode from that of the shorter poems and with a different degree of success, *The Faerie Queene*, too, undertakes a theodicy of Cupid. This theodicy becomes crucial in Book III, but Cupid's inconsistent roles in Books I and II introduce his power and benevolence as imaginative and moral problems. Archimago's false Una blames her wantonness on Cupid's compulsion (I i 47, 51); but this imitation of the old abuse that deifies private desire follows the poet's own association of Cupid with his heroic theme (proem 3) and is countered when, after a dream similar to Redcrosse's, Arthur attests his faith in Cupid's providential role (ix 8–12). The poet seems to share this faith when he compares the angel who watches over Guyon to Cupid (II viii 6), but other references to the god keep the question open. Phaedria abuses the connection between *eros* and *heros* (II vi 35; see Plato's *Cratylus* 398C–D); Medina denies it (II ii 26, 30); Charissa hates '*Cupids* wanton snare' (I x 30); Belphoebe quenches Cupid's 'lustfull fire' and breaks his 'wanton darts' (II iii 23), but – and the contradiction can stand for the way that Books I and II pose the problem of Cupid's divinity – in the next stanza, the poet judges Belphoebe's forehead suitable 'For Love his loftie triumphes to engrave, / And write the battels of his great godhed.'

Book III divides the problem of Cupid's divinity into two issues traditional in theology: if a god is benevolent, why do his servants suffer? and if he is omnipotent, why does he permit evil to exist? Book III returns two kinds of answer to the first issue, one historical, imaged in Britomart's family tree (ii 17, iii 22), and the other natural, imaged in the flowers of the Gardens of Adonis. Britomart's glorious progeny will redeem the sorrows of her love, which Cupid benevolently inflicts to achieve the 'destined descents' purposed by 'divine foresight' (iii 2–3, 21–4). The Cupid who plays unarmed in the flower garden of Adonis (vi 49–50) affirms that inside the world where courtiers, citizens, and rustics complain of Cupid's doings (vi 13–15) – at the secret ground of its natural processes – the pains of love, like those of time and death, are necessary and benign.

The poem as a whole answers the second issue: if Cupid is omnipotent, why is he not responsible for base lusts and false loves? Among all its lovers, the poem reserves Cupid's darts (and bridle) for its true lovers and heroes: Arthur, Britomart, Calidore, Marinell, Scudamour, Amoret. Of its false lovers, only the false Una mentions Cupid, and she is lying. Cupid's associations with places in Fairyland follow the same pattern. He is present in the house of Alma and the Gardens of Adonis, but (in defiance of literary tradition) absent from the Bower of Bliss. Spenser's fiction therefore bears out the distinction in III iii 1–2 between brutish lust and the noble love that Antiquity deemed a god.

This defense of Cupid's divinity rests, however, solely on the poet's godlike power over his story. In actuality, the poet rather than the god chooses Cupid's victims; and Book III tests this arbitrariness by two inconsistencies that in canto xii finally transform the poem's attempted theodicy into iconoclasm. At Castle Joyous, Malecasta's courtiers re-create orgies after 'the antique worldes guize,' and the poet adds, '*Cupid* still emongst them kindled lustfull fires' (i 39). This line clearly does not refer to Cupid's literal presence; perhaps it reflects the neopaganism of this brand of courtly love. But how can readers know whether to take the line as a statement about Cupid or about Malecasta's court? How can the poet be sure that he has not abused his power over his story to exalt the pagan god of lust? These questions arise again in canto x when the poet, about to relate Paridell's seduction of Hellenore, addresses Cupid as 'False love,' a pagan deity with power and omniscience, but without benevolence: 'Thou seest all, yet none at all sees thee; / All that is by the working of thy Deitee' (4). Nevertheless, the next stanza reports the invisible: that Cupid smiled upon Paridell's amorous arts. By contradicting himself so conspicuously, the poet concedes that poetical gods are controlled by mortal poets and implies that a poetic theodicy can never do more than justify a poet's ways with his fictions.

The attempt to make a poetic theology of Cupid falters here but returns transformed in the next episode, where the house of Busirane is a temple to the pagan Cupid acknowledged in canto x as well as the means of undoing that acknowledgment. Busirane has made nearly the whole tradition of Cupid's poetic theology into a 'fowle Idolatree' (xi 49), whose manipulative artifice Britomart iconoclastically destroys.

Cupid plays a diminished and disconnected role in the last three books, perhaps because of the poet's discovery in in Book III that a theology of Cupid can only be either a pious fiction or an enthralling idolatry. The Mirabella episode (VI vii-viii) is Cupid's only appearance in the later books. It contrasts Busirane's dangerous mythopoeia and affirms Cupid's justice; but its tone concedes its nature as only a pious fiction, perhaps one written long before (see E.B. Fowler in *Var* 6:223–4). The poet has not ceased to question Cupid's divinity (IV vii 1–2) or to justify his ways, but he writes now with a disenchanted regret at the limitations of poetic theology. Still, the last mention of Cupid in the completed books of *The Faerie Queene* expresses the poet's faith, radical because minimal, in the chief of his poetical gods. Unmingled joys of love would be a blessing too great for mortal men; 'Therefore the winged God, to let men weet, / That here on earth is no sure happinesse, / A thousand sowres hath tempred with one sweet, / To make it seeme more deare and dainty, as is meet' (VI xi 1).

THOMAS HYDE

DeNeef 1979; Donno 1974; Hyde 1986; Nestrick 1975.

Cybele The Phrygian Great Mother Cybele is an Asiatic fertility goddess often identified with Rhea, who was traditionally depicted as enthroned in a lion-drawn chariot and as wearing a crown of city towers to recall her gift of civic fortification. Eunuch priests and orgiastic rites were associated with her and with her Adonis-like consort, Attis. Once she had been absorbed into the more austere maternal deities of Greece and Rome, she became for Lucretius a figure of nature (2.598–654), for Virgil and Ovid a patron of *Romanitas* (*Aeneid* 6.784–7, *Fasti* 4.179–372), and for Boccaccio and succeeding mythographers a symbol of earth and city (*Genealogia* 3.2; Cartari 'La gran Madre'; Conti *Mythologiae* 9.6). The figure inherited by the Renaissance was the 'mother of the Gods' (*FQ* IV xi 28) and men, of nature and civilization, of wilderness, farmland, and city. She expressed an aggregate of vastly different meanings, of forces which pull in opposite directions: the raw, untapped energy of nature as well as the impulse to tame and civilize it.

Spenser mentions '*Cybeles* franticke rites' (I vi 15) when describing the 'woodborne people' who would make a divinity of Una, but the goddess' one overt representation in the poem occurs as a simile in the account of the marriage of Thames and Medway (IV xi 27–8). Here Thames wears a crown 'In which were many towres and castels set,' like the crown of 'Old *Cybele*' (see Roche 1964:182). Spenser is here imitating Virgil's *Aeneid* 6.784–9, where in the fields of Elysium a comparable simile advances the myth of Rome's divine origin and Trojan succession. The allusion links Spenser's epic to Virgil's, the vision of Thames and Medway to Aeneas' vision in Elysium, and Thames' Troynovant (London) to ancient Troy and Rome. The effect of the simile is to transfer the crown of civilization from the east to Troy's second rebirth in Troynovant.

The goddess thus signifies Britain's new ascendancy, but this very notion of a succession of reborn Troys suggests a continuing risk of decay and supplantation. Spenser pursues this idea in *Ruines of Rome* (stanza 6), where he translates a meditation from du Bellay's *Antiquitez de Rome* in which Cybele (Virgil's 'Berecyntia mater,' Spenser's '*Berecynthian* Goddesse bright') presides over the fall of Rome just as she once presided over its rise.

While IV xi is Spenser's one direct appropriation of Cybele in *The Faerie Queene*, she may also inform other characters within the poem and contribute to their iconography and allegorical meaning, less as a figure of historical process than as a reconciler of oppositions. The likeness to Cybele is most apparent in Cambina, who calms fraternal strife while dressed in oriental garb and riding a lion-drawn chariot (IV iii 38–52). The Cybele/Attis pairing is comparable to Venus/Adonis (III vi) and Isis/Osiris (V vii), as well as to the figure of Britomart, who embraces both male and female in her own identity while anticipating a paired relationship with Artegall. Finally, strong thematic connections may be seen between Cybele and Dame Concord (IV x 34ff), Mercilla (especially V ix 33), and that 'great Grandmother of all creatures bred / Great *Nature*' (VII vii 13). PETER S. HAWKINS

Fowler 1964:185–6; Peter S. Hawkins 1981 'From Mythography to Myth-Making: Spenser and The *Magna Mater* Cybele' *SCJ* 12.3:50–64; Nohrnberg 1976:648–50; P.A. Parker 1987.

Cymoent, Cymodoce The Nereid Cymoent (Gr *kyma* wave) first appears at *FQ* III iv 19 as the mother of the wounded Marinell. Later (IV xi 50, 53), she appears as one 'that with her least word can asswage / The surging seas, when they do sorest rage,' now named Cymodoce (Gr *kyma* + *dokeō* 'wave-tamer'; cf Hesiod *Theogony* 252–4). In classical tradition, Cymodoce, daughter of Nereus, is little more than a name suggesting the waves of the sea (see *Iliad* 18.39), and she so appears in the catalogue of sea nymphs at the end of *FQ* IV xi.

As mother of Marinell, Cymoent/Cymodoce is modeled on Thetis, mother of Achilles: each is a sea nymph impregnated by a mortal in her underwater bower, and each attempts to protect her son from his fate (cf Ovid *Metamorphoses* 11.217–65, 13.162–4; Conti *Mythologiae* 9.12; see also R.N. Ringler 1963 on relation to Statius' *Achilleid*). Cymoent attempts to circumvent the destiny prophesied by Proteus, that Marinell would be harmed or killed by a woman (III iv 25), by keeping him from love and thereby from fulfilling his nature. An overprotective, even narcissistic mother, she sees Marinell as a 'Deare image of my selfe' (iv 36; see Berger 1969b:242 and Nohrnberg 1976:431–2), even though, as the son of the mortal Dumarin ('of the sea'), he is made of 'living clay.' Cymoent inhabits an idyllic pastoral landscape, enclosed, protected, reflecting and answering to her desires (Alpers 1967b:31, 122, 380–7). Her son's wounding by Britomart brings the threat of death into that world, and like Venus in the Gardens of Adonis, she laments the aspects of experience that even the gods cannot control (vi 40, iv 36–9). Britomart's complaints (iv 8–10) and hers reveal the contrast between the human and pastoral worlds: Britomart faces a stormy sea within and without; Cymoent, though unable to control Marinell, can control the seas and her emotions with an ease remote from the human context. Her change of name at IV xi may signal her changed relationship to her son: after the marriage of Thames and Medway, she yields to Marinell, albeit reluctantly, and assists his union with Florimell. Her legalistic appeal to Neptune for Florimell's release is based on 'equitie' (IV xii 31) and thereby anticipates the subject of Book V. EVA GOLD

See also Goldberg 1975–6; Lotspeich 1932:51; Roche 1964:184–9, on parallel of Achilles and Marinell.

Cynthia Another name for Diana, goddess of the moon and the chase, champion of virginity. Cynthia is so named because 'she was bred and nurst / On *Cynthus* hill,' a mountain on the island of Delos (*FQ* VII vii 50). As lunar deity, her dominion over the sea made her a natural figure for Elizabeth after the defeat of the Spanish Armada in 1588 (E.C. Wilson 1939:273–320). Following the example of Raleigh's fragmentary *Ocean to Cynthia*, Spenser frequently refers to this association (Letter to Raleigh, *FQ* III proem 4, *FQ* Raleigh Sonn). Cynthia as Elizabeth figures most prominently in *Colin Clouts Come Home Againe*, where Spenser praises her glory and greatness (332–51, 590–615) and pledges his steadfast service and devotion (628–47) at the same time that he satirizes life at court (680–730, 749–94) and alludes to her unfair treatment of Raleigh (164–7).

As the planetary deity of the moon (though still with allusions to Elizabeth), Cynthia appears most prominently in *FQ* VII. There she is presented initially as a ruling, ordering, and guiding figure of stability (she 'raignes in everlasting glory' vi 8). Yet she is a complex and ambiguous representative of eternal order. She is the first object of Mutabilitie's attempt to control the heavens: her status is questioned and her vulnerability exposed when her light is darkened by the threatening Titaness. Mutabilitie points out the irony that the moon, a conventional image of change, should be considered a figure of constancy or control (vii 50); the paradox of her position is that she sits in her throne yet 'never still did stand' (vi 8): she is in a state of constant, but consistent, change.

This paradox is highlighted by the various forms Cynthia takes in *FQ* VII. In the story of Arlo Hill (vi 37–55), she appears as the virginal goddess of the chase, Diana, who is spied upon by Faunus while she is bathing naked (an echo of the myth of Actaeon). Diana not only punishes Faunus and his accomplice Molanna, but also abandons Arlo Hill, her favorite haunt, and in anger departs with a curse that opens the land to defacement by wolves and thieves. Earlier, Spenser mentions Hecate (vi 3), a Titaness of Mutabilitie's race and another form of Cynthia/Diana. The triple and changeable identity of Cynthia (Boccaccio *Genealogia* 4.16), her constancy through change, and her actions as Diana question whether she is to be seen as an image of earthly mutability or as the embodiment of constancy that ultimately rules over and through change, as articulated in Nature's final decree. JACQUELINE T. MILLER

Cyparissus When Una is rescued from Sansloy by the fauns and satyrs of the Salvage Nation, she is brought before their leader, 'old *Sylvanus*' (*FQ* I vi 14–17). This ancient wood god, leaning on a 'Cypresse stadle,' is struck by her beauty and reminded of his 'ancient love, and dearest *Cyparisse*.'

The reference here is to the transformation of Cyparissus into a cypress tree. Ovid's version (*Metamorphoses* 10.106–42) belongs to a long line of literary works dealing with grief over the accidental killing of a tame deer (D.C. Allen 1968:94–7). In Ovid, one of the trees attracted by Orpheus' lyre is the cypress, formerly the boy Cyparissus who had been loved by Apollo. He had accidentally killed his own tame stag and had begged the god that he might mourn his pet forever; the cypress into which he was transformed became an emblem of mourning. Spenser's list of trees in the Wood of Error, ultimately derived from Ovid's catalogue, includes 'the Cypresse funerall' (I i 8). The cypress also adorns the grave of Mortdant and Amavia (II i 60) and grows in the Garden of Proserpina (vii 52).

In associating Sylvanus rather than Apollo with Cyparissus, and in suggesting that Sylvanus himself killed the deer (now a 'gentle Hynd'), Spenser is probably following Boccaccio and Conti (*Genealogia* 13.17, *Mythologiae* 5.10; see also Lotspeich 1932:51, Starnes and Talbert 1955:80). The 'Cypresse stadle' is reminiscent as well of the uprooted cypress carried by Silvanus in Virgil's *Georgics* (1.20). *Stadle* may be the trunk, the entire standing tree, or a staff or walking stick. In this passage, it has been variously interpreted as an emblem of the rooted or fixed condition of the satyrs and as a sign that Sylvanus' life is still rooted in his love for Cyparissus. Although he is stimulated by Una's beauty, Sylvanus cannot reconcile his glimpses of her as Venus and as Diana into a single unified perception, and so he is carried back to his old pagan love, and not forward to possession of the Christian truth that Una represents. Ironically Una leaves the satyrs forever when they have gone 'To do their service to *Sylvanus* old' (I vi 33). CALVIN R. EDWARDS

D

dance Dancing was important in Elizabethan life, being integral to rural festivals, court entertainments, and other kinds of social gatherings. *Jig*, *hornpipe*, and *hay* were generic names for country dances, many of which were performed as rounds (hands linked or unlinked) or longways (the dancers in two files, partners usually facing each other). Morris dancers with bells on their legs took part in seasonal rituals. Sophisticated court dances included stately pavans and almains, lively galliards, voltas, and corantos. Choreographers were employed to devise special dances for masques and other shows. Dancing was both a daily exercise and a social grace; and Richard Mulcaster, Spenser's headmaster at Merchant Taylors' School, was among many writers on education who advocated it as a gentlemanly accomplishment. His pupils performed masques and interludes before Queen Elizabeth, herself a notable dancer into her old age.

As a courtier, Spenser may have had some practical knowledge of the dance; as a reader and a poet, he would have known its symbolic value. He names only two dances specifically, the bransle, in which the dancers move sideways instead of forward (*FQ* III x 8, referring to the music, however, not the dance) and the 'Heydeguyes' (*SC, June* 27), derived from *hay* or *hey*, a winding dance in which the performers weave in and out among one another in regular sequence. E.K. notes that the 'Myllers rownde' is 'a kind of daunce' (*SC, Oct* 52); but any dance in a ring could be called a 'round,' and since this is the only known reference, Spenser may have invented the name.

Though specific references are few, dancing is important to Spenser both positively and negatively. In cities and courts, it is often linked with wantonness. For example, there is 'Dauncing and reveling both day and night' at Castle Joyous (*FQ* III i 39); and the Ape at court 'could play, and daunce, and vaute, and spring' (*Mother Hubberd* 693). In *FQ* I v 47, Antiochus is said to have danced on the altars of God, a wanton act that suggests his extreme pride (cf 2 Macc 6.4–5). Curiously, in *The Faerie Queene*, Spenser plays down the dance element of masques, making them more like allegorical pageants. Dancing in *Epithalamion* is appropriate both to the festivity of marriage and to the emblematic presentation of order the poem celebrates in its structure.

Spenser's pastoral scenes use dance most extensively. Hellenore's dancing with the satyrs in *FQ* III x symbolizes the licentiousness into which she falls after her adulterous elopement with Paridell. With their horns, goats' legs, and hoofs, satyrs were associated with unbridled passion and rural disorder; here they dance 'with great lustihed,' accompanied by 'bagpipes shrill' and 'shrieking Hububs.' More positively, dancing is performed by shepherds, its regularity and relationship with music representing the ideal life of the Golden Age. Daphne leads 'The Shepheards daughters dauncing in a rownd' (*Daphnaïda* 310), and Astrophel 'could pipe and daunce, and caroll sweet' ('Astrophel' 31). In *The Shepheardes Calender*, Willye says that Cupid should be wakened so he can 'leaden our daunce' (*March* 24); and Perigot has learned a 'newe daunce,' meaning he has left behind (what the Wife of Bath in Chaucer calls) 'the old dance,' the dance of love (*August* 11); Colin Clout's song in *Aprill* introduces the Graces, who 'dauncen deffly' (111) and whose number is increased from three to four when they are joined by Queen Elizabeth. *November* provides a negative parallel, for now 'death doth leade the daunce' (105).

Aprill looks forward to *FQ* VI x, in which Calidore sees on Mount Acidale a beautiful maiden, crowned with a rosy garland, around whom the three Graces sing and dance (so enacting two potent symbols of harmonious order), themselves the center of a dancing ring of 'An hundred naked maidens lilly white' (11). They dance to Colin Clout's piping; but when Calidore approaches, wishing to know more, the vision vanishes.

In this dance, it is not clear whether two Graces face us with one turned away, or one faces us with two turned away, or whether the dance is in a continuous movement or backwards and forwards. Both movements are combined in the Burgundian bransle, which can be danced in a ring and proceeds by sideward movements, two steps to the left, one to the right, two to the left, and so on. These ambiguities could be intentional since Spenser is presenting a mysterious vision. Such movement often duplicates the perfect form of the garlands, rings, and circles found in several passages (eg, I vi 13, III iv 44, VI ix 8).

The philosophical commonplace that love is the motive force of the dance of order, given nimble expression in Sir John Davies' poem *Orchestra* (1596), is extended by Spenser to embrace the whole idea of art and its creator. ALAN BRISSENDEN

Thoinot Arbeau 1948 *Orchesography* (1589) tr Mary Stewart Evans (New York); Alan Brissenden 1981 *Shakespeare and the Dance* (London); Mabel Dolmetsch 1949 *Dances of England and France from 1450* to 1600 (London); James Miller 1986 *Measures of Wisdom: The Cosmic Dance in Classical and Christian Antiquity* (Toronto).

Daniel, Samuel (1562–1619) Born in Somerset and educated at Magdalen Hall, Oxford. Few details of his early life can be established with certainty, but it is known that he traveled in Italy, that he met Guarini, author of *Il pastor fido*, and that he made himself well acquainted with the poetry of the Italian Renaissance. It became his ambition, as it was Spenser's, that England should produce writers who would 'overgo' the Italians. By 1592, he had entered the household of Sidney's sister, the Countess of Pembroke, at Wilton and had come under the influence of a literary circle which owed its prime inspiration to Sidney. In 1591, 28 of his sonnets were published in a pirated edition of *Astrophil and Stella*. When Daniel brought out the first authorized version of his *Delia* sequence in 1592, he dedicated it to the Countess; and some years later, in 1603, he was to describe Wilton as 'my best schoole,' in which he had learned his poet's craft (*A Defence of Ryme*).

Spenser, who had known Sidney personally, was already within the orbit of the Pembroke circle. In 1594, Daniel links 'great *Sydney* and our *Spencer*' in the dedicatory poem to *Cleopatra* which he addressed to the Countess. He longs for a day to come when the English tongue will be known outside the confines of 'our sweete Ile' and these twin giants may show the world 'how far Thames doth out-go / The Musike of declined *Italy*' (75–8).

Spenser's influence on the young Daniel may have been considerable. *Delia* contains a few sonnets written in the rhyme scheme Spenser developed for *Amoretti*, although Daniel was not comfortable in this and preferred the Shakespearean form. On another area of his work, however, Spenser made an important impact. In *Colin Clouts Come Home Againe*, he welcomes Daniel as one who 'doth all afore him far surpasse' (417) and, evidently referring to *Delia*, urges him to rise above the level of 'loves soft laies and looser thoughts delight' and take up more serious and ambitious themes (423). Though *Delia* is an important and much-admired sequence, Spenser rightly discerned that it did not represent the full compass of Daniel's gifts. In 1594, Daniel published *The Tragedie of Cleopatra*, a closet (non-theatrical) drama in the tradition of French Senecanism, a work which revealed what Spenser had perhaps learned from personal acquaintance, a vein of mature, thoughtful, and sympathetic reflectiveness which was henceforth to be the distinguishing note of Daniel's poetry.

Temperament and early influence together made Daniel a Spenserian. He shared Spenser's belief in the noble status of poetry and in its mission to foster moral refinement and an enlightened national culture. Harvey links his name with Spenser's as among those who employ 'their studious endevours ... in enriching and polishing their native Tongue' (Letter 3 in ed 1922); and other contemporaries testify to his success, with epithets such as 'well-languaged Daniel' (William Browne) and 'sweet honey-dropping Daniel' (*The Return from Parnassus*). In his poem *Musophilus* (1599), he makes 'a generall Defence of all Learning' against the attacks of the Philistines of his day and a specific defense of poetry as the supreme form of the 'Powre above powres, O heavenly Eloquence' (939). His noble account of the humane and civilizing power of poetry, and his claim for it as a branch of knowledge worthy of the highest honor, are among the finest things he wrote.

After Spenser's death, his contemporaries saw Daniel as the surviving guardian of the ideals and practices embodied in his work. Yet for all their affinities, there were notable differences between them, as reflected in the character of their writings. Daniel himself realized this early, as he writes in *Delia* (Sonnet 55 in ed 1885–96):

Let others sing of Knights and Palladines;
In aged accents, and untimely words:
Paint shadowes in imaginary lines,
Which well the reach of their high wits records.

The lines pay tribute to Spenser, but they disclaim any intention on Daniel's part to walk the same ground. Daniel was a lyric poet, capable of delicate and beautiful music, but he was also a man for whom the past could never be a matter of chivalry and romance. His approach to history was critical and scholarly, as he seems to have discovered to his increasing discomfort while composing his long and uncompleted poem, *The Civil Wars*. How scholarly and critical were his attitudes is evidenced by the fact that towards the end of his life he was working on a prose history of England which has earned the praise of modern historians. The moral interests which he found in the study of history were characteristically expressed in his work through searching and subtle treatments of real, not allegorical, people.

In middle life, Daniel wrote eloquently on moral and political themes, in a variety of forms, often movingly and invariably rewardingly. He moved with less assurance in areas where a freer play of imagination was called for – in masques, for example, or pastoral drama, at both of which he tried his hand. The sweetness of his love poetry notwithstanding, his deepest passion was roused by things of the intellect, and the qualities of his own character had fullest play when he turned his serious attention to the checkered patterns of experience presented by his reading or observed in life. His poetry is not sensuous, nor is it infused with religious feeling, but prose and verse alike light up when he speaks of intellectual integrity and the need for humility in the pursuit of learning. The moral virtues which he most commends may be seen as counterparts of these intellectual qualities: inner strength or self-containment, and the extension of compassion and sympathy towards others.

Daniel could create no second world sustained by its own imaginative energies, as Spenser could. Neither did he have Spenser's experience of and commitment to the world of action. He could no more have served under Lord Grey in Ireland than he could have created the figures and landscapes of *The Faerie Queene*. But his responses to life and his reflections upon it produced a sober, thoughtful poetry which deserves esteem and affords a keen and enduring pleasure. It is part of our inheritance from the Spenserian tradition of moralized song and is, as he claimed, 'Worthy the reading, and the worlds delight' (*Musophilus* 200).

JOAN REES

Daniel ed 1885–96; Daniel ed 1930; John Pitcher, ed 1981 *Samuel Daniel: The Brotherton Manuscript. A Study in Authorship* Leeds Texts and Monographs, ns 7 (Leeds); Joan Rees 1964 *Samuel Daniel* (Liverpool); Svensson 1980.

Dante Alighieri (1265–1321) There is good reason to suppose that Spenser was acquainted with Dante's reputation and, in all probability, with the text of the *Divine Comedy* itself. He would have seen evidence of Dante's influence on Chaucer and on the Italian poets whom he followed most closely, Ariosto and Tasso. Texts of the *Comedy* were readily available, and both Sidney and Harvey knew Dante's work (Tosello 1977). Moreover, Dante's political opinions, as expressed in both the *Comedy* and *De monarchia*, had been cited in the Protestant cause throughout the English Reformation (Friederich 1950).

The fact remains, however, that Spenser himself makes no explicit allusion to Dante, except perhaps in *The Visions of Bellay* which describes a vision that had appeared 'to that sad *Florentine*' (13.2). This silence may itself be significant, possibly suggesting Spenser's unwillingness to challenge a poet whom he could not hope to outdo. That much, however, is speculation; and evidence of direct influence is not needed to justify a critical comparison of the *Comedy* and *The Faerie Queene*. The two works are products of a common culture; indeed, that culture constitutes in good part the subject matter of each. Both Dante and Spenser planned their poems quite consciously as works which would simultaneously investigate the intellectual traditions of Christian Europe and criticize or celebrate its achievements. That one poet is a medieval Catholic and the other an Elizabethan Protestant is less significant than that their poems are located within the tradition of literature and philosophy that began in Greece and Rome. It is also less significant than their remarkably unanimous confidence in modern vernacular literature. In romance, both Dante and Spenser discovered a repertoire of images (notably those of the Lady and the quest) and likewise a range of literary techniques (in particular allegory and narrative) which each could adapt quite deliberately to express those Christian truths of greatest concern. Both may plausibly be said to have attempted to write a form of Scripture; both, however, perceived that in doing so they must not repress but rather admit and redirect the sophistications of contemporary culture.

Important as such similarities are, the dissimilarities in thought and poetic procedure between the two poets are no less significant. For quite apart from any of the inevitable differences occasioned by time and place, each poet conceived it essential that he should make an independent and distinctive contribution to the culture he had inherited. Each casts himself as the defender of the Christian faith and, in his own way, attempts a systematic expression of religious and ethical thought. Yet each is also concerned to assert the prestige and intellectual competence of his native language and literature; and this entails a whole range of differences in the handling of language, narrative, and allegorical method. Unless one admits as much, one will do no justice to the originality of either, or to the spirit in which each wrote his poem.

It is a clear sign of how directly concerned both poets were with the task of teaching their contemporaries and fellow citizens that, while each possessed a religious sensibility that verged upon the mystic, each is nonetheless at his most vigorous in the philosophical examination of those virtues which were thought to ensure happiness in the earthly life. In this regard, both acknowledge themselves to be the heirs of Aristotle; and the conclusions they draw from him are closely comparable.

For Dante and Spenser as for Aristotle, no morality can ever be purely private. The virtues both need and supply the support of friendship – of a small, sane society of like-minded individuals pursuing a common ideal of justice. While Dante's tone is often one of embattled individualism, his first move as poet in *Inferno* I is to reveal the weakness of any single-handed approach to righteousness: Virgil is a necessary companion if the protagonist is to advance beyond the dark wood. From the outset, Dante portrays friendship as a virtue in the relationship between the protagonist and Virgil; and this virtue contributes directly to the pursuit of justice, which Virgil, as an embodiment of Empire, is also designed to represent. Similarly for Spenser, the virtue of friendship of *FQ* IV is the means by which the aspiration towards goodness displayed in the love and chastity of Book III may be translated into the justice of Book V. Friendship is the offspring of Concord (IV x 34); and for Spenser, as for Dante, friendship makes it possible for the pursuit of goodness to be located at the center of civilized life.

Like Aristotle, however, both poets place the responsibility of learning to be virtuous upon the individual: neither is interested in accidental or untried innocence; both are the heirs of Aristotle in accepting enthusiastically the curriculum of particular virtues which he defines, and in agreeing that virtue is the result of intelligent training. Thus, in constructing their profoundly systematic poems, each is conscious of how systematic he must be in order to fulfill his educative project. Each poem centers around a journey as an image of learning; and in constructing that image, each poet displays in his own art the power of intelligent analysis necessary in the training of the virtues. Accordingly, Dante begins 'nel mezzo del cammin di nostra vita.' Behind this line lies the long discussion in the *Convivio* of how certain virtues are appropriate to each of the four ages of man; the protagonist of the

Comedy has reached the age when he must consciously perfect and employ the strengths which are natural to him if he is to bring to fruition that pattern which nature has stamped in his life. Similarly, *The Faerie Queene* begins, 'A Gentle Knight was pricking on the plaine': like the protagonist of the *Comedy*, the Red Cross Knight is perceived in the middle of an action; though he wears old armor, he is still callow and must prove – as he is eager to do – his fitness to wear that armor.

It is characteristic of the differences between the two poets in their treatment of analogous images that Dante should emphasize – in his image of a path with a middle and therefore a beginning and end – a clear and conclusive sense of moral pattern, while Spenser draws attention to a process which becomes increasingly diffuse as *The Faerie Queene* develops. Nonetheless, both poets are concerned with the realization that the order which governs the life of the individual is consistent with, and sanctioned by, the laws of the physical universe as expressed in patterns of growth and causal consequence. In both, virtue promises a reconciliation with the order that underlies the universe at large; and while to assert this is to go beyond Aristotle himself, both poets take it as an essential part of their philosophical project to defend that position. Thus the first piece of sustained doctrine in the *Inferno* (Canto 7) demonstrates that Fortuna, far from being evidence of the cruelty and disorder of the world, can be seen as an indication that the order and justice of providence extend to the sphere of physical matter and worldly splendors. This order will be apparent only to those who have the intelligence to praise the principle of change as it deserves; but in this light, disorder is nothing more than a test of ethical and intellectual mettle. In *The Faerie Queene*, similar discussion is delayed until the *Cantos of Mutabilitie*, by which time the mettle of the English gentleman has been thoroughly proved. But here, too, one is asked to see that chance is properly neither more nor less than natural change: 'For, all that moveth, doth in *Change* delight: / But thence-forth all shall rest eternally' (viii 2). On such foundations, neither Dante nor Spenser would hesitate to affirm that ethical imperatives can be discovered in the facts of the natural universe.

The response of each poet to Aristotle represents only one strand in the intellectual program which each is pursuing; yet even when they depart from him, they move initially in a similar direction, along a route marked out by the passage of Christian thinking through Neoplatonism to a remote literary conclusion in the language of courtly love. Both concern themselves more than Aristotle ever could with the problems of sin and evil; as a consequence, each points to conversion as a necessary part of the spiritual life. Also, in responding to the commonplaces of courtly love, both characteristically develop an ethical conception of courtesy which goes much further than anything that the Aristotelian notion of *eutropia* might have suggested; Aristotle could hardly have admitted the ethical gravity which attaches to Dante's love of Beatrice or Spenser's devotion to Gloriana.

In their treatment of sin and evil, which is no less precise than their treatment of virtue, the two poets attribute to the human mind a capacity for perversion as great and subtle as its capacity for good. The *Inferno* at large bears witness to this on Dante's part, while Spenser's knights are invariably assailed at the tragic point where their virtues themselves have exposed them to danger. Some significant differences, however, are discernible here, even allowing for the incompleteness of Spenser's poem. In the *Comedy*, after only a third of his poem the poet does reach a stage at which evil – in the figure of Satan – can be revealed once and for all as emptiness and banality. Evil for Spenser may be no less an illusion – hence the collapse of Orgoglio. Yet *The Faerie Queene* is so structured as to allow illusion in the form of Archimago a protean vitality which admits of no final reckoning in this life. *The Faerie Queene* conspicuously lacks that sense of finality which the *Comedy* expresses not only through the mastery exerted over Satan but also through the trust which Dante reposes in the sacramental acts of confession and penance, and in his expectations of the coming of the Day of Judgment.

This sense of finality does not preclude Dante's strong insistence, found also in Spenser, upon conversion as an essential and, paradoxically enough, unending prerequisite for the enjoyment of truth. In the *Comedy*, those who enter Purgatory are those who have shown themselves capable of a 'new life'; this capacity is sharpened by penance in preparation for the life of Paradise which will be perpetually 'new.' Correspondingly, in *The Faerie Queene* no virtue would be possible were it not founded upon an unremitting appetite for the good and upon that holiness of seeing which Redcrosse acquires on the Mount of Contemplation. Here Spenser might indeed serve as the interpreter of Dante's procedure in writing the *Comedy*; for on Dante's own account, the engagement with practical questions of sin and virtue would not have been possible had it not been preceded by the vision of a new life which he gains in his love of Beatrice.

In regard to ethics, we come finally to the place which both poets accord to courtesy in the spiritual life. The extent to which Dante can grant ethical status even to such marginal aspects of sensibility as charm is well illustrated by his canzone 'Poscia ch'Amor'; and Spenser, placing courtesy after justice in his spectrum of virtues, is at one with him in recognizing that courtesy can institute a rule which transcends or transfigures justice; for in courtesy, the rule is an inward law or measure which allows heart and emotions to be no less educated than reason.

In both poets, a devotion to courtesy is paralleled by a fear of barbarism. The courtly and chivalric culture from which they drew some of their most important images had grown up in the wake of the Dark Ages. But Dante and Spenser are well aware that a decline in courtesy could herald a return to barbarism, be it in the Ireland of *FQ* VI or in the Tuscany and Romagna of *Purgatorio* 14, and both write with acute nostalgia for the passing of an age of ideal knights and ladies. This negative aspect, however, is outweighed by the strength of moral engagement which the Lady inspires. The Lady, whether Beatrice or Gloriana, is certainly distant from her lover; however, that inspires not regret but an unceasing exercise in self-refinement. In the face of the loved object, be it the Lady or ultimately God, the lover remains a humble swain; but he also realizes that humility is the logical condition under which the active pursuit of perfection must proceed. Thus Dante and Spenser both picture the reconciliation of humility and spiritual grace in scenes which represent the apotheosis of the Lady; in this respect, Colin Clout on Mount Acidale may be compared directly to Dante meeting Beatrice on the summit of Mount Purgatory. Against all expectations, the first move that Beatrice makes in that encounter is not to welcome Dante but to insist that, even after the experiences of Purgatory, he is still morally distant from her. The speechless, childlike Dante of *Purgatorio* 30 is as humble as Colin Clout; and Dante the poet understands as well as does Spenser the moral value of adopting that persona.

Both poets aim to refine the minds of their readers; and at first sight, the means they adopt are closely comparable. Both choose to address themselves to a coterie or elite. Accordingly, in the proem to Book II, Spenser wishes to exclude 'witlesse man' from his readership as Dante might be thought to exclude those who follow him in a 'little bark' in *Paradiso* 2: both authors are concerned to test the acumen of their readers, and, theoretically at least, Dante understands as well as Spenser that the veil of allegory may constitute such a test.

Yet there are decided differences in the conception of the elite and in the application of allegorical method. Thus, while Dante's earliest work is addressed to a coterie in the strictest sense (the 'fedeli d'amore' of the *Vita nuova*), the notion of the elite shifts in the course of his career until, in *Paradiso* 14.106–8, he can address himself to those who, in taking up the Cross and following Christ, are elect in the sense that any true Christian may be. On the evidence of the proem to *FQ* II, Spenser appeals to an audience which is more specifically qualified in terms of intellectual aspirations and literary skill. For him, there are mysteries in the world which unroll slowly in the course of time: myths, legends, and unknown continents await the explorer; and against this, he envisages a peculiarly enterprising and creative power of intelligence which can penetrate the hidden truth. We need not deny that Dante would have sympathized with such a conception; yet his time was hardly ripe for it. Only with Petrarch and the Boccaccio of the *Genealogia* is the wisdom of the ages consigned to the hands of the scholar; and it is upon the example of these authors and of the allegorists who followed them, that Spenser tends to draw.

The differences between the two authors in the handling of allegory are of radical importance. If Dante can usefully be called an allegorist at all, his allegorical method characteristically insists upon the primacy of literal reading, as is especially clear from his comments on allegory in the *Convivio*. Yet even in the *Vita nuova*, his great achievement (according to his own interpretation of the central canzoni) is to realize that love need not be conceived of in terms of literary personification, as if it were some separate substance; love is a reality in the person of Beatrice (as finally in God himself), and the poet must find a language in which to engage that reality directly. In a similar way, death in the *Vita nuova* ceases to be a mere trope for the anguish of the lover; Dante is obliged to consider it as an actual fact of human existence when Beatrice dies. It is precisely because he achieves a literal understanding of both love and death that he can proceed to the moral realism and rigorously technical analysis of religious issues which characterize the *Comedy*.

But Spenser would be nothing without his allegory. His essential concern is not with the linguistic problems that accompany the representation of reality but rather with the pure activity of intelligence as it plays upon the correspondences between one thing and another. To the mind which can contemplate the essential allegorical relationship of 'one thing in terms of another,' the truth is that all things are eternally present. So, for Spenser, the general subject of glory may indeed find particular expression in his praise of Gloriana: 'And yet in some places els, I doe otherwise shadow her' (Letter to Raleigh). The mind itself will be glorious only if it responds to all manifestations of glory and sees in them all the workings of an eternal principle. When Dante treats glory, it is precisely to insist upon the principle of individuation which is expressed in the reality that God has created. The first terzina of the *Paradiso* speaks of the glory of God which 'shines in some place more and elsewhere less'; *glory* is here used with technical precision to denote the creative power which has established a universal hierarchy of individual beings. Thus in Paradise even the Christian philosophers are not content to contemplate the pure idea; they may temporarily be eternal flames, but they still long to return to their dead bodies which at the resurrection will become flesh, glorious and sanctified (*Par* 14.43–66). It is in the individuality of the glorified body that they will finally boast the fullness of their existence.

From the differences in their attitudes toward allegory flow most of the particular differences in procedure, structure, and linguistic surface between the two poets. Dante is concerned – most obviously in the *Inferno* – to engage the mind in judgment upon particular cases. Francesca, for example, challenges the reader no less than the protagonist to sustain clear moral judgments in the face of confusing evidence. Dante writes 'for profit of the world that lives ill' (*Purg* 32.103), but his purpose is not merely to communicate a set of moral precepts. On the contrary, and in a way alien to Spenser, he speaks in the language of historical particularity and demands that his reader construe the spiritual grammar that underlies history by an unceasing activity of moral discrimination. Spenser teaches by raising the mind to the contemplation of delightful example, which in itself is a strenuous course to pursue, for the contemplative act is a consummation, not an evasion, of intellectual activity. The Bower of Bliss episode, for instance, demands that the reader see through the meretricious surface of false nature to the confusion that it conceals. But we view the scene from the frame that Spenser's own measured stanzas have erected. His description is not itself ambiguous or meretricious (as Dante sometimes allows his own to be): it is the aesthetic demonstration of his concern with the good and beautiful. Dante requires us to act out judgment. (Only in the last moments of the *Purgatorio*, when he sits with Beatrice to witness the Masque of the Corrupt Church, can he take anything like a Spenserian delight in the display of evil.) Throughout his poem, Spenser invites intelligence to cultivate an aesthetic and contemplative detachment.

These differences of procedure require different forms of both narrative and language. Thus the greatest of Dante's achievements as narrator is the creation of the canto form. Though the *Aeneid* is avowedly his model, he abandons the long epic unit of the Virgilian book. The form he creates is entirely capable of sustaining a narrative line; but it also admits the intensity of the short lyric. Spenser, by contrast, not only returns to the longer unit but, profiting from the virtuosity of Ariosto, develops a form in which the crises of the moral life are dissolved by interlocking patterns of narrative line which cross even the boundaries between one book and the next. For Dante, the vision of God is itself seen as a crisis, underlined by the tense but decisive silence which ends his poem as the mind judges itself to have reached its proper limit; Spenser's silence at the end of *The Faerie Queene* resonates with possibilities, as well as with some weariness that the vitality of the mind should enjoin upon the writing hand the unending pursuit of these possibilities.

Finally, in regard to language, much might be made of the difference between a writer who admitted into his 'comedy' all registers of language from the colloquial to the scientific, and one who wrote with a deliberate and scholarly eye for the pleasing archaism – between one who meant his reader to 'scratch where the itch is' (*Par* 17.129), and one who in part is as evasive in diction as Petrarch (whom Spenser certainly did acknowledge as a model) and anticipates Keats and Hopkins, in mouthing words 'to flesh-burst' on the tongue. Consider the following passages:

L'altro ternaro, che così germoglia
in questa primavera sempiterna
che notturno Arïete non dispoglia,
perpetüalemente '*Osanna*' sberna
con tre melode, che suonano in tree
ordini di letizia onde s'interna.

(The next triad that thus flowers in this eternal spring which nightly Aries does not despoil perpetually sings Hosannah with three melodies which sound in the three orders of bliss that form the triad.)

(*Par* 28.115–20)

There is continuall spring, and harvest there
Continuall, both meeting at one time:
For both the boughes doe laughing blossomes beare,
And with fresh colours decke the wanton Prime,
And eke attonce the heavy trees they clime,
Which seeme to labour under their fruits lode:
The whiles the joyous birdes make their pastime
Emongst the shadie leaves, their sweet abode,
And their true loves without suspition tell abrode.

(*FQ* III vi 42)

Even at this high point in the *Paradiso*, Dante adopts a technical language: his 'ternaro' specifies a grade in the hierarchy of angels and needs no affective qualification. Likewise, his 'primavera sempiterna' is no piece of wordplay; to speak of spring, the season of growth and renewed process, as eternal is to create a conceptual tension, but this tension exactly reflects his view of Paradise as life in a state of continual renewal. Spenser, by contrast, *is* conceited, softening the intellectual impact of the first 'continuall' by the relish with which he produces the repetition after the line break, while in his 'wanton Prime' there is a spectrum of ambiguity which includes sexual innuendo and liturgical reference. Dante's 'sberna' may be as choice as Spenser's 'wanton Prime'; but here again there is technicality, for the word has behind it a Provençal original denoting the passage from winter to spring. Though Dante pictures the mystic recreation of the schemes of nature, he uses his phrases (including the richly imagistic 'che notturno Arïete non dispoglia') with a clear sense of their normal application in denoting change in the world of natural phenomena. Spenser's phrases deliver another world.

Similar points of contrast are evident in the rhythmic effects of the two passages, as when the tension of Dante's lines breaks through in a sudden, almost nervous 'Hosannah'; but the moment of mystic exaltation is immediately controlled by a return to enumeration and technicality. In Spenser, the sheer breadth of his stanzaic form in contrast to the terzina allows space to each phrase, so that it may be contemplated as a phrase – almost to the obliteration of syntax, as in 'their fruits lode' – until the underlying patterns of the stanza produce the pleasure of a metrical conclusion.

Utterly distinct as Spenser and Dante may

be in point of linguistic form, comparison of their respective linguistic practices provides the most satisfactory way of revealing the characteristics of two writers much concerned with the functions and textures of language. Robin Kirkpatrick

Dante Alighieri ed 1966; Dante 1970–5 *The Divine Comedy* tr and ed Charles S. Singleton, 3 vols in 6 (Princeton).

Josephine W. Bennett 1952 'Genre, Milieu, and the "Epic-Romance"' *EIE 1951* ed Alan S. Downer (New York), pp 95–125; Robert C. Benson 1972 'Elizabeth as Beatrice: A Reading of Spenser's *Amoretti*' *SCB* 32:184–8; Charles Dédéyan 1961–6 *Dante en Angleterre* 2 vols (Paris); Werner P. Friederich 1949 'Dante through the Centuries' *CL* 1:44–54; Friederich 1950 *Dante's Fame Abroad, 1350–1850* (Chapel Hill); Melvin Goldstein 1968 'Spenser and Dante: Two Pictorial Representatives of Evil' *JAE* 2:121–9; Hamilton 1961a; Kostić 1969; M. Pauline Parker 1963; Parker 1968 'The Image of Direction in Dante, Spenser and Milton' *EM* 19:9–23; Matthew Tosello 1977 'Spenser's Silence about Dante' *SEL* 17:59–66.

Daphnaïda (See ed 1912:527–34.) First published in quarto in 1591, *Daphnaïda* was not entered in the Stationers' Register (Johnson 1933 no 13); only three copies are known to survive. It was next printed in a 1596 quarto.

This original, gloomy elegy commemorates the death in August 1590 of Douglas Howard, wife of Arthur Gorges. Member of a Devonshire family distantly related to the Howards, Gorges was a gentleman-pensioner at court and a poet; he also translated Lucan into English verse, Bacon's *Wisedom* into English, and Bacon's essays into French. In 1584, he had married Douglas, a considerable heiress who was only thirteen years old, against the strenuous objections of her father, Henry Howard, second Viscount Bindon, but with the support of her mother. Despite the ensuing litigation by the father, Douglas and Arthur Gorges appear to have been happily married. They had a daughter, Ambrosia, in 1588.

Daphnaïda may have been written soon after Douglas' death. The dedication to Lady Helena, Marchioness of Northampton (Arthur's aunt by her marriage to Sir Thomas Gorges), is dated London, 1 January 1591, but if this date is given in the Old Style, by which the year began in March, the date is 1592. It is unlikely that the date is Old Style, for the dedication to *Colin Clouts Come Home Againe* is dated from Kilcolman on 27 December 1591, and it is hardly possible that Spenser was in London five days later. More likely, the date is New Style, indicating that *Daphnaïda* was written sometime between August and the end of December 1590 (see de Sélincourt in Spenser ed 1912: xxxi).

The dedication stresses Spenser's familiarity with Gorges and with the Howard family (whose genealogy he briefly recounts), but not with Douglas Gorges, of whom he can say only that he has heard of her 'great good fame.' Despite his expression of the 'particular goodwill' he bears toward Arthur Gorges, however, nothing is known for certain about their relationship. Gorges was cousin and close friend to Sir Walter Raleigh, and it is possible that Raleigh brought his two friends together during Spenser's visit to England in 1589-90. Later, in *Colin Clout*, he mentions Gorges under the name Alcyon as a gifted poet who has been diverted from his poetry by continuing grief for his wife: 'And there is sad *Alcyon* bent to mourne, / Though fit to frame an everlasting dittie, / Whose gentle spright for *Daphnes* death doth tourn / Sweet layes of love to endlesse plaints of pittie' (384-7). He urges him to 'Lift up [his] notes unto their wonted height' by continuing his 'sweet Eglantine of *Meriflure*' (389-90). Apparently Gorges returned the compliment, for what seems to be a surviving fragment of this poem contains a verbatim quotation *FQ* III v 52; and Gorges' elegy on Prince Henry, *The Olympian Catastrophe* (1060-88), repeats words Spenser assigned him as Alcyon (ed 1953:124-5, 237-8; cf *Daph* 215-92).

In this century Spenser's poem has found few admirers.

It is a highly original work but also a gloomy and forbidding one; its form and meaning have only recently become the subject of sustained critical discussion. *Daphnaïda* is a reworking of Chaucer's dream-vision, the *Book of the Duchess*, which it frequently echoes and which it follows in placing the customary lament of elegy within a narrative frame. The narrator of each poem meets a grieving, black-clad mourner, questions him, and hears eventually that he mourns his dead beloved. The poems share several motifs: the mourner attempts initially to evade the narrator's questions with a riddling response, and after a complaint against the mutable world expresses his desire to die; moreover, the narrator himself suffers from melancholy and acts as a foil to the mourner.

Yet the poems are entirely different. Chaucer's work is programmatically varied in tone, moving from comedy to pathos, remembered joy to present pain. Its complex juxtaposition of springtime renewal and individual death quietly reminds the reader of the necessary mixture of joy and sorrow attending life in a fallen world. Spenser's poem avoids this variation, simplifying both structure and mood. The dream-vision which frames Chaucer's poem is discarded, as are most of his digressions; the bereaved Alcyon's long lament occupies a considerably larger portion of the whole. And in the place of Chaucer's contrasting moods, the poem focuses on Alcyon's intense and unchanging grief, insisted upon in an opening which banishes the Muses and announces that 'here no tunes, save sobs and grones shall ring' (14).

Spenser has also altered the genre of Chaucer's poem, recasting it as a pastoral eclogue; the change sets Alcyon in the context of other sad shepherds in a tradition stemming ultimately from Theocritus (Idylls 1, 3, 11), Moschus ('Lament for Bion'), and Virgil (Eclogues 2, 5, 7, 10). Renaissance pastoral conventions distinguish two kinds of plaintive eclogues and with them two kinds of shepherds: mourners and lovers. The mourners of pastoral elegy are treated seriously: they suffer and question as representative mortals, faced with the fact of death. In Christian pastoral elegy, they are often granted a consoling vision of the dead shepherd or shepherdess in heavenly bliss. Colin attains such a vision in *SC, November*, as the speaker of *Lycidas* was later to do. Shepherds grieving for love, on the contrary, are often presented with comic detachment: they tend to be obsessive, self-absorbed, and at times boorish. Spenser's Colin as he usually appears in the *Calender* is such a figure, and his morbid, unresolved sestina in *August* typifies his mood. In *Daphnaïda*, Spenser conflates the two eclogue conventions. Although Alcyon grieves for a death, he does so with the self-concern typical of *August*, not *November*.

Alcyon's extremity is heralded in his name, a masculine version of Alcione, the devoted Queen who – in the version of the myth with which Chaucer prefaces the *Book of the Duchess* – learns her husband has drowned and dies of grief. Alcyon is equally violent and less sympathetic. Rude, impatient, and self-absorbed, he tends to dramatize his own plight and sees himself as unique, 'the wretchedst man that treades this day on ground' (63). He appears as an epitome of the impulse to self-absorbed grief, blaming the heavens for his 'undeserv'd distresse,' and refusing to submit his will to God's. The narrator compares him to a 'stubborne steed' unwilling to be restrained by the bit: his long complaint is a 'breaking foorth' (531, 194–6).

Alcyon's willful misvaluation of his world appears in one of the most curious of Spenser's Chaucerian borrowings, his initial riddling evasion as to why he grieves. He tells the story of a lioness he has found and tamed to guard his flocks; but she, the delight of all, has been slain by a 'cruell *Satyre*' (156). Because the white lion (also mentioned in the dedicatory epistle) is part of the Howard coat of arms, the figure is appropriate for Douglas Howard; yet the story also serves to characterize Alcyon, for it envisions an unreal, paradisal setting in which the lion becomes as mild as a lamb (120–6): a fantasy of human happiness which the world (as embodied by Death the 'Satyre') will not allow (Harris and Steffen 1978).

Alcyon's seven-part complaint of 49 stanzas (197–539) accuses the world of failing to live up to his expectations. Its most important moment comes in the second part when he reports Daphne's last words – words which show her fully reconciled to her death (252–308). In contrast to her shepherd she acts as a model Christian, ready to go 'unto the bridale feast' (268), commending their daughter to him: 'In lieu of mee / Love her: so shall our love for ever last' (288–91). Alcyon disregards this command to brood over her remembered weakness and pallor, and this emphasis suggests again his withdrawal from the active life befitting a good father and a good Christian (DeNeef

1982:48). The vision of blessedness Daphne articulates usually marks the end of a pastoral elegy; here it marks the numerical center, and through the rest of the poem Alcyon remains blind to the truth he has heard and reported.

After describing Daphne, Alcyon falls into the ill will typical of disappointed shepherds, cursing the natural world (including his sheep), wishing for death, and hating earthly creation. It has been argued that in the central, twenty-fifth stanza of the complaint (365–71), Alcyon realizes his own sinfulness and abandons his selfish questioning of God's justice for a penitent renunciation of the world (Røstvig 1963:83–4). Such a reading seems unlikely, however, given his continued insistence in the latter part of the poem on his 'undeserved paines' (522) and his tendency to brag of his self-inflicted sufferings (372–85). Rather, it seems that the lament is one of Spenser's treatments of the complaint mode as an expression of human impatience with divine will.

Why Spenser should paint such an unflattering portrait of his friend can only be matter for speculation; perhaps *Daphnaïda* represents his attempt to rouse Gorges from grief by presenting him with a picture of its extremity (Oram 1981). The narrator claims to feel 'like wofulness' which gives him 'like cause' (66) to weep with Alcyon: if Spenser had recently lost his own first wife, Machabyas Chylde, the likeness between the two poets would temper the implied criticism of Gorge's fictional double. The narrator does contrast with Alcyon in the poem for, although he mourns at the opening of the work, he nonetheless manages to control and transcend his own melancholy. His active sympathy as he attempts to help Alcyon recalls the loving care of Daphne: both demonstrate a Christian charity that rises above personal misfortune.

Daphnaïda's experimentation is not isolated. With 'Astrophel,' *Colin Clouts Come Home Againe*, and *FQ* VI, the poem is one of a series of pastoral experiments which Spenser composed in the early 1590s. These poems create fictional versions of four actual poets, Gorges, Sidney, Raleigh, and Spenser himself, in order to investigate the poet's vocation and the nature of his art (Cheney 1983). In this context Alcyon appears (unlike the narrator) as a poet whose art is paralyzed, limited to mere repetition of his 'endlesse plaints of pittie' (*CCCHA* 387).

Daphnaïda is elaborately patterned: there are 81 seven-line stanzas in a modified rhyme royal borrowed from Chaucer, with the rhymes of fifth and sixth lines transposed to avoid the easy chime of a final couplet. These are divided into an introduction of 28 stanzas (4 × 7), a lament of 49 (7 × 7), and a coda of 4 (which total 28 or 4 × 7 *lines*). The careful patterning is obvious, its interpretation less so. 7 and 28 are traditionally associated with judgment and penance (see Røstvig 1963:83–7), which would suggest that Alcyon undergoes a penitential reformation. Agrippa calls 7 'the number of blessedness, or of rest' (*Three Books of Occult Philosophy* 2.10), citing the sabbath; 28 is also associated with perfection, from the completion of the moon's cycle. The idea of final rest would be appropriate to Daphne's blessed condition; and as a glimpse of a 'Sabaoths sight' it would have an ironic relation to Alcyon's own complaint, quietly insisting upon the ultimate order of the universe as it appears in the patterning of the poem itself.

WILLIAM A. ORAM

DeNeef 1982:41–50; Arthur Gorges 1953 *Poems* ed Helen Estabrook Sandison (Oxford); Harris and Steffen 1978; Oram 1981; Pigman 1985; Røstvig 1963; Helen Estabrook Sandison 1928 'Arthur Gorges, Spenser's Alcyon and Ralegh's Friend' *PMLA* 43:645–74; Spenser ed 1929.

Daphne Ovid's story of Daphne and Apollo (*Metamorphoses* 1.452–567) provides a model for the love chase which appears repeatedly in *FQ* III and IV. Whereas Cupid's golden arrow inspires Apollo with love for Daphne, his leaden arrow inspires her to flee: the virgin huntress becomes the hunted. As in Ovid's stories of Arethusa and Atalanta, the maiden's beauty is enhanced by her flight ('auctaque forma fuga est' 1.530), and love seems to be a natural predatory instinct like that of hound for hare. When Daphne is transformed into a laurel tree to evade her pursuer, Apollo makes her branches his personal symbol, the 'meed of mightie Conquerours / And Poets sage' (*FQ* I i 9). Stimulated by hints in Ovid's story and most significantly by Petrarch's poems to Laura (see Cottino-Jones 1975), poets made Daphne a figure of the ways in which lovers and poets alike confuse the literal and figurative objects of their pursuit: the sense, as Andrew Marvell would put it, that '*Apollo* hunted *Daphne* so, / Only that She might Laurel grow' ('The Garden' 29–30; cf Rees 1971).

Spenser playfully adapts these themes in *Amoretti* 28 (possibly on the model of Ronsard's *Astrée* II; cf Lotspeich 1932:52–3). Addressing his lady who is wearing a laurel leaf, the speaker reminds her that the laurel is a symbol of the poet's power as well as of Daphne's pride; he urges her to 'fly no more fayre love from Phebus chace, / but in your brest his leafe and love embrace.' Since *leafe* can refer to the poem itself as well as the symbol of the poet's power, embracing his leaf is the same as accepting the argument of the poem. With its echo of *lief* 'beloved,' the leaf also expresses both the love of the pursuer and the reaction of the one pursued. In his mock-serious warning to the lady, the speaker changes Ovid's story by saying that Daphne was transformed by 'the gods in theyr revengefull yre' rather than by her father Peneus in answer to her plea.

In *The Faerie Queene*, two chases are explicitly associated with Daphne's flight from Apollo, as well as with Myrrha's flight (for very different reasons) from her angry father whom she has tricked into lying with her (*Met* 10.311ff). Florimell flees the hyena-like beast sent in pursuit of her by the witch (III vii 26), and Amoret flees Lust (IV vii 22). Florimell especially is similar to Daphne, for both preserve their virginity by flight and unwittingly invite pursuit because flight makes them more desirable. (Florimell's pursuit is called 'beauties chace' in III i 19; the pun in the argument to III i, 'faire Florimell is chaced,' implies that she is chased because she is chaste.) Particularly reminiscent of Daphne's flight is Florimell's from Guyon, Arthur, and the rude Foster (i and iv). Spenser uses Ovid's simile of a hare fleeing from hounds (iv 46, *Met* 1.533–4), and he has Arthur try to assure her that he means no harm. In what might almost be taken as a comment on Florimell's experience with Proteus in III viii, Golding calls Daphne a 'myrror of virginitie' who achieves fame and immortality by not yielding to fear, force, or flattery (Epistle to his 1567 translation, Ovid ed 1904:2); his remark follows a line of interpretation found earlier in the *Ovide moralisé* (1.3215–60).

In describing the tapestry in the house of Busirane, Spenser says that Cupid caused Apollo to love Daphne by wounding him with a leaden (rather than golden) dart; Apollo's 'sad distresse' in loving Daphne was his punishment for revealing Venus' affair with Mars (III xi 36). This version seems to conflate the Daphne myth with the story of Apollo and Leucothoe (*Met* 4.171–97). Spenser's comment here on Apollo's love for Daphne ('Yet was thy love her death') relates a recurrent theme in *Metamorphoses* 10 to the perversion of love in the house of Busirane: in one way or another, lovers destroy and lose the objects of their love.

More problematic is the relevance of the Daphne myth to Spenser's *Daphnaïda*. Although the primary significance of the title lies in the fact that Gorges' own poems refer to his wife as Daphne, the poem does liken her to a tree (239–42); and there may be an implied allusion to the Petrarchan myth (Cheney 1983:11–12).

CALVIN R. EDWARDS

Boccaccio *Genealogia* 7.29; Marga Cottino-Jones 1975 'The Myth of Apollo and Daphne in Petrarch's *Canzoniere*: The Dynamics and Literary Function of Transformation' in Scaglione 1975:152–76; Ovid ed 1904; Rees 1971.

Daunger The allegorical figure Daunger appears three times in *The Faerie Queene*, each time with subtleties of depiction by no means obvious to the modern reader but evidently inherent in the etymological and semantic complexities of the word as it had developed in English from its Old French sources from the thirteenth century onwards.

Daunger first appears among the erotic personifications of the 'maske of Cupid' in the house of Busirane (III xii 11). Uncouth and ferocious in manner, clad in a rough bearskin, he seems to represent, oddly enough in respect of the medieval associations of the figure, nothing more erotic than a generalized ferocity, with a 'rustie blade' to threaten his foes and a net, 'his friends ment to enwrap.' Though in the romance tradition an affair would frequently involve the lover in physical danger, this would normally take the form of a chivalric encounter between knightly rivals, rather than the sordid or treacherous assaults implied here. Such perils hardly seem an essential element of the love relationship depicted in the masque of Cupid as represented in the personified qualities that precede Daunger in the procession, with Fancy, Desire, and Doubt all portrayed in terms appropriate to the erotic life.

Daunger's appearance here may be based on a certain etymological ambiguity. When Chaucer in the *Parliament of Fowls* writes of the peril to the lover of the 'mortal strokes of the spere / Of which Disdayn and Daunger is the gyde' (135–6), he is clearly referring to *danger* in the established medieval sense of 'resistance offered to a lover by his ladylove: disdain, aloofness, reluctance, reserve ... anything or everything that frustrates a lover' (*MED* 4.a, b). This meaning derives from the classic depiction of Daunger in Guillaume de Lorris' *Roman de la Rose* (c 1325) as the surly and potentially violent custodian of the rose garden in which the dreamer-hero of this famous courtly allegory seeks Love's rose. But such a meaning may have been dying out in the late sixteenth century (in the *OED*, the last citation of the general meaning of 'reluctance' is dated 1526). In 1590, Spenser may have decided to place the figure of Daunger in its traditional erotic context while changing its significance to that of 'peril' in general, a later development from the stem meaning of 'domination' (L *dominium*), that had, however, been available at least since Chaucer's Shipman (*General Prologue*, *CT* I [A] 402).

As a justification for Daunger's somewhat awkwardly nonerotic character, Spenser integrates the personification into the linear flow of the procession by pairing him with Doubt. He is followed by the equally nonerotic personification of Fear, who is terrified even by the glitter of his own weaponry and cowers behind his shield, his frightened gaze fixed upon Daunger's threatening presence. At the same time, something of the traditional style and appearance of Daunger from the *Romance of the Rose* tradition is given to a later character in the procession, Suspect, 'foule, ill favoured, and grim, / Under his eyebrowes looking still askaunce' (15). Yet Suspect here has no function parallel to the gruff gardener Daunger in the *Romance*, who frustrates the Lover's attempts to possess the Rose of Love, thus representing the Lady's rebuff of the Lover's pretensions.

A second depiction of Daunger, however, as the guardian of the Gate of Good Desert leading to the Island of Venus (IV x 16–20), does evoke the older erotic sense. Here Daunger is preceded by his old associate Doubt, but now there is an intermediate character, Delay, a chatty beldame who represents a more amiable manifestation of the Lady's reluctance than the hostility associated with Daunger. This time he is at least as fearsome as the Daunger of the masque, and certainly larger, 'An hideous Giant,' a rough and aggressive protector of the sanctuary; he may, however, be more frightening in show than in reality. At all events, he clearly represents something other than physical danger, since doughty warriors faint at no more than the sternness of his glance while known cowards manage to get past him by 'gifts, or guile.' By using the enchanted shield, Scudamour overcomes this ferocious porter with little difficulty, which may suggest that the bride has no right to display 'Daunger' towards her appointed husband. In this respect the episode prepares us for the later moment when Scudamour carries off Amoret from the Temple, quelling her reluctance, her 'tender teares,' and her 'witching smyles' by showing the enchanted shield (57). And in the following stanza, the incident is echoed on the level of personification allegory when, on his exit from the Island, Scudamour reports, 'No lesse did *Daunger* threaten me with dread' (58); but the enchanted shield once again wins him a way through.

One feature of Daunger here may not seem relevant to Scudamour's immediate situation (though it might be interpreted as foreshadowing the menace of Busirane): once the knight gets past Daunger, he is able to see that his hindparts 'Much more deformed fearefull ugly were ... For hatred, murther, treason ... lay in ambushment there' (20). This distinction between an openly threatening menace and a more dangerously hidden, treacherous source of peril appears in all three manifestations of the figure, even in his third appearance, brief and otherwise rather unremarkable, as defense witness at the trial of Duessa (V ix 45): 'And then came *Daunger* threatning hidden dread,' a line that compresses both these aspects of the personification into a striking oxymoron.

The distinction within *danger* between open peril and hidden treachery, unrecognized by *OED* or *MED*, is seldom found in literature, though there are analogues. Daunger with his net to entrap his friends (III xii 11) may suggest something of the classical retiarius. A further parallel is found in Alciati's Emblem 50. With its motto 'Dolus in suos' ('Treachery towards one's own'), it depicts two fowlers hidden behind a tree watching a decoy lure ducks into a net. The epigram translates, in part, 'Captive birds cry out, but the decoy, itself a joint conspirator, is silent. The treacherous bird has defiled itself with kindred blood, obliging to others, fatal to its own.'

Similarly the ominous hindparts of the figure of Daunger on the Island of Venus probably owe something to the medieval tradition of the lady fair in front but foul behind. For example, Nature in Hawes' *Example of Virtue* (lines 519–32) is of 'merveylous beaute,' but, the poet reports, 'behynde ... I sawe all the pryvyte / Of her werke and humayne kynde / And at her backe I dyd then fynde / Of cruell deth a dolfull image' (see Bernheimer 1952, ch 2).

PAUL PIEHLER

A late-15th-c analogue to the guardian Daunger on the Island of Venus occurs in the anonymous Scottish poem *King Hart*, where Dame Danger acts as jailer to Hart until Pietie rescues him when Danger is asleep (text in Gavin Douglas 1874 *Poetical Works* ed John Small, 4 vols [Edinburgh] 1:92, 95, 120). See also E.B. Fowler 1921:91, 127; Lewis 1936:364–6.

Davies, John (1569–1626) Writing in 1697 'Upon the Present Corrupted State of Poetry,' Nahum Tate complained of the absence of '*Spencer's* Strength, or *Davies*, who sustain'd / Wit's Empire when Divine *Eliza* reign'd' (*Sp All* p 307). Davies' first work was a collection of epigrams printed with Marlowe's translation of Ovid's *Elegies*. In a more severely didactic vein, he wrote *Nosce Teipsum* (1599), a long philosophical poem consisting of two 'elegies': 'Of Humane Knowledge' and 'Of the Soule of Man, and the Immortalitie Thereof.' His *Hymnes of Astraea* is a sequence of 22 acrostic lyrics presented to 'Elisabetha Regina' as an Accession Day tribute in 1599. Davies may have adopted the structure of *Teares of the Muses* (separate speeches by each of the nine Muses) for his *Epithalamion* (1594–5), and *Amoretti* may be parodied in his 'Gullinge Sonnets' (cf *GS* 4 with *Am* 1, 18, 30).

At the conclusion of his best-known work, *Orchestra, or A Poeme of Dauncing* (written c 1594, pub 1596, 1622), in addition to recognizing Homer and Virgil as his classical sources, Davies alludes to Chaucer and Spenser, linking his poem to a specifically English literary tradition: 'O that I could old *Gefferies* Muse awake, / Or borrow *Colins* fayre heroike stile' (ed 1975:124). The rhyme royal of Chaucer and of Spenser's *Ruines of Time* and *Fowre Hymnes* is employed, and there are generic affinities with *Muiopotmos* as well as verbal resemblances to *Hymne of Love* and *Hymne of Beautie*. *Orchestra*, in a manner characteristic of the Ovidian epic, is introduced as an incident which Homer forgot to include in the *Odyssey*: Antinous, a suitor for Penelope's hand, tries to persuade her to dance, insisting that dancing is the principle underlying cosmic order. Ostensibly a compliment to Elizabeth's orderly reign, the poem ends ambiguously, suggesting a threat to future order in the uncertainty over the succession (Brink 1980).

Davies served first as Solicitor General and then as Attorney General in Ireland. He and Spenser shared an interest in history: they knew and were influenced by Camden, the great antiquarian; and while in Ireland, they collected Irish historical materials for their political assessments of Anglo-Irish relations in *Vewe* and in *A Discoverie of the True Causes Why Ireland Was Never Entirely Subdued untill His Majesties Raigne* (1612).

JEANIE R. BRINK

Davies ed 1975 is a standard edition. The 1869–76 *Works* ed Alexander B. Grosart, 3 vols (Blackburn) includes the prose. See also Jeanie R. Brink 1979–80 'Sir John Davies's *Orchestra*: Political Symbolism and Textual Revisions' *DUJ* 72 (ns 41):195–201; Hulse 1981.

Dee, John (1527–1608) Philosopher, mathematician, astrologer, and magus; a controversial but major figure of the Elizabethan cultural revival (French 1972, Yates 1979).

Little can be documented of Spenser's

direct contact with Dee; the strongest evidence is a remark in one of Harvey's letters to Spenser: 'Would to God in heaven I had awhile ... the mysticall and supermetaphysical philosophy of Doctor Dee' (ed 1884:71). Yet, since Dee was known to many of Spenser's literary friends, it is reasonable to assume that he was also part of the poet's intellectual milieu.

Born of London gentry, Dee studied at St John's College, Cambridge, where he read in natural sciences and philosophy. Later he went several times to the continent 'to speake and conferr with some learned men, and chiefly mathematicians' (quoted in French 1972:24–5). By the 1550s, he was a respected mathematician and astrologer (on his early scientific achievements, see Clulee 1977 and Shumaker in Dee ed 1978). He lectured in Paris in 1550 and became acquainted with the philosophers Ramus and Guillaume Postel. At the time of Elizabeth's accession, 17 November 1558, he was invited to decide her coronation date on the basis of astrological divination. From then on, he remained in contact with court circles and with the Queen herself.

Dee seems to have been the first Englishman to have discovered and brought to England a new type of Renaissance outlook, represented by Hermetic Neoplatonists such as Ficino, Pico della Mirandola, and Agrippa. In 1562–3, he visited the Low Countries, Switzerland, Italy, Austria, and Hungary. Inspired by his reading of Trithemius at this time, he wrote his most famous treatise, the *Monas hieroglyphica* (Antwerp 1564), which describes a magic seal or formula composed of geometrical and alchemical symbols expressing the unity of the world according to Hermetic doctrines. His best-known work is the *Mathematicall Praeface* to the 1570 English edition of Euclid's *Elements*. It is more philosophical than strictly scientific (Clulee 1984), and one of its merits is that it translates into the vernacular the achievements of ancient scholars and Neoplatonic thinkers. The *Praeface* may have had some influence on Elizabethan theater construction by reviewing Vitruvian principles of architecture (Yates 1969); possibly it also influenced Sidney's *Defence of Poetry* (French 1972:135–59), and it could have provided the model for Spenser's castle of Alma (Hopper 1940:966, Fowler 1964:265–84). Dee's treatise on navigation, *General and Rare Memorials* 1577, is a patriotic call for British imperialism, an important forerunner of Hakluyt's famous compilation.

Dee's influence on English intellectual life was strongest during these years: his major works were published, and his library, of some 2500 volumes and several hundred rare manuscripts, as well as various pieces of his scientific equipment were made available to explorers, students, and men of letters. His *Private Diary* reveals a long list of Elizabethans as his clientele, and numerous other sources also mention his relations to members of the court and contemporary intellectuals. Names of persons close to the Areopagus appear frequently (Phillips 1965). Thomas Moffet writes that Sidney 'pressed into the inner-most penetralia of causes; and by that token, led by God, with Dee as teacher, and with Dyer as companion, he learned chemistry, that starry science' (1940:75). During 1570–1, Dee was tutor to the families of Leicester and Sir Henry Sidney. In 1577, Sidney, his friend Dyer, and Leicester consulted Dee in his house before Sidney's diplomatic mission to Emperor Rudolf's court; in 1578, Daniel Rogers visited Dee's home, Mortlake; in 1579, Dyer became godfather to Dee's firstborn son, Arthur; and in June 1583, Sidney escorted the Polish magnate Olbrach Laski to Dee's home after they had met Bruno in Oxford.

From 1583 to 1589, Dee lived in Central Europe, where he was received by Polish, Czech, and Hungarian nobility. He performed alchemical experiments and angel conjurations before the Habsburg emperor Rudolf II and the Polish king, Stephen Bathory (Evans 1973, Szőnyi 1980). After his return to England, he remained an advocate of Hermeticism. Although he kept in contact with Elizabeth and her court until her death (he dined with Raleigh in October 1595, not long before Spenser came to court for the second time), James did not take to him, and he spent his last years in oblivion as a college warden in Manchester.

György E. Szőnyi

John Dee 1842 *Private Diary* ed James Orchard Halliwell, Camden Society (London); Dee 1964 'Monas hieroglyphica' tr C.H. Josten *Ambix* 12:84–221; Dee 1975 *The Mathematicall Praeface to the Elements of Geometrie of Euclid of Megara (1570)* ed Allen G. Debus (New York); Dee 1978 *John Dee on Astronomy: 'Propaedeumata Aphoristica' (1558 and 1568)* tr and ed Wayne Shumaker (Berkeley and Los Angeles).

Nicholas H. Clulee 1977 'Astrology, Magic, and Optics: Facets of John Dee's Early Natural Philosophy' *RenQ* 30:632–80; Clulee 1984 'At the Crossroads of Magic and Science: John Dee's Archemastrie' in Vickers 1984:57–71; R[obert] J.W. Evans 1973 *Rudolf II and His World* (Oxford); Peter J. French 1972 *John Dee: The World of an Elizabethan Magus* (London); Hopper 1940; Thomas Moffet 1940 *Nobilis, or A View of the Life and Death of a Sidney* ed V.B. Heltzel and H.H. Hudson (San Marino, Cal); Phillips 1965; György E. Szőnyi 1980 'John Dee, an Elizabethan Magus and His Links with Central Europe' *HSE* 13:71–83; Frances A. Yates 1969 *Theatre of the World* (London); Yates 1979.

Deguileville, Guillaume de (1295–post 1358) His dream-vision trilogy, consisting of *Le Pèlerinage de la vie humaine* (in two versions of 1331, 1355), *Le Pèlerinage de l'âme* (1355–8), and *Le Pèlerinage de Jhesus Crist* (1358), is the best-known doctrinally inspired encyclopedic allegory of the late Middle Ages. These poems provide one of the clearest examples of how medieval allegory works: rather than presenting static personifications of characters and concepts, Deguileville explores the significance of ideas, and thereby leads the reader to 'knowing' by sharing the process of recognizing the revitalized meaning of conventional lore understood within the context of personal experience (see Tuve 1966).

Deguileville's most popular pilgrimage was *Vie*. According to the first version, the poet, asleep after reading the *Romance of the Rose*, has a vision of the New Jerusalem towards which he directs his pilgrimage. After nine months of being 'housed,' he meets his spiritual guide, Grace of God, who insists he be washed (baptized), instructed at her house by Reason, Moses, Nature, Penance, Charity, Wisdom, and Aristotle, and taught the sacraments. The Pilgrim is then armed with a scrip of Faith, a staff of Hope, and a doublet of Patience. Brute Understanding challenges him but is routed by Reason. Then the Pilgrim, encouraged by Body, chooses the easy path instead of the one involving hard labor and suffering, but soon meets the seven deadly sins; he escapes through help of Grace of God, prayer to the Virgin Mary, and washing in water from a rock. Coming to a sea where Satan fishes for sinners, he endures tests by Heresy and Tribulation and then enters the Ship of Religion where he meets the gracious ladies Charity, Discipline, Chastity, Sobriety, Obedience, and Abstinence. Attacks of Old Age, Infirmity, and Death are eased by Mercy and Grace of God. As his soul is about to be drawn from his body and he glimpses the New Jerusalem, he is wakened by the matin bells.

English versions include a fifteenth-century prose translation of the first version and an embellished octosyllabic couplet rendering of the second, attributed to Lydgate (c 1426). French poetic versions exist in hundreds of manuscripts; also popular was a French prose version first printed in 1485.

According to Padelford (1931), there are many parallels between *Vie* and *FQ* I, including the arming of the pilgrim and Redcrosse; their respective encounters with Brute Understanding and Error, the seven deadly sins, and Satan and Orgoglio; their delivery through Heavenly Grace; and their subjection to discipline in a religious household. He notes specific sources in *Vie* for Kirkrapine (*FQ* I iii 16–22), the Gulf of Greediness (II xii 3), the Whirlpool of Decay (20), and Envy and Detraction (V xii 28–42). *Ame*, too, elucidates Spenser's allegories, especially in the character of Syndérèse (Remorse), the analysis of penance, and the anatomy of the soul, which combines Aristotelian and Augustinian modes. If Spenser did not know Deguileville directly, the allegories may have influenced him by way of Chaucer and Langland.

Joan Heiges Blythe

The French texts were edited by Jakob J. Stürzinger for the Roxburghe Club: *Vie* (London 1893); *Ame* (London 1895); *Jhesus Crist* (London 1897). Deguileville ed 1899–1904 is the Lydgate version. The prose *Pylgremage of the Sowle* (Westminster 1483) has been reprinted (Amsterdam and Norwood, NJ 1975; also ed Katherine Isabella Cust, London 1859). Studies include Joan Heiges Blythe 1974 'The Influence of Latin Manuals on Medieval Allegory: Deguileville's Presentation of Wrath' *Ro* 95:256–83; Edmond Faral 1962 'Guillaume de Digulleville, moine de Chaalis' *HLF* 39:1–132, historical background and description of Deguileville's works; and Frederick Morgan Padelford 1931 'Spenser and *The Pilgrimage of the Life of Man*' *SP* 28:211–18. Tuve 1966 treats 'Guillaume's Pilgrimage' (ch 3) and *Vie*'s influence on Spenser (ch 5, on 'Romances'). Siegfried Wenzel 1973 'The Pilgrimage of Life as a Late Medieval Genre' *MS* 35:370–88 is a general analysis of the form.

Dekker, Thomas (1572?-1632) Dekker, prolific playwright and pamphleteer, was, like Spenser, born and reared in London. He began to work for the stage while very young, and has been associated with Shakespeare in writing *Sir Thomas More* in the 1590s. From 1598 he worked for Philip Henslowe. He was mainly a collaborative playwright, having a hand in over 60 plays; during times of trouble for the theater he wrote pamphlets. From 1612 to 1619, he was in the King's Bench prison for debt; but following his release he began again to write plays and pamphlets, and also several pageants for the City of London. His last work was a revision with additions of his most popular rogue pamphlet, *Lanthorne and Candlelight*.

Dekker obviously admired Spenser, though he is unlikely to have known him personally. In *A Knights Conjuring* (1607), he names him as one of the inhabitants of the Chapel of Apollo in Elysium: '*Grave Spencer* was no sooner entred into this *Chappell of Apollo*, but these elder *Fathers of the divine Furie*, gave him a *Lawrer* and sung his *Welcome*: *Chaucer* call'de him his Sonne, and plac'de him at his right hand. All of them (at a signe given by the whole *Quire* of the *Muses* that brought him thither,) closing up their lippes in silence, and tuning all their eares for attention, to heare him sing out the rest of his *Fayrie Queenes* praises' (*Sp All* p 112). He shared several traits with Spenser, including love of country and of London, and a propensity for emblem and allegorical personification.

It is not easy to find direct verbal connections, except in *The Whore of Babylon* (1607). This strongly Protestant play has both general and specific connections with Spenser. 'With respect to the Spenserian theme of England's destiny, Dekker is offering in drama a counterpart to *The Faerie Queene*' (Price 1969:69); the opening sentence of the preface is phrased in a Spenserian manner: 'The Generall scope of this Drammaticall Poem, is to set forth (in Tropicall and shadowed collours) the Greatnes, Magnanimity, Constancy, Clemency, and other the incomparable Heroical vertues of our late Queene' (Dekker ed 1953–61, 2:497). In this play, he presents England as Fairyland ruled by a Fairy Queen, whose antagonist is the Empress of Babylon, and he borrows three Spenserian names: Florimell, Paridel, and Satyrane. His Satyrane is a Spanish king unrelated to Spenser's character, but Florimell is a counselor to the Fairy Queen, Titania, and Paridel the treacherous Dr Parry. Such eclecticism is typical of his borrowings from Spenser. Florimell's account of the kings of England in 1.2 owes something to *FQ* II x 71–6 and uses the name Oberon for Henry VIII, though Henry VII is called Elfiline rather than Spenser's Elficleos; the account of the plight of the Netherlands in 2.1.234–56 is influenced by *FQ* V x, though where Spenser's Belge has 'seventeene goodly sonnes' (7) Dekker's Netherlands 'have but seventeen daughters young and faire.' *The Whore of Babylon* 4.2, where the reluctant Titania is urged to sign a death warrant for the Moon who has attempted to usurp her power, draws on Duessa's trial in *FQ* V ix; and the scene where the Empress of Babylon musters her Spanish armada to attack Fairyland (4.4) may relate to the Souldan and Adicia in *FQ* V viii.

Dekker shares Spenser's habit of combining political with moral allegory. Elizabeth as 'Dread Queene of Fayries' is also referred to in the prologue to *Old Fortunatus* (1599), where he compliments her under the alternative names of Gloriana, Belphoebe, and Astraea, and fleetingly introduces the patriotic theme. His city pageantry may be indebted to Spenser for some iconographical details, particularly from the wedding feast of Thames and Medway (*FQ* IV xi). The most Spenserian pageant, *Troia-Nova Triumphans* (1612), generally recognized as his best, draws on a range of Spenserian imagery in its emblematic device of Forlorne Castle, also called 'a cave of Monsters' (ed 1953–61, 3:238), commanded by Envy, a pallid, snake-haired hag, who is overcome by the brilliant shield held up by Vertue.

Dekker's prose pamphlets resemble Spenser in their manner of describing emblematic personifications, as in *The Seven Deadly Sinnes of London* (1606), but without close verbal parallels. His sins are conceived in contemporary terms and eschew the traditional attributes used by Spenser. The feeling for London, and especially for the river Thames, in *Time*, *Prothalamion*, and *FQ* IV xi is more intense and elaborate in Dekker, who uses his birthplace as his subject in many pamphlets. There are connections between these pamphlets and Spenser's poems, though few and of limited significance. In *The Dead Tearme* (1608), the Thames is personified as in *FQ* IV xi, though as feminine. The elegiac strain in *Time* may be recalled in *Worke for Armourers* (1609), where Dekker like Spenser laments the loss of past glories, and where the commotion caused by the armies of Poverty has similarities with the activities of the 'rablement' who besiege the castle of Alma (*FQ* II xi 8), though Dekker's sympathy towards this guerilla-like band is quite opposite to Spenser's feeling.

Although verbal echoes are fewer than one might expect, despite many similarities of allegorical detail, Dekker's work as a whole provides clear evidence for the popularization of Spenser's allegorical method in the years immediately after 1590. The two writers shared important habits of mind, which are especially evident in their use of emblematic imagery as a mode of embodying moral truths. SANDRA S. CLARK

Thomas Dekker 1884–6 *Non-Dramatic Works* ed Alexander B. Grosart 5 vols (London); Dekker 1953–61 *Dramatic Works* ed Fredson Bowers, 4 vols (Cambridge).

Larry S. Champion 1985 *Thomas Dekker and the Traditions of English Drama* Frankfurt-am-Main; Hoy 1980; M[arie] T[hérèse] Jones-Davies 1958 *Un Peintre de la vie Londonienne: Thomas Dekker* 2 vols (Paris), with full detailed biography; Irving Ribner 1957 *The English History Play in the Age of Shakespeare* (Princeton), useful on the context of *The Whore of Babylon*; George R. Price 1969 *Thomas Dekker* (New York).

---

demons The Renaissance understanding of demons combines both classical (especially Platonic) and Christian traditions. According to Plato, *daimōnes* are beings, such as Love, intermediate between the divine and the human. Mortals, awake or asleep, communicate through them with the gods (*Symposium* 202E; Plutarch *Moralia* 416–17; Apuleius *De deo Socratis*). The wise and good become daemons after death, and may also in this life be called daemons (Plato *Republic* 540C, *Cratylus* 397E, referring to Hesiod *Works and Days* 121–3; *Moralia* 361, 415a-b; *De deo Socratis*). Each person is allotted an individual daemon as witness and guardian through life and beyond (Plato *Phaedo* 107D, *Republic* 617E; *Moralia* 588–93 on the *daimonion* of Socrates). The daemon which is the supreme form of soul within man (Plato *Timaeus* 90A; cf *Moralia* 591E) Apuleius calls the *genius*. According to Plutarch, daemons do not assist everyone, but they especially help those emerging from worldly ordeals (*Moralia* 593F; cf Guyon in *FQ* II viii). Apuleius places daemons in the middle region between earth and ether and says they have aerial bodies not normally visible. Some daemons are mortal and some evil (*Moralia* 360F, 361C, 415–19).

Calcidius' commentary on the *Timaeus* identifies etherial daemons with Hebrew angels (119–36), as does Ficino, contrasting them with evil aerial daemons (*Convivium Platonis, sive De amore* 6.3 in ed 1956:201–3; *Theologia platonica* 10.2, 13.2, 18.7, 18.10 in ed 1964–70, 2:56, 206–7, 3:140–1, 198–9, 228). The prevailing Christian tradition, however, is represented by Augustine, who identifies pagan daemons with biblical demons such as those of Luke 4.35 (where a man is possessed by a *daimonion*), Ephesians 6.12, 1 Corinthians 10.20, and Revelation 16.14; these demons, with hell as their center of power, are angels, rebels against God, perturbers of human life, and the source of magic (*City of God* 8.14–10.32, with Vives' important commentary, 1522; see Augustine ed 1610). Aquinas and Hooker take similar views (*Summa theologiae* Ia 63.4, 64.1 etc; *Laws* 1.4.3).

In *The Faerie Queene*, good and evil operate through angelic and demonic spirit-agents, and 'the children of faire light' are opposed by 'great *Nightes* children' (I v 23–4,

III iv 59). Individual moral conflict and growth are so given spiritual and cosmic dimensions, and human figures have a potentiality to become angelic or demonic. Thus, Malbecco becomes 'an aery Spright' (III x 57) and the embodiment of jealousy; Amoret under enchantment is 'like a dreary Spright, / Cald by strong charmes out of eternall night' (III xii 19), but later becomes angelic (IV, v 13).

The Faerie Queene draws its throngs of demonic beings from various literary sources: from classical myth come divinities and heroic energies under 'the God of Sabbaoth'; from romance come fairies, witches, magicians, and their attendant sprites; from allegory, concentrated cosmic and psychic powers, personified virtues and vices; from Christian writings, celestial and infernal forces. Syncretic conflation is characteristic of *The Faerie Queene*, so the classical Fury Erinnys is a 'cursed evill Spright,' Duessa a 'feend,' and Ate 'an incarnate devill' (II ii 29, IV ii 3). The winged Angel who comes to 'succour, and defend' Guyon appears as 'a faire young man,' yet resembles Cupid and is Guyon's good genius (II viii 1–2, 5–8); Archimago appears as 'A bold bad man' (I i 37), though he acts as the evil genius of Redcrosse. Spenser's demons hold together the personal and the cosmic: Genius is both 'celestiall powre' in charge of life and generation (II xii 47, III vi 31–3) and 'our Selfe,' through whom enlightening vision comes (II xii 47; cf Britomart's 'heavenly spright' V vii 12). Genius' evil opposite is a deceptive source of error (II xii 46, 48–9). The Genius of Verulam is similar to the 'Romaine Daemon' of Spenser's translation of du Bellay (*Time* 19, *Rome* stanza 27).

KITTY SCOULAR DATTA

Augustine ed 1610; E.R. Dodds 1951 *The Greeks and the Irrational* (Berkeley and Los Angeles); Marsilio Ficino 1956 *Commentaire sur le banquet de Platon* tr and ed Raymond Marcel (Paris); Ficino ed 1964–70; Fletcher 1964; Frank Kermode 1954 'Ariel as Daemon and Fairy' in William Shakespeare *The Tempest* ed Frank Kermode (London) app B:142–5; Lewis 1964; I.G. MacCaffrey 1976; Rasmussen 1981; D.P. Walker 1958.

Despair Spenser's metaphor for the Christian soul's struggle with despair (*FQ* I ix) is a tour de force of narrative suspense. Redcrosse stops a bareheaded fugitive wearing a noose around his neck (Trevisan), who reluctantly discloses that a lovelorn friend (Terwin) has been persuaded by a man named Despair to give up hope and kill himself. Redcrosse finds it incredible that mere 'idle speach' could turn people against themselves (31). In the ensuing debate with the tempter, who appears in the deceptively vulnerable guise of a gaunt and ragged churl, the knight's scorn for others' weakness is punished by an inglorious display of his own. Idle speech turns out to be powerful enough to bring him to resolve 'to worke his finall smart'; and he is rescued from suicide only by the intervention of Una, who rebukes him for being 'faint harted' and gives him a reassurance he could not find in himself (51–3). Even in bare outline, it is a compelling story.

The heart of Redcrosse's dramatic encounter with Despair is the debate, dominated by the tempter's shrewd advocacy of suicide. Despair's argument unfolds in five principal stages. (*a*) He takes advantage of Redcrosse's ill-chosen emphasis on justice and vengeance rather than mercy (37): Terwin's death was punishment for his guilt, and the classic formula for justice is 'to each his due' (38; see Justinian *Digesta* 1.1). (*b*) Having defended himself against the charge of injustice, Despair takes the offensive: he says that Redcrosse is angered by Terwin's suicide because he envies it; at the same time, he takes foolish joy in a wretched life (39–40). (*c*) To Redcrosse's objection that men should not usurp God's right to decide the moment of death, Despair replies that they not only should not, but cannot; all deeds ostensibly done by human beings are really done by God and could not have failed to occur (41–2). The deterministic move is a palpable hit; it is a commonplace of sixteenth-century Protestant divinity that reflecting too curiously on the mystery of predestination can lead to despair (eg, see 39 Articles 17), and the major Reformers are at one in their affirmation of that mystery (see Luther *De servo arbitrio*, Calvin *Institutes* 3.24.12–17). In this respect, they differ little from those among their Roman adversaries who inherit the views of Thomas Aquinas (*Summa theologiae* 1a 23.8 *ad* 3). (*d*) Redcrosse has already been surprised by his opponent's 'suddeine wit'; now he is struck dumb, and Despair presses his advantage by arguing that the knight's military calling is necessarily involved with 'bloudshed' and 'avengement.' To live the active life is to be doomed to repeated sinning and ever-mounting guilt. Redcrosse has only to recall his defeat by Orgoglio and his betrayal of Una (43–6). Again, a palpable hit: a Protestant Redcrosse of Spenser's day, however moderate his views, would be painfully aware that depraved humanity has nothing to contribute to its own salvation: 'If any strength we have, it is to ill' (x 1). It is only a short step to Despair's clinching argument: (*e*) Redcrosse's guilt is already too flagrant for God to overlook and be just; it is better to carry out than to delay the punishment of death required by justice (47). In (*c*) and (*d*), Despair assails vulnerable elements of the Protestant outlook. With equal adroitness, he distracts attention from other elements that would undermine his own case: the presumptuousness of taking God's justice into one's own hands and the possibility that one is predestined to mercy and not justice. Redcrosse is rescued when Una assures him that this possibility for him is a certainty. Still, the demon has done a masterly job with the resources at his disposal. He represents a grave sin – by some accounts, the gravest – and a powerful temptation (on the gravity, see Isidore of Seville *Sententiae* in *PLat* 83 col 617; *Glossa ordinaria* in *PLat* 113 col 1107; Cassian *De coenobiorum institutis* in *PLat* 49 cols 357, 360; see also Becon *The Sick Man's Salve* in ed 1844:156–7; Hooper *A Declaration of the Ten Commandments* in ed 1843:422–3). Spenser has given him rhetorical cunning to match the terrible ensnarement he represents.

Despair's forensic repertoire can be conveniently surveyed under these traditional rubrics in order of increasing subtlety.

Verbal schemes: a bitter end – 'The further he doth goe, the further he doth stray' – is conjured rhetorically into a hopeful beginning – 'Then do no further goe, no further stray' (43–4) – by linking repetition (*anadiplosis*). A madly self-defeating climb toward disaster is dramatized by a sequence of linking repetitions (*climax*, or the 'ladder' Puttenham 1589, 3.19): 'The lenger life, I wote the greater sin, / The greater sin, the greater punishment' (43). Each of a list of accusatory terms improves in gravity or length on its predecessor (*incrementum*): 'strife, and bloud-shed, and avengement' (43). The spiteful caprice of Fortune is brought home by a random heaping of terms (*coacervatio*): 'Feare, sicknesse, age, losse, labour, sorrow, strife, / Paine, hunger, cold, that makes the hart to quake' (44). Antithetical terms of abuse are balanced against each other with mocking elegance (*isocolon*): 'Most envious man, that grieves at neighbours good, / And fond, that joyest in the woe thou hast' (39). The reference to God's 'equall eye' (47) repeats the preceding notion (of God as just beholder) in parallel order, but with an energy born of compression; 'equall' has been vividly displaced from beholder to eye (*hypallage*).

Schemes of thought: in his rejoinder to Redcrosse's opening attack, Despair not only mimics the cadence of Redcrosse's rhetorical question ('What justice ... What franticke fit' 37–8) but goes on to play subversively on Redcrosse's term *justice* (*antanaclasis*). The same strategy reappears when Redcrosse's metaphor of the Christian sentinel's 'watchfull sted' is deftly turned against him (41). The manipulation of an opponent's terms is only a special case of a more general and pervasive strategy: Despair's misappropriation of Christian terms like *grace* (39), and especially of the traditional homiletic theme of contempt for the world, with its associated metaphors of straying or wandering (39, 43; cf i 10) and warfare (40, 41, 43; cf Job 7.1 Vulgate, Isa 40.2). More subtly still, Despair seductively combines verbal schemes with the debater's trick of false analogy; thus, *isocolon* (systematic parallelism) gives a lulling impression of rightness to his equation of spiritual suicide or defection with bodily rest: 'Sleepe after toyle, port after stormie seas, / Ease after warre, death after life does greatly please' (40; note the sudden metamorphosis of sense marked by the inner rhyme 'seas-ease,' and the ironic inversion of the inevitable homiletic formula 'life after death'). Similarly, in Despair's peroration (47), *chiasmus* (arrangement of corresponding terms in the pattern *abba*) confers a delusive symmetry on his equation of forgiveness with complicity: 'thy sins [*1a*] up in his knowledge fold [*1b*], / And guiltie be [*2b*] of thine impietie [*2a*].' Again, the spurious universality of spiritual death is equated by *chiasmus* with the genuine universality of physical death: 'Let every sinner [*1a*] die [*1b*]: / Die [*2b*] shall all flesh [*2a*].' By *chiasmus* yet again, suicide is treated as merely a kind of dying that improves by freedom and activity on the constraint and passivity of natural death: 'needs [*1a*] be donne [*1b*] ... doe [*2b*] willinglie [*2a*].' Spenser is aware that rhetoric is as dangerous a resource as it is subtle and potent; in this art, he has made the enemy of hope an evil virtuoso.

The suicide Despair advocates is (by synecdoche) any expression of the refusal to hope for salvation; indeed, despair is etymologically the opposite of hope. It is a spiritual suicide that Trevisan has already committed unawares by giving up his Pauline helmet of 'the hope of salvation' (1 Thess 5.8). One commits it by yielding, like Terwin, to worldly disappointments as if they mattered supremely, for 'the worldlie sorowe causeth death' (2 Cor 7.10). And one commits it, as the elect Christian barely escapes doing here, by inferring one's damnation, and the futility of moral effort, from the actual and habitual sinfulness that even a Redcrosse cannot avoid (ix 48). In one especially relevant medieval classification (Hugh of St Victor *De fructibus carnis et spiritus* in *PLat* 176 col 1001, Chaucer *Parson's Tale* 686–785), despair is a branch of sloth, which has already put in a significant appearance as Lucifera's chief privy councilor (*FQ* I iv 8). The essence of sloth is a state of moral paralysis or acedia (Gr *akēdeia* uncaring) in which the Christian soldier destroys himself by shrinking from the battle. This uncaring is the faintness of heart that 'enrages' Una when she finds her knight succumbing to it (52–3). One might think that despair so conceived is the polar opposite of the presumption or spiritual pride to which, in the person of Orgoglio, Redcrosse has already succumbed (vii 10) – the sin of demeaning God's justice by expecting to be forgiven without repentance (Aquinas *ST* 2a2ae 21.1). Sin, however, is wrongdoing deliberately chosen; one is hardly guilty if one does not know that what one is doing is a sin (Augustine *De trinitate* 12.12.17; Aquinas *ST* 2a2ae 156.3 *ad* 1). To be a mortal sin, presumption has to include some awareness, however unacknowledged, that one's arrogant claims are empty. Yet this awareness, combined with unrepentance, is precisely the state of despair 'Puft up with emptie wind' (vii 9). Hence the theological acuteness of the narrative detail that pride's dominion over Redcrosse does not merely precede but coincides with imprisonment in despair, the dungeon from which he calls for a 'happy choyce / Of death' (viii 38).

It is a tribute to Spenser's penetration and candor that in his Protestant vision of spiritual crisis despair should seem, to the naked eye, to enjoy even a temporary victory, for in the dominant Protestant view of his day, whether harshly laid down by Calvin or mildly by Hooker, the elect are often troubled, but never give up hope for God's forgiveness (*Institutes* 3.2.19; Hooker *A Learned and Comfortable Sermon of the Certainty and Perpetuity of Faith* in ed 1888, 3:473–4). 'Extreme despair,' says Hooker, is among the sins from which 'God shall preserve the righteous, as the apple of his eye, forever' (*A Learned Discourse of Justification* 26 in ed 1888, 3:519). Despair is the worldly sorrow that 'causeth death'; it should not be confused with loathing of one's sinfulness and despair of earning salvation by works; these are the marks of godly sorrow or repentance (2 Cor 7.10). Even Luther, who endorses despair in this benign sense as an agonizing but necessary step toward repentance, warns the sinner not to speculate about his lack of free will lest he fall into the despair that is a mortal sin (*Lectures on Romans*, in reference to Rom 9.16). The elect are protected from the loss of all hope by 'assurance': the conviction, sustained by the Holy Spirit, that the promises of the Gospel apply to them; Una rescues Redcrosse by bringing him just such an assurance. Paradoxically, these would-be consolations only add to the burdens of the Protestant conscience. It is not helpful to insist that the despair of Saints is merely apparent, that 'they seem stone-dead, who notwithstanding are still alive unto God in Christ' (Hooker *Discourse of Justification* 26 in ed 1888, 3:517); the difficulty is precisely the absence of vital signs. How is one to tell Redcrosse's apparent despair in Orgoglio's dungeon from the real thing? How, for that matter, is one to tell the wavering assurance of the elect from the nearly identical state that, by Calvin's admission, is often taken for assurance by the reprobate (*Institutes* 3.2.11, 3.24.8)? It is notable that Redcrosse was rescued once before from a form of despair, not by Una but by her evil twin Fidessa (v 12). Indeed, from Redcrosse's first entry into the Wood of Error, *FQ* I is filled with stories of illusion, misunderstanding, and mistaken identity – with reminders of how frail is the human claim to certainty. Redcrosse's escape from despair makes its own ironic contribution to this pattern: his restored belief in his salvation is warranted and will be fulfilled; but considered simply as 'evidence of things which are not sene' (Heb 11.1), it falls short of the unambiguous knowledge that is supposed to underlie assurance. At least twice in later cantos, it will seem to fail again, in highly ironic circumstances. To Una's 'great perplexitie,' Redcrosse persists in 'Disdeining life, desiring leave to die' even after such feelings have outlived the function of godly sorrow by prompting him to learn how to take 'assured hold' on hope's anchor (x 22); far from being redemptive, these lingering griefs are mere symptoms of a 'disease' to be cured by 'trew' repentance (23, 29). Still later, Redcrosse is forced by the heat of the Dragon's breath to unlace his helmet, the hope of salvation (xi 26, 1 Thess 5.8). This is no blessing in disguise; it is a disaster from which he must again be rescued at the last minute. In effect, Spenser's Legend of Holiness says of assurance what the Tudor homilist (adapting Prov 24.16) says of works: 'the just man falleth seven times a day' ('A Sermon of the Miserie of Mankind Part 1' in *Certaine Sermons or Homilies*). There is a certain courage in this imaginative willingness to live with precariousness.

In the end, the hope with which Una is made to reply to Despair is precisely courage, not assurance. That is the point of the angry reproach and sarcasm with which she begins: this 'faint harted knight,' no less, has boasted of his coming battle with the Dragon (ix 52)! She goes on to appeal to his 'manly hart' and 'constant spright' (53). Despair is cowardice, so hope is courage. This rehabilitation of personal initiative seems to reflect the traditional view that, unlike desire, hope is essentially 'irascible' or aggressive, and that its typical object is not merely a good but an arduous good (Aquinas *ST* 1a2ae 45.1). Hope thrives on difficulties.

The stress on initiative is no mere bow to tradition. It has been woven into the fabric of the allegory. *FQ* I ix begins with a glimpse of Arthur, who has freed Redcrosse from captivity and talked Una out of a state very much like despair (vii 41). The canto ends with another act of rescuing. Redcrosse's own mission is to rescue the captives of sin, in a reenactment of Christ's Harrowing of Hell. This pattern of chivalric rescuing is Spenser's pervasive metaphor for good works. In Pauline terms, it is the husbandry of souls (1 Cor 3.9) that gives Redcrosse the name *Georgos* and defines his calling (x 66). Yet the chivalric metaphor is fundamental: Christian knighthood, in all its rigor, is for the poet the ultimate rejoinder to despair. (See also *Aylett.) HAROLD SKULSKY

Kathrine Koller 1964 'Art, Rhetoric, and Holy Dying in *The Faerie Queene* with Special Reference to the Despair Canto' *SP* 61:128–39; Ernest Sirluck 1949–50 'A Note on the Rhetoric of Spenser's "Despair"' *MP* 47:8–11; Skulsky 1980–1; Susan Snyder 1965 'The Left Hand of God: Despair in Medieval and Renaissance Tradition' *SRen* 12:18–59; Torczon 1961.

Despetto, Decetto, Defetto As allegorical extensions of the Blatant Beast, Despetto, Decetto, and Defetto devise a plot to destroy Timias by defaming him (*FQ* VI v 12–24), seeking to impugn for a second time the honor and renown signified by Timias' name, first compromised when Belphoebe, 'misdeeming' his relationship with Amoret, denied him her grace (IV vii 36–viii 17). They enlist the Beast in their plot, just as Envy and Detraction had enlisted it in their attack on Artegall (V xii 41), and use it as bait to lure Timias into their covert trap set in the forest. The story is analogous to Serena's being wounded by the Beast and is narrated as a flashback during that episode. Subsequently, Arthur takes both Timias and Serena to the Hermit to be cured of the inner wounds of shame which infamy has fixed in them (VI vi 1–15).

Like Reproach, Repentance, and Shame, Timias' three adversaries are 'All three to each unlike, yet all made in one mould' (III xii 24). Despetto, who exceeds the others in 'powre and hight,' is spite (Ital *dispetto*); like Disdain and Mirabella, he openly despises. Decetto is deceit or deception, the principle of furtive malice that accounts for the ambush which entraps Timias by 'slight.' Defetto, the third brother, is detraction (Ital *difetto* 'a fault, a want, an imperfection, a vice'; see Florio 1611); defective both in proud might and in cunning, he is the most troublesome of the three (VI v 20). Like the Blatant Beast, which is offspring of three-headed Cerberus and thus a hellhound (i 8, vi 12), these three villains dog Timias with infamy (v 19).

The trio is a parody of Neoplatonic triads: in v 20, the disposition of Timias' graceless assailants anticipates Spenser's description of the three Graces on Mount Acidale. All without guile, the Graces appear so 'That two of them still froward seem'd to bee, / But one still towards shew'd her selfe afore' (x 24); Defetto and Decetto creep behind Timias and 'circumvent' him, while only Despetto fronts him (Fowler 1973:64–7). Bitten from behind by the Beast, Timias learns too late to guard against 'backeward onset' (v 16, 18). Spenser thus reflects on the insidious practices of backbiting, as he does with Sclaunder, Corflambo, Envy, and Turpine, all of whom attack from the rear (IV viii 36, 41; V xii 39; VI vi 26).

The third line of *FQ* IV viii 18 is recalled almost verbatim in the narrator's comment that, after reconciliation with Belphoebe, Timias had lapsed into carelessness, 'Nether of envy, nor of chaunge afeard' (VI v 12). 'Heedlesse' and drawn 'Unwares into the daunger of defame,' carefree Timias is akin to Serena (iii 23) and Clarion (*Muiopotmos* 377–84), both victims of envy. In the poem's moral allegory, Timias' misadventure exemplifies the sentence that concludes *Visions of the Worlds Vanitie*: 'For he that of himselfe is most secure, / Shall finde his state most fickle and unsure.'

Since Timias shadows Raleigh, this episode also hints at the latter's problems with calumny. Raleigh's expeditions to Virginia, his affair with Elizabeth Throckmorton (called Serena in his poetry), and his reputation for atheism made him vulnerable to 'wounds of spightfull envy' (Raleigh ed 1951:24). Just as Timias' encounter with the Foster and his brothers at the ford in III v points to an exploit that helped make Raleigh's name – the defeat of the Desmonds in Ireland – so his encounter with the Blatant Beast in VI v points to Raleigh's injured reputation at court (Bednarz 1983).

RONALD B. BOND

---

dialect When all literature is written in dialect, as in the time of Chaucer, the fact is of no literary interest. It is only when a standard form of language is used for literary works that dialectalisms are foregrounded: they obtrude. This was the position when Spenser wrote. By the early sixteenth century, there existed a standard type of both written and spoken English. For a courtly poet to sprinkle his work with dialect was as striking as speaking today of 'Euclidizing' the 'one and one and one' of the Trinity to 'nowt but a nowt.' To assess the contemporary impact of his practice, two things need to be done: the extent of dialect use has to be established, and its inclusion in particular poems explained. Neither is easy.

The clearest evidence for dialect is provided by words which had a different form of pronounciation in standard English: forms like *gate* 'goat,' *glitterand* 'glittering,' *hale* 'whole,' *han* 'have,' *ligge* 'lie,' *thous* 'thou art,' *wae* 'woe,' *warre* 'worse,' are, like *hame* 'home' in Burns, immediately recognizable. With words like *frowie* 'musty,' *garre* 'cause,' *totty* 'dizzy,' *wimble* 'active,' the evidence has to be based on the incomplete record of dictionary citations which appear to show occurrence in texts written in a particular area. It is best to ignore all but the most probable examples of these.

It is striking that the highest number of likely dialect uses (more than 40 different words occurring over 100 times) are found in *The Shepheardes Calender*. They include *cragge* 'neck,' *dirke* 'dark,' *dirks* 'darkens,' *earnd* 'yearned,' *gang* 'go,' *heme* 'home,' *her* 'he/him,' *kirke* 'church,' *mirke* 'obscure,' *narre* 'nearer,' *pousse* 'grain,' *sike* 'such,' *sicker* 'surely,' in addition to those mentioned above. This along with the brevity of the work, makes them an obtrusive feature of its language. The clear dialectalisms cluster most heavily in *Maye*, *Julye*, and *September* (see Ingham 1970–1). This throws light on their function. They can scarcely serve the purpose of 'suggesting rusticity' (McElderry 1932:150). Such a reading belongs to a later period, not the sixteenth century; to Hardy and his Wessex rustics, not to Spenser. If Spenser's aim were this, E.K. might well feel that he needed defending; pastoral poetry was not then regarded as simple scenes from rural life, either by poets or by critics. Alexander Barclay, a sixteenth-century writer of eclogues, and George Turbervile, the translator of Mantuan, recognized their moral aspect and the intellectual nature of the shepherds' discussions. They recommend plain language, by which they mean one unadorned by rhetorical figures, not an imitation of rustic speech. Puttenham states clearly that the eclogue is an 'artificiall Poesie' written 'not of purpose to counterfait or represent the rusticall manner of loves and communication: but under the vaile of homely persons ... to ... glaunce at greater matters' (*Arte* 1.18). Only after Spenser, and presumably because of him, dialect became a feature of English pastoral poetry.

It is usually forgotten that, compared with standard English, dialect was regarded as 'barbarous' by scholarly writers like Edmund Coote (*The Englishe Scholemaister* 1596) and Alexander Gil (*Logonomia Anglica* 1619, 1621). This explains the significance of the concentration of dialectalisms in *The Shepheardes Calender* in the satirical, or as E.K. says, the 'Moral' eclogues (Gen Arg). For such satires as these, with their rough meter, Puttenham (and other rhetoricians) recommends 'rough and bitter speaches' (*Arte* 1.11). It must have been dialect that helped to create the necessary roughness, evident in the opening of *September*. An interesting variant of this view is that the roughness is meant to create an effect of parody (Berger 1969–70).

Aside from *The Shepheardes Calender*, the only significant use of dialect is in *The Faerie Queene*, where it is much more limited: about 13 dialectalisms in 40 occurrences. These include *garre*, *ligge*, *mister* 'be needful,' *sperre* 'lock,' *totty*, *warke* 'work,' *warre*. The most frequent are *glitterand* (4), *ken* 'know, see' (11), and *mickle* 'great' (18). The most important point here is that these uses, like those in *The Shepheardes Calender*, are Northern or North Midland. That must have been driven home to the contemporary reader by 4 occurrences where rhymes on the past tense *rade* 'rode' (eg, with *made*, VII vii 41) indicate a pronunciation which results in modern Scots *hame* 'home' rhyming with *shame* and not with *dome*. Such forms were not likely to be confused with Chaucerian archaism. That was of a Southern or Midland kind, from Dunbar onwards through the sixteenth century. Whether Spenser knew Northern dialect because of possible Northern connections is immaterial. However he learned it, the inclusion in a courtly epic requires an explanation not provided by theories of foreign influence, whether Italian (from Bembo) or French (from the Pléiade). These writers suggested enriching the vernacular to make it suitable for the higher forms of literature and recommended, among other things, the use of certain valued kinds of dialect to do so. This would explain Chaucerian forms in Spenser and elsewhere, but for his use of specifically Northern dialect, the poet had virtually no precedent. Further, the use of a relatively small number of dialectalisms spread over a work as long as *The Faerie Queene* has a very different effect from that in *The Shepheardes Calender*. In the longer work, they obtrude less: they are absorbed into a general impression of deviance from the prose norm created by many archaisms, neologisms, arbitrary modifications of existing forms, numerous compounds, and an excessive use of rhetorical figures. In this context, dialect becomes one more feature of an obtrusively odd language, and unless this is to be read as a merely mechanical and ineffectual 'enrichment,' dictated by external 'influences,' further consideration is needed.

If such language seemed appropriate to Spenser, the explanation probably lies in a rather revolutionary notion of decorum. This is akin to his boldness in writing an epic in the vernacular at all. The kingdom about which and in which this strange and exotic language is used is ambiguously located. It is 'England, in the historical allegory; the Celtic Otherworld in the fairy aspect' (Greenlaw in *Var* 1:352). The proem to Book II, addressed to Queen Elizabeth, asserts that the land of 'Faery' is, though unknown, not mere fancy. Like the once unknown Amazon and Peru, this land too men may one day 'find.' Equivocation on the word *find* is revealed by the reference to 'certaine signes here set in sundry place' which may help in the discovery: Elizabeth may recognize her own realms 'in lond of Faery.' This is England and not-England, and it needs a language which cumulatively is English and not-English. Jonson was perhaps paying the poet an unwitting compliment when he said that Spenser 'writ no language.' In *The Faerie Queene*, we have a new language for a new kingdom – standard and nonstandard – and the incorporation of dialect into such a medium suggests that it is felt to possess the necessary exotic quality. It is here that the fact of Spenser's using specifically Northern dialect becomes relevant, for it had, unlike the others, a strong literary tradition familiar from Middle English onwards. Some of the medieval romances thought to be sources of *The Faerie Queene* existed in Northern versions. Undoubtedly, the poet Surrey drew on the Scots forms in Douglas' *Aeneid* when he too translated the poem in the mid-sixteenth century. From this one may infer that, though all spoken forms of dialect were thought of as rough and uncouth, the Northern type could be drawn on to add a slightly alien literary quality.

That dialect should be regarded in *The Shepheardes Calender* as barbarous and rough and yet in *The Faerie Queene* as adding to a generally exotic effect are two logically irreconcilable views. But an ambiguous attitude to dialect is a common feature of those like Hardy who include it in otherwise standard English works. That such ambivalence was possible even at this early period can be clearly demonstrated. Gil's *Logonomia anglica* gives the fullest account of English dialects around this date. In general, Gil recognizes and condemns vulgar speech and dialect. He scathingly dismisses Western speech, for instance, as so barbaric as scarcely to be English at all. Yet, in a belated rider, he allows that poets may sometimes use Northern forms for special purposes because it is 'the most pleasing, oldest, and purest, being closest to the speech of our ancestors' (1619:18–19). Gil may have had Spenser in mind, for he admired him greatly and transcribed passages of his poems into phonetic script. If a phonetician of Gil's standing could have this dual attitude to Northern dialect, it seems that Spenser, a linguistic innovator of the first order, could do so too.

Spenser's use of dialect in *The Faerie Queene* is not a matter only for the philologist but for the sensitive reader prepared to delight in a strangely mixed language as fitted to his Fairyland as newspeak is to Airstrip One in Orwell's *Nineteen Eighty-Four*.

PATRICIA INGHAM

Berger 1969–70; N. Bøgholm 1944 'On the Spenserian Style' *TCLC* 1:5–21; E.J. Dobson 1955 'Early Modern Standard English' *TPS* pp 25–54; Ingham 1970–1; McElderry 1932; Charles Bowie Millican 1939 'The Northern Dialect of *The Shepheardes Calender*' *ELH* 6:211–3; Rubel 1941.

dialogue, poetic Little notice has been taken of dialogue in Spenser, despite its considerable presence. The reason is perhaps the modern reader's tendency to associate dialogue with characterization and dramatic presentation, neither of which figures largely in his poetry. His use of dialogue is directed rather towards theme and allegory.

The Shepheardes Calender is a series of dialogues in the tradition of the classical eclogue. Here dialogue is less a way to represent individual characteristics of the speakers (who are often indistinguishable in their speech) than a technique to mirror conflicting arguments, for example, on the nature of pastoral and the right behavior of ministers. The same is generally true of *Colin Clouts Come Home Againe*, which consists almost entirely of dialogue between Colin and his companions. A dramatic situation is evoked to some extent – Colin surrounded by inquiring friends who ask questions and listen eagerly – but the verbal exchanges are used principally to highlight his observations about court life. When Hobbinol interrupts with the claim that court life cannot be all bad, Colin is prompted to explain his views more fully (731–70); the next interruption, by Corylas, allows him to speak of love at court (771–822); Cuddie's amazement at such deep insight inspires him to speak of love as a cosmic power beyond the reach of human understanding (823–94). The voices are not individualized. The dialogue form and the dramatic frame serve the central (thematic) purpose: Colin's report of what he has discovered during his travels.

In *The Faerie Queene* there is a range of dialogue as well as indirect or reported speech. The displacing of the narrative voice from time to time by dialogue introduces variety into the poem and is one technique for bringing the characters to life. There is a relatively dramatic use of dialogue in the stories of Malbecco, Hellenore, and Paridell, and of Britomart, Artegall, and Radigund. The *Cantos of Mutabilitie* provide some of the most sustained scenes of dialogue in the poem with the 'haughty *Titanesse*' Mutabilitie as the dominant speaker. The temptation scenes with Despair and Mammon are especially dramatic. However, allegorical figures, since they shadow forth abstractions, cannot be read as though they were characters in a play or novel, and *The Faerie Queene* is (as Tuve 1966 and Alpers 1968:437 claim) primarily allegorical and radically undramatic.

What we find in *The Faerie Queene* are dramatic interludes or effects which serve the overriding allegorical and thematic purpose. The 'fabliau' of Malbecco is a notable instance, being part of Spenser's anatomy of love in Book III. On a smaller scale is the episode where Duessa and Ate goad Scudamour to jealousy by telling him that Amoret is enjoying a new lover (IV i 44–ii 3). Duessa begins in a coaxing voice; Ate follows aggressively in the tones of a gossiping shrew: 'I saw him have your *Amoret* at will, / I saw him kisse, I saw him her embrace.' Blandamour and Duessa then take over in gloating, taunting accents until Scudamour erupts in a torrent of words against Glauce. In trying to pacify Scudamour, Glauce is less a character than an agent of concord and the 'Musicke' of 'wise words.' Book IV treats human relationships, specifically how discord flares easily from what people do to one another; hence the dialogue in this scene illustrates discord, functioning as an allegorical image.

Book V has pronouncements of Artegall as judge but relatively little dialogue – significantly, Talus is dumb. Book VI, however, has a high proportion as well as reported conversations, one reason being that a chief theme of the book is speech (both good and bad). The romance narrative unfolds in poetic dialogue to illustrate this theme. For similar thematic reasons, Arthur uses dialogue whenever he appears, exemplifying the idea that speech can bind society together and comfort and aid the individual. He resorts to force only when dialogue will not work, as with Pyrochles and Cymochles (II viii 23–31), and occasions some of the most charming and civilized scenes, such as his conversation with Una in which he gently saves her from despair (I vii 38–52), a dialogue related thematically to the debate of Redcrosse and Despair.

That debate (ix 37–47) is powerfully oriented towards theme and allegory and represents Spenser's finest use of poetic dialogue. Through parallels between the descriptions of Redcrosse emerging from the dungeon (viii 40–1) and Despair in his cave (ix 35), he prepares us for the doppelgänger effect of the episode. Redcrosse comes face to face with himself and, in the book which is centrally concerned with the problem of how we *know*, the 'unweeting' knight here falls into the ultimate deception, self-deception. The two voices of the dialogue are deliberately intermingled to suggest two voices within his own mind; the ambiguity of 'Quoth he' (41) and the similarity in manner and matter across 41–3 contribute to this effect, so that from 44 on the voice speaking seems to belong at once to Despair and to Redcrosse. What we witness is a process or a mental and emotional state which is despair itself. The brooding over what is done and cannot be undone, the repeated self-cross-examination that leads to a kind of dementia or division of the self, which can lead eventually to destruction of the self – all this is despair in action. The entire debate is an allegorical image of the most powerful kind.

Comparable in power is a dialogue which shows temperance in action, the debate between Guyon and Mammon (II vii). Here Spenser creates two contrasting voices: Mammon's, expansive and magnanimous, at times incantatory, and Guyon's, sententious, declarative, and frequently brusque. The interplay of speeches images temperance in action: a right knowledge and an alert self-control repeatedly maintained in acting upon that knowledge.

To be treated fully, dialogue in *The Faerie Queene* would require statistical analysis of the text to answer several important questions: how much converse (direct and indirect speech) is found, in what proportions, in which books and where? How much direct dialogue is there in relation to indirect speech and how are these disposed in the poem? Here statistics might be an effective aid to literary interpretation.

BEVERLEY SHERRY

Alpers 1968; Freake 1977.

dialogue, prose Spenser apparently first wrote *Vewe of Ireland* as a treatise, then revised it as an expository dialogue, a conversation between two characters: Irenius (cf 'Irena' *FQ* v i 4, an anagram of Ierne, the classical name of Erin or Ireland; 'peace' from Gk *eirēnē*), an Englishman just returned from Ireland, and Eudoxus ('of good repute, honored' from Gk *eudoxos*), who wishes to know more about Ireland. From an analysis of the manuscripts, Renwick conjectures that the first version was not in dialogue form but consisted of historical notes (*Vewe* ed 1934 [rev 1970:199–200] in *Var Prose* pp 509–10).

With only the barest fiction of conversation, no setting, and few digressions, the two thinly characterized speakers move methodically through an agenda: uncovering the chief evils in law, custom, and religion infecting the Irish commonwealth, suggesting means to redress these evils, and recommending a permanent cure. While Eudoxus suggests a moderate regimen, Irenius urges radical surgery. Eudoxus helps Irenius' argument by asking questions, offering suggestions, and seeking clarification; he summarizes each part of Irenius' plan and finally endorses it. The dialogue form enables Spenser to present a structured exposition through the apparently objective and reasonable Irenius who knows Irish history and has the benefit of Spenser's experience but need not be identified with him. In the remarks of Eudoxus, Spenser anticipates potential objections and deals with them on his own terms, an especially important strategy for a counselor advocating the reformation of Ireland.

Spenser's choice of the dialogue form may have been influenced by *Solon His Follie* (1594), a plan for reforming Ireland by Richard Beacon, the royal attorney for Munster (1586–91). This work and *Vewe* are the only two published late Elizabethan dialogues which attempt to advise the monarch about pressing affairs of state. (Two earlier dialogues of this kind are Thomas Wilson's *Discourse uppon Usurye* [1572] and Thomas Smith's *Discourse of the Commonweal ... of England* [c 1549, rev c 1578, printed 1581].) Like Smith's *Discourse* and Thomas Starkey's *Dialogue between Reginald Pole and Thomas Lupset* (c 1535), Spenser's *Vewe* was intended for a limited audience and circulated in manuscript.

As a direct expository dialogue, *Vewe* has no Socratic dialectic, no Ciceronian urbanity, and no Lucianic humor shown in the classical exemplars of the form. Nor have the continental Renaissance dialogues (eg, Castiglione's *Courtier*) or German Reformation dialogues influenced Spenser's choice of form. Instead, his practice is closest to the traditional catechistical method of dealing with instructional material in dialogue form, as exemplified in Book 2 of Ascham's *Toxophilus* and other Tudor works. Of the more than 120 other original works in dialogue form printed or composed during Elizabeth's reign, most are instructional or religious dialogues intended to educate the 'unlearned' English populace in all manner of practical topics (surveying, fishing, heraldry, navigation), to engage in religious controversy, or to edify the laity through the pious conversation of the speakers. Notable late Elizabethan works of these kinds are Thomas Morley's *Plaine and Easie Introduction to Practicall Musicke* (1597), Francis Savage's *Conference betwixt a Mother a Devout Recusant, and Her Sonne a Zealous Protestant* (1600), and Arthur Dent's *Plaine Mans Pathway to Heaven* (1601). Less numerous are literary Elizabethan dialogues reminiscent of the early Tudor dialogues of More, Elyot, and Ascham. These include Thomas Lodge's belletristic and moral *Catharos: Diogenes in His Singularitie* (1591); Robert Greene's parody of Puritan dialogues, *A Disputation betweene a Hee Conny-Catcher, and a Shee Conny-Catcher* (1592); Thomas Nashe's final work in his quarrel with Gabriel Harvey, *Have with You to Saffron-Walden* (1596); and many of the short prose works of Nicholas Breton.

JOHN T. DAY

Roger Deakins 1980 'The Tudor Prose Dialogue: Genre and Anti-Genre' *SEL* 20:5–23 provides background and preliminary discussion more fully than does Elizabeth Merrill 1911 *The Dialogue in English Literature* (New York), although his claim that the typical Tudor dialogue is an anti-genre remains questionable. The standard history is still Rudolf Hirzel 1895 *Der Dialog* 2 vols (Leipzig). K.J. Wilson 1985 *Incomplete Fictions: The Formation of English Renaissance Dialogue* (Washington, D.C.), with full notes and bibliography, discusses the dialogue form through the early Tudor period. Important contemporary treatises on the form are by Carlo Sigonio (1561) and Torquato Tasso (c 1587). See also the discussion in Grennan 1982 on agricultural and medical imagery. For further bibliography, see **Vewe of Ireland*.

Diana The Latin name for Greek Artemis, goddess of the hunt. As Cynthia, Lucina, or Phoebe, sister of Phoebus Apollo, Diana rules the moon; as Hecate, she rules in Hades. Because of her three functions, she is sometimes called the 'three-formed goddess' (*diva triformis*); allusions to her in one form often include the other two. Above all, she is said to be constantly changing (for mythographical background, see Boccaccio *Genealogia* 4.16, Conti *Mythologiae* 3.17 'De Luna' and 3.18 'De Diana'). In her various forms, she appears throughout Spenser's works.

In the *Aprill* eclogue of *The Shepheardes Calender*, Colin says that Eliza is more beautiful than Phoebe, though he breaks off with a grim reminder of what happened to Niobe when she made a similar claim about her children (64–90). The moon is again referred to as Phoebe in *June* 31 and *December* 84, and as Cynthia in *August* 89–90. In *Julye*, Morrell mentions Phoebe as the captor and seducer of Endymion (63–4).

The goddess and her names appear infrequently in the rest of Spenser's shorter poems. Not until *Colin Clout* do Phoebe and Cynthia appear again, the former to designate the new moon, the latter again to compliment the Queen. This Cynthia, 'the Ladie of the sea' (166), is praised for her power, wisdom, and mercy rather than for Diana's usual chastity: her ill treatment of Raleigh, the Shepherd of the Ocean, is cautiously chided. In *Epithalamion*, the bridegroom asks Cynthia not to envy the married lovers, but to remember that she once loved Endymion and to bless the new union with fertility.

Diana is one of the presiding deities of *The Faerie Queene*. The goddess herself appears in Books III and IV, and stories are told about her in I and II. Her adopted daughter Belphoebe shares her traits and brings them directly into the narrative. In contrasting 'hard' and 'soft' aspects of primitivism, Spenser associates the former with the discipline and self-denial practiced and demanded by Diana, and the latter with the pleasure and fecundity of Venus. He frequently attempts to reconcile these two impulses in such heroines as Belphoebe and Britomart, as well as in the cooperation between Diana and Venus themselves when they search for the truant Cupid in Book III, and find the infants Belphoebe and Amoret instead.

Even so, the associations and behavior of Diana in *The Faerie Queene*, under her various names and in her various rhetorical uses, are increasingly negative. Whether this is because Spenser chooses to extol love over discipline or because the discipline exacted by the deity is sometimes too painful to be humanly borne, the fact remains that Diana endangers or punishes or is associated with harm almost every time she appears in the poem.

In Book I, the moon tends to be associated with the powers of night, shining in Morpheus' house when Archimago's sprite comes to find a distracting dream (I i 39). The goddess both saves and destroys in the story of Hippolytus (v 39–40); by persuading Aesculapius to revive the young huntsman, she causes the physician's damnation. Also in Book I, Spenser tells the story of how Diana punished a lazy nymph, transforming her into an enervating spring (vii 5). In Book II, another of Diana's fountains refuses to wash the blood off a baby's hands (ii 8–10). Belphoebe, a glorious Venus-Virgo with attributes of both goddesses, first appears in this book, scorning the would-be courtiers Trompart and Braggadocchio in a scene that echoes Aeneas' encounters with both Dido and his mother Venus (iii 31–2).

Diana and her adopted daughter have larger roles in Books III and IV, roles that contrast with those of Venus and her foundling Amoret. In the story of Venus' search for Cupid (III vi 11–28), Diana is angered at the suggestion that he might be hiding among her nymphs; their quarrel continues until they find the twin girls and each takes one of the babies. Diana raises Belphoebe to be like herself; both figures compliment

Elizabeth, Spenser's maiden queen. In Book III, Belphoebe rescues the young squire Timias and awakens his love. In IV, she jealously misinterprets his attentions to her sister and nearly kills him with disdain (vii 36), while literally killing the monster Lust who had threatened Amoret. Britomart, the enamored patroness of the Legend of Chastity who figures largely in Books IV and V as well, is named for one of Diana's virgin nymphs, but only once is she compared directly with the goddess, when her face is said to be as lovely as Cynthia's when the moon gives light to weary travelers (III i 43). In V, the moon is worn by the tyrannical Amazon Radigund. The goddess reappears in two manifestations in the *Cantos of Mutabilitie*: as Cynthia, ruler of the ever-changing, cyclical moon, and as Diana, the outraged huntress who destroys Arlo Hill with 'an heavy haplesse curse' (VII vi 55).

Spenser's Diana is the antithesis of Venus. In her opposition to lust, the dark side of love, she provides a necessary check to the abusive tendencies in the erotic impulse. But her opposition to love in any form sets her apart from the generative 'kindly flame' which is a positive image in the poem. Like her foster child Belphoebe, and like Elizabeth herself, she becomes an increasingly problematic figure of 'dearest dred,' 'inburning wrath,' and 'imperious feare' (I proem 4; IV proem 5, viii 17). ANNE SHAVER

Dido A legendary Phoenician queen, also known as Elissa. After her husband was slain by her brother, she fled to Africa and founded the city of Carthage. To avoid marriage with a neighboring king, she committed suicide and thereby became a model of chaste widowhood. Her story, preserved in Justin's *Epitome* of Pompeius Trogus' universal history (18.4–6), was cited with approval by authors from Tertullian and Jerome to Petrarch and Boccaccio (Allen 1962, Lord 1969). It was most notoriously and influentially adapted by Virgil in the *Aeneid*, where Dido combines the dignity of Trogus' queen with the passionate barbarism of his principal literary model, the Medea of Apollonius Rhodius' *Argonautica* (see Otis 1963:62–96).

Virgil, probably following earlier Roman writers, altered chronology to arrange a love affair between Dido and his hero Aeneas. Shipwrecked near Carthage, Aeneas is warmly received by the queen and tells the story of the fall of Troy and his subsequent wanderings. Although the narrative is cathartic for him, it enflames her, and they begin an ambiguous sexual relationship: she calls it marriage, but he does not (Williams 1968:374–87). When he abruptly leaves for Italy, she commits suicide. Her curses against the departing Aeneas foretell the Punic Wars between Rome and Carthage; and when he later encounters her shade in the underworld, she turns away from him to rejoin her husband Sychaeus.

The *Aeneid* is a poem of historical transition, 'of threatened but preserved continuities' (Greene 1982:66). Dido's tragedy, which is at once a tragedy of desire and one of narrative implication, defines Aeneas' distance from the Homeric ideals of action and individual will, and moves him towards Virgilian ideals of suffering and the sublimation of individual will to the good of the state. Any account of Virgil's influence on Spenser, especially as regards the story of Dido, should both note echoes of language and incident and consider how they are translated into Spenser's own idiom.

Spenser's reminiscences of Virgil's story of Dido are comparatively few and frequently indirect, but they are of potentially central importance (Bono 1984:61–79). They range from the certain (his appropriation of Virgilian language to characterize Elisa and Belphoebe: *SC, Aprill* 162–5, *Aeneid* 1.327–8; *FQ* II iii 31, *Aeneid* 1.491–501), to the indefinite (the name Dido in *November*; see McLane 1961:47–60), to the suggestive (parallels between Dido's and Amavia's suicides: *FQ* II i 35–6, *Aeneid* 4.450–705; or between Dido's and Britomart's suffering in love: *FQ* III ii 30–52, *Aeneid* 4.1–53, 478–521; or between Aeneas' narration and those of Guyon, Paridell, and Britomart, *FQ* II ii 45–6, III ix 32–52). These examples suggest that Spenser's allusions to the story of Dido translate Virgil's tragedy of erotic abnegation into a romance of rectified desire, at the center and periphery of which is the image of Elizabeth.

In *The Shepheardes Calender*, Rosalind, the Elisa of *Aprill*, and the Dido of *November* variously present the Virgilian problem of desire, which remains unresolved in the *Calender* but is further explored in *The Faerie Queene*. Elisa is celebrated for her virginity; but *Aprill* concludes with two 'Emblemes' derived from a particularly ambiguous moment in the *Aeneid*, when the shipwrecked Aeneas encounters his mother Venus, disguised as a Diana-like huntress, in the woods outside Carthage. Herself seemingly virginal and self-sufficient, she tells of Dido and awakens his interest. She is a Venus-within-a-Diana, a *Venus virgo*, insinuating those desires which Aeneas and Dido will tragically enact.

These emblems celebrate Elisa, but they also complicate our response to the poem's objects of public and private desire. We are told that Colin's song to Elisa was composed before he was frustrated in love by Rosalind. Virgil's *Venus virgo* introduces a chaste Elissa masking a passionate Dido; Spenser's Elisa may come to focus his poetry's more urgent desires. *Aprill* thus suggests the problem openly discussed in *October*: can love be other than destructive?

Colin's elegy to Dido, a mysterious 'mayden of greate bloud,' epitomizes the poetry he can still write. Numerous similarities link this dead heroine to the Elisa/Eliza of *Aprill*: both are daughters of great shepherds, intimately associated with flowers, and beloved of the Muses and shepherds. If the poem is a covert and indirect warning against Elizabeth's proposed marriage to Alençon, so that the Queen is being urged not to imitate Virgil's Dido but to sublimate her womanly desires for the good of her people, Spenser avoids offense and fulfills the generic imperatives of elegy by having his Dido – unlike Virgil's who wanders the Mourning Fields – 'enstalled nowe in heavens hight ... in *Elisian* fieldes so free' (177–9, with a possible pun on *Elisian/Elisa*). The resolution of this elegy contrasts with the despairing condition of Colin as the *Calender* closes on a note of frustrated desire: he hangs up his pipe and longs for 'dreerie death' (*December* 141–4). The *Calender* only partially revises Virgil's epic, for it has not determined whether love can exert a positive force in this world.

Spenser associates the success of his epic, *The Faerie Queene*, with the problem of right and wrong loving suggested by Virgil's story of Dido. Repeatedly, he invokes Elizabeth as both the source and ideal audience of his efforts, his 'dearest dred' (*FQ* I proem 4). The narrative reveals a profound uncertainty whether this desire is transcendent; what is clear is that it cannot be ignored. Spenser's explicit reminiscences of Virgil's Dido in those 'mirrors' of Elizabeth, Belphoebe and Britomart, suggest the diffusion of the Virgilian problem of desire throughout the poem.

In Book II, both Amavia's death and Guyon's description of it at the castle of Medina recall aspects of Dido's story: the former her bitter suicide, the latter her invitation to Aeneas to tell the tale of his misfortunes and wanderings. Both reminiscences, however, seem to reveal limitations in Spenser's hero. Guyon, though passionately moved by Amavia's suicidal furor in love, quickly moralizes it as a spur to temperance (i 57–8). He resists Virgil's structure of narrative implication, and unlike Dido holds himself aloof from Amavia's tale of misfortune. But the Virgilian allusion encourages a skepticism towards his detachment which is heightened by the complexity of our reaction to Belphoebe.

Belphoebe develops the density of Spenser's Virgilian allusion in *Aprill*. Like *Venus virgo* and Virgil's Dido, she provokes both awe and desire in the beholder. The confusing blend of majesty and eroticism in her blazon (iii 21–31) is matched by the adaptation and conflation of two Virgilian moments. Like Dido before the temple, Belphoebe is compared to Diana; yet she is also compared to Penthesilea, the doomed Amazonian queen pictured there. Despite the glory in both images, Spenser modulates what is already Virgilian irony even further towards a sense of vulnerability: his Diana is wandering alone, and his Penthesilea is slain. Braggadocchio's reaction, in leaping to embrace Belphoebe, comically exaggerates Aeneas' plea to that other *Venus virgo*, his disguised mother, that he be allowed to clasp her hand and speak unambiguously with her (iii 32–46, *Aeneid* 1.314–410). Braggadocchio's intemperate response is rejected, as is the noble Timias' erotic attraction to her.

However, neither Belphoebe, nor for that matter Elizabeth, denies Virgilian implication in desire. Majestically disdainful here, in Book III the huntress softens to feel pity for the wounded Timias; the change imitates

Virgil's similar modulation of the imagery of hunting (cf v 27–30 with *Aeneid* 4.68–73). Restoring Timias to favor after he has been rendered inarticulate by her disdain (IV viii 1–17), she reminds us of the proem to Book IV where the poet places himself in a similarly abject position toward his sovereign, dependent on her love for the sustenance of his words. The narrative interdependence of Virgil's Aeneas and Dido provides us with a subtle and powerful means of access to the problems of Spenserian textual production and intertextuality.

Belphoebe raises erotic problems that Guyon's classical temperance cannot resolve. Book III points towards their resolution through a neo-Virgilian strategy of combining Aeneas and Dido in Britomart and thereby crafting a dynastic epic-romance. Britomart's love and Glauce's attempt to exorcise it recall the relationship of Dido to her sister Anna, and the rites of the Massylian priestess. But in canto iii, in a sequence modeled on Anchises' prophecy to Aeneas in *Aeneid* 6, Merlin foretells Britomart's famous progeny up to Elizabeth. This prophecy inspires her in canto ix to supplement Paridell's lackluster and self-serving narration of the Trojan past (he is using it to seduce Hellenore and enact a burlesque version of Dido's banquet and the fall of Troy), offering in its place her own enthusiastic praise of the third Troy, English Troynovant. There is no clearer indication of Spenser's attempt to depart from Virgil's portrait of narrative implication and erotic tragedy in the first third of the *Aeneid* than this contrast between Paridell's illicit love and diminished history and Britomart's heroic love and sense of redemptive history. In place of the sharp divisions of Virgil's poem, where Dido repeats the past and Aeneas painfully sublimates it, Britomart, united through heroic effort with Artegall, proposes to transcend these differences.

Whether this promise is fulfilled and the poem finds a stable relationship to the contemporary events that so powerfully conditioned it, is problematic. In Books IV-VI, specific allusions to Virgil's Dido fade as generalized allusion to the *Aeneid* becomes more diffuse. It is arguable that even rectified desire is experienced there as a lack, so that Britomart's quest is eroded from within by the dense intertextualities of Book IV, and we are left with strained justifications of power in Book V and pastoral nostalgia in Book VI – Virgilian themes indeed. But whether the reader is absorbed by the internal drama of desire or seeks its resolution by emphasizing firmly its dynastic frame, Virgil's influence on Spenser cannot be seen as a series of 'misappropriated' passages. That influence to a large extent engendered the poem, much as Aeneas' tale to Dido engendered the *Aeneid*.

BARBARA J. BONO

Don Cameron Allen 1962 'Marlowe's *Dido* and the Tradition' in *Essays on Shakespeare and Elizabethan Drama* ed Richard Hosley (Columbia, Mo) pp 55–68; Berger 1957; Barbara J. Bono 1984 *Literary Transvaluation: From Vergilian Epic to Shakespearean Tragicomedy* (Berkeley and Los Angeles); Bush 1963; Fichter 1982; Greenblatt 1981; Greene 1982; Hughes 1929; Mary Louise Lord 1969 'Dido as an Example of Chastity: The Influence of Example Literature' *HLB* 17:22–44, 216–32; McLane 1961; Brooks Otis 1963; Otis 1969 'The Originality of the *Aeneid*' in *Virgil* ed D.R. Dudley (London) pp 27–66; Virgil 1955 *Aeneidos, liber quartus* ed R.G. Austin (Oxford) and Virgil 1971 *Aeneidos, liber primus* ed R.G. Austin (Oxford), both with useful commentaries; Gordon Williams 1968 *Tradition and Originality in Roman Poetry* (Oxford); Wind 1958.

Digby, Everard (fl 1590) Perhaps the most distinguished philosopher and teacher of philosophy among Spenser's Cambridge contemporaries. While there is no evidence that the two men ever met, they shared a constellation of intellectual concerns.

Digby entered St John's College, Cambridge, receiving the BA in 1571; he was a fellow of the College from 1573 to 1587. In 1579, he published in Latin the *Theoria analytica*, a long and ambitious (though highly derivative) volume of metaphysics. Over the next two years, he engaged in a Latin pamphlet war with William Temple over Ramus, whom he saw as a corrupter of modern learning. In 1588, he left St John's after a dispute in which he was accused of papism. The support of his patron, Sir Christopher Hatton, who intervened with Burghley, had only postponed his departure. About 1589–90, he published a polemical treatise on the economic problems of the church in which he attacked the Puritans.

It has been argued that Spenser may draw upon Digby's *De arte natandi* (*On the Art of Swimming* 1587) in *FQ* V ii 14–17 (West 1973), but the parallel will strike few readers as close. Digby's real interest for students of Spenser lies in the insight his *Theoria* affords into currents of syncretic Neoplatonist scholarship and speculation in mid-Elizabethan Cambridge. In this work (dedicated to Hatton), his intuition of the presence of many great 'mysteries' in Aristotle's *Posterior Analytics* leads him to develop a theory which conflates technical logic with a vast mass of Neoplatonic and Cabalistic lore taken (not always with acknowledgment) from Ficino's translation of Plotinus and from the Cabalistic dialogues of Johannes Reuchlin.

Digby's *Theoria* has much in common with *The Faerie Queene*. Both works appeal to ideas of analogy between different layers of reality (with the *Theoria* making explicit the Cabalistic basis of a threefold world comparable to that implied by the names of Triamond and his brothers in *FQ* IV ii-iii); both are consciously archaistic in language; both show evidence of composition in accordance with numerological theory; and both are explicitly devoted to forming or fashioning a man – in the *Theoria*, a master of philosophy rather than a gentleman. Also, both works fuse Platonic and Aristotelian materials, each starting from an Aristotelian base (of analytical and ethical theory, respectively) and introducing Platonic concepts of emanation and return.

EUGENE D. HILL

Schmitt 1983a; Michael West 1973 'Spenser, Everard Digby, and the Renaissance Art of Swimming' *RenQ* 26:11–22.

Digby, Kenelme (1603–65) Equally well known in letters and politics, Digby was a career diplomat and naval commander, an author of numerous literary and philosophical works, and an amateur scientist of some standing. His *Two Treatises ... Of Bodies [and] Of Mans Soule* (Paris 1644) present Digby's views in comparison to those of his acquaintance Descartes (whose *Discours de la méthode* Digby introduced to England by sending a copy to his friend Thomas Hobbes). He was a founder of the Royal Society. His most striking literary work is the semi-autobiographical romance *Loose Fancies*, based on his courtship of Lady Venetia Stanley.

Digby was known as a patron of literature and a collector of books; one of his favorite authors was Spenser. Jonson (whose 1640–1 *Workes* Digby was to edit) wrote an epigram to Lady Digby in which he expressed the hope that her husband will not only love his verses, but 'will looke / Upon them, (next to *Spenser's* noble booke,) / And praise them too' (*Underwood* 78 in ed 1925–52, 8:263). Digby seems to have done as requested: in an essay he wrote on Spenser he compliments both authors as successive wearers of the 'Laurell crowne': 'when divine SPENCERS sunne was noe sooner sett ... in JOHNSON a new one rose with as much glory and brightnes as ever shone withall' (*Sp All* p 213).

For Digby, Spenser was skilled in decorum: 'certainely, weight of matter was never better joyned with propriety of language and with majestey and sweetnes of verse, then by him' (p 212). Moreover, he commends Spenser's knowledge and expression of complex philosophy: 'SPENCER in what he saith hath a way of expression peculiar to him selfe; he bringeth downe the highest and deepest misteries that are contained in human learning, to an easy and gentle forme of delivery: Which sheweth he is Master of what he treateth of; he can wield it as he pleaseth ... His knowledge in profound learning both divine and humane appeareth to me without controversie the greatest that any POET before him ever had, Excepting VIRGIL' (p 213). What is so striking about this learning is the subtlety by which it is presented: 'if one heed him not with great attention, rare and wonderful conceptions will unperceived slide by him that readeth his works, and he will thinke he hath mett with nothing but familiar and easy discourses but let one dwell a while upon them and he shall feele a straunge fulnesse and roundnesse in all he saith' (p 213).

Digby is most attracted to Spenser's 'solide and deepe insight in THEOLOGIE, PHILOSOPHY (especially the PLATONIKE) and the MATHEMATICALL sciences' (p 213) in another work, his pamphlet entitled *Observations on the 22. Stanza in the 9th Canto of the 2d. Book of Spencers Faery Queene* (London 1624), written as an informal letter to his friend, Sir Edward Stradling. This, the first published and certainly the most learned early criticism of Spenser's verse (though not the first commentary; see *Dixon, *Raleigh), is a line-by-line analysis explaining the allegory of the castle of Alma as a geometrical human figure. Digby begins by drawing attention to a sudden complication introduced into the allegory by *FQ* II ix 22, a single stanza that is 'evident testimonie' that Spenser was 'thoroughly verst in the Mathematicall Sciences, in Philosophy, and in Divinity,' yet a stanza that leaves 'Readers to wander up and down in much obscuritie' (*Var* 2:472). Digby's task is to unravel the lines, to approach as closely as possible 'the Authors intention,' which is 'to describe the bodie of man inform'd with a rationall soul' that together 'frame a compleat Man' (p 473). By the circle is meant the soul, the center of which is God. The triangle refers to the body, for a triangle is the 'lowest of all Figures' – 'for as the Circle is of all other Figures the most perfect and most capacious: so the Triangle is most imperfect, and includes least space' (p 473). The circle is – in Spenser's words – 'immortall, perfect, masculine,' the triangle, 'imperfect, mortall, foeminine.' The 'quadrate' at the base is 'the foure principall humors in mans Bodie' (p 475; see *medicine). So long as the humors are proportioned, 'the soul and bodie dwell together like good friends' (p 476). They are proportioned 'equally by seven and nine,' which means, according to Digby, proportioned according to 'the *Starres*' or 'seven Planets' in the body and the nine angelic 'Hierarchies or Orders' in the soul. Spenser's line 'Nine was the circle set in heavens place' Digby explains as the perfection of the highest sphere of the Intelligences which move the heavens (p 477). Finally, the 'goodly diapase' is that 'most perfect Harmony' that arises when the parts of the body and the soul are in 'due time' or properly ordered in relation to one another.

Digby's interpretation shows familiarity with Neoplatonic doctrine; his application of this doctrine to Spenser is one of the earliest and most astute examples of practical criticism in English. Modern analysis of the stanza (summarized by Hamilton in *FQ* ed 1977) still begins with Digby's full and informed commentary, though it goes beyond it both in historical range and in seeing the stanza within the full context of Book II. ARLENE STIEBEL

A biography based on early sources is R.T. Petersson 1956 *Sir Kenelm Digby: The Ornament of England 1603–1665* (London). The *Observations* is rpt in *Var* 2:472–8; the variously titled essay on Spenser is found in BL Add Ms 41846 and Harleian Ms 4153, the latter rpt in *Sp All* pp 211–14. Digby's copy of the 1617 folio of Spenser is in the library of Wellesley College in Massachusetts. For discussion of the *Observations*, see Wurtsbaugh 1936:14–17, and Fowler 1964:260–88, with full commentary on II ix 22.

Disdain The allegorical figure Disdain first appears in *The Faerie Queene* as the awesome and belligerent keeper of the portals guarding the court of Philotime (wordly ambition) in the house of Mammon (II vii 40–3). Brief though his role may be, he is among the more subtly developed of Spenser's personifications. On his manifestation hinges a major theme of the canto, the contagious nature of disparagement. Like Ate in Book IV, Disdain is a transpersonal force, infecting human relationships like a disease of the emotions.

This force is first manifest in a relatively inert and abstract form in the phrase 'great disdaine' (II vii 7), describing Mammon's response to Guyon's perturbed, aggressive questioning on their first encounter. Although the term is not mentioned again at this point, it is clear that Guyon, the temperate (or would-be temperate) knight, in his turn accepts with somewhat similar disdain Mammon's offer to visit his underground realm. But in the underworld of myth to which Mammon conducts him, inner qualities are projected into external objectification very freely; and it is not long before Disdain appears as an independent personification.

Guyon has just been shown the last of Mammon's treasure rooms and with 'bold mesprise' (great disdain) has rejected his 'idle offers' of worldly pelf (39). Mammon then decides to use other tactics and conducts him through a 'darksome narrow strait' where he is threatened by Disdain in the form of a gigantic man of gold (in the 1596 text; iron in 1590), armed with a great iron club. But before the equally incensed Guyon can join battle, Mammon stays Guyon's 'hasty hand,' telling him that the giant cannot be overcome (or even wounded) by force of arms. A brief word from Mammon seems sufficient also to calm Disdain himself, and the knight passes on into the court of Philotime without further ado.

Nonetheless, the incident seems to have shaken Guyon, who now abandons the persistent arrogance with which he had earlier invariably addressed the Money God. Indeed, he seems a model of courtesy when declining the honor of Philotime's hand in marriage (50) or simply asking Mammon's leave to depart (65). He seems to have learned the lesson that disdain, however justified, breeds only further disdain, and can never be overcome by such aggressive outbursts.

The thematic structure here, one common enough in Spenser and other allegorists, may be termed a 'seminal image' (Piehler 1971:15). Allegory in this respect functions as an extended metaphor in which an image or other key phrase is used first in a limited, inert manner, but under the stress of visionary or similar experience is transformed into full experiential reality as, for example, a personification or allegorical landscape.

The second appearance of Disdain, in Book VI, is considerably more sustained. Intimated in vi 16, he is on scene from vii 27 to viii 30; and although now serving Cupid rather than Mammon, he seems to be the same character, for here, too, he is a giant, is associated with the giants of classical mythology, bears an iron club, has a body (or at least feet) of gold, and is (perhaps in rather a different sense) invulnerable. The principal difference, however, is that while previously he functioned as the general guardian of Philotime's court, now he is attached to one specific person, Mirabella, as her peripatetic jailer and minister of penance and punishment.

Mirabella is the heartless fair lady who exploits her charms to torment and destroy her would-be lovers. Disdain (quality) has become so deeply ingrained within her that she has been sentenced by Cupid to live permanently under the lash of Disdain (personification) until she atones for her misdeeds. She seems in fact to have established a kind of symbiotic relation with him, for when he is finally brought low by Arthur, Mirabella has to plead for his life, since his death would bring about hers also (viii 17). In terms of relationship between character and personification, this seems to represent a penultimate stage of absorption – Malbecco, the jealous husband who is actually transformed into the personification 'Gealousie' (III x 60), representing the final stage. The incident serves also to illustrate the potential danger to Guyon, should he not have succeeded in separating himself from his own quasi-obsessive disdain of the Money God. PAUL PIEHLER

E.B. Fowler (1921:127) describes an allegorical entertainment at which a Castle of Love is defended by Disdain and Dangier, and similar allegorical ladies, against the assault of Ardent Desire and other allegorical lords. Other uses of the name are found in Hawes ed 1928, lines 4949ff, where Graunde Amoure's courtship of La Belle Pucelle is temporarily impeded by the machinations of Dysdayne, 'the crafty sorceres'; and in William Nevill 1930 *The Castell of Pleasure* ed Roberta D. Cornelius, EETS os 179 (London) lines 562–745, in which the lover, Desire, wins his lady, Beauty, in spite of the opposition of Disdayne, who opposes the lover's suit in a somewhat slow-moving debate with Pyte. John Donne, in 'The Dampe,' urges his lady, 'First kill th'enormous Gyant, your *Disdaine*.' For Spenser, see Hankins 1971.

Dixon, John The first reader of *The Faerie Queene* who left a record of his response, Dixon made notes in the margin of a copy of the 1590 edition of *FQ* I-III, now in the possession of the Earl of Bessborough. His annotations can be dated 1597, for in his note to I xii 36 he refers to the 39 years of peace that England had enjoyed since the accession of Queen Elizabeth (1558), which he understands as allegorized in the wedding day of Una and the Red Cross Knight. Beyond the marginalia and his name, which appears on the title page of the volume in the same hand and ink as the annotations, nothing is known of him, but the provenance of the volume points to a John Dixon of Hilden, near Tonbridge, Kent.

Dixon's annotations are valuable in showing how one educated, patriotic, Protestant, but not notably literary Englishman read *The Faerie Queene* in the 1590s. He is keenly interested in the religious allegory of Book

I, is perceptive of scriptural allusions, and provides some significant notes to historical allusions he felt to be present. The cantos of chronicle history in II x and III iii elicit his most minute and detailed annotations, but he does not appear to notice imitations of Ariosto, Tasso, or the classical poets. In Book III, he has difficulty dealing with the variety of characters and episodes: at various points, he mistakes Florimell for Belphoebe, the Foster for Braggadocchio, Duessa for Malecasta, Scudamour for Artegall, and Amoret for Belphoebe. A modern editor concludes that Dixon 'is indifferent to the courtly and romantic aspects' of the poem and that 'it is the Protestant divinity, the ascetic morality and the national history' that primarily concern him (Hough 1964:1).

Dixon's most interesting notes are on Book I. Especially significant is his perception of the continual relevance of the Book of Revelation to the narrative: he marks more than twenty references to it. Since the Geneva Bible interpreted Revelation as achieving an historical fulfillment in the Reformation, Dixon's notes to contemporary history are a suggestive complement to his understanding of the way Spenser used Revelation as the basis of his myth (see *Apocalypse). Two of these historical notes may appear somewhat eccentric: in cipher, Dixon identifies Redcrosse with Leicester (at i 2) and Arthur with the Earl of Cumberland (x 65). But more plausible are his notes linking Una with Elizabeth (iii 2, 7; xii argument, 36, 40); this is especially suggestive in that he has no difficulty in associating Elizabeth with Gloriana as well (i 3, and x 59). He appears to see Una's tribulations in Book I as alluding to Elizabeth's during the reign of Mary.

In Books II and III, he is most concerned with the chronicle histories (II x, III iii). These cantos evoke in him a keen interest in the history and legend fused there; and it appears that the poem sent him back to his books, specifically Robert Fabyan's *New Chronicles of England and France*, to look up specific details which he then recorded in the margins. His notes on II xi indicate he appreciated the allegory of the human body in the castle of Alma, and he follows Guyon's overthrow of the Bower of Bliss with relish. In the Amintas of III vi 45, he finds an allusion to Sidney.

MICHAEL O'CONNELL

A selection of Dixon's annotations has been edited by Hough and privately published by the Earl of Bessborough (Hough 1964; see also Graham Hough in *TLS* [9 April 1964]:294). Other early annotations in copies of *The Faerie Queene* have also been reported on over the past 30 years. An anonymous scholar described notes, including historical identifications in *FQ* V, in a Cambridge copy of the 1596 edition ('MS Notes' ed 1957). Other annotations in copies of early editions in Oxford and London, while sparse in historical identifications, show evidence of emblematic interpretation (Alastair Fowler 1961 'Oxford and London Marginalia to *The Faerie Queene*' *N&Q* 206:416–19). There are marginalia concerned with Raleigh in the copy owned by his son, including some by his wife and others perhaps by Raleigh himself (Oakeshott 1971). Fowler and Leslie 1981 reports on annotations of the poem by William Drummond, whose interests in literary imitations show him to be an opposite sort of reader to Dixon. For early seventeenth-century notes in a Belfast copy of the 1611 edition of Spenser's *Works*, see John Manning 1984 'Notes and Marginalia in Bishop Percy's Copy of Spenser's *Works* (1611)' *N&Q* 229:225–7. These early commentaries show that *The Faerie Queene* was closely read, though often for personal reasons. See also the commentary of Digby on *FQ* II ix 22 and William Austin's remarks in his *Devotionis augustiniae flamma* (1635; see Ernest A. Strathmann 1937 'William Austin's "Notes" on *The Faerie Queene*' *Huntington Library Bulletin* 11:155–60).

Dolon On her way to rescue Artegall from Radigund, Britomart meets the treacherous though seemingly courteous older knight Dolon, who invites her to stay the night in his house (*FQ* V vi). She watches the whole night, refusing to lie in her bed, which shortly after cockcrow falls through a trapdoor into the room below; Talus, on watch outside her room, drives off two knights and a 'raskall rout' who try to break in shortly afterward. We learn that Artegall killed one of Dolon's three sons, Guizor, before attacking Pollente on the bridge (V ii); taking Britomart to be Artegall because she is escorted by Talus, Dolon has attempted revenge. His remaining sons meet Britomart in battle and fall to the heroine's spear on the same bridge (rigged with a trapdoor like the bedroom) where Artegall encountered Pollente.

Dolon's name is from Greek *dolos*, 'craft' or 'treachery,' as suggested by reference to his 'slie shiftes and wiles' (32). This scene of nighttime adventure and deception derives from the episode of the spy Dolon in *Iliad* 10 (see *Virgils Gnat* 536): those of Nisus and Euryalus in *Aeneid* 9, Medoro and Cloridano in *Orlando furioso* 18, Clorinda, Argante, and Tancredi in *Gerusalemme liberata* 12. In Roman law, *dolus malus* or 'malice aforethought' is the chief nemesis of equity (it is synonymous with *malum ingenium*, hence Malengin in *FQ* V ix, also routed by Talus; see Fletcher 1971:233). The nocturnal setting recalls a mythological tradition that Dolus, or Deceit (along with other abstractions like Envy, Fear, and Fraud), was born of Erebus and Night, a genealogy construed by Boccaccio to mean that deceit originates from the concupiscence of a sick heart (*Genealogia* 1.20). Like the perilous bridge, the trapdoor in the bedroom is conventional in romance.

The possibility of political allegory has attracted many commentators, the episode recalling efforts to overthrow Elizabeth. There was even a Dolon-like conspirator, Leonard des Trappes, who wanted to blow up Elizabeth in bed (Graziani 1964a:387–9). Dolon's son Guizor and his two brothers may allude to the Duc de Guise, instigator of the massacre of French Protestants on St Bartholomew's Day in 1572, and his two brothers; Dolon himself might then represent Philip II of Spain, close political ally of the Guise family (*Var* 5:211).

In its violation of hospitality, Dolon's attempt is near sacrilege: his false hospitality recalls, although here in a knightly form, the welcome given by that arch-fraud Archimago to Redcrosse and Una in *FQ* I i. Britomart has been seen as turning aside from her mission through a defect of vision comparable to the spiritual blindness of Redcrosse when he strays into the Wood of Error and Archimago's house (Dunseath 1968:166–9). Yet critics are not agreed that she is at fault in this episode. The curious allusion to St Peter's betrayal of Christ at cockcrow (vi 27) has been taken as a suggestion that Britomart typifies *agape*, and that the ultimate victory in Book V is that of 'the true Christian logos ... over a more ancient, darker form of worship,' Catholicism (Bieman 1968). Alternatively, the episode may stress the threats to Elizabethan stability posed by abusing the letter of the law: 'unlike Sir Artegall, Britomart can *experience* the error of *dolus malus* in an experimental fashion so that, unlike him, she will not fall into the trap of excessive legalism' (Fletcher 1971:233).

RICHARD F. HARDIN

Donne, John (1572–1631) Modernist literary theory has cast Donne as the implicitly anti-Spenserian hero of English poetic tradition. Thomas Carew's elegy on him (1633) makes Donne a sort of Guyon in the bower of romance: 'The Muses' garden with pedantic weeds / O'erspread, was purged by thee; the lazy seeds / Of servile imitation thrown away / And fresh invention planted' (25–8). Actually, one might be hard put to decide whether the smooth line of Jonson or the strong line of wit stemming (in the modernist histories, at least) from Donne veered more sharply away from Spenserian mythopoetic modes. Indeed, only Milton, by eschewing (after some juvenilia) either of these genera, and Marvell, who seems to combine them, emerge as Spenser's major heirs from among the more doting Spenserians like Drayton, Browne, and the Fletchers. It is, however, certainly the sons of Donne whom Henry Reynolds accuses, in *Mythomystes* (1632), of having chosen to read and study 'in the best of their Authors ... meerely his stile, phrase and manner of expression,' they who 'imbrace assembled cloudes with *Ixion* and beget only Monsters' (C1v-C2r).

A recent book on Donne, unpurged of this narrow modernism, remarks that if *The Progresse of the Soule* had been completed, and 'if it, rather than Spenser's *Faerie Queene*, had come to be recognized as the great Elizabethan epic[, i]n place of Spenser's dreamy conservatism, we should then have had ... a work which was not only progressive and contentious in its intellectual cast, but also wedded to immediacy and the real world' (Carey 1981:157). As with Professor Carey's seventeenth-century namesake, not only the qualities for which Donne is praised, but more interestingly, the very tropes in which the protest is framed – the garden purged, the 'wedding' of a poem to 'the real world' – are themselves unwittingly Spenserian.

Donne's anti-mythopoetic stance, his fondness for the dramatic monologue whether in lyric or in elegy, his lack of concern for the kind of progress and contentiousness in its intellectual cast that goes with parables of questing, all help to polarize Spenser and Donne. It is all the more curious, then, to observe one egregious instance of the Spenserian in Donne, both half-avowed and brilliantly averted even in its formal structure. *The Progresse of the Soule*, which Donne abandoned by 1601 (otherwise titled *Metempsychosis* and *Poema Satyricon*), is an unfolding account, through the trope of Pythagorean metempsychosis, of the subsequent history of that soul which originally inhabited the apple in Paradise. The chronicle moves along the scale of creation as the soul passes through one embodiment to another. At the conclusion of the first 'Song,' or canto, the soul is about to enter the race of Cain, and the promised account of its later career in the lives of Luther, Mahomet and 'this great soule which here amongst us now / Doth dwell' (61–2) was never written. Akin to such chronicles as those in *FQ* II x or III iii, the obliquely Spenserian character of this anomalous poem is apparent in a stanza like this one (6):

> But if my dayes be long, and good enough,
> In vaine this sea shall enlarge, or enrough
> It selfe; for I will through the wave, and fome,
> And shall, in sad lone wayes a lively spright,
> Make my darke heavy Poëm light, and light.
> For though through many streights, and lands I roame,
> I launch at paradise, and I saile towards home;
> The course I there began, shall here be staid,
> Sailes hoisted there, stroke here, and anchors laid
> In Thames, which were at Tigrys, and Euphrates waide.

The not-quite-Spenserian stanza form (ten lines rhyming *aabccbbddd* with the terminal alexandrine which had become a Spenserian signature), the romance trope of writing a long text as sea-voyage, the use of the rivers, the probably allusive 'darke heavy Poëm' underlined by the *méchant* punning, all bespeak a complex stance towards the Spenserian mode. This stance cannot be easily reduced to notions such as 'parody,' and perhaps one might observe that in this uncompleted project Donne uses elements of romance for ambitious, but ambivalent satiric purposes. R.C. Bald (1970:124) acknowledges Spenserian 'influence' on this poem, but the course and shape of that 'influence,' the contours of the attitudes it generates, remain to be mapped.

Donne's 'Epithalamion Made at Lincolnes Inne' has been singled out for its relation to Spenser. It has an alexandrine refrain, 'To day put on perfection, and a woman's name,' which changes, for the second four of its eight strophes, to the nocturnal form 'To night put on perfection.' (It is almost as if A.K. Hieatt's discoveries about *Epithalamion*'s numerical structure might have been known to Spenser's contemporaries. Even the anti-Spenserian Ben Jonson has an epithalamion – *Underwood* 65 – with an alexandrine refrain, and commences with what reads as, among other things, a self-conscious statement of belatedness vis-à-vis the midsummer moment of *Epithalamion*: 'Though thou hast passed thy summer standing, stay / Awhile with us, bright sun, and help our light.')

In the Donne poem, 'Daughters of London, you which bee' (13) has been thought to be an echo of *Epithalamion* 167, 'Tell me ye merchants daughters did ye see,' and Donne's opening line associated with Spenser's line 20. David Novarr (1956) argues that Donne's poem was broadly parodic of Spenser, and was probably written in 1595 as a piece of spoken entertainment, at the time that Donne was reading law at Lincoln's Inn. Another view, somewhat more sophisticated in its conception of allusive relations between poems, is that of Heather Dubrow Ousby (1976).

Of Donne's two other epithalamia, one on the Lady Elizabeth and Count Palatine being married on St Valentine's day also has eight stanzas and an alexandrine refrain, varied at each return, as closure. The other one might be thought of as deliberately skewing this formal allusive relation, having eleven stanzas, each with a subtitling rubric and a closing fourteener refrain. But in general, Donne's role remains antithetical to Spenser's, and whether or not 'An Essaie of Valour,' first printed as Donne's in 1562, is indeed his (ed 1980 prints it as 'Dubia'), it excludes Spenser in all but name from its own canon of modernity: 'before this age of witt, and wearinge Black broke in upon us, Their was no way knowne to wyn a Ladye, but by Tyltinge, Turnynge, and riding through Forrests' (ed 1980:64).

JOHN HOLLANDER

John Donne 1967 *Satires, Epigrams and Verse Letters* ed W. Milgate (Oxford); Donne ed 1980. Bald 1970; John Carey 1981 *John Donne: Life, Mind and Art* (New York); Novarr 1956; Ousby 1976.

Doughty, Charles M. (1843–1926) No English poet more freely proclaimed his discipleship of Spenser than Doughty, the son of a Suffolk clergyman, who read geology at Cambridge and from an early age combined scientific interests with extensive reading and study of sixteenth-century English literature and Teutonic languages. His studies were directed toward preparing himself for writing an epic of the beginnings of the British people, a task fulfilled in the publication of a poem somewhat 'less in bulk than *The Faerie Queene*,' *The Dawn in Britain* (in 6 vols 1906, 1-vol 2nd ed 1943). The prose work for which he is best known, *Travels in Arabia Deserta* (1888, 2nd ed with intro by T.E. Lawrence 1921), he considered a necessary preparation for the epic. His shorter poems include two imaginative recreations of the early times of the world and of man, *Adam Cast Forth* (1908) and *The Titans* (1916); two prophecies of invasion of England by Germany, *The Cliffs* (1909) and *The Clouds* (1912); and a dream allegory, *Mansoul* (1920, rev 1923).

Doughty claimed Spenser as his nearest master. In the 'Post Illa' to *The Dawn in Britain*, he asserts that it was only to Spenser that the Muses 'revealed their own golden intimate tongue; and taught him without spot or stain, to devoutly perceive the harmony of the Spheres' (6:242). In *The Clouds*, he writes, 'Dear Master Edmund, since from thy pined flesh, / Thou was unbound; is fallen thy matchless Muse; / Alas the while! on many evil days: / Wherein, as waxed untuneable; can mens ears, / Now, no more savour thy celestial lays!' (p 10). And in Mansoul's Dream-City, Spenser is 'Edmund, my lodestar ... Whose Art is mine endeavour to restore' (1920:179).

Both Doughty's poetic ideal and his dissatisfaction with later literature were expressible in terms of Spenser and his art. This is not a matter of verse technique: here he is remote from Spenser, indeed disapproving of his use of 'medieval riming.' His borrowing of Spenserian vocabulary, however, is a sign of deep affinity. Doughty was a follower of Spenser, but he was also widely read in Renaissance literature and history, and intimate with Italy and the Mediterranean. It was because he was able to arrive at Spenser's outlook independently of him as well as through him that he was able to write as if anticipating him and to create the feeling that Spenser's world is actually beginning in his own verses. Doughty does not speak of Spenser as one 'Whose Art is mine endeavour to explain,' as he might legitimately have done, but 'Whose Art is mine endeavour to restore' – another matter altogether. He finds in Spenser and other early poets a 'Fulness of Vision, and diviners' Art' (*Mansoul* 1920:180).

Doughty's continuing and lifelong regard for his original is discernible in everything from the details of his diction to his use on occasion of fully worked-out allegory. As his 'Word Notes' show, he associated all his thoughts, discursive or imaginative, with specific words; and his whole endeavor as poet and moralist is to counter the 'vility of language' he saw and heard about him. Without desiring archaism or rusticity as a 'colour,' as Spenser did, Doughty like him chooses words patriotically and morally; the words he chooses include 'tottic of the must,' 'louting in clownish sort,' and (a Spenserian phrase beloved of Keats and of Virginia Woolf) 'sea-shouldering whales.' Single images, such as 'silver streaming Thames,' and extended tableaux and processions also derive quite openly from Spenser: the procession of the Months and Hours in *Adam Cast Forth*, the procession of kingly and patriotic figures in *The Cliffs*, the shepherds in *Mansoul*, the song and dance of the shepherds in *The Titans*. So too some of the persons in Doughty recall Spenserian originals – Palarge in *Dawn in*

Britain Book 4, for example, is a more sinister Braggadocchio – but this should not be pushed too far: it is indeed astonishing that a poet who regularly evokes Spenser should glancingly and unnecessarily refer to a certain Britomart, son of a Cantian king. As an allegorist, finally, Doughty is closer to Langland in *Mansoul* or to Phineas Fletcher's *Locusts* in the Vision of Hell (*Dawn in Britain* Book 7) than he is to Spenser.

Every student of Doughty will have read Spenser; every reader of the Spenserian tradition in English poetry will need to add the name of C.M. Doughty to 'Fames eternall beadroll.'

BARKER FAIRLEY AND WILLIAM BLISSETT

William Blissett and John Arthur Tucker 1983 *British Poets, 1880–1914* ed Donald E. Stanford (Detroit) pp 137–48, incl bibliography (vol 19 in *Dictionary of Literary Biography*); Barker Fairley 1927 *Charles M. Doughty: A Critical Study* (London) ch 10; Ruth M. Robbins 1980–1 "The Word Notes of C.M. Doughty' *Agenda* 18:78–98.

Douglas, Gavin (c 1475–1522) Scottish poet, famous throughout the sixteenth century in England as well as Scotland for his translation of Virgil's *Aeneid* (1513), the first translation of a major classical poem into any form of English. This work circulated in manuscript and print (London 1553), and influenced two of Spenser's predecessors, Surrey and Sackville. Although not certainly known to Spenser, the translation and the original prologues that accompany each book contain much that would have been congenial to him: impressive natural description (Prologues 7, 12, 13), discussion of Virgil's artistry and significance (Prologues 1, 5, 6), and an ambition to achieve in the vernacular a poem of epic proportions. Douglas is stylistically an interesting forerunner of Spenser. He uses the same *topos* of the 'little heard groomes' (cf Prologue 7.77–8 with *SC, Feb* 35–6); and his diction is strongly alliterative, marked by archaism and Chaucerian forms, by a liking for etymological wordplay and sonorous Latinisms.

Spenser may also have known an earlier work by Douglas, *The Palice of Honour* (c 1501), which was available in an English edition (c 1553). This allegorical poem raises questions of great interest to the sixteenth century: what is honor, and how may it be attained? Douglas follows homiletic tradition in distinguishing true honor from earthly glory, and in presenting it as the reward of virtue. He celebrates in particular the heroic concept of honor: for him, Honor is 'a god armypotent,' and his court contains courageous warriors and patriots (cf *FQ* II iii 40–1). But the poem also has much to say about love and poetry; like Spenser, Douglas stresses the role of poets in conferring immortality (cf *Time* 425–7). *The Palice of Honour* has some resemblances to *The Faerie Queene* – in its decorative processions, its palace presided over by a personified abstraction, and its style, rich with rhetorical ornament and mythological allusion. But Douglas' allegorical technique is simpler and less interwoven than Spenser's. The poem is framed by a dream, and is indebted for some motifs to Chaucer's *House of Fame* and *Legend of Good Women*. As an impressive late example of the medieval dream poem, it is not strictly a source of *The Faerie Queene* but forms an important link in the tradition of courtly allegory that stretches from Chaucer to Spenser.

PRISCILLA BAWCUTT

Gavin Douglas 1964 *Selections* ed David F.C. Coldwell (Oxford); Douglas 1967 *Shorter Poems* ed Priscilla J. Bawcutt, STS 4th ser 3 (Edinburgh); Virgil ed 1957–64.

Priscilla Bawcutt 1970 'Gavin Douglas and Chaucer' *RES* ns 21:401–21; Bawcutt 1976 *Gavin Douglas: A Critical Study* (Edinburgh); Charles R. Blyth 1970 'Gavin Douglas' Prologues of Natural Description' *PQ* 49:164–77; Gregory Kratzmann 1980 *Anglo-Scottish Literary Relations 1430–1550* (Cambridge); A.K. Nitecki 1981 'Gavin Douglas's Rural Muse' in *Proceedings of the Third International Conference on Scottish Language and Literature* (Stirling) pp 383–95; Penelope Schott Starkey 1973–4 'Gavin Douglas's *Eneados*: Dilemmas in the Nature Prologues' *SSL* 11:82–98.

dragon, Cupid's In the house of Busirane, Britomart sees a dragon blinded by shafts in both eyes, lying beneath the idol of a cruel Cupid at whose altar all the denizens of the house worship (*FQ* III xi 47–9). Recent scholarship has argued that Cupid's dragon should be interpreted in terms of Alciati's emblem *Custodiendas virgines* ('Virgins must be protected' in his *Emblemata* 1534:46).

(See **dragon, Cupid's** Fig 1.)

In this emblem, Pallas Athena (Roman Minerva) is accompanied by a dragon that, according to the verses, symbolizes the sleepless care needed to preserve the virginity of unmarried girls against the ubiquitous snares of love. Glossed by reference to this emblem and other traditional uses of the dragon as wakeful guardian (eg, in the Garden of the Hesperides), Spenser's dragon is apparently a symbol of vigilance; but because it has been blinded by Cupid, that vigilance has been undone by erotic passion. To emphasize further the mischief of Cupid's forces, the dragon's tail is wrapped around the left (L *sinister*) foot of the idol.

LINDA R. GALYON

Hieatt 1975a:127–8; Lewis 1967:22–3; Jean MacIntyre 1966 'Spenser's *The Faerie Queene*, III, xi, 47–48' *Expl* 24: Item 69; Nohrnberg 1976:485–6.

dragons Most of Book I of *The Faerie Queene* may be read as the Red Cross Knight's preparation for the battle in canto xi with 'that fire-mouthed Dragon, horrible and bright' (ix 52), that has wasted Eden, the kingdom of Una's parents. It is first named in I i 3 as 'a Dragon horrible and stearne.' Before we meet this ultimate adversary, the enemy of Christian faith, 'that old Dragon' (xi argument; cf Rev 20.2), Redcrosse's adventures involve two other serpent-dragons, also possessing characteristics of the apocalyptic dragon of Revelation: Error, the half-woman, half-serpent, which he kills, and the 'dreadfull Beast with sevenfold head' (vii 18) that Duessa rides in triumph and Arthur wounds in seeking to free him from Orgoglio's dungeon.

(See **dragons** Fig 1.)

The image of 'filthie' Error (i 14) is compounded from the traditional monsters of classical literature (eg, Hesiod's Echidna in *Theogony* 295–305 and Pliny's description of spawning adders in *Natural History* 10.82), medieval bestiary lore (cf Bartholomaeus Anglicus 18, esp 18.95), emblem literature (as Alciati's *Impudentia*, Emblem 68), the antipapal writings of the Reformation where Rome is the 'great seven headded beast' (*Time* 71; cf also *Bellay* sonnet 8), and most significantly the Bible. She is the serpent (L *draco* serpent, dragon) in the Garden of Eden (traditionally figured from Peter Comestor [d 1179] onwards as having a woman's face); she is also the dragon in Revelation, for her 'huge long taile' (I i 15) is one of the principal signs of the apocalyptic beast (Rev 12.4; for its 'mortall sting,' cf the scorpions of Rev 9.10; cf also Geryoneo's monster with its 'Dragons taile, whose sting without redresse / Full deadly wounds' V xi 24), and the 'dreadfull Dragon with an hideous trayne' that lies under Lucifera's feet in the house of Pride (iv 10).

Even closer visually and conceptually to the horrifying apocalyptic beast is Duessa's dragon, whose tail throws the stars to earth (vii 18; cf Rev 12.4). Duessa, clad by Orgoglio in 'gold and purple pall' (16) is the 'purple and skarlat' woman riding on a 'skarlat coloured beast ... which had seven heads' (Rev 17.3–4). Her dragon is compared to the Lernaean Hydra, 'that renowmed Snake ... Whose many heads out budding ever new' bred such 'endlesse labour' for Hercules (cf Ovid *Metamorphoses* 9.69). Although a contemporary such as Topsell might ingenuously claim that there could not be 'such a Serpent [as the hydra] with seven heads,' he allowed the existence of a dragon so huge that mounted riders could not see over it, and another 'a hundred and twenty foot long' (in Gesner 1551–8, vol 4, sv Dragon, Hydra). That it is 'bloudie mouthed with late cruell feast' (I viii 6) suggests that like its rider it has been drinking 'the blood of Saintes, and ... Martyrs of Jesus' (Rev 17.6), and its fieriness even suggests the hellmouth of leviathan (Job 41). Although the dragon is associated with hellfire ('every head with fyrie tongue did flame' viii 6), one of its heads is struck off by Arthur, and it is overcome by the 'flashing beames' of his 'sunshiny shield' (20). Arthur's role as a dragon fighter has already been suggested by the heraldic device of his helmet (vii 31–2): a golden dragon whose mouth seems to emit 'bright sparkles fierie red' is surmounted by the plumage which is likened to 'an Almond tree ... On top of greene *Selinis*' (a sign of victory; cf Virgil *Aeneid* 3.705).

The final battle in *FQ* I recapitulates the earlier struggles, though in a more protracted and profound manner. For this narrative, Spenser turns back to representations of the sustaining legend of Book I: the St George story of the *Legenda aurea* by Voragine, *The Life of St George* by Barclay, and the popular English and religious mythology. Within the old tale are echoes of the angel Michael in Revelation, who 'toke the dragon that olde serpent, which is the devil, and Satan, and he bounde him a thousand yeres' (20.2), and of Christ who 'the great Dragon strongly doth represse' (*Heavenly Beautie* 157). As a type of Christ in the Harrowing of Hell (for the Dragon is 'Bred in the loathly lakes of *Tartary*' at vii 44 and 'hell-bred' at xi 40), Redcrosse has been seen to reenact one of the fundamental patterns of the Christian faith (Kaske 1969). Indeed, the Dragon's mouth, an 'infernall fournace ... gaping wide' (xi 44, 53) fits the common iconography of hell-mouth and suggests that the knight harrows hell to defeat death. In I xi, the visual imagery recalls the many medieval and Renaissance illustrations of dragons and dragon fights. Yet, in *The Faerie Queene* there is a difference. Whereas in medieval art dragons tend to be small or middle-sized and easily speared, Redcrosse's enemy is staggeringly immense. There is also nothing in secular literature like Spenser's vast dragon ('that like was never' known [xi 26]) in the imaginative literature available to him, except the huge but comparatively lesser serpent fought by Ovid's Cadmus (*Metamorphoses* 3.31). The great dragon of Revelation, with its imaginative potential realized and much developed, is related to the popular, small, humorous, and homely St George dragon of pictures and dramatic festivals.

BELINDA HUMFREY

drama, medieval The Latin liturgical or church music-drama appeared as early as the tenth century and continued to be performed, mainly in cathedrals and monastic churches, until the Reformation, when it was suppressed. Though the twelfth century seems to have been the high point in the development of these Latin plays, their history can no longer be seen in terms of simple evolution from simple to more complex forms, nor did they demonstrably form the basis for subsequent vernacular religious drama, which was spoken rather than sung though it was often interspersed with vocal and instrumental music.

The English vernacular religious drama may be divided into at least three genres: the biblical drama, often but not always presented in cycles, based on history, legend, and religious myths; the saint or miracle play, of which only two English examples, the Digby *Mary Magdalene* and *Conversion of St Paul*, are extant; and the morality play, such as *The Castle of Perseverance* and *Everyman*.

Production of plays, most often sponsored by civic authorities or civic guilds, utilized either pageant wagon or place-and-scaffold staging. The evidence of dramatic records suggests that wagon staging, favored for the cycle drama in cities such as York and Chester, probably was related to the use of *tableaux vivants* in civil and religious processions and to pageantry generally. Although the religious plays were suppressed under Queen Elizabeth (eg, the last performance of the Coventry cycle was in 1579), the traditions of pageantry continued through Spenser's lifetime. Such a common stage device as the hell-mouth (noted in a York inventory as early as 1433, but a common stage property as late as Marlowe's *Doctor Faustus*) seems echoed in Spenser's comparison of the mouth of the dragon to 'the griesly mouth of hell' (*FQ* I xi 12). More important, however, Spenser, like the anonymous medieval dramatists who prepared texts for the civic cycle plays which for subject matter took in all of Christian history from Creation to Doom, tended to think in terms of visual units arranged around an iconographic center – units that are described in *Ruines of Time* 489–90 as 'strange sights ... Like tragicke Pageants seeming to appeare.'

The morality play, like much civic pageantry, introduced allegorical actions with a particular liveliness and presumably energetic acting style. Spenser's practice, especially in *The Faerie Queene*, likewise involves sharply visualized allegorical scenes that are appropriately comparable to scenes in allegorical drama, which commonly presented personifications of virtues and vices in conflict (see *psychomachia). Many of his characters (eg, the seven deadly sins in *FQ* I iv or Mammon in II vii) are remarkably similar to characters in the morality plays (eg, the Deadly Sins in *The Castle of Perseverance* or Goods in *Everyman*). Although the plays participated in a broader literary and visual tradition which was very strong in England and Europe, it is clear that they established a kind of theater that would have been particularly congenial to Spenser.

The saint play was essentially a devotional genre that also, because of its frequent termination in a scene of martyrdom, influenced the form of the Elizabethan tragedy which only fully emerged during Spenser's lifetime and to which he alludes in a passing reference to Ease appearing 'as on the ready flore / Of some Theatre ... Yclad in costly garments, fit for tragicke Stage' (*FQ* III xii 3). Of the saints dramatized on the medieval stage, one of the more popular was St George (see *Var* 1:389–90). Plays or 'ridings' of St George were presented in both the large cities (eg, London) and smaller towns (eg, Bassingbourne in Cambridgeshire), most commonly on his feast day, 23 April, an appropriate time also for a spring celebration because of its proximity to May Day.

With the St George plays and pageants, the line between religious drama and folk expression must have been blurred from an early date, as the identification of the princess as 'the May' in the York presentation will indicate (cf Una being crowned with 'a girland greene ... twixt earnest and twixt game' *FQ* I xii 8). There were also the so-called mummers' plays, which, though no texts are extant earlier than the eighteenth century, frequently include a St George figure as part of a combat routine. Folk drama, known to have existed from Anglo-Saxon times, is part of the context of game and play of the medieval vernacular stage in England. Redcrosse may owe something to the hero of the early folk play on his entry (I iv 13; see Preston 1969), and Duessa may be modeled on the female – ugly but seen by the other actors as beautiful – who is known in subsequent folk drama as the 'Molly.' Such popular drama may also lie behind Britomart's lament when she discovers Artegall in Radigund's dungeon dressed as Maid Marian in woman's clothes – 'What May-game hath misfortune made of you?' (V vii 40) – and the description of June 'arrayd / All in greene leaves, as he a Player were' (VII vii 35).

While Spenser's debt to the medieval drama perhaps cannot be gauged with precision, there is no doubt that his handling of narrative structure, character, and allegory owes much to the traditions shared by the various dramatic genres of the Middle Ages.

CLIFFORD DAVIDSON

Richard Axton 1974 *European Drama of the Early Middle Ages* (London); Chambers 1903; Clifford Davidson, C.J. Gianakaris, and John H. Stroupe, eds 1982 *The Drama of the Middle Ages* (New York); Davidson ed 1986 *The Saint Play in Medieval Europe* (Kalamazoo); Alexandra F. Johnston and Margaret Rogerson, eds 1979 *York* (Records of Early English Drama) 2 vols (Toronto); Thomas Pettitt 1985 'Approaches to Medieval Folk Drama' *EDAM Newsletter* 7:23–7; Michael J. Preston 1969–70 'The Folk Play: An Influence on the "Faerie Queene"' *AN&Q* 8:38–9; William Tydeman 1978 *The Theatre in the Middle Ages* (Cambridge).

Drayton, Michael (1563–1631) The earliest important Spenserian poet, Drayton was born in Warwickshire, his childhood and youth being spent there as page to Sir Henry Goodere the elder, a country gentleman who provided him with a tutor. Although he acquired wide learning, he did not attend university. During a long career, he supported himself by writing and patronage, attempting almost every kind of poetry in vogue. Some works by this popular poet appeared in a dozen or more editions during his lifetime. He was buried near Spenser in Westminster Abbey.

Drayton was acutely aware that he was following Spenser in writing pastoral, heroic, and satiric poetry: 'Deare *Collin*, let my Muse excused be, / Which rudely thus presumes to sing by thee, / Although her straines be harsh untun'd and ill, / Nor can attayne to thy divinest skill' (*Endimion and Phoebe* 993–6). In *Colin Clout*, Spenser praises 'A gentler shepheard' named Aetion, 'Whose *Muse* full of high thoughts invention, / Doth like himselfe Heroically sound' (444–7). Of the writers proposed as Aetion, Drayton seems the most likely (*Var* 7:472–3). His pastoral name, Rowland, has an heroic sound; and 'high thoughts' may refer to the mystical passages of *Endimion and Phoebe*, published in 1595.

Drayton gained notice as Spenser's disciple with *Idea: The Shepheards Garland* (1593), dedicated to Robert Dudley, only son of Spenser's former patron, the Earl of Leicester. As in *The Shepheardes Calender*, meter and rhyme vary widely. The nine eclogues begin and end with a complaint by Rowland, imitating the first and last eclogues of the *Calender*. The second includes a debate between a young and an old shepherd (resembling *Februarie*, with a nod to its fable of the Oak and the Briar, and *March*); youth and age are again treated in the seventh eclogue. The third poem is a dialogue framing a lyric in praise of 'Beta' (Elizabeth). Eclogues 4 and 5 recall the defense of poetry in *October*, and 5 is an elegy for Sidney that shows careful study of *November* and its source in Marot. The true poet is a 'Spel-charming Prophet, sooth-divining seer' (62); false poets deal in flattery, emotionalism, and slander. Only the sixth and eighth poems are thematically independent of the *Calender*. As in Spenser, Latin mottos follow most of the eclogues.

Drayton's diction closely follows Spenser's. Besides dozens of archaisms, there are such Chaucerianisms as the participial *y-* prefix and the present-plural ending *-en*. Only Peele's *Eglogue Gratulatorie* (1589) had imitated this feature of Spenser's pastoral style before Drayton. The third eclogue and Spenser's *Aprill* nicely exemplify Drayton's imitativeness. Drayton's poem, briefer and simpler, compresses Spenser's comparison of Elizabeth with the sun and moon (*Apr* 64–81) into one perfunctory stanza lacking the rich implications of the original. The two flower catalogues are verbally similar, and Drayton even uses the same flowers as rhyme words. Both Elisa and Beta are associated with the peaceful symbolism of the olive, attended by nymphs, and crowned with a 'coronall.' In Drayton's poem, however, there is nothing like the thematic density of the mysteries of Pan, Syrinx, and Latona. Instead, the actualities of Queen and nation are celebrated: the birds and flowers are English, and Beta is specifically Queen of the Thames. Typically, Drayton is the realist – less a *vates* than a would-be laureate.

The young pastoralist follows Spenser in hoping to move beyond pastoral to 'sing in honor of some worthies deede' (Eclogue 5.165). While experimenting with other poetic models (Sidney for his *Idea* sonnets, Horace and Ronsard for his odes), he was clearly in awe of the mature Spenser of *The Faerie Queene*. The epyllion *Endimion and Phoebe* blends Spenserian sensuousness with Chapman-like metaphysics. In language that evokes Spenser but avoids the many specific borrowings of the pastorals, the poem tells the fable of the love of the moon goddess for the chaste shepherd. The earthly paradise of Latmus discloses birds 'Tuning theyr trebbles to the waters fall' while 'gentle *Zephyre* murmuring among, / Kept tyme, and bare the burthen to the song' (57–60). These lines may recall *FQ* II xii 71, but keeping time with the fall of water is a familiar Spenserian conceit (cf *Apr* 36, *June* 8, *Bellay* 10, *FQ* VI x 7). Hints of the Bower of Bliss and the Garden of Adonis run throughout the topography of Latmus. The description of Phoebe and her nymphs also recalls *The Faerie Queene*, especially Belphoebe (compare Spenser's 'In gilden buskins of costly Cordwaine,' II iii 27, with Drayton's 'In branched Buskins of fine Cordiwin' 783). The inset myth of the nymph and her lover changed into flower and fountain (583–610) is substantially original, but it may derive from similar digressions in Spenser's narrative (*FQ* I vii 5, II ii 7–9). Phoebe's transporting of the slumbering Endimion may be modeled on Cymoent's of Marinell (*FQ* III iv 31–42). As Drayton's nearest approach to allegorical narrative, this poem, like *Muiopotmos*, renders a moral Platonic fable in an Ovidian style, sacrificing narrative detail to richly symbolic description.

In his third eclogue, Drayton complains that Spenser has laid 'his pipes to gage, / And is to fayrie gone a Pilgrimage: / the more our mone' (14–16), perhaps implying regret over Spenser's residence in Ireland. During the last Elizabethan decade, Drayton chiefly wrote historical poetry, starting with verse 'legends' in the vein of *The Mirror for Magistrates*. Addressing Elizabeth in *Matilda* (1594), he admits that he cannot write of chastity as did Spenser in Britomart because he lacks his art, perhaps referring to Spenser's art of allegory. In the 1619 preface to his revised legends, Drayton writes of Spenser as the first 'who transferred the use of the word, LEGEND, from Prose to Verse [ie, the Legends of *FQ*]: nor that unfortunately; the Argument of his Bookes being of a kind of sacred Nature, as comprehending in them things as well Divine as Humane' (ed 1931–41, 2:382); but his own legends are linked to Spenser's only superficially.

In one sense Drayton did try to incorporate something of the divine into his human poems. The mythology of sacred love underlies his highly successful *Englands Heroicall Epistles* (1597–9), twelve pairs of verse epistles between famous lovers in English history, from Henry II and his mistress Rosamond to Lady Jane Grey and Guildford Dudley (brother of Spenser's patron, executed for trying to overthrow Mary Tudor). More important than the occasional echo (such as Richard II's allusion to Spenser's Despair, 59–60) is Spenser's idea that love effects 'The fatall purpose of divine foresight ... in destined descents' (*FQ* III iii 2). The poems are partly meant to show providence fulfilling England's destiny through heroic love. Just as the marriage of Britomart and Artegall will culminate in the reign of the 'royall virgin' (*FQ* III iii 49), the sequence of lovers leading up to Grey and Dudley paves the way for a queen who 'shall extirpe the Pow'r of *Rome*' (181) and bring England to greatness. A version of the Tudor myth recalling Merlin's prophecy in *FQ* III iii appears in Owen Tudor's marriage proposal to Henry V's widow, Katherine.

Another historical poem shows Drayton more technically Spenserian in dealing with lovers. His *Mortimeriados* (1596), on the civil wars of Edward II (recast as *The Barons Warres* in 1603), portrays the adulterous love of Queen Isabel and Roger Mortimer in a tower bedroom decorated with mythological paintings (2311–94, 2521–41). The pictures comment on the action much as do the tapestries of Castle Joyous or Busirane's house (*FQ* III i 34–8, xi 29–46) or, following the comparison to '*Arachnes* web,' the tapestries in *Muiopotmos* (273–336). They show the destruction caused by a god's erotic passion (Phoebus and Hyacinthus, Jove and Io, Mercury and Hebe), foretelling the results of Mortimer's adultery with the Queen. Phaeton (as in *FQ* I iv 9) hints at the social disorder resulting from ungoverned passion, also a Spenserian theme (cf III xi 35, 46). The moral tone of Isabel's bedroom also owes something to the Bower of Bliss (compare Drayton's 'The naked Nymphes, some up, some downe discending' with the naked damsels in *FQ* II xii 66). Unlike the early pastorals, however, this episode shows Drayton less dependent on Spenser's phrasing than on a wide set of images associated with him, incorporating Ovidian myth, delight in artifice, playful irony, and reflective scene painting.

The episode in *The Faerie Queene* that Drayton most often imitates is the marriage of the rivers (IV xi). *The Tragicall Legend of Robert, Duke of Normandy* (entered for publication in November 1596, ten months after *FQ* IV-VI) opens with a personification of Isis, Thames, and Medway. (This part of *Robert* also owes much to *Time* and *Prothalamion*.) The passage is a foretaste of the extensive use of the river-marriage conceit throughout the huge *Poly-Olbion* (1612–22), a county-by-county description in alexandrine couplets of the topography and history of England and Wales. About 1630, perhaps without Drayton's knowledge, the poem was issued entitled *The Faerie Land*. In addition to personified rivers and frequent locality myths of nymphs and satyrs, as in Spenser's Faunus and Molanna episode in *FQ* VII vi, there are the marriage of Tame and Isis (Song 15, part of which is called a 'Prothalamion'), a specific allusion to Spenser's river marriage (Song 18.108) and the Spenserian names of the sea nymphs (Song 20).

In the seventeenth century, this long-lived poet abandoned some of his Spenserian habits. (Freeman 1983 discusses the forgeries long thought to be Drayton's notes on Spenser.) The 1606 *Pastorals* were heavily revised to exclude the archaic diction of 1593, though the hymn to love ending the seventh eclogue (new in 1606) echoes *Colin Clout* and *Fowre Hymnes* in describing the 'holy and resistlesse fire' that holds in harmony the chain of nature (167). *Endimion and Phoebe* was also revised as the shorter, rather clumsy, Jacobean satire 'The Man in the Moone' (1606), then again, in considerably different form, as the delicate Caroline 'Quest of Cynthia' (1627). Symptomatic of the change is the fairy poetry of 'Nimphidia' (1627) and the eighth pastoral of *The Muses Elizium* (1630), where we see not the human-sized fairies, the *longaevi* (long-lived ones) of Spenser and the Middle Ages, but the miniature folk of Herrick and after. The 1619 preface to the pastorals announces that 'SPENSER is the prime *Pastoralist* of *England*,' who 'had done enough for the immortalitie of his Name, had he only given us his *Shepheards Kalender*, a Master-piece if any'; and the delightful 'Shepheards Sirena'

(1627) sings of 'COLLIN on his *Shalme* so cleare, / Many a high-pitcht Note that had, / And could make the Ecchos nere / Shout as they were wexen mad' (145–8). Yet Drayton had moved with the taste of Stuart England to the familiar epistle, love elegy, lyric dialogue, biblical narrative, and even (though he professed to abhor it) the metaphysical poem.

Drayton always shared Spenser's love of British antiquity. In *Mortimeriados* (1933–2009) the imprisoned Edward II studies his past in an English chronicle as Arthur had (*FQ* II x). Song 16 of *Poly-Olbion* personifies Verulam in an extended lament for lost glories, full of echoes of *Ruines of Time*. The poem often recalls the myth of Arlo Hill in lamenting natural beauty now devastated by the sins of man. The two poets also reflect the same aversion to the fashions of the court, evident in Drayton's 'Moone-Calfe' (1627), containing a lively set of satiric fables told by old women, recalling *Mother Hubberds Tale* (a witch and an ape replace Spenser's fox and ape at 957–1036). Spenser's didacticism and his 'high' art are uppermost in the elderly Drayton's tribute during the roll call of poets in the 'elegy' to Henry Reynolds (1627, 79–84):

Grave morall *Spencer* after these came on
Then whom I am perswaded there was none
Since the blind *Bard* his *Iliads* up did make,
Fitter a taske like that to undertake,
To set downe boldly, bravely to invent,
In all high knowledge, surely excellent.

The brief history of English poetry in this elegy reminds us that both poets shared an interest in defending native poets (cf Spenser's tribute to Chaucer, *FQ* IV ii 32). Spenser's image of defiling the sacred springs and trampling the Muses' garden (*Teares* 271–6) appears often in Drayton (*Pastorals*, 'Shepheards Sirena,' *Elegies*). The frequent coupling of Drayton's name with Spenser's (by Meres, Camden, Wither, and others; see *Sp All*) may have convinced him that he had inherited the older poet's mantle as custodian of Helicon.

Drayton manages to follow Spenser without imitating him too closely. He shared Spenser's belief in the poet as prophet and in writing the long poem demanded by that role, though he had less attention from the sovereign than did Spenser and seems to have despised James I. Unlike Spenser, though, he wrote many occasional poems and lyrics that suggest an interest in craft apart from any large design. Although he believed, like other Spenserians, in what he calls the 'fine madnes' of poetic inspiration ('To Henry Reynolds' 109), his narrative work is more historical than mythic, inclining toward statement not suggestion. His style manages to avoid the extremes of metaphysical plainness and pseudo-Spenserian decoration, the pitfalls of many minor poets in the early seventeenth century. Often in *Poly-Olbion* (for example, in the Cotswold sheep-shearing feast of Song 14), we are reminded that Drayton was first and last a pastoralist – a role temperamentally suited to a man who hated London and the court, who spent as much time as possible in the rural England from which he came. Along with his patriotism, this inclination toward pastoral identifies the essence of Drayton's Spenserianism. RICHARD F. HARDIN

Drayton ed 1931–41; Dorangeon 1974; Arthur Freeman 1983 review of Dewey Ganzel 1982 *Fortune and Men's Eyes: The Career of John Payne Collier* (Oxford), *TLS* (22 Apr):393; Grundy 1969; Richard F. Hardin 1973 *Michael Drayton and the Passing of Elizabethan England* (Lawrence, Kans); Bernard H. Newdigate 1941 *Michael Drayton and His Circle* corr ed 1961 (Oxford).

---

dreams While dreams and dream lore pervade Spenser's poetry, his chief work on this subject, itself titled *Dreames*, is counted by E.K. among his 'divers other excellent works ... which slepe in silence' (*SC* Epistle). Spenser's friend Harvey praised *Dreames*, implicitly for its kinship with the Revelation of St John which contained the 'jollyest conceited *Dreames* or *Extasies*, that ever were devised' and explicitly for its savor of 'extraordinarie veine and invention' equal to that of the 'most delicate, and fine conceited Grecians and Italians' (*Three Letters* 3). Scholars still debate whether *Dreames*, *My Slomber*, and *A Senights Slumber* (perhaps alternate titles for the same work) ever existed, were completed and then lost, or were subsumed by Spenser into other poems which, on the basis of dates of composition and presumed similarity of content, have been variously identified as *Ruines of Time*, the visions poems in *Complaints* (see **Complaints: Visions*), and *The Faerie Queene*.

Just as the titles of the three 'lost works' are divided between two processes, dreaming and sleeping (slumber), so the topic of dreams in Spenser needs to be similarly divided and to be distinguished from vision. Blurring distinctions among these phenomena would suggest a fundamental contiguity which is not sustained in Spenser's poetry. In Old English, one word stands for both dream and sleep; in Middle English, two different words are used interchangeably. By the sixteenth century, however, *dreme* and *dremen* in the modern sense had supplanted all other terms and were used, as in Spenser, with a meaning exclusive of sleep and with connotations of deception and illusion.

Spenser often associates dreams with endangerment, using such epithets as diverse, deadly, fearful, troubling, idle, and, most important, false and feigning. In *Amoretti* 77, the dream's potentially misleading ambiguity of representation is contrasted with the certain clarity of waking perception: 'Was it a dreame, or did I see it playne?' Even in the lovely classical metaphor for dawn's arrival in *Epithalamion*, the dream's potential for clouding what should be clear is unequivocally expressed: 'My love is now awake out of her dreame, / And her fayre eyes like stars that dimmed were / With darksome cloud, now shew theyr goodly beams' (92–4). The poem's final stanzas comprise a litany of the horrors of night and the invocations necessary to ward off all the possible disruptions of sleep.

Dream in *The Faerie Queene*, like sleep, appears in a context of paradoxical ambiguity, with both malevolent and benign aspects, and in an atmosphere which privileges movement across the states of waking, sleeping, and dreaming over the nature of those states. In this way, the boundaries between all states and their modes of experiencing, perceiving, and reporting are dissolved (Anderson 1976:26–40), and, along with them, the boundaries between truth and falsehood, reality and illusion, memory and prophecy, outer world and inner world. Thus, in contrast to many of his predecessors, contemporaries, and successors who attempt to resolve, ignore, or circumvent the inherent ambivalence in dreams, Spenser chooses to heighten their contrariety. The central pattern of action in *The Faerie Queene* is occasioned by its second episode, a false dream brought to the Red Cross Knight by Archimago (I i 46–55). Two other dreams, Arthur's of the Fairy Queen (I ix 13–14) and Britomart's in Isis Church (V vii 12–16), are crucial narrative, dramatic, thematic, and allegorical moments. These and other dream episodes also contribute significantly to the mode of liminality, of transitionality, which is one of the poem's most prominent features.

Spenser could have read about dreams in Renaissance treatises such as Girolamo Cardano's *Somniorum synesiorum* (1562), but only Macrobius appears in his works: E.K. mentions him in his General Argument to *The Shepheardes Calender* and in the March gloss. Macrobius was the leading authority on dreams in the Middle Ages, through his widely known *Commentary on the Dream of Scipio*; his influence on Chaucer is extensively documented. Following Artemidorus' *Oneirocritica* (a 2nd-c AD Greek handbook on dream interpretation which influenced both Freud and Jung), Macrobius identified two main types of dreams (ed 1952:87–92): the enigmatic, which includes the prophetic and oracular, having implications for the future and hence value, and the nightmare-apparition type resulting from conditions in the dreamer's life (day residue): 'The things that day most minds, at night doe most appeare' (IV v 43). The nightmare apparitions, Macrobius claims, are not worth interpreting, since they have no significance, importance, or symbolic meaning. Yet it is this type of dream, with erotic components, which is featured in critical moments in *The Faerie Queene*: not only the three central episodes but also Britomart's dreams after seeing the image of Artegall in Venus' mirror (III i 8, ii 28–9) and Scudamour's dream in the house of Care of betrayal by Amoret (IV v 43).

Arthur's dream and Britomart's crocodile dream belong also to Macrobius' category of the prophetic dream – but only the latter is given oracular and enigmatic dimensions, characterized by appearance of a revered figure with a message for the future and concealment of the content through an ambiguity that requires interpretation. Even here Spenser stops short of giving her a 'vision,' or full oracular dream in which the revered figure reveals the future and recommends a course of action to the dreamer. These figures and functions Spenser places outside her dreams, when first Merlin and then the Priest of Isis are called upon to interpret her experience.

The central dream episodes in *The Faerie Queene* also occur within an epic tradition begun as early as the Babylonian epic *Gilgamesh* (c 3000 BC) and continuing through the major and minor Greek and Latin epics, Ariosto's *Orlando furioso*, Tasso's *Gerusalemme liberata*, and Camoens' *Lusiads*. The tradition may be said to culminate in Eve's diabolical dream in *Paradise Lost* 4.799–803, 5.26–94, although the conventions are also found in seventeenth-century Christian 'epics' by Cowley, Crashaw, and the Fletchers, as well as in *Paradise Regained* (2.260–83, 4.407–9, 4.422–31).

Further precedents for dreams in poetic narratives are provided by Dante's *Divine Comedy* and by medieval dream-vision poems, including the Old English 'Dream of the Rood,' the *Romance of the Rose*, *Pearl*, Langland's *Piers Plowman*, and poems by Chaucer, Froissart, and Machaut (see **Hypnerotomachia Poliphili*). The dream-vision is framed by a narrator falling asleep and dreaming, a frame which some scholars have seen as implicit in the initial, initiatory dream of Redcrosse.

In *The Faerie Queene*, Spenser retains unchanged many conventions of dream lore. That the gates of ivory and horn distinguish respectively between true and false dreams is mentioned at I i 40, echoing *Aeneid* 6.893–8. Use of the dream in simile or metaphor to capture analogically certain human experiences occurs notably in the epic simile of Britomart compared to a child with bad dreams at v vi 14, but a more typical use occurs at I xi 50: 'But lay as in a dreame of deepe delight.' Reference to physiological etiologies for sleep and dreaming is made: 'As one then in a dreame, whose dryer braine / Is tost with troubled sights and fancies weake' (i 42). The token left behind by a dream figure to prove the 'reality' of the remembered dream (and in ancient theory authenticate its visionary status) is found in the pressed grass beside Arthur where the Fairy Queen has been (ix 15). Britomart enacts an ancient practice called incubation, where sleeping in a sanctuary elicits a prophetic dream, especially when accompanied by appropriate rituals such as prayer (v vii 12).

But even when dream is used in simile or allusion, Spenser's chief interest is in the passage into sleep, or swoon – often the result of exhaustion from quest or combat – and the passage back to wakefulness – usually abrupt and harsh, caused by bad dreams, external disturbances, or a resurgence of combative energy. Some characters who experience this process are Amavia, Pyrochles, Cymochles, Satyrane, Hellenore, Blandamour and Paridell, Triamond, Calidore, and Radigund.

Despite Spenser's evident fascination with dreams, sleep as word and as experience occurs in his poetry far more often. For him, sleep paradoxically offers respite from physical and mental stress, while at the same time it may be the condition in which stress-creating disturbance is most profoundly felt – the kind of contradiction Shakespeare represents in *Macbeth*. Sleep is not only care-less, delightful, gentle, kindly, silver, sound, sweet, and timely; it is also deadly, dull, heavy, slothful. It is a medium in which one is most often said to be drowned. When invoking Christian doctrine or classical myth (see *Morpheus, *Night), Spenser emphasizes the kinship of Sleep and Death (II vii 25), the sleep of lovers disturbed by 'deluding dreames [and] dreadful sights' (*Epith* 338), the equation of sleep with the sin of sloth, the imprisoning effects of a sleep like Endymion's (*SC, Julye* 64 gloss), and, finally and most alarming, the sleeper's relaxation of moral vigilance and consequent susceptibility to evil influences.

Alongside these malevolent aspects of sleep, however, Spenser invokes many Christian and classical precedents for its benign influence, especially its restorative power and rest from care. Versions of the proverb 'Sleep takes away all cares and woes' appear in *FQ* II v 30 and *Daphnaïda* 470–4, echoing Homer, Euripides, Ovid, and other ancient poets (C.G. Smith 1970:241). It is one of the two pillars – food being the other – that 'upbeare ... this fraile life of man' (II vii 65). In *The Faerie Queene*, Spenser depicts the passage between sleep and wakefulness more often than the state of sleep itself, just as he does when treating dreams.

Spenser uses *vision* only occasionally, with varying connotations, and often accompanied by such adjectives as strange, wondrous, celestial, and dreadful. In the poem's most visionary episode (v vii 1–24), the narrator uses only *vision* to describe Britomart's experience. The priest, however, even while sanctioning the experience as having originated with 'th'immortall Gods,' uses only *dream*. And his interpretation, like Adam's of Eve's dream in *Paradise Lost*, is quite inadequate to the event. Thus Spenser appears to invoke the central premise of pagan and Christian oneiric tradition – dreams come from the gods and their principal function is divination – while actually transforming this tradition by moving the expected valorizing of Britomart's *vision* from the spiritual realm and the voice of the priest to the realm of the imaginal and the voice of the narrator. Sometimes *vision* is used pejoratively, as in II ix 51, where it is lumped with all the other deceitful contents of Alma's chamber: 'idle thoughts and fantasies, / Devices, dreames, opinions unsound, / Shewes, visions, sooth-sayes, and prophesies; / And all that fained is, as leasings, tales, and lies.'

All of the dream and sleep episodes in Spenser are congruent in their parts with traditions of literature, oneirology, theology, physiology, and philosophy current in sixteenth-century England. Spenser's emphasis is singular, however: within his inclusive, almost encyclopedic representation of dream lore, he exaggerates, rather than trying to reconcile, the contradictions and profound ambivalence which pervade traditional views. The same few questions haunt him that haunt all seekers after knowledge about dreams: Are they divine or demonic? mental or physical? magic or madness? sexual or spiritual? literal or symbolic? of past, present, or future? Spenser both underscores the ambiguity of traditional answers to these questions and undermines the process of questioning itself by transforming all phenomena in his poetry, including language itself, into processes known usually to us only as mentation during sleep. He does this not by presenting his poem in the frame of a dream, nor by excluding conventional 'dream' episodes. Instead he uses dream convention to foster the dissolution of levels, phases, and stages of referentiality, to demonstrate and insist on the indeterminacy and Protean flux of all 'reality.' Thus his poetry, especially *The Faerie Queene*, comes to us not as a dream, but as a quality of experience which many have called dreamlike. No reader has described this quality so effectively as Coleridge: 'You will take especial note of the marvelous independence and true imaginative absence of all particular space or time in the Faery Queene. It is in the domains neither of history or geography; it is ignorant of all artificial boundary, all material obstacles; it is truly in land of Faery, that is, of mental space. The poet has placed you in a dream, a charmed sleep' (ed 1936:36).

CAROL SCHREIER RUPPRECHT

Anderson 1969; Artemidorus 1975 *The Interpretation of Dreams* tr Ralph J. White (Park Ridge, NJ); Patricia J. Boehne 1975 *Dream and Fantasy in 14th and 15th Century Catalan Prose* (Barcelona); Markus Fierz 1983 *Girolamo Cardano, 1501–1576* tr Helga Niman (Boston); Constance B. Hieatt 1967 *The Realism of Dream Visions: The Poetic Exploitation of the Dream-Experience in Chaucer and His Contemporaries* (The Hague); Thomas Hill 1576 *The Moste Pleasaunte Arte of the Interpretacion of Dreames* (London); Hough 1962; William B. Hunter, Jr 1946; Hunter 1948 'Prophetic Dreams and Visions in *Paradise Lost*' *MLQ* 9:277–85; Lewis 1964; Thomas Nashe *Terrors of the Night, or A Discourse of Apparitions* (1594), in ed 1904–10, 1:337–86; Foster Provost 1975 'Treatments of Theme and Allegory in Twentieth-Century Criticism of *The Faerie Queene*' in Frushell and Vondersmith 1975:1–40, 217–22; Carol Schreier Rupprecht 1986 'Dreams and Literature: A Reader's Guide' in *Sleep and Dreams: A Sourcebook* ed Jayne Gackenbach, pp 359–77 (New York); A.C. Spearing 1976 *Medieval Dream-Poetry* (Cambridge); Thorndike 1923–58; Manfred Weidhorn 1965 'Dreams and Guilt' *HTR* 58:69–90; Weidhorn 1967a 'The Anxiety

Dream in Literature from Homer to Milton' *SP* 64:65–82; Weidhorn 1967b 'Eve's Dream and the Literary Tradition' *TSL* 12:39–50; Weidhorn 1970 *Dreams in Seventeenth-Century English Literature* (The Hague); B.A. Windeatt, tr and ed 1982 *Chaucer's Dream Poetry: Sources and Analogues* (Cambridge).

Drummond, William, of Hawthornden (1585–1649) The most talented Scottish poet of the early seventeenth century, Drummond chose to remain on his estate near Edinburgh when so many other men of letters followed James VI south to the court in London. The isolation he felt is often expressed in his letters. Scottish writers, after a long period of distancing themselves from English traditions, were now anxious to reverse the trend. As Ben Jonson noted, Drummond belonged to the Spenserian group which included Drayton, Fairfax, and Giles and Phineas Fletcher; and for that reason Jonson judged his work 'smelled too much of the schooles' (Jonson ed 1925–52, 1:135), forgetting that what seemed outdated in England was really a new vogue in Scotland.

Spenser's influence on Drummond is expressed in many ways. His library contained copies of *Amoretti*, *Fowre Hymnes*, *The Shepheardes Calender*, and *The Faerie Queene*. A voracious reader, he read *The Faerie Queene* in 1610 after perusing *Orlando furioso*, *Gerusalemme liberata*, and *La Franciade*. There is no doubt that he was highly impressed, and his enthusiasm expresses itself not only in direct echoes (compare *Teares, on the Death of Moeliades* 130ff with *FQ* I i 8–9) but also in the annotations he made to his own copy. His marginalia, which are confined to VI ix 7–xii 18 and VII vii 28–53, note sources for certain of Spenser's imitations, chiefly in Tasso. For instance, where Meliboe describes his pastoral contentment (VI ix 20), Drummond writes 'all this is Tor. Tassos can. 7.1 Gier.' Next to the passage of Pastorella's recognition through her 'rosie marke' (VI xii 15), Drummond notes 'See Tassos Rinaldo ca. II St. 90 of Florindo'; this is a likely source (though not the only one brought forward by subsequent scholarship). In addition to his notes on imitation, Drummond also has a comment on scansion and many marginal indicators showing his attention to the general structure of Spenser's allegory (see Fowler and Leslie 1981).

Clearly, Drummond considered Spenser to be one of his mentors. He follows him in rich, sensuous description, in his love of pastoral settings, and in his eulogies and satires. In his many borrowings from English lyrical verse, however, he usually calls upon Sidney and Daniel in preference to Spenser. The reason for this is Drummond's surprising reaction to *Amoretti*. While praising the Englishman's art as a love poet, he adds, 'As to ... his *Amorelli* [*sic*], I am not of their Opinion, who think them his; for they are so childish, that it were not well to give them so honourable a Father' (*Sp All* p 154).

R.D.S. JACK

William Drummond of Hawthornden 1711 *Works* (Edinburgh) pp 226–7; Drummond 1913 *Poetical Works* ed L.E. Kastner, 2 vols (Manchester); Fowler and Leslie 1981.

Dryden, John (1631–1700) Two of Dryden's personal copies of Spenser survive, and one indicates the range of his reading, but not Spenser's substantial influence on his career and works. Although his copy of the 1611 folio, preserved in Pope's library, is unannotated, a 1679 edition later owned by his publisher, Jacob Tonson, and now at Trinity College, Cambridge, bears annotations almost throughout the Spenser canon. Investigation of the Trinity copy shows most annotations to be minor textual corrections and emendations (see also Osborn 1940:241–5). Following *FQ* VII vii 12, however, Dryden has written 'Ground work for a song on St Cecilias Day,' which suggests that Spenser's 'celestiall song, and Musicks wondrous might' led to similar emphasis in the 1687 St Cecilia ode.

This instance is representative of Dryden's use of Spenser for details, of which there are many from early to late career: echoes of *Hymne of Heavenly Beautie* 53 and *FQ* IV xi 13 in *Heroique Stanzas* 55–6 and 69–70, a borrowing from *FQ* IV x 46 in the Lucretius translation (1.18–19) in *Sylvae*, and a reference to *Mother Hubberds Tale* in *The Hind and the Panther* 3.1–15. 'Much of Dryden's alluvial and marine detail' in *Albion and Albanius* can be found in *FQ* IV xi (see Miner in Dryden ed 1956–, 15:327); and Dryden's catalogue of trees in *Palamon and Arcite* 3.959–65 follows both the Chaucerian original and *FQ* I i 8–9. The content of these allusions is most often pictorial: Dryden recognizes Spenser both as a pictorialist after his own poetic temperament and as an obvious master of ecphrasis. He also recognizes in him the justification for his own technical innovations, as when he defends his fondness for the alexandrine (preface to *Aeneis*) and his revival of obsolete words (*Discourse concerning Satire*). Indeed, most of the 22 references to Spenser in his critical prose deal with stylistic and technical issues such as diction and versification. In his judgment, 'the *Shepherd's Calendar* of Spenser is not to be matched in any modern language' (ed 1962, 2:220). Spenser is variously named 'inimitable,' the author of 'that immortal poem called the *Fairy Queen*,' and, with Homer, Virgil, and Horace, 'the top ... of all poetry' and one of his 'masters' (1:277; 2:82, 150, 237).

Dryden's sustained account of Spenser in the *Discourse concerning Satire* (1693) summarizes his technical concerns. Spenser is praised for his genius and learning and the varied harmonies of his verses ('only Virgil ... has surpassed him among the Romans') but censured for avoiding the Aristotelian rule of unity of action, and for his undifferentiated heroes, obsolete diction, and 'ill choice of his stanza' in *The Faerie Queene*. The poem is not 'of a piece ... because the model was not true' (2:83–4). However, the judgment indicated here involves more than technique. Dryden in late career does not willfully misunderstand Spenser's project; rather, he seems to be articulating his indebtedness to, and departure from, a model which has been formative for him but also in part inappropriate to his post-Restoration poetics.

In the preface to *Aeneis* (1697), Dryden again praises Spenser's genius but faults the disunity of action in *The Faerie Queene*, as if the poem were a species of heroic drama. Nevertheless, there is strong evidence that his usual process of borrowing is at work in his plays (Ringler 1963, 1968). There is also evidence that as early as 1672 (*Of Heroic Plays*) he considered *The Faerie Queene* in terms of his own heroic drama. He defends the use of spirits and visionary objects in such plays, citing the 'noble' example of the Bower of Bliss episode that matches English poetry with the 'ghost of Polydorus' in Virgil and the 'Enchanted Wood' in Tasso (1:160–1). This defense was one aspect of his attempt in the 1660s and 1670s to create a species of heroic drama appropriate to his time by accommodating the epic form to the demands of the stage. The mediating factor is romance, which he could have derived from his reading of French prose heroic romances (eg, de Scudéry or La Calprenède) but more likely from *The Faerie Queene*. His mature heroic dramas (*Conquest of Granada*, *All for Love*, *Don Sebastian*) resulting from this mediation have aspects of a romantic structure strongly resembling Spenser's. First, Spenser is the great English predecessor for Dryden's new conjunction of love and pathos. Second, *The Faerie Queene* provides clear models for his lawless and duplicitous female characters: compare Duessa, Acrasia, or Malecasta with Zempoalla (*Indian Queen*), Lyndaraxa (*Conquest of Granada* part 2), or Nourmahal (*Aureng-Zebe*). Third, and most important, Spenser provided Dryden with one method of reconciling the classical and Christian conceptions of the hero, as in his characterization of Almanzor as a heroic and romantic Christian knight (*Conquest of Granada*).

Dryden's greatest 'Spenserian' hero might have been King Arthur, had he written the epic he planned under Charles II. His comments on it in the *Discourse concerning Satire* point to his reading *The Faerie Queene* as more of an historical allegory than we do now ('the Original of every Knight, was then living in the Court of Queen *Elizabeth*' ed 1956–, 4:14): Dryden's characters would represent friends and patrons, the events would predict future ages. Instead he produced an opera, *King Arthur*, originally intended as a political allegory. Much of this is obliterated in the published play (1691), but Spenserian influence remains. Arthur is a British Christian hero functioning in a romance context. Part of Act 4 imitates the Bower of Bliss: Dryden's Arthur encounters a silver stream with two naked 'Syrens' in it to tempt him, but 'Honour calls.' Unlike Spenser's, Dryden's Arthur is conceived as an overtly nationalist, political character; but politics is leavened by Dryden's 'Fairy kind of writing, which depends only upon the Force of Imagination' (dedication to *King Arthur* ed 1932,

6:242). Because it looks back to his reference to 'enthusiastic' poetry and *The Faerie Queene* (*Of Heroic Plays* ed 1962, 1:160), this important remark (and the whole context of spirits, magic, and myth in this play) demonstrates that Dryden found in Spenser not simply a source for allusions but a model for some aspects of his poetics.

One such aspect is allegory. *Absalom and Achitophel* (1681) and *The Hind and the Panther* (1687) show Dryden as the most distinguished poetic allegorist after Spenser. The latter poem, a discontinuous allegory of the Catholic and Anglican faiths in a beast fable, also enunciates a shift for which Spenser's authority may be partly responsible. Citing *Mother Hubberd* as his example (see 3.8), Dryden establishes a general relation between Spenser's allegorical process and his own. After the mid 1680s, he moved away from a concern with religious and historical typologies to write for a mixed audience, with moral parables for the general reader combined with a more complex allegorical rendering of life for those of 'truest understanding' (preface to *Aeneis* ed 1962, 2:244). This is not Spenser's process, but Dryden's continuation of the allegorical method he saw proceeding from him.

This continuation finds its fulfillment in Dryden's most Spenserian work, *Fables Ancient and Modern* (1700). Here, the complex mosaic of heroic narratives allegorically construing a code of morality for the good life is analogous to the scheme of the twelve moral virtues projected for *The Faerie Queene*. Besides much contemporary political and theological matter cloudily (sometimes clearly) enwrapped throughout, he resorts to 'that Fairy kind of writing' in his Spenser-influenced versions of *The Flower and the Leaf* and *The Wife of Bath Her Tale*. In the preface to *Fables*, he places Spenser centrally in the line of English heroic narrative writers which begins with Chaucer, continues with Milton, and leads to Dryden himself (*Sp All* p 311). It is this statement of filiation which most clearly asserts the continuity from Spenser's to Dryden's works.

Reginald Berry

Dryden 1808 *Works* ed Walter Scott, 18 vols (London); Dryden 1931–2 *Dramatic Works* ed Montague Summers, 6 vols (London); Dryden ed 1956–; Dryden ed 1962. James M. Osborn 1940 *John Dryden: Some Biographical Facts and Problems* (New York); Richard N. Ringler 1963 'Two Sources for Dryden's *The Indian Emperour*' *PQ* 42:423–9; Ringler 1968 'Dryden at the House of Busirane' *ES* 49:224–9.

Duessa Deceivers of various kinds operate throughout *The Faerie Queene*; but in the figure of Duessa, Spenser presents the principle of falsehood itself: 'I that do seeme not I, *Duessa* am' (I v 26). Her name (L *duo* two + *esse* to be) means two-ness, doubleness, and duplicity, in contrast to the One Truth of which she is the division and attempted destruction. A line in du Bartas summarizes this Renaissance topic: 'Th'Unitie dwels in God, i'th'Fiend the Twine' (*The Divine Weeks* 2nd Week, Day 4, 2.1327). The exploits of falsehood in *The Faerie Queene* are finely adjusted to the particular theme of the book in which they occur: in I Duessa embodies religious falsehood, in II she acts a part calculated to disturb the equilibrium of the temperate man, in IV she reflects the falsehood of friendship between libertines, in V she propagates political falsehood with the aim of overthrowing a just queen. But her meaning remains constant throughout. Though intrinsically ugly, she regularly appears in 'faire' guises until the facts are discovered, in line with Spenser's sense that untruth often presents itself with an alluring surface.

In the creation of this figure, Spenser combines several literary traditions. The classical enchantress Circe (*Odyssey* 10, *Metamorphoses* 14) stands behind his witch with her cup of poison (I viii 14) and her ability to transform or imprison her lovers, although the Italian Renaissance versions of Circe, especially Alcina in *Orlando furioso*, have a more direct influence. In particular, Ruggiero's encounter with Astolfo transformed into a myrtle tree by Alcina (*OF* 6) is the model for Redcrosse's encounter with Fradubio transformed into a tree by Duessa's sorcery; and the exposure of Alcina's ugliness (*OF* 7) makes important contributions to the scene of Duessa's disrobing at I viii 46–8. The distinctive identity of Duessa, however, derives from Spenser's bold fusion of the sinister enchantress with the biblical Whore of Babylon described in Revelation 17 and 18. This is not to deny that the Whore of Babylon had on previous occasions been labeled a Circe (for instance, by Heinrich Bullinger and William Fulke); but Spenser in Book I develops the casual link into an inseparable fusion. The literary figure and the biblical figure possess characteristics in common which give their poetic fusion a very Spenserian appearance of inevitability: both are witches, both are seductive, both wield poisonous cups, both are shown at last in their essential ugliness. Other sources also contribute to the episode of Duessa's exposure, particularly Isaiah 3.17, 24 and 47.1–3, which speak of the discovery of a scabby head, baldness, and a foul smell (Hankins 1971:101–2). Spenser may also be remembering medieval descriptions of personified falsehood, for example, in Alanus de Insulis' *De planctu Naturae*, where Falsehood includes baldness and old age among her attributes.

The Whore of Babylon is regularly interpreted by sixteenth-century Protestant commentators as an image of the Roman Catholic religion and the Roman Catholic church (eg, John Bale *The Image of Bothe Churches* 1548, Bullinger *A Hundred Sermons upon the Apocalips* Eng tr J. Daus 1561, Fulke *Praelections upon the ... Revelation of S. John* tr Gyffard 1573, van der Noot *Theatre*; see Bennett 1942:111–12). Bale, in particular, emphasizes the contrast between the two women of Revelation, the Woman Clothed with the Sun and the Whore of Babylon. Spenser builds this contrast into Book I, where the activities of Una and Duessa in relation to Redcrosse are sharply juxtaposed and contrasted. The former seeks to teach him true faith (i 19) and assists in his rescue after his captivity; the latter brings him to the house of Pride, subsequently seduces him (vii 4–7), and causes his imprisonment. Duessa's flirtation with the knight, and her seduction of him, are to be understood as the literal adventures of a morally imperfect traveler and as allegorical images of the spiritual enticement of an imperfect believer into false religion.

A narrower interpretation of Duessa as a personification of the Roman Catholic Mass has been proposed (Waters 1970), based on the argument that Spenser was influenced by the satirical personifications of 'Mistress Missa' in a group of tracts of the late 1540s and early 1550s by William Turner, John Bradford, and others. Although when Duessa flourishes her golden cup of poison (viii 14) there may be an allusion to the harmful psychological effects of the Mass, the wide range of her activities suggests that the broader interpretation of her in Book I as the Roman Catholic church is appropriate. The false church lures Fradubio and Redcrosse into spiritual whoredom; her monstrous pride is exposed when she allows Orgoglio to deck her in temporal pomp and the triple crown of the papacy. The seven-headed Beast which she rides was usually interpreted by Protestants as Rome with its seven hills and hence as the power of the Roman Empire which had been transferred to the Pope. The false church's role in the persecution of the godly emerges when Arthur finds the slaughtered innocents in Orgoglio's castle (viii 35). Her disrobing (45–9) reveals her true ugliness, and perhaps also alludes to the stripping of pomp and possessions from the Roman Catholic church in England (see Hume 1984:92–6). These episodes dramatize Spenser's bitter critique of the Roman Catholic church and his hope that in England at least it has been defeated.

In Books II and IV, there are few references to false religion; and with his usual flexibility, Spenser makes plain that what is now at issue is the general principle of falsehood. The consistency of Duessa as an imaginative creation is vigorously maintained throughout *The Faerie Queene* by ensuring that her two dominant personal characteristics are in evidence at all times – untruthfulness and lechery. She adopts misleading roles with great facility: in Book I the role of Fidessa, whose very name (L *fides* faith + *esse*) is an imposture, in II i the role of a chaste damsel allegedly raped by Redcrosse. She lies fluently and irrepressibly, claiming to have been betrothed to the meek prince, Christ (I ii 23), and inventing a remarkable tale of Redcrosse's ill-treatment of her (he has kept her 'in darksome cave' iv 47), for the sheer pleasure of lying, it seems. Her letter to the King of Eden concerning the knight's former liaison with her is adorned with extravagant phrases ('Witnesse the burning Altars, which he swore' xii 27) which carry the special stamp of her mendacity. In Book IV, the book of concord, her lies are calculated to destroy relationships: her manner to Scudamour is seemingly soothing even while she introduces a disturbing lie about

Amoret ('Ne be ye wroth Sir *Scudamour* therefore, / That she your love list love another knight' i 46). In the trial scene in v ix, the reader learns that her lies have recently become seditious and treasonable.

Her lechery is equally persistent. In Book I, she has seduced Fradubio before the main action begins; on her entry into the narrative, she is seen in 'dalliaunce' with her lover Sansfoy (ii 14). After flirting with Sansjoy (iv 45–8) and seducing Redcrosse, she is ready for the most rapid of all her couplings, that with Orgoglio: 'So willingly she came into his armes, / Who her as willingly to grace did take' (vii 15). In Book V, the crimes she has committed appropriately include the 'Adulterie' for which she has a predilection (ix 48).

Spenser's art ensures that Duessa is a vitally imagined figure in the fiction, and also personifies a universal principle, significantly found in alliance with other destructive powers, especially Night, Pride, discord, and Sedition. Renaissance literary witches tend to invoke the aid of Night, but Spenser has made Duessa the direct descendant of the ancient power of darkness which hates the sons of Day. As 'the daughter of Deceipt and Shame' and granddaughter of Night, Duessa is the cousin of the Saracen brothers (the sons of Aveugle and grandsons of Night), a fact which signals the relationship between followers of the Pope and followers of Mahomet, the two forms of false religion felt to be most menacing by sixteenth-century Protestants. With regard to discord, it is Duessa who has fetched Ate, chief enemy of Book IV's presiding virtue, up from hell (i 19). The two travel together, Duessa providing the lies which Ate elaborates and extends in order to create strife (i 47). In Book V, the pair are found to have worked together again, this time in the cause of treason (ix 47). Finally, Duessa is accused of a whole sequence of malignant activities: Murder, Sedition, Incontinence, Adultery, Impiety (ix 48). All the personifications linked with Duessa reveal facts about the nature of falsehood.

In V ix, however, Spenser also portrays the actions, trial, and condemnation of Mary, Queen of Scots. The specific historical allusions are neatly connected with Duessa's personal characteristics established earlier in the poem. Elsewhere in *The Faerie Queene*, also, she briefly carries historical meanings: she may signify Mary Tudor in particular as well as the Roman Catholic church in general when she joins with the seven-headed Beast and Orgoglio in persecuting believers; and she may represent Mary, Queen of Scots, when she claims by letter at I xii 26 that Redcrosse (here an image of the English nation) belongs to her and not to Una (the true church and momentarily Elizabeth I), an identification first noted in 1597 by John Dixon (see Hough 1964:10). Spenser is expert in pointing up and then discarding historical allusions. Indeed his whole treatment of Duessa exhibits imaginative energy and flexibility, in that she functions simultaneously as a vital character, a powerful personification, and on occasion an historical individual.

ANTHEA HUME

Bennett 1942; Fowler 1964; Hamilton 1961a; Hankins 1971; Hume 1984; Nohrnberg 1976; Roberts 1978; Waters 1970.

dwarfs The four dwarfs of *The Faerie Queene* usually serve as attendants of female characters, two (Una's and Florimell's) of virtuous maidens beloved of virtuous knights, two (Poeana's and Briana's) of vicious accomplices of evil knights.

In the antecedent action as described in the Letter to Raleigh, Una's dwarf is said to have followed Una to Fairy court 'leading a warlike steed, that bore the Armes of a knight, and his speare in the dwarfes hand.' At the beginning of Book I, he follows bearing her 'needments.' He accompanies Redcrosse after the knight is separated from Una, warns him to flee the house of Pride, witnesses his defeat by Orgoglio, bears his armor to Una, revives her from her faint at the sight of it, and finally brings Una, Arthur, and Timias to deliver him from Orgoglio's dungeon.

Florimell's dwarf, Dony, who has served her at court, searches for her through the forest; later he is joined by Arthur, whose quest for Gloriana merges temporarily with the dwarf's for Florimell (III v 3–12). In Book V, as he hastens to Florimell's wedding at the Castle of the Strond, he is stayed by Artegall and directs him to Pollente, who bars the bridge leading to the castle (ii 2–10). His name has been derived from the Italian *donzello*, a page or squire, and also from Adonio, a knight in Ariosto's *Orlando furioso* 43.66. The humor in giving a dwarf a name that is a diminutive of *Adonis*, if that be a source, may not have escaped the Elizabethan reader.

The dwarfs of Poeana and Briana assist their mistresses in overcoming good knights, as jailer and messenger, respectively (IV viii 38–ix 8, VI i 29–31). Like Jonson's Nano in *Volpone* (whose character, like theirs, may owe something to the Renaissance tradition of the dwarf as monster and butt of humor), they are efficient in the service of evil.

An original of Una's dwarf and, to a lesser extent, of the others is the dwarf accompanying Sir Gareth and Lady Lynette in Malory's *Morte Darthur* 7. The lady's dwarf is a familiar figure in medieval romance, particularly in the Fair Unknown story from which Malory's tale derives (eg, the Anglo-Norman *Ipomedon* of Hue de Rotelande, c 1190, and the anonymous Middle English *Lybeaus Desconus* c 1350). Jonson remarks that 'Dames, and Dwarfes,' are part of 'The whole summe / Of errant Knight-hood' ('An Execration upon *Vulcan*' 66–7).

The attributes of shortness, slowness, and serviceability may associate Una's dwarf with discursive reason, which in a Christian theological context is subservient to revealed religion and faith. For Florimell's dwarf, they may imply the limited power of reason to apprehend ideal or heavenly beauty, which, in Neoplatonic thought, must ultimately be spiritually perceived. The activities of Poeana's and Briana's dwarfs may imply that a perversely servile reason impedes, just as a properly subordinated reason aids, the achieving of virtue or the escape from an enslaving vice. The association of dwarfism with the subordination of reason, either properly to divine revelation and ideal beauty or improperly to the passions, is supported by the appearance of dwarfs in every book of *The Faerie Queene* except Book II, in which reason, exercised by the Palmer, is given a more decisive role in moral choice.

RONALD A. HORTON

For general background, see Vernon J. Harward, Jr 1958 *The Dwarfs of Arthurian Romance and Celtic Tradition* (Leiden); E. Tietze-Conrat 1957 *Dwarfs and Jesters in Art* tr Elizabeth Osborn (London) (on the 16th and 17th centuries); and E.J. Wood 1868 *Giants and Dwarfs* (London). See also Bernard W. Bell 1968 'The Comic Realism of Una's Dwarf' *MSE* 1:111–18; Richard C. Frushell and Bernard J. Vondersmith 1978 'The Redcrosse Dwarf in Book I of *The Faerie Queene*' *LJHum* 4:52–8.

Dyer, Edward (1543–1607) Poet, courtier, and diplomat, Dyer is now chiefly remembered as a friend of Sidney and one of the 'Areopagus' mentioned in the *Letters* between Spenser and Harvey. Spenser seems to have been a welcome member of this literary circle when he was in London between October 1579 and August 1580. He writes that Sidney and Dyer 'have me ... in some use of familiarity' and tells Harvey that he means to dedicate his (lost) work *My Slomber* to Dyer (*Var Prose* p 6). Dyer was praised as one of the best early Elizabethan court poets, though few of his poems now survive. Modern commentators have tried without any firm evidence to identify him with one of the shepherd poets Spenser includes in his pastoral works – as Cuddie in *The Shepheardes Calender* or Corydon in *Colin Clout* (382). (See further Sargent 1935.)

L.G. BLACK

E

E.K. Author of the Epistle to Harvey, General Argument, Arguments, and glosses to *The Shepheardes Calender*, and of a lost commentary on Spenser's *Dreames* (*Nov* 195 gloss, *Three Letters* 1). His identity remains matter for speculation. Apart from the academic and poetic interests that can be deduced from his commentary, identification can be based only on the initials and his claim to friendship with both Spenser and Gabriel Harvey (a claim supported by his knowledge of their unpublished writings). A Cambridge connection seems likely, in which case E.K. is probably Edward Kirke (1553–1613), who became a sizar at Pembroke Hall in 1571 (Spenser matriculated as a Pembroke sizar in 1569; Harvey was elected a fellow of Pembroke in 1570). Kirke received his BA in 1575 and MA in 1578 (two years after Spenser, and perhaps four years after Spenser left Cambridge), and then became rector at Risby, Suffolk, in 1580 (*DNB*, Judson 1945:39–40). Spenser's reference of 16 October 1579 to having been that morning at 'Mystresse *Kerkes*' (*Two Letters* 1) provides some slight support for the identification.

The claim has also been made that E.K. is Spenser himself, assuming the dual roles of author and critic of the *Calender*, but E.K.'s emphases suggest a textual presence distinct from Spenser's. It is difficult, for example, to imagine that Spenser, who brought to the *Calender* an attentive and fruitful reading of Marot, would manifest E.K.'s desire to denigrate the French poet (*Jan* 1 gloss, *Nov* Arg), or that the future author of *The Faerie Queene* would share E.K.'s distaste for the 'rancke opinion' of fairies and elves (*June* 25 gloss) and his view of Arthurian romance as the product of 'fine fablers and lowd lyers' (*Aprill* 120 gloss). It is difficult, too, to attribute to Spenser E.K.'s one-dimensional reading of the *Calender*'s ecclesiastical allegory, which obscures in its antipapist bias the poem's extensive indictment of Anglican abuses (eg, *Maye* 121 gloss, *Julye* 173 gloss – though such interpretations may admittedly involve an element of protective camouflage). Similarly, most readers have been unable to accept that Spenser would resort to the kind of self-praise implied by his authorship of the commentary. While he was certainly not averse to proclaiming the value of his poetic achievement ('Loe I have made a Calender for every yeare' envoy), it is difficult and even embarrassing to imagine him as responsible for such local expressions of delight as 'a gallant exclamation moralized with great wisedom and passionate wyth great affection' (*Nov* 153 gloss), whereas E.K.'s remarks of this kind are themselves rather delightful when viewed as the record of an enthusiastic early reading of the poem.

E.K.'s learning, like most in the Renaissance, is more indebted to handbooks than he acknowledges and often falls victim to reliance on an imperfect memory. He is also not proof against the lure of a digression into classical mythology or (with the aid of Holinshed) into British history. His eye is nevertheless on Spenser's text rather than his own self-presentation. When he observes, for example, of *Januarye* 61–2, 'a prety Epanorthosis in these two verses, and withall a Paronomasia or playing with the word,' his reference to two commonplace figures could scarcely seek to impress an audience almost universally well versed in the art of rhetoric. Rather he is inviting the reader to share in a moment of particular pleasure in the experience of the poem – a delight in language, and particularly in Spenser's use of language, which is a dominant note throughout the commentary: 'rough and harsh termes enlumine and make more clearly to appeare the brightnesse of brave and glorious words' (Epistle).

E.K. says of Spenser's eclogues that 'by meanes of some familiar acquaintaunce I was made privie to his counsell and secret meaning in them' (Epistle). In fact, he solves few of the mysteries that have intrigued those attracted to the *Calender*'s historical allegory: he refuses, for example, to offer more than tantalizing hints as to the identity of Rosalind (*Jan* 60 gloss, *April* 26 gloss). He does nevertheless have valuable secrets to reveal. Not only does he provide some indication of the ways in which the poem would be read by a sympathetic Elizabethan reader with an enthusiasm for English poetry, but more important he offers a glimpse into the literary attitudes and aspirations that led to its actual creation.

E.K. knew and was undoubtedly influenced in his commentary by Spenser's lost *English Poete*, a brief but valuable record of which is preserved in the *October* Argument. He was, moreover, almost certainly a participant, perhaps jointly with Harvey, in prepublication discussions about the *Calender*. Some evidence of such discussions is preserved in E.K.'s remark that the identity of Dido is 'to me altogether unknowne, albe of [Spenser] I often required the same' (*Nov* Arg). Less tangible but more pervasive evidence of these discussions and their influence on the commentary is the very content of the commentary, particularly in Epistle. E.K. is almost certainly not Spenser, but in his description of pastoral as only the first step toward epic, in his expression of the humanist belief in the potential of good letters to preserve 'an eternall image of antiquitie' while 'discoursing matters of gravitie and importaunce,' in his linguistic nationalism and his dismay at the current state of English poetry, and above all in his faith in the promise of 'this our new Poete,' who, 'so soone as his name shall come into the knowledg of men, and his worthines be sounded in the tromp of fame ... shall be not onely kiste, but also beloved of all, embraced of the most, and wondred at of the best' – in all these we surely hear an echo, indeterminate but precious nonetheless, of the voice of the youthful Spenser himself, as he took his first firm steps toward his goal of epic achievement for himself and his nation. It is perhaps E.K.'s greatest achievement that his voice first helps to define for us Spenser's own.

DAVID R. SHORE

echo, resonance Natural resonance often figures a community within nature, or uniting man and nature; the word *concord* still has meanings that carry this figurative extension of the acoustic. The ability to excite the landscape to resonant or echoic response is a traditional mark of poetic skill: since to respond or echo is the best nature can do toward perpetuating human utterance, such response is taken as an act of natural homage. The most accomplished of Virgil's pastoral singers, the shepherd Tityrus, is discovered at the opening of the *Eclogues*, 'teaching the woods to resound with the name of "Amaryllis."' In this respect, as in many others, Colin Clout is the heir of 'Romish *Tityrus*': in *The Shepheardes Calender*, *Colin Clouts Come Home Againe*, and *The Faerie Queene*, Colin's potent song elicits the harmonious response of the landscape. Sometimes the pastoralist's power over the landscape is rather greater than his power over his beloved, and so he may find himself seeking out the echoic landscape as an appropriate spot for amatory lament, as Colin does in *August*. In a sense, Echo sings descant to all erotic song, be it celebratory or doleful.

Resonance, then, has a traditional association with pastoral eroticism. Even where there is no Tityrus-figure to sing the praises of his beloved, Spenser will often describe a spontaneously echoing natural scene as an 'image' (etymologically, as much an acoustic term as a visual one) of nature's inherently erotic disposition (eg, *Amoretti* 19).

Sometimes the acoustics of a particular location signal that its erotic disposition is to be distrusted. In Acrasia's Bower, 'all that pleasing is to living eare, / Was there consorted in one harmonee, / Birdes, voyces, instruments, windes, waters, all agree.' Harmony and resonance blend here as 'Th'Angelicall soft trembling voyces made / To th'instruments divine respondence meet: / The silver sounding instruments did meet / With the base murmure of the waters fall' (*FQ* II xii 70–1). Spenser carefully marks the dangerous allure of this acoustic eroticism, not only by a pun on *base* and the ominous connotation of *fall*, but chiefly by recalling the resonance with which nature responds to the vicious song of the sirens a few stanzas earlier: 'the rolling sea resounding soft, / In his big base them fitly answered' (33).

Thus, the incidence of acoustic response not only signals generic associations; it also raises moral problems. (Spenser often suggests that a poet's decision to write a particular kind of poem entails *ethical* choices.) If resonance is a sign of the community of man and nature, the ethical value of that community is complicated. In translating a phrase of Petrarch (or rather, translating Marot's translation of Petrarch) at the beginning of his career, Spenser described a condition of perfect pastoral mimesis, in which a group of Muses and nymphs 'sweetly in accord did tune their voyce / To the soft sounding of the waters fall' (*Petrarch* 4): this vocal music is a counter-version of echo, in which animate singers reproduce the inarticulate soundings of nature. As his career unfolds, Spenser repeatedly figures his own plaints as similarly tuned to this liquid music – such tunings become one of the poet's signatures. Yet this signature is often unclear: in these counter-echoes, nature does not rise to answer the poet; the poet instead descends to match the voice of nature. This brings the celebration of concord to an extreme, to an epitome of pastoral that marks it as a mode to be transcended.

Where celebratory resonance has flourished and failed or been found wanting, more haunting echoes almost inevitably obtrude. In *Teares of the Muses*, the decline of poetry is described in terms of just such a transformation in the acoustic environment: 'th'hollow hills, from which their silver voyces / Were wont redoubled Echoes to rebound, / Did now rebound with nought but rufull cries, / And yelling shrieks throwne up into the skies' (21–4). Spenser narrates a similar transformation in *FQ* VI, where a devastated pastoral world is haunted by 'ecchoes vaine ... Where wont the shepheards oft their pypes resound' (xi 26). In both this passage and *Teares*, the transformation of resonance owes something to an old tradition in which Echo also functions as a special assistant to lamentation, as in the pastoral elegies of Bion and Moschus, or in Spenser's own *Daphnaïda*. Plutarch subtly adjusted this tradition when he described how a disembodied voice prophesied the death of the god Pan and how news of that prophecy roused the landscape to keening resonance (*De defectu oraculorum*; quoted in E.K.'s gloss to *Maye* 54). The similar prophecy of Sidney's death in *Ruines of Time* (594–8) also exploits this tradition.

That resonance is both erotic and elegiac, and that the Muses' celebratory resonance can suffer transformation into a 'feeble *Eccho* [who] now laments and howles' (*Teares* 285), no doubt account for the ambivalence with which Spenser handles his most famous address to natural echo, in the refrains of *Epithalamion*. He claims the poetic power and amatory good fortune of Tityrus when he insists that 'The woods shall to me answer and my Eccho ring' (18; cf Colin's celebratory song in *FQ* VI x 10). This refrain may be usefully compared with that of *Prothalamion*, for the request 'Sweete *Themmes* runne softly, till I end my Song' is a declaration of the *limits* which hedge the singer of that wedding poem; in *Epithalamion*, the claims are larger. For most of the poem, the refrain renders its own status *as* refrain thematic, so that its recurrences are shown to be authorized by the acoustic recurrences that animate the world. The echo-refrain suggests a voice poised between nature and culture, and serves as a sign of ideal marriage, in which natural impulse is blessed by the civility and sanctity of English Protestant culture. The ominous aspects of echo are not heard during the stanzas celebrating the wedding day; but when night falls and the time for a physical union with the bride approaches, the singer no longer aspires to the power of Tityrus. He calls for an end of natural echoing, abjuring not only nature's resonant erotic chorus, but also the 'lamenting cryes' (*Epith* 334) which regularly threaten a landscape when wonted celebratory resonance ceases. Thus, instead of desiring the immediate satisfaction of acoustic persistences, the poet now asks for the blessings of progeny, a more substantial means of self-perpetuation – a means represented as entirely within the province of divine grace, undisturbed by the clamorous nature of the pastoral world.

Joseph Loewenstein

John Hollander 1981a; Hollander 1987 'Spenser's Undersong' in *Cannibals, Witches, and Divorce: Estranging the Renaissance* ed Marjorie Garber (Baltimore) pp 1–20; Loewenstein 1984; Loewenstein 1986.

---

ecphrasis (Gr *ekphrazein* to speak out, tell in full) In its loose sense of 'vivid description' or *enargeia*, *ecphrasis* was a highly desired element in Renaissance literary aesthetics, contributing to distinctness, clarity, and emotional impact on the audience. Much of Spenser's poetry, particularly his descriptions of persons and places, can be called ecphrastic in this sense.

In a narrower sense, it is the most commonly used term for a literary description of a real or imagined work of visual art. Subjects range from statuary, painting, and tapestry to decorated armor and utensils such as cups and bowls. (Hagstrum 1958:18 n 34 uses *icon* for this device; the *Oxford Classical Dictionary* and Bender 1972 use *ekphrasis* or *ecphrasis*, though confusion is possible because the term is generally used for any pictorially vivid description, even of natural objects or persons.) In this narrower sense, Spenser's most notable extended ecphrases are the descriptions of tapestries in *Muiopotmos* 257–352, *FQ* III i 34–8 and xi 28–46, and the description of the Bower of Bliss (II xii 42–87), especially the ivory gate depicting the history of Jason and Medea (44–6), and the fountain (60–1).

These passages have a literary genealogy stretching back to Homer's description of the shield of Achilles (*Iliad* 18.478–616). In imitation of Homer, literary epic came to include such passages as a matter of course. Virgil depicts the wars of Troy on the walls of Juno's temple at Carthage and describes the shield of Aeneas (*Aeneid* 1.453–97, 8.608–731). Classical examples are not limited to epic. Hesiod has a description which takes up nearly half of his *Shield of Heracles* (139–317); Catullus 64 tells the story of Ariadne abandoned by Theseus as it was embroidered on the bridal coverlets for the marriage of Peleus and Thetis; Theocritus describes a cup offered as prize in a shepherds' singing match, and has two spectators admire vividly realistic tapestries (*Idylls* 1, 15). Ovid provides later poets with a host of models. Most notable in connection with Spenser is the description of the tapestries woven by the contending Pallas and Arachne in *Metamorphoses* 6.70–145 (cf *Muiopotmos* 257–352 and various details in Busirane's tapestries). Lucian and Philostratus both composed prose works entitled *Eikones*, epigrammatic descriptions of real or imagined works of graphic art, exploiting the *topos* in another genre.

Medieval poets frequently embellished their poems with ecphrastic descriptions, especially in dream-visions and romances. While many instances appear to exist merely to conform to classical models, others contain a new element of allegorical imagery. Notable examples are the paintings and carvings on the walls of the garden in the *Romance of the Rose* (lines 129–464 in ed 1971) and the interior mural decorations and statues in the temples of Diana, Mars, and Venus in Chaucer's *Knight's Tale*. Here the moral content of the pictorial images is primary, and their conceptual meanings illuminate the themes and conflicts of the narratives in which they appear.

Renaissance advances in the technical capacities and prestige of the visual arts intensified pressure for ecphrasis to serve as implicit *paragone*, or comparison of the sister arts (see **ut pictura poesis*). More than that of any intervening period, Renaissance use of this type of ecphrasis captures the aesthetic sophistication of Alexandria and later antiquity. The contending arts were more equally matched than they had been in Dante's time, for example; and while the medieval doctrine that images are signs was not forgotten, the poets were stimulated by the striking achievements of Renaissance painting in color, perspective, presentation of character and emotion – in short, in the imitation both of nature and of rediscovered classical art. Always a potential excuse for a rhetorical tour de force in the hands of alert and skillful poets, ecphrasis became a means for testing and defining the limits of the representational techniques and affective powers of the visual and verbal arts. The device could be used to highlight whatever self-consciousness the poet possessed about the nature and role of art itself. It could become a means for exploring art's relation to nature. It might examine the moral import of the sensible world. An expanded repertoire of more-or-less subtly introduced mythological, iconological, and occult significances further heightened the appeal and expressiveness of this *topos*. Ecphrastic descriptions were still used both as literary formulas imitating classical models and as an indication of the wealth and status of fictional settings and persons. The best Renaissance instances, however, embody complex explorations of relationship and limits, and become artistically significant reflections on their narrative context.

Spenser's ecphrases (especially the tapestries in *FQ* III i and xi) may be compared to Marlowe's depiction of Hero's dress and Venus' temple (*Hero and Leander* 1.9–36, 135–56); to Daniel's description of 'a Casket richly wrought' (*The Complaint of Rosamond* 372–413); to Drayton's lengthy portrayal of the wall paintings in the chamber of Mortimer and Queen Isabel (*Mortimeriados* 2311–94); and to Shakespeare's description of the wall paintings of the Fall of Troy, contemplation of which provides the ravaged Lucrece 'means to mourn some newer way' until her husband returns (*Lucrece* 1366–1582). All were published after *FQ* III had first appeared in 1590. Like Spenser's tapestry ecphrases, these descriptions comment on the activities and aspirations of the characters in whose stories they are set. All give particular attention to vivid descriptive detail, and all explicitly remark on art striving with nature in the workman's cunning (see *nature and art). Again, all are heavily indebted to Ovid, often as a source of characters and incidents, but more generally as a pattern of tone and rhetoric.

Yet Spenser's ecphrases are both more Ovidian and more medieval than his contemporaries'. They are more informed with a sophisticated understanding of the capabilities and limits of language in imitation, and they are more pregnantly suggestive of a 'hidden sense' behind the sumptuous surface. In this rhetorical device, so peculiarly suited to the means and tastes of the Renaissance, no English poet outdoes Spenser's richness and complexity of visual evocation and emotional resonance. His exploitation of ecphrasis is a striking instance of his ability to respond sensitively and fully to the wide range of possibilities available in his literary tradition.

MICHAEL L. DONNELLY

Bender 1972; Curtius ed 1953; DuBois 1982; Hagstrum 1958; Hulse 1981; Murray Krieger 1967 'The Ekphrastic Principle and the Still Movement of Poetry; or *Laokoön* Revisited' in *The Play and Place of Criticism* (Baltimore) pp 105–28; George Kurman 1974 'Ecphrasis in Epic Poetry' *CL* 26:1–13; Pamela L. Royston 1984 'Unraveling the Ecphrasis in Chapman's *Hero and Leander*' *SAB* 49.4:43–53; R.R. Wilson 1986.

Eden From Genesis 2.4–4.4 derives the Christian theology of original sin and redemption, figured in six images: a man and woman, a serpent and lamb, and symbolic trees and water. God sets Adam, the first human being, in a perfect garden in the land of Eden, watered by four rivers sustaining the plants, including the Tree of Eternal Life. Eve, created from Adam's rib as his mate, is tempted by the serpent. After the couple eat the forbidden fruit of the Tree of the Knowledge of Good and Evil, they lose paradise and must endure toil and death in the world, though God still cares for the righteous, such as Abel, who sacrifices his sheep devoutly.

Spenser fuses these six images with their parallels in the New Testament (John 4.14, 1 Cor 15.21–2, 1 Pet 2.24, Rev 2.7, 12.1–17, 19.1–21, 21.1–22.2) and in the St George legends. As a consequence, the narrative of *FQ* I refers to Adam's Fall and Christ's redemption at the same time as it anticipates final salvation in a heavenly Eden. The Red Cross Knight anchors these themes in England.

Una's father, 'most mighty king of *Eden* faire' (I xii 26), though never named, is either Adam (vii 43–4, xi 46–7) or his descendant (i 5). Once his rule of '*Eden* lands' (II i 1) extended from East to West like the early church admired by English reformers, but now it oversees only the East (I i 5, ii 22, vii 43), where the garden is placed by most exegetes and the Geneva Bible map (A. Williams 1948:99–102). The mention of only three rivers (vii 43) may allude to the triangular shape of Britain, as in stanzas 23–4 of Joseph Hall's *Kings Prophecie* (1603), where England appears 'a second Paradise.' Spenser's Eden still contains the baleful Tree of Knowledge (xi 47) as well as the hill mentioned in Ezekiel 28.13–14 (4). The 'brasen towre' (3) defending Eden recalls a descendant of wicked Cain, Tubal-Cain, a brassworker (Gen 4.22). Una's lamb (i 4), symbolizing the truth found in Eden before the Fall, suggests Abel's sacrifice, the Lamb in Revelation 19.6–9, and the virgin's lamb in the St George legend.

The papist Archimago may hate Una 'as the hissing snake' (ii 9), and Error is half serpent (i 14), but the great enemy is 'that old Dragon' (xi argument) of Revelation 12.1–6 against which Una brings Redcrosse. As Adam (Hebrew *'adam* man, mankind) was created from earth (Hebrew *'adamah*) and tilled the soil (Gen 2.7, 3.17–19), Redcrosse's name Georgos (x 66) means 'ploughman' in Greek, while the first syllable of the name of this 'man of earth' (52) echoes the Greek for 'earth' (*gē*). Corrupted by original sin, he lapses several times in *FQ* I.

In the first day of the fight with the Dragon, Redcrosse falls near the Well of Life, the *fons* (well) of Genesis 2.6 and John 4.14 (Vulgate). The waters, purging sin and revivifying the dead, represent baptism (*FQ* I xi 29–30, 34, 36; *Glossa ordinaria* on Rev 22.1), 'spiritual grace' (Geneva gloss on John 4.14), and 'the worde of Salvation' (van der Noot *Theatre for Worldlings* 1569: fol 88, on Rev 22.1).

Following 1 Corinthians 15.47 ('The first man is of the earth, earthlie: the seconde man is the Lord from heaven'), Redcrosse is called 'Right faithfull true' (i 2; cf Rev 19.11), like the heavenly Lord whose arms he bears. After the second day's battle, he falls under the Tree of Life with blood-vermilion apples, which symbolizes the Eucharist (Fulke 1589, on Rev 22.2), the tree of the Cross (1 Pet 2.24), the 'Balme' of extreme unction (xi 46, 48, 50; cf 2 Esd 2.12), 'faith and participation of [God's] spirit' (Fulke), and 'the two testamentes of the Lorde' (*Theatre* fol 89). As the tree bestows everlasting life (xi 46; cf Gen 3.22, Rev 2.7, 22.2), Redcrosse triumphs on the third day, his weapon driving itself into the Dragon's maw, a figure for hell-mouth. He releases the King of Eden, just as in the *Gospel of Nicodemus* Christ harrows Hell, leading Adam and his company through brazen gates to a restored Eden (James 1924:132–40).

Though *FQ* I xii 13 recalls Christ's triumphal entry into Jerusalem (Matt 21.1–9) and medieval advents where kings were greeted as the Messiah entering the heavenly Jerusalem, the book ends with the betrothed Redcrosse returning to serve Gloriana by destroying the pagans (18). The consummation in a heavenly Eden is delayed. As in *Theatre*, the New Eden is the reformed church – for Spenser, the English church. Similarly, Greene in *The Spanish Masquerado* (1589: sig E3v) rejoices over the ruin of the popish Armada, while 'God maketh ENGLAND like EDEN, a second Paradice.'

ALEXANDER GLOBE

David K. Cornelius 1970–1 'Spenser's *Faerie Queene*, I, xi, 46' *Expl* 29, item 51; J.M. Evans 1968 *'Paradise Lost' and the Genesis Tradition* (Oxford); Fowler 1960b; William Fulke 1589 *The Text of the New Testament ... with a Confutation* (London; *STC* 2888); *Glossa ordinaria* in *PLat* 114; Montague Rhodes James, tr and ed 1924 *The Apocryphal New Testament* (Oxford); Ernst H. Kantorowicz 1944 'The "King's Advent" and the Enigmatic Panels in the Doors of Santa Sabina' *ArtB* 26:207–31; Kaske 1969; Esther Casier Quinn 1962 *The Quest of Seth for the Oil of Life* (Chicago); Walter Raleigh 1614 *The History of the World* 1.2–4 (London); John M. Steadman 1968 *Milton's Epic Characters: Image and Idol* (Chapel Hill) pp 82–9; D. Douglas Waters 1969–70 'Spenser's "Well of Life" and "Tree of Life" Once More' *MP* 67:67–8; A. Williams 1948.

Egypt Spenser and other sixteenth-century humanists distinguished two Egypts: the evil Egypt of biblical tradition and the venerated ancient Egypt of Horapollo's recently discovered *Hieroglyphica* and of the Hermetic renaissance.

The evil Egypt is first alluded to in *Theatre for Worldlings* (sonnet 3), the apparent subject of which (to judge by the accompanying woodcut) is an Egyptian obelisk, complete with hieroglyphics, treated as an emblem of the vanity of human wishes. It also appears in *The Faerie Queene*, when Error is connected with the Nile, and her vomit and brood of young serpents with the Nile's sun-bred monsters (I i 21); later, weeping Duessa is identified with the hypocritical Nile crocodile (v 18). In the first instance, there is a suggestion that Redcrosse's encounter with Error is a type of the Egyptian bondage as well as a passing encounter with the lusts of the flesh (for Egypt as lust, see Valeriano 1602:213, sv 'Temperantia'). In the second, mention of 'seven-mouthed *Nile*' invites an additional identification with the seven deadly sins and Duessa's seven-headed

Apocalyptic beast of vii 16–17. The pharaoh from whom the Israelites escaped was understood to be Busiris, the prototype for tyrannical Busirane (cf I x 53, III xi-xii). Thus, the 1590 *Faerie Queene* is framed by Egyptian allusions, those in Book I relating to the true church's bondage and liberation, and those in Book III functioning as tools to explore psychological oppression.

At III vi 8 and IV xi 20, however, Spenser mentions the Nile's fertility as a force for good, a cliché behind which we may perhaps detect the influence of Horapollo and his followers. Similarly, Una's lion in I iii may recall (along with many other meanings) the rising of the Nile portrayed as a lion (*Hieroglyphica* I.21). Una, the English church-as-Truth, is thereby identified with ancient Egyptian wisdom, in contrast to the evil Nile and false church of Error and Duessa; her stole (i 4) recalls the emblem of royalty in Horapollo (I.40).

Egyptianism helps to shape *The Faerie Queene*'s overall religious and political allegory, too: Spenser would have been influenced in this respect by Ficino's Latin translation of the *Corpus hermeticum*, in which ancient Egypt is the center of the world and the seat of religion and wisdom, and by Bruno's use of the Hermetic *Asclepius* dialogue, with its climactic vision of an Egypt fallen prey to evil but restored by God's grace to its former position of religious and philosophical supremacy. This vision is a primary motif in Bruno's works on pan-Christian reform, especially the *Expulsion of the Triumphant Beast* (1584). He visited England in the 1580s and dedicated his reforming *Expulsion* and *Heroic Frenzies* (1585) to Sidney, presumably because he felt that his own ideas on reform harmonized with Elizabethan notions of Protestant imperial reform (Elizabeth is praised in the prefatory 'Argument of the Nolan' ed 1964b:65).

If Bruno and the *Asclepius* anticipate the restoration of Egypt to its former glory and the banishment of present corruption, this explains why forces of both good and evil are often Egyptian in *The Faerie Queene*. In V vii, for example, Britomart/Elizabeth visits Isis Church and thus becomes a type of Isis as a prelude to our recognizing Mercilla/Elizabeth as another manifestation of Isis. This recognition has been anticipated in I vi, where Una's ass recalls the ass of the Isis mysteries (as in Apuleius' *Golden Ass* II), and in IV xi 24, through the personification of the river Isis as female.

The mythological Isis is daughter of a river god and associated with Nile-induced Egyptian fertility (see 'Diana' in Cartari 1571:118). She is the Egyptian moon goddess and her husband Osiris the sun god (*FQ* V vii 4); thus, from the perspective of Book V, they are archetypes of the poem's lunar heroines (Una, Diana, Belphoebe and Britomart, etc) and solar heroes (Redcrosse, Arthur, Artegall). Moreover, since Isis' search for her dead husband was equated with Venus' quest for Adonis and with Ceres' for Proserpina (Macrobius *Saturnalia* I.21.11), the governing myths of Books III and IV are retrospectively open to an Egyptian interpretation: the Proteus who imprisons Florimell (III viii 30ff, IV xi-xii) in imitation of Busirane's imprisoning of Amoret (III xi-xii) shows that he is not just a sea god but the Egyptian prophetic king of that name (Ross 1648:371).

Catholic Geryoneo, whose church at V x-xi opposes Isis' church, may be the poem's final evil Egyptian, since his church has a sphinx-like guardian monster. Admittedly, Spenser draws a parallel with the sphinx of the Oedipus legend (xi 25); but Egyptian and Greek Thebes were frequently confused, and iconographers rarely distinguished the Greek from the Egyptian sphinx (eg, Ross 1648:393–4). Geryoneo's sphinx is an emblem of ignorance. Yet the sphinx is also the emblem of the deep mysteries of Isis and of Hermeticism (Plutarch *Isis and Osiris* 354C). Here we have a beautiful example of the possible Asclepian aspects of Spenser's Egyptianism: Roman Catholicism appropriated and corrupted the original Christian faith now restored by Elizabeth, just as the evil angels and barbarians corrupted the Egypt of the Hermetic *Asclepius* but were then purged, restoring Egypt to its pristine state. Through Elizabeth/Isis, Spenser celebrates England as Egypt and as center of apocalypse. DOUGLAS BROOKS-DAVIES

Bruno ed 1964b; A.J. Festugière 1967 *Hermétisme et mystique païenne* (Paris); Hermes Trismegistus ed 1924–36; Erik Iversen 1961 *The Myth of Egypt and Its Hieroglyphs* (Copenhagen); Alexander Ross 1648 *Mystagogus Poeticus, or The Muses Interpreter* (London; rpt New York and London 1976); Valeriano 1602; Yates 1964.

---

elegy, pastoral A type of poem common to both classical and Renaissance literature in which a herdsman mourns the death of his fellow and nature joins or is invited to join the lament. The elegy may be part of a pastoral sequence, like Spenser's *November*; it may take its place among other funeral offerings, like 'Astrophel: A Pastorall Elegie'; or it may stand alone, like *Daphnaïda*.

The Greek Alexandrian poet Theocritus (3rd c BC) wrote the first pastoral elegy known to Renaissance writers. In his first *Idyll*, a shepherd, Thyrsis, sings the lament of dying Daphnis, who calls on nature to turn upside-down at his death: 'Pines may grow figs now Daphnis dies, and hind tear hound if she will, / And the sweet nightingale be outsung i' the dale by the scritch-owl from the hill' (135–6). Nature's sympathy for man is limited, however: although the nymphs love the mortal Daphnis, they cannot save him. There is no primitive merging of natural and human states in Theocritus; his poetry is the sophisticated product of a sophisticated age. Nor is there any explicit consolation for death beyond the implicit sweetness of the pastoral world in which the lament is rehearsed.

Two later Alexandrian laments, usually included in editions of Theocritus, also influenced the Renaissance convention. Bion's *Lament for Adonis*, through Ronsard's imitation, was a model for Spenser's 'Astrophel.' As well Moschus' *Lament for Bion* provided an important new motif to the Renaissance convention: the sense of a difference between the natural and human worlds was now registered explicitly, in the contrast of nature's annual cycle of renewal to a single human life span.

Virgil's fifth *Eclogue* established one dominant pattern for pastoral elegy by adapting to the lament the Theocritean singing match in which one herdsman's verse answers another's. Here Mopsus' song of Daphnis' death is answered by Menalcas' celebration of his deification. But Virgil leaves Daphnis marveling at the threshold of Olympus, and turns to describe a regenerated pastoral world below, where 'the wolf plans no ambush for the flock, and nets no snare for the stag; kindly Daphnis loves peace' (60–1).

Both classical and Renaissance commentators identify Julius Caesar with Virgil's Daphnis, who becomes custodian of the whole pastoral world; and to later commentators Daphnis is also a type of Christ. Thus when a Christian elegist assumes the guise of a simple herdsman to mourn his friend, his fellow poet, or his sovereign, he mourns one whose death and redemption participate in those of his Saviour; and he is consoled for death by the comforts of this world and a better one. Many Renaissance pastoral elegies, particularly those of the early humanists, conclude by turning from the earthly setting toward the idealized heavenly landscape.

The form of the classical pastoral elegy gives the Renaissance poet a framework within which to explore his personal response to loss. In fact, that framework provides consolation through both the pastoral setting and the element of conventionality itself, allowing the poet to express more freely his own, seemingly inconsolable loss.

Many Renaissance pastoral elegies written in vernacular tongues look back to earlier Renaissance prototypes as well as to classical sources. In this respect, Spenser's *November* is typical in evoking Theocritus and Virgil by way of the French poet Marot's eclogue on the death of Louise de Savoie. If not unique among Renaissance pastoral elegies in its desire to accommodate classical and Christian consolations for death, Spenser's *November* is remarkable for the ease with which it makes that accommodation. Dido's death, the death of 'The fayrest May ... that ever went' (39), participates in the *Calender*'s assurances of renewal even as it threatens to undo 'Dame natures kindly course' (124). The Christian poet's lament for the 'trustlesse state of earthly things' (153) has no counterpart in Marot but many echoes in his own later poetry. In *November* he places it within a cosmic vision that takes us down to hell and then, triumphantly, up to heaven. Particularly fine is the adaptation of the *Lament for Bion*, contrasting the course of nature's life and that of man. Spenser reminds us forcefully of our participation in nature even as he qualifies it: nature's flowers spring up fresh in the new season, 'But thing on earth that is of most availe, / As vertues braunch and beauties budde, / Reliven not for any good' (87–9). Milton's *Lycidas* is doubtless more comprehensive than Spenser's *November*; but Milton's knowledge of the gulf between man and nature is not joined in this intimate way to a knowledge of their connection, one which Spenser emphasizes again in *Daphnaïda* when he describes the subject of that lament as one who 'fell away against all course of kinde ... fel away like fruit blowne downe with winde' (242–4). As the pastoral setting remains primary for Spenser, so does the pastoral elegist's way of understanding death by placing it in a naturalistic setting. In 'Astrophel,' he translates the erotic atmosphere of Bion's (and Ronsard's) lament into a healing pastoral one. *Daphnaïda* is better read as a pastoral elegy which seeks but does not find pastoral consolation, rather than as an inferior medieval lament on the model of Chaucer's *Book of the Duchess*.

Sidney's 'Since that to death' (ed 1962, *Old Arcadia* 75) and Spenser's *November* are the earliest examples of formal pastoral elegy in English. Spenser's poem became the model for the English tradition, and *November* was often imitated in the last decades of the sixteenth century (eg, by Drayton's fourth *Eclogue* [1593] and in poems in the *Astrophel* volume). By the early seventeenth century, however, pastoral's naturalistic setting seemed to falsify rather than clarify human sorrows, and the notion that one might express those sorrows through a highly stylized form seemed less possible and less desirable. As a result, the pastoral elegy began to atrophy and decline. The great exception to this decline is, of course, Milton's *Lycidas* (1637), in which we see a radical revision as well as the culmination of a tradition inaugurated in England by Spenser's *November*.

ELLEN Z. LAMBERT

Donker and Muldrow 1982:74–7; Thomas Perrin Harrison, Jr 1939 *The Pastoral Elegy: An Anthology* (Austin, Tex); Ellen Zetzel Lambert 1976 *Placing Sorrow: A Study of the Pastoral Elegy Convention from Theocritus to Milton* (Chapel Hill); Panofsky 1955:295–320; Pigman 1985.

elements The traditional four elements are earth, water, air (see *winds), and fire. They are formed out of chaos and are the building blocks of the material world (cf *FQ* VII vii 25). In classical physics, they are often arranged in an ascending series or pairs of interlocked contraries which continually pass into one another. Each element manifests certain inherent qualities: earth is cold and dry, water is cold and moist, air is hot and moist, and fire is hot and dry. Galen held that these qualities are distributed in the human body through the action of natural, animal, and vital spirits, and that imbalance in their distribution produces a person's characteristic humor: the choleric temperament has a predominance of hot and dry, the sanguine of hot and moist, the phlegmatic of cold and moist, the melancholic of cold and dry.

According to the Neoplatonic doctrine adopted by Spenser, love brings the elements together. Cupid, nurtured by Venus in the Garden of Adonis, is the first god (*Colin Clout* 806); his task is to reconcile the qualities of the four elements so that they can bring forth 'other kynds' (841–86). In *Hymne of Love* (57–91), Love tempers the 'contrary dislikes' of the elements by showing them how to mix. The world's birth from chaos is developed in a complex allegory of physical generation and mutability (*FQ* III vi). In nature's original harmony during the Golden Age of Saturn, justice ruled; then the Fall caused the world to 'runne quite out of square,' so that its condition 'growes daily wourse and wourse' (V proem 1–2).

In *Hymne of Heavenly Beautie* (48–9), the elements are shown to be arranged in ascending order, increasingly pure: after the earth amid the sea, 'Ayre more then water, fire much more then ayre.' But at the end of time, they will revert to the first chaos: 'The bands of th'elements shall backe reverse / To their first discord, and be quite undonne' (*Rome* 22). The Giant with the scales finds the elements in disorder and wrongly attempts to restore the original balance (*FQ* V ii 30–49). Conti (*Mythologiae* 4.9) interprets the Titans' overthrow (and with it the loss of the Golden Age) as a collapse of the elements into random fluctuation; Spenser's Mutabilitie, who claims descent from the Titans, asserts her power over 'these fower' constantly at war (VII vii 17–25).

In the *Cantos of Mutabilitie*, as in *FQ* V, the perversion of nature's original rule causes the world to grow 'daily worse' (VII vi 6). Yet the poem also renders the designs and achievements of concord, perennially in tension with the reversion of the elements toward chaos, the domain of 'griesly *Night*' (I v 20). Thus, the concord between Marinell and Florimell, and between the sea and land of *FQ* III and IV, suggests elemental equilibrium wherein water and earth are presented as beneficent as well as potentially destructive. Concord tempers the elements, for 'Else would the waters overflow the lands, / And fire devoure the ayre' (IV x 35). The friendship between Triamond, Cambell, Canacee, and Cambina suggests a balance of the elements; and the four false friends (Paridell, Blandamour, Duessa, and Ate), the contrary imbalance.

Within the human body, where a mixture of elements produces the four humors, a correct proportion is necessary for health, as in *FQ* II, where the virtue of temperance requires a balance among the humors. The castle of Alma is constructed from three geometrical figures traditionally representing the human being, and the 'quadrate' (ix 22) stands for the humors (see Kenelm *Digby, *Hermeticism). These constantly change, so that the achievement of form is always under threat of dissolution. This condition is shown in the figure of Proteus, who changes his shape and yet must tell the truth if held. He was thought to allegorize the elements and to suggest their receptivity to form (eg, Conti *Mythologiae* 8.8). Thus, though he captures Florimell, he also preserves her. By contrast, Spenser's evil shape-changers (Archimago, Duessa, the false Florimell, Malengin) are Protean but not nurturing figures. Archimago is compared to Proteus (I ii 10), and his changes into bird, fish, fox, and dragon suggest the four elements; but he seeks to destroy the balance among the humors and thereby the virtues.

Spenser's sensitivity to the delicate preservation of form through moments of transformation is reflected in his allusions to weather phenomena, or 'meteors.' These are caused by the interaction of the elements, especially in the middle region of air – 'Thelement,' as Spenser calls it (*SC, Feb* 116), perhaps indicating its special connection with human vitality. So life is a delicate 'bubble glas of breath,' a 'vapour' (*Time* 50, 56), and beauty is a mixture of 'complexions' (humors) which fade like a 'sommers shade' (*Hymne of Beautie* 67–8).

Spenser's information on the elements and their connection to the humors most likely derives from widespread Galenic and Neoplatonic traditions. Specifically, he could have learned about the common physics and physiology of his time from such readily available sources as Sir Thomas Elyot's *Castel of Helth* (1541), John Jones' *Galen's Bookes of Elements* (1574), Philip Barrough's *Methode of Physicke* (1583), and *Batman uppon Bartholome* (1582), a translation of Bartholomaeus Anglicus' *De proprietatibus rerum*.

PATRICK GRANT

Evelyn May Albright 1929 'Spenser's Cosmic Philosophy and His Religion' *PMLA* 44:715–59; Bamborough 1952; Fowler 1960a; Greenlaw 1920; Hankins 1971:260ff; Heninger 1960; Kocher 1953, esp pp 146–50; Milne 1973; Nohrnberg 1976:583–6 et passim; Brents Stirling 1934 'The Philosophy of Spenser's "Garden of Adonis"' *PMLA* 49:501–38; Temkin 1973.

Elizabeth, images of The traditional view of Elizabeth Tudor gives her long reign (1558–1603) the character of legend. It shows an enigmatic Virgin Queen dexterously negotiating the perilous milieu of national and international politics, adored by her peaceful people, inspiring universal wonder. This myth of Elizabeth is largely the product of her government's effort to promote her regime. It became Elizabethan history when Camden in the *Annales* (1615) read her era retrospectively in terms of the myth – as if her motto *semper eadem* (always the same) were fact. Until recently, histories of her reign have commonly fallen in behind Camden as does the most influential biography of this century, J.E. Neale's *Queen Elizabeth* (1934). Recent revisionist historians, however, have begun to query the extent of Elizabeth's achievement and to suggest that the gap between fact and a rather modest statement of the myth may be wide. (The introduction to Haigh 1984 surveys this scholarship usefully.) Both views are relevant to Spenser studies for, although *The Faerie Queene* is a major expression of the Elizabeth myth, some critical assessment of her regime darkens its later books.

It is a helpful simplification to see this

reign as four roughly decade-long phases: the uncertain, formative 1560s; the myth-making 1570s; the Armada-*Faerie Queene* period of the 1580s; and the restive, depressed years before 1603.

the formative period At its beginning, two great problems augured against the success of Elizabeth's rule. One was the religious dilemma she inherited. At Henry VIII's death (1547), there was a national church obedient to the crown rather than the Pope, still Catholic in practice yet undergoing the first tentative steps toward reform. The regents for the child-king Edward VI (1547–53) carried a Protestant reform through energetically, but then his sister Mary (1553–8) restored obedience to Rome. Her burning of some 500 Protestants (giving her the epithet 'Bloody Mary') exacerbated religious tension. Thus Elizabeth's first major act was necessarily a Settlement of Religion – a compromise church moderately reformed but traditionally episcopal in structure and so frustrating to both Catholics and Geneva-style Protestants. Since a majority outside the main cities remained Catholic in sympathy, however, there was real doubt that any such fragile settlement could hold. That Mary, Queen of Scots, was both Catholic and Elizabeth's likely successor made its future even more tentative. At the same time, even though Elizabeth had symbolically embraced the English Bible on formally entering London in 1559, Protestants rightly felt insecure about her devotion to their cause.

More immediately perturbing was the fact of Elizabeth's sex. In theory it was assumed that a woman monarch contradicted the law of nature (in 1558, John Knox had entitled his polemic on this subject *The Monstruous Regiment of Women* (see defense of *women); in practice it was assumed that no woman was competent to manage the essentially male business of state. Until Elizabeth married, as her sister Mary had done and as Parliament now insisted that she do, her regime had to be regarded as provisional.

Such were the misgivings early in the reign. But by about 1570, it began to appear that not only was her regime succeeding but the Queen herself, though unmarried, was proving a competent ruler who had kept England free from war. 'God gave us Queen Elizabeth,' wrote Bishop John Jewel in 1570, 'and with her gave us peace, and so long a peace as England hath seldom seen before' (Jenkins 1959:158).

Essential to her success was her shrewd counselor William Cecil, now Lord Burghley. Working together, they had successfully confronted foreign and domestic threats. While the menace of a Catholic successor remained, Mary Stuart was fugitive from Scotland under house arrest in England. Elizabeth's government had crushed the rebellion of the northern Catholic earls (1568–9) and foiled the plots of the papal agent Ridolfi (1570–1) – both actions centered on Mary's cause. As for marriage, the problem had stalemated and was beginning to seem irrelevant: overtures from foreign princes had foundered or were in abeyance; and Elizabeth's dalliance with the dashing *arriviste* Robert Dudley, now Earl of Leicester, had not resulted in marriage or disgrace but in a *modus vivendi* of royal lady and romantic 'favorite.' But Elizabeth's tacit toleration of English Catholics who were quiescent yet loyal had become a scandal in Rome. The result in 1570 was Pius V's bull excommunicating 'that Pretended Queen of England' and absolving the English from obedience to her. This one stroke made English Catholics and Catholic Europe – especially Spain – Elizabeth's enemies and so served to excite and focus the English sense of their queen as bulwark between them and disaster. (On this first decade, see Erickson 1983, MacCaffrey 1968.)

the cult-forming period Like any Renaissance ruler, Elizabeth had been from the first routinely praised in sermons, poems, and pageantry. Such praise was rationalized as indirect counsel: 'there is surely no more effective method of reforming princes than to present them with a pattern of the good prince under the guise of praising them' (Erasmus ed 1974–, 2: Letter 179). Idealization as a strategy of influence underlies much of the celebration of Elizabeth in the uncertain 1560s. Thus to exalt her as 'the handmaid of the Lord' was to encourage her identification with the Protestant cause. But in the celebrations of the 1570s and 1580s, this didactic impulse generally yielded to an excited vision of the historically unique, mythical, quasi-divine Virgin Queen – a figure more to be wondered at than counseled.

A popular manifestation of the altered perception of the Queen after her excommunication were local celebrations of her Accession Day, 17 November, as a major countrywide festival during which sermons looked back to 1559 as the time of Englishmen's 'deliverance from the powers of darkness' and reminded them that 'only ... while God's holy handmaiden ruled' would they continue to be shielded from the 'chaotic hordes of the Antichrist of Rome ... It was an atmosphere charged with these thoughts that generated the fervent cult of the Queen' (Strong 1977:126–7). Behind such celebrations lay manipulation of public opinion by such spokesmen for the regime as the Bishops Jewel and Foxe and courtiers like Sir Henry Lee who during the 1560s had developed a mythology of the Queen as national savior and quasi deity who could be properly represented only through cultic metaphors.

Cults. These were of four basic types. (1) The earliest identified Elizabeth with the national heroines of the Old Testament – Judith, Esther, and the righteous judge Deborah. The day before her coronation, Elizabeth rode in public procession through London and received the city's tribute in pageants that combined adulation with instruction. The last depicted Deborah as an English queen 'in Parliament robes' who would lead 'God's People' by the sword from foreign 'bondage,' while a speech exhorted Elizabeth to follow this pattern (J. Nichols 1823, 1:53–4).

From now on, Old Testament heroines become the staple of Protestant celebration of the Queen in sermons, popular broadsheets, and civic receptions. In these cults (unlike those that follow), the strain of counsel is overt.

(2) The most surprising cult transferred features from the late medieval veneration of the Virgin Mary to the Virgin Queen. Though offensive to Catholics, it caught the sense of Elizabeth after 1570 as a figure whose life had become infinitely precious and who was ruling successfully though unmarried – as Calvin had suspected, a divinely ordained exception to male rule.

(3) An intensely important cult focused on a more secular devotion to Elizabeth as the remote beloved of the sonnet sequence, addressed by the male lover with less hope than despair. Raleigh's poems are central expressions of this cult, and his sonnet 'Methought I saw the grave, where *Laura* lay' salutes *The Faerie Queene* for making obsolete Petrarch's praise of Laura. Laura overlapped with the remote lady of late medieval romance whom knights made it their goal to honor, or the more otherworldly fay or fairy queen who was the chaste mistress of some virtuous knight. (See Wilson 1980:21–6.) However derived, the cult of the Queen as focus of erotic devotion was essentially a matter of court etiquette, one aspect of the game of sexual politics that Elizabeth played with her courtiers.

(4) Given Renaissance classicism, cults identifying Elizabeth with Greek and Roman goddesses were a necessary tactic for courtiers and scholars. Diana as the virgin goddess of chastity furnished an inevitable antique expression of the Virgin-Queen cult; but she also served as a ruler-figure, not only as goddess of the hunt but also in her identification with Luna, Cynthia, or Phoebe, moon goddess and sister of the sun god Phoebus Apollo. This Diana, as Conti says, has great power over things of the lower world and mediates to them something of the Divine Mover (*Mythologiae* 3.18).

Complementing Diana was a cult of Elizabeth as Venus, goddess of love and beauty, who gave focus to the court's adulation while her attributes of fertility could point allegorically to Elizabeth bringing peace and prosperity. Given the Renaissance monarch's function as agent of justice, an inevitable cult-figure for Elizabeth was Astraea, goddess of ideal justice who fled to heaven at the waning of the primeval Golden Age and became the constellation Virgo (the Virgin).

The most complex cult was a Diana-Venus or Virgo-Venus paradox nicely suited to a queen who projected conflicting images of herself, with its Virgo aspect enfolding a range of unspecified mythical allusions to virginal figures. Spenser makes frequent use of this cult (see *Belphoebe, *Britomart, *Gloriana, *Isis, *Mercilla, *Una).

According to standard encomiastic strategy, Elizabeth must not only reflect but surpass each deity. Sometimes she outdoes them in groups as in Peele's *Araygnement of Paris* (1584) or in the 'Hampton Court' painting (1569) showing her astonishing and dismaying Juno, Minerva, and Venus – the deities of rule, political wisdom, and beauty (Strong 1987: no 53). Latin verses on the frame describe the situation: 'Here are Juno great in her scepter and Minerva in clearness of mind, while Venus' beauty glows from her rosy lip; but when Elizabeth comes on the scene Juno flees away astonished, Minerva is struck dumb, and Venus blushes red.' In their surprise all three have dropped their proper symbols: Juno her scepter, Minerva her sword, and Venus her roses – now not only red but also white, ie, the Tudor sign of having brought to an end the Wars of the Roses. Thus the goddesses' attributes are properly only Elizabeth's. This is the first of what was to be a long series of allegorical depictions of the Queen.

Entertainments. The growth of mythologizing cults coincided with the development in the 1570s of imaginative entertainments glorifying Elizabeth. These are of three basic types. (1) The royal entry. The Queen's entry into London in 1559 set the pattern for subsequent official urban receptions. Borne in a procession meant to suggest a Roman triumph, Elizabeth would pause to view historical or moral tableaux and hear their reference to her expounded. From the beginning, she improvised (or seemed to improvise) responses to such addresses, thus imparting a dramatic element to a static form and showing sensitivity to her reign as theater. Some notable entries were at Warwick (1572), Bristol (1574), and Norwich (1578).

(2) The Accession Day tilts. The brainchild of Sir Henry Lee during the 1570s, these tournaments continued to the end of the reign. Though tilting no longer had martial relevance (see *chivalry), Lee developed its late medieval aspect as an athletic display in honor of one's lady, in this case the Queen. The imaginative impact of such honorific tilts can be felt in the frame-story Spenser gives *The Faerie Queene* where strange knights appear at Gloriana's 'Annuall feaste' (Accession Day?) and receive quests in which they can express her honor.

(3) Progress entertainments. Beginning in the 1570s but continuing through the reign, Elizabeth staged summer 'progresses' in the countryside with prolonged stays at great courtiers' houses. The most famous of these took place in 1575 at Kenilworth, where Leicester entertained the Queen for nineteen days. Arthurian motifs ran through the entertainment scripts (by Gascoigne) beginning when a Lady of the Lake welcomed Elizabeth as a figure of Arthur returned to effect acts of liberation. In Lee's reception of Elizabeth at Woodstock later that summer, partly scripted by Gascoigne, a blind hermit Hemetes involved her in a pastoral romance with the happy resolutions of its plot effected by her mere presence. A Faery Queen appeared to salute Elizabeth, apparently the first association of such a figure with her. In 1578, Leicester received Elizabeth again at Wanstead, for which Sidney wrote the *Lady of May*, a complex pastoral romance. These three progress entertainments of the late 1570s with their acted-out deifications of the Queen not only caught the sense of her invaluable, if problematic, uniqueness that had developed in this decade, but used her involvement in acted-out fictions as an oblique strategy of counsel.

the Armada period During the 1580s, the figure of Elizabeth served to focus an intensified patriotism in face of imminent invasion by Spain. In 1584, such a Spanish fleet had tried to set sail, and its famous successor was famously dispersed in 1588. Several portrait images from 1585 comment allegorically on the impending war in 'Briton fields ... Twixt that great Faery Queene and Paynim king' (I xi 7). For instance, the Sieve portrait (Strong 1987: no 84) shows a sober Elizabeth holding the sieve of the Vestal Virgin Tuccia, thereby implying the Virgin Queen's imperial claim and concomitant challenge to Spain. In the Ermine portrait (Strong 1987: no 111) a 'crowned litle Ermilin' (Artegall's device in III ii 25) and an unsheathed sword indicate a militant Virgin Queen ready to defend her just right.

(See **Elizabeth, images of** Figs 1–3.)

The most allegorically intricate of all images of Elizabeth, the Armada portrait of 1588 or 1589 (Strong 1987: no 138) presents a semi-sacred icon of God's victorious handmaid enthroned in earthly power and glory. Behind her on the left is an accurate depiction of the Armada approaching in tight-packed formation but about to be broken up by fire tugs from the French coast and then picked off by the technically advanced English ships flying the standard of St George. Beneath this scene the closed imperial crown sits above the royal hand which rests on a globe: altogether, a claim to New-World empire backed by naval superiority. On the other side the famous storm, read in England as sign of divine favor, finishes the Armada off, while below a carved mermaid adores Cynthia, the revealed queen of the sea. Elizabeth's dress is black and white, not only her personal colors as worn by her champions in jousts, but also the colors of Hercules – for the Renaissance the archetype of the altruistic hero who cleanses society of the monstrous. In nearly every portrait Elizabeth wears 'a bushel of pearls' (as Horace Walpole remarked) but here in conspicuous abundance to adumbrate vast wealth from Britain's emerging maritime empire. Among them are strands of 'black' pearls said to be like 'black muscat grapes,' important here for their rarity among jewels of the sea but more so as the one-time jewels of her late would-be successor Mary, Queen of Scots. (On Elizabeth's acquisition of these pearls, see Fraser 1969:348 and Jenkins 1959:136).

The Armada would have made ideal topical material for the 1590 *Faerie Queene*, especially Book I, but by 1588 the first two books at least were apparently already in manuscript circulation. Spenser seems to have projected an Armada allusion in I proem 3 where 'triumphant *Mart*' joins Venus '*After* his murdrous spoiles and bloudy rage' (italics added). But his creation of *FQ* I-III during the 1580s and its publication at the beginning of 1590 make it very much an Armada poem with its celebration of Elizabeth utterly in harmony with 1580s patriotism. One of Elizabeth's Armada medals, inscribed *tandem bona casta triumphat* (at last the virtuous virgin triumphs), would aptly summarize Book I. (On this medal, see Strong 1958:92–3.)

the close of the reign In the decade preceding her death in 1603, two attitudes had developed toward the aged Queen who was the last of her line. One was a decadent courtly cult promulgating the fantasy of perpetual youth that Elizabeth herself had cultivated. Its visual realizations took on what Strong has called a 'mask of youth' aspect. In contrast to Nicholas Hilliard's portrait images of the Queen in the 1570s (eg, Fig 4), his late portrait images show a girlish April Eliza (Strong 1987: nos 162–5), and Davies' *Hymnes of Astraea* (1599) apostrophize an ideal and changeless queen of unending spring. The last major image, the Rainbow portrait of c 1600–3 (Strong 1987: no 172), gives the Queen the mask-of-youth face but adds emblems of experience that sum up the myth of the reign: the rainbow of peace which requires the royal sun; the eyes and ears on the dress, signifying an all-knowing Minervan cognizance in matters of state; and on the sleeve a serpent with a heart dangling from its mouth to signify wisdom controlling emotion.

(See **Elizabeth, images of** Figs 4–6.)

But the decade's cult of the Queen's youth was at odds with the resentment of a now-aging generation of Spenser's contemporaries who saw their early expectations of success and advancement blocked by the rigidities of the regime (see Esler 1966). Spenser seems to have shared this late disillusionment in part, as evidenced by the Fairy court's frustration of Artegall's quest in Book V, the apology for omission of Gloriana in VI x 28, and Diana's spiteful destruction of Arlo in VII vi 37, 54–5.

Thomas H. Cain

The voluminous literature on Elizabeth and her age is made manageable by the short annotated bibliographies in Christopher Haigh, ed 1984 *The Reign of Elizabeth I* (London) and Paul Johnson 1974 *Elizabeth I: A Study in Power and Intellect* (London). Among the throng of biographies, Neale 1934 is the classic idealization. Carolly Erickson 1983 *The First Elizabeth* (New York), Wallace T. MacCaffrey 1968 *The Shaping of the Elizabethan Regime* (Princeton), and MacCaffrey 1981 are more detached.

For the entertainments, the basic collection of texts is J. Nichols 1823, still indispensable and the sole source for some scripts. Bergeron 1971 is an effective survey, while Jean Wilson 1980 *Entertainments for Elizabeth I* (Woodbridge, Eng) has a valuable introduction and additional texts. For the iconography of Elizabeth, the seminal study is Frances A. Yates 1947 'Queen Elizabeth as Astraea' *JWCI* 10:27–82 (rpt in Yates 1975). See also Roy C. Strong 1958 'The Popular Celebration of the Accession Day of Queen Elizabeth I' *JWCI* 21:86–103; Strong 1963; and Strong 1977.

Studies that deal at length with Spenser's

representation of Elizabeth include Cain 1978; Kermode 1971; McLane 1961; O'Connell 1977; and Wells 1983. See also Erasmus *Correspondence ... Letters 142 to 197* vol 2 in ed 1974–; Anthony Esler 1966 *The Aspiring Mind of the Elizabethan Younger Generation* (Durham, NC); Elizabeth Jenkins 1958 *Elizabeth the Great* (London); and Roy Strong 1987 *Gloriana: The Portraits of Queen Elizabeth I* (London).

Elizabeth and Spenser Elizabeth was born 7 September 1533 and ascended the throne 17 November 1558. For the 25 years of her girlhood, adolescence, and young womanhood, she lived in the court of her father Henry VIII, her brother Edward VI, and her older sister Queen Mary. She studied with Grindal and Ascham, learning to read, compose, and speak Greek and Latin, French and Italian (and later Spanish). With her teachers she conned her Greek Testament, her Church Fathers, her Melanchthon. From instructors she learned to delight in music and in dance, in hunting and in sewing. But her true nurse and abiding tutor was the court.

The court of the 1530s and 1540s was coarse in passion, refined in appearance, ablaze with the hunger for power. Wyatt said it was where men cloaked vice with the nearest virtue. She learned at court how to seem, how to avoid, how to choose the public show over the private need. Watching the shifting, ever-changing inner circles, with all men seeking, like a cloud of gnats over the great bog of Allen, to rise to the royal sun that spawned them, she learned to trust only her own powers, those innate and those derived, and to place her faith in nothing beyond what she possessed in herself.

She learned patience and delay. As she said much later, she learned, especially during her sister's reign, so stiff with terror and tears in the service of the Old Religion, 'how to keep silent.' When she was twenty years old, in all likelihood she scratched in the windowpane during confinement at Woodstock: 'Much suspected by me, / Nothing proved can be.' At court, by watching and waiting, she developed the instincts, the habits, and the style that later became her motto: *Taceo et video – I see and am silent.* Under Mary Tudor she learned how to give, as she would in the matter of Mary Stuart, an 'answere answerelesse.' She learned she had no one to answer to if she was sufficiently self-possessed.

She learned self-possession by watching the court and learning about power. Her innate powers of mind and character were developed so diligently that when she was sixteen Ascham could write a friend: 'Her mind has no womanly weakness, her perseverance is equal to that of a man, and her memory long keeps what it quickly picks up.' By watching, she also learned about public power. She learned that public power is a pure derivative of some overmastering idea to which all people agree; it is the force that accrues from some transcendent principle, the potency available for use in some bargain men make with heaven. The word *virtue* contains both the meanings: neutral force and the transcendent, moral compact.

She learned that power derived from such an overarching idea can only be held if one becomes the embodiment of the idea oneself. Only by complete self-absorption can one contain the grand principle and the force that therefrom derives. She learned that to hold power she first had to deny herself – deny herself the ordinary delights of body and of spirit that otherwise disperse potency and principle. She early chose to deny those forms of dispersal represented by sex, by marriage and family, by the sense of wonder. She learned to deny that delicious, delightful human capacity to be smitten by anything outside of oneself. Wonder, a luxury she never tasted, would be for others, who adored and feared her.

She learned not only that power is derivative and that it must be held close; she also learned that those who share in one's power are forever bound by something stronger than love. They are bound by need – the need to be defined by power's beautiful and mysterious clarity. Those who come to, or get close enough to be shaped by, the sovereign's power never forget it. They also never forgive power its clarifying coherence and they grow in resentment if the source of power recedes. She learned there is no one more dangerous than an intimate who fears exile.

And she learned about power that it is at bottom concerned only with the maintenance of itself, which is to say, that true power only answers to its source, to the principal idea whence it derives. At 25 she would have thought the notion that absolute power corrupts absolutely a sentimental axiom of a time grown blurred. Absolute power is nonexistent; power is only proximate, and circular, and can no more corrupt than light or wind can corrupt. If the first idea, the supreme fiction everyone agrees defines reality, is inward sound and invulnerable to the worms of doubt or fear, then whatever derives from that idea can be mishandled or lost but power itself can never spoil or be spoiled.

She learned of the grandeur of power and that the handling of power derived is not grand. She saw how using power is a domestic activity: how it is gathered and stored and apportioned in local, intimate, homely, daily moments; she saw how the careful cultivator of power, like a good housewife wise in the vicissitudes of weather and time, always stores more than enough, keeps much in reserve, never wastes, uses the power of others so as to conserve one's own. She learned never to dilute the larder. By watching, she learned that others will always waste their small portion eagerly enough on one's behalf if they are sufficiently enthralled by their sovereign. She learned therefore never to be enthralled precisely by what she would most burnish – her gorgeous, glittering self.

At court, she learned that power often resides where the world believes it does not dwell: she learned that power grows in not doing; that it can flourish in silence, gathering to itself more of itself. She learned that it must be used without doubt as it has been aggregated in men's minds, by deliberation. Above all, she learned that power lies in seeming. Power, she learned, is merely the strength of a systematic self-delusion on the part of the many about the primacy of some one grand idea no one has ever seen. She learned all the secrets the court could tell.

Of the court, Raleigh would spit in the 1590s: 'Say to the Court it glowes, / and shines like rotten wood' ('The Lie'). Spenser would spend three years there in the 1570s and later hammer out his hatred of the place, where a man expends his spirit only 'To fawne, to crowche, to waite, to ride, to ronne, / To spend, to give, to want, to be undonne' (*Mother Hubberds Tale* 905–6). But to Elizabeth, the court was nurse and tutor and university: its factions, her toys; its intrigues, her girlish pastimes; its backbiting, her lute; its shifting savageries, her spaniel; its endless, glittering glaze, her stay against time; its awesome magnificence, merely the movable cart that served her as a stage, the platform on which she played first to her countrymen and then to the world her multiple roles of prince, politician, goddess, woman. She played Bess of the ballads, Eliza of the sonnets; Deborah the good ruler of Judges 4–5; Astraea the Virgin Queen, derived from Virgil's fourth eclogue; Pandora, who knew all; Cynthia. Raleigh would see her, he told the younger Cecil, 'riding like Alexander, hunting like Diana, walking like *Venus* ... sometime playing like Orpheus.' She was called a new Constantine bringing a new religious dispensation, despite all the tensions with Puritan and Papist; she was called a new Augustus bringing a new era of peace, despite all the incessant wars to the north, the wars in and across the Channel. She was the bringer of unity to England; Fulke Greville in *Caelica* saw 'a Virgin sit, / The red, and white Rose quarter'd in her face; / Starre of the North, and for true guards to it, / Princes, Church, States, all pointing out her Grace.' Sir John Davies saw in her 'the Propp of Belgia, Stay of France, / Spaine's Foyle, Faith's Shield, and Queene of State.' As she gathered in her country's recent past, and all of Europe's woes, Thomas Churchyard saw 'she that sits in reagall Throne, / With Scepter, Sword, and Crowne. / (Who came from *Arthurs* rase and lyne).' He thus affirmed an essential strand in the Tudor myth, that her Welsh descent made her Arthur's heir, Queen in whom England's greatest King was caught up and made holy again.

All the roles she played were Gloriana, the single, sole and abiding fountainhead and goal of Unity. She *was* the grand idea: division – of religion and party and blood and region and level of society – would be in her healed into oneness, and from her transcendent oneness would come her awesome force, the tremendous power to draw all to her and to make all wish to be reconciled and reformed by her. Her people's hunger for unity became the celestial bargain: they would believe she embodied their ideal and submit, if she would deny everything except their need and thereby weld them together.

She understood her people and the nature of the compact between them as few monarchs ever have. She allowed her people to deify her in so many guises in order that she might be both source and instrument of power – a Phoenix, self-generating, self-absorbed, unique, mysterious, eternal. In this way, what she wanted most – that nothing essentially change in England – might be accomplished by her own untiring, absolute presence. Where is the evidence for this profoundly conservative goal? Simply the last sentence of her first proclamation as Elizabeth I, announcing her accession:

> And further we streightly charge and commaund, all maner our sayd subjectes of every degree, to kepe themselves in our peax, and not to attempt uppon anny pretence the breache, alteration or chaunge of any ordre or usage presently establyshed within this our Realme, upon payn of our indignacion and the perilles and punishment which thereto in anywise may belong.

While these words were meant to calm the turbulence after Mary, they also represent her basic goal.

Toward this goal, all her cunning, her ruthless ebullience, her dilatoriness, her life as supreme actress on the stage of court and kingdom, shot. Toward this goal, her self-fashioned mythological persona as the principle of unity tended. Above all, for this goal, she created and publicized herself, and caused herself to be adored, as Virgin. Her fabulous virginity, probably not the result of sexual fear or disability, probably real, was the consequence of a calculated political choice. Her virginity was a conscious stratagem of self-denial that successfully tapped the twin impulses to idolatry latent in the idealizing platonists, and the puritans – finally all the same large tribe – and in the adherents of the active, and the vast residual, Roman Catholicism. It was a stratagem that transformed those hungers for a living, forceful abstraction into the vision of a singular, inviolable, unified woman – divine, distant, breathing and visibly dazzling. Her virginity, like her emblem the Phoenix, promised and required devotion to an abiding ideal. Elizabeth held England together – through inflation, famine, war, religious tension, fears about invasion and succession, threats of civil war, crop failure, and plague – by making it promise to worship unity and constancy in her. It was her most brilliant performance and it was lifelong.

The single, overwhelming fact of her life was that she was a woman. By the alchemy of her political genius, she transmuted into seemingly inexhaustible strength a fact her contemporaries regarded as a fatally debilitating weakness. In the year of her ascension, 1558, John Knox coincidentally proclaimed to the world that the rule of women was a sign of the Fall, that it was 'monstriferouse.' In his *First Blast of the Trumpet against the Monstruous Regiment of Women*, Knox assured the world that a woman's reign 'is repugnant to nature, contumelie to God, a thing most contrarious to his reveled will and approved ordinance.' He also said that women were 'weake, fraile, impacient, feble, and foolishe.' For all the things she was, she was never any of these. In the year of the Armada, speaking to her troops, she seemed to remember Knox as she asserted what she had become in 30 years: 'I know that I have the Body of a week and feeble Woman, but I have the Heart and Stomach of a King, and a King of *England* too.' She was, the younger Cecil would say, 'more than a man, and (in troth) sometyme less than a woman.' The bejeweled icon of the later portraits showed, at last, the androgyne, another Renaissance image of unity and model of self-possessed power.

All the women she seemed to be, the ancient and the modern, the British and the Greek, the international coquette and the English virgin, were displayed in the greatest poem to celebrate her, or to celebrate England, in our language. Spenser's *Faerie Queene*, massive, intimate, melancholy, is a petition to her and a hymn to women. Though Helen and Penelope and Roma and Beatrice – awesome feminine presences – are central to the greatest poems of our tradition, no other poem in the West is so suffused by the role and power of women as *The Faerie Queene*. In that epic, the poet adds his power to Elizabeth's, idealizing her idealization of herself so that he might finally associate with her endless capacity to clarify and shape reality his imagination's power to simulate a coherent and unified world. We believe much of what we believe about Elizabeth, and so did most of her literate contemporaries, because of Spenser's platonizing drive to deify her. More than any other poet or publicist of the age, he made her into the idea whence derived her power. And more than any favorite, councilor, or suitor, he was dashed in his expectations of reciprocity, in his hopes for a role in reality commensurate with the role he realized for her. Spenser came to learn that you do not strike bargains with living goddesses; the poet can supplement her mystery, but he is always her subject. Much as he has the power to exalt her, she has the greater power to remain indifferent to him and beyond his reach.

To understand how and why the poet wished to exercise his power, we must step back and look at the role of poetry in Spenser's time and poem. A summation of the role of poetry is offered us by Queen Elizabeth's godson, Sir John Harington, in the 'Brief Apology for Poetry' prefixed to his translation of *Orlando furioso* (1591). Poetry, says Harington, should 'be studied and imployed, as was intended by the first writers and devisers thereof, which is to soften and polish the hard and rough dispositions of men, and make them capable of vertue and good discipline.'

'Vertue and good discipline' echoes Spenser's own statement concerning the role of poetry set forth in the Letter to Raleigh appended to Books I-III in 1590. There, Spenser lays out the purpose and plan of *The Faerie Queene* and tells the reader that 'the generall end ... of all the booke is to fashion a gentleman or noble person in vertuous and gentle discipline.' This language echoes yet another preface. In 1485, William Caxton printed Sir Thomas Malory's *Morte Darthur* and told the reader he wished 'noble men' to 'see and lerne the noble actes of chyvalrye, the jentyl and vertuous dedes that somme knyghtes used in tho[se] dayes.'

Poetry, therefore, was assumed to present paradigms. These paradigms were meant to teach moral lessons in order to instill the desire for proper behavior and civil society. The audience for the didactic moralizing of poetry was men, men already fitted to be receptive. Yet Spenser also has a 'noble person' in view; he will not only 'fashion' or shape his traditional audience, but will also aim at his Queen. She is as much the object of his poem as she is the subject. He wishes to influence her as he deifies her, to shape the state as much as to construe the state's ruler as a model for the individual.

Caxton's 'Jentyl and vertuous dedes,' Harington's 'vertue and good discipline,' Spenser's 'vertuous and gentle discipline' all implicitly assert the delimiting power of paradigmatic images. That is, these formulas assume human behavior will spin out of control if not presented with models that contain our tendency to formlessness. Like the fixed commonplaces of rhetoric, models for proper behavior bring boundaries to human activity, limits by language that will contain the rush to shapelessness that is the result of the Fall. In the word *discipline* (derived from L *discipulus* and finally *discere* 'to learn'), with its overtones of penitence and punishment, Spenser and Harington posit the goal of self-control and self-government. *Gentle* is the moderating word, softening the strict, forceful moral constraint while at the same time (its root being identical to Dante's *gentile*, from *gens*) bearing the meaning of the human stock that is susceptible to becoming an aristocrat of manners and civil behavior. For all three – printer, translator, and poet – the word *vertue* carries the double meaning of a moral or transcendent pattern for behavior and (as in Machiavelli's *virtù*, at whose root is *vir*) of force or potency.

The fifteenth- and sixteenth-century commonplaces for the role of poetry carry complex meanings and indicate the seriousness with which poets, and others, regarded poetry. They viewed it as having a moral force for individual control and social betterment similar to the political power for containment and reform exercised by the good ruler. And while the worlds of poetry and politics would ultimately remain separate and unavailable to each other, it is nevertheless understandable why the poet could believe his power like the prince's, and why the prince would wish to have her poets tractable and domesticated. It is not so hard to understand why Essex and his bravos would stage *Richard II* right before their attempted coup; they all believed language, if shaped, was capable of shaping reality.

Spenser believes he can shape his times by presenting paradigms of Elizabeth in his poem; he also believes he can influence Elizabeth's acts and deeds by way of his poem. He chooses, he tells Raleigh, the history of Arthur as the most excellent and fit whereby to teach, and he then lays out a plan for a poem in twelve, perhaps twenty-four, books in which Arthur, inspired by a vision of the Fairy Queen, seeks throughout Fairyland to find her. 'In that Faery Queene,' Spenser says, 'I meane glory in my generall intention, but in my particular I conceive the most excellent and glorious person of our soveraine the Queene, and her kingdome in Faery land.' She will be Gloriana, the paradigm for us all.

The paradigm for her is Arthur. Spenser presumes to instruct his first principle by presenting her with the only husband he could safely propose and she could safely take, Arthur who is the history and future of England. 'In the person of Prince Arthure I sette forth magnificence in particular, which vertue for that (according to Aristotle and the rest) it is the perfection of all the rest.' Arthur, here prince because he is not yet at one with the Fairy Queen and therefore not yet King, embodies all the virtues that will be severally displayed, each in its own book of the poem, each under the aegis of a knight who leaves her court to better the world. The fiction is that all twelve knights will be gathered back into her court at the end when, though the poet does not say so, Arthur too will come home and find her. Redcrosse is the knight of Holiness in Book I; Guyon the knight of Temperance in Book II; Britomart the knight of Chastity in Book III.

So much Spenser told Raleigh in 1590. In 1596, when the second three books were added to the first three, Book IV, Of Friendship, has a number of heroes, Britomart chief among them; Artegall, whom she seeks, is the knight of Justice in Book V, and Calidore is the knight of Courtesy in Book VI. There the poem stops. The poet dies in 1599. In 1609, two cantos of the Book of Mutabilitie, numbered vi and vii, and two stanzas of viii, were published as a coda. So the great scheme, projected in the 1580s, broke down. The poet never saw Arthur marry his Fairy Queen; he never saw all the knights home. Decay and change were in reality too strong. Formlessness, the poem's deepest fear, won again. Exile, the condition of life for the poet in Ireland, for the virtuous knights seeking to return to Gloriana's court, remained the constant state. The world finally is never shaped or saved.

The grand idea of twelve, much less twenty-four, books was never realized. Yet the massive plan, placing such tremendous pressure on structure to convey meaning, is sufficiently realized to tell us what Spenser hoped for. If we look at the poem as it remains, and consider it a ruin of time, fragmentary but projecting the ideal pattern, we can see what Spenser means to teach us and his Sovereign Queen.

We have six books of twelve cantos each, and a seventh of two cantos. We have a poem about overcoming exile and returning to the center, about pursuing an ideal vision and making it flesh, about division in the world and the need for healing, about placing boundaries around change and containing the mad rush to moral dissolution that is our fallen condition. We have a poem that sees us all, like Redcrosse, 'Pourd out in loosnesse on the grassy grownd, / Both carelesse of his health, and of his fame' (I vii 7), if we do not submit to moral mastery. We have a poem where Arthur has a vision in sleep of the one whose reality will redeem us. 'When I awoke, and found her place devoyd, / And nought but pressed gras, where she had lyen ... From that day forth I lov'd that face divine; / From that day forth I cast in carefull mind, / To seeke her out with labour, and long tyne, / And never vow to rest, till her I find' (I ix 15). The constant note of care, of travail, permeates the poem as completely as does Arthur's quest for the ideal reality that pressed the grass that night.

These deep tides running through the poem are shaped by the overarching structure. As I have suggested elsewhere (see Giamatti 1975), in all six books, cantos i and ii establish, through the act of some force concentrated in a dwelling or house, the principles of division and discord, and this divisive energy holds sway over the first six cantos of each book. Then, usually by canto vii, always by canto viii, Arthur appears and begins to heal the wounds or to restore the losses suffered in the first six cantos. If Arthur does not appear by canto vii, some grand vision usually does – as it does at III vi, the vision of flux and fecundity in the Garden of Adonis, or at V vii, when Britomart envisions Concord in her dream at Isis Church; if the redemptive Arthur does appear by vii, the grand vision often appears in canto x, as at I x, when Redcrosse sees Jerusalem from the Mount of Contemplation, or at IV x, when Scudamour recounts his vision of Concord in the Temple of Venus, or at VI x, where Calidore sees Colin and the maidens on Mount Acidale. There is also in the ninth or tenth canto of each book another structure or dwelling, answering the place of discord at the outset of the book, and concentrating the preoccupations of the book: the house of Holiness (I x) or of Alma (II ix); Malbecco's castle (III ix) foreshadowing the house of Busirane; the Temple of Venus (IV x), the palace of Mercilla (V ix), and the cottage of Meliboe (VI ix). Containment of energy and focusing of force are constant imperatives in a poem about moral shapeliness.

At the end of each book, the agent of division and deformation – the Dragon in I, Acrasia in II, Busirane in III, Grantorto in V, the Brigands in VI – is challenged or defeated, while in IV, Proteus and his hall are mastered by the poet, who absorbs the protean energies to transform and makes them his own in the marriage of Thames and Medway. The poet thus displays the self-mastery that each hero has had to learn. And after overcoming the power of debate, decay, and dissension, the twelfth canto then ends with redemption, variously figured as betrothal, marriage, rescue, or right restored. In Book I xii, Una is restored to her parents, the King and Queen, who shadow Adam and Eve; their kingdom, Eden, is redeemed, and Una is betrothed to Redcrosse. And out of Book I xii, flow the versions of restoration and unity that animate the other books. As a girl is restored to her parents in I xii, so also is a girl restored to hers in VI xii; as a land is redeemed from evil and restored to its rightful condition in I xii, so also is a kingdom restored aright in II xii and V xii; as there is a betrothal very like a spousal in I xii, so also is a bride redeemed in III xii, so also do a betrothal and a marriage occur in IV xii.

There are innumerable patterns in this poem but the deepest are those concerned with restoring relationships – of child to parent, a people to its land, lover to beloved. Those are the sacred paradigms in the poem, all versions of romance's drive to re-establish Edenic, or at least ideal, sentiments and landscapes, and to show unity and oneness in the realm where it is hardest to accomplish, in history. The healing of the divisions in history are here figured by the immensely satisfying reunion of the generations. The embrace of parents and children, each enacting the other's part, shows the poet's deepest hope, the victory in time, in the span of our human time, over the force of time that will always dissolve the bands of love and sunder us each from each.

By the structure of his poem which promotes reconciliation and reunion, Spenser desired to teach his sovereign. He would teach his Queen to overcome the debates of religion, the division of party, the dangers of foreign war, the discontinuity of childlessness, and to win for her people and her land the unity she embodied. He also presumes to show her, within the body of his poem, how the poet's power was in its way as splendid as hers. He asserts, again and again, his own hegemony over an empire as vast and turbulent as hers, the empire of language. He wishes her to understand that he too is a sovereign, though in fact he came to believe less and less in the efficacy of his potency as monarch while she, from all one can tell, scarcely noticed him or his power at all. Let us see how he says it.

In the proem to Book II, the poet's confidence is high. He addresses the Queen directly, and directly challenges what he knows some detractors will say of his poem: 'this famous antique history, / Of some th'aboundance of an idle braine / Will judged be, and painted forgery, / Rather then matter of just memory.' But what he says is true, true even if unseen, true in the realms that lie beyond the outward eye. Do not wonders like the Indian Peru, the Amazon, 'fruitfullest *Virginia*,' exist even if hitherto beyond view? 'Why then should witlesse man so much misweene / That nothing is, but that which he hath seene?' Reality is what the mind apprehends beyond the limits of this world. 'Of Faerie lond yet if he more inquire, / By certaine signes here set in sundry place / He may it find.' The poet asserts that his power to set 'certaine signes' both reflects a reality that lies beyond and creates for the reader a palpable image of that reality. 'Signes' are everywhere, in the paradigms, rhetorical figures, blazons or devices – in the very words themselves. Behind any theory of knowledge is a theory of language; behind the platonizing surge of the poem lies the conviction that language moors or grapples the transcendent reality of ideas to our fallen state, shadowing what awaits us, ordering the chaos that surrounds us. To believe a word can shadow the grand reality beyond is to know that a sign may be truly reflective of reality – but it is also to know that a 'signe' may be only a 'scene,' may be only 'seen.' It is to fear that the medium for grappling or mooring transcendent reality to our fallen state may only make a misleading illusion, may fashion only a counterfeit.

Though Spenser will offer many examples of the misleading power of language, the insubstantiality of words, he focuses our attention very early on his power truly to signify and he returns us to that view very late in the poem. In Book V vii, Britomart enters Isis Church and sees an idol that shows force in the service of truth and restraint. Britomart falls before her and prays: 'To which the Idoll as it were inclining, / Her wand did move with amiable looke, / By outward shew her inward sence desining' (8).

The idol is language used as Quintilian said it was in allegory, as *alieniloquium*, a sign that means other than what it appears to mean. By designing an idol who 'as it were' moves, Spenser figures a figure for poetic language, an artifact that is alive with significance. He asserts his power to link paradigms and energy, to make a shape that is ideal and charged with moral meaning. Idols that act like words, words that are idols – these are the signs that make Fairyland and show us how to live ideal lives.

If his poetry is palpable moral abstraction, what can his poetry do? In the first two stanzas of IV ii, he tells us:

Firebrand of hell first tynd in Phlegeton,
By thousand furies, and from thence out throwen
Into this world, to worke confusion,
And set it all on fire by force unknowen,
Is wicked discord, whose small sparkes once blowen
None but a God or godlike man can slake;
Such as was *Orpheus*, that when strife was growen
Amongst those famous ympes of Greece, did take
His silver Harpe in hand, and shortly friends them make.

Or such as that celestiall Psalmist was,
That when the wicked feend his Lord tormented,
With heavenly notes, that did all other pas,
The outrage of his furious fit relented.
Such Musicke is wise words with time concented,
To moderate stiffe minds, disposd to strive:
Such as that prudent Romane well invented,
What time his people into partes did rive,
Them reconcyld againe, and to their homes did drive.

All *The Faerie Queene* is here: discord and division, and all-consuming fire, to be slaked only by the 'God or godlike man,' the poet – whether secular or divine, whether ancient like Orpheus or David in 1 Samuel 16.23 or Agrippa in Livy's *History* (2.32) or modern like himself. Healing and reconciliation can be brought by 'wise words with time concented [harmonized]'; such moral music will civilize 'stiffe minds, disposd to strive.' It is instructive that Spenser's definition of poetry and its power follows upon the divine examples of Orpheus and David and proffers, as it were, the example of Menenius Agrippa, the civic example of a polity unified. He is always teaching us and his Queen, always celebrating his awesome lineage and potency as a poet, claiming quasi-divine status for the poet and for his moral art.

He could not sustain this superb optimism, or innocence, for he had to face the consequences of his faith in his art. And that meant facing what had been implicit all along – that his poetry was perhaps not a sign of the supernal, but might in fact be only a 'painted forgery' (II proem 1), only a 'painted show' (VI x 3), or worse. In the figure of the hag Sclaunder, the poet faced up to the horror language could wreak (IV viii 26):

Her words were not, as common words are ment,
T'expresse the meaning of the inward mind,
But noysome breath, and poysnous spirit sent
From inward parts, with cancred malice lind,
And breathed forth with blast of bitter wind;
Which passing through the eares, would pierce the hart,
And wound the soule it selfe with griefe unkind:
For like the stings of Aspes, that kill with smart,
Her spightfull words did pricke, and wound the inner part.

Because he knows that words can bring forth evil as well as good, monsters as well as moral shapes, he gradually loses faith in his signs, in his system of allegorical 'other speech' by which he creates paradigms to reform the spirit in each of us. He never loses faith in virtue, he loses faith in his power to project its image. At the very outset of Book VI, he confesses, 'vertues seat is deepe within the mynd, / And not in outward shows, but inward thoughts defynd' (proem 5). The power to make reliable imagery has failed; there is no coherent 'outward shew ... inward sence desining,' no trustworthy set of signs to make or mirror the moral life.

By the end of his poem, the poet has given up on his power. Perhaps that is why he stops. The last woman in his poem is Dame Nature, who combines in herself all, male and female, order and energy, ideal form and the stuff of life. She is his last version of Elizabeth. He cannot encompass her: 'for, well I weene / That this same day, when she on *Arlo* sat, / Her garment was so bright and wondrous sheene, / That my fraile wit cannot devize to what / It to compare, nor finde like stuffe to that, / As those three sacred *Saints*, though else most wise, / Yet on mount *Thabor* quite their wits forgat, / When they their glorious Lord in strange disguise / Transfigur'd sawe; his garments so did daze their eyes' (VII vii 7).

We recall that in the seventh canto of each book a vision of redemption, or the figure of Arthur, usually has appeared; here, in the seventh stanza of the seventh canto of the seventh book, where the final Revelation should be (if we have read the poem, and the Bible's final book, closely), we find the last goddess. And we find the poet able to limn her only by reference to the Gospels of Matthew and Mark. His own words fail; only God's words can accommodate his first and last goddess. A godlike man, the poet, can transform our ideals into a lifelike reality; only the word of God can transfigure in reality. The power of the poet is an innate power, derived only by analogy but not directly from the idea of the Word that was made flesh. The poet's power cannot make flesh out of ideas and his power cannot approach his Queen's, which is between his and God's. Poetry finally cannot do more than aspire to a condition like political power. They are separate worlds.

The poet died on 13 January 1599. Jonson told Drummond of Hawthornden that after the Irish rebels burned his house and a little child new born, 'he and his wyfe escaped, and after, he died for lake of bread in King street, and refused 20 pieces sent to him by my Lord of Essex, and said, he was sorrie he had no time to spend them.' Camden tells us he 'was buried at *Westminster* neere Chawcer, at the charges of the Earle of *Essex*, all Poets carrying his body to Church, and casting their dolefull Verses, and Pens too into his grave.' In the final falling away, the poet of Elizabeth became the care of Essex.

She died four years later, cruelly wasted, lying on cushions on the floor, her court in constant touch with her successor, James, power ebbing from her. Yet she kept enough so that Camden could tell of her end in all the ideal ways she, and her poets, had taught an age.

On the 24. of *March*, being the Eve of the Annunciation of the Blessed Virgin, she (who was born on the Eve of the Nativity of the same Blessed Virgin) was called out of the Prison of her earthly Body to enjoy an everlasting Country in Heaven, peaceably and quietly leaving this Life after that happy manner of Departure which *Augustus* wished for, having reigned 44 Years, 4 Months, and in the 70. Year of her Age; to which no King of *England* ever attained before ... No Oblivion shall ever bury the Glory of her Name: for her happy and renowned Memory still liveth, and shall for ever live in the Minds of men to all Posterity, *as of one who* (to use no other then her Successour's Expression) *in Wisedome and Felicity of Government surpassed* (without Envy be it spoken) *all the Princes since the days of* Augustus.' A. BARTLETT GIAMATTI

Reprinted, by permission, from *The Yale Review* 73(1984):321–37, copyright Yale University.

Elizabethan age The Elizabethan age, like the Victorian, may be divided into two halves – but even more decisively; for with the Elizabethans, the decades up to 1580 were a period of cautious consolidation, of exploration, feeling their way outwards in various directions, both in body and mind, of preparation for the astonishing flowering that was to come. It must never be forgotten that England was a latecomer to the Renaissance. The clue to its achievement is that the English were a small people, some five million strong, inhabiting only half an island on the northwestern shelf of Europe, essentially backward compared with the countries that led in the Renaissance: Italy above all, France and the Netherlands, Spain and Portugal, the Rhineland and the cultivated cities of southern Germany.

One may visualize the Renaissance impulse as a series of stones thrown into a pool, creating ever-widening ripples which spread until they reach Scotland, northern Germany, Denmark, and Scandinavia. But what accounts for the speed of backward little England in catching up? For that is the most striking characteristic of the phenomenon – especially after the disturbed and dismal black decades of mid-century, the 1540s and 1550s, covering the later years of Henry VIII, the disappointed promise of Edward VI's reign, the reaction without hope of Mary's brief hiatus.

Internally, the first two decades of Elizabeth I's reign, the 1560s and 1570s, saw on the whole a considerable measure of *apaisement*, if not actual appeasement, a spirit of tolerance and lenity in government of which the Queen was justifiably proud. Inevitably, the dynamic of the Reformation was resumed (not wholly to her liking), but in less sharp and divisive terms than under Edward VI. Nevertheless, the earlier Elizabethans – Burghley, Bacon, the Dudleys, Matthew Parker – were really Edwardians: it is curious to think that, if the promising young Edward VI had lived his full span, we should have been talking about the Edwardian age.

The impulse at work was continuous. The Reformation experience – a revolution in itself – was being absorbed into the nation's tissues. The lands of the monasteries and a good deal of the wealth of the church had been redirected much more productively into secular channels, taken up and developed by the rising gentry and middle classes, as vigorous younger sons founded expanding families. Expansion was the word. Everywhere one could see Reformation families – like the Raleighs, Grenvilles, Drakes, Eliots, Rashleighs, Champernownes – putting the profits from church lands into shipping, commercial, then colonial enterprise, from Ireland to the New World.

In the 1560s Elizabeth's able administrators set on foot the systematic nourishing of the marine and fishing industries, the exploration and development of the country's natural resources. When they took over a defeated and distracted England in 1558–9, the island was dependent on foreign countries for the new armaments: brass cannon, firearms, gunpowder. A search was instituted, the necessary ores discovered. By the end of her reign, England was the leading exporter of cannon in Europe. The superior gunnery of the English fleet against the Armada of 1588 spoke eloquently to the outer world: a first-class naval power had arisen.

Externally, the discovery of America made the fortune of England – as it had done for Spain – but more decisively and lastingly. For the arrival of a whole New World upon the horizon tipped the balance of Europe away from the Mediterranean to the Northwest, and the British Isles were now at the strategic nub of the shortest Atlantic crossing. Economically the most efficient society in Europe (after the fatal blow to Antwerp and the southern Netherlands in 1576, from which London profited hugely), England was well placed to make the most of her opportunity, and proceeded to do so. Eventually, the more North America developed and prospered, the more did Britain.

The 1570s were filled with oceanic voyages, deliberately and boldly conceived, forecasting what was to come. The Elizabethans followed in Edwardian tracks to make the first oceanic contacts with, and for, Russia, expanding trade down the Volga to the Caspian and Persia. Later penetration of the Mediterranean in force led to the Levant Company and to trade with the Near East. Attempts to find a Northwest Passage to the Far East led to voyages of exploration – to Labrador, to Hudson's Bay, up the Davis Strait – and to eventual possession of Newfoundland. Drake's voyage around the world – the most successful in the history of navigation – not only penetrated the Spanish preserve of the Pacific and yielded immense returns in geographical knowledge, but ultimately directed attention to the East Indies. Some of the specie found its way to the East India Company, founded in 1600, from which eventuated an Empire.

Meanwhile, the Atlantic voyages piloted planned settlement on the coast of America – *Virginia* to the Elizabethans. The intellectual propagandist for this was the leading geographer, Richard Hakluyt (the fantastic Elizabethan spelling for the recognizable Herefordshire name of Hacklet), who worked in close association with the practical leaders of colonial enterprise, Sir Humphrey Gilbert, Raleigh, Grenville, Sir Ferdinando Gorges, and others.

In the year after the Armada, all this activity received its timeless expression in what has been called the prose epic of Elizabethan literature, Hakluyt's *Principal Navigations, Voyages, and Discoveries of the English Nation* (1589). This immense and classic work was deliberately conceived to catch up with the record of other peoples, Italians, Spaniards, Portuguese, French. It provides a precise, and notable, example of our theme – and with it we are over the threshold of the 1580s.

In the 1580s, everything comes together, the culmination of those previous decades of preparation and exploration, of trials and hesitations, along with deliberate planning and bold ventures. It is difficult, if not impossible, to account for movements of the spirit, but the historian can at least observe comparable concatenations of circumstances. Coruscating periods in civilization appear to arise at times of strenuous testing – especially when a small people confronts a great power and comes through successfully. 'Look, we have come through,' in D.H. Lawrence's phrase, or 'they are people such / That mend upon the world,' in Shakespeare's. The inspiration runs through the veins and finds expression in many forms: compare fifth-century Athens after her successful confrontation with the Persian Empire, or the golden age of Rembrandt's Holland after it emerged from the long struggle with Spain.

Similarly with Elizabethan England: it is as if the heightened tension raised self-awareness and its various forms of expression to a higher power and fused them in the heat. One can *feel* the rising temperature, the sense of urgency, the excitement, in the state papers and documents of the 1580s. Francis Drake to the Queen: 'We trust so to handle the matter that the Duke of Medina Sidonia will wish himself at St Mary Port among his orange trees'; or again, as the danger of the Armada came nearer, 'The Lord of all strengths is with you.' And of course the Queen herself responded and gave inspiration, riding on her white horse among the troops at Tilbury, with a long plume flying from her headdress: 'I know I have the body of a weak and feeble woman, but I have the heart and stomach of a king, and of a king of England too, and think foul scorn that Parma or Spain, or any prince of Europe should dare to invade the borders of my realm.'

It must have been an unforgettable occasion for the thousands of menfolk who got a glimpse of the famous woman who gave her name to the age. Again, the fact that the sovereign was a woman had its own psychological importance in the appeal she exerted – we see her exploitation of it in her speech. The adulation expressed in the literature of the time, the portraiture, the music – *The Triumphs of Oriana* – is perfectly sincere, we should realize, and not be anachronistic about it. Then, too, Elizabeth was the supreme actress of the age, always appealing to the gallery and showing herself constantly to her people in London and the populous South, in regular progresses and on state occasions – openings of Parliament, processions, thanksgivings, Accession Day tilts and tournaments, feasts of the Order of the Garter, and suchlike.

The diaries of Burghley and Walsingham show her constantly on the move, not only traveling among her own many palaces – Whitehall, St James', Greenwich, Richmond, Hampton Court, Windsor, Nonsuch, Oatlands – but quartering herself and her court upon her subjects (a devastatingly expensive honor). We find her frequently enough visiting or stopping at Leicester House on Thames-side – where Spenser himself would have had the opportunity of seeing his sovereign close at hand.

All this naturally went with a good deal of patriotic boasting, well into the 1590s – one hears it in the earlier historical plays of Shakespeare, in the speeches of John of Gaunt, in *King John*, right up to the reverberating capture of Cádiz in 1596. We note this boasting as a recurring feature among youthful, emerging peoples today; and anyway, the Elizabethan English did capture Cádiz (Donne was there, Spenser wrote about it, Shakespeare noted it) – the Spaniards never captured Plymouth.

The lasting expressions of the experience of the age are in culture, in literature and the arts – notably in Shakespearean drama – in which all can share across the world today, though naturally, those who speak the language of Shakespeare can share most intimately, with the most feeling.

The language itself offers prime evidence of the expansive spirit of the age – we might even say the expansion of spirit. For the language was reaching out to colonize new words – primarily from Latin and Greek, but also from modern languages – to express the crowding experiences the Elizabethans underwent, and the new knowledge of every kind which they were so rapidly acquiring. In the course of the age, the Elizabethan vocabulary must have doubled. It is reckoned that Shakespeare's vocabulary of some 8000 words is double that in average use today. Spenser, who was criticized for his resort to archaic forms and usages, is not an exception, for he is also *adding* to the language by reviving old words. All the commentators on the subject, such as Puttenham, are aware of this movement of the spirit, and they are aware of it as something *new* and also characteristic of the time.

No art is more visually revealing of the character of an age than its architecture. We can *see* its ambition in the palaces Elizabethan courtiers built for themselves, the immense size of Burghley House at Stamford or Hatfield, though Lord Burghley's Theobalds and Sir Christopher Hatton's Holdenby (which have disappeared) were even larger; so too Audley End, of which only one range remains. And we can appreciate the fantasy of the age in the skyscraper of a hall at Wollaton or in the soaring turrets of Hardwick, built by the ambitious daughter of a small Derbyshire squire, who became the ancestress of three or four dukedoms.

Scores, if not hundreds, of manor houses attest the taste and increasing prosperity of the age, while lower down the scale in that hierarchical society took place 'the Great Rebuilding,' in which yeomen and farmers rehoused themselves in markedly greater comfort the length and breadth of the land. In the churches, thousands of monuments – altar-tombs, effigies, busts, tablets, heraldic sculpture – were erected, ocular evidence of the rise of the gentry, the most significant social feature of the time, and the most energizing class in the spectrum. These monuments also bear witness to the more secular character of the age: local gentry in the places where stood the medieval altars, shrines, and statues of the saints.

Art historians recognize portraits and portraiture as the characteristic Renaissance development in the arts, for it goes along with the increased self-awareness which is of the essence of the Renaissance experience. Thousands of representations of greater and lesser personages of the time have come down to us; in them, we can read the wide variations of human expression, as in the drama, from the regal splendor of the Queen's portraits, the symbolism of her attributes (as in *The Faerie Queene*), the politic wariness and reserve, to fantasies of love and war or plain housekeeping domesticity. In portraiture, the summit of refinement and sensibility was achieved in the miniatures of Nicholas Hilliard and Isaac Oliver, with which we may correlate the sonnet sequences of the time. Again, the note is a secular one, for, in Protestant England, the visual representation of Counter-Reformation religious sensibility – sometimes almost orgiastic (as in the Bodleian portrait of Nicholas Harpsfield) – was censored.

Even the jewelry gives us the note, as does the music. The Queen's jewelers were partly English (like the poet Herrick's grandfather) and partly Italian. Their designs show the native inspiration in the simple love of flowers – rose, lily, woodbine (as in Shakespeare's songs) – along with elaborate designs of more sophisticated foreign artists. As again with Verzelli glassware, Venetian-inspired.

We now know that the madrigals – which began in England at the same moment as the war with Spain – were inspired from Italy, seedbed of the Renaissance in general. The earlier Tudor period had produced the splendid church music of Taverner, Tye, Shepherd, and others – a last flowering of medieval music going back to Dunstable. The Reformation imposed a change and gave a new inspiration with the ending of the Latin rite and the new vernacular liturgy. In this, we glimpse something of the subtle interpenetration of Renaissance and Reformation influences, for what was characteristic of the music of the Renaissance was the dominance of the word – of which late medieval polyphony had taken little consideration.

These new developments fused with those from abroad, essentially Italy – cultural contacts with which were of the utmost significance for the Renaissance – to produce the golden age of English music. William Byrd was recognized by his contemporaries as its leading spirit, his accomplishment prolific in all fields. The dual character of his work bears witness to the 'duplicity' of the age: the blithe and positive quality of his writing for the Anglican rite, the timeless *Innerlichkeit* of his Latin Masses and Corpus Christi motets. For he was a Counter-Reformation convert to Catholicism, though protected by a cultivated Queen, no fanatic, whose organist of the Chapel he was.

Thomas Tallis of the previous generation, Henry VIII took over from Waltham Abbey at its suppression for his Chapel Royal. It is not generally known that he became a conforming Anglican; it is thus appropriate that his music has remained customary through the centuries for the services of the English church.

It is impossible to do justice here to the proliferation or the quality of Elizabethan music, for it penetrated into every corner of the national life. But at the summit, we observe again the cross-fertilization of Renaissance England with Italy, for the Queen's musicians were half English and half foreign, Ferraboscos, Bassanos, and Laniers. Byrd enjoyed friendly rivalry with Alfonso Ferrabosco I, and Jonson was a close friend of Alfonso Ferrabosco II. For a time, Shakespeare lived in the same street in Bishopsgate as Thomas Morley, who wrote the music for at least one of his songs and whose madrigals exemplified the lighter Italianate school. The close interweaving of music with drama needs no further illustration than the plays of Shakespeare, most musical of them all. (His musical 'Dark Lady' was born a Bassano, daughter of one of the Queen's Italian musicians. Her protector, Lord Chamberlain Hunsdon, patron of Shakespeare's company, had a number of musical compositions dedicated to him; his daughter-in-law, Elizabeth Spencer, was a patroness of Edmund. That the poet was an offshoot of the Spencer clan is evidenced by the fact that he was recognized as such by all of them. Spelling with *s* or *c* is quite interchangeable in Elizabethan spelling, and has not the slightest importance – it is merely a minor irritant.)

It is usually held that the characteristic science of the Renaissance was geography, and this is convincing when one reflects that the world itself was expanding before men's astonished eyes. How inspiring that is! – contracting monotonously in ours, no stimulus to the imagination. The voyages led to a vast increase in geographical knowledge and improvements in map-making. The real importance of John Dee has been exaggerated: Mercator was much more reliable and in touch with the seamen in London, which he visited; Molyneux constructed his globes at Lambeth and 'the new map with the augmentation of the Indies.' Marked advances were made by practical craftsmen in relation to the compass, cross-staff, and nautical and astronomical instruments.

Thomas Hariot, Raleigh's adviser and tutor in navigational matters, was the leading algebraist in Europe, along with Viète. But he was an all-round scientist, whose importance is realized fully only today, because he did not publish but left a mass of esoteric papers. He possessed a rudimentary telescope, with which he observed Jupiter's satellites contemporaneously with Galileo and astonished the Indians of Virginia. His *Brief and True Report of the New Found Land of Virginia* shows him as the first English anthropologist, as John White's depictions of the flora and fauna fix him as the first watercolorist. Hariot made observations in other fields as well, in meteorology, statics, physics.

The greatest physicist, however, was Dr William Gilbert, president of the Royal College of Physicians; his *De magnete*, based on two or three hundred experiments, explored the alluring subject of magnetic attraction. Viewing the earth itself as a great magnet may be seen as a stage on the way to Newton and the theory of universal gravitation. Contemporaneously, Bacon was clearing the ground of a great deal of unilluminating teleology, making way for advances in empirical science which were eventually institutionalized in the Royal Society.

Perhaps the subtlest inspiration to susceptible minds, though impossible of diagnosis, was just the element of dubiety, of uncertainty: knowledge was advancing, the frontiers being pushed back – but into what region? Not to know was in itself stimulating to the imagination, as we see in Shakespeare no less than in Montaigne. What did Shakespeare really believe about ghosts and spirits, or the influence of the planets? Sun and moon exerted obvious influence on the earth: why not the stars? Elizabethans hardly distinguished between astronomy and astrology, between chemistry and alchemy. Lord Keynes, no historian, was surprised to find from Newton's secret papers how much of a magus he was. But an historian is not surprised; he watches the process of disentangling the rational from the irrational, the stimulus to the imagination of realms of human experience about which one cannot be sure, the dialectic between conscious and unconscious, reason and mystery. No wonder Shakespeare's plays exhibit archetypal situations, intuit the findings of supranormal psychology.

Literature is the prime expression of the English-speaking peoples in the arts. At the same moment as the war with Spain and the arrival of the Italian madrigal came the new poetry and the new drama. Naturally there were precursors and foreshadowings, but the creators of the new modes were conscious that they were making something new.

Sidney was familiar with Europe – where he was everywhere received like a prince as the heir not only of the Sidneys but of the Dudleys, Warwick and Leicester. He deliberately set out to create a literature which could compare with the Italian, his model. The aim is expressed in the preface to Spenser's *Shepheardes Calender*, the hope that 'in this kind, as in other we might be equal to the learned of other nations.' Sidney may be said to have achieved his aim by his own work in poetry and prose, both creatively and in criticism, by example and by patronage. Court and aristocratic patronage was of the first importance for the arts in Renaissance society. We may remark also that Elizabethan literature was the creation of a younger generation – think what more might have been accomplished by Sidney, dead at 32, Marlowe at 29, Greene at 37; Kyd, Peele, Watson, Nashe all died in their thirties. Even Shakespeare ceased to write before he was 50; Spenser died at 46.

However, Spenser lived long enough to accomplish what Sidney had designed, and to be accepted as *the* poet of the age – as his epitaph in Westminster Abbey called him, 'the Prince of Poets in his tyme.' A portrait of the age could be constructed – almost, if not quite – from his work; even his prose work (like his life) relates to a chief problem for the Elizabethans, Ireland. His poetry highlights the leading personages; the dedications of *The Faerie Queene* present a roll call of most of the outstanding figures. We can hardly call it an official work, but we can say that it was symbolically representative and has a 'recognized' character. The Queen, it is said, proposed a reward: a pension of £100 a year, unique for a writer. If her Lord Treasurer halved it to £50, it was remarkable that the old Polonius allowed it at all, considering what Spenser had written about him. But Burghley didn't like poets much; he preferred scholars.

The glittering figure of the Queen is at the apex of it all. She appears in much of Spenser's work; but in *The Faerie Queene*, her personality occurs as a leitmotif all through, helping to knit the work together, as Proust uses the musical theme of the Sonate de Vinteuil in *A la recherche du temps perdu*. One sees her in various aspects: as Una (a symbolic name) in contrast to the false Duessa (Mary, Queen of Scots), as Belphoebe in her personal relation to Raleigh, as Gloriana the queen and empress. This last title reflects Raleigh's specific influence, through whose friendship Spenser came closest to her. It is all there in the dedication, 'To the most high, mightie and magnificent Empresse renowmed for pietie, vertue, and all gratious government Elizabeth by the grace of God Queene of England Fraunce and Ireland and of Virginia.'

In Spenser's roll call of the age in the dedicatory sonnets to *The Faerie Queene* and in his minor poems, we naturally hear most intimately of Raleigh; but they are all there: Leicester, Sidney, Hatton, Essex; Lord Admiral Howard, the privateering Earl of Cumberland, those leading soldiers the Norris brothers; Arthur, Lord Grey of Wilton, much to the fore as Spenser's admired leader in Ireland, along with the Earl of Ormond; the Earl of Oxford, Sir Arthur Gorges; Sir Edward Dyer and Thomas Sackville, Lord Buckhurst, courtiers who also wrote poetry; the Queen's two principal ministers, Walsingham and even (in the second version of the dedicatory sonnets) Burghley. Among the Queen's ladies appear the three Spencer sisters and her favorite, Anne, Countess of Warwick; also, of course, Sidney's famous sister Mary, Countess of Pembroke. Among literary figures in the roll call we find Sidney's half-Italian friend Bryskett, Cambridge's Gabriel Harvey, and those who served a while in Ireland, Barnaby Rich, and Barnabe Googe; among scholars, the great Camden and Mulcaster, the distinguished headmaster of Spenser's own school, Merchant Taylors'. A whole bevy of churchmen are there, too: Archbishop Grindal, Bishops Aylmer of London, Young of Rochester, Piers of Salisbury, Davies of St David's (Diggon Davie).

Spenser was capable of sharp satire, as we know, and was no more subject to illusions than Elizabethans were in general: they were realists about life, well aware of its dangers and essential insecurity, and knew that life was a struggle. However, they mostly struggled upwards; and Spenser, whose nature was a religious one and highly ethical, preferred to present an ideal portrait of the age. This was in keeping with Sidney's idealism, whose own life exhibited a noble chivalry which his end broadcast far and wide. There was, somewhat paradoxically, an element of ethical idealism in the age, related to the curious revival of medieval chivalric notions; *The Faerie Queene* is its classic expression, along with Sidney's sonnets and his *Arcadia*.

Something of this idealized chivalry has its visual expression in such plaster reliefs as that of the knight at rest under a tree at Grenville's Buckland Abbey, or the famous large miniature of a Herbert at Powys Castle. Again, we must impute much of this to the strict rule of a maiden lady: its most popular expression was in the Accession Day tilts and tournaments, with all their Renaissance pageantry accompanied by song, music, and poetry, which arose spontaneously as an annual tribute to her. Whatever views we may hold as to the Elizabethan court, under the scrutiny of an authoritarian woman, it was a paragon compared with the courts of the Valois and Philip of Spain with their murders and assassinations, of Mary Stuart and her son in Scotland, or of the papacy until the Counter-Reformation wrought its reform.

We can see what the new poetry meant to the young men of the time from these inspired lines of Marlowe in the 1580s:

If all the pens that ever poets held
Had fed the feelings of their masters' thoughts,
And every sweetness that inspired their hearts,
Their minds and muses on admirèd themes;
If all the heavenly quintessence they still
From their immortal flowers of poesy,
Wherein as in a mirror we perceive
The highest reaches of a human wit:
If these had made one poem's period,
And all combined in beauty's worthiness -
Yet should there hover in their restless heads
One thought, one grace, one wonder, at the least,
Which into words no virtue can digest.

We know what Shakespeare felt, for, in his magpie fashion and with his actor's memory, he annexed the penultimate line and adapted it for himself.

Naturally the drama was in touch with more sides of the nation's life, more widely and popularly expressive of it, like music itself; and it caught up much more of native traditions and customary modes. In attaining new heights, it did not turn its back on what had gone before. For it was a national activity, from simple parish mummings and Whitsun pastorals, town and guild moralities and miracle plays, school and university Latin comedy and tragedy, to court interludes, masques, and chronicles.

All this fused in that decade of heightening tension and inspiration to produce the characteristic Elizabethan drama – one of the great periods in the world's dramaturgy: to my mind, richer than that of ancient Athens. For it was more varied, less categorized, with its mixtures of tragedy and comedy, history and folklore, as in life itself. It was less regular, more proliferating and ebullient, perhaps even more fertilizing – as we see from its progeny in the novel, particularly the historical novel, and in music, opera, and the visual arts.

The drama took up into itself far more of traditional English writing, incorporating everything – balladry and bawdry, chronicle and legend, morality and farce, patriotic propaganda and rant. Only one element of prime significance was censored: political and religious issues were too dangerous. Nevertheless, Shakespeare's plays have their constant political morals: the urgent insistence on the necessity of social order, authority, and obedience, the observance of degree, the proper fulfillment of function. This applies as much to rulers as to subjects, perhaps even more: witness what happened to Richard II and Richard III, King John and Henry VI, Macbeth and King Lear. It is all in accordance with the Book of Common Prayer and the Homilies. Shakespeare saw eye to eye with the Queen on these matters: his was an upper-class point of view, conservative of order, fundamentally conforming – with no use for the Puritan challenge to the established order.

The Elizabethan religious settlement had finally been arrived at, in keeping with the irresistible Reformation dynamic, after two decades of conflict, insurrection and rebellion, executions and burnings. It proved the one practicable form of consensus, such as neither Catholicism nor Puritanism on either flank could have achieved; and it worked. So there is no need for historical partisanship on the issue – the Queen was reasonably opposed to discussion of religious issues as divisive; too many people were at each other's throats on such matters. Her constant emphasis was on unity – Spenser would have had that in mind in giving her the name Una. And indeed, the unity of the nation in the dangers of the time was the absolute condition of the success and prosperity it achieved, as against the religious and civil wars that devastated France and the Netherlands, or the static division within Germany which ultimately erupted in the Thirty Years' War and impeded its progress to power for two centuries. The Elizabethans were conscious of their luck and appealed to the prosperity of the regime as its sanction – as did Edmund Bunny, for instance, in his controversy with the Jesuit Robert Parsons, who sought by every means to upset it.

Elizabethans were very conscious of the terrible consequences that ensue from undermining, let alone overthrowing, the social order. To them, the anarchy of the Peasants' Revolt in Germany, with all its killings and its ludicrous experiment in communism, bore a message similar to that of the Bolshevik Revolution earlier in this century. On the threshold of the sixteenth century, there had been the dastardly killings of the Wars of the Roses: it was the Queen's grandfather only, Henry VII, who had brought that to an end with his wise and wary, authoritarian and humane, rule. The generation after Shakespeare's death saw the even worse, far more destructive experience of the Civil War and the Puritan Revolution. A sensitive and skeptical mind like Shakespeare's, with his view of human nature without illusions, realized that overthrowing social order brought about far more human suffering than any promise of bettering it. All societies need a continuous process of gradual, empirical reforms, and piecemeal reforms are safer than wholehogging. Spenser's idealism would lean to reform; Shakespeare's skepticism, conscious of the dangers of upsetting the apple cart, to conservation and conformity. Perhaps we may see them as two sides of the Elizabethan coin.

Elizabethan drama exemplified the integration of society under the pressure of external danger. When this was relaxed, things began to fall apart. The stage itself became increasingly divided on class lines: the court and upper class went to élite Blackfriars, more mixed and popular audiences to the Globe and Fortune. And this is reflected in writing for the theater.

Up to about 1600, during the sad last years of the Queen, the tension and exigencies of war held the strains within society without bursting the integuments. The Puritans were a challenge to the Elizabethan settlement; but they could not surmount the fact that Elizabeth (who detested them) pursued a Protestant policy abroad, and was the linchpin (as well as the paymaster) of the anti-Spanish, antipapal forces in Europe. After her death, peace and the equivocal policies of the Stuarts allowed divisions to rip ahead and come to the fore, and the long years of Stuart peace permitted the revolutionary challenge of Puritanism to make headway. The result was the Civil War.

People looked back on Elizabeth's reign as a blissful period of prosperity – even Oliver Cromwell did. Shakespeare paid tribute to it as such, after it was over, in Cranmer's prophetic speech at her christening in *Henry VIII*. There need be no doubt or discussion as to the fact of the achievement. When Elizabeth I came to the throne in 1558, England was a defeated and distracted country of the second rank; by the end of her reign, it was the first naval power in Europe, had fought the world empire of Spain to a standstill, and was poised to found settlements in North America which ultimately made her a power in the world.

Elizabeth's government was indubitably the ablest of its time – everybody abroad, from Pope Sixtus V downwards, paid tribute to its ability and its skillful, judicious conduct of the country's affairs, as it threaded its way warily through the reefs and shoals of the Reformation and Counter-Reformation. Earlier, the Queen had been cautious about taking risks; later, when she was stronger and had built up reserves, she became bolder (in her support for Drake's aggressions against Spain, for example, as against Burghley's cautious opposition), though always calculating the consequences. Like her grandfather, Henry VII – and unlike her father, Henry VIII – she was a born calculator, and her government, though financially strained, the only one in Europe that did not go bankrupt. (Philip II, with all the treasure of the Indies, overstrained Spain's strength, to achieve bankruptcy twice.) Elizabeth's government carefully considered undertakings in relation to resources.

Like all societies of the time, it was hierarchically ordered, rationally in accordance with function; but unlike most others, it was flexible to a degree. One could go up or down in it; one could make a fortune, one could also lose one. Drake and Shakespeare, each starting from nothing much, made their fortunes; the Earls of Huntingdon and of Oxford lost theirs; the latter – a gifted ass – ruined his family. Initiative, energy, achievement were its keynotes; incentive was often rewarded. All these factors helped to make it the most efficient society in Europe, and worked together, with time and luck, to make it most productive and creative, with astonishing results for a small people.

To this evaluation, we must add that the Queen personally emphasized the motive of winning renown. She frequently cited that in writing to thank subjects for notable services on the field or at sea, or in condoling with parents on their loss. It was without doubt her own prime motive in working at her job as sovereign, to leave a name to posterity as a famous ruler. History has acknowledged her endeavors and justly rewarded her. A.L. Rowse

Shakespeare's England; Neale 1934; A.L. Rowse *The England of Elizabeth: The Structure of Society* (London 1950), *The Expansion of Elizabethan England* (London 1955), *The Elizabethan Renaissance: The Life of the Society* (New York 1971), *The Elizabethan Renaissance: The Cultural Achievement* (London 1972).

emblematics The study of the arts of both the emblem and the device (Fr *devise*, Ital *impresa*). A device, the immediate predecessor of the emblem, consists of a motto and a picture to express its bearer's heroic or amorous aspirations. To the motto and the picture, an emblem adds an explication in either verse or prose to inculcate a universal moral.

Although in theory the emblem and the device are separate genres, in practice they are often regarded as conjoint, especially by those who ignore the differences in both form and name (eg, Georgette de Montenay *Emblemes, ou Devises chrestiennes* Lyons 1571, Gabriel Rollenhagen *Nucleus emblematum selectissimorum quae Itali vulgo impresas vocant* Arnheim 1611, Henry Peacham *Minerva Britanna, or A Garden of Heroical Devises, Furnished, and Adorned with Emblemes and Impresa's* London 1612; see Daly 1979:23, 25). In appearance as well device collections are seldom without explications of one form or another, having the same three parts as emblems. Moreover, despite their functional differences (private versus public), the two genres have in common many ideals derived from classical and contemporary poetry and painting (Clements 1960:61–72, 173–82, 225–36); and they also share textual and pictorial sources with these other arts.

If Spenser's imagery often appears 'emblematic,' therefore, it is not that he has necessarily borrowed from emblem or device books; rather, he has either 'invented' his images according to mimetic ideals common to both poetics and emblematics, or based them on sources common to both poetry and emblems, for example, natural history, Aesop's fables, proverbial lore, and mythology (cf Daly 1979:9–36 'Forerunners of the Emblem'). These sources were either emblematized or assimilated into emblem and device books during the last quarter of the sixteenth century and the first quarter of the seventeenth. For instance, Joachim Camerarius' four-volume *Symbola et emblemata* (Nuremburg 1590–1604) is an emblematized natural history of plant and animal lives in 400 emblems; W[illiam] B[arret]'s *Fables of Aesop* (London 1639), Gilles Corrozet's *Hecatomgraphie* (Paris 1540), and Gabriele Simeoni's *La vita e metamorphoseo d'Ovidio* (Lyons 1559) represent respectively emblematized fables, proverbs, and mythology. The vogue was prompted by Alciati's *Emblemata* (first ed 1531, last supervised ed 1550), which assimilated all of these sources along with devices, heraldic arms, epigrams, symbols, and personifications.

Three examples of Spenser's 'emblematic' imagery may be cited. In *FQ* IV viii 39 and *Amoretti* 49, the basilisk or cockatrice that kills with a look may be based on such popular natural historians as Pliny, Aelianus, or Solinus, on bestiaries (eg, T.H. White 1954:168–9), or on proverbial lore (C.G. Smith 1970, no 40 'the basilisk's eye is fatal' and no 109 'the cockatrice kills with its look'), rather than on emblems like those of Maurice Scève (*Délie* 1544, no 21), Battista Pittoni (*Imprese* 1562, vol 1 no 11), or Camerarius (vol 4 no 79). Unlike the emblematists who picture the basilisk facing a mirror and thus directing its lethal power against itself (Fig 1), Spenser chooses the simpler version in natural history and proverbs.

(See **emblematics** Fig 1.)

Similarly, when he mentions the greedy dog losing the bone ('flesh') for its reflection in the river (*SC, Sept* 59–61), the image owes more to bestiaries than to emblem books. Although this fable from Aesop (ed 1952, no 133) was assimilated by Joannes Sambucus (*Emblemata* Antwerp 1566:228), Nicolas Reusner (*Emblemata* Frankfurt 1581, vol 2 no 23; see Fig 2), and Geoffrey Whitney (*A Choice of Emblemes* Leyden 1586:39), Spenser's moral – 'To leave the good, that I had in honde, / In hope of better, that was uncouth' – seems to echo that found in the bestiaries: 'Because it leaves the true food in the river out of greed for the shadow, it symbolizes those silly people who often leave that which is peculiarly of the Law out of desire for some unknown thing' (White 1954:67).

(See **emblematics** Fig 2.)

The proverb 'to seize occasion by the forelock' (C.G. Smith 1970, no 777; Erasmus *Adages* 1.301.34) is treated extensively and untraditionally by Spenser in the person of Occasion (*FQ* II iv 4–13). There are numerous emblematic portrayals of Occasio: Alciati 1531: fol A8 (based on *The Greek Anthology* 16.275) (Fig 3), Guillaume de La Perrière *Théâtre des bons engins* (Paris 1539) no 63, Corrozet *Hecatomgraphie* (Paris 1540) sig M2v, Achille Bocchi *Symbolicae quaestiones* (Bologna 1555) book 3 no 71, and Whitney 1586:181, to name only those Spenser could have seen. Rather than following any of these, he retains only the proverbial forelock, which represents for Guyon the opportunity to restrain wrath (see Manning and Fowler 1976). This instance exemplifies his practice of inventing images in an 'emblematic' mode.

(See **emblematics** Fig 3.)

This practice is the result of Spenser's 'imitating' in the 'tenor' and the 'vehicle' of his images the metaphorical relation between the motto and the picture of an emblem, a relation seen in most emblems where the metaphors or similitudes are made explicit by the verses below the pictures. For example, in Whitney's *In occasionem* (p 181), Occasion's forelock is explained by these two lines: 'What meanes longe lockes before? *that suche as meete, / Maye houlde at firste, when they occasion finde.*' Here, the intelligible 'occasion' (tenor) is revealed in the visible 'forelock' (vehicle); the universal is revealed in the particular. The author's meaning – to seize occasion by the forelock – is revealed by the resemblance in the two significations with which a metaphor appears to our understanding. We are to transfer the meaning from the picture to the motto, from the vehicle to the tenor, from the visible to the intelligible (see the definition of metaphor in Estienne *The Art of Making Devises* tr Thomas Blount [London 1646], and cf Aristotle *Poetics* ch 21; for the emblem's relation to wit, enigma, and conceit, see Praz 1964:14–23 and Steadman 1974:195 n 36 and 210). Such a realization of the particular in the universal or of the visible in the intelligible has long been the mimetic ideal of poetic imagery.

Another common ideal is the Horatian 'utile dulci miscere' ('to mix the pleasurable with the useful'). In applying this ideal to the metaphorical relation between motto and picture, many theorists compare them with body and soul. Just as the picture (equated with the body) pleases the eye (*dulce*), so the motto (equated with the soul) feeds the mind (*utile*). Similarly, in poetic imagery, the vehicle (picture or body) must please the eye or the imagination so that the tenor (motto or soul) will feed the mind. It follows that the more the picture pleases the eye by striking it with the most vivid details, achieving the kind of rhetorical effect called *enargeia*, the greater will be its didactic impact upon the mind. Hence the corollary ideals of *enargeia*, *ut pictura poesis*, and imitation. *Enargeia* is produced when the picture or image is so vivid or visualizable that it is true to nature or verisimilar to the model it imitates. From *enargeia* come the doctrine of *ut pictura poesis* and its corollary formula, 'painting is mute poetry; poetry is speaking picture' (see Trimpi 1973).

Verisimilar or natural picture painting in verbal art is not, however, the highest ideal, according to Aristotle (*Rhetoric* 3.11). To him, the apex is represented by the homonymous *energeia*. 'Poetry possesses *energeia* when it has achieved its final form and produced its proper pleasure, when it has achieved its own independent being quite apart from its analogies with nature or another art, and when it operates as an autonomous form with an effectual working power of its own' (Hagstrum 1958:12). These qualities are essentially the same as those produced by imitation. To Aristotle, an ideal imitation enables the artist to 'invent' a new reality that transcends its model and has its own organic life. Similarly, the reality created by *energeia* transcends the merely visible or the verisimilar and realizes it in the intelligible or the universal.

These ideals can be seen in Spenser's Occasion. By retaining only the traditional forelock, Spenser transcends his model which usually portrays a naked maiden with winged feet standing on a globe in the midst of a sea and holding a razor in her hand (Fig 3). Spenser changes Occasion into a lame old hag whose tongue must be locked and arms bound, after her forelock has been seized, before Guyon can overcome Furor (*FQ* II iv 13–15). The descriptions of her person and actions achieve the kind of verisimilitude *enargeia* calls for (4–5, 9); but the image achieves *energeia*, its organic reality, only after the metaphorical transference is made, as explained by the Palmer: that to stop wrath one has first to stop its occasion (10–11).

The Graces' dance in *FQ* VI x 24 is a more nearly perfect example. The motto, 'That good should from us goe, then [than] come in greater store' dictates the details of the picture, especially of how the three Graces move: 'That two of them still froward seem'd to bee, / But one still towards shew'd her selfe afore' (ie, two go away from and one returns towards the viewer; Fig 6; cf Wind 1958, Figs 17–19). The way they dance, which is the central metaphor, is compared to the lesson they teach: 'how to each degree and kynde / We should our selves demeane, to low, to hie; / To friends, to foes, which skill men call Civility' (23). To be civil and gracious in this context means to bestow unmerited favor, to give more than to receive. As the allegorical core of Book VI, the Graces' dance also controls the Legend of Courtesy by this motto, in that both Calidore and Calepine are paragons of courtesy because they give more than they receive (Tung 1972). In choosing this motto, Spenser transcends the traditional model, which shows two Graces facing toward and one going away from the viewer (Figs 4, 5, 7) and inculcates the opposite moral of giving in order to receive more in return.

(See **emblematics** Fig 4–7.)

Thus, in the Graces' dance Spenser 'invents' an image in an emblematic mode, not by borrowing from emblem books but by imitating in the tenor and the vehicle of his image the same metaphorical relation that exists between the motto and the picture of an emblem, and by realizing the mimetic ideals common to both poetics and emblematics. Such a conclusion does not deny the influence of emblem books. It does affirm, however, that this influence has been overestimated. If this is true of Spenser, it may also be true of many other authors, including Shakespeare, Donne, Herbert, and Milton (see, eg, Daly 1975). The truth is that the emblematists were latecomers to the literary scene, and they drew their inspirations and materials from the same classical and medieval resources which had for some time served all arts and letters. MASON TUNG

Many of the principal sixteenth-century emblem books are indexed in Henkel and Schöne 1967; see also *Alciati. The most accessible example for English readers is Whitney 1586. Contemporary emblem theory is found in Henri Estienne 1645 *L'Art de faire les devises* (Paris) tr T[homas] B[lount] 1646, rpt (in ed of 1650) New York and London 1979; and Paolo Giovio 1559 *Dialogo dell'imprese militari e amorose* (Lyons) rpt with the 1585 tr by Samuel Daniel, Delmar, NY 1976. The principal critical discussions in English are Robert J. Clements 1960 *Picta Poesis: Literary and Humanistic Theory in Renaissance Emblem Books* (Rome); Peter M. Daly 1975 'Goethe and the Emblematic Tradition' *JEGP* 74:388–412; Daly 1979; Graziani 1964b; Hagstrum 1958; Manning and Fowler 1976; Praz 1964; Steadman 1974; Trimpi 1973; Tung 1972; Tung 1984; Wind 1958.

---

emblems The Renaissance emblem has been defined by modern scholars as a picture with motto and verse; sometimes the 'emblem proper' has been defined as the picture alone. According to these definitions, there are no emblems in Spenser. *Theatre for Worldlings* has woodcuts and verses but no mottos; the 'Emblemes' of *The Shepheardes Calender* have only mottos. To be useful in Spenser criticism, the term *emblem* needs to be defined in terms that Spenser's contemporaries would have recognized and understood.

The major sixteenth-century writers on emblem theory – Sambucus, Junius, Aneau, and Mignault on the continent, Fraunce and Whitney in England – distinguish the emblem from the other forms of symbolic representation described by the general term *device* (see *emblematics). All agree that the distinctive concern of the emblem is moral: all emblems, declares Whitney in his 'To the Reader,' 'doe tende unto discipline, and morall preceptes of living' (1586: sig **4r). The means of instruction is indirect: Junius advises that truth be subtly concealed, enfolded in pleasing obscurity, as if covered by a veil (1565:65); Sambucus advises that the emblem should describe something rather obscure ('aliquid obscurius') which demands further thought and explanation (1564:3). The puzzle is intended to attract the attention of readers, delight them when it is solved, and so arouse their enthusiasm for virtue.

All these theorists derive *emblem* from Greek *emballo* or *emballesthai* (to put or place in), and affirm that it is 'something set in for the sake of ornament' ('quicquid inseritur ornatus causa'). The allusion is to mosaic or inlay, or to small ornamental images that could be attached to plate or vases for decoration. Whitney explains that the term properly refers to 'suche figures, or workes, as are wroughte in plate, or in stones in the pavementes, or on the waules, or suche like, for the adorning of the place.' However, our sixteenth-century theorists do not define their emblems as images. They apply the term metaphorically to a particular kind of poem which describes an image, statue, or work of art, and explicates its meaning: 'Here Emblems are metaphorically called poems, in which images, statues, paintings, and such kind of other works are learnedly and elegantly described in various ways.' ('*Metaphoricos* hic Emblemata vocantur carmina, quibus imagines, agalmata, pegmata, et id genus alia scite adinventa, varie et erudite explicantur'; Mignault 1573 'Syntagma de Symbolis,' quoted from Alciati ed 1621: lxiv.) Fraunce in England quotes this sentiment exactly (1588: sig N2). Thus Alciati, the founder and foremost practitioner of the genre, declares 'we have written a book in verse with the title *Emblemata*' ('nos carmine libellus composuimus, cui titulus est Emblemata' 1530:97); and Aneau defines emblems as 'kinds of epigram' ('especes de Epigramme' in Alciati ed 1549:11). The hallmark of the emblem style is denseness and brevity: Mignault calls it 'crammed speech' ('oratio referta'), while Aneau states that it 'includes great thoughts in few words' ('en briefve parolle concluans tresample sentence'). Each word is to be highly polished; in the phrase repeatedly quoted from Lucilius, each word takes its place like a tile in a mosaic design ('ut tesserulae omnes arte pavimento atque emblemate vermiculato' *Remains of Old Latin* 3:28).

Images were, of course, never far from the author's thoughts, for the epigram described in detail some real or imagined work, such as an artist had made or might devise. 'Indeed,' admits Mignault, 'we will acknowledge that the cogency of the emblem depends upon the symbol' ('Fatemur Emblematis quidem vim in symbolo sitam esse' in Alciati ed 1621: lxiii). But, as Fraunce explains, 'In the emblem, the words describe the image' ('in emblemate vox figuram exponit' 1588: sig N3r). The provision of illustrations was in many cases the printer's responsibility, not the author's. Steyner, the printer of the first emblem book (Alciati's *Emblematum liber* 1531), seems to have added cheap cuts on his own initiative as a way of making the author's meaning plainer and, perhaps with an eye to sales, accessible to a wider readership. The learned, he apologizes, will know what the author means anyway ('quod docti [intentionem authoris] per se colligent' sig A1). Somewhat later, de La Perrière adopts a similar attitude towards the pictures: 'if the verse be any thing obscure, the Impresas or pictures make it more lively, and in manner actual' (ed 1614: sig A5). The cultivated brevity and obscurity of the verse, it seems, defeated the less learned members of the reading public, who gained access to the author's intention by means of the woodcuts. The pictures, then, were meant as no more than a faithful representation of the author's words ('convenantes à la lettre' Aneau in Alciati ed 1549:4). By the mid-seventeenth century, Menestrier could, without fear of contradiction, define the emblem as a moral painting ('ce mot Grec est a present universellement receu parmy les scavans pour une peinture d'instruction' 1662:14); and Tesauro could list *Figura* under the essential parts of the perfect emblem (1682:403; 'degli Emblemi' first appeared in the 3rd ed, 1663).

Central to Spenser's practice is the emblem's minute, significant description, self-conscious mysteriousness, and teasing obscurity which invites and demands explication. The erudite imagery stored in the emblem books provides Spenser in many cases with models and sources. Much of his imagery in *The Faerie Queene* accords with the contemporary definition of emblem: brilliant descriptions of tapestries, 'painted imagery,' and other objects of curious workmanship exist 'for the sake of ornament,' while the intrusion of apparently perverse, irrelevant material exemplifies the emblematic 'something set in.' Often the narrative halts completely while the significant parts of an image are fully anatomized, exactly in the manner of the emblem book.

For example, the enigmatic dragon that lies beneath Cupid's feet has an emblematic provenance (*FQ* III xi 47–9; Lewis 1967: 22–4). Alciati's emblem *Custodiendas virgines* ('Virgins must be guarded') describes a dragon who attends the goddess Minerva, patroness of chastity. Its traditional function is to guard things, and its vigilance is essential for the protection of unmarried girls, since Cupid sets his snares everywhere. However, Spenser's Cupid has disqualified it from performing this office by shooting out its eyes. Spenser's displacement of Minerva by Cupid suggests that the unmarried girl has been overcome by passion, and that the dragon's close supervision, appropriate to virgins, is now redundant. The triumphant Cupid certainly indicates masculine, passionate aggression; perhaps it also alludes to the marriage of Amoret to Scudamour, '*Cupids* man.'

Traditionally we would expect Venus, not Cupid, to be the patron deity of marriage. Several emblems contrast unmarried Minerva with married Venus, as Plutarch states succinctly: 'Beside the statue of Athena Pheidias placed the serpent and in Elis beside the statue of Aphroditê the tortoise, to indicate that maidens need watching, and that for married women staying at home and silence is becoming' (*Isis and Osiris*, *Moralia* 381E-F). From this, Junius derived his emblem *Virginem pudicitiae, matronam domus satagere* ('The unmarried girl should be totally occupied in keeping her chastity, the wife in keeping her house'). The iconography of Spenser's statue of Venus (IV x 38–41) identifies her as a perfect exemplum of matrimonial union, which exposes and corrects the male-dominated view implied by the image of Cupid.

The fact that Venus is 'covered with a slender veile afore' alerts us to the enfolding of some emblematic mystery. Together with the fast binding of her feet and legs, it identifies her as *Venus Morpho*, an ancient symbol of marital concord. 'The story is,' says Pausanias, 'that the fetters were put on her by Tyndareus, who symbolized by the bonds the faithfulness of wives to their husbands' (*Description of Greece* 3.15). Junius adopts this ancient statue of the veiled and fettered Venus in his emblem *Uxoriae dotes* ('The endowments of a wife') to illustrate that chaste modesty, constancy in love, and attendance to household duties are fitting for a wife. In his notes, he interprets the fetters as 'the close and indissoluble bond of conjugal love' ('indissolubilis vinculi conjugalis et arctissimi amoris significationem habent' 1565:87). But where the traditional iconography shows Venus bound with fetters, Spenser binds her not with stocks or chains but 'with a snake, whose head and tail were fast combyned.' The serpent whose tail is hidden by its head, or who bites its own tail, is an ancient hieroglyph of eternity (Horapollo ed 1950, I.I; Mignault on Alciati, Emblem 133: *Serpens in se revolutus, aeternitatem designat* 'The serpent bending itself into a circle signifies eternity'). It was also seen as symbolizing the machinery of the universe (Macrobius *Saturnalia* I.9.12, Horapollo I.2). Of particular relevance to the statue of Venus is the sexual significance of the serpent: the symbolic accretions imply that the universe is sustained and the ravages of time repaired through the process of procreative generation within the bonds of conjugal love (Fowler 1964:164).

It is apparent from these two examples that Spenser treats his emblematic 'sources' with considerable freedom. He modifies, substitutes, combines, and adapts traditional materials to meet the demands of his poem. His changes do not indicate his disregard of the emblem but rather attest to his fidelity to the best traditions of emblematic writing. Mignault praised Alciati not only for choosing examples of wit and sense from the best authors but also for his imagination which allowed him to construct completely new ones, or to refurbish the old and present them in fresh garb ('de plusieurs endroits des meilleurs ouvriers il a en partie choisi quelques devises pleines de bon sens et invention: et en partie aussi en a basty d'autres a sa fantasie, qu'il a revestues de nouvelle parure' 'De l'embleme' in Alciati ed 1587: sig a10). There is nothing mechanical about Spenser's procedure: he combines emblematic commonplaces with a range and freshness (occasionally tinged with cunning deviousness) of invention, which is always logical, yet always manages to surprise.

There is teasing, sportive wit in his presentation of Occasion (*FQ* II iv 4–5). Alciati, de La Perrière, Whitney, and others all present emblems of *Occasio*. But in all save the long forelock and bald occiput, Spenser's hag differs from the young, vital, comely figure in the emblem books. It is as if Spenser sets his readers a puzzle by his radical departure from this commonplace image. Once again he shows his fidelity to the traditions of emblematic presentation, devising an image which, being obscure at first sight, demands further thought and explication.

Spenser's ability to fuse and combine several different emblematic figures may also be seen in his presentation of Cambina, in whose figure are deftly juggled the attributes of several ancient gods, goddesses, and moral personifications (IV iii 38–44). Although one response has been to obscure all her symbolic accretions under a general definition of Concord, Spenser's symbolism works in almost the opposite direction, leading not to generalized but to precise meaning. Cambina occupies simultaneously Cybele's lion-drawn chariot and Cupid's, shown in Alciati's emblem *Potentissimus affectus Amor* ('Love, the most powerful emotion'; see Roche 1964:23–8); the cup and caduceus are attributes of Civic Concord in Nicolas Reusner's emblem *Pulcritudo civitatis, Concordia* ('Concord, the beauty of the state'). The aggregation of symbolic detail indicates that the subject of Book IV is the ultimate harmonizing of personal and civic ambition, of love and the public good. Cambina acts as love, as civilization, as a composer of family differences, and shows that these impulses need not be mutually destructive.

Since Spenser's avowed interest was in 'vertuous and gentle discipline,' it would be surprising if he neglected a technique which was so germane to his purpose, especially one which was, in Sambucus' phrase, 'covert, witty, and delightful' ('tecta, arguta, jocunda'). JOHN MANNING

Andrea Alciati 1530 *De verborum significatione* (Lyons); Alciati ed 1531; Alciati ed 1549 *Emblemes d'Alciat* tr Barthélemy Aneau (Lyons); Alciati ed 1587 *Emblemata latino-gallica* (Paris); Alciati ed 1614 *Emblemata* ed Claude Mignault (Lyons); Alciati ed 1621; Barthélemy Aneau 1552 *Picta Poesis* (Lyons); Theodore Beza 1580 *Icones* (Geneva); Fraunce 1588; Junius 1565; Guillaume de La Perrière 1539; La Perrière ed 1614 *The Theatre of Fine Devices* tr Thomas Combe (London; rpt San Marino, Calif 1983); Claude-François Menestrier 1662 *L'Art des emblèmes* (Lyons; rpt New York and London 1979); Georgette de Montenay 1571 *Emblemes, ou Devises chestiennes* (Lyons; rpt Menston, Yorks 1973); Reusner 1581; Sambucus 1564; Emanuele Tesauro 1682 *Il cannocchiale aristotelico scelta* (Venice; ed Ezio Raimondi, Turin 1978); Whitney 1586.

Horapollo ed 1950; Macrobius ed 1969; Lucilius in *Remains of Old Latin* (Loeb ed).

Berger 1957; Burchmore 1981; Daly 1979; Fowler 1960a; Fowler 1964; Freeman 1948; Lewis 1967; McManaway 1934; Manning and Fowler 1976; Hessel Miedema 1968 'The Term *Emblema* in Alciati' *JWCI* 31:234–50; Praz 1964; *Reallexicon zur deutschen Kunstgeschichte* 1937– ed Otto Schmitt, et al (Stuttgart) sv 'Emblem, Emblembuch'; Roche 1964.

envy Spenser formally describes envy (L *invidia*) twice in *The Faerie Queene*, first as a character in the procession of sins (I iv 30–2) and then at V xii 27–43, where the composite figure of Book I appears as the paired, complementary characters Envy and Detraction. His depictions are very much in the manner of Whitney's emblem 'Invidiae descriptio' (1586:94; for iconographical sources and analogues, see Chew 1962:109–11 and Aptekar 1969:201–5). In these passages, envy is both a debilitating recognition of others' superiority (the habit of viewing resentfully our happy, famous, or virtuous neighbors) and the defamatory verbal stratagems that aim to diminish excellence by blotting good report with blame. Crucial to this conception are Envy's evil eye (an etymological deduction from Latin *in + videre*) and its poisonous mouth (a detail from Ovid *Metamorphoses* 2.777, that links envy with calumny and evil speaking). Envy's clothing is 'ypainted full of eyes' that presumably 'looke askew' (I iv 31; cf V xii 29), and 'corrupt envies' are among the 'monstrous rablement' that besiege the 'bulwarke of the *Sight*' at the castle of Alma (II xi 8–9). Moreover, as *FQ* VI testifies, Envy's bite is almost worse than its basilisk-like glance, thanks to its chawing, leprous maw, infected with poison from frogs and snakes. Spenser's metaphors realize the traditional affinity between envy and evil speaking; they help to create the envious and railing characters conspicuous elsewhere in the poem, such as the Blatant Beast, Ate, Sclaunder, and Corflambo – all of them invidious opponents of amity (Tuve 1966:129).

(See **envy** Fig I.)

During the Renaissance, as self-fashioning individualism became more pronounced and as opportunities for social advancement increased, poets, dramatists, and artists were intensely interested in examining how and why human aspirations and achievements evoke envy and its constant companion, slander (see, eg, Whetstone 1586, Cast 1981). Their main ways of explaining this process may be traced to a constellation of Greek and Latin texts on envy and calumny and to the still-vital medieval Christian tradition of the seven deadly sins, which ranked envy second only to pride. Frequently cited authors in the classical tradition were Lucian, Plutarch, Hesiod, Statius, Horace, and Ovid. *Metamorphoses* 2.768–82 is particularly important because it begets the Ovidian iconography of envy found in Renaissance emblem books and reflected in *The Faerie Queene*. In the Christian tradition, the notion that the devil's envy brought death into the world (Wisd of Sol 2:24) gave point to discussions of *invidia* as an especially demonic sin in commentaries by Cyprian, Gregory, Thomas Aquinas, and others (Bloomfield 1952). Spenser draws liberally on both classical and Christian considerations of envy and analyzes its workings at personal, social, and cosmic levels.

When 'Immerito' fears at the opening of *The Shepheardes Calender* that envy will bark at his little volume, he invokes a *topos* frequently found in prefatory material. Equally formulaic is his accompanying hope that a patron will shelter the work. Spenser later uses the same motif in asking the Earl of Oxford to defend *The Faerie Queene* from 'foule Envies poisnous bit' and Lord Buckhurst to ward off the backbiting of Zoilus, Homer's scourge and type of the envious critic (*FQ* ded sonn). But such protection will inevitably be futile: the ravages of Envy in the house of Pride reach a climax with his biting 'the verse of famous Poets witt' (I iv 32); and *FQ* VI ends with the concession that the Blatant Beast, at liberty again, is triumphant: 'Ne spareth he most learned wits to rate, / Ne spareth he the gentle Poets rime, / But rends without regard of person or of time' (xii 40). The vaunting Horatian poet seeks to build an enduring monument (*SC* envoy) to which neither age nor envy shall lay waste (*Time* 406); but he acknowledges in *FQ* VI at the end of his career that his whole artistic enterprise is vulnerable to misinterpretation – what he elsewhere calls '*Envies* false surmise' (I v 46). Spenser's insecurity about the poet's vocation may be related to the likely calling-in of *Mother Hubberds Tale* and to the failure of 'Stoicke censours' to understand his praise of love (IV proem 3).

'Freedom from envy is a main character of all Spenser's Utopias' (Hughes 1926:564). This freedom is an aspect of erotic and pastoral wish-fulfillment: it belongs to those lovers in the Garden of Adonis and at the entrance to the Temple of Venus (III vi 41, IV x 25–8). In the less utopian context of *Amoretti* 85–6, the envious outsider of troubadour poetry appears as he does in other Renaissance sonnet sequences, only to be humorously exorcised in *Epithalamion* when all 'false whispers,' 'deluding dreames,' and 'drery accents' are dispelled (334–52). In the *Hymne of Love*, 'gnawing envie' and 'false reports,' along with other afflictions, threaten to make 'a lovers life a wretches hell' (259–72). As in a diptych by Giotto in the Capella degli Scrovegni, Padua, Envy sets its sad face against Charity and maligns love. Blame's feeding on the essentially blameless is an aspect of the world's vanity. (See **envy** Fig 2.)

It is to courtesy that Spenser primarily opposes envy (*FQ* VI). He incarnates envy in the Blatant Beast; but it is also visible, for example, in Despetto, Decetto, and Defetto, in Mirabella (Disdain is sometimes Envy's alter ego, as in Medwall's *Nature*), and in the savages who cannibalize Serena with their eyes. In deriving *courtesy* from *court* (VI i 1), Spenser shares with his contemporaries a conviction, developed in the vigorous genre of anti-court satire, that courts breed envious place-seeking. He had earlier expressed reservations about envy at court in *Colin Clouts Come Home Againe* (680–730), and in *SC, Februarie* and *Muiopotmos*. In Belphoebe's misdeeming of Timias (*FQ* IV vii 36–viii 17), he had even convicted the Queen of invidious misconstruction. In *FQ* VI, courtesy itself is tinged with envy. When Calidore envies Meliboe's lot and in turn elicits Coridon's envy (ix 19, 38–41), he introduces envy into a pastoral domain that had hitherto been immune to it. As he spies the gracious circle that Colin has called forth, 'even he him selfe his eyes envyde' (x 11). Spenser's involuted formula here reminds us that envy feeds on itself (V xii 31).

Destructive of fame, love, justice, and civil conversation, and ranging freely through all degrees and states, envy takes on a cosmic significance. In *Ruines of Time*, 'envies cruell tort' colludes with 'fortunes injurie' and 'times decay' (166–8); in *Muiopotmos*, Aragnoll's resentment against Clarion merges with heaven's so that fortune and envy become interchangeable (Bond 1976:146; see *Arachne). Especially during the later books of *The Faerie Queene*, fortune and the heavens begrudge human felicity, as Spenser dramatizes the inexorability of divine envy (cf III iv 39, IV viii 16, V v 36, VI iv 31 and xii 38). It is fitting, then, that in *FQ* VII, Mutabilitie's aspirations should rest on an envious desire to supplant Cynthia (vi 10–11). But Nature's verdict delivers a consoling truth that leads us away from the deprivations of envy, contention, and disorderly change. In eternity, envy ceases, as Spenser asks that the misseeings and misdeemings of the fallen world be succeeded by 'that Sabaoths sight.'

RONALD B. BOND

Bloomfield 1952; Ronald B. Bond 1976; Bond 1981; Bond 1984 'Vying with Vision: An Aspect of Envy in *The Faerie Queene*' *Ren&R* ns 8:30–8; Cast 1981; Cheney 1983; R.B. Gill 1979 'The Renaissance Conventions of Envy' *M&H* ns 9:215–30; Hughes 1926; Whetstone 1586.

---

epideictic In two of his works, Spenser ascribes to the poet an epideictic function: Colin's ode in praise of Eliza in *SC, Aprill*, and *The Faerie Queene*, which not only celebrates Queen Elizabeth under several mythological disguises but in its opening stanza announces its intention 'To blazon broad' the gentle deeds of knights and ladies.

Epideictic originally comes from the Greek *epideiktikós* 'fit for displaying,' but more specifically refers to a rhetorical genre that uses praise and blame in the treatment of a subject. In this respect, it differs from two other rhetorical genres, the judicial or forensic which deals with accusation and defence, and the deliberative or political which is devoted to the alternatives of admonition and dissuasion. As a type of rhetoric that is more concerned with formal display than practical debate, it prefers the decorative devices of *elocutio* to the argumentative logic of *inventio*. The epideictic or demonstrative genre proves most successful under a feudal regime whose legitimacy it strives to justify by celebrating its prominent representatives. In transferring the norms and techniques of this kind of rhetoric to literature, poets sought to pursue essentially the same aim. The purpose of Spenser's courtly epideixis is the creation of an ideology that confirms Elizabeth as the ideal ruler of an elect nation.

Rhetorical praise of a person or thing observes a strict order of 'places' (*topoi*) usually through the two orders of *effictio* (physical description) and *notatio* (moral description). Thus the celebration of a noble person must take account of his descent: native land, ancestors, parents; his gifts of fortune (eg, wealth), body (eg, beauty), and mind (eg, virtues); his childhood (upbringing), youth (study), manhood (deeds), and old age (wisdom). Each of these places allows numerous subclassifications and applicative varieties, so that Spenser had to make an individual selection appropriate to the subject of his praise. Thus, in the *Aprill* eclogue he lays particular emphasis on the parents ('*Syrinx* daughter,' '*Pan* the shepheards God'), the ancestors ('heavenly race'), the bodily excellencies ('angelick face'), and the spiritual accomplishments ('heavenly haveour') of the Queen which underline her hereditary and personal rights to the throne. He applies three epideictic techniques in order to embellish his royal panegyric: *comparatio* (with mythological figures such as Phoebus and Cynthia), *divisio* (Eliza's admirers: Muses, Graces, Nymphs, 'sheapheards daughters'), and *descriptio* (catalogue of flowers). Finally, the author's feigned protestation of his literary incompetence enables him to raise his subject to the heights of unassailability. This occurs in the exordium of the *Aprill* eclogue no less than in the prologue to *The Faerie Queene*.

Of the poetic genres used by Spenser, the ode, hymn, elegy, sonnet, and epic serve epideictic purposes. Whereas the epideictic origins are self-evident in the other kinds of poem (praise of a ruler, a virtue, a dead poet, an adored lady), the literary ancestry of the epideictic epic seems obscure. Two theoretical aids encouraged the Elizabethan author to venture out on this literary field of experience: the allegorical interpretation of Virgil's *Aeneid* as a work written in praise of its hero (Donatus, Fulgentius, Bernard Sylvestris), and the medieval misunderstanding of Aristotle's conception of poetry as being based on the two effects of praise and blame (Averroes, Hermannus Alemannus). Both traditions were continued in the Renaissance, as is testified by Puttenham's epideictic system of poetic genres. This literary context furnished Spenser with an epideictic dualism in his conception of figures: icons of virtue (eg, Una, Mercilla, Britomart), which deserve to be praised, contrast with icons of vice (eg, Duessa, Archimago, Acrasia), which deserve blame. The equation of living creatures with virtues and vices reveals a characteristic feature of Spenser's epideixis: its ethical substratum. The poet assumes the role of a moralist who teaches philosophical precepts by means of praiseworthy and blameworthy examples. Apart from Virgil's *Aeneid*, the other classical precedent for this procedure is Xenophon's *Cyropaedia*, an idealized biography of Cyrus the Elder referred to in the Letter to Raleigh. The Renaissance author followed such models in the firm conviction that the praise of virtue would kindle in the reader the desire to imitate that virtue and shun its opposite.

Praise of Elizabeth in *The Faerie Queene* reveals yet another aspect of epideixis in courtly literature: hyperbolic mimesis, which is not primarily understood as a set of stylistic devices but rather as the mythical iconography of the monarch. The encomiastic identification of Elizabeth with Gloriana, Una, Belphoebe, Britomart, and others bestows on her the dignity of a superhuman being, rendering her practically unassailable to any kind of Blatant Beast. This mythographic idealization becomes even more complex by the application of the typological method known from scriptural exegesis. Thus it becomes possible for Spenser to 'shadow' (identify) Elizabeth as the Virgin Mary, the second Eve, Christian faith, the true church – even as Diana, Venus, and Penelope. Under various disguises, therefore, she appears as one and the same – that is, as Una. The difficulties of converting the living paragon of virtue into polysemic icons of poetic praise (and vice versa) are illustrated in Spenser's ironic address in III proem 3: 'But O dred Soveraine / Thus farre forth pardon, sith that choicest wit / Cannot your glorious pourtraict figure plaine / That I in colourd showes may shadow it, / And antique praises unto present persons fit.'

HEINRICH F. PLETT

Theodore C. Burgess 1902 'Epideictic Literature' *UCSCP* 3:89–261; Cain 1968; Cain 1978; A. Leigh DeNeef 1973 'Epideictic Rhetoric and the Renaissance Lyric' *JMRS* 3:203–31; Hardison 1962; Brian Vickers 1983 'Epideictic and Epic in the Renaissance' *NLH* 14:497–537; Wells 1983.

---

epigram Spenser's contribution to the genre of the epigram is slight, and, according to the modern conception, somewhat eccentric. His only poems entitled 'Epigrams' are six pieces of twelve or fourteen lines each, plus a four-line envoy, which first appeared anonymously in the English version of van der Noot's *Theatre for Worldlings* (1569), when Spenser was about seventeen. These 'epigrams' were originally the six stanzas and the envoy of a canzone of Petrarch (*Rime sparse* 323, 'Standomi un giorno'). Clément Marot had translated the canzone into French earlier in the century as *Des visions de Petrarque*, and in 1568 van der Noot published this version and his own Dutch version in *Het theatre* with an accompanying etching for each stanza. Marot had retained the continuous form of the canzone in his translation, so it was evidently van der Noot who decided to treat each stanza as an 'epigram'; clearly what he had in mind was the etymological sense of the term, a 'writing in or upon,' here for verse accompanying the emblems of *Het theatre*.

Spenser's epigrams, then, like the French and Dutch versions, are not 'epigrammatic' in the modern sense: they have neither the sharp, witty 'turn' that closes Jonson's epigrams nor the explosion of wonder that characterizes the best of Crashaw's. They are epigrams in the broad sense typical of the diverse short poems in the Planudean *Greek Anthology*, which influenced Renaissance love poetry and the reflective lyric, and which provoked considerable discussion about the relationship between the sonnet and the epigram. Most continental theorists saw them as parallel forms, although some, most notably Minturno, insisted on a sharp tonal and thematic contrast (Colie 1973:68–75; Fowler 1982:138, 183, 197). The association of the sonnet with the epigram led to the pointed, sometimes dour sonnets of du Bellay's *Regrets* and the hundreds of witty, satiric sonnets by the seventeenth-century Spanish poets Lope de Vega, Góngora, and Quevedo. As late as 1648, the critic Baltasar Gracián could use the terms *soneto* and *epigrama* almost interchangeably in his *Agudeza y arte de ingenio*.

In England, however, the sonnet and the epigram came to be regarded as antithetical by the last decade of the sixteenth century, and this view seems to have influenced Spenser. When he republished his translation in *Complaints* (1591), he dropped the rubric 'Epigrams,' adapted from Marot the title *The Visions of Petrarch*, and turned the canzone into seven fourteen-line sonnets. Although this change probably means that he no longer thought of the poems as epigrams, their tone and texture still show the inspiration of the *Greek Anthology* which, especially as mediated through the Pléiade, is pervasive in his poetry of complaint. His Anacreontics furnish another clear example of this influence. (See also **Amoretti*, *anacreontics.)

R.V. YOUNG

Colie 1973; Fowler 1982; Heyt Hopewell Hudson 1947 *The Epigram in the English Renaissance* (Princeton); James Hutton 1935 *The Greek Anthology in Italy to the Year 1800* (Ithaca, NY); Hutton 1946 *The Greek Anthology in France and in the Latin Writers of the Netherlands to the Year 1800* (Ithaca, NY); van der Noot 1569; van der Noot ed 1953; Barbara Herrnstein Smith 1968 *Poetic Closure: A Study of How Poems End* (Chicago); T.K. Whipple 1925 *Martial and the English Epigram from Sir Thomas Wyatt to Ben Jonson* (*UCPMP* 10.4; Berkeley).

Epithalamion. See ***Amoretti, Epithalamion***

---

epithalamium (Gr 'before the bridal chamber') A poem about a wedding; the term applies to a wide range of works, from lyrics that merely praise or congratulate the couple to those that describe the occasion itself. Though little information about it survives, a long tradition of folk epithalamia apparently lies behind literary instances of the genre such as Spenser's *Epithalamion* (see **Amoretti*) and *Prothalamion*. Influenced by the widespread assumption that the Bible is a compendium of all literary forms, Renaissance writers would have been aware of scriptural antecedents for the epithalamium: both the Song of Solomon and Psalm 45 are poems about weddings. Major Greek poets, including Sappho and Theocritus, contributed to the genre, and Greek rhetoricians codified rules for it.

Renaissance writers derived their primary models, however, from Latin literature. Especially influential were Catullus 61, 62, and 64. Catullus 64, like Claudian 10 and Statius *Silvae* 1.2, exemplifies what is sometimes termed the 'epic' epithalamium – a narrative based on mythological stories. Catullus 61 is one of the most successful and renowned instances of an alternative sub-genre, the 'lyric' epithalamium, which is the type that Spenser's *Epithalamion* exemplifies and extends.

Both guest and stage manager at the ceremony, the speaker of Catullus 61 describes the day's events in chronological order. He invokes Hymen, invites the nymphs and other wedding guests to participate in the festivities, details such Roman wedding customs as sprinkling wine in the house, praises the couple, refers to the dangers their marriage will confront, and offers prayers for children. Catullus' chronological structure, the particular events described within it (including allusions to the Roman customs), and his use of a refrain were all to be imitated in continental and English versions of the lyric epithalamium. The poem emphasizes the passage of time during the wedding day (one refrain is 'sed abit dies' ['but the day is passing']) and reminds us that one can achieve a type of immortality by producing heirs – a juxtaposition of mutability and immutability that no doubt helps to explain why the genre appealed to the author of *The Faerie Queene* and to many of his contemporaries.

The models that Catullus and other Latin writers had established found few imitators in the Middle Ages; weddings did inspire ephemeral light verse during that period, however, and many religious poets adapted the language of epithalamia when describing mystical spiritual marriages. The continental Renaissance witnessed a resurgence of interest in the genre. Scaliger analyzes it at length in his *Poetices libri septem* (1561, 3.101). Some Neo-Latin poets (including George Buchanan) composed epithalamia, as did members of the Pléiade. The fact that many of these French epithalamia were written for royal weddings testifies to the interrelationship of literary and social factors that contributed to the rise of the genre. The genre may also have been popular because it provided a safety valve for Petrarchism, a forum in which sexuality could be discussed more freely and fully than the sonnet tradition normally permitted (Forster 1969:84–121).

Despite the popularity of the genre in

other cultures, comparatively few English epithalamia precede Spenser's. Among the earliest are 'On Gloucester's Approaching Marriage' by Lydgate (1422) and 'The Thrissil and the Rois' by Dunbar (1503). A wedding poem is also included in *A Courtlie Controversie of Cupids Cautels* (1578), Henry Wotton's translation of a work by Jacques Yver. Epithalamia with extensive pastoral imagery appear in Sidney's *Old Arcadia* (circulated in manuscript in the early 1580s; his 'Let mother earth now decke her selfe in flowers' [*OA* 63] has been called 'the first formal epithalamion in English': Ringler in ed 1962:411) and in Bartholomew Yong's translation of the continuation Gil Polo wrote for Montemayor's *Diana* (completed by 1583, pub 1598). The pastoral motifs in these and other epithalamia may reflect a fundamental though often implicit preoccupation of the genre: the reconciliation of natural forces, especially sexuality, with the demands of society. Other native antecedents to Spenser's epithalamia include an incomplete masque, dated 1588, by James VI of Scotland, and an anonymous translation of Theocritus' Eclogue 18 in *Sixe Idillia* (1588). Though he concentrates primarily on folk customs rather than literary versions of the genre, Puttenham devotes a chapter to the epithalamium in his *Arte of English Poesie* (1.26). He distinguishes three kinds of 'Epithalamies' or 'ballades at the bedding of the bride,' according to the times at which they are performed. The first is 'at the first parte of the night when the spouse and her husband were brought to their bed': it is chiefly noted for its noise, to drown out 'the skreeking and outcry of the young damosell.' The second ballad is performed around midnight, 'to animate new appetites with cherefull wordes,' and the third when it is broad daylight, 'a Psalme of new applausions, for that they had either of them so well behaved them selves that night.'

Spenser writes about marriage frequently in his major and minor works, invoking the formal characteristics of the epithalamium on a number of occasions. In a letter to Harvey (*Three Letters* 1), he describes a lost work, the *Epithalamion Thamesis*, which may have influenced his portrayal of the marriage of Thames and Medway in *FQ* IV xi. His description of the betrothal of Una and Redcrosse, like Catullus 61 and *Epithalamion*, refers to the custom of sprinkling wine during the festivities (I xii 38). Even the *Aprill* eclogue in *The Shepheardes Calender* has been described as an epithalamium (Tufte 1970:167–78), though that reading is controversial.

Spenser's principal contributions to the epithalamium tradition are his *Prothalamion* and *Epithalamion*, which develop several conventions of the genre and effect radical changes in it (Greene 1957). For example, like Catullus 61, these lyrics employ a refrain; the *Epithalamion* also evokes a procession of human and superhuman wedding guests. The 24 stanzas of *Epithalamion* seem to allude to the hours of the day and hence underscore the concern for time that is present in many earlier epithalamia (Hieatt 1960, 1961; Welsford 1967:191–206). *Epithalamion* presents one striking innovation in the genre: the bridegroom is the poet himself.

Epithalamion and *Prothalamion* inspired few imitations during the remainder of the sixteenth century. The paucity of Elizabethan epithalamia has been attributed to Elizabeth's image as the Virgin Queen and her disapproval of courtiers who married. Donne, however, offers an exception: his 'Epithalamion Made at Lincolnes Inne,' modeled on Spenser's, was probably composed in 1595, the same year *Epithalamion* was published (Novarr 1956, Bald 1970:77, Ousby 1976).

The genre became popular in seventeenth-century England, when Donne, Jonson, Carew, and Herrick contributed to the tradition and Suckling even composed a mock epithalamium. Parallels have been traced between seventeenth-century wedding poems and the masque tradition to which they are so closely related, Shakespeare's *Tempest* IV i providing a notable example (McGowan 1972). HEATHER DUBROW

Forster 1969; Greene 1957; Margaret M. McGowan 1972 '"As Through a Looking-glass": Donne's Epithalamia and their Courtly Context' in *John Donne: Essays in Celebration* ed A.J. Smith (London) pp 175–218; Novarr 1956; Ousby 1976; Tufte 1970.

Erasmus, Desiderius (c 1466–1536) Spenser never refers to Erasmus by name, nor does he quote or echo him except in a few passages; nevertheless, a sense of what Erasmus thought and wrote is important for a historical reading of his poetry.

Erasmus was the greatest humanist scholar of his age. Born in Rotterdam, he traveled widely and wrote extensively. He had a vast influence on the intellectual and religious life of Europe, especially England, throughout the sixteenth century. Practically every educated person knew some Erasmus, though few could claim to have read him all: his many works on education, morality, piety, including satires; translations, annotations, and paraphrases of the New Testament; editions of classical authors and Church Fathers; many apologiae defending his own works and attacking his critics; and his extraordinary correspondence (much of it published during his lifetime). His achievement was remarkable, for he set new directions in theology, philology, and education in Reformation Europe and even – although his books were banned – in Counter-Reformation countries. He was one of the great revivers of the new learning, of the return to ancient literature and the renewed texts of the Bible and the Church Fathers; he was a promoter of careful reading and of careful style (although he could be extremely hasty in some of his own work); he attacked social pretensions and false learning in his satires. In part because he was an ironist and a complex thinker, his works were read for quite conflicting reasons. Thus he was admired for preaching a message of peace and compromise in an era of extreme religious discord, yet hated for this same reason by those who sought him out to join their factions. He was himself extraordinarily fractious and uncompromising in some areas of his theology, especially in his attacks on religious abuses.

Erasmus spent part of his early career teaching at Cambridge, but his main impact on English culture was through his books, either in Latin or in their many translations, which taught a whole generation. This generation flourished during the reign of Edward and left an indelible mark on the religious and intellectual life of England; its legacy was passed on to Spenser's generation through the schools, universities, and religious establishment. To those writing and reading during the 1590s, Erasmus was still a potent force. In Nashe's *Unfortunate Traveller* (1594), Jack Wilton and the Earl of Surrey travel out of their way to Rotterdam to visit Thomas More and his friend 'that abundant and superingenious clarke, *Erasmus*' (ed 1904–10, 2:245). Spenser's contemporaries knew Erasmus best as the author of *The Praise of Folly*; Sidney in his *Defence of Poetry* compares Agrippa on the 'vanity of science' with Erasmus on the 'commending of folly' (ed 1973b:100). Yet they also knew the less familiar works: Harvey owned and annotated the *Parabolae*, a school text of sayings by Greeks and Romans mostly out of Plutarch, and Jonson quoted from *Hyperaspistes*, the work in which Erasmus attacks Luther's doctrine of the bonded will and sets forth his own doctrine of its freedom.

Spenser would have encountered Erasmus' writings at Merchant Taylors' School or at Cambridge. We do not know which of the works he read. He might have known any or all of the *De copia* on variation and abundance in Latin style (see *copia), the *Parabolae*, *Adagia*, and *Apophthegmata* (all collections of sayings, the *Adagia* with extensive commentary), and the Latin dialogues called *Colloquia*. All were popular and are listed in many curricula of the period. He may also have read in the *Paraphrases* of the New Testament, either in Latin or English, for this work had been translated in Edward's reign and placed by royal injunction in all churches. The curriculum Spenser followed, its texts, its techniques of rhetorical composition and variation, even its methods of ethical, religious, and philological explication, were all strongly Erasmian in orientation.

The relations between the texts of Erasmus and Spenser are closest in three areas: adages, similitudes, and catch phrases; moral satire; and Christian themes. The first of these is the most obvious: Spenser uses many proverbs and proverbial expressions that have sources in classical literature and that are often in Erasmus' vast *Adagia*. For example, when Paridell offers to fight in the place of Blandamour, he explains his service with a proverb – 'the left hand rubs the right' (*FQ* IV i 40) – given in Erasmus as 'manus manum fricat' (ed 1703–6, 2:240D) with a short essay on its Greek origins in the pseudo-Platonic dialogue *Axiochus* and in Menander and its transmission in Seneca and Petronius. Whether Spenser knew this proverb of 'mutual convenience' from Erasmus seems beside the point (after all, he is thought to have translated *Axiochus*) – yet it is quite likely that Erasmus' collection was the source for its use in England (Tilley 1950, H 87) and that his analysis of it might have been known to some of Spenser's readers. As reported by Erasmus, the proverb has high classical authority; hence its use by the unworthy knight Paridell to the equally unworthy Blandamour is heavily ironic. Many of the other proverbs in *The Faerie Queene* can as well be read as classical *testimonia* by reference to Erasmus and his exegetical tradition (C.G. Smith 1970).

That this procedure was actually followed is suggested by E.K.'s playful explication of the second emblem of *SC, Februarie*. He claims, incorrectly, that the Latin version of the emblem, 'Nemo Senex metuit Jovem' ('No old man fears Jupiter') appears in the *Adagia*, and that Erasmus has misinterpreted it. The adage is usually held to mean that experienced persons have no fear, that old men (having seen everything) no longer fear God and are therefore blasphemous. According to E.K., Erasmus takes it otherwise: experienced old men do not fear a *false* god (Jupiter) and are therefore models of probity and wisdom. E.K. implies that Erasmus, 'a great clerke and good old father,' is really just defending other old men from the charge of blasphemy; yet 'it is plaine, to be gainsayd, that olde men are muche more enclined to such fond fooleries, then younger heades.' E.K. refutes Erasmus, an 'old father' and author of a *Praise of Folly*, on the grounds of his old age and foolishness. Although somewhat refined, the joke would not have been lost on the educated reader, who might also have seen the joke in relation to the whole of *The Shepheardes Calender*, a work that favors wise youth over foolish old age. That the adage is not in Erasmus' collection hardly seems to matter; the point is the overthrow of authority by the young.

E.K.'s mocking shows the tables being turned on the most famous satirist of the age. Even so, Spenser's satires share with *The Praise of Folly* and the *Colloquies* a deep distrust of ecclesiastical abuse, the falsity of court life, and indeed all formally regulated but meaningless behavior. The attacks on corrupt clergy in *SC, Julye* and *Mother Hubberd* and the rejection of court life in *Mother Hubberd* and *Colin Clout* seem colored by Erasmian satire. In part, for both authors, social abuse is also abuse of language. One of the strongest echoes of Erasmus in all of Spenser is the description of the Blatant Beast in *FQ* VI xii 23–5: the beast roams 'Through all estates,' 'into a Monastere,' and finally 'into the sacred Church' before it is finally 'Rencountred' by Calidore. In Erasmus' *Lingua*, one of the worst abuses of language is calumny (*lingua calumniatrix*) which can be seen traveling 'per domos privatas, per collegia, per monasteria, per aulas principum, per civitates, per regna' ('through private houses, colleges, monasteries, the halls of princes, cities, kingdoms' ed 1703–6, 4:417, first noted by Thomas Warton). Calumny or detraction is also said by Erasmus (who follows the Bible and the Church Fathers) to be a plague, a poison, something that wounds and infects – all of which describe the Blatant Beast. *Lingua* is literally 'the tongue' as well as 'language'; the many tongues of the Beast are referred to several times in *The Faerie Queene* (V xii 41; VI i 9, xii 27). The power of calumny to wound or poison its victim, a theme found in many humanist writings, is given point and force in both Erasmus' treatise and Spenser's poem. Likewise the power of language to heal is also found in both works: for Erasmus, the greatest curative is the language of Christ; for Spenser, it is 'civill conversation' (VI i 1), the kind of 'good counsell' given by the Hermit to heal the wounds of Timias and Serena (VI 13).

The most complex area shared by the two authors is theological. Although *FQ* I seems to have much in common with Erasmus' notion of the Christian knight who bears a 'sure and impenetrable sheld of faith' (*Enchiridion militis christiani*, tr by William Tyndale as *The Manuell of the Christen Knyght* 1533: sig A2r), the theology of both authors is far from simple. Spenser is a Protestant of the Elizabethan Settlement (with its Calvinist bias and belief in the primacy of faith over works); Erasmus, though highly critical of the Church of Rome, remained faithful to its key tenets, especially the possibility of human agency in seeking divine grace. *FQ* I shows the inability of the Christian knight to do good without divine grace; the *Enchiridion* demonstrates how the human will may do good under adverse circumstances. A comparative reading of the two works offers some interesting parallels (see Wells 1979), but ultimately there is a great gap between them. Spenser and Erasmus seem closer when they are read in the light of a shared literary and ethical humanism.

WILLIAM W. BARKER

The works are printed in Erasmus ed 1703–6; a modern text, *Opera omnia* gen ed C.M. Bruehl, is published in Amsterdam and London (1969–). The letters are printed in ed 1906–58 *Opus Epistolarum*. Erasmus ed 1974– is a modern English translation; see also Olin 1965 and M.M. Phillips 1964. For earlier English translations, see E.J. Devereux 1983 *Renaissance English Translations of Erasmus: A Bibliography to 1700* (Toronto). There is a vast modern commentary on Erasmus, but little on Spenser and Erasmus: besides a number of notes in the Spenser *Variorum*, there are Starnes 1942 (which argues for a close relationship between *Teares of the Muses* and Erasmus' colloquy 'Conflictus Thaliae et Barbariae' dramatizing a debate between the Muse Thalia and barbarism), and Robin Headlam Wells 1979 'Spenser's Christian Knight: Erasmian Theology in *The Faerie Queene*, Book I' *Anglia* 97:350–66.

Error The first episode in the first canto of *The Faerie Queene* (stanzas 6–28) centers on the serpent-woman Error and her lair in the midst of the Wandering Wood. After a violent rainstorm has compelled the Red Cross Knight and his companions to seek shelter in a nearby grove, he successfully overcomes the monster and her brood. The episode concludes with their successful departure from the wood. Both the wood and the monster at its center – the forest-labyrinth with its winding paths and the serpent-woman with her winding coils – are symbols of error, the logical contrary of the truth that the knight has pledged himself to defend.

As champion and patron of 'true Holinesse,' the knight faces a double danger: losing his way in the labyrinth and losing his life in Error's coils. Only gradually, however, does he become enmeshed in error and realize his increasing peril. Initially he is deceived by appearances, and even Una is partly deceived; the grove 'seemes' to offer 'Faire harbour' from the tempest, and the travelers are not aware of its true nature as a dangerous labyrinth leading to a monster's lair. Admiring the beauty and variety of the trees, and led forward by pleasure and delight, they 'beguile the way' until the storm is overblown; only then do they discover that they have *lost* their way and that the pleasant grove is a cunning and deadly snare, as Una recognizes it for what it is: 'This is the wandring wood, this *Errours den*, / A monster vile, whom God and man does hate.'

This episode provides the first test of the knight's prowess and his first use of the Christian soldier's spiritual armor. It combines conventional images of the classical labyrinth and the dark wood with images of the serpentine hybrid, half human and half viper. Two of the principal analogues of Spenser's wood of error are found in Ovid and in Dante: the Cretan labyrinth designed by Daedalus for King Minos (*Metamorphoses* 8.159–68), and the shadowy wood ('selva oscura') in which Dante loses his way (*Inferno* 1.2). Though these motifs attracted a variety of interpretations, they were frequently regarded as symbols of the world and of human life. In various commentaries, the labyrinth symbolizes the vanity, ignorance, and false wisdom of the world; and in the *Convito* (4.24.12), Dante mentions the wandering wood of this life ('selva erronea di questa vita'). The double senses of the Greek *hyle* (wood or matter) and the Latin *silva* (forest, miscellany) reinforce the symbolism of the forest-labyrinth in terms of matter and multiplicity, Plato's realm of opinion.

In elaborating this symbol and some of its conventional associations, Spenser also exploits the familiar Platonic imagery of the dark cave (Error's den) as an image of the world, and of earthly ignorance and false knowledge. His use of the conventional tree list as an epic catalogue serves to emphasize the concepts of multiplicity and variety, in addition to suggesting the varied pleasures of the senses. The variety and multiplicity of the delights that the forest offers reinforce the poet's emphasis on the multiplicity and variety of ways and paths, and on their contrast with the single Truth and the one true way.

In choosing the well-trodden path 'that beaten seemd most bare, / And like to lead the labyrinth about,' the travelers are following the principle of *consensus gentium* (majority opinion) as a criterion of truth. Ironically, this path plunges them into still greater error, for it leads them to the lair of the deadly monster Error herself. Upon leaving the forest, they reverse their path in a retrograde movement analogous to the reversed movements in rites of disenchantment, but also in a direct reversal of the principle of *consensus gentium*.

Instead of a Minotaur, part man and part bull, Spenser's labyrinth contains a monster: 'Halfe like a serpent horribly displaide, / But th'other halfe did womans shape retaine, / Most lothsom, filthie, foule, and full of vile disdaine.' As a serpent-woman, Error resembles the hybrid Echidna in Hesiod's *Theogony* 294–306 and other similar hybrids: the Libyan beast described by Dio Chrysostom, the Scythian queen described by Herodotus and Diodorus Siculus, the monster Campe in Nonnus' *Dionysiaca*, the she-dragon Delphyne in Apollodorus' *Library*, the description of *Adikia* (Unrighteousness or Improbity) in Conti's *Mythologiae*, and, of course, Duessa herself (*FQ* I viii 46–9). Classical giants were portrayed with serpentine legs; and in Alciati's *Emblemata*, human wisdom is depicted as half man and half serpent. Error's speckled tail recalls that of Hesiod's Echidna, while her scorpion-like sting is also characteristic of Nonnus' Campe. The behavior of Error's brood, who take refuge inside her body but subsequently drink up her blood, represents a variation on superstitious natural history concerning the unnatural and unfilial behavior of the female viper (*echidna*) and her young. The female allegedly slew the male, while the young in turn slew their mother by gnawing through her body.

The serpent who seduced Eve was often depicted with the face of a woman or even with a woman's arms and bust. In medieval natural history, this figure was sometimes identified as *draconcopes* ('serpent-footed'). The books and papers that Spenser's Error spews forth have been compared to the books that Philologia vomits up in Martianus Capella's *De nuptiis Philologiae et Mercurii*; they also recall visual imagery from the anti-Catholic propaganda of the Reformation.

Though Error is partly modeled on Echidna, they are not linked genealogically. Elsewhere in *The Faerie Queene*, however, Spenser introduces Hesiod's monster as the mother of other monsters: The 'two headed dogge, that *Orthrus* hight' is 'begotten by great *Typhaon*, / And foule *Echidna*, in the house of night' (V x 10); in Flanders, the monster under the altar is 'Borne of the brooding of *Echidna* base, / Or other like infernall furies kinde: / For of a Mayd she had the outward face, / To hide the horrour, which did lurke behinde' (xi 23); and the Blatant Beast is an offspring of 'foule *Echidna*' and 'Cruell *Typhaon*' (VI vi 9–12). Echidna herself is described as 'a Monster direfull dred,' who displays the 'face and former parts' of a 'faire young Mayden, full of comely glee; / But all her hinder parts did plaine expresse / A monstrous Dragon, full of fearefull uglinesse' (vi 10).

In portraying Error in her cave in the midst of the Wood of Error, Spenser combines the conventions of personification allegory with those of moral topography and allegorical landscape (see allegorical *places). He thus provides an 'imperfect definition' of Error, while simultaneously defining Truth more clearly through juxtaposition with its logical contrary. The contrast extends even to the cave in which the monster dwells; and the way Error is drawn forth from her cave suggests an ironic parody of a familiar Renaissance motif, the teasing out of Truth from a hidden place.

In this initial episode, Spenser subjects the typical forest setting of the romance and the conventional wandering knight (*cavaliere errante* or knight-errant) to significant, even radical, reappraisal. The delights of the forest's wide variety of trees and the motif of wandering at leisure through a seemingly idyllic sylvan landscape are almost immediately converted into symbols of error. The seemingly leisurely narrative moves with surprising rapidity to the presentation of a moral emblem: the verbal icon of the knight and his shield caught in Error's toils. The ethical significance of this emblematic scene is immediately emphasized by a moral *sententia*: 'God helpe the man so wrapt in *Errours* endlesse traine' (I i 18).

The episode invites comparison not only with the exploits of warrior saints but also with monster-quellings by medieval knights-errant or by classical heroes. Heroic analogues familiar to Spenser's readers would have included mythological worthies like Hercules and Theseus, Perseus and Bellerophon, and also romantic heroes such as Orlando and Ruggiero in Ariosto's romance epic.

Redcrosse's struggle with Error is in part both paradigmatic and proleptic. As St George he is to be the patron saint of England and patron of the Order of the Garter; but he is also a pattern of the *miles Christianus*, the spiritual warrior fighting valiantly against the deceptions of the world, flesh, and devil. His ordeal is in a sense an heroic apprenticeship, for the knight's spiritual arms are new to him, and he requires exercise and practice to prepare for his ultimate duel with the dragon of Eden. Una assists him in his combat with Error by exhorting him to 'Add faith unto [his] force, and be not faint,' but she also warns him against exposing himself to Error too recklessly. Subsequent events justify her admonition; although victorious against learned Error, the knight is soon separated from Truth by Hypocrisy and Falsehood. Relying on faith and the armor of the gospel, and accompanied by Truth, he overcomes the erroneous wisdom of the world and the perils of heresy and false religion. Nevertheless, while the Error episode foreshadows his defeat of the Dragon in canto xi, it also provides a basis for his (still unsuspected) separation from the true faith and his subjection to falsehood and pride.

In addition to the personified Error of *FQ* I i, there are references to 'error' in *Teares of the Muses*. These are complemented by the imagery of moral and spiritual genealogy: familial ties of darkness and blindness, ignorance and worldly wisdom. As such, they invite comparison with the genealogical images of *The Faerie Queene*, with the lineage of Night, Darkness, Blindness, Falsehood, and their moral progeny. In *Teares*, Euterpe complains that 'monstrous error flying in the ayre, / Hath mard the face of all that semed fayre' (257–8). Terpsichore similarly laments that ignorance has confounded the kingdom of the Muses, supplanting them in the hearts of men with his own 'accursed brood, / By him begotten of fowle infamy; / Blind Error, scornefull Follie, and base Spight, / Who hold by wrong, that wee should have by right' (315–18). In turn, Urania exclaims that man bereft of the 'heavenlie light of knowledge' and the 'ornaments of wisdome' resembles a beast: 'Then wandreth he in error and in doubt, / Unweeting of the danger hee is in, / Through fleshes frailtie and deceipt of sin' (487–92).

JOHN M. STEADMAN

Roland B. Botting 1937 'Spenser's Errour' *PQ* 16:73–8; Hamilton 1961a; Joan Larsen Klein 1978 'From Errour to Acrasia' *HLQ* 41:173–99; P.A. Parker 1979; John M. Patrick 1956 'Milton, Phineas Fletcher, Spenser, and Ovid – Sin at Hell's Gates' *N&Q* 201:384–6; Patrick 1960 *Milton's Conception of Sin as Developed in 'Paradise Lost'* (Logan, Utah); J.D. Pheifer 1984 'Errour and Echidna in *The Faerie Queene*: A Study in Literary Tradition' in John Scattergood, ed *Literature and Learning in Medieval and Renaissance England* (Dublin) pp 127–74; Steadman 1979:159–84, 280–90; J.B. Trapp 1968 'The Iconography of the Fall of Man' in *Approaches to 'Paradise Lost'* ed C.A. Patrides (London) pp 223–65; *Var* 1:182–3.

---

eschatology (Gr *eskhatos* last) The doctrine of the universal last things: the end of the world, the Second Coming, the Last Judgment, and the resurrection of the dead. Eschatological speculation flourished in the Elizabethan period, and Spenser is very much a man of his time, as indicated by his early version of themes from St John's Apocalypse in *Theatre for Worldlings* and the Red Cross Knight's vision of the New Jerusalem in *FQ* I x 53–5.

Eschatological doctrine is particularly influential in *FQ* I. For instance, Una wanders in a 'wildernesse,' like the Woman Clothed with the Sun, who represents Christ's church (iii 3; cf Rev 12.14). Duessa has a beast with seven heads and is finally stripped to reveal her spiritual ugliness, like the Whore of Babylon (the false church), who is also rendered 'desolate and naked' (vii 18, viii 46–9; cf Rev 17). Since Una represents the true Protestant Church of England and Duessa, its Roman Catholic antagonist, Spenser is portraying contemporary historical conflict in eschatological terms.

Redcrosse is also part of this eschatological allegory. On different levels, he represents both St George and Christ-in-man, the warrior-Christ who will struggle with Antichrist and whose victory will inaugurate the millennium (the thousand-year reign of Christ). Spenser's poem reflects one phase of this conflict (the fall of Babylon) when Redcrosse fells the Dragon (xi 54; cf Rev 14.8). Again, Cleopolis is an earthly counterpart of the New Jerusalem, which will appear on earth at the millennium as the Christian's final paradise and reward (x 59; cf Rev 4, 21.10). Redcrosse is given a vision of the New Jerusalem because he will be St George, one of the chosen saints for whom it is prepared and a symbol of England's national 'pilgrimage' towards the end of time (x 61). By his vision Redcrosse is brought to realize that the private virtue of holiness should achieve a dynamic relationship with the universal process of glorification in the millennium (x 61–3).

In eschatological doctrine, the last day is preceded by a period of degeneration and decay. Spenser, like some of his contemporaries, identified that period with his own age, sounding the theme of *omnia vanitas* in poems like the *Amoretti* and the *Complaints*. (Cf *FQ* I x 63, where Redcrosse repudiates the temporal world in longing for 'that last long voyage' to the New Jerusalem.) Spenser's solution to worldly transience is poetic immortality: poetry provides an analogy to the eternity that supervenes upon the world's last end.

In the *Cantos of Mutabilitie* (as at the end of *Epithalamion*), however, Spenser seems to reach beyond poetic immortality to an eschatological life eternal. The poem ends with the end of time, and 'that Sabaoths sight' of Book VII's last stanza corresponds to the seventh and last day, or age, of the world, the age of 'rest.' *The Faerie Queene* characteristically aspires to this stasis and the visionary New Jerusalem. (The millennium itself may also be inferred from the binding of the Blatant Beast [VI xii 38; cf Rev 20.1–3], although Spenser's treatment of it is not millenarian.) The poet, like Redcrosse, has come to 'loath this state of life so tickle.' But instead of returning to the consolation of poetic immortality, he closes the poem with a vision 'of Eternity, / That is contrayr to *Mutabilitie*' and reverts to silence. MARGARITA C. STOCKER

Bennett 1942; Hankins 1945; Kermode 1964–5; Stocker 1986; see also observations by Upton in *Var* I.

Essex, Robert Devereux, second Earl of (1566–1601) At first sight, the life of Essex has the shape of a medieval tragedy: a young man of great family and high blood (the Devereux), raised to the heights of fortune and popular esteem by his prince, then thrust down by a combination of fate and a flaw (of impetuousness) in his otherwise impeccable character.

Essex rose from relative obscurity in the mid-1580s to become Queen Elizabeth's favorite by the end of the decade, successor at court to his stepfather, the Earl of Leicester (d 1588). Like Sidney (whose widow he married), Essex was regarded as the '*Mercury* of peace, the *Mars* of warre' (Daniel 1595 *Civill Wars* 2.127), an ideal patron of arts and sciences and an heroic soldier in the field. By the end of the 1590s, he had known a decade of personal victories, but also frustrations and failure. In 1596, he was joint commander (with Raleigh and Howard of Effingham) of the sea and land attack on Cádiz, a brilliant operation which disabled Spanish preparations for a second Armada; but less than three years later, his campaign against the rebels in Ireland was a disaster in which the English lost both troops and reputation. At court and with the Queen, Essex had kept alive an anti-Catholic, anti-Spanish war policy (part of his political and Protestant inheritance from Leicester and Sidney); but he had been outmaneuvered repeatedly by the Cecils, father and son, whose style of prudent, patient bureaucracy would inevitably confound him.

The beginning of his end came in September 1599 when he deserted his Lord Lieutenancy in Ireland after just six months and rushed home to the Queen. Following treasonable utterances and questionable behavior, he was placed under house arrest for many months and kept apart from his family and friends before being tried by the Privy Council. The severe penalties – he was banned from the Queen's presence and deprived of income – maddened him. Eventually, in February 1601, backed by 300 swordsmen, he stormed the City of London and tried to raise the citizens. The rebellion failed, and he was executed on Ash Wednesday, 25 February.

It seems likely that Spenser had something of the pastoral, heroic, Protestant, and courteous Essex in mind when he created Calidore and Artegall. In 1590, in the *Faerie Queene* dedicatory sonnet to Essex, Spenser promises that in a future part of the poem his Muse will 'make more famous memory' of the Earl's 'Heroicke parts.' It has been alleged that in *FQ* V and VI, there are general, and in some places minutely exact, parallels with Essex's career. For example, in V xi, Artegall's rescue of Burbon from a 'rude rout him chasing to and fro,' is taken (by Heffner 1936) to allude to Essex's championing and supporting Henri IV, the Bourbon King of France, against the Holy Catholic League. (For other allusions, see *Variorum* index.)

Prothalamion (1596) refers directly to Essex, when the bridal party arrives on the Thames, near the London law courts and adjacent to the 'stately place' (Essex House) once owned by Spenser's patron, the Earl of Leicester. Sadly, that 'great Lord' is dead; but in the same house there now lives another 'noble Peer,' Essex, 'Great *Englands* glory and the Worlds wide wonder, / Whose dreadfull name, late through all *Spaine* did thunder, / And *Hercules* two pillors standing neere, / Did make to quake and feare' (137–49). This passage compliments Essex on the victory at Cádiz, the city adjacent to the Strait of Gibraltar (and the Pillars of Hercules). Moreover, Cádiz stands beside the Pillars and Strait as Essex House stands beside the Thames (not far from an English landmark, London Bridge); but Cádiz is Catholic and conquered, while Essex House is Protestant and triumphant. More important, when Essex makes the pillars quake, he is challenging Spanish imperial rule (the Pillars were the impresa of both Emperor Charles V and his son, Philip II of Spain), as well as the ancient Mediterranean limits to journeying out into the Atlantic and the New World. Hence Spenser depicts Essex House as a place not only for betrothing lovers, but also for wedding England to its own Protestant imperial future, as the successor of defeated Spain. Through the endeavors of Essex, in wars and weddings, 'great *Elisaes* glorious name may ring / Through al the world' (157–8). We glimpse the same vision of England, the new way out to the Americas, when Essex himself writes that 'Seated betweene the olde world and the newe, / A Land there is no other lande may touche, / Where regnes a Queen in peace and honor true; / Storyes or fables doe describe noe suche' (ed 1980:44).

It is clear that about 1596 Spenser was actively seeking Essex's patronage, not only in his literary writing but in *Vewe of Ireland* as well (at lines 5245–8, Spenser recommends that Essex be given the Lord Lieutenancy; see also Gottfried 1937). No documentary evidence has been uncovered to show that Essex became his patron, and there is only the well-known tradition that the Earl sent the dying poet twenty pounds, which he refused, and that Spenser's funeral expenses were paid by Essex (see Carpenter 1923:61, 70; *Sp All* p 178). JOHN PITCHER

The standard but not entirely adequate biography is still G.B. Harrison 1937 *The Life and Death of Robert Devereux, Earl of Essex* (New York); some of the facts are corrected in Oxford and Essex ed 1980:14–22. Lytton Strachey 1928 *Elizabeth and Essex: A Tragic History* (London) transforms Essex into a literary character. See also Ray Heffner 1933; Heffner 1934 'Essex, the Ideal Courtier' *ELH* 1:7–36, which draws parallels between Essex and Calidore; and Heffner 1936 'Essex and Book Five of the *Faerie Queene*' *ELH* 3:67–82, on Essex and Artegall. Heffner's conclusions are questioned and tempered by Charles E. Mounts 1958 'Spenser and the Earl of Essex' *RenP 1958, 1959, 1960* pp 12–19. Rudolf B. Gottfried 1937 'Spenser's *View* and Essex' *PMLA* 52:645–51 argues that *Vewe* was written as part of this bid for patronage. The significance and occasion of *Prothalamion* is considered in Fowler 1975, ch 4. See also Millar MacLure 1953–4 'A Mirror for Scholars' *UTQ* 23:143–54 for an account of Henry Cuffe, secretary (and evil genius) of Essex and executed with him.

etiological tales Curiosity about how something comes into existence is subject in the natural sciences to methodical investigation, which consists of framing and testing hypotheses about it. Those hypotheses which survive attempts to disconfirm them are held to be true only until superseded by others which in turn are tested systematically. In prescientific times, however, speculation is controlled by satisfaction, and the sort of myths we call etiological attempt to explain, in satisfying ways, the cause (*aitia*) of something whose origin intrigues or worries people. For example, the knowledge that everybody in the world has been produced from the sexual conjunction of male and female promotes speculation about the origin of the 'first' male and female, and related questions such as whether one of the sexes came first, and if so, which. In a patriarchal society like that which produced the Book of Genesis, the first person on earth is said to be male and to have been created by a male God; a matriarchal society, by contrast, would favor the female as the originating principle. One way of transcending the problem of priority in the etiology of sexual dimorphism is to propose that the originating principle is neither male nor female but both, as Spenser does in describing such veiled and androgynous figures as Nature (*FQ* VII vii 5) and Venus Genetrix, who 'hath both kinds in one, / Both male and female' (IV x 41), and who therefore emblematizes, through the resolution of sexual difference into sexual unity, that greater resolution of discord into concord which is celebrated in *FQ* IV.

Etiological tales can be used to explain anything, from how the leopard got his spots to why nothing grows in winter or why a landscape looks the way it does. Spenser appears to have had little interest in those trivial etiologies which turn up in many sixteenth-century sonnets, and which are exemplified in the Sidneian conceit that Cupid's bow originates in Stella's eyebrows (*Astrophil and Stella* 17). The closest he comes to that kind of subject matter is in his pastoral elegy on Sidney, 'Astrophel,' which is a rewriting of Ovid's story of Venus and Adonis (*Metamorphoses* 20). For just as Ovid's account of how Adonis metamorphosed into an anemone can be read as an explanation of how there come to be such flowers as anemones in the world, so, too, Spenser's poem makes the love and death of Astrophel and Stella the origin of a red and blue (but botanically unidentified) flower called Starlight or Penthia (193–4). The usual displacement of emphasis occurs here: what is nominally the thing to be explained is dwarfed by the circumstantial narrative of its *aitia*.

Etiological tales are a boon to writers of narrative verse, for they provide opportunities for seemingly digressive embellishments in the form of tales within tales, which swell the pages and create the illusion of inexhaustible narrative abundance. Etiologizing in the tradition of Ovid is characteristic of Elizabethan epyllia such as Marlowe's *Hero and Leander* (1598), especially the Mercury episode. But (perhaps for generic reasons) it is not characteristic of Spenser's epic poem which, strictly speaking, contains only one etiological tale, namely the Faunus and Diana episode. It explains how Arlo Hill ceased to be a pleasance inhabited by nymphs and satyrs, and was transformed by an angry Diana into a waste land where 'Wolves and Thieves abound' (VII vi 55). Although prefaced by misgivings about the generic decorum of incorporating a story of 'hilles and woods, mongst warres and Knights' (37), the episode proves to be only a pseudo-digression, for the tale it embodies – how Faunus angered Diana by intruding on her privacy while she was bathing – in fact recapitulates (as an elegant variation in the pastoral mode) two previous stories: Mutabilitie's territorial invasion of the moon, and Calidore's interruption of the dance of the Graces.

Spenser's myths can be called etiological only in a broader sense than the Ovidian. They tend to be less spectacular and more deliberate than the metamorphic kind, which record swift and inscrutable transformations. His diagrammatic style of allegory permits a more detailed and explicit account of why things are as they are. A typical instance is the presentation of Britomart, a virgin who intends to marry and have children by Artegall, whom she has glimpsed in Merlin's mirror (III ii 22–6). The ambivalence of Britomart as a representative of Elizabeth – not only as virgin but as the sexually fulfilled woman she would become if she were to marry – obliges Spenser to create an etiological myth to explain the unexplored potential in his heroine's character. So we are given the story of Belphoebe and Amoret, the twins who emblematize Britomart's actual and potential nature. Belphoebe embodies 'perfect Maydenhed' (vi 28) and is brought up by the goddess of virginity, Diana, which is the allegorist's way of differentiating the secondary *aitia* of nurture from the primary one of nature. Amoret, on the other hand, embodies 'goodly womanhed' and is reared by Psyche (on Venus' behalf) in that center of procreative sexuality, the Garden of Adonis, before Scudamour takes her away. The ultimate unity of apparent opposites in the characters of Belphoebe and Amoret is signaled by the fact that as twins they are daughters of the same mother, the 'golden born' Chrysogone, who conceived them immaculately while lying naked in the sunshine (5–7) – that is, by parthenogenesis, which symbolizes a mystic reconciliation of the antithetical states of virginity and procreativeness. Hence the doubleness of Belphoebe and Amoret, virginity and chaste sexuality, is shown to derive from a reconciling singleness in Chrysogone, herself the daughter of a doubleness, Amphisa (4), whose name denotes her double nature (Gr *amphis*). Infolded in the character of Britomart, therefore, are the characteristics of the twin sisters; or to put it the other way around, the actual condition of the unmarried Britomart is unfolded mythically in Belphoebe, and her potentially married condition in Amoret. This etiological myth is sufficiently comprehensive and flexible to accommodate any development in Britomart's way of life (or in Queen Elizabeth's, for that matter).

The fact that no topic is too complex to have etiological tales told about it is shown in the Garden of Adonis episode (III vi 29–50), which assimilates a fairly technical philosophical vocabulary into a mythopoetic account of how life is perpetuated in a world subject to mutability and death. The Garden is 'the first seminarie / Of all things, that are borne to live and die, / According to their kindes' (30). Every created thing is said to have a form which is susceptible to change and decay and a constituent substance which is not. So although the forms of things 'are variable and decay' (38) and therefore wither and die in this 'chaungefull world' (33) of ours, nothing is ever lost because the 'substance is eterne' (37). It is this substance or matter – miraculously conserved despite the depredations of time and mortality – which is recycled in the Garden, where it is refitted with new forms before being sent out once more into our universe of death. The procreative analogue to this is the sexual penetration by Adonis, 'the Father of all formes' (47), of Venus, who is the 'mother' (40) or *mater* of all matter, and whose prolific fertility repairs the damage done by time and death, thus ensuring that the natural world will continue to exist 'eterne in mutabilitie' (47).

If the Garden of Adonis is the most comprehensive of Spenser's etiological myths, his most ambitious may well be a political one, namely his justification of the Tudor monarchy. Traditional problems in bridging the gap between events and descriptions of events have led historians to adopt tactics which are reducible to rhetorical devices, and which poets and novelists can use in order to make their pseudo-histories sound like genuine history. Spenser's appropriation of the genealogical table as an authenticating device (II x) is a case in point. In the house of Alma, the two books which Arthur and Guyon borrow from Eumnestes' study constitute a double genealogy of Queen Elizabeth. One of these, the *Antiquitie of Faerie lond* (ix 60), traces her lineage back through Henry VIII, 'the mightie *Oberon*' (x 75), to an Adam and Eve called Elf and Fay 'Of whom all *Faeryes* spring' (71). In the other book, *Briton moniments* (ix 59), Arthur reads prophetically about the ancient lineage of a woman who will become his future descendant, Queen Elizabeth, and who is allegorically the Fairy Queen he is searching for. The purpose of these two books is to situate Elizabeth Tudor at the confluence of two venerable traditions, one Arthurian and 'British,' the other 'Saxon,' and in this way to perpetuate the myth (encouraged by Henry VII and promoted by myth-making imperial chroniclers) that the Tudors' Arthurian links legitimated their claim to sovereignty. To the extent that *The Faerie Queene* is shaped by this imperial myth, the whole poem constitutes an etiological tale whose function is to justify a polity by explaining how the Tudors come to have an inalienable right to the power they possess.

K.K. RUTHVEN

etymology Speculation about the origin of words has resulted in two rival conceptions of the way in which language relates to reality. The one favored by descriptive linguistics is 'conventionalist' and treats the relationship between words and things as arbitrary, thus supporting the view that a rose by any other name would smell as sweet. But the one favored by Spenser and many other poets is 'naturalist,' insofar as it holds that words denote the natures of the things they refer to.

Both conceptions of language are articulated in Plato's *Cratylus*, where Hermogenes argues the conventionalist case against Cratylus, who favors the naturalist view epitomized in the Elizabethan proverb, 'Names and natures do often agree' (Tilley 1950, N32; cf 1 Sam 25.25). Unlike modern lexicographers, who do not believe that words have 'correct' meanings which etymology can retrieve, naturalist etymologizers like Spenser regard etymons as vehicles of truths obscured by the duplicities of everyday language; etymology therefore promises linguistic restitution, the consequences of which are moral and epistemological. Just as the universe appeared to Spenser to have decayed visibly since antiquity, so words had decayed; and the consequent mismatch between words and things was an index of moral confusion: for what 'men then did vertue call, / Is now cald vice' (*FQ* V proem 4). To retrieve the etymons would be to repair the original bond between words and things on which are predicated epistemological distinctions between truth and falsehood and moral distinctions between good and evil.

To Spenser, etymology is a category of thought with forensic uses; and *figura etymologica* is a rhetorical device not only for representing persons and places but also for structuring narrative incidents. Because abstract qualities are personified in *The Faerie Queene*, etymological inquisitiveness frequently takes the form of probing the significance of personal names. For if names reveal natures, they are prognosticatory; and the ability to decode them etymologically is worth cultivating, since to be forewarned is to be forearmed: 'Know it by the name,' Amavia instructs Guyon when warning him about the Bower of Bliss (II i 51). 'How hight he ... ?' (II iv 41) is an important question to ask of an enemy whose nature is immediately manifest to those adept at spotting the veridical etymon concealed under the integument of an opaque name. Because Spenser represents attributes or behavior before naming the characters who display them, the appositeness of an etymologizing name often strikes us with probative force: 'Therefore *Corflambo* was he cald aright' (IV viii 49), we are told of the man whose 'false eyes' send 'secret flakes of lustfull fire' into the 'harts' of women (48), and whose hybrid name combines 'heart' (L *cor*) with 'torch' (Fr *flambeau*).

Spenser's most striking use of forensic etymology occurs in the debate between Nature and Mutabilitie, and focuses on the meaning of a relatively new word: *universe* (VII vii 56). The *OED*'s earliest citation is from Puttenham (1589), who glosses it as 'the whole of created or existing things regarded collectively,' an interpretation which erases the implications of its derivation from L *unus* (one) and *versus* (from L *vertere* to turn). Etymologically, a *universe* is a 'oneturning,' a derivation which raises the question of whether or not the word matches the thing. Mutabilitie regards it as a misnomer, for everything in a world subject to change goes awry, 'turned by transverse' (56). According to Nature, however, the etymology of *universe* describes exactly the type of unidirectional change to be expected in a world whose history is shaped providentially. Things change, but not 'by transverse,' for they end up 'turning to themselves ... againe,' uni-versely (58); the etymology of *universe* therefore provides incontrovertible evidence from the world of words about the nature of the world of things.

Naturalist etymologizers remedy discrepancies between names and natures by renaming. Thus the poet who is nailed by his tongue to a post for publishing slanders against Mercilla has his name changed from Bonfont to Malfont – 'Eyther for th'evill, which he did' (in which case the derivation is from Fr *faire mal* 'to do evil'), 'Or that he likened was to a welhed [L *fons* fount] / Of evill words' emanating from the printer's font (V ix 26). The tolerance shown here for complementary etymologies is characteristic of Spenser's interest in names whose multiple significances collectively invite multiple perspectives on the narratives in which they are embedded. Even the simplest etymologies generate significant details. For example, Envy appears 'to looke askew' (V xii 29) because the Latin word for envy is *invidia*, which derives from *invidere* (to look awry); and Cymochles wades through 'waves of deepe delight' in the Bower of Bliss (II v 35) because his name derives from Gr *kuma* (wave). Generative etymologizing is a form of wit. The terrified Trevisan, who is 'staring wide / With stony eyes' when the Red Cross Knight first meets him, and whose hair is 'Upstaring' (I ix 22, 24), is 'thrice looking' (L *ter* thrice + *visi* I have seen) and therefore encounters Despair three times: once in the company of Terwin, again when 'looking backe' (25) in fear that Despair is pursuing him, and last when he is leading Redcrosse to Despair's cave. As puns indicate, the eye which 'looks' at Despair is 'unlucky' (26); and Trevisan is 'luckie' (30) to have looked and lived.

Although the evidence adduced in an etymological inquiry is linguistic, allegorists may present the results in nonlinguistic forms such as family trees and emblems. To have the blustering Orgoglio fathered by the god of winds (I vii 9) merely displaces a fascination with origins from etymology into genealogy, perhaps inevitably in a poem which personifies its key terms. Again, instead of simply saying that Scudamour's name means 'shield of love' (Fr *escu d'amour*), Spenser depicts him carrying an emblematic 'shield ... On which the winged boy ... Depeincted was' (III xi 7).

Ambiguous names offer many narrative opportunities, especially when a multiple etymology is believed to signify a multifaceted truth. If Orgoglio is 'pride' (Ital *orgoglio*), he will be 'arrogant' (I vii 10); but for all his vanity, he will fight 'in vaine' against Arthur (viii 21). If his name denotes swelling with wind (Gr *orgaō*), it is appropriate to have him fathered by 'blustring *Aeolus*' (vii 9), and to let him overcome Redcrosse with the 'wind' of one of his blows (12); and it is comically apposite that, when Arthur has killed him, Orgoglio should be spoken of as mortally punctured, 'like an emptie bladder' (viii 24).

Complementary etymologies raise problems of interpretation, however, which Spenser manipulates for ironic effects, and nowhere more successfully than in *FQ* VI, where the question of Calidore's 'truancy' from his quest is intimately related to the significance of the place he frequents while truant, and which (Spenser assures us) 'rightly cleeped was mount *Acidale*' (x 8). But in what sense 'rightly'? Because Acidale is said 'to overlooke' the surrounding landscape, a derivation from L *acies* (look) is likely; but other etymologies link it positively with Gr *akēdēs* (free from care) and negatively with L *accidia* (sloth). Despite the standard etymology – 'Of Court it seemes, men Courtesie doe call' (i 1) – the knight of Courtesy finds the virtue he exemplifies represented in a pastoral community; and his discovery of a mismatch between word and thing has some bearing on whether Acidale signifies *akēdēs* or *accidia*. A close inspection of Spenser's etymologizing practices reveals the remarkable extent to which they shape the writing and structuring of *The Faerie Queene*. K.K. RUTHVEN

Belson 1964; Alice Fox Blitch 1965 'Etymon and Image in *The Faerie Queene*' diss Michigan State Univ; Craig 1967; K.K. Ruthven 1969 'The Poet as Etymologist' *CritQ* 11:9–37.

Europa A maiden loved by Jove, who disguised himself as a bull and carried her off to sea on his back; the child of their union was Minos of Crete (Ovid *Metamorphoses* 2.833–75, Moschus *Idylls* 2, Boccaccio *Genealogia* 2.62). In *Muiopotmos*, Arachne depicts Europa's abduction in the tapestry she weaves in her contest with Pallas. Lines 277–84 closely follow Ovid's description of Arachne's tapestry (*Met* 6.103–7), and Spenser's 'true Sea, and true Bull ye would weene' translates his 'verum taurum, freta vera putares.' Lines 285–8 recall Ovid's earlier description of Europa's trembling on the bull's back as she sees the shore receding (*Met* 2.873–5), but the reference to 'a wilde wildernes of waters deepe' gives the scene a primitive terror not in Ovid. Spenser similarly emphasizes terror when mentioning Europa in the tapestry found in the house of Busirane (*FQ* III xi 30).

Spenser identifies the bull that abducted Europa with the zodiacal sign of Taurus, probably following Ovid (*Fasti* 5.605–22, *FQ* V proem 5, VII vii 33); a similar identification with the Cretan bull in the labors of Hercules may suggest zodiacal or Herculean patterns in *FQ* V (Aptekar 1969:160–1;

Nohrnberg 1976:397, 591). Other elements of the Europa myth appear at one or more removes in the story of Florimell, who is similarly carried over the waters and loses her girdle thereby, if not the virginity it traditionally signifies. Moschus' Europa is gathering flowers with her friends when she is carried off, and so anticipates the seasonal myth of Proserpina which is central to Florimell's story and name. The abandoned girdle appears in Ovid's treatment of Proserpina (*Met* 5.468–70); and it may be his development of resemblances between the Europa and Proserpina myths that lies behind Spenser's feelings for the emotional resonance of Europa's story, as well as his mythic union of land and sea in the Florimell-Marinell story. Ariosto's Angelica is similarly indebted to Ovid, while providing further elements in Florimell's story.

CALVIN R. EDWARDS

F

fables In a note to *Februarie* 102 in *The Shepheardes Calender*, E.K. disputes Spenser's identification of Chaucer as his model for the fable of the Oak and the Briar, declaring that it is 'cleane in another kind, and rather like to Aesopes fables.' The distinction seems specious, since Chaucer's *Nun's Priest's Tale*, like Spenser's tale, is an elaborate expansion of an Aesopian fable. E.K.'s note was not aiming at accuracy, however: it alerted the reader to the vital link between pastoral and fable as rustic or primitive forms, suitable both for a poet in training and for a spokesman of the common man. *Februarie*, *Maye*, and *September* imitate Aesopian fables, *Maye* (95–102) also refers briefly to 'The Ape and Her Young,' *Julye* (221–6) to 'The Eagle and the Shellfish,' *September* (61) to 'The Dog and His Shadow,' *October* (11–12) to 'The Grasshopper in Winter,' and *November* (25–6) to 'The Nightingale and the Titmouse.' In *Vewe of Ireland*, Spenser refers to 'the Tale in Aesope of the wilde horse' and to the fable of 'the frozen Snake' (*Var Prose* pp 167–8). E.K. adds to this already heavy fabulist emphasis a note in *Februarie* on the meeting of the ape with the lion, and his Epistle compares writers who are biased against 'their owne country and natural speach' to the dog in the manger and the complacently blind mole. In *Mother Hubberds Tale* (pub 1591 but possibly written much earlier), Spenser stretched the fable to what was, for him, its absolute limits of form and meaning. Thereafter he abandoned the genre.

(See **fables** Fig 1.)

The fable is an ancient form of fiction and primitive allegory in which beasts and occasionally plants behave in human ways from which a moral can be drawn. The genre is still associated with the name of Aesop, traditionally a hyper-intelligent Greek slave of the sixth century BC. His historical existence is supported only by one brief mention in Herodotus; and the earliest 'Life' dates from the first century AD, as do the two collections in which his work was believed to survive, the Greek verse fables of Babrius and the Latin verse fables of Phaedrus. These were transmitted to the Middle Ages through two further intermediaries, the 'Romulus' prose redaction of Phaedrus and Avianus' Latin verse translation of Babrius. In the twelfth century, Walter Anglicus is believed to have turned the Romulus collection back into Latin verse, in an influential text that was probably the base for Marie de France's vernacular translation. In the fifteenth century, Italian humanists rediscovered Phaedrus and Babrius, along with the oriental Bidpai fables. Steinhöwel's German edition (1477) printed Romulus, some of Avianus, and a selection from other humanist sources; it was reproduced at least 27 times in several languages before 1500. Also widely known in sixteenth-century England were the Greek prose text (c 1480) and the school anthology by Martin van Dorp. By 1484 Caxton had published an English version with a Life of Aesop and 167 fables from various sources dating from the late fourth century to the mid-fifteenth.

By Spenser's time, therefore, 'Aesopes Fables' meant a genre rather than a definitive text, a genre constantly accumulating new examples, in which different versions or adaptations of individual fables were taken for granted. Henryson's late-fifteenth-century *Morall Fabillis of Esope* (printed in 1570, 1571, 1577) provided a recent example of selection from, expansion on, and addition to the corpus, with Aesop himself appearing as the author's personal mentor.

As well as by natural accretion, the fable tradition was influenced by other systems of animal or plant symbolism. Scripture, especially *Judges*, *Job*, *Proverbs*, and *Ecclesiastes*, provided emblematic status for the briar, lion, ant, and grasshopper. From the late Middle Ages, political prophecy had featured animals in its enigmatic style. So, of course, had heraldry. Medieval bestiaries, Renaissance emblem books, collections of proverbs – all overlapped with the fable (see *emblematics). One of the most important convergences was with the French cycle of tales about Reynard the Fox, grouped with the Aesopic fables by Marie de France and Steinhöwel, but published separately by Caxton in 1481. Where the classical fable was essentially brief, the Reynard tale expanded narrative, characterization, and dialogue in the interests both of humor and of brutal satire. The fox himself became recognized as a figure for the hypocrisy, greed, and rhetorical cunning of medieval clerics, a tradition that Spenser adapted effectively, in *Maye* and *Mother Hubberd*, to contemporary anti-Catholicism.

The study of rhetoric helped to make fables more popular. Aristotle had recommended Aesop's fables to orators (*Rhetoric* 2.20). Quintilian required pupils to paraphrase, abridge, and embellish them (*Institutio oratoria* 1.9.2). In 1563, Richard Rainolde explained the eight-point amplification of the fable that Spenser uses in *Februarie* (*Foundacion of Rhetorike* fols 4v-12r). In many schools, very likely including Merchant Taylors', Aesop's fables in either Latin or Greek were part of the curriculum; and to produce an English version was primarily, of course, to demonstrate one's skill in the vernacular.

But Spenser's fascination with the fable in his early poems cannot be explained solely on rhetorical grounds. Aesop was reputed to have been a counselor to kings. Phaedrus, like Aesop a freed slave, had claimed that the fable was invented by slaves as an oblique medium of expression for those who could not speak openly. This obliqueness was generally recognized; as Sidney said, 'the poet is indeed the right popular philosopher, whereof Aesop's tales give good proof: whose pretty allegories, stealing under the formal tales of beasts, make many, more beastly than beasts, begin to hear the sound of virtue from these dumb speakers' (Sidney ed 1973b:87). It seemed natural that political readings or versions of fables should evolve side by side with more generally ethical ones. Thus Sidney, to whom Spenser dedicated *The Shepheardes Calender*, wrote two beast fables with political reference for the *Old Arcadia* (1580). One tells of how the swan was silenced for imprudent criticism of the other birds, who called a parliament and 'statute made he never should have voice' (Sidney ed 1973a:78–9), presumably a reference to the 1581 'Statute of Silence' (23 Eliz Cap II) passed by Elizabeth's parliament. The other, introduced by Sidney's own persona Philisides (ed 1973a:256–9), is a radical revision of the fable of the frogs desiring a king. The tyrant is not now a stork (or, in some versions, a water serpent) but man, created by the beasts and endowed with their own characteristics. In addition, they unwisely agree that he alone should have freedom of speech. Sidney's poems are therefore metafables, which ironize by reversing the human desire to give animals our own bad traits, and which explain the connection between fabling and censorship. When Sir Roger L'Estrange published his *Fables of Aesop and Other Eminent Mythologists* in 1692, his preface defined the fable's role in implying 'by *Hints*, and *Glances*' what 'neither the *Pulpit*, the *Stage*, nor the *Press*, Dares so much as Touch upon't' – '(Who shall say to a King, What Dost thou?)' (sig B1r).

Unfortunately, hints and glances that were originally enigmatic for safety's sake become still harder for later readers to interpret with certainty. In Spenser's longer fables in *Complaints*, specific identification of persons and events has proved notoriously difficult; yet we can probably assume that they all speak, sometimes generally, sometimes pointedly, to the political situation in England in the 1580s. Like Sidney, Spenser was certainly disturbed by Elizabeth's marriage negotiations with the French and Roman Catholic Duc d'Alençon, by the presence of his persuasive agent Simier (coincidentally 'the monkey'), by Leicester's loss of favor at court, and by Burghley's dominance. When Dryden published *The Hind and the Panther* in 1687, he included in the beginning of the Third Part a definition of the beast fable that serves indirectly as a gloss on Spenser's (ed 1956–, 3:161):

Much malice mingl'd with a little wit
Perhaps may censure this mysterious writ
...
Let *Aesop* answer, who has set to view,
Such kinds as *Greece* and *Phrygia* never knew;
And mother *Hubbard* in her homely dress
Has sharply blam'd a *British Lioness*,
That *Queen*, whose feast the factious rabble keep,
Expos'd obscenely naked and a-sleep.

With Dryden's guidance to *Mother Hubberd*'s contemporary reception, we can understand why the *Complaints* volume is suspected of having been 'called in' or censored after publication; and if we apply similar assumptions to the fables in *The Shepheardes Calender*, Spenser's campaign for what is native and natural to his 'owne country' acquires an interesting political dimension.

Annabel Patterson and Ann Coiro

T.W. Baldwin 1944, 1:607–40; Friedland 1937; David G. Hale 1972 'Aesop in Renaissance England' *Library* 5th ser 27:116–25; Annabel Patterson 1987 'Fables of Power' in *Politics of Discourse: The Literature and History of Seventeenth-Century England* ed Kevin Sharpe and Steven N. Zwicker (Berkeley and Los Angeles) pp 271–96, 348–50; Anthony G. Petti 1963 'Beasts and Politics in Elizabethan Literature' *E&S* ns 16:68–90.

fabliau (or *fablel*, OF from L *fabulellum* 'a little story') A generic term variously applied in modern criticism to three distinct but related literary manifestations of the comic spirit: the extant corpus of over 150 short, frequently bawdy, comic tales in French verse, composed in northern France between the late-twelfth and mid-fourteenth centuries and preserved, some in several versions, in 36 manuscripts; analogous prose and verse tales from many other cultures and periods or in other medieval languages; elaborations or adaptations of such stories embedded in more ambitious, learned, or self-consciously artistic medieval and Renaissance narratives. Underlying these categories is a venerable Indo-European oral tradition, still vigorous today, of earthy, cynical, or irreverent short tales or jokes that mock or invert established values and exploit social stereotypes for comic, rather than corrective or satiric, purposes.

Although the fabliau (in all its senses) is often called 'realistic,' to distinguish it from the idealizing tendency of courtly or sentimental literature, it is anything but a transcript of social or personal reality. In the fabliau world, people are simplified to professional, class, ethnic, or sexual stereotypes; they exist either to get the better of others or to be made fools of. Institutions and values become unavailing restraints imposed on, or hypocritical disguises for, basic desires. Love is reduced to sex, intellect to trickery and selfish problem solving. The stories embodying this comic inversion of civilized values completely subordinate description and character to plot; all components of the tale are manipulated to bring about the comic climax: a reversal, comeuppance, outburst of random or retributive violence, or triumph of cleverness. Elements of this form developed out of the earlier Old French fabliau into the well-known stories of Boccaccio, the anecdotes of Poggio Bracciolini and the tales of Chaucer. In Spenser's time, these were popular in their original forms, in prose or verse redactions, or in the jestbooks (for instance, *The Merie Tales ... by Master Skelton* that Spenser gave Harvey [Stern 1979:240]; cf the 'merry tales' that Phaedria tells Cymochles [*FQ* II vi 6]).

Spenser's two forays into fabliau plot and atmosphere – the Squire of Dame's search for chaste women and the story of Malbecco, Hellenore, and Paridell – show an adaptive mastery comparable to Boccaccio's and Chaucer's, but indebted also to comic narratives of Ovid and Ariosto. *Orlando furioso* contains several fabliau-inspired episodes treated with characteristic irony by being juxtaposed to other stories that have quite different views about women and sexuality. Its most notorious tale, for instance, concerns two extraordinarily handsome men, each of whom discovers his wife betraying him with a man of far inferior looks and station (canto 28). The two husbands, Astolfo and Giocondo, subsequently travel the world together, seducing women and proving to themselves that there is no woman strong enough to resist their adulterous charms. This tale and its variants were well known to Elizabethan readers, and form a basis for Spenser's narrative of the Squire of Dames. (Cf Harington's comment, 'The hosts tale [in *OF* 28] is a bad one: M. *Spencers* tale ... is to the like effect, sharpe and well conceyted' *Sp All* p 22.)

The Squire of Dames (*FQ* III vii 53–61) first appears as a prisoner of the giantess Argante, who intends to kill him if he does not succumb to her insatiable lust. Rescued by Satyrane, he recounts the two quests he had undertaken at the command of his mistress. First he spent a year wandering about offering 'service unto gentle Dames' and returned with 'Three hundred pledges for my good desartes, / And thrise three hundred thanks for my good partes.' The quibble on *partes* makes clear the sexual nature of the Squire's service, as does his mistress' reaction: she dispatches him again, forbidding him to return until he has found an equal number of women who refuse his service (ie, remain chaste). After a search of three years, he has found only three: a prostitute who demands payment, a nun who fears discovery, and 'a Damzell ... of low degree,' the only one who is chaste. The narrative, especially in the word *service*, shows a crucial link between the conventions and rhetoric of the fabliau and those of courtly love. The rituals of courtly love, far from subjugating desire to nobler ideals as they pretend, constitute a game that encourages sexual indulgence while appearing to oppose it. If the Squire can discover only one chaste woman, perhaps the fault lies as much with masculine 'service' as with feminine weakness. Spenser modifies and moralizes his inherited fabliau so that, more than an occasion for cynical laughter at the expense of women, it becomes a vehicle for passing judgment upon licentious courtly attitudes (and their valorizing rhetoric) that justify dalliance, exploit sexual attractiveness, and promote unchastity in men and women alike.

In the tale of Malbecco, Hellenore, and Paridell (III ix-x), Spenser undertakes a more ambitious synthesis of fabliau elements and material from other literary kinds and traditions. The story in its barest outline conforms to the enduring fabliau plot of the lusty young wife who cuckolds her rich, jealous, old husband. In Spenser's treatment, the story begins with this traditional situation, but as it develops it becomes increasingly symbolic, with the main character finally transformed into an abstraction (Malbecco 'Forgot he was a man, and *Gealosie* is hight' x 60). Malbecco has clear antecedents in the medieval fabliau; his semiblindness (symbolizing both his unavailing jealousy and his avarice) may descend from Chaucer's *Merchant's Tale*, where the blindness that seizes old Januarie after his marriage to 'fresshe May' is equally emblematic and leads to the same outcome. Hellenore and Paridell may receive their names from great lovers of antiquity, but they dramatize the trivialization of the traditions of love and honor. Indeed, the interaction of these three types of failed love endows Spenser's fabliau with powerful moral impact appropriate to its placement within the Legend of Chastity. R.W. Hanning

Two collections are Anatole de Montaiglon and Gaston Raynaud, eds 1872–90 *Recueil général et complet des fabliaux des XIIIe et XIVe siècles* 6 vols (Paris); and Willem Noomen and Nico van den Boogaard, eds 1983– *Nouveau Recueil complet des fabliaux* (Assen). Robert Harrison, tr 1974 *Gallic Salt: Eighteen Fabliaux* (Berkeley and Los Angeles) is a selection with English translation. Studies include Joseph Bédier 1925 *Les Fabliaux* 5th ed (Paris; first pub 1893); R. Howard Bloch 1986 *The Scandal of the Fabliaux* (Chicago); Thomas D. Cooke and Benjamin L. Honeycutt, eds 1974 *The Humor of the Fabliaux* (Columbia, Mo); Peter Goddall 1982 'An Outline History of the English Fabliau after Chaucer' *AUMLA* 57:5–23; Philippe Ménard 1983 *Les Fabliaux: Contes à rire du moyen âge* (Paris); Charles Muscatine 1976 'The Social Background of the Old French Fabliaux' *Genre* 9:1–19; Muscatine 1986 *The Old French Fabliaux* (New Haven); Per Nykrog 1957 *Les Fabliaux: Etude d'histoire littéraire et de stylistique médiévale* (Copenhagen; rev ed Geneva 1973); Roy J. Pearcy 1976–7

'Investigations into the Principles of Fabliau Structure' *Genre* 9:345–78; Jean Rychner 1960 *Contribution à l'étude des fabliaux* 2 vols (Neuchâtel); Mary Jane Schenck 1976 'The Morphology of the Fabliau' *Fabula* 17:26–39.

The Faerie Queene (See ed 1912:1–2, 211.) FIRST ED 1590; quarto in eights; Johnson 1933 no 9, *STC* 23080, 23081, and 23081a – Reel 1220 (film of 23081). This ed appeared in three different forms which have been distinguished as 'issues' in the past, but which are really various levels of correction within a single issue. One distinction is the presence or absence of the Welsh words on sig X7v; a second is the spacing of the date on the title page; and a third, the only one which might really constitute a new 'issue,' is the two versions of the Dedicatory Sonnets at the end of the volume (a set of 10 or a set of 15 which includes the first 8 of the series of 10). This last variation came about through a failure to cancel leaves 2P6 and 2P7 and to replace them with a *cancellandum* signed 2Q. Copies exist with only the original series of 10 sonnets, with only the new set of sonnets on 2Q (without 2P6 and 2P7), and with all three leaves. This ed was clearly set from Spenser's manuscript, and he may have seen it through the press. For further discussion of the textual history, see critical *bibliography.

SECOND ED 1596; quarto in eights; Johnson 1933 no 10, *STC* 23082 – Reel 332. The second ed of Books I-III is a page-for-page reprinting of the 1590 ed with a few revisions which may be authorial. The dedication to Elizabeth I is changed, and the final five stanzas of the 1590 Book III are here revised to three. The Letter to Raleigh, Commendatory Verses, and Dedicatory Sonnets are not reprinted, except for two sonnets by W.R. and the poem 'To the learned Shepheard' by Hobynoll.

THIRD ED 1609; folio; Johnson 1933 no 12, *STC* 23083 – Reel 1716. The first ed to print the *Cantos of Mutabilitie* and also the first to print the stanzas of *FQ* in double columns. This ed set the style of the physical presentation of this work which has continued to the present day. It was sufficiently different to require the publishers, Waterson and Lownes, to reenter the work in the Stationers' Register on 3 September and 5 November 1604. It was set from a copy of 1596, except for the *Cantos of Mutabilitie*, although 1609 may have been slightly corrected from some source. Like the second ed, it omits the Letter to Raleigh and the other supplementary matter from the first. Nevertheless, some copies of 1609 include this material, bound in from the 1611 collected folio.

FOURTH ED between 1612 and 1617; folio; Johnson 1933 no 19.II.B and 19.III.B, *STC* 23083.3–4 – not filmed. (For a full description of the peculiarities of this ed, see Johnson.) A page-for-page reprint of 1609. However, the unsold sheets of the last three books ran out before the first four books, and it became necessary to reprint Books IV-VII; they were given their own title page dated 1612 (a few copies bear the date 1613). In 1609, the first leaf of the book had the title page on the front and the dedication to Queen Elizabeth on the back; when Books I-III were reprinted, the first leaf was left blank. There has always been great confusion between the 1609 (third ed) and the 1612/1617 (fourth ed) of *FQ* because, from 1612 onwards, sheets from all three printings were sold in mixed sets according to what the bookseller or printer had on hand. But the fourth ed can be distinguished by its lack of ornamental initial letters at the beginning of each canto in Books I-III; moreover, only the first three leaves of each gathering are signed, whereas the third ed is signed on the first four. Also, one gathering in Books IV-VII is signed 'Z' in the fourth ed, whereas this letter is not used in the signing sequence in the third ed.

Clearly, all authority for the text ceases with the third ed of 1609, but the fourth ed has been included here because anyone working with the old copies will frequently encounter it in conjunction with the third. It is also important to note that the Letter to Raleigh and the Commendatory and Dedicatory Verses, almost all of which had not been reprinted since the first ed in 1590, were reprinted in 1611 in a single eight-leaf folio gathering (Johnson 1933 no 19.IV.A) and again in 1617 (Johnson 1933 no 19.IV.B) when supplies of the first printing had been exhausted (see Johnson for distinctions between these two printings). These materials can be found in any of the 1609 or 1612/1617 folio eds or any permutations thereof.

Best modern eds: *Variorum* 1–6, J.C. Smith (1909; rpt by Hamilton in ed 1977), or Roche (1978). Note: Smith, Roche, Hamilton are three good reading editions, but the *Variorum* presents the fullest textual evidence to date.

WILLIAM PROCTOR WILLIAMS

***The Faerie Queene*, Book I** 'The Legende of the Knight of the Red Crosse,' or St George (as he is named at ii 11–12); also the book 'of Holinesse.' Holiness signifies devotion to God, the urge to conform to his will and, as far as is possible in a state of mortality, the accomplishment of that urge. Ideally, holiness results in spiritual perfection and, as such, becomes equivalent to sanctity. Etymologically, *holy* derives from Old English *hal* (whole) and signifies completeness, the integrity of one's spiritual and moral nature, the union of flesh and spirit. Moreover, if holiness is equivalent to sanctity, then *saint* signifies the posthumous canonization of a person of holy life and also, as in the New Testament, one of God's elect. Holiness is at once the foundation of virtue (as it validates the existence and the pursuit of virtue by justifying it in relation to God) and the goal of the Christian's life, election by God to the army of his saints. Holiness is the foundation, therefore, of Spenser's poem; and it provides the fitting subject of Book I, because the number one, the monad, is identified with God's single being (Gal 3.20).

All this is implied in the title to Book I; and the holiness that Redcrosse quests for – in part expressed in the figure of Una – is at once private (the assurance of his individual holiness) and public (as Redcrosse is England, his attainment of holiness is England's). Holiness on both levels is achieved through the union in betrothal of Redcrosse and Una in canto xii.

As an individual, Redcrosse is also a Christian Everyman; and his journey to holiness is archetypal in that it explores the anguish of all human beings confronted with a spiritual ideal and only too aware of their frailty. He is a novice in battle who must grow old by experience: the fact that his armor is ancient and dented (i 1–2) and is 'the whole armour of God' of Ephesians 6.13 (Letter to Raleigh) cannot guarantee immunity from the forces of evil, merely protection if used correctly. At the beginning he is 'faithfull true,' a phrase which, in various forms, sounds throughout the book and announces exactly the goal of holiness set for him, for it alludes to the militant Christ of Revelation 19.11, seated on a white horse signifying 'triumph over his enemies' according to the Geneva gloss: 'Faithful and true, and he judgeth and fighteth righteously.' As we meet it at the opening of the book, the phrase announces a hope for achievement. The book of holiness will be about the attainment of that faith (Fidelia) without which Christ may not 'dwell in your hearts' (Eph 3.17) by confrontation with its opposite (the infidel Sansfoy, the corrupt Fidessa), and about the attainment of truth (Una) by confrontation with its opposite (Duessa). Redcrosse will learn to distinguish false from true so that he, too, may fight righteously in killing the Dragon of canto xi and become betrothed to Una. That betrothal marks his attainment of holiness in the sense that he is now dedicated to God and his spiritual and physical wounds have been made whole. But the marriage itself must wait while he continues to fight the pagan enemies of God (xii 18): complete holiness and spiritual perfection may be achieved only in the New Jerusalem, the corresponding image at time's end of human time's beginning in Eden.

The myth of Eden dominates Book I, for Redcrosse's mission is to release Una's parents from imprisonment by 'that old Dragon' (xi argument; cf Rev 20.2). Her parents are the King and Queen of Eden, Adam and Eve (i 5, vii 43ff). To liberate them is to restore Eden; hence the rejoicing in canto xii and the old king's recognition of Redcrosse's achievement and suffering (xii 13–17). The restored Eden is an emblem of the garden of the virtuous individual soul watered by grace, which is attainable only by arduous battle against sin. Redcrosse, now worthy of his red cross, supersedes the old Adam because he has embraced the second Adam: 'For as in Adam all dye, even so in Christ shal all be made alive' (1 Cor 15.22). But the restored Eden of the individual soul is a tropological image (see *allegory, *Bible). Although it is rightly read anagogically by many critics as the New Jerusalem (glimpsed more directly in canto x), the anagogical level is not the most important in this canto, as Redcrosse himself recognizes when he replies to the king's invitation to 'ease and everlasting rest' (xii 17, a tempting echo of Despair's offer of 'Ease after warre' at ix 40) with the reminder that he is still of the world, still attempting to fulfill the demands made on him as a soldier of Christ. He is committed by 'faith' to go and fight for the Fairy Queen (xii 18): 'Faithfull ... he ... fighteth righteously' (Rev 19.11). At the end of Book I, he returns to Fairyland; and in the beginning of Book II and even in the Castle Joyous episode at the beginning of Book III, he is still doing and suffering; the 'ease [of] everlasting rest,' of death and the eternal sabbath, is not yet his. Even Dame Caelia herself spends 'all the day in *doing* good and godly deedes' (x 3).

Redcrosse's essential problem, then, is that he, like the church militant, is time-bound. Time, in the sense of mortality, began with the Fall; the passing of time is measured precisely in Book I, but nowhere more so than by Lucifera's ominous dial that, in the canto of the sins, 'told the timely howres' (iv 4). Holiness, however, as the fulfillment of one's spiritual self, exists beyond time since it has as its model the imitation of Christ who sojourned on earth but then returned to eternity. The knight of Holiness is caught between time and eternity: he is committed to knighthood, the pursuit of the active life, because he has been chosen by God to fight against evil; and yet he yearns for the timeless which he seeks impatiently through death many times, for example, in Orgoglio's dungeon (viii 38) and when Despair tempts him to suicide (ix 49–51). Redcrosse must learn not only patience but also that there are varieties of holiness. Hence Despair's polar opposite follows in the next canto: the life- and body-denying Contemplation, whose asceticism has led to such an enlargement of Mind (that fragment of the divine which the holy person has within himself) that on the top of his mountain he, like Moses, sees God. But Contemplation is also within Redcrosse, whose experience in the house of Holiness has granted him an epiphany, an atemporal vision of the divine, to confirm the goal of his holy life. Just as Moses had to descend from the mountain, however, so does Redcrosse. Only after his earthly battles have been won may the knight begin his 'painefull pilgrimage' to the New Jerusalem (x 61). Contemplation is part of the Protestant Christian's life, not a way of life in itself. Contemplation is an old man, to signify that the youthful Redcrosse is now old in Christian experience. He is also old like Una's Adam-father, heading towards death like Despair, and, with his age and hermit dwelling, a double of the aged hermit Archimago (i 30ff). The difference between Archimago and Contemplation shows how far Redcrosse has traveled in the book, but the similarity is ominous. Redcrosse wants to stay, and Contemplation has to tell him to go. But he has been tempted to stay and tempted to die to a world which needs not only his faith but his strength as a warrior.

We have so far considered the account of Redcrosse's quest as it leads him to attain holiness as a private virtue. As a statement about public virtue, it draws heavily on the St George legend, in which dragon, princess, king, and queen all appear. From this point of view, Book I concerns the gradual revealing to Redcrosse of his name and identity: alluded to as the 'true *Saint George*' in his absence at ii 11–12, he finally learns his name and nation from Contemplation at x 60–6: he will be called 'Saint *George* of mery England, the signe of victoree.' Identification of Redcrosse with the nation's patron saint is not a simple theological statement that perfected holiness is sanctity but an affirmation that Redcrosse is England itself in its quest for holiness. That is, Book I is in the technical sense of the word allegorical of England's return to Christ under Elizabeth and her Protestant church: 'Saint' George reminds us that England saw herself as the divinely elected leader of Protestant reform in late sixteenth-century Europe. This was probably Book I's main meaning for contemporaries who could remember the emphasis (in the tableaux which greeted her during her coronation entry) on Elizabeth's redemption of England from the tyrannical Catholicism of Philip and Mary (see *Dixon). The first three books of *The Faerie Queene* appeared only two years after the 'providential' defeat of Philip's Armada.

On the level of historical allegory, Redcrosse's history is inextricably bound up with Una's. As the 'One,' she is Elizabeth, *semper eadem* and *semper una*; as a virgin, she is Elizabeth, virgin queen and single head of the reformed, Protestant religion, the pure (*casta*) religion. Protestant contemporaries would not have needed reminding that their church returned to the true religion, to primitive Christianity as derived from Christ and brought to Britain from the Holy Land by Joseph of Arimathea (the intimate relationship between Britain and Jerusalem continues from Book I into Book II in another figure whom Archimago parodies, the Palmer, whose name declares that he has been to the Holy Land). The ancient church, it was believed, had been corrupted by the arrival of popish St Augustine of Canterbury. Spenser's readers would not have needed reminding, either, that the first Christian Roman emperor, Constantine the Great, who had united the eastern and western empires, was British on his mother's side: from Constantine, Elizabeth derived in part her imperial claims in defiance of equivalent papal claims. This explains why the respective empires of Una's and Duessa's parents are opposed at i 5 and ii 22.

Thus, near the beginning of Christian time, Redcrosse and Una were 'one.' But under the influence of Augustine and later medieval Catholicism, England betrayed its ancient religion and deviated into the arms of Una's double, Duessa (or Fidessa as she is known for most of the book), an image of Catholicism as an anti-Christian pagan force – hence her '*Persian* mitre' (ii 13), which places her in symbolic as well as actual alliance with the Saracen anti-trinity of Sansfoy, Sansjoy, and Sansloy. The betrothal of Redcrosse and Una marks England's return to the true church of Christ on earth (Rev 20.9) in anticipation of the church of Christ and his saints in heaven which will be achieved with their marriage after the defeat of the 'Paynim king' (xii 18).

Una is thus a manifestation of Elizabeth as Protestant emperor, temporal and spiritual ruler. Hence the solar imagery attached to her (iii 4, xii 23), symbolic both of monarchical authority (as it is for her other Persian parody Lucifera at iv 7–8) and of divine truth and grace (Christ as the 'Sunne of righteousnes' Mal 4.2). She is further unfolded as Fidelia, the first of the three theological virtues in the house of Holiness, who, like Una, has a sunny face and is dressed in 'lilly white' (x 12–13; cf xii 22). Accordingly, she holds the Bible, the book of faith. She and Una are one iconographically because Una/Elizabeth's church is the church of the true faith. Hence Una's opposite is Duessa, the Catholic church; and the opposite of Una-as-faith (Fidelia, the Anglican communion) is Duessa as Fidessa (false faith, the Roman Mass). Redcrosse's opposite is Archimago, who actually disguises himself as St George for part of the book (ii 11ff) and is the symbolic progenitor of Catholic Duessa.

Another embodiment of Catholic tyranny is Orgoglio, who takes Duessa-Fidessa as his mistress in canto vii and mounts her upon a seven-headed dragon. In canto viii, the dragon is killed by Arthur, who then proceeds to kill Orgoglio and strip Fidessa of her papal finery, thus announcing the defeat of papal authority in England. Like Una, Arthur is an emblem both of monarchy and of divine grace. His defeat of the dragon anticipates Redcrosse's defeat of a different dragon in canto xi as, indeed, it recalls Redcrosse's slaying of the serpent-woman Error in canto i. These three dragon slayings are narrative equivalents to the legendary St George's killing of the dragon interpreted as England's defeat of the papal dragon, and they probably relate specifically to Elizabethan Garter symbolism. Elizabeth, as head of the order, used the annual St George's Day Garter procession to glorify the monarchy and the pure faith it represented. The order's patron saint is George; his killing of the dragon, depicted on the Garter medallion (the 'George'), was interpreted as the vanquishing of the papal dragon. Some portraits of Elizabeth from the mid-1570s onward depict her with her Garter 'George.' Perhaps we should sense as presiding over Book I's statement of England's holiness one of these familiar portraits of the Queen as head of the Knights of the Garter, whose order was founded in imitation of Arthur's band of Round Table knights, and who were sworn to the discipline of obedience to their heavenly and earthly sovereigns. From this point of view, Lucifera is a parodic Garter Elizabeth (historically, some suggest, a Mary, Queen of Scots), enthroned as she is with a 'dreadfull Dragon' beneath her feet (iv 10). (See Strong 1963, paintings 28–30, 39–40.)

From what has been implied about the

book's indebtedness to the Book of Revelation and what has been said about its culmination in a betrothal, it will be gathered that it is possible to detect two main biblical sources for Book I. The first is the Protestant interpretation of Revelation as shown in the 1560 Geneva Bible and other propagandist texts: Duessa-Fidessa is the Whore of Babylon as the papal Antichrist riding her seven-headed beast of Rome and the sins (Rev 17); Una is the 'woman clothed with the sunne' of Revelation 12, the Protestant 'Church which is compassed about with Jesus Christ the Sonne of righteousnes' and is exiled in the wilderness until the defeat of the dragon, interpreted as persecution by 'Antichrist' (Geneva gloss on 12.1; see verse 6 for the wilderness, and cf Una in the wilderness, cantos iii and vi). Revelation ends with preparation for the marriage of Christ (the Lamb) to the Heavenly Jerusalem (and the church); Book I ends with preparation for the marriage of Redcrosse and Una. The second source for Book I is the Old Testament type of these parts of Revelation, the Song of Solomon, in which lover and beloved praise each other's beauties and in which the woman searches for the man (Song of Sol 5). Catholics and Protestants alike allegorized this epithalamium as celebrating 'the faithful soule or ... Church, which [Christ] hathe sanctified and appointed to be his spouse, holy, chast and without reprehension' in her relation to Christ (Geneva prefatory argument to Song of Sol). Una is thus seen allegorically and anagogically as the church in her tribulations and final union with Christ, and Redcrosse as a type of Christ.

Book I, then, opposes false and true, an opposition traceable to Eve's choice to know good and evil in Eden (a point remembered in xi 47, where the trees of Life and Knowledge are described and remind us that the two trees of the metamorphosed Fradubio and Fraelissa of ii 28ff dominate a cursed Edenic landscape). Postlapsarian history is a wandering from the right path into captivity and the worship of false gods or graven images: a forgetting of good, and a willed espousal of evil which is always a pale imitation or fragmentation of the original good or God. The Fall brings spiritual blindness and a high probability of making the wrong choice. The symbols for the fallen state include woods and labyrinths (Error's wood is labyrinthine at i 11), darkness (we meet Night herself, who saw 'the secrets of the world unmade' v 22), and blindness (eg, Corceca, 'blind heart' or ignorant Catholic superstition, canto iii; cf Aveugle, v 23). Spenser thus chooses to depict in Book I the psychological processes which lead, in our fallen world, to the choice of evil rather than good.

The crucial faculty involved here, according to Renaissance theory, was the imagination, located in the front cell or ventricle of the brain and, together with judgment (reason) and memory, an attribute of the sensitive soul (see II ix 49ff). When not balanced by memory and judgment, and especially during sleep, the imagination releases and conceives strange images, false idols within the brain which become, as it were, the internal equivalent of western humanity's historical struggle for and against the true God, particularly as embodied under the Old Dispensation; or, worse, it lies open to the operative power of Satan himself. This is why canto i and the opening of canto ii depict a sleeping and dreaming Redcrosse. A key biblical gloss on this episode states that God sends afflictions to man to 'kepe backe his soule from the pit,' 'in dreames and visions of the night, when slepe falleth upon men' (Job 33.15–18). God speaks through dreams and visions but so might 'the devil also practise his divinations by dreams' in imitation of the divine (Raleigh *History of the World* I.II.3; ed 1829, 2:392). In Book I, the devil's surrogate is Archimago, who commands the dream to abuse Redcrosse's fantasy 'with false shewes' (i 46). Evil is most successful when it masquerades as good. The way to truth is demonstrated in this book of holiness by the juxtaposition of truth with its false imitation, and by complementary images of unveiling or revelation (Una's face in cantos iii and xii, Arthur's shield in canto viii). The means to apprehend truth are rational control of the appetites, the direction of one's mental faculties by an uninfected will, and the possession of divine grace.

The Redcrosse whom we meet at the beginning is a novice. He has, we are to assume, been baptized; he knows his catechism; he has not (because he is young) undergone the full test of faith. The first half of canto i (28 stanzas of a total of 55) offers him an easy victory: he can recognize and defeat doctrinal error (books and papers) when he sees it. Error, however, can take many forms; and Redcrosse remains unaware of the warning implicit in the simile which compares her numerous offspring to molesting gnats (i 23), for winged insects are also traditional emblems of the delusions of the imagination: in the second half of the canto, Spenser compares Archimago's evil demons to 'little flyes' (38). One kind of error, the inhabitant of a cave, is vanquished. But doctrine can in itself offer no guarantee against other forms of error, testaments to fallen human nature, embodied in the figure of Archimago, inhabitant of a 'hidden cell' (30, like a cave and also like the *cellula phantastica* within the brain), 'seeming' and 'shewing' in order to deceive Redcrosse with two nocturnal visions of a harlot Una, from which he escapes full of anger and sexual jealousy. The irascible and concupiscible faculties of his soul have been so activated that, awake, he can no longer see: his 'eye of reason was with rage yblent' (ii 5); and his spurred horse, emblem of the uncontrolled passions directly released by reason's failure to control imagination's images, becomes the direct opposite of Christ's horse of Revelation 19.11. Irascibility will be subdued with the killing of the wrathful Dragon of canto xi; concupiscence will be eradicated when Duessa is abandoned for chaste Una, Caelia, and the three female theological virtues (canto x). In the meantime, the direct result of the dreams is that Redcrosse takes the place of faithless Sansfoy as knight-protector of the harlot of doubleness in the *second* canto.

Book I begins with a wood and Error; it ends with another dragon and the restoration of paradise. Exactly halfway through we are presented with a diptych. Canto vi contains the woodland episode of Una and the satyrs; canto vii begins with a false paradise in the shade of which Redcrosse removes the Christian armor he had so proudly worn in canto i. He is immediately joined by Duessa, who thus again displaces the Una who had accompanied him in the first canto; and he drinks from the enervating fountain which is the spiritual opposite of the 'living well' required to redeem Fradubio and Fraelissa in ii 43, of Fidelia's chalice of wine and water in x 13 (itself the double of Duessa's cup of poison in viii 14), and of the virtuous water and 'streame of Balme' in xi 29 and 48. (We may note in passing that Redcrosse's refuge from the sun's heat at this midpoint of the book recalls his earlier refuge in the shade offered by the 'two goodly trees,' recalling those of paradise, at ii 28–9. On both occasions he is escaping unwittingly from the blazing heat of the midday sun of justice, not realizing that there is healing 'under his wings' [Mal 4.2], and falling into the snares 'of the plague that destroyeth at noone daye' [Ps 91.6].)

In the wood, Una is rescued from Sansloy by the wood gods, whose dance of rejoicing as they lead her to Sylvanus reverses the mock-epithalamic dance in Redcrosse's first dream at i 48 and is an anticipation of the Christian rejoicing at xii 6ff. The lion has responded instinctively to Una by submitting to her in canto iii; the wood gods adore her in canto vi. Natural law and reason, the state of nature rather than of grace (and also of the Old Law rather than the New), prevail at the end of this first half, suggesting on the theological level the necessary interaction of nature and grace, and on the historical level the Renaissance belief in the tradition of early theologians who held that some ancients at least had enjoyed partial revelation. As reflected here, this respect for Una testifies to a spiritual integrity far greater than that of Sansloy (willful lawlessness that attacks truth even though it has the opportunity, because it lives under the New Dispensation, for full revelation) and of Redcrosse himself, who has betrayed Una with comparable lawlessness. Una's tale is thus one of the true church sequestered and then justified by increasing degrees of recognition which at once mark stages within Redcrosse's spiritual consciousness and historical phases as well: the lion, wood gods, Satyrane, and finally Arthur are all surrogates for Redcrosse as individual and as England. (The lion, emblem of Christ, St Mark, and justice, is historically the emblem of Brutus, legendary founder of Britain and ancestor of Elizabeth; Arthur's rescue of Redcrosse in canto viii gives the knight

Arthurian-British power and signifies the restoration of unity, through Tudor Elizabeth, to the realm.)

The above account of the shape and allegory of Book I began with Redcrosse's dreams, since the book, like the poem as a whole, is related to the medieval tradition of dream romances; and so we should notice that Sylvanus-Pan is wakened by his followers when they approach to show him Una (vi 14), and that he then takes her for a goddess. That he has been sleeping reminds us that the Legend of Holiness occurs within Christian time, and that with Christ's birth Pan slept (or died) and the ancient oracles ceased. This figure of antique nature now awakens as a guarantee to the abandoned Una that lawlessness is not the order of nature, and that the forces of good can preserve truth until the fallible earthly instrument of revealed truth, embodied in Redcrosse, has learned faith. Redcrosse awoke to falsehood; Sylvanus, to a truth partially veiled to him. At ix 13–15, Arthur narrates to Una his dream of the Fairy Queen, a manifestation of divine truth. It recalls Diana's appearance to the sleeping Endymion (the queen of fairies was identified with the moon goddess; Una herself is dressed in silvery white at xii 22), a myth interpreted by Renaissance mythographers as suggesting the immortal bliss that lies beyond death, the striving of the mortal to attain the divine. The myth was linked in turn with the beginning of the Song of Solomon, 'Let him kisse me with the kisses of his mouth,' itself interpreted as an expression of the yearning to die into Christ. All this would suggest that although Arthur's dream might well have temporal fulfillment in union with Gloriana, its ultimate fulfillment will be in eternity, as will the fulfillment of Redcrosse's parallel quest for Una, whose kissing of Redcrosse in the house of Holiness (x 29) is not just the kiss of salutation in the early church or the kiss of charity (Rom 16.16, I Pet 5.14) but a promise of eternal union to come.

Spenser leaves clues to the relationship between Una and Arthur's Fairy Queen. Arthur says of the vision which appears to him as he sleeps on the ground, 'So faire a creature yet saw never sunny day'; and on awakening he finds her impression on the grass where she lay all night. At the opening of canto iii, Una, alone, lies 'on the grasse' and reveals her sunlike 'angels face' to 'the shadie place' (4; note also the anticipation of Redcrosse's abandoning himself to Duessa in the 'cooling shade' of vii 3). Although her pose anticipates the pose of the sleeping Arthur, she does not actually sleep here; she is the truth that is revealed by revelation. As we move through Book I, then, we encounter Archimago-induced false dreams (cantos i, ii), the true object of a dream as revelation (iii), Sylvanus' waking to a partial recognition of Una's true value (vi), Arthur's revelation (ix), and finally Contemplation's revelation to Redcrosse of the 'new *Hierusalem*,' the goal of his life's pilgrimage and, as the bride of Revelation 19, the ultimate image to which Una, Gloriana, and all the poem's objects of good are referable (x). Despair's false visions 'painted in a table plaine' (ix 49) are a last attempt of the deceiving imagination to suppress Contemplation's visions of salvation. But with Contemplation, Redcrosse leaves imagination's images behind to participate for a moment in the pure realm of Mind and enjoy the ultimate gift of the Holy Spirit, wisdom.

Redcrosse's dalliance in the shade with Duessa begets Orgoglio, who erupts from his prone (fallen) self as a gigantic – even apocalyptic – emblem of pride carrying an oak tree to mark him as a demonic wild man of the woods (as such, he is the opposite of the wood-knight Satyrane of canto vi and of Contemplation, who is compared to an oak at x 48). Redcrosse is thus possessed by a tree-man and fulfills the prediction symbolically made by the tree-man Fradubio in canto ii. In canto vii, he is imprisoned in Orgoglio's dungeon, the equivalent in the book's second half of Lucifera's dungeon in cantos iv and v. Some critics, detecting the familiar schema of temptations by flesh, world, and devil in Book I, identify Lucifera as worldly pride (though as a false Venus she is also a temptation to the flesh) and Orgoglio, her grotesque counterpart, as a manifestation of spiritual pride, or of the rebellious pride of life, an ultimate inner corruption manifesting itself as the devil. The dungeon of Lucifera's palace contains the founder and kings of Babylon, the worldly opposite of Jerusalem; and Redcrosse's habitation of Orgoglio's dungeon makes him, too, a prisoner of Babylon, as indicated by the presence of the scarlet whore Duessa and the key-keeping ignorant Ignaro, aged antithesis of Contemplation and complement to Archimago.

Rescued by Arthur from Orgoglio's dungeon in an episode which inverts Duessa's intervention with Night to obtain Sansjoy's regeneration in canto v, Redcrosse nevertheless yields to joylessness (the 'worldlie sorowe' which is the opposite of the 'godlie sorowe [which] causeth repentance unto salvacion' in 2 Cor 7.10). Recognition of his sin in generating Orgoglio leads to self-disgust and a loss of faith culminating in Despair (canto ix), by a spiritual process epigrammatically described at vii 41: 'griefe ... breedes despaire.' Despair inhabits a cave that symbolically amalgamates the cave of Error, Archimago's cell, and the dungeons of Lucifera and of Orgoglio, and that marks the nadir of which Contemplation's mountain is the zenith. Despair, a denial of one's worthiness for salvation, is also a failure to recognize that God can save one, and thus is pride masking as false humility (true Humility is porter to the house of Holiness). As Spenser describes him, Despair is melancholic, an embodiment of the extreme life-denying temperament, an absorption of joylessness into the very depths of Redcrosse's being, and a symbolic focus for all the references to sadness throughout the book (eg, i 2, 4; vi 17; xii 5). Redcrosse is rescued from Despair by Una's reminder of God's election of his 'chosen' by justice and grace (ix 53), a timely reminder that Despair's (and Sansjoy's) Old Law ethic that 'bloud must bloud repay' (ix 43) is true not as an argument for suicide but as a typological admission of salvation through Christ's 'pretious bloud' (x 57).

But salvation has to be earned by mortification of the very flesh that, inherited from earthly Adam and embodied in the name Georgos (the second syllable recalls Orgoglio), induced Redcrosse to sin in the first place. This mortification in turn involves a recapitulation of earlier situations: Caelia's house in this tenth canto (the number of completion and the Commandments [Brooks-Davies 1977:92] and the fourth canto of the second half of the book) undoes Lucifera's palace of false holiness (a house built on sand) in canto iv. Here the knight suffers like the inhabitants of Lucifera's dungeon, repents, and is attended by the seven Bead-men (the corporal works of mercy), thereby undoing the effects of the seven sins embodied in Lucifera's court and in Fidessa's seven-headed beast. He then merits the ultimate vision granted to the faithful at the top of Contemplation's mountain, which is high enough to cancel out Lucifera's 'loftie towres' (iv 4), the presumptuously towering, Babel-like Orgoglio (viii 23), Duessa's dragon whose tail reaches to heaven (vii 18), and the mountainous Dragon (xi), and to remind the Christian reader that God 'wil exalt the humble, and wil abase him that is hie' (Ezek 21.26).

As Redcrosse descends from the mountain, his flesh and spirit (disjunct at its peak as he views the New Jerusalem) unite in a wholeness that he has never known before. His body is now the true vessel of his spirit, whole and holy, so that he can achieve his quest of liberating Adam and Eve into the paradise of his regenerate soul and of England. Even for the knight of Holiness, this battle is not easy. The Christian man, with Christ in him, takes three days to kill the dragon of the sin that remains in the holiest of mortals, to remind us that his anagogical equivalent, Christ himself, took three days to harrow hell. The Dragon dies because Redcrosse is aided by the salvific well and tree; structurally, this fifth canto of the book's second half transcends the pagan Aesculapius' healing of Sansjoy in canto v. Anagogically, the Dragon is dead forever; from the tropological viewpoint, it will revive within Redcrosse's soul, because the battle against evil is perpetual until the end of time. From the viewpoint of simple structural aesthetics, however, its death certifies the defeat of the serpent Error, the dragon under Lucifera's feet, and the beast on which Fidessa rides – deaths which have already been homeopathically assured by the serpent in Fidelia's cup and by the golden dragon on Arthur's helmet, both reminders of Christ as serpent (John 3.14–15) and of the dragon of Britain, emblem of Arthur's father, Uther Pendragon.

In the house of Holiness, the last of the theological virtues to be encountered is Charissa, suckling her babies. She is the culminating and joyful expression of the trinity of virtues that undo the triad of the Sans brothers; in herself, she symbolically obliterates the memory of Error with her brood and Orgoglio's killing of babies (viii 35), and she anticipates the time beyond the end of the book when Una and Redcrosse will beget a holy progeny for their new land – a progeny like 'the fry of children young' who greet the still virginal Una at xii 7. The young knight (Letter to Raleigh) ages into holiness with experience, but leaves his book with the promise that can be given only to youth: 'Suffer the litle children ... to come to me: for of suche is the kingdome of heaven' (Matt 19.14). It is they who will be embraced by the 'Jerusalem, which is above [and] is the mother of us all' (Gal 4.26).

DOUGLAS BROOKS-DAVIES

Alpers 1967b; Brooks-Davies 1977; Brooks-Davies 1983; Cain 1978; Cheney 1966; Crampton 1974; *Critical Essays on Spenser from 'ELH'* 1970 (Baltimore); Cullen 1974; DeNeef 1982; Evans 1970; Fichter 1982; Fowler 1964; Freeman 1970; Giamatti 1975; Goldberg 1981; Gross 1985; Guillory 1983; Hamilton 1961a; Hamilton 1972a; Hankins 1971; Hieatt 1975a; Horton 1978; Hough 1962; Kermode 1971; Kouwenhoven 1983; Leslie 1983; Lewis 1967; I.G. MacCaffrey 1976; Nelson 1961; Nohrnberg 1976; P.A. Parker 1979; Quilligan 1979; Quilligan 1983; Rose 1975; Waters 1970; Wells 1983; Whitaker 1950; K. Williams 1966; Yates 1975.

***The Faerie Queene*, Book II** Like most books in *The Faerie Queene*, Book II is thematically self-contained. New literary directions give it its own poetic identity and expand the philosophically ambitious image of the nature of man it fashions. When Spenser compares the discovery of faerie to the way explorers are daily discovering new regions (proem 2), he is both reassuring the literal-minded about the reality of his world behind theirs of everyday appearance and summing up his ongoing project of poetic world-making. The New World allusions accurately signpost the direction of the book: nature, or more specifically human passions, and their need to be controlled. The Legend of Holiness had been a drama of grace and sins played out against the symbolic landscapes of the spirit: saint's life, Revelation, and the older moral poetry had been assimilated to newer elements of Italian epic, myth writing, and Protestant polemic – all on a base of chivalric romance. But with analysis of moral life and human nature as his business, Spenser no longer needs to draw extensively on the Bible and the church for imagery, and after Book I religion no longer dominates poetically. The new impetus in Book II is humanism, and its teachers are the philosophers and the poets. Hence the perceptible shift of intellectual and literary bases to classical ethics, history, natural philosophy (ie, science), Virgil, Tasso, and erotic poetry. As Spenser mirrors the Renaissance's synthesis of cultures with his own innovative poetic technique, even the vocabulary of chivalric incident loses its earlier medieval appearance to take on the look of the century of Dürer and Titian.

The altered perspective takes some time to establish, however, and in the opening canto the magical world of romance seems little altered from Book I as Archimago begins another deception. The young knight Guyon hears a whining tale of the Red Cross Knight's sexual assault on the virgin Duessa. His haste to avenge her is rash since he knows only good about Redcrosse, but his ears and eyes are fooled. In his anger, he charges to the fray, leaving behind his traveling companion and mentor, the Palmer. The incident proves that he needs drill in temperance, the virtue being fashioned in Book II.

Guyon's quest The progress of the knight of Temperance is shown in a brilliantly imaged sequence of scenes. After Guyon is saved from his rage by seeing the cross on Redcrosse's shield, he witnesses a tragedy that shows human passion at its most deadly along with fallen human nature's ineradicable concupiscence (Mortdant, Amavia, and Ruddymane). His next adventure introduces a rational solution to self-destructive excess (Medina and her sisters). Back in the thick of random events, he applies his newly experienced lesson of moderation with mixed results, saving one victim whose rage is fueled by sexual jealousy (Phedon) but only exacerbating that of another who is too far gone (Pyrochles). Moderation also proves effective for him against enticements to waste leisure in play and idleness (Phaedria), but when sexual fantasy and aggression flare up as well (Cymochles), their challenge is evaded or at least postponed. Reason and moderation seem to work against the temptations of riches, status, and glory (Mammon, Philotime), for Guyon resists with triumphant superiority. Yet this adventure turns out inconclusively in the sense that his opponent is not defeated, thus precipitating the crisis of his faint which opens the door to an outrageous assault. This setback reveals the hero's innate flaw to be fallen human nature that makes him powerless against the passions (Pyrochles and Cymochles) without special divine assistance (Arthur). Then Guyon is reeducated in the house of Alma concerning his make-up, the healthiness of temperance, and the need of grace both for the individual and for nations in the endless vicissitudes of their history (the British chronicles). He learns that the soul and reason are of divine provenance (the Elfin chronicles). Arthur opposes all the evils and pains inimical to life (Maleger) and raises temperance to an heroic level through fortitude and Christian patience. Guyon in his turn proceeds on his final journey to establish rational control over desire, now aware that he needs the Palmer's supernatural powers (xii 40–1) to resist the might of the passions successfully. He frees nature and the senses from the false glamour cast over them by imagination possessed by concupiscence (Acrasia). Excesses are rejected and fantasies shattered when temperance and reason confront Acrasia's illusory fabrications (the Bower of Bliss) so that finally man is restored to rational dignity.

This brief outline shows that the unity of Book II derives more from theme and image than from a plot based on the hero's behavior or psychology. One cannot call the narrative plotless, in view both of the quest and of the complications developing through cantos iv-viii as Guyon is embroiled in the affairs of Pyrochles and Cymochles and, from trying to help one control his rage, ironically finds himself becoming the main object of the other's fury. Yet since he lies in a coma throughout their attack, he is not involved dramatically in their states of passion. To see their applicability to him, we must read allegorically, for the allegorical structure, not dramatic plot, is the major shaping force of the book. This is specially clear in the episode where Guyon faints (vii). The narrative gives the simplest cause-and-effect explanation – Guyon faints from lack of food and sleep – but on the level of thematic significance, a striking peripeteia follows when his strength against Mammon is ironically revealed as utter powerlessness. This irony is the pivot of the structure.

Guyon's temperance provides the continuity of Book II. Although he is often dramatically upstaged by high-powered passions set in their own landscape, the book is readable as the portrait of a young man learning to master the disorder of his nature. His inclination to temperance is constitutional (i 6), but to possess the virtue he needs to build it up until it becomes a habit or disposition. Experiences accrue, and he changes from an untried beginner-in-life to someone alert in self-discipline. With the Bower of Bliss, the threshold of maturity is reached, though any development follows only rough-and-ready psychological phases – scorn of mindless entertainment and instant riches comes before the control of erotic daydream – and goes more by topics. The decisive structure is synchronic, made up of opposites of pain and pleasure and irascible and concupiscible passions. In these, one reacts to Guyon both as a character and as an allegorical figure. As he wrestles with Furor, he does not seem to be subduing anger in himself but embodying the temperance that Phedon needs – the classic psychomachia. Again, Guyon's leaving the Palmer behind can usually be interpreted allegorically to mean that his hold on rationality is still intermittent (as with Duessa and Phaedria). But this meaning is not fixed: the absence of the Palmer during the temptation by Mammon does not signify the absence of reason so much as lack of something else connected with the Palmer's Christian identity.

The Palmer's role raises the question of how to view the relation between classical temperance, which is self-sufficient, and Christian temperance, which depends on grace. Does Guyon generally act as natural man, or are nature and grace sequential, the one exhibited by a classical temperance in Guyon's deeds before the faint (Berger 1957), the other revealing a superior Christian heroic virtue afterwards (Kermode 1960)? Certainly in the first canto we cannot mistake the way Guyon's virtue is activated by a Christian symbol. His charge is halted by the sight of the red cross, not by reason.

The Christian symbol generates the symbol of temperance, the reins and bridle that signify a horse brought under control. The other symbols of temperance appear in due course: the 'golden squire,' the pouring of water into wine, the midplace between extremes, and the connection with education and the arts. Christian meanings in turn inform such crucial symbols as the nymph's fountain and the bloody babe, Arthur's wound, and Maleger's death by water. Four sets of emblems mainly compose Spenser's Christian temperance. First, water, which expresses both the absence, dilution, or purification of passion, and the libido and generative power per se: the main symbolic link is with the appetitive or concupiscent part of the soul. Second, net, curbs and chains, and an equivalent human figure, the wrestler, which express discipline and control. These and the next symbols link particularly with the spirited part of the soul located in the breast. Third, blood, the heart, and their red color, which symbolize both passion and pain, but also link temperance to Christ's atonement in the Passion. Redeemed human nature is kept in sight from the time of Guyon's initiation by the cross to the moment he is saved from death by Arthur, who takes a Christ-like wound 'Red as the Rose' in his right side (viii 39; Hamilton 1961a:99). Finally, the symbols of the authority of the rational part, along with its products: the Palmer's staff, the book, the house, and the city.

Christian truth acts in concert with classical philosophy to make Book II a distinctly Christian humanist creation. Room for mysteries and paradoxes beyond reason's reach is always made, but reason sets the prevailing tone: 'How brutish is it not to understand,' Arthur says about reading his country's history (x 69), and his remark sums up a guiding principle in the selection of materials, literary models, and strategies (imitation of other poets, for instance, and irony) which follow typical humanist preferences. Humanism had no precise program or terminology to identify it but was nevertheless fairly clearly distinguished by its many rallying points: classical culture (especially in the arts and *litterae humaniores*), the slogan 'Know thyself,' the rule of reason, *eloquentia*, and confidence in knowledge. Thus understanding, which was of minor concern in Book I where the aged idiot Ignaro represents lack of it within the church (viii), assumes a key position in Book II and provides its summation when Guyon reflects on Acrasia's victims and their bestial form (xii 87).

With this humanist accent, it is hardly surprising that Book II is the most didactic, though its instruction is by fiction and imagery in the mode of delightful teaching required of poetry by Horace and Sidney. Special to the book is the quantity of dramatized discourse and debate. In Book I, the spoken word rarely goes beyond ordinary romance usages – Despair's eloquent rhetoric is the exception, a great set piece kept separate from the complementary Boschian symbolic landscape. In the Mammon episode (II vii), the treatment is much freer, allowing description to blend with dialogue. Throughout Book II, Guyon, the Palmer, Belphoebe, Phaedria (in song), Mammon, and Arthur comment and analyze with easy facility and, within the limits set by the music of the Spenserian line, with convincing naturalness. These articulate arguments contribute perceptibly to the book's humanist tone.

cantos i-ii Guyon's quest properly starts when he comes upon a lover's tragedy caused by Acrasia: Amavia has stabbed herself in grief at the magical poisoning of her erring husband, Mortdant. Spenser's immediate concern is to assemble a 'Pittifull spectacle' for the mimesis of grief. Amavia's 'deadly shrieke' establishes the sphere of the tragic muse as she sees 'men depriv'd of sense and minde' (*Teares of the Muses* 151–72). But the family's experiences are also an epitome of human nature, for they represent both 'forward' and 'froward' passions (Nelson 1963:182–203). The former (eg, love) are congenial with the vital flow from the heart, the latter (eg, fear) work against it, both being harmful in excess. Mortdant's adultery is forward, Amavia's grief froward, and between them the dead pair makes a typical 'image of mortalitie.' The tragic waste would have been avoided had temperance moderated the excesses. This states a major theme developed in the Medina episode, which is modeled on Aristotle's definition of virtue (*Nicomachean Ethics*). The tragic phase, however, is taken up again in canto iv with the vengeful Phedon's love tragedy. Spenser depicts the intractability of the destructive passions with great feeling, and at intervals through the book his heroes treat the tragedy makers with unendearing sternness. Nevertheless, the mood is not entirely stark: Amavia's babe is smiling, which is both a fearful irony and a portent of renewal (Evans 1970:119). Guyon's experience includes an education in pity, which is proper 'at the right times, with reference to the right objects, towards the right people, with the right aim, and in the right way' (*Ethics* 2.6.1106b), or, as Aristotle in the *Poetics* calls it, *catharsis*. Aristotle's 'mean' is frequently the tacit criterion of temperance after canto iii.

Mortdant's death is caused by an oracular charm which cryptically pinpoints immoderateness, an enigma that the rational Palmer cannot quite explain and that requires more myth-making. In Ruddymane's blood-stained hands (the Elizabethans frequently used 'blood' for 'passion') which the mystically pure water of the nymph's fountain will not cleanse, Spenser finds an arresting symbol for his Christian mystery. (But as he is content to leave it enigmatic, explanations may remain tentative.) After pure water touches the tainted cup Mortdant dies, just as the Old Man of Sin dies in baptism (Rom 6.6). The babe's stained hands and the combination of innocence (ii 10) and blemish stem from the doctrine of original sin. Baptism effaces only sin, not concupiscence, which is not a sin but a stigma, a byproduct of original sin that operates by disordering the lower parts of the soul. That concupiscence is the mode in which original sin is transmitted accounts for the near-equivalence of Duessa (sin) and Acrasia (concupiscence). Concupiscence passes to man with life (not with the soul) through male seed; hence Mortdant is named as the one who 'death does give.' Grace annihilates sin but is incompatible with the carrier, concupiscence. The unwashable blood shows Amavia and the babe sharing a disorder implanted in all mankind. The Acrasia force is thus inescapable, and it remains to be seen how it may be controlled by temperance.

The fountain resembles a weeping woman who symbolizes the human lot of suffering, particularly woman's share. Amavia's childbearing and loss of her husband are typical. Just as significant are the scientific data: the nymph became a rocky fountain of cold water first because she was afraid (science classified fear as cold), then because virtue is immovable like stone and also cold. Hot lustful pursuit and cold virtue resemble elemental opposites like fire and water and forward and froward impulses. In fact, if any features speak generally for the method and concerns of Book II, it is emblems like the nymph's fountain and Amavia's bleeding heart. Heart and blood (for Aristotle the heart was literally the fountain of the blood, *Parts of Animals* 3.4.666a) and all images of the body are meaningful for their literal import. Phedon is a descendant of *Cor*adin. The crowd in the house of Alma's 'goodly Parlour,' the heart, with its royal (red) arras, are the emotions: of the two fully described, Shamefastnesse and Praysdesire, each possesses its identifying physical symptom, blushing and hot and cold flushes. Spenser draws tirelessly on nature, the elements and their qualities, the body and its humors, the soul and its faculties, as he coordinates the physical world with moral significance. The eye in particular seems to have a life of its own, though this is true of all the senses. Thus Phaedria's element is air: she sings and laughs a lot and uses her lungs lustily 'that nigh her breth was gone,' though at other times, beautifully observed, she laughs at the 'shaking of the leaves light.' Airiness is a metaphor of her frivolity and giddiness, but she is also associated with water in its placid moods.

Spenser is also something of a humanist social critic in Book II, where the ideological implications extend considerably beyond private virtue. Socially, temperance was a timely topic: the ideal of gentlemanly restraint was in the making at the time, but Stone (1965:225) reminds us of another norm when he documents one knight who bit an opponent's nose off in a brawl. Hudibras and Sansloy (ii 16–26) give the impression that brawling is a private sport. Later Guyon, who was used to 'faire defence and goodly menaging,' is surprised to be put on his back by an opponent who 'smot, and bit, and kickt, and scratcht, and rent' (iv 6). Knights are specially prone to wrath, the Palmer and Phaedria observe: Spenser meant it literally. He gives horsemanship (a traditional symbol of control) a strong class accent, mentioning it as one of a triad of innate gifts of the 'noble seed': 'feates of armes,' 'love to entertaine,' and 'chiefly skill to ride.' Thus Braggadocchio's baseness is obvious even to Guyon's horse Brigadore because he cannot ride him properly. Here the 'skill to ride' is metaphorical and means that virtue is the proper basis of knighthood and true nobility. This is not to say, however, that virtue joined to social position is not the combination Spenser preferred.

For the late-feudal nobility, temperance had only minor status as a virtue, and when Spenser put temperance before freedom of action (cf Rabelais' Thélème), he challenged traditional aristocratic values. The application is broader, of course: the impulsiveness of the noble class was typical of the violent ways of the era (Huizinga ed 1924). These reach their peak when Pyrochles and Cymochles invoke the honor code of family revenge (viii 28) to justify mutilating Guyon. Arthur's intervention shows, among other things, a prince exercising control of private violence, an important ideal of Tudor policy even if usually rather feebly executed. In promoting measure as the virtue befitting civil life, Spenser is adopting a humanist emphasis found in Vives, Castiglione, Skelton, and Lyly (Hughes 1944). The image of Gloriana's face on Guyon's shield should be read as both a private and a public symbol, for it draws attention to the peace and political moderation and stability Elizabeth represented as well as to virginity (ii 42) and personal modesty (ix 43). A peacemaking role is symbolized in Medina's Sabine-like separation of combatants, and the theme of the intemperance of war reappears when Spenser quotes Virgil's emblem for the abolition of war in Guyon's chaining up of Furor (iv 14, *Aeneid* 1.294–6). All this suggests that Spenser was setting up temperance as a national ideal.

Some of these moral, social, and political implications are packed into the Medina episode, a face-value didactic exposé. Medina and her sisters (Elissa and Perissa) and the sisters' lovers (Huddibras and Sansloy) objectify concepts from Aristotle and Plato. One is that virtue consists in keeping a middle position between hostile extremes (*Ethics* 2.9.1109a-b). As well as operating throughout the moral allegory of Book II, this concept also affects the book's structure: the themes of the cantos are arranged symmetrically on either side of the midpoint of the book (Hieatt 1975a:209). The other basic concept is Plato's division of the soul into three powers: reason, a spirited part (*thumos*), and desires or appetites (*Republic* 4.439–41). Here Medina's composure embodies the rational power, and with it she restrains one moody and one flighty sister, the former curbing impulses too much, a distortion of the spirited part, the latter giving way unrestrainedly to the appetitive or impulsive part. The textbook distinctions translate effectively into characterization by humors and into comedy of manners. The lovers Huddibras and Sansloy display excesses, the one of the spirited part through a froward angry nature, the other forward lawlessness of appetite. Huddibras is given to rash projects and is a melancholiac with his irascibility turned inwards. His opposite, the insolent Sansloy, enjoys his inordinateness to the hilt; positive love of excess marks him as concupiscent. Medina, who mediates their hostilities, is not out to eradicate passions – an impossibility – but to moderate them. Her compassion for the damage their egos inflict on themselves sets the tone of an important side of temperance and the benefit it brings to war-torn man. Spenser's narratives go on to follow the harmful side of the spirited element as it escalates in wrath, but Arthur and even Guyon will also be shown drawing on their thumos as guardians of rational order.

canto iii The analysis of the irascible emotions is interrupted by the meeting between Braggadocchio and Belphoebe – both go their separate ways in later books. Braggadocchio is a braggart with no real spirit: his 'baser brest' harbors a 'pleasing vaine of glory vaine' which stirs up appetite. This exposure of a posturing coward and his lechery makes a fine piece of moral comedy. He has big ideas of making a show at court, figuring that is what courts are all about (5). He finds a wayside idler to impress: 'kisse my stirrup,' he commands, and the simple flavor of the *miles gloriosus* acquires tartness as the crafty Trompart obliges with groveling servility – new gentry sometimes have a poor idea of how to behave to inferiors who know how to profit from it. Something close to a burlesque of chivalry and feudal relations follows, but Belphoebe's appearance makes it clear that disparagement of honor and the institution of nobility is not intended. The low parodic characters are there as an anti-masque to offset the lady-huntress who shows us the real thing. Every beautiful feature of her appearance is imbued with moral energy. The boaster reveals his fear by creeping under a bush as she approaches; further fear makes him come out. While she disparages 'pleasure' and 'ease' and prescribes 'perill' and 'paine' as the way to honor, his baser spirit lusts only after her 'wondrous beautie' and he attempts to embrace her. The drama of desire thus begins on a resoundingly comic note which continues with Phaedria and can still be heard in Grill (xii 86–7).

cantos iv-vi Although anger is probably not what readers remember most about the book, it is its most intensively treated subject. Guyon is at close quarters with it from the first flare-up over Duessa to the finale when his virtuous wrath executes sentence on Acrasia's Bower. Irascible passions dominate the earlier cantos (while the later ones are given over to concupiscence: this is the basic thematic structural division of the book). In the joint attack on Guyon by Pyrochles and Cymochles, anger is being shown receptive to motives like prestige and greed, added from concupiscence while it is being demonstrated underground with Mammon, and these turn it into sadistic savagery when it resurfaces (viii).

An epic subject if not *the* epic subject (*Iliad* 1.1), anger's many embodiments also exercise the poet's versatility in literary modes. Phedon is a true likeness of maniacal vengefulness 'imitated' from Ariosto's well-made tale of Ariodante and Ginevra, but Ariosto is reconstructed with the duped victim's tormented mind as the new center of interest. To accentuate the psychological core of basic emotions – wrath, jealousy, grief, and love – Spenser throws away Ariosto's realism of setting and motivation, along with his elaborate plotting, and substitutes a false-friend motif to add to the surrealistic irrationality. Exploiting personification's capacity to capture the autonomy of passions and appetites, two eye-catching figures express first anger's physical grip, full of hair-pulling and facial disfigurement (Furor) and next its hair-trigger sensitivity to reactivation (Occasion). Guyon saves Phedon by locking Occasion's tongue and chaining Furor. Then Pyrochles comes on unmotivated and looking for trouble, hardened in his vice and bent on finding excuses and opportunities for it. (His progress into madness is reminiscent of *Republic* 9.572–3). Guyon brings him temporary relief by forcibly restraining Furor, but this simply encourages Pyrochles to play out the grim comedy of double-talking himself back into his habit and releasing Furor once more (v 16–24). Spenser works him up to impotent fury with a combination of drama and elemental symbolism. 'O how I burne with implacable fire,' he cries as he wades flaming through the sluggish waters of a shallow lake. With water's failure to put out fire, we are back with its failure to wash blood from Ruddymane's hands. The disordering of nature through elemental malfunction gives warning of total reversion to chaos.

Where Pyrochles' anger is painful to him, his brother Cymochles is not only possessed by rage but also given over to lust, so that we see anger becoming enjoyable. When we first encounter him (v 26–38), he is dreamily indulging libertine fancies among the fleshly delights of the Bower, a spot saturated with sugary, voluptuous promise and lecherous stealth. He too seems to embody Plato's insights into the tyrannical character, drawn towards complete license (*Republic* 9.572). He is Acrasia's 'Leman' and is in his element in both kinds of intemperance, turning to 'daintie delices, and lavish joyes' whenever 'his fiers hands he free mote find.' When he is called to avenge his brother, he rises flamelike out of 'waves of deepe delight.' He takes his name from the restless energy of water (Gr *kuma* a wave), the element symbolizing generative force, and in his final phase assumes the cruelty associated with the sea. The brothers' attack while Guyon lies in a coma (canto viii) may be connected with Plato's choice of a dream setting for desires of the very worst type, which may break free and take over in real life (*Republic* 9.572). As a Christian, Spenser finds a similar state of corruption among the passions, and the only answer to Pyrochles and Cymochles is redemption and grace, symbolized in Arthur.

Cymochles' way from lust to atrocity lay through idleness, and this is Phaedria's domain. Her mirth and 'carelesse ease' can be traced back to the courtly Garden of the Rose (via hints from Tasso *Gerusalemme liberata* 14–16), but there are differences, especially in the bellicose rivalry Phaedria excites. She is obsessed with being amusing and her ideas of recreation are soporific and brainless. Sometimes her laughter seems equivalent to what Sidney called 'scornful tickling' (*Defence*). Spenser's correction appears with Alma, who offers good reading (history and poetry). However, one should not overlook the poetic delight that buoys up the satiric comedy at her expense, for the editor of *Englands Parnassus* (1600) was surely right to anthologize the silly but artful vi 13. It is a pity, nevertheless, that Spenser (or is it only Guyon?) has the same low opinion of 'merry tales' and popular buffoonery as Puttenham (6, *Arte* 2.9). Notwithstanding, Phaedria's lyrics praising genteel courtship, 'present pleasures,' and the philosophy of leaving everything to nature vindicate a more sophisticated kind of comedy; her song is enriched by subtle irony and turns out to be a pirated version of the parable of the lilies of the field (Matt 6.28). The whole experience marks the point where 'foes of life' (froward states like grief and wrath) give way to joy-bringing pleasures, which can be just as dangerous to the temperate life (vi 1).

canto vii Phaedria's shallow manner leads logically to full immersion in worldliness as Guyon meets Mammon, who offers him riches, position, and immortality of a sort. Guyon is appalled by Mammon's world, but Spenser also registers that the extremes of materialistic desire are beyond the hero's youthful grasp. Its baleful aura barely penetrates Guyon's chivalric keenness, or only like a troubling dream. The extravagant offer of all he can desire is mythic and does not reflect Guyon's personal subconscious. He disposes of the world by intellectual rebuttal based on earlier lessons. But he is all the time passing through a series of cryptlike spaces evoking cave, dungeon, mine, foundry, and tomb (with hints of grander interiors reminiscent of the guildhalls, the court, and perhaps recently discovered ruins like Nero's *domus aurea*). The whole situation is riddled with irony. The pursuit of wealth is driven by the appetitive part of the soul, and its goals include bodily comfort and pleasure. Yet Mammon excites sordid desires regardless of the ugly cheerlessness and utter absence of 'joyous pleasure' – the Bower of Bliss is a sensationally agreeable opposite and the house of Alma is the healthy middle. Here there is everything to appall the senses: dirt, poisonous plants, ghastly apparitions, sweating fiends. Passing by a silent group that includes 'rancorous Despight' and 'hart-burning Hate,' Guyon 'with wonder all the way / Did feed his eyes, and fild his inner thought.' As the poet's moral vision dictates the scene, the gap between his and Mammon's viewpoints produces the profoundest irony, for Mammon's enticements are Spenser's chamber of horrors, with Guyon somewhere in the middle. The total impression is of human appetites drawn down half-reluctantly to incarcerate themselves in material craving, oblivious to the fact of descent. At the same time, while Mammon is indubitably one of the 'foes of life,' his offerings are not without their desirable side. Under its surface grime, his treasure glistens with a secret drawing power (vii 4). The trick of half-concealment works for gold in much the way it works for nudity in the Bower (Lomazzo ed 1598, 2:51): Guyon is greedy to see more. He is tempted to make trial of the earthy element and venture on a battle of wits with Mammon. His reason and will are equal to the test, but the secret workings of the place (literally the lack of food and rest) subtly undermine his strength and on escaping he faints, and we are left with a sense of some riddle connected with his reactions yet to be solved.

Spenser sees to it that Guyon's noble assumptions do not go unchallenged (18), and in his meeting with Philotime we have a bleak vision of humanity obsessed by ruthless place-seeking. 'Honour and dignity' drive the crowd to clamber the chain of Ambition, implying a Spenser skeptical about courtiers pursuing nothing but honor. Possibly he found support in Plato in whose timarchic or honor-loving society ambition coexisted with 'a fierce and secret passion for gold and silver' (*Republic* 8.548–9). Spenser does not voice this point directly, but he leaves us in no doubt that Philotime's honor is nullified by her clients' dog-eat-dog competitiveness (vii 47). Guyon rejects her as a bride and follows Mammon outside to two further temptations, a silver seat in the shade and apples of gold. In the Garden of Proserpina where these are, nature's gifts have nether-world duplicates, as though from the dark portion of the moon whose light side is Belphoebe. The silver seat makes an insidious appeal to rest and security as the driving forces behind worldly effort. (Yet Spenser leaves this archetypal prohibition thematically open, like many other details.) Proserpina's monumental tree would seem to hold out prizes: fortune, eminence, happiness, and immortality. The supporting mythologies tell of desires fulfilled but to be followed by misfortune, as though catastrophe must go with earthly success. Some see a resemblance to the Tree of the Knowledge of Good and Evil, specifically the temptation of curiosity in the sense of desire for forbidden knowledge, an aspect of greedy desire to which Renaissance man was especially prone. Yet the Tree of Life, which also stood in the middle of the Garden of Eden (I xi 46, Gen 3), seems a truer opposite for this chthonic parody. Proserpina's tree offers false promise of *fruitio*: perfect fulfillment of human desire through earthly satisfactions, somewhat in the sense of Marlowe's 'sweet fruition of an earthly crowne' (*1 Tamburlaine* 2.7.29). The tree gives special prominence to the appetite for secular fame and immortality, like that envisaged, for instance, in Petrarch's 'Triumph of Fame,' specially pertinent to Arthur and, perhaps, the poets.

Guyon refuses the golden fruit, and his stay in Mammon's underworld confirms his dependence on the nourishment divine bounty (*bonté* goodness) alone supplies through nature: food and rest. Emerging after three days without these, he faints. He also needs sustenance on the spiritual level, and like all 'creatures bace' (viii 1), he does not deserve the grace he receives. The fault lies mostly in his species, but some blame attaches to his attitude or so it seems. His virtuous rejection of Mammon had been on the wrong footing – the personal appeal and ethical merit of temperance, not love of God. Indeed, three figures might have reminded him of what man owes to God: Tantalus, who offended and blasphemed the gods; Pilate, who had 'delivered up the Lord of Life to die'; and Socrates, who had made death the occasion of his 'last Philosophy' (52) concerning man's duty to the gods (*Euthyphro*) and on the soul's immortality (*Phaedo*). It may not be precisely 'pagan self-sufficiency' Guyon is guilty of (Berger 1957), but he does seem to have forgotten to count himself one with 'wicked man': he has not called out to God from the depths. The flaw is not in the same class as Redcrosse's reliance on his own efforts to maintain spiritual wholeness. Guyon is not corrupted and does not have to suffer, though his utter helplessness and humiliation are dramatized. The grace that preserves him is an effect of a divine love that transcends his rational understanding. The key literary effect is irony. Virtue's solo efforts are neutralized by natural gracelessness. The turning point is not unlike the ironic outcry from Duessa that carried Redcrosse to Pyrrhic victory (I v 11–12).

In fainting, Guyon is overcome by the 'too exceeding might' of 'vitall aire' when he is brought to 'living light,' and he may be likened to Plato's cave dweller who is overwhelmed by the sunlight missing from his former existence (this allegory was not as familiar as it is now, but it is occasionally alluded to in the Renaissance). The Eros-like angel who protects Guyon manifests God's love for man, drawing Guyon finally to a love of wisdom (cf *Heavenly Beautie*), which takes the form of greater self-knowledge learned in the house of Alma. The celebrated alternatives of gaining the world or saving one's soul (ie, Alma; Matt 16.26) are obviously structural here. The divine love works on Guyon without his becoming a lover himself; being virtue-bounded in fact makes him the odd-man-out among *The Faerie Queene*'s leading figures.

cantos viii-xi These cantos dwell on the strength and frailty, the beauty and deformity of man. After Arthur providentially rescues Guyon from the passion of the brothers, it is imperative for Guyon to understand his place in nature better. Spenser's castle of the body allows the heroes to comprehend their composition and final purpose. The building and its operation exhibit the workings of a tripartite soul. Individuality is reflected by characteristic passions such as Prays-Desire and Shamefastnesse which reveal Arthur's and Guyon's inmost selves; they complement each other as expressions of the aspiring and the curbing sides of the spirited part of the soul. To tie the whole human and divine nexus together, Spenser devises a stanza (ix 22) of supreme concentration giving the blueprint of man's nature – physical, biological, mental, ethical, and spiritual.

The body becomes a symbol of the divine order – a Renaissance commonplace – however, this is balanced by the contrasting images of forces seeking its disintegration (Barkan 1975). Defended by virtue and grace, Alma's beauty and functionality go hand in hand. Spenser encourages a down-to-earth feeling about the body and the uninflated scale of its everyday experience: Alma's practicality subsequently gives Guyon a standard by which to judge Acrasia's glitzy production. She fosters an attainable ideal of happiness measured to man's natural state. The rational spirit that rules reminds one of More's Utopians and their idea of pleasure as a 'calm and harmonious state of the body, its state of health when undisturbed by any disorder.' Alma's 'bounteous banket' is very sober, but she makes provision for the spirit, and the readings raise the poet's strain to heroic. The chronicle of Britain is a macro-version of the evils threatening the microcosm of Alma. Spenser often symbolizes antirational forces as monsters or giants, and in Arthur's book the aborigines of Albion are 'a salvage nation ... Of hideous Giants, and halfe beastly men, / That never tasted grace, nor goodnesse felt, / But like wild beasts lurking in loathsome den' (x 7). These are conquered by the Trojan Brutus, but in fact the struggle remains a perennial one against the chaotic in man. The best gloss is Guyon's reading matter, a Genesis-like history of Faerie but without the Fall. There the dispelling of brutishness by the light of reason is the work of the Titan Prometheus, who created Elfe, founder of the Elfin dynasty – 'A man, of many partes from beasts derived' – and who 'stole fire from heaven, to animate / His worke.' Prometheus' soul-infusing role resembles Orpheus' role as the poet, 'the first light-giver to ignorance,' who civilizes 'stony and beastly people' (Sidney *Defence* in ed 1973b:74). Temperance's link with the arts is customary, and Guyon is specially susceptible to the animating Promethean fire, as Arthur is to heroic example.

Examining his own makeup at the house of Alma restores Guyon. But though they see the point, modern readers may react coolly to the ideal of good order it may seem to endorse. We are not as horrified at disorder as the Elizabethans were: chaos may mean energy for us. Spenser does not seem to notice the exploitive side of 'civilized' discipline as Shakespeare does in *The Tempest*. To understand Spenser, however, one must look to Book III, for instance, where the magical, divine power of love produces an instant revaluation of rational control per se, and the *Cantos of Mutabilitie*, where earlier certainties about order and degree have been destabilized. And even with Alma, complacency about a well-regulated world is precluded by its beleaguered condition. A rabble of villains looking like an artist's fantasy of a peasant uprising surrounds the castle. These are all moral corruptions, with those deforming the five senses especially singled out. It is hard to assess what political overtones there are, but the siege image is fundamental to Spenser's vision of life as a battleground. The first two books are rarely free of background static emanating, if one may adapt a term from Auerbach (ed 1953:246–50), from creaturalism, an awareness of everything wrong with transitory human existence, part Christian, part folkish gloominess, part the sort of guardedness about expecting much from life that Petrarch's *De remediis* sums up, and part the result of Spenser's life as a colonist in Ireland (ix 16). Against this background, anything 'faire and excellent' takes on a special poignancy, making its protectors true paladins succoring a hard-pressed maiden. But something else emerges as the victory over the castle's assailants expresses a note of humanist confidence.

Arthur defends Alma's house with the noble steadfastness against adversity and evil that belongs both to the cardinal virtue fortitude and to Stoic *constantia*. (The resemblance of Spenser's battle outside an anthropomorphic castle to an engraving of *Fortitudo* after Brueghel is truly uncanny.) It takes a Herculean spirit to resist all the blows and failures within that human nature faces. Arthur undertakes it, as he does most of the conventionally heroic actions of the book. His earlier defense of Guyon's body is the bloodiest *aristeia* of the poem (viii 32–52) and enacts a critique of Achilles' fury against Hector's corpse (*Iliad* 22). An imperial destiny like Aeneas' lay ahead of him, and he has an intimation of his future role as he read the British chronicle and its record of faction, civil war, foreign harassment, and 'dayly spectacle of sad decay' (x 62). History reinforced the theme that the 'stubborne' human heart continually suffers from 'fraile infirmity' (xii 28). This major correction of the heroic idea is exemplified when Arthur comes to fight Maleger and needs help: 'So feeble is mans state, and life unsound ... That had not grace thee blest, thou shouldest not survive' (xi 30). The 'dead-living' Maleger introduces a principle that 'farre exceeded reasons reach,' and so cannot be left to Guyon. Maleger sums up all sickness of body and soul, the arch-foe of man alive (to borrow a term from Lawrence). Using the language of paradox familiar in love poetry, Spenser shows that his wasting forces have more strength than healthy bodies have: 'fiercer through infirmitie / Of the fraile flesh,' 'a bodie without might, / That could doe harme, yet could not harmed bee' (xi 1, 40). The struggle enters a more interiorized phase when the hags Impotence (inability to control passions) and Impatience grapple with Arthur and make him experience his own unsoundness intimately: here the dreaded *melancholia* seems to be in question. The honor impelling the Prince's action is invested with Christian value (xi 30) – the train of thought is one that develops through the rejection of Philotime and the comparison of Guyon's angel to a pursuivant (viii 2). Man's chief honor is to be made in the divine image (ix 22), and this is the basis of a Christian humanist confidence in the dignity of man and its own constructive ideology (Trinkaus 1970). It is not the least important effect of 'grace' that it helps Arthur confront the sense of defeatism that Maleger and his hags embody (counterparts to Despair in I ix).

The poetry keeps underlining the greatness of the action and the mystery of a force unbeatable by natural means: the heroic and the supernatural. But other literary combinations also coalesce: the poet's reinterpretive *mythopoesis* in the Antaeus motif, the assimilation to heroic action of du Bartas' Lucretian poetry about physical nature and Pauline texts on the warring of spirit and flesh: 'Who shal deliver me from the bodie of this death,' a foe 'of the earth, earthlie' (Rom 7.24, 1 Cor 15.47). The Prince's final recourse against a deadness that draws its strength from the earth (Arthur himself is fiery, II xi 32) is to elevate the body, crush the breath out of it, and throw it into a stagnant mere. This drowning of evil in water is a grace symbol that balances the finding of irremoveable concupiscence in the bloody babe (ii 4, 10).

canto xii Guyon is less orthodox a hero than Arthur, and he does not overawe the reader as does Belphoebe. It makes sense, of course, not to have a hero of temperance scoring gory victories over vice. (In the *Psychomachia*, Sobrietas' defeat of Luxuria is incredibly brutal.) Spenser may have envisaged Guyon as relatively young – Elyot thought seventeen was the age a young man was ready for the *Nicomachean Ethics* (*Boke Named the Governour* I.11 in ed 1883:91–2). To see Guyon in an heroic light means going to the humanist viewpoint. Moral perception and moral strength become the cornerstones of a revised concept of the heroic. Ulysses and Hercules (read selectively) become the favorite heroic models (Waith 1962). The side of the Ulyssean hero that emerges most fully in Guyon is the one Thomas Wilson summed up: 'In the Odissea is set forth a lyvely Paterne of the minde' (1553; ed 1982:388), later rounded out by Chapman as 'the Mind's inward, constant and unconquerd Empire, unbroken, unalterd with any most insolent and tyrannous infliction' (*Odyssey* 'To the Earle of Somerset' 1614). Guyon is not quite up to this. But his quest of rational control puts him into the class described by Bryskett: 'divine creatures, who apply themselves to live according to reason. And such have auncientl y bin called *Heroes* ... For they put all their endevours to adorne and set foorth that part of man which maketh him like unto the divine nature ... which may conduct him to the highest and supreme good. This part is the minde' (1606; ed 1970:153).

When Guyon makes his final sea journey as the Ulyssean hero, the earlier adventures fall into place and the general direction of the poem emerges more clearly. His adventure ends with the capture of a Circe while the poem proceeds towards the Penelope-like marriage ideal. A sex-for-pleasure enchantment is blocking the way to the bliss of human love, a complex, passionate state that finds its ideal form in marriage (III and IV). Married love in turn lies along the (right) road to Arthur's union with Gloriana, Spenser's symbol of human desire's highest goal. Yet it is natural for Acrasia to lie where she does. Human desire naturally seeks to return to its first principle and continually mistakes substitutes for its real object (see Dante *Convivio* 4.12).

Guyon's voyage begins in a burst of epic energy that continues to invigorate the moral-satirical mode of its allegory. The life-threatening or softly seductive episodes tend to recapitulate Guyon's past 'maistries.' The captions for the itinerary (the Gulf of Greediness, etc) read like an older-style allegory by Barnabe Googe, but the keynote is a voice speaking simple and obvious truths, a moralist in the native tradition unimpressed by a newer sensibility geared to pleasure. Guyon safely negotiates rocks, whirlpools, and quicksands, but is still susceptible to beauty and sentiment. Yet temperance is now a steady disposition, more or less, and quickly bridles indiscretions and allays monstrous fears (xii 26). As his boat nears the island, poetically fresher images of sea birds, deep-sea creatures, and 'all the nation of unfortunate / And fatall birds' bring to mind the nameless inner menace of disordered lower nature. These shocks and fears are meant to push Guyon into wanting to take things easy, but they could create a need for rest and pleasure. 'Here may thy storme-bet vessell safely ride,' the sirens call out to him. Such invitations sometimes intimated that rest amid sensual pleasures was a hero's rightful reward (eg, Camoens *Lusiads* 9). For Spenser, however, the way to earn the bliss of love is to suffer its pains (*Hymne of Love*, *Heavenly Love*), and of course neither Guyon nor those in the Bower have done that. Guyon, approaching the long-awaited enemy, resists all the attempts to lull or charm him as he moves in on Acrasia's inner sanctum. The demands of the quest narrow his character, but this is not where the reader's attention is directed which is the extraordinarily enticing quality of Acrasia's promotion of the sensual nature.

The trouble with Acrasia's exploitation of sensuous beauty is that it leaves nothing for the divine aspirations of man but leads only downward. Spenser's embodiment of beauty in harmony with the soul is Belphoebe, in whom beauty coexists with higher powers: 'Kindled above at th'heavenly makers light,' 'Hable to heale the sicke, and to revive the ded,' 'the temple of the Gods' (iii 22–8) – the Graces especially are a touchstone of the divine dimension. Beauty, moreover, is a rational quality involving proportion, as well as a matter of sense impression (Castiglione ed 1928:81–2). Sensual beauty by itself nevertheless has extraordinary power. A most effective rendering of beauty assailing the eye is provided by two damsels who vie for Guyon's attention in an ornamental pool. Spenser spectacularly avoids lubricity as total erotic awareness is poised against harmonious verbal composition of bodies, water, and the yellow of hair (65, 67).

This makes Guyon feel his concupiscence rising and writing its signature in his 'sparkling face.' But the effect is short-lived as reason 'rebukt those wandring eyes of his.' The damsels' beauty serves the great mystery of procreation (65), but their shamelessness makes them unworthy of it. Also, its humid origins are Spenser's indication of contrast with the 'sacred fire' of love that moves Britomart in the next book (III iii 1). If a more specific point is being made, it is that the damsels would put their show on for anybody with the indiscriminateness common in animals; man, however, has 'the sparke of reasons might, / More then the rest to rule his passion,' and his love is ordained to await 'the fairest in his sight' (*Colin Clout* 867–9).

Another sort of beauty Acrasia taps is that which artists create out of attractive materials, as in the decoration of the fountain where rich metalwork deceives the eye with an illusion of real ivy (see *nature and art). The main gate is likewise embellished with a scene beautiful to the eye, though it is ironic that the artist's 'admirable wit' has transformed the blood of Medea's child murders into an aesthetic effect. Tasso's subjects for his gates had been Hercules and Omphale, and Antony at Actium. Spenser's Medea, Jason, and Creusa alter the theme from the hero-become-effeminate to criminal passion. Also at work is the popular contrast of overdone ornament with plain truth. Acrasia's magic is called 'art' so many times that the attention drawn to art suggests that the chief defect of the Bower may be its artificiality: art on a level with unlived sex and voyeurism (Lewis 1936:332). It certainly does not reflect what nature ordains, though it has pretensions to act in nature's name, after the fashion of Armida who sings, 'This wisdom is, good life and worldly-bliss, / Kind teacheth us, nature commands us this' (*GL* 14.64, tr Fairfax).

Another way of looking at the art of the Bower is to see it in the light of attacks on poetry, especially by Plato. Spenser adopts Sidney's line of defense: it is not art itself but the abuse of art that must be driven out. This may be the point of the etiology of the sirens (31), whose mermaid form was a consequence of defeat by the Muses in a song contest, though they retained 'their sweet skill in wonted melody; / Which ever after they abusd to ill.' Guyon destroys all Acrasia's works somewhat as a censor might, but mainly because they obscure what is truly desirable. Her works cloud the true intent of sexual union because imagination can be distorted by concupiscence and material impurities. This aspect of imagination is most explicit in the 'guilefull semblaunts' which the false Genius 'makes us see' (48). Fantasy may 'breede *Chimeres* and monsters in mans imaginations' (Puttenham *Arte* 1589, 1.8). But a sound imagination is the source of many new and rare things, 'a representer of the best, most comely and bewtifull images or apparances of thinges to the soule and according to their very truth.' While Acrasia disorders the imagination to produce monsters, the poet gives his account of her according to its 'very truth.' Guyon's opposition to Acrasia's illusions, which might seem at first sight to strike at the essentially illusionist nature of the whole Faerie world, thus emerges as a way of freeing that world for true imagination. The poet audaciously imitates Acrasia's abuse of art, but then states his correction through the Palmer and Guyon. He counters Plato's accusation that the poet's 'appeal is to the inferior part of the soul ... and by strengthening it tends to destroy the rational part' (*Republic* 10.6.605B) by rendering reason's restraint of these lower elements in poetic images. But he curtails Acrasia's dramatic role, probably to make her less morally dangerous to the reader, because it was the empathy created by dramatic impersonation that Plato feared most. Spenser further implies that the pleasurable fictions of the poet are not ends in themselves. Looked at in the light of literary theory, Acrasia and her Bower propose pleasure (48.8) as poetry's principal end (the view of Robortello and Castelvetro comes close to this). Against this, Guyon brings the classic complementary idea that poetry's function is to teach, in effect to teach virtue – one recalls how the *utile* characterizes Alma. Both viewpoints combine in the Spenserian synthesis: poetry is to teach by delighting. Perhaps the most important thing to emerge is Spenser's deeply felt responsibility towards his art (Evans 1970:148).

When Acrasia eventually appears in two painterly tableaux, she blends with her setting, as in some allegory by Luini. Spenser's 'faire Witch' is as unlike Circe or Armida as a sibling can be, neither a goddess giving in gracefully to her lover's homesickness, nor a doting mistress roused to fury as she is abandoned. Spenser's first description places her beside her sleeping lover tremulously savoring his beauty in a moment of sinisterly overshadowed post-coital tenderness, and surrounded by 'Many faire Ladies, and lascivious boyes' who 'pleasauntly did sing' (72). The second tableau sums up all that 'hungry eies' and 'Fraile harts' can ask for (78). As object of desire, she practically ceases to be flesh and blood: her semi-transparent nudity is a subtle trap, particularly for sight and touch (the spider). Here and everywhere, the poet is concerned with what is wrong with Acrasia as well as with conveying her appeal.

When we look closely, her Bower of Bliss reveals an ironic marriage subtext: nature is given the look of an overdressed bride (50), and the false Genius cheats those who enter of progeny. Images associated with wedding poems keep appearing: the ivy on the fountain is sterile metal; Excess' vine is so overloaded 'That the weake bowes ... Did bow adowne, as over-burdened,' recalling a common marriage emblem of the vine that needs the support of the elm. The rose song is reminiscent of the one in Catullus 62 sung by the chorus of girls, though Spenser's words follow Tasso's (one of whose reasons for introducing a song may well have been the popularity of Ariosto's 'La verginella è simile alla rosa' [*Orlando furioso* 1.42] as set by numerous composers). Most curious of all is the combination of the sea track of the Argo (44) with the damsels' exhibitionism (63–8). Together these reproduce the *aetia* from Catullus 64 on the marriage of Peleus and Thetis, where it was in order to see the marvelous Argo that the modest nymphs first showed their breasts above water and so caused a mortal to fall in love with and marry one of them. The marriage motif brings the canto into line with most of the other endings of the poem's books.

As Guyon passes through the Bower, the reader's perception tenses with his hostility. Guyon dashes several sybaritic invitations aside, and his touch of roughness throws the ingratiatingness of it all into high relief. Moral stricture produces a deliberately jarring note as the word *crime* wrecks the fragile lyricism of the 'Virgin Rose' lay (a more amusing spoiling effect is the line about Guyon's arousal by the damsels: 'On which when gazing him the Palmer saw'). Spenser one moment enters haunting pleas to 'Gather the Rose of love, whilest yet is time' and then goes on with the moralist's answers in the next. The two sensibilities, sensual and critical, never work together better than in the stanza picturing Acrasia with Verdant (73). However, some readers find the moralist seriously at odds with the poet (Saunders 1952), and others see the sensuousness of moments like this riddled with ironies and totally compromised (Hieatt 1975a). Guyon, at any rate, can resist the pathos of lower nature's subjection to time through having had, at Alma's, a poet's vision of the soul's constructive undertakings.

One clearly defined defect of the Bower is enervation, so much so that one critic has renamed it the Bower of Sloth (Evans 1964). Introducing Verdant asleep in the Bower was one of Spenser's most significant changes. More generally, the absence of tension in the Bower offends a Renaissance perception of life's *discordia concors* or necessary dynamism of opposites, forcefully present elsewhere, as in pleasure-pain or male-female. This dynamism belongs especially to love (eg, the Temple of Venus, IV x 31–5, or *HL* and *HHL*) and its absence in the Bower is noteworthy. *Love* and *lover* are hardly used in this canto, and where they are it is in delimiting senses that reduce emotional content to near zero. The point is one Spenser's image structure elicits through having the Bower's erotic fountain, where 'naked boyes ... them selves embay in liquid joyes,' contrast with Amavia's heart that spurted like a fountain at her suicide (and had her baby playing in it). This passionate and dangerous side is excluded from the sex of the Bower. For passion's purification with heavenly fire, the reader must wait until Book III, as he must for a vision of generation that comes to terms with time and death (Gardens of Adonis).

As its name implies, the Bower is proffered as a substitute for the soul's bliss with God (cf III v 35), and an essential feature of the copy is its static quality, because this imitates the truly divine pleasure of rest (*Nicomachean Ethics* 1154b 26–31). Spenser's attitude to action was complex, but clear to him was the unattainability in this earthly life where 'all that moveth, doth in *Change* delight' of that 'Sabaoths sight' (VII viii 2) of the soul's rest in God (Heb 4.1–11). So we see that the image of Acrasia and Verdant 'Whose sleepie head she in her lap did soft dispose' – the repose of sexual fulfillment – is one of a succession of misrepresentations of true rest: Amavia who 'slyding soft, as downe to sleepe her layd, / And ended all her woe in quiet death' (i 56), Braggadocchio's pursuit of 'ease' (iii 39–41), Cymochles beside the soporific streamlet of the Bower (v 30) or with his head in Phaedria's lap (vi 14), Mammon's offer to Guyon of Proserpina's silver stool 'To rest thy wearie person, in the shadow coole' (vii 63), the Sirens' promise of a 'Port of rest from troublous toyle' (xii 32), even Arthur who after being tempted not to resume the struggle rouses himself vigorously 'As one awakt out of long slombring shade' (xi 31). The answering image to the temptation to sleep is to be found in Spenser's explanation of the name Elfe, the first man of Faerie, 'to weet / Quick': in other words, living, alive, vigorous (*OED*), and in the activity attributed to him of 'wandring through the world with wearie feet' (x 71). The motif dominating the narrative of Book II is thus no accident: the adventurous travels of Guyon are themselves a symbol of alert engagement with living.

After the climax of his drama of the mastering of concupiscence when Guyon and the Palmer capture Acrasia, Guyon annihilates all Acrasia's pleasant bowers 'with rigour pittilesse': 'Ne ought their goodly workmanship might save / Them from the tempest of his wrathfulnesse, / But that their blisse he turn'd to balefulnesse: / Their groves he feld, their gardins did deface, / Their arbers spoyle, their Cabinets suppresse, / Their banket houses burne, their buildings race, / And of the fairest late, now made the fowlest place' (II xii 83). Many readers see this as overkill, and blame Guyon for 'vindictive hostility,' 'Puritan frenzy,' and being a 'self-righteous prig.' Is the meaning ironic, a reflection against Guyon? The poetic impact is considerable. Guyon's act is morally intelligible and at the same time ultra-personal. The hero acts as the instrument of God. His tempest of wrath foreshadows the Judgment and divine reprobation of all who will not change while time allows. Ambivalence about Guyon seems as inevitable here as it is about Henry's severity to Falstaff on the coronation route in Shakespeare's *2 Henry* IV. The devastation is another similitude of Babylon, the fallen city, expressed earlier as the fall of a mountain and the death of a dragon (I xi 54). Guyon's destruction of a pleasure garden reformulates anathema in the language of this particular book. (An epic equivalent would be Ulysses' execution of the suitors and the maids.) Guyon also happens to be carrying out a legal sentence of 'waste' (*OED*; see also Blackstone ed 1962:454–5) against a murderess, Acrasia. There is a natural logic in the image of a demolition accompanying the raising of a fairer Temple (Prudentius' concluding motif), that is to say, the 'goodly frame of Temperance' (xii 1) and the chaste love of Book III.

Slavery to the senses produced 'monstruous' minds (85) as Verdant, Grill, and the others lost awareness of their higher potential. Guyon's final comments sound like Pico della Mirandola contemplating man's freedom and rational dignity: 'See the mind of beastly man, / That hath so soone forgot the excellence / Of his creation, when he life began, / That now he chooseth, with vile difference, / To be a beast, and lacke intelligence' (87). He is in effect liberating the soul for the spheres of love, friendship, justice, and courtesy that follow.

The image of travel had served the humanist to try out new ideas and scrutinize the near and familiar, as we see in More, Rabelais, Sidney, Nashe, Bacon, and Cervantes. Guyon's travels, too, cover much Renaissance ground, intellectual and literary. But the poet has reservations about Guyon and temperance as keys to the full measure of man. Passions need to be made safer, yet life also depends on them. Hence, though not too diagrammatically, Book III reinstates some of the energies repressed in Book II. Guyon's journey in discipline is necessary for survival, but it does not round him out into a complete man in the way suggested of Redcrosse, Britomart, or Calidore.

The Faerie Queene is a visionary poem in the great tradition of the poet 'having all ... under the authority of his pen' (Sidney *Defence* in ed 1973b:89). Overviewing Book II, one takes in its self-sufficiency as a cosmos. The boundaries stretch from Ruddymane's birth to Maleger's shadowing of death. Completeness is symbolized by Alma's microcosmic body flanked by Mammon's hell and Acrasia's would-be heaven. From this point on, the poem's landscapes fan out and render the earthly scene in such a variety that faerie-land almost seems to displace the Fairy Queen. Yet one assumes that everything will eventually converge again to a final point and that all the poem's buildings would merge with the 'pillours of Eternity' (VII viii 2, Ps 84.2) in the final city image, fulfilling the one that Guyon read about in this book. RENÉ GRAZIANI

Robert Allot 1913 *Englands Parnassus ... 1600* ed Charles Crawford (Oxford); Alpers 1967b; Barkan 1975; Berger 1957; William Blackstone 1962 'Of Judgment and Its Consequences' in *Commentaries on the Laws of England: Of Public Wrongs* ed Robert Malcolm Kerr (Boston) pp 444–59; Bryskett ed 1970; Cain 1978; Camoens ed 1952; Carscallen 1967–8; Cullen 1974; Dante Alighieri 1966 *Il convivio* ed Maria Simonelli (Bologna); Antoinette B. Dauber 1980 'The Art of Veiling in the Bower of Bliss' *SSt* 1:163–75; Davis 1981; Maurice Evans 1964 'Guyon and the Bower of Sloth' *SP* 61:140–9; Evans 1970; Fowler 1960a; Fowler 1960–1; Giamatti 1966; Madelon S. Gohlke 1978 'Embattled Allegory: Book II of *The Faerie Queene*'

ELR 8:123–40; Hamilton 1961a; Hieatt 1975a; Homer ed 1967; Hoopes 1954; Merritt Y. Hughes 1943; Hughes 1944 'England's Eliza and Spenser's Medina' *JEGP* 43:1–15; Huizinga ed 1924; Sean Kane 1983 'The Paradoxes of Idealism: Book Two of *The Faerie Queene*' *JDJ* 2.1:81–109; Kaske 1976; Kaske 1979; Kermode 1960; Kermode 1971; Kostić 1969; Giovanni Paolo Lomazzo 1598 *A Tracte Containing the Artes of Curious Paintinge, Carvinge and Buildinge* tr Richard Haydocke (London; rpt Amsterdam and New York 1969); I.G. MacCaffrey 1976; MacLachlan 1980; MacLure 1961; Lewis H. Miller, Jr 1971 'The Ironic Mode in Books I and II of *The Faerie Queene*' *PLL* 7:133–49; Geoffrey A. Moore 1975 'The Cave of Mammon: Ethics and Metaphysics in Secular and Christian Perspective' *ELH* 42:157–70; Nellist 1963; Nelson 1963; Nohrnberg 1976; O'Connell 1977; Pollock 1980; Puttenham 1589; Roche 1964; Rossky 1958; J.W. Saunders 1952 'The Façade of Morality' in William R. Mueller and Don Cameron Allen, eds 1952 *'That Soueraine Light': Essays in Honor of Edmund Spenser: 1552–1952* (Baltimore) pp 1–34; Sirluck 1951–2; Stone 1965; Tonkin 1973; T. Wilson ed 1982; Woodhouse 1949.

The Faerie Queene, Book III The third book of *The Faerie Queene* presents the virtue of chastity, 'That fairest vertue, farre above the rest' (proem 1). Classically, chastity was a branch of temperance, treating the uses of sexuality and over the centuries endlessly readjusted as a commentary on Paul's injunction in 1 Corinthians 7.9: 'But if they can not absteine, let them marie: for it is better to marie then to burne.' The apparent opposition in this text is between abstinence and marriage. The medieval church, characterized by a celibate clergy, tended to place emphasis on abstinence (or virginity), even though it granted matrimony the status of sacrament. The Reformers, having disposed of the ideal of a celibate clergy, deposed matrimony from its sacramental status.

This seesaw balance between abstinence and marriage has left chastity as a virtue largely undefined except by specifying limits. It does not fit into the Aristotelian modality of defect and excess, any more than holiness will fit that procrustean grid. Yet we cannot be left in this matter with nothing (abstinence) or all (marriage) because the opposition does not square with reality; therefore, one writer of the Renaissance defined the virtue thus: 'Chastity is the beauty of the soule and purity of life, which is onely possessed of those who keepe their bodies cleane and undefiled; and it consisteth eyther in sincere virginity, or in faithful matrimony' (John Bodenham 1597 *Politeuphuia: Wits Common Wealth*). The adjectives used here to describe the limits of chastity are interesting in that they relate the virtue to individual integrity ('sincere') and to communal understanding and objectives ('faithful') that encompass the proper uses of sexuality.

Within such a wide range of limits it would be hard to find a single myth or figure to carry the burden of exposition of such a virtue. Spenser found single heroes to carry forward his embodiments of holiness and temperance; but no Isabella from *Measure for Measure* could sustain the journey that Spenser's chastity must exemplify, and therefore Book III of *The Faerie Queene* differs strikingly from the first two.

Part of the difficulty may be seen in Spenser's description of Book III in the Letter to Raleigh: 'The third day there came in, a Groome who complained before the Faery Queene, that a vile Enchaunter called Busirane had in hand a most faire Lady called Amoretta, whom he kept in most grievous torment, because she would not yield him the pleasure of her body. Whereupon Sir Scudamour the lover of that Lady presently tooke on him that adventure. But being unable to performe it by reason of the hard Enchauntments, after long sorrow, in the end met with Britomartis, who succoured him, and reskewed his love.' Almost nothing of this narrative occurs in the poem as written. Britomart does meet Scudamour after leaving Malbecco's castle and does rescue Amoret in canto xii, but the suggestion that Scudamour is 'the knight' of Book III jars with its title: 'The Legend of Britomartis, or, Of Chastitie.' That Spenser had in mind the poem he wrote is more than adequately represented in the Letter by the comments he makes on the events that do happen in the book: 'But by occasion hereof, many other adventures are intermedled, but rather as Accidents, then intendments. As the love of Britomart, the overthrow of Marinell, the misery of Florimell, the vertuousness of Belphoebe, the lasciviousnes of Hellenora, and many the like.' These 'intermedled' adventures do constitute the major episodes of the poem we have, almost in the order in which they occur.

Spenser's narrative plan as disclosed in the Letter was to depict each virtue as a quest bestowed on a knight by the Fairy Queen, the accomplishment of which was to show the nature of that virtue: Redcrosse expresses holiness by rescuing Una's parents from the Dragon; Guyon sets forth temperance by defeating Acrasia. Presumably the other knights were to have their quests imposed by Gloriana, yet that is not the way the narrative works in Book III. Scudamour appears only in canto xi; Britomart, the titular heroine, has not even seen the Fairy Queen. She is in search of Artegall, and her search intersects with Scudamour's only in canto xi. The narrative of Book III meets up with Spenser's expressed plan only in the final adventure of the book.

This is no more accident than Ariosto's imposing the madness of Orlando as a title around the Virgilian dynastic romance of Bradamante and Ruggiero, the progenitors of his patrons the Este just as Virgil created his epic to celebrate Augustus. Spenser may have thought of imitating Ariosto when his patron Leicester might still have become the consort of Elizabeth, thus following the intentions of his Italian predecessors Ariosto and Tasso; but those intentions were defeated by Leicester's death in 1588, at which point Spenser found himself in the position of Virgil writing his epic celebrating Augustus and his successor Marcellus long after that heir of Augustus had died. If Arthur was to marry Gloriana at the end of the poem in the properly dynastic match, then Spenser's Arthur (like Virgil's Marcellus) had 'prevented' his triumph and any possibility of marriage between his patron and patroness. History in the form of mortality had defeated his narrative scheme; and probably for this reason he included a stanza about the fate of Arthur's armor when he died (I vii 36), a poignant reminder of the fate both of patron and of poem.

Although Leicester's death canceled the possibility of a dynastic marriage between Arthur and Gloriana, and Scudamour's participation in the third book does not fulfill the expectations set by the Letter, the poem does have a logical narrative structure, resembling the *entrelacement* of medieval romance and Ariosto.

The book begins with Britomart's meeting Guyon, Arthur, and his squire Timias. After an initial defeat of Guyon and a speedy reconciliation with him, the action is interrupted by the flight of Florimell from a 'griesly Foster,' or forester. Arthur, Guyon, and Timias pursue them, and Britomart proceeds alone. The consequences of this encounter and immediate separation constitute the narrative frame of the first eight cantos.

Book III can be seen as a triptych of four cantos each. The first four tell of Britomart's encounter at Malecasta's castle, of the inception of her love for Artegall and Merlin's prophecy about that love, and finally her defeat of Marinell. Cantos v–viii resume the adventures of Arthur and Timias in their pursuit of Florimell and the Foster respectively. In canto v, Arthur is told why Florimell fled the court; and Timias, wounded by the treachery of the Foster and his brothers, is rescued by Belphoebe, who inflicts on him the even greater wound of love. Canto vi relates the miraculous birth of Belphoebe and of her twin Amoret, who is taken to the Garden of Adonis. Canto vii picks up the adventures of Florimell at the witch's hut and her escape; canto viii describes the creation of the false Florimell and Florimell's plight at sea first with the old Fisher and then with Proteus. The third group of four cantos returns to the exploits of Britomart, first at Malbecco's castle and then at the house of Busirane.

Thus the first and last four cantos surround the four that deal with the consequences of Florimell's flight, both for herself and for her would-be rescuers. Each of these three parts separately throws light on Spenser's notions of *accident* and *intendment* and on his skillful use of flashback techniques. Florimell's flight is central to the narrative: it is the primary cause of the action to follow, providing adventures for Arthur and Timias, and, more important, leaving Britomart alone. After the departure of Arthur, Timias, and Guyon (with the Palmer), Britomart rides on until she encounters the six knights guarding Malecasta's castle and attacking Redcrosse (i 20). Once inside the castle she is wooed by Malecasta, slightly wounded by Gardante, and helped by Redcrosse to trounce them all. Riding away from the castle, Britomart gets Redcrosse to comment on a knight named Artegall, whom she secretly loves. The rest of cantos ii and iii are devoted to the flashback story of the inception of her love for Artegall and Merlin's prophecy about their future marriage. At the end of canto iii, Redcrosse departs, never to be heard of again in the poem. Canto iv begins with Britomart again riding off, alone again, this time towards the seacoast where she laments to the sea about the vagaries of fortune, after which she is accosted by and wounds Marinell, whose mother, Cymoent, comes to rescue him and lament his harm, with another flashback to the history of Marinell and his mother. The canto ends with the reentry of Arthur, who in despair at his failure to find both his Fairy Queen and Florimell complains to the power of night, a parallel to Britomart's complaint at the beginning of the canto.

The placement of these episodes in the first four cantos displays a morally thematic decorum: we move from the pain and danger of love (Florimell's flight) to Britomart's first awareness of love as play (Malecasta's castle), to the inception of love and its high potentialities (vision of Artegall and Merlin's prophecy), to the rejection of love (Marinell). These first four cantos make moral and thematic sense, but are structurally problematic: in canto v Arthur meets Florimell's dwarf, who tells that her flight was precipitated by the news that her unrequiting love, Marinell, had been wounded five days before. Yet this is the action we have just seen accomplished by Britomart in canto iv.

Spenser must juggle the discordant facts that Marinell's wounding is the cause of Florimell's flight so far as the action of the poem is concerned, and that his wounding represents an important stage in Britomart's initiation into love. That we learn about the relationship between Florimell and Marinell only after his wounding is even more important. An analogous situation is the way we learn about the circumstances of Amoret's abduction by Busirane only at the beginning of Book IV after we have experienced his masque of Cupid in III xi-xii. The dwarf's relation to Arthur of Florimell's love for Marinell is a very important readjustment of the story of cantos i-iv because the initial description of Florimell and her flight unmistakably calls up a similar flight of Ariosto's heroine Angelica. In canto v, we learn that the fickle and clever Ariostan heroine is not to be duplicated in this poem because the cause of her flight is unrequited love from a man who will not love, has now been wounded, and is likely to die; this radical readjustment of Angelica's reasons for fleeing Charlemagne's Paris is amply noted in the central cantos v-viii.

Canto v brings both Arthur and Timias back into the action of the poem after their separation at the flight of Florimell in canto i. Timias in v 13–25 defeats but is wounded by the Foster and his two brothers; he is rescued by Belphoebe and cured, only to receive from his benefactor the more grievous wound of love.

More important for understanding Spenser's narrative is that this rescue continues the imitation of Ariosto's Angelica, whose adventures were first imitated in the flight of Florimell and are now imitated in the figure of Belphoebe. In Ariosto, Angelica's flight precipitates her through a series of encounters with helpful but self-seeking knights and a randy but impotent friar, until she comes upon the beautiful and wounded groom Medoro, whom she cures and marries. This is the cause of Orlando's madness, the putative subject of Ariosto's poem; but Spenser cannot imitate the reciprocal love of Angelica and Medoro because of the nature of the characters who play the roles that Ariosto created. Timias' love cannot be reciprocated by Belphoebe because the Letter to Raleigh has presented her as that 'most vertuous and beautifull Lady,' as opposed to 'our soveraine the Queene, and her kingdome in Faery land' – the private versus the public persons of Elizabeth – and in her first appearance in the poem (II iii), she is cast in the role of Virgil's Venus, who appears to her son in the guise of Diana (*Aeneid* I). This figure of a loving Diana and a chaste Venus precludes the simple amorousness of Angelica, and is complicated by Spenser's equally historical treatment of Timias.

It has long been accepted that the continuation of the Belphoebe-Timias story in IV vii tells of the historical disgrace of Raleigh for secretly marrying Elizabeth Throckmorton, one of Elizabeth's ladies-in-waiting (Roche 1964:142–8). More recently it has been suggested that Timias' defeat of the Foster and his two brothers is an equally historical rendition of Raleigh's heroic defeat of the three Desmond brothers in Ireland, which made him a national hero in the early 1580s (Bednarz 1983). If these suppositions are true, then even in the 1590 *Faerie Queene* Spenser was representing his friendship with Raleigh through the figure of Timias. If in 1588 he had lost the possibility of a patron who might marry the Virgin Queen, he was not about to lose the opportunity of displaying the heroism of the friend and neighbor who was going to introduce him to her court. Canto v is important not only for reintroducing Arthur and Timias but also for enmeshing current historical realities in the fiction.

Canto vi broadens the philosophical implications of Spenser's Ariostan imitation through a flashback genealogy of the birth of Belphoebe and her twin Amoret, who is now introduced and whose plight will be the climactic action of this book through the agency of Britomart. The canto is based on the opposition of Venus and Diana, which repeats the contrary roles of these goddesses in the earlier characterization of Belphoebe. Here Venus and Diana are Renaissance versions of two major Olympian deities who fight out their conflicting claims in a sprightly debate; both goddesses are deprived of their usual attributes, for Venus searching for her lost Cupid comes upon Diana bathing without her buskins, quiver, and bow. The encounter is an imitation of Moschus' *Eros drapetēs* ('Runaway Cupid'), and Venus reenacts the myth of Actaeon in coming upon Diana, although the ensuing quarrel does not change Venus into a stag. Both goddesses set out to find Cupid and instead come upon the nymph Chrysogone who has just given birth to Belphoebe and Amoret, conceived through the power of the sun. Diana takes Belphoebe; Venus brings Amoret to the Garden of Adonis, now described in the great creation myth of canto vi. Just as in the first four cantos Spenser moves from the present state of his heroine Britomart in love to narrate the inception of her love and prophesy its outcome, so in these cantos he moves from the present action of Timias and Belphoebe to describe the conception of Belphoebe and her relationship to the world of generation as represented by the Garden of Adonis.

In cantos vii and viii, Spenser picks up the flight of Florimell which initiated the action of the book and describes her progressively more straitened circumstances as she meets and escapes from the witch and her churlish son, to the dubious safety of the boat of the old Fisher, and finally to her captivity by the sea god Proteus. Here the imitation of Ariosto in this book ends.

It might be well to speculate why Spenser should model Britomart, Florimell, and Belphoebe on characters and actions taken from Ariosto. Explanations range from his inability to deal with the virtue of chastity, to the necessity of hastily assembling a third book in order to complete the first segment of his poem for publication, to his attempt to 'overgo' the helter-skelter of Ariosto's prodigious invention of story. Fortunately, such explanations appear less plausible now that *Orlando furioso* is credited with the respect its architectonic splendor deserves, and moreover now that Spenser's virtue of chastity seems less a cloistered virtue.

Josephine Waters Bennett, in tracing the evolution of *The Faerie Queene* (1942), claims that Book III is the most Ariostan of the poem and that it was also the earliest book conceived and written. Her evidence for these statements is not likely to be disproved or superseded, but her notions of Ariosto and of poetic genesis and influence should be revised. Of Ariostan influence on Book III there can be no question. Florimell's flight in canto i strongly recalls *Orlando furioso* I, in which the beauteous Angelica escapes from the siege of Paris to try her own luck. Both her escape and her adventures are carefully buttressed by Ariosto's irony, and we fear neither for Paris nor for Angelica because of the foolishness of the knights who pursue her. Spenser's Florimell rides into *The Faerie Queene* pursued by a 'griesly Foster,' unprovided with irony or chivalric delicacy of any sort, and his own chivalric knights, also unprovided with irony, must be sent off to rescue her. The difference between Ariosto and Spenser is enormous: smiles of a summer night in the former, and danger in the latter; comic play in the one, and sturdy pursuit in the other. Spenser totally changes the tone of Ariosto, almost as if he did not understand it. The humor has gone, and in its place are a sobriety and intensity that characterize Book III.

Part of this change occurs because the characters arrive on scene in full allegorical array. Even before we know that Britomart is modeled on Bradamante, we know that the 'Legend of Britomartis' is also the Legend of Chastity. Even before we see the flight of Florimell, we see the confrontation of Britomart and Guyon, in which she defeats the hero of the preceding book by the magic of her enchanted lance; and this confrontation, presented in the language established as the norm in the first two books, domesticates the ensuing Ariostan imitations even before they occur. Spenser hints at much darker realities for his Florimell than Ariosto's poem could sustain for Angelica, who is in control and always eludes her pursuers until she is smitten by love's arrow for the lowly but beautiful Medoro. Spenser's division of this episode between Florimell and Belphoebe complicates Ariosto's story by suppressing the comic tone and making the pursuit of Florimell a most serious adventure; she is in real danger, and her would-be rescuer, Arthur, questions whether this damsel might not be his own vanished Fairy Queen (III iv 54). Spenser's handling of Arthur's pursuit of Florimell begins in selfless derring-do and ends in a self-questioning that no pursuer of Angelica could abide. Arthur's pursuit pushes Spenser's readers into questions of the nature of human desire, which cannot be afforded to Ariosto's welter of doughty knights. Florimell ends up imprisoned by Proteus, the god of change, who universalizes the story that Ariosto told through the figures of many knights pursuing one woman as a simple object of desire, wanted but not understood except as the projection of male desire.

The further transformation of the Angelica story into that of Timias and Belphoebe also distances Ariosto's narrative from both because of the historical agents Spenser uses (Raleigh and Elizabeth) and because of the enormous weight that his earlier depiction of Belphoebe as Virgil's Venus dressed as Diana gives to the serious moral import of this imitation. His choice of Ariosto's coy and evasive heroine who settles on an unworthy love suggests something of Sidney's desperation at Elizabeth's possible union with d'Alençon; it echoes his own more judicious criticism in *The Shepheardes Calender* and puts his friend Raleigh in the role of aggrieved servant. Nonetheless, Spenser's depiction of Elizabeth as Belphoebe extends beyond historical identifications because he universalizes once more the narrative to the philosophical issues of love and chastity, within which he can still praise the Virgin Queen, and his depiction of Raleigh as Timias becomes subsumed in the fabric of Renaissance idealism. Spenser tampers knowingly with Ariosto's seamless narrative by pushing his source beyond the limits that Ariosto would allow. Yet whether he did 'overgo' Ariosto is a question that probably should not be asked.

The last four cantos return the reader to the adventures of Britomart, who once more must depose a knight to gain entry into the poem, as she did Guyon in canto i. This time it is Paridell outside the castle of Malbecco, whose story we hear in cantos ix and x. Paridell's seduction of Hellenore is another retelling of the Paris and Helen story in Spenser's inimitable anachronistic style, and is included at this point of the narrative to link up with the creation of the false Florimell in canto viii where his model is not Ariosto but the alternative myth of Helen, which relates that she was not taken to Troy but was kept by King Proteus of Egypt, who substituted a living idol that deceived both Paris and the other Trojans. The false Florimell, created by the witch to soothe her lovesick son, is an allusion to this myth, which leads on to the reenactment of the Homeric story in the escapade of Paridell and Hellenore.

The linking of these two episodes is signaled by two short but crucial framing passages. In the first (vii 37–61), Satyrane, who with Florimell's girdle has just bound the beast that killed her palfrey, is startled by the sudden appearance of the giantess Argante carrying a squire bound up with wire and pursued by another knight. Satyrane joins the chase and is knocked unconscious. When the other knight approaches close, Argante throws down the squire and rides off still pursued by the other knight. When Satyrane revives, he unbinds the squire, who identifies himself as the Squire of Dames and tells the story of Argante and her incestuous conception by Typhoeus and Earth and her incestuous relations with her twin brother Ollyphant in their mother's womb and after. That name refers to the Olifaunt of Chaucer's *Sir Thopas*; in the 1590 version of this stanza Spenser mentions 'Chylde *Thopas*' but deletes it in 1596 because he is not continuing Chaucer's tale. Nonetheless, Ollyphant reappears in the second framing passage (xi 3–6), pursued by Satyrane and Britomart, who have just left Malbecco's castle. In the pursuit, Satyrane and Britomart are separated, and she finds not Ollyphant but Scudamour lamenting outside Busirane's castle. Thus, Satyrane enters this book at the point where Florimell has abandoned herself to the sea and disappears just at that point where Britomart meets Scudamour. In 1590 Spenser apparently wanted to make some allusion to Chaucer's ribald *Sir Thopas*, a supposition that becomes more pertinent as the Squire of Dames tells the story of his cruel Columbell, who sent him to do service to ladies for twelve months before she would accept him. Having obtained 300 'pledges' and 900 'thanks' for his services, he returns only to win the further punishment of finding an equal number of ladies who would refuse his services; at the point where he is picked up by Argante, he has found only three – a whore, a nun, and a country girl. This sad but funny fabliau is important because it too has a literary pedigree of equal importance to the Chaucerian reference.

The Squire's story is a version of Giocondo's from *Orlando furioso* 28. Popularly known as the most scurrilous story in Ariosto, it was the first to be translated by Harington, and it so displeased Elizabeth that she is said to have banished him until he completed a translation of the whole poem. On the completion of that Herculean task (1591), Harington mentions Spenser's use of the story in his commentary: 'The hosts tale ... is a bad one: M. *Spencers* tale ... is to the like effect, sharpe and well conceyted' (*Sp All* p 22).

Why should Spenser introduce these stories into his already fragmented narrative? Just at the point where Satyrane loses his chance to find Florimell and to control the beast meant to kill her, Spenser distracts him with the fleeing Argante. Between Florimell's disappearance and Britomart's discovery of Scudamour, Satyrane is an active and ever-present participant in the action of the poem. He and the Squire of Dames are the first to arrive at the walls of Malbecco's castle. They are joined shortly by Paridell and thereafter by Britomart, who immediately defeats Paridell. The four enter the castle, where Paridell and Britomart take front stage with Satyrane playing a mere supporting role; the Squire of Dames is totally left in the wings, of no further use to Spenser. The next day, Satyrane and Britomart leave Paridell behind to complete his 'rape' of Hellenore, while they proceed to their meeting with Ollyphant.

This framing device is meant to contrast the two halves of Book III: in the first half, sexuality is a shadowy possibility; in the second, a perverted reality. The solidarity of the group in canto i is immediately shattered by the flight of Florimell. Guyon fades out of the poem; Britomart rides on through her discovery of love and defeat of Marinell; Arthur and Timias reappear in canto v. In canto vi we see the birth of the twins Belphoebe and Amoret. In canto vii Florimell again appears and again flees; this time the knight searching for her hears of a set of twins who make a striking contrast to those of canto vi, whose parents were the sun and Chrysogone. The latter twins are the outcome of the incestuous union of Typhoeus (wind) and Earth. One set represents the options open to human sexuality; the other, the ultimate perversion of that gift. They are born of wind and earth; in the second half of the book the element of water imprisons Florimell, and the element of fire keeps Scudamour from claiming his Amoret.

The knight of Chastity must reclaim one of the four heroines of Book III from the element of fire, and this is the story of Britomart's single-handed rescue of Amoret from the house of Busirane in xi-xii. As the exemplar of chastity, Britomart wins the day for Amoret and brings her out of imprisonment to a reunion with Scudamour in 1590 and to a continued separation leading to further adventures in Books IV and V in 1596.

There has been less than general agreement about the cause of Amoret's imprisonment by Busirane. Some critics feel that it is the overboldness of Scudamour's attempt to take his bride. Others have suggested that it is Amoret's own fears of sexuality that imprison her in the abusive power of Busirane. Perhaps these questions take us too close to the psychological realism demanded by a certain kind of modern reading and too far from the moral dimension of the world in which Spenser lived. The wall of fire that prevents Scudamour from entering the house of Busirane need not be part of the symbolism of his psyche or Amoret's reticence. It is part of the raging fire of human desire that must be subdued by the stalwart Britomart, who forges in with sword pointing straight on and shield defending her face, like a thunderbolt piercing a cloud. Yet when she enters the house, it is filled with images, not people. Without benefit of other human intervention, she studies the images on the tapestries, derived from the battle of Minerva and Arachne in Ovid. There, images of gods are transformed to satisfy their desires, which, when satisfied, do not end with that act but further transform the nondivine participant into some object of the world as we know it, some flower or animal. The initial desire always results in a degrading of the hierarchy of being. Britomart sees these depictions, but her reactions are not revealed. Likewise, her reaction to the masque of Cupid is also kept hidden. The images that emerge from the inner room, led by Ease, followed by six couples – Fancy and Desire, Doubt and Daunger, Fear and Hope, Dissemblance and Suspect, Grief and Fury, and Displeasure and Pleasance – have been described as typical sonnet metaphors, here brought to play in the torment of Amoret, the woman who has given in to love, whose heart has been cut out and is carried in a silver basin. This entire triumphal masque is superintended by Cupid who slyly lifts the band from his blinded eyes to see the whole procession. Britomart again does not, or is not allowed to, comment on the proceedings. The images alone must convey the meaning. The triumph of chastity is manifest in Britomart's forcing Busirane to unsay his unspecified charms. Once the charms are unsaid, Amoret's chains are dissolved and Busirane bound with those very chains. The enchantment of his house is gone, the house itself with tapestries and masquers disappears, and Britomart and Amoret emerge through a now-no-longer-fiery porch. In the 1590 conclusion of the canto, Scudamour waits to meet his rewon bride. In the 1596 conclusion, no one waits, but the triumph has occurred in spite of the deferment of reunion.

Britomart has progressed from the tapestries of Malecasta's castle through those of the house of Busirane and has effaced their images, destroyed their force, as firmly as Guyon destroyed the Bower of Bliss; she has moved from her own involvement in Malecasta's mistaken view of her to a selfless defense of Amoret, whose rescue represents little definite progress in her search for Artegall. Taken as a man in the earlier episode, she is now a woman acting out the part of a man so that she may rescue a woman subjected to the images created by a man.

A choice or resolution of the two endings of Book III, whether we want to call one happy (1590) or the other without closure (1596), does not answer the question that Book III poses. In terms of Britomart's narrative, the book is complete with either of its endings. With the original ending of 1590, Spenser announces an epithalamic triumph to his Legend of Chastity. In 1596, he projects further complications to the adventures of Scudamour and Amoret, complications returned to in Books IV and V; yet he does not renege on the triumph of Britomart in those last cantos of Book III.

Nonetheless, Britomart has as limited a victory as Redcrosse over the Dragon, as Guyon and the Palmer over Acrasia, as Artegall in his freeing Irena, as Calidore in his binding the Blatant Beast. All these are limited victories, in that the subject to which Spenser addresses himself cannot be objectified or brought to closure, not at least until we come to the closure of *The Faerie Queene* in the canto 'unperfite,' those two stanzas at the end of the *Cantos of Mutabilitie* where he throws his whole poetic endeavor up to that totally demolishing Being, who would efface all our false images. Spenser knew that his treatment of love under the guise of chastity would not be superseded because it presented an image of the process of living virtue as complete as the image of Adam and Eve, 'with wandring step and slow,' walking out of the closure of *Paradise Lost* into a complicity with the lives of all readers. That complicity may be in part authorial intention and in part the broad intellectual and emotional issues already in the reader from nonliterary sources, which are struck into action and light by the images projected by the poem. Milton manages to enclose his Adam and Eve within his poem, yet directs them, doggedly, toward the latter-day workaday world we know. Spenser never gives such finality, such suspension, but poises his images between a literary completeness and the knowledge that any literary victory would be merely verbal in a real world that must fight daily for those same victories.

THOMAS P. ROCHE, JR

Bednarz 1983; Bennett 1932; Bennett 1942; Berger 1960–1; Berger 1969a; Berger 1969b; Berger 1971; Brill 1971; Gilbert 1947; Hieatt 1962; Hieatt 1975a; Roche 1964.

The Faerie Queene, Book IV

introduction: analogical coherence The Legend of Friendship initiates the second half of the present *Faerie Queene* by introducing Ate – strife – the evil genius of the poem's social installment. But Ate is a Janus-figure, and Book IV also looks back to Book III, the narratives of which it extends, recycles, updates, culminates, or prolongs, and the happy ending of which it begins by deferring. The last canto begins by lamenting the poet's having undertaken an endless work; but since it presents the second, social half of the poem's central duplex on love, Book IV actually supplies major evidence of closure in the poem overall: it balances Book III as the second installment will balance the first. Nonetheless, Book III's happy ending is never explicitly restored: thus Book IV represents to us the fact that *The Faerie Queene* as a whole realizes only half of the poet's stated intention, and that the second installment often fulfills objectives and expectations projected from the first in merely intentional form. Book IV implies a deflationary critique of those expectations: where the narrative of the first installment was ambitiously prophetic – reformist, expansionistic, and desirous – that of the second is rueful, dilatory, retrospective, double-minded, and self-neutralizing. In Book I Redcrosse recovered Eden, but in Book VI one doubts whether Calidore saves Arcadia or destroys it.

Stories begun in III are dilated in IV, and even beyond. However, the two independent stories in IV – those of Triamond and Amyas – are begun and ended within a much shorter compass than that of the legend as a whole. These two stories are grafted onto a more extended narrative where characters intercept many of the notably chronic figures of the poem (Duessa, Satyrane, Arthur, Amoret, Belphoebe), as if the exclusive groupings of close friends were in need of further socializing. In the second of the double-couple stories Arthur will intervene on behalf of each of the four principals, and in IV more of the poem's characters cross with each other, and with the poem's dynastic heroes and their proxies, than in any other book. Thus Arthur's original introduction into the poem's heroic personnel, through his befriending of Redcrosse, also introduces the image of a 'golden chaine' linking both the virtues and virtuous men's hearts, and mutualizing their endeavors (I ix 1). In IV the chain is recognized as the work of Concord (i 30).

The network of Book IV's narration illustrates that 'Friendshippe is a vertue, or joyneth wyth vertue ... [It] is none other thyng, but a perfect consent of al thinges' (W. Baldwin ed 1557, 4.5). Thus this legend answers a traditional question – Is friendship a virtue in its own right? – by promoting relatedness as this virtue's distinguishing quality. A marriage-union of the virtues must take place in the ideally integrated personage the poem sets out to fashion, and in no other legend are so many marriages contracted, whether or not they are finished. With its plurality of heroic protagonists, congenial alliances among the worthy characters, and sharing of prominence, Book IV projects the consensus of the virtuous and the virtue of consensus. Canto xi varies the formula of the other legends: while it celebrates no victory over any antagonist other than the bride's own previous reluctance, the marriage of Thames and Medway becomes a triumph of consensus. And a triumph of repletion – or closure – over its own riverlike dilation and open-endedness.

An episode-by-episode comparison between *FQ* III and IV can show a running analogy between the legends for sexual and social love, which exhibit similar internal contiguities. But a sort of contagion across the parts of a Renaissance analogy tends to draw them closer together in a process of mutual emulation. Book IV is not only similar to III, but contiguous with it as its continuation. Yet Book IV can tell the same story differently, not proleptically but retrospectively. Book IV can know the two books' analogy, or reflect it. Book IV suggests analogies for *The Faerie Queene*'s analogies, friendship itself principal among them.

The most notable analogical friendship in Book IV – that of Cambell and Triamond – is consolidated by means of an archetypal marriage of convenience in the Renaissance sense of the term: each marries the other's sister, thus affirming the likeness of things pre-likened by the sharing of boundaries or adjacency. Plato's *Timaeus* (32B-C) says that a double mean analogizes and proportions the four elements and promotes the spirit of friendship in the body of the world; Spenser's four characters are held together in their tetradic relationship by the double bond of matrimony and friendship, even while it holds them apart from the tautologies and redundancies of homosexuality, incest, promiscuity, and self-love. The marriage quaternion converts the illicit attractions into permissible attachments, by means of the four factors of sameness and difference of sex, and propinquity and compatibility of blood (see *tetrads). The resultant combinations are twinship (same sex, same blood), friendship (same sex, different blood), kinship (different sex, same blood), and wedlock (different sex, different blood). The world of Triamond is united by sympathy between twins, emulation between friends, convenience or adjacency between kin, and analogy between each character as the spouse of the friend's sibling of the opposite sex. Cambina resorts to magic to conclude the contest between Triamond and Cambell, but her name makes her a 'combiner' or 'exchanger': Agape's daughter, Triamond's sister, and Cambell's potential wife, three in one person. Her magic is the art of supplying the deficient element in the combinations of nature: 'to work magic is nothing other than to marry the world' (Pico della Mirandola *Conclusions on Magic* no 13).

As combination expresses agreement in the first quaternion (Triamond et al), substitution expresses likeness in the second (Amyas et al). The appearances of the two squires agree to such a degree that Poeana herself can scarcely be undeceived, as to 'whether whether weare' (ix 10). A substitution motif runs throughout the legend. The false or unstable friends Blandamour and Paridell are paired with 'two companions of like qualities' (i 32) – and like divisiveness. Neither knight can win the love of the biblical helpmeet, 'a fellow for your ayd' (33). Paridell substitutes for Blandamour in challenging Scudamour, and wishes himself in Blandamour's place with the false Florimell rather than with the Duessan paramour Blandamour has lent him. Meanwhile, Duessa and Ate confuse us with their apparent interchangeability in the legend's initial mock-tetrad. Britomart substitutes her female identity for her male one at the castle of couples; she converts from a knight for Amoret to an Amoret for a knight. The Hag in the cave of Lust substitutes sexually for Aemylia. Cambell and Triamond fight in each other's arms on the second day of Satyrane's tournament. Corflambo's corpse substitutes for Corflambo, which allows him to die to Placidas and Poeana on different occasions. In the death-and-substitution pattern of the Pri-Di-Triamond story, the brothers' friendship does not so much prevail over death (*pace* x 27.7–9), as survive collectively the extinction always implicit in individuality. Self-sacrifice proves conservative here, for it endows the trust provided by Agape for the group. Poena's affection obtains a new lease on life for Amyas, owing to his identical substitute's capacity to reciprocate and to conserve an otherwise promiscuous combination.

the tale told by storytelling *FQ* IV renews the narrative of *FQ* III. The received nature of much of the story in the later book results in an apperception of relatedness: to the story told in the earlier book, to its own telling, to its teller. Stories in Book IV define themselves as unfinished, continuing, long to tell, needing to be perfected or retold. And characters define themselves as having a story that wants relating, as they want or need friends or relations.

Spenser shows great virtuosity in making storytelling so much of his story. Some stories get repeated merely to tell us where the poet last left off. Other stories require their being shared with otherwise uninformed characters. Britomart reports to Scudamour her loss of Amoret in IV vi; as if merely for the pity of rehearing this, Spenser repeats the story at the opening of the next canto. (The sequence would make more sense if the poet were renewing the story of Florimell, from the same canto in Book III, as he is in IV xii.) Aemylia tells Amoret her story, to bring Amoret up to date on the place in which Amoret now finds herself. Later she relates it to Belphoebe 'at large' (vii 34) – and later still Amoret and Aemylia 'told all' of it to Arthur (viii 21). Sclaunder then takes occasion blatantly to misinterpret the sympathetic relation in question. At the insistence of the receptive Britomart, Scudamour takes the story of his own relation to Amoret back to its inception at the Temple of Venus, in the next canto (x). This canto is the poem's only case of a hero's educational experience at his house or sacred site being recounted either retrospectively or in the first person. A virtual apotheosis of recounting and retailing follows, in the literal form of Spenser's counting and tallying the catalogue of guests mustered by the nuptials of Thames and Medway.

Virtually every canto in Book IV contains some reference to its own telling or to the previous telling of its story. Ate's den is a great collection of strife-tales, and storytelling is not only enlarged upon by Book IV but also perplexed. At the outset, Amoret has been delivered from Busirane – but to what effect, if she is no longer delivered to Scudamour? The union of the lovers – ecstatic, hermaphroditic, and coital – has been reversed into the sobering discovery that Amoret is an oxymoronic 'virgine wife' (i 6). Womanhood and Belphoebe both 'said no more' regarding Amoret's violation by her protectors (x 55, vii 36); Scudamour's step-by-step courtship of Amoret contrasts with the lurid, Ariostan tale of her wounding by a reckless Timias, yet arrives at the same impasse, as the sequel shows.

Other stories also leave things hanging. Rejected by Belphoebe, an uncouth Timias is unrecognized first by Arthur, then by Belphoebe. Spenser has decomposed a crucial sequence from Ariosto into separate motifs. Belphoebe, like Angelica befriending Medoro, has ministered to the wounded Timias, but not sexually. Timias, like Medoro, has carved his love on the trees, but unavailingly. Arthur, like Orlando, has come to read those trees, but not comprehendingly. And Timias, like Orlando, is grief-crazed by his rejection, but not by jealousy of anything but his former status as a frustrated or emasculated Medoro. Despite its sense of amnesia, lost originals, and inverted roles, the story has not forgotten the sources of action in the *romanzi*: it is as if Timias and Arthur had drunk of the fountain of infatuation, and Belphoebe and the Fairy Queen of the fountain of disdain.

Some stories in Book IV seem deliberately to defeat their own point: any irony at the expense of Timias' or Raleigh's conceits for the Queen as the Cynthian must also be at the expense of Spenser's following his friend's lead. In the story of Cambell and Triamond on the second day of the tournament, Cambell fights for the wounded Triamond in his friend's armor, to save his friend's honor. But Cambell gets into trouble on the field, and Triamond – now in *his* friend's armor – must disregard his wound to rescue his friend – or else to recoup whatever remains of his own reputation, his other 'other self.' Similarly, the substitution of Placidas for Amyas in prison allows for Amyas' temporary enlargement, but the more Poeana is captivated by the more available captive, the more the doubles are endangered by her father. Friends, so to speak, are hostages to their friends, as lovers are to their sensibilities. Marinell's Adonis-like wound is dressed with the 'heavenly food' of nectar in *FQ* III iv 40, treated by a god, reported cured in *FQ* IV xi 7, and yet has made him thrall to his overprotective mother, who brings him to the house of Proteus to see the socializing of the gods. But being mortal, 'He might not with immortall food be fed' (xii 4), an exclusion that leads back to Florimell and the recurrence of his wound.

Stories that discover their own frustration may be compared to stories that tend to become their own refrain. The legend's most distinctive myth, Agape's descent to the underworld, re-enrolls the Fates in the somewhat mindless machinery of copy-making, otherwise a function of Agape's own womb; perpetuation-through-repetition becomes the essential mechanism of the story thereafter. Pri-Di-Triamond must fight Cambell in three incarnations because traditionally only a knight who had prevailed thrice in the lists had proven himself worthy of a lady's love. The tyranny of this fairytale rule of three is extended to Satyrane's tournament, where the pyramiding, triplex structure and descriptions of confrontations are similar. Each day recapitulates, enlarges, and reverses what has previously occurred. The result of Britomart's final improvement upon all preceding records, however, undercuts everyone else's effort, when she rejects the prize, the false Florimell, who thereupon awards herself to Braggadocchio, who is never said to have participated in the tournament at all.

Fate is a mechanism, and apparently the spinning of story after story can become one too. Britomart tends to be the master of her fate in *FQ* IV, and to cut across the more chronic stories to which other characters are addicted: Timias' repeatedly getting himself into trouble, the multiple comebacks of Agape's triplets, the recurring illusion that Amyas and his friends can attain a degree of freedom greater than their limited self-mastery and their straitened circumstances will permit, Marinell's perennial vulnerability to his own delaying development, and the reversals in the fortunes of the Knights of Maidenhead on the field.

The chronic nature of the story in Book IV reminds us that half the cantos end with the narrator's deferring completion of his narration until further occasion. Chaucer's *Squire's Tale* is a prototype, not only because the famous acts of its heroes are nowhere to be found (ii 32), but because the Squire shows few signs of being able to find them (cf 'I sey namoore ... ye gete namoore of me' *CT* V 289, 343). Spenser's project of enlarging upon such a prolix but barren narrator results in a rigidly teleological narrative intending to perfect the Telamond of the title page by blessing his replacement Triamond with the 'perfect love' of his friend's sister and 'a long and happie life' (iii 52). Amyas and his three friends are also finally and 'perfectly compylde' (ix 17). The friends and lovers in Venus' Elysian park there enjoy an 'endlesse happinesse' (x 28) comparable to the 'eternall happinesse' given by Cambina's potion of nepenthe (iii 43–4). Love worked his own perfection as of old (cf *Colin Clout* 805); Love the perfecter perfects these happy endings accordingly.

Yet the happy souls in Elysium would think theirs a 'lesser happinesse' – and the lovers' a greater – if they should 'happen' to behold the scenes that Scudamour sees at the Temple of Venus (x 23). Happiness and unhappiness seem to be things that just happen to happen; thus the frequency in *FQ* IV of happy and unhappy accidents, and of the refrain 'it so befell' and its congeners (i 19, ii 25, iv 1–2, vii 24, viii 50, ix 41, xi 8). Yet the lucky accident of happiness, in the possession of others, may seem their 'lot' (cf vii 14–15; III ii 26, x 4). Happy or unhappy, love is also both a matter of luck, and one's lot. A beautiful woman is a 'lucky lot' (x 4; cf v 25–6); an 'unlucky lot' is a terrible mate like Lust (vii 14) or a Hag (iv 9–10). Lust's own lot, indeed, is a Hag.

Spenser's lovers are typically alloted happy endings, even if one cannot be entirely sure what has happened. An amnesia seems to be enforced upon these endings, like the drink of nepenthe that washes away the memory of former cares at the end of the battle between Cambell and Triamond (iii 48). We forget that Triamond now has only one life left, and that it was not to be long (ii 50). We assume Scudamour will be reunited with Amoret, since he says he now beholds her as he begins his terminal narration of his original quest (x 4; cf 'this' at x 3.3). Yet the narration itself is what preoccupies him, as if it were produced from an ecstatic state in which he beholds Amoret mentally, rather than in the flesh. Instead of this elusive, human union, *FQ* IV offers the conjunction of Thames and Medway, where ambrosia replaces nepenthe as the stuff of immortal bliss (xii 4, xi 46; III iv 40). Since the persons are rivers, theirs is a courtship that is always proceeding, a wedding that never ends, and a marriage continuously consummated in extinction. Book IV surprises its proper end in an unending ending.

Thus Spenser avoids the teleology of earlier legends, which conclude with the successful achievement of a culminating adventure designed to show a virtue achieving its end. He begins by lamenting Amoret's and Florimell's stories ever having been written, and rebegins in his last canto by exclaiming over the 'endlesse worke' he has undertaken in recounting the seas' generations (i 1, xii 1). Just as he must reopen the stories of the imperiled women, he cannot close them: Amoret will not embrace Scudamour, Florimell's story the poet will leave 'to another place ... to be perfected' (xii 35). Unlike Florimell's, Amoret's marriage cannot perfect her story – it being the place from which her story begins – except by reappearing. But this is to return to the scene of trauma and impasse, as in the chronic pattern of a neurosis. Scudamour finds the story painful to recall.

Nonetheless, Spenser uses paradisal images of pleasure for the Temple of Venus itself. Aristotle says that the end of virtue is happiness (*Nicomachean Ethics* 1095A), ideal friendship is long-lasting, and its legend certainly merits a happy ending. Indeed, friendship seems like happiness itself – a reward for virtue – more like virtue's end than a means to some other end. Thus Spenser condenses the quest of Scudamour to the Temple itself, a house of recognition where happiness is the thing there to be recognized. This canto is terminal for the 'legend' of Scudamour, because it is twelve cantos from his introduction in III xi. It is all the *telos* Scudamour properly has: a lover's bliss at his acceptance as a lover, at his being befriended by Venus. Thus the motif of the arming of the knight, a typical point of departure for a knight-errant, stands in place of his fulfillment of the quest. Scudamour claims his shield and his love in the same momentum: the object of his quest is his identity and recognition as a lover. He has no other.

A second telos explicitly reconceived by this legend is also Aristotelian. This is the telos of *physis* or nature, which seeks completeness of form and fulfillment of function. This desire is represented by Agape, who combines purposes of nature and love. She seeks out the Fates on behalf of her sons, 'desirous th'end of all their dayes / To know, and them t'enlarge with long extent' (ii 47): in the first generation of Boccaccio's *Genealogia* (1.3), the Fates are given to nature to assist her in bringing births to completion. Nature would enlarge her progeny – Agape wishes her sons fullness of life. Yet a natural life may be long without being happy: Agape's purpose of prolongation may be perverse.

Similar ambiguities have penetrated to the telos of storytelling itself; the 'hap' or haphazardness of happy endings is in doubt, and even if all worthy things be either ended or begun in love (IV proem 3), it is hard to determine where the extended stories of the Januslike sequel book properly begin and end. Some stories end abruptly; others just tail off inconclusively. Or they are 'long to tell': the tedious havoc of the battle between Triamond and Cambell is a 'Great matter growing of beginning small' (ii 54), requiring a separate canto; the continuation of their story thereafter does not have a real terminus. Scudamour's tale of his winning Amoret 'harder may be ended, then begonne' (x 3), a succinct statement of the very problem Spenser is here finessing, by ending with the tale's beginning. Scudamour echoes what the poet said of strife at the outset: strife 'harder is to end then to begin' (i 20), a moralization of the Virgilian descent into hell (which is easier to get into than out of; cf *Aeneid* 6.126–9). Scudamour compares himself to Orpheus leading Eurydice out of the underworld (x 58), it being easier for him to tell how he got his escutcheon and his start, than to recover Amoret in the end, that is, at the house of Busirane in the 'sequel.' Did he lead her out, or in?

At the opening of the legend, Ate is found breeding the 'seminal reasons' of strife, the words 'which most often end in bloudshed and in warre' (i 25). The lengthening of stories towards confusion might polarize resistance to telling them: Book IV accumulates an impressive number of stories almost too long to tell (see i 24, vii 47, x 3, xi 9, 40, 53, xii 3). Yet even as Florimell complains that her woes have been suffered to go on too long (xii 9), the dilation of her complaint is proving the means to end it, since in the last canto it is at last being heard. The poet's list of rivers has been on her side after all. The maundering in Timias' approaches to Belphoebe makes her wrath subject to 'delay' (viii 1); the ambassadorial dove can then lead her towards Timias 'with slow delay' (viii 11). Conversely, dispatch may curtail development. Diamond, 'disdeigning long delay' (iii 17), thereupon gets himself killed.

The violent engagement between Britomart and Artegall threatens 'to make their loves beginning, their lives end'; they postpone consummation until their marriage (vi 17, 41), but the marriage has been deferred indefinitely.

Thus the problems of storytelling in Book IV are entangled with those of the characters themselves. Chronic stories suggest chronic problems, untellable stories failure of nerve, happy endings obliviousness. Strictly controlled stories suggest greater powers than the self; mechanical or indeterminate stories suggest a devalued personal effectiveness. In Book IV, nonetheless, to have a character is to have a story.

Why should character be particularly 'storied' in a legend of friendship? An important model for *FQ* IV is Chaucer, whose spirit in Spenser – 'through infusion sweete' (ii 34) – analogizes the friendship of the poets to the Pythagorean metempsychosis promoted by Agape among her sons. Spenser's interest in the *Squire's Tale* does indeed have its charitable aspect, and if scenes of weaving can also be scenes of storytelling, then it is logical that the continuation of Chaucer's story dates from Agape's intervening with the Fates to participate in the process of the story's being made up. Spenser begins with the first line of Chaucer's first storyteller, the Squire's father the Knight, and thus suggests the Chaucerian 'knotte why that every tale is toold' (*SqT* 401). Each of Chaucer's narrators is attempting to secure his or her audience, and to make his or her case, as it were, for pardon. This confessional and self-justificatory end is transformed into a more sociable and communicative purpose by *FQ* IV: a story is told to find a sympathetic hearer, and to collate its teller with a commiserative companion 'of' his or her care. An example is Timias with his dove: the dove 'likewise late had lost her dearest love' and is moved with compassion for Timias' analogous plight (viii 3–4). Chaucer's Canacee can feel gentle pity for the distress of the bird in the *Squire's Tale* because 'Nature' has set 'Compassion' in her 'principles,' and because of their 'similitude' (480–7). The bird, in contrast to the Squire, really does have a story to share, and Canacee has the language of the birds. A trace of this skill is retained by Spenser's Canacee (IV ii 35.6), for reasons that make her a natural magician (see below).

Friends share and share alike, if what they share is like stories. Storytelling owes its privileged place in *FQ* IV to this feature of sharedness – shared over some length or in some depth. The feigned friendship that begins and ends upon occasion – the occasion when it is opportune to have a friend – is as much like enmity as friendship, for enmity is also occasioned: Ate and Occasion actually cause some temporary alliances. The truer form of friendship entails a consensus of lives and experience through time. Thus the stories of *FQ* IV are designed to bring the various friends and lovers to a likeness or correspondence through like and parallel stories, such as Marinell's and Florimell's comparable thralldom in the sea. Similarly, a jealous Scudamour is hosted by Care while Amoret fears the worst from her male protectors: Amoret and Scudamour each discover the sex of the alleged offender – Britomart – with some relief. Again, Placidas shares Amyas' imprisonment while the captives Aemylia and Amoret commiserate; Poeana, party to the same story, is imprisoned in her turn, and thus made eligible for their company. Cambell joins Triamond in friendship when Triamond's previously unseen sister emerges from her machine with a power of enchantment comparable to that of Cambell's own sister.

In comparison to these sharers of symmetrical stories, the false and feckless friends have no story, for they have no genuine attachments. Blandamour and Paridell cannot give friendship, only borrow it; the Duessa they share has likewise borrowed her beauty (i 31). Paridell has traded on his Homeric lineage in seducing Malbecco's wife, but he has abandoned this history – and Hellenore herself – before Book IV begins. Blandamour takes his name from a lover (Scudamour) and a flatterer (Blandina). The false friends' attempt to win Amoret implies their need to borrow from Britomart the character they lack. They are used by the false Florimell, whose imposture easily imposes on their vanities. But she finally matches herself with Braggadocchio, because she is loyal, in her fashion, to her own brand of pretentiousness: shallow hearkens unto shallow.

It follows from their being in a legend of friendship that the marriages contracted in *FQ* IV are companionate, and symbolize (in the language used for the Graces as a type of *amicitia*) the attracting, ingratiating, and retaining of a friend. 'Womman sholde be felawe unto man,' as Chaucer's Parson explains the marriage ideal, and in Book IV marriage symbolizes the collateral dilation of one for whom it is not good to be alone (*Parson's Tale* in *CT* X 928; IV i 33.9). Of course it is exactly when the partners are apart that their stories are likeliest to be dilated upon – where there is separation to be abridged. Absence, if it makes the heart grow fonder, also makes it grow more echoic: hence the resonance of stories told in caves, the poignance of names carved on trees, and the distortion of imaginations left in the dark. When the wretched Timias hears the name Belphoebe read back to him, he brightens to kiss the ground she has deserted. Arthur can only guess at the history of the tongue-tied madman who was once his second; but after Britomart is revealed to be a woman, she and Amoret can share their bed and bemoan each other's story all night. Later Amoret will hear Aemylia moaning in the dark, Aemylia will warn Amoret of her 'like ... plight,' and Amoret will pity Aemylia's as her own (vii 10, 19). Care, in contrast, is deaf to Scudamour, the mirror of 'the man ... dismayd with gealous dread' (v 45), as the forsaken, mute Timias is himself the mirror of Care. It is appropriate that *FQ* IV end with a reconstruction of the myth of Echo and Narcissus, the story of the enamoring of Marinell upon his hearing the enthralled Florimell's complaint. Florimell thinks she counts her cares alone, yet she does so 'hoping griefe may lessen being told' (xii 6). A sympathetic echo is awakened in the self-enclosed Marinell. Excluded from the wedding party, he can stumble upon the castaway; hospitalized at length by his mother, he has known captivity. Eventually he too learns to share his story, for until he tells his mother about his new love, he cannot be cured of his old wound.

Even the rivers contribute to telling this story. Their destined descents to the house of Proteus (a 'house' requiring two generations to establish it), the nationality of the various rivers, the etymologizing of their names – all suggest the archival kind of history at the head of a narration, where no story remains apart from layers of ancestral names. But what audience does this roll call design to conscript? Cymoent takes her son to the fecund house of Proteus to behold 'the Seas posterity' – 'the fomy sea' that Venus continuously replenishes and restocks (xii 1–2). Marinell's name suggests he will not marry, and thus the vast progeny of rivers must be a kind of lesson in the purposes of matrimony for one of mortal seed. The proem to Book IV strongly hints that the heirless Queen should read the same lesson, with the pious wish that Cupid touch her with the ambrosial dew that bedecks the bridal and the bride (xi 46).

the legend of friendship as a legend of loneliness Characters in *FQ* IV are defined by having a story to tell, by having a psychic 'sharer' or counterpart, and by having a secret. Insofar as a character's story remains undisclosed, it is the secret of the character, or of the counterpart. Examples are Britomart's sex and her masked vulnerability, Marinell's recurrent wound, the exchanges of Amyas' double in imprisonment, Poeana's secret love of Amyas, Triamond's supply of supplementary lives, Cambell's magical aid from his sister, the occult knowledge possessed by Agape and Canacee and Cambina, Timias' former position at Arthur's side and in Belphoebe's favor, the enthralled Florimell's fancy-free double, and Aemylia's sexual surrogate in the Hag. Scudamour's loneliness behind the shield of love, suggested by his nighttime self at the house of Care, also qualifies as such a secret burden.

These secrets throw into relief the social pretenses and social needs of a self at the very moment when it finds itself thrown upon its own resources. Loneliness works in two ways here: it makes the subject doubt his relatedness to others, even while cutting him off from feelings of personal wholeness or well-being – Aristotle's happiness again. The self-disliking and self-abandoned Timias is only the most extreme example of the isolation that overtakes Scudamour tossing at the house of Care (who looks like Timias), Aemylia moaning in the cave of Lust, Poeana complaining to her rote, and Florimell and Marinell suffering their grievances at the wedding. Loneliness is the self's ill-kept secret.

The heroes of some of the greatest assemblages and social occasions in the poem are unknowns, or are snubbed or disregarded. Public isolation is generally caused by the ignorance of the many in Spenser, but private loneliness as exposed to others is the particular province of Book IV. The events in the cave of Lust offer a deeply pessimistic interpretation of sexual intimacy, for example. Amoret is made aware of her situation in the cave through overhearing Aemylia's groans. Like the darkness in which it takes place, the story works towards defining the potential solitariness of the sex act. The monster's physiognomy is an allegorical anatomization of the male genitalia, and thus the 'wonted sinne' to which Lust yields in the presence of Amoret may well be masturbation, 'spredding over all the flore alone' (vii 20). Amoret flees from the monster like a 'Gelt,' and he is finally and emasculatingly dispatched by the celibate maid Belphoebe: her 'wonted joy' – the chase – is a means 'To banish sloth' (vii 21, 23), idleness being the hotbed of sins of the self-pleasing kind. Given the potentially autogenic character of sexual activity, the ogre's phallic selfishness might well be the wonted sin of much of it. Thus what appears to be a shared situation (Amoret's captivity shared with Aemylia, Aemylia's sexual service supplied by the Hag) in fact allegorizes the part played in coitus by self-regard and fantasy substitutes. Lust can also be the husband in a marriage of male sexual convenience, with the wife the bondslave of a fruitless copulation (the Hag), and the prisoner of sex (Aemylia). Such a union may be what Amoret is shown dreading at the house of Busirane.

A number of sexually restless beds is found in the Legend of Chastity, and the emphasis in its stories is on what leads to the bedroom. That is also the import of Scudamour's taking of Amoret by the hand to lead her from the Temple of Venus in *FQ* IV, as the parallel with Paridell's rape of Hellenore in *FQ* III shows: the original scene of the man leading the woman to the bed is the one enforced on Helen by Aphrodite (*Iliad* 3.380–448), Paris repeating, as it were, his rape. Post-Homeric tradition had Paris abduct Helen from a temple of Venus. But despite this marked allusion to male urgency, the more general force that draws characters toward each other in *FQ* IV is not sexual, but social: the need for companionship.

The proof lies in an essential feature of the male initiatives in *FQ* IV: they are less like the impulse of Paris than the purpose of Menelaus, which is recuperative. Scudamour is less like Paridell raping Hellenore than like Malbecco trying to get her back. Scudamour's recounting of his adventure at the Temple of Venus shows him recovering Amoret virtually: he compares himself to Orpheus, and in one version of that story the singer succeeded only in recovering an image of his lost bride. The missing Florimell sought by the Knights of Maidenhead as a group is recovered in virtual form, first by society and then by Braggadocchio, in the person of her simulacrum. Amyas and Aemylia, and Florimell and Marinell, may be said to get each other back; even Lust and Corflambo try to get their captives back. Agape's sons seek Canacee to strengthen the bond among themselves, and thus recover their original fraternity.

Much in the Temple of Venus canto suggests that Scudamour originally sought Amoret as the prize of male aggressiveness, the boldness that gets him the shield of love at the outset. The courtly love personifications of the figures of Delay, Daunger, and Welcome (suggested by the open gates) imply the knight's success with either a deserving demeanor or the arts of the seducer. A companion for his care and a mother for his children hardly seem his object: he regards his adventure as a test of courage and a proof of worth. But while he is a lover bent on proving himself in his story, he is also a narrator who has suffered remarkable reverses in the eyes of his audience. In his motion toward possession he passes through the paradises of companionate unions, and he never seems to come their way again.

Scudamour's audience includes both Paridell and Britomart, and while each would regard Scudamour as relating an initiation ritual in the form of an adventure, they might have very different interpretations of what was being initiated. Even as Scudamour is rendering his experience as a romance, Paridell may be translating it back into the story of an affair, and Britomart may be translating it forward into the story of a marriage: the hermaphroditic Venus of the Temple may represent the temporary conjunction of a Paridellenore, or the dynastic union of a Britomartegall. Spenser has taken the courtly love imagery of a court of love (where lovers take their suits, as in Lydgate's *Temple of Glas*) and a figurative garden and keep (which the lover seeks to enter, as in the *Romance of the Rose*), and he has boldly digested this imagery to the main stages of the fulfillment of a suitor's licit desires in a marriage contract. He has, in fact, combined the account of Scudamour's courtship with the marriage service itself, as otherwise found in his own *Epithalamion*. The narration accommodates both sides of Scudamour's audience, but in a way that makes each interpretation seem a purposed blind for the other. Thus the shield can represent the lover fixing on an object of desire, or his declaration of his honorable intentions (his 'clame' x 11). Doubt and Delay are the woman's hesitations, or objections of her family (cf 'impediment' 11; impediments are allowed for as late as the marriage service itself). The Gate of Good Desert is her acceptance of his advances or the officializing of the engagement. Daunger is her resistance to further advances or his guarded response or her modesty. The Elysian park is her favors or the festive period of anticipation during the engagement. Concord is her agreement to pursue the affair or the final terms of the marriage contract. The Temple itself is the pleasures of intimacy (eg, hot tubs) or the culmination of the preparations for the wedding. The idol of Venus is the final revelation of the lady's sexuality and the lover's embrace of it, or the 'one flesh' of the marriage service itself. The 'Antheme' might seem to belong to the wedding alone (cf *Epith* 221), though the preceding prayer adapts a pagan hymn (x 44–7; Lucretius *De rerum natura* 1.1–28); it stands in place of either the lover's drive to consummation, or the text of the priest. The bevy of maidens are all virtues, but they can be either the mistress' amorous delay and final reluctance, or the bride's embarrassment and her bridesmaids. Amoret herself can be the act of love or the loveliness of the bride. The matron Womanhood, who lets her go, can be loss of maidenhead in the making of a woman, or the purpose of matrimony in maternity. The taking of Amoret's hand can be coital, or it can be the fulfillment of the promise of the porch of Concord – the giving of the bride's hand in marriage. Venus' amiable laughter can cover both Cupid's tricks and the blessing of the marriage. The comparison to Orpheus can point to the deathly house of Busirane, or to the lover-narrator who has written his own wedding poem (cf *Epith* 16–17). The sequel tells us that Amoret became a wife: thus Scudamour's successful advances make him surprise his own marriage, and transform a courtly lover into a husband.

Since Britomart requests this canto, the double-entendre in question must address her condition. The common factor in the two readings, formal courtship ritual, pertains to either the stages of a seduction (as at Malecasta's castle), or the order of a marriage (as in the masque of Cupid). Scudamour's marriage service presents the bride only upon his marrying her, and she is as suddenly lost. But the engagement of the poem's most fully realized character – Britomart – extends from her fixing upon an object of desire at the opening of *FQ* III to the dynastic union emblematized by Isis and Osiris in V vii. This long engagement is aptly and formally contracted in the center of *FQ* IV: Book IV's ideal of companionate marriage mediates between opposed answers – that is, the ancient and modern ones – to the question of the relative value of ancient friendship and modern love.

Britomart is in large possession of what we mean by a self in this poem, necessarily an engaged self. Book IV implies that the self cannot be wholly itself until it finds its likeness in someone else. Alone, a character like Scudamour is not adequate to himself. A sense of this deficiency – the Penury who begets Eros on Plenty (in Plato *Symposium* 203) – may itself be what an individual would impart to another. In the first installment, a doubtful Redcrosse is impersonated by Hypocrisy, a self-conscious Guyon finds himself checked by an exteriorization of his own Shamefastnesse, and a fascinated Britomart adopts the sex and martial persona of the future lover she sees projected in her father's mirror. In *FQ* IV one finds a natural basis for these various allegories of the self in the self's motion to make itself its own object through another, and thus to recapture and befriend its likeness unselfishly. This re-adequation of the self, when the self can find itself the object of another's love and care, becomes the theme of the final canto. The self-preoccupied Marinell, as Narcissus, is awakened to the frustrated love of Florimell when he hears her repeating, like Echo, the unavailingness of a love of which the object is heedless. Hearing this echo of his own obtuseness, feeling pity for one so despairingly enthralled, his hearkening has made him a reconstructed Echo. Florimell, conversely, is a reconstructed Narcissus – an image under the water of her double above. The acknowledging of her reality by Marinell is the principal condition for dispersing the illusion of the *alter* Florimell's substantiality. When he espouses Florimell, her narcissistic, self-taken, redundant double will evaporate. 'Forgetfull of his owne, that mindes anothers cares,' *FQ* I moralizes the danger of a careless and heedless Redcrosse (v 18); 'Selfe to forget to mind another, is oversight,' Aemylia warns an equally imperiled Amoret (IV vii 10). Yet that is how a Marinell might well 'learne to love, by learning lovers paines to rew' (xii 13). Resisting the solace of a sympathetically attuned Arthur, the tearful Una says 'great griefe will not be tould,' but an aggrieved Florimell will try anyway, 'hoping griefe may lessen being told' (I vii 41, IV xii 6). In *FQ* IV a story is told to dispel a grievous solitude and to quicken in an audience a capacity to mind another's care and loneliness.

love and will, love and necessity in the stories Two stories are unique to Book IV, that of Triamond and company, and that of Amyas and company. The confederation presented by the first allegorizes the basis of union in a common psychic participation; the combinations arrived at by the second allegorize the basis of attraction in something not unlike 'likeness.' Let us begin from the second basis.

According to Plato's *Lysis*, the source of attraction in friendship is neither solely similarity, nor solely dissimilarity. In friendship there is the desire to find one like oneself, yet also to find one whom one can like – that is, one whom one would like to be like, or liked by. Yet one also wants the good of friendship itself, not merely the vicarious supplementation of one's deficiencies through psychic appropriation. In a poet where all of the virtues are like Platonic patterns, the love of virtue common to two friends is easily identified with the appreciation of the virtue of friendship itself. The paramours Blandamour and Paridell do not know what this good is, and are not motivated to possess it. Though a pair, they do not share the 'one patterne seene somewhere' by means of which Amyas and Placidas have been 'made a paragone to be' (IV ix 11).

The sympathizing of two selves leads to their likening, but also to their liking. As likeness is a mean between sameness and difference, so liking is a mean between compulsion and indifference – or between urgency and disability in caring. The story of Amyas and Aemylia begins from two characters doing what they want, which is to elope against the wishes of their friends. The prayer of the lover at the Temple of Venus, that he might not miss his love (x 47), is surely theirs as well. Yet miss they do. Aemylia is carried off by a phallic Lust: not so much lust narrowly meant, as lust in the sense of what an independent member wills or lists to do. Amyas is carried off by Corflambo (heart + torch, the symbol of the rape of Helen), so both lovers are made captive to a concupiscence lurking in their original impulse to elope. Amyas is cast deeper into the situation he lusted to escape, for his captor's daughter, like Aemylia, defies her parent to be with a lover: Poeana does not want to miss her chance for love either.

Both Amyas and Aemylia avoid the unwanted attentions of their captors and preserve a limited self-determination by means of a substitute. The serviceable friend Placidas does duty for Amyas with Poeana; the enslaved Hag serves Lust's lusts in place of Aemylia. The angel of Aemylia's welcome deliverance from this arrangement is Belphoebe, the free-spirited woman not attached to men. The freelance Arthur also intervenes to restore the friends to freedom – freedom of choice included. But it is hard to deny a love that has fallen in with the care of its object, and so Poeana's advances towards Amyas are rewarded with the responsiveness of his look-alike. Poeana, taken captive by Arthur, now resembles those fated to love, rather than those 'led with selfe delight' (i 46). Her penal servitude frees her to join the others in the double marriage that will bind their likes and likenesses together into a society.

When Amoret races from the cave of Lust, Love revolts against Compulsion. The most distinctive allegory of Book IV, if indeed it depends upon Agape's negotiations with the Fates, makes the relation between Love and Necessity a prime consideration. The story takes its beginning from Agape's visit to the realm of Daemogorgon, and so suggests the cosmic dimension of her sons' threefold predestination to love; they all are fated to maternal care, erotic attraction, and fraternal sympathy. Family love, sexual love, and the common love of virtue shared by friends is a progression said to govern the story of Amyas et al (ix 3), but it also suggests the three worlds of the Mond-brothers: Agape's solicitude for her sons, their challenge for the love of Canacee, and the survivor's friendship with Canacee's brother Cambell.

The story makes the three sons three souls. A soul may love a body, or another soul, or an idea; thus the word *soul* appears as a mean in the stanzas describing the three loves. IV ix 2 also speaks of the soul as ruling the earthly mass, in which case the World Soul may be implied, since it rules the world's body. In Plato's *Timaeus* 35, the Demiurge makes the World Soul out of three portions: sameness, otherness, and the existence common to both. Pico della Mirandola, in his *Commentary on a Canzione of Benivieni* 1.10, identifies the three sons of Cronus – who drew the three lots for the rule of sky, sea, and underworld (*Iliad* 15.187–93) – with the three parts of the World Soul: celestial, mundane, and elemental. The soul of Triamond, made up through Agape's twining of the threads of her sons' three lives, is similarly composed of three lots. Thus one could address to Agape Boethius' salute to the Creator-Craftsman: 'Entwining the all-moving Soul through all the harmonious members of the cosmos, you release it as a medium of threefold nature' (*Consolation of Philosophy* 3 metrum 9).

The World Soul in the philosophy of Ficino is also triple: like a vegetal soul, it promotes life in the inanimate; like the animal or sensitive or fiery soul, it provides a mean between body and mind, and is locomotive and spiritous; and, like the rational soul, it is immortal and contains the forms of all things. In scholastic thinking on the human soul, the functions of the two lower souls are assumed by the rational soul at the time of its infusion into the womb: the lower souls in effect die, to prevent the individual from having more than one soul. The brothers' unanimity is charitable as well as psychic, and charity is an infused virtue. Their story, beginning from Agape's womb, illustrates a universalized consensus deriving from an original coinherence. But why is the World Soul charitably derived? Why is Agape a Venus, the mother of three Cupids?

In explaining why Venus is said to have dominion over the three Fates, Ficino's *De amore* 5.11 explains how Love can be said to rule before Necessity. The Orphic Hymn to Venus is cited against the one to Night. In the former, Venus is said to rule the three Fates – all the kinds in sky, earth, and sea – while the latter gives the rule of all things to Necessity. (Pico reconsiders this question – from Plato *Symposium* 195C, 197B – and glances at the Middle Platonic distribution of the three Fates among the three cosmic strata, corresponding to the three Chronides' portions – *Commentary* 2.22; *Heptaplus* 1.3 in ed 1965:89–90.) Agape must negotiate the impasse between Love and Necessity in consulting the Fates: their 'direfull distaffe' is a 'rocke' (ii 48), and hence the adamantine spindle of Plato's Necessity (*Republic* 616C). Agape makes it possible for one son to survive strife by providing for him a kind of charitable trust, whereby individual death is collectively postponed. Duessa's consultation with Night for the purpose of extending the animus of the three Sans-brothers intends a similar untying of 'the chayne of strong necessitee' (I v 25): the agreement whereby Triamond's life is enlarged by twining it with the lives of his twins, trebling their 'thrids' and affiliating their filaments, is a traditional story, whether of predestined dynastic perpetuation or of necromantic reanimation. It not only makes Agape a witch, but Venus a Fate: a late example of the classical type known as Spinning Aphrodite. Nonnus' Harmonia – coeval with the universe – is found by this Aphrodite, weaving a fabric designed with the cosmos; she acknowledges Aphrodite as the one 'at the bidding of whose spirit the unbending Fates do spin their complicated threads' (*Dionysiaca* 41.315–8).

In Boccaccio's *Genealogia* 1.3, the three Fates born of the primal Daemogorgon (invoked upon occasions like Agape's descent to the underworld) preside over development, having Pan or nature for their brother. In Spenser's story the three world-brothers have a protective mother, sister, and future spouse. Each is a 'carefull Fay' (ii 53) promoting one of the three kinds of love: family love in the womb (Agape), amorous love on the field (Canacee), and friendly or virtuous love infused with nepenthe (Cambina). All three are natural magicians with the art 'Of secret things,' the knowledge of 'every secret worke of natures wayes' (ii 44, 35; see *magic). The same occult participations underlie the 'secret feeling' moving Diamond to continue for Priamond, or the 'secret counsels' uniting the final quaternion (iii 14, ii 30). The secret in question is the invisible power of sympathy that draws all things together into one and into love, that is, the 'secret sence' or quasi-magnetic sensitivity of *Colin Clout* 886.

In the realm of Daemogorgon, Agape also beholds 'the secret of the life of man' (ii 49). This means a kind of Renaissance man, who is celebrated for his miraculously containing the forms of all things and making present to the world its unity and connectedness. Writers like Pico in his *Heptaplus* and Leone Ebreo in his *Dialogues on Love* describe man as epitomizing and reflecting a three-storied universe (like the one found in Spenser's *Heavenly Beautie*) by means of his own tripartite nature and soul. Much ingenuity was spent in elucidating analogies between the Neoplatonists' supercelestial, celestial, and mundane spheres, and man the microcosm of all three. Such a project was built into Pico's system: 'Because of the mutual containment of the three worlds, bound by the chains of concord, they all exchange natures as well as names with mutual liberality ... From this principle ... flows the science of all allegorical interpretation': the early Fathers' training in 'the hidden alliances and affinities of all nature' inspired them to symbolize 'the natures of one world by those which they knew corresponded to them in the other worlds' (*Heptaplus* proem 2 in ed 1965:78–9). Pico ends this work (pp 173–4) saying the three confederated worlds of the macrocosm should be copied by the microcosm so that we may likewise be united in mutual charity – in these lights an Agape might well prevail in a vale of ontogenesis.

The depths Agape penetrates are also figured by the places confining Amoret and Florimell. In the cave of Lust Amoret cannot tell up from down, and in the Stygian darkness of Proteus' cave where day is not divided from night, Florimell thought it all one night (vii 9, xi 4). These increate places remind us of the Daemogorgon's hall in I v 22, where Night 'sawst the secrets of the world unmade.' Yet Florimell sheds light into the realm of Proteus, and Amoret shows kindness in the cave of Lust. In the aboriginal darkness prior to creation in the *Hymne of Love*, the Fate Clotho wakes Cupid and Venus lends him light (63, 73). Yet if Cupid is elder than his own nativity (54), Love is indeed in some sense prior to Necessity. (For the allegory of the three worlds, see Roche 1964:15–31, and for that of Agape and the three Fates and the triple World Soul, see Burchmore 1984. Burchmore cites the Neoplatonic material above extensively and observes the comparable positions of the Fates' distaff, or coven, and Amoret's temple placement, p 52; see below.)

antithetical symbols in a legend of consensus Sympathetic relations are assimilative, yet presuppose antipathetic relations as their shadow and twin. Thus the order of the world imposes on 'contrary dislikes with loved meanes' (*Hymne of Love* 86), but also does the reverse. Accordingly, almost every symbol in *FQ* IV will qualify for an antithetical reading of its manifest implication. This is especially true for the symbols of consensus and concord: Scudamour's half-missed marriage and its happiness, the merely nominal union of Scudamour and Amoret 'both under one name' (x 41), the riotous advent of the peacemaker's Cybelean chariot, the pacification of Artegall's disarmed Mars by Britomart's armed or martial Venus (he must turn to marshalling the Venerean passions she has inflamed), the golden chain of Concord (Gr *harmonia* 'fastening') which is no less the adamantine chain of Necessity or *heimarmene* (Gr 'fate'; the wordplay is ancient), Canacee's narcotic amnesty, and the temple of the goddess of *love*, where *arms* are claimed (as once in Sparta they were retired there, to form the classical image of *Venus armata*: Venus' Spartan shrine was military, like the one where Britomart originally claimed her arms). Symbols of antipathy and discord are equally ambiguous: Ate's garden of strife is a conservatory, and Ate regularly shows up at weddings; Florimell's chastity belt or *zona virginitatis* is provocative and inflammatory, while Care's divisive wedges are otherwise joiners – the pins, in fact, of Horace's goddess Necessity (*Odes* 1.35, 3.24). The etymology of *world* (viii 31) cuts both ways: it 'warre old,' because it waxed worse ('warre') as it aged; and yet, if the name is ancient too, the world was in a state of *werre* (ME 'confusion'), or decrepit, from of old. Biune Venus and schismatic Ate are the same principle in different guises, or vice versa: no matter how effective as poetry, the antithesis between Concord and Discord at IV i 29–30 is rhetorical. Concord enforces her will on Love and Hate alike (x 33), and this commensuration of opposites tells us that although Concord built the Temple of Solomon (x 30), and Discord the tower of Babel (i 22), a great ruin is a great work. This idea haunts the 1596 edition of *The Faerie Queene*, from Book IV on.

Reading *FQ* IV in terms of its own doubleness is complicated by its doubleness with *FQ* III, and the results are not the same. For example, the idol of Venus might originally stand for the idolatry in which lovers are engaged – the crowds before the image of Cupid in *FQ* III xi 49 'oft committed fowle Idolatree.' Such idolatry controls the three major story lines in *FQ* III's second half: the witch, on behalf of her smitten son, literally idolizes Florimell; Malbecco closets up Hellenore on the analogy of the idol of his money (x 14), and while he voyeuristically watches, the satyrs worship her as if she were the classical 'Helen of the Tree' (Theocritus Idyl 18, Pausanius 3.15.3); Busirane's house enshrines the love idol in question, where the dragon is transfixed in the eye and Amoret through the heart. These fixations also metamorphose the ladies' frustrated and fantastical suitors: Proteus changes form to impose on Florimell, Malbecco is scapegoated and dematerialized in pursuit of Hellenore, and the love-smitten gods in Busirane's tapestry are bestialized and materialized.

In the second half of Book IV, the governing image of evil fixation and possession is progressively dispelled: Belphoebe transfixes a devouring Lust through the throat; Arthur stuns Corflambo – who fixes on his victims with basilisk-like eyes – with his Medusan shield; Scudamour, armed with a shield showing Cupid 'with his killing bow / And cruell shafts' (x 55), fixes his eye on Venus and obtains her favorable response; and a hearkening Marinell's hardness melts with ruth, anticipating the dissolution of the idol of Florimell. Thus when Venus smiles on Scudamour's suit, she ceases to be an idol. She now symbolizes the living presence of lovers to each other in their mutual embrace and responsiveness. Yet these terms are taken from the original ending of *FQ* III, and not from the complementary scenes one might cite from *FQ* IV.

Scudamour's penetration to the altar of Venus to lay claim to Amoret in the name of love and desire – placed at the center of the last four cantos – can be compared to the penetration of Agape to the primal scene of cosmogenesis to enlarge her sons' lives in the name of charity and mutual love, which is placed at the center of the first four cantos. Each of these two scenes, in turn, finds a quizzical or somewhat antithetical counterpart elsewhere in its own half of the legend. The scene where Venus favors the claim of Scudamour may be contrasted with the scene in which Belphoebe is revolted by Timias' violation of Amoret and which turns Timias into the picture of Care. Womanhood let Scudamour take Amoret, 'And said no more' (x 55), but Maidenhead, in the person of the shocked Belphoebe, flies from the scene of her twin Amoret's desecration by Timias as if it were her own: 'Is this the faith, she said, and said no more' (vii 36). The comparable scene for the one in which Agape beholds the work around the spindle of the Fates is the scene in which Scudamour beholds the work around the anvil of Care: both scenes have cosmogonic backdrops, and the cosmic adamantine spindle of Necessity in the one scene is comparable to the cosmic iron wedges (pins) of Necessity in the other. Agape, Amoret, Scudamour, and Timias all care, but – antithetically – they are victims of care as well. Thus Amoret's wound may be given on the sacred altar of

Venus, but also in the savage wilds. While showing great love, Agape also joins the Fates in Care's manufacturing of anxiety.

Evidence of a quasi-Timaeic artifex can be found throughout *FQ* IV. The joiners and separators on Care's 'Andvile' (v 36) are the labors of a demiurge, and so is the workmanship of Cambina's chariot, Florimell's girdle, and Venus' tabernacle. The nodal knot on Cambina's caduceus is both conjugal and cosmic, like the bond honored by Florimell's girdle: nature itself is traditionally bound by such a bond. The Cybelean chariot is the vehicle of the cosmos, and its charioteer strikes her universal peace from a kind of universal machine. The noise of Care's smithy cannot wholly drown out what its numbers and proportions convey, the mathematical and therapeutic harmonics of Pythagorean-Platonic world-building.

To maintain the service of the Great Goddess in Book IV, Scudamour must rob the church; to consummate his marriage, he must sanctify a sacrilege. The mysterious glassy substance of Venus' altar is scarce to be understood (x 39), but it is not altogether insubstantial: it is hymeneal (Nohrnberg 1976:477–8). The most complex of Book IV's antithetically coherent symbols, maidenhead is an inheritance from the Legend of Chastity, where it was treated like a maternally cherished child, as in Belphoebe's protégée-like virginity. But in Book IV, maidenhead is treated like a critical node in the artifact of the cosmos – a cosmos subject to wear and tear. Florimell's girdle is now an enshrined relic; it can tear asunder; it was forged by Venus' cuckolded husband Vulcan. In the very canto where we learn these things (v), a Vulcanlike Care – with diamond-rending force – beats out the wedges of divisive thoughts with hammers of jealousy. How different from the cherishing of Belphoebe's fresh flowering maidenhood in the same canto of Book III!

At the juncture of the two legends, Britomart as *Cinxia Juno* – the patroness of the wedding night – undoes the virgin knot otherwise untied by the Roman husband in the bridal bed. Amidst effects of breakage, Amoret's wound will close and she will find herself 'perfect hole' (III xii 38). Yet Spenser's new legend is preceded by the poet's own sacrifice of the very hermaphroditic reunion here made possible. The similitude of Amyas and Placidas tells us that the two selves of friendship are better than one. The psychic solidarity of Pri-Di-Triamond tells us that the threefold cord of charity will not easily be broken. But the sundered embrace of Scudamour and Amoret tells us that whatever in Book IV will be made sole or whole must first be rent.

JAMES NOHRNBERG

***The Faerie Queene*, Book v** The Legend of Justice has been for many modern readers the least-liked book of *The Faerie Queene*. Partly because of its subject matter and partly because it comes closest to Spenser's own political experience in Ireland, the book is hard-edged and uncompromising. Justice is a virtue that demands decisions of right and wrong, guilty and not guilty, even in areas of human experience variously shaded in gray. The operations of justice, or at least of the law, are most often negative: it must punish and correct the failures of people to live together in civilized harmony. Spenser spent most of his adult life as a colonial official in a country where these failures were impressive. Justice to such an official, as he clearly tells us through Irenius in the *Vewe of Ireland*, meant the imposition of English law on the recalcitrant Irish population. And justice, being so narrowly conceived, failed utterly in Spenser's experience of Ireland. C.S. Lewis expressed this relation between the life and the poem most strongly: 'Spenser was the instrument of a detestable policy in Ireland, and in his fifth book the wickedness he had shared begins to corrupt his imagination' (1936:349).

In Book v, Spenser's art undergoes a profound crisis, which involves some of his most central poetic impulses: his commitment to the Elizabethan imperium, his desire to direct his poem outward toward history, and his preoccupation with the sources of morality within the individual and society. Elizabeth remains for him the ideal ruler he had first celebrated in the *Aprill* eclogue of *The Shepheardes Calender*. In the proem to *FQ* v, she is the 'Dread Soverayne Goddesse' who as God's vicar presides over her people 'with magnificke might and wondrous wit.' So she appears in Mercilla sitting in judgment over a Duessa who figures Mary, Queen of Scots (ix). But the book portrays a world grown harsh and dangerous in which the accomplishment of justice is by no means certain. The virtue is typically imposed by means of the sword or through the violence of Talus, a Superman-like wish fulfillment who ferrets out and punishes malefactors. (He is an Elizabethan's dream of an as-yet-nonexistent police force; he looks more sinister in a world where he actually exists.) An undercurrent of skepticism about the operations of justice surfaces from time to time, and in the end, Artegall, the 'instrument' of the Queen's justice (v proem II), is himself assailed by Envy, Detraction, and the Blatant Beast.

Such a tainting of Artegall's victory suggests doubt in the poet's mind about the course of Elizabeth's judgment of her own officers. Spenser's Irish experience did not give him confidence that justice would be done to the instruments of justice, and whether or not he quite intends us to see it this way, we are left with this impression. *Vewe*, which Spenser wrote shortly after completing the second three books of his heroic poem, expresses explicit doubts about the efficacy of English law to bring order and justice to his adopted home. There Irenius asserts that English law, though good in itself, has no positive effect and sometimes indeed works unintended evil. Only massive military power, he believes, would be effective in bringing order to the country. This melancholy conclusion must have been lurking in the poet's mind as he created Talus and showed his relationship to Artegall as the instrument of Elizabethan justice. Though Artegall's subordinate, Talus often seems the truly effective partner.

The proem, which is the longest and most elaborate in the poem, betrays some of this ambivalence about contemporary justice and law. Spenser at first goes against his usual practice of finding the virtue in question dazzlingly embodied in his Queen. The first four stanzas insist that a cosmic and moral entropy has caused the world to grow 'daily wourse and wourse.' There follows an amusing animated cartoonlike picture of the signs of the zodiac falling one against the other like dominoes until the whole cosmos seems about to grind to a halt. Is this a serious lament about injustice, we wonder, or just an elaborate posturing? In the final stanza, he addresses Elizabeth as 'Dread Soverayne Goddesse' and announces that his subject is her 'great justice praysed over all.' In effect Spenser seems to have it both ways: his subject is the antique ideal of justice, not the present corruption, *and* it is the contemporary justice over which the British Astraea presides. He may want us to expect that his poetic treatment of law and justice will be more abstract and jurisprudential than concerned with the specific operations of justice in the actual world.

But some ambivalence about the subject matter remains in the development of the book. Artegall, like the other knights of the poem, travels through an antique Fairyland populated by giants, monsters, caitiff knights, distressed (and distressing) damsels. But a goodly portion of this population now bears resemblance to situations and events of the contemporary world. A majority of the episodes of the book in fact make at least general reference to actual situations, and in the last five cantos, the historical references actually structure the fiction – to produce what is generally termed historical allegory. In Books I-III, Spenser's practice was to direct his moral allegory toward the contemporary through brief allusions. In the second half of Book v, however, as historical references become more explicit, certain episodes ask to be interpreted according to the events they portray. This creates some thematic difficulty, perhaps the very difficulty Spenser wished to avoid when he spoke in the proem of contemporary justice as 'corrupted sore' (3). Inasmuch as the episodes are designed to reflect contemporary events, the justice portrayed depends on those events. Though the operations of justice in Spenser's day may not necessarily have been corrupted more sorely than in other times, many of them, especially those concerned with Ireland, are not likely to strike a modern reader as unassailable examples of justice. As a consequence, instead of attaining the level of moral and psychological persuasiveness that the poem at its best achieves, some episodes – and among them the climactic ones of the book – assert the problematic, even dubious justice of contemporary political events. The problem lies partly with our reaction to those events, but the poem invites our reaction in its insistence on the justice of particular cases.

These conceptual problems admitted, Book v nevertheless impresses by the clarity of its structure and the inventiveness of many of its episodes. In the opening stanzas of canto i, Spenser links Artegall with Bacchus and Hercules as primordial conquerors of lawlessness who established peace in the East and the West. Artegall's quest assigned by the Fairy Queen (in this, the book agrees with the plan described in the Letter to Raleigh) is to rescue Irena (Gr 'peace') from the 'strong tyrant' Grantorto (Ital 'great wrong'). Since Irena's specific plight has little to do with the action until the last canto (we scarcely hear of her again until the middle of xi), we should see this quest as also figural in meaning: Artegall's role is to preserve the Queen's peace from threatened lawlessness.

Structurally, the book falls into three unequal sections. The first section (cantos i-iv 20) is concerned with illustrating what we call the Common Law. The second (iv 21–vii) explores the limitations of law and the necessity of its being supplemented by equity. The third (viii-xii) demonstrates the role of the Queen's justice beyond the borders of England, in the conflict with Spain in the Netherlands, in Ireland, and in the trial of Mary, Queen of Scots. The thematic movement of the book, then, is outward from the common operations of English law to the place of England in establishing justice among nations.

In the first section of the book, Artegall's adventures comprise five episodes that illustrate in summary fashion the scope of the Common Law. In these episodes, he resembles a traveling justice of the assizes who rides in circuit with his very efficient iron sheriff Talus. On his docket is a mixture of criminal and civil cases, or more properly stated in terms of Elizabethan jurisprudence, crimes against the 'law of reason primary' (mainly crimes against the person, such as murder, battery, breaking of the peace, perjury, deceit) and those against the 'law of reason secondary' (involving property). The first episode, in which Sanglier is convicted of murder, displays the law discovering and punishing the most basic crime against the person. Artegall is shown to be Solomon-like in his judicial wisdom – though we may wonder if it would not be simpler (not to say more legal) if he just took the testimony of the lady who witnessed the crime instead of offering to cut her in two. The next two episodes portray in a general manner contemporary political problems. Pollente (L *pollens* powerful) alludes to the extortionate power of holders of monopolies; in the specific monopoly of the toll bridge, Spenser appears to refer to the abuse of a variety of monopolies on commodities and public facilities such as roads, ferries, and bridges. (The Commons would petition the Queen to end these burdensome monopolies in 1597 and again in 1601.) Pollente's wife, Munera (L 'gifts'), suggests that such power is supported by bribery.

The second episode of canto ii refers to a threat at the other end of the political and social spectrum: the Giant with the scales, who attracts a crowd of common people with his schemes of redistributing wealth and leveling rank, may refer to the radical Anabaptists (see *radicalism). If Spain was the leading military challenge to Elizabethan society, the Christian socialism of the Anabaptists was seen as the dominant philosophical threat, a threat far out of proportion to their actual numbers. The real danger of the Giant's preaching (and of Anabaptist social doctrine) is that it may be put into rebellious practice. The Elizabethan fear of rebellion appears in the fact that Talus does not wait for an order from Artegall before pushing the Giant over the cliff; juridical process yields to force in the face of such a threat.

The next two episodes center on offenses against property. Canto iii, in returning to the story of Florimell and Marinell from Books III and IV, has something of the feel of those earlier books. Artegall's judicial function comes in the second half of the canto when he exposes Braggadocchio for the imposter he is, shows up the false Florimell by confronting her with the true, and restores Guyon's horse, which Braggadocchio had stolen in II iii. A thematic connection between Books II and V occurs when Guyon must moderate Artegall's anger against Braggadocchio, showing the necessity of temperance to the judicial temperament. The first half of canto iv also portrays law dealing with property. Artegall must now venture into admiralty law to decide a case between two brothers, Amidas and Bracidas, who have unwittingly exchanged land for jewels through the action of the sea. He decides the case by applying equally the same legal principle of alluvion to each.

In the second section of the book (cantos iv 21–vii), the narrative becomes less episodic, and we sense an ampler romantic design at work. The influence of Ariosto and Tasso becomes again evident, and the poem now appears less of a programmatic illustration of law. Perhaps most significantly, the historical dimension is now expressed in terms of romance fiction. In Artegall's captivity by Radigund, the narrative illustrates a limitation of the Common Law and the necessity of its being supplemented by the principle of equity. Radigund, in her beauty and in the separate system of law to which she holds Artegall hostage, alludes to Mary, Queen of Scots, and the perplexity in which she, as a foreign queen, entangled English law. But this meaning unfolds gradually, and only in the allegorical core of the book, when Britomart visits Isis Church and hears the priest interpret her reciprocal relationship to Artegall, do we sense the legal principles at issue. There Artegall is linked to Osiris, the Egyptian god of justice, while Britomart is identified with his wife, Isis, who is said to shade 'That part of Justice, which is Equity' (vii 3).

In Elizabethan jurisprudence, equity was understood as a supplement to the ordinary operations of the Common Law; it emanated from the judicial authority of the monarch and was institutionally embodied in the Court of Chancery. Equity gave relief in the absence of Common Law or in the absence of Common Law jurisdiction. Perhaps because his own sovereign was a woman, Spenser is able to suggest the 'feminine' nature of princely equity: it is the legal principle which complements the masculine rigidity of the Common Law and allows justice to be done in extraordinary situations which elude the Common Law. In theory, equity was not bound to precedent and could consider 'respect of person' in making judgments. Though it could extend mercy where the letter of the law denied it, it is not to be confused with mercy. Equity was in fact invoked in the extraordinary (and not finally merciful) trial of the Queen of Scots. Elizabeth required that Parliament establish a special commission to try Mary and also that it ratify the commission's final judgment. She herself was concerned to emphasize that Mary was not tried by Common Law, and that Mary's princely rank forbade such a proceeding.

What Britomart learns in Isis Church concerns her own immediate history and her typological role as ancestor and prefigurement of Elizabeth. As the embodiment of princely equity, she alone can save the justiciar who is the usual instrument for maintaining the Queen's peace in the extraordinary situation of his imprisonment by another princess. When we compare this episode to the later allegorizing of Mary's trial in the trial of Duessa at Mercilla's court, we notice that the combat of Britomart and Radigund not only looks more like an episode in a romance epic but also places the typological figures for Elizabeth and Mary on an equal footing. Not a pathetic defendant like Duessa, Radigund more nearly catches the proud defiance of the artful Queen of Scots. The combat also portrays more aptly the ferocity and dangers of the twenty-year duel between the two queens. After the publication of the second half of *The Faerie Queene*, James VI of Scotland (later James I of England), Mary's son, expressed to Elizabeth his distress over the portrayal of his mother in Duessa and asked for Spenser's punishment. But there is nothing he could object to in Radigund. Spenser has Britomart end the struggle as Elizabeth ended hers with Mary: she strikes off the head of a still proud and defiant rival. Radigund's complex femininity in comparison with Britomart's gives the cantos the greatest imaginative interest in the book, and in the historical dimension, she stands as a worthy portrayal of Elizabeth's most dangerous competitor for rule. We may also sense how that contemporary conflict stands just behind the numerous contests of female power in the poem. Not only does the battle between Britomart and Radigund gesture toward contemporary history but it also climaxes the polarities of Una and Duessa,

Belphoebe and Acrasia, Britomart and Malecasta, Cambina and Ate, and the two Florimells.

One subsidiary episode in these cantos also suggests Britomart's typological relation to Elizabeth. In canto vi, she takes shelter in the castle of Dolon (Gr 'fraud, deceit'), a knight 'Well shot in yeares' (19). While there she narrowly escapes death or captivity in the middle of the night when the bed in which she was to sleep suddenly drops into a lower chamber. Talus then routs a band of armed men who attempt to ambush her. The incident appears to reflect the numerous plots against Elizabeth's life connected with Mary's pretensions to the English throne, including one to blow up her bedchamber. Dolon's age and the fact that he lives a 'little wide by West' may indicate that Philip II is shadowed.

Having vindicated the workings of British justice in the domestic sphere, the poem opens out in its third section (cantos viii-xii) to assert its international role. Artegall is joined in canto viii by Arthur, and the two manifest British power against foreign injustice. By bringing Arthur to the titular knight's aid at this point, Spenser follows the structural pattern he established in the first two books and, with certain differences, in Book IV. But Arthur's role here differs significantly from that in the earlier books. As the representative of some higher or integrative virtue, he had there rescued the knights in their moment of greatest need; here he teams up with Artegall more as an equal. (Artegall's name, Art-egal, may indeed express this equality with Arthur.) Britomart has already performed the usual Arthurian role in rescuing her knight from Radigund's housework and restoring his manly dignity.

The episodes in this final section of the poem show ingenuity, but the conceptual design becomes problematic. Much of the difficulty lies with Spenser's desire to represent and justify England's foreign policy. The episodes are now constructed to reflect actual situations and events, not to allude to them from within an independently conceived romance world. The result is large-scale historical allegory for the first time in the poem. Unlike those of the first four cantos, these episodes do not appear to be tied together through the development of an idea about law or justice; only the reference to international politics provides thematic connection. In fact, the *idea* of justice is not advanced at all. Except at the trial of Duessa, Artegall and Arthur do not judge cases or arbitrate right and wrong. Instead, they both take on Talus' function and become executive forces. Any moral or legal issues, we must assume, are already decided; the injustice of the Souldan, Malengin, Geryoneo, and Grantorto must be taken as a given. Like the sheriff in a western, Artegall and Arthur face tactical problems, not legal or moral ones.

Arthur's victory over the Souldan and Adicia illustrates both the strengths and weaknesses of this section of the book. The Souldan's historical reference is clear from the start. As a mighty foe devoid of faith and religion who seeks to subvert the crown and life of Mercilla, 'mayden Queene of high renowne' (viii 17), he must refer to Philip II and Spanish power generally. That his wife is named Adicia (Gr 'injustice') delivers a verdict on that power sufficient for Spenser and his contemporaries. Indeed, no further weighing of the Souldan's case seems necessary *because* he refers to the Spanish. If historical reference simplifies the moral issues, the allegory itself is inventive. The Souldan's high war chariot aptly portrays the turreted Spanish galleons of the Invincible Armada and at the same time cleverly plays on Philip II's emblem of Apollo driving his chariot of the sun toward the west, a reference to the westward advance of his empire. Arthur's removal of the cover from his blinding shield suggests (as in Book I) God's grace protecting England, here in the storm which scattered the Spanish fleet. Instead of Apollo, the Souldan becomes Phaethon, Apollo's son, whose horses flew out of control when he attempted to drive his father's chariot. Like the scattered Armada, the Souldan is torn apart and left in pieces on the battlefield.

Similar allegorical inventiveness is evident with Malengin (guile) in canto ix. Malengin, who changes his shape like Proteus in the *Odyssey*, portrays the shiftiness of the Irish guerrillas who effectively eluded the English forces hunting them. In stanza 10, Spenser assigns him the 'glib,' the long bushy style of hair worn by Irish men, and the rugged cloak which doubled as bed and blanket for sleeping outdoors (both are mentioned in *Vewe*, eg, *Var Prose* p 99). His final capture and destruction by Talus represents Spenser's fondest wish for his adopted homeland. The episode is grounded on the reader's presumed agreement about Malengin's villainy, and no attempt is made to persuade us of Mercilla's case against him.

The final half of canto ix contains what looks like another allegorical core of Book V. If jurisprudential issues predominate in Isis Church, the court of Mercilla in canto ix may be understood as the political core of the book. Britomart shadows Elizabeth's legal role as the ground of equity; Mercilla is the clearest representation in the entire poem of the Queen as center of authority and object of veneration. Iconically, the two allegorical cores are connected: in Isis Church, the image of the goddess had stood controlling a crocodile beneath one foot; Mercilla has the heraldic British lion under her feet. In each case, the animal suggests the source of power and the necessity of firm control over it. The court of Mercilla gives the appearance of wanting to tie together various strains of the allegory. Her name leads us to suppose that here mercy is reconciled with justice. Her attendants suggest a compendium of the virtues leading to beneficent rule. The picture of Mercilla enthroned in her court makes us expect some judgment to show the union of mercy and justice and the resulting political harmony.

What Spenser gives us, however, is a close allegorization of the trial of Mary, Queen of Scots. The Radigund episode, curiously, has not laid the issue of Mary to rest, and the poem returns to it to justify further Elizabeth's proceedings against her. The result illustrates one difficulty with historical allegory. Thematically, this allegorical core leads the reader one way, while the historical element pulls in quite another direction. For whatever the trial of Mary was, its conclusion was not a notable reconciliation of justice with mercy. Rather than draw back from history to pursue his apparent thematic intentions, Spenser gives us much of the ambivalence and difficulty which beset the actual trial, including Elizabeth's own vacillation about Mary's sentence. When he must acknowledge the execution that was finally carried out, he does so in so oblique a way as to suggest something like embarrassment: after three stanzas at the beginning of canto x praising Mercilla's mercy, we learn that 'strong constraint' forced her to some unspecified action ('thereto') that required her to pay last honors to Duessa's corpse. The allegorical core stubs its toe on the politics of the actual world.

The Geryoneo and Burbon episodes similarly show the poem growing closer and closer to actual history. With Geryoneo, as with Duessa, Spenser doubles back to give us another portrayal of one of Elizabeth's enemies. Geryon was a triple-bodied Spanish monster slain by Hercules, and his son's similar triplicity refers to the three parts of Spain's empire. Like the Souldan, then, Geryoneo refers to Philip II and Spanish aggression. The oppressed damsel is now called Belge, and her seventeen sons are the provinces of the Low Countries. Arthur's aid to her portrays the military aid to the Protestant cities which was sent by Elizabeth after the mid-1580s. Though the historical focus has changed from aggression against England directly in the Armada to aggression against a neighbor, the narrative pattern remains similar: Arthur rescues a symbolic damsel from a tyrannical monster – or rather two monsters, since the Souldan's Adicia is now doubled by the monster of the Inquisition.

In the brief story of Burbon's discarding of his shield in order to win back Flourdelis, the poem comes down once again on the side of historical fact, and thematic purpose falters. Burbon refers to Henri de Navarre (Henri IV), who gave up his Protestantism to take the throne of France ('Paris is well worth a Mass' is the cynical *mot* attributed to him). In the allegory, Burbon discards his shield, claiming it has won him more enemies than friends. But when Artegall scolds him for this, he ignores the rebuke and enlists his aid in rescuing Flourdelis. Artegall seems to forget about the discarded shield and complies. So, too, Elizabeth rebuked Henri for his recantation of Protestantism but did not break her agreement to aid him. When Flourdelis is recovered, Artegall lectures her about her faithlessness, but Burbon, still shieldless, eagerly takes her up onto his horse and rides off. If there is a moral to this, it must be that you listen politely to someone like Artegall, then do the politic thing. This is rather Henri's lesson – and history's – and not, we assume, Spenser's.

In the argument to the final canto, we see evidence of some last-minute revision of the book. The verses refer to Burbon and his shield, though the episode actually appears in canto xi. Spenser evidently transferred it there from canto xii, making canto xi unusually long, perhaps because he was adding other material to canto xii. If so, the melancholy conclusion to the book, in which Envy, Detraction, and the Blatant Beast assail Artegall, may well have been added while the poem was in press. Artegall's victory over Grantorto and the subsequent attack by the scandalmongering trio have sometimes been thought to reflect the Irish experience of Lord Grey of Wilton, the Lord Deputy whom Spenser served as secretary until the former's disgrace in 1582. But the allegory of Artegall's aid to Burbon and his hasty voyage to save Irena more nearly fit the more recent military experience of Sir John Norris, a leading general who had served in Ireland and the Low Countries in the 1580s and from 1591 to 1594 had campaigned in aid of Henri IV in Brittany. In early 1595, Norris was sent to Ireland to crush the rebellion of the Earl of Tyrone. It may be that Spenser originally wrote of Artegall and Grantorto with Lord Grey in mind, then revised to make the episode reflect the recent and continuing Irish experience of Norris. If the verbal assaults of Envy, Detraction, and the Blatant Beast were last-minute additions, they represent Spenser's fears that what had happened to Grey would also happen to Norris, that Ireland's bogs would swallow yet another bright military reputation. Sir Sergis, the 'aged wight' (xi 37) who presses Artegall's hasty journey to rescue Irena, appears to allegorize someone in particular. If Artegall is identified with Grey, Sergis would very likely be identified with Henry Sidney, Philip Sidney's father, who had been thrice Lord Deputy and advised Grey before his appointment to that office. But certain details make Sir Henry Wallop a more likely candidate for Sergis. Wallop had been concerned with Irish affairs since 1579 and returned there in 1593 as treasurer of the wars to pay and provision troops.

After all the other single combats in Book V, the battle with Grantorto must seem anticlimactic. As a foe, he lacks the pizazz of Radigund and the technological advantages of the Souldan and Geryoneo. Though Spenser is asserting the political ideal nearest his heart, the pacification of Ireland, his imagination seems less than totally engaged in its representation. Except for his name, there is no indication why Grantorto should be the final foe of the knight of law and justice. Not only does the combat itself appear conceptually thin as a portrayal of the role of English law in maintaining justice and social order, but it is offset by a dismal sense of defeat: ten stanzas describe Grantorto and Artegall's victory over him, while eighteen stanzas narrate the efforts of Envy, Detraction, and the Blatant Beast against Artegall.

While we may be disappointed in such a drab and anticlimactic closure and see in the allegorizing of specific political situations a narrowing of poetic vision, there is a certain melancholy honesty in the way the Legend of Justice ends. Having determined to show the workings of justice in the actual world, Spenser follows its twistings and turnings even when they lead him, as in the case of Mercilla and Burbon, away from where he intended to go. If he explicitly asserts the victory of English policy and rule in Ireland, the tone of the episode belies the triumph and makes us suspect that one part of him knew he was whistling in the dark. There is something obsessive in the way the historical allegory keeps returning to certain themes: the justice of Elizabeth's case against Mary, the monstrousness of Spanish power, the necessity of proceeding swiftly and ruthlessly against rebellion in Ireland. It is as if the poet keeps trying to fasten closure on these issues, but cannot, and in one sense the book itself remains unconcluded: Artegall himself will not find justice. If Lewis was right that Spenser's imagination begins to be corrupted in Book V, it is still honest enough to suspect inadequacy in the justice it seeks to portray.

The best defense of Book V finally is its relation to Book VI. Like Books I and II and Books III and IV, V and VI form a pair that mutually illuminate one another. At first their relationship may seem one of antithesis. Book VI contains no historical allegory, or for that matter any serious allusions to history. It has an amplitude and sense of ease that contrast strikingly with Book V. Calidore moves in a world where decisive victories are impossible and somehow irrelevant. But the beginning of the Legend of Courtesy makes clear that Calidore's quest is a continuation of Artegall's, for he pursues the Blatant Beast which robs Artegall of the fruit of his victory. When they meet, Calidore tells Artegall, 'where ye ended have, now I begin / To tread an endlesse trace' (i 6). Certain episodes early in Calidore's quest remind us of moments in Artegall's (particularly VI i of V ii and VI ii of V i). And like Artegall's, Calidore's adventures show him as a version of Hercules; both conform to the Renaissance idea of Hercules as a bringer of civilization. Courtesy complements justice, completing the process of ordering human life and conduct. Calidore's victory will also be inconclusive, but explicitly so, and this in itself seems to acknowledge the implicit incompletion of the victories of justice.

Most importantly, the imaginative freedom of Book VI seems to depend on the rigidity and austerity of Book V. The fact that Spenser directs his poem outward in Book V toward politics, law, and history frees him in Book VI to explore the inwardness of poetry, his own imagination, and more intimate human relationships. In Book V, Ireland is a dangerous land populated by the treacherous guerrillas imaged in Malengin and subject to the tyranny of Grantorto. In Book VI, we see its pastoral side. When that pastoral peace is destroyed by the Brigands in VI x, we understand that the danger and fragility continue. But now we know what Artegall was fighting to preserve throughout his arduous quest.

MICHAEL O'CONNELL

Until recently, Book V has received less critical attention than other books of *The Faerie Queene*. Bennett 1942 discusses the structure of the book and what she sees as the strata of its composition and Spenser's revisions; she also argues for the relevance of Sir John Norris and Sir Henry Wallop to the concluding historical allegory. In the renascence of Spenser studies in the 1960s, Book V is frequently accorded a chapter-length discussion. Hamilton 1961a, K. Williams 1966, Sale 1968, and Freeman 1970 consider the difference between Book V and the earlier books in terms of tone, allegorical character, and poetic success; all find it flawed to a degree. Nelson 1963 reads the book in terms of Renaissance ideas of justice and equity. Cheney 1966 describes the relation of V to VI through the contrasting nature of their heroes.

Three book-length studies from the end of the sixties argue a revisionist assessment of the book. Dunseath 1968, believing Book V a success, describes it as a *Bildungsroman* in which Artegall must successively purge himself of flaws which keep him from achieving his role as a model justiciar. Aptekar 1969 also insists on its success; through an illustrated study of the emblem tradition that stands behind the allegory, she argues that its meaning is frequently ironic. The most challenging of these longer studies is Fletcher 1971, which suggests that Spenser, through an historicist myth, illustrates the development of justice from its prelegal social state to contemporary legal and political structures. The historical allegory was largely neglected in the 1960s. Only Graziani 1964a considers again the relation of the poem to contemporary history with a detailed argument that the legal issues of Elizabeth's decision to execute Mary are portrayed in Isis Church.

More recently, the historical allegory is considered in three studies analyzing it in terms of Spenser's general treatment of history in the poem. O'Connell 1977 finds that the allegorizing of history, rather than allusion to it, subverts the poet's mythmaking by subjecting his prophetic moral intent to the dubiety of history. Cain 1978 similarly sees Spenser's intentions to write praise of Elizabeth undermined by the representation of intrusive political elements. By focusing on the dynastic promises expressed in Britomart and Artegall, Fichter 1982 can claim success for the mythmaking of the book, but he admits Spenser must idealize the history he engages.

***The Faerie Queene*, Book VI** 'The Legend of S. Calidore or of Courtesie' is the last of the completed books of *The Faerie Queene* and occupies the final section of the 1596 edition. As the proem implies, in tone and mood it differs from earlier books of the poem. It links the chivalric mode, in which knights ride out to do battle with adversaries in a cruel and hostile natural world, with the pastoral mode, which emphasizes the beneficence of the natural world and its regenerative powers. The combination of these two modes in a single book raises numerous problems of interpretation. Book VI may be regarded as less overtly allegorical than its predecessors, but its narrative is complex and dense. Its pastoral character is evident not only in the structure of its final episodes but also in the inclusion of figures from folk legend: a wild man, a baby in the jaws of a bear, a group of cannibals, a band of brigands.

Although the central episodes treat other characters, the book as a whole is concerned with Calidore's pursuit of the Blatant Beast, a fierce doglike creature which slanders innocent people and first appears at the end of Book V pursuing Artegall. The first section begins with a meeting of Calidore and Artegall, which resembles meetings between Redcrosse and Guyon at the opening of Book II and Guyon and Britomart at the opening of III. Calidore subsequently encounters Crudor and Briana (canto i), Tristram (ii), Priscilla (ii-iii), and Calepine (iii), at which point he pursues the Blatant Beast, and our attention turns to Calepine and Serena. These two are attacked by the discourteous and cruel Turpine (iii-iv), and rescued by the Salvage Man (iv); Calepine in turn rescues Matilde's baby from a bear (iv). In canto v, the Salvage Man and Serena meet Arthur and Timias; Arthur, accompanied by the Salvage Man, wreaks vengeance on Turpine and his lady Blandina (vi-vii). From here we turn to the story of Mirabella (vii-viii) and to Calepine's rescue of Serena from the cannibals (viii).

The central cantos are followed by the concluding and climactic section of the book, which again starts with the appearance of the Blatant Beast, which Calidore pursues into the community of peaceful shepherds (ix). There he meets and falls in love with the beautiful Pastorella, apparently the daughter of the old shepherd Meliboe. Wandering away from the shepherds, he witnesses the Graces dancing to the music of Colin Clout, Spenser's alter ego (x). On his return, he finds the homes of the shepherds devastated by Brigands, and Pastorella and Meliboe led into captivity. Meliboe is killed in a dispute among the Brigands (xi), but Pastorella is rescued by Calidore. She turns out to be the long-lost daughter of Sir Bellamour and his lady Claribell, with whom Calidore leaves her (xii) before riding off to capture the Blatant Beast, which nonetheless breaks free again in the final lines of the book.

The difficulties of interpretation arise primarily because the answers to the problems faced by Calidore and Calepine appear to lie in the countryside, away from cities and courts. It is a Hermit who cures Serena and a Salvage Man who rescues Calepine; and it is in the country that Calidore finds Pastorella. The countryside provides a setting for the love of Calepine and Serena, and of Aladine and Priscilla; and there is little sign that the narrator disapproves of their relationships, even though Aladine and Priscilla defy her parents by meeting. The opening of canto i declares that 'Of Court it seemes, men Courtesie doe call,' but much of Book VI seems dedicated to exposing the inadequacy of this etymology since it is outside the court that most of the courtesy in this book is revealed. The Hermit was once a knight, however; Pastorella is a lady; and there is even a hint that the Salvage Man was once a member of courtly society. In short, Spenser is interested in exploring the complex relationship between courtly ideal and courtly reality, for courtesy is 'now so farre from that, which then it was, / That it indeed is nought but forgerie' (proem 5). All too frequently, the creatures of the natural world know more about courtesy than supposedly civilized knights like Crudor or Turpine; and the true courtiers have, for one reason or another, fled a court where corruption rather than courtesy rules. Calidore, his surrogate Calepine, and Arthur are practitioners of a virtue that is valid despite its frequent debasement. They are cast in the role of mediators as they seek to reconcile opposing forces: Priscilla and her parents, Crudor and the knightly ideal, even Mirabella and her captors. Their mediation stands in contrast to the clear-cut oppositions of Book I.

The appearance of Colin Clout in the midst of the dance of the Graces indicates a strongly self-reflexive element in Book VI. The proem, in which the speaker addresses his readers on the beauties and variety of the imaginative world of his poem, begins the process. It comes close to equating the world of the poem and the kingdom of Fairyland. Certainly several of the characters and episodes offer illustrations of the workings of poetic language. Mirabella's fault lies in mistakenly applying the metaphors of love poetry literally; and the Salvage Nation of cannibals indulges in a similar misprision of the 'blason' in praise of female anatomy, in effect making what ought to be a love poem into a menu. But such critiques of the uses of poetic language are not new in this poem. They are apparent throughout, particularly in Book III in the episodes of Malecasta and her knights early in the book, and of Busirane at its conclusion. If this uneasiness about the role of poetic language (an uneasiness shared by many of Spenser's generation and later, notably by Sidney and Herbert) runs all through the poem, it becomes central only in Book VI, where the presence of Colin Clout brings the courtly ideal rooted in action into rude confrontation with the poetic ideal associated with contemplation. Can the poet really have an effect on the world of affairs? Can the world of affairs possibly learn from poetry? Has the former so corrupted the latter as to render it impotent? The notion of a binary ontology, in which metaphor and reality interact successfully because the one is clearly distinguishable from the other, or in which court and country complement one another because the two are clear and distinct yet interactive, or in which poetry and politics occupy clearly defined and carefully separated domains nonetheless conjoined – this notion is called into question. Also called into question are the chivalric ideal and the quest structure, since they too depend on clear distinctions between good and evil, responsibility and truancy, that seem harder and harder to sustain in this book of shifting values and problematic choices. Hence Book VI becomes, at least in part, a critique of *The Faerie Queene* itself.

It is appropriate that the villain here is a creature which slanders the right-living and the decent. The Blatant Beast, with its 'thousand tongs empight,' uses language to wound and destroy: it is opposed both to men of action and to poets. Calidore's quest is, at least in part, the redemption of poetic language.

Accompanying this extension of the concerns of the poem is a broadening of the definition of courtesy. An unwary reader might be led to believe that courtesy is no more than Calidore's 'gentlenesse of spright ... manners mylde ... comely guize ... And gracious speach' displayed along with his military and athletic prowess (i 2). The virtue is not so much graceful behavior as it is 'the ground, / And roote of civill conversation' (i 1), by which Spenser appears to mean social harmony, the quality which makes possible the organization of society itself. He borrows the term 'civill conversation' from Stefano Guazzo, author in 1574 of a courtesy book of that title, translated into English in the 1580s. In the proem, we are presented with an image of a well-functioning court, in which 'Lords and Ladies' circle in dancelike fashion around their sovereign. The image is reminiscent of contemporary representations of rulers as the earth around which the planets revolve, or as the *primum mobile*. 'Grace,' then, is the quality that makes possible the harmonious functioning of the state, which is itself a microcosmic representation of universal harmony or a mirror of nature.

Book VI in relation to the other books The first three books of *The Faerie Queene* are concerned with the private virtues related to the right conduct of the individual: holiness, temperance, and chastity. Books IV-VI deal with social or public virtues related to the interaction of the individual with others in friendship, justice, and courtesy. The six books may be seen to form pairs: holiness and temperance dealing with the proper management of the individual, chastity and friendship with the management of personal relations, and justice and courtesy with the management of society. As Book IV suggests that the chastity of Book III is not possible without the mutual respect and support of friendship, so Book VI suggests that the government of nations requires a kind of social intercourse, a courtesy, which makes possible the structures of justice. Hence the appearance of the Blatant Beast in the concluding episode of Book V, and the meeting of Artegall with Calidore at the beginning of Book VI. Despite being attacked by Envy, Detraction, and the Beast, Artegall as a good judge 'for nought would swerve / From his right course' (V xii 43). Yet it is evident that his assailants can create an untenable political environment for justice (as happened to Lord Grey, the historical figure behind Artegall). Courtesy, or 'civill conversation,' is a prerequisite for justice. The two virtues may also form a pair in the sense that Book VI tempers the severity of Book V: despite the presence of Isis and Mercilla, the emphasis in Book V is on retribution, while in Book VI it falls on reconciliation and rehabilitation (Cheney 1966:176–96).

The meeting of Artegall and Calidore sustains a continuity of purpose among the major figures of the work: as Redcrosse meets Guyon, so Guyon meets Britomart; as Britomart is united with Artegall, so Artegall salutes Calidore. However, the nature of the fiction in Book VI differs profoundly from that in earlier books; there is a certain whimsical quality, with 'repeated touches of realism' and a 'deliberate casualness in Spenser's treatment of narrative and character' (Tonkin 1972:66–7, Berger 1961b:38). The openness and diversity implied in the proem are realized in the treatment of narrative and episode. Notably absent are the personified abstractions of earlier books: the closest we come to them are Despetto, Decetto, and Defetto, the three villains who attack Timias (v 13–22), and Disdain and Scorn who accompany Mirabella. None of these figures engages Calidore himself, and none has the narrative importance of Lust in Book IV or Despair in Book I. Equally absent are the sharp historical and political referents of Book V, in which parallels between episodes in the poem and historical events in Spenser's Europe are obvious and inescapable. Book VI may be regarded as the least allegorical of the books, but it is perhaps more accurate to suggest that the nature of the allegory has changed. Of all the books, it is 'closest to romance with its aura of manifold, mysterious meanings conveyed in a "poetic" context' (Hamilton in *FQ* ed 1977:621; see also K. Williams 1966:190–1); and the 'irreducibly ambiguous' nature of some of its most important passages suggests that the 'ambivalences of romance itself' are the book's true subject (P.A. Parker 1979:105).

At the same time, Book VI suggests a return to Spenser's stated purpose, 'to fashion a gentleman or noble person in vertuous and gentle discipline.' While the curriculum he lays out to that end begins, hardly obviously, with holiness, it is only in Book VI that he focuses on what might be regarded as the obvious virtue in such an effort: courtesy. Although the entire poem has some of the earmarks of a courtesy book, it seems that only after we have been led through the other virtues are we ready to deal with the broad and exalted definition of courtesy presented here. Hence, the six books end where we might have expected them to begin: the poem is cumulative and retrospective as well as linear and progressive. Furthermore, the emphasis in Book VI on Elizabeth's court (as suggested in the proem) makes it a fictionalized mirror of Elizabethan society, while its reprise of so many of the themes and motifs of the literature of its age renders it an epitome of Elizabethan culture. Book VI 'sums up and evaluates the driving purpose of the whole poem' (Tonkin 1972:11); but in some measure, the evaluation undermines the summation.

Book VI as conclusion While many of the concerns of the work as a whole coalesce in Book VI, it ends on a distinctly negative note. In what looks like a typical ending to a pastoral romance, Pastorella is restored to her parents; but the Blatant Beast breaks loose from its bands and 'raungeth through the world againe' (xii 40). We may argue that Book VI is only a way station in a larger enterprise, which Spenser did not live to complete, and that the balance might have been redressed in subsequent books (Lewis 1936:353). Perhaps he intended to end the 1596 edition negatively, much as he ended the 1590 edition positively, by rounding out the story with a few stanzas at the end that could be removed when he was ready to continue. The removal of the four final stanzas would leave the Blatant Beast still in captivity. Furthermore, the ambivalence of the ending of Book VI is not wholly different from that at the end of Book I, where, though the Dragon is slain, Archimago is still at work with his spells. In fact, the figure of Archimago has much in common with the false poet who weaves false and misleading spells out of thin air and subverts the true purpose of poetry.

Yet it is hard to imagine how Spenser might have continued beyond Book VI. The *Cantos of Mutabilitie* deal with a world so radically different from the first six books that their relationship to the poem is questionable. Much of Book VI is concerned with the gap between poetry and action, and its emphasis on pastoral questions the chivalric premise of the poem as a whole: Calidore has been seen as a failed hero unable to understand Colin's poetic vision (Neuse 1968), and the book's ending taken as 'a kind of twilight of the gods' (Nohrnberg 1976:697). Any assumption that Book VI is just one more episode in a larger structure needs to recognize the degree to which the structure itself has been put in doubt. Coupled with this is a certain renunciatory quality, as though Spenser through Colin were bidding farewell to his role of public poet, much as Shakespeare through Prospero seems to bid farewell to the stage. The 1596 poem has been seen, therefore, as giving way to self-doubt, as it 'returns to the blatant beast and to its own dissolution' (Berger 1961b:74).

the principal episodes *Calidore's early adventures* The initial episodes in the book, leading up to the temporary disappearance of Calidore from the action in canto iii, are carefully arranged in rising order of difficulty for Calidore and in descending order of success. The triumphant success of the initial episode is less evident in the later ones, until finally Calidore himself is partial cause of the misfortunes of the characters he meets. These episodes link courtesy with using power properly, avoiding exploitation, and cooperating in the face of misfortune. Where Book V begins with a variant of an Old Testament story, Book VI begins with a variation on a Celtic legend. To win his love, Crudor obliges Briana to capture passing travelers so that she may present him with a mantle lined with 'beards of Knights and locks of Ladies' (i 15). After defeating Crudor, Calidore responds to his pleas for mercy, forces him to give up his cruel condition, and reconciles him to Briana. He thereby breaks a chain of exploitation (Crudor's of Briana, Briana's of travelers) and replaces it with one of obligations based on mutual respect and love.

The episode of Tristram in canto ii is somewhat more compromising for Calidore. Meeting a young man on foot fighting a knight on horseback, he finds that what appears to be an offense against the rules of chivalry (the young man, himself no knight, should not fight with a knight) turns out to be justified: the knight was ill-treating his lady when Tristram came to her rescue. This knight, traveling with his lady in the forest, had come upon another knight and his lady, 'in joyous jolliment / Of their franke loves' (16). Seized with desire, he attacked and wounded the knight, while the lady escaped into the forest. He then proceeded to vent his frustration on his own lady. The story again illustrates the need for 'courteous' behavior of men toward women, and suggests that initial appearances, or 'outward shows,' may belie reality: Tristram's behavior was indeed proper, and his outward appearance (decked in the garments of a woodsman) contrasted with his chivalrous and courteous behavior.

As for the wounded knight, Aladine, Calidore restores him to his father, Aldus. He also escorts the lady, Priscilla, to her parents. But since they disapprove of her liaison with the less nobly born Aladine, Calidore is obliged to tell only part of the story and to take responsibility for slaying the knight killed by Tristram. While his conduct saves a lady from shame, it also involves a compromise with the truth. We witness here a tension between Calidore's championship of love and the rules of society (no dalliance in the forest, no attachments between people of differing rank).

In the next episode, it is Calidore who offends, albeit unwittingly. He interrupts the lovemaking of Calepine and Serena by chancing upon them in the 'covert shade,' and he seeks to rectify what 'was his fortune, not his fault' by engaging Calepine in manly conversation (iii 20–2). But Serena wanders off and, like Proserpina at the hands of Pluto, is seized by the Blatant Beast. Calidore forces the beast to relinquish her and gives chase, leaving her wounded. The episode emphasizes the vulnerability of the individual to chance and misfortune, and the need for courteous conduct towards all. Calidore's neglect of Serena leads to her falling victim to the Beast. Book VI puts repeated emphasis on fortune, 'the pressure of a power that circumscribes and limits the human will' (I.G. MacCaffrey 1976:371–93). Also implied in the episode is the constant risk of scandal that lovers run: the physical attack of the Beast on Serena is a metaphor for an attack on her reputation.

Calepine The central episodes of the book provide a series of examples of courtesy and discourtesy. They begin and end with Serena as victim: initially of the Blatant Beast (iii) and finally of the Salvage Nation (viii). Calepine functions as surrogate for Calidore. By isolating Calidore from the episode with Turpine, Spenser is able to show how low a courteous knight may come as a result of discourtesy and abuse of power, yet also allow his readers to keep their respect for Calidore. As Cali*dore* meets Cru*dor*, so Cal*epine* meets Tur*pine*, a discourteous knight who refuses (despite the pleas of his lady Blandina) to assist Calepine and the wounded Serena, locks them out of his castle, and attacks them the next day. Calepine, who initially challenged Turpine to a duel, is so hounded by him that he must hide behind Serena and finally is desperately wounded. From this abject condition, he and Serena are rescued by a 'salvage man, that never till this houre / Did taste of pittie, neither gentlesse knew' (iv 3). His arrival at this point in the narrative emphasizes that courtesy, rooted in the natural world, 'though it on a lowly stalke doe bowre, / Yet brancheth forth in brave nobilitie' (proem 4).

Although the Salvage Man can find no cure for the wound that the Blatant Beast has inflicted on Serena, he restores Calepine to health. Going forth 'To take the ayre, and heare the thrushes song' (iv 17), Calepine meets a bear with a baby in its mouth, forces it to drop the child and, lacking his sword, kills the beast with a stone. Encumbered with the child, miraculously he meets Matilde lamenting her lack of an heir to protect her and her husband, Sir Bruin, from the ravages of the giant Cormoraunt. The child, according to a prophecy, will 'Be gotten, not begotten' (32). While affording a measure of comedy, this fantastic story also serves a number of narrative and thematic purposes. It demonstrates Calepine's powers of regeneration after being humiliated by Turpine, it again suggests that the natural world may yield gifts of courtesy strong enough to overcome great enemies, and it provides an example of how cooperation can yield miraculous results. As Calepine and Serena were rescued by 'natural' forces, so are Matilde and the dynastic succession.

Calepine cannot find his way back, and Serena and the Salvage Man are left to fend for themselves. The arrival of Arthur in canto v provides a link with earlier books and particularly with the story of Arthur's squire Timias, who is himself an example of a nobleman who takes to the woods out of despair in love, becoming so hirsute and bedraggled that even his own master does not recognize him (IV vii 43). He is later attacked by three enemies, Despetto, Decetto, and Defetto who are aided by the Blatant Beast (VI v 12–21). Since he is wounded, Arthur and the Salvage Man leave him and Serena in the care of a Hermit, a former knight who is skilled both in medicine and in spiritual and moral discipline. It is the latter that Timias and Serena require.

Arthur's revenge on Turpine comes in two stages. The first (VI vi) parallels Turpine's attack on Calepine: he is reduced to hiding behind his lady Blandina. It also parallels Calidore's showing mercy to Crudor: Arthur spares Turpine's life. But here the parallels end: though Crudor, the cruel, ultimately belies his name, Turpine, the base, remains so. In canto vii, he seeks to overcome Arthur by subterfuge, but helped by others, Arthur seizes him and hangs him by his heels (see *baffling).

Serena and Timias meanwhile meet Mirabella, who having scorned many suitors is condemned by Cupid to wander through the world accompanied by Disdain and Scorn until she has 'sav'd so many loves, as she did lose' (vii 37). She is the physical embodiment of the cruel lady of Elizabethan and Italian sonnet sequences (eg, *Amoretti* 10). Her error lies in taking the metaphors of these sonnets quite literally and seeking to act them out; but the attempts of Arthur and Timias to rescue her are also misguided, for her punishment is just. Like Briana and Crudor, she has misused her power and beauty to create disharmony and conflict. Implicit in her story is a critique of the imagery of love poetry, or, rather, a reminder of the fact that metaphor is effective only when it is clearly recognized as such. In a work where *reading* and *interpretation* are all-important, Mirabella is in effect condemned as a poor 'reader.'

Equally poor 'readers' are the Salvage Nation of cannibals, who attack Serena after she has run away from Timias' fight with Disdain and Scorn (viii). Their preparations to consume her are a parodic, gastronomic representation of Petrarchan imagery that builds on the Mirabella episode. These two examples of abuse, redolent with literary echoes and antecedents, are a reminder of the parlous state of poetic language as well as of courtly behavior. It now remains for Spenser to offer an occasion for regenerating both, in the episode of Pastorella.

the pastoral episode and conclusion With canto ix, Calidore returns, pursuing the Blatant Beast from the court to cities, towns, country, and through farms to 'open fields' where 'the Heardes were keeping of their neat, / And shepheards singing to their flockes' (4). There, he accepts the shepherds' hospitality, and sees Pastorella seated on 'a litle hillocke' and 'Environ'd with a girland, goodly graced, / Of lovely lasses' (8). He is overcome by her beauty and readily accepts Meliboe's offer of lodging. The quest for the Blatant Beast is abandoned.

During his stay among the shepherds, Calidore conducts himself with his wonted courtesy, deferring to Coridon, a manifestly unsuitable rival for Pastorella's love. While here, he comes to Mount Acidale, where he sees three ladies dancing around a fourth figure and surrounded by 'An hundred naked maidens lilly white' as Colin Clout pipes (x 11–12). All disappear when Calidore breaks in, and Colin is left alone. As in the earlier encounter with Calepine and Serena, Calidore apologizes and seeks to make amends by engaging Colin in conversation. What, he asks, was the meaning of this dance? Colin's explanation echoes Renaissance mythographers: the three ladies were the Graces, who present a perfect pattern of courteous and civil behavior, symbolizing the notion of giving and receiving, of reciprocity and support. They are ideal representations of the cooperation that has played so important a role in the book. They are also symbols of the threefold life, the division of experience into the realms of action, contemplation, and pleasure. It was one of these three realms that Paris had to choose in his famous judgment, just as Hercules had to choose between action and pleasure (Panofsky 1930, Tonkin 1972:264–80, Wind 1958). The choice and the judgment are conflated in this complex vision, which presents to Calidore and the reader a central dilemma of the book, in which neither the chivalric choice of action over pleasure nor the pastoral choice of pleasure over action provides an adequate path to courtesy. If Calidore had remained faithful to his quest, he would not have been vouchsafed this vision; but by abandoning or postponing it, he leaves the world vulnerable to the Blatant Beast.

The separation of poet and knight, Colin and Calidore, as the one seeks to communicate to the other the meaning of the vision, is itself symbolic of a widening gap between poetry and politics, contemplation and action. The lady in the center of Colin's vision is not Elizabeth or Gloriana but Colin's own beloved, poised in the center of the dance much as Pastorella was surrounded by a 'girland' of shepherdesses. Colin feels constrained to beg his sovereign's forgiveness; but the incongruity of centering this grand vision of courtesy, the courtly virtue par excellence, on Colin's own mistress will not be lost on the reader. The poem has turned in upon itself.

But it is harmony and reconciliation rather than distinctions and differences that ultimately dominate in this miraculous vision. This is arguably Spenser's supreme statement of order and harmony. Nor do the answers to its meaning lie wholly in the glosses that Colin Clout provides: such glosses are to courtesy as the bare instructions in a courtesy book are to the truly courteous man – and Spenser repeatedly emphasizes in this book that courtesy, while it can be improved by instruction, is something innate and natural. The most arresting characteristic of this vision is the harmonious complexity of its meaning.

Whether, like the house of Holiness for Redcrosse in Book I, Mount Acidale is Calidore's place of education, or whether he is already equipped to bring the Blatant Beast to bay, is never explained in specific terms. Although he does indeed overcome the Beast, dragging it through Fairyland for all to behold, it escapes, and, like some eraser out of Robbe-Grillet, threatens to destroy the poem that has brought it to life. The question that remains is whether Colin's vision, had it been wholly accessible to Calidore, would have enabled him to imprison the Beast forever, or whether, like Orpheus, the poet sings on in spite of his knowledge of loss.

conclusion The initial episodes of Book I have been widely recognized as a lesson in the reading of allegory (eg, by Quilligan 1979:33–42). As the poem progresses, it becomes evident that the education in virtue proposed in the Letter to Raleigh is also – indeed, may be the same as – an education in the correct interpretation of the text. Just as Spenser presents the poem's initial episodes in a rising scale of complexity, so his allegory increases in complexity. As the work progresses, he redefines allegory in a way that goes beyond the simple one-to-one correspondences of medieval allegory to embrace a consciousness of the multivalency of the text (Tonkin 1972–3). His grandest statement, or vision, of this allegory is arguably the dance of the Graces. This dance of a hundred maidens, the Graces in their center, is less easy to describe visually than we at first imagine. Is the lady in the center one of the Graces, and dancing with them, or is she, like Venus in Botticelli's painting (Wind 1958), separate from them? 'Who is the maid in the middle? Pastorella? Elizabeth? Rosalind? Florimell? the Muse? No matter, one name will do for another' (Goldberg 1981:170). These dancing figures seem to symbolize the movement of poetry itself, a whole universe turning on a single point, and the whole conjured up by the piping poet.

Parallels have been discerned between Book I, with its emphasis on the Word and divine grace, and Book VI, which stresses a somewhat different grace and language: 'If Book I ... may be said to present the romance of the gospel, Book VI presents the gospel of romance' (Nohrnberg 1976:676; see also Woods 1977). While it would be a mistake to see Book VI as a kind of secular theology, it is certainly possible to view the Dance of the Graces as representing the power of poetry and its ability to bestow a kind of grace upon humankind (Osgood 1941:69).

Ironically, however, this vision lacks the authority, the universal recognizability of those structures of meaning that Spenser chose for his opening book. Though the established church, the destiny of England, and individual salvation may not seem like the same thing, Spenser was able, in his artful narrative, to hold them together; but any suggestion that the order of poetry, of society, and of the individual are the same comes undone in the separation between Calidore and the poet. The final vision of allegory is a personal rather than a patriotic one; private poet and public poet seem to have parted company.

The reappearance here of Colin Clout, associated with the opening stages of the poet's career and with his role of provincial outsider (as in *Colin Clout*), may come as a surprise. We might speculate that Book VI was being completed while Spenser's involvement with Elizabeth Boyle was beginning. If *Amoretti* and *Epithalamion* are indeed a fictional representation of that relationship, *Amoretti* 80, with its celebration of the completion of six books of *The Faerie Queene* and its request for leave 'to sport my muse and sing my loves sweet praise,' would seem to imply as much. It is in the context of questioning the political effectiveness of humanist learning, rather than in a narrowly autobiographical context, that the personal turn taken in Book VI is particularly interesting. The gap between Calidore's knowledge and Colin's, Calidore's ultimate inability *both* to rescue Pastorella *and* to keep the Blatant Beast permanently chained (he succeeds with the first but not with the second), may be Spenser's way of recognizing that his poet's calling can no longer bridge the personal and the public. Ultimately, Spenser's efforts to make sense of the world around him bring him circling back to himself and his own beloved. The ingenious reader might note that some of this ambivalence has been present since the beginning: in the criticism of the court in Book I, for example, and in Spenser's concern for the relationship of the sexes which he explores with such sensitivity in the middle books. The fact that the hero of Book III is a female knight may imply a criticism of the male-oriented chivalric theme itself, rather than an attempt to make it all-inclusive. It is in Book VI that the adequacy of the chivalric theme is most directly questioned.

Spenser's choice of pastoral as the emergent mode of Book VI may seem less surprising in light of recent criticism which has argued that the pastoral analogy, with its emphasis on hierarchy, on humility, and on gifts freely given, 'was a particularly apt ideological instrument for a government trying to subordinate the wills of all subjects to the will of their Queen' (Montrose 1980:164). Equally important in the context of Book VI is the fact that pastoral offers a device for the exaltation of poetry: the pastoral world may *become* the world of poetry. In some measure this is surely what occurs in Book VI. Glorying in the richness of the literary tradition that he has inherited, Spenser boldly reaches out beyond the already broad confines of dynastic epic to write, also, for himself: 'So Orpheus did for his owne bride, / So I unto my selfe alone will sing' (*Epithalamion* 16–17).

HUMPHREY TONKIN

Berger 1961b; Bernheimer 1952; Blitch 1973; Cain 1978; Cheney 1966; H. Cooper 1977; Gross 1985; Hamilton in *FQ* ed 1977; Horton 1978; Javitch 1978; Lewis 1936; I.G. MacCaffrey 1976; Montrose 1980; Neuse 1968; Nohrnberg 1976; O'Connell 1977; Charles Grosvenor Osgood 1941 *Poetry as a Means of Grace* (Princeton); P.A. Parker 1979; Quilligan 1979; Spenser ed 1965b; Stanley Stewart 1984 'Sir Calidore and "Closure"' *SEL* 24:69–86; Tayler 1964; Humphrey Tonkin 1972; Tonkin 1972–3 'Some Notes on Myth and Allegory in the *Faerie Queene*' *MP* 70:291–301; A. Williams 1967; K. Williams 1966; Wind 1958.

***The Faerie Queene*, Book VII** Read as the seventh and last-published book of *The Faerie Queene*, the *Two Cantos of Mutabilitie* seem problematic: amusing at times, sublime at others, though apparently afterthoughts. They are allegorical, but in an unprecedented manner; climactic in tone and theme, but fragmentary – perhaps only another stage on the way to the twelfth book promised in Spenser's Letter to Raleigh. Yet when read apart from the rest of the poem (as they almost always are at first), the *Cantos* are clear and self-sufficient, among the most moving and accessible of Spenser's allegorical fictions. Both their uncertain relationship to the rest of *The Faerie Queene* and their excellence in themselves are central themes of Spenser scholarship and criticism.

The *Cantos of Mutabilitie* include two cantos (numbered vi and vii) of 55 and 59 stanzas respectively, and a third of only two stanzas (numbered viii), labeled 'unperfite.' They first appear with Books I–VI of *The Faerie Queene* in the 1609 folio edition published by Matthew Lownes. A cautious headnote states that 'both for Forme and Matter, [they] appeare to be parcell of some following Booke of the *Faerie Queene*, under the legend of *Constancie*.' The *Cantos*' two narratives and the prayer in canto viii, while relevant to the idea of constancy, are equally relevant to other virtues and give us no figure comparable to a Redcrosse or a Guyon on whom to center a legend. The numbering of the *Cantos* as vi, vii, and viii remains unexplained, although it has been suggested that eight – the number of baptism or resurrection in numerological lore – was an appropriate place to stop (Fowler 1964:53). The two stanzas of canto viii, which are a moving prayer for eternal rest and divine communion, hardly suggest the label of 'unperfite.' There is no doubt, however, that for form – Spenserian stanzas at the extreme of musicality, and allegorical narrative – and for matter – a characteristic intertwining of the moral with the psychological, and the historical with both – these *Cantos* are indeed 'parcell' of *The Faerie Queene*.

The *Cantos* consist of two narratives and a devotional response to them. The major narrative, serious but with comic undertones, relates Mutabilitie's attempt to displace Jove as ruler of the heavens (vi). Her rebellion ends after the trial of her case and a cryptic judgment by Nature (vii). In the minor narrative (interpolated in vi), Faunus bribes Molanna to help him peep at the nakedness of her mistress, Diana. Unlike the Actaeon of myth, who was changed into a deer and killed by his hounds, Faunus is merely draped in deerskin and exhausted in the chase. The two narratives are linked not only as upstairs-downstairs instances of the violation of order, but as complementary pictures of what is ordered: the vast cosmos and the local countryside.

In manner and materials the *Cantos* recall other parts of *The Faerie Queene* and some of Spenser's earlier works. Spenser formalizes narrative movement and makes argument concrete through pageant, which is his way of pleasing the senses while making fine intellectual distinctions. In the seasonal pageant which is Mutabilitie's 'evidence' of her power, he also employs the motif of the calendar, his method for encompassing human time and for suggesting through the idea of the cycle a spiritual timelessness beyond it. The setting of the *Cantos*, too, is calculated to be not only metonymic but encompassing: planetary vastness for Mutabilitie's incursion, Arlo Hill for Nature's judgment, its woods for Faunus' trespass. The poet gives us not only heaven and earth, but his spiritual home as well as his 'real,' emotional home in Ireland, for Arlo Hill is both a type of Eden and a favorite mountain near Spenser's Kilcolman estate. The action, too, is topical, since in the two narratives the immediate objects of attack are Cynthia and Diana, both of whom are moon goddesses and complimentary poetic surrogates for Queen Elizabeth. At deeper thematic levels, both narratives embody (as does the whole poem) Spenser's master idea of the Creation as a continuing process in which permanence and change are united. The difficulty of this idea is progressively alleviated as one examines the *Cantos* in detail; alleviated, but not entirely dispelled, for intellectual difficulty was thought the garb of wisdom, and without mystery there could be neither faith nor the need for revelation.

Canto vi begins with Mutabilitie's determination to be recognized as governor of the heavens. She invades the Circle of the Moon and demands that Cynthia leave her throne. Fearing the return of Chaos, Jove dispatches Mercury to quell the rebel, but Mutabilitie is immune to his mace. Taking advantage of surprise, she enters an emergency council of the gods and claims Jove's throne by right of her descent from Titan. Like the other gods, Jove is impressed, as much by her beauty as by her boldness, and his rebuke, though firm, is gentle. Mutabilitie appeals for judgment to the God of Nature; reluctantly, Jove agrees to submit to a verdict on Arlo Hill. When the story resumes in canto vii, it is not quite the God of (ie, over) Nature who presides at the assembly of all Creation which gathers to hear the verdict on Arlo Hill. Dame Nature, a vicar of God and a symbol of his creative power, is in the tradition of the goddess Nature in Chaucer's *Parliament of Fowls* and in Alanus de Insulis' *De planctu Naturae* (*The Complaint of Nature*). She is both young and old, sexually ambiguous, solar, leonine, draped in garments like those of the transfigured Christ on Mount Tabor (Matt 17.2) – in short, a figure of mystery and power to whose judgment Mutabilitie submits. Mutabilitie argues her case as a legitimate descendant of Titan, and as acknowledged mistress of change in man and beast and in the four elements of fire, earth, air, and water that constitute the world. She summons a procession of mute witnesses testifying to her power: the four seasons and the twelve months, each of them part of a vignette combining sensuous immediacy, classical allusion, and moral import. The pageant continues with the antithetical figures of Day and Night, and the Hours (Jove's daughters), and ends with Life and Death: all of them apparently embodiments of change. In rebuttal, Jove asserts that although Mutabilitie does achieve changes over the course of time, the gods control Time itself. Mutabilitie's positivist response is that she will not credit a power she cannot see; in any case, she continues, Cynthia and the other planetary gods also change in appearance and in orbit and hence are subject to her power. Nature's judgment, given after a suspenseful pause, is that, deeply considered, nothing is altered from its nature at the Creation; change in time and space is a process of 'dilation' or a progressive unfolding through which the essential qualities of all things are fully realized and revealed. Thus 'over them Change doth not rule and raigne; / But they raigne over change, and doe their states maintaine' (VII vii 58). With this, Mutabilitie's claim is denied and Nature vanishes.

Nuances of meaning will escape any interpretation of Nature's judgment if only because one cannot simplify or fix the complex relationships between the One and the Many. Several points seem clear, however. Nature's judgment attempts not only to reconcile the world of change and the unaltered spirit, but to insist on their distinctness and integrity. The Months of Mutabilitie's pageant demonstrate seasonal change, yet they also undercut the case for change. Not only do they, like the Hours and Day and Night, circle to their beginnings in a stable pattern, but the 'year of grace,' which begins in March with the Annunciation, mirrors the divine redemptive pattern. In short, seasonal change embodies God's unchanging will. But change in time is not presented as illusory; each vignette is distinct and memorable, and also both beautiful and of value. Even Death, though composed of negations, is neither an illusion nor merely the end of something. This is perhaps the central point the *Cantos* make about mutability: change does not put an end to prior states nor is it their goal. Mutability is only the means by which the unchanging essence of things is revealed.

This reconciliation of the One and the Many, here divine intent and temporal change, is the doctrine paralleling Spenser's celebration of life in process; together they constitute the main discursive motif and emotional tone of *The Faerie Queene*. The *Cantos* thus cap and summarize the whole poem. They suggest a reconciliation of opposites in a variety of ways. Both *Canto* narratives begin with violations of order, both end with the co-option – not the destruction – of the violators, and the violations themselves are a testing and subsequent definition of order. The main narrative is a culmination of the calendrical forms glimpsed in Spenser's *Amoretti* and *Epithalamion* and fully realized in his *Shepheardes Calender*, where the theme of grace emerges in the September repentance of Diggon Davie. The zodiac, seen with Mutabilitie's wholly temporal eye, is evidence of the power of temporal change. However, seen with Nature's insight – a spiritual outlook 'natural' to humanity – it is evidence of an eternal, unchanging grace.

The theme of reconciliation is also suggested in Spenser's protean and hermaphroditic figures. Elsewhere in *The Faerie Queene*, he gives us shape-shifting opposites like the evil Archimago and benign Merlin. Mutabilitie is a culmination of such figures, sometimes sponsoring nature's beauty and plenty, at other times championing vicissitudes like the Fall. Therefore, change in itself is ethically problematical unless subject to control. In the *Cantos*, the controlling figure, Nature, has neither the settled but limited character of most of the poem's other symbolic persons – or indeed ourselves – but is a figure in whom change is transcended through a uniting of contraries. Like the Venus seen by Scudamour in IV x 41, she is veiled and of both sexes. One mystery (the veil) shields a further mystery (hermaphroditism), a paradox in which generation requires a uniting of opposing principles. *The Faerie Queene* does not tolerate the extremes of mere flux, exemplified by Proteus in Book IV, or of mere termination, exemplified by the figure of Death in the *Cantos*; their powerlessness is revealed in the continuing processes of nature, which does not employ arbitrary change and which renews all things, but mitigates opposites in reconciliation.

In the comic minor plot (VII vi 38–55), Faunus, a wood god, is overlord of the forest, like the Latin Pan. He promises Molanna the love of Fanchin if she will help him see her mistress Diana bathing. Faunus is discovered when he laughs, 'for great joy of some-what he did spy.' He is taunted and harried by Diana and her maidens, but preserved from death or gelding because the 'Wood-gods breed ... must for ever live.' Faunus informs on Molanna, who is punished by stoning, but, transformed into a stream (the river Behanagh), she joins her beloved Fanchin (the river Funcheon) in his watery bed. The Irish landscape also prospers, for though Diana in anger leaves the Arlo forests to the wolves, the countryside is still rich, the streams teeming with fish.

This episode is charming and light-hearted, but it is related to the weightier main tale by the motif of disorder and indecorum vanquished and subdued to higher ends, and by the motif of an unexpected symbolic reconciliation (the joining of the rivers). Differences in tone are appropriate to differences in meaning. Mutabilitie's story is told in the cool, debunking manner of Lucian's *Dialogues of the Gods*, with Spenser's own addition of moments of lofty beauty; the Faunus episode is a reworking of three stories from Ovid's *Metamorphoses*: Actaeon and Diana, Diana and Callisto, and Alpheus and Arethusa. Both of Spenser's tales are enriched in detail and phrase by classical allusion, typically (as in the Faunus-Actaeon analogy) by Spenser's conscious departure from literary antecedent, both to underline a new meaning and to please the reader with ingenious transformations. The distinctive contribution of the Faunus episode is its topicality, first in its detailed references to the countryside near Spenser's home in Kilcolman, and second in its regret that the 'lands in-dwellers' find it full of wolves and thieves. Clearly Spenser has in mind the Irish uprisings of the 1590s, which were to drive the poet himself back to England after Kilcolman was looted and burned to the ground in 1598.

A date of composition after April 1595 has been urged on the grounds that Spenser possibly knew and used the details of an actual eclipse (Meyer 1983). Whether or not one accepts this argument, the urgency and force of the prayer seem a response not only to perennial religious reflection and to the mutability of Spenser's life, in which political uncertainty and a disappointing career must have been felt at least as keenly as the comforts of a good marriage and undeniable literary achievement. But the question remains: does the prayer's loathing of 'this state of life' and its longing for eternal rest with the 'God of Sabbaoth' represent an orthodox reflection on the Last Things, with an appropriate choice of heavenly salvation over earthly transitoriness, or does it represent Spenser's new distrust of human effort and great quests in the earlier books of his *Faerie Queene*? Read in isolation, the *Cantos* seem to bear out the orthodox view which he had expressed at least as early as *Ruines of Time*, that 'deeds doe die, how ever noblie donne' (400). There is no loathing implied in the world of beauty, mischief, and transcendence Spenser gives us in the *Cantos*. There are, moreover, intellectual parallels – all pointing toward orthodoxy – between the *Cantos* and such antecedent works as Chaucer's *Parliament of Fowls*, Alanus de Insulis' *De planctu* (to both of which Spenser refers), and Boethius' *Consolation of Philosophy*.

In Book VI x, however, Colin Clout (Spenser's sobriquet) pipes to a hundred naked maidens dancing about the Graces and to his own beloved. Until the mountain vision on Arlo Hill, this is the last of a series of ideal visions of reconciliation and fruitfulness that includes the Garden of Adonis, the Temple of Venus, and Isis Church. The Mount Acidale vision reconciles motion and stillness, the actual and the desired; but it vanishes as Calidore approaches. Even though Spenser's visionary moments are fragile and complex, some readers emphasize the growing futility of human enterprise (especially in Book VI) and read the prayer of the *Cantos* as a recantation of the optimistic striving of the whole poem (especially of Books I-IV). This interpretation provokes thought, although it neglects the sunlit assurance of the verdict on Arlo Hill. It does, however, raise again the three questions the answers to which would indeed help us decide finally how the *Cantos of Mutabilitie* relate to the rest of *The Faerie Queene*. When were cantos vi and vii written? Was the prayer written at the same time? What, if anything, had Spenser conceived or written beyond Book VII? Unfortunately, these questions seem unanswerable. Yet this problematic relationship of the *Cantos* to *The Faerie Queene* as a whole only underscores the thematic integrity and artistic completeness that place the *Cantos* among Spenser's highest achievements.

SHELDON P. ZITNER

Berger 1968b; Blissett 1964; Hawkins 1961; Meyer 1983; Nohrnberg 1976; R.N. Ringler 1965–6; Spenser ed 1968; Judah L. Stampfer 1951–2 'The *Cantos of Mutability*: Spenser's Last Testament of Faith' *UTQ* 21:140–56; K. Williams 1952.

The Faerie Queene, children's versions From 1779 to the present, over 30 English-language adaptations of *The Faerie Queene* have been published for children and young adults, including 3 in multiple versions. Of those specifically for children, 26 appeared between 1829 and 1929. These adaptations (like other contemporary children's versions of historical romance, fairy lore, classical myth and legends, and English classics) are often moralizing, bowdlerized, archaic-sounding, and didactic. Spenser ranks with Chaucer and Malory in the number of children's versions written in the period, although adaptations of both Shakespeare and the legends of Greece and Rome are far more numerous.

The dual function of these children's versions of *The Faerie Queene* is stated in most of their introductions or prefaces: to introduce young readers to a work of great literature and to afford moral instruction. Of the authors who preface their work, only six claim to retell Spenser's poem for amusement or story-value alone; all the others stress the beauty and difficulty of the original and the purpose of its moral allegory. The adaptations are essentially non-scholarly; only a few contain notes or a brief glossary, extracts of Spenser's works, or brief biographical information; only one has a bibliography. Clearly, they were intended to precede later study of *The Faerie Queene*, so they complement rather than compete with the many contemporary readers and other school editions, complete with scholarly apparatus, that confirm Spenser's popularity.

Despite this popularity of children's versions of *The Faerie Queene*, and despite the fact that several versions saw more than one edition (some on both sides of the Atlantic), bibliographies of children's literature are curiously silent on this matter, and extant copies are hard to find. Of the 34 versions described in this article, copies of 24 are at the British Library, 14 at the Newberry Library, and 9 at the Library of Congress. Public lending libraries in North America collectively own more copies than universities; Cleveland, New York, and the Free Library of Philadelphia have the most. (Current locations where copies were consulted are indicated in parentheses at the end of each entry.)

The earliest version explicitly for children is Eliza W. Bradburn's *Legends from Spenser's Fairy Queen, for Children* (London 1829). It consists of two dialogues between a mother and three children, the first about Book I, the second about Book II. Bradburn is the first of many nineteenth-century adaptors to stress the moral allegory at the expense of the narrative (Osborne Collection, Toronto Public Library). Seven years later appeared the first American version, *Holiness, or The Legend of St. George: A Tale from Spencer's Faerie Queene, by a Mother* (Boston 1836). Its author, Mrs Elizabeth (Palmer) Peabody, renders Spenser's poem in fairly archaic language without noticeable omissions (Newberry).

In 1846 in the Home Treasury series of 'Felix Summerly' (Sir Henry Cole), a humorless and extremely simplified adaptation of the legends of Redcrosse, Guyon, Artegall, and Calidore appeared, entitled *Tales from Spenser's Faerie Queen* (Westminster 1846). The Preface, signed by a 'Charles Cole' (probably Sir Henry), states that Book III has been omitted because it is 'unsuited to the mind of a child' and IV because it is too complex and interwoven to redact (British Library, Newberry).

Equally simple is *Knights and Enchanters: Three Tales from The Fairie Queen* (Salisbury and London 1873), in which the anonymous author retells the stories of Redcrosse, Guyon, and Britomart, omitting all allusions to anything sexual (British Library).

Presumably disagreeing with Cole concerning Books III and IV, M.H. Towry in *Spenser for Children* (London 1878, 1885) covers Books I through V, untangling III and IV into three separate chapters. This version is the most amusingly bowdlerized: Lust is omitted completely from the parade of Sins, but Error's vomit is described in lavish detail. Each of the five illustrations by Walter J. Morgan is accompanied by an appropriate quotation from Spenser's original (British Library, Newberry).

The Story of the Redcross Knight from Spenser's Faery Queen by R.A.Y. (London and Edinburgh 1885, London and New York 1891) is illustrated anonymously. It has nine chapters in all, with the story of Book I worked into a continuing frame: 'Aunt Alice' tells the story to an eager group of nephews and nieces, who comment on how exciting it is as they go along (British Library, Kent State University).

An obviously popular version was Sophia M. Maclehose's *Tales from Spenser Chosen from The Faerie Queene* (Glasgow 1889). It was reedited in 1890 and 1892, then again in 1893 and 1894 as part of the Macmillan's School Library Series, and finally in 1905 for a different Macmillan series, this time in slightly reduced version (with accompanying questions) as a school text (London and New York 1905). The author chose the eleven self-contained stories she felt were most interesting to children, taking them from all books except II, but making most extensive use of III and IV (British Library all editions, Newberry 1890 only).

In 1897 appeared the first version of all six books, *Stories from The Faerie Queene* by Mary Macleod (London 1897). Like Maclehose's, this adaptation enjoyed great success, being reedited in New York in 1905 and in London in 1908, and also issued in a shortened version. Macleod concentrates on Books I, II, and III, often translating names to explain the allegory. Drawings are by A.G. Walker, introduction by John W. Hales (British Library, Newberry). In 1908, the stories of Redcrosse and Guyon were published separately with Walker's illustrations under the title *The Red Cross Knight and Sir Guyon, from Spenser's Faerie Queene* (London) (British Library).

Two years after Macleod's version first appeared, E. Edwardson published his *Courteous Knight and Other Tales* (Edinburgh and London 1899), drawing on both Spenser and Malory for his seven tales. Three are taken from *The Faerie Queene* ('The Courteous Knight,' 'The Wooing of Canace,' and 'The Treasure House of Mammon'), while one retells *Mother Hubberds Tale* ('The Sham King'). Edwardson tells Calidore's story in nine chapters and includes the procession of seasons from the *Cantos of Mutabilitie* as a dream. This is the only children's version to use the *Cantos* or indeed any of Spenser's poetry other than *The Faerie Queene*. It is illustrated by Robert Hope (British Library).

In 1902 came two more versions of the six complete books of *The Faerie Queene*, one by Edward Brooks and the other by Clara L. Thomson. In *The Story of The Faerie Queene*, illustrated anonymously (Philadelphia 1902, 1903, 1908), Brooks retells the poem in a didactic but not unpleasant tone, rejecting most of Book IV as 'unsuited to young people' and omitting the Calepine sections of VI, as well as Colin's vision. Books I, II, and III occupy over two-thirds of the text (British Library, Columbia University). Thomson's *Tales from The Faerie Queene*, illustrated by Helen Stratton (Shaldon and London 1902), is intended to serve as an introduction to the whole poem, although it offers complete tales only from I and II. Despite its claims to fidelity, it makes the usual omissions: sexual allusions, the religious significance of the Abessa episode, and the Fairy Chronicles (British Library).

Three years later, Andrew Lang published his *Red Romance Book* (London, New York, and Bombay 1905), a collection of fairy tales written by his wife, Leonora Blanche Lang, which includes two stories from *The Faerie Queene*: 'Una and the Lion' and 'How the Red Cross Knight Slew the Dragon.' The first retells (with omissions) the story of Una as found in *FQ* I i-iv; the second, Redcrosse's adventures as they unfold in cantos v-xii. Lang is relatively faithful to Spenser's original narrative and style. She translates many of his phrases and images into the modern idiom but retains the flavor of the original by occasionally using Spenser's own vocabulary. Illustrations, two in color and six in black and white, are by H.J. Ford (British Library).

(See ***Faerie Queene*, children's versions** Fig I.)

Although it offers excerpts from Books I and II, *Una and the Redcrosse Knight, and Other Tales from Spenser's Faery Queene* by N[aomi] G[wladys] Royde-Smith (London and New York 1905, London 1927) is primarily a version of the Legend of Holiness; less than a fifth is devoted to Guyon. About a third of the whole is direct quotation, and the prose is archaic: *eftsoones* and *bethinkings* abound. The four illustrations by T. H[eath] Robinson are up to that illustrator's usual high standard. A reduced version of this text was used for the Temple English Literature Series for Schools (London 1905) (British Library, Cleveland Public Library, Newberry).

Jeanie Lang simplifies and moralizes eight stories that span and rearrange the chronology of Spenser's poem in *Stories from The Faerie Queen, Told to the Children* (London and Edinburgh [1906], New York 1906). Rose Le Quesne provides one uninspired drawing for each tale, four of which come from Books III and IV, two from I, and one each from II and VI. Lang's book appeared in the Told to the Children Series edited by Louey Chisholm in 38 volumes (London and Edinburgh 1905–9) (British Library).

Also in 1906 appeared *The Faery Queene, First Book, Rewritten in Simple Language* by Calvin Dill Wilson (Chicago), in the series Old Tales Retold for Young Readers. Like Lang, Wilson simplifies; but he is more faithful to both Spenser's tone and narrative. He omits the House of Holiness episode but keeps Redcrosse's vision as revealed by a nameless figure obviously based on Contemplation. Ralph Fletcher Seymour is the illustrator (Newberry).

The years 1908–9 saw no fewer than four disparate versions of *The Faerie Queene*. The Reverend Alfred John Church is the author of the anonymously illustrated *The Faery Queen and Her Knights: Stories Retold from Edmund Spenser* (London 1910 [1909], New York 1909). Twice as many pages are devoted to Redcrosse as to any other knight. The language is consciously archaic, and sexual allusions are pointedly avoided: Redcrosse's dreams, 'as to what these were, 'tis best not to tell' (British Library, Cleveland Public). Lawrence H. Dawson's *Stories from The Faerie Queene; Retold from Spenser* (London 1909 and 1910, New York [1910] and 1911) comprises 42 chapters and is illustrated by Gertrude Demain Hammond. One of the most complete children's versions, it ranges in much detail over all six books, giving most space to Book I and least to V. Unlike Church, Dawson makes no attempt to sound archaic (British Library, Newberry). In sharp contrast is R.W. Grace's cloying and condescending *Tales from Spenser* (London 1909 [1908]). Omissions are manifold and some peculiar shifts take place: Lust becomes Quackery, and Arthur is renamed Magnificence. An epilogue reminds the young – male – reader of the knightly virtues and ends with an appeal for him to follow his leader Jesus as the knights followed their Gloriana. The book is illustrated by Helen Kück (British Library).

After Grace's edition, *The Quest of the Red Cross Knight, a Story from Spenser's Faerie Queene* by Mrs F.S. (Henrietta O'Brien) Boas (London 1911) appears refreshingly free of moralizing. It explains difficult words in a glossary and intermingles prose and extracts from the original to draw the young reader to Spenser's poem (British Library).

Similar in intent and tone are Emily Underdown's four versions of Spenser's poem. The first was published two years earlier than Mrs Boas' and was entitled *The Gateway to Spenser: Tales Retold by Emily Underdown from The Faerie Queene of Edmund Spenser* (London 1909). It comprises four sections centering on Redcrosse, Guyon, Britomart, and Calidore. The author adds a marriage and honeymoon to Book I but balances such poetic license with frequent direct quotations from the original. She also provides a simple introduction to the poem. Illustrations are by F.C. Papé. Subsequent editions appeared under different titles and underwent some content changes. The 1912 *Stories from Spenser Retold from The Faerie Queene* (London), listed as anonymous in the British Museum Catalogue, removes all extracts from the original and omits the stories of both Guyon and Britomart as well as the author's introduction. Papé's illustrations remain. The following year came *The Red Crosse Knight: The Story of Una and St. George Retold from Spenser's Faerie Queene* (London 1913), published in the series The Children's Bookcase. As its title suggests, it retells only Book I. Again, there are no direct quotations or introductory materials, but Papé's illustrations are retained. Underdown's final version, *The Approach to Spenser: Prose Tales by E. Underdown* (London 1925), was published as volume 7 in the Teaching of English Series. It returns to the form of the 1911 version but lacks Papé's illustrations. Despite these changes, the redacted text of all four editions remains that of Underdown's original 1911 version. Unlike previous works, in both tone and content it is a faithful rendition that glosses over neither the sexual allusions nor the religious allegory (British Library all editions, Newberry 1911).

By far the most faithful and scholarly adaptation of the period, however, is Minna Steele Smith's *Stories from Spenser* (Cambridge 1919), intended for 'young readers,' older children or young adults. Nothing is omitted from Book I and little from either II or from Britomart's story as recounted in III and IV. The critical apparatus is unusual in including analysis of the original, explanation of the religious and historical as well as moral allegory, appendices, and notes. Also unusual is the replacement of modern illustrations with reproductions of medieval and Renaissance paintings (British Library).

Within the next decade, five more retellings of *The Faerie Queene* appeared, two American and three British. 'Una and the Red Cross Knight' is in Olive Kennon (Beaupré) Miller's *From the Tower Window of My Bookhouse* (Chicago 1921), which was published as Book 5 in The Bookhouse for Children Series and reissued four times (1922, 1932, 1936, 1937). It uses archaic-sounding language and much direct quotation; and it includes all the episodes, even adding a narrative based on the Letter to

Raleigh to explain how Redcrosse's quest began (University of Kansas, Lawrence). Grace Adele Pierce's *The Red Cross Knight and the Legend of Britomart* (New York 1924) is an awkward mix of simple and ornate language with ponderously drawn morals. Henry Pitz provides decorations and pictures (Newberry). In the same year appeared in England *The Knights of The Faerie Queene: Tales Retold from Spenser* by Mary Sturt and E.C. Oakden (London 1924), part of the Kings Treasuries of Literature Series edited by Sir Arthur Quiller-Couch. Of its six chapters, four retell selected stories from Books I-VI while two are original to the authors rather than to Spenser: one elaborates the setting at Gloriana's court, and the other brings Arthur and Gloriana together. The language is very old-fashioned and much is made of the moral allegory (British Library, Harvard University).

Two anonymous retellings end this spate of children's versions. *Una and the Red Cross Knight and Other Legends. Retold from Spenser's Faerie Queene* (London 1928) was published as Number 28 in the Brodie Books. Its prose is a little more felicitous than that of Sturt and Oakden, and the moralizing is done with a lighter touch. The stories of Redcrosse, Britomart, and Cambell, Triamond, and Canacee are quite closely rendered (British Library). This was followed in 1929 by *Stories from The Faerie Queene* (London), published as Number 7 in the Epworth Children's Classics. This version scantily covers half of Book I, ending with Una's meeting with Arthur. R.B. Ogle's illustrations are particularly unattractive, and both author and illustrator have confused Error with the Dragon (British Library).

Since 1929, children's versions have appeared in 1945, 1963, 1980, and 1984. Sister Mary Charitina (Hilburger) in *The Adventures of the Redcrosse Knight* (London and New York 1945, London 1946) offers a pleasant rendition which sometimes stops to moralize and explain, but which omits all anti-Catholicism. Jeanyee Wong illustrates (British Library; University of Colorado, Boulder). *Saint George and the Dragon, Being the Legend of the Red Cross Knight from The Faerie Queene* is the only rendering of Spenser's work in poetry rather than prose (Boston 1963). In adopting varied forms of free verse along with occasional rhymes, Sandol Stoddard Warburg hopes to lead the young reader to Spenser's own 'special and much more beautiful constructions.' The version is very faithful to the original in content, while its tone is pleasantly unpretentious. Drawings are by Pauline Baynes (Chicago Public Library; University of Nebraska, Lincoln). Douglas Hill's *Illustrated Faerie Queene* (New York 1980) is meant for older children or young adults. Although it lacks the *Cantos of Mutabilitie*, it is the only children's version of all six books of Spenser's poem to have appeared since that of Sturt and Oakden in 1924. Its language is plain, retaining Spenser's similes only in descriptions of battles. The book is lavishly illustrated with medieval and Renaissance art captioned to fit the narrative. Margaret Hodges' *Saint George and the Dragon* (Boston and Toronto 1984) is a redaction of Book I that eliminates almost everything but the dragon fight; it is redeemed by Trina Schart Hyman's illustrations, for which it won the Caldecott Award.

Other adaptations not intended especially for children include the early two-volume prose allegory *Prince Arthur: An Allegorical Romance* (London 1779), published anonymously but in fact the work of Alexander Bicknell (British Library, Newberry); a dense prose version by J.E. Rabbeth, *The Story of Spenser's Faerie Queene* (London 1887) (British Library, Newberry); a retelling by Mary E. Litchfield of Britomart's story which excerpts stanzas from Books III, IV, and V, published first as *Spenser's Britomart* (Boston and London 1896) (Case Western Reserve University) and then as *Britomart* (Boston and New York 1906) (Newberry); a British play, *Lady Una and the Red Cross Knight: A Fairy Tale in Three Acts* (London 1806), published anonymously but written by Lady Bradshaw and later republished with three other plays as *Dramas* (Manchester 1826) (British Library, Newberry); and a second British play, *The Red Cross Knight: Scenes from Spenser's Faerie Queene* (London 1913) by William Scott Durrant (British Library).

Finally, two early children's works should be mentioned, although they are imitations, not versions, of *The Faerie Queene*. In 1785, Lucy Peacock published *The Adventure of the Six Princesses of Babylon, in Their Travels to the Temple of Virtue* (London), an allegorical romance modeled on Spenser's poem, as the author admits in her preface. Peacock followed this work, apparently a best-seller in its time, with an equally didactic one inspired by Book II: *The Knight of the Rose* (London 1807), in which the hero's mission is to destroy Excess (British Library, Pierpont Morgan Library).

Most of these children's versions of *The Faerie Queene* are concentrated in the nineteenth and early twentieth centuries and are very much a product of their times. With the exception of Thomson, Maclehose, and Royde-Smith who all edited selections from *The Faerie Queene* for school use, their authors published nothing else on Spenser. A dozen or so, however, were quite prolific writers of children's literature, and were also adaptors of Chaucer, Malory, Shakespeare, and even Milton (eg, Bradburn). What attracted them to Spenser was primarily the moral power of his fiction – for as Ruskin says in Letter 95 of *Fors Clavigera*, his stories were a 'suitable source' for teaching children. In these retellings, Spenser's humor is lost, as is much of his charm (although it is sometimes resupplied by the illustrators). Despite the shift from poetry to prose, some authors have obviously attempted to reproduce some of the beauty of Spenser's lines; but many have simply approximated his diction in that archaic-sounding parlance which Victorian and Edwardian re-creators of the past believed authentic. As for selection, some of the adaptors draw on six books of *The Faerie Queene*, some on several books (I and II are the most popular, III and IV the least), and others on Book I only. Within each individual book, the choice of episodes and characters is very uniform. Omitted or scantily presented are sexual matters (Redcrosse's dream, Lust, Acrasia's Bower, Malecasta), some of the specifically religious or historical topics (Kirkrapine, many of Book V's stories), and many of the figures drawn from mythology. As if to compensate for the omissions, many authors add episodes or characters to Spenser's narrative, the favorite being an elaborate wedding at the end of Book I.

Although it is difficult to assess the popularity enjoyed by these versions in their time, their number suggests they attracted a keen audience. Three went through several editions within a short time (Maclehose, Macleod, Underdown), eight were published on both sides of the Atlantic (R.A.Y., Maclehose, Macleod, Royde-Smith, Jeanie Lang, Church, Dawson, Hilburger), and ten appeared as parts of various popular series. Today, the versions that have survived in the largest number of library copies seem to be those of Maclehose, Andrew Lang, Miller, and Dawson.

BRENDA M. HOSINGTON AND ANNE SHAVER

***The Faerie Queene*, commendatory verses and dedicatory sonnets** (See ed 1912:409–13.) When *FQ* I-III was first published in 1590, some items were printed at the end of the volume that one would expect to appear as prefatory matter: the Letter to Raleigh, the commendatory verses, and the dedicatory sonnets.

Commendatory and dedicatory verses, which are common in Elizabethan works, have different, though related, purposes. Commendatory verses are usually supplied by friends of the author who, with the privilege of a preview, have written a short poem of tribute, saying what a fine work it is and how much they admire it. Their commendations act as seals of approval, indicating that the work has already found favor with discriminating readers who recommend it to a wider audience.

Dedicatory verses are supplied by the author. He offers his work for the approval and protection of an actual or prospective patron, hoping to be suitably rewarded, and in return providing a type of fame, a tribute to the patron's generosity: if the work lives forever, so too will the name of its patron). It was normal for a work to be dedicated to one person, as *The Faerie Queene* is dedicated to Queen Elizabeth on the reverse of its title page. Yet Spenser's poem is remarkable for the number of subsidiary dedications at the end: sixteen to influential figures, and one to all the ladies of the court. Both kinds of verse thus serve as does a modern publisher's puff: they advertise the work, praise it, and associate it with the names of the great.

commendatory verses The 1590 *Faerie Queene* contains seven commendatory verses.

CV 1, 'A Vision upon this conceipt of the *Faery Queene*,' is a sonnet beginning 'Me thought I saw the grave, where *Laura* lay.' *CV 2*, 'Another of the same,' is a sonnet, in poulter's measure, beginning 'The prayse of meaner wits this worke like profit brings' and signed 'W.R.' Both are by Sir Walter Raleigh, whose authorship is confirmed in his son's copy of *The Faerie Queene*, where the poems are marked with a marginal note by Lady Raleigh: 'bothe these of your fathars making.' The first strikingly develops a typically Spenserian vision, picturing Spenser in competition with Petrarch and Homer (poets of love and war) and judging him supreme. It is appropriate that Raleigh heads the list of commenders, for he seems to have been instrumental in encouraging Spenser to come to England to publish the first part of the poem (see *Raleigh). His own credit with the Queen provided Spenser an entree to the court, and perhaps he hoped to gain further favor with the Queen by championing a major poem dedicated to her. Certainly he was a sympathetic reader: his second sonnet shows him alert to the treatment of virtue and beauty, chastity, and temperance in the poem.

CV 3, 'To the learned Shepheard,' is a poem in six six-line stanzas, beginning 'Collyn I see by thy new taken taske,' and signed 'Hobynoll,' the pastoral name of Spenser's friend, Harvey. His poem salutes Spenser's change from pastoral to heroic poetry, and expresses his hope that the Red Cross Knight will be victorious in England 'which thou doest vaile in Type of Faery land.'

CV 4 is an untitled, ten-line poem, beginning 'Fayre *Thamis* streame, that from *Ludds* stately towne,' and signed 'R.S.,' who remains unidentified. He hails Spenser as a 'Bryttane *Orpheus*,' who sings 'deepe conceites ... in *Faeries* deedes.'

CV 5 is an untitled, ten-line poem beginning 'Grave Muses march in triumph and with prayses' and signed 'H.B.,' also unidentified, though he was apparently close enough to the author to play with his name when he refers to him as 'this rare dispenser' of the Muses' graces. He hopes the Queen will reward the poet appropriately, as Augustus did Virgil.

CV 6 is an untitled poem of four six-line stanzas beginning 'When stout *Achilles* heard of *Helens* rape' and signed 'W.L.,' likewise unidentified. This poem emphasizes Spenser's connection with Sidney, who is said to have first penetrated his disguise (a probable reference to *The Shepheardes Calender* which was dedicated to Sidney but not published under Spenser's name) and encouraged him to write something more heroic, in praise of the Queen.

CV 7 is another untitled poem of four six-line stanzas beginning 'To looke upon a worke of rare devise' and signed 'Ignoto,' a common pseudonym (and appropriately still unidentified).

These seven commendatory verses praise the excellence of the work and the author. As well, they remind readers of Spenser's first pastoral work; they provide subsidiary compliments to the Queen, suggesting that, like Augustus, she should reward the poet who celebrates her so finely; they point out Spenser's interest in heroism and in virtue; and they celebrate him as a great national poet, who has at last brought English literature into competition with Homer, Virgil, and Petrarch. In the 1596 and 1609 editions of *The Faerie Queene*, only *CV 1-3* were reprinted (at the end of Book III), but all seven appear again in the 1611–17 folio editions.

dedicatory sonnets Following the commendatory verses in the 1590 edition come the dedicatory sonnets, what Nashe, criticizing Spenser for omitting his patron Amyntas (Lord Strange), calls 'that honourable catalogue of our English *Heroes* ... Whom he as speciall Mirrours singled fourth, / To be the Patrons of his Poetry' (ed 1904–10, 1:5, 243). There are two versions. At first the printer set only ten sonnets on pages 601–5 (sigs 2P6–8): those to Hatton, Essex, Oxford, Northumberland, Ormond, Howard, Grey, Raleigh, Lady Carew, and the Ladies in the Court. At the end of these, he printed 'Finis' and, on page 606 (2P8v), the list of errata. He then stopped the press after a few sheets had been printed and reset the sonnets, adding seven new ones and reusing eight of the original series, lifting the type settings complete and rearranging them in a new order together with the new sonnets. All fifteen sonnets were then printed on a new quarto sheet, with the signature 2Q but no page numbers. The new order has sonnets to Hatton, Burghley, Oxford, Northumberland, Cumberland, Essex, Ormond, Howard, Hunsdon, Grey, Buckhurst, Walsingham, Norris, Raleigh, and the Countess of Pembroke. It seems clear that the printer intended this new sheet to cancel pages 601–4 (2P6–7) of the original printing and to be followed by the last leaf, containing the sonnets to Lady Carew and to the Ladies in the Court (which had not been reprinted), so forming a series of seventeen sonnets. Some copies of 1590 exist in this form, but others have only the first series of ten sonnets, and others have both the ten-sonnet version and the fifteen-sonnet version bound together. The 1611–17 folio editions of Spenser's works reprint only the fifteen sonnets of the revised series.

The seventeen dedicatory sonnets address some important Elizabethan patrons, military and naval heroes, favorites of the Queen, and high officers of state. *DS 1* is to Sir Christopher Hatton (1540–91), a patron of literature, and a favorite of the Queen. As Lord Chancellor, he heads the list in precedence. Spenser hopes that as the works of Ennius (the first Latin epic poet) pleased Scipio Africanus the Elder, and as Virgil pleased Augustus, so *The Faerie Queene* may delight Hatton.

DS 2 is to Sir William Cecil, Lord Burghley, Lord Treasurer and virtual first minister to the Queen, whom Spenser sees as bearing the burden of government like Atlas, who bore the world on his shoulders. Since Burghley seems to have favored serious and useful works, Spenser here emphasizes the morality and seriousness of his poem, in striking contrast, for instance, to the sonnet to Raleigh (*DS 14* below).

DS 3 is to Edward de Vere, seventeenth Earl of Oxford, hereditary Lord Great Chamberlain of England, a poet himself, and a patron and supporter of poets. Spenser suggests that he will find the glory of his own family 'under a shady vele,' but no clear allusion has been identified. Possibly Spenser intended a general shadowing of the Elizabethan nobility rather than anything more specific.

DS 4 is to Henry Percy, ninth Earl of Northumberland (1564–1632). A friend of Raleigh's, he was 'the noble Progeny' of a famous military family, though he was primarily known as the 'Wizard Earl' for his interest in alchemy and other early sciences.

DS 5 is to George Clifford, third Earl of Cumberland (1558–1605), a naval and chivalric figure who became the Queen's official Champion in 1590 and so was responsible for fighting on her behalf at the tilt.

DS 6 is to Robert Devereux, second Earl of Essex, Master of the Horse, and a poet, patron, and soldier. In the 1590s, Spenser seems to have especially sought his patronage. This sonnet hints that Essex will have a part to play in later books of *The Faerie Queene* (see also *Prothalamion).

DS 7 is to Thomas Butler, tenth Earl of Ormond (1531–1614) and Lord Treasurer of Ireland. He had been brought up at the English court and was the most anglicized of the Irish nobility. He was a Boleyn relation of the Queen, and Spenser praises his military prowess and his loyalty. Spenser was with Lord Grey when he visited Ormond's castle at Kilkenny, here described as a refuge of art and learning. *The Faerie Queene* is memorably described as 'wilde fruit,' bred in the 'salvage' and 'wasted' soil of Ireland.

DS 8 is to Charles, Lord Howard of Effingham (1536–1624), the Lord Admiral and also a cousin of the Queen. He was a hero in the defeat of the Armada, 'those huge castles of Castilian king.'

DS 9 is to Sir Henry Carey, first Lord Hunsdon (c 1526–96), Lord Chamberlain and Governor of Berwick. He was the Queen's cousin and trusted servant; his victory in 1570 pacified the 'Northerne rebels.'

DS 10 is to Arthur, fourteenth Lord Grey of Wilton, addressing him in very personal terms as the pillar of the poet's life and 'Patrone of my Muses pupillage.'

DS 11 is to Thomas Sackville, Lord Buckhurst (1536–1608), the Queen's cousin, and influential both as statesman and poet. His 'golden verse' includes *Gorboduc* and the 'Induction' to the *Mirror for Magistrates*.

DS 12 is to Sir Francis Walsingham (c 1532–90), the Queen's principal secretary. Spenser compares him (perhaps hopefully) to Maecenas, the great Roman patron under Augustus.

DS 13 is to Sir John Norris (c 1547–97), Lord President of Munster in Ireland. He fought with the Huguenots in France and with Leicester in the Netherlands, and together with Drake commanded the expedition to Portugal ('the Lusitanian soile') in 1589.

DS 14 is to Sir Walter Raleigh, Captain of the Guard from 1587, sea captain, and poet. Spenser's sonnet is attractively personal, addressing him as 'the sommers Nightingale' and alluding to his poem to Elizabeth, *The Ocean to Cynthia*. Though his star was in decline, Raleigh was still a favorite to be reckoned with in 1590.

The final three sonnets are addressed to women. *DS 15* is to Mary Sidney, Countess of Pembroke. She is here greeted mainly as Sidney's sister, though she was a translator and an important patroness. Spenser writes of her again as Urania in *Colin Clout* and as Clorinda in 'Astrophel.' *DS 16* is addressed to Lady Carew, probably Elizabeth Carey (d 1618), wife of Sir George Carey, son and heir to Lord Hunsdon (see *DS 9*). She was said to be a poet and a translator of Petrarch, and Spenser claimed kinship with her as she was one of the daughters of Sir John Spencer of Althorp. *Muiopotmos* is dedicated to her, and she is praised as Charillis in *Colin Clout*. *DS 17* ends the series with a sonnet to 'all the gratious and beautifull Ladies in the Court.'

Spenser addresses his prospective patrons in rough order of precedence, starting with the high officers of state, then earls, barons, knights, and ladies; for this reason, the introduction of new sonnets required a new order. He appeals to most of those who might be expected to favor a new work such as *The Faerie Queene*. Some had Irish connections, and several were well known for their military or naval prowess in modern crusades such as Leicester's campaign in the Netherlands and the campaign against the Armada. Ten were Knights of the Garter, and a number were prominent performers at the Accession Day tilts – both institutions of chivalry and knighthood not far removed from Spenser's heroic world.

But nearness to and favor with the Queen were important features, and most of those addressed were well placed to advance Spenser's cause with her. Though he needed the support of lesser patrons, he clearly hoped also to impress the Queen and win some recompense for glorifying her in his poem. Her grant to him, in 1591, of an annual pension of £50 may indicate that his hopes were not in vain. L.G. BLACK

The ordering of the dedicatory sonnets is discussed in detail in Johnson 1933:15–16. The aspect of precedence is analyzed in Stillman 1984. Judson 1945 looks at Spenser's relations with some of the named patrons. See also F.B. Williams 1962 and *patronage.

***The Faerie Queene*, geography of** The geography of *The Faerie Queene* includes all the places that compose its setting. Most conspicuous among these is Fairyland, the allegorical, time-inclusive world of chivalric and erotic adventure in which most of the action occurs. But Spenser situates Fairyland within a cosmology stretching from heaven to hell, and within a specific spatial and temporal terrestrial geography in which locations outside Fairyland represent various heroic settings in political history. These include sixth-century Britain (Wales and Cornwall), sixteenth-century Ireland and Western Europe, and the political dimensions of Cleopolis and Mercilla's court. Since Spenser writes a Christian poem, he anchors it in religious history by setting the climax of Book I in a composite theological realm he calls '*Eden* lands' (II i I).

The universe of *The Faerie Queene* includes a horizontal dimension of spatial and temporal political geography and a vertical dimension of topographical and cosmological geography (see *cosmogony, *space, *time). The horizontal – the earthly setting in the fallen world – intersects the vertical – an ontological spectrum extending from heaven to hell – on the plain in Fairyland where much of the action of the poem occurs (see allegorical *places). In general, vertical shifts in the setting – up a mountain, down into a valley or a cave, up or down into a building – reflect changes in the ontological status of the events portrayed, usually accompanied by an increase in allegorical intensity roughly proportional to the distance of a particular setting from the plain. At the upper limit of Fairyland lie what C.S. Lewis named the 'allegorical core[s]' (1936:334), such places as the Mount of Contemplation, Alma's castle, the Garden of Adonis, the Temple of Venus, Isis Church, and Mount Acidale. At the lower limit, their demonic counterparts are such places as the dungeon of Orgoglio; the caves of Error, Despair, Ate, Malengin, and the Brigands; and the houses of Mammon and Busirane. The narrative of Fairyland unfolds between these vertical poles; any place higher than the Mount of Contemplation (I x 55–9) or deeper than the house of Mammon (II vii 56–7) exists in heaven or in hell.

Descent into hell proper – that is, travel across one of the four rivers of Hades – occurs at least once (I v 31–41), and probably on two other occasions (i 39, IV ii 47). The divine world enters the narrative when Redcrosse views the New Jerusalem (I x 55–7) and when an angel descends from its 'silver bowers' to protect Guyon after he faints (II viii 1–2, 5–8). In general, Spenser's heaven is a syncretic creation with Christian, classical, and astrological associations. Venus leaves her 'heavenly hous' to search the earth for Cupid (III vi 12–16); Cymoent ascends 'Unto the shinie heaven' to bring back Apollo to cure Marinell (IV xii 25); Astraea returns to her 'everlasting place' in heaven (as the constellation Virgo) when she retreats from the fallen earth (V i 11); and Mutabilitie travels 'To *Joves* high Palace' (VII vi 7–8, 23).

Spenser ties his poem to national history by making Fairyland part of a larger political geography. From this perspective, Fairyland occupies the political space of Elizabethan England or 'Logris land' (II proem 4, IV xi 36); across the sea to the west is the land of 'fayre *Irena*,' Artegall's destination (V xii 4, 10); across the sea to the east is the land of 'Belge,' where Arthur goes on Mercilla's behalf (x 7, 25); directly to the north, across the Tweed, lies Picteland or Albany (II x 14, IV xi 36, VI xii 4); and to the southwest, across the Dee, the Severn, and the Tamar, lie the Celtic lands of Wales and Cornwall, the Britain of *The Faerie Queene* (II x 14; IV xi 31, 39). From Britain, the Briton knights enter Fairyland: Arthur travels from North Wales (I ix 4, 15) and Britomart from South Wales (III ii 18, iii 62); Artegall and Redcrosse are brought to Fairyland as changelings, Artegall from Cornwall (III iii 26–7) and Redcrosse, the only Saxon hero in the poem, from somewhere in '*Britane* land' (I x 65). The temporal dimension of this political geography allows the poem a multiple relation to history: the time in the Low Countries, France, and Ireland (except in the *Cantos of Mutabilitie*) is the sixteenth century; the time in Britain is the sixth century; and specific historical references tie Cleopolis and Mercilla's court to Elizabethan London. Eden, distanced in space and time, is associated with its traditional setting (I vii 43) and the time of biblical myth.

In Fairyland, where various historical, legendary, and mythical times coexist, past, present, and future must be treated as relative, not absolute, terms. Since Spenser frees Fairyland from the burden of any particular time, he can use it to coordinate the historical circumstances of the epic quests, the political and religious events that occur and are destined to occur in the places that make up the political geography surrounding Fairyland. When his heroes enter Fairyland, they gain access to the whole of history, which enables their quests to move across both time and space. The major quests originate either in sixth-century Britain or in sixteenth-century Cleopolis. At her annual feast in Cleopolis, Gloriana assigns to the Fairy knights, Guyon and Calidore, moral and social quests that take place entirely within Fairyland; to the knights of Britain, Redcrosse and Artegall, she assigns religious and political quests that conclude outside Fairyland, the one in Eden and the other in sixteenth-century Ireland. The quests of Britomart and Arthur emerge directly from sixth-century Britain, an heroic realm of political conflict and mimetic realism (I ix 2–16, II x 1–69, III ii 17–iii 62), and are destined to conclude in Britain and Cleopolis, respectively. Together, the quests create a pattern of temporal mediations among sixteenth-century English, ancient British, biblical, and prophetic history

Spenser creates three parallel epic quests representing three temporal perspectives on Tudor history, and he anchors them in Britain, Cleopolis, and Eden, which form a political and religious historical frame around the moral, erotic, and social allegory of Fairyland. Upon their return to Britain, Britomart and Artegall, like Aeneas, would begin to build a nation out of chaos; they would establish the Tudor line as Aeneas had established the Augustan (III iii 27, V vii 23). Upon reaching Cleopolis, Arthur may, by serving and marrying Gloriana, initiate the prophetic nation of Tudor legend. The realization of Arthur's quest would have taken Anchises' prophecy to Aeneas one step further, beyond the poet's own time into the future of an apocalyptic third Troy. Redcrosse, whose quest parallels in religious history that of Arthur in political history, is destined to return to Eden (I xii 18–19), where by marrying Una he may establish the redeemed earth. Spenser creates an innovative political and ontological geography capable of accommodating the momentous heroic poem he never completed.

WAYNE ERICKSON

***The Faerie Queene*, proems** The proems preceeding each of the six completed books of *The Faerie Queene* exist at a juncture between the poem and the 'real world,' neither fully in the fiction of Faery nor wholly outside it. Although the speaker in the proems is less fictionalized than he is within the cantos, we cannot assume that he is Spenser speaking in his own voice. All the proems end in praise of England's Queen, and so emphasize the encomiastic aspect of *The Faerie Queene*; but the Elizabeth of the proems is more than an historical monarch. Semi-divine, she plays the roles of muse, patron, protector, idealized reader, and dedicatee of the poem. The proem to Book III announces that she is mirrored in Gloriana and Belphoebe, and she is fictionalized as a descendant of the characters who appear in the chronicle of Briton kings in II x. Like *The Faerie Queene* generally, the proems have many literary forebears, but that to Book I particularly insists upon the patrimony of Virgil and Ariosto: the first four lines imitate the opening verses of Renaissance editions of the *Aeneid* (now regarded as spurious) and the fifth line is a variant of the opening of *Orlando furioso*.

It is frequently asserted that, with the exception of the first, the proems introduce the subjects of the books that follow them. Yet only the fifth discusses the titular virtue of its book in significant detail; the introductory function of the others is generally indirect. The first proem opens *The Faerie Queene* as a whole; less obviously, it anticipates goals and problems that will arise in the narrative of Book I. The others, more specific to the books that follow them, also comment upon the whole poem.

Ostensibly introductory, the proems condition the reader's understanding of the following narratives; at the same time, our understanding of the proems is altered retrospectively by the development of the books that follow. The proems announce the speaker's attitude toward the poem, but his attitude becomes as much a point of departure as a fixed point of reference. Similarly, the pressure that they exert to define an explicit or implied ideal reader both shapes and is shaped by the further definition of the reader-within-the-poem as the narrative proceeds. The proems offer fertile and compact areas for considering such issues as the character and status of the narrator of the epic, the multiple framings of the poem, its relation to the historical and fictional materials it incorporates, and, broadly, what we mean and what Spenser may have understood by the elusive entity that we call the text of *The Faerie Queene*.

The six proems are remarkably various in rhetoric and subject. Announcing *The Faerie Queene* in its entirety, the first contains, as we would expect, an invocation to the Muse (2), either Clio or Calliope, or possibly both to mark the poem as both history and epic. While it mentions neither holiness nor Redcrosse, its concerns are analogous to those of the following 'legende.' The quest on behalf of and for Gloriana/Elizabeth sets the poet a task parallel to that of Redcrosse, whose quest is also on behalf of Una and for her, in that he must recover her after they are separated. Like the knight, the speaker will need divine grace and 'wit' to complete his task. His second invocation, of Venus, Cupid, and Mars (3), anticipates the central role of love in Book I and the book's martial themes. Redcrosse's strength comes from his love of Una – and hers for him – but much of his vulnerability also results from his youthful passion.

The proem to Book II raises the question of how to locate and interpret the truth of the poet's fiction. It offers two answers. The more playful consists of the kind of argument we associate with Hamlet's famous 'There are more things in heaven and earth, Horatio, / Than are dreamt of in your philosophy.' The second speaks of mirroring the real world in the fictions of Faery, which at once expose and conceal truth. The proem does not introduce temperance directly, but does address the issues of interpretation and of appearance versus reality, both of which will be central concerns for Guyon.

The topos of poetic inadequacy and an extended allusion to Raleigh's *Ocean to Cynthia* dominate the third proem, which has little to say specifically about chastity beyond mentioning the names of Belphoebe and Gloriana. The allusion to Raleigh, however, and the promise of 'mirrours more then one' anticipate the diffuse, digressive, 'Italian' narrative techniques that first appear in Book III.

In the proem to Book IV, the speaker considers the social consequences of his poem, a new subject which signals the shift from the private virtues of Books I-III to the public ones of IV-VI. He counterattacks with notable acerbity an unnamed critic of *The Faerie Queene*, generally assumed to be Lord Burghley, the most powerful person in England after the Queen. If this identification is correct, the temerity of Spenser's gesture is hard to overestimate. In stanza 4, he turns his back on his critics to sing to 'that sacred Saint my soveraigne Queene' whom he characterizes as the 'Prince of peace.' In the book that follows, those who 'cannot love' (including those who reduce love to lust) head the forces of social disruption, while those who do love bring about peace and concord. By turning from hostile to sympathetic readers, the speaker anticipates the emphasis on compatibility of 'kind' which assumes central importance in the portrayals of friendship in Book IV.

This proem strikes for the first time a note of personal grievance that reappears in the proems to Books V and VI as despair about the 'state of present time' and as poetic weariness. The tone of the proems in the second installment of *The Faerie Queene* probably contributes to the widespread perception that Spenser became more sour and cynical between 1590 and 1596. The rhetorical stance appropriate to a social commentator, however, may with decorum contain more 'Satyrical biternesse' (as E.K. calls it in the General Argument to *SC*) than that of an arbiter of private morality. The latter risks appearing sanctimonious, while the conventions of social satire largely exempt the former from such accusations. The disciplines 'Of vertue and of civill uses lore' (V proem 3) require different rhetorical stances.

The only proem that specifically discusses the nature and conditions of the titular virtue of the book to follow, the fifth is also the longest. It presents an important strain of Renaissance moral and historical thought, the decay of the world since the Golden Age. At the same time, it serves in part as a foil to the more complicated understanding of justice that we arrive at by the end of Book V. As the retributive justice of Talus is finally inadequate to the complex shadings of morality in a fallen world, so the dismissive indignation of the speaker in the proem fails to give proper place to the only real cure for human iniquity: justice tempered with mercy and love. Like Artegall, he lacks an understanding of the complicated intersection of the fallen world, human frailty, justice, and mercy that the Renaissance sometimes called equity. The astronomical stanzas 5–8 support the speaker's contention that the heavens and 'all this world with them amisse doe move.' What the speaker does not yet see, however, is that the consequent departure of Astraea from earth is partly regrettable, partly fortunate in that it provides occasions for mercy and forgiveness.

After his pessimistic appraisal of the present, the speaker has a logical problem in moving to his concluding praise of Elizabeth, who must somehow be dissociated from the corruption of justice in the 'stonie' age. His response is to associate her with an earlier, undecayed time, '*Saturnes* ancient raigne' when 'all the world with goodnesse did abound.'

Still 'ravisht' by Faery but admitting to some 'decay of might,' the speaker in the proem to Book VI asks the Muses to show him the 'silver bowre' in which virtue grows. The imagery of stanzas 3 and 4 anticipates Calidore's pastoral interlude, which leads to the thematic center of Spenser's conception of courtesy. The weary poet, like Calidore, discovers his direction in pastoral indirection.

As in the proem to Book V, the speaker laments the state of the modern world, doubting that true virtue can exist among its 'fayned showes.' As a result, he once again faces the contradiction of claiming as an exemplar of virtue a Queen who lives in a time that he has accused of being incapable of true courtesy. He responds to this dilemma more directly than he did in the fifth proem, by asserting that his sovereign and her court are the very pattern of courtesy and exceed 'all Antiquity' in that virtue. Compounding his apparent self-contradiction is the fact that the imagery of praise in stanzas 6 and 7 strikingly resembles that of dispraise in 4 and 5.

Although the proem contains little specific discussion of the titular virtue of Book VI, the rhetorical 'career' of the speaker, as is usual for all the proems, anticipates crucial themes of its narrative. In this case, the apparent contradictions within stanzas 4–7 reflect similar contradictions within the book itself. Courtesy, in both the proem and book, consists not in logical consistency but in meliorating gestures. It leads to reconciliation of conflict, rather than to resolution in favor of one side or the other.

LESLEY BRILL

Cain 1978; DeNeef 1982; Goldberg 1981.

fairies By the late sixteenth century, various strands of classical, romance, and folk mythology had become inextricably intertwined in stories pertaining to fairies, elves, nymphs, and sprites. In his *Discoverie of Witchcraft* (1584), Reginald Scot lumps together 'spirits, witches, urchins, elves, hags, fairies, satyrs, pans, faunes, sylens [*sileni*, or figures of the wood god Silenus], tritons, centaurs, dwarfs, giants, nymphes ... and other such buggs' (7.15). In Shakespeare's *Midsummer Night's Dream*, Oberon (from a 13th-c *chanson de geste*, *Huon of Bordeaux*) is found with Puck (the Robin Goodfellow of English village folk mythology) in a wood outside ancient Athens during the time of the legendary Theseus and Hippolyta, Queen of the Amazons. Indeed, it is partly under the influence of this play and Mercutio's Queen Mab speech in *Romeo and Juliet* that a coherent English tradition of fairies and fairy lore is generated in literature out of various traditions, so that in poems like Drayton's *Nimphidia* or Herrick's several fairy poems, there begins to be found a recognizably modern image of fairies and elves as little people – sometimes clear embodiments of evil (Burton calls them 'terrestrial devils ... which as they are most conversant with men, so they do most harm' *Anatomy of Melancholy* 1.2.1.2 in ed 1893, 1:219), sometimes mischievous tricksters who might steal no more than a bowl of milk. In Elizabethan England, there are records of individuals put on trial for conversing with or successfully impersonating the king and queen of fairies (Thomas 1971:727). Belief in a spiritual life, with its hierarchy of angels and invisible though potent forces, has with it a belief in the force of evil, of which fairies and elves may be the least noxious manifestation. Thus, when Milton compares Satan's hordes to 'faerie elves' (*Paradise Lost* 1.781), he diminishes Satan's power at the same time he tells the reader that this power may be found in seemingly innocent nature spirits.

The various kinds of fairies who as the *longaevi* or long-livers dwell between air and earth led to various theories of their nature: as a rational species distinct from angels and men, as angels who fell with Lucifer though not into hell, as the dead, and as devils (see Lewis 1964, ch 6). Confusion over their spiritual source and destination also extended to their names. *Elf* and *fairy* were sometimes interchangeable (or even, as in Milton, merged into a single 'fairy elf'), though elves were often held to be more evil or were presented as servants to fairies. *Nymphs* were usually classical creatures (female spirits of wood, fountain or stream; see *Nereids), yet the Latin *nymphae* was to be translated as 'elfes' or 'women of the fayrie' according to a standard dictionary (Elyot 1538), so that often the categories of nymph, fairy, and elf were merged or blurred. All of them are terrestrial spirits (*spirits*, or *sprites*, was an inclusive term, though with a special meaning in some authors). According to the anonymous author of *A Discourse concerning Devils and Spirits* (appended to the 1665 edition of Scot's *Discoverie*), they may be categorized 'according to the places which they occupy, as Woods, Mountains, Caves, Fens, Mines, Ruins, Desolate places, and Antient Buildings, calld by the Antient Heathens after various names, as Nymphs, Satyrs, Lamii, Dryades, Sylvanes, Cobali, etc. And more particularly the Faeries, who do principally inhabit the Mountains, and Caverns of the Earth' (Latham 1930:59). Yet most authors, including Spenser, did not maintain these clear distinctions.

In the minor poems, Spenser confuses the categories of fairies, elves, and nymphs. When Hobbinol says that here are no 'elvish ghosts' but rather 'frendly Faeries ... many Graces, / And lightfote Nymphes' (*SC, June* 24–6), he is banishing the bad spirits in favor of those who might be seen as part of a benign and acceptable paganism. E.K., however, reacts strongly against even the mention of these spirits: 'the truth is, that there be no such thinges, nor yet the shadowes of the things, but onely by a sort of bald Friers and knavish shavelings so feigned' – a heavily ironic dismissal of a Christianized paganism found throughout *The Shepheardes Calender*. Elsewhere in the poem, nymphs and fairies are found in pastoral locations with the Graces and goddesses of classical antiquity: in *Maye* 30–2, 'A fayre flocke of Faeries' attend Flora, the May Queen, and in *Aprill* 37–40, nymphs of the brook help to sing Elisa's praise. An interesting merging of the language of romance with classical mythology is found in *Aprill* 120, where 'Ladyes of the lake' is glossed by E.K. as 'Nymphes,' which 'certain fine fablers and lowd lyers, such as were the Authors of King Arthure' believed were goddesses of fountains. Generally, though, Spenser keeps nymphs distinct from fairies, although in *Virgils Gnat* 177–9, wood gods, satyrs, and dryads (ie, wood nymphs) are seen dancing on the green 'With many Fairies.' Nymphs are part of Cynthia's retinue in *Colin Clout* (459–60, 577–8). The clearest vision of nymphs anywhere in Spenser's poetry, though, is found in *Prothalamion* (19–36), where the poet sings of the 'lovely Daughters of the Flood' who gather their baskets of flowers in order to bless the swans as they proceed along the river.

The same concepts of nymphs are found in *The Faerie Queene*. They are tutelary spirits of fountains (such as the one in which Guyon tries to wash his bloody hands at II ii 3–10; see also *Faunus); they attend Diana in the woods (III vi 17–19); they are Nereids (IV xi 48–52). In other words, they are the recognizable entities of classical mythology, however modified.

For elves and fairies, though, Spenser moves from village lore to romance. His elves and fairies are of human stature, principal agents in the poem, most noticeably in the figure of the Fairy Queen. After Harvey read some part of Spenser's poem, he referred mockingly to 'that *Elvish Queene*' and accused Spenser of having allowed '*Hobgoblin* [the village fairy prankster] runne away with the Garland from *Apollo* [the classical god of poetic inspiration and prophetic utterance]' (*Three Letters* 3). Yet, the image of the Fairy Queen had a source in popular imagery which was also, at the time, being used to praise Elizabeth (Baskervill 1920–1). Strong hints of this appear in the pageant at Kenilworth, in which the Lady of the Lake, accompanied by two nymphs, presumptuously offered 'the Lake, the Lodge, the Lord [ie, Leicester]' to the visiting Elizabeth. The theme was picked up and worked even more strongly at Woodstock in the same year: a beautiful arbor was presented to the Queen, the arbor of the Fairy Queen, a 'Lady in whom inhabiteth the most vertue, Learning, and beauty, that ever yet was in creature.' The Elizabethan Fairy Queen was derived from romance – from the queen of the isle of Avalon in *Huon of Bordeaux*, the good Dame du Lac of the *Prophecies de Merlin* (14th c) who also appears as Arthur's protector the Lady of the Lake in Malory's *Morte Darthur*, Gloriande in *Tristan de Nanteuil* (14th c), and the fairy queen Gloriande in *Charles le chauve* (14th c). Although Spenser clearly knew *Huon of Bordeaux* (tr Lord Berners, 1534) and Malory, the transmission of Gloriana the Fairy Queen from these other sources to his own work is obscure (see Rathborne 1937, ch 4). Yet he has retained many characteristics of the fairy queen of medieval romance – her mysterious location, her beneficent guidance and rule, her special powers (in Spenser given more a moral than a magical cast), and her reputed beauty.

The meaning of *elfe* or the designation *elfin* is very mixed in *The Faerie Queene*. In certain instances, the terms clearly refer to the noble ancestry and powerful line of the ancient elves – as when, for instance, Guyon is said to be 'an Elfin borne of noble state, / And mickle worship in his native land' (II i 6; the passage asserts that he was knighted by Sir Huon and came to Fairyland with King Oberon). The Red Cross Knight, by contrast, is Saxon born, but was carried away by a fairy and given to a plowman for upbringing; in his place, the fairy left 'her base

Elfin brood' (I x 65), implying that it is better to be born a hearty Saxon than a good-for-nothing elf. Another usage is less common in Spenser though it is found in contemporary writers: when the narrator refers to Pastorella as 'wofull wretched Elfe' (VI xi 19), he means only that she is an unhappy creature (*elf* as 'being or creature, living entity'). Usually *elf* and *elfin* are applied to noble characters, though sometimes merely as a statement of their origins, not as a compliment – as when Sansloy mistakenly identifies Satyrane (the son of a satyr) as a 'misborne Elfe' (I vi 42). That he is blind to Satyrane's origins is again apparent when he calls him 'foolish faeries sonne' (47). Similarly, Despair mistakenly names the Saxon Redcrosse a 'faeries sonne' though he was a changeling (ix 47; x 60, 64–5).

The word *fairy* also is mixed in meaning, though far more rarely than *elf* or *elfin*, for which it is often a synonym. It almost always refers to the race, person, or kingdom of Gloriana. Thus, 'this Faery knight / The good Sir *Guyon*' tells us simply that he is from Fairyland and an elf by race (II proem 5). So, too, when Artegall is referred to simply as 'The fayrie' (V v 55, although earlier Merlin had informed Britomart that Artegall, like Redcrosse earlier, 'is no *Fary* borne, ne sib at all / To Elfes, but sprong of seed terrestriall, / And whilome by false *Faries* stolne away' III iii 26), he believes he is a fairy knight though he is actually of Cornish extraction, and a Briton (on the distinctions between Britons and elves, see Hume 1984, ch 7).

In the reference to 'false *Faries*,' we have a glimpse of the folkloric fairy (eg, Puck) as mischievous spright or evil spirit, an aspect of fairy lore that hardly ever appears in *The Faerie Queene*. The other sense of fairy, as a kind of benign wood or water nymph, is given at *FQ* VI x 7 and 17, when Calidore sees 'Nymphes and Faeries' sitting on the banks of the stream on Mount Acidale.

Finally, although they are not called fairies, Duessa, Lucifera, Acrasia, and Phaedria are related to the learned fairies, or fays, of medieval romance. Morgan the Fay is a learned clerk in necromancy in *Morte Arthur*, who acts against King Arthur with an especial malignancy. In *The Faerie Queene*, Agape is a fay who 'had the skill / Of secret things, and all the powres of nature, / Which she by art could use unto her will, / And to her service bind each living creature' (IV ii 44). Although she is more benign than Acrasia or Phaedria or Lucifera, she is in league with subterranean powers of darkness: she travels to the underworld to learn about her sons' lives, rather than seeking guidance from above. These fays are related to evil powers, but they have many of the same qualities as the Fairy Queen: they are retiring (they live 'in privie place' IV ii 44), they are lovely, they exert power over men, they have a court or retinue, and they have access to supernatural powers. EDITORS

Two useful surveys of background and citations of 16-c writings on fairies are Katharine M. Briggs 1959 *The Anatomy of Puck: An Examination of Fairy Beliefs among Shakespeare's Contemporaries and Successors* (London); and Latham 1930. Thomas 1971 sets fairy lore in the context of social relations and religious beliefs. The fullest discussion of Spenser's fairy lore is Rathborne 1937, though see Baskervill 1920–1 for the Fairy Queen in the pageants of 1575 and Greenlaw 1918 for the claim that *fairy* is *Welsh* and a discussion of the political significance of Fairyland. Hume 1984, ch 7 argues that the categories of Briton and Elf correspond to the historical and fictional worlds of *FQ* respectively, and that by using the 'two sets of antiquities' of British history and elfin lore, esp at II x, Spenser 'takes the opportunity of pointing up the profound difference between history and poetry as literary modes' (p 156).

---

fairyland Spenser derived his notion of fairyland principally from two heroic cycles, one of which concerned Huon of Bordeaux, the other Roland or Orlando. The first was an Old French verse cycle, written mostly in the thirteenth century, consisting of *Auberon*, the *Huon* proper, *Esclarmonde*, *The Crowning of Huon*, and further continuations. Spenser would have known the cycle through its prose version (1454), of which there were many editions and an English translation by Lord Berners (1534). He refers explicitly to *The Crowning of Huon* at *FQ* II i 6. Although *Auberon* was not included in the prose version, its plot has parallels in *FQ* I: it includes a version of the St George story which has the hero woo a princess in Mesopotamia, which is also Una's homeland. In addition, Spenser's Orgoglio episode resembles the closing story of *Auberon*, where the giant Orguilleus catches the Fairy King resting with his armor off and takes possession of his castle but spares his prisoner. The giant next finds a mistress, as does Orgoglio. The second cycle was an Italian verse romance begun by Boiardo's *Orlando innamorato* and concluded by Ariosto's *Orlando furioso*. Scholars have long recognized that the *Furioso* is the greatest single source for *The Faerie Queene*, especially for Books III and IV; and although there is no conclusive evidence, Spenser probably also read Boiardo.

The poets of these cycles took the old *chanson de geste* and revitalized it with fairy marvels commonly associated with Arthurian romance. Sometimes the romancers were explicit about this: Boiardo says that he is using Arthurian material for a Charlemagne story (*OI* 1.1.1–3, 2.8.1–3, 2.18.1–3). This practice further allowed poets to bring Arthurian characters into their poems. Morgan le Fay, Arthur's sister and frequent enemy, gives birth to Oberon, the Fairy King, in the *Huon*; she is also the most important of Boiardo's fays. Ariosto has Merlin in his poem. Spenser achieves a similar generic mixture, though he begins differently. He is writing an Arthurian romance but imitating the Matter of France with its wars of Moslem and Christian, so he has Saracens in *FQ* I and V.

This mixed genre combines characters from different stories and, therefore, from different times. In *The Crowning of Huon*, Oberon (a child of Julius Caesar), Arthur, and Huon (a younger contemporary of Charlemagne) all meet in the fairy city of Monmur. The whole plot of *Auberon* consists in such anachronisms. The Italians downplay this aspect of the genre, and few readers of the *Furioso* would know that Angelica, daughter of the Grand Khan (13–14th c), Norandino (12th c), and Charlemagne (8–9th c) could not be contemporaries. Spenser brings this anachronistic mingling of characters back to the foreground and has Arthur rescue St George.

Each new romance built on its predecessors, and this practice led to a habit of cross-reference. The prose *Huon* relates its action to that of other *chansons de geste*, and Spenser in turn refers to *Huon*. This habit creates a sense that fairyland is larger than its development in any single poem (Murrin 1980:140), and in fact the poets of these cycles assume it is a place that can be found on the map.

Fairyland exists just beyond the boundaries of the known. *Huon* locates it beyond Palestine, and the continuations (*Esclarmonde*, *The Crowning of Huon*) move it to Persia, conceived as the edge of the world. Monmur, the fairy capital, is in the mountains of North Persia. Geographers normally called this zone India, as do Chaucer (Lowes 1905–6:18) and the later romancers. Boiardo's Angelica has a fortress in Turkestan, which the poet calls both Cathay and India (1.1.52–3, 6.42, 10.14). Spenser follows this tradition when he has Elfin rule over 'all *India*' (*FQ* II x 72).

In romances of this kind, the heroes come to fairyland from Western Europe. The main characters of the Huon and Orlando cycles are Franks, and Spenser's Arthur and Britomart travel there from Britain. Heroes who travel suggest tales of travel and voyages, and these romances have parallels in Marco Polo, Mandeville, and Hakluyt.

This connection to travel literature helps to explain the wonders of fairyland. Spenser bases much of his wonder on a traveler's experiences, for his heroes and heroines, even fairies like Guyon, perceive and judge people and places that they have never encountered before. The narrator, with his constant hyperbole, increases this wonder and makes fairyland a 'golden world.' Other English poets also emphasize this quality of wonder. In the *Squire's Tale*, Chaucer has the King of Arabia and India send magical gifts to the Tatar Khan: a brass horse which flies, a mirror which reveals friends and foes, a ring which gives understanding of bird songs, and a sword which alone can heal the wounds it gives. Milton refers to this passage in *Il Penseroso* 109–15 and elsewhere recalls Boiardo's India and the siege of Albracca (*Paradise Regained* 3.337–44).

Travel likewise provides a useful analogy when a poet wishes to defend the wonders of his fairyland. He can argue that the reader should recognize that many surprising things exist in faraway lands and, furthermore, that the zone of the known includes only part of the world. Hence Ariosto defends the wonders of the fay Alcina (*OF* 7.1–2), and Spenser works out a similar defence in the proem to Book II. This kind of argument also indicates an important characteristic of fairyland: since it represents the area beyond the known, it changes location depending upon variations in European knowledge of the world.

Legend perhaps determined its initial location. Fairyland began in the East, often near the Caspian or the Pacific. For the former location, there was the fact that two of the four rivers of Paradise were the Tigris and Euphrates, and native tradition equated the Gihon with the Jayhun (Oxus) and the Pison with the Sayhun (Jaxartes) (Le Strange 1905:434). Spenser follows this tradition: Una's parents once controlled the lands by the Euphrates, Phison, and Gehon, and the dragon came from Tartary or Tatary, the steppe zone to the north which had salt marshes and lakes (*FQ* I vii 43–4). Milton likewise puts Paradise in Armenia, over the Tigris (*Paradise Lost* 9.69–73). Geographers, on the other hand, placed Paradise in the uttermost East, beyond India (Pullé 1905:11–12). There the poet of the *Esclarmonde* has Huon find the Tree and Well of Life, which Spenser borrowed for his dragon fight (*Huon* ed 1882–7, chs 121–2; *FQ* I xi 29–30, 46–8). Gower assumes this location in his *Confessio Amantis* 7.568–71. The place, however, did not always have to be in the East. The Portuguese thought Prester John lived in Ethiopia, and Ariosto accordingly moved him there as well as the terrestrial paradise.

Over the centuries, fairyland mostly drifted eastward. It started as an undefined zone beyond Palestine, floated to northern Persia, and then to central Asia, as more and more travelers took advantage of the *pax Mongolica* or visited the Timurid courts of Khorasan and Turkestan. The zone of the unknown shifted with the movements of explorers and sailors. In the sixteenth century, Europeans experienced a sudden widening of the known beyond any expectation, as the Portuguese sailed to India, Columbus to America, and Magellan around the world, and fairyland receded farther and farther away. Ariosto takes Alcina, a fay who lived by the Black Sea in Boiardo's *Innamorato* (2.13.55, 2.14.10), and puts her in the East Indies. Spenser continued the process of placing fairyland in ever more distant areas, for his fairies rule India and America (*FQ* II x 72). By this time, fairyland existed both East and West, and he could speculate about possible worlds in the stars (II proem 3).

The poets gave to fairyland a splendor like that found in the *Arabian Nights*. The courts of the Mongols and Timurids, visited by European ambassadors, partially explain this emphasis. Marco Polo, for example, described the grand palace of Cambalu (Beijing), a large hall covered with silver and gold which gleamed from afar (ch 71). More importantly, the East was famous for the luxury goods it exported to the West. Marco Polo talked of the rubies and sapphires of Badakshan (ch 35) and the pearls of Malabar, which he considered the richest province in the world (ch 151), and geographers associated the Eastern islands with gold and silver as well as with spices (Caramella 1923:53, 130). Spenser looked to America, where the Conquistadors found gold and Philip II an endless supply of silver. The romancers express this wealth mythically: in *Esclarmonde*, Huon finds by Paradise a river which has precious stones for gravel (*Chanson d'Esclarmonde* ed 1895, ch 122). The prose version has the Castle of Adament which defines its locale by the precious materials used to construct it: it possesses what the European must import (chs 108–11, 116). Boiardo makes the economic basis for such fantasies explicit. He turns Morgan le Fay into a treasure fairy who owns a field of gems and pearls. She presides over wealth in its raw state, the silver and gold found in mines (*OI* 1.25.5–7). Spenser's comparable figure is Mammon, who takes Guyon on a tour of his caverns (*FQ* II vii 28–37). Milton evokes this vision of the East when he describes Satan as an oriental despot, sitting on a raised throne, 'which far / Outshone the wealth of Ormus and of Ind, / Or where the gorgeous East with richest hand / Showers on her Kings barbaric pearl and gold' (*PL* 2.1–4).

Fairyland serves two functions: political and philosophical. The political develops out of the real and imagined wars between Christians and Moslems. It expresses and imaginatively fulfills the wish for an ally beyond the Saracens (see *Paynims). The Crusaders could not defeat Ayyubid and Mamluk Egypt, so the poet of the *Huon* imagines that Oberon and a fairy army come to help the Franks capture 'Babylon' (Cairo). Spenser similarly envisages a war with infidels where Gloriana will help the British confront the Saracens (*FQ* I xi 7). Such fantasies occurred normally when the Mongols were active in the East, fighting the same enemies who troubled Christians in the Levant. Whether the Ilkhans of Persia (13th c), the Timurids (15th c), or perhaps the Moghuls of India (16th c), these powers made their presence felt at a distance, and the West looked to them for aid against both Mamluk and Turk. In the romances, however, this ally had to be Christian or a convert to Christianity, since the warfare was religious. Ariosto's Prester John sends a Christian army to Barbary. In *Esclarmonde*, the ally is originally Moslem but is converted when their aged admiral miraculously recovers his youth. He then leads his subjects on a crusade. This vision of a benevolent but non-Christian ally obliged the poet to imagine, however sketchily, a foreign religion.

Renaissance authors followed the practice of the *chansons de geste* and regarded foreign religions as variants of Greek and Roman practices. The Saracens of the *Song of Roland* worship Apollo (1.8), and Boiardo's Rodamonte espouses an Epicurean agnosticism. Spenser follows the same tradition when he classicizes the Tatars, introducing Daemogorgon, the Fates, nepenthe, and the caduceus into his version of Chaucer's *Squire's Tale* (*FQ* IV ii 32ff), and when he consigns the Saracen Sansjoy to a classical hell (I v 29–44). The allies beyond these Moslems could similarly begin as Saracens who worship classical deities. In his *Amoryus and Cleopes* (1448–9), a redoing of the story of Pyramus and Thisbe, John Metham has the Persians worship Venus before their conversion. This method fits standard Renaissance practice, for both Ariosto and Spenser, though they inherited a medieval form, turned to the classics for many of their scenes and marvels.

Spenser changes the function of this political fantasy. He does not look for an ally beyond the Ottoman Empire, since his nation feared Roman Catholic Spain much more than a distant Saracen power. Instead he wishes to compete with the Spanish, and dreams of a colonial empire (see *New World). In *The Faerie Queene*, he talks of Virginia (II proem 2) and encourages an expedition to Brazil (IV xi 21–2). The ally comes to resemble a transplanted Englishman, and Spenser has his fairy rulers mirror the Tudors. This new political interpretation in turn requires a new artistic and philosophical understanding of fairyland.

Traditionally, writers established a contrast between the ordinary world of the West and an idealized fairy kingdom where both good and evil exist in purer forms. Charlemagne's imperfect kingdom contrasts both with Oberon's model government in the Huon cycle and with the evil gardens of Boiardo's fays. Spenser preserves traces of this tradition, for the chronicle which Guyon reads in the castle of Alma shows a uniformly successful fairy government, while Arthur finds a mixture of good and evil in English history. Ariosto has both good and evil figures in his fairyland, which may be exaggerated to the point that they become personifications like Logistilla. Her story is an isolated episode in the *Furioso*, but Spenser uses personifications regularly: Una and Duessa, extremes of good and evil, struggle over the Red Cross Knight. Moreover, the semi-anarchy of the periphery, that portion of fairyland in which most of the events of *The Faerie Queene* occur, likewise contrasts with the idealized government in Cleopolis, which no one ever visits. In all these things, Spenser follows and develops tradition.

He departs from tradition when he drops the normal world from his plot. The Huon and Orlando cycles contrast fairyland and France, but Spenser has almost no action occur in the West. Artegall travels in that direction to save Irena (V vi 7, 22). There is also Britomart's visit to Merlin, but the poet uses that story to explain her presence in fairyland and her conversation with Redcrosse. The West, that is, our Western culture, exists allegorically, not literally. As a result, fairyland and therefore the whole romance become allegorical, and Spenser argues that fairyland mirrors England (I proem 4, II proem 4). Boiardo and Ariosto had invited allegorical readings of fairy episodes, but the English poet applies this method to his entire poem.

In one place, Spenser shows how a reader might interpret fairyland. When he completed Chaucer's *Squire's Tale*, he departed from his normal practice, promising to give the meaning rather than reproduce the literal details of his original (*FQ* iv ii 32–4). He interprets Chaucer and so provides his reader with a paradigm for the interpretation of his own poem. The magic ring, for example, becomes Canacee's natural knowledge of herbs and birds (35), and Chaucer's Tatars with names like Cambyuskan and Cambalus become Scots like Cambell. The logic is geographical. In Chaucer, the King of Arabia and India sends fairy gifts to the Golden Horde, the nomads who live in the steppe north of the Middle East, the zone of wonder. For Spenser, the Golden Horde must mirror the Scots, since fairyland to the south mirrors England. By similar thinking, the kings of fairy resemble Tudor monarchs and Duessa, Mary Stuart. The reader can do for the rest of *The Faerie Queene* what Spenser does to Chaucer. Fairyland functions as a mirror only when the reader interprets the text.

Although fairyland existed beyond the known world, romancers prior to Spenser made it a land partially continuous with our own. Knights sail or ride to it, and fairyland operates according to laws similar to those of our own world. When Spenser sets his whole poem in this beyond, the laws governing ordinary experience disappear as well. Guyon, for instance, takes a sea voyage in a rowboat. Spenser signals this change when he drops the specifics of the traveler's tale. Previous romancers had to make fairyland believable, since their heroes also fought in France. They therefore gave precise itineraries and geographical locations for Eastern adventures. In Spenser, place and time become vague. He does not give a specific location for Cleopolis, nor does he say what routes Arthur and Britomart followed to come to fairyland. References to time occur but not often enough to establish a chronology of events. This phenomenon led Coleridge to equate fairyland with a mental space independent of all particular space and time. Spenser would have expressed this insight Platonically, and the philosophy of the Academy with its stress on memory more accurately explains the practice of these romancers. Stories of fairies are all of long ago, of the days of Arthur and Charlemagne. Spenser strengthens this retrospective sense by his archaic spelling and rhymes. The reader can never forget that this is a story of the past. Spenser especially appeals to memory rather than the imagination because he considers the present age corrupt (v proem, vi proem) and looks to the past for models. His fairyland recalls an older and better time. Recollection awakens us to superior values and restores our better selves. Literally, fairyland is beyond the horizon, but allegorically its poet wishes to lift us to the stars. Michael J. Murrin

Chanson d'Esclarmonde 1895 ed Hermann Schäfer (Worms); [*Huon*] 1882–7 *The Boke of Duke Huon of Burdeux* tr John Bourchier, Lord Berners, ed S.L. Lee, EETS es 40–1, 43, 50 (London); *Huon de Bordeaux* 1960 ed Pierre Ruelle (Brussels); *Le Roman d'Auberon* 1973 ed Jean Subrenat (Geneva).

Berger 1957; S. Caramella 1923 'L'Asia nell'-*Orlando innamorato*' *Bollettino della Reale Società Geografica Italiana* ser 5, 12:44–59, 127–50; G[uy] Le Strange 1905 *The Lands of the Eastern Caliphate* (Cambridge); John Livingston Lowes 1905–6 'The Dry Sea and the Carrenare' *MP* 3:1–46; Murrin 1980; Marco Polo 1954 *Il libro di Marco Polo detto Milione* tr Giulio Einaudi, ed Daniele Ponchiroli (Turin); Francesco Pullé 1905 'La cartografia antica dell'India' Part 2 *Studi Italiani de Filologia Indo-Iranica* 5:1–139; Rathborne 1937.

falconry References to hawking and figures of speech using the terms of this field occur in English literature of all periods, but especially the Renaissance. Spenser uses such terms with exceptional frequency and accuracy even for his time, usually in metaphors or similes, which may give difficulty to those unfamiliar with the vocabulary and its common figurative associations. Many hawking terms have become dead metaphors and some were largely used in transferred senses as early as the fourteenth century, but there is almost invariably a hint of the original context in Spenser's uses. (An exception is *gorge*, which he does not seem to use as 'hawk's crop,' 'a cropful of food,' and so forth.) In *FQ* iv x 49, Womanhood uses no 'luring baytes.' To *lure* is to train a hawk to come to the falconer's lure, a feathered apparatus on which a bait of meat is placed. Thus Womanhood is favorably contrasted to those who allure lovers, as falconers lure hawks, with false pretenses.

Similarly, while others had for some time used *mew* with little implication of its original sense, Spenser always seems to mean by the noun 'a cage or room for a hawk' or by the verb 'to confine or hide in such a place.' When the 'fouler' Guyle captures the 'Damzell' Samient in his net, as falconers sometimes capture hawks, we are told he 'Ran with her fast away unto his mew' (v ix 13–14), the proper place to safeguard a newly captured falcon. That Acrasia keeps her victims in 'yron mewes' (ii v 27) implies that she, too, acts as a falconer caging her catch. Although Spenser does not use the original sense of the verb *mew*, to moult, he suggests it once: Night 'forth comming from her darkesome mew' has been hiding 'her hated hew' as a moulting bird might do (i v 20). Editions which gloss *mew* as 'to confine, secrete' or as 'prison, den' overlook the implied metaphor.

One significant use of *mew* tells us that Malbecco will not allow anyone near Hellenore, 'But in close bowre her mewes from all mens sight' (iii ix 5). In the next two stanzas, Satyrane makes a point about women that could equally well be made of falcons, who cannot be tamed by overt force: 'But fast good will with gentle curtesyes, / And timely service to her pleasures meet / May her perhaps containe, that else would algates fleet.' In the next canto, Spenser develops the comparison of Hellenore to a falcon, casting Paridell as a thieving falcon fancier. Once he and his stolen bird have fled 'free from all mens reclame,' 'having filcht her bels, her up he cast ... and let her fly alone,' 'loose at randon left' (x 16, 35–6). *Reclaim* is the act of recalling a hawk; bells are fastened on the hawk's feet so that the falconer may find her if she flies to a hiding place; *cast* is the proper term for letting the falcon loose to fly; and a hawk flying *at random* is following her quarry wherever it may happen to fly, not making moves directed by the falconer.

This extended metaphor is one of several in *The Faerie Queene* which compare men to falconers and the women they pursue or wish to control to hawks, which is much the most common application of falconry in medieval and Renaissance literature. (It is the dominant metaphor of Shakespeare's *Taming of the Shrew*, which culminates in Kate's retrieval of two lesser 'birds' for whom her 'keeper,' Petruchio, has dispatched her; see iv i 197 and v ii 46–7, 146.) The association was a natural one, since the hawks preferred for falconry are females; males are called tercels, not hawks.

In *The Faerie Queene*, however, we more often find women depicted as the actual or potential prey of men, who are then the figurative hawks. Examples include Florimell, who flees the Fisher as from a 'sharpe [hungry] Hauke' (iii viii 33), and Aemylia, who describes how Lust, 'trussing' her [snatching in talons], made her captive and 'mewed' her (iv vii 18, 34). The classical comparison of fighting men to hawks is also an analogy more used by Spenser than by most of his contemporaries. He often describes Arthur and other heroes and/or their opponents as falcons. Arthur is a heron attacked by 'a cast [pair] of Faulcons,' Turpine's confederates (vi vii 9). Redcrosse is a 'hardie fowle' escaping a 'hagard [untamed adult] hauke,' the Dragon, who has 'rousd himselfe' like an eagle (shaking his feathers) but will soon be unable 'to stye [rise, as a hawk] above the ground' (i xi 4, 9, 19, 25). Later in the same canto, Redcrosse is 'newborne' as an 'Eyas hauke,' a nestling (34). Elsewhere, the newborn Time has 'eyas wings' (*Heavenly Love* 24); and Una, in need of renewal, wishes her eyes 'seeled' (sewn together) like those of an eyas being tamed (*FQ* i vii 23).

Another common association shows women as falcons preying on men. Radigund is compared to a goshawk balked of her *quarrey*, Terpine, by the eagle-like *souce* (pouncing attack) of Artegall, which tears the prey from her *pounce* (talons) (v iv 42). In v v 15, she is a 'Puttocke' or 'foolish Kyte' (birds valueless for falconry) beating against a 'gentle Faulcon' (Artegall), and 'With many idle stoups [swoops from a height] her troubling still' (note the use of the feminine pronoun for a hawk). In a more comic vein, Braggadocchio is first a *kestrell* (another hawk of no value) stealing Guyon's horse, then demoted to a 'fearefull fowle' driven 'out of his nest,' the bush in which he is 'mewed,' by the 'soaring hauke' Belphoebe. Recovering, he begins 'her [ie, his] feathers ... Proudly to prune [preen, trim with the beak]' (ii iii 4, 34–6).

A fairly widely used metaphor is the human mind or spirit as falcon. When Spenser writes in *Amoretti* 72, 'Oft when my spirit doth spred her bolder winges,' he refers to a hawk's wings, for he adds that, drawn 'with sweet pleasures bayt' (his beloved's heavenly beauty), his frail fancy 'doth bath in blisse and mantleth most at ease.' A hawk *mantles* after bathing, stretching first one wing then the other over the corresponding leg. The same association provides an extended metaphor in *Heavenly Beautie*: first the poet describes his spirit's desire to rise above the world by learning from the 'soare faulcon' (26: a fledgling hawk in its first plumage); that is, he wishes to learn to 'fly' from a fellow neophyte. He later exhorts the reader to follow this example and 'To impe the wings of thy high flying mynd, / Mount up aloft' (135–6). To *imp* the wing of a hawk is to graft feathers into it, a procedure usually required because the hawk's own feathers have been weakened by malnutrition. Spenser thus implies that human spirits may be too malnourished to rise above worldly matters without assistance. (See also *birds).

CONSTANCE B. HIEATT

For further information about falconry in Spenser's time, see the facsimiles in the *Theatrum Orbis Terrarum* 'The English Experience' series (Amsterdam): [*The Boke of St Albans*] 1486 (London; rpt London 1901, Amsterdam and New York 1969; *STC* 3308), invaluable for its definitions; William Gryndall 1596 *Hawking, Hunting, Fouling, and Fishing* (London), another version of the same work; George Turbervile 1575 *The Booke of Faulconrie or Hauking* (London), the fullest treatment of the subject in the period, drawing on continental sources; Symon Latham 1615 *Falconry* (London; rpt Amsterdam and Norwood, NJ 1976), a reliable English account. See also Emiliu C. Delmé Radcliffe 1910 'Falconry' *Encyclopaedia Britannica* (11th ed). For a fuller discussion of literary uses of falconry, especially in Renaissance England, and including Chaucer, Shakespeare, and Spenser, see Constance B. Hieatt 1983 'To Stoup at a Simile: Some Literary Uses of Falconry' *PLL* 19:339–60.

Fall and Restoration of Man The theological doctrine of the Fall of Man attests to one of the fundamental truths about the human condition, that we are all innately imperfect. Generously confirmed by our common experience, it is best summarized by St Paul: 'I do not the good thing, which I wolde, but the evil, which I wolde not, that do I' (Rom 7.19).

Within the Judaeo-Christian tradition, the experiential reality of the Fall – our 'fall' – invariably reverts to the account of Adam and Eve in Genesis 2.7–3.24. As annotated by Paul (Rom 5.12–21), the account adumbrates man's proclivity toward sin or, in other words, toward a consistent deviation from obedience to the behests of God. The Christian doctrine of *original* sin – the hereditary transmission of Adam's sin to his descendants – was constructed by inference rather than by direct reference to the Scriptures. First argued by Tertullian (c 160–c 220), it posits the existence in us all of 'an antecedent, and in a certain sense natural, evil which arises from its corrupt origin' (*De anima* 27, 41; *De carne Christi* 2). The doctrine was much more fully developed by Augustine (354–430), who attributed the biological propagation of Adam's sin primarily to man's will. According to him, God 'made man upright: who being willingly depraved and justly condemned, begot all his progeny under the same deprivation and condemnation: for in him were we all, when as, he being seduced by the woman, corrupted us all' (*De civitate Dei* 13.14, ed 1610). More than a millennium later, Luther was even more unequivocal: 'Whatsoever is in our wil,' he wrote, 'is evil: whatsoever is in our understanding, is errour. Wherefore in spirituall matters man hath nothing but darknes, errours, ignoraunce, malice, and perversenes both of wil and understanding' (*A Commentary ... upon ... Galatians*, anon tr pub 1575, fol 82). For his part, Calvin redefines the Augustinian doctrine of original sin as 'the inheritably descendynge perversnesse and corruption of our nature, poured abroade into all the partes of the soule.' 'Adam,' he adds, 'was not onely the progenitour, but also the roote of mans nature, and therefore in his corruption was all mankynde worthelye corrupted' (*Institutes of the Christian Religion* 1.15.4, 2.1.4–8, 2.2.6, 2.5.19; tr Thomas Norton 1561).

The impact of Calvin on Tudor England was profound. Even more profound, however, was the impact of the modified Calvinism advanced partly by Theodore Beza (who succeeded Calvin in 1564 as head of Geneva's theocracy) and partly by the numerous theologians who erected Protestant equivalents of the massive 'cathedrals of the mind' characteristic of medieval Catholicism (eg, Gulielmus Bucanus, Heinrich Bullinger, Wolfgang Musculus, Lucas Trelcatius, Zacharias Ursinus, Pietro Martire Vermigli). Not always resident within the strict boundaries of Calvin's formidable *Institutes*, these theologians evolved a flexible, even 'liberal' Calvinism, its broad premises apparent generally among Spenser's contemporaries and particularly in Spenser himself. It should be remarked, however, that the doctrine of sin, including its hereditary emphasis, was accepted equally by all: the Fall of Man is both a historically datable calamity and an ever-recurring reality.

Spenser nowhere directly reiterates the Fall of Man as related in Genesis. Even though he bypasses the Garden of Eden, except as the setting for the Red Cross Knight's battle with the Dragon, he creates other terrains whose contours suggest the presence of that prototypical garden and, even more to the point, the prototypical occurrences within its confines and eventually within our own world. The allegory of *The Faerie Queene* rests firmly on the tendency of mankind to do the evil that it would not. The poem's mighty panorama parallels Augustine's vision in *De civitate Dei* of the diametric opposition between centrifugal love as represented by the City of God and centripetal self-love as represented by the City of Man. Likewise, the dichotomies espoused by Spenser – agape and eros, grace and nature, eternity and time, good and evil, order and chaos, concord and discord – most urgently argue that he did not underestimate the infinite attraction of evil; and because he did not, his interrogation of reality is attended by an implicit warning that we must transcend the poetry in search of the reality beyond. Where we may prefer the phantasmagoric house of Pride to the austere house of Holiness, or the luxuriant Bower of Bliss to the measured Garden of Adonis, Spenser insistently reminds us that the presence of hypocrisy in our midst constantly severs reality from appearance. His protagonists, ever misled by the superficially attractive because they are prone to 'evil which derives from its corrupt origin,' reenact the Fall – that is, attest to man's innate imperfection – to such an extent that one generalization appertains to them all: they are 'never without sin' (Evans 1970:3). The display of that most cardinal of sins, 'outragious pride,' is not confined to monsters like the Dragon (see I xi 53); it is also habitually exemplified by every human agent, arguably including even Arthur himself. Not at all coincidentally, moreover, several of Spenser's protagonists fall especially when they fall in love. The Blatant Beast rages, and will rage to the end of time, as a demonic force at once external to man and internal to the innermost recesses of his being.

The Fall is thus allegorized in *The Faerie Queene* as an omnipresent human experience. Spenser's somber conception, however, is much qualified by an optimistic strain, in line with the emphases of the Christian tradition at large. Man does indeed incline to do the evil that he would not; but he is also empowered to say with Paul, 'I can do all things through Christ' (Phil 4.13). The restoration of man by Christ, accomplished at a specific moment in history and promised to the believer for ever after, is not delineated by Spenser in the explicit fashion of the mystery plays, of Giles Fletcher's *Christs Victorie, and Triumph*, or of Milton's *Paradise Lost*; yet it is, for all that, a reality equally as omnipresent as is the Fall. In cosmic terms, this restoration involves the progress of history along the great gap of time until the dissolution of the globe itself, when 'all shall rest eternally / With Him that is the God of Sabbaoth hight' (VII viii 2). In national terms, it asserts with an urgency reminiscent of *De civitate Dei* that temporal entities like Augustine's Rome or Spenser's London are to be annihilated, their palpable glories dismantled. In human terms, it confirms the abrogation of the fallen individual's self-centeredness in favor of a state of mind receptive to the initiatives of divine grace. The experiences of the Red Cross Knight are in this respect crucial to the entire context within which *The Faerie Queene* unfolds: our 'natural' proclivity to credit that we can 'do all things' terminates in our 'falling' before Lucifera 'on lowly knee' (I v 16), and in our concomitant inability to defeat the agents of evil, save where the dispensation of grace through its visible signs, the sacraments, empowers the individual to eradicate the demons both within and without (I xi 36–55). The general principle is stated lucidly enough: 'many perils doe enfold / The righteous man, to make him daily fall ... Were not, that heavenly grace doth him uphold' (I viii I).

Spenser's optimistic strain pervades his poetry. It informs the gaiety that attends *Muiopotmos* and *Virgils Gnat*, it sustains the fecundity that molds *The Shepheardes Calender*, and it justifies the exuberance that in the *Fowre Hymnes* issues in a single if fourfold doxology on the unity of the created order. In his major poem, finally, Spenser weaves the optimistic strain within the poetry qua poetry, notably in the assurance that the stanzaic form intimates and the concord that the resonance of the well-tuned sounds evinces. The Fall of Man remains throughout a Cimmerian reality; and so does the judgment certain to come, whether within history or at the end of time. But the poet's emphatic concern with restoration transcends fallenness to suggest that each moment of time constitutes, through Christ, a new beginning. History is not the nightmare from which Joyce's Stephen Dedalus would in our time endeavor to awaken. Spenser permits a vision of the New Jerusalem only from afar, true; but his several knights, like his readers generally, emerge from Fairyland vigilant of the present because cognizant of the past, and unafraid of the future because admonished by both.

C.A. Patrides

The general theological premises of Protestantism are delineated in J.S. Whale 1955 *The Protestant Tradition* (Cambridge); for attitudes in England, consult Patrides 1966, chs 4–5. Two collections of primary sources, alike entitled *Reformed Dogmatics*, are ed Heinrich Heppe, rev Ernst Bizer, tr G.T. Thomson (London 1950) and tr and ed John W. Beardslee, III (New York 1965); also see Thomas F. Torrance, tr and ed 1959 *The School of Faith: The Catechisms of the Reformed Church* (New York) and Theodore G. Tappert, tr and ed 1959 *The Book of Concord: The Confessions of the Evangelical Lutheran Church* (Philadelphia). For a wide-ranging list of primary and secondary sources relevant to the Renaissance, see C.A. Patrides and Raymond B. Waddington, eds 1980 *The Age of Milton* (Manchester) pp 379–83, 408–10.

Fanchin, Molanna The comic tale of the rivers Fanchin and Molanna in the *Cantos of Mutabilitie* (*FQ* VII vi 38–55) is inserted by the narrator to explain why Arlo Hill changed from being 'the best and fairest Hill' in the range of hills near Spenser's Kilcolman Castle in Ireland to 'the most unpleasant, and most ill.' In some ways similar to the etiological tale of Bregog and Mulla in *Colin Clout* (104–55), this tells how the wood god Faunus manages to spy on Diana by bribing her nymph Molanna by an offer of union with her beloved Fanchin. Faunus sees the naked goddess, but reveals himself by his sudden, gross laughter at the sight of her 'some-what.' For his indiscretion, he is punished and pursued by the angry goddess and her nymphs; Diana, 'full of indignation,' decides to abandon the 'delicious brooke' and surrounding woods, leaving the area to 'Wolves and Thieves.' The tale foreshadows Nature's judgment of Mutabilitie, who attacks the moon goddess Cynthia. Both violate the cosmic order: Mutabilitie desires 'To see that [what] mortall eyes have never seene' (vi 32); Faunus forbiddenly gazes on Diana's 'lovely limbes' (45).

Ovid's Actaeon is changed into a stag and torn apart by his own hounds (*Metamorphoses* 3.155–252); Faunus is merely clad in a deerskin and chased by Diana's hounds, which soon weary. Ovid's Callisto is turned into a bear and almost slain by her son as punishment for betraying Juno (2.401–507); Molanna is only 'whelm'd with stones,' (explaining why the river is 'so shole' [40] or shallow). Ovid's Arethusa escapes the pursuit of the stream Alpheus (5.572–641); Molanna is wedded with 'her beloved *Fanchin*' through the implied agency of Faunus as a reward for betraying Diana. Although the episode is redolent with echoes of these Ovidian tales of pursuit and violent revenge, the punishments in *The Faerie Queene* are muted or entirely averted, heightening the comedy and at the same time enforcing a parallel with Mutabilitie, who is never forced to suffer for her rebellion. The only dark side of the episode is Diana's desertion of Arlo Hill.

Fanchin (so named to suggest a connection with Faunus which means 'foolish one') is the river Funsheon (or 'Funchin' *Colin Clout* 301) which rises in the Galtymore (Spenser's Arlo) and runs for nearly thirty miles before joining the Blackwater (Allo) about ten miles east or downstream of the Awbeg (Mulla). The name Molanna is a compound of 'old father *Mole*' (Ballyhoura and Galty Mountains) and Behanna (Behanagh), a stream rising in the Knockaterriff to the west of the Galtymore. Running for about four miles, it joins the Funsheon at the hamlet of Kilbeheny about eighteen miles northeast of Kilcolman Castle. Spenser's description of this lovely stream accurately corresponds to the local features.

Shohachi Fukuda

Fanshawe, Richard (1608–66) Diplomat, poet, translator, Cavalier, and husband of the memoirist Anne Fanshawe (1625–80), Fanshawe was considerably influenced by Spenser, especially at the beginning of his poetic career in the later 1620s when he translated the metrical portions of Boethius' *Consolation of Philosophy*. These poems (in BL, Add Ms 15,228) contain several clear Spenserian echoes. His translation of Metrum I.I begins, 'Lo I, that whilome lusty notes did rayse' (cf *FQ* I proem I), and alludes throughout to the *December* eclogue of *The Shepheardes Calender*; Metrum 5.5 borrows a line from *FQ* III iv 49.

A sonnet by Fanshawe, entitled 'A Dreame' (ed 1964:77), bears an obvious debt to Spenser's *Prothalamion*. It is a compliment to two daughters of Lord Aston, and begins 'I saw two swans come proudly downe the streame / Of Trent, as I his silver curles beheld; / To which, the doves that draw fayre Venus' teame, / And Venus selfe must beauty's scepter yield. / Jove was not halfe so white, when he was one.' His revision lessens the debt (Huntington Library HM116): 'Two stately swans sayle downe the Trent I saw / (Like spotless Ermynes charg'd on silver field) / To which the Doves which Venus chariot drawe, / And Venus selfe, must beauties scepter yeild.' This process of removing the Spenserian borrowings does not, however, indicate any slackening of interest in Spenser. In 1648 he published a miscellany of English and Latin poems as a supplement to the second printing of his translation of Guarini's *Il pastor fido*. Among these is a Spenserian allegory entitled 'A Canto of the *Progresse of Learning*,' in which the figures of Wit and Craft plead before the bar of Nature the relative merits of utilitarian and humane studies, a dilemma felt by Fanshawe in his own hesitation between the law and poetry. The form and style of the *Cantos of Mutabilitie* are imitated throughout this piece, which begins 'Tell me O Muse, and tell me *Spencers* ghost, / What may have bred in knowledge such decay ... ?' The poem is notable 'for the ease with which he uses the Spenserian stanza, which he was the first of a long and distinguished line of poets to adopt' (Buxton 1967:111).

In the same collection, a translation of Virgil's *Aeneid* 4 into the Spenserian stanza succeeds both as a continuous narrative and especially in Fanshawe's expressive use of the alexandrine: 'Did I not loath the Nuptiall Torch and Bed, / To this one fault perchance, perchance I might be led' (ed 1964:39). His choice of form suggests that he was attempting a thorough translation and sought the form of an accepted English epic to naturalize his Latin original.

Fanshawe's version of the *Aeneid* represents the height of his involvement with Spenser. After 1648 he published only translations from the Latin, Spanish, and Portuguese (most notably, Camoens' *Lusiad*) in which Spenserian influence is less apparent, though in a postscript he refers to 'the Greek Homer, the Latin Virgil, our Spencer' (*SP All* p 240).

Peter Davidson

John Buxton 1967 *A Tradition of Poetry* (London) ch 6; Richard Fanshawe ms HM 116 quoted by permission of The Huntington Library (San Marino, Calif); Fanshawe ed 1964; *Sp All* pp 236, 240–1.

fantasy literature *The Faerie Queene* may be considered the first major work of fantasy in the Western world. Successor to but distinct from medieval romance in which elements of fantasy conventionally infuse the primary world, the poem establishes fantasy as an autonomous secondary world. Ariosto's *Orlando furioso*, with which it is often compared, mingles human and superhuman elements but largely contains its action within the identifiable map of Europe. Coleridge, who noted the remarkable absence of specific time and place in Spenser's poem, identified this secondary world as a mental landscape (ed 1936:36). Spenser's Fairyland is a visionary world which, like a dream, follows its own strange laws and moves in its own wondrous ways. In this world, magic is operative, and spirits lurk in wood and well. Characters frequently possess magical powers and inspire awe or fear. Of particular importance is the figure of the wizard, whether projected positively as Merlin or negatively as Archimago. Events deal with archetypal themes such as coming of age, struggles with monsters, death and rebirth. The narrative structure, particularly in the first three books, is a physical journey which is also a spiritual quest. Ultimately the landscape of Fairyland offers a mirror of the human imagination, and the reader's experience there represents an inward journey.

In the nineteenth century, a resurgence of interest in the secondary world of the imagination brought *The Faerie Queene* into focus as a paradigm of fantasy literature. Two significant writers of fantasy, William Morris and George MacDonald, were indebted to Spenser both for a concept of Faerie and for particular details of adventures in that perilous realm.

Morris' *Wood beyond the World* (1894) and *The Well at the World's End* (1896) reveal Spenser's influence. The hero of the first romance undertakes a journey over sea and land pursuing a recurring vision of a maiden, a lady, and a dwarf, the two female figures representing respectively chastity and sensuality. The chaste maid, an enchantress, kills the lady, an evil witch-queen, and marries the hero. These three characters parallel Una, Duessa, and the Red Cross Knight. Morris' later romances also borrow many Spenserian elements including the allegorical landscape. They adopt romance formulas in which the hero undertakes a quest that leads him through the Wood Perilous to the Castle of Abundance, and eventually to the wondrous well which endows him with special gifts of ability and longevity; he then returns home to be made king.

Spenser's informing spirit is even more apparent in MacDonald's *Phantastes* (1858), which not only borrows its title by way of Phineas Fletcher's *Purple Island* from Spenser's character in the castle of Alma episode (*FQ* II ix 52) but also quotes from the poet in chapter headings. Cast as a dream-vision, *Phantastes* concerns Anodos' journey through Fairy Land, where he undergoes remarkable encounters with ogres, giants, dragons, goblins, and tree spirits. Throughout this work the atmosphere evoked is one that C.S. Lewis later identified as holiness, thus connecting it in mood and theme with *FQ* I.

The twentieth-century psyche has responded overwhelmingly to the lure of Faerie, and it is no coincidence that some of the most popular writers of fantasy have been readers of *The Faerie Queene*. Closest in spirit to Spenser is C.S. Lewis. In his Chronicles of Narnia and in his space trilogy, Spenserian motifs abound. In *Perelandra* (1943), the second in the trilogy, the hero's death struggle with the Unman, a totally degenerate evil scientist, is analogous to Arthur's victory over Maleger in *FQ* II: the hero Ransom tries in vain to kill the seemingly indestructible Unman by throwing a stone at him, and finally, like Arthur, succeeds by throwing his enemy into water.

In the Narnian novel *The Magician's Nephew* (1955), the hero recalls Guyon as he is tempted by a tree bearing golden apples. The most extensive parallel to the story of Guyon, however, occurs in *The Silver Chair* (1953), where the chair corresponds to the silver seat used to tempt Guyon in the house of Mammon (II vii 53, 63). The setting of Lewis' silver chair is at once a subterranean location and the site of a spiritual ordeal, as is Mammon's dwelling for Spenser's knight. Guyon's implied refusal to accept Mammon's reductive view that the material world is an end in itself has its counterpart in the temptation presented to Lewis' character Puddleglum. This gloomy but heroic figure resists the hypnotic words of the green witch claiming that there is no sunlit world above the dark underground prison with its silver chair holding the prince captive under its grim spell. When the prince is stirred to challenge his enchantress, he is subjected to the startling revelation that one whom he had seen as a beautiful woman is actually part serpent. The scene of her gradual exposure, as her lower limbs transform into the coils of a serpent, closely resembles the scene in which the monstrous underparts of Duessa are exposed to Redcrosse (*FQ* I viii 46–9).

Although J.R.R. Tolkien in his trilogy *The Lord of the Rings* (1954–5) writes largely in an Anglo-Saxon heroic mode, he is indebted to Spenser for his conceptual grasp of Faerie, relating its appeal to the joyous Christian belief in an ultimately happy ending (Tolkien 1966). He finds the profound satisfaction of fantasy literature in its offering of recovery (regaining a clearer view of reality), escape (from the prison of material reality), and consolation (joy beyond the walls of the world). Parallels to *The Faerie Queene* include the depiction of a warrior maiden, Eowyn, who strongly resembles Britomart, particularly in the description of her hair tumbling from under her helmet.

Contemporary fantasist Ursula K. LeGuin also suggests a Spenserian influence in *The Beginning Place* (1980). The climactic scene in this quest narrative of two young people forced to fight a dragon is strongly reminiscent of Redcrosse's struggle with the monster Error. LeGuin's monster is also female, although not depicted with young; and it is summoned from its cave by the young woman who taunts it while encouraging her adolescent male companion, a most unlikely St George figure, to strike the death blow. Although not named as an abstraction, the repulsive monster is clearly an allegorical representation, not of moral but of psychological error.

Spenser's work has also been the subject of comic and parodic imitation in modern fantasy. In their story 'The Mathematics of Magic' in *The Incomplete Enchanter* (1941), L. Sprague de Camp and Fletcher Pratt offer an anachronistic parody based largely on the last four books of *The Faerie Queene*, with two time travelers from the twentieth century visiting Fairyland and meeting Britomart, Amoret, Belphoebe, the Blatant Beast, and others. In this comic pilgrimage, the older traveler plays a double role of palmer and magician while the younger strives to become a hero, eventually winning a combat for Gloriana and being rewarded with the love of Belphoebe. Also parodic is the novel *Gloriana* (1978) by Michael Moorcock, which adopts both Spenserian characters and figures from Elizabethan drama and history.

These borrowings suggest a profound relevance of Spenser's poem to certain contemporary writers and readers. Although most recent works of fantasy and science fiction may not seem as explicitly allegorical as *The Faerie Queene*, the nature of fantasy as a visionary mode is implicitly allegorical. Essentially the quest is always the one quest, however its manifestations may vary, and the wizard, whatever his name, is always the archetypal Wise Old Man. The inward journey which the reader experiences as he travels with Gloriana's knights moves through the same spiritual landscape as in the imaginative worlds of Lewis' Narnia, Tolkien's Middle Earth, and LeGuin's Earthsea. The reader of contemporary fantasy will find in *The Faerie Queene* the enriching experience of discovering an inspiring source. Conversely, the reader of Spenser will find in fantasy literature the excitement of the renewed spiritual quest in the ever-shifting, yet ever-the-same, landscape of the imagination.

CHARLOTTE SPIVACK

Roger C. Schlobin ed 1982 *The Aesthetics of Fantasy Literature and Art* (Notre Dame, Ind); Charlotte Spivack 1981 'The Perilous Realm: Phantasy as Literature' *Centennial Review* 25:133–49; Ann Swinfen 1984 *In Defence of Fantasy: A Study of the Genre in English and American Literature since 1945* (London); J.R.R. Tolkien 1966 'On Fairy Stories' in *The Tolkien Reader* (New York) pp 3–84; Gary K. Wolfe 1975 'Symbolic Fantasy' *Genre* 5:194–209.

Fates From Latin *fatum*, 'that which has been spoken,' and thus, by extension, destined. In Boccaccio's *Genealogia* 1.5, the three Fates – Clotho, Lachesis, and Atropos – are identified as daughters of Daemogorgon and also of Erebus and Night (cf *SC, Nov* 148 gloss). These three sisters, traditionally represented as spinning, measuring, and cutting the thread of life (see T. Cooper 1565, sv 'Parcae'), are associated with the dark underworld and with chaos, out of which the world was held to be created. Boccaccio indirectly, and other Renaissance mythographers directly, record Plato's interpretation of the Fates (*Republic* 10) as the daughters of Necessity.

The word *fate* occurs more frequently in Spenser's poetry than related words like *destiny* or *necessity*. In some contexts, it is used almost formulaically with *chance* and *Fortune* to mean a mishap (eg, *Virgils Gnat* 361–3, *Muiopotmos* 417–21, *FQ* VI xi 31). In other contexts, it refers to the three Fates or to the working of Christian providence in the natural world, particularly as described by Boethius in *The Consolation of Philosophy*. In *The Faerie Queene*, *fate* rarely has the classical meaning of 'necessity,' except in relation to demonic figures who wish to restrict or deny God's providence (eg, Night in I v 25, who speaks of the 'chayne of strong necessitee,' and Despair in I ix 42, who speaks of the 'eternall booke of fate').

The Fates are mentioned conventionally in the early poems (eg, *Ruines of Time* 17–18, 309), though atypically when Clotho is said to awaken Love in order to create the world out of chaos, and when they lament Dido's untimely death: 'The fatall sisters eke repent, / Her vitall threde so soone was spent' (*SC, Nov* 148–9). Their story is told at *FQ* IV ii 47–52. To save the lives of her sons, Agape descends into the abyss where the Fates dwell and where Daemogorgon, confined 'in dull darkenesse,' keeps the 'hideous *Chaos*.' The Fates are linked with destiny and perhaps providence when Agape learns that the length of her sons' lives is 'ordained by eternall fate.' Lachesis tells her that the decrees of the Fates are fixed: 'for what the Fates do once decree, / Not all the gods can chaunge, nor *Jove* him self can free.' Agape requests and receives the promise that the spirits or 'lives' of Priamond and Diamond, who are destined to die young, will pass into her third son, Triamond. In this way, Spenser suggests that love can affect if not altogether change destiny.

Fate is specifically related to the providentially ordered processes of love and generation in nature and society in the story of Britomart and Artegall, in ways that seem indirectly indebted to Boethius. Boethius calls God's providence ('purveaunce'), that foresight which exists in the mind of God. What the pagan world called destiny, he writes, is providence working itself out within the created universe (see Chaucer *Boece* 4 prosa 6). In the *Genealogia*, Boccaccio quotes Cicero's statement that fate is the 'eternal cause of things' and adds the relevant passages from *The Consolation of Philosophy*, thus reemphasizing Boethius' understanding of pagan fate as Christian destiny (see also Cartari 1571:301–2).

Spenser writes that divine love, 'pourd into men,' directs their actions 'aright' and thus fulfills the 'fatall purpose of divine foresight' (III iii 1–2). Accordingly, Merlin tells Britomart that when she fell in love with Artegall's image in a mirror, fate ordained her love, their marriage, and their subsequent history (21–8). Using the Boethian distinction between providence and destiny, Merlin tells her that it was 'the streight course of heavenly destiny, / Led with eternall providence, that has / Guided thy glaunce, to bring his will to pas.' Therefore, he says, she must submit her will to providence 'And do by all dew meanes [her] destiny fulfill.' Men's 'good endevours,' in other words, should confirm their fate, 'And guide the heavenly causes to their constant terme.' For Britomart, this good endeavor reaches its first conclusion when, after their battle, she sees and loves Artegall. Glauce witnesses what 'secret fate hath in this Ladie wrought' (IV vi 30; see Klein 1973).

The concept of providentially ordered (fated) love and generation is given its grandest affirmation in the Garden of Adonis and in the debate between Mutabilitie and Nature. (Since the Fates were concerned with birth as well as death, they were also sometimes considered goddesses of birth.) Here the underlying processes of natural creation are fostered and maintained by the same 'Almightie lord' who first created this Eden (III vi 34) and bade all things 'to increase and multiply.' Genius, perhaps an agent of Boethian destiny, fulfills this command as he 'letteth in [and] out ... Such as him list, such as eternall fate / Ordained hath' (32).

Fate is again identified with the working out of God's providence in the conflict between Mutabilitie and Jove. Although Mutabilitie claims dominion over the created universe and Jove himself, both she and Jove must submit to the higher authority of Nature, who is revealed as that providence which moves the created universe to seek through change its own perfection. Nature rules that, although 'all things stedfastnes doe hate,' they all move through change towards the final perfection which was fated before their beginnings: 'They are not changed from their first estate; / But by their change their being doe dilate: / And turning to themselves at length againe, / Doe worke their owne perfection so by fate' (VII vii 58).

Joan Larsen Klein

Fathers, Greek John Welles, BD, who died at Pembroke Hall in 1569 (the year of Spenser's matriculation), left in his study an 'Opera Crisostomi. 5. voluminibus,' an 'Opera Basilii I volumine' and a 'Lexicon grecum'; from this we may infer the possibility that Spenser had some acquaintance with the Greek Church Fathers. Welles is representative of 176 Cambridge scholars who died in residence between 1535 and 1599: inventories (in Cambridge University Archives) reveal that they owned 277 copies of editions of the following Greek Fathers: 21 copies of Athanasius, 24 of Gregory of Nazianzus, 5 of Gregory of Nyssa, 32 of Basil, 18 of Cyril of Alexandria, 2 of Cyril of Jerusalem, 9 of Dionysius the Areopagite, 16 of Irenaeus, 25 of John of Damascus, and a surprising 125 of John Chrysostom. These figures show that Spenser was educated in a milieu in which Eastern patrology was probably influential.

Interest in the Greek Fathers was not peculiar to Cambridge. Almost the entire corpus of Greek patristic writing was published in Western Europe in the sixteenth century – in Greek, in Latin, and a few works in English. Most of the editions were from the houses of the great Renaissance scholar-printers, such as Froben, Estienne, Aldus, and Chaudiere. Pirckheimer, Billius, Musculus, and Erasmus were among the editors and translators. These were books to attract attention, and evidently they did. Many works were printed several times, including Petrus Nannius' translation of Athanasius, Erasmus' Greek Basil and his Chrysostom in five volumes, a Greek collected works of Cyril of Jerusalem as well as Grodecius' Latin version, Erasmus' Latin Irenaeus, and Jacobus Billius' texts of John of Damascus. There is every indication that the Greek Fathers were popular in the sixteenth century, almost as widely printed as the Western Doctors and the Reformers. English patristic publication before 1600 was scanty, but the Cambridge inventories testify to English acquisition of the continental editions (Haugaard 1979).

So, too, do frequent references to the Greek Fathers in English Reformation literature. For instance, in *An Apology of the Church of England*, John Jewel cites or quotes Athanasius, Basil, Cyril of Alexandria, and Gregory of Nazianzus; in his *Actes and Monuments*, Foxe invokes Athanasius, Basil, Chrysostom, Irenaeus, Gregory of Nazianzus, Gregory of Nyssa, and Cyril of Alexandria; and in his preface to the Great Bible, Cranmer quotes extensively from Chrysostom and Basil. The Reformers use the Greek Fathers against Roman Catholicism, appealing against alleged Latin aberrations to the ancient and undivided church – a church governed by an emperor rather than a pope. In view of Spenser's representation of the Eastern emperor in *FQ* I, and his identifying Una (the true church) with the East and Duessa and false Christianity with Western Christendom (i 5, ii 22), we may infer his familiarity with that interpretation of ecclesiastical history and thus with the arguments from Greek patrology which sustained it (see also Kermode 1964–5). The humanist motive for Eastern patristic publication may also have attracted Spenser. Recovery of the Fathers was a part of the humanist endeavor, as dear as the recovery of classical texts to scholars like Erasmus. To the extent that Spenser was affected by the northern European Renaissance, he is likely to have been influenced as well by the Eastern Fathers.

None of this proves Greek patristic influence upon Spenser; there is no conclusive evidence. Perhaps none is needed. Resemblances and echoes may be enough to establish that Spenser is writing within a tradition hospitable to patristic imagery and interpretation. Thus, he describes Redcrosse's fornication with Duessa (*FQ* I vii 7) in phrases used by Chrysostom to characterize the slothful and lustful Christian who, as Redcrosse has done, lays aside the Pauline armor of Ephesians 6 (Chrysostom 1581 *An Exposition upon the Epistle of S. Paule the Apostle to the Ephesians*; Weatherby 1982). Redcrosse's baptism and subsequent unction with balm from the Tree of Life (*FQ* I xi 29–34, 48–50) closely resemble Cyril of Jerusalem's descriptions of baptism and postbaptismal chrismation in his *Mystagogical Catecheses* (Weatherby 1987b). The comparison of Dame Nature with the transfigured Christ amounts to a veritable Eastern signature in the *Cantos of Mutabilitie*

(*FQ* VII vii 7), since the Greek Fathers consistently interpret the Transfiguration as both manifesting and effecting the deification of nature. (Note that the authoritative Eastern treatise on the subject had been newly published in the West in a Greco-Latin text in John of Damascus *Opera* tr Jacobus Billius Prunaeus [Paris 1577]; see Weatherby 1984.) These passages suggest that Spenser's theology and thus his allegory may have been shaped by Greek as well as by Latin and Reformed Christianity.

HAROLD L. WEATHERBY

William P. Haugaard 1979 'Renaissance Patristic Scholarship and Theology in Sixteenth-Century England' *SCJ* 10.3:37–60; E.S. Leedham-Green 1986 *Books in Cambridge Inventories: Book-Lists from Vice-Chancellor's Court Probate Inventories in the Tudor and Stuart Periods* 2 vols (Cambridge); Harold L. Weatherby 1982; Weatherby 1984; Weatherby 1987a; Weatherby 1987b 'What Spenser Meant by Holinesse: Baptism in Book One of *The Faerie Queene*' *SP* 84:286–307; Weatherby 1988 'Two Images of Mortalitie: Spenser and Original Sin' *SP* 85:321–52.

Fathers, Latin Orthodoxy, holiness, antiquity, and ecclesiastical approval – these words mark the theologians who guarded the deposit of faith (1 Tim 4.6) during the first eight centuries of Christianity, though the title of Father extends to others who defended the church as it faced the world it was to evangelize in a time of schism and heresy. In the course of their defense, the Fathers adapted pagan learning – what they called 'the spoils of the Egyptians' – to the Christian context, thereby making possible the Renaissance outlook we know as Christian humanism.

Patristic authority was quoted freely and extensively by Reformation humanists of every persuasion who, like Calvin, boasted that 'Augustine is completely on our side.' Erasmus' editions of the Greek and Latin Fathers helped make the writings of the church available: the four great Latin Fathers – Ambrose (c 339–97), Jerome (c 342–420), Augustine (354–430) and Gregory (c 540–604) – were consulted by most undergraduates in Spenser's time, together with other patristic theologians who, variously, offered models of prose style (eg, Lactantius, c 240–c 320, called by Pico della Mirandola 'the Christian Cicero'), models of allegorical poetry (Prudentius, 348–c 410), and pictures of corporate worship in the early church (Cyprian, c 200–58). Their greatest influence lay in doctrinal and dogmatic controversy where they appealed to Protestants anxious to restore the church to the less speculative and more practical duties of men and women to God described by the Latin writers of Christian antiquity. Yet their renewed appeal should not overshadow the fact that the patristic tradition, with its extension in the twelfth century (see *Alanus de Insulis), shaped medieval thought and expression authoritatively, and was mediated to Spenser's generation in every way, in the sermons in the village church as much as in humanist treatises. Because of the number, complexity, and ubiquity of the works of the Latin Fathers, any particular indebtedness to them by Spenser is likely to remain doubtful.

On a broader scale, however, there are special reasons for identifying the works of Augustine, the exemplar of the Christian philosophical tradition, as an essential context in which *The Faerie Queene* may be read. An argument for his importance to Spenser begins with a consideration of the change in perspective of the Virgilian epic after Augustine (see *heroic poem before Spenser).

The epic traditionally invokes a consciousness of history as moving toward the founding of a just society based on a dynasty. Augustine's vision of the relationship between the earthly city and the heavenly city gave a new impetus to this dynastic theme, with the Christian epic poet substituting the earthly city 'ruled by the love of ruling' (*City of God* 14.28) for Virgil's Carthage, and marriage in the heavenly city for Virgil's consecration of Rome. Augustine's own journey from Carthage to Rome, suggestively if not self-consciously paralleling that of Aeneas (see *Confessions* 1.13), assimilates the pagan 'wanderings' to a destiny beyond time. Commentaries on Virgil by Fulgentius (6th c), Bernard Sylvestris (12th c), and Cristoforo Landino (15th c), together with the popular 'Thirteenth Book of the *Aeneid*' by Mapheus Vegius (15th c) see in Virgil's epic an allegory of the progress of the soul through material existence, and so help amplify a tradition which construes Aeneas as having a potential for completion in the life of Christ. The fame that is the reward of the classical hero becomes the earthly anticipation of heavenly glory (*City of God* 5.14–16), as Cleopolis is a mirror of the New Jerusalem in *FQ* I x 58–9. The Augustinian metaphor of marriage (of body to soul, of the faithful to Christ) extends the dynastic theme beyond the unresolved state of affairs at the close of the *Aeneid*, with the classical choice between personal love and obligation to empire, between passion and reason, transcended by the Christian historical destiny in which love and duty, body and soul, are one (*City of God* 14.28).

The apocalyptic impulse given to the epic quest by Augustine finds smaller but sharper focus in the realm of individual moral action. Contemplating the collapse of Roman civilization in AD 410, Augustine sees in classical philosophy the failure of materialism, which he describes as a mentality bound to the exterior object projected by the will to power and accepted by the intelligence as real and natural. The polarities of character versus destiny, duty versus desire, soul versus body that bedeviled the Roman quest for 'empire without end' (*Aeneid* 1.279) arise when the exterior object is invoked as the necessary obstacle to the will's need to endure and conquer. Augustine everywhere laments these fatal polarities in the classical vision.

A perspective of habitual and illusory conflict is given explicitly pagan reference in these Augustinian terms by Spenser, beginning with his own Augustinian meditation in *Ruines of Time* and *Ruines of Rome*. The symmetrical battle between Artegall and Radigund in *FQ* V v is his most vivid picture of the classical fallacy of character as virtue pitted against *fortuna*, and of the captivity of the unregenerate will to nature. The futile debate between freedom and necessity in the persons of Mutabilitie and Jove magnifies what Augustine perceives as the error of *scientia* in its identification of knowledge with power and its obsession with ruling an exterior object. For Augustine, any effort of self-realization without obedience to God leads inevitably to self-righteousness (*City of God* 19.25), seen in Redcrosse. The illusion of moral self-sufficiency which classical ethics engenders forever tempts the individual into 'the desire of making trial of his own power' (*On the Trinity* 12.11), seen in Guyon. Redcrosse's relapse into sin is particularly detailed, following Augustine's observation that sin originates in a passion for independence and develops as a result of the physical satisfactions it then enjoys until it is confirmed by habit (*On Patience* 14). The behavior finds expression in ignorance or blindness (*ignorantia*, *caecitas*), the 'error' that permits the shadow of the self to interfere with vision, and in *difficultas* or *necessitas*, an increasing inability to resist the seduction of sense (*On Free Choice* 3.19.53, *On Nature and Grace* 81). The condition of sin is depicted in *The Faerie Queene* in naturalistic and pagan settings. When Redcrosse, with a Virgilian resigned melancholy, fights Sansjoy, and there follows a list of pagan rulers imprisoned through Lucifera's pride and earthly glory, the chief context is probably Augustinian.

Augustine's philosophical response to the self-defeating contests which the unregenerate will sets for itself is to adduce the principle of hierarchy. By separating the Creator from creation, by relating visible to invisible things as surface to interior, he breaks open the arena of classical materialism. Distinct from a fatalistic view of history based on the cycles of nature, he asserts providential history (*City of God* 12.14). Distinct from the piecemeal obsession with 'objects' in 'nature,' he celebrates the pattern of eternity evident in the passage of visible change (*Confessions* 4.10). Distinct from the divided soul of classical ethics, he points out that the life of the soul and the life of the body 'are not two different things, but one and the same thing, viz., man living according to man' (*City of God* 14.4).

These teachings apply particularly to *FQ* V. Artegall's training in natural law, his obsession with mastery, his corresponding repression of *eros* for *furor*, mark him as a hero in the classical mold. Britomart's dream in Isis Church (vii 12–23), however, portends an apocalyptic turning to membership in the divine society, with the passions of the Typhonic beast who is both Osiris and crocodile liberated and redirected in the man of reason through his union with the woman of spirit, and with the linking of body and vision through will in the dynamic Christian personality who can say, 'For I am, and know, and will' (*Confessions* 13.11, *On the Trinity* 10.11.17; cf Hooker *Laws* 1.11.3). Augustine identifies human willfulness, swollen and driven by desire, as the central force in the integration of body and soul; the crocodile symbolizes this voracity which is the spur toward complete being, uniting the outer and inner person, *scientia* and *sapientia*, Artegall and Britomart, through the *ardor caritatis* ('heat of love') or *ignis voluntatis* ('flame of the will') which, for Augustine, represents the working of grace as a natural law (*Retractions* 2.42). Referring by analogy to the dynamics of sense perception, Augustine describes the uniting through the will of body and understanding as coming about in a manner so violent that it can only be described as desire, passion, or lust (*On the Trinity* 11.2). In the protracted and fierce joust of the two dynastic heroes, which occurs in the presence of Scudamour, the knight of eros (*FQ* IV vi), is pictured divine grace working through the very willfulness that persistently opposes it.

Where the will loving its own power relapses from a universal to a private good, there is no possibility of regeneration except through grace. And grace comes to the Spenserian hero once he has exhausted himself in efforts of self-realization. For Augustine, a good will is the greatest gift of God to man and woman, and grace is 'prevenient,' supplying energy to the will that is good. The providential and naturalistic world of Book VI especially elaborates Augustine's assertion that the order of grace is not opposed to the order of nature, but the means through which nature is liberated and controlled (*Retractions* 2.42). The 'heavenly seedes of bounty soveraine' (proem 3) and the dance of the Graces (x) illustrate this dispensation, which is earlier shown by physical details in the 'Infinite shapes of creatures' of the Garden of Adonis (III vi 34–6). Created all at once and pre-existing, yet going out into the world one by one and increasing and multiplying in obedience to the divine command, the forms are identifiable with what Augustine, following late classical philosophy and Genesis 2.4–5, termed the 'seminal reasons' or 'reason principles' (*Commentary on Genesis according to the Literal Sense* 5): 'the model, according to which the creature is fashioned, is in the Word of God before the creature is fashioned' (2.8).

With the signs of the Creator found in all created things, it is vital for lovers to refer the beauty they perceive to its divine source (*Hymne of Beautie* 211–31). Such visionary perception marks a return in spirit to the home of all beauty, which in the metaphors of Augustine's influential *On Christian Doctrine* (1.4.4) is a native country from which humanity is exiled in its pilgrimage through time. When Sidney mentions the kind of love against which his passion for Stella is an aberration, he quotes Augustine ironically: 'True, that on earth we are but pilgrims made / And should in soul up to our country move' (*Astrophil and Stella* 3). Spenser, typically, quotes Augustine with sincerity: 'But mindfull still of your first countries sight, / Doe still preserve your first informed grace' (*HB* 166–7).

SEAN KANE

For the English translations of the Latin Fathers, see *STC* under their names; all were widely available in the 16th c in collected Latin editions and in separate publications of individual works. The texts are assembled for modern readers in *PLat* and its reprints. Two series present English translations: the 19th-c Library of the Fathers and the 20th-c Fathers of the Church. For Augustine, there are many editions and translations of his works; a useful collection is Augustine ed 1948; see also *On Christian Doctrine* tr D.W. Robertson, Jr (New York 1958) and *On Free Choice of the Will* tr Anna S. Benjamin and L.H. Hackstaff (Indianapolis 1964).

Little has been written on Spenser and the Fathers, though some discussion is found in Rathborne 1937 (the two cities in relation to *FQ* I), Ellrodt 1960, Nelson 1963, Hankins 1971 (the reason principles in the Garden of Adonis), Nohrnberg 1976 (various topical allusions), Fichter 1982 (dynastic epic), and Kane 1989 (the critique of classical materialism and the psychology of sin).

Faunus, fauns Fauns are classical woodland deities, often portrayed as part man, part goat, and frequently indistinguishable from satyrs except in name. Conti identifies both as children of Faunus but suggests that fauns offer protection to workers in the country (*Mythologiae* 5.9). They are usually more benign than the sexually aggressive satyrs.

Spenser seems to have had no set view of their temperaments, however, and presents them as either benign or bestial. The fauns in *SC, Julye* are 'holy' (77); as E.K. notes, they 'be of Poetes feigned to be Gods of the Woode.' In *Virgils Gnat*, they form part of an untroubled pastoral landscape (145–52). *FQ* I pictures them 'dauncing in a rownd' with the satyrs (vi 7) and taking part in the rescue of Una. In the *Theatre for Worldlings* (sonnet 10), they are a 'naked rout' of unclean beings who chase nymphs with 'hideous cry.' *Teares of the Muses* also presents them as brutish and beastly (268–70).

Faunus, who appears in *FQ* II and VII, lives up to the character given him by Horace as the god who chases nymphs (*Odes* 3.18.1). In Book II, the nymph he pursues prays to Diana and is changed into a stone from which issue two streams, 'As from two weeping eyes' (ii 7–9; cf Ovid's accounts of Daphne in *Metamorphoses* 1.452–567 and of Arethusa in 5.572–641). The nymph's story is told by the Palmer to explain why the well does not clean the hands of Ruddymane; here, Faunus is one of the many figures in Book II who demonstrate the nature and effect of concupiscence.

Spenser's original myth of Faunus and Diana (*FQ* VII vi 37–55), while having most of the elements of an Ovidian narrative, lacks any metamorphosis except perhaps that of the landscape. Faunus, who conspires to see Diana naked, is clothed in a deerskin and pursued by hounds, but he is allowed to escape rather than being changed into a beast and killed as in the parallel Ovidian myth of Actaeon and Diana (*Met* 3.138–252, Conti 6.24), a myth allegorized by Fraunce as a warning against excess curiosity, 'spying and prying into those matters, which be above our reache' (ed 1975:109). Through this burlesque or parody of Ovid, Spenser turns a potential tragedy into a comedy. In doing so, he also offers a pastoral counterpart to the main action of the *Cantos of Mutabilitie*, Faunus' attempt on Diana being a farcical version of Mutabilitie's attack on Cynthia. Since Faunus had been confused in Roman and later mythology with Pan, the Greek god of nature, he is also associated with the figure of Nature in the main plot. Nature and Mutabilitie are thus symbolically united in this comic character before they are revealed to be part of the same cosmic whole in the main action.

Spenser's pastoral interlude is also a myth of the Fall, but Faunus' action is not an intrusion of satanic evil into a paradisal world, despite his gifts of 'Queene-apples, and red Cherries.' Rather, he is merely 'Foolish God *Faunus*' and is treated accordingly; his very name, according to Servius, derives from the same sources as *Fatuus*, the foolish one (Nelson 1963:300). His gross sexuality, for all the problems it causes, is something which even the virgin Diana may not destroy, since 'the Wood-gods breed ... must for ever live' (50). Though he seems to be nothing more than a peeping Tom, Faunus may symbolize our human sexual appetites, comic but necessary and indestructible.

This episode is related to other Ovidian myths: Callisto and her banishment by Diana, Alpheus and Arethusa, and the rape of Omphale by Faunus (*Met* 2.401–507, 5.572–641, *Fasti* 2.267–358; see R.N. Ringler 1965–6). In addition, Faunus may be related to the figure of Momus, who appears in Lucian and later classical literature (Nohrnberg 1976:751–2; cf vi 49). He can be seen as the product of 'medieval modes of imagination,' and the episode taken as the middle term of a pagan-to-medieval-to-Renaissance transformation of modes within the *Cantos* (Berger 1968b:148). Since his comic trickery and his presence in a nature myth concerned with Arlo Hill suggest a folkloric mode of imagination at work, Spenser's Faunus may in part derive from Irish folk or fairy tales (see R.M. Smith 1935a).

RICHARD D. JORDAN

Berger 1968b; Doyle 1973; Friedmann 1966; R.N. Ringler 1965–6

Ferryman In the allegory of temperance, Alma's Ferryman who rows Guyon and the Palmer to Acrasia's island represents the will that enables one to carry out the actions dictated by reason. He thus complements the Palmer, with whom he alternates in advising Guyon about the perils of the voyage (*FQ* II xii 3–37). Since he embodies the active principle – stamina, bodily strength – he is described in physical terms; and four of the five objects he warns against represent physical dangers: the Gulf of Greediness, the Rock of Reproach, the Whirlpool of Decay, the Quicksand of Unthriftyhed (Nellist 1963). Thus, great emphasis is placed on his 'puissance,' 'brawnie armes,' oarsmanship, and navigational skills. His allegorical significance as the will is figured forth in his 'stedfastnesse'; 'wary' and 'heedfull' of danger, he holds to his course even when tired. It is therefore no accident that the fifth danger he descries is the Wandering Islands: because they constitute temptation rather than physical danger, avoiding them demands resoluteness.

The Ferryman's warnings against the Wandering Islands also point up the contrast between him and Phaedria, who reappears presently. This contrast is reinforced by verbal echoes of canto vi in the description of the water and boat, but more strongly by the fact that they both 'ferry' passengers across water – although Phaedria is anything but a steadfast navigator and her boat is without oars.

For his Ferryman, Spenser possibly drew on the classical Charon (suggested by Guyon's calling him 'old Syre') or on later interpretations of him as confidence in God's mercy helping one navigate the sea of error (Conti *Mythologiae* 3.4). By contrast, in the Homeric episode which serves as a model for Spenser's Gulf, Rock, and Mermaids (*Odyssey* 12), Odysseus' oarsmen prove wanting in both navigational and moral strengths, a fact not lost on later commentators. They thus stand in sharp contrast to Spenser's capable and resolute oarsman, skillfully navigating his moral waterscape. (See also Lotspeich 1932:21–2.)

BRENDA M. HOSINGTON

Ficino, Marsilio (1433–99) Florentine scholar, philosopher, psychologist, and theorist of magic, Ficino became the father of Renaissance Neoplatonism. He was patronized by three generations of the Medici, with whom he was on intimate terms and over whose circle of poets, diplomat-scholars, and intellectuals he presided. He served as the informal leader of the 'Platonic Academy,' which was not an organized institution, but a group of gifted and influential men with a shared enthusiasm for philosophical and theological discussion, for the arts, particularly music and poetry, and for the cultivation of friendship and the inner life. They assembled regularly in the villas of the Medici and other Florentine patricians for recitals, lectures, conversation, and banquets, and thought of themselves as recapturing the spirit of Plato's original Academy. Ficino was their Plato reborn. There was a curious mixture of jocosity, studied courtesy, and high seriousness in all this, but obviously one that spoke to the age, for the fame of the Platonic Academy quickly spread throughout Europe and inspired a number of academies, especially in Italy and France, but including the Sidney circle's Areopagus.

Ficino is an interesting thinker who developed, within the context of an inherited scholasticism and as a result of his grasp of a number of newly discovered texts from antiquity, a philosophical system that reflects attitudes and emphases now deemed characteristic of the Renaissance. Nevertheless, he is chiefly famous as the champion and interpreter of the rediscovered Plato whom he saw through the eyes of Plato's rather distant successors, the third-century Plotinus and his fourth- and fifth-century followers, Iamblichus, Proclus, and Pseudo-Dionysius. We now think of these successors as the ancient Neoplatonists, but Ficino thought of them simply as the Platonists, the standardbearers of a unified and essentially theological tradition that stemmed directly from Plato and what they all interpreted as his monistic metaphysics. Ficino was the first to render the whole of Plato into Latin (including several dialogues we now regard as apocryphal). He thereby made the dialogues available to the West for the first time in a millennium, and to this day his remains the chief Latin translation and a monument of Renaissance erudition. It, or other Renaissance versions indebted to it, were Spenser's Platonic sources. Spenser may have also known the long and extraordinarily rich and suggestive commentary on the *Symposium*, entitled *De amore*, which Ficino had composed by July 1469 and included in his Plato edition of 1484, along with briefer introductions and epitomes with comments for the other dialogues. He conceivably read some of these treatises directly, but he was certainly acquainted with many of their ideas indirectly, given their wide diffusion and profound impact on the intellectual and cultural life of the fifteenth and sixteenth centuries.

In 1492, Ficino published his equally impressive rendering into Latin, again with epitome and commentary, of Plotinus' *Enneads*, a series of philosophical treatises. Given the terminological and conceptual difficulties, the prestige that Plotinus enjoyed in the Platonic tradition and in Ficino's eyes as the second Plato, and the compatibility, from a Renaissance viewpoint, of many of his leading ideas and motifs with Christian philosophy, the Ficinian Plotinus is possibly of even greater significance for readers of Spenser than the Ficinian Plato; parts of it, notably its renderings of 1.6, 3.5, 5.8, and 6.9, deserve careful study. In addition, Ficino translated into Latin the first fourteen treatises of the Greek *Corpus Hermeticum* that purported to be authentic writings of the 'thrice-great Hermes' of the ancient Egyptians (see *Egypt, *Hermeticism). We now regard these and other *Hermetica* as derivative theosophical tracts of late antiquity by various, and often contradictory, hands. But Ficino and his contemporaries believed them the genuine work of the earliest Egyptian sage, one just three or four generations younger than Moses and invested with a lesser but similar authority. Finally, Ficino also translated other Neoplatonic extracts and treatises that he saw as crucial for a full understanding of the Platonic tradition, and commented at length upon them and others already accessible in Latin, such as the works of the Pseudo-Dionysius (whom he identified with St Paul's Areopagite). Since he wrote in a lucid, if repetitious, Latin, since his translations were, by contemporary standards, both accurate and elegant, and since he had a thorough grasp of the complexities of the Platonic philosophical tradition, he became, and to a large extent remained, the Renaissance authority on all Platonic matters and the personal embodiment of Platonic values.

Ficino was much more, however, than the interpretative voice for Plato, Plotinus, and Hermes Trismegistus: he was also the first in a succession of Renaissance magi interested in theology and speculative philosophy, but even more deeply in magic, theurgy, demonology, mystical mathematics, astrology, and ultimately in the secret paths to gnosis, to the knowledge that enables man to recover former quasi-angelic powers and become again a prelapsarian Adam. Less flamboyant, assuredly, than Pico, Agrippa, Paracelsus, Bruno, or Dee, Ficino nevertheless was the principal Renaissance theorist both of the soul and of the spirit that binds the soul to the body, and of the World Soul and the World Spirit, the source of nature's magic. Since he deftly managed to confine his pneumatological, demonological, and magical theories within the boundaries tolerated by the liberal Catholicism of his day, Ficino succeeded in pointing the way for other speculative thinkers intent on accommodating the dogmas of orthodoxy and the Christian philosophical heritage with the philosophy and religion of pagan antiquity, and even with what was known about antiquity's demon and star magic, as well as its natural magic. The implications for our understanding of Spenser's notions of an enchanter, of Fairyland, of Nature herself, are many.

Equally profound was the impact of Ficino's notion of a natural Platonic theology. Like Origen, St Basil, Augustine, and other Church Fathers, but to a more radical degree, Ficino became fascinated by the ways in which ancient sages, always viewed as culminating in or deriving from Plato, had seemed to anticipate the truths definitively revealed by Christ. In contrast to the Aristotelians (if not to Aristotle himself), the Platonists, by use of their highest reason and by way of 'natural' revelation, had arrived at a theosophical wisdom that may have been derived from, but was certainly complementary to, the Mosaic wisdom of the Hebrews and that was treated as an alternative, albeit subordinate, religious tradition with its own scriptures in the works of the poets and the sages. This sympathetic perspective on the ancient 'theologians' came to be shared by many Renaissance apologists, Catholic and Protestant alike, and it was demonstrably the view of Sidney and probably Spenser. Not only does it help us to understand Spenser's presentation of himself as Colin Clout in his pastoral poems and of initiatory moments in natural or mythological settings, it also helps us to enter into the realm of the *Fowre Hymnes* with their subtle explorations of the ways which lead from pagan to purely Christian conceptions of beauty and of love, from a natural to a revealed theology, from the Platonism of Hermes, Orpheus, and other pre-Platonic sages, via the Platonism of Plato himself and of the great Plotinus, to the Platonism of St John and Pseudo-Dionysius.

More specifically, many scholars feel (Ellrodt 1960 is a signal exception) that Spenser was indebted to, or at least influenced by, three aspects of Ficino's thought: his mythologizing, his philosophies of beauty and love, and his psychology of the soul.

Classical, including Egyptian, myth occupied a special status for Ficino and the Platonists he studied. More than acknowledging that the myths, rightly interpreted, contained profound theological or metaphysical truths, he developed a methodology for interpreting them Platonically. Proclean in inspiration, it was his own notwithstanding, and was subsequently transmitted to theorists in the ambiance of the French Pléiade and thence to its English admirers. Ficino's understanding of the Platonic deployment of myth was predicated on the assumption that all the Platonists (whether before or after Plato) were dedicated monotheists who had called upon the plural conceptions and images of polytheism by virtue of their commitment to what Ficino himself thought of as the 'Orphic' principle: the principle that the one God is in all the gods, and all the gods in the one God, each in his own way. With this principle, Ficino was able to approach a host of familiar Greek, Egyptian, and Roman myths Platonically: he felt justified, that is, in viewing any one myth as a variation on the central motifs found in all myths and concerned with the stages in the descent from and the ascent to the One. Like Spenser after him, he was convinced that myth is preeminently theological and treats therefore of origins and causes, beginnings and ends, and hence of theogony, cosmogony, anthropogeny, and their attendant eschatologies. While reflecting the many manifestations of the descent from and ascent to the ultimate unitary reality of God, and thus the variety, plenitude, and multeity of the unfolded world, myth strives to apprehend the indwelling unity. This should help us to understand the commitment of Ficino and Spenser to triadic formulas, for the Platonic interpretation of a myth must see it in terms of movement away from, conversion towards, and movement back into the One. Critics have unraveled such triadic rhythms in Spenser's portrait of the dance of the Graces on Mount Acidale in *FQ* VI (eg, Wind ed 1967, Geller 1972, and Nohrnberg 1976), but they underlie his presentation of a number of classical myths, either directly or in his characteristic variations on their treatment by other poets.

While Ficino has some interesting analyses of particular myths, it is the hermeneutical principles he devised for transforming them Platonically that allow us to appreciate more fully Spenser's habitual elaboration and replication of mythological situations, his fascination with mirroring events (see *mirror), his piling up of mutually reflective episodes. In fundamental if surprising ways, Spenser emerges as Ficino's ideal poet and mythographer, exploring unity in multeity and multeity in unity, and orchestrating the triadic rhythm of unfolding, folding, and infolding that underlies Ficino's basic conceptions of both metaphysics and the inner life. From this perspective, *The Faerie Queene* much more than the *Fowre Hymnes* is Spenser's Platonic masterwork. However indebted to such mythographers as Cartari, Conti, and Giraldi, with their profuse and diffuse Neoplatonic allegorizing, Spenser was more profoundly indebted to Ficino for his basic conceptions of what myth signified, even if this indebtedness was by way of various French disciples and admirers of Ficino. Myth was the instrument which enabled him to portray the mystery of man's relationship to the One or God, and to approach that mystery again and again in episode after episode, myth after myth, figure after figure, in the playful and yet serious conviction that man, as the cosmic amphibian inhabiting both the sensible and the intelligible worlds, is empowered to apprehend but not to comprehend, to glimpse but not fully to perceive the One in the profusion and complexity of the Many. The luxuriance and digressiveness of *The Faerie Queene* are thus as illustrative of Ficino's understanding of Platonism as its idealism and certain of its image clusters. Recognition that the One is every high poet's ultimate theme was a Renaissance commonplace; but it was the never-ending process of attempting to glimpse the One in the ever-changing shapes of the Many that constituted the philosophical challenge presented, explicitly or implicitly, by that age's poetry in what is also its Platonic variety and copiousness. Critics have merely begun to tap the rich veins of this relationship, however mediated, between Elizabethan poet and Florentine philosopher, in part because scholars are still engaged in the task of anatomizing Ficino's complicated mythography and hermeneutics.

For Spenser's debt to Ficino's theories of beauty and of love, we must turn to *De amore*, first written in Latin and then translated by Ficino himself into Italian. By the late sixteenth century, two French translations had also appeared, one of them in three editions, and many of the commentary's ideas and formulations had become incorporated, often without acknowledgement, into numerous treatises on love and courtly behavior, the most well known instance being the sustained meditation that Castiglione gives to Bembo at the conclusion of *The Courtier*. In *De amore*, Ficino is primarily concerned with establishing a metaphysics and ethics of beauty and not an aesthetics as such. He attributes beauty to God, and at times he also thinks of it as an Idea in the Platonic sense. Usually, however, he defines it as the 'splendor' that radiates from the Ideas as they exist collectively in the Mind of God. All inferior beauties are reflections of, or Platonically speaking participations in, this divine splendor. Since it is the radiance of Truth itself, Beauty is the light of intelligible Being and must accompany the lower manifestations of that Being. In the commentary, Ficino expands on the notion that the universe is intrinsically beautiful (*formosus*); hence its name in Greek, the *cosmos*, meaning originally 'that which has been endowed with form.' Chaos conversely is that state of being ugly (*informis*) which precedes the imposition of form, and with it of beauty, though Ficino believes that such a state is always longing for form and is always desirous of beauty (*eros* being, in Socrates' definition, the desire for beauty). Later Ficino explores the Plotinian theory that cosmos and chaos, beauty and the desire for beauty, Venus and Cupid, are universal states of being; and that cosmoses and chaoses are everywhere in nature and in man, each chaos perpetually longing for the act of becoming beautiful, of being formed into a cosmos. It is here that the *Fowre Hymnes* and the Garden of Adonis episode in *FQ* III come immediately to mind. Both focus on Beauty as cosmically creative, and both look back to Ficino's two most important sources outside the *Symposium* and the *Phaedrus*, the opening of Genesis and the first part of Plato's *Timaeus*. Spenser's heightened awareness of the mystery of beauty, its generativeness and immanence as an idea and an ideal, and his probing sensitivity to the ceaseless yearning of all lovers for that beauty, are Ficinian in spirit, though in all probability only indirectly indebted to particular passages in *De amore*. For both, the mysteries of beauty and love were not confined to aesthetic or even ethical considerations, but centered on the metaphysics of being from the most sublime to the most material realms and thus on theogonies and cosmogonies. Even so, the nature and extent of Spenser's debt to Ficino in these matters also remains largely unexplored.

The role of Ficino's psychology is equally problematic, perhaps more so since it is itself dependent principally on the common stock of late medieval notions about the faculties and their mutual relationships and about the processes of perception, ratiocination, and recollection. Nonetheless, Ficino's ideas about the human soul and its mobility and immortality were enormously influential and widely disseminated, and his championship of Plato introduced a number of recognizably Platonic terms, images, and distinctions into an arena hitherto dominated by Aristotle and the Galenists. Of special interest are the roles Ficino assigns to intuitive intelligence (*mens*), as contrasted with discursive reason (*ratio*), and the intelligence's crown, (*apex* or *unitas*). Plotinian in origin, *unitas* is thought both to unite us inwardly, to bind our disparate parts into a concordant whole, and then to unite our finite beings with the infinite oneness of God, first during those transient moments of ecstasy which prophets, priests, true poets, and true lovers experience here on earth when enraptured by one of the four divine madnesses or *furores*, and second eternally at the Resurrection. But these two degrees of union are both intimately intellectual (given that *unitas* is the apex of intelligence), and both signify an intellectual love, a coming together of intellect and will in visionary fire.

Ficino's Platonic psychology was thus especially keyed to the theory of the soul's ascent and eventual beatification, and it provided the best available conceptual system and terminology for propounding the theory of the divine madnesses, including those of poetic and erotic ecstasy. In particular, it brought into sharp focus Plato's compelling figure in the *Phaedrus* of the soul as a charioteer striving to control the twin steeds of mettlesome wrath and rebellious desire. As set forth by Plato and interpreted on sundry occasions and at length by Ficino in the light of a complex tradition of interpretation, the figure became the Renaissance's major paradigm for the notion of the tripartite soul, and, more significantly, for the notion of the soul in motion, either ascending under Jupiter's leadership to a transcendent vision of God and his Ideas, or descending, in an agonizing struggle with the black steed of misdirected desire, into the night of terraqueous existence. Again the implications for Spenser are multiple but in need of careful analysis.

Other aspects of Ficino's encyclopedic range of interests may also be pertinent: his numerology, demonology, medical, and astrological theories, his theories of friendship, music, medicine, and magic, to name just a few. But with regard to his views on Platonic mythologizing, on beauty and love, and on the soul's cyclical motions away from and towards union with the divine within itself and with the absolute divine, there is general recognition of their significance for Spenser, though many questions concerning specific indebtedness and lines of transmission or influence remain unanswered. In short, Ficino and the kind of Platonism he propounded constitute one of the three most important (though imperfectly researched) sources, besides the Bible and Virgil, for our understanding of Spenser's fundamental cast of mind, and for our sense of him as a poet who strove triumphantly to be other – and much more – than the English Ariosto. MICHAEL J.B. ALLEN

EDITIONS AND TRANSLATIONS OF FICINO *Opera omnia* 1576 (Basel; rpt Turin 1959, 1962) is the standard, though defective, ed of Ficino's works, few of which have been tr into English. The *De amore* has been edited, with French tr, by Raymond Marcel (Paris 1958), and tr into English by Sears Jayne as Ficino ed 1985. Ficino's commentaries on the *Philebus* and *Phaedrus* have been tr and ed by Michael J.B. Allen respectively as *Marsilio Ficino: The 'Philebus' Commentary* 1975 and *Marsilio Ficino and the Phaedran Charioteer* 1981 (Berkeley and Los Angeles). Books 1, 3, 4, and 5 of Ficino's interesting letters have been tr into English by Members of the Language Department of the School of Economic Science in London as *The Letters of Marsilio Ficino* (London 1975, 1978, 1981, 1988); further books are scheduled to appear. Ficino's major work of philosophy and apologetics, the *Platonic Theology*, has been ed with Fr tr by Raymond Marcel 1964–70; and his major work on psychology and magic, the *De vita libri tres*, has been tr into English and ed by John R. Clark and Carol V. Kaske (Binghamton, NY 1988).

The two full-length studies of Ficino are Kristeller 1943, the standard work; and M.J.B. Allen 1984, keyed to the *Phaedrus* Commentary. See also M.J.B. Allen 1980 'Cosmogony and Love: The Role of Phaedrus in Ficino's *Symposium* Commentary' *JMRS* 10:131–53. For a skeptical assessment of Ficino's influence on Elizabethan literature, see Jayne 1952. For a complete bibliography of secondary literature, including references to his own many important essays, see the second appendix to Paul Oskar Kristeller 1986 'Ficino and His Work' in *Marsilio Ficino e il ritorno di Platone: Studi e documenti* ed Gian Carlo Garfagnini (Florence).

Of interest is Ellrodt 1960, an effective revisionist attack on the sometimes insufficiently discriminating attribution of Neoplatonic sources to Spenser.

---

fire Since fire is the purest and most rarefied of the four elements, its region is farthest from earth and nearest heaven (*Heavenly Beautie* 36–49; Elyot *Governor* I.1). It is therefore the last element through which the titaness Mutabilitie passes in her ascent to the moon (*FQ* VII vi 7–8). Spenser follows Conti 2.6, 8.19 in making Vesta goddess of ethereal fire, while Vulcan, whose flames are relatively impure and therefore visible, is god of the fire 'with us so usuall' on earth (vii 26). This earthly fire strives constantly to rise upwards to its native sphere (II xi 32; see also *Batman uppon Bartholome* 10.4, where further properties of fire are enumerated). The soul contains a beam of divine fire and accordingly seeks to mount to heaven, its natural abode (Sir John Davies *Nosce Teipsum* 583–8, 1329–80; cf Cicero *Tusculan Disputations* 1.19.43–5). In Neoplatonic love theory, the soul is set on fire with heavenly love and ascends by degrees to enjoy divine bliss (Castiglione ed 1928:316–20).

Fire in Renaissance imagery and symbolism is ambivalent. It burns in the abode of the gods (the Empyrean) as well as in the infernal regions: the classical Tartarus is surrounded by the fiery river Phlegeton (Virgil *Aeneid* 6.550–1), and the biblical hell has its burning lake (Rev 21.8). It is a symbol of vitality and also of destruction. Flames define both pure love and lust (in Thomas Cooper's *Thesaurus*, the entry for *Ignis* includes 'Love' and 'an harlotte').

Spenser similarly invests fire with positive and negative connotations. In *Amoretti* and *Fowre Hymnes*, love is a fire which, once kindled from the divine flame, urges man to seek beauty and virtue (see esp *Amoretti* 3, 7, 22; *Heavenly Love* 106–12, 186–210). In *The Faerie Queene*, fire imagery portrays the chaste love of Una for Redcrosse and Arthur for Gloriana (I vii 27, ix 8–10). Since love incites desire for virtue, its fire provides the energy for heroic endeavor. 'Most sacred fire ... ykindled first above' inspires knights to noble deeds (III iii 1). So Redcrosse is 'full of fire' as he encounters Error, he is restless with 'flaming corage' awaiting his battle with Sansjoy, and when he confronts Despair he is burning with 'firie zeale' (I i 14, V 1, ix 37).

Elsewhere, however, fire is not life-giving but life-devouring. Its destructive (and self-destructive) characteristics are emphasized in Mutabilitie's argument (VII vii 24). Imagery of fire is prominent in the depiction of evil passions, particularly anger since fire is the element appropriate to the choleric temperament. Wrath and Furor have burning brands and fiery eyes, which are emblems of anger (I iv 33; II iv 15, v 22). The irascible Pyrochles (his name means 'inspired or moved by fire') has flames on his shield, and his armor throws sparkling fire about him as he rides (II iv 38, v 2). The motto on his impresa, 'Burnt I do burne,' suggests that his passion afflicts himself as much as others. Fires of wrath rage like furnaces in men and monsters; and the flames which burn internally are emitted through mouth, nose, eyes, and entrails. Cerberus and Duessa's many-headed beast have flaming tongues, and the Dragon casts flames from every aperture of his body (I v 34, viii 6, xi 14, 22, 26, 45). Lust also is a fire which consumes a person from within. Its flames ransack the veins of Malecasta and spread through her bones like poison, lust burns the bowels of the witch's son, and Corflambo shoots infecting beams of fire from his eyes (III i 47, 56, vii 16; IV viii 39).

Imagery of fire is used to identify the infernal origin of evil passions. The smoky and sulfurous flames emitted by the Dragon and by the fires at the entrance of Busirane's house suggest hellfire (I xi 13, 44; III xi 21), as do the furnaces of Mammon which are tended by his fiery-eyed fiends (II vii 35–6). Firebrands brought from hell suggest the devilish influence of a passion: Despair, discord, and lust are referred to as hellish firebrands (I ix 53, IV ii 1, *HB* 169–70); and brands are carried by Wrath, Furor, Impatience, and Fury (I iv 33; II v 22, xi 23; III xii 17). The Stygian 'fire brond' given to Pyrochles by Furor appropriately brings its recipient to a fate akin to that of a damned soul in the fiery river of Phlegeton as he burns in water which will not slake his flames (II v 22, vi 44–50). The firebrands of hell which arouse the passions may be contrasted with the moon and stars, the torches of heaven which lend 'desired light' to men in darkness (*Epithalamion* 409–12).

The potential of fire to break out of control is always evident in Spenser. The kitchen of the house of Alma has a 'mighty furnace' which creates great heat, but there are bellows to provide 'cooling breath' to temper the flames (*FQ* II ix 29–30). The destruction by fire of Malbecco's house serves as an emblem of Hellenore's unquenchable lust and Malbecco's insatiable jealousy; it is analogous to the greatest instance of destruction in classical legend, the burning of Troy (III x 12–13). Generally, in Spenser's universe the divinely inspired fire of love of beauty and virtue burns quietly and kindly; the flames of demonic passion are turbulent, uncontrollable, and ultimately self-consuming. GEOFFREY G. HILLER

Gaston Bachelard 1964 *The Psychoanalysis of Fire* tr Alan C.M. Ross (London); Jean-Pierre Bayard 1973 *La Symbolique du feu* (Paris).

Fisher Florimell encounters a 'fisher old and pore' in her flight from the witch's beast (*FQ* III vii 27). She is about to throw herself in the sea when she discovers his cock-boat, placed there (the narrator tells us) by God's ordinance. She leaps into the boat and pushes it off while the Fisher sleeps. When the episode is resumed a canto later, the pathos of the scene (Aeolus restrains the winds out of pity as the boat drifts with the tide) is intensified when the Fisher awakes and, aroused by her beauty, attempts to rape her (viii 20–9). Florimell is comically unaware of his sexual intentions, or of the sexuality inherent in the terms of her situation: 'Have care, I pray, to guide the cock-bote well, / Least worse on sea then us on land befell. / Thereat th'old man did nought but fondly grin' (24). The narrator stresses her helplessness and distance from all rescue in an apostrophe reproaching her absent suitors; and when she is saved from the Fisher by Proteus, he again attributes her rescue to the intervention of divine grace. Yet Proteus in turn attempts to seduce her.

Readers see this episode as a physical and spiritual turning point in Florimell's adventures, variously placing it in Neoplatonic, archetypal, psychological, and Christian contexts. Neoplatonists interpret Florimell as ideal beauty or as the soul achieving its union with matter, and take her sexual encounter with the Fisher to represent a stage in her descent into the material world necessary for her cosmic union with Marinell. Beauty is able to reanimate even the dead wood of nature represented by the Fisher (Bahr 1965, Lewis 1967, Roche 1964). Those who note the archetypes stress the sexuality of the episode and see it as the first stage of Florimell's metamorphosis, a yielding to the fecund sea which is necessary for her cosmic union with Marinell (Hamilton 1961a). Read psychologically, the Fisher is a stage in her descent into the depths of fear of male sexuality, which she must overcome to marry Marinell (Giamatti 1975). A Christian interpretation sees Florimell undergoing a spiritual metamorphosis in which she discovers her inability to defend chastity by purely human means and is renewed by grace which gives her the spiritual strength to withstand Proteus. The episode is comic because its framing by the interventions of providence makes her safety beyond question and mocks her reliance on her own weak powers to overcome lust (Benson 1985).

The sensuality of the episode is its most striking feature, for now Florimell is forced to stop her flight from male sexual desire and to experience it directly and in an uncivilized form. How completely she experiences it is suggestively unclear. Before entering the boat, she loses her girdle (later, a symbol of chastity at the tournament in IV v); and the drifting boat suggests uncontrolled passion. The old man's 'drie withered stocke' and 'frozen spright' are restored to potency, and he throws her down and defiles her 'garments gay' with scales of fish. Although the substitution of the defiling of her clothing for the violation of her person preserves her honor, his sexual force cannot be denied; he and his fish scales present her first contact with male fecundity and the sea which are ultimately to be represented positively by Marinell.

Heaven's sanctioning of such a brutal sexual encounter may be explained not only by the positive connotations of fertility but by the change the experience works in Florimell's spiritual state. Despite the trials she has endured, her appeal to heaven when she is overwhelmed by the Fisher is her first admission of her complete helplessness. This delay is unique among Spenserian heroines threatened with rape. Both Una and Serena waste not a moment in calling on heaven. Florimell's delay suggests an excessive self-reliance, but the immediate response of divine grace to her plea suggests both a literal physical rescue and spiritual renewal.

The primary source of the details and the comic tone of this episode is Ariosto's *Orlando furioso* 8, in which an old hermit magically leads Angelica (Florimell's prototype as a maiden repeatedly in flight) across the sea, where he puts her to sleep and attempts to rape her. Yet there are significant differences. The lascivious sea breezes caress Angelica, whereas they hold back from Florimell out of pity; and the hermit is impotent, so that no allegorical connection is made between the sea and sexuality. The comedy derives primarily from the contrast between the man's desires and his inability to act on them, although he tries all night. Because Angelica continues to sleep, the adventure has no effect on her; her rescue is a true piece of bad fortune and, in contrast to Florimell's, moves her no closer to her final happiness. Spenser's apostrophe to absent heroes is taken instead from Angelica's next adventure, her exposure on the rock in Ebuda (*OF* 8.68).

A possible source of the character of the Fisher and his actions is Antoninus Liberalis (*Metamorphoses* 40; first pub 1568), in which Britomartis escapes from Minos' lust in a fisherman's boat but must leave it when he attempts to rape her. Although Antoninus' story is very brief, it reinforces the suggestion that Florimell and other figures of chastity in Book III are aspects of Britomart.

PAMELA JOSEPH BENSON

Howard W. Bahr 1965 'The Misery of Florimell: The Ladder of Temptation' *SoQ* 4:116–22; Pamela Joseph Benson 1985 'Florimell at Sea: The Action of Grace in *Faerie Queene*, Book III' *SSt* 6:83–94; John D. Bernard 1983 'Pastoral and Comedy in Book III of *The Faerie Queene*' *SEL* 23:5–20; Giamatti 1968; Murtaugh 1973; Nohrnberg 1976:595.

Fletcher, Phineas and Giles The two Fletchers were early imitators of Spenser, Phineas having been called by one admirer 'the *Spencer* of this age' (Fletcher and Fletcher ed 1908–9, 2:8).

Phineas (1582–1650), the elder son of Giles Fletcher the elder, was educated at Eton and King's College, Cambridge, but left his college fellowship in 1615 to serve as a pastor in rural Norfolk. John Fletcher the dramatist, who imitated Spenser in *The Faithful Shepherdess* (1610), was his elder cousin. His early poems include a Spenserian pastoral in a memorial volume published on the death of Queen Elizabeth. His Latin verse includes an anti-Catholic satire, *Locustae, vel Pietas Jesuitica*, later revised in English as *The Locusts, or Apollyonists* (the Latin and English versions appeared in a combined edition of 1627).

Although these works contain only echoes of Spenser, others show clear imitation. *Venus and Anchises* is a verse narrative first published in 1628 as *Brittain's Ida*, a pirated edition in which the publisher claimed the work to be by 'that Renowned Poët, Edmond Spencer.' The poem, which even has a Bower of Bliss in its second canto, exaggerates certain features of Spenser's style: patterns of repetition, opposition, and, most excessively, parenthesis. It begins (in the printed version) 'In *Ida* Vale (who knowes not *Ida* Vale?)' – a direct echo of Spenser's famous '*Arlo-hill* (Who knowes not *Arlo-hill*?)' (*FQ* VII vi 36) – and continues throughout to evoke the lines and images of the master. Lines such as 'With all she starts, and wondereth withall' (4.1), following 'Withall she laughed, and she blusht withall' (II xii 68), show Fletcher's attraction to Spenser's rhetorical figures (in this instance to his use of *epanalepsis*, beginning and ending a line with the same word). Fletcher, however, tends to load his verse with such devices, causing his style to become highly idiosyncratic. The heavy reliance on figures and images is also accompanied by a less determined moral vision than Spenser's; the poem in places delights in its own sensuousness. The same weakening of moral vision is also apparent in the determinedly erotic 'Epithalamium' (extant only in manuscript and not printed until this century; see ed 1926). Even the *Piscatorie Eclogs* (1633), which include the traditional complaints on church corruption, earthly and heavenly love, and the state of poetry, miss the moral tone of Spenser's verse while here and there showing its influence.

Phineas' most ambitious work is *The Purple Island, or The Isle of Man*, twelve cantos allegorizing man's physical and spiritual state. It contains a tribute to 'Colin' (identified in a marginal gloss as 'Spencer') who, 'Discourag'd, scorn'd, his writings vilifi'd' (1.19), illustrates England's failure to patronize poetry. The first half of the poem expands the conceit of Spenser's house of Alma, even borrowing the circle-quadrate-triangle image (1.44; cf *FQ* II ix 22). The procession of vices (cantos 7–8) and virtues (cantos 9–10) amplifies briefer scenes from *FQ* I and II. Compared with Spenser's anatomical descriptions, Fletcher's are greatly extended: where Spenser gives two lines to the 'goodly Beacons' of the eyes, Fletcher provides fifteen stanzas on the optic nerve, muscles, and fluids of the 'two watching towers' (5.23–37). Like Spenser, Fletcher places the mental faculties (canto 6), Phantastes, Judgment, and Eumnestes, in the front, middle, and rear of the castle; he gives Gluttony a crane's neck and puts Covetousness in rags. Parthenia ('Chastitie in the single') closely resembles Belphoebe, but the cantos on the virtues are less obviously Spenserian than the rest. Canto 12, owing something to the Red Cross Knight's battle with the Dragon, depicts Christ as an apocalyptic hero in a final battle of good and evil. (For many other parallels, see *Sp All* pp 189–91.)

Giles Fletcher (c 1586–1623) studied at Westminster and Trinity College, Cambridge; relinquishing his college fellowship and a briefly held readership in Greek, in 1619 he took up a living in Suffolk from Francis Bacon. He is remembered for his one long poem, *Christs Victorie, and Triumph in Heaven, and Earth, over and after Death* (1610; rpt 1632, 1640), a blend of allegory and gospel narrative that shows in subject matter an enthusiasm for the works of du Bartas and Spenser (whom he terms in his preface those 'two blessed Soules' of poetry). In modified eight-line Spenserian stanzas (rhyming *ababbccC*, the final line an alexandrine), the four-book poem celebrates Christ's birth, temptation, crucifixion, and resurrection. Book I, 'Christs Victorie in Heaven,' anticipates Milton's Nativity Ode in the personifications of Justice and Mercy and the cessation of oracles. The many resemblances to Spenser (see *Sp All* pp 120–2) show Giles' desire to use diction and image in such a way that *The Faerie Queene* and *Christs Victorie* comment on each other. This reciprocity occurs far less fruitfully in Phineas' poetry.

The temptation in the wilderness borrows details from Mammon's temptation of Guyon. Personifications of Despair and Vainglory (recalling Philotime in *FQ* II vii 43) also appear. The luxurious depiction of Christ's physical beauty and his enticement into Pangloretta's garden exemplify a 'sexual feeling masquerading as religious and moral concern' (Grundy 1969:182), present in the work of both brothers (at least until they left Cambridge and married). In both, the Spenserian style is heightened by a baroque or high baroque tendency toward antithesis and a fondness for lively color. Giles seems to be the stronger poet, more in control of his art than his prolific brother.

The Fletchers passed their decoratively rhetorical brand of Spenserianism to the mid-seventeenth century. Francis Quarles and Edward Benlowes (in whom imitation becomes plagiarism) were both friends of Phineas, both Cambridge men; other Cambridge imitators were Thomas Robinson and Joseph Beaumont. Robinson's *Life and Death of Mary Magdalene* (c 1620) closely adheres to Giles, using his stanza; scenes like the Cave of Melancholy (based on the cave of Despair) return for their inspiration to Spenser. Beaumont's *Psyche* (1648) begins with an infernal council like that in *The Locusts*. The psychomachia recalls the house of Alma; there is a version of the house of Pride, a pageant of the seven deadly sins, and (from *FQ* VII vii) of the seasons. Spenser and the Fletchers also touched the formative years of two greater Cambridge poets, Crashaw and Cowley. Cowley may be the 'A.C.' who commended Phineas' *Purple Island* in 1633 (Langdale in ed 1908–9, 2:10), the year that his first book was published at age fifteen. Such evidence hints that the 'school of the Fletchers' was in the main a vogue of gentlemen amateurs from Cambridge. It made its one permanent mark in suggesting a few scenes to their greatest Cambridge contemporary, Milton. One reason for these poets' notably narrow borrowings from Spenser may be that they had already begun to lose sight of Spenser's own medieval and Renaissance influences. This particularly applies to the Fletchers' often heavy-handed religiosity. Not understanding the spirit, they were too often left with only the letter. RICHARD F. HARDIN

The standard edition is Fletcher and Fletcher ed 1908–9; see also Phineas Fletcher 1926 *Venus and Anchises (Brittain's Ida) and Other Poems* ed Ethel Seaton (London), which gives manuscript readings not in ed 1908–9. Some texts, with valuable commentary and introductions, are given in William B. Hunter, ed 1977 *The English Spenserians: The Poetry of Giles Fletcher, George Wither, Michael Drayton, Phineas Fletcher, and Henry More* (Salt Lake City). Still worth consulting is Herbert Ellsworth Cory 1912 'Spenser, the School of the Fletchers, and Milton' *UCPMP* 2:311–73. Abram Barnet Langdale 1937 *Phineas Fletcher: Man of Letters, Science and Divinity* (New York) is the standard life; see also R.J. Fehrenbach 1985–6 'The Marriage and Last Years of Giles Fletcher, the Younger' *MP* 83:395–8. Significant criticism includes James Bobrick 1979 'The Numerological Structure of Giles Fletcher's *Christs Victorie, and Triumph*' *TSLL* 21:522–52; Jerome S. Dees 1976 'The Narrator of *Christs Victorie and Triumph*: What Giles Fletcher Learned from Spenser' *ELR* 6:453–65, which shows Fletcher's debt to Spenser's narrator in *FQ*; Grundy 1969, esp pp 181–203; and Lee Piepho 1984 'The Latin and English Eclogues of Phineas Fletcher: Sannazaro's *Piscatoria* among the Britons' *SP* 81:461–72.

Florimell (L *flos* flower + *mel* honey) One of the four principal female characters in the middle books of *The Faerie Queene*. Her adventures begin with her flight from Fairyland in III i and end with her marriage to Marinell in V iii. Along with Amoret and Belphoebe, she supports and supplements the role of Britomart with specifically female characteristics to offset the martial exploits of the male knights.

Florimell's escape imitates Angelica's flight from the Paris of Charlemagne in Ariosto's *Orlando furioso* I. Yet her further adventures owe little to Ariosto, and her character is developed very differently from Angelica's. Thus Ariosto's episode of Angelica's love for the young knight Medoro, whom she cures of his wounds and by whom she is wounded in love (*OF* 19), is transferred by Spenser to Belphoebe, who likewise cures Timias in *FQ* III v. In his portrayal of Florimell, Spenser limits his imitation of Angelica to her role as the pursued woman whose beauty is threatened by desire and lust.

Florimell's flight from the 'griesly Foster' in III i scatters the coalition previously made between Guyon and Britomart. Guyon and Arthur set out to succor Florimell, not knowing who she is, while Timias pursues the Foster and Britomart rides on alone to her trial at Malecasta's castle. In III vii, Florimell arrives at the cottage of the witch, whose idiot son becomes enamored of her. In fear, she escapes, only to be pursued by a hyena-like beast ('That feeds on womens flesh' 22) created by the witch, who meantime furnishes her son with an image of Florimell, the false or snowy Florimell. The beast follows Florimell until she abandons her palfrey to escape in a small boat with an old fisherman asleep in it. The beast devours the horse, leaving behind only Florimell's girdle. In the boat, she is again attacked, this time by the Fisher, and saved by Proteus, only to be imprisoned in the latter's watery house.

While Florimell is thus held under the sea, the narrative takes up the problem of her girdle or cestus. The history of this golden belt is the reader's only knowledge of Florimell's genealogy (IV v 2–6): it was made by Vulcan as a gift to Venus 'to bind lascivious desire, / And loose affections streightly to restraine; / Which vertue it for ever after did retaine.' When Venus began her adulterous affair with Mars, she left it behind on Mount Acidale with the Graces. Florimell, fostered by the Graces, brought it with her to Gloriana's court. It is a symbol of chaste love protecting and adorning beauty. When she abandons herself to the sea for protection, the cestus becomes a material replacement for her and is debased and misused until it is returned to her by Artegall at V iii.

First mentioned just after Florimell's embarkation on the boat at III vii 31, the girdle is discovered by Satyrane, who uses it to subdue the witch's beast, until he is interrupted by Argante. Satyrane had helped Una in Book I and is the natural person to help Florimell; but chaste love cannot be imposed on a beast, and Argante's interruption suggests a deeper problem for the union of chaste love and beauty. Released from his struggle with Argante, Satyrane finds the cestus held by Paridell. By IV ii 25, Satyrane wears the cestus as a memorial to Florimell, and by iv 15, assuming that she is dead, has placed it in an 'arke' as prize for the winner of the tournament. After a series of disappointing encounters involving most of the major characters of Book IV, it is finally awarded to the false Florimell, who then gives herself to Braggadocchio when none of the virtuous knights will accept her. The unjust outcome of this tournament is resolved in V iii at the tournament following the marriage of Florimell and Marinell, in which Braggadocchio is disgraced and the false Florimell melts away, leaving only the girdle behind. Appropriately the girdle is restored to Florimell by Artegall, the exemplar of justice in Book V.

Book III showed Florimell being pursued in several dehumanizing and debasing episodes. Book IV shows the debasement not so much of Florimell as of her chief attribute, the girdle, especially when it falls to the false Florimell. This surrogate character masquerades as Beauty throughout Book IV and fools all who place their perception of beauty primarily in their senses, especially the sense of sight. The rescue of the true Florimell by Marinell (IV xii) brings out this distinction of the senses brilliantly: he *hears* her declaration of love for him and his indifference to love and beauty is overcome, but he does not *see* Florimell until after he has suffered for his love and his mother has wrested her from Proteus' prison. (On Florimell's lament, cf Britomart just before she wounds Marinell on the Rich Strond, despairing for her love whom she, like Florimell, has not seen; III iv 8–10). That Marinell is won by Florimell's words is important for the pattern of Books III-IV. We never hear Florimell speak – we only see her pursued – and she is rescued only when she speaks to someone of whose presence she is unaware. She does not speak – indeed is never described – again, even when Cymodoce brings her to Marinell (IV xii) or when she is married to him (V iii).

In his depiction of Florimell, Spenser tells us something important about his perception of the place of physical beauty in the world. Just as Venus is born from the sea, so Florimell is retrieved from the sea to be married to Marinell, who in turn is the recipient of the riches of the sea as birthright from his father Dumarin and maternal grandfather Nereus. Spenser's allegory of beauty in Florimell thus relates her to the realm of Venus, to desire and pursuit, and finally to the imprisonment of beauty in this world figured by the Protean nature of the sea. Her desirability, figured as feminine weakness, draws all the male characters, even Arthur. The union of beauty and strength, whereby each is seen to reflect the characteristic of the other, is a goal which the poem repeatedly bodies forth but fails to display as fully attained.

THOMAS P. ROCHE, JR

flowers Spenser mentions some 125 plants, including trees, fruits, and spices, for which he uses 140 names. (The corresponding figures for Shakespeare are 170 and 190, respectively.) Of these – some 70 of which are common to Spenser and Shakespeare – about 80 are flowers (in the popular sense) or herbs (see *plants). As with many Elizabethan writers, the two flowers most often mentioned are related to love and sometimes to death: the rose and the lily.

Although a learned poet like Spenser would have turned to works of natural history and herbals for information about flowers (eg, Lyte's *Niewe Herball, or Historie of Plantes* 1578; see Arber 1931, Wrenn 1943), he is less concerned with taxonomic exactness than with the literary and moral significance of plants found in the works of other Renaissance poets, such as Marot, Ronsard, and du Bellay, who often refer to flowers found in classical sources such as Virgil (*Eclogues* 2), the pseudo-Virgilian *Culex*, Claudian (*Rape of Proserpina*), and Ovid (*Fasti, Metamorphoses*). Spenser could also have turned to medieval writers and works, especially Chaucer and the *Romance of the Rose*.

Each flower in Spenser's poetry bears some special significance, even in the simple catalogue in *Prothalamion* of flowers 'cropt' by the Nymphs to celebrate the approaching bridal day: 'the Violet pallid blew, / The little Dazie, that at evening closes, / The virgin Lillie, and the Primrose trew, / With store of vermeil Roses' (30–3). The 'pallid' violets, emblematic of faithful love, and the contrasting 'vermilion' rose of passion are mixed with a Christian symbol (the lily) to note the sanctity of marriage. The primrose may be associated with nascent love, the daisy with 'manifest pleasure' (Bellot 1580). Yet their associations may vary. In *FQ* II iii 22, Belphoebe's cheeks appear 'Like roses in a bed of lillies shed'; in Acrasia's Bower of Bliss, Cymochles lies 'On a sweet bed of lillies' (v 32) while she lies 'Upon a bed of Roses' (xii 77).

Since the floral garland in the *SC, Aprill* eclogue is made in praise of the Virgin Queen, its flowers carry strong symbolic associations. The olive branches are emblematic of 'peace, / When wars doe surcease,' the bay leaves of honor and victory, the pansy of thought and care, the columbine (*Aquilegia*) and the carnations (cf Rydén 1978) of love. Carnations (which also have implications of crowns and royalty in Spenser's spelling *coronations*) are identifiable in Elizabeth's dress in the Rainbow portrait (c 1600). The eclogue also displays the poet's interest in native flower names, gathered either from his general reading, from contemporary herbals, or from personal familiarity, for example, *cowslip, kingcup*, and *sops-in-wine*, and including fanciful formal modifications or etymologizings like *daffadilly* and *daffadowndilly*.

Yet, despite his playfulness with names, Spenser's description of plants is conventional, as his color epithets indicate. Occasionally, however, he attempts more distinct characterization, as in depicting thyme as 'Bees alluring' (*Muiopotmos* 191). The setwall (*Valeriana*) is described as 'drink-quickning,' the poisonous poppy as 'Dull' ('making dull' *Mui* 196) and 'Dead sleeping' ('causing death' *FQ* II vii 52). Sometimes he gives us glimpses of old seasonal customs associated with flowers, such as the decking of churches on May Day 'With Hawthorne buds, and swete Eglantine, / And girlonds of roses and Sopps in wine' (*SC, Maye* 13–14).

Usually, he gives current English plant names, most of which would have been well established. Only about one-tenth of those identified are first attested in his time or slightly earlier (eg, *kingcup* or *pink*). Some come from Latin or Greek, like *cicuta, moly, panace* (a heal-all), and *tetra* (L *taeter* horrible, loathsome). Spenser's curiosity about words and his delight in etymology, or the 'true' and 'original' meanings of words, are also evident in his plant names: for example, *arboret* and *busket* (both first evidenced in Spenser). His *rosmarine* comes from the Latin *ros marinus* (sea-dew), and *queen* in *queen-apple* (another first use) conflates *queen* and *quine*, a singular form of *quince* (Wrenn 1943). Also due to fanciful etymologies or implications are his names for the iris: *flowre Delice* and *flowre-deluce* (cf *OED*). Spenser's *saulge* (for *sage*) is an example of etymological spelling, a reflex of the Latin *salvia*.

Most of Spenser's flower names are well known, but some are difficult to identify, for example, *chevisaunce* (*SC, Apr* 143), which may be a misprint for *cherisaunce*, a name found in Lyte's *Herball*. This book, which seems to have been his chief botanical source, may also have provided names like *caprifole, coronation*, and *sops-in-wine*. In certain contexts, the precise botanical reference is obviously subordinate to the associations linked with the word as such, for example, *amaranthus* (*FQ* III vi 45) as an emblem of immortality. The detailed description of *astrophel* ('Astrophel' 181–98), also named *penthia* (from Gr 'to lament'), and *starlight* may be linked to passages in Lyte's *Herball* (Harrison 1946). Also unidentified is *bellamoure* in *Amoretti* 64, occurring with half a dozen other 'sweet' and 'fragrant' flowers in a list of similes.

Spenser's names for flowers, however, are often not mere markers of botanical reference but part of his verbal craftsmanship and imaginative range. An example is found in Phaedria's artful lily-song at *FQ* II vi 15–17:

> The lilly, Ladie of the flowring field,
> The Flowre-deluce, her lovely Paramoure,
> Bid thee to them thy fruitlesse labours yield,
> And soone leave off this toylesome wearie stoure;
> Loe loe how brave she decks her bounteous boure,
> With silken curtens and gold coverlets,
> Therein to shrowd her sumptuous Belamoure,
> Yet neither spinnes nor cardes, ne cares nor frets,
> But to her mother Nature all her care she lets.

Phaedria's subtle and profane argument uses the erotic image of the lily mating with a phallic fleur-de-lis (traditionally portrayed with upright petals between two pliant lip-like leaves on either side) and echoes Matthew 6.28 ('Learne, how the lilies of the field do growe: they labour not, nether spinne') in order to suggest that her dalliance with Cymochles may be pleasurable, harmless, and even approved by God (see Hieatt 1975b, esp pp 102–6). The lovely song of the rose in the Bower of Bliss (II xii 74–5) shows a similar ironic use of natural beauty for the ends of artful and decadent pleasure: the 'Virgin Rose' peeps forth 'with bashfull modestee,' yet the burden of the song is the conventional *carpe florem* injunction memorably expressed by Herrick: 'Gather ye Rosebuds while ye may, / Old Time is still a flying.' In the songs of both the lily and the rose, the conventional imagery of love and nature is set on edge: the beauty of the imagery is retained, but its seductiveness is examined closely. MATS RYDÉN

A. Arber 1931; Jacques Bellot 1580 *The Englishe Scholemaistre* (London; rpt Menston, Yorks 1967); H.N. Ellacombe 1908 'The Flowers of Spenser' *GC* 3rd ser, 43–4(20 June-22 Aug); Thomas Perrin Harrison, Jr 1946 'Flower Lore in Spenser and Shakespeare: Two Notes' *MLQ* 7:175–8; Otten 1985; Vernon Rendall 1934 *Wild Flowers in Literature* (London); C[aroline] Ruutz-Rees 1936 'Flower Garlands of the Poets, Milton, Shakespeare, Spenser, Marot, Sannazaro' in *Mélanges offerts à M. Abel Lefranc* (Paris) pp 75–90; Mats Rydén 1978 *Shakespearean Plant Names: Identifications and Interpretations* (Stockholm); Rydén 1984 'The Contextual Significance of Shakespeare's Plant Names' *SN* 56:155–62.

folklore Properly defined, the term *folklore* describes a social group's traditional expressions, practices, and beliefs that are preserved and transmitted outside official or institutional structures – most often orally or by demonstration – acquiring variant states in the process. To designate as *folklore* that which is merely old-fashioned, rural, childish, untrue, fantastic, or archetypal is to use the term imprecisely.

Examples of such imprecision are the usual mentions of 'Celtic folk tradition' and 'Irish folklore' in commentaries on Spenser. For him, as for his readers, the British traditions concerning King Arthur and the lore of elves and fairies were preponderantly derived from books. Likewise, the lore and legends of Ireland in Spenser's poetry tend to have an air of the quaint rather than the popular; they probably came to the poet from his antiquarian studies. The same bookishness characterizes Spenser's use of plant, bird, and beast lore, astrology, sorcery, and even superstitions, aside from those embodied in proverbs. It is noteworthy that E.K., glossing *Maye* 230, felt the need to validate the portentous 'stomble at the threshold flore' by citing chronicles – even though the expression was already proverbial (T 259 in Tilley 1950), and the superstition must have been current, as it is today.

Folklore and bookish learning are often difficult to distinguish for the sixteenth century because of the voluminous residue of orality that characterized schooling and literary craft (Ong 1965). Proverbs, similes, apothegms, fables, and jests traveled back and forth between print and oral tradition as schoolboys mastered their recitations and authors picked the flowers of rhetoric. Besides, scholars and poets then as today constituted their own folk groups as well as belonging to other groups, each of which possessed its own folklore. Thus, for purposes of studying the sixteenth century, John Ashton (1957) advocates broadening the definition of folklore to include 'folk materials drawn from written sources, or more often, based on a combination of the oral tradition and printed reports of or statements about that tradition,' for 'at no time in the history of English literature has there been a more complete blending of the literary impulse and the native and derived folk material than in Elizabethan England.' He calls *The Faerie Queene* 'one of the greatest repositories of folk materials' (pp 10–11). However, since most of those materials are derived or drawn from written sources, their function in the poet's creative process or in the reader's response is very much like the function of any other esoteric learning appropriated from books.

One important category of folklore is the beast fable. Its oral and popular character was reinforced during the Middle Ages by the use as pulpit exempla and during the Renaissance by Latin and vernacular collections widely employed as textbooks. Even jestbooks often contained 'Aesopic' fables. Their popularity is evident from the number that were epitomized in proverbs, the category of folklore that Spenser uses most extensively; for example, 'An ass in a lion's skin' (Tilley A 351), 'A dog in the manger' (D 513), 'Sour grapes' (F 642), 'To blow hot and cold' (M 1258), and 'A bosom serpent' (V 68). Spenser could have assumed his readers' familiarity with the fables more confidently than he could have depended on their detailed knowledge of classical mythology or Celtic legend.

With fables and proverbs, as with other kinds of folklore, the challenge for a modern reader is not only to recognize instances but also to appreciate the creative use. Little seems to be gained by the mere identification of folktale motifs having parallels in *The Faerie Queene*; for example, 'Unpromising hero' (motif L 100 in S. Thompson 1955–8), 'Magic forest seems to stretch farther as mortals travel within' (D 1368.5), 'Snake body – woman's head' (B 29.2.3), 'Transformation: man to tree' (D 215), 'Girl saved by lion from ravishment' (B 549.1), 'Tabu: drinking from certain fountain' (C 261), 'Loss of strength from broken tabu' (C 942), 'Magic shield' (D 1101.1), 'Magic knowledge of identity of stranger' (D 1810.0.13), 'Dragon fight in order to free princess' (B 11.11.4), 'Magic well heals wounds' (D 1503.7), and so on through the other books. Individual motifs are not distinctive to folktales but are shared with histories, scriptural episodes, literary epics, romances, and plays. The significant considerations are where the author got the materials and how the reader's recognition of folk materials in literary contexts affects the response. For example, the legend of St George has long lived in European oral traditions (Szövérffy 1955). The reading public's familiarity with the legend, partly attributable to its currency in folklore ('The Dragon-Slayer,' type 300 in Aarne ed 1961), would have influenced Spenser's plotting of the events leading up to the apocalyptic battle in *FQ* I xi and his presentation of the battle itself.

A more subtle instance of a folktale analogue affecting a reader's response occurs at *FQ* II iii 17, which echoes 'The Brave Tailor' (Aarne type 1640), best known in the English tradition as an episode of the 'Jack'-cycle. Jack, on impulse or by accident, kills seven flies in a single swat. From flaunting the motto 'Seven at one stroke,' he gains a reputation for great valor and prowess. Spenser's Braggadocchio boasts how 'with one sword seven knights I brought to end.' As so often in Spenser, the real force of the analogy lies in the differences. Whereas both characters are braggarts and cowards, Jack is clever, Braggadocchio foolish; Jack equivocates, Braggadocchio simply lies. Jack's boast initiates a series of unintentionally heroic achievements; Braggadocchio's leads him finally into total embarrassment (see *baffling).

FQ III is particularly rich in folktale echoes; their proliferation in its last six cantos resembles the clustering of proverbs at *FQ* I vii 41. At the beginning of III vii, the reader enters a world strikingly familiar from nursery tales. Like many another maid of childhood memory, Florimell flees through a nightmare landscape (motif S 143 'Abandonment in forest') and unluckily seeks refuge at the cottage of a witch (motifs G 236 'Witch lives in forest,' G 401 'Children wander into ogre's house'), a character that has been called 'the most complete witch in the regular English tradition' (Briggs 1962: 75–6).

Its folktale valence thus established, the narrative moves on to two jocular tales. The Squire of Dames recounts, to the laughter of Satyrane, his hopeless efforts (motifs H 1371 'Impossible quests,' Q 512 'Punishment: performing impossible task') to locate 300 chaste women (vii 53–61). Again, with Satyrane expressing satiric amusement, canto ix prepares the reader for an old and widely known tale about a one-eyed dotard and his lusty wife (Aarne type 1419C 'The Husband's One Good Eye Covered'). In the traditional conclusion of that short tale, the adulteress enables her paramour to escape by kissing, bandaging, or medicating the cuckold's remaining eye, which in Malbecco's case is 'blincked' or dimmed (5). To anticipate the customary resolution in Spenser's episode, however, is to be surprised – as if the poet himself, having set up the reader, pulls a joke by winding the expected brief jest through a complicated series of narrative and amorous devices, some of them reminiscent of the international folktale 'The Enchanted Pear Tree' (type 1423), best known from Chaucer's *Merchant's Tale*. Even the subsequent discovery and entertainment of Hellenore by the satyrs (III x 36–52) seems like a bawdy burlesque of 'Snow-White' (type 709).

Spenser's most pointed use of a folktale, other than fables, occurs at the end of canto xi. When Britomart reads over the doors in Busirane's castle, 'Be bold' and 'Be not too bold' (50, 54), the messages strikingly parallel inscriptions in an old tale 'Mr Fox,' an English version of 'The Robber Bridegroom' (type 955). 'Mr Fox' was first printed (from a transcript by the antiquary John Blakeway) in Edmond Malone's variorum *Plays and Poems* of Shakespeare (1821, 7:163–5) to identify an allusion in *Much Ado about Nothing*. Apparently James O. Halliwell was the first to recognize the connection with *The Faerie Queene* (Shakespeare 1855

Works 4:35). Typically, however, beyond merely noting the parallel, commentators until recently have not interpreted it.

In the tale, young Lady Mary is charmed by, then betrothed to, the mysterious Mr Fox. Uninvited and unannounced, she visits his castle, entering portals successively inscribed 'Be bold, be bold,' 'Be bold, be bold, but not too bold,' and 'Be bold, be bold, but not too bold, / Lest that your heart's blood should run cold.' The last door opens into a chamber where she finds 'bodies and skeletons of beautiful young ladies all stained with blood.' When Mr Fox arrives dragging his latest victim, Mary hides, then escapes, and finally exposes the horrors of 'the Bloody Chamber.'

Structurally and psychologically, the association between the tale of this English Bluebeard and Spenser's episode are striking. The preeminent (if sometimes submerged) theme of nursery tales or *Märchen* is personal growth, as a youthful protagonist struggles symbolically toward social and sexual maturity – toward an integrated adult personality that Spenser would have designated *chastity*. According to the psychoanalyst Bruno Bettelheim, a *Märchen* of the type to which 'Mr Fox' belongs tells the juvenile hearer or reader that 'sexual feelings can be terribly fascinating and tempting, but also very dangerous'; like all 'fairy stories ... [it] teaches deep down a higher morality or humanity': that 'the person ... who experiences sex only in its destructive aspects' will be 'deservedly undone' (1976:302). Such an analysis is not greatly at variance with the terms in which readers may interpret the adventures in Busirane's castle and elsewhere in *FQ* III-IV. Britomart and Amoret can be said to divide Lady Mary's roles: 'a spectator in the lonely castle' and 'the one who only narrowly avoids the fate in store for those who put themselves in the power' of a figure like Mr Fox (Nohrnberg 1976:476). Further, Amoret can be identified with another immature *Märchen* protagonist, Briar-rose, 'the comatose princess in the fairytale' (pp 450, 477–8; the character is the Grimms' *Dornröschen*; cf Aarne type 410 'Sleeping Beauty').

With his genius for synthesis and analogy, Spenser garnered his materials widely and eclectically. Some of those materials were folklore, though not so large a portion nor exactly the same materials as sometimes supposed. The uses of folklore complement Spenser's literary and historical allusions. In some forms, such as proverbs and fables, folklore implies a common-sense norm by which to assess the mysteries and perversities of the fictional and the real worlds. In other forms, such as *Märchen*, it gives psychological depth or reality to exotic occurrences. Ashton may exaggerate when he says of *The Faerie Queene* that 'the folk materials are made a substantial and integral part of the whole work from beginning to end' (1957:12), for compared with Chaucer and Shakespeare, Spenser was not a prolific adapter of folklore for literary purposes, except for his abundant and brilliant use of proverbs. Nevertheless, the reader who comprehends the uses of folklore will better appreciate the poet's art.

CHARLES CLAY DOYLE

Antti Aarne 1961 *The Types of the Folktale* tr and enl Stith Thompson, 2nd rev ed (Helsinki); Ashton 1957; Bruno Bettelheim 1976 *The Uses of Enchantment: The Meaning and Importance of Fairy Tales* (New York); Briggs 1962; Walter J. Ong SJ 1965 'Oral Residue in Tudor Prose Style' *PMLA* 80:145–54; Joseph Szövérffy 1955 'The Master of Wolves and Dragon-Killer (Some Aspects of the Popular St. George Traditions)' *SFQ* 19:211–29; S. Thompson 1955–8; Tilley 1950.

For an outline of Elizabethan folklore, see Katharine M. Briggs 1964 'The Folds of Folklore' *ShS* 17:167–79. For observations on method in the analysis of folklore material in literature, see also Roger D. Abrahams and Barbara A. Babcock 1977 'The Literary Use of Proverbs' *JAF* 90:414–29; Richard M. Dorson 1957 'The Identification of Folklore in American Literature' *JAF* 70:1–8; Alan Dundes 1965 'The Study of Folklore in Literature and Culture: Identification and Interpretation' *JAF* 78:136–42; Dundes 1976 '"To Love My Father All": A Psychoanalytic Study of the Folktale Source of *King Lear*' *SFQ* 40:353–66; Wolfgang Mieder 1974 'The Essence of Literary Proverb Studies' *Proverbium* 23:888–94; Bruce A. Rosenberg 1982 'Literature and Folklore' in Jean-Pierre Barricelli and Joseph Gibaldi, eds *Interrelations of Literature* (New York) pp 90–106; Francis Lee Utley 1963–4 'Arthurian Romance and International Folktale Method' *RPh* 17:596–607; Utley 1965 'Some Implications of Chaucer's Folktales' *Laographia* 22:588–99; Utley 1974 'Boccaccio, Chaucer and the International Popular Tale' *WF* 33:181–201.

Fortune For Spenser and his contemporaries, Fortune embodies change and contingency; hence he refers to her 'mutabilitie' (*Gnat* 560) and 'chance' (*FQ* VI i 41). From antiquity, Fortune had been personified as a mercurial woman, often accompanied by a turning wheel and turbulent sea, both symbolic of inconstancy. Her image, pictorial or verbal, is found nearly everywhere in Renaissance culture. The popularity of this once-pagan deity in a Christian world testifies to the persistent effort to explain the phenomenon of unmerited adversity, which Fortune's change and chance could inflict.

In Spenser's minor poems, Fortune is most often a source of adversity. Although he mentions her 'guifts' (*Amoretti* 74), more characteristically he speaks of her 'scorne,' 'injurie,' and 'threate' (*Time* 28, 166, 465), her 'freakes' and 'spight' (*Teares* 130, 303). Taking a perverse pleasure in menacing and thwarting mankind, she may be overtly 'froward' (*Mother Hubberd* 66), or she may conceal her true nature for a time: Spenser speaks of 'false Fortune' (*SC, Maye* 198) and 'the guile of fortunes blandishment' (*Colin Clout* 671). In either case, Fortune may destroy man's felicity by suddenly changing his external circumstance. These references are incidental and conventional, for Spenser is not interested in her naturė or iconography, although he does refer to her wheel (*Daphnaïda* 498, *FQ* V x 20).

More varied and extensive is the treatment of Fortune in *The Faerie Queene*, undoubtedly because it is a romance, a genre that customarily gives prominence to her (see Culp 1971a). As in his other poetry, she frequently proves hostile: 'Tempestuous' (I vii 25), 'wilde' (50), 'fierce' (II xi 30), 'wicked' (III ii 44), and 'straunge' (viii 20). Spenser refers to her 'cruell freakes' (I xii 16), 'doome unjust' (II v 12), and 'wrackfull yre' (VI ix 27). Most of his epithets for chance similarly suggest adversity: 'direfull' (II i 44), 'cruell' (III vii 45), 'gracelesse' (IV iii 8), 'deadly' (VI v 28), and 'fatall' (xi 31). Yet Fortune or chance at times proves helpful. For instance, 'It fortuned (as faire it then befell)' that the Red Cross Knight should fall into the waters of the Well of Life, as also 'It chaunst (eternall God that chaunce did guide)' that he should fall near the Tree of Life (I xi 29, 45).

These last two citations point to the most problematic aspect of Fortune and chance in *The Faerie Queene* – their relation to God's providence. That relation seems variously conceived even within a single episode. Fortune appears subservient to benevolent providence when the narrator says, 'It fortuned (high God did so ordaine)' that the fleeing Florimell should come upon a boat, permitting escape from her pursuer (III vii 27). But when she is nearly raped by the Fisher, a malign Fortune is deemed responsible: 'that cruell Queene avengeresse ... Did heape on her new waves of weary wretchednesse' (viii 20). Two (not mutually exclusive) explanations for the apparent contradiction seem likely. The first regards the assertions of providential intervention as having a rhetorical purpose: 'at particular points in the poem, Spenser uses them to direct and extend the reader's emotional responses and awareness of issues'; they should not be interpreted as 'literal claims about a world' (Alpers 1967b:27). They intensify the reader's sense that providence is operative in the narrative. The second explanation involves Fortune's disparate characterization in medieval and Renaissance tradition. Some writers (eg, Dante) portray Fortune as an executrix of providence; and she is at times conflated, poetically and pictorially, with Nemesis, the classical goddess of justice. Other writers portray her as a temptress in league with the devil (Klein 1973); Fortune is often cunning and cruel in Petrarch, Boccaccio, and Guillaume de Machaut. Both concepts appear together in Lydgate's *Fall of Princes*, the *Mirror for Magistrates*, and also in *The Faerie Queene*.

FQ VI, which contains more references to Fortune than any other book, epitomizes the anomalous relation of Fortune to providence. In the stories of both Calepine and Calidore, it would seem that the change and contingency embodied in Fortune serve the ends of providence. Calepine is aided by 'wondrous chaunce' at one point (iii 51), and by 'fortune' at others (iv 21, viii 46). Yet Fortune seems not so much an executrix of providence as a force of wanton destruction, who malevolently singles out the innocent and vulnerable for the worst adversity. Thus 'False Fortune' betrays Serena, and the Brigands come upon her 'by fortune blynde' (viii 34, 36). Fortune shatters the pastoral world: the relationship of Calidore and Pastorella continues 'Till fortune fraught with malice, blinde, and brute ... Blew up a bitter storme of foule adversity' (x 38). The reader may recognize intellectually that chance and change are part of a providentially ordered world yet feel, as many Renaissance poets and thinkers did especially when they doubted or despaired of the world's design, that Fortune not only frustrates human felicity generally but also specifically thwarts those whose lives are most worthy. In this respect Fortune, as in much Renaissance literature, seems antithetical to providence.

This impression is supported elsewhere in *The Faerie Queene* by Fortune's opposition to Virtue, Justice, and Nature, personifications commonly identified with God's providence. Guyon, for example, tells Arthur, 'Fortune, the foe of famous chevisaunce / Seldome ... yields to vertue aide, / But in her way throwes mischiefe and mischaunce, / Whereby her course is stopt, and passage staid' (II ix 8). As she hinders virtue, so too is she inimical to justice. The outcome of the battle between Bracidas and Amidas is said to be 'doubtfull' because governed by Fortune: 'Ne other end their fury would afford, / But what to them Fortune would justify' (V iv 6). If Fortune may be identified with Mutabilitie in *FQ* VII (traditionally she symbolizes mutability, turns a wheel such as Mutabilitie controls, and elsewhere in sixteenth-century literature opposes Nature), she is rebuffed by a divinely ordained Nature. Each of these oppositions suggests an underlying struggle between Fortune and forces identified with providence.

In view of this struggle, it is interesting that the evil characters employ Fortune as a kind of protective coloration. They invoke her to make themselves seem more vulnerable and hence less threatening to the virtuous characters. Thus Duessa tells Redcrosse that she is 'Captiv'd to fortune' and that 'fortune false betraide me to your powre' (I i 52, ii 22). Calculation of a slightly different kind is evident when a defeated Pyrochles pleads for mercy, shrewdly suggesting that Fortune – not Guyon – has caused his plight and thus the victor should behave with restraint: 'Ne deeme thy force by fortunes doome unjust, / That hath (maugre her spight) thus low me laid in dust' (II v 12). Despair's invocation of Fortune is deliberate, too, as he urges Redcrosse to recall that 'ever fickle fortune rageth rife' (I ix 44). Rarely do the virtuous invoke Fortune's name in so obviously purposeful a manner. Una, however, perhaps to ease the guilt of the imprisoned knight, speaks of being victimized by Fortune rather than by Duessa: 'fie on Fortune mine avowed foe, / Whose wrathfull wreakes them selves do now alay' (I viii 43).

The prominence that Spenser accords Fortune in *The Faerie Queene* and his rich pictorial sense make all the more curious his indifference to her iconography; there is no real equivalent in Spenser to Fluellen's speech on Fortune in Shakespeare's *Henry V* (III vi 30–8) or to the Poet's and Painter's speeches in *Timon of Athens* (I i 63–77). The blazon on the shield of an evil knight – 'A Ladie on rough waves, row'd in a sommer barge' (VI ii 44) – may suggest the image of Fortune (Anderson 1972), but only in Britomart's comparison of herself to a boat does Spenser give memorable and apparently original expression to a topos involving Fortune: 'The whiles that love it steres, and fortune rowes; / Love my lewd Pilot hath a restlesse mind / And fortune Boteswaine no assuraunce knowes' (III iv 9).

If Occasion represents misfortune (ie, Fortune in her unpleasant aspect; see Burchmore 1981:95), she would constitute a striking visual image of Fortune. Although Fortune and Occasion were often conflated in the Renaissance, nowhere else in Spenser is the conflation apparent. The character who evokes Occasion by saying 'fortune friends the bold' (IV ii 7) is Blandamour who uses the adage to justify his penchant for violence. Also, the references to personified misfortune in the poem (II iv 17; IV iv 24, viii 14; V vii 40; VI i 12, xii 16) bear no resemblance to the portrait of Occasion in Book II. Occasion's features derive rather from Penitence, a figure sometimes portrayed along with Fortune in emblem books (see Manning and Fowler 1976).

Spenser's Fortune is characteristically medieval, being implacable rather than tractable. The twofold strategy he suggests for dealing with Fortune is not that appropriate for wresting advantage from Occasion (ie, aggressive cooperation with circumstance). Rather, it is one of mournful acceptance and aid for those already afflicted. In the words of Calidore, 'All flesh is frayle, and full of ficklenesse, / Subject to fortunes chance, still chaunging new; / What haps to day to me, to morrow may to you' (VI i 41).

Spenser's reluctance to conflate Fortune and Occasion points to his essential conservatism. Despite the many references to Fortune in *The Faerie Queene*, he makes no effort to define afresh her nature or to reconcile the inconsistencies in the traditional figure he inherits. FREDERICK KIEFER

Anderson 1972; Kenneth Borris 1986 'Fortune, Occasion, and the Allegory of the Quest in Book Six of *The Faerie Queene*' *SSt* 7:123–45; Burchmore 1981; Dorothy Woodward Culp 1970–1 'Courtesy and Fortune's Chance in Book 6 of *The Faerie Queene*' *MP* 68:254–9; Frederick Kiefer 1983 *Fortune and Elizabethan Tragedy* (San Marino, Calif); Klein 1973; Manning and Fowler 1976; Howard R. Patch 1927 *The Goddess Fortuna in Mediaeval Literature* (Cambridge, Mass).

Foster A Foster, or forester, appears at *FQ* III i 17 chasing Florimell, 'Breathing out beastly lust her to defile.' Timias pursues him while Arthur and Guyon chase Florimell. The narrative is resumed in canto v: ambushed by the Foster and his two brothers at a narrow ford in a wooded glade, Timias slays all three but is himself wounded in the left thigh with an arrow (13–25). Subsequently he is found by Belphoebe, who cures his wound but pierces his heart with love.

Although the Foster is not named, his essential qualities are well defined: he is a lawless creature of the woods (see *Salvage Man); and Spenser insists upon his sinfulness, associating him with lechery, specifically the lust of the eye; the three brothers together suggest 'the luste of the flesh, the luste of the eyes, and the pride of life' (1 John 2.16; Bloomfield 1952:165). Spenser also stresses the shame involved in the brothers' acts, and the 'renowne' that Timias wins by killing them. Timias' original decision to pursue the Foster rather than Florimell, and his subsequent wounds, have been variously interpreted. In the moral allegory of the poem, the Foster has been seen as lust, an uncivilized force threatening unprotected beauty, a force that Timias can defeat but to which he is also susceptible – hence his wound in the thigh (Nohrnberg 1976:598). The Foster may anticipate the figure of Lust, who attacks Amoret, fights with Timias, and is killed by Belphoebe (IV vii). He and his brothers also prefigure the attack on Timias by Despetto, Decetto, and Defetto in VI v. In terms of the historical allegory, Timias' encounter with the foresters has been associated with Raleigh's role in quelling the rebellion in Ireland (1579–83) led by the three Desmond brothers (Bednarz 1983). DAVID O. FRANTZ

foundlings An ancient narrative formula used often in the Renaissance, the typical foundling plot includes a noble child who is exposed, saved by peasants, raised in primitive surroundings, discovered through a talisman or birthmark, and returned, usually just before marriage, to his or her real parents, thereby restoring a threatened dynasty. In *The Faerie Queene*, foundlings include the Red Cross Knight, Arthur, Ruddymane, Satyrane, Amoret, Belphoebe, Merlin, Artegall, Pastorella, Tristram, the Salvage Man, and the baby whom Calepine rescues and gives to Matilde and Bruin.

Though their stories approximate the formula to varying degrees, none reproduces it fully. Only the story of Redcrosse comes tantalizingly close to completing the formula as he learns of his descent from Saxon kings and his saintly destiny, triumphs over his enemies, and celebrates his betrothal to Una; yet he does not marry her. (For conflicting interpretations of their union, see Hamilton 1961a:104 and Nohrnberg 1976:281.) Pastorella is restored to her family; and her name, sojourn with Meliboe, tearful reunion, and rosy mark fit the foundling paradigm. But like Una, she too is left behind when her knight returns to his quest. Adopted by Venus and raised by Psyche in the Garden of Adonis, Amoret is never reunited with Chrysogone or (in the 1596 poem) with Scudamour. Artegall, for whom Merlin predicts marriage with Britomart, remains unaware of his ancestry; and he is no sooner rescued by her than (as Redcrosse leaves Una) he leaves her 'Full sad and sorrowfull' (v vii 44). The poem's tendency to defer marriage becomes a means of avoiding it.

Why does Spenser begin these foundling plots but refuse to complete them? One answer may lie in elements of the plot itself. Renaissance writers were attracted to it both because it made for a good story and because it could treat the relationship between nature and art. Art is represented in the claim that the found child and adoptive family are superior to the conventional nuclear household, a view that Calepine summarizes when he tells Matilde that she 'may enchace / What ever formes ye list there to apply' in the 'spotlesse spirit' of the baby that fortune has given to her (vi iv 35). Similarly, the twins Amoret and Belphoebe are the products of their separate upbringings, of nurture not nature. Nature is represented by the biological parents who first lose and then regain their child, whose marriage guarantees their family's continuity. The plot allows an exploration of artistic possibility even as it affirms the validity of the family in the natural order. But by prolonging the separations and circumventing the reunions and marriages, Spenser implicitly sides with art rather than nature.

Elsewhere, Spenser even redefines nature to make it seem more artistic. In the Garden of Adonis' idealized vision of nature, Adonis is 'by succession made perpetuall,' constantly replaced and replicated like the flowers themselves (iii vi 47). Similarly, the androgynous Venus 'Begets and eke conceives, ne needeth other none,' unlike humans and other animals seeking 'to quench their inward fire' (iv x 41, 46). The cool self-sufficiency of the generative principle, contrasted with the fiery torments and furies of sexual pairing, appears again on Mount Acidale, where Colin's celebration of his lady is interrupted by Calidore and yet (the narrator suggests in his apostrophe to Colin) is recurrently present as Adonis had been, in the copia that art enables: 'Pype jolly shepheard, pype thou now apace ... Thy love is present there with thee in place' (vi x 16). Keeping alive through his piping the denying shepherdess, the poet resolves the art-nature controversy in his own way, making Colin's regenerative song an imitation of the fecund Genius of the Garden and the androgynous Venus of Book iv. Although he persistently denies closure to his stories of foundlings, Spenser suggests that the poet's art accommodates the psychological need for reconciliation with origins and the biological desire for connections to the future.

Barbara L. Estrin

Barbara L. Estrin 1985 *The Raven and the Lark: Lost Children in Literature of the English Renaissance* (Lewisburg, Pa); Ivy Pinchbeck and Margaret Hewitt 1969–73 *Children in English Society* 2 vols (London); Lawrence Stone 1977 *The Family, Sex and Marriage in England, 1500–1800* (London). On the relationship of medieval foundling tales to Redcrosse, see Tuve 1970:39–48.

fountains Spenser's fountains are not usually architectural structures: they are springs, wells, sources, where the play of water itself engages our attention. At such places, the symbolic properties of the water that circulates through *The Faerie Queene* in many guises become particularly manifest, both in the lives of the characters and in the reader's understanding (see *Idle Lake, *rivers, *sea).

Fountains are manifestations of a radical mutability. Water wells, bubbles, gushes, springs, tumbles, trickles, drizzles; above all, it flows. But fountains are also associated with the clarity of what is seen through or reflected within them. If they are a drowsy murmur, they are also silver mirrors, 'cleare as cristall glas' (*FQ* i vii 6). If they are a perpetual flowing away, they are also the spring of whatever comes to be and, hence, an image for the very principle of origin (as in Spenser's 'fountains' of modesty, eloquence, beauty, etc: ii ix 43, iii vi 25, *Hymn of Beautie* 186, *Heavenly Beautie* 21).

This paradoxical union of flow and form explains the multiplicity of allegorical meanings associated with fountains and accounts for their tendency to cluster into antithetical pairs, as now one and now the other element is emphasized. In classical literature, fountains are the site of metamorphosis, dissolution through love or grief (see *Ovid); but they are also places where lovely forms become manifest in naked splendor: Diana, Venus, or the lesser nymphs who nourish all mankind 'with their waters clere' (*FQ* iv xi 52). Similarly, the many allegorical waters in Scripture are all extensions of the fundamental opposition between the turbid waters of the dragon of the deep (Ps 74.13; cf Job 38.8–11) and the 'fountaine of living waters' (Jer 2.13; cf John 4.10, Rev 22.1) by which, in baptism as in the original Creation, the dragon's power is subdued (Lundberg 1942:64–166). But the most magical fountains seem to promise, or demand, an interplay of flow and form – as if the brightness of their forms were reserved for those willing to submit to their shadowy flow.

Spenser's fountain allegories derive from this underlying dialectic. In *The Faerie Queene*, there is a basic opposition between fountains associated with dissolution or the loss of form, and those associated with birth or the manifestation of form. To the first category belong the fountains of Duessa (i vii 2–7), Acrasia (ii v 30, xii 60–8), and Scudamour (iii xi 7); closely aligned is the 'drizling' bower of Morpheus (i i 39–41), whose murmurous illusions threaten to melt Redcrosse's manly vigilance. These tend to be shadowy places, shut away from the sun's informing light, where the quester's spiritual armor is set aside and, in the very 'middest of the race' (vii 5), he succumbs to a dangerous 'loosnesse' – whether through lust (Acrasia's victims), excessive grief (Scudamour), or the sort of spiritual sloth of which Redcrosse appears to be guilty. For Duessa's fountain, Spenser constructs an Ovidian myth of a lazy nymph whose fate recalls Salmacis (*Metamorphoses* 4.286); but he also alludes to the scriptural 'corrupt spring' before which 'a righteous man fall[s] downe' (Prov 25.26). Hence, Duessa's fountain is set over against the Well of Life, where the Dragon who 'Defyld' its waters with bloodguilt (i xi 29) is finally defeated. The dyad ('Duessa') of matter and the simple flow ('Una') of grace are the two rival 'sources' of Redcrosse's spiritual life. Acrasia's fountain, which is in the 'midst' of her realm to epitomize its 'liquid joyes' (ii xii 60) – joys which melt the bather to liquidity (eg, Cymochles in v 28–36; cf *Gnat* 233–48) – stands in a similar relation to the fountain of the chaste nymph at ii ii 7–9: the one a sleep-inducing murmur (v 30), the other an unstainable purity.

Spenser's immediate model for this pair seems to have been the waters of concupiscence and conscience in Trissino's *Italia liberata* 5 (cf Armida's fountains in Tasso's *Gerusalemme liberata* 14.55–61 and Alcina's in Ariosto's *Orlando furioso* 6.24–5). The ancestor of all these enchantresses is Circe; and Acrasia's fountain is emblematically the source of those poisonous drinks that turn men to beasts and that Neoplatonists were fond of allegorizing (eg, in the cup of Bacchus: *FQ* ii xii 49, 56–7) as the surrender of soul to matter. (*Hyle* was the Greek term for matter and Hylas the victim of fountain nymphs: Spenser uses him in the masque of Cupid, iii xii 7–8, to represent the mutability of Fancy.) Scudamour 'wallows' and 'grovels' beside his fountain in a way that may remind us of Byblis, whose grief turned her into a fountain (*Met* 9.450–665), although his tears are without the penitential value they sometimes acquire in such tales (eg, the chaste nymph of *FQ* ii ii 9). Britomart too finds that her complaint carries her to the margin of watery dissolution (iii iv 6–10).

Other fountains suggest the generative power of water. Sometimes, as in the case of Chrysogone (vi 6–9), Agape (iv ii 45), and Maia (*Epithalamion* 307–10), there are actual births. Chrysogone's nude body, 'mollifide' by its immersion in a 'fresh fountaine,' becomes as transparent to the informing virtue of sunlight as the crystalline water itself. Belphoebe's birth is said to be 'of the wombe of Morning dew' (iii vi 3), which, in its echo of Psalms 110.3, suggests an analogy to the Incarnation. Like the spring on Mount Acidale (vi x 7), Chrysogone's fountain is unmarred by the 'slime' that makes most earthly waters imperfectly receptive to the divine light (cf Pyrochles' ineffectual 'lake of mire' ii vi 44). Her Nile-like fertility, stirring with 'fruitfull seades,' thus presages the 'eternall moisture' of the Garden of Adonis (iii vi 34), where what is celebrated is the loving union, the fitness (9), of matter and form. This fecundity, 'eterne in mutabilitie' (47), is contrasted both with Adonis' fountain in Castle Joyous (i 35–6), where the boar triumphs, and the 'liquid joyes' of Acrasia's realm, whose Genius is a sterile progenitor of images rather than of forms, and whose fountain (the only one of its kind in *FQ*) is an elaborately sculptured artifice, its 'Infinit streames' (II xii 62) mere 'guilefull semblaunts' (48) of Nature's own fruitful waters (ii 6).

Even where there is no actual birth, the presence of a nymph beside or within a fountain is often a token of its fruitfulness. On Acidale and Arlo Hill, classical goddesses (the Graces who attend on Venus; Diana) are assimilated to the fairy lore that makes fountains gateways to other worlds (see *Var* 6:282–3). Sometimes the traditional play of crystal waters and golden tresses (eg, IV ii 45) suggests that the emergent nude is simply the most manifest form of water's capacity for brightness. Spenser cites the seaborn Venus as an emblem of water's fruitfulness (xii 1–2), and she is parodied by the maidens of Acrasia's fountain (II xii 65) – teases who leave the onlooker as unsatisfied as Tantalus in the river of hell (vii 58). Diana and her avatars, on the other hand, suggest how fleeting such moments of illumination must be in a mutable world; and allegorizations of Actaeon's fate often remind us of the dangers of presuming beyond mortal capacity. Faunus' presumption (anticipating that of Mutabilitie herself) may bring about a sort of Fall, but the tale of his useless bribe ('Queene-apples, and red Cherries from the tree' VII vi 43) alludes as well to the motif of the maiden/goddess wooed by the insufficient gifts of mutable earth (Polyphemus and Galatea in Theocritus' Idyll 11; the satyr and nude Silvia in Tasso's *Aminta*; cf the polluted spring, recognizably Diana's, in *Bellay* 12; also *Teares* 271–88). Faunus' gifts are enough to secure Molanna (whose mutability is indicated by her watery fate), but the real goddess of the fountain eludes his grasp. What can be caught is only a poor replica, like the giggling beauties of the Bower of Bliss, or the false Florimell at large while true beauty is locked in the sea's Protean embrace.

Hence, the elusiveness of the nudes on Acidale is the measure of their authenticity. Acidale was originally a fountain, and Calidore's approach is by way of a stream to whose flow not sleep but heavenly harmonies are tuned (VI x 7; cf *SC, Apr* 35–6) and whose 'silver' clarity may distantly reflect the imaging power of Narcissus' well (*Met* 3.407: 'nitidis argenteus undis'; cf note to VI x 7.2 in *Var* 6). Although the Graces (offspring of Ocean, Spenser explains: VI x 22) are no longer in the fountain, their behavior obeys its dynamics: they manifest themselves like Venus (Florimell, too, was nurtured on Acidale: IV v 5) and disappear like Diana. Colin Clout's presence aligns Acidale with Helicon's 'learned well' (*Apr* 42) and with the 'speaking streames of pure *Castalion*' on Parnassus (*Teares* 273). Such allusions are not merely formulaic in Spenser. Fountains and the language associated with them designate whatever wells up – blood, tears, divine or poetic inspiration – from below or beyond the realm of conscious intention. (Rhetorical tradition, allegorizing Helicon and Castalia as the 'fountains' of the poet's and orator's copiousness, suggested that language itself is such an originating source; hence, Chaucer as the 'well of English undefyled' [IV ii 32] and his opposite, Malfont, a lewd poet, 'welhed / Of evill words' [V ix 26].) The gifts of the Graces are such as 'seeking cannot fynd' (VI iv 28). They are accessible only to those who have at least temporarily doffed their 'bright armes' (ix 36: in this Calidore is like the victims of less auspicious springs), and they flee from any attempt to possess them (Calidore as a more courteous Faunus).

The same interplay (rather than simple opposition) of flow and form characterizes the Well of Life (I xi 29–34) and may help distinguish its operation from the failure of the chaste nymph's fountain in *FQ* II to cleanse the baby's bloody hand. The allegorical intentions of this latter fountain have been much disputed (see *Amavia; also Kaske 1976). But what is crucial in the behavior of the fountain is its refusal of any admixture of the baser streams of wine (i 55: washing Bacchus was supposed to temper his fiery effects; cf *Greek Anthology* 9.331) or blood (ii 9–10; cf Ezek 16). The waters that spring from the nymph's helpless grief (an Ovidian motif, but also an emblem of penitence) are 'cold through feare' (ii 9), rejecting corruption rather than purging it. Like medieval chastity tests, they only reveal what they are unable to remedy. The Well of Life is more active. It seems to be related to the Tree of Life, with its blood-red fruit and springing balm (I xi 46, 48), as baptism is to the Eucharist, original to actual sin. (The trees and stream on Acidale are perhaps a secular parallel, while the tree over the river Cocytus in Persephone's grove, II vii 58, is a demonic parody.) Both baptism and the Eucharist suggest that purification is not mere washing but dissolution from which new form emerges: the death of the Old Adam and the birth of the New. Redcrosse 'falls' into the well just as his armor has become a fiery trap, and he topples again into the stream of balm. He is 'drenched' (I xi 34), 'bathed' (ii 43), thoroughly immersed. Here as elsewhere, water is associated with the collapse of will, surrender to unseen chance, the extinction of light, sleep. But this Fall (like Calidore's dereliction) is a happy one. Redcrosse rises eaglelike from the waves (xi 34; cf Ps 103.5), 'new-borne' as is the sun itself (33: in the Easter Vigil, baptismal water is purified by the submersion of the paschal candle); and eventually – a happier Actaeon – he opens his eyes (as Dante does, emergent from Lethe and Eunoè: *Purgatorio* 31–3) upon the unveiled beauty of his lady (xii 21–3).

TERRY COMITO

Terry Comito 1978 'Beauty Bare: Speaking Waters and Fountains in Renaissance Literature' in *Fons Sapientiae: Renaissance Garden Fountains* ed Elisabeth MacDougall (Washington, D.C.) pp 15–58; Kaske 1976; Grace Warren Landrum 1941 'Imagery of Water in *The Faerie Queene*' *ELH* 8:198–213; P. Lundberg 1942 *La Typologie baptismale dans l'ancienne église* (Uppsala).

Fowre Hymnes (See ed 1912:585–99.) First published in 1596, in a quarto volume that also contained a second edition of *Daphnaïda*. The late date of *Fowre Hymnes* suggests that it contains some of the last verse written by Spenser. The first two hymns present love and beauty in human and cosmic perspectives, drawing upon the poetic theologies traditionally associated with Cupid and Venus; the second two present divine love as incarnated in Christ, and heavenly beauty as an adjunct, or more probably an aspect, of the godhead. Taken as a whole, the series sets forth a comprehensive, complex, and sometimes puzzling vision, by turns self-consciously learned and deeply moving.

In the dedicatory epistle, dated from Greenwich, 1 September 1596, Spenser purports to explain the history of the four poems. The first two, he says, were written in the 'greener times' of his youth. Yet *An Hymne in Honour of Love* and *An Hymne in Honour of Beautie* were unsatisfactory to some critics: pleasing only to younger readers ('those of like age and disposition' as the poet) and too unsettling in their moral effect (they did 'rather sucke out poyson to their strong passion, then hony to their honest delight'). Spenser claims he was asked to recall the poems by one of the 'two most excellent Ladies' to whom the *Fowre Hymnes* are dedicated: the sisters Margaret, Countess of Cumberland, and Anne, Countess of Warwick (erroneously called 'Marie' in the text by Spenser or by Ponsonby, his publisher). Yet too many manuscript copies had been 'scattered abroad' for the lady's request to be granted. So the poet 'resolved at least to amend, and by way of retractation to reforme them' by adding *An Hymne of Heavenly Love* and *An Hymne of Heavenly Beautie*.

This brief epistle raises questions for the critic: about the poet's reason for allowing the publication of the improper 'earthly' hymns with the later pair, about the date of those 'greener times' of the earlier composition, and about the possible revision before publication of the first two poems that rendered them the conventional and utterly inoffensive hymns they appear to be. Although the epistle indicates that there is a qualitative difference between the first pair and the second, the large number of parallels and consistencies suggest that the four are meant to be read as a group. Why then the suggestion of such a difference between them? The notion of a retractation does not clarify the interpretive problems for it does not suggest a rejection of the earlier poems so much as a request that they be reinterpreted. Such gestures in the later writings of Petrarch and Chaucer may be so understood: they wrote retractions of their love poems so that they would be reread (a sense of the Latin *retractatio* found in Christian literature from Paul and Augustine onwards; Oates 1983).

Although the dedication suggests a split between the two pairs, the connections among the hymns certainly indicate a wholeness and a continuity, whether these qualities resulted from a single period of composition or of two (or more?) periods of composition and revision. There is no absolute dichotomy between the poems. Although some critics have pointed out sharp contrasts between the two pairs, for instance in the descriptions of the descent and rule of Cupid and the descent and service of Christ (Bjorvand 1975, Ellrodt 1960: 153–93), they concede, as others affirm, that these contrasts are established as a series of parallels (Hyde 1986, Nelson 1963:99). All who are less inclined to find a sharp split between an order of nature and an order of grace stress the evidences of progression through the quartet, as in the movement from the 'disjunctions' of the *Hymne of Love* to a later refiguring and transvaluation of the initial experience of the Petrarchan lover (Comito 1977), or in evidence of a growth in psychological awareness (Oates 1983). There is, then, a forward and upward movement in the series by which the earlier pair leads into the later; earthly love is never left behind in favor of heavenly love, but exists in polar and dialectical relation to it. *Eros*, the love that 'ascends to get' is set in relation to *agape*, the love that 'descends to give' (Nygren 1953, Welsford 1967). In the dynamic and constant movement of love throughout creation, agape gives itself to be transformed into responsive eros, to be transformed again upon return to its source into divine love. The completion of any instance of the cycle is premised on the absence of interference by sin, fate, necessity, or chance, any one of which can divert towards disaster the power and energy of love.

Although the movement in *Fowre Hymnes* is essentially indivisible (and accessible to human understanding only in rare moments of intuition), to be presented in human language it must be broken down into units accommodated to the imperfect capacities of human comprehension. In telling stories about such units, narrative is capable of drawing an interpreter into dynamic and imaginative release from the limitations of dogma and individual experience. The hymns function as a complex glass through which the dynamism of divine creativity may be apprehended. The celebrants of the hymns are drawn into a process that leads back to God. This form of celebration is traditional: hymns had from the earliest time been the vehicles for celebrations of the divine, especially in the early Neoplatonic tradition (Orphic hymns, the early Christian hymns of Synesius), and well into the Renaissance (see D.P. Walker 1958:12–29, Puttenham *Arte* I.12, and for an interesting parallel with Spenser, the *Hymnes* of Ronsard).

The structure of each of the four hymns follows a generic pattern: an invocation to each deity, descriptive praise of the genealogy and function of each, and a culminating suit, or exhortation to enter into the suit, for enjoyment of grace.

In the *Hymne of Love*, the deity invoked initially is the cruel Cupid of Petrarchan tradition. He recalls the masque of Busirane (*FQ* III xii) and the more complaining of the early *Amoretti*, the suffering of Timias for love of the unattainable Belphoebe (*FQ* III v), and the woe and pain Britomart feels when she knows Artegall only as mirrored through Merlin's art (ii). Cupid is later shown in a softer and more sensuous light as a babe in the lap of Venus enjoying 'her ambrosiall kisse' (*HL* 25). The love celebrated as the sections of praise begin (43) 'reign[s] in the mynd' even as he works mightily in the macrocosm. This account reflects Ficino's 'Commentary' on Plato's *Symposium*; its tone and significance accord also with the description of forces at work in the Garden of Adonis, with the celebration of wholesome loves at the Temple of Venus, and with the great figure of Concord there (*FQ* III vi, IV x). One 'moved' by this love 'To multiply ... Not for lusts sake, but for eternitie' (*HL* 99–104) feels the same motive force as the lover at the end of *Epithalamion* and as Arthur in pursuit of Florimell (*FQ* III i). At this point, the first hymn anticipates the less problematic praise offered in the second hymn to Beauty, the beloved goal who draws love to herself. But the cruelty of Cupid as described by lovers' plaints reappears: jealous earthly lovers must oscillate in torment between visions of anticipated joy and present pain. As the *Hymne of Love* prepares to yield to the praise of Beauty, the lover begins to see his pains as purgatorial. He promises that if he is granted his taste of an earthly paradise he will celebrate, in a heavenly hymn, 'My guide, my God, my victor, and my king' (305). The lover's hope to be 'embosomd' with his beloved, and his vision of her as '*Venus* dearling' among the favored 'folke' who enjoy their 'hurtlesse sports, without rebuke or blame' in the bosom of Pleasure (*HL* 249, 278–93), verbally anticipate the vision in the final hymn of Sapience, 'soveraine dearling of the *Deity*' sitting 'in his bosome' (*HHB* 183–4).

The Venus invoked as Beauty in the *Hymne of Beautie* encompasses both the goddess and the mistress who participates in her power. Spenser's blurring of the lines of demarcation between Venus and the singer's lady, and between both and the Cupid they resemble in 'dart[ing] fyre into [his] feeble ghost' (24) has led to the suggestion that he is an unphilosophic poet (Nelson 1963:115, Welsford 1967:47–8), but it is quite in keeping with the philosophical tradition upon which he is drawing. Ficino, following Plotinus, stresses the power of love to overcome the distinction between loving subject and beautiful beloved object by elevating their two souls to the intellectual level upon which they interpenetrate as spiritual beings (Kristeller 1943:264, A.H. Armstrong in Loeb Plotinus pp xx-xxi). Leone Ebreo, a successor to Ficino, melds the biblical affirmation of procreative love to the older Platonic paradigm of ascent, hallowing earthly love by declaring its participatory resemblance to the unfolding of the divine creativity (Ebreo ed 1937; see Ellrodt 1960:185–93).

In leaving behind the more lustful complaints of the pained Petrarchan lover, the lover pleads for 'one drop of dew reliefe' to cure his pain and 'restore a damned wight from death' (*HB* 284–7). This near-equation of the joys of love to the baptism of grace risks condemnation as blasphemy from those who do not share the biblicized Neoplatonic perspectives, but it prepares effectively for the lofty opening of the third hymn and for the due descent of heavenly love in Christ in response to human need.

Love's 'golden wings' in the opening line of *Hymne of Heavenlie Love* recall the 'golden plumes' of love in *Hymne of Love* 178, which also bear the lover to 'the purest skie,' and effectively counter the discursive echoes of the 'retractation' that follow (*HHL* 8–21). The account of creation which begins appropriately at line 22 (the number of the letters in the Hebrew alphabet, and the line paralleling that in which the babe Eros is introduced in *HL*) is marked by a specifically Christian piety achieved through biblical diction and image, but it is fully congruent with the Platonism of the first two hymns. As the Son comes forth like a Plotinian emanation from the overflowing godhead, the word *begot* (30) preserves the impression of orthodoxy. His purity, 'voide of sinfull blot' (32), resembles that of the paschal lamb and the bride of the Song of Solomon. In the blending of biblical and Greek thinking which he sustains throughout *Heavenly Love*, Spenser participates in a Christianity which cannot be disentangled from the Platonism in the language of the New Testament and Apocrypha and of the Church Fathers (Nelson 1963:114).

The strongest impulse in *Heavenly Love* to a loving response in the reader stems from the narration of the earthly suffering and death to which the Son proceeds when he leaves the heavens where he has been attended by the 'trinall triplicities' (64) of the angelic orders. One who feels the 'most unspeakeable impression / Of loves deepe wound, that pierst the piteous hart / Of that deare Lord' (155–7) may be initially too deep in meditative piety to recall the Petrarchan pains of the lover in *Heavenly Love*, of Britomart (*FQ* III ii 37, iii 16, iv 8), or of the suitor in the early *Amoretti* sonnets. Yet Spenser perhaps does not forget them in using language that identifies the redemptive sufferings of 'that most blessed bodie, which was borne / Without ... reprochfull blame' (*HHL* 148–9) with the sufferings of Cupid's targets. Thereafter, contemplation of the earthly suffering of the Lord of heavenly love leads to an apostrophe of grateful bliss (169–75), then to an exhortation to the reader in turn to reflect gratitude in loving service to humanity (197–217; cf *Am* 68). Finally the singer promises that at last the 'ravisht soule ... shall plainely see / 'Th'Idee of his pure glorie, present still / Before thy face' – a vision that mystics may enjoy even before death through love 'Kindled through sight of those faire things above' (281–7).

The design traced by the third hymn makes a full circuit: it describes the heavenly begetting of Christ, plunges with the account of the Incarnation and Passion to the nadir of human sin and Love's death on the Cross, and with the resurrection account rises in return to the source of all. There has been, of course, no inappropriate suggestion of an eddying love between singer and lady at the earthly level, but the injunction to brotherly love and the verbal echoes demonstrate that Heavenly Love incarnate applies to human love.

The cumulative effects of much recent study suggest that the process unfolding in the sequential reading of the hymns leads by the *Hymne of Heavenly Beautie* to an infolding of retrospective understanding. Some readers suggest that this last hymn should be seen also in terms of meditative and contemplative traditions stemming from the biblical religions.

Heavenly Beautie locates itself finally, and with it the meditative consciousness of singer and reader, in the highest heaven. But significantly in line 22 – the same structurally important position that he has used for fresh beginnings in *Love* and *Heavenly Love* – Spenser indicates that he is anchoring the final vision to its bases in earthly experience by 'Beginning then below.' In the ensuing ascent, the singer passes quickly through the celestial cosmic regions that parallel the poetic setting for the *Cantos of Mutabilitie* to image forth the higher heavens 'farre above' and 'farre exceeding' (*HHB* 64–5) those below the starry firmament. The orderly levels he describes depart from the hierarchical orders codified by Pseudo-Dionysius, of whose number and arrangement he has shown himself aware in the 'trinall triplicities' of angels attending the Son in *Heavenly Love*. Like Hooker (*Laws* 1.3–4), he salutes the Dionysian writings current in medieval Catholicism but chooses not to follow them precisely. His supracelestial orders range upwards from 'happy soules' beholding 'still' the divine face, past a level manifesting 'those *Idees* ... which *Plato* so admyred' 'Enraunged' with 'pure *Intelligences* from God inspyred' (78–84). The abstruse language seems to be describing the Neoplatonic level ranged above 'Soul,' the level of *Nous* or 'Intellect' in which individual minds are contemplating individual mental objects, the multiple Platonic forms. In the mystical tradition upon which he is drawing, the distinction between subject and object suggested in 'Idees' and 'Intelligences' is regarded as a necessary accommodation to human discursive reason: on that high level, divisions and distinctions of any sort do not properly apply. The abstruse terms have little devotional effect upon the reader, and seem to have no more for the singer. Yet they are curiously conspicuous as interposed between the fairly conventional reference to a heaven of felicitous Christian souls and two subsequent stanzas (85–98) which contain their own puzzling departures in describing what seem to be four heavens enlivened by six angelic orders. The upward motion of the imagination is clear enough, but the confusions in detail serve to effect the abdication of erstwhile limitingly logical habits of thinking.

Attained after this long approach, the vision of Sapience in the bosom of the deity is the culmination of *Heavenly Beautie*. Although her significance in the hymns as a whole is not grasped easily, her position suggests that she may be expected to subsume all that has gone before. The conjoined and indistinguishable biblical and Cabalistic imagery, with the echoing of the earlier hymns, invites the understanding of Sapience as divine being, but with strong suggestions of an analogy to human sexuality. She is the 'soveraine dearling' of a 'great *Deity*' (184, 145) whom the poet leaves unnamed – prudently, if he has in mind the first male emanation from the highest unknown godhead. Awesomely enthroned, she is 'hid in his owne brightnesse' (178) from unworthy eyes. The worshiper who sees God's 'owne Beloved' (241) enjoys by highest grace the sum of 'joy,' 'blisse,' and 'happinesse' (241–3). The language transfigures lesser experiences of earthly love and beauty.

There are analogies between the last two hymns and the final stanzas of the *Cantos of Mutabilitie*. *Heavenly Beautie* figures forth in universal rather than personal terms the vision invoked there in the 'Sabbaoth' prayer. The androgynous figure of Nature in the *Cantos* suggests a divine persona who is as close to the hidden godhead as the heavenly lovers, the unnamed 'Deity' and Sapience of *Heavenly Beautie*. Both hymn and *Cantos* play the mind retrospectively over what has gone before, and point in contemplative wisdom, beyond the poetic language that has served its anagogic purpose, to that state where 'tongues ... cease' (1 Cor 13.8).

ELIZABETH BIEMAN

For editions of *Fowre Hymnes*, see Spenser *FH* ed 1907, Spenser ed 1929, and Welsford 1967; for a concordance, see Bjorvand 1973. Studies include Bennett 1931c; Bennett 1935; Bjorvand 1975; Blondel 1976; Terry Comito 1977 'A Dialectic of Images in Spenser's *Fowre Hymnes*' *SP* 74:301–21; DeNeef 1974; Leone Ebreo (Leo Hebraeus) 1937 *The Philosophy of Love* tr F. Friedeberg-Seeley and Jean H. Barnes (London); Ellrodt 1960; Galyon 1977; Hyde 1986; Sears R. Jayne 1972 'Attending to Genre: Spenser's *Hymnes*' *SpN* 3.1:5–6; Paula Johnson 1972 *Form and Transformation in Music and Poetry of the English Renaissance* (New Haven); Nelson 1963; Anders Nygren 1953 *Agape and Eros* tr Philip S. Watson (London); Oates 1983; Plotinus ed 1966; Jon A. Quitslund 1969; Quitslund 1985 'Spenser and the Patronesses of the *Fowre Hymnes*: "Ornaments of All True Love and Beautie"' in *Silent but for the Word: Tudor Women as Patrons, Translators, and Writers of Religious Works* ed Margaret Patterson Hannay (Kent, Ohio) pp 184–202, 281–3; Rollinson 1971; Paul R. Smith 1977 'Rhyme Linking Techniques in Spenser's *Fowre Hymnes*: Another Aspect of Elizabethan Rhymecraft' *CCR* 2.1:39–48; D.P. Walker 1958; Wind 1958.

Foxe, John (1516–87) Martyrologist. In the vicissitudes of Una and the Red Cross Knight at the hands of Duessa, Archimago, and their allies, Elizabethan readers would have recognized intermittent allusions to the historical vicissitudes of the church. Particularly in Redcrosse's final victory over the Dragon and the apotheosis of Una as his bride (*FQ* I xi-xii), they would have seen the triumph of Protestantism: the burning of the Reformation martyrs during the reign of the papist Mary had been followed by the accession of the Protestant Elizabeth, her triumph reaffirmed in the victory over the Spanish Armada (see *Dixon). With Elizabeth as Queen, the nation had been freed from false religion and united with the One True Church.

This view was familiar from the definitive English Protestant version of ecclesiastical history, Foxe's *Actes and Monuments* (also known as the Book of Martyrs, first English pub 1563), which was dedicated to Elizabeth. Returned from exile under Mary, Foxe was ordained priest by Grindal, his old friend and fellow exile, and lived as writer and preacher, mostly in London. Widely disseminated and required from 1571 in all cathedrals, Foxe's book became one of the best-known works of English Protestantism. With copious documentation, Foxe traces the history of the Church from apostolic times, more particularly in Britain, advancing the thesis that through the Middle Ages the true church was continually undermined and supplanted by a false church, the power of the Christian emperors such as Constantine usurped by an imperial papacy, and the gospel corrupted by a false doctrine of priesthood and sacrament. Protestantism is the true church resurgent, its triumph in England heralded by the work of Wycliffe and the Lollards (among whom Foxe would include Langland, other 'Piers Plowman' poets, and even Chaucer), and its victory achieved in the Elizabethan Settlement under a Queen who is the Constantine of her day. Elizabeth herself had been imprisoned under Mary, and the story of her liberation from the Tower to the Throne is the last of the martyr-histories in Foxe's book.

In seeing the life story of a nation or an individual as a struggle between truth and falsehood as historical and moral entities, Foxe's history and Spenser's *FQ* I are influenced by the Revelation of John with its presentation of Jerusalem and Babylon, and also by the 'Image of both Churches' of John Bale (1495–1563), who, together with Foxe, had pioneered in England a Protestant historiography, interpreting Revelation as a prediction of the events of the Christian centuries. The presentation of Una and Duessa at many points in *FQ* I assumes an understanding of the historical role of Foxe's true and false churches, also presented graphically on his title page – the one church 'persecuted,' the other 'persecuting' – the two contrasted in their worship, their witness on earth, and the verdict pronounced on them at the Last Judgment. (For further parallels between Foxe and Spenser, see Hankins 1971, Kermode 1964–5, and Sandler 1984.)

FLORENCE R. SANDLER

John Foxe 1563 *Actes and Monuments* (London; *STC* 11222–8, including later eds rev by Foxe), ed George Townsend 1843–9, 8 vols (London). The work was popular into the nineteenth century and was often updated, so many post-sixteenth-century editions are unreliable. Olsen 1973 traces Foxe's life; King 1982 gives literary background. William Haller 1963 *The Elect Nation: The Meaning and Relevance of Foxe's 'Book of Martyrs'* (New York) is a principal study, although certain of his theses have been questioned by later scholars; see Olsen 1973 on Foxe, and Bauckham 1978 and Firth 1979 on apocalyptic tradition. Bibliography in Warren W. Wooden 1981 'Recent Studies in Foxe' *ELR* 11:224–32.

Fradubio In *FQ* I ii 28–45, Redcrosse encounters the two lovers Fradubio and Fraelissa transformed into 'two goodly trees.' Fradubio cries out when Redcrosse plucks a bough from him to weave a garland for Duessa, and, bleeding from the wound, goes on to recount the circumstances of his transformation at Duessa's hands. The motif of the bleeding, speaking tree has a long literary pedigree that enables Spenser to demonstrate his mastery of an epic convention while illuminating his protagonist's character. Furthermore, it reinforces a dramatic and rhetorical pattern that will dominate Book I.

Key texts by Virgil, Ovid, Dante, Ariosto, and Tasso elaborate the motif of the speaking tree, the animistic component of which suggests primitive mythological origins. In *Aeneid* 3, Aeneas encounters a bleeding and speaking myrtle bush that identifies itself as the Trojan Polydorus, slain for his wealth by the avaricious king of Thrace. Virgil recounts Aeneas' *pietas* toward his mutilated countryman; but Ovid mocks that response in *Metamorphoses* 8.742–76, where the impious Erysichthon cuts down an oak tree sacred to Ceres. As the tree bleeds, it warns him of disasters that await him. In applying this motif to Redcrosse, Spenser conflates Aeneas' piety and Erysichthon's obduracy. Redcrosse, for example, reverently buries the bleeding bough after it finishes speaking; but he does so for the possibly self-protecting reason that 'from the bloud he might be innocent.' 'Too simple and too trew' to understand the application to his own case, he resumes his journey with the false Duessa.

Dante's use of the motif in the Wood of the Suicides, *Inferno* 13, underscores the aptness of Pier della Vigna's transformation into a bramble as punishment for his sin of suicide. The canto also dramatizes Dante's sentimental pity for the sinner and his moral failure to heed Virgil's advice. For Spenser, the issue of Redcrosse's moral failure is likewise important; but Fradubio's sin is infidelity to his beloved. In this respect, the episode recalls the examples of Ariosto and Tasso. In *Orlando furioso* 6, Ariosto uses the motif to depict both Astolfo's punishment for erotic dalliance on the Isle of Alcina and Ruggiero's failure to heed Astolfo's advice. Tiring of her lovers, the Circean enchantress transforms them into animals and plants. Having become a myrtle bush, Astolfo warns Ruggiero that a similar fate awaits him. Ruggiero nonetheless ignores his advice, succumbs to Alcina's charms, and requires powerful intervention to be released. Finally, in *Gerusalemme liberata* 13, Tasso uses the motif to suggest the psychic consequences of an ill-fated troth. There the Christian knight Tancredi encounters a bleeding and speaking tree that projects the ghost of his beloved pagan Clorinda, whom he has unwittingly slain. In fleeing from the enchanted wood, he flees from an image of the past that he knows he cannot remedy.

All these literary antecedents illuminate Redcrosse's character. So, too, do general associations that link the shadowy forest with Spenser's own Wood of Error in I i. The latter in turn evokes the garden of mundane delights and the diverse biblical traditions related to Adam and Eve (see Nelson 1963:160–4, Nohrnberg 1976:158–66). Taken together, these references create an allusive context for Redcrosse's moral drama. When Redcrosse encounters Fradubio and Fraelissa, he is already a victim of duplicity. He has recently abandoned the faithful Una because Archimago has deceived him with an image of the false Una's erotic debasement. He has just attacked and defeated Sansfoy; but he is now paired with the latter's mistress, the false Duessa who calls herself 'Fidessa.' Although Fradubio tells how Duessa led him to doubt Fraelissa's beauty (whence one Italian meaning of his name, *fra dubbio* 'amidst doubt'), Redcrosse fails to associate Fradubio's witch with the woman who now accompanies him; nor does Fradubio enlighten him. The stage is set for Redcrosse's descent into sin.

Careful rhetorical patterning links Redcrosse with Fradubio. From the beginning of Book I, Redcrosse appears prone to the doubt implicit in Fradubio's name. After entering the Wood of Error in i 10, for example, he finds himself 'in diverse doubt.' Elsewhere his doubt amounts to misplaced faith. In i 53, the 'doubtfull words' of false Una 'made that redoubted knight / Suspect her truth'; but because Redcrosse has no real reason for suspicion, he soon dismisses his doubt. The word *doubt* (from L *dubitare* 'to waver or hesitate') relates to the word *fear*; according to the *OED*, the sense '"to fear" ... was an early and very prominent sense ... cf. *Redoubt*.' In this sense, Redcrosse, 'Full of sad feare and ghastly dreriment' (ii 44), is Fradubio's 'brother in doubt' (whence another Italian meaning of Fradubio's name, *frate dubbio* 'brother doubt').

Fradubio's first words to Redcrosse with their emphatic rhyme on *feare* suggest the knight's relation to Fradubio's own plight: 'fly far hence away, for feare / Least to you hap, that happened to me heare.' Redcrosse's response, 'doubting much his sence' and listening with 'doubtfull eares,' further links him to the tree (ii 31–2). Earlier, his own 'wonted feare of doing ought amis' (i 49) led him to reject the false Una; but Archimago tortured him 'with fearefull frights' until he 'wandred far away' in flight from 'gealous feare' (ii 4, 12). His doubts about Una are reflected in Fradubio's turning against Fraelissa (whose name suggests the frailty of human nature). Both knights are confronted with Hercules' choice at the crossroads, and both choose the path of vice. The irony is that Redcrosse wishes to appear as proof against fear and doubt. On the verge of disaster, he urges Fidessa-Duessa to 'put feare apart' (21). With her, he sits in Fradubio's shade where 'fearefull Shepheard ... never sat' (28). Fradubio's tale nonetheless foreshadows Redcrosse's doom. Ignoring its implications, the knight departs with his 'Fidessa': 'At length all passed feare, / He set her on her steede, and forward forth did beare.' Turning his back on Fradubio, Redcrosse behaves as though he has fairly escaped any bloodguilt in this episode – even, that he has succeeded in repressing his own 'wonted feare of doing ought amis.' But he is not yet out of the wood, and his future remains doubtful. Like Fradubio, he cannot realize his humanity until he is 'bathed in a living well' (ii 43; cf xi 31). WILLIAM J. KENNEDY

W.J. Kennedy 1973; Quilligan 1979:109–14.

France, influence and reputation in The very name of Spenser seems to have been unknown in France until the eighteenth century, and his work did not meet with due recognition until 1864. Up to that time, his name appears only in translations from English critics and in passing allusions by French writers.

The first translation of a life of Spenser, extracted from Theophilus Cibber's *Lives of the Poets*, came out in the *Journal étranger* (May 1755) edited by the Abbé Prévost. In the *Nouveau dictionnaire historique et critique* (1750–6), the supplement to the dictionary by Pierre Bayle, J.G. de Chauffepié had a patchwork item on Spenser from various English sources, mainly John Hughes. Spenser is presented as a victim of court intrigues, in prose translations from *Ruines of Time* (449–69), *Teares of the Muses* (469–72), *Mother Hubberds Tale* (894–905) and *The Faerie Queene* (VI xii 40). On *The Faerie Queene*, Chauffepié reports judgments ranging from the censorious to the laudatory (Temple, Rymer, Dryden) and centered on its value as an epic poem. Parts of this article were used again in the 1759 edition of Moreri's *Dictionnaire historique*. The *Journal anglais* (1775) included another 'Vie d'Edmond Spencer,' probably translated from the anonymous life in volume I of Church's edition of *The Faerie Queene* (1758). The last translated biography was published in 1818: A.M.H. Boulard's version of J. Aikin's preface to the 1806 edition of Spenser's works. In a footnote, Boulard quotes Chauffepié as the authority on Spenser in France (p 8). In addition, an 1860 university thesis on *The Faerie Queene* by Carl Mayer 'de Berlin' reports the views of English critics together with the first summary of the poem in French.

Infrequent allusions show that if Spenser's name had reached various French authors, they knew him only by hearsay. The first of them, the Abbé Prévost, mentions him as one of the great English poets along with Milton in *Mémoires et aventures d'un homme de qualité* (1728–31). Voltaire cites Spenser twice: in the *Essai sur les moeurs* (1756), he states that 'Spencer avait ressucité la poésie épique'; but in his article 'Epopée' (under the heading 'De l'Arioste'), which appeared in *Questions sur l'Encyclopédie* (1771), he writes that in England 'on l'estima, et personne ne le put lire.' At the turn of the century, in her essay *De la littérature* (1800), Madame de Staël is resolutely hostile: Spenser's *Faerie Queene* is 'ce qu'il y a de plus fatigant au monde.' In *Génie du christianisme* (1802), Chateaubriand equates Spenser with the Spanish poet Ercilla, both having 'fait des stances et imité l'Arioste.' In 1836, in the *Essai sur la littérature anglaise* published in the same year as his translation of Milton's *Paradise Lost*, though acknowledging Spenser's 'imagination brillante' and 'invention féconde,' he deems him 'glacé et ennuyeux' and declares he prefers *Vewe of Ireland* to *The Faerie Queene*.

The first valuable French assessment is found in Hippolyte Taine's *Histoire de la littérature anglaise* (1863–4; tr Edinburgh 1871), where he enthusiastically extols Spenser's Platonism, his dreamlike quality, and his painter's sensibility. The three longest passages of *The Faerie Queene* which he translates into prose show these aspects (II iii 22–30, vii 28–46, xii 53–78). In his conclusion, Taine declares that in Spenser's poetry he sees 'l'apparition du paganisme dans une race chrétienne et le culte de la forme dans une imagination du Nord.'

The period since 1864 has been outlined by Wilson (1973), who contrasts Taine's praise with Jusserand's severe criticism of Spenser's 'Incoherence' (1903). But what Jusserand actually censures is Spenser's elitist obscurity and his conjunction of eroticism and moralization. Wilson shows that Taine's and Jusserand's conflicting views are at the root of most judgments on Spenser in the dictionaries and histories of literature he surveys. Even the first book-length survey in French of Spenser's life and work presents him as an artist more than a philosopher, arguing that one must not judge *The Faerie Queene* for its moral value, depth of thought, or sentiment (Legouis 1923). According to Legouis, the poem is a succession of 'paintings' unified through a prevailing atmosphere that is engendered by the 'powerful and monotone harmony of the stanza' (336).

The few attempts at translating Spenser are recent. Fernand Henry's translation of *Amoretti* (1914) tries to comply with Spenser's prosody; his preface and notes stress Spenser's debt to French poets, mainly Desportes. Legouis' rendering of *Epithalamion* in rhymed alexandrines and fourteeners in 1921 is included as an appendix to his study of 1923. Paul de Reul translated part of *The Faerie Queene* into prose in 1933, with summaries linking selected passages from the seven books. In 1950, Michel Poirier translated *The Faerie Queene* I i entirely, together with extracts from II, III, VI and VII, using unrhymed alexandrines whenever possible.

Works of scholarship parallel these allusions and translations. Legouis' doctoral thesis in Latin, *Quomodo Edmundus Spenserus* ... (1896), demonstrates Chaucer's influence on Spenser's verse in *The Shepheardes Calender*. Articles by Etienne Taboureux (1899) on the Spenserian stanza and its influence, and by Jusserand (1905–6) on the Aristotelian source of Spenser's 'twelve private morall vertues,' have a distinguished place in the tradition of international scholarship on Spenser. Twenty years later, Denis Saurat studied the connection between the Cabala and Spenser's thought (1924, 1926; tr 1930).

The most important recent contribution to Spenser studies in France is Robert Ellrodt's *Neoplatonism in the Poetry of Spenser* (1960), a study of the poet's intellectual heritage (medieval Neoplatonism, Petrarchism, certain forms of Renaissance Platonism and Protestantism). In 1972, he finds in Spenser's thought and sensibility 'no effort towards synthesis or even syncretism ... coexistence rather than any conscious pursuit of agreement, however artificial' (p 7).

Spenser's reputation in France, though very slow to take shape, is now confirmed but restricted to university specialists (see Blondel 1976, Dorangeon 1974, Gasquet 1974, Lecocq 1969, Maguin 1980, Moreau 1964). His influence on French poetry has always been, and still is, nonexistent, perhaps because, as Malezieu has claimed, 'les Français n'ont pas la tête épique'.

BERNARD TANNIER

Blondel 1976; Dorangeon 1974; Robert Ellrodt 1960; Ellrodt 1972 'Les Structures fondamentales de la pensée et de la sensibilité dans l'oeuvre poétique de Spenser' *Etudes anglo-américaines* (Nice) 18:5–16; Gasquet 1974:343–53; Fernand Henry 1914 *'Amoretti' d'Edmond Spenser, traduits en sonnets avec introduction, texte anglais et notes* (Paris); J.J. Jusserand 1903 'Edmond Spenser' *Revue de Paris* 10(May):58–95; Jusserand 1905–6; Louis Lecocq 1969 *La Satire en Angleterre de 1588 à 1603* (Paris); Emile Legouis 1896 *Quomodo Edmundus Spenserus ad Chaucerum se fingens in eclogis 'The Shepheardes Calender' versum heroicum renovarit ac refecerit* (Paris); Legouis 1921 'L'*Epithalame* d'Edmund Spenser traduit en vers français' *RLC* 1:398–415; Legouis 1923 *Edmund Spenser* (Paris; tr New York 1926; rev ed 1956); J.M. Maguin 1980 *La Nuit dans le théâtre de Shakespeare et de ses prédécesseurs* (Lille) 2:868–72 and passim; Carl Mayer 1860 '*La Reine des Fées*: Poème allégorique d'Edmond Spenser, étude littéraire et historique' (diss Univ of Paris); Joseph Moreau 1964 'Introduction à la lecture des *Hymnes* de Spenser' *RTP* 3rd ser 14.1:65–83; Michel Poirier 1950 *Spenser, 'La Reine des Fées,' extraits* (Paris); Paul de Reul 1933 *Edmund Spenser: Introduction, traduction et notes* (Paris); Saurat 1930; Etienne Taboureux 1899 'The Spenserian Stanza' *RELV* 15:499–505 and 16:14–21, 112–18, 163–72; Hélène Tuzet 1987 *Mort et résurrection d'Adonis* (Paris) pp 128–43 (tr of 'garden of Adonis' *FQ* III vi 29–49); R.R. Wilson 1973.

Fraunce, Abraham (c 1558–1633) As a member of the Sidney circle, Fraunce shared many of Spenser's interests – including emblems, mythology, allegory, and experimental versification – and actively promoted his poetry. Like Sidney, he was educated at Shrewsbury School; through Sidney's patronage, he went to St John's College, Cambridge, matriculating in 1576, Fellow in 1580, and MA in 1583. He entered Gray's Inn in 1583 and was called to the bar in 1588. In 1591, he failed to be appointed Queen's Solicitor, despite the Earl of Pembroke's backing, but continued to practice as barrister. As late as 1633, he may have been in the service of the Earl of Bridgewater.

Fraunce seems to have acquired from Spenser his interest in pastoral, and he imitates the rustic dialect of *The Shepheardes Calender* in his *Amintas Dale* (1592); he cites the *Calender* throughout his *Lawiers Logike* (1588) and quotes *The Faerie Queene* from manuscript in *The Arcadian Rhetorike* (1588). While his references may illustrate the Sidney circle's continued interest in Spenser through the 1580s, we know little of Spenser's interest in him beyond two conjectures: that 'Corydon' in *Colin Clout* 382–3 refers to Fraunce (Todd and Malone, in *Var* 7:465–6), and that he may possibly be one of the 'sweet Poets' who have commemorated the death of 'Amintas' in *FQ* III vi 45.

Fraunce's interests were wide and varied: he promulgated the ideas of Ramus, championed quantitative verse in English, advanced the art of interpreting myth and symbol, and helped popularize pastoral. His works are notable for the strikingly original and occasionally eccentric ways in which they combine these interests; all of them were dedicated to members of the Sidney family. His earliest work is the Latin comedy *Victoria*, written at Cambridge. His first published work is *The Lamentations of Amyntas* (1587), a translation into English hexameters of Watson's Latin *Amyntas* (1585); here he shows himself valiantly continuing the verse experiments that had so interested Sidney, Spenser, and Harvey (see *Three Letters*). Although his efforts earned him Jonson's verdict that 'Abram Francis in his English Hexameters was a Foole' (Jonson ed 1925–52, 1:133), he was highly regarded as a poet by Meres, Nashe, Peele, and Harvey.

Fraunce's first work of interpretation, *Insignium, armorum, emblematum, hieroglyphicorum, et symbolorum ... explicatio* (1588), is a Latin treatise in three books. A manuscript (c 1580) contains an earlier version of the third book and a fourth on 'symbolica philosophia' (Maidstone, Kent Archives Office, Ms De L'Isle and Dudley U1475 Z16); a related manuscript contains 40 emblems beautifully drawn by Fraunce (Oxford, Bodleian Lib, Ms Rawl D.345.1, c 1582).

The first of his two expositions of Ramus (to which, as he tells us, he was set by Sidney) was *The Lawiers Logike* (1588). It draws examples of invention and disposition both from law cases and (surprisingly) from *The Shepheardes Calender*, and it contains an interesting logical analysis of Virgil's second eclogue (spoken by 'Corydon' – hence, possibly, the identification of Fraunce as 'Corydon' in *Colin Clout*). There are 97 direct quotations from the *Calender*, many of which illustrate syllogisms, occasionally making the point that even shepherds can use logic and method. An earlier draft, *The Shepherd's Logic* (c 1585) similarly draws its examples from the *Calender*; the manuscript includes two short treatises by Fraunce on logic.

The Arcadian Rhetorike (1588) completes the Ramist program by treating elocution. It is as much an anthology of pastoral literature from Virgil to Sidney as it is a handbook of schemes and tropes. Especially noteworthy are Fraunce's brief comparison of Sidney's and Spenser's handling of the sestina and the first appearance in print of a stanza from *The Faerie Queene* (II iv 35, quoted by book and canto, suggesting that the poem was organized in final form by 1588, at least to this point in the text). In these two works, Fraunce was establishing Spenser as a norm of eloquence for English verse.

Fraunce was concerned throughout his career with exploring how poetry works. The way it expresses modes of thought and illustrates the varying of expression occupied him in the 1580s; in the 1590s, his attention turned to basic matters of the creation and interpretation of poetry. The center continued to be pastoral. In 1591 appeared *The Countesse of Pembrokes Emanuel*, hexameter poems on the life of Christ with translations of some psalms. In the same year appeared the first of his two final works dedicated to Sidney's memory, *The Countesse of Pembrokes Ivychurch* (Ivychurch being one of the Earl of Pembroke's country estates). It contains an adaptation of Tasso's *Aminta* and Fraunce's early *Lamentations* mentioned above, with appended hexameter translations from Virgil and Heliodorus. His last and in many ways most interesting publication was *The Third Part of the Countesse of Pembrokes Yvychurch, Entituled, Amintas Dale* (1592). Within its framework of a commemoration of Amintas' (Sidney's) death, various nymphs and shepherds tell of the transformations of the gods in songs which are in turn explicated. The book thus combines a set of pastoral poems, a dictionary of myth, and a work of allegorical exegesis. It is valuable for interpreting mythological allusions in Spenser and also for indicating how a contemporary writer worked with allegory. Often mining etymology and iconography for clues, Fraunce strove for interpretation in three senses: literal, moral, and mystical.

WALTER R. DAVIS

The best account of Fraunce's life and works is G.C. Moore Smith's introduction to Fraunce's *Victoria, A Latin Comedy* in vol 14 of W. Bang 1906 *Materialen* (Louvain). Modern editions of his works include *The Shepherd's Logic* c 1585 (facs ed of BL Ms Add 34361; rpt Menston, Yorks 1969); *The Lamentations of Amyntas* in Watson ed 1967; *Insignium ... explicatio* 1588 ed Stephen Orgel (New York 1979); *The Arcadian Rhetorike* 1588 ed Ethel Seaton (Oxford 1950); *The Third Part of the Countesse of Pembrokes Yvychurch* in Fraunce ed 1975.

French Renaissance literature France, said Spenser, was a land 'fruitfull of brave wits' (*Rome* envoy). He would naturally have been interested in those 'wits,' for when he was a boy, the Renaissance had long since come to France, bringing an increased awareness of Italian letters, the publication of many classical texts, a new confidence in the French language itself, and, despite bloody religious and political turmoil, a flurry of literary experiments accompanied by frequently justified claims that an age of recovery and renewal had dawned.

Spenser's introduction to French literature came early, for his headmaster at Merchant Taylors' School, Richard Mulcaster, had almost certainly read du Bellay, whose *Deffence et illustration de la langue françoyse* (1549) offered his colleagues in what was to become the Pléiade a program for linguistic innovation and literary improvement (Renwick 1922a, 1922b). While still Mulcaster's pupil, Spenser was asked to translate some verses for van der Noot's *Theatre* (1569), an illustrated indictment of Catholic Rome. Among the poems were eleven sonnets on the collapse of ancient Rome, taken from du Bellay's *Songe* (1558).

During Spenser's university years and early adulthood, he made some friends who knew French writers well: Harvey, who admired Ramus, Ronsard, du Bartas, and Rabelais; Fraunce, who quoted du Bellay and du Bartas; Arthur Gorges, whose verse in large part derives from du Bellay and Desportes; Sidney, who translated the Huguenots Mornay and du Bartas; and Buchanan, who knew everybody and had ties to the Leicester circle known to Spenser. Spenser's friend Daniel Rogers, furthermore, had attended the meetings in Paris among Ronsard, Baïf, Tyard, Pibrac, and others; out of those meetings grew the *Académie de poésie et de musique* (1570), dedicated to the arts and to semihermetic and Neoplatonic hopes for moral and spiritual revival through the harmonies of syncretic encyclopedic learning, metrical experiment, and philosophical or poetic rapture (van Dorsten 1970, Phillips 1965, Prescott 1978). In their correspondence, Harvey and Spenser refer to an 'Areopagus' or 'Senate' designed to promote English quantitative verse (*Var Prose* pp 6, 442). Most scholars dismiss this exchange as a passing pleasantry, but the references do suggest that Spenser knew of those Parisian gatherings. One possible sign that his friends kept an eye on such proceedings is E.K.'s story of Timotheus, which he may have read in Tyard's *Solitaire second* (1555), a Neoplatonic dialogue connected with the early 'academic' movement in France (Carpenter 1956); this legend of music's occult effects, though, is also found in St Basil, eds 1557 and 1567[?] (*STC* 1543.5 and 2729).

True, the political and religious situation in France sometimes angered Spenser; and when in the late 1570s Elizabeth seemed willing to marry the Duc d'Alençon, he was among many Englishmen disturbed by the prospect of an alliance with what they thought a murderous and tyrannical Catholic regime. But neither Elizabeth's perhaps feigned affection for her 'frog' Alençon nor the later conversion of Henri IV (*FQ*'s Burbon) diminished Spenser's liking for French writers. Thus, Bodin's political thought probably affected his *Vewe of Ireland* (Kliger 1950). He also knew Le Roy's *La Vicissitude ou variété des choses* (1575; Lievsay 1944), and he used the mythographical dictionaries of Robert and Charles Estienne (Starnes and Talbert 1955). There is no evidence he looked at Rabelais but a little to show he read Montaigne (McNeir 1954). Not surprisingly, Spenser focused particularly sharply on French verse. Certain passages in his poetry show he knew, among others, Claude Buttet, Jean Dorat, Rémy Belleau, and Marguerite de Navarre; but from these he borrowed only conceits or phrases (see McPeek 1936, Prescott 1985). It was Marot, du Bellay, Ronsard, Desportes, and du Bartas who provided more than the opportunity for intermittent search and seizure.

Spenser may first have heard of Clément Marot (c 1496–1544) when he used his translation of Petrarch's 'Standomi un giorno' for the *Theatre for Worldlings*. A decade later, E.K. tells us, Spenser included Marot among his models for *The Shepheardes Calender* (although E.K. doubts 'he be worthy of the name of a Poete,' perhaps implying that Marot was too much the author of courtly trifles). *November* imitates Marot's elegy on the death of Louise de Savoie. To Spenser, the loss of a great lady brings more general thoughts of the 'trustlesse state of earthly things,' and the poem's position in a circling calendar bends its energies and significance to engage those of other eclogues; Marot's poem is less richly entangled. *December* follows Marot's complaint to François I 'soubz les noms de Pan et Robin.' Both shepherds lament the withered spring; but Marot turns this to a witty request for funds whereas Spenser leaves his Colin shaken and, for the moment at least, silent. After 1579, Spenser's work shows little trace of Marot except for two of the Anacreontics: 'I saw in secret' translates 'Amour trouva celle qui m'est amere,' and 'As Diane hunted' is loosely based on 'L'Enfant Amour.'

Spenser's response to du Bellay went deeper. For his *Complaints*, he reworked his translation of the *Songe* and Englished du Bellay's *Antiquitez* (1558) as *Ruines of Rome*. The poetry is not Spenser's best; but together with *Ruines of Time*, much influenced by the *Songe*, it shows what Spenser found in du Bellay: emblematic imagery, an ambivalent admiration of fame and glory, and an awareness of both mutability and continuity at work in time. Du Bellay's melancholy and nostalgia (sometimes for inner realms of nymph-haunted greenery) have a homesickness that recalls Spenser's feelings while in Ireland. And cutting across this perception of time as the ruin of pride is a belief that rebirths are possible, especially in a commonwealth led by those dedicated to the restoration of learning. In *Teares of the Muses*, Euterpe's speech shows traces of du Bellay's 'La Musagnoeomachie,' a celebration of France's triumph over cultural darkness. No wonder that in the envoy to *Rome* Spenser praises du Bellay as France's eternally famous 'first garland of free Poësie.' Here du Bellay seems fresh, leafy, liberated from a stuffier or narrower past; he offers hope that verse can outlast the monuments of mere power. Indeed, it was just this interrelationship of poetry, material structures, and time that Spenser found significant when writing a dynastic epic, for phrases from *Rome* appear in the historical passages of *FQ* II x and III ix, and du Bellay's Great Mother goddess Cybele (*Rome* 6) has left the Tiber for the Thames in *FQ* IV xi 27–8.

Spenser borrowed from Ronsard's 'Un Enfant dedans un bocage' for Thomalin's account of Eros in *SC, March*, and *Astrophel* owes something to his 'Adonis.' Furthermore, the two poets shared much: a liking for the inwardness or source of things (for example, the young Muses in Ronsard's ode to Michel de L'Hospital are led to the ocean depths to view the 'seeds' of the world), a distrust of a sublimated sexuality that denies the flesh (although Spenser's affirmations in this regard are more domestic and respectable than Ronsard's), and an ease with the allegorical significance of ancient myth. Above all, Spenser had in Ronsard a near contemporary keenly aware of authorship as both career and vocation, convinced that poetry is a matter not merely of discrete moments of intensified discourse but of prolonged and public stance, obligation, and spokesmanship. Although Virgil and Ariosto provided the chief models for *The Faerie Queene*, the self-promotion, the links through modern dynastic epics to ancient Trojan or Celtic heroes, the prophetic voice and nationalistic claims, even the later doubts and waverings, were all more immediately present in Ronsard. The poets' range of genres is similar, and even E.K.'s annotations have a parallel in Muret's commentary on Ronsard's *Amours* (Adams 1954, Prescott 1978).

Yet the differences are also striking (Terence Cave, private correspondence). Ronsard shared the Pléiade's rejection of the native French tradition, whereas Spenser, despite some humanist innovation, retained ties to Chaucer and to medieval romance; Ronsard is far more exuberant and wide-ranging in his borrowings from Greek, Latin, and Italian poets; he was happier with shorter forms, finding difficulty with large-scale structures. And Ronsard's allegorical imagination is likewise more sporadic, as a comparison of the four seasonal hymns of 1563–4 with the Garden of Adonis episode in *The Faerie Queene* shows: his myths of generation and natural recycling are discontinuous, attractively wayward, and partly burlesque; Spenser's allegory is both more coherent in itself and integrated into a larger allegorical frame with greater moral emphasis.

Some *Amoretti*, such as 15, 22, and perhaps 69, recapitulate conceits found in the clever love poetry of Philippe Desportes (1546–1606); and other sonnets treat the lady as a cruel beauty in terms very like the French poet's pained and sometimes semi-mocking elaborations on eyes, smiles, pride, cruelty, and thralldom. These sonnets adopt almost to the point of parody attitudes of passivity, suffering, and captivity while playing with a conceit until all its facets have flashed in turn. Yet Spenser's sonnets differ from Desportes's in having greater emotional resonance, success after 'weary chace,' and a lady whose initial hardness is modified by her goodness and wit. The difference can best be seen in *Amoretti* 15, a reworking of Desportes's *Diane* 1.32: Desportes describes his mistress in glittering detail, but Spenser also praises 'that which fairest is, but few behold, / her mind adornd with vertues manifold' (Prescott 1978:150–1).

According to Harvey, Spenser admired the Fourth Day of *La Sepmaine*, a long hexameral and encyclopedic work by du Bartas. Spenser's *Teares of the Muses* may owe something to du Bartas' 'L'Uranie,' for his own Urania flies to see the heavens and tell of the world's creation (Campbell 1935, Lotspeich 1935, Snare 1969). And at the end of *Rome*, Spenser says, 'gins *Bartas* hie to rayse / His heavenly Muse.' The two poets are radically unlike, however, for although du Bartas used Greek myth and emblematic imagery, his chief desire was to show God's works and Word in their unveiled splendor, whereas Spenser was most at home in allegory. Spenser wished du Bartas 'never dying fame,' but he did not often imitate him.

Spenser, in sum, knew some French prose and scholarship and knew contemporary French verse especially well. He would have noted, particularly in Ronsard, an extreme self-consciousness and a talent for self-publicizing by no means alien to his own temperament and tactics. And in much of the Pléiade's poetry, he would have found a useful model for his own easy mixture of classical and local scenery, an affectionate if respectful familiarity with ancient symbols of cosmic and natural energies quite different from later preciosity on the one hand or demands for straight fact or doctrine on the other. To move from reading the Pléiade to reading Spenser is to move to a nearby province of the same country. The landscape is more soberly cultivated than parts of Ronsard's territory, and one has left behind du Bellay's gentler sweep into distant prospects, the lower slope of his hills; but the terrain is still familiar, even if its allegorical nature is more clearly posted and its temples wear a reformed look.

Anne Lake Prescott

Marjorie Adams 1954 'Ronsard and Spenser: The Commentary' *RenP 1954* pp 25–9; Lily B. Campbell 1935 'The Christian Muse' *HLB* 8:29–70; Nan Carpenter 1956 'Spenser and Timotheus: A Musical Gloss on E.K.'s Gloss' *PMLA* 71:1141–51; Deborah Cartmell 1985 '"Beside the shore of siluer streaming *Thamesis*": Spenser's *Ruines of Time*' *SSt* 6:77–82 with response by Anne Lake Prescott in *SSt* 7:289–94; M.W. Ferguson 1984; Samuel Kliger 1950 'Spenser's Irish Tract and Tribal Democracy' *SAQ* 49:490–7; John L. Lievsay 1944 'An Immediate Source for *Faerie Queene* Bk. v, Proem' *MLN* 59:469–72; Henry Gibbons Lotspeich 1935 'Spenser's Urania' *MLN* 50:141–6; Waldo F. McNeir 1954 'The Behaviour of Brigadore: "The Faerie Queene" v, 3, 33–34' *N&Q* 199:103–4; Manley 1982; O'Connell 1971; Patterson 1986; Prescott 1978 contains references to many sources omitted here; Prescott 1985; W.L. Renwick 1922b 'Mulcaster and Du Bellay' *MLR* 17:282–7; Satterthwaite 1960.

G

game Literary games have been defined as 'any *playful*, self-conscious and extended means by which an author stimulates his reader to deduce or to speculate, by which he encourages him to see a relationship between different parts of the text, or between the text and something extraneous to it' (Hutchinson 1983:14). *Metafiction*, for example, refers to the author's playfulness: a literary work's modes of play, the varieties of game incorporated into it, its 'gamelike' structure, and the way it imposes rules of a new game that the reader must learn to play. Although the existence of game and play, in many diverse forms, has been acknowledged only in the modern period, it does not follow that earlier literature was without its playfulness or was not gamelike. All literature, simply in being literature, must manifest some of the modes of play and game. Renaissance literature, and certain writers in particular, may be seen to embody many playful and gamelike stratagems. For instance, the plays within Shakespeare's plays, all of which are reflexive in nature (and thus metafictional), show that literary playfulness is a Renaissance preoccupation.

Play and game elements abound in Spenser's writing in at least four ways: in wordplay; in the numerous accounts of festivals and chivalric tournaments; in a number of narrative episodes involving entrapment in which a temporarily superior character employs cunning and advantage to trick other characters (in such situations the trickster may be said to have devised elaborate rules that the entrapped character must play); and in reflexivity, which is the self-conscious flaunting of either the work's status as fiction or its specific range of conventions. Since these ways are unmistakably metafictional, the modern term fits Spenser with justness.

Renaissance rhetorical theory distinguishes several types of wordplay. Paronomasia is not simply punning in the modern sense. When E.K. glosses *SC, Januarye* 61, 'I love thilke lasse, (alas why doe I love?),' as 'Paronomasia or playing with the word,' he apparently means that it is an instance of *traductio*, or repetition of homonyms, in which multiple signification counts for less than multiplication of similar sounds. Polysemous wordplay, in the more familiar sense of the pun, is frequent throughout Spenser's poetry. In *Amoretti* 10, there is a common play between *hart* and *heart* in order to establish a correlation between courtship and hunting. In *FQ* I x 9, Caelia greets Una paronomastically when she inquires, 'Hast wandred through the world now long a day; / Yet ceasest not thy wearie soles to lead, / What grace hath thee now hither brought this way?' As the church, Una leads human souls in their earthly pilgrimage to salvation; this play upon the sense of *soles* seems, in its plainness, almost disconcerting. Often Spenser's wordplay is extremely sophisticated. In *The Shepheardes Calender*, Thenot begins *November* with the query, '*Colin* my deare, when shall it please thee sing, / As thou were wont songs of some jouisaunce?' E.K.'s gloss of *jouisaunce* as 'myrth' allows an elementary wordplay since Thenot may mean either songs about mirth or songs that cause mirth. (When the term is used at *Maye* 25, E.K. glosses it as 'joye.') Moreover, the word suggests a larger play of signification than the gloss admits: it may mean pleasure, or (if the word is allowed its possible French associations) sexual pleasure. The latter sense would be consistent with the love themes of *The Shepheardes Calender* and with Renaissance treatments of love generally. It is quite possible to see further polysemy in the hidden senses of joviality, jolliness, Jove-likeness and even youthfulness (L *iuventas*, Fr *juvénilité*). Etymological wordplay is pervasive in *The Faerie Queene* (see *etymology). A name always signifies some aspect of a character's true nature. Generally, not only does a knowledge of the relevant etymon behind a name supply an insight into a character's significance but, since it is a kind of secret wit, it also draws the reader into an elaborate game with the author (see Craig 1967).

Although tournaments and festivals usually associated with chivalric romance (whether in their courtly or their carnivalesque aspects) do not figure prominently in *The Faerie Queene*, occasionally they are introduced as points the characters in their quests move towards or away from. In the Letter to Raleigh, Spenser says that the whole poem will culminate in the Fairy Queen's annual twelve-day feast (from which, in historical time, the adventures begin). In Book V iii, the 'spousals of faire Florimell' provide a locus towards which the characters move, and in which a number of diverse narrative threads are gathered. All such festivities are occasions for spending 'joyous dayes and gladfull nights' with 'all deare delices and rare delights' (iii 40). Spenser's insight into the conventions of courtly play and festival laughter is illustrated when Britomart spends a night in Castle Joyous: as the evening festivities begin, each knight and squire 'Gan choose his dame with *Basciomani* gay, / With whom he meant to make his sport and courtly play'; then they engage in dancing, gambling, wooing, and merriment, as 'diverse wits to divers things apply' (III i 56–7). In canto ix, Paridell and Hellenore share the festivities of the unwilling Malbecco's table, at one point playing *cottabus* (see *games). Later Paridell and Britomart exchange tales of adventure, genealogy, and courtly grace, discoursing 'diversly, / Of straunge affaires, and noble hardiment' (53). Here Spenser presents a moment of laughing exuberance, intricate playfulness, and complex courtly banter aided by '*Bacchus* fruit' (30). Festivities are both an occasion for the release of carnivalesque impulses and themselves a mode of play.

Narrative episodes in which one character falls into a snare set by another character, or is otherwise entrapped or deluded, may be called 'godgames.' Although the term is modern, it accurately describes a recurring narrative and dramatic situation in Renaissance literature, for example, in Shakespeare's *Tempest*, Cervantes' *Don Quixote*, and, the most famous of all, Calderón de la Barca's *La vida es sueño* in which the hero has been so thoroughly deluded by his father, Basilio, King of Poland and his subordinates that he cannot tell whether he is sleeping or waking. A number of episodes in *The Faerie Queene* involve situations in which the hero confronts another character who has a temporary advantage, who creates a delusion concerning the true state of things, and who (in effect) imposes a set of rules that the hero must master in order to escape. Godgames test the hero's intelligence and moral qualities, for example, in Archimago's stratagem by which he deludes Redcrosse into accepting a 'seeming body of the subtile aire' as the true Una (I ii); Duessa's entrapment of Redcrosse by her illusory form of Fidessa, the high point of which occurs in the house of Pride when he seems unable to penetrate any of the complex illusions and is, for the moment, overplayed; the house of Mammon, within which Guyon is repeatedly tested by the labyrinthine illusions that Mammon creates (II vii); the Bower of Bliss in which Acrasia entraps a number of knights, including Mortdant and Verdant (xii); Castle Joyous in which Britomart is subject to, and tested by, several illusions (III i); the house of Busirane in which the magician entraps Amoret and tests Britomart by a number of powerful and dangerous illusions (xi-xii). In these episodes, which illustrate the salient features of a godgame, a powerful, controlling character creates illusions that threaten to entrap the hero.

Reflexive play makes the literary work its own subject. It is a highly self-conscious mode of discourse in which a writer calls attention to the work's literary status (and to the ontological problems that surround its status) and thrusts the work's conventions self-referentially into the foreground. It has been argued that rhetoric, in elaborating the distance between *topoi* and expression, constitutes an essentially reflexive mode of discourse (Lanham 1976). *The Faerie Queene* often seems to comment on its own fictional status and on the arbitrariness of its literary conventions. For example, the proem to Book II begins with an address to Elizabeth in what appear to be mock-confessional tones: 'Right well I wote most mighty Soveraine, / That all this famous antique history, / Of some th'aboundance of an idle braine / Will judged be, and painted forgery, / Rather then matter of just memory.' In other places, the narrative appears to denigrate the conventions of chivalric romance (a type of reflexivity already pervasively present in Ariosto) or to develop them into ludicrous hyperbole (Nelson 1973). The Dragon in I xi is described in physically incongruous terms: not only are its wings like sails but the individual feathers are like 'mayne-yards, with flying canvas lynd' (10). Other descriptive passages overplay the conventions of romance and, in so doing, call attention to their status as artifice.

A common type of reflexive play in Renaissance literature is the technique of embedding in one narrative other narratives in which characters tell stories or in which stories are read or even (as paintings and tapestries) observed. Embedded narratives covertly underscore the act of narration as well as the conventions of narrative, thus making the narrative itself an important theme. *The Faerie Queene* is rich in the sophisticated form of such playfulness in which characters recall adventures or recount genealogies. In Book III, Paridell narrates his genealogical history (ix 33–51); and in II x, during their stay in the house of Temperance, both Guyon and Arthur read their genealogies in Eumnestes' library. Densely allusive embedded narratives are made possible by ecphrasis. Britomart and Redcrosse observe tapestries that express 'The image of superfluous riotize' through the tale of Venus and Adonis (III i 33–9). Although ecphrasis necessarily reduces a tale to its essential sequence of incidents, it is nonetheless narrative; indeed, its minimal nature calls attention to the discursively elaborated properties of the literary narrative that contains it.

The degree of elaboration in embedded narratives does not constitute narrative but only the presence of incidents possessing some recognizable order (not necessarily chronological) among themselves. Spenser occasionally embeds the most minimally narrated tales conceivable: those which are not narrated but only mentioned. For example, as Triamond and Cambell ride with Blandamour and Paridell, they speak of 'deeds of armes abrode, / And strange adventures' (IV iv 5). No such adventures are actually narrated, but the allusion to a body of story ('of courtesies and many a daring feat') that could be narrated, even if left empty, makes the point that tales and tale-telling are traditional aspects of chivalric romance. All the instances of embedded narrative, whether as tales actually told or as pictorially represented, or even as reduced to bare allusiveness, make the nature of narrative an integral aspect of *The Faerie Queene*'s complexity (R.R. Wilson 1986). As with other kinds of reflexive play, these make the primary narrative and its conventions its own subject. Far from being translucent or invisible, the conventions of the literary work become precisely what must be considered. Whatever the forms it displays, Spenser's reflexive play is invariably allusively dense and intricately provocative.

R. RAWDON WILSON

Elizabeth W. Bruss 1977 'The Game of Literature and Some Literary Games' *NLH* 9:153–72; Roger Caillois, ed 1967 *Jeux et Sports* Encyclopédie de la Pléiade, 23 (Paris); Craig 1959; Craig 1967; J[ohan] Huizinga 1949 *Homo Ludens: A Study of the Play-Element in Culture* (London); Linda Hutcheon 1980 *Narcissistic Narrative: The Metafictional Paradox* (Waterloo, Ont); Peter Hutchinson 1983 *Games Authors Play* (New York); Richard A. Lanham 1976 *The Motives of Eloquence: Literary Rhetoric in the Renaissance* (New Haven); Nelson 1973; Olson 1982; Shormishtha Panja 1985 'A Self-Reflexive Parable of Narration: *The Faerie Queene* VI' *JNT* 15:277–88; Mihai Spariosu 1982 *Literature, Mimesis and Play: Essays in Literary Theory* (Tübingen); Bernard Suits 1978 *The Grasshopper: Games, Life and Utopia* (Toronto); R. Rawdon Wilson 1982 'Godgames and Labyrinths: The Logic of Entrapment' *Mosaic* 15.4:1–22; Wilson 1986.

games, Renaissance In *Mother Hubberds Tale*, Spenser distinguishes the martial games which befit a courtier from the 'thriftles games' of the modern court gallant (737–52, 797–823). The belief that martial games were justified because they prepared the body for war was held in ancient Sparta, and may be found in Plato and Aristotle no less than in a military theorist like Vegetius. Though not without classical precedents, the view that modern aristocratic education represented a sad falling-away from the discipline of the ancients was more typically medieval: 'auncient noble men,' writes Christine de Pisan, 'made not theyre children to be norisshed in kyngis and prynces courtes for to lerne pryde, lechery, nor to were wanton clothing'; rather, they were sent to 'propre scoles' which taught them to 'wrastle, lepen, and playe one with other, moeving theyre bodyes' (ed 1932:28–9). This utilitarian view is echoed in the works of the Elizabethan educational writers Elyot, Ascham, and Mulcaster, all of whom strongly supported games of physical prowess, and it explains why Spenser refers infrequently to mere pastimes or amusements (never to backgammon, and only indirectly to chess [*FQ* I ix 12; *SC, Dec* 53], though both games were very popular in the Renaissance), and then disparagingly. Similar disparagement is reflected in his description of the Ape who 'could play, and daunce, and vaute, and spring, / And all that els pertaines to reveling' (*MHT* 693–4; see *dance). For him, the principal games are the praiseworthy 'knightly feates,' such as running, swimming (see Everard *Digby), horseback-riding, wrestling, and archery as practiced by the 'brave Courtier' in *Mother Hubberd* or, in a very similar passage, by Astrophel ('Astrophel' 73–84). 'Now the nigh aymed ring away to beare' (*MHT* 742) alludes to the sport of running at the ring, a form of tilting in which the jouster sought to impale with his lance a small metal ring attached to a post; this sport was particularly popular in the sixteenth and early seventeenth centuries (Strutt 1903:112–13). At *FQ* III vii 41, the vivid image of an Olympic charioteer clipping the marble course-marker (the *meta*) on the turn (an image apparently taken from Horace's first Ode) shows that Spenser shared the common misconception that the Olympic games were held on Mount Olympus.

Spenser alludes four times to the game of prisoner's base. When Britomart and Satyrane pursue Ollyphant, they 'boldly bad him bace' (III xi 5). The two knights who pursue Samient and are pursued by another knight are said to 'bene at bace, / They being chased, that did others chase' (V viii 5). Mount Acidale serves as a place where nymphs and fairies choose either to dance 'Or else to course about their bases light' (VI x 8). Cuddie's reference to 'bydding base' in *SC, October* 5 may refer not to the literal game but, by a common metaphorical extension involving a pun on *base/bass*, to a poetic or musical competition (Larrabee 1936). Still played by schoolchildren in England, prisoner's base is first recorded as early as the fourteenth century (Opie and Opie 1969:143–6); in France it is known as *la partie de barres* (from which *base* is probably derived by folk etymology) and is mentioned by writers from Froissart to Proust. It has even been recorded in North America. Though there are many local variations, the game always involves two teams, each of which has a 'base' and a 'prison,' normally located at diagonally opposed corners of the playing area. Play is initiated by a player approaching the other team and challenging (the Elizabethan term is 'bidding') one of its members to catch him before he can return to base; once this challenge is responded to, the respondent is himself open to pursuit by a second member of the challenging team, who becomes himself at risk as soon as he takes the field, and so on, alternately, throughout both sides (see Opie and Opie 1969; Strutt 1903:67–9; Gomme 1894–8, 2:79–83).

Among those 'thriftles games' of the modern court gallant in *Mother Hubberd* are mumming and masking, dice, cards, billiards (one of the earliest references to this game in English), and shuttlecock (801–4). All these are included in a list given by Robert Burton of 'the ordinary recreations which we have in Winter' (*Anatomy of Melancholy* 2.2.4). He is less censorious than Spenser, however, regarding only cards and dice as morally suspect. Spenser seems less concerned about the games themselves than their potential for encouraging licentiousness among the players; the masking which is seen as a culpable activity for the Ape is regarded as 'joyance innocent' by Astrophel ('Astrophel' 25) – presumably a phrase which might also be applied to the games played by the shepherds in *FQ* VI x 33. Since the third of Malecasta's knights is called Jocante, it is not surprising that after the banquet some of her guests turn to dicing (*FQ* III i 57). Riddling, mentioned frequently by Spenser, was another pastime open to abuse. Riddles, like verses, might be innocent in themselves ('Clorinda' 43–6); but when Paridell devises 'purposes,' 'riddles,' and 'verses vaine' for Hellenore (III x 8), he is employing a well-tried weapon in the seducer's arsenal.

Paridell and Hellenore also engage in an even more venerable game of flirtation when they read covert messages in wine spilled on the banquet table (III ix 30–1). Spenser seems to have taken this episode from Ovid, who represents Paris writing Helen's name, followed by the word *amo*, in just this manner (*Heroides* 17.87–8), and who describes a faithless mistress in *Amores* entertaining her new lover at a table scribbled over in wine (2.5.17–18). A somewhat strained comparison has been made between this game and the Greek *cottabus* (see Upton in *Var* 3:280), described by Athenaeus (*Deipnosophistai* 15.665–8) as an all-male after-dinner game in which dregs of wine were tossed into a basin. In Spenser, however, the 'game' is shown to be a blasphemy of Holy Communion: 'A sacrament prophane in mistery of wine' (30; see Tuve 1947:221). Spenser's one use of a popular game occurs when Britomart sees the defeated Artegall dressed in woman's clothes; her lament – 'What May-game hath misfortune made of you?' (*FQ* V vii 40) – alludes to the game of disguising a man in May Day celebrations.

RICHARD FIRTH GREEN

Philippe Ariès and Jean-Claude Margolin, eds 1982 *Les Jeux à la renaissance: Actes du XXIIIe colloque international d'études humanistes, Tours, juillet, 1980* (Paris); Christine de Pisan 1932 *Book of Fayttes of Armes and of Chyvalrye* tr William Caxton, ed A.T.P. Byles, EETS os 189 (London); Alice Bertha Gomme 1894–8 *The Traditional Games of England, Scotland, and Ireland* 2 vols (London); Stephen A. Larrabee 1936 'Bydding Base ("October" 5)' *MLN* 51:535–6; Iona Opie and Peter Opie 1969 *Children's Games in Street and Playground* (Oxford); Joseph Strutt 1903 *The Sports and Pastimes of the People of England* rev ed J. Charles Cox (London).

gardens Spenser's gardens have provided almost as much difficulty for his commentators as they do for some of his characters in *The Faerie Queene*. How may one adjudicate the moral implications of their necessary involvement in both nature and art?

Although in interpreting Spenser's gardens it is essential to begin with literary prototypes, it is also useful to relate them to actual gardens. It is not a question (scarcely to be answered) of what garden theory and practice influenced him directly but rather how we may bring to bear upon a reading of his work our considerable knowledge of sixteenth-century garden art. We know, for example, that the most advanced examples of gardens were Italian, and that their Renaissance designs were slowly spreading northwards. They were known through visual and verbal descriptions and also through actual gardens. In late sixteenth-century England, the gardens at Theobalds and Nonsuch Palace, among others, displayed sophisticated Italianate features.

Phaedria's island, the Bower of Bliss, the Garden of Adonis, and the gardens of the Temple of Venus are each convincing representations of an Italian Renaissance garden. Their components are exactly those on which northern visitors to Italy commented with delight: 'arbers' (*FQ* II xii 83) and pergolas; water, both in natural streams and formal fountains, and 'pumy stones' (the pumice decoration of waterworks, II v 30); architectural garden features such as arches, temples, and banqueting houses, often adorned with elaborate iconography for the visitor to read (see the ivory gates to the Bower of Bliss wherein 'all the famous history / Of *Jason* and *Medaea* was ywrit' II xii 44); sculpture, cabinets, and other smaller divisions of the garden space; and larger features such as groves, grottoes and caves, labyrinths, the chiaroscuro of light and shade, and what Sir Henry Wotton later called 'severall *mountings* and *valings*' (*Elements of Architecture* 1624:108–9).

Individual features, such as fountains, arbors, and the 'pleasauns,' may have been found in earlier gardens, but the skillful organization of Spenser's ensemble is distinctly Italianate and fashionably up-to-date. The fountain in the Bower of Bliss has characteristically Italian imagery, similar to that which visitors admired at the Medici villas of Pratolino and Petraia (II xii 60–2). In the behavior of the 'naked Damzelles' (63–8), it is perhaps not too farfetched to see either those animated figures that worked hydraulically in the Pratolino gardens and elsewhere, or the stationary fountain figures in Italian Renaissance gardens and in those at Nonsuch in England which seemed to move (see Waldstein ed 1981:159–63).

Like all gardens, Spenser's are the result of the activities of nature and art. The gardens and groves of the Villa Lante at Bagnaia (1568 onwards) took as their theme the rivalry of nature and art in the Golden Age and after. Yet the ideal Renaissance garden was usually admired as a balanced collaboration of the two, rather than as a war between them. Both ways of relating nature to art can be seen in Spenser's gardens. In the Bower of Bliss, art tries to overgo nature (as would happen in the Mannerist gardens of the late sixteenth and seventeenth centuries). In the Garden of Adonis, nature is dominant, though not in sole control: despite the assertion that 'Ne needs there Gardiner to set, or sow, / To plant or prune,' each kind of plant is arranged 'in a sundry bed / Set by it selfe, and ranckt in comely rew' (III vi 34–5), strongly suggesting the organization of botanic gardens created for scientific study throughout sixteenth-century Europe. This imitation of botanic gardens is clearly appropriate for 'the first seminarie / Of all things' (30). The Garden of Adonis, unlike the Bower of Bliss, is essentially an ideological garden: a version of Golden Age gardening, of a prelapsarian nature (except for the presence of time and the boar, although they too are of the natural world). Only in the gardens of the Temple of Venus do nature and art collaborate as they should in the post-Edenic world, 'Art playing second natures part' (IV x 21); but even here the harmony is precarious, as it must be in all gardens after the Fall.

By the second half of the sixteenth century, many gardens had at least rudimentary iconographical programs. Some, like the villa at Castello, simply announced the virtues, power, and attributes of their owners, thus alerting the visitor to the particular *genius loci* (on Spenser's two garden Geniuses, see *Genius). Others, such as those of the Villa d'Este at Tivoli (1550–72), presented in elaborate form a choice of Hercules: visitors following one set of clues and paths reached a grotto of voluptuous pleasure; those pursuing alternative paths arrived at that of virtuous pleasure and chastity. Their parallel to the gardens of *The Faerie Queene* is clear, though there was no obvious formal difference between the two parts of the gardens at Tivoli. As for Spenser's characters, some of whom do 'not well avis'd it vew' (II xii 61), the onus was on the right reading of the signs. Such ambiguity belongs to the very nature of a garden, real or literary, as shown in Spenser's Bower of Bliss, contemporary garden practice, and in the literary gardens found in Ariosto's *Orlando furioso* and Tasso's *Gerusalemme liberata*. Yet the elaboration of ambiguity in the Bower of Bliss and the imperative of correct moral choice, which have much puzzled critics disturbed at the destruction of such an apparently beautiful garden, are perhaps Spenser's own contributions to contemporary gardening. Ambiguity in the Villa d'Este is educative but harmless if ignored or misunderstood, whereas in Spenser's world of quest and pilgrimage any mistake is crucial.

By the end of the sixteenth century, Italian garden art contained some beautiful, straightforward designs, notably in the northern and Florentine territories, as well as more elaborate, Mannerist examples, such as the Villa d'Este and several in Rome itself. The wickedness of some Spenserian gardens with their deceptive beauty is suggestive of the latter. Phaedria's island is inhabited by tuneful songbirds, but the harmony of their song is described in a rhetorical progression that seduces the unwary: 'No bird, but did her shrill notes sweetly sing; / No song but did containe a lovely dit: / Trees, braunches, birds, and songs were framed fit, / For to allure fraile mind to carelesse ease. / Carelesse the man soone woxe' (II vi 13). Some Roman gardens contained similarly deceptive birds, such as the owls at Tivoli, which were hydraulically operated automata, enticing both visitors and real birds with their song. Phaedria's island garden is but a prelude to the more radical seductions of the Bower of Bliss, in which Spenser notes more decisively the attractiveness of apparent harmony and the discrepancy between the deceiving fancy and moral truth. The destruction of the Bower, and the reader's forced acquiescence in it, may refer to and rebuke the more lavish, indulgent, and fantastic illusions of Mannerist and papal garden art.

Other aspects of Spenser's gardens are illuminated by contemporary practice. Simple iconographical schemes were often maintained even throughout a whole demesne so that garden and grove would participate in a shared meaning, as at the Villa Lante and Nonsuch in England. (Compare Phaedria's garden with its stream and grove, *FQ* II v 29–31.) Italian and Italianate gardens were particularly esteemed for their spatial excitements, which were discoverable only by moving through them. Spenser's gardens distinguish themselves as Renaissance and Italianate partly by requiring characters to explore them and by exploring to learn their nature. Although it may seem that Spenser describes Acrasia's bower only at the moment of its destruction, through his listing its 'groves,' 'arbers,' 'Cabinets,' 'banket houses,' and other features (II xii 83), we have, like Guyon and the Palmer, been slowly discovering its variety and meaning through several dozen stanzas.

Spenser directly and indirectly acknowledges his literary and mythic debts for gardens: the historical garden of Eden in Genesis and the metaphorical garden of the Song of Solomon; a variety of groves and gardens from classical sources, particularly Ovid's *Metamorphoses*; the medieval love-gardens of such works as the *Romance of the Rose* and *Hypnerotomachia Poliphili*; and the allegorical gardens of Italian Renaissance epic, notably *Orlando furioso* and *Gerusalemme liberata*. Spenser deliberately signals his indebtedness to these precursors (eg, *FQ* II xii 52), and recognition of them is essential to our full enjoyment of his poem. Thus Acrasia's enrapturement of Verdant owes much to Tasso's narrative of Armida and Rinaldo. Yet we are likely to read the description of the Bower of Bliss more attentively and profitably if we are also aware of actual Renaissance gardens that drew their own inspiration from literature (eg, the use of the *Orlando furioso* in the garden at Bomarzo), or that provided imagery for painters. Jan Soens' *Rinaldo and Armida in the Enchanted Garden* exactly captures both the delights of a Renaissance garden and the different perspectives of a Guyon aware of its intemperance or Acrasia's victims.

(See **gardens** Fig 1.)

JOHN DIXON HUNT AND MICHAEL LESLIE

Strong 1979 is a full and well-illustrated history of the development of English gardening during the sixteenth and seventeenth centuries. John Dixon Hunt 1986 *Garden and Grove: The Italian Renaissance Garden in the English Imagination: 1600–1750* (Princeton) discusses late-16th-c English interest in Italian garden art. David R. Coffin 1960 *The Villa d'Este at Tivoli* (Princeton) is a major study of a celebrated Renaissance garden. For the garden as a literary ideal, see Comito 1978 and Giamatti 1966, both of which contain extensive additional bibliographical information. Zdenek Brtnicky,

Baron Waldstein 1981 *The Diary of Baron Waldstein: A Traveller in Elizabethan England* tr and ed G.W. Groos (London) describes Renaissance English gardens.

garlands A complex and recurring image in Spenser's poetry. Osgood's *Concordance* lists over 80 occurrences (including *ivy-garland, laurel-garland*, and *olive-garland*), with *chaplet, coronet, crown*, and *wreath* as synonyms.

Garlands are mentioned throughout classical literature (though not as early as Homer), and their varied uses are amply illustrated in vase-paintings, sculpture, and engravings. The vernacular *garland* renders the Latin *corona*, the wreath of metal, leaves, or flowers worn on festive occasions and given as a reward for distinction in war, government, and the arts. In classical and vernacular pastoral, garlands and garland making are stock images for innocent golden-age pursuits. The flower garland is commonly a love token (suggested by the garland Pastorella gives to Calidore, *FQ* VI ix 42). Garland making is a metaphor for the poet's craft: in *SC, June* 45, the 'gaudy Girlonds' Colin gave to Rosalind signify the love poetry he wrote for her; hence in *December* 109–14, he laments the withering of flowers in his garden which should have made a garland for her. In the woodcut to *October*, Cuddie is shown crowned with laurel; in *November*, Thenot crowns Colin with the poet's bays. *Prothalamion* makes elaborate play with the motifs of spousal garlands and garland making (Fowler 1975:61–77), and *Epithalamion* arguably shows a similar 'resonance between structure and imagery' with the poem itself figuring as bridal crown (Fowler 1970b:169–70). (See ***Shepheardes Calender***, Fig 2: *November*.)

Garlands of foliage probably had their origin in religious rites, especially sacrificial rites (*FQ* III iv 17, VI viii 39), certain trees being sacred to specific divinities, as the ivy to Bacchus, the oak to Jupiter, the myrtle to Venus, and the olive to Minerva. Spenser exploits these classical associations to enrich his allegory in *The Faerie Queene*. In the Red Cross Knight's dream, 'freshest *Flora*' seems to crown Una with an 'Yvie girlond' (I i 48), the appropriate adornment for a Bacchante (see E.K.'s gloss on 'wild Yvie' in *Oct* 111) and for Gluttony in the house of Pride (I iv 22), while the naive but discerning satyrs crown Una with a garland of olive, Minerva's plant (vi 13), and listen to her 'wise beheast.' Insofar as the garland is made of materials which have a traditional emblematic significance (eg, gold, lilies, roses), it reveals the nature of its wearer. Alma's virginal state is indicated by her being 'crowned with a garland of sweete Rosiere' (II ix 19).

As might be expected, Spenser's garlands do not merely follow classical precedent: garlands were (and still are) widely used in popular seasonal festivities. In England, the practice of Maying survived until after the Restoration; Spenser describes the custom in *Maye* 11–14: 'And home they hasten the postes to dight, / And all the Kirke pillours eare day light, / With Hawthorne buds, and swete Eglantine, / And girlonds of roses and Sopps in wine.' Elizabeth herself kept Mayings, and there was a vogue in contemporary literature which celebrated her as the Spring Queen (see Sidney's *Lady of May* and Spenser's *Aprill*; the vogue is discussed in H. Cooper 1977:193–213). In *Colin Clout* 641–3, Spenser evokes a rustic dance with garlands and singing to commemorate Cynthia's 'bountie.' Other associations of garlands, song, and round dance occur in *Daphnaïda* 309–15 and *FQ* VI ix 7–8 (the revels surrounding Pastorella). The imagery provides a perfect formal and expressive resource in Calidore's vision of the Graces (x 12–14) where the dance, with its 'girlond' of dancers and central Damzell crowned with a 'rosie girlond,' is compared to a heavenly nuptial crown, Ariadne's Crown. Through the garland images, Spenser links the dance of the Graces to the starry dance, the revolution of the spheres.

Spenser several times stresses the appropriateness of the garland as an ornament for a 'mayden' or 'virgin' queen (*FQ* I xii 8, *Teares* 309, *Epithalamion* 157–8); in *Colin Clout* 337–43, it becomes an emblem for the Virgin Queen herself. The passage draws upon Elizabeth's personal iconography to create a rich triple garland image: Cynthia is likened to a bride's nuptial crown of lilies, to the iridescent 'circlet' of the colors around the neck of the turtledove, and lastly to the 'garlond' of radiance around the moon. As these garlands become increasingly ethereal, Spenser ascends Platonically to the idea of 'pure perfection' evoked by the garland's circular shape. Here the garland becomes the central emblem in his most impassioned (and most impersonal) praise of Elizabeth as Empress. (See also 'Couronne' in de Tervarent 1958).

DEBORAH JOHNSON

Gascoigne, George (1534?-1577) Remembered by E.K. as 'the very chefe of our late rymers' (*SC, Nov* 141 gloss), Gascoigne dedicated *The Complaynt of Phylomene* (1576) – mentioned by E.K. – and other poems to Lord Grey of Wilton, whom Spenser later served as secretary. His earlier poetry (collected in *A Hundreth Sundrie Flowres* 1573) reflects a tempestuous life in quest of patronage; his later work becomes more pious. He was something of an innovator, and explained his aesthetic of versifying in *Certayne Notes of Instruction* (1575). Though inspired by Italian poets (mainly Ariosto and Petrarch), he favored a metrical regularity which encouraged a monosyllabic English style; his archaisms anticipate Spenser's (Johnson 1972:75).

Sylvanus' tale in Gascoigne's *Princely Pleasures at Kenelworth Castle* (pub 1576) is a possible source for Spenser's Oak and Briar in *Februarie* 102–238 (Friedland 1954, Prouty 1942:222n). The Ariostan figure of Suspition in his *Adventures of Master F.J.* (ed 1907–10, 1:421–4) is a likely source for Malbecco (Nelson 1953, but see McNeir 1959).

Gascoigne's composition shows a symmetrical design in *Master F.J.* and in some of his devotional poems (Anderau 1966:76–82; Eriksen 1984, 1985). In this he may be following his favorite author, Ariosto; similar patterning has been found in Spenser as well (see *topomorphical approach).

ROY TOMMY ERIKSEN

George Gascoigne ed 1907–10; Gascoigne 1982 *George Gascoigne, the Green Knight: Selected Poetry and Prose* ed Roger Pooley (Manchester). Alfred Anderau 1966 *George Gascoigne 'The Adventures of Master F.J.': Analyse und Interpretation* Schweizer Anglistische Arbeiten 57 (Bern); Roy T. Eriksen 1984 'Two Into One: The Unity of George Gascoigne's Companion Poems' *SP* 81:275–98; Eriksen 1985 'Typological Form in "Gascoignes De Profundis"' *ES* 66:300–9; Louis S. Friedland 1954 'A Source of Spenser's "The Oak and the Briar"' *PQ* 33:222–4; Ronald C. Johnson 1972 *George Gascoigne* (New York); Waldo F. McNeir 1959 'Ariosto's Sospetto, Gascoigne's Suspicion, and Spenser's Malbecco' in *Festschrift für Walther Fischer* (Heidelberg) pp 34–48; Nelson 1953; C.T. Prouty 1942 *George Gascoigne: Elizabethan Courtier, Soldier, and Poet* (New York); Nancy Williams 1986 'The Eight Parts of a Theme in "Gascoigne's Memories: III"' *SP* 83:117–37; Susanne Woods 1978 'Aesthetic and Mimetic Rhythms in the Versification of Gascoigne, Sidney, and Spenser' *SLitI* 11.1:31–44.

gender Spenser inherited traditional Western conceptions of gender whereby men are associated with power and the public realm, and women with love and the private realm. This division of sex-roles arises from certain beliefs: that women are biologically bound to nature and men are not; that men are therefore able to control nature and women; that men who do not exercise control are unmanly. Like other poets of his age, Spenser attempted to envision a moral structure that could integrate the two realms without undermining the sexual-political structure of society, to create a morality that could heal the split between private virtue and public power.

Spenser's intention was 'to fashion a gentleman or noble person in vertuous and gentle discipline' (Letter to Raleigh). His intention can be read as a wish to teach those with power, who had standing in the public realm, to understand, value, and defend love and other beneficent 'feminine' qualities. Because the morality of his period was divided by ideas about gender, gender – that is, sex roles – and the sexual-political relations of Elizabethan society lay at the very heart of his argument. To separate power and virtue is to decree virtue powerless and to license power to ignore virtue with impunity. Almost inevitably, those with power seek greater power, and no mere poet has the power to dissuade them. Spenser's approach is oblique, aimed at teaching readers to see the beauty of 'feminine' ends and the nobility of placing 'masculine' power at their service.

The characters of *The Faerie Queene* may be divided into two kinds: types and humans. The distinguishing mark of humans is a capacity for error. The very notion of error assumes the possibility of correction, of change. Types cannot err or change their nature: they represent absolute moral states; their meaning is fixed, whether it be holy or wicked. Their behavior is an acting out of an unalterable identity: they exist in a realm lacking freedom. Since types cannot err, they cannot learn. Yet allegory is about learning.

Spenser's types are conventional, that is, stereotypes. Figures who represent emotional states are often female; those who represent intellectual qualities are invariably male. Female types who express rage are likely to be merely verbal, impotent to act; those who act are likely to do so under direction of a male or out of lust – yet Lust incarnate is male. Spenser's types are vivid and comic, and provide much of the fun of the poem; but they do not challenge our moral preconceptions.

Human figures may also bear allegorical significance; like types, they may embody a particular state or quality. Yet simultaneously they undergo experience; they suffer and can change. They are neither absolutely good nor absolutely evil, but morally uncertain: they exist in ignorance and freedom. But because they can learn, we can learn with and from them.

If we distinguish in this way between types and humans in the poem, we become aware that Spenser's 'human' females exist in a realm somewhere between the two. They undergo experience, they suffer. Hypothetically, they exist in moral incertitude and freedom and are capable of change – but they *may not err*. It is virginity that provides the ground of the moral interest of the significant human females in the poem. Yet it is implicitly understood that they may not lose their virginity and remain within the ranks of the 'human.' Indifference to chastity is the mark of evil women; and in this poem, such women are types. Malecasta and Hellenore may begin with a human (morally unclear) appearance, but they end locked into viciousness. Because virtuous female humans have significance largely because of their virginity, and because they must retain that virginity, we cannot learn from them. Their function is not to teach but to gain our sympathy.

The qualities that draw our sympathy are their beauty and powerlessness, which are connected. Beauty is a great force in the poem, but it is not a force at the disposal of its possessors. Beauty can spur men to action or draw them like a magnet, but it cannot be used as an agent of a woman's will without becoming an instrument for evil. Only evil women, like Malecasta or Duessa, consciously use their beauty to attract or seduce. To use one's beauty, a 'feminine' quality, to fulfill one's will is to exercise power, and to pervert the proper moral arrangement of beauty and power.

Women may fix their hearts on particular men – Florimell may seek the wounded Marinell, Britomart may charge through Fairyland dressed as a knight in search of Artegall – but they cannot *win* men by active behavior. They must wait for men to reach toward them: until Marinell is softened by awareness of Florimell's fidelity, suffering, and love; until Artegall sees Britomart's face and adores it. Women cannot assert their feelings; they must abide in constancy until men are able to perceive the virtue inherent in their beauty. Thus, women's only worldly power, beauty, is not subject to women's volition: whether it evokes disaster or felicity depends upon the man it attracts. It is a power for which women are responsible but over which they have no control. It is a power that symbolizes their powerlessness.

Female 'humans,' then, exist in an intermediate realm. They are human, with a capacity to fail, to err, to change; but they may not do so and retain their human status. They are not, like types, conceived as absolutes: they are morally required, as women, to be absolute.

The male humans of the poem err in ways that stimulate our curiosity. What sort of pride causes Redcrosse to fall victim to Orgoglio? Why does Guyon become helpless after escaping from Mammon? Britomart, the major human female in the poem, has been the subject of similar scrutiny; but such scrutiny is singularly unfruitful. For although she is a human figure and can learn from experience, she is also female and cannot seriously err. She cannot fail, as the male heroes do, in the very virtue she incarnates. For her to fail in chastity, even for a moment, even in her imagination, would be to fall into obloquy. Thus Britomart is more type than human; we are intended less to judge her behavior than to judge males by their response to her.

There are female figures in the poem who are permitted power-in-the-world; but each of these has, implicitly or explicitly, received special dispensation from a divine power, has been lifted from woman's condition to 'lawfull soveraintie' (V v 25) by the heavens. Women who rule without such dispensation may claim it (like Lucifera) or challenge or deny the necessity for it (like Mutabilitie or Radigund), but such females are clearly evil. All virtuous women of power in the poem are divinely appointed virgins because, for Spenser, the full worldly power of women precludes marriage. Therefore, Belphoebe is a virgin demi-goddess; and the throne of the virgin queen Mercilla is upheld by Jove himself. Britomart is also marked by the hand of God, resembling 'the maker selfe' (IV vi 17) in her features. She is the 'heavenly image of perfection' (24), and both Merlin's predictions and her dream in Isis Church suggest why she has been so marked. Even powerless heroines possess an aura of divinity: Amoret is, like her twin, semidivine; and Florimell's extraordinary beauty seems celestial. Indeed, the witch's son worships her as divine, and she owns a magic girdle.

Spenser predicates another, spurious, kind of beauty in the false Florimell and Duessa. The difference between true and false beauty lies in the character's regard for chastity. Beauty linked with chastity signifies the moral stance Spenser conceives as appropriate to women. By refusing to use her beauty as a power, a woman demonstrates that she volitionally abjures power-seeking. By maintaining her chastity even though she may feel desire or fear, a woman demonstrates that she understands the nature of love.

Properly defined, love is mutual attraction and companionship. Desire expressed coercively, either as rape or ownership by a male, or as seduction by a female, is lust; but even mutual desire fails to create love if the parties involved are unequal. Since the sexes *are* unequal politically, a bond of mutuality can be created between them only if they both feel the kind of love that causes them to defer to each other. This mutual deference annuls the difference in their worldly status, and supersedes it by moral and emotional equality, friendship.

Women who fail to insist upon this ideal love lack faith in the ideal or in themselves. From fear or lack of self-respect, Duessa, in various guises, panics and surrenders herself to men with power. Women like Duessa are willing to trade faked love for male protection or some worldly good, or to fulfill desire without demanding friendship. The failure of such women is more than personal: by refusing to maintain their own integrity, they fail society at large, and the cosmic purpose for their existence, which is to teach men respect – indeed adoration – of 'feminine' qualities, to teach them the true value of love.

As the Knight of Chastity, Britomart alone of the 'human' figures fully understands the nature of love. Because she possesses 'masculine' power, she can defend herself and others against the many threats to chastity in Fairyland, threats symbolizing worldly pressures that tend to make women give up hope for an integrated life. She is an instrument of divine purpose. Although in speaking to the male knights she claims to desire fame and glory as they do, she knows her destiny is to attain glory in a 'feminine' way, to bring forth a 'Lion' (V vii 16), first of a line of heroes. Britomart uses power in order to reach love: her quest is not fame, but Artegall. She incorporates both gender principles in proper alignment: she uses power as a means to the proper ends of life – love, bonding, and fruitfulness. She is never tempted to use her power to coerce love, and never conflates love with power; thus she is able to destroy Busirane's house, a monument to love compelled, love as mastery.

FQ III and IV examine the cruelties that result from conflating love and power, that is, the consequences of perverting the proper relation between those values. For Spenser, the two are and must remain distinct; and power must be used only as a means to uphold love and 'feminine' values. Britomart's unvanquishable spear is a symbol of her clarity about this moral truth. In Book III, the spell cast by a notion of love as dominance is unwoven by a variety of plots; in Book IV, that notion is superseded by a redefinition of love as friendship, mutuality.

Book V, however, contains the core of Spenser's thinking about gender. The Legend of Justice is set specifically in the world of time, the real world. Men have become stone, they no longer recognize virtue and vice, and justice must be maintained by force. The central events of the book are Artegall's surrender to Radigund, Dolon's attack on Britomart, Britomart's vision in Isis Church, and her rescue of Artegall. Artegall's submission to the Amazon is his only real error: Radigund is a perverted (not divinely appointed) woman of power, who uses power to gain power and uses power against Artegall to compel love. Spenser depicts Artegall's error as injustice against himself and other males, rather than as Adam-like disobedience to a divine decree. He takes the further unusual step of having a woman rescue him.

Male supremacy is central to earthly justice. Spenser emphasizes this within the structure of *The Faerie Queene* by his placement of the stanza affirming that Nature itself decreed women's subordination to men except when divine decree intervenes: it appears at V v 25, and 5 is the number of justice (Fowler 1964:34).

Artegall's failure and Britomart's restoration of 'true justice' – male supremacy – frame a central vision which appears to contradict this version of sexual politics. In Britomart's dream in Isis Church, the crocodile which lies at the feet of the idol of Isis swallows a fire that threatens her, but then offers to swallow her as well. Isis, associated with clemency, restrains him with authority; he humbles himself and curls around her in a sexual embrace that will result in the birth of a significant progeny, a lion. In this vision, the *male* represents sex, emotion, unreason, and acceptance of subordination, as well as power and aggressiveness; and the *female* represents order, control, restraint, as well as mercy. She also possesses a power higher than his.

From these scenes, we can deduce Spenser's attitudes toward gender in their complexity. On this earth as it is, power is the supreme value. It is *necessary*, like nature itself, a fact of life. Because males are identified with power, male supremacy is necessary, though Spenser emphasizes that it is not rooted in actual male superiority. Britomart reestablishes male supremacy after she has been taken for Artegall and attacked in an underhanded way, and after she has thoroughly defeated Artegall's enemies. The political structure she restores is not the inevitable result of an inadequacy, powerlessness imposed on women by nature. Indeed, elsewhere Spenser affirms that in 'antique times' many women bore 'the girlond' for deeds of arms. Men's envy and fear of 'their rules decay' led them to exclude women from these activities and to excise women's deeds from history. But women still excel in 'artes and pollicy' (III ii 2).

The 'shamefast band' (V v 25) placed on women by nature signifies their special role, their identification with divine 'feminine' qualities. 'Feminine' qualities create 'feminine,' Astraean, worlds. But in this iron age a 'feminine' world cannot uphold itself: it may easily be eradicated by hostile 'masculine' onslaughts, as is the shepherds' world of Book VI; it may also decay into a Bower of Bliss. A 'feminine' world must be protected by 'masculine' power. Men of power must be in control.

But in the divine realm – from an overarching perspective on human affairs – 'feminine' values dominate. Indeed, throughout *The Faerie Queene*, love is the greatest force on earth. It is a cosmic principle of harmony, but it is also a humanizing principle. Falling in love teaches people they are not self-sufficient, not in full control of anything, not even themselves. It is love that leads men and women to embrace their subordination to, which is actually participation in, cosmic order. Women are the earthly guardians of this order; it is women who have been appointed the moral guides of the human race. This is why women must be absolute, and why virtuous women are happy to give up power-in-the-world in favor of a sacred role. Only women can uphold chaste love, the true meaning of which is an unwavering insistence on full mutuality of desire and companionship; only they can redeem the human race by teaching and preserving love and those values associated with it. On women depends the moral well-being of the entire human race.

What makes Spenser's treatment of gender remarkable is not really Britomart – the androgyne who can retain her masculine power so long as she remains virgin, unmarried, and, by Spenser's standards, unfulfilled – but rather his conception of this 'feminine' role. For Spenser, the highest end of human endeavor is not the limited goal of people of power – personal fame and glory – but the vision given to Colin Clout on Mount Acidale: a vision of grace, harmony, and generosity entertained with full knowledge of men's lack of control. Colin's piping may draw the dancers, but he cannot summon or dismiss them. He cannot command this most ecstatic of experiences; like women and their beauty, he can present himself and his gift – his piping – and then simply, passively, await response. Understanding of divine purpose comes not to those who exercise control, but to those who yield it, and themselves, to that purpose.

This understanding was crucially important to Spenser; in *The Shepheardes Calender*, he records the process by which Colin arrives at it. A hero to Hobbinol, lauded by the shepherds for his excellent piping, Colin is an important figure in his world. But he falls in love with a woman who does not love him, and his consequent sorrow and frustration force him to confront mortality and recognize the fact that he does not control his world, other people – like Rosalind – or even his own life. Love teaches all who are capable of feeling it (those who cannot are doomed) that they are 'women' in the face of the cosmic forces governing human life.

Women in patriarchal societies are born to subordination; they know that they are subject to men and that, to be virtuous, they must preserve their virginity for the 'right' man despite intimidating assaults upon it: the entirety of the freedom they are granted lies in that single choice. In exchange for loss of the freedom to err, however, they are granted participation in what Spenser conceives as divine purpose. Love teaches men the limits of their power, teaches them that they, too, are subordinate and vulnerable in a situation in which worldly power is irrelevant. Spenser does not find this dimension of the female role constricting, nor does he consider men's discovery of human limitation a demeaning or emasculating lesson. Rather, it is liberating.

The poet Spenser is also excluded from power by his nature and position in society rather than by his sex. An outsider, lacking the illusion of control, he can perceive the delusions and limits of power but cannot express his awareness openly in his society. He uses indirection to suggest that surrender of control allows one to perceive life more broadly, to experience the radiant harmony of divine purpose, and to attain the celestial perspective from which one sees the contentions of the world fused by love and grace into an eternal vibrant concord.

MARILYN FRENCH

Genius The word *genius* (from L *gignere* 'to give birth') suggests ideas of generation and protective nurture; a Genius is either the guardian of a place or person, a daemon (see *demons), as he was conceived by the ancients; or a universal deity of procreation, Nature's Priest, as he was most often styled in the Middle Ages. Spenser's sources for his ideas of Genius may include Alanus' *De planctu Naturae*, the *Romance of the Rose*, Gower's *Confessio Amantis*, Boccaccio's *Genealogia*, Conti's *Mythologiae*, and Lydgate's *Reason and Sensuality*.

Spenser twice casts Genius in his classical role, as 'th'auncient *Genius* of that Citie' (*Time* 19) and as 'the *Romaine Daemon*' (*Rome* 27.12), but he is more inclined toward the medieval conception. Thus, although Genius in *Epithalamion* retains his ancient office as spirit of the 'geniall bed' (399), his duties also embrace the general care of 'fruitfull progeny' (403). And in the Garden of Adonis, he is wholly universalized. Like the Genius of the *Tabula of Cebes*, especially as depicted in Holbein's title-page illustration (see Roche 1964: frontispiece, 121), the Garden's porter has 'a double nature': he first clothes all souls with mortal flesh in order to send them 'into the chaungefull world,' and then readmits them to the Garden (*FQ* III vi 31–3).

Spenser's treatment of Genius is problematic. In the Bower of Bliss, the evil porter whom 'They in that place ... *Genius* did call' (II xii 47) is distinguished from the good Genius, Agdistes. The former is 'The foe of life, that good envyes to all, / That secretly doth us procure to fall' (48) – a tempting demon or bad angel. The latter seems to combine both medieval and classical attributes. He is a 'celestiall powre, to whom the care / Of life, and generation of all / That lives, pertaines' (the medieval Genius), and also 'our Selfe, whom ... each doth in him selfe it well perceive to bee' (the classical Genius). Although attempts have been made to read the passage in such a way as to keep the distinction between the two (Lewis 1936:361–3, 1966:169–74, 1967:57–9), their conflation was commonplace in the Renaissance, as Vives' commentary on *The City of God* suggests: 'The sonne of the gods and the father of men, begetting them: and so it is called my *Genius*. For it begot me' (quoted in *Var* 2:375). It seems likely, then, that 'Pleasures porter' should be taken as not merely the evil genius of a particular place, or a figure of an individual's bad angel, but as the Genius of evil generally, opposed to the good Genius in both traditions. Conversely, Spenser conceives the individual genius of each human life, not as one of a distinct class of beings, but as an instance or manifestation of the principle of life at work in the universe at large. JOHN C. ULREICH, JR

Kahin 1941; E[dgar] C. Knowlton 1920 'The Allegorical Figure Genius' *ClassP* 15:380–4; Knowlton 1924 'Genius as an Allegorical Figure' *MLN* 39:89–95; Knowlton 1928 'The Genii of Spenser' *SP* 25:439–56; DeWitt T. Starnes 1964 'The Figure Genius in the Renaissance' *SRen* 11:234–44.

genres The organization of literary works into genres tends to dominate both classical and Renaissance critical theory. Even the Muses originate in and reflect generic categories (see their complaints in *Teares* about the poor state of the arts). The Renaissance inherited various lists and groupings from Greek and Latin sources. Some genres were named for their verse form, but each was normally expected to express a certain kind of content (eg, the elegiac or iambic) – though there were exceptions. Others were named for their subject matter, setting, content, or attitude; but each was usually written in one verse form (eg, satire, pastoral, and heroic poem, all in hexameters) – also with exceptions. These two traditional kinds of identification – by form and by matter – resulted in overlappings and inconsistencies in the classical lists and in classical poetic practice, which generally remain and recur in the Renaissance.

Quintilian, for example, treats as separate genres the epic, pastoral, elegy, satire, iambic, lyric, comedy, and tragedy (*Institutio oratoria* 10.1.27–72). Giovanni Viperano, a skillful Renaissance theorist who is thoroughly generic in orientation, drops the elegiac and iambic but adds the dithyrambic to his essential list of genres (*De poetica libri tres* 1579). Du Bellay, the most important vernacular theorist of the French Renaissance, lists epigrams, elegies, odes, letters, satires, sonnets, eclogues, hendecasyllabics, comedies, tragedies, and heroic poems (*Deffense* 1549, 2.4). In antiquity and the Renaissance, however, there are mixed genres like pastoral satires (eg, *Colin Clout*, and probably *Virgils Gnat* for which the bitter dedicatory sonnet implies a satiric intention) and satiric pastorals (eg, the 'moral' eclogues of *SC*). Elegy and pastoral similarly overlap (as in *Daphnaïda*, 'Astrophel,' and *SC, Nov*). The pastoral especially could include a wide range of poetic subjects, attitudes, and (in vernacular poetry like *SC*) verse forms.

While usually restricted in verse form, the sonnet, a vernacular species of the lyric, came to be similarly capable of expressing a wide variety of subjects. Spenser began his career translating sonnets. Including the translations and paraphrases, they embrace many different attitudes and subjects (*Theatre, Rome, Vanitie, Bellay, Petrarch, Amoretti*, and the *FQ* dedicatory sonnets). The first six sonnets appearing with woodcuts in *Theatre* are even identified as epigrams, while the eleven immediately following are entitled 'Sonets.'

The *Shepheardes Calender*'s eclogues are also illustrated with woodcuts; along with the six sonnets in *Theatre*, they reflect the influence of the emblem, a new Renaissance genre which in its fullest form includes three parts: a picture, an appropriate epigrammatic motto, and a text (as exposition, explanation, or story). Each eclogue in *The Shepheardes Calender* has, in order, a woodcut, a prose plot summary, a poetic text, and an epigrammatic motto (usually one for each character) which is identified as an 'embleme.' The source for several sonnets in *Vanitie* is Alciati's *Emblematum liber* (1531), the first collection of emblems.

The Renaissance was concerned not only with the sharing and blurring of component traits in the genres, but also with the question of which genres were proper vehicles for genuine artistic endeavor. As a point of artistic decorum, there was a marked tendency to reject the vernacular genres of the later Middle Ages in favor of classical Greek and Latin genres which had the authoritative sanction of antiquity, a time assumed by most to have been vastly superior intellectually and artistically to the benighted 'Dark Ages.' The *Fowre Hymnes* and *Epithalamion* reflect this kind of artistic commitment. Their titles explicitly name their classical models: hymn and epithalamium. For *Prothalamion*, Spenser cleverly varies the Greek *-pro-* (before, in front of) rather than *epi-* (at, in the presence of) + *thalamos* (the bridal chamber) – to entitle his celebration of the double betrothals, rather than the marriages, of Elizabeth and Katherine Somerset.

His use of Greek titles in two other works recalls their classical generic origins. *Muiopotmos, or The Fate of the Butterflie* (*muia* fly + *potmos* destiny) is a mock-heroic struggle harking back to the *Batrachomyomachia* (*Battle of the Frogs and Mice*) frequently attributed to Homer in antiquity. *Prosopopoia, or Mother Hubberds Tale* has the same pattern: the Greek title followed by an alternate in English. In rhetoric, *prosōpopoiia* is the making (*poieō*) of a *prosōpon* (a look, countenance, mask, or character); it is usually reserved for personification, the giving of speech and character to things which normally lack them (eg, cities, the dead, or abstractions). The fable of personified animals in *Mother Hubberd* goes back to the Latin poetic fables of Phaedrus; significantly, the function of all beast fables in antiquity and later seems to have been in some measure satiric.

The genre of romance also originated in antiquity with Apollonius Rhodius' love-epic, the *Argonautica* (3rd c BC), and in subsequent prose stories, which especially flourished in the second and third centuries AD. The principal elements of romance are the complicated, often fantastic adventures of young lovers, who finally overcome incredible hindrances to their union. Following Boiardo in the Italian Renaissance, Ariosto's *Orlando furioso* (1516) again elevates romance to epic stature. The simultaneous interest in and influence of Aristotle's *Poetics*, which stresses a unified plot, led to continuing literary controversy in the sixteenth century whether the diffuse, multiple plots of romance were inherently inferior to Homeric and Virgilian unity. Defenders of romance frequently insist that the epic-romance of *Orlando furioso* is a natural development from the heroic genre of antiquity, and that the Aristotelian norm of unity does not apply to romance. Later in the century, Tasso defends love as a proper heroic theme and equates epic and romance. Spenser clearly agrees, since the opening stanza of *The Faerie Queene* claims as subjects of the poem both love and war (I proem 1), and the whole plot, which obviously owes more to Ariosto than to Homer, is carefully structured on twelves, the common factor of the epic (the *Aeneid* and *Thebaid* in 12 books, and the *Iliad* and *Odyssey* in 24).

The opening of Book I also refers to one of the commonplace generic organizations of the typical poetic career (in imitation of the opening lines of Renaissance editions of Virgil's *Aeneid*), which attempts the pastoral before the heroic. Earlier, in *The Shepheardes Calender*, Piers had urged Cuddie to take the same step in his career (*Oct* 37–48), and Cuddie had responded by referring to the complete, three-stage paradigm, based on Virgil's career and related to three basic rhetorical styles of writing: pastoral, low; georgic, middle; and heroic poem or epic, grand or high style (55–60). The Epistle to Harvey also refers to the anonymous author's appropriately beginning his poetic career with the pastoral. Such ideas about sequence in poetic career may even bear on the date of composition of *Muiopotmos*, since the most influential sixteenth-century poetics, Vida's *De arte poetica* (1527), suggests that the mock epic is an appropriate genre for young poets after they have finished with the pastoral (1.459–65).

Among the major genres (and depending to some degree on which list is chosen), Spenser's poetic achievement is impressive, missing only dramatic comedy and tragedy (though he may have written some comedies among his lost works). His prose works include letters, a translation of a dialogue attributed to Plato in the Renaissance (*Axiochus*), a discussion of the Irish problem in dialogue form (*Vewe of Ireland*), and a treatise analyzing and making recommendations about Tyrone's rebellion (*Brief Note*). All these forms have classical precedent. Like most vernacular writers of the Renaissance, Spenser was greatly influenced by classical genres and genre theory, especially as worked out in Renaissance theory and practice. (See also *allegory, *anacreontics, *catalogues, *chronicles, **Complaints*, *courtesy books, *dialogue, medieval *drama, *elegy, *emblems, *epigram, *epithalamium, *fables, *fabliau, *fantasy literature, *georgic, *heroic poem, *hymn, *letter, *Ovidian epic, *pastoral, *proverbs, *romance, *satire, *science fiction, *sestina, mottos in **Shepheardes Calender*, *song, *sonnet, *tragedy, *visions, lost *works.)

PHILIP B. ROLLINSON

Key Renaissance texts are Vida ed 1976, du Bellay ed 1948, and Julius Caesar Scaliger 1561 *Poetices libri septem* (Lyons; rpt Stuttgart-Bad Cannstatt 1964); du Bellay has been translated by Gladys M. Turquet as *The Defence and Illustration of the French Language* (London 1939). The Italian debates over genre are analyzed in Weinberg 1961. Principal English writings on genre are gathered in G.G. Smith 1904, with a useful index to various genres. See also Colie 1973; Heather Dubrow 1982 *Genre* (London); Fowler 1982; Lewalski 1986; Renwick 1925; Hallett Smith 1952.

Geoffrey of Monmouth (c 1100–55) Although they disagreed among themselves about the reliability of his work, nearly all Tudor poets, antiquarians, and historiographers regarded Geoffrey of Monmouth as the basic source of pre-Saxon British history. In his *Historia regum Britanniae* (c 1139), Geoffrey, a secular Augustinian canon at Oxford, had provided the first coherent account of what has traditionally been called the Matter of Britain. His book fixes the career of King Arthur in an historical perspective informed by earlier writers such as Gildas, Bede, Nennius, Henry of Huntingdon, and William of Malmesbury, but elaborated by his own imaginative grasp of Celtic myth and by a genuinely sophisticated patterning of the rise and fall of dynasties and the relating of historical currents to the moral and political functioning of individual personalities.

The *Historia* is organized chronologically, and is traditionally divided into twelve books, although current opinion doubts that the division is Geoffrey's own. Matters relating to Arthur occupy five books, of which Book 7 contains the prophecies of Merlin, an earlier account by Geoffrey interpolated into the *Historia* to the great interest of later writers – including Spenser, who has it in mind in *FQ* III iii where Merlin allows Britomart a vision of her own and the nation's future.

For sixteenth-century English readers, however, the most interesting parts of the *Historia* were its beginning with the legendary Trojan origins of Britain and its end in the death of Arthur and the prophecies granted to Cadwallader about the continuance of his line. These stories and especially the genealogies in Geoffrey's work had taken on a highly political significance. They were closely tied up with political claims of the Tudor monarchs, whose propagandists pointed to Henry VII's Welsh ancestry as evidence of the alleged Tudor continuance of true Authurian stock and thus as fulfillment of the prophecy Geoffrey relates (see Greenlaw 1932).

This interpretation of Geoffrey's material was ridiculed by Polydore Vergil and defended with equal zeal by Leland and others. A canceled passage in *Vewe of Ireland* indicates that Spenser was himself a skeptic (see *Var Prose* p 86); but his political application of the history is more than evident in the chronicle of *FQ* III iii, where Arthurian and Tudor genealogies are specifically linked to anticipate the eventual union of Arthur and Gloriana (Greenlaw 1932). In Spenser's pre-Arthurian chronicle in *FQ* II x, Geoffrey's history is ultimately the main source for both content and sequence (Harper 1910); and it may have contributed to Spenser's development of the motif of dynastic rise and fall. (See also legend of *Arthur, *Arthur in Middle English romances, *chronicles, *Troy.)

JERRY LEATH MILLS

Spenser could have read the *Historia regum Britanniae* in the Paris editions of 1508 or 1517, or in *Rerum Britannicarum scriptores* (Heidelberg 1587). Harper 1910 speculates that spellings of proper names may indicate use of one of several extant versions in manuscript and print. A standard modern edition is that tr Richard Ellis Jones and ed Acton Grissom (London 1929); there are many translations, eg, *History of the Kings of England* tr Sebastian Evans, rev Charles W. Dunn (New York 1958). Geoffrey's relationship to his sources and to Tudor historiography is discussed in Tatlock 1950; see also Hanning 1966.

George, St The patron saint of England and, as the Red Cross Knight, the protagonist-hero of *FQ* I. (See ed 1912:68.)

The origins of the St George legends are obscure. Originally an Eastern saint, he was by the sixth century accepted into the roster of saints of the Church of Rome. His popularity and association with chivalric prowess grew during the Middle Ages, especially during the time of the Crusades. The popular *Legenda aurea* of Jacopus de Voragine, an early medieval lectionary of saints' lives, established from a wide variety of earlier sources a basic structure and interpretation for the legend that persisted into the Renaissance, chiefly through Caxton's redaction in *The Golden Legend* (c 1483). According to Voragine, 'George is sayd of *geos* / whiche is as moche to saye as erthe and *orge* / that is tilyenge / so george is to saye as tilyenge the erthe / that is his flesshe ... Or George may be sayd of *gera*: that is holy / and of *gyon* that is a wrasteler / that is an holy wrasteler. For he wrasteled with the dragon. or it is sayd of george that is a pylgrym / and *geyr* that is cut or detrenched out and *us* that is a counseyllour. He was a pylgryme in the syght of the worlde / and he was cut and detrenched by the crowne of martyrdome / and he was a good counseyllour in prechynge' (in Barclay ed 1955:112; italics added). George's name is derived principally from Greek *gē* (earth) and *ergon* (labor), which together signify the humility of this warrior before God. A nobleman of Cappadocia (here Voragine identifies him with the 4th-c Arian bishop George of Cappadocia), he is said to have been a tribune in the Roman army during the late Roman Empire. His two greatest exploits are to have rescued a town from a dragon and to have resisted the cruel persecutions of Dacian, the virulently anti-Christian prefect of Rome.

Although the latter account may have the firmer historical basis, the former (with its echoes of the myth of Perseus) is the one that passed into popular legend. In Voragine, a dragon threatened the citizens of Silene in Libya; to appease the creature, they fed it two sheep every day. Soon, however, the supply of sheep began to dwindle, and they were forced to sacrifice a youth along with a single sheep, the youth being chosen by lottery. The king's daughter was finally chosen. (Caxton adds that she was accompanied by a sheep; cf Una's lamb.) When George passes by and sees her predicament, he wounds the dragon (which is spitting out fire, according to Caxton) and tells the maiden to subdue it by throwing her girdle over its neck (cf Florimell's girdle, which Satyrane uses to subdue the witch's hyena, III vii 36). She leads the dragon to the city, and the 15,000 inhabitants are so grateful that they are willing to be baptized by George. Only then does he kill the dragon. The king builds a church from which there flows a spring with the power to heal all kinds of illness; George instructs him in proper religion, and then leaves without marrying the princess.

George was early seen as a type of Christ. His red cross on a white field, his associations with the archangel Michael who triumphs over Satan and with Christ who triumphs over the dragon of the Apocalypse, and his military skill reveal him to be a type of Christ as soldier and victor, one through whom is attained the triumph of the covenant of mercy over that of justice, of grace over sin and death, of Christianity over paganism, of St Paul's new man over the old. In Redcrosse, Spenser enforces the parallel; as the antiquary John Selden says, 'some account [St George] an allegory of our Saviour Christ; and our admired *Spencer* hath made him an embleme of Religion' (note to *Poly-Olbion* Song 4, in Drayton ed 1931–41, 4:85).

Yet Spenser's George also subsumes other qualities of a more distinctly political nature. Even before Edward III declared St George to be the patron saint of the Order of the Garter (c 1345), he was already known as the patron saint of England. By the fifteenth century, he was a popular figure in mummers' plays, pageants, and processions, honored with a feast day (23 April), and portrayed in numerous murals, carvings, and paintings. In addition to his recognition by the church as a saint, he had a role in popular culture similar to that of Robin Hood or King Arthur. Yet even with the rise of Protestant hostility to saint cults, George persisted in England; when other saints' days were removed from the calendar during the revisions of Henry VIII, his was kept. Spenser recognizes the patriotic enthusiasm for this English knight, and makes him a figure not just of a single holy individual but of an entire nation and its religion.

Spenser may have known numerous versions of the St George tale – not only those by Voragine and Caxton but also the rhymed tale by Lydgate (who records that 'This name George by Interpretacioun / Is sayde of tweyne, the first of hoolynesse, / And the secound of knighthood and renoun' ed 1911:145) or even the Latin *Vita sancti Georgii* of Mantuan, with its elaborate hellish description of the dragon (Padelford and O'Connor 1926). The history of Redcrosse's obscure origins and arrival at court (see Letter to Raleigh) may be indebted as well to tales of Gareth or the Fair Unknown (*Var* 1:391–5). In merging the old tales, Spenser endows them with expanded meanings. George's name is thus associated not only with his humility but also with the plowman who reared him in plowman's state after finding him as a baby hidden in a furrow (I x 66), and it ultimately becomes a sign of his inheritance from Adam (Hebrew *adamah* earth) and thus of his fallen nature. Though Redcrosse begins his quest as fallen man, he is potentially a saint (I x 61); his successful defeat of the Dragon not only frees him from bondage to sin but also anagogically enacts Christ's rescue of mankind from death and establishes the New Jerusalem.

HUGH MACLACHLAN

David Scott Fox 1983 *Saint George: The Saint with Three Faces* (Windsor Forest, Berks); Peter Heylyn 1631 *The Historie of ... St. George of Cappadocia* (London; *STC* 13272); Hume 1984:72–4; Grace Warren Landrum 1950 'St. George *Redivivus*' *PQ* 29:381–8; John Lydgate 1911 *Minor Poems* ed Henry Noble MacCracken (London) EETS es 107:145–54; Nelson 1963:147–52; Padelford and O'Connor 1926; *Var* 1:379–95; *Sp All* pp 84, 208; Strong 1977:164–85; Voragine ed 1900 'The Life of S. George' 3:125–34; Voragine 1941 'Saint George' in *The Golden Legend* tr and adapted Granger Ryan and Helmut Ripperger (London) 1:232–8; Voragine 1955 'The Lyfe of Saynt George' in Barclay ed 1955:112–18; Weatherby 1987a.

georgic (Gr *gē* earth + *ergon* work) A literary genre deriving from Virgil, who wrote his *Georgics* between the *Eclogues* and the *Aeneid*, and supposedly read it aloud to Augustus' courtiers in Greece in 30 BC, just after the battle of Actium that ended the civil war with the defeat of Mark Antony and Cleopatra. In four books, Virgil describes the agricultural labors to which Rome now calls her citizens. His famous phrase from the *Eclogues*, 'omnia vincit Amor' ('Love conquers all' 10.69), becomes in the *Georgics* 'labor omnia vicit' ('Toil conquered all' 1.145). Fierce work, compelled by necessity, once conquered all; and Virgil implies that necessity will again drive the Romans to new lands, new labors, and, by extension, the new imperium. Cultivation of the landscape is placed in a larger context of the *translatio imperii*. When he later describes the building of the new city of Carthage (*Aeneid* 1.435), he repeats his image of the communal activity of bees from *Georgics* 4, with its background in the renewal myth of Aristaeus.

Spenser's first and most direct reference to the *Georgics* appears in the *October* eclogue of *The Shepheardes Calender* (55–60) where Cuddie discusses the Renaissance commonplace that the poet should imitate the pattern of Virgil's career (the *rota Virgilii*). Cuddie charts a progression from pastoral ('Oaten reede' and 'flocks') through georgic ('laboured lands to yield the timely eare') to epic ('sing of warres and deadly drede'). Mantuan (Spenser's immediate source for *October*) defines the Virgilian career as a sequence of 'rura, boves, et agros et Martia bella' (*Eclogues* 5.87), in which pastoral and georgic tend to merge; and E.K. may reflect this conflation when he mistakenly glosses the *October* passage by using two names for Virgil's pastorals: 'For in teaching his flocks to feede, is meant his Aeglogues. In labouring of lands, is hys Bucoliques.' But his mistake emphasizes the functional aspect of the *Georgics*' transformed pastoral landscape.

The influence of the *Georgics* may also lie behind Spenser's treatment of the redemption of Una's homeland in the first book of *The Faerie Queene*. At the climax of Redcrosse's visit to the house of Holiness, he learns the significance of his given name, George. Stolen by a fairy in his infancy and left in a furrow, he was discovered by a plowman 'As he his toylesome teme that way did guyde ... Whereof *Georgos* he thee gave to name' (I x 66). It is as 'Saint *George* of mery England' that he will be known in times to come, as a consequence of his victory over the Dragon (61). The fact that the poet calls on his muse to 'let downe that haughtie string' of epic, 'And to my tunes thy second tenor rayse' for the description of that dragon fight (xi 7) may similarly reflect the tradition that georgic sought a middle style, between pastoral and epic. A comparable muting or tempering of the high style will also appear in *Paradise Regained*, Milton's four-book poem of 'Eden raised in the waste wilderness.' The most important echoes of georgic tradition in the English Renaissance seem to be found in these works, where the heroic is redefined and redirected toward redeeming a land and a history from the effects of time's disorders.

WILLIAM A. SESSIONS

Ettin 1982; Alastair Fowler 1986 'The Beginnings of English Georgic' in Lewalski 1986:105–25; Antony Low 1983 'Milton, *Paradise Regained*, and Georgic' *PMLA* 98:152–69; Michael C.J. Putnam 1979 *Virgil's Poem of the Earth: Studies in the 'Georgics'* (Princeton); William A. Sessions 1980 'Spenser's Georgics' *ELR* 10:202–38.

Germany, influence and reputation in Although Spenser is highly esteemed in German-speaking countries, he is rarely read. He has never been, as in England, the poet's poet, but rather the poet of linguists, philologists, and those interested in the history of language or sources. Very few others have read him carefully. A slight influence can be detected in the work of the Baroque author and diplomat Georg Rudolf Weckherlin who was resident in the English court from 1625 to 1648 (see his *Gedichte* ed Hermann Fischer [Darmstadt 1968] 2:473, 478, 491–3, 509). Since writers of the age of Goethe and of the Romantic movement were fascinated by the Elizabethans, some read *The Faerie Queene*. A number of stanzas were translated in *Der Teutsche Merkur* of 1788, the journal edited by Christoph Martin Wieland. August Wilhelm Schlegel is known to have read *The Faerie Queene*; Johann Gottfried Herder called Chaucer and Spenser the 'morning stars' of English poetry (*Sämmtliche Werke* ed Bernhard Suphan, et al [Berlin 1891–2] 5:647, 8:417). Yet Spenser never received even a fraction of the homage given to Shakespeare at that time.

Despite the poor reception given Spenser by German writers, within the academic community his poetry proved to be a rich quarry for dissertations and specialized studies, especially by the end of the nineteenth century when it was seen as a philological curiosity by historians of the transition from Late Middle to Early Modern English. Thus we find studies of Spenser's participles (Fritz Hoffman, diss Berlin 1909), his archaisms (Karl Reuning, Strasbourg 1912), his pronouns (Hugo Düring, diss Halle-Wittenberg 1891) and his word stress (G. Günther, diss Jena 1888). As well, Spenser is usually mentioned in the hundreds of other linguistic studies on Elizabethan language, and brought forward as a key example in more literary studies: in histories of rhetoric, literary motifs, the pastoral, Petrarchism, the sonnet. For the academic community, Spenser ranks among the important writers of world literature.

Since his poetry in Germany has never had much influence outside the fairly narrow academic world, there is no 'German Spenser' in the sense that one may speak of a 'German Shakespeare.' The historians of language and literature have always had an eye on the contemporary English criticism so that a separate German figure could never really emerge. Of course, at the end of the nineteenth century, when English critics tended to treat Spenser's poetry as an unhistorical and highly romanticized object, German critics went even further: for certain writers, he was a 'king in the realm of romanticism,' a harbinger of a 'fairy land detached from the world.' Even the Spenserian stanza was praised as a 'genuine child of romanticism ... like all blooms of romanticism tender and sensitive' (Hedwig Reschke 1918 *Die Spenserstanze im neunzehnten Jahrhundert* [*Anglistische Forschungen* 54, Heidelberg] p 20).

Spenser's influence in Germany has been limited in part because he has never been fully translated. Some stanzas of *The Faerie Queene* were translated in 1788, as noted above; 'Spensers Feenkönigin, I i. Probe ein-er Ubersetzung, von Eschenburg' appeared in *Deutsche Monatsschrift* in 1795 (February, pp 313–31); *FQ* VI i was translated in 1810 by Karl Ludwig Kannegiesser in the Leipzig journal *Pantheon* (1:58–74); and *FQ* I i-v was rendered in a free metric version by G. Schwetschke (*Fünf Gesänge der Feenkönigin* [Halle 1854]), who claims to avoid the long-windedness of Spenser's narration and his moralizing parts. (He removes evidences of Spenser's 'naiveté,' especially if they 'cause physical nausea,' and he modifies the mythological names as he wishes: eg, 'Chaos' becomes 'Aveugle.') This sad performance is the best that has been done for *The Faerie Queene*. To a certain extent, the failure of German translators is due to the awkwardness of the Spenserian stanza in German: von Zedlitz, translator of Byron's *Childe Harold's Pilgrimage*, noted that the form requires a 'great artist of the language' to render its rhymes and internal structure effectively (see his preface to *Ritter Harold's Pilgerfahrt* [Stuttgart 1836]). The sonnets of *Amoretti* have had better fortune: a complete and on the whole successful translation was made by the traveler and orientalist Joseph von Hammer-Purgstall (Vienna, 2nd ed 1816); the well-known poet Richard Flatter also translated many of *Amoretti* in his collection *Die Fähre: Englische Lyrik aus fünf Jahrhunderten* (Vienna 1936).

WERNER BIES

Lawrence Marsden Price 1953 *English Literature in Germany* (*UCPMP* 37; Berkeley and Los Angeles); Mary Bell Price and Lawrence Marsden Price 1934 *The Publication of English Literature in Germany in the Eighteenth Century* (*UCPMP* 17, Berkeley).

Geryoneo A 'strong Tyrant' in *FQ* V, son of the Spanish Geryon conquered by Hercules. This latter-day or 'neo'-Geryon becomes protector of the widowed Belge, and subsequently sacrifices twelve of her seventeen sons to a 'dreadfull Monster' hiding beneath an altar bearing 'an Idole of his owne, / The image of his monstrous parent *Geryone*' (x 6–13). Arthur is sent by Mercilla to rescue Belge and does so in a protracted adventure, first killing Geryoneo's Seneschall (18–39) and three evil knights, then Geryoneo himself (xi 1–17), and finally the monster (18–35).

Arthur's triumph over Geryoneo is modeled on one of Hercules' twelve labors, in which he steals a herd of purple cattle from the triple-bodied Geryon, whom he defeats after killing the cowherd Eurytion and his dog Orthrus. Geryoneo's monster resembles Dante's serpentine Gerione (*Inferno* 17.1–33), with specific details from Conti's description of the Sphinx (*Mythologiae* 9.18). In emblem books, Geryon is often depicted as a three-bodied king representing unity (eg, 'concordia insuperabilis' [unconquerable concord] in Alciati ed 1621, Emblem 40); but Spenser's Geryoneo is presented as wholly negative, a 'demonic parody of the power of just concord' (Aptekar 1969:149) and a figure of the tyrannical idolatry of Catholic Spain.

Spenser's purpose in describing Arthur's defeat of Geryoneo is to justify England's military intervention in the Low Countries. To this end, he selects the brightest period in Leicester's campaign (which extended, with one interruption, from December 1585 until November 1587): Arthur's slaughter of the Seneschall in 'a Castle huge' near 'a Citie farre up land' (x 25) celebrates the Earl's capture of the Veluwe fort near Zutphen in the final months of 1586. Spenser magnifies this achievement by making it appear that the city under siege was actually Antwerp and that Leicester had defeated the governor appointed by Philip II. Thus the episode provides a vision of what Elizabeth is to accomplish once she has fulfilled Merlin's prophecy and extended 'her white rod over the *Belgicke* shore,' smiting 'the great Castle' which will 'shortly learne to fall' (III iii 49).

The second and third parts of Arthur's adventure complement the historical allegory by furnishing symbolic victories over Spanish power and the Catholic church in the Low Countries. Geryoneo's defeat foretells the end of Philip's rule, and the monster's death the lifting of 'the yoke of inquisition' (V x 27). Charles V had created a papal inquisition in the Low Countries and had decreed in 1550 that heretics should, in Belge's words, be 'burnt in flame; / With all the tortures, that he could devize, / The more t'aggrate his God with such his blouddy guize' (xi 19). Through the Duke of Alva's 'Council of Troubles,' commonly known as the 'Council of Blood,' Philip executed thousands of Protestants, who are represented in Spenser's narrative as victims of human sacrifice (in an episode that parallels the offering of Ammonite children to Molech, in Lev 18.21). Arthur's destruction of the monster underneath the Idol of Geryon, worshiped by Geryoneo, terminates this sacrifice, which originates in the son's idolatrous reverence for his dead father – the imputed motive behind Philip's persecution of Dutch Protestants. Arthur's final triumph thus recapitulates in specific detail and general intention the Red Cross Knight's defeat of the Dragon.

JAMES P. BEDNARZ

Giant with the scales In *FQ* V, Artegall and Talus encounter a large assembly of people flocking to 'a mighty Gyant' holding a pair of balances in his hand (ii 29–54). Believing the world to be suffering from inequalities and lacking any distributive justice, the Giant proposes an ambitious project of cosmological, geological, and political reform. With his balance, which as a symbol of justice makes him a parodic version of Astraea, he will begin by weighing the four elements to see which has encroached upon the others and then will level hills and mountains. The real point of the episode comes, however, in the political and social leveling he intends: he will suppress tyrants 'And Lordings curbe, that commons over-aw; / And all the wealth of rich men to the poore will draw' (38).

In a general way, all the giants of Book V recall the rebellion of the Titans against Jove in classical literature. Abraham Fraunce allegorizes the Titans as 'seditious and rebellious subjects in a common wealth, or schismaticall and haereticall seducers in the Church' (ed 1975:23–4). But the richness of scriptural allusion in this episode points to the Bible as Spenser's real model. Weighing the winds, the waters, and the earth in a balance is an image of impossibility and a rebuke to human arrogance in a number of biblical passages (see Job 28.23–5, Isa 40.12, Jer 31.37). Most immediately relevant is the apocalyptic vision in Revelation 6.5 of the rider on the black horse (glossed as famine in the Geneva Bible) carrying 'balances in his hand,' and in 2 Esdras 4, in which the prophet is mocked for his moral presumption. In the latter, in a dialogue strikingly similar to that between Artegall and the Giant, the angel Uriel asks the prophet if he can weigh the fire or measure the winds. The Giant's end, moreover, recalls the mortal illness of Antiochus in 2 Maccabees 9.7–8 (which Spenser uses even more explicitly in the death of the Souldan in V viii): 'And thus he that a litle afore thoght he might commande the floods of the sea (so proude was he beyonde the condicion of man) and to weigh the hie mountaines in the balance, was now cast on the ground.'

Spenser requires the support of such biblical allusion because the Giant embodies egalitarian principles which were felt to be deeply threatening to the orthodoxy of hierarchical social order in the sixteenth century (see *radicalism). Insofar as these principles found contemporary expression, it was mainly by the Anabaptists, ancestors of the modern Mennonites, who preached a radical Christian vision of equality and anarchy. Their name, originally applied in scorn (from the Greek for 'rebaptizers'), referred to their denial of infant baptism and the belief that the sacrament should be conferred only on adult believers. Early in Elizabeth's reign, Anabaptists had come to England among the Dutch refugees fleeing Spanish persecution. In 1568 a proclamation ordered them to be expelled if they did not renounce their heretical beliefs. Article 38 of the Thirty-nine Articles, while stressing the duty of charity, specifically condemned their communist teaching. Although it is unlikely that underground Anabaptists represented any threat to the political order in the 1590s, their social doctrine continued to be feared. In *The Unfortunate Traveller* (1594), Nashe satirizes them in a savage portrayal of the Münster debacle of 1534. There an extremist group of Anabaptists under John of Leiden established a theocracy practicing communism and polygamy until the city was retaken and the leaders of the sect executed. Thus for both Protestant and Catholic Europe, the extremism of the Anabaptists of Münster came to typify the sect, especially in its social and political doctrines.

Although the perceived threat of Anabaptist ideology may stand at some distance behind the Giant, more immediate anxieties of the mid-1590s are likely to have brought the apocalyptic vision of 2 Esdras to Spenser's imagination and caused him to make the Giant represent to Artegall so monstrous a danger. The purchasing power of agricultural workers in England had been declining steadily through the century, reaching its lowest point in the 1590s. Beginning in 1594, unseasonable weather in spring and summer brought four bad harvests in a row. Unprecedented shortages caused grain prices to double in 1594 and again in 1595. Because two-thirds of the population lived at the margin of poverty, the threat of starvation immediately endangered social order. Food riots were widespread in 1595, and there was an attempted insurrection among the artisans of Oxfordshire. The Giant clearly personifies the social threat this human misery represented to the political order of the kingdom.

The immediacy of this threat may explain why the episode ends as it does. Spenser gives Artegall some of the most rhetorically impressive poetry in Book v to defend the established social order; the biblical cadences and allusions of stanzas 41–3 express that order as divinely ordained and imaged in the unchanging course of nature. In effect, the Giant is a rebel not only against the political order but against God himself. When he proves stubbornly literal-minded about the metaphor of the balance, however, Talus, with no command from Artegall, shoulders him off the cliff and he drowns in the sea. A reader may expect that Talus, as mere executive power, should wait upon judicial authority, but the iron man is not rebuked by Artegall (or by the narrator), and an incipient rebellion seems to justify the Giant's summary execution. The contemporary threat of insurrection seems to have made Spenser less interested in such legal distinctions.

The episode has troubled many readers, most notably Keats and Shelley. Declaring himself 'of the Giant's faction,' Shelley told Thomas Love Peacock that the Giant has the better of the argument; the conclusion, he felt, represents 'the usual way in which power deals with opinion' (ed 1964, 2:71n). In order to bring the ending of the episode into line with later political history, Keats wrote a Spenserian stanza (perhaps the last verse he composed and, according to his close friend Charles Brown, 'till then, he never wrote a line of a political tendency' ed 1935, 4:232) and inscribed it at the end of *FQ* v ii in a copy of Spenser's poetry he gave to Fanny Brawne:

In after time a sage of mickle lore,
Yclep'd Typographus, the giant took
And did refit his limbs as heretofore,
And made him read in many a learned book,
And into many a lively legend look;
Thereby in goodly themes so training him,
That all his brutishness he quite forsook,
When, meeting Artegall and Talus grim,
The one he struck stone blind, the other's eyes wox dim.

While modern readers are likely to sympathize with Keats's revisionary ending, in the sixteenth century, Typographus – and the poets – more often supported the Elizabethan status quo. MICHAEL O'CONNELL

Dunseath 1968; Duncan B. Heriot 1933–9 'Anabaptism in England during the Sixteenth and Seventeenth Centuries' *Transactions of the Congregational Historical Society* 12(1933–36): 256–71, 312–20, 13(1937–9): 22–40; Keats ed 1978:535, 680–1 (and rev ed 1982:408, 484–5); Frederick Morgan Padelford 1913 'Spenser's Arraignment of the Anabaptists' *JEGP* 12:434–48; Buchanan Sharp 1980 *In Contempt of All Authority: Rural Artisans and Riot in the West of England, 1586–1660* (Berkeley and Los Angeles).

---

giants Spenser's giants have a complex ancestry. In part they derive from classical giants, sons of old Earth sprung, some say, from the blood of the conquered Titans or from that of castrated Uranus. Urged by their angry mother to rebel, they piled up hills to reach the heavens but were defeated at Phlegra by Jove and an army of gods including Minerva and one mortal, Hercules. (Like others before him, Spenser often confuses these giants with the earlier Titans.) Renaissance mythographers agree that giants are unkempt, impious, tyrannical, thieving, envious, violent, cruel, oversexed, greedy, armed with rocks and clubs, terrible-eyed, and snake-footed (a detail Spenser ignores). Their rebellion also signifies the struggle of trapped air to escape in volcanoes and earthquakes; one giant, Osiris' enemy the monster-engendering Typhon or Typhoeus, lies under Etna. Jove's victory reestablished the rule he had wrested from older gods, reaffirming an evolution towards justice and order. Some giants lingered, but many of these succumbed to Bacchus or Hercules; meanwhile, a few Titans joined Jove on Olympus.

(See **giants** Fig 1.)

Equally wicked were biblical giants, interpreted as tyrants and 'mightie men' (Gen 6.4 and gloss), rebels against God (and thus useful in Reformation polemic; Catholic enemies were 'giants,' and Spenser's Orgoglio, Geryoneo, and Grantorto signify Spanish and Roman tyranny; see Iredale 1966). Commentators said they were descended from Cain and, after the flood, from the cursed Ham, and called them proud and oppressive men, sunk in the flesh, given to robbery, atheism, heresy, mockery, boasting, and even cannibalism. Others called them demons. Some of these mighty men were also literally giants, for King Og was about nine cubits and Goliath six. The original giant inhabitants of the Promised Land were conquered by the Israelites with the help of God, but their rebellious race remained, threatening the new dispensation. Goliath was one such rebel, and so was the hunter Nimrod, often considered a giant, who built the proud tower of Babel.

Before the Trojan Brute could civilize the land now called Britain, he too had to rid his new territory of giants, who were cannibals ignorant of law, agriculture, or sexual restraint. One was Gogmagog (Spenser's Goëmot), who later reappeared in London pageantry, often standing on London Bridge or Temple Bar with his conqueror Corineus. Like the famous Antwerp giant who cut off the hands of travelers refusing to pay a toll, and whose defeat made way for the founding of that city, Gogmagog survived in affectionate memory, as though civic celebration required his presence: foundation ritual is commemorative, not conclusive. (Spenser's teacher Richard Mulcaster contributed to such a pageant in 1559; see Fairholt 1843–4, passim, and Anglo 1969:346.) The Renaissance saw increasing disbelief in giants; but skeptics could examine great bones like those at Antwerp, and voyagers reported fifteen-foot porters in China. Elizabeth herself had a 'giant' porter at Hampton Court.

Classical giants appear in Spenser's shorter poems, especially the *Complaints*; in *The Faerie Queene*, however, all the traditions concerning them work together to give multiple associations to his many giants, some of whom resemble those in earlier epic and romance. This eclecticism was encouraged by his authorities' tendency to see classical myth, biblical story, and legendary history as interconnected.

Most of Spenser's heroes must confront giants (though Calidore, the knight of Courtesy, chases only their relative, the Blatant Beast). Two are associated with ancient giant-quellers: Britomart with Minerva (if also with the good Titaness, Bellona), and Artegall with Hercules. As dynastic founders and makers of justice, they must dominate what giantry represents: tyranny, lawless violence, sexual confusion, and the rebellion of the concupiscible and irascible powers in the soul and cosmos. The champion is Arthur, for when human might fails, grace fights on our behalf. As for technique, giants are best attacked from below, especially when their arrogant wrath leads them to misdirect their blows.

Although Spenser's giants sometimes own castles, they also dwell in woods, rocks, and caves and are themselves club-wielding and crude, demonstrating their emanation from the least cultivated part of the soul and the most archaic times. They are angry boasters whose blasphemies reveal them as enemies of God. Some, recalling the figures of hell in medieval iconography, have big mouths which like Earth herself threaten to swallow human beings back into darkness. Some hoard treasure; Disdain is even made of 'golden mould' (II vii 40). Some burn with sexual fury, although Daunger and Mirabella's Disdain oppose sexual union. Giants tyrannize like Orgoglio and Grantorto but they also rebel like the Giant with the scales. Some, like Corflambo, have the fiery eyes of classical giants; several are called 'mighty' like the biblical giants; and since the toll-collector Pollente bears a name meaning 'mighty,' he too recalls the giant tyrants of Scripture.

Argante, Ollyphant, and Lust (hunters like Nimrod) pursue their victims; others stand at passageways impeding progress. In either case, the result may be slavery or deviation. As the Vulgate Bible had said, those who stray from the path of wisdom will dwell in the assembly of giants (Prov 21.16). (The Geneva version reads *of the dead* where the Vulgate has *gigantum* 'of giants'; but for the imprisoned Redcrosse, both words apply.) Just as a giant like Orgoglio may block or divert a quest, the Giant with the scales obstructs due process, and Goëmot, Grantorto, or Cormoraunt fight history and succession. Contributing to the poem's exploration of legitimacy and descent in religion and politics, many giants in *The Faerie Queene* have lineage involving incest or monstrosity and show a perverted relationship with their mother Earth. Goëmot's giants pollute the 'gentle soyle' (II x 9), Orgoglio rips his club out of her bowels, Antaeus-like Maleger falls incestuously into her womb in a quasi-biblical parody of rebirth, and the defeated Grantorto feeds on her. Geryoneo, too, precludes natural succession by sacrificing children to his father's image. Such opposition to the natural order of the generations suggests the giants' hope to close off areas of space or time in which to tyrannize.

Yet giants are paradoxical, for they also represent necessary roles or energies. They block bridges, fords, and gates, and in this way act as agents of rites of passage, which require obstacles. As phallic children of Earth, they show her fertility as well as the impulse her daughter Mutabilitie inherits to rise above her station. Hence, only half of the giants in *The Faerie Queene* are killed; the others have some needed and continuing function. Therefore, although the lust-filled Corflambo dies, he leaves a daughter who is capable of love. Nor are giants utterly unlike heroes, however much they inflate or distort heroic nature. They carry clubs but so did Hercules. They glory in their ancestry but so do Britons (although, significantly, the Britons also glory in their descendants). They seek power through violence – like Jove, David, Aeneas, Brute, and Henry Tudor. They are earthy, but so is St George, and so was Adam. Heroes subdue and reshape such 'earthly slime' (I vii 9) but cannot permanently abolish it. The knights and giants thus play out a continuous drama in the 'unperfite' world of Spenser's poem.

In fact, as Spenser might have known from writers like Pulci and Rabelais and from biblical comparisons of God to a giant (eg, Isa 42.13), or even from the gentle Polyphemus of classical pastoral, giants can be neutral or benign. Some of Spenser's giants merely need braving, like Mammon's Disdain or Cupid's Daunger; and even painful Care recalls the Cyclopes, Jove's helpers. Good giants guard Alma's house and Mercilla's palace, and Artegall's descendant Malgo is 'like a Gyaunt in each manly part' (III iii 32). Nature herself is a supergiantess: terrible, calm, huge, powerful, and fertile, she shows what good giantry can be like.

ANNE LAKE PRESCOTT

The giants in classical literature are found in such works as Apollodorus *Library* 1.6.1; Ovid *Metamorphoses* 1.150–62, 181–4; Claudian *Gigantomachia*; and Philo Judaeus *On Giants*.

On historical and legendary giants: Jean de Chassanion 1580 *De gigantibus* (Basel) and Harrison's chapter on British giants in *Description of England* 1.5 (in Holinshed ed 1807–8, 1:14–22). On English giants, see Frederick W. Fairholt 1843–4 *Lord Mayors' Pageants* (London); and Fairholt 1859 *Gog and Magog: The Giants in Guildhall* (London). Iredale 1966 looks at giants in *FQ* V; and see entries on individual giants. See also Nohrnberg 1976:140–59; Susan Stewart 1984 'The Gigantic' in *On Longing: Narratives of the Miniature, the Gigantic, the Souvenir, the Collection* (Baltimore) pp 70–103.

Glauce Nurse and companion to Britomart in *FQ* III-IV. Her name may derive from the Greek *glaukē* 'gray' or from *glaukos* 'owl,' referring to age (her characteristic epithets are *aged* or *old*) and to the bird of Minerva, whose qualities of wisdom and nocturnal vigilance she shares. Glauce is also a name of the mother of Diana (Cicero *De natura deorum* 3.23.58), who like Minerva is Britomart's mythic ancestor.

The scene in which the sleepless and lovelorn Britomart confides in Glauce echoes the pseudo-Virgilian *Ciris* 220–378, where aged Carme (mother of the nymph Britomartis and nurse to Scylla) hears Scylla's confession of love. Such nurse-confidant figures have many analogues in classical and medieval literature; but unlike Glauce, they are often morally ambivalent in character, cunning rather than wise. Dame Brusen in Malory's *Morte Darthur* 11–12, for example, uses enchantment to assist Elaine's love for Lancelot; and Myrrha's nurse in Ovid (*Metamorphoses* 10.382–464) and Phaedra's in the *Hippolytus* of both Euripides and Seneca encourage their charges to pursue the 'filthy lust, contrarie unto kind' (*FQ* III ii 40), which Glauce needlessly fears for Britomart. Closer to Glauce than these is the old nurse in Boccaccio's *Fiammetta*, who first counsels her mistress against an adulterous love affair but later colludes with her to further it.

Glauce's probity emerges through her role as wise woman: her use of spells to cure Britomart's love-melancholy may be implicitly contrasted with the amatory magic of the witch and Busirane (III vii 21, xii 31–8). As companion in male disguise to Britomart on her quest for Artegall, Glauce is a version of the comic squire, her disguise adding to the humor of her alliterative vehemence and melodramatic manner (ii 32–3, 50). Love for her mistress makes her courageous; though she is almost killed by the jealous Scudamour (IV i 50–4), she remains faithful and does not betray the secret of their disguise. Appropriately, she makes her last appearance at the fight between Artegall and Britomart and is the means by which the lovers discover each other's identity (vi 25–38). When Glauce has thus fulfilled her vow to see Britomart through her quest, she disappears from the poem.

SANDRA S. CLARK

Gloriana The Fairy Queen, also known as Tanaquill, daughter of Oberon; from her court at Cleopolis originate the adventures described in *The Faerie Queene*. The 'glorious flowre' and culmination of the elfin line whose origins can be traced back to Prometheus (II x 70–7), she is explicitly identified with Queen Elizabeth (see Letter to Raleigh and III proem 5).

Her names are given early in Book I: Tanaquill in proem 2 and Gloriana at i 3. The first comes from Latin antiquity: Caia Tanaquil, wife of Lucius Tarquin, was noted for her chastity, industriousness, and sadness. From the accounts of her by Livy, Cicero, and Ovid, she became a figure of much repute in the Renaissance, chiefly through Boccaccio and Vives. Her name was first flatteringly applied to Elizabeth in a Latin panegyric by Thomas Drant (*Carminum sylvae* 1578; see also *Sp All* pp 77, 86–7, 100–1, 190–1). The more descriptive 'Gloriana' for this 'greatest Glorious Queene of *Faerie* lond' echoes Gloriande, a lady at the court of Oberon, king of the fairies, in *Huon of Bordeaux*. The vision of a fairy queen found in the Elizabethan court entertainments at Kenilworth and Woodstock in 1575 is linked to other romances. Such a queen is chaste, has remarkable magic powers, and stands apart from normal human activity. As such, she associates Elizabeth with mysterious powers as flattering to her as the chastity and industriousness of Tanaquil. Although these names have an eclectic literary background, they are directly related to the presence of Elizabeth in the poem. They evoke a woman strong in character, beautiful, diligent, mysterious, chaste, and in some ways delightfully moody.

Gloriana is also part of the tradition of protagonists whose influence on the action of their poetic world is manifest through a kind of negative capability: by their absence or uninvolvement, or through the indirect influence of a god or supernatural force. Service to her brings hope of glory, especially to Arthur. The memory of her image and the quest for her glory are presented as two forces driving him, though allegorically they are one. In the poem, Arthur says that she appeared to him in a vision (I ix 13–15), her image appears on Guyon's shield (II ix 2–4), and occasionally we are told the latest news from her court (III viii 46) or hear of meetings there (II i 31, V xi 37); but we learn little about her. In using his other knights and ladies to adumbrate Gloriana and her court, Spenser makes his praise of Elizabeth part of a Christian, patriotic Platonism by which he and the reader can apprehend the 'glorious type' of the ideal Christian woman and prince. Associations of her with Pauline motifs of the mirror and the veil (2 Cor 3.11–18, *FQ* II proem 4) and with grace (eg, I proem 4, i 3) inform the reader that her absence is not merely prudent artistry but (as part of the poem's religious and moral design) Protestant artistry.

It is specifically in the context of the influence of the unseen Gloriana that Spenser speaks most directly about the method and meaning of his poem. The fullest view of her is given in the Letter to Raleigh. Here Spenser tells of the Fairy Queen's twelve-day annual feast which provides the occasions of the twelve adventures undertaken by the twelve knights in the proposed twelve books of the poem. He further explains that Arthur had a dream-vision of Gloriana and, ravished by her beauty, resolved to seek her out. Spenser explains that 'in that Faery Queene I meane glory in my generall intention, but in my particular I conceive the most excellent and glorious person of our soveraine the Queene, and her kingdome in Faery land.'

Since Gloriana bears two persons – 'the one of a most royall Queene or Empresse, the other of a most vertuous and beautifull Lady' – Spenser develops two characters, Belphoebe who represents the Queen's private self as perfect chastity and Britomart who represents her public and feminine self (although this latter identity is not made explicit). In thus fragmenting her image and removing the character of Gloriana from the poem, Spenser is able to turn his encomiastic form to the larger design of instructing noble persons in virtuous behavior. A depersonalized portrait of Elizabeth allows him to explore more fully his themes of the sexuality of power and the power of sexuality, and the ways in which public and private aspects of character interact and influence one another.

For all this, Gloriana's name is not mentioned in the Letter; she is always the 'Faery Queene.' We first hear that she bears the name Gloriana at I i 3, and its associations with 'great,' 'glorious,' and 'grace' recur with each use, thereby calling attention not only to her public and private identity but also to her combined spiritual and secular roles.

Infrequently as the name Gloriana appears, it is an essential addition to her other titles. That of 'Faery Queene' with its echoes of Chaucer's *Sir Thopas* and *Huon of Bordeaux* falls short of epic *gravitas*, and the classical associations and historical particularity of Tanaquill emphasize a secular private virtue to the exclusion of explicitly Christian qualities. Thus, when we imagine the end of Arthur's quest, we need to remember that it must be his union with a woman (Tanaquill), a queen, and a 'heavenly Mayd' (II i 28). It will thus represent the realization of another of his qualities, divine grace and graciousness associated specifically with Gloriana. While the Letter to Raleigh speaks of the Queen's 'two persons,' the alliterated presentation of Gloriana suggests the three aspects figured by her three titles: goodness, glory, and grace.

W.H. HERENDEEN

Baskervill 1920–1; Greenlaw 1918; Millican 1938–9; Nohrnberg 1976; Rathborne 1937.

glossing The editorial practice of adding notes to explain foreign or difficult words in a text, through methods of definition ranging from grammatical analysis to historical discussion. The practice occurs in Greek and Latin before the Christian era but is most common in the lexicographers of the late Roman Empire. For the Renaissance, the most outstanding ancient examples of the glossing of poetry were the commentaries of Servius (4th c AD) on Virgil and of Porphyrion (early 3rd c AD) on Horace. By the sixteenth century, glosses almost always accompany editions of canonical texts, such as Virgil's *Eclogues*. The glossarial practices of Paulus Manutzio (1558) and Clément Marot (1555) provide a relevant background against which to observe the procedures of E.K. in *The Shepheardes Calender*. Both editions of the *Eclogues* provide the basic linguistic helps to Virgil's Latin, often with elegant etymological analyses; furthermore, they identify historical characters they take to be allegorized under pastoral names in the text, explain mythological allusions, historical events, and places, define figurative phrases and metaphors, and urge the moral truths they find to be implicit in the poems.

Renaissance glosses are commonly found in editions of classical rhetoric (Quintilian), the classical poets (Homer, Virgil, Ovid, Horace), the major medieval poets (Dante, Petrarch, Chaucer), civil and common law, history (Livy), philosophy, theology, and, of course, the Bible. Of the vernacular translations, Chapman's Homer and Harington's Ariosto are both accompanied by commentaries that seek to interpret the work; Sandys' translation of Ovid (1621–6) is a slightly later example. Yet very few original, contemporary works of English literature appeared with glosses; the significant exceptions are *The Shepheardes Calender*, Thomas Watson's *Hekatompathia* (1582), several of Chapman's poems, including *The Shadow of Night* (1594) and *Ovids Banquet of Sence* (1595), and Whitney's *Choice of Emblemes* (1586).

Renaissance glosses often observe a common scheme: first appears the lemma (the word under discussion), then a definition which is followed by a paraphrase of its general sense, a brief interpretation and, finally, a personal commentary. Especially in the last two stages of this scheme, the glossator will often quote a similar usage in another author and add a series of analogues. This procedure is related both to the pedagogical practice of the Latin grammar school, which with other techniques also favored translation, definition, paraphrase, and commentary, and to the standard rhetorical practices of the day: first the *verba* (words and matters of style), then the *res* (the subject matter). E.K. himself notes these procedures in his Epistle to Harvey. The gloss will often note the author's exemplary rhetoric, his profound learning, and his moral rectitude by alluding at length to history, ethics, literary theory, Scripture, common superstition, local flora and fauna, and much else. Glosses of considerable amplitude are not at all unusual. Spenser speaks of his lost *Dreames* 'being growen by meanes of the Glosse, (running continually in manner of a Paraphrase) full as great as my *Calender*' (*3 Lett* I, *Var Prose* p 18).

The glosses to *The Shepheardes Calender*, by their very presence, claim for the poem a status usually conferred upon an old, not a new poet. But while the poem may be new, the glosses themselves are conventional in the ways sketched above. E.K. defines 'old wordes and harder phrases,' notes Spenser's rhetorical propriety (the 'many excellent and proper devises both in wordes and matter'), and comments on the argument and moral content of the poems.

The practice of glossing offers some hints about the habits of a generally learned reader in the Renaissance: an intense grammatical interest in words, their derivations, and how they are used in rhetorical structures; the tendency to look upon texts as compendia of general historical knowledge and style; the expectation of learned allusion and of multiple meanings and significations implied in historical usage or in the etymology of the words or metaphors at hand; and, finally, the tendency to derive an ethical or religious inference from the subject or narrative.

GERALD SNARE

Gnat, Virgils. See Complaints: Virgils Gnat

God In spite of Spenser's general eclecticism, his God is essentially Christian. God's transcendence (throughout Spenser's work), his provision of salvation through the work of Christ (eg, *Amoretti* 68, *Heavenly Love* 127–54), and his omnipotence within the logical principle of noncontradiction (God cannot 'doe ... that, which cannot be donne' *FQ* III ii 36) are all orthodox tenets of Christian theology.

Spenser is thoroughly traditional in the many references to God throughout *The Faerie Queene*, from 'the Lord of life and light' in the opening canto (I i 37) to 'that great Sabbaoth God' in the concluding line; and to God chiefly as creator, for example, 'the mightie word, / Which first was spoken by th'Almightie lord, / That bad [all things] to increase and multiply' (III vi 34), creating man in his image (I x 42, V x 28), or planting the Tree of Life in Eden (I xi 46). *Heavenly Beautie* is a hymn praising God's love for man traced from the creation of all things to the crucifixion of Christ. Spenser refers frequently to God's grace (I x 38, IV viii 15, V vi 34, VI iv 10, viii 38), and most movingly to God's love for man: 'But O th'exceeding grace / Of highest God, that loves his creatures so, / And all his workes with mercy doth embrace, / That blessed Angels, he sends to and fro, / To serve to wicked man, to serve his wicked foe' (II viii 1). His references to Christ are also thoroughly traditional: Christ is 'the Lord of life' (II vii 62), the 'heavenly spouse' (I x 42), 'that unspotted lam' (57). In referring to the life of Christ, he emphasizes the Incarnation (II x 50), the Crucifixion (I x 57), the Harrowing of Hell (40), and the Epiphany (VII vii 7). For a thorough listing, see Shaheen 1976.

Spenser's doctrine of the Trinity is also orthodox in its substance, though in some respects Neoplatonic in flavor and mystical in spirit. Its clearest statement refers to the Father's begetting of the eternal Son 'Before this worlds great frame ... found any being place,' to the Son's being 'with equall honour crownd,' and to the 'Spright' who is 'derived' from Father and Son and shares with them the epithets 'Most wise, most holy, most almightie' (*Heavenly Love* 22–42). In this account, Spenser's language agrees precisely with that of the Nicene Creed regarding both Son ('begotten of the Father before all worlds ... begotten not made') and Holy Spirit ('who proceedeth from the Father and the Son'). However, in *Heavenly Beautie*, although Spenser invokes the Holy Spirit as the source of 'wit and knowledge' (9–10), the figure of Sapience should probably be interpreted not as the third person of the Trinity, but rather as one of 'those essentiall parts' or attributes of God, which include 'His truth, his love, his wisedome, and his blis, / His grace, his doome, his mercy and his might' (109–11; see also *FQ* v x 1).

A further divine attribute identified by Spenser is justice, 'Most sacred vertue she of all the rest, / Resembling God in his imperiall might' (v proem 10). In thus associating God's justice with his power, Spenser engages one of the most important questions of theodicy: is God's power 'absolute,' or is it 'ordinate' (ie, conditioned by something other than his sheer will; not arbitrary)? Some Scholastics and some Calvinists would have answered, 'absolute.' But Calvin himself rejects this 'voluntarism,' 'for it is easier to dissever the light of the sun from its heat ... than to separate God's power from His righteousness' (*Concerning the Eternal Predestination of God* 10.13). Like Calvin, Spenser envisages an integral relationship between these attributes, with justice being primary: 'For powre is the right hand of Justice truely hight' (*FQ* v iv 1). By contrast, Jove in *FQ* VII, who is *not* God, can be seen as embodying might without right after the fashion of the pagan god Zeus in Aeschylus' *Prometheus Bound*.

Spenser seems also to assume the Calvinist analogy between knowledge of God and knowledge of self (*Institutes of the Christian Religion* 1.1–5). Both are arrived at indirectly, by means of signs and images which must be read correctly and distinguished from false ones (see *idols, idolatry). In this way, both the created world and the world of Spenser's works point beyond themselves to the transcendent God (*HHB* 113–33, *FQ* VII viii 2), 'the elegant structures of the world serving us as a kind of mirror, in which we may behold God, though otherwise invisible' (*Institutes* 1.5.1). So, too, Spenser's characters (eg, in *FQ* I ix 3 and III iii 24), as well as his readers, undergo a process of coming to apprehend identities and destinies that ultimately lie beyond the action itself. It is precisely this epistemological dimension that establishes the significance of the action, of history both actual and poetic. The world is a theater (*Amoretti* 54), God's theater; and in it persons truly do act (*FQ* III iii 25), be they character, author, or reader, 'dilating' their beings (VII vii 58) and, if they read the signs faithfully, having revealed to them the very character and purposes of God. (See also *providence.)

DENNIS DANIELSON AND STEPHEN DE PAUL

---

gods and goddesses Spenser repudiates any literal belief in the divinity of the 'heathen Gods,' describing their worship as 'prophane' (*FQ* IV x 30) and their existence as 'fained' and 'invented' (xii 2, VII vii 46). Yet he venerates myths, the products of 'sage Antiquity' (II xii 48), as repositories of ancient learning, and believes them to have been devised by the earliest theologians and philosophers, 'antique wisards,' who imparted their wisdom under the veil of fiction. Their story of Venus' birth from the 'fomy sea' is on a literal level nothing more than a fable, but Spenser sees through the fiction to the scientific fact behind the myth, which for him expresses the natural phenomenon of the sea's abundant fertility (IV xii 1–2).

Spenser's treatment of Isis and Osiris (V vii 2–4) exhibits his attitude to myths more fully. Here he dismisses the trappings of ancient religious ceremonial, the 'altars,' 'temples,' and 'heavenly honours,' as the product of vulgar superstitious reverence, and concentrates on the factual basis of the myth. Osiris was not divine but a mortal, 'The justest man alive, and truest,' and therefore after his death was worshiped as a god. Many of the ancient gods, Spenser implies, were in reality men and women reverenced for their exceptional achievements and beneficence. Alternatively, their virtues might be regarded as divine: in this instance, Justice is 'a God of soveraine grace,' and Osiris is its personification and preeminent exemplar. In stanza 4, Spenser offers yet another interpretation: Osiris and Isis personify forces of nature, the sun and the moon. There is no sense of strain in explaining the myth first in euhemeristic, then in moral terms, and finally as a symbolic presentation of natural phenomena, for it accommodates all these interpretations, which were shaded 'cunningly' by the priests of the Temple. This metaphor of shading implies that such wisdom was delivered covertly – 'cunningly' may also suggest a deliberate subterfuge to keep the truth from the vulgar. If so, Spenser would seem to credit the theory that myths, like the Egyptian hieroglyphics, were veiled expressions of mysteries. This shrouding of knowledge is also alluded to in the Temple of Venus, where the priests 'labour'd to concele' the real meaning of the goddess' statue 'From peoples knowledge' (IV x 41). Nevertheless, what the myth-makers conveyed was essentially true though delivered in obscure and riddling fashion beneath a veil of fiction. The fables which embodied some edifying, factual truth concerning the secrets of nature, philosophy, or morality, were called 'physical,' since they had some firm, factual basis. Most of Spenser's myths are of this kind.

As for Osiris, gods may be no more than mortal men of great virtue and exceptional achievement. 'Famous men' and 'worthies of the earth' are 'made gods' because of 'their high merits and great dignitie' (IV iii 44). When Spenser has the Muse Calliope proclaim her 'powre to deifie' mortal men (*Teares* 460), what he means is that poetry has the resources to praise in the highest possible terms the excellence of those who deserve it most. Bacchus, Hercules, and Charlemagne are cited as notable examples. Those admired for excellent and unusual virtues are called gods or goddesses, or the sons or daughters of the gods, since they might be considered the inheritors of such perfection as could only spring from heaven itself. Thus Spenser's beloved mistress is styled 'a goddesse graced / With heavenly gifts from heven first enraced' (*FQ* VI x 25). Queen Elizabeth is frequently addressed as a 'Goddesse' or a 'Goddesse heavenly bright' because of her virtues. In *SC, Aprill* (50–4), she is provided with gods as her progenitors, because, as E.K. explains, the author 'could devise no parents in his judgement so worthy for her.'

Benefactors of humanity are similarly called gods. The ancient world made a god of anyone who contributed something to the betterment of life. E.K. repeats the story of the goddess Flora: she was 'a famous harlot' who 'made the people of Rome her heyre: who in remembraunce of so great beneficence, appointed a yearely feste for the memoriall of her, calling her, not as she was ... but Flora: making her the Goddesse of all floures' (*SC, March* 16 gloss). Elsewhere the gods are described as the authors of some beneficial discovery: Apollo is both the 'King of Leaches' (physicians) and the 'god of Poets' (III iv 41, IV xii 25; VII vii 12); Jove is the exemplar of 'true justice' and 'righteous lore' (V vii 1). Similarly, anything excellently done is seen as the work of the gods: the task of describing the sovereign's glory is seen as a task 'worthy of great *Phoebus* rote' (II x 3); works of exceptional industry and outstanding craftsmanship are seen as wrought by Vulcan, the artificer of the gods (see *Bellay* 4.11, *Muiopotmos* 369–74, *FQ* IV v 4).

In other cases, some exceptionally potent force, for good or evil, might be called a god (see Cicero *De natura deorum* 2.23.61). Genius, who is a 'celestiall powre,' was wisely made a god by 'sage Antiquity' (*FQ* II xii 47–8). Love deserves the godhead bestowed upon him by 'Antiquitie,' because it 'over mortall minds' has 'so great might' (*FQ* III iii 2). In recognition of this might, many gods are given ensigns of power: Jove a thunderbolt, Neptune a trident, Diana a bow and arrows.

As in the 'well invented' myth of Venus' birth, many fables of the gods can properly be understood only as poetic allegories of nature, and the gods as personifications of natural order. Spenser divides these gods into two categories: 'those that are sprung of heavenly seed,' and those that 'fill' this earth, who 'rule both sea and land unto their will' (VII vii 3). In the first category, the 'heavenly Powers,' are the planets: the Moon (called Cynthia), Mercury, Venus, the Sun (also called Apollo or Phoebus), Mars, Saturn, and Jove (see 50–3). These dwell in '*Joves* eternall hous' (III iv 51) or 'high in heaven' (I iv 11), and are ruled by 'heavens king' (I v 43, VII vii 1), 'sky-ruling Jove' (VI x 22). In this class, we might also include the zodiacal signs, such as Astraea and the lesser attendant divinities of heaven: the Muses, the Graces, and the Hours.

Spenser distributes the sublunary sphere among those deities who have 'rule and soveraintly' over the elements: Vulcan of fire, Vesta of 'the fire aethereall,' Ops 'of the earth,' Juno 'of the Ayre,' Neptune 'of Seas,' and the Nymphs 'of Rivers all' (VII vii 26). Well might he say that deities 'fill' the created world, when we consider the catalogue of all the 'watry Gods' and the fifty 'daughters of old *Nereus*' (IV xi 11–53), the rustic deities, Pan, Sylvanus, the fauns and satyrs, Diana and her crew of 'wooddy Nymphes,' and Aeolus, who helps control the realm of air by keeping his winds in 'his hidden threasure' (ix 23).

Spenser's mythology not only covers the created universe but traces the creation back to its first beginnings in primeval darkness to discern 'the secrets of the world unmade' (I v 22). Here Daemogorgon, 'Prince of darknesse' (i 37), presides accompanied by Aeternitie (II iv 41) and 'The hideous *Chaos*' (IV ii 47), and Cybele, mother of the gods (xi 28). From these are born Night and Erebus, the 'sonne of *Aeternitie*' (II iv 41), and Earth, 'great *Chaos* child,' 'Grandmother magnifide / Of all the Gods' (VII vi 26). From these 'Stygian gods' spring the principles of darkness, evil, and confusion in the universe: the Fates, daughters of Erebus and Night (*SC, Nov* 148 gloss), who 'weave the direfull threds of destinie' (*Daphnaïda* 17); the Furies, 'the Authours of all evill and mischiefe' (*SC, Nov* 164 gloss); Ate, the goddess of discord; Philotime, whom the envious gods cast from heaven (*FQ* II vii 49); and the giants, 'th'Earths cursed seed' (VII vi 20), the forces of rebellion and confusion, who war against the celestial gods.

The gods and goddesses in Spenser's poetry range from the depths of hell to the heights of heaven. They were inherited only in part from the classical poets, for classical, medieval, and Renaissance works of moral philosophy, natural science, theology, antiquarianism, and literary criticism shaped his attitudes to them and made them fit vehicles for his own moral and cosmological allegory. JOHN MANNING

Golding, Arthur (1536–1606) Prolific Elizabethan translator, best known for his vivid, colloquial rendering of Ovid's *Metamorphoses* (1565, 1567); also translated Caesar's *Commentaries* (1565), sermons by Calvin, and many religious tracts from the continent. Golding belongs to the generation of translators immediately prior to Spenser who rendered the Latin classics into English.

Spenser and Golding both secured patronage from the Earl of Leicester, but there is no evidence that they knew each other. Golding has been identified with 'Palemon' (*Colin Clout* 396–9), but this dubious honor seems to belong instead to Thomas Churchyard (*Var* 7:469). An indirect link between Spenser and Golding occurs outside the Ovidian context. In his one original piece, *A Discourse upon the Earthquake*, Golding, like other pamphleteers (including Churchyard and Anthony Munday), maintained that the tremor which shook London on 6 April 1580 was a divine omen. In *Three Proper Letters* 2, Harvey ridicules the conclusion of these 'counterfaite, and reasonlesse *Orphei*' (*Var Prose* p 459) and argues for a natural cause. Topical interest in this controversy is partly responsible for publication of the Spenser-Harvey correspondence.

Close scrutiny of Ovidian imitations in *The Faerie Queene* fails to show that Golding's translation had a significant influence on Spenser's poetry. For example, the house of Morpheus is the first major imitation of the *Metamorphoses* in *The Faerie Queene* (I i 39–44); but instead of using Golding's text, Spenser amplifies material from Ovid's eleventh book with Chaucerian and classical analogues. Unlike Shakespeare, whose writing reflects a familiarity with both Ovid's original phrasing and Golding's English rendering, Spenser is unaffected by his contemporary's diction. Indeed, even though the two are remarkably flexible in their use of language, their most characteristic modes are antithetical. Golding excels in manipulating a racy vernacular, while Spenser cultivates an elevated, slightly archaic style.

In spite of their independence, however, *The Faerie Queene* shows certain philosophical parallels to Golding's dedicatory Epistle to Leicester (Bennett 1932). The description of the Garden of Adonis blends Genesis and Platonism at III vi 34, as Golding had done (Epistle 354–8). Spenser's subsequent account of birth as the combination of form and substance (stanzas 36–7) can also be found in the Epistle 346–54.

Golding's *Metamorphoses* and Spenser's *Faerie Queene* are both important contributions to the medieval *Ovide moralisé* tradition, which systematically expanded allegorical passages in Ovid and emphasized the didactic import of his text. Both are also contributions to the larger humanistic goal of translating and emulating classical texts in the vernacular. Yet the language of Golding's 'English Ovid' is distinctly British; for example, he renders Roman minor gods (*dii*) as *elves* and uses the words *Nymph* and *Fairie* interchangeably. His precedent anticipates the fusion of classical and Celtic sources characteristic of Spenser's poetry. JAMES P. BEDNARZ

Louis Thorn Golding 1937 *An Elizabethan Puritan: Arthur Golding* (New York); Ovid ed 1904; Ovid 1965 *Ovid's Metamorphoses* tr Arthur Golding, ed John Frederick Nims (New York).

Googe, Barnabe (1540–94) A poet, translator, and a gentleman in rank whose work and life anticipate and parallel Spenser's in several ways. His *Eglogs, Epytaphes, and Sonettes* (1563) is the first collection of short personal poems in modern English to be published by a single author in his own lifetime, and the work can be seen as giving a precedent for the gentleman poet to publish. Sheidley sees Googe as 'more a professional writer than a courtly amateur,' though one less dedicated to poetry as a primary occupation than was Spenser (1981:117).

Apart from Barclay's, his eclogues are the only earlier English analogue to *The Shepheardes Calender*. Their unifying theme of the problems and dangers of love is explored through discussions between older and younger shepherds, through narratives of the unhappy experiences of Dametas, Faustus, and Selvagia, and through the contrast of human and divine love. The pastoral frame of seasons and animals reinforces the theme, and the familiar criticism of urban pride, vice, and cruelty comments on contemporary ecclesiastical problems. In combining the moralistic attitudes of Mantuan with translations from the Arcadian romance of Montemayor, Googe paves the way for the synthesis of different pastoral modes which Helen Cooper sees as giving *The Shepheardes Calender* 'its inherent excitement' (1977:154). (Greenlaw 1911:426–7 sees Googe's eclogues as an influence not only on *The Shepheardes Calender* but also on *Colin Clout*, *Heavenly Beautie*, *Heavenly Love*, and *Mother Hubberd*.)

In 'Cupido Conquered' in the same volume, Googe combines the old forms of dream allegory and the battle of vices and virtues, together with borrowings from Ovid and Montemayor, to show the Muses rewarding the Renaissance poet with a vision of conquered love. Googe's poetic self-consciousness, and his efforts to explore for his own time questions that had engaged Chaucer in his dream-visions, provide a useful preview of Spenser's experiments in *The Shepheardes Calender* and other minor poems. His vivid picture of the great lubber Excess, with his nose like a turkey cock, is not unworthy of some of Spenser's more grotesque figures, such as the crane-gaited Disdain of *FQ* VI. Another of his original poems, 'The Ship of Safegarde' (1569), an allegory of the voyage through the sea of life, in general type and in many details is suggestive of Guyon's voyage to the Bower of Bliss (*FQ* II xii). It incorporates a lengthy quotation from Chaucer's translation of the *Romance of the Rose* describing the image of Pope Holy, an instance both of his reverence for 'learned Chaucer that gem of Poetrie' (sig D7v), and of the Elizabethan view of Chaucer as an early voice of the Reformation.

The work which Googe seems to have considered his chief contribution to learning and poetry, and for which he is most often praised by his contemporaries (among them Gabriel Harvey) is his translation of Palingenius' *Zodiake of Life*. He published the first three books in 1560, the first six in 1561, all twelve in 1565, and a revised edition in 1576, reprinted in 1588. Tuve has argued that Spenser knew and echoed Googe's translation, finding it congenial both in matter and manner: 'it fulfilled the high function of Christian philosophical poetry; it treated of great matters – of God, Nature and Man: his end on earth, his temptations, his virtues, and his possible helps. And it presented these in ways which Spenser approved of and often used – astronomical framework, didactic allegory, quests, dream-visions, gardens-of-love, and all the familiar devices of mediaeval romance' (1935:19). The prefatory and dedicatory material shows Googe intensely concerned with the calling and function of the poet: of particular interest in the 1560 edition are the poetic preface describing the vision of the Muses and the amusingly deprecatory poem 'The Translatour to the Reader,' and in the 1561 edition, the epistle to his kinsman and patron Cecil (later Lord Burghley) which provides an embryonic poetic manifesto perhaps akin to the concerns that prompted Spenser to write 'The English Poete.' Like Spenser, Googe enjoyed mottos and emblems, and the final word of the 1565 *Zodiake*, 'Non nobis Domine sed nomini tuo' (not unto us, O Lord, but unto thy name [be the glory]), is in the spirit of 'Merce non mercede' at the close of *The Shepheardes Calender* (see J.M. Kennedy 1980).

Googe's two other major translations also show parallels with Spenser's activities. His translation of Kirchmeyer's violently antipapist poem *The Popish Kingdome* (1570), like the *Theatre for Worldlings* in 1569, is dedicated to Queen Elizabeth. This volume included two books of Kirchmeyer's 'Spirituall Husbandrie'; in his next translation, Googe turned his attention to this earth, with Heresbach's *Foure Bookes of Husbandry* (1577). It is pleasant to think that Spenser could have found this practical, readable, and frequently reprinted handbook useful in managing Kilcolman. Through its translation of verses from Virgil's *Eclogues* and *Georgics* (interspersed with advice on how to get rid of moss in pastures and the pip in chickens) and through Googe's personal additions, it gives a charming picture of gentlemanly rural life.

Googe served three times in Ireland. On the two later occasions (1582–3, 1584–5), Spenser was also there and probably knew both Googe and Barnaby Rich, for whose *Allarme to England* (1578) Googe wrote a prefatory epistle, warning that without 'skilfull and well trayned souldiers,' England would follow the course of Rome, which remains 'a spectacle of miserable ruine to the universall world' (cf *Complaints*).

Like Spenser, Googe was gentleman, scholar, and poet, intensely Protestant, dedicated to serving his country through both his writings and his actions. His writings show a sound classical training combined with a lively interest in current continental literature and in the native English tradition, particularly Chaucer. The claim made by Saintsbury a hundred years ago is large, but still contains truth, that 'without the study and experiments which Googe represents Spenser could not have existed' (1887:27). JUDITH M. KENNEDY

Mark Eccles 1985 'Barnaby Googe in England, Spain, and Ireland' *ELR* 15:353–70; J.M. Kennedy 1980; George Saintsbury 1887 *A History of Elizabethan Literature* (London); Sheidley 1981; Tuve 1935.

Gosson, Stephen (1554–1624) Humanist and Protestant critic of poetry; also an actor, dramatist, and author of a romance. He was educated at the King's School, Canterbury, and Corpus Christi College, Oxford, where he studied under John Rainolds. From 1584, he was a preacher for the established church and was awarded some of the most lucrative livings in and around London.

His most popular work is *The Schoole of Abuse* (1579). Published the same year as *The Shepheardes Calender*, it is a pamphlet addressed both to 'Gentlemen that favour learning' and to 'all that wyll follow vertue' (title page). Stressing music and drama, Gosson argues that poetry should instruct by presenting only virtuous models of action; abusive art arouses emotions and suggests or teaches evil. Immoderation and the misuse of reason should be avoided in drama, or else plays must be abandoned altogether. Metaphor helps Gosson to restate his arguments that poetry should awaken thoughtful response, teach right and wrong, point out correct modes of behavior, expose ill practices, and warn of future threats by acknowledging hidden dangers. He dedicated the work to Sidney, as someone who would agree with such moral precepts.

But Gosson's pamphlet was often misconstrued, and to many it seemed to attack all poetry indiscriminately. Spenser wrote to Harvey in 1579 that 'Newe Bookes I heare of none, but only of one, that writing a certaine Booke, called *The Schoole of Abuse*, and dedicating it to Maister *Sidney*, was for hys labor scorned: if at leaste it be in the goodnesse of that nature to scorne. Suche follie is it, not to regarde aforehande the inclination and qualitie of him, to whome wee dedicate oure Bookes' (*Two Letters* 1, *Var Prose* p 6). Sidney, like Spenser, misunderstood Gosson, and wrote his *Defence of Poetry* partly in reply (c 1580, printed 1595). Through jest, parody, and oblique counterstatements, Sidney attempts a full response; but he is unable to answer Gosson's chief complaint that if a work portrays both good and evil, given mankind's fallen nature, there is no assurance the reader will choose the good.

Gosson stated his position more clearly in *An Apologie of the Schoole of Abuse* (also 1579 and dedicated to Sidney). *Playes Confuted in Five Actions* (1582), his best work, argues against drama by examining it through each of the four Aristotelian causes; here the argument is more scholastic than humanist. Spenser may have sensed this line of development in Gosson's thought when he dismissed his first work. In fact, however, both *The Shepheardes Calender* and *The Faerie Queene* support the moral program for poetry set forth by *The Schoole of Abuse*; and in requiring poetry to serve a moral purpose, Gosson also anticipates the indestructibility of an Archimago, a Grill, or a Blatant Beast, so that didactic poetry is forever possible. ARTHUR F. KINNEY

Stephen Gosson 1579a *An Apologie of the Schoole of Abuse* appended to his *Ephemerides of Phialo* (London; rpt New York and London 1973) pp 80–[94]; Gosson 1579b *The S[c]hoole of Abuse* (London; rpt Amsterdam and New York 1972, New York and London 1973); Gosson 1582 *Playes Confuted in Five Actions* (London; rpt New York and London 1972).

J. Bronowski 1939 *The Poet's Defence: The Concept of Poetry from Sidney to Yeats* (Cambridge); Arthur F. Kinney 1967 'Stephen Gosson's Art of Argumentation in *The Schoole of Abuse*' *SEL* 7:41–54; Kinney 1972 'Parody and Its Implications in Sydney's *Defense of Poesie*' *SEL* 12:1–19; Kinney 1974 *Markets of Bawdrie: The Dramatic Criticism of Stephen Gosson* (Salzburg) with texts of the critical writings, and notes; William R. Orwen 1937 'Spenser and Gosson' *MLN* 52:574–6; William A. Ringler, Jr 1942 *Stephen Gosson: A Biographical and Critical Study* (Princeton).

Gower, John (1330–1408) The extent of Gower's influence on Spenser is an open question, since Spenser refers to him neither directly, as he does to Chaucer, nor even obliquely, as he does to Langland. (Initially he may have been attracted to him by Chaucer's dedication of *Troilus and Criseyde* to 'moral Gower' [5.1856].) Nevertheless, there is much circumstantial evidence to indicate that he knew and used the *Confessio Amantis*, and perhaps other poems by Gower. Black-letter editions of the *Confessio* were readily available: William Caxton's of 1483, and Thomas Berthelet's of 1532 and 1554. (There may have been a 1544 edition by Berthelette, but no copy survives.) Very likely it was in one of these printed volumes that Spenser's friend Harvey discovered 'sage Master Gower' (Harvey ed 1884:134).

Spenser may also have read the *Confessio* in one of the many manuscripts circulating in the sixteenth century, some of which can be traced to his acquaintances, and not impossibly one to his own hand: Anne Russell, a dedicatee of *Fowre Hymnes*, owned the manuscript now in the Bodleian (Bodley 902), among the sixteenth-century annotations of which appears one bracketed 'Spenserus' (Tuve 1940:152 and 1964; her claim is not generally accepted: see *handwriting). Two other manuscripts (BL, Royal Ms 18.C.22 and CUL, Mm.2.21) were in the possession of Margaret Stanley, sister of George Clifford, Earl of Cumberland, to whom a dedicatory sonnet to *The Faerie Queene* is addressed and whose wife was one of the dedicatees of *Fowre Hymnes*.

Spenser is further linked to Gower by his contemporaries. E.K. notes in his gloss to *SC, Julye* 177 that *glitterand* is 'a Participle used sometime in Chaucer, but altogether in J. Goore.' In his *Garden of Eloquence* (1593), Henry Peacham connects the onomatopoeia of the *Calender* with the work of Chaucer and Gower (*Sp All* p 34; see also pp 72, 137–8, 158).

Gower may have influenced Spenser in three ways. First, like him, he was a poet who recognized the reforming power of moral narrative. More didactic than Chaucer in applying his tales to moral ends, and doubtless more polished, from Spenser's point of view, than Langland, Gower would have provided Spenser a valuable precursor in his national tradition. Again like Spenser, and certainly unlike Chaucer, he wrote poetry of social purpose, addressed to the great figures of the kingdom, replete with political analysis and advice about just government of soul and state only lightly veiled under fiction.

Second, Gower's attempt to reshape his sources imaginatively, melding versions and inventing new details and new myths when it suited him, is analogous in purpose and scope to Spenser's. Behind the moral method of *Mother Hubberds Tale*, Gower's legacy is visible; and insofar as *The Faerie Queene* must be read not simply as a collection of exempla but rather as a didactic fantasy – a category of writing characteristic of the Italians and one which C.S. Lewis sought to isolate in Gower and Spenser from their similar understandings of 'the fairy way of writing' and 'romantic epic' (1936:210, 299–305) – Spenser's poem resembles Gower's *Confessio Amantis* on the related levels of conception and execution.

Third, Gower may have influenced Spenser in specific passages. His Anglo-Norman *Mirour* 841–948 may have suggested the procession of the deadly sins in *FQ* I iv: there are suggestive similarities between the animals that the sins ride, the object each carries, and the malady each endures. The Genius of the *Confessio* may be the direct source for Spenser's Genius, though Spenser was doubtless acquainted as well with the *Romance of the Rose* and the *De planctu Naturae* of Alanus de Insulis.

At times Spenser seems to have been influenced by Gower and Chaucer jointly. For example, his source for the house of Morpheus in *FQ* I i was Ovid's *Metamorphoses*, as it was for both Chaucer (*Book of the Duchess* 153–94) and Gower (*Confessio* 4.2989–3033); and in the lines of all three English poets, one can hear the same soporific meters, rhymes, and diction working toward an identical effect. Again, Spenser's anatomy of true gentilesse at *FQ* VI iii echoes Chaucer's *Wife of Bath's Tale* (*CT* III 1170), but may have been influenced by Gower's version of the loathly lady story, his 'Tale of Florent' (*Confessio* 1.1407–882), which makes a point about pride and humility that affirms and illuminates Chaucer's discourse, and would have sharpened the moral issue for Spenser had he known both versions. Also, Spenser's continuation of Chaucer's *Squire's Tale* in *FQ* IV iii has further connections with Gower's version of the Canacee story (*Confessio* 3.142–360), which, unlike Chaucer's, is brought to a conclusion.

The punishment of Mirabella (*FQ* VI vi) may derive from Gower's 'Tale of Rosiphelee' (*Confessio* 4.1244–1446), the most likely immediate source for Spenser's version of the story of the 'purgatory of cruel beauties' (see Neilson 1900:89–90, Tonkin 1972:87). Una's lament at her unkind desertion by Redcrosse and the more generous treatment of wild beasts in *FQ* I vii may draw upon *Confessio* 5.5424–6 (or upon Chaucer's *Legend of Good Women* 2198). Other interesting parallels are Arthur's strange slothfulness when overcome by Maleger (*FQ* II xi 31; cf *Confessio* 4.3389–3423); Artegall's overpowering pity for Radigund and its dire consequences, which likely have as background Gower's carefully developed royal virtue of hardiness, a manly forcefulness neither sanguinary nor yielding (*FQ* V vii; cf *Confessio* 7.3572ff); Paridell's rape of Hellenore (*FQ* III x), with its analogue in Scudamour's leading Amoret out of the Temple of Venus (*FQ* IV x), both of which may be indebted to Gower's account of Paris' rape of Helen from Venus' temple (*Confessio* 5.7469–590), told as an example of sacrilege, a sub-sin of avarice (Nohrnberg 1976:271, 318, 383, 641).

Despite Spenser's silence about Gower, then, it is possible that he read the *Confessio Amantis* and found matter in it of some importance. In temper, in tastes in reading, even to some degree in habits of life (for Gower, too, was a partly public man who yet loved privacy), Spenser had much about him that we recognize in Gower from his life and works. Both men found life a strenuous, though worthwhile, enterprise; both were sparing in their use of irony; both hoped to reform their nation through a poetry addressed to sovereign and sinners alike. In the growing Elizabethan consciousness of literary historicity, Spenser may have found in Gower a subtle, morally unexceptionable poetic intelligence that he could claim as kindred, depend upon as probative source, and ultimately supersede as the greatest reforming fabulist of English letters.

R.F. YEAGER

Gower 1899–1902 *Complete Works* ed G.C. Macaulay, 4 vols (Oxford) is the standard edition. There is a valuable introduction to the *Confessio Amantis* in the 1968 abridged edition of Russell A. Peck (New York). A useful survey of the reception of the author and his text is Derek Pearsall 1983 'The Gower Tradition' in *Gower's 'Confessio Amantis': Responses and Reassessments* ed A.J. Minnis (Cambridge) pp 179–97. The manuscript tradition is treated in Macaulay's edition and by John H. Fisher 1964 *John Gower: Moral Philosopher and Friend of Chaucer* (New York) pp 303–12. On Gower and Chaucer, see J.A. Burrow 1971 *Ricardian Poetry: Chaucer, Gower, Langland and the 'Gawain' Poet* (London); Russell A. Peck 1978 *Kingship and Common Profit in Gower's 'Confessio Amantis'* (Carbondale, Ill); and further Lewis 1936; Lewis 1967; John Livingston Lowes 1914 'Spenser and the *Mirour de l'Omme*' *PMLA* 29:388–452; William Allan Neilson 1900 'The Purgatory of Cruel Beauties' *Ro* 29:85–93; Renwick 1925; Tonkin 1972; R.F. Yeager 1987 '*Pax Poetica*: On the Pacifism of Chaucer and Gower' *SAC* 9:97–121.

Graces (Gr *Charites*, L *Gratiae*) In Greek and Roman antiquity, the Graces personified grace in person, social behavior, and moral action (see esp Pindar *Olympian Odes* 14.5–7). Usually three in number, although sometimes referred to singly or in great numbers (as hundreds of Graces), they bestowed beauty, nobility, skill, and wisdom on human beings. Spenser writes that 'all gracious gifts' come from them, 'Which decke the body or adorne the mynde' (*FQ* VI x 23). They are often pictured joined in a dance with linked hands: as the Renaissance mythographers describe them, two Graces facing and the third turned away; as Spenser describes them, 'two of them still froward ... But one still towards' (24). In *De beneficiis* 1.3–4, Seneca says they are symbols of liberality or generosity, their dance signifying the giving, receiving, and returning of favors or benefits. E.K., in his gloss to *SC, Aprill* 109, follows Senecan tradition by seeing them as representations of the 'three sundry Actions in liberalitye' (his gloss is probably taken from Thomas Cooper 1565, in turn from the *Dictionarium* of Charles Estienne 1561). For Spenser, their dance signifies 'That good should from us goe, then come in greater store' (VI x 24). Although classical poets usually describe the Graces dancing clothed, the mythographers (eg, Boccaccio *Genealogia* 5.35 and Conti *Mythologiae* 4.15) say they dance naked, their nudity indicating open and honest dealing. Spenser, following Conti and Cartari, says they are mild, gentle, and always smiling, and also naked 'that without guile / Or false dissemblaunce all them plaine may see' (VI x 24).

Homer mentions a single Grace, but Hesiod (*Theogony* 907–11), Spenser's probable source, names three: Aglaia, Thalia, and Euphrosyne, daughters of Zeus (Jove) by Eurynome, a daughter of Ocean, begotten, as Spenser adds, when Jove was returning from the wedding of Peleus and Thetis (VI x 22). The mythographers record different names and parentages for the Graces, as well as different numbers; E.K. mentions a fourth Grace, Pasithea, found in Homer. The names of the Graces have literal meanings: Aglaia, splendor, Thalia, prosperity or growth, Euphrosyne, happiness; but the triad was symbolically interpreted in Neoplatonic circles as beauty, love, and pleasure, beauty, intellect, and pleasure, or beauty, love, and chastity, interpretations which may have relevance to the triad of chaste ladies in *FQ* III and IV, Florimell, Amoret, and Belphoebe, two of whom (Florimell and Belphoebe), Spenser tells us, were nurtured by the Graces (IV v 5, III vi 2), and all of whom share the heritage of celestial or all comely grace (III vi 4, V iii 23; see Wind 1958, Geller 1976).

Sappho associates the Graces with Aphrodite (Venus), as does the Homeric Hymn to Pythian Apollo, which describes them dancing with linked arms with the Horae, Harmonia, and Hebe (194–6); in the *Cypria* (fragment in Athenaeus 15.682 D, F), the Graces are handmaids of Aphrodite. Renaissance mythographers picture them carrying Venus' symbols, the rose and the myrtle. Some say that Venus and Bacchus were the parents of the Graces, others that the heavenly Venus was the mother of both the Graces and the Hours (Seasons). Neoplatonic theory suggests that Venus as heavenly beauty gave birth to the Graces as the gift of divine love or bounty. In *Hymne of Beautie*, Spenser describes the thousands of Graces who attend the heavenly Venus to deck her beauty (253–66). Although at one point in *The Faerie Queene* he calls the Graces sisters to Cupid, hence daughters of Venus (II viii 6), elsewhere he makes them handmaidens of Venus and her associates on Mount Acidale, which he describes, as its name signifies, as a place free from all care (VI x 8–9). Greek tradition placed their earliest temple in the city of Orchomenus in Boeotia, where King Eteocles first instituted their worship and where the mythographers also locate the Acidalian mountain or spring (eg, Giraldi 13.30, Conti 4.15). Spenser makes Acidale a special retreat for Venus, where she reposed or sported with the Graces and where she left her cestus or girdle (IV v 5, VI x 9). Florimell was fostered there (IV v 5) and Calidore sees the Graces dancing and singing on Acidale to Colin's pipe (VI x 12).

Ancient poets identify the Muses as associates and sister goddesses of the Graces. Hesiod places the Muses' homes and dancing-places next to those of the Graces and Himerus (Desire), with whom they live in delight (*Theogony* 64–5). Pindar invokes both throughout his odes and describes the Graces in *Olympian Odes* 14 as queens of song and orderers of the festivals in heaven and on earth. As fellow patronesses of the arts, both Graces and Muses are connected with Apollo, the god of poetry and music; the mythographers picture the Muses at his side and the Graces, as was true of the ancient statue of the god at Delos (Callimachus *Aetia* 114), dancing in his right hand. He is the leader of the Muses, as Mercury (Hermes) is of the Graces. In *SC, Aprill* and *June*, the Graces dance to the musical accompaniment of the Muses. In *FQ* VI, Spenser joins the Graces and the Muses as inspirers of poetic composition. The Muses, invoked in the proem, guide and assist the poet; in canto x, the Graces prompt him while he creates his song.

Repeatedly, Spenser describes the Graces not only as handmaidens of Venus but also as attendants on earthly ladies of great beauty or position. In *Aprill*, both Muses and Graces wait on Eliza, who becomes a 'fourth' Grace. The three Graces are among the bride's attendants in *Epithalamion*, who sing and dance to her and array her in their own graces (103–8, 257–8). In the parodic epithalamion of *FQ* I i 48, the Graces in Redcrosse's dream sing and dance while bringing Una to his bed. Many 'graces' attend the chaste ladies of *The Faerie Queene*, and the three Graces themselves come to attend Colin's love, the simple country lass, and encircle her with their dance, as they in turn are surrounded by 'An hundred naked maidens lilly white, / All raunged in a ring' (VI x 11–12). Employing once more the tradition of the fourth Grace used in *Aprill*, a tradition dating from Callimachus' epigram honoring Queen Berenice as a fourth Grace (52), Spenser describes Colin's love as 'a goddesse graced / With heavenly gifts' (VI x 25): 'Another Grace she well deserves to be, / In whom so many Graces gathered are' (27). To describe his beloved in *Amoretti*, Spenser adapts a classical description attributed to the legendary poet Musaeus and cited both by E.K. (*June* 25 gloss) and Conti (4.15); describing Hero, Musaeus says that her smiling eye begets a hundred graces. Spenser adapts this as 'on each eyelid sweetly doe appeare / an hundred Graces as in shade to sit' (*Am* 40).

Whereas throughout Spenser's poetry the Graces personify feminine beauty, charm, and graciousness, they become in *FQ* VI the emblem for the virtue courtesy. Calidore's vision of the Graces in canto x demonstrates that true courtesy is a heavenly gift both of body and of mind. There the Graces not only sing sweetly and dance, not only serve as handmaidens to human and divine beauty, but also instruct human beings in friendly offices that bind man to man: 'They teach us, how to each degree and kynde / We should our selves demeane, to low, to hie; / To friends, to foes, which skill men call Civility' (23). STELLA P. REVARD

For the gloss to *SC, Aprill* 109, see W.P. Mustard 1930 'E.K.'s Note on the Graces' *MLN* 45:168–9. Excellent background is also given in DeWitt T. Starnes 1942, showing Spenser's reliance on the dictionaries: 'Spenser and the Muses' *TexSE* 22:31–58. See also Gerald Snare 1971 'Spenser's Fourth Grace' *JWCI* 34:350–5. For a general history of the image, see Wind 1958, ch 2; see also Geller 1976.

Grantorto (Ital 'great wrong') The giant from whom Artegall, the knight of Justice, must free Irena in *FQ* V – a task for which he is chosen in canto i 4 and which he accomplishes in canto xii. The magnitude of the lawlessness he represents is suggested by his name, with the specifically legal resonance of *tort*, a wrong or injury to a person or property. He oppresses and disinherits Irena (Gr *eirēnē* 'peace'; cf *Ierne*, the classical name of Ireland). His gigantic stature places him in a tradition of lawless giants such as those of Genesis 6, glossed by the Geneva Bible as 'tyrants ... Which usurped autoritie over others,' and the rebellious and blasphemous Titans who threatened to cast Jove out of heaven (Ovid *Metamorphoses* 1.151–62). Artegall kills Grantorto with Chrysaor, the sword which Jove used to quell the Titans (i 9). Like the 'monstrous tyrants' that Hercules subdued with his 'club of Justice' (i 2), Grantorto is an embodiment of lawlessness and injustice. As the quest to free Irena frames Book V, so Grantorto himself provides a fitting culmination to the tyranny, rebelliousness, and blasphemy of all the other overmighty wrongdoers with whom the knight of Justice must deal.

In cantos xi and xii, Spenser gives the general moral significance of Grantorto a vivid and disturbing particularity for his sixteenth-century English readers by associating him with the combined threats of rebellion and Roman Catholic aggression in contemporary France and Ireland. The sequence of events evokes the sense of continual crisis which beset Protestant England in the 1580s and early 1590s. While Arthur defeats the Spanish threat in the Netherlands, Artegall goes to aid Irena (Ireland), spurred to a new urgency by the warnings of her representative, Sergis (xi 37). But before he can reach her, he must attend to Burbon's claim that Grantorto has defrauded him of his betrothed Flourdelis. The names point clearly to the crisis in France in the early 1590s in which England intervened with money and troops. The French throne was withheld from its legitimate possessor, the Protestant Henri (Bourbon) de Navarre, by the Catholic League, a rebellious faction within France aided by Spain. Grantorto represents this combination of usurpation, rebellion, and Spanish intervention (see *Geryoneo).

In canto xii, Grantorto again embodies the combined evils of tyranny, rebellion, and Roman Catholic aggression. The details of the episode closely echo Spenser's account of the Irish situation in *Vewe of Ireland*, which expresses attitudes widely held by his contemporaries. Irena dwells in a 'salvage Iland,' thrall to a tyrant whose injustices must be curbed by Artegall's sword (i 3, xi 38–9, xii 23). Through delay, her affairs have reached a point of crisis (xi 39–40). In *Vewe*, Spenser calls Ireland a 'salvage nacion,' oppressed by the depredations and rebelliousness of its own Catholic lords, often actively supported by the Pope and Spain (*Var Prose* pp 43, 161–2, 198). He advocates the use of martial law and accuses England of habitually failing to act with resolution, thus precipitating avoidable crises (pp 146–8). Grantorto's appearance, on foot wearing a shirt of mail with a steel cap and carrying a poleaxe, resembles contemporary descriptions of the mercenary Irish gallowglass soldiers (xii 14; cf *Vewe* p 123, Quinn 1966:40, 92). More specifically, the possible identification of Artegall with Lord Grey, Lord Deputy of Ireland from 1580 to 1582, associates Grantorto with the second Desmond rebellion (1579–83), which Spenser experienced at first hand and which was given papal and unofficial Spanish support. (For a contemporary identification of Grantorto as 'Giraldus Comes Desmond', see 'MS Notes' ed 1957:513.) On one occasion, the rebels marched into battle behind the papal banner (Holinshed ed 1807–8, 6:416).

The Elizabethan horrors of rebellion and of papal/Spanish aggression are combined in Grantorto, justly making him the culminating evil of Book V. But Artegall is not wholly successful in his confrontations, either with Burbon or with Grantorto. Burbon is rescued, but not before he has abandoned his shield; and his reconciliation with Flourdelis is far from complete. Artegall succeeds in killing Grantorto, but he is recalled before he can reform Irena's 'ragged common-weale' (xii 26–7) and then accused by Detraction of cruelty and treachery (xii 40), in an echo of contemporary complaints that effective officials in Ireland were recalled too early and were too often rewarded by ingratitude and blame (*Vewe* pp 159–60, 228). The harm worked by Grantorto cannot easily be undone. At the end of the Book of Justice, we are reminded of the pessimism, the insistence on the fallenness of 'present dayes, which are corrupted sore' (proem 3), with which Spenser began Book V. ELIZABETH HEALE

Iredale 1966; Knight 1970; 'MS Notes' ed 1957; Quinn 1966.

Gray, Thomas (1716–71) As a scholar, Gray was interested in Spenser. In his plan for a history of English poetry, he includes Spenser as an allegorical and romantic poet influenced by Ariosto and Tasso, and the 'school' of Spenser as including Drayton,

Phineas Fletcher, Phaer, and Milton. In a footnote to 'The Progress of Poesy,' he further specifies that 'Spenser imitated the Italian writers; Milton improved on them' (Lonsdale 1969, line 66n). In 'The Bard,' he refers to Spenser and the revival of poetry under the Tudors in the lines 'Fierce war and faithful love, / And truth severe by fairy fiction dressed' (126–7; cf *FQ* I proem 1). Spenser's metrical inventiveness provided much of the material for Gray's analyses of English meters ('Observations on English Metre' rpt in ed 1884, 1:325–60; Jones 1937:84–107; Martin 1934:220ff).

As a poet, however, Gray was not influenced by Spenser. He is Spenserian (and Miltonic) in believing that 'the language of the age is never the language of poetry' (ed 1935, 1:142), but his diction is never Spenserian. Any Spenserian words he uses occur also in Milton or Dryden, Pope or Thomson. He does not write 'Spenserian' poems, in the sense that in subject, form, mode, meter, or diction one feels the presence of the earlier poet. Though he read intensively and widely, his 'debts' are casual. Very occasionally, in a passage involving personification or allegory, one might suspect a Spenserian debt; but in the 'fury Passions' section of the 'Ode on ... Eton College' (61ff), for example, his debt is more immediately to Thomson's *Spring* and ultimately to the *Aeneid* (6.273–81), and possibly to Dryden, Pope, and Statius. Gray is conscious of competing with other poets who have listed the passions in this way; he is not merely under the influence of Spenser.

Yet Spenser was important to him. Norton Nicholls tells us that 'Spencer was among his favourite poets'; Gray 'never sat down to compose poetry without reading Spencer for a considerable time previously' (ed 1935, 3:1290). Presumably this experience attuned his ear to a rich rhythmic language, but the very small number of phrases (set out in detail in Lonsdale's edition) that might have been suggested by Spenser show that it was not for specific borrowings of diction or imagery that he was reading.

ARTHUR JOHNSTON

Thomas Gray 1884 *Works* ed Edmund Gosse, 4 vols (London); Gray 1935 *Correspondence* ed Paget Toynbee and Leonard Whibley, 3 vols (Oxford). William Powell Jones 1937 *Thomas Gray, Scholar* (Cambridge, Mass); Lonsdale 1969 (an edition of Gray, Collins, and Goldsmith); Roger Martin 1934 *Essai sur Thomas Gray* (Paris).

Greene, Robert (1558?-1592) Writer of prose fiction, playwright, and pamphleteer, Greene was a close contemporary of Spenser and like him was educated at Cambridge (BA St John's College 1580, MA Clare Hall 1583, MA from Oxford 1588). His short but varied literary career had begun by 1580, when his *Mamillia* was registered, the first of several euphuistic tales; it ended with a spate of colloquial prose pamphlets in the hectic months before his death. Some part of his literary life was spent in London where he formed friendships with writers such as Nashe, Lodge, Thomas Watson, and Peele and became notorious for his bohemian style of life. He antagonized Spenser's friend Gabriel Harvey by attacking his family and his use of hexameters, in the pamphlet *A Quip for an Upstart Courtier*, to which Harvey responded by defaming Greene after his death in *Foure Letters and Certaine Sonnets* (1592). Harvey disparagingly ascribes Greene's great popularity to the poor taste of readers who (because of his use of pastoral and chivalry) long above all for '*Greenes* Arcadia ... *Greenes* Faery Queene' (*Sp All* p 25).

Greene's literary success was largely due to his ability to cater to and extend the prevailing tastes of his time, both in his romances and in his pamphlets of prodigal life and the London underworld. His romances and plays were influenced more by the pastoralism of the 1580s in general than by any individual writer; but a possible allusion to *The Faerie Queene* in *Menaphon* (1589) suggests that he knew it before publication ('Our *Arcadian* Nimphs are faire and beautifull, though not begotten of the Suns bright rayes' *Sp All* p 12; cf *FQ* III vi 6), and the prologue to *Alphonsus, King of Aragon* (c 1587) might conceivably respond to the pessimistic view of the contemporary status of poetry expressed in *Teares of the Muses*. Other hints and allusions link Greene and Spenser as kindred figures in the Elizabethan literary world. Nashe in his preface to *Menaphon* praises Spenser along with Greene and others as true poets and scholars as contrasted to unlearned playwrights. The anonymous author of *Greenes Funeralls* (1594) imagines Spenser ('Colinet') paying tribute to the dead Greene; and Robert Allott, compiler of *Englands Parnassus* (1600), ascribes to Greene three passages from Spenser (the opening lines of *Mother Hubberd* and two short sections from *Virgils Gnat*).

SANDRA S. CLARK

Greene ed 1881–6; Greene ed 1905; René Pruvost 1938 *Robert Greene et ses romans (1558–1592)* (Paris).

Greville, Fulke, first Lord Brooke (1554–1628) We have no record of direct personal contact between Greville and Spenser, a somewhat surprising fact given that Greville was Sidney's closest friend and that Spenser was associated with the Sidney circle. In his 1580 letter to Gabriel Harvey, Spenser claims 'some use of familiarity' with Sidney and Sir Edward Dyer (*Two Letters* 1, *Var Prose* p 6). He does not mention Greville, though we know from one of Sidney's poems that Greville, Sidney, and Dyer were members of a 'happy blessed Trinitie' who wrote and talked about poetry together (Sidney ed 1962:260). Greville may have been abroad during the period referred to by Spenser, when Sidney and Dyer were eagerly pursuing experiments in classical scansion – a major topic of the Spenser-Harvey letters, but one for which Greville, apparently, had little enthusiasm. He did, however, include two such experiments in *Caelica* (6 and 37). If Spenser missed Greville at that time, he might have met him through his acquaintance with Samuel Daniel, who early in his career was a member of the Countess of Pembroke's household. Spenser encouraged Daniel in this early period; later, Greville too became an important figure in Daniel's life, offering him practical support when he left Wilton and exerting a lasting intellectual influence on his poetic outlook. Whether or not Spenser and Greville met, Sidney's interest alone would certainly have been enough to ensure that Greville would be attentive to the career and aspirations of this socially humbler but greatly gifted 'new Poete.'

A consideration of Greville's work and intentions as a poet alongside Spenser's reveals some piquant contrasts. Spenser sought deliberately to enlarge the scope and increase the capabilities of English poetry; so did Greville, but in a very different way. For Spenser, poetry is a self-justifying activity; but for Greville, poetry and music are 'Arts of Recreation.' They are not 'pretious in their proper kind' but only in their application. The highest function of words is 'not to flatter, or beseech, / Insinuate, or perswade'; rather, it is to declare, as forcefully and directly as possible, 'What things in Nature good, or evill are' (*A Treatie of Humane Learning* ed 1939, stanzas 110–15). 'O what an honor is it, to restraine / The lust of lawlesse youth with good advice,' Piers exclaims to Cuddie (*SC, October* 21–2); but the sort of influence which he describes the poet as having – holding his audience spellbound by the enchantments of his verse – is not the influence which Greville seeks. Rather, he strives to distinguish good and evil in their proper natures and as they appear in deceptive guises in the world of mortals. This for him is an activity which demands a strenuous and sustained intellectual exertion on the part of both poet and reader, with few appeals to sensory pleasure or emotional warmth. During Sidney's lifetime, Greville made some concessions to the 'golden' world of poetry, and handled with skill and even charm the love rhetoric of the day. Yet even at his most courtly, in the first 76 poems of the *Caelica* sequence, the wit is frequently biting, and the gaze turned on the love situations is often sardonic. *Caelica* 3 which has close links with *Amoretti* 8 is among the exceptions.

Several poems in *Caelica* appear to be companion poems to sonnets in Sidney's *Astrophil and Stella*, and the pairings tend to show Greville making ironic comments on Astrophil's sanguine claims for the values of romantic love. Later works give stronger expression to Greville's belief that this world is a place to be endured not enjoyed, and that hope of salvation in another life lies only in keeping one's sense of spiritual absolutes uncontaminated by worldly taint. 'All worlds glorie is but drosse uncleane,' Spenser writes in *Amoretti* 27. He shares Greville's Puritan insistence on 'frayle corruption, that doth flesh ensew' (*Amoretti* 79) but tempers it with a belief that human love and beauty can be sanctified by divine blessing. Thus, at the beginning of *FQ* IV, he engages in a defense of love against detractors who complain that he makes too much of it.

In Greville, however, the Puritan insistence on corruption is accompanied by a sharp sense of the deep division between this world's values and those of the spiritual kingdom; and it is tempered only by a belief that those who are not among the front rank of the elect (those who 'livinge in the world, yet of it are not,' according to *A Treatise of Religion* ed 1965, stanza III) must both 'know the world and believe in God' (as Greville said of himself). In other words, those excluded from the special band of 'Gods owne elect' have a duty to study the world and master its ways in order to achieve whatever degree of truth, compromised as it may be, is possible to our fallen natures.

Spenser's language is a rich amalgam of direct and indirect reference to a background of learning and well-pondered moral concerns, together with visual and musical delight in abundance. Greville's language is also distinctive; and on the theme of personal and national sin and the need of grace, he can write with power and fully charged feeling. More typically, the language of his poems written after Sidney's death is elliptical and knotty, forcefully and rigorously analyzing themes such as fame and honor, war, or the political constitution of states. At its most impressive, as in his Senecan drama *Mustapha*, it becomes a form of double statement, a palimpsest. On the most obvious level, the play is an account of human passion and ambition; but running through it as an under-writing is a commentary on human behavior in terms of the demands of supernatural law. The double meaning of the language exposes the 'wearisome condition of humanity' in all its weakness, contradiction, and futility. Such work engages the whole power of Greville's temperament. He was a man who both thought and felt deeply about his experiences as private individual and public figure, and the combination of energies produces remarkable effects. His epitaph, composed by himself, is both striking and characteristic: 'Fulke Greville, Servant to Queene Elizabeth, Concellor to King James, and Frend to Sir Philip Sidney. Trophaeum Peccati' (Rees 1971:25).

Sidney encouraged Spenser and praised *The Shepheardes Calender*. He was intimate with Greville from boyhood and, for Greville's part, their friendship was probably the relationship which meant most to him in the whole course of his long life. Both Spenser and Greville owed a debt to that humane and cultivated young man who prized poetry as worthy of 'the highest estimation of learning' (*Defence of Poetry*) and thought it a better teacher than history or philosophy. The ways in which their poetry developed after the early Sidneyan influence are nevertheless sharply divergent. We cannot know whether Sidney himself, had he lived, would have been drawn more to the richness of Spenser or to the austere world view of Greville. What is certain is that, whatever our final assessment of their respective achievements, Spenser and Greville are both resonant voices from the late-Elizabethan world (though Greville lived into the reign of Charles I, his Elizabethan experiences color all that came later); and no account of the period and its poetry can be complete unless it makes full recognition of both.

JOAN REES

Fulke Greville ed 1939 (incl *A Treatie of Humane Learning*); Greville 1965 *The Remains* ed G.A. Wilkes (London); Greville 1973 *Selected Writings* ed Joan Rees (London); Greville ed 1986. Ronald A. Rebholz 1971 *The Life of Fulke Greville, First Lord Brooke* (Oxford); Joan Rees 1971 *Fulke Greville, Lord Brooke, 1554–1628* (Berkeley and Los Angeles); Richard Waswo 1972 *The Fatal Mirror: Themes and Techniques in the Poetry of Fulke Greville* (Charlottesville, Va).

Grey, Arthur, fourteenth Baron of Wilton (1536–93) Son of William, the thirteenth baron, who had acted for Henry VIII, Mary, and Elizabeth as a senior commander in France and Scotland. Grey served with his father from youth and wrote a colorful memoir of his life for inclusion in Holinshed's *Chronicles*. Like his father, whom he succeeded as baron in 1562, Grey was regarded from the outset as a semiprofessional soldier. Briefly considered for the Irish viceroyalty during the first Munster rebellion (1569–73), he was passed over as the crisis subsided in favor of a more irenic nominee. His candidacy was again promoted by the Earl of Leicester after the outbreak of the second Munster rising in 1579, and Elizabeth somewhat reluctantly appointed him Lord Deputy in July 1580.

The Queen's hesitancy reflected the expediential character of the appointment. Whereas most of his predecessors had taken office with comprehensive and clearly conceived programs for the general reform of Ireland's political and social problems, Grey assumed the viceroyalty with no further objective than the suppression of rebellion by force. A man of no previous experience of Ireland who openly confessed his ignorance of the origins of the broils he came to quell, he preferred to leave these deeper issues to one side. Such was the man to whom Spenser became private secretary, presumably arriving with him in Ireland on 12 August 1580.

Grey's direct and simplistic approach to government was soon revealed in his attempt to cow the rebellious Gaelic clans of Wicklow. On its trek through the vale of Glenmalure, his large and unwieldy campaign army was relentlessly harassed by the O'Byrnes, sustaining heavy losses on its first outing. The ordeal at 'balefull Oure' (*FQ* IV xi 44) carried immense implications for the rest of his service. While it greatly encouraged the Munster rebels and their sympathizers by revealing that the new impulsive governor was by no means invincible, it also compelled Grey to seek a spectacular success to compensate for his loss of reputation. Thus, at a stroke, Grey's commitment to a military solution and the rebels' determination to resist him were greatly intensified.

His desperately needed opportunity was provided by the landing of an Italian and Spanish expedition in support of the Munster rebels at Smerwick harbor in County Kerry in September 1580. After a brief investment by land and sea, Grey secured the surrender of the fort and had its entire complement, save some fifteen individuals, massacred: around 700 men and a number of Irishwomen and children who had flocked to the fort died. This massacre, which Spenser almost certainly witnessed – in the *Vewe*, his mouthpiece Irenius offers a vivid description of it – continues to arouse dispute, though the latest researches appear to support the conclusion that some unsavory deal was arranged in advance with the commander who survived unharmed. But even in the short term, the consequences of the bloodletting were ambivalent. Grey recovered his flagging reputation: he was congratulated by Elizabeth and secured her permission to dismiss the Earl of Ormond, of whose conciliatory tactics as commander in Munster he had roundly disapproved. Yet Grey's mercilessness and the common assumption of his perfidy only increased his immediate difficulties as those already compromised by rebellion decided to stay out.

The limits of ruthlessness were further demonstrated when, upon his return to Dublin, Grey was presented with evidence that appeared to link the Earl of Kildare and the Baron Delvin, the two leading nobles of the Pale, with the young Viscount Baltinglass who had rebelled ineffectually in June 1580. The evidence revealed nothing other than the fact that Kildare and Delvin had had some ambiguous foreknowledge of Baltinglass' intentions. But Grey, who was convinced that a much larger conspiracy existed, committed both men on a charge of high treason. His action had the effect of forcing into existence among their relatives and dependents the very plot that had hitherto been merely imagined. The hastily formed conspiracy was soon exposed, and a spate of arrests and trials ensued which touched many of the leading families of the Pale. At the same time, the lands of the accused were seized and granted away, by the viceroy alone, to a select coterie of captains, even before the trials had been completed. These highly irregular proceedings provoked massive protests to the Queen from the Pale and even from some members of the Dublin government. Elizabeth responded quickly, ordering the suspension of trials and the granting of a general pardon before many had perished. But the whiff of corruption surrounding this affair combined with his insistence on maintaining a costly and ineffective strategy in Munster finally determined Gray's recall. He returned to England under a cloud (for Spenser's treatment of this moment, see *FQ* V xii 27–43) to face an official inquiry by the privy council in August 1582.

Like many of his contemporaries, Grey combined genuine scholarly tastes – he was a noted linguist – with a keen enthusiasm for adventure; but his Irish service displayed only the most distasteful aspects of his character. He was more like Talus than Artegall; and his summary of his own achievements boasted neither of peace restored nor of laws revived, but merely of the killing of 1500 gentlemen and of churls 'the account of which is beyond number' (PRO, SP 63/95/82). Yet Grey was in time to be vindicated in a rather perverse manner. The universal bitterness which his conduct aroused fostered an already existing deep suspicion of all English government throughout Ireland. Thus when his successors attempted to return to the reformist methods of the past, their efforts were drowned in a sea of mistrust. Mutual misapprehension and frustration mounted until, in the mid-1590s, they resulted in a general conflagration.

It may seem odd that the unattractive figure depicted here should have been such an inspiration to Spenser's poetic imagination. But Spenser's celebration of Grey (see *Var* 5:312–13, 318–19) and his unqualified defense of Grey's conduct in Ireland are explicable on a number of levels. There was, of course, the personal connection as Grey was the one figure within English government to extend real political patronage to the poet. But there were deeper reasons also. As a scion of an ancient (if minor) noble house, Grey was acutely conscious of his long heritage of feudal service. He had written of his father's services in France deliberately in the manner of a *chanson de geste*, and he clearly conceived of his own doings in Ireland in similar terms. A member also of an aristocratic family which had, unlike many others, wholeheartedly embraced the Reformation in its political and doctrinal forms, Grey was himself an intensely committed Protestant who had argued strongly, and at some personal risk, for the rigorous enforcement of religious conformity in the parliaments of 1572–89. Most of all, it was Grey who in Ireland had confronted and repelled the threat which haunted so many of Spenser's contemporaries: invasion from Catholic Europe. In so many ways, therefore, Grey appeared to Spenser as the apotheosis of that morally engaged noble warrior who is at the center of *FQ* v. But writing amidst the tumult of the 1590s, Spenser could not see that the danger now posed to England from Ireland was not one which Grey in his time had averted, but one which he had helped to create. CIARAN BRADY

Richard Bagwell 1885–90 *Ireland under the Tudors* 3 vols (London) chs 37–8; Crinò 1968; *DNB* sv; Arthur Grey, Baron Grey de Wilton 1847 *A Commentary of the Services and Charges of William Lord Grey of Wilton, K.G., by His Son Arthur Lord Grey of Wilton, K.G.* Camden Society (London); Henley 1928; Jenkins 1937; H.S.V. Jones 1919; Alfred O'Rahilly 1938 *The Massacre at Smerwick (1580)* ed Philip de Malpas Grey-Egerton (Cork; first pub *JCHAS* 42 [1937]).

Grill (Gr *gryllos* hog) One of Acrasia's lovers, transformed by her into a hog and restored to human shape by the Palmer (*FQ* II xii 86–7). When he repines at his restoration, Guyon and the Palmer deplore, but cannot remedy, his degeneracy.

Grill's name and bestial preference derive from Plutarch's dialogue *Beasts Are Rational* (*Moralia* 986B), where Gryllus, one of Ulysses' companions transformed into swine by Circe, declines to be restored to humanity, arguing that beasts possess intelligence and excel man in natural virtues, notably temperance. Plutarch's purpose may be satirical, but his paradoxical encomium inspired the 'theriophily' of Renaissance writers like Montaigne, who commend animals over men (Boas 1933, Levin 1969:80–3). Erasmus' Folly prefers Gryllus to Ulysses (ed 1974–, 27:108; see also p 83).

Plutarch's theme was notably reworked in Gelli's *Circe* (1549, Eng tr by Henry Iden 1557), where all Circe's animals refuse reconversion, except the philosophic elephant who recognizes man's freedom and dignity. There is no pig in Gelli, but Plutarch's hog reappears in Machiavelli's fragment, *The Golden Ass* (1517), with supportive arguments from Pliny (*Natural History* 7 proem). Wallowing in mud (like his classical predecessors), Machiavelli's beast is happier than a god.

Spenser confines Plutarch's happy pig within a tradition of moral allegory where Circe represents lust and Ulysses *sōphrosynē* or temperance, and where his companions suffer transformations which reflect their vices (Heraclitus *Homeric Allegories* 72.2, Conti *Mythologiae* 6.6). The Grill episode completes Acrasia's associations with Circe. Grill is a moral exemplum, forgetting his higher, human nature in bestial irrationality. His restoration breaks the spell of physical metamorphosis; but man's true shape is his soul, and Grill's inner swinishness persists: 'But it is come unto them, according to the true proverbe, The dogge is returned to his owne vomit: and, The sowe that was washed, to the wallowing in the myer' (2 Pet 2.22). Grill's defiant, Rabelaisian corporeality is potentially comic, but Spenser makes him a tragic reflection of man's fallen nature.

(See **Grill** Fig 1.)

This moral view is paralleled in Petrus Costalius' *Pegma* (1555:176), where Gryllus represents degenerate hedonism. Spenser's Grill delights in filth and incontinence. Plotinus says that 'the unclean loves filth for its very filthiness, and swine foul of body find their joy in foulness. What else is Sophrosyne, rightly so-called, but to take no part in the pleasures of the body, to break away from them as unclean and unworthy of the clean?' (*Enneads* 1.6.6). Swine were traditionally associated with gluttony and lechery; some of Maleger's troops are fashioned 'Like swine; for so deformd is luxury, / Surfeat, misdiet, and unthriftie wast' (*FQ* II xi 12). Significantly, Grill cannot be reformed (cf Rev 22.11: 'He which is filthie, let him be filthie stil'), and Books II and V both end in illustrations of unregeneracy. Temperance and justice regulate man's fallen nature, but they cannot change a reprobate will. SUPRIYA CHAUDHURI

George Boas 1933 *The Happy Beast in French Thought of the Seventeenth Century* (Baltimore); Lovejoy and Boas 1935; Giovanni Battista Gelli 1963 *Circe* tr Thomas Brown (1702) and ed Robert M. Adams (Ithaca, NY); Hughes 1943; Levin 1969.

Grindal, Edmund, Archbishop of Canterbury (1519?-1583) Shortly after Archbishop Parker's death in 1575, Lord Burghley urged Queen Elizabeth to appoint Grindal as his successor. Grindal held an MA from Cambridge and was a Marian exile; his work on the *Bishops' Bible* and Foxe's *Actes and Monuments* would have been familiar to Spenser. He was also a close friend of John Young, Bishop of Rochester, who employed Spenser in 1578. Within a year of his selection on 10 January 1576, however, Grindal aroused the Queen's wrath by refusing to obey her directive to abolish the so-called prophesyings (clerical meetings for discussing Scripture). In a long, eloquent response dated 20 December 1576, he cautioned Elizabeth that she was 'a mortal creature' tampering in divine things, and declared that he could not 'assent to the suppressing of the said exercises' (ed 1843:389). Nevertheless, convinced that prophesyings were a forum for the Puritan faction of the church and angered by Grindal's defiance, she directed the bishops to ban the meetings; in June of 1577, she suspended the Archbishop for noncompliance. Elizabeth considered forcing Grindal's complete deprivation, but she was finally swayed by the advice of his friends on the council and by Whitgift, the then Bishop of Worcester, who refused to supplant him. Having endured several years of diminished power, Grindal was finally reconciled with the Queen and fully restored to favor by the end of 1582. Suffering from failing health and about to resign, he died on 6 July 1583.

Through the anagram *Algrind*, Spenser alludes to Grindal on two occasions in *The Shepheardes Calender*. Piers approvingly voices Algrind's belief that the clergy should not be concerned with amassing wealth for their heirs, since they 'Mought not live ylike, as men of the laye' (*Maye* 76). Grindal is again quoted as an authority on the proper behavior of the clergy when Thomalin tells Morrell (the haughty Bishop Aylmer of London) that, contrary to current practice, the first prelates, like Abel and Aaron, were humble, pious, and 'lived with little gayne' (*Julye* 128). At the end of this eclogue, Thomalin relates the most transparent ecclesiastical allegory in *The Shepheardes Calender*, documenting Grindal's sequestration through the fable of the Eagle and the Shellfish (215–28): sitting on a hill, Algrind, a great shepherd, was 'bruzd' (ie, crushed) by a shellfish (the Puritans) dropped by an eagle (Elizabeth). Spenser reveals his concern for Grindal's fate in Thomalin's lament for the man whose 'hap was ill' and who 'lyes in lingring payne' (228–9). His fable is an implicit criticism of Elizabeth's censure of the archbishop as well as a Senecan reminder of the dangers attendant upon aspiration and high estate.

JAMES P. BEDNARZ

Peter Clark et al, eds 1979 *The English Commonwealth 1547–1640* (Chatham, Eng); Collinson 1967; Collinson 1979; Grindal ed 1843; Joel Hurstfield and Alan G.R. Smith, eds 1972 *Elizabethan People: State and Society* (London).

Guarini, Giovanni Battista (1538–1612) Court poet at Ferrara after the imprisonment of Tasso, and later at Florence and Mantua. His enormously popular pastoral tragicomedy *Il pastor fido* (*The Faithful Shepherd*) was first published in Italy in 1589 (title page dated 1590); by conservative estimate, it was in its twentieth printing by 1602. An Italian edition was printed in London in 1591, followed by English translations in 1602 and 1647 (the latter by Fanshawe). Jonson's allusion to the play suggests its influence and popularity, greater even than Tasso's *Aminta*, during the 1590s and the first decade of the seventeenth century: 'All our *English* writers, / I meane such, as are happy in th'*Italian*, / Will deigne to steale out of this author, mainely' (*Volpone* 3.4.87–9).

The complex plot of *Il pastor fido*, its multiplicity of intrigues and episodes, and its technique of interruption to build suspense, may have influenced Spenser's narrative strategies in the later books of *The Faerie Queene*. Although Spenser clearly was imitating Ariosto, his serious tone and severity in treating his themes are very unlike Ariosto's playful irony and may owe something to *Il pastor fido*. Guarini's Neoplatonism, his theory of love and of feminine dominance, his reconciliation of pleasure and virtue, and the delicacy and eroticism of his pastoral scenes may have influenced Spenser's assimilation of Ariosto.

The pastoral of shepherds, nymphs, and satyrs in *FQ* VI seems to owe a general debt to the Italian pastoralists, and possibly, then, to Guarini. A specific parallel is the riddling prophecy concerning Sir Bruin's 'sonne / *Be gotten, not begotten*' (iv 32). The plot of *Il pastor fido* depends on a similar quibbling prophecy concerning 'two of race divine,' on the subsequent mistaken identities, and on confusion caused by the oracle's words. The Serena episode (viii 35ff) of interrupted sacrifice with its elaborate ritual detail is analogous to the final act of *Il pastor fido* (Staton 1966).

KAREN NEWMAN

Louise George Clubb 1965 'The Moralist in Arcadia: England and Italy' *RPh* 19:340–52; Giovanni Battista Guarini 1964 *A Critical Edition of Sir Richard Fanshawe's 1647 Translation of Giovanni Battista Guarini's 'Il Pastor Fido'* ed Walter F. Staton, Jr, and William E. Simeone (Oxford); Guarini 1976 *Il pastor fido* tr Richard Fanshawe, ed J.H. Whitfield (Austin, Tex).

Guyon The name of the hero of *FQ* II may be derived from Gihon, one of the four rivers of Paradise and traditionally associated with temperance (Fowler 1960b); but it could also refer to Guy of Warwick, the legendary hero of chivalric romance (Nelson 1963:179–80), or to Guy of Burgundy (called 'the good Gyoun' in *Firumbras* ed 1935:465). The name also has been derived from *guido* or 'guide' (see Camden 1605:82); in the *Golden Legend*, it is said to signify 'wrestler' (quoted in Barclay ed 1955:112; cf Snyder 1961).

Guyon is 'an Elfin borne' (i 6), and his ancestry is contained in the '*Antiquitie* of *Faerie* lond' which he reads in the castle of Alma (canto x). He is not, then, an historical hero elevated into myth, like Arthur or the Red Cross Knight, but a fiction created to embody heroic virtue. Yet, he is not simply an abstract virtue but a character whose temptations and adventures demonstrate the nature and practice of his virtue. Spenser's method of presenting him, however, is allegorical: like Redcrosse, Guyon is fragmented, and his qualities, impulses, and states of mind are personified to provide a moral analysis of the action as it proceeds. Accordingly, he goes to Acrasia's island in a boat rowed by the Ferryman and steered by his Palmer, signifying that to complete his quest he needs the strength of a temperate body and the guidance of reason. When he reaches land, he proceeds only with the Palmer because the temptations he will encounter now are aimed specifically at the mind. The Palmer is the most extensive personification of a human faculty in the book. Like Una in Book I, he represents the spark of right reason remaining in man after the Fall, but looking downwards now to the problems of earth instead of upwards to the mysteries of faith. Parted from the Palmer, Guyon lacks the intuitive recognition of good and evil which reason provides, and is liable to fall into error. It is important to recognize that by his complex allegorical methods, Spenser is describing normal human behavior through his moral abstractions.

Of all the heroes of *The Faerie Queene*, Guyon has provoked the most disagreement. Perhaps the contradictory accounts of the origin of his quest expressed in the story of Mortdant and Amavia (i 61) and in the Letter to Raleigh are a reason for this; but the nature of temperance itself has been a contributing factor. The ability to control the passions, which makes temperance possible, is not the hallmark of the classical hero; and of all the quests in *The Faerie Queene*, Guyon's is the one least involved in heroic battle. Moreover, temperance is so strongly associated with Aristotle that readers have always been tempted to force upon the text a more rigid interpretation of the mean than it will in fact support.

The main debates about Guyon have centered on the kind of virtue he is pursuing: whether his quest is concerned exclusively with the world of nature as opposed to grace, whether his story demonstrates the inadequacy of a purely classical temperance, or whether his concern is with the kind of temperance possible in a fallen world. The choice of definition here dictates the answer to the questions habitually asked about the Mammon episode: should Guyon have entered Mammon's house without his Palmer, and do his adventures there represent a triumph or a fall? His destruction of the Bower of Bliss has been both praised as a victory and censured as an unhealthy asceticism.

The evidence of Book II, as well as the pattern of heroism throughout the whole poem, indicates that Spenser's concern is with Christian temperance. Guyon begins where Redcrosse leaves off, with 'like race to runne' (i 32), secure in the strength of faith which his predecessor has established, so that he checks his charge as soon as he sees 'The sacred badge of my Redeemers death' on his opponent's shield (26–7). The pageant of Guyon committing the babe with its bloody hands to the care of Medina (iii 2) is emblematic of his quest: his dedication of sinful human nature to the rule of temperance (Hamilton 1958b, 1961a:95). His quest must be achieved in a fallen world, where there is no place for pagan self-sufficiency, where the supreme horseman is without his horse and the Palmer cannot control the passions once they take hold (iv 34).

The episode of Furor and Occasion in canto iv demonstrates that, in view of the weakness of human nature, the only hope of escaping intemperance is to avoid the occasion of it: the Palmer's prayer (iv 10–11) says, in effect, 'Lead us not into temptation.' The code of virtue which Guyon attempts to follow throughout his quest is defined by Belphoebe in canto iii. It is related specifically to the penalty of Adam, and its basic assumption is the need to labor unceasingly in the sweat of one's brow: 'Who seekes with painfull toile, shall honor soonest find ... Before her gate high God did Sweat ordaine' (40–1). One of the deadly sins is sloth, the giving up of the quest as does Verdant (xii 80). Guyon's quest demands sustained moral effort and eternal vigilance, and therefore the temptation by which he is most frequently assailed is that of sloth. It comes to him in many forms: in Phaedria's advice to live like the lilies of the field (vi 15–16), in the Sirens' song wooing him to forsake his quest and take refuge in 'The worlds sweet In, from paine and wearisome turmoyle' (xii 32), and most of all, from the pressure to relax which Acrasia's garden exerts by presenting a world in which nothing apparently needs to be put right.

Guyon follows the Palmer's advice to avoid a direct confrontation with Furor by binding Occasion, perhaps because such a course is congenial to his natural human preference for a quiet life; and once having overcome Furor and Pyrochles by this means, his resulting complacency (18) encourages him to relax. Later he leaves the Palmer behind to board Phaedria's 'litle Gondelay' (vi 2) on the Idle Lake, although her idle mirth offends him. On her island, he battles Cymochles but soon is persuaded to a truce. Cymochles' nature is to fluctuate between extremes of sloth and anger, and Guyon has taken on this quality, wavering in his quest in direct contradiction to the steady and unremitting effort advocated by Belphoebe.

On escaping from Phaedria's soporific island, Guyon goes to the other extreme of activity and presses forward on his quest again. With no Palmer to guide him and no sense of absolute moral values, he can direct his way only by the memory of what has worked successfully in the past (vii 1–2). (One can imagine how the Palmer would have denounced so obvious a figure of evil excess as Mammon, and how he would have steered Guyon away.) Lacking this moral intuition, Guyon seems not to recognize Mammon for what he is but to mistake him for the ordinary riches of the world with which temperance must come to terms. He inquires, therefore, whether all these goods 'well be got' (vii 19) and enters the house to find out. To his credit, he soon discovers Mammon's true nature, and his values stand firm against all that Mammon rather contemptuously offers him. Mammon's goods are irrelevant to his quest for honor and do not tempt him as, for example, he is tempted by the very different delights of Acrasia's garden. But his immunity must be paid for: though not tempted, he is weakened by his stay in the presence of uncongenial and hostile values. It is as though, having fed his eyes on the unwholesome vittle of the underworld and grown accustomed to the unnatural smoke and darkness, he is unfitted when he comes to the surface to breathe the 'vitall aire' which is his proper element. The physical limitations of mortality, embodied elsewhere in Maleger, have taken their toll and he faints. The image of sleep which Spenser uses (viii 4) is linked to sloth and is the opposite of the 'wakefull watches ever to abide' of Belphoebe's manifesto (iii 41). Guyon is claimed by Pyrochles and Cymochles: in effect, he is taken over by his intemperate passions and can no longer control them.

This is Guyon's fall, and the subsequent episode is an allegorical statement of his struggle and ultimate success in seeking to regain self-control. Spenser's treatment of the process is a theological one which places the hero firmly in the Christian tradition. The Angel who comes to his aid is the love of God which, though not itself saving, offers the means to salvation by recalling Guyon's Palmer to him. Reason cannot itself control the passions, but it can turn to faith for help, and Arthur is therefore at hand when he is needed, as he is for Una when Redcrosse is imprisoned by Orgoglio. Arthur symbolizes the external figure of Christ crucified, by whose blood mankind is redeemed; but he is also a power within Guyon himself which reason can invoke, the new Adam restored by faith within the old Adam. Arthur cannot conquer Pyrochles and Cymochles until his own blood has been spilled in the fight – 'Wyde was the wound, and a large lukewarme flood, / Red as the Rose, thence gushed grievously' (II viii 39) – but at this point, he conquers with Guyon's own sword. By the use of his reason and in the strength of his faith, Guyon is redeemed and rises out of his sleep, a temperate man again.

After confronting Maleger and his forces and passing through the castle of Alma, he is now ready to face his final test, which comes in two stages. The first, the journey across the sea to the Bower of Bliss, is a test of his moral and physical stamina in face of the varied distractions and appeals with which sloth can confront him. On this occasion, Phaedria gets short shrift from the Palmer. The second and more difficult test is Acrasia, the aspect of fallen nature to which these temptations appeal and from which they ultimately derive. We are shown something of her power on the voyage in the hideous swarm of sea monsters (xii 22–6) which, as the Palmer demonstrates, are created by her but have no real existence. Acrasia's power is to play on the imagination and create illusions which can blind the eye of reason and be mistaken for reality. Her garden is an illusion which she has created, where everything is more beautiful and desirable than things can ever be in the real world. The Genius at the gate is 'of stature tall, / And semblaunce pleasing, more then naturall' (46); and throughout the garden, art improves on niggard nature to produce a world apparently unfallen and eternally temperate. Such a world is all false, as Spenser continually reminds the reader in many ways, and derives entirely from the tendency of the sensual imagination, when uncontrolled, to distort our perception and make us see the things which in our human weakness we want to see.

The Bower of Bliss projects all of the erotic fantasies, the wishful thinking, the nostalgia for a lost age, the escapist impulses which all of us experience but especially Guyon because his moral fervor has forced him to repress more than most of us. They must be repressed and the Bower ruthlessly destroyed because they inhibit action and become a substitute for it. By replacing reality with dreams and allowing us to regard everything in the garden as beautiful, they make us forget the Fall and the need to repair its ruins. Verdant's slumbering is one example of our forgetfulness, and Grill's contentment with his animal state another. Acrasia, the source of human passion, cannot be killed, but she must be strictly bound and subjected to reason; and in mastering her, Guyon masters his own passions and establishes as the basis for all subsequent moral action the ability to see things as they really are in the fallen world.

Guyon is one of the great masters of reality. Of all the heroes of *The Faerie Queene*, he is perhaps the nearest and dearest to Spenser himself, for like the poet, he is the supreme creator of fantasies. It is Spenser's achievement to have given full vent to this impulse in Book II and at the same time to have neutralized the dangers inherent in these fantasies by turning them into an allegory about themselves – and about us.

MAURICE EVANS

Anderson 1970b; Barclay ed 1955; Berger 1957; Evans 1970; *Firumbras and Otuel and Roland* 1935, ed Mary Isabelle O'Sullivan, EETS os 198 (London); Fowler 1960b; Fowler 1964; Gang 1959; Hamilton 1958a; Hamilton 1961a; Hamilton in *FQ* ed 1977, esp pp 163–8; Hoopes 1954; Hough 1962; Hume 1984, ch 4; Kermode1960; MacLachlan 1983; Nelson 1963; Snyder 1961; Stambler 1977; K. Williams 1966; A.S.P. Woodhouse 1949.

H

hair A lady's hair in Spenser's poetry is always conventionally long and golden, though admired coiffures range from braided (*FQ* II ii 15, ix 19) and netted (*Amoretti* 37) to loose, in which state it may be 'crisped, like golden wyre' (II iii 30, IV vi 20, *Time* 10, *Epithalamion* 154) – a convention parodied by the false Florimell's tresses of gold wire (III viii 7) – or designedly or accidentally entwined with flowers (*Epith* 154–6, II iii 30, IV xi 46). Queen Elizabeth's hair, being red-gold and 'crisped,' doubtless influenced Spenser's choice. A dramatic moment (borrowed from Ariosto's *Orlando furioso* 32.79–80 and twice repeated) is that in which Britomart reveals her sex by releasing from her helmet her ankle-length hair, whose silky sheen is compared to the aurora borealis (III ix 20–1, IV i 13; Jortin in *Var* 4:167). The fleeing Florimell's hair streams backward like the tail of a 'blazing starre' or comet (with a play on *stella comata* 'hairy star' III i 16). Sea nymphs have green hair (IV xi 48). Would-be rapists drag ladies by the hair. Hair is aesthetically crucial in ugly anthropoids, whether absent (I viii 47, V ii 6), snaky, or standing up in uncombed clumps. In others, hair standing on end registers fear; tearing one's hair, grief; white hair, venerable old age. Cutting hair from the survivors and throwing it into the grave – a ritual which Guyon and the Palmer perform at Mortdant's and Amavia's burial (II i 61) – is agreed to be an exclusively pagan practice (Puckle 1926:269, Rush 1941:212 and note 37, eg, *Iliad* 23.135–6; cf Upton in *Var* 2:195) here expressing identification of the living with the deceased (whose locks are also collected) and sealing Guyon's vow of vengeance.

Just as hair symbolizes the sexual identity of females, so beards symbolize the sexual identity of males. Most though not all Elizabethan men wore beards. In *The Faerie Queene*, facial hair is so common that Alma's castle-body sports a 'wandring vine' over its maxillary door (II ix 24). To be shaved is humiliating (V iii 37, VI i 13–14; cf 2 Sam

10.4, Isa 50.6); even scantiness of beard is a butt for jokes (VI i 19), though peach fuzz enhances an adolescent's charm (II xii 79). Beards indicate virility, maturity, or unfulfilled lust, as in the 'gotish beard' on both Malbecco and Faunus (VI i 19, ix 13; III x 47; VII vi 49). Sexual identity is at stake in the highly traditional episode of the castle whose custom is the exaction of the beards of men and the hair of ladies to compile a mantle (*FQ* VI i 12–15; cf Malory *Morte Darthur* I.26). In the dragon fight, however, Redcrosse's beard becomes a hindrance, serving as tinder (L *fomes*) for a spark from the Dragon which so increases as to burn the knight inside his armor (I xi 26). This beard has been interpreted as the *fomes peccati* or proneness to sin inherent since the Fall – natural and yet something of an excrescence, susceptible to trimming but not eradication (Kaske 1969). St George, Redcrosse's model in the dragon fight, is originally and indeed usually portrayed without a beard, which suggests that Spenser's use of it here is purposeful.

CAROL V. KASKE

Kaske 1969; Kaske 1979; Bertram S. Puckle 1926 *Funeral Customs: Their Origin and Development* (London); Alfred C. Rush 1941 *Death and Burial in Christian Antiquity* (Washington, D.C.); L. Sommer 1912 in *Real-Encyclopädie* sv 'Haaropfer'; Carl Winter 1949 *Elizabethan Miniatures* rev ed (Harmondsworth).

Hall, Joseph (1574–1656) Sometime fellow of Emmanuel College, Cambridge (one of the chief centers of Elizabethan Puritanism), and later successively Bishop of Exeter and of Norwich, Hall was best known in his own time as a writer of contemplative and devotional literature. Although his defense of episcopacy angered Parliament and embroiled him in the Smectymnuan controversy with Milton, his meditative and casuistical works remained popular throughout the Interregnum.

Hall first achieved fame in formal verse satire a year before the publication of Marston's *Scourge of Villanie*. In the first three books of *Virgidemiarum* (1597), he attacks what he considered to be the moral and stylistic failings of contemporary literature but expressly excepts Spenser from his strictures: 'But let no rebell *Satyre* dare traduce / Th'eternall *Legends* of thy *Faery Muse*, / Renowmed *Spencer*: whome no earthly wight / Dares once to emulate, much lesse dares despight' (ed 1949:16). Spenser is thus set apart from his contemporaries both morally and aesthetically as the supreme Renaissance poet, preferred before Ariosto and du Bartas, and effective allusion is made to such episodes from *The Faerie Queene* as the marriage of Thames and Medway and the metamorphosis of Grill (pp 12, 25).

Spenserian diction is detectable throughout Hall's poetic canon. On one occasion, for example, he refers to heaven as the '*Boure* of *Blisse*' (cf *FQ* III v 35), and on another he alludes to Talus with his 'flayle of lead' (ed 1949:4, 50). Other familiar phrases include 'Pagan vaunt,' 'rufull plaint,' 'lucklesse peeres,' and 'fortune fraile' (pp 12, 17). His 'Defiance to Envie,' which serves as a preface to *Virgidemiarum*, seems to imitate Spenser's style – 'Come Nimphs and Faunes, that haunt those shadie Groves, / Whiles I report my fortunes or my loves' – although Hall denies any intention to 'scoure the rusted swords of Elvish knights, / Bathed in Pagan blood: or sheath them new / In misty morall Types' (pp 8–10). This passage has sometimes been interpreted as critical of Spenser but the context makes it clear that such subjects would be inappropriate to 'lowly *Satyres*,' and Hall proceeds to acknowledge the inferiority of his own early pastorals (not extant) to those of Colin at whose feet he symbolically throws his 'yeelding reed' (pp 9–10). He was also familiar with *Complaints*, undoubtedly attracted by its strongly satiric ethos, and he makes a passing reference to *Ruines of Time* in his satiric dystopia *Mundus alter et idem* (1605?, tr 1609 as *The Discovery of a New World*; see *Sp All* p 99, Hall ed 1937:25).

Hall was much offended by the apparent lack of deference shown to Spenser after his death. His account of the poet's last days corroborates Jonson's. In a poem to Camden in which he compares the merits of Sidney and Spenser, he complains of the latter's untimely end through 'want' and of his subsequent lack of a suitably inscribed tomb (p 105). On another occasion, he hails as Spenser's poetic heir William Bedell (putative author of *A Protestant Memorial, or The Shepherd's Tale of the Pouder-Plott: A Poem in Spenser's Style*, a work which includes commendatory verses by Hall, and which remained in manuscript until 1713; see *Sp All* p 98), again insisting upon the straitened circumstances of the poet's death, poignantly remarking that his 'Relicks' lie 'Under unwritten Stones, that who goes by / Cannot once Read, *Lo here doth* COLLIN *lie*' (ed 1949:123).

RICHARD A. MCCABE

Joseph Hall 1937 *The Discovery of a New World* tr John Healey, ed Huntington Brown (Cambridge, Mass); Hall 1949 *Poems* ed Arnold Davenport (Liverpool); Hall 1981 *Another World and Yet the Same: Bishop Joseph Hall's 'Mundus Alter et Idem'* tr John Millar Wands (New Haven) p 26. Frank Livingstone Huntley 1979 *Bishop Joseph Hall 1574–1656: A Biographical and Critical Study* (Cambridge); Richard A. McCabe 1982 *Joseph Hall: A Study in Satire and Meditation* (Oxford); *Sp All* pp 54–5, 66–7, 98–9, 140.

handwriting, Spenser's Autographs are more plentiful for Spenser than for most other Elizabethan literary figures. They comprise over a hundred items, being roughly equivalent in quantity to 120 folio pages of continuous writing, and include eleven authentic signatures. However, no autograph survives from the Spenser canon, the only literary document of any kind being a single-leaf transcript of a Latin letter on poetry from Erhardus Stibarus to Erasmus Neustetter and two Latin poems from Lotichius' *Poemata* (1576) (item *B58* below). Fifty-four items are official letters and documents written out by Spenser as secretary first to Lord Grey and later to Sir John Norris; another forty are merely addresses or endorsements of similar documents not otherwise in Spenser's hand. Of the rest, one – the earliest autograph – is a rental receipt made out by him as secretary to John Young, Bishop of Rochester, 23 November 1578 (*B1*). Three others are the most personally related to Spenser: an undated grant of land from him to McHenry; his answer to the commissioners for attainted lands, May 1589 (*B55*); and the latest dated example, his bill against Lord Roche, 12 October 1589. Finally, there are three isolated signatures of attestation (*A4*, *A5*, *A8*).

(See **handwriting** Figs 1–2.)

Spenser's autographs are located mainly among State Papers Ireland in the Public Record Office, the Additional and Cottonian Manuscripts in the British Library, and the Cecil Papers at Hatfield House, Hertfordshire. The first to be identified and published in facsimile was the McHenry grant found among the Roche papers, though the discoverer thought only the signature was Spenser's (*GentM* 102 [1832]:305). The grant was condemned as a forgery by John Payne Collier (himself a forger) and then by Grosart, who accused Collier of the forgery. But with the publication of the *Calendar of the State Papers Relating to Ireland* (esp vols covering 1574–92, pub 1867–85), other Spenser autographs came to light for comparison, and the document was eventually accepted as genuine.

The pioneers of Spenserian paleography in this century include Hilary Jenkinson, who laid some of the groundwork; H.R. Plomer, who settled the forgery debate and provided a short description of Spenser's 'secretary' hand; and W.W. Greg, whose extensive treatment included confirming the identity of Spenser's 'italic' hand. Assiduous research by Raymond Jenkins produced a large number of new autographs, while Roland M. Smith made further discoveries and produced the first extensive catalogue of Spenser documents. Despite their excellent work, some of Jenkins' attributions seem wrong (eg, SP 63/78/29) or doubtful (eg, *C18*, *C31*, *C32*, and SP 63/85/36), and five Latin letters should be deleted from Smith's list (Table 1, nos 3, 11, 16, 17, 23) for reasons stated below. New autographs continue to appear, such as the rental receipt, the Latin letter and poems (first noted by Beal), and two letters and three endorsements (*B3*, *B4*; *C10*, *C11*, *C12*) discovered during the research for this article.

Spenser uses two different scripts: an Elizabethan secretary hand for English texts, and an italic 'mixed' with secretary graphs for Latin texts, some marginalia, and a few endorsements; an 'unmixed' form of the same style of script is employed for signatures and attestations. Presumably he learned penmanship at Merchant Taylors' School, and his italic may have been influenced by styles current at Cambridge. Wherever he learned to write, he perfected two hands which combine clarity, elegance, and speed – assets both in government service and in his literary career.

The prevailing script of the documents is

an Elizabethan secretary script similar in style to the 'facile' form described and illustrated by Martin Billingsley (1618?) and in popular use, especially in Chancery depositions. It is quite regular, is even-spaced, slopes at an angle of 45 degrees, and is fine-nibbed, except in some early examples (*B2*, *B3*), or when the paper is porous (*B57*). The bodies of linear letters are small; the downstrokes of *f* and long *s* are contrastingly long, sometimes descending below the next line. Of the vowels, *a* is often open or spurred or both; *o*, too, is frequently open and shaped like *v*, and when combined with *f* is merely a semicircle, losing half its body in the *f*'s shaft. Among the distinctive consonants are the split *B* with lobes like a curtailed *3*; an open, looped, and upright *d*; *g* with a tail running parallel or diagonal to the line and thickened at the end, or crossing over itself from right to left and moving upwards to close the head of the letter. Double *l* has small rounded loops, the second usually shorter and leaning backwards; *p* is sometimes like a secretary *x*; *r* has four different forms: Greek *e*, twin-stemmed, *2*, and *v*; and *y* has a tail often extending well above the line, also representing *y^e* (for *the*). The abbreviation for *es* is usually heavy and elongated, resembling an unlooped *g* with a small head. Though individually these characteristics are not especially idiosyncratic, combined they are marked indications of Spenser's hand.

(See **handwriting** Fig 3.)

Relatively little of Spenser's italic has survived: the Miler Magrath letter (*B10*), the Latin letter and poems (*B58*), the marginalia on the Nugent confession, the occasional endorsement (eg, *C1*, *C8*, *C12*), and the signatures, often prefixed by 'copia vera' (eg, *A1*, *A2*). In general appearance, the hand seems a cross between the angular and semicursive *littera antiqua* and the more rounded and looped italic scripts. It exhibits the same regularity and slope as the secretary, but downstrokes are usually much shorter and tend to be clubbed. When 'mixed,' the italic contains the following secretary graphs: reversed *e* (sometimes alternating with italic *e* or Greek *e*), the *r* 'flat-topped' form of *c*, and *t* with low cross-stroke linked to the stem. Among the distinctive italic graphs are the thick-stemmed *p* with a hooked loop and bowl angled upwards, and *r* with a heavy foot-serif.

The italic hand ascribed to Spenser by Smith is a chastened form of *testeggiata* and markedly different from his known 'mixed' italic or the pure italic of the signatures. Having perfected one form of italic completely adequate for his secretarial duties, he would hardly have made an occasional switch to a totally different one for no apparent reason. Smith's attributions are based mainly on orthography, but derive from a totally unsupported suggestion, first made by Renwick (*Vewe* ed 1934:285) and echoed by Jenkins, that the Smerwick letter from Grey to the Queen (12 November 1580, SP 63/78/29) is in 'Spenser's most careful and beautiful Italian hand.' Among other italic examples which must be rejected for lack of evidence are the 'Spenserus' inscription in a Gower manuscript (Bodl Ms 902, fol 184r, supposed by Rosemond Tuve to have a similarity to the Smerwick letter, 12 November 1580), and two inscriptions in the Folger copy of George Sabinus' *Poemata* (1563), which have been discounted by Beal.

Though Spenser gives his name in full as 'Edmond Spenser' or 'Edmund Spenser' when simply writing it in secretary (*B55*, *B57*), he invariably abbreviates his signature to 'Ed: spser' or 'Edm: spser,' with the loops on the *d* and *sps* acting as marks of abbreviation. Signature graphs, including *e*, are entirely italic; *E* is cursive, with an introductory arc at its head; and *r* has the characteristic heavy foot-serif. Aesthetic symmetry is provided by the three upper and lower loops and the two brevigraph loops; the bowls of *d* and *p* are similarly counterbalanced.

ANTHONY G. PETTI

CHRONOLOGICAL LIST OF AUTOGRAPHS (unprefixed nos = State Papers Ireland [SP 63]) *Signatures* **1581**: *A1* 81/20 (11 Mar); *A2* 81/36 I (13 Mar); *A3* 81/36 II (16 Mar); *A4* 83/6 I (29 Apr); *A5* 83/6 II (29 Apr?); *A6* 84/14 (10 Jul). **1582**: *A7* 93/64 I (May/Jun); *A8* 94/107 (29 Aug). **1589**: *A9* 144/70 (May); *A10* 147/16 (12 Oct); *A11* BL Add Ms 19869 (1589?).

Letters and documents **1578**: *B1* Univ of Kansas, uncatalogued ms North 2C:2:1 (23 Nov). **1580**: *B2* 75/75 (29 Aug); *B3* 75/84 (31 Aug); *B4* 76/1 (2 Sept); *B5* 76/10 (4 Sept); *B6* BL Add Ms 33924, fol 6 (28 Nov); *B7* 78/68 (30 Nov); *B8* 79/24 I (22 Dec). **1581**: *B9* 81/15 (7 Mar); *B10* 81/20 (11 Mar); *B11* 81/36 I (13 Mar); *B12* 81/39 (20 Mar); *B13* 83/47 (10 Jun); *B14* 84/13 (10 Jul); *B15* 84/14 (10 Jul); *B16* 84/28 (18 Jul); *B17* Cecil 12/16, no 1078 (28 Nov); *B18* Cecil 12/19, no 1081 (28 Nov); *B19* 87/64 (29 Dec). **1582**: *B20* 88/2 (3 Jan); *B21* 88/12 (12 Jan); *B22* 89/18 (5 Feb); *B23* 89/30 (13 Feb); *B24* 89/35 (18 Feb); *B25* 90/1 (1 Mar); *B26* BL Cotton Ms Titus B.XIII, fol 364 (23 Mar); *B27* 90/31 (24 Mar); *B28* 90/48 (27 Mar); *B29* 90/52 (28 Mar); *B30* 91/11 (4 Apr); *B31* 91/26 (12 Apr); *B32* 91/38 (19 Apr); *B33* 91/52 (30 Apr); *B34* 91/53 (30 Apr); *B35* 92/9 (7 May); *B36* 92/10 (7 May); *B37* 92/11 I (9 May); *B38* 92/30 (11 May); *B39* 92/46 (16 May); *B40* 93/64 I (May/Jun); *B41* 92/85 (28 May); *B42* 93/64 (29 Jun); *B43* 94/28 (16 Jul); *B44* 94/46 (28 Jul); *B45* 94/47 (28 Jul); *B46* 94/61 (31 Jul). **1585**: *B47* 115/13 (7 Mar); *B48* 115/14 (7 Mar); *B49* 115/15 (7 Mar); *B50* 115/16 (7 Mar); *B51* 115/41 (31 Mar); *B52* 115/42 (Mar). **1588**: *B53* 135/66 (1 Jul). **1589**: *B54* 140/37 (22 Jan); *B55* 144/70 (May); *B56* 147/16 (12 Oct). **Undated**: *B57* BL Add Ms 19869 (1589?); *B58* Folger, x.d.520.

Endorsements and addresses **1580**: *C1* 79/26 (23 Dec). **1581**: *C2* 81/1 (1 Mar); *C3* 81/4 (2 Mar); *C4* 81/27 (14 Mar); *C5* 81/42 (23 Mar); *C6*? 82/6 (6 Apr); *C7* Cecil 11/91, no 970 (6 Apr); *C8*? 82/16 (7 Apr); *C9* Cecil 11/94, no 976 (22 Apr); *C10* 83/6 I (29 Apr); *C11* 83/6 II (29 Apr?); *C12* 83/6 III (10 May); *C13* 83/6 (12 May); *C14* 83/43 (9 Jun); *C15* 83/45 (10 Jun); *C16* 84/3 (5 Jul); *C17* 84/12 (10 Jul); *C18*? 85/6 (10 Aug); *C19* 85/13 (12 Aug); *C20* Cecil 11/113, no 1026 (26 Aug); *C21* Cecil 11/114, no 1029 (30 Aug); *C22* 85/37 (12 Sept); *C23* 86/51 (6 Nov); *C24* 86/53 (6 Nov); *C25* 87/32 (10 Dec). **1582**: *C26* 88/9 (7 Jan); *C27* 88/15 (13 Jan); *C28* 88/40 (27 Jan); *C29* 89/11 (4 Feb); *C30* 89/55 (Feb); *C31*? 91/17 (8 Apr); *C32*? 91/22 (12 Apr); *C33* 92/25 (10 May); *C34* 92/26 (10 May); *C35* 92/52 (22 May); *C36* 92/86 (28 May); *C37* 93/34 (21 Jun); *C38* 93/46 (22 Jun); *C39* 94/15 (10 Jul); *C40* 94/62 (31 Jul).

BIBLIOGRAPHY (facsimiles are indicated in parentheses): Beal 1980, 1.2:523–31 (*B58*); Martin Billingsley 1618? *The Pens Excellencie* (London; rpt Amsterdam and Norwood, NJ 1977); Carpenter 1923:286–8 (*B8*); W.W. Greg 1925–32 *English Literary Autographs, 1550–1650* 3 pts (Oxford) 39–40 (*B10*, *B15*, *B22*, *B55*); Raymond Jenkins 1935 '*News out of Munster*, A Document in Spenser's Hand' *SP* 32:125–30 (*B26*); Jenkins 1937 (*B6*); Jenkins 1938 (*B53*); Hilary Jenkinson 1923 'Elizabethan Handwritings: A Preliminary Sketch' *Library* ser 4, 3:1–34, esp 33–4 (*B55*); Anthony G. Petti 1977 *English Literary Hands from Chaucer to Dryden* (London) 74–5 (*B11*, *B57*); Henry R. Plomer 1923–4 'Edmund Spenser's Handwriting' *MP* 21:201–7 (*B8*, *B15*, *B22*, *B31*, *B43*, *B47*); R.M. Smith 1958 (*B8* and ascribed italic autograph); Tuve 1964. Some general introductions to Elizabethan paleography are Giles E. Dawson and Laetitia Kennedy-Skipton 1966 *Elizabethan Handwriting 1500–1650: A Manual* (New York) and Petti 1977; R.B. McKerrow's 'Note on Elizabethan Handwriting' (appended to McKerrow 1927 and Gaskell 1972) summarizes the main points.

Harington, John (1561–1612) Harington's *Orlando Furioso in English Heroical Verse* (1591) is one of the landmarks of Elizabethan translation. The product of a prominent courtier, epigrammatist, occasional soldier, and Rabelaisian author of *The Metamorphosis of Ajax* (1596), the Ariosto volume is elaborately produced and embellished with fine plates for each of the 46 cantos; it presents a version of Ariosto that, in spite of many omissions, compressions, and some wholly unwarranted expansions, is still vigorous and highly readable. Published the year after *Faerie Queene* I–III with a dedication to Harington's godmother, Queen Elizabeth, it reveals him sharing with Spenser not only an expected absorption in Ariosto but also the conception, recently expressed in Sidney's *Defence of Poetry*, that epic occupies the highest place in the hierarchy of poetry, as much for its comprehensiveness as for its ability to inculcate moral values through pleasurable means. There is an overt compliment to Spenser's poem in Harington's notes to canto 43, in which he mentions the fabliau ('to the like effect') of the Squire of Dames (*FQ* III vii 53–60).

Both the format of the volume and its critical commentary are influenced by Italian models, although Harington throughout attempted to adapt them to an English audience's particular interests, often by substituting English for Italian exempla and anecdotes. For the format's chief elements, though not for their arrangement, Harington relied mainly on the Venice text of 1584 annotated by Ruscelli, with its scholarly apparatus: 'arguments' and annotations for each canto, an advertisement to the reader, various essays, a life of Ariosto, and an index of names and places. Especially important is the 'Preface or rather, a Briefe Apologie of Poetrie,' in which Harington claims an elevated role for the epic poet similar to Spenser's: 'I beleeve that the reading of a good Heroicall Poeme may make a man both wiser and honester.' In order to demonstrate that the epic is essentially allegorical and hence not frivolous, Harington appends a four-part interpretation to the end of each canto. This includes, first, 'The Morall,' involving some fairly primitive and platitudinous moralizing 'approving vertuous actions and condemning the contrarie'; second, 'The Historie,' an explication of actual historical elements underlying the romance narrative; third, 'Allegorie,' differing from 'The Morall' in attempting more complex and sophisticated interpretation on a relatively more continuous level; and (rather more rarely) 'Allusion,' which identifies the occasional elements of classical mythology to which Ariosto refers.

The translation demonstrates the accessibility of the Italian allegorical tradition that had grown up around Ariosto's text in the years since 1542. Harington gives evidence throughout of having closely consulted both the readings of the allegorizers, who provided brief bits of moralizing commentary at the headings of cantos in various editions, and also (in his 'Briefe and Summarie Allegorie') the more extended allegories suggested by Bonomone for the 1584 edition, itself heavily influenced by Simon Fornari's two-volume interpretation of 1549–50, *La spositione ... sopra l'Orlando furioso*. Harington's translation is sometimes directly affected by these allegorical readings. A case in point is the Ruggiero-Alcina narrative, where the diction and tone, heavily pejorative and gnomic (perhaps ironically so), show all too clearly certain negative moral aspects of the allegory as it had been belabored by the heavy-handed allegorizers; see, for instance, Harington's interpolation of three very un-Ariostan stanzas (7.35–7). Both Spenser and Harington treat Ariosto's text very freely, the first re-creating it in a spirit of intense literary rivalry common among all epic poets, the second adapting and altering a great original for the delectation of a courtly public. Perhaps the chief value of Harington's translation resides in its reflection of social and critical principles rather than in its fidelity to Ariosto or its ability to convey the splendor of his language. That would at once 'place' his *Orlando* and qualify the remorseless charge, leveled against it by the unyielding Ben Jonson, of being 'under all translations ... the worst' (ed 1925–52, 1:133).

The Metamorphosis of Ajax contains two allusions to Spenser. With reference to the recent publication of the 1596 installment of *The Faerie Queene*, the 'Apologie' records that 'They descanted of the new Faerie Queene and the old both, and the greatest fault they coulde finde in it was that the last verse disordered their mouthes, and was lyke a trycke of xvii. in a sinkapace.' Addressing Sir John Spencer, brother of Lady Elizabeth Carey, Harington states, 'You have a learned Writer of your name, make much of him, for it is not the least honour of your honourable family' (*Sp All* p 49).

PETER V. MARINELLI

Ariosto ed 1591; D.H. Craig 1985 *Sir John Harington* (Boston); Judith Lee 1983 'The English Ariosto: The Elizabethan Poet and the Marvelous' *SP* 80:277–99; Townsend Rich 1940 *Harington and Ariosto: A Study in Elizabethan Verse Translation* (New Haven); Alfonso Sammut 1971 *La fortuna dell'Ariosto nell'Inghilterra elisabettiana* (Milan).

Harvey, Gabriel (1552–1631) A longtime friend of Spenser, Harvey was the eldest son of a well-to-do yeoman family of Saffron Walden, Essex. His father, a rope-maker, took an active part in civic affairs, becoming Walden's chief official in 1572. Gabriel himself had multiple careers: as a scholar as shown in his *Ciceronianus* and *Rhetor* while praelector or professor of rhetoric at Cambridge, writer of Latin and English verse and prose tracts, civil lawyer at the Court of Arches, bibliophile, and writer of marginalia.

Spenser and Harvey became acquainted at Pembroke Hall, where Harvey seems to have recognized Spenser's very special gifts and became his mentor, urging him to acquire the academic background which he felt was essential for a serious poet. By 1573 when Spenser was a sophister and Harvey in his first year of graduate study, these intellectually avid youths were already firm friends. Although opposites in temperament, they were alike in altruistic ideals and subsequently in practical aims: to obtain positions at court through which they could thrive and exert a beneficial influence.

Some of their earlier writings seem intended to promote their admission to court. Harvey's *Gratulationes Valdinenses* (1578) is a group of Latin poems in praise of the Queen and her chief nobles; his unpublished 'Anticosmopolita, or Britanniae Apologia' (written c 1579, apparently not extant) was a long British epic in Latin verse. Spenser's *Shepheardes Calender* (1579) was meant to establish him as England's 'new Poete.' The little 1580 volume of Spenser's and Harvey's letters likewise seems to have been instigated by the desire to bring them to public notice, even though Harvey claimed (not altogether convincingly) that it was printed without his acquiescence. In Harvey's *Letter-Book* (ed 1884) are drafts of early letters to Spenser which also reveal their relaxed intimacy with occasional banter (eg, Harvey addresses Spenser as 'young Italianate signor and French Monsieur') and exchange of serious ideas. When they failed to obtain any position at court, some of their later works became admonitory and corrective.

Harvey's inscription in his copy of Jerome Turler's *The Traveiler* (1575) indicates that it was a gift in 1578 from Spenser, then secretary to John Young, Bishop of Rochester. Marginalia of Harvey's in *Howleglas* (c 1565) show that it and three other 'foolish' books were given him by Spenser in London on 20 December 1578, with the proviso that Harvey read them before 1 January or else forfeit his four-volume Lucian (ed 1913:23). The gift may have been to celebrate Harvey's receipt two days before of a fellowship to study civil and canon law at Trinity Hall, Cambridge.

There are possible traces of Harvey's influence in some of Spenser's writings. Harvey's 1577 *Smithus, vel Lachrymae Musarum*, a group of Latin elegies eulogizing his patron Sir Thomas Smith who had died that year, consists of a series of verse laments uttered by each of the Muses in turn. Spenser's 1591 *Teares of the Muses* uses this same format, although in other respects the two works are very different. *The Shepheardes Calender* opens with an epistle 'To the most excellent and learned both Orator and Poete, Mayster Gabriell Harvey' in which E.K. offers to him 'the maydenhead of this our commen frends Poetrie' and urges him to defend the poem 'with your mighty Rhetorick and other your rare gifts of learning.' In the gloss to *September* 176, E.K. informs the reader that Colin Clout is the author himself, then discusses Colin's 'especiall good freend Hobbinoll ... or more rightly Mayster Gabriel Harvey,' and lists the titles of five unpublished works. Hobbinol appears or is mentioned in five eclogues and plays an important role as the wise friend who deplores Colin's crippling love for Rosalind and highly commends his 'piping' (*Dec* 45–8).

The year after the *Calender* was published, there followed five Spenser-Harvey letters titled *Three Proper, and Wittie, Familiar Letters ... Touching the Earthquake in Aprill Last, and Our English Refourmed Versifying* and *Two Other, Very Commendable Letters ... Both Touching the Foresaid Artificiall Versifying, and Certain Other Particulars* (1580). The letters date from the time when both Harvey and Spenser were enthusiastic about quantitative verse, although their interest apparently ended once they realized the awkwardness of classical meters for English poetry. It is evident from postscripts to several of the letters that they considered Sidney and Dyer their literary mentors and seem to have had periodic contact with them, Spenser more directly since he was then at court in Leicester's service. There are references in the 1580 volume to an 'Areopagus,' which probably alludes to an elite literary-philosophical circle; but whether the group is literal or figurative is a moot question.

Harvey was taken to task for two satires in his letters to Spenser: the attack on pseudo-learning at Cambridge as portrayed in the earthquake letter (*3* Lett 2), and the poem 'Speculum Tuscanismi,' which attacks the Italianate Englishman and very probably was a caricature of Edward de Vere, Earl of Oxford, for whom Harvey had little love. Harvey was close to serious trouble; but after profuse apologies to Cambridge and the Earl, and assurance to the latter that he was really not the subject of the poem, the agitation subsided. Harvey became chary of publishing further satire and until 1592 held his tongue regardless of provocation. But when Greene attacked his family in the first issue of *A Quip for an Upstart Courtier* and died so soon afterwards that no legal action could be taken against him, Harvey's anger burst forth into print. In *Foure Letters*, he alludes to invectives that are too bold and satires that are too presumptuous (ed 1922:15).

After bitterly assailing Greene, he made mild sallies at Greene's young friend Thomas Nashe who at this time Harvey believed was merely a misguided talented youth. Harvey radically changed this tolerant view when he began to smart under Nashe's persistent lacerating attacks, for the clever young man had discovered that his writings were eminently salable when he made the learned Dr Harvey the butt of his wittily distorting pen. As Nashe continued his abusive lampoons, Harvey became more and more peppery and caustic. Intense and ambitious, he had already been made ultrasensitive and acerbic by Greene's attacks and earlier by those of Cambridge classmates jealous that one from a middle-class background should excel. As Harvey now saw his hard-earned reputation being ravaged, he realized that the most dangerous enemy was a witty one.

Among 'presumptuous satires,' Harvey also mentions 'with the good leave of unspotted friendship' Spenser's *Mother Hubberds Tale* (1591), which apparently had caused some commotion of its own. The protagonists of this tale may have evolved from discussions between Harvey and Spenser, for there are early marginalia of Harvey's which refer to a fox and an ape in much the same terms as in *Mother Hubberd*. Toward the end of Harvey's copy of John Florio's *Firste Fruites* (1578), in the margin adjacent to a printed text treating of 'La Lingua Inglese,' is a note in Harvey's hand about Stephen Gardiner (Bishop of Winchester and later Lord Chancellor of England) and Nicholas Wotton (Henry VIII's Principal Secretary): 'Dr Gardiner of manie surnamed the Foxe: Dr Wootton the Ape, Wootton had the text, and glosse of the lawe bye hart verbatim: Gardiner the matter, and substance. Two pregnant advocats in anie dowtfull or subtile case of whatsoever importance' (Stern 1979:154). Because of craftiness and deceit, Gardiner was frequently characterized by his contemporaries as a fox; but the linking of a fox and an ape (in this case Wotton) as two shrewd and designing 'advocats' suggests a relationship to *Mother Hubberd* some years in advance of its publication, for Harvey annotated the Florio volume in 1580 and 1585.

At the end of *Foure Letters*, there is a commendatory sonnet by Spenser (in ed 1912:603) addressed 'To the right worshipfull my singular good Frend, M. Gabriell Harvey, Doctor of the Lawes,' dated 18 July 1586 from Dublin. The salutation was very likely in response to the happy news that eight days earlier Harvey had been incorporated at Oxford as Doctor of Civil and Canon Law. The sonnet itself seems to have been written as preface for Harvey's contemplated volume of satires. It praises him as 'the happy above happiest men,' and is signed 'Your devoted frend during life, Edmund Spencer.'

After Spenser left for Ireland in August 1580, he would have had no direct contact with Harvey except through letters and Spenser's very occasional visits to England. Nevertheless, their friendship seems to have continued, as can be surmised, on Spenser's part, from the 1586 sonnet and the expressions of love and esteem for Hobbinol that appear in *Colin Clouts Come Home Againe* (written in 1591 or shortly thereafter) and, on Harvey's part, from his 'To the learned Shepheard' which first appeared in the commendatory verses to the 1590 *Faerie Queene* and his various praises of Spenser and his work in *Pierces Supererogation* (1593), in *A New Letter of Notable Contents* (1593), and in marginalia.

When Harvey was first sent some part of *The Faerie Queene* by Spenser, he was disappointed with it, calling him '*Hobgoblin* runne away with the Garland from *Apollo*' (*Var Prose* p 472). The final version of the poem was, however, very much to his liking, as attested by his high praise of it in his Chaucer marginalia, where he ranks it among 'owre best Inglish, auncient and moderne' (ed 1913:232), and in *New Letter*, where he writes, 'is not the verse of M. *Spencer* in his brave Faery Queene, the Virginall of the divinest Muses, and gentlest graces?' (1593: A4v).

Harvey's influence on Spenser probably was to spur him toward more disciplined study, turning it to pragmatically useful results, and also to temper his idealism with an appreciation of the present age (for Harvey the golden age was now rather than, as for Spenser, in the past). Spenser's influence on Harvey seems to have been to stress the need for compromise between ideal values and the expediencies of the everyday world, encourage tolerance for human foibles, and indulge in occasional whimsical playfulness. VIRGINIA F. STERN

Gabriel Harvey 1593 *A New Letter of Notable Contents* (London; rpt Amsterdam and New York 1969, Menston, Yorks 1970); Harvey ed 1913; Harvey ed 1945.

Austin 1947; Eccles 1982; McLane 1961; Stern 1979 (from which some of the above is derived by permission of the Clarendon Press, Oxford); Harold S. Wilson 1948 'The Humanism of Gabriel Harvey' in *Joseph Quincy Adams Memorial Studies* ed James G. McManaway, et al (Washington, D.C.) pp 707–21.

Hawes, Stephen (1475? – 1523?) There is a tradition that *The Faerie Queene* was probably influenced by Hawes' allegorical poems *The Example of Virtue* (1504?) and *The Pastime of Pleasure* (1509). The origins of this tradition are unclear: the *Variorum* ascribes it incorrectly to Thomas Warton's *History of English Poetry* (1774–81). But it seems first to have been explicitly formulated by Elizabeth Barrett Browning, who called the *Pastime* one of 'four allegorical poems, on whose foundations is exalted into light the great allegorical poem of the world, Spenser's *Faery Queen*' (Browning 1842:520, in *Var* 1:415).

Yet there is little to justify any claim that Hawes directly influenced Spenser; parallels between them remain tenuous or commonplace. Their major similarity lies in their combination of allegory and romance. Hawes appears to have been the first English poet to attempt to fuse the two forms; but the romance element in his poems remains subordinate, almost incidental, and his main stress falls on inert, didactic allegory.

It is not likely that Spenser read Hawes' poems: *The Example of Virtue* was last published in 1530 and *The Pastime of Pleasure* in 1555, and neither was reprinted until the nineteenth century. Nor did Hawes have sufficient reputation in the sixteenth century to make it likely that Spenser would have sought out his works. Despite C.S. Lewis' claim that 'it is probable that Spenser had read the *Pastime*' (1954:128), it seems most likely that Hawes' poems are interesting analogues to *The Faerie Queene*, but not direct sources. A.S.G. EDWARDS

Hawes ed 1928; Hawes 1974 *Minor Poems* ed Florence W. Gluck and Alice B. Morgan, EETS 271 (London); Carol V. Kaske 1989 'How Spenser Really Used Stephen Hawes in the Legend of Holiness' in Logan and Teskey 1989:119–36.

Hawthorne, Nathaniel (1804–64) Among the Hawthornes, there was a family story that *The Faerie Queene* was the first book that the young Nathaniel bought with his own money. We cannot know if the story is true, nor even just when Hawthorne first read the poem, but in early letters to his wife, both dated in June of 1840, he mentions that he has the poem at hand. Shortly after, in 1842–3, during his first winter at the Old Manse, he and his wife passed the evenings reading it to each other, and later, in England, they would reread it again to their children. In the meantime, several of the poem's figures had become household terms: the Hawthornes drew upon Spenser's fiction for the name of a daughter, Una, called her dog 'Una's lion,' and referred to George Bancroft, Polk's Secretary of the Navy, as 'the Blatant Beast.'

If *The Faerie Queene* formed part of the fabric of Hawthorne's everyday life, it still more pervasively influenced his literary imagination. From the earliest of his tales through the manuscripts of his late, unfinished romances, the Spenserian undersong is profound and varied. Hawthorne doubtless knew Spenser's shorter poems as well, but it was *The Faerie Queene* that remained central. It provided not only a model for moral allegory and psychological romance, but also a kind of handbook of emblematic technique and rhetorical gesture.

An examination of Spenser's general influence may profitably begin with *The American Notebooks*. Covering the period 1835–53, the entries in these notebooks can usefully be divided into two categories.

They are part lengthy, rambling passages about whom Hawthorne has seen and what he has done, and part shorter, epigrammatic entries which include but are not comprised exclusively of ideas for stories. This latter group belongs to an imagination that began and remained highly susceptible to the allegorical significance of nearly everything it lit upon.

How much this tendency owes to Spenser and how much to inherited modes of typology is difficult to determine, but, frequently enough, the story suggestions are markedly Spenserian. In the early 1840s, for example, Hawthorne writes: 'To allegorize life with a masquerade, and represent mankind generally as masquers. Here and there, a natural face may appear'; 'Visits to Castles in the Air – Chateaus en Espagne etc – with remarks on that sort of architecture'; 'To personify If – But – And – though – etc'; 'An eating-house, where all the dishes served out, even to the bread and salt, shall be poisoned with the adulterations that are said to be practised. Perhaps Death himself might be the cook' (ed 1962–, 8:240, 242, 252). The interest in pageantry, procession, and personification, in the architecture of dreams, in the potentially moral aspect of situations and objects, these are literary concerns that Hawthorne would return to throughout his career and that he surely associated with Spenser. It is worth noting, however, that these concerns extend well beyond Hawthorne's jottings for future tales and characterize the majority of his remarks, such that it is often difficult to distinguish what is meant as material for a story and what is more randomly observed. What the journals then make clear above all else is Hawthorne's habit of reading his daily existence as if it, too, were a canto in *The Faerie Queene*.

Despite this pervasive Spenserian mode of perception, the direct allusions to Spenser in the tales and novels are few. In the 'Hall of Fantasy,' the poet himself is described as 'meet guest for an allegoric structure'; and in 'A Virtuoso's Collection,' the narrator is rebuked for having 'but carelessly read Spenser' (in *Mosses from an Old Manse* ed 1962–, 10:174, 478). 'A Select Party,' itself a highly Spenserian tale, refers to 'the unwritten cantos of the Fairy Queen' (10:69); and a single passage from *The Blithedale Romance* makes mention of the masqueraders as 'allegoric figures from the Faery Queen' (3:209). It is not surprising that the majority of these references occur in the early forties, at the time that George S. Hillard, a boarder in the Hawthorne household, edited the first American edition of *The Poetical Works of Edmund Spenser* (1839), and just before Hawthorne is known to have given the poem another careful reading.

Perhaps because the overt allusions are sparse, scholarship has been slow to recognize the very deep sense in which Spenser exerted a shaping force on Hawthorne's imagination. It was Herman Melville, in his 1850 review of *Mosses*, who first remarked the Spenserian cast of Hawthorne's fiction, but only recently has scholarship focused its full attention on the relation between Spenser and Hawthorne. A large part of this criticism has devoted itself to tracing Spenserian echoes in specific tales. It is widely noted, for example, that Hawthorne's description of Lady Eleanore and her mantle in 'Lady Eleanore's Mantle' relies heavily on Spenser's stanzas about Lucifera and the house of Pride (see *FQ* I iv 10–14, v 53), or that certain qualities of Hawthorne's villains, such as Dr Rappaccini of 'Rappaccini's Daughter' and Chillingworth of *The Scarlet Letter*, derive from the figure of Archimago (see *FQ* I i 29). The list of tales that contain distinct parallels with *The Faerie Queene* extends throughout Hawthorne's career, from early stories such as 'The Gentle Boy' and 'Young Goodman Brown' through middle works such as 'Egotism; or, The Bosom Serpent,' 'A Select Party,' and 'The Birthmark' to a late masterpiece like 'Feathertop.'

Such parallels are no less pertinent to certain scenes in the longer romances. But perhaps more significant than any specific textual parallels are the lessons in rhetoric that Hawthorne learned from Spenser. Above all, Hawthorne seems to find in Spenser a particular mode of allegorical romance. It is, however, misleading to think of Hawthorne's allegorical bent as a tendency towards didacticism, for the tales and novels suggest that his reading of Spenser was highly sophisticated. Despite occasional tendentiousness, Hawthorne refuses to predicate meaning on the direct correspondence between a representation and an abstraction. We may remember a period in Spenser studies, perhaps best exemplified by Ruskin's reading of Book I, in which each character and episode is reduced to its abstract equivalent. Hawthorne, however, seems to have construed the moral dimension of allegorical romance rather more nebulously. As he writes in the preface to *The House of the Seven Gables*, 'when romances do really teach anything, or produce any effective operation, it is usually through a far more subtile process than the ostensible one' (ed 1962–, 2:2). A very Spenserian proposition, this is simply to say that the 'lesson' of any story cannot be stated but rather inheres in the process of reading, in what the poet teaches the reader about reading, whether the text be that of *The Faerie Queene* or of the world itself.

This understanding of allegorical romance helps to explain Hawthorne's further interest in Spenser's emblematic technique. One of Hawthorne's chief devices of characterization, for example, whereby spiritual qualities are externalized in objects that attach to a person, may be called emblematic. The gesture in both Spenser and Hawthorne would seem to be based on the belief that a character's physical appearance corresponds to the state of his soul. Hence Talus carries a flail, just as Hawthorne's minister is defined by his black veil, or Hester, by the letter she wears. *The Scarlet Letter*, however, also carries emblematic technique beyond characterization and into the service of narrative. The scaffold scenes in particular are constructed as pictorial metaphors similar to the personified processions that run through Spenser's poem. Here, the letter *A* is the motto, the scene described, the device, and the interpretations given by the onlookers, the stanzas beneath the device.

In a general sense, and perhaps because of their emblematic nature, Hawthorne seems to favor the processional moments of Spenser's poem. It is important to remember, however, that these pageants always occur in particular places – the house of Pride, the Bower of Bliss, Busirane's castle – and Hawthorne does not overlook this. Although he often employs the emblem for purposes of characterization, he seems finally to have understood Spenser's fiction as a mode of romance that creates place rather than character. Much as Spenserian heroes may be defined by the places they pass through and by their reactions to those places, Hawthorne's characters, too, become the essence of the places in which they find themselves. The late story 'Feathertop,' itself a version of the false Florimell episode in *FQ* III, provides a compact example. In Mother Rigby's romance world, the scarecrow can indeed be brought to life. A hodgepodge of odds and ends, Feathertop has no distinctive qualities of his own, except those that Mother Rigby gives him. When she sends him into the realistic life of a New England town, he passes briefly as a fine gentleman, but finally is exposed as illusory, even as the townsfolk are themselves illusory. The tale is an incisive parable, both about the relation between romance and realism and about the constitutive character of place, however abstract that place may be.

This tale, like much of Hawthorne's work, shows both a deep and deeply personal sense of Spenser's poetic. It helps to illustrate, too, that Hawthorne's relation to Spenser is parallel rather than revisionary. He undoubtedly does revise, merely in seeing as and what he sees; but when he turns and returns to Spenser, it is less as antagonist than as unflagging student.

PAMELA SCHIRMEISTER

Nathaniel Hawthorne 1962– *The Centenary Edition of the Works* ed William Charvat, Roy Harvey Pierce, and Claude M. Simpson (Columbus, Ohio). Melville 1850; Randall Stewart 1933 'Hawthorne and *The Faerie Queene*' *PQ* 12:196–206.

Hazlitt, William (1778–1830) Hazlitt's most considered judgment of Spenser appears in the lecture 'On Chaucer and Spenser,' the second of his eight *Lectures on the English Poets* (1818, in ed 1930–4, 5:19–44). He starts by contrasting Chaucer, a 'masculine' poet, with Spenser, a poet of 'effeminate' temperament, of luxurious enjoyment and unrestrained indulgence, of an ease apparently detached from the common interests of life, and always on the brink of voluptuousness. 'The love of beauty ... and not of truth, is the moving principle of his mind.' In the third lecture, 'On Shakspeare and Milton,' Hazlitt goes on to identify romance as Spenser's proper domain, as distinct from nature for Shakespeare, manners for Chaucer, and morality for Milton. This afterthought shows how far from censorious his initial judgment was meant to be. A strength, not of dramatic intensity or elevation, but of 'melting harmony, dissolving the soul in pleasure, or holding it captive in the chains of suspense,' is for him a strength nevertheless. He connects the 'suspense' of *The Faerie Queene* with the narrative conventions of romance, and also with a deliberateness of style peculiar to Spenser.

Allegory for Hazlitt is an ideal language that finds its appropriateness in the record of associations through which each individual mind must interpret it. That record, however various our lives in other respects, exhibits a sufficient number of common features: Spenser 'paints nature, not as we find it, but as we expected to find it; and fulfills the delightful promise of our youth.' Once again, Hazlitt says this neither to praise nor to blame, but to mark the qualities of one kind of poetry. He was free of the romantic prejudice against didactic books, and it is not clear in any case that he would have regarded Spenser as affording simple moral instruction. He admits that Spenser's is a poetry of ideas – indeed, a poetry in which the author's ideas 'seem more distinct than his perceptions' – and yet, from Hazlitt's point of view, ideas may have for poetry a reality no less striking than that of perceptions. 'A gentle Husher, *Vanitie* by name' (*FQ* I iv 13) would have seemed to him a conception as perfectly realized and as fully poetic as Wordsworth's 'A violet by a mossy stone, / Half hidden from the eye.' To the charge that in *The Faerie Queene* the image and the idea fail to coalesce permanently for the reader, he replies: 'It might as well be pretended, that we cannot see Poussin's pictures for the allegory, as that the allegory prevents us from understanding Spenser.' He agrees with the verdict of several generations of readers, that 'in point of interest' Spenser cannot bear comparison with Shakespeare. Among other allegories, however, he finds only *The Pilgrim's Progress* more interesting, and he adds that 'a fairer comparison would be with Comus; and the result would not be unfavourable to Spenser.' If ease, pleasure, and luxuriance are the chief traits of Spenser's poetry, it is remarkable too for its passion and steady power. Spenser is 'the poet of our waking dreams,' and these include the dreams of moral virtue which no history can cancel or place entirely beyond our grasp.

Hazlitt read the whole of *The Faerie Queene* when young, knew and spoke highly of other poems, and retained to the end of his life a precise memory of details. He seems to have admired Books I and II above the rest (to judge by quotations from them elsewhere, as well as by what he says of them in his lectures), and was responsive in particular to the eloquence of two episodes, the Cave of Despair and the house of Mammon. Of all modern poets, he concludes, Spenser is 'the most poetical.' This description is in keeping with his more general refusal to separate the work of persuasion from the work of imagination. Because poetry always affects us as rhetoric, a poem of ideas may influence a reader's life as easily as a poem of perceptions. Every emotion which we are capable of experiencing as a conviction is itself poetry. Hazlitt first made this assertion in his lecture 'On Poetry in General,' and supported it with a Spenserian catalog of animating ideas: 'Fear is poetry, hope is poetry, love is poetry, hatred is poetry; contempt, jealousy, remorse, admiration, wonder, pity, despair, or madness, are all poetry.' DAVID BROMWICH

heaven Spenser's major predecessors in representing a Christian or Christianized heaven were Dante and Tasso, the latter in *Il mondo creato* and at the end of the *Gerusalemme conquistata*, in the vision of Goffredo. Petrarch's *Africa* includes a scene in which Jove hears the pleas of Carthage and Rome in the court of heaven; Sannazaro's *De partu virginis* and Vida's *Christiad* present brief views of heaven. Chaucer and Ariosto had little to offer Spenser in this regard. While the traditional Christian heaven never assumed the central importance for Spenser that it did for Milton, it figures significantly in his minor poems and in *The Faerie Queene*. In his translation of the last of four sonnets on the Apocalypse in *Theatre for Worldlings* (sonn 15), Spenser describes the 'holy Citie of the Lorde' according to Revelation 21 and 22: square, with twelve gates of pearl, houses of gold, jeweled pavement, and with the clear waters of the river of life, bordered by the tree of life, running through its center. Yet the New Jerusalem of Revelation does not appear in Spenser's own poetry until the Red Cross Knight is shown a vision of the Christian heaven at the end of his sojourn in the house of Holiness (*FQ* I x 55–8).

Spenser first describes heaven in Colin Clout's elegy for Dido in *SC, November* 177–89. Renaissance pastoral elegies frequently conclude with a *consolatio* in which grief yields to celebration as the person mourned is translated to heaven, often represented in pastoral terms (see Ronsard's first eclogue and Boccaccio's 'Olympia' eclogue). Spenser's Dido is 'enstalled' in a pastoral heaven that is a perfected version of the familiar natural world, with 'The fieldes ay fresh, the grasse ay greene' (cf the conclusion of Milton's *Lycidas* 172–81). This heaven owes more to classical than to Christian tradition: its '*Elisian* fieldes so free' are Virgilian, its nectar and ambrosia Homeric. Yet Spenser would have expected his readers to understand this as a version of the Christian heaven, as his easy mingling of classical and Christian terminology suggests: 'She raignes a goddesse now emong the saintes.' Elysian fields, nectar, and ambrosia appear again in *Ruines of Time*, where Spenser imagines Sidney in the heaven of poets; and the 'Lay of Clorinda' in *Astrophel* pictures Sidney enjoying 'everlasting blis' in a lush celestial paradise with beds of flowers and caroling birds (68–85).

At the conclusion of *Epithalamion* (409–23), Spenser introduces a more obviously Christian heaven that blends into the poem's mythological texture, much as his Christian wedding with angelic alleluias follows naturally from pagan rituals. The stars of the night sky suggest a 'thousand torches flaming bright' in the 'high heavens'; they catch the poem's festive tone and offer a comforting hint of divine protection from the 'dreadful darknesse.' Spenser invokes the 'powers' of heaven not only to ensure a fruitful temporal union but also to depict a stable, timeless world beyond the poem. He is finally able to rest in the hope that his progeny ultimately will join the company of 'blessed Saints' in their 'heavenly tabernacles.' This vision of heaven exorcises fears aroused by the night and extends the scope of the poem to encompass the end of human activity (see *eschatology).

Whether fully represented or not, heaven in Spenser's poetry suggests an ideal beauty and purity contrasted to the imperfection and corruptibility of earth. Characteristically, he praises feminine beauty by associating it with the perfection of heaven. The lady of *Amoretti* 61, for instance, is described as 'The glorious image of the makers beautie' and is said to be 'divinely wrought, / and of the brood of Angels hevenly borne.' In *Amoretti* 79, 'true beautie' argues the lady 'to be divine and borne of heavenly seed.'

Spenser explores the nature of beauty, and of heaven, most thoroughly in the *Fowre Hymnes*. It is here that the Neoplatonism which underlies his praise of beauty and moral virtue in *Amoretti* and elsewhere receives its fullest expression, although it remains subordinate to the fundamentally Christian world view of the hymns (Ellrodt 1960, chs 7–9). In both pairs of hymns, heaven is the source of true love and beauty and the object of human aspiration. The image of celestial light pervades the poems: love lifts one up to the 'flaming light of that celestiall fyre' (*HL* 186) which unpurified lust cannot endure, and the beautiful are 'lively images of heavens light' (*HB* 163). Participation in this radiance becomes a measure of progress from earthly imperfection to heavenly perfection. Heaven itself remains largely undefined in the first two hymns, except insofar as it is represented by the heaven of love to which Cupid leads lovers 'through paines of Purgatorie' (*HL* 278). The lovers' reward is to enjoy the rarefied sensuous pleasure of gods and goddesses who feed on nectar and recline on ivory beds. This heaven of lovers offers the bliss and rest of the Christian heaven but more nearly resembles a secular paradise like the Garden of Adonis (*FQ* III vi).

The two 'heavenly' hymns picture a distinctly Christian heaven inhabited by angels who behold God's glory and carol hymns of love. Like Milton, Spenser stresses attributes of heaven that defy normal expectations of time and space: 'eternall blis,' 'illimitable hight' (*HHL* 62, 57). As in the heaven of Revelation, day never ends. Light becomes Christ's 'celestiall beauties blaze' (277), which dazzles the senses while it illuminates the spirit and kindles a love of God. In both these hymns, heaven is the home of celestial patterns or Platonic ideas that earthly forms imitate. It is also the source of a power that inspires the 'sweete enragement' of the love of God (*HHL* 286) and the ecstatic contemplation of divinity (*HHB*).

Spenser had offered a simple version of 'heavens great *Hierarchie*' in *Teares of the Muses* (505–16), as part of Urania's effort to establish a heavenly perspective against which to measure human insufficiency. In *Heavenly Beautie*, he offers his most elaborate vision of heaven, basing it upon the traditional Pythagorean concept of concentric spheres extending from earth to the sphere of the prime mover (Heninger 1974:114–32), but he complicates this tradition by introducing a succession of heavens, or subdivisions of heaven, beyond the visible one. The multiple heavens of *Heavenly Beautie* share characteristics of the Christian heaven: 'infinite in largenesse and in hight, / Unmoving, uncorrupt, and spotlesse bright' (67–8). In the poem's lowest heaven, souls enjoy the sight of God; above it we find the heaven of Platonic ideas, then others for different angelic orders until we reach the highest, 'farre beyond all telling' (101). This fundamentally Platonic approach to divinity by degrees of fairness and brightness underscores the inexpressibility of divine perfection and the difficulty of approaching God. It prepares for Spenser's introduction of Sapience (183), the contemplation of whose face inspires the ecstasy in which the 'thrise happie man' (239) hears heavenly carolings (260–2) and transcends the cares and delusions of this 'vile world' (299). The quintessential element of the heaven that Sapience inhabits and the ultimate source of its purity and power is 'that soveraine light, / From whose pure beams al perfect beauty springs' (295–6).

Spenser frequently reminds us of heaven in *The Faerie Queene*, even though he describes it fully only in the vision that Contemplation shows Redcrosse. He causes us to feel the benevolent influence of the visible heavens (which he characterizes as '*Joves* eternall hous,' with a porch, windows, and a 'golden Orientall gate' through which the sun rises: III iv 51, I v 2), and to recognize heaven itself as the place where 'all goodnesse is' and where the saints find 'blisse and everlasting rest' (III ix 2, viii 8). We see the agency of heaven in the angel's descent to protect Guyon after his swoon and, indirectly, in the 'blazing brightnesse' of Arthur's shield, surpassing 'heavens light' (II viii 3–9, I viii 19). Its presence is felt in the mysterious 'heavenly noise' that accompanies the betrothal of Una and Redcrosse (I xii 39).

In representing Redcrosse's vision, Spenser draws heavily upon Revelation, stressing the inconceivable splendor and strength of the New Jerusalem and also the joy of the 'gladsome companee' of angels (I x 56). Conventional elements of the Christian heaven here take on added force when contrasted to Redcrosse's experience in the house of Pride with its false glory and spurious fellowship, and in the cave of Despair with its desolate solitude. His attraction to the 'goodly Citie' is so great that Contemplation must insist in good Protestant fashion that he return to his task in the world (55, 63). This vision establishes a standard against which Cleopolis, earth's 'fairest Citie' (58), can be measured; and it defines the goal of the journey for which Redcrosse's stay in the house of Holiness has prepared him.

Spenser returns to the idea of heaven in the *Cantos of Mutabilitie* where Jove and the other gods and goddesses inhabit a shadowy, ostensibly changeless Olympian world of towers and palaces. The chief drama of the cantos arises when Mutabilitie tries to touch their 'celestiall seates' with 'earthly mire' (VII vi 29). Spenser's most powerful image of heaven occurs in the final stanza's haunting evocation of the sabbatical rest of the saints. The time 'when no more *Change* shall be, / But stedfast rest of all things firmely stayd / Upon the pillours of Eternity' can be imagined only in connection with a place that embodies unassailable stability and order. Spenser leaves his Christian readers with the promise that they will find rest in a heaven beyond the reach of time, unchanging and incorruptible.

John R. Knott, Jr

Roland Mushat Frye 1978 *Milton's Imagery and the Visual Arts* (Princeton); Greene 1963; John R. Knott, Jr 1970 'Milton's Heaven' *PMLA* 85:487–95; Patch 1950; Patrides 1966.

Hecate Goddess of the underworld, Hecate is named only twice in *The Faerie Queene*. At I i 43, when Archimago's messenger-sprite cannot awaken Morpheus, god of sleep, he 'threatned unto him the dreaded name / Of *Hecate*,' which frightens him into attention. At VII vi 3, after the defeat of the Titans, Hecate, like Bellona and others of Titanic descent, 'obtain'd / Great power of *Jove*, and high authority.' In Hecate's 'almighty hand, / He plac't all rule and principality, / To be by her disposed diversly, / To Gods, and men, as she them list divide.'

Evidently Spenser carefully read the related group of articles in Conti on Night, Sleep, Death, Proserpina, Luna, and Diana (*Mythologiae* 3.12–18). All are treated as dark or bright aspects of the same powers. Conti (3.15) interprets Hecate as an ancient symbol of the mystery of fate or the divine will, referring to Hesiod (*Theogony* 411–52; Lotspeich 1932:67). Spenser follows Hesiod in emphasizing that she exercises her power in earth, sea, and heaven under Jove and along with the other gods, a power first given to her as one of the Titans, though Jove later assigned her role as patroness of warriors to Bellona. She acts by Jove's permission, in contrast to the self-assertive aspirations of the Titaness Mutabilitie. Like others of Titanic descent (including the sun, Spenser's 'Titan'), Hecate has her place in the natural order.

As daughter of Night, she has links with the dark powers in *FQ* I. Archimago's night-magic includes invocation of Proserpina, Queen of Hades, sometimes identified with Hecate. As patroness of witchcraft, she was traditionally invoked by Circe and Medea, euhemerized in Conti as her daughters, whom she taught the art of making fatal drugs. Accordingly, the underworld Garden of Proserpina (II vii 51–5) contains plants associated with sleep, poison, melancholy, madness, and death. As *trivia* or *triformis* (threefold), she is also identified with Diana and Luna, or the moon's three phases, and rules over sky, earth, and underworld. Euripides calls Hecate 'phosphor' (*Helen* 569), rendered by Conti 'Lucifera,' the name of the daughter of Proserpina and Pluto (*FQ* I iv 11). Lucian's Hecate (Loeb ed 3:355) has a female head and serpent hindparts like Error (i 14). Hecate's magic links her with Duessa, 'a false sorceresse,' granddaughter of Night (I v 26–7). Night, who takes the wounded Sansjoy down to Avernus, owns barking dogs (v 30) as does Hecate in Apollonius Rhodius' *Argonautica* 3; her chariot resembles Hecate's, and she 'in hell and heaven had power equally' (v 34). Compare *Aeneid* 6.247, where before Aeneas' descent to Avernus, Hecate is invoked as 'caeloque Ereboque potentem' (supreme both in heaven and hell).

Kitty Scoular Datta

Excellent sources for Milton's Hecate in *Comus* 135, 534 are given in Hughes, et al 1970–, 2.3:879; many of these would have been known to Spenser.

hell As both a physical place and a state of damnation, hell appears in *The Faerie Queene* with its full Christian moral force. It occupies a space as real as that of Spenser's imagined realm of faerie: Duessa visits it in *FQ* I v, and Mammon's house lies within its precincts (see esp II vii 24). It is also the place from which Archimago's spirit fetches a salacious dream to torment the Red Cross Knight (I i 38–43). Lucifera's name and retinue (the seven deadly sins) indicate her kinship with the ruler of hell, as she is the daughter of the King and Queen of hell (iv 11). Hell and its manifestations in Fairyland become significant places in Spenser's moralized landscape (see allegorical *places). It provides one of the few moral absolutes in *The Faerie Queene*, a fixed pole of spiritual and psychological reference: it is inhabited by fiends, and villains like the vicious Sansfoy are condemned to it after death (ii 19). Almost anything designated *hellish* or *infernal* is a creature or object literally derived from hell (eg, Despair as 'A man of hell' I ix 28; the 'Firebrand of hell' that causes discord IV ii i).

Spenser's readers would have known about hell from a variety of popular, learned, religious, and literary sources. From the Bible, they knew it as a place of punishment for sin, the outer darkness or the fiery furnace, where there is weeping and gnashing of teeth, where the fire is not quenched and the worm never dies (Matt 13.42, 25.30; Mark 9.43–8). Following Augustine's *City of God* (21.9–11), Protestant divines taught that hell was both a real place (though just where was a matter of conjecture) and a condition. Its pains, therefore, were of two sorts: psychological and physical, the pain of loss and the pain of sense. Bishop Hugh Latimer's description is succinct and graphic: 'Painters paint death like a man without skin, and a body having nothing but bones. And hell they paint with horrible flames of burning fire ... But this is no true painting. No painter can paint hell, unless he could paint the torment and condemnation both of body and soul; the possession and having of all infelicity. This is hell, this is the image of death' (Seventh Sermon Preached before King Edward VI, 19 April 1549, in ed 1844–5, 1:219–20). Moreover, hell is eternal: doubters and quibblers, like Marlowe's Faustus who banters with Mephistopheles about the real nature of hell, all come at the end to Faustus' fate and realization: 'No end is limited to damned soules ... mine must live still to be plagu'd in hell' (ed 1973, lines 1963, 1971).

Spenser's account of hell derives mostly from secular sources, such as Homer's *Odyssey* 11, Ovid's *Metamorphoses* 4, 10, and especially Virgil's *Aeneid* 6, which provided the paradigm for the descent to hell, a narrative motif that assumed great importance in epic poetry from the impetus of Christian teaching, Neoplatonic allegorizing, and the example of Dante. Sackville's 'Induction' to the *Mirror for Magistrates*, for example, provided a notable exemplar for adapting Virgil's underworld to English poetry.

Spenser's poetic practice in *The Faerie Queene* typically fuses the pagan and Christian elements of hell into a single place of damnation peopled by both 'feends' and classical figures like Aesculapius (I v 32, 36). He makes one major change in classical orthodoxy: except for the passing reference at IV x 23, he omits all mention of the Elysian fields (the abode of blessed spirits, as in *SC, Nov* 175–9), thus selecting only those classical images which are compatible with the Christian view of hell as a state of damnation for sin.

In most of his underworld details, Spenser follows Virgil fairly closely. He mentions the conventional Virgilian rivers of the underworld: Acheron and Phlegethon (I v 33), Cocytus (II vii 56), and Styx (IV xi 4). He follows convention in making Erebus, traditionally the lowest region of hell, the husband of Night (II iv 41 and III iv 55). According to Charles Estienne's *Dictionarium historicum, geographicum, et poeticum* (Paris 1596), Erebus is a god of the underworld and his name is often used to denote the underworld itself. In Boccaccio, Erebus is identical with Tartarus, the classical place of punishment (*Genealogia* 1.14). Whatever his sources, Spenser attributes considerable importance to Erebus and Night: from the moment that Night meets Duessa (*FQ* I v 20), he links darkness, night, and Erebus to hell and evil. He twice refers to '*Limbo* lake,' which he identifies as the abode of a 'damned Ghost' (I ii 32; cf III x 54), following Virgil, who speaks of the Styx (the *limbus* 'border' of the underworld) indifferently as river, marsh, and lake, or Elizabethan translations of Virgil (see Lotspeich 1932:78).

In *FQ* II vii 25, Spenser seems to be following tradition and a hint from *Aeneid* 6.273–8 in placing the entrance of the cave of Sleep immediately beside the entrance of hell, for his catalogue of personified abstractions imitates Virgil's list of spirits before the gates of hell. As elsewhere in *The Faerie Queene*, he refers here to hell as '*Plutoes* griesly raine' (21). In Boccaccio and Conti, Pluto was confused with Plutus, the god of riches (see Lotspeich 1932:102), as Spenser does in the allegorical geography of Fairyland: 'but a litle stride ... did the house of Richesse from hell-mouth divide'; 'Here Sleep, there Richesse, and Hel-gate them both betwext' (24–5).

Christ's harrowing of hell is mentioned only once in *The Faerie Queene* (I x 40; cf *Amoretti* 68) in a context that links Christ's actions with the ransoming of prisoners. Yet it is 'imitated' in actions as diverse as Redcrosse's quest to free Adam and Eve from imprisonment by the Dragon (I x), Arthur's rescue of him from Orgoglio's dungeon (viii), and Calidore's rescue of Pastorella from the Brigands' cave (VI xi). It is a recurrent motif in the poem, for figuratively each hero is first harrowed from hell and then goes on to harrow hell.

THOMAS E. MARESCA

Anderson 1969; Raymond J. Clark 1979 *Catabasis: Vergil and the Wisdom Tradition* (Amsterdam); Cullen 1974; Latimer ed 1844–5; Maresca 1979; *Mirror* ed 1938; Patch 1950; C.A. Patrides 1964 'Renaissance and Modern Views on Hell' *HTR* 57:217–36; D.P. Walker 1964 *The Decline of Hell: Seventeenth-Century Discussions of Eternal Torment* (London).

Hellenore As her name suggests, Hellenore plays a diminished, latter-day Helen to the degenerate Paris of Paridell, who steals her from Malbecco in the elegant fabliau of *FQ* III viii-x. This licentious creature (whom the narrator ironically calls 'This second *Hellene*, faire Dame *Hellenore*' at x 13) parodies the chaste Britomart's virtue and her relation to Troy. The subplot of Hellenore begins as a traditional bawdy tale and ends in an Ovidian transformation when her husband becomes Jealousy itself, and when Hellenore realizes her own nature as the common woman of a band of satyrs.

Hellenore's story begins when Britomart, Satyrane, and Paridell gain entrance to the castle of Malbecco, an aging, one-eyed niggard who counts among his treasures his young, restless wife. Her desires for 'kindly joy and naturall delight' (ix 5) are left unsatisfied by her impotent husband, and she participates willingly in the courtly seduction which Paridell begins at dinner and completes after Britomart and Satyrane depart. First setting fire to the castle, the two lovers abscond with much of Malbecco's wealth; but Paridell soon discards Hellenore, who is picked up by satyrs and remains with them, rejecting Malbecco's pathetic plea to return. After hearing a satyr make love to her nine times, even her jealous husband is forced to admit that 'not for nought his wife them loved so well, / When one so oft a night did ring his matins bell' (x 48).

Although the story of Hellenore has a comic tone, her classical prototype recalls the potentially monumental destructiveness of adultery. Renaissance readers were likely to regard Helen less as 'the face that launch'd a thousand ships' (Marlowe *Dr Faustus* 18.99) than as the epitome of a faithless wife. The narrator invokes this view by emphasizing Hellenore's 'fancie,' fickle 'will,' 'fraile wit,' and 'weake hart' (ix 6, 52; x 8). Yet he is chivalrous (as Spenser's narrator often is to beautiful women) and attempts to shift the blame to Paridell. This attempt leads to the ludicrously misapplied epic simile which begins 'No fort so fensible, no wals so strong' (10). Hellenore's enforced chastity ill fits this conventional image of a fort of virtue, as the narrator himself concludes a stanza later: 'So readie rype to ill, ill wemens counsels bee.'

Hellenore and her various consorts collaborate in transforming her into what we would now call a sex object. Malbecco hoards her. Paridell steals her and then throws her away. The satyrs take her home and discover, to everyone's pleasure, a feminine lechery as insatiable as their own. Hellenore's happiness with her semibestial lovers comes as poetic justice of a sort, but it also testifies to the inevitable degradation of people who allow themselves to be overrun by their desires. At the same time, it shows by bad example the necessity in human life of the titular virtue of the Legend of Chastity. LESLEY BRILL

Henryson, Robert (c 1425–c 1500) Very little is known about the life of this important fifteenth-century Scots poet except that he was master of the grammar school in the abbey at Dunfermline. His longest work is the *Fables*, which contains a prologue and thirteen Aesopic and Reynardian fables, each divided into a narrative and a *moralitas*. Two other long poems by Henryson survive. *Orpheus and Eurydice*, another narrative followed by a *moralitas*, is based on a short poem in Boethius' *Consolation of Philosophy* (3.12) and the allegorizing commentary on it by Nicholas Trivet. *The Testament of Cresseid*, in some sense a sequel to Chaucer's *Troilus and Criseyde*, tells how Cresseid, abandoned by Diomede, blasphemes against Venus, is punished with leprosy, and dies penitent. Twelve short poems are also ascribed to Henryson, though the attributions are not always certain.

Spenser is not likely to have come across Henryson's *Orpheus*. While it was printed in Edinburgh circa 1508, there is no evidence that the poem was known in England. His *Fables*, on the other hand, was not only printed in Edinburgh in 1570 and 1571 (there is evidence for other lost Scottish editions), but was also 'translated' (unskillfully anglicized and modernized) and printed in London in 1577 by Richard Smith. Smith's version is not attractive, and there is no evidence that Spenser read it.

The work by Henryson which Spenser is most likely to have read, though without knowing that it was by Henryson, is *The Testament of Cresseid*. Besides some sixteenth-century Scottish prints (of which only one survives), it appears in an anglicized version immediately after *Troilus* in Thynne's 1532 edition of Chaucer, and similarly in each of the four subsequent sixteenth-century editions of Chaucer. Although line 64 ('Quha wait gif all that Chauceir wrait was trew?') might lead one to suspect that the *Testament* was not by Chaucer, there is no indication of authorship in the English prints, and it was apparently taken as Chaucer's by all sixteenth-century readers. It is safe to assume that most people who read *Troilus* in the second half of the sixteenth century read it in one of these collected editions, and that most of them went on to read the *Testament*. But nothing in Spenser's works suggests that he was in any way influenced by the *Testament*: the parallels which have been proposed are unconvincing.

While Henryson and Spenser are coheirs of Chaucer, the two later poets are so unlike that Spenser might have found little in Henryson to learn from. Henryson is a diverse and subtle poet, so any simple description of his work is bound to be misleading, but one might venture that he is characteristically terse, austere, ironic, impersonal, moral, uncourtly, and, especially, medieval – there is hardly any sense in which he can be thought of as a Renaissance poet.

DENTON FOX

Douglas Gray 1979 *Robert Henryson* (Leiden); Henryson ed 1981.

heraldry A system of hereditary symbols used chiefly on shields and banners, heraldry developed in the Middle Ages and retained its fascination and importance for Elizabethans partly as the result of a revived interest in chivalry, of which *The Faerie Queene* is itself a product. Its visual symbolism identified and distinguished those of noble or gentle rank, and in doing so referred to many of the factors crucial for success in an unstable and competitive society: family, dynastic, and marital alliances; nobility and antiquity of race (whether real or fictional); royal favor and connections; and the wealth implied by all of these. Heraldic images were central to the art of display which was essential to princely magnificence, and they figured prominently in the splendid pageantry surrounding Queen Elizabeth and her court, on which Spenser drew so heavily. During the late sixteenth century, heraldic designs could decorate almost any object or available surface, including books, paintings, and buildings, from the seals validating Acts of Parliament to the wool weights used in country markets. From the 1550s onwards, many explanatory treatises were published. Heraldry was so ubiquitous that Elizabethan authors could employ its images and conventions in the sure knowledge of their audience's comprehension; and such writers as Shakespeare, Sidney, Marlowe, and Nashe, as well as Spenser, found in it a versatile and expressive language.

Visual symbolism appealed to the educated Renaissance mind, and part of heraldry's revived and continued popularity probably stems from its similarity to the arts of emblem and impresa. Like these, the heraldic device wedded visual and verbal in its image and motto. The coat of arms, the central image in heraldry, could also act as a rebus (a kind of pun in which a word or phrase is represented by a visual image), especially in canting heraldry in which the device plays upon the name of the bearer. Heraldry's supposed antiquity (even the ancients and figures from the Old Testament were thought to have borne coats of arms) and its elaborate and arcane language made it seem something of an English equivalent to the continental art of the emblem, counterbalancing the emblem's European origins and aura of Neoplatonic symbolism and pseudo-Egyptian hieroglyphics with an heroic, military, and often English vocabulary of images. This is not to say that heraldry was absent from the rest of Europe, or that emblems were not created and enjoyed in England; but the Arthurian cycle of the Matter of Britain and the preeminence of the English Order of the Garter among European orders of knighthood endowed heraldry as an expression of chivalry with a special appropriateness in the neo-medieval culture of Elizabethan England. Spenser therefore found in heraldry both visual and verbal wit and a species of symbolism suited to his interest in chivalry and national history.

Spenser uses heraldry's visual symbolism in two ways: he alludes to people and events outside his works by their heraldic devices, and he uses heraldic images and conventions in creating his own chivalric symbols, especially in *The Faerie Queene*. He draws both on contemporary devices and on those traditionally associated with ancient and medieval heroes. However, he rarely alludes to the complicated quarterings of arms which were becoming normal in the sixteenth century; instead, the heraldry he uses is of the simplest and richest kind. The devices he gives his knights in *The Faerie Queene* are normally unelaborate and made up of common heraldic charges, such as St George's red cross or Britomart's 'Lion passant in a golden field' (III i 4). While such simplicity is partly for ease of comprehension, Spenser has other reasons. First, his poem is set in an heroic past when heraldry was supposed to have been simpler. Second, and herein lies the paradoxical richness of his simple heraldry, he selects from the available vocabulary of images the most ancient, striking, and pervasive of charges. In fact, his devices are more often derived from heraldic badges and banners than from coats of arms themselves, because these are usually simpler and more readily recognizable, as in older heraldry. These traditional charges, like the red cross and the lion, tend to have acquired multiple and resonant associations on which Spenser can draw for complex and subtle expression.

In his heraldic descriptions or 'blazons,' Spenser often uses the technical vocabulary of the heralds: Tristram's clothes, for instance, are 'paled part per part' (VI ii 6), that is, with vertical bands of color. Pyrochles' shield, borne by Atin, appears to be described in terms that are fairly general but in fact are specific: it shows in 'colours fit' – that is, in correct heraldic tinctures – a 'flaming fire in midst of bloudy field,' this *field* being the background color of a coat of arms (II iv 38). His device resembles that of Disdain in Ariosto's *Orlando furioso* who bears 'flames of fire all in a yeallow field' (42.51.4, tr Harington). 'Burnt I do burne' is written as a motto 'round about the wreath' (38). Here Spenser may mean that a wreath or garland is represented visually on the shield; but in heraldic terminology, a wreath is a narrow band around the edge of a shield, so that he more likely means that the words are inscribed therein. By and large, he obeys the somewhat arcane rules of heraldry, although Upton criticizes him for the device borne by Braggadocchio at Marinell's tournament, which shows 'the Sunne brode blazed in a golden field' (V iii 14). Unless otherwise stated, the sun in heraldry is always golden; so this shield shows gold on gold. Upton is correct in saying that in the sixteenth century ''tis a fault in blazoning to lay colour upon colour, or metal upon metal,' and it may be, as he tentatively suggests, that Spenser 'on purpose falsely blazoned his shield, as he was a false and recreant knight' (*FQ* ed 1758a, 2:616).

Pyrochles' shield shows a fire, its device and motto obviously playing upon his name, as in canting heraldry (Gr *pyr* fire). Similarly, Scudamour's shield 'On which the winged boy in colours cleare / Depeincted was' (III xi 7; cf IV i 39, x 55) is an *escu d'amour* like that of the Scudamore family. Usually there are close connections between the shield and its bearer – Satyrane's shield bears 'a Satyres hed' (III vii 30) – although they are not always as simple as in canting arms. Sanglier's shield bears 'A broken sword within a bloodie field; / Expressing well his nature' (V i 19). But as the Elizabethan theorists often assert, the device a man bears is in some ways part of him and the loss or desecration of his shield is highly significant. Verdant's fall from honorable manliness in Acrasia's Bower of Bliss is signified by having his shield 'fowly ra'st, that none the signes might see' (II xii 80); Burbon's voluntary abandonment of his red cross shield (V xi 46–56) signifies his abandonment of true religion; and Braggadocchio's forcible expulsion from the company of knights, and from the poem, is rendered as a chivalric degradation, in which Talus 'blotted out his armes' (V iii 37).

In all these examples, Spenser draws on the convention that the whole coat of arms expresses the bearer's honor and nobility. Each of the charges and tinctures that compose the device has its own meaning as well – or rather, its many meanings, for heraldic symbolism is complicated. In general, Spenser avoids problems of interpretation by using only major and well-known devices (a notable and still inadequately understood exception is the device of the knight whose shield shows 'A Ladie on rough waves, row'd in a sommer barge' VI ii 44). But this does not mean that the well-known devices are simple in meaning. For example, the dragon in Prince Arthur's crest may allude to *King* Arthur's traditional dragon-crest, said to have been inherited from his father, Uther Pendragon (thus canting); or it may allude to the Dragon of Cadwallader, used by the Tudor dynasty as an heraldic badge and as a supporter to their coat of arms, emphasizing their Welsh and ancient British origins. (*Supporters* are animals – often mythical – or human beings one on each side of a coat of arms represented as holding it up, such as the Lion and Unicorn used from the Stuarts to the present day on the royal arms of British monarchs.) The advantage of the dragon-crest for Spenser is that these associations would be readily recognized by his readers.

In using well-known heraldic images as part of his poetic vocabulary, Spenser creates larger and more complex meanings through combination and cross-reference, as with Arthur's crest, of which the dragon is only part; he draws out and alludes to the various meanings of his heraldic symbols at different points in his poem; and he renders every detail significant. In his description of the dragon, for example, the head is 'close couched on the bever' (I vii 31); but the correct heraldic term (used elsewhere) is *couchant*. This variation draws attention to the dragon's unusual posture – a *couchant* animal lies with its head and tail erect, but this animal's head is hung low down on the helmet and its 'scaly tayle [is] stretcht adowne his backe full low' – and so may anticipate Redcrosse's victory over 'that old Dragon' in canto xi, as well as alluding ironically to an epic prototype in the triumphant dragon on the Sultan's crest in *Gerusalemme liberata*.

The device borne by Redcrosse is also traditionally connected with King Arthur, but has many other well-known and complex associations. Spenser makes its significance emphatically explicit in *FQ* I i 2: the 'bloudie Crosse' on the knight's breast and shield is the badge of 'his dying Lord.' In the Middle Ages, Christ was given his own heraldic arms (the *arma Christi*), which were composed of the various instruments and implements of the Passion, chiefly the cross. Their use as his device is based on the convention that the coat of arms may refer to the events which resulted in the ennobling of the bearer and his descendants. The instruments stand for Christ's 'battle,' often presented as a chivalric joust; and in images of the Harrowing of Hell, he is frequently shown bearing the *crux invicta* (cross of victory) in a banner or pennon. Spenser follows tradition in giving Christ's own heraldic device to Redcrosse as he imitates him in defeating the Dragon and freeing Adam and Eve, Una's parents.

In canto xi, the poet again refers to this device in heraldic terms, in invoking the Muse that 'I this man of God his godly armes may blaze' (I xi 7). In the context of 'armes,' *blaze* means more than merely 'proclaim'; it has the sense of 'describe in words an heraldic device.' By emphasizing the instruments of the knight's victory – the personified sword, the 'weapon bright,' kills the Dragon – Spenser defines the charge borne by Redcrosse. Besides this direct association with Christ, the red cross device may connect the knight with the Crusaders (especially in his battles with 'Paynims' and 'Sarazins'), and with various other knights in literature who bear red cross shields, including the hero of the Old French *Perlesvaus* and Sir Galahad in Malory's *Morte Darthur*, the 'good knight' who achieves the Quest of the Grail. Here, as with Spenser, the red cross is connected with Joseph of Arimathea, and thus with the Passion.

Through the simple device on the shield, then, Spenser links his hero with Christ, with militant Christianity, and with various quasi-religious heroes of the Middle Ages. But St George is also the patron saint of England and the red cross forms his country's flag. Both saint and flag are also central to the symbolism of England's chief chivalric institution, the Order of the Garter, alluded to in the Order of Maidenhead (*FQ* I vii 46; II ii 42, ix 6, etc). The red cross figures prominently in national symbolism; and in the years immediately preceding the publication of *FQ* I-III, the struggle for national and religious integrity was particularly intense. Spenser's dragon in the moral allegory no doubt represents sin and death; but the scales of its tail are like 'shields of red and blacke' (I xi II), colors that predominated in the arms of Philip II of Spain. As they advanced up the English Channel in 1588, the ships of his invading Armada flying ensigns of red and black at their sterns were met and defeated by English ships flying the red cross of England. In the battle between Redcrosse and the Dragon, Spenser may be using the heraldry of these two fleets to interweave the narrative with his religious and national themes.

Spenser seems to refer to Philip in describing the Souldan in *FQ* V. Instead of using the king's coat of arms as the basis for an allusion, he plays wittily upon his impresa. The impresa, though not heraldic, is similar to the badge in being a personal (ie, not familial) sign, frequently taking the shape of a shield. Philip used an image of Phoebus Apollo managing the horses of the sun; in contrast, the careering Souldan is compared to Apollo's presumptuous son Phaethon, who failed to control them. The Souldan's fate thus contradicts the vainglorious boast of Philip's device.

In general, Spenser's knights bear devices more similar in construction to impresas than to contemporary coats of arms. For example, Sansfoy's shield, consisting purely of the bearer's name (I ii 12), is unheraldic but would be permissible in an impresa. By using the impresa (which was increasingly popular in England in the late sixteenth century), Spenser broadens the range of images and devices available to him.

The class of heraldry to which Spenser most often refers is associated with Elizabeth: her royal heraldry as English monarch, her family heraldry as a member of the Tudor dynasty, and her personal symbolism as an individual ruler. Mercilla's court is the obvious example of royal heraldry: the decoration of her throne, 'all embost with Lyons and with Flourdelice' (V ix 27), is composed of the charges of the English royal coat of arms. As previously mentioned, Arthur's crest may refer to the Dragon of Cadwallader, one of the badges of the Tudors and a supporter to their coat of arms; Artegall's 'couchant Hound' (III ii 25) may refer to another, the Tudor or Beaufort Greyhound. Artegall's shield contains an ermine, which may be associated with Hercules through its relative the weasel, but is more likely to echo one of Elizabeth's personal emblems, adopted because of its associations with chastity and purity. Alternatively, the hound and ermine may allude to the familial heraldry of the Earl of Leicester through his ancestors, the earls of Warwick.

Britomart's shield contains a 'Lion passant' (ie, a lion walking and looking to the right, with the front right foot raised). Three lions passant are the basis of the English royal coat of arms, the lion being its most common supporter. But Britomart's arms may refer to those of the Trojan Brutus, the eponymous founder of Britain, for from that 'race of old ... she was lineally extract: / For noble *Britons* sprong from *Trojans* bold' (III ix 38). From her first anonymous entry, then, her shield forms an heraldic link with her own and her nation's origins in the heroic myth of Troy, as well as pointing forward to her progeny, the Tudor kings of England. Traditional heraldry thus establishes connections which are at the heart of the poem's praise of Elizabeth. The other heroic, royal myth is Arthurian; and although Spenser's Arthur does not use any traditional symbol apart from the dragon-crest, some Arthurian heraldry may be present elsewhere in *The Faerie Queene*. The charge on Guyon's shield, later said to represent Gloriana, at first remains ambiguous: 'that faire image of that Heavenly Mayd' and 'the Saint' (II i 28, V II) inevitably suggest the Virgin Mary, whose image appeared on King Arthur's shield, Pridwen (see Geoffrey of Monmouth *Historia* 9.4).

The shorter poems allude to several prominent figures through their heraldic symbols. In *Mother Hubberds Tale*, Spenser alludes to the Earl of Leicester's marriage, which was resented by Elizabeth, through his badge of a bear chained to a ragged staff: 'But his late chayne his Liege unmeete esteemeth; / For so brave beasts she loveth best to see, / In the wilde forrest raunging fresh and free' (628–30). Typically, he is not content merely to mention the device but makes it function poetically by interpreting its constituent parts. He uses the same device in *SC, October*, where Piers sings of 'the worthy whome shee loveth best, / That first the white beare to the stake did bring' (47–8). E.K. comments on this allusion to Leicester's relationship with Elizabeth in his gloss: 'he meaneth (as I guesse) the most honorable and renowmed the Erle of

Leycester, whom by his cognisance ... rather then by his name he bewrayeth.' This remark indicates how well known and understood such 'cognisances' were.

(See **Leicester** Fig 1.)

The term *heraldry* originally included all the functions of heralds, who acted as referees at tournaments, as they do in the joust between Redcrosse and Sansjoy at the house of Pride (I v 15). It was also their job as genealogists and artists to recognize and record coats of arms (hence the name 'heraldry'). Thus, in describing Marinell's tournament, Spenser refers to 'worke fit for an Herauld, not for me' (V iii 3). He makes the costume and ambassadorial role of the herald the basis of *Amoretti* 70: using the medieval conception of the god of love as a young prince rather than the more classical naked baby, he calls spring 'the herald of loves mighty king.' His 'cote armour' (the herald's tabard or short coat bearing the armorial device of his employer) is composed of 'all sorts of flowers' whose 'goodly colours' recall the tinctures or blocks of bright colors characteristic of heraldic art. The herald Spring is sent to summon the beloved to the court of the king of love; and the sonnet's humor depends on writer and reader pursuing this initial heraldic metaphor. The same is true of an episode in the *Cantos of Mutabilitie*, where the assembly of the gods is presented as a medieval court rather than as a classical senate. Mercury, the messenger of the gods, thus becomes 'Heavens Herald,' sent by Jove the king on an 'Embassie,' and returning to Jove's 'principall Estate' (ie, a royal throne and canopy, normally decorated with heraldic symbols, VII vi 19, 23; cf Mercilla's court in V ix 27). Spenser's periphrasis for Mercury's caduceus, his 'snaky-wreathed Mace' (18), in this context allows one sixteenth-century meaning of *mace* – a herald's rod of office – to add humor to the episode.

MICHAEL LESLIE

John Bossewell 1572 *Workes of Armorie* (London; facs rpt Amsterdam and New York 1969); Favyn ed 1623; John Ferne 1586 *The Blazon of Gentrie* (London; rpt New York 1973); John Guillim 1610 *A Display of Heraldrie* (London; rpt Amsterdam and Norwood, NJ 1979); Gerard Legh 1562 *The Accedens of Armory* (London); Sir William Segar 1590; Segar 1602 *Honor, Military and Civill, Contained in Foure Bookes* (London); John Selden 1614 *Titles of Honor* (London).

Berman 1983; *Boutell's Heraldry* 1978 comp C.W. Scott-Giles, rev J.P. Brooke-Little (London); Gerard J. Brault 1972 *Early Blazon: Heraldic Terminology in the Twelfth and Thirteenth Centuries, with Special Reference to Arthurian Literature* (Oxford); Paul C. Franke 1980–1 'The Heraldry of *The Faerie Queene*' *Coat-of-Arms* 4th ser, vol 4.116:317–23; Graziani 1964b; Leslie 1983; Richard Marks and Ann Payne, eds 1978 *British Heraldry: From Its Origins to c. 1800* (London); Anthony Wagner 1967 *Heralds of England: A History of the Office and College of Arms* (London).

Herbert, George (1593–1633) Since Herbert was less than six years old when Spenser died, he could not have known him directly, although their mutual friends and shared experiences are so numerous that he must have been reminded of him often. Lancelot Andrewes, who had studied with Spenser at Merchant Taylors' School and Pembroke Hall, was one of those who elected Herbert to Westminster School in 1605; the two remained friends until Andrewes' death in 1626. A similar kind of indirect contact also may have occurred through Anne Clifford, Countess of Dorset. Her mother and aunt were among Spenser's patrons (*Fowre Hymnes* was dedicated jointly to them), and she erected the monument to Spenser in Westminster Abbey in 1620. A longtime friend of Donne, she knew Herbert certainly by 1630 when she came to Wilton as the wife of Philip Herbert, fourth Earl of Pembroke; a quite cordial letter to her from Herbert, dated 1631, survives. Nicholas Stone, the sculptor of the Spenser monument, also laid out the elaborate grounds for the Chelsea home of Herbert's mother and stepfather, where Donne stayed with Herbert during the plague of 1625. Examples of strictly historical propinquity could be multiplied. The shadow of Spenser, its greatest poet, extended over the Cambridge of Herbert's day; moreover, the greatest influence of both poets was undoubtedly the Sidneys and their circle.

Herbert never refers directly to Spenser. Perhaps the most straightforward allusion, in 'Jordan' (I), appears to show some acquaintance with *FQ* I vii 5–7. In other poems, too, he implies a rejection of pastoral allegory (as well as courtly metaphors), and about the closest he will come to pastoral narrative – and that is not very close at all – is in a poem like 'The Pilgrimage.' But despite this difference in subjects, their basic assumptions about the nature of poetry have much in common. Both show a concern for the essential nature of metaphor and the way that metaphoric identifications – which inevitably emphasize differences as well as equivalences – can illuminate the division between sense experience and religious meaning. Such concern is manifest also in the choice of images that are fully congruent at all points with the intellectual argument at hand, and the subsuming of every detail to its proper place in the design of the whole.

As for contrasts, in Herbert we see a habit of allegorical thinking with referents firmly anchored in everyday life; in Spenser the same habit more typically finds referents in poetic tradition and the social conventions of the court. For both poets, though, the poem itself is a repository of sacred meaning; and its final end, as Sidney says in the *Defence*, 'is to lead and draw us to as high a perfection as our degenerate souls, made worse by their clayey lodgings, can be capable of' (ed 1973b:82). For both poets it follows that as a poem is made of words and words may be invested with numinous properties, its very form may also possess in itself a hieroglyphic significance, be it accessible through numerological analysis, as in *Epithalamion*, or ocular inspection, as in 'Easter-wings.'

Stylistically, Spenser and Herbert exhibit the same impulse to the serial elaboration of images in direct, even muscular syntax: Coleridge linked Chaucer, Spenser, and Herbert as masters of a direct style 'in which every thing was expressed, just as one could wish to talk, and yet all dignified, attractive, and interesting; and all at the same time perfectly correct as to the measure of the syllables and the rhyme' (*Biographia Literaria* ch 19). But while both poets value a clear prose sense in their poetry, they also may be the two great masters of stanzaic form in English poetry. It is true that the Sidney psalter provides a wider inventory of prosodic forms than do Spenser's lyrics, but Spenser and Herbert completely integrate a highly complex argument with the movement of syntax and meter. The varied lyric forms of *The Shepheardes Calender* may bear a superficial resemblance to some of Herbert's work, but seldom do they show the thorough technical control, working through fully articulated ideas, which appears throughout *The Faerie Queene* and *Fowre Hymnes*.

In studying technique, the reader of Spenser should turn to Herbert, the better to see how Spenser had anticipated the full control of the stanza as a unit of thought (see Miner 1969:237). A Herbert lyric such as 'The Agonie' may be said to present *in parvo* the sinews and inner contours of a Spenserian stanza, with its gathering tensions in an alternately rhymed quatrain extended in a fifth line, which is also the first line of a couplet drawing out the final thought in a long, pausing motion. Such stanzas, like those of 'Even-song,' for example, offer a kind of X-ray of the *Faerie Queene* stanza; similarly, in the three ten-line stanzas of 'Church-rents and schismes,' with their brief allegories each moving steadily toward a conclusion in a couplet, one may see how a later poet adapted Spenser's stanzaically contained plots with all their gathering complexities and resolutions.

A more specific aspect of allegorical thinking that the two poets share appears in their use of emblems. For Spenser, the practice begins early with the three series of visions in *Complaints*; the concreteness and brevity of the emblems in these early works are different from the later visual-aid effusions of Quarles, Wither, and the rest, and point ahead rather to the practice of Herbert. Both poets are largely visual but differ from the emblem poets in that they never confine themselves to the description of a representation and the expansion of a tidy thesis; rather they are interested in the moral valences that may inhere in objects themselves. Herbert's 'Humilitie' is a case in point: as in Spenser's early emblem poems, picture, interpretation, and application are all condensed directly into the image, which has moral weight. Emblems offer a system of symbolic correspondences based upon

Scripture (or prior to it, archetypal critics would say), and unlike later poets who might be described as 'emblematic,' Spenser and Herbert consistently employ intrinsic symbols rather than arbitrary or personal ones; for both, the emblematic habit of thought allows them to disinfect the poem of a personal self and instead draw strength and meaning from liturgical sources.

Allegorical thinking and the use of emblems should be distinguished from the use of allusion. Spenser is a master of classical allusion, and his ability to draw from his own formidable reading list could take on some of the character and power of the allegorical habit of mind. Herbert begins writing in this mode but eventually pares it away: while it is a commonplace that *The Temple* eschews references to classical myth, Herbert freely employs classical allusions in his Greek and Latin poetry as well as in his orations. For him, the culminating effort is to draw back to the liturgy and its place in the symbolic imagination.

Herbert indeed reaches so deeply beyond a self that his poems have been rightly described as self-consuming: for him, the annihilation of both author and artifact may be the final aim of religious art. What permits this final step is the resolution and propriety with which the image is employed as a source of meaning, and that resolution in turn originates in the conviction (shared with Spenser) that objects and persons may have holy and transcendent purposes. Thus the student of Herbert should read Spenser to be disabused of the notion that Herbert is a 'seventeenth-century writer' or a 'metaphysical' in some narrow textbook sense of the terms; by the same token, the student of Spenser should read Herbert to appreciate how self-conscious and sophisticated the emblematic habit of mind could be in the poet writing a generation earlier. Some specific illustrations: Herbert's 'The Flower' draws together whole clusters of floral emblems with overlapping and even conflicting significances, as does Spenser's Wandering Wood (*FQ* I i) or the episode of Amavia and Mortdant (II i); the condensation of a highly generalized emblem can permit the dreamlike concentration and consistency of both a brief poem like 'Redemption' and an extended scene like the cave of Despair (I ix); and the use of a more surreal emblem can permit something like a visual pun: the emblematic planting of man as a tree may yield Fradubio (I ii) as well as the ambiguities of Herbert's 'Employment' (I) and 'Affliction' (II). Yet to be fully explored is the similar way the two poets use images related to music and elaborate that trope in rich and intricate forms.

Spenser and Herbert have much in common in terms of their religious and philosophical temper. Both show a persistent concern for courtly love as parody and as *caritas*, and both are alert to the uses of ironic inversions of the convention, as in Paridell's seduction of Hellenore (III ix 30) or in the briefly suggestive account given in Herbert's 'Dulnesse.' Both reiterate the need for a truly catholic form of devotion that is older than, and frequently opposed to, the established church as an institution. Alongside Spenser's critical vision of the church one might set such poems of Herbert's as 'The British Church' and 'The Church Militant'; any notion that Herbert had retreated to a pietism that takes no account of the realities of politics and worship should be dispelled by the last of these, which foresees not only the translation of the true church to America but also its eventual decline into a repeated cycle of sin and renewal.

Both poets also hold the 'Empedoclean' acceptance of the humanist and Stoic ideal of humanity trapped in a disintegrating system but still capable of moving toward salvation. From a more strictly theological point of view, it was the received opinion for some time that their sympathies lay with the more conservative element of the English church (Lewis 1936:328 refers to Spenser's doctrines as 'that fine flower of Anglican sanctity which meets us again in Herbert or Walton,' and Whitaker 1950:69 sees Spenser as 'the religious fellow of Hooker and ancestor of Herbert'); but recent revisionist interpretations of Spenser place him in the fore of an intellectually aggressive Puritanism (eg, Hume 1984), a position imputed to Herbert since the 1970s (eg, Halewood 1970, Lewalski 1979). Nonetheless both poets show a certain wariness regarding Calvinist doctrines of grace, and more strictly Augustinian notions are much in evidence: Redcrosse is aided in his final battle not so much by grace (Arthur's shield) as by the sacraments of baptism (the Well of Life) and the Eucharist (the Tree of Life; see Ellrodt 1960:201), and the theology of these two rites also supports the fabric of *The Temple* (see Strier 1983). Finally, both poets appear to endorse that strand of Christian Neoplatonism which holds that the human soul has come from elsewhere and is imprisoned in the body (*FQ* IV is clearly pertinent here, with its passages on friendship and the nature of the soul, esp ii 43, vi 31, and x 26–7). But unlike a number of poets and divines who absorbed Cambridge Platonism, neither poet can be called a mystic in any real sense, and both are always ready to describe the ineffable: as Stein 1968:109 dryly remarks, *The Temple* is the spiritual record of a man who was unable 'to hold [his] peace' ('The Altar' 13, the first poem in *The Church*).

The differences between the two are more interesting and finally more illuminating. Unlike Spenser, Herbert rejects the idea of human love as being analogous in any way to divine love. Sensuality is not the issue, but rather misplaced love as a form of idolatry. This is simply another way of saying that Spenser is able to accommodate certain Neoplatonic dualisms that Herbert emphatically rejects: human nature, in Herbert's view, cannot be transcended by any form of love within nature (Tuve 1970:206). For Spenser, nature is a great mediating system, and any discussion of 'Spenserian ecology' (Kane 1983) must take account of both divine love and the world of fallen nature. Every aspect of Spenser's *oeuvre* moves between those poles, including his distinction between a poetic vocation and a poetic career. The cost and pathos of that dualism is everywhere present in the later Spenser; and the deep gravity of his tone, as he contemplates the endless accommodation that must be made between the two, resembles most the tone of Herbert as he ponders how, from every side, the poet and even poetry itself are cut away as the soul moves toward God. COBURN FREER

George Herbert 1945 *Works* ed F.E. Hutchinson, 2nd ed (Oxford). Stanley E. Fish 1972 *Self-Consuming Artifacts: The Experience of Seventeenth-Century Literature* (Berkeley and Los Angeles); William H. Halewood 1970 *The Poetry of Grace: Reformation Themes and Structures in English Seventeenth-Century Poetry* (New Haven); Hume 1984; Lewalski 1979; Earl Miner 1969 *The Metaphysical Mode from Donne to Cowley* (Princeton); Nohrnberg 1976 (on the handling of sacred metaphors in Spenser and Herbert); Arnold Stein 1968 *George Herbert's Lyrics* (Baltimore); Richard Strier 1983 *Love Known: Theology and Experience in George Herbert's Poetry* (Chicago); Tuve 1947; Tuve 1970, 'Herbert and *Caritas*' and 'Sacred "Parody" of Love Poetry, and Herbert.'

Herbert family The Herberts were a major force in literary patronage from 1551, when William Herbert became first Earl of Pembroke, until the death of his grandson, Philip, the fourth earl, in 1650. They were regularly associated with the Sidneys during the reigns of Elizabeth and James, and the presidency of the Council of Wales was held by Sir Henry Sidney and the first two earls of Pembroke. The first earl was a native Welsh speaker who had little familiarity with reading or writing English; however, his influence at court attracted the dedications of translations and religious works between 1552 and 1570. His son Henry was more thoroughly educated, and was addressed by translators and by authors of medical, poetic, and dramatic texts in Italian, Welsh, and English. In 1577, he married Philip Sidney's sister, Mary, who attained considerable social distinction by becoming Countess of Pembroke. The Sidneys became her regular guests at Wilton House; and Simon Robson remarked that Pembroke and the two Sidney brothers, Philip and Robert, were united 'in an indissoluble band of amitie and fraternitie' (*The Choise of Change* 1585, dedication). This family intimacy was preserved during James' reign by William, the third earl, and Robert Sidney, Earl of Leicester.

John Aubrey assumed, but without conclusive evidence, that Spenser visited Wilton (ed 1847:89). Spenser was probably aware of the Herberts during the compilation of the *Astrophel* elegies on Sidney, and it is probable that he, rather than the Countess herself, depicted her sorrow in the 'Lay of Clorinda.' He appears to encourage Mary Herbert to follow her brother's example in literary patronage and praises her reputation in a *Faerie Queene* Dedicatory Sonnet, in the address prefacing *Ruines of Time*, and in lines describing her as '*Urania*, sister unto

Astrofell' in *Colin Clouts Come Home Againe* (486–91). *Peplus* (1587), an Oxford University volume of elegies on Sidney, indicates (in its dedication to the second earl) that both the Countess and her husband were expected to continue Sidney's patronage. During the 1590s, Spenser was only one of many poets, including Breton, Daniel, Fraunce, and Harington, who were attracted by the literary atmosphere of Wilton House. During this period, the stationer Ponsonby also provided an indirect but significant contact between the Herberts and Spenser.

In the seventeenth century, William and Philip Herbert, the third and fourth earls, are remembered as the 'incomparable paire of brethren' of Shakespeare's First Folio. They also received the dedications of a wide range of texts, including translations, poetry, courtesy books, religious volumes, and plays. They were familiar with Donne, Jonson, Middleton, Massinger, and many other writers. These later Herberts were frequently urged to preserve the tradition of literary patronage fostered by their illustrious mother and uncle, and they became the natural focus for the group of Spenserian poets which included Browne, Drayton, Smith, and Wither.

MICHAEL G. BRENNAN

John Aubrey 1847 *The Natural History of Wiltshire* (1685) ed John Britton (London; rpt with intro by K.G. Ponting, Newton Abbot 1969); Brennan 1988; Lamb 1981; F.B. Williams 1962.

Hercules In the mythology inherited by Renaissance poets and readers, Hercules was an even more complex figure than in antiquity. Although still the hero of the twelve labors (and therefore an example of the just prince), he was also known for his madness and his temperance, for his brutishness and his eloquence, for his choice at the crossroads of virtue rather than vice (cf *FQ* I iv 1–2), and as a pagan who prefigured Christ. The contradictory elements of the Renaissance Hercules have their beginnings in classical literature (eg, Euripides *Heracles*, Seneca's two Hercules plays, Ovid *Metamorphoses* 9), but show the transformations typical in the history of mythological figures who are redrawn to suit the interest of Christian interpreters. By the Renaissance, Hercules is portrayed fully Christianized in such works as Coluccio Salutati's *De laboribus Herculis* (early 15th c), Ronsard's *Hymne de l'Hercule chrestien* (1555), and Cintio's *Dell'Ercole* (1557).

For Spenser, Hercules is above all 'that great Champion of the antique world' (*FQ* I xi 27), also known by familiar epithets as 'Alcides,' the '*Tirynthian* swaine,' 'that great Oetean Knight,' or even 'th'*Amphytrionide*.' He is the hero of the twelve labors (see I xi 27; cf III vii 61) – the choice of labors can vary considerably. Besides those to which Spenser refers explicitly, he may allude to others: Busiris (a tyrannical king of Egypt who sacrificed strangers on his altar until slain by Hercules) may be figured in the tyrant Busirane (III xi-xii), and the Erymanthian boar in the Sanglier episode (V i 13–30). In performing these labors, Hercules is like the knight undertaking a series of quests; his patience and persistence can be contrasted with the violence needed to overcome his enemies. It is his strength (physical but also moral) in overcoming his enemies that is often compared to the strength of knights. Thus, when Redcrosse feels the blast of the Dragon's breath, the pain is compared to that felt by Hercules 'When him the poysoned garment did enchaunt / With *Centaures* bloud, and bloudie verses charm'd' (I xi 27), an allusion to the shirt poisoned by the blood of Nessus, and given to Hercules by Deianira. At his death, Hercules is transformed to a god in a Christlike apotheosis on Mount Oeta. Redcrosse not only shares the pain and heroic strength of Hercules but is also transformed during his three-day battle.

Yet Hercules works his way further into *The Faerie Queene* than by the tangential form of the simile. Although the poem is no *Herculeid*, six episodes especially resonate with his presence. The battle between Arthur and Maleger (II xii) is a direct echo of Hercules' encounter with the giant Antaeus. Four Herculean episodes appear in Book V. In canto v, Radigund enslaves Artegall just as Omphale (called 'Iola' by Spenser) enslaves Hercules – by making him take the place of a woman and forcing 'His mightie hands, the distaffe vile to hold' (V 24). In canto viii, the Herculean comparison is shifted to Arthur: as Hercules defeats Diomedes who fed guests to his horses, Arthur defeats the cruel Souldan, the defender of Adicia. In canto ix, he encounters Malengin, tricking him much as Hercules tricks Cacus. In canto x, Arthur kills Geryoneo and his monster just as Hercules kills Geryon (Geryoneo's father) and his dog Orthrus. Hercules appears throughout Book V because he is the traditional enemy of tyrants and the great representative of ancient justice (see Dunseath 1968). Hence Artegall is compared to Hercules, 'Who all the West with equall conquest wonne, / And monstrous tyrants with his club subdewed; / The club of Justice dread, with kingly powre endewed' (i 2). Yet by the end of the book, it is apparent that Artegall is also like Hercules in his weakness for women, whereas Arthur is like him in his strength and cleverness. Together they make up the picture of justice.

Book VI ends with an enforced parallel with Hercules. Calidore overcomes the Blatant Beast as successfully as the 'great *Alcides*' cropped the heads of the 'hell-borne *Hydra*' (xii 32). Then he is compared to 'that strong *Tirynthian* swaine' who brought Cerberus 'the dreadfull dog of hell' up to the earth's surface (35), the most challenging of Hercules' labors. Although both similes recall the classical Hercules, Calidore is related to the Renaissance Hercules, the eloquent speaker who 'had all men linked together by the eares in a chaine, to drawe them and lead them even as he lusted' (preface to Thomas Wilson *Arte of Rhetorique* 1560). For 'every deed and word, that he did say, / Was like enchantment, that through both the eyes, / And both the eares did steale the hart away (VI ii 3).

ANTHONY WOLK

For general discussion, see Galinsky 1972. For the Renaissance Hercules, see Bush 1963 passim, Marc-René Jung 1966 *Hercule dans la littérature française du XVIe siècle* (Geneva); Panofsky 1930; Marcel Simon 1955 *Hercule et le chrestianisme* (Paris); and Waith 1962. For Spenser, see Aptekar 1969; Cain 1978; Dunseath 1968; MacIntyre 1966; and Victor Skretkowicz 1980 'Hercules in Sidney and Spenser' *N&Q* 225:306–10 on the Iole/Omphale confusion.

Hermaphrodite The 1590 *Faerie Queene* concludes with a rhetorically complex reference to the Hermaphrodite as a figure of the union between Scudamour and Amoret: 'Had ye them seene, ye would have surely thought, / That they had beene that faire *Hermaphrodite*, / Which that rich *Romane* of white marble wrought, / And in his costly Bath causd to bee site: / So seemd those two, as growne together quite' (III xii 46). The embracing lovers are likened to the Hermaphrodite by a process of ecphrasis and allusion that calls attention to the distance between reader and text ('Had ye them seene') and to the maze of sources underlying the image. The marble statue has never been identified satisfactorily; since Spenser's description more closely resembles pictorial representations of an embracing couple (Hermaphroditus and Salmacis) than it does Hermaphrodite statues, which portray a single androgynous figure, his text may be pointing deliberately to a wholly fictitious work of art. The 1590 ending of *The Faerie Queene*, in which Britomart, her own quest unfulfilled, is merely an onlooker, half envying the bliss of others, seems all the more problematic because the reader is teased about what he cannot see, both because the reference to Scudamour and Amoret is conditional ('Had ye them seene') and because the statue the reader would have called to mind may be purely imaginary.

To compound the problem, the last five stanzas of Book III were canceled and replaced in 1596 with the present stanzas xii 43–5. The new stanzas delete all reference to the Hermaphrodite and substitute a wholly inconclusive ending in which neither Amoret nor Britomart is united with her lover. Why Spenser should have altered the conclusion remains a major critical question. The cancellation of the five stanzas lends itself to contradictory explanations: either he repudiated the stanzas, the Hermaphrodite, or, perhaps, his own power to create poetic closure (Goldberg 1981:1–4, Paglia 1979), or the last three books of *The Faerie Queene* supersede the partial conclusion of 1590. Other readers have suggested that Spenser meant to include the canceled stanzas in the complete poem (Lewis 1967:36).

More general questions arise concerning the place of the Hermaphrodite in Spenser's text: its relationship to other, single figures of the androgyne (Venus in IV x 40–1, Nature in VII vii 5, Britomart and other martial maids, the transvestite Artegall in V vii 37–40), and the intertextual relationship between Spenser's figure and its sources, principally Plato's *Symposium* (189E-92E) and Ovid's *Metamorphoses* (4.285–388), and the traditions deriving from each. Aristophanes' fable in the *Symposium*, of primordial double beings or *androgynoi* compounded of male and female, gave rise to a positive tradition of interpreting the Hermaphrodite as an emblem of spiritual union. The Neoplatonic hermaphrodite became a symbol of Christian marriage when associated with verses in Genesis describing male and female created in the image of God (1.27) and husband and wife as one flesh (2.24; Roche 1964:134–6). Undoubtedly, spiritual union and Christian marriage are part of the hermaphrodite image that concludes Book III. However, such Neoplatonic theories of hermaphroditic spiritual union transcending physical limitation and sexual difference fail to recognize that Aristophanes' fable, by positing purely corporeal origins of desire, attributable to females as well as males, introduces both physicality and sexual difference to the *Symposium* (Brenkman 1982). This revisionary aspect of Aristophanes' myth may also contribute to the conclusion of Book III. Perhaps the fact that the union is observed by a third party, half envying their bliss, provides an alternative to the simple restoration of two halves to a single whole, an alternative that respects and preserves sexual difference and corporeality (Cheney 1972).

A more problematic, skeptical view of the Hermaphrodite, which focuses on the threat of dissolution, derives from Ovid's story of Salmacis and Hermaphroditus. Hermaphroditus' loss of shape in the fountain of Salmacis, merged with the nymph who is tutelary spirit of the fountain, was interpreted by mythographers as a cautionary tale warning that sensuality results in effeminacy (Arnolph d'Orléans 3.13, *Ovide moralisé* 4.2284–311, Sabinus, Charles Estienne). While the Ovidian mythographic tradition emphasizes the dangers of losing oneself in sensuality and in union with another, Ovid's own text is more ambiguous. Coincident with Hermaphroditus' apparent loss of shape and manhood is the creation of the Hermaphrodite, a figure of sexual consummation and an expression of the two parents, Hermes and Aphrodite, who have produced the boy. Accordingly, the final embrace of Amoret and Scudamour is described in terms that emphasize the positive values of that consummation (Silberman 1987; Nohrnberg 1976:606–7 notes the hermaphroditism of many of Spenser's couples, eg, Britomartegall, Scudamoret, Thamedway).

The negative elements of the Hermaphrodite tradition appear in the illicit coupling of Duessa with the Red Cross Knight (I vii 1–7). The Hermaphrodite of 1590 alludes to this earlier episode, both by shared imagery and by shared reference to Ovid's text. The image of Amoret's 'pour[ing] out her spright' (III xii 45) echoes the earlier reference to Redcrosse 'Pourd out in loosnesse on the grassy grownd' (I vii 7). In addition, the fountain from which he drinks while being seduced is identifiable by its origin and effect with the well of Salmacis (cf *FQ* I vii 5, *Met* 4.302–4.307). The cause Spenser gives for its enfeebling properties, the curse placed on it in retribution for the laziness of its attendant nymph, echoes the mythographic interpretations of the Hermaphrodite in which Salmacis is an emblem of moral laziness. The effect that drinking from the fountain has on Redcrosse recalls the more physiological interpretation of the Hermaphrodite as a warning against sexual overindulgence. Both sexual misconduct and moral lassitude are part of his transgression. Because he is 'carelesse of his health, and of his fame' (I vii 7), he falls into an overt sin which initiates the process of his punishment and redemption. The conclusion of the 1590 *Faerie Queene* redeems this image of the Hermaphrodite.

LAUREN SILBERMAN

John Brenkman 1982 'The Other and the One: Psychoanalysis, Reading, the *Symposium*' in *Literature and Psychoanalysis: The Question of Reading: Otherwise* ed Shoshana Feldman (Baltimore) pp 396–456; Cheney 1972; Goldberg 1981; Lewis 1967; Paglia 1979; Lauren Silberman 1986; Silberman 1987 'The Hermaphrodite and the Metamorphosis of Spenserian Allegory' *ELR* 17:207–23; Woodbridge 1984.

Hermeticism Originally, the traditions deriving from the *Hermetica*, mystical writings of the Hellenistic period attributed to Hermes Trismegistus, the mythical archpriest and descendant of the Egyptian god Thoth.

The Hermetic teachings show a blend of Neoplatonism and early Christian influences complemented by elements of nonclassical and non-Christian tenets. Babylonian and Egyptian philosophy and Jewish Gnosticism contributed the beliefs that chaos can be a source of life, that creation is a recurrent process, and that man is divinely creative and can be exalted to the level of God (Feinstein 1973, Shumaker 1972:201–51, Yates 1964). Since in the *Corpus hermeticum* the creation-myth of the first man (Anthropos) bears some resemblance to the story of Adam in Genesis, these texts gave rise to a Christian interpretation as early as the time of the Church Fathers (Hermes Trismegistus was thought to have lived in the time of Moses), but it was the Renaissance Neoplatonists who drew special attention to Hermeticism.

Ficino's translation of the Hermetic texts in 1471 gave impetus to a theological-philosophical trend which elicited a synthesis of 'high magic' (consisting of Neoplatonism, alchemy, astrology, and the Cabala) and the new, man-centered doctrine of the Renaissance. Perhaps because of this syncretism, Hermeticism now is commonly treated as synonymous with the 'occult,' that is, with a wide range of topics from astro-alchemy, magical medicine, primitive rituals, to 'angel spiritism' and some other parapsychological activities. There are common elements in the two systems, but without a clear distinction between them, the term *Hermeticism* becomes meaningless. Occult elements occur in virtually all philosophy before the seventeenth century, and the Renaissance was still far from systematically separating the ideas we consider rational and irrational.

Renaissance Hermeticism emerged in the context of an animistic concept of the universe and became a distinct trend with the following main tenets, as deduced from the writings of Ficino, Pico della Mirandola, Trithemius, Reuchlin, Agrippa, Guillaume Postel, Dee, and Bruno: (1) a special reverence for the writings of Hermes Trismegistus, (2) a firm belief in the harmony of the world, (3) the ambition to learn about this harmony through a reformed theology and philosophy based on ancient Hermetic teachings as well as the current findings of the natural sciences (often called *magia naturalis*), and (4) the ultimate goal of recovering man's primordial unity with himself and with the supernatural.

The second tenet in particular has led to the notion that Hermeticism was largely responsible for the emergence of modern science in the seventeenth century (Yates 1967 and Burke 1974; but cf Rossi 1975 and Westman 1977). Hermeticism as a self-contained system of thought and a mentality was responsible at least in part for the Renaissance exaltation of man. Instead of associating it with natural science, one may explain it as a way of thinking alternative to rationalism, and heavily dependent on metaphoric expression and analogies, which has coexisted with discursive logic up to the present (Vickers 1984a:6).

This explanation calls attention to poetry, a way of thinking also often understood as an alternative to 'scientific' reasoning. Accordingly, most recent studies of Hermeticism have tried to detect the relationship among esoterism, white magic, alchemy, and Renaissance poetry (Niculescu 1981, Gill 1982).

Traces of these Hermetic ideas are apparent in Spenser's intellectual milieu as well as in his poetry. In England, the most outspoken exponent of Renaissance Hermeticism was Dee, who explored secret correspondences between the macrocosm and the microcosm and who mixed patriotic Protestantism with irenicism. Spenser had access to his ideology since both belonged to Leicester's circle, though the Hermetic ideas in his poetry may well have come from other sources (Feinstein 1968, Mulryan 1972). For example, the Astraea myth and British imperialism are topics common in the work of many Elizabethans, including Spenser's patron Raleigh (Yates 1975). The harmony of the spheres, another idea which had been incorporated into Hermeticism, informs some of the numerological patterns in *The Faerie Queene* and astral or planetary patterns in its themes (Fowler 1964). Giorgio's *De harmonia mundi totius* (1525), an Hermetic text, has been used as a cipher-key to the number symbolism of *The Shepheardes Calender* (Røstvig 1969); this text has also been used to illuminate one of

Spenser's darkest conceits, his description of the human body in *FQ* II ii 22 (Hopper 1940, Fowler 1964:260–88, Szőnyi 1984).

Other Hermetic elements in Spenser include the use of Egyptian lore and eastern cosmogonies (Fletcher 1971:121–9). Cambina's rod of peace entwined with serpents recalls the caduceus of Hermes-Mercury, the occult meaning of which was a subject in most Hermetic-esoteric treatises of the Renaissance (Brooks-Davies 1983:11–85). The vision of the hermaphroditic Venus (IV x 41) may be associated with Hermetic teachings about the dual nature of God the Creator (Lewis 1967:42). Spenser's most complex esoteric metaphor is undoubtedly the Garden of Adonis (III vi), the conception of which is by no means wholly classical: it includes father, mother, and time deities (Feinstein 1968); and correspondences between God, Venus, Adonis, chaos, and flowers relate to the deities of the *Chaldean Oracles*. The cycle of generation with the references to chaos as the major supplier of 'substance' for nature's progenies points beyond orthodox Platonism to an Hermetic syncretism.

In the seventeenth century, Hermetic books became lavishly illustrated with diagrams and depictions of the occult universe, some of which help to clarify Spenser's 'darke conceit[s].' For example, an engraving from Tobias Schütz's *Harmonia macrocosmi cum microcosmi* (1654) shows a human figure standing in a circle with arms and legs outstretched. This symbol refers to the correspondences between the celestial world and the human microcosm through astrological connections. On either side, diagrams show the four elements (square) and the three principles (triangle), as in Spenser's description of the house of Temperance. Also shown are portraits of Hermes Trismegistus and Paracelsus, authorities for this interpretation of the universe.

Spenser was a poet, however, not a philosopher: his imagination was largely syncretic, inspired by many ideas that include but are not limited to Hermeticism. Though biblical, Virgilian, or Ovidian traditions of prophecy provide the main strength and substance of his vision, the 'Hermetic mode of thought provides a measure of his style and visionary intensity' (Fletcher 1971: 129). GYÖRGY E. SZŐNYI

Brooks-Davies 1983; John G. Burke 1974 'Hermeticism as a Renaissance World View' in *The Darker Vision of the Renaissance* ed Robert S. Kinsman (Berkeley and Los Angeles) pp 95–117; Blossom Feinstein 1968; Feinstein 1973 'Hermeticism' in *DHI* 2:431–4; J.S. Gill 1982 'English Hermeticism: A Critical Study of Contrasting Responses to Hermeticism in Renaissance and Seventeenth-Century English Literature' diss Loughborough, Eng; Hermes Trismegistus ed 1924–36; Mulryan 1972; L.I. Niculescu 1981 'From Hermeticism to Hermeneutics: Alchemical Metaphors in Renaissance Literature' diss UCLA; Paolo Rossi 1975 'Hermeticism, Rationality and the Scientific Revolution' in *Reason, Experiment, and Mysticism in the Scientific Revolution* ed M.L. Righini Bonelli and William R. Shea (New York) pp 247–73; Szőnyi 1984; Vickers 1984a; Robert S. Westman 1977 'Magical Reform and Astronomical Reform: The Yates Thesis Reconsidered' in *Hermeticism and the Scientific Revolution* ed Lynn White, Jr (Los Angeles) pp 1–91; Frances A. Yates 1964; Yates 1967 'The Hermetic Tradition in Renaissance Science' in *Art, Science, and History in the Renaissance* ed Charles S. Singleton (Baltimore) pp 255–74; Yates 1975; Yates 1979.

hermits As one might expect, Spenser's heroic poem is not heavily populated with hermits, those prime literary avatars of the contemplative life. In fact, there are only two authentic examples, in *FQ* I x and VI v-vi. Archimago is disguised as a hermit at his first appearance (I i), and Arthur mistakes the hut in which Timias lies for the abode of 'some holy Hermit' (IV vii 42). In the house of Holiness (I x), the ancient hermit Contemplation instructs the regenerate hero so persuasively that the knight exclaims, 'let me here for aye in peace remaine' (63). The most representative figure of the traditional hermit is the wise healer to whom Timias and Serena repair in VI v-vi to be cured of the bites inflicted by the Blatant Beast; the details of his presentation adapt several conventions of the hermit figure to illuminate major issues in the poem.

Like the other hermits, the figure in Book VI lives in solitary isolation. His hermitage is 'Far from all neighbourhood, the which annoy it may' (v 34), much as the disguised Archimago abides 'Far from resort of people' (I i 34) and Timias as putative hermit is assumed by Arthur to shun 'resort of sinfull people' (IV vii 42). The hermitages of Archimago, Contemplation, and this hermit all have chapels next to them in which to offer their devotions. The genuine hermits of Books I and VI reluctantly but courteously interrupt their prayers to receive their guests. Most notably, the hermit of VI is a retired knight. Of gentle demeanor, he is said to have been a 'man of mickle name, / Renowmed much in armes and derring doe,' who in old age has hung up his armor, sloughed off 'all this worlds incombraunce,' and exchanged the 'grace and glory' of battle for the serenity of the hermitage, 'In which he liv'd alone, like carelesse bird in cage' (v 37, vi 4). His career may recall the career of Redcrosse prophesied by Contemplation (I x 60–1).

A strategy of retirement and avoidance informs the Hermit's treatment of Timias and Serena. After examining their wounds, he concludes that only a strict austerity can protect them from the Blatant Beast. Warning them that the Beast's venomous tongue is the source of their malaise, he advises them to 'learne your outward sences to refraine' from all sensory stimulation, to 'avoide the occasion of the ill,' to 'Abstaine from pleasure, and restraine your will,' to speak only 'in open sight,' and in other ways to avoid furnishing the occasion for scandal (vi 7, 14). His counsel effects a quick though temporary cure. Keeping 'well his wise commaundements' (15), they soon find their wounds healed and depart. But their subsequent encounters, Timias' with Scorn and Disdain in canto vii and Serena's with the cannibals in viii, suggest the difficulty of acting out the Hermit's counsel in the world.

Spenser's Hermit blends several strains of the complex Renaissance conception of the contemplative life. Humanist culture in general favored the active life but acknowledged valid exceptions. The Roman rhetorical-philosophical tradition allowed early retirement either to pursue scientific knowledge or to escape the tyranny of an unjust ruler (Seneca *De otio* 2.1, 3.3; *De tranquillitate animi* 5.5). It also laid great stress on rest after labors (Tacitus *Annales* 14.55), viewing retirement in old age as the crowning reward for a life spent in active public service (Cicero *Pro Sestio* 98). Though Seneca and others sometimes identified contemplation and self-reflection as forms of active service to the state, the dominant view of approved retirement passed down by the Romans to the Renaissance is that exemplified by Spenser's Hermit: a self-imposed withdrawal from the world at the end of long heroic activity.

If the Hermit's career mirrors the classical ideal of dignified retirement, his name and circumstances evoke a familiar pattern in medieval culture. The appellation 'Hermit' strictly denotes one of two well-distinguished types of Christian contemplative: 'solitary wandering Hermits, or pent-up Anchorets,' in the words of Giraldus Cambrensis (c 1215; in Darwin 1944:83). As opposed to the normally enclosed anchorites (descendants of the 'desert fathers' who exemplified a static asceticism), hermits were free to move about as they performed a variety of more active functions. In literature, the term may be used of either type. The ascetic hermit, whether stationary or mobile, appears in English saints' legends from about the eighth century. This type is dominant in the various Guy of Warwick romances, a ballad version of which was printed in London as late as 1592. In this story, a page wins his lord's daughter in marriage through a series of heroic exploits, only to leave her at once in order to do penance as a pilgrim. After further adventures he retires, unknown, to a cave. On his deathbed he sends for his faithful wife, reveals his identity at last, and dies in her arms.

In the thirteenth century, the hermit as religious contemplative begins to evolve into a noble counselor and friend of the oppressed. Chivalric romance knows both the 'pure' type and the aged, retired knight who, among other roles, acts as host, counselor, and healer. All of the latter are exemplified in Malory, who reflects the fifteenth-century revival in England of hermit literature, spurred by the invention of printing. Hermits cure Lancelot's wounds (12.3, 18.22) and persuade him to forswear his adultery with Guinevere (13.19–20). Malory's hermits frequently interpret his heroes' visions or dreams. Lancelot learns in this way that he is Galahad's father (15.3), and Gawain and Ector learn that they are unworthy to achieve the Holy Grail (16.3–5). Two of

Malory's reclusives have retired from more exalted stations in the world: Percival's aunt, an anchoress and former Queen of the West Lands (14.1); and the banished Bishop of Canterbury, now a hermit, who receives the supposed remains of King Arthur and presides over the burial of Lancelot before being restored to his bishopric, only to have his place taken by the repentant Bedivere (21.6, 10ff). In Caxton's *Book of the Ordre of Chyvalry* (1484), a retired knight in his solitary woodland hermitage is interrupted by a wandering squire, to whom he narrates the whole 'order of chivalry' that forms the bulk of the book.

The sixteenth century witnessed an increasing secularization of the hermit's literary image. Ariosto's lascivious hermit (*Orlando furioso* 8) bequeathes his false seeming to Spenser's Archimago and his comic lust to the old Fisher in *FQ* III vii. Tasso's Peter the Hermit is the presiding spiritual genius of the Crusade in *Gerusalemme liberata* (1.29–32; 10.73–8; 11.1–15; 14.17, 29–30). Another hermit, a converted pagan in whose cave all the world's rivers have their sources (14.38), derives from one of Ariosto's hermits the power to reveal to the dynastic hero (Ruggiero in Ariosto, Rinaldo in Tasso) the glories awaiting him and his progeny (*OF* 41.52–67, *GL* 17.66–94). Spenser assigns a similar function to his Contemplation, but with a notable slackening of the Ferrarese poets' dynastic, though not their prophetic, ardor.

Despite the decrease in actual hermits in England following the dissolution of the monasteries in the 1530s, and their virtual disappearance by 1570, they remained popular in literature to the end of the century. Increasingly, however, the hermit-counselor gives way in this period to the hermit-philosopher, who is frequently associated with the renewed debate about the active versus the contemplative life. In Lyly's *Euphues and His England* (1580), for example, a prosperous merchant's wastrel son hears a cautionary tale against indiscriminate travel from his late father's once-prodigal brother, who is now a hermit. The youth rejects his uncle's advice but later returns to his cave to confess his folly and, to his surprise, receive his patrimony.

The new secular-philosophical hermit is also connected with the cult of Elizabeth in the 1570s and after. Examples are Gascoigne's retelling of the tale of Hemetes the Hermit presented to the Queen at Woodstock in 1575, and the 'Hermit's Speech' written by Peele for her visit to Burghley's estate at Theobald's in 1591 (in Peele, ed 1888, 2:305–14). In Gascoigne, a story of love and adventure is consummated by the hermit-narrator's regaining his sight in the presence of the Queen. Peele's verses (commissioned and delivered by Burghley's son, Robert Cecil) excuse Burghley's quasi-monastic retirement from public life following the deaths of his mother, wife, and daughter, and urge the Queen to command his reemergence.

Spenser's hermits reflect these cultural shifts. Despite the anti-Roman Catholic portrait of Archimago as a false hermit and the poet's Protestant skepticism concerning a lifetime spent in contemplation, the hermit-counselor-healer of Book VI combines worldly wisdom with a genuine religiosity, while his hard-won knowledge of the ways of court echoes *Colin Clout* and other anticourt satire of the period. The severe discipline that the Hermit practices and preaches does justice to the world he has left. Though his 'cure' is too vague to be useful (and seems little more efficacious than that of Friar Lawrence in *Romeo and Juliet*), his character and the general tenor of his advice imply a growing unworldliness in Spenser's outlook characteristic of the tendency toward withdrawal in his later poetry. In the face of the detraction, scandalmongering, and corruption of language associated with the Beast whose wounds he undertakes to heal, the Hermit is exemplary more perhaps in his elected life of retirement than in the counsel he gives. JOHN D. BERNARD

Jean-Marie André 1966 *L'Otium dans la vie morale et intellectuelle romaine* (Paris); Rotha Mary Clay 1914 *The Hermits and Anchorites of England* (London); Francis D.S. Darwin [1944] *The English Mediaeval Recluse* (London); Charles P. Weaver 1924 *The Hermit in English Literature from the Beginnings to 1660* (Nashville).

hero Although Spenser writes that the 'generall end' of his *Faerie Queene* is to 'fashion a gentleman or noble person' (Letter to Raleigh), he treats of heroes, and thereby places his poem in the line of heroic poetry from Homer to Tasso and his knights in the tradition of heroes from Achilles to Rinaldo. The glory Arthur seeks is the object of all heroic quests. The word *heroic* is among Spenser's highest and most frequent terms of praise, one he uses in an almost technical sense in relation to the 'old *Heroes*' (*FQ* III iii 32, IV xi 13): the 'famous founders ... Of puissant Nations' such as Albion (IV xi 15); literary and mythical heroes among whom are Orpheus, Odysseus, Hercules, and Aeneas; and what Puttenham calls 'the gods, halfe gods or *Heroes* of the gentiles' (*Arte of English Poesie* 1.11), a category in which Spenser includes Isis, Osiris, Bacchus, and many others.

This curious medley of literary, mythological, and historical heroes results from the euhemeristic interpretation of pagan mythology current from the fourth century BC and throughout the Middle Ages to the Renaissance. Euhemerism is the belief that the gods and heroes of pagan mythology were originally historical heroes, lawgivers, civilizers of nations who were first venerated for their benefactions to humanity and eventually elevated to godhead and worshiped by posterity. Spenser often refers to this belief in *The Faerie Queene*, notably in his account of the divinity of Osiris and Isis (V vii 2–3), and in Mutabilitie's sneer at Jove's human origin (VII vii 53).

The principal means for transforming historical figures to mythic heroes was the poet, especially the writer of hymns or heroic poems, as Puttenham explains in his chapter describing 'In what forme of Poesie the great Princes and dominators of the world were honored' (*Arte* 1.16). It was through the poets, 'the trumpetters of all praise,' that 'Bacchus, Ceres, Perseus, Hercules, Theseus and many other ... thereby came to be accompted gods and halfe gods or goddesses (*Heroes*).' This function of the poet as mythmaker underlies Sidney's *Defence of Poetry*, as well as the common Renaissance claim (as in Shakespeare's sonnets, for example) that the poet has power to immortalize his beloved. For his ability to preserve and transmit heroic values, the poet was awarded an extraordinary status in the Renaissance, and the heroic poem was credited with almost superhuman authority. Puttenham was voicing a commonplace in his chapter headed 'How Poets were the first priests, the first prophets, the first Legislators and polititians in the world' (*Arte* 1.3).

That Spenser was familiar with this concept of the poet's responsibility is shown in *Ruines of Time* 421–7 and more fully in *Teares of the Muses* 457–62, where Calliope, the Muse of epic, describes very precisely her euhemeristic function: 'Therefore the nurse of vertue I am hight, / And golden Trompet of eternitie, / That lowly thoughts lift up to heavens hight, / And mortall men have powre to deifie: / *Bacchus* and *Hercules* I raisd to heaven, / And *Charlemaine*, amongst the Starris seaven.' In *The Faerie Queene*, the Muse most commonly evoked is Clio, Muse of history (I xi 5–6). Consequently, Spenser describes himself and the line of heroic poets as 'Poets historicall' (*FQ* Letter).

The term *historical* was used with less rigorous precision in the Renaissance than now, and implied a type of subject rather than strict factual veracity. Poetry itself was, by definition, fiction, and historical poetry allowed anything from an accurate account of historical fact to a free improvisation upon the qualities associated with an historical figure. The Renaissance hero comes somewhere between an historical personage and a purely literary creation.

Spenser fully exploits the poetic freedom which euhemerism allowed. In the dedicatory sonnets, he tempts possible patrons with the offer of traditional glory: to Essex, to 'make more famous memory / Of thine Heroicke parts'; and to Howard, to 'Make you ensample to the present age, / Of th'old Heroes, whose famous ofspring / The antique Poets wont so much to sing.' For the Queen herself, he augments her contemporary mythology by celebrating her glory, her virginity, and her mercy under the guise of Gloriana, Belphoebe, and Mercilla (*FQ* Letter). In Arthur and Redcrosse (St George), he redefines for his own moral purposes historical characters who had already attained the status of myth. In Artegall, he creates a new myth out of a minor historical figure, relating his exploits to those of Hercules and of Lord Grey in Ireland – at the same time raising Lord Grey himself to the level of a Hercules. In Guyon, Britomart, and Calidore, he creates fictional heroes, but patterns them on figures already established in myth, particularly Odysseus, Minerva, and Hercules. In a fundamental way, euhemerism shapes both the purpose and the literary strategies of *The Faerie Queene*.

Since the hero carried an almost religious significance for the Renaissance, the poet's conception of heroism had to be sound. The nature of true heroism was the matter of much debate, provoked by the changing intellectual framework of the period and by humanist interest in classical epic and heroic romance. The essentially heroic virtue in both classical and medieval poetry was courage in battle, with or without the spur of love: the hero, whether an Aeneas or a Lancelot, was first and foremost a fighter. This martial ideal runs counter to Christian ideals of humility, patience, and charity, whether expressed by medieval moralists or by Renaissance humanists such as Erasmus and Ascham in their attacks on the old military values and in their insistence that true heroism lay in the conquest of self. There were, of course, attempts to produce Christian heroes, such as Galahad to rival Lancelot; but Galahad belongs with the saints rather than the heroes, and the logic of Christian heroism ends in martyrdom. Tasso's *Gerusalemme liberata* was written a little earlier than *The Faerie Queene* as a Christian epic, but it largely evades the problem by employing normal pagan epic virtues in a Christian cause.

The medieval answer was to turn pagan myths into Christian allegories and to interpret battles with monsters as conquests over the devil or unruly passions. In this way, Hercules and his labors were absorbed into the Christian typological tradition; and Aeneas, the hero of classical epic most easily reconciled with Christian values, became *pius Aeneas* indeed. The knowledge of classical myth became more extensive in the Renaissance, and such syncretic allegory became even more common, as can be seen most obviously in the iconography of Cartari or Cesare Ripa, in Harington's preface to his 1591 translation of *Orlando furioso*, or in Chapman's comments on Homer's heroes, 'In one [Achilles], Predominant Perturbation; in the other [Odysseus], over-ruling Wisedome' (Homer ed 1967, 2:4).

By the sixteenth century, however, the wider knowledge of classical philosophy and new Reformation theology had polarized classical and Christian values in ways which made their reconciliation more difficult than in the Middle Ages. The Neoplatonism of Pico della Mirandola's very influential *Oration on the Dignity of Man*, for example, assumes an almost limitless potential for human nature; and the new and fashionable 'Senecan man' has a self-sufficiency beyond the reach of a Christian. At the other extreme, Luther and Calvin represent human nature as totally corrupt, lacking free will and devoid of all merit, wholly dependent on God's grace and incapable of any virtuous action unless predetermined to it by God. The traditional epic goals of honor and fame become meaningless. A further challenge to the possibility of heroism was the rising tide of skepticism in the sixteenth century, with its distrust of human reason, as expressed by Montaigne or, a little later, by Bacon. Machiavelli helped to dilute the heroic ideal by insisting that in a less-than-heroic world the fox is as necessary as the lion. The old-style hero was something of an anachronism in the new complex society of the seventeenth century, and *Don Quixote* is his obituary.

These conflicts of attitudes towards heroism led to a wide variety of literary treatments of the hero in Spenser's age. The problem was particularly acute for the writer of the heroic poem, since the form inherited so many conventions associated with traditional epic values; but to use the heroic vein in any form was to be faced with certain basic questions. Marlowe, for example, was obviously attracted by the great aspiring hero, although accepting that in the nature of things he was bound to overreach himself. Sidney's *Defence of Poetry* shows that he believed in the necessity of the heroic ideal, although his other writings suggest that he was skeptical about the possibility of heroes in real life. Chapman's Bussy d'Ambois demonstrates the vulnerability of the heroic lion in a world of foxes. Only Milton assumes the full Christian position in *Paradise Lost* by giving the epic values of courage, pride, and defiance to Satan and endowing his Adam with patience and humility.

As a Christian humanist writing an heroic poem, Spenser was fully aware of the problem, and he defines it clearly in the most traditional Christian terms. When the Red Cross Knight climbs the Mount of Contemplation and sees afar the New Jerusalem, he must acknowledge the worthlessness of the heroic quest and the pursuit of earthly fame when set against the scale of eternal values: 'But when thou famous victorie hast wonne, / And high emongst all knights hast hong thy shield, / Thenceforth the suit of earthly conquest shonne, / And wash thy hands from guilt of bloudy field: / For bloud can nought but sin, and wars but sorrowes yield' (I x 60). Yet he cannot enter the Holy City until he has completed his quest upon earth. The heroic virtues are in their nature sinful; but in some form they are necessary and appropriate to the fallen world of man, although among the saints there will be no further need for battles and 'loose loves.' Spenser never defines his position in relation to the great Reformation debate about 'merit,' and he never makes it clear whether heroic deeds are the cause or the result of salvation. He assumes, however, what would be accepted by all shades of Christian belief, that man is fallen and in need of grace, and that the Christian's duty is, as Milton believed, to repair the ruins of the Fall. This is achieved by overcoming sin as far as corrupt human nature will allow, and by defeating death through procreation, ensuring that life is 'eterne in mutabilitie, / And by succession made perpetuall' (III vi 47).

The Faerie Queene redefines the virtues necessary for Christian regeneration; it is almost a handbook of heroism in its analysis of their constituent parts, their relationship to each other, and the temptations to which they are most vulnerable. The separate facets of Christian virtue are demonstrated by the individual heroes, and Arthur embodies the perfection of them all. This combination of heroic action and moral statement is possible only because of the traditions of allegory available to Spenser. The Renaissance allegorizing of pagan myths and their application to internal conquests gave him both his theme and his method; the labors of Hercules in particular provide the model for many of his episodes. All his heroes at some point of their quests have to face the choice of Hercules, between the easy and the difficult way.

The heroic virtues even of the Christian are not self-sufficient: unless they spring out of faith, the noblest actions have the nature of sin (Article 13 of the Thirty-nine Articles). Therefore, holiness – the achievement of faith and the understanding of its powers – comes first, since without it, no other virtue is possible. Redcrosse, the knight of Holiness, sets off on his quest wearing battered Christian armor but with very little recognition of its properties. His aims are the traditional knightly ones – 'For all for prayse and honour he did fight' (I v 7) – but he is quickly lost in a world which offers none of the simple choices facing the usual knight of romance, and he sinks by way of Orgoglio's dungeon into the cave of Despair. Only then is he in a position to recognize his total dependence on grace and on the strength which faith alone gives him to get up again after every fall. In this strength, he can rise again each time the dragon of sin strikes him down. All other forms of Christian heroism are also based upon this: all other heroes, because they too are fallen, will fall in pursuit of their quests and need the power of regeneration. For this reason, Spenser makes Redcrosse the first of his exemplary knights and identifies him with St George, the patron saint of his country. He is aware, however, that the pattern of Christian victory does not accord with that of the traditional heroic poem; and he draws attention to the fact that he is treating the fight with the Dragon in a less heroic style than he would use for the treatment of 'warres and bloudy *Mars*' (I xi 5–7).

Once the lesson of holiness has been established, Spenser's other heroes can explore the nature of their particular forms of heroism; but their virtues are humbler than those of the traditional heroic poem, and geared specifically to Christian ends. The first, temperance, is not a virtue normally associated with the battlefield, nor is it the self-sufficient temperance of the golden mean. For Spenser, it is the rational self-control and resolute application which makes any moral action possible; and his emphasis is always upon the ability to keep straight on without being deflected from one's purpose – above all, the willingness to endure the sweat and toil of Adam and to forswear the sloth which is the chief enemy of heroism. Temperance is defined in Belphoebe's great speech at II iii 40–1, which is a central text of the poem and the recipe for virtue throughout. To achieve this virtue demands a knowledge of the limitations of one's own physical and moral strength: the most dangerous villain of Book II is Occasion, and wisdom lies in knowing when to avoid her and how to recognize in time the little sparks which, if left, will grow into uncontrollable fires. Guyon learns this lesson and so reaches Acrasia, whose capture is the object of his quest. It is significant that Spenser models him upon the prudent Odysseus rather than the fiery Achilles who, in the form of Pyrochles, symbolizes a type of excess which Guyon must try to conquer.

Book III moves from sin to death and deals with the role which sex plays in human regeneration. The variety of attitudes towards sex prevalent in Spenser's day ranged from the still-surviving medieval belief in the inherently sinful nature of all sex, to its complement, the Neoplatonic idealism which aimed to transcend the physical and ascend to the spiritual by means of the 'ladder of love.' In between was the new Protestant ethic which asserted the sanctity of sex within marriage (Rose 1968:7–34), a belief most powerfully expressed by Spenser in *Epithalamion*, although in *Fowre Hymnes* he meditated on the Neoplatonic concept and in *Amoretti* on the Petrarchan. In *The Faerie Queene*, however, where his subject is heroic love, his position is unmistakably the Protestant one in defense of marriage. For Spenser, the flesh was made holy by the Incarnation – 'love is the lesson which the Lord us taught' (*Amoretti* 68) – and procreation is the answer to death which entered the world with the Fall. This thoroughly traditional assumption is found at the ending of the *Romance of the Rose*, except that in *The Faerie Queene* the pleasure inextricably involved with the act of love is itself sinless because sanctified by its religious purpose. Spenser's figure embodying heroic love, therefore, is a woman, Britomart, whose task is to raise 'Most famous fruits of matrimoniall bowre' (III iii 3), and whose quest is to find the fitting husband to father her child through whom the heroic line will continue. Her achievement in Book III is to establish sex as something holy and innocent, as it is shown to be in the Garden of Adonis, and to destroy all the mythology of Ovid or medieval *Fine Amour* which down the ages had presented love as something guilty and to be feared. She does this by freeing Amoret from the torments to which Busirane has subjected her, and by restoring her to the blissful sexual embraces of Scudamour at the end of the 1590 *Faerie Queene*.

But this, although the basis of sexual heroism, is only the first stage in its achievement. The sexual passion once admitted is especially liable to excess or perversion, as the Palmer recognizes (II iv 34); and Book IV shows how it may be tempered and directed into the ways of concord instead of those of Ate by fusion with the moral and spiritual values of friendship. This reconciliation of eros and agape is demonstrated by Cambina when she makes peace between Cambell and Triamond (IV iii 42–9), and by Belphoebe when she rescues Amoret from Lust (vii 29–33). Only when this harmony has been achieved can the great pageant of married fertility proceed, the marriage of Thames and Medway. Even this is not the end of Spenser's treatment of the theme, however, and the final stage of heroic love consists in the establishment of the true nature of marriage itself. Spenser's position, like Milton's, is the traditional one which defines marriage as a hierarchy of which the husband is the head: having found her husband, therefore, Britomart has to educate him and herself in the proper relationship of the sexes in marriage. Artegall's weakness is a tendency to set up his lady on a Petrarchan pedestal and worship her, whether she is Radigund or Britomart herself – a fault which Britomart cures by ruthlessly slaying Radigund and her warrior maidens, and relinquishing her own warrior status: 'And changing all that forme of common weale, / The liberty of women did repeale, / Which they had long usurpt; and them restoring / To mens subjection, did true Justice deale' (V vii 42). It is an ideal not easy to accept today, and even Spenser may have had his doubts about it, for at the conclusion of the same passage he describes how all the people adored Britomart as a goddess for her wisdom in doing this. It is, however, the orthodox concept of truly heroic love; and because it concerns what properly belongs to love and marriage, Spenser treats it under the heading of justice in Book V.

Books V and VI deal respectively with the most characteristic virtues of epic and heroic romance, namely justice and courtesy, but both are redefined. Artegall is introduced as the generic hero 'Ay doing things, that to his fame redound, / Defending Ladies cause, and Orphans right' (III ii 14), and he is modeled more closely than any other hero on Hercules. Yet his exploits follow the pattern of Hercules' ignoble servitude to Omphale, not only his heroic labors; and the virtue he professes is less simply heroic than the traditional one. Spenser's justice includes cunning as well as courage: it softens the strict letter of the law with equity, but it is also suspicious of a mercy which can weaken into sentimentality. In Book VI, courtesy too is modified. It is given a more idealistic vision than in the courtesy books, and vested with almost redemptive properties; but it is hostile to an easy idealism and needs the sword of justice to become effective.

These are Spenser's virtues, the pursuit of which constitutes heroism as he understands it, although none of them conforms to the conventional heroic pattern. They are, in fact, the domestic virtues of everyday life, more like those of Jane Austen than of the epic; and they are heroic only because they are difficult to achieve and because much depends on them. They are, however, capable of attainment, unlike those of Sidney's Arcadian heroes. Although Spenser writes within romance conventions, he is the great realist of the period. By means of these virtues, the world will carry on its regular cycle; and mutability, though indestructible, can be controlled and used. The Garden of Eden and the Golden Age are gone forever, but Jove's Silver Age is still possible, where order and decency prevail.

One other aspect of the heroic must be considered, namely the sort of heroism which Spenser considers appropriate for the poet. *FQ* VI is the book most explicitly concerned with poetry, and its vision of the Graces (which only the poet, Colin Clout, is allowed to see) provides a transcendental ideal of harmony which parallels that of Spenser's heavenly Jerusalem in Book I. In the proem of Book VI, Spenser invokes the Muses' aid to describe the poet's task in terms which echo those used for the quests of his hero-knights. Although it is not defined until Book VI, a sense of the poet's heroic role runs throughout the poem.

The poet, for example, must oppose mutability in his own way, by resisting the ravages of devouring time which would destroy the memory of heroic deeds and erode the works of literature, and even the language itself. Spenser's tale of Cambell and Cambina in Book IV is explicitly designed to restore what 'Dan *Chaucer*, well of English undefyled' originally wrote 'With warlike numbers and Heroicke sound,' but which has now been defaced by 'wicked Time' (ii 32–3). Even the use of archaic English in *The Faerie Queene* is an attempt to keep the past alive in the present. Besides creating new myths, the poet must sustain the great traditional moral myths by giving them modern applications and demonstrating their contemporary relevance; equally important, he must identify and reject any perversions of mythology which have crept in and could corrupt mankind. The Bower of Bliss embodies all the erotic fantasies which lust has inspired in poetry and iconography from Ovid to Tasso, and Spenser exposes its essential sterility. Busirane's Ovidian tapestries and masque of Cupid offer a vision of sex as something to be feared, and Britomart forces Busirane to forswear his 'wicked bookes' and 'bloudy lines' (III xii 32–6). Even the Arcadian vision of *FQ* VI ix, described in terms of traditional literary pastoral, presents an ideal which is dangerous because it might make us, as it makes Calidore for a time, forget that the Fall ever happened. Spenser exposes its fragility by means of the Brigands.

Three major quests of *The Faerie Queene* – those of Guyon, Britomart, and Calidore – are directly involved in the destruction of potent but corrupting literary myths. The poet Bonfont earns by his 'lewd poems' the name Malfont, the 'title of a Poet bad' (V ix 25). The ultimate enemy of the good poet is the Blatant Beast with his many evil voices; and Colin Clout, as well as Calidore, must do battle with him if he is to fulfill his heroic function as prophet, civilizer, and mythmaker for mankind (see role of *poet). That the Blatant Beast breaks his chains at the end of Book VI could perhaps indicate Spenser's loss of belief in the poet's heroic mission, and account too for the abrupt ending of *The Faerie Queene*.

MAURICE EVANS

D.C. Allen 1970; H. Baker 1947; Bolgar 1975 in Burns and Reagan 1975:120–44; Norman T. Burns and Christopher J. Reagan, eds 1975 *Concepts of the Hero in the Middle Ages and the Renaissance* (Albany, NY); Sukanta Chaudhuri 1981 *Infirm Glory: Shakespeare and the Renaissance Image of Man* (Oxford); Dunseath 1968; Evans 1970; Galinsky 1972; John Harington 1591 *Preface, or Rather, A Briefe Apologie of Poetrie* prefixed to his translation of *Orlando furioso* 1591, in G.G. Smith 1904, 2:194–222; Homer ed 1967; Bernard F. Huppé 1975 'The Concept of the Hero in the Early Middle Ages' in Burns and Reagan 1975:1–26; Richard S. Ide 1980 *Possessed with Greatness: The Heroic Tragedies of Chapman and Shakespeare* (Chapel Hill); Pico ed 1948; Rose 1968; Seznec ed 1953; Steadman 1967; Steadman 1975 'The Arming of an Archetype: Heroic Virtue and the Conventions of Literary Epic' in Burns and Reagan 1975:147–96; Waith 1962; Bruce W. Wardropper 1975 'The Epic Hero Superseded' in Burns and Reagan 1975:197–220.

heroic poem before Spenser The Renaissance concept of the heroic poem differs from our own. We think of the heroic poem as a long verse narrative about spectacular exploits in a heroic age, and of epic as a particular genre whose norms derive from the classical tradition of Homer, Virgil, and their emulators. Renaissance theory was vague about this distinction. Epic evoked a specific prosody, the six-foot dactylic line that William Webbe called *Hexametrum Epicum* (*A Discourse of English Poetrie* 1586, in G.G. Smith 1904, 1:281). Harvey identified this meter as 'the soveraigne of verses and the high Controwler of Rimes' (*Third Letter* 1592, in Smith 2:230). Yet epic was also heroic poetry, as Harington implied in the preface to his translation of Ariosto's *Orlando furioso* (1591): 'the *Epopeia*, that is the heroicall Poem.' With Aristotle's idea of the epic in mind, Harington grounded the heroic poem in history, verisimilitude, and *peripety* 'which I interpret an agnition [recognition] of some unlooked for fortune either good or bad, and a sudden change thereof' (in Smith 2:216). Some years earlier, Puttenham had conflated heroic poems with epic when he described the former as 'long histories of the noble gests of kings and great Princes entermedling the dealings of the gods, halfe gods, or *Heroes* of the gentiles, and the great and waighty consequences of peace and warre ... whereof *Homer* was chief and most auncient among the Greeks, *Virgill* among the Latines' (1589, in Smith 2:26). For Sidney, the primary quality of heroic poetry was its capacity for elevated moral instruction through narrative exempla: 'for as the image of each action stirreth and instructeth the mind, so the lofty image of such worthies most inflameth the mind with desire to be worthy, and informs with counsel how to be worthy' (*Defence of Poetry* ed 1973b:98). Spenser, too, deemed this quality paramount.

Elizabethan theory acknowledged the preeminence of Homer and Virgil within the classical tradition, as classical scholarship in England and on the continent uncovered more information about the Greek and Roman past. With the dissemination of Aristotle's *Poetics* after 1548, English writers more and more celebrated Homer as the exemplar of the heroic poet. They did so in part by appropriating insights from a growing body of Italian literary theory on epic and romance. For this theory, the most important problem was to evaluate romance digressiveness against the unity of action perceived in classical epic. In English scholarship, however, a good firsthand acquaintance with Homer's texts was rare. Nor were the latter translated into English directly from Greek until Chapman's renditions of the *Iliad* (1598–1611) and the *Odyssey* (1615). Even more rare was a philological knowledge of other ancient epics, including reassembled fragments of an early Greek narrative cycle on the Trojan war that provided a context for Homer's composition. Renaissance scholars certainly did not recognize Homer's relation to oral poetry, nor did they perceive that he had composed his verse in an oral formulaic mode quite different from that of writers in later ages.

The literary context for Virgil's *Aeneid* was more widely understood. Since the mid-fifteenth century, scholars had begun to glean this context from such Greek poems as Hesiod's genealogy of the gods, the *Theogony* (8th c BC), and Apollonius of Rhodes' epic account of Jason's voyage, the *Argonautica* (3rd c BC). Moreover, they possessed fragments of texts by Virgil's Latin predecessors: Naevius' chronicle of the First Punic War (3rd c BC), Ennius' hexameter *Annales* (2nd c BC), and, since Poggio's rediscovery of it near St Gall, Lucretius' philosophical *De rerum natura* (1st c BC). They nonetheless failed to estimate the radical nature of Virgil's attempt to transpose Homer's oral formulae to the level of his own highly wrought subjective style.

Renaissance readers did, however, locate the achievements of Virgil's other successors in their Roman context. They greatly enjoyed the poetry of Ovid, though they tended to depreciate the radical nature of his attempt to acculturate the most disparate Homeric and Virgilian myths to the epic framework of his *Metamorphoses*. They recognized the efforts of Lucan (AD 39–65) to shape his epic *Pharsalia* on events of recent history stripped of conventional mythic epic machinery, though some theorists questioned whether it were not simply versified history rather than heroic poetry. Few Renaissance poets in either Latin or the vernaculars imitated the style of later Virgilian emulators such as Statius (c AD 45–96), who wrote the *Thebaid* and an incomplete *Achilleid*; Silius Italicus, who composed *Punica*, an epic about the Punic Wars; and Valerius Flaccus (late 1st c AD), who produced an *Argonautica*. Instead, the humanist movement of the fifteenth century repeatedly asserted the primacy of Virgil's style at the expense of lesser imitators.

It did so with good reason. The classical Virgilian form of the epic had disappeared almost entirely in the late Empire. Claudian's descriptive narrative, *De raptu Proserpinae*, subverted it with the bombastic artifice found in his poems sycophantically addressed to his patrons. Prudentius' *Psychomachia* (c 400) signaled the beginning of a long tradition of philosophical and theological allegory that would later dominate such narratives as Alanus de Insulis' Latin *Anticlaudianus* and the vernacular *Romance of the Rose* of Guillaume de Lorris and Jean de Meun or the *Divine Comedy* of Dante. Boccaccio's *Filostrato* and *Teseida*, both in ottava rima, imposed upon medieval romance forms a classicizing narrative structure with a minimum of allegorical decoration. Chaucer's adaptation of those poems in his *Knight's Tale* and *Troilus and Criseyde* extended the possibilities into English rhyme royal. To the later humanists, however, any replication of Virgilian grandeur demanded a return to Virgil's language and to Virgil's texts themselves. Yet, beginning with Petrarch's *Africa* (1338–41, an unfinished epic on the Punic Wars), the history of attempts to compose a new Latin epic on the Virgilian model recounts general failure. Humanist devotion to the surface of Virgil's style resulted in technically proficient, often ingenious, but sometimes arid imitations of the master's diction, syntax, and elocutionary figures. Prominent examples include Francesco Filelfo's unfinished *Sphortias* (1473) about the author's patron, Francesco Sforza; Mantuan's slender *Parthenice* (1488) about the lives of seven saints; Jacopo Sannazaro's *De partu virginis* (1526) about the birth of Christ; Marco Girolamo Vida's *Christias* (1535) about the life of Christ; and Girolamo Fracastoro's *Joseph* (1553) about the Old Testament hero.

All of these Neo-Latin epics owed a tremendous debt to the textual and philological scholarship displayed in early printed editions of the ancient classics. Virgil and Lucan appeared in print in 1469, Ovid, Statius, and Silius Italicus in 1471, Lucretius in 1473, Valerius Flaccus in 1474, and Claudian in 1483. The Greek texts generally became known in Latin translations. Homer entered the western Renaissance through Leontius Pilatus' prose translations sent to Petrarch in 1364. More sophisticated but still only partial verse renderings of Homer into Latin came from Pier Candido Decembrio in 1440, Lorenzo Valla in 1442, Carlo Marsuppini in 1447, and Angelo Poliziano in 1475. The *editio princeps* of the *Iliad* and *Odyssey* in Greek was not issued until 1488. Printed editions of Hesiod and Apollonius of Rhodes first appeared in 1496.

Just as important as accurate editions were the interpretive commentaries on Homer, Virgil, and Ovid appended to various editions. They established a hermeneutic tradition, a context of understanding that shaped the Renaissance reception of texts. Some of these commentaries harked back to ancient times; others were contemporary and reflected the increasing movement of sixteenth-century exegesis away from medieval methods of systematic allegorical interpretation towards a freer, more flexible mode of comprehending different levels of meaning in a single text. Ancient Neoplatonic readings of Homer by Dio Chrysostom, Didymus, Porphyry, Proclus, and Heraclitus appeared in print between 1488 and 1554, as did specifically Christian readings such as the anonymous *Moral Interpretation of the Wanderings of Odysseus* and the early Byzantine commentary of Eustathius of Thessalonica. Commentaries on the *Aeneid* generally amplified the late classical ones of Servius and Donatus with the accretions of such editors as Cristoforo Landino (1488), Antonius Mancinellus (1490), Badius Ascensius (1500), and Pierius Valerianus (1523). Even greater in number and diversity were the commentaries on Ovid's *Metamorphoses*. In the sixteenth century, the new, comparatively modern concern with philological and historical problems in the text supplemented and eventually supplanted the medieval tradition of the *Ovide moralisé* (14th c) that attempted to justify pagan myths as Christian allegories. Notable commentators were Raffaello Regio (1493), Petrus Lavinius (1512), Georgius Sabinus (1555), Antonio Trifonio (1560), Giuseppe Horologgio (1563), Francesco Turchi (1572), and Ercole Ciofano (1575–8).

These editions and commentaries had an impact on many Renaissance poets before Spenser. The first wave of their influence on the vernacular heroic poem crested in the late fifteenth and early sixteenth centuries. Materials from the French *Chanson de Roland* (c 1100) and the medieval romances about King Arthur's knights merged with classical motifs to produce in Italy a series of chivalric epics about the heroes of Charlemagne's time. Such prose accounts as Andrea da Barberino's *Reali di Francia* (*France's Noblemen* c 1400) led to Luigi Pulci's *Morgante maggiore* (1483), an epic in ottava rima about a giant in Charlemagne's employ. Pulci's epic contributed to Boiardo's *Orlando innamorato* (1494), also in ottava rima, narrating the disastrous effects of Roland's love, and to Ariosto's continuation of that poem, *Orlando furioso* (1532). Pulci, Boiardo, and Ariosto were deeply steeped in the classical tradition, and each replicated the classical epic in unique ways. Most powerful was their emphasis on historical, dynastic, and nationalistic motifs. Just as Virgil had exploited the patriotic dimension of his myth about the founding of Rome and its potential for greatness, so the Renaissance poets exploited a similar dimension in their chivalric epics. Their heroes and heroines became progenitors of illustrious Italian contemporaries, and their exploits foreshadowed remarkable events in the present age.

A second wave of classical influence on the sixteenth-century heroic poem followed from the discovery of Aristotle's *Poetics* and a renewed appreciation of Homer. Latin translations of the *Poetics* in 1498 and 1536 and its first Greek edition printed by Aldus Manutius in 1508 had little impact, but Francesco Robortello's emended Latin translation and commentary in 1548 gave it new prominence. Aristotle's ideas about Homer in turn enhanced Homer's prestige. While Vida's *De arte poetica* (1527) still extolled Virgil's artful regularity over Homer's amplitude, later Italian theorists extrapolated an Aristotelian concept of epic that favored Homer. Trissino's *Poetica* (pub 1562, but composed largely in 1529) elevated Aristotle's theory to normative status. Giraldi Cintio's *Discorso intorno al comporre dei romanzi* (1554) stressed the merits of the modern chivalric romance, and Antonio Minturno explored the possibilities of accommodating its norms to the Aristotelian epic model in his *L'arte poetica* (1563); Tasso endorsed those possibilities by praising Ariosto's romance-epic in his *Discorsi dell'arte poetica* (1564, pub 1587).

The result of this classical influence was to expand contemporary awareness of epic's narrative, stylistic, allegorical, and historical qualities. After the publication of Aristotle, the ideas of length, proportion, and unity of action became increasingly important, while the relationship of allegorical motifs to historical verisimilitude generated intense discussion. These concerns emerge directly and indirectly in the Letter to Raleigh, where Spenser describes the structure of *The Faerie Queene* according to a scheme of exemplified virtues. The general inclination of vernacular epic in the late sixteenth century, however, was to favor historical rather than allegorical narrative. In Italy, the most significant attempts to compose historical epics were Trissino's 27 books of blank verse narrating the Emperor Justinian's repulsion of the Goths, *L'Italia liberata dai Goti* (1547–8), and Tasso's ottava rima epic about the First Crusade, *Gerusalemme liberata* (1581). A major contribution in France was Ronsard's incomplete *Franciade* (1572), an epic in alexandrines about the founding of the French nation (see *French Renaissance literature); and in Portugal, Camoens' *Lusiads* (1572), an epic in ottava rima about the explorations of Vasco da Gama.

Spenser shows his engagement with classical and Renaissance heroic poetry more in his poetic practice than in his critical theory. Imitations of classical similes, extended descriptions, mythic ornamentation, and complex grammatical constructions occur on every page of his work, even in his shorter poetry. The envoy ('To His Booke') of *The Shepheardes Calender*, for example, echoes Statius' *Thebaid*; *Ruines of Time* refers pointedly to *Aeneid* 6; *Teares of the Muses* summons the catalogue of muses from Hesiod's *Theogony*; *Mother Hubberds Tale* recreates the description of the Golden Age in Ovid's *Metamorphoses*; *Ruines of Rome* evokes Lucan's *Pharsalia*; *Muiopotmos* includes an imitation of Ovid's tale of Arachne in *Metamorphoses*; and *Epithalamion* echoes motifs from Claudian's epithalamium for Honorius.

The Faerie Queene naturally reveals Spenser's deepest experience of classical and Renaissance heroic poetry. Ariosto's *Orlando furioso* opened by far the richest mine of inspiration, but other Italian epics afforded noteworthy materials. From Boiardo's account of the Palazzo Gioioso in *Orlando innamorato* 1.8 came Spenser's account of Castle Joyous in *FQ* III i; from his narrative of Mandricardo and the shield of Hector in *OI* 3.2–3 came the narrative of Scudamour and the Shield of Love in *FQ* IV x. From Trissino's *Italia liberata da' Goti* 4–5, where Belisarius' knights rescue their comrades imprisoned in Acratia's garden, Spenser derived the framework for Guyon's mission to rescue fellow knights imprisoned in Acrasia's Bower of Bliss (*FQ* II xii) . Other details of Acrasia's Bower echo Tasso's account of Armida's garden in *Gerusalemme liberata* 16, and Phaedria's song in *FQ* II vi echoes the siren's song in *GL* 14. Also from Tasso came the pastoral motif of Calidore's sojourn among the shepherds in *FQ* VI ix, which parallels Erminia's sojourn in *GL* 7.

The Italian Renaissance epic ultimately mediated much of what Spenser adapted from the classical epic. Guyon's voyage to the Bower of Bliss in *FQ* II xii, for example, recalls aspects of Ulysses' voyage to Ithaca in the *Odyssey*, but it evokes Tasso's and Trissino's borrowings from Homer more than the Homeric text itself. The Fradubio episode of *FQ* I ii alludes to the fate of Polydorus in *Aeneid* 2, but only through Ariosto's imitation of Virgil in his tale of Astolfo on Alcina's isle in *Orlando furioso* 6. Nonetheless, Spenser's direct references even to the lesser classical epics are strong. Merlin's incantations in *FQ* III iii, for example, recall the magicians' activity in Lucan's *Pharsalia* 6; the description of Ate's house in *FQ* IV i recalls the description of the Temple of Mars in Statius' *Thebaid* 7.34–63; the lover's complaint in *FQ* IV x closely follows the invocation to Venus at the beginning of Lucretius' *De rerum natura*; the description of the Souldan in *FQ* V viii recalls that of Aegis in Valerius Flaccus' *Argonautica* 6.

No English poet before Spenser appropriated quite so many diverse materials from the classical and Renaissance tradition of heroic poetry. In so doing, Spenser established himself as both the Homer and Virgil of sixteenth-century English poetry and, as Harvey remarked, the modern master who overwent Ariosto and all the Italians.

WILLIAM J. KENNEDY

Recent general studies of the epic tradition include Bowra 1945; Durling 1965; Giamatti 1966; Greene 1963; W.J. Kennedy 1978, ch 3; Murrin 1980; Steadman 1967; Tillyard 1954. For further reading on individual poets and their epic poems, see *Homer, *Virgil, *Ovid, *Ariosto, *Tasso. For allegorizations of Homer, Virgil, and Ovid in the Renaissance, see D.C. Allen 1970. One example of a medieval allegorization of Virgil (c 1136) is Bernard Sylvestris ed 1977, translated in ed 1979. IJsewijn 1977 is an excellent survey of publications on Renaissance commentary and Neo-Latin epic. Excerpts with translations from Neo-Latin epics appear in F.J. Nichols 1979. For a discussion of the tradition, see William J. Kennedy 1983 *Jacopo Sannazaro and the Uses of Pastoral* (Hanover, NH). One example of the genre is Marco Girolamo Vida 1978 *The Christiad* (1535) tr and ed Gertrude C. Drake and Clarence A. Forbes (Carbondale, Ill); see also Mario A. Di Cesare 1964 *Vida's 'Christiad' and Vergilian Epic* (New York). Some important Renaissance treatises are gathered in Bernard Weinberg, ed 1970–4 *Trattati di poetica e retorica del cinquecento* 4 vols (Bari); partial translations are in Gilbert 1940. The theory is surveyed in Weinberg 1961, esp ch 19–20 for the quarrel over Ariosto and Tasso. See also Tasso ed 1973. English writings are found in G.G. Smith 1904.

heroic poem since Spenser The term *heroic poem* refers to an extended verse narrative displaying valued human qualities. The 'heroic' consists of the qualities honored by an age in its great men; those qualities do not remain constant from age to age. In almost all ages, poets have embodied their ideals of human greatness in epic heroes within such poems; the poetic structures chosen for heroic narratives do not remain constant from age to age. Indeed, the term *heroic poem* itself scarcely survived the eighteenth century. In Spenser's time, it was used interchangeably with *epic* or *historical*, as in Puttenham's 'a Poet Epick or Historicall' (*Arte of English Poesie*), or Sidney's 'The most notable [denominations of poetry] be the heroic, lyric, tragic [etc]' (*Defence of Poetry* 1973b:81). There is no reason why we should not use these terms interchangeably as well; the interesting questions about the development of heroic poetry after Spenser are not questions about generic nomenclature. They have to do with genre theory and history, or with tradition and change. Nevertheless, from Spenser's day to ours the terms *epic* and *heroic* when used of poetry increasingly apply less to a strictly defined genre than to a loosely conceived mode. The suggestion that in the nineteenth century much of the heroic impulse moved from poetry into the novel has received much popular and some scholarly assent, however (Tillyard 1958, Vogler 1971, Maresca 1974). Critics writing in English have been less willing than some continental critics to extend the term to such long dramas as Goethe's *Faust* or Hardy's *Dynasts* (but see Merchant 1971).

With respect to genre theory, the problem of discussing epic is easily stated. Critics since Spenser have periodically pointed out that what has been defined as heroic poetry in one age neither does nor ought to turn up quite the same thing in the next age. They have therefore presumed that the genre has died or ought to die (Foerster 1962, Fowler 1982, Hägin 1964), or even that the concept of genre itself has outlived its usefulness (Hernadi 1972). Frequent obituaries, however, have not prevented subsequent poets from writing heroic verse in which a narrator speaks in the first person and then allows his characters to speak for themselves in such a way as to display the qualities considered essentially worthy of human beings. Because such poems persist to dignify human endeavors, scholars have continued to write generic history, distinguishing a series of historical stages in the development of epic. The stages usually noted are the high Renaissance (allegorical, Christian; Spenser, Milton), the neoclassical (national, satirical; Cowley, Dryden, Pope, Blackmore), the Romantic (subjective, psychological; Blake, Wordsworth, Keats, Byron, Whitman), the later nineteenth century (novelistic, historical; Melville, Browning, Tennyson, Doughty), the modernist (experimental, fragmented, decentered; Crane, Stevens, Pound, Williams), and the post-modernist (Jones, Berryman, Lowell); some would distinguish the American long poem as a separate category (Vogler 1971, Wittreich 1975; Pearce 1961). Historians of the genre notice the epic in continuous change and are reluctant to call its survival into question, even when they are inclined to agree that as time goes on fewer works central to the canon bear many of the earmarks of previous versions of the literary kind.

The question then becomes how those earmarks are to be regarded. The heroic poem has always been seen to be composed of a number of formal, thematic, mimetic, prosodic, and linguistic elements or conventions or, in some periods, 'laws.' How many of them out of the full repertory must be present in a poem to admit it to the tradition? Is the history of epic to be traced in terms of its conventions of form, which would include admixture of genres, the bard, the invocation, the epic question, high style, commencement *in medias res*, epic simile, and epic catalogue? Or is epicality to be defined as a matter of theme or content, which would involve the cosmic setting, the national hero, the military action, the quest or test, the romantic interlude, the descent to the underworld? Or is the heroic determined by its affect, which would incorporate wonder at the sublime, instruction through example in the culture's value system, and national celebration or warning? Or does the heroic inhere in its origins and foundation structures, which would embrace oral formulae, ritual, myth, and archetype? (For other qualities, see Abrams ed 1988, Frye 1957, Swedenberg 1944, Wellek and Warren ed 1956, Wilkie 1965.) To approach the problem in slightly different terms, do we know an epic by its heroic spirit or its epic rules – by its inner form (or generic function) or its outer form (or awareness of traditional practice; see Vogler 1971)? Modern criticism tends to identify all these *topoi* or conventions merely as variable elements in an heroic agenda, some number of which present in some combination marks a particular epic. Although heroic poetry achieves a clear identity in historical moments, that sharp sense of definition soon dissolves and an evolution or transformation occurs before another kind of identity emerges. Thus the tradition is reconstituted by those subsequent poets whose work rearranges our sense of the tradition (see Eliot ed 1950). The presence of so many elements so variously combined in the past and combinable in the future makes it difficult either to proscribe future change or to endorse any critical procedure that effaces the genre or mode from serious consideration.

The history of the heroic poem after Spenser, then, can be seen as the history of the transformation and recombination of the formal, thematic, mimetic, affective, and generative elements – both those recognized by him and those subsequently found valuable, often drawn from parts of the tradition Spenser ignored. From Spenser's practice in *The Faerie Queene* and theory in the Letter to Raleigh, we can isolate several conventions, to which future epic poets would add others. To examine the whole heroic repertory is impossible here, but it is possible to choose one topic from three of the constituent aspects (formal, thematic, and affective) to suggest epic's post-Spenserian life. Topics central to each of these three areas are (1) for form, the announcement of genre or epic intention; (2) for content, the nature of the bard and of the hero and their relationship; and (3) for affect, the shifts of expectation among readers involved in incorporating allegorical morality, satire, and current history in the epic.

announcement of genre In both *The Faerie Queene* and the Letter to Raleigh, Spenser announces his genre as allegorical heroic. The Letter proclaims a 'general intention,' aligns it with that of 'all the antique Poets historicall,' and says that to be 'plausible and pleasing' the work will be 'coloured' with 'an historicall fiction.' He notes that there are precedents in the heroic tradition for either one or many heroes and chooses for his poem the multiplication of heroes 'for the more variety of the history,' beginning *in medias res* because it 'maketh a pleasing Analysis of all' when 'a Poet thrusteth into the middest.' In *FQ* I proem 1, he identifies his audience as a 'learned throng' including Elizabeth, his bard as 'all too meane' but determined to 'blazon broad' 'gentle deeds ... Whose prayses [have] slept in silence long,' and his mimesis as 'Fierce warres and faithfull loves.' Spenser sees heroic poetry as a genre telling the truth to its own times in an imaginative guise, and delightfully but critically communicating the highest values of those times.

Subsequent heroic poets typically relate their major works to the tradition, not always taking the title 'epic poet' but usually referring to some of these signals of heroic intention. Thus Milton says of *Paradise Lost* that its argument is 'not less but more heroic' than that of the ancient epic poets (*PL* 9.14). Dryden claims that a part of *The Hind and the Panther* has 'the Majestick Turn of Heroick Poesie' and that another part makes use of 'the commonplaces of satire' ('To the Reader'); in *A Discourse concerning Satire*, he holds that 'Satire is undoubtedly a Species' of 'Heroique Poetry it self,' implying an epic claim for both *The Hind and the Panther* and *Absalom and Achitophel* (see Budick 1974). Blake's epic intentions in the prophetic books are clear. His meter for *The Four Zoas* is the 'march of long resounding, strong heroic Verse' ('Night the First' 1.2); and although he disowns 'Homer and Ovid' as models in the preface to *Milton* by choosing instead to imitate the 'consciously & professedly Inspired Men' who wrote 'the Sublime of the Bible,' he thereby stakes a claim to be writing in the scripturally heroic vein. Wordsworth calls *The Prelude* only the 'portico' to epic, but speaks in Book 1 of intending 'glorious work,' 'immortal verse,' 'holy services,' and 'noble theme' (158, 233, 13, 129), so as to make heroic claims even while denying them. With Byron the claims are both directly made and mocked in *Don Juan* (1.200.1–2): 'My poem's epic, and is meant to be / Divided in twelve books.' Whitman declares his heroic intention in an anonymous self-review of the first edition of *Leaves of Grass* printed in *The United States Review* and appended by him to the second edition of the poem. Identifying himself as the new bard of the New World, he names his poem indirect super-epic: 'It is to be indirect and not direct or descriptive or epic. Its quality is to go through these to much more.' Tennyson not only denies the heroic title to his composite and ironic poem about heroic failure, *Idylls of the King* ('Calling the Idylls an epic, which they are not, is a misnomer'), he says that to write any version of the heroic is impossible in his own day ('I should be crazed to attempt [an epic of King Arthur] in the heart of the 19th Century').

To regret that one's times cannot support epic, however, is tantamount to confessing an intention to write it aslant. One might compare Milton's fear that he too may write in 'an age too late' (*PL* 9.44). Melville does much the same sort of silent urging when he calls *Clarel* 'A Poem and Pilgrimage.' Wallace Stevens attempts the 'supreme fiction' of 'heroic children,' 'moments of awakening,' and 'major man,' as 'an heroic part, of the commonal' in *Notes towards a Supreme Fiction* ('It Must Be Abstract' 5, 7, 8, 9). Pound comments of his *Cantos*, 'For forty years I have schooled myself ... to write an epic which begins "In the Dark Forest", crosses the Purgatory of human error, and ends in the light' (in 'An Introduction to the Economic Nature of the United States' 1960:15). In the preface to *The Anathemata* (1952), David Jones calls himself 'the maker' of the poem and says it is written 'sub specie aeternitatis' to deal with 'things set up, lifted up, or in whatever manner made over to the gods'; his wish for inspiration and his holy vision recall a good number of the heroic poets before him, and his concern for the fragmentary nature of his poem recalls a constant problem for the epic poet from Spenser's day to his. Finally, John Berryman makes heroic claim for *The Dream Songs*, remarking to Peter A. Stitt in an interview, 'I was aware that I was embarked on an epic' (*Paris Review* 53[1972]:177–207).

Not all epic poets either signal or pointedly deny their heroic intention, of course. And while most of these poets making heroic claims would appear, along with others, on most historical critics' lists of epic poets, unanimity can neither be hoped for nor found about who should be included or which of their long narratives. One might mention Southey, Morris, Hardy, Eliot, and Pound as contested figures and Dryden's *Absalom and Achitophel* or *The Hind and the Panther*, Keats's *Hyperion* or *Fall of Hyperion*, Browning's *Ring and the Book* or *Sordello*, Tennyson's *In Memoriam* or *Idylls of the King*, Stevens' *Comedian as the Letter C* or *Notes towards a Supreme Fiction* as contested alternatives (see Webber 1979). Hence, to make or not to make an epic claim does not assure membership in the genre or mode. Literary history is strewn with poets who attempted the heroic and are not considered to have succeeded; some instance Abraham Cowley, Edward Arlington Robinson, and Hart Crane. Other heroic poets have seemed what Dryden called the 'last great Prophet[s] of Tautology' (*Mac Flecknoe* 30) for insisting on outer form over inner; Joel Barlow, Joseph Cottle, Ossian, and Scott come to mind.

the hero, the bard, and heroic virtue Spenser's heroes grow from inexperience into possession of the virtues they represent; as his heroes grow, he as bard shadows their growth from an expressed inadequacy to an expressed confidence like that of a captain sailing his ship into harbor. He acknowledges that the increase in confidence arises not so much from his own skill as from the power of an inspiration that comes to the aid of his poetical inventions (see Guillory 1983). Only in Book VI does Spenser the bard make himself an actor in the body of his own epic, under an earlier poetic pseudonym, Colin Clout. His heroes are multiple and presented in *entrelacement*; they represent single virtues, save for Arthur in whom all are joined. The bard himself is not shown acquiring the virtues appropriate to private and public life, he but admires their growth in his heroes. Nonetheless, the bard doubles in his own person the processes of growth, often delayed and sometimes turned from. This pattern of relationship, as well as the virtues extolled in heroes and the sources of poetical authority claimed by bards, is subject to change throughout the history of epic. Sometimes the change in bard or hero or their relationship is signaled by a recollection of Spenser, or of other English predecessors, as Spenser placed himself in relation to Chaucer to suggest the kind of romance-epic he intended: 'through infusion sweete ... I follow here the footing of thy feete' (*FQ* IV ii 34). Acknowledged disciples or persistent echoers of Spenser in narrative poems of heroic turn include Milton, Dryden, Blake, Keats, Shelley, Byron, Browning, and Eliot.

Milton's bard is drawn as one of Adam's fallen sons, who has suffered blindness and public defeat, and who is enabled by inspiration to defend God's ways to man. In *Paradise Lost*, the double heroes (man and 'one greater man' 1.4) and the antihero (Satan) show that true heroism is not military prowess or royal rule but 'Patience and Heroic Martyrdom' (9.32). The transformation of the bard and the transvaluation of heroism in Milton is accompanied by an honoring of Spenser, 'whom I dare be known to think a better teacher than *Scotus* or *Aquinas*' (*Areopagitica*) as the poet of temptation overcome. (Dryden wrote that 'Milton has acknowledg'd to me, that Spencer was his Original'; and of his own indebtedness, that 'At last I had recourse to Spenser, the author of that immortal poem called the *Fairy Queen* and there I met with [the turns of words and thoughts] which I had been looking for so long in vain' *Discourse concerning Satire*).

Dryden's poetic persona in *The Hind and the Panther* is even more self-critical than Spenser's and more sardonically aware of being fallen than Milton's. The heroic virtue of faith or of trusting obedience to the church that Dryden would extol is given to the Hind both to exemplify and to teach, since the bard well knows that only as a prodigal son has he any claim to grace. The relationship between bard and hero is ironical: the hero is a heroine and an animal, the bard is aware of being too worldly to embody heroism in himself or even to see it in any human being.

Blake's mythology is everywhere indebted to his close study of *The Faerie Queene* that long antedated his drawings for it. In *Milton* his bard is actually the over-hero of an epic in which under-heroes are allegorical projections of qualities the bard struggles to unify in the human imagination. At the same time, the work presents a stage in the history of Albion, an historical national hero conceived somewhat on the lines of Spenser's Arthur. The bard-hero imagines himself as a reborn Milton attempting to reconstitute his epic poem, since the history of poetry like the life of man is a struggle to correct temporal errors through 'mental fight' ('And did those feet') and to achieve completeness.

Wordsworth's bard-as-hero is conceived even more autobiographically than those of Milton and Dryden. In *The Prelude* he enters on a quest for the right course of life and poetry. His invocation, 'O welcome Messenger' (1.5), announces a serious work of heroic scale. Wordsworth conceives of the highest heroic virtue not as heroic martyrdom but as imaginative self-fulfillment, and his religion is not of the Christian God revealed to Spenser but of the divine reciprocity of imagination and nature. Direct Spenserian influence on the Romantics can be seen in Blake's archetypes, Byron's 'fierce loves and faithless wars' (*Don Juan* 7.8.1), and the moral landscape of Shelley's *Witch of Atlas*; but the virtue extolled in all is vitalistic imagination.

Moving on to the later nineteenth century, we need cite only one instance, and that an American one, of the epic as a long noveletic poem, in order to indicate the objectification of the bard and scaling down of the hero that take place in the next stage of the form's modification. In *Clarel* Melville effaces the bard into the third person but allows himself to enter his poem autobiographically, disguised as a choral character Rolfe. His hero is not at all gigantic in conception; he is a divinity student whose God has left the world. The qualities Melville presents as heroic through him are not Promethean but sadly humanistic, courage in the face of despair and loss. Although the poem has a central hero, of democratic ordinariness, it represents a group of characters on a journey; characters, journey, and symbolic moral landscape are treated both naturalistically and allegorically.

The modernist epic is as fragmented and experimental with respect to the bard and hero as with respect to most of its thematic considerations. Wallace Stevens, confessing that 'My interest in the hero, major man, the giant has nothing to do with [Nietzsche]; in fact, I throw knives at the hero' (ed 1966:409), presents an abstract hero in *The Comedian as the Letter C* and as bard-theorist discusses his value in *Notes towards a Supreme Fiction*; in both cases the heroic capacity extolled is the power of admitting the fictiveness of all conceptions of reality. Pound, Eliot, and William Carlos Williams constitute their epics autobiographically, the bard entering the poem as a character (such as Dr Paterson) virtually indistinguishable from the poet, or through reference to other heroic poets (like Browning who begins Pound's Canto II), or as the nameless deployer of allusions forming a heroic mosaic (the personal-impersonal voice of *The Waste Land*). Modernist value structures are seen as ironically inadequate, well represented by the collage and fragmentation the modernist heroic poet tends to use. Post-modernist heroic continues to find its materials in subjectivity, the responses of the poet-speaker to his cultural and personal experiences being the essential material for Berryman's *Dream Songs* as for Lowell's *History*. The autobiographical bard mulls over the experiences of other men seeking and more often than not failing to find values unassailable enough to denominate heroic. He tends to use a new variety of stanza forms to achieve sequence in his explorations, rather than to draw on blank or heroic or free verse to suggest a unified journey, test, or quest (see Rosenthal and Gall 1983). The variableness of the conceptions of bard and hero in the long evolution of the heroic poem since Spenser is one reason for resisting the proposal that after the eighteenth century the epic impulse passed from poetry into the novel; another reason is the difficulty of finding canonical novels so impelled towards epic that they do not aspire to the condition of experimentation and subjectivity to be found in modern poetry.

allegory, history, and satire in epic The large genre *epic* or mode *heroic* not only accommodates a repertory of variable formal and thematic elements; as the principal member of the *genera mixta*, it also encompasses by tradition numerous other genres, each carrying a number of reader expectations. A reader may expect to find within an epic the tragic, the comic, the pastoral, the encyclopedic, for example, together with all the emotions and responses appropriate to each. Again the history of the genre combinations and consequent reader expectations of epic is very rich. Spenser is a particularly genre-conscious poet and instructs his audience to see *The Faerie Queene* as allegorical-romance-epic. The interpretative fluency expected by that poem becomes something of a general rule to writers influenced by it; heroic poets feel themselves authorized by it to create their own genre combinations, and *The Faerie Queene* thereby becomes paradigmatic for a number of interesting sub-genres of the heroic to which it does not always bear very precise resemblance: the verse romance (Keats, Browning, Tennyson, E.A. Robinson, Charles Doughty), the long religious poem (Auden's *For the Time Being* or Eliot's *Four Quartets*), the allegorical heroic (Whitman's *Passage to India*, Crane's *Bridge*). Similarly, other imitative mock- or counter-genres cannot be written until the heroic genre is formally constituted: the epic of current history (Cowley's *Civil War* and *Davideis*, Joel Barlow's *Columbiad*, Sandburg's *The People, Yes*) or heroic mockery (Dryden's *Absalom and Achitophel*, Pope's *Dunciad*, Byron's *Don Juan*; see Lord 1977).

The affective variety of *The Faerie Queene* from book to book, so that one book shadows or comments on another by structurally echoing it, has also set an example of the possibilities of emotional diffusion as well as concentration to subsequent poets of the heroic. One has only to think of Blake's deliberate playing off of *Milton* against *Paradise Lost*, Wordsworth's similar evocation of Milton in *The Prelude*, or Pound's equivalent deployment of Dante's *Divine Comedy* in his *Cantos* to see the increase in affective richness that placing oneself in the heroic tradition has brought. Not irony alone, but satire, caution, pathos, awe, and even dread inhere in the devices of heroic allusion to an emotional agenda.

Mary Ann Radzinowicz

M.H. Abrams 1988 *A Glossary of Literary Terms* 5th ed (New York); Sanford Budick 1974 *Poetry of Civilization: Mythopoeic Displacement in the Verse of Milton, Dryden, Pope, and Johnson* (New Haven); T.S. Eliot 'Tradition and the Individual Talent' in ed 1950:3–11; Anne Davidson Ferry 1963 *Milton's Epic Voice: The Narrator in 'Paradise Lost'* (Cambridge, Mass); Donald M. Foerster 1962 *The Fortunes of Epic Poetry* (Washington, D.C.); Fowler 1982; Frye 1957; Guillory 1983; Peter Hägin 1964 *The Epic Hero and the Decline of Heroic Poetry* (Bern); Paul Hernadi 1972 *Beyond Genre: New Directions in Literary Classification* (Ithaca, NY); E.D. Hirsch, Jr 1967 *Validity in Interpretation* (New Haven); Lewalski 1986; David Lodge 1977 *The Modes of Modern Writing* (London); George deForest Lord 1977 *Heroic Mockery* (Newark, Del); Thomas E. Maresca 1974 *Epic to Novel* (Columbus, Ohio); Paul Merchant 1971 *The Epic* (London); P.A. Parker 1979; Roy Harvey Pearce 1961 *The Continuity of American Poetry* (Princeton); Ezra Pound 1960 *Impact: Essays on Ignorance and the Decline of American Civilization* (Chicago); M.L. Rosenthal and Sally M. Gall 1983 *The Modern Poetic Sequence: The Genius of Modern Poetry* (New York); Steadman 1967; Wallace Stevens 1966 *Letters* ed Holly Stevens (New York); H.T. Swedenberg, Jr 1944 *The Theory of the Epic in England: 1650–1800* (Berkeley and Los Angeles); E.M.W. Tillyard 1954; Tillyard 1958 *The Epic Strain in the English Novel* (London); Thomas A. Vogler 1971 *Preludes to Vision: The Epic Venture in Blake, Wordsworth, Keats, and Hart Crane* (Berkeley and Los Angeles); Joan Malory Webber 1979 *Milton and His Epic Tradition* (Seattle); René Wellek and Austin Warren 1956 *Theory of Literature* (New York; 3rd ed 1963, first pub 1949); Wilkie 1965; Wittreich 1975.

heroine In *Mulierum virtutes* (*Moralia* 242E–263C), Plutarch argues eloquently that the virtues of men and women are identical and not to be distinguished by gender. To illustrate his thesis and record for posterity the heroic deeds of exemplary women, he offers a catalogue of tales that celebrate female heroism. In this endeavor, he represents one side of the ancient debate on the virtue of women. The early representative polarities are established by Plato, who argues that feminine virtue is indistinguishable from its masculine counterpart, and by Aristotle, who maintains that virtue is defined by gender and that 'the courage of a man is shown in commanding, of a woman in obeying' (*Politics* 1.13). Aristotle's position became fundamental to the classification of gender in Western metaphysics; eloquence, sovereignty, and masculinity were opposed to silence, subjection, and femininity. Woman's capacity for heroism resided in her ability to exemplify the negative virtues of silence, obedience, chastity, and passivity, qualities which Aristotle is reluctant to count among the true virtues, designating them instead as 'imperfect' (*Nicomachean Ethics* 4.9, 7.7; I. Maclean 1980:51). The very imperfection of the virtues allowed to woman because of her physiology was destined to exclude her both from the socially exalted male versions of active heroism and from whatever fame those exploits might confer. Aristotle thus maintains that 'silence is a woman's glory' (*Politics* 1.13), a glory that helps to relegate her accomplishments to oblivion and exiles her from heroic literature except in a marginal capacity. His position is echoed in numerous misogynist treatises of the late Middle Ages and Renaissance, an anti-feminist tradition that is nurtured by Pauline doctrine and by scholastic and Renaissance commentaries on Aristotle. Yet the opposing tradition, the praise of the heroic female following Plutarch, is also voiced in works by Christine de Pisan, Boccaccio, Sir Thomas Elyot, J.L. Vives, and others.

The philosophic and poetic tradition of female heroism inherited by Spenser presents several difficulties for the project that he had undertaken: to write an English epic with the Troy story as its central classical subtext yet dedicated to his female sovereign Elizabeth and designed to celebrate her power. Clearly, silence and subjection were qualities inappropriate to a monarch, just as the act of immortalizing her fame in verse was out of keeping with the opinion of many classical authorities who declared that the best woman was the one about whom the least was said. Furthermore, the Troy story as represented by Virgil seemed to reinscribe the problematic place of woman in epic through the figure of Dido, the queen whose alluring seductiveness caused Aeneas to defer and almost forget his dynastic quest. Dido becomes the dangerous alternative or impediment to the dynastic imperative, the incarnation of a private, erotic satisfaction that is the antithesis of the public, political goals of the hero's quest. Yet even for her, power is inextricably linked to chastity, for her private pleasure is achieved at the expense of her political power.

Tasso, in *Discorso della virtù feminile e donnesca* (1582), addresses the problem of reconciling feminine virtue to female sovereignty; he asserts that each sex has a dominant virtue – for women, chastity; for men, courage – and that constellated around this dominant characteristic is a series of complementary qualities, in the case of women, economy, silence, and modesty. But he distinguishes moral from political virtue, arguing that the moral virtues appropriate to a woman in a private context are different from the qualities a woman of royal blood ought to possess. In the case of a princess or queen, she should forsake the virtues of her sex, preferring to practice the heroic, manly virtues appropriate to her political status (Maclean 1980:62). To be a female sovereign on these terms entails denying the very qualities that constitute femininity: since the terms female and monarch, heroic and woman seem mutually exclusive, Spenser must attempt to resolve these apparently opposed qualities in a representation that incorporates both power and femininity.

Spenser's treatment of the female hero in *The Faerie Queene* can be seen as an attempt to expand the boundaries of female heroism beyond such exemplars of 'negative' heroism as Lucretia and Griselda to encompass a vision of the feminine that also incorporates power. In the Letter to Raleigh, he identifies the earlier heroic poems by their heroes: just as Homer embodied virtue in the central figures of Agamemnon and Ulysses, so did subsequent epic poets celebrate heroic qualities in a central male figure. (The very etymology of *virtue*, from L *vir* 'man,' points to the masculine nature of heroic virtue.) Although Spenser designates Arthur as the hero of *The Faerie Queene*, Arthur's image is 'perfected' in 'private morall vertues,' which have as their champions knights who incarnate those particular qualities. Notable among them is Britomart, the hero of Book III and the knight of Chastity, the only virtue of the six books to be embodied in a woman. In the Letter, Spenser states that his Queen is represented by Gloriana, the Fairy Queen, and by Belphoebe: the first is a figure of power who presides over the Fairy court but is not an integral part of the poem's narrative; the second, a version of Diana, is an emblem of chastity, the poet's flattering reference to his Virgin Queen. Yet Britomart is most closely associated with the idea of female heroism, for she embodies both power and chastity. Several times in Book III, Spenser alludes to famous female heroes who serve as models for Britomart and who provide a genealogy of woman's heroism in general. Even though the word *heroine* did not enter the English language until the seventeenth century, Britomart is clearly the culmination of a tradition of specifically feminine heroism (see also defense of *women).

The tradition that Spenser invokes is less fully documented in literature than its masculine counterpart, and he laments the paucity of references to heroic women in the records of antiquity (III ii 1):

Here have I cause, in men just blame to find,
That in their proper prayse too partiall bee,
And not indifferent to woman kind,
To whom no share in armes and chevalrie
They do impart, ne maken memorie
Of their brave gestes and prowesse martiall;
Scarse do they spare to one or two or three,
Rowme in their writs; yet the same writing small
Does all their deeds deface, and dims their glories all.

A recurrent theme of Book III is attention to the suppressed tradition of feminine glory, a theme that is often expressed as an elegiac sorrow for what has been lost ('Where is the Antique glory now become, / That whilome wont in women to appeare?' iv 1). Spenser ascribes the effacement of women's deeds from the record of history to the heroic stature of their exploits; men, 'fearing their rules decay,' began to create laws to curb the 'liberty' of martial women (ii 2). Yet when women laid aside their warlike arms and turned their attention to 'artes and pollicy,' their excellence in these arenas spurred men to new envy. Spenser's attention to the exclusion of heroic women from legend and his attempt to write a revisionary epic figuring a martial maid at its center is clearly designed at least partially in praise of the Queen who is his audience, for his attention to the exploits of legendary women almost always appears in conjunction with an address to his sovereign. Out of his recognition of what has been erased in the poetic tradition grows his determination to rectify the errors of his predecessors. As long as the heroines of antiquity are not dead but only sleeping, their fate can be reversed (iv 1), and Spenser takes it upon himself to 're-verse,' that is, to sing again the praises of feminine heroism.

At the beginning of Book IV, Spenser says that the 'brave exploits which great Heroes wonne, / In love were either ended or begunne' (proem 3), a reference not only to the erotic foundation of heroic action but to a common philological root. The *locus classicus* of the etymology is a passage in Plato's *Cratylus* (398D) where Socrates tells Hermogenes that in old Attic the name *heros* is only a slight alteration of *Eros*, signifying that the heroes were born of love. In the classical poems that Spenser names as his poetic precursors (*Iliad*, *Odyssey*, *Aeneid*), both the place of woman and the value of love are problematic, relegated to subsidiary positions in the action. Women are depicted either as the Penelope figure who waits, representing the home from which the hero has been exiled and to which he must finally return, or as the Circe or Dido figure, the seductive woman whose love causes the hero to defer his journey and his political or dynastic ambitions (Giamatti 1975:20). Woman also appears as a female warrior (Penthesilea or Camilla), exemplary for her courage and participation in traditionally male exploits but limited by her predilection for battle to a minor place within the epic poem. Spenser's feminine figures in *SC, Aprill* and *November* begin to confront the dilemma incorporated in Dido (chastity/eroticism, power/impotence, public/private), especially as the problem is encountered when the poet depicts and celebrates his Queen. Yet it is in *The Faerie Queene* proper that he ultimately reconciles the conflicting demands of eroticism and female heroism.

In addition to classical epic, Spenser drew on medieval romance and Ariosto and Tasso for his representation of the female hero, for romance as a genre had traditionally accommodated women more easily to its central action than had epic. The Renaissance epic diverged from its classical counterpart in exalting love and admitting the erotic into heroic action; Sidney in his *Defence of Poetry* observes that 'even to the heroical, Cupid hath ambitiously climbed' (ed 1973b:103). In the Middle Ages, lovesickness was sometimes referred to as the malady of *hereos*, which was transformed in the Renaissance to 'heroical love,' a sentiment clearly appropriate to heroes (Lowes 1913–14, Mark Rose 1968:11). Britomart displays the classic symptoms of the disorder (as catalogued by Burton's *Anatomy of Melancholy*) after she sees Artegall in the magic mirror: she languishes, becomes melancholic, suffers from insomnia, and begins to waste away (III ii 27–9). Unlike the Ovidian heroines Spenser alludes to who are similarly afflicted and whose erotic longings are incestuous or even monstrous (41), her illness can be resolved only through heroic action, that is, a quest for Artegall, who is the goal of both her heroic and her erotic yearnings. Although male heroes in *The Faerie Queene* may also be victims of heroic love, their erotic desire is almost always subsumed into another quest that transcends the private world of love. Britomart's heroic destiny, however, begins and ends with and is indistinguishable from her erotic impulse; both will result in the establishment of the Tudor dynasty. In Britomart, then, the rupture so prevalently and disturbingly displayed in the *Aeneid* begins to be healed, for through the integration of private love and public power in *The Faerie Queene*, female heroism can be accommodated within the structure of dynastic epic.

While embodying figures both of the dynastic wife and the alluring maiden, Britomart is also related to the female warrior or Amazon (see *Radigund). When she sets out to seek Artegall, Glauce counsels her to disguise herself in 'feigned armes,' a heroic attire whose trappings of 'dreadfull speare and shield' will teach her 'weake hands ... new strength' (iii 53). In fact, the armor that she dons belongs to Angela, the Saxon queen and warrior who is described as 'No whit lesse faire, then terrible in fight' (56) and from whose invented name Spenser derives the English race (Angles). She thus assumes, in both sartorial and poetic terms, the legacy of the maiden warrior. Having armed her body, Glauce gives Britomart a genealogy of feminine heroism to 'inflame' her courage: 'Bards tell of many women valorous / Which have full many feats adventurous / Performd, in paragone of proudest men: / The bold *Bunduca*, whose victorious / Exploits made *Rome* to quake, stout *Guendolen*, / Renowmed *Martia*, and redoubted *Emmilen*' (54). Britomart's bodily arming is simultaneous with her psychological preparation, for just as she dresses herself in the legendary Angela's armor, so too does her mind begin to transform itself: Glauce's 'harty words so deepe into the mynd / Of the young Damzell sunke, that great desire / Of warlike armes in her forthwith they tynd, / And generous stout courage did inspire' (57), infusing it with 'manly' virtue just as her body is transformed by the knightly apparel of the hero.

Unlike the Amazon of classical epic, however, whose bared breast announces her gender (*Aeneid* 1.492, 11.803), Britomart conceals her feminine nature beneath the surface of her armor. Clothes, as the most visible sign of sexual difference, demonstrate how strongly responses are determined by assumptions about gender. Britomart is a kind of transvestite hero, revealing herself as female only when she removes her armor: 'Faire Lady she him seemd, like Lady drest, / But fairest knight alive, when armed was her brest' (ii 4). Her male disguise renders her sexually ambiguous and attractive to both sexes, as likely to invite the advances of Malecasta as of Paridell. On the one hand, her male exterior and female interior allow her to fulfill her feminine desires by means of the strength and freedom she acquires through her disguise, since her armor liberates her from the fate of a passive female protagonist (such as Florimell), enabling her actively to seek her traditionally feminine destiny. On the other hand, her equivocal sexual identity points to the problem of the feminine role in the heroic context and to the difficulty of reconciling their conflicting demands. It could be argued that Britomart's voyeuristic pleasure in the hermaphroditic union of Amoret and Scudamour in the 1590 ending of Book III represents a desire not only for union with Artegall but also for an integration of the characteristics of both sexes within her own body. The image of the Hermaphrodite is an image of power in *The Faerie Queene*, as in the hermaphroditic Venus of Book IV or the sovereign in the proem to Book VI, who is simultaneously a queen and a prince (see also *androgyne).

Despite his celebration of female heroism in Britomart and in his catalogues of famous women, Spenser ultimately endorses the conventional Renaissance sexual hierarchy that makes woman subject to man's dominion. His disquisition on sexual equality (or inequality) is located (appropriately according to Renaissance thought) in Book V, the Legend of Justice. The mechanism of its revelation is parody and inversion. If Britomart represents the heroic image of the maiden warrior, Radigund is its parodic extreme, an Amazonian virago whose hatred of men is inspired by a man's rejection of her love (ix 30). Exiled from her natural impulses and from the natural order, she is an emblem of thwarted desire, who acts out her vengeance by repeatedly inflicting her wishes on men by force. She is the means by which Spenser reveals the dangers of transvestism, which are presented in this episode as parody. Far from being disguised by her male attire, Radigund's feminine love of ornament and color is simply transposed to masculine trappings; her purple silk dress woven with silver, quilted with white satin and trailing with ribbons, betrays both her gender and the erotic nature of her battle with Artegall. Although they initially fight like men, Artegall is overcome not with her force but with her face; when he unlaces her helmet to give her the death blow, he discovers her female beauty. Confronted with the image of woman, he is literally mollified; and in an act of specular transposition, they virtually exchange genders, Artegall becoming feminized and Radigund responding with increased masculine fury and strength. When Artegall finally submits to her, the language of his concession is couched in erotic terms: he is not overcome, but yields of his own accord, promising 'To be her thrall' and do her 'service' (v 17). These 'warelesse' words proleptically announce the domestic tyranny to which he will be subjected, for her revenge on the knights she defeats in battle is to despoil them of their armor and dress them in 'womens weedes,' forcing them 'to card, to sew, to wash, to wring' (iv 31).

The consequence of Amazonian rule or female sovereignty is that it metaphorically converts men into women, for when women usurp the role of ruler men must become subjects. Unlike Britomart, and unlike Belphoebe (who is associated with Radigund through her dress; see Nohrnberg 1976:457), Radigund's embodiment of both masculine and feminine characteristics is seen as a source not of strength but of perversity. Even more unnatural is her imprisoning Artegall in 'womanishe attire,' which unlike Britomart's assumption of armor is a 'lothly uncouth sight' (vii 37), for 'womans weedes' are 'to manhood shame' (v 20). This inversion of the natural order expressed by Radigund's supremacy is designed not to celebrate women's heroism but to demonstrate its perils. When Britomart frees Artegall from his demeaning state, she also restores balance to Radigund's Amazonian kingdom, returning the women who had usurped power to 'mens subjection,' thus establishing a reign of 'true Justice' (vii 42). Britomart's encounter with Radigund, as a parodic version of herself and a perverted example of female heroism, shows that heroism in women is laudable when it serves (and is subservient to) male heroism, since only the proper balance between the sexes (and between eroticism and heroism) can result in the harmonious marriage that will ensure the future of the Tudor dynasty. As Spenser tells us, Radigund and her kingdom represent 'the crueltie of womenkynd, / When they have shaken off the shamefast band, / With which wise Nature did them strongly bynd, / T'obay the heasts of mans well ruling hand, / That then all rule and reason they withstand, / To purchase a licentious libertie. / But vertuous women wisely understand, / That they were borne to base humilitie, / Unlesse the heavens them lift to lawfull soveraintie' (v 25). Spenser is clearly in dangerous territory here, and redeems himself only in the final line when he makes an exception for his Queen. Heroism for him is still the province of men and accessible to only the most exceptional of women. Even so, however conventionally hierarchical the final vision of the relation between the sexes, the figure of his female sovereign haunts his poem, infecting his images of power with ambivalence. ELIZABETH D. HARVEY

S. Davies 1986; Ferguson, et al 1986; Angeline Goreau 1985 *The Whole Duty of a Woman: Female Writers in Seventeenth-Century England* (Garden City, NY); Katherine Usher Henderson and Barbara F. McManus 1985 *Half Humankind: Contexts and Texts of the Controversy about Women in England, 1540–1640* (Urbana); Lisa Jardine 1983 *Still Harping on Daughters: Women and Drama in the Age of Shakespeare* (Brighton, Sussex); Kleinbaum 1983; Madeleine Lazard 1985 *Images littéraires de la femme à la Renaissance* (Paris); John Livingston Lowes 1913–14 'The Loveres Maladye of Hereos' *MP* 11:491–546; I. Maclean 1980; P.A. Parker 1987; Mary Beth Rose, ed 1986 *Women in the Middle Ages and the Renaissance* (Syracuse); Silberman 1986; Woodbridge 1984.

Hesiod (fl 720–700 BC) Regarded by the Greeks with the legendary poets Orpheus and Musaeus, and with Homer as one of their oldest poets, Hesiod was a member of the Boeotian school of epic and didactic poetry. Three works were attributed to him by antiquity and the Renaissance: *Theogony*, *Works and Days*, and *Shield of Heracles*. (A number of fragments attributed to him also survive, eg, *Catalogue of Women*, which is often attached to the end of the *Theogony* in manuscripts and printed texts.) Printed editions appeared from 1474 on, including the Aldine in 1495 published with the Bucolic poets, and Trincavelli's in 1537, which printed the scholia. He was well known in England; Sir John Cheke possessed a manuscript of the poems which he apparently sent to Birchman to edit. Spenser probably knew him in one of Birchman's editions that appeared in Basel in 1542, 1544, 1564, and 1574 (Bennett 1931b), or possibly in Estienne's popular large folio edition of the major Greek poets, *Poetae Graeci principes* (Paris 1566).

Hesiod, especially in the *Theogony* but also in *Works and Days* and *Shield*, provided Renaissance mythographers and poets with standard versions of the genealogies of the classical gods and with basic accounts of many classical myths. He is so important as a source for mythographers such as Boccaccio, Conti, and Cartari that it is often impossible to decide whether Spenser has drawn a mythic detail from them or directly from him.

The *Theogony* narrates the generation of the Earth, Erebus, and Night from Chaos, along with Earth's generation of Heaven and (after her union with him) of the Titans, the youngest of whom, Cronos (Saturn), castrates his father and assumes power. It tells next of the birth of the Olympians from Cronos and Rhea, Zeus' (Jove's) assumption of power, his quarrel with Prometheus, and his victory over the Titans after a fierce battle in which the giant children of Earth, the hundred-handers, assist him. Zeus establishes order after defeating Typhoeus, yet another monstrous child of Earth; and he begets the youngest race of gods. The *Theogony* includes genealogies for these gods, for minor deities, for monsters, and for deities of the underworld.

Either because of his respect for Hesiod's reputation among the ancients or perhaps because of the accessibility of Hesiodic genealogies in Boccaccio and Conti, Spenser often follows the *Theogony*'s genealogies and versions of myths not only for the principal gods but also for a host of lesser figures. From it, he draws the names and parentage of the Graces (*FQ* VI x 22; cf *Theog* 907–11) and the Litae (V ix 31–2; cf the Horae in *Theog* 901–3); those of the Nereids (IV xi 48–52) may come from Hesiod directly (*Theog* 233–64), from the Latin verse translation in Birchman's editions, or from Conti's catalogue (*Mythologiae* 8.6) based on Hesiod (see *Var* 4:273–5). Other of Spenser's catalogues, while not closely following Hesiod, are modeled on him (eg, the sea and river gods of IV xi 12–21; cf *Theog* 337–45, 364–70). Spenser follows him (as do Plato and the Neoplatonists) in making Eros (Love) the eldest of the gods and an agent of the world's creation (*Theog* 120–2; *Colin Clout* 799–806, *Hymne of Love* 50–98). He frames his description of Night and her progeny in *FQ* I v 20–34 and III iv 55–8 from *Theog* 123–5, 211–25; and his description of Ate in IV i 19–30 is based on that of Strife and her offspring in *Theog* 226–32. Several of Spenser's monsters go back to Hesiodic models: Typhaon, Echidna, and their monster brood appear in *Theog* 295–332, 821–35. Spenser makes Typhaon (whom he probably distinguishes from Typhoeus-Typhon; see Lotspeich 1932:113) and Echidna the parents of Orthrus and the Blatant Beast (V x 10, VI vi 9–12); and Geryoneo's monster (V x 11) is said to be 'Borne of the brooding of *Echidna* base, / Or other like infernall furies kinde' (V xi 23). The form of the monster Error has a long history which has been traced back to Hesiod's Echidna.

With Ovid, Virgil, and Lucretius, Hesiod is an important source for the *Cantos of Mutabilitie*, providing Spenser with an account of the struggles of the Titans against Uranus and Jove's victory over them. Spenser closely follows *Theog* 411–52 in making Hecate the only Titan to be given great power and high authority by Jove (VII vi 3). He also follows the Hesiodic view of the Muses more closely in vii 1–2 than in his earlier poetry. Hesiod claimed a close personal relationship with the Muses as inspiring deities. In the proem to the *Theogony* (1–115), he numbers nine goddesses, names them individually (the first poet to do so), and tells how they came to him when he was herding his sheep on Helicon, taught him song, and commanded him to sing of the generation of the gods. While Spenser assigns the Muses their Hesiodic names and number throughout his poetry, in the last books of *The Faerie Queene* he also assigns the Muses the Hesiodic parentage (Jove and Memory) and appeals to the Muse, as Hesiod does, to assist him to tell of heavenly matters: 'things doen in heaven so long ygone; / So farre past memory of man that may be knowne' (VII vii 2).

Works and Days furnishes Spenser with fewer specific details of classical mythology than does the *Theogony*; but it contains a second version of Prometheus' deception of Jove and the creation of the first woman, Pandora, and the earliest account of the five ages of man (Ovid's *Metamorphoses* and Virgil's *Georgics* provide later versions; see Levin 1969). Hesiod's concept of a 'fall' from the Golden Age, his notion of bad and good strife (the first leading to war, the second to work and achievement; see *Works and Days* 11–24), and his definition of justice as divine ordinance seem to influence *FQ* IV and V. In Book IV, Ate, defined (as in *Theog* 230) as a daughter of Strife, stirs up dissension: Artegall, like Hesiod's Zeus, attempts to establish justice and to rule by law. Spenser alludes several times to Jove as the divine force that quelled the insolence of the Giants or the Titans and established divine right or justice (V i 9; vii 1, 10). Artegall bears Chrysaor, the sword that Jove used to put down the Titans (its name is borrowed from *Theog* 281). Spenser also echoes the work ethos of *Works and Days* 287–92 in lauding the power of work to promote virtue: 'Before her gate high God did Sweat ordaine, / And wakefull watches ever to abide: / But easie is the way, and passage plaine / To pleasures pallace' (II iii 41).

Shield of Heracles, the third work attributed to Hesiod, recounts Heracles' birth and his fight with Cycnus; it also describes at length (140–317) the shield used in the fight and is a special genre of poetry, the ecphrasis, a literary description of sculpted or pictured representations on a work of art. It describes a series of scenes, some allegorical (the depiction of Fear, Pursuit, Flight, and Strife as personified beings), some purely descriptive (the picture of a safe harbor or of the gods in Olympus), and some narrative (the pictured representation of Perseus killing the Gorgon). While none of these scenes served Spenser directly, the *Shield* was undoubtedly a general model for the kind of allegorical description that he so often assays in *The Faerie Queene* and for the descriptions of sculpture, tapestries, and other works of art that so often adorn places such as the Bower of Bliss and the house of Busirane. STELLA P. REVARD

Hesiod ed 1966; Hesiod 1970 *Theogonia, Opera et dies, Scutum* ed Friedrich Solmsen (Oxford).

hieroglyphics By the middle of the sixteenth century there had developed a widespread belief that semantic content could be conveyed by means of quasi-pictorial signs, or ideograms. This belief was based upon a crude understanding of Egyptian hieroglyphs, which had not yet been deciphered. Although Spenser did not use hieroglyphics per se in his work, he seems to have been especially receptive to similar semiotic modes where gnomic wisdom is encoded in some extraordinary item or event involving both verbal and visual statement, such as emblems (*FQ* I x 30–1), imprese (III ii 25), apocalyptic visions (*Vanitie*), and charms (*FQ* III xii 31, 36). Wittkower argues 'that hieroglyphics and the broad stream of Renaissance allegory and symbolism merge' (1972:90).

The hieroglyphical technique inherited by the Renaissance is grounded in the Platonist dichotomy between the realm of insubstantial essences, which is the true reality, and its replication in our natural world, which is a congeries of physical objects that are merely reflections or shadows of the absolute ideas residing in the transcendent realm of essences. The physical object conveys semantic content because it represents the idea which it embodies. As a consequence, each item in nature becomes a hieroglyph, its name being a symbolic representation of its meaning. In the Hermetic tradition, the god Thoth (Hermes Trismegistus) assigned names to things in order to render knowable their inner significance (cf Plato *Phaedrus* 274C–E). Similarly, in the Judeo-Christian tradition, Adam's first task was to name the creatures in accord with their natures predetermined by God, thereby creating a verbal universe analogous to the physical universe created by God. In both traditions, we are enjoined to read 'the book of nature' because there we will learn about the attributes and intentions of the deity. Nature becomes a vast hieroglyphical system available for our perusal, so that Shakespeare's Duke Senior 'Finds tongues in trees, books in the running brooks, / Sermons in stones' (*As You Like It* II i 16–17).

Frequently in Spenser's work, the items of nature assume an almost hieroglyphical significance. In the opening episode of *The Faerie Queene*, for instance, when the storm drives Una and Redcrosse into the forest and they arrive at a cave, Una accurately interprets the meaning of the place: 'This is the wandring wood, this *Errours den*' (I i 13). Other well-known examples include the Bower of Bliss and the Garden of Adonis.

The knowledge of hieroglyphs in the Renaissance was based largely upon Iamblichus' well-known *De mysteriis Aegyptiorum* and a classical text rediscovered in 1419 and assigned to a shadowy author known as Horapollo. This tradition was enriched by the writings of Plutarch, especially his essay on Isis and Osiris (upon which Spenser drew for the episode of Britomart's visit to Isis Church, *FQ* V vii 1–24), and the writings of Philo Judaeus, especially his exposition of the hexaemeron, *De opificio mundi* (whose much less distinct influence has been discerned in the *Cantos of Mutabilitie*; see Williamson in *Var* 6:423). Also supplementing this tradition was a collection of fables about animals characterized by certain distinctive qualities inherent in their nature. This animal lore had originated among the sacred priests of Egypt, but by the late classical period had become so popular that it verged upon folklore. It persisted throughout the Middle Ages in the pages of bestiaries such as the *Physiologus*, and Spenser utilized it for the tale of the Fox and the Kid in *SC, Maye* and for *Mother Hubberds Tale*.

Following the syncretic impulse of Plutarch, the Florentine humanists (particularly Poggio, Alberti, and Ficino) accumulated and extolled all this exotic material, so that by the sixteenth century it carried considerable authority. It was comprehensively codified by Pierio Valeriano in a profusely illustrated folio entitled *Hieroglyphica, sive De sacris Aegyptiorum literis commentarii* (1556, etc). Through illustrated editions of Horapollo's *Hieroglyphica*, this reputedly Egyptian wisdom was closely allied with the genre of emblem books (see Daly 1979:11–21). Because of its linkage with Hermetic philosophy, the hieroglyphical technique sometimes occurred in the occult sciences, such as astrology and alchemy; and because of Philo, it enjoyed an ancient association with Hebraic wisdom and the Cabala.

S.K. HENINGER, JR

D.C. Allen 1970:107–33; Daly 1979; Liselotte Dieckmann 1970 *Hieroglyphics: The History of a Literary Symbol* (St Louis); Horapollo ed 1950; Ludwig Volkmann 1923 *Bilderschriften der Renaissance: Hieroglyphik und Emblematik in ihren Beziehungen und Fortwirkungen* (Leipzig); Rudolf Wittkower 1972 'Hieroglyphics in the Early Renaissance' in *Developments in the Early Renaissance* ed Bernard S. Levy (Albany) pp 58–97.

history Guyon and Arthur in the house of Temperance visit an aged man in a room 'hangd about with rolles, / And old records from auncient times deriv'd' (*FQ* II ix 57). While Guyon reads the '*Antiquitie* of *Faerie* lond,' Arthur reads an ancient book of *Briton moniments*, containing the history of the land from its first settlement by Trojan Brutus to the death of his own father Uther Pendragon, and 'ravisht with delight' praises his 'Deare countrey' (x 69). In III iii, following an invocation to Clio, the Muse of history, 'That doest ennoble with immortall name / The warlike Worthies, from antiquitie' (iii 4), Merlin tells Britomart the glories of her progeny beginning with the reign of Arthur's half-brother Artegall and culminating in the reign of Queen Elizabeth I. In canto ix, Spenser completes the narrative by returning to the Trojan history from the fall of Troy to the founding of Troynovant. In these three sections, Spenser narrates the entire mythological history of Britain except for the time of Arthur himself, which is the subject of his poem.

In his chronicles, Spenser includes some of the most popular stories from Geoffrey of Monmouth's *British History*, such as the discovery of the island by Brutus and his followers, the tale of King Lear and his daughters, and the misfortunes of Gorboduc. While retaining much of Geoffrey's thirteenth-century narrative, Spenser adopts the early Tudor myth of political history first propagated by the Italian Polydore Vergil. In traditional fashion, Polydore thought of history as providing examples for moral behavior, but he differed from his English predecessors in using his theory of exemplary history to construct a framework for the political history of the fifteenth century. By adopting the biblical idea that punishment for evil might extend down to the third generation, he was able to show that Henry IV's usurpation of Richard II's throne was punished by the eventual deposition of his grandson, Henry VI, and that Edward IV's lies and treachery in seizing the kingdom from Henry VI were in turn punished by the death of his son, the young Edward V, and by the collapse of his dynasty with Richard III's defeat by Henry Tudor. Thus the accession of the Tudors represented not only the restoration of order after nearly a century of turmoil but also the workings of divine providence. Polydore's ordering of the recent past was adapted by the Henrician chronicler Edward Hall, by the popular chroniclers Richard Grafton and John Stow who succeeded him, by Raphael Holinshed, and by such poets as Shakespeare and Spenser.

Another 'Tudor myth' was embodied in the ecclesiastical history used to defend the Church of England and could be found most spectacularly in Foxe's *Actes and Monuments*, popularly known as the Book of Martyrs. Foxe argued that the history of post-Nicene Christianity was one of decline, caused by an increasing dependence on the Roman Pontiff rather than on Christ, and accelerated by the elevation of the monk Hildebrand, Pope Gregory VII, who consolidated such 'abuses' as transubstantiation and celibacy of the clergy. Foxe claimed that the English had resisted the papacy from the beginning and were always the last to accede to papal demands; it was only to be expected, then, that resistance to Antichrist would begin in England with John Wyclif, the real precursor of the Reformation, and would culminate with Henry VIII's throwing off the Roman yoke. The English, as the nation that had always adhered most closely to Christ's commands and continued to do so, were God's chosen people, their kings and queens, God's chosen rulers. Queen Elizabeth, as both defender of the kingdom from internal disorder and external attack, and defender of the faith, embodied in her own person both Tudor historical myths.

Spenser links Elizabeth to the mythic Arthur, who had saved Britain a thousand years earlier, and (in *FQ* I) uses the Red Cross Knight to symbolize Britain's progress on the course mapped by Foxe. Yet he did this just when the Tudor historiographical consensus was about to collapse. Exemplary history had come under attack, not least by Sidney, for failing to demonstrate that God regularly punishes the wicked and rewards the good: the historian, tied to his 'old mouse-eaten records' (ed 1973b:83), was an unpersuasive moralist. At the same time, the antiquaries, led by Camden, began to query the existence of Brutus, thus undermining the veracity of Geoffrey of Monmouth and therefore the legends of Arthur. Moreover, the first signs of a new approach to history, in which the past was made to teach political rather than moral lessons, could just be discerned. This approach was associated with the study of the Italian historians and political thinkers Machiavelli and Guicciardini and with the revival of the Roman historian Tacitus; it was centered on the intellectual coterie surrounding the Earl of Essex whose patronage, for a time, Spenser sought.

In the *Vewe of Ireland*, Spenser shows himself able to use the latest antiquarian scholarship. Not only does he cite Camden and the Scots humanist historian, George Buchanan, but in his analysis of the reliability of Irish tradition and of the Irish bards, he shows himself more subtle than either. Where most of his contemporaries would have tried to establish the origin of the Irish by way of strained etymologies, Spenser shows their connection to the Gauls, the Spanish, even the Scythians by a careful comparison of their various customs – an altogether more plausible method. Moreover, he studies Irish history for the sake of political rather than moral examples, that is, in order to learn from it which solutions to the Irish problem might be successful. So, when recommending that the English reestablish order by transferring the institution called the tithing (wherein the population is divided into groups of ten men, each of whom is responsible for the others), he has to face the question of how such an institution could be moved. He does so by remarking that tithings had first been imposed on the English by one of the Saxon kings, at a time when 'Englande was verie like to Irelande as it now standes' (*Vewe* in *Var Prose* p 202). Finally, all his analyses are controlled and tempered by a study of the works of the contemporary French historian and political theorist Jean Bodin, and probably by a reading of Machiavelli as well.

In *Vewe*, Spenser uses at least occasionally the new, 'politic' history; but in *The Faerie Queene*, he remains determinedly old-fashioned, casting himself not in the role of an historian but in the far different role of a 'Poet ... historicall.' Unlike the historian, who is forced to an orderly discussion of affairs as they occurred, the poet can thrust himself into the very middle of things, wherever it best suits him. As Sidney argues, the historian 'being captived to the truth of a foolish world' must tell things as they are while the poet may freely create from historical materials a golden world of things as they should be. Spenser takes advantage of his freedom. He chooses to write of Arthur, not only because that story is 'most fitte for the excellency of his person, being made famous by many mens former workes, and also furthest from the daunger of envy, and suspition of present time,' but also because the authenticity of the history of Arthur is a little dubious, and thus malleable. His model is not a modern historian like Holinshed or Polydore Vergil, nor even an ancient one like Livy, who had historicized the glorious tales of early Rome, but Virgil, the epic poet who had transformed those stories into myth. (See also *eschatology and historical *allegory.) F.J. LEVY

For surveys of Tudor approaches to earlier British history, see Kelly 1970; Kendrick 1950, Levy 1967, and May McKisack 1971 *Medieval History in the Tudor Age* (Oxford); some of this historiography is summarized by Geoffrey Shepherd in Sidney ed 1965:39–42. For Spenser and history, see Robert E. Burkhart 1975 'History, the Epic, and the *Faerie Queene*' *ES* 56:14–19, Fichter 1982, Mills 1978, and O'Connell 1977. See also C.A. Patrides 1964 *The Phoenix and the Ladder: The Rise and Decline of the Christian View of History* (Berkeley and Los Angeles); Patrides 1972 *The Grand Design of God: The Literary Form of the Christian View of History* (London).

Hobbinol A shepherd and friend of Colin Clout in *The Shepheardes Calender* and *Colin Clouts Come Home Againe*. Like the name Colin, Hobbinol has slightly comic and rustic associations. Probably, as the *OED* suggests, the name is a combination of *hob*, a familiar form of Rob (Robert or Robin), used generically to mean a rustic or clown, as in Shakespeare's *Coriolanus*, and *noll*, which refers to the crown of the head and has pejorative (but not ill-natured) overtones, as in *FQ* VII vii 39, where the tipsy October's 'noule was totty of the must.' Hob, which had the meaning of 'sprite,' 'elf,' is also a short form of *hobgoblin*, an association with folklore which may have suggested the references to 'elvish ghosts' and 'frendly Faeries' in Hobbinol's description of his pastoral paradise in *June* 24–5. In this connection, it is interesting to recall Harvey's 1580 description of *The Faerie Queene* as '*Hobgoblin* runne away with the Garland from *Apollo*' (*Var Prose* p 472).

In the *Januarye* gloss, E.K. describes 'Hobbinol' as 'a fained country name, whereby, it being so commune and usuall, seemeth to be hidden the person of some his very speciall and most familiar freend.' Possibly Spenser appropriated a name in popular use, but there are no recorded uses of the name earlier than the *Calender*, and though by 1600 it was being used for a typical rustic (*OED*), such later uses are probably traceable to Spenser – Peele, for example, shows the influence of the *Calender* when, in *The Arraignment of Paris* (1584), he associates the name with shepherds called Digon, Thenot, and Colin, while in *The Honour of the Garter* (1593) he uses the name apparently in allusion to Spenser himself; Nashe clearly follows Spenser's lead when he refers to Harvey in *Strange Newes* (1592) as 'Gamaliel Hobgoblin ... Poet Hobbinoll' (ed 1904–10, 1:289). The name, too, seems more a pastoral equivalent to such epic coinings as 'Marinell' and 'Paridell' than an example of popular use. Probably, then, Spenser invented the name, and E.K. was simply responding to his familiarity not with the name as a whole but with its parts.

It is also possible that the name originated in the Spenser-Harvey circle at Cambridge, whether or not by Spenser's invention, and that it was associated with Harvey – identified with Hobbinol in the *September* gloss – before Spenser made use of it in the *Calender*. We know from Harvey's *Marginalia* that he was fond of assuming personae in his private annotations, and possibly he adopted a similar practice with close friends such as Spenser. In any case, the comic element in the name, nicely at odds with the serious and self-important face Harvey presented to his academic colleagues at Cambridge, is appropriate to that lighter side of his nature which surfaced in his relationship with Spenser, as reflected in the Spenser-Harvey correspondence, for example, and in his record of Spenser's gift in December 1578 of a number of jestbooks on condition that he read them 'before the first of January immediately ensuing: otherwise to forfeit unto him my Lucian' (Stern 1979:228).

Harvey twice refers to himself as Hobbinol in a 1580 letter to Spenser (*Var Prose* pp 471, 476) and uses the name to sign his commendatory poem to *The Faerie Queene*. And Spenser confirms the identification in *Colin Clout* when he has Hobbinol say of Cynthia's court, 'I my selfe was there, / To wait on *Lobbin* (*Lobbin* well thou knewest)' (735–6) – a clear reference to Harvey's (brief) service as secretary to Robert (Robin) Dudley, Earl of Leicester. Harvey's use of the name does not, however, extend beyond occasions which allude to his friendship with Spenser, and it is unlikely that Spenser intended Hobbinol in the *Calender* as a more detailed portrait of Harvey (McLane 1961:237–61).

Hobbinol's philosophy of moderation – 'Such il, as is forced, mought nedes be endured' (*Sept* 139) – is not at odds with what we know of Harvey's own views concerning ecclesiastical abuses, and is also in accord with Spenser's praise of Harvey as a stoic spirit in 'Ad ornatissimum virum.' But Hobbinol's adherence to pastoral tranquillity – 'Content who lives with tryed state' (*Sept* 70) – scarcely accords with Harvey's well-known ambition, and nothing in the text justifies an appeal to irony in order to force a biographical allusion. Reflections of Harvey's attitudes towards women in Hobbinol's disapproval of Colin's love for Rosalind are slender speculation indeed, while the omission of anything which could be taken as praise of Harvey's academic achievements would seem to argue conclusively against the view that the allusion to Harvey determined the treatment of Hobbinol.

Hobbinol's primary function in *The Shepheardes Calender* is not to serve as a portrait of Harvey but to embody pastoral conventions. In *Januarye*, the gifts with which Hobbinol tries to win Colin's love away from Rosalind recall the world of pastoral contentment which Colin is losing; in *June*, Hobbinol's possession of that world is explicitly set against Colin's own discontent ('O happy *Hobbinoll*, I blesse thy state, / That Paradise hast found, whych *Adam* lost' 9–10); and in *December*, Colin's reaffirmation of his friendship for Hobbinol suggests, in the midst of his disappointment, a glimpse of a former pastoral contentment ('Adieu good *Hobbinol*, that was so true' 155). As an inhabitant of the pastoral pleasance, Hobbinol in *Aprill* appropriately recites the song in praise of Elisa which Colin made before he left. In *September*, the only eclogue in which his role is defined apart from any mention of Colin, Hobbinol again acts as spokesman for the values of the pastoral ideal when he sets the tranquillity of his own pastoral existence against the uncertainties of urban corruption: 'who will seeke for unknowne gayne, / Oft lives by losse, and leaves with payne' (72–3). Hobbinol is neither Harvey's spokesman nor Spenser's, but he does help to define a central region of the imaginative world the *Calender* creates.

Though always a subordinate character, he appears or is mentioned in more eclogues than any character except Colin himself, and his relation to Colin, like Colin's to Rosalind, gives an important element of unity to the poem. In *Colin Clout*, he plays a less important role and one with no dramatic complications; but the role is recognizably similar, characterized by mutual friendship (12–15, 48–50), by Hobbinol's admiration for Colin's art (16–31), and by his regret for the sorrow Colin has suffered for love of Rosalind. Here, as in the *Calender*, Hobbinol belongs to and in part defines the pastoral realm from which Colin's (now very different) journey begins and to which he returns. DAVID R. SHORE

holiness The nature of holiness as expounded by theologians of the sixteenth-century Reformation in England clarifies our understanding of the spiritual allegory of *The Faerie Queene* Book I. The Reformation redefined not only 'justification' and 'salvation' but 'sanctification' or 'holiness.' The Roman Catholic doctrine of the Atonement was 'exemplarist': one could not be justified merely by having faith in Christ's atonement for sin because faith erased original sin but not subsequent sins. These had to be purged and sinful inclinations overcome by following Christ as exemplar in a life of holiness devoted to God and goodness. The Catholic polemicist Cardinal Pole explains in his *Treati[s]e of Justification* that 'Faith alone justifieth no man, without the helpe and working of charitie' (Louvain 1569:36).

In contrast, reformed theology, which followed a 'sacrificial' view of atonement, maintained that a person's justification was possible only by faith in Christ's sacrifice on the Cross, and never by good works. Justification was obtainable immediately upon acceptance of God's free and merciful forgiveness to sinners because of this sacrifice. Salvation did not depend on holiness because, as Luther says, 'a Christian has no need of any work or law in order to be saved since through faith he is free from every law and does everything out of pure liberty and freely' (ed 1958–75, 31:361).

Reformed theology made clear, however, that though holiness was not required in order to be saved, Christians still needed to strive to be holy in order to prevent proud self-interest and preserve a constant awareness of divine guidance. Though Richard Hooker maintained that justification came solely by faith (*Of Justification* 31), he nonetheless stressed that 'if we look to stand in the faith of the sons of God, we must hourly, continually, be providing and setting ourselves to strive' (*A Learned and Comfortable Sermon of the Certainty and Perpetuity of Faith in the Elect* in ed 1888, 3:480). Unless we live a holy life, an official Elizabethan homily cautions, our faith is 'not a right, pure, and lively faith, but a dead, divelish, counterfaite and feigned faith' ('Sermon on the Salvation of Mankind'). Personal holiness was considered so important that Hooker even warns that 'none shall see God, but such as seek peace and holiness, though not as a cause of their salvation, yet as a way through which they must walk that will be saved' (*Of Justification* 20, in ed 1888, 3:506).

Many Protestant treatises and devotional manuals of the late sixteenth century in England redefine holiness in its new Protestant context and suggest ways to be holy. In 1576, John Woolton reminded believers of Paul's words that Christ 'hath not called us to uncleanness and filthiness of life, but to holiness' (ed 1851:6). Around 1590, John Norden described holiness as an attempt 'to take order with our affections, wills, and dispositions, that our conversations be in such decent, comely, sweet, and comfortable order disposed, that our souls be not annoyed with the filth and stink of our corruptions' (ed 1847:161). Preachers like Henry Balnaves (*The Confession of Faith* 1584), Andrew Kingsmill (*A View of Man's Estate* 1574), and Richard Rogers (*The Practicse of Christianitie* 1603) suggest practical methods of holiness, including exhortations to serve God and one's neighbor, avoid sloth and vanity, read the Bible, pity others' miseries, and give thanks. Some devotees even kept daily diaries to record their spiritual advances or failures, though this seems largely to have been a post-Elizabethan tendency.

In this theological context, Spenser wrote Book I, the Legend of Holiness, which addresses the issue of the need for holiness in the life of a person saved by faith. In the story of the Red Cross Knight's quest to win the grace of the Fairy Queen, Spenser fashions the virtue of holiness to show that even clothed in the armor of God we must still do our best to defeat the dragon that holds us captive. When Redcrosse appears with Una, his armor shows that he has spiritual aid on his side, as his subsequent battles with Error, Sansfoy, and Sansjoy confirm. But once he is diverted from his quest by falling prey to duplicity, pride, and despair, the path of holiness cannot easily be discerned: 'how many perils doe enfold / The righteous man, to make him daily fall?' (viii 1). He is easily deceived by Archimago disguised as a model of holiness. By trying to remain chaste and flee Una, whom he believes to be unchaste, he is led away from the truth which could help guide him in decisions. Unlike medieval poems on salvation or morality, Spenser's Legend of Holiness does not simply present the choice between God and Satan, or good and evil, but involves the much more complicated task of determining divine will on earth.

Reformers taught that the life of holiness involves not merely moral choices, but choices made always with an awareness of God's presence and aid in order to avoid pride: 'There is no man's case so dangerous as his, whom Satan hath persuaded that his own righteousness shall present him pure and blameless in the sight of God' (Hooker *Of Justification* 7, in ed 1888, 3:492). From what he says and does, it appears that Redcrosse only imperfectly discerns the need to depend on God for strength and guidance, and thereby is drawn toward a belief in his own self-sufficiency; he therefore does not recognize that God's spiritual armor wins every battle, even when Sansfoy directly tells him it is the cross on his armor that makes him invulnerable (ii 18). Self-will would seem to cloud his assigned purpose until he comes close to physical and spiritual death in Despair's cave.

Redcross's spiritual health is restored at the house of Holiness, where his experience is designed to show that 'If any strength we have, it is to ill, / But all the good is Gods, both power and eke will' (x 1). The Christian virtues embodied in Caelia's house comprise Spenser's fullest definition of holiness: a life full of humility, zeal, reverence, faith, hope, patience, charity, repentance, penance, obedience, mercy, and contemplation. Here, Redcrosse is taught the doctrinal and disciplinary requirements for holiness. He is so 'Greev'd with remembrance of his wicked wayes' and 'prickt with anguish of his sinnes' that he falls into despair until Speranza and Patience aid him. 'Trew *Repentance*' follows, to rid him of 'Inward corruption, and infected sin.' Then Charissa demonstrates the value of 'well to donne' (see *Bead-men) and Mercy guides him to Contemplation, who shows him the rewards of the saintly life. Redcrosse emerges with enough spiritual knowledge of divine guidance to become an effective defender of the church on earth. Subsequently, at the three-day battle with the Dragon, his increased understanding of holy living enables him to draw upon Christ's power in an interplay between human effort and divine aid which symbolizes the way life should be lived daily.

The sixteenth-century concept of holiness is faith in action: the attempt, despite human failings, to do battle as a knight of the Cross, recognizing human limitations and the sufficiency of God. After Redcrosse's initial quest is over and he meets Guyon, his humble deflection of praise for victory over the Dragon shows how much he has learned about the virtue of holiness: 'His be the praise, that this atchiev'ment wrought, / Who made my hand the organ of his might; / More then goodwill to me attribute nought: / For all I did, I did but as I ought (II i 33).

DEBRA BROWN SCHNEIDER

Homilies ed 1623; Hooker ed 1888; Luther *The Freedom of a Christian* (1520) in ed 1955–75, 31:327–78; John Norden 1847 *A Progress of Piety* Parker Society (Cambridge); John Woolton 1851 *The Christian Manual, or Of the Life and Manners of True Christians* Parker Society (Cambridge).

Holiness, house of In *FQ* I x, the three stages of the Red Cross Knight's regeneration in the house of Holiness provide the poem's most comprehensive image of human identity – a saintly perfecting of body, heart, and mind which subsumes the educative houses of subsequent books.

This spiritual castle is a remarkable synthesis of allegorical edifices from ancient philosophy, the Bible, and medieval romance. In particular, it draws upon medieval courts of love and temples of fame and honor as moralized in later romances and pilgrimage literature (eg, Deguileville's *Pilgrimage of the Life of Man*, Chaucer's *House of Fame*, and Lydgate's *Temple of Glas*). It unites the classical temple, the medieval church, and the feudal castle. Throughout the house, the rigors of penitential discipline are combined with 'comely courteous glee,' though 'no courting nicetie.' Charissa's rejection of '*Cupids* wanton snare' (30), though disparaging, enforces the comparison between her teaching and the courts of love; and similarly, the conversation between Redcrosse and heavenly Contemplation about chivalric fame (57–63) places the tradition of the temple of fame (an important theme of the poem) within the larger context of heavenly glory. In its three hierarchic stages, the house also shows indebtedness to the philosophic castle of the body, deriving especially from Plato's *Timaeus* but idealized and spiritualized by Neoplatonic and Christian philosophers who treated the human form as a spiritual body fitted for the heavenly realm of pure ideas.

Most important is the specifically religious castle or city of Jewish wisdom literature (eg, Prov 9.1) and the New Testament (eg, 1 Cor 3.10–17). Drawing from such texts, patristic and medieval writers portrayed the human form as God's temple or the body of the Blessed Virgin as a sanctified *castellum* into which Christ entered as divine love (eg, numerous homilies for the Feast of the Assumption based on Luke 10.38); and they portrayed the human soul as a fortress assailed by vices and defended by virtues, divine grace, and the Christ-knight (eg, Prudentius' *Psychomachia* and the 'hous unitee, holy chirche on englissh' in Langland's *Piers Plowman* B 19.328) or as a place of the *unio mystica* where the soul dwells in God and God in the soul (eg, St Teresa's *Interior Castle*).

In contrast to the lush dreamlike setting of the courts of love and fame, Spenser's spiritual house is a plain, unornamented edifice. Its simplicity suggests the curtailing of sensuous, worldly pleasures in favor of inward spiritual joys. Its locked, closely watched door and 'streight and narrow' entrance lead to a 'spacious court' within. Redcrosse attends its 'schoolehouse' of faith, and in some 'darkesome lowly place farre in' endures a repentant, ascetic period of fasting. He is nurtured by charitable love, regally ornamented, but his rigorous training continues as he is led by Mercy through a 'narrow way, / Scattred with bushy thornes, and ragged breares' to the seven Bead-men's hospital, where he learns of their good works before he proceeds up a steep hill topped by a 'litle Hermitage' to meet the blind 'heavenly *Contemplation*.' Only in Charissa's 'fruitfull nest' and in Contemplation's spiritual vision of 'that most glorious house' in heaven does Spenser celebrate the beatific pleasures of this mystic architecture. The strait and narrow entrance, passed with difficulty but leading to a spacious interior, and ultimately to the limitless freedom of the heavenly city contrasts with the broad, much-traveled highway leading to Lucifera's house of Pride (iv 2–3), entered with ease but ending in a dungeon (v 45–51).

The ample and courteous welcome to Caelia's house by Humiltà, Zeal, and Reverence contrasts with that given by the porter of Lucifera's castle (Malvenù) and of Orgoglio's castle (Ignaro). In earlier figurative castles (eg, Deguileville's *Pilgrimage*), the porter is 'Drede off god' (*timor domini*), the first gift of the Holy Spirit, related to the 'poore in spirit' (Matt 5.3), who gain the kingdom of heaven (see Chew 1962:123, Tuve 1966:93–4); and in later allegories, humility is the castle moat (eg, Bernard's Castle of Sapience, Cartigny's School of Repentance). The matron of the house is Caelia, whose daughters represent the three theological virtues, faith, hope, and charity. Redcrosse's three stages of regeneration in her house are a precise and elaborate formulation of the three stages on the mystical way to God (see Collins 1940:193–203): purgation or mortification in Fidelia's schoolhouse and Patience's 'house of *Penaunce*,' illumination or vivification in Charissa's throne room and in the seven Bead-men's hospital, and future rapturous union promised in the vision from the Mount of Contemplation. As a structuring device for the Christian pilgrimage, these three stages appear in Dante's *Divine Comedy*, Chaucer's *House of Fame*, and Langland's *Piers Plowman*. As a structural principle for education, they are apparent in Deguileville's House of Grace-Dieu (Dames Penance, Charity, and Sapience), in Cartigny's School of Repentance (Ladies Repentance and Remembrance, the preacher Understanding), and, more broadly, in Cartigny's overall sequence of regeneration (School of Repentance, Palace of Virtue, tower vision of New Jerusalem).

That Fidelia initiates the process of regeneration, that she carries the sacramental cup and the Scriptures whose mysteries she clarifies by preaching, and that she gives Contemplation the keys to the kingdom of heaven all indicate the staunch Protestantism of this part of the allegory (see Calvin *Institutes* 1.9.3). Unlike Deguileville's horned Moses, she does not administer the cup in priestly fashion but preaches to clarify and support belief, suggesting that she is less an external priest than a reflection of the knight's own faith. Her leech, Patience, completes the initial phase of purgation, first by confession and absolution, then by the subordinate activities of Amendment, Penance, Remorse, and Repentance. The naming of Patience, stressing inner response rather than priestly authority, suggests a distinctly Protestant revision of medieval doctrine and symbolism, for in earlier allegories this ministrant is called Confession or Shrift (eg, *Everyman*) or Penance (eg, Deguileville's *Pilgrimage*, Cartigny's *Wandering Knight*).

The illuminative phase of the house of Holiness focuses on vivification of the heart by Charissa. If Fidelia and Patience are relatively new figures, she is traditional in medieval spiritual castles, often playing a central role in the regenerative process (between penance and sapience) and her love actively expressed as the seven works of mercy. Although the essential sources of Charissa are from the New Testament (eg, 1 Cor 13), Spenser hints at an analogy with Venus and the courts of love. The knightly lover, having confessed his wrongdoings to the leech (as in Gower's *Confessio Amantis*), now learns from Charissa the statutes of true love before finally moving up the Mount of Contemplation to learn the true meaning of fame and honor. Charissa is 'founderesse' of the hospital of seven Bead-men, whose seven corporal acts of mercy are the 'good and godly deedes' of Caelia. By working to restore 'The images of God in earthly clay,' 'The wondrous workemanship of Gods owne mould,' they manifest the redemptive love of Christ.

Mercy, as Charissa's best manifestation, guides the knight to Contemplation, the unitive stage of regeneration. Spenser's ecstatic mountain vision appears in much romance-pilgrimage literature (eg, *The Wandering Knight*), its main images having been developed by medieval mystics and allegorists. The New Jerusalem (Rev 21) and Jacob's ladder (from Gen 28.12) are commonplace, the former an essential symbol of the unitive stage (see, eg, Chaucer's *Parson's Tale*). Contemplation helps the knight to see Cleopolis and its temple of Panthea within the purview of that heavenly city with its register of saints.

Fuller understanding of the house of Holiness comes from examining the extensive parallels with the house of Pride: the differing guides, Duessa and Una; the contrary moral landscape, architecture, porters, and presiding female figures; the development from exultation to joylessness in one, from mortification to beatific joy in the other; Lucifera's tyrannous dragon versus Fidelia's healing serpent; the frustrated leech Aesculapius who sustains the sinful flesh versus the leech Patience who mortifies and cures it; the vengeful combat for worldly honor versus the charitable works leading to true glory; the seven deadly sins versus the seven works of mercy; Night's hellish realm versus Contemplation's heavenly vision.

An equally instructive and elaborate parallel exists between Caelia's house and Alma's castle in Book II, clarifying the difference between the saintly perfection of the spiritual or mystical body and the temporal virtues of the natural body. (Caelia represents the soul *sub specie aeternitatis*; Alma, the soul *sub specie temporis*.) In the three hierarchic stages of the house of Holiness, the analogous levels of Alma's castle (belly, heart, brain) are purified and transformed: Fidelia and Patience mortify the belly's fleshly appetites, Charissa and the works of mercy chasten and illuminate the feelings of the heart, and Contemplation turns the intellect toward union with God. Of particular interest is Spenser's analogy between the ambivalent passions which inhabit Alma's parlor of the heart, where Cupid plays, and the pure steadfast emotions fostered by Charissa. Equally important is the parallel between Alma's brain turret where the working of natural reason is displayed, and Caelia's Mount of Contemplation where the eagle-vision of superior reason takes flight. Alma's three sages are purified and fulfilled in Contemplation, whose mount is associated with Moses on Sinai looking back to the Old Law, Christ on Olivet unfolding the present covenant of grace, and the poet on Parnassus representing man's imaginative vision as a continuing instrument of divine revelation (53–4). The house of Holiness episode thus presents the most comprehensive allegorical center in *The Faerie Queene*, fashioning man in the image of God.

ROBERT L. REID

Collins 1940; Cornelius 1930; Nohrnberg 1976; Reid 1981–2; Whitaker 1950.

Homer '*Spenser*, whose hart inharbours *Homers* soule' (Charles Fitzgeffrey, in *Sp All* p 48). We have no certain knowledge of the poet called Homer. That he was a blind singer of tales from Ionia, working around the eighth century BC before the rise of general literacy in the classical era, that he performed in the courts of aristocratic patrons who identified their ancestors with his heroes, and that he was the author of the first and the greatest epics in our literary tradition are for some scholars reasonable conjectures, but by no means for all. The biographical picture has been made up largely from Homer's portrait of the blind poet Demodocus, who sings a tragic tale of the war at Troy and a comic tale of the adultery of Ares and Aphrodite (*Odyssey* 8). Traditions informing us of Homer's hairy thighs (Heliodorus) and of his suicidal frustration in attempting to solve a riddle about lice (Pseudo-Plutarch *Vita Homeri*) have, for the present, no modern adherents.

The subject of the *Iliad* is the wrath of Achilles, which is seen against the background of the Trojan War. The subject of the *Odyssey* is the return of Odysseus from Troy to his kingdom in Ithaca. While the

Odyssey does not pick up the narrative where the *Iliad* leaves off, references to intermediate events, such as Agamemnon's murder and Orestes' revenge, are scattered throughout the poem, a fact that in some measure explains why all stories connected with the Trojan War are implied in the epics of Homer. Subsequent works of literature from this tradition of stories were seen, in a phrase attributed to Aeschylus, as 'slices from the banquet of Homer.'

Many events barely mentioned in the *Iliad* and the *Odyssey* are elaborated by later poets of the 'epic cycle'; and the climactic destruction of Troy by the famous stratagem of the Trojan horse, briefly alluded to in the *Odyssey*, is best known in the brilliant description in the second book of Virgil's *Aeneid*. Likewise, many of the most famous events connected with Homer – the birth of Clytemnestra and Helen from Leda's egg, the marriage of Peleus and Thetis, the judgment of Paris, the rape of Helen, the feigned madness of Odysseus, the sacrifice of Iphigenia, the battle with the Amazons, the death of Achilles – are not directly treated in the Homeric epics. It was in this body of tales that romantic developments began to appear, notably the tale of Troilus and Cressida, elaborated by Chaucer and Shakespeare, and the tales of the founding of the nations of Europe by escaped Trojan princes or their descendants, one of whom is Brute, the eponymous founder of Britain and remote progenitor of Spenser's Arthur.

In the Middle Ages the Troy story was best known in the narratives of the pseudonymous authors Dictys Cretensis and Dares Phrygius, who claimed to have been participants in the war. A more substantial achievement is the *Bellum Troianum* of Joseph of Exeter (Sedgwick 1930), the quality of whose classical hexameters prompted Milton to call him 'the only smooth Poet of those times' (*History of Britain* in ed 1953–82, 5.1:15). Joseph's poem is the source (through intermediaries) of Caxton's *Recuyell of the Historyes of Troye* which, like Lydgate's *Troy Book* (based on the *Roman de Troie* of Benôit de Sainte-Maure), was widely read in Spenser's time. Geoffrey of Monmouth recounts the Trojan ancestry of the Britons through Brute, the story is repeated by Wace and Layamon, and it is accepted in Holinshed's *Chronicles*.

While the accumulated Homeric legends are omnipresent in the literature of Spenser's time, none of his contemporaries gives evidence of being deeply affected, as Milton would be, by the Homeric epics themselves. Chapman's translation (too late to influence Spenser) captures some of the energy of the originals and Jonson's knowledge of Greek was thorough; but no poet before Milton could appreciate at first hand Homer's artistic subtlety and formal integrity. Because Spenser is the first English epic poet to read Homer in Greek, it is interesting to estimate how well he did so.

Although Greek studies in England had declined from the days of Ascham and Cheke, Spenser was fortunate to attend Merchant Taylors' School, which imitated the great humanist school of St Paul's in its emphasis on Greek. The boys in the senior year were examined in Homeric Greek, and a list of books in use at the school (dating shortly after Spenser's time) includes the great dictionary of Henri Estienne. It has not been ascertained what text was commonly used, for the *Iliad* was not published in England in a Greek edition until 1594. One particularly attractive continental edition, which Chapman used, is the Greek text of Homer with Latin translation and commentary by Jean de Sponde (1583). Greek studies at Cambridge were at their lowest when Spenser was there; but he was friends with the very considerable scholar Gabriel Harvey (D.C. Allen in Meres ed 1933:102–5). Although E.K.'s commentary on *The Shepheardes Calender* is liberally sprinkled with Greek quotations, few Englishmen would have attained to the level of continental scholars and poets. Spenser would not have shown himself, as Ronsard does in a sonnet, forbidding his servant to interrupt him for three days while he reads through the *Iliad*; nevertheless Spenser was reputed to be 'perfect in the Greek tongue' (Bryskett ed 1970:21).

There are moments in Spenser's poetry that may indicate a direct experience of Homer, notably the invocation before the catalogue of rivers (*FQ* IV xi 9–10), a passage that is modeled partly on Virgil (*Aeneid* 7.645–6) but principally on Homer's invocation before the catalogue of ships (*Iliad* 2.484–93). (For further instances, see *FQ* ed 1977 and *Var* passim.) There are occasional moments in *The Faerie Queene* where Spenser seems not to be quoting from but responding to the spirit of the Homeric text, for example, his treatment of Marinell and his mother, Cymoent (cf Achilles and Thetis in *Iliad* 1.348–427, 18.22–147). Such moments suggest a maturer acquaintance with Homer than is seen in more superficially Homeric contemporaries, such as William Warner and George Peele. Still, in the main, Spenser is a son not of Homer but of the Homeric tradition: explicit Homeric details such as the chain of Philotime (II vii 44–9) and the Odyssean voyage of Guyon (xii 2–38) are built up out of subsequent allegorical commentary on these stories and not out of Homer directly. Rather than absorbing and transfiguring Homer as Milton does, Spenser is content to give *The Faerie Queene* a Homeric patina by means of descriptive Greek names, such as *Philotime* or *Cymodoce* (IV xi 53; cf *Iliad* 18.39), and by means of Homeric figures like Atē (IV i).

Many stylistic features of *The Faerie Queene* can be traced ultimately to Homer, although they come to Spenser by way of Virgil, Ovid, Ariosto, and Tasso. These include the epic simile (I v 8, 18), the mythopoeic description of sunrise (2), the formalized account of a single combat, the insulting of a defeated enemy (13), the rescue of a combatant by a god who spirits him away in a cloud (13), the use of cosmological symbols such as the golden chain suspended from Jove's throne (25), the reluctance of supernatural agencies to aid mortals because of the anger this might provoke in more powerful gods (42), and of course the very presence of the Greek gods. As this list is taken from a single canto, it is apparent that Homeric features are so completely woven into the fabric of Spenser's epic that it is useless to tag them. The Homeric style, passed down through so many intermediate poets, provides the underlying system of images, conceits, and relations for European narrative verse up to the nineteenth century.

Thus while Homer is the culmination of a long oral tradition that is unknown to us now, he stands also at the beginning of the tradition of written epics in the West; and he has been acknowledged as the sovereign of that tradition even by poets, such as Dante, who could not have read him. Attempts, such as J.C. Scaliger's, to place Virgil on Homer's throne have failed not only because of Homer's superiority but also because Homer was, as Johnson observed when measuring Milton against him, the first.

To appreciate the influence on Spenser of a more self-conscious Homeric tradition, we must divide that tradition into three parts: first, the ancient practice of allegorically interpreting the Homeric epics; second, the medieval tradition, deriving in part from Geoffrey of Monmouth, in which Europe is imagined to have risen out of the ashes of Troy; third, Renaissance neo-Aristotelian poetics, wherein the epics of Homer are brought into a systematic theory of the ideal aesthetic structure, and the ideal moral function, of heroic poetry. (For the first of these, see *allegory.)

The key passages in *The Faerie Queene* recounting the story of the Trojan origins of Britain are (*a*) the conversation at Malbecco's table (III ix 33–51), where Paridell (a diminutive of Paris, whose lust caused the Trojan War) tells of the fall of Troy and of Brute's founding a new Troy (identified as London in stanza 45) in a new land: 'For noble *Britons* sprong from *Troians* bold, / And *Troynovant* was built of old *Troyes* ashes cold' (38); (*b*) the Briton chronicle, wherein the story is brought forward from Brute to Arthur's father, Uther (II x 5–69, esp 46), a story worthy of Homer's pen or, as Spenser calls it, the '*Moeonian* quill' (3); and (*c*) the prophecy of Merlin, which carries the Trojan line into the future from Britomart to Elizabeth: 'from thy wombe a famous Progenie / Shall spring, out of the auncient *Troian* blood' (III iii 22–50, esp 22). Here Spenser gives Elizabeth the same form of authority that Virgil gives Augustus: just as the Roman emperor's lineage is derived from Trojan Aeneas, so the English Queen's lineage is derived from Trojan Brute.

A more mysterious connection to the story of Troy is made when Britomart, looking into the 'glassie globe,' sees Artegall wearing the divine arms of the principal hero of the *Iliad*: 'Achilles armes, which Arthegall did win' (III ii 25). By this Spenser may have meant that, though the Greeks (Achaeans, as Homer calls them), led by Achilles, had conquered the Trojans, the descendants of those Trojans would at length win supremacy. This may follow Virgil's suggestion that Rome's rise to greatness fulfills the prophecy of Poseidon (*Iliad* 20.307–8) that the power of Aeneas shall rule over the Trojans in all the generations of his sons – and, Spenser would add, of his daughters.

The importance for Spenser's contemporaries of the fable of the Trojan ancestry of the Britons (and of the fable of Arthur, which depends partly on it) is very great. The legend had been an essential element in the legitimation of Tudor power under Henry VII, and its political importance is evident in works such as Peele's *Tale of Troy* and *Arraignment of Paris*. One of the most conspicuous celebrations of the theme is the interminable *Albions England* (first two books appeared in 1586) of Warner, whom Francis Meres styled the 'English *Homer*' (ed 1933:76). That this accolade is given without irony suggests that to be the Homer of a nation does not here imply the attainment of an aesthetic ideal. Rather it implies that the poet has established the consciousness of his nation in the story of Troy, thus asserting the community of the British with other nations of the same stock, and preeminently with Rome. This is Spenser's purpose in relating the Trojan origins of Britain: like Virgil, he intends to create a national consciousness out of the ashes of Troy.

A more sophisticated conception of Homer, however, one based not on ancient hermeneutics or on medieval legend but on the Renaissance revival of learning, was beginning to emerge in Spenser's time. This can be seen in the Letter to Raleigh, where Homer is set forth as the first in a tradition of 'antique Poets historicall' whose didactic aim is to make princes good governors and virtuous men – though Homer's Agamemnon is a far cry from a 'good governour,' and Odysseus is not scrupulously moral. Nevertheless, Sir Thomas Elyot spoke for the times when he said that princes should read of the heroes in Homer 'that they most fervently shall desire and coveite, by the imitation of their vertues, to acquire semblable glorie' (ed 1883, 1:59). By offering a story of Prince Arthur acquiring the virtues as he moves towards Gloriana, Spenser seems to enact Elyot's proposition in narrative form.

Whether Homer intended his epics to provide a mirror for princes we cannot know; certainly he accomplished much more. Yet some such idea does seem a reasonable description not only of the complex, mediated, Renaissance picture of the Homeric epics but also of Spenser's purpose in writing *The Faerie Queene* – though he too accomplished much more. Naive as such narrowly didactic ideas of Homer would appear to the more accurate scholarship of the following century, they help us to understand why it would be reasonable for Milton's schoolmaster, Alexander Gill, to call Spenser 'our Homer.' GORDON TESKEY

For background, see Bolgar 1954; Bush 1952; Bush 1963; Curtius ed 1953; F.W.M. Draper 1962; Hermann Dunger 1869 *Die Sage vom trojanischen Kriege in den Bearbeitungen des Mittelalters und ihre antiken Quellen* Programm des Vitzthumschen Gymnasiums 8 (Dresden); Georg Finsler 1912 *Homer in der Neuzeit von Dante bis Goethe: Italien, Frankreich, England, Deutschland* (Leipzig); Gilbert Highet 1949 *The Classical Tradition: Greek and Roman Influences on Western Literature* (Oxford); Lemmi 1929; George deF[orest] Lord 1956 *Homeric Renaissance: 'The Odyssey' of George Chapman* (New Haven); Francis Meres 1933 *Francis Meres's Treatise 'Poetrie': A Critical Edition* ed Don Cameron Allen (*ISLL* 16.3–4; Urbana); Walter Bradbury Sedgwick 1930 'The *Bellum Troianum* of Joseph of Exeter' *Spec* 5:49–76; Arthur Tilley 1938 'Greek Studies in England in the Early Sixteenth Century' *EHR* 53:221–39, 438–56; Tillyard 1954; H.B. Wilson 1814; Arthur M. Young 1948 *Troy and Her Legend* (Pittsburgh).

---

homiletics Protestantism in the sixteenth century was a 'preaching' religion: the first duty of its spiritual leaders was to proclaim the Word of God. And though the Church of England purported to subordinate preaching to prayer and the liturgy, the Elizabethan period was a time of great preachers, from Hugh Latimer to Henry Smith and Lancelot Andrewes. Elizabethans not only listened avidly to sermons; they read them voraciously. A conservative estimate suggests that over a thousand were on the market in Elizabeth's reign, and the actual number may have been double that (Herr 1940:117). Great numbers of homiletic treatises, or *artes concionandi*, describing how to construct and deliver sermons were published in Latin, English, Italian, Spanish, French, and German; and many, like collections of sermons, went to several editions. Ancillary aids to sermon making, such as collections of exempla (brief narratives illustrating moral points) and books of commonplaces (topics for argument derived from scripture), were also widely published: Phillip Melanchthon's *Loci communes* received many editions between 1521 and 1577. Larger churches might provide daily 'lectures' and more than one Sunday sermon to hearers who were trained listeners, who often took extensive notes, and who might, even against the preacher's wishes, reconstruct and publish them (see *homilies). The sermon was a vehicle not only for instruction in the faith, but for controversy and the refinement of theological doctrine. As a student at Cambridge, Spenser might have heard preached on the morning and afternoon of the same day 'pure Canterbury' followed by 'pure Geneva' (Fuller 1662:423). Through hearing, reading, analyzing, and discussing sermons, probably throughout his life and certainly as a schoolboy and university student, he would have absorbed many of the rhetorical and epistemological principles which inform his poetry generally but most pronouncedly the narrative of *The Faerie Queene*.

Preaching in Spenser's time meant more than a speaker addressing a group of passive listeners. The *artes praedicandi* agree that the audience must actively participate in the sermon, the preacher mediating divine truth to a community of receptive listeners. Since truth has been recorded in time by human intellect and can therefore be misunderstood, the preacher is a man walking 'by faith and not by sight' (Augustine *De doctrina christiana* 1.37, quoting 2 Cor 5.7; see Latin *Fathers). Since his grasp of truth is often tentative, he imparts it indirectly by way of his own 'answering' to its imperatives; his preaching is thus an act of 'becoming' through personal response to a perceived reality. By gradually fulfilling a responsibility to divine inspiration, he provides an 'ensample' for his auditors. As Andreas Gerardus (Hyperius) expresses it in one of the most influential sermon treatises of the day, 'Before all thinges,' the preacher must 'conceyve such lyke affectations in his mynde, and rayse them upp in himselfe, yea, and ... shewe them forth to be seene unto others, as he coveteth to be translated into the myndes of his auditors' (*The Practis of Preaching* ed 1577: fol 43r). To accomplish this end, the preacher often adopts the personae of members of his audience, inviting them to discover for themselves through imaginative identification what the sermon 'means.' Although in William Burton's words 'the Minister is the mouth of God unto the people,' it is finally they who 'must say, *So be it*' (*Davids Evidence* 1592, in ed 1602:360). This process of discovery and assent is most frequently called 'trying the word,' and as Henry Smith indicates, it is an act of choice almost tangible in its intensity: 'Now, when we have tried the word which is truth, and which is error, what shuld we doo then? ... We must keep and hold the truth, as a man gripeth a thing with both his handes' (ed 1593:316–17).

Such conditions obligate us to understand the commonplace notion of 'applying' the sermon as a reciprocal process, involving a dramatic relationship between preacher and hearer. In Donne's words, 'It becommeth me ... to infuse the Word of God into you, as powerfully as I can, but all that I can doe, is but a small matter, the greatnesse of the worke lieth in your Application ... quickned by [God's] Spirit' (ed 1953–62, 8:272–3). This concept of application lies at the heart of Renaissance preaching. It makes the sermon not so much a form to be defined by spatial notions of structure as a strategy enlivened by varied but concerted efforts to involve the listeners through 'trying' and 'proving' in a spiritual community whose aim is an ever-increasing recognition and showing forth of their human and divine potentialities.

The Faerie Queene continually reflects this dynamic conception of preaching. Like the preacher, the narrator must transmit and within his powers open to his readers' understanding a 'historye' revealed by a 'sacred Muse' so that they may be confirmed in lives of gentle and virtuous discipline. The muse constrains him to a sometimes trying effort to apply to a diverse audience the moral doctrine residing in his narrative. His interpretive commentary is often inadequate, and, like the preacher, his understanding is tentative; but as his fable progresses, he becomes more conscious of the complexities inherent in human endeavors toward perfection. Such a development is most apparent in the formal comments at the beginnings of cantos. For example, the introductory stanzas to *FQ* I iii-v evolve from a sentimental courtly sympathy for distressed beauty to the deeper philosophical concept of a noble life grounded in vigorous pursuit of a virtuous ideal. In cantos vii-x, the narrator's guiding assumptions change. In contrast to his more rational, detached earlier stanzas, these are emotionally charged and sway from elation to depression in reaction to Redcrosse's religious experience. By altering his perspective, the narrator conforms to Gerardus' injunction to 'rayse ... upp' and 'shewe forth,' as he seeks to understand better and to induce his reader to confront more effectively the experiential implications of their shared history. Similar changes occur in Books II, III, V, and VI.

As mediator of a revealed 'historye,' the narrator, like the preacher, invites our trust, either explicitly in assurances that what may seem 'missayd' is not really so, or implicitly in his serious tone and authoritative manner. In turn, our faith in him rests on his willing acceptance of his 'dewtie.' We respond to his efforts as he tries to surmount his own shortcomings through faith in the importance of his poetic purpose. We actively participate in a constantly varying relationship between himself and his fable, and the 'meaning' of the poem becomes for us a kind of personal discovery – not something we are 'told' or 'shown,' but rather something that we find. Spenser's narrator assumes that we are like accomplished sermon listeners who 'try by the word' in order to 'keep and hold the truth.'

Renaissance preaching thus exerts its most profound influence on the epistemological assumptions governing the narrative strategies of *The Faerie Queene*. But there are other, more immediate influences. In attempting to accommodate homiletics more closely to classical rhetoric, Erasmus expanded the three classical rhetorical genera (deliberative, judicial, epideictic) into five 'orders of preaching': persuasive, exhortative, admonitory, consolatory, and laudatory (*Ecclesiastes, sive De ratione concionandi* ed 1703–6, 5:758–92). Reformed theorists rename these orders variously, but most commonly as the *didascalick*, which seeks to confirm a doctrine; the *redargutive*, aimed at refuting error; the admonitory, designed to 'bring the hearer to an exercise of Christian duties to God and man'; the corrective, directed against 'corruption in manners, vice, and wickedness'; and the consolatory, which seeks to raise the spirits of the downcast (Gerardus ed 1577: fols 17v-20v, see also Hemmingsen *The Preacher* ed 1574: fols 17v-18v). Such distinctions provide a consistent means for classifying Spenser's rhetorical intentions. For example, although the comments at I x I, III iii 1–3, and V x 1–2 differ greatly in subject, they are all *didascalick* and therefore formally related in ways that contribute to the poem's Christian humanist synthesis. Although some commentary is also *redargutive* (eg, II proem 2–3, III iv 8), most is admonitory (eg, I iv 1), corrective (III ii 1–2), or consolatory (III i 7–8; this category, interestingly, always aimed at characters within the poem and not directly at the audience). *Didascalick* and *redargutive* comments appeal to the intellect, the last three to the emotions, corresponding to Erasmus' division of preaching into instruction and persuasion. This proportion suggests an important truth about Renaissance preaching and Spenser's poetry: whether the aim be salvation or fashioning a gentle person, what is at stake is the person's whole being. The mind's apprehension of one's condition becomes efficacious only with the heart's assent.

In Spenser's day, a sermon might take one of several prescribed forms; common to all, however, was a deep structure implied by the preacher's desire to save souls. This is what modern theologians call the pattern of 'salvation history,' embodied in both the epic shape of the Bible and the individual's spiritual progress. Renaissance preachers usually conceived of this structure as spiritual warfare or pilgrimage, two of the chief structural images in *The Faerie Queene*. The theology of the sermons that Spenser would have heard was predominantly Calvinist. Calvin's language is imbued with the concepts and images of medieval romance, and words like *honor*, *majesty*, *homage*, *combat*, *contest*, *alliance*, *fealty*, *fidelity*, *prince*, and *tyrant* go far toward giving his thought narrative form. This form was then assimilated into the sermons influenced by it, where in turn it was made available to the poetic imagination. For the principles which shape his authorial stance in *The Faerie Queene*, Spenser was probably as much influenced by sermons as by medieval romances or classical moral treatises. JEROME S. DEES

William Burton 1602 *Sermons and Treatises* (London); Donne ed 1953–62; Erasmus ed 1703–6; Andreas Hyperius [Gerardus] 1577 *The Practis of Preaching* tr J[ohn] Ludham (London; *STC* 11758); Niels Hemmingsen [Nicolaus Hemmingius] 1574 *The Preacher, or Methode of Preaching* tr J[ohn] H[orsfall] (London; rpt Menston, Yorks 1972); William Perkins ed 1616–18 *The Art of Prophecying* in *Workes* 2:643–73 (London); Henry Smith ed 1593.

J.W. Blench 1964 *Preaching in England in the Late Fifteenth and Sixteenth Centuries* (Oxford); Harry Caplan 1970 *Of Eloquence: Studies in Ancient and Mediaeval Rhetoric* ed Anne King and Helen North (Ithaca, NY); Th.M. Charland 1936 *Artes Praedicandi: Contribution à l'histoire de la rhétorique au Moyen Age* (Paris); Stanley Fish 1967 *Surprised by Sin: The Reader in 'Paradise Lost'* (Berkeley and Los Angeles) pp 7, 20, 52; Alan Fager Herr 1940 *The Elizabethan Sermon: A Survey and a Bibliography* (Philadelphia); Heinrich F. Plett 1975 *Rhetorik der Affekte: Englische Wirkungsästhetik im Zeitalter der Renaissance* (Tübingen); James Michael Weiss 1974 '*Ecclesiastes* and Erasmus: The Mirror and the Image' *ARG* 65:83–108.

---

homilies The official homilies are two collections of simple sermons written by bishops and other learned men for the common people and imposed on the whole realm by royal injunctions that required most ministers to read a homily or part thereof each Sunday and holy day in the year. The 'homely' homilies, as Latimer called them (ed 1844–5, 1:121), were the steady diet fed to Edwardian and Elizabethan parishioners by unpreaching pastors, those 'dumb dogs' (cf Isa 56.10) whose ability to purvey the Word had been impaired by either lack of education or governmental control. Sometimes regarded as texts inspired by the educational ideals of Christian humanism, the homiles also allowed the authorities to 'tune the pulpits' (as Elizabeth put it) in their campaign to create uniformity of belief.

The first book of homilies (1547) contains twelve sermons; it ushered in the theological reformation undertaken during Edward VI's brief reign (1547–53) in the aftermath of Henry VIII's repudiation of papal supremacy. The second, Elizabethan book (1563) supplemented the first with twenty sermons that further reveal the official concerns and chief preoccupations of the Tudor Protestant establishment. The Book of Common Prayer (1549) secured a place for the homilies in a new English liturgy; Articles 11 and 35 of the Thirty-nine Articles affirmed their doctrinal significance; Jewell, Hooker, and even Donne asserted their usefulness in the pastoral mission. For Herrick, the homilies had a distinctive place among the ceremonies of the church in England: even fairies 'have their Book of Homilies' ('The Faerie Temple, or Oberons Chappell' line 83). Five homilies are particularly important and influential declarations of what Article 35 calls 'godly and wholesome doctrine': the three sermons, now known to be Archbishop Cranmer's, which define the process of justification by treating in turn salvation, faith, and good works; and the two propaganda pieces on obedience and disobedience (the second of which was occasioned by the Northern Rising of 1569 and suffixed to the second book). Literary critics (esp since Hart 1934) have acknowledged the importance of the homilies in considering the religious background to Elizabethan writing.

Spenser knew the homilies and the controversies their use entailed. That fact seems plain from a passage in *Mother Hubberds Tale* (pub 1591, though possibly composed in the late 1570s when Spenser was secretary to John Young, Bishop of Rochester; see Long 1916, Judson 1934). Spenser complains satirically about the illiterate clergy and alludes sardonically to the reading of homilies as a facile alternative to a preaching ministry (382–95):

For read he could not evidence, nor will,
Ne tell a written word, ne write a letter,
Ne make one title worse, ne make one better:
Of such deep learning little had he neede,
Ne yet of Latine, ne of Greeke, that breede
Doubts mongst Divines, and difference of texts,
From whence arise diversitie of sects,

And hatefull heresies, of God abhor'd:
But this good Sir did follow the plaine word,
Ne medled with their controversies vaine.
All his care was, his service well to saine,
And to read Homelies upon holidayes:
When that was done, he might attend his playes;
An easie life, and fit high God to please.

Read beside a later passage (431–8), this excerpt hints at Spenser's Puritan leanings; his 'Homelies' may anticipate Milton's 'lean and flashy songs' which fail to satisfy the hunger of the expectant flock (*Lycidas* 123–4).

The ecclesiastical turmoil of the 1570s makes it likely that Spenser would have offended the Queen if the passage quoted above had appeared at the time. The Puritan wing of the church had begun to criticize the homilies during the *Admonition* controversy of the early seventies, when it was promoting a preaching over a reading ministry (Padelford 1913–14:89–91). In 1576, Edmund Grindal, recently translated to Canterbury, decried the Queen's preference for the homilies in a famous letter (ed 1843:376–90) and for his audacity was sequestered from the archiepiscopal see.

Although Spenser seems to have agreed with Grindal that the homilies are but half a loaf, these sermons do clarify some aspects of the poet's work. Along with the Articles and Nowell's *Catechism*, they are evidence that Spenser, while supportive of further reform in church discipline, adheres to the principal tenets of the Elizabethan settlement and inclines toward theological moderation rather than strict Calvinism (Whitaker 1950:31–9). Like the homilies, his poems virtually ignore the doctrines of election and predestination, but the nature of *The Faerie Queene* requires him to establish the relation of faith to good works. If the poem's end and subsuming virtue is magnificence, or the doing of great deeds, how can the poem also be founded on the austere Lutheranism of justification by faith alone? *The Faerie Queene* achieves the necessary reconciliation between ethical and religious understandings of human conduct precisely as the homilies achieve it: in both, man's misery is relieved by a lively faith that trusts in God's love and brings forth a temperate life charitably disposed to others, as a tree bears fruit (Wall 1976; cf *Heavenly Love* 190–217). The homilies concentrate first on faith alone, the thing essential for salvation, before they attack antinomianism and 'carnal liberty' in sermons on charity and almsgiving and on whoredom, gluttony, and idleness. Likewise, Spenser predicates the later books of his epic on the first: virtuous action and 'civill conversation' depend on grace apprehended through faith.

The homilies supply a helpful context for the structure and for various episodes and images in *The Faerie Queene*. Those on faith and good works may have given Spenser metaphors to sustain a doctrinal allegory in *FQ* I: for example, Cranmer describes the sequence of man's lapsing into sin as 'errors, superstitions, idolatry and all evil'; this phrase reflects the impediments to holiness embodied in Error, Archimago, Duessa, and Despair (Kane 1981). The same homilies distinguish a lively from a dead faith and the conduct of the truly faithful Christian from the behavior of the ethically virtuous, but spiritually deficient, natural man; they thus pertain to Spenser's depiction of Guyon's inadequacies prior to his fainting in II vii 66 (MacLachlan 1983). The lengthy homily exposing the 'peril of Idolatry' denigrates veneration of both images and idols in a way that explains Guyon's iconoclasm in the Bower of Bliss; it enlarges the biblical understanding of idolatry as spiritual fornication (an idiom typical of *FQ* I) and criticizes a practice associated throughout the poem with Archimago, principal maker of the false and meretricious. The homily on declining from God treats the twin temptations of pride and despair and concludes with a passage on the uncertain date of man's death (cf IV ii 52, iii 1–2; Skulsky 1980–1 applies this homily to I ix 41–2 as well). 'Against Excess of Apparell' denounces 'glittering show' worn in lieu of the Pauline armor. It pertains to Lucifera's gorgeous array (I iv 8, 17) and to the ostentatious attire of other vicious characters such as Duessa (I ii 13), Perissa (II ii 36), Acrasia (xii 77), and Munera (V ii 10); its excursus on reasonable need can be compared with I x 39. In V vi 2–3, 'Artegall's constancy and Britomart's lack of faith illustrate [a misogynistic sentence from] the Homily "Of the state of matrimonie"' (Hamilton in *FQ* ed 1977:567). Later, in V ix 39–49, Zeal versifies 'Against Rebellion' in his attack on Duessa (Fletcher 1971:237–8); but Spenser here distills the homilist's method more than his matter. Like the Rogation week homily in honor of God the creator and the homily advocating obedience, the sermon against rebellion displays attitudes to the natural appointed order that Spenser seriously parodies in *FQ* VII.

The homilies, then, articulate some theological and cultural commonplaces that appear in Spenser's poetry in a considerably more mature and complicated form. They are best regarded less as sources than as part of a religious tradition on which he drew and to which he contributed.

RONALD B. BOND

Church of England 1547 *Certayne Sermons, or Homilies* (London; *STC* 13639); 1563 *The Second Tome of Homelyes* (London; *STC* 13663); *Homilies* ed 1623; 1859 *Two Books of Homilies Appointed to Be Read in Churches* ed John Griffiths (Oxford); 1987 *'Certain Sermons or Homilies' (1547) and 'A Homily against Disobedience and Wilful Rebellion' (1570): A Critical Edition* ed Ronald B. Bond (Toronto). Grindal ed 1843; Latimer ed 1844–5.

Ronald B. Bond 1978 'The 1559 Revisions in *Certayne Sermons or Homilies*: "For the Better vnderstandyng of the Simple People"' *ELR* 8:239–55; Collinson 1979; Alfred Hart 1934 *Shakespeare and the Homilies and Other Pieces of Research into the Elizabethan Drama* (Melbourne); Sean Kane 1981 'Spenser and the Frame of Faith' *UTQ* 50:253–68; Long 1916; MacLachlan 1983; Padelford 1913–14; Skulsky 1980–1; Wall 1976; Wall 1983.

Hooker, Richard (1554–1600) A Protestant theologian who was an exact contemporary of Spenser and, like him, wrote his major work in the 1590s. *Of the Laws of Ecclesiastical Polity* (Books 1–4, 1593; Book 5, 1597) is the most important English philosophical and theological work of the later sixteenth century, and one of the most significant of all treatises on natural law. There is no recorded connection between Hooker and Spenser, no measurable influence in either direction, and no direct reference by one to the other. Yet Spenser would have been comfortable with Hooker's ideas (especially with Hooker's position regarding authority as derived from the Bible, reason, and tradition); and Hooker could have found magnanimity and the rule of right reason well expressed in Spenser, especially in *FQ* I and VI.

Queen Elizabeth is as essential to Hooker's work as she is to *The Faerie Queene*. Hooker refers to that terrible age 'of discomfort and darknes' during Catholic Mary's reign before God caused in Elizabeth 'a most glorious starre to arise, and on hir head setled the Crowne, whome him selfe had kept as a lambe from the slaughter of those bloudie times' (*Laws* 1.14.7). There are other, more fleeting references to the Queen (as at the end of the dedication of Book 5 to Archbishop Whitgift), always with implicit belief in her authority and just government. Indeed, the *Laws* clarify and defend Elizabethan supremacy and order; and the Queen, though not the inspirer of his work and object of his praise like Spenser's Gloriana, is for Hooker the essential and implied arbiter of secular law.

Of the literary works of his time, Hooker refers only to Shakespeare's *Julius Caesar* (see his marginal notes on his copy of *A Christian Letter*, in ed 1977–, 4:77–8), an indication not of what he must have known or read but rather of the specialized demands of polemical writing. Spenser reveals much more awareness of general religious concerns than Hooker does of literary ones, though he does not mention contemporary controversialists such as Hooker himself or Bishop John Jewel, nor does he usually define ecclesiastical positions.

In the role given to Arthur in *The Faerie Queene*, Spenser comes closest to depicting the harmony of laws supernaturally revealed and by necessity enforced in 'politique societies.' These laws are conveyed by means of God's grace in order to check errant human nature. Herein lies the ground where Spenser and Hooker meet. Arthur's 'goodly reason, and well guided speach' to Una (I vii 42) reveal those 'lawes of well doing [which] are the dictates of right reason' (*Laws* 1.7.4).

Hooker would also have agreed with Spenser's presenting Redcrosse's abandonment of the one true church as an abandonment of reason: 'The eye of reason was with rage yblent' (I ii 5). Later, when Redcrosse enters the house of Holiness, he renews his knowledge of 'the exercise of Christian religion, and the service of the true God' (*Laws* 1.1.3), that very 'celestiall discipline' which enables him to continue on his adventures (I x 18). This 'Patron of true Holinesse' who sets the course of *The Faerie Queene* is literature's best expression of the operation of '*natures* law' and 'that light of reason, whereby good may be knowne from evill' (*Laws* 1.3.1, 1.7.4). PAUL G. STANWOOD

Hooker ed 1977–; W. Speed Hill, ed 1972 *Studies in Richard Hooker: Essays Preliminary to an Edition of His Works* (Cleveland).

Hopkins, Gerard Manley (1844–89) English Jesuit and poet; his poems are notable for compact expression and innovations in rhythm. Hopkins' home had a five-volume edition of Spenser (London 1842), a birthday present to his poet father from his mother (House 1974:38), who copied passages into her own commonplace book (Family Papers). A 'glorious copy of Spenser' was one of the few books of English poetry in his Highgate School library (Skeat 1896: x). His earliest poem, 'The Escorial,' is in Spenserian stanzas; but Milton proved a greater influence. Aiming at maximum compression and impact, Hopkins classed nearly all *The Faerie Queene* as 'Parnassian' (poetic, but below the language of inspiration); he said the same of 'much ... in *Paradise Lost*,' and thought the 'lost books' of *The Faerie Queene* among the 'fortunate losses of literature' (ed 1959:38, 49; ed 1956:216–20). Asked by Canon Dixon how important he considered Spenser's experiments with sonnet structure, he recalled no details of *Amoretti*; but he confessed the charm of Dixon's 'quaint medley of Middle-Ages and QueenAnnery,' which pleased him as Spenser did, though alien to his own style (ed 1935:82–3). However, Hopkins himself often revived rare words for which the *OED*'s latest quotation is a century or more earlier. Stanza 5 of his 'Penmaen Pool,' where Charles' Wain is said to be 'brighter shaken' in the rippling water, seems one of his clearest debts to Spenser (ed 1967:65; cf *FQ* II xii 78). NORMAN H. MACKENZIE

Gerard Manley Hopkins 1935 *The Correspondence of Gerard Manley Hopkins and Richard Watson Dixon* ed Claude Colleer Abbott (London); Hopkins 1938 *Further Letters* ed Claude Colleer Abbott (London, rev ed 1956); Hopkins 1959 *Journals and Papers* ed Humphry House and Graham Storey (London); Hopkins 1967 *Poems* ed W.H. Gardner and N.H. MacKenzie (London); Madeline House 1974 'Books Belonging to Hopkins and His Family' *HRB* 5:26–41; Walter W. Skeat 1896 *A Student's Pastime* (Oxford).

humanism A loosely unified group of attitudes common among European intellectuals between 1300 and 1650. Its most typical features are its approval of classical antiquity and its hostility toward the Middle Ages. It derives its name from the interest of humanists in *litterae humaniores* ('the humane letters,' ie, the humanities), usually in contrast to the writings of the scholastics, which the humanists considered overly technical, remote from general human interests, and corrupt in style.

The points which recur most often in humanist writing are the liberalizing influence of Greek and Roman philosophy, literature, and political thought; the narrow dogmatism of the thought of the scholastic period; the importance of education as a means of reforming society; and the superiority of rhetoric, philosophy, history, and poetry to logic and theological disputation. It should be emphasized that 'humanism' in this sense is an historical movement closely related to the culture in which it flourished and entirely different from what is loosely termed 'secular humanism' in contemporary American society.

Given the looseness of the complex of attitudes called humanism, it is not surprising that there is considerable difference of opinion as to its essential definition. It has been considered a reassertion of pagan secularism (Burckhardt ed 1945); a program to revive classical antiquity (Voigt 1893); an attempt, in its initial phase, to liberalize the civic order (Baron 1955); a movement to foster the arts of communication, especially rhetoric and poetry, and to use them to instill wisdom (Clark 1922, 1948; Seigel 1968); a philosophy of practical common sense that was incapable of appreciating the momentous advances of the age in mathematics and physics (Sarton 1927–48, Randall 1961); an educational reform movement dominated by scholars (Woodward 1897, T.W. Baldwin 1944); and an effort to liberalize Christianity without sacrificing its essential ethical values (Bush 1939). Justification can be found for all of these descriptions, and each of them applies to some part of Spenser's works. But none of them is adequate for all his poetry and prose, or for the entire concept of humanism, or for any particular humanist.

Although they admired antiquity and the antique world, humanists were seldom as pagan as Jacob Burckhardt made them out to be in *The Civilization of the Renaissance in Italy* (1860). They tended to be practical Christians more interested in the ethical than the mystical message of the Bible. They preferred historical and philological methods of biblical interpretation to the four-level allegorical method of the Middle Ages, which they often satirized. Somewhat paradoxically, they generally welcomed moral, and later (under the influence of Florentine Platonism), mystical allegorizations of pagan myth. This sort of interpretation is the foundation of the first great humanist defense of poetry, Boccaccio's *Genealogia* (D.C. Allen 1970, Boccaccio ed 1930).

The humanists were skeptical of the value of monasticism and tended to favor the active life or the life of studious leisure rather than the contemplative life (see *triplex vita). They sought a synthesis of classical and Christian values applicable to relations among individuals and to the reform of education, law, and government. The central thrust of the idea of the dignity of man as formulated by Pico della Mirandola in his famous oration on the subject is that man is not an abject creature hopelessly mired in sin, but the central glory of divine creation destined to work God's will in the world (in Kristeller, et al 1948). They admired the early Latin and Greek Fathers for their breadth of learning and their avoidance of the chop-logic and exegetical ingenuities of the Schoolmen. Most were pious, but they scorned fanaticism and dogmatism, which they often attacked with dogmatic zeal.

These attitudes characterize humanism in general but appear in different combinations in the writings of its various schools. Italian humanism was deeply influenced in the fourteenth century by the mysticism of Dante and the medieval Platonism of the poets of the *dolce stil nuovo*. In the mid-fifteenth century, the influx of Greek scholars after the fall of Constantinople (1453) encouraged a quickening of interest in ancient Greek literature. Later in the century, the so-called Platonic Academy, established in Florence under the patronage of the Medici family and centered in the translations and commentaries of Ficino, led to a revival of ancient Neoplatonism. Northern humanism adopted Platonic trappings but remained somewhat detached from the strain of mysticism that Ficino introduced into Italian humanistic thought. In the North, the influence of Florentine Platonism is evident chiefly in love poetry like Spenser's *Amoretti* and related literature, and in allegory like *The Faerie Queene*. Spenser's *Fowre Hymnes*, which are explicitly Neoplatonic, are exceptional rather than typical for the period, although their tone would recur in seventeenth-century England in the writings of the Cambridge Neoplatonists. For the most part, the Plato of the northern humanists of the sixteenth century was the Plato of the *Republic* – that is, the philosopher of temperance, education, and civic responsibility.

If humanism is considered an effort to combine the best values of Christianity and antiquity, it is as old as Christianity. Humanists were fond of citing St Paul's allusions to the classics (Acts 17:28, 1 Cor 15:33) to show that there was nothing radical about their enterprise. They approved – and edited and translated – writers like Jerome, Chrysostom, and Augustine, with the emphasis in England on the latter two. These writers were still in contact with the full range of both the classical and the apostolic heritage. They wrote before what the humanists considered the dark night of the Gothic invasions and the equally dark night of scholasticism. In fact, however, the humanism of the early Fathers continued throughout the Middle Ages (Bolgar 1954). It is evident in the writing of Cassiodorus, Rabanus Maurus, Bernard Sylvestris, and Richard of Bury, among others. It was temporarily eclipsed in the thirteenth century by the scholasticism of the universities, but there is a sense in which fourteenth-century humanism is the revival of a dominant medieval tradition rather than the revolutionary movement that the humanists themselves and their nineteenth-century admirers made it out to be. From this perspective, the hostility of Renaissance humanists to the Middle Ages can be understood as hostility primarily to such entrenched defenders of the scholastic tradition as the Dominican order and the faculties of the northern universities. This interpretation is fully confirmed by studies of literary quarrels among the early Italian humanists and their Dominican adversaries (Greenfield 1981); for most of the fourteenth through sixteenth centuries, humanism did not so much supplant scholasticism as coexist with it.

The prototypical humanist is Petrarch, whose influence shaped Italian humanism and, through it, all later varieties of the movement. He was a scholar, a searcher-out of manuscripts of lost pagan works, an ardent admirer of Cicero and Virgil, a moral philosopher, the author of a Latin epic, *Africa*, which imitates the *Aeneid*, a masterful propagandist and letter writer, and the exemplar for the entire Renaissance of the poet of love through his *Canzoniere*. He was also a sincere if imperfect Christian, who confessed his real sins of pride and concupiscence to an imaginary St Augustine in the dialogue entitled *The Secret*. Petrarch's humanism was often fervently patriotic but not nationalistic in the modern sense of the word. He regarded himself as the prophet of an international movement led by a European elite sharing the values of *litterae humaniores*.

For northern Europe and for England in particular, the prototypical humanist is Erasmus. He was overtly international in outlook and considered the intensifying nationalism of his age a chief cause of war and human suffering. Since this nationalism would, in the wake of the Reformation, become the basis of the network of alliances and hostilities that resulted in the modern European nation-state, and with it the wars that have been endemic in Europe from the Thirty Years' War to World War II, his concerns were valid.

Erasmus was more interested than Petrarch in education, and many of his works have an explicitly pedagogic function. He was an admirer of Cicero but not a fanatic, and he advocated eclectic imitation of the ancients rather than slavish copying (see *Ciceronianism). As a scholar, he edited the works of Jerome (his favorite Christian author) and of other early Fathers. His greatest contribution in this area was his Greek edition, with Latin translation, of the New Testament. He believed that this translation would restore the values of early Christianity to an age sorely lacking in them, in part because of centuries of dependence on Jerome's Latin (Vulgate) translation; and he felt that vernacular translations to be made from his Latin would spread Christianity among the common people.

Ironically, instead of aiding the cause of Christian unity, Erasmus' translation played a central role in the Reformation. Because it challenged many readings of Jerome's Vulgate, on which medieval theology had rested, it was welcomed by Luther and other reformers but aroused the hostility of Catholic conservatives. Although Erasmus refused to follow Luther, his fellow Catholics continued to regard him with suspicion. In fact, he had attacked medieval Catholicism in a devastating satire, *The Praise of Folly*, which mercilessly ridicules all kinds of ignorance, especially the pretentious ignorance of the scholastics. It is no accident that Folly comes onto the stage of the book dressed in the robes of a medieval professor. The work is filled with the aggressive humility and ironic skepticism which Erasmus found in the comments of Socrates in Plato's dialogues. This satirical humanism, which recurs in the writings of Montaigne and Swift, has affinities with Spenser's *Mother Hubberds Tale* and other similar, late sixteenth-century works, but it is not prominent in the writings of sixteenth-century English humanists.

The friendship of Erasmus with John Colet, founder of St Paul's School, helped to shape the course of English education throughout the sixteenth century; and his friendship with Sir Thomas More, commemorated in the Latin title *Moriae Encomium* (*Praise of Folly* or *Praise of More*), encouraged More to write his masterpiece, *Utopia*. In spite – or because – of these achievements, Erasmus died an embittered man attacked by Catholics for having given ammunition to Protestants through his translation of the New Testament, and rejected by radical reformers on the continent for having led the way to the truth and then having refused to follow it. His major legacy to theology may be the ideal of compromise reflected in what was later called the *via media* of the Church of England.

The influence of Erasmus in England can be traced in the work of Thomas Elyot, John Cheke, Roger Ascham, Thomas Cranmer, Richard Mulcaster, Hooker, and a host of other humanistic writers. The internationalism of Erasmus, however, was generally ignored by his English followers. The idea of a community of intellectuals transcending national boundaries was a victim of the Reformation, if it had ever been viable in the first place. England was under siege from Catholic Spain during the latter third of the sixteenth century, and the resulting tensions discouraged the sort of idealism exhibited by Erasmus.

English humanists were for the most part intensely patriotic. They were committed to elevating their culture through education and imitation of authors, especially the ancients, much as the Italians had tried to do in the fifteenth century. When they turned to political issues, they were staunch and frequently strident nationalists, a point amply illustrated by the anti-Catholic satire of *FQ* I and by the *Vewe of Ireland*, which attacks the Irish rebels with a vehemence reminiscent of Luther's vitriolic blast against the German Anabaptists, who were also attacked by Spenser in *FQ* I. In addition, the tensions of the Reformation and Counter-Reformation led many of the later humanists to a violent religious intolerance which is the opposite of the ideal of religious accommodation espoused by some earlier humanists (Olin 1965). This position is characteristic of English Protestants, including those who gave lip-service to the ideals of Erasmus; and it is clearly evident in both the 'moral eclogues' of *The Shepheardes Calender* and the anti-Catholic sections of *The Faerie Queene* (see *Church of Rome).

For Spenser, the most important aspect of Erasmian influence was probably in the field of education, specifically, the curriculum and pedagogical methods of Merchant Taylors' School, which he attended. The curriculum of English grammar schools of the sixteenth century is well known (T.W. Baldwin 1944). It emphasized the Latin language and the reading of classical Latin (and later, Greek) literature, combined with exercises in rhetoric based on imitation of Cicero in prose and Virgil in verse. Mythology was taught chiefly from Ovid, conversational Latin and dramaturgy from Terence, and moral philosophy and history from a mélange of excerpts and wise sayings (*sententiae*) of the ancients – often indebted to the *Adagia* (*Adages*) of Erasmus – and excerpts from Caesar, Livy, and other ancient historians. Spenser's studies at Cambridge introduced him to more advanced topics, including a good deal of residual Aristotelianism of the sort that Milton was still dealing with in his *Prolusions* in the 1620s. Religion was a central interest at Cambridge, and it is almost certain that he owed much of his knowledge of Reformation – and especially Calvinist – theology to the Cambridge years. He would also have deepened his knowledge of classical authors and contemporary developments in Italian and French literature.

Although poetry was far from the center of interest of the Cambridge curriculum, Spenser's friendship with Harvey and his own personal interests encouraged him to begin thinking seriously about artistic questions. Their letters touch on the place of poetry in society, the need to elevate English culture by introducing poetic forms equivalent to those which ennobled Greek and Roman society, and the corollary need for an English system of versification as expressive as the quantitative prosodic system of the ancients. The letters show further that before Spenser emerged as a major poetic talent he had experimented with drama and had written several poems which are either preludes to, or parts of, his major works.

The Shepheardes Calender reflects humanistic interests in several ways. Its format is that of a humanist edition of a classical author, with its text supplemented by the learned introduction and scholarly apparatus of the unidentified E.K. In content it is partly an imitation of Virgil's *Eclogues*, supplemented by imitations of Mantuan and other Renaissance cultivators of pastoral. It is filled with experiments in prosody designed to expand the range of English versification. It attempts to define a specifically

English poetic tradition beginning with Chaucer, and to establish a sense of national identity and national achievement through a definitive work of art based on that tradition. In *Complaints*, Spenser pays homage to Virgil and Petrarch by translation; in *Amoretti*, he expresses his indebtedness more deeply by creating the most nearly Petrarchan sonnet cycle of the English Renaissance.

The Faerie Queene is the major poem of sixteenth-century English humanism (its counterpart in prose being Sidney's *Arcadia*). It objectifies the humanistic tradition in its generalized bid to become the definitive English epic, its philosophical seriousness, its effort to teach by creating examples of moral virtue, its generally secular emphasis, its rhetorical inventiveness, and its idealized patriotism. The Letter to Raleigh, which is intended to explain the method of *The Faerie Queene*, is a curious mixture of medieval and humanistic attitudes. Its claim that the poem is 'a continued Allegory, or darke conceit' would have been understood perfectly by Dante. Yet the object of the poem is instruction in the secular virtues: 'to fashion a gentleman or noble person in vertuous and gentle discipline.' In proper humanist fashion, Spenser chooses a figure from legendary history – 'Arthure, before he was king' – and notes that the precedents for such a choice are not only Homer and Virgil but also Ariosto and Tasso. Arthur will represent 'magnificence' understood as the sum of the individual virtues represented by each of the protagonists of the individual books, 'the twelve private morall vertues, as Aristotle hath devised.' While the humanism of this description is obvious, no one has been able to identify satisfactorily the source in Aristotle that Spenser has in mind. Aristotle makes no reference, for example, to holiness, which is a Christian, not a pagan, virtue. Spenser is probably drawing on a commentary on the *Nicomachean Ethics* rather than on Aristotle's text. Holiness, in particular, seems to have little to do with the *Ethics*.

In several ways, *The Faerie Queene* departs from the typical attitudes of northern humanism. Northern humanists generally accepted allegorical explanations of ancient myth, but they favored moral and natural, rather than mystical, interpretation. Spenser is more complex. The religious allegory of Book I is pietistic and Protestant and, as such, well within the range of religious interests transmitted by Erasmus to English humanism. However, its hard edge of religious intolerance comes from Puritan England, most probably from Cambridge, rather than from Erasmian humanism. Its technique also draws heavily on such medieval traditions as psychomachia, typology, multivalent signification, and the complexly folded time of dream-allegory. Dream-allegory is associated in the Middle Ages with love poetry (Lewis 1936), and this type of allegory is prominent in *FQ* III and IV.

In addition to drawing on medieval allegorical traditions, Spenser imitates – even extensively adapts – plot material found in Ariosto's *Orlando furioso* and Tasso's *Gerusalemme liberata*. His treatment of erotic love has an Italianate flavor most obvious in the sensuous style of the Bower of Bliss episode in *FQ* II xii. Elsewhere, the sensuousness has echoes of the medieval eroticism typified by the *Romance of the Rose*. Whether medieval or Renaissance-inspired, however, it is quite different from the sober, rather pedestrian view of the relations between the sexes found in humanistic marriage manuals.

In the same way, Spenser's Platonism is closer to the fervent, quasi-mystical Platonism of the Italians than to the didactic and ethical Platonism of northern humanists. Finally, his *Cantos of Mutabilitie*, which have traditionally been considered fragments of an incomplete book of *The Faerie Queene*, are reminiscent of the twelfth-century naturalism of Alanus de Insulis. Mutability was a common theme in English Renaissance literature, but when set against other poems on the theme (eg, Shakespeare's many sonnets on time and decay), Spenser's *Cantos* seem intentionally anachronistic.

Books II, V, and VI of *The Faerie Queene* are the most obviously humanistic. The second book is modeled on the quests of Odysseus and Aeneas, as well as those of the heroes of Italian romance, and based on the Aristotelian definition of virtue as a mean between two extremes. Book V treats a favorite humanistic theme: the need for order in society, and the role of law, including the harsh punishments meted out by the law, in maintaining this order. Book VI treats the humanizing effect of the social amenities on culture. Courtesy transcends the barriers of the social order and saves it from becoming an inhuman construct maintained by force. In this sense, Book VI is a humanistic critique of Plato's *Republic* based on recognition that a common humanity unites all members of the social order. The fact that the Blatant Beast, the enemy of all of the values symbolized by courtesy, escapes at the end of the book is an ironic expression of the idea of original sin which would have been much enjoyed by the author of *The Praise of Folly*: even the effort to compensate for the imperfections of original sin is frustrated by original sin.

Is Spenser, finally, a humanist? The answer clearly depends on which works are being considered and from what point of view. Humanistic themes and strategies are present in all his major works, and these works are unimaginable without the influence of humanism; but when compared to Erasmus or Montaigne or Ascham, Spenser seems more medieval, more flamboyant, more Platonic (or Neoplatonic) than the typical humanists of his age. In short, he seems more a poet than a rhetorician, and at least as much an artist as educator and social reformer. O.B. HARDISON, JR

D.C. Allen 1970; T.W. Baldwin 1944; Hans Baron 1955 *The Crisis of the Early Italian Renaissance* 2 vols (Princeton); Boccaccio ed 1930; Bolgar 1954; Alan Bullock 1985 *The Humanist Tradition in the West* (London); Burckhardt ed 1945; Bush 1939; Donald Lemen Clark 1922 *Rhetoric and Poetry in the Renaissance* (New York); Clark 1948; DeMolen 1978; W.K. Ferguson 1948; Greenfield 1981; Kristeller 1943; Kristeller 1955; Kristeller 1964; Kristeller, et al 1948 (includes Pico's *Oration on the Dignity of Man*); Lewis 1936; McConica 1965; Olin 1965; John Herman Randall, Jr 1961 *The School of Padua and the Emergence of Modern Science* (Padua); George Sarton 1927–48 *Introduction to the History of Science* 3 vols (Washington, D.C.); Seigel 1968; Charles Trinkaus 1970; Trinkaus 1979 *The Poet as Philosopher: Petrarch and the Formation of Renaissance Consciousness* (New Haven); Trinkaus 1983 *The Scope of Renaissance Humanism* (Ann Arbor); Georg Voigt 1893 *Die Wiederbelebung des classischen Alterthums* 2 vols (Berlin); Weiss 1941; William Harrison Woodward 1897 *Vittorino da Feltre and Other Humanist Educators* (Cambridge).

hunt A traditional motif prominent in Spenser's poetry, beginning with *Theatre for Worldlings*, in which two 'egre Dogs' pursue and kill a beautiful hind, symbolic of the brevity of human life. To this allegorical vision (based on Petrarch and Marot) may be added a long array of literal and figurative uses of the hunt in *The Faerie Queene*, ranging from hackneyed metaphors to complex mythological images, which evoke or embody major thematic concerns and comment obliquely on minor scenes and issues.

In contrast to medieval poets, who often take a keen interest in the technical aspects of the hunt, Spenser does not describe actual procedures in detail. He does, however, employ such terms as *bring to bay*, *flush*, and *quarry*; and the hunt is a narrative device of striking visual and dramatic force in *The Faerie Queene*. At intervals, characters burst on to the scene, one pursuing the other; sometimes the effect is enhanced by an onlooker joining the chase, not necessarily aware of the identity of the participants (eg, III i 15–18, vii 37–8; IV vii 24–5, viii 38–41; VI iii 46–51). On occasion, such pursuits refer explicitly to prisoner's base, a children's game in which two teams take turns pursuing each other (III xi 5, V viii 5, VI iv 8; see *games). A subcategory of this kind of pursuit is the use of famous flights and pursuits from Ovid's *Metamorphoses* (eg, III vii 26 and IV vii 22, where the predicaments of Myrrha and Daphne are applied to Florimell and Amoret). A conflation of Ovid's accounts of Daphne and Arethusa seems to underlie II ii 7–9, where a hunting nymph is observed by Faunus, who is aroused to engage in 'beauties chace' and pursues her only to see her transformed into a well. Thus one kind of hunt results in another, which in its turn anticipates a major theme of *FQ* III and IV.

The thematic basis of the hunt in *The Faerie Queene* is the *discordia concors* of Diana and Venus. The struggle of these two deities forms the subject of many medieval débat poems; in Spenser it is acted out by their protégés (with the exception of III vi 16–28, where Venus herself comes to look for the fugitive Cupid among Diana's nymphs). Traditionally, Diana is the champion of the 'hard hunt' of boars, symbolic of virtue and honor, while Venus prefers the 'soft hunt' of rabbits and hares which do not expose the hunter to danger (cf *Met* 10.543–52, where Venus advises Adonis against chasing boars, a warning repeated in *FQ* III i 37). The more prestigious stag hunt is the province of both Venus and Diana. In medieval and Renaissance poetry, it is often synonymous with the love chase, associated with the Actaeon myth by Petrarch in *Canzoniere* 23.147–60. In this kind of hunt, the hunter (identified with the lover as early as Plato *Sophist* 222D) often becomes the hunted. Such is the fate of the speaker-huntsman of *Amoretti* 67 whose 'gentle deare' surrenders in a way that implies that the lover is the real quarry.

The antithetical ideals of Diana and Venus suggest the basic meanings of the hunt in *The Faerie Queene*. Arthur and Guyon set out 'To hunt for glorie and renowmed praise,' thus opting for the hard hunt (III i 3; cf I iv I, V iv 29). Yet they are quickly diverted to 'beauties chace,' an activity later qualified as 'chace of beautie excellent' (III i 19, iv 45). At the extreme of this latter pursuit is the wanton Faunus, who is identified with Actaeon (II ii 7–9, VII vi 42–53); the poem's heroes are frequently so tempted: thus Calidore, temporarily deflected from his quest by his love for Pastorella, becomes a hunter in the woods and Pastorella his 'game' (VI x 2).

Another version of the motif of the sensual hunt is presented by Venus and Adonis, whose liaison is the subject of the tapestry at Castle Joyous (III i 34–8). Spenser's Adonis, like Shakespeare's, is a reluctant lover, enjoyed in secret by Venus but 'bent ... To hunt the salvage beast in forrest wyde' (37), that is, longing for the hard hunt. Adonis plays a symbolic role in the poem: while his passivity as a lover recalls that of the languorous Verdant seduced by Acrasia (II xii 72), his fatal wound anticipates the sexual wounds inflicted on some of the characters of *FQ* III (notably Marinell at iv 16 and Timias at v 20–6; cf also i 65, vi 48, and V v 9).

In a more complex way, Adonis also recalls Hippolytus, the hunter of 'the foming Bore' who is associated with the hard hunt and whose very refusal of his stepmother's invitation to the soft hunt leads to his destruction (I v 36–8).

As one turns from mythological exempla to the main actors of *The Faerie Queene*, the hunt takes on yet wider meanings. At II i 4, Archimago's designs on Guyon are those of a crafty hunter; his 'stales,' 'snares,' and 'bait' hint at his affinity with other guileful protagonists such as Malengin and Radigund (and at the rhetorical and iconographic tradition in which hunting gear is the basis of metaphors of guile and deception; cf Inganno in Ripa *Iconologia*). But the hunt is also important to the making of a perfect gentleman. Thus Tristram begins his career in the woods, realizing that his 'unryper yeares ... unfit / For thing of weight' make the 'salvage chace' a natural occupation (VI ii 9). In passages such as these, the hunt often suggests the overcoming of brutish instincts, as when Satyrane masters the wild beasts of his wood at I vi 24–6, indicating that a 'natural' man too may possess restraint. Similarly, Belphoebe, described as a huntress with a boar spear at II iii 29, exemplifies the pursuit of honor and virtue. The most obvious instance of this wider meaning of the hunt is Calidore's quest for the Blatant Beast, consistently referred to as a chase taking him through forests, cities, courts, and monasteries (see, eg, VI ix 2–4, xii 24–5). It also appears in 'Astrophel' 79–120, where Sidney's participation in the wars is evoked in terms reminiscent of Adonis fighting the boar.

LARS-HÅKAN SVENSSON

Despite the pervasiveness of the hunt theme in Renaissance literature, relatively little has been written on it. For a slightly earlier period (though ending with Tudor lyrics), see Marcelle Thiébaux 1974 *The Stag of Love: The Chase in Medieval Literature* (Ithaca, NY). Michael J.B. Allen 1968 'The Chase: The Development of a Renaissance Theme' *CL* 20:301–12 touches on Spenser. Valuable background information on the hunt is provided by D.C. Allen 1968:42–57, 165–86; see also [George Turbervile?] 1575 *The Noble Arte of Venerie or Hunting* (London; *STC* 24328).

Hunt, Leigh (1784–1859) Proud to brand himself a 'Spenser-ophilist' (ed 1862, 2:264) James Henry Leigh Hunt was important in shaping Spenser's reputation during the early nineteenth century. Although now considered less notable than the major Romantics, he exerted considerable influence in his own day as a political journalist, theater reporter, literary critic, editor, occasional essayist, novelist, playwright, and poet. A versatile and well-known man of letters, he was most significant for nurturing the young second-generation Romantics – Keats, Shelley, and to a lesser extent Byron. He was also Spenser's most vocal champion in the early nineteenth century, and his enthusiastic criticism helped awaken the younger poets to Spenser's imaginative and sensuous capacities. His critical and poetic revisions of Spenser also help us to understand how the younger Romantics used Spenser to dramatize their own conflicts of visionary and realistic perception. These distinct effects of Hunt's Spenserian activity developed from his lifelong habit of investing Spenser with his own most troubling aesthetic division – a split allegiance to realistic and escapist art.

Although Hunt read Spenser in an 'odd volume' at school (ed 1949:77), his earliest idea of Spenser's art came from Thomson's eighteenth-century imitation, *The Castle of Indolence*. Its second canto of insistent didacticism particularly appealed to his youthful interest in moralistic art. Thus inspired, he composed two adolescent poems in Spenserian stanzas – a lost effusion at twelve called 'Fairy King,' and a more substantial work at sixteen, *The Palace of Pleasure*, which headed his first publication (*Juvenilia* 1801). This later poem closely follows *The Castle of Indolence*, quoted on the opening page, in its title, narrative structure, and sermonizing account of vice's false allure. Despite such links, Hunt claimed Spenser as his model and thereby transformed Spenser's more subtle allegory into his own concept of stark moralism.

Several years later, Hunt refashioned Spenser in a new projection of his shifted emphasis on poetic enchantment. This response followed his distressing incarceration for political libel (1813–15), during which he sought refuge in the descriptive and lyrical bounty of remote, imaginary landscapes, whose dreamy charm anesthetizes pain. Such effects became Hunt's ideal of poetic function, outlined specifically in the preface to his 1832 volume of collected poems, and he devoted much of his career to identifying representative examples throughout literary history. From his prison cell, the lush sounds and images of Spenser's fairy gardens beckoned strongly. He subsequently read Spenser anew in Todd's 1805 variorum edition (Hunt's annotated copy, now at the Victoria and Albert Museum Library, is hereafter cited as Todd) and remade Spenser the moralist into Spenser the enchanter. He thus made several lists in Todd of Spenser's 'Beautiful sequestered scenes' and penned this 1814 annotation of *The Faerie Queene*: 'Finished reluctantly, and with gratitude for many hours which it has almost abstracted from disease, my second regular reading of this divine poem.'

Hunt's own verse rapidly incorporated this new Spenser as a dominant model. His 1815 sonnet 'The Poets' favors the rich style and imaginative subjects of Spenserian enchantment. Similarly, his 'Epistle to Charles Lamb' (1816) applauds Spenser's balmy remoteness, which 'wraps you, wherever you are, / In a bow'r of seclusion beneath a sweet star' (ed 1923:31–2). *The Story of Rimini*, begun in prison, features hidden bowers whose delicious portraiture and music recall Spenser's Bower of Bliss. Similar retreats, their distance enhanced by a new mythological aura borrowed from Spenser, fill *The Nymphs* (1818).

Hunt popularized this view of Spenser throughout his prolific critical works, presenting it most forcefully in two extensive 1833 studies of Spenser: 'A New Gallery of Pictures: Spenser' and 'Spenser Recommended' (ed 1956:420–56). Both essays dismiss intellectual substance in favor of the dream-inducing music and portraiture of Spenser's remoter haunts. This preference leaves Hunt arguing the irrelevance of allegorical design and narrative continuity in Spenser. 'A New Gallery' dallies instead with isolated scenes of pictorial charm in *The Faerie Queene*. 'Spenser Recommended' champions the bewitching sounds of Spenser's language, which has the quality of 'a fine, lazy, luxurious, far-off majestic dream' (ed 1956:447). Both essays find that such effects make Spenser the most delightfully removed of all poets from the shocks of reality, especially in those passages – also heavily marked in Todd – on which Hunt dwells most rapturously: the garden of *Muiopotmos*; Cupid's appearance in *SC, March*; the masque of Cupid, the descriptions of

Una, and the vision on Mount Acidale in *The Faerie Queene*; and foremost of all the Bower of Bliss.

This exclusive love of Spenserian intoxication both characterized and helped develop the most prominent feature of Spenserian criticism among the second-generation Romantics. Though Wordsworth and Coleridge liked Spenser's dreaminess, they also stressed his moral truths; but Hazlitt, in an 1818 claim seconded by Keats, Reynolds, and most of the young poets clustered around Hunt, urged readers to imbibe Spenser's luxury by not 'meddling' with his allegory (ed 1930–4, 15:38). Hunt's direct role in shaping this response can be traced in Keats's early sonnet 'Written on the Day that Mr. Leigh Hunt Left Prison,' which commends Hunt for straying in 'Spenser's halls ... and bowers fair, / Culling enchanted flowers' (9–10). More generally, the bias in Hunt's criticism toward brief, colorful scenes helped enhance Spenser's popularity among England's early nineteenth-century reading public.

As early as Hunt's incarceration, however, a latent compulsion toward realism made him leery of Spenser's enchantment. As his doubts about escapism increased, his attitude toward Spenser grew increasingly reflective of his own divisions between fancy and realism. Thus while still in prison he warned against the 'tramels' of Spenser's ornate style (*The Feast of the Poets* 1814:69). Later, he avoided composition in the Spenserian stanza and, as a rule, shunned lengthy discussion of the Bower of Bliss for fear of being entrapped by its luxuries. As Hunt's division between escapist and realistic art intensified, this ambivalence toward his former idol grew more pronounced. In 1833, for instance, he published his approving studies of Spenserian enchantment; yet only a year before, sensitive to reviewers' caution against escapism, he had excluded 'The Poets' from his collected poems. Such conflicts of response became critical in 1844 when he issued two essays on Spenser, both of which make contradictory claims for Spenser as realist and enchanter: the Spenser chapter of *Imagination and Fancy* (pp 49–96) and 'A Jar of Honey from Mount Hybla' (*Ainsworth's Magazine* 5:536–43 to 6:79–86 in 12 parts; rpt London 1848).

These essays project the conflict of realism and escapism onto a Spenser who begins to seem blameworthy of Hunt's own fanciful excesses. The preface of *Imagination and Fancy* outlines a new poetic ideal of psychological realism, termed 'Imagination,' which is held above enchantment, labeled 'Fancy.' Yet this preface dwells, perhaps too zealously, on examples of 'Fancy' in manifestation of Hunt's lingering attachment to the art he wishes to subordinate. A similar conflict emerges in his treatment of Spenser. The preface, citing Una's lament over Redcrosse's desertion, compares Spenser's pathos favorably with Shakespeare's (p 39). This new emphasis then receives broader treatment in the Spenser chapter, which discusses mental truth in the Despair, Mammon, and Malbecco episodes. The same chapter, however, returns more fully to Hunt's unqualified love of Spenserian transport. Paeons thus abound to the 'excess of ... luxury' in Spenser's descriptions, the 'perpetual honey' of his versification, and the general 'remoteness' of his art. A special section is devoted to Spenserian portraits, like the bathing nymphs of Acrasia's bower, that receive high praise for their intoxicating beauty. Such contradictory Spensers – remote and realistic – embody Hunt's own divided impulses; and his more sanguine presentation of the dreamy Spenser implies his persisting bondage to enchantment. The difficulty of rejecting it moved him, in the same year, to another projection that made Spenser guilty of his own excesses.

'A Jar of Honey' thus finds Spenser mistakenly allowing fantasy to subvert realism. It specifically attacks the false archaisms and rude diction of *The Shepheardes Calender*, which seem unrealistic given the intelligence of the speakers; and its unusually mean language (the 'needless perversity' and 'rudest crab-apple' of Spenser's diction are condemned; 5:540, 6:80) suggests the uneasy projection of Hunt's own sense of excess. This projection is quite obvious in his interpretation of Colin Clout's broken pipe (*FQ* VI x 18), which he sees representing Spenser's petulance against Sidney's injunction to quit pastoral for epic. Such a reading makes Spenser guilty of Hunt's unwillingness to reject enchantment. It further implies that he is at fault for giving Hunt a luscious pipe that must be repudiated upon the demand of Hunt's own critics – and yet, Hunt has no epic harp like Spenser's to take up instead. Hence the edge to his language, his transformation of Spenser's muse into beguiling siren, and a temporary distancing of himself from Spenser. Though Hunt never rejected him absolutely, he did markedly limit references to him in his writings of the next decade. He excluded Spenserian works like 'The Poets' and *The Nymphs* from his 1844 volume of collected poems, and he gave dramatic writing in a realistic vein new priority. His withdrawal persisted until the late 1850s when he formulated his last and most complex idea of Spenser.

This conception integrated Hunt's divided aesthetics by making a model of Spenser as both enchanter *and* political poet who confronts worldly suffering in his art. Two developments inspired the breakthrough: a new urgency for aesthetic pleasure and relief balanced with a fresh conviction that Spenser's art expresses a painful struggle against temporal authority. The deaths of Hunt's favorite son (1852) and his own wife (1857), reminding him of the distress he experienced in prison, brought him back to the consolation of Spenser but also made him keenly aware of the political duress he shared with a grief-stricken Spenser. The new identification was provoked by two lectures (1856–7) in which Cardinal Wiseman, England's Catholic primate, condemned Spenser's sensuous style. Hunt saw an insidious political attack in this judgment, directed against Spenser's anti-papal Protestantism in a new display of the political oppression under which Spenser had labored. He thus noted in Todd how Spenser had written against popery's 'scandal on religion' and had thereby incurred the wrath of 'corrupted readers' from his own time to Wiseman's. Freshly reminded of his own political sufferings, Hunt felt moved to refute Wiseman in an essay that defends Spenser's luxury while sympathizing with his fight against intolerance (Hunt 1859).

This essay shapes the distinct image of a Spenser who, as combined enchanter and realist, speaks powerfully to Hunt's own condition. It specifically endorses Spenser's remoteness as balm against the personal griefs his allegories render; and in a concurrent annotation of George Craik's 1845 edition of Spenser (*Spenser and His Poetry* 3 vols; Hunt's annotated copy of this edition, now in the Brewer-Hunt collection of the University of Iowa Libraries, is hereafter cited as Craik), Hunt links this suffering with his own political miseries. He thus writes 'Ah memory' beside a Spenserian line on sorrow (*FQ* IV x 28) that he once underscored in prison. Such an identification with the Spenser of enchantment and suffering left Hunt appreciating a new poignance in Spenserian art. It also helped reconcile his own aesthetic conflicts of realism and fantasy in a balance projected onto Spenser as the supreme poet of joy and sorrow.

This view informs Hunt's lively return to Spenser in his last years. Reading Craik in 1857, he consistently marked the editor's references to Burghley's designs against Spenser. He similarly distinguished numerous allegories of personal suffering, such as Thenot's acceptance of pain ('But gently tooke, that ungently came' *SC, Feb* 22) and the Care sequence in *The Faerie Queene*. Yet he also noted his old easeful favorites, such as the Bower of Bliss and the masque of Cupid. The next year found him rereading *The Faerie Queene* in Todd for the old relief he characterized with this new annotation: 'my third regular reading of the divine poem ... I seem to possess it like a property, to which I have recourse whenever I wish to shut myself away ... from care and sorrow.' Such enchantment now seemed wedded, however, to the political Spenser's suffering, which Hunt emphasized by updating his earlier annotations of Todd. He thus crossed out several commendations of Spenserian romance, revalued *Complaints* with a fresh set of sympathetic notes, and criticized Todd's minimizing of Spenser's hardships. Holding this emphasis on suffering in balance with Spenserian enchantment, he stressed above all the profundity of what he termed Spenser's 'grave and gay' outlook. This blend struck him most forcefully in the dirge of Sidney's sister, the Countess of Pembroke, whose description he vigorously marked in both Craik and Todd: 'Sorrowing tempered with deare delight' (*Time* 319). Her music of joy and sorrow figures prominently in Hunt's last tribute to Spenser, *The Shewe of Faire Seeming* (1858).

His first poem since boyhood in Spenser's stanza, *Shewe* projects Hunt's final aesthetic balance of realism and enchantment onto a

Spenserian context; it also catalogues his lifelong response to Spenser. Its treatment of vice's false allure recalls the naive moral allegory of his own *Palace of Pleasure* – allegorical masquers first attract and then repel when they turn their foul posteriors. Hunt alters his eighteenth-century design, however, with a new severity in the anguish of the masquers. The change suggests his own progression beyond simple moral allegory to more complex evocations of grief. He also exposes vice successively, instead of blasting the charade at the work's conclusion as he did in the eighteenth-century manner of his earlier poem. This gradual and increasingly final rejection of tempting façades points to the major shift in Hunt's response to Spenser. The poem concludes, however, not in disdain of luxury but rather in a union of enchantment and pain figured by Sidney's sister. Seated amid a 'bowery nook,' she radiates lustrous beauty and chants a sweet lyric; but the sweetness of her song is 'grief-taught,' and her face interchanges grave and gay looks. Her bittersweetness represents Hunt's ultimate aesthetic balance, and its appropriation from *Time* encapsulates the way he finally received Spenser to help express his own 'Sorrowing tempered with deare delight.'

Hunt's overall reaction to Spenser is significant in several ways. It affected the second-generation Romantics most directly in shaping their love of Spenser's imaginative and sensuous beauties. Its complex formulation of the real/ideal Spenser influenced the younger Romantics even more subtly and helps explain to us their typical appropriations of Spenser. Keats, for instance, in *The Eve of St Agnes* uses Spenserian contrasts to dramatize his own conflicts between visionary and realistic perception. Hunt's response, in its popularization of Spenserian enchantment, also suggests one cause of Spenser's increasing appeal throughout the early nineteenth century. Yet this same recognition of his charm led to a relative decline in his popularity among Victorian readers, like Macaulay, who saw a trivial Spenser in Hunt's rhapsodic praise and vowed resistance. GREG KUCICH

Francis Willard Emerson 1958 'The Spenser-Followers in Leigh Hunt's Chaucer' *N&Q* 203:284–6; James Henry Leigh Hunt 1859 'English Poetry versus Cardinal Wiseman' *Fraser's* 60:747–66; Hunt 1862 *Correspondence* ed Thornton Hunt, 2 vols (London); Hunt 1923 *Poetical Works* ed H.S. Milford (London); Hunt 1949 *Autobiography* ed J.E. Morpurgo (London); Hunt 1956 *Leigh Hunt's Literary Criticism* ed Lawrence Huston Houtchens and Carolyn Washburn Houtchens (New York); Greg Kucich 1988 'Leigh Hunt and Romantic Spenserianism' *KSJ* 37:110–35.

Hurd, Richard (1720–1808) Educated at Cambridge, Bishop Hurd pursued careers in both letters and the church. The third of his *Dialogues Moral and Political* (1759) and the twelve *Letters on Chivalry and Romance* (1762; rev with substantial additions 1765; 5 further eds before 1800) developed the first fully historical reading of *The Faerie Queene*. His work may be seen as culminating just over a decade of renewed interest in Spenser, beginning in 1751 with Upton's *Letter concerning a New Edition of Spenser's 'Faerie Queene'*, and including Birch's edition (1751), Warton's *Observations on the Fairy Queen of Spenser* (1754), a series of notes and letters in *The Gentleman's Magazine* (vols 25 and 28, 1755 and 1758), and the editions of Church (1758–9) and Upton (1758).

Hurd went beyond the cliché that an author should be judged in relation to his era and presented detailed information on feudalism and chivalry, derived from the French medievalist La Curne de Sainte-Palaye. He believed that medieval romance faithfully depicted chivalry, albeit with some distortion or metaphor, for example, presenting tyrannical lords as giants. Since conditions in ancient Greece resembled feudalism, Homer's 'heroic' epics are not opposed to 'gothic' romances but resemble them in many points: enthusiasm for military affairs, games, and adventures; the distractions of alluring women; tolerance for robbery, piracy, and bastardy; refined hospitality and courtesy; encounters with savages, giants, and monsters. Hurd even claims that gothic manners, polity, and religion are better suited than classical to the highest poetic purposes, namely to move feeling and stimulate imagination.

In Letter 8, Hurd outlines for *The Faerie Queene* 'the idea, not of a classical but *Gothic* composition.' Spenser's plan reflects a real chivalric custom: a feast where knights are assigned adventures. Lacking the unity of a single action, the poem yet has 'unity of *design*,' for all the stories have the same origin and end. Spenser interweaves stories from book to book and follows classical precedent by introducing a central hero, Prince Arthur. To reinforce these structural unifying devices, he adds an allegorical moral: the hero of each book exemplifies a single virtue, while Arthur encompasses them all. These shifts to strengthen unity, however, merely show the 'violence of classic prejudices.' By contradicting the gothic form, they produce a confused mixture. For Hurd, 'the more sublime and creative poetry' rests on 'poetic truth,' which readily admits marvels presented with 'consistent imagination' and based on popular belief (Letter 10). Chivalry fell into disfavor because the early romances were badly written. By Spenser's time, chivalric customs had all but disappeared, persisting only in the form of royal entertainments. Spenser had to pretend that his pictures of antique manners allegorically concealed profound wisdom. But reason and ignorance of history soon drove out romance: 'Henceforth, the taste of wit and poetry took a new turn: And fancy, that had wantoned it so long in the world of fiction, was now constrained, against her will, to ally herself with strict truth, if she would gain admittance into reasonable company. What we have gotten by this revolution, you will say, is a great deal of good sense. What we have lost, is a world of fine fabling' (Letter 12).

Here and in the *Dialogues*, Hurd comes close to recognizing explicitly that precisely because they pictured only vanished customs, chivalric images and romance forms could be used by Elizabeth and her supporters to legitimize her reign by connecting it symbolically to native tradition. Always a neoclassical rationalist, he became convinced that the feebleness of mid-eighteenth-century poetry demanded renewed stress on feeling and imagination, precisely the qualities attributed in his era to Elizabethan literature. DONALD G. MARSHALL

Richard Hurd 1811 *Works* 8 vols (London; rpt New York 1967) is the standard ed; the *Dialogues* are in vols 3–4 and the *Letters* in vol 4. The *Letters* of 1762 have been edited by Edith J. Morley (London 1911; includes the third *Dialogue* from the edition of 1788); there are facs rpts in 1963 (Augustan Reprint Society 101–2; Los Angeles) and 1971 (New York), the former with excellent intro by Hoyt Trowbridge. For Hurd on Spenser, see Stephen J. Curry 1965 'The Use of History in Bishop Hurd's Literary Criticism' *TWA* 54:79–91; Johnston 1964:60–74; Donald G. Marshall 1980 'The History of Eighteenth-Century Criticism and Modern Hermeneutical Philosophy: The Example of Richard Hurd' *ECent* 21:198–211; Audley L. Smith 1939 'Richard Hurd's *Letters on Chivalry and Romance*' *ELH* 6:58–81; Hoyt Trowbridge 1943 'Bishop Hurd: A Reinterpretation' *PMLA* 58:450–65. For the broader context, see Lionel Gossman 1968 *Medievalism and the Ideologies of the Enlightenment: The World and Work of La Curne de Sainte-Palaye* (Baltimore) esp pp 153–71, 273–98, 327–48; and Wellek 1941, esp pp 102–4.

Hyacinthus In *Virgils Gnat* 670, the 'purple Hyacinthe' is one of the flowers the shepherd teaches to grow around the gnat's tomb; and in the Garden of Adonis, 'Fresh *Hyacinthus*, *Phoebus* paramoure' is one of the sad lovers transformed into flowers (*FQ* III vi 45). An early model for such elegiac flower collections is Flora's garden in Ovid's *Fasti* (5.223–8), in which Hyacinthus, Narcissus, Crocus, Attis, and Adonis appear as flowers; similar collections appear in Ausonius' *Cupid Crucified* and Politian's *Stanze* 1.79 (Nohrnberg 1976:513–14).

In Ovid's version of the myth (*Metamorphoses* 10.162–219), Hyacinthus, a beautiful Spartan youth, is accidentally killed when a discus thrown by his lover Apollo rebounds from the earth and strikes him. In other versions, the west wind (Zephyrus) or north wind (Boreas) is a jealous lover who blows the discus off course to kill the youth. In the Garden of Adonis, Hyacinthus and the other flowers are sheltered from both '*Phoebus* beams' and '*Aeolus* sharp blast,' in a possible echo of Boccaccio's interpretation (*Genealogia* 4.58) by which the sun and wind are named as the two lovers (although in Boccaccio's version the sun tries to protect the youth and the north wind kills him). Hyacinthus' fate parallels that of Adonis, another mortal fatally loved by a deity and himself lying 'Lapped in flowres' (46): according to the traditional story which Spenser revises here (eg, Ovid *Met* 10.519ff),

Adonis, too, was accidentally killed and turned into a flower.

In the tapestry at the house of Busirane (III xi 37), Hyacinthus appears again, as one of three lovers accidentally killed by Apollo. Here he is transformed idiosyncratically into a 'Paunce' or pansy, not a hyacinth. The change may be expressive of Busirane's emphasis on the casual destructiveness of love: the pansy was known to the Elizabethans as 'love-in-idleness,' and Shakespeare makes it the agent of amorous mishaps in *Midsummer Night's Dream* II i 168. Busirane's tapestry echoes a recurrent paradox in Book 10 of the *Metamorphoses*: the two poet figures, Orpheus and Apollo, unintentionally kill those they love.

CALVIN R. EDWARDS

---

hymn The artistic structuring of Spenser's *Fowre Hymnes* is largely determined by a well-developed classical and Renaissance tradition of literary (ie, nonliturgical) hymns. In ancient Greece, hymns which had a liturgical function in public worship of the gods were lyrical in form, but another important tradition developed in hexameter verse. Although the brief *Orphic Hymns* may originally have had a liturgical function, they came to be read solely for their literary value, and the *Homeric Hymns* seem to have served as literary-religious preludes to epic recitations.

Like its secular equivalent, the ode which originally celebrated a victory at the Olympic or other games, the hymn became one of the basic poetic forms. Some developed into poems of several hundred lines. The Alexandrian poet Callimachus imitates the longer Homeric hymns, preferring the elegiac couplet to the hexameter and expressing an erudite, witty sophistication rather than religious feeling. Classical Latin poets occasionally imitate Greek lyric hymns.

Some hymns, for example, those by Proclus (5th c AD), are distinctly philosophic, usually Stoic or Neoplatonic. Some are written in prose, for example, those by Julian the Apostate; the long discussion of literary hymns by the rhetorician Menander (third century AD) makes no distinction between verse and prose. While his contemporary St Jerome was developing the Christian liturgical hymn, the Christian poet Prudentius continued the literary tradition of the hymn in both hexameters and lyric verse forms, one being over 1000 lines long (*Peristephanon liber* 10).

The classical pagan and Christian literary hymn usually has a three-part structure. Most often, there is an opening invocation and apostrophe. The main body may evoke a traditional story or describe some attribute or implication – moral, philosophic, or scientific – of the divinity invoked. The poem normally concludes with some kind of prayer, entreaty, or farewell. The tone is usually serious and the style elevated, whether rhetorically elaborate as in Callimachus, or more restrained as in Homer.

Renaissance writers imitate the classical literary hymn in all its variations. Particularly important for Spenser are the Neo-Latin poets Marullo (late 15th c) and Vida (16th c). Marullo's *Natural Hymns* imitate the Proclean philosophic hymns while Vida's *Hymns* treat Christian subjects, but both poets use hexameters and lyric verse forms, with hexameters usually reserved for the longest, most formal pieces, for example, Marullo's opening hymn to Jupiter and Vida's initial hymn to God. Subsequent sixteenth-century imitations of the classical literary hymn tend to divide along the lines established by them. Marullo follows Callimachus in his rhetorical embellishment and allusive display of mythological knowledge. Vida's hymns are also rhetorically elaborate but make sparse use of classical allusions. The critical theorist Julius Caesar Scaliger also wrote Christian literary hymns like Vida's, but they are heavily allusive and, after the pattern of Homer, more rhetorically restrained. Scaliger's *Poetics* (which severely criticizes Marullo's hymns) shows the importance of the literary hymn as a genre. In his influential system (reflected in Sidney's *Defence of Poetry*), the hymn is highest in the order of poetic excellence.

Like Spenser after him, Ronsard wrote literary hymns on both pagan/philosophic and Christian topics. Two years before the publication of Spenser's *Fowre Hymnes*, there appeared two long literary hymns by Chapman written in the philosophic tradition of Orphic Neoplatonism (*The Shadow of Night* 1594, with Latin titles for the individual hymns praising Night and Cynthia). Spenser, however, follows Ronsard in exploiting Renaissance developments in treating both pagan/philosophic and Christian subjects.

Aside from other implications, Spenser's pairing of two 'earthly' hymns (also described as 'natural' in a Marullian echo) with two heavenly ones reflects the generic tradition of the Renaissance literary hymn. The first two celebrations of love and beauty reflect his adoption of the Marullian kind of hymn with non-Christian philosophical themes. The third and fourth hymns follow Vida and Scaliger in treating Christian objects of praise.

Stylistically, both pairs are more restrained than those by Callimachus, Vida, and Chapman. The most rhetorically elaborate, *Heavenly Love*, excludes classical allusions as do Vida's hymns. In addition to many traditional conventions of the genre, the first two *Hymnes* are indebted for rhetorical *topoi*, images, and motifs to Proclus' hymn 'To Love,' two Orphic hymns (55, 57), the Homeric 'To Aphrodite,' and especially two Marullian hymns praising Love and Venus (1.3, 2.7). Their fictional frame of the unrequited Petrarchan lover recalls Callimachus and Prudentius. Both the heavenly hymns lack such a well-developed frame, but the poet still intrudes in the first person, and the conclusion of *Heavenly Beautie* applies the lesson of the central praise to the poet himself (295–7). Also conventional is the fiction that the poet's work is being recited by a group, a fiction that Spenser exploits in both earthly hymns (40–2 and 269–73, respectively). His choice of rhyme royal reflects the traditional non-lyric decorum of the heroic hymn with its elevated subject and serious tone. Chapman had chosen pentameter couplets (perhaps influenced by Ronsard, who prefers decasyllabic couplets or alexandrines for his hymns), but Spenser's choice is reflected in Gascoigne's remark that rhyme royal 'is a royal kind of verse, serving best for grave discourses' (*Certayne Notes of Instruction* in ed 1907–10, 1:471, 473).

PHILIP B. ROLLINSON

Philip B. Rollinson 1969 'The Renaissance of the Literary Hymn' *RenP 1968* pp 11–20; Rollinson 1971.

Hypnerotomachia Poliphili Printed in Venice by Aldus Manutius in 1499, *Hypnerotomachia Poliphili* is 'Poliphilus' strife of love in a dream,' a dream-vision highlighting the imagination as powerfully as does *The Faerie Queene*. The work is generally believed to be by Francesco Colonna (1433–1527), although his authorship is disputed. Published with extremely beautiful woodcuts by an unknown artist, it is in a prose made up of Italian, Latin, and Greek, thus belonging to an Hermetic tradition in which a mélange of languages simultaneously hides and expresses mysteries.

Poliphilus, in love with Polia, falls into a dream in which he loses his way in a wood, encounters strange adventures, and meets various allegorical figures through whom he comes to a nymph resembling Polia. Together they witness triumphs, go through love rituals in a temple of Venus, and are taken by Cupid to Cythera, where Polia tells her story after seeing a triumph of Cupid. As Poliphilus offers to embrace her, she vanishes, and he wakes alone on 1 May 1467.

Certain features are familiar from tradition, such as the wood, denoted by a tree catalogue comparable to *FQ* I i 8–9 (see also *gardens). Many others are unexpected, not least that the Dominican author reveals in an acrostic that 'Fra Francesco Colonna desperately loved Polia,' who herself is identifiable as a member of a Treviso family. Colonna also desperately loved art, particularly that of antiquity, and the *Hypnerotomachia* is full of rhapsodic descriptions of triumphs and works of art, especially ruins, such as temples, statues, and obelisks.

Its influence was strong and pervasive, with two French translations in 1546 and 1600, and a translation of the earlier part into English, dedicated to Sidney's memory (*Hypnerotomachia: The Strife of Love in a Dreame* tr R.D., 1592). It stimulated the taste for ruins and the fashion for emblems through what the Elizabethan translator calls its 'Aegiptian Hyerogliphs' (sig C3r). Text and woodcuts became a source for artists in France and Italy. There is plentiful evidence that it was popular in England (see ed 1973: vi-xvii). Jonson owned a copy (now in the British Library). Whether the English, still by and large provincial in their tastes in the visual arts, were responsive to the visual beauty of the book and its illustrations is debatable.

The Faerie Queene seems to echo the

work, though precise links are hard to substantiate. Arguably, Spenser is indebted to Colonna for the singular importance of the triumph (Fowler 1970b:47–57) and for the arithmological stanza of II ix 22 (Cummings 1967; see *Alma). Colonna's taste for emblems would have been congenial to Spenser, though not his often frank eroticism. Probably a significant precedent for *The Faerie Queene* would have been the descriptions in which Colonna celebrates both physical beauty and a Platonic ideal, such as his account of Polia (ch II; ed 1980, I:133ff; 1592: fols 77v-9) which, in this respect, can be compared with the account of Belphoebe in *FQ* II iii 21–31.

LUCY GENT

Francesco Colonna 1499 *Hypnerotomachia Poliphili* (Venice; rpt London 1963 with intro by George Painter); Colonna ed 1592 *Hypnerotomachia: The Strife of Love in a Dreame* tr R.D. (London; rpt Amsterdam and New York 1969; Delmar, NY 1973 with intro by Lucy Gent; New York and London 1976); Colonna 1980 *Hypnerotomachia Poliphili* ed Giovanni Pozzi and Lucia A. Ciapponi, 2 vols (Padua). R.M. Cummings 1967 'A Note on the Arithmological Stanza: *The Faerie Queene*, II.ix.22' *JWCI* 30:410–14; Fowler 1970b; Dudley Wilson 1986 '*The Strife of Love in a Dreame*, an Elizabethan Translation of Part of the First Book of Francesco Colonna's *Hypnerotomachia*' *BSRS* 4.1:41–53.

I

identity Identity in Spenser's poetry (here limited to *FQ*) is extremely various. There is no single formula that will serve to explicate the way in which the social situation of Spenser's characters – their objective position in a network of obligations, roles, status hierarchies, kinship bonds, and possessions – is coordinated with their particular perceptions, desires, and actions. This is not to say that each character possesses a unique and irreducible core of selfhood; on the contrary, nothing is more familiar in *The Faerie Queene* than the linked narrative principles of interchangeability and duplication (whereby, for example, Sansfoy, Sansloy, and Sansjoy all seem, in effect, versions of one another and of the characters they encounter). But these allegorical fragments of identity coexist and interact with far more complex, nuanced characters who arouse in the reader the moral discriminations and identifications that are among the familiar pleasures of literary realism.

Virtually all mimetic art requires such conjunctions: Hamlet chats with the court water-fly Osric, and the most subtly conceived characters in a novel by George Eliot negotiate their experience among cardboard cutouts. But there is in such fictions the theoretical presumption of ideal fullness: we assume that even the wretched Osric, if Shakespeare had wished, could have existed for us more completely; while George Eliot achieves one of her finest moments in *Middlemarch* when she suddenly insists that Casaubon, who had begun the book in the role of a conventional comic *senex*, has his own intense needs, fears, and desires. There is, moreover, in the tradition of mimetic art an allied presumption of uniform ethical and physical agency: we are far more interested in Hamlet than Osric, Dorothea than Raffles, but they all possess in our view the same mode of being in the world. Violations of this presumption are dilemmas that the characters themselves feel driven to explain: hence the status of the ghost is as much a problem for Hamlet as it is for ourselves; and when Dickens has a choleric character melt, in allegorical fashion, he feels compelled to provide a scientific explanation.

There is no place in *The Faerie Queene* for either of these presumptions. We precisely must *not* imagine that, had Spenser the inclination or we the patience, he could have given Ollyphant or Sansfoy the same complexity of identity as that of Britomart or the Red Cross Knight. To do so would be to read against the poem, to transform its moral judgments into a nightmare of fanatical violence. What we are not told about a character in Spenser's poem does not hover, as it were, on the margins of the narration (as does, for example, the untold personal history of Iago or Malvolio); in *The Faerie Queene*, what is not narrated simply does not exist. No one, to my knowledge, has attempted to imagine the girlhood of Duessa.

At the same time, we must resist the conclusion that only a few characters in Spenser possess any identity at all – as if identity itself were a moral achievement or a gift conferred by grace upon the virtuous and the noble. While the protagonists are, not surprisingly, given a density of character denied to the minor figures of the poem, it is impossible to establish a clear boundary or even a stable set of degrees between their form of identity and that given to the swarm of lesser beings around them.

There is no orderly hierarchy of identity that leads from relatively complex, full characters like Redcrosse, Guyon, and Britomart to near cyphers like Gardante, Parlante, and Jocante. If Britomart's identity, for example, seems to depend upon experiences that are unusually subjective and inward – as when she is depicted suffering the intense pangs of love – the same experiences are scattered through the depiction of lesser characters. Thus Malecasta is shown suffering the identical sleepless nights: the crucial difference lies not in the intensity of subjective experience but in its moral meaning and hence in its end. Malecasta 'was given all to fleshly lust, / And poured forth in sensuall delight' (III i 48); Britomart's longings, by contrast, are completely honorable: 'Not that she lusted after any one; / For she was pure from blame of sinfull blot, / Yet wist her life at last must lincke in that same knot [ie, marriage]' (ii 23). The contrast here is not between an evil woman who experiences desire and a good one who does not: Britomart too comes to know the power of sensual delight. But while Malecasta's desires are poured out loosely and promiscuously, Britomart's are channeled toward the holy 'knot' of matrimony.

Identity, then, is not defined by subjective experience, nor does it depend upon any self-consciousness that the characters may possess about the significance of their actions. Self-consciousness is not by itself a defining moral trait for Spenser: virtuous figures like Fidelia, Speranza, and Charissa are less self-reflexively concerned with the grounds of their own being than are the wicked Archimago or Duessa. Consequently, Spenser seems indifferent to the distinction between allegorical agents defined in the most restrictive sense and literal agents upon whom is conferred a substantial density of character. Such a distinction, as we have already seen, exists in practice in the poem – exists indeed in the most absolute form, since there is no implied aura of unexpressed experience around each character – but it does not seem to have interested Spenser. Hence, without the slightest hesitation, he conjoins his most complex characters with his most one-dimensional personifications: Redcrosse fights with Sansfoy, Guyon describes his quest to Medina, Arthur bandies blows with Disdain. To a later poetic (and critical) tradition, such encounters could only be a kind of grotesque comedy, since they yoke figures presumed to be 'real' with personified abstractions and hence threaten both the literary conception of identity and the ethical conception of agency.

These conjunctions do not trouble Spenser – they do not threaten the aesthetic or moral coherence of the poem – precisely because identity is for him quite distinct from the subjectivity and self-consciousness that we tend to associate with it. In *The Faerie Queene*, identity is a given, very much as a name is a given; indeed, the two are closely linked because names are not arbitrary designations of persons set apart from them but rather true and precise expressions of particular, distinct identities.

Wicked characters can, of course, assume false names; but their actual and accurate names remain, to be revealed in the end. Certain characters, moreover, seem to grow into new names: we are told, for example, that Malbecco 'Is woxen so deform'd, that he has quight / Forgot he was a man, and *Gealosie* is hight' (III x 60). Yet even this new name is less the designation of a change in his identity than a disclosure of its original essence. Finally, in the most complex instances in the poem, characters seem to achieve their names through long trial and adventures – hence Redcrosse learns his name, George, only near the end of his quest – but here, too, the name already exists as the true essence of his character; and the hero's experiences, though necessary, do not actually create an identity which has already been, as Contemplation says, 'ordaind.' As Contemplation's language suggests, this conception of identity is bound up with a theology that at once demands vigorous human action and regards the outcome of that action as already divinely determined. STEPHEN GREENBLATT

Idle Lake With details conflated from Tasso's Asphalt Lake (*Gerusalemme liberata* 10.62, 16.71), Dante's Stygian Marsh (*Inferno* 7), Virgil's Cocytus (*Aeneid* 6.132, 323, 438–9), and the biblical Salt Sea (Gen 14.3, glossed as 'the dead Sea, or the lake Asphaltite nere unto Sodom and Gomorah'), the Idle Lake (*FQ* II vi) constitutes a richly significant image. In its physical aspect, it warns against idleness, moral stagnation, and withdrawal from the world of action into superficial pleasures as represented by its inhabitant, Phaedria. This warning is stressed throughout the canto by the repeated word *perilous* (10, 19). The lake constitutes one of the major symbols of sloth in Book II, with its 'sluggish,' 'griesly' (in 1590, 'griesy'), mud-laden waves (46, 18). It has the color and viscosity of mud; and it has an ominous, gruesome effect on those whom its waves 'agrise' (46; a verb with the double sense of rendering horrible and of terrifying: cf III ii 24, IV viii 12).

The lake shares Phaedria's characteristics, in being withdrawn not only from the world of action but also from that of nature, its waters being impervious to wind and tide. It denies nature's laws by failing to perform two of water's natural functions, to quench fire and to drown by letting 'weightie' things 'sinke downe to the bottome there' (46); in this, it is as shallow as Phaedria. A further allegorical significance, social as well as moral, is suggested in the lake's other name, 'Inland sea' (10), probably a literal translation of *Mediterranean*. Along with the 'gondelay' (11) of Phaedria, the name helps to evoke an association between Italy and a life of idle pleasures. In his *New Age of Old Names* (1609), Joseph Wybarne, in castigating those whose 'wils had drowned themselves in the dead sea of pleasure,' tells his reader to 'see the Legend of Phaedria in the 2. booke of the Fayerie Queene' (*Sp All* p 120).

The Idle Lake both constitutes an allegorical image complete and rich in itself and plays a structural role in the first two books of the poem. It provides a counterpart to the fountain of sloth in I vii (placed in a similarly central position); in Book II, it is framed by the comparably moralized waters of the chaste nymph (ii 3–10) and Acrasia (xii 2–33); and it provides a contrast with the 'standing lake' in which Arthur is able to drown Maleger (xi 46).

BRENDA M. HOSINGTON

idols, idolatry The Old Testament sin of worshiping other gods in violation of the first commandment and of making graven images in violation of the second is redefined by the psychological understanding of *eidōlon* (Gr 'phantom, image idol') given by the early church and repeated by Calvin. An idol may be an internal mental image that perverts spiritual vision by focusing on material phenomena. Since 'the inventing of idoles [is] the beginning of whoredome' (Wisd of Sol 14.11), or adultery (Eph 5.5, Rom 2.22, Col 3.5), and under the new law, adultery may be committed in the heart (Matt 5.28), idolatry may be found even in one who does not worship 'graven images.'

According to St Augustine, sin occurs when the soul ignores the indwelling image of God for an obsession with the mental pictures formed from sensory stimuli: 'wrapped up in their images, which it has fixed in the memory, [the soul] is foully polluted by fornication of the phantasy' (*On the Trinity* 12.9). For Calvin, the nature of man is 'a perpetual factory of idols' such that man 'conceives an unreality and an empty appearance as God,' leading him to express this phantom in the manufacture of actual exterior idols (*Institutes of the Christian Religion* 1.11.8, in ed 1960:108). *Eidolon* in this psychological definition has an analogy in Plato's discussion of an image of something that is neither wholly real nor utterly nonexistent (*Sophist* 239C–40C). Maleger, 'lifelesse shadow' and 'dead-living swaine,' answers this definition of a phantasm when he assaults the soul as it struggles against 'crowds of contradictory phantasms' (*FQ* II xi 44, Augustine *Confessions* 7.17).

The question of when a spiritual image becomes an idol vexed theologians, from the iconoclastic movement in the eighth- and ninth-century Eastern church against the veneration of holy pictures to debates in the Reformation over church ornaments and ceremonies. The psychological definition of idolatry does little to resolve this question. Orthodox and Catholic teaching has always allowed for legitimate use of images in public worship and private devotion according to the understanding, best articulated by G.K. Chesterton, that 'saints and angels are not worshipped, for the simple reason that they are themselves represented in the act of worshipping' (1950:182). Protestant and Reformed opinion is divided: the Lutheran tradition kept many aids to devotion, the Calvinist rejected them. William Fulke's *Defence* (1583, in ed 1843:100ff) tended to equate images and idolatry, seeing in the disputed ceremonies of the English church (the wearing of the surplice, kneeling at Communion, the sign of the Cross in Baptism) the 'impotent and beggerlie rudiments, whereunto as from the beginning ye wil be in bondage againe' (Gal 4.9).

In England from 1540 on, the term *idolatry* was used to refer mainly to the Roman Mass: 'this wicked idol the mass, that glorious and gorgeous strumpet,' 'whorishe idolatrie,' 'meretricious ornaments ... alluring men to spiritual fornication,' 'popysh adultery,' and the 'idolatrous masse' are typical phrases from the 1570s. The rhetoric achieved official statement in the homily 'Against Perill of Idolatrie' in *The Second Book of Homilies* (1563): 'Bee not the spirituall wickednesses of an Idols inticing, like the flatteries of a wanton harlot? Bee not men and women as prone to spirituall fornication (I meane Idolatrie) as to carnall fornication?' (*Certaine Sermons or Homilies* ed 1623:61–2). Shrines, images and 'monuments of feigned miracles, pilgrimages, idolatry, and superstition' were to be removed from churches in accordance with the Royal Injunctions of 1559 that enforced the Acts of Uniformity and Supremacy; but the ancient instruments of worship could never be eradicated.

The beast fable in *SC, Maye* tells how a fox 'Bearing a trusse of tryfles at hys backe, / As bells, and babes, and glasses in hys packe' (239–40) – 'the reliques and ragges of popish superstition' in E.K.'s gloss – misleads a simple Christian victim. In *FQ* I iii 11–20, Kirkrapine gives the spoils from the churches he robs to 'blind Devotions' daughter Abessa, 'With whom he whoredome usd,' an act which suggests that the material trappings of religion are not things indifferent to salvation but rather the very substance from which idolatry develops. Idolatry is Redcrosse's fate when he accepts Duessa as his companion. In her ornaments, in the mists she stirs up to becloud reason, and in her playing on the victim's fears (of which she is in part composed), she represents the idolatry that follows upon 'errours' (the monster Error) and 'superstition' (Archimago) in the struggle against sin described in the homilies ('The Third Part of the Sermon of Faith' *Certaine Sermons or Homilies* ed 1623:28). In particular, she represents the Mass, identified conventionally in the Protestant imagination with the Whore of Babylon of Revelation 17.4 (cf *FQ* I viii 14), holding forth the 'Cupp of fornicacion with which the purple Harlott had then made all nacions drunken' (*Vewe* 2640–1, in *Var Prose* p 137).

Perhaps idolatry comes easily to the champion of *FQ* I: the lover fixated on his lady as a revered object is also an idolater, and Spenser takes care to show that courtly love is founded upon seemingly innocent rituals that deify the beloved. The false Una, 'So lively, and so like' her original (i 45), appears in Redcrosse's imagination as a garlanded May queen. The false Florimell, 'So lively and so like' the true (III viii 5), is also associated with the pagan rites of Flora, considered by Piers in *SC, Maye* 37–54 to be dangerously frivolous. The slide from such innocent naturalism into the pagan error of investing the mysterious powers of the universe with personality is swift, as John Jewel warns, speaking of the Mass: 'They turned the remembrance of the death of Christ into a May-game: they made the people commit horrible and open idolatry, to worship the creature instead of the Creator, which is God blessed for ever' ('An Exposition upon the Two Epistles of St Paul to the Thessalonians' in ed 1845–50, 2:911).

In this light, Petrarch's response to Laura as 'my idol carved in living laurel' (*Canzoniere* 30.27) – like Spenser's 'My soverayne saynt, the Idoll of my thought' (*Amoretti*

61) – is ironic, for obsession with a phantasm of the beloved is what distinguishes the narcissist, enslaved to his own projections, from the spiritual lover who witnesses God's truth and beauty in his lady. Idol worship is the enemy of spiritual vision in the Legend of Chastity, not just in the 'fowle Idolatree' before Cupid's statue in the house of Busirane (III xi 49) but also in the cult that surrounds the false Florimell, twice identified as an 'Idole' (viii 11, IV v 15). Like an *eidōlon*, she 'stirreth up the desire of the ignorant: so that he coveteth the forme that hathe no life, of a dead image' (Wisd of Sol 15.5). The behavior of the pantheistic wood folk shows how easily divine truth and beauty are deflected into sensible substitutes: mistaking Una for a May queen, they make her 'th'Image of Idolatryes' (I vi 19; cf Acts 14.15, 18, Rom 1.20–3, Exod 20.5).

The consequences of relapse into heathen ceremony become clear in the Legend of Justice. The tyrant Geryoneo devours the sons of Belge 'And to his Idols sacrifice[s] their blood' (V x 8), in the cause of a renewed Roman imperialism based, so it seemed to Protestants, on the Mass as a primitive propitiary sacrifice. A whole empire can be sustained through the manipulation of images, as attested by the broken idol envisioned by the speaker in *Ruines of Time* (491–504).

How, then, does one distinguish the legitimate image of truth from the misleading idol? As an allegorist, Spenser seems to treat idols as images, for example, in describing the statue of Venus (IV x 39–40), where the context is benign. As a Protestant writer, he treats images as idols, for example, in the beast fable of *Maye*, where the context is sinister. In so doing, he follows the homily against idolatry in making the terms interchangeable (see *Rome* 70). Such arbitrariness indicates that idolatry is a question no less political than theological. As a political writer, Spenser is free to set against the idol worship of Spain the figure of Gloriana as 'th'Idole of her makers great magnificence' (II ii 41), and against Munera (who is chopped up by Talus in the manner of the golden calf in Exod 32.20), the silver idol of Isis (V vii 6–8).

As a Christian writer responsible to a truth that poetry can only imperfectly embody, Spenser is apprehensive about mere surface appeal such as we find in the fantastic and sensual décor of Castle Joyous and the house of Busirane; he is fond of clear figurative expression which, as in the tapestries of the castle of Alma, is 'easie to be thought' (II ix 33), suggesting that, for him, images become free of idolatry when they do not blind the perceiver to some form of 'Sabaoths sight.' SEAN KANE

William Fulke 1843 *A Defence of the Sincere and True Translations of the Holy Scriptures into the English Tongue* (1583) ed Charles Henry Hartshorne, Parker Society (Cambridge); John Jewel 1845–50 *Works* ed John Ayre, 4 vols, Parker Society (Cambridge).

Hume 1984 analyzes *Maye* as a fable warning of the subversive behavior of English clergy who urge retention of Roman ceremony. Kane 1989 treats the significance of the phrase 'errors, superstitions, idolatry and all evil' in the psychological structure of *FQ* I. D.W. Robertson, Jr 1962 *A Preface to Chaucer: Studies in Medieval Perspectives* (Princeton) discusses the terms *adultery* and *idolatry* in the patristic exegetical tradition. Waters 1970 quotes post-Reformation characterizations of the Mass and demonstrates its personification in Duessa. Gross 1985 examines iconoclasm, idolatry, and magic as motive forces in *FQ* in the context of post-structuralist literary theory. Ernest B. Gilman 1986 *Iconoclasm and Poetry in the English Reformation: Down Went Dagon* (Chicago) analyzes the impact of iconoclasm on pictorial poetry from Spenser to Milton. Broader historical studies of the status of images in the Reformation include John Phillips 1973 *The Reformation of Images: Destruction of Art in England, 1535–1660* (Berkeley and Los Angeles); King 1982; and Patrick Collinson 1986 *From Iconoclasm to Iconophobia: The Cultural Impact of the Second English Reformation* (Reading). Edwyn [Robert] Bevan 1940 *Holy Images: An Inquiry into Idolatry and Image-Worship in Ancient Paganism and in Christianity* (London) presents a temperate and learned discussion of the place of images in Christian worship.

Ignaro As Orgoglio's foster father, Ignaro (Ital 'ignorant') is keeper of his castle, ignorance and pride being proverbially akin. In his dotage and blindness, he is unable to prevent Arthur from liberating the imprisoned Red Cross Knight (*FQ* I viii 30–4). Historically, he may allude to the Catholic bishop Edmund Bonner, who, under Mary Tudor, kept a private prison at Fulham and was notorious for his persecution of dissenters (see Foxe's *Actes and Monuments* 1563). Ideologically, he represents the decrepitude and obscurantism of the old religion: sixteenth-century Protestant thought commonly equated popery with spiritual ignorance.

Many anti-Catholic interludes personify ignorance as an old, reactionary, and deceitful popish priest (eg, *The Nature of the Four Elements* c 1519, probably by John Rastell, and the anonymous *New Custom* 1573). Other interludes depict ignorance as a senile and depraved braggart (eg, William Wager's allegorical comedies of the 1560s, *The Longer Thou Livest, the More Foole Thou Art* and *Inough Is as Good as a Feast*). As a rule, these stock characters suffer from blindness or bad sight. In the popular anonymous interlude *Lusty Juventus* (c 1540), 'old blind ignorance' is repeatedly contrasted with 'godly new knowledge.' In John Redford's *Wit and Science* (written in the 1530s or 1540s), Ignorance appears as an idiot boy, son of Idleness, whose typical answer 'Ich can not tell' anticipates Ignaro's unvarying response: 'He could not tell: ne ever other answere made.'

The outward appearance and behavior of Spenser's Ignaro owe more to this domestic tradition than to conventional representations of Ignorantia in continental mythography and iconography, where that vice usually figures as a lady (Donna Ignoranza), sometimes as a jester, and occasionally in the guise of an ape, ass, or other animal. Such portrayals are based on the tradition of describing ignorance by metaphors of blindness and imprisonment.

This unholy trinity of ignorance, blindness, and the imprisonment which they bring can be traced back to patristic, classical, and biblical sources. It was familiar to Renaissance writers from collections of pertinent quotations in various thesauri and commonplace books. Among them, Peter Martyr Vermigli's *Loci communes* is particularly interesting, since Spenser seems to have known this rich compendium of Protestant theology (Eng tr by Anthony Marten as *The Common Places* 1583). Undoubtedly he knew Palingenius' very popular *Zodiacus vitae*; in Book 9 of the English edition, man is delivered from the dark prison of ignorance by grace, much as Redcrosse is delivered by Spenser's Arthur.

Ignaro's backward-turned face has been related to the punishment of sorcerers and soothsayers in Dante's *Inferno* (20.13) and its possible source in Isaiah 44.25; but Ignaro is not a wizard, nor can we be sure that Spenser read the *Divine Comedy*. His backward-turned face has been identified as a traditional representation of bondage to the old law and the Old Testament (*FQ* ed 1965a:36), but Ignaro is blamed for his allegiance to papistry rather than for adherence to the Old Testament. Double-faced figures with (sometimes aged) faces looking backwards (as Trevisan is seen at I ix 21) can be found in many iconographic works; however, they personify not Ignorantia but Prudentia (wisdom), as represented by Janus. Imprudent Ignaro is a reduced Janus deprived of his younger, forward-looking face (ie, foresight, circumspection), for he is given a staff and keys, the typical emblematic signs of Janus. These are also papal insignia, so Ignaro's inability to make proper use of them also indicates the decay and incompetence of papal authority. Spenser thus visualizes the ambiguous aspects of images commonly held in high esteem, specifically the latent opposite idea that (according to Jung) is inherent in every archetype.

Ignaro becomes even more abhorrent when the reader recognizes him as a mock impersonation (like Archimago) of the true *senex doctus* seen in Contemplation. In his blindness and ignorance, he may be compared to Corceca who cannot speak and her mother, the blind Abessa, who is named 'blind Devotion' (I iii argument). As a stupid and powerless guard, Ignaro has much in common with the janitors (*archontes*) in gnostic and Hermetic systems of the soul's ascent. Spenser couples ignorance and darkness twice more, in *The Teares of the Muses* 68, 181–90. The noun *ignaro* as a generic name for an ignoramus survived in England until the end of the seventeenth century. WILHELM FÜGER

Wilhelm Füger 1971 'Ungenutzte Perspektiven der Spenser-Deutung: Dargelegt an "The Faerie Queene" I.viii.30–34' *DVLG* 45:252–301.

illustrators Next to the plays of Shakespeare and the poems of Milton, Spenser's poetry has provided more subject matter for visual artists than the work of virtually any other English poet. From the very beginning, he practiced his craft for publication in a format designed to accommodate both word and pictured image. His translations in van der Noot's *Theatre for Worldlings* (1569) share page space with emblem woodcuts designed (it is thought) by Marcus Gheeraerts the elder or Lucas de Heere; and his own *Shepheardes Calender* in 1579, unique for its time in English publishing, includes woodcuts at the head of each of the twelve eclogues (see **SC*, printing and illustration). The intimate relationship of these texts to the cuts elevates their status far beyond that of mere decoration. They show specific textual detail, commenting upon and thereby expressing in visual terms the message of the poems. Though, excepting the lone woodcut of the Red Cross Knight between Books I and II in 1590, *The Faerie Queene* was not an illustrated book at the outset, Spenser's powerful sense of the visual made it all but certain that visual artists would ultimately mine the poem for subjects and that many subsequent editions would be illustrated.

illustrated editions Such was the case in 1715 when Jacob Tonson purchased rights to Spenser's works and published them in six volumes. For the eighteen illustrations, he engaged Louis du Guernier, who evidently worked closely with the editor, John Hughes. The episodes and selections discussed by Hughes in his 'Essay on Allegorical Poetry' appear to have determined the artist's selection of details.

In 1732, John Ball published *The Shepheardes Calender* with Spenser's text facing Bathurst's Latin translation and illustrated with twelve engravings newly designed by Peter Fourdrinier. Some of the designs deviate radically from the originals of 1579 while others retain the iconography verbatim. Fourdrinier dresses his shepherds in eighteenth-century costume and uses a vertical rather than horizontal format, thus altering picture space considerably.

At about the same time, Queen Caroline engaged Robert Bridgeman to design Merlin's Cave at Richmond, her favorite residence. A thatched, mock-gothic building, the Cave housed a library (presided over by the poet, Stephen Duck) as well as a kind of diorama that included Merlin, Britomart, and Glauce. Considered a curiosity even in its own time (see Colton 1976–7), the Cave is the first known instance of Spenser illustration independent of a published book. Pictures of the Cave were engraved for *Merlin: A Poem* (1735), *Merlin, or The British Enchanter* (1736), and John Vardy *Some Designs of Mr Inigo Jones and Mr William Kent* (1744). A 'raree-show' replica of the diorama is described in an undated broadside, *Merlin in Miniature, or A Lively Representation of Merlin in His Cave, as in the Royal Gardens at Richmond, Being, a New and Entertaining Piece of Moving Machinery, Such as Never before Appeared in Public*. Contemporaneously, Viscount Lord Cobham engaged William Kent to design and build the Temple of Venus at Stowe, within which the painter, Francesco Sleter, included fresco illustrations of the Hellenore and Malbecco episode. Described in William Gilpin's *Dialogue upon the Gardens ... at Stowe* (1748) and in Benton Seeley's eighteenth-century guides to Stowe, the paintings would seem to have been mildly risqué, an inference supported by Cobham's reputation for indecent storytelling and the remark by the third and last Duke of Buckingham and Chandos (about 1880) that he was glad the paintings were fading because of their off-color subject matter. No trace of them remains.

Before his death in 1748, Kent completed thirty-two illustrations, which John Upton and Horace Walpole savagely criticized, for a new edition of *The Faerie Queene* by Thomas Birch and published in London in 1751 by J. Brindley and S. Wright. Of the original pen-and-ink drawings, twenty-six are at the Victoria and Albert Museum and one at the Huntington Art Gallery. Also at the Victoria and Albert is a single sheet with four unpublished drawings and one sheet with an unpublished drawing of the Salvage Man. John Bell's edition of Spenser, eight volumes in the Poets of Great Britain series published in 1778, contains eight illustrations engraved by Sharp and Grignon from designs by John Hamilton Mortimer. Four original pen-and-ink drawings survive in the British Museum, while Mortimer's large, brooding, banditti-inspired painting, 'Sir Artegal and Talus,' is at the Tate Gallery.

A six-volume *Poetical Works of Edmund Spenser* edited by John Aikin from Upton's text appeared in London in 1802 with twelve engraved illustrations cut by John Heath from designs by Thomas Stothard. Two of Stothard's remarkably fresh watercolor designs survive at the Pierpont Morgan Library, while two of his oil paintings illustrating Spenser have recently passed through the auction houses: 'Britomart Disarming' (Sotheby's 1973) and 'Una and the Satyrs' (Christie's 1983). Stothard also contributed four additional designs for Aikin's six-volume *Poetical Works* (1810), the engravings having been cut by John Romney, Charles Pye, and F. Engleheart. In 1819, the firm of Suttaby, Evance, and Fox published a two-volume *Poetical Works* with four designs by Richard Westall, engraved by L.H. Robinson, R. Rhodes, and A. Raimbach. (Westall exhibited 'Una, a Portrait of Miss Esten' at the Royal Academy in 1804.) Beginning in 1859, George Routledge published the first edition of his 'red line poets' *Faerie Queene* with illustrations designed by Edward Corbould, a friend of the royal family. The volume was reprinted numerous times until 1893, and documents in the Routledge archive testify to the profitable nature of the Spenser in particular, as well as to the 'Parlour Library' concept in general. There was clearly a substantial popular audience for Spenser during those years. Corbould's designs were engraved by the Dalziel brothers, but only one of the original paintings has come to light, 'Belphoebe and the Turtle Dove' (Sotheby's Belgravia 1973).

The final decade of the century saw a greater sustained interest in illustrated editions of Spenser. *Epithalamion ... with Certain Imaginative Drawings by George Warton Edwards* (New York 1895) is a handsome *art nouveau* production in which each stanza is set within a rich pictorial frame. William Morris' Kelmscott Press edition of *The Shepheardes Calender* in 1896 gave A.J. Gaskin opportunity to create an entirely new set of designs in a Pre-Raphaelite style; the relation of text to illustration in this edition bears no relation to that in the 1579 original. Walter Crane's illustrations for Harper and Brothers' *Shepheardes Calender* (New York 1898) is another matter; in keeping with his scholarly instincts, Crane's designs employ and reinterpret the original iconography. In 1897, J.M. Dent published a two-volume *Faerie Queene* with 26 black-and-white illustrations by Louis Fairfax-Muckley. This edition, however, pales before that published by George Allen (London 1894–7), which was edited by T.J. Wise and profusely illustrated with 88 frontispieces, 55 tailpieces, 7 half titles, and 7 title pages in all six folio volumes by Crane. Issued in unbound fascicles so that collectors might bind their volumes to suit their tastes, the Wise-Crane *Faerie Queene* stands as the most ambitious single effort to offer visual commentary on Spenser's allegory. These illustrations are a fitting climax to the interest in Spenser generated by the gothic revival. But as the George Allen archives testify, poor sales were the result of the publisher's failure to see that the market for such goods had already peaked.

William Butler Yeats edited a *Poems of Spenser* published by T.C. and E.C. Jack (Edinburgh 1906), and there is a revealing compatibility between his now-famous introductory essay and the charming illustrations by the Glasgow artist, Jessie M. King. In 1928, John Lane at the Bodley Head published *Epithalamion* with somewhat rough and uninspired illustrations by Maud Wethered. There is also an edition of *The Wedding Songs* illustrated in colored woodcuts by Ethelbert White (Golden Cockerel Press) listed in Christie's catalogue of 26 July 1978 no 180. In 1930, the Cresset Press issued a new *Shepheardes Calender* with intelligent and thoughtful illustrations by the Camden town artist, John Nash. Three special copies were printed on white vellum and then hand-colored by the artist; they are outstanding examples of the bookmaker's art and an impressive vehicle for Nash's interpretation of the poems. Unlike Gaskin, who rejected the iconography established by Spenser's first and anonymous illustrator in 1579, Nash retained some pictorial features of the original. *Thalamos, or The Brydall Boure*, published privately in 1932 with designs by Lettice Sandford, contains five of the most tasteful and delicately erotic illustrations ever given the wedding poems. During the late thirties, George Macy engaged John Austen to illustrate a projected Limited Editions Club *Faerie Queene*. Papers from the Macy Archive (Univ of Texas) contain a poignant record of Austen's careful preparation, of the hardships he suffered during World War II when bombs fell nightly about his house, and of the stroke which paralyzed his arm and prevented completion of the drawings. The commission was passed to Agnes Miller Parker, and her illustrated *Faerie Queene* came off the Oxford University presses in 1953, fifteen years after the project was initiated. (See also *FQ, children's versions.)

eighteenth-century paintings Paintings illustrating characters and episodes from Spenser done independently of publishers' commissions became popular during the eighteenth century. One of the earliest such 'history paintings,' William Dawe's 'The Red Cross Knight in the Cave of Despair,' was exhibited at the Free Society of Artists in 1764. Five years later, Henry Fuseli did a pen-and-ink drawing of the same subject (Chicago Art Institute) and a pen-ink-watercolor, 'Arthur's Dream of the Faerie Queen' (Oberhaufen, Kanton Bern, Frau Beatrice Ganz). An oil painting by Fuseli on this theme (Basel, Kunstmuseum) appeared in 1788 and was engraved by P.W. Tomkins for Thomas Macklin's *British Poets* scheme. During the 1770s, Benjamin West painted 'Una and the Lion' (Wadsworth Atheneum), 'The Cave of Despair' (Yale Center for British Art and Duxbury Art Complex), and the magnificent 'Fidelia and Speranza' (Timkin Art Gallery). Sometime during the decade, James Jefferys did an impressive pen drawing of 'Pride Led by the Passions' (Maidstone Museums). A portrait of Jefferys by his father, William, depicts the younger artist at his drawing table with an open book of 'Spenser' beside him (also Maidstone), a painting reminiscent of that by Michael Dahl of the poet Matthew Prior, who poses with a volume clearly marked 'Spenser's Works' (Knole, Kent). A self-portrait by Jefferys in pen and brown ink shows him before a sketch for 'Pride Led by the Passions' (Yale Center for British Art). In 1791, Elias Martin painted 'Amoret Rapt by Greedie Lust' for Macklin's *British Poets*, while Charles Grignon, Jr, exhibited 'The Charge Which God Doth unto Me Arret' at the Royal Academy in 1775, and Joseph Barney exhibited 'Una' at the Society of Artists in 1777 (and was later to paint 'Mercy and the Red Cross Knight Entering the Cave' in 1827). Robert Fulton (the American inventor) exhibited 'Priscilla and Alladine' at the Society of Artists in 1791, John Graham painted 'Una' for exhibition at the Royal Academy in 1783, and Mary Moser exhibited 'Belphoebe' at the Royal Academy in 1778. In 1783, a 'Una and the Lion' by Angelica Kauffmann was engraved by Thomas Burke; Sylvester Harding's 'Belphoebe' was engraved in 1786 by J. Delatre. At the Royal Academy in 1783, John Taylor exhibited a painting titled 'Busirane, Enchanting Amoret, Is Surprised by Britomartis.'

The last twenty years of the eighteenth century saw many more Spenser paintings. Fuseli continued his fascination with Spenser, doing a 'Una and the Lion' (Staatliche Museen, Berlin), 'Red Cross Slaying the Dragon' (drawing, Kunsthaus, Zürich), 'Malengine Appears from His Cave Observed by Arthur, Artegal and Talus' (Oberhaufen, Kanton Bern, Frau Beatrice Ganz), another 'Malengine' drawing, and 'Britomart Freeing Amoret' (both Kunsthaus, Zürich). A different version of the 'Britomart' is at the Staatliche Museen, Berlin. Richard Cosway painted a 'Sans Loy Killing the Lion' about 1780; Thomas Daniel, best known for landscapes based on his travels in India, painted 'Prince Arthur Defeats the Souldan,' 'The Red Cross Knight and Una,' and 'Sir Artegal' for exhibition at the Royal Academy in 1780 (all unlocated), while Francis Daniel exhibited 'The Babe with Bloody Hands' (unlocated) in 1781. Sir Joshua Reynolds painted 'Miss Beauclerc as Una' (Fogg Museum) in 1780 (engraved by T. Watson and then by S.W. Reynolds); in 1782, George Stubbs painted 'Isabella Saltonstall as Una' on an unusual ceramic plaque (Fitzwilliam Museum). Catering to similar tastes for portraits in literary guise, Maria Hadfield (Mrs Cosway) did a dramatic painting of Georgiana Spencer as Spenser's 'Cynthia' (Chatsworth, Derbyshire; engraved by Bartolozzi); she also painted 'Astraea Instructing Artegal' (unlocated). About 1780, Lady Diana Beauclerc, who designed engravings for an edition of Dryden's *Fables* (1797), executed five watercolor drawings illustrating Una with the satyrs, Redcrosse at the Cave of Despair, Britomart rescuing Amoret, Britomart revealing herself to Artegall, and Belphoebe and Amoret (all in the Lewis Walpole Library, Farmington, Conn). John Singleton Copley painted a large and dramatic 'Red Cross Knight with Fidelia and Speranza' (c 1789), using his children as models (National Gallery, Washington, D.C.), while John Opie did 'The Freeing of Amoret by Britomart' for Macklin (engraved by Bartolozzi) and 'Sir Calepine Rescuing Serena,' the latter exhibited at the Royal Academy in 1798 (unlocated). Henry Singleton exhibited 'Sir Calepine Rescuing Serena from Salvage Men' at the British Institution in 1791 (unlocated), while J. Mowson – following what appears to be a general interest in distressed damsels – exhibited 'Serena Carried off by the Blatant Beast' and 'Calidore Chaining the Blatant Beast' at the Academy in 1797 (both unlocated). George Romney drew an undated 'Study of Una' (Fitzwilliam) and Alexander Runciman drew 'Sir Satyrane' (private collection, London) as well as 'Una and the Lion' (National Gallery of Scotland), both undated. A 'Satyrane' by John Runciman is unlocated, as is a 'Una' by Thomas Burke.

nineteenth- and twentieth-century art From 1800 to 1900, a large number of paintings, drawings, stained-glass windows, Parian-ware figurines, sculptures, and prints testify to the very considerable popularity of Spenser's poetry, a popularity grounded in the perception that his heroes and heroines, often particularly the latter, exhibited the qualities of Christian commitment that were much on nineteenth-century minds. At Cheltenham Ladies' College, for example, a large set of stained-glass windows depicts features of the Britomart episodes of *FQ* III and IV while an additional window extols the virtues of Una. These windows, originally begun by Frederick Shields but completed by an unidentified artist, offer visual confirmation of ideas discussed by the college founder, Miss Dorothea Beale, for whom Britomart was a symbol of womanly ideals ('Spenser's Ideal of Woman, as Set Forth in Britomart' *Cheltenham Ladies' College Magazine* 1882:212–33; see Farmer 1988).

Paintings illustrating Spenser were done during the early decades by Henry Howard ('House of Morpheus' Royal Academy 1821 at Petworth, Sussex, and 'Dream of the Red Cross Knight' unlocated, Royal Academy 1800), Stephen Rigaud ('Dream of the Red Cross Knight' Royal Academy 1803 and 'Belphoebe' Royal Society for Painters in Water Colours 1807, both unlocated), John Halls ('The Salvage Man Rescuing Sir Calepine and Serena' unlocated, Royal Academy 1801), J. Mowson ('Calidore Chaining the Blatant Beast' and 'Serena Carried off by the Blatant Beast' Royal Academy 1797 as well as 'The Spirit Bringing Archimago' Royal Academy 1801, all unlocated), B. Greathead ('The Cave of Despair' unlocated, Royal Academy 1803), Samuel Shelly ('Britomartis Frees Amoret' Royal Academy 1806, sketch at the Victoria and Albert), Henry Thomson ('Death of the Dragon by the Red Cross Knight' unlocated), George Jones, William Martin ('Serena Rescued from Suraza' Royal Academy 1807 and 'Serena Falls into the Hands of the Savages' Royal Academy 1812, both unlocated), John Cawse ('The Adventures of Sir Calepine' unlocated, Royal Academy 1809), and William Bewick, whose 'Una' (unlocated) was painted for John Fleming Leicester, Baron De Tabley, in 1820. Thomas Stothard painted 'Britomart' in 1786 (Sotheby's) and, after 1800, 'Una and the Satyrs' (Christie's) and 'May Morning' (in the McCormick Collection, Chicago, until 1920; now unlocated).

Among more prominent artists, William Blake painted 'Characters in Spenser's *Faerie Queene*' (executed c 1825 Petworth, Sussex) much as he painted Chaucer's pilgrims, while J.M.W. Turner included a drawing of 'The Red Cross Knight at the Cave of Despair' in his *Liber studiorum* (1807–19) and painted 'The Cave of Despair' (Tate Gallery). Joseph Severn, Keats's friend, won the Royal Academy First prize in 1819 with his 'Cave of Despair' (Christie's 1963). In the same year, Coleridge's friend Washington Allston painted 'Flight of Florimel' (Detroit Institute of Art), and two versions of 'Una in a Wood' (one in the Dana Collection, Cambridge, Mass, and the other in a private collection, Baltimore). Meanwhile, William Hilton began a series of Spenser paintings which carried him well into the 1830s: a 'Red Cross Knight' (unlocated, exhibited Royal Academy 1809) and a 'Una and the Satyrs' (unlocated, exhibited Royal Academy 1818). In 1820, he painted the large and impressive (6′ × 8′) 'Venus in Search of Cupid Surprises Diana at the Bath' (Wallace Collection), a painting exhibited with some acclaim at the Royal Academy owing to the artist's formal debt to Titian's 'Diana and Acteon' then hanging in the Stafford Gallery. Additionally, Hilton painted 'Sir Calepine Rescuing Serena' (decayed from the use of unstable pigments, but engraved by T. Williams for *The Art*

Journal 1855:253) and 'Una Entering the Cottage of Corceca' (unlocated, exhibited British Institution 1832, engraved by W.H. Watt). The British Museum Print Room holds drawings of 'Archimago Overcome by Sansloy' and 'Una and the Satyrs,' as well as a drawing by Richard Doyle called 'Richard Doyle and Friends Looking at Hilton's Picture, "Sir Calepine Rescuing Serena."' Leigh Hunt writes of Hilton's desire to paint a 'gallery' of Spenser illustrations 'among his other meritorious endeavors' (ed 1844:106).

In 1820, Sir Thomas Lawrence, President of the Royal Academy, did a portrait of 'Lady Leicester as Hope' (at Tabley House, Cheshire; engraved by H. Meyer in 1823), with reference to *FQ* III xii 13. In 1824, Fuseli returned to the subject of 'Britomart Freeing Amoret from Busirane' (Goethe Museum, Frankfurt); and in 1827, Samuel F.B. Morse painted 'Una and the Dwarf Showing Arthur the Castle of Orgoglio' for a pleasure-boat, *The Albany*, belonging to a Colonel Stevens of Hoboken, New Jersey (Toledo Museum of Art). A major work by Sir Charles Eastlake, 'Una Delivering the Red Cross Knight from the Cave of Despair,' was commissioned by Sir John Soane in 1829 and may still be viewed at Soane's Museum, London. Also during the decade, William Etty found the subject 'Phaedria and Cymochles on Idle Lake' quite suited to his extraordinary ability to paint nudes (one version at Princeton University Museum, another in Forbes Collection, New York). But his best-known Spenser painting is the colorful and dramatic 'Britomart Redeems Faire Amoret,' painted in 1833, now at the Tate Gallery.

During the 1840s, Marshall Claxton exhibited 'Spenser Reading *The Faerie Queene* to his Wife and Sir Walter Raleigh' at the Royal Academy (unlocated) and painted 'Una and the Lion' (unlocated). Eleven cartoons for proposed frescoes illustrating Spenser appeared in the Westminster Hall Exhibition sponsored in 1843 by the Fine Arts Commission (*The Art Union* 1843:88–9, 207–12, 219–24, 231–4). William E. Frost's 'Una Alarmed by the Fauns and Satyrs' won a premium of £100, while Frank Howard submitted 'Una Coming to Seek the Assistance of Gloriana' (engraved by Frank Howard), E.V. Rippingill submitted 'Una and the Red Cross Knight Led by Mercy to the Hospital of the Seven Virtues' (engraved by Frank Howard), Joseph Severn submitted 'Marinell in a Swoon,' and William John Montaigne submitted 'Cymochles Discovered by Atin in the "Bowre of Bliss."' Other submissions that cannot be identified by artist include one from a passage in Spenser's *Epithalamion*, a 'Una and the Lion,' a 'St. George Immediately after the Death of the Dragon' and another 'St. George after the Death of the Dragon,' a 'Fauns and Satyrs Bringing Una to Sylvanus,' and a 'Cymochles in the Bowre of Bliss.' In the 1844 Westminster Hall Exhibition, F.R. Pickersgill exhibited 'Sir Calepine Rescuing Serena,' while to the 1845 Exhibition William Cave Thomas submitted 'Justice' based on *FQ* v. None of these is located. When Severn's subject was rejected, George Frederick Watts was invited to paint 'The Triumph of the Red Cross Knight' in fresco in the new Parliament building, but by 1854 the painting had blistered badly and was subsequently destroyed.

William Frost, in addition to his Westminster Hall cartoon, painted 'Una: "The Woody Nymphs, Faire Hamadryads, etc"' (H.M. The Queen, Kensington Palace; engraved by P. Lightfoot) – a drawing for which is at the British Museum – a 'Phaedria and Cymochles' (unlocated, Royal Academy 1871) and a 'Serena, Found of Salvages' (unlocated, Royal Academy 1874). Frank Howard, who wrote 'An Essay on Historical Allusions in Spenser' (*The Artist and Amateur's Magazine* 1843:106–8, 163–4), backed it up with a painting called 'Spenser's "Faerie Queene," Containing Portraits of Elizabeth and Her Court, as Allegorized in Spenser's Poem' (unlocated, British Institution 1842). And William Montaigne painted 'The Wounded Knight' (unlocated, Royal Academy 1854). But among those who submitted Spenser paintings to the Westminster Hall Exhibitions, F.R. Pickersgill produced more additional paintings on Spenserian subjects than any of the others: an 'Amoret Delivered from the Enchanter, Busyrane' (unlocated, Royal Academy 1841), 'The Salvage Man, Having Rescued Sir Calidore ... Crouches at the Feet of Serena' (unlocated, British Institution 1841), 'Florimel in the Cottage of the Witch' (unlocated, Royal Academy 1843), 'Amoret, Aemylia, and Prince Arthur in the Cottage of Sclaunder' (Tate Gallery, Royal Academy 1845; engraved by G.A. Periam), 'Phaedria, a Personification of Idleness' (Sotheby's Belgravia, British Institution 1847), 'The Contest of Beauty for the Girdle of Florimel: Britomart Unveiling Amoret' (Christie's, Royal Academy 1848), 'The Dance to Colin's Melody' (Christie's, c 1854), 'Britomart Unarming' (unlocated, Royal Academy 1855), 'A Little Gondelay' (Manchester Art Gallery) and 'The Pearl Boat,' which may be another version of the same motif, or another of 'Phaedria.' A watercolor sketch is also extant, 'Una and the Lion Leaving the Cottage of Abessa' (Austin, Tex, private collection, undated).

Other representations of Spenser include those by Charles W. Cope ('Pastorella' unlocated, Royal Academy 1846), John James Chalon ('Serena among Savages' unlocated but described in *The Art Union* 1847:190), William Gale ('Phaedria' unlocated, Royal Academy 1846; 'Florimel in the Witch's Cottage' unlocated, Royal Academy 1848; 'May' unlocated, Royal Academy 1849; and 'The Wounded Knight' unlocated, Royal Academy 1854), and Thomas Uwins ('Sir Guyon ... Destroys the Enchantments' Tate Gallery, damaged by the flood of 1928). Joseph Noel Paton did drawings of 'Cymochles Discovered in the Bowre of Bliss by Atin' (Forbes Collection) and 'The Cave of Despair' (National Gallery of Scotland); three etchings by G.P. Jacomb-Hood, 'Una and the Wicked Magician,' 'A Gentle Knight Was Pricking on the Plain,' and 'The Combat of St George and Sansfoy,' appeared in *Portfolio* (1880).

In the 1850s, William Leitch's 'The Birth of Belphoebe and Amoret' was commissioned by Prince Albert, who gave the work as a birthday gift to the Queen (Royal Collections). It has been suggested that Rudolphe Bresdin's 'Comédie de la Mort' (lithograph, 1854) was directly inspired by Spenser's Cave of Despair (Slee 1980). Meanwhile, in 1855, Alfred Stevens began an ambitious project to provide paintings of Spenser's heroines for the drawing room at 11 Kensington Palace Gardens, a commission offered by Don Cristobal de Murietta. Numerous preparatory drawings are at the Tate Gallery, Fitzwilliam Museum, Victoria and Albert, and Royal Institute of Architects, one of the most interesting of which shows a decorated urn displaying Britomart rescuing Amoret (Fitzwilliam). Stevens' nine paintings themselves have been recently rediscovered (Courtauld Institute). Other works of the decade include George Cattermole's two watercolor sketches of Britomart's rescue of Amoret (Glasgow Museums and Art Gallery); William Bell Scott's fresh, Pre-Raphaelite 'Una and the Lion' (National Gallery of Scotland); Samuel Palmer's 'Sir Guyon Tempted to Land on the Enchanted Island' (private collection, Baltimore); George Paten's 'The Graces, Daughters of Delight' (unlocated, Royal Academy 1839) and 'The Bowre of Bliss' (unlocated, Royal Academy 1858); and George Landseer's 'Una Sleeping by Moonlight' (unlocated, Royal Academy 1855). Emphatic corroboration of mid-century interest in Spenser appears in Joseph Pitts' Parian-ware figurines 'Vision of the Red Cross Knight,' 'Britomartis Unveiling Amoret,' 'Britomartis Releasing Amoret,' and 'Sir Calepine Rescuing Serena.' Further, the Ascot Cup for 1852 is a dramatic sculpture of Redcrosse, Una, and the Lamb. Finally, the Chesterfield Cup for the Goodwood Races in 1864 was a large silver and bronze statue of 'The Red Cross Knight' designed by H.H. Armstead.

Sometime during the 1860s, a monumental lead statue of 'Una and the Lion' by John Thomas was installed at Hazelbank House, Edinburgh. In 1862, the photographer Henry Peach Robinson made one of his most highly acclaimed 'composition pictures' on the *Maye* eclogue of *The Shepheardes Calender* (*The Photographic Journal* 1863:235–6). Sometime during the seventies, Sir Edward Coley Burne-Jones painted a mural on 'The Masque of Cupid' on commission from R.H. Benson, still at Chiswick Hall, London; two sketches for the mural are at The National Museum of Wales, one is at the Tate, and six pencil drawings on wood are at Birmingham. In 1871, Robert Thornburn exhibited 'The Orphan' with reference to *FQ* II viii 1 (Sotheby's Belgravia 1973). At about the same time, Paul Falconer Poole painted 'Sir Guyon and the Palmer at the Bower of Bliss' (Sotheby's Belgravia), while Thomas Uwins painted another version of the same subject (Victoria and Albert). A third painting of Guyon and the Palmer had been done in 1848 by William Denholm Kennedy (unlocated). Sixteen drawings by Charlotte Morrell Schreiber for *The Legend of the Knight of the Red Cross, or Of Holiness* (London 1871) are now at Erindale College, University of Toronto.

In 1878, George Frederick Watts painted his magnificent 'Britomart and Her Nurse' (Birmingham, with a small, altogether-different version at Castle Museum, Norwich, and a sketch at Watts Gallery, Compton, near Guildford). Watts also painted 'Mammon' (Compton) and 'The Red Cross Knight and Una' (Perth, Australia). Walter Crane, mentioned above as a book illustrator, painted 'The Red Cross Knight in Search of Una' in the sixties and a 'Britomart by the Sea' in the nineties, which seems to have been done in two versions, one oil and the other watercolor (all unlocated). In about 1886, Sir John Gilbert painted 'The Slain Dragon' (Walker Art Gallery); and in 1890, Rubert Bunny painted 'Una and the Fauns' (Queensland Art Gallery). Between 1890 and 1894, the Belgian artist Fernand Khnopff painted a triptych called 'L'isolement' (Barry Friedman, Ltd, New York). The outer images, which owe a debt to Khnopff's friend Burne-Jones, depict Acrasia on the left side and Britomart on the right. About 1885, John Strudwick painted an impressive 'Acrasia' in the sharply defined Pre-Raphaelite manner (Fine Art Society, London); and in 1902, the Royal Academy declared 'The Masque of Cupid' the subject for the annual competition. (The minutes of the Royal Academy meetings give no indication why the subject was chosen.) Paintings were submitted by A. Lawson Chaplin, Elsie Gregory, John Hodgson Lobley, Osmond Pittman, W.E.G. Solomon, and Frank Eastman; reproductions appeared in *The International Studio* (1902:30–7), but only the Eastman can now be located (Christie's, Feb 1976). The most recent paintings to come to light belong to a series of twelve watercolor designs by T. Erat Harrison in 1885 depicting each of the months from *FQ* VII (private collection, Austin). These designs were the basis for the Zodiac windows at Betteshanger House, near Deal, Kent, which are still in place. Other paintings at this time include 'Una' (unlocated) by Briton Riviere (whose father, William, had painted 'The Legend of Guyon' in 1827, also unlocated), 'Florimell' (unlocated) by Henry Ryland, and 'Britomart' (unlocated) by Mary F. Raphael.

The last major project to paint episodes from *The Faerie Queene* began in the 1930s when Lee Woodward Zeigler was commissioned by the trustees of the Enoch Pratt Free Library, Baltimore, to execute seventeen large murals for the second-floor reading room. These murals offer a distinguished range of pictorial commentary on Spenser's vast allegories and testify eloquently to the fact that Spenser has, since the mid-eighteenth century, been the 'poet of the painters.' *The Faerie Queene* has been called 'a series of moving pictures full of color and action' (Osgood 1945:5). The power of Spenser's poetry to 'move' its readers has been demonstrated no less by the artists who have undertaken to comment on it through pictorial images than by the critics who, from E.K. to John Hughes to the present, have responded to Spenser's imagination with gloss and commentary.

NORMAN K. FARMER, JR

Laurel Bradley 1979–80 'Eighteenth-Century Paintings and Illustrations of Spenser's *Faerie Queene*: A Study in Taste' *Marsyas* 20:31–51; Judith Colton 1976–7 'Merlin's Cave and Queen Caroline: Garden Art as Political Propaganda' *ECS* 10:1–20; Norman K. Farmer, Jr 1986; Farmer 1988 'Dorothea's Disagreement' *Country Life* 182.2:58–9; Hind 1952–64; Krieg 1985; Charles Grosvenor Osgood 1945 *Murals Based upon Edmund Spenser's 'Faerie Queene' by Lee Woodward Zeigler* (Baltimore); Philip R. Rider 1978 'Samuel F.B. Morse and *The Faerie Queene*' *RS* 46:205–13; Jacquelynn Baas Slee 1980 'A Literary Source for Rodolphe Bresdin's "La Comédie de la Mort"' *Arts Magazine* 54.6:70–5; Jean Vialla 1983 *Les Pickersgill-Arundale: Une famille de peintres anglais au XIXe siècle* (Paris).

imagination Spenser uses the word *imagination* only twice, both times in *Vewe of Ireland* to suggest a wild or unfounded conjecture (*Var Prose* pp 104, 131). He uses the verb *to imagine* four times in *The Faerie Queene* meaning 'to represent to the mind something not present to the senses.' He designates the faculty of imagination by *fantasy* or, more frequently, by its contraction *fancy*. Both words also carry the *OED* senses of 'a particular mental image, usually a delusion' (*SC, Feb* 211, *Amoretti* 78), of 'taste or preference in matters of art' (*SC, Dec* 16, *FQ* II xii 42), or of 'sexual desire' (I iv 24, V v 26).

The concept of *phantasia* had already acquired, before entering the vernacular, the stigma of a dangerous source of error (Bundy 1927:278). It survives in Elyot's reference to *fantasy* as a word of reproach (ed 1883, 2:384). Spenser apparently shared the widespread distrust of, and contempt for, the fantasy and its operations. E.K. claims that in *The English Poete* Spenser argues that poetry is celestially inspired (*Oct* Arg). In *Teares*, bad poetry is called 'the fruitfull spawne of ... ranke fantasies,' a 'monster' made by the 'fantasie' of vulgar charlatans who are themselves 'begotten of fowle Infamy; / Blind Error, scornefull Follie, and base Spight' (313–22, 558). The similarity between these terms and those describing Error (*FQ* I i 14–15) and Geryoneo's monster, guardian of the Idol produced by 'his owne vaine fancies thought' (V xi 19), reveals the close contemporary association of fancy with poetry, fiction, falsehood, and even heresy. Nor does lyric poetry escape censure: love lyrics are held to contaminate the imaginations of their hearers, alluring 'Chast Ladies eares to fantasies impure' (*Mother Hubberd* 820).

In Phantastes' chamber (*FQ* II ix 49–52), 'tales' are associated with dreams and lies as typical products of the fantasy which are allegorized as buzzing flies. Dreams exhibit the vulnerability of the fantasy to manipulation when Archimago abuses the Red Cross Knight's fantasy with a false dream (I i 46). In contrast, Britomart's true prophetic dream in Isis Church appears not to any of her earthly faculties but to her 'heavenly spright'; and when, on waking, she tries to interpret it 'With thousand thoughts feeding her fantasie,' she fails (V vii 12, 17). *Fancy* and *fantasy* in Spenser are usually accompanied by disparaging modifiers such as *fond, frail, vain, weak, falsed, feigning, wandering, light, lustful, idle*. Yet the persistent dominance of fantasy in human affairs, its influence on the heart (V vi 7) and the will (*Hymne of Beautie* 222), wrings from the poet the occasional admission that 'fantasie is strong' (*Mother Hubberd* 1326).

It was commonplace to charge the fantasy with misrepresenting reality by arbitrarily recombining the partial reports of the senses into imaginary hybrid creatures 'such as in the world were never yit' (*FQ* II ix 50), although it did not follow that the poet was required to describe reality. The truths most valued in Spenser's day were transcendent and hence, on the model of Revelation, quite properly conveyed in nonrealistic, visionary images. Thus Calidore approaches Colin Clout (VI x 18) to learn the 'truth' embodied in the vision of the Graces summoned by the poet's art. Colin's inability to restore the vision confirms Spenser's commitment to the doctrine of inspiration; but the poet, unlike the dreamer, retains the use of his earthly wits and can expound its meaning, at least to the satisfaction of the knight. What role the poet's fantasy plays in the reception, transmission, and explication of the vision is left unclear; and there seems little doubt that, whatever his private, possibly disabling misgivings and reservations, Spenser continues to defend, at least officially, the view of poetry as divinely inspired rather than 'gotten by laboure and learning' (*Oct* Arg).

In the sixteenth century, a strong association developed between fantasy and sexual desire. It was most marked in the use of *fancy*, as indicated by the formation of the verb *to fancy* meaning 'to be attracted by' (used once by Spenser at *FQ* VI ix 40), and was primarily a feature of literary writing, particularly poetry. Except in poetry, *fantasy* was less affected by the association with desire, being used most frequently in the senses of 'imagination' and 'unsubstantiated opinion.' Thus, by Spenser's day, the two words, though related and often used as synonyms, were sufficiently differentiated in sense to allow for ambiguity and wordplay. Because other writers used *imagination* as a synonym for *fantasy* and with equal frequency, the association with desire colored the whole concept.

At best fancy was an equivocal and ambiguous experience, being common to the onset of love and lust. Thus Britomart on seeing Artegall is 'full of fancies fraile' (III ii 27), and Paridell seduces Hellenore by feeding her fancy (x 8). As love develops, fancy is followed by desire; but false love remains on the level of desire, while true love advances to a higher plane. Thus the fancy of the unchaste Malecasta (i 47), being easily vexed, ignites the 'hasty fire' of desire so that she is entirely consumed by passion, and that of the insatiable nymphomaniac Argante demands continual feeding 'with delightfull chaunge' (vii 50).

Two activities metaphorically ascribed to fancy are 'flitting' and 'feeding.' Flitting harks back to the association between the arbitrariness of both sexual attraction and fortune; feeding comes from the tendency to see the characteristic operation of the fancy or fantasy as the pursuit of sensual gratification stimulated by the appetites rather than the orderly transmission of images from the senses to the judgment. Pleasure and delight are fancy's preferred food (*Amoretti* 72, *FQ* VI x 30). The pleasurable fancies themselves may then become food for the 'hungry soule' for which they can never afford 'satietie' but only 'false beauties flattring bait' (*Heavenly Beautie* 279–91).

Some implications of the difference in sense and connotation between *fantasy* and *fancy* are shown in the personifications of Phantastes and Fancy (*FQ* II ix 49–52, III xii 7–8). Phantastes is depicted as unprepossessing, with 'beetle browes' and 'sharpe staring eyes'; Fancy is a 'lovely boy' comparable to Ganymede and Hylas. The former seems doomed by the baleful influence of Saturn to solitary confinement in his fly-ridden turret chamber; the latter is accompanied by his son, Desire (who paradoxically seems of riper years), and is followed by the whole cast of the masque of Cupid. Although the masque becomes as sinister as the chamber of Phantastes, Fancy is disturbing only by his ambivalence. He fuses the images of child and parent, lover and beloved. Dressed in feathers and carrying a 'windy fan,' he also seems part bird, like the poet's fancy in *Amoretti* 72 which, on sight of his beloved, 'fed with full delight, / doth bath in blisse and mantleth most at ease'; as such, he seems fleeting and 'fraile.' Throughout the century, the emergent concept of fancy tends to be personified either as a parent (Breton's 'Dame Fancie's School' in *A Floorish upon Fancie* 1577) or as a child (in Skelton's *Magnyfycence* c 1530, Fancy is a boy who cannot grow up; in Shakespeare's 'Tell me where is fancy bred?' [*Merchant of Venice* III ii 63], he is a short-lived infant). In depicting Fancy as a boy who is nonetheless a father, Spenser merges both images, thus legitimizing desire and linking it to the universal experience of procreation. This sociable, desiring, parental Fancy projects a more generous image. Poets as celestially inspired seers are necessarily a minority and suffer the loneliness and disregard complained of in *October* and *Teares*. Poets as lovers and parents, however, articulate common experience and are more readily heard and widely appreciated. It is as Colin Clout, the lover-poet, that Spenser chooses to present himself in *The Shepheardes Calender*, *Colin Clout*, and especially *FQ* VI.

The disadvantage of associating imagination and desire was that it seriously impaired the plausibility of the poet's claim to truth. Poetry, Bacon writes, 'doth raise and erect the mind, by submitting the shews of things to the desires of the mind; whereas reason doth buckle and bow the mind unto the nature of things' (ed 1857–74, 3:343–6). Defense of the nature of Spenser's imagination had to wait upon general acceptance, about the time of the Romantics, that poetry is a product of a unique, autonomous imagination.

FELICITY A. HUGHES

Murray Wright Bundy 1927 *The Theory of Imagination in Classical and Mediaeval Thought* (Urbana); Guillory 1983; I.G. MacCaffrey 1976; Rossky 1958.

imitation The theory of poetry as mimesis (an art of imitation) and the question of what and how poets do or should imitate are elaborated by Plato in the *Republic* (597–9, 602) and other dialogues. Poetry and painting, he suggests, are thrice removed from reality, copying nature as nature copies the ideas: they imitate appearances or fantasies rather than truth. In his *Poetics* (ch 5), Aristotle discusses the subject more systematically and more sympathetically, primarily in relation to tragic drama. Arguing that men naturally delight in works of imitation, he distinguishes sharply between two different kinds of poetry: the graver poets imitate noble actions by noble persons, the meaner imitate the actions of the ignoble.

Although the mimetic theory of art was never entirely abandoned, it was partly displaced during much of the Middle Ages and early Renaissance by other theories, in particular, the equally ancient concept of poetry as allegorical fable or myth. In sixteenth-century Italy, the mimetic theory underwent a significant revival and elaborate development after the rediscovery and publication of the *Poetics*, and gradually made its way through northern and western Europe. Since most critics read Aristotle's treatise in the light of other and more familiar traditions, their mimetic theories were usually eclectic – sometimes more Horatian or Platonic than Aristotelian in emphasis – and often diverged significantly not only in their interpretation of Aristotle's views but in their attitudes toward modern, nonclassical genres such as romance.

How much of this critical theory was known to Spenser is uncertain. His treatise *The English Poete* is lost, though we do know that he discoursed 'at large' on the poet's divine *enthousiasmos* and 'celestiall inspiration' (*SC, Oct* Arg) – a concept discussed in Plato's *Ion* and *Phaedrus* but easily accessible in many later authors. E.K. mentions Plato's *Laws* on the origin of poetry (*Oct* 21 gloss). Though there is no evidence that Spenser knew Aristotle's *Poetics* and though he does not specifically mention Plato's doctrine of poetry as mimesis, it would be rash to infer that he was altogether unfamiliar with their theories.

The subject also attracted the attention of other Elizabethan authors. In *The Scholemaster*, Ascham defines imitation as 'a facultie to expresse livelie and perfitelie that example: which ye go about to folow.' The 'whole doctrine' of comedies and tragedies is a 'perfite *imitation*, or faire livelie painted picture of the life of everie degree of man' (ed 1904:264, 266). According to Puttenham's *Arte of English Poesie* (I.1), the poet is 'both a maker and a counterfaitor: and Poesie an art not only of making, but also of imitation.' As 'a follower or imitator,' the poet 'can expresse the true and lively of every thing is set before him, and which he taketh in hand to describe.' Sidney similarly defines poetry as 'an art of imitation, for so Aristotle termeth it in the word *mimesis* – that is to say, a representing, counterfeiting, or figuring forth – to speak metaphorically, a speaking picture – with this end, to teach and delight.' The distinctive office of the poet consists in 'feigning notable images of virtues, vices, or what else,' with 'delightful teaching' (ed 1973b:79–81).

Although Ascham (and apparently Spenser himself) uses the term *imitation* in restricted senses, Sidney and many Italian critics, following Plato and Cicero, give it a much more comprehensive meaning; and for theorists like Jacopo Mazzoni, it covers the entire range of the poet's representational modes. We do not know whether Spenser had access to Sidney's *Defence* in manuscript; but even if it is not a demonstrable influence, it is valuable as a synthesis of various contemporary ideas on the nature of the poet's mode of representation and its relation to reality. In particular, it restates the concept of 'ideal' imitation, which may be regarded as a major strand in Renaissance poetic theory. Like many continental theorists, Sidney fuses Aristotelian and Platonic notions of imitation with the Horatian ideal of teaching delightfully by example, with the classical view of poetry as speaking picture (see *ut pictura poesis*), and with traditional conceptions of *poesis* as fictive invention ('making' and 'feigning'). With Aristotle he argues that poetry is more philosophical and more serious than history because it deals with the 'universal consideration.' With Horace he affirms the superior efficacy of the poet's exemplars over the philosopher's precepts: by coupling 'the general notion with the particular example,' the poet yields to the 'powers of the mind an image of that whereof the philosopher bestoweth but a wordish description' (ed 1973b:85). Sidney also adapts to the doctrine of poetry as an imitation of ideas the Platonic commonplace that 'who could see virtue would be wonderfully ravished with the love of her beauty,' for 'poetry ever sets virtue so out in her best colours ... that one must needs be enamoured of her' (pp 98, 90). Arguing that a feigned example has as much force to teach as a true one, he asserts the virtual independence of the poet's invention, his freedom to soar beyond nature and fact into the 'divine consideration of what may be and should be' and to produce a second and superior nature: things 'either better than nature bringeth forth, or, quite anew, forms such as never were in nature' (pp 81, 78).

Although Spenser alludes frequently to the exemplary aspects of poetry and to its association with types and allegory, his explicit references to imitation are comparatively few. In *Teares*, he commends 'Our pleasant *Willy*' (unidentified) as 'the man, whom Nature selfe had made / To mock her selfe, and Truth to imitate, / With kindly counter under Mimick shade' (205–10). This reference occurs, significantly, in the immediate context of Thalia's lamentation over the decline of comedy and apparently echoes the familiar definition of comedy attributed to Cicero by Donatus: 'imitatio vitae, speculum consuetudinis, imago veritatis' ('imitation of life, mirror of custom, image of truth'; Spingarn 1908:104). Spenser could have encountered it as a schoolboy in editions of Terence. Elsewhere in his own writings, he normally prefers the alternative terms *image*, *mirror*, and the like to *imitation*. In *The Faerie Queene*, he sometimes treats imitation pejoratively. Archimago fashions a counterfeit Una out of an idle dream (I i 45–6); for this false Una, the poet uses *imitate* primarily in the sense of dramatic impersonation. Having 'made a Lady of that other Spright, / And fram'd of liquid ayre her tender partes / So lively, and so like in all mens sight, / That weaker sence it could have ravisht quight,' the enchanter teaches this new creature 'to imitate that Lady trew, / Whose semblance she did carrie under feigned hew.' Similarly the witch creates a false Florimell, who is so marvelously contrived that she puts Nature herself to shame, and animates this statue with a wicked spirit skilled in 'counterfeisance' (III viii 5–9): 'Him shaped thus, she deckt in garments gay, / Which *Florimell* had left behind her late, / That who so then her saw, would surely say, / It was her selfe, whom it did imitate, / Or fairer then her selfe.' Imitating, in either a favorable or a pejorative sense, is thus a kind of feigning or counterfeiting; and Spenser's terminology in most of the passages cited above (*counter*, *counterfet*, *counterfeisance*, *lively*, *like*, *semblance*) is reminiscent of the language that his own fellow countrymen – Ascham, Puttenham, Sidney – had applied to mimetic theory in general.

In part at least, Spenser's imagery of imitation and counterfeiting is reminiscent of Ovid's poetry. In his description of the house of Sleep (*Metamorphoses* 11.592-649), Ovid describes the god Somnus surrounded by dreams which imitate various forms. Juno's messenger Iris bids Sleep to counterfeit a dream 'that shall seem true form.' Morpheus is described as 'a cunning imitator of the human form,' skilled in imitating human beings in gesture and gait, garb and speech. His brothers are likewise specialists at imitation. One of them concentrates on imitating birds, beasts, and reptiles; another, in imitating inanimate objects. Spenser alludes to such imitation of nature by art in *FQ* II xii 42 in describing the site of Acrasia's Bower of Bliss: 'A place pickt out by choice of best alive, / That natures worke by art can imitate' (on their rivalry, see *nature and art).

The primary emphases of Aristotle's mimetic theory – the single, complete action as the object of imitation; the plot as the soul of the poem; probability, necessity, and verisimilitude in the arrangement and connection of incidents – are tangential to Spenser's romance, just as they are largely irrelevant to the romances of Boiardo and Ariosto. Both of these Italian poets had written before the development of neo-Aristotelian critical theory in their country, and had thus managed to escape its tyranny. A generation or two later (as Spenser may have been aware), Italian critics were debating the relevance of Aristotle's 'rules' to romance, and especially to Ariosto's *Orlando furioso*.

Spenser shows greater affinities with those critics who (like Sidney) had assimilated Aristotle's concept of imitation to Horatian views, combining the ideas of poetry as image, moral example, and speaking picture. With Horace and Sidney, he affirms the superior efficacy of 'ensample' over precept (Letter to Raleigh). In Ulysses, according to Horace, Homer had fashioned an exemplar of virtue and wisdom, teaching the principles of morality more effectively than the philosophers Chrysippus and Crantor (*Epistles* 1.2). Sidney similarly lauds the heroic poet as one who 'teacheth and moveth to the most high and excellent truth ... For as the image of each action stirreth and instructeth the mind, so the lofty image of such worthies most inflameth the mind with desire to be worthy, and informs with counsel how to be worthy' (ed 1973b:98). Spenser's remarks on the principal hero of his romance belong to this predominantly Horatian tradition. Declaring his intention of portraying the moral and political virtues in the person of Arthur (the 'image of a brave knight' and subsequently of an ideal king), he claims to be following the precedent of earlier 'historicall' (ie, narrative or epic) poets, both ancient and modern.

The nature and qualities of Spenser's imitation vary widely, from realistic to ideal and from sensuous to abstract. Its most striking feature is the carefully realized, imaginative presentation of conceptual structures through a judicious choice and arrangement of significant particulars: 'fitting' details selected in accordance with the principles of decorum and vividness (*enargeia*) and applied to the description of persons, places, and actions. Many of these descriptions are allegorical or exemplary, and they often bear a viable relationship to the symbolic pageants, tournaments, masques, fetes, and figurative castles associated with Renaissance court and civic spectacles. (Spenser himself refers to his poem and its books as a 'Pageaunt' in the dedicatory sonnet to Howard.) Behind these verbal tableaux lie the traditions of Renaissance mythographical and iconographical literature and the descriptions of characters, landscapes, and personifications left by Virgil and Ovid, Ariosto, Chaucer and Langland, and other poets. JOHN M. STEADMAN

For Renaissance concepts of imitation, see John D. Boyd, SJ 1968 *The Function of Mimesis and Its Decline* (Cambridge, Mass); Doran 1954:53–84, 404–9; Greene 1982; Spingarn 1908; Steadman 1974; W[illem] J[acob] Verdenius 1949 *Mimesis: Plato's Doctrine of Artistic Imitation and Its Meaning to Us* (Leiden); Weinberg 1961. For imitation and 'counterfeiting,' see Miskimin 1975:35–80, 132–55. See also Auerbach ed 1953.

imitation of authors *Imitatio auctorum* is not to be confused with the more general theory of poetry as mimesis, imitation of nature. Although the two traditions sometimes converged (as in neoclassical concepts of art as a more perfect nature and a better model for imitation than nature itself), they usually involved different notions of imitation and underwent separate, though not entirely independent, development.

The imitation of authors served both as an aesthetic principle and as a pedagogical technique. Well-established in the rhetorical schools of the Roman Empire, it played a major role in shaping the theory and practice of humanist educators in Renaissance Italy, especially after the rediscovery early in the fifteenth century of a complete text of Quintilian's treatise on the education of the orator. With the diffusion of humanist pedagogical ideas, it became a standard method in most of the Latin grammar schools of western and northern Europe; at Merchant Taylors' School in London, Spenser would have acquired firsthand experience of it.

Both the *Rhetorica ad Herennium* and Quintilian's *Institutio oratoria* (*The Education of an Orator*) were utilized as textbooks in Renaissance schools. The former included imitation along with art (ie, precept) and exercise or practice as essential elements in an orator's education. The latter advised imitating the best authors – thus complementing the three conventional requirements for oratorical excellence: natural talent, art, and exercise. It also encouraged the formation of a personal style, and warned against subservience to one author.

Ascham's *Scholemaster* distinguishes three distinct kinds of imitation in 'matters of learning'. The first is the mimetic theory of drama. The second is 'to folow for learning of tonges and sciences, the best authors': this entails a decision as to 'whether, one or many are to be folowed: and if one, who is that one.' The third is closely related to the second: 'when you be determined, whether ye will folow one or mo, to know perfitlie, and which way to folow that one: in what place: by what meane and order: by what tooles and instrumentes ye shall do it.' On this point, the Strasbourg humanist Johann Sturm is the best guide, showing who and what should be followed and explaining 'by what way and order, trew Imitation is rightlie to be exercised.' In imitating a given author, the follower might either treat different material in a similar manner or handle the same material in a different way. Thus Virgil followed Homer, 'but the Argument to the one was *Ulysses*, to the other *Aeneas*.' Similarly, Cicero persecuted Antony 'with the same wepons of eloquence, that *Demosthenes* used before against *Philippe*' (Ascham ed 1904:266–71).

Besides its value as a formal pedagogical

technique, *imitatio auctorum* was also recognized as an aesthetic principle. Horace had urged the Latin poet to study carefully the masterpieces of Greece: 'handle Greek models by night, handle them by day' (*Ars poetica* 268–9). Longinus had proposed the 'imitation and emulation of the great prose writers and poets of antiquity' as a source of inspiration and an aid to elevation in style (*On the Sublime* 32). Cintio advised youthful poets to study and imitate the best narrative poets in order to develop their own critical judgments and to recapture the 'enthusiasm' (divine inspiration) of the masters. Minturno stressed the importance of selecting as models for imitation the comparatively few poets of greater merit, and urged that the imitator learn to disguise his borrowings so skillfully 'that what is borrowed seems to have sprung up in your own garden and not to have been transplanted from that of another' (see Gilbert 1940:163–4, 265–7, 301–2). In their admiration for Virgil, both Vida and Scaliger carried the principle of imitating the ancients to still greater extremes; it became (as Spingarn comments) 'the chief and almost the only element of literary creation.' 'All the things which you have to imitate,' Scaliger declared, 'you have according to another nature, that is Virgil' (see Spingarn 1908:131–4).

Spenser's imitation of earlier authors in *The Shepheardes Calender* is of particular interest to E.K.; he uses the word *imitate* exclusively in this sense. Noting that Spenser had followed the example of both classical and modern poets in exercising his fledgling genius in the eclogue, E.K. cites the precedent of earlier poets such as Theocritus and Virgil: so flew 'divers other excellent both Italian and French Poetes, whose foting this Author every where followeth, yet so as few, but they be wel sented can trace him out' (Epistle to Harvey). His commentary singles out passages imitated from several of these authors, as well as echoes of Hesiod and Horace, the epitaph of Sardanapalus, and even a common proverb. He observes that the *November* eclogue 'is made in imitation of Marot his song, which he made upon the death of Loys the frenche Queene. But farre passing his reache' (*Nov* Arg). In his gloss to the envoy, E.K. notes that Spenser is 'folowing the ensample of Horace and Ovid' in making a calendar 'That steele in strength, and time in durance shall outweare.'

Spenser overgoes Marot, and his original hope 'to emulate, and ... overgo' Ariosto in *The Faerie Queene* (as Harvey says in *Three Letters* 3, *Var Prose* p 471) reflects the same Renaissance version of *imitatio auctorum*: mastering an art by close, judicious imitation and adaptation of earlier authors, but avoiding servile copying and allowing ample scope for one's own peculiar genius and for freedom of invention – and aspiring to equal or even surpass such models, both ancient and modern. Thus Sidney urges that in imitating earlier writers poets should 'devour them whole, and make them wholly theirs' (*Defence* ed 1973b:117). A more general instance of the same principle appears in Spenser's conception of Arthur as exemplary warrior and ruler. In thus fashioning a hero perfected in both private and public virtues, he claims in the Letter to Raleigh to 'have followed all the antique Poets historicall': the ancients Homer and Virgil as well as the moderns Ariosto and Tasso.

Spenser's adaptations and imitations of his predecessors include Greek and Latin, French and Italian and English authors: Homer and Theocritus and Hesiod, Virgil and Ovid, Ariosto and Tasso, Marot and the Pléiade, Chaucer and Sidney. One must admire the skill with which he has assimilated his borrowings – material, formal, and stylistic – from other writers and (in particular) the combination of imitation and free invention in *The Shepheardes Calender*, *Daphnaïda*, and *The Faerie Queene*. His wide range of literary echoes, allusions, and adaptations helps to establish the continuity of these works with genres notable for their variety as well as for their international character and their antiquity. Evoking both the pastoral tradition and that of heroic poem and romance, he has to a degree 'naturalized' the genres, assimilating them to the native poetic tradition and giving them a British identity and context.

JOHN M. STEADMAN

For discussion of Spenser's indebtedness to earlier poets, see articles listed in Spenser's *reading. See also Greene 1982; O.B. Hardison, Jr, ed 1963 *English Literary Criticism: The Renaissance* (New York) esp pp 59–64; G.W. Pigman, III 1979 'Imitation and the Renaissance Sense of the Past: The Reception of Erasmus' *Ciceronianus*' *JMRS* 9:155–77; Pigman 1980 'Versions of Imitation in the Renaissance' *RenQ* 33:1–32; Spingarn 1908; H.O. White 1935.

imitations and adaptations, Renaissance (1579-1660) *The Shepheardes Calender* and *The Faerie Queene*, Spenser's most frequently imitated works, became literary models for very different reasons. The *Calender*'s appearance in 1579 started a trend in experimenting with the 'base' and 'homely' pastoral genre and its forms. Epic poetry, however, was no mere testing ground for aspiring writers; and *The Faerie Queene* gave this genre an English authority and identity. Even though going out of fashion in the seventeenth century, it provided a native model for translations of foreign epics, for England's new heroic poetry, and for poets who wished to revive and supplement it during the troubled reign of Charles I.

In the late sixteenth and early seventeenth centuries, the *Calender* exerted a strong influence on writers who wanted to test a new type of English verse. Many works imitated the *Calender*'s verse forms, pastoral themes, and diction, including Drayton's *Idea: The Shepheards Garland* (1593) and Lodge's *Phillis* (1593). Other writers borrowed names from Spenser, for example, Henoch Clapham's 'Pastoral Epilogue, betweene Hobbinoll, and Collin Clout' (1608:102–3) and John Davies of Hereford's 'Eclogue between Yong Willy, the Singer of His Native Pastorals, and Old Wernocke His Friend' (1614; in Davies ed 1878, 2: m17–22). During the Stuart reign, Spenserian pastoral was generally scorned, though some writers based their entire careers on it. William Browne's *Shepheards Pipe* (1614) borrowed some of the *Calender*'s verse forms; his *Britannia's Pastorals* (1613–16) used Spenserian episodes, characters, and language, as did Phineas Fletcher's *Piscatorie Eclogs* (1633) and *Sylva poetica* (1633). In his *Kalendarium humanae vitae: The Kalender of Mans Life* (1638), Robert Farley moved away from the Spenserian style, presenting instead both a Latin poem and – on facing pages – an English translation in iambic pentameter couplets. By beginning his twelve-poem sequence in March rather than January, he departed further from Spenser. Francis Quarles' *Shepheardes Oracles* (1646) and William Basse's *Pastorals* (1653) returned to the imitation of the *Calender*'s style and structure. Many of these imitative works represent poetic trials for their authors, who also often used the pastoral to escape from a difficult era (under an aging queen or an incompetent king) and return to the golden age of the *Calender*.

If Spenser wrote *The Shepheardes Calender* to show that the pastoral form of Theocritus in the Greek language and of Virgil in the Latin could be rendered in English, Latin translations indicate that some missed the point. An anonymous writer translated the *Aprill* song as *Hymnus pastoralis in laudem serenissimae Reginae Elizabethae* (c 1600; BL Ms Harleian 532); John Dove translated the whole poem in *Poimenologia, que vulgo calendarium pastorum appellatur e versu Anglicano in latinum traducta* (c 1584; the manuscript is at Gonville and Caius College, Cambridge), and so did Theodore Bathurst in *Calendarium pastorale* (c 1608; two manuscripts are in the British Library; another is at Pembroke College, Cambridge; the work was printed posthumously in 1653, 1679, and 1732). That the translators did not have these works printed in their lifetimes suggests that the Latin verses were conceived as exercises (Bradner 1935–6).

As the *Calender* provided a model for English pastoral, *The Faerie Queene* provided a model for the diction, style, and syntax of epic translators. Chief among the translations were Harington's of Ariosto's *Orlando furioso* (1591), Edward Fairfax's of Tasso's *Gerusalemme liberata* (1600), Joshua Sylvester's of du Bartas' *La Sepmaine ou création du monde* (1605), and Fanshawe's of Camoens' *Lusiads* (1655). Others attempted original heroic verse using *The Faerie Queene* as a model. Barnfield's *Cynthia* (1595) may have been the first work to use the Spenserian stanza; and Spenser's style and epic quest served as a model for patriotic poems such as Daniel's *Civil Wars* (Books 1–5, 1595) and Drayton's *Poly-Olbion* (1612), and for romance epics such as Patrick Gordon's *First Booke of the Famous Historye of Penardo and Laissa* (1615), Phineas Fletcher's *Purple Island* (1633), and William Davenant's *Gondibert* (1650). Still others used Spenser's techniques to create a new kind of religious epic, such as Giles

Fletcher's *Christs Victorie, and Triumph* (1610), Thomas Robinson's *Life and Death of Mary Magdalene* (c 1620), Cowley's *Davideis* (1656), and most notably Milton's *Paradise Lost*. All these epics – patriotic, romantic, and sacred – received their authority from *The Faerie Queene*, which taught aspiring epic poets that English was a dignified language for serious narratives.

Other original poetry found its source in episodes from *The Faerie Queene*. In the preface to his *Tale of Two Swannes* (1590), William Vallans alludes to a Latin *Epith. Thamesis*, which may be the lost work by Spenser thought to have been adapted for the marriage of Thames and Medway in *FQ* IV xi. In *Spencers Squiers Tale* (1616), John Lane completed the story of Cambell, Cambina, Triamond, and Canacee (IV ii 31–5), which Spenser had already inherited from Chaucer. Unoriginal but historically significant, the anonymous *Faerie Leveller* (1648; Wing F81, S4967) reprinted Spenser's episode in which Artegall and Talus defeat the Giant with the scales and scatter his rebellious mob (V ii 29–54). The preface argues that Spenser's tale of the 1590s is 'propheticall' because (as the 'key of the work' explains) Artegall represents Charles I, Talus stands for the King's forces, Munera symbolizes the 'intolerable Tax-raisers,' and the 'Gyant Leveller' is Oliver Cromwell. Spenser's episode thus reveals 'the dangerous doings' of the Levellers. The author claims that he is reviving *The Faerie Queene*'s story 'for the undeceiving of simple people,' thus echoing Spenser's estimation of the Giant's unruly followers (V ii 33).

The Faerie Queene inspired not only translators and authors of original epics but also direct imitators. In *A Fig for Fortune* (1596), Anthony Copley turned *FQ* I into a Roman Catholic allegory. Ralph Knevet's unpublished *Supplement of the Faery Queene* (c 1633) attempted to complete Spenser's epic by adding Books VII–IX. These books present the legends of Albanio, or Prudence (James I); Callimachus, or Fortitude (Gustavus Adolphus II, Sweden's Protestant champion in the Thirty Years' War); and Belcoeur, or Liberality (who, like Spenser's Calidore, has little connection with the political allegory). The reactionary Knevet followed Spenser's stanza structure, archaic diction, allegorical character types, episodes, and chivalric world – though with limited artistic success.

Political instability in the 1630s and 1640s also led Samuel Sheppard to revive Spenser's age of supposed calm, heroism, and nationalism. In *The Faerie King* (c 1650), he did not use Spenser's stanza form, characters, or diction but wrote instead a six-book antiheroic epic for his own age, an historical allegory evaluating Charles I and the events that led to his execution. Like Copley and Knevet, Sheppard was a man of limited poetic skills; but he offers an interesting, ambiguous portrait of England's leaders and political climate during the Civil Wars. Although imitation of Spenser's pastoral in the 1590s had the spirit of experimentation, by the time of Charles' reign authors turned to Spenser the established poet and tried to preserve his view of an orderly world ruled by a wise monarch. PAUL J. KLEMP

C.R. Baskervill 1913 'The Early Fame of *The Shepheards Calender*' *PMLA* 28:291–313; Bradner 1935–6; Greenlaw 1911; Greenlaw 1913.

COLLECTIONS, EDITIONS, AND REPRINTS William Basse 1870 *Pastorals and Other Works* (London); Basse 1893 *Poetical Works* ed R. Warwick Bond (London); Theodore Bathurst 1653 *Calendarium pastorale* (London); Henoch Clapham 1608 *Errour on the Left Hand: Through a Frozen Securitie* (London); Anthony Copley 1883 *A Fig for Fortune* (1596) Publications of the Spenser Society 35 (Manchester); William Davenant 1673 *Works* (London; facs rpt New York 1968); John Davies of Hereford 1878 *Complete Works* ed Alexander B. Grosart, 2 vols (Edinburgh); Fletcher and Fletcher ed 1908–9; Ralph Knevett 1955 'An Edition of Ralph Knevett's *Supplement of the Faery* Queene (1635)' ed Andrew Lavender, 2 vols (diss New York Univ); Knevett 1966 *Shorter Poems* ed Amy M. Charles (Columbus, Ohio); John Lane 1887–90 *John Lane's Continuation of Chaucer's 'Squire's Tale'* ed Frederick J. Furnivall, Chaucer Society Publications 2nd ser 23, 26 (London); Francis Quarles 1880–1 *Works* ed Alexander B. Grosart, 3 vols (Edinburgh); Thomas Robinson 1899 *The Life and Death of Mary Magdalene* ed H. Oskar Sommer, EETS es 78 (London); Samuel Sheppard 1984 *The Faerie King (c. 1650)* ed P[aul] J. Klemp (Salzburg).

---

imitations and adaptations, 1660-1800 After Milton and before Shakespeare, Spenser was the English Renaissance writer most often imitated in the eighteenth century. Faced by a rising enthusiasm for Spenser, Samuel Johnson expressed dissatisfaction over the imitation of his style, particularly of his diction and stanza, a practice which, at mid-century, 'by the influence of some men of learning and genius, seems likely to gain upon the age' (*Rambler* 121, May 1751). And some 30 years later, when he came to write *The Lives of the Poets* (1779–81), Johnson did not change his mind. In his Life of Gilbert West (a skillful imitator of Spenser), Johnson praises West's imitations for 'the metre, the language, and the fiction,' three aspects that contemporary commentators on Spenser always addressed; but he adds that such works

> are not to be reckoned among the great achievements of the intellect, because their effect is local and temporary; they appeal not to reason or passion, but to memory, and pre-suppose an accidental or artificial state of mind. An imitation of Spenser is nothing to a reader, however acute, by whom Spenser has never been perused. Works of this kind may deserve praise, as proofs of great industry and great nicety of observation, but the highest praise, the praise of genius, they cannot claim.

Despite Johnson's animadversions, the imitation of Spenser occupied the talents of a wide range of poets, all of whom were perhaps content to fall short of 'the praise of genius,' but whose work is nonetheless an extraordinary testimony to the 'great industry and great nicety of observation' of the age.

The vogue for imitating Spenser in the period 1660–1800 began in 1706, the year of Matthew Prior's 'An Ode, Humbly Inscrib'd to the Queen.' Before Prior, there were only a handful of Spenser imitations (see below); after 1706, Spenser imitations multiplied rapidly. The most intense period of imitation was around 1746 to 1758, though imitations are found in abundance throughout the eighteenth century. Of some 250 verifiable imitations and adaptations (not including works only influenced by, or alluding to, or echoing Spenser), at least 50 come from this short period of the mid-century, so it is little wonder that Johnson wrote as he did in his *Rambler* essay of 1751. The thirteen years produced James Thomson's *The Castle of Indolence* (1748), one of the best imitations, and the writings of Moses Mendez, one of the most authentic imitators of the age. Also from this same brief period came the imitations of the influential anthologist Robert Dodsley, himself a minor Spenser imitator, whose collections of *Poems* (6 vols, 1758–63) contain 12 Spenser imitations which are at once reprises of the efforts of earlier imitators and harbingers of the kinds of imitations to appear in the second half of the century. During these few years, there were at least 19 imitations of *The Faerie Queene* totaling some 700 Spenserian stanzas. There were at least 7 more that adopted the quasi-Spenserian stanza which Prior introduced in his 'Ode' of 1706: *ababcdcdeE*, the final line an alexandrine. There were imitations of Spenser's sonnet form by writers such as Thomas Percy, a mysterious Dr P., and Thomas Edwards, who in 1748 wrote his Sonnet 8 'On the Cantos of Spenser's Fairy Queen, Lost in the Passage from Ireland.' Other Spenserians imitated *The Shepheardes Calender*, *Epithalamion*, *Amoretti*, *Fowre Hymnes*, *Time*, and *Mother Hubberd*. There was also a 1758 blank-verse adaptation of *The Shepheardes Calender* by one 'Philisides.' This concentrated output at mid-century shares many characteristics with other imitations and adaptations of the years from 1660 to 1800.

The middle years of the century produced imitations in several major categories: (1) allegorical imitations, (2) 'new' or substitution cantos, (3) continuation cantos, (4) bucolic and 'seasons' poems, (5) elegies and panegyrics, (6) political and satiric pieces, (7) school or education poems, and (8) major-author imitations. These divisions do not include miscellaneous adaptations of Spenser such as Blake's 'Head of Spenser' (c 1800; see, too, his tempera entitled 'The Characters in Spenser's *Faerie Queene*' c 1825); the anonymous *New Occasional Oratorio* (with the text of recitative and chorus adapted from Milton and Spenser), 'rehearsed at Handel's lodging' and performed 14 February 1746 at Covent Garden; a prose rendering of *The Faerie Queene* called *Prince Arthur: An Allegorical Romance* (1779, 2 vols in I); or *Colin Clout's Madrigal, on the Auspicious First of March 1727–8* (1728); and the anonymous *The Cestus: A Mask* (c 1783?), a three-act imitation of Spenser's *FQ* II, IV and Milton's *Comus* (BL, Egerton Ms 3507).

Like their fellows throughout the century, mid-century imitators were fond of generalized or partial allegories. For example, in 1747, the Reverend Robert Bedingfield published 'The Education of Achilles,' a passable imitation of *The Faerie Queene*'s form and diction; the content, however, is strictly eighteenth century. In this poem, Thetis takes her son Achilles to the famous centaur Chiron, in a wood where Aesculapius, Jason, and her husband Peleus were educated. Modesty lives nearby, close to Temperance, Fidelity, Benevolence, Experience, Contemplation, even Exercise. 'The fond parent left her darling care' with this group to learn discipline. In the final stanza (14), after 'The stern-brow'd boy in mute attention stood' to learn his lessons from the sages, he ends up shaking his shield 'And braves th'indignant flood, and thunders o'er the field.' Seemingly all that instruction did little to teach Achilles control. There is nothing Spenserian here, not even the slight situational humor. A synecdoche of sorts for all imitations of this type, Bedingfield's piece is characterized by feeble, transparent allegory, absence of literary ornamentation, emphasis on instructive elements, and roots which cannot be tied to any specific episode, character, or meaning in Spenser.

None of the many eighteenth-century allegorical imitations like Bedingfield's are of the first rank except James Thomson's *Castle of Indolence* (1748), with its Spenserian sensuousness and its clash of seemingly opposite personifications of Indolence and Industry, the former superior to the latter portrait. Even its wry humor is reminiscent of Spenser. Second to Thomson's *Castle* in excellence but equal in influence on later Spenser imitators is James Beattie's more philosophically murky *The Minstrel, or The Progress of Genius* (1771, 1774), in two books totaling 123 Spenserian stanzas; Wordsworth was impressed by its hero, Edwin, the nature lover.

'New' or substitution cantos are exemplified by John Upton's *New Canto of Spencer's Fairy Queen* (1747), curiously in 42 Prior, not Spenserian, stanzas. Seen occasionally throughout the century, this sort of imitation is usually an ambitious effort to copy authentic Spenserian detail and to adhere to Spenser's stories. In a quite non-Spenserian touch, however, Upton includes scholarly notes to explain his allegory. His motto promises a tale indebted to *FQ* I, but he uses Book III as well: 'From Ill to Ill, through various Scenes, / Led is the Fairy Knight: / Him Arthur Heav'n directed saves, / From Archimago's Spite.' Upton's fairy knight is Sir Paridel rather than Redcrosse, perhaps because Paridell had also been saved by Arthur (*FQ* IV ix). He also has some of the sensualism of Spenser's Paridell (III ix-x).

Closely related to substitution cantos are 'continuation cantos.' Both types are represented in works by Samuel Croxall, Moses Mendez, and William Julius Mickle. Croxall, the first masterly imitator of Spenser's stanza, diction, and pictorialism, wrote two important imitations early in the century: *An Original Canto of Spencer, Design'd as Part of His Fairy Queen, but Never Printed* (1713), and *Another Original Canto of Spencer* (1714). Both are topical pro-Whig allegories in verse startlingly similar to Spenser's own. An important transitional imitator writing at mid-century, Moses Mendez helped turn the fashion away from more purely political-allegorical content and manner with his emphasis on description and narration. Especially noteworthy are *The Squire of Dames* (1751) and *The Blatant Beast* (c 1755), his loose imitations of *The Faerie Queene*. The former poem is in two cantos, the second of which is much better, especially in its Castle of Bon-vivant and L'Allegro episodes. *The Blatant Beast*, also in two cantos, shows Sir Pelleas' adventures and misadventures with the Blatant Beast, Peter the Eremite, Talus, and Florella; it is a good imitation of Spenser's diction, form, and humor.

Another practitioner of the continuation canto is William Julius Mickle, who revised his popular *The Concubine* (1767, 4 eds by 1772) into *Sir Martyn, or The Progress of Dissipation* (1777) in two cantos totaling 136 Spenserian stanzas. This piece is noteworthy for its tongue-in-cheek humor and its imitation of Spenserian similes, antique diction, and painterly descriptions. It is a domestic tale of Sir Martyn and his domineering Lady Kathrin, who is perhaps the model for Tabitha Bramble in Smollett's *Humphrey Clinker* (1771). Canto I is a good imitation of Spenser, and canto 2 has attractive bucolic scenes and an able imitation of a Spenser cave scene in its Cave of Discontent; but Mickle's fable of Martyn's dissipation in canto 2 is digressive.

Bucolic imitations (including rural-life and pastoral poems), and 'seasons' imitations (including 'days' and time poems) are amply represented at mid-century in Robert Potter's 'A Farewell Hymne to the Country' (1749), Moses Mendez's 'The Seasons' (1751), Thomas Warton, Jr's 'A Pastoral in the Manner of Spenser' (1753), and William Vernon's 'The Parish Clerk' (1758). Among the century's finest poems in imitation of Spenser is William Thompson's *Hymn to May* (c 1740, 75 stanzas *ababccC*). The poem is a paean to May with Popean echoes, and with some surprising images, diction, and descriptions of moods, flowers, and creatures such as the bee (stanza 25) and fairy elves (34). Thompson's May is no time for owl, raven, ghost, witch, 'Ponk,' rumor, misery, or martial trumpet. Rather, it celebrates patriotism, innocence, simplicity, shepherds, and Venus' birthday. Ianthe is invoked in an excellent stanza beginning 'Come then, Ianthe! milder than the Spring' (61), and later, 'Ianthe! now, now love thy Spring away; / Ere cold October-blasts despoil the bloom of May' (68).

Other noteworthy bucolic and seasons imitations are anticipated if not influenced by Ambrose Philips' *Pastorals* (1708–9). (Pope's *Pastorals* of the same date were strongly influenced by Spenser but are not strictly imitations.) John Gay humorously combines the bucolic and seasonal in *The Shepherd's Week* (1714). The conduct and quality of rural life figure in imitations such as Moses Browne's *Piscatory Eclogues* (1729), William Melmoth's 'The Transformation of Lycon and Euphormius' (c 1743), as well as Robert Fergusson's 'The Farmer's Ingle' (1773), and its literary offspring, Robert Burns' 'The Cotter's Saturday Night' (1786). Other anonymous imitations include 'The Country Parson' (1737, published with its parody 'The Country Curate'), *Thames: A Canto ... in Imitation of Spenser* (1741), 'A Pastoral Digon Davy and Colin Clout' (1743?), and *The Progress of Time, or An Emblematical Representation of the Four Seasons and Twelve Months ... in Imitation of Spencer's Fairy Queen* (1743). A more *Sturm und Drang* nature setting is part of Andrew Macdonald's two 1782 imitations, *Velina* and 'Minvela.'

Rural-life imitations were written through the end of the century, among them Samuel Hoole's 'Edward, or The Curate' (1787), three imitations in 1788 by Gavin Turnbull ('Pastoral I,' 'The Bard,' and 'The Cottage'), Richard Polwhele's *The Influence of Local Attachment* (1796), John Bidlake's well-received *The Country Parson* (1797), John Merivale's continuation of James Beattie's poem *The Minstrel* (c 1798), and two end-of-century anonymous imitations, the first of Burns' poem called 'The Peasant's Sabbath,' and the second, *The Village Sunday: A Poem Moral and Descriptive, in the Manner of Spenser* (both c 1799).

Since most eighteenth-century readers and imitators of Spenser considered him a dignified, moral, and instructive poet, it is not surprising to find him adopted or adapted in several elegiac and panegyric pieces, most written before mid-century, some concerning events and persons of some moment, and some about persons long dead. Two of these poems, both written in 1706, are noteworthy. Thomas Warton, Sr's elegy, 'Philander: An Imitation of Spencer, Occasioned by the Death of Mr. William Levinz,' is significant only because of its author and its early date of composition, though it was not published for 42 years.

Matthew Prior's much more significant 'An Ode, Humbly Inscrib'd to the Queen' has already been noted for its 10-line adaptation of Spenser's stanza. Largely concerned with the battle of Ramillies (1706) and the Duke of Marlborough's puissance, it is also a panegyric of Queen Anne. Its adaptation of Spenser for panegyric, patriotic purposes was the century's first. Reading the 'Ode' as a satiric attack, William Atwood in 1706 severely reviewed it in *A Modern Inscription to the Duke of Marlborough's Fame*. But Prior's piece was not hindered. It was often reprinted (*Grub-Street Journal* 153, 30 November 1732, uses lines from it for its motto), and its stanza form was clearly influential.

No elegies imitative of Spenser were written after 1754, except for Robert Burns'

'Stanzas on the Same Occasion' (ie, the prospect of death) (1784) in three Spenserian stanzas of little distinction. Panegyrics faded even earlier – the final one was published in 1748 – partly because the fashion for such praise had greatly declined. Imitative panegyrics include Prior's 'Colin's Mistakes' (c 1717), William Thompson's 'An Epithalamium on the Royal Nuptials' of Frederick and Augusta (1736), Samuel Boyse's 'The Olive: An Heroic Ode' (1736), his equally poor 'An Ode, Sacred to the Birth of the Marquis of Tavistock' (1740), and William Hamilton's 'On Seeing a Lady [Mary Montgomery] Sit to Her Picture' (1748).

The Spenserian elegies are more substantial, beginning with William Mason's partly imitative *Musaeus: A Monody to the Memory of Mr. Pope* (1744). Pope's death in 1744 was also the occasion of Robert Dodsley's 'On the Death of Mr. Pope,' part of which imitated *The Shepheardes Calender*. Four more elegies come from the early fifties: in 1751, the anonymous 'Thales: A Monody, Sacred to the Memory of Dr. Pococke' and Thomas Warton's 'Elegy on the Death of the Late Frederick Prince of Wales'; in 1752, Thomas Blacklock's 'Philantheus'; and in 1754 another monody, Thomas Denton's 'Immortality, or The Consolation of Human Life.'

Most political and satirical imitations were written before mid-century. Although often the two types cannot be separated, a few works are more one than the other. Alexander Pope's 'The Alley' (c 1706) is possibly the earliest eighteenth-century satirical imitation. Its 6 Spenserian stanzas are a puerile burlesque of Spenser and a treatment of noisome experiences in alleys along or near the 'silver' Thames. It is a poor indication of Pope's respect for and indebtedness to Spenser; its few imitators include Shenstone (in muted fashion) and the more scurrilous 6 Spenserian stanzas of Christopher Pitt's 'The Jordan' (1747). A better satire is Richard Cambridge's 'Archimage' (1742), a buoyant mock-heroic piece of 29 Spenserian stanzas, replete with old diction, about a boat trip with a belle. Mark Akenside's 'The Virtuoso' (1737), in 10 Spenserian stanzas of fossilized and overdone diction, is a youthful spoof of that type of projector called the virtuoso. Nonetheless, it is the best of this group, all of which made some fun of Spenser, as Henry Mackenzie was to do in the mid-sixties with his companion poems in Prior stanzas, 'The Old Batchelor' and 'The Old Maid.'

Political imitations, which also touch upon religion and patriotism, lack the satires' mocking tone. Of the 13 political poems, excluding Prior's 'Ode,' 8 were published before 1752 and are better imitations than the largely patriotic examples following Thomas Denton's 1762 attack on the Catholic church, 'The House of Superstition,' which is reminiscent of Spenser's den of Error episode. Other late political imitations are the anonymous *Land of Liberty* (1775) in 2 cantos totaling 120 Spenserian stanzas, the anonymous 'Liberty' (1783) in Prior stanzas, Richard Polwhele's 'The Ancient and Modern Patriot Contrasted' (1795) in 6 Spenserian stanzas, and Sir James Burges' incredibly prolix *Richard the First* (1800) in 1849 Spenserian stanzas.

The political poems before mid-century are characteristically specific, for example, Robert Lloyd's 'The Progress of Envy' (1751), 30 Spenserian stanzas on the occasion of William Lauder's attack on Milton in 1747. After Prior's 1706 'Ode,' an anonymous imitator wrote a political satire in couplets on the Earl of Oxford's administration: *A Protestant Memorial, or The Shepheard's Tale of the Pouder-Plott* (1713). In that same year and the next appeared Samuel Croxall's two *Canto* poems. *An Original Canto* (1713), in 46 fine Spenserian stanzas, was immediately popular; it lightly purports to be a lost canto by Spenser himself – a claim made by few of Spenser's imitators. The motto of Croxall's poem indicates its content: 'Archimage with his Hell-hounds foul / Doth Britomart enchain: / Talus doth seek out Arthegall, / And tells him of her Pain.' *Another Original Canto of Spencer* (1714) is in 54 Spenserian stanzas of somewhat lesser quality than *An Original Canto*; its motto hints that the later poem may be a covert political satire: 'Archimage goes to Faction's House, / Deep delved under Ground: / The Hag adviseth how he may / Fair Britomart confound.' Both are good Spenser-like yarns, which the Whigs gleefully read as attacks on the Tories, 'party' being specially important in 1713–14. Three additional political imitations are an anonymous, supposedly Jacobite, parody of Spenser's *Mother Hubberd*, 'Mother Hubbards Tale of the Ape and Fox' (1715), an anonymous elegiac-panegyric-patriotic effort called 'The British Hero ... Sacred to the Immortal Memory of ... Marlborough', and Samuel Boyse's dismal 'Albion's Triumph' (1743).

School or education imitations include poems written by university students – some writing prize poems – as well as a small group of poems dealing directly with education. At least nine student pieces date from mid-century, beginning with Thomas Warton, Jr's 'Morning' and the anonymous 'An Imitation of Spenser,' both published in 1750 in *The Student, or The Oxford and Cambridge Miscellany*. Warton's stanza rhymes *ababcC*; the anonymous poem is in 6 Spenserian stanzas. Two others are Lewis Bagot's 'Imitation of the Epithalamion' (1755), published in *Gratulatio Academia Cantabrigiensis*, and the anonymous 'Morning: An Ode, Written by a Student Confined to College' (1772, *ababcC*), published in *The Gentleman's Magazine*. Five other school poems were Cambridge Prize winners published in the 1808 *Musae Seatonionae*. Beilby Porteus' 'Death' (1759) is in blank verse; the rest are in Prior stanzas: James Scott's 'Heaven: A Vision' (1760, in 31 stanzas indebted to the Bower of Bliss episode), James Scott's 'An Hymn to Repentance' (1762), Samuel Hayes' 'Hope' (1783), and Charles Philpot's 'Faith: A Vision' (1790). Clearly, Spenser's own university continued to be mindful of its famous son.

The four major imitations about education are longer, more substantial poems. Two of them are less important: Reverend Robert Bedingfield's 'The Education of Achilles' (1747, discussed above), and Thomas Ager's 'The Schoolmaster' (1794), an imitation of an imitation by Shenstone. The other two are quite good as Spenser imitations and as poems in their own right: William Shenstone's justly celebrated 'The School-Mistress' (1737, 1742, 1748) and Gilbert West's quite competent *Education: A Poem, in Two Cantos, Written in Imitation of the Style and Manner of Spenser's Faery Queen* (1751). A call for educational reform away from total adherence to antiquity, West's *Education*, in 96 Spenserian stanzas, is one of the better imitations of the century. Shenstone's school piece is one of the century's five or six best imitations of Spenser's stanza (even if not diction) and one of the age's better minor poems. 'The School-Mistress' began as an imitation of Pope's 'The Alley,' then expanded in subsequent editions from 12 to 28 to 35 Spenserian stanzas while adopting a tone somewhere between Pope's 'Alley' and Thomson's *Castle of Indolence*; its gentle burlesque of Spenser and tastefully humorous treatment of the schoolmistress are appealing. Exceedingly popular, Shenstone's poem led to other Spenser imitations. Although no enthusiast for the type, Dr Johnson approved of both West's and Shenstone's imitations.

Little work has been done on the major-author category. Except for Pope's youthful 'Alley,' neither he nor Dryden wrote imitations of Spenser – although both (and particularly Pope) were influenced by Spenser and used him in their own works. Dryden admired Spenser and learned much from him; but his age preferred to imitate or 'paraphrase' the Psalms, classical authors such as Pindar, Virgil, Homer, Horace, Anacreon, Ovid, and Martial, and 'moderns' such as Milton, Butler, Dryden, and even Defoe. In 1679, however, Samuel Woodford wrote an imitation of Spenser called *Epodē: The Legend of Love*, in 3 cantos of 189 Spenserian stanzas; and in 1687 appeared an anonymous adaptation of *FQ* I titled *Spencer Redivivus; Containing the First Book of the Fairy Queen* in some 4600 couplets.

Swift and Dr Johnson wrote no formal imitations of Spenser, and his influence on them is difficult to assess. Blake, on the other hand, was clearly interested in Spenser and adapted his stanza in 'An Imitation of Spenser' (early 1780s). All the major British Romantics were serious readers of Spenser, some lifelong; and a few revered him. Some were influenced by him in their own work, and some wrote imitations before 1800. Wordsworth's *Guilt and Sorrow*, in 74 Spenserian stanzas, was written in the early 1790s and partly published as 'The Female Vagrant.' Coleridge's two short imitations date from the mid-1790s: the lighthearted 'Effusion XXIV, in the Manner of Spenser' and 'To the Author of Poems' (Joseph Cottle), both in 5 Spenserian stanzas. Lamb openly revered Spenser; and his romantic 'Vision of Repentance' (1797), a dream-vision in 6 stanzas *ababcC* and 23 octosyllabic couplets, is at least as Spenserian as most late-eighteenth-century dream-vision poems, even those written in Spenser's *Faerie Queene* stanza.

Lesser eighteenth-century imitators of Spenser include Christopher Smart ('Hymn to the Supreme Being' 1756), William Cowper ('Anti-Thelyphthora' 1781), and Thomas Chatterton (several of the Rowley poems, possibly late 1760s). The Lonsdale 1969 edition of William Collins' poetry shows how imitative are his *Persian Eclogues* (1739) and his *Odes on Several Descriptive and Allegoric Subjects* (1746); and the same edition demonstrates how indebted the scholarly Thomas Gray was to Spenser, whom he steadily read. Gray reportedly told a friend that he never wrote poetry without first reading Spenser at length.

A final category can only be termed miscellaneous imitations on a broad range of subjects. In mid-century, Glocester Ridley's *Psyche* (1747) is a 51-stanza mix of Spenserianisms. *Psyche* is also the title and subject of 372 Spenserian stanzas by Mary Tighe (1795), perhaps the most influential of the nine eighteenth-century women who imitated Spenser. The others were Anna Barbauld, Jane Bowdler, Miss Hunt, Mary Leapor, Mary Robinson, Anna Seward, Elizabeth Smith, and Elizabeth Thomas.

Other subjects of imitations are hope (William Bowles 1796, an imitation of Spenser's masque of Cupid), pain and patience (Samuel Boyse c 1740 and Robert Dodsley 1742), the sun (Elijah Fenton 1707), music (George Sewell c 1710), taste (Alexander Thompson 1796), sickness (William Thompson 1745, in blank verse), the sexes (Samuel Wesley 1723), traveling (Gilbert West 1739, whose Redcrosse is an English xenophobe), and suicide (Alexander Wilson 1790). More specific miscellaneous imitations include Thomas Morell's 'Verses on a Silk Work' (1742), William Rider's 'Westminster Abbey' (1735), and William Thompson's 'The Nativity' (1736). Three good allegorical imitations complete this list: William Wilkie's 'A Dream in the Manner of Spenser' (1759) in 18 Spenserian stanzas, Hugh Downman's *The Land of the Muses* (1768) in 85 Spenserian stanzas (recast in couplets in 1791), and the anonymous 'The House of Care, in Imitation of Spenser's Faery Queen' in 8 stanzas. The various nature of many of the century's imitations is typified by Thomas Dermody's 14 imitations in several Spenserian measures, written from 1792 to the turn of the century about the pleasures of poetry, enthusiasm, ignorance, joy, pedantry, hope, fancy, the Reverend Mr Sterling, the Countess Moira, winter's night, and even coffeehouses.

The great number of Spenser imitations and adaptations between 1660 and 1800 leads to several generalizations. First, the imitations follow the changing styles and emphases of eighteenth-century poetry generally. Second, received opinion about the best imitations still holds true; but the names of Croxall, Edwards, Mendez, Mickle, Thompson, and West – and perhaps even Downman and Wilkie – should be added to such worthy imitators as Akenside, Beattie, Burns, Shenstone, and Thomson, for belletristic or historical reasons, or both.

Third, most imitators were college men, many educated at Spenser's own Cambridge University. A surprising number were schoolboys at Westminster or Winchester; many of the better imitators were educated at Eton. There is no doubt that encouragement came from teachers or fathers or other Spenser imitators, resulting in literary genealogies such as Downman-Blacklock-Fergusson-Burns or Warton-West-Thomson. (There were at least 16 Scots among the nearly 100 imitators, and many Irishmen.) The playfulness of some works is perhaps explained by the fact that nearly all imitators were young men who were attracted to Spenser – some via school exercises – in a spirit of stanzaic experimentation and poetical adventurousness, away from the strictures and conventions of couplet verse. Favorites such as Pope were never abandoned, however.

Finally, many imitators of Spenser's stanza still have the couplet feel, and imitations of Pope or the ancients are occasionally combined within Spenser imitations throughout the century. Except for Croxall, Thomson, Mendez, and Mickle, most imitators did not succeed in approximating Spenser's diction. Many did not *want* to imitate his diction. When they attempted 'old' words at all, they randomly sprinkled their archaisms around a text. Eighteenth-century imitations of Spenserian measures were much more successful. A few writers caught something of his incidents and 'types.' Judging from their comments as well as their imitations, most seemed to like Spenser's seriousness, pictorialism, and poetic virtuosity. Eighteenth-century readers did not seem to care as much for Spenser as fabulist or allegorist, and many enthusiasts even found the *Faerie Queene* stanza metronomical; but Spenser was never ridiculed, very seldom burlesqued, but often played with.

The imitations tell us part of the story of Spenser's reputation during the Restoration and eighteenth century. They show that many writers – and not only the so-called pre-Romantics – cared about and for him. He was considered a useful, moral teacher. He was read, admired, commented on, and imitated throughout the period and not just in the second half of the century. There are no appreciable lacunae in these practices. Scholars have yet to ascertain Spenser's place in the eighteenth century; but when that position has been determined, imitations of Spenser will figure large.

RICHARD C. FRUSHELL

The following list includes about 70 percent of some 250 known imitations and adaptations for the period 1660–1800. It is complete for the first 40 years; it is nearly complete for the first 60 years of the eighteenth century and thus gives evidence that the latter part of the century was not the only active time for Spenser imitations. Because of space limitations, the list is selective for the last 40 years and includes from 10 to 20 items for each decade.

The information here is often incomplete since many imitations were reprinted, some many times. A typical entry includes author's name (if known); date when written or first published; author, date, and title of a work in which it appeared (most often the one I saw or know it in) if not published separately; place of publication; statement on its form and other annotations. Page numbers are for the most part omitted.

OTHER BIBLIOGRAPHIES For fuller lists, see the Spenser bibliographies of William Sipple 1984 (for studies 1900–36), Waldo McNeir and Foster Provost 1975 (for 1937–72), and *SpN* 1970–. See also Phillips G. Davies 1973–4 'A Check List of Poems, 1595 to 1833, Entirely or Partly Written in the Spenserian Stanza' *BNYPL* 77:314–28, and Julius Nicholas Hook 1941 'Eighteenth-Century Imitations of Spenser' diss Univ of Illinois. Other unpublished theses and dissertations that touch or center on the topic include those of George Linnaeus Marsh 1899 University of Chicago, Herbert Cory 1910 Harvard University, Karl Reuning 1911 University of Giessen, Edna Bell 1928 University of Oklahoma, C.D. Yost 1936 University of Pennsylvania, Norman Dreyfus 1938 Johns Hopkins University, D. Sen 1952 University of London, and Charles E. Mounts 1941 Duke University. I am indebted also to remarks and leads from scholars, especially my colleague Joe Weixlmann, *ESTC* editor R.C. Alston, and Donald Cheney. I am grateful to the librarians of the Harvard, Boston Public, Johns Hopkins, Folger, Library of Congress, Illinois, and Lilly libraries for being helpful hosts as I pursued Spenser and Spenserians in the eighteenth century on several research trips since 1977 (two partly underwritten by Indiana State University Research Committee funds), including a two-month Indiana University summer research fellowship in the Lilly Library several years ago for study of Spenser imitations 1700–54.

MAJOR SOURCES Spenser imitations are included in collections published under titles like *Poems on Several Occasions*, collected works of individual imitators, and periodicals such as *The Gentleman's Magazine* (abbreviated here as *GentM*) and *The European Magazine* (*EurM*). The other major repository is anthologies, important and convenient collections of poetry which long have been recognized as barometers and shapers of taste and poetic fashions. The Dodsley collections (continued by Pearch) are primary examples. Over 50 Spenser imitations were published in the collections of (alphabetically) Robert Anderson, John Bell, Alexander Chalmers, Robert Dodsley, Moses Mendez, George Pearch, and Samuel Whyte. The following anthologies are cited more than once in the accompanying list: John Bell 1789–90 *Classical Arrangement of Fugitive Poetry* vols 10–11 (vol 10 titled *Poems in the Stanza of Spencer*, vol 11 titled *Poems Imitative of Spenser; and, In the Manner of Milton*) (London); Alexander Chalmers 1810 *The Works of the English*

Poets from Chaucer to Cowper 21 vols (London); Robert Dodsley 1751–63 *A Collection of Poems in Six Volumes, by Several Hands* (5th ed, London); George Pearch 1783 *A Collection of Poems in Four Volumes, by Several Hands* (London); James Ralph 1729 *Miscellaneous Poems, by Several Hands* (London).

INDIVIDUAL IMITATIONS Mark Akenside 1745 *Odes on Several Subjects* (London). Several odes are reminiscent of Spenserian and Prior stanzas. 'Ode VIII: On Leaving Holland' is in 4 stanzas, *ababcdcdC*, an adaptation of the Spenserian stanza. 'Ode to Sleep' (rpt in Pearch 1783 vol 3) is in 6 Prior stanzas. Akenside 1737 'The Virtuoso' *GentM* 7:244. 10 Spenserian stanzas.

[John Armstrong] 1748 'An Imitation of Spencer Written at Mr. Thomson's Desire, to be Inserted into the Castle of Indolence' in *Miscellanies, by John Armstrong, M.D. in Two Volumes* I (titled *Imitations of Shakespeare and Spencer*) (London 1770). 4 Spenserian stanzas, the final ones for Thomson's *Castle of Indolence* canto I (see Thomson 1748, below).

[Cornelius Arnold] 1755 *The Mirror: A Poetical Essay, in the Manner of Spenser* (London). 44 Spenserian stanzas.

['W.B.'] 1789 'Fragment, in the Style of Spenser, Being an Introduction to an Intended Continuation of the Canto of Mutability, Left Unfinished by That Author' in *A Collection of Poems, Mostly Original, by Several Hands* (Dublin) 2:176. Spenserian stanzas.

Lewis Bagot 1755 'Imitation of the Epithalamion' *Gratulatio Academiae Cantabrigiensis* (Cambridge).

James Beattie 1771 *The Minstrel, or The Progress of Genius: A Poem, Book the First* (Edinburgh). 60 Spenserian stanzas. Beattie 1774 *The Minstrel, or The Progress of Genius, the Second Book* (London). 63 Spenserian stanzas. 4 eds of Book I by 1774, when Book 2 was pub. Rpt of Books 1–2 in Bell 1789–90 vol 10.

Joseph Beaumont 1702 *Psyche, or Love's Mystery, in XXIV. Cantos: Displaying the Intercourse betwixt Christ, and the Soul* (Cambridge) 2nd ed (first ed 1648, in 20 cantos). Spenser imitation in stanzas *ababcc*.

Robert Bedingfield 1747 'The Education of Achilles' in Bell 1789–90 vol II. 14 Spenserian stanzas. First pub in *The Museum* 3(1747).

[Alexander Bicknell?] 1779 *Prince Arthur: An Allegorical Romance; The Story from Spenser, in Two Volumes* (London). Prose. Donald Cheney has determined that, aside from title-page differences, this is the same work as *Una and Arthur* 2 vols in 1 (Cambridge 1779).

Thomas Blacklock 1746 'Hymn to Divine Love' in his *Poems on Several Occasions* (Glasgow). *ababbcc*. Blacklock 1754 'Philantheus' in his *Poems* (Edinburgh). *ababbcc*.

William Blake 1783 'An Imitation of Spenser' in his *Poetical Sketches* (London). 6 near-Spenserian stanzas.

Jane Bowdler 1786 'Envy: A Fragment' in her *Poems and Essays by a Lady* (Bath). 14 Spenserian stanzas.

Henry Boyd 1780a *Orlando* (London). 92 Spenserian stanzas (part of this poem is appended to his 1785 tr of Dante's *Inferno* [London]). Boyd [1780]b *The Woodman's Tale, after the Manner of Spenser* (London 1805). 325 Spenserian stanzas.

[Samuel Boyse] [1736]a *The Olive: An Ode, Occasion'd by the Auspicious Success of His Majesty's Counsels, and His Majesty's Most Happy Return, in the Stanza of Spenser* (London 1737). Prior stanzas. Boyse [1736]b 'Part of Psalm XLII, in Imitation of the Style of Spenser' in his *Translations and Poems, Written on Several Occasions* (London 1738). *ababcc*. [Boyse] 1740a 'The Character and Speech of Cosroes the Mede: An Improvement in the Squire's Tale of Chaucer, in the Manner of Spenser, Inscrib'd to George Ogle, Esq' *GentM* 10:404–5. 18 Prior stanzas. [Boyse] 1740b 'An Ode Sacred to the Birth of the Marquis of Tavistock' *GentM* 10:83–4. 12 Prior stanzas. Boyse [c 1740] 'The Vision of Patience, Sacred to the Memory of Mr Alexander Cuming, A Young Gentleman Unfortunately Lost in the Northern Ocean on his Return from China, 1740' in Bell 1789–90 vol II. 26 Prior stanzas. [Boyse] 1743 'Stanza's from Albion's triumph: An Ode, Occasioned by the Happy Success of His Majesty's Arms on the Maine' *GentM* 13:378. 5 Prior stanzas, nos 13–15 and 19–20 of *Albion's Triumph ... in the Stanza of Spencer* (London 1743); this poem is mostly in Prior stanzas also. [Boyse] 1748 'Irene: An Heroic Ode, in the Stanza of Spencer' *GentM* 18:517. 3 Prior stanzas, part of a longer *Irene: An Heroic Ode, in the Stanza of Spencer* (London 1748). Boyse [c 1783] 'Stanzas Occasioned by Mr. Pope's Translation of Horace, Book IV, Ode I, Addressed to the Honourable Mr. M-' in his *Translations* (1738; see Boyse [1736]b above). Prior stanzas.

Samuel Boyse and George Ogle. See Joseph Sterling.

The British Hero, or The Vision: A Poem, Sacred to the Immortal Memory of John, Late Duke of Marlborough 1733 (London). *aabbccb*.

Moses Browne 1729 *Piscatory Eclogues* (London). Couplets and varying stanzas.

Sir James Burges 1800 *Richard the First: A Poem* (London). 1849 Spenserian stanzas.

Robert Burns 1784 'Stanzas on the Same Occasion [ie, the prospect of death]' in *Poems, Chiefly in the Scottish Dialect, by Robert Burns, the Third Edition* (Edinburgh 1787). 3 Spenserian stanzas. Burns 1786 'The Cotter's Saturday Night, Inscribed to R.A.****, Esq' in *Poems, Chiefly in the Scottish Dialect, by Robert Burns* (Kilmarnock). 21 Spenserian stanzas.

Richard Cambridge 1736 'The Marriage of Frederick' in Chalmers 1810 vol 18. Prior stanzas. Cambridge [c 1740] 'Archimage' in Chalmers 1810 vol 18. 29 Spenserian stanzas.

Samuel Taylor Coleridge 1795 'Epistle IV, to the Author of Poems Published Anonymously at Bristol, in September, 1795' in his *Poems* (1796; see Coleridge [1796?] below). 5 Spenserian stanzas. Called 'Lines Addressed to Joseph Cottle' in the 2nd ed (1797). Cottle, Coleridge's friend, was a poet who wrote 'Monody on John Henderson' in Spenserian stanzas. Coleridge [1796?] 'Effusion XXIV, in the Manner of Spenser' in his *Poems on Various Subjects* (London 1796) [very rare]. 5 Spenserian stanzas, addressed to the Rev W.L. Bowles, himself a Spenserian.

Colin Clout's Madrigal, on the Auspicious First of March, 1727–8, Being the Anniversary of Her Majesty's Birthday 1728 (London).

William Collins 1739 *Eclogues* (London 1742). Rpt in 1757 as *Oriental Eclogues* and in Pearch 1768 *Collection of Poems*. Collins 1747 *Odes on Several Descriptive and Allegoric Subjects* (London). Lonsdale 1969 demonstrates how imitative of Spenser are Collins 1739 and Collins 1747.

William Combe 1775 *Clifton: A Poem, in Imitation of Spenser* (Bristol). 30 Spenserian stanzas. Cf Henry Jones 1773 *Clifton: A Poem, in Two Cantos* 2nd ed (Bristol).

'The Consolation' 1729 *The Flying-Post, or Weekly Medley* (12 Jul). 4 Prior stanzas.

Joseph Cottle. See Samuel Taylor Coleridge.

'The Country Curate' 1737 *GentM* 7:52–3. 12 stanzas *ababbcC*.

'The Country Parson' 1737 *GentM* 7:52–3. 12 stanzas *ababbcC*.

'The Court of Excess' 1800 *EurM* 38:128–30. 21 stanzas *ababcdcD*.

'The Courtier' 1729 in Ralph 1729. 7 pp of blank verse.

[William Cowper] 1781 *Anti-Thelyphthora: A Tale in Verse* (London). Couplets.

[Samuel Croxall] 1713 *An Original Canto of Spencer, Design'd as Part of His Fairy Queen, but Never Printed, Now Made Publick, by Nestor Ironside, Esq* (London 1714). On dating, see D.F. Foxon 1975 *English Verse 1701–1750: A Catalogue* (Cambridge) p 154. 46 Spenserian stanzas. See *The Examiner Examin'd, in a Letter to the Englishman: Occasion'd by the Examiner of Friday Dec. 18*, 1713, upon the Canto of Spencer [by Samuel Croxall] 1713 (London). [Croxall] 1714a *Another Original Canto of Spencer, Design'd as Part of His Fairy Queen, but Never Printed, Now Made Publick, by Nestor Ironside, Esq* (London). 54 Spenserian stanzas. Croxall 1714b *An Ode Humbly Inscrib'd to the King, Occasion'd by His Majesty's Most Auspicious Succession and Arrival, Written in the Stanza and Measure of Spencer, by Mr. Croxall, Author of the Two Original Canto's, Etc* (London). Dedicated to the Rt Hon Thomas, Earl of Wharton, Lord Privy Seal. 42 Spenserian stanzas. Croxall [c 1720] 'On Florinda Seen While She Was Bathing' in *The Fair Circassian: A Dramatic Performance ... to Which Are Added Several Occasional Poems* (London 1720).

Thomas Denton 1754 'Immortality, or The Consolation of Human Life: A Monody' in Dodsley ed 1758–63 vol 5. 31 Prior stanzas. Denton 1762 'The House of Superstition: A Vision' in Bell 1789–90 vol II. 13 Prior stanzas.

Thomas Dermody 1792 *Poems Consisting of Essays, Lyric, Elegiac, Etc* (Dublin). Includes 3 imitations. (1) 'Sonnet.' 1 Spenserian stanza against hunting. Poetic diction perhaps reaches its nadir with 'fatal tube' for gun. In his 'Postcript' to 'Memory: A Poem' in this volume, Dermody's sentimentality is clear. After confessing to copying the 'language of sweetness' of Spenser's age, he allows that 'One tear [shed over his poem on 'Memory'] from the ey[e] of feeling, is, in my opinion, more precious than the superfluous plaudits of a million.' (2) 'Sonnet, to the Rev. Mr. Sterling.' 2 Spenserian stanzas. (3) 'To the Right Honourable the Countess of Moira [nee Lady Elizabeth Hastings, his patron].' 1 Spenserian stanza serving as dedication to the volume. Dermody published his poems in several editions from 1792 to 1802. Many of his many imitations are in the 2-vol ed of his works, titled *The Harp of Erin* (London 1807). Dermody [c 1792]a 'The Enthusiast' in his 1802 *Poems on Various Subjects* (London). 16 Spenserian stanzas. This series of 'delightful dreams' and 'faery scenes' has been read as a satire on liberalism. Dermody [c 1792]b 'The Pleasures of Poesy, in Spenser's Stanza' in his *Poems on Various Subjects* (1802; see Dermody [c 1792]a above). 16 Spenserian stanzas.

[Robert Dodsley] 1744a *Melpomene, or The Regions of Terror and Pity: An Ode* (London 1757). *ababccdD*. Dodsley 1744b 'On the Death of Mr. Pope' *GentM* 14:447. *ababcC*. 2 stanzas of 1 section are imitative of *SC*. Dodsley 1745 'Pain and Patience: An Ode' in his *Trifles* (London). 17 stanzas of *ababcC*.

Hugh Downman 1768 *The Land of the Muses: A Poem in the Manner of Spenser, with Poems on Several Occasions* (Edinburgh). 85 Spenserian stanzas, changed to couplets in his *Poems* 1791.

Philip Doyne 1763 *The Triumph of Parnassus: A Poem on the Birth of His Royal Highness the Prince of Wales* (London). Noteworthy only because in both Prior and Spenserian stanzas.

'Y.E.' 1787 'To the Authoress of the Victim of Fancy' *GentM* 61(Mar):260. 6 stanzas *ababacc*. Signed 'Y.E.'

Thomas Edwards 1765, 1780 sonnets in *The Sonnets of Thomas Edwards* (1765, 1780) ed Dennis G. Donovan, Augustan Reprint Society 164 (Los Angeles 1974). Four of Edwards' 52 sonnets are in the Spenserian *ababbcbccdcdee*; most are Petrarchan. Among the 'irregular' sonnets is 'Sonnet VIII: On the Cantos of Spenser's Fairy Queen, Lost in the Passage from Ireland' in Robert Dodsley 1748 *A Collection of Poems in Three Volumes, by Several Hands* 2nd ed (London) vol 2.

[Charles Emily] 1755 'The Praises of Isis: A Poem, Written MDCCLV, by the Same' (ie, by same author as the previous poem *Death*; see Emily 1762, below) in Pearch 1783 vol 1. Blank verse. Emily 1762 *Death* in Pearch 1783 vol 1. 18 sonnets considered by Hook to be imitative of Spenser; their rhyme scheme, however, is *ababcdcdefefgg*.

Thomas Enort 1797 'Sonnet to the Sky-Lark, by Thomas Enort' *EurM* 32:40. 1 Spenserian sonnet.

'Epithalamium' 1729 in Ralph 1729. Couplets.

'Epithalamium, by the Same' [c 1758] in Dodsley ed 1758–63 vol 5. Irregular stanzas.

Andrew Erskine 1757 'Ode to Fear' *GentM* 27:228. 10 ten-line stanzas, some of which are Prior stanzas.

'W.F.' 1800 'Sonnet to Sleep' *EurM* 38:368. 1 Spenserian sonnet. Signed 'W.F.'

[Elijah Fenton] 1707 'An Ode to the Sun, for the New-Year, 1707' *Poems on Several Occasions* (London 1717). Several of the 24 stanzas, numbered from 1 to 3 cyclically throughout, are Prior stanzas.

Robert Fergusson 1773 'The Farmer's Ingle' in his *Poems* (Edinburgh). *ababcdcdD*.

Giles and Phineas Fletcher 1783 *The Purple Island, or The Isle of Man: An Allegorical Poem, by Phineas Fletcher, Esteemed the Spenser of His Age; To Which Is Added Christ's Victory and Triumph: A Poem, in Four Parts, by Giles Fletcher, Both Written in the Last Century* (London). Rpt of 17th-c Spenser imitations.

'Fragment of Horace's Ode, in Praise of Pindar' 1771 *GentM* 41:327. *ababcC*.

John Gay 1714 *The Shepherd's Week, in Six Pastorals, by Mr. J. Gay* (London). Couplets. Cf Lady Mary Wortley Montague 1747 *Six Town Eclogues with Some Other Poems* (London) (in the manner of Gay's Monday-Saturday approach, but quite distant from Spenser), pub as *Town Eclogues* in 1716.

Thomas Gibbons 1750 'An Elegiac Ode' in his *Juvenelia* (London?). *ababcC*.

Thomas Gray 1742–68 *Poems by Mr. Gray* (London 1768). Lonsdale 1969 shows how imitative of Spenser Gray was in his hymns, *Elegy*, and odes (both 'regular' and Pindaric). Especially impressive is Gray's detailed knowledge of Spenser's works other than *FQ*.

[William Hamilton] 1748 'On Seeing a Lady Sit to Her Picture, in Imitation of Spencer's Stile' *Poems on Several Occasions* (Glasgow). *abab*.

Samuel Hayes. See James Scott.

Henry and Minerva: A Poem 1729 (London). Couplets.

[John Holywood?] 1797 'The Trumpet-Call – 1794' *GentM* 81(Apr):324. 6 Prior stanzas.

'The House of Care, in Imitation of Spenser's Faery Queen' 1786 *GentM* 60(Aug): 696–7. 8 Spenserian stanzas.

Leigh Hunt 1786 'The Palace of Pleasure' in *Juvenalia, or A Collection of Poems, Written between the Ages of Twelve and Sixteen* (London 1801). 130 Spenserian stanzas.

Miss Hunt 1786 'On Visiting the Ruins of an Ancient Abbey in Devonshire, September, MDCCLXXXVI, by a Young Lady' *GentM* 60(Oct):885. 6 Spenserian stanzas.

An Hymn to Harmony, in Imitation of Spencer 1729 (London).

'An Imitation of Spencer's Fairy Queen: A Fragment, by a Gentleman of Twenty' 1729 in Ralph 1729. Decasyllabic couplets rendering *FQ* VII vii.

'An Imitation of Spenser' 1750 *The Student, or The Oxford and Cambridge Monthly Miscellany* 5(31 May):198–9. 6 Spenserian stanzas.

'Industry and Genius, or The Origin of Birmingham: A Fable, Attempted in the Manner of Spencer, to Mr. Baskerville' 1751 *The London Magazine* 20:37. 7 Spenserian stanzas.

Henry Jones. See William Combe.

Charles Lamb 1797 'A Vision of Repentance' in *Poems, by S.T. Coleridge, Second Edition; To Which Are Now Added Poems by Charles Lamb, and Charles Lloyd* (London). 6 *ababcc* stanzas and 23 octosyllabic couplets.

Mary Leapor [c 1743] 'The Temple of Love' in her *Poems upon Several Occasions* (London 1748). Couplets.

Charles Lloyd 1794 'A Poetical Effusion, Written after a Journey into North Wales' in his *Poems* 3rd ed (London 1819). Dated Feb 1794. 6 Spenserian stanzas. This is the first poem in this volume quite reminiscent of Wordsworth. A 4-stanza version of it is in *Poems, by S.T. Coleridge* 2nd ed (see Lamb 1797 above). Lloyd 1799 'Lines to a Brother and Sister, Written Soon after a Recovery from Sickness' in his 1819 *Poems*. Signed '6th April, 1799.' 10 Spenserian stanzas. Lloyd 1797 *Oswald: A Poem* (Carlisle) in his 1819 *Poems*. 46 Spenserian stanzas.

Robert Lloyd 1751 *The Progress of Envy: A Poem, in Imitation of Spenser, Occasioned by Lauder's Attack on the Character of Milton, Inscribed to the Right Honourable the Earl of Bath* (London). The dedication identifies the Earl of Bath as 'Patron of Milton, and his Vindicators.' Poem in 30 altered Spenserian stanzas: *ababcdcdD*.

Robert Lowth 1747 'The Choice of Hercules' in Bell 1789–90 vol 11 (first pub in Joseph Spence 1747 *Polymetis* [London]). 27 Prior stanzas.

[William Mason] [c 1744] *Musaeus: A Monody to the Memory of Mr. Pope, in Imitation of Milton's Lycidas* (London 1747). The first 2 stanzas of Colin Clout's speech 'as they relate to Pastoral, are written in the measure which Spenser uses in the first eclogue of the *Shepherd's Calendar*; the rest, where he speaks of Fable, are in the stanza of the *Faery Queen*.' See Mason as imitator in William Rider 1762 *An Historical and Critical Account of the Living Authors of Great-Britain* ed O.M. Brack, Jr, Augustan Reprint Society 163 (Los Angeles 1974).

William Melmoth [c 1743] 'The Transformation of Lycon and Euphormius' in Bell 1789–90 vol 10. Previously pub in *Fitzosborne's* [Melmoth's pseudonym] *Letters* 2 (London 1749). 19 Spenserian stanzas.

Moses Mendez [c 1748] Spenserian stanza on Thomson in *EurM* 22(1792):517. 1 stanza. Mendez 1751 *The Seasons* (London, rpt [anonymous] Dublin 1752). 35 Spenserian stanzas (8 for each season and 3 more as an introduction which testily strikes at critics of the four seasons to follow). [Mendez] [c 1751] 'The Squire of Dames: A Poem, in Spenser's Stile' in Robert Dodsley 1755 *A Collection of Poems in Four Volumes, by Several Hands* 4 (London) rpt in Dodsley ed 1758–63. 82 Spenserian stanzas in imitation of *FQ* III vii. Mendez 1752–8 'The Blatant Beast: A Poem, in Spenser's Style' *EurM* 22(1792):331–6, 417–22. Canto 1 in 48 Spenserian stanzas, canto 2 in 46.

John H. Merivale [c 1798] 'The Minstrel' in his *Poems Original and Translated* (London 1808). 69 Spenserian stanzas. In this volume are 2 other of his imitations (both in variant Spenserian stanzas): 'St. George and the Dragon' and 'St. Denis and the Mulberry Tree.'

[William Julius Mickle] 1767 *The Concubine: A Poem, in Two Cantos, in the Manner of Spenser* (pub separately at Oxford and Cambridge). At least 4 editions by 1772; rev as *Sir Martyn: A Poem, in the Manner of Spenser, by William Julius Mickle* (London 1777). In 2 cantos of 73 and 64 Spenserian stanzas. Mickle c 1770 'An Inscription on an Obelisk at Langford' in Chalmers 1810 vol 17:523. 1 Spenserian stanza. Mickle 1776 'On the Neglect of Poetry' in Chalmers 1810 vol 17:553. 8 Spenserian stanzas.

J. Miller 1754 'The Sloe-Ey'd Maid: A Pastoral' in his *Poems on Several Occasions* (London). Couplets.

Thomas Morell [c 1747] 'To Mr. Thomson, on His Unfinished Plan of a Poem Called the Castle of Indolence, in Spencer's Style' in Chalmers 1810 vol 12:467. Spenserian stanzas.

'Morning: An Ode, Written by a Student Confined to College' 1770 *GentM* 40:232. *ababcC*.

Mother Hubbards Tale of the Ape and Fox, Abbreviated from Spencer 1715 (London). 8 pp. Supposedly a 'Jacobite parody of Spenser's poem' according to British Museum Catalogue. Octavo ed 'with the obsolete words explained' pub London 1784.

A New Occasional Oratorio, As It Is Perform'd at the Theatre-Royal in Covent-Garden, the Words Taken from Milton, Spenser, Etc. and Set to Musick by Mr. Handel 1746 (London). On the 'suppression of the Rebellion' according to British Museum Catalogue.

'On Happiness and Palinodia' 1731 in James Husband *Miscellany of Poems by Several Hands* (London). *ababcC.*

'Dr P.' 1755 'Sonnet, by Dr. P-, Occasioned by Leaving B-X-N, July 1755, the Author Telling the Ladies "He Looked upon Himself in a Worse Situation than Adam Banish'd Paradise," Was Enjoined by Them to Give His Reasons in Verse' in Pearch 1783 vol 3. *ababbcbccdcdee.*

'A Pastoral: Digon Davy and Colin Clout' [1743?] in Timothy Silence, ed 1764 *The Foundling Hospital for Wit, Intended for the Reception and Preservation of Such Brats of Wit and Humour, Whose Parents Chuse to Drop Them, Number V* (London).

'A Pastoral, in Imitation of Spenser' 1741 *The Publick Register, or The Weekly Magazine* (7 Mar): no page. 22 stanzas *ababcc.*

Thomas Percy [c 1755] 2 Spenserian sonnets in Pearch 1783 vol 3.

Ambrose Philips 1709 *Pastorals* in Jacob Tonson *Poetical Miscellanies: The Sixth Part, Containing a Collection of Original Poems, with Several New Translations, by the Most Eminent Hands* (London). (Also includes Pope's *Pastorals.*) 6 pastorals of decasyllabic couplets in imitation of *SC.*

['Philisides'] 1758 *The Shepherds' Calender, Being Twelve Pastorals Attempted in Blank Verse, the Subjects Partly Taken from the Select Pastorals of Spenser and Sir Philip Sidney* (Dublin). Blank verse.

Charles Philpot. See James Scott.

'A Pindarick Ode in Imitation of Spencer's Divine Love, Inscrib'd to Mrs. Katherine Bridgemann, Unfinish'd' 1726 in *Poems on Several Occasions, by a Lady* (London). *ababb.*

[Christopher Pitt] 1747 'The Jordan' in *Poems by the Celebrated Translator of Virgil's Aneid; Together with The Jordan: A Poem, in Imitation of Spenser, by –, Esq* (London 1756). 6 Spenserian stanzas.

Richard Polwhele 1795–6 'The Ancient and Modern Patriot Contrasted, 1795' in his *Poetic Trifles* (London 1796). 6 Spenserian stanzas. Contains 4 other imitations in Spenserian stanzas including, in 2nd ed, Polwhele 1798 'The Influence of Local Attachment, with Respect to Home: A Poem, in Seven Books.' 166 Spenserian stanzas.

Alexander Pope [c 1706] 'The Alley' in Motte 1727 *Miscellanies in Prose and Verse* vol 4 (London). 6 Spenserian stanzas.

Beilby Porteus. See James Scott.

Robert Potter 1749 *A Farewell Hymne to the Country, Attempted in the Manner of Spenser's Epithalamion, by Mr. Potter* (London). 19 irregular stanzas, most long. Potter 1758 *Kymber: A Monody to Sir Armine Wodehouse* (London). Long stanzas.

Matthew Prior 1706 *An Ode, Humbly Inscrib'd to the Queen, on the Glorious Success of Her Majesty's Arms, 1706,* Written in Imitation of Spencer's Stile (London). For a long explication of this ode, see his *Miscellaneous Works* vol I of 2 (Dublin 1739?). Prior's ode, a panegyric of both Queen Anne and Marlborough, is in 35 Prior stanzas: 10 lines *ababcdcdeE*, the last alexandrine. For a contemporary attack on Prior's influential *Ode*, see William Atwood 1706 *A Modern Inscription to the Duke of Marlborough's Fame, Occasion'd by an Antique, in Imitation of Spencer* (London). Prior [c 1718] *Colin's Mistakes, Written in Imitation of Spenser's Style* (London 1721). 11 Prior stanzas.

The Progress of Time, or An Emblematical Representation of the Four Seasons and Twelve Months ... in Imitation of Spencer's Fairy Queen 1743 (London).

A Protestant Memorial, or The Shepherd's Tale of the Pouder-Plott: A Poem in Spenser's Style 1713 (London). Couplets; imitation of *SC.*

James Ralph 1729 'Zeuma' in *Miscellaneous Poems, by Several Hands* (London). One section of canto 3 imitates *FQ* II xii 60–1. Blank verse.

William Rider 1755 'Westminster Abbey' *GentM* 25:373. 10 stanzas *ababbccC.*

Glocester Ridley 1747 'Psyche, or The Great Metamorphosis' in *The Museum* (London); rpt in Bell 1789–90 vol 10. 51 Spenserian stanzas. Ridley [c 1772] *Melampus, or The Religious Groves: A Poem in Four Books, with Notes* (London 1781). 260 Spenserian stanzas.

Mary Robinson 1806 *Poetical Works* (London). Includes 'The Cavern of Woe' 1:49. Near-Spenserian stanzas. Also includes 'The Foster-Child' 2:52 (c 1790). 53 Spenserian stanzas.

'The Ruins of Time' 1729 in Ralph 1729. *abab.*

St. James's Miscellany, or The Lover's Tale, Being the Amours of Venus and Adonis, or The Disasters of Unlawful Love 1732 (London). Four parts in couplets: pt 2 House of Sleep; pt 4 Dungeon of Despair. Although the preface says that Virgil and Homer are 'the noblest Patterns for our Imitation,' the Morpheus and Despair sections may be considered imitations of Spenser.

James Scott 1761 'Ode on Sleep' in his *Odes on Several Subjects* (London). *ababcC.* Scott [1761?] 'A Spousal Hymn, Addressed to His Majesty [George III] on His Marriage' in Pearch 1783 vol 3. 19 Prior stanzas. See Scott's award-winning (Cambridge University) imitations, 'Heaven: A Vision' (1760) and 'An Hymn to Repentance' (1762), both in Prior stanzas, in *Musae Seatonionae* 1808 vol 1; this collection also contains Beilby Porteus' 1759 'Death,' a blank-verse imitation. Prize imitations in Prior stanzas in vol 2 are Samuel Hayes 1783 'Hope' and Charles Philpot 1790 'Faith: A Vision.'

George Sewell [c 1710] 'The Force of Musick: A Fragment after the Manner of Spenser' in his *A New Collection of Original Poems, Never Printed in Any Miscellany, by the Author of Sir Walter Raleigh* (London 1720). Couplets.

William Shenstone 1737 'The School-Mistress: A Poem, in Imitation of Spenser' in Robert Dodsley 1748 *A Collection of Poems in Three Volumes, by Several Hands* 2nd ed, vol 1 (London). 35 Spenserian stanzas.

Christopher Smart 1752 *Poems on Several Occasions, by Christopher Smart, A.M. Fellow of Pembroke-Hall, Cambridge* (London). Includes 'Epithalamium.' Smart 1756 'Hymn to the Supreme Being on Recovery from a Dangerous Fit of Illness' in Robert Anderson 1795 *The Works of the British Poets* (London) 11:136. *ababcc.*

'Sonnet, by Spenser, Never before Printed' before 1727 in Curll 1727 *Miscellanea, in Two Volumes, Never before Published* 1 (London). 11 couplets.

'Sonnet, to a Lady of Indiscreet Virtue, in Imitation of Spenser' [1755?] in Pearch 1783 vol 3. *ababbcbccdcdee.*

[Robert Southey] 1800 'St. Juan Gualberto' in *The Annual Anthology* vol 2 (Bristol). *ababcc.*

Spencer's Fairy-Queen, Attempted in Blank Verse, Canto I 1774 (London). 18 pp of blank verse.

Spencer Redivivus; Containing the First Book of the Fairy Queen; His Essential Design Preserv'd, but His Obsolete Language and Manner of Verse Totally Laid Aside, Deliver'd in Heroick Numbers, by a Person of Quality 1687 (London). Paraphrase in some 4600 couplets of *FQ* I.

Spenser's Fairy Queen Attempted in Blank Verse, with Notes, Critical and Explanatory 1783 (London). Blank-verse version of *FQ* I i-iv.

Joseph Sterling [1782?] 'La Gierusalemme Soggettita' in *The Poetical Register for 1805* (London 1807). 56 Spenserian stanzas. See Sterling's sonnet imitations in his *Poems* (Dublin 1782). Sterling 1785 *Cambuscan, or The Squire's Tale of Chaucer, Modernized by Mr. Boyse, Continued from Spenser's Fairy Queen, by Mr. Ogle, and Concluded by Mr. Sterling* (Dublin). In Prior stanzas, as was its prototype: Samuel Boyse and George Ogle 1741 'Cambuscan' in Ogle's *Canterbury Tales of Chaucer Modernis'd* (London).

Jerome Stone 1755 'Albin and the Daughter of Mey: An Old Tale, Translated from the Irish, by the Late Mr. Jerome Stone' in Moses Mendez 1767 *A Collection of the Most Esteemed Pieces* (London). Prior stanzas.

'N.T.' 1783 'To Dr. Beattie' *GentM* 54(Oct):870. 6 Spenserian stanzas. Headnote signed 'N.T.'

[John Tait] 1775 *The Land of Liberty: An Allegorical Poem, in the Manner of Spenser, in Two Cantos, Dedicated to the People of Great Britain* (London). 120 Spenserian stanzas.

'Thales: Sacred to the Memory of Edward Pococke, D.D.' 1751 in Bell 1789–90 vol 11. 16 stanzas *ababbccc.* First pub as *Thales: A monody, Sacred to the Memory of Dr. Pococke, in Imitation of Spenser, from an Authentic Manuscript of Mr. Edmund Smith* (London 1751).

'Thames: A Canto, on the Royal Nuptials in May 1737, in Imitation of Spenser' 1737 *The Publick Register, or The Weekly Magazine* (May):296–9. 25 Spenserian stanzas.

Isaac Thompson 1731 'An Epithalamium,' 'Colin's Despair,' and *A Pastoral Ode* in his *A Collection of Poems Occasionally Writ on Several Subjects* (Newcastle-upon-Tyne). The 7 pastorals of the *Ode* are 'Spring,' 'Parting,' 'The Pensive Swain,' 'The Complaint,' 'Friendship,' 'The Letter,' and 'Absence.'

William Thompson 1736a 'An Epithalamium on the Royal Nuptials' in his *Poems on Several Occasions* (London 1758). 25 Spenserian stanzas. Thompson 1736b 'The Nativity' in *Poems on Several Occasions* (London 1758). 20 Spenserian stanzas. Thompson 1740 *An*

Hymn to May, by William Thompson, M.A. of Queen's College Oxon. (London, nd). Includes an important preface. 72 stanzas *ababccC* (adaptation of *Fowre Hymnes*), expanded to 75 stanzas in Bell 1789–90 vol II. See also Thompson's Spenserian sonnets (c 1768) in his *Poetical Works* (1807).

James Thomson 1748 *The Castle of Indolence: An Allegorical Poem, Written in Imitation of Spenser* (London and Dublin). 158 Spenserian stanzas.

'To Mr Urban, on the Conclusion of His Vol. XIII for the Year 1743' 1743 *GentM* 13: no page. 10 Prior stanzas.

'To Samuel Rogers, Esq. Author of the Pleasures of Memory, on His Ordering a Short Great Coat Called a Spenser' 1795 *EurM* 27:418. 3 Spenserian stanzas. Signed 'P,' who says that Sam Rogers is better as a Spenserian than either Mason or Shenstone.

Gavin Turnbull 1788 *Poetical Essays* (Glasgow). Includes 'Pastoral I,' 'The Bard,' and 'The Cottage.' Couplets, 22 Spenserian stanzas, and 4 Spenserian stanzas, respectively.

Untitled Spenserian stanza [1756]. On flyleaf of *Universal Visiter and Memorialist* 1756.

[John Upton] 1747 *A New Canto of Spencer's Fairy Queen, Now First Published* (London). 42 Prior stanzas.

William Vernon 1758 'The Parish Clerk' in Pearch 1783 vol 2. 28 stanzas *ababcc*.

'Verses on Hope, in the Manner of Spencer' [1741] in *The Polite Correspondence, or Rational Amusement* (London, nd). 1 stanza *ababcdcd*.

Thomas Warton, Jr [c 1745] 'Morning' *The Student, or The Oxford and Cambridge Miscellany* 1(1750). *ababcC*. [Warton] 1753 'A Pastoral in the Manner of Spenser' in *The Union, or Select Scots and English Poems* (Edinburgh). 6 stanzas *ababcc*. Warton 1777 'Sonnet in Imitation of Spenser' *GentM* 47:500.

Thomas Warton, Sr 1706 'Philander: An Imitation of Spencer, Occasioned by the Death of Mr. Wm. Levinz, of M.C., Oxon, Nov. 1706' in his *Poems on Several Occasions* (London 1748). *ababcc*.

[Samuel Wesley] 1723 *The Battle of the Sexes: A Poem* (London). 46 Prior stanzas. Revision in 50 Prior stanzas in Wesley 1736 (see below). *Guardian* 52(1713) supposedly presents the argument for Wesley's stanzas. Wesley 1736 *Poems on Several Occasions, by Samuel Wesley, A.M. Master of Blundell's School at Tiverton, Devon, Sometime Student of Christ-Church, Oxford; and Near Twenty Years Usher in Westminster-School* 2nd ed (London). Includes 'The Iliad in a Nutshell, or Homer's Battle of the Frogs and Mice, Illustrated with Notes' (in 75 Prior stanzas) and 'Pastoral' (in couplets), both written before 1736.

[Gilbert West] 1739 *The Abuse of Travelling: A New Canto of Spenser's Fairy Queen* (London). Also pub as *A Canto of the Fairy Queen, Written by Spenser, Never before published* (London 1739). 58 Spenserian stanzas. West 1751 *Education: A Poem, in Two Cantos, Written in Imitation of the Style and Manner of Spenser's Fairy Queen, by Gilbert West, Esq.* (London). Half-title adds, 'Inscrib'd to Lady Langham, Widow of Sir John Langham, Bt.' 96 Spenserian stanzas.

John Whaley 1745 'Prothalamium' in his *A Collection of Original Poems and Translations* (London).

William Wilkie 1759 'A Dream in the Manner of Spenser' in his *Epigoniad* 2nd ed (Edinburgh). 18 Spenserian stanzas.

Alexander Wilson [1790] 'Suicide' *The Scots Magazine* 53(1791):138. 10 Spenserian stanzas.

Samuel Woodford 1679 *Epodē: The Legend of Love* in his *A Paraphrase upon the Canticles, and Some Select Hymns of the New and Old Testament, with Other Occasional Compositions in English Verse* (London) pp 54–118. 189 Spenserian stanzas.

William Wordsworth [1791–4] 'The Female Vagrant' in *Lyrical Ballads, with a Few Other Poems* (Bristol 1798). 26 Spenserian stanzas. This poem was pub in revised form as *Salisbury Plain* in 54 stanzas, and then as *Guilt and Sorrow* in 74 stanzas (1793–8).

'Written in Mr Stanyan's Grecian History, by a Gentleman Lately Deceased, to the Rev. Thomas Burton, A.M. Student of Christ Church, Oxford' 1755 *GentM* 25:420–1. 7 Prior stanzas.

Ireland, the cultural context Spenser's Irish experiences affect both his poetry after 1580 and his *Vewe of Ireland*. Both show evidence of strong, if contradictory, responses to the alien landscape, society, and culture, and to the experiences of exile and government service. Ireland figures, too, in his antiquarian interests and in the development of his autobiographical theme.

Spenser may have visited Ireland as early as 1577 for his spokesman in *Vewe* claims to have seen the execution of Murrough O'Brien in that year. In 1580, he accompanied Lord Grey as his secretary and probably witnessed the massacre of papal troops at Smerwick and the horrors of the Munster famine at the end of the Desmond rebellion. Though the *Vewe* was probably written in 1596, these early experiences are its most memorable personal testimony. In the 1580s, he was an active servant of the Dublin administration, and a thriving one – he acquired large properties around the provinces of Munster and Leinster. Although he was writing *The Faerie Queene* throughout the decade, there are few identifiable Irish references in Books I-III, published in 1590. His residence at Kilcolman began about 1588; its surroundings and Ireland's affairs figure prominently in parts of *FQ* IV, V, and VII, and in *Colin Clouts Come Home Againe*. Ireland is the setting for *Epithalamion* and perhaps some of the *Amoretti*.

Exile in *Colin Clout* expresses the religious and philosophical theme of man's distance from the divine, and reflects the poet's separation from the center of his own culture. The knights of *The Faerie Queene*, too, have left Gloriana's court to travel through a wilderness inhabited by alien forces. Some of these forces are seductive: thus, Spenser complains in *Vewe*, Gaelic Ireland has so contaminated the descendants of English colonists that they 'quite forgett theire Countrie and theire owne names' (2002–3). Others – Despair, Maleger, Malengin – are grotesque or illusory, recalling the 'Anotomies of deathe' he had seen in the Munster famine, or loathsome in their strangeness like the long-haired fighting men he recoils from (*Vewe* 3261, 1657, 2230). The siege of the castle of Alma in *FQ* II xi and the Brigands' raid on the peaceable shepherds of VI x (a *buaidhreadh*; cf 'bodrags' *Colin Clout* 315, 'bordragings' *FQ* II x 63) are examples of the repetitive disorder which the poet, as both colonist and moralist, denounces. The simile of the gnats in the bog of Allen (II ix 16) gives Alma's besiegers an Irish background.

The most direct political references to Ireland in *The Faerie Queene* occur in Book V. Among its many topical allusions, Irish events and individuals are less particularized than international ones, however, perhaps because the English reader would be more likely to recognize Henri IV of France or Philip II of Spain than an Irish rebel. Identifications such as that of Pollente with Sir John of Desmond or of Sir Sergis with Sir William Pelham are doubtful. Even Artegall becomes recognizably Lord Grey only when he is recalled from the Salvage Island, his work half-done, and is slandered by Envy and her crew (V xii 27–43) – a link passage introducing the theme of Book VI. The focal figure is Ireland itself, personified as a lady, Irena, to be rescued. The context of her introduction in V i is the narrator's insistence that justice involves the use of force to repress wrong and civilize the savage. In the opening stanzas, 'furious might' and conquest bring the benefits of peace; Artegall, the hero, is compared to Hercules, conqueror of 'all the West' (i 2–3). His quest to save Irena from the tyrant Grantorto is not a quarrel between individuals; rather, it confronts the lawlessness of the native aristocracy with Ireland's hopes of peace. (The name Irena, especially in the 1596 variant spelling Eirena, puns on Gr *eirēnē* 'peace,' and on the Gaelic name of the country, Éire, genitive Éireann.) Canto i emphasizes the sword of justice and presents Artegall as protector of the weak and lowly: warlike justice is shown as truly merciful to the wronged and innocent. In Book V, whole masses of people are condemned; the iron man Talus, in Ireland as elsewhere, piles up corpses which lie 'As thicke as doth the seede after the sowers hand' (xii 7). The poet balances his approval of the rage of justice with a repeated movement of intervention by a controlling figure who stays the carnage (vii 36–7, xi 65, xii 7–8).

The same pattern is envisaged in *Vewe* as the one way to establish English civilization in Ireland. Irenius (his name continuing the pun) plans widespread slaughter, famine, and expropriation to break the Gaelic aristocratic regime; he provides also for offers of mercy, for some limitation of the suffering of ordinary people, and for an ultimate goal of civilization and its products: peace and true religion. He fears only the clemency of Elizabeth who, like Mercilla/Elizabeth at the trial of Duessa/Mary, Queen of Scots (V ix 50), may relent at the 'lamentable image' of her subjects' distress (*Vewe* 3293–316).

Justice in *FQ* V is presented as beyond the reach of established systems of legal tradition. *Vewe* similarly dismisses formal law, whether English common law, parliamentary statutes, or Irish Brehon Law. Along with this humanist distaste for the tangle of archaic or medieval survivals which made up the Irish status quo, Spenser inherits the centuries-old hostility of English officials towards Gaelic culture: customs, clothing, surnames, and poetry. The Gaelic language he regards as doomed to give way to the conqueror's English (*Vewe* 2091–3). He argues from the meaning of some Gaelic words, but his treatment, for example, of *cumairce* ('Cummericke' 1435) and *faire* ('Farragh' 1690) lead one to assume he knew the language only sketchily. He paraphrases a poem in praise of a dead chieftain, translated for him by someone – perhaps a member of those bilingual Anglo-Irish families who had been notable as Gaelic poets for generations – and notes the 'studied ambiguity' of bardic compliment (Bergin 1970:161). Bardic poetry is treated as naive art, praised for the 'prettie flowers of [its] owne naturall devise' but found lacking in 'the goodlie ornamentes of Poetrye' (*Vewe* 2314–42). Spenser fails to recognize the virtuosity and deliberate archaism of the professional poets, but he was right in regarding them as enemies. While in the centuries since the original conquest many Gaelic poets had complimented Anglo-Irish lords and even referred civilly to the court in London, in the 1590s they called their compatriots to arms against the foreigners and relished the thought of houses set ablaze like Spenser's Kilcolman.

Spenser's planned work on Irish antiquities never materialized. *Vewe*, however, shows an intellectual approach to Ireland which stresses the primitive, inquires after origins, and blends with the antiquarian disposition which led him to set *The Faerie Queene* in a British past vouched for by chronicles. He dismisses the works of Irish historians and in turn was to be attacked by the seventeenth-century historian Geoffrey Keating as a traducer of the Irish. His poetic fictions, however, show Ireland not only as the home of sixteenth-century rebellion and savagery, but also as a pastoral Eden belonging to a past which is legendary rather than historical.

Spenser's use of Irish landscape in pastoral is subtly related to his autobiographical theme. Pastoral convention assumes that the poet is anchored in his countryside. But in *The Shepheardes Calender*, the London-born poet has already become Colin Clout, 'the Southerne shepheardes boye' (*Apr* 21) because of his employment by the Bishop of Rochester. When his career takes him to Ireland, the pastoral name reappears naturalized in the title, *Colin Clouts Come Home Againe*. The phrases 'who knowes not *Colin Clout*?' (*FQ* VI x 16) and 'Who knowes not *Arlo-hill*?' (VII vi 36) stress familiarity and neighborhood; by them we trace Spenser's travels from England to Ireland via Fairyland.

Two river stories of Spenser's Kilcolman neighborhood appear in *Colin Clout* 92–155 and the *Cantos of Mutabilitie*. The former especially associates the poet with a particular landscape: Bregog is 'my river,' as in *FQ* IV xi 41, 'Mulla [is] mine, whose waves I whilom taught to weep.' The rivers are Colin's theme because at this point he knows of no greater waters. They are 'mine' for Spenser the colonist because they run through his land, 'mine' for the poet because he has appropriated them as poetic capital. In *FQ* IV, Mulla (the Awbeg) is not in North Cork but appears with other Irish rivers among the guests in Proteus' house at the marriage of Thames and Medway. The Irish landscape turns out to be no more stable than the shepherd who in *Colin Clout* had wandered as far as London in search of fortune. The opposites of pastoral content and worldly ambition meet in the river, symbol of both mobility and permanence. The humble, unknown Awbeg (Ir 'small river') appearing as a guest among famous rivers at the nuptials represents Spenser in his combination of modesty and determination to equal the greatest heroic poets.

The second Kilcolman river-tale, of Molanna and her love for Fanchin, like the first mixes the serious theme of vengeance for guilt with a comic conclusion (VII vi 40–53). The river nymph sins by allowing Faunus to see her mistress Diana naked. She is punished by being overwhelmed by boulders, but Faunus brings about her confluence-marriage with Fanchin all the same. Her crime causes the angry goddess to abandon the whole district to savagery, suggesting the condition of all Ireland in the later 1590s, about to revert to war. Yet by ending with a marriage, the tale, like the other river stories, expresses a belief in underlying peace and harmony.

Arlo Hill, location of this drama, is also the setting for Nature's judgment on Mutabilitie's case against the planetary gods. Mutabilitie's chief witnesses, the laboring Months with their aura of georgic festivity, figuratively recolonize the wilderness. The selection of North Munster as background enables Spenser to offset his cosmic drama with the perfect example of the particular and familiar. Arlo is pastoral and remote from both London and Gloriana's court which the reader of *The Faerie Queene* never visits. Privately renamed by the poet, it sums up an irony both personal and cosmic, the coexistence of permanence and fluidity.

Eiléan Ní Chuilleanáin

Line references to *Vewe of Ireland* are from the ed by Rudolf Gottfried in *Var Prose* pp 39–231.

Osborn Bergin, tr 1970 *Irish Bardic Poetry* comp and ed David Greene and Fergus Kelly (Dublin); James Carney 1967 *The Irish Bardic Poet* (Dublin); Anne Cronin 1943–4 'Sources of Keating's *Forus Feasa ar Eirinn*: I. The Printed Sources' *Eigse* 4:235–79; David Greene 1982 'The Bardic Mind' in *The Pleasures of Gaelic Poetry* ed Seán Mac Réamoinn (London) pp 35–45; Grennan 1982; Jenkins 1937; Jenkins 1938; Brian Ó Cuív 1976 'The Irish Language in the Early Modern Period' in Moody, et al 1976:509–45; Quinn 1966.

Ireland, the historical context The last half of the sixteenth century witnessed a series of efforts by the English government to establish its authority in Ireland. Experience revealed that a forceful attempt to assert government influence in all quarters of the country would prove altogether more arduous and expensive than Queen Elizabeth would countenance, but those soldiers and officials who had been introduced to the country in the forays of the mid-century were anxious to pursue an aggressive forward policy that would present them with the opportunity to seize and develop land in areas controlled by Gaelic Irish families. Because of their manifest greed, these soldiers and officials can be likened to Drake, Raleigh, and the other English adventurers who were then trying to colonize Virginia, and like them too they were strongly motivated by Protestant zeal.

An increasing involvement with continental affairs from the 1570s on persuaded Elizabeth that she should quell the ardor of those who had been appointed to represent her interests in Ireland, and she sought to regain the confidence of the so-called Old English population. These were descendants of Anglo-Norman settlers who had established control over a considerable part of the country in the twelfth and thirteenth centuries, and who were still powerful in the sixteenth century in the more fertile lands of the east and south of the country and most especially so in the small fertile area known as the Pale which surrounded Dublin and Drogheda. Most of the Old English had remained loyal to Catholicism, but their leaders were anglicized in appearance and were historically the upholders of English influence in Ireland against the onslaughts of their Gaelic adversaries whom they had always represented as barbarians. It became the Queen's hope that these Old English would combine with her recently appointed officers to bring the Gaelic population to accept English authority by means of persuasion, but mutual antagonisms were by then too great to allow for any such combination of effort. Instead, the leaders of each group found fault with the other until eventually, in 1579, some sections of the Old English community, led respectively by the Earl of Desmond in Munster and by Viscount Baltinglass in the Pale, entered into open rebellion against crown authority in Ireland. These revolts seemed to support the contention that the seemingly civil Old English were no more reliable as subjects than the allegedly barbaric Gaelic Irish, and they persuaded the Queen that she should again seek to establish her authority in Ireland by force of arms. The man assigned to this task was Arthur, Lord Grey of Wilton, who, backed by 8000 soldiers, was sent in 1580 as governor to Ireland.

Spenser went to Ireland in August 1580 as secretary to Grey and, after Grey's recall in 1582, stayed on, first as registrar of Faculties in the Irish Court of Chancery, then as deputy to the Clerk of the Council of Munster. About 1588, during the disposition of the Earl of Desmond's properties, he received an estate in Munster of some 3000 acres, and there, at Kilcolman Castle (County Cork), established a small colony, containing at one time six households. He held various administrative positions as well. Spenser's life as a landholder was disturbed by recurrent legal challenges to his title, and it was severely marred in 1598 when Kilcolman was destroyed by some of the dispossessed Irish who had made common cause with the Ulster lord Hugh O'Neill, Earl of Tyrone, who had then risen in arms against the crown.

The basic facts relating to Spenser's life in Ireland are assembled in Henley 1928, and there is little to be added to what is said there. Yet it is possible to offer a fresh appraisal of his career in relation to the group of English-born officials and adventurers to which he belonged and who forced the pace of the Elizabethan conquest of Ireland from the mid-1560s to the end of the sixteenth century. It appears that the ideas underlying both *FQ* v and *Vewe* were shared by this group and sharpened by the poet's association with these English careerists in Ireland, especially those who worked closely with him on the provincial council in Munster. To this extent, it is possible to obtain a better understanding of Spenser's involvement with Ireland by considering it in the broader context of the Elizabethan conquest of the country.

English-born officials were conspicuously present in Ireland from the late 1530s on, but these were few enough to be readily absorbed into the previously anglicized population who resided in Dublin and the surrounding English Pale. Furthermore, these officials pursued a policy which enjoyed the support of the traditionally loyal community, a policy that sought to extend an anglicized social order to all parts of Ireland through gradual means. Most of those who were appointed from England before the mid-1560s were loyal to whatever religion was designated by the state, but in this, they were no different from the leaders of the loyal community in Ireland who were also willing to conform to the state religion. These Englishmen, like officials everywhere, were anxious to enrich themselves through the acquisition of land and office in Ireland. Their appetites were, however, satisfied from the dissolved monastic properties in the anglicized areas, and their willingness to share these spoils with the leaders of the local community served to ease the tensions that briefly surfaced when the confiscation policy first began.

Relations between English-born officials and the loyal Old English community in Ireland became more difficult after the mid-1560s, and we can trace to that decade the emergence of a distinctive, self-conscious group of English-born officials with clearly defined personal and policy objectives. The significant increase in the number of English officials serving in Ireland helps to explain why they stood out from the community at large, but they also became isolated as a group because they were now engaged upon a policy which had been defined in England without any reference to the Old English community in Ireland. The policy in question involved the extension of English authority to all parts of Ireland by more forceful means than had been previously approved: the expulsion of those lords who proved recalcitrant and the appointment of English colonists to take their place. Tension between English officials and the Old English community became acute when it became clear that only Englishmen would profit from the newly devised scheme of government. The scheme itself was bitterly opposed once it emerged that the loyal community would be compelled to bear a substantial part of the cost of its implementation through the crude extension of the prevailing practices of purveyance and billeting.

The hostility which these developments aroused within the Pale, and the concerted efforts of the Old English community to counter the efforts of the government by lobbying support at the English court, forced the officials in Ireland to close in upon themselves and defend their actions against the criticisms of their Old English adversaries. This involved them in the composition of treatises which were circulated in England with a view to persuading the Queen and her privy council of the propriety of the scheme that was being embarked upon. The most competent of these early authors was Edmund Tremayne (later clerk of the English privy council), who served for some years in Ireland as personal secretary to Sir Henry Sidney, the governor most closely associated with the new aggressive program of government. The statements composed by Tremayne during the mid-1560s when the new scheme was first launched were stated by him to have been based upon the speeches delivered in Ireland by Sidney and underlined the conservative rather than the radical aspects of the proposed policy. Attention was drawn to the deficiencies of Irish society in quite graphic language, but the essential point was that, while admitting their backward or degenerate condition, most of the Irish were open to persuasion, and the severe measures being proposed would apply only to those perverse individuals who would never come to order.

The essentially moderate tone of these discourses failed to counter the offensive of the spokesmen from the Pale, and the English officials in Ireland became increasingly frustrated as their efforts were repeatedly stymied by the lobbying of the Old English. But some of the Old English in the provinces went even further to achieve their ends, engaging during the years 1569–72 in a series of studied revolts that finally persuaded the Queen to withdraw support from the policy of the Dublin government in preference to provoking a general revolt. The governor and those associated with him were understandably outraged, and the authors among them engaged in the composition of a second wave of discourses aimed at recovering some lost ground. These discourses confronted the Queen with the choice of governing the country 'after the Irish manner as it hath been accustomed' or reducing it 'as near as may be to the English government.' Furthermore, they stressed the difficulties that would be encountered in achieving acceptable order even in those parts of the country that were apparently civil because, as Tremayne put it in 1573, even the Old English were attracted by the tyrannical rule of the Irish in which 'point of usurpation ... there is very few of them any different at all from the Irishry' ('Discourse at the Request of Sir Walter Mildemay, December 1573' Huntington Library, Bridgewater and Ellesmere Ms 1701).

In 1573 Tremayne was hoping to win the Queen's support for the pursuit of some forward policy to bring the country closer to a civil condition. He believed that only Englishmen could be trusted to implement such a policy, and his opinion was shared by almost all English-born officials who had served in Ireland or who went to serve there over the next two decades. These officials came progressively to regard themselves as the only people capable of promoting civility in Ireland, and as a distinctive group engaged upon a unique mission the purpose of which was as dimly understood in England as it was vehemently opposed in Ireland. Furthermore, these new officials came from a society which had recently become decidedly Protestant, and they were shocked by the extent to which loyalty to the old religion endured even in the supposedly obedient areas of Ireland. Concern over the continued Irish attachment to 'papistry' and 'superstition' was prominent in the treatises of the 1570s; but it became dominant in the tracts composed after 1579 when two Old English lords, the Earl of Desmond in Munster and the Viscount Baltinglass in the Pale, entered into revolts which were justified in purely religious terms. The occurrence of these outbreaks at a time when Philip II of Spain was known to be plotting against England provided the New English authors with a welcome opportunity to discredit the entire Old English population in the eyes of the crown, and to recommend a comprehensive program of reform that would leave control of the country in the hands of English-born Protestants.

At this juncture, when a coherent, radical policy was being formulated by the English officials serving in Ireland, Spenser first arrived as personal secretary to Lord Grey. Grey had no previous experience in Ireland, but he had taken advice from Sir Henry Sidney, and he was determined to root out the rebels in a comprehensive fashion such as Sidney had been constrained from doing in the aftermath of the earlier rebellions of 1569–72. Although clear as to his objectives and fully supported by the English army and officials in Ireland, Grey proved dilatory in the field, both against the Leinster rebels who inflicted an initial defeat on him at Glenmalure in August 1580, and against Desmond and his adherents in Munster. Grey's inability to produce the quick victory that the Queen had expected of him provided his Old English opponents with an opportunity to regroup and to lobby in England for his recall. The Old English leader on this occasion was Thomas Butler, Earl of Ormond, who was, conveniently, an irreproachable Irish Protestant and a cousin of the Queen. Ormond had a particular cause for grievance because he had been in charge of the military operations in Munster before Grey's arrival, and he now contended that Grey's unwillingness to offer mercy to any of the rebels explained why the conflict in Munster had become too prolonged and expensive for the crown to bear. Arguments from cost always worked with the Queen, especially when they were combined with charges of dishonesty. The Palesmen contended that the land which had come into crown possession following the overthrow of the Leinster rebellion had been disposed of by Grey to a small group of personal followers, and at rents prejudicial to the crown's interests. The Queen harkened to these charges, Grey resigned his office in August 1582, and Ormond was restored to command of the military campaign in Munster.

The English officials who had pinned all their hopes on Grey were shattered by these developments, and none more so than Spenser, who had accompanied the governor on his military excursions in Leinster and Munster. The recall of Grey was regretted because it represented a tactical success for the Old English, and emphasized that the Queen would never be persuaded to maintain any consistent policy for Ireland. The New English were further alarmed when they saw much of the land in Munster that might have been forfeited to the crown being frittered away by Ormond who, in their opinion, proved excessively generous in granting pardon to the lesser rebels. Their hopes for a coherent plantation in Munster, which would advance the cause of civility while enriching themselves, were also set back by Ormond's insistence that the 'English by blood' should receive equal consideration with the 'English by birth' when the rebels' land came to be confiscated. However, the most severe reverse suffered by the English officials was the decision to remove the disposition of those lands from the Dublin administration to the London government.

This sequence of events meant that the death in rebellion of the Earl of Desmond in the winter of 1583 came as something of an anticlimax for the English officials in Ireland, and their worst fears materialized when grants of the forfeited lands in Munster came to be made. Dublin-based officials were generally overlooked in the distribution of property; the principal grants went to Ormond, who had brought the military campaign to a satisfactory conclusion, and to Englishmen who were in favor at court. Of those Englishmen who had rendered service to the crown in Ireland, a mere handful were rewarded: these included Sir Thomas Norris, Jessua Smythes, Richard Beacon, and Spenser, all four of whom served on the provincial council in Munster.

While these four might have considered themselves fortunate to have been included among the grantees, they remained outspoken over the failure of the government to implement the scheme as originally conceived by the officials. As they perceived it, the existence of Irish proprietors in the midst of the planted land would always represent a threat to the colonists, and those Englishmen with no previous knowledge of Ireland would lack the motivation to bring the plantation to a successful conclusion. Many, it was feared, would be principally concerned with immediate profit, and would therefore succumb to the barbarous condition of their Irish neighbors. A few of the recently arrived settlers, notably William Herbert, agreed with these propositions and joined the officials in bewailing the shortcomings of the plantation effort. This discussion led in turn to the production of formal treatises, and Munster of the 1580s became a remarkably productive place for the generation of ideas relating to civil and religious reform.

The existence of a provincial council in Munster presented these officials and planters with frequent occasion to discuss their common problems. Besides such meetings, which would have occurred in the normal conduct of business, it is possible that these individuals and their associates in Dublin occasionally came together to engage in formal discourse such as that described by Bryskett in *A Discourse of Civill Life* (1606) as having occurred in 1585 in his Dublin residence. Even without such discussions, the Munster officials could have readily agreed upon a common line of argument because the English officials serving in Ireland had already arrived at a consensus on how best to reform the country. What occurred in Munster was that some officials and planters refined these common assumptions and engaged upon an active program of propaganda designed to impress the validity of their case upon the government in England.

Much of what was written was intended to redeem the reputation of Lord Grey and of those Englishmen in Ireland who had emulated him, but we can also accept that the several authors were not satisfied that a secure framework of government had been established in Munster. They therefore feared for the safety of their lives and property in the event of future rebellion, and they concentrated on the defects of what had been accomplished and prophesied doom if these defects were not remedied. The most comprehensive of these analyses is Spenser's *Vewe of the Present State of Ireland* (1596), but the significant fact is that his opinions in this discourse enjoyed common currency among the Munster officials during the previous decade. Thus, for example, the basic propositions around which *Vewe* is organized are the same as those isolated for discussion in Richard Beacon's *Solon His Follie* (Oxford 1594). Like Spenser, Beacon praises Elizabeth and her predecessors for the steps taken to introduce civility to Ireland, but he insists that the work was but well begun and that Ireland like all 'such commonweales which in all the parts thereof are found corrupted and declined from their first institution may not by profitable laws ... be reformed' (1594:4). What is needed, avers Beacon, is a forceful military policy aimed at crushing the power of the great lords who, he claims, oppress the commonalty and divert them from loyalty to the crown. When, in the pursuit of such a policy, the military governors in Ireland find it necessary 'in cases of great extremities' to proceed against the rebels 'without observing the usual ceremonies of law,' this 'may not be deemed any part of tyranny' (p 16). Beacon anticipates Spenser in making use of this occasion to defend the actions of Lord Grey, and he also justifies the use of extralegal measures against the Irish rebels by reference to the frequent wars in Ireland which 'proceed from the greatness of the nobles and the lords' (p 76).

The distinction which Beacon draws here between Irish nobles and lords indicates that he includes the apparently civil Old English within his blanket condemnation of the Irish condition, and this becomes all the more evident in the third section of his discourse treating the 'causes of decline in commonwealths.' His discussion of 'decline,' like Spenser's in *Vewe*, is intended to reveal the extent to which the Old English population in Ireland had become 'corrupted' by their environment; but it is also designed to illustrate his concern that those Englishmen being settled under the plantation scheme would become degenerate in turn if appropriate measures were not taken by the state. These included imposing a penal code under which the lords who oppressed the people would be chastised, recalling all offices into the hands of loyal English-born Protestants, and appointing forceful rulers in the provinces who would enjoy the unqualified support of the Queen in their efforts to undermine the authority of the Irish lords.

Beacon is not as specific as Spenser in detailing the program of action that he thinks necessary, but his dissatisfaction over the government's failure to pursue a coherent policy in Ireland emerges as clearly from his composition as it does from the *Vewe*. Perhaps his fear of government retaliation for such specific criticism explains why *Solon His Follie* is presented in allegorical form, and perhaps it also explains why he succeeded in having his work published in 1594, whereas Spenser's *Vewe*, which was entered in the Stationers' Register in 1596, was not published until 1633, and even then only in a truncated form.

This summary of Beacon's discourse makes it clear that the opinions favored by Spenser were shared by those English officials and planters who were associated with him in Munster during the subjugation of that province. They and their colleagues were conscious that their opinions would appear radical to readers in England, but they derived a certain grim satisfaction from the events in 1598 when the nascent colony in Munster was uprooted by rebellion. This, at any rate, is the tone of *A Brief Note of Ireland*, a petition written in the aftermath of that rebellion and often attributed to

Spenser, who may have presented it to the Queen in 1598. The responsibility for that rebellion, the author claims, lay principally with the ineptitude and even greed of those governors who had put private interest before public trust, but also partly with the Queen herself, who had preferred her 'wonted milde courses' to the comprehensive conquest of the country that had been recommended by the New English (*Brief Note* in *Var Prose* line 253). The settlement in Munster had been defective from the outset, he claims, because it had relied excessively on the potency of example in achieving reform of the Irish population, a manifestly hopeless plan, given that the Irish 'have ever bene brought upp licenciouslie' (175). The author now recommends that the Queen adopt a firm resolution 'to make an universall reformacion of all this Realme' (240).

This petition shows confidence, even in the face of adversity, that the long-sought ambition of bringing civility to Ireland could be attained, and it explains the rebellion of 1598 as an act of providence 'to stirre upp' the Queen to more vigorous effort. But while clinging to a consistent argument, the petition fails to admit that the rebellion was due also to the insufficiency of planters with the means to meet the conditions that had been stipulated by the government. In this respect, no group had been more delinquent than the Munster officials who had been favored by the government in the allocation of land. The various surveys of the plantation taken before the rebellion of 1598 provide no convincing evidence that these officials had done anything more than occupy their lands, and in this respect we may take the performance of Jessua Smythes as typical of the group. Smythes, who had passed his patent for 6000 acres, assured the commissioners that none of the previous Irish occupiers had been retained on the land and that he would 'rather set fire in the nest than such birds should roost in any land of his' ('Answer ... to the Commissioners, May 1589' Public Record Office, State Papers 63/144/69). While asserting his self-righteousness in this respect, he was forced to admit that the lands lay entirely vacant and undeveloped, and that he had done no more than extract promises from 'a sufficient number of gentlemen and others of good ability' in England that they would take leases of his land. The likelihood of their ever fulfilling this promise was extremely remote in 1589 when Smythes had still to divide his lands into tenancies and to 'build houses meet for them to come unto.'

This example from 1589 shows that Smythes and other officials like him could never bear the cost that was involved in plantation along scientific lines, and that they would in the end have to dispose their land 'to some such as have been soldiers in this land and now out of entertainment.' Many besides Smythes are likely to have resorted to such expedients, but even then the total population of English settlers in Munster seems never to have exceeded 3000 in the years previous to 1598, despite the minimum of 8000 that had been stipulated under the plantation conditions. This deficiency in numbers, as well as the shortfall in the erection of defensible buildings, explains why the planters in Munster were not better able to defend themselves in 1598, and none was so brazen as Spenser – if he is the author of *Brief Note* – in seeking to have the Queen disregard their failure as a factor contributing to their ultimate overthrow. While the outraged tone of this propaganda did not convince the Queen, it did satisfy the settler population of the sixteenth century, as well as several generations of their descendants, that their difficulties and even shortcomings could always be accounted for in terms of English neglect or misunderstanding.

To this extent, it is possible to trace the development of the Anglo-Irish ideology of *Vewe* and *Brief Note* to Spenser's experience in Ireland, and this account should also assist us in understanding *FQ* V. His strong attachment to Ireland emerges as clearly through his poetry as in his prose, but so also does his belief in the capacity to impose order upon chaos, particularly when the protagonist is supported consistently by a farsighted prince who recognizes 'his right course' (V xii 43). NICHOLAS CANNY

Brendan Bradshaw 1979 *The Irish Constitutional Revolution of the Sixteenth Century* (Cambridge); Bradshaw 1987; Ciaran Brady 1981 'Faction and the Origins of the Desmond Rebellion of 1579' *IHS* 22:289–312; Brady 1986; Nicholas P. Canny 1976; Canny 1983 'Edmund Spenser and the Development of an Anglo-Irish Identity' *YES* 13:1–19; Canny 1987a *From Reformation to Restoration: Ireland 1536–1660* (Dublin); Canny 1987b 'Identity Formation in Ireland: The Emergence of the Anglo-Irish' in *Colonial Identity in the Atlantic World 1500–1800* ed Nicholas Canny and Anthony Pagden (Princeton) pp 159–212; Canny 1988 *Kingdom and Colony: Ireland in the Atlantic World, 1560–1800* (Baltimore); Canny and Brady 1988; Henley 1928; Judson 1947; MacCarthy-Morragh 1986; Moody, et al 1976; David B. Quinn 1966 'The Munster Plantation: Problems and Opportunities' *JCHAS* 71:19–40; Anthony J. Sheehan 1982; Sheehan 1982a 'The Population of the Plantation of Munster: Quinn Reconsidered' *JCHAS* 87:107–17.

Isis, Osiris Egyptian deities who preside over Britomart's visit to Isis Church in *FQ* V vii. The goddess Isis, whose symbol is the moon, is said to signify 'That part of Justice, which is Equity,' while her consort Osiris, the sun, signifies justice itself (2–3). In Britomart's dream as interpreted by the priest, Osiris is associated with Artegall and (by implication) Isis with Britomart, and both thereby with the Tudors.

Spenser derives his knowledge of the Egyptian gods and their cult from Plutarch's *Isis and Osiris* (in *Moralia* 351–84) and from Diodorus, Apuleius, and Renaissance mythographers, most notably Conti. Plutarch and Diodorus provide a wide range of identifications of Isis and Osiris: as the female and male generative powers, earth and water, moon and sun, Hera and Zeus, Demeter and Bacchus, and as patrons of death, fertility, justice, and monarchy. Like Diodorus', Spenser's Isis and Osiris were an actual royal couple, deified in recognition of their virtues as rulers. Such euhemeristic interpretation would have appealed to him as a precedent for shadowing Elizabeth and her possible consort in Gloriana and Arthur. Plutarch, in contrast, rejects euhemerism as reductive and subversive to piety.

Isis is identified with the moon by both Diodorus and Plutarch, who share an interest in synthesizing Greek and Egyptian myth. She is another Diana/Phoebe figure, and so readily assimilable to Spenser's other images of the English Cynthia, Queen Elizabeth. Less obviously, as a goddess of childbirth, marriage, and the female generative principle, she is related to marriage, sexuality, and the proper balance of female and male power treated in *FQ* III-V.

Another symbolic dimension of Isis relates her to the Virgin Mary. A cult statue of Isis with her son Horus was regarded by Christians as an image of Mary and the infant Jesus, an association strengthened by Plutarch's allusions to Horus' miraculous conception and Isis' flight into the wilderness with him (cf Rev 12.5–6). Moreover, Isis, Mary, and the Woman Clothed with the Sun (Rev 12) are portrayed as either standing upon or crowned with the moon.

Osiris' role in Spenser's allegory is relatively straightforward. Plutarch and Diodorus both identify him with Bacchus and Hercules as a civilizer of primitive man, a role assigned to Artegall in the proem to Book V. Spenser says that Bacchus, Hercules, and Artegall spread order by the use of a 'strong hand' and 'The club of Justice dread' (i 1–3). Plutarch's Osiris is also a model of the poet, for he reforms savage peoples by the use of eloquence: 'he civilized the whole world as he traversed through it, having very little need for arms, but winning over most of the peoples by beguiling them with persuasive speech together with all manner of song and poetry' (356A-B). Together with Isis and their son Horus, he serves as a founder and patron of monarchy (the pharaohs were viewed as incarnations of Horus); and so it is particularly appropriate that Britomart's dream should reveal the dynasty of British monarchs.

Plutarch offered Spenser more than a convenient compilation of Egyptian mystic lore, for his *Isis and Osiris* is in large part an explication and defense of allegory. He takes pains to emphasize that legends and rituals which appear grotesque or absurd to the uninitiated conceal a deeper sense, and his frequent criticism of unthinking adherence to taboos would appeal to Protestants concerned with combatting papist superstition. CAROL A. STILLMAN

Brooks-Davies 1983; Plutarch ed 1970.

Isis Church The temple of Isis visited by Britomart (*FQ* V vii) before she rescues Artegall from the Amazon princess Radigund forms one of the two iconographic centers of Book V (the other is the court of Mercilla in ix 21–50). Although this church is pagan, Spenser tells us that worship of Isis, like devotion extended to her spouse Osiris, involves a 'true case' hidden under the 'fayned colours' of her cult (vii 2). Though ostensibly used for pre-Christian worship, Isis Church is an appropriate setting for Britomart's vision which will reveal her future marriage and Queen Elizabeth's ancestry. Her vision also unveils important aspects of the relationship between justice (the subject of Book v) and equity.

The church, which represents sacred space where such knowledge can be communicated, is itself a 'goodly building' supported by 'stately pillours, all dispred / With shining gold, and arched over hed,' a Gothic or Romanesque form of architecture with aisles and arched pillars. Central to the temple is the statue of the goddess Isis, an 'Idoll ... framed all of silver fine' and wearing 'a Crowne of gold.' Its function distinguishes it from false idols such as Geryoneo's deceitful image (v xi 19–33). The statue of Isis clothed in linen and with one foot on a crocodile is an iconic image (ie, one which signifies an aspect of reality but also participates in that reality) that will demonstrate the necessity of 'clemence ... in things amis' and of equity as a factor which tempers justice.

When Britomart spends the night in the temple, she sees a 'wondrous vision' in which she participates first as a votary of Isis and then as the goddess herself. Her devotion to the statue causes her to become Isis in her dream: she is serving at the altar when she sees herself transformed into Isis but wearing the royal robe. The crocodile awakens, devours the flames which threaten to destroy the temple, and threatens to eat Isis/Britomart until it is driven back by her rod. Then it seeks her 'grace and love,' she yields, it impregnates her, and from their union she gives birth to a lion. As the Priest explains, the crocodile is Osiris (the Egyptian god of Justice) who sleeps under the feet of Isis 'To shew that clemence oft in things amis, / Restraines those sterne behests, and cruell doomes of his' (22), and who shows thereby the proper relation of justice and judgment to equity. The Priest also explains to Britomart that the crocodile is Artegall, 'The righteous Knight,' who will settle the storms and 'raging flames, that many foes shall reare' and restore to her the heritage of her throne, and who will give her a 'Lion-like' son (23), the new British monarchy of the Tudors.

The crocodile is a symbol both of guile and of a regeneration that will affect future history. As guile, its relation to Isis is reminiscent of Vice figures under the feet of triumphing Virtues in medieval art. An iconographic association between the crocodile in its demonic aspect and medieval saints' legends derives ultimately – and significantly for Spenser – from the classical figure of Britomartis (Miskimin 1978). In Plutarch's *Isis and Osiris* 50, it is linked to Typhon, the enemy of justice and order, while in Renaissance iconographic tradition it is often symbolic of the need for prudence (for one must be prudent to avoid the wily crocodile). Cesare Ripa's *Iconologia* (sv *Lussuria*) shows the nude Luxury (or Lechery) seated upon a crocodile, an interesting analogy to its phallic sexuality in Britomart's dream. Yet along with these primarily negative associations, there are also positive ones in the crocodile's identification with Osiris/Artegall/Justice and in the implication that Isis/Britomart/Equity is incomplete without her partner. The image contains its own contradictions, unresolved by the Priest.

The priests of Isis Church are depicted with a deliberate ambiguity that in part identifies them with unreformed Christian and heathen religious practices, although their leader is accepted as one able to reveal good and useful knowledge to Britomart. After her vision, she finds them on a lower level of the building where they are preparing their 'holy things' to celebrate the first Mass of the day. This ritual, part of their 'rites and daily sacrifize,' seems to be Roman Catholic. Yet it may be the 'sacrifice of praise and thanksgiving' of the Book of Common Prayer rather than the Roman Catholic 'sacrifice' in the Mass which was condemned by the Thirty-nine Articles as 'blasphemous' (Article 31; cf *FQ* v xi 19–20); and this 'Mas' may refer to a ritual compatible with the Protestant religious rite.

The priests of Isis are dressed 'in linnen robes with silver hemd,' while 'on their heads ... They [wear] rich Mitres shaped like the Moone' which, in contrast to Duessa's demonic '*Persian* mitre' (I ii 13), symbolize the sacerdotal function of Isis' votaries; and their moon-shaped design is linked to the iconography of Isis, who traditionally wears clothing or headgear bearing the symbol of the moon (eg, see Cartari *Imagini*). The description of the linen vestments is derived from classical writings (see esp Plutarch *Isis and Osiris* 3). When Britomart in her vision is 'deckt with Mitre on her hed, / And linnen stole after those Priestes guize,' the word *stole* indicates the kind of garment worn by Isis' priests and not the ecclesiastical stole, which was reintroduced in the Church of England only during the nineteenth century. (See **Isis Church** Fig 1.)

The depiction of the priests' hair also seems deliberately ambiguous. Unlike Plutarch, who describes their heads as being shaven, Spenser says they have 'long locks comely kemd.' (Cf Ezek 44.20: 'Thei shal not also shave their heades, nor suffre their lockes to growe long, but round their heades'; the Geneva gloss on this passage associates long hair with 'infideles and heathen.') Possibly their long hair nevertheless reflects a Protestant bias: it prevents them from being seen as tonsured Roman Catholic priests.

Isis' priests are restrained and ascetic in their behavior: they are vegetarians and abstain from alcohol, and they practice celibacy as well as whatever austerities may serve 'to mortify' the 'proud rebellious flesh.' They recognize that the correct attitude in the presence of the idol and altar of Isis is humility. For this reason, Talus' unthinking and mechanical imposition of justice – a justice untempered by equity – makes him unsuitable as a visitor to the temple, while Britomart appropriately enters 'with great humility,' an attitude that is also important for her role as the feminine liberator of Artegall, victim of the proud Radigund. Justice must be restrained from excess by the principle of equity, a classical quality which will be transformed at the court of Mercilla (v ix) into the Christian virtue of mercy. CLIFFORD DAVIDSON

Aptekar 1969:88–107; Clifford Davidson 1969 'The Idol of Isis Church' *SP* 66:70–86; Graziani 1964a; Hieatt 1975a:135–49; Kermode 1964–5; Miskimin 1978; Plutarch ed 1970; Stump 1982; D. Douglas Waters 1979 'Spenser and the "Mas" at the Temple of Isis' *SEL* 19:43–53.

Italy, influence and reputation in The first known mention of Spenser in Italy occurs in the manuscript *Relazioni d'Inghilterra dell' anno 1667* written by Count Lorenzo Magalotti (perhaps the first Italian 'anglofilo' or 'anglomane'). A passing reference lists 'Spens' among the English poets (Magalotti ed 1972:151), although in translating Waller's *Battle of the Summer Islands* Magalotti omits lines 11–12 of canto 3 where Talus is mentioned, which means that he was not acquainted with Spenser's work.

A second mention of the poet in Italian, the first in a printed book, occurs nearly a century later in the preface to *A Dictionary of the English and Italian Languages* (1750, rev ed 1760) by Giuseppe Baretti (1719–89), the well-known Italian author of *La frusta letteraria* (*The Literary Whip*). In his *Dictionary* (for which Samuel Johnson wrote a dedication), Baretti encourages his countrymen to study the English language. He also praises English literature:

> Quanta carta però non mi converrebbe scarabocchiare per darvi solo una malabbozzata idea d'uno Shakespeare, d'uno Spenser, d'un Milton, d'un Dryden, e di molt'altri divini spiriti, che accozzando chi più chi meno alla schiettezza della poesia Greca la venustà de' Latini, la vaghezza degl' Italiani, e la nitidezza de' Francesi con la robustezza e la fantasticaggine della Sassonia e delle Gaule, hanno prodotto una maniera di pensar poetico, della quale noi ... non ci curiamo ancora quanto dovremmo fare.
>
> [How much paper however I would need to scribble on to give you even an ill-sketched notion of a Shakespeare, a Spenser, a Milton, a Dryden, and many other divine spirits, who – more or less by uniting to the integrity of Greek poetry the grace of the Latins, the delight of the Italians, and the clarity of the French, with the strength and whimsicality of the Saxons and the Gaul – have produced a manner of poetic thought which we ... have not yet taken into account so much as we should.]

Baretti appreciates English poetry and regrets that the best English and English authors are unknown in Italy. He also realizes how challenging and awkward it is to translate English poetry into Italian, and he modestly notes that he is unable to translate well some of the most impressive passages for his countrymen.

The translation of Spenser into Italian was first undertaken by the learned English scholar Thomas James Mathias (c 1754–1835; see *DNB*). He rendered *FQ* I in ottava rima as *Il Cavaliero della Croce Rossa* (1826, rpt 1830) and *FQ* VII as *La Mutabilità* (1827). For all his efforts and enthusiasm, Mathias' translation is the scholarly work of a foreigner who has learned Italian extraordinarily well but who lacks the *disinvoltura* and genius to enliven his verse translation. His choice of ottava rima is unfortunate, because it is a shorter stanza than Spenser's, and Italian is notoriously a language that needs many more words than English to say the same thing. Moreover, in several cantos he simply omits stanzas from the original. His work unfortunately did not give Italians a good idea of Spenser's poetry or make Spenser popular in Italy. Neither did the next effort, which is in better Italian but rather prolix: *La vergine Una* (1831), a translation of *FQ* I in terza rima by Giovan Battista Martelli (a lawyer, friend of the poet Vincenzo Monti).

After Martelli, no one translated anything else for more than a century, when Tarquinio Vallese rendered the first canto of *FQ* I as an appendix to his *Spenser: Studio critico della poesia di Edmund Spenser* (1947). Only apparently in verse, this is actually a pedestrian, word-for-word translation into Italian prose for student use, printed in line-for-line groupings to look like Spenserian stanzas. In 1954, Carlo Izzo translated *FQ* I as *La Regina delle Fate*, using ten-line stanzas in which the first eight lines are *versi sciolti* (ie, unrhymed hendecasyllables) followed by a couplet. This edition includes the Italian translation with facing English text, an introduction, a glossary, and a bibliography; on the whole it is not a great success.

Until the mid-twentieth century, only portions of *The Faerie Queene* had been translated into Italian. Spenser's shorter works were completely ignored until Anna Maria Crinò published a verse translation of *The Shepheardes Calender* with the English text printed on facing pages (1950). Other translations followed: *Amoretti* and *Epithalamion* (1954), *Colin Clouts Come Home Againe* (1956), and *Mother Hubberds Tale* (1957). Selections from Spenser (in English) were published for Italian university students in *Antologia spenseriana* (1966), with an introduction, notes, glossary, and bibliography.

Most Italian Spenser studies deal with the influence of Tasso and Ariosto, of which the best by far is Alberto Castelli's study of Tasso and Spenser (1936). Spenser's relation to Ariosto is treated in Ida Turrini's modest essay (1891), by Alice Galimberti (1903, 1938), and by Anna Benedetti (1914). The studies by Viglione (1937) and Vallese (1947) are less reliable. Crinò 1968 presents evidence on the relationship of Spenser and Lord Grey of Wilton.

Now that English and English literature are widely studied in Italy, one hopes that more attention and study will be given to Spenser, whose work, if known, might well prove particularly attractive to Italians, for in *The Faerie Queene* they would find an allegory interestingly different from Dante's and a romantic epic comparable to those of Ariosto and Tasso. ANNA MARIA CRINÒ

Spenser 1826 *Il Cavaliero della Croce Rossa, o la leggenda della Santità, poema in dodici canti* tr Thomas James Mathias (Naples, rpt 1830); Spenser 1827 *La Mutabilità, poema in due canti* tr Thomas James Mathias (Naples); Spenser 1831 *La vergine Una, canti dodici* tr Giovan Battista Martelli (Milan) rpt in *Parnaso straniero* 17 vols (Venice 1834–51) vol II; Spenser 1950 *The Shepheardes Calender* (an Ital metrical tr) tr Anna Maria Crinò (Florence); Spenser 1954a *'Amoretti' and 'Epithalamion'* (an Ital metrical tr) tr Anna Maria Crinò (Florence); Spenser 1954b *La Regina delle Fate* tr Carlo Izzo (Florence); Spenser ed 1956; Spenser 1957 *Prosopopoia, or Mother Hubberds Tale* (an Ital metrical tr) tr Anna Maria Crinò (Florence); Spenser 1966 *Antologia spenseriana* ed Anna Maria Crinò (Verona).

Giuseppe Baretti 1750 *A Dictionary of the English and Italian Languages* (London; rev ed London 1760, Venice 1787, etc) 2 vols; Anna Benedetti 1914 *L'"Orlando furioso' nella vita intellettuale del popolo inglese* (Florence); Castelli 1936; Crinò 1968; Alice Galimberti 1903 'L'Ariosto inglese' *NA* 190:407–18; Galimberti 1938 *Edmondo Spenser: l'Ariosto inglese* (Turin); Lorenzo Magalotti 1972 *Relazioni d'Inghilterra 1668 e 1688* ed Anna Maria Crinò (Florence); Ida Turrini 1891 *L'Orlando furioso e La Regina delle Fate* (Piacenza); Tarquinio Vallese 1947 *Spenser: Studio critico della poesia di Edmund Spenser* (Naples); Francesco Viglione 1937 *La poesia lirica di Edmondo Spenser* (Genoa); R.R. Wilson 1973 (summarizes Spenser's reputation, although most native speakers would disagree with his assessments of the several Italian translations).

J

James I of England (James VI of Scotland) (1566–1625) While he was King of Scotland, as Robert Bowes wrote to Lord Burghley in 1596, James 'conceaved great offence against Edward Spencer [*sic*] publishing in prynte in the second p[ar]t of the Fairy Queene and ixth chapter [ie, *FQ* V ix] some dishonorable effects (as the k. demeth thereof) against himself and his mother deceassed.' Although Bowes assured the King that Spenser had not published 'with previledge of her ma[jes]t[ie]s Commission [-er]s' or official sponsorship, James 'still desyreth that Edward Spencer for his faulte, may be dewly tryed and punished' (Carpenter 1923:41–2).

In *FQ* V ix 38–50 Spenser represents Mary, Queen of Scots, as Duessa, 'A Ladie of great countenance and place, / But that she it with foule abuse did marre; / Yet did appeare rare beautie in her face, / But blotted with condition vile and base, / That all her other honour did obscure.' In the narrative, Zeal, the prosecutor, accuses her of many heinous crimes, including murder and adultery, and urges that she be punished for plotting to deprive Mercilla (ie, Elizabeth) of her throne. The merciful queen weeps with pity for her, 'Though plaine she saw by all, that she did heare, / That she of death was guiltie found by right.'

James was deeply offended by this characterization and, besides his request that the English authorities punish Spenser, seems also to have encouraged Walter Quin (a young Irishman in Edinburgh who later wrote a Latin defense of James' title to the English throne) to respond to 'Spencers booke whereat the K[ing] was offended' (Carpenter 1923:42). Yet James' remonstrance came to nothing; and later, after he became King of England in 1603, he allowed several new editions of *The Faerie Queene* to be printed. It has been argued that James was less interested in the characterization of his mother than he was in the implied suggestion that, as the son of a traitor, he might have no proper claim to the English throne (J.E. Phillips 1964:201–3, 212–13). The poem never presents Duessa as a mother, however, and there is nothing in it that bears on James' title to the throne.

Other proposed relationships between Spenser and James seem unlikely. Though James' *Essayes of a Prentise* (1584) uses a sonnet form similar to that favored by Spenser, there seems to be no direct influence (Markland 1963). Likewise, the suggestions that James appears in allegorical guise in the poetry (as the Kid in *SC, Maye*, the Ape in *Mother Hubberd*, or Alcon in *Colin Clout*) are unsubstantiated. MARK ECCLES

James I ed 1955–8; Markland 1963. The standard biography is D. Harris Willson 1956 *King James VI and I* (London). Goldberg 1983 discusses Spenser's relation to royal authority; see also *Bonfont.

Japan, influence and reputation in Spenser's name was first introduced to Japan in 1853 by Kennosuke Araki's Japanese version of *Egeresu Kiryaku* (*A Survey of England* Tokyo), originally by the Chinese writer Chen Feng-heng, which mentions Shakespeare, Milton, Spenser, and Dryden as four representative English poets. Serious studies began in 1937, when Sadao Toyama published the first Japanese translation of *FQ* I (*Senjoo* Tokyo); he resumed periodical publication of his translation in 1950, but regrettably left the work unfinished at *FQ* VI iii.

In 1969, seven scholars at Kumamoto University (Yuichi Wada, Shohachi Fukuda, Masato Kimura, Masanori Yoshida, Chiyoshi Yamada, Yoshihiko Fujii, and Yoshifumi Hirado) published their joint translation of *The Faerie Queene* (*Yosei no joo* Tokyo), which received the prize for the best translation of the year from the Japan Society of Translators. The same group published their translation of *The Shepheardes Calender* in 1974 (*Hitsujikai no koyomi* Tokyo) and of the other shorter poems in 1980 (*Spenser shokyokushu* Tokyo). Thus, this Spenser Circle of Kumamoto University made practically all of Spenser's poems accessible in Japanese. No Japanese poet, however, seems to have been influenced by Spenser. While Shakespeare and Milton have become widely known in various circles of Japanese readers, interest in Spenser is confined to scholars.

Among several thousand scholars of English literature in Japan publishing about 1000 books and articles each year, only about 30 show continuing interest in Spenser, publishing five to ten items every year, mostly interpretations of Spenser's allegory. The poet's treatment of love, nature, and time especially attracts Japanese readers, while many of them feel unfamiliar with his religious and political ideas. The first important work of Spenser scholarship was Itsuki Hosoe's annotated edition of *FQ* I (Tokyo 1929); his extensive notes (in Japanese) are unique for their minute philological explanations of Spenser's vocabulary and syntax. Saburo Oita published *Edmund Spenser* (Tokyo 1936), a short critical biography. Torao Taketomo's *Spenser to sono shui* (*Spenser and His Influence* Osaka 1952) was the first study to pay serious attention to the poetic tradition formed by Spenser and his followers. Haruhiko Fujii's *Time, Landscape and the Ideal Life: Studies in the Pastoral Poetry of Spenser and Milton* (Kyoto 1974) was the first book on Spenser written in English by a Japanese scholar; it was followed by Motohiro Kisaichi's edition of *Epithalamion* (Kyoto 1982) with an introduction and annotations in English. Shohachi Fukuda and Alexander Lyle edited *Spenser Meishisen* (*Selected Poems* Tokyo 1983) with Japanese notes. Herbert W. Sugden's *The Grammar of Spenser's 'Faerie Queene'* was translated into Japanese (slightly abridged) by Michio Masui (*'Faerie Queene' no bunpo* Tokyo 1959); and Rosemary Freeman's *Edmund Spenser*, by Haruhiko Fujii (Tokyo 1970). The first symposium on Spenser, 'Aspects of Love in *The Faerie Queene*,' was held in 1968 at the fortieth annual meeting of the English Literary Society of Japan, with Yuichi Wada as chairman, and panelists Yukinobu Nomura, Susumu Kawanishi, Shohachi Fukuda, and Haruhiko Fujii.

HARUHIKO FUJII

Kazuyoshi Enozawa and Miyo Takano 1979 *Bibliography of English Renaissance Studies in Japan: I, 1961–1970* (Tokyo); [Hugh Maclean] 1983 'Spenser in Japan: Signs and Portents' *SpN* 14.1(Winter):20–2; Haruhiko Fujii 1985 'Spenser in Japan' *SpN* 16.1(Winter):16–19.

Jerusalem, New Spenser inherited from medieval exegesis a fourfold notion of the New Jerusalem as the antitype of the historical city in the Holy Land, the Bride of Revelation who is the allegorical figure of the Church, the moral representation of the Christian soul, and the anagogic image of heaven itself. He rarely refers to Jerusalem in his works; but when he does (as in *Theatre* and *FQ*), it appears as the celestial city envisioned in the biblical Apocalypse (Rev 21–2), the ultimate perfection of human life and anagoge of paradise. Spenser's preference for the transcendent New Jerusalem over the actual historical city as the final goal of the Red Cross Knight's quest contrasts with Tasso's treatment in *Gerusalemme liberata* (1581), where the besieged Jerusalem of the First Crusade is the symbolic center of the epic and is glossed by the author (in his 'Allegory' to the poem) as signifying the achievement of 'civil happiness' which may come to a Christian after he has climbed the hill of virtue. Although 'sacred Salem' appears once in *The Faerie Queene* in a catalogue of ancient 'Great cities ransackt' (IV i 21–2), even here Spenser treats it suprahistorically. It is the divine paradigm of civic life against whose standard all earthly communities ultimately must be judged – and be found wanting.

In *FQ* I x 55–64, Contemplation gives Redcrosse a vision of the 'new *Hierusalem*' after his purgation in the house of Holiness. Spenser's biblical subtext is clear: as in Revelation, a heavenly guide presents a mountaintop view of an indescribable city to an abashed mortal. The matchless sight that Redcrosse glimpses not only contrasts with Lucifera's antithetical Babylon (I iv) but also surpasses the noble splendor of Gloriana's Cleopolis. When the knight wants to enter the heavenly city without further delay, Contemplation tells him that he may do so only after serving the 'royall maide' Una. Although the New Jerusalem may be his life's final goal, it can be reached only through faithful commitment to the 'mery England' of which he here discovers himself to be not merely a citizen but proleptically a patron saint.

This implied connection between earthly and heavenly realms, seemingly confirmed by the divine music that accompanies the betrothal of Redcrosse and Una (I xii 39), occurs again in II ix 47, where the tower of Alma's castle is likened to God's citadel in heaven. However, it does not survive the poem: by the end of the *Cantos of Mutabilitie*, the poet is left looking forward to the secure foundation of an eternal rest wherein the 'Sabbaoth God' reigns supreme. The New Jerusalem glimpsed in *FQ* I x becomes a vision which the poet finally can only pray for, a reality that transcends and eludes 'this state of life so tickle' (VII viii 1). Having begun his poem in the optimism of Christian civic humanism, Spenser seems to end with an almost Augustinian pessimism about the rapport between God's Jerusalem and the earthly city.

PETER S. HAWKINS

Hankins 1971; Kaske 1975; Nohrnberg 1976; Rathborne 1937.

Johnson, Samuel (1709–84) Johnson never wrote at length on Spenser; his scattered, sometimes contradictory remarks are almost always made either with reference to other writers or on their authority. As an undergraduate, he probably used the 1679 edition of Spenser's works, and at his death owned the six-volume Hughes edition (1715 or 1750) and a set of *The Faerie Queene* and other works (either the 1751 edition with a life by Birch, or the 1758 edition by Upton). According to his biographer Hawkins, Spenser was one of several authors – including More, Ascham, and Hooker – who formed his style. What *style* means here is unclear, but it is likely that the richness of Spenser's language impressed him. In his 'Preface to Shakespeare,' he credits Spenser and Shakespeare with first discovering 'to how much smoothness and harmony the English language could be softened'; and in the Preface to his *Dictionary* (1755), he recommends Spenser and Sidney as resources for the 'dialect of poetry and fiction.'

As a lexicographer and philologist, Johnson was committed to documenting and elucidating the vagaries of English usage, for which he found Spenser useful. In his notes to Shakespeare, for example, he glosses words such as *wappen'd* from *Timon of Athens* with *awhape* from *Mother Hubberds Tale*, and *impossible* from *Much Ado about Nothing* with *importable* from *The Faerie Queene*. Although such allusions are few, they prove that he knew Spenser well. In the *Dictionary*, he cites his poetry and prose at least 2,878 times (2.9% of the total number of illustrations), drawing most heavily from *Vewe of Ireland* and the early works, in which the language is more frequently archaic and irregular.

However, when Johnson the critic writes of Spenserian imitations, he censures the same qualities he considers valuable from a philological point of view. He calls Spenser's style 'vicious,' 'darkened with old words and peculiarities of phrase,' and 'remote from common use'; and he cites with apparent approval Jonson's opinion that Spenser wrote no language (*Rambler* 121). He did not approve the use of language that was already obscure, whether by Spenser or, worse, by his eighteenth-century imitators.

Johnson also attacks the Spenserian stanza as 'difficult and unpleasing, tiresome to the ear by its uniformity, and to the attention by its length.' Designed in imitation of Italian poetry, it is incompatible with the 'genius' of English, where rhymes are scarce; it therefore leads to arbitrariness. Citing Milton's general dislike of rhyme, he maintains that the 'long concatenations' of this stanza oblige poets 'to express their thoughts in improper terms' for the sake of rhyme alone (*Rambler* 121). Elsewhere, in his satiric portrait of Dick Minim, the facile young critic of the coffeehouses (*Idler* 60, 61), he shows how Spenser's detractors are as mindless and faddish as his imitators. Since Minim's strictures parrot some of his own, we may assume that Johnson's judgments were more flexible than they appear. He was aware that Spenser's historical context must be carefully reconstructed before his work can be accurately assessed. Praising Warton's method of illuminating 'our ancient authours' by directing readers 'to the perusal of the books which those authours had read,' he suggests that a genuine appreciation of Spenser and his contemporaries requires a thorough knowledge of sixteenth-century literary and intellectual history, an aim he promotes in the *Dictionary* (Boswell ed 1934–50, 1:270).

Johnson's description of pastoral as 'easy, vulgar, and therefore disgusting' (*Life of Milton*) has become notorious. He accepted realistic pastorals grounded in what he considered the actual experience of rural life; but as an advocate of invention, he was nonplussed by the deliberate artificiality of traditional pastoral and impatient with the contradictions of pastoral theory (*Rambler* 36–7). He considered the genre at best as an acceptable, if not particularly inventive, literary exercise for the apprentice poet (*Life of Pope*), and at worst as too conventionalized and implausible to engage one's attention. Spenser's pastorals seem to have fallen into the latter category. Since he demands internal consistency, Johnson objects to joining 'elegance of thought' with 'coarseness of diction.' Like Pope in *Guardian* 40, he ridicules the 'studied barbarity' of *September* 1–4 and, noting how the shepherds here discuss the corruptions of Rome, quips, 'Surely, at the same time that a shepherd learns theology, he may gain some acquaintance with his native language' (*Rambler* 37). His later criticism of Milton's *Lycidas* suggests another, possibly more damaging objection to Spenser's pastorals: their mingling of 'trifling fictions' with the 'most awful and sacred truths.' His logical and religious temper balked at an overlay of pagan and Christian material, finding Christian truth 'polluted' by 'irreverent combination' with the myths it has displaced (*Life of Milton*).

Johnson also brought rigorously logical standards to bear on allegory, and again his comments on Milton illuminate what presumably was a problem in his reading of *The Faerie Queene*. On moral grounds, he approves imitating Spenser's 'fiction and sentiments' and grants that allegory is a pleasing vehicle of instruction (*Rambler* 121). However, his strictures on Milton's allegory of Sin and Death indicate a strict definition of allegory that precludes multivalency and prohibits dropping and then resuming an allegorical fiction. He does not object to investing 'abstract ideas' with 'form' – he does as much himself in *Theodore* and in several issues of the *Rambler* – but he will not allow them to have any 'real employment' and 'material agency.' Sin and Death may show the way to hell, but they may not 'facilitate the passage by building a bridge.' To ascribe 'effects to nonentity' in this way is to break the allegory and thereby to 'shock the mind' with absurdity (*Life of Milton*). Johnson finds, then, that the conceptual references of extended allegory restrict rather than enlarge a poet's field of invention. It is likely that he would have objected to the plotting of *The Faerie Queene*. He appears to have concurred with Dryden that Spenser's plots lack unity, for he quotes his remarks favorably while criticizing Butler's *Hudibras* on the same count (*Life of Butler*).

Johnson's comments on Spenser often follow other eighteenth-century writers. He is always an exacting and dauntless critic; but his harshness towards Spenser can be attributed partly to his impatience with Spenserian (as with all) imitations, and partly to demandingly empirical assumptions which are unsympathetic to the genres and techniques Spenser employs. It is worth noting, however, that when he censures Spenser, he generally does so indirectly, through the medium of another poet: Milton on rhyme, Jonson on diction, Dryden on unity. Such obliqueness is uncharacteristic and suggests that he may not have identified fully with the judgments he cites.

If many of Johnson's written comments on Spenser are critical, other evidence attests to an abiding admiration. For example, he encouraged Thomas Warton's study of *The Faerie Queene* (in which the 'admirable authour of the Rambler' is acknowledged); and Hannah More reports that he tried to include Spenser in his *Lives of the English Poets* but was thwarted by the booksellers sponsoring the project (*Memoirs* 1.174). More and Boswell also report that he eventually declined an invitation by George III to write Spenser's biography because of the lack of new information about his life (Boswell ed 1934–50, 2:42 n 2, 4:410). This evidence suggests that his occasional remarks do not represent his last words on Spenser. He would probably have praised Spenser's invention and morality; he certainly commends him for creating a literary language and for initiating a formidable national literary tradition in the process: 'We consider the whole succession from Spenser to Pope, as superiour to any names which the continent can boast' (*Idler* 91).

Claudia L. Johnson

Boswell ed 1934–50; John Hawkins 1961 *Life of Samuel Johnson LL.D.* ed Bertram H. Davis (London); Samuel Johnson 1926 *Critical Opinions* ed Joseph Epes Brown (Princeton); Johnson 1897 *Johnsonian Miscellanies* ed George Birkbeck Hill, 2 vols (Oxford); Johnson 1958– *Works* ed W.J. Bate, et al (New Haven).

Bernard L. Einbond 1971 *Samuel Johnson's Allegory* (The Hague); Donald Greene 1974 'The Proper Language of Poetry: Gray, Johnson, and Others' in *Fearful Joy* ed James Downey and Ben Jones (Montreal) pp 85–102; Greene 1975 *Samuel Johnson's Library: An Annotated Guide* (Victoria, BC); Jean H. Hagstrum 1952 *Samuel Johnson's Literary Criticism* (Minneapolis); Maxine Turnage 1970 'Samuel Johnson's Criticism of the Works of Edmund Spenser' *SEL* 10:557–67; Wasserman 1937; W.B.C. Watkins 1936 *Johnson and English Poetry before 1660* (Princeton).

Jonson, Ben (1572?-1637) During most of his life, Jonson looked on Spenser much as he did on Shakespeare, with a mixture of admiration and disapproval. It is unlikely, though not impossible, that the two men ever met. Drummond, in *Conversations* (1618–19), records Jonson as saying that the Irish burnt Spenser's house over his head, together with 'a litle child new born' and that the poet died 'for lake of bread in King street and refused 20 pieces sent to him by my Lord of Essex and said he was sorrie he had no time to spend them' (Jonson ed 1925–52, 1:137). It was a story that made an impression on Jonson, a man particularly sensitive both to the deaths of children and to society's neglect of poets, but it does not suggest any direct, personal knowledge of Spenser or of the circumstances surrounding his death.

Jonson shared Spenser's convictions about the moral responsibilities and high calling of poets. He was well aware of Spenser's own greatness. According to Drummond, he knew that Spenser had sent an explication of the allegory of *The Faerie Queene* to Raleigh, and his own copy of what he called '*Spenser*'s noble booke' (*Underwood* 78) was filled with marginal annotations. (Unfortunately, Jonson's copy of the 1617 edition of Spenser's works, sold at auction in 1884, cannot now be traced; see McPherson 1974:91.) The printed text of Jonson's *Masque of Queens* (1609) praises 'grave and diligent Spenser' – a formulation Milton may have remembered when he spoke of 'sage and serious Spenser' – and quotes four lines about 'Bunduca *Britonesse*' from *Ruines of Time* (ed 1925–52, 7:310). In another Jonson masque, *The Golden Age Restored* (1615), Spenser is one of the four sons of Apollo (the others being Chaucer, Gower, and Lydgate) who accompany the goddess Astraea when she returns to earth and takes up residence in King James' Britain.

Yet Spenser's artistic achievement often made Jonson uneasy. The clash here was partly temperamental. Jonson was preeminently a dramatist, and Spenser is the least dramatic of all the great English poets. Again, although Spenser is far from humorless, his subtle and subdued sense of fun is very different from that which animates *Volpone*, or the boisterous antimasques in Jonson's court entertainments. The younger Jonson especially liked to think of himself as the champion of classicism against 'degenerate' Elizabethan ways of writing. He was impatient with romance literature, the idealization of women, and Tudor medievalism, all of which lay near the center of Spenser's art. Even in nondramatic verse satire, a form exploited by both men, Jonson's faithful adherence to the Roman models provided by Juvenal, Horace, and Martial sets his work off sharply from *Colin Clouts Come Home Againe* or *Mother Hubberds Tale*.

Most of Jonson's criticisms, however, were leveled at Spenser's style. He himself believed that couplets were the best kind of rhymed verse, largely because they allowed content to overrule form in determining the length of the poem, and he had a particular dislike for the 'forced' modes of the sonnet and stanzaic verse. It is possible that Drummond misrepresented the latter part of what

Jonson said when he recorded that 'Spencers stanzaes pleased him not, nor his matter' (ed 1925–52, 1:132). More probably, Jonson had softened his earlier judgment when, in his prose work *Timber, or Discoveries* some years later, he advised young men to read Spenser precisely 'for his matter' (8:618). But he never seems to have reconciled himself to the Spenserian stanza.

The same passage from *Discoveries* goes on to counsel that Spenser should be read 'as *Virgil* read *Ennius*.' Ennius was an early Latin poet whose work was revered by his successors but also considered somewhat rustic and old-fashioned by comparison with later, Augustan literature. Some of Spenser's earliest commentators declared that Spenser was the Virgil to Chaucer's Ennius (Fitzgeoffrey 1601: sig D5r, Cokain 1658:8). For the Jonson of *Discoveries*, however, Spenser was Ennius: an important but stylistically primitive writer who should be respected by future poets, but not imitated. In saying this, Jonson was thinking particularly about Spenser's use of archaism. It was his own view that writers should be equally wary about coining new words, or fetching them 'from the extreme and utmost ages ... the eldest of the present, and newest of the past Language is the best.' Spenser, he asserted, 'in affecting the Ancients, writ no Language' (ed 1925–52, 8:618, 622).

Arguably, Spenser's influence on Jonson was more pervasive than the younger poet knew. The spirit behind many of the great masques Jonson wrote for King James and (briefly) for Charles I was learned, allegorizing, and concerned to synthesize classical, Christian, and Renaissance ideas. It often seems very Spenserian. Jonson carried a good deal of Spenser's poetry in his memory. Drummond heard him recite Colin's encomium on wine, from *SC, October* (1:136), and his plays and poems are filled with conscious and unconscious Spenserian echoes. (See the commentary on individual works in ed 1925–52.) In his later years, however, Jonson like many of King Charles' subjects found himself looking back on the reign of Elizabeth as a vanished golden age. His attitude to the literature of his youth, in particular to the work of Shakespeare, Spenser, and Spenser's disciple, the once-despised Michael Drayton, underwent a significant change. Not only did he come to value this literature more highly, he made a series of attempts to come to terms with it in his own writing.

There is a world of difference between casual Spenserian references like the one to 'prety *Pastorella*' in Jonson's early comedy *The Case Is Altered* ([1597] ed 1925–52, 3:128) and the use made of Spenser in *The Sad Shepherd*, the pastoral that Jonson left unfinished at the time of his death. Two passages rework lines from *The Shepheardes Calender* and *Colin Clout* in a way that Jonson clearly meant to be recognized (ed 1925–52, 10:368–9), while the story of Earine shadows that of Spenser's Florimell. Like *A Tale of a Tub* (1633), moreover, and *Love's Welcome at Bolsover* (1634) and *The King's Entertainment at Welbeck* (1633), *The Sad Shepherd* employs archaisms, including some that had been used by Spenser himself. In 1638, Jonson's friend and editor Kenelm Digby spoke of Jonson as Spenser's admirer, a poet 'who being himself most excellent and admirable in the judicious compositions that in several kinds he hath made, thinketh no man more excellent or more admirable than this his late predecessor in the laurel crown' (in Alpers 1969:59–60). There is no reason to doubt Digby's testimony. The older Jonson was quite capable of such praise, as the younger was not.

ANNE BARTON

Aston Cokain 1658 'A Remedy for Love' in *Small Poems of Divers Sorts* (London); Norman Council 1980 'Ben Jonson, Inigo Jones, and the Transformation of Tudor Chivalry' *ELH* 47:259–75; Fitzgeoffrey 1601; Jonson ed 1925–52; David McPherson 1974 *Ben Jonson's Library and Marginalia: An Annotated Catalogue*, *SP* Texts and Studies 71.

Jove (also called Jupiter though never by Spenser) The supreme god in Roman mythology, the god of gods, identified with the Greek Zeus. As god of the sky, he is often shown wielding a thunderbolt. Different accounts explain how he overthrew his father Saturn (Chronos) to become the ruling god. According to Hesiod's *Theogony* and most classical mythology (much of which was transmitted through Boccaccio *Genealogia* 2.2), it was prophesied that Saturn would be deposed by one of his children; to prevent this, he devoured each at birth. When Jove was born, however, his mother Rhea saved him by giving Saturn a stone which he swallowed thinking it was the infant; Jove thus survived to fulfill the prophecy. According to the less popular account (in Conti *Mythologiae* 2.1 'De Jove' and 6.20 'De Titanibus'), Saturn reigned only under an agreement made with his elder brother Titan that he destroy his progeny so that Titan's could inherit the throne. The difference between these two accounts is significant. In the first, Jove's position as the highest god is justified as the fulfillment of prophecy; any attempt to prevent this is futile. The second suggests that Jove's position is itself a usurpation.

In *The Faerie Queene* and elsewhere, Spenser frequently refers to Jove as 'father of the Gods' (VII vi 15), 'highest *Jove*' (*SC, June* 66; *FQ* I proem 3, II vii 60, V vii 1, VII vi 12), 'sky-ruling Jove' (VI x 22), 'great *Jove*' (*Teares* 69, *FQ* III xi 35), and 'king of Gods' (VII vi 14), acknowledging him as a figure of ruling authority and power. In *FQ* VII, however, he also makes the unusual choice of having Mutabilitie present the less popular account of Jove's rise to power, suggesting that Jove rules heaven 'injuriously' and has gained his position 'by unjust / And guilefull meanes' (vi 27). Jove claims his inheritance is just: 'we ... by eternall doome of Fates decree, / Have wonne the Empire of the Heavens bright' (33), but Mutabilitie remains unconvinced. Grudgingly, he agrees to have their case judged by an even higher power, Nature, 'Father of Gods and men by equall might' (35).

Spenser's presentation of Jove as the highest god is also complicated by questions about his vulnerability. Mythological accounts tell various stories of Jove defeating the many enemies who rise against him. The Titans, whom he had displaced, waged long battle against him and were driven out of heaven. Later, Typhon sought to usurp his position, but he too was defeated. Ovid tells how the giants of the earth assailed the kingdom of the gods (*Metamorphoses* 1); they too were destroyed. Since their progeny, the human race, was just as rebellious and violent, Jove all but eradicated it and created a new one.

Occasionally Spenser presents Jove as the ultimate and eternal ruler analogous to Jehovah, capable of maintaining his position and quelling rebellion. In *Ruines of Time*, he is called the 'father of eternitie' (369; Lotspeich 1932:76 cites Boccaccio II.1). In *Mother Hubberds Tale*, he is 'high *Jove*, in whose almightie hand / The care of Kings, and power of Empires stand' (1225–6); once he becomes aware that the Ape and Fox are usurping the Lion's crown, he works immediately to restore the proper rule. In *FQ* V i 9, by conflating the giants and the Titans 'that whylome rebelled / Gainst highest heaven,' Spenser exalts Jove's victory: his sword was 'Well prov'd in that same day, when *Jove* those Gyants quelled.' In *FQ* V vii 1, he speaks of 'highest Jove, who doth true justice deale / To his inferiour Gods, and evermore / Therewith containes his heavenly Common-weale.'

More frequently, Spenser presents Jove as vulnerable to attacks from foes whom he cannot quell, and as insecure about his own authority. In *Visions of the Worlds Vanitie*, the Eagle, the 'kingly Bird, that beares *Joves* thunder-clap,' is so plagued by 'the simple Scarabee' that Jove concludes, 'Lo how the least the greatest may reprove' (4). In describing Rome's burgeoning greatness in *Ruines of Rome*, Spenser presents Jove as 'fearing, least if she should greater growe, / The old Giants should once againe uprise'; hence he 'Her whelm'd with hills' (4).

Questions about Jove's power are again raised in the *Cantos of Mutabilitie*. Although he had deprived the Titans of their rule, 'Yet many of their stemme long after did survive' (vi 2). When he hears Mutabilitie's challenge, he explains it to the other gods in words that recall the earlier rebellion when 'th'Earths cursed seed / Sought to assaile the heavens eternall towers.' His language conjures up an image of the gods themselves feeling vulnerable: 'And to us all exceeding feare did breed.' He triumphantly recalls their victory but adds that it was not complete (vi 20). Even before he learns the specific cause of the present disturbance in heaven, his initial response is to review past victories that no longer seem final: 'Doubting least *Typhon* were againe uprear'd, / Or other his old foes, that once him sorely fear'd' (vi 15). Spenser presents a Jove who battles constantly against old enemies to maintain his position and anticipates rebellion with discomfort, unease, and fear. His position is further questioned when he is superseded by Nature as highest authority, and when he is depicted as subservient to the Fates (IV ii 51).

In Ovid, Jove appears as a lusty lover of young nymphs and maidens, often transforming himself into various earthly, human, and animal forms to achieve his ends. Spenser provides an ambiguous perspective on Jove as lover in his description of the tapestries in the house of Busirane (III xi 29–35). The framing story of the tapestries tells of Cupid's battles against the gods to enlarge his own empire. Jove abandons his heavenly kingdom in pursuit of love, leaving his throne open to Cupid who quickly occupies it: Jove's indulgence of his lust leads to Cupid's victory and usurpation. The tapestries picture Jove metamorphosed into various shapes, ravishing his mortal lovers. Some readers conclude that Spenser debases the god and pictures love as bestiality (eg, Roche 1964:84); others see him maintaining Jove's godlike quality even in his transformations and lust (eg, Sale 1968:135–7). That Jove raises love rather than lowering himself by his participation in such actions is suggested when Venus rebukes Diana for scorning 'the joy, that *Jove* is glad to seeke' (III vi 22). Jove's lust is put into a gentler context, and the greatness of his progeny emphasized, in *Epithalamion* 326–31. Yet his fondness for women is given a more insidious cast when Diana, disrobed and innocently bathing at Arlo Hill, is described as 'for *Jove* a likely pray' (VII vi 45). His susceptibility to beauty is shown earlier in his response to Mutabilitie, when the sight of her beauty transforms his stern authority to mildness (VII vi 30–1). Here Spenser may be either disclosing a weakness in Jove's character or alluding to his godly nature, since Jove explains his change in words that echo biblical comments on divine forbearance (Gen 6.3 and Ps 78.39; cf *Var* 6:280–1).

Jove figures in Spenser's poetry, sometimes simultaneously and sometimes alternately, as the highest god, an illegitimate ruler, a vulnerable leader, and a figure of somewhat indiscriminate lust. He seems to embody the poet's ambivalent attitude toward authority and order: the godlike standard-bearer of stability is also a renegade usurper, a figure of power who is open to attack, and a male predator who, himself ruled by passion, is likely to neglect his position and to violate rather than protect, maintain, and rule his subjects.

JACQUELINE T. MILLER

Joyce, James (1882–1941) Spenser is one of many writers upon whose life and works Joyce drew to weave the webs of allusion which pervade *Finnegans Wake* (1939). The most important relationship between the two authors is not found in the few direct references, but in the multilayered narrative mode they share. In *Finnegans Wake*, 'Joyce, like Spenser, wrote a dream vision of history, fitting the techniques of metamorphosis and transvaluation and fragmentation to the operations of the liberated fancy, liberated in the one case by allegory as in the other by sleep. Both heightened the vision with experimentally evocative and unfamiliar language' (Greene 1963:334).

Of the allusions noticed by Joyce scholars, not all are equally convincing. Even so, one sees something of Spenser in such coinages as 'colinclouted' (maybe referring also to Skelton), 'marchant Taylor's fablings,' and 'our fiery quean' (*FW* pp 49, 61, 328; see Atherton 1974:206, 282ff and Glasheen 1977:270). *Ulysses* (1922) mockingly alludes to *Epithalamion* (14.253) and indirectly compares Bloom with Malbecco (4.257; see Füger 1986:210–12).

On the whole, Joyce shows little fondness for Spenser; because of the unflattering portrait of the Irish in *Vewe of Ireland*, Spenser has traditionally had few friends in Ireland. Nevertheless, Joyce did read him at least in part. Although he does not name him other than peripherally ('oddman rex' in *FW* p 61), in his early rough notes on English literature and drama he copied out almost three stanzas from *FQ* IV xi 23–30, the description of the marriage of Thames and Medway, seeing it as an analogue to *Hamlet* IV vii (Cornell Ms *Notes for Hamlet* fols 52v-3r; reproduced in Joyce ed 1979, 2:268–9).

Of greater significance to the relationship of Joyce and Spenser are certain analogous techniques of narrative. In the only extended comparison of the two writers to date, Honig (1948) compares the religious quests of the Red Cross Knight and Stephen Dedalus in *A Portrait of the Artist as a Young Man* (1916). He sees both authors intentionally choosing anachronistic forms and superimposing classical mythology. For him, Spenser's characters come to life in spite of the author's technique, whereas Joyce's break away from naturalism to become symbolic.

The affinities between Spenser and Joyce are even more striking when one compares *The Faerie Queene* to *Ulysses*. Both works are essentially comic narratives that gather within themselves a comprehensive repertory of ways of speaking and presenting reality. Spenser works mainly within a tradition of romance and legend and models of virtuous behavior; Joyce works from a later development of narrative art and less virtuous models of behavior; but their scope is equally various: it includes bits of melodrama, popular fiction, clichés of conversation, proverbs, and songs. Both are highly allusive writers who attempt to incorporate through their allusions the previous history of their genres. Both structure their works around characters who remain unaware of their own symbolic significance as well as of their archetypal situations. The characters move through symbolic landscapes in both works, and stop at various 'houses' of thematic import. Behind both *The Faerie Queene* and *Ulysses* is the presence of Homer's *Odyssey* and the epic tradition. A close study of *Ulysses* may help one to read *The Faerie Queene* with greater insight, and vice versa.

WILHELM FÜGER AND RICHARD D. JORDAN

James Joyce 1979 *Notes, Criticism, Translations, and Miscellaneous Writings* facs arranged Hans Walter Gabler, intro Michael Groden, 2 vols (New York). James S. Atherton 1974 *The Books at the Wake: A Study of Literary Allusions in James Joyce's 'Finnegans Wake'* 2nd ed (Marmaroneck, NY); Wilhelm Füger 1986 'Bloom's Other Eye' *JJQ* 23:209–17; Adaline Glasheen 1977 *Third Census of 'Finnegans Wake'* (Berkeley and Los Angeles); Edwin Honig 1948 'Hobgoblin or Apollo' *KR* 10: 664–81.

Juno The queen of heaven in Roman myth, the wife of Jove (Jupiter); identified with the Greek Hera. Not a major figure in Spenser's poetry, she appears infrequently, usually in her conventional forms as 'Queene of heaven' (*FQ* I v 35), as ruler of the air (whose position is claimed by Mutabilitie in VII vii 26), and as patron of marriage and protector of women during childbirth (*Epithalamion* 390–7; *FQ* II i 53 and III vi 27 refer to her in this function by her epithet Lucina). Equally notorious for her jealousy of Jove's infidelities and her vengefulness against his host of female lovers, she is named in Busirane's tapestries as the deceiver of Semele (III xi 33) and in the description of the Wandering Islands as the angry pursuer of Latona (II xii 13). She is also associated with pride when Spenser compares her to Lucifera: Lucifera's pride is evoked by her attempt 'to match ... Great *Junoes* golden chaire'; but Juno's own pride is then suggested in the description of her chariot as 'Drawne of faire Pecocks, that excell in pride' (I iv 17, based on Ovid *Metamorphoses* 2.531–4). Spenser follows classical tradition in identifying the peacock, a symbol of pride, as '*Junoes* Bird' (*Muiopotmos* 95; see Lotspeich 1932:76).

JACQUELINE T. MILLER

justice and equity As the moral virtue fashioned in *FQ* V, justice is associated with the Golden Age of Saturn, when the uncultivated earth, in a continuous spring and autumn together, brought forth all that humanity needed, and there were neither laws nor punishments. Ovid recounts (*Metamorphoses* 1.89–150) that an original harmony with nature allowed everyone to enjoy a sufficient portion of earthly goods without encroaching upon any neighbor or invading the earth itself. But when Jove overthrew Saturn, inaugurating the Silver Age, seasons arrived, seeds had to be planted, and labor began. Soon the aggressive instincts of the Bronze Age manifested themselves, and thereafter deception, shamelessness, greed, and violence. In the fourth, Iron Age, men left their homes, felled trees, mined the earth, and carried war to distant shores, transgressing even filial and domestic boundaries. Then Astraea, virgin goddess of justice, fled to heaven. It is this fallen world, which has lost the fundamental juristic principle of due measure and further degenerated into a 'stonie' age, that Spenser laments in the proem to *FQ* V.

The notion that justice consists in maintaining proper boundaries between the elements that constitute an organism appears early in Greek physics and ethics. 'The sun will not overstep his measures,' says Heraclitus; 'if he were to do so, the Erinyes, handmaids of Justice, would seek him out' (Frag 94, in Wheelwright 1966:79). In Plato's ethical theory, justice in the soul – the necessary complement to justice in the state – occurs only when reason, assisted by the spirited element, is in control of the passions so that each power can do its proper work for the benefit of the whole man (*Republic* 4.441–4). It was Aristotle, however, who developed the ethical notion of due measure most familiar to the Renaissance. He defined virtue as a mean of behavior situated between two extremes – a mean not strictly arithmetical, but relative to the kind of person performing a given action. Thus, the amount of fear appropriate for a trained soldier in wartime might be three on a scale from one to ten, while for a woman or child it might be six or eight. Justice is the mean directly concerned with determining an individual's fair share of the goods of life and may be measured in two ways. Distributive justice apportions the wealth and honors a person may acquire through social interaction, and is based on the system of value governing a particular society. Like the relative mean itself, it is a proportionate principle of division, and does not necessarily aim at an equal distribution of goods. Corrective justice acts on a strictly arithmetical basis to restore the balance disturbed when one individual takes more than his or her share from another. If initially *A* and *B* each owns ten sheep and *A* takes three from *B*, raising his portion to thirteen while *B* is left with seven, corrective justice will restore the original equality (*Nicomachean Ethics* 5.3–4). The Giant with the scales in v ii 29–54 reveals his judicial ignorance when he attempts to apply an arithmetical corrective justice to a universe constituted on the principle of proportionate distribution. Unaware that all things were created 'In goodly measure, by their Makers might,' he offers to equalize the four elements, heaven and hell, mountains and valleys, lords and commons, as though each created thing 'had encroched uppon others share' and needed rectification. His impious presumption, which draws upon scriptural images of false measurement (Dunseath 1968:97–107), is matched by his ethical insipience, for he also insists upon balancing right with wrong and truth with falsehood, under the illusion that each pair is a set of extremes, capable of quantitative adjustment to one another; he does not understand that right, as also truth, is actually a mean – neither defective nor excessive – and therefore 'ever one.' His unfitness as a judge is most evident in his reliance upon the mechanical scales: as a moral virtue, justice must abide in the mind, as truth and falsehood must be weighed by the ear. Only a just man can act justly, Spenser reminds us – a point he repeats with some irony when Guyon has to mitigate the wrath of Artegall, 'our judge of equity,' following the trial of Braggadocchio (iii 36–7).

Artegall encounters a case in real need of corrective justice when he meets the fighting brothers Bracidas and Amidas (iv 4–20). Each had inherited an island of equal size, but the sea has gradually washed land away from Bracidas' island and deposited it on Amidas'. When Philtera, Bracidas' fiancée, abandons him for his wealthier brother, Amidas' betrothed, Lucy, attempts to drown herself but is wafted to Bracidas' island upon a shipwrecked trunk containing Philtera's rich dowry. Spenser mingles Aristotelian theory and English practice in Artegall's settlement of the conflict. By the law governing alluvion, Amidas has the right to his new land, while Philtera's trunk, as *wreccum maris*, falls under the royal prerogative and may be granted at the crown's pleasure (Hall ed 1875: app xxiii-xxxix; cf *FQ* IV xii 31). Artegall restores equality between the brothers by assimilating the cases under a single rule – 'That what the sea unto you sent, your own should seeme' (v iv 18) – following an equitable maxim frequently invoked by sixteenth-century justices when extending a statute or common law rule: 'For equall right in equall things doth stand' (19; cf Hake ed 1953:108–9). Amidas and Philtera seem displeased by the judgment, yet 'each one had his right' (20).

Policing the borders is but one way to be just; an equally important activity is nurturing relations among the elements that compose microcosm and macrocosm, for the concept of justice is related to the notion of 'binding,' as in the Latin cognates *jus* (right, law) and *jungo* (join, fit, tie together) (Barker 1951:94). Although the communal function of justice was discussed by Plato and Aristotle, Cicero's notion of justice as a system of ethical relationships was more widely disseminated in the Middle Ages and the Renaissance. Cicero conceived of justice as an internal harmony that subsumes many other virtues and flows outward to bind all mankind in solidarity. Moral goodness originates in the four cardinal virtues – justice, prudence, temperance, and fortitude – but the duties of justice presuppose those of the others (*De officiis* 1.43.152–5). Elyot makes the hierarchy explicit in *The Boke Named the Governor* (1531), where fortitude guarantees the constancy of justice, prudence the ability to discern right from wrong, and temperance the means of fitting the punishment to the crime (3.1). Other virtues are also linked within Cicero's constellation of justice – religion, filial piety, gratitude, obedience, and truthfulness – and good faith is its foundation (*De inventione* 2.53.160–1, *De officiis* 1.7.23). Late classical and Christian commentators supplemented and interpreted these various categories (Tuve 1966:66–73), so that by the late Renaissance the iconography of justice can easily include such figures as Temperance, Reverence, and even Mercy herself, who, as Mercilla, presides at Duessa's trial (v ix 31–2).

Cicero's definition of justice as the preservation of human society, the rendering to each his due, and the faithful discharge of assumed obligations (*De officiis* 1.5.15) encouraged the translation of these associated virtues into judicially related ethical duties. Acting justly meant religiously rendering God his due, mercifully assisting the wretched, paying respect to one's parents, venerating one's superiors, giving amicably what is owed to equals and giving, without condescension, to inferiors – thereby involving the individual ideally in a network of social, political, and spiritual obligations that bind man to man and to God. But to render each his due is not a simple matter in practice. Both Plato and Aristotle recognize the necessity of ensuring the fulfillment of mutual obligation and fair dealing through the establishment of uniform standards to which citizens can appeal for justice. Law inculcates and reinforces this virtue. In itself, however, it is no guarantee of justice. As Aristotle observes, the problem lies in the incompatibility between the nature of law and of human behavior. While laws must be formulated in very general terms, human actions are infinitely varied; it is impossible for a legislator to foresee every contingency and devise laws that will cover all possible situations. When, therefore, a particular case arises whose peculiar circumstances would make the application of the relevant general law inappropriate, the judge is to exercise the principle of equity by considering what the lawmaker himself would have said if he had been present and knew of the case. In this sense, equity is considered a rectification of the law; strictly speaking, the law is neither incorrect nor unjust, but defective due to its necessarily universal formulation (*Ethics* 5.10).

Equity mitigates the law by examining the internality of an action – the defendant's motives and background, the circumstances attending his act – and also the interiority of the law itself, by referring to the intentions of the legislator (Aristotle *Rhetoric* 1.13). In sixteenth-century England, the concern with legal interiority was reflected in the practice of common law judges who often repeated Aristotle's words when determining whether a given statute ought to be applied in a case not expressly mentioned in the law. They would try to construe the legislator's intention, the sense of the law, or the historical conditions leading to its enactment (*A Discourse upon ... Statutes* ed 1942:56–64). In Saint Germain's famous dialogue between a doctor of divinity and a student of the laws of England (1523–31), equity is an exception understood to lie within positive laws should these contradict the laws of God and nature, and a righteousness that considers all circumstances of a deed, tempered with the sweetness of mercy (ed 1974:95–7).

In Spenser's time, equity was most frequently associated not with the common law courts – Common Pleas, King's (or Queen's) Bench, Exchequer – but with the prerogative courts of the crown, especially the Chancery. For centuries, this court had been known as a court of conscience because unlike the common law courts, where the alleged fact was tried (in accordance with strict forms of action) by oath-swearing and jury verdict, the Chancery could examine the consciences of the parties to determine motive, character, and circumstance, and base its judgment on this information. Moreover, the Lord Chancellor, who presided, framed his decree in accordance with his conscience. In the view of theologians and canon lawyers, conscience was the instrument of judgment God placed in man to enable him to know whether a particular action was consonant with divine and natural law; and in the pursuit of justice, conscience might find a defendant innocent who would be judged guilty at common law. When this happened, the party would be granted relief, though the Chancery was not supposed to set aside judgments already made in common law courts. Common law reaction to such equitable incursions may be reflected in Radigund's fury at Artegall's rescue of Terpine, 'that did her judg'ment breake' (V iv 40).

In *FQ* V, equity is figured primarily in Isis, Britomart, and Mercilla. Although Artegall is taught by Astraea to measure equity 'According to the line of conscience,' he is more 'Like to *Osyris* in all just endever' (i 7, vii 22). Britomart, however, clearly acts in the manner of equity when she turns from jealous rage at the news of Artegall's submission to Radigund to an inquiry about the circumstances of his entrapment (vi 12–15). She eludes the plot of Dolon (vi 19–35), who is associated with a cunning that takes unscrupulous advantage of the law by adhering strictly to the letter (Fletcher 1971:233), and following her visit to Isis Church rescues Artegall from the Amazon's conditional bond, which, Spenser hints, was offered in guile (iv 31, v 27; cf Jones 1967:440–8). Her action is represented symbolically in Isis' restraint of the righteous crocodile.

Equitable procedure did not always result in exoneration, as the trial of Duessa (ix 38–50) reveals. Historically, Mary, Queen of Scots was told that she would be heard 'according to Equity and Reason, and not upon any cunning Niceties of Law' (Camden ed 1970:244), and, however manipulated the actual event may have been, Spenser presents Duessa's trial as one in which both hard evidence and ameliorating personal and political considerations are weighed. He is careful here to distinguish between the merciful disposition the equitable magistrate ought to possess (cf iii 36) and the larger view of justice she must always hold before her. Elizabeth was warned repeatedly not to mistake a self-destructive 'cruel mercy' for true equity (Graziani 1964a). Mercilla lets fall 'Few perling drops from her faire lampes of light' in token of her natural remorse, but consents to Duessa's execution.

Spenser's portrayal of Mercilla as judicial executor in a court of conscience brings into focus a theme he recurs to intermittently in the preceding cantos and develops more fully in the concluding Belge and Irena episodes: justice as an imperial virtue. In the dedication to *The Faerie Queene*, he addresses Elizabeth as 'magnificent Empresse,' a title she inherited from her father, who had claimed 'that this realm of England is an empire, and so hath been accepted in the world' ('Act of Appeals' in Elton 1960:344). In declaring himself possessed of an imperial crown, Henry had sought to legitimize his assumption of supreme power in matters both secular and spiritual, and drew upon a tradition that went back to the first Christian emperor, Constantine the Great. This tradition had legal, political, and religious implications: the emperor received his power directly from God, and therefore was the mediator between divine and human justice. In England, this had long raised the question of where the king stood in relation to law. From the imperialist point of view derived from the Roman civil code, he was both author and executor of law, though the medieval jurist Bracton had insisted that the very prerogatives granted him by the law depended upon his submission to it (ed 1968–77, 2:33–4). From the common law point of view, however, the laws of England originated in immemorial custom, and extended to the monarch certain prerogative powers, including that of equitable relief, in recognition of his preeminence as preserver and defender of the people. Throughout the Tudor period, there was tension between the imperialist and common law views of the prerogative (Kermode 1971:49–59). When, in 1587, Lord Chancellor Hatton remarked that 'it is the holy conscience of *the Queen*, for matter of equity, that is in some sort committed to the Chancellor' (thus suggesting that Chancery was the court of the Queen's conscience), he made explicit the imperial monarch's position as the medium through which divine justice flows (Spence 1846–9, 1:414). This was an opinion endorsed by Spenser (V proem 10, vii 1); its corollary, that the prince must delegate wide discretionary powers to her executive officers, is given expression in V iv 1 and *Vewe* (*Var Prose* pp 228–30), where it is clear that 'mightie hands' are needed to carry out just judgments lest justice itself be mocked.

The 'kings and kesars' who prostrate themselves at Mercilla's feet recall the political mission of the emperor, who, in imitation of Constantine and – even more particularly – of Augustus, is to conquer faction with the sword of justice and reduce the world to universal peace. The Augustan empire was intimately associated in the European imagination with the restoration of the Golden Age. Virgil had announced in his fourth eclogue the imminent return of Astraea and the reign of Saturn, and this was widely interpreted as signifying that the Roman emperor was to usher in a new era of justice. Imperial reform is specifically alluded to in the efforts of Artegall and Britomart at Pollente's bridge (ii 28), Radigund's court (vii 42), and in Irena's kingdom (xii 26–7).

For Christians, Astraea's return had a special resonance. Virgil's eclogue celebrating the birth of a child, during whose lifetime the new age will unfold, was read as a Messianic prophecy since Christ was born in the reign of Augustus. Thus imperial reform became associated with religious reform, Astraea with the Virgin Mary, and the Golden Age with Christian piety. The concept of a sacred empire was later used by the Holy Roman Emperors in their propaganda wars against the popes and became a common theme of the English Reformation (Yates 1975:29–87). Its conflation of myth, history, and poetry was reinforced by the Tudor claim of descent from Troy and Rome, and the allegedly British origin of Constantine. In the Elizabethan configuration, the returning Astraea was the Virgin Queen, bringing with her the purified religion of the Church of England and the imperial mission of reform abroad. It is in this context that Belge's sons appeal to Mercilla, the embodiment of mercy, for armed intervention in behalf of their mother – thereby releasing the invincible might of Arthur upon Geryoneo and his monster. Elizabeth's mercy could take strange forms (Phillips 1969–70:115–20). Spenser himself asks, at the beginning of canto x, whether mercy is a part of justice or divinely distilled from it, and praises mercy for acting in its own capacity to save without ever departing from righteousness. One answer to this mystery is found in a parliamentary petition of 1572. The Queen's mercy, it cautions, must be directed 'towards Gods People and her good Subjects, in dispatching those Enemies that seek the confusion of Gods cause amongst us, and of this noble Realm ... Mercy oftentimes sheweth itself in the Image of Justice' (D'Ewes 1682:210). JOEL B. ALTMAN

Henry de Bracton 1968–77 *On the Laws and Customs of England* tr Samuel E. Thorne, 4 vols (Cambridge, Mass); Camden ed 1970; Simonds D'Ewes 1682 *The Journals of All the Parliaments during the Reign of Queen Elizabeth* (London; rpt Shannon, Ireland 1973); *A Discourse upon the Exposicion and Understandinge of Statutes with Sir Thomas Egerton's Additions* 1942 ed Samuel E. Thorne (San Marino, Calif); Edward Hake 1953 *Epieikeia: A Dialogue on Equity in Three Parts* 1600 ed D.E.C. Yale (New Haven); Robert Gream Hall 1875 *Essay on the Rights of the Crown* ed Richard L. Loveland, 2nd ed (London); Christopher Saint Germain 1974 *Doctor and Student* ed T.F.T. Plucknett and J.L. Barton (London); Philip Wheelwright, ed 1966 *The Presocratics* (New York).

Carleton Kemp Allen 1964 *Law in the Making* 7th ed (Oxford); J.H. Baker 1971; Ernest Barker 1951 *Principles of Social and Political Theory* (Oxford); Elton 1960; W.J. Jones 1967 *The Elizabethan Court of Chancery* (Oxford); George Spence 1846–9 *The Equitable Jurisdiction of the Court of Chancery* 2 vols (London).

Aptekar 1969; Bradshaw 1987; Dunseath 1968; Fletcher 1971a; Graziani 1964a; Kermode 1971; Knight 1970; Phillips 1969–70; Tuve 1966; Yates 1975.

K

Keats, John (1795–1821) The first and last poems written by Keats were imitations of Spenser, the first in 1814 when he was still a schoolboy and the last in the summer of 1820. These 'imitations' are characteristic of the way in which Keats, throughout his brief poetic career, passionately responded to whatever reading his swift empathic imagination fastened on and at the same time fought to prevent his keen literary sympathies from imperiling the discovery of his individual poetic voice. By 1819 it seemed to him that of those who 'have ever been the food / Of my delighted fancy' (from the sonnet of early 1816, 'How many bards gild the lapses of time!'), the most strongly influential were Shakespeare (whom in April 1817 when embarking on *Endymion* he had already begun to think of as his true 'Presider'), and Milton, from whom he struggled to free himself. 'English ought to be kept up,' he said in the autumn of 1819 (ed 1958, 2:167), now claiming that the language of the tribe remained pure and undefiled only in the early English tradition celebrated by Chatterton. Towards the end of his creative life, then, whether consciously or not, Keats reaffirmed a stance associated with Spenser, the poet who was uniquely responsible for first setting his poetic career in motion, and whose presence is felt here and there all along the way like – appropriately – an undersong.

Yet it is abundantly clear from the start that Keats's response was instinctively selective and that it was Spenser's richness of language, imagery, and stanzaic skills, not his moral themes, that captured his youthful enthusiasm and quickened his sense of his own potential poetic genius. Only later, in that year of 1819 when his growing command of a personal idiom was reinforced by powerful and conflicting emotional experiences recently undergone, did his poetry come to carry overtones reminiscent of certain kinds of Spenserian ambivalence. Even then, his use of narrative remained essentially un-Spenserian, being as always characteristic of his own age in its personal, lyrical, and reflective expressiveness. (It is significant that he was not at home with his epic conception in the unfinished *Hyperion*, transforming it in *The Fall of Hyperion* into a personal 'dialogue of the mind with itself,' a sign of the modern spirit, as Matthew Arnold recognized in the preface to his *Poems* [1853]).

Keats was introduced to *The Faerie Queene* in 1814 by Charles Cowden Clarke, his admirable teacher at Enfield School, who tells us he went through the poem 'as a young horse would through a spring meadow – ramping,' was bowled over by 'the felicity and power' of the epithets, and '*hoisted* himself up, and looked burly and dominant, as he said "what an image that is – *sea-shouldering whales*!"' (*FQ* II xii 23, saluted in *Endymion* I.529–30: 'saw the horizontal sun / Heave his broad shoulder o'er the edge of the world'; see also C. and M. Cowden Clarke 1878:126). Keats's gratitude is expressed in 'To Charles Cowden Clarke' (September 1816), the verse letter which celebrates – albeit in un-Spenserian pentameter couplets – 'one who had by Mulla's stream / Fondled the maidens with breasts of cream; / Who had beheld Belphoebe in a brook, / And lovely Una in a leafy nook, / And Archimago leaning o'er his book,' and who 'first taught me all the sweets of song,' among them 'Spenserian vowels that elope with ease, / And float along like birds o'er summer seas' (34–7, 53, 56–7). It has been rightly noted, however, that these lines sound like Pope and that the next two lines, which are about Milton – 'Miltonian storms, and more, Miltonian tenderness; / Michael in arms, and more, meek Eve's fair slenderness' – sound more like Spenser's own voice and are indeed alexandrines (John Hollander, private communication).

Charles Brown, another friend, records that Keats at once fell in love with the Spenserian stanza, 'attempted to imitate it, and succeeded,' this first trial of his awakened 'genius' being 'Imitation of Spenser' written in his eighteenth year (Rollins 1965, 2:55–6). The poem, consisting of four Spenserian stanzas, describes a lakeside scene at sunrise and aims at a delicate opulence obviously inspired by Phaedria's island and the Bower of Bliss in *FQ* II vi, xii. But the piece is already characteristically Keatsian in gathering 'unnumbered sounds' from 'many bards,' in this case Milton's *L'Allegro*, Book 6 of the *Aeneid* (Keats's single classical passion then), and less felicitously the derivative diction of eighteenth-century Spenserians earlier studied at school, such as Beattie, Thomson, and Mary Tighe (who captured Keats's youthful attention for a while). He used the Spenserian stanza four times again: momentously five years later in *The Eve of St Agnes* (Jan 1819), amusingly in the three *jeu d'esprit* stanzas of 'He is to weet a melancholy carle' addressed to Charles Brown (Apr 1819), with touches of wit in the otherwise misjudged satire 'The Cap and Bells' (Nov-Dec 1819), and didactically in – by a strange irony – his last composition, a single stanza written during his final illness when he was 'marking the most beautiful passages' in his copy of Spenser for Fanny Brawne, the woman he had hoped one day to marry (ed 1958, 2:302). 'In aftertime a sage of mickle lore' is prompted by the Giant's 'undemocratic' behavior in *FQ* V ii 29–54 and expresses 'this *ex post hoc facto* prophecy, his conviction of the ultimate triumph of freedom and equality by the power of transmitted knowledge' (Milnes in Keats ed 1848, 1:281).

Such explicit comment is untypical. Keats's running debates with the poets he challenges while acknowledging their strength are usually conducted obliquely, as in his reply to Shelley's 'Alastor' in *Endymion* or to Wordsworth's 'Expostulation and Reply' in 'O thou whose face hath felt the winter's wind.' His finest 'Spenserian' poem, *The Eve of St Agnes*, suggests the intimate connection between such debates and the continuous inner dialogue about the conflicting claims of 'sensation' and 'thought' which attended his lifelong search for poetic mastery. The richly textured central stanzas, celebrating erotic love in a charmed setting radiant with warmth, color, music, and a feast which delights every sense, are framed in other stanzas which evoke age, sickness, death, and the remorseless erosions of time. The central stanzas celebrate qualities first quickened into poetic expression through that affinity spontaneously recognized in 1814 and soon confirmed by further Spenserian reading. The framing stanzas direct us to the 'burden of the mystery' which the harsher realities of existence lay upon those entering the dark passages beyond what Keats, in a famous metaphor, calls the Chamber of Maiden Thought. In the poetic program set out for himself in *Sleep and Poetry* (1817), he pleads for ten years to dwell in 'the realm ... Of Flora and old Pan' before turning to nobler, darker themes inspired by 'the agonies, the strife / Of human hearts' (101–2, 124–5).

But the innocent pastoral pleasures that Spenser taught him to sing cluster in a mere handful of very youthful poems such as the February 1816 valentine for his pretty acquaintance Mary Frogley ('Hadst thou liv'd in days of old'): he portrays her as the chaste Britomart of *FQ* III; her hair like 'globes that rise / From the censer to the skies' (21–2) seems to be inspired by the 'rolling globes' of incense at *Colin Clout* 608–11, while his descriptions of her breasts 'like twin water-lilies born / In the coolness of the morn' and of 'the little loves' that flutter round them 'with eager pry' (29–30, 33–4) seem to arrive directly from *Epithalamion* (eg, 176, 357–9). Numerous other early echoes include the direct quotation in 'To George Felton Matthew' ('And made "a sun-shine in a shady place"' 75; cf *FQ* I iii 4), as well as the reference to chivalric fantasies inspired by 'knightly Spenser' and the pastoral scene inspired by *Colin Clout* 640–4 in 'To My Brother George' (24–36, 81–8; see ed 1970:27, 50, 51–2).

To the same brief untried period belong the unfinished companion pieces 'Calidore' and its 'Induction,' which unsuccessfully attempt 'a tale of chivalry' with the 'Courtesie' of *FQ* VI in mind. Their style and diction suffer from the debilitating effects of Keats's current enthusiasm for his new friend and patron Leigh Hunt. The Spenserian 'luxuries' are refracted through the loose heroic couplets and sentimental eroticism derived from Hunt's popular *The Story of Rimini* but without its narrative verve. The latest Spenserian passages in this short sojourn in 'the realm of Flora' appear in some parts of *Endymion*, notably the bower of the sleeping Adonis (2.389–427). This garden of pleasure with its 'chamber, myrtle-walled' guarded by Venus' cupids emulates the pictorial charm, though not the moral perspective, of the Garden of Adonis, where a 'grove of mirtle trees' shelters 'a pleasant arbour, not by art, / But of the trees owne inclination made' (*FQ* III vi 42–5).

Endymion, whose fortunate hero both eats and has his cake by winning earthly love with his Indian maid and enjoying immortal passion with his moon goddess, is Keats's last sustained effort to fend off the troubling perplexities surrounding his highly individual Romantic contribution to the process of reconciling the ideal and the actual. In early 1818, in his sonnet 'On Sitting Down to Read *King Lear* Again,' he bade farewell to 'golden-tongued Romance with serene lute' (ed 1970:295). By the end of the year, we find him journeying still further along the 'dark corridors,' his imagination further quickened by increasing familiarity with Shakespeare, Wordsworth, and Dante, and his sensibility wrought upon by the emigration of one brother to America and the death of the other (portending his own fatal illness), and by his first experience of passionate love.

The next year opened with his one celebration of happy love in *The Eve of St Agnes*, whose Spenserian delights are nevertheless encompassed by what is not delightful at all. Thereafter, the gentle loved one vanishes forever, to be dramatically replaced by the Spenserian antithetical image of the fatal enchantress. This ambiguous figure focuses the destructive power of passion in 'La Belle Dame Sans Merci' (Apr 1819) and *Lamia* (Jun-Sept 1819), which reflect Keats's now deeply conflicting feelings about the relationship between love, death, and poetic creativity. In the earlier poem, the 'lady in the meads / Full beautiful, a fairy's child' (13–14) owes much to earlier ballads such as 'Thomas the Rhymer,' Chatterton's medieval rhymes, and 'La Belle Dame Sans Merci' by Alain Chartier (c 1385–1433); but her nearest relatives are Spenser's Duessa, false Florimell, and Phaedria, who share her 'garland' and 'fragrant zone,' her sighs 'full sore' and 'sweet mone,' and her power to hold men 'in thrall' (cf *FQ* I ii 28–30, 45; II vi 2–18; III vii 17; IV viii 64).

Her sister enchantress in *Lamia* was discovered by Keats in Philostratus' story as retold in Burton's *Anatomy of Melancholy*. Any remaining traces of a Spenserian poetic style retreat before the oddly mixed tone of his Drydenesque couplets and incidental details drawn eclectically from various sources including studies of Greek antiquities, the Arabian Nights, and verse tales by Coleridge and Peacock; but the presence of the Elizabethans is still diffusely felt in echoes from Marlowe and Sandys' Ovid. More importantly, the flavor of Spenser's false enchantresses continues to haunt the ambivalent appeal of this Lamia transmogrified into 'a real woman,' though now with tragic consequences for herself as well as her lover when their enchanted dream fades in the cold light of reason.

The ambiguous relationship between dream and reality in *Lamia*, as in 'La Belle Dame Sans Merci' and ágain in the odes ('Was it a vision or a waking dream?': 'Ode to a Nightingale' 79), is altogether different from the 'prefigurative' dreaming of *Endymion*, Keats's early experiment with the long poem. The relationship has now acquired the resonance of Spenser's ambiguities, such as those in Arthur's dream of the Fairy Queen (*FQ* I ix 13–16) and in *Amoretti* 77, 'Was it a dreame, or did I see it playne ... ?' (Allott in Keats ed 1970:516). To these last writing months (illness prevented him from working consistently after December 1819) also belongs Keats's revision of *Hyperion* which shows Milton in retreat, the spirit of Dante presiding over his new purgatorial 'vision,' and his impressive personal manner resuming its progress after his major 1819 accomplishments in *The Eve of St Agnes*, 'La Belle Dame Sans Merci,' the experimental sonnets, and the great odes. The poetic structure in the odes is shaped by the familiar Keatsian movement from painful actuality to intense delight in a 'waking dream' of idealized sensuous experience from which real awakening is as inevitable as its accompaniment of baffling questions.

If the nature and status of the 'waking dream' is at the heart of Keats's most celebrated reflective poems, then Spenser is there, too, his presence encouraged by memories of Hazlitt's description of him as 'the poet of our waking dreams ... he has invented not only a language but a music of his own for them ... lulling the senses into a deep oblivion of the jarring noises of the world, from which we have no wish to be ever recalled' (Hazlitt ed 1930–4, 5:44). '"Load every rift" of your subject with ore,' Keats advised Shelley in August 1820, quoting ironically from Spenser's description of the house of Mammon (*FQ* II vii 28), for '*an artist* must serve Mammon – he must have "self concentration" selfishness perhaps' (ed 1958, 2:323). He followed his own advice in his 'waking dreams,' loading with ore the leisured stillness of the opulent scenes in Madeline's bedchamber in *The Eve of St Agnes*, the fragrant pastoral setting for the vision or waking dream in 'Ode to Psyche,' the 'verdurous glooms' and 'embalmèd darkness' brimming with the scent of mid-May's fruits and flowers in 'Ode to a Nightingale,' the dense magnificences transforming 'the melancholy fit' ('Ode on Melancholy') into a state of intense poetic creativity. Such ore, it is hardly too much to say, was mined first in the 'realms of gold' which, even before he discovered the 'pure serene' of Chapman's Homer in October 1816, excited the imagination of Cowden Clarke's brilliant schoolboy, and were still poignantly captivating him six years later when to delight his beloved Fanny he singled out the 'most beautiful passages' as he sat alone and ill, reading *The Faerie Queene* for the last time. MIRIAM ALLOTT

John Keats 1848 *Life, Letters and Literary Remains* ed Richard Monckton Milnes, 2 vols (New York); Keats 1958 *Letters 1814–1821* ed Hyder Edward Rollins, 2 vols (Cambridge, Mass); Keats 1970 *Poems* ed Miriam Allott (London); Keats ed 1978.

John Barnard 1987 *John Keats* (Cambridge); Charles and Mary Cowden Clarke 1878 *Recollections of Writers* (London); Robert Gittings 1954 *John Keats: The Living Year, 21 September 1818 to 21 September 1819* (London) reviewed by F.W. Bateson in *EIC* 4(1954):432–40; Hazlitt ed 1930–4; Greg Kucich 1983 'Spenserian Versification in Keats's *The Eve of St. Agnes*' *Michigan Academician* 16:101–8; Hyder Edward Rollins, ed 1965 *The Keats Circle: Letters and Papers, 1816–1878* 2nd ed, 2 vols (Cambridge, Mass).

Kilcolman Castle *Location*: Republic of Ireland, County of Cork (roughly halfway between the cities of Limerick and Cork); 3¼ miles NNW of Doneraile; some 600 yards on the left of the road from Doneraile to Charleville. *Data*: Kilcolman Middle Townland; Doneraile Parish; Fermoy Barony; Imphrick District Electoral Division; Mallow County Division. *Ordnance Survey*: sheet I7, 1:10,000 (6 inches to 1 mile); plan 6, 1:2500 (25 inches to 1 mile); trace 3; 1:10,000 County Sheet Coordinates: 413mmE, 381mmN; National Grid Coordinates: R 581 113.

(See **Kilcolman Castle** Fig 1: location maps.)

topography The castle is situated close to the south of the western termination of the Ballyhoura Mountains, a geological and physical extension of the larger and higher Galty Mountains further east. These mountains are of extreme age, being of Old Red Sandstone of the Devonian period, with Silurian outcrops (Geological Survey 1979). The flat land on which the castle is built consists of Lower Carboniferous Limestone, a rock occurring over much of the great low central plain of Ireland. The extensive plain on which the castle is located, approximately 30 miles east-west by 10 miles north-south, is bounded, at successively further distances, by the Nagles Mountains to the southeast, the Boggeragh range to the southwest, the Mullaghareirk Mountains to the west, and the Knockmealdown Mountains to the east. The plain is drained by several rivers, principally the Blackwater, flowing west to east along the southern side, while the Awbeg curves southwards from the northwest to meet it, passing about 2¼ miles to the west of Kilcolman Castle, and 1¾ miles to the south. The Bregoge flows from north to south to join the Awbeg, passing one mile to the east of the castle. Further to the east the Funshion flows southwards to meet the Blackwater, while to the west the Allow flows south to join the Dalua and the Blackwater.

In Spenser's time, the champaign country surrounding Kilcolman Castle abounded in trees, adding beauty and interest, and was referred to by Charles Smith as 'a most pleasant and romantick situation' (ed 1774, 1:333; quoted in Spenser ed 1805, 1: l-li). A local tradition exists that the woods extended to Buttevant, three miles distance (Bartlett 1842, 1:81). Spenser knew and loved this countryside, and reproduced its features in his poetry, with the Ballyhoura and Galty Mountains becoming the Mole, while the highest of them, Galtymore, became Arlo Hill. Rivers include the Blackwater or Awmore or Awniduff, the Brackbawn (a small upstream tributary of the Funshion) which became the Molanna, and most notably the Awbeg, which Spenser appropriated to himself by the name of Mulla. This name was extended to include the plain on which the castle stood, which became Armulla Dale.

Larger towns in this area include Kanturk, Mallow, and Fermoy; other towns include Mitchelstown, Liscarroll, and Glanworth, the latter two having large early castles which Spenser must have known and visited. (See Fig 1, left location map.) Kilbolane Castle at Milford is also of importance, and there are a number of fortresses picturesquely sited along the banks of the Blackwater. Medieval ecclesiastical establishments in this area include Ballybeg Friary, near Buttevant, Buttevant Friary which Spenser acquired c 1597 (Henley 1928: 68–70), Bridgetown Priory, between Killavullen and Ballyhooly and which was owned by Spenser's friend Lodowick Bryskett, and Castlelyons Friary.

There are a number of medieval castles close at hand to Kilcolman which Spenser must also have known. Ballinguile Castle (some 2 miles 800 yards west from Kilcolman) is situated on the west bank of the Awbeg. Originally an ancient castle of the Stapletons and erected after the reign of King John (Smith ed 1893, 1:292), it now consists of a ruin of two periods. Almost the same distance to the east of Kilcolman, 2 miles 125 yards, lies Castlepook, a lofty square, massive tower with walls 8 feet thick. (For an early illustration, see Windele Mss 191.) It was probably erected at the same period as Kilcolman and is situated on a similar rocky outcrop. The name 'pook' (from the Irish 'Phooka' a wild bestial phantom) could have associations with an adjacent cave, known as Castlepook Cave, one of the largest in Ireland, which was excavated in 1904 (Scharff, Seymour, and Newton 1917–19). The cave contained, among other things, bones of mammoths, giant Irish elks, bears, hyenas, and reindeer. There is no evidence to show that it was known in Spenser's time, although it had been entered previous to the excavation.

Almost the same distance to the south, 2 miles 780 yards, is Richardstown Castle on the extreme border of Spenser's seignory, which he acquired (Henley 1928:61) but covenanted to a Mr Fienny (Smith ed 1893, 1:345–6). Unfortunately, the castle was knocked down by lightning in 1865 and only a large mound remains to show its location (White 1911–19, 24:175), but a bawn and castle are mentioned in the covenant. Another castle that Spenser had acquired, probably about 1597, and some 9 miles away to the southeast, near Bridgetown Priory, was Renny (Henley 1928:67–8). It was located near the Blackwater River on the edge of a cliff, and was constructed originally by the Fitz-Geralds (Smith ed 1893, 1:317). It is marked as the site of a castle only on the first edition of the 1:10,000 Ordnance Survey of 1841, although Windele (1897: 260) states that a fragment remained in his time and O'Flanagan (1844:117–18) refers to the ruins of the old castle. This late acquisition was for his sons to inherit, and Sylvanus made over the lands to Peregrine after his inheritance (White 1911–19, 21:270). In the nineteenth century, 'a very old oak tree still [threw] its branches over the river, called Spenser's Oak, under which he is said to have written part of the Faery Queen' (O'Flanagan 1844:118). For short periods Spenser acquired other medieval structures, including Enniscorthy Friary (gone) and Castle, and the Augustinian Friary (gone) at New Ross, both in County Wexford, and the Franciscan New Abbey at Kilcullen in Kildare (Henley 1928:37–8).

site The castle is situated in level, arable countryside on the extreme southeast edge of a long limestone ridge, some 20 feet high and 170 by 270 yards in size, the longer axis running east-west. Owing to the flat nature of the terrain, this rocky outcrop forms a noticeable feature in the landscape, enhanced in this respect by the prominent remains of the castle tower, which forms a conspicuous object at the eastern termination. To the south, the castle is slightly west of the north-south axis of a large oval bog, some 1000 yards north-south by 730 yards east-west with an extension of some 170 yards to the west in the southwest quadrant. This bog may originally have been a permanent lake although now it is reduced to a narrow strip of water along the shore of the northeast quadrant, where it extends outwards to some 70 yards from the shore at the northeast. The water level in the remainder of the marshland varies according to the season, and floods almost completely during prolonged heavy rainfall. The earliest accurate plan, the Ordnance Survey map of 1841, shows a larger area of permanent water, with an extension down to the east side of the bog. At approximately the center of this shoreline, there was a rounded promontory extending into the lake with a dairy farm; this is now at the southeastern end of the lake, and the buildings have been converted into a residence. Charles Smith, writing in 1750 (ed 1893, 1:311), describes the castle as 'situated on the north side of a fine lake, in the midst of a vast plain,' which might authenticate the shrinking of the lake in recent times, although it could have been the flood season at the time of his visit. It was very likely partially overgrown even in Spenser's time, as he refers to it as a 'rushy lake' (*Epithalamion* 60). It may also be the 'little bog' mentioned in the survey of 1622 (Dunlop 1924:144), but its exact whereabouts remains uncertain. However, the Petty map (1685) of the area indicates a small bog of the correct shape and size, and which, being the only one in the vicinity, may verify the description of 1622, although the area of permanent water might have been larger, since the bog appears to have been drained. That marshland was in the area may be suggested by Spenser's reference to 'th'unpleasant Quyre of Frogs' on his wedding night (*Epith* 349).

Some 180 yards from the castle, to the northwest, at the bottom of the limestone ridge, a cave or 'subterraneous passage' is indicated on Ordnance Survey maps (for 1937 and 1841; see Fig 1, upper site plan). It has a wide, high entrance partially blocked by a low, modern stone wall, and narrows down gently, penetrating deeply into the rock until the roof contacts the present ground level. Excavation would undoubtedly penetrate further, since the floor level has been considerably raised by the use of the cave as a cattle pen.

history The earliest evidence for the occupation of the site of Kilcolman Castle is provided by archaeology and tradition. Traditionally, the limestone ridge on which the castle was built was the site of an ancient Irish fort named Cathair Gobhaun or 'the fort of the Smith' (Lynch 1908:7, L[ynch] 1912:109), belonging to the Ui Rossa of the race of Mogh Ruith. In the earliest period, these forts were built beside lakes and rivers, and this lake site would have appealed to the Dairine kings as most suitable for the smiths of Ross na Righ (a short distance to the south of Kilcolman). Thus the lake could be archaeologically fertile. An English Royal Bard is connected with the district of Kilcolman, further substantiating occupation at this period of time.

Irish forts were in use from the Late Bronze Age (c 750 BC) to the end of the seventeenth century, although the great fortbuilding period was the Iron Age, lasting from c 500 BC to the Early Christian period, which commenced when St Patrick introduced Christianity into the country in the fifth century and extended into the twelfth century. If a fort was constructed on this ridge, it would have come under the general category of a hill-fort or, more correctly in this instance, a promontory or ridge-fort, where the rocky outcrop was utilized to assist in the artificial defenses, which here would have consisted of a large stone wall enclosing the area of the ridge-top. The use of the rocky ridge would have rendered unnecessary the customary digging of a ditch, for the edge of the outcrop was of sufficient height to provide the protection required. The greatest occupation of this type of site would seem to commence around the time of Christ, and to continue well into the Early Christian period.

There are the remains of many ring-forts, mounds, enclosures, and so forth in the area; and evidence for early occupation in the district is also provided by the concentration of *fulachta fiadh*, there being no less than ten (and possibly more unmarked) within roughly a mile radius around Kilcolman Castle as indicated on modern Ordnance Survey maps, where each is marked *Fulacht Fian*. The names indicate that these were deer roasts or cooking places of the Fianna, and they consisted of a horseshoe-shaped mound of burned stones with its opening towards a stream or small lake. In the hollow of the mound was a hearth of flat stones where a fire was built, and between it and the water supply was a wooden trough filled with water. The meat, placed in the trough, was boiled by heating stones in the fire and rolling them into the trough; the mound was formed of discarded stones which had split and become brittle. Dating of these sites depends on the finds, which are sparse, but suggests that they began in prehistoric times, certainly in the Bronze Age, and continued into historic times. Two *fulachta fiadh* are located on the south shore of Kilcolman bog (or possibly lake in this period). A pillar stone is recorded at Kilcolman (Windele Mss 171) which could suggest a marker for a Bronze Age burial, but not all examples served this purpose, if indeed the stone was from this period.

There is evidence of Early Christian activity in the Kilcolman area, since 1720 yards to the south of the castle lie the ruins of Templetaggart Church. This ancient church, located close to Kilcolman bog in a southeast direction near Rossagh, has an old graveyard attached to it. The name means 'the Priest's Church,' and it is also called Thoumpaleenhulmane ('small church of Colman') or Thoumpaleenawane (possibly 'small church of the monks'); it is supposed to have been founded by St Colman in the sixth century (Jones 1910:56). The *Annals of the Four Masters* mentions that St Column Mac Lenine died in 600. This church gave its name to the district and castle, since Kilcolman means 'church of Colman,' although boundaries have been changed so that it is now in the townland of Rossagh East. The churchyard was in use in 1910, stillborn children being traditionally buried there (Jones 1910:57). A raised, roughly circular enclosure is shown on the Ordnance Survey maps immediately to the south of the church (on the other side of the road), which may have been connected with it.

During the medieval period, a castle was built by the earls of Desmond. It was held by Sir Philip Sidney (one of Spenser's first patrons) for some time in 1568 (Jones 1901:239). When the vast estates were confiscated in 1583, the escheated lands were surveyed and undertakers were solicited from England to run the seignories and make them profitable. The plantation of Desmond lands in Munster involved dividing the profitable land into various sizes. The seignory around Kilcolman Castle with the manor and town involved 3028 English acres (1226 hectares) including 'a great quantity of mountain' (Dunlop 1924:143–4). The castle seems to have been allotted in 1586 to Andrew Reade (Henley 1928:56), but he did not take possession and the castle and various lands formed part of the grant made later to Spenser, the patent not being passed until 1590. It is probable that Spenser bought the title of the estate from Reade since both their names appear officially for the same lands on the same date, Spenser's name appearing in the Articles for the Undertakers. Some doubt exists as to when Spenser arrived in Cork to administer his seignory, but in July 1586 he addressed a letter from Dublin, where he held a post in the Court of Chancery, and his name appears in 1587 in the list of those in arrears with the First Fruits (Henley 1928:45) so he must have held the living, which was prebendary at Effin, County Limerick, for at least a year. Effin is close to his seignory at Kilcolman, so he could have moved south from Dublin towards the end of 1586.

In 1598, insurgents attacked and burned the castle, where some fighting is inferred since it is recorded that an Irishman was killed at the spoil of the castle (Henley 1928:158), but Spenser with his family escaped to Cork and then to England. After his death in the following year, his wife and children returned to Ireland. The seignory descended to Sylvanus and the stone house (an addition to the castle?) built by Spenser was re-edified but again lately consumed by fire (1622) and replaced by a 'convenient English house' (Dunlop 1924:143–4). Upon his death, a fee-farm grant was made of the lands in 1638 to his son Edmund (Henley 1928:201). When Edmund died tragically in 1640, being thrown from his horse, his brother William, aged six, inherited the lands. Since William was brought up as a Roman Catholic, the lands were lost to the Spenser family in 1654, going to a Captain Courthope. William's appeal to Cromwell was successful, but the land he was then granted was near Ballinasloe, County Galway, though he eventually recovered Kilcolman (Henley 1928:208). Kilcolman must have passed into obscurity some time later, since the Petty map of 1685 shows no trace of name or structure on the site, and finally in 1738 it passed out of the Spenser family to Elizabeth, Lady Meade.

evidence of the site The principal remaining portion of Templetaggart Church is the north wall, 29 feet long. A central round-headed door is in good condition, with a 4-foot-long hole for sliding the bar when the door is open. The heights are 6 feet 2 inches to the soffit of the arch, and 2 feet 10 inches to the springing of the arch. The east wall is missing, while the west wall has collapsed and is overgrown. The south wall has two portions remaining, that to the west being 5 feet long and that to the east 7 feet (White 1911–19, 25:190). A good portion of the stones of the church were removed to build a laborer's cottage (Jones 1910:57). A road of large blocks of stone runs from the church and fort towards the east and Brough.

Since the rock ridge on which the castle was built has been used for grazing for many years, the feet of the cattle have blunted its contours; also the details of the rocky edges are obscured by falls of earth and stone. However, it is apparent that the west end of the ridge was cut off by a deep rock-cut fosse at some earlier period. There are humps and hollows running over parts of the summit, suggesting previous occupation – perhaps a much larger castle or possibily a small, medieval settlement. In the field below the castle was a churchyard or cemetery (Windele Mss 179), a bush being said to mark the site of Kilcolman Church, which was 100 yards to the north of the castle (Power 1932:122). Another ancient church traditionally associated with the castle, Cill Colman Grec (ie, Kilcolman), once stood in the castle field some 300 yards to the northwest of the castle ruin (Power 1932:124–5); the term Grec derives from *gar* 'the voice' referring to the singing of St Coleman, who was famed for his poetry (L[ynch] 1912:109) – like a later famous site occupant! – and was poet-royal or poet-laureate in AD 550 (Jones 1901:238).

(See **Kilcolman Castle** Figs 2–8.)

Various modern structures exist or existed on or near the castle. The Ordnance Survey of 1841 marks the cave as a 'subterraneous passage' and shows a limekiln slightly to the east. A cottage with an outhouse is marked to the southwest of the castle at the extreme western end of the lake. Further away, to the southeast, a cottage and a limekiln are shown on the shore of the lake and appear in the foreground in the Bartlett engraving (Fig 5), while further away lies the dairy farm. On the 1937 1:10,000 map, the buildings are similar except that the cottage and limekiln shown on the Bartlett engraving have gone, and the cottage to the southwest has another outhouse. The cottage adjacent to the limekiln was still present in 1903 during the survey for the 1:2500 maps, but the limekiln had been removed.

the castle structures As the ruins were extensively repaired and altered in the middle of the nineteenth century, the following list of earlier views is given in chronological order.

(A) An oil painting, c 1820, by William Sadler (1782–1839), an accomplished landscape artist. From the northwest (Fig 3).

(B) A lithograph from a sepia painting, 1821, by T. Crofton Croker, published in Croker 1824. From the northwest.

(C) A sketch, 1883, by Samson Carter, presented to the Royal Society of Antiquaries of Ireland in 1856. Unlocated.

(D) An engraving, 1840, by J.W. Archer from a sketch by F. Lush, title page to Spenser ed 1840. From the northwest.

(E) An engraving, 1841, after a sketch by T. Crofton Croker. From the northwest (Fig 4).

(F) An engraving, after W.H. Bartlett 1842. From the southeast (Fig 5).

(G) A pencil-and-crayon sketch, c 1845, by William Denny, National Library Collection, Dublin, Number 1971 TX (mislaid and presumed lost).

(H) Ink sketches, 1850, by John Windele 12I10. From the southwest (Fig 6); and p 185, sketch of upper window. These sketches were copied by W. Frazer, National Library Collection, Dublin, Number 1975 TX (32).

There are a number of other views published around the middle of the nineteenth century in topographical works, and so forth, but they are copies of the views listed. The engraving in Savage (1878:457), for instance, is roughly copied from Fig 5 although some 25 years earlier the castle had been partially rebuilt. The castle was heavily shrouded in ivy previous to the repairs, which left it ivy-free. Perhaps the best illustration of the castle after the repair work and before the re-advance of the ivy is from Lovett 1888 (Fig 7), for the engraving was taken from an early photograph. This can be compared with Croker (Fig 4) taken from a similar viewpoint. Soon after the ivy took hold again, until at present, apart from a few feet of masonry visible at ground level, the remainder of the structure is completely hidden (Fig 8, and esp de Breffny 1977:147).

For an impression of the appearance of the castle before being repaired, these views need to be scrutinized carefully. They more or less agree that the main block of the castle is ruined down to the stone vault and that the stair tower and south wall are still standing to a taller amount of their full height. However, details vary. The earliest depiction, view A (Fig 3), is artistically distorted, for the vault is shown open to resemble an arched gateway and is facing the artist when it should be at an angle, and the doors in the tower are too far apart. Also the south wall is practically nonexistent and the window is therefore omitted. It does show the upper door before its collapse, and that it was pointed in shape, and the open vault also indicates that the north and south walls are of comparable thickness. A number of unlikely features crept into views B and D, such as square-headed windows instead of a door on the upper level, and a projection on the north wall of the main block. View E (Fig 4) corrects these errors but continues in other ones shown, such as the short south wall of the main block and a string course running along the north wall of the stair tower, while all the views omit the splay on the northwest angle of this tower. The Bartlett view (Fig 5) is notable in that it is the only one taken from the southeast, but it is artistically dramatized and the main block seems to be incorrectly projecting in front of the stair tower. Perhaps the most faithful view is Windele (Fig 4), who has also taken a fresh viewpoint, the southwest. The profile of what could be part of the bawn wall is also indicated twice. Since Windele was an antiquarian as well as an artist, he would have been unlikely to try to misrepresent the castle in any way. Apart from Windele (whose sketch is from the wrong side), all the views indicate to a greater or lesser extent a projecting mass of masonry high up on the northeast angle of the stair tower. Lovett (Fig 7) shows an indication of this before the ivy concealed it.

A contemporary account of the repair work is given by Windele (Mss 183):

> 22nd July 1858 I was informed that Mr Barry the tenant of Kilcoleman, wishing to preserve this interesting ruin from further injury has been causing repairs to be made wherever most needed, erecting Buttresses etc. In digging outside the Castle to underpin a failing wall, they discovered a pipe of antique fashion ... Mr Barry has the good taste to eschew all idea of renovation or restoration ... The object in this case is merely to preserve and guard against further dilapidation a monument venerable from its age and interesting from its associations.

Jones (1901:239) states that Philip Harold Barry repaired and strengthened what remained of the castle in 1850, and that during the repairs a very curious chalk or pipeclay instrument was found. This pipe is also mentioned in Henley (1928:73n) where it becomes 'a number of curiously-shaped tobacco pipes ... also some deer bones ... the pipes were removed, I have been told, to the National Museum.' No record of these can be traced and the present owner of the castle, Mr Charles Harold-Barry, has no knowledge of them, so what might have been an interesting link with Spenser appears to be lost. Henley also says that one of the walls was buttressed, but rather more than that was achieved (1928:73n). Refer to section and floor plans, Figs 1, 2 (where the modern work is shown hatched), to assist with the following architectural description.

If one walks around the ground floor from the outside, it becomes apparent that all the masonry has been buttressed, with the exception of parts of the stair and garderobe tower. The original work is in limestone ashlar, roughly squared and semicoursed, while the quoins are large, hammer-dressed, and alternate in direction from the arris. Occasionally the purplish Old Red Sandstone occurs, sometimes decoratively, as in the stairwell, where courses are built in between the ground floor and the floor above the vault. The new masonry is also limestone and is composed of large squared blocks *en bosse*, that is, with a slightly raised, roughened surface, mixed with rubble work. Where the rectangular garderobe chute has been broken into, it has been incorrectly repaired as a window with brick and stone jambs. The chute continues downwards and should discharge lower down. The projecting portion containing the garderobe is an addition and straight joints are visible, probably indicating a design change during building. All the external openings on this level have been renewed and are not original. The present doorway in the south wall replaces what would have been a loop; similarly in the north wall a loop has been replaced by a square-headed window. The doorway in the east wall is in the correct position for the entrance but is completely new, and is provided with a flat lintel as are all the new openings. Both new doorways have spud stones with a pivot hole and bolt holes for doors. Rather more undisturbed masonry exists inside the castle, and an original aumbry remains at the north end of the west wall. The stair and garderobe tower projects into the interior space, the arris having been rebuilt and rounded. The linteled doorway leading to the stair is original work, badly spalled on the arrises by intense heat. Some original projecting stones survive above and to the left of this door. Inside it is rebated for a door, and there is a tiny lobby for the door swing before the spiral stone stair starts climbing up to the left, an unusual direction as most castle stairs spiral up to the right, so that a defender on the stair facing downwards has room to use his right arm to wield his sword.

The next level, under the vault, is not reached from the spiral stair, and access must have been obtained from a wooden stair or ladder. This area for storage or sleeping space is lit by one small, narrow, flat-headed loop set in a long embrasure whose flat soffit is cranked down to meet the vault arch in the south wall. (Since the loop is concealed by ivy on the exterior and blocked with loose rubble on the interior, information is taken from the Windele drawing; dimensions on section A-A and plan 2 [Figs 1, 2] have been estimated.) The continuous stone vault, running east-west, is a drop-pointed arch, and a socket for a beam survives at the east end of the north wall. At this level, the stair is lit by a square-headed loop with a dished sill and drainhole for slops; it is provided with a long, narrow, flat-headed embrasure, which just avoids the adjacent rectangular garderobe chute. The straight joints noted on the ground floor are still apparent, and some original masonry projects forward on the outside over the main door, largely hidden by ivy, so that its purpose is not readily discernible.

The third level is reached after fifteen steps, and entry is made to the area over the vault through a drop-pointed arched doorway rebated to open into the floor space. (For this and some other views, see White 1911–19, 21: photographs facing pp 266, 268). Apart from the stair tower and the south wall, the remaining parapet walls are modern. The south wall, badly cracked near the stair tower, possesses the most decorative item of surviving architecture, a cusped lancet window set in a segmentally arched embrasure provided with a window ledge, and stone seats, one on either side (Fig 9; the sketch on Fig 2 is the inside elevation). The seats die into the splay of the embrasure jambs, which commences halfway along their length. The arched embrasure soffit is turned over wickerwork centering, and the centering holes remain, two on either side. This south-facing embrasure is known as the bower, or Raleigh's window, where traditionally Spenser used to sit with his friend and smoke the new tobacco. Entry to the stair to the upper floors is by a drop-pointed, arched doorway, rebated on the inside, with a tiny lobby for the door swing. The facing stone spiral stairs turn upwards, again to the left, while on the right above the first two steps a small linteled doorway, rebated on the inside for a door, leads, via a small lobby for the door swing which curves to the right, to the garderobe or privy. This is provided with two small flat-headed loops, one in the south wall and one in the west, the latter being provided with a slop sill and drain hole. The stone seat for the garderobe is missing. Halfway up the stairs, facing to the east, a flat-headed loop lights the stair, its northern jamb missing.

(See **Kilcolman Castle** Fig 9.)

The upper level is reached after fourteen steps, the lobby being damaged. The stair continues up two steps and one flag riser into a short corridor heading in a northeasterly direction which opens into a small chamber, now badly ruined and choked with ivy. This was once provided with a loop facing north (Croker sketch B, and see E [Fig 4]). Facing south from the lobby is a small wedge-shaped room; its doorway is missing, apart from the eastern jamb, which has a small bar hole, and it has two linteled windows in splayed linteled embrasures, one in the east wall and one in the south. A large aumbry is positioned at the east end of the north wall, and this room, with its segmental arched roof turned over wickerwork centering, would have made a pleasant bedchamber. The door into the main chamber is missing, although part of the bottom part of the north jamb survives. From Sadler's painting (Fig 3), this door would probably have had a drop-pointed arch, while from the Windele sketch (Fig 6), there was a south-facing window in the south wall of the main block where it meets the stair turret. This would have lit a small lobby, perhaps the beginning of a straight stair in the south wall leading to the top levels; part of its east jamb remains.

Outside the tower, to the south, is a wall running off to the east, now largely ruined, with upstanding pieces of masonry at either end. Its profile in 1850 is shown in two sketches by Windele (Fig 6) which indicates a possible window towards the east end. This returns northwards, denoting the corner of a building. The remains of these walls are very overgrown, and they may be represented by the wall to the rear of the tower in Croker's lithograph (B) and Lush's sketch (D), or this may be a continuation of this existing wall to the west, although this feature does not occur on the other views, possibly because (apart from Sadler) they are of a later date when this wall may have been destroyed.

conclusions The castle was undoubtedly of the tower-house type, a late medieval fortalice that was built in great numbers in Ireland, Scotland, and the north of England when social conditions were unsettled. They were intended to repel bands of marauders, although many of the larger examples held out successfully against military forces. They usually consisted of a strong tower, protected by enclosing walls surrounding a bawn, an area where cattle could be driven to be protected at night. The bawn could be protected by corner towers or a gatehouse or both. They were built from the end of the fourteenth century to the middle of the seventeenth, and in Ireland there were strong concentrations in some western counties, especially Limerick and Galway (Johnson [1985]:13). The tower could be especially strong, with stone barrel vaults over some floors for strength and protection against fire. The wall head was provided with battlements, machicolated galleries, and turrets for defense, while larger windows were kept to the upper stories, the lower stories being provided with gun loops and shot holes. Such a castle is shown under attack in Fig 10, which represents the siege of Glin Castle during the Elizabethan wars. Kilcolman could have superficially resembled this castle in appearance, and have had a similar type of bawn, the lake taking the place of the river in the illustration. Of course, Kilcolman could have had better defenses, being built on a limestone rock.

(See **Kilcolman Castle** Fig 10.)

With regard to the architectural details, Fig 11 shows a section through Blarney Castle, situated some 22 miles due south of Kilcolman. The similarity to Kilcolman can be seen, especially the very thick walls supporting the vault. Blarney is said to carry a date stone marked 1446, although the great tower is credited to Cormac Laider the Strong, who died in 1494 (Leask 1941: 113–).

(See **Kilcolman Castle** Fig 11.)

Jones (1901:239) states that Kilcolman was built in 1347 by the first Earl, and Henley (1928:72) follows this; Jones also mentions that the sixth Earl of Desmond received the property from an uncle in 1418, and de Breffny (1977:146) prefers this date for the erection of the castle. The middle of the fourteenth century was a time of strife and plague during which little or no building work was carried out, and the style and detailing of the castle, as far as can be seen from what remains, is of the fifteenth century. A date for the commencement of the building of the castle in the 1420s could therefore be advanced with some confidence.

The buttressing or cladding of the lower walls in the 1850s, which so successfully arrested the decay of the castle, does not seem to have respected the original thickness of the walls, especially the north wall which should correspond roughly to the south wall. The rock upon which the castle is built seems to have been dressed vertically in two places outside the western end of the south wall (see floor plan 1, Fig 2), which could mark the original wall thickness where it was bonded to and above the rock; similarly, the projecting masonry to the east just over the present entrance to the tower, could have formed part of the original wall thickness. As for the west wall, although Sadler shows the vault broken completely open (Fig 3), he must be indulging in artistic license: although Croker suggests this slightly by shading on the north edge of his 1821 lithograph (B), in his much more accurate 1841 representation (E), the arch is again shown but without any deep shading to suggest an opening. The voussoirs of the vault arch would normally extend into the end walls in this type of construction, and they could be revealed if the outer skin were removed and the corework disturbed. That Windele (Fig 6), an antiquarian draftsman, shows no opening broken through (not even the arch is indicated) would seem to confirm this, as does the appearance of the actual internal face of the wall, which shows no definite sign of new work or disturbance.

The limekiln shown on the 1841 Ordnance Survey and in the foreground of the Bartlett view (Fig 5) has completely disappeared in the 1903 edition – possibly it provided the masonry for the 1850s repair work.

On all the views (esp Figs 4 and 5), the projection shown at an upper level on the northeast angle of the stair tower corresponds with the position of the ruined chamber at the end of the short corridor on the upper floor. The projecting masonry could represent the remains of a machicolated gallery or box machicolation at this level to protect the entrance door underneath – a standard feature on tower-houses.

The original height of Kilcolman is open to question: it could have had only two floors above the vault, but Blarney has three, and a total of six floors was not uncommon in the south and west of Ireland. The probability that the tower was considerably taller has to be seriously considered. That the upper staircase terminates does not necessarily mean that the castle went no higher: it was customary to change the position and type of stair at various levels as a means of defense. Perhaps an upper stone vault was incorporated, over the second highest floor, which would not be uncommon, since the lord's hall was on the top floor for security, and larger windows were possible since they were the furthest from the ground, and a stone floor was fireproof.

That the castle was burned shows in the spalling of the arrises of the original stonework in various places, especially on the door leading to the stairs on the ground floor.

The possibility exists that the remains of a wall to the south and east of the tower represents a bawn surrounding the tower. This could also perhaps incorporate at the east end the remains of the stone house or the convenient English house referred to in the 1622 survey (Dunlop 1924:143–4), or it could have been a church or hall which formed part of the castle complex, or merely a corner tower of the bawn. From the traces left on the site, there was definitely a rectangular structure to the southeast of the tower (see lower site plan, Fig 1). The masonry shown to the west (under the north point in this drawing) is a chunk that has fallen from the tower and rolled intact to its present position, which illustrates the strength of the mortar in use at the time. The area of disturbed ground to the east of the castle could also be the site of the churchyard, in which case the rectangular building in this area would have been a church.

White (1911–19, 17:178) mentions an underground passage between Burton House and Kilcolman Castle, which is not possible, since Burton House is over five miles away and any passage would have to go under rivers and bogs. Another passage from the castle, called the Fox Hole, is noted in the Ordnance Survey Field Book for 1840, possibly referring to the 'subterraneous passage' that may have led from the large cave in the northeast part of the limestone ridge to the castle, along which Spenser and his family could have escaped in 1598 (White 1911–19, 21:273). However, there is no visible evidence of an entrance to a passage in the castle ruins.

How could the most delicate portion of the castle, namely the stair tower with its thin walls, remain, while the massive walls of the main portion of the castle have gone? The explanation must lie with the two limekilns that used the limestone ridge as a quarry, one of which remains to the north of the castle. The castle must have been systematically dismantled and fed into the kilns, the stair being spared to allow access to the upper parts for the wreckers. That there are no loose stones at all on the site bears this out. Perhaps it is rough justice that one of the kilns may have been similarly dismantled and used for the 1850s repair work.

One may conclude, then, that the castle was taller than now, and was surrounded by a bawn and other buildings. That it was higher is supported by Windele (Mss 186) who states 'the present remains of Kilcoleman Castle are far inferior to their original height.' It is possible that Smith, normally a shrewd observer, writing c 1750, also knew this when writing of the castle, which would explain his rather misleading statement that 'the castle is now almost level with the ground' (ed 1893, 1:311; ed 1774, 1:333 quoted in Spenser ed 1805, 1: l). It is on a ridge that was once an Iron Age fort, and part was cut off by a fosse to provide a citadel. That the castle was not located on this part of the ridge is puzzling, but the citadel could have fallen into disuse many years before the erection of the castle. Signs of occupation on the ridge and the tradition of churches and a graveyard suggest that a small settlement could have existed there. Since the 1591 grant to Spenser mentions the manor, castle, town, and lands of Kilcolman (Smith ed 1893, 1:345), perhaps the manor consisted of a small medieval settlement along the ridge adjacent to the castle.

Removal of the ivy from the castle and archaeological excavation would be needed to confirm or refute some of these possibilities. The former should be carried out without delay, for the main south wall of the castle is cracked through above the vault with ivy stems and needs immediate attention to prevent collapse.

Spenser, by coming to Ireland and especially by living in a castle in Kilcolman as an undertaker, was transported from a relatively peaceful environment into an area where he found that castles were still very necessary. His chivalric world of 'fierce warres and faithfull loves' was for him partly reality. In England the vast popularity of *The Faerie Queene* in particular caused a sympathetic reaction, strongly boosting the current preoccupation with chivalric pursuits, and wealthy landowners and merchants who had developed a desire to be knights-errant began to build massive castellated structures in more accurate simulation of earlier castles. These had the appearance of great strength but their thin walls and anachronistic lucid large windows belied this suggested power. This Elizabethan chivalric style, which peaked in the closing years of the sixteenth century and the first quarter of the seventeenth, is often labeled Spenserian (Girouard ed 1983:223–4; Platt 1986:183), and one of the first advocates of this more realistic baronial revival was Sir Walter Raleigh himself, whose castle at Sherbourne in Dorset, begun in 1594 as a three-story rectangular block, was provided with four large polygonal corner towers of four stories after 1600. Nearby Lulworth in Dorset – an embattled cube with massive cylindrical corner towers built by Viscount Bindon – followed around 1608, and its twin, Ruperra, Glamorganshire, was erected by Sir Thomas Morgan in 1626. Among others perhaps the most notable is Bolsover, Derbyshire, built by the prodigy house-architects Robert and John Smythson for Sir Charles Cavendish and begun on the ruins of a genuine castle in 1612. This spectacular fantasy castle stands high on a hilltop, the architectural climax being provided by a dramatic simulation of a Norman donjon modeled on examples such as Castle Rising, Norfolk, and Castle Hedingham, Essex. This is a high, massive, almost square crenelated block with narrow angle towers capped by a great staircase tower which soars some hundred feet into the sky. Paradoxically, it is known as the 'Little Castle.'

While most of these Spenserian castles are still fondly tended, it is ironic that Kilcolman, the poet's castle and the indirect inspiration for much of this revival, lies mutilated and abandoned. D. Newman Johnson

W.H. Bartlett, illus 1842 *The Scenery and Antiquities of Ireland* text by J. Stirling Coyne and N.P. Willis, 2 vols (London); Brian de Breffny 1977 *Castles of Ireland* (London); J[ames] C[olman] 1894 *JCHAS* os 3:89–100; T. Crofton Croker 1824 *Researches in the South of Ireland* (London); Robert Dunlop 1924 'An Unpublished Survey of the Plantation of Munster in 1622' *JRSAI* 54:128–46; Geological Survey 1979 *Geological Map of Ireland* Ordnance Survey (Dublin); Girouard ed 1983; Mr and Mrs S.C. Hall 1841–3 *Ireland: Its Scenery, Character, etc* 3 vols (London); Henley 1928; D. Newman Johnson [1985] *The Irish Castle* (Dublin); Walter A. Jones 1901 'Doneraile and Vicinity' *JCHAS* 2nd ser 7:238–42; Jones 1910 'The Munster Ros-na-Righ and Its Traditions' *JCHAS* 2nd ser 16:53–9; Harold G. Leask 1951 *Irish Castles and Castellated Houses* (Dundalk); Richard Lovett 1888 *Irish Pictures Drawn with Pen and Pencil* (London); J.F. Lynch 1908 'The Ford of Ae' *Irish Independent* 2 Oct:7; J.F. L[ynch] 1912 '[Notes and Queries:] St. Coleman Grec' *JCHAS* 2nd ser 18:108–10; James R. O'Flanagan 1844 *The Blackwater in Munster* (London); Ordnance Survey 1840 *Field Book* Ordnance Survey Mss (Dublin); William Petty 1685 *Hiberniae delineatio* (London); Colin Platt 1986 *The National Trust Guide to Late Mediaeval and Renaissance Britain: From the Black Death to the Civil War* (London); Patrick Power 1932 *Crichad an Chaoilli: Being the Topography of Ancient Fermoy* (Cork); John Savage 1878 *Picturesque Ireland* (New York); R.F. Scharff, H.J. Seymour, and E.T. Newton 1917–19 'The Exploration of Castlepook Cave, County Cork' *PRIA* 34B:33–72; Charles Smith 1893 *The Ancient and Present State of the County and City of Cork* ed Robert Day and W.A. Copinger, 2 vols (Cork); James Grove White 1911–19 'Historical and Topographical Notes etc on Buttevant, Castletownroche, Doneraile, Mallow, and Places in Their Vicinity' *JCHAS* 2nd ser suppl 17:1–128, 21:181–292, 24:109–180, 25:181–220; John Windele [1830s-50s] Mss *Topography Co. Cork, W and N.E.* Royal Irish Academy Number 12110; Windele 1897 'Windele Manuscripts (Continued)' *JCHAS* 2nd ser 3:246–63.

On Spenserian architecture, see further William Anderson 1970 *Castles of Europe from Charlemagne to the Renaissance* (London) p 289; Clive Aslet and Alan Powers 1985 *The National Trust Book of the English House* (Harmondsworth) p 124; Lord Montagu of Beaulieu 1987 *English Heritage* ed P.H. Reed (London) p 109; Olive Cook 1974 *The English Country House: An Art and a Way of Life* (London) p 71; Mark Girouard 1978 *Life in the English Country House: A Social and Architectural History* (New Haven) p 103; Girouard 1981 *The Return to Camelot: Chivalry and the English Gentleman* (New Haven) p 17; Girouard ed 1983:209, 223–5; J. Alfred Gotch 1909 *The Growth of the English House ... from 1100 to 1800* (London) pp 138–40; Christopher Hussey 1951 *English Country Houses open to the Public* (London) pp 14, 73; Platt 1986:183, 185, 187; Summerson 1953:51 and n 6.

L

labyrinths, mazes Of these two terms, *labyrinth* is the more literary, being derived from the intricate subterranean structure built by Daedalus in Crete to hide and house the Minotaur (see Virgil *Aeneid* 6.14–30, Ovid *Metamorphoses* 8.155–68). The term *maze* (with related forms such as *amazement*) is closer to everyday language and experience: topiary mazes in gardens and pavement or turf mazes in churches and churchyards were commonly seen in Spenser's day.

If a way of life or course of events is traced, its path describes a maze. The image is especially insistent for a knight errant (L *errare* to wander) who pursues his quest through places of danger, testing, and reward. In choosing errantry as a controlling metaphor in *The Faerie Queene*, Spenser doubtless recalled the elaborate civic and royal processions winding through the streets of London from station to station. In literature, he would have found a prototype of all wandering in Homer's Ulysses, and of descents to a lower world in Virgil's Aeneas. The Bible imprinted on his mind Israel's 40 years of wandering in the wilderness together with backsliding and exile as sign and punishment of sin; the New Testament picks up wandering by the way as an image of sin but combines it with the assertion that the elect are 'strangers and pilgremes' in this world 'with no continuing citie' (Heb 11.13, 13.14; see also 1 Pet 2.11). Medieval literature, sacred and secular, makes explicit the pilgrimage and the quest.

There are few images of labyrinths in Spenser's shorter poems. E.K. says of the poet that 'his unstayed yougth had long wandred in the common Labyrinth of Love' (*SC* Epistle to Harvey), Hobbinoll speaks of 'my wandring mynde' (*June* 2), and Colin looks back over his wandering in 'wastefull woodes' when he was 'wont to raunge amydde the mazie thickette' (*Dec* 20–5). In *Daphnaïda* 372–3, the grieving Alcyon intends to 'walke this wandring pilgrimage / Throughout the world from one to other end'; *Virgils Gnat* 542 refers to the whirlpool Charybdis, and *Ruines of Rome* 22 to the Cretan Labyrinth; in *Muiopotmos* 358–60, the spider Aragnoll lurks in a cave at the center of his labyrinthine web.

In *FQ* I, the Red Cross Knight's first appearance with his companions on the plain is emblematic; as soon as something happens to establish his errantry, he leaves the plain for a grove full of turnings which is explicitly called a 'labyrinth' and leads to a cave (i 11). 'This is the wandring wood, this *Errours den*,' cries Una; and the monster herself is an embodiment of both cave and labyrinth, with her 'huge taile ... in knots' with its 'folds' and 'endlesse traine' (13, 15–18).

Guyon's two main adversaries in *FQ* II are Mammon and Acrasia, who menace him with amazement and loss of bearings. The deeper he descends into the house of Mammon in canto vii, the more it becomes a vast labyrinthine realm with diminishing prospect of egress. The long twelfth canto of the voyage and the Bower of Bliss is differently arranged: except for the resolved will of Guyon as guided by the Palmer, everything is prearranged by Acrasia, the spider at the center of the web (xii 77; cf vii 28). The earliest manifestation of her power is the Gulf of Greediness, a watery labyrinth with 'th'huge abysse of his engulfing grave' (xii 5). The culminating peril of the deep, 'threatning to devoure all,' is the Whirlpool of Decay, which is called a 'restlesse wheele' and a 'wide *Labyrinth*' (20–1). Since the labyrinthine voyage is preparation and forewarning for the Bower itself, Guyon and the reader are steeled to resist the 'wanton wreathings intricate' of the witch's world of seductive illusion (53).

In the middle books, the Ariostan manner of interrupted narrative may be described metaphorically as a maze or knot or interlace, as many incidental phrases suggest: the hunt for glory 'through wastefull wayes,' the following of 'false Ladies traine,' the sea's 'hollow bosome' and 'greedie gulfe,' the 'wandring forrest,' and 'miswandred wayes' (III i 3, iii 11, iv 22, vi 26, vii 18). What is a drawn-out torment in Book III is delay in access in Book IV. The profusion of plurals and pairs in the Temple of Venus leads up to a phrase which in another context would certainly be menacing but here stands safe under the sign of innocency, ardor, and self-discovery: 'False Labyrinthes, fond runners eyes to daze; / All which by nature made did nature selfe amaze' (IV x 24).

In Book VI, Calidore must 'tread an endlesse trace' in pursuit of the Blatant Beast (i 6, 37). The characteristic movement of Calidore and Calepine is deeper into the forest, and the Brigands and the Salvage Nation carry Serena and Pastorella into tenebrous thickets. Such groping 'through this worlds wyde wildernes' (vii 37) makes the pastoral episode especially welcome, with its culminating vision of the dance of the Graces on Mount Acidale (x 5–18). The dance is labyrinth in clear air and full sight, maze without danger, the knot that holds but does not constrain, the fully answered riddle. It must end, however, for the same reason that the Beast must escape its bonds and errantry resume. Similarly, Mutabilitie can be silenced only when her pageant – and with it the vast intricate labyrinth of Spenser's poem and Nature herself – disappear into 'that Sabaoths sight' which is not of this world (VII viii 2).

WILLIAM BLISSETT

Blissett 1989; Janet Bord 1976 *Mazes and Labyrinths of the World* (New York); Angus Fletcher 1971; Fletcher 1983 'The Image of Lost Direction' in *Centre and Labyrinth: Essays in Honour of Northrop Frye* ed Eleanor Cook, et al (Toronto) pp 329–46; Lima de Freitas 1975 *O labirinto* (Lisbon); Hermann Kern 1982 *Labyrinthe* (Munich); W.F. Jackson Knight 1936 *Cumaean Gates: A Reference of the Sixth Aeneid to the Initiation Pattern* (Oxford); Gertrude Rachel Levy 1948 *The Gate of Horn: A Study of the Religious Conceptions of the Stone Age, and Their Influence upon European Thought* (London); W.H. Matthews 1922 *Mazes and Labyrinths: A General Account of Their History and Developments* (New York); D'Orsay W. Pearson 1977 'Spenser's Labyrinth – Again' *SIcon* 3:70–88; Paolo Santarcangeli 1967 *Il libro dei labirinti* (Florence).

Lamb, Charles (1775–1834) Testimony from acquaintances leaves no doubt about Lamb's devotion to Spenser's poetry. In 1836 Walter Wilson remembered that 'Spenser and Shakespeare were to him as household-gods' (ed 1934:147), and in 1844 Leigh Hunt thought he remembered that his friend Lamb had titled Spenser the 'Poet's Poet.' Although the phrase is more likely a compressed variation on Hazlitt's 'Of all poets, he is the most poetical' (ed 1930–4, 5:34; already quoted by Hunt more than a decade earlier, 1833:161), the mistake is itself significant: Hunt knew enough about Lamb's high regard for Spenser to attribute the phrase to him.

Despite the superlatives, what Lamb did not do with Spenser is at least as remarkable as what he did do. In 1797 he encouraged Coleridge to write an 'Epic' in the spirit not only of Milton but of Spenser, and in 1815 he urged Wordsworth to write 'more criticism, about Spenser etc' (Lamb and Lamb ed 1975–8, 1:87, 3:149), but so far as we know Lamb himself attempted neither. He does mention Spenser by name in the early verses 'To the Poet Cowper': 'with lighter finger playing, / Our elder Bard, Spenser, a gentle Name, / The Lady muses' dearest darling child, / Elicited the deftest tunes yet heard / In Hall or Bower, taking the delicate Ear / Of Sidney, and his peerless maiden Queen' (to Coleridge, 5 Jul 1796; ed 1975–8, 1:41). And Spenser influenced the subject and style of several other early poems, most evidently 'A Vision of Repentance.' Lamb dared to hope Coleridge might discern in the poem's imagery and diction 'a delicacy of pencilling [ie, brushwork] not quite unspencer like' (to Coleridge, 15 Apr 1797; 1:106–9). But the Spenserian influence faded with the enthusiasms of Lamb's early poetic period.

His prose, where the standard units of Spenser criticism are the glancing allusion and the telling phrase, is similarly unencouraging. It is characteristic of Lamb to drop the phrase 'golden vapour' into the middle of a letter of 1802 (2:52; cf *FQ* III ix 20); to write out Spenser's Harvey Sonnet in a fourteen-shilling copy of the 1679 folio that he had located for Wordsworth (to Wordsworth, 1 Feb 1806; 2:206); to report whimsically in the same letter the story of an associate who mistook Lamb's reference to Spenser (who 'generally excites an image of an old Bard in a Ruff, and sometimes with it dim notions of Sir. P. Sydney and perhaps Lord Burleigh') for a reference to an acquaintance, William Spencer, who had written a monody on his wife's death (2:206; the story was later incorporated into Lamb's essay 'On the Ambiguities Arising from Proper Names'); or, without the aid of a concordance, to advise a correspondent correctly in 1815 that Spenser does not use the word *air* to mean 'song' or 'tune' (3:202). But only once in his life does he expound to the length of a paragraph. We can compensate for his reticence in two ways: by extending metaphors he never extended, and by drawing on his associates to establish a context that he never established. Only in the context of his associates' views of Spenser can the coherence of Lamb's be seen, but nonetheless his view stands apart in certain key respects from theirs.

If Walter Wilson's memory of Lamb's pairing Spenser with Shakespeare is accurate, it is not quite typical of Lamb's circle, the first rank of whose pantheon is monopolized by Shakespeare and Milton. Spenser tends to appear in second-order rankings as the opposite of Chaucer, the poet supposedly closest to the gritty realism of everyday life. His ranking usually comes tagged with the corollary that he lacks some essential quality, as in Coleridge's assertion that he has 'imaginative fancy' but not 'imagination, in kind or degree, as Shakespeare and

Milton have' (Coleridge ed 1936:38). Hazlitt's essay 'Of Persons One Would Wish to Have Seen' (1826), which takes the form of a remembered hearthside conversation dominated by Hazlitt and Lamb, shows the typical characterization of Spenser in action. Hazlitt proposes Chaucer as a candidate for recall from eternity. Lamb asks if Spenser might not be added. Hazlitt thinks not: worldly Chaucer deserves extradition back to the world, but otherworldly Spenser is in eternity where he belongs. If Lamb would extradite them both, it is presumably because he sees their opposition as complementary – divergent poets who converge at the center where real life is carried on (Hazlitt ed 1930–4, 17: 126–7).

Put another way, Hazlitt's opposition is vertical, with Chaucer below, while Lamb's is horizontal, with earthdwellers stationed between Chaucer and Spenser. As different as these orientations are, Hazlitt and Lamb differ more in their portraits of real life and the place of Spenser in each than in their portraits of Spenser, which are constructed from an archive of metaphors in general use. For example, the innocuous stock phrase with which Lamb reinforces his suggestion that Coleridge write an epic, 'by the dainty sweet and soothing phantasies of honey tongued Spencer' (to Coleridge, 8 Jan 1797; ed 1975–8, 1:87), ties, in the way that was common among Lamb's associates, Spenser's rhetorical pleasures to sensual pleasures through the organs that they share. When paired with *sweet*, *dainty* opens the possibility of the female poet that Coleridge, also singling out Spenser's 'sweetness' but leaning on the association of tastes with temperaments rather than sounds, finds in Spenser's 'feminine tenderness and almost maidenly purity of feeling' (ed 1936:38). In turn, this female personification supports Lamb's characterization of Spenser's Harvey Sonnet as 'Manly and rather Miltonic ... with nothing in it about Love or Knighthood' – and thus, 'as a Sonnet of Spenser's,' rather 'curious' (to Wordsworth, 1 Feb 1806; ed 1975–8, 2:206).

It is no surprise that the metaphor of the female brings with it *in potentia* the conventional pleasures and burdens of that role, including children. Both Hazlitt and Hunt hint poetically of a nanny Spenser. As a figure of the relationship between poetry and audience, Spenser-as-female suggests that the poetry may have a role in early education analogous to the pedagogical role of women in the family – 'all manner of pitiable storys, in Spencer-like verse – love – friendship relationship etc. etc.' (to Coleridge, 5 Feb 1797; 1:97) – reserving the manly Milton for a later stage when men take over as teachers, and locking Chaucer away until the time comes for terminal lessons in the school of experience.

Though it would be anachronistic to dismiss altogether the notion of introducing children to life and poetry through Spenser, in practice the application of the metaphor usually took a somewhat different turn to accommodate the adult reader. In that instance, Spenser's poetry addresses the child in the adult. In 'To the Poet Cowper,' Spenser, though 'Our elder Bard,' is 'a gentle Name' and 'The Lady muses' dearest darling child.' Reopening childhood, Spenser becomes the poet of memory, speaking the (archaic) language of the past to satisfy the yearning for retrospection and nostalgia. Since the childhood that Spenser can help us remember is, as it were, shut away in a sleeping compartment of our brains, his poetry is identified with night, sleep, dream – 'mental space ... in a dream, a charmed sleep,' says Coleridge of *The Faerie Queene* (ed 1936:36) – and, insofar as dreaming is a means of escape from daylight cares, with leisure. Out of this line of identification, which Lamb shares with Hazlitt, Hunt, and Coleridge, comes the honey-tongued Spenser who creates 'phantasies' and is easily assimilated to the retrospective rhetoric of Lamb's most retrospective productions, the essays of his persona Elia. He opens one of the most nostalgic, 'The Old Benchers of the Inner Temple' (1821), by using the eighth stanza of *Prothalamion* to tie his own past, as a child born and raised in the Temple, in a triple knot to the city's past and to the poetry of the past – 'There whylome wont the Templer knights to bide' (Lamb and Lamb ed 1903–5, 2:82). When Elia's subject is woven from strands of childhood memory, night, and dream, as in 'Witches, and Other Night-Fears' (1821), no poet can bind the fabric of association better than Spenser: 'What stops the Fiend in Spenser from tearing Guyon to pieces ... we have no guess. We do not know the laws of that country' (2:65–6). The country is of course dreamland – 'What dreams must not Spenser have had!' (2:354n) – and its laws are mental laws for mental space: 'we have absolutely no place at all, for the things and persons of the Fairy Queen prate not of their "whereabout." But in their inner nature ... we are at home' ('Sanity of True Genius' [1826]; 2:188–9).

If the story is stopped here, as it generally is, then the creation of the sweet and dreamy nineteenth-century Spenser, though coherent, seems entirely unmotivated. Motivation is supplied, however, by the dangers of poetry and the perceived failure of allegory. The dangers emerge in the very imagery that seems to make *The Faerie Queene* safe for children. The airy-fairy Spenser is distilled from only one side of the logic of association, while complications seep from the other side. Freeing the dream, for instance, reveals a connection with enchantment and delusion. Freeing the female reveals the adult sensuality hidden in the maiden, as her honey-tongued sweetness matures into license and luxury.

These dangers have been the perennial concern of the most significant negative tradition of Spenser criticism, which Lamb's generation lodges in the palpable undercurrent of suspicion flowing from the unstable metaphors of Coleridge, Hazlitt, and, despite his escapism, Hunt. The most reliable critical stabilizer, well illustrated by John Hughes' essay on Spenser (prefixed to Spenser ed 1715), had always been the 'two senses' of allegory, a critical category long regarded as sufficiently powerful to contain the excesses of imagination in a balanced economy of sense translated into thought. But for the early Romantic generation, allegory had lost much of its remedial power to increasing fears of abstraction or of the senses, both, curiously, involved with the supposed tyranny of the eye. As either didactic child's poet or enchanting optical despot, Spenser cannot win. 'What to do with the allegory?' becomes a standard question in Spenser criticism. The first and perhaps most memorable in a nineteenth-century series of snappy responses, Hazlitt's figure of the allegory as a 'painted dragon' that readers, like children, need not 'meddle with' (ed 1930–4, 5:38), tellingly delivers child's play and adult allure simultaneously.

Lamb could hardly have avoided these issues, and his Spenser, which shores up an old foundation with new elements, is certainly created with them in mind. The metaphor that best focuses his conception is the venerable figure of *The Faerie Queene* as dream, traditionally two-sided: dream as the threshold of escapist fantasy, associated with romance, and dream as the threshold of deep truth, associated with allegory. Both retreat from everyday waking states of mind, but only the second insists on bringing the dream back into everyday life. Filtering the first through the second is so conventional a way of making romance respectable that romance and allegory have often seemed synonymous. Lamb, like his contemporaries, makes an almost automatic connection between nighttime dream and Spenserian 'dream,' or allegorical romance. His case for Spenser is based on the link between dream and a deeper reality. His most significant remarks occur in the Elian essay on the 'Sanity of True Genius,' which briefly develops the familiar paradox that dreams are more real than reality (ed 1903–5, 2:188–9). Here, the apparent madness of a great poet, manifested as the retreat to a dream world instanced by the house of Mammon episode, is 'hidden sanity,' while the apparent quotidian sanity of a modern novelist (William Lane, d 1814) is manifested outwardly as naturalism that cannot stand the test of coherence: 'The one turns life into a dream; the other to the wildest dreams gives the sobrieties of every day occurrences.'

The key to Lamb's position is the implicit identification of dream with mind, on the strength of which he can claim that Spenser reveals 'inner nature' by a 'subtile art of tracing the mental processes.' The similarity between an actual dream and a dreamlike episode in Spenser is that 'the transitions ... are every whit as violent'; the difference is that, in Spenser, 'the waking judgment ratifies them.' The deep truths revealed in Spenserian dreams refer to the internal rather than the external world, and they seem to be revealed more in plot, whose apparent external incoherence is really a psychological coherence, than in character (Lamb slides over allegorical characters such as 'the Money God' and his 'daughter, Ambition' as if they were Lord Glendamour and Miss Rivers). Spenser's allegory presumably represents the 'waking judgment' that 'ratifies' its dreamlike plot, giving the reader access to the public ethical significance of private psychological truths. Lamb is modern – and Romantic, if Romanticism characteristically substitutes psychological for religious explanations – in his emphasis on the internal rather than external truth of dreaming. He is traditional and even conservative in his plain faith in allegory.

Allegory was a stock target for attacks on moralizing poetry, and those persistent nineteenth-century attempts to certify a deallegorized *Faerie Queene* that would supply instruction-free pleasure can be partly explained as attempts to remove Spenser from the line of fire. Lamb, however, is strongly committed to the moral efficacy of literature – 'no book can have too much of SILENT SCRIPTURE in it' (to Bernard Barton, 23 Jan 1824; ed 1935, 2:415). Although he is equally averse to undramatized morality, he expresses no reservations about the effectiveness of allegory as a strategy for putting morality where it ought to be in a poem, 'wrought into the body and soul, the matter and tendency' (to Southey, 15 Mar 1799; ed 1975–8, 1:163). In this respect, his appreciation of Spenser is of a piece with his better-known appreciation of Hogarth. As a critic of Spenser, Lamb belongs in the line that runs through John Hughes and Edward Dowden ('Spenser, the Poet and Teacher' 1882, rpt in Dowden 1888: 269–304), readers who would recover Spenser's poetry for the purposes of real life by accepting the traditional estimation of the power and function of allegory.

MORRIS EAVES

Coleridge ed 1936; Leigh Hunt 1833 'A New Gallery of Pictures: Spenser, the Poet of the Painters' *New Monthly Magazine* ns 38:161–77; Charles Lamb and Mary Lamb 1903–5 *Works* ed E.V. Lucas, 7 vols (London); Lamb and Lamb ed 1935; Lamb and Lamb 1975–8 *Letters* ed Edwin W. Marrs, Jr, 3 vols (Ithaca, NY; must be supplemented by ed 1935 for letters after 1817); Walter Wilson 1934–5 'Some Recollections of the Late Charles Lamb. By One Who Knew Him Well' ed E.V. Lucas *London Mercury* 31:146–51.

Winifred F. Courtney 1982 *Young Charles Lamb 1775–1802* (London) discusses in passing Lamb's earlier interest in Spenser; J. Milton French 1933 'Lamb and Spenser' *SP* 30:205–7 gives minor additions to Hard 1931, who responds in *SP* 30:533–4; Frederick Hard 1931 'Lamb on Spenser' *SP* 28:656–70 compiles Lamb's significant references to Spenser.

Langland, William Alone of major poems in English, Langland's *Piers Plowman* afforded Spenser the model of a Christian allegory in narrative verse that is at once encyclopedic, exploratory, satiric, and visionary. Written in the 1370s and 1380s, Langland's profoundly searching and original poem had strong ripple effects – as prophecy, satire, and allegory – during the reigns of the Tudors. In 1550, Robert Crowley, a Protestant printer living in London, published in slightly modernized form three editions of the B-text of *Piers Plowman*, based on at least two different manuscripts; and in 1561, Owen Rogers issued a reprint of Crowley's final edition. These four printings made the poem readily accessible to Spenser and his contemporaries.

As analogue, precursor, and source, *Piers Plowman* is relevant both to Spenser's early poetic manifesto, *The Shepheardes Calender*, and to his fullest achievement, *The Faerie Queene*. In *Maye*, the name and character of Piers as good shepherd (ie, good parson) come from Langland's poem. More generally in *The Shepheardes Calender*, Spenser's intermittent use of the alliterative long line (*aaax*), his frequent deployment of persistent alliteration, his vigorously plainspoken moral satire, and his homely archaisms suggest both Langland's *Piers* and other works, like the late fourteenth-century *Plowman's Tale*, which derive from Langland's. In manner and matter, the *Calender* thus invokes the *Piers* tradition, Langland's legacy to the 'English Poete' (the title, presumably, of Spenser's lost discussion of poetry). The argument to *October* mentions this lost work explicitly, and the eclogue itself posits in a character named Piers the admonition, encouragement, and inspiration of Cuddie, in whom Spenser represents 'the perfecte paterne of a Poete' for his own time. The only Piers in literature who qualifies perfectly for this role is Langland's.

In the envoy to *The Shepheardes Calender*, Spenser refers to the two English poets whose steps he follows from afar – first Chaucer (Tityrus) and second 'the Pilgrim that the Ploughman playde a whyle.' The Pilgrim-Ploughman poet is Langland. (While there is also evidence in *SC* to suggest Spenser's knowledge of *The Plowman's Tale*, this work is a most unlikely referent for the Pilgrim-Ploughman, since sixteenth-century editions generally attributed it to Chaucer: Spenser specifies two poets as his precursors, and both cannot be Chaucer.) Although recently there has been general agreement that Langland is the second poet to whom Spenser refers at the end of the *Calender*, less agreement exists about the meaning of the line in which this reference occurs. Different explanations of how the line applies to *Piers* are tenable because the subject and object of the verb *playde* (performed, acted) are interchangeable syntactically. What matters, however, is that all possible readings of the line make sense as references to the author of *Piers Plowman*.

The most complex relationship between Spenser's poetry and *Piers Plowman* pertains to *The Faerie Queene* and ranges from an occasional verbal echo or explicit allusion to fundamental and far-reaching similarities in technique and conception. Langland's Lady Meed, for example, is 'Purfiled with Pelure, the fineste upon erthe,' and her robe is 'ful riche, of reed scarlet engreyned / With Ribanes of reed gold and of riche stones' (2.9, 15–16); Spenser's Duessa is 'clad in scarlot red, / Purfled with gold and pearle of rich assay' (1 ii 13). The archetype behind both women is the Whore of Babylon (Rev 17.4); but direct influence is indicated by the word *purfled* and the combination of *scarlet* (rich cloth) with *red* in both descriptions, neither of which is to be found in the Bibles Spenser is likely to have used. Similarly unbiblical is Duessa's headdress, a tiara 'with crownes and owches garnished'; it recalls suggestively the description of Meed, who is illicitly but emphatically 'Ycorouned with a coroune' (2.10). In *FQ* v, Lady Munera reincarnates Langland's Lady Meed yet again. *Munera* is merely a Latin form of *meed*, and Munera's 'golden hands' (ii 10) recall Meed's 'fyngres ... fretted *with* gold wyr' (2.11).

The most striking of Spenser's direct allusions to *Piers Plowman* occurs in Redcrosse's moment of self-recognition and discovery – self-recovery, to be exact – on the Mount of Contemplation in *FQ* I. Here Redcrosse learns that as a child he was stolen from '*Britane* land' (x 65) and transported to Fairyland, where he was found by a plowman in the furrow of a field and brought up in plowman's state until his own aspirations led him to Fairy court. Infolded in this allusion is a Spenserian myth of origins that includes Spenser's own origin as an English poet, and in it he again acknowledges the debt to *Piers Plowman* that underlies and informs his own courtly epic.

The deepest and most pervasive relations between *Piers* and *The Faerie Queene* involve the history of ideas and the literary history of allegory. The two poems feature remarkably similar treatments of the individual's efforts to reenact the historical Redemption in himself and in society, of the selfish greed and corrupting materialism that Mammon embodies, of the distance between received truth and earned understanding and the compelling quest to possess true wholeness, of the imagination's role in this quest, of the observable conflict between the complementary virtues of justice and courtesy, of the opposed realities of contemporary politics and poetic vision, and finally and movingly, of the poet's own presence in his poem. Held behind *The Faerie Queene* – 200 years behind it – and viewed with something approaching Spenser's historical imagination, *Piers Plowman* becomes a conceptual grid for Spenser's massive poem.

A host of more specific ties connects the two poems: for example, resemblances between Langland's Lady Holy Church and Spenser's Una and Contemplation, between 'Mede the mayde' (2.20) and the 'mayden Queene' Lucifera (1 iv 8), between envy and detraction throughout *Piers* and their quintessence in *The Faerie Queene*, the Blatant Beast; between the recurrent concerns in both poems with the creative and destructive powers of language; and between Piers and Arthur as symbols that evolve throughout the poems – symbols specially associated with divine grace and at times alluding specifically to Christ. Like Langland's use of the traditional dream vision, moreover, Spenser's is distinctive. Among medieval dream poems, a series of dreams, laced with inner dreams and with periodic waking intervals, is peculiar only to *Piers*. This structure not only influences directly Spenser's treatment of Redcrosse's dreaming in *FQ* I but also influences less directly other dreamlike qualities of the poem and the nature of the poet's presence in it, in particular his tendency to participate in – even to appear within – his characters' experiences.

Projection allegory – the representation of one character's state of mind or of an aspect of his identity in a second character – is also a striking feature of both poems and, as employed therein, another distinctive connection between them. When Langland's Dreamer meets Thought (8.70ff), for example, he finds his own thinking in a character who looks just like him and has been following him around for seven years; similarly, when Redcrosse meets Despair, he confronts a mirror image of the figure Arthur has rescued from Orgoglio's dungeon, that is, an image of himself. Sophisticated projection allegory in both poems extends to the merging of characters with other, less abstract, less simply personified ones (eg, of Hawkin or Piers with Will, Sansjoy with Redcrosse, Cymochles and Pyrochles with Guyon, or Colin with the poet of *FQ*), and it can include such highly distinctive details as the use of ambiguous, double pronominal referents to effect the merger.

Dialogue, essentially in the form of debate, to achieve through multiple perspectives evolving definitions of concepts, identities, or conditions, constitutes another major allegorical technique present distinctively in both poems. *Piers Plowman* is full of such debates, of which the exchange between Holy Church and the Dreamer affords a typical analogue to numerous debates in *The Faerie Queene*, such as those between Redcrosse and Despair or Contemplation, between Duessa and Night, between Guyon and the Palmer or Mammon, between Britomart and Glauce, between Calidore and Meliboe. A corollary to formal debating in both poems is the virtually continuous redefinition of key terms, such as nature and life.

Allegory, as it functions in these poems, is a distinctive habit of mind and a continuing process of reassessment. Above all it is a process organic to meaning. Definitively in both poems, it is a direct way of conceiving and conceptualizing reality.

JUDITH H. ANDERSON

William Langland 1975 *Piers Plowman: The B Version* ed George Kane and E. Talbot Donaldson (London). The Kane-Donaldson edition gives the variants for all three of Crowley's editions. Citations in the preceding article combine the Kane-Donaldson text with the readings of Crowley's third edition. Medieval þ in Kane-Donaldson has been modernized to *th*, and initial *v* to *u*.

Anderson 1976; William R. Crawford 1957 'Robert Crowley's Editions of *Piers Plowman*: A Bibliographical and Textual Study' diss Yale Univ; Greenlaw 1911; Hamilton 1961b; Barbara A. Johnson 1982 'From *Piers Plowman* to *Pilgrim's Progress*: The Generic and Exegetical Contexts of Bunyan's "Similitude of a Dream"' diss Brown Univ; King 1982; Miskimin 1975; Reid 1981b.

language, general, and resources exploited in rhyme (See also related articles on *archaism, *dialect, *etymology, *morphology and syntax, *names, *neologism, *pronunciation, *rhyme, and *versification.) Spenser is one of the most diverse, as well as prolific, of poets – a man to whose artistry in language almost universal tribute is paid, but whose language has received practically no attention during the last thirty years, when items for the Spenser bibliography have been pouring off the presses at an average rate of three a week. There is a long tradition of comment on certain linguistic eccentricities, especially in *The Shepheardes Calender*, and this preoccupation with selected aspects of his usage, especially diction, and notably archaism, dialect forms, loans, and inventions is a modern reflex of the almost contemporary view held by Jonson that he 'writ no Language.' There is also a tradition of exegesis, this, too, contemporary in origin. Systematic analysis, even a systematic attempt to relate his usage to the norms of his contemporaries, is wholly lacking. The reader of Spenser should approach the text as being in Spenser's language, which is a very different matter from reading him as if he were writing modern English with intermittent lapses into strange expressions which require glossing. The medium he forged is seen mature, and at length, in *The Faerie Queene*. If we hope to achieve even a provisional basis for generalization, we should start with that, and consider in a secondary way the more experimental forms he tried out and abandoned. Since the work is far too long for systematic analysis of the whole to be attempted, the most practical course is to undertake detailed study of a short sample: *FQ* I proem and canto i, a total of 59 stanzas, 531 lines, about 5000 words, consisting of two contrasted types of language use, which may be distinguished as invocation and narrative.

Since for those works which appeared more than once in Spenser's lifetime we do not know the measure of his control of textual detail, it does not seem profitable to lay too great stress on the sort of variable that might be due to the printer, or to worry too much about the choice of edition on which statistical tables are to be based (the figures in such tables must for other reasons be interpreted as approximate). Full textual details are available in the *Variorum* edition, which has been consulted on all points at issue; but of carefully edited single texts it is likely that the most widely current is that edited by J.C. Smith in 1909, which was incorporated in Spenser ed 1912 and taken as textual basis of *FQ* ed 1977.

We begin then with the media of transmission, realized in a printed text whose relationship to Spenser's intentions we cannot determine, and a phonological form we have to reconstruct from internal and external evidence. What can be said of the spelling and punctuation is said with conviction about the printer's practice, though they have a consistency of function, and an organic relationship to phonological patterning, that make it, at first sight, plausible that Spenser exercised considerable influence. Whatever can be reconstructed of the pronunciation of the past comes to us through the evidence of the written medium. That Elizabethan English differs from modern English in the repertoire of letters, their distribution, the degree of orthographic regularity, and the punctuation is obvious to any reader, and this is not the place for a systematic study. How much we can know of Spenser's personal usage is hard to say. There is clear evidence of an input from the printer to the spelling and punctuation as we know them. On the other hand, there are some signs of a Spenserian policy both in choosing among concurrent variants, and in adopting forms outside the range of normal Elizabethan usage. Most evident in Spenser's poetry is his concern for sound patterning, not only in his complex and varied metrical structures, but in the incidental features of alliteration, assonance, and sound symbolism. Related to this is his fondness for choosing or inventing spellings most suggestive of the sound structure (including the choice between alliterative pronunciations) of a particular passage. Thus, in rhyme with such words as *rest* and *best*, *breast* tends to appear as *brest*; and in rhyme with *red* and *garnished*, *head* and *overspread* tend to appear as *hed* and *overspred*, in contrast to where, in rhyme with *dead*, the *head* spelling appears. Likewise, with *Sarazin*, *been* will appear as *bin*, but with *greene* and *seene* as *beene*.

Spenser clearly liked rhyme forms to be visually matched even where pronunciation was not at issue; the inflection *-(e)s*, for instance, where it has no syllabic value, tends to appear either in adjacent rhyme words with *-e-* exclusively (*plaines/vaines/paines*), or, in other such adjacent words, exclusively without (*arts/imparts/harts/smarts*). Where words have longer or shorter forms, he prefers rhymes to make a consistent choice, even if one of the elements has to have an invented spelling and no difference in pronunciation is involved (*pas* [v]/*gras/was/has*, *lesse/wildernesse/blesse/distresse*). Distortion can go quite a long way, as when *told* is spelled *tould* to rhyme with *would*, which would sound like it only if an archaic pronunciation were revived (for the normal form, cf *hold/manifold/told/behold*).

What next concerns us is the rhythmical and metrical patterning of the spoken and written forms in the stanza he invented – a metrical form of exceptional difficulty in execution, and probably the most brilliantly original exploitation of the inherent possibilities of the language in the history of English versification.

In looking at Spenser's metrical technique, I shall confine myself to *The Faerie Queene*, so it is specifically the Spenserian stanza that concerns me. I shall concentrate on rhymes and look briefly at how the rhyme words get into the right places; I shall confine myself to masculine rhymes, since feminine ones (which in any case are rare) complicate the issue without in most cases adding any new light. It is hardly surprising that the qualities for which Spenser has been most admired have changed from century to century. But unwavering is the praise of his mellifluousness, his metrical inventiveness, ingenuity, and sustained facility. Yet there is a dearth of analyses of the technical demands made upon him, and of his precise methods of solving the problems he posed for himself. Commentators single out particular local effects for explanation and praise; historians of the language use his lines as evidence both of current pronunciation and of the existence of both spelling- and eye-rhymes. What I have not found anywhere is a careful look at what was involved in writing the longest poem in the language in an apparently demanding metrical form and a particularly difficult rhyme scheme, and in doing it in sixteenth-century English. Despite local attention to forms that were different then, the sense of wonder at his achievement is, I suspect, based on intuitions about what it would be like to achieve this feat now. There isn't even an account why, with all due respect to Pope, most readers find that the Spenserian stanza works, rhythmically and metrically, for them, though on all conventional patterns of metrical analysis it shouldn't.

The Spenserian stanza is a nine-line unit, the first eight lines being decasyllables, followed by an alexandrine, and linked by rhyme on the scheme *ababbcbcC*. Feminine rhymes, of which there is only one in the first three books, occur rather more often in the last three. The stanza uses lines of sharply marked identity, though there are instances of enjambment, even between stanzas. The rhyme scheme calls for a two-term (the two *a*'s in the scheme above), a four-term (4 × *b*), and a three-term (3 × *c*) rhyme pattern in every stanza. At only two points do these patterns constitute what in another context would be a couplet: between lines 4 and 5 where they help to prevent the eight decasyllabic lines splitting into two quatrains, and between lines 8 and 9, where they support the integration of the alexandrine with the decasyllabic lines in a unitary stanza.

Now, what characteristic resources and constraints did Spenser's English afford for the completion of his metrical task? I begin by asking questions about the repertoire of syllable-codas available to Spenser to form rhyme schemes: what did it consist of, how does it compare with that of modern English, and how fully did he exploit it so as to diversify his sound patterning? It is most convenient to start from present-day English, both because we know more about it, and because what we don't know about it may put our areas of ignorance about Spenser's English into perspective. I will accept Gimson's tabulation of present-day English syllable-codas (Gimson 1962). The most complex class of syllable-codas is those of -VCCCC structure (where - = preceding letters, V = one vowel, and C = one consonant), used only where an inflection is added to a base ending in a triconsonantal structure, as in *exempts* or *glimpsed*. Gimson does not list them, but I think there are about twenty; each type is realized in very few words, often only in one, which rules it out as an element in rhyme. Spenserian English was considerably richer in them, largely because of the survival of post-vocalic /r/, but Spenser never uses them in rhyme, and henceforth I shall leave them out of account. Even this negative point, however, may have the function of suggesting that he disliked them.

Next come the -VCCC structures, where we can speak rather more realistically of what is possible and what is done. Of these, on Gimson's analysis, the phonotactics of present-day English permit 912 in stressed syllables, of which 177 (about 19 percent) are used. Of these, 11 are marginal to the vocabulary, or stylistically improbable in poetry, or phonologically unique so that they cannot enter into rhyme schemes, or even all three. We might guess that not many over 155 (about 17 percent) belong to the real field of candidates for rhyming. I cannot begin to estimate how many billion words of running text, on various subjects, and in various styles, would be required to ensure that even 155 turned up.

The composition of Spenser's repertoire of stressed -VCCC syllable codas cannot be determined so precisely at that of modern English, if only because we do not know the limits of his lexicon with such precision, let alone the limits of the vocabulary suitable to his subject. Nor indeed can we fix exact limits to the possibilities and constraints of his phonotactics. Clearly, however, the repertoire would be different in total and in composition. He probably would have been working with a system of 13 stressed-syllable vowels (as against Gimson's 19), but all of them would have been able to precede clusters starting in /ŋ/ /nk/ and /r/ (for characters like these in the International Phonetic Alphabet, see introductory material in almost any standard English-foreign language dictionary), and the bisegmental status of /ŋg/ would make many of his clusters triconsonantal which for us are only -VCC. An educated guess is that there might have been about 250 realized codas of this class available in his English, of which perhaps 220 would have been serious candidates for rhyming. Of this possible total, he utilizes in rhyme at most 29, and this small set has distinct characteristics. First, the patterns that are used are not particularly rare and for the most part recur quite often. Second, 26 of them involve inflections – the same inflections that occur in four-consonant terminal clusters today. The remaining three are all questionable in one way or another. One is apparently imperfect: *world* on one occasion rhymes with *extold* (I xi 27) and on another with *introld*, *hold* and *told* (II ii 44). There are, of course, Early Modern English pronunciations of *world* in which the final cluster is simplified, but none are known involving both loss of /r/ and preservation of the /o(:)/ value of the vowel. The rhyme may be imperfect, but the most likely explanation is that it is conventional; if so, only the non-matching part of it perhaps has a three-consonant cluster, and if not, none of it has. The second example is unique, and appears from the spelling to have triconsonantal /ɪŋkt/ though it almost certainly represents /ɪnt/: *Hyacinct*/*extinct* (III xi 37) [ɪ = sound of first vowel in *finny*]. Finally, for the elements in *length*/*strength* (I v 29), two-consonant terminations are recorded from the seventeenth century – /lɛnθ, strɛnθ/ – and one might suspect that they were already known in the sixteenth century. Much attention has been paid to Spenser's archaisms, which are superficial and limited; the essential character of his poetic language is its modernity. In many features, it is ahead of its time, and rhyme could well be one of them.

There is then no entirely convincing case in which Spenser uses a triconsonantal terminal cluster in rhyme unless the last element in it is an inflection. This again looks like aesthetic preference, the more so in that his language favored heavily consonantal terminations more than ours. Impressionistically, one might suggest that a consonant whose function is grammatical, and which does not contribute to the word in its lexical function, is somehow reduced in prominence. And one notes that in Spenser, the status of -VCCC codas corresponds to the status of -VCCCC codas in present-day English.

We come now to the main body of rhymes, which belongs to the remaining three types of coda, -VCC, -VC, -V. For these, in stressed position, present-day English as a whole affords the following figures:

	Phonotactically possible	Realized	Real field for rhyming
-VCC	1121	566 (50%)	c 520-50
-VC	418	265 (63%)	c 220-45
-V	13	13 (100%)	13

To calculate Spenser's possibilities we have to take account of differences additional to those already mentioned, such as absence of final /ŋ/ and /ʒ/. As an educated guess we might postulate a certain total of phonotactic possibilities, of which we can be fairly confident that a certain number are realized in rhyme. What we find in *The Faerie Queene* is a very low rate of -VCC, with very high rates of -VC and -V:

	Possible	Realized
-VCC	c 942	c 162 (c 17%)
-VC	c 246	c 143 (c 58%)
-V	8?	8 (100%)

Considering that the sample is so small – about 11,700 patterns and three times as many words – the remarkable figure is that for -VC realizations. We are never likely to know whether the ratio of realizations to possibilities was the same in the sixteenth century as now, but the current figure is the only guide we have, and Spenser's percentage of realizations in a small sample nearly matches that of all English today. This observation gives a quantified basis to the impression that Spenser is astonishingly varied in the rhyme patterns he uses, but it limits the property to two of the possible types of coda, -VC and -V. In fact there are in this category some codas which Spenser employs out of rhyme, but not in rhyme (such as /ɪb/ in *sybbe*; /ɪg/ in *big, dig*; /ɪʃ/ in *dish, fish, wish*), but this is only to be expected since the population of non-rhyming stressed syllables is over four times as large as the population of rhyming stressed syllables, and over twelve times as large as the number of masculine rhyme patterns. There are accidental gaps in the evidence, and some gaps are shown by *FQ* VII as in the case of /ɛk/ in the rhyme *beck/check/speake/reck* (vi 22); *speake* is probably imperfect, but late medieval shortening to /ɛ/ cannot be ruled out.

Closer inspection reveals a further difference between -VC and -VCC realizations. In the -VC group, there is a negligible difference in the rate of take-up between one-mora vowels (V_1) [mora: generally, a metrical time-unit equivalent to one unstressed, or short, syllable; here, a short vowel] and two-mora [ie, long] vowels (V_2): (-V_1C, 57/94 = c 60%; -V_2C, 86/152 = c 57%). In the -VCC group the difference is striking (-V_1CC, 95/368 = c 25%; V_2 CC, 68/574 = 12%). It is likely then, as now, that the language had a lower utilization rate in the two-mora category, and possible that properties of my reconstruction tend to distort the difference. But in addition, there seems to be at least a possibility that Spenser preferred to avoid such sequences in positions as prominent as rhyme. This impression is strengthened if we look at the composition of the 68 clusters. Of them, 51 commonly have their second consonant by virtue of the same two inflections as enter into the -VCCC codas, though occasional uninflected forms may enter into rhyme patterns involving the same codas. The other clusters (which may each co-occur with more than one vowel) reduce to types, seven of which (when combined with different vowels) match the clusters incorporating inflections (/nd, nt, ld, lt, ns, rs, st/). This leaves only the liquid clusters /rn/ and /lv/, and in the latter the /l/ is doubtful. Once again we may suspect an aesthetic preference: in rhyme codas, Spenser tends to avoid structures consisting of two-mora vowel plus two-consonant cluster, unless either the cluster is one which could incorporate an inflection, or its first element is a liquid.

To sum up: generally the English available to Spenser was more heavily consonantal in its terminations than ours, but his selection of forms for prominent positions suggests a preference for forms which deemphasize this property. His deployment of final -CCC clusters is like that of general present-day English for -CCCC clusters; his of -Vi2CC or derived clusters is largely the same. His favored patterns for morphemically simple words are -V, -VC, -VCC, but his capacity for variation is demonstrated by the fact that up to the end of Book VI one is still recording new patterns.

Naturally the proportion of codas used is only half the story, both as to range and as to preferences and constraints. Rather more than 300 codas are distributed over nearly 12,000 pattern occurrences, so the average rate of coda recurrence must be high; and since the distribution is uneven, some codas will be very frequent indeed. The other half of the story depends on the words in which the codas are realized, and we may ask two things: are these varied or repetitive? and do they clarify the hints we have found of preference for certain types of coda rather than others? In our sample analysis of Book I, proem and canto i, there are 80 repetitions of the same element in the same grammatical function – more than one in seven, and if we were to slacken the definition to 'the same word,' there would be many more. This seems a high proportion. It is, for instance, more than the rate for a corresponding sample from the opening of the *Canterbury Tales*, in which the subject matter is more varied, and where the rhyme elements do strike me as repetitive. Spenser's seeming variety, I suggest, results from the variation in location and grouping of rhyme words, in twos, fours, and threes, elaborately interwoven, rather than from their actually being varied.

Finally, I return to the question of how difficult it was for Spenser to achieve his metrical smoothness, given what seem to be self-imposed optional constraints. It has, of course, long been recognized – at least since de Sélincourt – that Spenser made maximum use of the variability permitted by good Elizabethan English. In our sample analysis, I made a count of the forms for which he had alternatives available: they are nearly one in ten, and in many cases he had several variants at his disposal, which enabled one and the same item to hook into different chains of rhyme words. Aesthetic preference apart, he ranged with extraordinary freedom over the rhyming potential the language afforded. Of course, he lived in a century which afforded a greater range of acceptable variant pronunciations in a single city than any before or since, and he made full use of this. Among the -V patterns, the numerous common words in *-y* or *-ly* could be /i:/ or /I/. In only 55 stanzas (I i), pattern 3 links *harmony* to *sky* and *dry*; *victorie* to *lye* (v); *Armorie* to *enimie*; *Yvory* to *lye* (v), *enemy*, and *quietly*; *die* to *destinie* and *indifferently*; *fly* (v) to *fantasy*, *privily*, and *sly* (and in -VC *flyes* to *applyes*, *enimies*, and *lyes*); but pattern 1 links *perplexitie* to *bee* ('are') and *free*. Many *-ea-* words may have /ɔ:/,/əi:/, or /ɛ/ and so hook into three different populations of rhyme words; the domain of quantitative variation is extremely wide. All of this is too well known to require extensive exemplification. While Spenser makes use of this variability, he doesn't cheat. For instance, words like *is*, *his*, *has*, *was*, in their normal unstressed uses were already subject to Verner's Law – that is, their final consonant was voiced. But when such a word occurs in a masculine rhyme it is necessarily stressed, and the voicing does not take place. In every case where the rest of the rhyme provides a check, Spenser uses the unvoiced form. Thus we find *amis* with *his*, *is*, and *kis* and *alas* with *was* – there are no counter-examples. I would suggest there is a quality in Spenser's exploitation of variability that nearly always protects it from the appearance of license or mere contrivance.

This quality derives from something far less formal than a theory of language; perhaps we could call it a context of assumptions – the atmosphere his actual use of language breathes. It is most nearly overt in two linked areas, etymology and name-giving, in which Spenser's implicit views have rather a Platonic coloring. Characteristically, names are bestowed or revealed by the poet as name-giver, and are offered to us both as the culmination of, and check upon, our full comprehension of the being who has been introduced to us. It is essential that names be correct, and that we know enough to recognize their rightness before they are revealed to us. To this extent, the language of poetry is not arbitrary. These correct names (whether grammatically they are nouns or adjectives) typically operate etymologically – that is, they derive their meaning from a source other than contemporary usage, namely from an original or supposed original meaning which will often be suggested by the form of the word. *Original* is not really the right word, for the importance of etymology to Spenser and his contemporaries did not lie in the chronological dimension; it was nearer to what a twentieth-century philosopher would call analysis, that is, a way of getting at the irreducible elements of meaning in such a manner as to provide a correct interpretation which, because it is correct, is unchanging.

Only recently has the pervasiveness of this conception in Spenser's use of names and epithets been identified, but I will give an example which has always been recognized. Though *faerie* has earlier meanings in English which were revived after Spenser, its normal early Elizabethan meaning was rather like the modern *fairy* except that the little creatures were more sinister and more powerful. But etymologically, faerie is the realm of certain supernatural females, the Fates; the fusion of divinity, destiny, and womanly dominion makes it a correct and revealing name, or, as we would more usually say, symbol or image, of Elizabethan England, not as a temporal kingdom but as an unchanging idea. In each case, the etymological meaning is the immutable essence; vagaries through time, in form or meaning, are mere accidents. In proportion as the poet's goal is the permanent in language, variable surface realizations are functionally a matter of indifference. Contemporary variation in the standard language, advanced, even slangy colloquialisms, dialect forms, and archaisms are all on a par. To Jonson, this meant that Spenser writ no language, and in a surface sense this is undeniably true. But it is not a relevant sense. Spenser's exploitation of variation gives him great license, but the sympathetic reader does not perceive him as taking liberties or the easy way out because his freedom is in accord with a deep, pervasive, and coherent intuition about the nature of poetic language – at least for poetry of this kind. Comparison is often made with *The Shepheardes Calender*, where the linguistic eccentricities are not only more numerous and more extreme, but different in kind because they are different, more superficial, in function. The apt comparison is with Spenser's prose. There you see what language he writes when his object is to deal with matters of contemporary concern: classically correct sixteenth-century English. In *The Faerie Queene*, he is the poet of universal grammar, and he keeps constantly before the reader, who is also the hearer, the accidentalness of any surface structure chosen as the realization of the underlying forms.

BARBARA M.H. STRANG

Professor Strang had planned to contribute an article on 'Spenser and the English Language' that would treat in a unitive manner the separate topics of diction (sources, deployment, varying characteristics in different poems, preferred and foregrounded elements, relationship, and diction in *The Shepheardes Calender* especially with reference to E.K.'s comments); grammar (both morphology and syntax); spelling; pronunciation; prosody (rhythm and meter); and style. The drafts of what she had written on Spenser's exploitation of the reservoir of language for his rhymes were organized by Margaret Cooper at the University of Newcastle. A lengthy account of the general character of verse and prose meter has been omitted very reluctantly because it would have made sense only if the original scope of the article had been fulfilled.

Latin literature Latin was the commanding father tongue of the Renaissance, presiding over the vernacular mother tongues with the austere voice of distant authority. It had been the language of the Roman Empire, the older unity out of whose provinces and dialects the nations and languages of Western Europe had developed separately during the Middle Ages. Against this diversification, the church had preserved a sense of Europe's corporate identity, and had continued to do its business in Latin as the natural medium of such an identity. Much of the effort of Renaissance humanism was devoted to reaffirming that identity by strengthening that medium: restoring Latin to its classical norms, reasserting its associations with Roman civilization, and broadening its use by placing it at the center of an international program of educational reform.

So important was Latin's role in that program that even within the specialized field of classical scholarship Greek made relatively little headway; the most sophisticated classicists still saw antiquity largely through Roman lenses. The success of the humanist effort ensured that almost every Renaissance literary career, of whatever kind and in whatever language, began with an early encounter with Latin and its unique status. Not a dead language, since it was written and even spoken by all educated men, it was no one's native language either. Acquired by discipline and study amid the rigors of the schoolroom, it was preeminently the serious language, setting a standard of impersonal linguistic dignity and durability to which the vernaculars could only aspire.

Literary ambition of the time was often shaped by its dominance. Many writers chose Latin for their own mature careers; the substantial body of what is known as Neo-Latin literature is one of the significant features of the Renaissance landscape. Even for writers who returned to their native languages, the literature of classical Rome retained a privileged position. Contemporary literary theory was dominated by a concern with classical imitation, the means by which modern literature might be raised to the level of Latin precedent; and learning to read Renaissance literature involves learning to read the signals of that effort.

For instance, the opening lines of *The Faerie Queene* – 'Lo I the man, whose Muse whilome did maske, / As time her taught, in lowly Shepheards weeds' – are evidence that Spenser had read the reputed opening of the *Aeneid*: 'Ille ego qui quondam gracili modulatus avena / carmen.' They are also, for those who catch the allusion, a comparison of his career to Virgil's in order both to appropriate some of Virgil's prestige and to set himself a mark to reach; further, this is an announcement that the poem to follow is to be considered an epic, serving in English (the author hopes) something like the same purpose that the *Aeneid* serves in Latin. Subsequent intersections between Virgil's text and Spenser's evoke the same frame of reference, sometimes in complex ways. Virgil's comparison of the triumphant Cybele to Rome (*Aeneid* 6.784–7) was imitated by du Bellay in a poem about Rome's fall which Spenser translated (*Ruines of Rome* 6); both the Latin and the translated French seem to have been on Spenser's mind later when he compared Cybele's crown to Troynovant or London (*FQ* IV xi 28). But the *Aeneid* itself is about Rome as a 'new Troy,' about historical ruin repaired by a *translatio imperii*, a transfer of authority from one site to another; and the poem in which Spenser quotes Virgil is part of his effort to repair in a similar way the damage that du Bellay describes, to reestablish Roman dignity by English effort. Using classical texts this way to define and validate their own aspirations was almost second nature to Renaissance poets.

Nevertheless, the vitality of Renaissance classicism owes much to the unexpected lightness with which the paternal authority of the Roman heritage could be borne; by more severely neoclassical standards, Renaissance practice – and especially Spenser's – is often deceptive and irresponsible. Although *The Faerie Queene* begins with an implicit promise to be a Virgilian epic or heroic poem, it follows few of the overt rules of that genre. By the middle of its first stanza, Spenser has slipped out of the world of Virgil's *Aeneid* into that of Ariosto's *Orlando furioso*. His pledge to 'sing of Knights and Ladies gentle deeds' savors far less of Latin precedent ('arma virumque cano') than of Italian: 'Le donne, i cavallier, l'arme, gli amori, / Le cortesie, l'audaci imprese io canto' (*OF* 1.1). Spenser's poem as it proceeds bears a far more obvious resemblance to Ariosto's digressive *romanzo* and the vernacular medieval traditions of romance behind it than to any classical model. Major critical battles were fought in the Renaissance over the right of such a poem as Ariosto's to be called epic; but Spenser's practice seems characterized by the absence of any real sense of incongruity in what he is doing. Quoting Virgil in his opening lines is a significant homage as far as it goes, but it is not a long-term commitment.

Such untroubled mixing of classical and nonclassical elements is made easy, and almost inevitable, by the general practice of classical imitation in the Renaissance, which did much to detach specific quotations from the control of their original contexts. Not the least important part of imitation was the systematic excerpting of particular moments from ancient authors for separate display in commonplace books, rhetorical manuals, mythological compendiums, dictionaries, and similar reference books: by this route rather than being read in the original works Latin literature often found its way into contemporary writing. From such entry, particular *topoi* were capable of spreading so promiscuously that it can be impossible to be sure what a particular author had actually read. For instance, a modern researcher may think he has found Spenser's imitation of Catullus 7 in 'More eath to number, with how many eyes / High heaven beholds sad lovers nightly theeveryes' (*FQ* III xi 45): 'aut quam sidera multa, cum tacet nox, / furtivos hominum vident amores'; but he has probably turned up Spenser's imitation of Ariosto's imitation: 'e per quanti occhi il ciel le furtive opre / degli amatori a mezza notte scuopre' (*OF* 14.99). Here no evidence suggests a conscious or meaningful triangulation such as that with Virgil and du Bellay. The quotation has lost any felt status as a classical quotation; it has become part of an anonymous rhetorical repertoire of sentiments and turns of phrase on which a writer could draw for any number of unrelated purposes. Classical literature, so assimilated, combined with all other manner of possibilities; and amid the particularly wide range of materials with which Spenser worked – chivalric, biblical, historical – it quickly lost its privileged standing.

Even when Spenser wrote more closely within the confines of an identifiably classical genre, he was as likely to be following the modifications of later imitation as to be attending to the ancient exemplar. *The Shepheardes Calender* resembles Virgil's *Eclogues* somewhat more securely than *The Faerie Queene* resembles the *Aeneid*; but for the conception and details of his individual months, Spenser looked to the more recent models available in Neo-Latin and French pastoral, which are not merely conduits for their own classical sources. Mantuan, for instance, despite his name and a reputation as the 'second Virgil,' helped give Renaissance pastoral an ethical and satirical edge barely hinted at in Virgil, but one that Spenser found very much to his own purposes. On the other hand, generic watchfulness did not prevent the spirit of classical pastoral from invading other traditions. For his *Epithalamion*, Spenser went back to the prime representative of the classical marriage hymn in Catullus (61, with 62 and 64); but what many readers find most memorable in Spenser's poem is the evocation of an extravagant, natural, and even cosmic sympathy not to be found in the original: 'And hearken to the birds lovelearned song, / The deawy leaves among. / For they of joy and pleasance to you sing, / That all the woods them answer and theyr eccho ring' (88–91). Again, Spenser's cues are to be sought in exercises closer to home: 'Let mother earth now decke her selfe in flowers, / To see her ofspring seeke a good increase' (Sidney ed 1962:91, after Gaspar Gil Polo). The classical tradition in which Spenser can be placed is not one of definitive models and rules, but one of continuing experiment and change.

That disposition is perhaps unknowingly evident in Spenser's classical reading list itself, which includes a fair number of writers who do not exemplify the authoritative spirit of their language. Continental theory had already recognized that a significant narrowing of the classical canon was necessary to isolate and preserve that spirit, and had specified Cicero and Virgil as the preeminent, even exclusive, models for imitation. Subsequent neoclassicism would articulate a fuller theory of a golden age of Latin literature from which later works manifest a decline. Spenser's own reading included a generous share of Cicero and Virgil; but no theory of literary history seems to have constrained him to pay comparable attention to the other great practitioners of Augustan decorum like Livy and Horace, or to suppress an evident inclination for the more luxuriant and hyperbolic style of such later writers as Statius and Claudian (both of whom figure, for instance, in the epithalamic tradition). Some of Spenser's most significant mythological figures – Genius, Nature, Cupid, and Psyche – have their ultimate sources in the later antique milieu, where classical literature often verges on medieval allegory; and much of his sense of earlier Latin literature was filtered through the late antique sensibility of such commentators as Servius and Macrobius. Even the *Culex* and the *Ciris*, which he surely believed were by Virgil, and which are the Virgilian poems he imitated most closely and extensively (the former is expanded into *Virgils Gnat*, the latter supplies the model for *FQ* III ii 30–51), are almost certainly post-Virgilian, and are now treated by scholars as early specimens of the decadence. Some of Spenser's natural affinities are with the margins of the classical tradition.

Ovid, the most subtly marginal of these figures, provides points of reference around which some of the most complex tensions in *The Faerie Queene* are organized. He falls loosely under the rubric of golden-age Latin; but his gamesome and elusive facility is something different from Virgilian epic momentousness, and an aura of official disrepute as the poet of sexual license clings to his career. Yet he was in practice *the* classical poet for Elizabethans, and for Spenser no less than for his contemporaries; any census shows notably more Ovidian than Virgilian moments in his works. What is alluded to in the process, though, tends to be not, as with Virgil, an authoritative cultural value, but a source of danger to the moral order. Ovid, for instance, provides the standard catalogue of the gaudy metamorphic lusts of the pagan gods (*Metamorphoses* 6.103–28); Spenser virtually translates this passage in *Muiopotmos* 277–99, and uses it as the basis for the tapestries that Britomart sees in the house of Busirane (*FQ* III xi 29–46). The antique world in those tapestries provides some of the most violent yet enticing images of the sexual energies which threaten chastity, and which Britomart must learn both to confront and to master.

More generally, all the heroes in *The Faerie Queene* must confront and master the tumultuous mutability which challenges any sense of purpose and personal identity, even of reality itself, and which is also the titular theme of Ovid's *Metamorphoses*. At moments, the central visions of the two works can seem very close: 'Nec species sua cuique manet, rerumque novatrix / ex aliis alias reparat natura figuras: / nec perit in toto quicquam, mihi credite, mundo, / sed variat faciemque novat' (*Met* 15.252–5): 'That substance is eterne, and bideth so, / Ne when the life decayes, and forme does fade, / Doth it consume, and into nothing go, / But chaunged is, and often altred to and fro' (*FQ* III vi 37). The spectacle of constant change is more disturbing to Spenser than to Ovid, however, and the search for a definitive still point in the flux is far more urgent and complex in *The Faerie Queene* than in the *Metamorphoses*. A major effort of Spenser's poem is the attempt to bring the anarchic instability of which Ovid sings under the control of a firmer sense of moral direction; and the last section of his poem, the *Cantos of Mutabilitie*, makes unusually dense use of Ovidian material to articulate the most acute crisis of that effort. A certain ambiguity in the final resolution further witnesses an engagement with Ovid appreciably deeper and more serious than that with Virgil precisely because it is more unsettled.

One of the components of that unsettlement is a suspicion of Ovid's own cultural pedigree: all worldly authority is more vulnerable than it thinks, including the authority of the Latin language. Ultimately Spenser's work may illustrate the special place of that language in Renaissance literature less well than it does the contrary possibility of the submergence of Latin's prestige in the different authority that could be asserted by the vernacular. Humanist Latin in England never achieved the dominance that it did in continental culture; among the major Western European countries, England suffered the least significant break with her vernacular medieval past. Spenser's own Latin training at Merchant Taylors' School was under Mulcaster, distinguished among humanist educational theorists for his concern with the importance and dignity of English in its unregulated native vitality. Throughout his career, Spenser's sense of his vernacular heritage remained at least as strong as that of his classical heritage: Chaucer remained as magic a presence as Virgil, and the archaisms with which Spenser seasoned his diction are more Anglo-Saxon than Latinate. In no other Renaissance poem of comparable ambition is the classical background less prominent, more thoroughly mixed with native elements, than in *The Faerie Queene*. Indeed, a settling of linguistic family politics to the unusual advantage of the mother tongue is perhaps only what might be expected in the background of a poem that, in its amplitude and decorative fertility, and its concern with sources of power that are often androgynous when not actively feminine – with service to a queen – is probably the most maternal epic of its age. GORDON BRADEN

European classicism generally is most fully mapped by Bolgar 1954. For Renaissance Latin, see IJsewijn 1977; on the language's specially paternal authority and its relation to the vernaculars, see William Kerrigan 1980 'The Articulation of the Ego in the English Renaissance' in *The Literary Freud: Mechanisms of Defense and the Poetic Will* ed Joseph H. Smith (New Haven) pp 261–308. The reading list and methods of English humanist education are surveyed in T.W. Baldwin 1944; for scrutiny of Spenser's indebtedness to classical authors (with particular reference to his use of Renaissance dictionaries and mythographers), see Lotspeich 1932 and Starnes and Talbert 1955:44–110. Such material is assimilated into wider perspectives by Bush 1963:89–120 and Greene 1963:294–335. Discussions of Spenser's dealings with particular Latin authors are cited in their individual entries.

law, natural and divine For us, law is made by man; it is a product of judicial and legislative decisions that result from conflicting political forces seeking to maintain or enlarge domains of economic or social privilege. For Spenser and his contemporaries, law derived from God: it was real, absolute, and eternal, and it governed all orders in society and in the cosmos.

The Elizabethan 'realist' conception of law has a long history. Contending with the Sophists, Plato argued that laws are neither factitious nor arbitrary but reflect an underlying order that sustains the observable regularities of the cosmos. Focusing more directly on law's functions in society, Aristotle subsequently developed the idea that equity – the adjustment of general laws to specific circumstances – holds a place superior to law itself (see *justice). Later, the Stoics, Cicero, Seneca, the Roman jurists, and the canonists all contributed to the synthesis of legal theory produced by Thomas Aquinas, the central features of which received influential restatement by Hooker. With varying degrees of emphasis, medieval and Renaissance authorities subscribed to a patristic idea restated by Calvin: God's 'providence is an unchangeable law' (*Institutes* 1.17.2). Similarly, Hooker argues that law is grounded in providence, which he defines as 'the setled stabilitie of divine understanding' (*Of the Laws of Ecclesiastical Polity* 1.3.1, 1.3.4).

Law's immutable and indivisible essence, serially enacted in the temporal world, appears to human observers in a hierarchy of partial manifestations, which Hooker defines in words that echo recurrent earlier formulations and anticipate later ones (*Laws* 1.3.1):

> That part of [God's eternal law] which ordereth naturall agents, we call usually *natures* law: that which Angels doe clearely behold, and without any swarving observe is a law *coelestiall* and heavenly: the law of *reason* that which bindeth creatures reasonable in this world, and with which by reason they may most plainly perceive themselves bound; that which bindeth them, and is not knowen but by speciall revelation from God, *Divine* law; *humane* law that which out of the law either of reason or of God, men probablie gathering to be expedient, they make it a law.

As he concedes, '*Natures* law' and 'law of *reason*' are often conflated; in common parlance, therefore, to follow the dictates of reason is to obey natural law (*Laws* 1.8.9).

Hooker's idea of a hierarchy of distinguishable systems of lesser laws issuing from the divine mind leads to a number of significant inferences. To legislate truly, for instance, is to base human laws upon dictates of divine will: 'men ... learne in many things what the will of God is ... they by naturall discourse attaining the knowledge therof, seeme the makers of those lawes which indeede are his, and they but only the finders of them out' (*Laws* 1.8.3; cf 1.16.2). Even Christ's two 'great' commandments (Matt 22.36–40) can be discovered in 'axiomes and lawes naturall,' and this double law of what Spenser's age called charity ('love' is the preferred modern term) provides the broadest foundation of the legislation and administration of human law. Out of the first commandment – the injunction to love God with heart, mind, and soul – derive 'all offices of religion towardes God.' The second – 'that it is [our] dutie no lesse to love others then [ourselves]' – 'is the root out of which all lawes of dutie to men-warde have growne' (*Laws* 1.8.7; cf 1.8.5–6).

Likewise, Calvin held that the essence of moral law, which (in sixteenth-century English translation) he alternately calls 'charitie' and 'equitie,' ought to be 'the marke and rule and ende of all lawes' (*Institutes* 4.20.15, in Calvin ed 1561: fols 165v-6r). This use of 'equity' as a synonym for 'charity' provides another index of the link Spenser's contemporaries normally believed to exist between human laws and the higher ones that validate them. The usage was common: paraphrasing Christ's commandments, for example, King James bases ecclesiastical and civil government on 'the whole service of *God* by man ... which is nothing else but the exercise of Religion towardes God, and of equitie towards your neighbour' (*Basilicon doron* 1.29–31).

Although they share a common, transcendent origin and frequently make similar demands, human laws differ from divine ones chiefly because human law is more restricted in scope of jurisdiction. The salient Christian pronouncement on law, the Sermon on the Mount, teaches that sinful intentions are as culpable as actions. In the view of the divine judge, adulterous intent is equivalent to adultery; anger is equivalent to murder. But human judges, who cannot assess conditions of the soul, must confine their judgments to outward actions, and, when obliged to infer anything about underlying motives, they must observe the law of charity (Matt 5–7, esp 5.17–48).

While enjoined to show charity toward others, however, individual Christians are equally obliged to use divine law to bring severe judgments against themselves. Protestant theology insisted that the standards of both Old Law and New are too high for any mortal to satisfy. By equating intentions with actions, divine laws aim especially to display the individual believer's unavoidable sinfulness and utter dependence on grace (see *nature and grace). Faith in Christ's merits alone will bring salvation, though works of charity prescribed by the law offer outward assurances that one has the grace which brings salvation.

Since individual categories of law – divine, natural, rational, human – belong to a single comprehensive system (eternal law or providence), a poet's reference to one category can invoke the others, which become implicit contexts for themes immediately at issue. In *FQ* I iii 5, the lion that bursts from 'the thickest wood' and becomes Una's obedient protector may suggest the absolute obedience of nonrational nature to dictates of natural law (as Hooker defines that law), and hence also to the eternal law, or truth, that Una can also, at times, represent. When it destroys Kirkrapine (19–20), however, the lion may represent the power of the Tudor monarchs suppressing the Roman church's economic and social abuses. It may also represent the compatibility of the human laws that enacted those reforms with the divine law which, because it demands true love of God and neighbor, required suppression of the monasteries and their uncharitable legalism, which Spenser embodies in Corceca and Abessa. As the narrative movement allows or requires, the lion's varying meanings reflect different manifestations of a single comprehensive idea, eternal law or providence.

Una, who often speaks specifically for divine law in her exhortations to the Red Cross Knight, at times appears to personify this most ample truth, the eternal law, which subsumes all her specific demands for virtuous behavior (eg, I iii 4, xii 23). At such moments, she appears similar to Dame Nature, whose garment 'wondrous sheene' the poet compares to the garment of the transfigured Christ (VII vii 7). This comparison implies that the beautiful and regular patterning of the natural world represents a perpetual revelation of the divine mind – a revelation available through nature of meanings Christ himself embodied. Natural law reveals eternal law.

Such expansive Renaissance concepts of law clarify and enrich many passages in *The Faerie Queene*. For instance, when Despair asks 'Is not his [God's] law, Let every sinner die' (I ix 47), reason's law might agree; so too would those articles of divine law that are designed to display man's incapacity to merit salvation. But the most comprehensive implication of the phrase 'his law' includes a feature of eternal law (providential rescue extended gratuitously to the faithful) that reveals the sophistry of Despair's argument. Una later makes this explicit: 'In heavenly mercies hast thou not a part?' (53).

All features of law are treated directly in *FQ* V, where they inform, among many other things, the appearance and significance of both Isis and Mercilla. In vii 1–2, Spenser invokes the widest implications of the term, locating the foundation of lesser laws in the eternal law by which God (here represented by Jove) regulates his entire creation: 'For th'hevens themselves, whence mortal men implore / Right in their wrongs, are rul'd by righteous lore / Of highest Jove, who doth true justice deale.' In vii 3, the poet announces an intention to treat 'That part of Justice, which is Equity,' referred to later as 'clemence' (22). Both terms appear in contexts that recall the ideal foundation of all human law: that part of eternal law which is charity. Mitigating Talus' ire at vii 36, Britomart is moved to pity by her susceptibility to the fellow-feeling on which charity is based: 'Yet when she saw the heapes, which he did make, / Of slaughtred carkasses, her heart did quake / For very ruth, which did it almost rive.'

These consonant and overlapping terms – mercy, clemency, equity, 'ruth' – appear as central features of the Legend of Justice because each of them expresses in slightly differing ways a fundamental feature of eternal law: God's love toward us and our answering love (called charity and sometimes equity in Spenser's time) toward one another. Mercy, who in 'th'Almighties everlasting seat ... first was bred' is, like the highest forms of love, 'From thence pour'd down on men, by influence of grace' (V x 1; cf III iii 1). So too, *The Faerie Queene* recurrently implies, is the capacity to perceive and to heed every sort of law, natural, rational, divine, eternal, or human.

Darryl J. Gless

Calvin ed 1960; John Fortescue 1567 *A Learned Commendation of the Politique Lawes of Englande* tr Robert Mulcaster (London; rpt Amsterdam and New York 1969); Hooker ed 1977–, *Laws*; James I of England 1918 *Basilicon Doron* (1616) in *Political Works* intro Charles Howard McIlwain (Cambridge, Mass) pp 3–52.

Aptekar 1969; J.H. Baker 1971; Dunseath 1968.

Lear The Lear story derives from Geoffrey of Monmouth's *Historia regum Britanniae* (2.11–14). Spenser's version, which Arthur reads in the book of *Briton moniments* in the castle of Alma (*FQ* II x 27–32), fuses Geoffrey's account with details from the chronicles of John Stow, William Warner, John Hardyng, and Holinshed (*Var* 2:315). But Spenser is not concerned with historical accuracy alone. He transforms a story of division and internecine war into a moral and political exemplum illustrating the need for temperance in rulers.

Spenser's most significant departure from his sources is Cordelia's death by hanging, a change Shakespeare adopted in *King Lear* along with the spelling of her name (Bullough 1957–75, 7:276, 334n). Perhaps influenced by her 'tragic fall' in the 1574 *Mirror for Magistrates* where she is slain with a knife offered her by Despair (Bullough 1957–75, 7:330–2), Spenser turns Cordelia's death into suicide and thus into an emblem of despair, linking the Lear story both with the earlier Despair episode in I ix, and with Pellite's hanging (another change from the received text; *Var* 3:233) at III iii 36, in Merlin's chronicle of British rulers.

MARTIN COYLE

Leicester, Robert Dudley, Earl of (c 1532–88) The exact nature of Spenser's relationship with Leicester is complicated and problematic, but his contact with the Queen's leading courtier certainly left an indelible mark on his poetry. As John Florio wrote in *Florios Second Frutes* (1591) of the two men, 'so I account him thrice-fortunate in having such a herauld of his vertues as Spenser; Curteous Lord, Curteous Spenser, I knowe not which hath perchast more fame, either he in deserving so well of so famous a scholler, or so famous a scholler in being so thankfull without hope of requitall to so famous a Lord.'

At Pembroke Hall, Cambridge, Spenser met Gabriel Harvey. By 1576, Harvey was familiar with Leicester's nephew and heir Philip Sidney (Stern 1979:150), who had probably spent some time at Cambridge in the early 1570s after he had left Oxford (Wallace 1915:105–7). He would also have known one of the fellows, Humphrey Tindall, who as a chaplain to Leicester officiated at his wedding to Lettice Knollys in September 1578. Through these links, Spenser may have got the job of carrying dispatches between Leicester, Sir Henry Sidney, and the President of Munster in July 1577, but this is not certain (Judson 1945:46).

Having worked for John Young, Bishop of Rochester, Spenser probably joined Leicester's household in the spring of 1579, at about the same time as his new secretary Arthur Atey. The exact duties he performed for the Earl remain obscure, but he stayed until the summer of 1580 in his service at Leicester House. From there he wrote on 5 October 1579 to Harvey, enclosing a long Latin poem which announced he would soon be going abroad in 'his Honours service' and at Leicester's instigation (*Two Letters* I, in *Var Prose* p 12). The trip never came off, and its failure is probably related to Spenser's presumed marriage later that month and to his becoming secretary to Lord Grey, the newly appointed Lord Deputy of Ireland.

Spenser's poem and letter to Harvey form the earliest part of their correspondence, which was published in 1580. The letters (parts of which are related to Harvey's autograph notes in his letter book, preserved in BL, Ms Sloane 93) concern themselves, among other subjects, with Spenser's literary plans and were intended to promote interest in the recently published *Shepheardes Calender.* (High-spirited, laced with deliberate obfuscations, private jokes, and airy references, they represent a kind of humorous showing-off that would have been enjoyed in the sophisticated and 'cultivated' circles around the court; part of their intention is to imply that Spenser and Harvey were part of that milieu.) In his first full letter of 15 and 16 October 1579, Spenser reveals his doubts about the wisdom of dedicating the work and '*My Slomber*, and the other Pamphlets, unto his honor' (*Var Prose* p 6). Writing again at the beginning of April 1580, Spenser tells Harvey that he is more careful than to send out his *Stemmata Dudleiana* with its 'sundry Apostrophes therein, addressed you knowe to whome' (*Three Letters* I, in *Var Prose* p 18). Leicester is clearly intended as the recipient of both these lost works.

Spenser's two letters are both signed 'Immerito' – the pseudonym he used at the end of the little poem 'To His Booke' which prefaces *The Shepheardes Calender.* Although its title page carries a dedication to Sidney, the prefatory poem still bears the marks of its being intended for 'his honor' Leicester, 'him that is the president / Of noblesse and of chevalree.' The Oak in *Februarie* has been interpreted as representing Leicester (McLane 1961, ch 5), but this is by no means convincing. More plausible, and supported by E.K.'s gloss to *October* 47–8, is the association of 'the worthy whome shee loveth best, / That first the white beare to the stake did bring,' whom Piers urges Cuddie to celebrate, with Leicester and his badge of the bear and ragged staff. In the *November* eclogue lamenting Dido's death, the 'greate shepheard *Lobbin*' is a mourner (*Nov* 113). Leicester is probably intended, but as E.K. notes, 'The person both of the shepehearde and of Dido is unknowen and closely buried in the Authors conceipt' (*Nov* 38 gloss).

(See **Leicester** Fig 1.)

The Earl's presence in Spenser's first major work is shadowy and hard to detect, especially as it could have been written at any time before he came to work at Leicester House. His employment there gave him the chance to discuss poetry with Sidney and Dyer (whatever the real nature of the so-called Areopagus was), and to have access to Leicester's fine library and his even finer paintings, tapestries, and other works of art.

Why Spenser stayed for such a brief time in Leicester's service is not known, but it is most unlikely that he was sent to Ireland in disgrace for any supposed indiscretion, such as has often been connected with the writing of *The Shepheardes Calender* or *Mother Hubberds Tale.* Leicester was on close terms with Grey and would hardly have recommended someone who had recently offended him to Grey's service. In any event, they were never to meet again since by the time Spenser returned to England in 1589 Leicester was dead. Their subsequent relations can only be inferred from what Spenser published after his arrival in Ireland.

Before then, however, he had begun *The Faerie Queene*, and critics have sought to determine Leicester's role in it. One popular view holds that Spenser planned it to help Leicester ingratiate himself with Elizabeth after his fall from her favor during the second Alençon courtship of 1578–82. According to this view, Leicester may be associated with Arthur in his service of the Fairy Queen. His moment of triumph comes in *FQ* V, which reflects Leicester's expedition to the Low Countries as Governor General in 1585–7. This traditional interpretation has been strongly challenged (Bennett 1942:84–6, 95–100), and instead the knights Artegall and Guyon have been taken to compliment the house of Dudley since their names are those of famous and legendary Earls of Warwick. As with *The Shepheardes Calender*, *The Faerie Queene* was clearly the work of a poet familiar with and sympathetic to the political and religious views of Leicester's faction, but the Earl's own role in the epic is still a matter of debate.

The meaning and significance of *Virgils Gnat* are equally uncertain. The poem is said to have been 'Long since dedicated' to Leicester 'late deceased' and is accompanied by a sonnet in which the poet feels 'Wrong'd' by the Earl who is 'the causer of my care.' It has been connected with Spenser's supposed punishment of exile to Ireland for warning Leicester about the Alençon courtship (Greenlaw in *Var* 7:571–4). But the historical facts do not fit the poem and its allegory, while the closeness of its translation of the *Culex* makes a biographical interpretation problematic. It is possible that the poem reflects the episode before October 1579 which caused Spenser to call himself 'Immerito' in his letters to Harvey and in *The Shepheardes Calender.* The opening words of the gnat's speech in hell are 'what have I wretch deserv'd' (329). In his letter book, Harvey says that the name was assumed by Spenser 'since a certayn chaunce befallen unto him, a secrett not to be revealid.'

Gnat appeared in the *Complaints* volume of 1591, which also contained Spenser's tribute to the Earl in *Ruines of Time.* Whatever wrong Spenser thought Leicester had done him, as implied in *Gnat*, it had clearly been forgiven when he composed the later work. There Verlame mourns his unhonored death (183–238) – 'Of greatest ones he greatest in his place' – and laments the passing of 'his bounteous minde,' forgotten by poets and those who 'did goodnes by him gaine.' His patronage is remembered again in *Colin Clout* when Hobbinol reminds Colin of when he waited on '*Lobbin* (*Lobbin* well thou knewest) / Full many worthie ones then waiting were' (736–7) for him and Cynthia. Finally, at the very end of his career in *Prothalamion*, Spenser turned his thoughts once more to Leicester house: 'a stately place, / Where oft I gayned giftes and goodly grace / Of that great Lord, which therein wont to dwell, / Whose want too well now feeles my freendles case' (137–40).

H.R. Woudhuysen

Florio 1591; Alan Kendall 1980 *Robert Dudley, Earl of Leicester* (London); Rosenberg 1955; M.W. Wallace 1915; Derek Wilson 1981 *Sweet Robin: A Biography of Robert Dudley, Earl of Leicester, 1533–1588* (London).

Leland, John (c 1503–52) A major figure in antiquarian and topographical studies in early Tudor England; probably he influenced several of Spenser's works. Born in London, he attended St Paul's School under the mastership of William Lily, took the BA at Christ's College, Cambridge, and afterwards studied at Oxford and Paris. Soon after his return to England (c 1529), Leland became seriously engaged in antiquarian research. Prompted by his passionate loyalty to the king and nation, he spent over a decade traveling throughout England, visiting libraries and collecting historical materials. He had grandiose publishing ambitions, mostly concerned with British history, but very little apart from his poetry was published during his lifetime. In 1547 he became insane and died five years later. Although a significant number of his papers survived and were used by generations of scholars before they were first edited by Hearne and published in 1710–15, many others were badly damaged soon after his death, and some appear to have been lost or stolen.

Leland's researches and intended projects were major shaping influences on Raphael Holinshed and William Harrison; in particular, the latter's *Description of England* shows a considerable debt to Leland, as Harrison acknowledges. Leland was also an inspiration and a specific source for Camden, whose *Britannia* may be seen as a culmination of Leland's pioneering antiquarianism.

Leland was a patriotic supporter of Henry VIII, whom he saw as a modern reincarnation of King Arthur. As a strong nationalist and dedicated Protestant, he defended Geoffrey of Monmouth's version of British history and of the Arthurian legend against Polydore Vergil, a foreigner and a Catholic (for the debate between Leland and Vergil, see Greenlaw 1932: ch 1). His *Assertio inclytissimi Arturii regis Britanniae* (1544), translated by Richard Robinson in 1582 as *A Learned and True Assertion of ... Prince Arthure, King of Brittaine*, is a compilation of almost all the literary and archaeological evidence available in Tudor England on what would now be called the historical Arthur.

Leland's treatment of the Arthurian legend is the first example of a new way of looking at Arthur, one in which medieval romance has given way to a 'topo-chronographicall' mode (to use the term from George Wither's prefatory poem to Part 2 of Drayton's *Poly-Olbion*), For Leland, the landscape itself reflects the glory of the nation, its present king, and his famous ancestor. He sees a new kind of romance in historical fact and in close descriptions of actual landscape. His adulation of Arthur as a man, his sense of the almost numinous value of Arthurian sites, and his linking of contemporary monarch, nation, and Arthur prefigure many elements of the Renaissance Arthurian revival. The Arthurian world of *The Faerie Queene* is much closer to Leland than to Malory.

Modern scholars remember him for his prose remains; but Leland and his contemporaries regarded his Latin verse as equally important, and in certain ways he is the prototype of the glorifying national poet. Two of his major Latin works address themselves to the English countryside: *Genethliacon ... Eaduerdi principis Cambriae* (first pub 1543, reissued in *Principium ... in Anglia virorum, encomia ...* ed T. Newton 1589) and *Cygnea cantio* (first pub 1545, reissued 1658). The *Genethliacon* describes the celebrations in honor of Edward VI's birth: the Muses, Graces, and sylvan nymphs all sing praises, and then Wales, Cornwall, and Cheshire pay tribute in appropriate regional manner. Apart from its metrical virtuosity, the poem is remarkable for its precise topographical information and for the fascination with local custom it reveals. It is a literary ancestor of Spenser's marriage of Thames and Medway (*FQ* IV xi).

An even more important connection with Spenser is *Cygnea cantio*, a river poem with historical commentary by the author. Here, as in *Prothalamion*, the reader finds gentle Zephyr, banks of flowers, garlanded swans glimmeringly white of hue, and detailed descriptions of high towers from the perspective of the Thames. The similarities in imagery and tone are noteworthy, and it is likely, as Thomas Warton first postulated, that Spenser made specific borrowings (see Todd and Osgood in *Var* 8:667, 673). *Cygnea cantio* may also have been a model for Spenser's concept of an *Epithalamion Thamesis* (see lost *works). The singing swan of *Ruines of Time* 589–95, too, finds many parallels in Leland's poem and in his shorter verse.

Ultimately, though, Leland's attitude to the past and to landscape is very different from Spenser's. The greatest part of the *Cygnea cantio*, for example, is devoted to a prose commentary, an encapsulated history of all the sites which the swans had seen. Leland wishes to describe the past and the landscape accurately, not to illuminate them. He does not look for patterns of moralization in the physical world; ultimately his poetry becomes subservient to his interest in historical facts. For him, verse is a medium through which to convey specific information, not to create a mythology.

James P. Carley

Most of Leland's works and collections were edited by Thomas Hearne in *The Itinerary* 9 vols (Oxford 1710–12, 2nd ed 1744–5) and *Johannis Lelandi ... collectanea* 6 vols (Oxford [1715], 2nd ed 1760). A later edition of *The Itinerary* is ed 1907–10. The *Assertio* (1544) as tr Richard Robinson (1582) is appended to Christopher Middleton 1925 *The Famous Historie of Chinon of England* ed William Edward Mead (London, EETS os 165). For a general introduction to Leland, see Kendrick 1950: ch 4; see also James P. Carley 1983 'John Leland's *Cygnea cantio*: A Neglected Tudor River Poem' *HumLov* 32: 225–41; Carley 1984; Carley 1986 'John Leland in Paris: The Evidence of His Poetry' *SP* 83:1–50.

letter as genre In the Middle Ages, letter writing was a professional skill practiced by *dictatores*, masters of the art of Latin prose composition. The *ars dictaminis*, as it was called, adapted the rhetoric of the classical oration to the public documents of a feudal society. Like the oration, the medieval letter was divided into parts, usually five: greeting (*salutatio*), opening (*exordium* or *benevolentiae captatio* 'securing of goodwill'), statement of the situation (*narratio*), request (*petitio*), and conclusion (*conclusio*). Since etiquette required that the letter reflect the correspondents' social status, handbooks offered formulas for courteously addressing such dignitaries as the pope, bishops, abbots, kings, noblemen, and magistrates. The style was as artful as the *dictator* could make it, often employing the *cursus*, an accentual prose rhythm.

Before 1420, letters were seldom written in English. In the fifteenth century, families like the Pastons, who could afford to hire scribes but not the professional secretaries who served the nobility, modeled their private letters on official documents. The first English handbooks on letter writing, published in the sixteenth century for the merchant class, followed the medieval tradition: William Fulwood's *Enimie of Idlenesse* (1568), Abraham Fleming's *A Panoplie of Epistles* (1576), Angel Day's *English Secretorie* (1586), and John Browne's *Marchants Avizo* (1589). Not until the seventeenth century did such gentlemen as James Howell and Suckling break with professional formulas to create a new literary genre, the familiar letter. The roots of this change in epistolary style can be found, however, in the humanist movement, which reached England from Italy in the late fifteenth century. The published English letters of Spenser and Harvey are a late sixteenth-century landmark in the development of the genre.

Harvey paraphrases observations on letter writing by Cicero, Seneca, Demetrius, and other classical authorities when he writes in his manuscript *Letter-Book*, 'it makith no matter howe a man wrytith untoe his frends so he wryte frendlye; other praeceptes of arte and stile and decorum, and I know not what, ar to be reservid for an other place ... What ar letters amongst frendes but familiar discourses and pleasante conferences?' In letters to friends, he scorns 'affectinge the comendation of an eloquent and oratorlike style by overcurious and statelye enditinge' (ed 1884:76).

Ever since Petrarch had discovered a manuscript of Cicero's *Letters to Atticus* and had published his own correspondence following this great classical example, humanists had quoted the classical distinction between the private conversation of the familiar letter and the public discourse of the oration. The humanists were, however, 'the professional successors of the medieval Italian *dictatores*,' serving 'either as teachers of the humanities in secondary schools or universities, or as secretaries to princes or cities' (Kristeller 1979:23–4). Although they admired classical models, their professional expertise was defined by the *ars dictaminis*; and the elaborate medieval etiquette of letter writing resisted sudden change. Furthermore, the letter was a favorite composition exercise in schools, a miniature oration in which students practiced rhetoric before attempting longer, more complex assignments.

In their correspondence, the humanists gradually abandoned the *cursus*, purified the 'barbaric' Latin of the *dictatores*, and substituted simple Ciceronian expressions (*salutem dicit, vale*) for the fulsome medieval formulas; but letter writers who attempted wholesale imitation of Cicero were labeled extremists in Erasmus' *Ciceronianus* (1528). His influential *De conscribendis epistolis* (1522) categorized letters, like orations, as judicial, deliberative, and demonstrative, while treating familiar letters as an exception to the rule. Aside from Juan Luis Vives' *De conscribendis epistolis* (1533) and Justus Lipsius' *Epistolica institutio* (1591), humanist handbooks on letter writing paid little attention to the familiar letter. While conceding that not every letter needs five parts, they insisted that letters, like orations, should persuade; and they recommended rhetorical figures and other artificial devices of style. As late as the end of the seventeenth century, most humanist handbooks only modified medieval tradition.

In effect, the humanists could not altogether abandon the complexities of the *ars dictaminis* without undermining their professional status, and this problem became more acute as their employers became better educated. The humanist ideal, expressed in such English works as Elyot's *Boke Named the Governour* (1531) and Ascham's *Scholemaster* (1570), was the education of the governing class. By the end of the century, literacy had joined military prowess as marks of the gentleman. Not ponderous medieval formulas, however, but the intimate, witty conversation of the familiar letter expressed the effortless grace, the *sprezzatura*, the art concealing art that defined the Renaissance courtier. In private letters to his peers, the seventeenth-century gentleman could afford to adopt fully the Ciceronian model. Furthermore, he could distance himself from his Latin secretary by writing on personal or courtly rather than on official or scholarly topics, and in English rather than Latin. The aristocratic revival of the classical familiar letter was nevertheless made possible by the experiments of such humanist scholars as Spenser and Harvey.

The Spenser-Harvey letters illustrate the uneasy marriage of medieval tradition and classical models in humanist epistolography. Their purpose was professional. Harvey or Spenser probably initiated their publication in 1580 and very likely Harvey himself wrote the preface. Harvey's *Letter-Book* contains first drafts for a similar project. By their name-dropping, their tantalizing reports of work in progress, their learned discussions of poetry and natural philosophy, and their exchange of poems in both Latin and English, the letters were intended to enhance the reputations of two ambitious young scholars seeking court patronage.

Nevertheless, the correspondence of these 'two Universitie men' is advertised as 'proper, and wittie, familiar Letters.' Here *proper* means 'excellent' (as it does in the phrase 'proper and hable men with their penne' from 'the Preface of a wellwiller'), but it also implies that these are familiar letters proper; *wittie* suggests that they are intellectual. Together with the *Two Letters* that follow, the *Three Letters* self-consciously avoid formal structure. Frequent changes of topic and multiple postscripts make them seem unpremeditated. Their tone is intimate, excluding outside readers by alluding to unpublished letters and conversations and by recording the most personal messages in Latin (eg, Harvey's greeting to Spenser's wife, 'mea Domina Immerito, mea bellissima Collina Clouta' *3 Lett* 3, *Var Prose* p 476).

The letters are even more avant-garde in language than in form. Renaissance humanists customarily exchanged letters in Latin or Greek, the languages of the universities. To write a fellow scholar in English was uncommon, although not unprecedented; Ascham, for example, had recorded his continental travels in English for colleagues at St John's College, Cambridge, in the 1550s, probably to avoid censorship by foreign officials. Comments in Harvey's *Letter-Book* suggest, however, that even scholarly taste was changing. To Sir Thomas Smith, he expressed impatience with stock Latin phrases: 'when al is dun, I have nothing els to sai, but gratias ago habeoque, referat Deus, utinam par pari, and the like, for you ar well acquaintid with the stile' (ed 1884:178). He petitioned John Young, master of Pembroke Hall, for his MA both in Latin, as university custom required, and in English. For a subject so close to his heart, he seems to have found Latin inadequate – 'I culd not possibely ani other wai expres the matter as it is' (p 20) – and insincere: 'becaus it is commonly the manner of schollars, to write more in there lattin epistles, then thai profes in there commun talk, or show in there outward doings, and mani things often times mai sem to be spoken rather of cours and custum, then of ani inward affection, I thouht it not amis, or rather I thouht it mi duti, plainly and simply in flat Inglish to utter mi mind' (p 159).

Perhaps, though, both language and form are best explained by the intended audience. Courtiers ordinarily had not the inclination, if indeed the skill, to read Latin school exercises, so the two young scholars chose to present samples of their professional expertise (Harvey's discourse on earthquakes, their English poetic experiments, Spenser's Latin farewell, the translation exercises of Harvey's young brother John, and Harvey's own paraphrase of Latin verses on the mutability of all things but virtue) in the more playful context of familiar letters. As with their contemporary Lyly, whose similar intent produced the fictional *Euphues: The Anatomy of Wit*, the result was highly original. The Spenser-Harvey correspondence heralds the development of the English familiar letter in the next century.

JUDITH RICE HENDERSON

Bennett 1931a; Cecil H. Clough 1976 'The Cult of Antiquity: Letters and Letter Collections,' in *Cultural Aspects of the Italian Renaissance: Essays in Honour of Paul Oskar Kristeller* ed Cecil H. Clough (Manchester) pp 33–67; Harvey ed 1884; Helgerson 1983:55–100; Judith Rice Henderson 1982 'Euphues and His Erasmus' *ELR* 12:135–61; Henderson 1983a 'Defining the Genre of the Letter: Juan Luis Vives' *De Conscribendis Epistolis*' *Ren&R* ns 7:89–105; Henderson 1983b 'Erasmus on the Art of Letter-Writing' in Murphy 1983:331–55; Katherine Gee Hornbeak 1934 'The Complete Letter-Writer in English, 1568–1800' *SCSML* 15.3–4; William Henry Irving 1955 *The Providence of Wit in the English Letter Writers* (Durham, NC); Javitch 1978; Kristeller 1979, chs 1, 5; James J. Murphy 1974 *Rhetoric in the Middle Ages* (Berkeley and Los Angeles); Malcolm Richardson 1984 'The *Dictamen* and Its Influence on Fifteenth-Century English Prose' *Rhetorica* 2:207–26; Jean Robertson 1942 *The Art of Letter Writing: An Essay on the Handbooks Published in England during the Sixteenth and Seventeenth Centuries* (London); Snare 1970; Stern 1979; Whigham 1981; Louis B. Wright 1935 *Middle-Class Culture in Elizabethan England* (Chapel Hill).

---

letters, Spenser's and Harvey's (See ed 1912:609–41.) Spenser's extant correspondence consists of two letters among the five exchanged between him under his nom de plume Immerito and Gabriel Harvey, identified only by his initials. The letters were published in two parts in one quarto volume by Henry Bynneman in 1580 (registered on 30 June). For reasons never made clear, the two groups of letters were published in reversed chronology. *Three Proper, and Wittie, Familiar Letters*, dated 1580, contains an unsigned address 'To the Curteous Buyer' (dated 19 June), Spenser's letter to Harvey (from Westminster, 2 April), Harvey's reply (from Saffron Walden, 7 April), and a second letter from Harvey (also from Saffron Walden, 23 April). There follows *Two Other Very Commendable Letters, of the Same Mens Writing ... More Lately Delivered unto the Printer*, dated 1580, which contains a letter enclosing a Latin poem from Spenser to Harvey (written partly at Leicester House on 5 October 1579 and partly at Westminster and 'Mystresse *Kerkes*' on 15–16 October), and Harvey's reply (from Trinity Hall, Cambridge, 23 October).

The letters were issued to complement

the publication of *The Shepheardes Calender* by describing the literary and intellectual concerns of those associated with Leicester House. Their tone is familiar and intimate, knowing and rather joky, secret and yet clearly assembled with publication in mind. They are in Harvey's own words 'Patcheries, and fragments' (*3 Lett* 3), heavily edited and reworked from material at hand, some of which can be seen in its raw state in Harvey's *Letter Book* (see ed 1884). The letters caused some offense, and from his later quarrel with Nashe, we know that Harvey, who denied direct involvement in their publication, had to make some sort of public apology for what he had written.

The earliest part of the letters is Spenser's 'last Farewell,' the long Latin poem 'Ad ornatissimum virum' enclosed in *Two Letters* 1, hurriedly written the week before he was to go abroad in 'his Honours [Leicester's] service.' In the covering letter written a week and a half later, the promise of travel has disappeared, and he is concerned with the dedication of *The Shepheardes Calender*, which he has now decided to publish, and the practice of writing English quantitative verse, which Sidney and Dyer have been promoting in their Areopagus. Spenser says that 'they have me, I thanke them, in some use of familiarity,' and that he has been drawn 'to their faction.' Warned by the example of Gosson's tactlessness in dedicating his *Schoole of Abuse* to Sidney, he will be careful about presenting '*My Slomber*, and the other Pamphlets, unto his honor. I meant them rather to *Maister Dyer*.' E.K. sends his greetings. The first part of the letter closes here but is immediately resumed, for, having received Harvey's quantitative verses which he will show to Dyer and Sidney, he offers him an example of his own facility in the same style of writing, the 'Iambicum Trimetrum,' which he also asks him to keep 'close to your selfe, or your verie entire friendes, Maister *Preston*, Maister *Still*, and the reste.'

Harvey's reply (*2 Lett* 2) contains Latin and English verses by himself and his friends, but is chiefly concerned with responding to Spenser's news about the Areopagus, his love, and his continental travel. Evidently Harvey has reused material here that he had earlier sent to his friend when he was still expecting him to go abroad. While urging him to publish *The Shepheardes Calender*, he criticizes the metrics of the 'Iambicum.'

During the following gap in the correspondence, *The Shepheardes Calender* was published. Spenser refers to it in the 'Postscripte' to the letter he sent Harvey from Westminster at the beginning of April (*3 Lett* 1). Although dated 2 April, the letter contains a reference to the earthquake which took place on 6 April. This is probably an interpolated passage to prepare the reader for Harvey's next letter with its 'Pleasant and pitthy familiar discourse, of the Earthquake in Aprill last' (*3 Lett* 2). Although Spenser mentions 'that olde greate matter' which may be the Alençon courtship, his letter is mainly concerned with his literary projects, especially 'reformed Versifying.' He quotes a tetrastich (quatrain) and a distich (couplet) (which E.K. cites in his gloss to *Maye* 69) and asks Harvey either to give him his rules for versifying, or to follow his which Sidney gave him. He announces that he will soon issue the *Epithalamion Thamesis*, says his *Dreames* and *Dying Pellicane* are soon to be printed (*Dreames* with a gloss), so that he can get on with *The Faerie Queene*, which he asks Harvey to return with his 'long expected Judgement' of it. He adds that he will not send his *Stemmata Dudleiana* abroad.

Harvey touches on some of these works, his own writings, and the debased state of learning at Cambridge in his long reply (*3 Lett* 2); but most of his letter is taken up with a discourse on the earthquake. In this, he satirizes traditional Cambridge philosophy by juxtaposing it with his own Ramist, logical exploration of the scientific causes of the event. The piece is set in 'a Gentlemans house, here in *Essex*,' which is probably to be identified with Arthur Capell's home at Rayne near Braintree. It was, E.K. tells us in the gloss to *September* 176, at Arthur's father Henry Capell's house, Hadham Hall in Hertfordshire, that Harvey presented the printed text of his *Gratulationes Valdinenses* to the Queen. The letter ends largely in Latin with exclamations about poverty and learning, internal university disputes, and the decline in general of Cambridge. Harvey pictures himself sitting back, watching, and being amused by it all, much in the same way that Spenser describes him in his Harvey Sonnet ('Harvey, the happy above happiest men'). Once more he bids farewell and adds a tantalizing postscript that the letter may be shown only 'to the two odde Gentlemen you wot of,' who are presumably Dyer and Sidney.

In the final letter of the series (*3 Lett* 3), Harvey returns to the issue of writing English verse in classical meters, and shows off some of the poems he has written in this way including the 'Speculum Tuscanismi,' which satirizes the Earl of Oxford. He alludes to Spenser's service under Bishop John Young ('Imagin me to come into a goodly Kentishe *Garden* of your old Lords'), and quotes from *The Shepheardes Calender* and E.K.'s glosses to it. Once more he discusses Spenser's literary plans, mentioning his *Nine Comoedies* and offering his famous judgment of *The Faerie Queene* ('*Hobgoblin* runne away with the Garland from *Apollo*'), and tells him that the contents of the letter can be communicated to 'the two Gentlemen,' and to the diplomat and poet Daniel Rogers.

The Spenser-Harvey letters are interesting examples of the Elizabethan vernacular, familiar letter. They were essentially designed to draw attention to the London literary life in which Spenser was then involved and to publish Harvey's poetic and academic compositions. Their artificiality puts much doubt on the statement of the 'Welwiller of the two Authours' – possibly written by Harvey himself – that he acquired the letters at fourth or fifth hand from a friend who 'had procured the copying of them oute, at *Immeritos* handes.' Spenser's own interest in their publication is indeterminable. The rather oblique parts (often in Latin) dealing with love and travel may reflect on his imminent departure for Ireland after his first marriage. Certainly the correspondence is the most important, at times the only, source for Spenser's biography at this crucial time. The letters, despite their edited and sophisticated state, tell us almost everything that we know of his literary plans and projects from *The Shepheardes Calender* to the publication of *FQ* I–III. The information gained from them, however, should be treated with extreme caution: they are consciously self-promoting, a means of showing off the beginnings of the 'new' poetry and the literary and social milieu of London and Cambridge as the new decade began.

H.R. WOUDHUYSEN

The standard text is in *Var Prose*, which unsatisfactorily breaks the book down and prints Harvey's letters as an appendix; a more accessible ed is found in Spenser ed 1912. James H. Hewlett 1927 'Interpreting a Spenser-Harvey Letter' *PMLA* 42:1060–5, Judson 1945, Rosenberg 1955, and Stern 1979 give a largely biographical analysis of the letters. The relation of Harvey's Letter Book to the Harvey-Spenser correspondence is discussed in Bennett 1931a. Snare 1970 gives a more literary analysis. David McKitterick 1981 *Library* 6th ser 3:348–53 reviews Stern 1979 and prints Harvey's handwritten corrections in a printed copy of the letters.

Life and Death The last two figures in the pageant of Mutabilitie (*FQ* VII vii 46). Life is 'like a faire young lusty boy, / Such as they faine *Dan Cupid* to have beene'; Death is 'with most grim and griesly visage seene' yet is less a presence than an absence, 'Unbodied, unsoul'd, unheard, unseene.'

The personification of Death as an animated corpse comes from the later Middle Ages when the Dance of Death and the encounter between three living and three dead kings were popular themes in verbal and visual art. Related images of personified Death persist in the art of the Tudor period, although the typical medieval double tomb (where the body *au vif* surmounts the decaying cadaver) is displaced, as it had been in Renaissance Italy, by an emphasis on life not mortality. Like his predecessors, Spenser perceives the heterodox implications of the medieval figure: death, properly considered, is an absence not a presence, and is to be defined, like evil itself, in negatives.

The figure of Life is both medieval and classical in origin, related to portrayals of Cupid, the god of love. In the fourteenth century, Love began to be portrayed as a winged adolescent not unlike an angel (cf II viii 6). In representing Life as a 'lusty boy,' Spenser places the figure in the Renaissance tradition, where the clear-eyed Cupid of the ancients is distinguished from the blindfolded descendant of the medieval world: as spiritual, distinct from carnal, love (Panofsky 1939, ch 4).

Spenser's allusive use of these motifs ingeniously anticipates Nature's claim in stanza 58 that all things 'are not changed from their first estate; / But by their change their being doe dilate.' Interestingly, although Death is said by the narrator to be the last in the procession (cf III xii 25), Life is the last to be described. Similarly, the description of Day follows that of Night in stanza 44. The emphasis is on resurrection: on the New Testament (symbolized by Day or Life) following the Old (Night or Death), a common medieval conceit. The contrast is made emphatic by the imagery in stanza 46: Death is disembodied, a mere shadow of the mind, whereas Life is robust with color and vitality. The connection between Life and Death persists, but Life, like the *Eros funèbre* (the Cupid found on Renaissance tombs), is a power that frees the soul. As was said of Spenser's near contemporary, Lancelot Andrewes, 'yea, then his life did begin, when his mortality made an end.'

PHILIPPA M. TRISTRAM

Chapters on 'La Mort' in Emile Mâle 1908 *L'Art religieux de la fin du Moyen Age en France* (Paris), and Mâle 1951 *L'Art religieux de la fin du XVIe siècle, du XVIIe siècle et du XVIIIe siècle* (Paris). See also Philippa Tristram 1976 *Figures of Life and Death in Medieval English Literature* (London) esp ch 5; and for figures of Life and Death in Spenser, Whitman 1918.

light In the cosmology of *The Faerie Queene*, Jove is the ruler of light and supreme deity: he created day and constricted darkness to 'deepest dongeon' (I vii 23), and at his command the moon and stars light the world at night (VII vi 12, III i 57). In his continual conflict with Night, the infernal deity who works to undermine his rule, he favors the 'sonnes of Day' (I v 25) who will ultimately subdue darkness and win heaven (III iv 59; cf Eph 5.8, 1 Thess 5.5). The *Fowre Hymnes* describe God, the heavens, and angels in terms of glittering light (see esp *HHL* 55–74, *HHB* 92–7, 118–26); and the soul's relation to its divine source is defined by light imagery (*HB* 106–12).

The sun's brilliance is analogous to the divine radiance, dazzling to mortal eyes: the face of the unveiled Una (*FQ* I vi 4) and of Fidelia (x 12) burn and daze the beholder, and Contemplation sees God not with his eyes but with his 'spright,' which like the eagle can look directly into the sun (x 47). The sun serves as an image of God because it both creates and sustains life. It is the 'Great father ... of generation ... th'author of life and light' (III vi 9); and as its beams can create life by their action on the moist earth, it conceives Belphoebe and Amoret in the womb of the virgin Chrysogone (3–9). Since the sun is associated with physical health and spiritual life, the Red Cross Knight in Orgoglio's dungeon, the lovestruck Marinell in Proteus' hall, and Pastorella in the Brigands' cave wither like a plant deprived of light (I viii 41, IV xii 34, VI x 44). The sun's power to regenerate and heal is represented by Apollo, whose chief role in *The Faerie Queene* is as a physician (I v 43, III iv 41, IV xii 25).

Spenser often describes physical beauty in terms of light or brightness since it is an earthly manifestation of 'that soveraine light, / From whose pure beams al perfect beauty springs' (*HHB* 295–6): Rosalind is 'The beame of beautie sparkled from above' (*Colin Clout* 468), the beloved in the *Amoretti* radiates light from her eyes and smiles (9, 40), and Queen Elizabeth is likened to the sun in both her pastoral role as Eliza (*SC, Aprill* 77) and her heroic role as Gloriana (*FQ* VI x 28). All the heroines of *The Faerie Queene* shine with radiant beauty: for example, Una's face shines like the sun (I iii 4, xii 23), Belphoebe's eyes dazzle with their fiery beams (II iii 23), Florimell's hair streams like a comet (III i 16), and when her womanhood is revealed, Britomart's hair shines like the moon (i 43), the sun (ix 20), the aurora borealis (IV i 13), and golden sand (vi 20).

False beauty may also shine brightly since it strives to emulate the true. Lucifera (light-bringing) in her 'bright blazing beautie' (I iv 8) is a counterfeit morning star in contrast with Una the true one (xii 21), and the brightness of her house of Pride (iv 4) parodies that of the heavenly city (x 58) and of Mercilla's palace (V ix 21). The brightness with which evil beauty shines is never genuine: Duessa's light is 'borrowed' (I viii 49), Philotime's is 'wrought by art' (II vii 45), and the 'goodly glosse' of the false Florimell is forged (IV v 15).

The virtue of Spenser's knights is associated with the brightness of their armor. At the beginning of his quest, Redcrosse's armor casts a 'litle glooming light' by which he sees Error (I i 14); and at the end, its radiance fills heaven (xi 4). A dazzle of 'glitterand armour' is the first impression we receive of the approaching Arthur (vii 29). The brilliance of his unveiled 'sunshiny shield' paralyzes Orgoglio (viii 19–20) and defeats the Souldan (V viii 37–8).

The light of day promotes virtuous activity, while darkness is a time of passiveness and often of moral laxity. Night distorts vision and conceals crimes, as Arthur laments, while daylight 'discovers all dishonest wayes' and shows things for what they are (III iv 55–60). Accordingly, sunrise is greeted cheerfully: dawn 'maketh every creature glad' (II xi 3), and sunshine 'makes all skip and daunce' (VII vii 23). The sun itself was created 'mens wandring wayes to guyde' (I vii 23). At night, the moon and stars give comfort and direction to the seaman, the traveler, and the lover (I ii 1, III i 43; *Epithalamion* 288–90).

Appropriately Phoebus, whose light both reveals and guides, is also the 'god of Poets hight' (*FQ* VII vii 12). By a tradition descending from Hesiod (*Theogony* 25–104), the Muses were the daughters of Zeus, and Phoebus (Apollo) was their companion. Spenser, however, following a little-known passage in Conti (*Mythologiae* 4.10), makes Phoebus the father of the Muses (I xi 5, III iii 4; *Epith* 121) and so emphasizes that as the god of light he is also responsible for poetic enlightenment.

GEOFFREY G. HILLER

Lindsay, David (c 1486–1555) Scottish poet; courtier and herald to James V of Scotland. Lindsay was familiar to Elizabethan readers, but they did not take account of the works for which he is best known today: the romance *Squire Meldrum* (1550), the short burlesque poems, and the morality play *A Satire of the Three Estates* (1540–54). These were absent from sixteenth-century editions of Lindsay's *Works*, which were dominated by his longest, most serious work, *A Dialogue between Experience and a Courtier*, commonly called *The Book of the Monarch* (1554). Thomas Purfoote's three English editions of the *Works* (1566, 1575, 1581) are typical, in that numerous shorter poems (*de casibus* tragedies and 'mirrors for princes') are appended to this major work. English interest in Lindsay's *Monarch* was probably an offshoot of the growing popularity of the *Mirror for Magistrates* in the 1560s and 1570s.

The *Monarch* purports to be a survey of the four 'monarchies' of the ancient world: the Assyrian, Persian, Greek, and Roman empires (cf Geneva gloss to Daniel 2.28ff). His treatment is eschatological, showing how mankind has degenerated since Adam, through the monarchies and into the mock-monarchy of the papacy towards a now-imminent Judgment. The work is essentially controversial in attacking contemporary abuses of secular power by church and court. From the hindsight of the 1560s, the *Monarch* established its author as a forerunner of the Scottish Reformation.

While Scottish and English readers valued what the Edinburgh printer Charteris called Lindsay's 'hailsum and notabill counsellis and admonitionis to Princis, to Prelates, and to all estatis' (Lindsay ed 1931–6, 1:397), they must also have relished his vigorous prosody and diction. Lindsay looks to the previous generation of Scottish poets for his stylistic models, although he seems less centrally concerned than they with stylistic experimentation. Above all, he lauds Douglas, 'quhilk [which] lampe wes of this land, / Off Eloquence the flowand balmy strand, / And, in our Inglis rethorick, the rose' (*Testament of the Papyngo* 22–4, ed 1931–6, 1:57). With his rhythmic energy, ingenuity of rhyme, and persistent alliteration, Lindsay represents the maturity of the Scottish poetic tradition; he need no longer make the gesture of looking south for his models of eloquence. In fact, his characteristic expression of moral earnestness in selfconsciously, artfully rustic style may in turn have provided a model for southern poets in the 1570s, not least the author of *The Shepheardes Calender*. (See also *Scottish antecedents.)

DAVID PARKINSON

Lindsay 1931–6 *Works* ed Douglas Hamer, 4 vols, STS 3rd ser 1, 2, 6, 8 (Edinburgh).

lineage In *The Faerie Queene*, lineage is a historiographical and an allegorical device. It is the form that British history takes on the assumption that divine providence works through the royal blood line to determine England's political fortunes from one generation to the next. As an allegorical metaphor, lineage often signifies the interconnectedness of abstract moral principles: for example, Duessa, who personifies falsehood, is said to be the daughter of Deceit and Shame (I v 26).

Spenser's original audience believed that heredity determines one's proper place in a hierarchic social order. Lineage is correspondingly important in the aristocratic genre of chivalric romance, where, as a figment of class ideology, it justifies the economic and political power of the ruling class as a natural endowment, an ontological prerogative. To affirm the legitimacy of hereditary aristocracy, Spenser reinterprets a line from Chaucer ('he is gentil that dooth gentil dedis' *Wife of Bath's Tale* 1170) in such a way that its emphasis is reversed: 'gentle bloud will gentle manners breed' (*FQ* VI iii 2). This 'truth' is referred to often in *The Faerie Queene* (cf II iii 10, iv 1; III ii 33), especially in Book VI, which has several virtuous characters in lowly roles who turn out to be nobly born (cf ii 24, iv 36, v 2). Throughout the poem, lineage signals a character's importance and establishes who he or she 'really is.'

As an allegorical device, an appeal to lineage generates abstract definitions of moral concepts while giving these concepts the status of primeval cosmic powers. For example, Spenser's claim that Duessa is the daughter of Deceit and Shame helps to define the abstraction she personifies: falsehood is produced by deceit and is a thing of shame. Duessa's 'race,' of which Night is the 'root,' is a system of interrelated evils. The 'most auncient Grandmother of all,' Night (who ironically but appropriately fails to recognize her 'daughter' at first) is a primeval power, at war until the end of time with 'the sonnes of Day' (I v 22, 25–7). This lineage suggests that falsehood is part of the human condition in a fundamental and abiding way. Lucifera's lineage gives pride a comparable status in Book I: 'Of griesly *Pluto* she the daughter was, / And sad *Proserpina* the Queene of hell' (I iv 11). Lucifera lies about her ancestry in claiming to be descended from Jove; but her lie helps to define the sin she personifies, since pride consists in willful self-deception about one's proper place in the scheme of things. Lucifera's parents are pagan gods, whereas Duessa's are personified abstractions; but these were overlapping categories for Spenser and his contemporaries. As early as Roman antiquity, the classical pantheon had been infiltrated by personifications like Fortune; and the gods themselves often personified abstract principles such as love or justice.

Not only in Book I but in every book, the most formidable enemies of the virtue in question are linked by genealogies that trace their origins to the Titans, or to the giants of the Old Testament, or to the primordial Chaos that threatens to reassert itself through their actions. In Book II, Guyon's principal antagonists are Pyrochles, the choleric or fiery man, and his brother Cymochles, the lecherous or 'moist' man. At II iv 41, they are said to be 'sonnes of old *Acrates* and *Despight*'; Acrates (Gr *akrateia* intemperance) is the son of Jarre (discord) and Phlegeton (the burning river of hell, suggesting both the fire, Gr *pyr*, of Pyrochles and the watery nature, Gr *kuma* 'wave,' of Cymochles). Phlegeton, in turn, is said to be the son of Erebus and Night, and Erebus, the son of Eternity. Here again, personified abstractions are woven into a genealogical system based on classical mythology. This same system is invoked again briefly in Book III where Arthur addresses Night, the 'Mother of annoyance sad, / Sister of heavie death,' as wife of Erebus 'the foe / Of all the Gods' (iv 55). In Book VI, the Blatant Beast is 'a Monster bred of hellishe race'; its parents are said to be Cerberus, the dog that guards the entrance to hell, and Chimera, the monster that guards the outer gates; a subsequent account of its origins extends them a generation further back, by citing as its parents the hideous monster Echidna, whom the gods thrust down to the lowest depths of hell, and Typhaon, father of the winds (i 7–8, vi 9–11).

For allegorical characters, genealogy, the tracing of lineage, often amounts to etymology, the tracing of a word back to its original, 'truest' sense. For example, Orgoglio is 'An hideous Geant horrible and hye,' whose mother is said to have been 'The greatest Earth' (I vii 8–9). In other words, this 'Geant' is etymologically derived from Gaea, the goddess Earth in Greek mythology. The Red Cross Knight is also linked to the earth by an etymological lineage. Contemplation explains to him that although sprung 'from ancient race / Of *Saxon* kings,' he was brought to Fairyland as a changeling and hidden in a furrow, where a ploughman found him and named him Georgos, which in Greek means 'tiller of the earth' (I x 65–6). The knight's Saxon lineage establishes that he has a predestined role to play in English history. His allegorical, 'fairy' lineage establishes that his sainthood as St George consists not in repudiation, but in acknowledgement and transformation, of one's earthly nature. The stupid boastfulness of the 'Geant' Orgoglio is from this point of view a demonic parody of the knight's saintly self-acceptance. (For a more extended treatment of these etymologies, see Craig 1967.)

Most of the heroes and heroines of *The Faerie Queene* are either British or Elfin/Fairy. As with Redcrosse's fairy lineage, the lineage of the Elfin/Fairy characters is apt to be quasi-mythological and allegorically suggestive. Satyrane, for example, is the son of a satyr who raised him up to assert humanity's natural supremacy over the lower animals. Amoret and Belphoebe were begotten upon 'the faire *Chrysogonee*' by the rays of the sun; and their grandmother, a fairy 'of high degree,' is named Amphisa, a Greek word that means 'of double nature' or 'equally both' (III vi 4). (Hamilton in *FQ* ed 1977 cites J.W. Draper 1932 and Lewis 1966 for these etymologies.) Amphisa's name foreshadows the miraculous birth of her daughter's opposite-natured twins: Belphoebe is supremely aloof and self-sufficient, Amoret is supremely amiable and dependent, and 'twixt them two' they share 'The heritage of all celestiall grace.' In contrast to the heroes and heroines whose lineage gives them a predestined role to play in British history (Redcrosse, Arthur, Britomart, Artegall), the Elfin/Fairy characters tend to be simpler figures whose nature is more allegorically transparent and whose capacity for growth and change is virtually nil (Cheney 1966:9).

The difference between the two races emerges most clearly when the British Arthur and the Elfin Guyon are given their nations' histories to read (II x). *Briton moniments* is a chronology of the rulers of Britain that traces Arthur's (and thereby Queen Elizabeth's) ancestry back to the nation's founding father, Trojan Brutus. The *Antiquitie of Faerie lond* meanwhile tells how the first man, called Elfe, was created by Prometheus with stolen fire, and how he married Fay, a native of the Garden of Adonis, 'Of whom all *Faeryes* spring, and fetch their lignage right' (71). Culminating with the reign of Gloriana, the Elfin chronicle gives Elizabeth a mythical ancestry that is conspicuously glorious, straightforward, and unproblematic. Spenser generates the line of Elfin kings etymologically by inflecting the original king's name: Elfin, Elfinan, Elfiline, and so forth. (Elferon's untimely death brings Gloriana's father Oberon to the throne; this one slight irregularity in the lineage calls attention to the link with Elizabeth.) Whereas Elizabeth's claim to the throne had been fragile on several counts at the time of her accession, Gloriana's title to rule not just England but Europe, America, and Asia – 'all the world' (72) – is as crystal clear as the tower Panthea in Fairyland's capital city of Cleopolis. At stake in the Fairy/Briton distinction is the degree to which an originating purpose or principle can be seen to inform a nation's history or an individual's life (Roche 1964:31–50).

In *FQ* III, British history itself becomes transparent to a providential design. Merlin's prophecy speaks directly to Britomart of her own family tree, 'Whose big embodied braunches shall not lin, / Till they to heavens hight forth stretched bee. / For from thy wombe a famous Progenie / Shall spring, out of the auncient *Trojan* blood' (iii 22). By casting this stretch of British history as prophecy, Spenser claims providential authorization for the political power of the Tudor royal dynasty. Dynastic mythmaking is a convention of Renaissance epic: Ariosto, Tasso, and Spenser took their cue from *Aeneid* 6.713–892, where Virgil traces the origins of Augustus' Roman empire. Later in Book III, Britomart demonstrates that she has internalized this understanding of her nation's history when she corrects Paridell's account of the outcome of the Trojan war. Boasting of his descent from Paris, he laments that Troy is 'now nought, but an idle name' (ix 33). Britomart is a better etymologist and genealogist, however; and at her urging, Paridell recalls that 'of the antique *Trojan* stocke, there grew / Another plant' (47), so that Troy now lives again as Troynovant. His descent from Paris finally means only that history repeats itself in a sterile and idle way: his theft of Hellenore from her miserly old husband is a petty domestic scandal without any effect on world history. Britomart, by contrast, experiences her own and her nation's history as part of an organic cycle whereby Trojan civilization is continually reborn, analogous to the cycle that perpetually renews the human species in the Garden of Adonis. JANE HEDLEY

Fichter 1982; Hinks 1939.

Lodge, Thomas (1558–1625) Poet, romancer, dramatist, satirist, pamphleteer, translator, adventurer, Catholic recusant, exile, physician. Second son of Sir Thomas Lodge, Lord Mayor of London (1562), he served in the household of Henry Stanley, fourth Earl of Derby, attended Merchant Taylors' School (1571–3) while Mulcaster served as headmaster (but after Spenser) and Trinity College, Oxford (BA 1577). He was admitted to Lincoln's Inn in 1578 and was still signing himself 'of' the Inn as late as 1595. His literary career proper lasted from about 1579 until 1597, when, having publicly avowed his Catholic allegiance, he left England to study medicine in Avignon. He remained abroad, practicing medicine in France and the Low Countries, for most of the next fifteen years; he then returned to England and, being exempted from prosecution for recusancy, established a successful practice in London's Catholic community. Appointed plague physician in 1625, he died in September of that year. Writing remained an avocation in later life; he produced medical treatises, devotional works, and monumental translations of Josephus (1602), Seneca (1614), and French Calvinist Simon Goulart's commentary on du Bartas (1621).

Lodge was a confirmed pastoralist, employing the mode variously in several prose romances, in his sonnet sequence *Phillis* (1593), and in a number of lyrics and eclogues scattered through other works and in anthologies. He was the principal contributor to *The Phoenix Nest* (1593), a partly pastoral collection; and evidence of his standing is his prominence in the best of the Elizabethan miscellanies, *Englands Helicon* (1600).

Spenser had the seminal influence on late Elizabethan pastoral, as Lodge bears witness explicitly and implicitly. His few direct references to Spenser are mainly in a pastoral connection. In the 'Induction' to *Phillis*, he addresses his verses, 'If so you come where learned *Colin* feedes / His lovely flocke, packe thence and quickly haste you; / You are but mistes before so bright a sunne, / Who hath the Palme for deepe invention wunne' (*Sp All* p 33). The first eclogue of *A Fig for Momus* (1595, the first collection in English of verse satires, epistles, and eclogues) is addressed 'To reverend Colin'; it is a dialogue between a young shepherd, Ergasto, and an old one, Damian (*Sp All* p 43), who sings a song ascribed to an absent musician, Ringde. The general model is *SC, Aprill*, though the subject, the decline of poetry, is nearer that of *October*; and Damian's song is a mythical fable vaguely reminiscent in theme of Thenot's tale of the Oak and the Briar in *Februarie*. The other three eclogues in the volume are on similar topics: poetry, patronage, youth and age. They are addressed to 'Menalcus' (?), 'Rowland' (Drayton), and Daniel; 'Golde' is Lodge. In the preface 'To the Gentlemen Readers,' he is no doubt alluding to E.K.'s glosses (and tacitly recognizing Spenser's preeminence in the genre) when he writes, 'For my *Eclogues*, I commend them to men of approved judgement, whose margents though I fill not with quotations, yet their matter, and handling, will show my diligence' (in ed 1883, 3).

Other eclogues show even more clearly the heritage of *The Shepheardes Calender*. In *Rosalynde* (1590), Lodge's best-known work, the old shepherd Coridon and his young companion Montanus speak 'a pleasant Eglog,' the older man chiding the younger for being in love, in the manner of *Februarie*. Coridon speaks in the *Shepheardes Calender* idiom: 'Say shepheards boy, what makes thee greet so sore? / Why leaves thy pipe his pleasure and delight?' and 'Ah Lorrell lad, what makes thee Herry love?' 'Coridons Song,' near the end of the tale, imitates *August* in its 'Heigh ho' echo refrain, and generally recalls *The Shepheardes Calender* in such lines as 'A smicker boy, a lyther Swaine,' 'she simpred smooth like bonny bell,' and 'Alas said he what garres thy griefe?' Lodge may allude to Spenser when he promises in the epilogue, 'assoon as I have overlookt my labors, expect the *Sailers Kalender.*' *Phillis* contains 'Egloga Prima Demades Damon,' a dialogue, also on the theme of age versus youth (*Sp All* p 15). Demades, the elder, admonishes Damon, 'For shame cast off these discontented lookes, / For griefe doth waight one life, tho never sought, / (So *Thenot* wrote admir'd for Pipe and bookes)' – an allusion to *Februarie* 11–16. In the Ovidian narrative poem *Scillaes Metamorphosis* (1589), the procession of '*Furie* and *Rage*, *Wan-hope*, *Dispaire*, and *Woe*' is comparable to the descriptions of the seven deadly sins in *FQ* I iv and of Despair in I ix; both come from a long tradition of similar descriptions. Other so-called allusions appear to be no more than general resemblances due to both poets' use of conventional *topoi* and imagery (*Sp All* pp 12–13).

Lodge mentions Spenser once by name. In *Wits Miserie, and the Worlds Madnesse* (1596), calling upon 'divine wits' to join forces in resisting detractors, he includes 'SPENCER, best read in ancient Poetry' (*Sp All* p 50); the others are Lyly, Daniel, Drayton, and Nashe. Spenser may allude to Lodge as 'Alcon' in *Colin Clout* 394–5 (see Paradise 1931:110–11).

While Lodge's familiarity with and admiration for Spenser is evident, it would be misleading to classify him as a Spenserian. Some of his pastoral romances and lyrics are inspired by others: Sidney, Montemayor, the French Pléiade, and the Italian Petrarchists. His other works suggest yet other contemporary influences: Golding, Marlowe, Greene, Nashe, Lyly, and Daniel. Lodge was an eclectic assimilator, a borrower, an imitator, but also frequently an experimenter and innovator. He has been attacked for unoriginality and plagiarism because he translated and adapted French and Italian poems without always naming his sources. His debt to Spenser was modest but significant, and he generously acknowledged it.

CHARLES WALTERS WHITWORTH, JR

Lodge ed 1883, still the only collected edition. Many of the literary works are available in separate editions. A standard study is N. Burton Paradise 1931 *Thomas Lodge: The History of an Elizabethan* (New Haven), but see also Helgerson 1976:105–23 for the pattern of Lodge's career; Wesley D. Rae 1967 *Thomas Lodge* (New York); and Charles W. Whitworth 1973 'Thomas Lodge, Elizabethan Pioneer' *CahiersE* 3:5–15. The most recent and thorough study is Eliane Cuvelier 1984 *Thomas Lodge: Témoin de son temps (c. 1558–1625)* (Paris).

logic Logic in Tudor England was central to education, and Spenser would have spent at least one of his years at Cambridge studying the standard texts of the art. Literary men often took more than a passing interest in the subject: both Abraham Fraunce and Milton, for instance, published logic texts of their own. Conversely, late sixteenth-century logics routinely illustrate their procedures with examples drawn from literary figures ranging from Virgil, Homer, Cicero, and Ovid to du Bellay, Ronsard, and Spenser. This relation between logic and literature may seem surprising today since the modern discipline called logic differs markedly from Tudor 'logic' or 'dialectic' (the terms were interchangeable). Modern logic is associated with the specialized and formally precise notation appropriate to science and mathematics, so that 'logical' and 'poetic' modes of thought may even be taken as antithetical, but sixteenth-century logicians declared their art to be nothing less than a general theory of discourse. John Seton, for example, author of a text widely used in the mid-Tudor period, defines his subject as 'the art of discoursing convincingly on any theme whatever'; and the French logician Peter Ramus defines logic even more simply as *ars bene disserendi*, 'the art of discoursing well.' Throughout these and other texts, the words used to describe logical procedures include *teaching*, *explaining*, *inventing*, *judging*, *organizing*, and *analyzing*, as well as what might seem to be the more likely terms, such as *disputing* or *arguing*.

Logic's concern with discourse developed in the fifteenth and early sixteenth centuries as part of a general reaction against what humanist scholars took to be the excesses of their medieval predecessors. Rejecting medieval logics as too narrowly directed towards abstruse philosophical problems, the humanists simplified the traditional logic course to make it more easily applied to the tasks of ordinary life. In practice, this meant that in addition to its traditional role as an art of disputation, logic also became the basis for teaching analytic reading and writing.

In this reorientation, perhaps the most

important change was the emphasis on 'the places of invention.' Long part of both the rhetorical and logical traditions, these places in essence comprise a set of conceptual categories such as *definition*, *genus*, *cause*, or *effect*, each of which names a particular kind of relationship which can hold between the subject and the predicate of a statement. For example, in the statement 'Man is a reasonable creature,' since the predicate defines the subject, the sentence would be said to have been taken from the 'place of definition.' Similarly, in the statement 'Man is an animal,' the predicate names the genus of the subject and therefore comes from the 'place of genus.' Rudolph Agricola's *De inventione dialectica* (1523) sets out 24 of these places, which collectively are supposed to provide for every possible relationship between any subject and any predicate.

In practice, the places helped to develop discourse by enabling a process of conceptual analysis whereby one's entire stock of knowledge on a given subject could be inventoried and applied. Typically, such an analysis began with a student's being given a 'question' to be thought through by means of the places. In *The Arte or Crafte of Rhethoryke* (1st ed 1530, 2nd ed 1532), Leonard Cox gives 'What is Justice?' as an example and shows his readers how to answer it through the logical places of definition, cause, effect, and division by parts. Students should 'visit' each place in turn, Cox advises, to search out appropriate statements which would develop the original question into a progressively more complex theme. The places thus provide a means of inventing subject matter sufficient to an entire discourse. Moreover, because questions often dealt with moral issues, a further result of such training was an analytic habit of mind whereby simple moral terms such as *justice* could be seen as conceptually complex entities whose full implications required a step-by-step unpacking into definitions, characteristics, opposites, causes, effects, and the like. This process mirrors the analysis of moral concepts in *The Faerie Queene*; when in the Letter to Raleigh Spenser promises a 'pleasing Analysis' of the moral virtues, his word *analysis* refers to precisely this kind of analytic thinking.

Beyond analysis, logic's interest in the places also extended to expository discourse, for once a student had surveyed the places appropriate to a given topic, and had thereby invented a range of subordinate statements, it was but a short step to writing them down. To move from analysis to discourse, however, an organizational theory was needed that would allow one to find a subject's clearest and most complete presentation. Rhetoric, of course, had long dealt with principles of oratorical organization; but its three traditional orders (judicial, deliberative, and demonstrative) were essentially audience-oriented. Each generally included an exordium, sections of proof and refutation, one or more digressions, and a peroration, none of which was appropriate to the relatively straightforward explication of concept which expository discourse required. In response, early sixteenth-century logics introduced to organizational theory the 'didascholic method,' an explicitly subject-oriented order. By midcentury, 'method,' as it came to be called, had become a usual logical concern; indeed, in Ramist logics, it subsumed all control of disposition, whether logical or rhetorical.

Of interest for Spenser studies are the discussions the logics developed concerning methods appropriate to different kinds of writing. For most discourse there was but one proper order, the so-called natural method of beginning a discourse with the most general statements and proceeding to those which were increasingly particular – that is, from issues of definition, through division, to specific examples. Though this natural method was generally regarded as the clearest of all expositional orders, some writers, poets among them, had license to use other orders. Historians, for example, substitute temporal in place of natural order; and poets often invert orders, subverting readers' expectations in order to surprise or to please. Spenser makes technical use of the term *method* in the Letter: the 'Methode of a Poet historical,' he explains, is not that of either the philosopher ('good discipline delivered plainly') or the historiographer ('affayres [presented] orderly as they were donne'), for 'a Poet thrusteth into the middest, even where it most concerneth him.' Here as for other organizational strategies in *The Faerie Queene*, Tudor logics provide useful contemporary glosses.

Finally, in addition to helping with the invention and disposition of discourse, the analytic procedures of Renaissance logic were also used to teach students the skills of close critical reading. Just as the places of invention could be used analytically to generate extended discourse from a single simple question, so the places could also be used as guides for parsing an extant discursive text into simpler parts. The explicit purpose of such parsings was to clarify an author's line of thought by isolating the elements of the argument in order to judge them for truth or falsity, but since such parsings required a close, word-by-word attention to the text, and the texts analyzed were often those which humanist educators took to be crucial elements of a liberal arts education, logical analysis became in practice a prototypical literary criticism. Such analyses were often classroom exercises; Gabriel Harvey's *Ciceronianus* provides an inspiring description of their ends and means.

Not many of these exercises survive, but of those which do, perhaps the most interesting is the analysis of Sidney's *Defence of Poetry* by William Temple, a Cambridge-trained logician who became Sidney's secretary in 1584. His 66-page *Analysis* systematically paraphrases Sidney's text in terms of its argumentative structure, it questions what Temple takes to be false or misleading statements, and it concludes with an evaluation of Sidney's method. Throughout, analyses like Temple's show Tudor readers actually responding to texts; and for this reason they make it possible to imagine, if only indirectly, what critical expectations readers and writers alike might have brought to literary works.

The humanist logics which dominated the sixteenth century lost influence in the seventeenth. The new science increasingly reclaimed logic for more technical purposes, and rhetoric absorbed those responsibilities for discourse which humanist logics had borne for almost two hundred years. Milton's *Artis logicae plenior institutio* (1672) was among the very last of the purely humanist texts; in this as in much else, Milton marks the end of an era. John Webster

Rudolph Agricola 1523 *De inventione dialectica* (Cologne, rpt Frankfurt am Main 1967); Cox ed 1899; Abraham Fraunce 1588 *The Lawiers Logike* (London; rpt Menston, Yorks 1969); Harvey ed 1945; Pierre de La Ramée 1964 *Dialectique (1555)* ed Michel Dassonville (Geneva); Milton *A Fuller Course in the Art of Logic Conformed to the Method of Peter Ramus* tr and ed Walter J. Ong and Carles Ermatinger, in ed 1953–82, 8:139–407; John Seton 1545 *Dialectica* (London); William Temple 1984 *William Temple's 'Analysis' of Sir Philip Sidney's 'Apology for Poetry'* tr and ed John Webster (Binghamton, NY); T. Wilson 1560; Wilson ed 1972.

In addition to introductions in the Harvey, de la Ramée, and Temple editions, the following are useful general studies of Renaissance logic: Neal W. Gilbert 1960 *Renaissance Concepts of Method* (New York); Howell 1956; Jardine 1974a; Jardine 1974b; Reichert 1963; Wilhelm Risse 1964 *Die Logik der Neuzeit* vol 1: 1500–1640 (Stuttgart); Cesare Vasoli 1968 *La dialettica e la retorica dell'Umanesimo* (Milan); John Webster 1981–2 'Oration and Method in Sidney's *Apology*: A Contemporary's Account' *MP* 79:1–15. Tuve 1947 considers the relation of logic and poetic imagery.

London At the beginning of the Tudor period, London was a medieval community of 50,000; by the mid-seventeenth century, when its population approached half a million, it was a rapidly changing metropolis that would soon become the largest and most powerful in Europe. Next to the English language, it was the greatest and most widely experienced artifact in England, and, like other Renaissance cities, it was also an idea, a compelling force in intellectual life. A variety of Tudor and Stuart literary works – lyrics, ballads, encomia, satires, sermons, speeches, chronicles, plays, and pageants – concern themselves with London; the most famous of these are perhaps John Stow's *Survey of London* (1598) and the city comedies of Jonson, Thomas Middleton, and their contemporaries. In Spenser's poetry, London appears in a few key images which form a coherent pattern and inform his treatment of history, public life, and political destiny.

(See **London** Figs 1-3.)

Only in *Prothalamion* does Spenser refer by name to 'mery London, my most kyndly Nurse' (128). There, the inns of court epitomize the city in a triumphal posture, as their 'bricky towres ... on *Themmes* brode aged backe doe ryde' (132–3). This image balances a hope for cultural endurance against the temporal decay and mutability associated with the river. Throughout his poetry, Spenser regards cities as symbols of human achievement, and he normally contrasts them with rivers in order to measure the power of this achievement to survive the ravages of time.

In several *Complaints* and elsewhere, Spenser juxtaposes the ghostly genii of cities with the rivers that flow relentlessly through their ruins. In *Theatre for Worldlings*, 'a wailing Nimphe,' the genius of Rome, sits complaining 'On that great rivers banke that runnes by Rome' (sonn 8, sonn 1); and in *Ruines of Rome*, the ancient city lies 'earth'd in her foundations deep' while nought 'save *Tyber* hastning to his fall / Remaines of all' (8, 3). The poet of *Ruines of Time*, walking beside 'silver streaming *Thamesis*,' encounters the wailing genius of Verulam, who recalls the time when she 'in the necke of all the world did ride' (1–2, 74). In *Prothalamion*, the triumphal posture of London riding the river's back thus indicates that in Spenser's imagination London expresses the more positive side of a generally ambivalent approach to cities.

Spenser's other major depictions of London are in *The Faerie Queene*, where Troynovant adopts the same triumphal posture. The mythical city fastens her foot on the 'stubborne neck' of wealthy Thames (III ix 45); rising on the princely Thames 'like to a Coronet' (IV xi 27), she becomes the crowning expression of a humanized time. Likened through her crown-like towers to Cybele, Troynovant reincarnates both 'Berecyntia mater ... turrita' ('the Berecynthian Mother, turret-crowned,' the Cretan cradle of the Trojan people from whom Virgil traces the founding of Rome in *Aeneid* 6.103–19, 785) and Rome itself (which Spenser, following du Bellay, personifies as 'the *Berecynthian* Goddesse bright ... with high turrets crownde' in *Rome* 6). Troynovant is thus heir to a legacy passed on from Rome; its triumph over the river, like that of London in *Prothalamion*, reverses the river-city imagery of the *Complaints*. More broadly, the triumphal image of Troynovant approximates the image of the New Jerusalem, which as the antithesis to Rome in *Theatre* stands as the foursquare eternal order through which time flows. Yet London's more precarious triumph, as it rides the river's back and with its bridge barely holds the river's 'roring rage' in check (*Proth* 133, *FQ* III ix 45), reflects a fundamental distinction between earthly cities and the City of God that Spenser draws from St Augustine and emphasizes in the contrast between the New Jerusalem and Cleopolis (I x).

For Spenser, then, London symbolizes historic achievement and cultural endurance. Drawing its main significance from the court (located in the London suburb of Westminster), it is first of all a seat of power, capital of the nation, center of empire, and heir to antiquity. Though Spenser never considers 'the City' of London as a civic or mercantile community distinct from the court, he seldom divorces the court from the civic stability and commercial support on which he believes courtly power is based. Britain will be 'sought / Of marchants farre, for profits therein praysd' (II x 5), and throughout *The Faerie Queene*, the historic meaning of Troynovant emerges through an allegorical struggle with such civic and economic concerns as profit and loss, excess and deficiency, justice and injustice, strife, order, marriage, family, property, and inheritance.

The two prophetic panels depicting Troynovant occupy the central books of *The Faerie Queene* (III ix 38ff, IV xi 28). They shade backward and forward to form a sequence that first locates Troynovant in history and then traces its gradual emergence. Troynovant is thus an arch-element in the poem's structure; it gives shape and direction to its epic thesis and thus balances its romance wanderings with a sense of purposeful progression. Exiled into Fairyland from a history still incomplete, the British heroes Redcrosse, Arthur, Britomart, and Artegall pursue a destiny that includes the triumph of Troynovant. The precedent for building an epic thesis on the praise and prophecy of a city Spenser found principally in Virgil, though he could also have found the procedure in such Renaissance epics as Petrarch's *Africa* (9.305–51), Ariosto's *Orlando furioso* (35.6–7), and Tasso's *Gerusalemme liberata* (17.70–92).

The myth of Trojan descent, which traces the founding of London to Brute (a descendant of Aeneas), comes to Spenser from Geoffrey of Monmouth via several sources, principally Holinshed (1577, 1586). Arthur was regarded as a descendant of Brute, and the Arthurian motifs and chivalric decorum belong in curious ways to the contemporary image of London. The sixteenth-century chivalric revival, which can be traced through Caxton to fifteenth-century economic connections between Burgundy and London's merchants, provided a language in which Londoners frequently expressed their civic pride. Arthurian motifs often colored the civic pageants and military societies of Tudor London, and a number of burlesques (from *The Tournament of Tottenham* c 1440 to *The Knight of the Burning Pestle* 1613) reflect the more improbable adaptations of chivalry to the urban sphere. The chivalric and romance decorum of *The Faerie Queene* is thus connected to a style of civic consciousness and to a myth about London's epic destiny.

Spenser fleshes out this myth through a series of contrasted cities. In Book I x, the ahistorical contrast between the New Jerusalem and Cleopolis, between the City of God and the ideal city of earthly fame, is relevant to London chiefly through the further resemblance of Cleopolis to Troynovant. In Book II x, when Spenser enters history by turning from the rectified soul to the rectified body and body politic, he contrasts the idealized 'history' of Fairyland with the strife-torn history of Britain. The building of Cleopolis, a key development in the legends of Fairyland, is both a model for the historic evolution of all cities and an ideal that, in its emergence, Troynovant must approximate. The three great monuments of Cleopolis – Elfiline's 'golden wall,' Elfant's tower of Panthea, and Elfinor's 'bridge of bras' (x 72–3) – correspond to the three landmarks of Troynovant (and implicitly of London): its wall, tower, and bridge (II x 46, III ix 45, IV xi 27–8). Moreover, the order in which the monuments of Cleopolis are built parallels the historical progression from Troy to Rome to Troynovant. Elfiline's wall evokes the walls built by Tros, Romulus, and Lud, and thereby symbolizes the common cultural foundations of all three cities. Elfant's addition, the tower of Panthea, alludes to both the Roman Pantheon and the Roman addition to Trojan culture, which is shared by London and symbolized in its Tower, traditionally built by Julius Caesar. Elfinor's bridge of brass, which completes the building of Cleopolis, points forward from Rome to Troynovant, whose bridge is accounted a 'wonder of the world' (III ix 45). Through this bridge, the personified 'foot' of Troynovant, Spenser builds the image of the city's triumph which reverses the images of ancient Rome and Verulam in the *Complaints*.

Having pointed forward to Troynovant as the successor to Rome, Spenser examines this succession in Book III ix, contrasting Troynovant with its ancestors by comparing two versions of Trojan history recounted by Paridell and Britomart. Just as Britomart's adventures exemplify the ideal course of love and contrast with the wayward eros of Paridell, so her prophecy of Troynovant corrects the sad and incomplete story of Troy, which Paridell fails to trace beyond the founding of Rome. In Book IV, which traces the further progress of love toward its culmination in social concord (perhaps following Plato's *Republic* 2–4), Spenser compares Troynovant not to its ancestors but to its contemporary British neighbors. By naming the major towns as well as rivers of Britain, and by linking Troynovant to the kingdom at large, he depicts the reciprocity and concord that make Troynovant the center of a renewed empire.

Troynovant disappears from the poem as Spenser moves closest to contemporary history in Book V and then furthest from it in Book VI. However, the fate of Belge's 'cities sackt' (V x 23), and especially of Antwerp, London's main trading partner and the scene of Arthur's triumphal entry (xi 34), continues to connect Spenser's epic thesis to contemporary urban life. Like Aeneas' visit to the site of the future Rome (*Aeneid* 8), or Dante's vision of the earthly paradise (*Purgatorio* 32), Spenser's return to the pastoral sources of civility in Book VI defines the ideals of an advanced civilization.

During Spenser's lifetime, London's population increased from 100,000 to roughly 200,000, and Spenser registers some of the city's troubled life in his moral allegory. The seven corporal works of Mercy's Bead-men (I x 37–44), the wordly care and carelessness of Mammon and Phaedria, the body politic of Alma, the civic discord of Ate, or the tempering of Love and Hate by Concord are matters of concern throughout contemporary literature on London. In some cases, London may contribute images to Spenser's allegory, for example, Mammon's hundred roaring furnaces and vast storehouse, the thronging highway leading to the house of Pride, or the riotous mobs of Book v.

To pass from the allegory to the physical world of *The Faerie Queene*, and from its heroes to its lesser creations, is to discover the poem's capacity to embrace common life. Spenser depicts or alludes to clerks, bailiffs, surgeons, schoolmistresses, beadsmen, cooks, watchmen, keepers, messengers, monks, priests, bargemen, boatmen, pilots, sailors, fishermen, merchants, butchers, blacksmiths, goldsmiths, footmen, tax collectors, widows, orphans, beggars, courtesans, and thieves. Towers and palaces dominate his architectural vistas, but his landscape also includes inns, churches, schools, a hospital, bridges, harbors, a storehouse, sheds, walls, pillars, steeples, gates, and streets. For this landscape there is a solid material substrate of bricks, mortar, timber, glass, nails, conduit pipe, brass, iron, steel, lead, copper wire, cheese, milk, bread, wine, tobacco, coaches, wagons, wheels, clocks, compasses, cobbled shoes, linen, arras, and silk.

At this level, as in its pageantry, prophecies, and political allegories, Spenser's *Faerie Queene* bears out Tasso's claim that an epic poem is like 'some noble city' (ed 1973:205). LAWRENCE MANLEY

The best account of Elizabethan London remains Stow ed 1908. A succinct account of the main developments may be found in Peter Clark and Paul Slack 1976 *English Towns in Transition, 1500–1700* (New York) ch 5 'London.' Recent historical scholarship is gathered in A.L. Beier and Roger Finlay, eds 1986 *London 1500–1700: The Making of the Metropolis* (London). For Spenser's images of London, see Manley 1982. A collection of Tudor and Stuart literature on London is Lawrence Manley 1986, ed *London in the Age of Shakespeare: An Anthology* (London).

Lucifera Named from Lucifer (Satan), Lucifera embodies Redcrosse's delight in worldly glory while he is under the sway of faithless and corrupt Fidessa-Duessa. Indeed, it is Duessa who bids him 'bend his pace' to Lucifera's palace (*FQ* I iv 3ff). Simply, Lucifera signifies worldly pride, claiming Jove or whoever else may be 'highest' as her father. The paranoia of pride is finely caught in her jealousy of what she sees as the competitive brightness of her own throne. The essential materialism of the worldly glory that is one of pride's goals is expressed in the description of her palace and in the horrifying physical condition of some of her prisoners ('Like carkases of beasts in butchers stall' v 49). Her chthonic and diabolical aspects are suggested by her name, by her infernal dungeon, by the fact that Duessa's visit to the underworld occurs during the Lucifera episode, and by her parents, Pluto and Proserpina, king and queen of hell. Her spiritually corrupting consequences are further disclosed through her male counterpart, the proud, rebellious giant Orgoglio to whom Redcrosse succumbs in his next adventure (vii-viii).

Lucifera's superficial brilliance and vainglory make her a parody of Gloriana (though it would not have taken a very astute courtly reader to notice a satiric equivalence between some of Lucifera's aspects and trappings and those of Elizabeth: eg, iv 14 and the parody of the Accession Day tilts at v 5ff). What Lucifera and her palace signify for Redcrosse is summed up in his fight there with Sansjoy for the shield of Sansfoy: Redcrosse's initial joylessness (i 2) is now firmly established; it will culminate in his encounter with Despair which is also the apogee of his Sansfoy-like faithlessness.

Lucifera's palace is covered in 'golden foile' (iv 4) because it is essentially a place of hypocrisy (in its traditional derivation from Gr *hyper* + *chrysos* 'overlaid with gold': cf Dante's 'painted people ... gilded on the outside so they dazzle' *Inferno* 23.58–64), a place which conceals its spiritual and moral paucity and corruption. She seduces Redcrosse with an image of vainglory and the sins of the world, particularly 'the luste of the eyes, and the pride of life' (1 John 2.16), traditionally identified with the temptations of the tower and the kingdoms (Matt 4, Luke 4; see Cullen 1974: xxviii ff). Her name and character suggest the identification (as in the Geneva gloss) of 'Lucifer, sonne of the morning,' with Nebuchadnezzar, king of Babylon, who exalted his throne, claimed to be 'like the moste high,' and tyrannically refused to open 'the house of his prisoners' (Isa 14.12, 14, 17); the 'mercilesse' dungeon of Lucifera's palace is filled with prisoners who 'live in woe, and die in wretchednesse' (v 46). Her palace thus assumes aspects of Augustine's Babel-Babylon, the earthly city in *The City of God*: it has Babel-like 'loftie towres' and is built on a sandy hill (iv 4–5; cf Babel, built 'on a plot of sandie ground' in *Ruines of Time* 508). Babel's builder, Nimrod (Geneva gloss to Gen 10.8, 11.2), is in Lucifera's dungeon together with Nebuchadnezzar (v 47–8).

Augustine opposes his earthly city to the heavenly one. Similarly, Lucifera's palace is the opposite of the New Jerusalem seen by Redcrosse, and is also the opposite of its ideal earthly manifestation, Cleopolis, Gloriana's city of fame and glory (x 55ff; at II x 72, Cleopolis is 'enclosd ... with a golden wall,' another reason for the gold over Lucifera's palace). This parody of Cleopolis and its connection to tyrannical Nimrod and Nebuchadnezzar confirm the enthroned Lucifera as a demonic parody of the benevolently absolutist Elizabeth. She shares Persian pride with Catholic Fidessa (ii 13, iv 7) and recalls either Mary Tudor or the recently executed Mary, Queen of Scots, or both. She doubles Elizabeth and Una in presenting herself as 'mayden Queene' (iv 8; cf the wanton 'virgine, daughter Babel' of Isa 47.1), while her palace's ostentatious splendor contrasts with the palace of Una's parents (xii 14), the 'bare and plaine' nature of which may offer passing praise for Elizabeth's parsimony. As the planetary Lucifer or morning star, she imitates Una as Venus-Lucifer and Elizabeth in her mythological role as queen of love (Strong 1963:63). Hence she carries a Venerean mirror of vanity (iv 10) which is also the mirror of pride, a detail possibly linking her with depictions of the Whore of Babylon (Rev 17; see Rush 1976). Her narcissistic self-viewing is also an attempt to undo Elizabeth as the 'Mirrour of grace' (I proem 4).

Lucifera's 'scornefull feete' trample a dragon in anticipation of Isis and Mercilla (iv 10; cf v vii 15, ix 33), in imitation of Elizabeth trampling the papal Antichrist (Strong 1963:119, 121) and of the dragon-monarch as cosmic ruler (Horapollo *Hieroglyphics* 1.61, ed 1950:84), and in parody of Elizabeth as head of the Order of the Garter which had dragon-killing George as its patron saint, though the primary and ironic allusion is to Luke 10.18–19, 'I sawe Satan ... fall downe from heaven. Beholde, I give unto you power to treade on serpents.' Moreover, as the chthonic counterpart of the serpent of wisdom (Matt 10.16), the dragon connects Lucifera with biform Error and with hell, which we visit while at Lucifera's palace in canto v. *FQ* I iv 11 tells us that Lucifera's parents are infernal Pluto (commonly identified with Plutus, god of riches, thus implying a further link between Lucifera and the Mammon of II vii) and Proserpina (already summoned by Archimago at I i 37). As ravisher of Proserpina, Pluto causes Ceres' grief and the world's winter desolation. Spenser here implies another attempt to eclipse Elizabeth, frequently portrayed as Ceres-Astraea (Yates 1975:29ff). Since Proserpina is the dark aspect of the moon goddess, often identified with Hecate, goddess of witchcraft, we may detect a conjunction between Lucifera and her 'wisards' (iv 12) and the witch Duessa and the black magician Archimago. Most terrifying of all, Lucifera eclipses Elizabeth by adopting for her own a name that belongs by right to the virginal moon queen, since Lucifera is a Greco-Roman epithet for the moon (Cicero *De natura deorum* 2.27; cf Hankins 1944, who cites Conti as source).

The 'broad high way' that leads to her palace associates it, and turns it into yet another encounter, with Error's forest, opposing it to Caelia's house of Holiness (i 7, x 5; cf x 55 and Matt 7.13), so that it becomes the destructive Catholic antithesis to 'heavenly' Protestantism, a false temple of Solomon (the original of which was 'overlaid ... with golde' 1 Kings 6.22, etc), and literally a church built on sand (Matt 7.26–7). It is constructed of 'squared bricke' (dressed, and therefore polluted, stone; cf Exod 20.25) to recall Solomon's 'foure square' house (1 Kings 7.5; it was commonplace to identify the English monarch with Solomon) and to parody the 'foure square' New Jerusalem as well as Aristotle's quadrate of virtue (Rev 21.16, *Nicomachean Ethics* 1100b).

Lucifera has affinities with seductive Circe via an allusion to Ariosto's Circe-like Alcina (*Orlando furioso* 6.59ff). As a charioteer accompanied by Fidessa and Satan and drawn by the six other sins, she is an anti-Prudence, since Prudence was traditionally charioteer of the virtues; and the procession is also a dynamic and proleptic unfolding of Fidessa's apocalyptic seven-headed beast of the sins (vii 17). As a quasi-solar figure inhabiting a palace like the sun god's, she is also a presumptuous Phaethon and imitator of Una's solar attributes (iv 8–9; cf Ovid *Metamorphoses* 2.1ff). She is like Titan because Hyperion the sun god was a Titan and because the Titans dethroned their father to become symbols of rebellious pride. Hence, too, she claims paternity from the usurper Jove and rivals Juno, the queen of heaven and enemy of Aeneas, Elizabeth's supposed ancestor. Lucifera disappears from the poem after canto v; but her defeat is later implied in canto vii when solar Arthur appears with his shield of faith and fortitude which 'exceeding' shines (34), thus answering and canceling out the Lucifera who 'exceeding shone' at iv 8–9.

DOUGLAS BROOKS-DAVIES

Brooks-Davies 1977:45–6; John E. Hankins 1944 'Spenser's Lucifera and Philotime' *MLN* 59:413–15; Richard R. Rush 1976 'An Iconographic Source of Lucifera' *SIcon* 2:121–5.

Lucretius (94?–55? BC) The only known work of Titus Lucretius Carus is *De rerum natura* (*On the Nature of Things*), a didactic epic in the tradition of Hesiod, Aratus, and Empedocles. In Latin hexameters, it presents the atomic theory and ethics of the Greek philosopher Epicurus, asserting the therapeutic value of a studied tranquillity or 'ataraxia' in the midst of a changing world. 'In observing universal mutation and the vanity of life, [Lucretius] conceived behind appearance a great intelligible process, an evolution in nature' (Santayana 1910:29). Although Christianity opposed Lucretius' materialistic Epicureanism, his poem became an influential part of western intellectual and literary history, as evidenced by Chaucer and Dante, among others.

Poggio Bracciolini's discovery of a new manuscript of *De rerum natura* in a Swiss monastery in 1418 led to renewed interest in the poem; influential Neoplatonists like Ficino and mythographers like Conti quoted Lucretius' words and ideas. The syncretism that marks all Renaissance imitations of the classics is particularly evident in adaptations of Lucretius, in which his overt naturalism is blended with the idealizing of mythic figures (most notably, Venus) and with Christian and Platonic themes.

Spenser's own didactic purpose, as outlined in the Letter to Raleigh, may have made Lucretius' example especially congenial. It has even been suggested that Lucretius' influence may have been greater than Plato's, that 'his feeling for this world that is caught in the whirl of change' made for a 'deeper communion of spirit ... between Spenser and Lucretius' (Renwick in *Var* 1:361). If we are to believe Bryskett, Spenser's knowledge of Greek and his command of Latin and Italian gave him firsthand access to sources, text, and new interpretations of the poem. Possible echoes of Lucretius have been found throughout Spenser's canon, as the *Variorum* demonstrates; but significant influence may be seen most clearly at three points in *The Faerie Queene*: the Garden of Adonis (III vi), the hymn to Venus (IV x 44–7), and the *Cantos of Mutabilitie*.

Lucretius' materialism has been seen as a source for Spenser's description of natural processes in the Garden; and the religious skepticism underlying the Roman poet's ethical concepts and his atomistic universe may inform the arguments and actions of Mutabilitie (see Greenlaw 1920). The extent of specifically Lucretian influence has been disputed, however (see *Var* 3:340–52, 6:389–432); and the controversy has revealed the breadth of Spenser's exposure to classical and contemporary philosophical texts, as well as the impossibility of isolating individual sources for widely available ideas.

Lucretius' influence is more direct in Spenser's hymn to Venus, which closely follows the opening lines of *De rerum natura*, where the goddess is similarly invoked as a universal figure of fertility, 'joy of Gods and men' (*hominum divomque voluptas*) and source of flowers from the 'daedale earth' (*daedala tellus*). Spenser may be indebted as well to Chaucer's opening lines of the *Canterbury Tales* for this panorama of springtime impulses, which includes birds 'Privily pricked with thy lustfull powres'; yet even here Chaucer's 'smale foweles ... So priketh hem nature in hir corages' translates the Latin 'volucres ... perculsae corda tua vi.' And although the context of Spenser's hymn, sung by an anguished lover craving relief from his 'fury' and 'inward fire,' is alien to the tone of Lucretius' *prooemium*, it is characteristic of the poem's later, more savage description of the sensory prickings of lust in the human body: 'Haec Venus est nobis' ('This is our Venus' 4.1058). Spenser's blending of these two, widely separate treatments of Venus is perhaps the strongest evidence of his familiarity with, and indebtedness to, Lucretius.

WILLIAM A. SESSIONS

Greenlaw 1920; George Depue Hadzsits 1935 *Lucretius and His Influence* (New York); George Santayana 1910 *Three Philosophical Poets: Lucretius, Dante, and Goethe* (Cambridge, Mass); David West 1969 *The Imagery and Poetry of Lucretius* (Edinburgh).

Lust *The Faerie Queene* contains numerous figures of sexual excess, where desire is transformed into obsession and the creative urge becomes a purely physical drive to possess another by holding, carrying off, unclothing, penetrating, battering, or devouring. Such obsessive individuals may be characterized by hot, swollen, or deformed organs (eg, the unveiled Duessa at I viii 46–8), or by being themselves swollen or oversized (Argante and Ollyphant at III vii and xi); they may change shape, often to animal forms ('that old leachour' Proteus at III viii 41), be covered with excessive hair (Lust at IV vii 7), or have rolling eyes or an undiscriminating gaze (Malecasta at III i 41); they may carry a stick or other phallic emblem (the Foster's 'sharp bore spear' III i 17). The figure of Lechery in the pageant of the seven deadly sins is typical: he rides a hairy walleyed goat; he seems outwardly pleasant in his clothes of green but his body is filthy (I iv 24–6). He captures 'wemens hearts' by singing and dancing, and he carries a 'burning hart' in his hand.

The most memorable figure of sexual obsession is named Lust, the ugly and ferocious monster who captures Amoret, exemplar of love, and is finally defeated by her sister Belphoebe, exemplar of chaste virginity (IV vii 4–32). He is hairy and has a 'wide mouth ... With huge great teeth' and a hanging lower lip large enough to store 'the relickes of his feast.' His 'huge great nose ... empurpled all with bloud' is like the trunk of an elephant (for a contemporary instance of the popular association of nose and penis, see Donne's Probleme II, 'Why doth the poxe soe much affect to undermine the nose?'). Like Lechery, he is clothed in green, and like the Foster he bears a staff 'Whose knottie snags were sharpned all afore.' The solitary possessiveness of his behavior is stressed by his cannibalism ('on the spoile of women he doth live' – the connection between eating and sexual activity is made emphatic by the rhyme *deflowre/devoure*), and by the implied masturbation ('Gan dight him selfe unto his wonted sinne') that precedes his assault on the women (Hankins 1971:160). With the aid of an old woman who distracts him and satisfies his appetites, Amoret escapes Lust but is recaptured (a fact suggesting her inability to escape concupiscence by her own efforts); Lust is held at bay by Timias (who is unable to kill him because he is an inconstant lover, being in a sense distracted from both Belphoebe and from his opponent by Amoret, whom Lust is using as a shield), and is finally killed by Belphoebe.

This figure of Lust is a compilation of images, an exaggeration of traditional motifs. He is more than the conventional lecher who is compared to a goat or other beast; like Malbecco, he seems to have crossed the line separating human from beast, and to be no longer merely *like* an animal. His oversized features may come from illustrated versions of travel literature, such as the *Travels* attributed to Sir John Mandeville (Bennett 1954:248–9). He is the outward figuring of a moral quality that is frequently referred to in Spenser's writings.

This lust is often presented in sharp antithesis to love (*Hymne of Love* 176–82, *FQ* III i 49). Yet it is hardly different from love: what the witch's son feels towards Florimell (III vii-viii) seems silly, harmless love, though Spenser declares that it is 'No love, but brutish lust' (vii 15). Its brutishness comes from the fact that it is felt by a lazy and stupid son of a witch, whereas Florimell is of noble birth and destined for Marinell. Love between persons of different social, and therefore moral, status is seen as impossible to fulfill in marriage, and therefore equivalent to lust. Thus the love of the Brigand captain for Pastorella (VI xi 4–8) and Timias' love for Belphoebe (III v 43–50, IV vii 37–47) are both condemned as lust.

Lust seldom attains its aim in *The Faerie Queene*: those who are possessed by it frequently advertise the fact so clearly that their victims are able to escape (eg, I vi 3–8, V v 26–57). On other occasions, carnal satisfaction is only illusory, as in Redcrosse's dream (I i 47–9) and in Blandamour's wresting of the false Florimell from Ferraugh (IV ii 6–11). When lustful actions do take place, the pleasure they give is insubstantial: in Castle Joyous, Britomart is entertained by six handsome knights representing six pleasures of lust, but 'to faire *Britomart* they all but shadowes beene' (III i 45). Ordinary people, however, may be deceived by lust's outward attractions, for like Lechery, it puts on a 'gowne ... full faire, / Which underneath [hides] his filthinesse' (I iv 25).

Lust reveals its horror in the consequences of its actions. In contrast to love from which 'spring all noble deeds and never dying fame' (III iii 1), lust draws good knights 'from pursuit of praise and fame' (II i 23). The ultimate stage of lust is well illustrated by Cymochles, figure of concupiscence in II vi-viii. He is killed by Arthur, and, like the soul of Lust in IV vii 32, his 'ghost ... to th'infernall shade / Fast flying, there eternall torment [finds]' (II viii 45).

From a theological point of view, lust is a form of concupiscence, an extreme desire for immediate temporal ends, usually those of the senses. According to Augustine, who echoes Paul's many injunctions against physical sin ('Let not sinne reigne therefore in your mortal bodie, that ye shulde obey it in the lustes thereof' Rom 6.12), the Fall left the human race in a weakened state, whereby the desires of the flesh are no longer subject to reason (*City of God* 19.27). Although later Roman Catholic theologians treated concupiscence as not being a sin in itself, Lutheran and Calvinist thinkers tended rather to treat it as direct and actual sin. So, too, in Spenser, there is no evidence that Lust has a weakened or deformed will; he is instead himself a powerful figure of the depraved human will.

SUSUMU KAWANISHI

Lydgate, John (c 1375–c 1448) The most prolific and popular of Chaucer's followers. Lydgate's oeuvre runs, at the most generous estimate, to over 150,000 lines, although this figure is certainly swelled by a number of spurious attributions. His longest and most important works were his *Troy Book*, an account of the siege and destruction of Troy, and *The Fall of Princes*, a compendium of tragedies deriving ultimately from Boccaccio's *De casibus virorum illustrium*.

Among the works less certainly his are two which may have influenced Spenser: an English version of Deguileville's *Pèlerinage de la vie humaine* in verse, a possible source for the story of the Red Cross Knight in *FQ* I, and the long allegorical poem *Reason and Sensuality*, a possible source for the portrait of Nature in the *Cantos of Mutabilitie* (Kahin 1941). The very limited English circulation of this second poem, as well as the rather tenuous parallels that have been drawn, make direct influence highly improbable.

A work certainly by Lydgate which has been urged as a source for *The Faerie Queene* is his *Life of St George* (Padelford and O'Connor 1926, *Var* 1:386–9), but in none of the points of correspondence is Lydgate a unique source (Schulze 1931). Equally tenuous is the claim that Lydgate's only prose work, *The Serpent of Division*, may be one source for *Time* (Orwen 1941): the argument rests solely on coincidences of date (Lydgate's work was reprinted in 1590) and theme (both works warn against civil strife and are preoccupied with the problem of succession). Again, any specific relation is difficult to establish. Yet Lydgate probably did have some general influence on Spenser: Lydgate's name was so frequently coupled with Chaucer's in the sixteenth-century that it would be hard for him not to be aware at least of his major works, which were still widely available in both manuscript and print.

Spenser may have been drawn to Lydgate's *Troy Book* by its patriotic linking of the Troy story to contemporary history, for he employs the Troy legend as part of the glorification of Elizabethan England. He probably knew *The Fall of Princes*, if only indirectly through its imitation in the *Mirror for Magistrates*. More generally, Lydgate was important as an imitator and transmitter of Chaucerian style and language, and thus a likely source for Spenser's consciously archaic vocabulary. His lexicographical and stylistic innovativeness, which expressed itself most distinctively in his Latin-based, polysyllabic, aureate diction, would probably have found a positive response in Spenser's often backward-looking sensibilities.

A.S.G. EDWARDS

Kahin 1941; William R. Orwen 1941 'Spenser and the Serpent of Division' *SP* 38:198–210; Padelford and O'Connor 1926; Derek Pearsall 1970 *John Lydgate* (London); Alain Renoir 1967 *The Poetry of John Lydgate* (Cambridge, Mass; cites *The Temple of Glas* as a source for Panthea in *FQ* II); Walter F. Schirmer 1961 *John Lydgate: A Study in the Culture of the XVth Century* tr Ann E. Keep (London); Ivan L. Schulze 1931 'The Maiden and Her Lamb, *Faerie Queene*, Book I' *MLN* 46:379–81.

Lyly, John (1554?-1606) Only one direct and unambiguous point of contact between Spenser and Lyly seems to be known. In *Euphues and His England* (1580), we find a near quotation from *SC, Aprill* 137–8: 'heere wil be Jilly-floures, Carnations, sops in wine' (2:134). That Lyly read *The Shepheardes Calender* soon after it was published need not surprise us. An aspiring writer looking for fashionable novelties could hardly be expected to ignore 'the new Poete.' In *Pierces Supererogation*, Harvey tells us that before the quarrel about *Speculum tuscanismi* (1580; Lyly had apparently persuaded Oxford that he was the object of Harvey's satire on an Italianate Englishman) he had loved Lyly, 'in hope praysed him; many wayes favored him, and never any way offended him' (Harvey 1593:68). We may suppose that if Harvey had praised Lyly before 1580, Spenser must at least have been persuaded to look into *Euphues: The Anatomy of Wit* (1578). London literary life in this period was not a widely dispersed affair; it seems certain that the two men must have had many contacts in common (to put the issue in its most conservative terms). Spenser may also have known Lyly through Thomas Watson: in 1582, Lyly wrote a preface for Watson's *Hekatompathia*; in the third of the *Foure Letters*, Harvey mentions Watson with approval (1592:48); and in his *Meliboeus* of 1590, Watson praises Spenser as 'noster Apollo' (*Sp All* p 20).

The whole question of literary contacts in this period is, of course, worm-eaten with sentimental speculation: it is as profitless to conjecture that Lyly is 'Our pleasant *Willy*' in *Teares of the Muses* (208) as to imagine that Watson is Alcon in *Colin Clouts Come Home Againe* (394). It is more important to recognize that all these writers were in London at the same time, bent on the same purpose, clinging to the coattails of potentially cultured aristocrats, sharing (we may say) the shameful trade in flattery and reversions, in promises evaded and pensions not paid. Their future careers, convergent or divergent, depended largely on the ways in which the patrons they secured used or rewarded them. Lyly's first book, *Euphues: The Anatomy of Wit*, was a runaway success and established him at once as the up-to-the-minute purveyor of a dazzling courtly dialect. His attachment to the Earl of Oxford allowed him to exploit this success and use the Earl's singing boys to present his witty comedies at court and so (as it were) speak directly to the Queen. The success carried, of course, its own stamp of failure. Theater (even courtly theater) was snared in the suspect world of public and commercial art; its functionaries were thought of as naturally using the servants' entrance. Moreover, the sharp definition of court comedy confined it to a narrow range of immediate effects, aimed to secure the attention of a small specialized audience whose tastes and limitations were inevitably inscribed on the work written for it. It proved impossible for Lyly to move, like Euphues, from 'wit' to 'wisdom.' At the end of his novel, Lyly imagines his hero, seated in his cell on a remote mountain, as a classical sage who has seen it all and seen through it all, and whose remaining role is to point out the follies of love and ambition. Without a lucrative sinecure, however, the Elizabethan sage had to descend into the marketplace, play the buffoon, and end by despising himself for having done so.

In his distancing irony and in the manipulative wit of his antithetical prose structures, Lyly (and his persona Euphues) stands opposite to Spenser (and his alter ego Colin), who is characterized rather by ardency and commitment. Lyly presents his material with the flourish of a prestidigitator; he is always doctrinally correct, but he gives no sign of religious enthusiasm or of romantic astonishment. For him, love is less a mystery than an occasion for wit. His court allegories (particularly *Endymion*) deal with hopeless passions; but these are organized through his standard technique of a series of short sharp exchanges, subjecting the subject matter (hopeless passion, for example) to a witty parody of scholastic *divisiones*. Technically speaking, it is hard to imagine anything less Spenserian. G.K. HUNTER

G.K. Hunter 1962; John Lyly 1902 *Complete Works* ed R. Warwick Bond, 3 vols (Oxford).

M

MacDonald, George (1824–1905) Scottish-born writer of poetry, novels, romances, fairy tales, criticism, and sermons, MacDonald is noteworthy as a critic of Spenser's art and as an artist who draws on the Spenserian tradition. Though most of his works are little read today, there has been a revival of interest in his romances and fairy tales since the 1940s, spurred largely by C.S. Lewis, who acknowledged a profound debt to MacDonald's writings. Lewis first read *The Faerie Queene* and *Phantastes* at the same time early in 1916, and MacDonald's narrative helped foster Lewis' lasting interest in the Spenserian tradition.

As a critic, MacDonald is firmly in the Romantic tradition. When he compares Spenser's rhythms to melodies in water, 'like a full, peaceful stream, diffuse, with plenteousness unrestrained' (1868:66), he is adopting a metaphor used by Coleridge and Hazlitt. He also shares some of Coleridge's ambivalence regarding allegory. In *England's Antiphon*, a critical history of English religious poetry, he acknowledges *The Faerie Queene* as a major work but regrets its reliance on 'antique effects' (1868:64). Though he is drawn to the imaginative suggestiveness of allegory, he is wary of reductive, codified allegorical readings. The very complexity of the poem, coupled with the range of interpretative keys it attracted, undercut the pleasure he took at the purely narrative level. True religious poetry, he says, must spring from true religious feeling, and he praises Spenser for embodying the Reformation spirit of personal moral responsibility. As might be expected from the subject of his book, he praises the third and fourth *Hymnes* more than the first two. Elsewhere, however, in his essay 'The Imagination: Its Functions and Its Culture,' he quotes *Hymne of Beautie* 117–33 to help explain the relationship between poetic thought and poetic form (MacDonald 1867).

Spenserian echoes occur throughout MacDonald's fiction, even in a late work such as *Lilith* (1895), but the echoes are clearest and most self-conscious in his first major prose work, *Phantastes: A Faerie Romance for Men and Women* (1858). The title is only a partial nod to Spenser, for the epigraph names Phineas Fletcher's *Purple Island* as the source of the name Phantastes. The spelling of 'Faerie' seems a clear allusion to Spenser, however, though within the narrative itself MacDonald reverts to the more usual Victorian phrase 'Fairy Land.' The work resists any systematic allegorical reading but the narrative is Spenserian in its episodic structure, symbolic settings, transformative imagery, questing subject, and emblematic naming (eg, the hero is called Anodos, from Gr 'upward path'). Spenserian types abound: characters in the form of trees, waning knights, Duessa-like false heroines, giants, dragons, and a wolf-like creature that represents the idol worshiped by a corrupt religion. Spenser is referred to twice through epigraphic quotation (though the second quotation is actually from Roydon's elegy on Sidney, not Spenser's as claimed in the first edition). *FQ* I v I is quoted to introduce Anodos' climactic encounter with a giant, and the hero seems to aspire to a Renaissance standard of chivalry throughout. Like Redcrosse, Anodos is easily deceived, waylaid, and defeated, and his quest is eventually seen to be subservient to a larger one. Despite these similarities, however, MacDonald is decidedly un-Spenserian in his post-Romantic interest in the individual character's inner life, adapting romance narrative conventions to the issues of nineteenth-century idealism.

Douglas Thorpe

George MacDonald 1858 *Phantastes: A Faerie Romance for Men and Women* (London); MacDonald 1867 'The Imagination: Its Function and Its Culture' *BQR* July, rpt in *A Dish of Orts* (London 1893) pp 1–42; MacDonald 1868 *England's Antiphon* (London); MacDonald 1895 *Lilith: A Romance* (London).

Machiavelli, Niccolò (1469–1527) 'That Spenser knew the works of Machiavelli is hardly a matter of doubt.' So claims one modern scholar (Gasquet 1974:343); yet apart from possible influence on *Mother Hubberds Tale* and *FQ* v, clear evidence for any indebtedness is found in a single citation in *Vewe of Ireland*. In urging that the governor under special circumstances should have absolute power, Irenius (Spenser's spokesman) adds, 'This I remember is worthelye observed by machiavell in his discourse uppon Livie wheare he Comendethe the manner of the Romaines governement in givinge absolute power to all theire Consulls and governours' (*Var Prose* p 229). He goes on to claim that Machiavelli condemned the modern statesmen of Italy for limiting the civil power of the magistrate in time of crisis, apparently alluding to *Discorsi* 2.33 which, however, makes no such specific condemnation.

Yet there are other passages which may reflect Spenser's awareness of Machiavellian doctrine, though perhaps at second hand. In *Mother Hubberd* 647–50, the mule offers a brief statement which the Elizabethan reader would recognize as Machiavellian hypocrisy: 'That men may thinke of you in generall, / That to be in you, which is not at all: / For not by that which is, the world now deemeth, / (As it was wont) but by that same that seemeth' (cf *The Prince* ch 18, 'It is not essential that a prince actually have the above-mentioned qualities; but it is very necessary that he should seem to have them'). Machiavelli said the ruler should exercise the strength of a lion and the cunning of the fox; Spenser's beast fable of the Ape and the Fox seems to parody that advice, though of course both authors are writing within a tradition of portraying rulers as animals.

Throughout his poetry, especially in *The Faerie Queene*, Spenser seems opposed to guile in statecraft and in religion, although in Book v he presents an analysis of justice that looks at topics also considered in the work of Machiavelli (the nature of the prince, the problem of social order, etc). Yet the one work in which more than vague parallels may be found is the *Vewe*. The whole work, indeed, seems to expand Machiavelli's claim that 'the acquisition of territory in a province whose language, customs, and laws have been corrupted, brings problems with it, and great luck and diligence are required in order to hold on to it' (*The Prince* ch 3). Like Machiavelli, Spenser refers to the 'violente ... medicine' that is sometimes needed to keep the state healthy (*Var Prose* p 77; cf *The Prince* 'medicine forti' ch 3, a phrase also found in Bodin and later writers on the body politic). (For these and other parallel passages in *Vewe*, see Greenlaw 1909–10 and commentary in *Var Prose*; but see the rebuttal in H.S.V. Jones 1919, ch 4.)

That Machiavelli is named only once by Spenser may be due to his notoriety in England. Although he was more acceptable earlier in the century (see, eg, the writings of William Thomas), by Spenser's time he was regarded as the worst kind of cynic, and Machiavellianism was associated in public discourse with atheism. He was nevertheless ever more widely read in the original by many Englishmen, including Sidney who praised him and Harvey who called him a 'poysonous politician' (ed 1913). Although neither *The Prince* nor the *Discorsi* appeared in English during Spenser's lifetime, there were translations of less controversial works, for example, *The Arte of Warre* (1560, dedicated to Queen Elizabeth) and *The Florentine Historie* (1595). Meanwhile, Harvey's printer John Wolfe published the major works in the original Italian under false imprints throughout the 1580s.

Edward Chaney

On the reception of Machiavelli in England with a chapter on Spenser, see Gasquet 1974, esp pp 343–53; see also Sydney Anglo 1966 'The Reception of Machiavelli in Tudor England: A Re-assessment' *Il Politico* 31:127–38; Norbrook 1984; and Felix Raab 1964 *The English Face of Machiavelli: A Changing Interpretation 1500–1700* (London).

magic A definition of magic is as problematic in Renaissance thought as its distinction from witchcraft (see *witches). Equally difficult is a literary distinction of magic from the marvelous, wonderful, or supernatural, which are characteristic of romance literature. Magic defined as 'the marvellous controlled by man' may serve as a working hypothesis (J. Stevens 1973:101).

Magic as human control of the marvelous to produce wonderful effects (*mira*) laid it open to suspicion by Renaissance orthodoxy. Such effects could not be *miracula*, as these were the prerogative of God or his angelic or human agents. Fidelia's operations are clearly miracles worked by God's power and all have biblical authority (*FQ* I x 20). This left as potentially licit the production of wonders by the manipulation of hidden virtues of the created world (*magia naturalis*, the 'magyk natureel' of Chaucer's *Franklin's Tale* in *CT* V 1125). 'Natural magic pretendeth to call and reduce [lead back] natural philosophy from variety of speculations to the magnitude of works' (Bacon *Advancement of Learning* 1.4.11 in ed 1857–74, 3:289). Alternatively, there was the enticing prospect that men, profound in their art and yet not damnable, could somehow compel spiritual assistance without necessary contract with or submission to spirits. Natural magic is examined in the first book of Agrippa's *Three Books of Occult Philosophy* (1533) and ceremonial magic (*theurgia*) in its third book, the first being the more neutral concept. The thirteenth-century writer Roger Bacon claims that strange things may be worked by art and nature: ships may be moved without rowers, men may walk under the sea (1597:64–5). Reginald Scot devotes the opening chapters of *The Discoverie of Witchcraft* Book 13 to natural magic and says that God has endowed nature with graces men have not yet discovered, and even the rigorous George Gifford allows great secrets in natural things (1593: sig G1v). The waters of the Well of Life have secret virtues to heal Redcrosse and also possibly harden his sword (*FQ* I xi 29–30, 36), but this is not magic as there is no operative manipulation of the hidden virtues: the knight's fortunate fall into the waters is providential.

Canacee's ring is almost as innocent of magic. The property of staunching blood seems to be the virtue of the ring or perhaps specifically of its inset stone (IV ii 39–40, iii 24). Among other stones, the heliotrope is reported by lapidaries and Scot to have this virtue. The emphasis is on the ring's virtue rather than Canacee's, for she is a natural philosopher rather than an operator, even though she is versed in the secrets of nature (ii 35). There is no evidence she made the ring, although she has skill and science quite foreign to her Chaucerian original.

Natural magic might escape censure on the grounds that it simply uses the properties of nature. Apologists for *theurgia* were beset with suspicions of their dubious and aspiring claims to command spirits, and their insistence that they were quite different from witches. 'And these deale with no inferiour causes: these fetch divels out of hell, and angels out of heaven ... These are no small fooles, they go not to worke with a baggage tode, or a cat, as witches doo; but with a kind of majestie' (Scot *Discoverie* 15.1). The usual suspicion was that a theurgist was but old witch writ large. James VI, in *Daemonologie* 1, entertains a distinction between magic and witchcraft only to deny it.

An additional problem in defining magic in the Renaissance is that learned opinion differs from popular, and continental ideas from English. *Magie*, explains *Daemonologie*'s Epistemon (1.3–7), is a Persian word meaning a contemplator of heavenly sciences, but this honorable style is unjustified. The popular distinction, that witches are servants of the devil and magicians his masters, is only true *secundum quid* (as Marlowe's Faustus finds that his conjurations raised Mephostophilis *per accidens*). The devil only appears to be commanded in order to betray the magician. Magic is attractive to the learned, especially those with restlessly curious minds. Its practice involves the paraphernalia of circles, diagrams, and words of power; its rudiments are the virtues of words, stones, plants and herbs, of astrology (see *astronomy), mathematics, and divination. The deeper the magician penetrates into the art, the more deluded and diabolical he becomes: the usual consequence is the pact, thus rendering him no different from the witch.

Archimago initially presents himself as a benevolent and helpful romance hermit, the recluse we may expect to have profound knowledge, insight, and possibly supernatural skills as do hermits in Arthurian romance and Italian *romanze* (cf also the cells of Prospero and Greene's Friar Bacon). Contemplation (*FQ* I x 46–67) and the Hermit who tends Serena (VI v 34–vi 15) are types of what Archimago first leads us to expect; but at night, he is revealed as a diabolical ceremonialist. His study, magic books, words of power, and evocation of spirits identify him as a magician, and his blasphemy as a diabolist (I i 36–46). His cursing and speaking shame of God are deliberate renunciation, rather than the incidental blasphemy that critics of theurgists saw in their use of divine names to compel spirits (cf Faustus anagrammatizing the Tetragrammaton in *Dr Faustus* 1.3.236–7 in ed 1973 and Agrippa's constant recommendation of divine names in magic). Certain of Archimago's conversations have already revealed him as a papist. His magical blasphemies are analogous to his Catholic devotions, as Protestant propagandists constantly describe Catholic ceremonies and practices as impious and magical (Thomas 1971 passim, Waters 1970: 21–61). In the days of popery, 'then did conjurers and witches, and enchanters abond. Then were al manner of charmes rife and common' (Gifford 1587: sig G2r). Scot has numerous comparisons between popish practices and charms; and for him, the pope is, like Archimago, an archconjurer (*Discoverie* 12.9). Protestants also claimed that historically many of the popes were actually conjurers (Kermode 1971:40–9). *The Shepheardes Calender* illustrates this context for Archimago: superstitious practices (*Feb* 207–11 and gloss), Roman pastors as wizards (*Julye* 197–200), and their boast to command the devil but only at the expense of their salvation (*Sept* 94–7 and gloss). The false illusions that the eremetical Archimago's amatory magic produces for Redcrosse are answered by the true visions shown him by Contemplation.

Merlin is a different commander of spirits. He has an involved and changing history from British chronicles through medieval romances to the Renaissance. His Britishness, dynastic prophecies, and traditional role as Arthur's adviser and helper made him attractive to propagandists for the Tudor monarchy. Bishop John Bale even cited him as a prophet of the Reformation, and *The Mirror for Magistrates* saw his prophecies as divinely inspired: 'And learned Merline whom God gave the sprite, / To know, and utter princes actes to cum, / Like to the Jewish prophetes' (ed 1938:228). His dynastic prophecies, magic, and birth from an incubus father are données Spenser took from chronicles and romances. Magical exploits uncharacteristic of Merlin are his attempt to wall Cairmardin with brass (*FQ* III iii 7–11), his magic mirror (ii 17–21), and his manufacture of magical weapons for Arthur (I vii 36, II viii 20). Magic mirrors and crystals abound in literature (eg, the *Squire's Tale* and romances about Virgil), but the object is particularly associated with Roger Bacon, originally on the strength of passages on optics in his *Opus majus* and other works, and subsequently in tradition and legend. Like the Bacon of tradition, Spenser's Merlin operates by compelling spirits: like Greene's Friar Bacon he delivers veiled prophecies of the coming of Elizabeth to her ancestor (in ed 1905, 5.3.2068–88).

The magical functions of Merlin are twofold. His prophecies are inherited from chronicles (esp Geoffrey of Monmouth's where Merlin is already famous in the kingdom for prophecy and artificial contrivances, 8.6), Arthurian romance, and Ariosto (where Merlin's spirit prophesies her progeny to Bradamante, *Orlando furioso* 3). His making of magical objects is partly accounted for by Bacon, and partly by Spenser's analogy of Merlin with Vulcan, the artificer of gods and heroes, whose products are wonderful machines: tripod automata, and the metal dogs for Alcinous (*Iliad* 18.373–7, *Odyssey* 7.91–4). Both make the armor of epic protagonists: Vulcan for Achilles and Aeneas (*Iliad* 18, *Aeneid* 8), Merlin for Arthur. Vulcan also made armor for the gods in their battle against the giants; so Arthur's armor is described before and first used in his battle with Orgoglio (I vii-viii). Vulcan's craftsmanship in *Aeneid* shows him to be a prophet (8.627), and the ecphrasis of Aeneas' shield is prophetic as it shows the descendants of Aeneas and the culminating triumph of Augustus; so Merlin's prophecy (III iii 26–50) tells Britomart of her descendants and future British history, culminating in the triumph of Elizabeth. Arthur's sword is made in Etna's flames where Vulcan's forge is located in *Aeneid*, and it is dipped in the Styx as Turnus' was by Vulcan.

Spenser depicts Merlin's magic in terms of the two definitions of the poet that Sidney offers in the *Defence*: he is *vates* and maker, a prophet and craftsman in magic (see Blackburn 1980). With this analogy in mind, we can see in his magic glass not only the magic mirror of romance, Bacon's perspective glass, and the scrying glass of such Renaissance magicians as John Dee, but also the poetic and allegorical *speculum* held up to nature. It has the property to show whatever the world contains, and its construction is 'Like to the world it selfe, and seem'd a world of glas' (III ii 19). Again an analogue with Vulcan's artifice is suggested, for the shields of Achilles and Aeneas and also the doors of the sun's palace (Ovid *Metamorphoses* 2.5–18) represent the encyclopedic imitativeness of Vulcan. Like the works of the allegorist, they are *summae* of their worlds. Merlin's glass offers a true image of love in Artegall (who is dressed in Achilles' armor) to Britomart, answering the false image of love in the false Una produced by Archimago for Redcrosse. Britomart's virgin purity may help her adventitious crystal gazing, 'For she was pure from blame of sinfull blot' (III ii 23), and virgins were the most successful and accurate scryers. The truth of the image in Merlin's mirror also contrasts with the falsity of the magic shows Britomart is to witness in the house of another enchanter, Busirane.

Spenser's Merlin evades the categorizations of orthodox theorists on magic. His magic in *The Faerie Queene* seems an art lawful as eating, even though he commands spirits. His favorable treatment in the romances and his special attraction for Protestants and monarchists meant a predisposition for sympathetic treatment in *The Faerie Queene*, as did Spenser's rendering of him in terms of Sidney's poet. Both poet and magician work on nature; and the wonders worked by the poet are close to miracles, for he is able to make another nature, in imitation of the heavenly Maker (Sidney ed 1973b:78). *Miracula*, according to writers on magic, involve a new creation, which distinguishes them from *mira*. Merlin, with his insistence on co-operation with 'eternall providence' (III iii 24) may be working in an area where magic becomes miracle, in a secular analogue to Fidelia's powers (Giamatti 1971, Hamilton in *FQ* ed 1977). In iii 12, magic has power, as in classical literature, to pull down the moon from the sky (cf esp Virgil *Eclogues* 8.69, where this is effected by *carmina*). This answers, but is subtly distinct from, Fidelia's power, which is that of Joshua to make the sun stand still.

Cambina is another learned magician with prescience and 'mightie art' (IV iii 40; see *Cambell). The complicated interrelationships of the tetrad of Cambina, Canacee, Cambell, and Triamond have a female magical aspect. Canacee is the natural philosopher; Cambina proceeds to magical operation. She brings Canacee's natural philosophy to Francis Bacon's 'magnitude of works.' Magical links between them answer those in the anticipatory parodic tetrad of Duessa, Ate, Blandamour, and Paridell; in the female half, Duessa is a witch and Ate the infernal spirit she evokes (IV i 18–9). In her magical operations to bring concord, Cambina is presented as a good Circe with cup and wand. Since one of the iconographic meanings of her caduceus is eloquence (Fowler 1964:157–9), we can see the continuing Spenserian likeness between pleasing words and magic art. GARETH ROBERTS

Agrippa [c 1600]; F. Bacon ed 1857–74, vol 3; Roger Bacon 1597 *The Mirror of Alchimy* [and] *An Excellent Discourse of the Admirable Force and Efficacie of Art and Nature*; George Gifford 1587 *A Discourse of the Subtill Practises of Devilles by Witches and Sorcerers* (London; rpt Amsterdam and Norwood, NJ 1977); Gifford 1593 *A Dialogue Concerning Witches and Witchcraftes* (London, rpt London 1931); R. Greene *Friar Bacon and Friar Bungay* in ed 1905; James VI ed 1597; Scot 1584.

Briggs 1962; P. Cheney 1985; Giamatti 1971; Shumaker 1972; Thomas 1971; Thorndike 1923–58; D.P. Walker 1958.

magic, amatory Renaissance magic extends from the high earnest theories of sympathy of Ficino and Pico della Mirandola to the fraudulent services offered by city quacks and the muddled charms of English village witches. It includes the efforts of Florentine Neoplatonists to draw down favorable planetary influences, Agrippa's secret philosophy and its practical operation, John Dee's conversations with ambiguous angels, the supposedly spectacular night flying and Sabbats of European witches, and old English women suspected of souring cream and killing goslings. It is not surprising, then, that Renaissance writers on magic devote large sections of their treatises to defining their subject and categorizing its varieties and practitioners. Reginald Scot's *Discoverie of Witchcraft* (1584) in part adopts a favorite method of proceeding with demonologists, offering exegesis of the Hebrew words for 'witch' in the Bible – an exegesis that ranges through poisoning and ventriloquism, philters and oracles, necromancy and divination. This suggests something of the variety and complexity of the subject.

The definition of magic and the attempts to delimit its efficacy bear crucially on love magic in two respects. First, the question of whether magic can affect the will had acute relevance to the possibility of its causing or taking away love. Second, the question of whether there are secret and wonderful properties in natural objects, or whether conjuration of these objects gives them magical efficacy, bears on the possibility of herbs, stones, or potions causing love. *Malleus maleficarum* asks whether witchcraft can sway the mind to love or hate (Sprenger and Krämer 1580:98–114). Pierre Le Loyer's treatise (Eng tr of Book I as *A Treatise of Specters* 1605) examines the arguments as to whether herbs themselves or their conjuration produce an effect. The same questions are raised in numerous English Renaissance plays, poems, and prose works. Lyly's influential *Euphues and His England* (1580) has an extended dialogue between Philautus and the magician Psellus in which it is emphatically asserted that magic has no power over love. Most works of English Renaissance writers agree. Rare exceptions include the temporary potency of a love charm deriving ultimately from Virgil's eighth eclogue in Middleton's *Witch*, and the power of Puck's juice (technically an amatory collyrium) to affect the passions through the eyes in *Midsummer Night's Dream*. In *Othello*, Brabantio considers whether magic can abuse a youthful mind (I i 171–4), whether witchcraft can inhibit natural response (ii 62–71, iii 60–4), and whether the effect is due to the potion itself or to its conjuration: 'That with some mixtures pow'rful o'er the blood, / Or with some dram (*conjur'd to this effect*)' (104–5; italics added).

Renaissance magic from high to low is as various as the hierarchy of Renaissance love. The mighty power of love descends from the skies, provoking virtue, nobility, and fame (*FQ* III iii 1–2), stirring the brave to reward and honor (V 1–2). In the first passage, it is sharply distinguished from base lust; in the second, sensual thoughts are a mere idle pageant. But Plato's Diotima also calls love a sorcerer (*Symposium* 203D); and in his commentary on Ovid's *Metamorphoses*, Sandys describes love as a deceiving enchanter who 'deludes the eye of the minde with false apparitions: making that seeme noble, delightfull and profitable; which is full of dishonour, affliction and ruine' (ed 1970:123). This is precisely the intention and technique of Archimago in *FQ* I i-ii.

Amatory magic cannot directly affect the reason or will: to do so is the prerogative of God alone, as authorities from Augustine (and Renaissance demonologists who cite him) to Lyly assert. Spirits can, however, tamper with the interior and exterior senses (Thomas Aquinas *Summa* Ia III, *De potentia Dei* q 6). Citing Ephesians 6.12 (6.11–17 is the source for Redcrosse's armor), Aquinas says that demonic assault may be on the fantasy and exterior senses, and may include demonic fabrication of aerial bodies (*Summa* Ia 114). These are Archimago's techniques. He is revealed as a ceremonial magician by his study, books, and words of power. He invokes two spirits, appropriate to the constant dialectic between false and true in *FQ* I, a dialectic discernible stylistically in the syntax of I i 38 when they appear. One interferes with Redcrosse's imagination, the other with his outward senses. The reader's confusion over their precise activities imitates the knight's disturbed confusions. One sitting at the sleeper's head interferes with his fantasy, as Milton's Satan interferes successfully with Eve (*Paradise Lost* 4.800–3) and unsuccessfully with Jesus (*Paradise Regained* 4.407); the other, taking an aerial body, acts as a succubus. In the latter case,

Archimago's operation anticipates that of the rustic witch who devises the false Florimell in III viii. She too animates a simulacrum of a chaste heroine; both magically miscreate a deceiving eidolon. The false Una parades before the knight and reader a collocation of literary love conventions, all of which Spenser himself uses: complaint, Cupid the subduer of chaste hearts, Venus, even an epithalamium (I i 47–8). The deceptive uncertainties of the demonic dream are imitated in ambiguities of syntax and mythological personage. Although profoundly troubled, Redcrosse resists the assault on his fantasy only to succumb to the delusion of his sight by the succubus masquerading as Una and an incubus as a squire. Continental writers, following Aquinas, admit the possibility of actual copulation with demons who assume aerial bodies, but deny them paternity, for any child generated was produced by seed stolen from a man. The copulation of Archimago's two spirits is thus doubly false, unreal, illusory, and unnatural. Redcrosse's reason is blinded by demonically produced sense data. Although demons cannot directly influence reason, their interference with lower faculties can dispose it in certain ways. The archimage and arch image-maker, by magically produced false images of love, divides Redcrosse from his true love and the knightly lover from Truth.

Magic assaults love three times in *FQ* III, and each time it fails. *FQ* I demonstrates the limits of spirits controlled by an enchanter. *FQ* III sees love resisting the efficacy of amatory techniques and objects. Glauce's attempt to uncharm Britomart inverts an important question mentioned earlier: can magic *take away* love? Her charms are comically eclectic, and her remedies appropriately hint at the village cunning-woman (ii 49–51). For them, Spenser draws mainly on the pseudo-Virgilian *Ciris*, and for details on Theocritus' Idyll 2 and Virgil's Eclogue 8, adding a list of English herbs. Upton's claim (*Var* 3:221) that the herbs are anaphrodisiac cannot be conclusively substantiated. Some herbalists describe calamint, camphora, and especially rue as abating venery, but dill usually as provoking it. Writers on philters describe the use of calamint and rue in provoking love. There is, however, substantial agreement among authorities that these herbs bring down the menses or help troubles of the womb. Glauce's oldwife impercipience misreads Britomart's symptoms, especially those in III ii 39, as greensickness. Her receipt, part herb lore and part charm, attempts to treat the high passion of love as if it were a complaint responsive to village cunning-lore. 'Colt wood' ('colt-mad') is added to the pot separately. All commentators follow Upton in reading this as an alternative form of *coltsfoot*, although the term is not recorded in the *OED*. Spenser may well mean us to think of the English coltsfoot, but he is also literally Englishing Theocritus' *hippomanes* (horse-madness) (2.48); this is an aphrodisiac herb, although for Pliny and Aristotle it is either a sexual secretion from a mare or a growth on a foal's forehead. Renaissance writers, who list it regularly as a philter, cite Pliny and Aristotle on its sovereign value. Glosses in Renaissance editions worry over conflicting classical authorities when commenting on the *hippomanes* in Theocritus, *Georgics* 3.280–3, and *Aeneid* 4.515–16. One may suspect the general influence of *Aeneid* 4.474–516 on the end of *FQ* III ii. Both modern and Renaissance commentators suggest that Dido's deception of Anna involves the fiction that her magical rites are to *loose* the queen from Aeneas' love (see 4.478–9, 487–8). The priestess, like Glauce, employs herbs and *hippomanes*: perhaps the 'many drops of milke' (*FQ* III ii 49) were suggested by a quick reading of the difficult 'pubentes herbae nigri cum lacte veneni' (*Aeneid* 4.514). Alternatively Ovid's Medea mingles blood and milk (*Metamorphoses* 7.245–7). Glauce's eclectic magic, culled from classical sources and herb lore, is ritualistic, comic in its exaggerated exhortation to determined spitting and in Glauce's dizzying widdershins turning, and ineffective. Spenser agrees with most theorists on magic and English writers of his time that love cannot be caused or removed by idle charms.

(See **magic, amatory** Figs 1–2.)

Like Glauce, the witch in III vii attempts to assuage love. But even her son's base affection for Florimell resists herbs and charms. She sends the Hyena, a monster which traditionally ransacks graves and 'feeds on womens flesh' (22), after Florimell. Pliny's statement that magicians value the hyena above all other animals is repeated by Lyly and Topsell among others, and his extended list of the aphrodisiac properties of parts of its body led writers on magic to call them philters. Johan Wier mentions its womb as a love charm (*De praestigiis daemonum* ed 1566, 2.53). Its commonplace reputation for changing its sex or being both sexes at the same time made it a symbol for homosexuality and explains its appearance in the same canto with Argante and Ollyphant. Iconographically, it also represents instability and inconstancy and thus is an ironic comment on the alacrity with which the witch's son transfers his affections from Florimell to the magically miscreated simulacrum. The artifice of the construction of the false Florimell has been compared in its details to those of Petrarchan poetry: snow, 'perfect vermily,' burning eyes, and golden wires (viii 6–7). The same details match those in amatory magic. Snow, 'fine' (refined?) mercury, and virgin wax parody a Petrarchan lady's chastity and suggest the insistence on purity of substances, instruments, and even the operator in some kinds of Renaissance magic. The complex tensions between purity and passion in Petrarchism, acutely realized in the makeup of the false Florimell, are inherent in love magic in its own valuation of purity. Some conjurations even paradoxically invoke Mary's virginity. The virgin wax can be paralleled from both Sidney's blazon in *Arcadia* (Hamilton in *FQ* ed 1977:376) and from Wier's mention of amatory image magic (*De praestigiis daemonum* 2.53). The false Florimell, like the false Una, is a succubus and eidolon; but unlike her airy predecessor, she is a more substantial incarnation and therefore more troublesome. The male animating spirit in the female carcass may parody the hermaphroditic Venus, thus linking the androgynous false Florimell to the Hyena, the witch's other instrument.

Busirane continues the analogy of love poetry and love magic: 'imitation' is a principle of both Renaissance love magic and Renaissance poetry, and both the false Una and the false Florimell suggest false imitation. Busirane has been seen as the imprisoning power of courtly love (Lewis 1936:340–1) or of Italian love conventions (Nohrnberg 1976:471–90). Renaissance English poetry explicitly uses metaphors derived from magic: persuasion of the mistress as the love magic of Eclogue 8, the lover's address as charm and conjuration, the mistress' cruelty as image magic. The operation of the mistress' eyes on the lover's heart, one of the basic *topoi* of Petrarchism, is based on the same physiological theory as that explaining *fascinatio* by witches. Spenser's own reaction to Petrarchism in *Amoretti* anticipates three ideas informing the house of Busirane: love the tyrant, love as pageant, and the operation of the mistress' eyes as a painful *fascinatio* (*Am* 10, 54, 49). Busirane's static Ovidian tapestries iteratively depict the piercing dart of love, anticipating the distress of Amoret. They give way to the moving illusions of the masque procession, spirits called by Busirane from the *Romance of the Rose* and Petrarch's poetry to enact his present fancies. Amoret's first appearance in the pageant itself is like a conjured spirit (xii 19). In the inner room, the pierced and bleeding heart, a crucial Petrarchan image, becomes painfully incarnate for Amoret. Spenser's final image is also the image of amatory image magic, for the pierced heart was a feature of amatory operations. Busirane's writing 'straunge characters' with Amoret's blood (31) can also be documented from love magic (eg, BL, Sloane Ms 3851, fol 59), although the magician usually uses his own. If he is writing these characters in his magic book, then Spenser is developing and varying in a magical context an image potentially present in *Amoretti* 1, the conventional 'Go, little book' sonnet: 'reade the sorrowes of my dying spright, / written with teares in harts close bleeding book.' Again in the Busirane episode, Spenser insists that magic cannot move steadfast love. At the insistence of Britomart's Ulyssean sword, Busirane reverses his Circean charms, and the illusions of amatory magic disappear. GARETH ROBERTS

For further reading, see *magic. See also Couliano 1987; M. Gaster 1910 'English Charms of the Seventeenth Century' *Folk-Lore* 21:375–8; W.B. Hunter 1946; Gareth Roberts 1979 'A New Source for John Lyly's *Euphues and His England*' *JWCI* 42:286–9; D. Douglas Waters 1966 'Errour's Den and Archimago's Hermitage: Symbolic Lust and Symbolic Witchcraft' *ELH* 33:279–98.

magnanimity, magnificence Despite their importance for an understanding of *The Faerie Queene*, Spenser seldom uses the terms *magnanimity* and *magnificence* (see Cumberland Sonnet, *FQ* II viii 23, Letter to Raleigh, *FQ* dedication to Elizabeth, II ii 41, V v 4). In the Letter, he tells us that 'in the person of Prince Arthure I sette forth magnificence in particular, which vertue for that (according to Aristotle and the rest) it is the perfection of all the rest, and conteineth in it them all, therefore in the whole course I mention the deedes of Arthure applyable to that vertue, which I write of in that booke.' Since in Aristotle, however, magnanimity, not magnificence, is the perfection of the virtues, Spenser's apparent confusion of the terms has raised problems of interpretation. Yet this may be not so much confusion on his part as a reflection of the contemporary knowledge of the virtues, which derived ultimately from Aristotle but had been elaborated in a Latin tradition extending from Cicero and Macrobius through medieval scholasticism and Renaissance humanism.

For Aristotle, magnanimity (Gr *megalopsychia*) is an habitual quality of mind which aspires to achieve honor through the manifestations of any and all of the virtues and works as an 'ornament' or 'crown' to them (*Nichomachean Ethics* 4.3). Magnificence (Gr *megaloprepeia*) is concerned with great (though not excessive) expenditure in all public-spirited acts done with a certain flair, whether it be furnishing a warship, paying for a sacrificial ceremony, or offering a golden ball to a child (*Ethics* 4.2). The connection between the two virtues is honor (*timē*), which is the goal of magnanimity (*Ethics* 4.3.10–11, 17–18) and the result of magnificence (4.2.10–11, 15).

Cicero's vastly influential ethical teachings draw an even closer connection between the two. First, he uses *magnanimitas* (the Latin equivalent of *megalopsychia*) for a different Aristotelian virtue, courage (*andreia*) in his *De officiis* (1.43.152, and see his explanation of the connection in the *Tusculan Disputations* 3.7). Then in a well-known listing of the four cardinal virtues (*De inventione* 2.54.163–5), *magnificentia* is one of four parts of courage (here as *fortitudo*). Magnificence 'is the consideration [*cogitatio*] and the putting into action [*administratio*] of great and lofty matters with a certain greatness of soul and noble purpose' (authors' translation).

Macrobius adds a further complexity. In his often-cited list of the virtues (*Commentary on the Dream of Scipio* 1.8), both magnanimity and magnificence are subordinated equally as two of seven parts of fortitude. The Macrobian solution is frequently reflected in literary works, as, for example, in Chaucer's *Parson's Tale*, where 'magnanimitee' or 'greet corage' is the attitude of mind that makes a person 'undertake harde thynges and grevouse thynges,' while magnificence 'dooth and perfourneth grete werkes of goodnesse' (*CT* X [I] 730–6).

Scholastic ethics, the basis of Spenser's education at Cambridge, conflates Aristotle's with the subsequent Latin treatment. Thomas Aquinas, for example, cleverly manages to accommodate the Aristotelian claim for the supremacy of magnanimity. While other virtues, including the four cardinal ones, are 'principal,' magnanimity is the most principal (*Summa theologiae* 1a2ae 61.3.1). The encyclopedic discussion of Vincent of Beauvais also distinguishes magnanimity from magnificence in an Aristotelian way while subordinating both under courage and magnificence under justice (*Speculum morale* 1.83–5).

Among hundreds of references to this extended treatment in the Renaissance, Castiglione's best seller, *The Book of the Courtier*, and Hoby's popular translation are interesting. For courage, Hoby uses *manliness*, an exact translation of Aristotle's Greek *andreia*. He then uses a 'stoutnesse of courage' for magnanimity, which attends and makes greater temperance, courage, and justice. These four are then directed by the fourth cardinal virtue ('wisedom') and are joined by a 'chaine' of other virtues beginning with liberality and 'sumptuousnesse' for magnificence (ed 1928:272–3).

Thus, Spenser had available to him an extended tradition of the virtues in which magnificence was frequently defined as the doing of great deeds for the sake of glory, and he may have seen magnificence as an expansion of Aristotelian magnanimity. Thus when he says that magnificence is the 'perfection' of the other virtues, he could mean that it is their 'completion,' their being brought into action – action of the highest order available to man – for the sake of honor or glory.

Spenser's stress on doing great deeds may seem more Roman Catholic than Protestant in its theological orientation, since justification by faith and not works was the cornerstone of the Reformation. Good works, however, also found a place in Protestant thinking, as a means not of gaining salvation but of verifying the existence of the necessary true and lively faith – a faith which itself was the basis of salvation.

HUGH MACLACHLAN AND PHILIP B. ROLLINSON

DeMoss 1918–19; Richard J. DuRocher 1984–5 'Arthur's Gift, Aristotle's Magnificence, and Spenser's Allegory: A Study of *Faerie Queene* I ix 19' *MP* 82:185–90; Greaves 1964; Hankins 1971; Harris 1965; Viola Blackburn Hulbert 1926 'Spenser's Twelve Moral Virtues "According to Aristotle and the Rest"' *UCAT* 5:479–85 (rpt in *Var* 1:353–7); H.S.V. Jones 1926; Jusserand 1905–6; Hugh MacLachlan 1976–7 '"In the Person of Prince Arthur": Spenserian *Magnificence* and the Ciceronian Tradition' *UTQ* 46:125–46; McNamee 1960; Moloney 1953; John Skelton 1980 *Magnificence* ed Paula Neuss (Manchester); Steadman 1967; Tuve 1966; D. Douglas Waters 1969 'Prince Arthur as Christian Magnanimity in Book One of *The Faerie Queene*' *SEL* 9:53–62; Woodhouse 1949.

Malbecco The central figure in an episode of sordid love intrigue in Spenser's Legend of Chastity (*FQ* III ix-x). He is the old, churlish, miserly, impotent, and jealous husband of the young and wanton Hellenore and is elaborately cuckolded by his urbane and unwelcome guest Paridell. To distract Malbecco's attention while the adulterous couple escapes from his castle, Hellenore sets fire to his treasury and then, as he tries to save his wealth, calls out for help as if she were being carried off against her will. Malbecco is torn between his 'loved Dame' and his 'liefest pelfe,' but the 'pelfe' wins out and he turns back to fighting the fire (x 12–16). After a long search, he traces Hellenore (whom Paridell has meanwhile cast off) to a camp of satyrs by whom she is content to be 'handeled' as 'commune good.' Blending into the satyrs' herd of goats thanks to his beard and cuckold horns, he manages to sneak close enough to Hellenore to beg her to come away with him. He is rejected, but his ensuing madness results less from this disappointment than from 'extreme fury' at the discovery that his buried treasure has meanwhile been stolen. The character that emerges from these details of plot is duly expressed in his Italianate name: he is not only a 'goat' or cuckold (*becco*) but a bad one (*malo*) who has brought his misfortune on himself by a foolish marriage, and whose attachment to his wife is a travesty of love.

In the obvious allusive pattern that underlies the story, Malbecco plays Menelaus to his tormentors' Paris and Helen, and there are a few reminiscences of Ovid's deflationary treatment of the affair in the *Heroides* (16, 17). In Ovid, however, Menelaus is all too trusting and generous, and even cynical Paris is redeemed by a stubborn constancy to his passion. In these and other respects, Spenser's characters and their circumstances diverge too sharply from their classical counterparts to be elements of an implicit unmasking of the Matter of Troy. But then why degrade epic into fabliau? The answer seems to lie in Spenser's fictive chronology: it turns out that Paridell is not Paris but one of his descendants. The pedigree ironically illustrates Paridell's own remark that Troy's glory has been disgraced by her latter-day offspring (ix 33). The decline of the house of Paris is presumably dwelt on because it is typical: whatever the moral imperfection of earlier generations, it is nothing to the mounting corruption of later ones. The transposition from epic to fabliau, in short, is a metaphor for a somberly antiprogressive vision of history. As Spenser writes, 'men themselves, the which at first were ... form'd of flesh and bone, / Are now transformed into hardest stone' (*FQ* V proem 2).

The jealous cuckold is a perennial stock figure of buffoonery already well entrenched in Western folklore and literature during the period of Greco-Roman mime (eg, Juvenal 8.197, Martial 1.92). The Middle Ages knew him as a staple of salacious anecdote and fabliau. In Spenser's day, he remained the horned man, a target for the general hilarity that the deluded Othello thinks of first whenever he imagines the life he believes he faces as a cuckold (*Othello* III

iii 166, IV i 60–2, IV ii 54–5). In the light of the sympathetic imagination, this mockery only intensifies the tragic potentialities of the jealous man, whose passion is both a chronic vice and a terrible punishment. Like Malbecco, Othello is eventually made to betray the fact that the core of jealousy is possessiveness; the jealous lover would rather be a toad than 'keep a corner in the thing I love / For others' uses' (*Othello* III iii 270–3). The 'thing' to be hoarded for one's own 'uses' (and here the impotent Malbecco cannot use Hellenore at all) achieves the status of treasure in the jealous man's eyes only by being denied the status of a person. The irony is that the degrader himself is the one who suffers degradation. To lose exclusive possession of the 'thing I love' is to be reduced to something lower than a toad – emblematic kin to the poisonous creatures that Malbecco makes his 'pasture' in his ultimate degradation (*FQ* III x 59).

All of this is in keeping with the standard analysis of jealousy available to Spenser in traditional moral commentary. In this view, the 'love' that succumbs to jealousy is a warped egoism (a perversion of sexual desire or *amor concupiscentiae*) in which another person is regarded only as an instrument of one's own gratification (Thomas Aquinas *Summa theologiae* 1a2ae 28.4). Jealous 'love' is the enemy of real love (*amor amicitiae*) because it commits itself to no one's happiness but its own. The result, shown by Spenser with unsparing clarity, is isolation and self-loathing (III x 55). According to the Bible, 'love is strong as death: jelousie is cruel as the grave' (Song of Sol 8.6).

Malbecco performs a complex function in the Legend of Chastity. His jealousy is the 'vilest' of human passions (xi 1) because it debases the noblest of them. The eerie metamorphosis with which his story concludes shows emblematically what the rage for Having can do to the possibility of Being. Stripped of possessions, Malbecco's 'substance was consum'd to nought' (x 57), and he turns from a jealous man into jealousy itself. (This detail seems to have been adapted from Ariosto's *Cinque canti* 2.15; see Skulsky 1981:132–3.) The metaphorical analogue of obsession here is abstraction: Malbecco's individuality is gone; what remains, ironically, is the perverse chastity, or absoluteness, of a fixed idea. In the perspective of his final transformation, Malbecco's story unexpectedly takes on the force of a compelling allegorical symbol.

HAROLD SKULSKY

Alpers 1967b:215–28; Berger 1969a; Nelson 1953; Skulsky 1981:129–34.

Maleger One of two climactic opponents of temperance in *FQ* II, the other being Acrasia or Pleasure (xii 1). While Guyon journeys to destroy Acrasia's Bower of Bliss, Arthur with the aid of his squire, Timias, slays Maleger, who with two lieutenants, Impatience and Impotence, leads the army of 'passions bace' or 'strong affections' (ix 1, xi 1) in a final assault on Alma's castle. That base passions and pleasure are the twin enemies of the temperate life is a commonplace of classical and Christian tradition: for example, *libidines* are the handmaids of *voluptas* in Cicero's influential *De officiis* (3.33.117), and the same doubling of *epithumiai* and *hēdonai* is found in Titus (3.3).

Spenser divides the victory over these two opponents between two equally conventional aspects of temperance. When Arthur and Guyon are entertained by Alma in canto ix, each is paired with a lady, Arthur with Prays-desire (36–9) and Guyon with Shamefastnesse (40–4), two alter egos who are the two integral parts of temperance in scholastic ethics – *honestas* and *verecundia*. Honestas in this context is the sense of honor and beauty of temperance which desires to do temperate things and be a shining exemplar of its rule; it is the aggressive, active side of the rule of temperance. Verecundia is the passive shame that avoids doing anything intemperate. Guyon needs verecundia to defeat Acrasia's temptations, while Arthur needs honestas to subdue Maleger and the army of the passions.

Maleger, the 'cruell Capitaine' (ix 15) of the army of the base passions, is identified in stanza 1 as 'misrule' and not, as he is usually taken to be, original sin, the effects of sin, or sin-created mortality. His misrule is the negation or perversion of temperance's government seen in Arthur's honestas. The opening stanza emphasizes the contrast between the tempering effect of the well-governed body and the distempering result of the incontinent misrule of the base passions, for in the tradition available to Spenser, temperance is directly concerned with the rule of the will (see, eg, Cicero *Tusculan Disputations* 4.31.65).

The willful aspect of the government of temperance explains the presence of Impatience and Impotence, two balanced aspects of misrule, one the concupiscible, the other its irascible counterpart. *Potentia*, the power or ability to control oneself, is intimately related to the power of restraint, which Arthur embodies in his honestas. Maleger is the negation of restraint, and *impotentia* or *incontentia* is part of the inability to control oneself. Impotence then is the aspect of misrule which cannot control the concupiscible part of the passions (love/hate, attraction/aversion, joy/sorrow). Impatience, on the other hand, commonly identified by the scholastics as a daughter of anger, cannot control the irascible passions (hope/despair, fear/audacity, and anger). Together they represent the total lack of control of the passions which are attacking the castle of the body under the appropriate leadership of misrule.

The surface details of the episode in canto xi, reinforced by allusive and iconographic implications, develop these abstract truths and relationships. Impotence and Impatience are two horribly unclean, unkempt hags. Both are extremely swift of foot, although the former is appropriately crippled (by unrestraint). The latter carries anger's 'raging flame' and appropriately overwhelms an angry and impatient Arthur frustrated by his inability to close with Maleger and by Impotence's (appropriate) practice of rearming misrule. Rescued by Timias (L *honor*) and 'prickt with reprochfull shame,' that is, both by the goal of honestas and by verecundia, Arthur continues the fight. Maleger is large, long-legged and looks like a risen ghost still half-wrapped in graveclothes. Pale, thin, cold, dry, and draped in canvas, he races into battle on a tiger (noted in the bestiaries for swiftness) with bow and arrows. His tactics are explicitly (and accurately) likened to those of the Russians' arch-enemy, the Tartars, who showered their opponents with a hail of arrows while speedily retreating on horseback.

Associated with death and the destructive Tartars, Maleger proves a supremely paradoxical foe when he is finally engaged by Arthur. Although severely wounded, he is bloodless and apparently cannot be killed: 'Flesh without bloud, a person without spright, / Wounds without hurt, a bodie without might, / That could doe harme, yet could not harmed bee, / That could not die, yet seem'd a mortall wight, / That was most strong in most infirmitee.' His nature has its roots in commonplaces of classical and Christian ethics. In classical ethics, intemperate behavior is the result of allowing the passions to pursue their own unreasonable goals, which are only apparent goods or what is believed to be good but really are evils leading to death (see Cicero *Tusculan Disputations* 4.6–7). In Christian ethics, living according to the flesh is commonly thought of as being dead already, and conversion is described as passing from death into life (see, eg, John 5.24, Rom 6.12–13).

Arthur is astonished at Maleger's deathlike life and imperviousness to death but finally remembers that Maleger's mother is the Earth who keeps restoring her son to vigor. He consequently holds his enemy aloft, squeezes the life out of him, and casts the corpse into a nearby 'standing lake' so that it will be unable to touch earth again.

The episode parallels Hercules' defeat of Antaeus, except that once dead, Antaeus stays dead when dropped on the ground. The lake as a fitting receptacle for Maleger may have been suggested by Pomponius Mela's description of Antaeus' tomb in Mauritania as a huge mound in the shape of a man: whenever any dirt was dug out of the mound, rain fell on that spot until it had washed enough dirt back in to refill the hole. More obvious is the ironic parallel to baptism. Here, in an inverted parody of Christian baptism (from death to life), a deathly influence on human behavior is baptized into continuing death in a body of stagnant, dead water (in contrast to Milton's living, 'profluent stream' *Paradise Lost* 12.442 and the 'living well' of *FQ* I xi 31).

The traditional reading of the Hercules-Antaeus story construed Hercules as virtue, the earth as the flesh, and Antaeus as *libido*: virtue is able to triumph over lust by separating lust from the flesh. Antaeus as libido relates to the etymological components of Maleger's name: *male* 'badly' + *aeger* 'diseased, sick,' referring to the attack on the body by both physical sickness and spiritual sickness of sin or fallen mortality. But aeger (and the noun *aegritudo*) refers also to mental and psychic illness: in the discussion of the diseases of the soul which threaten temperance in *Tusculan Disputations* 3–4, aegritudo (distress, dejection, or sorrow) is one of four major sources of willful disturbance which afflict and attack the temperate soul. Another is libido, but these two are contrasting (3.10) and on different sides of the two sources of the soul's problems – false conceptions of good (libido, a desire for an assumed good) and false conceptions of evil (aegritudo, the distress and suffering occasioned by the experience of what is thought to be evil). With the suggestion of libido from the Antaeus myth and the connection with aegritudo from aeger, Spenser includes under Maleger's misrule key representatives of all the disquieting passions which afflict the soul.

Other etymological explanations of Maleger's name are *male+regere* (to rule badly or wrongly) and *male+gerens* (evil bearing or behaving), but the most likely are *male +regere* and *aeger*, both being appropriate to his identity and nature as captain of the passions.

The organization of the attacking passions into twelve companies (xi 6, 14) suggests the five senses (7–13) but probably not the seven deadly sins attacking the gate (6). Obviously the five senses are instrumental agents in the assault of the base passions on the body. However, the attack on the gate of the castle, which is the mouth of the body (ix 23–5), may be based not on common physiological knowledge but on a commonplace biblical truth. In the New Testament, it is not what goes into the mouth which defiles but what comes out of it from the heart: 'evil thoghts, murders, adulteries, fornicacions, thefts, false testimonies, sclanders' (Matt 15.19). These seven may have suggested to Spenser the seven companies of base passions attacking the castle's gate. Philip B. Rollinson

Malengin (L *malum* 'evil'+*ingenium* 'wit'; documented since 1390 as an English noun: 'evil machination') On their way to Mercilla's court (*FQ* v ix 4–19), Arthur and Artegall use their guide, Samient, as a decoy to lure Malengin out of his lair. Seeing her apparently alone, dejected, and vulnerable, the larcenous master of 'legierdemayne' ventures out to distract her with 'pleasant trickes' until he has caught her in his fishing net. But finding the path to his cave blocked by the knights, he abandons his prey and tries to elude Artegall's iron bailiff Talus by assuming one borrowed shape after another. Each of his shifts is thwarted by an appropriate countershift until he is summarily battered to dust and gore by Talus' flail.

Spenser draws on several traditions for his graphic metaphor of the vice he calls *malengin*. With his 'long curld locks' and 'uncouth vestiment,' Malengin resembles the rebel Irish who wore 'mantells and longe glibbes which is a thicke Curled bushe of haire hanginge downe over theire eyes and monstrouslye disguisinge them' (*Vewe*, in *Var Prose* p 99). The ubiquitous folklore motif of avoiding capture by passing through a rapid sequence of magical transformations is embodied most notably in Proteus (eg, Ovid *Metamorphoses* 8.730–7). The Homeric Dolon ('guileful one'), son of Eumedes ('good at plotting'), is a mercenary spy garbed in a weasel-skin helmet and wolf-hide mantle; he is the classic deceiver deceived, trapped and killed by Diomedes and the artful Odysseus (*Iliad* 10.314–467). Virgil's Cacus, a giant cave-dwelling pillager and thief, is crushed to death by Hercules, a champion of justice (*Aeneid* 8.190–267). Like Malengin, the figure of Deceit in Cesare Ripa's *Iconologia* is equipped with hook and net. The principle that 'fraud deserves fraud,' or that 'nothing done to a feigned friend is a wrong,' is a staple of Renaissance emblem books (eg, Whitney 1586:124, 210, 226).

(See **Malengin** Fig 1.)

To call guile *malengin* ('wicked cleverness') is to remind us that, like other powers reckoned evil, it is the perversion of a good. The fundamental text is Aristotle's discussion of tactical acuteness, a trait that the prudent and the sly have in common, the crucial difference being the respective presence and absence of a morally valid aim (*Nicomachean Ethics* 6.12). There are, therefore, benign as well as malicious forms of 'legierdemayne.' A paradigm of this doubling is the ruse by which Malengin himself is entrapped. It takes an Odysseus to stop a Dolon.

The morality of entrapment is an issue in traditional discussions of legal ethics, and hence in Spenser's poetic vision of justice and equity. It remains a dispute over law enforcement: is it proper to catch a thief by tempting him to thievery? Or is one doomed to be contaminated by aping Malengin's tricks, even when one's victim is the master himself? In the next episode, the officer assigned to keep guile out of Mercilla's court is Awe (*FQ* v ix 22–3); but awe by itself seems an unpromising bar against the guile we have just met, a villain 'bold and stout' and 'unassaylable' in his 'dwelling place,' which is the malicious mind (ix 4, 5). Against the owners of such minds, Spenser's story implies, justice and its knights are in a state of war. To the justice of such a war, as Augustine says in his classic remark on the subject, it matters not at all whether one fights in the open or from ambush, so long as one tells no lie and breaks no promise (*Quaestiones in Jesum Nave* 10, *PLat* 34:780–1). The Puritan divine William Perkins echoes Augustine, with many illustrations of justified patriarchal cunning, in his answer to the question 'whether a man may lawfully and with good conscience, use Pollicie in the affaires of this life' (*The Whole Treatise of the Cases of Conscience* 1606, 3.2.2).

Spenser turns this resistant matter into poetry by imaginatively fusing the classical and Renaissance metaphors noted above and, characteristically, by introducing a final illuminating irony. Malengin is an offense against a custom of truthtelling on which malengin itself depends; the more extreme the offense, the more suicidal: 'So did deceipt the selfe deceiver fayle.' The ambiguous placement of *selfe* (which in Elizabethan idiom can either emphasize *deceiver* or make it reflexive), the ambiguity of climactic *fayle* (ultimately from L *fallere* 'deceive'), the mocking chime of *deceipt/deceiver*, and the mockingly reptilian sibilance of the line as a whole combine to produce a tiny masterpiece of moral discourse, in which the subtle voice of the ironist is clearly audible. Harold Skulsky

Malory, Thomas (fl 1470) Author of *Le Morte Darthur* (completed between March 1469 and March 1470), the first great prose narrative in English and, from the time of its printing by Caxton (1485), the best-known vernacular telling of the tales of Arthur and his knights. The *Morte*, which is 1260 pages long in the standard modern edition, is based principally on five thirteenth-century French prose romances (the *Suite du Merlin*, the prose *Tristan*, and the Vulgate *Lancelot*, *Queste del saint graal*, and *Mort Artu*) and two late-fourteenth-century English poems (the alliterative *Morte Arthure* and the stanzaic *Morte Arthur*). It begins with the begetting of Arthur and his rise to kingship and imperial power, narrates adventures of Lancelot, Tristram, and other knights of late medieval Arthurian tradition, recounts the quest for the Grail, and ends with the destruction of the Round-Table fellowship and Arthurian civilization. In his endearing preface to the work, Caxton tells how noble gentlemen urged him to print an Arthurian history and argued that such a king had indeed existed; the *Morte*, he says, will show noble men the acts of chivalry and virtuous deeds by which some knights came to honor in those days and how those who were vicious were punished.

Le Morte Darthur was reissued five times between 1498 and 1585, but the reactions of Tudor Protestants to the work were mixed, estimates of Malory no doubt being complexly affected by changing attitudes toward medieval romance, the debate over Arthur's historicity, and the usefulness of Arthur for sixteenth-century politics. Sidney draws on Malory in composing the *Arcadia*; E.K. expresses his contempt for 'the Authors of King Arthure the great and such like' in his gloss to *Aprill* 120. From Roger Ascham we learn that '*Morte Arthure* [had been] received into the Princes chamber'; but for Ascham himself, the *Morte* is a product of the bad old days of papistry, the pleasures of the book standing 'in two speciall poyntes, in open mans slaughter, and bold bawdrye' (ed 1904:231). Still, there can be no question that Spenser was acquainted with the *Morte*, and most readers assume he knew it well: the Malorian example in *Vewe of Ireland* (*Var Prose* p 111) is more likely a thing comfortably remembered than the fruits of special research. But the central question is what Malory had to do with Spenser as the poet of *The Faerie Queene*, and this is a difficult question to answer satisfactorily.

The Blatant Beast certainly appears to be drawn from Malory's questing beast, and Spenser tells us (VI xii 39) that the Blatant Beast will later be taken in hand by Pelleas and Lamoracke – both Malorian knights, but not the two who follow the questing beast in the *Morte*. The *Morte* is the most likely point of departure for the Tristram narrative (VI ii); Artegall's punishment of Sanglier (V i) recalls Lancelot's punishment of Pedyvere in the *Morte*; Una's first encounter with Redcrosse, described in the Letter to Raleigh, may owe something to Malory's tale of Gareth and Lynet. Other incidents in *The Faerie Queene* bring to mind things in the *Morte* – but then the *Morte* itself is built largely from traditional tales and motifs; and of most Spenserian 'borrowings' from the book, we can say only that if here Spenser did draw on memories of just one work (a most troublesome *if*), that work was likely Malory's.

When we turn to language, we find a similar state of affairs. In *The Faerie Queene*, the line 'Thus long they trac'd and traverst to and fro' occurs three times (IV vi 18, V viii 37, VI i 37; see also IV vii 28). Malory uses 'traced and traversed' and 'tracyng and traversyng' eighteen times, and Spenser likely remembered this pairing from the *Morte*. By and large, though, his language is no more like Malory's than their shared concerns would lead us to expect.

Is Spenser's acquaintance with *Le Morte Darthur* simply a trivial fact of literary history? One cannot prove it is more. But readers who respond to both narratives will likely feel the *Morte* truly mattered to Spenser. And here the vital thing is not motif or locution or structure but tone and sensibility. In its last sections, where Malory tells how the glory and heroes of Arthurian civilization were lost, the *Morte* is a work of marvelous plangency; and it is hard to imagine that Spenser, with his sense of the world 'runne quite out of square' (V proem 1), was unaffected by this vision of a noble order destroyed. Everywhere in the *Morte*, we feel Malory's belief in chivalry as the great good thing, an institution to be chronicled with sober respect. The *Morte* is not at all an urbanely knowing book: its dialogue is notable for a laconic, stiff-upper-lip irony, but its author does not wink slyly at his readers. In *The Faerie Queene*, we find again and again an answering gravity. We read two lines about Calidore – 'For he loathd leasing, and base flattery, / And loved simple truth and stedfast honesty' (VI i 3) – and we recognize not Malory's style of writing, but his earnestness, a style of feeling. In the *Morte*, we come upon 'What, said Sir Launcelot, is he a theef and a knyght and a ravyssher of wymmen? He doth shame unto the ordre of knyghthode and contrary unto his othe; hit is pyte that he lyveth' (Book 6.10 in Malory ed 1983), and we may think of Guyon's reaction to a tale of rape: 'How may it be, (said then the knight halfe wroth,) / That knight should knighthood ever so have shent? ... And lives he yet (said he) that wrought this act, / And doen the heavens afford him vitall food?' (II i 11–12). Guyon's incredulous indignation at such baseness in a knight moves us in the way Lancelot's does: we wish we, too, could be so simply shocked. But Guyon's reaction, unlike Lancelot's, is inadequate to its context: he is being tricked and ought not to be 'halfe wroth.'

Morally, the world of *The Faerie Queene* is far more complexly nuanced than Malory's. And Spenser's sense not only of moral but of literary possibilities and difficulties was far larger than Malory's seems likely to have been. Both writers intensely loved the simple truth of noble conduct; but for Malory that truth was easier to find, and he appears to have worried not at all that simple truth might be miscalled simplicity. The undistracted earnestness of the earlier writer was, one imagines, a source of deep refreshment for Spenser – refreshment touched, perhaps, with a little envy. For the epic poet, *Le Morte Darthur* may have represented the lyric stage of chivalric commemoration and a deep truth which had to be combined with other, complex truths. MARK LAMBERT

It should be noted that the standard modern edition of Malory – *Works* ed Eugene Vinaver, 2nd ed, 3 vols (Oxford 1967) – uses as its base text a manuscript first discovered in 1934. Spenser would have known a *Morte* descended from Caxton's edition; and the *Morte* itself seems a little more Spenserian when it has Caxton's divisions into numerous chapters and his preface, with its rubric for each chapter of the work and its strong sense of the *Morte*'s usefulness for moral education. See Malory ed 1983.

Mammon (Aramaic 'riches') Mammon, whom Guyon visits in *FQ* II vii, is a personification of wealth, as were Plutus, Pluto, and Dis according to the mythographers. His house therefore opens onto a combined Hades and hell, home of those who forget that 'ye can not serve God and riches' (Matt 6.24, Luke 16.13; in Bishops' Bible, 'Ye can not serve God, and mammon').

Mammon's first appearance (3–9) expresses emblematically what serving him means. He is 'salvage,' although money's value depends on social consensus, and ugly from works that bring no happiness or salvation. His melancholy anticipates the sorrow in Cocytus (56), and his eye trouble, traditional in the avaricious, accompanies visual gluttony (cf Matt 6.23). In costume, he is the typical miser: poor in show, hiding his riches. His iron coat rusts because his treasure is laid up on earth (Matt 6.19); it is made of metal associated with Mars because Mammon encourages irascible disdain and competition. The figure-covered gold lining (dusty like mortality and unused treasure) recalls the deceptive coat of Plutus in Lucian's *Timon*, while its grotesques befit a cave-like dwelling and a liminal moment (Evett 1982; see *thresholds). Mammon's double coat may also reiterate a familiar witticism: the real golden age is now, in the iron age, when all is for sale and, as Guyon laments, we wound the earth with steel to find gold (17). Like the gnomes of legend, Mammon fears being seen, hurrying his lucre into a hole; Freud would probably call him anal retentive (cf Horace *Satires* 1.1). He is a hoarder with an entangling spider web that, like the one in Isaiah 59.5, shows how the presumptuous wicked are 'profitable to no purpose' (Geneva gloss).

Mammon says he is god of the world. His arguments are literal-minded, like the equation of horses and armor with chivalry, for cupidity was traditionally thought to include sticking to the letter of the law, ignoring the spirit and charity. (The worldly make bad readers and worse judges.) Here is Guyon's subtlest, unspoken temptation – to find the world's terms sufficient, to understand the cosmos without reference to its Creator – and to some extent he yields. Mammon encourages this illusion through parodic usurpation. Like God he offers 'blis' and 'grace,' like Christ he says, 'Come ... and see' (John 1.38–9), and an iron door opens for him as for Peter (Acts 12.10). His workers mix fire and water in a parody of temperance; the golden chain of Philotime, herself a false Gloriana, parodies that of Zeus (*Iliad* 8.18–27) while slyly suggesting the courtier's chain of office or honor; the attempts of Tantalus and Pilate to eat or wash parody communion and baptism.

Mammon invites Guyon to look, but insight is difficult in a world darkened by covetousness (Matt 6.23) yet seemingly complete in itself and divided into four areas, the number of cosmic inclusion (Heninger 1974:79, W.R. Davis 1981). True, Guyon maintains a secular and habitual temperance, but he ignores Mammon's false metaphysics and confusion of signs with reality (Heinzelman 1980). Mammon forgets to love gold for the proper reasons: that it is pretty, God made it, and it can buy things of real value. Instead, he begets ambition for 'Honour and dignitie' without generating accomplishments for them to represent. Paradoxically, then, he is not a materialist at all, for he offers only endless excitement and desire in which money and glory are unrelated to anything beyond themselves and thus invite the secular equivalent of image worship.

Deprived of his Palmer, Guyon is literally 'led' into temptation. Is he unwise? Maybe. He never lusts for what he sees, but he does lust to see, demonstrating a dangerous curiosity. Although an exploratory descent suits an epic hero, unlike Aeneas he has no trusty guide; and he discovers a nightmare of early capitalism, not the future of his race (that sort of knowledge Spenser saves for Britomart in the cave of Merlin). Yet the Red Cross Knight, who makes a similar visit to Lucifera (I iv), is his partial namesake (the *Golden Legend* claims a double etymology for *George*: 'of gera: that is holy, and of gyon that is a wrasteler, that is an holy wrasteler'; Nelson 1963:180, and see Snyder 1961); perhaps Guyon must also witness what threatens him and thereby experience an initiation of some kind.

Jesus himself says, 'Make you friends with the riches of iniquitie' (Luke 16.9), a passage that appears in the Elizabethan Book of Common Prayer immediately after the statement that God 'wil not suffer you to be tempted above that you be able, but wil even give the yssue with the temtation, that ye may be able to beare it' (1 Cor 10–13). William Tyndale's *Parable of the Wicked Mammon* (1528) explains that Jesus meant we should use wealth to help the poor; the Geneva Bible's gloss agrees. Guyon, though, never suggests a charitable use for Mammon's gold, any more than he mentions a higher 'blis' than honorable achievement. He insists, rather, that riches are the root of evil, forgetting that Paul (whom Mammon parodies in stanza 19; cf 1 Cor 2.9) blames the *desire* for money (1 Tim 6.10). Guyon, that is to say, worries about the source of Mammon's wealth but never addresses the issue of 'right usaunce' or examines its relation to enjoyment, result, fruit (on *utor* 'use' and *fruor* 'enjoy,' see Augustine *On Christian Doctrine* 1.3–39, and esp 1.3–4). Even his prudent fasting and waking may entail a rejection of matter as such; and he forgets, though Mammon cruelly reminds him, that knights need money. Guyon dislikes this modern shabbiness (16–17), but in the Golden Age there were no knights at all, and no Gloriana.

Guyon takes on this adventure in a spiritually risky state. No Protestant could note his feeding on 'his owne vertues, and prayseworthy deedes' without dismay at such pagan or 'papist' confidence in human merit and works. Just as Redcrosse (as George, Georgos) has a hidden kinship with Orgoglio, his fellow in earthiness, so Guyon's diet implies a connection with Mammon, who calls him 'Sonne.' One feeds on virtue, the other on the sight of wealth, so no wonder the two meet in a wilderness: grain, literal and symbolic, has become self-congratulation or gold, comparable in its sterility and menace to the 'sandie graile' which is the site of Redcrosse's fall (I vii 6). Significantly, the grain maiden herself, Proserpina, is missing from her own garden (II vii 51–64). Spenser thus establishes an ironic pattern involving earth, gold, grain, fruit, nourishment, sight, and works – whether the frenzied labor of Mammon's servants (parodying fallen Adam, they sweat without bread amidst signs of death, the wages of sin) or Guyon's good deeds performed without acknowledging grace.

After refusing to serve Mammon (9), Guyon is subjected to three temptations lasting 40 stanzas (26.3–66.4; Hieatt 1975a:196) and three days, a reminder of Christ's fast and temptation in the wilderness as well as his descent into hell. The first is in two parts (32, 38), thus extending the triad of sin throughout Mammon's quadrate world; but exactly how the temptations are to be defined is much debated (Cullen 1974:68–96). Literally, Mammon proffers wealth, a marriage to unearned fame (49), and golden fruit together with a repose not earned by useful labor (63) – an untimely sabbath on a tarnishable silver seat suitable for a rich moon goddess in her infernal aspect, not true rest on one of the heavenly seats promised the faithful or on the throne Christ will share with the victors when 'The kingdomes of this worlde are our Lords' (Rev 4.4, 3.21, 11.15; but cf Kermode 1971:74–5). Morally, Guyon sees avarice, ambition, and impiety (including, perhaps, impious curiosity), as sins that intensify from foolish greed for inanimate metal to envious rivalry with men to deicide, while the creatures he notes change from demons to anonymous aspiring people to two named magnates, Tantalus and Pilate. The next step would be for Guyon to examine himself, but this he does not do. Spatially, he moves forward to see the fruit and result of worldliness, and also downward to see its source and cause: putting the self and its desires before God. Proserpina's apple tree, a perversion of the healing tree of life (Rev 22.2) set in the center of Book II, recalls the tragedy in Eden; and her black river might – except for Mammon's colleague Satan – have been living waters like, for instance, the river Gihon in Eden, symbol of temperance and one origin of Guyon's name (Fowler 1960b).

Guyon nobly resists Mammon, avoiding the fiend Disdain, who follows him through this world of infernal law and taboo (appropriate to worldlings unawakened to Christian freedom); but unlike Christ, he is as yet temperate to no purpose beyond self-control. His efforts leave him 'dead' in a much-discussed faint, for the flesh is frail; worse, from another perspective such merely moral triumph is fruitless and even 'wicked' (viii 1) if not derived from a lively faith that relies on God alone. Guyon's name can mean 'wrestler,' but 'if a man also wrestle, yet is he not crowned, except he wrestle lawfully' (2 Tim 2.5, Bishops' Bible). Are we to condemn him? Of course not, for the same radical and unclassical ethic that demands a choice between God and Mammon also forbids our judging others as Guyon so smugly if accurately judges covetous Tantalus. Spenser sets a trap for us: even in victory Guyon has failed, but if we merely blame him we too forget what the 'Lord of life' said and fall into a worldliness far worse than avarice.

As Guyon lies unconscious, unbought grace arrives without fanfare or the knight's deserving, in the form of an angel feathered with heavenly gold who helps him 'for love, and nothing for reward' (viii 2; cf Matt 4.11). Roused from his torpor as though newborn, and returned to his right reason, the hero can now move forward with clearer direction and act with sterner temper.

ANNE LAKE PRESCOTT

Cullen 1974; W.R. Davis 1981; David Evett 1982 'Mammon's Grotto: Sixteenth-Century Visual Grotesquerie and Some Features of Spenser's *Faerie Queene*' *ELR* 12:180–209; Fowler 1960b; Kurt Heinzelman 1980 *The Economics of the Imagination* (Amherst, Mass), pp 35–69; Heninger 1974; Hieatt 1975a; Kermode 1971; MacLachlan 1983; Nelson 1963; Snyder 1961.

Mantuan (Baptista Spagnolo Mantuanus) Author of ten Neo-Latin eclogues which were used as a school text throughout Europe in the sixteenth and seventeenth centuries, and which became a model for many Renaissance eclogues including Spenser's. Born Giovanni Baptista Spagnolo (or Spagnuoli) in 1448, he was generally known by his monastic name of Baptista Mantuanus. He entered the Carmelite monastery at Mantua, becoming Prior, Vicar-General, and finally (in 1513) General of the Carmelite Order. He died in 1516, and was beatified in 1885. His literary output in both prose and verse was vast, and included a poem on St George that is an outside contender as a source for *FQ* I. It was however his eclogues that had the most extensive influence, both on European culture in general and on Spenser in particular.

The first eight eclogues were originally written while he was a student at Padua in the 1460s, at a time when the eclogue was becoming a fashionable form in Italy. He published them, probably with extensive revision, in 1498 as the *Adolescentia* and added two more to bring their number to the Virgilian total of ten. Within a couple of years, they had been furnished with a commentary by that indefatigable glossator of Renaissance texts, Jodocus Badius Ascensius; it was in this form that they were most widely disseminated across Europe, often under the title *Bucolica*. The earliest surviving English edition was printed by Wynkyn de Worde in 1523. The eclogues were popular as a schoolbook because they were moral, Christian, and written in comparatively simple Latin, so they made easy and uncorrupting reading for the young. They appear on many of the known curricula of sixteenth-century English schools, including St Paul's; they were probably also used at Merchant Taylors', Spenser's own school.

Mantuan's eclogues came to rank beside Virgil's *Eclogues* as a model of pastoral poetry. Alexander Barclay, William Webbe, George Puttenham, E.K., and Francis Meres so acknowledge them, and Drayton speaks of his tutor's reading 'honest *Mantuan*' to him when he expressed a desire to become a poet ('To ... Henry Reynolds' 36, in ed 1931–41, 3:227). The eclogues continued to be printed and studied in England until the early eighteenth century, though they were little imitated after 1600.

Mantuan's greatest significance is that he reorients the eclogue towards the didactic and the realistic. His own sources include not only Virgil but also Petrarch's allegorical and frequently invective *Bucolicum carmen*, and wider European vernacular traditions of pastoral writing about the literal, rather than the poetic or allegorical, herdsman. Where other Italian ecloguists look back to idyllic classical traditions, Mantuan preserves the vision of medieval pastoral. The world of the *Adolescentia* is the fallen world, of winter and bad weather. Love is usually baffled, women are seen as thoroughly evil, poets are ill treated, all towns are corrupt and Rome especially so. Shepherds are favored by God, however, and the true pastoral countryside is to be found in heaven. The first six eclogues are insistently naturalistic in subject, homely in imagery, and rustic even in diction (despite being in Latin). The last four become increasingly allegorical. Altogether they provide a pattern for the eclogue totally different from either Virgil's artistry or Petrarch's obscurity.

By the time Spenser wrote his *Shepheardes Calender*, the *Adolescentia* were already the dominant model for the English eclogue. Two of the eclogues of Alexander Barclay (c 1513, rpt 1570), on the meanness of patrons to poets and the vices of cities, were adapted from Mantuan; and Googe's *Eglogs* of 1563 drew on Mantuan for their moralistic tone as well as for specific subjects, such as the unpleasantness of love and, again, urban corruption. Nine of the *Adolescentia* were translated into English by Turbervile in 1567, and all ten by Thomas Harvey in 1656. Francis Sabie drew on them extensively in the eclogues of *Pan's Pipe* (1595). Quotations from and allusions to Mantuan abound throughout the Renaissance and indicate how familiar his works were; these include a line cited by Harvey in *Two Commendable Letters* 2 ('Nec deus ... et error': Mantuan 1.52; *Var Prose* p 444, lines 124–5), and a famous reference by the schoolmaster Holofernes in *Love's Labor's Lost*: 'Ah, good old Mantuan! ... Who understandeth thee not, loves thee not' (IV ii 94–100).

Mantuan is one of the leading models for *The Shepheardes Calender*, along with Virgil and Marot. E.K. points out some of the most distinctive similarities in his glosses. The ecclesiastical eclogues all owe something of their tone to him, and *Julye* and *September* are particularly close parallels. *Julye*'s debate on the rival merits of hills and plains is based on a similar debate in his eighth eclogue; and its list of biblical and classical exempla of good and bad shepherds is taken from his seventh, though it was also a commonplace of vernacular pastoral. *September* is based on Mantuan's ninth eclogue, on the corruption of Rome. The complaint on the neglect of poets and poetry in *October* draws thematically on the fifth eclogue. The winter world of *Februarie* is also Mantuanesque, and Spenser includes an adaptation of his description of winter. Mantuan's unrequited lover, Amyntas, is one of many analogues for Colin Clout and Colin's love for Rosalind. His deliberate effort to achieve a rustic decorum of style was stressed by the commentators and may well have influenced Spenser, though Spenser's use of language and rhythm go much further in this direction than Mantuan could achieve in Latin hexameters. Mantuan's use of inset stories or fables, which relate metaphorically or as exempla to the framing eclogue, may also have contributed to Spenser's structuring of his own eclogues.

HELEN COOPER

H. Cooper 1977; Cullen 1970; Mantuan 1911 *Eclogues* ed Wilfred P. Mustard (Baltimore).

Marinell In lineage as in name, Marinell is associated with the sea. He is the son of Dumarin ('of the sea') and a mother called Cymoent in *FQ* III and Cymodoce in *FQ* IV, daughter of the sea god Nereus who showers riches on him at her request. On discovering from Proteus that 'of a woman he should have much ill, / A virgin strange and stout him should dismay, or kill,' Cymoent misinterprets the prophecy and 'bad him womens love to hate' (III iv 25–7). Through her zealous efforts, he becomes lord of the Rich Strond, the seashore where his treasure lies, until he is overthrown by Britomart. The mythological structure of the episode alludes to Achilles – his mortal father and Nereid mother, her over-protective care, the warning prophecy, and his eventual marriage to the object of his initial disdain (R.N. Ringler 1963).

One of the most mysterious figures in *The Faerie Queene*, Marinell appears in three episodes in Books III–V: in III iv he is defeated by Britomart, in IV xii he falls in love with Florimell, and in V iii he marries Florimell. In each episode, he is contrasted to other major figures and episodes of the poem. In his defeat by Britomart, he is a Narcissus or Achilles, the young man reluctant to love (his name possibly suggesting 'marry-nill'; Hieatt 1975a:94) and a counterpart to Malecasta, whom Britomart has overthrown at Castle Joyous. In IV xii, he falls in love with Florimell, whose long confinement in Proteus' watery prison parallels that of Amoret behind the fiery walls of Busirane's prison at the end of Book III. His marriage to Florimell, where he is championed by Artegall, combined with the fact that it was Britomart who had first defeated him, figures the dynastic marriage of Britomart and Artegall which is central to Spenser's poem, much as that of Bradamante and Ruggiero had been to Ariosto's *Orlando furioso*, or that of Aeneas and Lavinia to the *Aeneid*.

For a poem so concerned with the idea of marriage, *The Faerie Queene* is remarkable for its avoidance of direct descriptions of weddings. The Red Cross Knight and Una are only betrothed, and the interrupted wedding of Scudamour and Amoret occurs at some point between his winning her (narrated in IV x) and her capture by Busirane (briefly noted in IV i). The only wedding which is described in detail is that of the Thames and Medway (the occasion of Marinell's overhearing Florimell's declaration of her love for him). The marriage of Marinell and Florimell, with its overtones of the union of sea and land, is Spenser's closest approximation to a direct presentation of a wedding between human figures in the poem; but here the narrator forgoes any description of the spousals themselves as 'worke fit for an Herauld, not for me' (V iii 3), and concentrates instead on the accompanying tournament.

THOMAS P. ROCHE, JR

Marlowe, Christopher (1564–93) It is hard to think of a greater contrast than that between the personal styles of Spenser and Marlowe. To describe Spenser's verse, such epithets as delicate, gentle, harmonious, fluent, and leisurely may serve; but none of these describes 'Marlowe's mighty line' (Jonson 'To the Memory of ... Shakespeare') with its forward thrust and breathtaking urgency. The Prologue to Part I of *Tamburlaine the Great* promises the audience a tragedy which will be significantly different from the drama of the time, and a protagonist 'Threatning the world with high astounding tearms / And scourging kingdoms with his conquering sword.' The promise is fulfilled: the play was received with 'general welcomes,' and its sequel showed more of '*The Bloody Conquests of Tamburlaine*. With his impassionate fury, for the death of *his Lady, and love, faire Zenocrate: his fourme* of exhortation and discipline to his *three sons, and the maner of his own death*' (title page). His 'Conquests' include the merciless destruction of Babylon, when 'every man, woman, and child' is cast 'headlong in the cities lake' (5.1.161); his impotent 'fury' at the death of Zenocrate drives him to devastate the town in which she dies (5.2); part of his 'discipline' is the murder of Calyphas, the son who disappointed his father (4.1); and 'the maner of his own death' is an agony of frustration voiced in the repeated cry 'And shall I die, and this unconquered' (5.3.150).

Yet in the midst of brutality of deed and word, he wears the triumphal plume in his helmet, 'Like to an almond tree ymounted high, / Upon the lofty and celestiall mount, / Of ever green *Selinus* queintly dect / With bloomes more white than *Hericinas* browes, / Whose tender blossoms tremble every one, / At every little breath that thorow heaven is blowen' (4.3.119–24). Marlowe would not claim these lines as his own: the alexandrine acknowledges Spenser's authorship. Although slight alterations have been made, the passage is taken from *The Faerie Queene*, where it describes the crest on Arthur's helmet: 'Like to an Almond tree ymounted hye / On top of greene *Selinis* all alone, / With blossomes brave bedecked daintily; / Whose tender locks do tremble every one / At every little breath, that under heaven is blowne' (I vii 32). This is not plagiarism; it is not even simple borrowing. Tamburlaine is *quoting* Spenser – deluding himself that he belongs to the same medieval chivalric tradition as Arthur, and that his approach to Samarcanda is comparable to Arthur's relief of Una. (See *Wales.)

Since *Tamburlaine* Part 2 was written in 1587 (or, at the latest, 1588), and *FQ* I was not published until 1590, Marlowe must have read the poem in manuscript as it circulated among Spenser's friends. He must have been included, then, with such dissimilar spirits as Harvey and Sidney. The courtly, cultured circles of literary England at that time were very small. Their like-minded members, however different in individual temperament, had much in common; most especially, they shared a common heritage. Spenser and Marlowe inherited the same literary legacy but spent it very differently.

In *FQ* III xi 29–46, Spenser describes the tapestries in the house of Busirane; and in *Hero and Leander* (135–56) Marlowe describes the pavement of the temple of Venus at Sestos. Their inspiration was the same (Ovid's account of the embroidered web woven by Arachne in *Metamorphoses* 6.103–28), but a startling difference appears when each introduces his topic. Spenser is gentle, dignified, and leisurely: 'And in those Tapets weren fashioned / Many faire pourtraicts, and many a faire feate, / And all of love, and all of lusty-hed.' In contrast, Marlowe's couplet form encourages speedy reading, and the rhyme emphasizes the outrageous comedy: 'There might you see the gods in sundrie shapes, / Committing headdie ryots, incest, rapes.' Spenser examines the tapestries in detail, lingering over each scene with aesthetic enjoyment. With loving care, he recounts each episode and all the circumstances surrounding the loves of the gods, counterpoising beauty and violence: in stanza 32, for instance, he narrates the story of Leda, 'in daffadillies sleeping,' when Jupiter, metamorphosed into a swan and 'ruffing his fethers wyde,' took her by surprise and 'did her invade.' In the last two lines of the stanza, he complicates the picture of harmless innocence and sexual aggression by observing that 'She slept, yet twixt her eyelids closely spyde, / How towards her he rusht, and smiled at his pryde.' Marlowe's poem glances at different incidents but, in haste to further its narrative, seizes upon the single detail relevant to its own purpose: transformed into a bull, Jove is 'for his love *Europa*, bellowing loud'; but in the next line, she has been replaced by Iris, and he is 'tumbling with the Rainbow in a cloud.' Spenser lavishes tender care on the abduction of Ganymede, visualizing the whole incident with all its drama and danger, and he even imagines the spectators when Jove was seen 'in soaring Eagles shape' (34); Marlowe casts a sardonic glance at '*Jove*, slylie stealing from his sister's bed, / To dallie with *Idalian Ganimed*' (147–8), and passes briskly on to list the god's other intrigues.

Both poets endeavor to display the great gods in human situations; but while Spenser's gods are always the creations of classical legend, Marlowe's (in *Dido, Queen of Carthage* as well as in *Hero and Leander*) are a motley crew, full of quirks and perversities, and morally no better than the mortals who serve them. While Spenser finds beauty in the most violent acts, Marlowe discovers the comedy and indignity which are potentially present in the most heroic. In thus reducing his gods, he robs them of some of their allegorical capabilities which Spenser, by contrast, expands.

As well as a familiarity with the better-known stories and figures of classical mythology, both poets show a knowledge of some more uncommon aspects of the subject, in particular, one of the 'creation' myths. In *Hero and Leander*, Marlowe speaks of 'ougly *Chaos* den' from which, by some mysterious operation, the earth was 'up-wayd [raised]' (450). He seems rather vague about the process (the whole section of the poem is a digression from the main narrative); but help with the obscurity comes from Spenser's *Hymne of Love*, which describes how 'this worlds still moving mightie masse, / Out of great *Chaos* ugly prison crept' (57–8). According to Spenser, love was the motivating force; this notion is an integral part of the Neoplatonic doctrine expounded in much of his work.

Marlowe appears to have picked up some of the ideas of Neoplatonism, but his use of the ideas suggests that he does not subscribe to the philosophy. The theory that form indicates content is a Neoplatonic commonplace: 'For all that faire is, is by nature good; / That is a signe to know the gentle blood' (*Hymne of Beautie* 139–40). There is no irony here: Spenser expounds the philosophy to praise the thought. But the situation becomes more complicated in *Hero and Leander*, where the narrator observes that 'In gentle brests, / Relenting thoughts, remorse and pittie rests. / And who have hard hearts, and obdurat minds, / But vicious, harebrained, and illit'rat hinds?' (699–72). Marlowe is here recounting the story – entirely the creation of his own mythopoeic imagination – of Neptune's pursuit of Leander as the youth is swimming across the Hellespont. The god has been shown to be *unnatural* in his desires for the boy, as well as *supernatural* in his powers; but now the Neoplatonic doctrine is adduced to explain his hopes in the renewed assault. Earlier in the poem, the same doctrine was alluded to by Leander himself on his first attempt to seduce Hero: 'Be not unkind and faire, mishapen stuffe / Are of behaviour boisterous and ruffe' (203–4). But Leander has already been described as being 'like to a bold sharpe Sophister' (197); Marlowe uses this term in the sense of 'one who makes use of fallacious arguments; a specious reasoner' (*OED* 3).

This points to the essential difference between Spenser and Marlowe, a difference of which one becomes increasingly conscious the more one recognizes the heritage they shared. Spenser is Petrarchan and Marlowe Ovidian, in the sense that Spenser seems to assent to the medieval, romantic interpretation of the *Ars amandi*, whereas Marlowe shares Ovid's flippant, even cynical sensuality. Again, one might say that Spenser is reverent in all that he does, and Marlowe is skeptical. Above all, Spenser is an idealist, with the ultimate aim of 'Fashioning XII. Morall vertues' in *The Faerie Queene*. Marlowe would express no such purpose, and what he has to teach is contained in the much sterner 'message' of *Doctor Faustus*. ROMA GILL

The plays in the Revels editions (1962–) have good notes; see also Marlowe ed 1950 *Marlowe's 'Doctor Faustus' 1604–1616* ed W.W. Greg (Oxford). The poems are included in *Complete Works* ed Roma Gill (Oxford 1987–). For general background, see Frederick S. Boas 1953 *Christopher Marlowe: A Biographical and Critical Study* rev ed (Oxford); Clifford Leech 1986 *Christopher Marlowe: Poet for the Stage* (New York). For recent critical studies, see Lois Mai Chan with Sarah H. Pedersen 1978 *Marlowe Criticism: A Bibliography* (Boston). Parallel passages in Spenser and Marlowe have long been noted. They are drawn together in Georg Schoeneich 1907 *Der litterarische Einfluss Spensers auf Marlowe* (Halle). For a convenient summary, see John Bakeless 1942 *The Tragicall History of Christopher Marlowe* 2 vols (Cambridge, Mass) 1:205–8, to which may be added *1 Tamb* 5.2.60 and *FQ* I vii 43, 5.2.196 and I vii 22; *2 Tamb* 4.3.112 and I iv 4, 5.2.26 and II vii 13 (*1 Tamb* 1.2.173 'bound fast in iron chaines' and VI xii 35 'fast bound in yron chaine' may show, by contrast, Spenser borrowing from Marlowe, for *FQ* VI is believed to have been written after *2 Tamb*; see Jump 1964). T.W. Baldwin 1942 'The Genesis of Some Passages Which Spenser Borrowed from Marlowe' *ELH* 9:157–87 has by all present-day accounts got the debt backwards, but his analysis of the classical background to the passages in *Tamburlaine* is still excellent; see the response in W.B.C. Watkins 1944 'The Plagiarist: Spenser or Marlowe?' *ELH* 11:249–65. Further parallels have been indicated in Douglas Bush 1938 'Marlowe and Spenser' *TLS* (1 Jan):12 (on the sword image in *Dido* 548–9, its borrowing by Shakespeare in the Player's speech in *Hamlet*, and its source in *FQ* I vii 12); John D. Jump 1964 'Spenser and Marlowe' *N&Q* 209:261–2 (the 1604 text of *Doctor Faustus* ed 1950:244–7 'the gloomy shadow of the earth ... dimmes the welkin' and *FQ* III x 46 'Earthes gloomy shade / Did dim the brightnesse of the welkin round'); Roberts 1978 (see *Circe); and A.B. Taylor 1971 'Britomart and the Mermaids: A Note on Marlowe and Spenser' *N&Q* 216:224–5 (*Hero and Leander* 2.161–4 and *FQ* III iv 18–22).

marriage Few characters in *The Faerie Queene*, and none of the major ones, are married. Fairyland (like the world of romance quests from which it derives) is not conducive to domestic permanence, and the ladies whom knights take on their adventures are not their wives. The two eponymous couples of Book IV (Cambell and Cambina, Triamond and Canacee) are married, but their marriages are not shown in any detail; the point that they are representatives of friendship presumably applies to the relationship between the two men, and is not a point about marriage. Malbecco and Hellenore are clearly married, and are described as 'lincked' (III ix 4); Hellenore is Malbecco's 'Lady,' 'dearest Dame,' and 'wife' (ix 25, x 39, 49). Yet theirs is an insecure union between 'far unequall yeares, / And also far unlike conditions' (ix 4): Hellenore elopes with Paridell, and when Malbecco finds her among the satyrs, he is unable to persuade her to return to him. Since he is presented as possessive husband and cuckold, and subsequently allegorized into a figure of jealousy (x 44–60), we are not, presumably, intended to sympathize with his conduct, though in itself it could be seen as truly Christian in his readiness to forgive all, and touchingly uxorious. Bellamour and Claribell, the parents of Pastorella, are also married; but their story is cursorily told, and their only function in the poem is to be reunited with their long-lost daughter (VI xii). The same might be said of Una's parents in Book I.

It is clear, then, that the married state is not directly treated in *The Faerie Queene*. The poem's important distinctions between different kinds of love – Christian and Neoplatonic, carnal and spiritual, consummated and unconsummated – are not directly related to the question of whether the lovers are married. This is true of many of Spenser's sources: Ficino approves sexual union between lovers if the higher faculties are in play, but whether the union is blessed by the church is not a central issue (Ellrodt 1960:28). In both the courtly and the Neoplatonic traditions, the distinction between love and lust is by no means the same as that between marital and extramarital love.

It should not surprise us, therefore, that there is so little reference to marriage in *The Faerie Queene*; to look too hard for it is to reduce the poem to a moral treatise. C.S. Lewis interprets Britomart as a figure for married love, and takes her centrality in Books III and IV as evidence that the poem is replacing courtly with married love (1936, ch 8); but he does not mention the obvious objection that Britomart is not married. True, she is intended to marry, and her children are referred to in prophecy; but courtship is very different from marriage, both in fact, since it involves neither cohabitation nor sex, and in the literary tradition, since it uses so many traditional images of love.

Amoret's relationship to marriage is more complicated, and there is considerable disagreement about the significance of her imprisonment in the house of Busirane (III xi-xii). He carries her off by force from the wedding feast with Scudamour: is this to be read literally, as an assault from without, or allegorized as representing a flaw in Amoret herself? The former reading seems supported by the insistence on her loyalty to Scudamour and by her resistance to the 'vile Enchaunter,' but most critics have opted for the latter: it is then difficult to decide whether the flaw is lust, or fear of sex, or some awkward combination of the two (Hamilton 1961a, ch 4; Roche 1964, ch 2; Freeman 1970, ch 6, especially pp 222–3). After her release, Amoret is (in the 1590 version of Book III) embraced by Scudamour in a manner that clearly suggests sexual intercourse. This has been seen as a symbol of marriage (Lewis 1967:38, K. Williams 1961), but there is no hint of a ceremony before the lovers embrace. Book IV makes clear that the wedding has already taken place; but the 1596 edition, which includes Book IV, removes the embrace from the end of Book III.

The importance of constancy, not only in Redcrosse and Britomart, but also in many other lovers (Florimell, Timias, Scudamour) can be seen as at least hinting at the virtues of married love; yet the courtly lover is constant, too, and there may be a degree of bias against marriage in the fact that Amoret and Belphoebe are the issue of a virgin birth (III vi 3); several other births of important, and virtuous, characters either mention no father or attribute to him a purely generative function after which he disappears (Marinell, III iv 19–20; Priamond and his brothers, IV ii 41–5) – or else the child's mother does (Satyrane, I vi 23). In Fairyland, a young hero is far more likely to be a foundling than to enjoy the benefits of a two-parent, nuclear household.

Since marriage is a moral and social, even legal concept, we would not expect it to be prominent in Fairyland; but what we can expect are weddings. Of the two sustained weddings in the poem, one is purely allegorical, that of Thames and Medway in IV xi. Most of this canto is taken up with a list of the bridal guests, who are classical gods and nymphs, and rivers. The elaborate ceremony is clearly symbolic, either politically (the marriage of England to Elizabeth) or in a more general way referring to the unity of life and the significance of generation in nature; its elaborate lists of guests have been seen as numerologically significant (Fowler 1964:182–91). The placing of this wedding in the penultimate canto of the book, just before Marinell and Florimell are united, underlines the absence of a wedding ceremony for the latter, which is deferred until V iii and then elaborately described (see esp 2–3, 40). None of Spenser's other main pairs of lovers actually marry: Artegall and Britomart plight their troth, 'Till they with marriage meet might finish that accord' (IV vi 41), and Redcrosse celebrates a betrothal to Una that seems tantamount to a wedding and leads to his 'swimming in that sea of blisfull joy' before (like Artegall) he is called away to a new quest (I xii 41). (When that quest ends in six years and he returns, Una's father vows 'The marriage to accomplish vowd betwixt you twain.') In line with these deferred marriages is the story of Philemon whose intemperate fury that leads him to kill his beloved breaks out at the moment when 'There wanted nought but few rites to be donne, / Which mariage make' (II iv 21). Considering the importance of ritual in the poem, and the likelihood of its climax being a (probably multiple) wedding, we ought perhaps to take more seriously than recent criticism has done the possibility that it is genuinely unfinished.

Spenser's minor poems have more to say about marriage. *Amoretti* is the first sonnet sequence that we know to have been written by a poet to his bride. The evidence for this is only circumstantial: he married Elizabeth Boyle in June 1594, and the poems were published shortly afterwards; sonnet 74 tells us that the lady is named Elizabeth, sonnet 60 tells us his age, and a few references tell us that the courtship lasted a year and a half. These autobiographical touches would hardly have been clear to the general reader, however; the revolutionary step of transferring the conventions of the love sonnet from an adulterous to an honest wooing is less apparent than the similarly revolutionary step of treating a courtship apparently destined from the start to end in marriage. The content and style of the poems themselves are by no means revolutionary; they use many of the stock devices of the Petrarchan poet addressing his imaginary or already married mistress: the beloved is a tyranness, the poet humbly begs the favors she is too cruel to grant, and he continually refers to her as 'cruell' and uses the love-war conceit, as well as images taken from religion. One point, however, does convey to the reader the transition to marriage: the fact of their publication along with *Epithalamion*, a wedding poem written in the first person. Spenser thus joins two genres which had not been previously joined (Greene 1957, Hieatt 1960, Lerner 1979:125–30).

Prothalamion (1596) also celebrates a marriage, indeed a double marriage, as the title page makes clear. It is a 'Spousall Verse' in honor of the marriages of the daughters of the Earl of Worcester to 'the two worthie Gentlemen' whose names, in small type, bring up the rear of the long title, indicating that the groom, whatever his subsequent power, is far from the center of attention at such a ceremony. The speaker of this poem, in contrast to *Epithalamion*, is only a spectator, and there is neither the close involvement nor the careful unfolding of the day's successive hours that makes *Epithalamion* so memorable. It is even probable that what is being celebrated is not the wedding itself, but a betrothal (hence the title's nonce word, *prothalamion*, a pre-bridal poem). Here, as so often in *The Faerie Queene*, Spenser's subject is the promise of a marriage rather than its celebration.

LAURENCE LERNER

Marvell, Andrew (1621–78) In 1657, Marvell, Latin Secretary in Cromwell's government, was asked by the Lord Protector to contribute verses for a masque to be performed at his daughter's wedding celebration. He wrote two pastoral dialogues. Both the masque itself and his choice of pastoral myths and motifs were somewhat unusual. Although pastoral dialogues had appeared in Playford's *Select Musicall Ayres and Dialogues* (1652), masques were almost unknown in the palaces of the Protectorate, associated as they were with monarchy, courtly extravagance, secular allegory, and in particular the indulgences of the Stuart court.

Marvell's first dialogue looks back to Lyly, enacting the wooing of Cynthia the moon by the shepherd Endymion (reversing the usual situation); the second imitates the rustic manners of the speakers of *The Shepheardes Calender* and some of Marvell's own lyrics such as 'Clorinda and Damon.' Marvell's Hobbinol congratulates 'the Northern Shepheards Son' (the groom, Lord Fauconberg, from Yorkshire), as Spenser's Hobbinol had lamented the lovelorn fate of 'the Southerne shepheardes boye,' Colin (*Aprill* 21). Hobbinol and Tomalin display their Spenserian origins in their naive wordplay and their concern for languishing pastoral lovers.

Marvell cannot be called Spenserian as may Browne, Drayton, or the Fletchers: he shows little interest in long narratives, continued allegory or dark conceits, or the metaphorical identification of shepherd and poet. Nor is Spenser for him the moral mentor, the 'sage and serious' source of doctrine that he was for Milton. But the filiation between the two poets is revealed by more than churlish names and rustic manners: the influence of Spenser's emblematic narrative style and symbolic natural world is apparent everywhere in Marvell's poetry. The evidence for his having read Spenser closely is rather slight. There are verbal echoes like the recollection of *March* 16 (and gloss) or *FQ* II xii 50 in the blazoning of Flora ('Clorinda and Damon' 4); and the same poem rests part of its argument on the implicit identification of Pan with Christ, as glossed by E.K. in *Maye* (54).

But these are merely surface indications of deeper sympathies. One reader notes the consonance between Marvell's treatment of temptation in 'A Dialogue between the Resolved Soul and Created Pleasure' and Augustinian views on the mind's struggle against the lures of the world and the senses, a tradition central to *The Faerie Queene*, and compares the stages of temptation in Marvell's dialogic agon to the structure of *FQ* II, particularly of the Mammon episode (Kermode 1971:69–71, 84–7). The archetype for the drama of temptation is Satan's assault on Christ in Luke 4.13. Augustine comments on this passage in a homily on Psalm 8, where he relates it to the warning in 1 John 2.16 against 'the luste of the flesh, the luste of the eyes, and the pride of life' (*Enerrationes in Psalmos* 4.1; cf *Confessions* 10.30). In Marvell's scheme and in Spenser's, the enemy of virtue attacks the senses before going on to offer worldly power and forbidden knowledge in exchange for the will's submission. Both poets share a Christian tradition in which the natural world, one of the 'books' of divine creation (the other being Holy Scripture), is seen as the field of trial for both will and reason.

Both Spenser and Marvell render the delights of the senses in full measure, faithful to their understanding of the difficulty of living morally in a world governed by apparently conflicting imperatives. In Genesis, God gave Adam regency over the created world; but since the Fall, the world, the flesh, and the devil bar our path to salvation. Spenser and Marvell share a sense of the complexity of this dilemma and a fascination with the powers of evil, which lie precisely in its ability to make itself resemble the good. The line dividing a just and licit appreciation of the bounties of creation from sinful indulgence and submission to natural beauty is so fine as sometimes to be imperceptible. Augustine distinguishes firmly between the proper appreciation of God's gifts as signs of providential care and their improper 'use,' wherein they are valued for themselves (see *Christian Doctrine* 1.3). But for Spenser's questing knights, as for Marvell's shepherds and rusticated poet-figures, that distinction is often hard to formulate and even harder to maintain. The bunches of grapes 'hanging downe' from the porch that shelters Excess 'seemed to entice / All passers by, to tast their lushious wine, / And did themselves into their hands incline' (*FQ* II xii 54). The parodic exaggeration of this image of benevolent nature is repeated, perhaps with more conscious humor, in the predicament of the retiring denizen of 'The Garden,' who reports that 'The Luscious Clusters of the Vine / Upon my Mouth do crush their Wine'; going even further, 'The Nectaren, and curious Peach, / Into my hands themselves do reach.' Spenser's hero rejects such blandishments by exercising self-discipline and following the rational guidance of his Palmer, Marvell's by retreating into a meditative state. Yet both poets register the appeal of the natural world as strongly as its dangers.

Spenser shows us Guyon and Redcrosse embattled, entoiled, and sometimes bewildered in their encounters with embodiments of the world's temptations; Marvell, working in the more restricted mode of lyric, often represents such recurrent combats through the eyes and voices of naive speakers, a rhetorical device that permits him the use of irony which is fundamental to his view of the ambiguities of moral experience and judgment.

The complaints of the Mower Damon, for example, against the adulteration of nature in 'The Mower against Gardens' rehearse Perdita's purist argument against grafting (Shakespeare *Winter's Tale* IV iv) and make the traditional charge against artifice that it is unnatural. But Marvell comments implicitly on that argument by creating a persona whose passion is clearly excessive and whose comprehension of the philosophical tradition in which he is enmeshed is inadequate. The poet thereby questions the truth of Polixenes' counterassertion that 'art itself is Nature,' while enacting for us the absurdities of a moral position which rests upon the rejection of those abilities that define our uniqueness as human beings.

A related, but less exclusively ethical consideration of this endless dispute between nature and the numinous can be found by comparing the Garden of Adonis with the Bower of Bliss (*FQ* II xii, III vi). The threat as well as the allure of Acrasia's bower is unfolded in images that characterize human art as the corrupting emulation of nature's inherent beauties and virtues. The ivy that twines around the fountain is deplored because, though made of gold, it has been painted so cleverly in 'his native hew' that it is able to trick the unwary eye into believing that it is 'yvie trewe.' Spenser returns repeatedly, as does Marvell in the 'Mower' poems, 'The Coronet,' and elsewhere, to the difficulty of separating the value of the artist's disciplined skill in imitating divine creation from the condemnation that art earns by placing a substitute reality before the eye of the mind. The dilemma is as old as Plato's *Dialogues*; but it appears to have become newly poignant for many Renaissance artists, especially those attempting to compose devotional works at the service of theological or ethical doctrines. Marvell's horror at discovering the 'wreaths of Fame and Interest' in which his poetry is entwined in 'The Coronet,' and his prayer to be freed from the exigencies of his art, have some of the moral resonance of Redcrosse's appeal to the hermit Contemplation to be released from the obligations of his quest and allowed to pass directly to the New Jerusalem (*FQ* I x 63).

In his dialogues and in such explicitly religious poems as 'On a Drop of Dew,' Marvell expresses a more categorical dualism between the values of the world and the spirit than is usual in the generally diffuse Platonism of Renaissance English poetry. Like Spenser in the *Fowre Hymnes*, he does not characterize nature as the first step in a divinely ordered ascent from the perception of physical beauty, to the idea of beauty, and finally to the contemplation and love of the source of all beauty. Roses and dewdrops are neither simulacra nor shadows of heavenly forms of truth, but self-substantial entities, evidence of God's immeasurable beneficence and limitless creative power. Understood and used properly, they are given to man to sustain his life on earth. Loved for their own sake, they are lures that can overturn reason's sovereignty over the will, toppling man from his supremacy and subjecting him to nature, which should be subordinate. In Spenser and Marvell, nature is an arena of moral trial, however lovely and seemingly benevolent. In 'The Picture of Little *T.C.* in a Prospect of Flowers,' Flora threatens the little girl as she matures into full womanhood; and the crypto-Adam of 'The Garden' indulges in a fantasy of a world without human ambition or sexual passion.

For both Spenser and Marvell, pastoral involves a pervasive reference to the values and symbols that cluster around the mythology of the Golden Age: the time, as Hesiod and Ovid wrote, when nature and man were in complete nurturing sympathy, a sympathy that Genesis suggests did not survive the Fall of Adam and Eve (Gen 3.17–19). Spenser laments the descent from the virtue of the Golden Age in the proem to Book V; indeed, the initiating quest of Redcrosse to free Adam and Eve from the Dragon makes clear from the outset that the world of *The Faerie Queene* is the familiar fallen one. Marvell allows himself to be teased by the imagination of the unfallen: 'The Mower's Song' is sung by one who remembers the time when his 'Mind was once the true survey' of the meadows he identifies himself with, the speaker of 'The Garden' dreams that 'Such was that happy Garden-state,' and the ambulatory poet of *Upon Appleton House* imagines that he recovers the language of unfallen nature and reads 'in *Natures mystick Book*' (584).

Marvell's preferred poetic mode is the dramatic: he creates voices and personae, the images of minds that speculate about the relations between mankind, the created world, and transcendent reality. In his attitudes toward the power of the world to entice those minds, as well as to serve as the scene of moral discipline and growth, he reveals the influence of Spenser, as does Milton. In his recurrent choice of pastoral situations, characters, and motifs as the expressive means of his poetry, he also reveals the importance of the intellectually luminous quality of Spenser's images of things seen. The enclosed world of *Upon Appleton House* moves by in a kaleidoscopic succession of scenes, each one viewed with an intense clarity comparable to the visual focus of Spenser's descriptions of pageants, tapestries, or the myriad characters who traverse the landscape of *The Faerie Queene*. Marvell's poems, the 'fruits' which he says are 'only flowers' ('The Coronet'), are held together by sinews of argument and logical inference; but they are also filled with images of created nature: tears and flowers, birds' nests, trees, and oranges hanging 'Like golden Lamps in a green Night' ('Bermudas'). His world, like Spenser's, is fully substantial, yet instinct with meaning. For both of them, the poetry of pastoral is a way to grasp that meaning, to reveal the numinous beneath the alluring surface. For Marvell, the process of discovery is more fascinating, perhaps because the relation between symbol and significance became less stable in the half century after the publication of *The Faerie Queene*. The vision of Colin Clout piping to the ring of dancing maidens in Book VI may be thought of as Spenser's ultimate symbol of the source of pastoral and poetry. Marvell's garden-reverie of the mind, by contrast, finds utmost 'happiness' in 'Annihilating all that's made / To a green Thought in a green Shade' ('The Garden'), his cryptic comment on pastoral as the poetic link between consciousness and the world it attempts to understand. While the 'thought' remains 'green,' it fades indistinguishably into the surrounding 'shade.' DONALD M. FRIEDMAN

Andrew Marvell 1971 *Poems and Letters* ed H.M. Margoliouth, 3rd ed rev Pierre Legouis with E.E. Duncan-Jones, 2 vols (Oxford). Rosalie L. Colie 1970 *'My Ecchoing Song': Andrew Marvell's Poetry of Criticism* (Princeton); Cullen 1970; Kermode 1971; J.B. Leishman 1966 *The Art of Marvell's Poetry* (London).

Marx & Spenser Late in life, Karl Marx (1818–83) wrote detailed notes and commentary on Henry Sumner Maine's *Lectures on the Early History of Institutions* (London 1875), which drew heavily on Spenser's *Vewe of the Present State of Ireland* for its account of Irish institutions. Marx's judgment of Spenser is made in a comment on Sir John Davies:

> D. lumpacii affirmed the illegality of the *native Irish tenures of land* ... The lousy [*lausige*] Sir John Davis [Maine's spelling] was King James's Attorney-General for Ireland, and for this post, of course, a right kind of rascal [Ger *Lump*] was chosen – a similarly 'unprejudiced' and disinterested fellow [*Patron*] as Elizabeth's arse-kissing poet [*der Elizabeths Arschkissende Poet*] Spenser ('State of Ireland'). His remedy for the ills of Ireland, the employment of large masses of troops 'to tread down all that standeth before them in foot, and lay on the ground all the *stiffnecked people of that land*.' That war was to be waged, not only in summer, but in winter too; he continues: 'the end will be very short' and he describes in proof what he himself had witnessed 'in the late wars of Munster' etc. For further cannibalism of this poet see Haverty [ie, Martin Haverty *The History of Ireland, Ancient and Modern* Dublin 1860]. (Marx ed 1972:305; German passages tr Prawer 1976:362)

Spenser's apparent role as apologist for Elizabeth's Irish policy, characterized here as 'cannibalism,' provoked Marx into employing a contemptuous and possibly deliberately echoing variant of Spenser's traditional epithet, England's 'Arch poet.' He does so by using a motif identified by folklorists as the 'misdirected kiss' (cf S. Thompson 1955–8: K 1225), which usually results from deception, as in Chaucer's *Miller's Tale* (*CT* I [A] 3730–41), but may be deliberate, as in the thirteenth-century French fabliau, 'Bérengier au Lonc Cul,' in which the cowardly knight would rather kiss than fight, unaware that his opponent is his wife in martial disguise (Hellman and O'Gorman 1965:59–66). (See **witches** Fig 2.)

This *osculum infame*, when bestowed on Satan as a sign of fealty, figures among charges leveled against witches and heretics; a Papal bull of 1233 gave the charge official notice. The Knights Templar, whom Spenser describes as 'decayd through pride' (*Prothalamion* 136), were said to use this kiss in their initiation ritual. In *FQ* I viii 48, the Red Cross Knight's recognition of falsehood at the sight of Duessa's 'rompe ... with dong all fowly dight' – in effect a recognition of his earlier 'misdirected kiss' (see ii 45, vii 7) – shames him into accepting Una once more as his companion and guide.

Although Marx's phrase may seem extraordinarily vulgar, he often uses such language in his unpublished diaries and notebooks. Yet here his native German is curiously mingled with English: the correct orthography would be 'Arsch küssende.' Prawer's rendering, 'Elizabeth's arse-kissing poet Spenser,' does not do grammatical justice to Marx who uses a somewhat faulty extended modifier construction with the definite article (*der*) to suggest that 'the poet Spenser was (always) kissing Elizabeth's arse.' Moreover, the phrase is not as vulgar in German as in English, for in German-speaking countries the command or invitation to kiss (more accurately, to lick) one's arse/ass/behind/backside is still often heard, particularly in the phrase's native Swabia, where the words, in a suitable tone of voice, can express friendly astonishment. Further, the 'Swabian greeting' had been hallowed by Goethe in *Götz von Berlichingen mit der eisernen Hand* (1773): a knight hurls this insult at his besiegers before shutting his castle window. One may infer, then, that Marx's phrase, especially when used with the anglicism *kissend* in place of the expected *leckend*, may not be as crude as might first appear. Also, the most accurate rendering would almost certainly be the mildest of the three translations offered by Schramm 1960: 'backside kissing.' 'Ass-kissing' is too literal, for one cannot suppose that Marx is positing a degree of familiarity far exceeding what Spenser himself acknowledges when he records, without any elision, how the Queen graciously 'enclin'd her eare' to him as she heard him read *The Faerie Queene* (*Colin Clout* 360–2).

Since Spenser's *Vewe* challenges, rather more than apologizes for, official policy in Ireland, Marx might better be referring to *The Faerie Queene*, which is dedicated to Elizabeth in hope of her patronage. If he had read Book I, he would have identified her with Una, whose name expresses the royal motto, *semper eadem*; and if he had read the episode in which the satyrs 'Do kisse her feete' (vi 12), he may well have identified the poet living in 'the salvage Island' (VI i 9) with them, especially since Harvey had characterized Spenser as 'Hobgoblin' for daring to write his 'Elvish Queene' (Spenser ed 1912:628). Just possibly, this episode prompted Marx's phrase, for in their adoration of Una, the satyrs 'her Asse would worship fayn' (I vi 19). Since her ass had been described as 'more white then snow' but she 'much whiter' (i 4), Marx could have made the connection with Elizabeth, whose pride in her white skin led her to bare her belly, and of whom André Hurault, the ambassador of the French king, Henry IV, wrote appreciatively: 'her flesh is exceeding white' (ed 1931:25).

Of more general interest is Marx's reference to Davies, by way of Spenser, as a *Lump* or rascal. The German word may have been suggested by the Latin title of a decree issued by the Court of King's Bench that imposed English procedures on Irish laws of inheritance. That Spenser should serve as a prime example of English rascality seems inevitable from Marx's reading of the *Vewe*; but German *Lumpen* means 'rags' or 'clout,' and for Marx, the pastoral persona of the humble rustic Colin Clout who adores the Queen from afar becomes a model of the base, conniving rascal.

The harshness of Marx's reference to Spenser may express the disdain he felt for the entire class of *Lumpenproletariat* – that working-class trash content with things as they are. In a letter from the period of the *Notebooks*, Marx writes from Cannes to Engels in London: 'Nature is splendid, otherwise a desolate nest; it is "monumental", in that it consists of nothing but hotels; here there are no plebeian "masses", apart from the *Lumpenproletariat* of the *garçons d'hôtels, de café*, etc' (5 June 1882 in Marx ed 1979:385). For Marx, the Colin Clouts of the world who comprise the Cloutish proletariat will be the last to throw off their chains, for they have used too much ingenuity in forging them.

EDITORS AND ANTHONY W. RILEY

Karl Marx 1972 *The Ethnological Notebooks* ed Lawrence Krader (Assen); Marx 1979 *Letters* sel and tr Saul K. Padover (Englewood Cliffs, NJ).

Robert Hellman and Richard O'Gorman, tr 1965 *Fabliaux* (New York); André Hurault, Sieur de Maisse 1931 *A Journal 1597* tr and ed G.B. Harrison and R.A. Jones (London); S.S. Prawer 1976 *Karl Marx and World Literature* (Oxford); Simon Shepherd 1989 *Spenser* (Atlantic Highlands, NJ). Heinz-Eugen Schramm 1960 *L.m.i.A.* [ie, *Leck mich im Arsch*] *Des Ritters Götz von Berlichingen denkwürdige Fensterrede ... Handbuch zur weltweiten Pflege des Götz-Zitats für nachsichtige Zeitgenossen* (Tübingen) provides not only a glossary of the phrase with phonetic translations into some 60 languages and dialects so that a tourist in almost any country of the world need never be at a loss for words, but also discusses its use by Goethe, Schiller, and esp Mozart, who composed several canons to it (eg, K.231, 233, 559, 560a and b).

Mary, Queen of Scots (1542–87) After Queen Elizabeth, Mary Stuart is arguably the historical personage who bears most significance in *The Faerie Queene*. Critics early in this century who freely constructed historical allegories to match what they took to be Spenser's intentions in the poem saw Mary allegorized especially in the two Duessas (*FQ* I, V) and Amavia (II), as well as in Acrasia, Malecasta, Ate, and Radigund. A more judicious approach to the question of historical allusion and allegory will not sustain all of these characters as representations of Mary. Yet there is a certain plausibility in seeing a relation to her in the threatening figures of female malevolence in the poem. If Elizabeth presided over Spenser's political and religious world, Mary threatened its stability for most of his lifetime. When the first three books were published in 1590, Mary had been dead for three years; but the danger she represented remains one of the moral poles of *The Faerie Queene*. That the various female figures of virtue and strength are often opposed by corresponding female figures of deviousness, lust, and violence suggests the influence that the twenty-year contention of the two queens had upon the imagination of Spenser and his age.

The first clear reference to Mary in *The Faerie Queene* occurs in Book I xii. Disguised as a messenger, Archimago interrupts the betrothal of Una to the Red Cross Knight with a letter from 'Fidessa' claiming prior betrothal to him. 'Fidessa' (ie, Duessa) claims to be the 'wofull daughter, and forsaken heire / Of that great Emperour of all the West,' that is, the Pope (26). Jonson told Drummond that in a paper Raleigh had of 'the Allegories of [Spenser's] Fayrie Queen' – evidently some version of the Letter to Raleigh – by 'the false Duessa' was understood 'the Q. of Scots' (*Sp All* p 154). John Dixon (the earliest reader of *The Faerie Queene* to leave a marginal record of his reactions) penned into his copy the opinion that Mary's claims are alluded to in Duessa's letter: 'A fiction of a Challenge by Q: of s: that the religion by hir maintained to be the truth' (in Hough 1964:10). Since the betrothal of Una to Redcrosse alludes in part to the metaphoric marriage of Elizabeth to her kingdom, its interruption may also bear political significance. Duessa's claim suggests Mary's claim to the throne of England in 1559, which she expressed by quartering the arms of England upon those she assumed with her new but short-lived husband, Francis II. Duessa's threat in the letter that her claim 'shall find friends, if need requireth soe' (28) accurately reflects the danger in which Elizabeth and England stood early in her reign from the forces of Catholic Europe.

Because Books II-IV are not directly historical, Mary's relevance to them, though present, is more general than specifically allusive. In Protestant polemic, Mary assumed the character of a political enchantress; after the murder of Darnley and her marriage to Bothwell, she became Clytemnestra and Circe to Englishmen. As charges proliferated of her sexual immorality and complicity in plots against Elizabeth, her image as Circean seductress came to predominate; thus Lodowick Lloyd rejoiced at the end of the Babington plot that '*Circes* cup is falne' (Phillips 1964:82–3). This image is clearly related to Acrasia in Book II, especially as she parodies the vigorous and chaste Belphoebe/Elizabeth. Though the poem does not insist on the political dangers of seduction by Acrasia, such dangers stand behind the threat she represents to Guyon and the knights of Fairyland. The degree of political significance is even less in Books III and IV; but it is just possible to sense similar antitheses in Britomart and Malecasta, and in the true and false Florimells (III i, viii). Here the poem is dealing not with images of Mary but with a refracted sense of why she might be a lure even to loyal Englishmen.

The clearest and most sustained representation of Mary occurs in the trial of Duessa, which allegorizes the trial of the Queen of Scots with uncommon closeness (V ix 36ff). Mary's son, James VI of Scotland, recognized the allusion and, in a protest to Burghley, asked through his agent that 'Edward Spencer for his faulte, may be dewly tryed and punished' (Carpenter 1923:42). The closeness of the allegory, however, does not reside in the external or legal details: Elizabeth did not preside over Mary's trial, whereas Mercilla (the poem's most sharply etched portrayal of Elizabeth as ruler) presides over Duessa's; and the special commission of jurors who tried Mary is reduced to Artegall and Arthur. Yet the political argument against Mary is reproduced quite exactly, even in details that exceed the strictly legal case. Like Mary, Duessa is charged with treasonous plots against the crown; but the prosecutor, Zeal, brings up old charges that she has beguiled and corrupted many knights. Witnesses such as 'Kingdomes care,' 'the law of *Nations*,' and Religion are called against her. The 'Peoples cry and Commons sute' represent Parliament's prior appeal for Mary's execution. Stanza 45 describes Duessa's defense in terms of the same mixture of political and personal considerations that caused Elizabeth's hesitation to act decisively against Mary. Perhaps closest of all is the way Spenser represents Elizabeth's desire to separate herself from the judgment and execution of Mary: aware of Duessa's guilt and urged to judgment by Artegall and Arthur, Mercilla abruptly rises and leaves the court in pitying tears, which she both hides and reveals (ix 50); we learn of Duessa's execution only obliquely in x 4, after three stanzas of praise for Mercilla's mercy.

An earlier episode in Book V adumbrates Mary with a breadth and generosity truer to Spenser's epic intentions. Rather than the sustained historical allegory of the trial of Duessa, in canto iv he uses the allusive method he had earlier favored, to suggest that the single combat between Britomart and Radigund shadows the conflict of the historical queens. Here allusion works through an accumulation of details: Radigund is called 'A Princesse of great powre, and greater pride,' who has defied all the knights of Maidenhead (33); she presides over an alternate system of law (49) and eventually makes a prisoner of Artegall, embodiment and 'instrument' of English law (proem 11); much of her power over men rests in her awesome beauty (which acknowledges Mary's legendary beauty, even down to her golden tresses in viii 1).

The epic generosity of this episode lies in its suggestion of Mary as a worthy, genuine opponent of Elizabeth. In the fiction, Spenser sets Radigund on equal footing with Britomart and makes us see Radigund as almost a version of Britomart, perhaps even an 'infolding' of Britomart and Belphoebe. Their fierce combat seems a fitting representation of the twenty-year duel of nerves between the two queens, and when it ends, it ends not with an evasiveness like Elizabeth's propaganda but with Britomart striking off the head of her still proud and defiant rival. In her beauty, power, and pride, Radigund seems a fitting representation of Elizabeth's most dangerous rival.

Because Radigund appears like the figures mirroring Elizabeth, the reader is challenged to see significant differences and apply them to queenship. What distinguishes Radigund from Britomart is that she cannot accept the masculinity of the men who serve her; she uses her power to emasculate them psychologically. Radigund veers between femininity and a desire to dominate men utterly; femininity is not reconciled to the virtues necessary to rule, as it is in Britomart's developing sense of queenship. If this is Spenser's judgment of Mary as ruler, it appears shrewd indeed, for queenship and femininity were ever at odds in her tragic career. MICHAEL O'CONNELL

Fraser 1969; Greenlaw 1932; Kerby Neill 1935 'The *Faerie Queene* and the Mary Stuart Controversy' *ELH* 2:192–214; O'Connell 1977; Phillips 1964.

masque One of the most sophisticated of secular rituals practiced within the Elizabethan court, the masque is a pattern of theatrical festivity drawing on both indigenous and continental traditions. Since social theatricality was particularly various during the Elizabethan age, the terms used to describe it are unstable. Court revelry had no canonical form until the reign of James I when Inigo Jones' staging and Ben Jonson's scripts brought a standard and a pattern.

During the Tudor period, the term *masque* could be used quite loosely, although it was beginning to be used to specify the formal entrances of bands of costumed and frequently masked nobles (groups of men or of women, but seldom both together) who would perform elaborate dances before an audience of their peers. Often the group would disband temporarily after the choreographed dances, choosing partners from the audience for social dances, after which they would reassemble for a formal withdrawal from the scene of their performance. These performances had the status of ritual intrusions, sometimes interrupting another sort of theatrical entertainment, sometimes simply intruding upon normal social intercourse, 'By way of sport, as oft in maskes is knowen' (*FQ* IV i 3).

Participation in a masque brought complex satisfactions. A masquer enjoyed the license of self-disclosure that ritual disguise invariably carries with it. Lavish costumes displayed the performer's wealth; the dances, his or her physical graces. Allegorical costumes often showed the special moral authority of the performer, however hypothetically. Above all, masques had a class specificity, a particularly aristocratic character, that bound performer and viewer into a unity which triumphed over the regulated rift that inevitably opened between the fictive and the real.

Spenser's attitude to such revelry involves that ambivalence with which he treats nearly all representational activity. Surely he means to flatter when he remembers that Sidney 'seemd made for meriment, / Merily masking both in bowre and hall' ('Astrophel' 27–8). Yet when the nymph Verlame laments Sidney's death in *The Ruines of Time*, she urges the innocent to beware of social theatricality – 'when the courting masker louteth lowe ... All is but fained' (202–4). The metaphoric force of masquing is enlarged in *The Shepheardes Calender*, where it represents the festive allure ('wherein thou maskedst late') with which the 'barrein ground' of the world seasonally arrays itself (*Jan* 19–24): the seasons themselves embody the world's theatricality.

If Spenser often holds his hostility to courtly theatricality in check, it is because he recognizes that masquing, like all pageantry, shares common methods and many common lines of cultural ancestry with the allegorical procedures of his poetry, particularly in *The Faerie Queene*. He expresses his awareness that poetry itself involves the poet in fictive self-representation at the opening of his epic, when he identifies himself as 'the man, whose Muse whilome did maske, / As time her taught, in lowly Shepheards weeds' (I proem 1). The verb *maske* is used oddly here, for it slowly resolves itself as syntactically transitive: before the resolution in which Spenser becomes the passive recipient of the traditional generic investitures, there is a moment when the Muse appears to us as herself a costumed courtier, a festive reveler, and not as the instructor of the poetic novice. Distinguishing his poetics for the work of *The Faerie Queene*, Spenser dissociates his Muse from mere courtliness or mere pastoral festivity. Such a nervous resistance to social theatricality pervades the epic.

Perhaps the most fully analytical responses to the traditions of masquing may be found in the hymeneal masque of *Epithalamion* and in the masque of Cupid in *The Faerie Queene*. In his wedding poem, the singer attempts to rouse his sluggish bride, 'for Hymen is awake, / And long since ready forth his maske to move' (25–6). To represent the wedding as a masque in this way is to recur to one of the nagging themes of the poem: masque is a *courtly* form, yet the poverty which forces the poet to provide his own entertainment – by singing the wedding song – on an occasion at which he should be the entertained and not the entertainer, cuts him off to some degree from full participation in so elevated a form. He looks on Hymen's masque as if from a distance, excluded from that form of revelry which characteristically joins actor and audience into a community of shared wealth and nobility (Loewenstein 1986).

Not surprisingly, Spenser looks on the intrusions of masque from an even greater distance in *The Faerie Queene*. The pleasures of theatrical self-presentation, the binding of actor to audience, and the intrusions of the fictive upon the real appear in the masque of Cupid as considerable dangers to ethical integrity; such 'idle shewes' (III xii 29) reveal the dangerous powers of *implication* which courtly festivity carries with it. When (we are later told) the masque of Cupid was performed at the wedding of Amoret and Scudamour, the attentive bride lost her interpretive self-possession: 'as oft in maskes is knowen,' the viewer is 'Conveyed quite away to living wight unknowen' (IV i 3). The implicative force of the masque is obvious to the reader, who *does* know where Amoret was conveyed: in Book III, she was discovered as the suffering figure at the center of the courtly theatrical fiction. Having lost her detachment from the spectacle of courtly eroticism, she became the plastic, barren ground on which the torments of love were graven: 'She dolefull Lady ... Had deathes owne image figurd in her face, / Full of sad signes, fearefull to living sight' (xii 19). It is a sign of Britomart's self-possession and interpretive integrity that she can see the masque without being drawn into it: 'Plast / In secret shade' (27), she is detached from the courtly crowd which is the normal audience of masque. 'Expecting ever' (xii 1: the term implies watching, and warding, from a distance), her reality is protected from the intrusions of the fictive.

JOSEPH LOEWENSTEIN

masque of Cupid Britomart's adventures in *FQ* III culminate at the house of Busirane when she witnesses the masque of Cupid (canto xii). Her final achievement, liberating Amoret from her role in a masque, may seem somewhat inconsequential compared to that of her predecessors in the first two books, who between them liberate Eden (I xi) and destroy the Bower of Bliss (II xii). Yet the masque of Cupid recapitulates major themes of Book III; and together with the events surrounding it, it is charged with the kind of excitement and mystery that make them a fitting climax not just for Book III but also for the entire first installment of *The Faerie Queene* (1590).

The Elizabethan masque was an aristocratic entertainment whose immediate antecedents were the banqueting spectacles, mummings, and disguisings that formed an important part of European court ceremonial from the late Middle Ages on. It consisted of a procession of elaborately costumed and visored persons, among them usually members of the royal family or the nobility of the court. The procession as a rule had a rudimentary story connected with the occasion for the masque – a wedding, a birthday, or an investiture – and would conclude with the presentation of a gift or a dance in which the masquers mingled with the aristocratic audience and 'unmasked' by taking off their visors.

With few exceptions, the masque of Cupid at the end of Book III is faithfully modeled on contemporary masque performances, although it derives as well from allegorical literary masques such as those found in Petrarch's *Triumphs* or the *Hypnerotomachia Poliphili* (see E.B. Fowler in *Var* 3:353–9). The sudden trumpet blast before the beginning of the evening's entertainment, the thunder and lightning accompanied by stench of smoke and sulphur, and the other violent signs that the house is enchanted (xii 1–3) have their equivalents in the sound and stage effects which contemporary accounts describe as introducing a masque. After the appearance of the first character of the masque, who is named Ease, there is singing and then 'a most delitious harmony,' presumably of instrumental music, at times interrupted by blaring trumpets. Ease is the 'presenter' typical of the Elizabethan masque, and he mimes the 'argument' or plot of the pageant to follow. The fact that here and throughout the masque of Cupid not a word is spoken reflects the masque as spectacle with music, a contemporary emphasis quite different from that of the later Jonsonian masque. Even so, Ease behaves as though he is 'on the ready flore / Of some Theatre' and about to introduce a full-scale drama. He is, furthermore, 'a grave personage ... Yclad in costly garments, fit for tragicke Stage'; and he motions to his audience 'In signe of silence, as to heare a play' as if they were 'the vulgar' or groundlings in a public theater.

The incongruity of presenting the masque as if it were a tragedy on the public stage points to the greater incongruity that there is no audience at the house of Busirane to witness it, if we except the concealed Britomart. Without an audience, the masque obviously loses much of its character and point: there can be no concluding dance in which audience and masquers mingle, no noble or royal person in whose honor the masque is staged, and, above all, no occasion the masque can be said to celebrate. That last point may seem to be only partly true, since the masque has the appearance of being a 'triumph of Cupid' and therefore could celebrate something like the formal consummation of a courtship – an engagement, say, or (as we find out in Book IV) a wedding – that began in Ease, proceeded to Fancy and Desire, and so through the stages symbolized by the five other couples (7–18). Its culmination would be the appearance of the beloved damsel, followed by 'the winged God himselfe' riding in triumph on a lion (19–23).

This scenario, however, ignores the

strongly negative and unhappy implications of the figures in the procession, and especially of the damsel with 'deathes owne image figurd in her face' (19). Nor does it take into account the 'rude confused rout / Of persons ... whose names is hard to read' (25) that makes up the latter part of the pageant. This 'antimasque,' with its sixteen figures representing 'maladies' comparable to 'phantasies / In wavering wemens wit ... Or paines in love, or punishments in hell' (26), recapitulates the opening procession of sixteen masquers (Ease, the six couples, Amoret, the 'grysie villeins' Despight and Cruelty). The recapitulation suggests that what might have been an occasion for rejoicing becomes a nightmare of fears, scruples, and second thoughts. It thus makes explicit something that was implicit in the masque from the start: the absence of an audience has transformed the masque from a public celebration into something resembling a private obsession. In that transformation, the masque's conventional symbols, the 'public language' of pageantry (Giamatti 1975:83), are turned inward and experienced as a threat to the self.

This process is observable throughout the first part of the masque (it explains how even Ease can become a tragic character), but it is particularly evident in the figures representing the traditional attributes of the beloved lady, such as Despight and Cruelty who lead Amoret. According to the literary tradition on which the masque is founded, these are expressions or consequences of the lady's Daunger or 'standoffishness' (see Lewis 1936:364–6); but in this masque they are transformed into the threat of physical or mental violence. That Amoret feels the threat to be directed at herself appears from the deathlike state in which we see her, and above all by the further, wonderfully grotesque transformation of the emblem of the wounded heart into a literal attack on her physical existence (19–21).

It is now up to Britomart to interpret the masque in order to understand Amoret's predicament and by implication her own, since she, too, is 'masking' (in a suit of armor) at the behest of love. The following evening, when the brazen door opens and she enters the inner room 'Neither of idle shewes, nor of false charmes aghast,' she finds all the masquers gone except Amoret and, before her, Busirane. The impresario and his chief character, still in her emblematic role as love's sacrificial victim, now seem to compose the masque between them (31):

And her before the vile Enchaunter sate,
  Figuring straunge characters of his art,
  With living bloud he those characters wrate,
  Dreadfully dropping from her dying hart,
  Seeming transfixed with a cruell dart,
  And all perforce to make her him to love.
  Ah who can love the worker of her smart?
  A thousand charmes he formerly did prove;
  Yet thousand charmes could not her stedfast heart remove.

Suddenly, in the course of this tableau, the roles of Busirane and Amoret are reversed. He begins as the tyrannical master of her bleeding heart, but what he does is done in a hopeless attempt to move her steadfast heart. This crucial revelation of their interdependence – one being as it were the creature of the other – is perhaps not a direct result of Britomart's presence in the inner room, but the ensuing conflict between her and Busirane makes it dramatically clear. As she rescues Amoret from his attack (32), she in turn learns from Amoret that Busirane must not simply be killed, but that the cure of her painful condition depends on his reversing his charms (34–7). Only then can he be led away captive by his own great chain (41), in token of the fact that social conventions neither can nor should be eliminated from human existence. They must not control, but can rather be controlled by, the individual.

In this scene, then, Britomart represents first of all the witness or audience that was excluded from Amoret's masque, an audience that itself stands for a social realm where language functions to communicate and not just to enchant or wound. Secondly, she represents a sense of self independent of conventions: she is someone who has donned her mask consciously and freely and will take it off as freely. Precisely for these reasons she can liberate Amoret from her seven-month self-imprisonment in the form of the erotic emblem or cliché to which the masque reduced her (37–8). Through Britomart, she recovers or achieves at least some sense of autonomy independent of her role in the masque. The masque of life is neither enchantment nor ultimate reality but a social convention which can be sidestepped or violated, though never ignored, for the sake of some superior good. Having learned this, Britomart may at last know the difficult meaning of that integrity of the self confirmed by Spenser's Legend of Chastity.

Finally, the masque of Cupid represents a kind of hinge between the two installments of *The Faerie Queene* in 1590 and 1596. The beginning of Book IV picks up the story of Amoret and Scudamour; by way of recapitulation, it informs us that the masque of Cupid was staged at their wedding and was used as an occasion to abduct the bride, 'By way of sport, as oft in maskes is knowen' (i 3). No doubt this 'rape' of Amoret was intended as a joke on the bridegroom (Fowler in *Var* 4:165–6); but a further, more sinister implication remains a definite possibility: that Busirane here is also a 'double' of Scudamour and that his abduction of Amoret serves as a deliberate reminiscence of the ancient custom, current in parts of Europe until the nineteenth century, according to which the man was expected to abduct his wife-to-be. Scudamour did pretty much just that before he even knew Amoret, as IV i 2 reminds us and his narrative in canto x confirms: he won her in 'perilous fight when he with force her brought / From twentie Knights, that did him all assay,' an action that has the ritual quality of an established custom.

The masque at III xii, then, is quite different from the 'same' masque recalled at IV i 3; the difference is symptomatic of the change that occurs from the first three to the last three books of the poem. As in the masque without audience witnessed by Britomart, the emphasis of the first three books is introspective, focusing on the individual in relation to social masks which, like chivalric armor, function as projections of desire or aspiration and therefore can serve the cause of education or become a form of entrapment. In the last three books, social conventions and masks are themselves scrutinized for their value and ability to control and direct human impulses. It is surely ominous as regards its vision of society that the narrative of Book IV begins amid the ruins of a wedding masque. (See also *masques, *pageants.) RICHARD T. NEUSE

Alpers 1967b; Berger 1971; DeNeef 1979; Fowler 1964; E.B. Fowler 1921; Giamatti 1975; Goldberg 1975–6; Goldberg 1981; Hieatt 1975a; Felicity A. Hughes 1978 'Psychological Allegory in *The Faerie Queene* III. xi-xii' *RES* ns 29:129–46; Lewis 1936; Nestrick 1975; Nohrnberg 1976; Thomas P. Roche, Jr 1961 'The Challenge to Chastity: Britomart at the House of Busyrane' *PMLA* 76:340–4; Enid Welsford 1927 *The Court Masque: A Study in the Relationship between Poetry and the Revels* (Cambridge); Glynne Wickham 1980 *Early English Stages 1300 to 1660* 2nd ed, vol I: *1300 to 1576 (London).*

medicine Though many Elizabethan gentlemen knew a little medicine and owned one or two simple texts on how to treat illness and wounds, there are no clear indications that Spenser read any of the works by classical, medieval, or contemporary medical authorities, or, for that matter, books on anatomy. He may have glanced at some of the anatomical sections of Aristotle's works on animals, and it would be surprising if he had not read at least in part Pliny's *Natural History*, which includes several books on medicine. There is evidence that he knew Bartholomaeus Anglicus' encyclopedic *De proprietatibus rerum* with its anatomical and medical sections, which he might have read in Latin, in Trevisa's translation, or in Stephen Bateman's shortened adaptation in 1582, and likewise the popular, often-reprinted *Castel of Helth* by Sir Thomas Elyot (1539). And it seems probable that his reading of Ficino included the medical writings. Yet he may have read nothing by Hippocrates, Celsus, Galen, nor Joannitius' short *Isagoge* (still familiar in Spenser's time), nor anything by Avicenna, or the more recent Paracelsus, Vesalius, Fernel, Ambroise Paré, or sixteenth-century English authorities on the subject. For most if not all of his passages involving anatomy or physiology, disease, and therapy, what he knew he learned from ancient, medieval, and modern literary writers, philosophers, and compilers. By comparison with Shakespeare, Spenser's medical and anatomical passages are seldom detailed or precise. His descriptions are almost invariably literary, uninformed by direct observation and unconcerned about professional accuracy. In *The Faerie Queene*, they are fitted to allegorical romance.

parts of the body, physiology By far the most extensive account of the parts of the body in Spenser is the castle of Alma (*FQ* II ix), but the descriptions of organs and exterior parts are not in the least anatomical. He is not concerned with shape or structure. Alma represents the highest or rational part of the tripartite soul residing in the living human body. According to both Plato and Aristotle, the rational soul, together with the sensitive soul whose seat is in the heart and the natural or vegetative soul whose seat is in the liver, directs and shares in the faculties and operations of the body's chief organs, ensuring the temperate and harmonious functioning of body and mind. In stanza 22, the body's overall frame is conceived in Pythagorean terms as consisting of the circular head, quadrate trunk, and a triangle formed by the legs and the ground. The various parts of the body mentioned are prettily imaged: the 'Porter' in charge of the 'larumbell,' for example, is the tongue; '*Port Esquiline*' is the anus. Yet the list is quite incomplete: for instance, of the interior organs, only the stomach, bowels, lungs, heart, and brain are mentioned – not the liver, kidneys, spleen, gall-bladder, blood vessels; and of course not the sexual organs, the emphasis being on the body's upper parts. (Contrast the infernal house of Mammon in II vii, though there bodily analogies are less overtly developed.) Spenser does refer in stanza 31 to the threefold faculty of the stomach to concoct, digest, and eliminate food (a theory found in Galen and medieval writers). Yet his stanzas on the heart (33–5) ignore its shape and basic physiological functions, concentrating instead on it as the seat of the sensitive soul and of the nine affections or passions, the emphasis being on love passion. Later stanzas allegorize the three ventricles of the brain (seats of fantasy or imagination, reason and the judging faculty, and memory) as well as their functions (see *memory, *psychology).

According to Plato, man's primary organ is the brain, the seat of intellect and the rational soul. But Aristotle insisted on the primacy of the heart (eg, *Parts of Animals* 3.4): he believed that the brain exercises only relatively minor functions (eg, *Parts of Animals* 2.7) and assigned the seat of the rational soul to no particular place in the body (*De anima*, especially 3.4). Some of the Stoics, including Seneca, went even further and made the heart the organ of thought, not only of sensory impressions and movement. Galen, however, rejected Aristotle's view, proving by experiment the link between the brain and the nervous system, as well as the eyes and ears, though he preferred as a scientist to leave it to philosophers to decide where the rational soul may be housed in the body. Thomas Aquinas and other medieval Christian philosophers took cognizance of Galen's demonstration of the brain's basic functions yet rejected Plato's close association of the rational soul with the intellect. Nevertheless, Aristotelian and Stoic notions concerning the primacy of the heart persisted strongly and are often echoed in medieval and Renaissance literature. Thus Spenser inherited a confused tradition and inconsistency is not surprising. Indeed the issue was hotly debated by contemporary physiologists until William Harvey's famous discovery in 1628 put an end to it. As for Spenser, in *Amoretti* 50, his preference is clear and Senecan: 'is not the hart of all the body chiefe? / and rules the members as it selfe doth please.' In the castle of Alma, however, the organ of thought and judgment is definitely located in the brain (53–4), though the heart remains the organ that receives sensory impressions. (It is perhaps for this reason that Spenser does not mention Aquinas' 'common sense' in the first ventricle of the brain.) The 'royall arras' in stanza 33 may suggest that Alma, the soul, and not only its sensitive part, resides there, even though Spenser's emphasis here is on the affections, including love, rather than on thought.

Passages mentioning other organs are notably few and, following psychological and literary tradition, usually associate them with particular appetites, passions, or related humors: the swollen spleen with anger (I iv 35), the liver with such lower, undesirable passions as lust, greed, jealousy, and rage (II vi 50, xii 6), the swelling stomach with pride (*Mother Hubberd* 1103, a purely literary notion), the gall with rancor and noxious humors (eg, *FQ* III x 59). Further, when referring to the blood vessels or 'veins,' Spenser almost invariably speaks of them as filled with an overwhelming passion: grief or fear (which makes the veins cold), hot avarice (II vii 17), rage, or love passion (III i 47).

According to traditional doctrine, the four humors or liquids in the body are produced chiefly from nutritive chyle in the liver. But in Spenser, as in his contemporaries, *humor* often is the word for some other liquid (eg, 'dewy humour'); and applied to man, it is often synonymous with 'complexion' or temperament. The physiological state or humorous condition denotes a psychological or passionate state, and is usually its consequence rather than its cause. Here again, Spenser follows the tradition of moral philosophers and poets rather than of medical writers. Galen asserted that man's character and passionate condition are decisively influenced by his physical state, including the relative balance or imbalance of the humors (*That the Faculties of the Soul Follow the Temperaments of the Body*); and physicians through the centuries agreed. Because they found the doctrine difficult to reconcile with free will, however, medieval Christian philosophers rejected it, preferring Aristotle and the Stoics. Thus in Spenser, intemperate conditions with 'noxious' or 'malignant' humors which corrupt the body's organs (eg, Malbecco in *FQ* III x 59) are the consequences of sinful conduct or of yielding to excessive passion, the only notable exception being characters in the throes of lovesickness. Since lovesickness is due to the wounding of the heart by Cupid's arrow, man's will has little power over it; and even such strong and idealized characters as Arthur and Britomart can become its victims.

Each of the four humors, mixed in the body in different quantities of which blood is by far the largest, combines the qualities of two of the four elements: blood is warm and moist, phlegm cold and moist, red bile or choler hot and dry, black bile or melancholy cold and dry. Each performs essential functions, but for the living animal or plant, adequate moisture and heat are primary. Since moderate heat and moisture are life-sustaining and enhancing, any factor that causes either burning heat or extreme dryness and cold in the body, such as an excessive amount of choler or melancholy, is dangerous, especially when fostered by 'burning' passions or overwhelming grief or fear. When overheated, the blood itself may 'boil' and, mixed with 'corrupt' humors, turn into vapor or smoke, and so reduce essential moisture. Rising from the abdomen or heart, such vapor or smoke will affect dangerously various organs, vessels, and the spirits, and therefore cause violent perturbations, even frenzy or madness if it affects the brain. Such notions and terminology are common to much medieval and Renaissance medical and psychological writing (eg, Bartholomaeus Anglicus, Levinus Lemnius' widely read *Touchstone of Complexions* translated 1565, and Timothy Bright's *Treatise of Melancholie* 1586). Spenser's Arthur therefore checks his lovesickness, lest its fury and 'flames' cause the 'living moysture' to turn into smoke (*FQ* I ix 8). In contrast, water has restorative powers (cf the Well of Life with its medicinal virtues, I xi 29), and the Palmer tells Guyon that Dame Nature has infused some fountains with secret virtues of 'moisture deawd; / Which feedes each living plant with liquid sap, / And filles with flowres faire *Floraes* painted lap' (II ii 5–6).

Warmth and moisture also play an essential role in the generation of new life, whether through normal intercourse or by 'spontaneous generation,' a doctrine found in Aristotle's works on animals and still widely accepted in Spenser's time. Thus in *The Faerie Queene* Chrysogone conceives Belphoebe and Amoret by the effect of the sun on her womb, which had been 'mollifide' by bathing: 'But reason teacheth that the fruitfull seades / Of all things living, through impression / Of the sunbeames in moyst complexion, / Doe life conceive and quickned are by kynd' (III vi 8). However, since the humors or complexions are purely bodily, they are subject to mutability and death. So in *Hymne of Beautie* 65–70, Spenser asserts that true beauty is inward, while all outward beauty 'is nought else, but mixture made / Of colours faire, and goodly temp'rament / Of pure complexions, that shall quickly fade' (cf *FQ* III vi 38).

The ideally proportioned mixture of the four humors, rarely found, produces the perfect temperament. Belphoebe's constitution is informed by such a 'goodly mixture of complexions dew' (II iii 22). Her angelic beauty on which 'gazers sense with double pleasure fed' is 'Hable to heale the sicke, and to revive the ded.' (In endowing Belphoebe with Christ-like powers of healing and reviving the dead, Spenser here applies the old notion that the animal spirit, flitting between the brain and the eye, can through its rays also affect and fascinate the beholder.) A slight imbalance, with one or two humors in small excess or deficiency, is normal and still healthy, producing a sanguine, phlegmatic, choleric, or melancholic temperament, or one marked by the dominance of two humors. Each temperament shows an inclination to certain passion: melancholy, for instance, to grief or fear. A more serious imbalance makes man prone to extreme passionate states as well as to particular diseases, physical and mental, especially if 'corruption' from some cause has blocked the flow of the humors in their vessels or overheated them to the point of being 'burnt' or 'adust.' While all this was so familiar that Spenser must have known it, allusions in his work are few and vague. He nowhere clearly mentions burnt or adust humors. He uses *sanguine* as a mere synonym for the color of blood. By *choler* he usually means the passion. He nowhere mentions phlegm or its combination of moist and cold qualities. Like many of his contemporaries, however, he does describe in several passages various symptoms of excessive melancholy.

Besides the doctrine of the four humors, the Renaissance inherited from classical and medieval philosophers and physiologists the notion of spirits, that is, fine vaporous substances flitting in the living body through channels separate from those of the blood and other humors. The origin of this notion is probably the simple realization that air is essential to life. Thus the Hebrew account of the creation of man in Genesis tells how God bestowed the 'breath of life' as a separate creative act after forming the body out of earth, and Hippocrates speaks of 'spirit' (*pneumata*) simply in the sense of inbreathed air. But the pneumatological doctrine developed step by step until by the Middle Ages three spirits acted as intermediaries between the immaterial tripartite soul and the material living body in which it is housed: the natural or vegetative spirit, responsible for nourishment and generation, and produced in the liver; the vital spirit, formed from air and blood in the left ventricle of the heart, and moving through the arteries (the blood and natural spirit move through the 'veins'); and the animal spirit, further refined out of vital spirit in the *rete mirabilis* just below the brain, and moving nimbly through nerves or 'sinews' and other white vessels. The animal spirit looks after not only the faculties of the brain itself but also the functioning of the nervous system and the senses, particularly sight and hearing. Terms still in modern usage, such as *in good spirits*, *spirited*, and *dispirited*, echo this ancient physiological notion which was shattered by Harvey's demonstration of the blood's circulation through both arteries and veins.

While the absence of any mention of 'arteries' by Spenser marks his lack of interest in physiology, he is not alone among Elizabethan poets in never referring clearly to either the animal or the natural spirit. Sometimes, indeed, *spirit* or *spright* is synonymous with *soul* (and at other times with *demon* or *gnome*), but often he clearly has in mind the traditional meaning of vital spirit or spirits, and at least twice, the particular spirit responsible for the visual sense (see *Rome* 19; also Belphoebe, *FQ* II iii 22, discussed above). Fear, severe grief, melancholy, lovesickness, or lack of food can cause the vital spirit to become weak and cold (eg, *Time* 560, *FQ* II vii 65), dulled and 'deaded quight' (IV xii 20). Such notions are commonplace in medieval and later poetry (eg, Chaucer *Book of the Duchess* 489, *Knight's Tale* 1369). On the other hand, cheer revives the 'feeble spirit' with 'inly felt refection' (*FQ* IV xii 34). That the soul leaves the body at the moment when the vital spirits die is clearly stated in *Hymne of Beautie* 102.

diseases Among the major poets and other literary writers of the later Middle Ages and Renaissance, Spenser may well be the one who least reflects the variety of diseases then known, their chief symptoms, and how they were understood. The notable exception is his detailed description of the symptoms of lovesickness and attendant melancholy of several characters in *The Faerie Queene* (eg, Britomart, III ii 27–32) and Colin in *The Shepheardes Calender*. About other illnesses, Spenser nowhere is truly informative or precise in listing their symptoms, as Shakespeare is, for instance, in *King John*, in Mistress Quickly's account of Falstaff's final illness in *Henry V* II iii, and in several passages devoted to the effects of syphilis in *Troilus and Cressida* and *Timon of Athens*. What follows is therefore little more than a list of passages mentioning specific diseases or symptoms, with brief comments where appropriate. Spenser several times uses *disease* in the literal sense of 'dis-ease' (perturbation, being ill-at-ease; eg, *FQ* II x 17).

In the chief passage mentioning diseases (I iv 20–35), Spenser follows medieval ecclesiastical and literary tradition in conceiving of certain illnesses as fitting punishments for various sins or uncontrolled passions. Each of the six deadly sins accompanying Lucifera or Pride suffers from particular diseases, though not all are clearly identifiable since Spenser is sometimes content with naming all-too-general symptoms. Pleasure-seeking Idleness is subject to a continual 'shaking fever,' a symptom of several illnesses. Gluttony suffers from a 'dry dropsie,' dry because dropsy is caused by excessive drinking which in turn causes excessive thirst; traditionally this is a disease of the covetous (but as Upton suggested, the text should perhaps read 'dire dropsie'; cf Horace's 'dirus hydrops' *Odes* 2.2.13). Lechery is filled with 'reprochfull paine / Of that fowle evill, which all men reprove, / That rots the marrow, and consumes the braine,' probably syphilis – but possibly leprosy, widely thought to be transmitted venereally, yet by Spenser's time known in England only from report and literature (see also III v 14). Avarice suffers from gout in hands and feet, a disease appropriate to his grasping nature. Envy has 'cankred' or infected teeth, and spews 'spightfull poison ... From leprous mouth.' Finally, Wrath, subject to 'Frenzy raging rife,' has a 'swelling Splene,' traditionally the seat of anger and rancor, and prone to cause decay of the entire body as well as 'The shaking Palsey, and Saint *Fraunces* fire.' Palsy is marked by irresistible tremor and paralysis, and St Francis' fire is erysipelas, often called St Anthony's fire, a severe fever accompanied by virulent inflammation of the skin.

The other references to disease form a very small and mixed bag. *Julye* (24) and *Mother Hubberds Tale* (5–8) allude to the ancient notion, already found in Hippocrates, that the Sirian dog or dog-star corrupts the air during the hot season and thereby causes plague, pestilence, and many diseases – all very general terms. Perhaps for the same reason, Willye asks Perigot whether cramp has numbed his joints with ache (*August* 4). The 'murrins pestilent' (*FQ* III iii 40) refer to any kind of severe epidemic. In *Colin Clout* 313, the 'bloodie issues' or issue of blood refers to the discharge of blood from a suppurating sore, ulcer, or blister (cf Lev 12.7, and the woman 'diseased with an yssue of blood,' Matt 9.20, Mark 5.25, Luke 8.43). *Sore* in Spenser usually is an inner wound caused by love or slander. The polluted water Redcrosse unwarily drinks from a stream causes his blood to curdle, weaken, and swell 'like a fever fit' (*FQ* I vii 6) in a passage describing the debilitating effect of poison which produces alternating 'chill' and fever. Finally, Maleger exhibits some of the customary effects of excess melancholy. He is cold and dry, and his body 'seem'd to tremble evermore, and quake' (II xi 22).

physicians and leechcraft Several of Spenser's physicians or 'leeches' are gifted in curing physical wounds, but their remedies prove useless against the wound of the heart and soul caused by Cupid's arrow. That is the subject of *Amoretti* 50: cordials that can 'appease / the inward languour of my wounded hart ... passe Physitions art.' In general, those adept in the leechcraft of treating wounds prove helpless for any inward diseases of 'soul' or 'mind' unless they are also expert in the art of psychological and spiritual counseling after persuading their patient to relate the secret cause of his 'smart' or illness. In allowing that physicians can treat only outward wounds and bodily diseases but that lovesickness and illnesses of the soul require a religious mentor in whom the patient can confide, Spenser once more follows in the tradition of the medieval church, with which not all medical men were happy.

In the house of Holiness, for instance, the salves and medicines Patience applies to the 'soul-diseased' Red Cross Knight are of course purely spiritual – they include confession and repentance. The Salvage Man stops the bleeding of Calepine's wounds with juice from herbs and cures them, but he has no remedy for the inward wound of his soul (VI iv 12–16). Belphoebe with her expertise in herbs and general therapy cures Timias of the deep wound in his thigh but ironically infects his heart with love (III v 31–3, 41–50), and as Timias does not reveal his passion, all her persistence with restoratives and cordials proves in vain since she withholds from him the only 'Cordiall, which can restore / A love-sick hart' (50). In VI vi, Arthur leaves Timias and Serena, gravely wounded by the poisonous sting of the Blatant Beast, in the care of a hermit who does his best 'to tame / The poysnous humour' (2) with many kinds of medicines. But discovering that their wounds 'had festred privily' and that their 'inner parts now gan to putrify' (5), he realizes that his salves are in vain. Yet, as he is also experienced in spiritual psychology, he proceeds to counsel them to curb their passions with their will, and when they follow his advice, they are soon cured.

Even the god Apollo, expert in medicine and father of Aesculapius, knows that the cure of lovesickness in the heart and mind is beyond the art of any 'leech,' especially if the afflicted person keeps it secret. Thus for Scudamour's malady, '*Dan Phebus* selfe cannot a salve provide' (IV vi 1). Cymoent, Marinell's mother, and her sister nymphs, among them Liagore who learned her 'skill / In leaches craft' from Apollo himself (III iv 41), discover that some life is left in the gravely wounded Marinell. They take him to the bottom of the sea, where Tryphon, the leech of sea gods (III iv 43, IV xi 6–7), quickly restores him to health. Later when Marinell suffers a relapse, he is taken by Cymoent to Apollo (IV xii 19–25) who discovers the cause and reveals why all cures have failed: Marinell must first reveal his secret love-passion. Similarly, when Guyon stops the flow of blood from the badly wounded Amavia (II i 43), feels her pulse to assure himself that 'living bloud yet in her veynes did hop,' and repairs her wounds until she becomes conscious again, she throws herself down once more in her grief. Aware of the dangerous effect of such passion, he urges her to tell him the cause, for only that way can she hope to find relief for her inward illness.

Archimago, coming upon Pyrochles gravely and inwardly wounded by Furor, which has caused his liver to swell and his entrails to burn, knows how to examine his secret, to allay his inward fire 'with mighty spels,' and to restore him to health with balms and herbs (II vi 50–1). Spenser underestimates neither the infernal powers nor the psychiatric skill of this archenemy of Protestantism. After Redcrosse overcomes the fierce Sansjoy, he is cured of his wounds in Lucifera's castle by 'skilfull leaches,' who wash them 'In wine and oyle' and embalm them while 'heavenly melody,' played as he lies in bed, beguiles his mind 'of griefe and agony' (I v 17). Aesculapius saves Sansjoy's life in the underworld, but ironically he cannot cure himself of the continual wounds inflicted upon him by the angry Jove. In Spenser's Christian universe, classical gods expert in leechcraft cannot cure diseases of the soul.

Spenser's most detailed description of leechcraft or methods of therapy is Belphoebe's treatment of Timias in Book III v 31–41. After feeling his pulse and discovering life in him, she massages his temples and 'each trembling vaine' or artery. She then looks for medicinal herbs in the forest (a skill she learned in childhood from her nurse), crushes the 'soveraigne weede' between two plain 'marbles,' squeezes its juice into his wound, gently massages the surrounding flesh 'T'abate all spasme,' soaks the swelling bruise, and after examining it carefully binds it with a scarf. Later she dresses his wound daily, and when he deteriorates once more, persists in applying cordials and restoratives. In Spenser's time, many women, both simple and aristocratic, were expert in the remedies of herbal medicine and in general therapeutic techniques. The passage is a rare instance of a medical description in Spenser based on direct experience.

diagnosis, types of therapy, medicinal herbs Spenser's leeches are either physicians of the soul or employed in the cure of wounds. With the exception of lovesickness and 'corruption' caused by sin or a bad conscience, his works do not include a single passage where a doctor attempts to diagnose an illness. Doctors feel the pulse of their unconscious patients but do not examine their urine, an invariable procedure in Spenser's time (cf Dr Caius in *The Merry Wives of Windsor* with his urinal, and Falstaff in *2 Henry IV* who has his urine examined) – but one hardly suitable for allegorical treatment. Nor does Spenser allude to some of the most familiar methods of therapy of his day, such as phlebotomy from a vein (to remove excess or 'corrupt' blood), or purging either upwards by inducing vomiting with emetics or downwards with cathartics (to aid digestion and improve the balance of the other humors). He knew about these things from experience but considered them irrelevant or improper to his poetic subjects.

Other than the episode in which Belphoebe treats Timias, Spenser is vague on the subject of balms, herbs, spices, salves, antidotes, restoratives, and cordials. More than once, however, wine is applied to wounds, a good disinfectant, as is now known. During a cure, music can assist in soothing passions and pain. The dieting alluded to in Patience's cure of Redcrosse's inward illness (*FQ* I x) is of course spiritual, but diet had been an essential part of therapy since classical times. The catalogue of plants in *Muiopotmos* 187–200 includes (typically for Spenser's time) several whose medicinal virtues are briefly mentioned, such as cummin 'good for eyes,' vervain, which was widely used against erysipelas, and others. On the other hand, the aged nurse who attempts to cure Britomart's lovesickness with amatory magic combines herbs with such charms as drops of blood, spittle, three hairs turned into a lace, but to no avail (III ii 49–51). And the Garden of Proserpina into which Mammon leads Guyon includes poisonous herbs (II vii 52).

The Well of Life (*FQ* I xi 29–30), by which the gravely wounded Redcrosse is miraculously restored to health and strength, is the biblical well of water and spiritual grace (John 4.14, Rev 22.1), but Spenser interestingly states that its powers excel those of Siloam and Jordan in Palestine and of 'th'English *Bath*, and eke the german *Spau*,' as well as of Cephise, whose purifying waters are described by Ovid (*Metamorphoses* 1.369–70), and Hebrus, whose restorative powers are mentioned by Servius (gloss on Virgil *Eclogue* 10.65). The 'boyling Bathes at *Cairbadon*,' the city of Bath, are once more referred to at II x 26. Taking the hot and purifying waters at a spa, customary in classical Rome, was advocated by physicians in the sixteenth century, as in William Turner's *A Booke of the Natures and Properties of the Bathes in England* (1562, 1568), which was printed together with the second part of his famous herbal. Yet there is no clear evidence that Spenser read his work. Finally, one should mention Spenser's allusion to a folk remedy against headache in *Maye* 241: the clever fox, disguised as a pitiful peddler, wears a biggin or cap.

To conclude, Spenser's anatomical and medical allusions are seldom precise, and few can be attributed to a particular source, for they are part of a common heritage derived from biblical, classical, and medieval literature, and from such traditional encyclopedic works as those by Pliny and Bartholomaeus Anglicus. The moral allegory of *The Faerie Queene* and the nature of his other poetry explain why on the subjects of physiology, pathology, and clinical therapy, he offers rather less than Shakespeare, Jonson, or Donne. F. DAVID HOENIGER

The Renaissance medicine known by Spenser was based largely on texts by Hippocrates, Aristotle, and Galen. For Hippocrates, see the 4-vol Loeb edition, especially 'Nature of Man' with its influential statement of the theory of humors (in 4:11–13). Works by Aristotle (eg, *Parts of the Animals*, *History of Animals*, *On the Generation of Animals*, *On Respiration*, *On Youth and Old Age*, *On the Soul*, etc) are translated in Loeb editions. Much of Galen is not translated into English; see *Opera omnia* ed Carolus Gottlob Kühn in 20 vols (Leipzig 1821–33) with Latin translations. In English, see *On Anatomical Procedures, the Later Books* tr W.L.H. Duckworth, ed M.C. Lyons and B. Towers (Cambridge 1962); *On the Usefulness of the Parts of the Body* tr and ed Margaret Tallmadge May, 2 vols (Ithaca, NY 1968); and the Loeb edition of *On the Natural Faculties*. Temkin 1973 discusses the response to Galenic doctrine during the Middle Ages and sixteenth century. For contemporary books on medicine and further bibliography, see the sections on medicine, anatomy, herbals, etc, in *NCBEL* 1. The range of English writing is surveyed in Paul Slack 1979 'Mirrors of Health and Treasures of Poor Men: The Uses of the Vernacular Medical Literature of Tudor England' in *Health, Medicine and Mortality in the Sixteenth Century* ed Charles Webster (Cambridge) pp 237–73; this collection also includes other important essays. See also Bamborough 1952, John Erskine Hankins 1978 *Backgrounds of Shakespeare's Thought* (Hamden, Conn), and the reading list for *psychology.

Medina, Elissa, Perissa Placed prominently near the beginning of *FQ* II, the Medina episode gives an important account of the nature of temperance, after the deaths of Amavia and Mortdant have called attention to the dire consequences of intemperance.

In canto ii, Guyon and the Palmer (who is carrying Amavia's child, Ruddymane) arrive at a castle in which there is continual strife among the three half-sisters who have inherited it. Guyon is courteously welcomed by the gracious and youthful but serious-minded middle sister, Medina. Her sisters are angered when they hear of the visit; their suitors Sir Huddibras and Sansloy, whom they have been indulgently entertaining, rush to do battle with him but on the way fall into discord. Hearing their fray, Guyon tries to 'pacifie' them, but instead a fierce three-way encounter ensues. Only Medina is able, by 'gracious wordes,' to end their fighting, even getting them to sign a 'treatie' and partake of a banquet, in spite of her sisters' ill-concealed opposition. At the feast, which lasts well into the night, Guyon recounts his story; and in the morning, he leaves Ruddymane in the care of Medina to be reared 'In vertuous lore' (iii 2).

Medina and her sisters (called the 'golden Meane' and 'two Extremities' in II ii argument) are in some sense patterned after Aristotle's definition of virtue as a mean between vices marked by excess and deficiency (*Nicomachean Ethics* 2.6–9). Specifically, the pictured relationship of the sisters (and of their suitors) agrees with Aristotle's notion that each of the three dispositions is opposed to both the others, 'for the extreme states are contrary both to the intermediate state and to each other, and the intermediate to the extremes' (2.8). In general, however, Spenser's virtue of temperance is closer to Aristotle's more dynamic idea of continence (*Ethics* 7). This perhaps most Aristotelian part of *FQ* II is also Platonic in juxtaposing the rational Medina with her sisters representing the irrational irascible (Elissa) and appetitive (Perissa) principles, and in the degree to which she stands for health or order in the soul (*Var* 2:415–18).

As Ruskin noted (*Var* 2:414), temperance is in a sense not so much a virtue as a guide for the other virtues. In the castle of Medina, courtesy appears to be one main quality in which temperance and its defective and excessive alternatives manifest themselves – what is at stake is the reception of a visitor, and the culminating banquet pictures a *social* kind of temperance.

In addition to signifying moderateness (deriving her name from L *media* or *mediana* middle, central), Medina also represents the process or act of moderating or mediating (LL *medio* intervene, conciliate), as well as of restoring to health (L *medior* heal, remedy). Although the allegory of her castle may seem elementary, Medina herself is a vital figure. Rather sober and dignified for her 'youthly yeares' (14–15), she nevertheless springs to action heedless of coiffure and even of proper dress (27), her appearance recalling the Sabine women who 'with loosened hair and torn garments' (Livy 1.13) intervened between the warring Romans and Sabines and persuaded them to sign a treaty. Combining passion and 'pitthy words' (28) in the cause of reconciliation, Medina is a fit predecessor of Milton's Eve who, at perhaps her outstanding moment, comes to Adam with 'tresses all disordered' to end their futile quarreling and offer mediation (*Paradise Lost* 10.911).

Less individualized than Medina, her sisters are in a way almost a parody of the traditional positions of the three Graces. Perissa and Sansloy are classed as 'forward,' and Elissa and Huddibras as 'froward,' that is, 'fromward,' 'perverse' (38). Representing passions linked with pleasure and pain respectively (vi 1), these types tend to appear throughout *FQ* II. The name Elissa comes from Greek *elassōn* (too little, inferior), and Perissa from *perissos* (too much, excessive). Huddibras, a melancholy malcontent (ii 17, 37), is appropriately paired with the elder, Elissa, while the licentious Sansloy (who attacked Una in I iii, vi) is obviously a 'Fit mate' (II ii 18, 37) for the excessively self-indulgent Perissa.

Medina's sisters are named and the distinction made between them only near the end of the episode (34–8); and in some respects, they tend to share each other's qualities. When first mentioned they are 'Accourting each her friend with *lavish* fest' (16; emphasis added), and later they are both called 'froward,' for, disdainful yet hypocritical, 'both did at their second sister grutch, / And inly grieve' (34). Perhaps Spenser is suggesting that the harmful extremes of passion may after all be similar beneath their obvious differences, and, by describing *both* suitors as 'gay' and 'valiaunt' knights (19, 26), that both extremes have their appeal.

In addition to its moral and psychological significance, this episode may be read in ecclesiastical-historical terms. Medina's castle, 'Built on a rocke adjoyning to the seas' (12; cf Matt 7.24, 16.18), may represent the English church, and Medina herself the 'middle way' of that church (George Herbert may have taken hints from stanzas 14–15 for the clothing and grooming imagery in 'The British Church'). But the Elizabethan *via media* must be dissociated from some nineteenth-century notions. Elizabethan church theology was Protestant, poised between the Roman and the Anabaptist or extreme sectarian. The Puritans who conformed (like Archbishop Grindal) were actually near the center.

Accordingly, in ecclesiastical terms, neither of Medina's sisters represents Puritanism: Elissa, the elder, represents the Church of Rome, Perissa the 'lawless' Anabaptist extremists. That the sisters are 'children of one sire by mothers three' (13) recalls the marriages and divergent offspring of Henry VIII. On this level of interpretation, Elissa is Mary Tudor, discontent and austere, and Medina is Elizabeth, representing the moderate position of the church of which she was the Supreme Governor. The third child is not Edward VI, but a third queen who laid claim to the same throne, Mary, Queen of Scots – descended from Henry VII, Roman Catholic but married by a Protestant rite, and in the public mind associated with lawlessness (see the trial of Duessa, V ix 38–50).

Huddibras, who has been linked with Puritanism because of Butler's poem *Hudibras* or because some readers confuse malcontents with Puritans, fits better as Philip II of Spain, Mary Tudor's husband, 'great of name' indeed, but felt by the English (especially after the Armada of 1588) to be 'More huge in strength, then wise in workes' (17). Sansloy (in this episode) could stand for Bothwell, Mary, Queen of Scots' reported lover and third husband, ill famed among the English for lust and violence, and perhaps also for John of Leiden, leader of the notorious supposedly Anabaptist mob that seized Münster in 1533.

The moderation of the English church stood out clearly against such extremes; and Medina's 'treatie' may allude to the Thirty-nine Articles, which took a position between the Roman and the Anabaptist (Dickens 1964:252). Calvinist in theology (though not in liturgy or polity), this church was generally characterized by the moderation which Calvin himself counseled (Wallace 1959: 170–92). But Spenser may have gone beyond the customary Protestant and Roman Catholic teachings of his time by figuring forth in Medina not only moderation, but a generally neglected Christian virtue and calling – peacemaking (Matt 5.9).

DANIEL W. DOERKSEN

W.R. Davis 1981 relates the Medina episode to other episodes in *FQ* II; Daniel W. Doerksen 1984 'Recharting the *Via Media* of Spenser and Herbert' *Ren&R* ns 8:215–25, and Doerksen 'Spenser's *Via Media* Reconsidered' (forthcoming) examine the place of the church as *via media* in Spenser's poetry; Magill 1970 supports an ecclesiastical reading of the episode, based on the idea of the *via media*, but dissociates Elissa from Puritanism. See also Dickens 1964; Kerby Neill 1945 'Spenser's Acrasia and Mary Queen of Scots' *PMLA* 60:682–8; Phillips 1964; Ronald S. Wallace 1959 *Calvin's Doctrine of the Christian Life* (Edinburgh). For earlier scholarship, see *Var* 2:415–18.

melancholy This term (from Gr 'black bile') had a technical meaning in Renaissance medicine: it referred to one of the four humors of which human bodies were thought to be composed, as well as to the temperament associated with that humor. In Renaissance psychology, melancholy could refer to a pathological state or simply to a temperamental disposition: associated qualities were solitariness, avarice, uncommunicativeness, and a tendency to brood upon one's injuries. The socially dissatisfied malcontent, a popular figure on the Elizabethan stage, was generally portrayed as melancholic, opposed to the mirthful, gregarious temperament of the sanguine type. Iconographically, melancholy was associated with the earth (see *elements), with the color black, with night, and with the 'slow' planet Saturn. 'Pensive' melancholics, when portrayed sympathetically, could be studious and contemplative (Hamlet is the outstanding example); but their temperament was more commonly seen as antisocial and self-destructive, their cold, dry qualities inimical to the warmth and moisture necessary for life itself. (For general discussions, see Babb 1951; Klibansky, Panofsky, and Saxl 1964; Lyons 1971.)

Melancholy often showed itself as an exaggerated awareness of the passage of time and the transitoriness of earthly glory. Spenser's *Complaints*, especially *Ruines of Time*, belong in this tradition of melancholy, though the poet's vision of the immortality conferred by art makes his a hopeful variant of the theme. But his most extended treatment occurs in *The Faerie Queene*, especially in Book II. Temperance in the ethical sense and psychological good 'temperament' are related; hence Acrasia, the evil spirit of the Bower of Bliss, is opposed to *crasis*, the ideal blending of humors, as well as to continence. Book II is based on the oppositions (partly humoral ones) among Guyon's antagonists (see Nohrnberg 1976:296–8). Traits commonly associated with melancholy – solitude, self-denial, retentiveness – form one set of extremes, while mirth and lack of restraint form the other. Such oppositions involve the discontented Elissa and her suitor Huddibras ('Sterne melancholy did his courage pas' ii 17) at one extreme and the loose Perissa and lustful Sansloy (ii) or Phaedria and Cymochles (v and vi) at the other. Guyon's climactic temptation by Acrasia in the Bower is preceded by his encounter with Maleger ('badly diseased') whose mother, like that of mythical Antaeus, is the earth. Maleger himself causes Arthur to doubt reality and to have hallucinations (xi 39–41) and is thus also related to melancholic illness. Spenser's allegory of the human mind and body in the house of Alma identifies melancholy, as was traditional, with the imagination; Phantastes, therefore, was born under Saturn and has the 'swarth complexion ... That him full of melancholy did shew' (ix 52; see Fowler 1964:104). (See also the association of melancholy and 'fantasie' in Britomart's response to her dream in V vii 17.)

Love-melancholy was one of the most important subspecies of the condition and provided familiar types for literary writers. Lovelorn melancholics – Romeo, for example, when he is pining for Rosaline – were common on the Elizabethan stage, and the condition also affected the personae of many love poets (eg, *Amoretti* 50). The most sustained portrait of love-melancholy in *The Faerie Queene* is that of Arthur's squire Timias in Book IV. After Belphoebe scorns him, he retreats alone into the depths of the dark forest to a cabin 'covered all with shade / And sad melancholy' (vii 38). His sorrow turns him into a semi-brutish figure who, unkempt and uncommunicative, spends his days carving his mistress' name on every tree. His dishevelment and neglect of himself were traditional for a melancholy lover (cf *As You Like It* III ii 369–84). Other characters in *The Faerie Queene* who become ill for love include Britomart (III ii 27), who thinks she is suffering from some other ailment ('some melancholy'), and, to some extent, Priscilla in her love and fear for Aladine (VI iii 9). A less curable example than any of these is Malbecco, whose ingrained affinity with melancholy is expressed in his 'cold complexion,' in the cold-blooded animals (toads, frogs) on which he feeds (III x 59), in his avarice, and in the image of his final fate – only half-alive to dwell forever in an inaccessible cave.

Spenser seems to have distinguished humoral sadness from melancholy caused by religious hopelessness, while noting the connections between them. Although Sansjoy in Book I is not sad and passive, he possesses several characteristics often attributed to melancholics; and his visit to the doomed healer, Aesculapius, in hell focuses some of the book's preoccupations with religious despair (Maier 1975). His fury as an opponent of Redcrosse is vengeful, and on the morning of their fight, the entertainments in the house of Pride (wine and music) are those traditionally associated with efforts to 'drive away the dull melancholy' (v 3–4). (The same phrase in a genuinely mirthful context is used for the betrothal feast in Book I xii 38.) The most powerful description of religious despair in the book, and perhaps in all literature, is Redcrosse's encounter with Despair in canto ix.

Spenser depended on his readers' familiarity with humoral vocabulary and with the major iconographic attributes of melancholy. In *The Faerie Queene* especially, the state of melancholy acquires its richness from the associations generated within the poem itself. The 'careful' avarice embodied in Mammon is shown by Spenser's imagery to be related to melancholy as surely as it is, at discursive length, in Burton's *Anatomy of Melancholy* thirty years later.

BRIDGET GELLERT LYONS

Babb 1951; Raymond Klibansky, Erwin Panofsky, and Fritz Saxl 1964 *Saturn and Melancholy: Studies in the History of Natural Philosophy, Religion, and Art* (London); Bridget Gellert Lyons 1971 *Voices of Melancholy: Studies in Literary Treatments of Melancholy in Renaissance England* (London); John R. Maier 1975 'Sansjoy and the *Furor Melancholicus*' *MLS* 5.1:78–87.

Meliboe The aged shepherd who has raised the foundling Pastorella (*FQ* VI ix 13–33). His name derives from Greek 'with honey tone' and appears in Virgil's Eclogue 1, as well as in Chaucer's *Tale of Melibee* with its sententious colloquies and counsel of peace. In his conversation with Calidore about the benefits of the pastoral life, he echoes the similar conversation between the shepherd and Erminia in Tasso (*Gerusalemme liberata* 7.8–13). Like Tasso's shepherd, Meliboe in 'pride of youth' had journeyed to court and witnessed its vanities before returning to his sheep, and similarly refuses the gold offered him by the visitor from the great world. He is unlike Tasso's shepherd, however, in that his visitor is already desirous of joining the pastoral world, having fallen in love with Pastorella; Calidore is shown manipulating Meliboe's remarks so as to elicit the praise of the simple life that will justify his desire to remain (Cheney 1966:220).

In the episode with the Brigands, Meliboe is taken captive and slain together with his wife in the subsequent fight over Pastorella (xi 18). The contrast between his Boethian denial of fortune's power over human lives ('each unto himselfe his life may fortunize' ix 30; cf *Consolation of Philosophy* 4 prose 7) and his own unfortunate end has led to conflicting readings. His speech to Calidore has been taken as a model of humility and self-sufficiency (I.G. MacCaffrey 1976:365–70, K. Williams 1966:207–8), or alternatively as expressive of illusory escapism (Anderson 1976:178–84, Berger 1961b, Tonkin 1972:116–18, 143). He has been compared to Despair, whose speech to Redcrosse in the corresponding canto of Book I is similarly an expression of the hero's own desire to abandon his quest (Nohrnberg 1976: 717–18); and he has been taken as a negative counterpart of the Hermit (VI v 35–vi 15), who was a man of heroic achievement before retiring to the life of the spirit, and who recommends self-discipline over self-indulgence (Anderson 1972, Cain 1978: 173).

RICHARD MALLETTE

Melville, Herman (1819–91) A careful reader of Spenser, Melville responded to his work romantically and impressionistically as he wove it into his own. He exhibits a marked fondness for *FQ* I ix and x, II ix and xii, III vi, drawing on Spenser indirectly in his early 'Fragments from a Writing Desk' (1839) and later directly and extensively in *Mardi* (1849), *Moby-Dick* (1851), *Pierre* (1852), and several of *The Piazza Tales* ('The Encantadas,' 'The Piazza,' and 'The Bell-Tower' 1853–6). Sometimes he cites actual lines, such as the whaling simile from VI x 31 in one 'Extract' to *Moby-Dick*. He also quotes Spenser in most of the verse epigraphs to 'The Encantadas.' Sometimes, as in *Mardi*, *Moby-Dick*, and *Pierre*, he borrows the lushness of Spenserian imagery and structures plots following Spenserian paradigms, such as the quest for truth, St George fighting the dragon, the wicked and innocent damsels. Sometimes his characters refer to the search for Fairyland or Una and her lamb, as in 'The Piazza.' Occasionally, he simply mentions 'sweet Spenser,' as in *White-Jacket* (ch 84).

Although the Spenser text that Melville used in the 1840s and 1850s remains undiscovered, the Francis J. Child edition (1855) that he acquired in 1861 shows that he read Spenser closely. Many of the lines that he borrowed are underscored, particularly images of orderly beauty, death and destruction, the sea, and the transience of earthly glory.

Melville is explicit about his admiration for Spenser in 'Hawthorne and His Mosses' (1850), the most comprehensive statement of his aesthetics. Toward the end of this enthusiastic review of Hawthorne's short stories, Melville compares Hawthorne to Spenser, a writer as 'deep as Dante' whose 'sublimity' was often missed by the public. According to Melville, both were considered merely 'pleasant' writers; however, he argues, no man of genius who can soar to 'such a rapt height' can exist without also possessing 'a great, deep intellect, which drops down into the universe like a plummet.' He admired this 'dark' side of Hawthorne, as he did in Spenser and Shakespeare, who 'craftily' insinuate those bleak truths about the universe which only sensitive readers can grasp. In a passage that recalls Florimell's flight in *FQ* III, he explains the necessity for duplicitous writing: 'in this world of lies, Truth is forced to fly like a scared white doe in the woodlands; and only by cunning glimpses will she reveal herself ... though it be covertly, and by snatches.' Beyond *The Faerie Queene*'s usefulness as a storehouse of images, he was drawn toward the encoded nature of allegory that conveys meanings surreptitiously. He thought of Spenser in conjunction with the other early prophetic poets he admired, such as Shakespeare, Milton, and Dante, who dared to wrestle with the problem of evil. Often he chose from Spenser descriptions of delusion or ugliness, masked by a seductive surface; conventional readers could focus on the picturesque, but bolder ones would discern Melville's darker purpose.

An imaginative synthesizer and not a scholar, Melville looked for connections among the writers he was reading, even at the risk of failing to discriminate critically among them. For him, genius was sufficient to connect one great writer with another. In a characteristic passage in *Mardi*, the narrator claims to be a frigate 'full with a thousand souls,' hearing 'Homer's old organ' roll past him while 'sweet Shakespeare soars' and 'Milton sings bass'; among others, he lauds St Paul, Montaigne, Augustine, Plato, Proclus, and Virgil (ch 119). This eclecticism makes it difficult to delineate the extent of his interest in a particular writer: we can detect starting points, such as Spenserian allusions, but cannot say where Melville's expansive musings or eventual criticisms end. His interest in an enchantress like Acrasia, for example, cannot be separated from his fascination with other treacherous nymphs such as Keats's Lamia or Coleridge's Geraldine; though more skillful as he matured, Melville continually worked with convergent analogues.

The problem of assessing Spenserian influence is further complicated by Melville's narrators. When he wrote a story in which narration is consistent, like 'The Piazza,' we may be fairly certain that his characters' naive misreadings of Spenser are ironic. Occasionally, however, this ironic perspective is missing, as in the homiletic conclusion to 'The Bell-Tower,' so that the extent to which his reading of Spenser is consistent becomes an issue. Nonetheless, his borrowings are frequent, direct, and varied, usually altered to express his own emerging ideas about the nature of truth. Combined with his persistent use of Renaissance *topoi* such as the microcosmic ship of the world or the harmonizing power of music, allusions to Spenser recall their larger Renaissance context.

Initially, Melville turned to Spenser to define the epic ambitions he had in *Mardi*: eager to move away from adventure tales, he wanted to show the world that his '*real* romance' would be nothing like *Typee* or *Omoo*, but 'made of different stuff altogether' (letter to John Murray, 25 March 1848, in *Letters* ed 1960). He believed that Spenserian romance or epic would allow him to 'dive' after the truth like the writers he admired (letter to Evert A. Duyckinck, 3 March 1849; also *Pierre* ch 25). Rivaling Milton, Melville would take the 'world of mind' for his song, wherein 'the wanderer may gaze round, with more of wonder than Balboa's band roving through the Aztec glades' (*Mardi* ch 169). Taji is on a quest for Yillah, a Una figure who personifies truth, while, like one of Spenser's knights, he struggles with the philosophically and politically muddied waters of the world. Large sections of the book are discussions of art and truth carried on by King Media and his companions: the mystical philosopher Babbalanja, the venerable historian Mohi, and the poet Yoomy. Echoes of Renaissance allegory abound as these travelers visit various islands such as Serenia (Melville's castle of Alma) and Hautia's 'flowery Flozella' (an Acrasian Bower of Bliss). The wicked Hautia may be compared to Duessa and the false Florimell. As in *The Faerie Queene*, characters follow the 'broad shaded way' to Circean dangers or gaze dumbstruck at Yillah when she removes her veil. Melville even suggests at one point that the Mardian universe is a poem and every island a canto (*Mardi* ch 191).

Always ambivalent about philosophical idealism, Melville was increasingly drawn toward Spenser's images of evil, soon using allusions to Spenser for bleaker purposes than he had in *Mardi*. Ultimately he used *The Faerie Queene* to reject Spenser's belief in an ordered cosmos, focusing instead on the impossibility of epistemological certainty and the probably malignant nature of God. In *Moby-Dick* and *Pierre*, he depicts a world in which good and evil are intertwined and those who quest for truth, like Ahab and Pierre, are bound to fail. The doomed quest becomes his trademark, and despair his dominant *leitmotif*, as in 'The Encantadas.'

Pessimism finally led Melville away from Spenser. In *The Confidence-Man*, he uses two images from *The Faerie Queene* and one from *The Shepheardes Calender* (Moses 1978:16), and in *Billy Budd* he alludes to Spenser's Envy in developing Claggart (Matthiessen 1941:505n). Basically, however, he abandoned epic-romance. This abandonment, like his initial attraction to *The Faerie Queene*, must be seen in context: it was part of a larger despair, a quarrel with American transcendental assumptions about human virtue, and with Platonic and Neoplatonic ideas of the benignity and purposefulness of the universe.

Yet most of his writing shows a profound responsiveness to Spenserian allegory, little troubled by what modern critics have found to be a split between earlier allegory and modern post-Romantic symbolism. Paradoxically, his response to Spenser reconciles these contradictory views. His tendency to focus on particular Spenserian landscapes (eg, that of Despair, I ix) reflects the modern, symbol-making imagination for which he is acclaimed. Moreover, like contemporary theorists of allegory, he was sensitive to the genre's psychological and epistemological possibilities, even to depict elusive truths. He suggests, for example, that Yillah and Hautia are projections of Taji's goodness and evil: mysteriously connected, Yillah is his 'crown of felicity,' his 'heaven below,' while Hautia is his 'whole heart abhorred' (*Mardi* ch 191).

Melville also read Spenser with a decidedly Victorian sensibility, choosing descriptive nuggets or bits of wisdom which confirmed his own ideas. His library included some of the 'beauties of literature' that were popular in his day, such as *The Riches of Chaucer* and Charles Lamb's *Specimens of English Dramatic Poets* (Sealts 1966, nos 141, 318). Melville read the *Beauties of the Bible* in school, and contemporary criticism, such as Lamb's, when he grew up. Like Lamb, he looked to passages by Spenser and others for 'richness of poetical fancy' (Lamb, letter to Coleridge, 14 June 1796 in ed 1935:28), dignity of expression, scenes of passion, and moral insight. Similarly, he borrowed the language of the fashionable flower books when it appealed to him (Davis 1941). It would be a mistake, then, to approach all of his borrowings as if they reflected a commitment to modern, symbolic, 'organic' readings of Spenser. Rather, despite his own idiosyncratic genius, Melville's use of Spenser reflects the complexity of Spenserian allegory itself. PENNY LOZOFF HIRSCH

The principal texts include Herman Melville 1960 *Letters* ed Merrell R. Davis and William H. Gilman (New Haven); Melville ed 1967 (incl Melville 1850); Melville 1968– *Writings* ed Harrison Hayford, et al (Evanston; incl Melville 1850).

C. Sherman Avallone 1976 'Melville's "Piazza"' *ESQ* 22:221–33; Mary K. Bercaw 1987 *Melville's Sources [A Checklist]* (Evanston); Merrell R. Davis 1941 'The Flower Symbolism in *Mardi*' *MLQ* 2:625–38; James Duban 1977 'The Spenserian Maze of Melville's *Pierre*' *ESQ* 23:217–25; Michael T. Gilmore 1975 'Melville's Apocalypse: American Millennialism and *Moby-Dick*' *ESQ* 21:154–61, esp 156; Penny Lozoff Hirsch 1982 'Melville's Spenser Edition for *The Encantadas*' *MSEx* 50:15–16; Hirsch 1985 'Melville's Ambivalence toward the Writer's "Wizardry": Allusions to Theurgic Magic in *The Confidence-Man*' *ESQ* 31:100–15; John Hollander 1982 'Observations on a Select Party' *SSt* 3:193–8; Leon Howard 1931 'Melville and Spenser – A Note on Criticism' *MLN* 46:291–2 (identifies Spenserian epigraphs to 'The Encantadas'); F.O. Matthiessen 1941 *American Renaissance: Art and Expression in the Age of Emerson and Whitman* (New York); Carole Horsburgh Moses 1976 'Melville's Use of Spenser in "The Piazza"' *CLAJ* 20:222–31; Moses 1978 'A Spenserian Echo in *The Confidence-Man*' *MSEx* 36:16; Moses 1986a 'Melville's "Cunning" Readings of Spenser' *MSEx* 50: 5–10; Moses 1986b 'Spenser and the Structure of *Mardi*' *SNovel* 18:258–69; Moses 1987 '*Typee* and Spenser's Bower of Bliss' *ELN* 25.1:60–5; John O. Rees, Jr 1972 'Spenserian Analogues in *Moby-Dick*' *ESQ* 18:174–8; Merton M. Sealts, Jr 1966 *Melville's Reading: A Check-List of Books Owned and Borrowed* (Madison, Wis); Russell Thomas 1931–2 'Melville's Use of Some Sources in *The Encantadas*' *AL* 3:432–56; Mildred K. Travis 1968 'Spenserian Analogues in *Mardi* and *The Confidence-Man*' *ESQ* 50(supp):55–8; Nathalia Wright 1952–3 'A Note on Melville's Use of Spenser: Hautia and the Bower of Bliss' *AL* 24:83–5.

memory At the end of their tour of the house of Alma, Arthur and Guyon come to the human head with its traditional threefold division in terms of Renaissance psychology (*FQ* II ix 45–60). In the front chamber is Phantastes (the imagination); in the second room, a figure corresponding to reason; and at the back, Memory, who is depicted as an old man, Eumnestes (the 'well-remembrer'), attended by a little boy, Anamnestes (the 're-minder'), whose task is to find whatever is 'lost, or laid amis' and bring to memory whatever is needed (58).

The division of memory into Eumnestes and Anamnestes is based on Aristotle's distinction between memory and recollection (*On Memory and Recollection* 2). The contents of Eumnestes' library derive from an older tradition of memory, that of Hesiod's myth of Mnemosyne (*Theogony* 53–103), who by the love of Jupiter became the mother of the Muses (ie, all the arts are seen as children of memory). The book of 'Briton moniments,' which comprises the history of the British kings up to Uther Pendragon, belongs to Clio, the Muse of history, whereas the '*Antiquitie* of *Faerie* lond' traces the line of the 'old *Heroes*,' the great historical figures who for their benefactions to mankind have been raised to the level of myth; and for this reason it belongs to Calliope, the Muse of epic poetry, since it is by epic that they have been deified. In canto x, it is fitting that the historical Arthur should read the account of his own ancestors, while Guyon, a hero in the making, should turn to the line of the 'old *Heroes*' (III iii 32). History and myth alike exist in memory and depend upon it for their survival. It is typical of the vicious Paridell that he should have forgotten what 'aged *Mnemon*' told him about the noble Trojan line (III ix 47).

It is difficult for us, with our easy access to pen, paper, books, and electronic information retrieval, to conceive of the supreme importance of memory before any of these were available. Poetry, and especially heroic poetry, owed much of the reverence in which it was held even as late as the Renaissance to its mnemonic quality by which the record of human history and heroic myth were kept in memory. The poet's most valued gift was his ability to 'eternize,' and one of the explicit aims of *The Faerie Queene* is to preserve the 'famous moniment' against the ravages of 'wicked Time' (IV ii 33).

At a more practical level, a good memory was essential to the orator in making a speech or pleading a case; and from the earliest times, therefore, memory formed one of the divisions under which rhetoric was studied. Memory training was a basic part of education, and techniques devised by the Greeks for creating artificial memory survived to the Renaissance with little change (Yates 1966). The most accessible and influential primary text dealing with the subject was the *Rhetorica ad Herennium* (3.16–24), probably by a contemporary of Cicero.

Memory training assumed that the sight was the strongest of the senses and that visual impressions penetrated more deeply and remained longer in the memory than words or ideas. The theoretical basis for this assumption derived primarily from Aristotle's theory of the imagination, as defined in *De anima* 3.3. The imagination was conceived of as the human faculty which converts direct sensation into mental images without which memory or even thought itself would be impossible. The secret of memorizing, therefore, was to build upon this by translating whatever had to be remembered into mental images which should be striking enough to be memorable in themselves and at the same time able to bring to mind what they represented through logical, verbal, or personal association. Where many things were to be memorized, the orator should stock his mind with 'places,' that is, locations in a familiar or easily remembered sequence, such as a series of frames, niches, or empty rooms in numbered order, or landmarks along a well-known street, or specific features inside a church or a room. The orator should then visualize his images and, in his mind's eye, set up each one in its own 'place' as if it were a statue in a niche or a picture on a wall; and having done this, he had only to make a mental journey down the street or around his chamber to recall first his images in their 'places' and then the things of which they were the reminder. Sidney even suggests that a line of verse, on account of its meter and rhyme, can act as a sequence of memory places in which 'every word having his natural seat, which seat must needs make the word remembered' (*Defence of Poetry* ed 1973b:101). For this reason, verse is more memorable and hence a better teacher than prose. It seems a roundabout way of remembering things, but the method is still used in some modern memory systems such as Pelmanism, and with its aid the orators of the ancient world were able to perform prodigies of memory.

These techniques formed a part of the normal training in classical rhetoric. In the Middle Ages, however, memory was reclassified, and from being a part of rhetoric designed mainly to help the orator plead in law cases, it became a part of prudence, the first of the cardinal virtues defined as the knowledge of what is good and bad. Its moral status and responsibility, therefore, were enhanced, for it showed how to memorize images which would help one reach heaven and avoid hell (Yates 1966, ch 3). In this capacity, it was of the utmost relevance to preaching and to medieval religious art in general: the great body of medieval iconography was designed to imprint upon the memory images useful for the moral life. This strong didactic inheritance survived into the Renaissance, but the humanist rediscovery in the fifteenth century of the great texts of classical rhetoric such as Quintilian's *Institutio oratoria* restored rhetoric to its central position once more, and sharpened the interest in the relevance of memory to persuasion (Yates 1966, ch 5). Both traditions of memory, the classical and the medieval, were available to Spenser and influenced his poetry.

The relevance of the art of memory to poetry is twofold. In the first place, it encouraged men to think in visual terms, to embody concepts in images. The enormous range and variety of visual imagery throughout the Renaissance owes much to this fact. The vogue of the emblem which presents moral definitions in pictorial form, the prevalence of visual metaphor in poetry, the popularity of allegory embodying abstract concepts in visual terms, the large number of figures of rhetoric involving verbal pictures (eg, Puttenham's prosopopoeia, hypotyposis, icon, topographia), Sidney's defense of poetry as 'speaking picture' – all these in their form and function show their affinity with the memory image. In the second place, the habit of remembering by means of a sequence of 'places' conditioned the ways in which writers organized their material, particularly in didactic literature where the intention was to impress something upon the reader's memory. This is most obvious in Herbert's *Temple* where the church itself provides the 'places' – the altar, the windows, the pillars, the pulpit – to each of which the poet attaches an image evocative of the virtue or festival to be commemorated.

The Faerie Queene has often been called a picture gallery and, although this is clearly a gross oversimplification of its allegorical method, the visual dimension is basic. Its images resemble those of the memory tradition in form and content and in the way they are deployed. The description of Ate, for example, with her ill-matched ears and her feet moving in opposite directions (IV i 28), and of Envy chewing her venomous snakes (V xii 30), conform exactly to the recipe for memory images given in the *Rhetorica ad Herennium*, namely, that they should be striking, unusual, or grotesque (3.22.37). *The Faerie Queene* is composed of images of this kind: Guyon carrying the bloody-handed child (II ii 1), Amoret with her heart transfixed with a knife and borne before her in a silver basin (III xii 21), Una with her lamb or her lion (I i 4, iii 6), or the dying

Amavia, 'which the image art / Of ruefull pitie' (II i 44). Spenser's use of the tradition is, of course, highly sophisticated and exploits the fact that mental pictures can express more than physical ones. We cannot actually see that the gold which covers the palace of Pride is only thin foil, or that its back parts 'that few could spie' were in ruins but 'painted cunningly' (I iv 4–5); and it is not always easy to see in Spenser's poetry where the visual description ends and the commentary takes over. The combination, however, enables him to define the nature of pride by indicating the difference between appearance and reality.

Single images such as these stay in the memory, but where Spenser deals with a sequence, he deploys them in a traditional series of memory 'places.' In Guyon's encounter with Mammon (II vii), the images of temptation and warning are located in a succession of rooms and a garden; and Britomart's exploration of Busirane's castle takes her into rooms which act as frames for the pictures within (III xi). Spenser's frequent use of tapestries and pictures, such as those on the gates of the Bower of Bliss and around its fountain (II xii 44, 60), and those in the castle of Malecasta (III i 34), derives from the memory tradition. At times, he uses the episodes of a familiar story as the 'places' for his images, so that to remember the story is to recall the moral sequence; but in such cases, the episodes themselves are used as allegories in their own right – the 'places' and the images are one. In this way, Guyon's voyage to Acrasia's Bower is modeled on the first half of Odysseus' journey home, and each adventure – Scylla and Charybdis, the Sirens, and finally Circe – is used as an image of some form of intemperance. The whole of *The Faerie Queene* is in fact a great frame of memory, in which the familiar traditional features of the romance – the knights, dragons, monsters, and giants – are turned into definitions and reminders of the moral issues which are Spenser's concern. The poem is not especially memorable at the verbal level, but it is supremely so as a sequence of images.

The art of memory gave Spenser both methods and materials which he exploited more comprehensively than any other Renaissance poet. It is ironic that he should have done this through the medium of the printed book, the new kind of artificial memory which finally supplanted the old in the following century. MAURICE EVANS

Daniel C. Boughner 1932 'The Psychology of Memory in Spenser's *Faerie Queene*' *PMLA* 47:89–96; Evans 1970, ch 4 sec 2; Murrin 1969, ch 4; Frances A. Yates 1966 *The Art of Memory* (London). See also *Var* 2:458–64 'Elizabethan Psychology.'

Merchant Taylors' School In 1569, Spenser received a gown and a shilling for representing Merchant Taylors' School at the funeral of Robert Nowell, a well-to-do Londoner. This is the only record that Spenser went to Merchant Taylors', for his name is not found in its well-maintained register. We do not know when he began at the school, only that he left in 1569 and went from there to Cambridge University.

Merchant Taylors' School was one of many educational foundations set up during Elizabeth's reign as part of a public-spirited and Protestant movement to establish sound religious and humanist schooling in England. The founding statutes of 1561 (the year in which Spenser might have started there) indicate that it was intended to be self-supporting (many of the boys were required to pay fees), that it was large (250 boys with one master and three ushers or assistant masters made it one of the largest schools in England), and that the curriculum was left to the discretion of the master. The last point is of special interest to those concerned with Spenser's education.

The only sure detailed knowledge of what Spenser may have studied at Merchant Taylors' is based on the minutes of the guild regarding examinations held in 1562 and following and on the personal memoir of Sir James Whitelocke who went to the school in the 1580s. During one examination, boys were tested in their knowledge of Horace, Cicero, Homer, and the Hebrew psalms, and were required to vary phrases in the set texts (see *copia). The examiners were pleased with the boys' results, though critical of their pronunciation, which followed the northern accent of the masters (Spenser used various Northernisms in his archaistic style; some of these he could have picked up from his masters' English speech). In addition to the regular curriculum, according to Whitelocke, boys performed both theater and music under the headmaster, Richard Mulcaster.

Beyond these few hints, the rest of the course of studies is not known, though it probably followed a pattern typical of the day: in the lower forms Cato's *Distichs*, Aesop's *Fables* in Latin, dialogues in Latin by Erasmus and the Spanish humanist Vives and, in translation, by the Greek satirist Lucian; in the middle forms, Terence, Ovid's *Tristia* and *Metamorphoses*, Cicero's letters, and epigrams by various authors; in the higher forms, Virgil (*Eclogues* and *Aeneid*), Horace, Caesar, Lucan, and Cicero's *De officiis*. Such was the course at Eton in 1560 as taught by a former classmate of Mulcaster; it may well have been the same at Merchant Taylors', with the unusual addition of Greek for the last year or two, and the even more unusual addition of Hebrew for the senior boys. The course could vary from year to year (depending on availability of textbooks and the master's whim), so it is hard to say exactly what Spenser read. The pace was quite slow, however, and a great deal of time was taken up with numerous exercises in rhetorical composition. Prayers and religious instruction were also important.

During his time at the school, Spenser may have enjoyed the special favor of the headmaster. By the 1570s, Mulcaster had become a fairly influential figure in London intellectual circles, but in the 1560s he was just beginning his career. He was born (c 1531) a gentleman in Carlisle, went to Eton as a King's Scholar, received the BA from Cambridge and the MA from Oxford, served in Elizabeth's first Parliament in 1558–9, and in 1561 was appointed the first headmaster of Merchant Taylors', where he taught for 25 years. In 1596, he became High Master of St Paul's; he retired in 1608 and died in 1611. He wrote *Positions* (1581) and *The First Part of the Elementarie* (1582), the only two volumes in an ambitious and unfinished series of educational treatises; he also wrote Latin and English verses and Latin textbooks. For him, education was a function of politics, and his theories seek to justify a uniform secular system of public schooling for boys and girls of all social classes; his system was quite different from the private tutoring recommended by such earlier writers as Elyot and Ascham.

As the son of a merchant taylor and not by birth a gentleman, Spenser was typical of Mulcaster's students, many of whom rose to high position in church and state affairs (Bishop Lancelot Andrewes is the best known). It is difficult to say how Mulcaster influenced Spenser. His love of the English language (in *Elementarie*), his interest in Ariosto (in *Positions* and in his play *Ariodante and Ginevra*, now lost), his close reading of Aristotle's ethical and political theory (in *Positions*), and his love of pageantry (as writer of several city pageants and as a member of Prince Arthur's Knights, a group of prominent Londoners given to celebrating archery) may have been evident during the 1560s when Spenser was his pupil. Nevertheless, attempts to show that Spenser used Mulcaster's works or ideas as a source seem unsuccessful. C.S. Lewis (1954:350) points out a parallel between Despair's speech in *FQ* I ix 40 and Mulcaster's 'everie privat man traveleth in this world to win rest after toil, to have ease after labour' (*Elementarie* 1582: sig 2F4v), but does not mention the common source in Aristotle (*Politics* 7.15). As Roland Smith (1958) has shown, Mulcaster's elaborate spelling method set forth in *Elementarie* had no influence on Spenser's orthography. Furthermore, in *Positions* (1581:273) Mulcaster is rather suspicious of poetry, treating it as a sub-branch of both history and rhetoric.

Spenser never mentions his old master outright. Yet G.C. Moore Smith (1913) ingeniously shows that the reference to 'A good olde shephearde, *Wrenock*' (*SC, December* 40), may be an anagram of Mulcaster (Mast. Wrenock = Mowncaster, an alternative spelling). And there may be more than coincidence that Spenser's two children from his first marriage were named Sylvanus and Katherine: Mulcaster had a son named Sylvanus and both his wife and daughter were named Katherine (Millican 1939). Mulcaster may have encouraged Spenser at Merchant Taylors' by getting him the gift of money from Robert Nowell's estate and by putting him forward as translator of van der Noot's *Theatre* (through Emanuel van Meteren, a Dutch merchant in London). Whether either author read the other's books is not known, though Spenser's friend Harvey read *Positions* with interest (Harvey ed 1913:117, 182, 185, 187). Nevertheless, an enthusiasm for the vernacular, a love of classical literature, a staunch support of Elizabeth and the state religion are all general themes found in Mulcaster and expressed later in Spenser's poetry.

WILLIAM W. BARKER

On Spenser at Merchant Taylors' School, see Douglas Hamer 1947 'Edmund Spenser's Gown and Shilling' *RES* 23:218–25. For the school history, with statutes appended, see F.W.M. Draper 1962; see also H.B. Wilson 1814. More general background is given in T.W. Baldwin 1944, though there is a corrective study: Bolgar 1955. For Mulcaster, see Richard L. DeMolen 1975 'Richard Mulcaster: An Elizabethan Savant' *ShakS* 8:29–82; Forster 1967; Charles Bowie Millican 1939 'Notes on Spenser and Mulcaster' *ELH* 6:214–16; and G.C. Moore Smith 1913 'Spenser and Mulcaster' *MLR* 8:368.

Mercilla In *FQ* v ix, Artegall and Arthur visit the court of Mercilla (from Eng *mercy* or Fr *merci* plus, perhaps, *selah*, used in the Psalms to indicate emphasis or praise), 'a mayden Queene of high renowne' (viii 17). They have heard of her from her messenger Samient (perhaps from ME *sam* 'together' [cf I x 57], because the two knights first meet through her, or more generally because she seeks concord between Mercilla and her enemies, viii 21). The giant porter Awe guards her palace against attacks of 'guyle, and malice, and despight' (ix 22), recalling their previous victories over Malengin, the Souldan, and Adicia. Order, the marshal, leads the knights and Samient past the many suitors and the poet Bonfont (renamed Malfont), his tongue nailed to a post for slandering the Queen.

Artegall and Arthur sit on either side of the Queen as jurors while she hears the trial of 'A Ladie of great countenance and place' (38) – Duessa, last seen in IV i. The prosecutor, Zeal, charges that this 'now untitled Queene' has conspired with Blandamour and Paridell to seize Mercilla's throne. Defense is given by Pittie, Regard of womanhead, and other figures; but after corroborating testimony from Murder, Incontinence, and others, Mercilla must pass judgment. At first she refuses to have Duessa executed, but later 'strong constraint' (x 4) forces her to do so. The Queen then turns to the widow Belge's complaint against the tyrant Geryoneo, whose overthrow becomes Arthur's quest, while Artegall continues on his way to rescue Irena.

In Mercilla, readers have always recognized Elizabeth I, for there are many correspondences: the entrance to Mercilla's palace resembles that to Hampton Court, Elizabeth had a giant porter, the lions and fleurs-de-lis in the portrait recall the royal arms, the rusty sword suggests the ancient sword Elizabeth kept as a reminder of the peace of her reign (Nelson 1965), Duessa's trial resembles that of Mary, Queen of Scots, and the response to Belge is the mission to aid the Low Countries against Spain. A contemporary described Elizabeth enthroned in Parliament like Mercilla, attended by ladies and at her feet 'a Lyon and a Dragon glistering with Gold, made with wonderfull cunning, supporting the Queenes Armes' (Northrop 1972–3).

Except for Una's father (I xii), Mercilla is the only good monarch present in the poem. Her emblematic portrait fusing monarch with mercy attests the unity of the two in the Christian polity. Erasmus reflects the widespread belief in mercy as the defining role of monarchy: 'the king shows mercy in helping the oppressed, truth in judging honestly, and clemency in tempering the severity of the law' (Epistle to Sigismund I in ed 1906–58 no 2034; cf Prov 20.28, 'Mercie and trueth preserve the King: for his throne shalbe established with mercie'). The qualities of mercy and truth are observed in Mercilla, from the time she first appears, hearing pleas of the 'meane and base' (ix 36), to the tears that she sheds for Duessa (50), a form of clemency in showing meekness even though sentence must be passed. A passage by Sir John Davies employs the virgo, sword, and lion imagery, declaring that in Ireland the law should 'make her progresse and Circuit about the Realme, under the protection of the sword (as *Virgo*, the figure of Justice, is by *Leo* in the Zodiack)' (*A Discoverie of the True Causes Why Ireland Was Never Entirely Subdued* 1612:74). The clouds, sun, and angels in the portrait place the origins of mercy-tempered justice in heaven, suggesting also the biblical 'mercy seat' of God covering the Ark (Exod 25.17–18; cf Ps 97.2 for 'cloudes and darkenes' about the Lord). The Litae attending her at ix 32 (see *Iliad* 9.502–12; in Conti 4.16, they are fused with the Horae) are Justice, Good Law, and Peace – essentially three ascending levels of justice (Dunseath 1968:208–11). The lion may represent restrained force or perhaps hostile force kept in allegiance (Aptekar 1969:58–69).

Book v seems to have two houses of instruction, Mercilla's court and Isis Church. Both suggest the need to temper justice with mercy, a main theme in the book. Canto ix instructs in the ideal working of justice, with the Isis-Mercilla progression representing (historically) Elizabeth's predicament earlier and later in her career, and (mythically) a movement from silver- to golden-age justice. Both events center on equity, the means of overriding strict legal constraints with general principles of justice; but in Mercilla's court, an equity of greater magnitude is clearly envisioned. Just as equity is seen as essential to legal justice, so mercy is a basis of divine justice. Britomart thus prepares at a lower level what, at a higher one, Mercilla completes.

RICHARD F. HARDIN

For general discussion, esp on iconology, see Aptekar 1969 and Dunseath 1968. On Mercilla, see William Nelson 1965 'Queen Elizabeth, Spenser's Mercilla, and a Rusty Sword' *RN* 18:113–17; Northrop 1968–9 and 1972–3 on historical significance; and Stump 1982.

Mercury (Gr Hermes) Messenger of the gods, psychopomp or guide of the souls of the dead, god of language, interpretation, silence, and reason; also peacemaker, musician, shepherd god, leader of the dance, god of spring and of thieves. His main attributes are the snake-entwined caduceus and winged feet and helmet. All these qualities and characteristics are discussed, for example, in Conti's *Mythologiae* (1567, 5.5); Spenser alludes to many of them in his works, particularly *Mother Hubberds Tale* and *The Faerie Queene*.

(See **Mercury** Fig 1.)

As psychopomp and intermediary between heaven and earth, Mercury is entrusted with the task of bearing Sidney's ashes to heaven in *Ruines of Time* (666ff). *Mother Hubberd* mentions his 'cunning theeveries' (1287) and his invisibility (1280), a quality attributed to Mercury apparently only by Spenser and in this particular instance (see Lotspeich 1932:81). His role in this poem is quite complex. He is sent by Jove to recall the lion king to his empire in a passage which echoes Mercury's descent to remind Aeneas of his duty and destiny (*MHT* 1246ff, *Aeneid* 4.238ff). Spenser's allegory signifies the need for rational control of the kingdom: Mercury, god of reason (see Cartari 1571:329), awakens the lion from a 'traunce' in which his 'fantasie' has dominated his other faculties and caused him to lose his kingly status (*MHT* 1325ff). Mercury may here be acting out the ordering role of the poet in a chaotic society (Bryan 1972), but his significance as a political symbol probably takes precedence. In *Aeneid* 4, Mercury warns the future ruler Aeneas (supposed ancestor of Elizabeth); in *Mother Hubberd*, he is instrumental in purging the kingdom and becomes in effect a divine surrogate for the monarch, his helmet doubling the lion's crown, his caduceus doubling the scepter (*MHT* 1279–340).

In *The Faerie Queene*, Mercury receives his most extended treatment – though strangely (or perhaps not so strangely for this mysterious god of silence) he is mentioned or alluded to only seven times. At II xii 40–1, the Palmer's staff is described as being made of the 'same wood' as the caduceus, 'the rod of *Mercury*.' The caduceus can tame 'infernall feends'; the Palmer's staff can defeat 'charmes' and subdue 'monsters.' Since the monsters at II xii 23–5 recall those depicted in Phantastes' chamber at ix 50, the staff may serve as an emblem of reason controlling the excesses of the imagination which are themselves, because of the implied connection between monsters and underworld 'feends,' seen at least in part to be embodiments of the darker, chthonic aspects of the fallen self. In this connection, we recall that in the Mercurian Palmer's absence Guyon almost succumbs to the underworld temptations of Mammon, 'Prince' of tempting and ensnaring demons (Agrippa ed 1651, 3.18, p 399). As he emerges from Mammon's house, his need for Mercury is expressed as the need to be tended by the angel and the Palmer (for the identification of angels with Mercury, see Seznec ed 1953:181 and Cummings 1970).

If the Palmer's staff is made of the same wood as the caduceus, it must be white

(Cartari ed 1599: sig Q3r). The relationship between Mercury and the lion king in *Mother Hubberd* implies a further link between the staff and the 'white rod' (scepter) of the 'royall virgin' (Elizabeth) in III iii 49. The Mercurian Palmer pacifies the demons of the imagination with his staff; the virgin, Mercurian by virtue of her 'white rod,' brings 'sacred Peace' (for the caduceus as an emblem of peace, see Cartari 1571:313ff). There is another, retrospective, link with Book II: the Palmer's staff and the virgin's rod seem symbolically to derive from Gloriana's shining scepter with which she 'All Faery lond does peaceably sustene' (II ii 40).

Further complementing the royal virgin's rod of III iii is queenly Cambina's 'rod of peace,' elaborately compared to the caduceus (IV iii 42). Cambina, too, is Mercurian, fittingly dominating the first half of this fourth, Mercurian Legend of Friendship and concord (see Fowler 1964:156–91). She makes her entrance in a chariot drawn by lions (iii 39), which identifies her also with the earth mother Cybele (Fowler 1964:186n). Such an identification is not, however, incompatible with her Mercurian role: Macrobius, for example, gives a detailed account of the caduceus as an emblem of genesis (*Saturnalia* 1.19.16–17), and Pierio Valeriano explains that it signifies *earth* (*Hieroglyphica* 15).

Mercury's caduceus is entwined by two embracing serpents (cf *FQ* IV iii 42). Their kiss, says Macrobius (1.19.17), is the kiss of love. Cambina's rod in canto iii, then, may influence the third canto from the end of the book (IV x), where the legs and feet of the Mercurian bisexual Venus, *Venus hermaphroditos*, are 'together twyned ... with a snake, whose head and tail were fast combyned' (40). This is the familiar *ouroboros* (Gr 'tail-devouring [serpent]'), emblem of eternity and the serpent of matrimony (Ripa 1603:305–7); but it is also a reminder of the snakes bound together by their tails on Cambina's rod, especially since the temple of the hermaphroditic Venus is guarded by Concord (31–5), traditionally depicted with a caduceus (Cartari 1571:313ff).

If the Mercury of *FQ* IV is modulated into an hermaphroditic symbol of the mysteries of human and divine love, the Mercury of *FQ* V is once more associated with monarchy by being embodied, as the name suggests, in the figure of Mercilla. She is enthroned under 'a cloth of state ... like a cloud' because Mercury alone can part the clouds of mental obfuscation to reveal truth while respecting the veiled mystery of godhead (ix 28; cf Boccaccio *Genealogia* 12.62, Wind 1958:106–8). A further clue to Mercilla's Mercurian nature lies in her golden (sunlike) and silver skirts in the same stanza. In combining gold and silver, sun and moon, she suggests the Mercury (*Mercurius noster*) of the alchemists, frequently interpreted as the culmination of the alchemical quest (Jung *Alchemical Studies* vol 13:191–250 in ed 1953–79, Brooks-Davies 1983:60). As such, she is the climactic symbol of a book in which alchemical imagery has already been detected (Nohrnberg 1976:391). Furthermore, the introduction of a Mercury associated with occult traditions has already been prepared for by the information that Mercurian Cambina is 'learned ... in Magicke leare' (IV iii 40).

Since Mercury was god of shepherds as well as a musician (Cartari 1571:312, 335ff), Calidore's 'shepheards hooke' and Colin's pipe (VI ix 36, x 16–18) may represent metamorphosed caducei. When Colin pipes to the Graces in VI x, he assumes an additional Mercurian persona, for Mercury was leader of the Graces (Cartari 1571:564) and of the dance (cf Jonson *Pan's Anniversary* 176–8, Brooks-Davies 1983:92). Nevertheless, Mercury's presence in *FQ* V and VI can only be inferred.

In *FQ* VII, however, Mercury appears in person for the first time in the poem, as Jove's messenger sent to discover the cause of the darkening of Cynthia/Elizabeth's light. With his caduceus, he opposes Cynthia's attacker, Mutabilitie, who, as a black magician associated with Hecate, is equipped with a wand (vi 3, 13, 18). He is thus a white magician, defender of the true monarch. (Planetary Mercury is included in the procession of planets at vii 51; see Fowler 1964:114, 156–91 for a discussion of his astrological role in *FQ*.)

Presumably, Spenser connects Mercury with magic by conflating the Greco-Roman Hermes/Mercury with Egyptian Thoth, known to the Renaissance as Hermes (or Mercurius) Trismegistus, the legendary priest-king believed to have invented all the arts and sciences including the various branches of magic. It may be that in *The Faerie Queene* allusions to magic and Egypt combine with references to Mercury to create a Hermetic-Mercurian poem in which Elizabeth's England is associated with the pure Egypt of the Hermetic writings and especially the Hermetic *Asclepius*. Spenser's poem as we have it terminates with an appearance of Mercury as Jove's messenger and the defeat of the 'Giantesse' Mutabilitie, a defeat brought about through an assembly of the gods summoned by Jove. There are echoes here of Bruno's Hermetic *Expulsion of the Triumphant Beast*, a work heavily indebted to the *Asclepius* (see Yates 1964; Brooks-Davies 1983, ch 1). According to the title page of Bruno's *Expulsion*, Mercury is the 'revealer' of that work. Even if the god does not 'reveal' Spenser's *Faerie Queene*, he does help us to penetrate some of its mysteries.

DOUGLAS BROOKS-DAVIES

Brooks-Davies 1983; Robert A. Bryan 1972 'Poets, Poetry, and Mercury in Spenser's *Prosopopia: Mother Hubberd's Tale*' *Costerus* 5:27–33; Yates 1964.

Merlin Despite his claim to follow books that 'hath written bene of old' (*FQ* III ii 18), Spenser treats Merlin with characteristic and fruitful independence. Mentioned in *Ruines of Time* as the creator of an earthly paradise (523–5), Merlin appears in *The Faerie Queene* as artificer, magus, and prophet. He is the maker of Arthur's arms and armor (I vii 33–6, II viii 20–1) and of King Ryence's magic glass (III ii 17–21); he oversees Arthur's education and selects his tutor (I ix 5), commands demons to rear a wall of brass around Cairmardin (III iii 7), and is instrumental in bringing about the union of Artegall and Britomart, the fate of whose descendants he prophesies before disappearing from the poem (III iii 26–50).

A brief summary of the tradition clarifies the Merlin of Spenser's poem. He first appears as Myrddin Wilt (Merlin the Wild) in a Welsh poem of the ninth century. Nennius' *Historia Britonum* (c 796) tells of Ambrosius, a fatherless child with strange powers of prophecy. Geoffrey of Monmouth creates the Merlin of romance by identifying Nennius' Ambrosius with the Myrddin of Celtic folklore. His *Historia regum Brittaniae* and *Vita Merlini* established Merlin's reputation as a prophet throughout Europe.

Yet Merlin was considered by the Renaissance to be more than a prophet. By identifying Merlin's father as an incubus, Geoffrey created a magician who can possess occult knowledge without engaging in witchcraft or entering into a pact with Satan. In doing so, he prepared the ground for the great magi of the Renaissance. Continental romances, such as Robert de Boron's *Merlin* and the Vulgate *Lestoire de Merlin*, confirmed the magician's Christian orthodoxy and multiplied his feats of magic, completing his elevation from Welsh prophet to white magician of immense power. Though Malory avoids the surfeit of magic in his French sources, the Merlin of his *Morte Darthur* is substantially the Merlin of thirteenth-century French romances.

Although Merlin's traditional function is retained in *The Faerie Queene*, it alone does not account for every attribute of Spenser's figure. A comparison with the Merlin of Ariosto (whose influence Spenser acknowledges as he does not that of the medieval romances) illustrates how he overgoes both his medieval and his Italian predecessors. In *Orlando furioso*, Ariosto notes Merlin's feats of magic (26.30, 33.4), but he is interested in him only as a prophet. Echoes of Virgil and Ovid show that he associates Merlin with the Cumaean Sibyl, and that Merlin's function is that of the prophets and oracles in classical literature. His art is dismissed as sorcery, and the matter closed with the assertion that the secret of his magic has been lost forever (33.4–5).

Spenser's Merlin is not hedged with such pious caution. Though earlier writers find in him a prophet and a cornucopia of marvels, he is most important in *The Faerie Queene* as a figure for the artist. His most noteworthy creation is the magic glass he makes for King Ryence, which is also an image of the entire world (III ii 19):

It vertue had, to shew in perfect sight,
What ever thing was in the world contaynd,
Betwixt the lowest earth and heavens hight,
So that it to the looker appertaynd;

What ever foe had wrought, or frend had faynd,
Therein discovered was, ne ought mote pas,
Ne ought in secret from the same remaynd;
For thy it round and hollow shaped was,
Like to the world it selfe, and seem'd a world of glas.

This glass is unlike anything attributed to Merlin in extant medieval romances. Despite superficial debts to earlier works, Spenser's Merlin is an original creation, as seen in Arthur's arms. The Merlin of romance does occasionally make swords, but the arms which he makes for Arthur are unlike any Arthur ever had before. Both sword and shield are proof against enchantment; and the shield, 'all of Diamond perfect pure and cleene' (I vii 33), can distinguish the real from the illusory. More is to be learned by contrasting Merlin to Archimago or Busirane, Spenser's evil magicians, than by reference to his literary antecedents.

As the creator of a 'world of glas,' Merlin illuminates Spenser's view of art. This mirror is no ordinary crystal ball. Since it shows all things truly, it is an image of prelapsarian Eden, of a world free from illusion and error; it recalls Sidney's statement that Nature's 'world is brazen, the poets only deliver a golden' (ed 1973b:78). It offers a pattern for the good life: like Britomart, we can see in it what pertains to us and fashion our lives accordingly. Finally, Merlin's mirror is a symbol of true art. It shows only what is 'Betwixt the lowest earth and heavens hight,' yet it suggests that truth which is beyond time. It does not claim, however, to depict transcendental reality, for that would be idolatrous. Unlike the works of the evil magicians in *The Faerie Queene*, Merlin's mirror is not to be confused with what it reflects or imitates. In this, it resembles Spenser's other great structure of glass, Panthea, the tower in Cleopolis which Redcrosse finally understands truly when he beholds the New Jerusalem and sees how 'this bright Angels towre quite dims that towre of glas' (I x 58). (Cf Isis Church, where 'the Goddesse selfe' stands upon an altar 'like to christall glasse' (IV x 39); here again, glass brings together the transcendent and the terrestrial.)

The full significance of Merlin and his mirror is not revealed until the *Cantos of Mutabilitie*. Here Mutabilitie is restrained only by the advent of Nature, whose face never 'could be seene, but like an image in a glass' (VII vii 6). For Spenser, sound art is a medium in which things are revealed which would otherwise remain unseen. In the absence of the goddess herself, only the glass of art reminds us that chaos is illusory, and that Mutabilitie is 'firmely stayd / Upon the pillours of Eternity' (viii 2). Deep in the quicksand of time, art affirms the unchanging and persuades us of what we cannot see. Spenser's final plea is to be granted 'that Sabaoths sight,' for only what is beyond time can redeem the world of time. The most Merlin's glass can do is point to 'that same time when no more *Change* shall be'; but the temporal image is a true and sustaining reflection of the eternal. Merlin, artificer, magus, and prophet in the service of civility, is for Spenser a type of the true artist.

WILLIAM BLACKBURN

Blackburn 1980; Brooks-Davies 1983; Nikolai Tolstoy 1985 *The Quest for Merlin* (Boston); K. Williams 1966.

metamorphosis The mythical transformation of deities or human beings into animals, plants, rocks, and the like. Myths of metamorphosis, like creation myths (eg, Plato *Timaeus* 90–2), are often etiological, explaining the origins of natural phenomena by assuming primary anthropomorphism. In Ovid's *Metamorphoses*, drawing comprehensively on classical myths and legends, transformation becomes virtually the essence of myth, and the essential quality of the transformed character is preserved in the change. Apuleius' *Metamorphoses* (*The Golden Ass*) combines magic, religion, myth, and allegory in a story of metamorphosis followed by restoration to human form.

Euhemeristic or historical interpretation of myths reduced metamorphosis to mere fantasy based on fact, and Christian writers similarly rejected the possibility of actual transformation. But mythical metamorphosis was allegorized from antiquity by Stoic and Neoplatonic writers as symbolizing moral or spiritual change, or the changes of the physical elements. Spiritual allegory received impetus from Pythagorean and Platonic doctrines of the soul's transmigration after death into bodies befitting its conduct and nature (see *Republic* 10 [619–20]). In the fourteenth century, the *Ovide moralisé* and Bersuire's *Ovidius moralizatus* gave transformations scriptural or doctrinal meanings.

Interpretations of myths of metamorphosis were compiled by mythographers, dictionary makers, emblematists, and commentators on Homer and Ovid. In Dante, the *Romance of the Rose*, Petrarch, and Ronsard, transformation acquired complex poetic, moral, and psychological significances. Renaissance vernacular and Neolatin poets created 'myths of locality,' and mythological 'epyllia' were popular in England. Humanists such as Erasmus dwelt on the moral implications of transformation; writers on magic, alchemy, and witchcraft investigated its possibility. In Renaissance Hermeticism and Neoplatonism, metamorphosis symbolized man's changing nature, his intermediate position between gods and beasts, and his freedom to ascend or descend the scale of being (see Pico *Oration on the Dignity of Man* 1486). It was also used in the 'theriophilist' debate arguing the superiority of animals over men (see Gelli *Circe* 1549).

Spenser recalls these traditions, drawing on Ovid, Renaissance mythographers, and his predecessors Ariosto, Tasso, and Trissino. Metamorphosis is exploited for both imaginative and moral ends in *Muiopotmos* (113–44, 257–352) and *The Faerie Queene*, and incidentally elsewhere in the minor poems (*Time* 589–630, *Gnat* 197–224, 401–8, 677–80, 'Astrophel' 181–98, *Amoretti* 28). In *The Faerie Queene*, Spenser exhibits an Ovidian fascination with the physical process of transformation and the interpenetration of contrary qualities, as in the Bower of Bliss (II xii) and the Garden of Adonis (III vi). Illusion, deceit, and the protean nature of evil are manifested through shape-changers like Archimago, Duessa, and Malengin. Arthur's shield, unmasking deceits and transforming punitively (I vii 35), acts as a counter-charm. The transformations in the Fradubio episode (I ii 28–43) and in the Bower (II v 27, xii 84–7) show man forgetting 'the excellence / Of his creation,' letting passion usurp reason, and degenerating to vegetal or animal existence. Similarly degenerative transformation characterizes the troops of Maleger in their assault on the house of Alma (the human body; II ix 1, xi). For the transforming arts of Acrasia and Duessa, Spenser is indebted to classical and Renaissance treatments of Circe and other witches such as Ariosto's Alcina, Tasso's Armida, and Trissino's Acratia.

The two fountain-nymph stories (I vii 4–6, II ii 5–10), as well as the metamorphosis of Malbecco into Gealosie (III x 54–60) and of Adicia into a tiger (V viii 49) – terrifying, imaginative tours-de-force where a character is transformed into an emblem of a moral state – are original myths of change, however much they echo patterns in earlier literature. In episodes presenting outward alteration, Spenser plays with the idea of transformation: for example, in the Faunus-Molanna story (VII vi 37–55) actual transformation is evaded, though Faunus' punishment recalls Actaeon's change; Artegall, enslaved by Radigund (V v 20–4) as Hercules was by Omphale, wears female dress and does women's work; Timias, made unrecognizable by Belphoebe's anger (IV vii 37–47), recalls Elizabethan court myths of Cynthia's disfavor (cf Lyly's *Endymion*).

Classical and pseudoclassical metamorphoses are recalled in the minor poems in the contexts of love, grief, and art (and incidentally in *FQ* II xii 30–1; III ii 41, 44, vi 45; V proem 2, 5, vii 10–11; VI x 13; VII vi 45, vii 32–4). In *Time* 589–630 and 'Astrophel' 181–98 (where Astrophel and Stella become a flower), invented metamorphoses commemorate Sidney. In *Muiopotmos*, Spenser adapts classical sources to explain the origins of both spider and butterfly through stories of metamorphosis. He deviates from Ovid's account of the contest of Arachne and Minerva (*Met* 6.1–145) by making Arachne the loser, transformed through envy. Moral meanings, and the contrast between good and bad art, are conveyed through metamorphoses, but the passages communicate above all the imaginative richness of myth. In *The Faerie Queene*, describing Malecasta's tapestry of Venus and Adonis (III i 34–8) and Busirane's tapestry showing the gods transformed for love (xi 28–46), Spenser's moral criticism is sharper: metamorphosis expresses the reductive, predatory, and debasing qualities of sexual love.

Further, Busirane's tapestry resembles Arachne's in Ovid; Busirane and Acrasia (cf II xii 77) are like Arachne/Aragnoll, converting love's sweetness into venom.

The most important mythical subject of metamorphosis in *The Faerie Queene* is Proteus (see III viii 39–41), ambiguously symbolizing mutability in both moral and physical nature and finally eluding moral categorization. Spenser makes Adonis in his Garden (vi 47) also subject to perpetual transformations. Here the great creative transformations of nature are contrasted to the sterile transformations of art in Acrasia's Bower. As in the *Cantos of Mutabilitie*, Spenser here asserts a principle of permanence and continuity amidst change: Adonis, 'Transformed oft, and chaunged diverslie,' is yet 'eterne in mutabilitie' (III vi 47). But metamorphosis is linked to the central themes of mutability and decay in IV viii 32, V proem, and VII vi 1, 5–6, 37–55. The Faunus-Molanna episode is at the heart of the *Cantos of Mutabilitie*. Faunus escapes death or gelding: 'The Wood-gods breed ... must for ever live' (VII vi 50), but the natural setting is irremediably altered through moral fault. The goddess and her nymphs depart; the land becomes a wilderness.

Metamorphosis is basic to the allegory of *The Faerie Queene*. Often it externalizes essence and demonstrates the congruity between being and seeming, image and idea typical of pageant, masque, or emblem, while deceitful shape-changing indicates the ubiquity of illusion and the need for masks. Moral allegory and the mutability theme suggest that for Spenser metamorphosis is a sign of the Fall. But his knights, striving to become their virtues, seek the upward transformation towards divinity possible only through faith and grace. Moreover nature, though fallen, survives change, absorbing mutations into a cycle of renewal. In the physical allegory, pagan myth is charged with an Ovidian sense of natural creativity and abundance. But ultimately (VII viii), Spenser seeks to escape from the mutable world, nature and art, illusion and metaphor, and the poem itself, into unchanging rest in God. SUPRIYA CHAUDHURI

Barkan 1980; Barkan 1986:233–42; Pierre Brunel 1974 *La Mythe de la métamorphose* (Paris); Bush 1963; Paule Demats 1973 *Fabula: Trois études de mythographie antique et médiévale* (Geneva); Hankins 1971; Hughes 1943; Pépin 1958; Rees 1971; Seznec ed 1953; Skulsky 1981.

metaphor, simile Broadly speaking, the modes of comparison known as metaphor and simile have attracted two different kinds of analysis, one rhetorical and the other hermeneutic. Rhetorical analysis is addressed primarily to writers and offers advice on how to use metaphors; hermeneutic analysis is addressed to readers and attempts to theorize problems of interpretation caused by the presence of metaphor in all texts, literary or otherwise.

In the rhetorical tradition, the distinction between metaphor and simile is more formal than substantial, there being general agreement that a metaphor is a contracted simile and a simile an expanded metaphor (Aristotle *Rhetoric* 3.4, Cicero *De oratore* 3.39). It is also agreed that metaphor and simile are not constitutive of style but are merely 'ornaments' of it. As such, they are assumed to be completely under the control of writers who use them in order to achieve perspicuity, arouse emotion, and stimulate delight in a poetry which is supposed to teach by delighting, and to do so in a manner which bears some affinity with those arguments-from-likeness encountered in the neighboring discipline of logic. Unlike logical proofs, however, poetic metaphors are policed solely by the criterion of decorum, which accredits those deemed appropriate and censures the far-fetched. Metaphors are treated as a supplement to 'literal' language, which in turn is conceived of (somewhat improbably) as not only devoid of metaphor but also as a preexistent norm from which the metaphoric subsequently deviates.

The shift from an allegedly literal to a figurative use of language is conceived of traditionally as a 'turning' (Gr *tropos* 'trope') or a 'transference' (Gr *meta* 'over' + *pherein* 'to carry,' which gives us 'metaphor' – the term glossed as *translatio* by Quintilian in *Institutio oratoria* 8.6.4, and Englished by Puttenham as 'transport' in *Arte* 3.16). Figurative language is produced when an obligation to describe something is accompanied by a reluctance or inability to do so. Similes invite us to 'turn' from the thing itself and entertain a likeness of it ('Her paps lyke lyllies budded' *Epithalamion* 176); metaphors have already 'transported' such likenesses, and so take them for granted ('the sacred noursery / Of vertue' *FQ* VI proem 3). The common impression that Spenser was partial to similes is confirmed by the Osgood *Concordance*, which lists about 900 citations for *like* and a further 300 for *as*, not counting numerous entries under *as when* and so on. In form, they vary from brief comparisons arranged in rapid succession (such as the catalogue of the bride's physical characteristics in *Epith* 171–8) to more expanded comparisons like the one which compares writing *The Faerie Queene* to going somewhere by ship ('Whose course is often stayd, yet never is astray' VI xii 1), or the two 'heroic' similes that describe how the Red Cross Knight is almost overwhelmed by Error's vomit (I i 21–3). Spenser's metaphors range similarly from non-embellished incidentals ('the riches of his wit': 'Astrophel' 62) to the sustained kind known to contemporary rhetoricians as *allegoria* and exemplified by the final stanza of *FQ* I, where by means of what Puttenham would call a 'sence translative and wrested from [its] owne signification' (*Arte* 3.18) the characters included in that book are viewed as passengers who will disembark before the poem continues its 'voyage' into Book II.

To look upon metaphor as a condensed simile is to condone the practice of explicating metaphors by unfolding them as similes, as E.K. does for the line, 'My head besprent with hoary frost I fynd' (*SC, Dec* 135): he glosses *hoary frost* as 'A metaphore of hoary heares scattred lyke to a gray frost.' If such a metaphor is produced by an act of transference – a *translatio* from the so-called literal domain to the figurative – then the sort of reading done here by E.K. involves a *retro-translatio* which relocates the figurative in the literal. In such cases, similes constitute a kind of suppressed middle term between the humdrum of ordinary language and the novelties of the poetic. But as other comments by E.K. show, we usually pass from metaphor to interpretation without paying our respects en route to buried similes. So when E.K. reads in the fable of the Oak and the Briar that the briar's flowers have been often 'defast' by 'hoarie locks' cast down by the oak (*Feb* 181–2), he says the words *hoarie locks* are used 'metaphorically for withered leaves' – despite the fact that the oak is leafless: it has 'bared boughes' (112), a 'toppe ... bald' (113), and 'naked Armes' (171), the latter phrase being glossed by E.K. as 'the bare boughes, spoyled of leaves.' The case for seeing *locks* as a metaphor for *leaves* (rather than, say, bark or twigs) is less self-evident than E.K. assumes. Trivial in itself, this example illustrates the variance produced by metaphor as an expressive device, and provides a nuclear model of those larger misprisions created by the slippage between what is encoded in a metaphor and what different readers at different times take to be encoded there.

The hermeneutic tradition, therefore, concedes our desire to control the meaning of metaphors but doubts that it could ever be achieved, because any piece of figurative language always produces a surplus of meaning generated by all those things which have to be declared irrelevant, strictly speaking, to what is taken to be the main point of a comparison. So, for example, when we read about Una's 'sunshyny face' and the 'blazing brightnesse of her beauties beame' (*FQ* I xii 23), we may feel obliged to repress memories of an earlier description of the 'bright blazing beautie' of Lucifera, or argue that this 'mayden Queene' of pride (iv 8) merely travesties the maiden Queen Elizabeth to whom *The Faerie Queene* is dedicated. But what is thus repressed or explained away by commentary on discrete passages accumulates and returns to haunt readers of the whole poem as a hermeneutic problem, and to justify deconstructionist readings of *The Faerie Queene* which argue that the duplicities of its figurative language make the poem resistant to efforts by either Spenser or his readers to produce a totalizing meaning which transcends conflicting interpretations. The semantic indeterminacies produced by figural ambivalence can thus be considered in relation to other features of the poem such as polysemous names, 'superfluous' characters, 'digressive' episodes, and narrative 'loose ends,' all of which frustrate readers in search of a disambiguated and tidy poem. Yet what shocks the virtuous interpreter delights the chameleon poet, and may well have delighted a man who, knowing 'how doubtfully all Allegories may be construed' (Letter to Raleigh), decided nevertheless to capitalize on the ambiguities of *allegoriae*, and to produce in *The Faerie Queene* a poem guaranteed to say more than it could mean, and to mean more than it could say. K.K. RUTHVEN

DeNeef 1982; Maurice Evans 1953 'Metaphor and Symbol in the Sixteenth Century' *EIC* 3:267–84; Terence Hawkes 1972 *Metaphor* (London); Tuve 1947.

Milton, John (1608–74) Milton was undoubtedly a careful and enthusiastic reader of Spenser, as Dryden attests in the preface to *Fables, Ancient and Modern* (1700): '*Milton* has acknowledg'd to me, that *Spencer* was his Original' (*Sp All* p 311). Yet in his repeated approach to that origin, Milton seems to have become only more himself. As Hazlitt shrewdly observed, 'In reading his works, we feel ourselves under the influence of a mighty intellect, that the nearer it approaches to others, becomes more distinct from them' ('On Shakspeare and Milton' 1818). A description of the relation between Spenser and Milton must account, therefore, both for Milton's identification of Spenser as his poetic origin, and for the way in which he became ever more 'distinct' from his 'Original.'

Milton's (or possibly Dryden's) use of the term *original* deploys one of several possible systems of figures for representing relations between poets. It might be called 'causative' for it includes all figures of inspiration and influence. Familiar examples are astral figures, as in Jonson's praise of Shakespeare ('Shine forth, thou Starre of *Poets*, and with rage, / Or influence, chide, or cheere the drooping Stage' 'To ... Shakespeare' 77–8); natural, as in Spenser's acclamation of Chaucer ('The pure well head of Poesie' *FQ* VII vii 9); or supernatural, as in Milton's aspiring to prophetic inspiration on the model of Isaiah. Influence appears in these examples as a mysterious and irresistible force.

In the passage from the preface to *Fables*, Dryden also uses a figure with quite different associations: '*Milton* was the Poetical Son of *Spencer* ... for we [poets] have our Lineal Descents and Clans, as well as other Families.' In this 'familial' conceit, relations between poets are seen as close, and therefore very complex. Familial relations are a complicated system of action and reaction, alongside which the figures of influence seem hyperbolic or reductive. If Milton represented Spenser to himself at times as an origin or a father, neither figure surprisingly is the one he usually prefers. Typically, Spenser is a teacher, most notably the 'better teacher' of *Areopagitica*; and one may examine their relationship by seeing how Spenser is made to perform a pedagogic function in Milton's poetry.

Many examples of imitation in Milton's early works testify to his discipleship. He conspicuously adopts Spenserian vocabulary, archaism, and, most important, the alexandrine. Although not complex in themselves, these examples of imitation serve as counterpoint to the romance fluidity of his diction; Spenserianisms anchor his early poetry in the native tradition. Perhaps the most interesting example occurs in the line 'Under a star-ypointing *Pyramid*' ('On Shakespeare'). Spenser, however, never uses the prefix *y* before a present participle (Carey in Milton ed 1968:123). The slightly bizarre effect of Milton's 'false archaism' suggests something more than imitation. He may be remembering the passage (marked in his own copy of the work) in Browne's *Britannia's Pastorals* where the poet laments Spenser's lack of 'A *Piramis*, whose head (like winged *Fame*) / Should pierce the clouds' (*Sp All* p 146; also p 228). While it is difficult to say precisely what is implied by this echo of Browne, it is at least evident that Milton is not forgetting Spenser even while praising Shakespeare. This conclusion is consistent with a certain ambivalence in the poem despite the hyperbole of its praise: 'Then thou our fancy of itself bereaving, / Dost make us marble with too much conceiving.' For Milton, Shakespeare's very monumentality inhibits his followers as Spenser (by implication) does not.

The case of the alexandrine, or more generally of the Spenserian refrain, is perhaps more consequential, for here Milton's imitation is already beginning to emphasize difference. The Spenserian alexandrine is structurally crucial to the stanza of *The Faerie Queene*, where it functions (with great variety of specific effects) both as summation and transition. Milton seems eagerly to have adopted the hexameter for his stanzaic closes, as well as for his more canzone-like shorter poems; yet his alexandrines resist the function epitomized by the hexameter refrain of *Epithalamion* ('The woods shall to me answer and my Eccho ring') or the pentameter of *Prothalamion* ('Sweete *Themmes* runne softly, till I end my Song'), which keep the time of his songs, like a metronome. They may be compared to Milton's most exemplary hexameter: 'Triumphing over Death, and Chance, and thee O Time' ('On Time' 22). Its apocalyptic effect, canceling the suspension and temporal dilation characteristic of Spenser, is most remarkable in Milton's Nativity Ode, which is much indebted to the alexandrines of *The Faerie Queene* and to the lyric intensity of Spenser's great marriage odes. The alexandrine in the Nativity poem participates in that premature apocalypticism that almost brings the poem to an end at several points ('But wisest fate says no, / This must not yet be so' 149). This effect should not be overemphasized, since it is by no means implicit in the alexandrine itself. Yet here is an example of the disciple learning from the master something the master may not be teaching. Milton was drawn to the prosodic device that Spenser had transformed into a brilliant narrative figure; but in Milton's hands the device resists narrative itself, in reaching out to the full stop of eternity.

If Milton became only more himself as a student of Spenser's poetic technique, the same may be said of him as a student of Spenserian doctrine. The dominantly conservative strain of Spenser's Protestantism was in many ways incompatible with Milton's radical Puritanism (Frye 1965:89–90). Yet Milton did not need to confront a living Spenser's disagreement, whereas he did have to accept gradual alienation from the views of his Presbyterian tutor, Thomas Young. Thus he was free to re-create within limits a figure of Spenser who could be adjusted as his own opinions developed. In the companion poems *L'Allegro* and *Il Penseroso*, and in the masque *Comus*, a fictional Spenser emerges who not only teaches lessons of technique but also represents a higher kind of poetry, a higher poetic vocation. Milton aspired to write a poetry 'doctrinal and exemplary to a Nation' (*Reason of Church-Government* Book 2, preface); in this project, he identified his precursor as Spenser, an identification that results in an interesting tension between the actual 'doctrine' of the Elizabethan poet and the necessary skewing of that doctrine to suit the precursory and pedagogic function accorded him by his Puritan disciple.

The fiction of Spenser as teacher is part of a much larger narrative fiction we recognize as literary history. In his poetic self-presentations, Milton places himself within a vernacular tradition just beginning to take shape. By the time he wrote his companion poems, the 'tradition' was sufficiently rich and diverse that he could make strong evaluative distinctions within it and even begin to suggest the lineal genealogies that Dryden later traced. Both *L'Allegro* and *Il Penseroso* contain passages in which particular poets and genres in the English tradition are associated with the thematic complementarities of mirth and melancholy. In *L'Allegro*, the masque, comedy, Jonson, and Shakespeare are grouped in what might be called an associative complex. Such complexes are very useful even though they are obviously reductive or hyperbolic. The praise of Shakespeare as 'fancy's child, / Warbl[ing] his native wood-notes wild' scarcely does justice to the author of the great tragedies; and when tragedy is mentioned in *Il Penseroso*, Shakespeare's name is not. Milton goes on to remark the rarity of good tragedy in his own, later age; whether or not he would have considered Shakespeare one of the rare exceptions, the point of Milton's fictionalized literary history is not accuracy or comprehensiveness. At this moment, he is far more concerned to organize the tradition in a way that corresponds to the poetic alternatives set out in the two poems. In *Il Penseroso*, he associates mystical Platonism, tragedy, and what we now describe as allegorical romance with two other English authors, unnamed but easily identifiable: Chaucer and Spenser. The link between the two poets is the unfinished *Squire's Tale*, which Spenser continued in *FQ* IV. In his first poetic portrait of Spenser, Milton sets the tone for all his future fictionalized representations: 'And if aught else, great bards beside, / In sage and solemn tunes have sung, / Of tourneys and of trophies hung; / Of forests, and enchantments drear, / Where more is meant than meets the ear' (116–20).

This oblique portrait of Spenser is just as reductive as that of Shakespeare, even if Milton happens to value the 'sage and solemn' over the 'fanciful.' Spenser's poetry is hardly exhausted by the qualities Milton singles out, but they help define the 'prophetic strain' he is embracing as constitutive of his own poetic identity. Milton never wrote an allegorical romance like *The Faerie Queene* though he long entertained the project of an Arthurian epic that might have led him to the Spenserian terrain of 'forests, and enchantments drear.' When he discarded that project, he had already learned what he needed from allegorical romance, a mode of ambiguity 'Where more is meant than meets the ear.' A remarkable example of that mode occurs in the line after the passage quoted above, 'Thus Night oft see me in thy pale career' (121); the hypermetric pentameter line produces an effect not unlike that of the Spenserian alexandrine. More is meant by this anomaly than meets the ear, if Milton means to evoke the whole world of Spenser's poetry by this slender echo of the Spenserian prosody. Milton was to achieve by such a technique of allusion the depth his teacher achieved in his 'darke conceit.'

Allusion is the most prominent figurative device in the most Spenserian of Milton's early works, *Comus*. In this masque, the fiction of Spenser's pedagogy is so strong that the pupil who writes himself into an impasse can call upon his teacher to show him the way to a solution. Given the Spenserian resonance of the masque's thematic concern with chastity, it is not at all surprising that Spenser appears (invoked under the pastoral cover name of Meliboeus) at the moment of crisis. He is linked directly to the theme in its more radical (if also finally unsatisfactory) form: 'the sage / And serious doctrine of Virginity' (785–6). The relation between virginity and chastity is oddly confused in *Comus*, but the Lady's easy equation of the two concepts may be partly responsible. Spenser is at least ambivalent about his virginal figures, including the Virgin Queen to whom he addresses *The Faerie Queene*. It is again a Miltonic reduction of Spenserian doctrine to invoke him in support of a fetishized virginity, which now stands as a synecdoche for the Puritan ethos Milton is contrasting to the aristocratic prodigality of Comus. If we remember the 'sage and solemn tunes' of *Il Penseroso* (as another prefiguration of the 'sage and serious' Spenser of *Areopagitica*), we will recognize that the discriminations of literary history in the companion poems have been carried over into the debate between Comus and the Lady. Comus is also the exemplar of a more 'allegro' Elizabethan poetic; according to the Lady, he delights in 'dear wit, and gay rhetoric' (789). *Comus* is very much indebted to that rhetoric and Spenser is invoked to assist Milton in the project of constructing a new, chaster poetry.

It is testimony to the peculiar honesty of Milton's genius that Spenser not only comes to aid him in his general poetic project but also tempers its undue severity. Both the Lady and Milton have invested too much in a virtue too narrowly conceived. When the Attendant Spirit returns, then, to *The Faerie Queene* for a solution to the Lady's state of fixation, he returns not to the house of Busirane (III xi-xii) but to a very brief passage on the death of a virgin named Sabrina, from whom the river Severn takes its name (II x 19). Milton resurrects her as a river goddess, a more fully realized Spenserian figure than she is in *The Faerie Queene*. He turns to her (and not to Amoret) precisely because she is committed to virginity even to death. She is the Lady's double, except that her sacrifice permits the Lady herself to move on to a more temperate chastity, presumably a married chastity. Milton is learning to use Spenser, not simply as a representative ego ideal of the 'sage and serious Poet,' but fully as a teacher, someone who can correct a disciple's work in the excesses of its novitiate.

The reduction of Spenser to a more Puritan figure than he could have been is thus complemented by a possible recognition on Milton's part of the difference between himself and his teacher. Yet when he refers in *Areopagitica* to 'our sage and serious Poet *Spencer*, whom I dare be known to think a better teacher then *Scotus* or *Aquinas*' (ed 1953–82, 2:516), he seems deliberately to recall the earlier epithets in a context that invites the reader to associate the argument of *FQ* II with the argument of Milton's own polemical tract. The virtue of temperance exemplified by Spenser's Guyon is proposed as the internal governor of an otherwise unrestricted practice of reading. Milton may well have misunderstood the episode of the house of Mammon to which he alludes in this passage, for he writes that Spenser brings Guyon 'with his palmer through the cave of Mammon' (2:516), whereas it is crucial to Spenser's scheme that Guyon's habit of temperance be tested by a solitary experience of temptation (see Sirluck 1950–1 and Milton ed 1953–82, 2:516n). The currents of significance swirl about this passage with more than usual depth and complexity, but it suffices to point out that Milton needs Spenser here in perhaps the same way that Guyon needs the Palmer – as a teacher. At the same time, Milton is beginning to envisage and even desire his independence from his 'better teacher.' His desire for independence is also intimated in connection with the better teachers of Reformation theology: 'we have lookt so long upon the blaze that *Zwinglius* and *Calvin* hath beacon'd up to us, that we are stark blind' (ed 1953–82, 2:550). These teachers will be superseded in the 'reforming of Reformation it self' (2:553).

It is perhaps worth recalling the contexts in which Spenser himself tends to use *sage*, the epithet so favored by Milton. In *FQ* II, it usually refers to the Palmer or to his 'counsell.' In the castle of Alma (which is organized around the alimentary conceit that dominates *Areopagitica*), there appears Diet, a figure not unlike the Palmer himself: 'He Steward was hight *Diet*; rype of age, / And in demeanure sober, and in counsell sage' (ix 27). Spenser may be punning here on his own name (a 'spenser' is a dispenser or steward; see Hamilton in *FQ* ed 1977:252), a pun further complicated by the etymology of *sage* (L *sapere* to be wise; to taste), a fact with which both Spenser and Milton were doubtless familiar and delighted. Milton seems to have conceived of Spenser as he sometimes, though not always, conceived of himself: as a figure of guidance and restraint in a labyrinth of confusion and temptation. The Palmer is to Guyon as Spenser is to Milton.

When Milton descends to hell and to Mammon in *Paradise Lost* I, however, he does not in any conspicuous fashion take the Palmer along; perhaps we may say that the Palmer has been internalized as an aspect of Milton's narrative voice. He has become the voice that warns the reader, as the Palmer might have warned Guyon: 'Let none admire / That riches grow in hell.' Milton openly appropriates Spenser's Mammon for his infernal *mise en scène*; and, indeed, his borrowing from *The Faerie Queene* is surprisingly direct. His description of mining and smelting (684–709) is lifted, sometimes nearly verbatim, from *FQ* II vii (17, 35–6). Like Spenser's Mammon, Milton's teaches mankind to rifle 'the bowels of their mother earth'; and like him, Milton himself digs out the ribs of gold from *The Faerie Queene*. Dryden remembered this figure when he wrote his *Discourse concerning Satire* (1693): 'I found in [Milton] a true sublimity, lofty thoughts, which were cloath'd with admirable *Grecisms*, and ancient words, which he had been digging from the Mines of *Chaucer*, and of *Spencer*' (*Sp All* p 297). In the context of literary history, the figure of 'mining' a predecessor's work marks a subtle but consequential revision of Renaissance theories of imitation. In *Paradise Lost*, the figure may not yet carry the burden of a fully self-conscious meditation on relations between poets; but because it so vigorously asserts its narrative priority over other works of literature, *Paradise Lost* necessarily raises the question of the status of allusion. If Milton is now writing a work greatly exceeding in ambition that of his teacher, he is no longer likely to invoke him as *Comus* invokes Meliboeus.

It is scarcely surprising that Milton's allusions to Spenser in *Paradise Lost* 2 emphasize the most conspicuous difference between his mode of narration and his teacher's. To return to Hazlitt's observation, nowhere is Milton closer to Spenser than in the episode of Sin and Death, and nowhere are we more impressed by how different are master and disciple. This impression is only more pronounced if the reader finds Sin and Death as objectionable as did Johnson in his 'Life of Milton.' Today, Milton's readers are disposed to find much more than an unfortunate deviation into allegory, especially since Sin is modeled on Spenser's Error. Milton emphasizes the allegorical status of his character by linking the name Sin with the concept of a sign: they 'called me Sin, and for a sign / Portentous held me' (*PL* 2.760–1). This gesture is all the more remarkable, for Milton might have de-emphasized the allegory in order to integrate his characters more easily into his cosmos of agents affirmed as really existing. We may ask once again, 'What is Milton learning from Spenser?' We may also ask, 'What is he *saying* he is learning from Spenser?' Milton's allegory is not so much a clumsy exercise in a mode to which he was unsuited as it is a virtuoso display of his having absorbed and exceeded the lessons of his teacher. The allusion intimates that equation of sin and error which underlies the Miltonic redaction of the Fall (as in Adam's 'That error now, which is become my crime' *PL* 9.1181). In Spenser, moreover, the figure of Error personifies the 'wandering' narrative structure of his poem. Milton is inviting us to compare the narrative mode of his poem with the fundamental equation by which Spenser's allegory is structured. The figure of Sin taps into that fundamental structure but draws from it not the elaborate allegorical machinery but *only* the structure: wandering. Beneath the tragedy of the Fall is the romance of wandering. The narrative of *Paradise Lost* is punctuated with that word; indeed it is the poem's great concluding period: 'with wandering steps and slow.' The effect is to add a certain kind of depth which evokes but does not exploit the semantic levels of allegory, a strategy which has been described as allegory 'ploughed back into the soil' (Fletcher 1971a:145).

The episode of Sin and Death thus functions as a complex *allusion* to Spenserian allegory. If Milton achieves an allegorical effect by means of allusion, he also takes over from Spenser the most nearly allegorical of that poet's local rhetorical devices, the etymological pun. In Milton, such puns are micro-allegories, as in the line describing the angels' response to the birth of Sin: 'amazement seized / All the host of heaven' (*PL* 2.758–9). They may as yet know only that Sin is a sign, but they have already suffered its effect: sin is error, wandering, the world become a maze.

All of the differences between Spenser and Milton cannot be attributed wholly to Milton's peculiar genius, to his choices as a poet. Since *The Faerie Queene* and *Paradise Lost* are in some sense the representative poems of their times, the difference between the branching polysemy of Spenser's allegory and Milton's characteristic modes of indirection is a measure of how much had changed in English social and political life. Spenser is distanced in the Restoration world of Milton's last works. Although Milton alludes by yet another temptation narrative to the house of Mammon in *Paradise Regained*, the allusion is strangely generalized and dispassionate. The figure of Spenser as teacher no longer suits the severity of this poem, which accepts no guide but the 'inward oracle / To all truth requisite for men to know' (*PR* 1.463–4). In the same way, *Samson Agonistes* accepts no guide but the 'intimate impulse' (223). It is perhaps the most paradoxical tribute to Milton's 'Original' that his disciple so internalized his teaching that he no longer recognized a Spenserian (or any other) origin for his internal pedagogue: 'And what he brings, what needs he elsewhere seek' (*PR* 4.325).

JOHN D. GUILLORY

Harold Bloom 1975 *A Map of Misreading* (New York); Cullen 1974; Angus Fletcher 1971; Fletcher 1971a *The Transcendental Masque: An Essay on Milton's 'Comus'* Ithaca, NY; Northrop Frye 1965 *The Return of Eden: Five Essays on Milton's Epics* (Toronto); Guillory 1983; Helgerson 1983; Hieatt 1975a; Maresca 1979; Richard Neuse 1978 'Milton and Spenser: The Virgilian Triad Revisited' *ELH* 45:606–39; Quilligan 1983; Ernest Sirluck 1950–1 'Milton Revises *The Faerie Queene*' *MP* 48:90–6; Wittreich 1975.

---

miniatures Miniature painting ('painting in little' or 'limning') was considered by many of Spenser's contemporaries to be the highest form of painting. Nicholas Hilliard, who first became prominent in the 1570s, gained international fame and was the foremost limner during Elizabeth's reign (rivaled only by Isaac Oliver in the 1590s). It is likely that Spenser met Hilliard or at least saw some of his miniatures, for both enjoyed the patronage of Leicester and Essex, and Hilliard painted most of the prominent figures of Elizabeth's court, including Leicester, Essex, Raleigh, Hatton, Cumberland, Penelope Rich, and – many times over – Elizabeth herself. When Spenser returned to England in 1589, Hilliard's reputation was at its peak and poets had begun to praise him. Spenser's record of his visit (*Colin Clout* 384–91) commends Sir Arthur Gorges, whose *Vannetyes* (mostly composed c 1584) includes a poem ('Sonnett' 75) calling on Hilliard to paint his mistress. Spenser may also have read Constable's sonnet in the Todd manuscript version of *Diana* (c 1590) that praises Hilliard's miniature of Constable's (and Sidney's) sonnet mistress: 'To Mr. Hilliard upon occasion of a picture he made of my Ladie Rich.'

Miniatures were exchanged between friends and lovers, especially in youth, as tokens of affection (even Elizabeth's limned image is more that of beloved mistress than royal queen). The limner was himself 'amorous': 'Howe then,' asks Hilliard, can 'the curious drawer wach, and as it [were] catch thosse lovely graces wittye smilings, and thosse stolne glances which sudainely like light[n]ing passe and another Countenance taketh place except hee behould, and very well noate, and Conceit to lyke' (ed 1983:23). The limner, seeking to catch the intimacy of love, focused usually on the face, shoulders, and sometimes the hands of the loved one. (Full-length miniatures, which began to appear in the 1590s, foretold the form's decline.) The limner, however, caught this intimacy of love through an ostentatious and idealizing artifice that hid as much as it revealed. True to the miniature's roots in illuminated manuscript painting and goldsmithing, Hilliard painted in the fresh primary colors of flowers and gems, opposed shadowing (which 'smutted' the purity of colors), and extolled 'the truth of lyne' (ed 1983:29, 28). The decorative effect of the bright colors and calligraphic style was further heightened by lavish application of gold (burnished like a metal rather than simply painted on the vellum), and by imitation in relief of the actual jewels and textures of the sitter's apparel. The net result was a rich, delicate, jewel-like image that complemented the sugar candy and perfume often added to limning colors. Hilliard's miniature of an *Unknown Lady* indicates his formalized ornamental style. Minutely drawn curls and a complexly patterned ruff frame the lady's face in the shape of a heart, while the design of her ruff extends, metamorphosed, into the decorative tulips on her bodice and the looping gold thread on her sleeves. The ornament of self-display encircles and points to the lady's face within; but the unshadowed face itself remains plain, white, and nearly expressionless. Only the hint of a smile appears, creating a tantalizing effect.

(See **miniatures** Fig 1.)

The private self represented in Hilliard's ornament of self-display is suggested by the decorative leaves and buds painted on ladies' bodices, signifying secret, personal meaning; and especially in the late 1580s by a hand held over the heart or riddling mottos swirled in burnished gold leaf. Hilliard's masterpiece of this period, *Young Man among Roses*, is an early full-length, still small enough to be held in the hand, which displays the curling golden motto, *Dat poenas laudata fides*: 'Praised faith brings sufferings.' Beneath the decorative motto, thorny eglantine (emblem of chastity) curls around a lovesick courtier (possibly Essex), who leans against a tree. Little white roses are painted on the lover's black cloak, which is slung over one shoulder and covers most of his right hand, which in its turn covers his heart. What is decoratively represented is a mystery. The ornamental image and motto are only suggestive; full meaning remains as concealed as the lover's heart under his hand, his cloak, and the decorative eglantine.

(See **miniatures** Fig 2.)

The appearance at court, as early as the 1560s, of richly enameled gold lockets encasing miniatures confirms the idea that a miniature's private meaning is concealed as much as revealed by artifice. Like the limning itself, the ornamental lockets allowed the wearer to 'publish' personal feelings, to carry them into the public arena of the court while at the same time keeping them private and hidden. *Man against a Background of Flames* depicts such a lover. Standing in dishabille before gleaming flames, the youth reveals a gold, enameled locket which he presses to his heart, literally baring his burning passion. Symbolic of the inaccessibility of the private self is the playing card used to back the vellum of limnings: what lies behind the bared breast of this enflamed lover turns out to be not his burning heart but the ace of hearts.

(See **miniatures** Fig 3.)

Spenser's own sonnet sequence, *Amoretti*, exhibits the strongest connection between his poetry and Hilliard's miniatures. Elizabethan sonnets and miniatures flowered at almost the same time and belong to the same world: the private and passionate, yet also public and artificial world of the court and the love affairs within it. Like the miniatures, Spenser's love sonnets play the game of self-revelatory artifice. He gives them wholly to his lady in token of his sincere devotion to her, just as a lover would give his miniature. In sonnet 17, which specifically addresses the problem of painting a 'pourtraict' of his love, he voices Hilliard's aim to 'expresse the life of things indeed.' The artist must capture 'The sweet eye-glaunces, that like arrowes glide, / the charming smiles, that rob sence from the hart: / the lovely pleasance and the lofty pride.' Striving to represent verbally such brief intimacies, the poet, like the limner, focuses especially on his beloved's face, eyes, and often her hands. The sequence of sonnets as a whole constitutes a series of limnings of the two lovers: one brief, close-up image after another. As with Hilliard, love can be expressed only through ornament. The poet's rhetoric prettifies his loved one with the bright colors of 'pretious' gems (15) and 'fragrant flowres' (64). (These rich images seem naturally to burgeon into the ringing refrain of 'sweet' in 26 and 39, as well as the poet's description of his love as 'the worlds most ornament' in 53; cf 31 and 74.) '[S]weet is the Eglantine, but pricketh nere' (26) could be another motto for the *Roses* miniature. Hilliard's passionate *Flames* lover also finds his double in *Amoretti*'s conventional image of the lover burning in the flames of his passion: in 22, for instance, the poet declares that he will build an altar to his love 'and on the same my hart will sacrifise, / burning in flames of pure and chast desyre.'

The rhetoric of Spenser's sonnets mirrors the decorative patterning that characterizes Hilliard's truthful 'line.' The sonnets form stylized rhetorical patterns, modifying or elaborating a dominant rhetorical figure with others (as the anaphora of 26 – the repetition of *sweet* at the beginning of the first 7 lines – intertwines with *antitheton*, *epiphonema*, and *erotema*). Even more patterned is the rhyme scheme by which Spenser works his lines into a 'weave' (23) as intricate and delicate as the looping gold thread or the decorative lacework of Hilliard's *Unknown Lady*.

The poet, like the miniaturist, paints an 'ornament' of his sincere 'inward' love, and the result is a Hilliardesque sense of intimacy, of an 'Idea' of love. The lovers' true selves represented by the ornamental display – the public artifice of sonnet conventions – are never fully presented. This recalls the critical debate over whether certain sonnets describe 'real' or 'conventional' truths. The poet's rhetoric may allude to heartfelt emotions and real events (a separation, a quarrel, some calumny), but full meaning is hidden, wrapped in the very rhetoric that expresses it. Much as Hilliard developed a game of hiddenness, limning for his lovers secret golden mottos, Spenser secretively points to private meanings through the play of words, as perhaps in his hint at Elizabeth Boyle's family name (Nagle or Nangle) in his play on *angel* (61). Like the intimate glances of the limned lover, encircled by ornament and further enclosed within a bejeweled case, the poet's true love is protectively 'enchased' in the 'golden moniment' of his verse (82). 'Deepe in the closet of my parts entyre,' the poet declares, 'her worth is written with a golden quill' (85).

Patricia Fumerton

For Hilliard, see his *Treatise Concerning the Arte of Limning* ed R.K.R. Thornton and T.G.S. Cain (Ashington, Northumb 1981), also ed Arthur F. Kinney and Linda Bradley Salamon (Boston 1983); Erna Auerbach 1961 *Nicholas Hilliard* (London); Mary Edmond 1983 *Hilliard and Oliver: The Lives and Works of Two Great Miniaturists* (London); John Pope-Hennessy 1949 *A Lecture on Nicholas Hilliard* (London); Graham Reynolds 1947 *Nicholas Hilliard and Isaac Oliver: An Exhibition to Commemorate the 400th Anniversary of the Birth of Nicholas Hilliard* (London). For technique, see also Jim Murrell 1983 *The Way Howe to Lymne: Tudor Miniatures Observed* (London). For Hilliard and Sidney, with discussion of cultural setting, see Patricia Fumerton 1986 '"Secret" Arts: Elizabethan Miniatures and Sonnets' *Representations* 15:57–97. General studies of miniatures include 'Miniatures' in Mercer 1962; John Murdoch, et al 1981 *The English Miniature* (New Haven); Roy Strong and V.J. Murrell 1983 *Artists of the Tudor Court: The Portrait Miniature Rediscovered 1520–1620* (London), a catalogue of an exhibition; also three further works by Strong: Strong 1969 *The English Icon: Elizabethan and Jacobean Portraiture* (London), a catalogue of works including miniatures; Strong 1977, with treatment of historical setting; and Strong 1983 *The English Renaissance Miniature* (New York).

Mirabella (L or Ital *mira* + *bella* wonderfully beautiful) The proud, insolent beauty condemned by Cupid to wander 'through this worlds wyde wildernes' in penitential guise until she has 'sav'd so many, as [she] earst did slay' by her tyrannous cruelty (*FQ* VI vi 16–17, vii 27–viii 30). She is accompanied by the giant Disdain and the 'huge great foole' Scorn, who constantly humiliate and torment her with taunts and whipping. Yet Mirabella prevents the killing of her tormentors since she claims they are necessary to her own life; given freedom of choice and power over her own fortune by Arthur, she chooses to fulfill her penance.

Although she is 'of meane parentage and kindred base,' she has been accorded dignity, honor, and fame in Fairyland because of her admirable physical beauties, the 'wondrous giftes of natures grace.' She abuses her beauty by misjudging the worth of those who love her, careless of their pain, insisting with stubbornness and hardness of heart upon her own liberty, and boasting of near-divine power over life and death. Her arrogance provokes the laughter of 'the Gods, that mortall follies vew,' and leads to her arraignment before the court of Cupid, held 'each Saint Valentide' (vii 32; for the literary tradition of Cupid's court, see E.B. Fowler 1921). When arrested, Mirabella stubbornly refuses to answer for her rebellion against love, thereby acknowledging her guilt; but after judgment is passed, she falls down 'with humble awe' and cries for mercy.

The story of Mirabella combines popular aspects of medieval and Renaissance poetry. Her psychological attributes are personified in the manner of the *Romance of the Rose*, the court and judgment of Cupid recall Chaucer's *Parliament of Fowls* and Prologue to the *Legend of Good Women* as well as the pseudo-Chaucerian *Court of Love*, and Mirabella herself is like the 'Chaucerian' Belle Dame sans Mercy in whom 'is lost ... Al curtesy' (Chaucer ed 1894–7, 7:312). At the same time, she embodies the cruel lady of Elizabethan sonnets who 'lordeth in licentious blisse / of her freewill' (*Amoretti* 10). The successive vivid pictures that Spenser presents of Mirabella and her companions also associate the episode with emblem literature (vi 16; vii 27, 39–44; viii 22–4).

Although literary convention and artifice figure largely in the character of Mirabella, she remains psychologically true to life in ways dramatized by Shakespeare's 'Lady Disdain,' the Beatrice of *Much Ado about Nothing* (Potts 1958:40–1), and that other embodiment of a literary type, the scornful shepherdess Phoebe in *As You Like It*.

Thematically, the episode is central to *FQ* VI. Mirabella's baseness is reflected in her base deeds, since she lacks 'the gentle hart' which 'it selfe bewrayes, / In doing gentle deedes with franke delight.' Her selfishness denies the operation of grace; she loves 'her owne delight' (cf Narcissus) and does not understand 'That good should from us goe, then come in greater store' (x 24). Her rebellious and antisocial behavior is an example of ingratitude and injustice. Her self-love and pride oppose the care for others and lowly demeanor of courtesy.

Yet she herself is capable of salvation even though she has saved only two lovers in two years, a space of time in which earlier she had killed twenty-four. She recognizes justice and seeks mercy, feels compassion and contrition, and responds to the intervention of grace in the person of Arthur with a free acknowledgment of her continuing need for penance. Her converted state suggests the 'humble, lowly, penitent, and obedient heart,' ready to confess openly 'unto the throne of the heavenly grace,' but not yet absolved (*BCP* ed 1976:50). Her final words of courteous thanks to Arthur open the possibility that nature's 'plenteous dowre, / Of all her gifts' will not be wasted (Nelson 1963:287–8, Tonkin 1972:230n).

Judith M. Kennedy

The Mirror for Magistrates A work of composite authorship first issued in 1555, with another version in 1559. With the addition of Thomas Sackville's *Induction* in the 1563 edition, the *Mirror* achieved its permanent format, though not its final bulk, as a collection of verse monologues or 'tragedies' spoken by the ghosts of important historical figures. Unlike its predecessors – notably Boccaccio's *De casibus virorum illustrium*

(1355), and Lydgate's *Fall of Princes* (1431–8) to which it was conceived as a sequel – the *Mirror* selects its tragic figures only from English history. As its editor, William Baldwin, tells his readers in the 1559 preface, 'Howe [God] hath delt with sum of our countreymen your auncestors, for sundrye vices not yet left, this booke ... can shewe' (ed 1938:65). The number of tragic complaints was expanded through editions of 1571, 1574, 1578, 1587, and 1610. In each monologue, a character laments a fall from high to low degree and discusses its cause – sometimes fickle Fortune, as in the medieval analogues, but often moral deficiency, political misjudgment, or both. As a 'mirror,' the book as a whole is intended as a reminder, or warning, to the reader, much as the head of the pagan decapitated by Artegall is called 'a mirrour to all mighty men' (*FQ* v ii 19).

The *Mirror* is the first important literary work to liberate British history from the chronicles and to use it for the purposes generally applied to history at the time, specifically to show God's providential intervention in human affairs (see Campbell 1936). Its doctrine of tragedy goes beyond the medieval ideas of irrational Fortune and of retribution in the afterlife to include earthly retribution for sin. The nineteen poems of the 1559 edition may be divided into three groups: five tragedies of fate, fortune, or circumstance, twelve tragedies of divided responsibility, and two tragedies of retribution (Peery 1949). The variety suggests that the notions of tragedy and providential retribution are not entirely consistent in the work (Kiefer 1977).

The *Mirror* may have conditioned the reading public to read history partly with an eye to God's judgment, but its contribution to Spenser's concept of providence is probably not great. His ideas derive from more sophisticated sources (see *chronicles). The chronicle in *FQ* ii x is demonstrably influenced by the additions published by John Higgins in 1574 and Thomas Blenerhasset in 1578. Yet even in these additions, there is no doctrine of providence beyond the occasional visitation of God's wrath on individuals, whereas in Spenser it permeates the entire sweep of history.

The *Mirror* seems to have been a source for several episodes and figures in Spenser's poetry. In the chronicle of *FQ* ii, for example, it may have provided details of nomenclature, phrasing, and specific points of interpretation for Spenser's treatment of Locrine, Humber, Estrild, Sabrina, Madan, Bladud, Cordelia, Morgan, Donwallo, Brennus and Bellinus, Morindus, Nennius, 'Kimbeline' (ie, Cymbeline), Fulgent, Carausius, and Vortiger. Perhaps only for Cordelia and Fulgent, however, was it the chief source (Harper 1910).

Higgins' account of Cordelia apparently gave Spenser the idea for the major episode of *FQ* i ix, Redcrosse's confrontation with Despair. In this account, which interprets her fate as an admonition against suicide, the imprisoned Cordelia is visited by a wraith named Despair (or Dispayre) who urges self-destruction and offers her a choice of instruments of destruction and then a knife, with which he eventually kills her after obtaining her consent (see *Lear). In his chronicle, Spenser alters her death to hanging (ii x 32); but in Book i, he has Despair provide Redcrosse with 'swords, ropes, poison, fire,' and finally 'a dagger sharpe and keene' (ix 50–1). Despair's 'darkesome cave' and disorderly surroundings are highly suggestive of Higgins' setting for the temptation scene, a dark and filthy dungeon.

From the prose links that provide a framework for the tragedies in the 1578 additions to the *Mirror*, Spenser may have borrowed details for the castle of Alma: his descriptions of Eumnestes and Anamnestes correspond respectively to Blenerhasset's description of Memory as a wise but forgetful archivist and Inquisition as his diligent research assistant; both pairs gather up and present the materials of chronicle history (ii ix 58; see Mills 1968).

Sackville's *Induction*, which is generally considered the finest poetry in the *Mirror*, may have left its mark on *The Shepheardes Calender*. Similarities between its opening stanzas and the setting of *Januarye*, with the use in both poems of an extended analogy between a blasted, sterile landscape and the speaker's emotional state, strongly suggest Spenser's interest in Sackville's rhetoric and imagery, and perhaps also in his strongly alliterative line (Bradford 1974). Spenser addresses one of the dedicatory sonnets to *The Faerie Queene* to Sackville (Lord Buckhurst), praising his 'golden verse, worthy immortal fame.' Sackville may also be the poet complimented as Harpalus in *Colin Clout* 380–1.

The *Mirror* as a whole helped transmit to Elizabethans the tone, vocabulary, and, to some extent, the moral stance of the tradition deriving from Boccaccio's *De casibus*. Although these elements are too thoroughly diffused in Spenser to be individually traced, they occur generally in those works which stress the mutable and slippery nature of human affairs: from some of the early work represented in *Complaints*, through *The Shepheardes Calender* (esp *December*) and *The Faerie Queene* (where, eg, a miniature *Mirror* concludes the episode of the house of Pride in *FQ* i v 51–2, a passage replete with the formulaic language of 'wofull falles' and retributive justice), to Spenser's final treatment of the subject in the *Cantos of Mutabilitie*. JERRY LEATH MILLS

The standard editions are *Mirror for Magistrates* ed 1938, and *Parts Added to 'The Mirror for Magistrates'* 1946 ed Lily B. Campbell (Cambridge). *Parts Added* consists of the Higgins and Blenerhasset tragedies of pre-Saxon history. For a survey of criticism c 1936–78, see Jerry Leath Mills 1979 'Recent Studies in *A Mirror for Magistrates' ELR* 9:343–52. Important readings of the *Mirror* are Lily B. Campbell 1936 *Tudor Conceptions of History and Tragedy in 'A Mirror for Magistrates'* (Berkeley and Los Angeles); Farnham 1936; Frederick Kiefer 1977 'Fortune and Providence in the *Mirror for Magistrates' SP* 74:146–64; and William Peery 1949 'Tragic Retribution in the 1559 *Mirror for Magistrates' SP* 46:113–30. See also Alan T. Bradford 1974 'Mirrors of Mutability: Winter Landscapes in Tudor Poetry' *ELR* 4:3–39; Mills 1968 'A Source for Spenser's Anamnestes' *PQ* 47:137–9.

mirrors The widespread use in Elizabethan literature of the metaphor of the mirror is characterized by the variety and ingenuity with which conventions are combined to produce new effects. Ample evidence of Spenser's skill in this regard can be found in both *The Faerie Queene* and the minor poems (Grabes 1982 passim).

In *The Faerie Queene*, besides 'real' mirrors like Lucifera's 'mirrhour bright' (i iv 10), Merlin's magic looking glass (iii ii 18–21), and 'the fountaine shere' in which Narcissus views his face (44), we find metaphorical mirrors like the fair woman of high birth (Una, i vi 15; Belphoebe, ii iii 25), the human face (of Scudamour, iv v 45), the head of the slain Pollente (v ii 19), the 'curtesie' of the present age (vi proem 5), Elizabeth as 'Mirrour of grace and Majestie divine' (i proem 4; cf vi proem 6) – all of them conventional. The qualities of these mirrors are also conventional: the prevailing kind of courtesy is a flattering mirror letting brass appear as gold, the Queen's mind is a 'mirrour sheene,' and the splendor of 'great dame *Nature*' is so great that she can be seen only in an ontologically reduced form, 'like an image in a glass' (vii vii 6). What is quite original, though, is the shape of Merlin's mirror: being round and hollow, a 'glassie globe,' it 'seem'd a world of glas' (iii ii 18–21).

What mirrors show in *The Faerie Queene* is again largely conventional: to the proud Lucifera her own face, to Sylvanus the beauty of Una, to Braggadocchio Belphoebe's 'celestiall grace,' to King Ryence – as did the legendary mirror of Virgil in *The Seven Sages of Rome* lines 1955–2136 – the planned invasions and treasons threatening his kingdom from outside or inside (iii ii 21), and to Britomart her future lover and husband Artegall (i 8, ii 23–5). Nor are the traditional effects of mirror gazing neglected: the flattering mirror causes deception (vi proem 5) and the beautiful image in the mirror engenders love. Narcissus and proud Lucifera fall in love with themselves, Britomart with the 'comely knight' Artegall. The love-engendering mirror is therefore aptly called '*Venus* looking glas' (iii i 8). With this role in the story of Britomart and Artegall, Spenser gives the mirror a new and crucial function: it is only because Britomart has already seen Artegall in Merlin's mirror that she can later recognize him as her destined husband. This decisive role of mirror gazing for her future fate cannot be justified merely by recourse to the conventions of the magic mirror that reveals things distant, past, and future, of the mirror as young maiden's love oracle, and of the mirror of Venus engendering love. There has to be a higher, a divine design behind all this in a poem based on a providential world view: 'It was not, *Britomart*, thy wandring eye, / Glauncing unwares in charmed looking glas, / But the streight course of heavenly destiny, / Led with eternall providence, that has / Guided thy glaunce, to bring his will to pas' (III iii 24).

In *Amoretti* 7, the lover regards the eyes of his beloved as 'the myrrour of my mazed heart.' The phrase combines the notion of the eye as mirror of one's own heart with the more modish trope of the lover's reflection in the eye of the beloved. It further includes the convention that the lover's heart reflects the beloved and the medieval theory of vision in which the eye is said to reflect light-rays (thereby enabling the soul to form an image of the world). The beloved's eye is a mirror of the lover's heart because it sends forth burning arrows (both Cupid's darts and the light-rays of the Empedoclean theory of extramission) to inflame his heart. Effect reflects cause, cause effect; and the lover's heart is identifiable with the expression in the eyes of the beloved as she gazes at him.

Amoretti 45 affords an even more instructive example of Spenser's skill in using the mirror-metaphor conventions. The beautiful lady at her toilet glass, the lover's heart as a mirror of the beloved, the distorting glass of the passions – these are no more original poetically than the Petrarchan trope of the lady's looking glass as the lover's rival, the comparison (in Marot Elegy 16) between this looking glass and the mirror of the lover's heart, or the tarnishing of the mirror of the heart by the beloved's heartlessness (in Tasso *Rime* 2.24). Spenser combines these conventions to conclude with this powerful plea to his lady: 'But if your selfe in me ye playne will see, / remove the cause by which your fayre beames darkned be.' (On his use of mirroring sonnets, see **Amoretti*.)

Spenser does not always exploit the conventions he inherits. In *Colin Clout* 513, he only refers to Mansilia as 'mirrhor of feminitie'; and in *Epithalamion* 63–4, in urging the nymphs to behold their faces in the mirror of Mulla's water there is no suggestion of the myth of Narcissus. In *Hymne of Beautie*, however, he exploits a number of conventions. In lines 162–8, an image of divine beauty appears in the 'beauteous face[s]' of the 'faire Dames' – a Neoplatonic reflection that is then strengthened in lines 176–82 by mention of the light shed by the refined fire of love. The image of love and that of the fair countenance resemble one another as in juxtaposed mirrors: the beautiful face takes on the aspect of love itself, and love is revealed in the form of the lady's 'beauteous face.' The idea of the divine origin of love as transcendent beauty is linked with psychological insight into the state of being in love: beauty heightens love, and love makes the beloved seem yet more beautiful.

In lines 218–24, this phenomenon is used thematically once more in association with the mirror. Stimulated by the sight of his beloved's earthly beauty, the lover forms in his mind an image of heavenly beauty. The source of his delight is thus the product of his own amorous imagination: 'The mirrour of his owne thought [he] doth admyre.' In contrast to the conventional distorting glass of earthly passions, pure love does not generate a deceptive image or mere hallucination; on the contrary, it removes the distortion which divine beauty has been subjected to through 'fleshes frayle infection.' Similarly, in *Hymne of Love* 190–6, divine love, 'that sweet passion,' is said to make a 'mirrour of so heavenly light' of the 'fairer forme' arising out of the lover's subjective imagination. This form possesses an objective quality transcending the subjective and emotional.

In *Heavenly Beautie* 109–19, Spenser adapts the Pauline mirror of indirect knowledge of God (1 Cor 13.12). Not even the angels can behold directly the dazzling brightness of God's glory, let alone 'his creatures vile and base.' But God can be perceived obliquely through divine revelation (or through a glass darkly): in 'His truth, his love, his wisedome, and his blis, / His grace, his doome, his mercy and his might,' he offers daily 'th'image of his grace.' Spenser distances himself from the conventional doctrine in which the natural world or its human inhabitants (including, by the late sixteenth century, virtuous and beautiful women) function as a mirror of transcendent divinity.

The same conventional metaphor appears in *Teares of the Muses* 571–82 in combination with another: Elizabeth ('Divine *Elisa*') is a 'myrrour of her Makers majestie' not just because she is virtuous and beautiful but primarily because her status (as monarch by the grace of God) makes her an earthly image and exemplary mirror of his dominion. This latter convention derives from the *topoi* of praise (see Cain 1978:6–10), according to which monarchs, princes, and knights were termed mirrors.

Such areas of metaphoric usage may seem conspicuously elevated compared to *SC, Januarye* 19–24, where the barren ground of winter appears to Colin, the unhappily enamored shepherd, as a mirror of his emotional state. In fact, however, it is rare in English literature at this time (in contrast, perhaps, to the post-Romantic period) for a mirror metaphor to be applied to correspondences between psychological states and the superficies of the natural world. In *October* 91–4, too, the designating of ideal beauty as an 'immortall mirrhor' is the exception rather than the rule in Elizabethan literature, despite widespread familiarity with Neoplatonic thought. As in *Hymne of Beautie* and *Hymne of Love*, it is love which makes it possible to catch this glimpse of divine beauty. HERBERT GRABES

Herbert Grabes 1982 *The Mutable Glass: Mirror-Imagery in Titles and Texts of the Middle Ages and English Renaissance* tr Gordon Collier (Cambridge).

---

monarchy Spenser in his poetry assumes that rightful sovereigns rule by the grace of God. This is a traditional medieval view that was sharply reaffirmed in England after the Reformation and more particularly after the excommunication of Elizabeth in 1570 (see Figgis 1914, ch 5). Thus, Spenser rests his absolutist belief in a theory of divine right, exercised in an England seen as God's chosen nation. Elizabeth appears in most, if not all, of his poems, most notably in *The Shepheardes Calender*, *Colin Clout*, and *The Faerie Queene*, his great 'mirror for princes' which is an elaborate encomium on Elizabeth and her realm, and a repository of late Tudor commonplaces concerning monarchy (see Cain 1978). The poet celebrates the monarch by praising her race, country, parents, education, and parts (both physical attributes and moral qualities). From one point of view at least, this rhetorical scheme can be seen to govern the poem, though in a diffuse rather than formally schematic way. Spenser's ecstatic view of Elizabeth, present already in *SC, Aprill*, is fundamental to *The Faerie Queene*: the Virgin Queen is his muse, the 'holy Virgin' and 'Goddesse heavenly bright' of I proem 2 and 4, at once the Virgin Mary and the virgin Astraea. One suspects that for him the Queen embodied the Divine Feminine herself.

If we regard *The Faerie Queene* as monarchical panegyric or encomium, the preoccupation with race (L *gens*) accounts for the poem's Arthurian roots. As a Tudor, Elizabeth is Welsh and Arthur's descendant. Equally important is her supposed descent from the Ur-Briton, Brutus, great-grandson of Aeneas. As a Trojan-Roman by blood, she may lay claim not just to England and Wales but to the Roman empire itself. It is also carefully noted that Saxon blood flows in her veins. Elizabeth is, as monarchs ought to be, uniter and peace-bringer – hence the thematic and narrative importance of the histories and prophecies at II x and III iii. Other obviously epideictic elements include Una's revelation to Arthur of her own country and parentage (*patria et patres*) at I vii 43, which is significantly anticipated by Catholic Fidessa-Duessa's claim to imperial descent at ii 22; and the physical descriptions of the 'good' female characters, each of whom is to be understood allegorically as an aspect of Elizabeth. As well, and on a much larger scale, praise for the monarch is reflected in the virtues presented in the books of the poem. Although these virtues are directed to the 'gentleman or noble person,' they also, whether private or public, belong supremely to the monarch (on the necessity for virtue in rulers, see Aristotle *Politics* 3.2).

Within *The Faerie Queene*, then, is that familiar Renaissance ghost, the ideal prince (king, governor, magistrate) as perceived by Erasmus (*Institutio principis christiani*), Elyot (*The Boke Named the Governour*), James VI (*Basilikon doron*), Sidney (*Defence of Poetry*), and others: Christian above all (hence the poem opens with the Legend of Holiness), temperate (II), chaste (particularly for a Virgin Queen married to her realm: III), exemplar of friendship or *amicitia* (IV; see Elyot 2.11–12), just and merciful (V), and courteous (VI).

Also underlying *The Faerie Queene* is the general doctrine of the king's two bodies, the notion that the king, as an individual, is mortal and fallen, but as prince mystically partakes of the immortality of the divine and of the realm of which she or he is head. The Letter to Raleigh points to the significance of this doctrine for the poem: 'the Queene ... beareth two persons, the one of a most royall Queene or Empresse, the other of a most vertuous and beautifull Lady.' The latter is especially 'expresse[d] in Belphoebe.' It also informs other aspects of the poem. Thus Arthur, exemplar of grace, tutored by Merlin and described as a golden solar knight (I vii 29), suggests a magical, alchemical, and mystical view of monarchy that is supported by contemporary tradition and by other allusions in the poem, and not least by the ineffably bright and powerful Gloriana herself (Brooks-Davies 1983, ch I). Yet even Arthur is human, and in Books III and IV perhaps all too human. Some of his emblematic attributes are susceptible of a double interpretation consistent with the doctrine of the king's two bodies; the dragon on his helmet, 'dreadfull [and] hideous,' menacing and death-dealing yet also redemptive like the serpent in Fidelia's cup at X 13; and his helmet's plume 'Like to an Almond tree,' which recalls not only Aaron's budding almond of priesthood (Num 17.5–8) but also the almond as a symbol of old age (Geneva gloss on Eccles 12.5, 'the almonde tre shal florish': 'Their head shal be as white as the blossomes of an almonde tre'). If such ambiguities reflect Spenser's preoccupation with the doctrine of the immortal-yet-mortal monarch, they are probably also a response to the contemporary reality of a heavily cosmeticized and aging queen.

Perhaps more purely theoretical is the pairing of the chronicle of British monarchs in *FQ* II x with that of 'Elfin Emperours.' Since the first largely recounts fallibility and bloodshed (sparing only stanza 50 for the 'enwombing' of 'th'eternall Lord in fleshly slime'), and the second gives an idealized version of princely government devoted to imperial and religious reform (Yates 1948), we again seem to have a duality explicable in terms of the king's two bodies. Together they commend Elizabeth as the two-bodied immortal mortal, a symbolism supported by the setting in which the chronicles are read: Alma's castle, comprising both mortal and immortal elements (ix 22) is not just the castle of the body and spirit but an image of the body politic as well; and Alma, virginal and gracious, has iconographic affinities with Elizabeth.

It is in the figure of Britomart, however, that the nature of the king's two bodies is most elaborately unfolded. Britomart's tale, of the British maid who is also the British Mars, the woman disguised as the valorous male, tells of her education into her role as queen. But her disguise as a man, suggesting an androgyny or double nature paralleling that of Christ, makes her, too, a statement of the doctrine while also accommodating Elizabeth's own realization of the difficulties inherent in being a female prince ('I know I have the body but of a weak and feeble woman; but I have the heart and stomach of a king': Elizabeth to her troops at Tilbury, 9 August 1588). Yet Elizabeth rejoiced in and took advantage of those difficulties, so that in Britomart we have a compliment to Elizabeth as private woman as well as public ruler and, further, admiration for her manipulation of her gender into a factor of strength rather than weakness.

The Elizabethan reader would also have noticed allusions to the Accession Day tilts (I v 2–16, II ii 42, IV iii); to a familiar monarchical pageant motif in the river marriage (IV xi); to the cult of the Virgin Queen in its many manifestations in the Mercilla episode (V ix-x 4); to monarchical propaganda in the Lucifera episode (I iv-v) and Una's encounter with the lion (I iii; as an heraldic beast it is the emblem of Brutus, founder of Britain – hence Britomart's lion at III i 4). All of which is to repeat what readers have always known: Spenser's *Faerie Queene* is dedicated 'to the most high, mightie, and magnificent Empresse' Elizabeth and celebrates her monarchical power. Yet we should note the admission of hard unpalatable reality and disillusion in its last two books. In Book VI, we are reminded that one of the best ways of dealing with the problems of court life is to flee the court altogether. In Book V, Spenser clearly feels obliged to defend a just Elizabeth whose person and policies he is now distanced from and finds poetically repugnant. The description of her as embodiment of divinely ordained justice and mercy (Mercilla), with the martial sword of justice symbolically rusty, has moments of poetic and iconographic beauty; but in the actual trial of Duessa (Mary, Queen of Scots), Spenser has recourse to naive personifications and invective, while the remaining cantos of *FQ* V offer a thin allegorical defense of Elizabeth's foreign policy in the Low Countries, France, and Ireland, which is also a defense of the warrior aspect of monarchy. The mysterious aspect of monarchy disappears as he insists stridently on the absolute difference between his martial Protestant prince and those images of Catholic tyranny, the Souldan (viii) and Geryoneo (x-xi). STEVIE DAVIES AND DOUGLAS BROOKS-DAVIES

Aptekar 1969; Brooks-Davies 1983; Cain 1978; John Neville Figgis 1914 *The Divine Right of Kings* 2nd ed (Cambridge); Fletcher 1971; Gary R. Grund 1981 'The Queen's Two Bodies: Britomart and Spenser's *Faerie Queene*, Book III' *CahiersE* 20:11–33; Kantorowicz 1957; Northrop 1972–3; Wells 1983; Frances A. Yates 1948 'The Elfin Chronicle' *TLS* (3 July):373; Yates 1975.

Montemayor, Jorge de (c 1520–c 61) Author of the popular pastoral romance, the first in Spanish, *Los siete libros de la Diana* (1559?). In England (as in France and Germany), the 'Diana of Montemayor' included three distinct works: the original romance plus two independent continuations, the *Second Part of Diana* by Alonso Perez (1563) and *Diana enamorada* (*Enamored Diana*) by Gaspar Gil Polo (1564). An English translation of all three works was not published until 1598, although it was completed in 1583; and Spenser may have read the Spanish, as Sidney did, or one of the French translations. Shakespeare used it as a source for *Two Gentlemen of Verona*.

Of Spenser's works, *FQ* VI was the most obviously influenced by pastoral romance. Similarities with *Diana* have been noted, such as the figure of the shepherd-poet who suggests the author himself, and detailed parallels between the Pastorella-Calidore episode and the main story of Perez's continuation. Some broader concerns shared by both works are a highly conscious interest in the power of poetry, a strong sense of fortune's operation and the fragility of happiness, an examination of the nature of nobility, and a constant awareness of the importance of 'civill conversation,' that is, 'an honest commendable and vertuous kinde of living in the world' (Guazzo ed 1925, 1:56).

Similarities may also be found between *Diana* and Spenser's books of chastity and friendship. *Diana* presents 'not false shepherds, but real lovers,' and is primarily concerned with investigating 'the world of beauty and love ... especially the world of women in love' (Wardropper 1951:144). It celebrates chaste and faithful love, leading to 'the sacred bonds of chaste and lawfull mariage' (Montemayor ed 1968:189). A major destructive force in both courtship and marriage is jealousy. Among the many heroines in *Diana* are a martial maid seeking her beloved, like Britomart; a woman tormented by an unsuitable and jealous husband, like Hellenore; a maiden finding escape under water from an uncouth lover, like Florimell; and a woman who flees in scorn from her servant because she mistakes his attentions to another, like Belphoebe. Friendship is a major theme in *Diana*. In particular, the main story of Perez's continuation, which involves a quartet of related lovers and friends, suggests both the central legend of *FQ* IV and the story of Amyas and Placidas. Throughout *Diana*, rivers, springs, and fountains are important; but the most watery of the three parts is Gil Polo's, which has at its center the song of the river Turia which celebrates Spanish poets. The main content of this work is a celebration of marriage in festive mood. This confluence of image and theme may have moved Spenser in his choice of the marriage of Thames and Medway as the climax of *FQ* IV.

Gil Polo's song 'in memorie and joy of the new marriage between *Syrenus* and *Diana*' provides parallels in imagery and refrain to Spenser's *Epithalamion* (Montemayor ed 1968:378; see *Var* 8.485, 492, 494, 652–3). There are also parallels between *Amoretti* and the complaints of *Diana*'s heroes about the cruelty of their mistresses. In particular, the laments of Taurisus and Berardus, the not-too-serious suitors of *Diana enamorada*, suggest Spenser's amused treatment of the cruel-beauty theme (eg, *Amoretti* 10, 31, 49).

Spenser seems to have found himself very much at home in the *Diana*'s world of love and poetry, and to have borrowed from it with his customary eclecticism.

JUDITH M. KENNEDY

Jorge de Montemayor 1598 *'Diana' of George of Montemayor* tr B[artholomew] Yong (London); Montemayor 1968 *A Critical Edition of Yong's Translation of George of Montemayor's 'Diana' and Gil Polo's 'Enamoured Diana'* ed Judith M. Kennedy (Oxford). Edwin A. Greenlaw 1916 'Shakespeare's Pastorals' *SP* 13:122–54; T.P. Harrison 1930; Amadeu Solé-Leris 1980 *The Spanish Pastoral Novel* (Boston); Bruce W. Wardropper 1951 'The *Diana* of Montemayor: Revaluation and Interpretation' *SP* 48:126–44.

Morpheus In classical mythology, Morpheus, the god of dreams, so called because he shapes or fashions dreams, is the servant or son of Somnus, god of sleep (Ovid *Metamorphoses* 11.592–649); but Spenser, like Chaucer in *Book of the Duchess* 136–91, conflates the two.

The description of '*Morpheus* house' in *FQ* I i 39–41 may seem at first to be made up of disparate details gleaned from traditional accounts and arranged chiefly for ornamental purposes. The pleasingly somnolent atmosphere brought about by the 'trickling streame' and the 'murmuring winde' recall Ovid and Chaucer; however, the sleep enjoyed by Spenser's Morpheus is not nearly so sound as that accorded to Ovid's Somnus, and it becomes increasingly evident that the sound of gently trickling water is a danger signal (eg, at II v 30). The emphasis on the proximity of Morpheus' abode to water accords with Renaissance dream lore (the rising of humors to the brain being conducive to sleep); yet the god himself is 'As one then in a dreame, whose dryer braine / Is tost with troubled sights.' The Virgilian motif of the two gates of sleep is ominous, too: that the spirit sent by Archimago returns through 'the Yvorie dore' as does Aeneas on his return from the underworld (*Aeneid* 6.898) suggests that his 'fit false dreame' may be riddlingly prophetic as well. The spirit's difficulties in waking the god of sleep is an ironic touch evocative of Ovid and Statius (*Thebaid* 10.84–117). But Spenser's Morpheus does not command respect; there are no elaborate invocations of the kind addressed to Sleep in Latin epics (and later repeated by many sleepless Renaissance sonneteers) to ensure his assistance. Rather, Morpheus is ordered to provide a dream.

The significance of the Morpheus episode is suggested by an intricate system of internal cross-references. At I i 36, Redcrosse and Una are 'drownd in deadly sleepe' by a 'Sweet slombring deaw' reminiscent of the Lethean dew administered to Palinurus by Sleep before he drowns (*Aeneid* 5.854–6); subsequently, Morpheus is characterized as 'drowned deepe / In drowsie fit.' Similarly, the Wandering Wood, not 'perceable with power of any starre' (7; cf Statius *Thebaid* 10.85–6), anticipates the ensuing description of the house of Morpheus. At the threshold to the den of Error, Redcrosse recalls Ovid: 'his glistring armor made / A litle glooming light' (14) like Iris' illumination of the cave of Sleep as she enters it (*Met* 11.617–18).

This play on internal and external contexts makes Spenser's Morpheus a figure of the sleepy mind. Sleep is a dangerous state in which one is exposed to evil forces (36), and Morpheus, as supplier of false dreams, is a servant of Archimago, the arch dissembler (43). As a form of mental imprisonment, Sleep is treated punningly at iv 44, where Morpheus is said to have 'Arrested' the courtly company with his leaden mace. The danger of sleeping is shown in Book VI: while Arthur 'in silver slomber lay' (vii 19), he is almost the victim of Turpine's treachery; and while Serena 'in *Morpheus* bosome safe she lay' (viii 34), she is seized by cannibals. In his pastoral retreat, Meliboe boasts that 'all the night in silver sleepe I spend' (ix 22); later, however, his retreat is despoiled by Brigands and he is slain. Thus, the recurring use of the metaphor of being drowned in sleep points to the inherent risks of this unguarded condition of the will, though the exact nature of the danger may vary from one instance to another, and though sleep may also sometimes bring important revelations in dreams, as to Arthur (I ix 13–15) and Britomart (V vii 12–16), and be a positive complement to the fallen will.

Lars-Håkan Svensson

Mythographical discussion is found in Boccaccio *Genealogia* 1.31 and Conti *Mythologiae* 3.14. See also Anderson 1976:29–31; Brooks-Davies 1977:24–6; Cheney 1966:29–31; Cook 1890; Lotspeich 1932:82–3; I.G. MacCaffrey 1976:138–42; Nohrnberg 1976:122; Rose 1975:17–22; Svensson 1980:305–16.

---

morphology and syntax The study of a poet's morphology (internal structure and forms of words; grammatical form) and syntax (arrangement of words) must in present days be complicated by the use in literary criticism of these two grammatical terms (esp *syntax*) to refer to more inclusive stylistic concerns. An avoidance of the word *syntax* in discussing the relationship between sentence structure and poetic style (see Fenollosa 1962) has generally given way to the recognition that poetic syntax 'is wholly different from syntax as understood by logicians and grammarians' (see Davie 1955:148). This recognition may be helpful for a fuller understanding of Spenser's style.

More narrowly technical, Sugden's detailed account (1936) of the grammar of *The Faerie Queene* remains essential reading. Yet serious research needs to be done to update his work with precise statistical analysis. There is no point in re-presenting Sugden's ample observations in a brief article; however, his general conclusions may be summed up. The widely accepted assertion is that Spenser's grammar (form and syntax) conforms generally to standard Elizabethan usage. His morphology, as his diction, is rhetorically determined, but manifests a common tradition that began with Skelton and Barclay. Nonetheless, Spenser's distinctiveness is 'conditioned' by his theories of diction, by his eagerness to enrich the language of poetry, by the constraints of his subject matter, and by the demands of his stanza and rhyme scheme. The archaism of *The Faerie Queene* resides 'to some extent in the inflections, and only slightly in the syntax.' Spenser's 'conformity' to the usage 'of the day' may be further defined by (1) his differences from Shakespeare: Spenser is 'careful of his grammar,' rarely makes errors of case and concord. His grammar is more formal, more learned, more self-conscious; (2) Spenser's differences from Milton, 'with whom he has, oversimply, been linked as a baroque writer' (Emma 1964).

However, as Milton's 'Latinity' has been probed (Carey and Fowler in Milton ed 1968), so are Spenser's dialectal and archaic forms being reassessed. (H.S.V. Jones sounded a cautious note in 1930 in Ch 32 on 'Language and Versification' *passim*, but scholarship has moved slowly here.) Spenser could be as plain as a pikestaff: his *Vewe of Ireland* is 'written in very competent prose' (p 377); Strang calls it 'classically correct sixteenth-century English' (in *language, above). Any archaism of inflection and syntax, then, may fairly be understood as factors in Spenser's deliberately styled poems – not unintended aberrations, nor yet merely 'spontaneous' educated Elizabethan English.

Jonson's famous comment that Spenser 'writ no Language' was to do with vocabulary. As to syntax, what is now said of Milton's sentence structure in *Paradise Lost* may be said of Spenser's in *The Faerie Queene*: 'It is a native English coordinate structure, loose rather than periodic, paratactic rather than syntactic. The verse paragraphs [stanzas, in Spenser's case] do not keep us waiting, perplexed, for the sense, or force us to traverse a single long syntactic line of subordinated parts. Instead, the sense is "diffused throughout a larger block of words" than is common' (Milton ed 1968:431, Prince 1954:122).

Archaism of syntax (like Latinism) rarely inhibits such diffusion in *The Faerie Queene*. Sugden (1936:13) asserts that 'the following ... sounds quite as Latinate as anything in *Paradise Lost*: "Him therefore now the object of his spight / And deadly feud he makes: him to offend / By forged treason, or by open fight / He seekes" [*FQ* II i 3].' But this is to beg the question. We should remember that the word order of Milton's time (let alone Spenser's) had a very much greater freedom than is allowed for us (see Milton ed 1968:431, Emma 1964:140–6).

Furthermore, the object-subject-verb structure in this example has its own peculiar poetic justification that has more to do with rhetoric than with any 'rules' of English grammar. And we need not refer to the Latin *alius ... alius/alter ... alter* for a model of the distributive use of *some* (eg, *FQ* IV x 43; see Sugden 1936:47), for this structure based upon the naturalized figures of *anaphora* and *ploce* has a lively native function in, for example, Chaucer's *Knight's Tale*.

E.K. praises Spenser's syntax: 'Now for the knitting of sentences, whych they call the joynts and members therof ... what in most English wryters useth to be loose, and ... ungyrt, in this Authour is well grounded, finely framed, and strongly trussed up together' (Epistle to Harvey). There are times when this is not true in *The Faerie Queene*.

Emma often demonstrates a 'looseness' (the term is not used pejoratively) in Spenser, compared with Donne or Milton. Sugden shows how periphrastic *do/did* plus infinitive to make forms for the present and preterite can lead to a 'loose and free construction with no special emphasis' and is often used merely for the sake of meter or rhyme (1936:146–7). But are not meter and rhyme the poet's tools? The most sophisticated statistical analysis will surely confirm the reader's impression of Spenser's pervasive use of the figure of form that Puttenham called *surpluse*, that is, the addition of syllables to fill out the verse: the prefixes *a-*, *be-*, *dis-*, *em-*, *en-*, *for-*, *fore-*, *mis-*; the formative suffixes *-al*, *-ance/-aunce*, *-full*, *-head*, *-ish*, *-ment*, *-y*; the inflexional suffixes *-en*, *-ne*, *-and/-ant*. But we cannot, given sixteenth-century poetics, dismiss these forms as merely decorative and not functional.

Strang contrasts Spenser of the *Vewe* with Spenser of *The Faerie Queene*: 'he is the poet of universal grammar, and he keeps constantly before the reader, who is also the hearer, the accidentalness of any surface structure chosen as the realization of the underlying forms' (in *language). The statistically chartable features of Spenser's morphology and syntax simply instigate an understanding of, and do not identify, the poet's meaning. We may cite Hollander's interpretation of the syntax of *FQ* II xii 71: it represents 'the total undermining of modes of recognition ... through which the Bower's ultimately deadly attractiveness is manifested' (1971:238). On the contrary (one may argue and show), Spenser's syntax, expressing the figure *conformatio*, precisely identifies and intensifies Guyon's recognition of the particular canker in his sensibility. That is, the distinction no longer holds which obtained between his 'wonder' and 'delight' at stanza 53.

Such differences of interpretation will always attend the 'accidentalness' of Spenser's grammatical structures if we perceive his morphology and syntax as chosen surface structures. This seems to be a useful approach to the poet's work that calls now for critical rigor. AVRIL BRUTEN

Donald Davie 1955 *Articulate Energy: An Inquiry into the Syntax of English Poetry* (London); Ronald David Emma 1964 *Milton's Grammar* (The Hague); Ernest Fenollosa 1962 'The Chinese Written Character as a Medium for Poetry' in *Prose Keys to Modern Poetry* ed Karl Shapiro (New York) pp 136–55; Prince 1954; *FQ* ed 1977; Sugden 1936.

Mother Hubberds Tale. See ***Complaints: Prosopopoia, or Mother Hubberds Tale***

Muiopotmos. See ***Complaints: Muiopotmos, or The Fate of the Butterflie***

Munera, Pollente Artegall's encounter with Munera and Pollente (*FQ* v ii 4–28) deals with the evils of aristocratic violence in contrast to the plebeian challenge to distributive justice in the second half of the canto (29–54). The combination of Pollente (L 'powerful'), a mighty warrior who has 'great Lordships got and goodly farmes, / Through strong oppression of his powre extort,' his servant whose livery is a shaven head, and his daughter Munera (L 'rewards, gifts'), suggests particularly the evils of 'livery and maintenance' (the wrongful upkeep and protection from law of armed retainers by a powerful magnate) against which the Tudors repeatedly legislated. An example in the 1570s of the oppression and corruption of justice to which this practice led is that of Lord Chandos, who 'used armed retainers with guns at the ready to frighten off the under-sheriff, protected servants of his who robbed men on the highway ... and put in a high constable of the shire who used his office to levy blackmail on the peasantry' (Stone 1965:229–30).

In speaking of 'farmes' (a rent or tax, as well as land leased for cultivation), oppression and extortion, polling and pilling (*'lit.* to make bare of hair and skin too: to ruin by depredation and extortion' *OED*), Spenser echoes contemporary commentators. John Christopherson, for example, acknowledges that some 'be sore oppressed with taxes, and tributes, with pollinge and pilling, with rentes raised and with pastures enclosed' (*An Exhortation ... to Take Hede ... of Rebellion* 1554: sigs D5r). The shaven scalp of Pollente's groom (named Guizor at vi 33) denotes not only his bondage but also his function: 'Which pols and pils the poore in piteous wize' (ii 6).

Pollente's tyranny, like Lord Chandos', extends to both rich and poor. The importance of the social criticism in this episode is suggested by its juxtaposition with what follows. It was widely recognized that a major cause of the rebellion of the poor was their oppression by the rich. Robert Crowley attributes to the poor the claim that 'Cormerauntes, gredye gulles; yea, men that would eate up menne, women and chyldren, are the causes of Sedition!' (*The Way to Wealth* 1550; ed 1872:132). Artegall's response to such a claim on the Giant's part will be as orthodox as Christopherson's: 'such perhappes have cause to complaine, but no cause at all to make rebellion' (sig D5r). First, however, he has himself corrected the abuse by killing Guizor, Pollente, and Munera, burning their 'mucky pelfe' and casting the ashes into the brook, upstream from the point where he will meet the Giant.

The narrative of Artegall's encounter with Pollente is modeled on Ariosto's account of the Saracen Rodomonte, who forces travelers to fight with him for passage over a narrow bridge (*Orlando furioso* 29, 31, 35), though contemporary abuses of right-of-way and toll bridges by the overmighty provide a more immediate context (Neff 1934, Knight 1970). Milton may be recalling the detail when he refers in *Areopagitica* to 'a narrow bridge of licencing where the challenger should passe' (ed 1953–82, 2:562; see Hamilton in *FQ* ed 1977 on ii 6). Interestingly, in 1648 the writer of *The Faerie Leveller* interpreted the whole episode as illustrating the 'arbitrary oppressive power' of the Houses of Parliament (Pollente) used against King Charles (Artegall) (see *Sp All* pp 223–4).

Munera is based on Lady Mede in Langland's *Piers Plowman* (2.8–17). Her golden hands and her role recall Psalm 26.10, quoted by Langland in relation to Mede (3.249): 'In quorum manibus iniquitates sunt, dextera eorum repleta est muneribus' ('In whose hands is wickednesse, and their right hand is full of bribes'). In razing their castle, Artegall realizes the promise of Job 15.34: 'fyre shal devoure the houses of bribes' (Dunseath 1968:94).

This episode is linked to the story of Dolon (vi 19–40), whose son Guizor is identified as Pollente's groom (the name Guizor suggests 'the disguise of treachery'; see Hamilton in *FQ* ed 1977 on vi 33). Escaping Dolon's treachery which also involves a trapdoor, Britomart comes to Pollente's bridge where she defeats Dolon's two remaining sons (36–40). The names and actions of Pollente and Dolon (L 'guile, deceit') suggest that the two episodes together exemplify the commonplace that injustice is perpetrated 'by two meanes ... by violence or by fraude' (Elyot ed 1883, 2:214), though the distribution is not simple. In Pollente's violence there is deceit (the trapdoor in his bridge), while Dolon's fraud is accompanied by the violence of his sons.

ELIZABETH HEALE

Muses In Greek and Roman antiquity, the Muses are sister goddesses who preside over poetry, music, and the other arts. Spenser follows Hesiod, most classical poets, and Renaissance mythographers in designating them as daughters of Memory and Jove (*SC, June* 66; *Time* 368–9; *FQ* IV xi 10, VII vii 1). Elsewhere, however (perhaps following Conti *Mythologiae* 4.10), he calls them daughters of Memory and Apollo (*SC, Aprill* 41 gloss; *Teares* 2; *FQ* I xi 5, III iii 4; *Epithalamion* 121). Nine in number in *Teares of the Muses*, they mourn the decline of their arts. Spenser's order of presentation, with Clio first as 'eldest Sister of the crew' (53), may have been affected by Hesiod's in *Theogony* 77–9 or by that found in the mnemonic epigram 'De musarum inventis,' attributed to Virgil and included in medieval and Renaissance editions of his works (see esp the Dumaeus Virgil [Antwerp 1542], said to have been used by Spenser; see also Lotspeich 1935, Gregory 1974, 1975–6). Specific Muses are traditionally associated with particular genres of poetry (Melpomene with tragedy, Thalia with comedy, Clio with history, Calliope with epic poetry), specific arts (Thalia with geometry or agriculture, Urania with astronomy, Polyhymnia with grammar), or the invention of musical instruments (Euterpe the flute, Terpsichore the lyre or psaltery). These associations may be traced either to the verses of 'De musarum inventis' or to certain Renaissance mythographers or lexicographers (eg, Boccaccio *Genealogia*, Cartari *Le imagini de i dei de gli antichi*, Conti *Mythologiae*, Giraldi *De deis gentium*, Linocier *Mythologiae musarum libellus*, C. Estienne *Dictionarium*, Thomas Cooper *Thesaurus*). Spenser describes his

Muses singing and playing on musical instruments (violins in *Apr* 103, lutes and tambourins in *June* 59). In *Teares*, he makes them the source of humane learning as the 'brood of blessed Sapience' (72); and he alludes to Thalia's governance over comedy, Melpomene's over tragedy, Erato's over love poetry, and Urania's over knowledge of the heavens.

The Muses are invoked by Spenser to assist in poetic composition, sometimes together (eg, *Apr* 41–3, *FQ* VI proem 2, *Hymne of Love* 29, *Epith* 11), sometimes separately by name or merely as 'Muse.' Specific Muses invoked are Melpomene as 'mournefulst Muse' (*Nov* 53) and probably as 'Tragick Muse' (*Muiopotmos* 413); Clio in order to recount Elizabeth's ancestry (*FQ* III iii 4); and Calliope, asked to help Clio recount the story of Arlo Hill (VII vi 37).

The unnamed Muse of *FQ* I proem 2, invoked as 'holy Virgin chiefe of nine' and called upon also in I xi 5–6 and in IV xi 10, may be either Clio or Calliope. (The Muse cited in VII vii 1 as the 'greater Muse' may also be one of these two or possibly Urania, since she is urged to tell of heavenly things.) Clio, named first in the list of Muses in *Teares* and appealed to by name in Book III, would be an appropriate patroness for *The Faerie Queene* because, as the mythographers point out, her name in Greek (*kleio*) means 'fame' or 'glory'; hence she is a fitting guardian for Cleopolis, a celebrant of noble deeds and keeper of written records (I proem 2). Calliope, often designated in antiquity and the Renaissance as head of the Muses and so named by Spenser in *Aprill* 100, *June* 57, and in E.K.'s glosses, would also be an appropriate patroness because she is the Muse of epic poetry whom Virgil invokes in the *Aeneid*, and because Spenser describes her in *Teares* as the foremost singer of deeds of heroes.

For Spenser, the Muses are sacred goddesses who inspire sweetness and delight in human beings, mediate between the divine and human, grant vision to poets, and guard learning and the arts by keeping the immortal record which preserves famous deeds. Following such poets as Hesiod, Callimachus, Ovid, and Propertius, he describes them as nature deities who inhabit secluded woods, mountains, and springs. He associates them most frequently with Parnassus and the Castalian spring, although he also refers to their association with Helicon, where Hesiod said he first met them (*Theogony* 22–3). He even names the Muses '*Heliconian* maides,' a term used by Pindar (*Isthmian Odes* 8.58), and alludes to the nonclassical account of their rivalry with the sirens (*FQ* II xii 31). He associates Pegasus with them and says that those seeking immortality 'on *Pegasus* must ride, / And with sweete Poets verse be glorifide' (*Time* 426–7). Spenser pictures the Muses in their pastoral haunts, singing, dancing, and playing on instruments; as 'Ladies of delight' or 'Sweete Ladie Muses' (*Mother Hubberd* 761), they give joy to mortals. They are closely associated with nymphs, fairies, and the Graces, for whom they provide song and instrumental music for dance (see *Apr*, *June*).

Spenser seems to distinguish between rustic muses associated with pastoral poetry and the sacred muse or muses associated with epic. The term *sacred* is consistently employed in *The Faerie Queene*, where the muse is approached with reverential awe and called holy or sacred (I proem 2, I xi 5, VI proem 2). Moreover, the poet speaks more fully in these places than elsewhere of his relation to his muse. He asks her in Book I to help his 'weake wit' and sharpen his 'dull tong,' and in Book VI to guide him 'where never foote did use, / Ne none can find, but who was taught them by the Muse.' In Book VII, Spenser addresses the 'greater Muse' as his instructress in things heavenly, the one who upholds his poetic flight and grants him insight into things unknowable without her. His stance toward his muse resembles that of the early Greek poets, especially Hesiod and Pindar. The concept of the muse as a divine intermediary and revealer of secret knowledge goes back to the Greek and Roman heroic tradition (Homer, Virgil, Hesiod, Pindar), and to the French poet du Bartas, whom Spenser praises in the Envoy to *Ruines of Rome* for his devotion to the heavenly muse.

The Muses also function as guardians of culture: the Greeks attributed the invention of letters to Polyhymnia or Calliope (Giraldi *De Musis syntagma*). Spenser attaches the epithet 'learned' to the Muses (*FQ* I x 54, *Epith* 1) and praises them for warding off ignorance from the world and guarding the monuments of time. Clio and her sisters chastise the foes of learning in *Teares* and tell how in former ages they recorded the noble deeds of men. The unnamed Muse of *The Faerie Queene* keeps the 'antique rolles' in her 'everlasting scryne' (I proem 2) and preserves the 'records of antiquitie' (IV xi 10); and all the Muses care for the treasures of learning, which excel all worldly riches (VI proem 2). Actively spurring men on to those noble deeds she will memorialize, the Muse inspires 'martiall troupes' and 'harts of great Heroes' (I xi 6); she preserves those deeds that would die 'how ever noblie donne' (*Time* 400) by creating through poetry a monument that outlasts the pyramids of princes. Spenser here echoes a notion common among poets from Pindar, Horace, Propertius, and Virgil to Ronsard, Desportes, and Sidney: that the Muses alone grant true immortality and lasting happiness to men; and he warns that whoever scorns the Muse will 'Nor alive, nor dead be of the Muse adorned' (455).

The term *muse* is frequently used by Spenser to signify poetic talent or inspiration, and even as a synonym for poet or poetry. He speaks of sporting his muse (*Amoretti* 80) or waking a 'sleepie *Muse*' (*CCCHA* 48); he speaks of his muse being hoarse (*Dec* 140) and of his 'trembling *Muse*' flying low (*CCCHA* 420). He designates pastoral poetry as the 'rustick muse' (*Daphnaïda* 231). He calls the poets and writers who inhabit Cambridge 'many a gentle Muse, and many a learned wit' (*FQ* IV xi 34), and, referring to future poets, says 'some brave muse may sing / To ages following' (*Prothalamion* 159–60). STELLA P. REVARD

E.R. Gregory, Jr 1974 'Spenser's Muse and the Dumaeus *Vergil*' *SpN* 5.2:10–11; Gregory 1975–6 'More about Spenser and "De Mvsarvm Inventis"' *AN&Q* 14:67–71; Lotspeich 1935; Patrick O'Dyer Spurgeon 1970 'Spenser's Muses' *RenP 1969* pp 15–23; Starnes 1942. See also Lotspeich 1932:83–8; 'The Muse of the *Faerie Queene*' in *Var* 1:506–15, a summary of articles by F.M. Padelford (1930) and J.W. Bennett (1932).

Muses, The Teares of the. See ***Complaints: The Teares of the Muses***

music For poetry of the English Renaissance, *music* can refer to musical settings of texts, to instrumental music incidental to their presentation (plays, masques, etc), or to the effects of musical conventions and structures in texts written specifically for musical settings (odes, dialogues, etc). Or music in poetry can mean literal ('practical' in Elizabethan usage) vocal or instrumental music occurring in fiction as the subject matter of didactic verse, or as a realm of human activity and technology providing figures and conceits for poetic language. General cosmic order, music's rhetorical and curative powers, the correspondences and extended senses of *harmony*, and so forth, which came under the concerns of 'speculative music' (*musica humana*, *musica mundana*) are another musical matter, sometimes connected in poetry with instances of practical music, according to a fairly conventional paradigm. Classical mythology and biblical anecdotes and types (the figure of David in particular) provided another system of musical topics. Finally, there is the conventionalized figure, descending from classical antiquity, of 'music' as a trope for 'poetry,' whether epical chanting ('*cano*,' says Quintilian, 'is a synonym for *canto*, and *canto* for *dico*') or pastoral. Terms such as *lyre*, *pipe*, *harp* must be understood in many contexts as more or less standard emblems of poetic genres. (Thus, in *FQ* I proem 1, 'For trumpets sterne to chaunge mine Oaten reeds' signals a change from pastoral to epic.)

We have no evidence of Spenser's actual accomplishments in practical music, aside from concluding that he probably could not have escaped the 'singing and playing' which Richard Mulcaster, following his own recommendation, must have included in the curriculum at Merchant Taylors' School. Spenser's wordplay on such technical terms as *meane* and *base* (passim) – where the nonmusical senses of the two words are more or less synonymous, the musical ones differentiated – or *divide* (*FQ* III i 40), or the celebrated *minime* (VI x 28), or his use of words like *tenor*, *treble*, *descant*, *consort*, do not necessarily indicate more than minimal musical competence. Sometimes there is an absence of possible play on a musical sense of a word: the figure of Concord in *FQ* IV x is free of musical associations.

Of other possibly musical matters – the so-called music of poetic scheme, prosodic effect, echoic texture – nothing will be said here, all of these questions being more usefully considered without the distractions of musical metaphor (see *echo, *song).

To start with the relatively simple matter of musical settings of Spenser, Catherine Ing (1951:209–19) observes that Spenser's lyrical work was antagonistic to the addition of music. This is debatable, although between 1588 and 1632 we do find sixteen settings each of poems by Sidney or Fulke Greville compared to five madrigals made from Spenserian texts. The earliest of these are two six-part madrigals from George Kirbye's collection of 1597; numbers 22 and 23 set two strophes of Colin's lament for Dido (*SC, November* 53–62, beginning 'Up then *Melpomene*,' and 173–82, 'Why wayle we then?'). In the latter line, *then* is changed to *thus* in Kirbye's text, the better to integrate the two widely separated strophes as a sequential pair of madrigals, one with the 'O carefull verse' refrain, the second with 'O joyfull verse.' A nice bit of 'word-painting' occurs when, after a strongly polyphonic opening section, the voices line up homophonically in chordal fashion on the words 'And is enstalled nowe in heavens hight.' Richard Carlton set *FQ* V viii 1–2 as a pair of madrigals (numbers 9–10 in his 1601 collection), although the second of these makes far better sense sung in sequence with the first than separately. Carlton's settings, despite their date, are of the older-fashioned sort that Spenser himself might have known.

The important composer Orlando Gibbons set, with great sensitivity, *FQ* III i 49 as two separate madrigals, numbers 10 and 11 in his 1612 collection (a work dedicated to Sir Christopher Hatton, who probably selected the texts). Most interesting is Henry Lawes' declamatory setting of *Amoretti* 8 (deleting lines 9–12) for solo voice and continuo, quite unexpected among all the Cavalier lyrics that usually provided his song texts (BL, Add Ms 53723, probably dating from the later 1630s or 1640s). Perhaps his friend Milton's love of Spenser influenced Lawes' unusual choice here.

In the eighteenth century, we can find three bits of Spenser among the potpourri of texts that Newburgh Hamilton assembled from Milton and elsewhere for Handel's *Occasional Oratorio* (1714). In Part I, a bass aria sets *Hymne of Heavenly Beautie* 141–7 and 155–61 as two sequential strophes; in Part 2, the first four lines of *FQ* I viii 1 (with the first of these changed to 'How great and many perils do enfold'), and *Teares of the Muses* 115–20 (with 'the air so wide' in line 118) are both set as soprano arias. The well-known London musician Maurice Greene (1695–1755) published a book of solo settings of 25 of the *Amoretti* in 1739, remarking in a preface on their 'Simplicity and easy elegance.' The sonnets chosen, and their order, represent a sophisticated kind of anthologizing, as well as an attention to what would provide texts for generic sorts of aria. The order is as follows (omitting the 1–25 numbering of the settings in Greene's score): *Amoretti* 80(!), 1, 7, 15, 18, 19, 25, 28, 34, 37, 38, 39, 40, 42, 47, 49, 56, 59, 63, 67, 70, 75, 78, 86, 88.

The most important modern settings of Spenserian texts have been by Benjamin Britten in his *Spring Symphony* op 44 (1949), where *Amoretti* 19 appears among texts by Barnfield, Peele, Nashe, Herrick, Milton, Vaughan, Beaumont and Fletcher, Blake, and Auden; and by Ralph Vaughan Williams, in his *Epithalamion Cantata* (1957) which sets *Epithalamion* 19–36 and 390–408. There are other Spenserian settings by Lennox Berkeley, Edmund Rubbra, and Sir George Dyson. In general, it may be observed that until very recently strophic song and epigrammatic flavor have predominated in texts set by English composers (save for oratorio, etc), who have in most instances seemed not to know *The Faerie Queene* well enough to find all manner of possible texts: it would seem that *FQ* II xii 70–1 should otherwise have received a multitude of musical treatments.

Musical subjects and tropes in Spenser range from the conventional use in *Amoretti* 38 of Arion and the dolphin (Amphion, Apollo, Linus, and Orpheus appear elsewhere in his poetry), and the triad of sleep, food, and merry music in the 'Iambicum Trimetrum' (*Two Letters* 1), to the complex arrangements of mythological, figurative, and actual kinds of music in *Epithalamion*. There, the modulations of the refrain include Muses, nymphs, songbirds, Graces, attendants, minstrels, with 'The pipe, the tabor and the trembling Croud, / That well agree withouten breach or jar' (131–2), organ and choristers, angels, and croaking frogs. These, followed by the poet himself, are variously the subjects of the verb *sing* in the refrain, to which, invariably, the woods answer with the confirming echo that has authenticated poetic music in pastoral ever since Virgil. In *Epithalamion*, *sing* implies sixteenth-century polyphony, village music, natural sounds, inaudible angelic harmony, and, ultimately, the writing of poetry.

The many musical terms in *Teares of the Muses* may reflect some of the musico-poetic thought of the Pléiade. Like the trope of piping and singing (and the perhaps central, and certainly widely imitated, figure in *Aprill* 36, 'And tuned it unto the Waters fall'), they involve the convention of music-as-eloquence. A curious moment of proleptic mythmaking in *Ruines of Time* (603–16) revises Ovid's account of the harp of dismembered Orpheus, floating down the river Hebrus, emitting mournful sounds: 'th'Harpe of *Philisides* [Sidney] now dead' rises out of its analogous Thames on the way to becoming constellated as Lyra, and flies through the air, 'Whilst all the way most heavenly noyse was heard / Of the strings, stirred with the warbling wind.' This caused Thomas Warton to point out that Spenser had 'beautifully feigned' the Aeolian harp, a favorite emblem of eighteenth-century Spenserians but not invented until their own day (see Hollander 1971).

Music is performed and heard on a relatively small number of occasions in *The Faerie Queene*. In the house of Pride, 'many Minstrales maken melody' (in echoing allusion to Chaucerian 'smale foules'), joined by 'many Bardes, that to the trembling chord / Can tune their timely voyces cunningly' (I v 3). Later, 'most heavenly melody' – but only hyperbolically heavenly – is employed by Duessa to cure Redcrosse's wounds (v 17). A literally, truly heavenly music is heard at the betrothal of Redcrosse and Una, evoked in apparent response to the formal music at the ceremony (xii 38–9). This is in itself prefigured, in a pattern apparently later recapitulated in the various musics of *Epithalamion*, by the maidens with their timbrels 'In well attuned notes' (xii 7), and by the song of the populace 'With shaumes, and trompets, and with Clarions sweet' (these being specifically instruments of outdoor music in the sixteenth century), on the way to the palace (13). The 'most celestiall sound, / Of dainty musicke' produced by Arion at the marriage of Thames and Medway is of this sort (IV xi 23).

Most memorable is the music in the Bower of Bliss in Book II. It is first encountered in connection with Cymochles in II v 31, where the Bower's essential danger (art does not merely counterfeit nature, but the natural and the feigned are seductively mingled) is first revealed. Phaedria singing to herself in her boat in II vi 3 joins the choir of birds in the Bower at stanzas 24–5, and strives 'to passe ... Their native musicke by her skilfull art.' The full force of this fiction emerges only in canto xii, where, as Guyon and the Palmer approach Acrasia's bower, they hear how 'all that pleasing is to living eare, / Was there consorted in one harmonee, / Birdes, voyces, instruments, windes, waters, all agree' (70–1). Stanza 71 represents this blended music with remarkable skill, punning on *base* and *meet*, troping the interlocking of rhyme and the intertwining of syntax as the relations of vocal and instrumental polyphony in the Elizabethan 'broken' (mixed) consort:

The joyous birdes shrouded in chearefull shade,
  Their notes unto the voyce attempred sweet;
  Th'Angelicall soft trembling voyces made
  To th'instruments divine respondence meet:
  The silver sounding instruments did meet
  With the base murmure of the waters fall:
  The waters fall with difference discreet,
  Now soft, now loud, unto the wind did call:
The gentle warbling wind low answered to all.

This passage, suggested by the music in Armida's bower in Tasso's *Gerusalemme liberata* 16, seems to have become thematic in later English poetry, from the imitations of it by devout Spenserians like Drayton and Browne, through the parodic treatment of urban noise in Pope's youthful 'The Alley' (c 1706), the meditative representations of natural sounds in eighteenth-century poetry, and ultimately even to Wordsworth and Whitman. Later in this same canto, the drowsing Verdant's 'warlike armes, the idle instruments / Of sleeping praise, were hong upon a tree' (80); given the repeated musical sense of *instrument* in stanza 71, this may suggest a conflation with the harps abandoned on the trees – for Spenser, a biblical variant of the breaking of the pastoral pipe – in Psalm 137.

A later occurrence of music making, at Malecasta's Castle Joyous (III i 40), where music of unspecified origin in the Lydian mode condemned by Plato blends with the choiring of birds, follows the model of the music in the Bower of Bliss. So, too, does the music at the masque of Cupid (III xii 5–6), which echoes as well the activities of the minstrels, bards, and chroniclers of I v 3: the proto-operatic qualities of indoor theatrical music are represented in the contrasting effects of what is perhaps woodwind consort in 'a most delitious harmony, / In full straunge notes' and the succeeding 'shrill trompets.' Here as in Book II, hearing the music contributes to the moral undoing of the listener. It is interesting that there is no music in the Gardens of Adonis (III vi), the Temple of Venus (IV x), or Isis Church (V vii).

Only in the remythologized pastoral music of the scene on Mount Acidale (VI x) is there something beneficent, albeit fragile, about the music of illusion. In stanza 7, the trope from *Aprill* mentioned earlier returns, with nymphs and fairies 'to the waters fall tuning their accents fit.' And in stanza 10, Colin's piping and the drumming of the feet of the dancing ladies partakes of the music of dance itself, of order in motion, and of grace (Tonkin 1972:232–6).

JOHN HOLLANDER

Renaissance musical settings of Spenser are discussed in Germaine Bontoux 1936 *La Chanson en Angleterre au temps d'Elisabeth* (Oxford) pp 214–36; Elise Bickford Jorgens 1982 *The Well-Tun'd Word: Musical Interpretations of English Poetry, 1597–1651* (Minneapolis) pp 243–5; and Joseph Kerman 1962 *The Elizabethan Madrigal* (New York) pp 1–37, 122–3, 221–2. See also Hollander 1961; Hollander 1971; Catherine Ing 1951 *Elizabethan Lyrics* (London); P. Johnson 1972; Pattison 1948; Tonkin 1972.

Mutabilitie, Cantos of. See ***The Faerie Queene*, Book VII**

mutability A characteristic theme of literature and the main theme of Spenser's poetry. While fiction need not be about time and change, it must draw plot and character against a background of advancing time and changeable settings. Sixteenth-century Petrarchan lyrics place the natural world and human relations in similar relief, not as a line of action or character development, but as hypostatized images of a continuing process of growth and decay. In Shakespeare's sonnets, Time personifies a preoccupation with mortality: it is the destroyer of beauty and the limiter of eternal values. Spenser's, by contrast, has no such personality. It is an interval, 'an almost mathematical statement of the Katabolic/metabolic process, to be concluded at a time, in a moment, in the twinkling of an eye, at the last trump. Nature and her works and rhythms are straitened to an almanac in the *Calendar*; the *Amoretti* celebrates a year of love; and the *Epithalamion* twenty-four hours of marriage' (MacLure 1966:556). The legendary aspect of *The Faerie Queene* adverts to a time which cannot be measured against chronicles of historical events or fame, and the drama of human process in the work is heightened by fabulous characters and incidents in such emblematic settings as the Wandering Wood of Book I and Phaedria's floating island of Book II. The Red Cross Knight and Guyon must pass through a protean world and remain uncorrupted though altered by it.

Thus the interplay of mutability and permanence, inconstancy and constancy, begins in the fictional modes adopted by Spenser. Their experimental character may even have been designed to elicit readers' sympathetic understanding of the relationship between art and truth (see Teskey 1986). The protean world of *The Faerie Queene* stands well for the frustrations of that art which attempts to express visions of universal truth. In Book II, Guyon, who recognizes constancy as a human virtue challenging earthly mutability, must overcome the unnatural artifice of the Bower of Bliss yet cannot do so without rushing through the garden intemperately. In Book III, the ephemeral images of the Garden of Adonis need not be overcome: Time, momentarily characterized as the 'troubler' (vi 41), collapses into a continual meeting of spring and autumn. But the Garden of Adonis is merely an emblem of permanence, its fecundity an imitation of the eternity bespoken in *FQ* VII. When the idyllic pastoral vision in Book VI is revealed as, in Shakespeare's words, an 'insubstantial pageant,' Colin Clout shatters his pipe (x 18; cf *Teares* 598–9). In the poetic imagination, image must take the place of unimaginable reality, and even this is all too easily lost.

Spenser's self-conscious imagery incorporates a complex tradition. The gardens of *The Faerie Queene* derive from a biblical picture of paradise as the expression of providential design, marked by coincident growth and constancy. These contrary characteristics are also a feature of the classical *locus amoenus*, where change and continuity are reconciled in a perpetual spring. But Spenser also holds up for scrutiny the less optimistic philosophy of *carpe diem*, of plucking opportunities for pleasure from a life of uncontrollable inconstancy, in the pastoral imagery of the *Complaints*, *Colin Clout*, *The Shepheardes Calender*, and *The Faerie Queene* (eg, II xii 74–5). Finally, all attitudes are cast into doubt by *FQ* VII, where the presumption of inspecting God's plan is suggested by the outcome of Mutabilitie's suit. The last stanzas of the work admit to the significant providential role of Change, 'though she all unworthy were / Of the Heav'ns Rule,' in anticipation 'Of that same time when no more *Change* shall be, / But stedfast rest of all things firmely stayd / Upon the pillours of Eternity' (viii 1–2).

Spenser's reluctant acceptance of earthly change has many antecedents, notably Chaucer's *Boece* and, more immediately, the poetry of the Pléiade, for whom 'Rien sous le ciel ferme ne dure' (Ronsard 'A Melin de Saint Gelais' 19). Their acceptance of change did not prevent Neoplatonists like Ficino, Pico, and Bruno from theorizing about diurnal and celestial process, alteration, change, and eternity, but most accepted Thomas Aquinas' reading of Aristotle (*Physics* 8), that eternity excludes mutability (Hankins 1971:296).

Spenser takes from Ovid in particular a picture of the constantly changing physical estate of man looking back on a golden age, and from the Bible a picture of fallen man looking forward to salvation. In the *Metamorphoses*, change is fraught with its own apparent absolutism, linked inextricably to the forward march of 'days, and months, and years and ages' (2.25–6), and such attendant processes as we find in *The Shepheardes Calender* and again more pointedly in *FQ* VII vii. In Ovid, the supremacy of change is shown by the powerlessness of the gods against indeterminable fate. It is no coincidence that Spenser's Mutabilitie iconographically resembles the medieval Fortune, and she equates herself with fate by vying with the Olympians and Titans for supremacy. Conti reports an apposite tradition of Fortune rebelling against Jove (Lotspeich 1932:13, 85–6; Nohrnberg 1976:745–6). Though fortune is concerned with the flux of the human condition and the vanity of earthly expectation (eg, *Vanitie* 165–8), and fate with human mortality, both suggest the unhappiness of lapsarian existence, for Spenser a powerful emotion: 'O vaine worlds glorie, and unstedfast state / Of all that lives, on face of sinfull earth, / Which from their first untill their utmost date / Tast no one hower of happines or merth, / But like as at the ingate of their berth, / They crying creep out of their mothers woomb, / So wailing backe go to their wofull toomb' (*Time* 43–9). These lines bring together the conventional *contemptus mundi*, spiritual rejection of the sinful world, with something of Lucretius' eternal process (eg, *De rerum natura* 2.75–6) – untroubled by virtue, ethics, or moral rejection of sin – in the joining of the womb and the tomb. If the mutable world is sinful, Spenser nevertheless takes grim satisfaction in the measures of its change.

The ambivalent or ironic characterizations of *FQ* VII in particular are the work of a 'chameleon poet' (Blissett 1964:259). Mutabilitie may be seen as an embodiment of the sinful world and the inconstancy of Error. Her progress through the 'Circle of the Moone' (vi 8) recalls the conventional image of 'Luna, full of mutabylyte,' as Skelton put it (*Bowge of Courte* 3), and she may have been meant to take the place of Hecate, the classical figure of chthonic influences (see Brooks-Davies 1983:66–8). Her suggested identification with Erasmus' Folly (Nohrnberg 1976:753) adds substance to this view. Yet, Mutabilitie is also the embodiment of an apparently unmotivated but necessary process. She may be Spenser's brief indulgence in a Neoplatonic or Gnostic historical pageant (see Nohrnberg 1976: 740–1). She may point to a theology of human deification stressing death rather than sin as the consequence of the Fall and godly immortality as its opposite. While it makes for a difficult disjunction between the wayward inhabitants of *The Faerie Queene* and the theology of *FQ* VII, such a reading might find in the work a way of dealing with failing moral values in the sixteenth century, and failing doctrines about natural and cosmic laws at the time of the new philosophy (Weatherby 1984:113–35; see Harris 1949: 93–129). It is tempting, moreover, to entertain biographical readings of Spenser's poetry in light of the mutability of political and social structures in his age, and in light of the mutability of careers and taste. From his vantage point in Ireland during the 1580s and 1590s, he was well placed to see the effects of court 'newfanglenesse.' He saw first the waning influence of his own patron Leicester, and he treated of this in *Mother Hubberd*. In *Vewe of Ireland*, he was to support the Irish policy of Lord Grey against the 'common winde / Of Courts inconstant mutabilitie' (*MHT* 722–3). *The Faerie Queene* makes occasional reference to the changing shades of politics and court life, and the rare autobiographical localization of Arlo Hill in *FQ* VII is an appropriate allegorical reference to the theme of mutability and constancy (see O'Connell 1977:190–4).

To Spenser, the poet's immortality in verse set forth by Ovid in *Metamorphoses* 15 may have seemed a metaphor of hope that art might be a shield against time (E.K. says of the missing *December* motto, 'The meaning wherof is that all thinges perish and come to theyr last end, but workes of learned wits and monuments of Poetry abide for ever'; see Hallett Smith 1952:41). It is a common theme in sixteenth-century poetry, and Spenser takes it up in *The Shepheardes Calender* and *Amoretti*, where the act of writing poetry tends to stand not for the immortality of the author or his subject, but for an internalized spatial love relationship: 'Deepe in the closet of my parts entyre, / her worth is written with a golden quill' (*Am* 85). In sonnet 75, the immortalizing effects of verse are the subject of unresolved debate between the poet-speaker and his beloved (who remains ironically unidentified). Spenser knew that art necessarily looks backward to models and forward to visions of permanence shared with or adapted from these models (see Greene 1982:4–27). Poetry invests its meaning in forms and words. Spenser's indebtedness to Chaucer as a 'well of English undefyled' suggests the mutability of the word. His archaic language reaches back to a place and time that never existed. He was aware of the capacity of sea-change to wash away words and names written in sand (*Am* 75), but names stood merely for greater essences. For example, the gods of *FQ* VII are emblems belonging to classical anthropomorphic imagination, and are thus more limited than the abstraction Mutabilitie. That Mutabilitie finds greater philosophical tension with Nature illustrates a difference in form and purpose between the antique epic and *The Faerie Queene*.

As a poetic textbook of human virtues, it is not surprising that *The Faerie Queene* should take up constancy last. Thomas Elyot saw constancy as an end of taught virtues: 'if eyther by nature, or els by custome, [man] be nat induced to be all way constant and stable, so that he meve nat for any affection, griefe, or displeasure, all his vertues will shortely decaye, and, in the estimation of men, be but as a shadowe, and be soone forgoten' (*Boke Named the Governour* 3.19). While mutability and permanence are the expression of human suffering and religious vision throughout Spenser – in *Fowre Hymnes*, *Complaints*, *Shepheardes Calender* – they are most completely expressed and linked with practical Christian virtue in *The Faerie Queene*. JOHN LOUIS LEPAGE

Victor Harris 1949 *All Coherence Gone* (Chicago); Joanne Field Holland 1968 'The Cantos of Mutabilitie and the Form of *The Faerie Queene*' *ELH* 35:21–31; Millar MacLure 1966 'Edmund Spenser: An Introductory Essay' *QQ* 73:550–8. See also Cheney 1966, esp pp 239–49; Colie 1966; Hawkins 1961; Holahan 1976; Lewis 1936:296–360; Nelson 1963; Spenser ed 1968; K. Williams 1952; R.R. Wilson 1974.

Myrrha 'The daughter of kynge Cinyras, whiche loved hir owne father fylthyly' (T. Cooper 1565: Appendix), Myrrha appears in Ovid (*Metamorphoses* 10.311–518) as a powerful figure of a young woman's sexual awakening in its most demonic aspects. Milton's catalogue of idols in *Paradise Lost* (1.376–521) explains the horror of such father-daughter incest by showing its source and model in Satan's union with his daughter Sin (Flinker 1980). Since her passion leads to the birth of Adonis, she might be expected to figure prominently in the mythology of *The Faerie Queene*. At the poem's outset, 'The Mirrhe sweete bleeding in the bitter wound' is found in the Wood of Error (I i 9), an allusion to the resinous tree into which Myrrha is transformed while fleeing her father's wrath, and from which Adonis is born. Since this resin is traditionally an aphrodisiac (Fulgentius 3.8), it evokes the forbidden origins of her sexual desire.

Britomart's confused feelings for Artegall, whom she has glimpsed in Venus' magic mirror, are contrasted by her nurse Glauce with the 'filthy lust, contrarie unto kind' of 'th'*Arabian Myrrhe*' (III ii 40–1); but the contrast invites comparisons as well. Both Britomart and Myrrha experience an awakening desire for someone who seems hopelessly inaccessible, and both feel confused and guilty. Glauce's speech is drawn from *Ciris* (237–40), a work long ascribed to Virgil, in which the nurse Carme mistakenly fears that her charge Scylla is suffering from the passion of 'Arabae Myrrhae'; there, however, it is an opposite (but equally disastrous) love for the father's deadly enemy. Spenser's whole episode is unmistakably an imitation of *Ciris* (where the name Britomartis itself appears), but at certain points he follows Ovid's story of Myrrha as well. Britomart's reference to her love as 'My crime, (if crime it be)' echoes Ovid (*FQ* III ii 37, *Met* 10.322–3), and the speeches of Glauce closely parallel those of Myrrha's nurse (see Hughes in *Var* 3:334–6).

Elsewhere, Spenser couples Myrrha and Daphne, comparing their very different flights from lovers to the fearful flights of Florimell and Amoret (III vii 26, IV vii 22). For all three heroines, he uses classical myth to suggest difficulties of distinguishing guilt and innocence, natural and unnatural loves. CALVIN R. EDWARDS

mysteries The Eleusinian mysteries, originally celebrated at Eleusis near Athens, developed from the story of Ceres' grief for her daughter Proserpina when she was abducted in Sicily by Pluto, god of the underworld; they provided Spenser with opportunities for elaborating on the cults of Elizabeth as moon queen and as the fruitful corn goddess and mother Demeter-Ceres (Yates 1975:76–8).

Greco-Roman literature contains many references to these mysteries, all of them fragmentary or frustratingly riddling. They testify to processions and crowds, and to the fact that the mysteries were celebrated by night and involved initiation through an apparent descent into hell culminating in a vision of brightness, beatitude, and rebirth. The central figure was the maiden Proserpina, the Korē. The mysteries became associated with a lunar cult when they were amalgamated with the Egyptian mysteries of Isis, the moon goddess worshiped as the fruitful mother who contained all female deities. Isis was identified with Demeter (Diodorus Siculus *Bibliotheca historica* 1.13.5; cf 1.29.1–4); although in imperial Rome the imported rites of Eleusis and Isis were observed separately, they were frequently confused by initiates and outsiders alike. Indeed, Apuleius' *Golden Ass* (or *Metamorphoses*, the most elaborate statement of Isis worship available to Spenser) identifies the lunar Isis with Ceres as well as with Diana, Proserpina, Cybele, and other female deities. The fact that Proserpina was also commonly identified as a manifestation of the moon goddess (Martianus Capella *Marriage of Mercury and Philology* 2.161, Conti *Mythologiae* 3.16) further helped to assimilate the Eleusinian mysteries into a lunar cult.

The initial clue to the presence of the Eleusinian-Isiac mysteries in *FQ* I lies in the connection of Una with Isis through the iconographic details of the veil, black stole, and ass. Isis is seen to be important to the book's narrative structure once we associate Una's unveiling and her appearance to Redcrosse 'as freshest flowre' robed in lunar white and silver (xii 22) with Apuleius' vision of Isis as a flower-garlanded moon goddess (11.2), and see this manifestation of Una at the end of Redcrosse's quest as a structural complement to his dream of a false Una in her Isiac black stole at the beginning (i 47–9; cf *Golden Ass* 11.3 where Isis' white vestment is covered with a black robe). Arthur's vision of the 'Queene of Faeries,' too, recalls Apuleius' vision as much as it does Diana's analogous visitation of Endymion (ix 13–15). So does the sight of Fidelia, encountered by Redcrosse as the first and 'eldest' of the three theological virtues in the house of Holiness (x 12): she is dressed in white like Una and bears a gold cup with a serpent in it. Isis was known as 'ancient' and 'eldest' (Diodorus I.11.4, I.27.4), and when Apuleius sees her she is carrying 'a cup of gold, out of the mouth whereof the serpent Aspis lifted up his head' (11.4). At such crucial moments, Spenser softens Christianity's stern moral rigor by admitting into its mystery the beneficent power of woman as exemplified in the ancient mysteries.

Spenser's evil characters parody the mysteries or try to reduce them merely to their deathly underworld aspect. Thus Archimago's spell which produces the false Una awakens Proserpina, 'blacke *Plutoes* griesly Dame,' as a prelude to a nighttime descent to the underworld that mentions the moon goddess Cynthia, the lunar color silver; and 'swarming Bees' (i 37–41). The bees may be emblems of a deluded or overactive imagination (cf II ix 51); but in context they perhaps suggest the *Melissae* or bee maidens who were the priestesses of Ceres (Callimachus 'To Apollo' Hymn 2.110, Porphyry *Cave of the Nymphs* 18). Three cantos later, the underworld of the Isiac-Eleusinian initiate, which culminated in illumination by a midnight sun (*Golden Ass* 11.4), is mocked by the enthroned and sun-bright Lucifera, whose glitter conceals the blackness of sin and who is the daughter 'Of griesly *Pluto* ... And sad *Proserpina*' ((I iv 8, 11). Moreover, as the daughter of Proserpina, she is also the double of her maiden mother, the Kore of the Eleusinian mysteries: Lucifera is a 'mayden' (8), and her name is one of the names of the moon goddess. Not surprisingly, the Lucifera episode contains an underworld journey 'downe to *Plutoes* house' (v 32), based in part on Aeneas' journey to Hades. Servius suggests that Virgil was echoing Eleusinian ritual in the line 'adventante dea. "procul, o procul este, profani"' ('the goddess drew nigh. "Away! away! unhallowed ones"' *Aeneid* 6.258); he glosses the goddess as Proserpina, and the *profani* as 'qui non estis initiati' (you who are not initiated into her mysteries; ed 1878–87, 2:45).

The second half of *FQ* II is structurally determined by the mysteries since they appear in the symmetrically opposed cantos vii and xii and in the central cantos devoted to the castle of Alma. The fiend that pursues Guyon in Mammon's house (vii 27–8) is rather like the fury that pursues the suppliant in some accounts of the Eleusinian mysteries; the silver seat with which the knight is tempted (63) recalls 'the forbidden seat' in the mysteries, itself based on the stone upon which the grieving Ceres rested on her way to Eleusis (Kermode 1971:74–6, Upton in *Var* 2:268–9; for the forbidden seat, see Clement of Alexandria *Exhortation to the Greeks* 2.16–17). Moreover, the fact that Mammon's house is adjacent 'to *Plutoes* griesly raine' (21, 24) suggests a fundamental, Eleusinian-oriented difference between Mammon and Pluto: Mammon is lord of riches, his house a hell of sterile gold; Pluto is the god of underworld riches understood as seeds which, after burial, will become the gold of corn (representing Ceres rejoicing after Proserpina is restored to her: Conti 5.14 'De Cerere'). Significantly, Mammon's house contains furnaces like those of Vulcan (35–6) which were traditionally located under Etna (*Aeneid* 8.416ff), the volcano which warned of Proserpina's impending rape (Claudian *Rape of Proserpina* 2.7–8; cf 1.153–91). Finally, Mammon's daughter, the darkly shining and queenly Philotime, is at once a proud double of Lucifera and another parody of Proserpina, as Guyon's immediate move into the Garden of Proserpina itself suggests. (Here, incidentally, we find Ceres' benign poppy of oblivion, one of the props of the Eleusinian mysteries [Callimachus 'To Demeter' Hymn 6.44, Virgil *Georgics* 4.545], characteristically turned into malevolent 'Dead sleeping *Poppy*' [vii 52], and also the Hesperidean golden apples which Ceres passed in her quest for her daughter [*FQ* II vii 54; cf Callimachus, Hymn 6.10–11].)

Acrasia's Bower of Bliss, at the opposite pole from the house of Mammon in the second half of *FQ* II, contains equally corrupt perversions of the Eleusinian rites, which may be connected to the Orphic mysteries and in particular to the Orphic hymn 'To Proserpine,' where the Korē is described as 'vernal queen, whom grassy plains delight ... Whose holy form in budding fruits we view' (Hymn 29 but numbered 28 in Thomas Taylor ed 1969:241; the lines are quoted in Conti 3.16). Acrasia's bower is springlike with its 'faire grassy ground' and 'tender buds' (xii 50–1); and Acrasia, its lasciviously parodic Kore, is accompanied by the spring god Verdant (82). It also contains fruits in the shape of Bacchic grapes (54–6) because Proserpina is Bacchus' mother, according to the same Orphic hymn and other sources. (Since Verdant is also Bacchic [Fowler 1964:214], Acrasia's sexual relationship suggests, via the mysteries, the additional crime of incest.) But Bacchus was also responsible for making Ceres 'drink the draught' so that she might proceed on her search for her daughter (Clement *Exhortation* 2.18), and Ceres and Bacchus were intimately acquainted (Callimachus, Hymn 6.70–1); these are other possible reasons, again connected with the mysteries, for the presence of Bacchus in the bower.

Between the two parodic negatives of Mammon and Acrasia, Alma's virtuous castle mediates as an Eleusinian 'positive': Alma's name derives in part from the adjective bestowed by Virgil and others on Ceres ('alma Ceres,' *Georgics* 1.7, in an Eleusinian context); and her castle's porch is decorated with Bacchic ivy, while inside is a furnace hotter than Etna (II ix 24, 29).

In Isiac and Eleusinian initiation rituals, the suppliant was purified by bathing in the sea (*Golden Ass* 11.1). This custom may be responsible for the narrative prominence given to the sea in *FQ* III: Eleusinian symbolism is delicately suggested in the grieving mother Cymoent, who is gathering daffodils (the flowers of Proserpina) when she hears of her son's apparently mortal wound (iv 29; cf Conti 3.16), and in the fleeing heroine Florimell (L *flos* flower + *mel* honey), who is at once an embodiment of the vegetation myth that lies at the root of the mysteries and a bee maiden or *Melissa*. As in the original Ceres myth and the Eleusinian mysteries, the mother obtains the release of her 'daughter' (Florimell is to become Cymoent's daughter-in-law) from her underworld prison. Moreover, Claudian's Eleusinian *Rape of Proserpina* lists sea gods and river gods in connection with Proserpina's rape (3.1–17), thereby giving Spenser authority for associating Florimell with the sea god Proteus and for associating her release with the procession of water deities (IV xi; see also Blissett 1965). Significantly, too, the central canto of this great book in praise of love is given over to a version of the Venus and Adonis myth that ends with the tale of Cupid and Psyche, whose story first appears in Apuleius' *Golden Ass* 5–6 where it is a symbolic counterpart to the concluding Isis initiation (Psyche is Ceres' servant and refers to Eleusinian secrets in 6.2). Adonis rites were also frequently connected with the Eleusinian rites of the abducted Proserpina, as in Theocritus' Idyll 15.

The presence of Isis and her priests in *FQ* V hints at the continuing importance of the Isiac mysteries for the poem. In *FQ* VI, however, the focus is again firmly on the Eleusinian story-cycle. Serena is abducted by the Blatant Beast while gathering flowers (iii 23–4), so that he is Pluto to her Proserpina (indeed, her name is contained in Pro*serpina*'s). She is rescued only to be threatened again, this time by 'divelish' cannibals (viii 45). She is then symbolically subsumed into Pastorella, who is abducted by brigands and thrown into a cave as dark as hell where she fades like a sunless flower (x 39–44). Pastorella is rescued by Calidore, but (as in *FQ* IV and in the Eleusinian mysteries) it is a mother who is ultimately important: this maiden 'That long had lyen dead' is 'made againe alive' not so much by Calidore as by her long-lost mother Claribell (xi 50; see Tonkin 1972:310–14). Claribell is explicitly Ceres to Pastorella's Proserpina when she bestows 'her owne handmayd, that *Melissa* hight' upon her (xii 14). Pastorella's father-guardian, Meliboe (ix 16), is named from Greek *Meliboas* 'sweet-singing' or 'honey-voiced,' which confirms her bee-like associations. (Porphyry observes that Proserpina is called *meltitode* 'or delicious, alluding to the sweetness of honey' *Cave of the Nymphs* 18.) Connections have also been made between Melissa and the *Melissae* (Upton in *Var* 6:265), and between Pastorella and Proserpina (in Blitch 1973, who does not, however, mention the Eleusinian mysteries).

Possibly a final testimony to the importance of the Eleusinian mysteries in *The Faerie Queene* occurs in the *Cantos of Mutabilitie*, where Pluto and Proserpina are the only chthonic deities admitted to Jupiter's great assembly in defense of the moon queen Cynthia (VII vii 3). Spenser's inclusion of the Ceres story in his poem in praise of his monarch clearly leads us beyond myth to what the ancients regarded as the greatest mystery religion of all.

DOUGLAS BROOKS-DAVIES

Apuleius ed 1975; Blissett 1965; Blitch 1973; Brooks-Davies 1983; S. Davies 1986; C[arl] Kerényi 1967 *Eleusis: Archetypal Image of Mother and Daughter* tr Ralph Manheim (New York); Martianus Capella 1971–7 *Martianus Capella and the Seven Liberal Arts* by William Harris Stahl, et al, incl *The Marriage of Philology and Mercury* tr Richard Johnson with E.L. Burge 2 vols (New York); Johannes Meursius 1619 *Eleusinia, sive De Cereris Eleusinae sacro ac festo* (Leiden); Walter F. Otto 1955 'The Meaning of the Eleusinian Mysteries' in J. Campbell 1955:14–31; Paul Schmitt 1955 'The Ancient Mysteries in the Society of Their Time, Their Transformation and Most Recent Echoes' in J. Campbell 1955:93–118; Steadman 1958; Colin Still 1921 *Shakespeare's Mystery Play: A Study of 'The Tempest'* (London); Still 1936 *The Timeless Theme: A Critical Theory Formulated and Applied* (London); Thomas Taylor 1969 *Thomas Taylor the Platonist: Selected Writings* ed Kathleen Raine and George Mills Harper (Princeton); Wind 1958; Yates 1975.

myth, mythmaking Three senses of the word *myth* form the minimal units for understanding the range and stakes of Spenser's mythmaking. The first is the most common, and the hardest to define: 'myth' as an old tale, something told and re-told, part of a body of more or less anonymous tales which cohere in a mythology – cycles of stories about gods, demigods, and heroes, describing fabulous battles or unreal romances, or presenting visions of creation and metamorphosis. We recognize such stories as myths not merely by their supernatural or scandalous character but by their stark, almost preliterary quality, their transmissibility. Myths, as critics diverse as C.S. Lewis and Claude Lévi-Strauss assert, are that form of linguistic expression which most easily survives translation (Lewis 1961:43, Lévi-Strauss ed 1963:210). They are in a sense the simples of poetry, perhaps also of thought. Drawing on that eclectic array of fables which he inherited from classical and medieval tradition, Spenser was necessarily cut off from the primitive sources of myth (though he certainly possessed various theories about its origin in ancient superstition or occult wisdom). Indeed, given modern research into the social and psychological origins of primitive stories – their power to structure and rationalize the difficult facts of human life – those mythic materials out of which Spenser constructs his allegory may seem to us painfully artificial; to an anthropologist's eye, they might even seem an array of ghosts, the corpses of true myths from which the original, living ritual and spiritual contents had departed. But such corpses were animated, the ghosts blooded. Myths such as those of Narcissus, Venus and Adonis, Orpheus, Diana and Actaeon, came to Spenser enlivened by a history of literary elaboration and galvanized by the intellectual energy of religious and philosophical commentary. Renaissance readers, of course, saw them in the light of Christian Scripture; they could not be taken as in any way 'true histories' of gods and men. Yet even as the limbs or fragments of what had once been a whole body of fable (to use Boccaccio's metaphor, from his preface to *Genealogia*), classical myths offered the Renaissance poet a vast storehouse of materials for parable, romantic narrative, fictive etiology, and sophisticated parody. From this perspective, the business of the poet-mythmaker is retrospective, a matter not just of repeating but of reviving, even rivaling the anonymous, inherited stories, *re*-making myths so that they might continue to engage and speak of the world.

The second crucial sense of 'myth' is that of the Greek word *mythos*, plot or story. Here one wants to recall Aristotle's use of the word to describe the inner form or dynamic 'idea' of a dramatic or narrative work. Mythos in Aristotle is no simple thing, being a structure that is manufactured by the poet and imposed on the raw material of language and history, yet also a deeply natural thing, responding to or reflecting patterns of thought and action that are part of the *given* structure of the world. Whatever its ontology, however, the pragmatic reason for recalling Aristotle's sense of mythos is that it shifts our attention from Spenser the antiquarian to Spenser the maker of literary artifacts. It suggests the importance of narrative design in Spenser: his rearrangements of the traditional plots of battle and trial, death and rebirth; his contrived parodies of older stories; his subtle experiments with narrative voice; his ways of exploring the motives for storytelling itself; his use of mythic stories as extended metaphors for his major philosophical themes. It is precisely through his efforts in the making of mythoi that Spenser is best able to repossess the material of ancient myth. A study of his narrative structures, though it can appear drily formalistic, need not lead us to overlook the religious, political, or ethical concerns of *The Faerie Queene*. Rather, looking at how the poet frames his stories immediately commits us to examining how he appropriates and interprets for his own poem the kind of narratives that could shape or reflect the tensions of his historical moment – including both explicitly literary or folkloric traditions like that of Arthur and his knights, St George and the dragon, and the sort of conceptual plots that conditioned contemporary ways of looking at salvation, justice, love, and so on.

The idea of such a culturally engaged and reflective form of mythmaking will underline the relevance of the third important sense of 'myth' as deception, lie, superstition, idolatry. This sense refers to something we normally want to get rid of or expose, a limited, fantastic thing, or perhaps a once-valid idea that masquerades as something permanent or natural and does violence to the human or historical realms even as it helps to shape them. Such myths are usually opposed by an appeal to what is claimed as reality or truth. It is myth in this sense that Bacon anatomizes with such complexity in the *Novum organum* (1620), in his account of the four sorts of 'idols' embedded in human mind, custom, language, and philosophy. The derogatory usage is perhaps most common in nonliterary contexts, for example, in the accusatory rhetoric of politics. The word thus tends to carry a skeptical tone about it, something which comes through even in one scholar's sympathetic and clarifying comment that while *The Faerie Queene* 'may be mythical poetry ... its myths are the myths of English polity in the fifteen-eighties and nineties' (Kermode 1971:46). Thus, the 'myths' with which Spenser's writing is concerned are not only those which are old or fictive but also those which are destructively false, whether because they get a story or history wrong or because they constrict it (say, by trusting in the literal truth of a tale which must be taken as a partial metaphor). Spenser's sense of the danger of such myths, their tyrannical presence in language and mind, informs his work as a demythologizing mythmaker, an iconographer who is also an iconoclast. His struggle against the spiritual or political lie leads him to portray those stories, images, or ideas which he distrusts as the work of false magicians like Archimago or Busirane; it leads him to stage scenes of iconoclasm and disenchantment, and to point continually to the hypothetical quality of his own transfiguring stories; it enjoins him to complicate all apparently simple centers of meaning by showing the reader their ironic mirrors or doubles (giving us, for instance, the proud 'mayden Queene' Lucifera as well as the heavenly, invisible Gloriana and the hieratic vision of Mercilla). Spenser's use of myth, then, concerns problems of illusion as much as allusion; it involves a desire that his own poetry might offer some agency of disillusionment.

Roughly defined in terms of these three senses – myth as old tale, as plot, as lie – Spenser's mythmaking appears as a narrative art which appropriates and transforms older stories even as it seeks to overcome those forms of myth which have become false or empty. It involves both the remaking and the unmaking of myth. Hence we should not think of his mythic poetry as somehow naive or irrational, for all the mysteriousness of its forms. The dynamic mythoi of *The Faerie Queene* offer us neither plain fiction nor confirmed scripture; they produce no fixed code of divine or political truths, no canonical system of idols and answers. Spenser's mythmaking is rather a system of transformations and reflections – a search for forms of literary mediation that enrich and test the limits of human expression, for forms of power, knowledge, and pleasure that can refresh earlier forms which have become stale or habitual.

A problem remains here, however (even beyond that of making the poem seem freer and less historically conditioned than it is). The three senses of myth cited so far do help us focus on issues proper to Spenser and his period, but they in fact become common in English only much later (see *OED*). Indeed, Spenser never uses the word *myth* at all; he speaks rather of *history*, *fable*, or *tale*, as well as of *vision*, *shadow*, and *allegory*. The resonance of the word *myth* for us, and its odd inevitability in discussing a poet like Spenser, is little related to its after all relatively circumscribed place in sixteenth-century literary vocabulary. Much more important is that we inherit the word from the criticism and anthropology of Romanticism (whence, by the way, the influential Grecism *mythopoesis*, literally 'mythmaking,' a coinage of nineteenth-century philologists), and from the survivals of Romanticism in modern scholars like Aby Warburg, Ernst Cassirer, and Northrop Frye. The problem of myth has indeed obsessed a variety of post-Enlightenment thinkers who, disenchanted with both the revelations of religion and the pretensions of rational science, sought in the study of myth to define a mode of sacred or visionary discourse which nevertheless kept hold on the human and the historical. For Romantic scholars, the study of ancient myths entailed not only the belated investigation of forms of collective expression which were obsolete, but also, with varying degrees of skepticism and nostalgia, a study of what might with effort be revived. Insofar as the idea of myth might define the aspirations of literary artists, it seems to have located a threshold between the 'naive' expressions of primitive culture and the reflective sophistications of more 'advanced' ways of seeing. Paralleling this interest one can also find an incipient awareness that mythology was no random compendium of stories or superstitions, nor yet again a secret encyclopedia formed by ancient bard-philosophers. Rather, myths were recognized as parts of a cultural process, psychological and social tools, hence yielding writers a core of forms implicitly truer to the structures of human reality than any bare mimesis of historical life could aspire to. Hegel and Marx are perhaps the most powerful theorists of this position, but the romance of myth among enlightened readers emerged even in the earliest modern student of the problem, Giambattista Vico. His *Scienza nuova* (1725) describes myth not as artful or allegorical, but as the product of an imaginative violence in which primitive men came to know only those forms which they made to empower and terrorize themselves. The gods and their myths were the products of a 'magic formalism,' 'true histories' which were inescapably false, yet whose unacknowledged falseness had a power to bind, defend, and instruct quite beyond the comprehension of modern, disillusioned minds (Auerbach ed 1959:193). (From this point of view, the idea of myth could become both a focus for the work of disenchanted modernists and a rallying cry for the sentimental, mystifying ideologies of fascism.)

This bare sketch of the historical background of our own usage provides vistas on all three senses of myth cited above; it may also suggest reasons for the strong if divergent commitments which critics have to words such as *myth* and *mythopoesis*. Aspects of Spenser's work that have undoubted roots in Renaissance culture and literature look different when considered in light of this relatively modern interest in myth, for example, his concern with primitive or marginal forms of imagination, his coupling of poetic romance with the more authoritative shapes of biblical narrative, his meditations on the structure and power of political iconography, his proliferation of mythic analogies. Yet the different senses of myth may animate our attention to Spenser in important ways; the problem of myth may become a center for bringing together issues in his poetry that might otherwise be left scattered, disassociated, or misvalued. One might even claim that he opens himself up to a critical emphasis on the problem just because his poetry has helped define, for English readers at least, the very sort of thing literary mythmaking looks like. The following sections do not offer a unified theory of myth in Spenser, but attempt to see how various questions raised by the idea of myth provide useful contexts for examining the dynamics of his mythmaking.

mythmaking and allegory Spenser's use of classical fable is dependent on the long tradition of allegorized myth, which transformed the concrete, supernatural tales of gods and heroes into elegant, sometimes grotesque narrative exempla, dramatic metaphors for moral, metaphysical, or psychological ideas. The story of Narcissus was read as a warning against the dangers of self-love; the petrifying face of Medusa as a figure for the terror of death or a symbol for the terrifying chaos of rebellion; the rape and restoration of Proserpina as mythic image or explanation of the cycles of winter and spring. Spenser was perhaps influenced even more directly by later translations of this fundamentally rationalizing exegetical mode – applied to already canonical texts such as Homer or Ovid – into the synthetic techniques of literary allegories like Prudentius' *Psychomachia*, which describes a battle between supernatural, magical opponents whose conceptual, allegorical character is explicit from the beginning. In both these modes, the more purely fabulous or ornamental elements of mythic narrative are placed under strong, sometimes violent thematic control.

We should recognize, however, that an allegorical logic was not necessarily imposed on a mythic text purely and blindly. In the earliest classical texts, myth is already serving as a complex conceptual rhetoric in its own right. Rather than being narrowly attached to a cultic situation or serving merely as the unconscious vehicle for the projection of cultural values, mythic narrative provided a vocabulary of forms which allowed ancient poets cannily to explore or experiment with a variety of religious, political, and psychological themes. In Homer, for instance, myth is already 'demythologized'; freed from the limitations of cultic expression, his gods become vehicles of lyric hyperbole as well as of subtle psychological drama (as when Athena, in her guise as the spirit of wise restraint, checks Achilles' wrath against Agamemnon by tugging on his sacred, red-gold hair). Hesiod is even more explicitly allegorical, turning members of the pantheon into phantom personifications even as he divinizes abstractions into concrete, daemonic creatures with names like Love or Chaos. Though Plato often sees myth as a body of superstition, a sort of pervasive irrationality which sustains the public world of illusory opinion, he also uses fables about the gods as tools of philosophical speculation, as a means of describing the most exalted workings of mind and cosmos. Somewhat more playfully, Lucian turns eschatological myths about flights to heaven, descents to hell, or battles of gods and Titans into the narrative frameworks of his satirical accounts of philosophical and religious conflicts (a technique that leaves its mark even on the solemn, apocalyptic comedy of *FQ* VII). Ovid employs myths in ways that are often explicitly allegorical, not only bringing on stage complex personifications like Envy and Sleep but also using the mythic fiction of metamorphosis to show gods turning human beings into the bestial emblems of their moral lives. (Indeed, the allegorical world of *FQ* may be seen as a landscape filled with the animated results of such transformations.) Of course, Ovid's ironic or tragic transformations can be quite grotesquely arbitrary, just as their lack of rationale can mock both the moralizing motives of allegory and the poet's fiction of divine or providential control. But the questions raised by Ovid's use of allegory are not foreign to Spenser's poem, where strict personification is only one technique available to the poet, and where no single abstract meaning ever exhausts the implications of a mythic image.

Spenser may differ from Homer in his epic scope or from Ovid and Lucian in his use of comedy, but their precedent reminds us of the complex relations existing between mythic and allegorical structures. Thus, though the turns of his plots and the deeds of his agents tend to reflect an underlying thematic intention – rather than being in any measure realistic or dramatic – the pressure of the thematic control is not always steady. Sometimes he seems inclined to give autonomy to the more concretely mythic bits of his story, counterpointing them with other fragments of fable or suspending them among alternate allegorical reductions. And though Spenser is consistently syncretistic – that is, he uses his allegory to suggest thematic or symbolic connections between different myths, or between classical and scriptural history – he often juxtaposes myths to reveal their paradoxical differences as much as their obvious similarities of patterning. The fiercely dialectical quality of Spenser's syncretism comes through strongly in the account of the Garden of Adonis, his most ambitious exercise in the mythopoesis of place. Rather than constructing a harmonious, even if complex, ideal of paradise, this episode sets the whole idea of such a garden in motion, calling up all of the diverse and conflicting ways in which Western writers have transformed the myth of a paradise. In an effort to expose the diverse impulses to which our myths of gardens are responses, Spenser makes the Garden of Adonis both a prelapsarian Eden and a late apocalyptic home, a place both of origination and of return; it is natural and supernatural, human and more than human, a place of innocence and immortality as well as a landscape which recognizes the pressures of time and death. The dead and revived Adonis, the 'Father of all formes,' may seem both a fallen Adam and a version of the crucified and resurrected Christ, the second Adam; Spenser has suspended him between these identities, and further distinguished him from both. The Garden as a whole is thus as much a reflection on the myths and allegories that compose it as a circumscribed myth or allegory in its own right; it is a mythic home of order which challenges our whole idea of what order (in nature or poetry) should look like.

We may often think of *The Faerie Queene* as a poem of deep or hidden meanings. But although it is consistently oblique or elliptical, the metaphor of depth may be misleading. Both the mythic stories and the allegorical ideas which interpret them are things which lie open to us on the surface of the poetry. The sense of 'obscurity' is often a darkening of the reader's mind, a confusion as to how the diverse parts should be linked or emphasized. To say the least, Spenser reveals his mythic materials to be pragmatic tools or masks which he disposes at will – now with an eye on theological or philosophical irony, now out of need for a piece of epic ornamentation, now pointing a moral lesson or praising a monarch. His sovereign polymorphosity, the highly structured, but also the redundant, mosaic-like, fragmentary and often opaque quality of his allusive assemblages indeed helps justify Angus Fletcher's comparison of the poet's work to the studiously indecorous and randomizing devices of surrealist collage (1971:102). The analogy may make so obviously moralistic and scholarly a poet seem speciously modern. Still, to mark the possible likeness may remind us of the ludic and ironic intelligence that sustains the poet even in his search for occult correspondences between different myths and allegorical figures; it may also help us to see the difference between the complex seriousness of Spenser's work and the kind of bathos and solemn literalism that one often finds in other Renaissance or medieval students of myth.

This is not to say that mythographers such as Boccaccio and Conti did not provide a rich fund of possible ideas to read into classical fables, as well as an encyclopedic index of parallels between different mythic stories. Still, Spenser may have been aware both of the willfulness of some of the readings imposed by mythographers and of their frequent indifference to the philosophical drama and liberation of allegorical expression already implicit in many classical works. A more important precedent in the mythographers, perhaps, is that their allegorical readings tend to concentrate on the secular (ethical, psychological, political) senses of the supernatural fables. As opposed to the more abstracted astrological, theological, or liturgical meanings which medieval scholars tend to discover in classical myth, Renaissance mythographers reveal a basic reticence about making over the gorgeous and often cruel myths of pagan literature into anything other than stories about human beings and their fates. It is just this complex, reflective 'humanization' of myth that served Spenser in constructing what has been called his 'anatomy of imagination,' his use of myth to reflect on the human makers of myth (I.G. MacCaffrey 1976, esp pp 3–10). But the mythographers finally do less to solve Spenser's allegory than we might hope, not so much because they help us decode only some of its hidden senses, but because (despite the syncretism which he shared with them) they give us too limited a measure of the stakes and motives of his conceptual inventions.

myth, order, and the quest Moving now from literary-historical to more broadly structural issues, we see Spenser attracted to mythic narratives for their schematic structures of opposition – their heightened visions of battles between gods and demons, heroes and monsters, their starkly differentiated visions of paradise and underworld, temple and labyrinth – oppositions which frame myth's endlessly varied stories of trial, pursuit, and transformation. This aspect of myth provides the grammar for his 'dialectical imagery,' his poem's repeated polarizations of agency, his testing of his heroic questers against ever more complex and more radically defined forms of evil (Frye 1963:74). Spenser continually refines his vision of the evil to be fought, even as he refines his vision of the good to be won; these two ends entail one another, since the highest good can be defined only against its opposite, and fully recovered only after the latter's defeat or assimilation. There is thus an embattled, agonistic quality in Spenser's quests; even the questing lover of Book III must put on arms in pursuit of her beloved.

This play of opposed images is not merely formalistic. It can be put to starkly polemical or political uses, as when Spenser identifies an allegorical enemy with a particular historical entity: Orgoglio as the Roman church, Geryoneo as the power of Spain, Duessa (in Book V) as Mary, Queen of Scots. But he is no simple partisan propagandist, though he may use the materials of propaganda: he is seldom merely reinforcing historical or ideological conflict by translating it into the black-and-white terms of a timeless fairy tale. For one thing, no single opposition of hero and enemy, angel and devil ever completely serves. The poem multiplies its visions of opposition; it explores the endless metamorphoses of error or evil in diversely psychic, sexual, religious, and political realms. Each individual allegorical enemy will compass a variety of dangers or levels of evil, the questers tending to progress from relatively simple to subtler, stronger, often more hidden forms of opposition. Such opponents may threaten the quest not just as explicit blocking agents but also insofar as they imitate or parody the good to be pursued, or confuse the mythic measures of that good. Friends become enemies, apparent enemies become friends; something which seems good in one context becomes partial or limiting or regressive in another, in need of correction or supersession. In addition, the most potent, extreme images of fulfilled desire or good are themselves rendered obscurely, placed beyond the scope of many of the questers – with the result that, being so continually thrust into new situations, both readers and questers never quite know how to measure by comparison the scope of what they may rightly assume are deformed or parodic images.

The 'dialectical' quality of Spenser's mythic patterning creates a paradox. His narratives of conflict and trial expose his strong impulse to pit good agencies against evil, and thereby separate true and false forms of a virtue. A similar dynamic gives life to the quest. Yet from the beginning of the poem, Spenser suggests that battles between apparently opposite forces may in the end reveal the mutual contamination or mirroring of the opponents. The allegorical narrative suspends any simple moral polarities, so that the reader cannot always know where or whom to praise or accuse. We are not always sure whether a quester fights himself or another, or whether the confrontation may not turn him into a version of his enemy. This kind of irony is fairly obvious in scenes where the Christian Redcrosse battles 'pagan' enemies like Sansfoy and Sansjoy whom in retrospect we recognize as projected, and hence evaded, forms of his own doubt and pride. In such cases, as one critic suggests, he must pass beyond this stage of infantile projection and self-alienation before he can do battle with the apocalyptic, objective symbol of evil, the dragon who poisons the human Eden (Berger 1966–7:40). But the ambivalent terms of the allegorical battle become more problematic when a hero like Arthur both bears the emblems and echoes the gestures of Orgoglio, the inflated, rebellious, and destructive pride which he proposes to overcome (I vii 31–5).

Part of the labor of Spenser's dialectic is to achieve a clarifying confusion; his quest narratives tell us about the duplicity, the sliding of values and identities which are an aspect of all human efforts to gain an end. More radically, he also seems eager to expose the danger of attempts to oversimplify such duplicity. Even an ideal representation of an unmediated good may finally only block the effective achievement of that end, and allow for the secret projection of more questionable motives under the cover of so blank or abstract an ideal. Spenser's sovereign complexity thus aims to oppose 'the primitive fury to keep things simple, pure, the same' (Berger 1968d:15). And he does this not only because the primitive impulse finds its way into more advanced designs, but because the rage for purity may realize itself divisively in all too narrow an identification of one's enemies or victims. Such a dilemma goes far to explain why the poet, in response to this impulse, continually suggests the possible violence or partial failure that shadows the work of his heroic questers (as when Scudamour's 'successful' capture of Amoret from the Temple of Venus is compared to Orpheus' recovery of Eurydice from Hades, IV x 58).

This possibility, that in mythic narrative the representing of a perfect triumph or sacrifice may itself be a dangerous lure, helps explain why Spenser constructs progressively more ambivalent resolutions to his Books, creating enemies whose particular error or evil seems progressively less easy to define or reject, even in fiction. The apparently complete tearing down of a Bower of Bliss or a house of Busirane – after each has been described in absorbing detail – leaves us with no purer power or world to be set in their place, no promise that the infection they represent will not renew itself in a different form. Artegall's successful defeat of Grantorto is marred by the railings of Envy, Detraction, and the Blatant Beast. This last – an iconoclastic demon of envy and slanderous speech which strangely mirrors Orgoglio's beast – is left running wild through the world at the end of the poem's last completed book, only briefly captured by Calidore. Its random poison seems to know no differences, its barking and its rebellious babble seem to compromise any clear sense of the proper motives of praise and blame; hence it constitutes an impasse to all further unfolding of Spenser's allegory. The monster and the historical evil it represents (rather than any of Gloriana's knights) are left triumphant – unless we are to see Spenser's terrifying myth of his poem's reception as itself a paradoxical triumph over the divisive and delusive simplifications of the mythopoeic mode.

Although the poet does stage a final defeat of the enemy in *FQ* VII, here too the metaphysical threat of the Titaness Mutabilitie is not so much battled and agonistically put down as it is ruled out of existence by the noble legal sophisms of Nature, who argues that any abstracted idea of absolute change must be dissolved and reabsorbed by a more complex vision of dynamic order and process. And even this dialectical triumph is at best fragile; a darker, more elegiac and threatening vision of change returns in the fragmentary closing of the book, not redeemed by an harmonious image of natural process but rather moving the poet to conjure the distant prospect of an apocalyptic moment wholly beyond change. 'If faith is a refuge here, it is a lonely and bitter one. For the poet has no sight of God or of that hearsay Sabbath. He invokes, and waits, but he affirms only the reality of the Titaness' (Greene 1963:323). He is caught both by what we might call existential doubt and by a more specific distrust of the mythic motives of his poetry itself, a suspicion that even the subtlest stories by which we make sense of ideas of order and disorder and change and time are liable to seductive simplicities and reductive dualities.

mythmaking, parody, and allusion Spenser's interest in the parodying or degraded imitation of mythic images has already been mentioned. Such a literary intersection of mythic narrative and parody has a complex ancestry. Spenser's use of parody, for instance, recalls Virgil's attention to the failed and even comic efforts of some Trojan exiles to rebuild their fallen city as the 'Little Troy' of *Aeneid* 3.349–51, as well as his interest in grander constructs like Dido's Carthage, which rivals Troy and threatens to interrupt Aeneas' quest for Troy's providential, Roman mirror. Another precedent is visible in Ovid's and Lucian's burlesques of older cultic and heroic narratives (a technique common to Italian romancers like Ariosto as well). Equally important, however, is the precedent of Christian ideas about the manner in which men and demons create seductive, idolatrous, and ultimately parodic imitations of true worship and true divinity. This latter complex of ideas became especially urgent during the crisis of the Reformation, since Protestants were arguing that the work of the historical church was being usurped by a political and spiritual institution (the Church of Rome) which was in effect a demonic parody of the true church, its rituals and dogmas the empty allegories or poisonous mirrors of Scripture's true mysteries. This concern raises the moral stakes of Redcrosse's quest, with its intricate, romantic fascination with seductive illusion and mistaken identities.

It is useful in theory to distinguish instances of broadly literary parody from instances of demonic disguise represented as such within the fiction of the poem (for instance, in Archimago's dressing up as Redcrosse, I ii II, or in a witch's creation of a snowy double of the virgin Florimell, an artificial female animated by a male demon, III viii 5–8). In practice, however, different forms of parody and disguise tend to slide together, such that attempts at literal disguise or substitution often end by exposing degraded or parodic elements in the imitation itself. The complexity of the issue can be seen in the Bower of Bliss episode, which is both Spenser's extended parody of earlier poetic attempts to create an ideal, literary Eden and a gravely moralizing account of the way that human imagination, in its defensive efforts to deny change or hoard pleasure, ends up with deathly and frigid travesties of its original ideals. The fact is that Spenser is interested in parody mainly when it raises larger questions about the workings of human thought or art, rather than when it touches merely on circumscribed matters of literary taste and decorum.

A further complication is that while the reader may detect parodic intent in a certain form or image, the norm against which it is to be measured may not be clearly accessible, or may be revealed only partly. We may, for example, discern a parody of the Eucharist in the spilled liquor by which Hellenore signals her lust to Paridell, 'A sacrament prophane in mistery of wine' (III ix 30); we might even see a darker travesty of the love feast in Amoret's bearing her own bleeding heart in a silver bowl at the center of the ritualistic dream-procession that is the masque of Cupid (xii 21). Yet Spenser's own more benign or 'truer' visions of that sacrament remain problematic: the serpent-cup borne by Fidessa in the house of Holiness and the balm which heals Redcrosse during his fight with the Dragon (I x 43, xi 48). Despite their deeply biblical, typological resonances and their poetic vividness, such images scarcely give us any clear sense of the theology or liturgical shape of the ritual whose quality was so fiercely debated by Catholics, Calvinists, and sectarian Protestants of Spenser's time, and on which so many questions about religious and political authority hinged.

Allowing for whatever cowardly or politic wisdom may motivate Spenser's evasions, we might define the problem about how to read his parodic images in the following way: the poet puts us into a position where our struggle to discern the nature of such parodies can become the conceptual analogue of the labor of his questers, who seek to combat the illusions imposed on them by their enemies or themselves. There are many deceiving magicians and phantasms in the poem, but readers are not likely to be literally duped by what the poet clearly marks out as illusion or enchantment. Nevertheless, we *are* thrust into situations in which we may not be able to discern clearly the sources, structure, and scope of a disguise or an enchantment; and it is here that Spenser's parodic images put us on trial.

Questions about Spenser's treatment of mythic parody are deeply bound up with broader issues involving his use of mythic allusion. Even in cases where there is no obvious mockery of a source in his imitation, he tends to appropriate the images and narratives of prior texts with something of the abstracted, ironic freedom of a parodist. A sketch of the transformations of a single myth suggests the complexity of his method. At the outset of Book III, he displays on the ornamental tapestries in Malecasta's house the traditional episodes of the Adonis myth: the courtship, his death, Venus' mourning (i 34–8). The images are not parodic per se, yet we are conscious that they render the source myth with a strange, revealing mixture of the sensual, the sentimental, and the prurient. Spenser varies the opening image of the wounded lover/hunter throughout Book III, evoking the figure of Adonis in the story of the sheltered hero Marinell falling like a sacrificial beast under the lance of Britomart (iv 16–17), as well as in the story of Belphoebe curing Timias (struck in the thigh like Adonis, but by a boar spear rather than a boar, v 20–2), even as she wounds him in turn with her own beauty. We might want to claim that the image of Venus nursing and taking pleasure in the living-dead youth at the center of the Garden of Adonis (vi 46–7) is the 'true' or original type whose discovery redeems or corrects both the decadent versions of Malecasta's house and the more vicious parody of the lovers glimpsed in the description of Acrasia embracing the debauched youth Verdant at the center of the Bower of Bliss (II xii 77–80). Yet persuasive as it is, we must remind ourselves that Spenser's ideal couple compose what is itself a licit, erotic parody of the traditional image of the Pietà (Frye 1963:82). In such cases as these, 'parody' works in more than one direction; it may both corrupt and correct an ideal, degrade or subtly displace a myth. Spenser's repeated variations on a story like that of Adonis let him stretch its implications, or unfold more clearly its ambivalent potential in differing contexts and fields of analogy.

The radical strangeness of his strategy comes through most strongly in Spenser's 'redemptive parodies,' those instances of ironic misappropriation which nevertheless heighten rather than mock his originals. He thereby endows with a romantic and epistemological seriousness situations which authors like Chaucer or Ariosto treat with detached and urbane humor. Chaucer's comic account of Sir Thopas' dream of an elf-queen (itself a broad parody of popular folklore) gives Spenser the basis or pretext for Arthur's dream of Gloriana, an event which is arguably the constitutive visionary encounter of the entire poem, in that Arthur's quest for his dream-image is the measure of all other quests. His dream is not an unambiguous or a purely 'religious' experience, and the poet's 'redemption' of Chaucer's comedy is by no means simple. The complex responses we may have to Spenser's crossing of a comic and a heroic narrative may indeed be deeply appropriate to an episode which uneasily combines suggestions of romantic love, coy seductiveness, supernatural enlightenment, and political propaganda (since Gloriana is among other things an image of Elizabeth in her multiple roles as head of state, patron of the arts, defender of the faith, and courtly idol).

Likewise, Spenser takes the risk of giving elaborate mythic treatment to popular materials which his literary culture might have thought indecorous, and which the religious establishment might have thought both false and dangerous – for example, what E.K. himself speaks of as the 'rancke opinion' of fairies and elves, which he takes to be the products of popish superstition (*SC, June* 25 gloss). Spenser's rather Virgilian or Ariostan fairies have been pretty much stripped of superstitious coloring, of course; they have none of the preciosity or natural magic that we find, for example, in both the medieval *Sir Orfeo* and *A Midsummer Night's Dream*. But Spenser's literary choices, both brave and sly, remain difficult to evaluate. We may thus wonder how much he expected memories of a medieval or popish St George would color his readers' responses to the legend of Redcrosse; we may wonder what it means that he founded his most nearly Dantean vision of cosmic order and grace, the scene on Mount Acidale (VI x), on popular stories about elves who dance secretly on hilltops or in woods at night, dangerous or impossible for mortals to watch. Such examples at least illustrate a crucial point about the freedom and prophetic seriousness of Spenser's mythmaking. Even as we register the possibly subversive ironies of such allusions, we find there as well evidence of the poet's sublime disregard for certain merely normative, historical prejudices of literary decorum or religious authority, and by implication his sense that no form into which the human imagination has projected itself is either necessarily pure or inescapably corrupt.

primitivism and genealogy Spenser's allusions to and parodies of earlier texts point toward larger issues in his treatment of literary and cultural history, and the myths and narratives by which we make sense of those histories. The flexible, transmissible nature of myth has already been noted, as has its ability to order mental and cultural experience and give shape to their conflicts. Related to these capacities is another: myths look backward. As is evident in stories of the Creation and Fall, myths explain where we came from, what we were, what blessings or catastrophes made us the way we are now. They tell us about origins in order to explain what the present has lost, what it might retain or (through labor or grace) expect to recover. Myth's very detachment from the awkward, shifting, and contingent facts of history is what gives it some of its permanent appeal – though in practice myths tend to be deeply engaged in or part of history, since they may be used to re-create the past in order to account for or justify the present, or to simplify a complex historical moment by making the conflicting terms of some present situation into earlier or later stages of an unfolding history. Spenser co-opts and explores this retrospective aspect of myth in his poem with great energy. His 'famous antique history' is continually drawing the reader back toward ideal images of source and origin, to natural or supernatural birthplaces like the Gardens of Adonis, or to places of flood and fountain like the house of Proteus where we witness the marriage of rivers. Still, it is crucial to note that he chastens as much as he indulges our nostalgia for an ideal or mythic past. He continually reminds us of the tentative or obscure, if not wholly lost, nature of such original forms, multiplying nearly beyond count his own images of origin and raising shrewd questions about our human desire to seek a source or an authority in some time other than the present.

As poetic anthropologist, Spenser is capable of both 'soft' and 'hard' primitivism. He can imagine an ancient world filled with peaceful, gentle shepherds as well as one populated by ruthless cannibals and savages; he can people the forests of Fairyland with innocent, chaste nymphs and with wild, priapic satyrs. Indeed, he may give us both hard and soft versions of a single myth, as when he takes up the medieval myth of the hairy, forest-dwelling wild man, and translates it into figures like the phallic rapist Lust in IV vii and the gentle, wordless, and naturally 'noble' Salvage Man of VI iv. His critical view of myths of origin disallows any monolithic idea of progress or simple opposition of states: our human history has been a process of decline from some grand original as well as a process of evolution, a movement both away from and toward a complex ideal (Berger 1968e:6–7). Spenser's mythmaking, indeed, looks backward at our imagined origins in order to point to reversals and confusions of direction, haltings or radical discontinuities along an apparent line of progress.

Most notably, he often shows images in which the early and late are combined in one moment, or in which more primitive forms of expression occur alongside or 'below' what appear to be more sophisticated and 'civilized' expressions. Thus he calls up memories of a wedding feast defiled by the rages of drunken, half-human centaurs in the middle of his apostrophe to the ordered, celestial crown of Ariadne on Mount Acidale (VI x 13). In the house of Busirane, he exposes the anarchic elements of sexual terror and sadomasochism that saturate the civilized, erotic phantasmagoria of Petrarchan poetry (III xii). And in his account of the lost Serena gazed upon by a savage robber-band in looks that cross lust, hunger, and superstitious awe, Spenser describes the heroine herself in the delicately self-conscious terms of a courtly blazon – her body being figured in turn as a bed, a sacrificial altar, and a triumphal arch hung with the spoils of battle (VI viii 38–43).

These examples suggest that Spenser wants us to see that the present always bears traces of the past, that civilization is always haunted by ghosts of the 'primitive' it presumes to have transcended or sublimated. (Compare Montaigne's fascination in *Essais* I.30 with New World 'cannibals,' and his way of admiring their stern virtue even as he uses them as an ironic mirror to remind his time of its greater tendencies to organized cruelty and violence and to attack its myths of cultural advancement.) If we think that we have evaded the past, it may come back to trouble us the more strongly, since it may only be a portion of the present which we are trying to forget. Conversely, if we think that the past possessed a greatness wholly lost to us, we may in turn lose hold of what greatness can be repossessed or work accomplished in the present. In Spenser, the return to individual and cultural origins can be both strengthening and humbling, as in the case of Satyrane's regular return to the forest-dwelling satyrs who raised him, or in Redcrosse's discovery of his descent from a British plowman even at the moment when he learns the way of trial that will lead him to heaven (I vi 30, x 55–67).

Spenser rarely seeks to uncover any single, pure, or pristine center by which to measure the motivations or aims of a particular quest. He offers no simple, original event that we can wonder or weep at. Still, it is not simply a question of the sheer quantity of ways in which he repeats or varies his images of origin. More important is that his representations of the early or the original tend to thrust us into situations of conceptual crisis. They tend to frame an image of an origin or center which involves us in a dynamic confusion, where different levels of mind, experience, and cultural history overlay one another, and where we can no longer see clearly the differences between early and late, progression and regression. For example, Spenser confronts us variously with 'the premature and one-sidedly feminine fulfillment in the Gardens of Adonis; the archaic and unsatisfactory reconciliation of male and female principles, generative and courtly forms of erotic impulse, pagan and medieval institutions that are structured into the Temple of Venus,' or such 'primitive modes of harmony and resolution as we find in the Marriage of the Rivers' (Berger 1968c:9) – an episode which interweaves histories of Titanic rebellion and ancient tyranny along with images of primal nourishment and playful fluidity. Again, he may suggest that the imperial rule of Elizabeth finds its 'antique' original in the work of an ancient, Herculean justicer like Artegall. Yet he possesses a 'Machiavellian hardness of attitude towards the pieties of mythographic history' (Fletcher 1971:41); and in case we are inclined to take the greatness of Artegall too simply or literally, he reminds us that his ideal principles of justice must in the end be enacted by inhuman and murderous robots like the 'iron man' Talus. Likewise, in Britomart's dream in Isis Church, he exposes the buried, rebellious energies (possessing both sexual and political overtones) that haunt the hieratic emblems of justice and equity. Spenser can also mock the pretended mythic origins of others, as when he suggests that Orgoglio – an image of papal pride and false mystery, a figure for the usurped authority and specious timelessness of the Roman church – derives his power not from a heavenly source but only from an empty subterranean wind that both impregnates and destroys, a chthonic rather than divine spirit which issues only in idolatry and impurity.

One cannot define absolutely the proper tact with which to deal with such complex images of origin. The main point may be to recognize the doubled impulses which condition Spenser's use of them. He can compose his mythic histories with the gaze of a prophet-propagandist who seeks an heroic past to project onto the present or future, a past that can be the occasion of a Virgilian piety and fatalism as much as of a benign Christian hope. But he can also probe his own and others' stories with the critical eye of a psychoanalyst or Nietzschean genealogist, one whose subversive stories of origin serve mainly to cut through the illusions of older, more authoritative myths, showing what the present has buried as much as what it has lost. In the end, Spenser finds no present form so pure that it can be appropriated without qualification, nor any past image so trivial or degraded that it cannot be restored to some possible luster.

conclusion Words like *myth* or *mythmaking* may give *The Faerie Queene* some of the strangeness and authority lacking even in terms like *allegory* and *romance*. And yet they can lead us to over-idealize the poem as well, unless we carefully take the measure of its chauvinism, its evasions and exclusions, its often self-indulgent abstractness, its sentimentality and perversity. Intricate to the point of exhaustion, at once highly structured and strangely entropic, the poem may fail to satisfy our appetites for either strong spontaneity or determined formalism. No doubt it is hardly the swamp of indulgent vagaries, slippages, and decorative excesses found by G. Wilson Knight when he compared the poem as a whole to the frigid and deliquescent Bower of Bliss (in Alpers 1967a:329–44) – though the latter may be the poet's nightmare vision of his poem. Yet one must admit that Spenser never offers his readers the kind of linguistic compression and the intensified presentation of human life and choice that we find in Shakespeare, Dante, or Milton. Nor does he, for all the sustained inventiveness of his mythopoeia, bequeath us literary types of the originality and transmissibility of the absurd quester Don Quixote or the demystifying giant Gargantua. Despite its fluid and unsettling range, *The Faerie Queene* gives us no figures which can do what these do by way of enlarging or setting at risk our common concepts of mind, self, and culture. Even in embarking on the more conservative project of accommodating and embellishing the established icons of Elizabethan politics and religion, Spenser seems to work quite as hard at emptying these icons of any blind, persuasive power. *The Faerie Queene* may in the end appear to beg too many of the questions we ask of poetry, even as it seeks to provide alternative answers to them all.

Readers must decide for themselves the relative value they give to the discriminations and the muddlings of meaning that characterize Spenser's poetry; they must come to terms with both its scholarly difficulty and its often surreal or oblique playfulness. If it is mythic poetry, it is also a poetry which remakes and unmakes myth, just as it is a dream which frames, analyzes, and dissolves other dreams, both degrading and ennobling. If in its complicating of metaphorical and conceptual motives *The Faerie Queene* does yield us anything like true myth (with its non-reflexive, super-literary starkness), this may be visible primarily in the poem's ability to draw its readers into a momentary or hypothetical naiveté. *The Faerie Queene* is the kind of poem which 'comes to possess the reader ... naturalizes him in its own imagination and liberates him there' (W. Stevens 1951:50). Hence, one does not say of the Garden of Adonis that it is an allegory of nature, or sex, or generation, but rather that this is simply what nature and sex and generation look like. One says of the Blatant Beast, 'that is simply what slander looks like,' or of the house of Busirane, 'that is what Petrarchan poetry makes love look like.' Such episodes bring the reader to a condition of intensified attention where common ways of bracketing the poet's metaphors or fictions fail, where any exterior subject (whether a person, an event, or an ambiguous idea) seems nearly occluded by the poet's own absorbing constructs, where any frame of reality that is external to the poem seems likely to disappear. The science of Spenser's mythmaking is to bring us continually to the threshold of such failure and such disappearance. KENNETH GROSS

This list is at best a schematic guide for further reading. Omissions are inevitable, and many voluminous authors are represented here by only a single characteristic work.

SPENSER CRITICISM Almost any study of the poet will have to characterize his use of mythological allegory, political iconography, or supernatural fiction in ways that could contribute to a description of his 'mythmaking,' at least as this has been sketched out above. The following picks out primarily works of specific relevance to the preceding discussion. General accounts of Spenser's use of mythological allusion and analogy include Fletcher 1971:57–129; Frye 1963; Hamilton 1961a; Lotspeich 1932 (focusing particularly on the poet's use of Natale Conti's *Mythologiae*); Nohrnberg 1976; and K. Williams 1961. (See also *allegory and *mythographers, as well as entries under specific mythic figures.) On Spenser's narrative mode, see Alpers 1967b:3–69; Goldberg 1981 passim; and P.A. Parker 1979:54–113; see also Harry Berger, Jr 1966–7 'Spenser's *Faerie Queene*, Book I: Prelude to Interpretation' *SORA* 2:18–49. (See also *narrative and *romance.) On Spenser's relation to Elizabethan political mythology, see Aptekar 1967; Goldberg 1981:122–65; Kermode 1971:33–59; O'Connell 1977 passim; Quilligan 1983:175–85; Wells 1983 passim; and Yates 1975:69–74, 112–20. (See also *Elizabeth.) On Spenser's concern with idols and idolatry, see Greenblatt 1980:157–92; and Gross 1985 passim. (See also *idolatry.) On parodic transformations in Spenser's narrative, see Fletcher 1971:34–7. On the poet's complex treatment of the archaic and the primitive, see Berger 1968b; Berger 1968d; Berger 1968e; Cheney 1966; Giamatti 1976; and Guillory 1983:23–45. Kermode 1971:12–32 contains some useful and pointed comments on the problems of 'myth criticism' as applied to Spenser.

RENAISSANCE IDEAS OF MYTH The study of Renaissance mythography and iconographic tradition was pioneered by historians of art, among whom Panofsky 1939, Seznec ed 1953, and Wind 1958 are in particular worth consulting. Studies with a more literary emphasis include D.C. Allen 1970, Bush 1963, and D.J. Gordon 1975. Allen 1970 also contains an extensive bibliography of major classical, medieval, and Renaissance mythographers, and related scholarship. (See also *mythographers for descriptions of those specific works which most influenced Spenser.) Nohrnberg 1976:735–91 offers some suggestive comments on the larger ambitions of Renaissance mythmaking as they relate to Spenser. Among innumerable monographs, the reader might look at Hyde 1986 and Loewenstein 1984 for examples of what can be yielded by investigating the development of a single mythic figure in the literature of the period.

LATER DEVELOPMENTS The best introduction to important post-Renaissance students of myth is Burton Feldman and Robert D. Richardson, Jr 1972 *The Rise of Modern Mythology, 1680–1860* (Bloomington), which contains discussion of and extracts from numerous authors, including Vico, Lowth, Herder, Schelling,

Marx, and Müller, as well as excellent bibliographies. In addition to the massively influential (though deeply flawed) work on myth and ritual in James Frazer 1922 *The Golden Bough: A Study in Magic and Religion* (New York; 1-vol abr of 3rd ed 1907–13), exemplary modern studies include Ernst Cassirer 1955 *Mythical Thought* tr Ralph Manheim, vol 2 of *The Philosophy of Symbolic Forms* (New Haven); Mircea Eliade 1954 *The Myth of the Eternal Return* tr Willard R. Trask (New York); and Jane Ellen Harrison 1912 *Themis: A Study of the Social Origins of Greek Religion* (Cambridge). Different aspects of a psychoanalytic approach to myth are visible in Sigmund Freud 1918 *Totem and Taboo* (in ed 1953–74, 13:1–161); Otto Rank 1914 *The Myth of the Birth of the Hero: A Psychological Interpretation of Mythology* tr F. Robbins and Smith Ely Jelliffe (New York); and Carl G. Jung and C[arl] Kerényi 1963 *Essays on a Science of Mythology: The Myth of the Divine Child and the Mysteries of Eleusis* tr R.F.C. Hull (Princeton). Claude Lévi-Strauss' structuralist analyses of primitive myth, described schematically in *Structural Anthropology* tr Claire Jacobson and Brooke Grundfest Schoepf (New York 1963; first pub Paris 1958) and worked out most fully in the four volumes of *Mythologiques* (Paris 1964–71; Eng tr John and Doreen Weightman, New York 1969–81), have been extended to classical sources in Marcel Detienne 1977 *The Gardens of Adonis: Spices in Greek Mythology* tr Janet Lloyd (Hassocks, Eng); and Jean-Pierre Vernant 1983 *Myth and Thought among the Greeks* (London). More useful than any of these for the student of Spenser, however, might be the reflections on the history and hermeneutics of Near-Eastern, classical, and scriptural myth in Paul Ricoeur 1967 *The Symbolism of Evil* tr Emerson Buchanan (New York). More recent, revisionary studies include Walter Burkert 1979 *Structure and History in Greek Mythology and Ritual* (Berkeley and Los Angeles); René Girard 1977 *Violence and the Sacred* tr Patrick Gregory (Baltimore); and Victor Turner 1974 *Dramas, Fields, and Metaphors: Symbolic Action in Human Society* (Ithaca, NY). Some general surveys and commentaries on modern theories of myth can be found in G.S. Kirk 1970 *Myth: Its Meaning and Functions in Ancient and Other Cultures* (Cambridge); K.K. Ruthven 1976 *Myth* (London); and William G. Doty 1986 *Mythography: The Study of Myths and Rituals* (University, Ala), which also contains an extensive, if somewhat uneven bibliography. Two useful anthologies are Henry A. Murray, ed 1960 *Myth and Mythmaking* (New York) and Thomas A. Sebeok, ed 1958 *Myth: A Symposium* (Bloomington). The critical, historicizing, 'demythologizing' approach to religious myth that has characterized twentieth-century theology and hermeneutics, and has touched even sympathetic students like Ricoeur, is best exemplified by the essays of Rudolf Bultmann collected in 1984 *'New Testament and Mythology' and Other Basic Writings* tr Shubert M. Ogden (Philadelphia).

MYTH AND LITERATURE The most influential and controversial work in this area has been that of Northrop Frye, especially in Frye 1957 and Frye 1963. (Important responses are collected in Murray Krieger, ed 1966 *Northrop Frye in Modern Criticism* [New York].) Maud Bodkin 1934 *Archetypal Patterns in Poetry: Psychological Studies of Imagination* (London), Richard Chase 1949 *Quest for Myth* (Baton Rouge), Robert Graves 1948 *The White Goddess: A Historical Grammar of Poetic Myth* (London), and Philip Wheelwright 1954 *The Burning Fountain: A Study in the Language of Symbolism* (Bloomington) also make interesting, if somewhat eclectic contributions to the debate. Bloom 1959 is a particularly striking appropriation of ideas about mythic thought for the sake of commentary on a single author. Useful collections of essays include Joseph P. Strelka, ed 1980 *Literary Criticism and Myth* (University Park, Pa), and John B. Vickery, ed 1966 *Myth and Literature: Contemporary Theory and Practice* (Lincoln, Nebr), both of which contain good basic bibliographies. See also the reflections on myth and myth-criticism in Kenneth Burke 1966 'Myth, Poetry, and Philosophy' in *Language as Symbolic Action* (Berkeley and Los Angeles) pp 380–409; C.S. Lewis 1961 *An Experiment in Criticism* (Cambridge) pp 40–9; and Fredric Jameson 1981 'Magical Narratives: On the Dialectical Use of Genre Criticism' in *The Political Unconscious: Narrative as a Socially Symbolic Act* (Ithaca, NY) pp 103–50. It should be noted that, in contrast to the 1950s and 1960s, most recent practical and theoretical work in literary criticism has little interest in the terms 'myth' and 'mythmaking,' despite such late and fairly sophisticated attempts at recuperation as Albert Cook 1980 *Myth and Language* (Bloomington), Eric Gould 1981 *Mythical Intentions in Modern Literature* (Princeton), and John B. Vickery 1983 *Myths and Texts: Strategies of Incorporation and Displacement* (Baton Rouge).

---

mythographers As a schoolboy, Spenser would have become aware of the allegorical interpretation of Greek and Roman myth. Although the tradition of mythography extends from the earliest allegorizations of Homer, systematic treatments did not begin until the Renaissance (see D.C. Allen 1970, T.W. Baldwin 1944, Seznec ed 1953, Starnes and Talbert 1955). Boccaccio's *Genealogiae deorum gentilium libri*, the source of all later classifications and explanations of ancient myth, reflects the shift in Renaissance allegory from the cumbersome fourfold method of interpretation appropriate to biblical exegesis and to Dante's allegory, to a more secular threefold method focusing on specific approaches to knowledge: historical, physical (ie, natural or scientific), and ethical (Murrin 1969). Boccaccio's scheme assumes that the parent of all the gods was Daemogorgon (whose existence is based on a misreading of Statius' *Thebaid* 4.516; Allen 1970:216). Although this assumption limits its usefulness, the *Genealogia* remained a key text in the mythographical tradition.

The German Georg Pictor (c 1500–69) is the only non-Italian among the leading Renaissance mythographers. Although hardly as comprehensive as Boccaccio, he avoids Boccaccio's problems with genealogy by adopting an etymological approach to the pagan deities in his *Theologia mythologica* (1532), and by expressing iconographic materials in dialogue form in his illustrated *Apotheseos* (1558). His work marks a shift from allegorical explanation to etymological and iconographical concerns, and to a more specialized, tightly organized mythographical treatise.

The distinguished humanist Lilio Gregorio Giraldi (1479–1552) also wrote an etymological history of the gods (*De deis gentium*) in the manner of Pictor's *Theologia* and of a later work, the *De cognominibus deorum* (1541) of Julianus Aurelius (ie, J.A. Haurech). Giraldi is the most scholarly and historically accurate of the mythographers, but his dependence on etymology as the key to the meaning of ancient myth is a return to the euhemeristic derivations of Isidore of Seville (c 560–636) found in the eighth book of his *Etymologies*. Giraldi classifies the gods into thirteen groups (*syntagmata*) according to their powers and functions (Allen 1970:221, 223). Within each group, however, the gods are only very loosely related, and there is nothing very logical about the arrangement of the cognomens within each entry. While Giraldi is more accurate than Boccaccio, his material was almost inaccessible to seventeenth-century writers (Mulryan 1974); after the fourth edition in 1580, his *De deis gentium* was not reprinted until 1696.

Vincenzo Cartari (c 1531–70) continued the iconographic emphasis of Pictor's *Apotheseos* in his *Le imagini con la spositione de i dei de gli antichi* (1556, rev and illustrated 1571). The *Imagini* appeared in various languages and in many editions (12 in Spenser's lifetime), most of them illustrated. This popular mythography includes multiple indexes, lists of authors consulted, and various introductions emphasizing its importance to artists, poets, and scholars. Although known as a primarily visual source, it is immensely learned in its citations and allusions to almost the entire body of classical literature.

The most lucid and complete of the Renaissance mythographies is Conti's influential *Mythologiae*. First printed in 1567–8 (and 26 times thereafter, including 6 17th-century editions of a French translation by Jean de Montlyard), this compendium became the mythological source most frequently cited by Elizabethan writers (eg, Chapman, Bacon, Nashe; see Starnes and Talbert 1955). While all the Renaissance mythographers employ Boccaccio's threefold method of allegorical interpretation, Conti's application is the most sustained, systematic, and comprehensive. The tenth book is an epitome of the entire *Mythologiae*, based on the historical, physical, and ethical interpretations of the myths discussed in the previous nine books. The work is not illustrated, though some late editions interpolate illustrations from editions of Cartari. While Conti does pay some attention to iconographical matters, his main concern is with the ethical significance of the myths, what they have to do with promoting human values and a civilized way of life. The work grew to an immense compendium of mythological information as new editions added indexes, abstracts of earlier mythographies, annotations, Ovidian analogues, and selections from other works by Conti (including his entire *On Hunting*). It was the last significant example of mythography to appear during Spenser's lifetime.

Given the numerous editions of Boccaccio, Cartari, and Conti, Spenser could have had access to them, to Giraldi, and indirectly to Pictor through Giraldi. Conti's *Mythologiae* was used as a textbook at Merchant Taylors' School, although not necessarily while Spenser was a student (T.W. Baldwin 1944, 1:421). In any case, Spenser relied more on Conti than on any other Renaissance mythographer, probably using the Frankfurt 1581 edition, 1075 tightly packed octavo pages, with over 1700 quotations from classical authors. He often reproduces not only Conti's mythological details but also their order of presentation; and when Conti errs, Spenser errs with him (Lotspeich 1932).

Certain features of Cartari's *Imagini* may also have proved especially useful to Spenser. Its pictorial bias, for example, would have appealed to his own iconographical bent, and many depictions of the gods in *The Faerie Queene* seem indebted to him: the paraphrase and interpretation of Moschus' *Love the Runaway* (III vi 11–20); the Fates (IV ii 48); the caduceus of Mercury, which Spenser assigns to Cambina (iii 42); the image of Occasion and its relation to *kairos* (II iv 4); the veiled Venus (IV x 41–2); and Mutabilitie (VII vi 6). Cartari's images of time and of Mercury may have influenced *Epithalamion* and *Mother Hubberds Tale* respectively. The *Imagini* possibly influenced Spenser's iconography of Fortune and minor details in his depiction of other classical deities as well (Nohrnberg 1976).

Some of the creative etymologies of Pictor and Giraldi may also have proved useful to Spenser, notably in his passages on Aphrodite and the foam (II xii 65, IV xii 2). He is so close to Conti in selecting and arranging details of numerous myths that the *Mythologiae* is unquestionably his chief source (cf Lotspeich 1932:14–23). Yet he did not restrict himself to any one source, but drew freely from a vast array of Renaissance mythographies, emblem books, dictionaries, artifacts, and editions and translations of the classics. JOHN MULRYAN

D.C. Allen 1970; Bush 1963; Lotspeich 1932; John Mulryan 1974; Mulryan 1981 'Translations and Adaptations of Vincenzo Cartari's *Imagini* and Natale Conti's *Mythologiae*: The Mythographic Tradition in the Renaissance' *CRCL* 8:272–83; Murrin 1969, which discusses mythographers and the allegorical tradition; Nohrnberg 1976; Seznec ed 1953, a wideranging history of the tradition; Starnes and Talbert 1955, a thorough study of the manuals in relation to English Renaissance poets.

N

names, naming The study of Spenser's names leads directly to the characteristic difficulties and pleasures of his poetry. A rough initial taxonomy, mixing rhetorical and lexical categories, may indicate the range of the topic: there are personifications based on English or foreign nouns, sometimes with suggestively archaistic spellings (Envie, Slowth, Sclaunder, the Salvage Man); more subtle 'speaking names,' in which the root is motivated by some feature of the narrative (Una, Duessa, Ollyphant, Talus); names compounded of English simples (Kirkrapine, Prays-desire) or of classical or Romance roots (Corceca, Philotime, Radigund, Portamore); bilingual hybrids and paronyms (Belphoebe, Scudamour; Samient); names adopted from mythology and literature (the gods, Hellenore, Arthur, Tristram); pseudomythical coinages (Phao and Poris among the Nereids); emblematic and heraldic titles (Knight of the Redcrosse, Squire of Dames); pastoral names, genuine and ersatz (Coridon, Meliboe; Colin Clout); Irish toponyms, often domesticated or personalized (Arlo for Aherlow, Mulla for Awbeg); 'feigned name[s] ... counterfeicting the names of secret [or public] Personages' (*SC, Jan* 60 gloss) (Rosalind, Hobbinol; Gloriana, Malfont); doublets and serial names generated from a common phonemic base (Elissa, Perissa; Sansfoy, Sansjoy, Sansloy); patronymics (Satyrane, Geryoneo); pseudonyms (Fidessa for Duessa); transmutations (Malbecco to Gealosie, Cymoent to Cymodoce); anagrams (Terwin for Winter); rebuses (the 'gentle Bee' for Elizabeth *B*oyle in *Amoretti* 71); far-fetched or transumptive portmanteaus (the archaistic 'Authour' combining the names Arthur and Uther at II x 68, 'Sabaoth' evoking the compound etymology of Elizabeth at VII viii 2); and even significant anonyms (the nameless sage who dwells between Phantastes and Eumnestes, the Hermit who heals Serena and Timias from the wounds of the Blatant Beast, the 'Damzell' serenaded by Colin at the center of the ring of Graces). This omnium-gatherum has been a target for Spenser scholars from E.K. on, most notably for the line of inspired editors (Upton, R.E. Neil Dodge, A.C. Hamilton) whose glosses epitomize the kinds of intertextual options available to readers of the poem.

Perhaps the most striking feature of Spenser's name poetry, one he inherits from the tradition of chivalric quest-romance, is the carefully delayed revelation of a name. Beyond producing a common sort of narrative suspense, such delay opens a space of speculative trial for the reader, a studied uncertainty which enlarges the range of the allegorical figures. In Book I, for example, the 'wandring wood' is not so identified until questers and readers have succumbed to its dangers (i 13); the name Una is not revealed until the creation of a false double puts its meaning at risk (i 45); the giant Orgoglio, first defined by his genealogy, is not actually named until after his battle with Redcrosse (vii 14); and Redcrosse himself learns his own name George, identifying him as both warrior saint and fallen man (from Gr *gēorgos* 'plowman, worker of the earth'), only following the successful completion of his preliminary trials and purification at the house of Holiness (x 66). The force of these delays usually depends on some image (semantic or phonic) planted in the preceding narrative, which seems in retrospect to determine the name. Thus the 'blustring' wind god who fills the womb of earth with 'stormie yre' (vii 9) prefigures the name of Orgoglio, their 'Puft up' son (via Gr *orgaō* 'to swell with moisture [or lust]' and *orgē* 'passion, ire'), while the proleptic description of Maleger as 'leane and meagre' (II xi 22) provides not only an apt image of moral disease (L *aeger*) but a phonetic matrix for the withheld name.

In the teleological structure of the traditional quest-romance, a hero must earn or realize his name, which thereby becomes the celebratory mark of an achieved (and fixed) identity. In Spenser, however, the poem works as much to unname, to release identity from the iconic arrests which attend the fixation of proper nouns. The situation is especially complex since in *The Faerie Queene*, as in Ovid's *Metamorphoses*, we often rely on the illusion of continuous essence created by names to help us keep track of the narrative personae despite their endless transformations (Greene 1963:332). This dependence on nominal identity makes all the more disconcerting the instability of the names themselves, for in most cases the semantic content if not the form of the important names becomes more elusive the more closely we consider them.

To begin with, many of Spenser's names, delayed or not, suggest more than one allegorical derivation. The wizard Archimago is both the chief or 'arch' magus of the poem and the source or *archē* of many of its images, idols, and illusions. Mount Acidale suggests *accidens* 'mishap' and *accidia* 'sloth' no less than Greek *akēdēs*, the 'carefree' life adduced by the mythographers. Orgoglio, an Italian version of pride specifically identified with the Church of Rome, reminds us simultaneously of Orcus, the Roman god of the underworld (via Fr *ogre* and Ital *orco*) and of the hero who will send him there (via the shared element *orge* [Gr *ergon*] 'work' or 'tilth,' highlighted in the play on 'furrow' in I viii 8), even as he personifies the orgasmic 'swelling' already mentioned.

Precedents for such multiplicity abound

in the Middle Ages, from Fulgentius and Isidore to the popular tales of the *Legenda aurea* on which Chaucer drew for the etymologies of St Cecilia in the Prologue to the *Second Nun's Tale*. Although Spenser turns to the same source for the meanings of St George, he generally eschews the explicit and relaxed polysemy of the medieval *interpretatio*. (The one exception involves Malfont, who not coincidentally is the only figure in *FQ* to claim the 'bold title of a Poet' v ix 25–6.) More typically, the several meanings of a name have all to be inferred from aspects of the narrative situation and from subtle allusions – thematic and formal patternings which yield different senses depending on one's interpretive framework. We see this with particular clarity when Spenser chooses to animate some phonemic feature of a traditional literary name: Britomartis, for example, who is already associated with Diana or chastity in classical sources, becomes in her new context the martial Britoness (III ii 4, 9); Terpine, a popular name in medieval romance, becomes the 'unknightly' Sir Turpine (via L *turpis* 'base'); Timias, whose name should suggest honor (Gr *timē*), becomes in time a type of silent shame or 'timidity' (IV vii 44, VI v 24).

As these examples indicate, an obviously 'false' interpretation of a name may be as thematically or figuratively suggestive as a 'true' etymology; and indeed antithetical meanings may resonate successively or even simultaneously within a given section of narrative (see *puns). Some of the punning etymologies are sanctioned by exegetical or mythographic tradition (eg, the play on Gr *hēdonē* and Hebrew ᶜēden, both 'pleasure,' which links the Garden of Adonis to the biblical Eden), but most seem to be invented ad hoc like the names themselves. Moreover, allusions to Italian, Latin, or Greek 'roots' may be shadowed by one or more lateral puns – arbitrary contaminations which can attack any part of the etymological complex, from the root to the name itself. Narrative context and the criterion of thematic relevance help us discriminate among the possible combinations, hearing a music amid the babble, but thematic criteria are almost infinitely elastic. Harry Berger hears 'busy-reign' in Busirane (1971:100); others may simply hear the tyrant Busiris or an echo of 'abuse.' Irena (spelled Eirena in the 1596 ed) is derived from *eirēnē* 'peace,' but the homonym is also, ironically, the classical name for Ireland. The whole question of Celtic echoes remains unresolvable: are we to suppose, for example, that Spenser knew that the common Irish name Una means 'dearth' or 'poverty,' or that another Irish name, Dubhessa, might be translated 'black nurse' (R.M. Smith 1935b, 1946a, 1946b)?

The continual insistence of such borderline cases, like the inherent tendency of indeterminacies to breed beyond the control of any strict ratio, helps give to Spenser's work its unfettered exuberance, but it may also raise the specter of a primal chaos beneath the linguistic flux. At the limit, places, percepts, virtues, characters, indeed phenomena of any kind, occur only insofar as they are also something else, so that even as the poem offers itself to us as a chart, it ensures that the mapping process will be interminable. In Faerie, as in Borges' Tlön, 'the fact that no one believes in the reality of nouns paradoxically causes their number to be unending.' Within the phantasmagoric world of the text, names come to resemble the 'switch-words' or 'verbal bridges' of the Freudian dream work (Freud ed 1953–74, 5:340–1). Determined by a process of condensation, they are the poem's 'nodal points,' specific sites of intersection for an indefinite number of associative paths, some of which are motivated by phonetic, others by semantic echoes. And because they point backward and forward simultaneously, they exercise a continually unsettling effect on the progressive or teleological movement of the narrative.

Beyond this ready analogy with unconscious processes, the logic of Spenserian naming resists formalization. In the majority of cases, correspondence at the level of sound implies correspondence at the level of meaning as well; yet it is never clear on the basis of resonance alone whether these correspondent names should be allied or opposed. Calepine, for example, seems a fit surrogate for Calidore with whom he shares a syllable of his name, until we learn some stanzas later that he shares another with Turpine, his adversary (VI iii 27, 40). At times, the formal pattern seems to relegate all referential meaning to a subsidiary role, as in the pageant of interchangeable knights (Gardante, Parlante, Jocante, Basciante, Bacchante, Noctante) and the memorable triads (Sansfoy, Sansjoy, Sansloy; Despetto, Decetto, Defetto; Priamond, Diamond, Triamond), in which the significance of each figure derives largely from its place in the series. Spenser's fascination with the potential autonomy of sound is most apparent in the catalogue of the Nereids at the marriage of Thames and Medway (IV xi 48–51), where musical effects predominate, as though the endless possibilities for allusion and echo must ultimately yield to cantillation as to a more natural principle of order. And yet even here the descriptive epithets closely render the meaning of the Greek names ('Joyous *Thalia* ... milkewhite *Galathaea*'), implying a more conscious harmonization with temporal process, in which 'part of the point is that those phatic particulars, in whose flow we take such melopoetic pleasure, each come from somewhere' (Braden 1975:34).

The catalogue of Nereids is a limiting case, confirming that even the most transient names in *The Faerie Queene* are semantically saturated and historically resonant. Each is the title for the short poem or fable implicit in its etymology. Many students of Spenser tend to relate this resonance to the contemporary interest in a natural or adamic language and to the widespread belief that etymological research could uncover the true correspondence of words and things obscured by the fall or by the division of tongues at the tower of Babel (see Borst 1957–63:1048–1262). Drawing on the legacy of the Stoic grammarians, for whom *nomen* was *omen*, and on a lengthy tradition of scriptural exegesis which took names to be the transparent signs of sacred truths, such theories derived their greatest impetus in the sixteenth century from the recently recovered *Cratylus* of Plato, which became the meeting ground for a strange amalgam of Cabalistic, alchemical, and Hermeticist influences. On the continent, polyglot scholars like Guillaume Postel, Conrad Gesner, and Jean Bodin had established a powerful tradition of Cratylan research (see Dubois 1970); and in England, Spenser's teacher Richard Mulcaster felt obliged, despite the patently conventionalist argument of his *Elementarie*, to invoke Plato along with Adam's naming of the creatures as warrant for the importance of giving 'right names ... bycause the word being knowen, which implyeth the propertie the thing is half known, whose propertie is emplyed' (ch 24).

But the surprising coexistence of naturalist and conventionalist views within a single corpus (the same paragraph in Mulcaster also contains a reference to Aristotle and the 'voluntarie' – ie, arbitrary – nature of words) is more common than might be expected and should alert us to the rhetorical or ironic countercurrents in sixteenth-century onomastics. One could cite Camden, but for Spenser the lesson of the Pléiade poets was apt to have been more crucial. That du Bellay, for example, took a conventionalist position on the meaning of names in his prose writings did not prevent him from exploring in his sonnets the hidden significance of the name 'Olive,' chosen 'par destinée' (*L'Olive* 4), or from devoting an entire volume of Latin verse to the ancient technique, expressly linked to the *Cratylus*, of deducing a person's character from the etymology of his name (*Xenia, seu Illustrium quorundam nominum allusiones*). Such secret wit is clearly playful, as is the run of acrostics and anagrams, for all their 'antique nobility' (*Deffence* 2.8; see Rigolot 1977:129–54).

So too when George Peele derives English from 'Angeli' (*Arraignment of Paris*), or when Marlowe puns on 'Machevill' (*Jew of Malta*), or when Shakespeare predicts that 'a lion's whelp [Leonatus] shall ... be embrac'd by a piece of tender air [Imogen]' (*Cymbeline*), we begin to suspect that for Renaissance poets the much-heralded 'virtue' of names could be a highly artificial construct, and that its 'notation' through etymology was more often a topic of invention, as Aristotle and Cicero had asserted (*Rhetoric* 2.23, *Topics* 35), than a key to divine or original truths. Hence, the pertinence of Angus Fletcher's caveat against the 'misappropriation' of Renaissance Cratylism 'in the service of a moralizing theory of Spenser's "rhetorical mode"' (1971:104). Doubtless, Spenser is playing on the fantasy of natural motivation, of a correspondence between name and thing, when he writes 'His name *Ignaro* did his nature right aread' (I viii 31), or 'Her name is *Munera*, agreeing with her deedes' (v ii 9), or when he has Adicia (injustice) surpass the cruelty of the tiger 'To prove her surname true' (v viii 49); but such gestures, with their emphasis on the verbal medium of the poet's art, are more nearly parodic than restitutive.

Spenser recognizes the power of our primitive belief that names can determine or fix identity; it is this belief, after all, that animates even the simplest personification allegory, transforming a table of abstract nouns into a field of daemonic agents. But he also recognizes the danger latent in the overestimation of a name's mythic or conceptual force, and it is the danger that is most often dramatized. Redcrosse's pride, which renders him susceptible to the illusions of Archimago, begins with his failure to distinguish between a monster called 'Errour' and the many forms of error which continue to wander under other names, while the closest we get to a truly 'magical' identification of name and thing, or name and agent, is the pageant in Busirane's house, where the daemonized abstractions that torture Amoret are radical onomastic illusions, images of the tyranny that involuntary and unauthored words can exercise over body and mind.

Spenser's ultimate pragmatism in regard to names is best represented by the attitude of Eudoxus in the *Vewe of Ireland*, who attacks the excesses of philological divination characteristic of the antiquarians. Eudoxus dismisses the notion that the popular Irish battle cry 'Ferragh Ferragh' can be derived from 'Pharao' – an etymology purporting to show that the Irish descend from the Egyptian princess Scota – and mockingly pretends to derive the princess' own name from the Greek *scotos*, 'that is darkenes which hathe not let [such speculators] see the lighte of the truethe' *Var Prose* p 104). The task of philology here is not to recapture an authoritative or essential meaning but to dispel the illusion that names are the keys to hidden truths. For Spenser, the power of learned mystification is analogous to the power of the peasant cry itself, a form of Babelizing presumption or idolatry, whose real effects he knew only too well: 'a Terrible yell and Habbub, as if heaven and earthe woulde have gone togeather' (p 103). In *The Faerie Queene*, this scrupulosity is taken a step further when the chronicle of British kings preserved in the castle of Alma is broken off just before it reaches the name Arthur, thus warning us against the analogous dangers of genealogy and etymology, which, in binding the present to an authoritative source, may enslave it to a temporal idol. The transumptive pun that takes the broken idol's place, conflating the names of Arthur and Uther, transforms historical continuity into a more elusive promise, mediated by the self-effacing figure for Spenser's own project as 'th'Authour selfe' (II x 68).

In sum, Spenser's poetry reveals a complex awareness of the way that names or processes of naming can be dangerous and delusive as well as revelatory. His literary use of names may indeed be called 'magical,' for his language is a haunted medium in which buried or ghostly meanings are always being brought to light, displaying occult and at times grotesque connections between ordinarily divided realms of existence. Yet like the 'bad mixture' in Acrasia's cup, that name-magic inaugurates one quest only by cutting off another. Names and their etymologies may give us epigrammatic themes or motives for an episode, but these are invariably invitations to further reflection – questions which the narrative will have to explore rather than immutable conclusions or original truths. It is only by so continually reinventing the old etyma, by laying bare the persuasions embedded in words and thus exposing the naive and tyrannical forms of name-magic, that Spenser is able to fulfill the poet's office as legislator of names. His text, to borrow Plato's own figure in the *Cratylus*, is always a weaving, and naming is its shuttle. But 'right naming' in a world where 'all things ... in time are chaunged quight' (v proem 4) first requires the skeptical unweaving of the dialectician. Only when the old texts have been undone can the poet's task for an instant resemble Adam's.

HERBERT MARKS AND KENNETH GROSS

Joachim du Bellay 1974 *Xenia, seu Illustrium quorundam nominum allusiones* ed Malcolm Smith (Geneva); Belson 1964; Arno Borst 1957–63 *Der Turmbau von Babel: Geschichte der Meinungen über Ursprung und Vielfalt der Sprachen und Völker* 4 vols (Stuttgart); Braden 1975; Craig 1959; Craig 1967; J.W. Draper 1932; Claude-Gilbert Dubois 1970 *Mythe et langage au seizième siècle* (Bordeaux); Fletcher 1971:96–106; Alastair Fowler 1989 'Spenser's Names' in Logan and Teskey 1989:32–48; Hamilton 1972b; Hamilton in *FQ* ed 1977; François Rigolot 1977 *Poétique et onomastique: L'Exemple de la renaissance* (Geneva); Roland M. Smith 1935b; Smith 1946a 'Irish Names in *The Faerie Queene*' *MLN* 61:27–38; Smith 1946b 'A Further Note on Una and Duessa' *PMLA* 61:592–6.

Narcissus A youth who falls in love with his reflection in a pool (Ovid *Metamorphoses* 3.339–510); the reflection is in effect identified with Echo, the nymph who loves him but cannot speak for herself. This fable explores problems of self-knowledge and self-possession; medieval and Renaissance poets applied it to their lives and their art with nearly limitless variation (Cave 1979, Goldin 1967, Vinge 1967). The despairing cry of Narcissus appears as Diggon Davies' emblem in *September*: 'inopem me copia fecit' (*Met* 3.466, 'my plentie makes me poore' in Golding's 1567 translation). E.K. comments, 'This poesie I knowe, to have bene much used of the author, and to suche like effecte, as fyrste Narcissus spake it.' Spenser repeats the paradox in *Amoretti* 35 and *FQ* I iv 29.

The speaker in *Amoretti* 35 is satisfied neither with nor without the object of his 'hungry eyes,' the 'faire sight' of the lady. In her presence, his eyes are 'in their amazement lyke *Narcissus* vaine / whose eyes him starv'd: so plenty makes me poore.' The lady's presence is the plenty that makes him poor; his viewing her arouses a hunger through his eyes that she cannot satisfy. The last six lines of the sonnet make clear that her beauty represents for him a higher reality than the vain 'glory' and 'shadowes' of the world that he has previously accepted. He contrasts the contemplation of her beauty with the quest for illusory worldly glory traditionally identified with the allegorized figure of Narcissus (Rogers 1976). His problem remains, however, that the lady has left him dissatisfied with the shadow world, without satisfying the hunger that she has aroused for a higher reality.

The Neoplatonic overtones in this sonnet suggest Ficino's commentary on Plato's *Symposium* (6.17), where he follows Plotinus (*Enneads* I.6.8) in seeing Narcissus as a symbol of the human soul searching for its own beauty – a reflection of divine beauty – but unwittingly seduced by the reflection of that beauty in the body. Ficino's interpretation presumably would apply to any love relationship in which the lover tries to find his true self in a particular loved one, for any person is by Ficino's definition a shadowy reflection of the true self.

A striking parallel between the speaker in *Amoretti* 35 and the lover in the more explicitly Neoplatonic *Hymne of Love* makes the influence of Ficino seem even more likely. After relating how love fashions the mind into a 'fairer forme' in which the lover 'Admires the mirrour of so heavenly light,' Spenser describes the lover as feeding his 'hungrie fantasy' on the image: 'Like *Tantale*, that in store doth sterved ly: / So doth he pine in most satiety' (193–201). The apparent echo of the Ovidian motto in this passage links the Narcissus-like lover of *Amoretti*, the Tantalus-like lover here, and the personification of Avarice in the house of Pride, 'Whose wealth was want, whose plenty made him pore' (*FQ* I iv 29). That Spenser conceived of narcissistic love as a kind of avarice, a hoarding of the self, is apparent in *FQ* III.

Spenser's most important use of the Narcissus myth is in the episode of *FQ* III that explains the origin of Britomart's love for Artegall. After unwittingly falling in love with the image that she has seen in the enchanted globe given her father by Merlin, earlier called '*Venus* looking glas' (i 8), Britomart complains to Glauce that her situation is even more hopeless than that of Narcissus: 'I fonder, then *Cephisus* foolish child, / Who having vewed in a fountaine shere / His face, was with the love thereof beguild; / I fonder love a shade, the bodie farre exild' (ii 44). Glauce challenges the validity of the comparison; but although she is right that the image Britomart complains of is not literally a self-reflection, it is also true that Britomart has seen an idealized self-projection (Nelson 1963:232–3, de Gerenday 1976). She has moved from seeing a simple reflection in the 'mirrhour fayre' to using the globe's magic power to show her whatever 'mote to her selfe pertaine,' in this case the 'manly face' of her future husband (22, 24). Glauce herself suggests the subjectivity of this sequence when she tells Britomart that it is most reasonable 'To love the semblant pleasing most your mind' (40); Spenser makes it explicit later when Britomart muses on her 'lovers shape' as she rides to the sea: 'A thousand thoughts she fashioned in her mind, / And in her feigning fancie did pourtray / Him such, as fittest she for love could find' (iv 5). Spenser's pun on *feigning* (like Touchstone's in *As You Like It* III iii) underlines the connection of desire and fancy's creation.

The reflecting globe in this episode can be related to the Platonic mirror in *Phaedrus* 255D, to the mirror in Chaucer's *Squire's Tale*, and perhaps most significantly to the literary convention stemming from the *Romance of the Rose* which associates the fountain of Narcissus with the origin of love (Edwards 1977). The Dreamer in the *Romance* resembles Britomart, for both first see themselves in the mirror, then fall in love with the reflected image of someone else (the rose, the knight), and finally turn away from the mirror to find their real object. Their love has a narcissistic beginning, but both avoid the fate of Narcissus by finding an object of love other than a reflection of themselves.

Given the causal logic of allegory, the narcissistic beginning of Britomart's love makes it inevitable that she should shortly encounter a true Narcissus in Marinell. His treasure, hoarded on the seashore (III iv 22–3), symbolizes his character as 'loves enimy,' someone who will not share himself with another human being and who hoards himself as well as his treasure. Marinell's nature is underlined by Florimell's later appeal to the sea gods: 'And let him live unlov'd, or love him selfe alone' (IV xii 9). Marinell and Narcissus are both offspring of water beings, both are loved by others but do not love in return, and both have been the subject of cryptic prophecies to their mothers (Nohrnberg 1976:431–2, 645–6). Marinell is what Britomart might have become had she remained fixed before the mirror.

The figure of the transformed Narcissus appears in the Garden of Adonis in the company of Hyacinthus and Amaranthus (as in the flower catalog in *Virgils Gnat* 665–80), one of the 'sad lovers ... transformd of yore' into flowers: 'Foolish *Narcisse*, that likes the watry shore' (*FQ* III vi 45). Even here, Narcissus is characterized as 'foolish,' the same word Britomart had applied to him; but in his folly he has now become a symbol of longing for the impossible. Like Amaranthus, he is now one 'To whom sweet Poets verse hath given endlesse date.' He exists in a realm of the imagination, for he is not part of the cycle of generation like the other things planted in the garden, nor is he subject to Time that mows down everything outside this central grove 'Whose shadie boughes sharpe steele did never lop' (vi 43; Berger 1960–1). If Narcissus and the other transformed lovers in the Garden of Adonis escape time and death through metamorphosis, by the same token they fail to achieve fulfillment of their loves (Cheney 1966:134). One of Spenser's finest ironies is that Narcissus, a figure of eternally unfulfilled love, should be memorialized in a place that is a seminary of life. CALVIN R. EDWARDS

Terence Cave 1979 *The Cornucopian Text: Problems of Writing in the French Renaissance* (Oxford); Calvin R. Edwards 1977 'The Narcissus Myth in Spenser's Poetry' *SP* 74:63–88; Lynn de Gerenday 1976 'The Problem of Self-Reflective Love in Book III of "The Faerie Queene"' *L&P* 26:37–48; Frederick Goldin 1967 *The Mirror of Narcissus in the Courtly Love Lyric* (Ithaca, NY); William Elford Rogers 1976 'Narcissus in *Amoretti* XXXV' *AN&Q* 15:18–20; Louise Vinge 1967 *The Narcissus Theme in Western European Literature up to the Early Nineteenth Century* tr Robert Dewsnap, et al (Lund).

narrative Narration uses language to symbolize real or fictional events in temporal relation. The resulting *narrative* inseparably represents both the events and the act of narration itself. The sequence of events in a fictional narrative is called the 'story' or, technically, the 'fable.' The discourse that symbolizes the fable may imitate the voice of a characterized narrator, it may personify transient inflections or rhetorical postures without asserting a consistent narratorial identity, or it may appear as impersonal utterance. Spenser employs all of these forms of narration, but the latter two prevail in *The Faerie Queene*.

The first stanza of the poem recalls Virgil and Ariosto, both of whom unified their epics by speaking in the voice of a steadily maintained, omniscient narrator. Spenser emulates neither of them in this respect even though he begins with imagery of the poet as shepherd-singer and, through allusions that parallel his own literary career with Virgil's, invokes expectations that the narrative perspective will be bounded by a single consciousness. The proems that introduce successive books reassert this initial voice (albeit in progressively disillusioned moods beginning with Book IV; see *FQ, proems and arguments), and the poem ends with a very brief fragmentary canto that raises this voice in prayer.

Various attitudes of the narrator as a character are suggested in the proems, at the beginnings of cantos, and in other passages scattered throughout the text. Any account of a putative narrator must be based on such passages. The ways of speaking are primarily didactic (II proem 2) and homiletic (I x 1, II viii 1), but range from the encomiastic (I proem 4) to the vituperative (V ix 1), from the hortatory (I i 18) to the dissuasive (III ix 2), from the proleptic (II proem 4) to the retrospective (V i 1). Frequently the address is scholarly and authoritative (III ii 20). Yet, despite such learned sophistication, the traits that may be thought to qualify this narrator as a distinct character paradoxically find complete summation in *Colin Clouts Come Home Againe*, where the naive shepherd poet, appearing as the chief speaker among several pastoral figures, informs their dramatic interchange with humility, emotional empathy, unaffected grace, and bewildered outrage at worldly corruption. Colin Clout reappears in *FQ* VI and, because of autobiographical references connected with this name in *The Shepheardes Calender* and *Colin Clout*, is usually considered as Spenser's portrait of himself in poetic garb.

On the whole, however, Spenser's narrative in *The Faerie Queene* moves seamlessly among multiple perspectives, the fleeting adoption of which is integral to the peculiar quality of his allegory. This narrative is nondramatic, expository, conceptually ordered, and selectively focused; in contrast to *Colin Clout*, it is not structured on a continuous grid of temporal, spatial, and psychological phenomena capable of representing personal identity. The interpretive construct known as Spenser's narrator is a specialized kind of personification inscribed rhetorically within the text in the form of intermittent vocal responses to its imagined action. These responses are situational and limited – sometimes mistaken, often momentary or incomplete – and the personification by which we attribute coherent meaning to them, as with other personifications in the poem, becomes present as the allegory unfolds through the interplay of linguistic elements in the reader's awareness, not, as in the more specifically referential *Colin Clout*, through the illusion of dramatic presence. This interplay of linguistic signals enables us to grasp the allegory. Only occasionally does its meaning include the specific presence of a narrator personally identifiable as a character. Narrator and fable are no more than enabling devices that allow interpretation to proceed: both dwell equally, and always inseparably, in the narration. The discourse represents a sequence of utterances attributable at any instant to some speaker but not necessarily to a single, sustained consciousness.

The poem mimics natural diversity by fluidly representing the world from many perspectives: historical, mystical, national, ethical, moral, generic, personal, theological, spiritual. A novel, by contrast, may recreate the world from the continuous, unified perspective of an individual who is imagined to be real, tangible, and capable of action in the actual plot of the work. In the first three books of *The Faerie Queene* especially, the narration proceeds more as a ritual recitation or charismatic vocalization in tongues than as the personal utterance of an individual. The poem can be described as embodying intelligent awareness but not a central, directing will; it can be described, from the vantage of the novel, as a narration lacking a narrator.

Spenser's abandonment of Ariostan narration is perhaps the most striking symptom of his abdication of rigorously specified meaning in favor of process. The residues of omniscient narration that remain need to be read not as signs of a narrator everywhere present but rather as reminders of his absence. Distinctive among heroic poets, Spenser adopts scattered points of view, the very transience of which calls attention to the momentary, incomplete, phenomenal nature of human understanding. 'Point of view' implies a viewer and something to view – the term assumes a continuum of time and space – but *The Faerie Queene* presents an imaginative and transcendent world. Even the many familiar, workaday objects woven into its fabric are made strange by their depiction as elements in a fragmented, partially knowable, ultimately mysterious realm. Fairyland is a construct, 'deepe within the mynd' (VI proem 5), of a reality higher than any single personality and accessible only through Spenser's text.

Spenser assigns the role of maintaining interpretive coherence to the reader. *The Faerie Queene* aims to *educate* in the full etymological sense of that word: to *lead forth*. According to the Letter to Raleigh, the 'generall end therefore of all the booke is to fashion a gentleman or noble person in vertuous and gentle discipline.' The poem must be 'coloured with an historicall fiction' in order to reach 'a pleasing Analysis of all'; but as *coloured* implies (with its reference to the classical subordination of figures and tropes of speech to those of thought and judgment), Spenser does not give fable primacy of place either in theory or in practice.

He favors discontinuous geographic, historical, and topical references over Ariosto's explicit world geography and generally avoids the delineation of realistically precise temporal and spatial perspectives (see *FQ, geography of). The encompassing fiction of *The Faerie Queene* is that a world which exists elsewhere takes over the poetic will. This fiction requires the narration to proceed as if uttered in continual distraction. The effect is reminiscent of dream-visions in Francesco Colonna's *Hypnerotomachia Poliphili* and Chaucer's *Book of the Duchess*. Spenser adopts the conventions of medieval romance – *entrelacement* above all – as means to analytic and argumentative exposition. His narrative method is at one with his stress on 'a pleasing Analysis of all.' Ariosto, by contrast, manipulates romance conventions to create the appearance of character in his ironic, self-dramatizing narrator, the illusion of whose consciousness depends upon the obtrusive virtuosity with which he controls the narrative medium as if it were emanating from a single psychologized presence.

Although Spenser's habitual mode of narration continues in the last three books, the voice becomes somewhat more personal, the fable proportionally more prominent, and the narration more often dramatic – as when Scudamour, himself a character in the action, retrospectively narrates the Temple of Venus episode (IV x). Yet when Spenser's official poetic persona, the shepherd Colin Clout, emerges in *FQ* VI as a character with a role in the story, he is placed on Mount Acidale where his piping evokes an epiphany of dancing Graces (x 10–16) but cannot sustain their presence when Calidore intrudes. The Graces vanish and the shepherd, having first broken his pipe in fury, is left to explicate their meaning and to demonstrate gracious behavior towards Calidore rather than to experience the virtue as unmediated divinity (21–8). His poetic world, formed generically on pastoral romance and reflective song rather than on the public genre of the heroic poem, cannot accommodate the simultaneity of event and interjection that characterizes the narrative when it is untrammeled by personal presence. Colin's very standing as a character closely allied with the voice of *FQ* VI implies a move away from the earlier mode of narration towards the more personal forms of utterance like lyric.

Spenser's narrative method parallels the poem's multiplicity of structure, whereby each virtue is seen in its various aspects through the adventures of a different knight in each book. Arthur represents magnificence, the sum of all virtues, but we see him act only with respect to specific virtues. Similarly, Spenser refers to Elizabeth as Gloriana or the Fairy Queen, although we see her directly in the person of Belphoebe – who, in turn, is a type of Cynthia or Diana, and so forth. As with the largest structures of the poem, the groupings of individual stanzas that make up single cantos and sustained episodes reflect different points of view. Even single stanzas may reflect a shifting, multiple awareness (eg, II xii 35, 73).

Spenser does not use the term *narrative*, but rather calls *The Faerie Queene* a 'continued Allegory' (Letter). His primary stress lies on metaphoric relations (especially of linguistic elements) and on a process of interpretation recognized by Renaissance definitions which assume that allegory is as much a way of reading as a way of writing. Since contemporary descriptions of allegory view the form as a specific figure of speech, an extended metaphor, and consider its function chiefly at the level of single sentences, Spenser's application of the phrase 'continued Allegory' to his entire poem implies an awareness that he is doing something different: he is altering the emphasis of a received poetics founded on the hierarchy of value in rhetorical theory, where invention and judgment took precedence over metaphoric elaboration (which was considered as ornament), and laying a new stress on extended symbolic and linguistic interrelations while relatively diminishing the role of fable to that of ornament or 'color.' Where 'allegory' had traditionally been a figure of speech (one of the decorative colors of rhetorical language) and fable had been allied with invention (the primary process of composition), Spenser puts the process of figuration at the center and subordinates fable. He retains the traditional terms but inverts their relationship. The 'vertuous and gentle discipline' that he insists upon is none other than the process of reading. Instead of allowing a narrator to dominate the world of the poem and define its interpretation, Spenser leads us to discover transcendence within ourselves.

JOHN BENDER

Alpers 1962; Alpers 1977; Bender 1972; Dees 1970–1; Durling 1965; Goldberg 1981; Kouwenhoven 1983; Tuve 1966.

narrator of *The Faerie Queene* A dramatic projection of the implied author, the narrator of *The Faerie Queene* is an aspect of the poem's rhetorical structure, a facilitating means to its end of fashioning a noble person (Letter to Raleigh). Although we cannot assume that this narrating presence is dramatically consistent – he vacillates between authorial omniscience and a more limited subjection to the world of appearances – it is helpful to view him as a character who, like the poem's protagonists, is on a quest. He faces their problems of knowing and doing: he must determine where truth lies and confront the difficulty of bringing it into palpable form, and he must consider the obstacles that make it difficult for this form to affect human action. As a dramatic character, he is defined by how he addresses his audience and by what he says of his aims, his abilities, and the difficulties of writing his 'historye.'

The narrator's principal metaphors for himself, as mariner (I xii 1, 42; VI xii 1) and plowman (III xii 47 in 1590 *FQ*, V iii 40, VI ix 1), stress both adventure and quotidian labor. In criticizing the debased values of his contemporaries (III iv 1–3, IV viii 29–33) and, more specifically, their shortsighted political leaders (IV proem 1, VI xii 41), he places himself in the tradition of great poets who have shaped the cultural destinies of their nations – Homer, Virgil, Ariosto, and 'Dan *Chaucer*,' to whom in particular he expresses a close and tense relationship (IV ii 32–4, VI iii 1, VII vii 9). He is alert to, yet nervous about, an audience that includes Queen Elizabeth, 'gentle Ladies' of varying moral color (III v 53–4, ix 2; VI viii 1–2), idealistic, aspiring knights (I iv 1), hardheaded politicians (IV proem 1–2), 'devicefull' clerks (V x 1), and boasting British adventurers (IV xi 22). Unimaginative empiricists join listeners better attuned to poetry's indirections (II proem 2–4), and among those who will smile at the poem's supernatural indulgences will be one whose puritanical aversion to 'loose incontinence' must be placated (III iii 8–9, ix 1). Members of the rising middle or lower classes may punctuate this courtly gathering, by implication, in the crowds that gape upon the Dragon's carcass or the muzzled Blatant Beast. This diversity complicates the narrator's concern to differentiate false from sound principles, to anchor these sound principles in social, political, moral, and theological virtues, and to strengthen the efforts of people of good will toward moral reform.

For the narrator, truth lies ultimately in an objective, ideal, and transcendent world. It is effective, however, only if apprehended and applied in daily life. Yet in the process, it becomes fragmented, multiple, and its sources obscured. This condition is mirrored in the poem by the narrator's imputing the source of his narrative variously to a 'sacred Muse' (I ii 1–2, 4; III iii 4; IV xi 10), to 'antique records' (III proem 3, vi 6; IV i 1), and to folk wisdom (III iii 7–8; IV viii 1, ix 27, x 1), and by his adopting a stance of humility toward these sources (I xii 23, II x 50, III viii 43). But this characteristic posture often seems at odds with an optimistic, authoritative tone: we may feel that his confident desire to 'blazon broad' long-slumbering praises belies the self-effacement of 'Me, all too meane,' or suspect that he covertly regards his 'lowly verse' as quite equal to the 'haughtie enterprise' of chronicling 'Briton moniments.' Such incongruity opens a gap between two possible loci of authority: the 'history' itself and the poet's mediating presence. This gap is embodied in the distinction felt between the continually evolving mimetic fiction, and the interpretive commentary which often arrests that movement. The reader is left uncertain whether to accord authority to the mimesis – thus perceiving the narrator to be unreliable, falsely confident, impercipient, or overhasty in his assessment of what his tale shows of the complexities of lived human experience – or to privilege the narrator's reflective, sober, usually discriminating judgments.

The first stanza of *FQ* I x, ending 'But all the good is Gods, both power and eke will,' illustrates the problem. On the one hand, the stanza confirms a lesson that Una has just taught Redcrosse in the cave of Despair: 'Where justice growes, there grows eke greater grace' (ix 53); the questing narrator has been instructed by his tale. And as all learning is subject to refinement and qualification, we look for his rigid determinism to be modified as he accompanies Redcrosse through the house of Holiness. In retrospect, this comment seems inadequate. On the other hand, by its initial position and measured tone, and by its insinuation of scriptural authority (cf Eph 2.8–9, Rom 13.1, Phil 2.13), the statement has the ring of settled and certain wisdom; and we may feel that to subordinate this authority to the tale, and to view the narrator ironically, would be arbitrary. The extended generalizations of Spenser's canto openings are particularly vulnerable to this uncertainty: they condense the attained wisdom of the cultural tradition while allowing something of the special, idiosyncratic human instance to elude them. In such cases, it may be preferable to think of a 'provisional' authority neither fully in the teller nor the tale, an authority derived from the metaphysical, moral, and historical truths with which the narrator is intimately in touch, his comments speaking truth though never the complete truth.

In this provisional confidence, the narrator is much like the Renaissance preacher, whose sermon embodies simultaneously the strength of faith in his calling and a humility grounded in his fallen nature. Paradoxically, his spiritual authority as the means by which the redeeming Word is heard is qualified by his powerlessness actually to save; his sermon must be a responsive act of inducement, pointing the hearer toward goals that the hearer alone can attain. Similarly, the narrator's comments strategically involve the reader as much as they instruct him. The preacher's art, however, is a *sermo*, or familiar conversation with the *hearer* of the Word, whereas Spenser's narrator insists on the metaphor of reading. Forms of the verb *to read* with at least fifteen denotations appear over 130 times in the poem; his audience specifically includes readers (III ii 20, iv 2); and he designates his six books Legends (from L *legere* 'to read, to pass through, to follow the footsteps of'; perhaps also 'to choose'). The insistence on reading reflects conditions of Spenser's own time, in which the transition from the oral to the written tradition was still in process; but more importantly, it embodies the epistemological assumption that coming to know oneself and others is an act of reciprocity: the reader actively completes what the writer has written. This fact is just as true of hearing, but by using *read* when the sense is 'declare' or 'tell' (I viii 31), 'speak of' (IV xii 2), 'call' or 'name' (III vi 28), 'see' or 'discern' (V vi 8), or 'understand' (III xii 26) the narrator capitalizes on the full etymological range of the verb with its emphasis on judgment, discernment, interpretation, and counsel. To be fashioned is to fashion, no innocent act, but always one of interpreting, of seeing aright when one might as easily see wrong. The narrator will not permit his reader a passive role in the fiction-making process; the reader is as much on a quest as are narrator and protagonist.

Spenser's conception of the poem's making as a reciprocal enterprise accounts for the way he continually parallels his narrator with both his protagonists and their antagonists. As Redcrosse seeks to liberate Una's parents, Britomart to rescue Amoret, and Calidore to capture the Blatant Beast, so the narrator seeks to embody the meaning of his foreconceit in poetic images which will adequately mediate between his idea and the reader's act. The sailing metaphor applied to both narrator and protagonists (cf I xii 1 and 42 with I vi 1, III iv 8–10, and VI ix 31) underscores the central danger for both – the continual pressure to withdraw prematurely from the rigor of social action into havens of contemplative ease. For protagonist and narrator alike, rest must be hard won (I x 63, VI ix 24–5). The narrator also parallels the antagonists and is implicated continuously in the moral corruption which his images seek to combat. When he asks Clio to 'sharpen my dull tong' (I proem 2), what he asks may not readily be distinguished from Archimago's ability to 'file his tongue as smooth as glas' (i 35). If the methods of good intention are hard to tell from those of evil ones, how trustworthy are the narrator's claims to truth? Book V shows us in the image of Malfont, his original good name erased, his tongue nailed to a post for bold speeches and lewd poems, the potential fate of any narrator – this one included. How 'tickle' indeed may be the terms of the right poet's estate when his conscientious efforts to enrich memory, enable judgment, and enlarge conceit may meet on every side with misunderstanding and distortion, ranging from the outright malice of Ate's disciples to the misguidedness of state functionaries unable to imagine how rhymes might conduce to disciplined virtue. To recognize these perils of judgment is to understand and aid the narrator's efforts toward reform because we acknowledge complicity in the viciousness that impedes it. Our responsibility to read his images aright must match his responsibility to mediate the muse's truth through them.

Over the course of the poem, the narrator's initial optimism, his confidence in the educability of his audience, and his adventurous enthusiasm gradually sour. He turns inward, becomes self-reflexive, feels alienated from a 'wicked world,' wishes on one side to escape from it and the burden of his poem, and on the other to resolve their conflicts either in nostalgia for a simpler, more virtuous past or in hope for a future 'Sabaoths sight' and peace. He expresses a heightened sense of his own unworthiness (V proem 11), feelings of bodily and mental fatigue (VI proem 1), a disinclination to keep coping with the nuances of complex experience (VI x 2–3), and at times seemingly, a cynicism masking capitulation to despair (VI xii 41). These changes, set forth most cogently in the proems, are only in part a record of the emotional toll taken by his heroic efforts to compose a poem that will be 'exemplary to a Nation' (Milton ed 1953–82, 1:815). More importantly, they embody a profound self-examination and show the narrator confronting the most difficult philosophical and aesthetic questions of his age.

The Faerie Queene is a heroic testing of Sidney's belief that right poetry is able to reform readers in the image of God. Spenser asks searchingly, Does poetry 'draw us to as high a perfection as our degenerate souls made worse by their clayey lodgings, can be capable of'? (Sidney ed 1973b:82), and What are the limits of its power? In each proem, the narrator pursues these questions from a different angle, and with increasing skepticism (see **FQ*, proems). The first announces optimistically the Sidneyan mission: 'I the man,' heir of Virgil and Ariosto, am commanded by my Muse to 'blazon broad' the praiseworthiness of knights and ladies. The second proem acknowledges what became obvious only as Book I revealed the duplicitous power of an Archimago – that this poem, whatever its intent, can be read either as truth or lie, as 'matter of just memory' or 'painted forgery.' The proem to Book III goes further by admitting that the poet's images may not be capable of bodying forth reality 'in such excellency as he hath imagined [it]' (Sidney ed 1973b:79). The fourth recognizes that, even could the poet succeed in taming the slipperiness of language to his foreconceit, his best efforts are subject to imaginative failure or to willful misjudgment by readers.

Faced with these realizations, the narrator begins Book V with little of his initial optimism. The task ahead parallels Artegall's: as the hero must apply to a badly fallen world theories of justice formulated in a golden age, so must the narrator confront the political realities of a rapacious historical world, armed with the residual ideals of a mythical fairy realm, small proof against the onslaughts of envy and detraction. Unable in Book V to find the means to effect public reform, being frustrated in all his humanistic assumptions, the narrator no less than Calidore seeks in Book VI to forget his 'tedious travell' by withdrawing into pastoral myth, where he may discover 'the sacred noursery / Of vertue.' Questioning the source of courtesy, whether 'in outward shows' or 'deepe within the mynd,' he finds a provisional, ambiguous answer in the circular movement of courtesy's giving, transforming, and receiving. When Colin teaches Calidore on Mount Acidale that virtue is a process of transference, his efforts imply that in mysterious ways poetry is a source of virtue. But Colin's vision is vulnerable to Calidore's intrusion, and he breaks his pipe in despair, not knowing whether his gesture has had real effect on Calidore's subsequent public actions. Just so does the narrator, vulnerable to the predations of a newly escaped Blatant Beast, retire into cynical expediency: 'Therfore ... my rimes ... seeke to please' (VI xii 41). We may read this two ways: it may be the final capitulation of art to an overpowering inimical reality, or its abrupt silence may signal the moment of transference when the circle initiated by the poet's efforts to reform must be closed by our own responsive efforts to comprehend.

JEROME S. DEES

Alpers 1977; Anderson 1971b; Berger 1961a; Dees 1970–1; DeNeef 1982; Durling 1965; Helgerson 1983, ch 2; Stan Hinton 1974 'The Poet and His Narrator: Spenser's Epic Voice' *ELH* 41:165–81; K. Williams 1969.

Nashe, Thomas (1567–1601) Until recently, the history of sixteenth-century English literature has been written in such a way as to emphasize the differences between Spenser and Nashe, if only by implication. This emphasis is understandable, since the differences are manifest. A generation gap separates the two authors, Spenser having been born fifteen years before Nashe. Contrasts are abundant between the courtier poet and the vulgar prose writer, between the Neoplatonic idealist and the street-wise empiricist, between the 'sage and serious' teacher and the popular comedian, between the upholder of pastoral and epic decorum and the popularizing pamphleteer, between the Virgil of Elizabethan England and the would-be Juvenal. The poet writing under aristocratic patronage stands in contrast to the journalistic producer of instant copy; the Irish landowner and imperial civil servant, to the self-proclaimed outcast adrift in the city; the associate of Raleigh, to the friend of scandalous Marlowe and lamentable Greene. The Spenser whom Lodowyck Bryskett portrays taking part in civil dialogues might be contrasted with the Nashe who admits his own participation in the wild banquet of pickled herring that apparently brought on Greene's death. Finally, the respective attitudes of Spenser and Nashe to Gabriel Harvey reveal extensive differences of literary fashion and temperament: to Spenser, Harvey is professedly a respected academic mentor and literary confidant, whereas to Nashe he is a discredited pedant, perhaps known chiefly for his ludicrous devotion to English hexameters. 'Immortall *Spencer*,' writes Nashe, 'no frailtie hath thy fame, but the imputation of this Idiots friendship' (ed 1904–10, 1:282).

This tale of differences – of generation gaps, contrasting personae, aristocratic and bohemian literary settings – is too simple and dramatic. Not only did Nashe and Spenser share gentlemanly pretensions, a Cambridge education, and a wide range of humanist loyalties and assumptions, but both inhabited the world of Elizabethan cultural politics – of patronage networks, of a technology of printing that offered significant opportunities to authors of every kind (Spenser exploits the resources of the press and of a reading public no less than does Nashe), and of constantly shifting ideological and political alliances. Both Spenser and Nashe, for example, appeal to Lady Carey for patronage; and Nashe complains that Spenser has neglected to include 'Amyntas' (presumably a courtier and putative patron) among those praised in the dedicatory sonnets published with the 1590 *Faerie Queene* (1:243). Nashe no less than Spenser exalts the memory of Sidney, and he too makes a flattering bid for the Countess of Pembroke's favor in his preface to Thomas Newman's unauthorized 1591 edition of *Astrophil and Stella* (3:329–33). Nashe and Spenser do not, in short, inhabit totally separate worlds.

Overemphasis on the differences between Nashe and Spenser has resulted in a certain critical blindness to Nashe's enthusiastic lobbying for Spenser, or else rendered it inexplicable. Not only is Nashe's work peppered with eulogistic references to Spenser, but he writes as if the two have a common stake in seeing English literature flourish in their time. Some of his references constitute important (if unreliable) testimony to the facts of Spenser's career. It is Nashe, for example, who claims that Harvey, not Spenser, was responsible for the publication of the Spenser-Harvey letters (1:295–6), and who claims that *Mother Hubberds Tale* had provoked 'displeasure.' 'Who publikely accusde or of late brought *Mother Hubbard* into question ... ?' he writes in 1592, accusing Harvey of raking up a scandal that could once again harm the poet (1:281). Other references constitute important (though again unreliable) evidence about Spenser's reputation in the 1590s; they also help to establish some of the terms in which Spenser's poetry could be appreciated (and perhaps deprecated) during his lifetime.

Nashe must have known *The Shepheardes Calender* and the 1590 *Faerie Queene* almost from the start of his own career. Presumably, he would have become acquainted with Spenser's other volumes as they appeared, though he refers directly only to *Mother Hubberd* and *The Faerie Queene*. (There is also at least one reference to Colin Clout, and a possible allusion to *Virgils Gnat*.) His references are consistently laudatory, emphasizing Spenser's supreme 'wit' and philosophical power as '*Apollo* ... his *Socrates*' (3:323). (Perhaps it is generationally determined rather than fortuitous, however, that Nashe does *not* emphasize Spenser's character as pastoral poet, that genre not only having become unfashionable by his time but also having provoked one of his characteristic outbursts: '*Pan* sitting in his bower of delights, and a number of *Midasses* to admire his miserable hornepipes' 3:329.) In extolling Spenser as early as 1589 as the supreme glory of English poetry, Nashe not only testifies to his having established a significant public reputation but simultaneously attempts to ride the wave of his success. His promotion of Spenser is always inseparable from his attempts at self-promotion, and it is worth noting that the poet's name could be so conjured with in the early 1590s.

Nashe's advocacy of Spenser is an even more complex phenomenon than all of this suggests. For him, Spenser is a figure of uncompromised distinction who can be enlisted in the continuing defense of poetry against its many Elizabethan detractors. Spenser's own defense against censorious objectors and violent slanderers is thus repeated by Nashe, though not necessarily in terms or contexts of which Spenser would have approved. Indeed, Nashe gives a violently polemical turn to this defense, which becomes almost an antiphilistine crusade once he embarks on it. Both the reception and the defense of Spenser's poetry are thus 'transported' from an idealized courtly or aristocratic setting into one more public and contentious than Spenser might have wanted or acknowledged. Perhaps this helps to account for Spenser's own attempt to shield his poetic identity and fictional world from the ravages of the Blatant Beast (*FQ* VI).

In exploiting Spenser's name in the defense of poetry, Nashe suggests that Spenser is a national asset and places his work (and, to a lesser extent, Chaucer's) on the same plane as that of the great classical and Renaissance authors, claiming as early as 1589 that he would 'preferre divine Master *Spencer* ... to bandie line by line ... against Spaine, Fraunce, Italy, and all the world' (preface to Greene's *Menaphon* in Nashe ed 1904–10, 3:323). Nashe thus assimilates Spenser – as Spenser does himself – to an English linguistic and literary nationalism that becomes increasingly buoyant throughout the sixteenth century, finding its culminating expression in Meres' *Palladis Tamia* (1598). This nationalistic appreciation contributed significantly to the growth of Spenser's reputation during the 1590s; it also facilitated Nashe's strongly patriotic defense of both Spenser and English drama against Puritans and other detractors. For Nashe, however, one prerequisite of this literary nationalism is a capacity to distinguish English authors of real merit from a university-trained horde of 'mechanicall mate[s]' and 'triviall translators,' not to speak of 'hexameterly entranced' pedants like Harvey (3:311, 315, 37). The real stars, in other words, must be identified if serious comparisons are to be entertained between English literature and its Greek, Latin, or Italian counterparts. An opinionated 'practical criticism' and ranking of English authors thus becomes a notable feature of Nashe's writing. In contrast to Sidney's *Defence of Poetry*, which is a theoretical defense incorporating a brief survey of the English literary scene, Nashe's preface to *Menaphon* is virtually all contentious survey, informed by somewhat obscure canons of judgment.

Perhaps because of differing social opportunity and literary fashions, Nashe did not model his work to any significant extent on Spenser's. 'Spenserian' elements are admittedly visible: for example, the Chaucerianism of 'The Choise of Valentines,' the motif of the seven deadly sins in *Pierce Penilesse* and *Christs Teares over Jerusalem*, and the use of beast fable for purposes of political allegory in *Pierce Penilesse*. Yet none of these elements need have been borrowed directly from Spenser. Both authors had access to a common literary stock; but whereas Spenser's treatment is characteristically decorous, Nashe's is 'demystifying,' violently parodic, or even scurrilous. The pastoral prelude to 'The Choise of Valentines' merely sets the reader up for the humorous shock of a pornographic revelation, while in *Pierce Penilesse*, as in Marlowe's *Dr Faustus*, the personified sins are brought in to entertain, not instruct. The world of Spenser's noble fictions has been left behind. Yet even here, the writers' ways do not entirely part. The poet-protagonist of Spenser's *Prothalamion* (1596) divests himself of his own pastoral, heroic, and epithalamic fictions, emerging as a 'malcontent' who has finally come home to his own solitude – not in an idealized courtly setting, but in the city of his birth.

JONATHAN V. CREWE

Jonathan V. Crewe 1982 *Unredeemed Rhetoric: Thomas Nashe and the Scandal of Authorship* (Baltimore); Kelsie B. Harder 1955 'Nashe and Spenser' in *Essays in Honor of Walter Clyde Curry* (Nashville) pp 123–32; Helgerson 1976; G.R. Hibbard 1962 *Thomas Nashe: A Critical Introduction* (Cambridge, Mass); Donald J. McGinn 1981 *Thomas Nashe* (Boston); Nashe ed 1904–10; Charles Nicholl 1984 *A Cup of News: The Life of Thomas Nashe* (London).

natural history Elizabethan natural history was a complex amalgam of facts and fancies about the animal, vegetable, and mineral kingdoms recorded in various types of treatises, many of which Spenser could have consulted. Of the classics, Aristotle's biological texts were still regarded as the most 'scientific' works on animals though available only in Greek or Latin. Pliny the Elder's *Natural History* was far more popular. This vast reservoir of information on all aspects of the terrestrial world was the ultimate source of much lore transmitted to the Renaissance through medieval encyclopedias; an abbreviated version, *A Summarie of the Antiquities and Wonders of the World*, became available in English in 1566 and Philemon Holland's complete translation in 1601.

Three genres of medieval treatises exemplify various approaches taken to the natural world. Lapidaries, collections of lore about gemstones and minerals, contained magical spells and remedies (see precious *stones). Herbals, designed to serve the practical needs of doctors, apothecaries, gardeners, and interested laymen, contained long-tested recipes that exploited the special virtues of each *plant (see also *flowers). Bestiaries presented animals as symbols with religious significance and as exempla of human behavior: the organization of a beehive, for instance, was seen to reflect the ranks and customs of feudal society. Although bestiaries declined in popularity in the Renaissance, conventional ideas about the characteristics peculiar to certain creatures were perpetuated orally as well as through literary texts like fables and romances.

All these approaches and more were mixed together in the medieval encyclopedias. The most enduring encyclopedia, Bartholomaeus Anglicus' *De proprietatibus rerum* (c 1230), devotes three of its nineteen books to minerals, plants, and animals, assembling material derived from Pliny, Isidore of Seville's *Etymologiae* (c 625), and various medieval sources. The three English editions printed between 1495 and 1582 indicate its continuing popularity. John Maplet's widely read *A Greene Forest* (1567) is essentially a summary of Bartholomaeus' sections on natural history.

The best Renaissance naturalists, however, were not prepared to repeat old authorities parrot-fashion, and dared to criticize even Aristotle when firsthand investigation proved him wrong. William Turner's *New Herball* (1551–62) and Henry Lyte's English translation (London 1578) of Dodoens' herbal exemplify this approach. The Swiss humanist and physician Conrad Gesner, though he incorporated poetry, hieroglyphics, travel stories, and much more into his *Historiae animalium* (5 vols, Zurich 1551–8), also made a concerted effort to sift fact from fancy.

Even so, many Renaissance poets including Spenser continued to foster the conventional lore. Usually his allusions to fauna may be glossed by referring to Stephen Bateman's English adaptation of Bartholomaeus, *Batman uppon Bartholome* (1582). For example, Bateman's entry on badgers partly illuminates Spenser's allusion in *Ruines of Time* to a filthy and underhand attack on the Earl of Leicester, presumably by Lord Burghley: 'He [Leicester] now is gone, the whiles the Foxe [Burghley] is crept / Into the hole, the which the Badger swept' (216–7). Bateman observes that badgers 'hate the foxe, and fight oft times with him'; the fox usually retreats, then later sneaks into the badger's den 'and defileth his chamber with urin and other uncleannes: and the [badger] is squemous of such foule things, and forsaketh his house that is so defiled' (18.103).

Again, Bateman may help to unravel an allusion in *Amoretti* 2. The lover beseeches his 'Unquiet thought' to 'Breake forth at length out of the inner part, / in which thou lurkest lyke to vipers brood: / and seeke some succour both to ease my smart / and also to sustayne thy selfe with food.' According to Bateman, 'Vipera ... bringeth forth broode by strength: for when hir wombe draweth to the time of whelping, the whelpes ... gnaweth and fretteth the sides of their dam, and they come so into this world with strength, and with the death of the breeder' (18.117). Spenser seems to suggest that the released 'Unquiet thought' if unnoticed by the lady will cause the lover's death – a curious and rather difficult reworking of the old viper lore (see also the description of Error's brood in *FQ* I i).

In another application of animal lore, Duessa is compared to 'a cruell craftie Crocodile' who 'Doth weepe full sore, and sheddeth tender teares' to attract its prey (I v 18). This description of the crocodile was more than proverbial; a contemporary account records that the crocodile's 'nature is ever when he would have his praie, to crie, and sobbe like a christian bodie, to provoke them to come to him, and then hee snatcheth at them' (John Hawkins 'Second Voyage' to the Caribbean, in Hakluyt 1589:535; see also *Isis Church). Such supposedly factual firsthand travelers' reports kept many animal stories alive.

In characterizing his 'horrible Sea-satyre' as one 'that doth shew / His fearefull face in time of greatest storme' (*FQ* II xii 24), Spenser may be drawing on Gesner's account of the appearance of a sea-satyr in the midst of a violent storm (Book 4, p 1001). Moreover, Gesner's volume on aquatic creatures seems to have inspired Spenser's catalogue of eleven sea monsters which Guyon and the Palmer confront on their trip to Acrasia's bower (II xii 23–4). On pages 210–11, Spenser would have seen illustrated side by side his 'Ziffius,' 'Rosmarines,' and 'The dreadfull Fish, that hath deserv'd the name / Of Death,' (the Morsz); by turning back a page, he would have found the sea unicorn 'Monoceros' (see Robin 1932: 119ff).

See **natural history** Figs 1–3.)

Spenser also picked up nature lore from literary sources: Ovid's account of the innumerable forms of life spontaneously generated in the slime of the Nile delta when it is warmed by the sun (*Metamorphoses* 1.422–37) is used three times in *The Faerie Queene* (I i 21, III vi 8, VII vii 18).

Spenser's principal use of natural lore takes the form of comparison between man and an element of nature. He often compares fighting warriors to wild beasts, a common literary device in classical epic. For example, his comparison of Redcrosse and Sansfoy to fighting rams suggests Virgil's comparison of Aeneas and Turnus to fighting bulls (*Aeneid* 12.715–24). Such familiar animal imagery helps the reader to visualize the event, here transforming the battle into an emblem of unreasoning, bestial conflict. Similarly (in II v 10), the comparison of Guyon and Pyrochles to the lion and the unicorn brings to mind heraldic representations of the feud central to British mytho-history. The use of animal lore in the *Amoretti* is more distinctive. Here Spenser draws extended comparisons between the behavior of lovers and the characteristics traditionally associated with particular beasts. For instance, the desperate speaker of sonnet 53 compares the seductive yet unyielding behavior of his mistress to the panther, who, while hiding his cruel face, flaunts his colorfully spotted coat to attract his prey (cf *Batman* 18.82, *Var* 8:437). Comparisons of this kind derive from bestiaries which use the behavior of creatures as instructive emblems of religious truth.

Sometimes Spenser provides characters with animal attributes which symbolize their personal qualities, as in the allegorical figures of the sins in Lucifera's pageant (*FQ* I iv). Each of her six counselors rides an appropriate beast, and Lucifera herself (like Juno in Ovid, *Metamorphoses* 2.531–3) is drawn by peacocks, birds symbolic of worldly pride and vanity. Such typically medieval allegorical uses of animal iconography continued to be transmitted through Renaissance emblem books and mythological dictionaries. Thus, in Ripa's *Iconologia* (1611:29), Lady Arroganza is shown holding a peacock.

Another classical literary convention adopted by Spenser is the catalogue of plants or animals, as the tree catalogue in *FQ* I i 8–9 is modeled on Ovid's *Metamorphoses* 10.90–108. Though the catalogue traditionally served a didactic function, Spenser's often perform other roles. In *Muiopotmos* 187–200 where Spenser describes the virtues of 26 plants, he is by no means following the herbals of the day closely. Rather, his source is traditional lore, and his motive is to create a decorative picture of the garden's abundance. Other catalogues serve a narrative function. That of the sea monsters discussed above evokes a mood of horror and danger by naming strange-sounding creatures. The expansive form of the catalogue itself, which gives a sense that many more monsters than those listed lurk beneath the surface, contributes to the simulation of a world full of malevolent forces.

CATHLEEN HOENIGER

Maplet 1567 and Topsell 1607 are rpt in facsimile in the English Experience series (Amsterdam) nos 941, 561 (1979, 1973). For Bartholomaeus Anglicus, see John Trevisa's ME tr *On the Properties of Things* in a critical ed (ed M.C. Seymour, et al, 3 vols, Oxford 1975–88) and *Batman uppon Bartholome* 1582. See also T.H. White 1954, an annotated tr of a 12th-c Latin bestiary. Two most important sources are Pliny the Elder *Natural History* (tr Philemon Holland as *The Historie of the World*, London 1601) and Conrad Gesner 1551–8. H.W. Seager 1896 *Natural History in Shakespeare's Time* (London) contains extracts from Bartholomaeus, Pliny, and Topsell.

A. Arber 1912 (rev ed 1938) is the best book on herbals. General treatments of Renaissance natural history include F.D. Hoeniger and J.F.M. Hoeniger 1969a *The Development of Natural History in Tudor England* (Charlottesville, Va); Hoeniger and Hoeniger 1969b *The Growth of Natural History in Stuart England from Gerard to the Royal Society* (Charlottesville, Va); Charles E. Raven 1947 *English Naturalists from Neckam to Ray* (Cambridge); George Sarton 1955 *The Appreciation of Ancient and Medieval Science during the Renaissance (1450–1600)* (Philadelphia) pp 52–115; Sarton 1957 'Fourth Wing' in *Six Wings: Men of Science in the Renaissance* (Bloomington); and Svendsen 1956, ch 1, on the encyclopedic tradition. On the use of nature lore by Spenser and his contemporaries, see Carroll 1954; Madeleine Pelner Cosman 1963 'Spenser's Ark of Animals: Animal Imagery in the *Faery Queen*' *SEL* 3:85–107; Friedland 1937; Arthur F. Marotti 1965 'Animal Symbolism in *The Faerie Queene*: Tradition and the Poetic Context' *SEL* 5:69–86; and Robin 1932.

Nature Spenser often mentions Nature (or Kind) in his poems before she becomes a major figure in the *Cantos of Mutabilitie*. Whether as God, Christ, or the vicar of God, Nature is superior to the planets, the stars, and the earth with everything upon it. She, in turn, works through deputies and agents, the gods of myth and the poet's invention. She is often called generous, loving, mysterious, and skillful; but chiefly she is a creator and lawgiver.

As creator, she is 'mother Nature' (*FQ* II vi 16), who forms all living things out 'of a formelesse mas' (*Teares* 502), that is, from 'An huge eternall *Chaos*, which supplyes / The substances of natures fruitfull progenyes' (*FQ* III vi 36). In Eden before the Fall, 'all good things did grow, / And freely sprong out of the fruitfull ground, / As incorrupted Nature did them sow' (I xi 47). Her fecundity is wondrous in its plenitude and infinite variety. Thus Colin knows that Cuddie has not 'seene least part of natures worke' (*Colin Clout* 293). Explaining apparently spontaneous generation, Spenser reports that from the shores of the Nile alone 'Infinite shapes of creatures' spring, 'quickned' by Nature through sunbeams on seeds in the mud (*FQ* III vi 8). Onlookers seeing Placidas and Amyas together, and believing that no two things are alike, wonder whether Nature's 'skill, or errour' is responsible for their amazing similarity (IV ix 11).

Nature's method of accomplishing the continuing creative process is to instill a powerful attraction between the sexes, which is nearly impossible to suppress. Marinell's mother warns her son daily against the love of women but fails: 'A lesson too too hard for living clay, / From love in course of nature to refraine' (III iv 26). Yet unrestrained sexual activity, according to Glauce, is 'filthy lust, contrarie unto kind,' as is incest and bestiality (ii 40–1; see also vii 49). In fact, moderation in all things is an ideal of Nature. Although man's 'feeble nature' finds it hard to learn continence in pleasure (II vi 1), Guyon tells Mammon that men would be temperate if only they thought 'with how small allowaunce / Untroubled Nature doth her selfe suffise' (vii 15); similarly, Meliboe tells Calidore that nature taught him to be content with little (VI ix 20).

Since Nature is bounteous, death is her enemy: even the loss of one person is a 'waste' of her work and contrary to her 'kindly course' (*SC, Nov* 64, 124). Similarly, the narrator of *FQ* VII blames Mutabilitie for violating Nature's laws by introducing death into the world (vi 6). But since the Fall, Nature's system includes death (as the Garden of Adonis makes clear), aging (I viii 33), and monstrous creatures with such 'fowle defects' that they might make Nature afraid or ashamed (II xii 23).

Nature's first law was to abstain from tasting blood (VI iv 14; cf Gen 9.4), and because of her, creatures need food and rest (III ii 29, VI ix 3). The narrator and others in *The Faerie Queene* often assert that a character is what he is 'by kind,' that is, naturally: Cymochles lustful, knights kindly toward women, Cupid mild, Disdain stern, ladies soft and tender (II v 28; VI ii 14, vii 37, 41, viii 2).

A few characters reputedly know some or all of Nature's secrets, such as Canacee, skilled in 'everie science' and 'every secret worke of natures wayes' (IV ii 35), and the fairy Agape, who knows 'secret things' and can use 'all the powres of nature' (44). The Palmer tells Guyon that fountains and lakes have 'secret vertues' instilled 'By great Dame Nature, from whose fruitfull pap / Their welheads spring' (II ii 5–6). Idle Phaedria claims that generous Nature throws flowers out of her lap, 'how, no man knowes' (vi 15). The speaker in *Amoretti* 21 asks whether Nature or Art is responsible for the mixture of qualities in his lady's face, and in Sonnet 31 he wonders why Nature gave 'so hard a hart' to so beautiful a woman; yet in Sonnet 30 he presumes to know that 'Such is the powre of love in gentle mind, / that it can alter all the course of kynd' (see *nature and art).

In the *Cantos of Mutabilitie*, the narrator first speaks of Nature indirectly in describing how Mutabilitie corrupted and perverted the 'meet order' of Nature's creation and laws (VII vi 5). When Jove denies Mutabilitie's right to his throne, she appeals 'to the highest him, that is behight / Father of Gods and men by equall might; / To weet, the God of Nature' (vi 35). At the trial, all of creation fills up Arlo Hill and is disposed by Nature's sergeant Order (vii 4). Not God but the 'great goddesse ... great dame *Nature*,' appears with 'goodly port and gracious Majesty.' She is taller than 'any of the gods or Powers on hie,' yet because both her face and head are veiled, no one can tell 'Whether she man or woman inly were' (5). Although she has been referred to as female throughout Spenser's poetry, apparently her gender has been a mere convenience: she may encompass both sexes since she produces both in creation, and she is later described as combining other opposites: always young yet aged, always moving yet stationary, invisible yet seen by all (13). The narrator has heard that the veil may hide the terror of a face like a lion's or, equally unendurable, beauty a thousand times greater than the splendor of the sun. The latter idea seems better to him, for he can only compare the shining of Nature's garment that day to the garments of the transfigured Christ (6–7; cf Matt 17.2).

The importance of the tradition from which Spenser's vision of Nature derives appears when the narrator interrupts his description of her throne and pavilion (8, 10) to return to the matter of her clothing. Even Chaucer, he says defensively, dared not meddle with it in his *Parliament of Fowls* but referred readers to Alanus de Insulis, who described it well in *De planctu Naturae* (9). Chaucer provided Spenser with an image of Nature much of which suited him, and other writers offered additional perspectives, some indirectly.

For the Greeks, the universe was organic, a living animal, and the word *physis* (L *natura*) meant 'becoming,' 'being born,' 'growing,' 'movement.' From Plato's *Timaeus* (34B) came a reasoned idea of the likely origin of creation: the World Soul, an emanation of God, infused primal matter with spirit or soul which, by implication, longs to return to its origin. Aristotle summarized *physis* as 'the source of the movement of natural objects, being present in them somehow, either potentially or actually' (*Metaphysics* 5.4). The cosmos has an eternal portion (sky) and a sublunar one (*physis*) where matter moves towards form or 'nature' (*Physics* 2.1), ever impelled or inspired to reach perfection, the ideal of God.

Among the Romans, nature was regularly personified. Although Lucretius opens *De rerum natura* by adopting the name of Venus for the life-giving, generative functions of nature, he later refers to Nature as managing the universe by herself and being responsible for creating and perfecting everything (2.1090–1104, 1116–17). (The worshipers of Venus in *FQ* IV x 40–7 treat her as Nature: she is veiled, believed to contain both sexes, and praised for creating and repairing the world.) Ovid begins the *Metamorphoses* by saying that God or 'kindlier Nature' separated the confused elements of chaos to bring order to the universe. In the *Thebaid*, Statius repeatedly has characters appeal or refer to the goddess Nature, calling her 'mighty' and 'sovereign' (eg, 8.330, 11.466, 12.561). Claudian personifies an aged, yet ever lovely, Mother Nature in several poems as bringer of order to chaos, as patroness of the marriages of deities, and as passionate petitioner to her father Jupiter on behalf of mankind.

Macrobius, in his *Commentary on the Dream of Scipio*, gives the label 'nature' to all that the Platonic World Soul brought into being; but he follows Aristotle in dividing the material universe at the circle of the moon – all beneath it changeable, all above divine and unchanging. In a passage that became famous (1.2.17–18), he defends 'fabulous narratives' as necessary because Nature dislikes being exposed by philosophers for the same reason that she envelops herself in 'variegated garments': to prevent the crude senses of most men from understanding her. Spenser was thus encouraged to veil Nature and to write allegory.

Boethius' *Consolation of Philosophy* was a major influence on medieval writers and probably Spenser. Philosophy's appearance is partly that of Spenser's Nature: majestic, shining, aged, and of a height at times seeming to reach the top of the heavens. The essence of her message is, in effect, an answer to 'the problem of the mutability of human affairs' that Spenser's Nature echoes in her decision in *FQ* VII, which emphasizes the pattern of 'the cyclical return of man and nature to their divine origins' (Zitner in Spenser ed 1968:38, 40). For Boethius, Nature ensures the survival of species by multiplying seeds and giving living things the means and impulse to survive. He associates her with secrecy, moderation, and control of the world through laws.

Alanus de Insulis made Nature a central figure in *De planctu Naturae*, an encyclopedic moral allegory in which Nature complains that man alone of her creatures violates her laws, mainly by unproductive sexual practices. Alanus' *Anticlaudianus* has Nature, still unhappy over the fallen world, proposing and participating in the creation of a new and perfect man. He gives Nature a wealth of allegorical associates such as Noys (God's providence; Gr *nous*) and Genius, and imagines her as having over a dozen sisters, such qualities and virtues as Concord, Plenty, Goodwill, and Beauty. His description of the images on Nature's clothes (mentioned by both Spenser and Chaucer) is an elaborate survey of all living things.

After the twelfth century, Nature regularly appeared in vernacular allegories across Western Europe. The most notable instance occurs in Jean de Meun's portion of the *Romance of the Rose*, in which an incredibly beautiful Nature, God's vicar, is concerned almost entirely with promoting reproduction. In contrast, Guillaume de Deguileville's Nature in *Le Pèlerinage de la vie humaine* is a garrulous old woman whose allegorical limitations prevent her from understanding the miracles wrought by Grace and even that she is Grace's servant.

Chaucer's Nature in the *Parliament of Fowls* anticipates Spenser's in several respects. She is the beautiful vicar of God, seen by the narrator as a queen, 'ful of grace' (319) and, repeatedly, noble. Appearing in a finely fashioned bower of branches on a hill of flowers, she is surrounded not by all of creation but by all of the birds arranged by class. She presides over a trial of sorts, an unplanned debate among the birds over how love relationships and mating should be conducted. Yet she is less than magisterial when she allows the birds to take up the debate, solicits their advice about what to do, and adjourns without a decision. Allegorically, her power is limited to having established the natural laws: she says she instilled sexual appetite in the birds, and they have free choice in selecting mates. In the *Physician's Tale*, Chaucer's narrator imagines Nature's pride at fashioning the maid Virginia (as no artist could do) for the worship of God, the purpose for which Nature creates all things under the moon.

Although Spenser drew upon these examples, and especially Chaucer, his Nature is freshly imagined. Revered alike by ambitious Mutabilitie and the insecure planetary gods, Nature in *FQ* VII rules above and below the moon. Her veil, absent from all but a few earlier works (eg, Macrobius' *Commentary*), lends her mystery and inspires awe. Spenser shrewdly manages to present the whole trial without her having to speak, effectively keeping her from the give and take that draws Nature in Chaucer, Jean de Meun, and Deguileville into awkward, unflattering situations. After Mutabilitie's summation, Nature creates suspense by remaining silent for a long time. When at last she looks up with 'chearefull view' (vii 57), it may be that her veil has disappeared without mention – by revealing a profound truth, she in effect reveals her true appearance.

Because Nature's decision has been elaborately prepared for, it carries great force. The meaning of her answer to Mutabilitie has troubled many readers, but it seems much like the idea expressed by Plato, Aristotle, Boethius, Bernard Sylvestris, and others: that the movement of nature is towards its final state, perfection. Although all things hate 'stedfastnes,' 'They are not changed from their first estate; / But by their change their being doe dilate: / And turning to themselves at length againe, / Doe worke their owne perfection so by fate' (58). Mankind, however, will never perfect itself independently, a fact Nature implies by speaking of the eventual end of change – in Christian terms, the Last Judgment with its promise of grace for the faithful. Mutabilitie, whom Nature calls daughter, makes no reply because she can make none. She must continue to carry out part of Nature's functions (change, aging, death) but cannot comprehend the rest (order, cyclical movement, reproduction, the end of change), in part because she will not be convinced by what she cannot see (49). When Nature vanishes, not even Mutabilitie knows how or whither.

Proposals for Nature's identity have included God, Christ, Divine Love, Providence (Wisdom, Sapience), a veiled Mutabilitie, and God's vicar or viceregent. All these ideas have merit and may actually agree, each placing a different emphasis upon details and sources. To see Nature as God or an image of God, for example, one would insist on a literal response to Mutabilitie's appeal to 'the highest him' called 'Father of Gods and men' (vi 35), cite 'Kynde' as God's name in Langland's *Piers Plowman* (B Text 9, 11, 20), and refer to Calvin's grudging admission that saying 'nature is God' could be a reverent utterance (*Institutes* 1.5.5). To see Nature as God's vicar, one would focus on Spenser's acknowledgement that she is the same as Alanus' and Chaucer's Nature, the latter specifically called vicar of the Lord in the *Parliament of Fowls* (379; cf 'vicaire general' *Physician's Tale* [*CT* VI 20]). Whatever the interpretation, however, clearly Spenser, much like the Greeks, views the universe as organic: nature is not the mechanical, mathematical construct devoid of intelligence that late Renaissance philosophers were beginning to derive from the discoveries of Copernicus, but good because it is purposeful and a part of God.

JACK B. ORUCH

Alanus de Insulis 1973 *Anticlaudianus, or The Good and Perfect Man* tr James J. Sheridan (Toronto); Alanus ed 1980; Bernard Sylvestris ed 1973; Calvin ed 1960; Deguileville ed 1893; Langland ed 1975; Macrobius ed 1952.

For further reading, see R.G. Collingwood 1945 *The Idea of Nature* (Oxford); George D.

Economou 1972 *The Goddess Natura in Medieval Literature* (Cambridge, Mass); Stanley E. Fish 1963 'Nature as Concept and Character in the *Mutabilitie Cantos*' *CLAJ* 6:210–15; E[dgar] C. Knowlton 1920 'The Goddess Nature in Early Periods' *JEGP* 19:224–53; Knowlton 1921a 'Nature in Earlier Italian' *MLN* 36:329–34; Knowlton 1921b 'Nature in Middle English' *JEGP* 20:186–207; Knowlton 1922–3 'Nature in Old French' *MP* 20:309–29; Knowlton 1925 'Nature in Early German' *JEGP* 24:409–12; Knowlton 1935 'Spenser and Nature' *JEGP* 34:366–76; Milton Miller 1951 'Nature in *The Faerie Queene*' *ELH* 18:191–200.

nature and art These words, bearing associations no longer directly available today, are central to Renaissance thought. For Spenser and his contemporaries, 'nature and art' served to exhaust the possibilities in the subject under discussion, in much the same way that 'heredity and environment' or 'matter and energy' seem all-inclusive to modern thinkers. Spenser's reliance on 'nature' as a normative concept derives from the Greek preoccupation with *physis* (nature, having to do with growth, physics, physiology, physician, etc), which in medieval times became a preoccupation with *natura* (a goddess as well as a concept) and with the Germanic *kind* (nature, genus, genre). When the cluster of 'nature' words enters into combination with the clusters derived from *nomos* (convention, custom, law) and *technē* (art, skill, technique), the resulting aggregates function as conceptual archetypes or basic instruments of thought, which in various writers on various occasions may range from the complementary (art perfects nature) to the antithetical (art perverts nature).

Although Spenser was familiar with the classical precept that art imitates nature, his understanding of 'nature and art' is not limited to the fine arts. In common with other thinkers of the time, he begins by assuming that we inhabit not only the realm of nature but also that of grace. In the realm of grace, we are aware of ourselves as possessing immortal souls and we hope for salvation; the principles of this realm may be known in part through God's revelations, and the kind of experience appropriate to it is religious. As reasoning animals, however, we live, together with the rest of animate and inanimate creation, in the realm of nature; the principles of this realm appear in the regularities of physical existence, in secular morality, and in natural as distinct from revealed religion.

Spenser and his contemporaries think of the natural realm as itself divided into two main parts, into two clearly distinguished areas of experience that they customarily denominated 'nature' and 'art.' In *Ruines of Rome*, for example, the summary verses 'what ever nature, arte, / And heaven could doo' (stanza 5) refer first to the division within the natural realm ('nature' and 'arte') and then to the realm of grace (the power of 'heaven'). These lines, in other words, take in what Spenser assumes to be the totality of experience.

Although some Renaissance Christians regarded postlapsarian nature with suspicion (or worse), Spenser's emphasis falls on 'Nature nurse of every living thing' (*Daphnaïda* 337) and on the way God, in his grace, works through nature. Art for Spenser may be wondrous, almighty, learned, or goodly, but the term more often appears in neutral (*Bellay* stanza 12, *Amoretti* 21), ambivalent, or even pejorative contexts. Polyhymnia inveighs against poetry that exhibits 'vaine art or curious complements' (*Teares* 542); 'dissembling' courtiers employ a 'filed toung furnisht with tearmes of art' (*Colin Clout* 700–1); Busirane, that 'vile Enchaunter,' practises against Amoret with the 'straunge characters of his art' (*FQ* III xii 31); the false Florimell is 'mistresse of her art' (IV ii 10); Blandina has 'the art to please' of false courtesy (VI vi 43); the false Duessa shows herself 'Great maistresse of her art' (I vii 1); Philotime glows with a beauty not 'her owne native hew, / But wrought by art and counterfetted shew' (II vii 45); and Biblis and Myrrha 'used wicked art' in loving their 'native flesh against all kind' (III ii 41). Such examples illustrate the primitivist suspicion of art and represent one extreme of the ancient *paragone* or rivalry between nature and art. In *Muiopotmos* 161–6, for instance, 'lavish Nature' adorns the gardens while 'Arte with her contending' strives to 'excell the naturall, with made delights'; in *FQ* II v 29 'art striving to compaire / With nature, did an Arber greene dispred.' Art may even on occasion win the *paragone*, as for example in extraordinary paintings where 'oftimes, we Nature see of Art / Exceld' (*Hymne of Beautie* 83–4).

For most Elizabethans, including Spenser, the various permutations of these presiding terms devolve from an assumed norm that represents the ideal relation between nature and art. This normative relation is the subject of one of the illustrations in Robert Fludd's *Utriusque cosmi maioris ... et minoris ... historia* (Oppenheim 1617–21), where it is captioned (in translation) 'The mirror of prime Nature and the image of Art': the hand of God stretches forth from a cloud, grasping a chain linked to the wrist of a naked woman whose head reaches the stars and whose legs bestride land and sea; her other hand likewise holds a chain, this one linked to an ape squatting on the globe of the earth. The woman represents Nature, the simian stands for Art, and the chain of command is clear: God guides the operations of nature, and art apes or imitates nature.

(See **nature and art** Fig 1.)

Spenser exploits the traditional relation of nature to art for his own purposes in much of his poetry, usually in contexts that oppose or seek to reconcile the universal and natural to the local and conventional, the primitive to the sophisticated, the contemplative to the active, and the country pastoral to the courtly epic. This last opposition is particularly important, as it includes the genre, the pastoral 'kind' or 'nature,' that mirrors in literature the philosophical concern with nature and art. Of all the traditional genres, it is pastoral that raises most directly questions of the value of 'nature' (sheep, shepherds, rural life) in relation to 'art' (poets, courtiers, urban life). The philosophical awareness of the distinction between what is given (nature) and what is made (art), between what seems spontaneous and unreflective (nature) and what seems to be the result of acquired habit or conscious intellection (art), necessarily precedes the writing of pastoral, for the genre pretends to depict the simple 'art' and unspoiled 'nature' of innocent shepherds while self-consciously employing sophisticated artifice in order to appear natural. Such paradoxes are denied to those who know only natural simplicity. Since it is an art to sing of nature, the pastoral invariably deals, if only implicitly, with the philosophical division.

Although the philosophic controversy remains in the background of the earlier pastorals, Spenser makes explicit use of the terms in elaborating the main themes of the pastoral episodes in *FQ* VI. He affects to wonder whether the false courtesy of Blandina was 'given her by kynd' or whether she 'learn'd the art' (vi 43), but he commits himself immediately with respect to his protagonist: the virtues of Calidore, the knight of Courtesy, 'were planted naturall.' Although 'good thewes, enforst with paine' (good manners acquired through laborious art) must be taken into account, our greatest 'helpe' comes directly from 'dame Nature' (i 2, ii 2). The Salvage Nation pervert their nature through cruel actions 'gainst course of kynde' (viii 36), whereas the Salvage Man, 'obaying natures first beheast,' shows a kind of rudimentary courtesy in 'senselesse words, which nature did him teach' (iv 14, 11). The allegory has begun to instruct us. Nature comes first in importance, though it may then become perverted by art – but nature may also stand in need of art.

In the pastoral episode, where nature appears untutored as well as unspoiled by art, Calidore may abandon the courtly 'manner' of a knight and doff his 'bright armes' (ix 36) to win the fair Pastorella, but when the two leave the countryside he must reassume his manner and his arms, for the Blatant Beast will always escape its bonds, untutored nature will prove insufficient, and art will be used 'gainst course of kynde.' Spenser knows that idylls do not last. The most dazzling moment of 'natures skill' (x 5), the ideal union of nature and art as represented in the dance of the Graces upon Mount Acidale, may be glimpsed only fleetingly. This evanescent vision of nature as art, of art as nature, is the product of poetic art (Spenser self-consciously advertises his presence in Colin, the figure of the poet) and is, appropriately, interrupted by Calidore, whose virtue of courtesy must serve the real world of the court. The vision, inaccessible to all but the poetic imagination, may serve as a guide for future action but remains an ideal unattainable except in memory.

It will be apparent that Spenser exploits the poetic possibilities of the philosophical division in ways distinctively his own. Although his goddess Nature owes much to Ovid, Lucretius, Boethius, Chaucer, and others, she assumes a characteristically ambivalent aspect – hermaphroditic, mysteriously veiled – in *Cantos of Mutabilitie* (VII vii 5–6). Although his understanding of 'art' derives from commonplaces current since Aristotle, Spenser combines art with nature in ways carefully calculated to manipulate the imaginative responses of his readers. The Garden of Adonis (III vi), for example, explicitly invites comparison with the Bower of Bliss in the preceding book. Spenser has us approach the Bower, where we shall see 'art striving to compaire / With nature' (II v 29), through a 'fertile land' in the Idle Lake that seems 'As if it had by Natures cunning hand' been chosen 'for ensample of the best,' and Phaedria invokes 'nothing envious nature.' Yet the attribution to 'Natures cunning hand' is qualified by the cautionary 'as if,' and Phaedria proffers only 'false delights' (vi 12–15).

The Bower itself appears to be the 'choice of best alive, / That natures worke by art can imitate' (xii 42), but the insinuation of something illusory, even deceptive, continues to lurk behind the further (Ovidian) comment that 'The art, which all that wrought, appeared in no place' (58). Finally, Spenser uses the traditional *paragone* to move us toward the finer moral discriminations. Although 'One would have thought' that art and nature, 'striving each th' other to undermine ... did the others worke more beautifie,' and that 'nature had for wantonesse ensude / Art, and that Art at nature did repine,' we are made aware that 'Art, as halfe in scorne / Of niggard Nature' does not merely beautify but beautifies 'too lavishly' (xii 59, 50). The Bower counterfeits the ideal, art perverting nature. The Garden of Adonis, by contrast, is as 'faire a place, as Nature can devize.' It has a 'pleasant arbour' that is explicitly 'not by art, / But of the trees owne [natural] inclination made' (III vi 29, 44). When Scudamour recalls the landscape, he summarizes the ideal relation of art to nature that prevails in the Garden: 'For all that nature by her mother wit / Could frame in earth, and forme of substance base, / Was there, and all that nature did omit, / Art playing second natures part, supplyed it' (IV x 21).

In short, Spenser deploys the terms 'nature' and 'art' in significant combinations to encourage his readers first to compare, to perceive resemblances, and then to contrast, to discern the differences, among parts of the grand structure of analogical dissimilarities that make up the poem. The conceptual pair, always in the service of the poet's basic method of comparison and contrast, becomes an instrument of moral discrimination, allowing us to understand that the Bower represents the perversion of nature by art and the Garden the perfection of nature by art. The terms, in other words, function as modes of thought and discrimination as well as objects of inquiry. Since Spenser thinks *with* the philosophical concepts as well as *about* them, nature and art may be used flexibly and subtly as controlling terms within his poetic universe.

Edward W. Tayler

For further discussion and additional bibliography, see Lovejoy and Boas 1935; Hiram Haydn 1950 *The Counter-Renaissance* (New York) ch 8; Frank Kermode, ed 1952 *English Pastoral Poetry* (London) introduction; Tayler 1964. For Spenser, see MacLure 1961; and Tonkin 1972, chs 7, 8.

---

nature and grace These concepts, recurrently important in the history of Western thought, provide a perspective from which to comprehend both *The Faerie Queene* as a whole and a number of its significant episodes, especially in Books I and II. Modern discussion of nature and grace in Spenser usually begins with the influential 1949 article by A.S.P. Woodhouse, who argues that Spenser shared with his contemporaries an inherited 'frame of reference' by which he assigned individual elements of experience to the order either of nature or of grace (p 195):

> In the natural order belonged not only the physical world ... but man himself considered simply as a denizen of that world. The rule of its order was expressed not only in the physical laws of nature, but in natural ethics ... This order was apprehended in experience and interpreted by reason ... To the order of grace, on the other hand, belonged man in his character [as] supernatural being, with all that concerned his salvation ... The law of its government was the revealed will of God, received and interpreted by faith.

Opinions about the interrelation of these orders differed. Augustinians, Lutherans, and the major Reformed Protestant theologians (Bullinger, Beza, Bucer, Calvin, Martyr, Zwingli) emphasized the divergence between nature and grace; Thomists, certain later scholastics, and Christian humanists allowed them a greater degree of compatibility. Both the Reformed Protestants and the humanists influenced Spenser.

Sixteenth-century theologians and humanists, while assuming or asserting the existence of the orders of nature and grace, focus usually on man. They explore the functions of grace within human nature and the powers and limitations of human nature without grace. Most zealous on behalf of grace, Reformed Protestants (a category that included most sixteenth-century English believers, conformists as well as those desiring further changes in Elizabethan worship) insist that God must totally re-create the believer's nature before his good works can begin to meet the standard of absolute righteousness set down in God's law – before, that is, he can begin to participate in the realm of grace. But even after such rebirth ('regeneration') through grace, man's best works remain polluted by the flesh. The believer can be saved only because Christ's perfect virtues are ascribed ('imputed') to him by the charitable judgment of God.

Christian humanists are often said, by contrast, to consider grace a mere aid that assists man to seek spiritual goods of which, despite its postlapsarian degeneracy, his nature retains vestiges of knowledge and for which it can feel a degree of residual desire (see *humanism). Eager to assert that men must be responsible moral agents, Erasmus, the preeminent humanist champion of free will, never altogether rules out the possibility that natural powers alone might allow some feeble, preliminary steps toward salvation. But even in the view of this loyal defender, the contribution of human nature, in contrast to that of grace, remains minute. Erasmus inclined to favor Augustine's position, which had become official Catholic doctrine at the Council of Orange (AD 529), that men can do no truly righteous works until God grants them the gift usually called prevenient grace. By the Renaissance, the proceedings of the Council had been lost sight of, and Erasmus claimed for this view the status only of a probable one. Carefully scrutinized, his opinion of natural human powers was less than enthusiastic (*On the Freedom of the Will* in Rupp and Watson 1969:52–3; cf pp 10–12).

Hooker, who allows nature even less scope than does Erasmus, requires attention because he is often considered the preeminent defender of natural reason and of the belief that the realms of nature and grace, existing in harmonious hierarchy, differ little in essence. As Woodhouse reads him, Hooker thought that there was 'no interval' between nature and grace, that the ascent from nature to grace was 'steady and relatively unimpeded,' that revelation was 'merely supplementary,' directing man toward the perfection his very nature pursues but to which it can 'carry him only part of the way' (1949:196, 225).

Hooker's convictions about nature and grace conform remarkably well, however, with those of Reformed Protestants. He insists that 'all that wee of ourselves can doe, is not only nothing, butt naught'; that God should have all the glory for our good works, since by his grace alone 'wee have our whole abilitie and power of well doing.' Hooker is convinced, moreover, that the human will is so possessed by 'a native evill habit, that if Gods speciall grace did not aide our imbecilitie, whatsoever wee doe or imagine would be only and continuallie evill.' The interval between nature and grace is broad enough that men can, by 'naturall meanes,' know nothing whatever about the realm of grace. They can participate in that realm only by means of 'a way which is supernaturall, a way which could never have entered into the heart of man as much as once to conceive or imagine, if God him selfe had not revealed it extraordinarilie' through Scripture (*Of the Laws of Ecclesiastical Polity* Dublin Fragments 13, 1; I.II.5 in ed 1977–, 4:113, 101 and 1:115–16).

For both Hooker and Erasmus, the distance between the realms of nature and grace is great. But as part of a world view governed by the Reformed Protestants' lively sense of the omnipresent activity of grace, that distance is also constantly annulled. Grace works incessantly within the souls of faithful Christians in a created world that God's gracious immanence supervises and maintains, down to its slightest details. The preservation and normal functioning of nature is itself a quotidian miracle of grace.

In human nature as in the natural world, the works of grace were held to be manifold. Yet for Spenser's readers, two of its effects are especially important. From Augustine onward, many Christian thinkers held that once God has given a first variety or function (the theologians' terms are interchangeable) of grace, he also grants a second. The first renews the will, making it possible for the recipient to have faith, which in turn enables belief in true doctrine and desire to conform to its ethical demands. The second operation of grace works ('cooperates') with the believer's new will, giving it the power actually to pursue those things. Protestants usually called the first function of grace 'justification,' the second, 'sanctification.'

Reformed doctrine (whether stated by Calvin, Beza, John Bradford, William Perkins, or the Thirty-nine Articles of the Church of England) describes sanctification as a collaboration between grace and human will. It is a cooperative endeavor that results in 'holiness of life' – a progressive cleansing which mitigates, though it never completely extirpates, all of the sins flesh is heir to. So defined, holiness can be seen as the comprehensive Christian virtue *which is active in the realm of nature*. It subsumes the less comprehensive virtues which Spenser explores in *FQ* II-VI. Although holiness results from cooperation of human will with divine grace, God alone remains entirely responsible for salvation. No one can do anything to merit the first action of grace, and cooperation with the second contributes nothing that might merit salvation. Efforts to achieve holiness simply render visible the otherwise secret inner operations of predestined grace (see *predestination).

This view received authoritative statement from Hooker. In everything he teaches concerning man's natural capacities, he claims always to presuppose 'that there is no kind of faculty or power in man or any other creature, which can rightly performe the functions alotted to it, without perpetuall aid and concurrence of that supreme cause of all things' (*Laws* 1.8.11). Developing a similar thesis, Perkins states a conviction, widely shared among Reformed theologians, that virtues (like temperance, chastity, justice, and the rest) constitute works of which natural man, enabled by God's gracious interventions, can become capable. But good works done in a way that will please God, which must arise from true faith and seek God's own glory, can be achieved solely by means of the grace that justifies and sanctifies (*Workes* 1608–9, 1: sig 3C6r).

In sum, therefore, we can speak of a consensus, current in late sixteenth-century England, which asserted (1) that an immense interval separates the orders of nature and grace because the latter is infinitely superior to the former, and (2) that the pervasive and miraculous potency of grace constantly bridges the gap, causing a perpetual interaction between the two orders. In the elect, one consequence of this interaction is holy works; in natural man, the consequence can be no more than outward conformity to civil or ecclesiastical law.

Because *The Faerie Queene* concerns heroes engaged in arduous pursuit of individual virtues, Protestant views of grace – especially that which brings sanctification – frequently condition the poem's content and structure. Since the consensus differed significantly from Woodhouse's conception of it, we must adjust his application of the frame of reference he first showed to be useful in interpreting Spenser's poem. Although he notes that the realms of nature and grace are not mutually exclusive, Woodhouse draws an absolute distinction between them. He hardly allows for the constant interaction which enables human nature both to act naturally and, among the chosen, to participate in the order of grace.

Woodhouse's sharp dichotomy underlies his major theses about *The Faerie Queene*: (1) that Spenser distinguishes clearly between nature and grace, (2) that this is especially evident in the contrast 'between the motives and sanctions of virtue on the natural level and on the specifically religious,' (3) that 'Book I moves ... on the religious level, or ... with reference to the order of grace,' while 'the remaining books [move] ... on the natural level only,' and (4) that certain episodes prepare for a reconciliation between nature and grace, a resolution withheld for presentation in a projected final book (1949:198–200).

The first point is at once true and useful. The very preponderance of scriptural materials (allusions to Paul and the Gospels, as well as images, characters, and monsters drawn from Revelation) demonstrates that the concerns of Book I are often explicitly religious. Beginning with Book II, Spenser makes classical sources (eg, Platonic, Aristotelian, and Ciceronian ethics in medieval and Renaissance guise) primary both for themes and imagery. Book I stresses man's complete incapacity to contribute to his own salvation, for despite apparent early successes the Red Cross Knight's progress in cantos i-ix displays his own, and the reader's, desperate need for grace.

Readers attentive to theological cues will find that grace is omnipresent in Book I in frequent references to providential oversight of all human actions and in the conviction, implied by the ultimately beneficial consequences of Redcrosse's failings, that a major function of grace is to use the believer's own sins to demonstrate his need for divine aid (see *providence). All of the knight's real achievements, moreover, receive eventual religious sanction and are sought in response to religious motives. His quest, for instance, is to destroy a dragon which is at once a familiar scriptural symbol of evil and an epitome of Error (I i), of Duessa's seven-headed beast (vii 16–18), and of their numerous allies. During the battle in canto xi, we are to presume that Redcrosse's motive is to live the life of faith working through love, the motive he consciously and clearly apprehends for the first time during his education in the house of Holiness (x).

Nevertheless, the action of Book I moves to a significant extent in the realm of nature, and in so doing attests to the grace at work in its hero. Holiness is the result of sanctification, and in that process grace 'works with' human will. This, according to all major Reformed theologians, is what Paul means in Philippians 2.12–13, the passage echoed at *FQ* I x 1: 'If any strength we have, it is to ill, / But all the good is Gods, both power and eke will.' When God gives us the first kind or benefit of grace, rescuing us from a state of complete spiritual impotence, he provides a new will by which we can pursue the good in cooperation with the subsequent impulsions of grace (see Calvin *Institutes* 2.3.11; Bradford *Treatise of Election and Free-Will* in ed 1848–53, 1:218; Perkins 1608–9, 1: sig 3C5r).

This distinction between the justifying and the sanctifying functions of grace appears in the contrast between two key episodes in Book I. When Arthur rescues him from Orgoglio's dungeon, Redcrosse contributes nothing; his 'feeble thighes' are 'unhable to uphold / His pined corse' (viii 40). By contrast, when he is learning to undertake the works of charity that flow from faith, his dependence is less complete. God's Mercy ('both gratious, and eke liberall') leads him into the narrow way and 'ever when his feet encombred were, / Or gan to shrinke, or from the right to stray, / She held him fast, and firmely did upbeare, / As carefull Nourse her child from falling oft does reare' (x 34–5). This is the dependence of sanctification. Like a child learning to take its first steps, man contributes to his holiness insofar as human nature, feeble though regenerate, is able.

As careful reconsideration shows, the action of Book I, concerned with man's participation in the order of grace, focuses nonetheless on the ubiquitous activity of grace in the order of nature. Subsequent books explore virtues that act explicitly in nature but originate in and are persistently enabled by grace. Critics have rightly argued that Book II reveals persistent interaction between the orders of nature and grace, that Guyon shares in the regeneration Redcrosse has experienced in Book I (see Fowler 1960–1; Hamilton 1958a, 1958b; Hoopes 1954).

Although Guyon represents a virtue first defined by pagan ethics, he is most effective in the company of the Palmer, a term which, in its strict sense, suggests that he has been on pilgrimage to Jerusalem. As Redcrosse's experience on the Mount of Contemplation (I x) has reminded us, a visit to Jerusalem has potent symbolic overtones: it implies a vision available only to faith, the reassuring knowledge of the existence of the heavenly Jerusalem and of one's own citizenship in it. The Palmer may be taken, therefore, to represent not mere natural reason, but reason corrected and heightened by insights which gracious revelation alone can make available. He embodies the rational faculty, man's by nature, but rendered competent to deal with spiritual things and to deal sensibly with things of this world by the 'perpetual aid and concurrence' of grace (see *nature and art). Similarly intimate alliances between nature and grace might be suggested by phrases referring most directly to physical beauty or other gifts, such as 'native grace' (II ix 1) and 'wondrous giftes of natures grace' (VI vii 28); likewise, Dame Nature's beauty expresses by natural revelation (cf Rom 1.20) the divinity that created and sustains all natural things (VII vii). As the first two instances show, recipients can misuse or lose gifts of grace that are theirs by nature.

In contrast to the Palmer, Guyon is less purely allegorical. Like Spenser's other knights, he is above all a representative man seeking to live by the virtue of which he is patron. Intermittently, he symbolizes that virtue. The characteristic intermittence of Spenserian psychomachia predicts that Guyon has a mind of his own; the Palmer does not at all times represent the knight's reason. Hence, Guyon falls readily to Archimago's temptation and, possessed by 'fierce ire' (II i 13; cf 25), outruns his reason and rushes off to attack Redcrosse. His temperance returns only after he recognizes 'The sacred badge of [his] Redeemers death' (i 27). Clearly, this recognition brings his own rational faculty into play, suggesting that reason, awakened and empowered by faith, restores the virtue of temperance. That the Palmer embodies a more reliable wisdom becomes evident when he approaches and instantly has 'perfect cognizance' of Redcrosse, especially of his place among the saints (31–2).

Guyon's independence and the Palmer's superiority are implied more elaborately in *FQ* II vii-viii. There Guyon enters the house of Mammon deprived, like the pilot of vii 1, of heavenly guidance and thrown back on the useful but inferior resources of experience, the recollection of 'his owne vertues' (2). Like anyone whose portion of grace God chooses temporarily to reduce, Guyon is left alone, as was Christ when his human nature was submitted to temptation in the wilderness. But even this human nature depends on grace, as Guyon's fall on reemerging from the cave implies. The divine emissary who appears attests not only to his future aid, working in conjunction with the Palmer's and Arthur's, but also to his perpetual care: 'Yet will I not forgoe, ne yet forget / The care thereof my selfe unto the end, / But evermore him succour, and defend' (viii 8).

In Book II, Guyon's experience parallels closely Redcrosse's earlier progress. The knight of Temperance has 'like race to runne' (i 32) in the sense that he too participates in the process of sanctification which occupies Redcrosse in I x-xii. His particular virtue belongs to, and by synecdoche represents, his holiness. Nowhere are we invited to see Guyon or the central knights of later books as 'natural' in the sense that they can have divine aid sufficient to enable only outward conformity to the dictates of virtue. Like the virtues of subsequent books, temperance represents a particular manifestation of the comprehensive Christian virtue of holiness, just as, in the classical terms of the Letter to Raleigh, each individual virtue represents an element of magnificence.

Although the action of *The Faerie Queene* occurs always within the order of nature, readers alert to theological signals will find that truly virtuous activities within that order persistently reveal, in ways subtle or overt, that they owe their origin and successes to grace. The realms of nature and grace remain clearly distinct, but they are carefully interrelated throughout the poem.

DARRYL J. GLESS

John Bradford 1848–53 *Writings* 2 vols, ed Aubrey Townsend, Parker Society (Cambridge); Gang 1959; Hamilton 1958a; Hamilton 1958b; Hoopes 1954; Hume 1984, ch 4; Porter 1958, esp part 3; E. Gordon Rupp and Philip S. Watson, trs and eds 1969 *Luther and Erasmus: Free Will and Salvation* in *Library CC* 17 (London); D.D. Wallace 1982, chs 1–2; A.S.P. Woodhouse 1949; Woodhouse 1955 'Nature and Grace in Spenser: A Rejoinder' *RES* ns 6:284–8; Woodhouse 1960.

Nennio William Jones' English translation of Giovanni Battista Nenna's *Nennio* (first pub in Italian, Venice 1542) appeared in 1595 as *Nennio, or A Treatise of Nobility: Wherein Is Discoursed What True Nobilitie Is, with Such Qualities as Are Required in a Perfect Gentleman. Written in Italian by that Famous Doctor and Worthy Knight Sir John Baptista Nenna of Bari. Done into English by William Jones Gent. Printed by P[eter] S[hort] for Paule Linley and John Flasket* (rpt Jerusalem 1967). Prefacing the work are commendatory sonnets by Spenser, Samuel Daniel, George Chapman, and Angel Day, in that order (see *Var* 8:264, 506–7 and Spenser ed 1912:603). Little is known about Jones, who also translated Justus Lipsius and Francesco Guicciardini.

Spenser's sonnet praises both author and translator for showing readers how to 'attaine, / Unto the type of true Nobility.' The sonnet does not reveal whether Spenser actually read the work (though he observes that Jones 'truely it translated') but accords with it in valuing a virtuous mind over noble birth and ancestry. As does *Nennio*, Spenser asks readers to choose between the two types of nobility represented. In *Nennio*, Possidonio, a wealthy and arrogant lord, and Fabricio, a virtuous young man of modest family and means, engage in a spirited debate with their friends and fellow courtiers about who is the more noble. The contest is decided by the wise and objective Nennio, who declares that 'the nobilitie of the minde, is farre more true, and farre more perfect, then the nobility of bloud conjoyned with riches' (sig 96v). He compares historical examples of virtue and gentility, defining nobility in its different kinds and allowing that one kind is most commonly attributed to those of wealthy and noble lineage. But he concludes that 'he is worthy of farre more greater glorie who of himselfe becommeth noble, then hee who is simplie borne noble' (96v); and so the prize, Lady Virginia's ring, is awarded to Fabricio for his exemplary character. Demonstrating his virtue, Fabricio promptly offers the ring to his defeated opponent.

Nennio is one of a number of Renaissance treatises that attempt to define true nobility, including Castiglione's *Courtier* (Eng tr 1561), Lawrence Humphrey's *The Nobles* (1563), and Jeronimo Osorio's *Of Civill and Christian Nobilitie* (1552; Eng tr 1576). Such works provide relevant background to a poet who aims 'to fashion a gentleman or noble person in vertuous and gentle discipline' (Letter to Raleigh), and who claims that 'vertues seat is deepe within the mynd, / And not in outward shows, but inward thoughts defynd' (*FQ* VI proem 5).

CAROL A. STILLMAN

Neo-Latin poetry When vernacular literatures were on the rise, but not yet ready to supersede Latin, Neo-Latin poetry acted as a vehicle for humanist sensibility. Still the lingua franca of cultured people, it also served as a filter for vernacular currents from other countries; for example, Petrarchism made its progress through both the original texts and Neo-Latin intermediaries. Moreover, major Renaissance poets often distinguished themselves in both tongues (eg, Petrarch, Politian, Sannazaro, du Bellay, Campion, Herbert, Milton, and Martin Opitz) and most literary theory was written in Latin (see humanist *poetics). J.-C. Scaliger's *Poetice* (1561) was the most influential: it helped to classify and define genres, and promoted interest in the formal aspects of poetry, including pattern poetry, enigma verse, numerological concerns – all aspects that become prominent by the end of the sixteenth century. (In England, Richard Willes' *Poematum liber* [1573] is a good example of the headway made by pattern poetry in humanist circles.)

There is some Neo-Latin verse in England before the 1570s, but thereafter a marked quickening of tempo. Thomas More's epigrams became an international model; indeed in the early years his public was greater abroad than at home. His English followers – such as John Leland, Walter Haddon, and Thomas Chaloner – were more local in their readership and more limited imaginatively. These writers do not seem to have left any mark on Spenser, except possibly Leland.

In Spenser's formative years, knowledge of certain foreign Neo-Latin models was becoming common in England. Even before Elizabeth became queen, Marian exiles had come into contact with these models, for many traveled in the Low Countries, France, Germany, Switzerland, and even northern Italy. Later humanists absorbed much during their continental journeys. Moreover, a sort of triangular relationship developed in the last third of the century between France, the Low Countries, and England, due in part to the scholarly and literary reputations of Jean Dorat, Adrien Turnèbe, Denys Lambin, George Buchanan, Ronsard, du Bellay, and other members of the so-called Pléiade. The special politico-religious circumstances of that period of the Reformation intensified the relationships. The Sidney circle had close connections with the Low countries; and it is noteworthy that much Dutch (and German) Neo-Latin verse was dedicated or addressed to Elizabeth. The main Italian Neo-Latin poets were being republished in volumes that made their way across national frontiers, not only in collections of *opera omnia* but also in the ever-increasing number of anthologies. The influence of the 1546 Basel anthology of pastoral verse (*Bucolicorum auctores xxxviii*), for instance, was considerable, not simply because it brought together a large number of eclogues in convenient form but because of the particular authors represented. Another influential example is the *Carmina quinque illustrium poetarum* (Venice 1548) with poems by Bembo, Andrea Navagero (Naugerius), Castiglione (including the eclogue *Alcon*, so much admired by Milton), Joannes Cotta, and Marcantonio Flaminio. Finally, some authors were translated into English: epigrams appeared in volumes such as Timothy Kendall's *Trifles* (1577), and there were versions of more substantial compositions such as Googe's rendering of Palingenius' *Zodiacus vitae* and Turbervile's popular translation of Mantuan's *Bucolica*. The practice of Neo-Latin verse in England is concentrated in the Universities of Oxford and Cambridge, but also in certain other cultured circles such as the court. This Neo-Latin verse had its courtly and political uses to which Elizabeth was not blind, especially as she was learned in her own right. Spenser's friend Harvey wrote this kind of verse, for instance in the curious volume connected with Elizabeth's progress to Saffron Walden in 1578 (*Gratulationum Valdinensium libri quatuor*).

There are several Neo-Latin works which were well known in England by the time Spenser had embarked on a poetic career, and are more important in our context. The most obvious is Mantuan, whose *Bucolica, sive Adolescentia* enjoyed immense success that in some ways is surprising, considering the late-medieval cast of his mind. While Mantuan proved useful to Spenser, there were limits to his value as a model: his amatory themes, so medieval in character, could hardly appeal; his satire would not fit in readily with some of the aims Spenser had in mind in *The Shepheardes Calender*; and for courtly elements Spenser would need to turn to other models, such as Marot. Metrically, Mantuan followed tradition in using the hexameter – and it is noteworthy that when John Dove wrote his unpublished Latin version of the *Calender* (c 1590 and preserved in Gonville and Caius College, Cambridge), he did not seek to maintain Spenser's metrical variety but reverted to normal convention (apart from one or two songs). Finally, since sources for the life of St George are relatively limited, it is possible that Spenser drew on Mantuan's hagiographic poem *Georgius*. It is not clear whether he used the original Latin texts, for the poem was apparently not published after the 1530s, and never in England. Possibly he relied on the English version of Alexander Barclay, an early humanist who made a number of valuable works available to a wider public.

For *The Shepheardes Calender*, another contemporary Neo-Latin model may have been Palingenius, whose *Zodiacus vitae* was published in 1534. The work of what a contemporary called 'that most Christian poet' is not easily defined, though it can come under the rubric of philosophical poetry. It has a clear unity that in a sense belongs to a world not entirely dissimilar from that of Mantuan or *The Shepheardes Calender*. Palingenius traces the journey of the poet towards a greater knowledge of the universe but within the proper limits imposed by God; he takes a sharp look at *mores*, develops the satiric element, and attacks monks and other depraved members of the church. He sees the poet as an initiate who acquires a deeper knowledge of nature than the ordinary man; he stresses the moral purpose of poetry; and he praises the values of virtue, wisdom, and poverty. Pastoral elements are introduced, although they diminish as the poem advances, and there is a strong allegorical presence.

Spenser also owes something to the emblematic tradition (see *emblems). Alciati's pioneering and highly popular *Emblemata* appeared in 1531, and was often reprinted (and augmented) as well as translated into various languages. He may also have contracted a small debt to Pierre Coustau (Costalius) whose *Pegma* (in a Latin and a French version) first appeared in 1555. This type of literature may however be more important for its pictorial way of looking at things than for specific details.

Generally, traces of Neo-Latin poetry are more apparent in Spenser's earlier and 'minor' writings. For the other works, one will find many themes developed by Neo-Latin poets, but overlaps are usually in the nature of analogues, not of direct influence (eg, pastoral elements, and themes such as that of friendship). Critics have seen analogues with Petrarch, Pontano (whose European presence stems from the quality of his writing as well as from the range of his subject matter and genres), Buchanan, Sannazaro (both pastoral and religious poetry); but certain similarities (Buchanan or Vitalis) had already been assimilated by du Bellay, who is Spenser's model. It is however correct that the Neo-Latins often led in certain genres, some of which were of interest to Spenser: satire (especially religious), hymns, and psalm paraphrases. For marriage verse, Renaissance models supplemented the rather meager classical sources (see *epithalamium). In addition, the Neo-Latins performed a very valuable service with their verse renderings of Greek texts: it is a moot point to what extent Renaissance poets were really proficient in Greek, so that the work done by Erasmus, Buchanan, and Henri Estienne, to name a few, was of incalculable value. Neo-Latin verse is important because its poets develop themes and genres, sometimes ahead of the vernacular and often in more accomplished form, so that they become part of the *caisse de résonance* in which Renaissance humanists lived and worked. This general role is as important as, perhaps more so than, specific debts contracted by authors.

IAN D. MCFARLANE

Useful anthologies of some of the hard-to-find poems (with translations) are Pierre Laurens and Claudie Balavoine, trs and eds 1975 *Musae reduces: Anthologie de la poésie latine dans l'Europe de la Renaissance* 2 vols (Leiden); I[an] D. McFarlane, ed 1980 *Renaissance Latin Poetry* (Manchester); and F.J. Nichols 1979. See also W. Leonard Grant 1965 *Neo-Latin Literature and the Pastoral* (Chapel Hill). A bibliographical guide to the whole field is IJsewijn 1977; for England, see Leicester Bradner 1940 *Musae Anglicanae: A History of Anglo-Latin Poetry 1500–1925* (New York). For other background, see also Lawrence V. Ryan 1978 'Neo-Latin Literature' in *The Present State of Scholarship in Sixteenth-Century Literature* ed William M. Jones (Columbia, Mo) pp 197–257. Spenser's own Latin verse is found in the correspondence with Harvey (and translated in *Var Prose*); for Spenser and Neo-Latin verse, see Bradner 1935–6; Giuseppe Galigani 1976 'Una nota su Spenser e il Poliziano' *RLMC* 29:122–8; F. Kluge 1880 'Spenser's Shepherd's Calendar und Mantuan's Eclogen' *Anglia* 3:266–74; Tung 1972.

neologism For the purpose of this article, a neologism is any linguistic feature, morphological, lexical, or whatever, which, on the available evidence, would have seemed linguistically 'marked' to Spenser's contemporaries, even though the feature in question may have been of a familiar type, conforming (eg) to contemporary rhetorical practice. The Elizabethan period was one of intense and exciting experimentation with language, especially in forming new words; and Spenser was, in his way, as innovative as Shakespeare. He was the first major English poet after Chaucer to be essentially literary, addressing *The Faerie Queene* largely to an audience that would not recite but read. This accounts for certain differences between his neologisms and Shakespeare's, though there are many similarities.

Spenser's style is often highly individual, and many of his stylistic idiosyncrasies can be regarded as neologisms: in syntax, his inversions, his Latinate constructions, his frequent omission of definite and indefinite articles; in morphology, archaisms like *her* for *their*, the *-en* verbal suffix and the *y-* prefix; in vocabulary, the more unfamiliar of his archaisms and dialect words; in spelling, the 'dressing' of rhymes, exotic-looking usages like *mirrhour*, and pseudo-archaisms like *faerie* (see *OED*). Few of these, however, would have been wholly unfamiliar to Spenser's readers, and it is in the lexical field that we can talk most confidently of neologisms.

Spenser's innovations here can be divided into two main classes: first, new words based on existing English words. These include a large number formed by the addition of a prefix such as *a(d)-*, *dis-*, *em-/en-* (*im-/in-*), *re-* (eg, *accourting*, *addeeme*, *dispred*, *embrave*, *engore*, *redisbourse*); or a suffix such as *-age*, *-a(u)nce*, *-ant*, *-ful*, *-he(a)d*, *-ment* (eg, *pupillage*, *joyaunce*, *thrillant*, *gronefull*, *bountihed*, *jolliment*). Many of these have an archaic ring, some because they resemble familiar archaisms, others because they are probably Spenser's re-creations rather than genuine survivals. Archaisms cannot be entirely detached from the matter of innovation in Spenser. In the same category as the above, though less common, are words formed by the reverse process, that is, by the omission of a prefix or suffix. These include, for example, *bove* (for *above*), and *daint* (for *dainty*). Here again, it is often difficult to know whether we are dealing with new formations or archaic survivals.

Also under the general heading of new words from existing ones are noun compounds such as *forckhead*, and adjectival compounds such as *dead-doing*, *love-lavish*, *rich laden*, *sea-shouldring* and many others. There is also a small but characteristic group of portmanteau words. Some would deny the existence of such a category in Spenser and would assign such words to different headings; but there is little doubt that *scruze* 'to squeeze, crush' and *treachetour* 'traitor' are genuine Spenserian blends, the former of the verbs *screw* and *squeeze*, and the latter, though derived by the *OED* from a (rare) verb *trechet*, much more likely to be a blend of *treachour* 'traitor' and *tregetour* 'juggler, deceiver.'

In this class also are words used in a grammatically new way: an original noun as a verb (*equipaged* from *equipage*), or a verb as a noun (*throb*). This highly metaphorical type of coinage was especially popular in the Elizabethan period. Here also belong words used in the same part of speech, but in a significantly different sense. Choice of examples is necessarily more arbitrary than in the cases above, but Spenser is remarkable for many striking shifts in usage of a kind and degree which demands that they be considered as neologisms. Examples are the verb *revoke* 'bring back, recall' to mean either 'restrain' (*FQ* II ii 28) or 'withdraw' (viii 39), and *insolence* used in the sense of 'exultation' in *Colin Clout* 622. He made his neologisms intelligible largely from the context alone (as with *revoke*) or by providing other clues, such as by calling on a Latin meaning (as with *insolence*). He also gives new meaning to certain archaic or obsolescent words, for example, *dearnly* in Middle English meaning 'secretly' (III xii 34) but used by him to mean 'dismally, mournfully' (II i 35), and *chevisaunce* used to mean something like 'high chivalric enterprise or achievement' (II ix 8, and cf *SC, Apr* 143 where it is the name of a flower), whereas in Middle English it normally meant 'supplies, provisions' or 'bringing to a successful conclusion.'

There is a view that in these and other cases Spenser misunderstood earlier usage; but his knowledge of older English was clearly extensive and it is more likely that, at least in some cases, any 'misunderstanding' was deliberate. *Dearnly*, for example, probably combines the associations of withdrawal in 'secretly' with the melancholy and painful associations of *yearn*, while *chevisaunce* seems to call on the associations of *chev-*, *chivalry* together with the romance overtones of the suffix *-a(u)nce*. In other words, *chevisaunce* was too good a word to leave entirely to the world of business.

The second and more obvious class of neologisms in Spenser is the borrowing of words from other languages. His major sources are the same as those of other writers of his time, though rather wider ranging and again generally literary in character. The importance of intelligibility is reflected in the fact that most of his lexical borrowings have prefixes or suffixes of the familiar types mentioned earlier, which thus provide important clues to their meaning. Spenser's main source is French, and his adoptions from it include *amenance* 'conduct, bearing,' *disloign(ed)* 'distant,' *paravant* 'before,' *renverse* 'to reverse.' Very common also are loans from Latin and Italian, reflecting the prestige and influence of the classical and neoclassical languages and literature, including, from Latin, some recondite items like *caerule* (*caerulus* 'blue'), *crumenall* (*crumena* 'purse, pouch'), *subverse* 'to subvert' (*subvers-*), plus a few, such as *indignant*, *lucid*, *pallid*, which have become established in the language. From Italian, Spenser borrowed, among others, *belgard(s)* (*bel guardo* 'loving look'), *canto*, *drapet* (*drappetto* '[small] cloth'), *retrate* (*ritratto* 'picture'). Since in quite a few examples it is not certain whether the origin was French, Latin, Italian, or even Spanish, a definitive list cannot be compiled.

Most of Spenser's neologisms are literary in character, so it is not surprising that few have entered the colloquial language. Most of the examples already quoted, such as *canto* and *indignant*, should probably not be traced specifically to Spenser, since other writers were using them at about the same time. Two striking exceptions, however, are *blatant*, virtually a proper name in Spenser and invented (though of still-disputed origin) to describe the monster introduced in *FQ* V; and *derring-do*, based on an archaic form of *daring to do*, but transformed by Spenser's creative alchemy into a noun meaning something like 'knightly endeavour or prowess.' This kind of innovation should remind us that he was writing poetry for the enjoyment of an audience, and not a mere verbal experiment for the interest only of scholars. (See also *etymology, *language, *puns.) ALAN WARD

Craig 1959; Craig 1967; J.W. Draper 1932; Gans 1978–9; Hamilton 1972b; R.F. Jones 1953; Joseph 1947; Kostić 1959a; McElderry 1932; Frederick M. Padelford 1941 'Spenser's Use of "Stour"' *MLQ* 2:465–73; Pope 1926; Renwick 1922a; Rubel 1941; Sugden 1936.

Nereids All Nereids are nymphs, but not all nymphs are Nereids (a four-syllable word in Spenser's spelling, 'Nereides'). Spenser uses the word *nymph* with all the vagueness it had in classical antiquity to designate a young unmarried woman whose affinity with the forces of nature is manifest in her influence on man – his passions and his poetry. His nymphs are traditional in being associated with the spirit of a place. Friendly, loving, and generally known for chastity, they defend the youth of the locale, bless their marriages, and are linked with wisdom and the arts. Such mythic plurality dates from well before the age of specialization – that is, before Hesiod.

Although nymphs are found often in his poetry (see especially *Prothalamion* 19–36), Spenser refers only twice to the daughters of Nereus, the sea god – once in passing (*FQ* III iv 29), and a second time in cataloguing the 50 daughters at the marriage of Thames and Medway (IV xi 48–53). This latter episode is a concentrated example of how he uses allusion to create a subtext which is essential to the meaning of his narrative. In *SC, Aprill* 37 and *December* 47, he refers to nymphs without forcing specific literary models on his reader. Such unobtrusiveness, however, is not congenial to Nereids or to Spenser's objectives, for his catalogue calls special attention to itself and to its model in Hesiod's *Theogony* 240–64.

In early mythology, Muses, Nereids, Oceanids, hamadryads, and others are distinguished only by their domains. Hesiod, giving authority and coherence to a succession myth at the center of the *Theogony*, establishes a loose genealogy for these figures, naming and characterizing the 50 daughters of Nereus for the first time. Spenser emulates this poetic model in the marriage procession of *FQ* IV xi, apparently following closely his Greek-Latin text (of Boninus Mombritius) and turning to Conti (8.6) only for minor changes in the names and order of the Nereids (Hesiod ed 1966, Bennett 1931b, Lotspeich 1932:89–90).

In choosing the Nereids as Medway's bridesmaids and the culminating image of the marriage procession, Spenser provides a group of specially qualified nymphs who bring art and nature together in a moral context. Thanks to Hesiod, the Nereids make up a numerous but finite assembly well suited to Spenser's own myth of succession and its image of orderly multiplicity in nature and history. As the daughters of Nereus and Doris (daughter of Oceanus), they are, as he says, 'Sea Nymphs.' For him, as for Conti, they suggest the generative powers of nature (see xii 1–2), and thus the force of love or concord.

Spenser also wanted to end the procession with an image of moral order to complement the 'geopolitical' order conveyed by the grooms who attend Thames, and for this he need not have gone beyond Hesiod's text. This company of 'Sea Nymphs ... goodly damzels, deckt with long greene haire, / Whom of their sire *Nereides* men call' (xi 48), represents the forces of nature, but in a way very different from their more mundane male counterparts, the English rivers, whose habitation and sphere of influence is a more particular natural world. The Nereids, with the natural artfulness that makes female charm mythical, are from a poetic realm of quintessential nature and thus are an extension of Medway's celestial qualities (45) and of the contrast between her ethereal nature and the historical, worldly, and quotidian qualities of Thames and his retainers.

As in Hesiod, the Nereids particularize the moral qualities of their father Nereus, and Spenser does not miss the smallest moral nuance in his source. Nereus, who is firmly fixed in Spenser's own succession myth (18), is 'th'eldest, and the best' offspring of the elemental gods Oceanus and Tethys, who divide the sea and land between them and anticipate the polarity between Marinell and Florimell. Patterned after Hesiod's carefully identified figure, Nereus is 'upright,' 'sincere in word and deed,' 'voide of guile,' known for 'Doing him selfe, and teaching others to doe right,' and for his prophetic powers (18–19). His 50 daughters spread his benign influence throughout the world: in Spenser as in Hesiod, their names convey their virtues, and this conjunction between name and character is significant for both authors, who also use the names for maximum poetic effect. Among the 50, whose virtues, ideally, form the sinews of Spenser's nature, there are 'milde *Eucrate*,' 'Joyous *Thalia*,' 'wise *Protomedaea*,' 'chaste *Actea*,' '*Themiste* just,' '[*Evarna*] that vertue loves and vice detests,' '*Menippe* true in trust,' and '*Nemertea* [who] learned well to rule her lust' (48–51). The epithets accompanying the names are either traditional (Thalia is joyous because her name is that of the Muse of comedy; cf VI x 22), related to the Greek etymology (Eucrate comes from the Greek for 'mild temperament') or translated from the commentary in Mombritius' edition of Hesiod (see further Braden 1975, esp pp 31–3). Certain of the names set up echoes with names elsewhere in *The Faerie Queene*: the reader may wonder whether 'wanton *Glauce*' is a glimpse of Britomart's nurse before she entered service, and whether the description of Cymodoce as 'she, that with her least word can asswage / The surging seas, when they do sorest rage' (50) is a witty adaptation of Hesiod's lines to Marinell's mother and her unsuccessful attempts to assuage her son's surging passion. W.H. Herendeen

New World European adventurers made the exotic phenomena of the New World seem less strange by associating them with such items from familiar travelers' lore as Amazons, sea monsters, floating islands, mermaids, Indians (see *FQ* II xi 21, III xii 8), and the terrestrial paradise (see Elliott 1970, chs 1–2). Spenser uses much of this mythology in *FQ* II, in which the proem gives notice of American themes by referring to 'Indian *Peru*,' 'The *Amazons* huge river,' and 'fruitfullest *Virginia*.' If Book I, in political terms, focuses on Britain's recovery of independence from Spain and Rome, Book II expresses the Elizabethan desire for an American empire to rival Spain's – an empire claimed to have ancient precedent: Guyon learns that a Fairy empire predating Cleopolis itself once stretched from India to America (x 72). To refound this empire was the particular project of Spenser's associate Raleigh, who in 1585 named everything north of Spanish Florida 'Virginia' in honor of the Virgin Queen. Spenser's concept of temperance as 'goodly mixture' (Gr *krasis*) is an element in his description of Belphoebe (iii 22), a Virgin Queen and Diana figure with Amazonian features but also with hints of Venus. With its implicit mixture of opposite attributes, 'fruitfullest *Virginia*' furnishes the potential geographical complement to this royal temperance.

Mismanaged sensuality and material greed are the two main obstacles to empire in the Book of Temperance, which warns Elizabethans to avoid Spanish excesses in the Americas. Guyon's goal is to destroy the Bower of Bliss, a perversion of the American terrestrial paradise (Greenblatt 1980:180) and, in its lust and sterility, a vicious parody of 'fruitfullest *Virginia*.' By succumbing to Acrasia (Gr *a-krasis* no mixture), young heroes like Verdant forfeit empire. Spenser models the Bower on Armida's garden in Tasso (*Gerusalemme liberata* 15–16), a faintly American paradise that includes grapes that know no season. To these Spenser adds artificial gold grapes (xii 54–5), indicating his awareness of a unique American wonder: the ceremonial Incan gardens which intermingled real plants with goldsmiths' duplicates (Cain 1978:92–3).

The other major American episode – Guyon's adventure in Mammon's cave – may allude to the mystery of the vast Incan treasure supposed by the Pizarros to have been spirited away to a mythic golden city called El Dorado. When Guyon stumbles on Mammon and his treasure, Mammon tries to conceal it as did the Incas and Guyon, however piously, to seek it just as the conquistadors had done. Among the forms of Mammon's gold are 'great Ingoes' (vii 5). Although Spenser's pseudo-Chaucerian vocabulary allows *ingoes* as a supposedly archaic form of *ingots*, Elizabethans would recognize their own word for Incas (*Ingas*, as in Spanish). Guyon's faint at the end of this episode warns Elizabethan adventurers of the dangers of greed in the Americas, although Spenser's later salute to Raleigh's attempt in 1595 to ascend the 'Rich Oranochy' in search of 'that land of gold' is clearly positive (IV xi 21–2) (Cain 1978:93–8).

Thomas H. Cain

Cain 1978; Chiappelli 1976; J.H. Elliott 1970 *The Old World and the New, 1492–1650* (Cambridge); Giamatti 1976; Greenblatt 1980; Samuel Eliot Morison 1971–4 *The European Discovery of America* 2 vols (New York); John H. Wall, Jr 1985 '"Fruitfullest Virginia": Edmund Spenser, Roanoke Island, and the Bower of Bliss' *RenP 1984* pp 1–17.

Nicholas of Cusa (1401–64) Canon lawyer, humanist, mathematician, theologian, and ecclesiastic, Nicholas of Cusa (Cusanus) began his mature speculative career with *De docta ignorantia* (*Of Learned Ignorance* 1440), in which he argues that, because precise truth resides only in the infinite God and there is no proportion between the finite and the infinite, all rational effort must remain incomplete. His favorite symbol for this epistemological condition is the relationship between polygon and circle: no matter how many sides the polygon has, it never achieves the perfection of the circle. This condition, although central to his mysticism, does not lead exclusively to mystical abnegation. Rather, it encourages the mind's positive quest for wisdom; Nicholas joins the 'negative way' to an enthusiasm for human capabilities. The quest, therefore, takes two forms. One is represented by the 'coincidence of opposites' (*coincidentia oppositorum*), a symbol for the ineffable One behind all diversity and a reminder of the necessity of transcending even the most basic of logical laws, the law of contradiction, when confronting mystery. The other, which comes into prominence in Nicholas' second work, *De coniecturis* (c 1440–4), insists on the mind's creative freedom, its ability to shape metaphorical and symbolic schemes in its quest for unattainable precision. These schemes range from word games and conceits to painted images, mathematical diagrams, scientific experiments, and the fashioning of human institutions in general. All rational effort for Nicholas assumes the status of 'conjecture.' His work has evoked controversy primarily because of his questioning of the creative mind's access to exemplars (ie, 'Ideas') outside itself, or to stable quiddities definable in things. Although he assumes the objective orientation of thought, his emphasis on the mind as the measure of things, its power to unfold a conceptual world by projecting its own points of reference, raises new problems about the hierarchical structure of the cosmos, and about the mind's relation to extramental reality.

Knowledge of Cusanus in Renaissance England is uncertain: Foxe mentions him in *Actes and Monuments*, as does Donne; Bruno may also have brought word of him (see Wind 1958:181 and nn 3, 4). His importance for Spenser studies is nonetheless manifold. Mythographic studies may turn to him (as does Wind 1958) for background to explore Spenser's philosophical interest in the *coincidentia oppositorum* as a mystical symbol: the reconciliation of contraries (eg, Love and Hate at the Temple of Venus, *FQ* IV x 32–3) or of sexual contraries (eg, the hermaphroditic statue of Venus, stanza 41). Others, influenced by recent work in poststructuralist theory, will find in Cusanus an historical context for the open-endedness of Spenserian narrative. This theory, opposed to a reading of allegory that assumes the presence of stable, objective doctrine beneath the poetic surface, emphasizes Spenser's avoidance of closure and the way *The Faerie Queene* represents the impossibility of ever resting on a final, authorized foundation of truth: allegory as 'endlesse worke' (IV xii 1). The dual concentration in Cusanus on the infinite gap separating the mind from its goal, together with the mind's potentially endless fecundity of metaphor, allows students of Spenser to explore the possibilities of post-structuralist reading in relation to the philosophical activity of his own age. More fundamentally, Cusanus raises important questions about the metaphysical justification of allegory. While sometimes invoking Neoplatonic hierarchies and scholastic notions of quiddity, he represents a powerful revision of philosophical themes which are often crucial to a mode offering levels of meaning and analogical correspondences. His importance for Spenser studies, then, lies in the way he complicates our understanding of Renaissance philosophical contexts – contexts that illuminate both the period's aesthetic ideals and the problematic nature of those ideals – and so opens up a variety of approaches sufficiently rich to explore the complexity of Spenser's thought and poetic invention.

RONALD L. LEVAO

The standard edition is ed 1932– *Opera omnia* Iussu et auctoritate Academicae Litterarum Heidelbergensis (Leipzig). Many of the major works have been translated into English. Studies include Cassirer ed 1963; Michel de Certeau 1987 'The Gaze of Nicholas of Cusa' *Diacritics* 17.3:2–38; F. Edward Cranz 1953 'Saint Augustine and Nicholas of Cusa in the Tradition of Western Christian Thought' *Spec* 28:297–316; Jasper Hopkins 1981 *Nicholas of Cusa on Learned Ignorance: A Translation and an Appraisal of 'De Docta Ignorantia'* (Minneapolis); Ronald Levao 1985 *Renaissance Minds and Their Fictions: Cusanus, Sidney, Shakespeare* (Berkeley and Los Angeles); and Pauline Moffitt Watts 1982 *Nicolaus Cusanus: A Fifteenth-Century Vision of Man* (Leiden). Cusanus remains a controversial figure. International bibliographies of recent studies appear in *Mitteilungen und Forschungsbeiträge der Cusanus-Gesellschaft* (Mainz 1961–).

Night The infernal deity Night is the oldest of the gods and the evil demiurge of Spenser's cosmology. She is the 'most auncient Grandmother of all,' born in pre-creation chaos, '*Daemogorgons* hall' (*FQ* I v 22); she is the wife of Herebus, who is the 'sonne of *Aeternitie*' and 'foe / Of all the Gods' (II iv 41, III iv 55). She appears in *FQ* I v 20–44, mantled in black and driving an iron chariot pulled by black horses (cf VII vii 44). For his description of Night and her lineage, Spenser elaborates on Conti (*Mythologiae* 3.12) and on the classical writers he cites, particularly Hesiod (*Theogony* 116–25, 211–25), Virgil (*Aeneid* 5.721–39, 8.369), and Cicero (*De natura deorum* 3.17). (See Lotspeich 1932:91.)

Both the source and nourisher of evil, Night works persistently to return the world to its original chaos by destroying 'the children of faire light,' and 'The sonnes of Day' favored by Jove (I v 24–5), though she must acknowledge the supremacy of Jove who is her own offspring (22). Arthur's apostrophe to Night puts her origin and end into a Christian context (III iv 55–60). She was born in heaven but thrust down to hell. She is now the agent responsible for all the world's woe, the 'Sister of heavie death'; but the children of Day will ultimately subdue darkness (cf Eph 5.8, 1 Thess 5.5).

Among the lineal descendants of Night are the Sans brothers, Duessa, Despight (who may be identified with Despetto, VI v 13), Pyrochles, and Cymochles (I v 22–3, 26–7; II iv 41). Echidna, who dwells in the house of Night, is the mother by Typhaon of various monsters including the Blatant Beast (V x 10, xi 23; VI vi 9). In *Teares of the Muses*, Night is the mother of Sloth by whom she bore Ignorance (259–64). In a more general sense, almost all the evil characters of *The Faerie Queene* are related to Night through a complex network of imagery of ugliness, darkness, secrecy, and blindness, which are attributes of Night herself and of the rule she promotes.

Her kingdom is a demonic parody of Jove's. While Spenser's good knights need daylight for moral vision and activity, evil beings such as Error (I i 16) thrive without light and are bewildered and repelled by its presence. Night herself is at first fearful of the 'sunny bright' Duessa; but when she realizes that Duessa's identity, like her bejeweled brightness, is false, she greets her as her true kindred (V 21–7). The pity which Night shows for Duessa is a parody of heavenly grace, and her efforts to have Sansjoy cured in hell contrast with God's nourishment of Redcrosse by the Well and Tree of Life (I xi 29–30, 46–9).

The antagonism between Jove and Night appears incidentally in the periphrastic descriptions of the rivalry between Day and Night at sunrise and sunset, particularly in Book I (esp ii 1, v 2, xi 49–51). In such instances, 'joyous' Day is welcomed for its beauty and vitality, while 'noyous' Night is a time of gloom and sadness. The crimson robe of sunrise contrasts with Night's sable mantle.

The onset of night is frequently an indication that a knight has become complacent, incautious, mentally or spiritually lazy, so that unwittingly he encounters a challenge to his virtue. The knightly quest demands perpetual endeavor; but the weakness of mortal flesh makes this impossible, and night which brings rest also brings temptation. Thus Redcrosse succumbs to Archimago's nocturnal magic (I i 36), he sleeps in the house of Pride while Duessa incites Sansjoy against him (iv 44), and Britomart is vulnerable to Malecasta when she sleeps unarmed at night (III i 58–9). Later, Britomart remains watchful all night in the house of Busirane and the house of Dolon (III xi 55, V vi 24–6) and survives the ordeals unscathed. If a knight must surrender to human frailty and rest at night, he must be protected, as Redcrosse rests in his fight against the Dragon, watched over by Una (I xi 31–2, 49–50), and the unconscious Guyon, watched over by the Angel (II viii 1–8); or he must be in a state of assured security, as is Guyon in the house of Medina and the castle of Alma (II ii 46, ix 10–xi 2), and Britomart 'Under the wings of *Isis*' (V vii 12). Only in such circumstances is sleep invigorating. To fall asleep without protection is to submit to Night's rule and to worship her blasphemously (III iv 56). When Arthur lies 'in silver slomber,' he is exposed to Turpine's treachery (VI vii 19–25). Meliboe who boasts that 'all the night in silver sleepe I spend' (VI ix 22) is deluded by a false sense of security since he is soon captured by the Brigands and killed.

Night is held responsible for evil dreams and fantasies: Redcrosse's in Archimago's hermitage, Britomart's in her father's house, and Scudamour's in the house of Care (I i 36–9, III ii 28–9, IV v 32, 43). When a delightful dream or *visio* is experienced (eg, Arthur's vision of the Fairy Queen in I ix 13–14, or Britomart's in Isis Church in V vii 12–16), Night plays no active role as agent. She rarely offers opportunity for pleasurable or creative thoughts. In this Spenser differs from several of his contemporaries (see Bradbrook 1936). In Chapman (*The Shadow of Night* 1594), Drayton (*Endimion and Phoebe* 1595, and *The Owle* 1604), and William Browne (*Britannia's Pastorals* 3.1.335–697), darkness brings a pleasing melancholy which induces meditation; but Spenser's Contemplation is encountered in broad daylight and his spirit is lifted toward the sun (I x 46–7).

A dislike, even fear, of Night is evident in other works by Spenser. Night and darkness are associated with loss and sorrow (*SC, Sept* 3–6, *Nov* 67–9; *Daphnaïda* 482–3) and with the ignorance of a world rendered lifeless by its lack of appreciation of poetry (*Teares* 68, 106). In seven of the twelve eclogues of *The Shepheardes Calender*, Spenser adopts the convention of Virgil and later pastoral writers by concluding the poem at nightfall. This lends a melancholy strain to his pastoral (see esp *Jan, Apr, June, Aug*), which becomes much more pronounced and more sinister in the pastoral interlude of *The Faerie Queene*, where the shepherds are carried off by the Brigands 'in the covert of the night' and are imprisoned in a dark cave which bears analogies with hell (VI x 41–4).

Yet Night as a natural phenomenon must be accepted as participating equally with Day in the divine order. In *Epithalamion*, night is welcomed, for it brings wedded joys which will bear 'timely fruit' (315, 404). In the pageant of creation in *FQ* VII vii, Day and Night ride together 'with equall pase' (44). In each case, Night is made the parent with Day (Jove) of the Hours (Horae), which by tradition were the daughters of Themis and Jove. Yet even here Night remains sinister, and she is only grudgingly accepted. Her terrors, real and imaginary, haunt the bridegroom in *Epithalamion* 321–52. While all other elements of creation look directly into the face of Nature as they await her verdict (*FQ* VII vii 57), Night is the only one of the assembly who is veiled: her 'uncomely' countenance and mysterious identity seem too awesome to contemplate.

GEOFFREY G. HILLER

Noot, Jan van der Born in Brecht near Antwerp in 1538 or 1539, Jonker Jan van der Noot, an Antwerp alderman since 1562, joined the Calvinists in 1566 and fled to

England in 1567. He spent some time in Germany in the early 1570s, perhaps visited Italy, and returned to Antwerp in 1578 via France where, he claims, he met Ronsard. He died between 1596 and 1601.

He arrived in London in April 1567 as the leader of a group of Antwerp Protestants, with a safe-conduct signed by William of Orange and addressed to William Cecil. In England, he published French, Dutch, and English versions of his *Theatre for Worldlings*, and a collection of poetry, *Het Bosken*, printed by Bynneman in 1570 and dedicated to William Parr, Marquis of Northampton (to whose widow Spenser dedicated *Daphnaïda* in 1591). A German version of *Theatre* appeared in Cologne in 1572. His other publications include *Das Buch Extasis* (1576, French and Dutch versions in 1579), *Lofsang van Braband* (1580), and *Poeticsche Werken* (1584–95).

Van der Noot was the first major innovator in Dutch Renaissance literature. He not only experimented with metrics and prosody but also introduced several new genres, such as epic, pastoral, epithalamium, and the Pindaric ode. His interest in emblems and hieroglyphics is particularly evident in the symbolic engravings and woodcuts (some of them depicting the poet himself as protagonist) with which his books were illustrated. He became his own sales manager and often made up different versions of his published work, with or without a portrait of the author.

Jan van Dorsten

Van der Noot ed 1953 is a standard edition of the two works *Het Bosken* and *Het Theatre*. *Poeticsche Werken* ed Werner Waterschoot, 3 vols (Ghent 1975) is a facsimile with elaborate commentary.

There is little on van der Noot in English. Leonard Forster 1968 'Jan van der Noot und die deutsche Renaissancelyrik: Stand und Aufgaben der Forschung' in *Literatur und Geistesgeschichte: Festgabe für Heinz Otto Burger* ed Reinhold Grimm and Conrad Wiedemann (Berlin) pp 70–84 is the principal brief assessment of the poetry, though see also René Galland 1922 'Un Poète errant de la Renaissance: Jean Van der Noot et l'Angleterre' *RLC* 2:337–50; Reinder P. Meijer 1978 *Literature of the Low Countries: A Short History of Dutch Literature in the Netherlands and Belgium* rev ed (Cheltenham; first pub Assen 1971) pp 84–9; C.A. Zaalberg 1954 *'Das Buch Extasis' van Jan van der Noot* (Assen), with English summary.

number symbolism, modern studies in Renaissance humanism imparted new energy to the ancient tradition of numerology. The astrological and arithmological lore of early Mesopotamian cultures was rationalized by Pythagoras and Plato, then modified by the reintroduction of ancient Orphic, gnostic, and Judaic influences; it was given a literary focus by medieval exegetes, theorists, and encyclopedists such as Augustine, Martianus Capella, Macrobius, Rabanus Maurus, Isidore of Seville, and later Hugh of St Victor, before its renewed elaboration and consolidation in the Renaissance by synthesizers such as Giorgio, Reuchlin, Pico della Mirandola, Ficino, Agrippa, and Bongo. The extent of Spenser's familiarity and concern with the details of numerology is uncertain, but it is clear that he shared the fundamental assumption of the numerologists: that numbers are profoundly meaningful as expressions of divine order in the universe.

Since A. Kent Hieatt's *Short Time's Endless Monument* (1960), the study of number symbolism in Spenser's poetry has yielded important insights. In addition to Hieatt, Alastair Fowler and Maren-Sofie Røstvig have been the pioneers and chief practitioners. Spenser's number symbolism generally involves arrangement of elements – characters, themes, episodes, stanzas, lines, and words – in places or patterns that derive significance by reference to conventional arithmological meanings or to known astrological or calendrical patterns, or by the fact that their symmetry in itself suggests a higher order. Though numbers had accumulated a very wide (and sometimes contradictory) range of meanings, certain frequent associations constituted a standard numerological vocabulary. In general, 1, 3, 9, and 10 were associated with holiness, perfection, divinity, spirituality, and related concepts; 2 and 11 with physicality and sin; 4 with concord, friendship, and stability; 5 with justice and marriage; 6 with perfection and marriage; 7 with humanity and mutability; and 8 with regeneration or resurrection.

Though it is clear from the shorter, and hence more tractable, works that Spenser used number symbolism in subtle and detailed ways, decades of study have yielded an abundance of suggestive detail but no consensus about the extent and nature of number symbolism in *The Faerie Queene*. Two astrological schemes for its overall organization have been proposed which relate the books to planetary and zodiacal deities (Fowler 1964, Yates 1979); but they agree only in associating Book I with the Sun, IV with Mercury, and VI with Venus. Images of virtue or good fortune occur in the third canto of every book, but they sometimes occur also in the second or eleventh (III ii, IV xi). Arthur appears in the eighth canto of all books – except III; images of evil occur in the eleventh canto of all books – except IV. We find pairs of characters in II, quartets in IV, and quintets in V, but no such groupings in III or VI. Facts like these characterize Spenser's number symbolism in *The Faerie Queene*, as now understood: it appears to be pervasive but not sufficiently consistent or comprehensive to command universal acceptance as a determining structural principle.

There are indications of smaller-scale but more subtle number symbolism. Scholars have, for example, proposed numerological schemes for the British chronicle in *FQ* II x (Mills 1976), or noted the occurrence of significant events at the precise midpoints of some cantos and books, such as the downfall of Redcrosse in Book I (Bayback, et al 1969), or the phrase 'like race in equall justice runne' (V vii 4) describing the relationship between Isis and Osiris in Book V, or correlated the number of characters in selected episodes with the number of stars in thematically appropriate constellations (Fowler 1964). Such examples of numerological arcana will lead the skeptic, properly, to ask why so many third, seventh, and ninth lines or stanzas, so many midpoints, and so many astrologically significant totals pass by without especially significant events, and why so many significant events occur in numerologically insignificant places. Yet there is enough information of this sort that it cannot be disregarded entirely.

Finally there is the famous arithmetic stanza (II ix 22), which introduces the castle of Alma. The proportions described here have been variously related to Hermetic, Platonic, and Aristotelian traditions, in terms of arithmetic and plane geometry and, more recently, of solid geometry and music. After centuries of commentary, the interpretation of the stanza remains controversial; yet no one would deny that number symbolism is involved. Even in this most explicitly numerological of stanzas, Spenser's number symbolism is as indistinct as it is in *The Faerie Queene* generally, where it is one thread of a veil of allegory intended not, as he tells us in the Letter to Raleigh, to give us 'good discipline delivered plainly,' but to invite pursuit of a faintly and sporadically perceptible truth.

In several of the shorter poems, number symbolism serves as a central structuring device. *Epithalamion* consists of 24 stanzas marking the hours of a day. The 365 long lines represent the number of days in the solar year; the 68 short lines may plausibly be assigned to other temporal units: the total of weeks, months, and seasons. These universal temporal symbols are joined, by means of a symbolic astronomical detail, with the specific historical day of Spenser's wedding, presumed to have taken place on 11 June 1594. The occurrence of the phrase 'Now night is come' in stanza 17, line 4 corresponds to the 16-and-a-fraction hours of daylight on that day in southern Ireland, where the wedding took place. The division between day and night is reinforced by positive refrains in the first 16 stanzas and negative refrains in the last 8. There are strong indications in *Epithalamion* of a further symmetrical pattern of concentric matching stanzas centered on the wedding stanzas, 12 and 13; however, at least three different matching schemes have been proposed (Hieatt 1960, Wickert 1968, Fowler 1970b; see also Greene 1957, Hieatt 1961, Eade 1972, and Kaske 1978).

Calendar symbolism is a primary structural device in the first part of the *Amoretti-Epithalamion* volume as well, where it again links universal temporal and religious symbols with specific historical events. Sonnet 22, announcing 'This holy season fit to fast and pray,' may plausibly refer to Ash Wednesday, and sonnet 68 is an Easter sonnet; they are separated by the number of days between Ash Wednesday and Easter in any year. Sonnet 62 celebrates a new year six sonnets before the Easter sonnet, which was the interval in days between 25 March, the traditional beginning of the year in Renaissance England, and 31 March, the date of Easter in 1594, the year of Spenser's courtship; thus the correlation of calendrical pattern and sonnet placement epitomizes Spenser's allegorical vision of a world in which universal and spiritual values inform at all points the particulars of historical life. This arrangement also establishes a Lenten group of 47 sonnets centered in the sequence, with 21 sonnets preceding and 21 following. Although each sonnet of the central group appears to correspond numerically to a calendar day and several sonnets have strong liturgical/calendrical associations (Hieatt 1973a, W.C. Johnson 1974 and 1976, and esp Prescott 1985), no sonnet-by-sonnet thematic correlation has been demonstrated for the entire series. Likewise, despite the clear thematic coherence of the 1595 *Amoretti-Epithalamion* volume, readings of the volume including the anacreontic verses have not revealed comprehensive numerical or calendrical patterns that are compelling (Kaske 1978, Thompson 1985).

Daphnaïda (1591) and *Colin Clouts Come Home Againe* (1595) both show elaborate numerological structuring. *Daphnaïda* consists of 81 stanzas of 7 lines, including a structurally discrete complaint of 49 stanzas divided into 7 strophes (lines 197–539); the crucial realization that death is a reward comes in the central stanza of this complaint (Røstvig 1963). Preceding the complaint are 28 stanzas: 3 introductory, 11 describing the poet's meeting with Alcyon, 11 relating Alcyon's story, and 3 introducing the complaint. Four stanzas follow the complaint, bringing the overall total to 81. *Colin Clout* has at its center Colin's 52-stanza catalogue of the 12 shepherds and 12 nymphs of Cynthia's retinue (376–583). In the midst is Colin's passionate dedication to his own love, with its key lines (477–8) clearly marked by a chiasmus and placed at the numerical center of the whole work. His catalogue is preceded and followed by 93 stanzas, though 3 stanzas, including the first and last) are irregular.

Prothalamion and 'Astrophel' provide interesting examples of numerological allusion on a small scale. For instance, the peculiar 18-line stanza of *Prothalamion*, whose model has been sought in the Italian canzone, may have an astrological basis, deriving from the 18 stars of the constellation Gemini, which is the house of Mercury, a force reconciling and holding opposites in accord (Fowler 1964). Other fundamental decisions in the composition of the poem appear to have been based on the desire to feature 5, the number of marriage. Spenser names 5 flowers and 10 individuals, 5 female and 5 male; and he has 10 stanzas, 5 with refrains in the past tense and relating to the river Thames and the grooms, 5 with refrains in the present tense and relating to the river Lee and the brides (Fowler 1964). Not all numerological allusion was based entirely on ancient and arcane tradition. The 216 initial lines of 'Astrophel' (2 × 108) and the 108 lines of the 'dolefull lay' of Clorinda which follows, probably allude to the 108 sonnets of Sidney's *Astrophil and Stella* (Fowler 1970b).

Evidence of number symbolism in the remaining shorter works is spotty. Of the 9 works in *Complaints* (1591), *Teares of the Muses* offers the clearest evidence of numerological structuring. After a 9-stanza introduction, Spenser devotes 10 stanzas to each Muse except Euterpe, who receives an additional stanza to bring the total to 100 and the line total to 600 (Røstvig 1963). There is some suggestion of numerological connection among the complaints. The structure of *Ruines of Time*, for example, may be based on 2 and 7: its initial 70-stanza lament is divided into 2 equal parts (Røstvig 1963), and its line total (686) has been analyzed as $7^3 \times 2$. This is the same as the line total of the main body of *Virgils Gnat* (Fowler 1964). Four of the remaining complaints have 14-line stanzas. Studies of *The Shepheardes Calender* and *Fowre Hymnes*, two very complex works at the beginning and end of Spenser's career, have revealed no clear evidence of comprehensive numerological patterning, although the tetrad appears to be significant in the overall plan of both works, and *October* and *Aprill* show symmetrical patterning (Heninger 1962, Røstvig 1969, Bristol 1970, Heninger 1974, Cain 1978, Brown 1980).

From what we know of Spenser's number symbolism, it is clear that he regarded numbers as but one means of symbolic expression among the many indications of order underlying the various trials and experiences of human life. None of his works is exclusively or even primarily numerological. His use of numerology is not rigorously comprehensive or mechanically consistent, any more than is his use of mythology. At the same time, it is clear that numbers had special value in his allegorical vision of life and that he used them symbolically from the beginning to the end of his career, in both simple and complex works. (See also *topomorphical approach).

Alexander Dunlop

Bayback, et al 1969; Bristol 1970; Brown 1980; Burchmore 1977; Burchmore 1984; C. Butler 1970a; Butler 1970b; Cain 1978; Donald Cheney 1986 'Envy in the Middest of the 1596 "Faerie Queene"' in *Edmund Spenser: Modern Critical Views* ed Harold Bloom (New York) pp 267–83; Dunlop 1970; Dunlop 1980; Eade 1972; Fowler 1964; Fowler 1970b; Fowler 1975; Greene 1957; Heninger 1961; Heninger 1962; Heninger 1974; Hieatt 1960; Hieatt 1961; Hieatt 1973a; Hieatt 1973b; Hopper 1938; Hopper 1940; W.C. Johnson 1974; Johnson 1976; Jordan 1980; Kaske 1978; Mills 1973; Mills 1976; Oates 1983; Prescott 1985; Reid 1981–2; Røstvig 1963; Røstvig 1969; Snare 1969; C. Thompson 1985; Seth Weiner 1984 'Minims and Grace Notes: Spenser's Acidalian Vision and Sixteenth-Century Music' *SSt* 5:91–112; Wickert 1968; Yates 1979.

number symbolism, tradition of Numbers were used by classical philosophers to express aspects of reality. Thus 1 was taken to represent the creative monad, 2 matter (because of its divisibility), and 3 mind (because it cannot be divided). If pebbles are used for numbers, 2 represents a line, 3 a surface (triangle), and 4 a solid body (a pyramid on a triangular base). This way of thinking is associated especially with Pythagoras and Plato. The Pythagoreans explained creation by means of the number 4: there are 4 elements, 4 humors, 4 seasons, 4 directions, and so on, and perfection results when they are harmoniously balanced. But 4 is also the number of harmony because the first four numbers (1, 2, 3, and 4) establish ratios that create the basic consonances. Thus the ratio 1:2 creates the octave or diapason, which is an image of return, since the last note returns to the first, but an octave higher. The universe itself displays these ratios (for example, 1:2, 2:3, or 3:4) in the distance between the spheres – hence the idea of the music of the spheres.

Plato's more comprehensive formula consists of seven numbers arranged in the form of the Greek letter lambda:

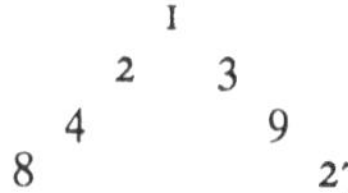

From the monad issue the two first numbers (2 and 3), and when these are squared (4 and 9) and cubed (8 and 27), a three-dimensional world is formed. The even numbers represent *matter* and the odd numbers represent *soul*; but two such different numbers as 8 and 27 can be related by inserting the mean numbers 12 and 18, which establish the same ratio between them all in the formula 8:12 :: 12:18 :: 18:27. (The ratio is $1\,^{1}/_{2}$, since 12 is 8 + $^{8}/_{2}$, 18 is 12 + $^{12}/_{2}$, and 27 is 18 + $^{18}/_{2}$.) The numbers in this formula (8, 12, 18, and 27) represent the 4 elements and the harmony imposed on them by the Creator. Plato saw too that the seven numbers define a musical scale.

The popular argument that the Greeks were indebted to Moses and the prophets made it legitimate to adduce classical number lore in commentary on the work of creation and restoration (see Augustine *On the Trinity* 4.2.4–4.6.10). In their capacity as signs, numbers were felt to be a purer language than words and much closer to reality.

Augustine favors the language of numbers both in his theology and aesthetic theory because he never separates the two. He refers the beauty of all the arts and sciences back to order, that is, to the use of number and proportion. When reason surveys the earth and heaven, beauty alone pleases it, and in beauty the figures, in the figures the dimensions, and in the dimensions the numbers. The regular course of the seasons and the circles of the stars and the intervals that separate them, all are entirely the reign of numbers (*On Order* 2.15.42–3).

Augustine uses this intellectual approach to creation as proof of the validity of the

Christian faith, and in his treatise *On True Religion* he conducts his whole argument in numerical terminology. Thus regeneration spells a return to the One or unity, which in its turn is the source of all concord (*omnis concordiae caput*). If we love what is mutable and temporal, we embrace death; but by loving God, we return from the mutable Many to the immutable One. Since the standard of all the arts is absolutely unchangeable, while our minds suffer the mutability of error, the standard called truth must be above our minds in the divine mind. By it, we perceive that beauty is harmony: 'In all the arts that which pleases is harmony [*convenientia*], which alone invests the whole with unity and beauty. This harmony requires equality and unity, either through the resemblance of symmetrically placed parts, or through the graded arrangement of unequal parts' (30.55). On perceiving the presence of balance in the universe or in a work of art, the mind is led back to God. It is the organization or structure which invests all spatial and temporal rhythms with beauty, regardless of their extension or duration. If stage spectacles please us, we should take even more delight in the art of God who imposed order on the theater of the world (Wisdom 8.1). Such is the message of Paul when he writes that the invisible things of God are understood through the things that are made (Rom 1.20), and this is how we may return from the temporal to the eternal and transform the old man into the new.

Augustine's concluding message cannot be put more plainly: his poetics, like his theology, is firmly based on organization or structures that unify by means of symmetrical or graded dispositions of parts. The juxtaposition of passages from Wisdom (8.1, 11.20) and Romans 1.20 is given equal if not greater emphasis in his most popular work, the *Confessions*, where the patterns woven through space and time by providence become a ladder of ascent to God (see esp Book 13).

Augustine defines the relationship between numbers and reality when he states that 6 is not perfect because God created the world in 6 days; rather, God created the world in 6 days because 6 is a number of perfection (*On the Literal Sense of Genesis* 4.7.14, cited by Bonaventura in *Collationes in Hexaemeron* 4.16). It is perfect because it is exactly equal to the sum of its aliquot parts (1, 2, and 3) so that the sum neither falls short of, nor exceeds, the number. God's creation is similarly marked by perfect fullness when all parts are added. His choice of the image or sign of the 6 days lifts the account in Genesis to a spiritual level, and the 'poem' of the world (his artifact) therefore obeys a highly intellectual law of decorum.

Biblical exegesis provides an uninterrupted tradition of numerical analysis which draws on a combination of classical and biblical number lore. Medieval and Renaissance commentaries on the creation, on the chariot seen by Ezekiel (Ezek 1, 10), and on the Psalms and Revelation are useful sources which illustrate the role played by numbers and balanced structures. Thus Pythagorean ideas were adduced to explain the vision of the chariot with its 4 wheels and 4 angels with 4 faces each and a man seated in the midst who is Christ, the Creator and Redeemer who harmonizes all the numbers of space and time. The week of creation was seen as a type of the seven ages that constitute all of time, and these ages are indicated also in the story of the book with seven seals (Rev 5). This symbolic number therefore connects the beginning and the end of the Bible. The beginning, middle, and end are joined by various other verbal and numerical signs: the tree of life in the midst of the garden, and the river which waters it and becomes four rivers (Gen 2.9–10), point forward to the tree of the Cross similarly placed in the midst (of space and time), and to the blood and water issuing from the side of Christ as told in the four Gospels. Another use of the number 4 was found in the 4 arms of the Cross itself. At the end of the New Testament, we read again about a tree of life and a river in the midst (Rev 22.1–2), and references to Ezekiel's chariot in Revelation 4 reintroduce the number 4 with all its classical and biblical connotations. But if one accepts the widely propagated view that the Greek philosophers were indebted to Moses and the prophets, the distinction between classical and biblical disappears. This explains why the Pythagorean argument that 4 equals 10 (as the sum of the first four numbers) was used to state the relationship between the two testaments: the 10 of the Decalogue points forward to the 4 of the Gospels since 4 (1, 2, 3, 4) equals 10.

In biblical exegesis, then, numbers were important types that set up links between parts of the narrative to establish unifying structures. The number 12 is a type which tells us that the months, the signs of the zodiac (types in nature), the tribes, the apostles, and the dimensions of the heavenly Jerusalem are coordinated, balanced parts in God's scheme for mankind. The meaning of the number tells us how the scheme will be realized: through the power of the Trinity (3), the Gospels (4) will be taken to the 4 corners of the earth. The meaning in this case is a matter of the meaning of the numbers which make 12 (3 × 4). Since 7 is 3 + 4, 7 and 12 could be used interchangeably. The number 40 provides yet another example of balanced patterns: the Flood lasted for 40 days, the tribes were in the desert for 40 years, Christ fasted for 40 days and was dead for 40 hours. 40 being 10 × 4 shows that salvation is achieved by means of the Law and the Gospels (both of them fulfilled by Christ). Since Christ rose on the eighth day after the beginning of Holy Week, 8 came to symbolize eternity, which explains why some baptistries, baptismal fonts, and churches are octagonal. The 15 Psalms of Ascent (and the 15 steps to the Temple), when seen as the sum of 7 and 8, have a structure which takes us from time (7) to eternity (8). The argument advanced by Cassiodorus in his commentary on the Psalms, that they were placed in a certain order to permit the meaning of the ordinal number to express the contents, gained wide currency. Among biblical numbers often used in Christian poetry are 15, 42 (the 3 × 14 generations listed in Matt 1), 33 (the age of Christ), and their multiples, because they lend themselves to divisions into 1:2. Number symbolism, therefore, is often found in close connection with the use of symmetrical and graded structural arrangements.

Most numbers, and especially those from 1 to 10, have a wide range of meanings that depend on context. Also the same number may be taken in a good or a bad sense according to general exegetical practice: 9 may represent either the angelic hierarchies or sin (because it falls short of the just number of the Decalogue).

In addition to Augustine and Cassiodorus, theologians and philosophers who transmitted this tradition to later ages include Macrobius (*Commentary on the Dream of Scipio*, c 400), Bonaventura (1221–74), Marsilio Ficino (1433–99), Pico della Mirandola (1463–94), Francesco Giorgio (*De harmonia mundi* 1525 and later eds), Pietro Bongo (*Numerorum mysteria* 1583–4 and later expanded eds), and Pierre de La Primaudaye (*The French Academie* 1586 and later expanded eds). Many of these divide their prose treatises into sections, the number of which is in keeping with the contents, and in so doing they explain the symbolic meaning, as in Cassiodorus (see *Introduction to Divine and Human Readings*, preface to Book 2), Pico (see *Heptaplus*, last paragraph of the Second Proem to the Whole Work), and Giorgio (passim). Among Christian poets, Rabanus Maurus (780–856) deserves special mention for his cycle of 28 poems entitled *De laudibus sanctae crucis*. Its intricate structures are carefully glossed and the subject of many of the poems is sacred numbers.

Number symbolism in poetry may be studied as a compositional technique capable of yielding pure aesthetic delight, of accompanying and making explicit what the words say, of providing an added semantic dimension, or of contradicting the contents. The counterpointing between form and content may be studied in *The Faerie Queene* where, for example, the apparently chaotic chronicle of Briton kings reveals a textual structure which spells the harmony imposed by providence on the course of time (II x; see Mills 1976). The number of textual units may be significant (books, cantos, stanzas, lines), as may character constellations (Sansfoy, Sansjoy, and Sansloy) and lists of various kinds. Thus the catalogue of trees in *FQ* I i 8–9 juxtaposes the earthly and the heavenly king. In stanza 8, the oak, 'sole king of forrests all,' is flanked by 4 and 2 trees (a graded arrangement of 2:1), while the 'Mirrhe sweete bleeding in the bitter wound' (ie, Christ) is at the center of 12 trees in stanza 9 (the sequence is 6–1–6). The 13th tree, which points forward to the description of Duessa's skin 'as maple rind' (viii 47), may possibly allude to Judas. One observes, too, that the rulers of earth (oak) and heaven (myrrh) are surrounded by 6 and 12 trees respectively, which yields another example of the ratio 1:2. The list, therefore, underlines the point that the forest is indeed the forest of life.

Many studies which consider the possible use of number symbolism are content with referring to the principle of decorum while providing little or no historical context for the symbolic import. Other studies reveal considerable familiarity with the sources of the tradition, while lending credibility to the analysis by identifying self-referring passages that serve as glosses on the meaning invested in the structure. As in *Epithalamion*, such glosses may be both explicit and emphatic once the textual structures are perceived. If the inspiration for a poem is a given structure or number, the whole poem becomes self-referring, as in Jonson's 'Epitaph on Katherine, Lady Ogle,' where the praise is given in terms of the many meanings invested in the number 8 (solidity, immortality, the circle, etc), and consequently the basic structural number is 8. Hence to consider the contents is to discover the form.

Some studies have argued the proof value of departures from an established norm. Thus in the *Hymne of Love*, stanza 33 in praise of Cupid fails to reach the stanzaic norm of 7 lines, a 'mistake' that suggests the inadequacy of earthly love – a view reinforced by the fact that it occurs in a stanza whose number alludes to Christ. A similar argument has been advanced concerning the last stanza of Giles Fletcher's *Christs Victorie, and Triumph* (1610), which fails to reach the stanzaic norm of 8 lines. The rhetorical patterning of this last 7-line stanza turns it into a circle in imitation of its subject, the ever-recurring cycles of days and weeks. The 7 lines, then, have been chosen to express time and by so doing reveal that the normal 8-line stanza symbolizes the eternal life gained for us by Christ's victory and triumph. Tasso explains his choice of an 8-line stanza for *Gerusalemme liberata* (1581) in his *Discourses on the Heroic Poem*: in its capacity as a cube of 2, 8 has fullness and weight; as the octave, it consists of odd and even (ie, 1 and 2 in the ratio 1:2, the octave or diapason), which represent the infinite and the finite; and it forms a solid web because it is made of a double quaternion or a quadruple binary or a double ternary and a binary. The rhyme schemes are responsible for these divisions. *SC, June* similarly has an 8-line stanza which is a double quaternion (*ababbaba*), and the circular arrangement of the rhymes expresses the idea of return so prominent in the eclogue.

The most recent development in number symbolism is the discovery that poets like Spenser and Daniel make their textual structures explicit by means of verbal repetitions, often in rhyme position. Both may use three or four identical rhyme words, repeated in inverse order, to mark the beginning and the end of a given structure. Verbal repetitions may also connect the beginning and the middle, the middle and the end, or all three points. This coexistence between verbal and numerical structures (including symmetrical and graded arrangements) shows that number symbolism is only part of many closely integrated structural phenomena. Hence some scholars use the term topomorphical to refer to the analytical method which includes them all.

The critical relevance of number symbolism has been shown in several studies, beginning with Hieatt's analysis of *Epithalamion* (1960). An interpretation of *The Shepheardes Calender* in terms of harmony restored as the cycle ends has been supported by the observation that the last eclogue relates to the first as 2:1. (Both eclogues have the same stanzaic form, and one consists of 26 and the other of 13 stanzas.) The harmony restored (it has been argued) is very much in a higher key, since Colin returns to his God in a spirit of penitence and rejection of all earthly goods.

Maren-Sofie Røstvig

Bjorvand 1975; C. Butler 1970b; Heninger 1977, esp ch 4 'The Pythagorean-Platonic Tradition'; Hopper 1938; John McQueen 1985 *Numerology: Theory and Outline History of a Literary Mode* (Edinburgh); Maren-Sofie Røstvig 1969; Røstvig 1969–70 'Ars Aeterna: Renaissance Poetics and Theories of Divine Creation' *Mosaic* 3.2:40–61; Røstvig 1970 'Structure as Prophecy: The Influence of Biblical Exegesis upon Theories of Literary Structure' in Fowler 1970a:32–72; Røstvig 1971 'Images of Perfection' in *Seventeenth-Century Imagery* ed Earl Miner (Berkeley and Los Angeles) pp 1–24; Røstvig 1980.

O

Occasion Guyon encounters a madman who drags a 'handsome stripling' by the hair and is incited by a 'wicked Hag,' ill-clothed, lame, and partly bald (*FQ* II iv 3–5). The three are identified as Furor, the squire Phedon, and Furor's mother, Occasion. Advised by the Palmer, Guyon locks Occasion's tongue, ties her hands to a stake, and then binds Furor. Phedon's story is interrupted by the sudden appearance of Atin, who reports that his master Pyrochles has sent him 'To seeke *Occasion*.' Later, at the behest of Pyrochles, Guyon foolishly unlocks Occasion's tongue and unbinds Furor. Ironically, the two turn on Pyrochles, who is overcome by Furor while Guyon stands and watches. In canto vi, Pyrochles throws himself into a lake to quench the burning wounds inflicted by Furor.

When the Palmer earlier describes the plight of Mortdant and Amavia as 'the image of mortalitie,' he concludes that temperance must find a middle way between the extremes of pleasure and pain: 'Neither to melt in pleasures whot desire, / Nor fry in hartlesse griefe and dolefull teene' (i 57–8). This concept of temperance derives from Aristotle (*Nicomachean Ethics* 2.7), but departs from him in focusing on those particular pains and pleasures which are the result of chance or luck. According to Boethius, 'You must carry on a fight in your soul against all kinds of fortune, lest the bitter oppress or the pleasant corrupt you' (*Consolation* 4 prose 7).

Guyon's encounter with Furor and Occasion concerns the proper means of dealing with emotions aroused by pain or misfortune. His subsequent encounter with Phaedria in canto vi concerns the passions aroused by pleasure or good fortune. He meets her after Phedon, Furor, and Occasion because, in Heraclitus' words which Spenser paraphrases at *FQ* II vi 1, 'it is harder to fight with pleasure than with anger' (quoted in *Ethics* 2.3). Guyon faces fortune's extremes of pain and pleasure in order of increasing difficulty.

Furor is the madness or frenzy caused by excessive passion, defined by Cicero as a 'blindness of the mind' and attributed to wrath, fear, or suffering (*Tusculan Disputations* 3.5.11). It is associated especially with wrath which disrupts the operation of reason (see Thomas Aquinas *Summa theologiae* 1a2ae 48.3). Thus Furor embodies many of the familiar attributes of wrath: grinding teeth, bloodshot eyes shooting fire, long reddish hair (Seneca *De ira* 1.1.3, 2.35.3–36.3, 3.4.1–3; John Chrysostom 'Homilies on John' 4, 26, 48 [*PGr* 59]; Gregory *Moralia* 5.14.79). He is not simply anger, however, but more properly the expression of passion – whether anger, grief, or fear – in action which is often vengeful. Aquinas writes that the 'first reaction of anger is called wrath; enduring anger is called ill-will; when it seeks an opportunity for revenge it is furor' (*Summa* 1a2ae 46.8 and 48.1 *resp*).

Guyon's initial inability to restrain Furor reflects Seneca's comment that anger must be prevented, not controlled (*De ira* 1.7.2–8.3), for otherwise it overcomes reason and enslaves the master (*De ira* 1.11). He must therefore turn to Occasion who represents those instances of misfortune which are the root cause of excess emotions.

Occasion's name and forelock derive ultimately from the classical figure Occasio. Her ugliness may be due to her conflation with other figures such as Envy, Discord, or Poena. Yet all her peculiar features – ugliness, old age, tattered clothing, reproachful tongue, staff, limp, and even her forelock – were attributes of Misfortune (Fortune in her negative aspect) in medieval sources well known to Spenser (eg, Chaucer, Lydgate). By the Renaissance, the original Occasio had been so thoroughly assimilated with Fortune that the two could be regarded as a single figure.

(See **Occasion** Fig 1.)

More particularly still, the fate of Spenser's Occasion reflects the story of the battle between Fortune and Poverty in Boccaccio's *De casibus virorum* 3, especially as it was presented in fifteenth- and sixteenth-century translations and illustrations. The story tells how Poverty, having overcome Fortune, ordered her to bind Misfortune to a stake so that she could escape only in the company of one who untied her. Like Fortune, Spenser's Occasion is thrown to the ground and her scornful tongue stopped; like Misfortune, she is then tied to a stake and left to be unbound by the heedless Pyrochles. One emblematic representation (from Corrozet's *Hecatomgraphie*) summarizes the moral significance of Boccaccio's story: 'Blame no one but yourself if any misfortune befalls you, for nothing prevails against you except through your own shortcomings.' Spenser echoes the title of this emblem, 'You are the cause of your own evil,' in his comment on Pyrochles' misfortunes: 'His owne woes authour, who so bound it findes, / As did *Pyrochles*, and it wilfully unbindes.' Guyon's struggle with Occasion, then, illustrates that only the man who can rise above fortune because he 'ever doth to temperaunce apply / His stedfast life, and all his actions frame' will be able to overcome the difficulties caused by 'rash *Occasion*' by preventing himself from sinking into despair or giving way to furor (iv 44, v 1).

In binding Occasion, Guyon overcomes misfortune and weakens Furor to a point where he can be restrained. Furor becomes like the anger described by Seneca, which 'has no enduring strength, but is a delusive inflation, violent at the outset ... Anger begins with a mighty rush, then breaks down from untimely exhaustion' (*De ira* 1.17.4–5). The chains with which Furor is bound are part of his traditional attributes as described by Virgil, who follows Homer (*Aeneid* 1.294–6, *Iliad* 5.385).

Occasion and Furor represent the general progression of emotional response to misfortune, from grief to wrath and the frenzied madness of fury; Phedon's story demonstrates a particular instance of this progress. He loves Claribell (famous or bright in beauty) and is betrayed by Philemon (love of self) and Pryene (from L *praiens* 'outstripping' or 'going before,' for she wishes to outshine her mistress, iv 25–26; or possibly from Gr *pyr* 'fire,' with overtones of 'praise,' because she is 'proud through prayse, and mad through love' iv 27). Love and betrayal occasion his grief from jealousy and shame (28). His grief then turns to wrath, which vents itself in vengeful murder. The murder of his beloved engenders more grief, more wrath, and more wrathful action until he is overcome by the frenzied madness represented by Furor. These passions assail other characters throughout *The Faerie Queene* but without the extreme effect they have on Phedon (cf II iii 3, iv 33, vi 1; III iv 12–13, xii 16–17; V vi 17).

That his passion for Claribell occasions Phedon's grief, wrath, and fury reflects the belief that love is the cause of all the other emotions (*Summa* 1a2ae 25.2 and 46.1 *resp*). In defining anger as an irascible rather than concupiscible passion, Aquinas states that 'anger is said to be composed of sorrow and desire, not as though they were its parts, but because they are its causes, and it has been said above that the concupiscible passions are the causes of the irascible passions' (1a2ae 46.3 *ad* 3). So, in the next canto, we find that Pyrochles, like Phedon, is 'captive' of a combination of passions – anger, discord, impatience, and love (v 16). The Palmer's careful analysis of the process of Phedon's passions traces them to their origins in jealousy, grief, and finally love. He advises that each emotion be controlled at its inception lest it grow too strong and through intemperance cause the overthrow of reason (iv 34–5).

The source of Phedon's name reflects the same warning against the subjection of reason to passion. According to Aulus Gellius (*Noctes Atticae* 2.18), Phedon was a handsome youth whom Socrates rescued from the slavery of forced prostitution and exhorted to become a philosopher. Ficino names him as one whom Socrates freed from the calamity of following base affections to pursue philosophy (*In convivium* 6.16).

Phedon is the son of Coradin, whose name comes from the Latin *cor* (heart) and the Greek *adunamia* (impotence, weakness). The name seems related to Guyon's explanation of the passions of Amavia and Mortdant: 'When raging passion with fierce tyrannie / Robs reason of her due regalitie, / And makes it servant to her basest part: / The strong it weakens with infirmitie, / And with bold furie armes the weakest hart; / The strong through pleasure soonest falles, the weake through smart' (i 57). As the son of 'weakness of heart,' Phedon suitably represents those who succumb to passion through occasions of misfortune.

The story of the deceived and betrayed lover parallels Redcrosse's deception by the false Una (I ii 3–6), where his reaction is similar to Phedon's. The same kind of story serves as the main plot in Shakespeare's *Much Ado about Nothing* and appears in many other Renaissance works. It is also related to tales about friendship destroyed by love, the best known of which is Chaucer's *Knight's Tale*, later dramatized by Shakespeare and Fletcher in *The Two Noble Kinsmen*. Spenser's direct source is Ariosto's *Orlando furioso* 4.51–6.16; but whereas Ariosto devotes his attention to external dramatic action, Spenser internalizes the events by having Phedon relate them from his point of view. Thus in Spenser's version the interest is not so much on the story itself as on the emotional effect upon Phedon, reflecting Spenser's technique of having the reader identify with the characters (Alpers 1967b:55–69).

The story of Cymochles and Phaedria extends the theme of fortune's temptations into the realm of pleasure or good fortune, providing in cantos iv and v a structural pairing of pain and pleasure analogous to the pairing of grief and lust found in Mortdant and Amavia, whose fate provides the main impetus for Guyon's quest.

David W. Burchmore and Susan C. Burchmore

Emblem book sources are discussed in McManaway 1934; his conclusions are modified in Manning and Fowler 1976 (who show how Spenser changed the traditional Occasion to correspond more closely to the allegorical iconology of Book II) and in Frederick Kiefer 1979 'The Conflation of Fortune and Occasio in Renaissance Thought and Iconography' *JMRS* 9:1–27 (who shows more of the close relation between Fortune and Occasio). Burchmore 1981 considers medieval sources. For additional discussion of the relationship of Occasion to Fortune, see Klein 1973.

occult sciences A discussion of occultism in Spenser's poetry is complicated by the variety of meanings given the term. In what follows, the occult will be considered as 'the hidden': knowledge that traditionally has either been passed down orally to a few chosen disciples or has been 'veiled' by cryptic exposition in the learned languages (usually Latin, often with sprinklings of untranslated Greek and perhaps Hebrew). The reason for secrecy was the authors' belief that the knowledge could be dangerous because it might be misconstrued or misused.

This sense of the occult excludes widely accessible notions like those taught at the universities: Aristotelian science, Galenic medicine, Christian theology, Greek and Roman mythology, even such little-known specialties as algebra. But there is also a second qualification: the occult is mysterious in a special way, as numerology differs from mathematics or witchcraft from medicine. Thus Egyptian religion had an aura lacking in the better-known pagan systems of Greece and Rome, and 'Platonism' (really Neoplatonism, or late Platonism as touched by Gnosticism and including an emanationist theory of the world's origin and government), interpreted by a series of Renaissance commentators headed by Ficino, was esoteric in a way Aristotelianism was not. The boundaries were sometimes thin between witchcraft and natural magic or astrology and astronomy and the like, but distinctions can usually be drawn with fair confidence between occult and nonoccult sciences.

It has been argued that Spenser was a Platonist and, if this is true, that he might be considered as a writer in the occult tradition (J.S. Harrison 1903; cf Ellrodt 1960). It will be convenient to begin by considering in special detail a single example (of many that might be brought forward): the alleged Platonic influence in *Hymne of Love*. There, in a borrowing from Apuleius' *Metamorphoses*, love is personified as Cupid, who not only preexists the formation of the world out of chaos but in fact creates it by separating the four elements. Cupid's own 'infused fyre' (97) awakens in all creatures a lust which causes them to multiply their species. Man, in contrast, because his immortal mind 'Seekes to enlarge his lasting progenie'

(105), wishes to embrace what 'seemes on earth most heavenly,' that is, 'Beautie, borne of heavenly race' (111–12). Cupid's darts, however, are tipped with a poison that can inflict 'consuming griefe' (126). Nevertheless, the poet celebrates love as a force that can expel 'all sordid basenesse' (191), refine the mind, and inspire the undertaking of brave exploits in the hope of pleasing. The lover who avoids 'That cancker worme, that monster Gelosie' (267), can rise from purgatory to paradise, where he may play with the daughter of Venus, Pleasure. If the poet should attain that result, he would honor only Love as 'My guide, my God, my victor, and my king' (305).

Is the hymn Platonic and, because Platonism was still the possession of a coterie, therefore occult? No easy answer can be given because the beauty that is praised might be either the Aristotelian universal capable of being predicated of many subjects or the Platonic archetype which has 'substance' (Gr *ousias* being, existence) independent of all subjects. The bed of which Plato writes in *Republic* 10 has a reality superior to any wooden or painted bed because it is permanent and perfect, whereas any other is imperfect and transitory. Whether the beauty of the hymn is Plato's abstraction or the loveliness that can be admired in many women of differing appearance (ie, Aristotle's universal) is not wholly clear.

A more important consideration, however, concerns the ladder of love described in Plato's *Symposium* and given prominence in 1528 by Castiglione's *Courtier* 4, that is, an ascent from the love of concrete beauty, through abstract beauty, to love of the divine which is God. The doctrine is missing in Spenser, for his poem ends with a love personified not as the supreme God but as the mischievous Cupid. The 'occult' quality of the poem may therefore be questioned. The doubtful relationship of the poetry to the occult is true of all four *Hymnes* (as Sapience in *Heavenly Beautie*), and calls into question claims that Spenser was profoundly influenced not only by the dialogues of Plato but also by 'the chief Italian commentators upon them, Bembo, Ficino, and Bruno' (de Sélincourt in Spenser ed 1912: ix). Perhaps Spenser knew some of these sources; there is a good chance, however, that he gained his knowledge through more popular channels (Ellrodt 1960:99), including such specifically literary texts as *The Courtier*.

What dominates the Spenserian corpus is not occultism but mythology and personification. The mythological details appear to come not directly from ancient sources but from Renaissance codifications, especially from Conti. In this respect, Spenser was typical of his age, in which mythology exfoliated with exuberance. As for personification, which developed easily into allegory, it was no more than a developed form of metaphor.

There are passages in *The Faerie Queene* that seem derived from an occultist background, if not directly from readings in occult literature. The best example is the famous stanza at II ix 22, in which Kenelm Digby found proof that Spenser was 'thoroughly verst in the Mathematicall Sciences, in Philosophy, and in Divinity.'

The frame thereof seemd partly circulare,
And part triangulare, O worke divine;
Those two the first and last proportions are,
The one imperfect, mortall, foeminine;
Th'other immortall, perfect, masculine,
And twixt them both a quadrate wasthe base
Proportioned equally by seven andnine;
Nine was the circle set in heavens place,
All which compacted made a goodlydiapase.

In this description of part of the castle of Alma, the Renaissance specialist will recognize three familiar plane figures, the circle, the triangle, and the square. The circle is identified with the immortal, perfect, and masculine – that is, God – and the triangle with woman. The circle, although commonplace in iconology, may also suggest the pseudo-Hermetic definition of God as a circle whose center is everywhere and whose circumference is nowhere; but the triangle is usually associated with the Trinity, and femininity with the figure two. Since one represents masculinity, three is often regarded also as the union of male and female in a new and more complex perfection. In the last four lines, seven is the number of the planets (including the sun and moon), eight the number of the diapason or octave produced by the revolution of the spheres, and nine the number of the spheres, including the fixed stars and the *primum mobile*. Although the shape of the house is not clear, representations in Renaissance texts of the body within a square, with the head touching the top and the feet in the two lower corners, suggest that the head is the circle, the trunk the quadrate or rectangle, and the legs, with their junction at the crotch, the triangle. This is a more literal interpretation, and an alternative to the mystical, Neoplatonic one. Whichever is preferred, the use of numerological and geometrical symbolism is obvious.

Digby's interpretation (see *Var* 2:472–8) combines elements of both interpretations. The circle represents man's mind, the triangle his body. The triangle, perhaps, represents also 'the 3 great compounded Elements in mans bodie, to wit, Salt, Sulphur and Mercurie, which mingled together make the naturall heat and radicall moysture, the 2 qualities whereby man liveth.' The source of the doctrine is Paracelsus. Similarly, man's body 'is compounded of the foure Elements which are made of the foure primarie qualities [cold, heat, moisture, dryness], not compounded of them ... but by their operation upon the first matter.' Taking all this together, we recognize that 'the admirablest work is the joyning together of the two *different* and indeed *opposite* substances in Man, to make one perfect compound; the *Soul* and the *Body*.' The body is imperfect and mortal like the feminine sex; the soul, immortal and perfect like masculinity and the circle. As for the quadrate, by this Digby believed Spenser meant 'the foure principall humors in mans Bodie, viz. *Choler*, *Blood*, *Phleme*, and *Melancholy*.' Although there is more, the stanza clearly derives from a numerological and geometrical mysticism for which the ultimate sources are Pythagoras and the most difficult of Plato's texts, the *Timaeus*.

In many other parts of *The Faerie Queene* there are echoes of occultist lore, but generally presented through allegory or mythology, both of which were independent traditions, however much they shared with each other and with the occult. Thus, such scenes as the Garden of Adonis (III vi) and the house of Busirane (III xi-xii) contain images from Platonic doctrine (in the theory of creation of the former) and esoteric iconology (in the wall of fire and the figure of Cupid of the latter), but they cannot be called sustained expositions of occult doctrine. Likewise, Spenser's magic (embodied in such figures as Archimago or the learned magus Merlin) is derived via Italian romances and popular imagery, not directly from the theoretical treatises of Agrippa and others. So, too, Spenser's numerology (in *Epithalamion*, *FQ*, and elsewhere) shares something of the occult; but because it is not consistently applied within a structure of metaphysics or cosmology leading to the ineffable, it should not be termed occult. What seems difficult in Spenser's poetry, and therefore possibly esoteric or occult, may seem so because we are unfamiliar with the prevailing popular imagery of his day, not because Spenser had access to a body of occult lore hidden even from many of his contemporaries. Spenser was not, like Lucretius, Dante, or Milton, deeply acquainted with philosophical texts. Or if he was – for his friend Lodowick Bryskett said he was 'very well read in Philosophie, both morall and naturall' (*Sp All* p 105) – he did not carry his reading of occult philosophy very far into his writings. (See also *alchemy, *Egypt, *Hermeticism, *magic, amatory *magic, *mysteries, *number symbolism, *Platonism, *Pythagoras, *witches.) WAYNE SHUMAKER

A number of writers argue in favor of occult readings of Spenser, eg, Yates 1979:95–108, who, although usefully drawing attention to specific passages that are certainly informed by the occult tradition, does not prove that Spenser was well read in occult literature. For the history of certain aspects of the occult, see J.S. Harrison 1903; Shumaker 1972; D.P. Walker 1958; Yates 1964.

Oldham, John (1653–83) A writer of satire, imitations, and occasional verse; highly praised by Dryden in 'To the Memory of Mr. Oldham' (1684).

Oldham refers most extensively to Spenser in his poem 'A Satyr. The Person of *Spencer* is brought in, Dissuading the Author from the Study of *Poetry*, and shewing how little it is esteem'd and encourag'd in this present Age' (ed 1987:238–46). Spenser's ghost appears 'all pale, and thin,' carrying a copy of *The Faerie Queene*. The poet says, 'Teach me (for none does better know than thou) / How, like thy self, I may immortal grow.' The ghost replies that he would now rather be anything but a poet: bad verse is prevalent, the favorite poems of one age are the waste paper of the next, and good poets get no reward. He advises the poet to seek any other profession: 'Be all but Poet, and there's way to live'; but if you persist in being a poet, 'May'st thou at last be forc'd to starve, like me.'

Oldham reuses the traditional legend (expressed by Jonson) that Spenser died of poverty and neglect. The Spenser he has resurrected is less the poet of *The Faerie Queene* than a satirist who speaks (as the ghost says somewhat misleadingly) 'In stile ... of *Mother Hubberd*.' The figure of the angry ghost would have brought readers sharply up against the gentler conventional image of Spenser as poet of pastoral and heroic deeds, thereby increasing the sense of loss and despair so central to the argument of the poem.

Elsewhere, Oldham refers to this other Spenser as the poet of 'Fame' ('The Enchantment,' an imitation of Virgil Eclogue 8) and as 'the Muses glory' who 'sung of Hero's, and of hardy Knights / Far-fam'd in Battles, and renown'd Exploits' ('Bion: A Pastoral, in Imitation of the Greek of Moschus, Bewailing the Death of the Earl of Rochester' pp 274, 131). In these direct references, Spenser is praised less for his language than as a model of the poet's proper career and subject matter. In his adaptation of the *Ars poetica* (pp 91–112), however, Oldham applies to Spenser Horace's praise of Cato and Ennius for enriching Latin with new terms: '*Spencer*'s Muse be justly so ador'd / For that rich copiousness, wherewith he stor'd / Our Native Tongue' (lines 100–2). Occasionally his use of Spenser's language suggests a close familiarity with *The Faerie Queene*. PAUL HAMMOND

John Oldham 1987 *Poems* ed Harold F. Brooks and Raman Selden (Oxford).

oracles Like apocalyptic literature, oracular literature is an aspect of prophecy, an utterance of the gods textualized by their spokesmen, and (because of its obscurity) a mystery to be unwrapped by interpreters. Popular in Britain from the twelfth century onward and an important locus for prophecy outside of the Bible, the sibylline oracles of antiquity provided a bridge between pagan and Christian revelation. Prophets to the Gentiles as David was to the Jews, the sibyls were disembodied voices, mediators of prophecies (often of doom), official seers of the state attuned to the fate of dynasties, and thus purveyors of prophecy with a freight of political and historical, apocalyptic and millenarian content. The sibyls were considered pagan witnesses to the truth of the Incarnation and, despite the gloom of their prophecies, heralds of a return of the Golden Age; they provided a pagan sanction for extrabiblical prophecy both before and after Christ.

For Spenser, as for any Renaissance writer, *sibyl* meant primarily the Sibyl of Cumae whose prophetic trance is described in *Aeneid* 6, and who accompanies Aeneas on his journey to the regions of the dead and the unborn. Other sibyls and sibylline lore attached themselves as ancillary to her or, more frequently, to apocalyptic writings, especially the Book of Revelation. John Napier's influential *A Plaine Discovery of the Whole Revelation of Saint John* (1593) addresses princes and rulers of nations not only as figures of state but as the best interpreters and implementers of prophecy. In the development of sibylline literature especially, there emerges from the desire for a human triumph in history the figure of a human savior or emperor who will accomplish a partial triumph before the final onset of evil and its extirpation by supernatural intervention. That is, sibylline literature encourages the view that God and man cooperate to overthrow evil and to establish a new heaven and new earth.

The sibyls provide a secular type and sanction not only for the oracular poet and the prophetess but also for the prophetic poet who would exalt a nation's ruler as being herself an oracle and agent in the apocalyptic drama of history. On two occasions, Spenser speaks of oracles, and, in each instance, in such a way as to reify the poet's status as prophet-seer. In *Teares of the Muses*, poets themselves usurp the role once reserved for princes and high priests, that 'secret skill' of relating and interpreting those 'deepe Oracles' with which their verses are full (560–2). In *Colin Clouts Come Home Againe*, Cuddie declares that 'some celestiall rage' now fills the shepherd's breast and 'powreth forth these oracles so sage, / Of that high powre, wherewith thou art possest' (823–6). The poet here assumes the role of the prophet uttering God's mysteries, and of the priest interpreting them.

In still another way, sibylline literature informs the poetics of Renaissance culture. The sibylline oracles are recorded on leaves, some of which when scattered are lost. The vision, the prophecy may be retrievable but only partially; fragments come together again and cohere, but they restore only a fraction of the total vision. Within this perspective, the fragmentary nature of *The Faerie Queene* as a whole, and especially of the *Cantos of Mutabilitie*, may seem both deliberate and meaningful. It may be Spenser's way of addressing the problems of prophesying, and the limitations of prophecy, in the modern world. (See also *Apocalypse, *visions.) JOSEPH WITTREICH

Orgoglio The Orgoglio (Ital 'pride'; cf Eng *orgueil*) episode in *FQ* I vii-viii may be reckoned among the finest in the poem. Spenser's account of the 'Gyaunt proud' who daunts and enthralls the Red Cross Knight, then with false Duessa tyrannizes over him until Arthur's bright power finally assures his fall and destruction, everywhere reflects the poet's masterful command of his allegory. The complex interlacement of folklore, fairy tale, and classical mythology, together with biblical doctrine and imagery (notably from the Book of Revelation), creates an extraordinarily comprehensive allegorical image that exerts a terrible power, yet quietly resists reductive or simplistic interpretation. To be able to 'read' (ie, to interpret, unriddle) the Orgoglio episode is to have found the green pathway into and through the forest of Spenser's art.

The evocative power of this episode derives from its 'imaginative ground-plot' (Sidney ed 1973b:103): the fairy-tale character of its literal narrative and the images from which relatively sophisticated levels or senses of allegory emerge. A modern editor's recognition that in some primary aspects Orgoglio 'is seen as a particular giant rather than as a particular kind of Pride' (Hamilton in *FQ* ed 1977:24) recalls Cowley's account of his youthful delight in 'the Stories of the Knights, and Giants, and Monsters ... Though my understanding had little to do with all this' ('Of My Self' in ed 1906:457). So this monstrous giant, who makes trees tremble and seems to shake the earth itself, all but takes possession of knight, poem, and reader too: these effects, which record Redcrosse's moral decline and alienation from truth, reverberate lastingly in the reader's imagination. It is relevant to note that Spenser's emphasis (vii 3–4) on the natural attractiveness of that refreshing grove where the knight gave way to sloth and lust reminds readers of their own everyday need for pleasing and restorative repose after wearying toil.

Not explicitly named before vii 14, Orgoglio is from his initial appearance described in terms that invite the reader to identify the ruling feature of this 'monstrous masse of earthly slime': stanzas 8–11 indicate the range of his presumptuous arrogance and draw attention to the sinful ambition it breeds, alluding ironically to the empty character (considered *sub specie aeternitatis*) of the pride that lugubriously swells mortality. By careful selection of word and image (and cf VI vii 41), Spenser contrives further to associate Orgoglio with the rebellious giants of classical myth, looking ultimately to Hesiod and Ovid and immediately to Conti's version of passion-ridden and ambitious earthborn figures who instinctively seek to topple the just gods themselves. In light of I v 48, it appears that the poet is sympathetic to the extension of these emphases by Renaissance historiographers to the giants of scriptural tradition, particularly to Nimrod (for commentators typically a warlike and rebellious figure) who was identified as 'the first Giant.' The account of Orgoglio's generation, suggesting that he personifies an earthquake, would also recall to Spenser's audience that of April 1580 (generally and even officially regarded as a sign of divine wrath; see Harvey in *Three Letters* 2, Heninger 1959), and also those punctuating Revelation (6.12, 11.19, 16.18) which foreshadow the Last Judgment. Revelation also provides a model for the description of Orgoglio's consort: Duessa, clad in purple and gold, and mounted on her seven-headed beast, figures the 'mother of whoredomes' (Rev 17.5) identified by Protestant readers with the sensually impious pomp and power of the Church of Rome. The full meaning of the pride that is

Orgoglio, so to speak, rests on these primary elements, represented by way of imagery pregnant with significant suggestion in 'natural,' mythical, and moral contexts that severally and in conjunction direct the reader toward larger, chiefly Christian, realms of being.

That the name of Orgoglio (whose 'uncouth mother' was Earth, vii 9) contains the root of the knight's name, Georgos (in the *Golden Legend* interpreted as 'tilling the earth, that is his flesh' ed 1900, 3:125) supports the view that Orgoglio is in some sense the fallen state of Redcrosse; yet in what sense the knight, at this nadir of his Christian quest for regenerate self-realization, may be said to fall through pride remains a vexing question, complicated by his earlier sojourn in Lucifera's house of Pride and by the fact that Orgoglio's entrance is directly consequent upon the knight's 'carelesse' dalliance with Duessa. By one arresting but somewhat reductive reading, the sexual intercourse of Redcrosse and Duessa, the curious fact that in *The Faerie Queene* only Orgoglio and Lust (IV vii) are equipped with 'snaggy' oaken clubs, and the association of *pride* with sexual desire, combine to identify Orgoglio as a form of Lust (Shroeder 1962). Again, in the historical allegory, with reference particularly to the attire, mount, and role of Duessa, it is arguable that Orgoglio's association with the 'false sorceresse' in some measure encourages the view that he chiefly figures the proud tyranny of the Church of Rome, especially of the Roman Mass (for Protestants a symbolic expression of whoredom and witchcraft). Another approach would transcend both historical and moral allegory: if allegory 'shadows and mirrors essences,' Duessa 'mirrors falsity pure' and Orgoglio becomes 'the very idea of ... radical Pride, usurping Godhead' (Tuve 1966:106). One may agree and yet feel uneasy with a reading that flies so high and so far beyond the imaginative groundplot of the poem, that delightful variety of matter enlivening the legend of the tall clownish young man found as a baby in a furrow, whose 'forces pryde' brought him at length to court and to his adventure.

On balance, and recognizing that each of these approaches contributes to the reader's comprehension of Orgoglio (and of Redcrosse's adventure), the contexts of the moral and spiritual allegory remain especially valuable to an assessment of Orgoglio that takes note of the knight's encounters with the world, the flesh, and the devil in the course of his 'imitation of Christ, the New Adam' (Kellogg and Steele in Spenser ed 1965a:30), as a directional narrative that looks before and after and a panoramic tableau of what happens to a Christian in a fallen world. Reductive identification of Lucifera with the pride of life and of Orgoglio with 'Carnal Pride' (as Ruskin claims, ed 1903–12, 11:253), or of Lucifera with vainglory and Orgoglio with grossly irrational and impious fleshly pride, or C.S. Lewis' distinction between pride within and without (1936:355), will not altogether serve; yet readers who listen to the poem are not likely to be persuaded that moral allegory requires no distinction between Lucifera and Orgoglio as two forms of pride.

A more subtle and perhaps more satisfying reading will recognize that the knight's service to Lucifera anticipates and prepares the ground for Orgoglio's triumph over him. The intoxicating glorification of worldly advancement that pulses through Lucifera's palace springs from, and masks, a self-absorbed and overweening aspiration (anticipating that of Milton's Satan) against which Redcrosse is not entirely proof (cf iv 15); as the knight slips secretly away from 'that sad house of *Pride*,' brutish and shameful heaps of corpses bear witness to the futility of the false glory that in Lucifera 'too exceeding shone.' Orgoglio duly overcomes and imprisons a Redcrosse who is in every sense 'Disarmd, disgrast, and inwardly dismayde': the telling pun emphasizes the knight's inner sense of futility and failure, while allusions to a remorseless Orgoglio's 'mercilesse' stroke hint at the knight's fearful expectation of a just vengeance. Orgoglio's triumph, then, figures the depth of the knight's fallen state: the subjection of Redcrosse to his own guilt as well as (given the name and nature of Orgoglio's foster father) to fear rooted in ignorance.

Yet the episode is finally more comprehensively complete than this. As Redcrosse came to Orgoglio by way of Lucifera's palace, only through Orgoglio may he, as an 'endeavouring Christian' (K. Williams 1966:21), be new-made by a Prince whose 'furious force' is matched and completed by 'pitty deare.' The deliverance of Redcrosse by Arthur fulfills the assurances of viii 1; more strikingly, it recalls Spenser's reminder, at the very moment when Orgoglio defeats Redcrosse, of that 'heavenly grace, that him did blesse' (vii 12). The wounding effects of sinful pride, which seem to promise death, do not at last oppose but become part of a larger power to enlighten, restore, and redeem.

'Reading poetry,' said Virginia Woolf, 'is a complex art' (ed 1966–7, 1:14). In the Orgoglio episode, Spenser's belief in his poem, as well as in the power of poetry to fashion a virtuous reader, shines through and ensures the delicate strength of a complex and many-layered pattern. The reader must be watchful, tolerant, quick-witted, malleable; readier to acquiesce, to believe in Spenser's way with the poem, than too abruptly to seize upon and declare the dominance of one or another aspect of the poet's art. Only so may the reader begin fully to realize the imaginative unity of the Orgoglio episode. HUGH MACLEAN

Var 1:248–64 and appendixes 1–6; Alpers 1967b:137–51; Brooks-Davies 1977:69–86; Cheney 1966:32–5, 53–4; Cullen 1974:52–7; Evans 1970:27–30, passim; Hamilton 1961a:71–9, passim; Hankins 1971:81–2, 99–127, 205–26, passim; Heninger 1959; Nelson 1963:134–5, 147–77; Nohrnberg 1976:261–81, passim; Shroeder 1962; Torczon 1961; Tuve 1966:106–8; Voragine ed 1900; Waters 1970:70–8; K. Williams 1966:18–25, passim.

Orpheus The son of Calliope, Muse of epic poetry, and Apollo. Orpheus was famous as a divine poet whose music had magical power over nature, as a singer of cosmogonic hymns, and as priest-prophet of a mystical nature religion. By accompanying the Argonauts, he ensured the success of their quest for the Golden Fleece, for he stopped their quarreling by singing a creation hymn (Apollonius Rhodius *Argonautica* 1.494–518; *FQ* IV ii 1). When his bride, Eurydice, died, he descended into hell to rescue her. He so charmed the infernal gods that she was released on condition that he not look back as she followed him out of hell; but he did look back and lost her for a second and final time. Bereft, he shunned human company, bewailing his loss so movingly that stones, trees, beasts, and birds gathered to listen. Subsequently, having been butchered by Bacchantes, his head and lyre floated down a river, singing and playing, and came to rest on a distant shore, where the head continued to sing oracularly and the harp was transformed into the constellation Lyra (Ovid *Metamorphoses* 10.1–147, 11.1–66; Virgil *Georgics* 4.453–558; Friedman 1970:1–12).

For Renaissance humanists, Orpheus became a hero of the arts. Renaissance Platonists regarded him as the source of all classical wisdom (Cain 1971, Walker 1953). Theologian and prophet, culture-bearer and civilizer, hero and lover, he was for Boccaccio, Conti, Ficino, Pico della Mirandola, and the poets of the Pléiade the primeval and archetypal poet. Accordingly, Spenser presented himself as the English Orpheus, a vatic poet of love whose visions would move his countrymen to virtuous action (Cochrane 1968, Jayne 1952).

Orpheus is a hero of love in *Virgil's Gnat*, a translation of the pseudo-Virgilian *Culex*. His boldness in daring to descend into Hades is praised (437, 449) and his failure to rescue Eurydice excused because he acted through love. In *Hymne of Love*, he is again found among those ancient heroes inspired to great deeds by love: 'daring to provoke the yre / Of damned fiends, to get his love retyre,' he is proof of love's rule of all creation (231–7). In *FQ* IV x 58, the hapless Scudamour compares his taking of Amoret from the Temple of Venus to Orpheus' recovery of Eurydice from hell. The allusion may be to the less common version of the story in which Orpheus recovered Eurydice, but the subsequent history of Scudamour's courtship parallels the tragic version: also overcome by desire, he loses Amoret (Hamilton in *FQ* ed 1977:507, Cain 1971:36–7).

Orpheus' ability to conquer hell by his music made him a symbol of the power of poetry even over death. In his elegy for Sidney in *Ruines of Time*, Spenser places Philisides 'in *Elisian* fields ... With *Orpheus*, and with *Linus*' (332–3), and urges princes to patronize poets if they want the Muses to grant them immortality as they had 'for pittie of the sad wayment, / Which *Orpheus* for *Eurydice* did make, / Her back againe to life sent for his sake' (390–2). To show his own vatic ability, he presents a number of visions, including one of a harp, now translated to the heavens as Lyra, which 'whilome seemed to have been / The harpe, on which *Dan Orpheus* was seene / Wylde beasts and forrests after him to lead, / But was th'Harpe of *Philisides* now dead' (604–9). In *Epithalamion* 16, the bridegroom determines to imitate Orpheus in singing a marriage song for his own bride. Here and in *Prothalamion*, the refrains of the stanzas command woods and river to obey the poet, showing his Orphic power to control the elements in the cosmos of the poem.

The Shepheardes Calender is a sustained advertisement of Spenser as an Orphic poet. The *Aprill* and *November* eclogues respectively show how poetry praises or immortalizes its subject. In the Argument to *October*, E.K. says that Spenser holds poetry to be 'no arte, but a divine gift and heavenly instinct not to bee gotten by laboure and learning, but adorned with both: and poured into the witte by a certaine *enthousiasmòs.* [enthusiasm] and celestiall inspiration.' In his gloss to Piers' reference to Orpheus' power, he explains how the vatic song inspires his auditors because 'the mynd was made of a certaine harmonie and musicall nombers' (27 gloss). Thus poetry is able 'to restraine / The lust of lawlesse youth with good advice' (21–2). In effect, the entire *Calender* presents Spenser as England's Virgil, as its new Orpheus, the vatic poet whose pastoral and heroic visions will fashion his readers in virtuous and gentle discipline.

JAMES NEIL BROWN

Thomas H. Cain 1971 'Spenser and the Renaissance Orpheus' *UTQ* 41:24–47; Kirsty Cochrane 1968 'Orpheus Applied: Some Instances of His Importance in the Humanist View of Language' *RES* ns 19:1–13; John Block Friedman 1970 *Orpheus in the Middle Ages* (Cambridge, Mass); Jayne 1952; Patricia Vicari 1982 'The Triumph of Art, the Triumph of Death: Orpheus in Spenser and Milton' in *Orpheus: The Metamorphosis of a Myth* ed John Warden (Toronto) pp 207–30; D.P. Walker 1953 'Orpheus the Theologian and Renaissance Platonists' *JWCI* 16:100–20; Wind 1958.

Ovid (Publius Ovidius Naso, 43 BC-AD 17) The Roman poet Ovid left a considerable legacy to later poets. His highly polished style in pentameter and hexameter lines set an ideal of elegant expression and provided rhetorical models for later schools. The worldly, cynical advice of his *Amores* and *Ars amatoria* established a tradition of wit in love that was greatly admired in the Renaissance. His major work, the *Metamorphoses*, traced numerous mythical transformations that joined divine, human, and natural shapes, usually under the force of love. Its *carmen perpetuum* (1.4) consolidated the principal Greek and Roman myths in a bravura presentation of linked or associated fables, and was regarded as an epic compendium of ancient lore. Later ages delighted in finding occult truths veiled behind its myths. Ovid's interest in myth, sacred ceremony, and ordered time appears in his *Fasti*, an unfinished work on the Roman religious calendar. Various aspects of the Ovidian legacy – the emphasis on style, the theme of love, myths of change, narrative ingenuity, the relation of sacred to profane time, even the existence of an unfinished work – all influenced Spenser throughout his career. Hence one can speak of an Ovidian matrix (Fletcher 1971:90–106), from which he continually drew forms, devices, themes, and even phrases for his own work.

Ovid and Spenser were courtier poets, necessarily affected by contemporary politics. Both careers were shaped by systems of aristocratic patronage that culminated in an imperial ruler who was simultaneously sponsor, subject matter, audience, and critic. Although Ovid abandoned a public career in law for poetry, he centered his writing career in the court of Augustus Caesar. Witty and cynical, he seemed destined to run counter to Augustan notions of the poet's proper civic role. In AD 8, for reasons still obscure, he was banished from Rome to Tomi, a primitive village on the Black Sea, from which until his death he regularly wrote verse epistles begging for pardon (*Tristia*, *Ex Ponto*). In contrast, Spenser remained within the Elizabethan system of patronage, dedicating his works to important court figures including the Queen. Although he seems to have angered certain persons in power (perhaps Lord Burghley) 'For praising love ... And magnifying lovers deare debate' (*FQ* IV proem 1), he continued his double career as both civil servant and professional poet. His service in Ireland may have forged a bond of sympathy with the exiled Ovid.

Literary influences are rarely pure or simple. Spenser could have read Ovid in any of the numerous Latin editions of his works, even (though this seems less likely) in English translations (eg, Golding's of 1567). He would also have found Ovid present in Chaucer (or Ariosto, to go abroad). In fact, the influence of Chaucer often merges with that of Ovid. For example, in *FQ* I i, the Red Cross Knight and Una take shelter in a grove whose various trees compose a literary catalogue that incorporates *Metamorphoses* 10.90–105, *Parliament of Fowls* 176–82, and *Knight's Tale* 2920–3). Ovidian metamorphosis and Chaucerian romance overlap and create metaphors for the progress of Spenser's knight, through whom we learn that the natural order can provide genuine shelter only when it is aligned with the true quest. Ovid is used with Chaucer to depict the start of an education in holiness.

Chaucer was not the only mediator between Spenser and Ovid. There was also a medieval tradition of allegorizing Ovid's myths to reconcile them to Christian ethics and doctrine. Ovid himself lent authority to a philosophical interpretation of the *Metamorphoses* by ending it with a Pythagorean account of the transmigration of souls, investing the previous fourteen books with a dignifying philosophy. He saw that we linger nostalgically over stories from the past and that our desires can transform them into other orders of meaning. This view of myth as a fiction of desire is not merely cynical or comic: Ovid displays a deep fascination for ancient stories, and by converting them into elegant poetry saves in art what had grown dull to opinion. Transforming stories is a constant in the Ovidian tradition.

Spenser extends what Ovid began and others continued. He uses Ovidian myth, with its commentary, to give his Fairyland a substrate of classical matter, suggesting that native British legends form a special outcropping of ancient myth. He also uses Ovid in ways that combine different elements in the Ovidian tradition. For example, the cuckold Malbecco flees from his adulterous wife into a waste land where he changes into jealousy itself (III x 60). Fully aware of the 'different' Ovids, Spenser can select among them for his own purposes. Here he joins together the author of the *Amores* who cynically observes sexual behavior, the narrator who describes metamorphic change, and the allegorist who converts rude myths into abstract moral emblems. The fate of Malbecco draws from and exhausts the entire Ovidian matrix.

In Spenser's minor poetry, Ovid generally does not receive the complexity accorded him in *The Faerie Queene*. *The Shepheardes Calender* invokes Chaucer, Virgil, and Theocritus; but Ovid is present only intermittently, usually (though not exclusively) in E.K.'s learned glosses. In *Aprill*'s hymn of praise to the Queen (46–54), the myth of Pan and Syrinx is revised considerably from *Metamorphoses* 1.689–712. Instead of Ovid's story of near-rape leading to metamorphosis, Spenser celebrates the sacred union of Pan and Syrinx leading to the 'flowre of Virgins.' The point of the changed myth is not so much a courtly allegory (despite E.K.'s explanation that by Pan is meant Henry VIII, Queen Elizabeth's father) as a poetic reference to a triumphant harmony between the new pastoral poet and the Virgin Queen; each emerges through the 'silver song' which unites Pan and Syrinx. Generally Ovid's wit is alien to the deliberate humility of Spenser's pastoral, although Ovidian materials can signal the high matters behind the veil of pastoral rudeness. For example, as E.K. observes, Diggon's emblem in *September* (*Inopem me copia fecit* 'plenty makes me poor') is said by Ovid's Narcissus (*Met* 3.466). Its transposition to Diggon measures the distance between Ovid's concern with passionate self-love and Spenser's concern with ecclesiastical abuse. Discontented at home, Diggon has traveled to Rome's great world (*copia*) only to find himself the more disillusioned (*inopem*) over the corruption of Roman pastors – a translation of narcissism into satiric complaint which has a rough wit, especially in this use of a classical Roman poet to mock Renaissance Rome.

Muiopotmos continues the calendar's pastoral concern for great things in small but now with Ovid at the center. Belonging to the late classical genre of the brief epic, it shows Spenser's command of the Ovidian spirit of 'delight with libertie' (210) as well as his understanding of that spirit's limitations. Its title (*muia* fly + *potmos* fate) and genre indicate the joining of high and low, serious and trivial. An essay in metamorphosis, the poem has a deliberately calculated instability of form, diction, and tone: at one moment, it rings with 'deadly dolorous debate' (1) and poses ancient epic questions ('And is there then / Such rancour in the harts of mightie men?' 15–16); at another, it depicts 'all the race of silver-winged Flies / Which doo possesse the Empire of the aire' (17–18). It moves easily from a catalogue of arms (57–8) or flowers (185–200) to various Ovidian myths of explanation (see *etiological tales). Spenser's inset story of Astery – a woman changed to a butterfly – varies Ovid's tale of Psyche (129–36) and explains the lineage of Clarion; it also prepares for his meeting with the spider Aragnoll and a version of the myth of Arachne (257–352; *Met* 6.5–145). There is a hidden literary point to the alignment of these stories: in Ovid, Astery is one of the abused women represented in Arachne's tapestry of complaints (6.108). Such literary allusions intensify the butterfly's fate: Spenser's explicit but fabricated allusion (Astery-Psyche) converts Clarion into the psyche or soul; the implicit but actual allusion to Ovid leaves Clarion-Astery within the enemy's craft. *Muiopotmos* then goes on to trace the story of Arachne in detail. Extended portions closely follow Ovid (eg, line 321 retains the Latin form *Aegide* from *Met* 6.79). Yet Spenser also changes Ovid's order: the sequence of competing tapestries is reversed, with the climax of the inset myth in *Muiopotmos* coming as Arachne gazes at Athena's work and knows that she is defeated. She becomes a grim emblem, lightly presented, both of artistic pride punished and of the ignorant butterfly's fate in spider nets.

Whether Spenser follows or revises Ovid, his shaping of sources is constant. *Muiopotmos* offers a free set of variations and inventions within a literary tradition whose sheer weight of texts, glosses, and commentaries would seem to deny any possibility of freedom. Losing 'delight with libertie' (210) and becoming 'the spectacle of care' (440), Clarion dies 'entangled' (425). Spenser, however, has won a new freedom, assimilating to his allegory the Ovidian techniques of recounting and inventing myths. *Muiopotmos* is an accomplished Ovidian performance, recapturing that literary past in the manner of assured detail so valued by the Renaissance. The command of the Ovidian vision is precise yet free, learned yet unhampered by any sense of anxiety's weight.

That vision receives full and subtle expression in *The Faerie Queene*. The interpolated myth of explanation, structurally the most prominent device in Ovid, can create a new atmosphere, clarify or alter themes, and foreshadow narrative developments. Spenser understood the value of Ovidian tales as expansive devices larger than the epic simile yet more compact than the intertwined subplots of Italian romance. A mythic story, loosely linked in the Ovidian fashion to the surrounding narrative, becomes an important way of multiplying narrative textures and of paralleling stories within the story; it can then indicate allegorical significances beyond the literal sense structurally as well as thematically. This treatment of Ovid, though precise, is not archaeological, for Ovid is most frequently used to mask Spenser's own inventiveness, the English poet seeming to disappear into the Ovidian tradition while actually re-creating it. *The Faerie Queene* does not simply record antique myths but freely invents its own, invoking literary traditions but quite consciously cloaking its mythopoeia. Ovid is the ideal stalking horse because as rhetorician and storyteller he dominates his materials so powerfully. His boast – as a poet who has completed his *carmen perpetuum* and concludes with the word *vivam*, 'I shall live' – enables Spenser to hide his own inventions with an artful humility, to avoid the fates of both Clarion and Arachne, the assertions of too little and too much.

Spenser's strategy appears most clearly in Books I–III, all of which start with episodes strongly marked by the *Metamorphoses*. The opening canto of *FQ* I presents an Ovidian natural world: the grove of trees noted above; an Ovidian imagery, associated with the monster Error, of Nile floods and muddy generation (i 21; *Met* 1.422–37, which introduces Ovid's story of Python); and an Ovidian dream world in the subterranean house of Morpheus (i 39–41, *Met* 11.592–615). Trees, up-welling water, and a careless or unready human consciousness all undergo various natural metamorphoses (eg, Fradubio), ending in Redcrosse's battle with the Dragon, an adversary joining Ovid's Python and Revelation's Old Serpent (Rev 12.9). There the Well of Life, the Tree of Life, and before the third day's battle a 'dreame of deepe delight' renew the knight (xi 29, 46, 50), permitting his victory and completing a pattern of Christian romance begun in canto i by Ovidian allusion.

Book II is not defined in Ovidian terms until canto ii, where Guyon's inability to cleanse the bloody babe is glossed by the Palmer's story of a pursued nymph transformed by Diana for intemperance into stone and stream (5–10). The account recalls various Ovidian myths of nymphs and fountains (Callisto in *Met* 2, Arethusa in *Met* 5) as well as Spenser's earlier treatment of the fountain of Salmacis (I vii 5, *Met* 4.285–515). The Palmer interprets the myth in the manner of the *Ovide moralisé*, that early fourteenth-century retelling of the *Metamorphoses*, heavily interlarded with interpretive moral and Christian commentary. He turns narrative details into moral signs (as when a purity of waves becomes a purity of self) and generates both images and meanings to join the drama of temperance throughout Book II. The virtue requires many trials of discrimination and contrary balance, and the Palmer's moralized Ovidian inset finds its matched opposite in the bathing scene of the two nymphs (xii 62–9), which draws directly from Ovid's bathing Salmacis (*Met* 4.310–12, *FQ* II xii 67). Guyon looks, slows, receives the Palmer's rebuke, and unchanged continues his 'earnest pace' toward Acrasia's Bower. Such liquid bliss is not the Well of Life.

In Book III, Spenser uses the myth of Venus and Adonis (*Met* 10.476–739) to define problems of love and chastity. The relationship between the virtues of Books II and III is suggested by structural similarities between the stories of Acrasia and Venus with their lovers. The latter myth, illustrating love's pleasures and consequent pains, is formally introduced in III i 34–8 on the tapestry which Britomart views at Castle Joyous. It presents in a visual art the contrary myth to the Legend of Chastity; it also indicates temptations which confront Britomart as well as experiences which are beyond her. Her innocent desires are confirmed in the discussion with Glauce about her love for Artegall (ii 30–46), in which there are hints of unchaste Myrrha and her aged nurse from *Met* 10.382–430). In canto vi, Spenser translates the Ovidian myth from the tapestry into his own account of Venus and Adonis in the gardens of natural generation. With this image of love's naturalness established, cantos xi and xii reveal the perverse corruption of love in the house of Busirane, where the masque of Cupid re-sets the tapestry's myth as theatrical ceremony and forms an extended variation on the triumph of Cupid in *Amores* 1.2. Book III displays Spenser's ability to assimilate Ovid's methods and materials.

Book III of the 1590 *Faerie Queene* ends with the lengthy embrace of Scudamour and Amoret, a passage cancelled in the revision of 1596. Spenser describes their physical union in a simile that combines Roman statuary art with Ovid's myth of Hermaphroditus (*Met* 4.373–9). In changing the familiar pool of Ovidian metamorphosis into a Roman bath, he presents a remarkable series of perspectives – the narrator's, the reader's, the heroine's – on the motionless pair:

Had ye them seene, ye would have surely thought,
That they had beene that faire *Hermaphrodite*,
Which that rich *Romane* of white marble wrought,
And in his costly Bath caused to bee site:
So seemd those two, as growne together quite,
That *Britomart* halfe envying their blesse,
Was much empassiond in her gentle sprite,
And to her selfe oft wisht like happinesse,
In vaine she wisht, that fate 'nould let her yet possesse.

These perspectives create a splendid sense of metamorphoses occurring in and around the lovers. The transformations extend from the united bodies in the narrative, to the inclusion through simile of one art within another, to the mingling of literary texts in allusion, to the translations of emotion that recall Britomart so keenly to her own contrary – though temporary – isolation. Although alluding to a specific Ovidian metamorphosis, Spenser expands the significance of metamorphosis into virtual equation with the movements of his poem.

The alert reader will see here the transformation of earlier episodes in *The Faerie Queene*, recollecting the various fountainside incidents in Book I, whether in Archimago's hidden dale (i) or on the plain in Eden (xii). In particular, Ovid's account of Salmacis and Hermaphroditus, most completely imitated in Redcrosse's fall into error 'foreby a fountaine side' (I vii 2), also links the final cantos of Books II and III in the loose, analogical fashion of the *Metamorphoses* itself, to discriminate the spectacle of lust before Guyon (II xii 65–9) from the view of love's complementary union before Britomart. Spenser's allusions make Ovid a means to measure the argument's progress. The necessary rigor of temperance avoids the errors but also the satisfactions of holiness, and it is followed and corrected by the inner yielding of chastity to proper passion as the myth of Hermaphroditus answers and supplants that of Venus and Adonis (see also *androgyne, *Hermaphrodite). This process of weaving intricately and linking distantly closes a sequence of books enriched by Spenser's varied uses of Ovid.

The last three books of *The Faerie Queene* differ in their use of Ovid, in a change heralded by the cancellation of the Scudamour-Amoret union. Spenser links the two sets of books by shifting the lovers' union from chastity's sphere into friendship's, in a redefinition of love that moves beyond Ovid's concentration upon virgins and victors. In Books V and VI, Ovid continues to provide important images of history's decline (V proem 2, *Met* 1.89–150) and of the earthly paradise or *locus amoenus* (VI x 5–9, *Met* 10.644–8), but he no longer provides major structural definitions for the separate books and virtues. Some comments on Book IV can illustrate this change. In *FQ* III vi, the Ovidian Venus joins with natural process in the garden and so moves beyond Acrasia's or Busirane's artifice. The Temple of Venus in Book IV is named not for Ovid's erotic deity of Paphos or Cyprus but for an older figure, the *magna mater* or 'great mother' of natural regeneration (x 5). This figure anticipates Dame Nature in the *Cantos of Mutabilitie*, who will finally doom but not end Mutabilitie, that rebellious incarnation of the Ovidian spirit of change for change's sake. In Isis Church, Spenser suggests the deep union of love and chastity, nature and justice, as well as his own evolved conception of myth. No one set of myths can be adequate to experience since the myths of one civilization emerge from those of another (Roman from Greek, Greek from Egyptian). In effect, Spenser turns the process of metamorphosis back upon its author. Changing classical materials into English forms, he becomes, like most of his major figures, a liberator. Through his practice, Ovidian myths are released from Ovid's powerful literary dominance and restored as emblems of nature rather than art. This is an important point in the catalogue of the world's rivers, Ireland's and England's above all, at the marriage of Thames and Medway (IV xi). At the close of this celebration of natural process and creation, Ovid stands excluded as Spenser turns deliberately to Hesiod, the first collector of myths and the original cataloguer of Ocean's nymphs (48–53). Ovid dissolves in his predecessor.

The *Cantos of Mutabilitie* restore Ovid to the center of Spenser's work, but only for a final dismissal. These apparent fragments of a seventh book present a number of complex problems. Central to them all is a sustained meditation on the history of Ovid's works and influence that ranges across classical antiquity and the Chaucerian Middle Ages to the Renaissance poet in the act of imagining his poem. The *Cantos* evoke the rich variety of that history: Ovid's mocking essays in epic as well as his urbane descents into pastoral, his delight in fantastic stories as well as his ironic, embellished treatment of them, his ability to give the sense that he has told all the stories, and brilliantly. Spenser's figure of Mutabilitie joins Ovid's themes of endless metamorphosis and complaint. Her adventures take her beyond the classical world of Olympus (canto vi) to the Christian world in its medieval and Renaissance phases.

At stake is poetic authority: which poet, which system, best defines the nature of things? For this reason, both the *Metamorphoses* and the *Cantos of Mutabilitie*, considered as the end to the *The Faerie Queene*, conclude with a poet-narrator's address to time and immortality; and we are asked to see behind Spenser's imitation of Ovid sharp differences. Ovid claims eternal life as his reward for completing his *carmen perpetuum* (*Met* 15.871–9). Spenser invokes this Ovid – the *Cantos* are laced with allusions to the *Metamorphoses* – but seems to subordinate him to the poet of exile whose religious calendar, the *Fasti*, was left unfinished. That poem as well as Spenser's own earlier calendar are evoked in Mutabilitie's pageant. The logic behind Spenser's use of Ovid allows us to see the Renaissance fragment as both natural and designed. Ovid completed his great book of changes, but could not finish his calendar of sacred time. Spenser ends rather differently: the calendar (both in *FQ* VII vii and in *SC*) is magnificently finished; Dame Nature's judgment – that change is a part of order – is delivered; but the poem itself is left 'unperfite' as all things must be until 'that Sabaoths sight' (see *closure). Spenser closes in prayer rather than boasting. He hopes for an immortality that follows after, not from, his poetry.

Like Milton, Spenser was steeped in Ovid, and it would be a mistake to emphasize only rejection. Spenser knew Ovid so intimately that to write poetry was to use him, even if that use led ultimately to the dismissal of 'flowring pride, so fading and so fickle' (*FQ* VII viii 1). Indeed, the knowledge was of such duration and depth that Spenser seems to have reshaped Ovid's career within his own, making possible there what was impossible for the exiled Roman poet. Some of the most delicate and precise allusions to Ovid in English literature may be found in Spenser's own marriage hymn, the *Epithalamion*. There Spenser had to resolve two nearly contradictory requirements. He had to be discreet since the bride was his own and the poem a wedding gift; but the traditions of the genre stipulated some erotic material. The resolution comes from Ovid. Ovidian tales of love are used, but with an element of surprise; they derive not from the *Metamorphoses* or the poems of love but once again from the *Fasti*, which breaks off in June, the month of Spenser's marriage. Spenser describes his bride's bedding by using the myth of Jove and Maia (307–10) to reveal and transform the eroticism of the genre (*Fasti* 5.85–8). His next stanza also draws from the May section of the *Fasti* (5.25–6) and addresses Night. But where Ovid saw Maia-Majesty as the May child of Honor and Reverence, Spenser invents a far more cosmic origin in the union of Jove with Night herself: 'lyke as when he with thy selfe did lie, / And begot Majesty' (330–1). Ovidian materials, authentic and invented, are woven together to transform details of love-making ('lie,' 'begot') into a dark conceit of cosmic splendor ('Majesty'). By this Ovidian allegory, Spenser honors with courtly grace his bride in Ireland and his sovereign in England, the Elizabeth he married and the Elizabeth he served. The most private of moments is infused with a sense of regal ceremony. Spenser ends his poem of marriage's sacred time as the exiled Ovid never did. He acknowledges the simple harmony of closure – the final quietness of woods, song, and echo – as well as the ineluctable accidents of time – the short period in which all endless monuments exist. In his poem, June is the proper month for ending. If the *Epithalamion* concerns marriages and unions and generations in more than the literal sense, then Ovid's 'happy influence' (416) has been to help create Spenser's calendar of love. Changed by Ovid through the use of him, Spenser returns that gift of transformation in his own quiet art. MICHAEL HOLAHAN

Ovid ed 1904; *Ovide moralisé*; Sandys ed 1970. Bush 1963; Madeleine Doran 1964 'Some Renaissance "Ovids"' in *Literature and Society* ed Bernice Slote (Lincoln, Nebr) pp 44–62; Fletcher 1971:90–106; Hermann Fränkel 1945 *Ovid: A Poet Between Two Worlds* (Berkeley and Los Angeles); G. Karl Galinsky 1975 *Ovid's 'Metamorphoses': An Introduction to the Basic Aspects* (Oxford); Holahan 1976; Daniel Javitch 1978 'Rescuing Ovid from the Allegorizers' *CL* 30:97–107; E.J. Kenney 1982 'Ovid' in *CHCL* 2:420–57 (and Martin Drury, pp 855–7 for bib); Lotspeich 1932; Brooks Otis 1970 *Ovid as an Epic Poet* 2nd ed (Cambridge); Hallett Smith 1952, ch 2; L.P. Wilkinson 1955 *Ovid Recalled* (Cambridge); K. Williams 1961.

Ovidian epic Among the classical models for Spenser and other Renaissance poets, Ovid's *Metamorphoses* was one of the most familiar, highly regarded, and troublesome. Sixteenth-century schoolboys were taught to admire it as an exemplar of elegant Latin style and as a storehouse of information about ancient history and religion. Yet poets and critics of the age had to struggle with its violence, eroticism, and cynicism, which challenged the common belief in the didactic aim of poetry as surely as its diffuse narrative technique challenged Aristotelian ideals of epic.

Overtly arranged as a chronological narrative running from the creation to the apotheosis of Julius Caesar, the *Metamorphoses* is divided into fifteen books, each of which contains several different episodes. At an uncertain date but probably in the fourteenth century, manuscripts of the poem were further subdivided by brief arguments inserted at the beginning of each episode. Almost all Renaissance editions use these subdivisions, changing Ovid's *perpetuum carmen* (perpetual song), as he calls it in his opening lines, into a loosely structured collection of short narratives. The effect on the narrative form is visible in the double nature of its influence on Renaissance literature. On one hand, the whole of the work, with its multiple plots, is the most important classical antecedent for the romance form of Ariosto's *Orlando furioso*, and so contributes significantly to the intricately interlaced form of *FQ* III and IV. On the other hand, a single episode may be developed as a self-contained short narrative, minor epic, or epyllion, in the manner of Shakespeare's *Venus and Adonis*, Spenser's *Muiopotmos*, or even the *Cantos of Mutabilitie*. Such short poems might in turn aspire to be miniatures of the whole, since their use of digressions, inset tales, and the like mimics Ovid's narrative strategy in little.

The importance of the *Metamorphoses* was recognized in Renaissance poetics from the middle of the sixteenth century. In his *Discorso dei romanzi* (1554), Giraldi Cintio singled out Ovid as the most modern of the ancient poets and recommended his poem as a model for those who, like Ariosto, would seek to rival the excellence of the classics without slavishly imitating the form or subject matter of Virgil's *Aeneid* or Homer's *Iliad*. While *FQ* I and II are deeply influenced by the *Aeneid*, the middle books elaborate the multiple plot-structure and amorous subject matter in ways much closer to the *Metamorphoses* and medieval Arthurian romance. The mingling of Ovid's narrative forms with the matter of romance redeemed each from humanist suspicions of immorality or formal inadequacy. Ovid's implicit challenge to the political, sexual, and literary orthodoxy of Augustan Rome could be used to dignify England's own Gothic literary heritage with a classical precedent. In turn, Arthurian romance provided more relevant native material for the rhetorical artistry Spenser learned from the *Metamorphoses*.

Throughout Books III and IV, the austere public values and the grand style of the *Aeneid* are lowered and turned into a private and sensual vein that derives from the *Metamorphoses*. The story of Malbecco and Hellenore in III ix-x epitomizes Spenser's method. A stranger, Paridell, forms a liaison with his hostess, as Aeneas does with Dido, Odysseus with Nausicaa, and Paris with Helen. His stirring recitation after the meal is in itself epic and noble, but within the greater schemes of history in the book, it charts the course from the untempered acts of the individual to the destruction of whole civilizations. Hearing the recitation, Britomart is, like Hellenore, stirred with passion, but her tempered sexuality, virtually unmarked by the other guests, will lead to personal happiness and the establishment of the Elizabethan empire in which Spenser himself holds office. This delicate balance of private and public feeling is underscored by the subtle narrative technique with which the episode is woven into the main narrative. The story ends with the transformation of Malbecco into Jealousy and the departure of Britomart and Paridell on their quest. Using skillfully the arts of transition and subordination that Cintio praised in Ovid, Spenser keeps his metamorphic narrative both closed and open, self-contained and multiple.

The description of the Garden of Adonis (III vi) explores in part the thematic potential of Ovidian epic. In this philosophical center of the poem, Spenser's language once again echoes both the *Metamorphoses* and the *Aeneid*. In *Aeneid* 6.727, Anchises explains to his son how a world spirit animates matter ('mens agitat molem') and souls are reincarnated in a perpetual cycle from which only a blessed few are released. In the *Metamorphoses*, 'nihil est toto, quod perstet, in orbe. / cuncta fluunt,' proclaims Pythagoras: 'there is nothing in all the world that keeps its form. All things are in a state of flux' (15.177–8). In Ovid, even Rome itself is in flux as it rises from a village to become the center of the world. To Arthur Golding, this 'oration of Pithagoras implyes / A sum of all the former woorke' which outlines a 'dark Philosophie of turned shapes' ('Epistle' in Ovid ed 1904:6, 1). Unable to reconcile metempsychosis with Christian resurrection or random historical flux with Christian eschatology, Ovid's Renaissance editors took the passage as a description of the pattern of Ovid's unfolding narrative. Similarly, Spenser's garden 'in the middest' defines his narrative in terms of forms that 'are variable and decay.' High and low, serious and sensuous, are mingled together in an art of ceaseless variety and endless transition.

If metamorphosis has primarily a benevolent and creative aspect in Book III, where it operates within the order of nature as a way of changing one form into another, its destructive force is shown in Book VII, where Mutabilitie becomes the destruction of form itself and of the principles of order. Even in this confrontation with the dark side of Ovid's vision, Spenser uses Ovidian poetic technique. The debate between Mutabilitie and Jove is set on Arlo Hill, near where Spenser himself lived. In passing he says that if the style of epic did not forbid it, he would tell the story of the hill, and of course goes on to do so. Perhaps his intent is to underscore further his digression from serious and public matter to Ovid's pleasing fictions. The hill, we are then told with outlandish incongruity, was anciently sacred to Diana. The story of how Diana was there revealed naked to Faunus comes from Ovid's tale of Actaeon. In his lowering of the epic tone, Spenser trivializes his story in good Ovidian fashion, comparing Diana at one point to a dairymaid. At the end, however, he reveals how the incident leads Diana to curse Arlo with wolves and thieves, 'Which too-too true that lands in-dwellers since have found' (VI 55). With his allusion to the Irish troubles that would soon consume his own Kilcolman Castle, Spenser turns the metamorphic tale back to the human implications of mutability, and prepares again for the higher strain of epic with which the poem would continue.

While *The Faerie Queene* explores the potential of Ovidian epic as an alternative form of the long poem, *Muiopotmos* takes the form of the short Ovidian narrative based on a single episode from the *Metamorphoses*. The generic identity of this short form is troublesome. Often it is called the *epyllion* (although the word is a nineteenth-century coinage) or *minor epic*, to suggest its relationship to the long forms. With no general or stable Renaissance account, the genre must be taken as fluid and experimental – appropriately metamorphic. *Muiopotmos* is included in *Complaints* (1591), 'Containing sundrie small Poemes of the Worlds Vanitie.' Most of these poems have separate title pages, making it difficult to know whether the designation complaint is Spenser's own or a conventional generic description. The texture of the poem is, like much of *The Faerie Queene*, embedded in the rival languages of epic derived from Virgil and Ovid, and so we may see the 'complaint' as a kind of 'minor epic.'

The opening and closing lines of *Muiopotmos* imitate the opening and closing of the *Aeneid*; but in between, Spenser follows the highest calling of the classicizing poet, which is to imitate by invention and variation in the style of the Latin poets. He accounts for the ancient rivalry between spider and butterfly in a series of mythological digressions that originate in the stories of Arachne in Ovid, and Psyche in Apuleius' *Metamorphoses*. Spenser's myths vary so freely from the originals, though, that they constitute new legends. The result is a poem with the unity demanded by Aristotelian or Virgilian notions of epic, and the luxurious variety so often praised in Ovid. Although the poem, like Ovid's, has been read as an allegory, it is perhaps best understood as another meditation on mutability, with a lightness of tone corresponding to its miniaturization of epic form.

If *Muiopotmos* was written about the time of the publication of *FQ* I-III (1590), it may justly be taken as a playful sporting, almost a parody, of the form of Spenser's own epic. It is, in any event, an excellent indicator of how Spenser's Ovidian epics set the tone for Elizabethan narrative poetry of the 1590s. Marlowe's *Hero and Leander* (1593) and Shakespeare's *Venus and Adonis* (1593) both attempt, like *Muiopotmos*, to compress the qualities of the *Metamorphoses* into the short form of the minor epic. Lodge's *Scil-*

laes Metamorphosis (1589), usually considered the first minor epic, and arguably too early to be influenced by Spenser's work even in manuscript, mingles the complaint form and mythological invention into a style which, like Spenser's, is simultaneously neo-Chaucerian and neoclassical (Chaucer was a thoroughly Ovidian poet). The first imitation of the Spenserian stanza is Barnfield's minor epic *Cynthia* (1595). Even the historical complaints, such as Daniel's *Complaint of Rosamond* (1592) and Drayton's *Matilda* (1594) (which are sometimes described as a species of minor epic), share with *The Faerie Queene* the Ovidian desire to interweave the private suffering of individuals with grand and impersonal schemes of history. As late as 1619, Drayton could still define such works as a 'species of heroic poem' (ed 1931–41, 2:382) and name them 'legends,' in emulation of Spenser. CLARK HULSE

Walter Allen, Jr 1958 'The Non-Existent Classical Epyllion' *SP* 55:515–18; Barkan 1976; Elizabeth Story Donno, ed 1963 *Elizabethan Minor Epics* (New York); Donno 1970 'The Epyllion' in Ricks 1970:82–100; Heather Dubrow 1987 *Captive Victors: Shakespeare's Narrative Poems and Sonnets* (Ithaca, NY); Hulse 1981; William Keach 1977 *Elizabethan Erotic Narratives* (New Brunswick, NJ); Paul W. Miller 1958 'The Elizabethan Minor Epic' *SP* 55:31–8.

Oxford, Edward de Vere, seventeenth Earl of (1550–1604) Lord Great Chamberlain of England (a prestigious, if largely ceremonial, hereditary office). An important royal favorite during the 1570s, Oxford was well known as a poet, although only sixteen of his lyrics can now be identified. By 1583, his profligate style of life had reduced him nearly to bankruptcy. This crisis was partly relieved in 1586 by an extraordinarily large grant of a £1000 annuity from the crown. Spenser probably addressed the third dedicatory sonnet to Oxford in recognition of his social rank (his earldom was the oldest in England) and to encourage his patronage of the arts, especially poetry (see **FQ*, commendatory verses and dedicatory sonnets).

Oxford's place in Spenser's allegory remains very problematic. The Briar (*SC, Februarie*) may represent Oxford, who supported the Catholic-French cause in the 1579 marriage negotiations between the Duc d'Alençon and the Queen (McLane 1961:61–76). Spenser's patron, the Earl of Leicester (the Oak), led the Protestant opposition to this match. In his dedicatory sonnet in *The Faerie Queene*, Spenser claims that 'th'antique glory of thine auncestry / Under a shady vele is therein writ,' though there is no likely identification of him with any character. He refers also to the love the Earl bears 'To th'*Heliconian* ymps, and they to thee' without mentioning his poetry.

STEVEN W. MAY

For Oxford's poems, see Oxford and Essex ed 1980. A.L. Rowse 1983 *Eminent Elizabethans* (London) pp 75–106 is a general treatment.

P

pageants Though the word *pageant* is of obscure origin, in the medieval period it had come to refer to the stages or wagons on which drama was performed. By Spenser's time, the term often referred to an entire entertainment, characterized by spectacle and colorful display. Scholars have often remarked on the ways in which *The Faerie Queene* in particular reflects the tone and practices of Elizabethan pageants, many of which were also designed to honor and praise the Queen in an emblematic manner. 'Just as a pageant or a masque is not completely dramatic, so Spenser's art is not completely narrative. Instead we are meant to *look* and to see the *shows* it presents' (Lewis 1967:3).

One broad category of Elizabethan pageantry can be designated civic pageantry: outdoor entertainments, typically accessible to the public, which focused on civic or national life and were frequently financed and produced by trade guilds and local governments. Civic pageants were planned entertainments with a clear dramatic purpose, responding to a specific occasion such as a coronation, the inauguration of a new mayor, or a summer provincial tour of the sovereign. In Elizabethan England, there were three major kinds: progresses, royal entries, and Lord Mayor's Shows.

English sovereigns had long made provincial tours to visit noblemen on their estates. By Elizabeth's time, the 'progress' or summer tour had become full-fledged drama, and entertainments were regularly associated with her visits. Several reasons prompted the sovereign to make such a progress: to escape unsanitary conditions in London during the summer, to enjoy the hospitality of noblemen and thereby reduce court expenses, to see and be seen – the political purpose of binding up the loyalties of the people was an essential part of Elizabeth's domestic policy. Not all such tours contained pageants, but many did, often stretching over several weeks. With their sprawling form, their diverse parts, and their Arcadian setting, they have obvious analogies to *The Faerie Queene*.

The most famous progress pageants in Elizabeth's reign took place during her visits to Kenilworth Castle and to Elvetham. As the Queen arrived at Kenilworth in July 1575 to be entertained by the Earl of Leicester, she was greeted by the Lady of the Lake floating on a movable island, and then crossed a bridge lined with gifts left by gods and goddesses. So began three weeks of entertainment planned by the Earl and written in part by George Gascoigne – the first identifiable poet to be associated with progress pageants. Citizens from nearby Coventry presented a historical show of a Danish battle against the English, and there was a mock marriage as well as the inevitable fireworks and hunting. The world of romance and mythology blends with a celebration of Elizabeth's mystical power. The Queen was greeted in the woods by a Savage Man (played by Gascoigne) and later on the river by Arion, floating on a mechanical dolphin filled with a consort of musicians. A basic theme recurs throughout the diffuse entertainment: in her person, Elizabeth brings the power to charm and to free; she is a regenerating and liberating force, seen in her responses to gods and goddesses, to the Arthurian world of romance, and to the Arcadian setting.

On the Earl of Hertford's estate at Elvetham, a special crescent-shaped pond was dug, creating the setting for a fierce battle between the wood gods led by Sylvanus and the sea gods led by Nereus. Arriving on 20 September 1591, Elizabeth was met by a Poet, who welcomed and praised her as six virgins (three Graces and three Hours) went before her, strewing the path with flowers and singing a song in six parts. The central dramatic event was the battle, with all the participants in elaborate costume and Elizabeth as spectator seated under a green satin canopy. The intense combat finally calmed when Nereus noticed the Queen and spoke of her as an enemy to war, a friend to peace. As in the Kenilworth show, so here in Elvetham: Elizabeth brings special power and virtue in her person. The closing day of the progress began with Elizabeth's being met by a Fairy Queen in the garden, a moment rich in its implications of fact and fiction, pageant and poem. In these progress pageants, one may see many elements of the exaltation of Elizabeth also found in *The Faerie Queene*.

The royal entry pageant, the official entry of a sovereign into a city accompanied by dramatic shows, can be traced back to thirteenth-century London. Obviously, many processions into cities involved no particular, formal entertainment; but coronations almost invariably elicited pageants. Typically, the sovereign was met outside the city by the mayor and other officials and escorted through the streets; dramatic tableaux were sometimes stationed along the way. One chief characteristic of the royal entry pageant was its processional form as the sovereign moved through city streets lined with spectators. Often special structures or stages were built on which the dramatic scene could be performed. Elizabethan royal entries took their subject matter from history, religion, mythology, and moral allegory.

Though Elizabeth made a number of official entries, the most stunning was her entry into London on 14 January 1559, the day before her coronation. (The surviving description of *The Quenes Majesties Passage* was prepared by Richard Mulcaster, Spenser's teacher at Merchant Taylors' School.) As she moved from the Tower through the city to Westminster, she confronted a number of tableaux performed on specially prepared scaffolds or arches. At Gracious Street, for example, a genealogical tree had been constructed, celebrating the union of the houses of Lancaster and York under the Tudors with persons representing Henry VII and his wife Elizabeth, Henry VIII and Anne Boleyn, and on the top stage Queen Elizabeth. Verses declaimed by a child pointed to the national accomplishment of unity. The pageant device at Cornhill celebrated the four virtues necessary for worthy governance: Pure Religion, Love of Subjects, Wisdom, and Justice. Each virtue trampled under foot its contrary vice. The device at the Little Conduit in Cheapside stretched across the street and displayed two mountains, the northern one illustrating a decaying commonwealth and the southern one, a flourishing commonwealth. They were portrayed as opposites in every detail. Between these hills was a cave from which emerged Time and his daughter Truth, who had been held captive. Truth presented Elizabeth with the Word of Truth, the English Bible. The political and religious implication is clear: the previous reign was oppressive, but now Elizabeth's government offers new hope and a pure religion. At one of the final arches the Queen saw Deborah represented, the ancient ruler of Israel to whom Elizabeth was likened. Themes of political union and royal instruction dominate the heavily didactic pageant. Royal entries into Bristol (1574) and Norwich (1578) differ in details but not radically in form, for they, too, honor the Queen's virtues.

For some time there had been processionals at the annual inauguration of the new mayor of London, but not until the mid-sixteenth century did the Lord Mayor's pageant become a permanent part of the festivities. Each 29 October, a new mayor, selected from one of the twelve principal guilds, was installed; and the guild to which he belonged sponsored a pageant. Rivalry developed among the guilds, each trying to outdo the others in expenditure and spectacle. Like the royal entry, the Lord Mayor's Show had a processional form as the new mayor made his way through London to the Guildhall or St Paul's. Sometimes there were also entertainments on the Thames.

The first Lord Mayor's Show for which speeches are recorded was in 1561. Since the mayor, Sir William Harper, belonged to the Merchant Taylors' Company (with which Spenser's father may have been associated), the young Spenser may have actually witnessed this spectacle, in which mythological and biblical characters dominate. (Again, some of the speeches have been attributed to Mulcaster, under whom Spenser may have just begun his studies; he wrote speeches for another Lord Mayor's Show in 1568, just before Spenser finished at Merchant Taylors' School.) The first mayoral pageant for which a printed text survives is that of 1585, written by George Peele; it marks the beginning of a long association of regular dramatists with these pageants. Thomas Nelson's 1590 pageant may be taken as typical in emphasizing the civic life of the guild through historical example. The opening speeches celebrate the glory of the city and commonwealth. Fame appears, sounds her trumpet, and instructs the mayor in maintaining the peace. Speeches by Peace of England, Wisdom, Policy, God's Truth, Plenty, Loyalty, and Concord – qualities that sustain a worthy government – stress the theme of peace.

Other kinds of entertainments do not easily fit these three broad categories of civic pageants. The Accession Day tilts honoring the accession of Queen Elizabeth each 17 November, continued a tradition of chivalric pageantry from medieval tournaments. Something of the same is true of the elaborate 1581 show in the tiltyard at Whitehall in which Sidney, Greville, the Earl of Arundel, and Lord Windsor, calling themselves the Foster Children of Desire, laid siege to the Castle or Fortress of Perfect Beauty, the residence of Elizabeth. Many Elizabethan indoor entertainments resemble the famous Jacobean court masques with their song, dance, and elaborate costume. All evidence indicates that the age was given to elaborate pageant entertainments, whatever their precise forms. Street shows and estate entertainments flourished in an era of peace and in an aesthetic world fully cognizant of symbol and metaphor.

Without insisting on specific indebtedness, one can see in Spenser many analogues to pageant entertainments of the Elizabethan age. In the *Aprill* eclogue of *The Shepheardes Calender*, for example, the unstinted praise of Elizabeth, the dialogue form, and references to the Graces and to the Ladies of the Lake evoke recollections of progress pageants. Its Arcadian pastoral world is analogous to the world created in the progress entertainments. Hobbinol's emblem, *O dea certe*, could readily symbolize the apotheosis of the Queen that is apparent through most of the Elizabethan pageants. She is the Fairy Queen of Spenser's poem and of the street and estate entertainments, the focus of devotion, the power that gives rise to such idealized fictions as Cynthia, Belphoebe, Deborah, Astraea, Britomart, the Fourth Grace, or her presumed ancestor, Arthur (see E.C. Wilson 1939).

Spenser is also capable of parodying the idealized status of the pageants. The description of Lucifera in *FQ* I v 5 seems a conscious parody of Elizabeth: with full 'royall pomp and Princely majestie,' the 'far renowmed Queene' is 'ybrought unto a paled greene, / And placed under stately canapee' to watch the tournament between the Red Cross Knight and Sansjoy. In this, Lucifera anticipates Elizabeth seated alongside the pond at Elvetham.

The portrait of Mercilla counters that of Lucifera and reflects positively on the idealized concept of the Queen in pageant and poem. Like the Elizabeth of the Elvetham pageant, Mercilla is a friend to peace and an enemy to war. In her gorgeous palace, she sits high and lifted up 'that she might all men see, / And might of all men royally be seene' (V ix 27). Such a position, at least as metaphor, is essential to Elizabeth's political purpose in the progress and royal entry pageants. As at Elizabeth's coronation pageant, Mercilla, surrounded by emblematic properties (eg, a rusty sword), is also accompanied by qualities crucial to good government (eg, Peace, Temperance, Reverence).

Spenser repeatedly adopts the processional form of the pageants. In *FQ* I iv, Lucifera and the seven deadly sins, each with appropriate emblematic properties, recall allegorical pageants as they move from palace to fresh flowering fields and back again, while 'Huge routs of people did about them band, / Showting for joy' (36). After Redcrosse has killed the Dragon, he is brought in a regal progress to the palace of Una's father, 'With shaumes, and trompets, and with Clarions sweet; / And all the way the joyous people sings, / And with their garments strowes the paved street' (xii 13). A comparable marriage procession is that of the bride in *Epithalamion* 129–66, who is similarly seen 'lyke some mayden Queene.' Arthur's victorious progress after defeating Geryoneo (V xi 34), and Calidore's after binding the Blatant Beast (VI xii 38) are similar public celebrations of virtue triumphant. One of the greatest processions in *The Faerie Queene* takes place on Arlo Hill in the *Cantos of Mutabilitie* (VII vii). Dame Nature is placed 'in a pavilion' not made by hands but by the Earth herself who has fashioned a canopy with trees. Here Nature watches processions of the Seasons, Months, Day and Night, Hours, Life, and finally Death. The processional form and the iconographical detail again resemble Elizabethan pageants, especially royal entries and mayoral shows.

In the house of Busirane in *FQ* III xii, Britomart witnesses the masque of Cupid, an entertainment in processional form with obvious affinities to the indoor pageants of the Elizabethan period. It is perhaps the most explicitly theatrical moment in *The Faerie Queene*. The figure Ease suddenly issues forth 'as on the ready flore / Of some Theatre' (3). Next comes a group of minstrels, and then 'a jolly company, / In manner of a maske, enranged orderly' (5). After the sounding of trumpets follows a gruesome procession of such characters as Daunger, Doubt, Grief, Fury, Suspect, Cruelty, all symbolically arrayed. Finally comes Cupid himself 'riding on a Lion ravenous' (22), reminding one perhaps of figures in Lord Mayor's Shows who often appeared on the backs of animals usually relevant to the guild. What Spenser offers is in many ways an anti-masque of grotesque figures who are the opposite of the idealized world that masques typically create. When Britomart gains entry into the room where the masquers have gone, she discovers that 'they streight were vanisht' (30). It is the nature of occasional drama, such as pageants and masques, for the actors to disappear abruptly, the spectacle revealing thereby its insubstantial quality.

Several attributes of the wedding festivities for the marriage of Thames and Medway in *FQ* IV xi recall pageant entertainments. The presence of Neptune and his wife Amphitrite echoes the appearance of sea gods and goddesses in a number of pageants (eg, the 1591 Elvetham progress), culminating in the crucial role of Neptune and Amphitrite in Anthony Munday's 1605 Lord Mayor's Show. Albion, the presumed son of Neptune, also appears in several pageants. Arion, 'playing on his harpe' (*FQ* IV xi 23), had also appeared in the 1575 Kenilworth pageant and in the 1561 Lord Mayor's Show. River symbolism is especially apparent in several Elizabethan mayoral pageants, and the river Thames is represented in Peele's 1585 mayoral entertainment. References to Brutus, mythical settler of Britain, in the Thames-Medway wedding account underscore Spenser's interest in national history and also recall the historical interest in pageants, especially in Lord Mayor's Shows in which Brutus is both mentioned and on occasion represented. In such wedding festivities, costume, song, and procession evoke masque entertainments that were associated with weddings.

At moments, it is not far-fetched to recognize some of the scenes in *The Faerie Queene* as pageants, dramatized moments of spectacle and meaning. Spenser and the Elizabethan pageant writers share much, beginning with a somewhat episodic, diffuse form. The emphasis in both cases is on theme reinforced by pictorial representation. The moral virtues treated in Spenser's poem are also apparent throughout the pageants. Britomart, for example, as the knight of Chastity would be at home in the part of the 1578 Norwich pageant which portrayed the victory of Chastity. Political virtues, those necessary for worthy governance, pervade both the pageants and *The Faerie Queene*. The quest for and maintenance of 'pure religion' is apparent in *FQ* I, as it is in the early civic pageants of Elizabeth's reign. National history is intertwined with Spenser's purpose and repeatedly celebrated in pageant. The romantic, allegorical world of his poem is similarly compatible with the pageants. Without self-consciousness, Time and Truth greet Elizabeth in the streets of London in 1559: pageant dramatists and poet share a similar vision of the world, one that allows for full operation of metaphor. Not surprisingly, Spenser refers to the visions in *Ruines of Time* as 'tragicke Pageants' (490), and has a poem entitled *Pageaunts* among his lost works. The knightly quests in *The Faerie Queene* are conceived as arising from the twelve annual feast days of Gloriana: Redcrosse addresses Guyon as one 'whose pageant next ensewes' (II i 33); Spenser himself calls the entire poem 'this same Pageaunt' (*FQ* Howard Sonn); and it is as a procession of characters that Blake presents the poem in his painting. The mystical, transcendental qualities of Elizabeth that inform *The Faerie Queene* permeate the pageant imagination also. Spenser's early readers would have been struck by how many details, how many ideas, were familiar to them from street or estate pageants and from other, indoor entertainments of the period.

DAVID M. BERGERON

R.T.D. Sayle 1931 *Lord Mayors' Pageants of the Merchant Taylors Company in the Fifteenth, Sixteenth and Seventeenth Centuries* (London) has the texts of several city pageants to which Spenser's teacher Richard Mulcaster, among others, contributed. Mulcaster's summary of the 1559 London pageant for Elizabeth has been reprinted several times; see, eg, James M. Osborn, ed 1960 *The Quenes Maiesties Passage* (1558) (New Haven), and the discussion in David M. Bergeron 1978 'Elizabeth's Coronation Entry (1559): New Manuscript Evidence' *ELR* 8:3–8. For descriptions of Kenilworth, see George Gascoigne's *A Briefe Rehearsall* in Gascoigne ed 1907–10, 2:91–131; and Robert Laneham 1575 *A Letter* (rpt Menston, Yorks 1968); for Elvetham, see the anonymous *The Honorable Entertainement Gieven to the Queenes Majestie at Elvetham* 1591 (London; *STC* 7583). J. Nichols 1823 contains the texts of these and many of the other important public spectacles of the period. Anglo 1969 and Bergeron 1971 together provide a full survey of the growth of Tudor pageantry; see also Strong 1977. Giamatti 1975:78–93 discusses 'Pageant, Show, and Verse' in Spenser. Yates 1975 is especially pertinent to Spenser, as are Baskervill 1920–1; Ivan L. Schulze 1935; Schulze 1938; Schulze 1944 'Blenerhasset's *A Revelation*, Spenser's *Shepheardes Calender*, and the Kenilworth Pageants' *ELH* 11:85–91. For a differentiation of *pageant* from *masque* and the meaning of the words in Spenser, see Lewis 1967:2–6.

Palingenius Marcellus Palingenius Stellatus is a pseudonym, probably of Pier Angelo Manzolli (c 1500–c 1543), about whom little is known. *Stellatus* suggests that he was born in Stellata, near Ferrara, though its meaning (adorned with stars) may allude only to the title of his twelve-book poem *Zodiacus vitae*, first printed c 1535 in Venice. That he was posthumously declared a heretic would have enhanced his reputation in England (see the dedication to William Cecil in the 1565 ed, tr Googe).

Although *Zodiacus vitae* is little read today, in its own time it was enormously popular, with some thirty editions by the end of the century. It was used as a Latin textbook in many English grammar schools; and in England by 1579, it had gone through five Latin editions and an English translation by Barnabe Googe (Books 1–3, 1560; 1–6, 1561; 1–12, 1565). Both the original and Googe's translation were frequently reissued, and were praised by Gabriel Harvey, Thomas Digges, Roger Ascham, and others. Circumstantial evidence, then, suggests that Spenser was familiar with the work; in addition to its popularity and availability as a school text, it deals with many of the ethical and cosmological issues that engaged him.

The work is an encyclopedia in verse, arranged in twelve books according to the signs of the zodiac, a compilation of traditional knowledge and beliefs described by the title of Googe's 1576 edition as *The Zodiake of Life, Written by the Excellent and Christian Poet, Marcellus Palingenius Stellatus. Wherein are Conteined Twelve Severall Labours, Painting Out Moste Lively, the Whole Compass of the World, the Reformation of Manners, the Miseries of Mankinde, the Pathway to Vertue and Vice, the Eternitie of the Soule, the Course of the Heavens, the Mysteries of Nature, and Divers Other Circumstances of Great Learning, and No Lesse Judgement*.

Since most of the ideas of *Zodiacus vitae* are commonplace, it is easier to find parallels with Spenser's poetry than any direct influence. Many have been suggested: with the Garden of Adonis (*FQ* III vi; *ZV* 9 in ed 1947:159; 12, pp 229–32); with the Garden of Proserpina (*FQ* II vii 51–5; *ZV* 6, pp 84–7); with the house of Pride, Bower of Bliss, and house of Philotime (*FQ* I iv; II vii, xii; *ZV* 3, pp 28–31); with ideas about love in the Garden and Temple of Venus (*FQ* IV x), the *Hymne of Love*, and *Colin Clout* (*ZV* 4, pp 47–51; 7, p 122; 8, pp 136–7); and the original Latin description of Pluto's palace (*ZV* 3) and the house of Pride (*FQ* I iv) (Bennett 1932; Tuve 1933, 1935; Beckwith 1983). *Zodiacus vitae* may also have influenced the twelve-part arrangement of *The Shepheardes Calender*, and perhaps as well the disposition of themes and topics in the eclogues.

J.M. RICHARDSON

There is no standard modern Latin edition of Palingenius; in English, see ed 1947, a facs rpt of the 1576 translation by Googe, intro Rosemond Tuve (New York; citations are to this ed). Two general studies are Luzius Keller 1974 *Palingène, Ronsard, du Bartas: Trois études sur la poésie cosmologique de la Renaissance* (Bern); Foster Watson 1908 *The 'Zodiacus Vitae' of Marcellus Palingenius Stellatus: An Old School-Book* (London). See also M.A. Beckwith 1983 'A Study of Palingenius' *Zodiacus Vitae* and Its Influence on English Renaissance Literature' diss Ohio State Univ; Bennett 1932; Sheidley 1981; Rosemond Tuve 1933 'A Mediaeval Commonplace in Spenser's Cosmology' *SP* 30:133–47; Tuve 1935; J.H. Walter 1941 '*The Faerie Queene*: Alterations and Structure' *MLR* 36:37–58.

Palmer A Palmer was a pilgrim who had returned from the Holy Land, his faith demonstrated and confirmed, in token of which he carried a palm branch or leaf. Although Guyon's Palmer carries no such token, his name implies that the reason which he embodies is firmly linked to the Christian faith: he recognizes at once the significance of Redcrosse's shield and asserts the Christian basis of temperance (*FQ* II i 31). Temperance in *The Faerie Queene* depends upon the control of the passions by reason, and the house of Alma is called 'the fort of reason' (xi 1). In making his Palmer an allegorical figure of reason, Spenser revives the full religious implications of the term in order to express his own conception of its function.

Like the other characters in Spenser's allegory, the Palmer has general and particular meaning: he expresses Guyon's inner moral debates and rational perceptions, and he also externalizes them, directing the reader's attention to their general moral implications. When Guyon is most completely governed by reason, as in the destruction of the Bower of Bliss, he is so fused with his Palmer into a single figure – the narrative voice alternates between 'he' and 'they' in describing the action – that it is difficult to tell them apart. When Guyon loses his Palmer, however, he has forsaken the path of reason, although he still attempts to maintain the habit of reason on an irrational course where success is ultimately impossible. The distinction is made in the opening lines of canto vii where, lacking his Palmer, Guyon must steer without the aid of the 'stedfast' Polestar and rely on the more experimental guidance of his own past and uncertain experience (1–2).

By *reason* Spenser means what the Renaissance knew as 'Right reason' or the 'erected wit' (Milton *Paradise Lost* 6.42, Sidney *Defence* ed 1973b:79), the spark of divinity still remaining in the human mind even after the Fall. It is, however, more clouded than in prelapsarian days: the Palmer avoids the dangers from the unruly horses of the passions, which he is no longer strong enough to control, by always traveling on foot, but his progress, in consequence, is slow. Nevertheless, like Christ he calms the sea with his staff (xii 26) and quells the wild beasts as with the caduceus of Mercury which the Platonists associated with divine wisdom (41; see Brooks-Davies 1983:33–42). He represents the same quality as Una in Book I and his adventures parallel hers, with this difference, that her eyes are directed upwards to the mysteries of faith and his usually downwards to the corruptions of earth which he must try to control by the light of reason. The fact that the one is dressed in white, the other in black suggests the different levels at which they must work: it is the Palmer who gives Guyon his quest to capture Acrasia (ii 43). Acknowledging the weakness of human reason against the passions once they have control, his advice to Guyon at IV 34–5 is strictly logical: the only way to avoid intemperance is to avoid all occasions of it, and thus prevent the passions from ever being aroused. Adam gives much the same advice to Eve in *Paradise Lost* before he allows her to leave his side (9.359–66). The Palmer speaks with the traditional voice of reason as heard, for example, in the *Romance of the Rose*.

Human beings, however, are not rational, and escape from the passions is neither possible nor perhaps desirable. Fallen man cannot always recognize occasion nor avoid it when he does so. The temptation Phaedria offers, for example, is the natural human instinct to relax after a hard-won victory, but it is enough to banish the Palmer, and it quickly deepens into the sensual indulgence of Cymochles. Mammon represents a kind of excess with which true temperance would not need to be concerned; but Christ as a man was tempted by Mammon, and Guyon is bound to explore the mortal dimension to which he belongs. By means of the habit of temperance and the not-always-relevant values and clichés of chivalry, he triumphs, but in winning the battle against Mammon, he loses the war.

At this point, the Palmer is too weak to conquer the intemperate passions by himself, but he knows the Christian answer to them. Once divine mercy restores him to Guyon, he turns for aid to the Christ figure of Arthur; and once the redeeming blood, 'Red as the Rose,' has been spilled, the battle can be won with Guyon's own sword (viii 39–40). The Palmer is the central figure in this process of regeneration: he is the channel through which God's love initially operates, and the human power able to recognize and make use of the strength which lies in faith (see *nature and grace). Through this, no fall need be final, but equally, of course, the battle on earth is never finally won. It is typical of Spenser's creed that Book II, like Book I, ends on a note of warning: having helped Guyon capture Acrasia and having restored her victims to human shape, the Palmer still advises Guyon to get out as quickly as possible, 'Whilest wether serves and wind' (xii 87).

MAURICE EVANS

Anderson 1970b; Brooks-Davies 1983; Hume 1984:63–5; Nohrnberg 1976 (see index).

Pan Although Spenser refers directly to Pan only once in his other works (*FQ* II ix 40), in *The Shepheardes Calender* he mentions him seventeen times in eight eclogues. These are mostly ceremonial identifications in which a personage is identified as Pan, in terms familiar from other Renaissance poetry but ultimately traceable to three lines from Virgil's second eclogue (31–3). The first two – 'With me in the woods you shall rival Pan in song. / Pan it was who first taught man to make many reeds one with wax' – identify Pan as the god or patron of pastoral poetry, the role that Colin adopts in *Januarye* (17–18, 67) but must, in *December*, ultimately reject. But the third line – 'Pan cares for the sheep and the shepherds of the sheep' – led via Rabelais to Spenser's numerous identifications of Pan with God (*Maye* 111), with 'Christ, the very God of all shepheards' (*Maye* 54 gloss), and with 'kings and mighty Potentates' (*Aprill* 50 gloss).

Spenser's concluding eclogue brings together, within a few lines (7–12, 46–50), two identifications of Pan (with the Christian God and with pastoral poetry) even less compatible with each other than were those with Henry VIII (*Aprill* 50–4, 91–4 and 68 gloss) and the Pope (*Julye* 179 and gloss), who were, at least, both 'mighty Potentates.' Rabelais' syncretic elaborations (*Quart livre* 28) showed Spenser how to combine a Pan who was 'All' (Gr *Pan* all) with one who means Christ. 'Mighty *Pan*' (*Julye* 144) is such a formulation, one clearly useful later to Milton in his Nativity Ode (88–90); another (from Rabelais's 'Pan le grand Dieu') is the formulation 'the great God *Pan*' (*Julye* 49), later made a cliché of Arcadian verse by Elizabeth Barrett Browning.

Twice Spenser reinforces these Virgilian-Rabelaisian motifs with tales from Ovid. Pan and Syrinx (from *Metamorphoses* 1.689–712) as the parents of Queen Elizabeth yield the ceremonial identification of Pan with Henry VIII (cf Jonson's identification of Pan with James I in *Pan's Anniversary* [1620]: 'Pan is our All'). Pan's unsuccessful musical competition with Apollo (*Met* 11.149–93; see also Virgil Eclogue 4.58–9) gives Colin grounds for moderating his own pastoral ambitions (*June* 68–70; also 30–1, *Nov* 8–10 and 38 gloss) and then renouncing them (*Dec* 46–8).

E.K.'s glosses suggest that he was familiar with more aspects of the Pan tradition than Spenser needed to use. He mentions the Orphic-allegorical Pan (the 'all or omnipotent' of Conti and many medieval and Renaissance mythographers, and the emblematic god of 'all' Nature in Alciati's Emblem 97, *Natura*) and gives (on *Maye* 54) a long account, taken from Ludwig Lavater's *Of Ghostes and Spirites Walking by Nyght* (1572), of Plutarch's story of the death of Pan (*De defectu oraculorum* 17, *Moralia* 419), widely known and used in the Renaissance to support identifications of Pan either with Christ or with Satan.

Spenser's most idiosyncratic reference to Pan is at *FQ* II ix 40, where Shamefastnesse holds a bird that is 'as yet ashamd, how rude *Pan* did her dight.' The bird has been identified tentatively with Jynx, daughter of Pan and Echo, metamorphosed by Hera as a punishment for a distinct *lack* of shamefastness (scholia on Theocritus *Idyll* 2.17; *Var* 2:295–6, but see Fowler 1961).

Neither E.K. nor Spenser mentions the shaggy Pan associated with sexuality; for such a figure, Spenser refers to fauns or satyrs. Spenser's metapoetical variations upon the ceremonial-pastoral identifications of Pan are intelligent, poetically vigorous, and influential. If they are not the equal of Milton's in their depth of significance, poetic resonance, or even (varied though they are) their variety, still they domesticated the Pans of Virgil and Rabelais for English poets and provide, especially in *Januarye*, *June*, and *December*, powerful clues to the interpretation of *The Shepheardes Calender* itself.

PATRICIA MERIVALE

Harry Berger, Jr 1983 'Orpheus, Pan, and the Poetics of Misogyny: Spenser's Critique of Pastoral Love and Art' *ELH* 50:27–60; Alastair Fowler 1961 'Spenser and Renaissance Iconography' *EIC* 11:235–8; Patricia Merivale 1969 *Pan the Goat-God: His Myth in Modern Times* (Cambridge, Mass); Montrose 1979; Moore 1975; John Mulryan 1980 'Literary and Philosophical Interpretations of the Myth of Pan from the Classical Period through the Seventeenth Century' *Acta Conventus Neo-Latini Turonensis* ed Jean-Claude Margolin (Paris) pp 209–18; Nohrnberg 1976.

Pandora The artificial woman sent by Zeus to Epimetheus in retribution for Prometheus' theft of fire. In Hesiod's *Works and Days* (47–105), her name (Gr *pan* all + *dōra* gifts) is said to be appropriate because each of the gods gave her a gift to plague men.

In the *Theogony* (562–612), Pandora herself is evil; in *Works and Days*, however, through curiosity she opens a jar which fills the world with evils of every kind; only hope remains within it.

The myth was much modified in the Middle Ages. Latin writers either ignore Pandora or her jar. Such Church Fathers as Origen (*Contra Celsum* 4, in *PGr* II:1086ff) and Tertullian (*De corona militis* 7, in *PLat* 2.84) regard her as a pagan distortion of Eve; Fulgentius (*Mythologiae* 46, 82) interprets her allegorically as the soul, 'the general gift of all'; and Erasmus furthers Pandora's rehabilitation by leaving ambiguous the question whether she or her husband opened the baleful jar (*pithos*), which Erasmus incidentally transforms into a box (*pyxis*; *Adages* 1.31).

In *Vewe of Ireland*, Spenser decries numerous 'evills' in 'lawes ... Customes ... [and] religion' that are 'hurtefull' to Ireland; he considers them 'countable with those ... hidden in the baskett of *Pandora*,' a usage suggesting the indirect influence of Erasmus (*Var Prose* p 45; cf Estienne 1561). In *Teares of the Muses*, he calls Elizabeth 'The true *Pandora* of all heavenly graces' (578), playing on the name's etymology, and perhaps contrasting the Queen with Hesiod's false enchantress, whom the Graces deceitfully adorn (*Works and Days* 73–4). Spenser here adopts the positive tradition that had clearly emerged by 1580, for example, in Dekker's *Old Fortunatus*, where Eliza is called Pandora, as well as Gloriana, Cynthia, Belphoebe, and Astraea (Prologue 2–4).

Spenser would have found a coherent summary of Hesiod's Pandora in Thomas Cooper (1565). Such a figure appears in *Ruines of Rome*, where the ancient city is said to have been 'Like a *Pandora* ... In which all good and evill was enclosed' (stanza 19). Spenser's translation of du Bellay thus suggests distant affinities both with Hesiod's epithet for her, *kalon kakon* ('good bad' *Theogony* 585), and with the Genesis account of the tree of knowledge. Hesiod's temptress is similarly present in *Amoretti* 24. Like her beautiful-evil prototype, Spenser's 'new *Pandora*' shows rare 'perfection of each goodly part' and yet causes the poet to suffer a 'bitter balefull smart.' Moreover, the lady's ambiguous influence is explained in the manner of Hesiod: like Pandora, she is sent 'into this sinfull world ... that she to wicked men a scourge should bee, / for all their faults with which they did offend.' Spenser, however, revises the ancient myth by deflecting blame from Prometheus and the woman to man himself (who is more sinned against than sinning in the classical texts), and by characterizing his mistress, in vaguely Christian terms, as an essentially faultless scourge of God, the innocent instrument of divine retributive justice. These modifications, for which precedent can be found in Fulgentius and Erasmus among others, seem consistent with Spenser's seriocomic introduction of Pandora into a Petrarchan sonnet.

The myth of Pandora also appears in the Spenser-Harvey correspondence, in Harvey's 'New Yeeres Gift' 12–15 (*Three Letters* 3; *Var Prose* p 465). There Harvey, in a strident assault on the myth of progress, denigrates 'many fruitlesse / *Artes*, and Craftes, devisde by the *Divls and Sprites*, for a torment, / And for a plague to the world: as both *Pandora*, *Prometheus*, / And that cursed *good bad Tree*, can testifie.' This poem is Hesiodic in its primitivism, and 'good bad' exactly translates Hesiod's *kalon kakon*. Harvey also implicitly accepts (with less acrimony) the view of Origen and Tertullian that pagan myth and Christian mystery share a family resemblance. For him, in fact, the Hesiodic and biblical accounts of the Fall are fully in accord: Prometheus provocatively resembles the 'Divls and Sprites' of Christianity, especially Satan in the serpent; his gift of fire is equivalent to the forbidden fruit; and in an extreme compression of the two myths, Hesiod's oxymoron is transferred to the sacred tree of knowledge of good and evil violated by Eve in Genesis 3. Although Spenser did not write these verses, they confirm his awareness of Hesiod, however far removed from the Greek original his immediate mythological sources may have been. Harvey's syncretism illustrates, moreover, the Renaissance commonplace found also in Spenser that certain Greek myths contain approximations of biblical truth and are explicable as God's partial revelation to the pagans.

PHILIP J. GALLAGHER

Dora and Erwin Panofsky 1956 *Pandora's Box: The Changing Aspects of a Mythical Symbol* (London) ch 6.

Panthea The Elfin emperor Elfant built the crystal tower of Panthea (Gr *pan* 'all' + *thea* 'goddess'; or *thea* 'sight,' ie, best of sights), the 'brightest thing' in Cleopolis (*FQ* I x 58, II x 73). Spenser drew on three traditions for this description: romance, allegory, and travel literature. Arthurian romance had Glastonbury (glass castle) on Avalon, a western island. There was also the Clere Toure with pinnacles of bright crystal in *Arthur of Little Britain*. The castles of medieval dream vision, whether Chaucer's beryl castle or that of Gavin Douglas, provided its allegorical association with fame (Rathborne 1937:44, 48, 195; see also the structure of 'shining Christall' in *Visions of Bellay* 2). Various sixteenth-century editions of the Roman guidebook *Mirabilia urbis Romae* suggested the classical model, the Pantheon. Panthea may also be identified with Westminster Abbey, where kings and nobles lay buried. In 1555 a tomb had been erected there for Chaucer, and Spenser later joined his predecessor in what has since become the poet's corner in England's temple of fame.

MICHAEL J. MURRIN

paradox A distinction should be made between paradox as a literary form and as a metaphysical concept. Popular from classical and medieval times, the Renaissance literary or rhetorical paradox is a witty, sophisticated form aimed at a coterie; it seeks through intellectual play or contrary notions to shock readers into a new way of looking at things or to make them realize a truth. In form it is like a small oration or an essay. Such paradoxes may take as their subjects arguments contrary to received opinion (Gr *paradoxa* 'beyond opinion,' hence 'unexpected, startling') and apparently undermining established truth; or they consist of false praise – mock or paradoxical encomiums, such as are found in Erasmus' *Praise of Folly* or Ortensio Landi's popular *Paradossi* (cf Sidney's *Defence of Poetry*: 'we know a playing wit can praise the discretion of an ass' ed 1973b:100). The basis of the rhetorical paradox is the metaphysical concept of paradox – the logical contradiction found in Zeno's denial of motion, in the Cretan's assertion that all Cretans are liars, and in various attempts to praise the unpraiseworthy. The nature of paradox is that a thing can simultaneously be and not be both in itself and in relation to that to which it is being related. In practice, both literary and metaphysical paradox were mixed.

Like Donne and Milton, Spenser writes within the Neoplatonic-Christian tradition and explores the paradoxes of the human condition. Unlike Donne, he does not exploit the rhetorical tradition of paradox. He is not interested in paradox for the sake of play; rather, like Milton he deals with metaphysical paradoxes such as time and eternity, being and becoming, life and death, and *dubia* concerning the nature of love and women, and creativity within a didactic and moral framework. Such deeper paradoxes appear throughout *The Faerie Queene* – in the very notion of the 'darke conceit' of the poem, in the contradictions found in characters and their depiction (eg, that the untried knight at I i I bears arms 'Wherein old dints of deepe wounds did remaine'), in contradictions of reason (eg, when Ruddymane's hands cannot be cleansed, Guyon is driven 'into diverse doubt' II ii 3–4), and in the religious paradoxes that are found from the beginning of the poem (where Christ is 'dead as living ever' I i 2) to the end in the contrast (only finally to be resolved) between 'Change' and 'Eternity' (VII viii 2). Central to the poem is the bringing together of unlikely opposites into a kind of unity (*discordia concors*), which represents one aspect of paradoxical thinking. For example, Redcrosse can both be the knight of Holiness and achieve the state of holiness; Duessa, an ugly hag, can appear fair, and her fair appearance may itself be foul because it is deceptive.

The Shepheardes Calender treats the paradox of time and eternity in relation to poetic creation. Dealing with changes in the seasons, the poem creates an image of eternity; and in it, Spenser displays both the pride of the creator and the humility of one who serves his creation. In the *Amoretti* and the *Fowre Hymnes*, he explores the paradoxical nature of love – that two who are two may nevertheless be one and that woman may be both inspiration and temptation. Although such paradoxes are inherent in the Neoplatonic-Christian tradition, Spenser uses them in a paradigmatic manner rather than as a writer who desires to exploit paradoxes as a rhetorical form. HELEN PETERS

The best-known series of rhetorical paradoxes was Ortensio Landi's *Paradossi cioè, sententie fuori del comun parere* (1543, etc), which was incompletely translated from the French version of Charles Estienne by A[nthony] M[unday] as *The Defence of Contraries* (1593 [*STC* 6467]; rpt Amsterdam and New York 1969); see also intro to Donne ed 1980. Colie 1966 analyzes the different forms of the paradox and, at pp 329ff, examines the 'metaphysical' paradox of the unity of becoming and being in *FQ*. Winifred G. Keaney examines the paradoxical function of courtly love in *FQ* VI in Nathaniel B. Smith and Joseph T. Snow 1980 *The Expansion and Transformations of Courtly Literature* (Athens, Ga) pp 185ff. Closely related to paradox is *discordia concors* (harmonious discord), for which see Wind 1958, esp pp 81ff.

Paridell As fickle lover and friend, Paridell is one of the many parodies and negations of virtue which enrich the moral texture of *The Faerie Queene*. After a major role in Books III and IV, he is last mentioned in V ix 41–2, a passage which suggests that he was executed when convicted of conspiring to replace Mercilla with Duessa. Although his name obviously evokes the Trojan Paris, his fate in Book V may associate him as well with Dr William Parry, who was executed in 1585 for treason against Elizabeth and appears as 'Paridel' in Dekker's *Whore of Babylon* (William Barker, personal communication 1984; for the historical allegory and Spenserian allusions in Dekker, see Hoy 1980, 2:300–83).

As a highly accomplished courtly lover in *FQ* III, Paridell is both attractive and dangerous. He is introduced as 'a knight faire pricking on the plaine' (viii 44; cf x 35), a description which suggests his importance because it recalls the description of Redcrosse at the opening of *FQ* I. On his breast, however, he wears not a bloody cross but a burning heart, an emblem indicative of his erotic aspirations. He and Britomart unhorse each other in a ludicrous dispute over shelter in a pigpen – few of Britomart's other antagonists have as much success. His seduction of Hellenore follows. A comic tour de force which shares the spirit of such fabliaux as Chaucer's *Miller's Tale*, the episode exemplifies Spenser's habit of defining virtue negatively: 'white seemes fairer, macht with blacke attone' (ix 2).

In recalling the adulterous Paris whose rape of Helen led to the Trojan war, Paridell contrasts both amorously and politically with Britomart, the chaste heroine of Book III. He is as experienced and faithless in love as she is innocent and constant. Eager to exploit rather than protect feminine weakness, he reverses the morality of a virtuous knight-errant. Paridell traces his Trojan ancestry to a bastard son of Paris and Oenone, the shepherdess abandoned for Helen. Britomart too descends from the Trojans; but her forebear is Aeneas, the heroic founder of Rome and, through his descendant Brut, of England.

In *FQ* IV, appropriately accompanied by the inconstant Blandamour, Paridell burlesques true friendship as he parodies true love in Book III. Along with Duessa and Ate, Paridell and Blandamour ironically mimic the group of true friends, Cambell, Triamond, Canacee, and Cambina. Paridell is defeated by Scudamour; he and Blandamour battle fiercely over the false Florimell, then proceed to the tournament for Florimell's girdle, where both are unhorsed by Ferramont. In IV ix, they appear in an alliance-shifting melee provoked by Ate and Duessa. The narrator accounts clearly for the weakness of their friendship when he observes that 'vertue is the band, that bindeth harts most sure' (ii 29). Lacking virtue in either love or friendship, Paridell forms his only stable connection with Duessa, falseness itself. LESLEY BRILL

Parnassus A twin-peaked mountain range in Greece, sacred to Apollo and the Muses (Ovid *Metamorphoses* 1.317, 2.221, 5.278); reference is made to its 'two hornes' in *Virgils Gnat* 22. Spenser invariably treats Parnassus as a metonym for the Muses. His reference to Mount Helicon as 'the learned well' which flows from Parnassus (*SC, Aprill* 42) shows the influence of Chaucer (*Troilus* 3.1809–10, *House of Fame* 521) and Chaucer's Italian sources (Dante *Purgatorio* 29.40, *Paradiso* 1.16–18; Boccaccio *Teseida* 11.63). Thus, Spenser's habitual spelling is the Middle English *Parnasse*, with its variant *Parnasso*.

From its association with the Muses and by virtue of its sacred wells, Helicon and Castalia, the mountain represents civilized life as opposed to 'brutish barbarisme' (*FQ* Ormond Sonn). It also stands for the elevated strain of heroic poetry, in contrast to the 'lowly grove' and 'savadge soyle' of pastoral (*June* 70, *FQ* Grey Sonn). The mode of 'learning' found on Parnassus is not acquired but infused by inspiration, and Spenser consistently uses Parnassus to suggest transcendent vision or 'goodly fury' (*FQ* VI proem 2). This conception underlies Spenser's invocations to the Muses (*Aprill* 41) and to Apollo (*Teares of the Muses* 58, *Virgils Gnat* 21).

Alternatively, Parnassus functions as a type of hill or *locus amoenus*. In a simple form, together with Eden it images the allure of the Bower of Bliss (*FQ* II xii 52). A more complex, syncretic fusion of myth and biblical history couples it with Mount Olivet, as in *Julye*, where the devious goatherd Morrell justifies his aspiring mind in a catalogue of such holy hills. Here the debate structure confines the effect of the pairing, but its force is developed in *FQ* I 54 where the classical Parnassus is linked with the Old Testament Sinai and the New Testament Olivet as types of the 'highest Mount' from which Redcrosse views the New Jerusalem. Each type adds its particular character, but all share a revelation from the divine. Thus, Spenser's allusions to Parnassus are bound up with the significant status he allows to the imagination as a means of divine instruction, in the spirit of humanist apologists for poetry from Boccaccio to Sidney.

DOMINIC BAKER-SMITH

pastoral In the Renaissance, *pastoral* as a literary term meant the use of the shepherd world as a metaphor or analogue for the real world. The countryside setting was a poetic fiction that often implied some contrast with the court or city. The metaphoric nature of pastoral allowed poets to use the mode for social, political, and religious comment, while the model of Virgil's *Eclogues* lent authority to its use as a symbolic pattern for poetic activity itself. Pastoral was thus a mode of almost limitless implication, but it had at its heart a close association with the very nature of poetry and the poet; and Spenser, more than any other English writer except perhaps Shakespeare, explored its full thematic range and potential. He wrote pastoral throughout his career, from *The Shepheardes Calender* in 1579 to the later cantos of *Faerie Queene* VI, with various individual eclogues or other pastoral poems in between.

Renaissance theoretical writings on the nature of pastoral stressed its allegorical and allusive potential, and also laid down some stylistic principles. Foremost among these is that, since shepherds are rustic, in order to keep decorum pastoral should be written in low style, at the opposite linguistic and rhetorical pole from the epic or heroic. Virgil's *Eclogues* and *Aeneid* were cited as models for this stylistic contrast (see, eg, Servius, Conrad of Hirsau, John of Garland, Boccaccio, Scaliger, etc). In practice, however, the *Eclogues* provided a pattern less of humble style than of high poetry. Spenser showed himself peculiarly alert to the possibilities of playing off the two, in the contrasting styles of the different eclogues of *The Shepheardes Calender* and in the synthesis of simplicity and sublimity found in the Mount Acidale episode of *FQ* VI x. The progression of Virgil's career from pastoral to epic furnished a model for the aspiring poet to follow, so it was not by chance that Spenser made his poetic debut with a series of eclogues; and in *October* he is already looking ahead to his future epic.

Theocritus, Virgil, Petrarch, Boccaccio, Sannazaro, Marot, and others had all made thinly disguised appearances in their own pastoral poetry; Spenser does the same. The pseudonym he chooses for himself, Colin Clout, relates him to pastoral traditions of various kinds. That he should make himself a central character at all recalls Virgil; the name 'Colin' had been chosen by Clément Marot for his supreme shepherd-poet who speaks the finely wrought elegy in his *Complaincte de Madame Loyse de Savoye* (1531); the full name, Colin Clout, recalls the plain-speaking satirist of Skelton's *Colyn Cloute* (1519). Spenser's choice of pseudonym therefore spans the classical, medieval, and modern traditions of pastoral; it encompasses both polemic and an 'allegory of poets.' The close relationship of pastoral with the making of poetry is crucial to Spenser: much of *The Shepheardes Calender*, part of *Colin Clouts Come Home Againe*, and, supremely, the Mount Acidale episode of *The Faerie Queene* explore the nature of poetry in pastoral terms. The metaphorical nature of pastoral enables the landscapes and settings of the poems to become landscapes of the poet's own mind. This is particularly clear in the *Shepheardes Calender* eclogues in which Colin himself appears (*Jan*, *June*, and *Dec*) and in his song in *August*; in *June*, it enables Colin and Hobbinol to inhabit different landscapes at the same time. The most idyllic example of Spenser's pastoral settings is Mount Acidale, which follows the widespread pastoral pattern of providing an ideal oasis within a wider shepherd landscape.

The close association of the shepherd with poetry and music was confirmed by the psalmist David's early career as a shepherd; Orpheus too was sometimes described as a shepherd (eg, *Oct* 28–30). The myth that Apollo, god of both music and (along with Pan) the care of flocks, had become a shepherd for a while, is used by other pastoral poets but gets only the briefest mention from Spenser (*FQ* III xi 39); most of his references to Phoebus as god of poetry are used to indicate a poetic level higher than the pastoral.

By the late sixteenth century, Spenser could draw on richly various pastoral traditions of both content and form. Certain myths were especially closely associated with pastoral. The most far-reaching of these was the myth of the Saturnian Golden Age, the age of Astraea, the maiden Justice (see Levin 1969). In that age, there was no seasonal change, the earth brought forth crops without labor, there were no cities or laws, and sea-travel had not been invented. It was an age of innocence and moral purity, and therefore was identified with the Garden of Eden in the paralleling of classical myth with Christian sacred history. The clear outlines of the myth made possible a series of conventions that enabled poets to locate their own pastorals immediately in relation to it. The winter setting of *Januarye*, for instance, or the reference to Astraea's departure at the opening of *Mother Hubberds Tale*, at once define the world of the poems as postlapsarian; and the trees' perpetual budding on Mount Acidale in *FQ* VI x removes the scene from the fallen world to the golden. The innocent shepherds who listen to Colin in *Colin Clout* have no experience of the sea, but Colin has crossed it to discover both an antipastoral world of courtly corruption and the suprapastoral world of Cynthia. Much Renaissance pastoral writing, including Spenser's, concentrates more on the fallen world than the golden; but the association of the Golden Age with pastoral was so strong that there is always an awareness of the perversion of an ideal order in dealing with the fallen world through the pastoral metaphor.

The generic forms pastoral could assume in the Renaissance were widely varied. The principal genre associated with the mode, and the only one unique to pastoral, was the eclogue. This genre dictated form rather than content (which could vary widely, occasionally even losing its shepherd associations). The eclogue form is essentially a shepherd monologue or dialogue; a third speaker occasionally appears (as in *August*) but takes only a minor part. The dialogue may take the form of responsive verses from the speakers (*amoebaeum carmen*), sometimes as a singing contest. There was a long tradition, going back at least to the ninth century, that the word *ecloga*, 'selected poem,' was properly *aegloga* (Gr *aig* + *logos*), meaning 'goatish speech' or 'goatherds' talk'; the unpleasant associations of the goat were taken to justify the satirical or polemical use of the genre. The correct spelling and derivation had become standard in classical dictionaries by the mid-sixteenth century, but the other form persisted in common usage and is defended by E.K. in the General Argument to *The Shepheardes Calender*. The oldest extant eclogues, the Greek idylls of Theocritus and his imitators, had been rediscovered early in the Renaissance; but although E.K. cites Theocritus in the Epistle to Harvey and in his glosses, Spenser probably had little firsthand acquaintance with the Greek pastoralists. Where he does appear to draw on their work, as in *March*, he was probably working from French or Neo-Latin translations.

Virgil's *Eclogues* furnished the supreme model for the eclogue. They had been read allegorically since classical times, and centuries of such readings had been incorporated into the glosses that often accompanied them. Typical Renaissance readings stressed the suffering of war described in the poems, the prince's patronage of the poet, and the messianic prophecy of Eclogue 4. The *Eclogues* emerged from all this as a work of deep social, political, and religious engagement. The series also contains an elegy on the death of Daphnis, taken to be a persona of Julius Caesar; the structure of this poem, in which the initial grief is transcended by rejoicing at Daphnis' new state in the heavens, was imitated by Spenser and by many other pastoral poets. The presence of death in the pastoral world perpetually counterbalances its tendency towards idealization.

Eclogues written after Virgil's drew heavily on all these aspects of his work, stressing particularly the elegiac and panegyric elements, and introducing a strongly polemic strain. The Virgilian singing match disappeared for some centuries and was replaced by the debate as a widespread eclogue form. *The Shepheardes Calender* contains all these forms: elegy in *November* and *December*, panegyric in *Aprill*, singing match in *August*, debate in *Maye* and *Julye*, polemic in the ecclesiastical eclogues. In the Middle Ages, allegory came to dominate the eclogue: when Petrarch wrote his *Bucolicum carmen* in the mid-fourteenth century, he could assert that the genre was so obscurely allusive as to be inexplicable without an authorial gloss. Many of Spenser's pastoral poems, including some of the *Shepheardes Calender* eclogues, *Colin Clout*, 'Astrophel,' and *Mother Hubberd*, are allusive, but not in this densely coded way. The moral patterns they set out always have a general significance of greater importance than any topical reference they may also contain.

Spenser could draw on Neo-Latin, French, and English models for his eclogues, as well as classical sources. Despite his concern to use native poetic traditions and subject matter, he adopted comparatively little from earlier English eclogues, though he continued their emphasis on social, political, and moral involvement, and on the state of the church. Alexander Barclay's five eclogues (c 1513, rpt 1570) were certainly known to Drayton and probably to Spenser; they include attacks on court and city life, and on the meanness of patrons (cf *Colin Clout*; *Mother Hubberd*; Meliboe's speech in *FQ* VI ix 22–5; *SC*, *Sept*, *Oct*). They are also the first eclogues to use an English setting; this technique is further developed by Spenser, though he never loses sight of the fact that the pastoral world is also the world of the imagination. Barclay is consistently moralistic, and occasionally also allusive; Puttenham's mid-century eclogue on Edward VI, now lost, may have carried allusion over into full-scale allegory (see *Arte* 3.13). Googe's *Eglogs* (1563) are also heavily allusive, with a strong anti-Catholic bias and a Puritan attitude toward love very different from the common inclination of pastoral. An increasing interest in the eclogue form in England in the later sixteenth century is suggested by these vernacular examples, along with English translations of Mantuan's eclogues by Turbervile (1567) and Virgil's *Eclogues* by Abraham Fleming (1575). A number of Anglo-Latin eclogues were also written at this period, again mostly allusive; the earliest examples, by Giles Fletcher, date from the 1560s. Sidney was writing pastoral in various forms, including eclogues, from the late 1570s. The increasing number of such works attests to a climate of interest that Spenser exploited in *The Shepheardes Calender* and that burgeoned in the later years of the century, partly as a result of his influence.

The two early Renaissance pastoral writers who influenced Spenser most extensively were Mantuan, in Latin, and Marot, in French. Mantuan's series of ten eclogues was at least as well known as Virgil's; he emphasizes the vision of the pastoral world as fallen, avoiding both idyllicism and, for most of the series, allegory. In the eclogues by Marot, or others ascribed to him, Spenser found models of high poetry, accounts of shepherd hardship, and the matching of the cycle of man's life with the cycle of the seasons. In writing *The Shepheardes Calender*, Spenser set out to follow the highest traditions of pastoral poetry, both classical and contemporary, and to prove that the English language could equal their achievements.

Romance, which after the eclogue is the most distinctive form taken by pastoral in the Renaissance, contributes less to Spenser's bucolic poetry. Pastoral romance itself has a history reaching back to the classical era; the late Greek *Daphnis and Chloe* of Longus was widely known in the Renaissance through Jacques Amyot's French translation and Angel Day's English version of the French (1587). The best-known continental Renaissance romances, Sannazaro's Italian *Arcadia* (pub 1504) and Montemayor's Spanish *Diana* (tr Bartholomew Yong, 1598), had little or no direct influence on Spenser, though Googe drew on Montemayor in his *Eglogs*; continental pastoral was too close to fantasy of the nymph-and-satyr variety to be adaptable to Spenser's concern with the real world. E.K. includes Sannazaro in his list of earlier eclogue writers, but he may have had in mind his piscatory eclogues rather than the *Arcadia*. Spenser does use a number of motifs from pastoral romance, but they tend to be so widely disseminated as to make the tracing of immediate sources impossible. The lost heiress brought up as a shepherdess is one such example, found in Longus and elsewhere, and in *FQ* VI ix and xii. Calidore's sojourn among the shepherds owes much to Tasso's *Gerusalemme liberata* 7, but the aristocrat's retreat to the shepherd world is a commonplace found also in Ariosto, Sannazaro, Montemayor, Sidney, and many other writers including Shakespeare. Colin's unrequited love for Rosalind in *The Shepheardes Calender* and *Colin Clout* probably also owes something to the romance tradition, though models could be found in eclogue and pastoral lyric as well. Virgil's *Eclogues* are as clear a source as the romance for defining one of the shepherd's roles as that of lover. The romance certainly encouraged the close association of pastoral with love – an association carried much further by other writers. Love in the romance, however, tends to follow courtly or Petrarchan conventions of suffering and long service; Spenser's portrayals of happy love, such as Calidore's for Pastorella or Colin's for the 'jolly Shepheards lasse' of *FQ* VI x 16, go back not to romance but to medieval traditions of pastoral (predominantly French but also known in England) that present love as joyous and fulfilled.

The interpretations of pastoral that developed during the Middle Ages contribute in many ways to Spenser's work, either directly or through intermediaries such as Mantuan, Marot, or commentaries on Virgil. The starting point for most medieval vernacular pastoral is the more or less realistic herdsman with all his responsibilities, sufferings, and hardships; this literalism in turn opens up new allegorical possibilities, though initially the shepherd may symbolize simply the common man. In a large number of works in English and other languages, the shepherd who cares for his flock is presented as the exemplar of the virtuous life, and thus as the figurative model for the good king or the good priest with his own metaphorical flock to keep. By contrast, the bad shepherd fleeces, starves, or slaughters his sheep; this image gives rise to a strong satiric tradition that links with ideas of the fallen world and, eventually, of the eclogue as 'goatish speech.' Biblical imagery of the Good Shepherd (see *Julye* 53), or even of sheep and goats, strongly influenced these developments of pastoral and is often explicitly cited. That Abel (127) and the Old Testament patriarchs (as Moses, 157) were shepherds, that shepherds were the first to hear the news of the Nativity (*HHL* 230), and that Christ called himself the Good Shepherd were taken as proofs of the close relationship between the shepherd and God; they were continually cited by pastoralists, including Spenser. The shepherd was taken as the type of the contemplative life as opposed to the active plowman; and this symbolism was combined with the metaphorical link between shepherd and priest, and with the fact that shepherds in their night vigils could watch the course of the heavens, to make the shepherd also the source of authoritative wisdom.

The notion that the shepherd could be the mouthpiece of instruction lies behind the work that gives *The Shepheardes Calender* its title. The *Shepherds' Kalendar*, based on the French *Compost et Kalendrier des Bergers*, was a kind of moral almanac loosely cast in the form of teaching by a master shepherd. Numerous editions were printed throughout the sixteenth century. The astronomical emphasis and didactic function of the *Kalendar* are picked up in the epilogue to *The Shepheardes Calender*: there Immeritô observes 'the starres revolution' and describes the function of his work as being 'To teach the ruder shepheard how to feede his sheepe.' The parallel Spenser draws in *The Shepheardes Calender* between the cycle of the seasons and the life of man also owes something to this work, as well as to Marot. The seasonal cycle, little stressed in classical eclogues, had been a recurrent theme of later pastoral since the eighth-century eclogue entitled *Conflictus veris et hiemis*, ascribed to Alcuin.

Spenser's first excursion into pastoral, *The Shepheardes Calender*, was an ambitious exercise that drew together most of the existing varieties of the mode. In the Epistle to Harvey, E.K. is at some pains to indicate how diverse these are, as he surveys the range of Spenser's subject matter from love to concerns of 'morall wisenesse,' runs through earlier great pastoralists from Theocritus to Marot and Sannazaro, and defends the rustic language and style on grounds of decorum. In the course of the eclogues themselves, Spenser exploits almost every aspect of the pastoral metaphor available to him: the shepherd as poet (especially in *Jan, Apr, June, Aug, Oct, Nov*, and *Dec*), as lover (*Jan, March, June, Aug*, and *Dec*), as priest (*Maye, Julye*, and *Sept*), as common man (most strikingly in *Feb*), and as sovereign (Eliza, daughter of '*Pan* the shepheards God,' in *Apr*; and Dido, 'the greate shepehearde his daughter,' in *Nov*). Although the eclogues are frequently allusive, Spenser breaks away from the straitjacket of allegory, so the poems are never limited to a single topical meaning. Some certainly contain such references, but they are more generally applicable in wider moral terms as well. It is this breadth of significance that enabled Milton to comment of *Maye* that Spenser wrote 'not without some presage of these reforming times' (*Animadversions ... against Smectymnuus* in ed 1953–82, 1:722).

Poetry is the single most important subject of the whole *Shepheardes Calender*, as is appropriate in a work acknowledged to signal the start of the golden age of Elizabethan literature. Spenser's choice of an eclogue series for his first excursion into poetry asserts his claim to be writing in the greatest classical and continental traditions; this emphasis is followed through in the detail of the work, partly in the discussions on poetry and the poet, partly in the way the *Calender* functions as a model of what English poetry can do. Accordingly, the homely singing match coexists with Colin's fine poems, celebration coexists with debate, beast fable with elegy, and the gaiety of *March* with the melancholy of *December*. The stylistic and generic range of the *Calender* is as great as its range of tone and theme.

After the *Calender*, Spenser's most fully pastoral poem is *Colin Clouts Come Home Againe*, which relates in pastoral terms a visit Spenser made to court from Ireland in 1589. The bulk of the poem consists of Colin's description of the court to a group of fellow shepherds and shepherdesses who know nothing about it. The poem abounds in allusions to contemporary court ladies, poets, and so on; but, like the *Calender*, it functions at a level beyond the topical. Spenser presents a double perspective on the court and country: the shepherds are innocent, but also ignorant; the court is corrupt, but can also be noble and courteous. Colin, the shepherd-singer whose songs can please both societies, alone has the experience to embrace both perspectives. Motifs of courtly corruption and of shepherds returning to the country are both traditional pastoral elements; so is the panegyric of the sovereign, here given the name Cynthia and herself portrayed as a shepherdess. Spenser extends his contrast of court and country to the questions of language and love. The court has the greater art, but it uses it as a substitute for truth; the country, with all its simplicity, can better preserve the true worship of Love. Spenser's handling of these paradoxes is a remarkable feat of poetic control. Cynthia and her followers remain untouched by the general corruption of the court, so Colin and his companions are united with her in a pastoral ideal of moral value which ignores distinctions of social rank.

A number of Spenser's other shorter poems contain pastoral elements. *Daphnaïda*, an elegy on the death of Lady Douglas Howard, is cast in the form of a shepherd's lament. 'Astrophel' is a pastoral elegy on Sidney, in which his death in the Low Countries is transformed into the shepherd Astrophel's death on a boar hunt. Astrophel, like Colin, is a shepherd-poet. The narrative element in the poem distinguishes it from the classic structure of pastoral elegy; the inset 'Lay of Clorinda,' in which his sister (herself described as a shepherdess) passes from lamenting at his death to rejoicing at his immortality, conforms much more closely to the conventional pattern which Spenser had used in *November*. Lodowick Bryskett's 'Aeglogue upon Sidney,' published in the same collection as 'Astrophel,' also conforms to this traditional structure.

Mother Hubberds Tale in *Complaints* is at a far remove from classical pastoral, but it nonetheless works within the Elizabethan definition. There is no shepherd framework, but it does fall within the aspect of pastoral Sidney describes in the *Defence of Poetry* as 'pretty tales of wolves and sheep' used for moral or allegorical ends. The inset fable of *Maye* and the first part of *Daphnaïda* are further examples of Spenser's use of pastoral beast fables. *Mother Hubberd* starts by establishing its setting firmly as *not* being in the Golden Age: it is an antitype of idyllic pastoral, as much of *The Shepheardes Calender* is. The various exploits of the Fox and the Ape as shepherd, pastor, and prince are finally judged, as in medieval vernacular pastoral, by the standard of the welfare of the sheep.

Recent criticism has tended to extend the meaning of pastoral to include any description of the beauty and harmony of the natural world. Since such themes are favorites with Spenser, this definition extends the possibilities of finding pastoral elements in other poems. There is no evidence that he would have thought of such themes as constituting pastoral in themselves, but they had long been associated with the mode, not least through its connection with ideas of the Golden Age. Spenser often treats the natural world mythopoeically, for instance in the marriage of Thames and Medway in *FQ* IV xi. This episode probably incorporates material from his earlier *Epithalamium Thamesis*, which is no longer extant as a separate poem. The *Cantos of Mutabilitie* are closely concerned with the same themes, *Epithalamion* and *Prothalamion* use them extensively, and they appear intermittently in other poems. *The Shepheardes Calender* itself tends to lay more stress on man's *dis*harmony with the natural world, or his harmony with its least pleasant aspects: cold and winter are associated with age and death, for instance. *The Faerie Queene* contains several idyllic landscapes, which often function as symbolic centers of the books in which they occur: the Garden of Adonis and the fully pastoral Mount Acidale are the most striking.

Spenser's treatment of the pastoral mode reaches its highest point in Calidore's sojourn among the shepherds in *FQ* VI ix-xii. Recent critical uncertainty over whether this episode is morally good or bad reflects a degree of ambivalence in the poem itself (see, eg, Hamilton in *FQ* ed 1977:623), but Spenser does make it quite clear that the shepherd world itself is a moral positive. Shepherd society here has all the innocence and joy long associated with it. The Blatant Beast of slander has never been heard of in this place of revels and dancing, where Calidore and Pastorella achieve for a while one of the poem's happiest love relationships. More importantly, and paradoxically, the shepherd world functions as the emblematic center of the Legend of Courtesy, the place where, for all the etymological and other associations of courtesy with the court, the values of courtesy receive their fullest expression. Here they grow naturally, without the threat of artificial perversion described in the court of *Colin Clout*.

Spenser does not set up the countryside as an absolute ideal, however. The loveliest of the shepherdesses is Pastorella; like Perdita in *The Winter's Tale*, she may belong to the pastoral world by nurture, but she is really of high birth. Similarly, the real shepherds cannot compete with Calidore, and Coridon is dismissed as being merely 'Fit to keepe sheepe' (VI x 37). The shepherds are finally destroyed by Brigands in one of the poem's most outrageous upsets of the moral order. The good often suffer, but elsewhere they normally finish up with a just reward; here, however, the shepherd world is left irrecoverably desolate. Their paradise is vulnerable to the onslaughts of evil just as Eden had been; and the only way that virtue can reassert itself in the fallen world, Spenser seems to suggest, is not through pastoral innocence but through the more active virtues of the heroic life.

Inset in the shepherd episode is Calidore's meeting with Colin Clout on Mount Acidale. It is only right that, as an encyclopedia of all human thought and action, *The Faerie Queene* should contain something on the nature of poetry and the poet, and Spenser finds in the pastoral mode the best way of giving to this topic the finest symbolic expression and his most searching definition. Even more than in *The Shepheardes Calender*, Colin here stands not only for Spenser himself but for any true poet. The idyllic setting and the dance of the Graces stress the sublimity of poetic inspiration, but Spenser is ready even here to call on homelier traditions, too. Thus, the instrument Colin plays is the rustic bagpipe; the lady in the center of the dance, whatever high symbolic resonance she possesses as the '*Idea* or fore-conceit' of his poetry (in Sidney's phrase) or as his model and inspiration, is also simply the shepherd's true love.

The relationship between this episode and the larger account of the shepherds helps to define Spenser's attitude to the pastoral mode. 'Real' shepherds, even with all the qualifications given to the term by their appearance in a moral allegory, are finally no more than sheep-herders. One has to move inwards, to the idyllic place within the beautiful landscape, to find the true heart of pastoral, which is concerned with love, poetry, and the imagination.

There are few pastoral themes in Spenser's works that are not derived from earlier writers. What makes him central to any study of pastoral literature, and what makes a study of his use of pastoral crucial to understanding his poetry, is the way he draws together all the multiplicity of earlier themes and interpretations to give the mode a new and unique importance. Some of his experiments, such as the use of rustic language in *The Shepheardes Calender*, were received by his contemporaries with caution. His language was imitated in George Peele's *Eglogue Gratulatorie*, a panegyric on the Earl of Essex; in an unpublished eclogue probably by Christopher Morley, Fellow of Trinity College, Cambridge (Bodleian Library, Ms Eng misc d.239; see Sukanta Chaudhuri 1988); and in some of the eclogues in Francis Davison's *Poetical Rhapsody*. Drayton, on the other hand, first wrote his own eclogue series, *Idea: The Shepheards Garland*, in a comparable style, but then revised it in the direction of standard English, as *Pastorals*. Poets who did not follow Spenser's linguistic example nevertheless followed him in other ways, from minor figures such as Thomas Blenerhasset, Richard Barnfield, and John Lane, to major poets such as Milton. By the early seventeenth century, the Italianate pastoral of nymphs and highly unrealistic shepherds was becoming increasingly popular in England, and pastorals came to have less and less connection with the real world; this interpretation eventually dominated the mode after the Restoration. Spenser's understanding of pastoral, however, was a stronger influence on the writings of Drayton, George Wither, Phineas Fletcher, William Basse, Thomas Randolph, Francis Quarles, and others; and his example is clearly perceptible in Milton's *Lycidas*. No other writer, however, realized so fully as Spenser the potential of pastoral to represent at once the fallen world, man's highest ideals, and the nature of poetry.

HELEN COOPER

Sukanta Chaudhuri 1988 'Marlowe, Madrigals, and a New Elizabethan Poet' *RES* 39:199–216; H. Cooper 1977; Cullen 1970; Levin 1969; Marinelli 1971; Annabel Patterson 1987 *Pastoral and Ideology: Virgil to Valéry* (Berkeley and Los Angeles); Poggioli 1975; Tayler 1964; Harold E. Toliver 1971 *Pastoral Forms and Attitudes* (Berkeley and Los Angeles); Tonkin 1972.

Pastorella While pursuing the Blatant Beast, Calidore arrives in the country of the shepherds. There he instantly falls in love with Pastorella, who is seated on a hillock, wearing a crown of flowers, and 'Environ'd with a girland, goodly graced, / Of lovely lasses.' Beneath her, shepherds sing her praises and pine for her as their sovereign mistress (*FQ* VI ix 4–12). The tableau looks back to a similar one in *The Shepheardes Calender*, in Colin's song honoring Eliza, 'Queene of shepheardes all' (*Aprill* 34). It also recalls the image of lords and ladies at Elizabeth's court forming a ring around their Queen (*FQ* VI proem 7), and it foreshadows the dance of the naked damsels around Colin's nameless lass on Mount Acidale (x 10–18).

No other Spenserian character sums up the dualities of the pastoral mode as neatly as does Pastorella. She is rustic and courtly, naive and sophisticated, humble and aristocratic, lass and queen. Her name insists on her rusticity, meaning in Italian 'a shepheardesse, a young prettie countrie wench keeping sheep,' according to John Florio's dictionary, *A Worlde of Wordes* (1598). At the same time, to an English ear the name suggests pastoral artifice, a connotation which reinforces her aloofness from the admirers around her: 'Though meane her lot, yet higher did her mind ascend' (ix 10). Even her birth sets her apart from the others, since she is a foundling, 'as old stories tell,' hinting at more than ordinary origins. Yet she herself regards Meliboe, the shepherd who discovered her abandoned in a field, as her father. To Calidore, Pastorella also seems beyond 'the meane of shepheards' and worthy 'To be a Princes Paragone esteemed.' In the midst of these reflections, he is 'unwares surprisd in subtile bands / Of the blynd boy,' Cupid.

In light of the ensuing courtship, Pastorella's name may well also allude to the pastourelle, a poetic genre of OF origin (Provençal *pastorela*, Ital *pastorella*) that describes a love affair generally between a knight and a shepherdess, emphasizing the social and intellectual disparities between them, often with critical or satirical intent (H. Cooper 1977:164). Yet Pastorella certainly lacks some of the characteristics of the typical pastourelle heroine: we never once hear her speak, often she is merely present while men fight over her, and rarely do we get a sense of what she thinks or feels. The country maid of the pastourelle, on the contrary, tends to have a definite character and viewpoint for which she argues, usually in a set debate, with her suitor, whose courtly pretensions she at times wittily exposes. Still, there are moments when Pastorella, displaying an unpredictable will of her own, fits the pastourelle pattern. Knowing herself destined for higher things than the bumpkins who adore her, she is nonetheless unreceptive to Calidore's courtship. 'His layes, his loves, his lookes' fill her with disdain; and she spurns his 'courtesies' in favor of Colin Clout's songs because she 'Had ever learn'd to love the lowly things.' Only when Calidore doffs his suit of armor and puts on 'shepheards weed' does he begin to win her (34–6).

At this point, it becomes difficult if not impossible to disentangle Pastorella's motives. Does Calidore's change of dress demonstrate to her that he too has 'learn'd to love the lowly things,' or only that he knows how to adapt himself to circumstances? Whatever the answer, she is no down-to-earth country lass doing combat with a courtly sophisticate, but a woman with an evident sense of the complexities and contradictions of life. If she does not belong in the pastourelle, neither does she fit into the mold of the romance heroine, though her story certainly shares many outward features with a character like Fawnia in Robert Greene's *Pandosto* (1588), the prototype of Perdita in Shakespeare's *Winter's Tale*. Both are exposed as infants by aristocratic or royal parents, both grow up ignorant of their origins in a society of shepherds, both are wooed by an aristocratic or royal suitor disguised as a shepherd, and both are eventually reunited with their true parents. What sets Pastorella apart from Fawnia and her romance sisters, and from her shepherd society, is an enigmatic ambiguity of character far removed from their spontaneity and openhearted nature.

Romance, according to Frye, is 'the mythos of summer' (1957:186). According to the same scheme, 'the mythos of winter' finds its literary expression in irony which parodies romance patterns (p 223). Both these archetypes seem applicable to Pastorella, whose imprisonment in the Brigands' cave (VI x 39ff) has often been regarded as a parallel to the descent into the underworld of the classical vegetation goddess Persephone-Proserpina. Like Proserpina, Pastorella is a figure of both summer and winter, but in such a way that, as with most of the narrative of Book VI, we can never be quite sure whether we are dealing with the summer world of 'pure' romance or its wintry, ironic parody. (The same ambiguity applies to Shakespeare's redaction of Greene's romance, significantly entitled 'the *winter's* tale.')

Pastorella's story has powerful elements of the 'wish-fulfilment dream' of romance (Frye 1957:186). Her rescue from the cave by Calidore (xi 43–50) has been described as a 'resurrection,' portending a rebirth of society and a promise of universal redemption (Tonkin 1972:312ff). Yet, although the Brigands' massacre of the shepherds is probably not to be lamented (their society seems as doomed from the start as the sheepfold left unfinished at the end of Wordsworth's *Michael*), Pastorella's 'redemptive' role is counterbalanced by the many unanswered questions with which her story concludes, not to mention the atmosphere of irony and even anxiety that characterizes the ending of Book VI.

A major question left unresolved by the end of the book concerns Pastorella's role in relation to Calidore's quest. Whether she is to be seen as the cause of his 'truancy' among the shepherds, or the inspiration for his final if temporary defeat of the Blatant Beast, their love does not lead to an epithalamic conclusion, like that of Redcrosse and Una, but comes to an end at Castle Belgard, when Calidore decides to resume his original quest (xii 13).

Another unresolved question concerns Pastorella's identity, which Spenser presents with deliberate mystification. When the old nurse recognizes her by her birthmark, a 'litle purple rose' (18) which was the inspiration for her original name, the reader is still left to guess what that name might be: probably Rose or some variant, most likely (in view of Spenser's use of the name elsewhere) Rosalind. The riddle of her name seems designed to arouse curiosity about her 'real' identity, and the story of her parentage surely serves the same purpose. Her parents, Bellamour and Claribell, marry secretly because Claribell's father, the 'Lord of *Many Ilands*,' wants to marry her to 'the Prince of *Picteland* bordering nere' (4). This precise geographical reference (Picteland = Scotland) in the context of dynastic politics has led readers since Upton to look for identifiable historical personages and events lurking behind the romantic narrative (see *Var* 6:262–4).

If her parents are part of an historical allegory, then Pastorella-'Rosalind' surely is, too. Since the Tudor rose was one of Elizabeth's emblems, she could well be another of those incarnations of the Queen so ubiquitous in Spenser's poetry. In that case, Bellamour and Claribell would be a highly idealized version of Elizabeth's parents, Henry VIII and Anne Boleyn, whose eventual marriage in defiance of papal interdict is here presented as the triumph of true love over parental tyranny. (At the same time, the 'Lord of *Many Ilands*' could, by the flexible logic and economy of poetry, allude to the more familiar Henry VIII, capable of treating his wives, including Anne Boleyn, with the brutality of a primitive despot.)

Pastorella, then, could well be Spenser's final tribute in *The Faerie Queene* to the Queen who served him as inspiration throughout his poetic career, from the ingenuous vision of *Aprill* to the increasing complexities of his heroic poem. If this identification is accepted, the Elizabeth we see in Pastorella is largely the emblematic, even hieratic, Muse and Petrarchan Queen rather than the active ruler of her people. Like Elizabeth, Pastorella knows something of the art of survival, as in her subterfuges with the Brigand captain, who woos her while she is his captive (xi 6–7). For the most part, however, she is a passive, even impassive bystander; and when the Brigands overwhelm the shepherd society over which she presided in Petrarchan fashion, she nearly perishes with it.

There may be an implied judgment of the Queen here, and of her inability or unwillingness to control what is happening in her society; though against hellish forces like the Brigands in league with the Merchants, any civilized order is likely to prove fragile. More plausibly, in Pastorella the poet is weighing his own (not necessarily past) ideals and aspirations. She harks back to the pseudo-naive ceremonial world of *The Shepheardes Calender*, but also to a more distant ancestor, the beautiful young woman who presides over the Earthly Paradise at the summit of the mount of Purgatory (Dante *Purgatory* 28). Dante the pilgrim's highly erotic encounter with her has been taken to recall the traditional pastourelle; and she reminds the pilgrim-poet of Proserpina at the time she was carried off to the underworld. Lastly, Matelda and the Earthly Paradise figure in Dante's historical and political allegory as the possibility of a perfect social order on earth. The pastoral interlude of *FQ* VI, in which Pastorella is not quite the center (she is, after all, excluded from the dance on Mount Acidale) would seem to be Spenser's comparable 'purgatorial' vision of what Elizabethan society might have been and what, Proserpina fashion, it may descend to. Or does her name of the Rose perhaps still hold a Dantean promise? RICHARD T. NEUSE

Blitch 1973; Cheney 1966; H. Cooper 1977; Evans 1970; Joan M. Ferrante 1984 *The Political Vision of the 'Divine Comedy'* (Princeton);

Hamilton 1961a; W.T.H. Jackson 1952 'The Medieval Pastourelle as a Satirical Genre' *PQ* 31:156–70; Poggioli 1975; Tonkin 1972.

Patience Traditionally, patience is that virtue which enables one to endure adversity. Rather than being conquered by external evils, the patient man, through his self-restraint (see Luke 21.19) – his inner harmony, self-control, and long-suffering – conquers his environment. Although outwardly the patient man appears passive, his patience is 'the truest fortitude' (Milton *Samson Agonistes* 654): 'he that ruleth his owne minde, is better then he that winneth a citie' (Prov 16.32).

The inner harmony of patience indicates a reciprocal relation between God and man. God both tests by tribulation and instills grace to meet the test; the patient man believes in God's support and love even as he loves his tormenting enemy. These mutual relations explain why patience must have its 'perfite worke, that ye may be perfite and entier, lacking nothing' (James 1.4), and why patient self-restraint is important throughout *The Faerie Queene*: Spenser follows tradition in associating this virtue very closely with constancy, moderation, and temperance (cf 2 Pet 1.5–7).

Spenser typically opposes the virtue of patience to two vices: 'Patience perforce; helpelesse what may it boot / To fret for anger, or for griefe to mone?' (*FQ* II iii 3). This opposition – to anger, fury, ire, and wrath, or to sadness, grief, 'teene,' and despair – recurs throughout the poem. Correspondingly, Spenser defines 'impatience' both as the inability to endure grief (v 16) and as the inability to repress anger (21). He inherits these oppositions from the late medieval septenary tradition (see Tuve 1966, ch 2). In this instructional pattern, the seven virtues are viewed explicitly as 'remedial,' as if they were drugs or a medical regimen to cure the sickness of the seven sins. To use the technical medieval language, the virtues extirpate the vices (cf *FQ* I x 25); penance, the sacrament of Christian renewal, provides spiritual medicine by which specific virtues enter the vacuum left by those vices they expel.

Within the septenary, patience routinely is the virtue which cures wrath and acedia. Wrath, the vice of the malicious persecutor, is in some respects a natural enemy of a patience which endures adversity: the 'soft answer' of the patient man 'putteth away wrath' (Prov 15.1), and his forgiving love conquers the occasion of anger. In contrast, acedia is opposed to patience, not because it is an unrestrained and overaggressive lack of self-control, but because this vice cannot endure hardship. (Since Cicero' s *De inventione*, patience had been considered a 'part' of the virtue fortitude.) Slothful behavior in *The Faerie Queene* typically takes the forms either of loose inanition resulting from lust or of despairing horror at the enormity of one's sins and at the apparent impossibility of atoning for them. In Book II especially, patience seems almost synonymous with temperance as that mental state opposed to the excesses of violence and despair represented by Mortdant and Amavia.

The only appearance of personified patience occurs in Book I x 21–52. As one might expect from the remedial context of the septenary, Patience is introduced in a context explicitly penitential and in the role of a wise physician. He comes to rouse the Red Cross Knight from his despair and to cure him both of his 'disease of grieved conscience' and of his fleshly earthiness.

Redcrosse has fallen in deserting Una, his true faith; wandering apart from her – 'Will was his guide, and griefe led him astray' (ii 12) – he eventually falls victim to Orgoglio, his pride in his own fleshly strength. His appalling consciousness of his fall produces despair, the 'sinfull horror' of a 'wounded hart' (x 23). The knight's sense of failure is extreme: he fears that he is utterly repugnant to God and thoroughly incapable of satisfying him.

Patience's leechcraft has essentially two stages – a soft verbal treatment succeeded by hard 'corrosives.' In the first stage Patience offers, in effect, good counsel: he encourages Redcrosse to tell his grief (ie, to confess) and comforts him. In this process, he fosters a patient equanimity, the ability to endure pain. However, this stage only prepares for a harsher healing – in this case of original sin, the bloated and prideful propensities of Redcrosse's flesh.

In this second healing, Redcrosse must confront directly the very nature of his enormity. The 'sad house of *Penaunce*' (x 32), the scene of his mortification, recalls in its dark lowness both Orgoglio's dungeon and Despair's cave; but this recapitulation of past action is constructive. Although Redcrosse behaves like a lion (28), he is no longer an aggressive and demonic 'roaring lyon' (1 Pet 5.8; *FQ* I iii 7) but one who roars because he voluntarily subjects his own flesh to mortifying pain. His roaring and the medical tearing of corrupted sin out of his flesh are mirrored in Una's rending of her garment, an act Spenser identifies as bearing all 'with patience.'

In the house of Penance, the language of Redcrosse's mortification signals a new movement in the poem. Although under Patience's direction he endures those violent physical rigors associated in medieval writings with the works of satisfaction, Spenser's language conveys a renewed and proper sadness, a true contrition. Remorse's nip represents the softening of Redcrosse's heart, the atonement for his past sins, and his openness to divine correction; Repentance's salt water represents Redcrosse's own tears and his hope never to sin again. The allegory is internal and psychological: for the first time in the poem, he appears patient, at peace within and properly directed toward God. At the end of the epidode, he is prepared 'Himselfe to chearish' (x 29) and is ready to meet Charissa, proper Christian love personified. RALPH HANNA, III

Alpers 1967b:37–8, 49–54; Auerbach ed 1965:67–81; Chew 1962:116–22; Crampton 1974:33–44, 118–30, 145–8; John F. Danby 1949 *Shakespeare's Doctrine of Nature: A Study of 'King Lear'* (London); Danby 1952 *Poets on Fortune's Hill: Studies in Sidney, Shakespeare, Beaumont and Fletcher* (London) pp 108–27; William O. Harris 1963 'Despair and "Patience as the Truest Fortitude" in *Samson Agonistes*' *ELH* 30:107–20; Harris 1965; William S. Heckscher 1970–1 'Shakespeare in His Relationship to the Visual Arts: A Study in Paradox' *RORD* 13–14:5–71; J[ohannes] H.L. Kengen, ed 1979 *Memoriale credencium: A Late Middle English Manual of Theology for Lay People* (Nijmegen) pp 89–100, 122–9, 181–97; Mary Ann Radzinowicz 1978 *Toward 'Samson Agonistes': The Growth of a Poet's Mind* (Princeton) pp 227–43; Gerald T. Schiffhorst, ed 1978 *The Triumph of Patience: Medieval and Renaissance Studies* (Orlando, Fla); Lorraine Kochanske Stock 1975 'The Thematic and Structural Unity of *Mankind*' *SP* 72:386–407; Tuve 1966:57–143.

patronage During Elizabeth's reign, patronage – 'the action of a patron in supporting, encouraging, or countenancing a person, institution, work, art, etc' (*OED*) – was a social institution of the first importance. As an instrument of the crown, it was a major force in transforming the great nobles and gentry from independently powerful local magnates into courtiers dependent upon the monarch. Like a vast web, the system extended from the Queen to her ministers and favorites (chiefly Burghley, Leicester, and Essex). Through their patronage, the nobles and gentry gained offices at court, in the Queen's household, in the government at Westminster or in Wales or Ireland, and in the church, army, or universities, as well as titles, grants of land, pensions, wardships, leases in the royal lands, fee-farming of commodities, and the like. In their turn, the recipients of such favors could dispense lesser offices and benefits to their petitioners. Literary patronage was part of this interlocking system whereby grants, offices, and honors were exchanged for loyalty, service, and praise.

Except for a few dramatists associated with the major theater companies, Elizabethan writers took up careers as courtiers, statesmen, civil servants, teachers, and divines. Writing as such was not a professional option: there were few readers and publishers of books, and poetry was commonly regarded as a social and courtly pastime. Writers like Sidney and Donne circulated their verses among coteries of friends, though Spenser broke this pattern by publishing his poems as serious works, doctrinal to a nation. However presented, poems were normally offered as gifts to actual or prospective patrons, with lavish hyperbole and high-flown rhetoric.

Literary patronage took various forms. A few Renaissance patrons and patronesses were well-educated humanists motivated by genuine literary interests; others sought chiefly to enhance their status through the service and the lavish praise of many clients. Writers might be educated as pages in noble families (eg, Drayton), or they might serve such households as secretaries, clerks, or tutors (eg, Daniel). Even the theater companies, which played to the public and were at least partly self-supporting, sought protection from and bore the names of noble patrons: the Lord Chamberlain's men, the Lord Admiral's men. Sometimes patronage extended beyond financial support: several writers and scholars (Spenser among them) enjoyed long- or short-term hospitality and literary exchange in the Sidney household at Penshurst or with the Herbert family at Wilton.

Spenser's career was advanced by several patrons. It began promisingly with a post as secretary to the Bishop of Rochester, Dr John Young, honored in *The Shepheardes Calender* as Roffy, the mild, wise, conscientious prelate. In 1579, Spenser was in London in the service of Leicester, leader of the Protestant court faction, whose bounty and 'goodnes' he acknowledged in 1591 in *Ruines of Time* (183–238). In 1580, however, his hoped-for advancement at court was blocked, in large part because his *Mother Hubberds Tale* satirized Burghley and the Queen's proposed French marriage, and he was forced to make his subsequent career in Ireland. After serving as secretary to the Lord Lieutenant, Lord Grey of Wilton, he gained through Grey's patronage several minor offices and leases of property which established him as a member of the landed gentry. Later, he made a bid for the patronage of Essex, who may have been instrumental in his appointment as Sheriff of Cork in 1598, and may have aided him when an Irish uprising destroyed his estate that year. That catastrophe, together with his continued failure to win office or reward in England, probably explains Phineas Fletcher's too-bleak summary of his fortune: 'all his hopes were crost, all suits deni'd ... Poorly (poore man) he liv'd; poorly (poore man) he di'd' (*Purple Island* 1633, 1.19). Essex stood the charge of Spenser's burial in Westminster Abbey.

Sidney's patronage was of special importance to Spenser's development as poet. In 1579, Spenser was part of the Sidney circle which included Sidney and his sister Mary, Countess of Pembroke, Dyer, Greville, and Raleigh; in addition to some financial assistance, they provided fellowship, encouragement, and aid in winning poetic recognition. Dedicating his anonymous *Shepheardes Calender* to Sidney, Spenser praises him as 'president / Of noblesse and of chevalree'; and Sidney honors the *Calender* in his *Defence of Poetry* as one of the very few English poems having 'poetical sinews in them' (ed 1973b:112). In 'Astrophel,' Spenser sings Sidney's funeral elegy; he exalts the dead Sidney above all living poet-shepherds in *Colin Clouts Come Home Againe*; and in the epistle to *Ruines of Time*, he refers to Sidney as 'the Patron of my young *Muses*,' extolling his poetic gifts, valor, and goodness. That epistle also praises the Countess of Pembroke as the repository of her brother's virtues and poetic gifts, and as one to whom he is 'bounden, by manie singular favours and great graces.' *Colin Clout* honors the Countess as Urania, greatest of Cynthia's nymphs, and also allegorizes Raleigh as the Shepherd of the Ocean, who visited Spenser in Ireland, enticed him to return to court, and aroused Elizabeth's interest in his *Faerie Queene*. That poem is dedicated to Raleigh for his 'singular favours and sundrie good turnes' – among them, two encomiastic commendatory sonnets.

Spenser made several general bids for patronage and favor, notably in the seventeen Dedicatory Sonnets appended to *The Faerie Queene*. Some of these honor major patrons: Lord Grey, 'the pillor of my life, / And Patrone of my Muses pupillage,' the Countess of Pembroke, and Raleigh. Others recognize specific relationships: Sir John Norris, Lord President of Munster, under whom Spenser served in Ireland; Thomas Butler, Earl of Ormond, whose 'brave mansione' Spenser found to be an oasis of learning and culture in Ireland; and his kinswoman Elizabeth, Lady Carey. Others are bows drawn at a venture, addressing the primary dispensers of patronage at court: Essex; Sir Christopher Hatton, Lord Chancellor; Lord Hunsdon, Lord Chamberlain; and Sir Francis Walsingham, Elizabeth's principal secretary, 'the great *Mecenas* of this age.' One sonnet attempts to placate the powerful Lord Treasurer, Burghley; others address the Earls of Cumberland and Northumberland (George Clifford and Henry Percy), the Lord Admiral, Charles Howard, and those noble poets and patrons of poets Edward de Vere, Earl of Oxford, and Thomas Sackville, Lord Buckhurst – all without apparent result. The final sonnet is an omnibus compliment 'To all the gratious and beautifull Ladies in the Court' (see **FQ*, commendatory verses and dedicatory sonnets).

In *Colin Clout*, Spenser draws encomiastic portraits of several court ladies, some of them his acknowledged patronesses. Pride of place is given to the Countess of Pembroke (Urania), and after her to the Russell sisters, Anne Dudley and Margaret Clifford, Countesses of Warwick and Cumberland (Theana and Marian). Spenser dedicated his *Fowre Hymnes* (1596) to them in gratitude for their 'great graces and honourable favours' shown to him 'dayly.' Favors in Ireland are acknowledged in the portraits of Galathea (probably Frances Howard, Countess of Kildare) and Neaera (Elizabeth Sheffield, Countess of Ormond). The compliment to 'Stella' refers here (as in the dedication to *Astrophel*) to Sidney's widow, Frances, now Countess of Essex, not to Penelope Rich; the gesture supports Spenser's earlier bid for Essex's patronage in the *Faerie Queene* sonnet and in *Prothalamion* (1591). The three Spencer sisters of Althorp receive an extended tribute, reiterating claims of kinship advanced in earlier dedications, and alluding to patronage received. Elizabeth, Lady Carey, dedicatee of *Muiopotmos* (1590), is Phyllis; Anne, now wife of Robert Sackville, dedicatee of *Mother Hubberd* (1591), is 'bountifull Charillis'; and Alice, Countess of Derby, is Amaryllis. Spenser had earlier addressed *Teares of the Muses* (1591) to Alice, expressing gratitude for 'particular bounties' and explicitly defining the mutual benefits of patronage and dedication: 'by honouring you they might know me, and by knowing me they might honor you.'

Finally, there is Queen Elizabeth, whom Spenser praised in poem after poem, and to whom he inscribed his *Faerie Queene* with a fine flourish: 'To the most high, mightie and magnificent empresse renowmed for pietie, vertue, and all gratious government' (see ed 1912:2). Spenser's admiration for Elizabeth was clearly genuine, but he also expected recompense from her, which he received after considerable delay in February 1591 in the form of a pension of £50. His delight is registered in the fulsome description of Cynthia's bounty to Colin Clout: 'For everie gift and everie goodly meed, / Which she on me bestowd, demaunds a day ... it duly to display' (*CCCHA* 592–5).

In its mundane aspect, literary patronage is an exchange of financial support for dedicatory praise. But major Elizabethan poets and patrons sometimes imagined and gave literary embodiment to its ideal form – a tribute to the highest virtue and a stimulus to the noblest art. Sidney articulates this ideal from the patron's perspective in the *Old Arcadia*: 'nothing lifted [the pastoral exercises] up to so high a key as the presence of their own duke who, not only by looking on but by great courtesy and liberality, animated the shepherds the more exquisitely to seek a worthy accomplishment of his good liking' (ed 1973a:56). Spenser exemplifies the ideal from the poet's side by creating transcendent versions of his greatest patrons in his poems. Lord Grey is shadowed as Artegall, knight of Justice, and his experiences in Ireland provide the substance for some of the historical allegory in *FQ* v. Sidney is the subject of *Astrophel*, and a primary model for Calidore, knight of Courtesy, in *FQ* VI. Elizabeth is celebrated as Eliza, royal shepherdess, in the *Aprill* eclogue of *The Shepheardes Calender*; she is Cynthia, Queen of shepherds and nymphs, in *Colin Clout*; and she is the symbolic center of *The Faerie Queene*, shadowed as Britomart, Belphoebe, Mercilla, and of course Gloriana. In Spenser's great epic, Fairyland is coextensive with, and an ideal form of, the England of Elizabeth.

BARBARA KIEFER LEWALSKI

SPENSER'S PATRONS Thomas Butler, Earl of Ormond and Ossory; Robert Devereux, Earl of Essex; Robert Dudley, Earl of Leicester; Sir Edward Dyer; Arthur, Lord Grey of Wilton, Lord Lieutenant of Ireland; Sir John Norris, Lord President of Munster; Sir Walter Raleigh; Sir Philip Sidney; Dr John Young, Bishop of Rochester.

SPENSER'S PATRONESSES Queen Elizabeth; Elizabeth (Sheffield) Butler, Countess of Ormond and Ossory; Elizabeth (Spencer), Lady Carey; Margaret (Russell) Clifford, Countess of Cumberland; Anne (Russell) Dudley, Countess of Warwick; Frances (Howard) Fitzgerald, Countess of Kildare; Mary (Sidney) Herbert, Countess of Pembroke; Anne (Spencer) Sackville, Lady Compton and Mountegle; Alice (Spencer) Stanley, Lady Strange, Countess of Derby.

Bradbrook 1960; Helgerson 1978; Helgerson

1979; Judson 1945; Lytle and Orgel 1981; W.T. MacCaffrey 1961; Conyers Read 1955 *Mr Secretary Cecil and Queen Elizabeth* (New York); Read 1960 *Lord Burghley and Queen Elizabeth* (London); Rosenberg 1955; Rowse 1971; Phoebe Sheavyn 1909 *The Literary Profession in the Elizabethan Age*, rev J.W. Saunders 1967 (Manchester); Stone 1965; Patricia Thomson 1952 'The Literature of Patronage, 1580–1630' *EIC* 2:267–84; F.B. Williams 1962.

Paynims An archaic form of *pagan*, used in the fourteenth century as either a noun or an adjective for 'heathen' or 'non-Christian.' Spenser uses it specifically to designate a Saracen knight emblematic of some wicked vice. The association of Paynim with Saracen is very old. In the Middle Ages, the nomads of the Arabian desert were thought to have descended from Abraham's wife Sarah, whence *Sara-cen*. The more they harassed the eastern borders of the Roman Empire, the more they acquired the reputation of being enemies of God and man. After their wholesale conversion to Islam in the seventh century, and especially after the Crusades began in 1096, they came to represent non-Christian belief, which for a Christian is no belief at all; like Sansfoy (without faith), they were thus 'infidels' opposed to the triumphant spread of the Christian faith. One of Spenser's Bead-men ransoms prisoners from Turks and Saracens (*FQ* I x 40), whose special curse is 'by *Termagaunt*,' the thrice-powerful Saracen God (II viii 30).

In an invocation to the Muse before Redcrosse's fight with the Dragon, the narrator requests a deferment of 'that mighty rage,' the 'dreadfull trompe' associated with martial epic, until he depicts another battle 'Twixt that great faery Queene and Paynim king' (I xi 6–7). The lines suggest that Spenser had planned such a battle as the climax of his completed epic of 12 (or 24) books. Redcrosse's conversation with Una's father in canto xii bears out the suggestion, for he says he is bound to serve the Fairy Queen 'six yeares in warlike wize, / Gainst that proud Paynim king' (18). In *FQ* II, Archimago warns Pyrochles and Cymochles about the approach of Arthur 'That hath to Paynim knights wrought great distresse, / And thousand Sar'zins foully donne to dye' (viii 18). In *FQ* III, Merlin reveals to Britomart that she will bring Artegall back to Britain 'to aide his countrey, to withstand / The powre of forrein Paynims' (iii 27; here, Paynims are Saxons; cf Octa and Oza, 52). Spenser may, therefore, have conceived of the poem's completed structure as Renaissance commentators conceived of the *Aeneid*'s. Its first half (either 6 or 12 books) would depict a series of allegorical wanderings in preparation for its second half (the remaining 6 or 12 books) that would stage a heroic conflict between Christian knights and Paynim King.

Despite, or perhaps because of, such a role for Paynims in the latter part of the poem's grand design, opponents specifically cited as Paynims in the existing books are few in number and inconsistent in designation. The brothers Sansfoy, Sansjoy, and Sansloy in I ii-vi are everywhere called 'Paynims.' In *FQ* II, however, Pyrochles and Cymochles, sons of Acrates and Despight, appear first as general figures for the concupiscible and irascible passions in cantos v and vi; only later, when they threaten to despoil Guyon who has fainted after his three-day visit to the house of Mammon and Arthur's intervention is required, do they gain specifically pagan identities as 'Two Paynim knights, all armd as bright as skie' (viii 10). In Book VI, Bruncheval is called a Paynim knight (iv 17).

In *FQ* V, Artegall encounters several Paynims. The first is Pollente (ii 13), who guards a bridge and extracts from travelers an unjust toll that he remits to his daughter Munera (bribery). The others are the Souldan, his wicked wife Adicia (injustice), and knights in their service, who mistreat Mercilla's messenger, Samient. After Artegall and Arthur rescue Samient from two Paynims, Artegall gains entry to the Souldan's palace by disguising himself in the dead Paynim's armor, and Arthur defies the Souldan directly (viii 11, 26–7). Once again, Arthur overcomes a Paynim threat, in a battle which is a type of the apocalyptic battle promised in I xi. The victories of the Legend of Justice remain qualified, however, by the poem's continuing deferral of that final battle.

WILLIAM J. KENNEDY

For background, see Samuel C. Chew 1937 *The Crescent and the Rose: Islam and England during the Renaissance* (New York); Norman Daniel 1975 *The Arabs and Mediaeval Europe* (London); and Dorothee Metlitzki 1977 *The Matter of Araby in Medieval England* (New Haven). See also William Wistar Comfort 1944 'The Saracens in Italian Epic Poetry' *PMLA* 59:882–910; and Graziani 1964b, which connects the Roman Catholic Philip II to the pagan Souldan.

Peacham, Henry (1578–1644?) Best known for his emblem book *Minerva Britanna* (1612) and for his courtesy book *The Compleat Gentleman* (1622), Peacham often alluded to and imitated Spenser. His father, also named Henry, praised Spenser in *The Garden of Eloquence* (1593) as a master at imitating 'ancient speech' in *The Shepheardes Calender*. The younger Peacham praised him more highly, numbering him in *The Compleat Gentleman* among those who had greatly 'honoured Poesie.' In *The Truth of Our Times* (1638), he recounts a version of Spenser's death recorded by Camden, that 'hee dyed but poore' and that Essex 'sent him twenty pound, either to relieve or bury him.'

Peacham chiefly admired Spenser as the creator of emblematic personifications. In *Graphice* (1612), he refers the gentleman who would draw Fear to the figure 'described by our excellent *Spencer*' and tells whoever would draw Dissimulation to remember Spenser's figure 'looking through a lattice' (*FQ* III xii 12; at 15, Dissemblance's companion, Suspect, peeps through a lattice). Anyone depicting August should draw a young man, wearing 'at his belt (as our *Spencer* describeth him) a sickle,' though it is Spenser's July who carries the sickle (VII vii 36). (References by both Peachams are cited from *Sp All* pp 34, 129, 132–3, 144, 157, 167, 203.) One emblem in *Minerva Britanna* is based on a line in *The Faerie Queene* (Sehrt 1968:491), and possibly two others (Freeman 1948:81–2). Its commendatory poem signed 'E.S.' is so close to versions of a passage in *Theatre*, *Bellay*, and *Time* (8–12) that one early editor supposed it was by Spenser himself (Waldron 1792:9–12).

(See **Peacham** Fig 1.)

Peacham's other poetry also demonstrates Spenser's influence. *The Period of Mourning* (1613) consists of six 'Visions' reminiscent of *Bellay* and *Petrarch* in subject matter and style, *Nuptiall Hymnes* (1613) echoes *FQ* IV xi 48–51, *Prince Henrie Revived* (1615) includes a dedicatory poem in Spenserian stanzas, and *An Aprill Shower* (1624) provides examples of dependence upon *Time* and *Petrarch*. In *Thalias Banquet* (1620), Epigram 81 is entitled 'Upon Grantorto' (Cawley 1971:92–5; Young 1979: 99–100, 105–6, 112).

Though a minor poet and remembered primarily for other things, Peacham belongs to that group of poets – among them George Wither, the Fletchers, and William Browne – who continued to imitate Spenser well into the seventeenth century.

ALAN R. YOUNG

Robert Ralston Cawley 1971 *Henry Peacham: His Contribution to English Poetry* (University Park, Pa); Freeman 1948; Sehrt 1968; Francis G. Waldron, ed 1792 *The Literary Museum, or Ancient and Modern Repository. Comprising Scarce and Curious Tracts, Poetry, Biography, and Criticism* (London); Alan R. Young 1979 *Henry Peacham* (Boston).

Peele, George (1556–96) Poet, dramatist, pageant writer, and 'University Wit,' Peele was educated at Broadgates Hall (now Pembroke College), Oxford, and subsequently at Christ Church (BA 1577, MA 1579). His contemporaries at Oxford included Lyly, Lodge, Dyer, Greville, and Sidney. His career as a dramatist seems to have begun there when he translated one of Euripides' *Iphigenia* plays into Latin. By the early 1580s he was in London, associating with other university men including Thomas Watson, George Buc, and Matthew Roydon. Although he married an heiress, he struggled to subsist in the professional literary milieu and, when ill in 1596, sent a copy of his *Tale of Troy* to Burghley, with a plea for help. The petition was in vain, and Peele died later in the year.

Of Peele's plays, the biblical drama *David and Bethsabe* and the short fantasy-comedy *The Old Wife's Tale* are the best-known; others are *The Battle of Alcazar* and *Edward I*. A number of other works, including his earliest, show clearly the influence of Spenser. Though not published until 1589, his narrative poem *The Tale of Troy* was probably written between 1579 and 1581. Spenserian archaisms abound: *whilom*, *mickle*, *wot, withouten, couth, mought*. When he describes Paris' sojourn as a shepherd in Ida, he lapses into an imitation of the *Sheppheardes Calender* idiom: 'So couth he sing his layes among them all, / And tune his pype unto the waters fall' (67–8; cf *Aprill* 36).

The Tale of Troy anticipates and was no doubt an immediate source for Peele's court entertainment *The Araygnement of Paris*, published in 1584. Written perhaps as early as 1581, it is subtitled 'A Pastorall,' the first English play so named. Pastoral informs not only the main plot of the judgment of Paris, which Peele turns to royal eulogy by having Diana, called in to arbitrate, award the golden apple to 'a gratious Nymphe,' Eliza, but also a subplot in Act 3, where Spenserian shepherds appear and Colin, 'thenamored sheepeherd,' sings a complaint, then dies for love of the unresponsive Thestilis; his faithfulness is contrasted to the faithlessness of Paris, who abandons another shepherdess, Oenone. Colin's friends, Hobbinol, Diggon, and Thenot, carry his hearse to Venus, who curses Thestilis. *Aprill*, in which Hobbinol and Thenot appear, is the *Shepheardes Calender* eclogue immediately behind this subplot. No allusion to Spenser himself seems to be intended, however (except insofar as use of the name 'Colin' can be construed as an allusion). When Peele does allude to Spenser in the prologue to *The Honour of the Garter* (1593), it is by another name. Lamenting the lack of patronage, he asks why all the poets have not fled to heaven: 'Why thether speede not Hobbin and his pheres? / Great Hobbinall on whom our shepheards gaze' (39–40).

Peele's closest imitation of *The Sheppheardes Calender* is *An Eglogue Gratulatorie* (1589), welcoming Essex back from Portugal. It is a pastoral dialogue between Piers and Palinode from *Maye*. Piers sings 'Io Paean' in praise of 'One of the jolliest Shepherds of our Greene,' and Palinode sneers at his presumption. The 173-line piece is entirely in the *Shepheardes Calender* idiom.

Peele employed pastoral devices frequently in his pageants, but did not always imitate Spenser. In *Descensus Astraeae* (1591), for the Lord Mayor, William Web, Astraea is a shepherdess; but the other characters are allegorical figures – Superstition, Ignorance, Charitie, Hope, Faith, Honor, Time – rather than shepherds. The lost play *The Hunting of Cupid*, known only in William Drummond's fragmentary transcription (1609) and a few excerpts in anthologies, is called a pastoral by Drummond. It contains a brief dialogue between Coridon and Melampus, reprinted in *Englands Helicon* (1600). There are pastoral allusions, but no Spenserian echoes, in Peele's last work, *Anglorum Feriae* (1595), for the Accession Day celebrations.

These instances show Peele to have been particularly responsive to Spenser's pastoralism; like other Elizabethan pastoralists, he bears witness to Spenser's preeminence in that mode. Occasional reminiscences of *The Faerie Queene* have been detected in his later works; that they are of the vaguest sort is not surprising, for his principal achievements were in genres distant from Spenser's epic.

CHARLES WALTERS WHITWORTH, JR

Peele ed 1952–70 is the standard edition; A.R. Braunmuller 1983 *George Peele* (Boston) is a concise introduction. For a comparison of Spenser and Peele, see Louis Adrian Montrose 1980 'Gifts and Reasons: The Contexts of Peele's *Araygnement of Paris*' *ELH* 47:433–61, esp the conclusion.

Peleus, Thetis Son of Aeacus (cf *FQ* VI x 22 where Peleus is called *Aeacidee*) and grandson of Jove, Peleus the king of Thessaly fathered Achilles on the Nereid Thetis. The story of their union is told in Ovid's *Metamorphoses* II.229–65; for allegorical interpreters, their marriage was the union of earth and water (Gr *pēlos* 'clay, mud'; see Conti *Mythologiae* 6.23 and cf the marriage of Florimell and Marinell in *FQ* V iii, another union of earth and water).

The wedding of Peleus and Thetis was especially significant in classical mythology because it occasioned the Trojan War. When all the gods had assembled for the wedding, the only uninvited guest, Ate, the goddess of discord, appeared and threw out a golden apple inscribed 'to the fairest' (cf *FQ* II vii 55). Paris (at that time a shepherd courting Oenone) was appointed judge in the ensuing conflict among three goddesses for possession of the apple and was offered power by Juno, wisdom by Pallas Athena, and the world's most beautiful woman (Helen) by Venus. His choice of Venus led eventually to the Trojan War, in which the child of Peleus and Thetis was to play such an important part.

The wedding of Peleus and Thetis is a central myth in the pastoral episodes of *FQ* VI. Anyone seeing Calidore when he assumed a shepherd's role in courting Pastorella, the narrator tells us, would have thought of Paris 'When he the love of fayre *Oenone* sought, / What time the golden apple was unto him brought' (ix 36). A few stanzas later, we learn that the Graces were begotten by Jove while returning from the wedding of Peleus and Thetis (x 22). The association of Calidore and Paris invites us to see Calidore's vision of the three Graces on Mount Acidale as analogous to Paris' judgment of the three goddesses. According to traditional allegorical interpretation, the gifts offered by the goddesses represented wisdom or the contemplative life (Pallas), power or the active life (Juno), and pleasure or the voluptuous life (Venus). Calidore in his pastoral sojourn may be seen as choosing between the active and contemplative lives, with the wooing of Pastorella implying 'a third alternative, a life of pleasure' (Nohrnberg 1976:722). That he sees the three Graces together on Mount Acidale suggests a harmonious vision of contemplation, action, and pleasure (Cheney 1966:224, Tonkin 1972:278).

Spenser associates the wedding of Peleus and Thetis with a second setting that suggests an earthly paradise, Arlo Hill, where all the gods assemble to hear Mutabilitie plead her case before Nature. The narrator comments that no occasion has been so joyous since the day when all the gods assembled on Haemus hill to celebrate the wedding of Peleus and Thetis (VII vii 12). In neither of his allusions to this wedding does Spenser mention the uninvited intruder who threw the golden apple; in effect, Mutabilitie has taken her place. Though he never directly explains the political implications of the myth, 'it was at this wedding that Jove was originally "confirmed in his imperial see"' (Frye 1963:85): Jove had restrained his own passion and ordered Peleus to woo Thetis after learning of a prophecy that her son would be greater than his father (Conti 8.2).

At two other points in *The Faerie Queene*, Spenser alludes to the golden apple that led to the Trojan War but without mentioning the wedding of Peleus and Thetis. It is one of the golden apples in the Garden of Proserpina (II vii 55), and it hangs appropriately in the dwelling of Ate (IV i 22). For Spenser, the wedding is ambiguously an event of joy and harmony which he associates with the birth of the Graces, and also an occasion for the strife that led to both the fall of Troy and the founding of Troynovant.

CALVIN R. EDWARDS

Pembroke, Mary Sidney, Countess of Translator of Psalms and works by Garnier, Mornay, and Petrarch, overseer of editions of works by her brother Philip Sidney after his death, and author of a few original poems, the Countess of Pembroke, is perhaps best known as the patron of the Sidney circle, a literary group which produced quantitative verse, closet drama, religious verse, and treatises on rhetoric and natural history. At Wilton, where she resided with her wealthy husband the second Earl of Pembroke, she apparently shared literary projects with Sidney's friends. This group included Thomas Howell, Gervase Babington, Daniel, Fraunce, Thomas Moffett, and probably Breton. Raleigh and possibly Dyer also visited Wilton. While heavily influenced by Sidney, this group may not have devoted itself entirely to any program to reform English verse and drama, as was once thought.

While there is no certain evidence for his presence at Wilton, Spenser had considerable literary contact with the Countess. Probably she first heard of him through Sidney, with whom he experimented with quantitative verse and to whom he dedicated his *Shepheardes Calender*. One of the *FQ* dedicatory sonnets praises the Countess for her resemblance to Sidney. Soon after, *Ruines of Time* alludes to her 'manie singular favours and great graces' in the dedication, and in the lament for Sidney asks, 'who can better sing, / Than thine owne sister, peerles Ladie bright' (316–17). In *Colin Clouts Come Home Againe*, his approval of '*Urania*, sister unto *Astrofell*,' for her 'brave mynd'

(487–8) is prominently placed before his commendation of eleven other ladies. In the *Astrophel* volume, the 'dolefull lay' of Clorinda (who is again praised for her resemblance 'in shape and spright' to her brother Astrophel) is projected as though by the Countess, but may be Spenser's.

There are some indications of contact between Spenser and members of the Countess' circle. Fraunce quotes *FQ* II iv 35 in his *Arcadian Rhetorike* (1588, 1.25) two years before its publication, suggesting circulation of early drafts at Wilton. Spenser's advice to Daniel in *Colin Clout* (427) to move from sonnets to 'Tragick plaints' parallels Daniel's actual practice in the period of the Countess' patronage. Barring new evidence, however, the exact extent of her influence upon Spenser is impossible to determine. MARY ELLEN LAMB

John Buxton 1954 *Sir Philip Sidney and the English Renaissance* (London); Herbert ed 1977; Lamb 1981; Lamb 1982; Waller 1979.

personification in *The Faerie Queene* Like its classical predecessors *prosopopoeia* and *conformatio*, personification is usually defined as the representation of a nonhuman or absent object by a fictitious person. Classical rhetoricians distinguished various types according to the object being personified: an imaginary, dead, or absent person; a nation or thing; or an idea. All of these occur in *The Faerie Queene*. Spenser states in the Letter to Raleigh that Belphoebe expresses an absent person, Queen Elizabeth; occasionally, material things, such as the Thames and the Medway, are presented as if human; Despair is a troll-like man, Charity a woman. Such unequivocal representations are particularly common in the central episodes of the books.

Outside these allegorical set pieces, however, personification in *The Faerie Queene* is problematic. We cannot always tell just what is being personified. Who or what is Maleger? Britomart? Florimell? the Blatant Beast? When we think we can make a firm identification, Spenser sometimes blurs it, as when he calls Una not Faith or Truth or the True Faith but Beauty (eg, I iii 1). Some agents, such as Duessa, refer to various objects, and we wonder which of these is (or are) appropriate to a given episode. Moreover, the apparent referents of many personifications bear either an undetectable or an ambiguous relation to most of the narrative. Does True Faith sleep whenever Una does? Does Belphoebe's abasement of Braggadocchio (II iii 21) represent some political triumph of Elizabeth? When Arthur and Guyon leave the castle of Alma, does the Soul bid them farewell (III i 1)? Does Guyon's swoon (II vii 66) reveal his imperfection in temperance, a limitation in temperance itself, or blameless human fatigue? Confronting such uncertainties, some readers accuse Spenser of inconsistency or lack of clarity.

Many writers on Spenser's allegory conclude that he rarely uses straightforward personification allegory – that readers should not even try to make consistent abstract identifications of most of the characters. Yet we may not abandon the search for extratextual identifications, for Spenser persistently encourages it. The Letter, the epigrammatic argument to each canto, the characters' quasi-abstract names, and the obviously improbable plot all proclaim that much of the poem is fabricated, a front for something more significant. That we cannot clearly identify ulterior meanings does not make them unimportant.

Nor does the complexity of his agents remove Spenser from the tradition of literary personification. In *prosopopoeia* as the rhetoricians defined it, the speaker substitutes a fictitious person for an absent or nonhuman referent that could have been named more directly; the astute listener reverses the substitution and recovers the original meaning. In literature, on the other hand, personifications are not substitutions but compounds. The personification is equally a person and a thing or idea, and it evokes, simultaneously or successively, various kinds of reality outside the text: ordinary people, historical figures, human institutions, components of the psyche, transcendent ideas. The balance among the referents varies throughout the narrative, but none is merely a signifier, and none is by itself the signified. Bunyan's Christian is not an individual who stands for a category; he is a categorical reconception of the individual. Likewise, Spenser's Charity is a divine reality manifested by grace in womanly form.

Within the tradition of personification, Spenser's compound agents are particularly subtle and fluid. Although the personifications in earlier texts bear complex and changing meanings, they achieve clarity and stability at the highest level of abstraction: Faith or Pride or Nature can subsume various human manifestations. Such semiotic resolution seldom occurs in *The Faerie Queene* because Spenser usually withholds or blurs – even while implying – the most general identities of his compound agents. Thus the poem's agents hover among various actual and potential meanings.

The result is not confusion but a range of particularly Spenserian effects, many of which arise from changes in level of reference. Spenser's clearest abstract identifications, for instance, produce allegorical epiphanies: this monster is Error; this place is the cottage of Sclaunder. A complementary effect is the withdrawal of an abstract identification previously established: when Alma begins to act like an ordinary courtly hostess, Arthur and Guyon reenter a realm of tentative and unstable meaning. The questing knights themselves seem to change repeatedly not only in character but in level of being. Setting out to rescue Florimell from a 'foule foster,' Arthur looks like Magnificence fortifying Chaste Beauty; later, when he expresses a preference for Florimell over that other incarnation of chaste beauty, Gloriana, he seems all too human (III i 18, iv 54). In shifting his focus from the unifying ideal of beauty to the accidental individuality of beauty's embodiments, Arthur has undergone a Platonic regression. The opposite movement occurs as well. Upon redefining his goal as the restoration of Florimell to Gloriana's court, Arthur reunifies his ideal and rejoins his virtue (III v 11). Similarly, after clarifying the nature of holiness painfully and gradually, the Red Cross Knight is suddenly merged with St George (I x 61).

Where an agent's abstract correlative cannot even be specified, its particular kind of ambiguity or indeterminacy bears meaning. Guyon faints as a man, as Temperance, *and* as a man defining temperance. His mortal limitations make him imperfect in the virtue, but we can see through him the limitation of the virtue itself – the insoluble paradox of absolute moderation. Similarly, if many of Britomart's adventures resist conceptual and moral identification, they reflect the difficulty of assigning clear meanings to sexual experience.

As these instances suggest, Spenser uses compound agency in part to evoke the complexities of human experience, particularly epistemological experience. It does not follow that his personifications are ultimately human beings. To reduce allegorical agents to people or to components of the psyche is no less fallacious than to translate them into didactic generalities. Moreover, human referents in *The Faerie Queene* are compounded not just with historical figures and with concepts that might be construed as psychological, but also with animals and elements of physical nature.

The passage on the marriage of Thames and Medway (IV xi) exemplifies the latter phenomenon, and with it some of the wider implications of Spenserian personification. We read that Thames had long wooed Medway to his bed and that for the wedding, the gods of the ocean, rivers, and brooks came to the house of Proteus (8–9). Expecting personifications to carry abstract significance, readers may be surprised to find these water deities presented literally – as bodies of water. In fact, all Spenser's personifications must be taken literally: they are not disguises but metaphoric compounds. As the Medway flows into the Thames, both retaining and losing its separate identity, and as the language of the passage conflates marriage bed and river bed, Spenser blurs the boundaries between the human, the natural, the transcendent, and the artificial. Personification in *The Faerie Queene* is a vehicle not for representing one thing by another but for exploring and manipulating the relationships among kinds of reality. CAROLYNN VAN DYKE

Quintilian's seminal definition of *prosopopoeia* is in *Institutio oratoria* 6.1.25, 9.2.29–37. On the classical rhetorical tradition, see Philip Rollinson with app by Patricia Matsen 1981 *Classical Theories of Allegory and Christian Culture* (Pittsburgh). For Renaissance rhetorical definitions, see Sonnino 1968.

The most useful context for Spenser's personification is provided not by rhetorical definitions but by studies of allegorical agency in classical, medieval, and Renaissance literature, eg, Barney 1979; Morton W. Bloomfield 1963 'A Grammatical Approach to Personification Allegory' *MP* 60:161–71; Bertrand H. Bronson 1947 'Personification Reconsidered' *ELH* 14:163–77; Donald Davie 1981 'Personification' *EIC* 31:91–104; Fletcher 1964; Robert Worth Frank, Jr 1953 'The Art of Reading Medieval Personification-Allegory' *ELH* 20:237–50; Honig 1959; W.T.H. Jackson 1964 'Allegory and Allegorization' *RS* 32:161–75; Quilligan 1979; Tuve 1966; Van Dyke 1985.

For Spenser, see Berger 1957; Hamilton 1961a; W.J. Kennedy 1973; I.G. MacCaffrey 1976; Teskey 1986; K. Williams 1966.

Petrarch, Petrarchism Petrarch (Francesco Petrarca), the greatest lyric poet of the Italian Renaissance whose work provided a model for Renaissance poets throughout Europe, influenced Spenser in many ways. Among Spenser's first published works was a translation of canzone 323 from Petrarch's *Rime sparse*, which appeared in van der Noot's *Theatre for Worldlings* (1569) along with unrhymed translations of du Bellay's *Songe*. He thought highly enough of it to republish it as *The Visions of Petrarch* in *Complaints* (1591). By then Petrarch's influence had already shaped parts of *The Faerie Queene*, especially its amatory episodes. Britomart's complaint in *FQ* III iv 8–10, for example, is a free translation of Petrarch's sonnet 189. Spenser's most sustained debt occurs in his *Amoretti*. The lineage of the sonnet sequence begins with Petrarch's *Rime* and includes the Petrarchan poetry of many of Europe's finest poets – Sannazaro, Ariosto, Tasso, du Bellay, Ronsard, Desportes, and others – all of whom provided Spenser with further models.

Petrarch was born in 1304 at Arezzo, the son of an exiled Florentine notary who after 1309 moved his family to southern France to seek employment at the papal court that Philip the Fair had established at Avignon. Petrarch studied law but found the pursuit of literature and scholarship more attractive. On Good Friday, 6 April 1327 at the Church of Santa Chiara in Avignon, he encountered Laura, the woman who inspired his poetic celebration of ideal love. In 1330, he took minor clerical orders and embarked upon an ecclesiastical career. He led an active life as a diplomat and outstanding scholar; but before the decade's end, dissatisfaction with curial politics at Avignon drove him to the solitude of Vaucluse in the countryside north of the papal center. There he built a modest home and retreated whenever he could to scholarship and his writing. On Easter Sunday, 8 April 1341, King Robert of Sicily crowned him with the laurel wreath on the Capitoline in Rome. Shortly afterward, Petrarch broke decisively with the curia and began a campaign to restore the papacy to Rome. The plague of 1348, which delayed his own plans to move permanently to Italy, claimed the life of Laura. Henceforth in his vernacular poetry Petrarch idealized his dead beloved as the object of intense unrequited desire. In 1353, he entered the service of the Visconti at Milan, where he remained until 1361. After serving at Padua and Venice for the next seven years, he settled at his own home in the Euganean hills near Arqua, where he died 18 July 1374.

Much information about Petrarch's life survives partly because he created his own autobiographical legend, and it in turn provided an example for later scholars and poets – not least Spenser – to emulate. In his letters, he fashioned a public image of himself as thinker, writer, and human being. In so doing, he imitated Cicero's letters to Atticus, a long-lost manuscript that he uncovered at Verona. The idea of self-presentation in these letters finds an echo in the Spenser-Harvey correspondence, as in many other published collections in the Renaissance. By the end of his life, Petrarch had assembled three major collections of letters written in Latin. They include his *Familiares* (familiar letters, 1345–66), *Sine nomine* (nameless letters, 1353–9), and *Seniles* (letters in old age, 1366–74). His other Latin writings include the *Epistole metrice* (verse letters, 1330?-1340?); a prose history, *De viris illustribus* (illustrious heroes, 1337–53); an epic in dactylic hexameter, *Africa* (1338–52); *Psalmi penitentiales* (penitential psalms, 1343); twelve pastoral poems, *Bucolicum carmen* (pastoral songs, 1346–66); three autobiographical tracts in prose: *De vita solitaria* (the life of solitude, 1346), *Secretum meum* (my secret, 1347–52), and *De otio religioso* (religious tranquility, 1357); *Invective contra medicum* (invective against physicians, 1355); *De remediis utriusque fortunae* (remedies for both kinds of fortune, 1354–66); and *De sua ipsius et multorum ignorantia* (his own ignorance and that of many others, 1367).

Petrarch assumed he would be remembered best for his Latin composition and not at all for his vernacular lyrics. His *Canzoniere* (songs), or *Rerum vulgarium fragmenta* (fragments in the vernacular) as he entitles them in the last codex, or *Rime sparse* (scattered rhymes) as he calls them in the first line of sonnet 1, 'Voi ch'ascoltate in rime sparse il suono' (you who hear in scattered rhymes the sound), nonetheless became the primary model for amatory poetry in Renaissance Europe. In his *Amoretti*, Spenser absorbed that model directly and, through many Petrarchan imitations, indirectly. In *Amoretti* 3, 8, 10, and 12, for example, the speaker falls captive to personified Love in the conventional terms that Petrarch had hallowed and others had echoed. Love ambushes the speaker, binds his eyes to the beloved's, and subjects him to a passion of oxymoronic contrarieties that she in her proud disdain will not requite. Petrarch derived these conventions from the love poetry of his own predecessors Guido Cavalcanti (1259?-1300), Dante Alighieri (1265–1321), and Cino da Pistoia (1270–1337), who in turn had appropriated them from their predecessors. They pervaded the love poetry of twelfth- and thirteenth-century Provençal troubadours whom Petrarch would have read during his years at Avignon, as well as the troubadour-inspired love poetry of Sicilians such as Giacomo da Lentini (1200–50?), who invented the sonnet form that Petrarch perfected. Above all, they informed the love elegies and epigrams of ancient Roman poets, especially Ovid and Propertius whom Petrarch emulated as classical masters. Petrarch imbues all these conventions with his own emotional intensity and stylistic elegance, and in the process he codifies the norms of the Renaissance love lyric.

Petrarch's inner turmoil affected his composition of the *Rime* in various ways. As early as 1342, he began organizing his youthful poems into a coherent cycle that would narrate his fall into love and his continuing obsession with Laura, but would also recount a growing awareness of his own moral insufficiency. Sonnet 1, composed in the mid-1340s, explains this awareness in its final line: 'che quanto piace al mondo è breve sogno' (that whatever pleases in the world is a brief dream). The penitential canzone 264, also composed at this time, 'I' vo pensando, et nel penser m'assale' (I go thinking, and in thought pity assails me), repudiates fleeting pleasure and false allurement, and a number of sonnets placed at the center of the sequence point further to his moral conversion. Spenser's *Amoretti* 67, 'Lyke as a huntsman after weary chace,' refers to one of these poems, Petrarch's sonnet 190, 'Una candida cerva sopra l'erba' (a white doe on the green grass). In that poem, the appearance of a white doe forecasts Petrarch's separation from Laura; though the speaker does not know it, an inscription on the doe's collar, 'Nessun mi tocchi' (let no one touch me), points to Laura's impending death. In Spenser's sonnet, however, the deer's yielding to her pursuer marks the moment of the beloved's change of heart towards the speaker. Spenser's resolution is finally a happy one, whereas Petrarch's is not, but emblematic echoes from the latter – especially those emphasizing the doe's purity – deeply enrich Spenser's poem.

Even before Laura's death in 1348, Petrarch had divided his sequence into distinct units corresponding to a change in his moral life. After her death, he divided his sequence into those poems conceived *in vita di Laura* (during Laura's life) and those conceived *in morte di Laura* (after Laura's death). Remorse now led him to write first about his heartbreak, then about his despair, and finally about his regeneration. *Amoretti* reflects these later poems in a curious way. At the end of Spenser's sequence, the lover is separated from the beloved for a brief interval after winning her consent to marriage. In the final sonnet, 'Lyke as the Culver on the bared bough,' the speaker laments this temporary separation by evoking Petrarch's sonnet 353, 'Vago augelletto, che cantando vai' (wandering bird, you who go singing). The difference between the sonnets is again profound. Whereas Spenser's speaker can look forward to a joyous reunion with the beloved at his journey's end, Petrarch's has no such consolation. Only God's grace and the passage of time can assuage his troubled spirit. Spenser's luminous reference to Petrarch expands the meditative range at the end of his sequence while yet leaving it open to the celebratory *Epithalamion* that follows.

Laura's death inspired Petrarch in 1352–3 to compose his other major Italian sequence, the *Trionfi* (triumphs), a series of dream-visions in terza rima that narrates Laura's triumph over temporal imperfection in the afterlife. Until the year of his death, Petrarch continued work on the *Rime* and *Trionfi*. He arranged a final selection of 365 poems and 6 triumphs covering 31 years from the date of his meeting Laura on 6 April 1327 to the tenth anniversary of her death on 6 April 1348. He added a final canzone, a hymn to the Virgin in which he repents of his earthly attachments and directs his will to heavenly concerns. The number and symmetry of poems in the *Rime* suggest that the cycle might have some calendrical significance corresponding to the liturgical year, but Petrarch deliberately kept that significance vague enough to resist any narrow interpretation. In a similar way, Spenser would construct his *Amoretti* sequence with pregnant references to 'New yeare' (sonnets 4, 62), spring (19, 70), Lent (22), the speaker's age (60), and Easter (68) without fully unfolding their significance. By restricting his sequence to the sonnet form with a single rhyme scheme, however, he did not imitate the variety of Petrarch's *Rime*. The latter comprise a highly diversified anthology of several forms that include 317 sonnets with ten different rhyme schemes; 29 canzoni each with a different stanzaic form, except for three 'sister' canzoni (71–3); nine sestine; seven ballate; and four madrigali. Petrarch's sequence owed much of its popularity in the European Renaissance to thematic and stylistic contrasts within the sequence, the balanced disjunctions that shift kaleidoscopically as themes and forms alternately converge and diverge.

Petrarch's Latin texts remained the best known of his works through the fifteenth century when *De remediis* held a favored position. Yet by the 1554 Basel edition of his *Opera omnia*, the Latin texts had begun to lose their readership. In England, though Henry Parker, Lord Morley, translated *The Tryumphes of Fraunces Petrarcke* in the 1540s (pub 1553–6?), attention was shifting to the Italian poetry. This shift had already occurred in Italy. From their earliest printed editions in the 1470s, the *Rime* and *Trionfi* were accompanied by extensive commentaries and annotations. Spenser and every other Petrarchan imitator of the sixteenth century approached the model through this web of commentary or through the myriad of imitations that they almost all tried. The first commentators, Antonio da Tempo and Francesco Filelfo (early 15th c, pub 1471 and 1476 respectively) attempted to identify figures, allusions, and mythic and historical references. Alessandro Vellutello (1525) rearranged most of the sequence in order to narrate a more coherent story. Sebastiano Fausto da Longiano (1532) and Antonio Brucioli (1548) interpreted the poetry from political and ethical perspectives betokening the spread of Lutheran ideas in Italy. Giovanni Andrea Gesualdo, author of the lengthiest commentary (1533), integrated a general stylistic appreciation with pointed moral interpretation. Bernardino Daniello da Lucca (1541) examined particular elocutionary devices and figures of speech that distinguish Petrarch's style, while Lodovico Castelvetro (1545? pub 1582) called attention to many subtle details of style and interpretation.

The *Rime* and *Trionfi* found wide and appreciative audiences and imitators throughout Europe for an entire century before Spenser encountered them. In Florence of the 1470s, Lorenzo de' Medici, Politian, and Boiardo echoed them with care. In Naples of the 1490s, Chariteo, Tebaldeo, Serafino Aquilano, and Sannazaro followed them with varying degrees of creativity and turgid fidelity. After Pietro Bembo canonized their diction and style as normative for Italian poetry in his *Prose della volgar lingua* (treatise on the vernacular, 1525), they became the model for slavish imitators everywhere in Italy. Some first-rate poets like Ariosto and Tasso renewed the model with their own vitality, and they in turn provided models for Spenser to imitate, but by the end of the century Petrarchism in Italy amounted to little more than a set of clichés. In France, Mellin de Saint-Gelais and Clément Marot tried their hands at translations and imitations before the late 1530s, and the major poets of Lyons in the 1540s, Maurice Scève, Pontus de Tyard, and Louise Labé, plotted fine lyric sequences imbued with Petrarchan fervor. Members of the Pléiade elevated Petrarchism to new heights outside Italy. After du Bellay conferred authority upon Petrarch's sonnets in his *Deffence et illustration de la langue françoyse* (defense and illustration of the French language, 1549), he and his associates evoked the *Rime* frequently – du Bellay somewhat austerely in *Olive* (1549), Ronsard with great ingenuity in several cycles of *Les Amours* (1552–78), and Philippe Desportes with bold extravagance in various sequences (1573–83). All three provided source texts for *Amoretti*. In Spain, Juan Boscán and Garcilaso de la Vega introduced Petrarchism in translations and imitations (1520s, pub 1543), and poets like Fernando de Herrera (1534?-1597) and Luis de Góngora (1561–1627) extended the tradition with their own innovations. Before the end of the sixteenth century, Petrarchism found its way into Portuguese, Flemish, Dutch, German, Hungarian, Polish, and Yugoslavian collections.

In England, Chaucer worked a free translation of Petrarch's sonnet 132 into *Troilus and Criseyde* 1.400–20, but otherwise Petrarchism made no mark for another century and a half. After Lord Morley's translation of the *Tryumphes*, both Queen Elizabeth and Mary Sidney, Countess of Pembroke, produced partial translations of the text. Following a visit to Italy in 1527, Wyatt introduced the sonnet form into English with translations and imitations of two dozen Petrarchan texts. A few years later, Surrey attempted some imitations. As the diverse collection of 'Songes and Sonettes' in *Tottel's Miscellany* (1557) implies, *sonnet* (little sound) originally meant any short poem or song, not necessarily the fourteen-line rhymed form of Petrarch. In 1582, for example, Thomas Watson published a collection of eighteen-line 'sonnets,' the *Hekatompathia*, the first lyrical sequence in English. A decade earlier, Gascoigne had included thirty sonnets in his *Hundreth Sundrie Flowres* (1573).

The floodgates of English Petrarchism opened with Sidney's *Astrophil and Stella*, published posthumously in 1591. This sequence inspired competitive cycles by Daniel (*Delia*, printed with *Astrophil and Stella* in 1591), Constable (*Diana* 1592), Giles Fletcher the elder (*Licia* 1593), Drayton (*Idea* 1594, 1619), and many more. Innumerable Petrarchan experiments pervaded the diversified work of Shakespeare, Donne, Jonson, and others in complex lyric and dramatic forms. By the time Shakespeare's sonnets appeared in print (1609, though composed in the 1590s), the Petrarchan vogue had crested in England. Spenser's *Amoretti* (1595) appeared during this high point.

William J. Kennedy

Oddly enough, there is no complete English translation of the *Rime sparse* until *The Sonnets, Triumphs, and Other Poems of Petrarch*, translated by various hands (London 1859). A careful modern bilingual edition is Robert M. Durling's *Petrarch's Lyric Poems: The 'Rime Sparse' and Other Lyrics* (Cambridge, Mass 1976). The *Trionfi* are translated by Ernest Hatch Wilkins, *Triumphs* (Chicago 1962). Among translations of the important Latin works are those by Thomas G. Bergin: *Bucolicum carmen* (New Haven 1974) and *Africa* (with Alice S. Wilson; New Haven 1977); Aldo S. Bernardo: *Rerum familiarium libri I-VIII* (Albany 1975) and *Letters on Familiar Matters ... IX-XVI* (Baltimore 1982); William H. Draper: *Petrarch's 'Secret'* (London 1911); and a selection of Latin verse by Fred Nichols in F.J. Nichols 1979. The best biography in English is Ernest Hatch Wilkins 1961 *Life of Petrarch* (Chicago). Excellent treatments of the life and works are Thomas G. Bergin 1970 *Petrarch* (New York); Kenelm Foster 1984 *Petrarch: Poet and Humanist* (Edinburgh); and Nicholas Mann 1984 *Petrarch* (Oxford). Greene 1982 contains a splendid critical examination. See also Roche 1974; Scaglione 1975; Ernest Hatch Wilkins 1950 'A General Survey of Renaissance Petrarchism' *CL* 2:327–42. A useful anthology with commentary on the English and French traditions is Stephen Minta 1980 *Petrarch and Petrarchism: The English and French Traditions* (Manchester); see also George Watson 1967 *The English Petrarchans* (London).

Petrarch, The Visions of. See ***Complaints: Visions***

Phaedria The figure of 'immodest Merth' whom Guyon meets on her Idle Lake (*FQ* II vi 2–38). With suggestions of 'glittering,' 'bright,' 'cheerful' in her Greek name, and with her Italianate 'Gondelay' reminiscent of the sirens of the *romanzi*, and with her resemblance to Idleness who admits the lover into the garden of delight in Chaucer's *Romaunt of the Rose* (531–628), she presents no trouble to the carebound Guyon. He is 'halfe discontent' with her frivolity during her main appearance in *FQ* II vi and, with the Palmer's help, rebukes her easily at her second, merely emblematic appearance during his voyage to the Bower of Bliss (xii 14–17). For Cymochles, however, she represents quick passage in a Petrarchan love boat to a floating island that anticipates Acrasia's 'wandring Island ... in perilous gulfe' (i 51) in locale as well as design (vi 12, xii 42). In fact, the Bower of Bliss seems to lie on 'the other side' (vi 19) of Phaedria's Idle Lake. If Cymochles represents Guyon's pleasure-seeking impulse, the brief battle between the hero and his passion in Phaedria's presence shows how quickly 'immodest Merth' leads into 'loose desire' (vi argument). The struggle to redirect a wavering desire disturbs her spell; both hero and temptress are relieved to see the other go; and an apparently innocuous encounter seems to end with a platitude: 'Excessive joy no lesse hath his defective and joylesse operations, the spleene into water it melteth; so that except it be some momentarie bubbles of mirth, nothing it yeelds but a cloying surfet of repentance' (Nashe ed 1904–10, 1:377). Phaedria hardly compares to Mammon as a tempter, yet something happens on the Idle Lake that deeply disturbs the narrative of Book II. At the end of the canto, Guyon has been separated from the Palmer, practically all of his troublemakers have concentrated in the place of sloth, and his state at the beginning of the next canto is like a pilot proceeding by dead reckoning.

There are two ways in which the larger context determines our understanding of this moment of ease. One is to read Book II as a straightforward exposition of the virtue of temperance (cf vi 1). Guyon wins a rational victory over 'immodest Merth,' identifiable with the superfluity of play mentioned by Thomas Aquinas as the excess of cheerfulness (*Summa theologiae* 2a2ae 168.2) as well as with the 'loose desire' or lust into which immodesty in play leads (*ST* 2a2ae 153.1), Phaedria being an avatar of Acrasia (cf vi 9). The term 'Continence' at vi 1 is associated with the willful restraint of the appetite for pleasure, and pleasure is harder to subdue than anger (Aristotle *Ethics* 2.3). What troubles this exposition is its conceptual austerity in relation to the complexity of the psychological event: what was Guyon doing at the Idle Lake in the first place?

Another way is to allow that the first eight cantos demonstrate the misleadingly partial successes of rational virtue. Aristotelian temperance creates an illusion of moral self-sufficiency and independence (vii 2): it identifies the self too intensely with performance as Archimago knows (i 8), it leads to pride in taking a risk at the house of Mammon, and it challenges experience in the spirit of mastering adversity, as in the battle with Furor when Guyon should have simply controlled Occasion. The classical conception of virtue as the willful management of extremes generates a tense balancing act at the house of Medina. Its abstraction of concrete experience segregates and polarizes into full-fledged passions (Pyrochles and Cymochles) the motions of the soul, where in their untroubled state the irascible is a temporary 'champion and defender' of the concupiscible (*ST* 1a 81.2), not its equal and opposite twin. But as Guyon is compelled to counterbalance an occasion of fury with an occasion of mirth, he must first let the concupiscible instinct slumber in order to control a moment of anger, then let the irascible instinct burn in repression (vi 44) while he enjoys a disdainful moment of pleasure. If Nicolas Coeffeteau's restatement of Aquinas is normative of Renaissance psychology, this is a picture of Guyon's soul towards the end of the Phaedria canto: 'The *Passions*, then raised, ride higher; are much more furious and ungovernable; for now indeed they are double: The [irascible motions] have come: and joyned [the concupiscible], and thus they back and sustain one another, by this Union and Mutual Consent' (1621:156).

From this psychological perspective, Phaedria is dangerously inviting not so much for whatever moral defect she represents as for her influence on a psyche already under stress. 'Refuse such fruitlesse toile, and present pleasures chuse' (vi 17) becomes a vicious sentiment when, in effect, it rationalizes as harmony a state of tensely balanced stress. In the Bower of Bliss everything is deadlocked in an enervating identity of opposites – woman versus man, nature versus art, passivity versus activity, coveting versus combat – producing a series of crises all serving to make stress seem normal and natural. As the prefiguration of Acrasia, Phaedria also exaggerates an inner division between *eros* and *furor* in order to achieve an artificial unity between them. '*Mars* is *Cupidoes* frend, / And is for *Venus* loves renowmed more' (35), she announces, using the Petrarchan and Ovidian language of the wars and the weapons of love. To Cymochles, implicated in the debased conception of a love which 'maketh warre' then 'maketh peace againe' (ii 26), the illusory quietism is appealing (cf I proem 3).

Phaedria also parodies the account of love in the Sermon on the Mount (Matt 6.25–34): 'The lilly, Ladie of the flowring field, / The Flowre-deluce, her lovely Paramoure, / Bid thee to them thy fruitlesse labours yield' (vi 16; cf Tasso *Gerusalemme liberata* 14.62–4). The lines do not express the Christian humility from which gentle love springs but promote the illusion that men and women are by nature self-sufficient. 'What bootes it all to have, and nothing use?' (vi 17) – a good point (Guyon will argue it against Mammon at vii 15), but its obviously partial and fragmentary appeal prompts one to ask: what is the unexpressed philosophy that so denatures Christ's teaching in the vacuum of canto vi?

Elizabethan readers might have identified Phaedria's sentiments with Lucretius, who offers as the basis of a kind of morality an imitation of the gods as ideals of tranquility (*De rerum natura* 1.36). Her detachment from all obligation, her imperviousness to fortune (vi 23), her emancipation from the anxiety of mythological illusion (10), her understanding that life is finally to be measured by the criterion of individual pleasure and pain (17), her emphasis on the tangible satisfaction of human relationships, all bespeak the gospel of 'taking no thought for the morrow.' Lucretian Epicureanism is based on the demystification of nature, revealed as nothing more than atoms stirring in a void; the random movements of Phaedria's skiff 'Withouten oare or Pilot it to guide' (5) suggest this scientific materialism, with its corresponding moral atomism displayed in the capriciousness of its owner.

Guyon escapes the seduction of inappropriate pleasure but not the vice of curiosity which is often its companion. Counting his moral victories (vii 2), he next meets in Mammon, counting his gold, the mirror image of that lonely self-sufficiency which continually requires adversity to test itself against.

SEAN KANE

J.C. Maxwell 1954 'Guyon, Phaedria, and the Palmer' *RES* ns 5:388–90 interprets the episode in Aristotelian terms. Lewis H. Miller, Jr 1964 'Phaedria, Mammon, and Sir Guyon's Education by Error' *JEGP* 63:33–44 is also typical of readings that see an education in virtue on the hero's part in the first half of Book II; for an ironic reading of the limitations of Aristotelian continence in *FQ* II, see Stambler 1977 and Kane 1989. Brian Crossley and Paul Edwards 1973 'Spenser's Bawdy: A Note on *The Faery Queen* 2.6' *PLL* 9:314–19 point to some bawdy associations of Phaedria's language.

Phaethon (Gr *phaos* light) The son of Apollo and a mortal mother, Clymene. He requests that his father permit him to guide the chariot of the sun; but he loses control, threatens to incinerate the earth below, and is destroyed. By the fourteenth century, Ovid's story (*Metamorphoses* 1.750–2.329) had been associated with that of the classical Lucifer (L 'light-bearer') or morning star and subsequently with the rebellious Lucifer of Christian tradition (*Ovide moralisé* 2.689–730, 914–1012).

(See **Adicia** Fig 1; **Phaethon** Fig 1.)

Accordingly, Spenser compares Lucifera to Phaethon, '*Phoebus* fairest childe,' in her excessive brightness and vain ambition (*FQ* I iv 9). Both Lucifera and Phaethon pervert the natural function of light, 'fire not made to burne, but fairely for to shyne.' An equally explicit but somewhat more complex allusion is found in Book V: the Souldan's runaway horses, terrified by Arthur's sun-like shield, are compared to the horses frightened by Scorpio during Phaethon's errant passage through the heavens; in adapting Ovid, Spenser transfers the fear from Phaethon to his horses (v viii 40, *Met* 2.195–209). Spenser not only contrasts the usurper Souldan with legitimate solar figures of justice like Arthur or Artegall (Aptekar 1969: 70–83); he also invites an ironic comparison with Philip II of Spain, whose impresa showed Apollo driving his horses (Graziani 1964b). To the Elizabethan poet, this Spanish Apollo is a Phaethon asking for destruction. Spenser also implicitly associates the Titaness Mutabilitie's assault on the heavens (*FQ* VII vi 8–15) with Phaethon's disastrous ride (Nelson 1963:298).

In three other allusions to Phaethon, Spenser stresses the viewpoint of those grieving at the youth's untimely fall (III xi 38, *Gnat* 197–200, *Teares* 7–12; cf Ovid *Met* 2.329ff). CALVIN R. EDWARDS

Conti *Mythologiae* 6.1; Graziani 1964b; Lotspeich 1932:99–100.

Philotime (Gr *philos* + *timē* love of honor) When Mammon tempts Guyon in the underworld, he offers him his daughter Philotime (*FQ* II vii 43–50). Her room is large and wide like a temple, with its golden pillars decked 'With crownes and Diademes, and titles vaine, / Which mortall Princes wore, whiles they on earth did rayne.' She is worshiped by a vast 'route of people ... Of every sort and nation.' Although her face is bright, her beauty is the result of art, and the narrator sees her as fallen (like Satan, in Isa 14.12, she has been thrust out of heaven into hell). In her hand she holds 'a great gold chaine' called Ambition ('every lincke thereof a step of dignity') rising from hell to heaven, up which her worshipers strive to climb and to force off, or at least restrain, fellow worshipers. The golden chain by which Zeus controls the created world (*Iliad* 8.18–27) is interpreted by Conti as ambition (2.4; cf Chapman: 'The golden chaine of Homers high device / Ambition is, or cursed avarice' *Hymnus in noctem* 159–60).

Guyon is told that 'Honour and dignitie' derive from Philotime alone and that she can advance him 'for workes and merites just.' In Spenser's Protestant allegory, Philotime is therefore seen to be both morally and theologically at fault, for justification by works alone is contrary to reformed religious doctrine. Guyon's response to Mammon's offer is ironic in its claims of unworthiness: he thanks him but adds that he is 'fraile flesh and earthly wight, / Unworthy match for such immortall mate,' and also that his love is 'avowd to other Lady late' and that 'To chaunge love causelesse is reproch to warlike knight.' Yet Mammon is superficially astute in offering Philotime, for at the beginning of the temptations, Guyon 'evermore himselfe with comfort feedes, / Of his owne vertues, and prayse-worthy deedes' (2): he is as familiar as any of Philotime's 'route of people' with this 'worldes blis / For which ye men do strive.'

In his rejection of Philotime, Guyon shows that he is a knight of magnanimity as well as temperance. One of the principal qualities of magnanimity is 'high recognition,' the fullest due acknowledgment of merit, which, according to Thomas Aquinas, is governed by two virtues: 'The first, which concerns modest recognition, has no proper name, being known by reference to its extremes, which are *philotimia* (love of recognition) and *aphilotimia* (indifference to recognition) ... Magnanimity governs high recognition ... [and] the magnanimous man strives for objects which are worthy of high recognition' (*Summa theologiae* 2a2ae 129.2).

Philotime represents the love of honor for objects not worthy of high recognition, such as vain titles, in contrast to the honor rightfully gained through the active life, as Belphoebe explains (iii 40–1). Guyon, however, strives successfully to perform great deeds for which honor is a proper reward.

The desire for honor is central to *The Faerie Queene*, from the beginning when the Red Cross Knight sets out 'To winne him worship' (I i 3), that is, honor. Arthur as magnificence (see *magnanimity) seeks Gloriana, whom Philotime in her 'glory' parodies. Guyon similarly carries Gloriana's image on his shield and has his 'trouth yplight' to her. In Alma's castle, Arthur meets Prays-desire, whose mood reflects his own 'great desire of glory and of fame,' and Guyon meets her opposite, Shamefastnesse, reflecting his own fear of shame or dishonor (II ix 39, 43). While worldly honor, the spur to virtue and its reward, is apparently allowed within bounds as the motivation of Spenser's knights, later that social code of honor is queried. His quest interrupted, Artegall may return to Fairyland disregarding Envy and Detraction whose slander 'his honour blent' (V xii 40); but in Book VI, the inability of the good man either to act honorably or to receive proper recognition for his deeds becomes painfully apparent. Contemplation's book of fame now seems closed, and far from virtuous action.

HUGH MACLACHLAN

Cain 1978; Greaves 1964; McNamee 1960; J.G. Peristiany, ed 1965 *Honour and Shame: The Values of Mediterranean Society* (Chicago).

pictorialism Spenser and his contemporaries were guided by a literary theory crystallized around the Horatian phrase *ut pictura poesis*, in which pictorial vividness was considered the essence of poetry because it assured that verisimilitude without which audiences would remain unmoved and, therefore, uninstructed. Renaissance writers use terms such as *enargeia*, *illustratio*, *descriptio*, *ecphrasis*, *icon*, *imago*, *exemplum*, *emblem*, *speaking picture*, and *allegory* to analyze the kinds of visualization that are possible in poetry. The general term *enargeia*, which in rhetoric designated an orator's power to evoke objects and scenes in the minds of his listeners by the use of vivid imagery, included the innumerable specific devices used to achieve it (Hagstrum 1958, chs 1–3). From antiquity onward, these terms entered literary criticism from rhetorical theory, which continued to shape their application to poetic practice (Curtius ed 1953).

Later writers have grouped the rhetorically derived schemes for visualization listed above, along with many other devices of Spenserian imagery, under the broad rubric *pictorialism*. The term is somewhat ambiguous because it also alludes to a particular kind of response to Spenser's poetry. A tradition of pictorialism extending from the early eighteenth century to the present imagines *The Faerie Queene* as a gallery of pictures from specific masters, schools, or historical styles (see *baroque, *visual arts). Although John Hughes, in 'An Essay on Allegorical Poetry' (1715), refers to Rubens' picture allegorizing the coming of age of Louis XIII to illustrate his claim that allegory resembles painting even more than other kinds of poetry, the notion of a Spenserian 'gallery' of characters and scenes was stated directly and in popular terms by the 70-year-old mother of Joseph Spence in 1744: after she had been read a canto of *The Faerie Queene*, she declared that her son 'had been showing her a collection of pictures' (Spence ed 1966, 1:182). Her notion has been developed by later critics, including Joseph Warton, Leigh Hunt, Hippolyte Taine, Edward Dowden, and W.B.C. Watkins.

The tradition of regarding Spenser as a poetic painter flourished during the eighteenth century, when, because of aesthetic considerations epitomized in Burke's *Philosophical Inquiry into the Origin of Our Ideas of the Sublime and Beautiful* (1757) and in Lessing's *Laokoön* (1766), literary criticism sought to distinguish clearly between the cognitive and illustrative functions of poetry which the earlier rhetorically derived criticism had attempted to unite. According to rules authoritatively summed up by Quintilian, the verisimilitude necessary to persuasion arose from the use of devices like *descriptio* which create *enargeia*, an illustrative vividness that 'makes us seem not so much to narrate as to exhibit the actual scene, while our emotions will be no less actively stirred than if we were present at the actual occurrence' (*Institutio oratoria* 6.2.32). In this tradition, narration and pictorialism could be considered technically as aspects of one another (Curtius ed 1953:70, 501; Trimpi 1983:291–4). They were, respectively, the general and particular means of moving audiences to action by inspiring visual images on the basis of verbal cues.

Twentieth-century semiotic theory has reasserted similarities between visual and verbal means of communication in terms parallel to but different from those of the Renaissance. Visual and verbal sign systems are now considered comparable, inextricably intertwined modes of cognition in fields as diverse as structural linguistics, the psychology of perception, and formal iconography. In the main, however, the dichotomy between cognition and illustration inherited from the eighteenth century has continued to dominate modern scholarship on Spenser's pictorialism and to focus debate on a question alien both to Renaissance thought about imagery and to Spenser's poetic mode: can poetry either represent or evoke any response properly called 'visual'? (Glazier 1955, Gottfried 1952, Sonn 1959). Arguments on this issue often oppose the visual to the rhetorical, neglecting or at times condemning Renaissance pictorialism because it assumed the validity of codifying visual and verbal sign systems together as modes of thought and communication.

The Faerie Queene adopts Renaissance pictorialist assumptions while thematically exploring questions they raise and scrutinizing them in the poem's distinctive line-by-line exposition of vision as subjective experience. It confronts the basic dilemma posed by the human use of signs and symbols: all language, all images may be considered either as natural signs that refer objectively to realities in the physical, mental, and spiritual universe outside the signs proper or as self-referential devices that allow us to constitute the world as existing meaningfully. Both views have been held throughout the Western tradition, but broadly speaking the first prevailed until the later Middle Ages; the other asserted itself powerfully during the Renaissance and has increasingly prevailed since. Although all 'periods' are actually times of transition, Spenser's poetry falls between these broad historical epochs, and in its pictorialism can fruitfully be understood as a meeting point between two ways of comprehending the relation of language to experience. *The Faerie Queene* in particular shows the poet struggling to define the very nature of signification: his subjective vision seems both to refer to an objective world and yet to treat that world as ineffable – to be realized only through the multiplication of visual and verbal explanations.

The Faerie Queene depends not on one way of seeing but on many. The poet often depicts the world of his poem as objective, natural, and capable of direct representation. His descriptions assume the translatability of signs into nature, nature into signs, and signs into signs, as did the rhetorically centered tradition of *ut pictura poesis*. His reliance on this tradition seems to imply that the experience he depicts is unified and continuous, that the terms in which it may be described are exchangeable, and above all that the world is objectively real and present to our view.

But, in almost every way, the major thrust of Spenser's genius runs counter to considering the world in this manner. His most striking poetic moments are those of struggle to comprehend, of evanescent visual or verbal experience, of transient forms so hard to grasp that, like the ever-changing Duessa, they may be captured only to escape again, returning perpetually with questions about the nature and concreteness of reality (see *appearance). In the Bower of Bliss (II xii), the house of Busirane (III xii), and many other episodes, Spenser thematically addresses the confusingly contradictory nature of signs, while employing language which maintains the reader's awareness that the representation of unknowability, strangeness, and mystification of experience is central to his effort.

A stanza from Spenser's account of Acrasia in the Bower of Bliss illustrates the distinctive stress his pictorialism lays upon perceptual contradiction (II xii 77):

Upon a bed of Roses she was layd,
  As faint through heat, or dight to pleasant sin,
  And was arayd, or rather disarayd,
  All in a vele of silke and silver thin,
  That hid no whit her alablaster skin,
  But rather shewd more white, if more might bee:
  More subtile web *Arachne* cannot spin,
  Nor the fine nets, which oft we woven see
Of scorched deaw, do not in th'aire more lightly flee.

Here, the imagination must remain in flux among different impressions of a single sight. *Alablaster* defines something that cannot be seen definitively – the whiteness of Acrasia's skin – because the veil both 'hid no whit' and 'shewed more white.' In the last three lines, Spenser's pictorialism easily comprehends a fusion of intellectual and visual 'sight' as the magical connotations of something weblike are enlarged. *Nets* anticipates the parallel of Acrasia and Verdant with Venus and Mars in Vulcan's net (81–2) while the final image completes the evanescent impression of the veil by reducing it to light sparkling in beads of water as they themselves disappear (Bender 1972, chs 1–2).

Usually Spenser does not preserve a strictly limited point of view through the eyes of a single character. Nor, except for special effects, does he map the world of his epic within any systematic projection of space like that of Italian Renaissance linear perspective (Kamholtz 1980–1). Usually he does not distinguish between visualization by the narrator and by characters (see *narrative). Techniques for doing so do not suit him because each regards a certain way of seeing as 'natural' and conventionally neutral; therefore, the steady adoption of any single one would cause the problematic character of perception itself to recede as an object of attention. Spenser has rightly been esteemed as one of the most pictorial of English writers because he employs every possible poetic means – including all of the rhetorical figures for maintaining *enargeia* as well as many devices of his own invention – to capture in visual terms the experiential struggle to hold together that world of direct correspondences assumed by the *ut pictura poesis* tradition. JOHN BENDER

For a general account of pictorialism, see Curtius ed 1953 and Wesley Trimpi 1983 *Muses of One Mind: The Literary Analysis of Experience and Its Continuity* (Princeton). Tuve 1966 and 1970 describe certain medieval traditions of allegorical pictorialism known to Spenser. Hagstrum 1958 outlines the traditional discussion about the relations of painting and poetry. The fullest study is Bender 1972; for particular discussion, see Dallett 1960; Judith Dundas 1981–2 'Fairyland and the Vanishing Point' *JAAC* 40:82–4; Dundas 1985; Farmer 1984; Lyle Glazier 1955 'The Nature of Spenser's Imagery' *MLQ* 16:300–10; Rudolph B. Gottfried 1952 'The Pictorial Element in Spenser's Poetry' *ELH* 19:203–13; Jonathan Z. Kamholtz 1980–1 'Spenser and Perspective' *JAAC* 39:59–66; Carl Robinson Sonn 1959 'Spenser's Imagery' *ELH* 26:156–70.

Pindar (c 518–c 438 BC) Greek poet widely admired in antiquity for his hymns and dithyrambs, and for four books of choral odes composed to commemorate victories at the Olympian, Pythian, Nemean, and Isthmian games. The epinician (victory) odes survive almost complete; the hymns and other poetry, only in fragments. Pindar was praised by Horace as inimitable (*Odes* 4.2) and by Quintilian as the prince of lyric poets (*Institutio oratoria* 10.1.61) – judgments often quoted in the Renaissance. Editions of the odes in Greek were first printed in Venice in 1513 and Rome in 1515. Later editions printed in Basel, Geneva, and Paris added Latin paraphrase and notes on the text and sometimes included ancient lives of Pindar and the Greek scholia. Two Latin commentaries on Pindar by Portus and Aretius appeared in the 1580s. Mythographers such as Conti and Giraldi frequently cite Pindar's odes for details about the gods or for other mythic references.

Pindar was regarded by the Renaissance as a vatic poet, admired for the morality, sentence, and religious devotion of his odes, and compared to David in the Psalms and Solomon in Proverbs. He was classified as a lyric poet by Scaliger, Minturno, and other commentators on classical poetics, and was compared to and contrasted with Horace. Imitations of his odes begin in Italy with Filelfo, Alamanni, and Lampridio, and continue in France until the end of the sixteenth century with Ronsard (*Odes* 1550) and other French poets. As a result of an imperfect understanding of Pindar's line and stanzaic form, however, Pindaric imitations in Italian and French usually have short lines and sometimes have stanzas of uneven length.

The metrics of Spenser's *SC, Aprill* seem to have been influenced by Ronsard's Pindaric experiments, but the description of and invocation to the attendant Graces and Muses may indicate a direct knowledge of Pindar's *Olympian Odes* 14 (see Van Winkle in *Var* 8:479). Hence, Spenser (rather than John Soowthern, despite the latter's claim in his *Pandora* 1584, Ode 1. Epode 3), may be the first poet in England to try to adapt the classical Pindaric ode to English. Interest in Pindar in sixteenth-century England is evident from allusions to him in Cooper's *Thesaurus* (1565), in Sidney's *Defence of Poetry* (ed 1973b:97) and *Astrophil and Stella* 3, and in Puttenham's *Arte of English Poesie* (1589, 3.22). Besides Soowthern, no English poet before Drayton and Jonson claims to imitate Pindaric ode directly. Since, however, the experiments in ode form that continued in France as a result of the popularity of Ronsard's Pindarics could not have been unknown to Spenser, it is likely that his own experiments in *Epithalamion* and *Prothalamion* were affected directly or indirectly by Pindaric influence.

Spenser knew Greek (see *Bryskett) and was probably introduced to Pindar by Gabriel Harvey, who owned an edition of the *Odes* dated 1600 but who (to judge from references in his prose and letters to Spenser) undoubtedly read Pindar much earlier (Stern 1979:230). Pindar would have impressed both Harvey and Spenser with his concept of the poet as mediator between the gods and men, his serious view of poetry as an inspired art, and his treatment of the Muses as divine beings who, through the poet, dispense fame to good men. In *October*, Spenser describes poetry as a divine gift, alludes to the great respect for poetry among the ancients, and regrets the neglect of poets and poetry in the modern age; in support, E.K. recounts the celebrated story of Alexander, who, out of respect for the poet, gave orders not to burn Pindar's house during the sack of Thebes (*Oct* 65 gloss). In *Teares of the Muses* and *Ruines of Time*, Spenser expresses sentiments much like Pindar's on the responsibility of the poet to preserve the good deeds of good men in his poetry. Spenser's invocations to the Muses and his treatment of the goddesses as personal agents of Jove (*FQ* VI proem, VII vii 1–2) argue for the influence of classical poets such as Pindar and Hesiod.

While details about classical deities such as the Muses and Graces could have come from a number of different sources (eg, other Greek and Latin poets or Renaissance mythographers), Pindar's vivid descriptions of the gods and his powerful narration of different myths in the digressions of the odes could not have failed to impress Spenser. Besides, Pindar used myth allusively, as Spenser does in *The Faerie Queene*, in order to illustrate a moral truth or convey an idea symbolically. Hence, his method of employing myth as well as his treatment of individual myths would have provided useful models for Spenser. We may compare, for example, the account of the Argonauts (*Pyth* 4.211–56, *FQ* II xii 44–5), the crime of Tantalus (*Olym* 1.54–64, II vii 58–60), and the founding of the Pillars of Hercules (*Olym* 3.43–4, *Proth* 148–9). Although there are few if any close verbal echoes of Pindar in Spenser, two phrases have been taken as possible direct recollections (*Var* 2:366, 7:307): '*Heliconian* maides' (*FQ* II xii 31, *Isth* 8.58) and 'I ... had rather be envied ... then fonly pitied' (*SC, May* 57–8, *Pyth* 1.85).

STELLA P. REVARD

Carol Maddison 1960 *Apollo and the Nine: A History of the Ode* (London); Robert Shafer 1918 *The English Ode to 1660* (Princeton).

places, allegorical Defined in accordance with its etymology, the elusive term allegory signifies 'other speaking.' During the long period extending from the rise of allegory in the first Christian centuries up to Spenser's own time, 'other speaking' can be defined more usefully as the employment of objective phenomena of the everyday world to describe the otherwise imperceptible and thus indescribable features of certain 'other' worlds, the transcendental world of the spirit and the closely related interior world of the mental, moral, and emotional life.

Spenser, like many of his predecessors, favored the heroic or chivalric quest as the heightened or romanticized objective experience most appropriate for allegorical delineation of these other worlds. The characters of *The Faerie Queene* thus encounter such border realms of the transcendent as Eden (I xi-xii), the Gardens of Adonis (III vi), and Nature's Arlo Hill (VII vii), as well as a profusion of traditional sinister forests, enchanted springs, alluring gardens, bowers, and suchlike allegorical places which collectively depict a spectrum of the fears, passions, and aspirations of humanity unequaled outside the *Divine Comedy*.

By what mysterious process is it possible for the external world to represent, as 'moralized landscape,' a 'place' in a transcendent or interior world that would seem beyond representation? Chiefly, the allegorist exploits the generally experienced fact that the natural world, in its varying configurations and 'moods,' does in some fashion stimulate corresponding human states of mind, though not any simple equivalence of place and mood. The endless forest (see *woods), for instance, that constitutes a kind of permanent backdrop to the heroic quests in *The Faerie Queene*, occasions such varied responses as anxiety and disorientation in the mind of the Red Cross Knight when he finds himself lost in the Wandering Wood (I i 7), or emancipation from the restraints of civilization as in Hellenore's self-abandonment to the sexual anarchy of the satyrs (III x 36), or the desire for the purity and seclusion of the woodland way of life by Belphoebe the virgin huntress (II iii 40–1).

These shifting relationships of inner and outer environment are equally discernible in such other Spenserian landscapes as mountains, caves, and lakes. They may be termed archetypal in that these fluid natural symbols, transcending all distinctions of period or culture, are also common in myth, folklore, and romantic poetry.

Allegorical landscapes always incorporate an archetypal element but add a dimension of meaning susceptible to more specifically rational interpretation, beyond mood, intuition, or emotion. Characteristically, such landscapes tend to incorporate human constructs such as gardens, buildings – castles and temples (see *architecture) – whose features are more susceptible to rational interpretation. Thus Acrasia's Bower of Bliss (II xii) embodies a far more complex representation of the libidinous instincts than the home of Hellenore's satyrs, for where the satyrs exhibit simple, earthy, almost innocent (because subhuman) sexuality, Acrasia maintains a whole culture subtly and intricately dedicated to alluring men into a state of deep and deadly sensual torpor through systematic and perverse exploitation of images in themselves wholesome and attractive, a type of complexity that tends to attract, naturally enough, much secondary elucidation from readers. Similarly, we may contrast the cave of the Brigands (VI x), the associations of which with the realms of the dead are fundamentally archetypal (though reinforced by a sprinkling of suggestive metaphors) with the house of Mammon (II vii), which embodies a specific, potentially intellectual analysis of the effects of worldliness on the human soul, conveyed through an elaborate reworking of the classical myths of the underworld.

Such allegorical interpretation is conveyed in many different ways: for instance, through elaboration of architectural features in the intricate arrangement of castle, bridge, and gatehouse guarding the island with the Temple of Venus (IV x 6–20) and depicting the mental and emotional barriers separating the lover from his wished-for lady. But the way to the Temple is also barred by the figures of Doubt, Delay, and Daunger, for Spenser's allegorical places are invariably associated with spiritual beings, gods, or personifications representing the more actively conscious or intellectual qualities of the place, an association that derives ultimately, no doubt, from the world of primitive animism.

This spirit of the place may communicate with the visiting hero simply on the level of action, friendly or hostile. At times, however, archetypal and allegorical aspects of a place are reinforced by the more intellectual mode of dialogue, as in Redcrosse's debate with Despair (I ix 37–54), Guyon's debate with Mammon (II vii 6–20), and Mutabilitie's with Jove (VII vii 48–9). But in general Spenser's places are less frequently explicated by dialogue than those of his predecessors in the allegorical tradition.

With or without the clarification of dialogue, the allegorical places of *The Faerie Queene* never fail to provide the reader with challenging problems of interpretation. Spenser's vast range of literary and iconographic reference, his discriminating skill in developing meaning from subtle correspondences and contrasts between the different allegorical places of his own epic, and his equally subtle borrowing from the allegorical locales of earlier poets, all make at times for baffling complexity.

Not that Spenser's own heroes are likely to be more alert to the significance of the places they visit than the reader, who has the advantage of being forearmed with the narrator's privileged explications of hidden dangers and treacheries seemingly unavailable to the knights. Thus we watch them learning the true significance of the places they visit through usually painful experience, as we must ourselves when we put aside the allegory and return (with whatever insights have come our way) to the unexplicated problems of our own lives.

Spenser's readers undoubtedly 'believed' in his allegorical places to a degree that is hard to imagine today without awareness of the contemporary visual arts: in particular, the Elizabethans enjoyed pageants that often featured elaborately wrought allegorical locales, as well as the magnificently decorated allegorical salons of the aristocracy, now difficult to find in England following the Puritan iconoclasm, but still grandly extant in such Italian monuments as Raphael's sublime Chamber of the Signature in the Vatican or Giulio Romano's grotesque and grandiose Room of the Giants in Mantua's Palazzo del Tè.

chief places in *FQ* *Book I* Wandering Wood with Error's den (i 7–27); Archimago's hermitage (34); house of Morpheus (39–44); unlucky ground (ii 28–44); Corceca's house (iii 12–21); house of Pride (iv-v); mew of Night (v 20); Pluto's house (31–5); cave of Aesculapius (36–44); Lucifera's dungeon (45–53); the wild forest (vi 3–33); spring of Diana's nymph (vii 2–6); Orgoglio's dungeon (15); Orgoglio's castle and dungeon (viii 29–40); cave of Despair (ix 33–54); house of Holiness (x 3–17) with its schoolhouse (18–24); house of Penance (25–8); Charissa's nursery (29–34); holy hospital (36–45); Contemplation's chapel and hermitage (46–52); Mount of Contemplation (53–68); vision of the New Jerusalem (55–63); the brazen tower in which Una's parents are imprisoned (xi 3); Eden's Well of Life and Tree of Life (29–34, 45–52); Emperor's palace (xii 13–41).

Book II forest (i 35–61); fountain of the chaste nymph (40, 55; ii 3–10); castle of Medina, Elissa, and Perissa (12–46); forest (iii 20–46); river of Phaedria (vi 2–4); Idle Lake (5–10, 19–22, 38–51); Phaedria's floating island (11–18, 22–37); Mammon's glade (vii 3–20); the ample plain (Pluto's vestibule, 21–3); gates of Pluto (24); house of Mammon (25–66) with its outer room (28–30), 'treasure' room (31–4), 'furnace' room (35–9), and gate of Disdain (40–2) leading to Philotime's room and throne (43–50); Garden of Proserpina with river of Cocytus (51–65); castle of Alma, with its wall, gates, porch, hall, kitchen, parlor, and turret with three rooms (ix 10–xi 3); siege of Alma's castle (xi 5–49); the sea with its Gulf of Greediness, Rock of Vile Reproach, Wandering Islands, Quicksand of Unthriftyhed, Whirlpool of Decay, Phaedria's island, bay of Mermaids, and harmful fowls (xii 2–38); Bower of Bliss, with the gate of Genius, porch of Excess, fountain of wanton maidens, and garden of Acrasia (xii 42–83).

Book III Malecasta's Castle Joyous (i 20–67); Rich Strond (iv 6–29, 34–42); Cymoent's bower (42–4); Belphoebe's pavilion (v 39–50); Gardens of Adonis with Venus' mount (vi 29–52); the witch's cottage (vii 5–18); Proteus' bower and dungeon (viii 37–41); castle of Malbecco (viii 52–x 18); wood of the satyrs (x 36, 43–53); house of Busirane, with its three rooms (xi 21–xii 43).

Book IV castle (i 9–16); house of the Fates (ii 47–53); the Martian field and Satyrane's tournament (iv 13–48, v 6–27); house of Care (v 32–46); cave of Lust (vii 8–20); Timias' forest retreat (38–47); Sclaunder's cottage (viii 23–34); Corflambo's castle and prison (51–61, ix 5–16); Island of Venus, with its castle, bridge, gates, garden, and temple (x 5–58); Proteus' hall with its dungeon (xi 3–xii 35).

Book V the perilous bridge (ii 4–12); Munera's castle (20–8); rock of the Giant with the scales (29–50); seashore with two islands (iv 4–20); Radigund's city, Radegone, with its prison chamber (iv 35–45, v 21–57); Dolon's house (vi 22–35); the perilous bridge (36–40); Isis Church (vii 3–24); Radigund's city (25–45); Souldan's castle (viii 26–51); Malengin's rock (ix 4–19); Mercilla's palace (ix 21–x 17); Belge's city, guarded by Geryoneo's castle with its chapel, altar, and idol (x 25–xi 35); Irena's land (xii 4–27).

Book VI Briana's castle (i 13–47); Aldus' castle (iii 2–16); house of Priscilla's father (17–19); Turpine's castle (37–43); the Salvage Man's glade (iv 13–16); Hermitage with its chapel (v 34–41, vi 1–15); Turpine's castle (vi 19–44); grove and altar of the Salvage Nation (viii 44–51); Meliboe's pastoral retreat (ix 5–46); Mount Acidale (x 5–30); Brigands' island and cave (41–xi 24, 41–51); Castle Belgard (xii 3–22).

Book VII Circle of the Moon (vi 8–13); Jove's palace (15–35); Arlo Hill with Nature's pavilion (36–vii 59). PAUL PIEHLER

Curtius ed 1953, ch 10; Giamatti 1966; Hankins 1971; Lewis 1936; Piehler 1971.

---

plants, herbs Spenser was familiar with plants and herbs, flowers, and trees of the classical world as well as with those of his contemporary world. In his day, herbals – books that gave the history of plants and described their botanical, medical, pharmaceutical, medico-magical, horticultural, and aesthetic properties – enjoyed general appeal and acceptance (see *natural history). The principal sixteenth-century writers of herbals on the continent were Otto Brunfels, Jerome Bock (Hieronymus Tragus), Leonhard Fuchs, and Rembert Dodoens. In England, there were William Turner, known as the father of British botany for his *New Herball* (2 parts 1551–62); Henry Lyte, *Niewe Herball* (1578), which Spenser may have known (Arber 1931) and which was a modified translation of Charles de l'Ecluse's French translation of Dodoens' *Cruydeboeck* of 1554; and John Gerard, *Herball, or Generall Historie of Plantes* (1597; enl by Thomas Johnson 1633, 1636). Although the English herbalists relied heavily on earlier herbals, they were especially eager to describe plants of the New World, as shown in the 1577 *Joyfull Newes out of the Newe Founde Worlde*, J. Frampton's English translation of an herbal by the Spaniard Nicolas Monardes.

harmful plants 'The power of herbs, both which can hurt and ease' derives from 'hidden' qualities (*SC, Dec* 88, 92). The noxious plants growing in the Garden of Proserpina (*FQ* II vii 51–2) show the indirect influence of classical mythology and of botany. The unspecified plants growing in 'griesly shadowes' are 'direfull deadly blacke both leafe and bloom, / Fit to adorne the dead, and decke the drery toombe.' Among the specified plants are 'Dead sleeping *Poppy*' (cf 'Dull Poppie' *Muiopotmos* 196), a potent soporific which could produce coma and death; 'Melampode' ('blacke *Hellebore*'), a powerful narcotic which could cause cardiac arrest (cf *SC, Julye* 85, 106); '*Cicuta* bad,' a deadly poison which could cause death by paralyzing the motor system (Lyte 1578:451); and 'Cold *Coloquintida*,' a violent and deadly cathartic, the seeds of which were used to preserve dead bodies (Gerard ed 1636:916). Heben may be henbane, known as a narcotic which procures sleep, as a poison which produces blurred vision, drowsiness, delirium, and convulsions, and as a plant used by witches, who made an ointment from its leaves (Gerard ed 1636:353–6). '*Tetra* mad' has been identified as Atropa belladonna (deadly nightshade), tetragonia (euonymus), and tetrabit or tetrabil (balm). It may well be Atropa belladonna, which was regarded as an insanity-producing drug whose bright, shining black berries 'troubleth the mind, bringeth madnesse if a few of the berries be inwardly taken, but if moe be given they also kill and bring present death' (Gerard ed 1636:341). Its popular names, Devil's Cherries, Naughty Man's Cherries, Devil's herb (Grieve 1931:583), hint at its diabolic instigation. 'Mortall *Samnitis*' may be the Savine-tree, 'arbor Sabina' (see Upton in *Var* 2:263), a tree in Greece but a shrub in Britain, known as an 'energetic poison leading to gastro enteritis collapse and death' (Grieve 1931:718).

healing plants In *FQ* II, Archimago is said to use 'balmes and herbes' to heal Pyrochles' 'secret wounds' (vi 51). In seeking to cure the lovesick Britomart, Glauce gathers rue, savine, camphor, calamint, and dill (III ii 49), all of which are standard herbal remedies with refrigerative, healing properties (Ferrand ed 1640:238, 264–73; see amatory *magic). In selecting plants to heal Timias' thigh wound, Belphoebe searches for three salvific plants 'whether it divine *Tobacco* were, / Or *Panachaea*, or *Polygony*' (III v 32). 'Divine *Tobacco*' (also known as 'Sacra herba' and 'Sancta herba' Gerard ed 1636:358) was held to cure wounds of 'hard curation' (Parkinson 1629:364) by a salve made from its leaves. Panachaea, known as All-Heal (cf Virgil *Aeneid* 12.419, Ariosto *Orlando furioso* 19.22), was used as a rapid cure for deep, bloody wounds (Gerard regards it as a miracle-cure that heals 'grievous wounds, and some mortall' ed 1636:1005–6). Polygony, or polygonatum, popularly known as Solomon's Seal, was regarded as effective in closing up 'greene wounds' (Gerard ed 1636:903–6).

aesthetic and practical use The 'gay gardins' of *Muiopotmos* (161–216) are typical of the gardens of Spenser's day which had three basic divisions: the physic garden, the garden of pleasure, and the kitchen garden. The epithets assigned to the list of culinary, salvific, and aesthetic plants are wide-ranging. Among the plants are those that facilitate digestion ('wholsome Saulge' [sage], 'Sound Savorie,' 'comforting Perseline' [parsley], 'Colde Lettuce'), raise spirits ('chearfull Galingale,' 'Bazill hartie-hale,' 'refreshing Rosmarine' [rosemary]), serve as efficacious healers and purgatives ('Cummin good for eyes,' 'drink-quickning Setuale' [valerian], 'hed-purging Dill'), are vulneraries ('Sharpe Isope [hyssop], good for greene wounds remedies,' 'Veyne-healing Verven' [vervain]), are aromatic ('Bees alluring Thime' [thyme], 'Sweete Marjoram,' 'Ranke smelling Rue,' 'Embathed Balme,' 'breathfull Camomill'), are long-lived ('Lavender still gray,' 'Orpine growing still,' 'Fresh Costmarie' [ageratum]). As the butterfly is enticed into the garden by nourishing plants, so the reader is led 'without suspition' into the mythological environment of Spenser's poem by familiar English garden plants.

magic use In his catalogue of plants that have their 'sweet' tempered with 'soure' (*Amoretti* 26), Spenser includes moly ('and sweet is Moly, but his root is ill'), the magical plant given to Odysseus to protect him from Circe (*Odyssey* 10.304, Ovid *Metamorphoses* 14.291–2). 'Wicked herbes and ointments' are used by the 'divelish hag' Duessa to overpower Fradubio (I ii 42). Spenser's magic use of plants includes demonifuges and those that resist enchantment, for example, the herb 'Medaewart' (meadowsweet) which, when mixed with the liquid metal of a sword, will prevent any enchantment from stopping its blow (II viii 20). Spenser's use of plants and herbs reflects the moral world of his poetry; even the epithet 'divine' in the phrase 'divine *Tobacco*' has its resonance in a moral cosmos. CHARLOTTE F. OTTEN

A. Arber 1912; Arber 1931; Jacques Ferrand ed 1640 *Erotomania, or A Treatise Discoursing of the Essence, Causes, Symptomes, Prognosticks, and Cure of Love, or Erotique Melancholy* tr Edmund Chilmead (Oxford); John Gerard 1597 *The Herball, or Generall Historie of Plantes* (London, rpt 2 vols, Amsterdam and Norwood, NJ 1974) ed 1633 rev and enl Thomas Johnson; M. Grieve 1931 *A Modern Herbal* (London); Lyte 1578; John Parkinson 1629 *Paradise in sole paradisus terrestris, or A Garden of ... Flowers* (London). See also Blanche Henrey 1975 *British Botanical and Horticultural Literature before 1800* 3 vols (London); Otten 1985.

Platonism The term means both the doctrines found in Plato's writings, and a tradition extending from pagan antiquity through the Christian centuries beyond the Renaissance. While Plato's dialogues do not offer a single coherent system, they have stimulated many philosophers and poets to build worlds of their own around ideas attributed to Plato. Our subject was known to Spenser as a profusion of opinions, not an 'ism.' Principles derived from Plato and the Platonic tradition were fundamental but mostly implicit and unexamined in his world view; he lacked our detachment from the tradition and our desire to distinguish between authentic Platonism and adaptations. In the sixteenth century, Platonic thought, like Christianity, was a protean phenomenon, known through many texts, interpretations, references to 'the Platonists,' and images available from many sources.

The Platonic doctrines which figure in Spenser's poetry – pervasive, elusive, significant but simply stated – indicate familiarity with several of Plato's dialogues and some knowledge of ancient Neoplatonism (the teachings of Plotinus, Proclus, and others), Jewish and early Christian adaptations of Neoplatonic doctrines, medieval philosophical traditions, Renaissance Platonism, and many literary uses of Platonic motifs.

There is evidence that as early as 1580 Spenser had assimilated Platonic attitudes toward love and beauty, but his borrowings from the tradition, as from other sources, were always eclectic and selective. A man with his education and experience was exposed both to philosophical texts and the fashionable idealism exemplified in Book 4 of Castiglione's *Courtier*. In his responses to this reading, Spenser was more receptive and imaginative than other Elizabethans. His education led him to the texts (such as Plato's *Timaeus* and *Phaedo*, Boethius' *Consolation of Philosophy*, Macrobius' *Commentary on the Dream of Scipio*, and the writings of St Augustine) on which medieval Platonism – part of the ground he shared with Alanus de Insulis, Dante, Boccaccio, Petrarch, and Chaucer – was based. To this he would add, apparently without any sense of incongruity between medieval traditions and Renaissance transformations, the Platonic bias of much humanistic and courtly literature, and some of the fruits of a century of scholarship which made available many texts (Plato, Neoplatonists, Christian Platonists) unknown in the Middle Ages.

Spenser's preparation for a career as an erudite poet began early and extended beyond his years at Cambridge. If like Sidney he studied Renaissance treatises on poetry, he found in some of them Neoplatonic responses to Plato's hostility to poetry, together with the idea that the poet, like Quintilian's orator (*Institutio oratoria* 1.10.5–7), must be familiar with philosophy. At an early stage, Italian influences were crucial to Spenser's development, and among these were some of the ideas of Ficino. Ficino's labors as a translator and interpreter of Plato and the Neoplatonists, together with the brilliant and controversial writings of Pico della Mirandola, had contributed to a revival of Platonism in both learned and courtly circles that spread from Florence throughout Europe, decisively influencing writers as diverse as Agrippa, Bruno, Castiglione, Conti, Dee, du Bellay, Giorgio, Leone Ebreo, and Tasso, each of whom contributed to Spenser's formation.

In philosophical and quasi-philosophical literature of the later sixteenth century, the strongest trend led away from systematic speculation such as Ficino's toward a combination of received opinions and reflections on experience. Arcane and eclectic learning became fashionable. Ideas and images traceable to Plato or to Platonists coexist in Spenser's poetry with others from sundry sources. In much of his poetry he seems committed to fashioning a synthesis out of the disparate elements of his reading and experience, but at times (esp in the post-1590 poetry) an alert reader encounters tensions and contradictions of which the poet must have been aware. Spenser found in the Platonic tradition both a basis for unifying all that he knew, and a recognition that things here and now are never whole, nor can our understanding of them be complete.

Much of the understanding Spenser sought was available from French translations of ancient texts and the principal Italian expositions of Platonic doctrines pertaining to love, beauty, the human soul, the cosmos, and poetry (see Ellrodt 1960). Editions of the pagan, patristic, and Renaissance Platonists were kept in print by publishers in Basel and Paris. Dialogues, discourses, and encyclopedias by French authors, several of which were translated into English, further disseminated Renaissance Platonism. In France as in Italy, 'academies' of poets and the literati encouraged study of Platonism and appreciation of 'Platonic sentiments' in Petrarch and other poets (see Yates 1947). Homer, Virgil, and Ovid were interpreted allegorically by Platonizing commentators. New interests in natural history and natural law, astrology and astronomy, alchemy, magic and other occult sciences, Paracelsian medicine, mathematics and number symbolism, music, ancient myths and cults, allegory, symbolic images, language, and the Cabala also went hand in hand with enthusiasm for Platonism. Sidney and his circle were alert to these developments, and to the religious position taken by the Huguenot leader Philippe de Mornay, for whom Plato and other spokesmen for the *prisca theologia* (the ancient religious tradition supposedly founded by Hermes Trismegistus; see *Hermeticism) offered support to Christianity. The publication of the Stephanus edition of Plato (Paris 1578) may have occasioned thoughtful study by Sidney and his associates (see Heninger 1983).

During his years at Cambridge, Spenser was probably aware of developments on the continent and of the philosophical learning possessed by such Englishmen as Everard Digby and John Dee. What he learned in his student days was augmented during the months of his association with the Sidney circle in 1579 and 1580. It has been argued that one poem from that period, later published as *Amoretti* 8, presents in mature form the Platonic conceptions of 'heavenly' beauty and virtuous love which mark much of his later poetry and distinguish it from *The Shepheardes Calender* (Quitslund 1973). Perhaps it was at this time that Spenser began studiously to assimilate the developments surveyed above.

From Platonism and kindred traditions he sought illumination of his muse's domain, which extends to heaven but has human affairs on earth at its center. What mattered most to him were God's creation as described in Genesis and the *Timaeus* (the work of the six days and the indwelling soul that sustains both macrocosm and microcosm through time in the image of an eternal pattern) and human analogues of God's work, ranging from mythopoeia and images of the cosmos to the making of poetry, and extending to self-fashioning and virtuous love. From his earliest poetry to the posthumously published *Cantos of Mutabilitie*, Spenser deals with themes that had been the property and legacy of Platonists: individual lives and moments of experience are seen in relation to seasonal and historical cycles; the human microcosm mirrors order and disorder in the cosmos; virtue and pleasure are to be found in harmony between the individual soul and cosmic processes, referred to their heavenly source and eventually returning to it; error and evil are understood as indifference to the higher order of reality and subversion of an upward-tending natural process.

Writers in the Platonic tradition had interpreted divine and human creativity systematically, subtly, and popularly, and it seems that to Spenser they offered keys to the world's labyrinth and a rationale for reconciling Christian and classical authorities. The poetry Spenser wrote in the 1580s and 1590s is all consistent with the teachings of Christian Platonists. Along with Sidney, he had learned from such authorities that the poet's 'erected wit' enjoys privileged knowledge of a 'golden' world, unfallen or restored, and that the poet's images are capable of moving the reader from shadowy types toward truth. Spenser emphasized much more than Sidney that the poet's creativity depends upon inspiration. (This doctrine, influentially expounded in Ficino's comments on Plato's *Ion*, is first found in *October* and E.K.'s apparatus.)

The more abstruse theories of the Platonists (celestial and supercelestial hierarchies, system-building logic) are not apparent in Spenser's poetry. Their ideas are used poetically, and more implied than stated even in the places most imbued with Platonism: the more idealistic of the *Amoretti* (3, 7, 8, 45, 61, 72, 79, 88); the symmetries and cosmic correspondences of *Epithalamion*; the mythology and psychology of love in *Fowre Hymnes*; the figures of Belphoebe and her twin Amoret; the mysteries of the houses of Mammon and Proteus, the Garden of Adonis, the Temple of Venus, and Isis Church; the symbolic (and symbolically situated) castle of Alma; the vicissitudes of Florimell; the schematic representation of friendship in the legend of Cambell and Triamond; the poet's reflections on his private access to Fairyland and the virtues, at once transcendental and 'deepe within the mynd' (see *FQ* VI proem); the divining dreams of Arthur and Britomart (I ix 13–15, V vii 12–23); the visionary experience granted Colin and Calidore on Mount Acidale (VI x 10–27); and Nature's image and message in *FQ* VII vii 5–13, 58.

Throughout *The Faerie Queene*, Spenser's representation of the virtues and vices and both the rational and irrational aspects of human nature combines Platonic and Aristotelian themes. In the *Republic* (4.430E–44E; cf 9.580D-3A), virtue is described as a harmony of parts in a hierarchy, the three parts of the soul being reason, noble irascibility, and concupiscence (see Reid 1981–2 for background on the tripartite soul; see also Platonic *psychology). To this, following interpreters of Plato's *Symposium* and *Phaedrus*, Spenser adds that, while concupiscence is base, in those worthy of it 'love does alwayes bring forth bounteous deeds, / And in each gentle hart desire of honour breeds' (*FQ* III i 49).

Several other Platonic principles are consistent with Spenser's vision and his allegorical mode. For him Plato's Ideas are found in heaven with the angels (*Heavenly Beautie* 82–4), and on a lower level the Garden of Adonis contains archetypes of 'all things, that are borne to live and die' (*FQ* III vi 30); similarly, in Ficino's 'Commentary' on the *Symposium* (2.3–5), the Ideas are one in God, plural in angelic intelligences, and then become reasons in the world soul, seeds in nature, and forms in matter. In Spenser's poetry, the world of the elements is only the lowest part of reality, full of illusions but receptive to heavenly light; both the cosmic and the ethical/aesthetic hierarchies are defined by degrees of permanence, noble purpose, and beauty; the human soul is heavenly in origin, and desires to enjoy heaven and heaven's analogues on earth; the soul ascends through virtuous love.

Spenser is most obviously indebted to the Platonists when he writes (as he often does) of love, which at its best he represents as the soul's access to itself in a harmonious relationship with the cosmos. Plato had said (*Phaedrus* 255D) that when love is reciprocated lover and beloved are mirrors to one another; Ficino had developed this idea and demonstrated how love makes possible full self-knowledge, since the proper object of love reveals the soul as it was before descending into a body ('Commentary' on the *Symposium* 2.8, 6.4–6). Exposition of these ideas is found in *Fowre Hymnes* (*HL* 99–119, 190–217; *HB* 190–238), and Spenser works with their implications elsewhere, sometimes using Plato's mirror metaphor.

Platonists find human nature mirrored in the cosmos; it is a theater designed by and for the soul. Plato's 'likely story' (*Timaeus* 29B-D) explaining the creation of the world's body and soul involves thinking of the nonhuman cosmos as if it were human, and in turn the cosmos is represented (41B-7E) as contributing substances to the formation of the human soul and body.

Plato's myth and the assumptions it entailed pervaded the anthropocentric world view of the Renaissance, and from Nicholas of Cusa to Bruno the subtlest philosophers pondered the relation of the human mind and soul to the cosmos (see Cassirer ed 1963). In the Platonists' system, built on analogies between microcosm and macrocosm, love unites the soul with the world; through love the soul can move both upward toward the intelligible world and God, and downward to admire or create beauty on earth. In the allegorical narrative of *The Faerie Queene*, nature is the basis for a moralized landscape, a stage set for the soul's education by trial and error and divine grace; the soul meets its own 'projections' and comes to terms with fallen reality, or is allowed access to manifestations of the ideal. Two examples of this dialectic will suffice. The giant Orgoglio who defeats Redcrosse in *FQ* I vii 7–15 personifies both an admonitory earthquake and the knight's own pride, which is the 'homebred evill' described by Archimago in I i 31–2. At the other end of the spectrum, in *FQ* VI on Mount Acidale Calidore is vouchsafed experience of the Graces, who are nymphs or goddesses associated with an unfallen natural order and also with Calidore's virtue, the 'skill men call Civility' (x 5–24).

The Platonists together with his own enabling genius gave Spenser an imaginative grasp of the order of reality which Plato had termed 'daimonic' – the planetary divinities, world soul, and nature in Ficino's scheme ('Commentary' on the *Symposium* 2.3–5, 5.4, 6.3–5, 6.7; see M.J.B. Allen 1984:8–34). Love, as Diotima explains (*Symposium* 202D-3A), is a great *daimon*, a mediator who interprets human actions to the gods and divine actions to men. For some later Platonists, daimons are agents of consciousness striving toward divinity; Spenser stresses receptivity to heavenly influence and grace flowing downward, and he represents the world as full of mediating entities through whom heaven and earth, spirit and matter, are united: for example, Cupid when benign (*FQ* I proem 3, III iii 1–3, V 1–2; *Colin Clout* 799–886; *HL* 43–119), Venus (*FQ* III vi 11–12 and 40, IV x 39–47; *HB* 29–56, 260–6), angels such as Guyon's guardian (*FQ* II viii 1–3), Genius (II xii 47–8, III vi 31–2, *Epithalamion* 398–404), and the Graces (*FQ* VI x 10–27). To the extent that Spenser fills the role of his prototype Orpheus, he is Plato's 'daimonic man' (*Symposium* 203A), capable of interpreting the world between heaven and hell and conducting willing souls toward the light.

Christianity teaches that Christ and the grace available through him mediate between God and mortals, and many Elizabethans believed that what Plato termed daimonic was in fact demonic and at odds with grace. Spenser's poetry lends some support to this view: there are infernal demons in every book of *The Faerie Queene*, and their power is great even though it is founded on illusion. However, we are repeatedly assured that the power given to 'The sonnes of Day' (*FQ* I v 25; cf III iv 59) is ultimately greater than that of darkness. Spenser's strategies for representing the world and the soul both illuminated by heaven show him to have been profoundly indebted to the broad stream with many tributaries termed Platonism. JON A. QUITSLUND

For background, see M.J.B. Allen 1984; Couliano 1987; Kristeller 1979; D.P. Walker 1972 *The Ancient Theology: Studies in Christian Platonism from the Fifteenth to the Eighteenth Century* (Ithaca, NY); Wind 1958; Frances A. Yates 1947 *The French Academies of the Sixteenth Century* (London). Two key texts have now been tr by Sears Jayne: Ficino ed 1985 and Giovanni Pico della Mirandola 1984 *Commentary on a Canzone of Benivieni* (New York).

For Spenser and Platonism, see Elizabeth Bieman 1988 *Plato Baptized: Towards the Interpretation of Spenser's Mimetic Fictions* (Toronto); Burchmore 1984; Ellrodt 1960; Fowler 1964; Fowler 1973; Hankins 1971; Hieatt

1975a; Hyde 1986; Kane 1983; David Lee Miller 1986 'Spenser's Poetics: The Poem's Two Bodies' *PMLA* 101:170–85; Nelson 1963; Nohrnberg 1976; Jon A. Quitslund 1973 'Spenser's *Amoretti* VIII and Platonic Commentaries on Petrarch' *JWCI* 36:256–76; Welsford 1967. See also S.K. Heninger, Jr 1983 'Sidney and Serranus' Plato' *ELR* 13:146–61.

Pleasure In the Garden of Adonis, Pleasure appears as the daughter of Cupid and Psyche (*FQ* III vi 50). Traditional interpretation of the Cupid and Psyche myth (transmitted to the Renaissance in Apuleius' *Golden Ass* 4–6 and discussed by Martianus Capella, Fulgentius, Plotinus, and others) glossed their child, Voluptas, as the eternal joy felt by the soul as it turns away from the flesh to embrace Divine Love (see Boccaccio *Genealogia* 5.22). Spenser, however, avoids any such stress on the otherworldly: he makes Pleasure the companion and foster sister of Amoret, associating her with earthly, sexual love (cf Milton *Comus* 1009–10 'Two blissful twins ... Youth and Joy'; Hughes, et al 1970–, 2.3:985–7). The Garden with its stress on generation recalls the 'Paradize / Of all delight' where the happy lovers play their 'hurtlesse sports, without rebuke or blame,' under the protection of Love's 'daughter *Pleasure*,' and anticipates the lovers in the garden outside the Temple of Venus who never 'for rebuke or blame of any balkt' (*Hymne of Love* 280–8, *FQ* IV x 25). In these visions, nature and pleasure are untainted: in all innocence, the lovers crown Pleasure 'their Goddesse and their Queene' (292).

The changed emphasis of the Cupid and Psyche myth is characteristic of Spenser, in whose work a Neoplatonic rejection of earthly delight is never strong. At times, the world's instability causes the poet to long for final rest as he does at the end of the *Cantos of Mutabilitie*; and there are many evocations of the pleasure caused by the vision of the ideal – the 'infinite delight,' for instance, that the vision of divine Sapience gives the visionary in *Heavenly Beautie* (256–9), or Colin's joy in his vision of the Graces (*FQ* VI x 11–16). But at the center of the Graces is a vision of Colin's earthly love: the praise of divine pleasures is continuous with the praise of earthly ones. One of the signs of a sick mind in Spenser's poetry is the inability to take pleasure in God's creation: in *The Shepheardes Calender*, Colin's solipsistic Petrarchism is partly signaled by his inability to enjoy the world around him, as is Alcyon's self-indulgent grief in *Daphnaïda*.

Spenser's stress on the goodness of earthly pleasure shares common ground with the Renaissance revival of interest in Epicurean thought. Lorenzo Valla's *De Voluptate* devotes most of its first two books to a praise of pleasure, More's Utopians find pleasure the greatest good, and Erasmus entitled one of his late colloquies *The Epicurean*. But as in Spenser, this Epicurean 'revival' tends to be Christian and conservative; and an exclusive concern with the pleasures of this world becomes the mark of a limited 'pagan' sensibility unaware of the deeper joys attested by Christian revelation. More's Utopians are virtuous pagans who demonstrate the capacity of reason unaided by Christian revelation to restore fallen human nature – and suggest as well the limits of that capacity; the third book of *De voluptate* incorporates and supersedes the first two, showing that the pleasures of divine love in the afterlife exceed all earthly delight; and the true pleasure of Erasmus' Epicurean turns out to be his serene confidence in salvation.

Had there been no Renaissance revival of Epicurus, Spenser's concern with earthly pleasure would still be consonant with the medieval and classical commonplace, often stressed by Erasmus, that the pleasures of the body have a real, if inferior, position in the hierarchy of goods. Physical pleasure throughout Spenser's poetry is worthwhile only if it does not hinder some greater good. At times, for example when Redcrosse relaxes with Duessa, or Verdant with Acrasia, earthly pleasure opposes virtue as in the choice of Hercules. More frequently, however, it appears a sustaining if at times ambivalent force associated with the world of process. The stanza that announces the presence of time in the Garden also insists that 'here all plentie, and all pleasure flowes' (III vi 41). When Venus possesses Adonis, she 'reape[s] sweet pleasure of the wanton boy' (46); the metaphor makes pleasure the fitting harvest of a world of generation.

Spenser's treatment of sexual pleasure in the less idealized context of normal experience stresses its ambivalent and troubling power. The poet of the *Amoretti* may assure his lady that 'spotlesse pleasure' builds his sacred bower in the tower of faith (65); but his desire for such pleasure often takes maculate form, most notably in the dream-blazon which turns the beloved into a table of 'juncats' (77). A similar tension appears in *Epithalamion* when the speaker's barely controlled imagining of 'greedy pleasure' in the bedding of the couple yields two stanzas later to a firm prayer invoking the Genius of generation who 'doest succour and supply' the 'sweet pleasures of ... loves delight.' The acts of pleasure need divine aid to yield their 'timely fruit' in this world (365–404).

Spenser's double stress on the goodness of pleasure and its liability to misuse appears in the pervasive and characteristic metaphor of food. His characters are ambivalently 'fed' with pleasures of both body and mind. The lover of *Amoretti* reduces his lady to a banquet in dream, but that lady is also his 'soules long lacked foode' (*Am* 1, 77). The ambivalence appears again when Sansloy 'feed[s] his fyrie lustfull eye' with Una's beauty (*FQ* I vi 4) and when Belphoebe's beauty feeds the 'gazers sense with double pleasure ... Hable to heale the sicke, and to revive the ded' (II iii 22). In both these contexts the pleasure deriving from an earthly expression of divine beauty merely excites lust. The work of the great poet is itself a pleasurable food: in *Teares of the Muses*, the right reader is 'With beawtie kindled and with pleasure fed' (364) – raised and sustained by the pleasures of art. But the art which tries only to 'please' resembles the pleasures which distract the hero from his quest; it is treated with contempt in *Teares of the Muses* and *Colin Clout*, and with disdainful irony in the closing lines of *The Faerie Queene*. WILLIAM A. ORAM

D.C. Allen 1944 'The Rehabilitation of Epicurus and His Theory of Pleasure in the Early Renaissance' *SP* 41:1–15; Fulgentius ed 1971; Nestrick 1975; Olson 1982; Edward Surtz, SJ 1957 *The Praise of Pleasure: Philosophy, Education, and Communism in More's 'Utopia'* (Cambridge, Mass); Lorenzo Valla 1977 *On Pleasure: De Voluptate* tr A. Kent Hieatt and Maristella Lorch (New York).

The Plowman's Tale A Lollard polemical poem of the early fifteenth century. Although reticent about such issues as the Eucharist, *The Plowman's Tale* mirrors much else that characterized Lollard belief in late medieval England and subsequently found favor with Henrician propagandists and Elizabethan Protestants. Its message, which emerges remorselessly from the lengthy speeches addressed by the Lollard Pelican to his ineffectual orthodox adversary the Griffon, is anticlerical, antiepiscopal, antimonastic, antimendicant, anticurial, antipapal, and proroyalist.

The poem was first printed in 1535 as part of a carefully orchestrated program of propaganda for the Henrician reformation supervised by Thomas Cromwell. Texts of demonstrable or plausibly assertable antiquity were particularly sought after to counter accusations of newfangledness in the king's doctrinal position. This explains the value of *The Plowman's Tale*, particularly after it had been furnished with a spurious and artless 52-line prologue, which enabled this anonymous and pallid verse tract to be included in William Thynne's 1542 Chaucer edition as a Canterbury Tale assigned to the Plowman of the *General Prologue*. England's most celebrated ancient poet thus became closely identified with the trenchant imperatives of the reformist cause; and Chaucer remained a Protestant poet in the eyes of readers who knew the editions by Stow (1561), Speght (1598; rpt 1602, 1687), and Urry (1721), or the texts of *The Plowman's Tale* printed separately as Chaucerian in 1545 and 1606. Of all the works of the Chaucer apocrypha, *The Plowman's Tale* exercised the most decisive influence on the poet's reputation, even after Tyrwhitt excised it from the canon in 1775.

Spenser was influenced by it in three ways. First, as Thomas Warton noted, phrases and lines from it appear in six of the *Shepheardes Calender* eclogues. Compare *PT* 14 'He was forswonke and all forswatte' with *Aprill* 99 'Albee forswonck and forswatt I am' (a doublet phrase not found elsewhere in Chaucer); *PT* 29 'To swete and swynke I make avowe' with *November* 154 'Of mortal men, that swincke and sweate for nought' (again, a doublet phrase occurring nowhere else in Chaucer); *PT* 53 'A sterne stryfe is stered newe' with *Februarie* 149 'Unto his Lord, stirring up sterne strife' (E.K. attributes 'sterne strife' to Chaucer, yet apart from *PT*, the phrase does not occur in his works); *PT* 96 with *September* 174 and *PT* 134 with *Julye* 177; and *PT* 756 'Suche myster men ben all mysgo' with *Julye* 201 'Sike mister men bene all misgone.' Second, the form of the ecclesiastical and moral eclogues suggests a more general influence from *The Plowman's Tale*. 'Tityrus' (Chaucer) is mentioned three times as an inspiration (*Feb* 92, *June* 81, *Dec* 4); of all the poems in the Chaucer canon, *The Plowman's Tale* is closest in form and spirit to the moral eclogues. Third, there is the possibility (it is no more) that Spenser's lost *Dying Pellicane* may have derived its title and substance from Pelican in *The Plowman's Tale*.

Tyrwhitt suggested that the line 'Nor with the Pilgrim that the Ploughman playde a whyle' (*SC* envoy) refers to *The Plowman's Tale*, whereas Warton believed it to be an allusion to *Piers Plowman*. Both views have received recent support. The Chaucerian 'plowman' in the tale does indeed 'play' the role of pilgrim, and E.K.'s glosses acknowledge the tale as a Spenserian model. Yet it is not clear why Spenser should have sought to differentiate this single work from the main canon of Chaucer, mentioned as 'Tityrus' in the preceding line. The reference seems more likely to be a separate work (*Piers Plowman*) by a different author (Langland) which together with *The Plowman's Tale* helped to shape the figure of Piers as the Protestant interlocutor in *Maye*. ANDREW WAWN

The text of *The Plowman's Tale* was regularly reprinted in the 16th c, following the ed of Thomas Godfray (c 1535; *STC* 5099.5); a facsimile of the text in the Chaucer 1542 *Works* is found in Chaucer ed 1969; a modern ed is Chaucer ed 1894–7, 7:147–90. For further discussion, see Anne Hudson 1983 '"No newe thyng": The Printing of Medieval Texts in the Early Reformation Period' in Gray and Stanley 1983:153–74; King 1986; Percy W. Long 1913 'Spenser and the *Plowman's Tale*' *MLN* 28:262; Andrew N. Wawn 1972 'The Genesis of *The Plowman's Tale*' *YES* 2:21–40; Wawn 1973–4 'Chaucer, *The Plowman's Tale* and Reformation Propaganda: The Testimonies of Thomas Godfray and *I Playne Piers*' *BJRL* 56:174–92. For general background, see Anne Hudson 1988 *The Premature Reformation: Wycliffite Texts and Lollard History* (Oxford), and King 1982; for the Renaissance Chaucer, see Miskimin 1975.

poet, role of the The role of poet changes from age to age and even from generation to generation, as does any social role; and in a complex society like that of Elizabethan England, the poet's role is as likely as any other to be riven by contradictory expectations. Renaissance literary theory, supported by the illustrious example of antiquity, made the poet a source of cultural authority second only to the monarch. As Jonson remarked, 'Every beggerly Corporation affoords the State a *Major*, or two *Bailiffs*, yearly: but, *solus Rex, aut Poeta, non quotannis nascitur* [only the king or the poet is not born each year]' (ed 1925–52, 8:637). Yet the actual practice and literary self-presentation of most Elizabethan poets, particularly those of Spenser's generation, suggest that the poet was considered a marginal figure, a delinquent, who, in his self-willed pursuit of love and beauty, departs from the ethical norms that ideally should govern both self and society. Spenser's presentation of himself as poet was caught between these conflicting notions. Though he sought to establish himself as a major national poet, the official literary spokesman of the newly emerging British empire, he shared the generic forms and the practical occasions of his poetry-writing contemporaries; and with those forms and occasions came a limiting idea of the poet and his career.

The high regard for poetry and the expectation that a great nation would produce a great poet owed much to Renaissance humanism. In his *Defence of Poetry*, Sidney regrets that 'from almost the highest estimation of learning [poetry] is fallen to be the laughing-stock of children' (ed 1973b:74); he speaks as a humanist, as one who holds before himself and his readers an image of supreme cultural accomplishment derived from the study of ancient Greece and Rome. We encounter the same attitudes in *The Shepheardes Calender* where Spenser recalls Virgil, 'the Romish *Tityrus*,' and laments that '*Mecoenas* is yclad in claye, / And great *Augustus* long ygoe is dead' (*October* 55–62). From the humanist's perspective, Virgil, Maecenas, and Augustus – the poet, the patron, and the ruler – formed an ideal triad that showed what kind of work the poet should do, how he should be supported, and what relation he should have to the power of the state. Already in the mid-fourteenth century, Petrarch, who had been crowned poet laureate in a magnificent ceremony on the Capitoline Hill overlooking the ruins of ancient Rome, had attempted to restore the classical triad. In subsequent years, many poets renewed the attempt, Ariosto, Ronsard, and Tasso most prominent among them. So firmly set was this Virgilian example that by the late sixteenth century England's failure to produce such a poet was becoming something of a national embarrassment. The humanistically educated thus rejoiced at the publication in 1579 of *The Shepheardes Calender*. Here at last England had a poet who knew what he was about. Like Virgil, the New Poet, as Spenser was called, had begun with pastoral, acknowledged a worthy patron, and paid proper homage to the monarch. Eleven years later, when the first installment of *The Faerie Queene* came out, the pattern seemed complete.

This familiar success story is, however, a little too easy and neat. In putting Virgil, Petrarch, Spenser, and the other great Renaissance poets together in this way, we ignore the difficulties that attended the revival of the ancient literary role. Petrarch was not, after all, best known as a humanist laureate. In the sixteenth century, his greatest fame and influence came from his *Rime*, love poems for which there was no obvious classical precedent. His *Africa*, the Latin epic on which his laureate pretension largely depended, was stillborn, as was the *Franciade* of Ronsard, who also gained his real reputation as a love poet.

Humanism did sound the call to which Petrarch, Ronsard, Spenser, and many others responded. But often it raised up these poets only to misdirect them, setting them to work on unsuitable projects or making them and their learned readers doubt the value of what they did best. Humanist ideas provoked controversy over Ariosto's *Orlando furioso*, made Tasso rewrite his *Gerusalemme liberata*, and started Sidney, Spenser, and the other members of their literary circle down a dead-end road of quantitative meters. Not even *The Shepheardes Calender* could escape reproach on such grounds, for, as Sidney, to whom the poem was dedicated, wrote, 'That same framing of his style to an old rustic language I dare not allow, since neither Theocritus in Greek, Virgil in Latin, nor Sannazzaro in Italian did affect it' (ed 1973b:112). Perhaps a new poet in a new age required precisely what the humanist, limited by his attachment to the standards of a long-departed culture, dared not allow. As C.S. Lewis (1954:19) has pointed out, 'humanism, with its unities and *Gorboducs* and English hexameters, would have prevented if it could' the great poetry and drama of the 1580s and 1590s, including *The Faerie Queene*, which combines the deviant archaism of *The Shepheardes Calender* with the unclassical narrative liberty of *Orlando furioso*.

Humanism, particularly as it emerged in Reformation England, cramped the poet as much as it did his poems. The humanist ideal of the active life left little room for the full development of a literary career. We see this most strikingly in such an expression of mid-century humanism as Roger Ascham's very influential *Schoolmaster* (1570), where poets are identified as 'quicke wittes': 'hastie, rashe, headie, and brainsicke' young men who, in his opinion, rarely prove 'either verie fortunate for them selves, or verie profitable to serve the common wealth' (ed 1904:189–90). Similar ideas are frequently repeated by the young men themselves. 'God helpe us,' Harvey exclaims to Spenser in a letter on poetry, 'you and I are wisely employed, (are wee not?) when our Pen and Inke, and Time, and Wit, and all runneth away in this goodly yonkerly veine: as if the world had nothing else for us to do: or we were borne to be the only *Nonproficients* and *Nihilagents* of the world' (*Three Letters* 3, *Var Prose* p 473). Here, as in Ascham, the poet appears a worthless donothing. Instead of expending his time and wit in the service of queen and country, as his humanist education directs him to do, he wastes both on what even Spenser (and in reference to *The Faerie Queene* itself) could call 'ydle rimes ... The labor of lost time, and wit unstayd' (*FQ* Burghley Sonn).

In Spenser's generation, this negative attitude toward poetry influenced the way poets actually presented themselves far more than did the exalted Virgilian model. In their many formal defenses of poetry, they remembered that 'Homer was no les accompted then *Humanus deus*,' that Aristotle thought poets 'the auncient Treasurers of the Graecians Divinity,' that 'Kinges and Princes, great and famous men, did ever encourage, mayntaine, and reward Poets,' that 'poets were the first philosophers, the first astronomers and historiographers and oratours and musitiens of the world,' and that poetry had long served 'to soften and polish the hard and rough dispositions of men, and make them capable of vertue and good discipline' (G.G. Smith 1904, 1:64, 206, 232; 2:8, 197). Yet they almost invariably forgot such ideas when speaking of their own work. Instead, they apologized for beginning and repented when they were finished. As a plaything of youth, a pastime for idle hours, poetry might be allowed. It might even serve to display abilities that once recognized and rewarded could be turned to more profitable ends. But as an end in itself, as the main activity of a man's life, poetry had no place.

When the humanist left school and turned courtier, as many did in the hope both of advancing themselves and of fulfilling the purpose of their classical education, these confining attitudes toward poetry were powerfully reinforced. Not that the court was opposed to poetry. On the contrary, courtiers were in many ways more receptive to aesthetic values than were humanists, and this receptivity contributed not only to the production of poetry but also to its status: 'poetry's ornamental features, its deceptive verbal tactics, its playful motives – all viewed suspiciously by factions in Tudor society generally hostile to artistic refinement – were bound to gain more respectability by being esteemed at the nation's center of power and fashion' (Javitch 1978:6). An easy and unaffected skill at verse making – an accomplishment recommended by Castiglione in *The Courtier* and made central to Puttenham's *Arte of English Poesie* – lent credit to the courtier capable of it; and when that courtier had the prestige of a Sidney, an Oxford, or a Raleigh, the credit was reflected on poetry itself. But for the courtier, poetry could be only an avocation, never a vocation. And as an avocation, it could not be practiced in such a way as to satisfy the expectations associated with the humanist idea of the great poet.

As humanist, the poet represented (or thought of himself as representing) a fixed standard of value. Through him, the eloquence and moral philosophy that had enlightened the ancient world would once again shine forth. As courtier, however, he was asked to supply entertainment and flattery, not learned instruction. He was 'the servant of his breeding and his sovereign, not of his understanding ... the tradition of practical learning and ethical preoccupation which brought the Humanists to the court was met with a requirement that they use their literary gifts and forget their ideals' (G.K. Hunter 1962:31). Thus, whether he remembered his courtly pretensions and spoke of his verse with playful disdain, or remembered his frustrated humanist principles and confessed to a more serious fault, the courtier poet respected boundaries too narrow for a man of Spenser's laureate ambition. Yet so prestigious were the greater courtiers that not even Spenser, himself a minor satellite of the courtly system, could disregard their limiting conception of the poet's role.

That conception found expression in three favorite Elizabethan literary personae: the shepherd, the lover, and the prodigal. Each allowed the gentleman-amateur to distinguish his serious and dutiful self from the erring self which was desirous of a temporary period of pastoral *otium* (leisure) or overmastered by the sway of some amorous passion or led astray by the passing folly of youth, and so made poems. Always implicit was the promise that the shepherd would eventually cast off his rural disguise, that the lover would renounce his passion, that the prodigal would return to the moral standard of his father, and that the poet would give up poetry – a promise most Elizabethans, particularly those of gentle rank, faithfully kept.

Spenser could not do likewise if he hoped to give England a laureate poet. Neither could he ignore the idea of the poet embodied in these various personae. Not only did that idea respond to pressures that weighed on him as they weighed on his contemporaries; it also gave poetry whatever structural autonomy it had outside the public theaters. The idea of the poet-amateur opened, however briefly, the space where the literary energies of Spenser's generation gathered. Spenser depended as much on the accumulated force of those energies as did anyone. The making of a great poetic career is never a wholly individual project. To transcend his age, the poet must first be of his age. This is true even of seemingly isolated figures like Blake or Hopkins, and it is still more true of a poet like Spenser who seeks to speak from the center of his culture. But in Elizabethan England, that very centering impulse made it difficult for the aspiring laureate to fit his ambitions to the role of poet as it was represented in the careers of his amateur contemporaries, for the amateur made of poetry an eccentric activity, one whose definition depended on its difference from the active life of service to the commonwealth.

Spenser's self-presentation thus required what might be called a double differentiation. Like the amateurs, he had first to distinguish himself from the more conventionally dutiful non-poets. This he did in many ways – most notably by adopting the pastoral guise of Colin Clout and by revealing in himself the familiar face of the prodigal youth beguiled by love. 'Onely this appeareth,' comments E.K. in explaining the motives that prompted *The Shepheardes Calender*, 'that his unstayed yougth had long wandred in the common Labyrinth of Love, in which time to mitigate and allay the heate of his passion ... he compiled these xii. Aeglogues' (Epistle to Harvey). Spenser himself later tells how 'in th'heat of youth' he made 'Many lewd layes (ah woe is me the more) / In praise of that mad fit, which fooles call love' (*Heavenly Love* 8–10).

Once having established the differences that put him in the category of poet, as he and his contemporaries understood that category, he then had to distinguish himself as laureate from the other poets of his generation. Again his strategies were many, though two stand out with particular clarity. One was to claim the poet's guise, the role of Colin Clout, not as a holiday mask, but as his fixed identity: 'A Shepeheards boye (no better doe him call)' (*SC, Jan* 1). The other strategy was precisely the opposite. He joined the amateurs in putting an end to his youthful delinquency, but unlike them, he returned to a duty that was itself literary. He abandoned his pastoral disguise and emerged as England's heroic poet.

Something of the complex interplay of these apparently contradictory strategies can be seen in the first lines of *The Faerie Queene*: 'Lo I the man, whose Muse whilome did maske, / As time her taught, in lowly Shepheards weeds, / Am now enforst a far unfitter taske, / For trumpets sterne to chaunge mine Oaten reeds, / And sing of Knights and Ladies gentle deeds.' Spenser here places himself in a laureate tradition. He echoes the opening of the *Aeneid* as found in Renaissance editions, thus reminding his readers that in moving from pastoral to epic he is following the Virgilian pattern. He also evokes Ariosto, who had also promised to sing 'of Knights and Ladies gentle deeds,' and perhaps Chaucer, whose diction and pose of authorial humility he imitates. But even as he establishes a connection to his greatest Roman, Italian, and English predecessors, he associates himself with – and dissociates himself from – his amateur contemporaries. Like them, he removes the pastoral garment of youth, but to become an epic poet, not a soldier, civil servant, or clergyman. He fulfills his duty and returns to the ethical and political center of his culture by writing a poem that will, as he puts it in the Letter to Raleigh, 'fashion a gentleman or noble person in vertuous and gentle discipline,' the very discipline the amateurs abandon poetry to practice. But there is a hint here too of the counterstrategy, for Spenser protests that this epic undertaking is 'a far unfitter taske' (*FQ* 1 proem 1); thus, he seems to suggest that the pastoral world is his true home, that he belongs to the native land of poetry in a quite particular way.

Through the early books of *The Faerie Queene*, the potential rift between these self-presentational strategies never opens. On the contrary, the two work together to help Spenser succeed in doing what no other poet of his generation could do: make the erring poetry of love into a poetry of heroic accomplishment, the kind of poetry that would support a laureate career. But in the last books of *The Faerie Queene* and in some of the shorter poems of the 1590s, that improbable but necessary union shows signs of breaking down. *Amoretti* 33 and 80 reveal a tension between Spenser's private love and his public poetic duty. *Colin Clouts Come Home Againe* distinguishes sharply between courtiers and shepherds and puts Spenser on the side of the latter. *FQ* v and vi set love and heroic endeavor in opposition to one another. Particularly significant is the reappearance in Book vi of the poet in the once-discarded mask of Colin Clout, piping not to Queen Elizabeth, as the epic poet had done throughout *The Faerie Queene* and as even Colin himself had done in the *Aprill* eclogue, but rather to his own love, in a vision that is destroyed by the arrival of Calidore, the knight of Courtesy. The knight and the shepherd, the man of action and the poet, are now seen as belonging to different worlds. To enter the pastoral world, the knight must abandon his quest. To enter the active world, the shepherd must expose himself and his poetry to the 'venemous despite' of that Blatant Beast who in the last stanzas of Book vi is menacing *The Faerie Queene* itself.

In reassuming the pastoral guise of Colin Clout, Spenser does not, however, return to the amateur pose of the literary delinquent that he had partly accepted in *The Shepheardes Calender*. Instead (in cautious and half-canceled ways, to be sure), he attributes delinquency to the active world with which his humanist upbringing had taught him to align himself. If poetry and power cannot be made concentric, it is because power has gone astray. The poet, with his access to 'the sacred noursery / Of vertue' (*FQ* vi proem 3), speaks from the center – a center represented by Spenser's own marriage in *Epithalamion*, by the pastoral world to which he comes home in *Colin Clout*, and by Colin's vision in Book vi. But despite these intimations, Spenser could not anticipate Shelley in declaring poets 'the unacknowledged legislators of the world' or Solzhenitsyn in seeing the poet as 'another government.' So profound a redefinition of the poet's role required Milton and a civil war. In Spenser's generation, the humanist idea of the great poet's relation to the monarch forbade it, as did the actual power structure of the age. But Spenser's career did show a way past the amateur dominance of poetry and, in doing so, gave England its first laureate. RICHARD HELGERSON

Helgerson 1976; Helgerson 1983; G.K. Hunter 1962, esp ch 1 'Humanism and Courtship'; Javitch 1978; Mallette 1979; David Lee Miller 1979b; Miller 1983; Montrose 1979; J.W. Saunders 1964 *The Profession of English Letters* (London).

poet's poet, the Although first used in 1822 by John Chalk Claris ('Arthur Brooke') in his *Elegy on the Death of Percy Bysshe Shelley* (stanza 13 'Thou poet's poet!' *TLS* 1 Jan 1925:9), for a century, this was the epithet by which Spenser was known and honored. It was first used in Leigh Hunt's *Imagination and Fancy* (1844), an anthology of English poetry with extensive commentary. Hunt attributed the phrase to Charles Lamb, to whom the honor of coining it has always been given. But it appears nowhere in Lamb's published writings or letters. Presumably (and perfectly plausibly) it was a remark in conversation, which Hunt, who had a talent for recognizing literary vitality, rightly recorded. It achieved a wide currency, for it seemed to many, as it did to James Russell Lowell, writing in 1875, that 'Charles Lamb made the most pithy criticism of Spenser when he called him the poets' poet.'

The phrase caught on because it encoded a particular aesthetic. Almost a century after Hunt launched it, the critic who initiated modern interest in Spenser called it into question. In *The Allegory of Love* (1936), C.S. Lewis objected to the epithet, claiming it had done 'incalculable damage.' It led readers to expect 'some quintessential "poeticalness" in the lowest and most obvious sense of that word – something more mellifluous than Shakespeare's sonnets, more airy than Shelley, more swooningly sensuous than Keats, more dreamlike than William Morris' (p 317). Bent on revising the Romantics' account of Spenser's poetic qualities, Lewis also proposed to revise the 'title' they had bestowed on him. Just as he drew attention to qualities of vigor, plain speech, and narrative energy in *The Faerie Queene*, he gave a plain prose account of 'the poet's poet': '[Spenser] is so called in virtue of the historical fact that most of the poets have liked him very much' (p 320).

It is true that Hunt liked pointing out how much Spenser was admired by later poets, but it seems clear that he cited Lamb's phrase in order to register the sense of Spenser's poetry that Lewis rejected. In introducing his selections from Spenser, Hunt says that his 'great characteristic is poetic luxury' and that of all poets he 'is the farthest removed from the ordinary cares and haunts of the world.' You must not go to him, Hunt tells his reader, for story, stylistic economy, pathos, or mirth. 'But if you love poetry well enough to enjoy it for its own sake,' you will be well rewarded: 'Take him in short for what he is, whether greater or less than his fellows, the poetical faculty is so abundantly and beautifully predominant in him above every other, though he had passion, and thought, and plenty of ethics, and was as learned a man as Ben Jonson, perhaps as Milton himself, that he has always been felt by his countrymen to be what Charles Lamb called him, the "Poet's Poet."' The force of all this is clear: what Hunt thought Lamb's epithet conveyed is what Hazlitt meant by saying of Spenser that 'of all the poets, he is the most poetical.'

It is inconceivable that anyone today would invoke Lamb's phrase to convey Spenser's essential qualities and merits. It remains only to ask whether the genitive noun in it is singular (*poet's*) or plural (*poets'*). There is no authoritative source, because Lamb never wrote the phrase down and one cannot distinguish the two forms when spoken. Hunt wrote the singular, but Lowell wrote the plural – as did Lewis, to support his argument about its meaning. Perhaps the decisive consideration is that other similar phrases in English tend to use the singular – for example, 'a man's man,' 'a soldier's soldier.' Thus the West Indian writer C.L.R. James says, in his great autobiography about cricket and race relations, 'If Spenser is the poet's poet, John was the fast bowler's bowler' (*Beyond a Boundary* 1963:81). PAUL ALPERS

poetics, Elizabethan Poetics in Spenser's time was less a coherent or systematic theory than an assortment of catch phrases and authorities. Notions of imitation, speaking picture, instruction and delight, feigning and counterfeiting, decorum, levels of style, and literary kinds or species all gathered around privileged names: Plato and Aristotle, Horace and Cicero, Scaliger and Sidney. To fix a pattern to this assortment would betray both the excitement and the urgency with which poets and critics tried to think seriously about their art. For this reason, it is better to consider Elizabethan poetics as a scene of competing claims and sometimes conflicting opinions.

At the center of this scene are three consistently repeated doctrines: that the poet's principal activity is imitation, that the poem is a speaking picture, and that the purpose of literature is to instruct and delight.

When Sidney asserts in *A Defence of Poetry* (1595) that 'poesy therefore is an art of imitation' (ed 1973b:79), he invokes a venerable formula susceptible of at least four interpretations. Imitation appears in Elizabethan treatises to explain the relations between the 'world' of the poem and the realm of nature, between the poet's formal idea of the work and the work itself, between the poet and his predecessors or between the poem and its literary genre, between the poetic model and its effect upon the reader. The first and third of these relations may be called external, for they situate the objects of artistic mimesis outside the poem itself. The second and fourth are internal insofar as they describe the origin and end of the poetic act.

Aristotle establishes the main tradition of poetic mimesis when he argues that poetry imitates actions, with agents who are necessarily either good men or bad (*Poetics* 2). So Ascham in *The Scholemaster* (1570) affirms that 'all the workes of nature in a maner be examples for arte to folow,' and that 'the whole doctrine of Comedies and Tragedies is a perfite *imitation*, or faire livelie painted picture of the life of everie degree of man' (ed 1904:264, 266). The same concept of art mirroring nature is repeated in William Webbe's *Discourse of English Poetrie* (1586): verse is said to originate 'in exercises of imitating some vertuous and wise man' (in G.G. Smith 1904, 1:248). Although the terms of these assertions are Aristotelian, Renaissance mimesis is heavily influenced by Neoplatonic assumptions that nature itself is a work of art, an 'image' of God's ideas. Poetry, therefore, imitates not only human actions but universal principles of divine creation. Its 'second nature,' the mimetic world of the poem itself, teaches the correspondences that obtain in God's poem, the world of nature. Elizabethan poetics thus develops two criteria for judging the mimetic success of a given poem according to its Aristotelian or Platonic bases: either the poem is subject to standards of natural probability (what is or could be) or to standards of ethical possibility (what should be or ought ideally to be).

The fullest elaboration of the ethical argument is Sidney's more radical theory of a mimetic relation between the poet's internal idea and the actual words of his text. The excellence of the poet, he claims, 'standeth in that *idea* or fore-conceit of the work, and not in the work itself' (p 79). Prior to Xenophon's *Cyropaedia*, for example, is an idea of right rule. In the work itself, Cyrus is not the historical founder of the Persian empire or any other 'natural' ruler, but the 'figuring forth' of this idea in words and plot is an imitation of the idea of what the right ruler should be. Although Sidney is here using Plato's terminology, his more likely source, as the argument continues, is Scaliger; but he revises Scaliger in order to emphasize that the poet is a maker comparable to 'the heavenly Maker.' The poet's imitation, therefore, is not limited to what he finds in nature, for he is free to create in a 'substantial' form anything he is capable of imagining. Such a thesis allows Sidney to internalize the doctrine of mimesis and to assert that poetry's principal lesson is the art of imitation itself – the process by which an abstract idea can be 'bodied forth' in particular human action.

At the end of the *Defence*, Sidney exhorts his contemporaries to study and imitate the ancients, thereby invoking a third sense of literary mimesis (see *imitation of authors). His scheme probably derives from Renaissance Ciceronians in general and Horace and Scaliger in particular. In his *Poetices*, Scaliger provocatively literalizes Aristotelian mimesis by arguing that poetry originates in verbal imitation of repeated human actions. Since weddings, for example, always follow the same formal patterns, they give rise to the mimetic genre of epithalamium; funerals, again following repeatable patterns, are imitated in literary epicedia. Once the 'natural' mimesis establishes the poetic kind, subsequent poets can copy that. They learned to write epithalamia not by observing or even conceptualizing weddings, but by mastering the conventions of the literary genre as manifested in the canonical works of Theocritus, Ovid, Catullus, and Claudian. In turn, this method of poetic 'invention' occasioned numerous commonplace books, lists of formal topics, even the kinds of structural models found in sundry rhetorical manuals which detail both the matter and the manner of various generic conventions. Mimesis, therefore, became a practical matter of the literary system itself, defining the obligations and options of a poet who chose to write in a particular poetic kind and ensuring him a place in that system if his poem fulfilled the conventions. This understanding of poetic imitation is explored most fully in Ascham's *Scholemaster*.

Elizabethan theory also extends the idea of generic mimesis in two directions. One is evident in the various hierarchic taxonomies of genre, while the other can be seen in the broader notion of the literary career. Although these are distinct emphases, they are related. The hierarchies of genre popular in Elizabethan treatises regulate correlative notions of subject, manner, and style. As Puttenham explains in his *Arte of English Poesie* (1589, I.II, I.19), the heroic poem, as the noblest of the genres, treats the noblest characters in the grandest style. This 'decorous' relation of style to subject or of kind of character to literary species is a consequence of appropriate imitation. Similarly, one may treat the mimetic character of a literary career by observing how laureate poets like Spenser and Milton consciously fashioned their poetic progress on Virgil. In the imitation of Virgil's career, there is a crossing of categories, for the mimetic progress *forward* (from poems of youth to those of maturity) is simultaneously *upward* (from pastoral, the lowest genre, to heroic, the highest). One final consequence of generic mimesis is that Renaissance emphasis on the tradition of literary kinds establishes not so much a rigid set of prescriptive rules as a horizon of reader expectations. Elizabethan authors could imitate their predecessors' conventions to frustrate, surprise, or gratify those expectations. Indeed, we might say that much of the 'wit' and excited urgency of Elizabethan poetry lies precisely in this kind of dialogue with the generic tradition (see Greene 1982). In order to appreciate such mimesis, the modern reader must become familiar with the commonly received generic codes.

The final mimetic relation, for which Sidney is perhaps the clearest spokesman, is between a poetic model and its effect on the reader. Xenophon's *Cyropaedia* was constructed 'not only to make a Cyrus, which had been but a particular excellency as nature might have done, but to bestow a Cyrus upon the world to make many Cyruses, if they [the readers] will learn aright why and how that maker made him' (p 79). The reader, in short, imitates the model of the literary image in refashioning his own moral actions. Behind this sense of ethical imitation lies the Renaissance insistence on poetry's didactic and moving faculties, but its center is the reader's ability to copy the poetic copy. Thus Spenser, in fashioning Arthur as 'the image of a brave knight, perfected in the twelve private morall vertues,' can expect in turn 'to fashion a gentleman or noble person in vertuous and gentle discipline' (Letter to Raleigh).

Spenser's description of Arthur as 'the image of a brave knight' also introduces the Renaissance notion of *ut pictura poesis*, or, as Sidney translates, 'a speaking picture.' Elizabethan use of the dictum emphasizes the sensory impression necessary both to delight and to affect the reader. In arguing the difference between the philosopher and the poet, Sidney constantly reverts to the claim that 'the philosopher ... replenisheth the memory with many infallible grounds of wisdom, which, notwithstanding, lie dark before the imaginative and judging power, if they be not illuminated or figured forth by the speaking picture of poesy' (p 86); or again, 'a perfect picture I say, for [the poet] yieldeth to the powers of the mind an image of that whereof the philosopher bestoweth but a wordish description, which doth neither strike, pierce, nor possess the sight of the soul so much as that other doth' (p 85). Here again we see how, in theory, *ut pictura poesis* buttresses Renaissance assumptions of ethical mimesis, for as the poetic picture 'speaks' through the image in the reader's mind, it shapes and directs moral action. Sidney draws this conclusion: 'as the image of each action stirreth and instructeth the mind, so the lofty image of [heroical] worthies most inflameth the mind with desire to be worthy, and informs with counsel how to be worthy. Only let Aeneas be worn in the tablet of your memory' and he will become an internal, imaginative 'speaking picture' of virtue in action (p 98).

While this theoretical understanding of *ut pictura poesis* is important in Elizabethan poetics, most allusions to the formula refer more narrowly to the 'ornaments' of poetry, such as notable images, visual analogies, emblems, conceits, and moral exempla. Yet this emphasis must not be taken as implying a separation of an essential idea from its purely decorative dress, but rather as attempting to articulate the graphic liveliness (*energeia* in Sidney's vocabulary) necessary to engage and involve the reader. It reminds us, therefore, that Elizabethan poetry is primarily visual and that at the heart of its tasks is the problem of how to make a conceptual idea substantially manifest to the senses.

The last of the three catch phrases is *utile et dulce*, a notion whose Renaissance locus is in Sidney's famous definition linking all three: 'Poesy therefore is an art of imitation, for so Aristotle termeth it in the word *mimesis* – that is to say, a representing, counterfeiting, or figuring forth – to speak metaphorically, a speaking picture – with this end, to teach and delight' (pp 79–80). The formula itself is Horatian, and the frequency with which it appears in Renaissance texts reminds us that both proponents and antagonists of secular literature presupposed a didactic function. This fact frequently puts Elizabethan poetry on the defensive: almost all its major critical texts are apologies for poetry or defenses against Puritan attacks that poetry is lewd and blasphemous at worst, antisocial and frivolous at best. Poetic theory, in reaction, continually argued that moral instruction was the primary end of literature.

Other subsidiary themes or strategies of Elizabethan theory are also conditioned by this defensive posture. The persistent search for sanctioned poetic origin (eg, the myths of Orpheus, Linus, Musaeus, and Amphion) is one such effect; constant citation of classical authorities (whether poetic, as Homer and Virgil, or philosophical, as Plato and Aristotle) is another. An extension of both is the broader argument that competing fields of knowledge like philosophy, history, and theology actually originated, as disciplines, in poetry. Poetry, therefore, can be seen as the foundation of all human sciences and as the 'fountaine,' as

Elyot argues, from which 'proceded all eloquence and lernyng' (*Boke Named the Governour* ed 1883, 1:58). Charges that poetry misleads untrained minds or licenses the immoral acts it sometimes portrays were usually met by the argument that its literal sense was but a veil hiding various allegorical or mystical truths – historical, philosophical, political, moral, and theological (see *allegory). In works like Harington's 'Brief Apology for Poetry' (1591), this argument assumes descriptive rather than defensive form, but we can still recognize its apologetic urgency (in G.G. Smith 1904, 2:194–222). Other conventional arguments about the esteem in which poetry has always been held, about how contemporary attacks reveal more about the corrupt nature of present society than about poetry, even calls for poetic reform or a coherent poetic theory were shaped by the fact that Elizabethan poets were on the defensive. They had to convince the reader that poetry was not a sportive pastime of a few would-be prodigals, but an enterprise at the very center of all human discourse.

Perhaps for this reason, Sidney extends the function of poetry beyond teaching and delighting to moving the reader to virtuous action: poets 'do merely [entirely] make to imitate, and imitate both to delight and teach; and delight, to move men to take that goodness in hand, which without delight they would fly as from a stranger; and teach, to make them know that goodness whereunto they are moved' (p 81). So Spenser argues in the Letter to Raleigh that poetry must be not only plausible and pleasing but also profitable. Its 'ending end,' for both authors, is action not knowledge, well doing not just proper understanding. To this extent, Renaissance didacticism is put to work in a broader context of humanistic reform, 'to lead and draw us,' as Sidney expresses it, 'to as high a perfection as our degenerate souls, made worse by their clayey lodgings, can be capable of' (p 82).

Sidney also extends the function of poetry to include moving the reader to virtuous action because of his fear, shared by others, that poetry will be misread. In the *Defence*, this fear occasions his worry over tyrants like Alexander Pheraeus, faultfinders like the *mysomousoi*, and naive literalists. Spenser, too, begins the Letter by acknowledging 'how doubtfully all Allegories may be construed' and misconceived. Such consciousness of the problems of poetic reading significantly affects poetic theorizing, and the implied reader becomes a frequent character in both literary criticism and in poetry. Here, too, we see a system on the defensive, although in this case the antagonist is not so much an active or disputative agent as an unaffected misuser.

Elizabethan poetic theory was related to other disciplines: to grammar, with its emphasis on methods of varying words and syntax; to logic, with its structures of development and argument; and to rhetoric, with its focus on embellishment, ornament, and other methods of persuasion. Although these three disciplines are frequently used to elaborate the poetic tasks of delighting, instructing, and moving, the extensive lists of grammatical variations (as in Erasmus's *De copia*), logical or illogical syllogisms (as in Richard Sherry's *Treatise of Schemes and Tropes*), and figures of rhetoric (as in Puttenham's third book, 'Of Ornament'), often overwhelm the modern reader with seemingly endless and pointless detail. But such lists testify to the seriousness with which Elizabethan theorizers and practitioners set about trying to articulate both the principles and the practice of poetry.

If, then, there is no coherent or systematic poetic available by the end of the sixteenth century, there is a concerted effort to erect such a doctrine and to explore the various implications of the literary system. The energy that drives this effort puts Elizabethan poetic theory in line with Renaissance thinking in general: an attempt to rediscover and to use the past – whether the classical past of Aristotle, Horace, Cicero, and Quintilian, or the more modern past of Vida, Minturno, Cintio, and Scaliger – in such a way as to inform and reform the present.

A. LEIGH DENEEF

Renaissance texts are cited from Ascham ed 1904; Elyot ed 1883; Puttenham ed 1936; Sidney ed 1973b; and G.G. Smith 1904. See also Margaret W. Ferguson 1983 *Trials of Desire: Renaissance Defenses of Poetry* (New Haven); Greene 1982; Tuve 1947; and humanist *poetics.

---

poetics, humanist Tudor poetics arising from humanist study – the conceptualization, function, and techniques of poetry, the concerns laid down in Aristotle's *Poetics* – grew directly out of the humanist trivium of grammar, rhetoric, and logic which Spenser studied at Merchant Taylors' School and at Cambridge. Although humanist poetics made some use of grammar, which taught the parsing and translating of Latin with some attention to prosody, the study of metrics and versification, and of logic, which taught syllogistic reasoning, it was primarily rooted in humanist rhetoric. This in turn derived from classical rhetoric: Aristotle's *Art of Rhetoric* (in Latin and English redactions), Cicero's *De inventione*, *Orator*, *De oratore*, and *Brutus*, and, the most popular of all handbooks, the *Rhetorica ad Herennium*, also thought to be Cicero's. Often the rules found in such manuals were reinforced by Quintilian, whose *Institutio oratoria* gained in authority throughout the sixteenth century. Humanist training promoted the close relationship of such rhetoric and what we think of as poetics so that it is often difficult to separate the orator from the poet, a distinction most Tudor writers did not make as clearly or decisively as did later writers. Indeed, for such Tudor schoolmasters as Colet and Mulcaster, poetry remained a branch of rhetoric and was rarely studied for its own sake.

As taught in Tudor schools and universities, rhetoric had three major concerns: invention (or 'finding places of argument,' often following rules of definition by genus, species, properties, adjuncts, or contrarieties), organization (or disposition of facts, illustrations, and arguments), and style. Each of these divisions brought to Tudor humanist poetics distinctive habits of thought and forms of writing.

Invention, for instance, made considerable use of endless varying of words and word patterns, as in Erasmus' *De copia*, to show art by the fertility of a writer's presentation (see *copia). Consequently, works of art proceeded at a leisurely pace, characterized by self-conscious ornamentation and complexity of expression.

Rhetoric also taught two primary means of presentation: the classical oration (used in descriptions and reports) and the disputation or debate (which encouraged, through training in writing colloquies, the use of dialogue). For Aristotle, orations had four basic parts (exordium or introduction, narration, proof, and conclusion); Cicero added division and refutation (and later digression); and in 1553 Thomas Wilson, in *The Arte of Rhetorique*, added an eighth part (the proposition). These parts always formed a paradigmatic pattern which assured definition, clarity, cogency, and persuasive power, whether an arrangement of parts (introduction, definition or proposition, division into issues, confirmation, dispensing of negative arguments, digression, conclusion, and often peroration) was immediately apparent or not. Variation was furthered by applying this organization to all three kinds of orations (judicial, deliberative, and demonstrative) depending on whether the purpose was accusation or defense, support or denial, or praise or blame. Nor were rhetoricians limited to formal speeches or descriptions; all acts of writing (narratives, reports, even letters) followed the rhetorical outline, the creativity coming in the choice and arrangement of commonplaces and illustrations within each major division of the work.

Students of humanism learned not only from rule books and from endless practice but also by *imitatio*, the close imitation of models such as those collected by Richard Rainolde in his *Foundacion of Rhetorike* (1563), where orations take the form of fable, narration or tale, *chria* or biography, or character portrayal (see also *imitation of authors). Such short (or occasionally long) exercises, employing 'artificial' arguments (traditional places intrinsic to rhetoric) or 'extrinsic' arguments (drawing on experience) show how orations, even when keeping to form, could vary sufficiently to allow for individual maneuvering and voice. The disposition of statements in *Fowre Hymnes*, the arguments of Archimago (*FQ* I i 30–3), and the description of Britomart (II iii 21–31) all derive from this pattern, as does the arrangement of entire episodes and books of *The Faerie Queene*, such as Book I, which first states the Red Cross Knight's mission (to free Una's parents and gain the grace of the Fairy Queen), and then presents definition, analysis, support, denial (through temptations and obstructions), and final success in both tasks.

Style was also a primary concern of humanist rhetoric; and later, under Ramus (whose reorganization of studies into logic dealing with matter and rhetoric dealing with manner was strongly advocated by Gabriel Harvey), style became its only subject. In the course of the sixteenth century, humanists developed their use of *copia* by 'figures,' clearly defined tropes and schemes of syntactic and metaphoric expression. Figurative rhetoric by Abraham Fraunce and Henry Peacham became immensely popular in Spenser's time (as seen in the descriptions of Mount Acidale and Colin Clout). Also increasingly popular among humanist rhetoricians (and so humanist poets) were emblem books in which gnomic sayings (brief sententiae or apothegms such as those collected by Erasmus) were paired with symbolic pictures, as in Daniel's translation of Alciati's *Emblemata* (1585, by way of Paolo Giovio) and Geoffrey Whitney's collections of words and pithy sayings (1586). The pictorial quality of Spenser's poetry thus also derives from humanist lessons by which rhetoric served as both basis and agent of poetry.

Interest in style is illustrated in Richard Sherry's *Treatise of Schemes and Tropes* (1550?), which taught 'effiguration' or the techniques of *prosopographia* and *prosopopoeia*, the description of feigned events or persons or the art of feigning (we would say 'imagining' or 'creating') to make a point. (Spenser uses this rhetorical concept as the title and underlying idea of *Mother Hubberds Tale*.) Such practices led to a concentration on examples further to define and persuade particular positions, as Spenser advocates in the Letter to Raleigh when he prefers Xenophon's *Cyropaedia* to Plato's *Republic*: 'So much more profitable and gratious is doctrine by ensample, then by rule.' It is Spenser's particular emphasis on concrete details which also elicits Milton's praise in *Areopagitica* for 'describing true temperance under the person of *Guion*, bring[ing] him in with his palmer through the cave of Mammon, and the bowr of earthly blisse that he might see and know, and yet abstain' (ed 1953–82, 5:16).

The second of the two primary means of presentation taught by rhetoric is the disputation, which consists of opposed orations, by which students were tested and for which they were awarded university degrees; it led also to the practice of eristics, in which winning debates was the chief objective and any clever means was desirable if it led to victory. Logic and syllogistic reasoning were thus handmaidens not of truth but of persuasion. Archimago, Spenser's arch-magus, depends on such an understanding of rhetoric and logic which he abuses because his ends (and means) are evil; at the same time, his arguments are easily recognized and even initially attractive to Redcrosse and Una because of their form and conventions. The abuse of rhetoric led to wary skepticism as much as to dogged tradition. Like poetry, or like our concept of fiction, rhetoric by its very nature promoted possibilities, but not necessarily fact or truth. Thus, for Leonard Cox, rhetoric is 'right pleasaunt' but as 'a persuasible art.' 'We hold many doctrines as probable which we can easily act upon but can scarcely advance as certain,' Cicero notes (*Lucullus* 2.3.7–8). Renaissance writers including Spenser show repeatedly their awareness that persuasion may rest not with the truth of statements but with the ability of speakers to make good impressions or play on the emotions, presuppositions, or desires of their audiences by the use of Aristotelian *ethos* or *pathos*, a contrived persona or situation. Aristotle was aware of such possibilities, and Cicero in the *De oratore* teaches students how to practice what we would call deception.

In this more abusive sense of rhetoric, the search for topics and images by which to build seductive or compelling arguments depended on ingenuity and resourcefulness; and eloquence came to be defined either as that golden language of a good and wise man, as Quintilian proposes, or as the deceitful manipulation of words if it misused the principles or models of rhetoric. Sophists, such as Gorgias, who told the classical world that he could prove anything he wished, traded on such practices. But Tudor humanists made it clear that such sophists as those described by Plato and defended by Sextus Empiricus were resorting to *euchéreia* (dexterity) and *agchinoia* (sharp-wittedness) rather than to reason and logic, practices which only seemed to align *sophia*, 'wisedome,' to sophistry, 'a craftye and deceytefull sentence, an Oracyon or invention, whiche seemeth to be trewe, whan it is false,' as Thomas Elyot defines these terms in 1538 in the first Tudor dictionary. Thus the age of rhetoric that taught the Tudors poetry also taught them to read closely and shrewdly, while pointing out the dangers of hasty reactions and judgments. Archimago in his evil feigning and Redcrosse in his quick acceptance of Archimago's statements show the twin dangers of the abuse of language in a rhetorically oriented culture – how the poet who should be Bonfont may become Malfont (*FQ* v ix 26).

In advancing rhetoric as the basis of learning, humanist study thus produced for Spenser's day a culture in which the poet and orator used similar or identical means for similar or identical ends – ends involving the definition of the perfectibility of man (the chief subject of humanist philosophy) and the beauty of language. Humanists believed that human reason was trained by the use of words, as Sidney says in the *Defence of Poetry*, and that the right use of language honed the mind while focusing on higher concerns. In Tudor England, humanist poetics was the property of orator and poet alike, for the difference between Cato's *vir bonus dicendi peritus* (the good man, skilled at speaking) and Coluccio Salutati's *vir optimus laudandi vituperandique peritus* (the best man, skilled at praising and censuring) was largely a matter of emphasis. Both, according to Puttenham in his *Arte of English Poesie* (1589), meant to teach, and by teaching, to civilize. This too is both the purpose and achievement of Spenser's work.

With this historical understanding of the basically verbal culture of the Tudors, we can appreciate the qualities of their art: their delight in words and wordplay; their interest in experimentation in form, vocabulary, and variation; and their endless parades of illustrations, similes, metaphors, analogies, and even syllogisms, some quite extravagant. There is genuine joy in varying traditions, too, as Spenser draws on and away from pastoral conventions for *The Shepheardes Calender*, philosophic concerns for *Fowre Hymnes*, and heroic conventions for *The Faerie Queene*.

ARTHUR F. KINNEY

Donald Lemen Clark 1957 *Rhetoric in Greco-Roman Education* (New York); Greenblatt 1980; Greenfield 1981; O.B. Hardison, Jr 1971 'The Orator and the Poet: The Dilemma of Humanist Literature' *JMRS* 1:33–44, rpt in his *Toward Freedom and Dignity: The Humanities and the Idea of Humanity* pp 59–83 (Baltimore 1972); Howell 1956; Javitch 1978; G.A. Kennedy 1980; W.J. Kennedy 1978; Arthur F. Kinney 1976 'Rhetoric as Poetic: Humanist Fiction in the Renaissance' *ELH* 43:413–43; Kinney 1986 *Humanist Poetics: Thought, Rhetoric, and Fiction in Sixteenth-Century England* (Amherst, Mass); Kinney 1989 *Continental Humanist Poetics* (Amherst, Mass); Walter J. Ong, SJ 1968 'Tudor Writings on Rhetoric' *SRen* 15:39–69; Vickers 1988.

Ponsonby, William (c 1547–1604) A London stationer, described as 'the most important publisher of the Elizabethan period' (McKerrow 1910:217–18); remarkable chiefly for publishing most of Spenser's and Sidney's works during the 1590s. Ponsonby's imprint is found on the 1590 and 1596 editions of *The Faerie Queene*, and on *Complaints*, *Daphnaïda*, *Amoretti and Epithalamion*, *Colin Clout*, *Fowre Hymnes*, and *Prothalamion*. He established a close and lasting professional relationship with Spenser, beginning with their collaboration in the production of *The Faerie Queene* (1590) and *Complaints* (1591). He added his own preface to *Complaints* in which he promised to publish several of Spenser's lost works, 'disperst abroad in sundrie hands, and not easie to bee come by, by himselfe.' He also dedicated *Amoretti* to Sir Robert Needham of Shropshire when Spenser was in Ireland. Ponsonby was one of a rare breed of Elizabethan stationers who blended their commercial instincts with genuine literary discrimination. In his publications, the chance of a quick financial return was secondary to a perceptive selection of volumes calculated to advance his own reputation. He limited himself almost exclusively to belles-lettres and politically motivated texts which were connected with influential court circles, particularly that of the Dudley and Sidney families.

Ponsonby traded throughout his career at the Bishop's Head, St Paul's Churchyard, and entered his first book in the Stationers' Register in 1577. During the early 1580s, he published two prose romances by Greene, but most of his other books were staunchly Protestant tracts which seem closely allied to the political interests of Robert Dudley, Earl of Leicester. In 1586, he made the most important business contact of his career. The death of Sidney in October had stunned the whole nation and aroused the commercial instincts of several members of the Stationers' Company. In November 1586, Ponsonby informed Sidney's trusted friend Fulke Greville that an unnamed stationer was planning a pirated edition of the *Old Arcadia*. Greville describes the meeting: 'one ponsonby a booke bynder in poles church yard, came to me, and told me that ther was one in hand to print, Sir philip sydneys old arcadia asking me yf it were done, with yor honors co[n]s[ent] or any other of his frends' (Sidney ed 1962:530). In August 1588, Ponsonby was rewarded with a commission to publish the authorized version of 1590. Sidney's friends and his sister, the Countess of Pembroke, continued to place their trust in him, and he became their recognized stationer. He published the 1593 *Arcadia*, the Countess' own translations of Mornay and Garnier, the authorized *Defence of Poetry* (1595), and the first collected edition of Sidney's works (1598). Ponsonby played an important role in suppressing various pirated editions of Sidney's compositions and also published volumes dedicated to the Countess of Pembroke by Fraunce and Watson.

Ponsonby held high office in the Stationers' Company and was elected a Warden (the Master's deputy) in 1598. He continued publishing high quality editions of various authors (including Machiavelli, Guicciardini, and Plutarch) until his death in 1604. He never owned a printing press himself but used those of such noted printers as Field, Windet, Orwin, Wolfe, and Creede. He was best known by Elizabethans as a bookseller. John Ramsey, an enthusiastic collector of Spenser's works, was one of his regular customers in the 1590s and left a fascinating description of his bookshop (Strathmann 1931). Ponsonby's career demonstrates how essential it was for a bookseller who wished to succeed to be associated through his publications with some of the influential political, religious, and literary groups of the day. However, the key to his preeminence in the trade lay in his virtual monopoly over the publication and selling of the works of Spenser and Sidney. MICHAEL G. BRENNAN

Michael G. Brennan 1984 'William Ponsonby: Elizabethan Stationer' *AEB* 7:91–110; R.B. McKerrow, ed 1910 *A Dictionary of Printers and Booksellers ... 1557–1640* (London); Paul G. Morrison 1950 *Index of Printers, Publishers and Booksellers ... 1475–1640* (Charlottesville, Va) p 58; Sidney ed 1973a:xl; Strathmann 1931.

Pope, Alexander (1688–1744) ''Tis easy to mark out the general course of our poetry. Chaucer, Spenser, Milton, and Dryden are the great landmarks for it' (Spence *Anecdotes* 410 in ed 1966, 1:178). This judgment by Pope in 1736 drew on an affectionate familiarity with Spenser's poems which lasted from his childhood to the end of his life. 'Spenser has ever been a favourite poet to me,' he wrote to John Hughes on 7 October 1715; 'he is like a mistress whose faults we see, but love her with 'em all' (ed 1956, 1:316). Spenser was for him a landmark in a tradition running through the Renaissance from the Ancients.

Before he was twelve, Pope's favorite poets were Waller, Spenser, and Dryden. A little after, his juvenile epic *Alcander* sought to blend – Pope smiled to recall – 'the beauties of the great epic writers' and the styles of Spenser, Cowley, and Milton (*Anecdotes* 43, 36–40 in 1:18–19).

Pope's edition of Spenser was the 1611 Folio; on the title page he wrote, 'E Musaeo Jo. Drydeni' and 'Alex: Pope./Pret: 7ss.' His annotations may belong to 1700–10. He liked *FQ* I i 8, saying 'This fine Description of the Trees is imitated from Chaucer's Assembly of Foules.' At I iii 21 he wrote, 'Ulysses with Calypso,' and at IV x 44 'This Mr. Dryden has copy'd in Palamon and Arcite. book 2. pag.' His comment on *The Shepheardes Calender* (otherwise insignificant) shows knowledge of other editions. At *Time* 281–7, Pope recognized the object of Spenser's tribute: 'Sr. Philip Sidney.' This book is preserved at Hartlebury Castle, Worcester, UK (Mack 1982:441–2).

Praising Pope's yet unpublished *Pastorals*, on 9 September 1706, William Walsh said he had compared Pope with Virgil and Spenser and thought he stood up to the test (Pope ed 1956, 1:21). The intimacy of the *Pastorals* with Spenser is seen in their adaptation of the refrains from *Prothalamion* and *Epithalamion* (*Spring* 3, *Summer* 16) and their bow to *Januarye* 1–2 at the beginning of *Summer*. In his *Discourse on Pastoral Poetry* (1717), Pope sets Spenser with Tasso as the best modern writers of pastoral but is inclined to question his use of lyric measure, allegory, blend of antique and rural diction, and the length and repetition entailed by the calendar concept. Yet he praises the latter innovation as 'very beautiful,' and in his blend of Virgil's Eclogue 10.69 with *FQ* VII vii 47 to give 'Time conquers All, and We must Time obey' (*Winter* 88) he helps us hear a note which sounds repeatedly in his work: the eternal note of sadness at the mutability of earthly things (Pope ed 1939–69, 1:59, 73, 71, 30–2, 95).

A more complex response is suggested by 'The Alley: An Imitation of Spenser' (1727; written before 1709). Its comedy lies chiefly in a deployment of the *Faerie Queene* stanza and idiom to mock the antique diction and the incidence of the low, lewd, and ludicrous in Spenser's heroic poem. Obloquy is described as follows: 'Her Dugs were mark'd by ev'ry Collier's Hand, / Her Mouth was black as Bull-Dogs at the Stall: / She scratched, bit, and spar'd ne Lace ne Band, / And Bitch and Rogue her Answer was to all' (37–40). But the poem rises to a noble prospect at the end: 'All up the silver *Thames*, or all a down; / Ne Richmond's self, from whose tall Front are ey'd / Vales, Spires, meandring Streams, and *Windsor*'s tow'ry Pride' (52–4; ed 1939–69, 6:44). Pope's mixed response to Spenser found expression in a poem whose mingling of low and lofty, and Thames-side setting, point forward to *Dunciad* 2.

When Pope came to compose *The Dunciad*, it was a stanza from *The Faerie Queene* that he considered as an epigraph: I i 23. Spence recalled seeing it 'writ down in this first manuscript copy for the *Dunciad*,' and judged that it hit 'the little impertinent poets that were brushed away by that poem very well' but was less apt in giving Pope 'clownish hands.' Pope may also have rejected it as too long (*Anecdotes* 420 and n in 1:182).

In the mid-1730s, Pope planned 'a discourse on the rise and progress of English poetry' considering the nondramatic poets only. He divided English poetry into six schools: of Provence (ie, Old French); of Chaucer; of Petrarch; of Dante; of Spenser, the Italian sonneteers and other translators from the Italian; and of Donne. In the School of Spenser he included Browne's pastorals, Phineas Fletcher, Alabaster, Daniel, Raleigh, Milton's juvenilia, Robert Heath, and William Habington (Ruffhead 1769:328–9). Earlier, Pope had also named Drayton and Fairfax as imitators of Spenser (*Anecdotes* 433 in 1:187).

Pope's interest in the history of English poetry found expression in his Epistle *To Augustus* (Horace Epistle 2.1 imitated) of 1737. Spenser is twice mentioned in relation to the taste of the time, first to illustrate old-fashioned and defective judgment: 'One likes no language but the Faery Queen,' later as the object of impartial modern criticism: 'Spenser himself affects the obsolete' (39, 97). In the same year Pope, imitating part of Horace's *Odes* 4.9, celebrated Spenser, Milton, Waller, and Cowley as poets of Britain who had conferred fame (ed 1939–69, 4:197, 203, 159).

This detached and consciously modern view of Spenser was not to the fore in Pope's later thought. In the last year of Pope's life, Spence reported that, on his having read part of *The Faerie Queene* to his old mother, 'she said that I had been showing her a collection of pictures.' 'She said very right,' Pope replied, 'and I don't know how it is but there's something in Spenser that pleases one as strongly in one's old age as it did in one's youth. I read the *Faerie Queene* when I was about twelve with a vast deal of delight, and I think it gave me as much when I read it over about a year or two ago' (*Anecdotes* 419 in 1:182). The casual phrase 'about a year or two' perhaps allows Pope's rereading of *The Faerie Queene* to coincide with his composition of *The New Dunciad* (pub March 1742), later *Dunciad* 4, which contains several Spenserian allusions. These are concerned with the linked ideals of epic heroism, humanist adventure, and political rectitude.

Among the 'lazy, lolling sort,' the poet discerns one he holds in 'great affection': 'Thee too, my Paridel! she [Dulness] mark'd thee there, / Stretch'd on the rack of a too easy chair' (337–46). Pope's note specifies the 'wandering Courtly "Squire"' from *The Faerie Queene* but the exact reference is defective ('Lib. Can. 9'). The Twickenham editor plausibly proposes III ix, where as guest of the inhospitable Malbecco Paridell tells Britomart the story of the transfer of empire through the refugees from fallen

Troy. This would be consistent with the broad allusion of *The Dunciad* to the *Aeneid*. It refers also to Brutus, mythological founder of Britain and hero of the blank verse epic which was the project of Pope's last months. Pope's Paridell has not so far been satisfactorily identified.

In the beautiful satire on the butterfly-courtier and butterfly collector (421–36), the note directs us to *Muiopotmos* 17–18. By contrast with Pope's 'child of Heat and Air,' Spenser's Clarion is an emblem of vigor and adventure; like the bee in Swift's *Battle of the Books*, he tastes every flower. He does not destroy but meets destruction. Pope's butterfly is collected and preserved, 'Fair ev'n in death!'

Finally, in a note to the great, 'truly Homerical' yawn which ends *The Dunciad*, it is remarked that such an ending is not 'without Authority, the incomparable Spencer having ended one of the most considerable of his works with a *Roar*, but then it is the *Roar of a Lion*, the effects whereof are described as the Catastrophe of his Poem' (4.606n). This reference to *Mother Hubberds Tale* 1337–84 also stresses contrast: at the end of Spenser's poem a kingly beast (Leicester-Elizabeth) punishes the knavery and injustice of the cunning Fox and usurping Ape. Here the Goddess Dulness concludes with a song which sends the whole of creation to sleep. It is not surprising that Pope should have admired *Mother Hubberd* (admitting as much through his comic notes), and if Spenser's political allegory may be thought to have been redirected by Pope, Walpole is the Fox, George II the Ape, and the Lion the Patriot King (ed 1939–69, 5:376–7 and n, 383–4, 403).

These moments in *The Dunciad* are marks of a broader affinity with Spenser deserving of critical exploration. It involves the evolution of a poetic mode highly mobile between the comic and the sublime, capable of remarkable visual and aural beauty, especially in the setting forth of temptation and danger, reaching often towards the emblematic and allegorical, using marvels and metamorphoses for strongly moral and religious ends.

HOWARD ERSKINE-HILL

Alexander Pope 1939–69 *Poems* ed John Butt, et al 11 vols (London); Pope 1956 *Correspondence* ed George Sherburn, 5 vols (Oxford). Owen Ruffhead 1769 *Life of Alexander Pope, Esq* (London; rpt New York 1974); Spence ed 1966; Maynard Mack 1982 *Collected in Himself: Essays Critical, Biographical, and Bibliographical on Pope and Some of His Contemporaries* (Newark, Del). On Pope's division of English poetry into schools, see James M. Osborn 1949 'The First History of English Poetry' in *Pope and His Contemporaries* ed James L. Clifford and Louis A. Landa (Oxford) pp 230–50, and Austin Warren 1929 *Alexander Pope as Critic and Humanist* (Princeton). See also Kathleen Williams 1974 'The Moralized Song: Some Renaissance Themes in Pope' *ELH* 41:578–601.

predestination In the Thirty-nine Articles of the Church of England, Article 17 says that predestination 'is the everlasting purpose of God, whereby (before the foundations of the world were laid) He hath constantly decreed by His counsel secret to us, to deliver from curse and damnation those whom He hath chosen in Christ out of mankind, and to bring them by Christ to everlasting salvation.' In one form or another, this now unfashionable doctrine was held in Spenser's time by all branches of the Church. Augustine and even Thomas Aquinas had taught it, but the Protestant reformers gave it new emphasis.

The English Articles, however, avoided extreme formulations, such as reprobation (predestination to damnation). Though logically predestination seems to preclude human choice (and radical predestinarians flatly deny free will), it is a case of paradox, not contradiction. In practice all Christian writers on this topic, even the most extreme, recognize human responsibility for choices – as does St Paul, whose letter to the Ephesians, for example, proclaims predestination (1.5, 11) yet abounds in exhortations. Spenser's contemporaries saw predestination not as an eccentric theory (although they gradually realized how divisive it could be), but as a practical and biblical teaching 'full of sweet, pleasant, and unspeakable comfort' (Article 17), giving believers strength, confidence, and perspective in the face of difficulties.

It was natural that Spenser should involve the doctrine of predestination in the climax of *FQ* I ix and imply it elsewhere. When Redcrosse is led by Despair to consider the 'eternall booke of fate' (42), he is heedless of the church's warning against 'curious and carnal' thoughts on this subject, and is 'thrust ... into desperation' (Article 17). But then Una, echoing language elsewhere in the same Article, declares that he is 'chosen.' Her intervention is an actual instance of deliverance 'from curse and damnation' and of the *calling* 'in due season' of which the Article speaks.

As in the Scriptures, so in *FQ* I, predestination is not a constant topic. Instead, it is implied by the hero's Christian armor and hinted at by references to 'grace' (vii 12, viii 1) before being explicitly recognized under difficult and challenging conditions (as in Rom 8, Eph 1, 2, and 6, and 1 Pet 1), where the assurance it gives is most needed. Knowing he is chosen gives Redcrosse a glimpse into the spiritual dimension of life (cf Herbert's 'Coloss. 3.3. *Our Life Is Hid with Christ in God*'), and by calling attention to God's initiative helps him pursue a middle way between the two extremes of undue self-preoccupation with which he has been tempted – first pride, and then despair. 'All the good,' says the narrator, 'is Gods' (x 1). In keeping with both the Scriptures and Article 17, knowledge of election does not paralyze Redcrosse or make him smug but helps prepare him for 'good workes, which God hathe ordeined, that we shulde walke in them' (Eph 2.10).

Elsewhere in Spenser (eg, *FQ* II viii 1 and *Heavenly Love* 214, 257), allusions to 'grace' or 'mercy' can be taken to imply predestination, but the poet seems to have reserved for *FQ* I his fullest use of this mysterious doctrine 'hard to be understood' (x 13, 19).

DANIEL W. DOERKSEN

Daniel W. Doerksen 1983 '"All the Good is God's": Predestination in Spenser's *Faerie Queene*, Book I' *C&L* 32.3:11–18; Lewalski 1979; Whitaker 1952.

pride Occasionally in Spenser's poetry, *pride* denotes something commendable, as a proper sense of one's own worth (eg, *Amoretti* 5) or a display of excellence or natural splendor (*FQ* VII vii 34), but usually it is a sin. In traditional Christian doctrine, inordinate self-esteem is a major offense, for all human beings are fallen and have no claim to personal merit: 'If any strength we have, it is to ill, / But all the good is Gods, both power and eke will' (I x 1). Accordingly, pride of even the most innocuous kind compounds a number of faults: ignorance of one's true nature, lack of proper humility toward fellow sinners, failure to rely on divine grace, and ingratitude toward God. It also encourages tyranny over subordinates and rebelliousness toward superiors. Traditionally, pride is the first sin of Satan and the source of disobedience in Adam and Eve and in mankind generally.

In *The Faerie Queene*, the paradigm of the vice is Lucifera. Following a tradition established by Gregory the Great in his *Moralia in Job*, Spenser separates pride from other offenses, treating it as the root of all evil and the queen of the seven deadly sins (see Bloomfield 1952). Lucifera's name suggests that Pride is the first daughter of the Devil (see Deguileville *Pilgrimage of the Life of Man* 14,030). The 'foggy mist' and the 'sculs and bones of men' that lie about her palace (I iv 36) depict the traditional consequences of pride: spiritual blindness and death (see Crossett and Stump 1984:210). That she is dazzlingly beautiful, though the other sins are ugly, indicates that pride is especially tempting: the Red Cross Knight scorns the others but kneels to her.

In Lucifera, Spenser also embodies several of the traditional 'daughters' of pride: vanity, ambition, arrogance, and presumption. Vanity appears, for example, in Lucifera's usher (13) and elsewhere in the poem in Braggadocchio (II iii), ambition in Philotime (II vii 44–9) and in the Giant with the scales (V ii 30–50), arrogance in Disdain (II vii 40–2), and presumption in Orgoglio, who relies on his own merit rather than on the grace of God (I vii 8–10). Although Redcrosse escapes the house of Pride, he later falls into the presumption represented by Orgoglio and ultimately into despair, a sin traditionally allied with pride (see Blythe 1972).

The dangers of pride are a major theme in the *Complaints*, where many of the 'tragicke Pageants' (*Time* 490) of decay and human loss seem designed to illustrate the proverb 'pride goeth before a fall.' One example is ancient Rome, which Spenser treats as an embodiment of 'all this worlds pride,' concluding that it attained greatness only that it might 'fall more horriblie' (*Rome* 421–34). The vanity of worldly achievements and the delusory nature of pride are also central concerns in the *Cantos of Mutabilitie*. In *FQ* VII viii 1, Spenser dismisses all things that are not of heaven as mere 'flowring pride.'

DONALD V. STUMP

primitivism Since the term may refer to a complex range of perspectives and attitudes in Spenser's poetry, it is useful to begin by distinguishing between *chronological primitivism*, the celebration of an original or much earlier historical period, and *cultural primitivism*, the celebration of what are assumed to be simpler, less sophisticated, less advanced conditions of human life. These two modes of primitivism may overlap, for both imply a contrast between uncivilized vitality and present circumstances.

Chronological primitivism, a belief that human culture has declined from an ideal order established in antiquity, is fundamental to the Renaissance and represents the dark underside of Renaissance confidence in and optimism about present achievements. With the Reformation in northern Europe, this belief was reinforced by the Protestant emphasis on returning to earlier and simpler forms of Christian worship. Such primitivism is an organizing principle in *The Faerie Queene*: it underlies Spenser's elaborate archaizing diction and is evident in the way each of the six proems initiates a process of measuring the Elizabethan present against values conveyed through 'this famous antique history' (II proem 1). Yet Spenser's primitivism is complicated, shifting, and anything but straightforward. His poem praises Elizabeth and her age even as it holds them to the standards of an idealized mythic past. Spenser's perspective is simultaneously 'retrospective' and 'evolutionary' (Berger 1968b); he matches 'primitivism with historical destiny, a perfect past with the promise of a second Golden Age' (Tonkin 1972:5–6). The myth of the Golden Age is the most persistent expression of chronological primitivism, and Spenser's evocation of it in the proem to *FQ* V may signal his pessimism about the restoration of Astraea's ancient justice to the world; but the identification of Astraea with the astrological Virgo (V i 11) holds forth the prospect that the goddess has indeed returned to earth in the idealized potential of England's Virgin Queen.

For Spenser, 'antiquity is a state of mind; a symbol of the Ideal as it exists before passing through the distorting lens of the Actual' (Cheney 1966:150). Chronological primitivism is a self-consciously manipulated artistic stance in Spenser's poetry, and this is even more conspicuously the case with cultural primitivism. Satyrs and wild ('salvage') men appear throughout *The Faerie Queene* as evidence of his familiarity with classical and medieval images of primitive life and with reports in sixteenth-century voyage literature of encounters with savage people (Pearce 1945). But his approach to these figures is shifting and ambivalent. The satyrs who rescue Una from Sansloy display a spontaneous capacity to respond to her beauty, but their worship quickly descends into idolatry (I vi). While the satyrs who welcome Hellenore as their 'housewife' and 'May-lady' appear as figures of healthy sexual vitality in contrast to Malbecco's twisted obsession (III x), their sexuality is clearly limited within the context of the entire book. Both these images of primitive passion are grimly parodied in VI viii, where Serena is held captive by a 'salvage nation' of cannibals whose idolatrous desire for her body is viewed from a perspective characterized as 'anti-primitivism and anti-Petrarchanism' (Cheney 1966:98–116). A related but reversed shift in the handling of primitivistic conventions appears when we compare the 'wilde and salvage man' who captures Amoret to the 'salvage man' who rescues Calepine and Serena from Turpine (IV vii, VI iv). The former is a predatory rapist and cannibal, but the latter shows himself capable of pity and gentleness – not surprisingly, since we learn at the beginning of the next canto that 'certes he was borne of noble blood' (see *Salvage Man). Nowhere are the limits and strategic function of Spenser's interest in cultural primitivism more apparent.

Chronological and cultural primitivism converge in pastoral, which offers a fiction of innocence and simplicity that was presumably universal during the Golden Age and may still be imagined to survive among rustic people uncontaminated by decadent civilization. Spenser's approach to the range and complexity of pastoral is consistent with his attitude towards other forms and traditions of primitivism.

WILLIAM KEACH

Don Cameron Allen 1938 'The Degeneration of Man and Renaissance Pessimism' *SP* 35:202–27; Berger 1968b; Lovejoy and Boas 1935; G. Ant. Borgese 1934 'Primitivism' in *Encyclopaedia of the Social Sciences* ed Edwin R.A. Seligman, et al (New York) 12:398–402; Cheney 1966; Giamatti 1984:89–100, 158–61; Thomas Perrin Harrison, Jr 1940 'Aspects of Primitivism in Shakespeare and Spenser' *TexSE* 20:39–71; Levin 1969; Pearce 1945; Tonkin 1972; H. White 1972.

Prior, Matthew (1664–1721) An important diplomat and a stylish and highly influential occasional poet. His work was praised by Congreve, Pope, and Lady Winchelsea, and the subscription list to his *Poems on Several Occasions* (1718) reads like a 'social register' of the period (Eves 1939:370). Yet this quintessentially Augustan poet was a great enthusiast for Spenser. His copy of the 1679 *Works* is full of his underlinings and admiring comments and contains his own index of favorite passages such as the Temple of Venus and the masque of Cupid. The evidence of the handwriting shows that he used the edition throughout his youth and maturity (Godshalk 1967), and this confirms what Prior says of himself in *Colin's Mistakes*: 'And much he lov'd and much by heart he said / What Father *Spenser* sung in *British* Verse' (Prior ed 1959, 1:545).

In his *Ode, Humbly Inscrib'd to the Queen, on the Glorious Success of Her Majesty's Arms, 1706*, Prior inaugurated the eighteenth-century vogue for imitating Spenser. He uses his own version of the Spenserian stanza (*ababcdcdee*, with the last line still alexandrine), adding one verse to make 'the Number more Harmonious.' The imitation is not very thorough, however, for Prior avoids 'such of his Words, as I found too obsolete,' and merely includes a few Spenserisms such as *I ween* and *whilom*. He says patronizingly, 'I hope the *Ladies* will pardon me, and not judge my MUSE less handsome, though for once she appears in a farthingal' (1:231). Yet his poem had an immediate influence, and he wrote in a letter that same year, 'As to Spencer, my Lord, I think we have gained our point, every body acknowledges him to have been a fine Poet, thô three Months since not one in 50 had read him: Upon my Soul, tis true, the Wits have sent for the Book, the Fairy Queen is on their Toilette table, and some of our Ducal acquaintance will be deep in that Mythologico-Poetical way of thinking' (2:896).

The real significance of his imitation lies not in its minor Spenserian trappings but in the fact that Prior is attempting to write high public verse and links Spenser with Horace as a model in this respect. 'Both have a Height of Imagination, and a Majesty of Expression in describing the *Sublime* ... Both have equally That agreeable Manner of mixing Morality with their Story' (1:231–2). His attitude shows how misleading is the conventional notion of an opposition between Augustan neglect of Spenser and 'pre-Romantic' admiration. Addison's appreciation of Spenser as an exponent of the 'Fairie way of Writing' (*Spectator* 419) in fact represents a divergence from the high public Renaissance tradition that still survives in Prior, though Prior's political situation made meaningful use of it impossible.

In the later imitation *Colin's Mistakes* (1721), Prior presents himself as the poet Colin; but the piece turns into little more than a compliment to Lady Cavendish-Holles-Harley, who is compared to Britomart and Belphoebe. Even here, however, he conveys a very genuine admiration for Spenser and the sense that to imitate him is not a superficial thing: 'Who reads that Bard desires like Him to write, / Still fearful of Success, still tempted by Delight' (1:545). In the Welbeck Abbey manuscripts, he writes in a similar vein: 'But when Thou bidest me Imitate Spencer I drop my Pen. / As well I might go out with Arthurs Sheild or Edwards Sword' (2:990). Prior was buried at his own request at Spenser's feet in Poet's Corner in Westminster Abbey, and this was obviously no mere whim but the fitting end to a lifetime of devotion.

THOMAS M. WOODMAN

Matthew Prior 1959 *Literary Works* ed H. Bunker Wright and Monroe K. Spears, 2 vols (Oxford). Charles Kenneth Eves 1939 *Matthew Prior: Poet and Diplomatist* (New York); William Leigh Godshalk 1967 'Prior's Copy of Spenser's "Works" (1679)' *PBSA* 61:52–5; Frances Mayhew Rippy 1986 *Matthew Prior* (Boston).

Prometheus The Titan of Greek mythology who stole fire from the sun and gave it to man in defiance of Zeus. For this crime, Zeus chained him to a peak in the Caucasus and sent an eagle to torment him by devouring his liver. (Some Renaissance authorities, however, say the heart, eg, Thomas Cooper 1565; cf *FQ* II x 70.) For accepting fire, man, too, was punished: Pandora, the first woman, was sent to Epimetheus and opened a mysterious jar from which sprang all evils, only hope remaining within (cf Harvey's 'New Yeeres Gift' 14, *Three Letters* 3; *Var Prose* p 465).

The earliest versions of the myth (especially Hesiod, *Theogony* 507–616 and *Works and Days* 47–105) depict Prometheus as a foolish trickster whose name (Gr 'forethought') is ironic and whose fate is justly deserved. Ancient redactors, notably Aeschylus in *Prometheus Bound*, interpret the gift of fire as a symbol of human progress, and Prometheus' punishment as a tragic apotheosis. Later mythographers suggest that Prometheus was *vir prudentissimus* (Estienne 1561) and allegorize his torment, 'by the whiche is signified, that he was studious, and a great astronomer' (T. Cooper 1565).

E.K.'s gloss on *Maye* 142 identifies Spenser's 'Geaunte' as Atlas, the brother of 'Prometheus who ... did first fynd out the hidden courses of the starres, by an excellent imagination.' This confused interpretation, which euhemerizes both Titans and associates Atlas (*Theogony* 517–20) with his brother, is found almost verbatim in Cooper, from whom E.K. appears to have borrowed it.

Spenser refers once to a trickster Prometheus, when Jove mentions Procrustes, Typhon, Ixion, and 'great *Prometheus*, tasting of our ire' as types of the hubris of Mutabilitie (*FQ* VII vi 29). By including him among other justly punished overreachers, Spenser may be alluding indirectly to the figure of Tityos in Homer (*Odyssey* 11.576–81) or Virgil (*Aeneid* 6.595–600). Horace seems even closer to Spenser's practice: in *Odes* 1.3.25–40, a bon-voyage salute to Virgil, the poet condemns sailing (cf *Works and Days* 236–47), a technological advance that he blames on such excessive pride as Prometheus'. Horace's figure, however, is presented ambivalently (he somewhat resembles the Aeschylean culture hero), whereas the Titan punished by Spenser's Jove has no redeeming features and seems cast in an essentially Hesiodic mold.

Spenser's fullest treatment of Prometheus occurs at *FQ* II x 70. At the beginning of his brief Elfin chronicle, the poet describes the Titan's creation of the eponymous ancestor Elf. This motif, analogous to the traditional notion that Prometheus made the human race, derives ultimately from Plato's *Protagoras* 320–2. There, the otherwise insufficiently motivated theme that Prometheus risked incurring the wrath of Zeus by giving fire to Epimetheus is explained by the Titan's partiality to a creature of his own making. Spenser's Promethean artificer has come to him through several sources: Ovid, who says that he may have made man by commingling earth and water (*Metamorphoses* 1.78–88); Horace, who says that the Titan adds to the new creature parts taken from every animal (*Odes* 1.16.13–21); Fulgentius, who says that he steals fire from the celestial regions to animate the work he has made (*Mythologiae* 2.9); and Conti, who catalogues Spenser's 'many partes from beasts derived' (*Mythologiae* 4.6). Many of these details are summarized by Cooper, though Spenser seems to have invented the notion that for his offense Prometheus was 'by *Jove* deprived / Of life him selfe.' The standard Renaissance interpretation is given by Sandys (ed 1970:58): 'But to conforme the fable to the truth: *Prometheus* signifies Providence, and *Minerva* Heavenly Wisdome: by Gods providence therefore and wisdome Man was created. The celestiall fire is his soule inspired from above.'

PHILIP J. GALLAGHER

---

pronunciation Spenser wrote in a period in which there was no single 'correct' pronunciation of English. Strang (1970:154) transcribes 'And first of the wordes to spẹake, I graunt they be something hard' (*SC*, Ẹpistle to Harvey) as '/ən(d) fırst əv ðə w*ɑ́*rdz tə spɛ:k, əı graʊnt ðe: bi:sʊmθiŋg hard/' and comments, 'any one transcription involves arbitrary selection between concurrent variant forms.' We cannot for certain reconstruct Spenser's own speech any more than we can reconstruct Shakespeare's. 'We do not even know how Shakespeare pronounced his own surname' (Cercignani 1981:1). Though Spenser's name is a simpler phonological problem, the variant spellings Spenser/Spencer warn us to expect inconsistency in the written evidence (and that is all we have) of the pronunciation of his time. Alexander Gil, discussing English consonants in his phonetic alphabet in his important and informative *Logonomia anglica* (1619, 1621), writes 'we exclude *c* because it is an inappropriate letter' (1621:8). Yet he chooses to illustrate his work with numerous lines from *The Faerie Queene* by Spencer or Spenser.

Rhymes may not be a reliable guide to Spenser's pronunciation, and are certainly not to any general pronunciation in his time. Dobson's assertion of the latter (1968:626) reflects many critics, such as John Hughes, in 'Remarks on the Writings of Spenser' (in Spenser ed 1715: cxi): '*Spenser* himself is irregular ... and often writes the same Word differently, especially at the end of a Line; where ... he frequently alters the Spelling for the sake of the Rhime, and even sometimes only to make the Rhime appear more exact to the Eye of the Reader.' So, *bin* rhymes with *Sarazin*, but *beene* with *greene* and *seene*.

Special factors may enter Spenser's usage. Linguists (eg, Wyld 1923, Zachrisson 1913) note his rhyme *seates/states*. This /ē/ :/ā/ rhyme was in London usage unusual and argues, since fronting of ME /ā/ was earlier in the North, a Northern pronunciation. Gil (1621:16) notes that Northerners often use '*ea* for *e*, as *meat* for *mët* "food"; and for *o*, as *beað for both* "both"' – related to Northern ME *bāþ*. He thus indicates ME /ē/ and ME /ā/ in a dialectal pronunciation where in each case diphthongization develops with [ə] after the vowel.

The possibility of Northernisms in Spenser may be supported by the understanding that his family was of Northern origin, that after Cambridge he had a year in the North, and that he attended Merchant Taylors' School, where his headmaster was the Northerner Richard Mulcaster, author of *The First Part of the Elementarie* (1582). The Minutes of the Court of the Merchant Taylors' Company from 16 August 1562 record of the ushers at the school 'that being northern men born, they had not taught the children to speak distinctly, or to pronounce their words as well as they aught' (Dobson 1968:125).

Gil's phonetic transcriptions of *The Faerie Queene* are often inconsistent. This may be owing to printer's errors in 1621 from 1619, but may sometimes show Gil's local interest in expounding rhetorical figures rather than concentration on consistency of phonetic transcription. So, he cites *FQ* I ix 17 in his chapter 'De figuris sententiae,' exemplifying *synchesis* and *hypallage*, in three differing transcriptions. This rhetorical interest which at times obscures Gil's phonetics nonetheless chimes with his identification (in ch 6) of six principal dialects in English. (We should understand *dialect* in Suetonius' sense of 'a manner of speaking.') The six are General, Northern, Southern, Eastern, Western – and Poetic. Of this last, Gil remarks, 'because poets maintain their dialect by no license [departure from a norm] except metaplasm, enough will be said of it when we get to prosody.' *Metaplasm* refers here to a figure whereby words, tone of voice, or grammatical and syntactical sequences may be altered for the sake of elegance and metrical effectiveness. Various types in Spenser include *diaeresis*: 'wündes, kloudes, handes, for wündz, kloudz, handz'; *antistoechon*: 'fön, ein, hond, lond, for föz, eiz, hand, land.' As an example of 'rhetorical accent' that affects pronunciation, Gil gives 'If yi bi âl thïvz, what höp hav J?' ('If ye be *all* thieves, what hope have I?') and comments that 'vowels long by nature are strongly distorted in yï, bï, häv, in what is stressed for need in âl, and in J' (1621:133). Many examples of such rhetorical shortening occur in Spenser. Also relevant to his poetic is Dobson's observation (1968:152) from Gil that 'in poetry the final syllable of a proparoxytone [word stressed on the third syllable from the end] in *-i* is often accented, with the result that the vowel of that syllable becomes long, as in *mizerj*.' So should we read *cunningly* at *FQ* I iv 5, for example.

It is of central importance to take Gil's point that the 'dialect of poetry' is, in its phonology, governed by the license of rhetorical metaplasm. Because this is so, a neat and systematic account cannot and should not be proposed of the sounds of Spenser. His decorum is not that of phonological exactness but of aesthetic verisimilitude. Sir Thomas Pope Blount's comment (*De re poetica* 1694), that '*Spencer* has endeavour'd [Theocritus' *Dorick* Dialect] in his *Shepherds*

Calendar; but neither will it succeed in English' (*Sp All* p 302), is quite true. On another level of linguistic decorum, though, Pope is poetically wise to observe the 'unusual and elegant Manner' of Diggon in *SC, September* 3–4: 'Hur was hur while it was Day-light / But now hur is a most wretched Wight' (*Guardian* 40, 27 April 1713).

Bearing in mind the fact that Spenser's 'dialect' is 'poetic,' the following may serve as a guide to his pronunciation. For convenience, the passage is *FQ* IV x 24.1–8, reproduced from Gil (both 1619 and 1621) in Dobson (1968:135):

Fresh shadöuz, fit tu shroud from ʃuni rai;
Fair laundz, tu täk ðe ʃun in ʃëzn dv;
Swït ʃpringz, in wich a thouzand nimfs did plai;
Soft rumbling brüks, ðat ʒentl ʃlumber drv;
Hjh rëred mounts, ðe landz about tu *v*v;
Löu lüking dälz, disloin'd from komon gäz,
Deljtful bourz, tu ʃolas luvers trv;
Fair laberinths, fond runerz eiz tu däz.

Suggested interpretation:
Freʃ ʃaedo:z fɪt tʊ ʃrəʊd ʃrʊm sʊnɪ rai
Fɛɪr lɔ:ndz tʊ tae:k ðə sʊn ɪn sɛ:zn dy:
Swi:t sprɪngz ɪn h(w)ɪtʃ ə ðəʊzənd nɪmfs dɪd plai
Soft rʊmblɪŋg brʊks ðaet dʒentɪl slʊmbər dry:
Həɪ(X) rɛ:rɪd məʊnts ðə laendz əbəʊt tʊ vy:
Lɔ: lʊkɪŋg dae:lz dɪslɔɪnd frʊm komən gae:z
Dələɪtfəl bəʊrz tʊ soləs lʊvʒrz try:
Fɛɪr laebərɪnθs fond rʊnʒrz əɪz tʊ dae:z

The readings [ae:] /tae:k, dae:lz, gae:z, dae:z/ and [y:] /dy:, dry:, vy:, try:/ perhaps ask for comment. Some commentators (eg, Strang) would transcribe not [ae:] but (tense) [e:]. However, Dobson shows (1968:145) that tense [e:] did not exist in Gil's speech, and the assumption is here made that Spenser too heard ME /ā/ as [ae:]. Cercignani (1981:171) judges that such rhymes in Shakespeare as *brake/take* (*Midsummer Nights Dream* III ii 15–16) and *blazed/gazed/amazed* (*Rape of Lucrece* 1353–6) 'should be taken to rest on [late] ME ā (normally [ae:]).'

The reading [y:] which might be doubted in favour of [ju:], again follows Dobson (pp. 144–5.) That Gil meant [y:] by Roman *v* 'cannot be finally proved'; that Spenser heard [y:] is an assumption, but likely. However, Cercignani would transcribe [*ɪʊ*].

The representation həɪ(X) reflects Gil's *h* and *r*, though in the process of becoming untrilled [ɹ], is especially in the language of poetry, still pronounced. The final *g* after [ŋ] is generally judged to be preserved in Spenser's time.

AVRIL BRUTEN

Fausto Cercignani 1981 *Shakespeare's Works and Elizabethan Pronunciation* (Oxford); E.J. Dobson 1968 *English Pronunciation 1500–1700* 2nd ed, 2 vols (Oxford); Gil ed 1621; Barbara M.H. Strang 1970 *A History of English* (London); Henry Cecil Wyld 1923 *Studies in English Rhymes from Surrey to Pope* (London); R.E. Zachrisson 1913 *Pronunciation of English Vowels 1400–1700* (Göteborg).

prophecies Prophecy is an important bond between the medieval and Renaissance worlds because they shared a common experience and sense of history. During the late sixteenth century, various forms of prophecy flourished – secular and sacred, pagan and Christian, astrological and apocalyptic, prophecies of doom no less than of millennial expectation. That they were ubiquitous and taken seriously, even in politics, is evidenced by the fact that during the reign of Elizabeth and at her instigation, there were edicts against prophesying. Those edicts were directed against 'prophesying' in both of its current senses: predicting the future by divine inspiration, and expounding the Scriptures by (usually Puritan) groups of readers claiming to be inspired by the Holy Spirit. Elizabeth herself may have commissioned from John Harvey *A Discoursive Probleme Concerning Prophesies* (London 1588), a work which by railing against Piers Plowmans, Merlins, and Colin Clouts seeks to discredit all forms of extrascriptural prophecy.

Spenser's use of prophecy in its various forms at once represents his age's distrust of prophecy and registers his own fascination with and allegiance to it. In donning the mantle of the prophet, he relates his poetry to a Christian paradigm of poetic development but also takes a stand different from the official position of the established church, which forbade prophesying and distrusted enthusiasm. At the same time, Spenser signals that his poetry is prophetic in a special sense: though not a conveyor of original prophecies, it is a commentary on existing ones, both secular and sacred. If not a representative of extremely conservative Protestantism, in his prophesying Spenser is at an extreme, expounding prophecy rather than enunciating it, but in this, still sustaining a tradition that was being threatened and that by some would be silenced. He clearly believed that, whatever its limitations and abuses, prophecy continued to provide an assured framework for understanding history. Prophecy was history anticipated, and history was prophecy fulfilled. Moreover, prophecy could not be fully interpreted until it had been fulfilled in history.

Spenser's posture toward prophecy is evident as early as *The Shepheardes Calender*, and in its crucial details illuminated by his correspondence with Harvey. The five published letters were probably a collaborative effort, written with each man looking over the other's shoulder. What Harvey says of the natural phenomenon of earthquakes is what Spenser himself would probably say of the supernatural phenomenon of prophecy. Their efficient cause is God, 'the Creatour, and Continuer, and Corrector of Nature.' They may themselves be 'terrible signes ... certaine manacing forerunners, and forewarners of the great latter day,' yet they do not all signify a 'fatall Action of God.' As a part of God's 'incomprehensible mysteries,' as well as an aspect of 'his eternall Providence,' what they really signify may remain uncertain: no one can 'definitively ... give sentence of his ... secret and inscrutable purposes' (*Three Letters* 2, *Var Prose* pp 454–5). Indeed, what the prophecy forecasts and what the prophet would actually foment often pull oppositely.

In *Ruines of Time*, a snowy swan sings 'the prophecie / Of his owne death in dolefull Elegie' (594–5). In *The Shepheardes Calender*, both elegy and pastoral are rendered in a prophetic key. The poem is a gathering of prophecies: Piers' of a time that will come; Morrell's of Algrind's restoration; Colin's of Elizabeth's, England's, and his own annihilation. Those prophecies collectively identify *The Shepheardes Calender* as a warning prophecy, Spenser knowing full well that the potential triumph of such a prophecy comes when it proves itself irrelevant – when impending disaster has been averted because the prophecy has been heeded. As Spenser depicts the historical situation, the Queen (Rosalind) is about to break her covenant with the people (Colin Clout). Her figurative death is the subject of the lament in *November*: it symbolizes the prophetic death which Elizabeth's impending marriage forebodes for England. It has been argued that in the death of Dido and the approaching death of Colin are figured the prophetic consequences of the Queen's marriage: her spiritual death, together with the death of the English church, of England, of the people; and the death of poets and of poetry as well (see McLane 1961, Wittreich 1979).

The prophetic element muted in *The Shepheardes Calender* is foregrounded in *The Faerie Queene*. Spenser's prophetic epic is framed by prophecies of the New Jerusalem (I x) and of a son being born who will dry up all the water and destroy the fiend (VI iv). More significant perhaps are the isolated prophecies scattered throughout the poem and especially those of its central books. In the castle of Alma episode, prophecies are numbered along with dreams and visions among the 'idle thoughts and fantasies' that encumber the mind (*FQ* II ix 51). Proteus appears as 'father of false prophecis,' foretelling that Marinell's 'decay should happen by a mayd' (III iv 37, IV xii 28). Yet Proteus also appears here as a foil to the true prophet Nereus, who 'voide of guile' teaches others to do right and 'expert in prophecies' unfolds 'the ledden [speech] of the Gods,' foretelling to Paris the fall of Troy (IV xi 18–19).

The Faerie Queene is a scanning of true and false prophecies by way of reaching toward the understanding that true prophecies rather than forecasting disaster seek to avert it, and that such prophecies are fulfilled only because they go unheeded. This lesson is driven home by Cymoent, mother of Marinell and daughter of great Nereus, who goes to Proteus, supposedly one 'with prophecie inspir'd,' to inquire of her son's destiny only to learn that her son will be dismayed or killed by 'A virgin strange and stout' (III iv 25). Yet Marinell does not die: his wound is healed, and what she really learns is that prophecies are fulfilled because wisdom comes too late.

The sharpest focusing of prophecy, and Spenser's most sustained reflection upon it, is provided by Merlin who is found 'Deepe busied bout worke of wondrous end' (III iii 14). Here prophecy itself is seen as a mirror on providence and history and as extending infinitely to encompass all things between heaven and earth. Merlin was traditionally thought to be blessed with special gifts of insight, wisdom, and prophecy; and during the Renaissance, his prophecies with their distinctly political hue were characteristically apocalyptic and millenarian. Instead of revealing prophecies in the moon and stars, Merlin reveals an evolutionary process within the cyclical patterns of history (III iii). Artegall, he says, not only will be the spouse of Britomart but will end his days in peace. After his time, woe will follow woe until the Britons are at last restored to rule, at which time enmities will disappear, divided nations will unite, and a reign of peace will be established: 'Then shall a royall virgin raine' (49). At that moment, Merlin ceases to prophesy, as one 'overcomen of the spirites powre' or by some 'other ghastly spectacle dismayd' (50). What he sees secretly he declines to divulge.

The figure who introduces apocalyptic to secular prophecy and imbues it with millenarian thought, here delivers an utterance that would dampen apocalyptic fervor and quiet millennial expectations: 'But yet the end is not' (50). Apocalyptic elements can be found in *The Faerie Queene*, most notably in Book I; but Spenser's procedure is gradually to subdue those elements within a prophetic perspective, thereby shifting attention from future to present history and then from the history of the world to the spiritual history of a chosen nation and chosen people. Apocalyptic utterances typically claim that God rules history and will wrest from it a glorious future regardless of human agency. Yet, perhaps out of frustration with this apocalyptic promise, Spenser attributes responsibility, at least in part, to his nation and her people. Evolution displaces revolution with God and man cooperating to achieve historical progress, and with Spenser himself becoming the emanative center of a vision that, by transforming individuals, could transform an entire nation and then the world.

If God is the architect of history, God's people are his draughtsmen and construction workers. Through human agency, an upside-down world can be turned right side up again. History is ongoing, and when prophecy invades history, it is to keep history moving on a course toward the apocalyptic consummation that lies in the distant future, not to predict that the consummation is at hand. For Spenser, prophecy is an agent of reformation, not revolution; it does not predict the future but rather addresses and hopes to alter the present to ensure that a future is possible. In this way, *The Faerie Queene* achieves the stature of a prophetic poem radiant with vision. (See also *Apocalypse, *oracles, *visions.)

JOSEPH WITTREICH

Fletcher 1971; Bernard McGinn 1979 *Visions of the End: Apocalyptic Traditions in the Middle Ages* (New York); McLane 1961; Marjorie Reeves 1969 *The Influence of Prophecy in the Later Middle Ages: A Study in Joachimism* (Oxford); R.W. Southern 1970–3 'Aspects of the European Tradition of Historical Writing' *TRHS* 5th ser, 20:173–96, 21:159–79, 22:159–80 ('History as Prophecy'), 23:243–63; Rupert Taylor 1911 *The Political Prophecy in England* (New York); Wittreich 1979.

Prosopopoia, or Mother Hubberds Tale. See ***Complaints: Prosopopoia, or Mother Hubberds Tale***

Proteus This sea god appears in two of Spenser's works: in *Colin Clouts Come Home Againe* 248–51, he is one of Cynthia's marine shepherds; in *The Faerie Queene*, he prophesies Marinell's fate and rescues Florimell from the lecherous fisherman only to abduct her to his cave, court her unavailingly, and imprison her for seven months in his rocky undersea dungeon (III iv 25–37, viii 29–42; IV xi 1–4). In *FQ* IV xi-xii, Proteus presides over the marriage feast of Thames and Medway. There Marinell overhears Florimell's lament that he does not love her; he falls in love and pines for her until his mother appeals to Neptune, who orders Proteus to release Florimell.

The iconography of Proteus, Neptune's herdsman and prophetic old man of the sea, derives chiefly from Homer (*Odyssey* 4.351–570) and Virgil (*Georgics* 4.387–529). Accordingly, in *Colin Clout* he is white-haired and bearded, driving a herd of 'stinking' seals and porpoises (cf *Odyssey* 4.441–3). Spenser independently makes him cold and frosty (*FQ* III viii 35). Homer and Virgil compare him to a shepherd, and Renaissance poets and mythographers similarly call him *pastor* (Sannazaro *Piscatory Eclogues* 3.62–5, Boccaccio *Genealogia* 7.9, Conti *Mythologiae* 8.8). In *FQ* III viii 30, his chariot is drawn by 'Phocas' or seals; this description is based on Conti's interpretation of Virgil's *equi bipedes*, mythical two-footed sea horses. In Virgil, Proteus dwells behind a rock in a mountain cave by the sea; in *FQ* III viii 37, his submarine cave is hollowed out of a rock.

Classical and Renaissance treatments give Proteus the paired attributes of shape-changing and prophecy: if pursued, he can change shape at will; but if he is captured and held securely, he will return to his own form and prophesy for his captor. His ability to change shape was proverbial. (Erasmus' *Adages* [ed 1703–6, 2:473b-4a] includes *Proteo mutabilior* 'more changeable than Proteus,' which is repeated in Cooper 1565; Tilley s 285 gives the English proverb 'As many shapes as Proteus.') His mutability was variously interpreted in the Renaissance. Following the Hermetic *Asclepius*, it could represent the mutable nature of man (Pico della Mirandola *Oration on the Dignity of Man* 1486, Vives *Fable about Man* c 1518 in Kristeller, et al 1948:223–54, 387–93). His false shapes could also represent the false opinions which thwart our search for the truth (Fraunce ed 1975:57–8).

Proteus is commonly called *vates* 'prophet' (Virgil *Georgics* 4.387, Ovid *Metamorphoses* II.249, followed by Renaissance mythographers). But his power of prophecy is linked to his capacity for deception; Augustine associates him with falsehood or the devil (*City of God* 10.10). More specifically, Plato connects him with the deceptive power of words (*Euthydemus* 288B-C compares two Sophists with Proteus; see also *Euthyphro* 15D, *Ion* 541E-2A). Spenser mentions the 'subtile sophismes, which do play / With double senses, and with false debate,' through which destiny, expressed in Proteus' prophecy, works itself out in mortal life (III iv 28). Another Renaissance tradition links Proteus, *vates* and word manipulator, to the poet (Giamatti 1984:122–7).

As prophet in *The Faerie Queene*, Proteus delivers a prophecy as ambiguous as himself. He tells Cymodoce that Marinell will be harmed by a woman, but she misunderstands him and reproaches him as 'father of false prophecis' (III iv 37). Yet the prophecy is doubly fulfilled, for Marinell is wounded physically by Britomart and psychologically by Florimell. Towards Florimell, Proteus is the agent of a destiny he seeks to thwart and whose purpose he expresses in 'double senses.' (By contrast, the poem's other marine prophet, Nereus, is sincere and upright in IV xi 18–19.) Despite the ambiguity of his prophecy, Spenser's Proteus does not change shape in order to avoid prophesying; rather, the incident recalls his voluntary prophecy to the sea goddess Thetis about her son Achilles, whom Marinell resembles (Ovid *Met* II.221–3, Lotspeich 1932:51). Sannazaro mentions the Nereid Cymodoce and Proteus mourning Achilles' death (*Piscatory Eclogues* 1.84–90). Proteus does transform himself in wooing Florimell (III viii 29–42), but it is in order to achieve a personal desire rather than to evade his divine function.

As 'shepherd of the seas,' Proteus is an instrument of heaven's grace when he rescues Florimell and punishes the lustful fisherman. But soon he becomes her unwanted lover, flattering her, transforming himself into pleasing or threatening shapes, and finally imprisoning her. This episode has two prototypes. Ariosto's *Orlando furioso* 8.52 describes a lustful Proteus who rapes an Ebudan princess. Euripides' *Helen* (drawing on Stesichorus' variant of the Trojan myth) casts Proteus as a benevolent king of Egypt who shelters the real Helen while the Trojan war is fought over a phantom; Proteus' son later threatens Helen's chastity. Spenser's Proteus combines the behavior of father and son; meanwhile, knights dispute over the counterfeit Florimell and Paridell's rape of Hellenore further debases the Trojan myth (III ix-x).

Spenser's Proteus resembles the enchanter Busirane and the shape-changers Archimago (compared to Proteus at I ii 10) and Malengin. Malengin, or guile, flatters and deceives like Proteus, who could be a type of the hypocritical flatterer (*Ovide moralisé* 2.25; see also Bersuire 1509: fol 66v). Proteus was sometimes thought to be a magician (Conti 8.8), like Archimago and Busirane. Further, Busirane imprisons Amoret for seven months as Proteus does Florimell. In these episodes, the captors display the cruel, frightening, and deceptive aspects of love; but their victims pass through their trials of chastity to a more fruitful relationship. Proteus' amorous shape-changing links him to the metamorphosed gods in Busirane's tapestry: Ovid advises the lover to be as cruel as Busiris, as versatile as Proteus (*Ars amatoria* 1.647–58, 755–70). Being inconstant himself, Proteus tempts Florimell to inconstancy. (The fickle lover and false friend in Shakespeare's *Two Gentlemen of Verona* is also named Proteus.) In the psychological allegory, Florimell, like Amoret, is subjected through love of Marinell to passion and vicissitude, here symbolized by Proteus since he traditionally could signify changeable passions, especially lust (Boccaccio *Genealogia* 7.9, Giraldi *De deis gentium* 1548:228, Erasmus *Enchiridion militis christiani* 7). After her erotic encounter with the fisherman, Florimell's descent into the sea with Proteus may therefore represent a fall into the passions.

More satisfyingly, Proteus may symbolize an aspect of physical nature. Since Florimell is replaced by a snowy or false Florimell during her seven-month confinement by a frosty Proteus, and since images of spring attend her union with Marinell, she is allied to Adonis and Proserpine (also a flower-maiden), vegetation deities confined underground through the winter. This analogy explains the wintry appearance of Spenser's Proteus. His behavior recalls the seasonal myth of Vertumnus, god of the changing year, who courted Pomona (goddess of fruit) in various shapes; and Erasmus links Proteus to Vertumnus in his *Adages*.

Proteus was anciently regarded as primal matter, his transformations proceeding through the four elements (Heraclitus *Homeric Allegories* 66.7). In *FQ* III viii 41, he changes to giant (earth), fiend (fire), centaur (air), and sea storm (water), recalling the way in which Archimago (I ii 10) is like him in being able to change to bird (air), fish (water), fox (earth), and dragon (fire). Proteus' cave and dungeon may be seen, then, as the abode of first matter, like the abyss of Chaos in the Garden of Adonis (III vi 36); his love for Florimell is the desire of matter for form, and Florimell is the Neoplatonic principle of beauty, or the soul, trapped and obscured by matter, fallen from the One into the Many. Alternatively, Proteus may be the giver of forms to matter (Orphic *Hymn* to Proteus; see also Conti 8.8) or the variety of those forms in nature (Giraldi 1548:228, citing Proclus). Fraunce calls him 'a type of nature' in *Amintas Dale* (ed 1975:58). In this interpretation, his love is the desire of the mutable natural world for ideal beauty. His cave parallels Homer's Cave of the Nymphs, which is allegorized by Porphyry as the world, dark because it contains matter but beautiful through its participation in forms and moist because it is generative.

At the marriage feast of the rivers (IV xi-xii), Proteus presides in his hall over the renewal of life and beauty, whereas in his dungeon he had seemed to constrain them. The feast is preeminently a symbol of concord amidst 'the seas abundant progeny,' the sea representing life or generation (Conti 8.1). Florimell withstands the diversity and mutability signified by Proteus, but he governs the world in which she will appear, like '*Venus* [from] the fomy sea.' Conti (8.8) also sees Proteus as a model of civic prudence, generating friendship by his flexible adaptability. His role as host thus forms a fitting conclusion to the Legend of Friendship. In *The Faerie Queene*, Proteus successively symbolizes various aspects of mutability in man and nature; but his last role is the most inclusive. SUPRIYA CHAUDHURI

Giamatti 1984:115–50; Nohrnberg 1976; Roche 1964; Wind 1958.

Prothalamion (See ed 1912:600–2.) The title page of the thin quarto published by Ponsonby in 1596 clearly announces that what follows is an occasional poem celebrating the double marriage of Elizabeth and Katherine Somerset, the two eldest daughters of Edward Somerset, fourth Earl of Worcester, to Henry Guildford of Hemsted Place, Kent, knighted shortly after the wedding, and William Petre, later the second Baron Petre of Writtle. The double wedding took place at Essex House on 8 November 1596. The poem was probably written to celebrate the betrothal ceremony which took place some time after the Earl of Essex' return to court by mid-August from his victory at Cádiz and before the court left Greenwich on 1 October – the end of September seems likely. The only contemporary evidence is Rowland Whyte's report, on 26 September 1596, to Robert Sidney: 'Tis sayd the 2 ladies of Somersett shall speedily be married to your cosen Gilford and Sir John Peters son' (Norton 1940:48).

In itself, the event was not sufficiently important either politically or socially to warrant Spenser's exquisite praise. The immediate cause may be found in the presence, at the occasion and in the poem, of Essex, whose patronage Spenser was seeking. Essex may have been called upon to be the host because of family connections: he was related to Worcester's wife, and his wife to Henry Guildford. Spenser uses his presence to lift the poem out of the private and into the public sphere.

The poem professes, as the occasion demanded, an optimistic faith in a promising future. In spite of their clear Roman Catholic leanings, the two husbands and the father of the brides seem to have done well for themselves under Elizabeth and James. Yet history has its ironies: only four years later, Essex fell out of favor with the Queen. During his abortive rebellion, the Earl of Worcester was kept a prisoner at Essex House but later served as one of the peers who condemned him to death for high treason.

Prothalamion is one of Spenser's most harmonious and melodious creations, full of beautiful phrases and with perfect control of both imagery and rhythm. In *Table Talk*, Coleridge praises 'the swan-like movement of [Spenser's] exquisite Prothalamion.' Both thematically and technically, it represents the poet's mature talents. Each of its ten eighteen-line stanzas is rounded off with the couplet (made memorable for the modern reader by T.S. Eliot's use of it in *The Waste Land*): 'Against the Brydale day, which is not long: / Sweete *Themmes* runne softly, till I end my Song.' The penultimate line shows some interesting variations, notably between the present and past tense, each used five times. The refrain focuses on the poem's major concern: to bring the poet's vision of the world as it ought to be into harmony with his knowledge of the world as it is. The mighty river, which has seen so much human triumph and misery, may comply with the poet's wish that it 'runne softly' and thus help to preserve the harmony of procession and poem. But the spell is only temporary, and the bridal day – the symbol of the harmonious union of opposites – 'which is not long,' will it also not last long?

If Spenser's vision refers to an actual event, the procession would seem to have begun somewhere on the river Lee, moved downstream to Greenwich, and then up the Thames to Essex House, which is located just upstream from the 'bricky towres' of the inns of court. The meaning of *Lee* in stanzas 3 and 7 has been disputed, since it may refer also to a meadow or to the lee side of a river. In both instances, however, the word is personified and seems to refer to the river Lee. That river is mentioned in two of Spenser's principal sources, Leland's *Cygnea cantio* (1545) and William Vallans' *Tale of Two Swannes* (1591); moreover, the pairing of Lee and Thames introduces the marriage of the rivers as a minor motif in the poem. An inconsistency remains, however, for the Thames is directly addressed in the refrain to every stanza; and in the transition from stanza 7 to 8, there is an abrupt jump from the Lee to London. Yet the sense of the real world in the poem is very strong: the final destination of the procession is Essex House, and stanza 8 refers to the inns of court, 'Where now the studious Lawyers have their bowers' (134). This line may refer to the affiliations of the two bridegrooms and their father-in-law with Inner and Middle Temples.

Although the betrothal poem can be found in classical poetry (eg, Propertius and Statius), in English poetry before Spenser (eg, Lydgate and Dunbar), and was in use in Elizabethan England as part of the betrothal celebrations, it never gained currency as a distinct genre. Spenser seems to have invented the title *Prothalamion* (Gr 'before [in time or place] the bridal chamber') for what he subtitles 'Spousall Verse.' It is arguable that he did so in order to deviate from the epithalamic convention. *Prothalamion* contains several elements which were uncommon or directly alien to the traditional marriage song, such as the poet's complaint and personal history in stanzas 1 and 8, his references to the history of the Temple and the loss of Leicester in 8, and the eulogy of Essex in 9. These deviations have led some readers to suppose that Spenser was trying to create a new genre, or a new sub-genre, by combining the traditional epithalamium with elements from the Chaucerian dream-vision (stanza 1), the river marriage (cf the union of Thames and Medway in *FQ* IV xi), the topographical antiquarian poem (the swan allegory and stanza 8), and the complaint (1 and 8).

Those who have complained that Spenser includes personal, historical, and political material in his beautifully phrased occasional poem, have applied too narrow a definition of that genre. Many modern readings have been directed towards a reinterpretation which allows us to see the so-called extraneous material as integral. Like much of Spenser's poetry, *Prothalamion* is concerned with the relationship between the poet and his vision, the actual and the ideal, the world of art and the world of time. The refrain is concerned not with the betrothal but with the poet's relationship with the river of time, which is not only potential enemy but also powerful ally. As it brings the brides to their future husbands, it also brings the poem towards its close. As the vision follows upon an escape from reality, it must eventually cease and effect a return to reality.

The betrothal described in *Prothalamion* clearly concerns the poet, and for this reason it concerns the reader. He is our representative, our emissary into the world of love, beauty, and nobility. As such, he could lead us on the road to envy and an intensified impression of our own failure, or to a romantic escape into the beauty and happiness of another, otherwise impenetrable world. Or he can present us with the vision as an enriching experience, leading us to accept our own situation, past, present, and future, as we move from the private sphere to the familial, social, national, and religious dimensions of marriage.

The temporary and precarious harmony of the poem is introduced by the conflicting forces of the wind and sun, Zephyrus breathing sweetly to 'delay' the 'Hot ... beames' of Titan. The burning sun often represents unpleasant actuality, and as a biblical image (eg, Ps 121.5–6) it was interpreted as worldly temptations from which one needed to be protected by grace. The contrast between Zephyrus and Titan, as well as that between the poet's unpleasant social past and his happy pastoral present, constitute the first pair in a series of contrasts. Thus the two swans seem to be angels and are compared to the swans of Venus; but they are 'bred of *Somers-heat*,' with an obvious pun on the brides' family name, Somerset, and also a reference to Titan's hot beams. With a characteristic pun, they are 'Fowles so lovely' (61), vulnerable to the 'foule' water (48) of the river of time which may soil their white purity.

Beneath the surface description of purity and chaste love are disturbing allusions to a violent sexuality. The description of the nymphs gathering flowers in the meadow in stanza 2 seems designed to recall the rapes of Proserpina and Europa and to prepare for the more direct reference to Zeus' rape of Leda in stanza 3.

There may be several reasons why Spenser chose to present the brides as a pair of swans. The Thames was famous for its many swans (Vallans' poem explains how they came to English rivers). The actual procession of the brides may have taken place in barges decorated to resemble swans; processions of this kind were not unusual in Elizabethan England, and to compare ships to swans was also a commonplace. Besides Leland and Vallans, Spenser may also have been influenced by Camden's 'De connubio Tamae et Isis' (1586), all of which refer explicitly to the classical idea – very popular in the Renaissance – of the poet as swan (see *Time* 589–602). In their roles as swans, the brides-to-be have therefore invaded a familiar mythical world.

John Hughes (1715) seems to have been the first to comment on the disappearance of the swans after stanza 7. When the two ladies reappear in 10, they are referred to as 'Brides.' The transformation is softened by the conventional and obvious pun on *birds/brides* (cf *Cymbeline* IV ii 197, *Taming of the Shrew* V ii 46); and by comparing the bridegrooms to the heavenly twins, Castor and Pollux, offspring of Leda, Spenser establishes a clear connection with the Leda myth in stanza 3.

If stanzas 1–7 are concerned with the private and pastoral spheres, stanzas 8–10 are concerned with the public sphere. Like stanza 1, stanza 8 clarifies the poet's relationship to his setting. As 4 alludes to the origin of the brides, 8 gives us the origin of the poet. In the mythic vision of 3–5, the bridal procession is seen to compare favorably with the classical past. In stanzas 8–10, the poet turns to the ability of present time to make up for the personal, moral, and national disasters of the past: the disappointed hopes of the poet, the fall of the proud Knights Templars, and the loss of 'that great Lord,' Leicester, whose memory is brought to mind as the procession reaches his former residence, Leicester House, now called Essex House and the residence of the Earl of Essex. By the end of stanza 8, Spenser is able to check his complaint, for the Knights Templars have been superseded by the 'studious Lawyers' and by the bridegrooms, who are described as 'Two gentle Knights of lovely face and feature / Beseeming well the bower of anie Queene,' and the tragic loss of Leicester is made up for by Essex whose martial triumphs, combined with the Queen's good government, provide for a secure and happy future for the married couples. A special celebration of Elizabeth is indicated in stanza 9, for the refrain may be taken to contain a reference to her Accession Day, which would be celebrated shortly after the double wedding, on 17 November, traditionally described as the day of her marriage to England.

The structure of *Prothalamion* is similar to, yet simpler than, the structure of *Epithalamion*. The conventional symbols of circularity – garlands and crowns – are given new significance by the cosmic image of the zodiac (line 174). From this perspective, the line total of 180 may suggest 'the 180 degrees of the sun's daytime course round half the circle of the heavens' (Fowler 1975:66), and this in turn may suggest other circular and astronomical symbols.

In the overall movement of the poem from discord to harmony, Spenser employs parallels and contrasts that may have structural implications. For example, the poet's 'discontent' because of his 'long fruitlesse stay / In Princes Court' in stanza 1 is contrasted to the 'hearts content' and 'fruitfull issue' promised to the brides in 6; the hot Titan in 1 is replaced by the radiant Hesperus of 10, even as the poet who 'walkt forth' to the river in his escape from 'Princes Court' in 1 is paralleled by the more stately bridegrooms 'forth pacing to the Rivers side' in 10. Just as the swans 'excell / The rest' of the river 'foule' (7) so the two 'gentle Knights' may be observed 'Above the rest' of the 'great traine' (10); and just as the swans seem 'heavenly borne' (4), so the bridegrooms also recall heavenly parallels. The nymphs who 'each one had a little wicker basket, / Made of fine twigs entrayled curiously, / In which they gathered flowers to fill their flasket' (2) are recalled in the description of Essex as 'Faire branch of Honor, flower of Chevalrie, / That fillest *England* with thy triumphs fame' (9).

Such verbal parallels and contrasts underscore the thematic movement as an escape from the actual world to a vision of the world as it should be, and, finally, to an acceptance of reality based on a renewed hope that the ideal may still blend with the real on some future 'Brydale day, which is not long.'

EINAR BJORVAND

Harry Berger, Jr 1965 'Spenser's *Prothalamion*: An Interpretation' *EIC* 15:363–80; Fowler 1975:59–86; Dan S. Norton 1940 'The Background of Spenser's *Prothalamion*' diss Princeton Univ; Norton 1944 'The Bibliography of Spenser's *Prothalamion*' *JEGP* 43:349–53; Norton 1951 'The Tradition of Prothalamia' in *English Studies in Honor of James Southall Wilson* (*UVS* 4, Charlottesville, Va) pp 223–41; J. Norton Smith 1959 'Spenser's *Prothalamion*: A New Genre' *RES* ns 10:173–8; Michael West 1974 'Prothalamia in Propertius and Spenser' *CL* 26:346–53; M.L. Wine 1962 'Spenser's "Sweete *Themmes*": Of Time and the River' *SEL* 2:111–17; Daniel H. Woodward 1962 'Some Themes in Spenser's "Prothalamion"' *ELH* 29:34–46.

proverbs In his *Second Frutes* (1591), John Florio remarks that proverbs are the 'pith, the proprieties, the proofes, the purities, the elegancies, as the commonest so the commendablest phrases of a language' (sig *2r).

As Erasmus comments, however, it is one thing to praise the proverb and another to define it (Intro to *Adagia* 1536, pub in *Opera omnia* 1540). His own tentative definition uses the triad of parts in medieval logic: 'A saying [the *genus*] in popular use [the species or *differentia*] remarkable for some shrewd and novel turn [the *particular characteristic*, in Erasmus' words].' As such, proverbs are to be distinguished from aphorisms (*sententiae*), fables (*ainoi*), quick witty sayings (*apophthegmata*), and facetious remarks (*skômmata*).

In *The Shepheardes Calender*, E.K. is aware of the proverb as Erasmus defines it. In his gloss to Cuddie's emblem in *Februarie*, he notes that Cuddie 'doth counterbuff' Thenot 'with a byting and bitter proverbe,' the Italian 'Niuno vecchio, / Spaventa Iddio,' spoken in contempt of old age. He also notes that Erasmus, 'a great clerke and good old father,' had rendered the proverb as 'Nemo Senex metuit Jovem' in the *Adages*, and had construed it favorably 'for his own behoofe' as 'old men ... be furre from superstition and Idolatrous regard of false Gods, as is Jupiter' rather than as 'old men have no feare of God.'

Spenser is less academic than E.K. in acknowledging proverbs. 'This reede is ryfe,' he may exclaim (*Julye* 11), or allow that he quotes 'an old sayd sawe' (98). Other times he introduces a proverb with 'Yet wisedome warnes' (*FQ* I i 13), or 'True he it said, what ever man it sayd' (IV x 1), or 'men use to say' (VII vii 50). Here he is following Erasmus' injunction on the need for 'careful introduction of a proverb' (*Adages* Intro, section 14) – 'an advance correction' such as used by the Greeks and Romans: 'as the old saying goes,' 'to use an old phrase,' 'as they say,' or 'as the adage has it.'

Spenser knew the 'many uses [to which] a knowledge of proverbs' could be put, such as 'philosophy' (the cracking open of thoughtful insights into old wisdom), persuasion and conviction, and pleasure in the decorative and structural effects proverbs can confer, for example, interest through novelty, delight by their concision and adaptability to all kinds of rhetorical figures, and conviction by their decisive power (*Adages* Intro, sections 6, 8). Even in the *Amoretti*, he shapes an entire sonnet (32) on the proverb 'The more you beat iron (the stone of Sicilia) the harder it grows' (Tilley I 96). In sonnet 18, he invents plausible variations on the proverbial theme 'Constant dropping will wear the stone' (D 618): the first quatrain contains the proverb as a basic fact, the second converts it to the unrequited lover's plea, the third reflects the mistress' quick perception of the rhetorical game, and the couplet reverses the original proverb in lamenting that the beloved has not been worn down. The proverb, true in inanimate nature, has been tested and found wanting in the world of human relations – a pattern of reversal which Spenser's 'counter proverbs' rely on with special effect.

Proof that Spenser was to the proverb born, and handled it with dexterity, daring, and complete mastery, comes in his willingness to vary the shape of a proverb (cf *Adages* Intro, section 12). He freely uses counter proverbs, such as 'Oft fire is without smoke' (*FQ* I i 12). Or he brilliantly reverses the proverb 'short pleasure, long lament (repentance, pain)' (P 419) in the sophistic speech of Despair, who seeks to persuade Redcrosse to contravene God's law against suicide: 'Is not short paine well borne, that brings long ease ... ?' (I ix 40). Or he twists the proverb 'That fish will soon be caught that nibbles at every hook (bait)' to indicate that Redcrosse has learned his lesson: having once nibbled, he will not bite again at Archimago's bait (II i 4; F 324, but cf T 316).

So completely is Spenser at home with proverbs that he often forms a new yet still familiar utterance by pairing essential yet incomplete elements of two common proverbs. Thus, after the sententious Thomalin rebukes the proud and pretentious pastor, Morrell, with 'an old sayd sawe,' 'To Kerke the narre, from God the farre' (C 80), he underscores the warning by fusing the introductory elements of two admonitory proverbs, one against celestial climbing, the other noting terrestrial falls: 'he that strives to touch the starres' (S 825) oft 'stombles at a strawe' (S 922, *Julye* 97–100). Similarly, at the marriage of Thames and Medway, 'To tell the sands' (S 91) or 'count the starres on hye' (cf Whiting S 681) is an easier activity than trying 'to reckon right' the wedding guests (*FQ* IV xi 53; cf Heb 11.12). In so doing, Spenser is again following Erasmus' counsel in *De duplici copia* about 'other methods' of varying proverbs.

The proverb's succinct form and its sense of long-shared, much-tried practical wisdom makes its use as a summary statement almost inevitable. Hence, ten 'emblems' for six of the months of *The Shepheardes Calender* are recognizably proverbial: two in English (*Mar*), two in Greek (a hexameter split in halves, *May*); three in Italian (*Feb* 2, *Aug*), and three in Latin (*Jul* 2, *Sept*). The final couplet or final line for five *Amoretti* are recognizably proverbial (11, 37, 42, 50, 74).

Proverbs also often appear in the summarizing or reflective alexandrine which closes the Spenserian stanza. With a skillful variant on 'plenty makes poor,' Spenser warns of the danger in Fidessa/Duessa's coy looks: 'so dainty they say maketh derth' (*FQ* I ii 27; cf Tilley P 427). A 'doubled proverb' in the alexandrine gives two reasons for Florimell's flight from the Witch's monster (III vii 26): 'Fear [which] gives wings' and 'Need (Necessity) [which] may make a coward valiant' (F 133, N 62). In his reply to Belge, 'That is the vertue selfe, which her reward doth pay' (V xi 17; cf Tilley V 81), Arthur uses a proverb which is a mature variation on the 'proverbial' claim by Redcrosse that 'Vertue gives her selfe light, through darkenesse for to wade' (I i 12).

In the microstructure of verse and stanza, Spenser knew how to expand the implications of a proverb, transforming it from didactic distillate to active metaphor. Thus the proverb 'The stream (current, tide) stopped swells the higher' is used by the Palmer to summarize his advice to Guyon on how to handle Furor through Occasion (II iv 11; S 929). Expanded to four lines (in III vii 34), this proverb becomes the first term of an epic simile that shows process rather than conclusion by describing the heroic energy that Satyrane must expend to restrain and finally subdue the monster that pursues Florimell.

The quiet advice and gentle rebuke of honey-tongued Meliboe to Calidore is an example of what might be called the bravura use of proverbs – delightful in itself and befitting the situation (VI ix 29–33). Meliboe's stanzas are based on Christian commonplaces and *sententiae*, and on three proverbs, 'It is the mynd, that maketh good or ill,' 'Wisedome is most riches,' and 'Every man is the architect of his own fortune' (M 254, W 526, and M 126 as augmented with examples 1533–94, *ODEP* 230a). In stanza 29, Meliboe implicitly rebukes Calidore for attributing too much to Fortune in describing his state and envying the pastoral retreat: 'each hath his fortune in his brest.' In stanza 30, by carefully picking the meat from two proverbial shells, he establishes the positive effect of the contented mind, converting Calidore's sophisms into the realization that 'each unto himselfe his life may fortunize.'

FQ VI vi 5 provides a fuller example of Spenser's tactics and strategy in using the proverb. Here the Hermit seeks to heal Serena and Timias of the rankling inward wounds inflicted by the Blatant Beast. Since their wounds are past help of herbs or surgery, he realizes that his patients need the counsel of 'sad sobriety' to rein in the stubborn rage of blind passion, a discovery underscored by Spenser's doubling proverbs in the alexandrine and varying them slightly but significantly: 'Give salves to every sore, but counsell to the minde.' The first half of the line is a variation of 'There is a salve for every sore'; the second half echoes '(Good) counsel is (the choicest, meetest) medicine' (cf Tilley S 84, C 683). Then the Hermit discusses at length the psychosomatic aspects of the lovers' predicament; he finally returns to his starting point, having explained how their wounds may not be physically salved, for they need instead 'wise read and discipline' (13). When Timias and Serena beg him for that counsel, he offers it in a bravura variation on two complementary proverbs: 'Avoid the occasion of (the) ill' and 'Take away the cause and the effect must cease' (O 8, C 202). The basic truths are stated in the first four lines of stanza 14 and a detailed therapeutic regimen spelled out in the remaining lines. Thus the problem of psychological 'advize' or 'counsell' posited in the proverb of stanza 5 is finally rounded off.

Typically, this episode reverberates with others, differing slightly in 'plot' and proverbial application, but awakening echoes and arousing memories of other heroes or heroines in other books or cantos, making visible for a moment the unbroken web of humanity toughly spun behind the six books and concluding cantos of *The Faerie Queene*. Guyon, for example, has been encouraged by his belief that 'goodly counsell ... Is meetest med'cine' to stir himself from stunned shock at the sight of Amavia and to offer her relief (II i 44). We sympathize, too, with the Hermit's realization of the physical limits of his pharmacopeia and his uncertainty in handling psychiatric tools when we recall Glauce's difficulties with lovestruck Britomart, smitten by the vision of Artegall (VI vi, III ii 24). Like the Hermit, the old nurse finds her medicinal cunning exhausted by her charge: nought will prevail, 'Nor herbes, nor charmes, nor counsell, that is chiefe / And choisest med'cine for sicke harts reliefe' (iii 5). Similar structural parallels obtain between the poet's admonition to 'Give salves to every sore, but counsell to the minde' (VI vi 5), the Hermit's confession that he, like the lovers, 'in vaine doe[s] salves ... applie' (6), and puzzled Glauce's superficially confident assertion to the fearful Britomart 'For never sore, but might a salve obtaine' (III ii 35).

The proverb is thus one of many ways of creating contrast and similarity, echo and recollection, and significant variation within repetition, by which Spenser generally articulates the large structure and meaning of *The Faerie Queene*. While not so substantial and impressive as a Bower of Bliss, a Garden of Adonis, or a Temple of Venus, the repeated proverbs weave important thematic strands into the larger tapestry of the poem.

In addition to offering various aspects of the major intellectual themes of the poem, proverbial elements contribute to characterization. The simplest proverbial materials – proverbial phrases or comparisons – quickly establish for the minor characters a minimal armature, or they rapidly convey fleeting impressions of abstract qualities. When Talus first appears, for example, he is said to be 'strong as Lyon' to represent enforcement of the law, but also 'swift as swallow' to represent the speed with which justice should be carried out (*FQ* V i 20; cf Tilley L 308, S 1023). Florimell is first seen on a milk-white palfrey (for gentle purity); her face is 'as cleare as Christall' but, through fear, as 'white as whales bone' (III i 15; cf C 135, W 279). At stanza 17, she is pursued by the grisly Foster who must chase her 'through thicke and thin' (her flight, his onrush) in hopes of attaining her 'by hooke or crooke' (his unrelenting lust). The spectral Maleger runs swift as the wind, his look as 'pale and wan as ashes,' his body 'leane and meagre as a rake' (II xi 20–2; cf W 411, A 339, R 22). The light and idly mirthful Phaedria sings as 'loud as larke'; her shallow vessel slides 'More swift, then swallow,' while she herself is 'more sweet, then any bird on bough,' and careless or fearless of 'how the wind do blow' (II vi 3ff; cf L 70, S 1023, B 359).

Spenser also uses patterns of proverbial speech to show the inadequacy of an inexperienced hero and the seasoned, at times startling, wisdom of his counselor, as in the exchange between Calidore and old Meliboe (VI ix 29–33), and in Una's warning to Redcrosse at the dark cave-mouth in the Wandering Wood (I i 12–13). Her first comment is a sententious warning that where Danger seems to lurk it is wisdom to provide beforehand (cf Henryson's aphorism in Whiting D 18). Then she adds a counter proverb from her higher wisdom, 'Oft fire is without smoke' (contrast 'There is no fire without some smoke' Tilley F 282; see Doyle 1972), supported by the accepted observation, 'And perill without show.' Redcrosse, young, zealous, and overconfident, resorts to his own variant, a conventional assurance that 'Vertue gives her selfe light, through darkenesse for to wade' (C.G. Smith 820, citing Ashley's contemporary work *Of Honour*; cf Tilley I 81, 'Innocency bringeth with her, her owne defence'). Redcrosse here as elsewhere has trouble differentiating between appearance and reality; as Una further urges, before he can prevail he needs to add to his force a faith tested by experience – 'the evidence of things which are not sene' (Heb II.I).

Una's reluctance to accept the conventional wisdom of proverbs is further shown in a marvelous stichomythic exchange of proverb and *sententia* between her and Arthur in I vii 39–42, 51. Brought almost to despair by Redcrosse's imprisonment by Orgoglio and the failure to free her beleaguered parents, for a while she fights off Arthur's comforting words. She is aware of the proverbial advice offered in *September* 12–13: 'gall not ... old griefe,' for it rips open causes for new woe (cf *FQ* I vii 39); but Arthur offers another form of the proverb of counsel that the Hermit offers Timias and Serena: 'counsell mittigates the greatest smart.' He adds, 'Found never helpe, who never would his hurts [griefs] impart,' a proverbial variant on a frequent topic in the mental world of Spenser's heroes and heroines, shepherds, knights and ladies (Tilley G 447). Una counters with a variant of the proverb 'Great griefs are silent; small sorrows speak' (S 664). With this utterance Spenser establishes a little structure within the canto as well as launching an exchange of proverbs and *sententiae* of counsel-in-grief. Through reason, Arthur is able to *persuade* Una to tell her sad tale and impart her grief (cf Erasmus *Adagia* Intro, section 7, 'Proverbs are a means to persuasion'). Una's grief subsides and she ends her account with her initial demurrer rephrased as 'This is my cause of griefe, more great, then may be told.' She is responsive to reason; and if at times skeptical, she does not abruptly dismiss the advice and comfort offered her. She and Arthur ultimately communicate with one another in a sort of proverbial shorthand mutually exchangeable.

It is tempting to connect Spenser's use of proverbs and *sententiae* with his desire to relate communal 'authority' and wisdom to individual apprehension (Cincotta 1980). For example, in the Error episode, readers are drawn up short with the poet's intrusion, 'God helpe the man so wrapt in *Errours* endlesse traine' (I i 18); we realize that we, too, are involved in error. Moreover, Una's counter-proverb, that fire indeed is often without smoke, provides salient advice along with her sententious imperative to add faith to force. Here Spenser predicates his own moral authority as a narrator upon the authority of commonly held wisdom; and, through freshly fashioned versions of that wisdom, he recreates his 'authorities' and manifests them as his own (Cincotta 1980).

In her conversation with Arthur, Una uses the power of the proverb to apply the intelligently sustained weight of the experience of the community to her plight. Nine closely related proverbs in three stanzas all contribute cumulatively to Arthur's 'goodly reason, and well guided speach' (I vii 40–2). Of equal importance is the weightiness of the alexandrine and the surprise of the counter proverbs which suggest authorial discontent with accepting ordinary proverbial lore in extraordinary circumstance. The alexandrines often emerge as proverb-like statements (when they are not actually proverbs), with their own authority and a new moral weight.

As William Baldwin observed in his *Treatise of Morall Phylosophie* (1547), 'although preceptes and counsayles be the most playne and easye, yet lacke they the grace of delyte, whiche in theyr Proverbes they have supplyed' – supplied 'so fynely and so wyttely, that they both delyte and perswade excedynglye' (sig M7r-v). When mixed with 'suche piththynes in wordes and sentence,' they give us occasion to muse and study. They become an important means of supporting the structure of a long narrative poem, a major way of enlivening and confirming a 'new' moral teaching, and a sympathetically new yet plausible teaching voice.

Robert Starr Kinsman

The principal indexes of proverbs are Tilley 1950 and Whiting 1968. Tilley tends to include commonplace wisdom as well as true proverbs and in this regard should be used with caution; otherwise, an excellent work. For corrected dates, missed examples, and newly legitimated proverbs, Tilley and Whiting should be supplemented by three recent works: *The Oxford Dictionary of English Proverbs* (*ODEP*) 1970 3rd ed rev F.P. Wilson (Oxford); R.W. Dent 1981 *Shakespeare's Proverbial Language: An Index* (Berkeley and Los Angeles); and Dent 1984 *Proverbial Language in English Drama Exclusive of Shakespeare, 1495–1616: An Index* (Berkeley and Los Angeles).

The outstanding early guide to classical proverbs (of which many English proverbs are simple translations) is Desiderius Erasmus *Adagia* (expanded in eds from 1509 to 1536), in ed 1703–6, 2; an English version is translated by Margaret Mann Phillips and annotated by R.A.B. Mynors in Erasmus ed 1974–, 31ff; this ed also contains Erasmus' introduction on the rhetoric of proverbs. Many of Erasmus' adages are cross-indexed with their English translations in Tilley and *ODEP*, though neither is complete. For Erasmus' own use of proverbs, see Clarence H. Miller 1978 'The Logic and Rhetoric of Proverbs in Erasmus' *Praise of Folly*' in DeMolen 1978:83–98. Spenser's proverbs have been studied in detail by C.G. Smith 1970, a work that unfortunately confuses *sententiae* and ordinary sentiments with proverbs. See also Charles Clay Doyle 1972 'Smoke and Fire: Spenser's Counter Proverb' *Proverbium* 18:683–5. The structural significance of proverbs in Spenser is examined by Mary Ann Cincotta 1980 'Community and Discourse in the "Faerie Queene": A Study in Literary History' (diss, Univ of California, Berkeley).

For additional background in English, see F.P. Wilson 1969 'The Proverbial Wisdom of Shakespeare' in his *Shakespearian and Other Studies* ed Helen Gardner (Oxford) pp 143–75. For the tradition and its development, see Archer Taylor *The Proverb* 1931 (Cambridge, Mass); also Natalie Zemon Davis 1975 'Proverbial Wisdom and Popular Errors' in her *Society and Culture in Early Modern France* (Stanford) pp 227–67; and John Heywood 1963 *A Dialogue of Proverbs* ed Rudolph E. Habenicht (Berkeley and Los Angeles).

providence As the guiding force of the Christian universe, providence was distinguished at an early stage from the classical concept of fate. According to Boethius, 'Providence is the divine reason itself which belongs to the most high ruler of all things and which governs all things; Fate, however, belongs to all mutable things and is the disposition by which Providence joins all things in their own order ... Thus Providence is the unfolding of temporal events as this is present to the vision of the divine mind; but this same unfolding of events as it is worked out in time is called Fate' (*Consolation of Philosophy* 4 prose 6, ed 1962).

In Spenser's time, the theory of providence received support from theologians as diverse in sympathy as John Knox and Richard Hooker and is clearly implied in the Thirty-nine Articles (17), the official profession of the Anglican church. Similarly, English historians from Foxe to Raleigh favored a providential view of human history, as did Milton (who endeavors to 'assert eternal providence' in *Paradise Lost*) and Spenser himself. In *Vewe of Ireland*, Irenius interprets the fall of Rome not as a cultural disaster but as an instance of how the 'singuler providence of god' works to convert pagan nations (*Var Prose* p 92). Nevertheless, the same speaker's initially deterministic view of Irish history is rejected by Eudoxus, who attributes the present state of the country not to 'anye suche fatall Course or appointment of god' but to the failure of human policy (p 44). By making man responsible for his own errors, Spenser guards against an obvious abuse of the providential concept while maintaining an ordered view of history.

Throughout *The Faerie Queene*, Spenser frequently calls attention to the providential pattern underlying an apparently fortuitous sequence of events. From a human viewpoint, for example, Redcrosse stumbles upon the Tree of Life by 'chaunce,' yet 'eternall God that chaunce did guide' (I xi 45). Similarly, 'Eternall providence exceeding thought' contrives a 'wondrous way' to rescue Una from Sansloy (vi 7). Speaking as God's viceregent, Nature informs Mutabilitie that time and fortune are merely the instruments of a grand design intended to restore creation to its original perfection. In effect, she subordinates fortune to fate but, still unsatisfied, proceeds beyond fate to a vision of a timeless and changeless state partaking of eternity (VII vii 58–9).

The poem's most striking instance of divine intervention is the dispatching of an angel to succor the fallen Guyon, an incident prefaced by one of Spenser's most explicit statements of the providential outlook: heaven's care of man is manifest in the 'exceeding grace / Of highest God' whose boundless love charges the spiritual powers with the protection of the church 'millitant' (II viii 1–2). Providence is usually associated with 'grace' even when the agency employed is human, as in Arthur's several interventions (eg, I viii 1) and his own deliverance by Timias (II xi 30).

Romance narrative with its multiple plots, coincidences, and accidents provides a particularly good vehicle for conveying the paradoxical idea of ordered contingency (see I.G. MacCaffrey 1976:372–6). The effect is greatly enhanced when the eventual resolution is foreseen at an early stage, since the artist's foresight may then be used to suggest God's 'wise foresight' (*Heavenly Love* 109): aesthetic order reflects providential order. Thus Britomart learns the full personal and national consequences of her love for Artegall before her quest has properly begun. However, since 'Providence heavenly passeth living thought' (III v 27), various vatic figures need to explain the plan to those concerned. The resulting insight assists these characters to come to terms with the problems of pain and disappointment (IV II). For example, Merlin advises Britomart to 'submit' herself to the will of providence (iii 24), and she in turn exhorts the despairing Scudamour to 'submit ... to high providence ... For who nill bide the burden of distresse, / Must not here thinke to live' (xi 14). Difficulties encountered on the quest hereby take on the status of spiritual trials. Through 'heavenly *Contemplation*,' we may grasp the concept of providence intellectually, but in the everyday course of events, we must endure the cruel vicissitudes of fortune: pain was an essential part of Christ's earthly ministry (I x 50).

Spenser associates the idea of providence with that of election, but their exact relationship was a central problem of contemporary theology. From Una (Truth), Redcrosse learns that he is 'chosen' (I ix 53), and his eventual sainthood is declared before the conflict with the Dragon (x 61). The 'Hierusalem' he glimpses is intended only for the 'chosen,' though Christ died for 'the sinnes of all the world' (x 57). As a result, an aura of mystery surrounds the workings of grace, making it unclear to what extent Spenser identified providence with predestination. The narrative presentation is balanced between apparently free and conscious acts of will and a strong element of spiritual determinism. Britomart 'submits' to God's will, but her love for Artegall is initially involuntary and occasioned solely by 'the streight course of heavenly destiny, / Led with eternall providence' (III iii 24). Whereas individuals remain responsible for their own failures, 'all the good is Gods, both power and eke will' (I x I). The 'sonnes of Day' are saved, while those of Night are apparently abandoned – for 'who can turne the streame of destinee, / Or breake the chayne of strong necessitee, / Which fast is tyde to *Joves* eternall seat?' (V 25).

RICHARD A. MCCABE

For the religious background, see Thomas 1971, ch 4, and Patrides 1966. The historical background is treated in Patrides and in Arthur B. Ferguson 1979 *Clio Unbound: Perception of the Social and Cultural Past in Renaissance England* (Durham, NC), and Kelly 1970. The connection between Spenser's Mutabilitie and providence is noted in Lewis J. Owen 1972 'Mutable in Eternity: Spenser's despair and the Multiple Forms of Mutabilitie' *JMRS* 2:49–68; see also Richard A. McCabe 1989 *The Pillars of Eternity: Time and Providence in 'The Faerie Queene'* (Dublin).

psychology The modern term psychology expresses a concept for which Spenser's nearest equivalent would be the doctrine of the bodily spirits; but in most medical opinion of the sixteenth century, the bodily spirits also accounted for what we would call physiology: they kept the body alive and working, accounted for the operations of the five senses, the brain, and for all movement, both physical and emotional. The elements of the doctrine derived originally from different traditions, both medical and philosophical; but by Spenser's day there was a reasonably unified and consistent body of thought.

It is important at the outset to understand that in all later medieval theory the bodily spirits within man differed fundamentally from the soul. The human soul was held to be immaterial, intellectual, and immortal; during life, it inhabited a body which was made up of the four material elements, insentient and doomed to decay. Between the two (Alma and her castle) was supposed to exist a middle term: the bodily spirit, whose substance was material but whose matter was so fine as to be imperceptible to the senses, like a gas. The spirit kept the body alive and endowed it with the powers of sensation and motion. Its departure broke the link which held soul and body together and thus caused death, but it was not itself immortal and would eventually decay into its elements.

The terms are confusing because they come from several different traditions. Paul speaks of the opposition of body and spirit (eg, Rom 8), which medieval writers would call body and soul. The notion of the bodily spirit comes from Stoic philosophy, in which *pneuma* (spirit) fulfills all the functions of the soul but is nonetheless a material substance. Medieval writers such as Avicenna (d 1037) accepted the Aristotelian definition of soul and body as form and matter and, at the same time, accepted from medical tradition the Stoic *pneuma* as a middle term between the two. Thus the term *spirit* may be used in religious contexts (eg, *Heavenly Beautie* 259) to mean the soul, but in medical and philosophical contexts, it is usually a technical term to define the soul's 'first instrument' and the body's subtlest part.

The theory of the bodily spirit was a necessity for medicine. Both Aristotelian philosophy and Christian belief maintained that the soul was incorporeal and the seat of reason and will; but it clearly could not be the same thing as life or the powers of sensation and motion: they may be interrupted, impaired, or lost without losing one's soul – for example, the insane were not without soul even though they seemed to be without reason. Hence it was necessary to postulate some other invisible agent – the bodily spirit – to account for the processes of life, sensation, motion, and the overt functioning of reason in man. This agent was regarded as corporeal because it could be damaged by material means – a blow on the head, for instance. Physicians did not concern themselves with the soul; but the bodily spirit – the instrument by which the soul communicated with the body and which was prone to all the mortal afflictions – was entirely within their province.

There is some dispute in the textbooks on whether the bodily spirit is essentially one or three. Avicenna holds that there is a single spirit, generated in the heart, which undergoes processes of differentiation in the brain, liver, sense organs, and genitals. Other medieval authorities, however, tend to write as if there were three different kinds of spirit, called 'natural,' 'vital,' and 'animal,' each one refined out of the one below. Haly Abbas (d 995), for instance, explains in detail how the food from the intestines is taken to the liver, and there converted into blood and endowed with natural spirit; the blood then takes the natural spirit through the veins to all parts of the body. The natural spirit is responsible for nourishment, growth, and the reproductive faculties. The great vein from the liver carries blood to the right ventricle of the heart. There the blood is heated, augmented by air drawn in by the lungs, and filtered through the septum of the heart into the left ventricle, where it is endowed with vital spirit. Arteries then carry vital spirit to all the organs of the body to give them warmth and life. The vital spirit in the heart is also the cause of 'passions': the emotions of joy and sorrow, wrath and fear. The carotid arteries carry some of the vital spirit to the base of the brain. There the spirit is again combined with air drawn in through the nostrils, filtered through the *rete mirabile* (a network of fine arteries), and refined until it turns into animal spirit. The animal spirit fills the 'cells' or ventricles of the brain and there operates the five senses and the inward wits; it passes thence down the spinal cord and through the nerves to bring sensation and motion to the various limbs and organs of the body. It was argued that the existence of animal spirit could be proved by the fact that a paralyzed limb loses sensation and motion but is still warm and alive: clearly, vital spirit can get to it but the nerve conveying animal spirit is broken or damaged. Loss of animal spirit results in what we would call a coma; loss of vital spirit means death.

Haly Abbas and Avicenna provide the clearest exposition of the theory of bodily spirit; but the theory was considered literal fact in Spenser's day, and references to it are widespread. Brief accounts may be found in popular encyclopedias (eg, Gregor Reisch *Margarita philosophica*, Bartholomaeus Anglicus *De proprietatibus rerum*) as well as in medical and quasi-medical handbooks (eg, Thomas Vicary *Anatomie* 1577, and seven other editions [this is in fact a reworking of a text written in 1392; see J.F. Payne *British Medical Journal* 1896 (25 Jan):200–3]; Lanfranc of Milan *Chirurgia parva* tr J. Halle 1565; Gratarolus *Castel of Memorie* 1562). Shakespeare refers to the 'nimble spirits in the arteries' (*Love's Labor's Lost* IV iii 302; see also Milton *Paradise Lost* 5.100–13, 479–90, 8.466; quotations in *OED* sv 'spirit' 16).

The natural spirit in the liver does not have implications for what we call psychology, but the vital and animal spirits explained a great deal to Spenser which would now come under that heading. Since the spirit was made up of the four elements, it was open to the same kinds of defects of temperament as the rest of the human body. Its quantity as well as its quality could affect a man; a person could be 'low-spirited' in a perfectly literal sense. Since the three spirits were either fundamentally all one, or were refined in stages out of the natural spirit, the quality of one could affect the quality of the others; and all depended on the nature of the blood, of the food and drink consumed, and of the surrounding air.

The chief function of the vital spirit in the heart and arteries is to preserve life and natural warmth. If the vital spirit goes out of the body completely, the creature dies. Spenser's most frequent use of the terminology of bodily spirits is in this context: when the shepherd brushes the gnat, 'streight the spirite out of his senses flew, / And life out of his members did depart' (*Gnat* 292–3); when Belphoebe splits Lust's throat with an arrow, 'all his vitall spirites thereby spild' (*FQ* IV vii 31). Since the spirit is nourished by blood, one can die from excessive bleeding: Priamond's 'streames of purple bloud issuing rife, / Let forth his wearie ghost' (IV iii 12). The 'litle rivers' of Triamond's 'vitall flood' (28) stream from his wounds and enfeeble him, but since he is magically endowed with the souls and spirits of his two brothers, he takes a lot of killing. He loses one 'living spright' through a throat wound, and another through a wound in the armpit; he is on his last 'spright,' his own, when he is reprieved by Cambina. Lack of food and drink naturally lead to lack of blood and hence a potentially fatal reduction in vital spirit: the Red Cross Knight, starved in Orgoglio's dungeon, has 'all his vitall powres / Decayd, and all his flesh shronk up like withered flowres' (I viii 41). Air, too, is required to 'feed' the vital spirit. Mutabilitie exclaims, 'O weake life! that does leane / On thing so tickle as th'unsteady ayre'; and she points out that the quality of the air affects the vital spirit directly: 'The faire doth it prolong; the fowle doth it impaire' (VII vii 22). Hence perfumed, temperate, or pleasant air has an immediate effect on the spirit: the paradise of flowers in *Ruines of Time* 521–2 is 'Such as on earth man could not more devize, / With pleasures choyce to feed his cheerefull sprights.' In short, death in Spenser is 'nought but parting of the breath' (*FQ* VII vii 46), when the vital spirit is literally expired or breathed out (*Hymne of Beautie* 102).

The other function of the vital spirit in the heart, as some of the above quotations show, is to express, or perhaps more properly 'suffer,' the passions. Usually classified as wrath, joy, sorrow, and fear, the passions were held to be the physical sensations resulting from the vital spirit's reaction to pleasant or unpleasant stimuli. Wrath, for instance, is produced when an exterior occasion of wrath (which can be an image in the mind) causes the spirit and blood in the heart to rush out suddenly to the extremities. It heats and dries the body, strengthens the power of choler or yellow bile, turns the eyes of an angry man red, and makes his face and body swell. A man whose temperament is naturally choleric will be more susceptible to the stimuli of wrath, and indulging in the passion will also dispose the spirit to receive the passion more easily the next time. Avicenna explains that since wrath occurs when the spirit is plentiful, clear, and hot, a person's proclivity to it will be increased when his blood has these same qualities; hence Haly Abbas prescribes rose water, camphor, vinegar, and fish as a suitable diet for the naturally wrathful and prohibits the consumption of wine.

The other passions are produced similarly: joy occurs when the spirit rushes out of the heart plentifully, but it is cooler than wrath and therefore less dangerous. Fear and sorrow occur when the spirit shrinks back into the heart; thin watery blood tends to produce fear; thick, cloudy, hot blood produces sorrow. Haly Abbas adds *verecundia* (shame) and care to the list of passions; many more could be added by postulating different combinations of temperament, volume, and movement in the spirit.

Spenser presents a whole array of passions dwelling within an arrased chamber (the heart and pericardium) in Alma's castle (II ix 33–44). Shamefastnesse, with her continual blushes, clearly has a common origin with Haly Abbas' *verecundia*; Prays-desire does not have a medical counterpart but is probably related to *audacia* (boldness). The poet's emotion in *Mother Hubberds Tale* 15–40 (and *Ruines of Time* 575) which makes his 'spirite heavie and diseased' is clearly *tristitia* (sorrow). The conflicting emotions of the ill-tempered Britomart when she first sees Marinell are compared to a sudden storm which clears the air: 'Her former sorrow into suddein wrath, / Both coosen passions of distroubled spright, / Converting' (III iv 12–13). The thick, hot dampness of her spirit in sorrow is converted to the clear heat of wrath, and she severely wounds Marinell. Similarly, when Pyrochles sees Arthur kill his brother, 'the stony feare / Ran to his hart, and all his sence dismayd'; when he rallies, 'vile disdaine and rancour ... gnaw / His hart in twaine' (II viii 46–50). When Malbecco gives himself up to jealousy and grief, 'all the passions, that in man may light, / Did him attonce oppresse, and vex his caytive spright' (III x 17).

An excess of any one of the passions can kill: the spirit may burst out of the body in joy or wrath, or shrink up to nothing in fear or sorrow. Una nearly dies of grief when she believes that Redcrosse is dead. Her dwarf has to struggle to keep her vital spirit within her body ('So hardly he the flitted life does win, / Unto her native prison to retourne'), and then Arthur's wise counsel is needed to remove some of the 'carefull cold' from her heart (I vii 21, 39). Redcrosse himself has been struck down by fear in the same canto: 'crudled cold his corage gan assaile, / And chearefull bloud in faintnesse chill did melt' (6).

The passions are not moral states but physical ones. The disposition to one passion or another is present in all men; but indulgence in any one passion strengthens the disposition to it rather than tempering it. Medical authorities, like moral philosophers, advocated the proper checking and balancing of passions so that they would not get out of control. Spenser's Hermit in Book VI could 'al the passions heale, which wound the weaker spright' (vi 3), and Guyon feels passions but masters them, but Furor is an embodied passion which may only be restrained, not destroyed.

When the vital spirit turns into animal spirit in the brain, it passes through the three ventricles of the brain, operates the organs of the five senses and the inward wits, and brings about voluntary motion by means of the nerves. The spirit in the sensory nerves transmits sensations from the eyes, ears, tongue, nose, and skin to the front ventricle, where sensation is actually effected. It was debated whether spirits went out from the eye to the object of vision, or the spirit in the eye received an impression from a visible object. Spenser, at least in his description of Corflambo, seems to believe that the eye casts out rays (IV viii 39; cf *Hymne of Beautie* 232–8). The primary function of the first ventricle or 'cell' was to receive and combine sense impressions and to hold them until judgment was passed on them by the power in the second ventricle. The power of movement received its impulse from this judgment: if it was favorable, the appetitive or concupiscible faculty moved the creature (animal or human) to seek or grasp the object; if the verdict was hostile, the irascible faculty moved the creature to attack or flee. The nerves then carried the message to the limbs, the vital spirit in the heart reacted with a passion, and the creature moved accordingly. The last ventricle was thought to be a storehouse where the results of these mental processes were stored up and remembered.

All these powers in the brain were properly held to be part of the sensitive soul, that is, common to man and animal. The human rational soul was supposed to rule over these powers; but, lacking an organ, it could operate only through them. The complicated (and, since the Fall, disorderly) relations between the rational and sensitive souls accounted for the human moral dilemma during life.

Medical writers approached the powers of the brain from a straightforward empirical tradition going back to Galen. He had described three case histories to illustrate what happens when each ventricle is damaged: the first patient suffered from hallucinations but was otherwise reasonable; the second perceived the world around him correctly but drew irrational conclusions from his observations; the third suffered from total amnesia. From these examples, Galen deduced that the first ventricle dealt with the mind's reception of the real world, the second with judgment, and the third with memory. This simple division runs throughout the whole medieval medical tradition and clearly underlies the three chambers in the tower of Alma's castle. The anatomical researches of Vesalius in the earlier sixteenth century had confirmed the number and positions of the ventricles but not their functions. Spenser disregards Vesalius' doubts and observes the older medical scheme, although he combines it ingeniously with other triads of the three parts of prudence and the three ages of man.

The first ventricle, the chamber of Phantastes (II ix 50–1), is the most interesting and complicated of the three. It houses the power which Aristotle calls *phantasia* (although he had placed it in the heart): it was the power responsible for receiving, combining, and holding sense impressions after the sense object had disappeared, and for producing the phenomena of dreams. Since for the Middle Ages Aristotle's fundamental dictum was that 'all our knowledge comes from sense impressions,' there was considerable interest in *phantasia*, which was frequently subdivided into a number of related powers known variously as *sensus communis* (the 'common' sense), *imaginatio* (imagination), *fantasia* (fantasy or fancy), or *vis imaginativa* (imaginative power; see *imagination). Physicians were less interested than philosophers in the subtleties of these distinctions and tended to talk as if there were one single imaginative power; they used a variety of names for it, but *phantasia* is perhaps the most common.

The first impression of Phantastes' chamber is one of confusion: a vast multiplicity of sense impressions pours continually into the front ventricle during waking hours – impressions which, for the most part, are not sorted or recorded but simply received. This is the function philosophers called *sensus communis*, where the evidence of all the five senses is collected together. Next, the front ventricle stores images or impressions after the object is no longer present to the senses; this function was sometimes called *imaginatio*, and was often compared to a kind of memory. The third important function of the power in the first ventricle was distinguished by the philosophers under the name *fantasia* or *vis imaginativa*. This was the ability to join and divide the *phantasmata* or sense impressions in order to produce, out of both fresh and stored impressions, new images to express or illustrate the processes of thought. *Fantasia* alters and combines, inventing chimeras and golden worlds 'such as in the world were never yit' ix 50) by using the evidence of the actual world in a selective and creative way. Dreams were the proof of the existence of *fantasia*: when the senses are shut off by sleep and the control of the rational soul is lifted, some power in the brain must be responsible for the 'reappearance' of images in peculiar combinations and sequences. (Sleep was caused by damp vapors rising to the brain; it was necessary to refresh the spirit and restore the bodily powers; cf *Daphnaïda* 470–4.)

Since all knowledge enters the soul through the senses, according to medieval Aristotelianism, even visions and prophecies have to be clothed in sense impressions before they can be apprehended; on a more mundane level, ideas about the future can be expressed only in terms of imaginary projections of what is known now. Hence Phantastes 'could things to come foresee' (49). He seems half crazy because his realm deals with experience as it happens before being interpreted, with all the 'creative' aspects of imagination but without judgment or selection, with dreams, and with inspired or merely dimly apprehended visions of what will come to be.

In animals, *phantasia* presents no particular problem. It presents an image on which *cogitatio* (here 'instinct') in the next ventricle passes judgment and arouses the motive powers: the sheep sees the wolf and runs away; the dog remembers the image of the bone and goes to dig it up. But man cannot obey his instincts so simply; his reason may, and often ought, to countermand his instinctive judgment (as Guyon finds in II i 8–31). Hence the quality and status of the images in *phantasia* become a subject of great anxiety. One may move too quickly to assent to a pleasing image: Arthur finds at the trial of Duessa that 'His former fancies ruth he gan repent' (V ix 49). The devil can manipulate images in imagination, especially in dreams, to tempt man to assent to sin 'And with false shewes abuse his fantasy,' as Archimago does (I i 46). Artegall finds he must beware of his imagination's tendency to free associate about Britomart; the severe beauty of her face 'his ranging fancie did refraine' (IV vi 33).

The creative activities of fantasy are dangerous in many other cases. Diseases like melancholy and disordered emotions like jealousy create disturbing images and to 'fayning fansie represent / Sights never seene, and thousand shadowes vaine, / To breake his sleepe, and waste his ydle braine' (*Hymne of Love* 254–6). This is what affects Scudamour in the house of Care and Britomart in Artegall's absence (*FQ* IV v 43, V vi 3–19). The sick poet in *Mother Hubberd* is comforted by friends 'With talke, that might unquiet fancies reave' (24). Poets, who dealt with the images of fantasy, were warned to beware that their images reflect something worthy, not something frivolous. The Muse Polyhymnia complains that contemporary poets 'Have mard the face of goodly Poësie, / And made a monster of their fantasie' (*Teares* 557–8); and the verses of the courtier Ape are 'sugrie sweete' to 'allure / Chast Ladies eares to fantasies impure' (*MHT* 819–20).

Most of Spenser's references to fantasy concern the phenomenon of falling in love. Amorous love was considered by medieval physicians to be a malady, the result of a disordered judgment on the sense impression derived from a particular woman (the textbooks consider it to be a male disease). According to Arnald of Villanova (d 1311), the spirit in the central ventricle gets overheated and falsely judges the sense object to be supremely desirable; the heat dries out the sense impression in the front ventricle so that it literally sticks to the brain, and the judgment cannot shift its attention elsewhere. Hence to 'have a fancy' for someone is really to have someone in mind; the insomnia, sighing, lack of appetite, and other symptoms which accompany love are all different symptoms of overheated bodily spirit.

In Spenser's poetry, this rather clinical view of love is affected by the grander Platonizing idea of love as a divine *furor* (madness). Yet characters as diverse as Britomart and Hellenore are guided by images in 'feigning fancie' (III iv 5, x 8), and Marinell's malady, 'which afflicted his engrieved mind,' displays all the classic symptoms of medieval love (IV xii 12–35). In the *Fowre Hymnes*, Spenser distinguishes the lower love or 'Weake fancies' felt by baseborn minds from the idealizing passion of the 'refyned mynd'; the beauty beloved by the latter is the 'mirrour of so heavenly light[,] / Whose image printing in his deepest wit, / He thereon feeds his hungrie fantasy, / Still full, yet never satisfyde with it' (*HHL* 263, *HL* 19, 196–9). Here the creative power of *phantasia* reaches its highest point: it is able to create an image of perfection out of the imperfect images received by the senses. Such an image then becomes the main moving force in the lover's life, since his whole being, his judgment and bodily spirits, move in accord with the reflection of divine beauty. The lover, seeing this image 'so inly faire,' finds it 'with his spirits proportion to agree,' and 'thereon fixeth all his fantasie, / And fully setteth his felicitie, / Counting it fairer, then it is indeede' (*HB* 225–30).

In the medieval scheme of things, the highest power is always *cogitatio*, which inhabits the central ventricle. It judges the images presented to it by *phantasia*, and judging is a higher faculty than combining or creating. Spenser presents *cogitatio* as an august ruler whose chamber is above all orderly, and full of laws and decisions. According to medieval philosophers, strictly speaking, human reason does not 'live' in the brain but merely acts through the power which operates instinct in animals. Physicians, however, tend to write as if reason actually dwells in the middle ventricle, just as it does in Alma's castle.

The last power, memory, inhabits the rear ventricle which slopes down, 'somewhat ... declind,' towards the spinal cord (*FQ* II ix 55). The memory stores up all the decisions and actions of *cogitatio*. Techniques for improving one's memory range from recipes to improve the organ and its animal spirit (eg, the consumption of ginger) to the practices of the art of memory, a system of organized recollection based on a sequence of ideas (Anamnestes). The memory, like the imagination, serves *cogitatio* by providing examples and precedents for sequences of thought – history, instead of imagination's poetry and sense impressions. The hierarchical structure of the powers of the sensitive soul, with its intrinsic principles of tempering and controlling, is reflected chiefly in the imagery of *FQ* II, where the temperate hero must learn to know himself and his powers before he can bind Acrasia.

E. Ruth Harvey

Arnald of Villanova 1585 *De amore heroico* in *Opera* (Basel); Avicenna 1564 *De viribus cordis* in *Libri in re medica omnes* 2 vols (Venice); [Costa ben Luca (d 923)] 1539 *De animae et spiritus discrimine liber* in Constantinus Africanus *Opera* (Basel); Haly Abbas ('Alī ibn al-'Abbās al-Majūsī) 1492 [*Regalis dispositio*] (Venice); Christopher Langton [1550?] *An Introduction into Phisycke* (London; rpt Amsterdam and New York 1970).

Babb 1951, ch 1; Bamborough 1952; E. Ruth Harvey 1975 *The Inward Wits: Psychological Theory in the Middle Ages and the Renaissance* (London); Rossky 1958.

psychology, Platonic In its literal meaning 'soul-study' and in its implicit allusion to the mythic figure of Psyche, the word *psychology* is more appropriate to medieval and Renaissance culture than to our own. From the seventeenth century to the present, psychology has shifted its focus from soul to mind and mental processes, from a transcendent conception of human nature to a materialistic physiological basis. The Elizabethans, however, still viewed the human soul essentially in mythic Christian-Platonic terms, as a transcendent entity engaged in a quest for moral and spiritual fulfillment.

In his *Timaeus* and *Republic*, Plato set the basis for Spenser's psychological model. (1) The soul, originating in an eternal realm of pure forms, has descended into the body at three levels (brain's reason, heart's irascible passions, belly's or liver's concupiscent appetites), comparable to the tripartite hierarchy of the social organism and cosmos. (2) The soul's highest power, intellect, is capable of grasping the Ideas of transcendent reality (including the Form of its own nature), dimly perceived in the shadowy appearances of sensory reality. (3) Mathematics and geometry provide special insight into the soul's essence and structural relation to the body. (4) Orphic myth and allegory, in spite of Plato's denigration of poetic fictions in *Ion*, contribute revealing parables of the human condition (the soul as winged, or as flying chariot, descending through the spheres into a confusing fleshly 'cave' or a divinely ordered 'castle,' and eventually reascending to the realm of pure Ideas). (5) The purpose of moral philosophy is to sustain the hierarchy of the embodied soul (ie, as 'castle') and ultimately to enable the rational essence to transcend its fleshly housing altogether.

The Platonic model, especially as adapted and transformed by Neoplatonic and Judeo-Christian tradition (Philo, Origen, Plotinus, Macrobius, Augustine, Boethius, 12th-c Chartrians, Bonaventura, 15th-c Italian Platonists, English Renaissance Platonists), is crucial to Spenser's allegories of the embodied soul. His characters are usually conceived in Platonic fashion, as philosophic essences more than as physiological or existential beings; they do not have distinctive physical features, except as symbolic indicators of their moral or spiritual natures. Spenser's heroes do not 'learn from experience,' but attain intellectual insight into the ideal human form by means of epiphanic moments when the hero is enlightened by divinely informed seers (Una, Heavenly Contemplation; the Palmer, Alma's sages; Merlin; Cambina, Concord-Venus; Isis' priests, Mercilla; the Hermit, Colin; Dame Nature). The iconographic centers of *The Faerie Queene*, especially the house or garden appearing in cantos ix-x of most books, reveal the ideal human form: the neat hierarchies and polarities of the soul's powers and operations, and its reflection of divinity – as order, life, love, or light. Of particular importance is the hero's perceiving and enacting the human form as a Christian-Platonic hierarchy of powers: triadic family groups, three-layered houses and gardens, sequences of triple temptation or triple challenge. Even more than Plato, Spenser uses traditional mythic figures (Psyche, Venus, Cupid, Proteus, etc) as well as original fictions (Caelia, Alma, Agape, Pastorella, Marinell, Cambell and Triamond, Scudamour, etc) to express the nature and operations, source and destiny, of the human soul. Following the composite psychology of Plato's *Republic* and of much subsequent Christian-Platonic allegory, Spenser's characters are thematically related, forming types, antitypes, or components of the hero. (See *allegory, *psychomachia.) The central Platonic myth, the soul's descent and ascent, is pervasive in *The Faerie Queene*: the hero descends into the shadows of Error's forest and den, Night's underworld, Orgoglio's dungeon, Mammon's subterranean dwelling, Proteus' underwater realm, Daemogorgon's lair, Lust's den, the Brigands' caves; and contrarily, the hero ascends to a vantage point in the bodily temple or landscape which affords a glimpse of transcendent reality: Contemplation's mountain, Alma's brain-turret, Venus' 'stately Mount' in the Garden of Adonis, or atop her Temple altar, Mercilla's lofty throne, Mount Acidale.

As is evident from many of these examples, Platonic features of the microcosm and the soul's moral struggle have been transmuted into a broader Christian perspective. First, Spenser's primary model of psychology is not Alma's castle, but the house of Holiness, where each of the triadic powers is turned toward a transcendent end by the three mystic ways: purgation of belly's appetites ('proud humors to abate'), illumination of heart's passions, and union of mind with God. Second, Plato's psychosocial organism in the *Republic* (philosopher as head, warriors as heart, workers as belly) is spiritually recast: Christ-like knight as head, radiant soul-maiden as heart, dwarf or child as belly or senses or 'hands.' Third, the Platonic symbolism of the soul's descent and ascent is subordinated to a Christian pattern of moral struggle. The carnal bondage in forests, caves, dungeons, and mutable underwater realms is caused not simply by the confusing shadows of sensory appearances but by the sinful rebellion of Adam and Eve; and Satanic powers sustain the varied effects of original sin in human psychology (Una's veil, Ruddymane's stain, Maleger's illness, Amoret's wound). The Platonic conversion of intellect (leaving its fleshly cave and turning upward to the sun of pure Ideas) is in Spenser's fable dependent not simply upon enlightenment by a philosophic sage, but upon redemption by the Christ-like Arthur (and in Books III-V, Britomart), whose armory (in Britomart's case, beauty) reflects the light of divine grace and truth. Redcrosse's vision of the heavenly kingdom establishes the end which is served by all subsequent legends; and the temples and gardens of Alma, Adonis, Venus, Isis, and Mercilla display various subordinate perspectives on the principles of divine life and harmony and power which are most fully revealed in the Christian microcosm of Book I. In sum, Spenser's portraits of moral and psychological crisis as a sinful darkening of rational vision, leading to fragmentation of the soul's three powers (and to demonic duplication of them); his emphasis on the soul's heavenly origin, nature, and destiny; and his subordination of physiological factors to this transcendent perspective – all express his fundamentally Christian-Platonic view of human nature.

In England after 1580, this concept of the microcosm was complicated by a flood of writings from the medical tradition, grounding psychology more emphatically on physiology (see *psychology). Drawing from the 'faculty psychology' of Aristotle and from the 'humoral psychology' of Galen, writers viewed the soul's actions as more closely dependent on the body's 'temperature' of its parts (the seven 'natural' factors: elements, humors, spirits, complexions, members, powers, operations), and also as dependent upon external conditions (the six 'nonnatural' factors: climate, diet, sleep, activity, digestion, passions). Lemnius' *Touchstone of Complexions* (tr 1576), Bright's *Treatise of Melancholie* (1586), Huarte's *Examination of Mens Wits* (tr 1594), Wright's *Passions of the Minde* (1601), Walkington's *Optick Glasse of Humors* (1607), Coeffeteau's *Table of Humane Passions* (tr 1621), Burton's *Anatomy of Melancholy* (1621), Reynolds' *Treatise of the Passions and Faculties* (1640) – all suggest a rising concern with the Aristotelian-Galenic model as a basis for moral and natural philosophy.

Aristotle rejected Plato's dominant concern with transcendent reality, with mathematics and geometrical forms, with mythic descents and ascents to express the soul's essential nature. Instead, drawing from his biological studies (*Parva naturalia*), he compared the soul's capacity for life, feeling, and sensation to similar potencies in plants and animals. In *De anima*, he repudiated Plato's three stages of rationality (concupiscent, irascible, rational) and instead described three incommensurate levels in man: vegetable, animal, rational. Aristotle's extensive empirical treatment of the 'vegetative' powers (nutrition, growth, reproduction, locomotion) differs profoundly from Plato's simplistic moral treatment of the belly's fleshly appetites (carefully controlling them lest they grow into a many-headed monster). He also treats the motive powers in more empirical and systematic fashion than Plato, placing both irascibility and concupiscence in the heart (in Spenser's terms, 'froward' and 'forward' passions), so that reason's task is to enforce the golden mean between them. Moreover, in contrast to Plato's depicting the brain as seat of divine reason, Aristotle describes the process of sensation (the five senses and the various inward wits in the brain) as 'animal' powers, like heart's passions. He complicates the microcosm further by locating the common sensorium (which receives the reports of the senses) in the heart, inducing the Stoics, Avicenna, and many medieval allegorists to associate the rational soul with heart rather than brain, center rather than summit (see *FQ* II ix 33).

In *FQ* II, where Spenser turns from a holistic to a temporal perspective, much Aristotelian influence is apparent in the depiction of the microcosm. In contrast to Redcrosse's fall from neglect of spirit, Guyon's faint in Mammon's house is depicted as the soul's proud neglect of its bodily needs: 'food, and sleepe, which two upbeare, / Like mightie pillours, this fraile life of man' (vii 65). Guyon acknowledges external circumstance (Occasion); he must act 'whilest wether serves and wind.' Alma's castle includes various Galenic features (the 'Concoction' of humors in the belly, lungs as bellows for cooling the blood, etc); and it is pervaded by Aristotle's principle of contrariety, crucial for dealing with mutable, temporal reality (see Anton 1957): in the belly, jolly Appetite versus sober Diet; in the heart, Prays-desire versus Shamefastnesse; in the brain, Phantastes' youthful indulgences versus Eumnestes' decrepit retentions (mediated by the middle wit of judgment). Throughout his quest, Guyon battles contrary extremes, especially of passion. The impact of bodily need, of sense, and of external circumstance (fortune) on the soul is apparent not only in Book II, but also in Book IV (where instead of Busirane's artful and spirit-infecting lust, Amoret is assaulted by a physical embodiment of Lust, shaped like the male genitals) and in Book VI (where the Hermit teaches Timias and Serena to 'learne your outward sences to refraine / From things, that stirre up fraile affection,' for from them 'The seede of all this evill first doth spring' vi 7–8).

But though Spenser gives special attention to the needs of body in II, IV, and VI, his focus is always on soul, rather than body, as moral cause. Redcrosse in despair, Britomart in love, Malbecco transformed by jealousy and Adicia by fury, show that passion is caused by moral misjudgment, or by God, rather than by humoral imbalance, which is merely a consequence. (Cf La Primaudaye *French Academie* 2.41–60; Wright *Passions of the Minde* chs 3, 8; Coeffeteau *Table of Humane Passions* ch 1.) Study of Spenser's love-psychology in Books III and IV has benefited from attention to humors and spirits (Busirane's tyranny causing 'burnt blood'; or the tetradic combats of Book IV being based on humoral and elemental conflict, which Concord resolves). But to understand Spenser's psychology of chastity and friendship one must also study the subtle sequences of *Romance of the Rose* and other medieval allegories of love, where passion is treated less in physiological than in moral and mythic terms. Thus, even in Alma's castle Spenser stresses the Christian-Platonic primacy of soul with its mystic hierarchy of powers. In the lowest region, he emphasizes the belly's appetites (ignoring Aristotle's diverse concern for reproduction, growth, and locomotion), and he stresses the rational 'order' enforced by Diet and Digestion even at this base level. On the intermediate level, he deals primarily with the heart's affections as motive assistants of reason. At the summit, the sages represent no 'animal' powers, but the highest working of reason within the natural order. The 'goodly frame' of the castle thus follows Plato's geometric and moral idealism in *Timaeus*. At each level, Spenser integrates notable features of Aristotelian physiology (crucial to his comprehensive vision), but he avoids the slavish profusion of the physical which one finds forty years later in Fletcher's *Purple Island*, which loses the Platonic vision of transcendent simplicity, mathematical order, and moral hierarchy in the body-soul relationship.

Spenser's allegory thus aligns itself with the early phase of English Renaissance psychology, which emphasized the socioethical and religious concerns of the soul more than its bodily housing: Elyot's *Of the Knowledge Which Maketh a Wise Man* (1533), Bartholomaeus Anglicus' *De proprietatibus rerum* (tr 1582), La Primaudaye's *French Academie* (tr 1586, 1594), Davies' *Nosce teipsum* (1599), de Mornay's *True Knowledge of a Mans Owne Selfe* (tr 1602), Charron's *Of Wisdome* (tr 1607). Though mingling Christian, Platonic, and Aristotelian principles in their depiction of the microcosm, these writers, like Spenser, primarily stress the soul's ability to 'know itself': its transcendent nature and dominion over the body, its moral and spiritual obligations, and its immortal end.

ROBERT L. REID

Ruth Leila Anderson 1927 *Elizabethan Psychology and Shakespeare's Plays* (Iowa City); John Peter Anton 1957 *Aristotle's Theory of Contrariety* (New York) ch 7; H. Baker 1952, chs 13–19; Bamborough 1952; Berger 1957, ch 3; Hieatt 1975a:171–214; Kocher 1953, chs 11, 14; Nelson 1963:183–98; Robert L. Reid 1981a 'Alma's Castle and the Symbolization of Reason in *The Faerie Queene*' *JEGP* 80:512–27; Reid 1981b; Reid 1981–2; P[ercy] Ansell Robin 1911 *The Old Physiology in English Literature* (London).

psychomachia The 'battle within the soul' between personifications of the vices and virtues was a favorite subject of medieval allegory and a method used extensively by Spenser. It may be traced to Peter's reference to 'fleshlie lustes, which fight against the soule' (1 Pet 2.11). In the fourth century, the Christian poet Prudentius formalized these 'lustes' as specific vices in his *Psychomachia*, a poem which presents a series of battles between Fides and Cultura Veterum Deorum (Faith and Worship of Old Gods), Pudicitia and Libido (Chastity and Lust), Patientia and Ira (Patience and Wrath), and so on. Each pair takes the field in turn, until the Virtues finally overcome the Vices. After the battle, Discordia (also called Heresy) slyly attempts to wound Concordia. After the Virtues tear Discord apart, they unite under the direction of Concord to construct a magnificent jeweled temple in which Sapientia (Wisdom) is enthroned. The poem concludes with a recognition that the rebellious side of man's nature, the flesh, can be controlled only with the aid of Christ. Elements of the *Psychomachia*, such as the battlefield descriptions, look back to Virgil's *Aeneid*. Prudentius' strongly Christian theme of soul warfare, however, lays a basis for a tradition of depicting allegorical conflict which descends through Martianus Capella and the scholastic epics of the twelfth-century Chartrians to Renaissance poets such as Petrarch, Boccaccio, Landino, and Tasso. It was also kept alive in morality plays, in the battles of virtues and vice found, for instance, in *The Castle of Perseverance*.

Spenser's allegory is very much part of this tradition, for example, in *FQ* I in the Red Cross Knight's fight with Orgoglio (Ital 'pride') and his subsequent defeat. Yet his allegory is more complex than Prudentius' and less reliant on a single fixed scheme of personification. His figures may be read against many operative schemes such as Aristotelian psychology, Protestant doctrine, Platonic psychology, and contemporary English history. Thus Orgoglio may be interpreted specifically as the pride of the Spaniards in conflict with the English at the time and as the pride of the Roman Catholic Church, as well as the general religious pride from which Redcrosse must be freed. Often it is hard to tell which scheme dominates, and usually a character's meaning is defined more by actions in the narrative than by reference to any external scheme. Sometimes in Spenser, as in Prudentius, a moral quality is split among several characters. For instance, Orgoglio is overcome not by Redcrosse but by Arthur, just as Superbia (Pride) is beaten by Mens Humilis (Humility) only with the aid of Spes (Hope).

As the tradition of the psychomachia developed, the conflict between vices and virtues was depicted as an internal struggle among the three faculties of the human soul: concupiscible, irascible, and rational. These were commonplace terms, comparable to id, ego, and superego in Freudian psychology. From the concupiscible faculty proceed the desires for food, drink, sexual satisfaction, and other sensual pleasures, which are destructive if not controlled. The rational faculty, of which conscience is a part, perceives the correct path to be followed, and is aided by an enforcer, the irascible faculty, an emotional impetus marked by generous indignation or firm determination, which holds in check the fleshly lusts of the concupiscible faculty. When the irascible faculty forgets the directions of the rational faculty, excessive or rancorous anger may itself become a cause of vicious conduct. All three faculties seek to influence the will, which finally determines a course of action.

Many characters in Spenser's allegory may be interpreted on at least two levels at once: as impulses of the soul and as exemplars of the various virtues and vices. Most of the giants, churls, beasts, and monsters may be interpreted as vices and as perturbations of the concupiscible faculty. The concupiscible faculty itself may be represented by Acrasia, and the irascible faculty by Satyrane, Una's lion, Guyon's boatman, and the Salvage Man. The rational faculty is represented by Alma. Through a sixteenth-century interpretation of Plato's *Phaedrus* 246, Florimell's white palfrey (*FQ* III vii 2–32) and Bruncheval (Fr 'dark horse,' Satyrane's opponent in IV iv 17–18) may also represent the irascible and concupiscible faculties respectively. (According to Piccolomini's *Universa philosophia de moribus* 1583, 9.21, Plato's skittish and erratic dark horse, the concupiscible faculty, is yoked in double harness with the white horse, the irascible faculty; the two horses keep each other in line with directions of the charioteer, reason.) Figures such as these are combined with the more obvious combats of virtues and vices in Spenser's application of the warfare within the soul throughout *The Faerie Queene*. JOHN E. HANKINS

On Prudentius, see Macklin Smith 1976 *Prudentius' 'Psychomachia': A Reexamination* (Princeton). For the tradition, see Lewis 1936, MacQueen 1970, Tuve 1966, and the reading list for *allegory. For an interpretation of Platonic psychomachia in Spenser, see Reid 1981a, 1981b, 1981–2. Anderson 1970b shows how the Palmer and Guyon's horse are psychomachic fragments of Guyon. On Spenserian allegory and psychomachia generally, see Hankins 1971.

punctuation While differing from modern practice, Elizabethan punctuation followed coherent principles, although it did allow greater freedom for individual idiosyncrasy. Following earlier traditions, it was basically concerned with indicating the length of time the reader was to pause, and with emphasizing the balance of rhetorical patterns. Punctuation of poetry was also much concerned with stressing metric and rhythmic patterns. In the century following Spenser, English punctuation developed in the direction of our modern emphasis on logical and grammatical patterns; but in the earlier Renaissance, this was a distinctly subordinate matter (Ong 1944).

Contemporary punctuation of Spenser's printed works generally follows the usage of his time. Although English printers sometimes respected the personal practice of individual writers (eg, Jonson and Donne), the somewhat varying punctuation of Spenser's poetry by different printers in his lifetime has led to the conclusion that the punctuation was likely due mainly to the compositors (*Var* 6:480–503).

The punctuation of Spenser's poetry is particularly aimed at reinforcing metrical and especially stanzaic patterns. The stanza is treated as the basic unit of meaning, and the punctuation is placed accordingly, although the departures from modern usage that this policy entails would not have surprised Elizabethan readers. The most important marks are the period, colon, semicolon (a recent addition to English punctuation), and comma, systematically indicating breaks of diminishing importance. When introducing subordinate clauses, these marks are chosen with considerable latitude and subtlety, according to rhetorical emphasis rather than the logical relationship of the subordinate clause to the main clause. The opening stanzas of *FQ* I as given in the *Variorum*, which reproduces the punctuation of the 1596 edition – the 1590 edition is less heavily punctuated – effectively illustrate the ways in which stops of different intensity skillfully reinforce and vary the stanzaic structure.

In other departures from modern usage, parentheses are freely used to set off material we would set off with commas, and commas are used more sparingly – or not at all – to set off vocatives. The punctuation of Spenser's poetry has been generally regarded as highly effective for reading aloud, as the poetry was certainly intended to be.

FRED J. NICHOLS

Dorothy F. Atkinson 1931 'A Study of the Punctuation of Spenser's *Faerie Queene*' diss Univ of Washington; Walter J. Ong 1944 'Historical Backgrounds of Elizabethan and Jacobean Punctuation Theory' *PMLA* 59:349–60; Mindele Treip 1970 *Milton's Punctuation and Changing English Usage, 1582–1676* (London).

puns Spenser's puns are not bright flashes of wit illuminating the surfaces of his texts but profound interpretive elements structuring the development of his narratives. While his wordplay may be studied most usefully in relation to the broadly extended narratives of *The Faerie Queene*, significant puns are to be found in his shorter poems as well. In *Amoretti* 10, for instance, wordplay such as *hart/heart* combines metaphors of the two veneries (hunting and courtship); a play in sonnet 28 on *leafe/lief* (the laurel leaf of the poet's fame, and the leaf or page of a book; the poet's 'life,' and his 'beloved') reveals that Spenser shared with Shakespeare and other Elizabethan writers a broad penchant for verbal play.

Such a penchant doubtless derives from the Renaissance attitude toward the possibly sacral autonomy of language – that world of words in which the ingenious explorer could discover unsuspected truths applicable to the world of things. The example of E.K. demonstrates that Spenser rightly assumed his readers would notice and appreciate his wordplay. Thus, E.K. comments on 'a Paronomasia or playing with the word, where he sayth (I love thilke lasse (alas etc.' (*SC, Jan* 61 gloss). E.K.'s terminology reveals the importance of the pervasive rhetorical training that prepared Spenser's audience to pause over his wordplay. The Renaissance had no catchall term like the modern *pun.* Punlike operations were classified by rhetorical figures such as *paronomasia* ('a lass, alas'); *adnominatio*, where the grammatical uses of a single word vary (as in 'Gay without good, is good hearts greatest loathing' *Mother Hubberd* 232); and *antanaclasis* or *syllepsis*, where the same word is used in two different senses (as in 'Thenceforth they gan each one his like to love, / And like himselfe desire for to beget' *Colin Clout* 863–4).

Allied to such play with the sounds of words is Spenser's complicated play with a word's history of meaning in etymological 'punning.' His typical procedures derive from the influential medieval misreading of Plato's *Cratylus* current in the Renaissance (see Craig 1959, 1967). Ignoring Plato's main point against the philosophical usefulness of etymology, prominent thinkers (such as Isidore of Seville) had argued that etymology was a means to discover the sacred origin of language, and thereby to read the language of the book of nature. Etymology and wordplay, therefore, provided not merely verbal wit but insight into divine purposes.

While Shakespeare's puns seldom aim at sacred wit, Spennser's frequently do. He is in the tradition of such medieval allegorists as Langland, Jean de Meun, and Alanus de Insulis; indeed, his pronounced polysemy may be less a product of the linguistic disposition of his own age than a trait caught from his medieval precursors in allegorical narrative. By recounting the actions of personifications (ie, of animated words), narrative allegory relies from its inception on a kind of wordplay. For example, the catalogue of rivers in *FQ* IV xi owes much of its animation to Spenser's 'stated and implied wordplay, much of it personifying the streams according to their names (aided by Spenser's unique etymology)' (Orange 1972). Thus, the Tigris is 'fierce' like a tiger, the Wylebourne has 'wylinesse,' the Mole runs underground, and the Humber, 'tossed with ... stormes' apparently owes its epithet to Greek *ombros* 'storm.'

Such local etymological play also extends over entire books. For example, courtesy derives from *court* (VI i 1), yet the narrative in *FQ* VI attempts to find the problematic origin of this virtue outside the court in the opposing pastoral landscape. So, too, play with the roots of the titular virtue of the incomplete Book VII, 'constancy' (L *stare* to stand), supplies the terms of Nature's solution to Mutabilitie's challenge: 'yet being rightly wayd / They are not changed from their first *estate* ... But they raigne over change, and doe their *states* maintaine' (vii 58; emphasis added). The image of 'turning to themselves at length againe' also enacts the etymology of *universe* 'a single turning.' In *FQ* I, Una, 'one,' is a fitting name for the heroine of a book which encompasses the 'whole' of 'holiness,' and in which Una's knight, after losing her, immediately meets an evil character named for the principle of doubleness, *Duessa*. The principle of doubleness is the basis of allegory (see Giamatti 1975). While wordplay should not be discounted in any of Spenser's works, it is most obviously structural in the allegorical narrative of *The Faerie Queene* where 'it is as if Spenser wanted every part, every feature, every partial form within the poem, to be a pun of some kind' (Fletcher 1971:105).

Critical interest in Spenser's punning is itself a significant question in literary history. While Milton was extraordinarily sensitive to Spenser's wordplay, borrowing numerous puns (as in the *fruit/fruitless* pun of *FQ* II vii 55; cf *Paradise Lost* 9.648), in subsequent centuries when puns were devalued as the lowest form of humor, authors and critics tended to ignore them. Renewed interest in Renaissance wordplay is a twentieth-century concern, inspired perhaps in part by Freud's influential discussion of the relation between parapraxis (verbal slips) and psychic truths, by the status of James Joyce's monument to the polyglot pun in *Finnegans Wake*, and by the critical writings of William Empson. Poststructuralist critical sensitivity to linguistic systems, especially the tendency of deconstructive analysis to proceed by punning analysis, may go even further in investigating Spenser's wordplay. However, earlier critical studies of Renaissance wordplay grew out of properly historical investigations into Renaissance attitudes toward language (eg, Mahood 1957; Craig 1959, 1967).

Spenser's puns may usefully be divided into two arbitrary but convenient groups, etymological and homophonic. The etymological pun can be based on either true or false etymology. For example, Spenser's use of *rede* commonly puns on *read* 'to peruse' and its historically accurate source, OE *raed* 'to give counsel'; yet he also follows Dante and medieval etymologies like the *Magnae derivationes* of Hugutio of Pisa, in fancifully deriving *hypocrisy* from Gr *hyper* + *chrysos* 'covered with gold' (*FQ* I iv 4). The homophonic or true pun derives from the similar sound of two words rather than from any historical connection between them (eg, *hart/heart*). In *The Faerie Queene*, both kinds serve the same structural function of organizing extended stretches of narrative.

A detailed look at some etymological puns will demonstrate how extensive and thematically significant Spenser's wordplay can be. In Book I, Una explains to her knight the name of the wood in which they are lost: 'This is the wandring wood, this *Errours den* ... Therefore I read beware' (i 13). Spenser is alerting his reader to the etymological significance of Error's name (L *errare* to wander); on this pivotal pun, he then builds the ensuing action of the errant knight's long wandering in a convoluted path – 'All in amaze' (ii 5) – that takes him ultimately to Orgoglio's dungeon, out of which he must be extricated by Arthur. The process by which Una and the Red Cross Knight find themselves in the wood in the first place unfolds through a related series of puns on an etymology of the word *doubt* (L *du[b]itare* to go in two directions); thus, they 'wander too and fro in wayes unknowne, / Furthest from end then, when they neerest weene, / That makes them doubt, their wits be not their owne: / So many pathes, so many turnings seene, / That which of them to take, in diverse doubt they been' (i 10). Etymologically, *diverse* also properly means 'two-turning.' Spenser has therefore doubled the wordplay by adding another word that has the same etymology as *doubt*.

The centrality of the word *doubt* to his description of the physical process of getting lost in the wood of Error is further amplified in the Fradubio episode (ii 30–44), where Fradubio's name means both 'Brother Doubt' and 'in doubt' (Ital *fra'* from *frate* 'brother,' *fra* 'between'). As a man turned into a tree, Fradubio is a repeated image of Error's forest; however, in being 'plast in open plaines' (33: ie, placed in more open spaces and there openly complaining of his misfortune), Fradubio makes clearer the more densely shadowed confusions of the original wood. There, Error had preferred to remain in darkness, 'Where plaine none might her see, nor she see any plaine' (i 16). The contrasting landscapes of plain and forest are intricately involved in the etymological play. Moreover, Fradubio mirrors Redcrosse's predicament: both have lost faith in their proper beloveds – and faith is the opposite of doubt. Both are enthralled by Duessa, who is finally revealed to be, like Error, a biform creature.

Despair's name is also falsely etymologized to reveal his kinship with doubt-engendering Duessa. *Despair* is properly derived from Latin *despero* 'to lose hope'; but Spenser also makes us see that just as Archimago has 'divorced in despaire' Una and her knight (iii 2), so Despair has *dispaired* a proper *pair* of testaments, forgetting the New Testament's lesson of love and insisting only on the Old Testament's law of justice. Spenser's extended play with *error*, and with the double sense of the physical and moral progress it names, ends only in canto x when Caelia greets Una and her knight in the house of Holiness, addressing her as one who ceases not 'thy wearie soles [souls] to lead,' and saying to him, 'Strange thing it is an errant knight to see / Here in this place ... So few there bee, / That chose the narrow path, or seeke the right' (9–10). Una had 'read' the name of the wood correctly, and so she was able to warn him of its dangers. In the house of Holiness, the Red Cross Knight is thus taught by Fidelia properly to interpret the New Testament 'That none could read, except she did them teach' (19). As the true text from which he should take counsel, the New Testament is thus opposed to Error's vomit of books and papers. Spenser makes the etymological puns very obvious in Una's first warning, as if to alert his reader to the fundamental importance of puns in the ensuing narrative. Her pun on *read* teaches the reader to read, and the pun on *error* structures the events of ten full cantos.

Although it is not unusual for Spenser to unfold a single bit of wordplay and interweave related puns over a long stretch of narrative, *The Faerie Queene* is also filled with innumerable puns at work in more confined ways, as in the description of the process of defecation in the house of Alma: waste 'was avoided quite, and throwne out privily' (II ix 32), *avoided* meaning both 'voided' and 'shunned,' the process taking place in 'privacy' by means of a 'privy.' Thus, both digestion and contemporary domestic architecture, the twin bases of Spenser's metaphor, are served.

A homophonic pun in Book III shows how Spenser's sense of the magic of language included what we regard as merely accidental similarity in the sounds of two words. When Scudamour meets Britomart, he laments 'Why then is *Busirane* with wicked hand / Suffred, these seven monethes day in secret den / My Lady and my love so cruelly to pen?' (xi 10). At first, *pen* means simply 'imprison'; but a second meaning – 'write with a pen' – is enacted in the climactic episode of canto xii when Busirane is revealed sitting before the enchained Amoret writing magic words with her heart's blood (31). *Pen* may also have a sexual resonance, indicating that Amoret's peculiar torture involves the productions of a sadistically phallocentric discourse (*pen*, from L *penna* 'feather,' is not related to L *penis* 'tail' – though *pencil* is – but the words share a significant syllable and a history of punning association). With this pun, Spenser literalizes the dangers of Petrarchism. Penned in passivity, suffering the torments of passion, Amoret is imprisoned in a metaphorical way of talking about love where one is always dying but never truly free of torment in a real death. Enchained in pernicious metaphor, neither she nor Scudamour can escape from the abuse of language literalized by Busirane's bloody verses until Britomart (a strong 'reader') breaks the 'spell' and forces Busirane to reverse (ie, to read backwards) those same bloody lines.

When Busirane chants the reversed verses, a strange magic occurs (38):

The cruell steele, which thrild her dying hart,
Fell softly forth, as of his owne accord,
And the wyde wound, which lately did dispart
Her bleeding brest, and riven bowels gor'd,
Was closed up, as it had not bene bor'd,
And every part to safety full sound,
As she were never hurt, was soone restor'd:
Tho when she felt her selfe to be unbound,
And perfect hole, prostrate she fell unto the ground.

Such postcoital-sounding magic answers female fears of sexual savaging by a bestial male lust; this lust is also imaged in the boar that Venus pens beneath her Mount in the Garden of Adonis at the center of Book III (and so Spenser says the wound heals 'as it had not bene bor'd'). At the same time, the moment of Amoret's collapse makes us aware of the legitimacy of female sexuality itself. By seeing *whole* without the *w*, we are made aware of the natural vulnerability of Amoret's virgin sexuality, a vulnerability she shares in the Book of Chastity with Britomart, who is also wounded twice (III i 65, xii 33).

The final pun in the canceled final stanzas of the 1590 Book III makes the nature of Amoret's 'wound' clearer. Britomart watches Amoret and Scudamour embrace, 'halfe envying their blesse' (xii 46a). Such enviable *bliss* is properly a 'blessing,' not only because their union is sacramental (as we learn in Book IV), but also because in sixteenth-century usage, *to bless* also meant 'to wound' (from Fr *blesser*). The bliss of such a blessed wound, the effect of sexual consummation for a female virgin, is the basis of chaste marriage – Spenser's subject in Book III. The pun on *(w)hole* underwrites the holy sacredness of female sexuality that he is inscribing in his culture *against* the virgin exemplar of his powerful first reader, Queen Elizabeth.

That Spenser canceled these stanzas, and complained in the proem to Book IV that his poem had been misread, may imply that here his sexual puns went too far. One could label such puns *cacemphaton*, 'such wordes as may be drawen to a foule and unshamefast sence' (Puttenham 1589:212). Spenser, however, appears not to find sexual issues shameful – either in puns such as these, or elsewhere, as in the anatomical landscape allegory of the Garden of Adonis. The sexual content of the first line of Book I, 'A Gentle Knight was pricking on the plaine,' may therefore be understood as an undeniably necessary element in the chivalric knight spurring his horse and filled with a phallic pride in his own prowess that will be hugely deflated by his loss to Orgoglio (Anderson 1985). We may still wish to resist the breach of epic decorum that such a pun implies; or we may realize, with the ease the text itself seems to assume about the entire range of human experience, that there are no repressed meanings in the poem, merely repressed readings of it. (See also *sex.)

The puns on *pen*, *(w)hole*, and *bless* in Book III are for Spenser neither obscene nor comic. While many of his puns are intended to be humorous, their meaning often goes beyond momentary laughter. When Archimago observes Pyrochles thrashing about in the lake and complaining of flames (II vi 49), his play with the similar sounds of *drent* and *brent* is a small joke that evokes a laugh at the expense of evil. But we are also meant to see that choleric burning and dissolute drowning are similar excesses, alike opposed to the *via media* of temperance.

Another extended series of homophonic punning, on *bear* the animal and *bear* 'to carry,' informs Spenser's meditation on the problems of nature and nurture in Book VI. When the pun first appears, *adnominatio* coalesces with *antanaclasis* to produce a very dense set of meanings for *bear* and *borne*. Turpine taunts Calepine who asks to ride with him as he guides Serena across a river: 'Perdy thou peasant Knight, mightst rightly reed / Me then to be full base and evill borne, / If I would beare behinde a burden of such scorne' (iii 31). Calepine knows, however, what Turpine forgets, that knights owe women a debt, for men are of women 'yborne' (41). In the next canto, Calepine happens on a seemingly unrelated incident when he sees 'A cruell Beare, the which an infant bore / Betwixt his bloodie jawes' (iv 17). After he rescues the infant, its cries for food 'greatly him offend' (25), so he happily rids himself of his 'offensive' burden by giving it to Lady Bruin, who is unable to conceive (ie, is 'barren'); with great joy, she 'bore it thence, and ever as her owne it kept' (37). She is further heartened by Calepine's assurance that even though the babe's lineage is not known, it may yet be raised to be a noble knight. Thus, the infant's possibly base birth may be overcome by her nurture.

Although Spenser elsewhere insists that blood is the only reliable basis of true nobility, the story of the bear-born baby implies the opposite: even though one is basely born, one may bear oneself nobly. It is not due merely to the accidental sound of the words that a bear 'bore' the child and that the lady who nurtures it is married to Sir Bruin. The pun names a fact in God's book of nature: bears were thought to be born malformed and needing to be licked into shape by their mothers (whence the proverbial phrase); they therefore emblematically represent the efficacy of nurture and discipline in child rearing. Such persistent play with *bear* finds its ultimate point when Arthur strips Turpine of his knightly accoutrements: 'for shame is to adorne / With so brave badges one so basely borne' (vi 36). Here *basely borne* no longer refers to base birth, but to having borne or behaved oneself basely.

As these examples suggest, puns are intricately involved in the narrative and thematic developments of all the books of *The Faerie Queene*. Play with the etymology of *concord* and terms related to it structure Book IV; an *antanaclasis* of the word *let* in V ix 50 says and unsays Mercilla's judgment on Duessa, speaking to the complicated relations between justice and mercy investigated throughout the book; in Book III, the punning fact that *chaste* sounds like *chased* fills the book with hunts and huntresses. Such puns show Spenser organizing narrative to investigate the truths dictated by the nature of the words he uses. As with his predecessors in allegory, the polysemy of puns is basic to his allegorical fictions. (See also *names.) MAUREEN QUILLIGAN

Craig 1959; Craig 1967; Joseph 1947; Lanham 1968; M.M. Mahood 1957 *Shakespeare's Wordplay* (London); Linwood E. Orange 1972 '"All Bent to Mirth": Spenser's Humorous Wordplay' *SAQ* 71:539–47; P.A. Parker 1979; Quilligan 1979; Sonnino 1968.

puritanism Spenser's relations with Elizabethan puritanism seem fundamental to the kind of poet he was, but they are problematic and disputed. Partly, this is because puritanism cannot be defined as any single position but must be seen rather as a range of attitudes to diverse aspects of religion and society, overlapping unevenly with the attitudes of protestantism at large, and changing with political circumstances (Hill 1964, ch 1; see *radicalism). Along with this difficulty in defining puritanism itself, relevant passages in the poems are often difficult to interpret, and Spenser's views seem inconsistent both towards the diverse aspects of puritanism and over the twenty years of his poetic career.

Most of the characteristics that have been attributed to Elizabethan puritanism can be shown to occur among protestants, and indeed Christians, at large. Nevertheless, the term is useful if it is regarded as a matter of emphasis and allegiance: puritans maintained certain positions with more urgency than other protestants and perceived themselves as the more godly and committed part of a protestant national church which, they believed, still required some further reformation. Puritans favored the repression of Roman catholics in England and Ireland and an active foreign policy to support protestants in other countries. They invoked as their model the *purity* of the beliefs and practices of the earliest Christians. (See *Church of England, *Church of Rome, *Reformation.)

In respect of doctrine, Elizabethan puritans were generally content with the Calvinist implications of the Thirty-nine Articles (finalized in 1571) and were eager to defend them against theologians like Peter Baro who, in Cambridge in the 1590s, spoke against predestination. The services of the Elizabethan church were criticized by puritans as retaining papist features, and some ministers were removed from their parishes for refusing to wear surplices and to use parts of the Book of Common Prayer (see *religious controversies). About church government, Elizabethan puritans held diverse opinions but most, though against extravagance and display, were in favor of or at least prepared to work with bishops (some of them *were* bishops). Presbyterianism and separatism developed strong followings only in the seventeenth century, when puritans found the establishment of the Stuart church and state moving decisively against them. Above all, Elizabethan puritans demanded an able and committed ministry to preach the gospel.

Because of the English Revolution of the 1640s, we tend to think of puritans as opposed to the existing social order. In Elizabeth's time some of them were, but for the most part those in the literate classes – for whom Spenser wrote – saw the state as a bulwark against catholicism, and their puritanism was intended to reinforce existing social controls. They were spearheaded by a court faction which included the Earls of Leicester, Warwick, Huntingdon, and Bedford, Sir Francis Knollys, and Sir Francis Walsingham; Philip Sidney was of this party, too. Such notables, and the gentry below them, presented themselves as godly magistrates who legitimated and were legitimated by the church (see Walzer 1965, chs 3, 7; Collinson 1982, ch 4). The difference between puritans and the Queen was in the main a matter of whether the social order would be better sustained by intensifying religious controls or by leaving things alone.

There is no necessary incompatibility, therefore, between puritanism and Spenser's manifest social and political conservatism. He explores the range and complexity of the political and ideological structure of his society – for instance, Gloriana is celebrated but not her court (*FQ* VI proem, *Colin Clout* 664–730). We may, however, discern a puritan orientation in his concern to complement 'good discipline delivered plainly in way of precepts, or sermoned at large' by fashioning 'a gentleman or noble person in vertuous and gentle discipline' clad in 'the armour of a Christian man specified by Saint Paul' (Letter to Raleigh). This project (and especially the word *discipline*) suggests the Calvinist ideal of the godly gentleman, zealous but sober, dedicated to his calling, and expressing his faith in the battle of life (see Siegel 1944).

In 1579–80, puritans thought the English church was threatened in two ways by Roman catholicism: through corruption among churchmen and through the proposed marriage of the Queen to the French catholic Alençon. The issues were fought out in the privy council, but also in writing, for Elizabethan politicians were very aware of the potential of publishing to organize opinion. *The Shepheardes Calender* and *Mother Hubberds Tale* may have been designed in part, either through conviction or because Spenser thought it would advance his career, to support the puritan party. *Mother Hubberd* criticizes the preferment of self-seeking pastors and fables the danger of the lion (Elizabeth) losing control of the kingdom to 'forreine beasts, not in the forest bred' (1119; see Padelford 1913–14, Greenlaw 1910).

The Shepheardes Calender was dedicated to Sidney and printed by the puritan Hugh Singleton. The main theme of *Maye*, *Julye*, and *September* is the inadequacy of the ministry: the worldliness of some pastors, the self-aggrandizement of certain bishops, the threat from catholics (wolves) and the presence of covert catholics (foxes). The issue was focused by the Queen's suspension of Archbishop Grindal, a moderate puritan who had refused to suppress 'prophesyings' – discussions among groups of clergy designed to improve their competence but offering, at least to the Queen's view, the beginnings of an alternative religious and political organization. Grindal is figured in the *Calender* as the good pastor Algrind, and an enigmatic passage in *Julye* suggests that the Queen mistook his courage and determination when she 'bruzd' him, and that 'his hap was ill' (213–30).

Because these eclogues are dialogues, they are particularly open to dispute about which position the author seems to endorse. Anthea Hume (1984:4) observes that critics' resistance to evidence of the link between the work and contemporary puritanism sometimes reflects 'personal preferences,' and Norbrook (1984:61) points out that such resistance goes along with the idea that 'poetry should transcend politics.' Both demonstrate that Spenser's imagery, rhetoric, and fables are constructed within a moderate puritan framework. Hume concludes that 'clerical worldliness in "Maye" together with an attack, in the fable, on superfluous ceremonies retained in the church; prelatical ambition and "lordship" in "Julye"; the serious menace presented by Roman Catholic missionaries in "September" coupled with an emphasis on the duties of the true pastor – coincide exactly with the major preoccupations of the moderate Puritan party' (p 40). However, insofar as the *Calender* leaves openings for alternative readings, we should perhaps not try to eliminate them and decide what Spenser 'really meant,' but rather perceive a studied indirection through which he sought to display a puritan commitment without incurring censorship or punishment. Attacks on Roman catholics and clerical abuses constituted puritan themes to which exception could hardly be taken: they were a safe way of establishing one's zeal (Lake 1982, ch 4). We cannot reliably infer Spenser's further religious outlook.

The puritan movement was active during Spenser's early years in Ireland but declined after 1588, mainly because of the defeat of the Armada and the death of Leicester (though Raleigh spoke up for imprisoned puritans in 1590; see Collinson 1967:444–5). Despite the apparent passing of the catholic threat, Spenser, perhaps because of his involvement in the English government's attempt to suppress catholicism in Ireland, harks back in *FQ* I to Edwardian and Marian themes and imagery. Through the figures of Archimago and Duessa, he depicts the papacy and its agents as virtually demonic powers, the repositories of every kind of vileness, the ultimate opponents of the English church and state.

It is unclear whether we should consider Spenser's vivid anti-catholicism puritan, and likewise his doctrines of grace and the sacraments. Here the Elizabethan church was broadly Calvinist, and whether there were distinctive puritan doctrines of grace and the sacraments has been doubted (see George and George 1961:5–8, 405). J.F.H. New (1964) believes that there were, and that the the differences were, once more, matters of emphasis. In respect of the doctrine of grace (see *nature and grace), he attributes to both puritans and Anglicans the common protestant doctrine that salvation is entirely the unmerited gift of God and that people cannot influence the divine decision – though New observes that some Anglicans 'softened the rigour of predestination' (p 13). Such softening is not apparent in *FQ* I vii 12, viii 1, ix 53, and x 1; even Whitaker who makes the case for Spenser's Anglicanism cannot deny the Calvinist slant of his doctrine of grace (1950:34–46).

New shows that puritans and Anglicans alike held that the sacraments 'were at one and the same time commemorations and participations in grace with a living Christ' (p 62), but that puritans emphasized the commemorative aspect whereas Anglicans attributed to the sacraments intrinsic efficacy as a means to grace. It may be argued that Spenser's apparent allusions to baptism and communion (I ii 43, xi 30, 48; IV iii 48–9) suggest that the sacraments possess intrinsic efficacy and therefore incline to the Anglican position (see Marshall 1959). On the other hand, in each of the passages specified, the access of spiritual power through the sacramental symbols seems independent of any merit in the recipient so that, contradictorily, the Calvinist doctrine of grace also seems to be present.

If Spenser's religious and political position in *The Faerie Queene* is not immediately coherent, that need not surprise us. The doctrines to which he was alluding were often internally contradictory and thoroughly entangled in current conflicts. Indeed, the emergence of a 'puritan' faction itself witnesses to the problems encountered in rendering protestant doctrine coherent in relation to other ideological formations and the actual power structure of the Elizabethan state (see Sinfield 1983). Spenser's extraordinarily ambitious and detailed treatment leads him to incorporate the disjunctions as well as the harmonies in the religious attitudes of his time.

The difficulty of pinning down his poems on doctrinal and political questions will lead many readers to identify his religious orientation more impressionistically, from the general tenor of his writing. But here again the evidence is conflicting. Although modern notions of puritans as kill-joys, hostile to what we call 'the arts,' have been set aside by scholars, puritans did tend to insist on a specific utility – religious, ethical, or practical – in cultural production (see Knappen 1939, chs 23, 26). In many ways, Spenser's poetry meets such criteria; but the decorous and ceremonial style, the sensuousness of some of the imagery, the indirectness and intricacy of the structure of *The Faerie Queene*, and the appeal to medieval motifs seem unpuritan. Two of the *Fowre Hymnes* are in honor of pagan love and beauty, but the other two are severely protestant, and the dedication – to two puritan ladies – retracts the first two. *Epithalamion* is elaborately ceremonious and seems to lean towards the sacramental view of marriage which protestants repudiated; but spiritualization of the family was characteristic of puritans, and the final stress on procreation 'Of blessed Saints for to increase the count' (423) sounds puritan in theme and phrasing. The Bower of Bliss is fulsomely evoked, but it is also destroyed.

Perhaps we should think of Spenser as crucially divided in himself over puritanism. But one component in his outlook *is* extremist: there is a streak of violence and fanaticism in his commitment to the English state, and this we might find puritan in tone (see Greenblatt 1980, ch 4). ALAN SINFIELD

Collinson 1967; Collinson 1982; George and George 1961; Greenblatt 1980; Greenlaw 1910; Christopher Hill 1964 *Society and Puritanism in Pre-Revolutionary England* (London); Hume 1984; King 1985; M.M. Knappen 1939 *Tudor Puritanism: A Chapter in the History of Idealism* (Chicago); Lake 1982; Marshall 1959; John F.H. New 1964 *Anglican and Puritan: The Basis of Their Opposition, 1558–1640* (Stanford); Norbrook 1984; Padelford 1913–14; Paul N. Siegel 1944 'Spenser and the Calvinist View of Life' *SP* 41:201–22; Sinfield 1983; Michael Walzer 1965 *The Revolution of the Saints: A Study in the Origins of Radical Politics* (Cambridge, Mass); Whitaker 1950.

Pyrochles, Cymochles The brothers Pyrochles and Cymochles appear in *FQ* II v-viii as opponents of Guyon, knight of Temperance, and of Arthur. Their names are derived from the Greek: respectively *pyr* (fire) and *kuma* (wave) with *ochleō* (to move, trouble, or disturb by tumult). The name Pyrochles therefore suggests volatility and wrathfulness, while Cymochles suggests dissoluteness and sensuality. The brothers' genealogy complements their generally troubled natures: among their progenitors are Despight and Acrates (linking them to Acrasia), Jarre and Phlegeton (the river of fire in the underworld), and Erebus and Night (iv 41).

Spenser uses Cymochles and Pyrochles to explore two distinct dimensions of the 'weakness of will' (*akrasia*) with which Book II deals. The chief images associated with Pyrochles are fire and dust. At his first entrance, his armor 'round about him threw forth sparkling fire, / That seemd him to enflame on every side,' while his steed he 'prickt so fiers, that underneath his feete / The smouldring dust did round about him smoke' (v 2–3). His motto, 'Burnt I do burne' (iv 38), captures his willful self-destructiveness; and even before Pyrochles himself appears, his squire Atin creates a picture of him as a knight who wills himself to act even when he has neither cause nor object. Thus while in canto iv Guyon had stopped the 'uprore' between Furor and Phedon by binding Occasion, paradoxically, with Atin's entrance that very binding results in a new demand for battle, for Atin announces that Pyrochles – unable to find the bound Occasion – has set out angrily 'To seeke *Occasion*, where so she bee' (iv 43). When Guyon explains he has bound her, Atin vows that Pyrochles will take vengeance for her having been subdued. Thus the binding of Occasion only encourages Pyrochles' strident willfulness.

When Pyrochles arrives in canto v, he makes good on Atin's boast, assaulting Guyon without so much as a word, while Atin flees to seek the aid of Cymochles. Guyon defeats Pyrochles, but having temperately spared his life, he then allows Pyrochles to convince him to unbind Occasion. Not surprisingly, the release of Occasion only occasions new strife: Furor and Pyrochles fall to battle, and the scene ends with Furor triumphantly dragging Pyrochles 'through durt and myre without remorse' (23). Pyrochles thus renders himself victim to his own willfulness, a point reiterated in canto vi when, still burning within with Furor's 'implacable fire' (44), he tries to quench his flames by drowning himself in the Idle Lake. Idleness, however, cannot be the willful man's lot; and though Archimago soothes his flaming parts with 'balmes and herbes' and 'mighty spels,' Pyrochles does not change (51).

Pyrochles appears again in canto viii where his willfulness takes one last ironic twist. There together with Cymochles, he tries to plunder the fallen Guyon's armor, but is stopped by the arrival of Arthur. In the ensuing battle Pyrochles is defeated, but when Arthur offers to spare his life, Pyrochles 'wilfully refused grace' (52), and thus forces Arthur to behead him, ironically realizing a phrase with which Pyrochles was introduced: 'His owne woes authour' (v 1).

In contrast to Pyrochles' unrestrained will for action, Cymochles' akrasiac weakness is an unrestrained will for self-indulgence – a willfulness which Spenser renders as paradoxically aimless, and which thus results in very little action at all. Images associated with Cymochles are those of water and sleep. Through word plays that link various liquid seepings with the moral condition of 'dissoluteness,' Spenser etymologizes Cymochles' 'incontinence' as an incapacity to hold himself (and his various liquids) in. Thus Cymochles has 'pourd out his idle mind / In daintie delices, and lavish joyes ... And flowes in pleasures, and vaine pleasing toyes, / Mingled emongst loose Ladies and lascivious boyes' (v 28).

Cymochles first enters the poem in canto v when Pyrochles' squire Atin seeks his aid for Pyrochles. Cymochles, however, prostrate in the Bower, is so dissolute that Atin must 'prick' him with 'his sharpe-pointed dart' to get him to move at all: 'Up, up, thou womanish weake knight, / That here in Ladies lap entombed art' (36). The double-entendre is clear: though the knight lies 'in Ladies lap,' he is nevertheless impotent and needs Atin's 'prick' to rouse him. Once 'up,' Cymochles arms himself to avenge his brother, yet he has trouble keeping the object of his quest in mind. He boards Phaedria's boat, and once they have arrived at her floating island, she sings a song that lulls him into a state of utter aimlessness: 'Why then dost thou, O man! ... Wilfully make thy selfe a wretched thrall ... Seeking for daunger and adventures vaine?' (vi 17). Without Atin's spurs of 'shame and wrong' at his side, Cymochles has no answer; his resolve slackens and he falls asleep. Cymochles awakes when Guyon arrives some ten stanzas later; he then begins a battle with Guyon that ends only when Phaedria, in an ironic parody of the temperate Medina (see II ii 27) intervenes and tempers their 'extremities of bloudie fight' (36).

Cymochles' final appearance is in canto viii when he dies battling Arthur. Interestingly, Spenser's language now abandons images of water and renders Cymochles instead through martial versions of self-destructiveness. In this respect Cymochles grows more like the warlike and similarly self-destructive Pyrochles. Unlike his brother, however, who dies because he 'wilfully' refuses Arthur's grace, Cymochles dies while striving with a confused and misdirected sense of honor: 'prickt with guilty shame / And inward griefe, he fiercely gan approch, / Resolv'd to put away that loathly blame, / Or dye with honour and desert of fame' (44). Our final image of Cymochles is thus of a mind disturbed less because it wills itself towards a dishonorable goal than because it can find no honorable object of will towards which to strive in the first place.

Possible sources for the two brothers are several, though none provides a fully satisfactory gloss. Plato's tripartite division of the soul into the reasonable, the high-spirited, and the appetitive (see *triplex vita) provides an analogue to the Palmer (reasonable), Pyrochles (high-spirited or, as Plato explains, that part of the soul with which one feels anger), and Cymochles (appetitive, or that part of the soul with which one seeks the pleasures of food, wine, and body [*Republic* 4.435–45]). The attractiveness of this scheme is obvious in cantos v and vi, but it breaks down when Pyrochles and Cymochles attack Guyon, for Plato is clear that the high-spirited and appetitive parts never act jointly against the reasonable (*Rep* 4.440b).

Aristotle's *Nicomachean Ethics* supplies quite different terms for the brothers. For Aristotle, virtues are means between vicious extremes, and temperance is the mean between too much and too little bodily pleasure. But while Cymochles displays the vice of concupiscence (*Ethics* 3.10), yet Pyrochles is not for Aristotle intemperate at all. Anger in the *Ethics* is an excess not of temperance but of gentleness (4.5).

A third tradition upon which Spenser may have drawn is the Renaissance theory of humors (see *medicine, *psychology). According to this system, different psychological states and dispositions result when the body is dominated by one or another of the four bodily fluids: blood, black bile, yellow bile (choler), or phlegm. From this perspective Pyrochles would be dominated by choler, a humor thought to be distilled from fire (hot and dry) and conducive to irascibility, and Cymochles would be dominated by phlegm, derived from water (cold and moist) and conducive to indolence. Yet while Pyrochles is surely choleric, Cymochles' battles suggest he is not as slow and lazy as what one might expect from a character of phlegmatic humor. Moreover his sensuality seems inappropriate to the phlegmatic type, who is too lazy and unmoved to pour out energies in sexual pleasure.

In sum, Spenser is eclectic with these traditions. As so often in the poem, his tactic with Pyrochles and Cymochles is to open commonplace materials to exploration and complication, not to hold himself and his readers to a single conceptual scheme.

JOHN WEBSTER AND RICHARD ISOMAKI

Berger 1957:56–62; Carscallen 1967–8; Hugh MacLachlan 1980 '"The carelesse heauens": A Study of Revenge and Atonement in *The Faerie Queene*' *SSt* 1:135–61.

Pythagoras Greek philosopher and mathematician of the sixth century BC. During the Renaissance, Pythagoras and his 'Italic school' held a place of honor in philosophy almost equal to that of Plato and of Aristotle. Although Spenser never mentions him by name, E.K. does, appropriately linking him with Plato (*SC, Oct* 27 gloss).

As a basic tenet, the Pythagoreans held that numbers as pure forms divorced from matter are the ultimate constituents of our universe (see entries on *number symbolism). They posited a benign deity who created our universe by imposing the forms of numbers on preexistent matter (cf *Hymne of Beautie* 29–40). The various items in physical nature are held together by a network of numerical relationships expressed in mathematical terms as proportions or in musical terms as harmonies. Pythagoras called the created universe *cosmos* because of its supernal beauty. Plato introduced this cosmology into the mainstream of Western culture, most concentratedly in the *Timaeus*.

The most fundamental and pervasive cosmic form is the *tetraktys*, a tetrad pattern comprising the four basic qualities: hot, cold, moist, dry. From these qualities derive the four elements, the four seasons, the four stages of man's life, and a multitude of correspondent systems. The *tetraktys*, in fact, underlies every level of creation. In *Hymne of Love* (78–91), Spenser describes the creation of cosmos out of chaos as Love organizes the elements into this tetrad pattern.

Pythagorean doctrine also underlay the aesthetics that saw proportion and harmony as the criteria for beauty. This is the aesthetics expounded in E.K.'s gloss on *October* and implied throughout the eclogue. Polyhymnia laments its decline in *Teares* 547–58.

The Pythagorean doctrine of metempsychosis operates in the Garden of Adonis as souls are repeatedly clothed in flesh for their sojourn in this world and then return to their point of origin (*FQ* III vi 32–3). It is also exemplified in the shared life of the three brothers Priamond, Diamond, and Triamond (IV iii). Although Spenser's works contain these several echoes of Pythagorean doctrine, he was probably less knowledgeable of its formulations in ancient texts than its reformulation in the various forms of Platonism in the Renaissance.

S.K. HENINGER, JR

Richard L. Crocker 1963–4 'Pythagorean Math-ematics and Music' *JAAC* 22:189–98, 325–35; Fowler 1964; Heninger 1961; Heninger 1974; Thomas Stanley 1687 *The History of Philosophy* 2nd ed, pp 491–576 (London; rpt New York and Hildesheim 1975), the best single source for how Pythagoras was viewed in the Renaissance; John M. Steadman 1964 'The "Inharmonious Blacksmith": Spenser and the Pythagoras Legend' *PMLA* 79:664–5.

Q

quantitative verse To a poet writing English verse in the 1570s with the aim of equaling the great achievements of Greece and Rome, the metrical forms available in the native tradition would have seemed limited and crude, rigidly based as they were on syllable count, rhyme, and the little-understood principle of accentual alternation. Humanist education in Latin, such as Spenser received at Merchant Taylors' School, inculcated an appreciation of meter as a complex patterning of syllables classified by precise rules and by the authority of earlier poets into 'long' and 'short.' These quantitative distinctions in Greek and Latin poetry were more a matter of syllable-structure than duration, but the theory which the Renaissance inherited was that the pronunciation of a long syllable took twice the time of a short syllable. In practice, however, the difference was not an audible one at all, since the Elizabethans pronounced Latin more or less as if it were English, and read Latin verse with a prose delivery. As a result, meter was conceived of as an intellectually apprehended formal arrangement, derived more from the visual characteristics of verse than from its sound. Given the humanists' desire to recapture the ancient union of music and poetry, and to create a verse-form that would be the exclusive preserve of the learned, it was inevitable that repeated attempts would be made to establish a quantitative tradition in English, and there is evidence that some 30 poets – including Spenser, Sidney, Greville, Greene, Lodge, and Campion – were attracted to this enterprise between 1576 and the end of Elizabeth's reign, by which time the poetic achievements of the native tradition had established its superiority beyond all challenge.

The earliest experiments in English quantitative verse were those of Thomas Watson, Bishop of Lincoln (not to be confused with the author of *Amyntas* and *Hekatompathia*) and Roger Ascham in the 1540s, though the full flood of classical versifying began with the collaborative project of Sidney, Edward Dyer, and Thomas Drant in the late 1570s. Drant died in 1578; but Sidney and Dyer were still trying to naturalize classical meters when Spenser, having secured the patronage of the Earl of Leicester (Sidney's uncle), encountered them at Leicester House in 1579. Evidence for Spenser's participation in their program for the 'generall surceasing and silence of balde Rymers' (*Var Prose* p 6) comes from two letters to Gabriel Harvey, written in October 1579 and April 1580, and published with Harvey's replies in the latter year (*Two Commendable Letters* and *Three Proper Letters*; see Spenser's and Harvey's *letters).

The first letter (*2 Lett* I; *Var Prose* pp 5–12) reveals that Harvey had already tried to interest Spenser in the quantitative verse project, but without success; 'then I thought,' writes Spenser in Latin, 'that you alone were wise with Ascham; now I see that the Court fosters excellent English poets.' With the added encouragement from the 'Areopagus,' as he jokingly calls the classicizing group, Spenser finds himself 'more in love wyth my Englishe Versifying, than with Ryming,' and he offers a 21-line specimen, entitled 'Iambicum Trimetrum.' In the second letter (*3 Lett* I; *Var Prose* pp 15–18), he adds four lines in elegiac couplets (see below), and reminds Harvey of a pair of hexameters 'which I translated you *ex tempore* in bed, the last time we lay togither in Westminster.' He also announces that he intends to embark on a book-length poem in quantitative verse entitled *Epithalamion Thamesis*; if this was ever written, it does not survive, though it may have served as the basis for the account of the marriage between Thames and Medway in *FQ* IV xi 8–53.

Spenser's quantitative experiments are characteristic of the movement in their disregard for the rhythm of the spoken language. What is important to him is that English 'versifiers' should agree on a set of rules based on those of Latin prosody regularly included in the standard Elizabethan grammars. The rules which Spenser follows were obtained from Sidney, 'being the very same which *M. Drant* devised, but enlarged with *M. Sidneys* own judgement, and augmented with my Observations' (*3 Lett* I). Sidney's rules have survived in manuscript (printed in ed 1962:391).

The most useful Latin rules were those which relied on orthography: the rule of 'position' (a syllable is long when the vowel is followed by two or more consonants) and the 'diphthong' rule (which means, given the Elizabethan mispronunciation of Latin, that a syllable is long when the vowel is spelled with two letters). The only rule that relied entirely on pronunciation was one which determined the quantity of the penultimate syllable of any word of three or more syllables: if that syllable is stressed, it is long; if unstressed, it is short. This rule was employed instinctively by Elizabethan prosodists, and was the cause of many of the apparent 'confusions' of accent and quantity. It posed particular problems when it came into conflict with one of the other Latin rules; and Spenser, in common with many other experimenters, is baffled by English words like *carpenter*, in which the second syllable is clearly long by position but short by the penultimate rule in its usual pronunciation. He therefore feels constrained to stress this syllable when using the word in quantitative verse, but complains that the result 'seemeth like *a lame Gosling, that draweth one legge after hir*' (*3* Lett I). Similarly, *heaven*, normally pronounced as one syllable, must receive two in verse because of its spelling, and the result is 'like *a lame Dogge that holdes up one legge*.' 'Rough words,' however, 'must be subdued with Use,' and time will soften the oddity; 'for, why a Gods name may not we, as else the Greekes, have the kingdome of oure owne Language, and measure our Accentes, by the sounde, reserving the Quantitie to the Verse?' – in other words, using special 'quantitative' pronunciations when reciting verse. (Harvey, in his reply, rightly takes Spenser to task for this high-handed approach to the English language, and insists that prosody must be based on normal pronunciation.)

Any syllable which is not subject to the established rules – and there will be many – can be scanned to suit the poet's metrical needs, there being as yet no body of authoritative verse to which to refer. Unlike many nineteenth-century imitators of classical verse (Coleridge, Southey, Clough, and Longfellow, for example), Spenser does not use stress as a substitute for quantity, but he does follow the classical practice of making the two features coincide at line ends. The following scansion of Spenser's elegiac couplets shows his observance of the rule of position (it must be remembered that *h* was not included among the consonants in Latin prosody), and, for the most part, the diphthong rule, though Spenser (or the printer) shows a somewhat cavalier approach in allowing *ee*, *ie*, and *oo* to count as short:

Metrical scheme:

— ⏖ | — ⏖ | — ⏖ | — ⏖ | — ⏑⏑ | — ⏓
— ⏖ | — ⏖ | — | — ⏑⏑ | — ⏑⏑ | —

S̄ee yĕe thĕ | blīndefōul | dēd prĕtĭe | Gōd,
 thāt | fēathĕrĕd | Ārchĕ̄r,
Ōf Lōv | ērs Mīsĕr | īes | whīch măkĕth | hīs
 blŏodĭe | Gāme?
Wōte yĕ whȳ, | hīs Mōoth | ēr wĭth ă | Vēale
 hāth | cōovĕrĕd | hīs Fācĕ̄?
Trūst mē, | lēast hĕ mȳ | Lōove | hāppĕlȳ |
 chāunce tŏ bĕ | hōlde.

Since there was no conception of any *inherent* quantity of vowels or syllables, there is nothing anomalous in Spenser's decision to scan the first syllable of *Lovers* as long, but the first syllable of *maketh* as short; other quantitative poets, however, Sidney among them, made stronger attempts to find an aural basis for classical meters in English.

In the same year as his involvement in the quantitative movement, Spenser's wish to match in English the formal rigor and intricacy of classical verse found an alternative expression in the varied exploitation of the native metrical tradition in *The Shepheardes Calender*. His apparent abandonment of quantitative versifying thereafter suggests that its main value to him was to reveal the insufficiency of a view of meter that, however well-grounded in classical authority, ignored the natural rhythms of the language he spoke. DEREK ATTRIDGE

Derek Attridge 1974 *Well-Weighed Syllables: Elizabethan Verse in Classical Metres* (Cambridge); G.L. Hendrickson 1949 'Elizabethan Quantitative Hexameters' *PQ* 28:237–60; Aage Kabell 1960 *Metrische Studien II: Antike Form sich nähernd* (Uppsala); Ronald B. McKerrow 1901–2 'The Use of So-called Classical Metres in Elizabethan Verse' *MLQ* (London) 4:172–80, 5:6–13; Sidney ed 1962: xxxi-xxxv, 389–93; Seth Weiner 1982 'Spenser's Study of English Syllables and Its Completion by Thomas Campion' *SSt* 3:3–56; G.D. Willcock 1934 '"Passing Pitefull Hexameters": A Study of Quantity and Accent in English Renaissance Verse' *MLR* 29:1–19.

quest In his *Observations on the Fairy Queen*, Thomas Warton writes that 'quest is a term properly belonging to romance, importing the expedition in which the knight is engaged, and which he is obliged to perform. It is a very common word with Spenser' (1762, 2:166). In fact, Spenser does not use the word at all in *FQ* I or II, and in the later books (except VI) less often than *adventure*, which he uses in the Letter to Raleigh. Though, as Warton implies, the quest – a journey to accomplish a particular task or to find or regain some object – is essential to romance, it is also an essential element of much narrative literature. The occasion of the action in Homer's *Iliad* is the rescue of Helen from the Trojans; Homer's Odysseus struggles to return to his home and reestablish himself as head of his family and country; Moses and Virgil's Aeneas search for new homelands; Christ seeks to redeem mankind; Chrétien de Troyes' Erec first leaves Arthur's court and then his own to seek adventure; Malory's Sir Gareth sets out to free the Lady Lyones from the Red Knight; Ariosto's Orlando searches for Angelica. The quest provides a reason for the action and motives for the actors, as it does in *The Faerie Queene*, where the narrative device of the quest is a central organizing principle.

A cyclical quest is found in many myths as a 'magnification of the formula represented in the rites of passage: *separation-initiation-return*' (J. Campbell 1949:30). In the monomyth, the hero answers a call to adventure, a formal challenge, or threat, and soon arrives at the threshold, the place of the first peril often guarded by a dragon or requiring a dangerous sea voyage. After passing over the threshold, he finds himself in an unfamiliar landscape or underworld, where, assisted by helpers, he undergoes further tests. At the nadir of the cycle, he faces his greatest peril, a supreme ordeal, but after his victory – or escape – he must return again to his own world with the 'elixir' or boon (often a magical talisman or special knowledge) he has obtained. After the proper application of the elixir overthrows the initial threat and restores the original order, the quest has come full circle.

Though this pattern may fit most mythological and many literary quests, some stories develop and elaborate one stage of the cycle, and reduce the others. The epic, for example, beginning in medias res, may omit the call to adventure and threshold-crossing at the start of the narrative but supply these stages later. It may present more than one hero, as in the *Iliad*, and more than one adventure, as in the *Odyssey*. The hero of the myth quest is usually a god or demigod; the epic hero, often the founder of a nation, usually undertakes his quest for his people with divine assistance. In romance, where the quest becomes progressively more digressive and episodic, the hero is a knight-errant who may undertake a personal quest, perhaps to find or free a lover, and the supernatural forces at play are most often magical, being wizards rather than gods. Unlike the myth quest, there is a tendency in romance for the conclusion to be deferred and a new adventure to succeed the last.

The romance quest may have three main stages in its completed form: the *agon* or perilous journey and preliminary adventures, the *pathos* or crucial struggle in which the hero dies or nearly dies, and the *anagnorisis* or exaltation of the hero. This threefold structure shows 'the passage from struggle through a point of ritual death to a recognition scene' (Frye 1957:187) and, like the myth quest, exhibits 'a cyclical movement of descent into a night world and a return to the idyllic world, or to some symbol of it like a marriage' (Frye 1976:54).

In *The Faerie Queene*, each quester visits a place or places of testing – often houses of anti-virtue – and then passes through a 'temple' of the particular virtue being fashioned, where the quester is perfected in the virtue and strengthened for the final, climactic battle (see Hankins 1971, ch 3). After that battle is over, each quest would have culminated – if Spenser had completed the poem – in a return to Cleopolis and Gloriana.

Arthur's search for Gloriana, which extends through all the books, provides the poem's unifying quest. It is comparable to Britomart's in that Arthur, too, undertakes his quest for a lover seen in a 'vision' outside Fairyland. According to the Letter to Raleigh, the other principal questers proceed from Gloriana's court and return to it at the end of their quests, completing a geographical cycle – though none does in the extant books. Arthur proceeds through *The Faerie Queene* in a linear fashion, demonstrating his mastery of each virtue rather than following an apparent quest cycle. In Books I and II, he plays the godlike helper, but his role in the later books becomes progressively more typical of the other questers.

Book I has a structure closer than any other in the poem to the monomyth, as does the biblical myth upon which it is based, and the total shape of the quest is central to the meaning of the book. Una arrives at Gloriana's twelve-day feast, according to the Letter, and issues the call to adventure by requesting a champion to restore the state which existed in Eden before its overthrow by a dragon. The crossing of the threshold begins when the Red Cross Knight, Una, and the dwarf enter a 'shadie grove,' the entrance to the 'wandring wood' (i 7, 13), which leads eventually to Error, the guardian of the threshold. Once it is defeated, Redcrosse enters the equivalent of the hostile underworld, a place inhabited by Archimago, Sansfoy, Duessa, Lucifera, Sansjoy, and Orgoglio. His descent takes him from Archimago's hermitage through the house of Pride and a 'gloomy glade' (vii 4) to the nadir of the cycle in Orgoglio's dungeon. He is rescued by the godlike Arthur, and then in Despair's cave is aided by Una, who guides him to the house of Holiness. Here he is perfected in the virtue of holiness, enjoys the vision of the New Jerusalem, and learns his identity. Thus strengthened, he continues to Eden, restores the original order by defeating the Dragon, after which he is betrothed to Una and prepares to return to Gloriana's court. The total shape of his quest – its story or plot – shows the fall through sin succeeded by redemption, regeneration, and final restoration through God's grace. Redcrosse's victory over the Dragon is essential to the whole quest and allegory of holiness because it imitates Christ's final defeat of sin and death in what Frye describes as 'perhaps the closest following of the Biblical quest-romance theme in English literature' (1957:194).

While the quest in Book I moves toward the completion of a major cycle, the episodes within the book – and much of *The Faerie Queene* – progress through a series of minor cycles, high points succeeding descents, defeats alternating with victories (see Nohrnberg 1976:202). The full shape of the quest, while present to a varying extent in each of the books, is of less importance as the poem progresses and the episodes, emblems, and illustrations of virtuous and vicious behavior take on more of the burden of fashioning the virtues.

Although the shape is not as important to the meaning of Book II as it is to I, Guyon's quest parallels Redcrosse's and follows a similar pattern. The call to adventure is described in the Letter – within the poem it is occasioned by Amavia (i 60–1) – and at i 24 Guyon enters the forest by an 'uncouth way.' That Guyon – like Chrétien's Lancelot – is forced to travel without a horse (iii 3–4) underscores his 'descent' and allows Braggadocchio's 'elevation' to knighthood for his own mock quest. Arthur must rescue Guyon also, acting again as a kind of *deus ex machina*. He accompanies him to Alma's castle, where both view the image of the temperate body and Guyon is perfected in temperance. While Arthur defeats the forces that threaten to destroy the castle, Guyon proceeds to the Bower of Bliss to fulfill his quest. The final episode reiterates many of the details of his journey as he successfully resists temptations already encountered in his quest.

Book III departs significantly from a simple quest structure. Its action and the action of the two succeeding books in which Britomart plays a principal role are more firmly placed in the world of romance. The reason for her quest, her love of Artegall, is a romance call to adventure, and her use of disguise, her enchanted spear, and her defeat of Busirane are all romance elements. What most distinguishes her story is the extension of her quest beyond the conclusion of Book III: her victory over a foe not mentioned until xi 10 is only another episode in her quest for Artegall. Spenser's portrayal of the virtue of chastity does not depend, then, on the shape of her quest; instead it is developed through the numerous episodes involving other questers – Belphoebe, Amoret, and Florimell – to illustrate 'in diverse minds, / How diversly love doth his pageants play, / And shewes his powre in variable kinds' (III v 1).

Book IV is also full of romance elements, and structurally it is the most distinctive of all the books. Unlike the others, the titular heroes Cambell and Telamond (Triamond), do not appear until halfway through canto ii; they have a minor role, neither being mentioned again after v 21. There is no overall quest, and the book ends not with the overthrow of some evil power but with the wedding of Thames and Medway and the union of Florimell and Marinell. Displacement and deferral dominate as Spenser moves farther from narrative conventions and mimesis towards a text which is 'open, endless, and reversible' (Goldberg 1981:10). In terms of a quest structure, Book IV continues Book III and shows the relationship of chastity to friendship. Spenser fills the book not with the enactment of a central quest but with a series of examples of the concord brought about by love and of the discord and strife which are the products of lust, frustrated love, and jealousy. Marriage and reunion replace the conflict which usually precedes the conclusion of a quest.

Book V returns to a more defined structure: Artegall is sent by Gloriana to right a great wrong by overthrowing the tyrant Grantorto (i 3–4). However, he has already begun his quest when he first appears at IV iv 39, and his quest in Book V is episodic. It begins with a number of parables of justice – his Solomon-like settling of the dispute between Sanglier and the squire, his treatment of Munera, and his encounter with the Giant with the scales – until he is defeated by Radigund. Britomart's encounter with Radigund – the final battle in her quest – also marks the nadir of Artegall's quest, as she is cast in an Arthur-like role in redeeming him. Once freed, Artegall is perfected in his virtue at Mercilla's court and continues his quest. His concluding battle against

Grantorto illustrates justice in action, but where the previous books leave their heroes triumphant, he is shown pursued by the Blatant Beast, Envy, and Detraction.

Book VI lacks a definite quest structure, and many of the elements of romance, such as magic and great deeds of arms, are absent or rare. Calidore quests without a companion or guide. Although he has a specific quarry, the Blatant Beast, his pursuit occupies little of the book: he disappears between cantos iii and ix, and reappears only to abandon his quest for a pastoral retreat. While this retreat, in which he risks 'great dishonour and defame' (ix 1), may be seen as a low point in his quest, it little resembles the hostile underworld or ritual death of other quests, for here he is rewarded by the vision of the Graces. His courtesy is not imperiled in the pastoral world but only his good name, a threat that exists in the discourteous opinions of others. He does not require assistance from a champion to escape from the pastoral retreat or to rescue Pastorella from her captors before he resumes his quest.

The various quests of *The Faerie Queene* have elements of myth, epic, and romance, but Spenser adapts the traditional form of the quest to suit the particular demands of the poem. The same pattern is not repeated in each book because the role of each quester changes according to the nature of the virtue presented. Because Spenser's first purpose is not to tell a story but to fashion the reader by way of a fiction, he does not confine himself within a particular quest form. The choice of the familiar romance device of the knight-errant, the searching wanderer, allows for a great variety of episodes, geographical backtracking, and encounters with other characters – the 'many other adventures ... intermedled' (Letter) with the principal story. He combines epic heroism and romantic variety to produce a work which is structurally unique, changing to reveal the changing allegorical meaning while retaining the essential element of all quests, the search or struggle to accomplish or attain some goal. ROBERT D. PITT

Arthos 1956; J. Campbell 1949; Frye 1957; Frye 1976; Hankins 1971; Joseph A. Johnson, Jr 1973 'The Journey of the Red Cross Knight and the Myth of the Hero' *SCB* 33:203–6; Miller 1979a; Moorman 1967; Neuse 1968; Nohrnberg 1976; Lydia Wevers 1979 'Quest as a Narrative Method: An Observation on *The Faerie Queene*' *Parergon* 25(Dec):25–31.

R

Rabelais, François (1494?-1553) French physician, Franciscan, humanist, and author of *Pantragruel* (1532?), *Gargantua* (1534?), the *Tiers livre* (1546), *Quart livre* (1552), and the probably unauthentic *Cinquième livre* (1564). In England, his influence was complicated by an anonymous comic romance about Gargantua at the court of Arthur and by other texts falsely attributed to him (Brown 1933; de Grève 1960, 1961; Prescott 1984).

Rabelais is famous for comic logorrhea and unbuttoned indecency, but recent critics have also stressed his sophisticated playfulness and his Erasmian piety. He is as learned as he is funny, and his obscenities have point. Such humor is readily misconstrued, especially when cultural changes make it seem merely nasty; many people in Spenser's time found it hard to connect Rabelais's earthy humor with serious religious suggestion and saw only his mockery. Furthermore, Rabelais enraged both Roman Catholics, who resented his satire and evangelical sympathies, and Calvin, who called him 'a Royster that casteth forth lewd scoffes against the holy Scripture' (Calvin ed 1583: sig Zz3). The result was that in England Rabelais projected a double image. To some he was at least funny, 'that merrie Grig' (Eliot 1593: sig B3r), that 'merry man' (Nashe 1589?, in ed 1904–10, 3:341). But others said that he 'derided the everlasting veritie of the true God' (Simon Patericke, dedicatory epistle of 1577 to Gentillet's *Discourse ... against Nicholas Machiavell* [1602], quoted in Brown 1933:33–4), called him an 'atheist' (Lodge *Wits Miserie* 1596 in ed 1883, 4:72), or believed that God punished his blasphemies with insanity so he died scoffing (Beard 1597: sig K3).

Yet, as Sir John Harington said, some who publicly objected to 'a litle scurrilitye' enjoyed reading Rabelais 'in theyr studyes' (cited in Hughey 1935:403n). Thus, when writing for publication, Spenser's friend Gabriel Harvey deprecated Rabelais's 'fantastical' raillery, while in his private marginalia he noted, 'In jest, Rabelais: in earnest, Bartas,' praising du Bartas for his 'divine frenzy' (ie, inspiration), Rabelais for his 'humanity,' and Chaucer for both (Harvey ed 1922:55, 67; Stern 1979:175).

We have no proof that Spenser read Rabelais, yet he must have had at least a secondhand awareness of so notorious a writer. The two authors, furthermore, share some strategies and interests. Both send their characters questing, and neither is comfortable with narrative closure. Both work with images of binding and release, investigating what it is that confines or liberates the body, spirit, and divine Word. Each is fascinated by the nature of signs and the abuse of language, although Spenser examines lies and false images and Rabelais particularly scorns the monopolizing jargon of clergymen, lawyers, and professors. Each explores physiology as well as psychology. Each treats marriage, generation, and lineage – whatever connects and perpetuates us. Each is royalist, antipapal, anti-Hapsburg. Like Spenser, Rabelais uses number symbolism (eg, in the Abbey of Thélème, *Gargantua* 52–8) and hints at the occult. Both writers welcome the grotesque and fantastic; true, Rabelais's fantasy is often less dignified (Spenser's Grill in *FQ* II xii prefers hoggishness, but not even he would fly around like the winged pig in *Quart livre* 41, dropping mustard and crying 'Mardigras!'). And Rabelais and Spenser are each hospitable to folk elements in their culture and to medieval forms and tones, whatever Rabelais's humanist devaluation of the romance and his antimonastic and antischolastic joking.

Yet there remain major differences. Rabelais is even more inclusive, for he is primarily writing Menippean satire, not epic, allegory, or romance; hence he shows an entire world (or a comic version of one) with lawyers, cooks, monks, privies, church bells, Parisians, dogs, tripes, professors, and urine. Spenser's sometimes indecent humor is discreet; Rabelais's is boldly obscene. The former's erudition may be deduced from his imagery and references, whereas the latter's splays all over the text's surface; even more than Spenser, Rabelais is bookish, and his comedy is sometimes exclusively verbal, edging into nonsense as a self-enclosed word game. Spenser is willing to violate our expectations; but Rabelais is often carnivalesque, turning a world upside down or inside out, playing with our perspectives.

This last difference is seen in the two authors' treatment of giants. Spenserian and Rabelaisian giants are generally impatient with restraint, earthy, and archaic in origin. But as rebels against reason and spirit, Spenser's almost always seek to destroy, disorder, and dishonor; those of Rabelais, like baby Pantagruel bursting out of his cradle (*Pant* 4), are comic and therapeutic, reversing and shaking a world too bound up for its own health. Doubtless Rabelais would sensibly reject Spenser's Giant with the scales (*FQ* V ii), but because of his position in a culture that he found in some regards repressive, in which to advocate even moderate religious reform was to risk censorship or worse, he was more open to the new and explosive – to the gigantic. To be sure, his young giants, violent, self-indulgent, and anal as they are, speedily mature into figures even St George could admire.

Rabelais has a few passages which seem to anticipate Spenser. For example, like other Christians Gargantua foresees the day when 'all generation and corruption will cease and the elements will escape continual mutation and the longed for rest will be perfected when all things are drawn to their end and first state' (*Pant* 8; cf *FQ* VII viii). Such parallels are rare, however, and although Spenser may have shared Harvey's liking for this great and complex writer, he apparently found nothing that required extended imitation or overt commentary.

ANNE LAKE PRESCOTT

Thomas Beard 1597 *The Theatre of Gods Judgements* (London); John Calvin 1583 *Sermons upon Deuteronomie* tr Arthur Golding (London; *STC* 4442); John Eliot 1593 *Ortho-epia Gallica: Eliots Fruits for the French* (London; rpt Menston, Yorks 1968); Ruth Hughey 1934–5 'The Harington Manuscript at Arundel Castle and Related Documents' *Library* ser 4, 15:388–444.

The standard edition is François Rabelais 1912–55 *Oeuvres* ed Abel Lefranc, et al 6 vols (Paris); there is a modern translation by J.M. Cohen (Harmondsworth 1955), although that of Sir Thomas Urquhart (Books 1 and 2, 1653; Book 3, 1693) and Peter Anthony Motteux (Books 4 and 5 with Urquhart's translation in a complete edition, 1694) has been often reprinted. The standard biography is Jean Plattard 1928 *Vie de François Rabelais* (Paris).

For the early reception of Rabelais, see Huntington Brown 1933 *Rabelais in English Literature* (Cambridge, Mass); Marcel de Grève 1960 'La Légende de Gargantua en Angleterre au XVIe siècle' *RBPH* 38:765–94; de Grève 1961 *L'Interprétation de Rabelais au XVIe siècle* in Etudes rabelaisiennes 3 (Geneva); Anne Lake Prescott 1984 'The Stuart Masque and Pantagruel's Dreams' *ELH* 51:407–30.

Critical studies include Mikhail Bakhtin 1968 *Rabelais and His World* tr Helene Iswolsky (Cambridge, Mass); Michel Beaujour 1969 *Le Jeu de Rabelais* (Paris); Lucien Febvre 1982 *The Problem of Unbelief in the Sixteenth Century: The Religion of Rabelais* tr Beatrice Gottlieb (Cambridge, Mass; first pub Paris 1942); Donald Frame 1977 *François Rabelais* (New York); M[ichael] A. Screech 1979 *Rabelais* (Ithaca, NY); and Florence M. Weinburg 1972 *The Wine and the Will: Rabelais's Bacchic Christianity* (Detroit).

---

radicalism in Spenser On two occasions, Spenser makes set-piece denunciations of lower-class communist ideas. The first is in *Mother Hubberds Tale* (155–66), when the Fox, harking back to 'the golden age of *Saturne* old,' says,

We will not be of anie occupation,
Let such vile vassalls borne to base vocation
Drudge in the world, and for their living droyle
Which have no wit to live withouten toyle
...
For they doo swinke and sweate to feed the other,
Who live like Lords of that which they doo gather,
And yet doo never thanke them for the same,
But as their due by Nature doo it clame.

The Fox combines traditional Golden Age ideas of primitive equality ('sith then we are free borne' 133) with a more modern dislike of wage labor. Spenser leaves us in no doubt that he thinks the root of such theories is reluctance to work.

In *FQ* v ii, he introduces an agitator, the Giant with the scales, who advocates an egalitarian communist society to a great assembly of 'the vulgar,' who 'cluster thicke unto his leasings vaine' (33). Holding a 'huge great paire of ballance in his hand,' the Giant proposes to weigh out everything equally, even 'heaven and hell together' (30–1):

For why, he sayd they all unequall were,
And had encroched uppon others share,
Like as the sea (which plaine he shewed there)
Had worne the earth, so did the fire the aire,
So all the rest did others parts empaire.
And so were realmes and nations run awry.
All which he undertooke for to repaire,
In sort as they were formed aunciently;
And all things would reduce unto equality.

(v ii 32)

When Artegall sees 'How he mis-led the simple peoples traine,' he tries to convince him that if men were made equal 'We are not sure they would so long remaine.' Then he warns that 'All change is perillous' (echoing both Eudoxus and Irenaeus in *Vewe, Var Prose* p 147), to which the Giant, not unreasonably, replies,

Seest not, how badly all things present bee ...
Were it not good that wrong were then surceast,
And from the most, that some were given to the least?

Therefore I will throw downe these mountaines hie,
And make them levell with the lowly plaine ...
Tyrants that make men subject to their law,
I will suppresse, that they no more may raine;
And Lordings curbe, that commons over-aw;
And all the wealth of rich men to the poore will draw.

(v ii 37–8)

Spenser must have heard someone talking like that.

Communist ideas had long existed in England. Langland's Envy argues that 'alle thinges under hevene oughte to ben in comune' (*Piers Plowman* ed 1975, 20.276). When William Tyndale said that every Christian is 'lord of whatsoever another hath,' John Foxe had to explain that the reformer was not advocating communism (Tyndale ed 1848:97–9). More's *Utopia*, which projects a commonwealth in which there is no private property, appeared four times in English translation during the sixteenth century. Thomas Lever and Robert Crowley at the time of the rebellions of 1549 had to combat communist talk, which (they said) resulted not from the Bible in English but from the shortage of learned ministers. Such ideas were bred of idleness, Lever (like Spenser) said; but they were also a reaction to the oppressive extension of commercial values to the countryside by London merchants (see Lever ed 1870:28–9; Crowley ed 1872:132–3, 164–7, etc; also cf *Vewe* pp 125–6, extending the same argument to poets, and *Mother Hubberd* 374–550, on the lack of good preachers). In 1572, the Presbyterian leader John Field found it necessary to denounce communism (quoted in Peel 1915, 1:87).

In the last three decades of Elizabeth's reign, Familist ideas spread in southern and eastern England, picking up something of the Lollard inheritance. Hendrik Niclas' *Terra pacis* (Eng tr 1575) described a society to be attained on earth in which 'noman ... claymeth any thing ... to his owne private use'; 'all whatsoever is theare, is free' (fol 54r-v). In 1589, Bishop Cooper attacked Anabaptists who – like Spenser's Giant – wanted communism and 'a general equality, most dangerous to the society of men' (ed 1882:148; cf Article 38 of the 39 Articles).

Behind this growing concern with communism was the fact that the economic changes of the later sixteenth century worked to the disadvantage of the poorest classes. In the famine year 1596, Oxfordshire rebels denounced wage labor in words that almost echo Spenser's Fox: '"Care not for work, for we shall have a merrier world shortly ... I will work one day and play the other" ... servants were so held in and kept like dogs, that they would be ready to cut their master's throats' (*Calendar of State Papers ... 1595–1597* pp 343–4). 'And henceforward all things shall be in common,' Shakespeare's Jack Cade had proclaimed a year or two earlier (*2 Henry VI* iv vii 18–19).

Spenser was associated with the Leicester-Sidney-Walsingham-Raleigh group at court – middle-of-the-road Protestants. He shared Sidney's hatred and fear of the lower orders: 'Vile caytive wretches, ragged, rude, deformd' (*FQ* ii ix 13; cf also Sidney's 'rascal company ... little better than beasts' in *Old Arcadia* ed 1973a:306–7, and see also *New Arcadia* 1.6 in ed 1987:33.20–40.24 passim). In one of the most openly political passages of *The Faerie Queene*, Burbon (Henri IV) calls upon Artegall for help 'Against these pesants, which have me opprest.' Talus and the knight of Justice make 'cruell havocke of the baser crew' and soon overthrow the 'raskall manie' (v xi 57, 59). Peasants were assumed to be opposed to the Huguenot party which, though it had to fight for its rights, was reassuringly nonrevolutionary.

In home as in foreign politics, Spenser was to the left of center. He (or E.K.) attacked 'Antichristian prelates' (*SC, Maye* 121 gloss) and 'dumb dogs' on the one hand, clergymen who favored presbyterianism and plunderers of the church on the other, praising the moderate Grindal. Men like Lever, Crowley, and Spenser had to dissociate themselves from extreme radicals: attacking egalitarian communism was one way of doing this. When the breakdown of the censorship in the 1640s allowed men like Winstanley, Walwyn, Coppe, and George Foster openly to advocate communism, they were combatted by Thomas Edwards (right of center) and John Lilburne (left of center). Yet the Giant episode in *The Faerie Queene* was reprinted in July 1648 as *The Faerie*

Leveller, or King Charles His Leveller Described in Queen Elizabeth's Dayes (see Frank 1968:209, King 1985:306).

CHRISTOPHER HILL

Calendar of State Papers: Domestic Series, Elizabeth, 1595–1597 1869 ed Mary Anne Everett Green (London); Thomas Cooper 1882 *An Admonition to the People of England (1589)* ed Edward Arber (Birmingham); Crowley ed 1872; Thomas Edwards 1646 *Gangraena* (London); Thomas Lever 1870 *Sermons 1550* ed Edward Arber (London); John Lilburne 1652 *An Apologeticall Narration* (Amsterdam); H[endrik] N[iclas] 1575 *Terra Pacis: A True Testification of the Spirituall Lande of Peace* (Cologne); Albert Peel, ed 1915 *The Seconde Parte of a Register, Being a Calendar of Manuscripts ... Intended for Publication by the Puritans about 1593* 2 vols (Cambridge); William Tyndale 1848 *Doctrinal Treatises* ed Henry Walter, Parker Society (Cambridge).

See also Nicholas P. Canny 1973 'The Ideology of English Colonialization: From Ireland to America' *WMQ* 3rd ser 30:575–98; Canny 1976; Canny 1983; Joseph Frank 1968 *Hobbled Pegasus: A Descriptive Bibliography of Minor English Poetry 1641–1660* (Albuquerque); Christopher Hill 1965 'The Many-Headed Monster in Late Tudor and Early Stuart Political Thinking' in *From the Renaissance to the Counter-Reformation: Essays in Honor of Garrett Mattingly* ed Charles H. Carter (New York) pp 296–324; John N. King 1985 '*The Faerie Leveller*: A 1648 Royalist Reading of *The Faerie Queene*, v.ii.29–54' *HLQ* 48:297–308.

Radigund The benighted, and ultimately beheaded, Amazon warrior in a dramatized exemplum spanning four cantos of the Legend of Justice (*FQ* v iv 21–vii 43). Radigund encounters first Artegall, then Britomart, in a series of parallel events which challenge those tendencies toward error which are inherent in the virtues of each. The episode's unambiguous dramatic reversals and inversions, its unusual finality of resolution, and the absence of gender-based mistaken identities indicate the gravity of Radigund's threat. At the same time, the frequently positive connotations accompanying her name, character, and actions indicate how difficult this threat is to counter or even to recognize, since it so closely resembles virtue and arises from the thwarting of great potential.

Radigund's name has been variously derived from Greek *radios* 'reckless' and *gunē* 'woman,' or from Latin *radere* 'to offend' (in connection with her role as a woman scorned by Bellodant; see iv 30). She has a namesake in the Persian princess Rhodogune, whom Plutarch identifies as the daughter of King Artaxerxes II and wife of Orontes (*Lives* Artaxerxes 27.4). Philostratus says that although 'her dress is not that of an Amazon ... she prays to conquer men ... for I do not think she loves to be loved' (*Imagines* 2.5). Sometimes conflated with her is another Rhodogune, presented in Cooper's *Thesaurus* (1565) as the daughter of King Darius who killed her nurse for persuading her to marry after her first husband's death. And a sixteenth-century French translation of Philostratus mentions a youthful eunuch named Rhodogune, a favorite of Nero, whom the emperor dressed in women's clothes (ed 1614:314–22, first pub 1578).

St Radegund, a virtuous queen of France (519–87), would have been familiar to Spenser through 'The College of Jesus, the Blessed Virgin Mary, St John the Evangelist, and St Rhadegund' in Cambridge, built on the site of an ancient convent of St Radegund's order. Her chastity and humility, including her reputed refusal to consummate an enforced marriage to a conquering prince, Clothar I, engendered the proverb 'as Saintlike as Saint *Radegund*,' used satirically by Spenser in *Mother Hubberds Tale* (497). In the *Acta sanctorum* (Venantius Fortunantis) and *Legenda aurea*, Radegund is known as a dragon-slayer, like St Martha, an antecedent of Britomart (Maury 1896:228–40, Miskimin 1978). And much as Radegund resists Clothar, Britomartis, in the pseudo-Virgilian *Ciris*, refuses to yield to another conquering king, Minos.

As an armed female like Britomart, Radigund shares in the contiguous traditions of Amazons, biblical heroines, poetic (especially epic) martial maids, and mythic figures of the *Venus armata* or *Venus victrix*, the armed or conquering goddess of love. It is as Amazon, however, that she is persistently identified. Most of the more than twenty explicit references to Amazons in *The Faerie Queene* involve Radigund, the only female character so labeled. All but three uses of the term *Amazon* occur in the Radigund episode; the others refer to the Amazon River (twice) and Penthesilea (once). In addition to contemporary travelers' tales like Raleigh's *Discoverie ... of Guiana* (1596), ancient and medieval writings known to Spenser were populated with Amazons whose most significant and invariable characteristic was their placement on the borders of the known world. New World discoveries merely extended those borders; hence, the 1540–1 exploration of the South American river whose name was misinterpreted as 'Amazon' (probably from a dialect phrase meaning 'river that flows upstream') led to stories of warrior women in the area. In *The Faerie Queene*, Spenser fancifully invokes the Amazon River's existence to lend plausibility to his newly created 'happy land of Faery' (II proem 1–2); and he stresses the valor of 'those warlike women' to shame British males to action, in a hortatory use of Amazon matter typical of epic (IV xi 21–2).

Elizabethans, including Spenser, gave varying degrees of credence to these widespread and contradictory accounts of Amazons; and their judgments of Amazons were similarly various (Wright 1940). Individual Amazons like Penthesilea (II iii 31, III iv 2; cf *Aeneid* 1.490–3) and Hippolyta (Shakespeare's *Midsummer Night's Dream*) achieved renown as admirable heroines, while Amazons in groups were regularly treated as savage misanthropists who copulated with men from nearby tribes only to acquire female offspring, male offspring being returned to their fathers, crippled and put to menial tasks, or killed. Their reputed mutilation of one breast to facilitate use of the bow was based on a false etymology from Greek *mazos* 'breast' and *a-* 'without.' They are always depicted in art with breasts intact, however; and their connection with the Ephesian cult of the many-breasted Diana suggests instead an augmentative prefix *a-*, implying a multiplication of female potential (Rupprecht 1974:284). Daughters of Ares and Harmonia, Amazons fought on horseback, bearing shields shaped like the crescent moon and double-edged battle-axes or bows and arrows.

Often invoked as barbarous primitive contrast to the civilized world of the writer, Amazons, like black-skinned Ethiopians, served in the sixteenth century as symbols of the unknown and were counted among such borderline phenomena as giants, unicorns, and centaurs. In the Radigund episode, Spenser draws primarily on two strands of Amazon legend: Hercules' ninth labor, in which he attacked the Amazons and won Hippolyta's cestus, subsequently becoming enslaved in female role and dress to Omphale; and Queen Penthesilea's aid to the Trojans after Hector's funeral and her death at the hands of Achilles, who loved her. Radigund is a highly original character, certainly Amazonian, yet deviating from central traditions in being a city-dweller, part of a love triangle (but cf Hercules-Omphale-Malis), betrayed by a handmaiden (Amazons were known for their loyalty to each other), and slain by another warrior woman. Like Gloriana herself, she is ruler of 'A goodly citty and a mighty one' (V iv 35); and numerous details suggest her role as an imitator of Elizabeth, who was frequently portrayed as armed, occasionally as an Amazon, especially around the time of the Armada.

In the original texts of most ancient and Renaissance epics including *The Faerie Queene*, however, armed females are rarely labeled Amazons. The indiscriminate use of that epithet by translators and scholars has thus been misleading. As epic convention, Radigund and Britomart are direct descendants of Camilla in Virgil's *Aeneid*, the warring Virtues and Vices in Prudentius' *Psychomachia*, and martial maids in medieval narratives of the Trojan War and in sixteenth-century Italian epics, where they are non-Amazonian participants in the lineage of the heroes and patrons of the poems: Bradamante and Marfisa in Boiardo's *Orlando innamorato* and Ariosto's *Orlando furioso*, and Clorinda in Tasso's *Gerusalemme liberata*. At *FQ* III iv 2, Spenser cites the biblical heroine Deborah (actually Jael: Judg 4.21), a common Renaissance precedent for armed females; but he omits the more frequently invoked Judith. Thus Radigund's name and background give her a context which ranges from the universally condemned to the unequivocally admired, in both pagan and Christian terms.

The affinity between Radigund and Britomart established by their common background turns into total fusion – and confusion – of the two during their duel, as a result of the ambiguity of pronominal references (v vii 26–7, 33–4) and the interchangeability of the women's roles in similes of combat (vii 30; cf iv 39). The duel suggests Britomart's confrontation with and conquest of her shadow, the unacknowledged and undermining tendencies within herself.

Radigund's major characteristic in love and war is pride (v 27–8, vii 32–3), which Britomart sets out specifically to attack (vi 18). Their duel imitates that of Bradamante and Marfisa (*Orlando furioso* 36), which sixteenth-century allegorists described as a victory of Virtue over Pride. Pride from thwarted erotic ambition (a reputedly typical Amazon motivation, in Radigund's case involving Bellodant) drove Radigund to vengeful misanthropy, although she had previously observed certain customs of combat and fulfilled her monarchal responsibilities. After her triumph over Artegall, however, she turns to a concupiscence which infects her subordinate Clarinda as well. Radigund 'chaw'd the cud of lovers carefull plight' for Artegall, but could not digest it (v 27). Although Britomart resembles Radigund in this respect, 'Chawing the cud of griefe and inward paine' (vi 19), her passage through the house of Dolon (vi 19–40) and Isis Church (vii 1–24), both episodes enclosed within the Radigund cantos, lead her beyond such incapacitating sentiments.

Radigund is further presented as a negative example when her defeat in battle is followed by the execution of Duessa, identified in the historical allegory with Mary, Queen of Scots. More generally, Radigund is a focus of the Elizabethan controversy over woman's right (by law) and ability (by nature) to govern (see defense of *women). John Knox expresses the Aristotelian position in this debate, denying governance to women unless special divine sanction exists wherein God imbues chosen women with the necessary capacities, a view echoed at *FQ* v v 25. Knox defines the issue thus: 'To promote a woman to beare rule ... is the subversion of good order, of all equitie and justice' (ed 1927:30).

Both Radigund and Britomart acquire the power to rule, demonstrating their ability; but Britomart declines to supplant Radigund, since Radigund's usurpation of authority from men is a form of injustice. Instead, Britomart 'did true Justice deale' (v vii 42) by restoring men to their former positions. Thus, Spenser does not indict all female warrior-rulers who take the initiative in courtship, but only those who go on to pervert the erotic-heroic union. This union is often represented in the Renaissance by the figure of *Venus armata*, a paradoxically harmonious balance of opposites. In iconographic representations of Justice as Mars united with Venus, the conjoining of masculine and feminine is a positive, even ideal, image (see *androgyne, *hermaphrodite). Radigund's radical perversion of this ideal is emphasized in the recurrent word *half*; she appears 'halfe like a man' (iv 36; cf iv 43, v 9). Her state is a one-sided imbalance of extremes which Britomart rejects, as she seeks the ideal balance for herself.

This balance begins to be possible when Britomart acts in direct opposition to Radigund, reversing all of her actions and securing her destruction. First, Britomart succeeds at each test that Artegall fails: she rescues the captive male, uses Talus effectively, refuses Radigund's terms, slays her, and restores equitable rule. Artegall still has much to learn as an exemplar of Justice and as symbolic progenitor. In preparation for his duel, Artegall identifies with his public role, Radigund with private sentiment: 'The Knight, as best was seeming for a Knight, / And th'Amazon, as best it likt her selfe to dight' (v 1). Both identifications are inappropriate and limited extremes. Artegall also participates in transvestism, an inversion of established order, like Hercules, whose myth underlies Book v, enslaved in female dress and role to Omphale (see *sex). By analogy, Radigund is both Iole and Omphale, two figures conflated in Renaissance texts who thereby suggest Radigund's dual nature as object of desire and as dominant female. Transvestism in Book v is typically 'uncouth,' strange or unusual enough to astonish (iv 21, vii 37; see Deut 22.5); and Britomart's first act is to divest Artegall of his womanly garments. Although Elizabethans shunned male transvestism, literary precedents existed: Achilles (a type for Artegall; cf III ii 25) hiding among the women in Lycomedes' court, and Hercules accepting voluntary, expiatory imprisonment under Omphale. These tales represent transvestism as an initiatory immersion in female experience necessary for the full education of the hero, not as the reprehensible subjection of the male to passion seen in the disguise of Pyrochles in Sidney's *Arcadia* (Rose 1964). Artegall must be released by a female who unites masculine and feminine in herself. Britomart has integrated her inner state with her outward actions, governance of her private self with governance of the public state. With Radigund dead, tendencies toward pride, pity, jealousy, and lust within Britomart and Artegall have been destroyed: justice can be infused with mercy and become equity, and chastity can merge with love in marriage, to further both private and public order.

With characteristic subtlety in gender representation, Spenser not only presents Radigund (a bad warrior woman, perverse even in her Amazonian associations) and Britomart (a good warrior woman who is not an Amazon); he also twice invokes Penthesilea (II iii 31, III iv 2). This Amazon, praiseworthy in legend for her union of martial force and beauty, is the heroine of Quintus of Smyrna's *Posthomerica, or The Fall of Troy*, itself a retelling of a lost Trojan epic, *The Aethiopis* or *Amazoneia* attributed to Arctinus of Miletos. Penthesilea 'of Thracian race, comes to aid the Trojans, and after showing great prowess, is killed by Achilles and buried by the Trojans. Achilles then slays Thersites for abusing and reviling him for his supposed love for Penthesilea' (Hesiod in Loeb *Homeric Hymns* p 507). Legend also holds that Eleanor of Aquitaine in the Second Crusade likened herself to Penthesilea (Auerbach ed 1965:210n).

Such ancient depictions and medieval perceptions of Penthesilea as powerful, positive, and beloved within the sexual politics of the Trojan War legend may underlie Spenser's representations of many female characters in *The Faerie Queene*. She has only one epithet, Queen of Amazons, in common with Radigund (v iv 33), and more importantly she is mentioned only in the Legends of Temperance and Chastity, where she is in the company of Diana (II iii 31) and Deborah and Camilla (III iv 2). She shares with Amoret a Thracian origin (IV vii 22) and with Amoret, Belphoebe, and Britomart a mode of dress and movement (Tuve 1940). Her unhelmeting and death, a favorite subject in ancient art and literature, was depicted by Propertius with a Penthesilea 'whose bright beauty conquered the conquering hero, when the helm of gold laid bare her brow' (*Elegies* 3.11) and was a convention of Renaissance epic appearing in two significant moments in *The Faerie Queene*: IV vi 19–22 and V v 11–13.

Carol Schreier Rupprecht

Knox ed 1927; Louis Ferdinand Alfred Maury 1896 *Croyances et légendes du Moyen Age* 2nd ed (Paris); Louis Adrian Montrose 1983 "Shaping Fantasies": Figurations of Gender and Power in Elizabethan Culture' *Representations* 2:61–94; Philostratus 1614 *Les Images* tr Blaise de Vigenère (Paris; first pub 1578); Mark Rose 1964 'Sidney's Womanish Man' *RES* ns 15:353–63; Carol Schreier Rupprecht 1974 'The Martial Maid and the Challenge of Androgyny' *Spring: An Annual of Archetypal Psychology and Jungian Thought* (Zurich) pp 269–93; Alex Shoumatoff 1986 'Amazons' *New Yorker* (24 March):85–107; W[illia]m Blake Tyrrell 1984 *Amazons: A Study in Athenian Mythmaking* (Baltimore); Celeste Turner Wright 1940 'The Amazons in Elizabethan Literature' *SP* 37:433–56.

Raleigh, Letter to (See ed 1912:407–8.) No part of the 1590 edition of *The Faerie Queene* has puzzled readers more than the appended Letter to Raleigh. Addressed to 'the Right noble, and Valorous, Sir Walter *Raleigh*,' it was apparently occasioned by Raleigh's request for some idea of the poet's 'general intention and meaning.' Accordingly, it promises to expound the poet's 'whole intention in the course of this worke' in order to give 'great light to the Reader, for the better understanding.' Unfortunately, for many readers, it offers only generalities, inaccuracies, and inconsistencies.

Critics in the eighteenth and nineteenth centuries were quick to identify the primary ways the Letter frustrates readers. Warton and Upton, for example, object that the intention to make Arthur the central, unifying hero does not agree with the secondary role he plays in the poem. Courthope complains that the Letter does not fulfill the poet's promise: it treats mainly the narrative and structural machinery (the 'plot' of the Fairy Queen's twelve-day feast) rather than the poem's moral or allegorical methods. Jusserand agrees, calling Spenser's allusion to

Aristotle's twelve private virtues 'misleading' and his statements on the allegory insufficient (see *Var* 1). Later criticism, unwilling to believe Spenser would deliberately mislead a reader, tried to argue that the Letter represents either a preliminary stage in Spenser's conception of the poem and that the actual writing significantly altered his plans, or that it represents a later stage but that Spenser did not have time to revise earlier portions of the poem to fit the newly conceived plan. In either case, it is assumed that the Letter was deleted from the 1596 edition because it did not accord with the text of the first six books. With a few notable exceptions, the Letter has been largely ignored by recent criticism.

Some have insisted, however, that the Letter is an invaluable guide to interpretation of the poem, not because it prescribes a particular critical approach but because it offers important authorial ground upon which many interpretive issues can be situated, such as the poem's genre, moral theme, allegorical manner, and narrative method. In the absence of his lost work *The English Poete*, it contains the fullest statement we have of Spenser's understanding of the tasks and ends of poetry. For these reasons, it deserves careful attention. Nor does its omission from the 1596 edition disqualify it as a statement of poetic intent, since its deletion may have been motivated by politics, not poetics.

In the Letter, Spenser's general plan for *The Faerie Queene* seems clear enough. In twelve books (the traditional epic number), the poet will recount the different adventures that befall twelve knights who attend the annual feast of the Fairy Queen and to whom (we learn in Book I xii 18, 41) they will return when they complete their adventures. Each of the twelve knights is a 'patrone' of one of 'the twelve private morall vertues.' Linking the knights are two figures: Prince Arthur, in whom Spenser displays the virtue of magnificence, 'the perfection of all the rest, and conteineth in it them all' (see *magnanimity), and the Fairy Queen, who displays glory, the final end of all virtuous action. This scheme accords with the conversation Bryskett reports in his *Discourse of Civill Life* of a meeting in his home during which Spenser, 'very well read in Philosophie, both morall and naturall,' was called upon to speak but declined: 'I have already undertaken a work tending to the same effect, which is in *heroical verse*, under the title of a *Faerie Queene*, to represent all the moral vertues, assigning to every vertue, a Knight to be the patron and defender of the same: in whose actions and feates of armes and chivalry, the operations of that vertue, whereof he is the protector, are to be expressed, and the vices and unruly appetites that oppose themselves against the same, to be beaten downe and overcome' (ed 1970:21-2).

So described, the poem would be a kind of allegorical romance in which the achievements of a central, 'infolded' hero are 'unfolded' in the adventures of his attendant knights. Arthur, as the general and complex ideal of magnificence achieving an equally general and complex end of glory, represents 'the image of a brave knight, perfected in the twelve private morall vertues.' In order to 'expresse' this conceit, Spenser 'analyzes' it by breaking it up into simpler elements, the twelve separate virtues. Through their sundry actions, the twelve lesser knights 'expresse' in turn the specific 'operations,' the ethical *praxis*, of the virtues. Such a plot is the narrative equivalent of logical analysis (see *logic), which divides and subdivides a general principle into subsidiary aspects and then explicates the particular applications of each. Finally, by showing 'the deedes of Arthure applyable to that vertue, which I write of in that booke,' Spenser attempts to abstract from the particular virtues the general 'perfection' of them all.

The Letter complicates this relatively straightforward plan by announcing that the moral scheme is the result of a prior conceptual division of virtues into private and public. The justification for such a division, Spenser explains, comes from the epic tradition, most notably from Homer, who depicts Agamemnon as the good governor and Ulysses as the virtuous man, and from Tasso, who portrays the virtues of a private man ('that part which they in Philosophy call Ethice') in Rinaldo and those of a public man ('named Politice') in Goffredo. Spenser promises that if the present poem be 'well accepted, I may be perhaps encoraged, to frame the other part of polliticke vertues' in the person of Arthur after he became king.

This private-public division may be the real, though usually unstated, objection many readers have to the Letter. Since our notion of virtue embraces both the private and the public, such a division seems arbitrary and falsifying. Spenser himself seems unable to maintain it, especially in the second installment of the poem: the virtues of justice, courtesy, and even friendship are hardly conceivable outside a political context. Is then the division of virtues in the Letter inapplicable to the poem? Or do we fail to understand Spenser's language? An important clue may be the clause 'as Aristotle hath devised.' Most criticism (eg, Hankins 1971) assumes that it refers to *twelve* moral virtues, and much energy has been devoted to counting that number in the *Nicomachean Ethics*. Yet it is not clear exactly what the clause refers to. If we recall that *devise* can mean 'to divide, separate, part' (*OED*), and that Aristotle discussed private virtue in the *Ethics* and public virtue in the *Politics*, the clause may refer more narrowly to the 'private morall vertues' as a way of separating morality in its private operations from morality in its public application. It is one thing, Aristotle argues in the *Ethics*, to be 'a good man' and quite another to be 'a good citizen' (5.2); yet virtue clearly applies to both human roles. Therefore, rather than referring to either a number of virtues or any specific virtues, the clause may direct us to a method of analyzing virtue in relation either to personal, individual lives or to the public body or commonwealth (see *Politics* 3.4). Certainly this is how medieval and Renaissance moralists wrote both treatises and poems.

We may compare, then, Spenser's own project of two twelve-book poems to Sir Thomas Elyot's plan in *The Boke Named the Governour* (1531) to write not one but two volumes: 'In the fyrste shall be comprehended the beste fourme of education or bringing up of noble children from their nativitie ... The seconde volume ... shall conteine all the reminant ... to the perfection of a juste publike weale' (ed 1883, 1:24). Like Spenser, Elyot never wrote the second treatise; but his proposed division is the same one Spenser sees in Homer, Virgil, Ariosto, and Tasso, and the same one we can see in the ethical tradition from Plato and Aristotle, through Macrobius, Cicero, and Thomas Aquinas, to various Renaissance conduct and courtesy books.

So interpreted, the Letter's reference to Aristotle will not help us to understand what twelve virtues Spenser had in mind, for the schemes of Aristotle, Bryskett, and even Francesco Piccolomini (the philosophers most frequently cited) do not accord with *The Faerie Queene* as we have it. Instead, we may assume that 'Aristotle' is Spenser's way of referring to a tradition of ethical exegesis that from antiquity through the Renaissance analyzed the qualities and characteristics of any one virtue by means of elaborate classification, division and subdivision, opposing vices, and contexts of operation, both private and public, individual and political. Such a method of explication, furthermore, is like romance narrative in the way it unfolds and infolds relations so that any single virtue, like any single romance 'character,' involves every other one (cf *Ethics* 6.13). The 'plot' of Renaissance narrative and analysis alike consists of articulating this complex web of ethical relationships.

To understand Spenser's announced moral plan in this manner may clarify as well what he means by calling the poem 'a continued Allegory, or darke conceit' that is 'coloured with an historicall fiction.' If one pole of the allegory is oriented toward private virtue, the 'history' points toward public virtue. We see this most clearly in the description of the Fairy Queen: 'In that Faery Queene I meane glory in my generall intention, but in my particular I conceive the most excellent and glorious person of our soveraine the Queene, and her kingdome in Faery land.' The 'history,' the narrative or story of the poem, is conceived as a particular public or political application of general private morality. History, human action portrayed or imagined in time (whether a mythical past or an actual present), puts individual virtue to public work. So Guyon, for example, may 'represent' or 'express' temperance; but once he is set to work in an 'historical' narrative, that virtue becomes a 'continued' set of private relationships and political consequences.

Such 'continued' relations also affect our understanding of Spenser's overall intentions. His general end, he says in the Letter, 'is to fashion a gentleman or noble person in vertuous and gentle discipline.' This, we might say, is a private effect of the power of the poem to educate and move an individual reader. But Spenser's humanism will not allow him to stop here. When he comes to discuss the historical frame – Arthur's search for the Fairy Queen and the adventures of the knights – he predicates, even before the poem itself refers to mighty wars 'Twixt that great faery Queene and Paynim king' (I xi 7), a grander social reform. The 'Poet historical,' by 'recoursing to the thinges forepaste, and divining of thinges to come, maketh a pleasing Analysis of all' – of all time, all history, all people. To be a 'Poet historical' is to accept the responsibilities of a national epic: to help reform society. To fashion a gentleman, therefore, is to make, or help to make, a country. Reunion with the Fairy Queen, glory, or even, in Christian terms, salvation may be the logical end of any of the poem's 'private' stories; but a reformed kingdom, Fairyland or England, is the necessary political counterpart of its 'history.' Like Milton's, Spenser's intentions embrace a work that would be 'doctrinal and exemplary to a nation.'

The Letter situates *The Faerie Queene* midway between two very different literary genres, romance and epic. Early criticism tended to treat the poem as romance and to interpret both its manner and its matter according to the generic conventions of works like Malory's *Morte Darthur* and Ariosto's *Orlando furioso*. Later criticism treated it as romance-epic, pointing to Renaissance amalgams like Tasso's *Gerusalemme liberata* and noting the difficulties such a mixed form occasions. Recent criticism has focused primarily on Spenser's epic conventions, especially on his links to Virgil (see *heroic poem before Spenser). Yet the generic complexities of *The Faerie Queene* have not been adequately explored. Romance, epic, courtesy book, history, allegory, ethical treatise, even the saint's life – participating in each, the poem as a whole still eludes generic description and definition.

If the Letter has important implications for Spenser's general plan and generic methods, it also raises particular questions about the poem's narrative and characters. These questions are especially important for modern criticism which, as a rule, takes one of these to be the function of the other. Narrative is taken to be the logical or 'realized' extension of character. But Spenser says his poem is 'coloured' with an historical fiction. To color, in this sense, is to embellish rhetorically or figuratively, and the coloring of narrative would thus be a function of the 'continued Allegory.' One consequence of taking narrative in this metaphorical or allegorical sense is that, rather than looking for a sequential, cause-and-effect logic to the progress of incidents, we would see each incident as an autonomous 'accident' or 'aspect' of the particular virtue a knight's actions express. When Spenser says of Book III, therefore, that he intermeddles many adventures 'rather as Accidents, then intendments,' he means that those adventures function as thematic attributes, not as effects or logical consequences. Incidents in the narrative line are to be read as changes to which a given virtue is subject according to various situations. The narrative, in short, is more like a set of grammatical inflections or declensions than the modern, novelistic notion of a syntactically complete sentence.

This notion of narrative inflection is valid only so long as the 'continued Allegory' of the 'historicall fiction' itself is underemphasized. It has been argued that the Letter denies any literal story or narrative in *The Faerie Queene* (Kouwenhoven 1983). Yet if the narrative is dismissed as illusory, private virtue becomes arbitrarily closed off from any social or even temporal extension. Such an argument deprives Spenser's poem of the double perspective allegory itself requires of perceiving thematic import in both segmented moments and narrative progress. Surely this is one reason that Spenser ends the Letter by focusing on such progress. Although he does not write as an historiographer, he speaks of past, present, and future, and his narrative 'history' is a significant part of the moral lesson he has to teach.

The same matter may be raised about character. Read strictly, the Letter implies that characters are personifications or representations. Gloriana is one aspect of Elizabeth; Belphoebe is another, with other aspects 'shadowed' in other figures. Character is thus figurative, and we cannot speak of intentions, feelings, or motivations: a given character is merely the trajectory of some unknown *x* mapped by an algebraic formula of relationships onto a functional grid. There can be no doubt that this view describes certain characters. Sansfoy, for example, is no more than a particular 'vice and unruly appetite' opposing the virtue of which Redcrosse is protector. Yet whether this is true of all characters is doubtful. The 'history' of a knight's or a lady's adventures cannot be dismissed as mere appearance. Indeed, the distinction Spenser draws between the value of an abstract rule and the profit of a particularized 'ensample' privileges the concept of person. To enact the operations of a virtue, some character or personality must be portrayed as acting in time. Character, like narrative, is both a shadow and a substance, to be read *through* and read *in*.

In Spenser's announced intention 'to fashion a gentleman or noble person in vertuous and gentle discipline,' to *fashion* means not only 'to represent or delineate,' but also 'to train and educate,' even 'to create or make.' The term *discipline* carries a similar complex meaning, for it refers both to moral teaching in general and, more specifically, to instruction which has as its aim the reformation of the pupil to proper conduct. The entire phrase, then, may be taken as referring narratively to Arthur, whom the poem will portray, and extra-narratively to the reader, whom it will attempt to fashion.

Once formulated in this way, both Spenser's assumptions about poetry's ethical effects and his setting forth an 'image' of a virtuous knight for the reader to imitate remind us of the arguments of Sidney, who asserts that the principal functions of poetry are to instruct, to delight, and to move a reader to virtuous action. Spenser allows that some may be displeased by his method of instruction, preferring 'good discipline delivered plainly in way of precepts, or sermoned at large' rather than 'clowdily enwrapped in Allegoricall devises' (here again he may mean 'divisions' rather than figurative 'devices'). But such readers forget that 'Xenophon [is] preferred before Plato, for that the one in the exquisite depth of his judgement, formed a Commune welth such as it should be, but the other in the person of Cyrus and the Persians fashioned a governement such as might best be: So much more profitable and gratious is doctrine by ensample, then by rule.' This is exactly the argument and the literary illustration to which Sidney consistently returns in the debate between the historian, the philosopher, and the poet: 'But even in the most excellent determination of goodness, what philosopher's counsel can so readily direct a prince, as the feigned Cyrus in Xenophon' (ed 1973b:86). Furthermore, as Sidney argues, poetry is ethically effective because it offers a credible historical model for a reader's imitation. It is not simply imaginative, like Plato's feigned Republic, 'but so far substantially it worketh, not only to make a Cyrus ... but to bestow a Cyrus upon the world to make many Cyruses' (p 79). Like Sidney, Spenser conceives of poetry as inciting the reader to remake and refashion himself according to the notable image of perfected virtue that the poem presents. In terms of its 'ending end,' the poem offers only 'an imaginative groundplot' for the reader's own profitable 'invention' (p 103).

Such a poetic end means that Spenser, like Sidney, must keep in constant view the possibility that a reader may misunderstand the poem. This privileging of the reader and of the risks to right reading may well be one of the least-appreciated aspects of the Letter. Perhaps for this reason, it begins not with Spenser's plan for the poem but with his fear that it could be 'doubtfully ... construed' by 'gealous opinions and misconstructions' or because it seems 'tedious and confused.' Spenser may have been led to this worry over the reader's misconstruing and misconstructing by Sidney's *Defence*, for there, too, the grand claims for poetry are always tempered by a recognition that some readers are either too dull or too hardened in vice to be properly affected by it. Spenser says he chose the history of Prince Arthur because it was 'furthest from the daunger of envy, and suspition of present time.' But as *The Faerie Queene* itself shows, whether in the 'rugged forhead' (IV proem 1) censuring Book III or in the Blatant Beast attacking the poet at the end of Book VI, the poem cannot be defended against the misconstructions of a calumniating reader. Still, the emphasis the Letter places upon the reader's task as interpreter does predict that

Spenser's efforts to expound his own intentions will not be limited to this appendix, just as it suggests that the 'implied reader' will be one of the poem's central characters.

A. LEIGH DENEEF

Alpers 1967b; Colie 1973; William Covell and Ralph Knevett in *Sp All* pp 41, 187–8; Fichter 1982; Goldberg 1981; Hamilton 1961a; Horton 1978; Kouwenhoven 1983; Tuve 1966.

Raleigh, Walter (1554–1618) Spenser's close contemporary, Raleigh was born in Devonshire of a seafaring family. To the end of his life, he was devoted to overseas adventure in competition with Spain in order to establish England as an empire. Yet exploration and colonization were only two of his many interests: he was a courtier, a poet, a historian, a warrior, even at times a scientist. His wide-ranging abilities and personal attractiveness made him the object of popular attention, and for some years he was a favorite of Queen Elizabeth. For Spenser, Raleigh was more than a patron. In the explanatory Letter to Raleigh of the 1590 *Faerie Queene* (ending with the salutation 'Yours most humbly affectionate'), in a dedicatory sonnet (where he is called 'sommers Nightingale'), and in the dedication and body of *Colin Clout*, there are suggestions of strong ties approaching a close personal friendship. Raleigh responded with two commendatory sonnets to *The Faerie Queene*.

After local schooling and perhaps a brief stay at Oxford, Raleigh went to France in a volunteer army supporting the Protestant faction in the wars of religion. He returned to Oriel College, Oxford, from 1572 to 1574, after which he became a student at the Middle Temple, a common route to court. From this period comes his first firmly dated work, a verse commendation of Gascoigne's *Steele Glas* (1576).

After an unsuccessful expedition to North America with his half-brother Humphrey Gilbert in 1578–9, Raleigh embarked on the first phase of his spectacular rise in the Queen's favor. He had been given a position in the retinue of Lord Grey of Wilton, Lord Deputy of Ireland, to command a force against the Munster rebellion. Since Spenser was Grey's secretary, the two very likely met then. Raleigh was in charge of the troops at the siege and massacre of Spanish, Italian, and Irish soldiers at Smerwick in 1580 (described in retrospect in *Vewe*); Spenser as Grey's secretary was responsible for the official report of the action. Raleigh served until late 1581 and then returned to court. There his attractiveness, intelligence, energy, and remarkable presence – as well as his uncompromising attitude towards the Irish – gained him notice. Within a few years, he became a knight, a Member of Parliament for Devon, the recipient of the Queen's patent for colonization in America, and Captain of the Queen's Guard.

Because of his rapid advancement, Raleigh was resented, ostensibly for his fairly humble origins though perhaps for his aloofness and independence. (In his *Brief Lives*, Aubrey says that Raleigh was known to be 'damnable proud' ed 1949:254.) Perhaps friction with the young Earl of Essex, one of his rivals, occasioned his temporary removal to Ireland in 1589. During that year, from July to November, he inspected the vast estates he had managed to accumulate after the confiscation of the lands of the Desmonds. At that time, Spenser was Clerk of the Council of Munster and lived at Kilcolman. There, on one or possibly more occasions, Raleigh came to see him. Their encounter is memorialized in *Colin Clouts Come Home Againe*.

In the poem, Colin tells his shepherd friends of a visit to him by the 'shepheard of the Ocean.' The narrative is a barely disguised account of Raleigh's visit to Spenser, their voyage to the court where Spenser presented *The Faerie Queene* to Elizabeth, Spenser's eventual disgust with the court, and his return to Ireland. The 'shepheard of the Ocean' is clearly Raleigh, who may by this time have begun work on some early version of a poem called *The Ocean to Cynthia* (1592?; only the purported 11th and 12th books – or, more likely, 21st and 22nd – see Clanton 1985 – have survived, if indeed the rest was ever written). Although Raleigh's poem, or part of it, may postdate the presumed composition of *Colin Clout* (1591?), Spenser's poem was not published until 1595, and may have been revised to include the reference. Of course, Raleigh may have been planning his poem long before. It is clear, though, that this was the period of their closest association. In *Colin Clout*, we get a picture of an unusually close relationship between poet and patron.

This picture is confirmed in the various references to Raleigh in the 1590 *Faerie Queene*: he is the recipient of the explanatory Letter; he receives one of the dedicatory sonnets, the strongest in its expression of personal feeling; he is referred to indirectly at III proem 4 as the 'gracious servant' who has written so well about Cynthia (Elizabeth); and he appears in a fairly transparent disguise as Timias, lover of Belphoebe, in III v. The last of these is perhaps of greatest interest, for the narrative of III v is taken up again in the 1596 *Faerie Queene* at IV vii-viii. The two-part story of Timias and Belphoebe offers a glimpse into Raleigh's fortunes at Elizabeth's court.

Belphoebe (an allegorical figure for Elizabeth, as both the Letter and III proem 5 explain), already present at II iii, returns at III v to save Timias. The young Squire has killed the three fosters at the ford; the historical parallel is Raleigh's famous defeat of the ambushing Irish on the road between Youghal and Cork in 1581 and, conflated with it, Raleigh's part in overcoming the revolt of the Earl of Desmond and his two brothers. Although Timias is victorious, he suffers a grievous wound. Belphoebe seeks out herbs to cure him (one of these herbs may be – the narrator is unsure – the 'divine *Tobacco*' [32], which Raleigh was celebrated for having introduced to court). Timias soon falls in love, now even more desperately wounded by an 'unwary dart' from Belphoebe's eyes (42). The historical allegory is complex. The wound by a character representing lust may be a warning to Raleigh. The cure by Belphoebe and Timias' subsequent passion indicate Raleigh's dependence on Elizabeth and what she stands for in the figure of Belphoebe: chastity and purity of conduct. Belphoebe's interest in the Squire suggests Elizabeth's known patronage and perhaps love for Raleigh.

The tale is picked up again at IV vii, where Amoret flees from Lust and is saved by Timias. Yet Timias cannot kill Lust; the monster may be defeated only by Belphoebe. It seems, however, that Timias for a moment succumbs to lust, for when Belphoebe returns from releasing Aemylia she finds him kissing and touching his unconscious 'new lovely mate' Amoret (35). His waywardness, her anger, his subsequent banishment, and their final reconciliation all have historical parallels. In 1591, Raleigh had secretly married Elizabeth Throckmorton, a lady-in-waiting to the Queen, and shortly after had become the father of their child. In her anger, the Queen imprisoned the offending couple in July 1592, releasing them only some months later. Raleigh's reconciliation with the Queen was in part effected by Arthur Throckmorton, Lady Raleigh's brother, who gave a ring containing a heart-shaped ruby to the Queen as a sign of the family's good will. In canto viii, a turtledove carries a 'Ruby of right perfect hew, / Shap'd like a heart, yet bleeding of the wound' from Timias to Belphoebe, then lures her back to him by refusing to give her the jewel (6–12). The narrative in cantos vii-viii would seem to reconstruct closely the events of Raleigh's disgrace. Yet Spenser does not come down firmly on either side. Timias/Raleigh is wrong for having wavered; Belphoebe/Elizabeth is excessive in rejecting her lover. Although Timias is represented as returning to Belphoebe, Raleigh returns to Elizabeth's somewhat diminished favor accompanied by the new 'mate' that Timias rejects in the poem.

Sir Walter and Lady Raleigh may also have a role in Book VI. Timias, now in the good favor of Belphoebe (v 12), has been rescued from Despetto, Decetto, and Defetto by Arthur, though during the episode he has been bitten by the Blatant Beast. Together they come upon the Salvage Man and Serena, who has likewise been wounded. The wounds of Timias and Serena begin to fester, and they are taken to the Hermit, who tells them the moral cure for this corrupting bite (vi 7–14). The episode suggests that Raleigh and his wife (named 'Serena' by him in a manuscript poem) are still subject to the detracting rumors of the envious and spiteful. The interesting parallel between the ambush of the fosters and of the three kinds of deceit (found respectively in canto v of the concluding books of 1590 and 1596) suggests that Raleigh still needs to exercise care. In each episode, however, he is vindicated (reconciled or cured). Yet in both instances, there is a strong implication that he has been partly at fault for his troubles.

By 1597, Raleigh was back in favor and

remained so until Elizabeth's death. Under James, however, his life underwent a sad change. For thirteen years, he was imprisoned for alleged involvement in the Main Plot of 1603. During these years he wrote his monumental *History of the World*, dedicated to the young and sympathetic Prince Henry. Unfortunately, Henry died in 1612. Raleigh published the *History* in 1614. In 1618 he was executed.

JERRY LEATH MILLS

The standard collected edition is still Raleigh ed 1829; for the poems, see Raleigh ed 1951. Perhaps the most generally useful of the biographies is J.H. Adamson and H.F. Folland 1969 *The Shepherd of the Ocean: An Account of Sir Walter Ralegh and His Times* (Boston); see also A.L. Rowse 1962 *Sir Walter Ralegh: His Family and Private Life* (New York; in London as *Ralegh and the Throckmortons*), which has details about the Throckmorton affair; and Greenblatt 1973, a study of some presumed relationships between Raleigh's life and art. The standard work on Raleigh's writing is Pierre Lefranc 1968 *Sir Walter Ralegh, écrivain: l'Oeuvre et les idées* (Quebec); for his religious and philosophical ideas, see Ernest A. Strathmann 1951 *Sir Walter Ralegh: A Study in Elizabethan Skepticism* (New York). The question of whether the surviving fragment of *The Ocean to Cynthia* constitutes books 11 and 12 or 21 and 22 would seem to be resolved (in favor of 21 and 22) by Stacy M. Clanton 1985 'The "Number" of Sir Walter Ralegh's *Booke of the Ocean to Scinthia*' *SP* 82:200–11.

The numerous studies relating Raleigh and Spenser include Bednarz 1983; Brink 1972, on Arthur Throckmorton's gift; H.M. English, Jr 1960 'Spenser's Accommodation of Allegory to History in the Story of Timias and Belphoebe' *JEGP* 59:417–29; Oakeshott 1960, esp pp 81–99; Oakeshott 1971, a description of a 1617 folio edition annotated by Lady Raleigh for her son, with numerous identifications of allegorical characters; and O'Connell 1977. Jerry Leath Mills 1986 *Sir Walter Raleigh: A Reference Guide* (Boston) annotates writings about Raleigh 1901–84; see also Christopher M. Armitage 1987 *Sir Walter Ralegh: An Annotated Bibliography* (Chapel Hill).

reader in *The Faerie Queene* Allegory even more than other modes of literature involves the activity of an interpreter, negotiating by whatever means the distance between the thing said and the other (Gr *allos*) thing meant. A definition of the reader who interprets the text is thus of crucial importance to any study of *The Faerie Queene*. Living in an age very self-conscious about the nature of reading (partly as a result of the growth of book-printing and therefore of literacy – for both men and women – in the vulgar and the learned tongues), Spenser seems to have been especially concerned with the activity of the reader, however that person may be identified.

With the publication of *The Shepheardes Calender* and E.K.'s glosses, Spenser presented his work accompanied by a reader's commentary and notes – almost as if the text would not be complete without evidence of at least one reader's activity. With his seventeen sonnets dedicating the first installment of *The Faerie Queene* to noble, would-be readers (including 'all the gratious and beautifull Ladies in the Court'), Spenser is exceptional among Elizabethan poets in wooing readers. *Amoretti* shows a similar concern for the reader in its opening sonnet: 'Happy ye leaves when as those lilly hands ... shall handle you ... And happy lines, on which ... those lamping eyes will ... look ... and reade.'

Although there are numerous recent critical theories which focus on the reader and offer useful terms to describe the active reading demanded by Spenser, one should begin by considering what he and his contemporaries appear to have assumed the reader's activity to include. The most direct comment we have from Spenser himself about the activity of his reader is his Letter to Raleigh. Its opening recognition of 'how doubtfully all Allegories may be construed' indicates at once that the reader is engaged in a difficult and risky process. To make his intentions clearer – and a reading of his poem easier – Spenser explains that his 'generall end' is 'to fashion a gentleman or noble person in vertuous and gentle discipline.' Such fashioning refers to the poem's presentation of Arthur and the other titular knights, but it also extends to the change Spenser expects in his readers: as they read the poem, they are supposed to become more 'vertuous' and 'gentle.' How he organizes his poem to effect this change is, of course, the main problem; but it is necessary to stress that, at least in the Letter, he does expect a change (for the better) to occur. He shares this sense of the power of poetry to move the reader to virtue with Sidney, who argues in the *Defence of Poetry* that the poet's image 'so far substantially ... worketh, not only to make a Cyrus ... but to bestow a Cyrus upon the world to make many Cyruses, if they will learn aright why and how that maker made him' (ed 1973b:79).

The Letter also implicitly defines two paradigmatic readers. The first is Raleigh himself, who in his remarkably broad range of relations to Spenser's text may represent the equally broad range of political positions involved in a contemporary reading of the epic. As fellow poet, fellow colonial administrator in Ireland, and successful courtier, Raleigh-as-reader embodies the underlying political nature of the reader's activity that Spenser addresses in his discussion of the various representations of Elizabeth within the poem.

The second reader indicated by both Letter and dedication is Elizabeth, whose reading is the one most actively signaled in the text itself, in the proem to each book. The dedication, consecrating the poet's labors 'to live with the eternitie' of her fame, not only acknowledges the special political nature of the poem's genre (which necessarily focuses on an imperial moment in history and that moment's 'empresse'); it also effectively includes within the posterity of readers a sense of gender difference. Historically speaking, then, Spenser's readers include both men and women, a fact borne out by the dedicatory sonnets to various ladies of the court as well as by specific addresses to women readers in Book III. We should not be surprised: Spenser's subject is dual – 'Fierce warres and faithfull loves' – and so the 'vertuous and gentle discipline' he seeks to effect in his readers incorporates not only martial valor but a gentleness born of a disciplined sexuality that includes the experiences of both sexes. Indeed, even 'prowesse martiall' is attributed to women as well as men (III ii 1–2).

Finally, the Letter also takes care to defend the singleness of the poem's action, in essence defending the Italianate interlace form of the romance-epic against an Aristotelian demand for unified epic structure. This defense of the poem's form also says something about its historical audience: a segmented, interwoven, carefully pieced structure is designed for the kind of slow-motion analysis of moral and political responsiveness necessary to a man or a woman involved in the weblike organization of the court. The poem's form may be said to reflect the interweave of aristocratic and landed-gentry dependencies among complexly interrelated family connections (based in sexuality) characteristic of Spenser's first readers.

Characterizing Spenser's readers by what can be gleaned from the Letter to Raleigh, we may say that the reader is engaged in a difficult activity where interpretation will often be doubtful, where mistaken 'construings' or interpretations will often take place, and where issues of sexual politics will be of central importance (and will include not only the imperial sexual politics of Elizabeth's regime, but sexual relations of a more intimate and less overtly political kind). The main question remains: how does Spenser attempt to 'fashion' his reader, to effect an ethical improvement?

One of his main narrative strategies is to create a homologous relation between the reader's experience in reading the text and the protagonist's experiences in the narrative. At its simplest, the reader may have difficulty in negotiating the grammar and rhetorical rhythms of the verse that parallels the protagonist's difficulty in traversing the landscape. For example, when Redcrosse and Una are interrupted in their quest by a 'suddeine' rainstorm that forces them to seek cover in what turns out to be the Wood of Error (I i 6), the sudden change in narrative direction is matched by an abrupt change in the organization of the stanza itself. The first three stanzas of the canto have described the knight, and the next two the lady. Stanza 6 begins with a description of the dwarf, and the reader will expect that with a comparable diminution, this whole stanza will be devoted to him. This expectation is thwarted, however: the description ends suddenly in the middle of the fourth line with a full stop at the caesura, a major rhythmic break reinforced by a trochaic inversion in the fourth foot: 'Of needments at his backe. Thus as they past.' This reversal of expectations replicates for the reader the sense of suddenness with which the rainstorm comes in the narrative. (That this rainstorm is described in sexual terms, with Jove raining into his 'Lemans lap,' hints at the sexual nature of ensuing surprises and narrative divagations.)

Spenser arranges even more complex homologies with the catalogue of trees that immediately follows. At the same time that Una and her knight become lost in the Wood of Error, the reader loses a sense of forward motion while negotiating the set piece of the tree catalogue that extends for a virtuoso thirteen lines, in which the poet displays for his learned reader his own ordering powers and vies with all the tree catalogues written by his precursors. If one may say that Una and the knight become lost in a dangerous wood because they cannot tell the forest for the trees (Cheney 1966:27), one may add that the reader will have experienced a similar error, analyzing the tree catalogue for its echoing of prior catalogues, and becoming as lost in a list of the names of earlier poets as the pair in the forest become in praising the trees themselves.

At the last item in the list, 'the Maple seeldom inward sound,' the reader may begin to suspect that the kind of poetic control displayed by a catalogue which privileges 'The Laurell, meed of mightie Conquerours / And Poets sage' (9), is misleading in what purports to be a Christian heroic poem, in which a truly sage poet ought to praise God rather than the conquering might of a human hero. The very process of being misled by traditional assumptions about heroism and heroic poetry is what reader and hero share in their parallel travels through the tree catalogue and the mental landscape it represents. The reader will necessarily assume – as do Una and Redcrosse – that once the hero cuts off Error's head he has vanquished her and they will no longer be subject to 'error.' Yet immediately afterwards they are tricked by Archimago, who dis-pairs them and sends them wandering in a convoluted and 'erroneous' path that does not end until Arthur extricates Redcrosse from Orgoglio's dungeon, repairing Una and her knight. (That the knight ends up in the dungeon after a series of sexual errors has much to do with the implicitly sexual content of his battle with Error.) Mistaken interpretations parallel the hero's mistaken judgments. Both reader and hero must learn to read the internal and external landscape more accurately.

In another example of the poem's homologies, Spenser tests the reader by providing an ambiguous reference. The reading of grammar (simply deciding which is the proper antecedent to a pronoun) becomes an ethical, theological, even eschatological choice. Thus, when Una celebrates Redcrosse's victory over the Dragon, Spenser writes, 'Then God she praysd, and thankt her faithfull knight, / That had atchiev'd so great a conquest by his might' (xi 55). Spenser's text invites the reader to decide whether the antecedent of *his* is *God* or *knight*. The problem posed by the ambiguous reference is the same problem the knight has learned to confront in all his trials and mistakings of the way: his own unaided strength can only end in accomplishing 'ill,' for 'all the good is Gods, both power and eke will' (x 1). Not to notice the ambiguity is an error readers may easily make; it means that they have neither understood the significance of Una's first cry to the knight to add faith unto his force nor seen how the narrative of the middle cantos has been explaining just what she meant. In such a way, the narrative not only insists that the reader make interpretive choices; it interprets those choices. Later, Redcrosse corrects Guyon's rather traditional heroic view of what the story of the 'Errant damozel' has meant: 'His be the praise, that this atchiev'ment wrought, / Who made my hand the organ of his might' (II i 33).

The problem with the pronoun in Una's prayer of thanksgiving is a more Miltonic either-or choice than Spenser usually offers. Unfortunately for the reader, things are seldom so clear in *The Faerie Queene*, especially in the later books which do not organize themselves along the eschatological lines of Book I. There are fewer signals that a given interpretation is right or wrong, just as there are fewer clear-cut victories for the protagonists. The heroes may be battling monsters and the reader the rules of grammar, but the ethical issues are comparable.

At the outset, Spenser indicates the homology between the experience of reading and the action of the narrative in the text itself when he characterizes Una and Redcrosse as readers. Error's vomit includes books, and the slimy creatures associated with her are 'blacke as inke' (i 22). Without losing a sense of the literal reality of such a hideous monster, Spenser signals the bookishness of the whole experience in which the knight is engaged; later, Archimago has such dangerous words in his book that Spenser directly tells his reader, 'Let none them read' (i 37). So, too, the knight gives Arthur a copy of the New Testament, the teachings of which he promptly forgets when he attempts to wreak an Old Testament revenge on Despair. Only in the house of Holiness is he taught how to read or understand that book; and finally his very identity is expressed in the vocabulary of reading, especially when he thanks Contemplation for having 'red aright' his name and nation (x 67). Other protagonists may be said to be readers as well: Guyon and Arthur take time to read history in Book II; and in Book III, Britomart confronts a powerfully evil poet in Busirane.

Britomart raises anew the problem of the reader's gender. At the opening of Book III, she becomes separated from the male knights with whom she has been traveling because she chooses not to pursue Florimell and the Foster. By this choice, Spenser establishes her subjective viewpoint as gender-specific. If the homology between reading and narrative experience is to hold, we must say that the reader is thereby asked to observe the action of this book from a specifically feminine viewpoint. Such a perspective does seem to be requested by Spenser's repeated addresses to specifically female readers. It may also help to explain the anomalous position of the Garden of Adonis, a place to which no character in the narrative travels – unless, as it seems fair to say, the reader is a character within the text. Addressed at the outset to those ladies who wish to know how Belphoebe 'So great perfections did in her compile' (vi 1), the canto purports to describe her training. Instead, we are given a vision of the Garden itself where (rather parenthetically) we are told that Belphoebe's twin sister Amoret was reared. The swerve away from Belphoebe suggests that Spenser is less interested in her Elizabeth-like virginity than in a female sexuality which is actively engaged with male sexuality, although the latter, as presented in the character of Adonis, is considered without its normal social characteristic of male dominance. Venus is in control of the pleasures of the Garden, and her power is presented as a maternal containment, the Garden itself a place of womblike security and 'everlasting joy' (49), outside of time and beyond the threat of anything the boar may represent in the Adonis story. Using a twentieth-century vocabulary, we may say that Spenser rewrites the myth of Adonis to suppress as well as he can Oedipal fears of castration; but we may also say that from the female perspective fears of such a wound are beside the point. The wound to be feared in Book III is figured in Busirane's rape of Amoret, a wounding and a fear that Britomart heals with her rescue of Amoret, achieved in great part because she is such a poor reader of Busirane's Petrarchan mottos. Britomart is 'bold' where the masculine-scripted discourse of Petrarchan (or courtly love) poetics would have her 'Be not too bold' (xi 54), that is, be restrained by a fear of sexuality represented in the character of Daunger, borrowed from the *Romance of the Rose*, an allegory which similarly deals with complicated questions of erotic desire and the cosmic purposes of sexuality.

The reader of Spenser's epic needs to be aware of all the contextual scripts within which Spenser writes his narratives. Moving from Genesis and Revelation in Book I, to Ovid and the *Romance of the Rose* in Book III, to contemporary history and politics in Books V and VI (and this list is just a start), he embeds other texts within his own, and makes it necessary to read his densely allusive narrative as a palimpsest of texts. But it is clear from his testimony in the Letter to Raleigh that we are not to assume that reading consists only in interpretation, in tracking down the sources of allusions, or labeling the features in his landscapes with the most abstract nouns that will serve. Instead, reading proceeds by a process of fits and starts, including constant revisions of prior judgments that are proved to be mistaken or at least incomplete. At times, more or less perspicuous moments of vision irradiate the dark places in the text; but we are always meant to be aware that our putting together of the often disparate pieces of Spenser's complex structure says just as much about us as readers as it does about the text Spenser has written. It finally reads us, not we it. (See also *narrator.)

MAUREEN QUILLIGAN

Goldberg 1981; Gross 1985; Quilligan 1983: Susan R. Suleiman and Inge Crosman, eds 1980 *The Reader in the Text: Essays on Audience and Interpretation* (Princeton); Jane P. Tompkins, ed 1980 *Reader Response Criticism: From Formalism to Post-Structuralism* (Baltimore).

reading, Spenser's The range and depth of Spenser's reading have not been precisely ascertained; and in the absence of definitive information, one should guard against the two extremes of exaggerating or underestimating the poet's erudition. As an alumnus of Merchant Taylors' School and a Master of Arts at Cambridge, Spenser undoubtedly received a generous education and (though his surviving Latin verses are undistinguished) a reasonable command of the Latin language. His contributions to van der Noot's *Theatre* reveal his knowledge of French at a relatively early age; and as early as 1580, he knew enough Italian to read Ariosto, whom he hoped to overgo. Yet, though reasonably well read, Spenser was hardly a polymath; and during his busy life in Ireland, his access to books would have been very limited. For his exploitation of classical (and in particular Greek) literature, he apparently relied to a considerable extent on secondary materials such as Renaissance dictionaries and the manuals compiled by the mythographers. Such reliance, however, does not preclude a limited knowledge of the primary sources themselves.

The extent of Spenser's reading has often been greatly exaggerated. In 'Spensers Belesenheit' (1908), Wilhelm Riedner gives a very inflated account of the poet's alleged debt to classical antiquity, extolling him as one of the most learned men of his time, with both an extraordinary range of reading and familiarity with major and minor authors of Greece and Rome. Few modern scholars would endorse these views, and recent scholarship generally takes a more conservative attitude toward Spenser's knowledge of classical authors. As Douglas Bush (1963) observes, scholars now 'speak less certainly than they once did of his familiarity with ancient literature. While his acquaintance with medieval and Renaissance writing has been extended his supposed classical learning has been reduced here and there.' There is 'hardly any evidence' that Spenser 'knew Plato at first hand. Doubtless, like most men of his time, he read Ficino and similar authors, and slighted the Greek.' Bush questions Spenser's direct indebtedness to Homer, arguing that the poet 'needed no more of Homer than he could find, translated and moralized in Comes and other higher critics.' He maintains that Spenser's 'chief models' in *The Shepheardes Calender* were 'Marot and the poets of the Pléiade, along with Chaucer and Mantuan.' Spenser certainly knew Conti's *Mythologiae*, and he was probably also indebted to Boccaccio's *Genealogia*.

In contrast to earlier scholars like Upton, Merritt Hughes (1925-6) finds 'no evidence that Spenser derived any element of his poetry directly from any Greek romance.' Although several motifs in the Pastorella episode ultimately derive from Longus or Heliodorus, 'all of them had become literary commonplaces when Spenser wrote,' and the 'use that he makes of them relates him as much to Ariosto, Tasso, Guarini, and Sidney as it does to the ancient romancers.'

In the opinion of both Bush and Hughes, the influence of Virgil's *Eclogues* on Spenser was 'slight, indirect, and distorted.' The *Georgics* 'left no, or almost no, trace in Spenser.' Nevertheless Spenser was 'attracted' by the pseudo-Virgilian *Culex* and *Ciris*, translating the former in *Virgils Gnat* and borrowing from the latter for the episode of Britomart's concealed love and her conversation with Glauce. Although he echoes the opening lines of the *Aeneid*, in most of the 'main parallels' between Virgil and Spenser, 'the borrower hardly ever approaches or perhaps quite understands the spirit of his original.' On the other hand, Ovid undergoes 'less alteration than Virgil' in Spenser's hands.

According to MacLure (1970), Spenser's 'formative reading' was 'mainly extra-curricular.' Built 'on a foundation of Cicero and Vergil,' it included 'the Bible, Ovid, Natalis Comes, Ariosto, Chaucer.' His Fairyland was compounded out of 'books and spectacles: the Apocalypse, Ovid, Ariosto, Tasso, the mysteries, masks, triumphs and entertainments ... Hellenistic pastoral romance, the *loci amoeni* of the classical rhetoricians, each shading into the other.'

Spenser revealed an early interest in French Renaissance literature. To van der Noot's *Theatre* he contributed a translation of Clément Marot's French version of Petrarch's canzone 'Standomi un giorno' and a series of visionary sonnets based on du Bellay's *Songe* for *Les Antiquitez de Rome*. He also published a translation of the *Antiquitez* among his *Complaints*. In the envoy of this work, he hails du Bellay as 'first garland of free Poësie / That *France* brought forth' and concludes with a commendation of du Bartas.

Spenser's *November* is partly indebted to Marot's *Complaincte de Madame Loyse de Savoye*, and his *December* to Marot's *Eclogue au Roy*. The influence of Philippe Desportes, Pierre Ronsard, and other French Renaissance poets has been noted in *Amoretti*.

In the Letter to Raleigh, Spenser mentions both Ariosto's *Orlando furioso* and Tasso's *Gerusalemme liberata*; the influence of both is apparent in *The Faerie Queene*. Parallels with the poetry of Serafino da Aquila, Tebaldeo, Petrarch, Tasso, and Agostino Cazza have been observed in *Amoretti*. Scholars have noted the influence of Mantuan's Latin *Eclogues* on *The Shepheardes Calender*. M. Paolina (M.P. Parker 1963) argues that Spenser knew both Dante's *Divine Comedy*, 'especially the *Inferno*,' and his *Convivio*. Lemmi (1928) examines the influence of Trissino's epic *L'Italia liberata dai Gotti* on *The Faerie Queene*. On the basis of alleged parallels between Boiardo's romance-epic and *The Faerie Queene*, Blanchard (1925) argues that 'Spenser had read the *Orlando Innamorato*.' In the *Fowre Hymnes*, scholars have detected the influence of various Italian writers: Castiglione, Ficino, Benivieni, Bruno, Pico, and Bembo. In *Mother Hubberds Tale* and *Vewe of Ireland*, Greenlaw (1909-10) finds parallels with Machiavelli's *Discorsi* and *The Prince*. Spenser refers directly to Machiavelli in *Vewe of Ireland*.

T.P. Harrison (1930) suggests that Spenser was acquainted with Alonso Perez's continuation of Montemayor's pastoral romance *Diana* and that this work influenced two episodes in *The Faerie Queene*.

Spenser praised Chaucer as the 'well of English undefyled' (IV ii 32), and *The Faerie Queene* shows indebtedness both to the *Squire's Tale* and to the *Tale of Sir Thopas*. His *Daphnaïda* reflects the influence of Chaucer's *Book of the Duchess*. Although scholars have questioned his familiarity with *Piers Plowman*, he would appear to have been acquainted with this work, for the context of his allusion to 'the Pilgrim that the Ploughman playde a whyle' in the envoy of *The Shepheardes Calender*, immediately after a reference to Chaucer ('Tityrus hys style'), makes it seem more likely that he is referring to Langland's poem than to the pseudo-Chaucerian *Plowman's Tale*. He derived the name Colin Clout from Skelton's poem *Colyn Cloute*, and the title of *The Shepheardes Calender* from the *Kalendar and Compost of Shepherds*, a translation from the French *Le Compost et kalendrier des bergiers*.

He knew the work of Holinshed, and Geoffrey of Monmouth's *Historia regum Britanniae* may have influenced the 'chronicle of Briton kings' in *FQ* II x. In the opinion of Renwick (1925), Spenser's discussion of Irish history in *Vewe* 'relies almost entirely on George Buchanan's *Rerum Scoticarum historia* ... Camden's *Britannia* ... and on Holinshed.' (See also *Agrippa, *Alanus de Insulis, *Alciati, **Amadis of Gaul*, *Apuleius, legend of *Arthur, *Boethius, *Camden, *Camoens, *Catullus, *Chrétien de Troyes, *Christine de Pisan, *chronicles, *Dee, *Deguileville, *Erasmus, *Gower, *Hawes, *Hesiod, **Hypnerotomachia Poliphili*, *Latin literature, *Leland, *Lucretius, *Lydgate, *Malory, *Neo-Latin poetry, *Rabelais, Spenser's *reference works, **Romance of the Rose*, *Statius, *Theocritus, *Trissino.)

JOHN M. STEADMAN

Red Cross Knight (See ed 1912:68.) The hero of *FQ* I, so called from the device he bears on his shield. His story is an allegorized chivalric romance, a quest to rescue the parents of the royal maiden Una, who has sought a champion for this purpose at the court of the Fairy Queen. After errors, hardships, a time of separation from Una, imprisonment, and ferocious combats, Redcrosse succeeds in his quest, killing the Dragon who has kept her parents exiled from Eden and captive in a brazen tower. He and Una are betrothed at the end of the adventure (xii). Redcrosse appears in less significant roles in the stories of Guyon (II i) and Britomart (III i-iv).

When he is presented to the reader in the Letter to Raleigh, Redcrosse is described as 'a tall clownishe younge man' who sits on the floor, 'unfitte through his rusticity for a better place'; but when he puts on the armor that Una brought with her to court, he is transformed into 'the goodliest man in al that company.' Una tells him that only in this armor may he succeed in his adventure, and Spenser identifies it as the armor of a Christian man specified by St Paul in Ephesians 6.10–17, that is, the whole armor of God, wherewith the Christian may be able to stand against the assaults of the devil.

Not until x 65–6 does Redcrosse (and the reader) learn his earlier history: he is descended from the Saxon kings who conquered Britain, and was kidnapped in infancy by a fairy who hid him in a furrow in Fairyland where he was discovered by a plowman and raised 'in ploughmans state to byde.' He was named Georgos ('earth tiller') and he will be remembered as St George, the patron saint of England (61).

Much of the imagery associated with Redcrosse derives from the Book of Revelation and from popular traditions of St George that were preserved in plays and paintings as well as in written legends (Padelford and O'Connor in *Var* 1:379–89). These traditions suggest a connection of St George with the plowman. For example, the folk plays and sword dances on Plow Monday (in early January) and St George's Day (23 April) were structurally similar, indicating a common origin in folk rites celebrating the death of winter and the rebirth of spring (Chambers 1903, 1:205–27).

Well before Spenser's time, the legends of St George had assimilated the myth of Perseus, in which the hero rescues a king's daughter from a devouring monster. They had come to include nearly all of the images associated with Redcrosse in the culminating scenes of *FQ* I xi: the city besieged by a fire-breathing dragon; the lamb and the maiden (sometimes St Margaret) intended as tribute to the dragon; the bones of earlier victims; the hero's fight, revivification, and ultimate victory; and the joyful celebration of the redeemed king, queen, and citizens.

Drawing on these associations, Spenser emphasizes both the mythic and the fully human nature of his hero, his earthly birth and his heavenly aspiration. Unlike most of the other knights in *The Faerie Queene*, Redcrosse is not a fairy. He is defined thematically, as are Spenser's heroes generally, in some part by the extended allegory of his whole story, especially in relation to his friends and foes. At his lowest ebb, languishing near death in Orgoglio's dungeon (vii), he is saved by Arthur, who returns him to the anxious care of Una (viii). She guides him through an allegorically explicit series of encounters that restore him to health and confidence (ix-x), in preparation for the culminating battle with the Dragon (xi).

Redcrosse's quest, considered as a whole, is most immediately understood as an allegory of the making of a Protestant saint, both the fall into sin once separated from Christian truth, and the gradual restoration, through the intervention of grace and the loving guidance of holy church, to spiritual health, wholeness, and conformity to the image of Christ. The hero's greatest foes are the magician Archimago and the falsely fair Duessa, who work toward his destruction through guile, duplicity, and false appearance, making evil seem good, folly wise, and foulness beautiful. The singleness and unity implied by Una's name is opposed throughout Book I by the duality and duplicity of Duessa, who illustrates a disjunction between truth and outward appearance that is the worldly milieu of the errant Christian and is everywhere exploited by Archimago.

The triumph of Redcrosse over the monster Error and the bookish errors of theology (i 14–26) does not leave him proof against the more insidious confusions forced on him when Archimago makes him dream that he is in bed with a lascivious Una or, in another magic spell, that she is in bed with another man (i 47–ii 5). Deceived by false appearances and overcome by jealousy and grief, Redcrosse deserts Una. Even though he is narrowly able to prevail over Sansfoy (ii 12–19), he is further beguiled by Sansfoy's companion, Duessa, who, calling herself Fidessa, is recognizable from Revelation 17.3–4 as the Whore of Babylon. Protected by his Christian armor, Redcrosse is capable (although barely so) of prevailing against overt attacks on his good sense, faith, and morality; but he is unable to interpret the external appearance of things to perceive their true condition, even when he hears his own story repeated in a slightly different version by Fradubio (ii 28–44).

That there were two churches, the Protestant and the Roman, one (in Spenser's view) true and the other false, accounts for much of the historical force of the allegory of Una and Duessa and Redcrosse's confusion of allegiance. In the domain of ethics, however, Christians of all persuasions acknowledged that deception and false appearance open the way to sin. Spenser's general allegory of sin, therefore, and of the means by which the sinner is cleansed and restored to health, is conventionally Christian. It can be understood as readily with reference to the thought of Thomas Aquinas and Augustine as to that of Calvin and Luther (Whitaker 1950).

In consequence of the various deceptions played upon him, his inability to see the falseness beneath a pleasing outward appearance, and his adherence to the company of Duessa, Redcrosse falls into a life of vanity and pride. The rich and complex imagery of the house of Pride (iv-v) suggests every form of sin, animated by demonic energy, and resulting inevitably in pain and damnation for the inhabitants. Even though Redcrosse defeats Duessa's secret lover Sansjoy (v 12), it is an empty, pointless, deeply ironic victory in a courtly entertainment. The lowest point in the fall of Redcrosse comes, however, after he and Una's dwarf have left the house of Pride, when he lays his armor aside to rest and makes love to Duessa. Yielding to physical and moral exhaustion is a particularly Spenserian temptation, and thus enervated, Redcrosse is unable to resist the giant Orgoglio, who enslaves him and accepts Duessa's suggestion that he also take her as his mistress (vii 1–18).

After his rescue by Arthur and restoration to the care of Una (viii), Redcrosse responds to his lady's beauty with increasing love. Romance and allegory reinforce each other. The fiction here, as throughout *The Faerie Queene*, cannot be understood primarily as one or the other. The love of Redcrosse and Una is a form of virtuous eroticism that serves to illustrate the relationship of the church to the righteous Christian, whose spiritual condition is both the church's care and her salvation.

As well, therefore, as being the product of a consistent allegory, the significance of Redcrosse's role in Book I is also determined in part by the immediate poetic context of each episode. Viewed in this way, his adventure consists of an accumulating series of highly complex poetic utterances, to an understanding of which the reader's entire response is relevant. One is aware of moral, historical, and eschatological allusions conveyed in a poetic language and imagery that simultaneously evoke universal psychological, physical, and cultural experience. The poem exists in the mind of the reader, where the monster Error, the seven-headed monster of Revelation 17.3–5 upon which Orgoglio sets Duessa, and the Dragon imprisoning Una's parents are in many respects, both fictionally and allegorically, the same monster, independent of an articulated order of presentation in the poem.

Holiness, the virtue of Redcrosse, is central to Spenser's conception of the secular. Morally, Christ is the pattern or 'type' to which the righteous person attempts to conform. The entrance of Christ into human history brought the possibility of salvation to everyone who had ever lived, from Adam onward. The life of the individual recapitulates both the history of mankind and a heroic choice of whether to risk death in service to the whole regenerate human community. In Redcrosse, therefore, we find aspects, as radically different as at first they seem, of universal human nature, of the Christian Saviour, and of the person in direst need of salvation.

ROBERT KELLOGG

---

reference works, modern Along with properly established texts, reference works are the most practical and essential aids to our understanding of authors. Yet indexes, concordances, dictionaries, and bibliographies are rarely mentioned in critical writing because they provide information and interpretation for particulars of the text, not for overall meanings. From their formal structure (as series of lists, tables, annotations, or alphabetized entries), reference works seem to stand outside of criticism even though they are part of it. Yet because they reflect critical biases, they must be consulted – and questioned – with the same attention demanded of any work of criticism.

Reference works specifically about Spenser began to appear during the rise of English studies during the late nineteenth century. They may be used with other more general works to answer a wide range of questions about his writings. This survey is divided into the following topics: bibliographies and reference guides; texts; language; names; proverbs, phrases, motifs; rhetoric and poetic forms; and history of Spenser's reputation and early criticism. For further reading, see also the lists appended to articles on particular subjects.

bibliographies and reference guides Still one of the important books for Spenser studies is Frederic Ives Carpenter's *Reference Guide to Edmund Spenser* (1923), which includes reference material from many different areas and periods and also early documentation and criticism. *Edmund Spenser: A Bibliographical Supplement* (1937) by Dorothy F. Atkinson covers subsequent criticism and adds material from earlier periods omitted by Carpenter. Inevitably both are incomplete, though they are excellent starting points for the unwritten history of Spenser's reputation. Both books are rendered obsolete in only one respect by William L. Sipple's *Edmund Spenser, 1900–1936: A Reference Guide* (1984) and that is in the listing of critical material from the early part of this century. The *Reference Guide* can be used as a companion volume with *Edmund Spenser: An Annotated Bibliography 1937–1972* (1975; 1st ed 1962, covering 1937–60) by Waldo F. McNeir and Foster Provost. Both the Sipple and the McNeir-Provost bibliographies are annotated and are extraordinarily full, including even marginal works (eg, Sipple lists MA theses). The result is a thoroughness that verges on the uncritical, and is most apparent in the sometimes frustrating indexes. Even so, these two works combined give a better picture of twentieth-century criticism for Spenser than is available for almost any other major English writer. A more selective, simpler, and – for scholarship before 1900 – fuller bibliography is A.C. Hamilton's guide in *The New Cambridge Bibliography* (*NCBEL*) ed George Watson (1974, 1:1029–47). Finally, there is in *Spenser Newsletter* vol 11 (1980) and later issues, a regular listing of the books, articles, and dissertations reviewed or abstracted in *SpN* from 1972 onwards. The *International Bibliography* published annually by the Modern Language Association adds little to the material in *SpN*, though it is usually the most up-to-date guide to recent publication about Spenser and other writers of the period.

texts Modern texts of older authors have the quality of reference books. By their use of standard line numbering and (in the more elaborate editions) their recording of variants and their annotations, they are meant to be consulted as well as to be read continuously. For Spenser's poetry, the principal modern editions are the Oxford English Texts of J.C. Smith for *The Faerie Queene* (2 vols, 1909) and E. de Sélincourt for the *Minor Poems* (1910); both are reprinted, with the Harvey-Spenser letters, in the one-volume Oxford Standard Authors edition (1912). Smith's text is reproduced without editorial apparatus but with full annotations in the Longman edition by A.C. Hamilton (1977). Further editions include *The Faerie Queene* (1978) edited by Thomas P. Roche, Jr, and *The Shorter Poems* (1989) edited by William A. Oram, et al. The *Variorum* edition (11 vols, 1932–57) also includes *Vewe of Ireland* and has a vast and fully indexed commentary from over 300 years of writing about Spenser.

The early texts on which these editions are based are catalogued in F.R. Johnson's *Critical Bibliography of the Works of Edmund Spenser Printed before 1700* (1933), which contains much information about printing and publishing. His list of copies may be supplemented by reference to the shorter but more recent record in the revised edition of A.W. Pollard and G.R. Redgrave's *Short-Title Catalogue ... 1475–1640* (*STC*; rev ed 3 vols, 1976–), a list of all English books printed in the period (most of which are now available on film from University Microfilms). For locating later editions of works by Spenser or his contemporaries, the principal guides are Donald G. Wing's *Short-title Catalogue ... 1641–1700* (Wing; 1945–51, rev ed 1972–88), *The British Library General Catalogue of Printed Books to 1975* (360 vols, 1979–87; an expansion of its predecessor *The British Museum Catalogue of Printed Books ... to 1955* 263 vols, 1960–6), and for the United States *The National Union Catalog pre-1956* Imprints (*NUC*; 754 vols, 1968–81, and supplements; the information in *NUC* is sometimes less accurate than that in other comparable works). There are also short-title catalogues for eighteenth- and nineteenth-century English printed books.

Compact introductory bibliographies for Elizabethan writers as well as Spenser are found in the *NCBEL* vol 1 and C.S. Lewis' *English Literature in the Sixteenth Century, Excluding Drama* (1954, Oxford History of English Literature). Douglas Bush's *English Literature in the Earlier Seventeenth Century: 1600–1660* (rev ed 1962, also OHEL) likewise has bibliographies for the slightly later period.

(For Spenser's manuscripts, see *handwriting.)

language Various historical senses of a word in Spenser may be worked out by the particular context, by his use of the word elsewhere, and by the practice of his contemporaries and predecessors. In the first instance, the notes to some of the editions may prove most helpful. There are extensive word notes in Hamilton's *FQ* ed 1977, in the selective editions of Robert Kellogg and Oliver Steele (1965) and of Hugh Maclean (2nd ed 1982), and in the editions of *Complaints* (1928), *Daphnaïda and Other Poems* (1929), and *The Shepherd's Calendar* (1930) all by W.L. Renwick, *Cantos of Mutabilitie* by S.P. Zitner (1968), *Fowre Hymnes* by L. Winstanley (1907), and *The Shepheards Calendar* by C.H. Herford (1895). The *Variorum* is rarely helpful for meanings of words, though disputed senses are sometimes given a note. Partial glossaries for Spenser's language are found in the one-volume Oxford edition (1912) and, for *FQ* I and II, by Alan Ward in P.C. Bayley's editions (1965–6). The *Concordance* of Charles Grosvenor Osgood (1915, corrected against the Oxford texts) is the standard word-list. There is also a computer concordance on tape at Cambridge University (prepared by John Dawson); its advantage over Osgood is that it can be used by specialists to find various combinations or patterns in vocabulary. There are also Einar Bjorvand's concordance to *Fowre Hymnes* (1973) and Herbert S. Donow's *Concordance to the Sonnet Sequences of Daniel, Drayton, Shakespeare, Sidney, and Spenser* (1969). For the historical context, the principal guide is the *Oxford English Dictionary* (*OED*; 12 vols, 1884–1928; 2nd ed, 20 vols, 1989); the supplements (1 vol 1933, 4 cumulative vols 1972–86), except under a few key headings for those words or senses formerly considered too rude for inclusion, do not add much for readers of sixteenth-century literature. A reader using the *OED* regularly should consult Jürgen Schäfer's *Documentation in the O.E.D.: Shakespeare and Nashe as Test Cases* (1980), an analysis of the datings for the Tudor and Stuart periods that shows a large number of citations may be pre-dated by as many as 50 years. Studies, historical grammars, and the like are listed in R.C. Alston's *Bibliography of the English Language ... to ... 1800* (1965–). General studies, such as A.C. Partridge's *Language of Renaissance Poetry* (1971) and Charles L. Barber's *Early Modern English* (1976), may answer questions about Spenser's language that even the dictionaries leave untouched (eg, grammar and syntax). The abundant citation of examples in the *OED* can also be supplemented by reference to the various concordances and indexes to Sidney, Shakespeare, Nashe, Lyly, Jonson, Donne, Milton, and others. A good Bible concordance is essential for certain kinds of word analysis (although citations should always be checked against historically appropriate translations; see reading list for *Bible). Sometimes the English word is explained by etymological reference to other languages; for Greek and Latin, standard modern sources are the *Greek-English Lexicon* of Liddell and Scott (9th ed, 1940, suppl 1968), the *Latin Dictionary* of Lewis and Short (1879), and the *Oxford Latin Dictionary* (1968), to which might be added the *Thesaurus linguae latinae* (1900–) and the *Glossarium* of Charles du Fresne, sieur Du Cange (10 vols, 1883–7). For Renaissance dictionaries, see *reference works, Spenser's.

names For proper names in Spenser's poetry, one may begin with the poetic context. As above, Osgood's *Concordance* is the principal aid, though it can be supplemented by Charles Huntington Whitman's *Subject-Index to the Poems of Edmund Spenser* (1918). Although Whitman's index is not always complete, it does offer something different from Osgood in its generous topic analyses of words and names of generic relationship that might otherwise be missed; it also alerts one to multiple appearances of characters not named directly (eg, where Cupid is called 'love' or 'a God'). In addition to Osgood and Whitman, the indexes to the *Variorum* volumes 1–8 and to *Variorum Prose* are guides to names in Spenser and the historical commentary. Explanations for names, as well as for words, is often provided in the smaller editions, too (most noticeably *FQ* ed 1977 and Douglas Brooks-Davies' *Spenser's 'Faerie Queene': A Critical Commentary on Books I and II* 1977). If the name has been the subject of critical discussion, it should be checked through the indexes to Sipple's *Reference Guide* (1984) or McNeir and Provost's *Annotated Bibliography* (1975), mentioned above, or through the indexes of critical studies (eg, Nohrnberg 1976).

For names of Spenser's own invention, in addition to the sources just mentioned, there is Joel Jay Belson's unpublished dissertation 'The Names in *The Faerie Queene*' (1964), though Hamilton summarizes most of its useful information in his edition. The way Spenser's contemporaries and later readers understood these names is shown in *Spenser Allusions in the Sixteenth and Seventeenth Centuries* ed William Wells, et al (2 vols, 1971–2) with its index of allusions to characters and passages in the poetry (pp 330–41).

For classical names, the best guides are Alice Elizabeth (Sawtelle) Randall's *Sources of Spenser's Classical Mythology* (1896) and, with reference to the Italian mythographers, Henry Gibbons Lotspeich's *Classical Mythology in the Poetry of Edmund Spenser* (1932). For this topic some of the best reference books are the Renaissance Latin and Italian works used by Spenser (see *mythographers, and *reference works, Spenser's). The less elaborate mythological handbooks and dictionaries of the Renaissance (eg, Thomas Cooper's English 'Dictionarium' appended to his *Thesaurus* of 1565) are also most useful in explaining the contemporary senses of a myth; these are analyzed in DeWitt T. Starnes and Ernest William Talbert's *Classical Myth and Legend in Renaissance Dictionaries* (1955). Modern compendia like the *Oxford Classical Dictionary* (2nd ed, 1970) or the massive German *Real-Encyclopädie* of A.F. von Pauly, rev by G. Wissowa (1894–, with supplements) can provide some assistance, but often do not point one to the sources known to Spenser as quickly or directly as the Renaissance works or even such works as Ebenezer Brewer's *Dictionary of Phrase and Fable* (1870 and many revisions) or William Smith's *Dictionary of Greek and Roman Biography and Mythology* (3 vols, 1849). A good index to Ovid is important; for Sandys' translation and commentary (1632) as edited by Karl K. Hulley and Stanley T. Vandersall (1970), there is an index by Christopher Grose (1981, vol 7 in the series Humana Civilitas). The indexes to the works of Lyly, Nashe, Jonson, Shakespeare, and especially Milton are essential guides to modern annotation of classical names in English writers. *A Milton Encyclopedia* ed William B. Hunter, Jr, et al (9 vols, 1978–83) and *A Variorum Commentary on the Poems of John Milton* ed Merritt Y. Hughes, et al (1970–) both overlap considerably with Spenser scholarship on many topics besides classical sources. Bush's *Mythology and the Renaissance Tradition in English Poetry* (rev ed 1963), while not specifically a work of reference, has a handy index to mythological figures in the works of Spenser and his contemporaries.

Names from British history (though not Spenser's contemporaries, for whom see below) may be located in Carrie A. Harper's *Sources of the British Chronicle History in Spenser's 'Faerie Queene'* (1910), in indexes for editions of the chronicles themselves (unfortunately, these indexes are often incomplete), and in the *Variorum* indexes. Some of the names appear in Malory (see 'A Dictionary of Names and Places' by Bert Dillon in Malory ed 1983:811–47).

proverbs, phrases, motifs Spenser uses many proverbs or proverb-like phrases in his poetry; these are imperfectly catalogued in Charles G. Smith's *Spenser's Proverb Lore* (1970), which should be supplemented by Morris Palmer Tilley's *Dictionary of Proverbs in England in the Sixteenth and Seventeenth Centuries* (1950) and *The Oxford Dictionary of English Proverbs* (*ODEP*; 3rd ed by F.P. Wilson, 1970); see reading list for *proverbs. A further and often surprisingly direct guide to catch phrases is Arthur Henkel and Albrecht Schöne's *Emblemata* (1967); see also *emblems, *emblematics. Henkel and Schöne, Guy de Tervarent's *Attributs et symboles dans l'art profane, 1450–1600* (1958), sometimes the *New Catholic Encyclopedia* (1967–79), and other works of Christian and medieval iconology, such as George Ferguson's *Signs and Symbols in Christian Art* (1954), can lead one to received significances of a creature or a thing (eg, an ass, a book, an oar). Sometimes the classical sources can be found through the index to commentaries in such works as Alciati's emblems (eg, ed 1621). Likewise, reference to standard collections such as Erasmus' *Adagia* or the *Lectionum antiquarum libri xxx* of Caelius Rhodiginus or to dictionaries of classical languages can also lead to early sources for a particular motif (see *reference works, Spenser's).

rhetoric and poetic forms Though Herbert D. Rix' *Rhetoric in Spenser's Poetry* (1940) outlines some of the principal techniques and W.L. Renwick's *Edmund Spenser* (1925) gives a survey of verse forms, there are no thorough guides to these topics in Spenser. General reference works like Richard A. Lanham's *Handlist of Rhetorical Terms* (1968), Lee A. Sonnino's *Handbook to Sixteenth-Century Rhetoric* (1968), Marjorie Donker and George M. Muldrow's *Dictionary of Literary-Rhetorical Conventions of the English Renaissance* (1982), and Alex Preminger, et al *Encyclopedia of Poetry and Poetics* (the 'Princeton Encyclopedia' 2nd ed, 1974) are, however, extremely helpful. For further works, see reading lists for *rhetoric and *versification.

history of Spenser's reputation and early criticism Early critical comments are indexed and often cited in *Spenser Allusions* (1971–2). Some of the same material is covered by R.M. Cummings' more general *Spenser: The Critical Heritage* (1971) and Paul Alpers' introductory *Edmund Spenser: A Critical Anthology* (1969), although Cummings and Alpers both quote extensively from commentary after 1700. William R. Mueller's *Spenser's Critics* (1959) is a general anthology of criticism from John Hughes (1715) to W.B.C. Watkins (1950). The early critical tradition is surveyed in Jewel Wurtsbaugh's *Two Centuries of Spenserian Scholarship (1609–1805)* (1936), which concentrates on textual history. A proper survey of Spenser's reputation and influence has yet to be undertaken, especially one that considers his popularity from the late eighteenth century onwards.

The works surveyed here, while fairly representative of what is directly available for Spenser, give only a hint of the labyrinth of information and interpretation surrounding his text. Often much of this information is not found through reference works anyway: a footnote to an article may provide more information on a particular subject than a general bibliography, the subject catalogue of a large library is sometimes the most direct route to a fact, a passage from a medieval theological work may be more relevant than the most elaborate modern aid for answering a question about an image. And finally, one should remember that questions of reference and information are often answered not from reference works but in classrooms, meetings, correspondence, or private conversation.

William W. Barker

reference works, Spenser's A reference book arranges or codes information for ready access. A writer might refer to such a work either to retrieve forgotten information (who were Priam's sons?) or to learn some new matter (what are the names of the English rivers?). The reference books of a culture will inevitably reflect its pedagogy: in Spenser's England, the chief users of such books were the students and masters at grammar schools and universities. The habit of reference is schoolish; the realms of knowledge compended by reference books are educational realms. An extended study of reference books available to Spenser (not undertaken here because of limited space; see also *reading), would explore in detail two areas: the practices of Tudor schooling, essentially the long shadow of Erasmus, and the technology of access, including the developing uses and formats of printing, the methods of indexing, and the growing ascendancy of the principles of alphabetization.

Spenser's resources for quick access to knowledge were much the same as ours. By the late sixteenth century, the art of indexing had developed practically to the level it still retains, so that many classical and modern texts were accessible both by means of their original arrangement and by means of an alphabetized table of contents or an index. Spenser used Latin-English dictionaries, principally that of Thomas Cooper, which are astoundingly full and accurate. He lacked only an encyclopedia as full and well-arranged as those that followed (and degenerated from) the great monuments of the eighteenth-century *encyclopédistes*; yet there were encyclopedias, of narrower scope than ours but some large and authoritative within their fields.

Many of the reference books available to Spenser have scarcely been studied, and even the dates of certain first editions are unknown. The whole subject needs considerable research.

dictionaries Medieval dictionaries were superseded but still used in the Renaissance. The landmarks are the *Elementarium doctrinae rudimentum* (c 1053) of Papias, alphabetized to the third letter of each entry but treating many words out of order; the popular *Magnae derivationes* of Hugutio of Pisa (1192–1201), again alphabetized only in part; and the dictionary portion of the *Catholicon* (1286) of John of Genoa (Joannes Balbus Januensis), a thoroughly alphabetized redaction of Papias and Hugutio. The *Catholicon* was among the first books printed, in 1460. These dictionaries, entirely in Latin and for the use of churchmen, concentrated, following Isidore, on (largely false) etymologies. The earliest English-to-Latin dictionary, the *Promptorium parvulorum*, was compiled about 1440 and issued in several printings (1499–1528). The first printed Latin-to-English dictionary was the anonymous *(H)Ortus vocabulorum* (1500); it contains about 27,000 entries.

Renaissance schoolmen wanted dictionaries that purged nonclassical Latin terms and elucidated classical texts. The first step was Nicholas Perottus' *Cornucopiae* (1489), a commentary on the epigrams of Martial so full it amounted to a lexicon. The major influence on sixteenth-century dictionaries was the Latin *Dictionarium* (1502) of the Italian Ambrosius Calepine, a large compilation still mainly medieval but partly humanist in its conception, reprinted through the seventeenth century and often accompanied by Conrad Gesner's *Onomasticon* or name-list. Calepine was the chief source of the principal dictionary used by Spenser, which had its origin in Thomas Elyot's *Dictionary* (1538), a mainly classical Latin-to-English dictionary that includes abundant phrases as well as single words, and preserves many proverbs and pointed sentences in English and Latin. Elyot revised his dictionary as the *Bibliotheca Eliotae* in 1542, using the *Dictionarium latino-gallicum* of Robert Estienne (Stephanus) (1538), which was an abridgement of Estienne's great *Dictionarium, seu Latinae linguae thesaurus* (1531).

From 1548, Thomas Cooper edited Elyot's dictionary, expanding and revising it by using the steadily advancing learning of continental scholars, including the 1552 edition of Estienne's Latin-to-French dictionary, which now, as the *Dictionariolum puerorum tribus linguis*, contained English. Elyot-Cooper appeared as Cooper's *Thesaurus linguae romanae et britannicae* in 1565, reissued at least five times by 1587. In 1587, Thomas Thomas published his *Dictionarium linguae latinae et anglicanae*, designed, with partial success, to supplant Cooper. John Legate (Legatt) edited, revised, and expanded versions of Thomas, which went through fourteen editions to 1644. Starnes and Talbert (1955) show that Spenser used Cooper's *Thesaurus*, which had become the acknowledged leader of all Tudor reference books, and they suggest but cannot conclude that he also used Calepine and materials from Charles and Robert Estienne.

Charles Estienne's major work was his Latin *Dictionarium historicum, geographicum, poeticum*, issued in twenty editions from 1553 to 1693. This was a dictionary, practically a brief encyclopedia, of proper names mainly from classical sources but including material from the Bible and church history. Cooper used it for the 1559 edition of the *Bibliotheca Eliotae*, and in his 1565 *Thesaurus* he included an appendix, *Dictionarium historicum et poeticum: Propria locorum et personarum vocabula breviter complectens*.

T.W. Baldwin (1944, 1:421) prints a list of books at Spenser's grammar school, Merchant Taylors' School, in 1599. Among these are Cooper's *Thesaurus*, a *Dictionarium poeticum* (doubtless that of Charles Estienne), and the monumental Greek-to-Latin dictionary, Henri Estienne's four-volume *Thesaurus graecae linguae* (1572–3). There is some evidence, then, that English schoolboys of the mid-century knew the lexicons of Cooper and the Estiennes.

encyclopedias Two ancient encyclopedias, both arranged by topic rather than alphabet, remained especially influential in the Renaissance: Pliny's *Natural History* (AD 77, translated by 'I.A.' in 1566 from the French) and Isidore's *Etymologiae* (c 630). Among medieval encyclopedias, besides the *Catholicon* the most important were Vincent of Beauvais' huge *Speculum maius* (c 1245–60), a 'greater mirror' containing three *specula* – of nature, arts and sciences ('doctrine'), and history – and Bartholomaeus Anglicus' *De proprietatibus rerum* (c 1240).

Bartholomaeus had a wide circulation and was translated into six languages. John Trevisa's translation (1396), modernized and revised by Stephen Bateman as *Batman uppon Bartholome* (1582), was known to Spenser. To the alphabetical list of authorities (ten quarto pages), Bateman adds a list of additional scientists whom he consulted: Gesner, Fuchs, Muenster, Mathiolus, Theophrastus, Paracelsus, Dodoneus, Agrippa, Ortelius. The book is especially full of naturalist lore, and displays an Isidorean interest in etymology. A long table of contents, arranged topically, provides access to its knowledge.

The French encyclopedic poem *L'Ymage du monde* (probably by Gossouin of Metz, c 1245) precedes Brunetto Latini's *Li Livres dou tresor* (c 1265) as the first vernacular encyclopedia. The *Ymage* would have been known to Spenser in Caxton's translation, from a French prose redaction, *Myrrour of the Worlde* (probably 1481), the first illustrated work printed in England. The tradition of didactic encyclopedic poetry includes *The Court of Sapience* (c 1450) and Stephen Hawes' *Pastime of Pleasure* (1509), both organizing information according to the scheme of the seven liberal arts. The tradition culminates in du Bartas' *Sepmaine* (1578–84) with the learned commentary by Simon Goulart (1583, 1588–9) which may have been known to Spenser. Among other influential encyclopedias should be mentioned the *Margarita philosophica* of Gregor Reisch (1503); the popular household encyclopedia, the *Shepherds' Kalendar* (1st Eng ed 1503); the various scientific and historical works of the polymath Conrad Gesner, especially the *Pandectae* (1548–9); and a digest of natural history, John Maplet's *Greene Forest* (1567).

Many sixteenth-century books have a scope too narrow to be called encyclopedias, yet clearly were compiled as reference works for their several disciplines, and not as specialized treatises exploring new ideas. Prominent examples of these can best be treated under the headings of history and chronology, science, the language arts, and mythography and emblems.

history and chronology Before the Renaissance, most historiography fell into the categories of chronicles and 'exemplary' histories, that is, lives of famous characters compiled for didactic and pedagogic purposes, often including their wise 'sayings.' Both forms were favored in Tudor England; their simple organization (according to the person described or according to the year) provides the ready access of a reference work. Some of the more popular exemplary histories were Diogenes Laertius' *Lives and Sayings of the Philosophers*, the historical information in Pliny, and the biographical collections of Valerius Maximus, Joannes Tzetze, Petrarch, and others. From these, and pedagogically simplified versions, Tudor schoolboys were to learn and imitate models of conduct and of wit.

Chronicles have always been ancillary to liberal learning; they are convenient for organizing archives arranged annalistically; they are the backbone of history, and in the Renaissance a favorite form even for polemical and speculative historiography. Standard continental chronicles were J.J. Scaliger's *De emendatione temporum* (1583) and Gulielmus Morellius' *Tabula compendiosa* (1580). Fundamental to English chronography were the various works published or reprinted in the sixteenth century by Ralph Higden, William Caxton, Robert Fabyan, Richard Grafton, and Humphrey Llwyd. Such works provided materials for the two master chroniclers of the period, both certainly known to Spenser: John Stow and Raphael Holinshed. Stow's *Summarie of Englyshe Chronicles* (1565), based on earlier authorities, includes a chronicle (with dates in the margin) to the year 1564, along with calendars, mileage charts, and other useful information. Revised editions appeared in 1580 (*Chronicles of England*) and 1592 (*Annales of England*). Spenser knew both the 1577 and the 1587 versions of Holinshed's *Chronicles*. In a letter to Harvey, he acknowledges that he used Holinshed for the names of English rivers (*Three Letters* 1, *Var Prose* p 17).

The special topic of 'British history,' the history of England including the legendary material of Troy, the Trojan Brut, and the Arthurian line, entered into the chronicles from an early time, and joined a vigorously developing line of historiography that may be termed 'antiquarian.' These early sources of legendary British history included Geoffrey of Monmouth's *Historia regum Britanniae* (c 1139) and Wace's *Roman de Brut* (1155, printed 1543, 1584), along with Bede (1525), Gildas (1568), and Giraldus Cambrensis (1585). Attacks on Geoffrey began as early as the twelfth century (William of Newburgh), and the question of the authenticity of the line of Brut and Arthur was much debated, especially under the Tudor monarchs, who claimed Arthurian ancestry.

Fifteenth-century antiquarians favoring Geoffrey were John Rous and William of Worcester. Most sixteenth-century historians followed suit, including Leland, Bale, and Stow, and culminating in the work of John Price (1573). The 1571 edition of the exemplary *Mirror for Magistrates* included figures from Geoffrey's history. Close to Spenser is a defense of the 'British history' by Gabriel Harvey's brother Richard in *Philadelphus* (1593). But the critics of Geoffrey were vigorous and included John Major (1521), Polydore Vergil (1534), John Twyne (1590), and, most authoritatively, Camden. Spenser himself disbelieved the legend of Brut (*Vewe* ed 1934:261), as did Sidney and Raleigh.

A final class of historical writing, more strictly for reference, are the Renaissance compilations of biographies and bibliographies of famous writers. Among these Gesner's *Bibliotheca universalis*, which aimed to catalogue nearly all writers in Latin, takes pride of place; it was epitomized and amplified (using Bale) by Josias Simmler (1574) and Joannes Jacobus Frisius (1583). Other great continental bibliographies are Michael Neander's *Anthologicum graecolatinum* (1556) and Frisius' *Bibliotheca philosophorum* (1592). Leland and Bale produced bio-bibliographies so learned and vast that they remain of service today. Leland's *Commentarii de scriptoribus britannicis* chronologically arranges *vitae* and lists of works of some 600 British authors through the fifteenth century. Although he was at work on the *Commentarii* in 1545, it was not published until 1709. Yet we know that Bale used it, that Stow transcribed it, and that it may well have been known to Spenser. Bale's *Illustrium maioris Britanniae* (1548, enlarged 1557, 1559) is roughly chronological in order, and an alphabetical index provides access to the authors treated. Its only sixteenth-century rivals in English historiography are Camden's works and Foxe's *Actes and Monuments* (Latin 1554; Eng revision and tr 1563), which from its 1570 edition contained a section on early British history.

science Although Harvey complained of Spenser's ignorance of astronomy, his works display some knowledge of science. Encyclopedic general works in natural history mentioned above were Pliny and Bartholomaeus; Caxton's *Myrrour* and Maplet's *Greene Forest* carried much of this lore to English readers. A popular form of scientific writing treated (quasi-historically) the 'inventors' of various arts and technologies, rites and customs; the most influential work of this kind was Polydore Vergil's *De inventoribus rerum* (1499). Aristotle of course remained important in Renaissance science. Other encyclopedic works which might have influenced Spenser directly or indirectly are Sebastian Verro's *Physicorum libri* (1581), Isidore's *De natura rerum*, Seneca's *Quaestiones naturales*, Gesner's *Pandectae*, du Bartas' *Sepmaine*, and Pierre de La Primaudaye's *French Academie* (part 1 tr Thomas Bowes 1586).

Much Elizabethan scientific thought centered on the exciting voyages of discovery and on cosmography, the general science of the movements of the heavenly bodies in relation to places on earth (comprising astronomy, geography, meteorology, and the computations of time found in calendars and almanacs); this was the most active English science in Spenser's time. By its nature, much of the work in cosmography took the form of reference books. In a letter to Spenser (*3 Lett* 2, *Var Prose* p 456), Harvey refers to Aristotle, Pliny, 'and other Meteorologicians' on the science of earthquakes. Baldwin (1944, 1:219) prints a list of scientific reference works recommended to Edward VI to aid his reading in history: among them are named Ptolemy, Strabo, and Pliny, and for 'chorography' (place-name guides), Heliodorus, Strabo, Pliny, and Herodotus. Aristotle was pre-eminent; the other principal authors were Theophrastus, Proclus, Sacrobosco, Pomponius Mela, and Roger Bacon. From these earlier writers, sixteenth-century readers might have turned to the 'moderns': Peter Apian, Oronce Finé, Copernicus, Ortelius, and Mercator. Some popular lore in cosmography came to England in Palingenius' *Zodiake of Life* (tr Googe). English writers, some of whom were sophisticated inductive scientists, included the 'magician' Dee, Anthony Askham, Leonard and Thomas Digges, and Robert Recorde. More popularizing English works in astronomy and meteorology were Thomas Hill's *Contemplation of Mysteries* (1571), William Fulke's *Goodly Gallerye ... of All Kynd of Meteors* (1563), and Abraham Fleming's *Treatise of Blazing Starres in Generall* (after 1577).

Geographical information is included in the historical writings of Higden, Caxton, Holinshed, and Camden, noticed above. For medicine, there is the treatise, ultimately based on Galen, by Thomas Elyot, *The Castel of Helth* (1539). Hippocrates, Galen, Avicenna, and Rhazes were in print, as was Gordon's *Lilium medicinae* (1542), Lemnius' medical treatise translated as *The Touchstone of Complexions* by Thomas Newton (1565), and the very popular commentary by Arnald of Villanova on the medical poem *Regimen sanitatis salerni*, translated (commentary only) by Thomas Paynell (1528). The first English arithmetic was Recorde's *Grounde of Arts* (1542).

language arts Because of their pedagogical uses, grammar books naturally assumed the shape of reference works. The most widely used Greek grammar in the schools was that of Clenardes; Michael Neander's *Graecae linguae tabulae* was another well-known school text. Erasmus and early English humanists produced Latin grammars to supersede such medieval ones as that prefixed to the *Catholicon*, more useful in sixteenth-century schools than the long-standard grammars of Donatus and Priscian. Notable examples are Thomas Linacre's *Rudimenta grammatices* (in English 1523?, later translated into Latin by George Buchanan); *A Shorte Introduction of Grammar* (in its earliest form, perhaps 1513) by William Lily and John Colet, which became the 'authorized grammar' in its many editions; and the several grammars of Robert Whittinton. Linacre had translated Proclus and Galen, and compiled three grammars, including a manual on Latin composition, *De emendata structura latini sermonis*. A beginning on a French grammar (with English glosses) was John Palsgrave's *Lesclarcissement de la langue francoyse* (1530).

Renaissance rhetoric derived from classical authorities, especially Cicero, Quintilian, and the *Rhetorica ad Herennium*, still falsely attributed to Cicero. Philipp Melanchthon's commentary on Cicero's *Topica* (1533) and his many rhetorics, including *De rhetorica* (1519) and *Institutiones rhetoricae* (1521), and Mosellanus' contribution to the venerable tradition of listing rhetorical figures, *Tabulae de schematibus et tropis* (1529) were influential continental works; later Joannes Susenbrotus aimed to replace Mosellanus with his *Epitome troporum* (1562). Medieval rhetorics were printed, including the brief lists of tropes in the *Catholicon*. The treatments of rhetoric in the fifteenth-century encyclopedic poems *The Court of Sapience* and Hawes' *Pastime of Pleasure* introduced the art into English. The chief English manuals of rhetoric include Leonard Cox's *Arte or Crafte of Rhethoryke* (1524, 1532), based on Melanchthon, the first book in English exclusively devoted to rhetoric; Richard Sherry's *Treatise of Schemes and Tropes* (1550), based on Mosellanus, and his *Treatise of the Figures of Grammer and Rhetorike* (1555) in English and Latin; most important, the first English rhetoric not a translation or paraphrase, *The Arte of Rhetorique* (1553) by Thomas Wilson, who also wrote the first English logic, *The Rule of Reason* (1551); Henry Peacham's *Garden of Eloquence* (1577), based on Susenbrotus and Melanchthon; and Fraunce's *Arcadian Rhetorike* (1588). Harvey gave a set of lectures at Cambridge in 1577 called 'Rhetor'; he was influenced by the organizational ideas in Peter Ramus' *Scholae* (1559). There were books on letter writing, prosody, and even orthography. (Harvey mentions a valiant effort to rationalize English orthography, Thomas Smith's *De recta et emendata linguae anglicae scriptione* 1568; there were many others.)

An abundant sixteenth-century tradition might be called the 'progymnastic': it consisted of exemplary lives (discussed above), especially as augmented by the wise sayings (sentences, adages, aphorisms, maxims, epigrams, chiliades) of notable men. The collections of sentences soon appeared separate from the lives, and included proverbs, epithets, and witty similes from any source. The purpose of these texts, increasingly arranged for ease of access, is obvious: they were the companions of schoolboys obliged to write compositions and poems on famous men and events, and obliged to lard their compositions with shrewd sayings and pointed turns of phrase.

To the 'lives' mentioned above, especially the most influential work of Diogenes Laertius, may be added Plutarch's *Lives* (tr Thomas North 1579), from which apophthegms were extracted, and two ancient textbooks, the *Progymnasmata* of Hermogenes (tr Priscian the grammarian) and of Theon. From these texts derived the most influential antique pedagogical text, Aphthonius' *Progymnasmata*, essentially an exercise book containing model speeches, illustrations of fourteen types of discourse, and analysis of the parts of oratory. The work was translated into Latin, was often reprinted, and was important in English schools. It was the base of Richard Rainolde's *Foundacion of Rhetorike* (1563).

Around 1400, Earl Rivers compiled *Les Dit moraulx des philosophes*, whose ultimate source was Diogenes Laertius. Together with the maxims of Publilius Syrus, the sentences by and attributed to Seneca, and the distichs of pseudo-Cato, these texts were at the head of a substantial Renaissance tradition of collections of sentences. *Les Dit* were translated by Caxton as *The Dictes or Sayengis of the Philosophhres*, distinguished as the first book printed in English (1477), followed in the same year by Caxton's version of pseudo-Cato's distichs. In 1498 appeared Polydore Vergil's *Proverbiorum libellus* (twenty editions before 1550), which was soon overtaken by Erasmus' monumental collection, the *Adagia* (1500), revised as the *Adagiorum chiliades*, 'thousands of adages,' with more than 3000 sayings, in 1508. This work was revised and expanded several times by Erasmus, and was largely influential both in its complete editions and in various epitomes and translations (Richard Taverner translated 178 adages in *The Proverbes or Adagies Gathered ... out of the Chiliades of Erasmus* 1539). Other compilations by other authors followed; in 1543, Gesner rendered Joannes Stobaeus' Greek *Sententiae* into Latin in parallel columns: the author's names are given in the margins, an alphabetical table of authors appears at the beginning, and running heads indicate the topics under which the sentences are arranged. This topical arrangement was standard, providing authoritative printed versions of the commonplace books boys were to compile at school. Pages of their notebooks would be titled with topics (justice, anger, leisure) under which they collected wise and witty sayings in order to flesh out their compositions with copiousness (see *copia).

Erasmus issued two kindred collections that likewise were of profound influence. His *Parabolae, sive Similia* was appended to his rhetorical guide *De duplici copia rerum et verborum*, itself a standard, in 1513, and his *Apophthegmata*, derived (1521) largely from Plutarch and augmented (1532) from Diogenes Laertius. The collection of similes again aimed to provide students with copiousness and wit. Sixteenth-century editors regrouped Erasmus' similes under commonplace headings or alphabetically. Similar to the *Parabola* was a series of collections issued by Joannes Ravisius Textor (Jean Tixier), such as his *Officina* (1503) and *Epithetorum opus* (1558), much reprinted and adapted. The latter amounted to collections of epithets and synonyms for various classical and biblical proper names, a handy aid for young poets struggling to fill their hexameters. Two other notable collections of epithets might have been known to Spenser: Montefalco's *De cognominibus deorum* (1525) and Conrad Dinner's *Epithetorum graecorum farrago* (1589), a copy of which was at Merchant Taylors' School in 1599.

Two books of Erasmus' *Apothegmes* were translated into English in 1542 by Nicholas Udall, who had earlier issued his *Floures* of Terence (1533) to aid the young in speaking Latin. Lycosthenes' *Apothegmata* appeared in 1555, and Thomas Crewe's English collection *The Nosegay of Morall Philosophie*, in 1580. Both John Stanbridge (1508) and Robert Whittinton (1520) issued texts named *Vulgaria*, common sayings, sometimes coarse, for schoolboys. In this tradition is John Heywood's *Dialogue of Proverbs* (1546, augmented 1562), a dialogue on marriage stuffed with 1267 English proverbs and proverbial epithets, which went through ten editions to 1598. Henri Estienne's *Les Premices* (1583), arranged by commonplace topics, worked French proverbs up into epigrams. All these texts influenced and were influenced by the great dictionaries with their arrays of sayings illustrative of uses of words.

Perhaps the most important and popular progymnastic work in English was William Baldwin's *Treatise of Morall Phylosophie, Contaynyng the Sayinges of the Wyse* (1547; enl Thomas Paulfreyman 1557). This presented in four parts lives of philosophers, precepts, adages, and similes: it is obviously indebted to Diogenes Laertius, Erasmus, and Caxton's *Dictes*. The sayings are arranged, as usual, according to commonplace topics. It is easy to see how a writer like Montaigne or Bacon could produce an essay largely by reflecting on a page of adages contained in such a copybook; and many Renaissance poems may be analyzed as a tissue of epithets, similes, and synonyms derived from the books of Erasmus, Textor, and others.

mythography and emblems The Renaissance mythographers vastly augmented the substantial work of their medieval predecessors, and added to the earlier genre of serial descriptions of the classical gods and heroes a new genre, emblem books, which rearranged mainly mythographical information often according to the principles of the collections of adages (see *emblematics).

Among the more important medieval mythographies that were printed in the Renaissance were the twelfth-century Albericus of London's (Alexander Neckham?) *Allegoriae poeticae* (1520); Boccaccio; and the fourteenth-century Pierre Bersuire's (Petrus Berchorius) *Metamorphosis ovidiana moraliter ... explanata* (1509), which was the basis for Colard Mansion's *La Bible des poetes* (1484). Editions of Ovid, often with elaborate commentary, constitute the core of Renaissance mythography. Later writers expanded the mythographical information in these commentaries, providing summary introductions to all of classical mythology. The major continental mythographers, probably all known to Spenser, were Conti, Pictor, Giraldi, du Verdier, and Cartari.

STEPHEN A. BARNEY

The books listed above illustrate but by no means exhaust the kinds of reference works available to Spenser, with some prominent examples of the kinds. The bibliography below lists some useful modern books, but reference should be made to several large series of facsimile reprints of Renaissance texts, which include many of the titles named above: two series edited by Stephen Orgel, 'The Philosophy of Images' and 'The Renaissance and the Gods,' published by Garland (New York and London); 'English Emblem Books' and 'Continental Emblem Books,' published by Scolar Press (Menston, Yorks); 'English Linguistics, 1500–1800,' edited by R.C. Alston, Scolar Press; 'Scholar's Facsimiles and Reprints' (Delmar, NY); 'The English Experience,' Walter J. Johnson, Inc, Theatrum Orbis Terrarum, Ltd, Da Capo Press (Amsterdam and Norwood, NJ).

D.C. Allen 1941 *The Star-Crossed Renaissance* (Durham, NC); Allen 1970; T.W. Baldwin 1944; Eustace F. Bosanquet 1917 *English Printed Almanacks and Prognostications: A Bibliographical History to the Year 1600* (London, suppl 1928, 1937); Crane 1937; Freeman 1948; Greenlaw 1932; Harper 1910; Heninger 1960; Heninger 1977; Henkel and Schöne 1967; Howell 1956; Johnson 1937; Kendrick 1950; Ong 1971; Praz 1964 (suppl includes list of emblem books by H.M.J. Sayles); Seznec ed 1953; DeWitt T. Starnes 1954 *Renaissance Dictionaries: English-Latin and Latin-English* (Austin, Tex); Starnes and Talbert 1955; Svendsen 1956; Eva G.R. Taylor 1930 *Tudor Geography 1485–1583* (London); A. Wolf 1935 *A History of Science, Technology, and Philosophy in the Sixteenth and Seventeenth Centuries* 2 vols (London; rev by Douglas McKie, New York 1950).

Reformation The Protestant movement of the sixteenth century was a revolutionary effort to change traditional practices of the Roman church considered to be incorrect or abusive. In northern Europe, the reformist movements led by Luther, Zwingli, and Calvin established various territorial churches. In England, the official Reformation extended from Henry VIII's political break with the papacy in the 1530s to the Protestant settlement under Queen Elizabeth. It centered at first on Henry's drive to impose royal authority on the church. Only during the minority of his son Edward VI (1547–53) did powerful Protestant lords collaborate with Archbishop Thomas Cranmer to introduce thoroughly Protestant doctrine and church ritual.

Born near the end of Edward's reign, Spenser was a child at the time of the Elizabethan religious settlement in 1559. He grew up knowing the doctrine and ritual of the Tudor Reformation, which were transmitted through the Thirty-nine Articles of Religion, and more generally through reading and hearing the Word of God in vernacular Bible readings, sermons, common prayers, sacraments, and other ceremonies that were based firmly on the Scriptures. Despite Mary Tudor's effort at counterreformation, service books authorized under Edward VI were again used in church services during Elizabeth's reign: the Great Bible, the Book of Common Prayer, and the primers (see Booty, et al 1981, King 1982, and Wall 1976). The authorized sermons in the books of homilies (1547 and 1563) expounded Cranmer's ideal of 'the life of active charity' in the public, social world. The homilies carefully linked this ethic to Pauline doctrines shared by all Reformed churches, namely, predestination, justification by faith alone, and man's natural and pervasive corruption.

Until the end of Elizabeth's reign, the broad, inclusive doctrine of the Church of England continued to accommodate early Puritans within the spectrum of acceptable Protestant theology. (It is anachronistic, though, to try to discover in the sixteenth century the radical sectarian divisions of the middle seventeenth century.) During Spenser's lifetime, there was general agreement on a predestinarian theology of grace, which, although compatible with almost any aspect of the Genevan church except ministry and discipline, essentially reaffirmed the largely Zwinglian settlement in religion imposed under Edward VI. The views of Zwinglian and Rhineland reformers such as Martin Bucer, Pietro Martire Vermigli (Peter Martyr), and Heinrich Bullinger are at the core of the English Reformation (see D.D. Wallace 1982). Although a deep religious cleavage did exist during the 1560s and 1570s, it divided those Protestants who saw themselves as 'godly' adherents to the Elizabethan Settlement from the multitude of the 'ungodly' (Collinson 1967).

During Spenser's adulthood, all Protestant groups were united in their opposition to the Church of Rome. The doctrinal articles of the Church of England express a Protestant consensus that denies key teachings of medieval Catholicism concerning papal supremacy, clerical intercession, purgatory, pardons, adoration of images and relics, invocation of saints, justification by good works, transubstantiation, and the concept of the Mass as a sacrifice (see *sacraments). Although some Puritans came to reject the Church of England's retention of vestments, episcopal authority, and kneeling at Communion as 'papist' vestiges, others agreed with Melanchthon and his English followers in accepting them as 'adiaphora,' things indifferent to salvation. The Elizabethan Puritan movement focused on matters of church polity rather than doctrine (see King 1985, *Puritanism).

Spenser's earliest publication reflects the Reformation use of the vernacular Bible as a model for poetry and art. It appeared in *Theatre for Worldlings* (1569), a militantly antipapal work by Jan van der Noot, a Flemish immigrant residing in London, whose four final 'Sonets,' modeled upon Revelation, are an apocalyptic attack on the Roman church and a prophecy of the Protestant Reformation. Their images of the Whore of Babylon, the beast with seven heads, the man sitting on a white horse, and the New Jerusalem recur prominently in *FQ* I. The Flemish compiler also dedicates to Queen Elizabeth, under the guise of Astraea, millennial prophecies dating from Edward VI's reign. The commentary identifies these dualistic images with the Reformation conflict between the 'true' and 'false' churches.

Spenser's conformity to the broad Elizabethan Protestant consensus helped him gain patronage from eminent members of the religio-political establishment at all stages of his career: John Young, Bishop of Rochester; Robert Dudley, Earl of Leicester; Sir Philip Sidney; Sir Walter Raleigh; and eventually the Queen herself, who was notoriously reluctant to reward poets. Although *The Shepheardes Calender* (1579) addresses fundamental Reformation concerns such as the problems of clerical greed and ignorance (by then conventional themes in pastoral literature), Spenser's service in 1578 as secretary to Young renders improbable contentions that the work endorses anti-prelatical attitudes. In all likelihood, Spenser wrote most of the *Calender* while serving this reform-minded cleric who is praised in *September* as the good shepherd Roffy. Although Spenser had planned to dedicate the work to Leicester, whose service he had entered by 1579, eventually he addressed it to Sidney, a proponent of the Protestant League and leader of a group of Protestant poets whose goal was to create a literary Renaissance in England.

The religious satires in the *Calender* (*Februarie*, *Maye*, *Julye*, and *September*) dramatize a problem that interested many Protestants: how to fulfill the clerical ideals of sincerity and obedience to the models for pastoral behavior set forth in the Scriptures. The work appeared in the aftermath of the earliest Puritan discontent (initially the 1560s protest over vestments and then the 1570s Admonition controversy; see *religious controversies), and it addresses issues of concern to religious purists. Nevertheless, the text itself offers little support for the seventeenth-century tradition that Spenser articulates a Puritan attack on the Elizabethan church settlement. Pastoral dialogue and disguise furnish instead a means to treat religious and ethical problems without taking sides in factional argument. The satirical fables allowed interpretation in terms of current ecclesiastical disputes, Puritan readers likely finding confirmation for their zeal in E.K.'s comment on 'the reliques and ragges of popish superstition' (*Maye* 239–40 and gloss). Yet most readers would have applied Spenser's generalized biblical paradigms to the concrete circumstances of contemporary history. The plain style and highly charged biblical imagery of the satirical eclogues were the common property of all Tudor Protestants, who agreed that sincere worship should be based upon the Scriptures and that ministerial integrity should avoid pride, avarice, and ignorance.

To label Spenser a 'Puritan' or a 'Catholic' is to ignore the antipapal concerns of *The Shepheardes Calender*, overlooking, for example, how Piers and Palinode dramatize the Reformation division between 'the protestant and the Catholique' (*Maye* argument), and the report that Palinode went on a pilgrimage to Rome (*Julye* 181–4). Even if E.K.'s reformist glosses represent Spenser's own views, both poem and commentary identify a rigorous standard of moral virtue and the clerical ideals of primitive Christianity with the good shepherd-pastors in the tradition of Piers Plowman, Chaucer's Parson, and the pseudo-Chaucerian Pilgrim and Plowman. Their probity contrasts sharply with the spiritual slackness of their companions. Spenser's choice of Piers as the name of a zealous pastor alludes to the Reformation interpretation of Langland's *Piers Plowman* as a proto-Protestant text (see **Plowman's Tale*). Diggon Davie, another rustic speaker descended from Langland's blunt visionary truth-teller, similarly attacks the 'abuses ... and loose living of Popish prelates' (*Sept* argument).

In their recapitulation of the biblical pattern of the Fall (eg, the fates of the Kid and Algrind), the satirical eclogues associate the conventional imagery of scriptural pastoral (shepherds, sheep, wolves, and foxes) with the reformist concern for ministerial integrity and sincere pastoral care. The account of Algrind in *Julye* alludes to the disgrace of Archbishop Edmund Grindal. Yet Spenser treats his fate not as a call to dissent but as an example of the political dangers of occupying high office. The commitment of Grindal, and other members of the progressive faction like Bishop Young, to continued reform of the ministry and church discipline kept alive the original Reformation ideals of thinkers like William Tyndale, Hugh Latimer, and Cranmer. Similarly, the fable of the Oak and the Briar in *Februarie* depicts a double tragedy that can be read not as a Puritan allegory but as a warning against both recusancy and Protestant radicalism (see King 1986).

The Faerie Queene treats central issues of

the Reformation: the individual process of religious and ethical reform in Book I, and the broad public and political sweep of the European Protestant movement in Book V. While the historical element may be subordinate to the moral allegory, these books praise Elizabeth's government and its program for reforming church and state. John Dixon's 1597 marginalia in the first edition of *The Faerie Queene* show how Tudor Protestants could recognize Book I's allusions to Revelation and interpret the allegory in terms of Elizabeth's restoration of reformist government after the persecutions of Mary's reign. A detailed examination of *FQ* I would show how Spenser portrays certain essential doctrines of the Reformation. Protestant theology pervades the Legend of Holiness, where Spenser embodies in the quest of the Red Cross Knight the doctrine of salvation as derived by Protestants from the letters of St Paul. This paradigm included the categories of election, calling, justification, adoption, sanctification, and glorification (see Lewalski 1979). The Letter to Raleigh indicates Redcrosse's election by stipulating that he wears the armor of God. Although original sin inherited from Adam and Eve leads him, like any Christian, repeatedly into error, the unmerited favor or grace of God manifested through election makes possible his justification and sanctification.

The primacy of individual faith in Protestant devotional life lies behind the indoctrination of Redcrosse in the house of Holiness (I x), where his tutor Fidelia ('faith') is older than her sisters Speranza ('hope') and Charissa ('charity'). The order of their births reflects the Protestant reordering of good works (charity) and faith in accordance with Pauline texts like Romans 3.19–26, which insists that the elect are justified by faith rather than by doing works prescribed by the Law. In contrast, the Church of Rome's emphasis on good works led to an elaborate system of absolution based upon private confession, almsgiving, penance, pilgrimages, indulgences, and the intercession of the Virgin Mary and saints. The fertility of Charissa and her 'multitude of babes' (31) is compatible with Cranmer's insistence in the homilies on the continuing importance of good works not as agents of justification but as 'fruits' of faith testifying to spiritual well-being. (Cf also Caelia's 'doing good and godly deedes' 3.) Spenser's seven Beadmen (36–43) mirror Cranmer's cautious traditionalism by honoring the seven corporal works of mercy.

The Reformation insistence on the accessibility of vernacular translations of the Bible as the basis for spiritual education is reflected both by frequent allusion to biblical texts throughout *FQ* I and by the relation between the two emblematic books in cantos ix-x. Although Redcrosse presents Arthur with 'his Saveours testament' (evidently the New Testament) at ix 19, the illiterate knight is as yet unable to read and understand the Scriptures as a model for human action. Bearing the same 'sacred Booke,' Fidelia alone can provide instruction in fundamental truths 'Of God, of grace, of justice, of free will' (x 19). Her teaching also instills an overwhelming sense of sin which leads Redcrosse once again to despair; but, like Una, Speranza counters this failure with the promise of salvation. Only through understanding derived from faith is the knight able to ascend the Mount of Contemplation and attain the spiritual insight necessary to defeat the Dragon that imprisons the human race through sin.

Theological and historical allegory overlap in Prince Arthur, who, as the embodiment of both divine grace and Tudor dynastic claims, typifies the fusion of church and state under Elizabeth. His defeat of Redcrosse's captors – Duessa (patterned after the Whore riding her seven-headed Beast) and Orgoglio (perhaps a type of papal or imperial pride) – recapitulates the apocalyptic battle of Revelation, commonly interpreted as a prophecy of the Reformation in works like van der Noot's *Theatre* (see Hankins 1971).

The pervasive anti-sacerdotalism of *FQ* I exemplifies how the Lutheran doctrine of the priesthood of all believers led to the Reformation attack on the Roman ecclesiastical hierarchy. For instance, polemical glosses in the Geneva Bible that identify Antichrist with the Pope (eg, Rev 17.1–4) underlie the portrait of Archimago as a necromancer and priest 'in long blacke weedes yclad' (i 29–35), as well as the satirical genealogy of Duessa as the Pope's daughter (ii 22). Roman vestments provide similar associations for Idleness: 'Arayd in habit blacke, and amis thin, / Like to an holy Monck' (iv 18). Although Henry VIII dissolved the monasteries during the 1530s, they remained attractive as symbols for continuing religious problems. Thus Kirkrapine personifies not simply Roman avarice but any form of 'church robbery.'

The Reformation issues in the ecclesiastical eclogues of *The Shepheardes Calender* and *FQ* I are found in most of Spenser's works, even those predominantly concerned with forms of behavior not explicitly religious. Because *FQ* II, for instance, is based on classical learning, biblical allusions are rare, and the handling of Protestant topics is enigmatic at best (eg, original sin or the nature of baptism, in the Ruddymane and Maleger episodes). Spenser may expect readers to approach it as a sequel that depends upon or extends the Reformation allegory of *FQ* I into the ethical sphere. Similarly, the antimonastic attack linked to the final triumph of the Blatant Beast (VI xii 23–5) recalls earlier religious satire. More closely linked to *FQ* I is the treatment of justice in *FQ* V, which refers explicitly to England's involvement in the international Protestant cause in cantos x-xii. The Burbon episode, for example, fictionalizes the experience of Henri IV as a Huguenot leader who eventually renounced the Protestant faith (xi 44–65). In these and many other cases, the reader must refer back to *FQ* I for a fully elaborated, extended coverage of Protestant topics and ideals. In that book and the religious eclogues, Spenser is most readily accessible as a Reformation poet.

JOHN N. KING

Booty, et al 1981 (on the worship books of Edward VI and Elizabeth I); Collinson 1967 (an indispensable history); Collinson 1982 (differentiates between Elizabethan Protestantism and nineteenth-century 'Anglican' assumptions about the Tudor Church of England); Dickens 1964 (a definitive history); Hankins 1971 (discusses *FQ* I and biblical commentary tradition); Hume 1984 (argues that Spenser is a moderate Puritan); King 1982 (on Spenser and his Protestant literary predecessors); King 1985 (argues that Spenser adopts the posture of a progressive Protestant); King 1986 (on Spenser's synthesis of classical precedent with the 'plowman' conventions of English Protestant satire); Lewalski 1979 (on Protestant poetic theory and the devotional lyric); Wall 1976 (on the official sermons as models for moral and religious reform); Wall 1983 (on *FQ* I and the reform program of Edward VI); D.D. Wallace 1982 (indicates the impact of the Rhineland reformers on the Elizabethan church); Whitaker 1950 (argues that Spenser is a conservative Anglican).

religious controversies Spenser's time at Merchant Taylors' School in London roughly coincided with the first decade of the 'religious settlement' under Queen Elizabeth and the outbreak of religious controversy involving the newly established Church of England with the Church of Rome and with Puritanism.

The first major controversy was provoked by the new Bishop of Salisbury, John Jewel, with his 'challenge' sermon (1559) and his *Apologie* (1562), both of which were answered by the Catholic theologian Thomas Harding from his exile in Louvain. These protagonists were joined by other writers, until by 1570 the number of printed items came to over 60. The dispute served to underline the main points at issue in the religious changes of the time; it was later recalled by Gabriel Harvey, in his *Pierces Supererogation* (1593), as a contest between 'two thundring and lightning Oratours in divinity,' the English equivalents of Demosthenes and Aeschines in ancient Greece.

Spenser's poetry echoes many ideas and even phrases from the *Apologie*. His description of the false Fox in *SC, Maye*, with 'bells, and babes, and glasses in hys packe' (240), agrees with Jewel's scorn of the 'superfluous ceremonies' of Rome. In *FQ* V iii 24, the disappearance of the false Florimell when placed beside her true exemplar may recall Jewel's assertion that the shadows of Rome vanish 'at the lighte of the gospell.' Yet the ironic reference in *Mother Hubberd* 478 to 'the Gospell of free libertie' may in turn recall Harding's frequent criticism of the reformers for preaching 'carnall liberty' (*Confutation* 1565). There is even some sympathy with the 'old faith' in the fable of the Oak in *Februarie* 207–8, 'an auncient tree, / Sacred with many a mysteree,' as contrasted with the upstart Briar with 'Colours meete to clothe a mayden Queene' (132).

While the poet maintains that 'sike fancies' as the sprinkling of the tree with holy water 'weren foolerie, / And broughten this Oake to this miserye' (211–12), he need not have approved E.K.'s reference to 'the reliques and ragges of popish superstition' (*Maye* 240 gloss).

Spenser's ambivalence appears above all in *FQ* I. He represents Archimago as a monkish hypocrite in 'an holy Chappell,' telling 'of Saintes and Popes' and strewing 'an *Ave-Mary* after and before' (i 34–5), and later introduces the false Duessa as a 'goodly Lady clad in scarlot red' and decked in a 'gold and purple pall' with a 'triple crowne set on her head full hye' (ii 13, vii 16; cf the Whore of Babylon of Rev 17). Yet he does not reject monks and hermits with all their 'holy things,' for he shows an ideal hermit, 'heavenly *Contemplation*' (x 46), as well as seven Bead-men, who stand for the seven corporal works of mercy in medieval piety (36–43). Further, when Spenser introduces Redcrosse, bearing 'on his brest a bloudie Crosse ... The deare remembrance of his dying Lord' (i 2), he possibly recalls John Martiall's *Treatyse of the Crosse* (1564), which was dedicated to Elizabeth because she retained the cross in her royal chapel. When this book was attacked by Alexander Nowell, Dean of St Paul's, in a sermon before her, she publicly reproved him for his abusive language.

Evidently Spenser distinguished between the old Catholic customs of England, which he often views with nostalgia, and the contemporary activities of the seminary priests from Douai. In *The Shepheardes Calender*, he compares these priests, who returned to England from 1574 onwards, to 'the false Foxe' (*Maye* 236) – glossed by E.K. as 'the false and faithlesse Papistes' – and to 'ravenous Wolves' (*September* 148). These comparisons have a contemporary echo in William Turner's anti-popish diatribe, *The Huntyng of the Romyshe Wolfe* (1555?), reissued in 1565 as *The Hunting of the Fox and the Wolfe*. Also, according to E.K.'s gloss, the Pope is included among those who 'gan to gape for greedie governaunce': this is 'meant of the Pope, and his Antichristian prelates' (*Maye* 121–2 and gloss). Spenser's antipathy to the Pope may have hardened on his arrival in Ireland in 1580, shortly after the failure of the papal expedition there in 1579, and about the same time as the arrival in England of the first Jesuits, Robert Parsons and Edmund Campion. While he was unaffected by the controversies they provoked in England, he knew the aftermath of the Spanish Armada of 1588 (supported by Rome) when many of its scattered ships were wrecked on the Irish coast. Events like these may help explain the antipapal vein in *The Faerie Queene*.

The first outbreak of Puritan protest, the vestiarian controversy of 1566, coincided with Spenser's schooldays. Its leader was Robert Crowley, prebendary of St Paul's, who had printed Langland's *Piers Plowman* in 1550 because of its criticism of popish abuses. In response to Archbishop Parker's insistence on the use of vestments in religious services, Crowley published *A Briefe Discourse against the Outwarde Apparell of the Popish Church*, strongly denouncing these 'remnants of the Romishe abhomination' and 'reliques of Romishe Idolatrie.' This controversy is echoed in Spenser's mention of the 'trusse of tryfles' carried by the false Fox (*Maye* 239–40), and even more clearly in E.K.'s gloss: 'by such trifles are noted, the reliques and ragges of popish superstition.' Yet in *Mother Hubberds Tale*, the poet seems nostalgic for the monks of old, 'Their service and their holie things ... besides their Anthemes sweete,' in contrast to the 'small devotion' of the new ministers who officiate only 'once a weeke upon the Sabbath day,' with 'free libertie' to enjoy their 'lovely Lasses' (449–51, 456–7, 476–8). In this he agreed with the Queen, who preferred her ministers, especially her bishops, to be celibate.

When Spenser went up to Pembroke Hall in 1569, he found himself at the center of religious conflict, for the University of Cambridge was the nursery of Elizabethan Puritanism. Already in 1565, the Puritans, led by William Fulke, later Master of Pembroke Hall (from 1578), had protested against the use of the surplice in chapel; and now in 1569–70, the new Lady Margaret Professor of Divinity, Thomas Cartwright, delivered his famous lectures on the Acts of the Apostles, in which he proposed Calvin's view of the early church as a model of presbyterian discipline. Owing to the intervention of John Whitgift, Master of Trinity, Cartwright was deprived of his professor's chair and his fellowship at St John's, and was eventually forced to leave the university. The antagonism between them soon appeared in print: in 1572 Cartwright wrote in support of the Puritan *Admonition to the Parliament*, and Whitgift responded with *An Answere to a Certen Libel*. In this controversy, the Puritans moved from their original protest against vestments to an open attack on the 'lord bishops' whose pride they contrasted with the humility of the apostles (see *homilies). It has been argued that Medina's appearance, being 'rich arayd ... In goodly garments' (II ii 14), reflects the Elizabethan church's approval of canonical dress (Magill 1970).

In Spenser's reaction to the issues of this controversy, we again find his characteristic ambivalence. His criticism in *Julye* 173–6 of those who 'bene yclad in purple and pall' and who 'reigne and rulen over all, / and lord it, as they list,' may be applied not only to 'the Popes and Cardinalles' identified by E.K. but also to some of the Elizabethan bishops, such as John Aylmer, Bishop of London, who may be identified as the Morrell of this eclogue. Here, too, like the Puritan authors of the *Admonition*, the poet looks back to a time when shepherds 'were lowe, and lief, / and loved their flocks to feede' (165–6). Yet he is vague about this time, which may be as well medieval as apostolic. In any case, *The Shepheardes Calender* bears ample testimony to the poet's good relations with many of the Elizabethan bishops. His hero is Edmund Grindal of Canterbury, who appears as 'good *Algrin*' in *Julye* 229. Further, John Young of Rochester, who employed the poet as secretary in 1578, is praised in *September* under the name of Roffy as 'meeke, wise, and merciable, / And with his word his worke is convenable' (174–5). John Piers of Salisbury is introduced as Piers in *Maye*, Richard Davies of St David's as Diggon Davie in *September*, and Thomas Cooper of Lincoln as Thomalin in *Julye*, where he is implicitly praised for remaining in 'the lowly playne,' in contrast to the proud Morrell on his hill. Of these bishops, only Cooper engaged in printed controversy, first (before becoming bishop) against the anonymous Catholic author of the *Apologie of Private Masse* (1562; *STC* 14615), one of the earliest responses to Jewel's challenge, and later (as Bishop of Winchester) against the tracts of Martin Marprelate, with his moderate *Admonition to the People of England* (1589). In *Mother Hubberd* 516–20, Spenser also defends the bishops and lesser clergy against the covetousness of courtiers. As he ironically remarks, at that time it was notorious that 'The Courtier needes must recompenced bee / With a Benevolence, or have in gage / The *Primitias* of your Parsonage: / Scarse can a Bishoprick forpas them by, / But that it must be gelt in privitie.' Here, however, he was on dangerous ground, for among the chief offenders in this respect were the Queen herself and his own patron, the Earl of Leicester.

In Ireland, away from the distractions of such controversy, Spenser was free to write *The Faerie Queene*, as it were in a hermitage of heavenly contemplation. In this poem more than in any other, he gives ample scope to his poetic nostalgia for the Middle Ages. If he criticizes the Pope and his adherents in such allegorical figures as Archimago and Duessa, he is no less outspoken against the radical reformers. In *FQ* VI xii 24, after describing how the Blatant Beast breaks into the monks' cloisters and finds 'filth and ordure' in them (as Cromwell's agents had claimed to have found in their visitation of the monasteries under Henry VIII), he adds that the creature himself is no less foul in the way he ransacks the cells, 'Regarding nought religion, nor their holy heast.' With his 'bitter termes of shamefull infamy' (33), the Beast recalls the portrayal of Martin Marprelate in Cooper's *Admonition*, as 'he that can most bitterly inveigh against bishops and preachers, that can most boldly blaze their discredits, that can most uncharitably slander their lives and doings.'

Another theological controversy broke out in Cambridge after Spenser's time, with important effects on the English church as a whole. The official orthodoxy had been that of Calvin (as vividly recalled by Richard Bancroft in his *Survay of the Pretended Holy Discipline* 1593); but under the influence of Peter Baro, who succeeded Cartwright as Lady Margaret professor in 1574, a more Catholic theology came to prevail, especially when the Lambeth Articles, which formulated the orthodox Calvinist theology of predestination and which had been proposed by the Regius Professor of Divinity William Whitaker and approved by Archbishop Whitgift in 1595, were refused the royal sanction. At that very time, Spenser's alma mater, Pembroke Hall, now under the mastership of Lancelot Andrewes (the poet's junior by two or three years at both Merchant Taylors' School and Pembroke Hall), was in the forefront of this opposition to Calvin; and here, no doubt, we may see where the poet's own sympathies lay.

PETER MILWARD, SJ

W.H. Frere 1904 *The English Church in the Reigns of Elizabeth and James I (1558–1625)* (London); Donald Joseph McGinn 1949 *The Admonition Controversy* (New Brunswick, NJ); Milward 1977; Harold Stein 1936 'Spenser and William Turner' *MLN* 51:345–51; Whitaker 1950.

Renaissance The term Renaissance (meaning 'rebirth' in Fr) has been applied to several periods of cultural renewal in European history, but since the nineteenth century has come to designate chiefly a resurgence of artistic, literary, and intellectual energy which began during the later fourteenth and earlier fifteenth centuries in Italy, and roughly a century later in northern and western Europe. The use of such a period term can mislead if it is taken to imply a quick, radical, historical change or to imply an identical change in several countries. The English 'Renaissance' in particular was a highly independent, native affair. Nonetheless England followed the continent in several significant respects.

One of the most important of these was humanism, which introduced the teaching, reading, and translation of ancient Greek texts and transformed the study of ancient Latin literature and culture. This transformation included a closer study of Latin style, as well as efforts to imitate ancient Latin works in Neo-Latin and the vernaculars, to establish more reliable texts in both ancient languages, and, aided by the development of printing, to disseminate these texts more widely. Renaissance philology was strengthened by a sharper awareness of the differences between historical epochs and thus an awareness of change itself. The complex relation to antiquity involved in varying degrees and in various stages awe for its achievements, humility before its greatness, regret for what was lost, inspiration for new endeavors, confident emulation of its modes, styles, and forms, resentment at its dominant status. There was also frequent anger at what was perceived as medieval indifference to, or even betrayal of, the ancient heritage.

The impact of rediscovered antiquity accompanied and in part produced changes in society, in government, in the arts, in values, in thought, and in religious experience. Society gradually became more secularized; the bourgeois class acquired more power; the use of money as a means of exchange increased. Government became more centralized; in Spain, France, and England, dynasties were consolidated which eventually resulted in the bureaucratic national state. Medieval precepts inculcating contempt for the world were counterpointed by voices praising life in this world. The active life in society gained ground in the minds of men and women against its traditional antithesis, the retired, contemplative life. The dignity of man was more widely perceived to stem from his activities as a creator and builder on earth. The pursuit of worldly glory was recognized as an honorable motive. (Spenser's fairy queen is named Gloriana, and her capital is Cleopolis, 'city of glory.') The ideal of a many-sided excellence displaying skill in a range of approved activities came to be cultivated.

The extraordinary flowering of the visual arts in Italy, especially during the fifteenth and sixteenth centuries, confirmed the power of human creativity, affirmed the value of beauty in itself, and raised the social status of the artist. Literature and even philosophy shared with the visual arts the values of harmony, proportion, and elegance. Of special importance for Spenser was the emergence of a Neoplatonic philosophy during the later fifteenth century in Florence. The central figure in this philosophical movement was Ficino, who translated all of Plato's works into Latin while composing original commentaries and treatises; Ficino's powerful influence spread throughout Europe and left its mark on many works, including Spenser's *Fowre Hymnes*, *Amoretti*, *Epithalamion*, and *Faerie Queene*.

Spenser rightly considered his major poem to stem from Italian epic romance, a Renaissance outgrowth of medieval chivalric narrative. The genre of romance was notable for its labyrinthine plot and large cast of characters, its dependence on chivalric adventure, its free use of the marvelous, the fantastic, and the magical, its mingling of Virgilian and Ovidian elements with medieval, and its organization by canto and *ottava rima* stanza. The principal poems in this tradition were Boiardo's *Orlando innamorato*, Ariosto's *Orlando furioso* (the single work most influential on the form of *FQ*), and Tasso's somewhat more regular epic, *Gerusalemme liberata*. Spenser read Ariosto in Italian editions with allegorizing commentary which presented the *Furioso* as more serious and moral, less ironic and skeptical, than it truly is. Still another influential current of the continental Renaissance was initiated by the French poets of the Pléiade, led by Ronsard and du Bellay. Their example of enriching the vernacular through imitation of prestigious models (see *French Renaissance literature) helped to determine Spenser's conception of his own poetic enterprise.

Although proto-Renaissance ideals can be found in England as early as the time of Humphrey, Duke of Gloucester (1391–1447), the English Renaissance entered its first important phase at the opening of the sixteenth century with a group of humanists whose dominant members were John Colet and Thomas More and who were in direct contact with the great Dutch scholar and writer, Desiderius Erasmus. During the second quarter of the century, Sir Thomas Wyatt and Henry Howard, Earl of Surrey, produced distinguished poetry deeply tinctured with continental conventions. A humanist flowering at Cambridge in mid-century, fostered by Sir John Cheke and Roger Ascham, preceptor to the future Queen Elizabeth, left a legacy which persisted at Cambridge through the seventies, when Spenser studied at Pembroke Hall; the influence of Ascham, for instance, can be traced in the Spenser-Harvey correspondence about quantitative meter. Despite these many anticipations, however, the English Renaissance first attained full maturity belatedly in the eighties and nineties, with the appearance of Sidney, Lyly, Marlowe, Shakespeare, Raleigh, and Spenser himself, among many others. English humanism was somewhat weaker than its continental counterparts; England's progress in painting and sculpture was slow; its considerable achievements in architecture could not match the finest work in Italy and France, but in music it did produce a superb school of native composers. The drama and poetry of the English Renaissance distinguish it as one of the supreme literary eras of human history.

Spenser exemplifies the Renaissance in many ways: his design of forming a complete gentleman (reminiscent of Castiglione's highly popular *Book of the Courtier*); his formal and prosodic experiments; his adaptations of Petrarch, Ariosto, Tasso, and others; his ambitious attempt to write a national epic; his use of classical mythology weighted by interpretations from continental mythographic compilations; and his aspiration to demonstrate that the English language and English genius could emulate the masterpieces of antiquity. Unlike many other Renaissance poets, Spenser never chose to cut his close ties with the Middle Ages, but he did feel deeply the desire for cultural renewal which was a governing passion of his period.

THOMAS M. GREENE

A classic definition of the Renaissance is given in Burckhardt ed 1945 (first pub 1860). Three important later works extend and analyze Burckhardt's thesis: W.K. Ferguson 1948; Federico Chabod 1958 'The Concept of the Renaissance' in his *Machiavelli and the Renaissance* tr David Moore (London) pp 149–200; and Erwin Panofsky 1960 *Renaissance and Renascences in Western Art* (Stockholm). The writings on the Renaissance are vast; perhaps the best introduction is in the first three volumes of *The New Cambridge Modern History* ed respectively by G.R. Potter, G.R. Elton, and R.B. Wernham 1957–68; although they do not cover all of the fifteenth century, they give excellent background for sixteenth-century Europe. For the continent, there is the vast study by Fernand ed Braudel 1972–3 *The Mediterranean and the Mediterranean World in the Age of Philip II* tr Siân Reynolds (London; first pub 1949 in French). For philosophy, see Kristeller, et al 1948; ample further discussion of philosophy and humanism can be found also in various works by Kristeller, Eugenio Garin, R.R. Bolgar, Roberto Weiss, and Douglas Bush, the last two treating England specifically in some of their books. The standard annual bibliography is *Bibliographie internationale de l'humanisme et de la Renaissance* 1965– (Geneva). See also reading lists for *humanism and *Reformation.

Reynolds, Henry (fl 1628–32) Almost nothing is known about Reynolds, one of the first critics to comment on Spenser, except that he wrote *Torquato Tasso's Aminta Englisht* (1628), contributed to Henry Lawes' *Ayres and Dialogues*, imitated tales from Anguillara's version of Ovid, and was the author of *Mythomystes* (1632). For this last (in which he mentions Spenser), he is often recognized as the greatest English disciple of Pico della Mirandola and author of the most important Neoplatonic poetics in Stuart England.

Appropriate to an age of metaphysical poetry, the neologistic title of *Mythomystes* refers to *myth* as both the story or fable of a poetic work and the parable which attempts to verbalize it and to *mists* as those things 'obscure' or 'hidden' and also 'mystical' or 'spiritual'; the progress of its argument, in fact, is from fable to mystery. This argument draws primarily on Pico and on Plato but also turns to philosophy and the Cabala to define the divine afflatus.

Briefly, Reynolds writes in *Mythomystes* that true poetry is divinely inspired, making poets into Tiresias-like prophets (p 19) so dazzled by their visions of the divine that they are blind to the mundane and earthbound. So acute are such visions that only those poets see the order of the world in such transcendent and hidden systems of meaning as the doctrine of numbers:

> The hidden workings of which wise Mistresse, could wee fully in all her wayes comprehend, how much would it cleare, and how infinitely ennoble our blind and groveling conditions, by exalting our understandings to the sight ... of God, or *those invisible things of God ... which are cleerely seene, being understood by the things that are made*; and thence instructing us, not sawcily to leap, but by the linkes of that golden chaine of *Homer*, that reaches from the foote of *Jupiters* throne to the Earthe, more knowingly, and consequently more humbly climbe up to him, who ought to bee indeed the only end and period of all our knowledge, and understanding. (pp 70–1)

His other two points follow: that unlike modern writers, ancient poets preserved their special knowledge by concealing it from the vulgar and unlearned – 'high and Mysticall matters should by riddles and enigmaticall knotts be kept inviolate from the prophane Multitude' (pp 29–30) – and that the uninitiated, in their ignorance, have no grounds to criticize such secret and inspired revelations. In this last, Reynolds is especially Hermetic, linking (through Moses) Rhea and Venus, for instance, with Eve and Noema (p 74). He joins his own versified translation of the story of Narcissus with his own prose explanation.

Reynolds praises only four English writers by name: Chaucer, Sidney, Daniel, and Spenser, of whom he writes, 'I must approve the learned *Spencer*, in the rest of his Poems, no lesse then his *Fairy Queene*, an exact body of the *Ethicke* doctrine: though some good judgments have wisht (and perhaps not without cause) that he had therein beene a little freer of his fiction, and not so close rivetted to his Morall' (p 8). Reynolds, who enjoyed mystical poetry best, would have been most comfortable with such visions as Spenser provides in the house of Holiness (*FQ* I), on Mount Acidale (VI), and in *Fowre Hymnes*, while he would have found *The Shepheardes Calender*, *Mother Hubberds Tale*, and *Muiopotmos* more bluntly moral and therefore inferior. As the author of a poetics of visionary art, Reynolds might have found *FQ* VII most to his liking with its consistent appeal to coded systems of knowledge. ARTHUR F. KINNEY

R[eynolds] 1632; modernized in J.E. Spingarn, ed 1908 *Critical Essays of the Seventeenth Century* 3 vols (Oxford) 1:141–79. See also A.M. Cinquemani 1970 'Henry Reynolds' *Mythomystes* and the Continuity of Ancient Modes of Allegoresis in Seventeenth-Century England' *PMLA* 85:1041–9.

rhetoric For Elizabethans, 'rhetoric' was defined in nearly all the contemporary manuals as an art or craft of verbal ornamentation. What we call rhetoric, namely a general theory of speaker/writer-audience interaction, was more usually dealt with under the rubric of 'eloquence.' Though this article also deals with rhetoric in the restricted Tudor sense, it is concerned primarily with eloquence, the end towards which both rhetoric and its sister art, logic, were directed.

Humanist rhetorical thought derived much of its force and most of its substance from classical oratory, chiefly the system, theory, and practice of Cicero. Humanists admired and emulated Cicero for several reasons: the model his life provided for the synthesis of action and contemplation, his status as a *novus homo* who rose (as many a humanist wished to do) above his origins, his proleptic embodiment of the humanist roles of scholar and teacher, and the stylistic range of his works. Perhaps most important, Cicero and his image of the orator were also idealized figures of the power to be gained by the scholarly and verbal tools to which the humanists alone had access. What humanists needed, and what Cicero's example supplied, was an example of how an almost exclusively verbal ability could be energized and transformed into an influential force in the world of action.

Even today's humanists, largely excluded from roles of political power but owners of a wide inventory of rhetorical and scholarly skills, can see the attractiveness of the Ciceronian ideal. 'It is the part of the orator,' Antonius says in Cicero's *De oratore*, 'when advising on affairs of supreme importance, to unfold his opinion as a man having authority; his is the duty both to arouse a listless nation, and to curb a frenzied one; his is the art by means of which mankind's offenses are brought to destruction, and mankind's honesty is brought to reward' (2.8.35). Here is the consummation devoutly wished by Renaissance humanists. Spenser's friend Harvey was only one of many who praised *De oratore* as a text crucial to the transformation of contemplative knowledge into political action.

Yet as attractive as the Ciceronian ideal was, much that the humanists valued in the life and the writings of Cicero was deeply embedded in the spoken, or performed, character of his classical art. His oratory depends for effectiveness both upon an actual physical presence before an audience and upon his being granted the authority and license with which to discourse on matters of the highest social significance. What, then, would happen when there was no central civic forum in which to perform? When, as an Italian humanist, you lived in a principate where deliberative oratory was neither profitable nor welcome?

In the long term, of course, there is no sufficient answer: modern culture does not often offer humanists the authority and occasion to address the republic on issues of great public importance. In the short term, however, Renaissance humanists found ways to retain the Ciceronian stance through what became exercises in the exegesis of Cicero's works, in which classical values were rewritten to fit Renaissance realities. The features of oratory which were irredeemably physical had to go, but the inspiring vision of what the oratorical art could accomplish was reinterpreted and preserved in other ways. For some, especially in Italy, this meant trying to achieve Ciceronian ends through imitating Cicero's style literally (see *Ciceronianism). For others, like Erasmus and Harvey, to whom stylistic imitation seemed only 'displaying a body that is surpassingly beautiful and lovely but deprived of sense and life' (Harvey ed 1945:87), it meant an effort to define the deeper underlying causes of Ciceronian greatness.

One significant result of these modifications of Ciceronian practice was that eloquence came to overshadow oratory as the privileged and most general term for invoking the high values of the classical system. Cicero himself had used the terms *ars eloquentiae* and *ars oratoris* synonymously; the humanists' adjustment of terminology shows them recognizing that while the values of Ciceronian *res humanae* were still worth pursuit, the means could no longer be the same. Given changed contexts (eg, printed texts) in which physical presence could no longer be imagined as an essential condition, oratory and eloquence could no longer be synonymous, but had to refer to two distinct, though related, entities.

To this point, we have dealt with eloquence; what Spenser's contemporaries called rhetoric, by contrast, was almost entirely a procedural art of the parsing of speeches and the conning of formal schemes. Thus in Melanchthon's *Elementorum rhetorices* (1542), one of the most popular of all the humanist rhetorics, we find a modest definition of 'the ends of rhetoric.' Students should be able 'to judge [when reading] of an extended speech what kind of sequence of parts it should have, what its members are, what its ornaments are; and, when speaking ... to be capable of making an oration with the proper parts and setting out serious matters not briefly, as logic teaches, but with the added light of words' (ed 1846: col 419). Nor, as he also makes clear, is a mastery of this subject by any means the equal to eloquence: 'The wise and skilled men who first discovered this art never believed that its precepts would make men eloquent, nor that they were sufficient to attaining eloquence. For eloquence first requires the highest natural capacity for speaking, and second an understanding of all the humane arts. In addition to [this book's] common rhetorical precepts, therefore, eloquence draws on many extensive helps both from nature and from learning' (col 417).

For Melanchthon, then, rhetoric per se is a limited art, but his view is by no means unique. His text served as a model for Leonard Cox's *Arte or Crafte of Rhethoryke* (c 1530), England's first vernacular rhetoric, and many English writers – Sherry, Peacham, and Fraunce, for example – treat rhetoric even more narrowly, defining and sometimes exemplifying extensive lists of schemes (figures of sound) and tropes (figures of speech), but omitting such matters as the nature and ordering of parts. The major English exception to this narrowing of rhetoric is Wilson's *Arte of Rhetorique* (1553), which attempts to provide a 'full' rhetoric, treating all five traditional divisions of the art – invention, arrangement, ornamentation, memory, delivery. But even Wilson excludes from rhetoric the handling of 'infinite questions,' by which he means any general topic such as 'whether it be best to marie.' These discourses he treats in his parallel treatise on logic, *The Rule of Reason*. The fact is that no humanist rhetorician ever imagined that a rhetoric was a complete treatment of the language arts; it was but one of the set of arts whose study, together with natural gifts and practice, might produce genuine eloquence.

As we review the range of Renaissance training in the verbal arts, it becomes clear that the values which first belonged to oratory in fact split in two, so that oratory's technical aspects were classed as rhetoric and its larger and more general ends as eloquence. Rhetoric, perhaps in compensation, got to call itself an art; eloquence, by contrast, was something like a general end to which all other arts were subordinate, and humanists of various specializations worked to reform their particular arts so that each might assume to itself this overarching, higher end. This process may be termed the rhetoricization of the humanist arts, although that term confuses our rather broad modern sense of rhetoric with the humanists' more restricted sense. A more precise (if barbarous) description would be that these arts are 'eloquent-ized,' or (as some have even said) 'Ciceronianized.' Eloquence was no longer the purview of any one art. It was, in a Sidneian word, an architectonic, and as such was something like a concept *in potentia* and waiting to be realized.

From the perspective of literary study, it is clear that the drift of these rhetorical events was no bad thing, for two things had happened which effectively put poetry at midstage. The first was that with eloquence no longer the property of one art, the major venue for the classical oratorical values shifted to the written page: if, in the absence of oratorical occasion, to speak eloquently in an empty room is to waste one's time, then by contrast, to write eloquently in an empty room merely allows better concentration, since books, unlike speeches, can supply their own occasions. Should a writer wish to address the state, in one place and at one time, he need only to set his mind accordingly and put pen to paper: to have books is thus to have replaced the Roman forum. Through books, literary eloquence could recover the stance of power which the culturally displaced orator had lost.

Yet if printing encouraged the oratorical values of eloquence to be relocated in literary contexts, it also helped to subordinate the otherwise independent trivium subjects (grammar, logic, and rhetoric) to whatever art could stake its claim to eloquence, and it is precisely this relegation of other arts to the role of 'serving sciences' that Sidney makes one of his primary tasks in the *Defence*. In a projection worthy of the best of alchemists, Sidney transmutes the central values which Cicero defined as those of oratory into those of poetry. Thus he begins by adopting for the poet the orator's unique and dominating position among the arts, borrowing from Cicero not just the conception of his argument, but his very terms. Further, in locating the poet's dominance in the power to move, Sidney again appropriates to the poet the chief Ciceronian office of the orator. But just as important, his argument for the special powers of poetic language is also very much the same claim which Cicero makes for the orator's special powers of *actio*. In Cicero, of course, these modes are primarily physical and formal; Sidney converts the idea of the orator's actual presence into the idea of the poet's putative presence, borrowing the orator's concept of *energeia* (the use of imagery and likeness to conjure up through mere words the sense and dimension of a fully realized experience) to argue the poet's need for 'forcibleness.'

This has been a brief treatment of a complex subject; and, when one finally comes to the question of how knowing rhetoric makes one a better reader of Spenser, there is no simple answer. It is not just a matter of knowing what schemes and tropes Spenser uses, or of what rhetorics he might have studied. These interesting questions encompass only a small part of what the classical oratorical tradition provided him.

The humanist poet's larger, more abstract rhetorical inheritance begins from what could be called the office of the orator, in the twofold classical sense of this word, both as a defined role to be fulfilled and as a social duty to which one is morally bound. Oratory supplies the poet an office in the first sense by defining for him a stance and authority from which to speak on the highest concerns of the state. In the second sense, the classical model enjoins on him the duty of deliberative as well as of epideictic speech. From a Ciceronian point of view, it is the poet's duty, and not just his choice, to advise the state as to future action. Finally, oratory also bequeaths to the poet a sense of position with respect to the culture he serves, for it becomes the poet's role as it once had been the orator's to act as the cultural nexus through which the best thoughts from the culture's wisest store can be brought to bear upon general public issues. A favorite Renaissance commonplace was Cicero's definition of eloquence as 'copiose loquens sapientia' (wisdom speaking with fullness; *Partitiones oratoriae* 79). Such a phrase would make no poor motto for the rhetorical achievement of *The Faerie Queene*. (See also *copia, humanist *poetics.)

JOHN WEBSTER

Cox ed 1899; Harvey ed 1945; Philipp Melanchthon 1846 *Elementorum rhetorices* in *Opera ... omnia* ed Carolus Gottlieb Bretschneider, 13: cols 417–506 (Halle); T. Wilson 1560.

Don Paul Abbott 1983 'Renaissance' in *The Present State of Scholarship in Historical and Contemporary Rhetoric* ed Winifred Bryan Horner (Columbia, Mo) pp 75–100; Alpers 1962; Dundas 1985; Hanna H. Gray 1963 'Renaissance Humanism: The Pursuit of Eloquence' *JHI* 24:497–514; Howell 1956; Joseph 1947; G.A. Kennedy 1980; Lanham 1968; Murphy 1983; Rix 1940; Seigel 1968; Nancy S. Struever 1970 *The Language of History in the Renaissance: Rhetoric and Historical Consciousness in Florentine Humanism* (Princeton); Tuve 1947; Vickers 1970; Vickers 1988; John Webster 1981 '"The Methode of a Poet": An Inquiry into Tudor Conceptions of Poetic Sequence' *ELR* 11:22–43. For bibliographies of Renaissance primary texts, see Abbot 1983, Howell 1956, Joseph 1947, and Lanham 1968. See also *logic.

rhetoric in Spenser's poetry Rhetorical analysis of Spenser's poetry has tended to focus primarily on identification of the tropes and schemes of *elocutio* (style and ornamentation), perhaps because this limited approach has the authority of long tradition. Renaissance theorists, themselves biased by tradition to stress the rhetoric of lawcourts, pulpits, and political assemblies, in their textbooks cited poets mainly as examples of style, and Spenser's first commentator, E.K., in his gloss to *The Shepheardes Calender*, limits his rhetorical observations to a random selection of often obscure figures. Renaissance poets, however, striving to emulate in vernacular literature the achievements of admired Latin models, also adapted the rhetorical principles of those models to their needs – adaptations involving more than devices of elocutio. Spenser's sense of occasion, audience, and subject dictates his choice not only of figures of ornament but also of *topos*, commonplace, method of proof, exemplum, and prosody – all according to criteria of appropriateness, or decorum. He expected his readers, schooled like himself in the disciplines of classical rhetoric, to discern his purpose by abstracting principles of decorum from details of elocutio and organization (*dispositio*) and to move from this base, by inference, to his conception (*inventio*).

In practice, however, such analytical inference proves complex and demanding. The rhetorical structure underlying Spenser's best work supports not one single network of decorous relationships but a dense mosaic derived from the poet's *copia* and his allegorical temper. Theorists traditionally classified *allegoria* as a trope, an element of elocutio, but Veltkirchius (in his commentary on an edition of Erasmus' *De copia* published in London 1569) classes it among other genres as an element of inventio. Spenser evidently made the same shift of status. As a rhetorical genre, allegoria functions both as a species of narrative in which one sequence of events alludes to others, thereby inviting multiple interpretations, and as a method of exegesis for such forms as prophecies, divinations, myths, and signs. Once a poet opts to use allegoria, he is committed by the demands of decorum to the conventions of the genre: to the formal and functional characteristics abstracted from admired models of allusive narrative or exegetical exposition. Spenser's debt to this tradition is well documented. Decorum also dictates, however, that the poet not simply adhere slavishly to his sources, but select and where necessary adapt or concoct topoi appropriate to his vision, enriching the rhetorical tradition he inherits. Implicit in both the configuration of one narrative sequence evocative of others and the notion of exegetical exposition is the common concept of a unity underlying apparent diversity, a concept central to the Neoplatonic strain in Spenser's Christian humanism. This evident affinity between allegoria and a primary focus of Spenser's vision accounts for his tendency to give this genre dominant status. By merging topoi of allegoria with those of other rhetorical genres (*elegia*, epithalamium, *fabula*, *heroica* [epic], *lyrica*, *pastoralia*, and sonnet) he subsumes all as species of allegoria, producing mosaics which, as the history of Spenserian commentary abundantly attests, engender multiple and diverse interpretations.

The rhetorical structures produced by Spenser's merging of genre capable of generating such a diversity of readings exemplify configurations abstracted from the concept of courtship. An analysis of the rhetorical motives in Castiglione's *Courtier* has adduced the following useful definition: 'By the "principle of courtship" in rhetoric we mean the use of suasive devices for the transcending of social estrangement' (Burke 1950:208). For Spenser, as for Castiglione and many other Renaissance artists, this principle has broad ramifications. Three motives for courtship correspond to three fundamental sources of perceived estrangement: those between sexes and between orders of being (man, nature, and God), as well as those between social classes. Patently, we find these estrangements intolerable and seek to overcome them. Each generates its own dynamic of courtship (erotic, transcendent, and social), creating three analogous rhetorical structures all conforming schematically to the hierarchical pyramid we associate particularly with models of social privilege: broad at the base where the masses dwell in the lowest stratum of power, narrowing to a small elite of nobility (Castiglione's courtiers), and converging to an apex, the seat of sovereignty. This social model patterns erotic and transcendent structures. In each, highly formalized strategies exist to ascend the hierarchy and approach identification with its apex, or 'ultimate term,' and the erotic courtier seeking physical union with his beloved, or the Christian courting spiritual unity with God, stand in relation to their respective objects of courtship as inferior to superior in the social model, traditionally adopting a stance of humility, supplication, and servitude. Because the structures are thus both formally and functionally analogous, any one of them may stand surrogate for the others, thereby providing Spenser with a source of considerable allegorical flexibility.

His exploitation of the rhetorical potential in this configuration reveals itself most readily in *The Faerie Queene*, where the narrative sequence of knightly quest provides a vehicle for interwoven progressions of erotic, social, and transcendent courtship. Book I will serve as a paradigm for his method throughout the poem. Rhetoric is the art of persuasion, and any effort to persuade another of our point of view both acknowledges an estrangement between us (we are not of 'the same mind') and seeks to overcome it. Spenser, functioning as rhetorician (quite apart from his probable role as courtier seeking preferment from Elizabeth), courts a meeting of minds between poet and audience to overcome their estrangement through suasive devices. In *FQ* I, the subject is holiness, and the 'Legende of the Knight of the Red Crosse' is Spenser's instrument of persuasion, constructed to forge an identification of perspectives and attitudes on this subject between his vision and that of his reader. In effect, he asserts a concept of holiness and sets out to prove it.

Traditionally, a rhetorical assertion is termed an *enthymeme* to distinguish it from a premise in logic. Logical systems, such as those of mathematics and metaphysics, are closed and permit the deduction of true and certain conclusions from premises if the rules of the system are followed consistently, unaffected by anything outside the system. Logical premises are either true or false with the certainty of a priori definition. Enthymemes, by contrast, are probable, not certain, and rhetoric is the alternative to logic as a source of comprehension and order in open systems where the certainty of logic is unattainable or suspect. Indeed, Renaissance humanists championed rhetoric in part because it provided a means of opening to fresh speculation and controversy issues long closed by scholastic philosophers within the formulaic protocols of Aristotelian logic. Spenser's choosing to treat holiness as a rhetorical issue reflects this humanistic influence, and commits him to 'alogical' methods of proof: *ethos*, *pathos*, and *logos*. Proof by ethos (ethical proof) occurs when we give our consent to an enthymeme either because of the respect due its source or because we are impressed by the performance of its advocate. Proof by pathos (pathetic proof) occurs when our consent is won by appeal to emotion. Logos (logical proof), despite its designation, is not deductive but demonstrative: it relies on examples (*exempla*) whose persuasive power depends upon decorum, our perception of their appropriateness to the enthymeme they purport to prove. Exempla also carry varying degrees of both emotional and ethical appeal. For Spenser and his readers, scriptural exempla were more authoritative than historical or literary (fabulous) exempla, and citations from classical authors outranked later sources.

Book I, however, is a secular fable on holiness, not a treatise or sermon, and decorum forbids Spenser's directly citing the kinds of exempla suitable to formal argument. Appeals to biblical, historical, or literary authority are indirect, or allusive, achieved through a suggestive phrase or detail of description, which are techniques of elocutio (style and ornament), not elements of inventio (the selection of topoi, enthymemes, and exempla appropriate to the subject). Spenser's inventio consists of mixed topoi, both those of genre already noted, and those of subject, the aspects of holiness as he envisions it. Each aspect is either praiseworthy (*eulogistic*) or blameworthy (*dislogistic*), generating enthymemes which, stated simplistically, conform to either the pattern '*x* is holy' or '*x* is unholy.' To 'prove' such enthymemes and conform to the topoi of allegoria and heroica, Spenser incorporates each aspect in characters whose actions, words, and description represent appropriately the nature of the particular aspect of holiness each embodies, be they eulogistic (eg, Una, Arthur, Caelia and her sisters, Mercy, Contemplation) or dislogistic (eg, Error, Archimago, Duessa, Lucifera, Orgoglio, Despair). Characters, in short, are Spenser's true exempla, some of whose characteristics may evoke scriptural, historical, or literary authority.

Spenser favors three schemes of elocutio to adduce such authority: *prosopographia* (the description of a person by form, stature, manners, studies, activities, and affections), *topothesia* (the description of an imaginary place), and *icon* (a specialized form of description by use of multiple comparisons to other persons or things). Some uses of prosopographia are extremely simple, involving little more than a suggestive name attached to an exemplum (eg, Fidelia, Zeal, Reverence, Repentance) or a detail of appearance (eg, the initial description of Redcrosse, I i

2, with its allusion to the 'whole armour of God' in Eph 6). Similar economy marks the topothesia of '*Morpheus* house' (i 39, 40) with its echo of passages from *Aeneid*, *Odyssey* and *Metamorphoses*. Other schemes are highly elaborate, involving both topothesia and prosopographia interwoven to produce a decorous relationship between place and person. The treacherous master of illusion, Archimago, for instance, is characterized by his monkish disguise and precious habitat, both conveying the exaggerated perfection that a stage manager might create to cater to conventional expectations of a hermit and his hermitage, and reflecting with exact decorum the hyperbolized cliché of his rhetoric: 'He told of Saintes and Popes, and evermore / He strowd an *Ave-Mary* after and before' (35). By contrast, Despair and his cave afford no disguise, but person and place (ix 33–6) reinforce each other in their appropriateness to the spiritual death they represent, 'Darke, dolefull, drearie, like a greedie grave.' Equally illustrative of decorum is Spenser's use of icon to depict Lucifera's counselors, the deadly sins. Their names evoke their religious significance, and every detail of description stands in appositional, sometimes synonymic, relationship to every other detail and to the abstract name. Another lengthy icon (vii 16–18) characterizes Duessa through a series of comparative identifications with the woman riding the seven-headed Beast of Revelation 17.3–4. Whether simple or elaborate, such strategies of elocutio, in their detailed copia disciplined by decorum, enrich the ethos of Spenser's exempla, enabling him to court, in his dispositio, recognition from his audience of deep moral import in this ostensibly secular fable of adventure.

Dispositio is the office of rhetorical practice concerned with the organization of the elements of inventio into their most persuasive form of argument. Spenser's argument is his plot, and its dispositio involves persuasive strategies of narration. Stripped to its fundamentals, the narrative sequence exhibits topoi of fabula, of romance, legend, and fairy tale. An untutored farmboy in borrowed armor undertakes a hazardous quest to rescue the parents of a mysterious princess whose castle is besieged by a dragon. Surviving encounters with monsters, wizards, witches, trolls, giants, and assorted other villains, he completes his mission, discovers his true identity as the patron saint of England, and is betrothed to the princess. Such tales are the stuff of daydream, self-pleasing and uncritically optimistic, and for the purpose of moral enthymemes the topoi of fairy tales are seldom effective as ethos or logos, although they exert a timeless pathetic effect, tending to captivate rather than to persuade. Like Sidney's poet, they give 'so sweet a prospect into the way, as will entice any man to enter into it' (ed 1973b:92). To entice the attention and sympathy of his audience is the first task of dispositio for the orator in his *exordium*, and the rhetorical elements of fabula allow Spenser to focus sympathetic attention on Redcrosse, who begins his quest as an exemplum, not of holiness or unholiness, but of the daydream-self in Everyman: well meaning, caught up in marvelous adventure, upward bound to success by dint of his good intentions and physical prowess alone.

Once established pathetically, Redcrosse is transmuted progressively into an instrument of ethical and logical proof. Unlike other exempla, he is not static in character but dynamic; neither saintly nor depraved, capable in potential of either holiness or unholiness, he thus attains the function of surrogate for general humanity even as, indeed because, his ethos as hero of fable is discredited by the manifest inadequacy of his good intentions and physical prowess over the first nine cantos. The narrator's *epiphonema* (summary moral) at x 1, drawn from these cantos, states as a discovered conclusion the enthymeme they seek to prove. Spenser's argument for the assertion in this stanza proceeds through a sequence of dramatic demonstrations in each of which the audience's surrogate exemplum, Redcrosse, 'takes on' a dislogistic exemplum – 'takes on' in both the dramatic sense of encountering as antagonist and the structural sense of manifesting the unholy aspect each exemplifies. He is enmeshed in Error, deluded by Archimago, wounded in his worldly pride by Lucifera, seduced by Duessa, conquered and dungeoned in darkness by Orgoglio, persuaded to self-destruction by Despair. Equally demonstrative of the enthymeme are statements within whose syntax Redcrosse takes on the countervalent eulogistic exempla, being comforted, rescued, healed, guided, and taught by Una, Arthur, the dwarf, the stream and tree of canto xi, and the figures of canto x whose names compose a lexicon of religious terms: Caelia, Fidelia, Speranza, Charissa, Humilitá, Zeal, Reverence, Obedience, Patience, Amendment, Remorse, Repentance, Mercy, Contemplation.

These names, like other devices of elocutio, mark the incursion of allegoria into the topoi of heroica and fabula, and serve to universalize both the exempla and the syntax of their relationship with Redcrosse. As the knight takes on successive exempla, he simultaneously moves toward the end of his quest; thus the structure of narrative sequence, by its very nature, proves through logos that each exemplum is necessary to, and has a place in, the attainment of that end. Led by Redcrosse and the narrator, readers discover that to accept the inefficacy of 'fleshly might' against 'spirituall foes' is a prior necessity for the attainment of grace. Each episode in the narrative demonstration is at once dramatically a step towards the goal and logically a derivative attribute of the goal; hence, structurally, it is an intermediate level in a hierarchical model with the goal as its apex. As each exemplum accumulates, through elocutio, attributes derived from religious, historical, and literary topoi, it becomes a constituent common to more than one such hierarchy. Thus Redcrosse, in completing his fairy-tale quest by killing a dragon, simultaneously reaches the apex of erotic, social, and transcendent structures, achieving identity as the betrothed of Una, a true knight of Gloriana, the patron saint of England, and recipient of salvation through grace.

Temporal simultaneity implies structural coincidence: all ultimate terms touch at the same point of convergence. Spenser prefigures this narrative point in graphic form as the physical summit of the Mount of Contemplation, a natural analogue for hierarchical structure, described in a topothesia using elaborate paraphrase (*paraphrasis*) to identify the place as Sinai, the Mount of Olives, and Parnassus (x 53–4), whose summits invoke associations with Moses and the dispensation of law, Jesus and the dispensation of mercy, and the classical Muses respectively. However we may interpret this episode allegorically, its rhetorical effect is to assert the identity of three apparently diverse mountains, making them analogous manifestations of a single entity. As Redcrosse climbs the mountain towards discovery of his identity as St George and his vision of the 'new *Hierusalem*' (55), both his quest for the summit and his function as courtier to Gloriana undergo an elaboration of ethos parallel to the accumulation of significance in his narrative encounters with exempla. Similarly, the narrative sequences culminating in the Dragon's death, by virtue of their common constituent exempla, the common figure of Redcrosse as courtier, and the coincident point of their ultimate terms, become, despite their apparent diversity, analogous manifestations generated from a single hierarchical structure of courtship.

Although they exhibit principles of decorum and generic topoi markedly different from those of *The Faerie Queene*, works throughout Spenser's canon reveal analogous strategies of rhetorical structure and proof. *The Shepheardes Calender* and *Amoretti* offer sufficient variety to illustrate both the continuity and flexibility of his rhetorical practice.

In *The Shepheardes Calender*, the figure of Colin Clout, the shepherd-poet, serves rhetorical functions similar to those of Redcrosse, and the presence of topoi from allegoria, here blended with those conventional to pastoral, creates interpretive potential of the type noted in *The Faerie Queene*. Particular readings of the *Calender* depend largely on how one identifies various characters in the poem, especially Colin and his 'faithlesse' beloved Rosalind. For the purpose of rhetorical induction, however, who or what these characters might be matters less than how they function in a formal structure. In the plaintive eclogues, Rosalind functions formally as the object of both poetic and erotic courtship, with Colin as the doubly frustrated courtier.

The key to Spenser's elaboration of this model is *October*, where Piers identifies the vocations of poet and priest: to guide 'lawlesse' youth with moral instruction to the 'good' regardless of the meager worldly rewards of which Cuddie complains. Piers' identification makes explicit the implications of rhetorical parallels between the plaintive and moral eclogues. Using a dispositio of debate in the latter, as opposed to that of complaint in the former, Spenser explores the faithlessness of shepherds who neglect their pastoral calling due to worldly corruption, a betrayal which, like Rosalind's, causes the flocks to suffer. The format of debate creates an amalgam of antithetical perspectives and complementary personalities. The debaters are not, in themselves, exempla of the moral alternatives for which they speak; figures designated as good or bad appear only as exempla used by the debaters: Algrind, Roffy, Tityrus, and the Oak are eulogistic, while the Briar, Fox, Wolf in sheep's clothing, and the Kid display dislogistic characteristics of folly, pride, falsehood, and neglect of duty. The debaters themselves, like Redcrosse, are neither saintly nor depraved, but median figures of equal ethical status serving as loci of conflicting moral alternatives.

In speaking for one alternative, each debater indicates a potential for good or evil, and Spenser gives all the advantage of logical proof to one of the antithetical perspectives coexisting in each eclogue. Diggon's attack on worldliness in *September*, for instance, uses the fabulous exemplum of Roffy and Lowder and his own experience as ample logical proof to undercut the homiletic complacency of Hobbinol (70–3, 152–3). *Februarie* displays a confrontation between pathetic and logical proof similar to *May*. Thenot cites the ethical exemplum of Tityrus and the fabulous case of the Oak and Briar to demonstrate the effects of imprudence and rash anger in refutation of Cuddie's emotional, ad hominem outbursts (51–4, 59–60). In each instance, the audience is invited to judge the issue, not the speaker, and to recognize, applying the rhetorical criteria for victory in formal debate, that one case has been proven while the other has not. The debaters, taken as a group, become an appropriate exemplum of common humanity struggling to mediate between antithetical alternatives, and Spenser's elocutio by antithesis in the moral eclogues is decorous with his combative dispositio which, in turn, reflects a Christian-humanist inventio of man balanced between conflicting moral polarities.

Piers' identification of priestly and poetic vocations in *October* merges this exemplar from the moral eclogues with Colin. Piers also invokes the Neoplatonic ideal of love, the recognition that earthly beauty is only an imperfect reflection of its heavenly counterpart, in answer to Cuddie's assertion that Colin's frustrated erotic passion prevents his raising poetry to its ancient heights (88–102). Colin thus becomes a synecdoche of poet, priest, and lover suspended, in each role, at a median point between the ideal and its worldly antithesis: a median figure striving for suasive union with the highest level in analogous hierarchies, not only the erotic and social structures of the plaintive eclogues, but also by functional identification, with the aesthetic and religious. Rosalind, as the object of Colin's courtship, thereby becomes the locus of multiple functions, equivalent to the ultimate term in each structure and thus capable of sustaining, like Colin, the multiple interpretations of allegorical analysis.

Within the Neoplatonic context, however, Rosalind is also a median figure, spirit and flesh, representing potentially the ideal Eliza of *Aprill* and the mutable Dido of *November*, both of whom transcend her as objects of successful poetic courtship, of praise and lament respectively. Insofar as she is a median figure, she is functionally identical with Colin; they are loci of antithetical values, poetic and antipoetic, within the same personality. Their courtship is equivalent to the courtship of debate through complementary voices in the moral eclogues, with Colin's struggle to overcome erotic estrangement informing a dispositio of internal struggle to resolve the antithetical demands of his vocation and those of the world. Through Rosalind, within the context of Neoplatonic love, Colin must, like the debaters in the moral eclogues, choose to court the heavenly or the earthly. His despair and sense of lost congruence with nature (*Jan* 25–30, *Dec* 19–138) are both proof that he has chosen wrongly and Spenser's means of courting our perspective in evaluating the same alternative. As the figure of courting shepherd common to multiple hierarchical structures, Colin has significance decorous to each setting, but whether he functions as lover, priest, or poet, like Redcrosse, he reflects Spenser's humanistic inventio.

Although its generic topoi are largely those of the Petrarchan sonnet rather than pastoral, *Amoretti* displays inventio, dispositio, and a functional relationship between its poet-protagonist and his object of erotic courtship virtually identical with the major rhetorical configurations of *The Shepheardes Calender*. Its dramatic fable of frustrated courtship again informs an inventio using, as topoi of subject, the antithetical polarities of Neoplatonic love – sacred and profane, rational and irrational – to generate a dispositio composing a collision of antithetical exempla focused within the protagonist's mind. Thus lover and beloved again function dialectically as complementary facets of a composite psyche, with the imagistic patterns of Spenser's elocutio defining the conflicting poles of this 'psychomachia.'

Images of tyranny and war (eg, 11, 14, 57), 'amazed' senses and blindness (3), storm (40, 62), nets and hooks (37, 47), sickness (50), and lost poetic power (33) are Neoplatonic commonplaces of irrational love attributed to his beloved, Elizabeth, as cause or source. She, however, is also, sometimes within the same sonnet, the locus of other, directly contrary, attributes: calm, peace, and inspiration. These contradictions within the lover's mind, epitomized by such *oxymora* as 'dying live' (14) and 'O mighty charm which makes men love theyr bane, / and thinck they dy with pleasure, live with payne' (47), prove by exempla the corrupting power of passion on intellect, but equally demonstrate that Elizabeth, like Rosalind, is potentially a source of both sacred and profane volition in her lover. The choice is his.

The apotheosis of Elizabeth in sonnet 74 to equal stature with mother and queen brings to explicit focus the implications of a cumulative attribution to her by devices of elocutio throughout both cycles, epithets denoting majesty, sovereignty, and divinity, beginning with 'soverayne beauty' in 3. She, like Rosalind, thus becomes the ultimate term in analogous structures, and the poet's courtship, ostensibly erotic, is simultaneously both social and transcendent. The seasons of his quest terminate in winter and despair because the erotic courtship remains unconsummated. Rhetorically, physical consummation would prove that through sexual union spiritual and social identification with God and sovereign also occur simultaneously and coincidentally. Despite their timeless pathetic appeal, such fairy-tale doctrines are wholly indecorous with Spenser's inventio and the Christian-humanist perspective it embodies. The protagonist of *Amoretti*, like Redcrosse and Colin, stands as surrogate and exemplar of man suspended between moral alternatives.

Spenser's persuasive strategies court our understanding that in only one state, that of holiness, are all fundamental estrangements, erotic, social, and transcendent, capable of resolution, and his rhetorical structures consistently define that goal as one common to all the elemental strivings of human life. MICHAEL F.N. DIXON

rhetorical criticism from E.K. to the present Modern rhetorical criticism attempts to understand Spenser historically in the context of an Elizabethan poetics different from both that of the classical period and our own. Classical Greece had developed an art of public speaking and a related but distinct art of poetry. Aristotle treated them separately in his *Rhetoric* and *Poetics*. Although this distinction was maintained by such Roman theorists as Cicero and Quintilian, rhetoric was later adapted to composition of all kinds: oral and written, prose and verse, public and private. By the late Middle Ages, sermons, letters, and poems all followed the rules of rhetoric.

The Renaissance inherited this fusion of rhetoric and poetics. For such Elizabethan critics as Puttenham and Sidney, the purpose of poetry, like that of the epideictic oration, was to move men to virtuous action by praising virtue and reproving vice (see humanist *poetics). To this end, poetry used the formal devices of argument, organization, and style developed for the oration. Their humanist education trained Spenser and his contemporaries both to write and to judge literature according to such rhetorical concepts as decorum, ornamentation, and imitation. Even though changes in the English language and in literary taste made Spenser's poetry increasingly remote to seventeenth- and eighteenth-century readers, they shared with him a poetics based on rhetoric.

Beginning in the late eighteenth century, the Romantic movement revolutionized poetics, severing its link with rhetoric. Education, too, underwent profound changes in adapting to the Industrial Revolution. In particular, rhetorical training, the foundation of the humanist curriculum, was weakened until by now it has been almost abandoned. Misunderstanding Spenser's rhetorical poetics, twentieth-century readers have often found his work inaccessible (see *rhetoric in Spenser's poetry). Accordingly, it has been recognized during the past fifty years that a developed rhetorical criticism is needed to foster a renewed appreciation of his art.

Not distinguishing between poetics and rhetoric, Spenser's contemporaries were necessarily 'rhetorical critics' of his poetry. Hence their debate about his style. Cicero had reserved archaic and other uncommon diction, such as dialect words and neologisms, to ornament the high style. Renaissance theory dictated the high style for epic, the low style for pastoral. Anticipating criticism of *The Shepheardes Calender*, E.K. asserts the new poet's 'dewe observing of Decorum everye where' (Epistle to Harvey). Whether 'Immeritô' used archaic diction in imitation of ancient authors, or because rough and obsolete speech is most suitable to shepherds, it gives 'great grace and ... auctoritie to the verse.' Such stylistic gravity is justified by the poet's 'morall wisenesse' in writing to persuade himself and others from the folly of love. 'Immeritô' has exceeded his predecessors in rhetorical skill: he has enriched the language by restoring good English words now out of fashion rather than by borrowing foreign words; his well-knit sentence structure has improved poetic language, which suffered from looseness; and he has avoided the excessive ornamentation of 'the rakehellye route of our ragged rymers.' Yet Sidney, to whom *The Shepheardes Calender* is dedicated, was not convinced: he criticized its 'olde rusticke language' because 'neither Theocritus in Greek, Virgil in Latin, nor Sannazzaro in Italian, did affect it' (*Defence* ed 1973b:112). The style of *The Faerie Queene* could be defended more easily on Ciceronian principles. The elder Francis Beaumont asserts that 'Maister *Spencer*, following the counsaile of *Tullie in de Oratore*, for reviving of antient wordes, hath adorned his owne stile with that beauty and gravitie, which *Tully* speaks of: and his much frequenting of *Chaucers* antient speeches causeth many to allow farre better of him, then otherwise they would' ('Letter to Thomas Speght' 1598; *Sp All* p 54). However, Daniel would 'Let others sing of Knights and Palladines, / In aged accents, and untimely words' (*Delia* 1592; *Sp All* p 23). Edward Guilpin summarizes the Elizabethan debate over language by noting that 'Some blame deep *Spencer* for his grandam words, / Others protest that, in them he records / His maister-peece of cunning giving praise, / And gravity to his profound-prickt layes' (*Skialetheia* 1598; *Sp All* p 58).

Spenser became accepted as a new model of poetic excellence (see *imitations and adaptations, Renaissance). E.K. glosses such rhetorical figures as *epanorthosis*, *epiphonema*, *fictio*, hyperbaton, *icon*, metaphor, paronomasia, periphrasis, proverb, syncope, and synecdoche. Logical, rhetorical, and grammatical treatises mined Spenser's poems for illustrations: Fraunce's *Shepherd's Logic* (ca 1585, rev as *The Lawiers Logike* 1588) and *The Arcadian Rhetorike* (1588), Henry Peacham the elder's *Garden of Eloquence* (rev 1593), Charles Butler's *Rhetoricae libri duo* (1598), and Alexander Gil's *Logonomia anglica* (1619). For more than fifty years after his death, excerpts from Spenser's poetry appeared in such collections of poetic 'flowers' and commonplaces as John Bodenham's *Bel-vedére, or The Garden of the Muses* (1600), Robert Allott's *Englands Parnassus* (1600), Daniel Tuvill's *Dove and the Serpent* (1614), and Joshua Poole's *English Parnassus* (1657).

Kenelm Digby, who wrote the most extensive seventeenth-century commentary on Spenser, praises his diction (*Discourse*; *Sp All* pp 211–14). However, Jonson's objection that 'Spencer, in affecting the Ancients writ no Language' (*Timber, or Discoveries* 1640; *Sp All* p 206) became dogma by the Restoration, not only because English neoclassicism grew more rigid but also because Spenser's language became more remote and perhaps more obscure with time. The 1679 Folio includes 'An Alphabetical Index of Unusual Words Explained.' The author of *Spencer Redivivus* (1687; *Sp All* 287) may have been overstating the case for translating *The Faerie Queene* into Restoration English when he wrote that Spenser's 'Stile seems no less unintelligible at this Day, than the obsoletest of our *English* or *Saxon* Dialect.' Dryden claimed that Spenser was 'still Intelligible, at least, after a little practice' (tr of Juvenal 1693; ed 1956–, 4:14). Nevertheless, Spenser was accused of obscurity as well as indecorum. Some argued that he attained grandeur in spite of, not because of, his diction: 'with all his Rustie, obsolete words, with all his rough-hewn clowterly Verses; yet take him throughout, and we shall find in him a graceful and Poetic Majesty' (Edward Phillips *Theatrum Poetarum* 1675; *Sp All* p 268).

In the eighteenth century, as the publication of major new editions and commentaries shows, Spenser continued to be read; also, he was frequently imitated by poets, even though his un-Virgilian epic form and subject matter offended neoclassical taste (see *imitations and adaptations, 1660–1800). By classical rules, *The Faerie Queene* lacked unity of theme, plot, and characterization in spite of the plan he had outlined in the Letter to Raleigh. His fairy knights, wizards, magic arms, dragons, and other romance elements were improbable; and he was accused of inconsistency, absurdity, occasional ugliness, and even impiety. The complex rhyme scheme of the Spenserian stanza, critics claimed, forced him into linguistic contortions and verbosity. In defending his art, Hughes (1715), Warton (1754, rev and enl 1762), and Hurd (1762) especially initiated historical criticism of Spenser by recognizing that he had followed the Elizabethan taste for Ariosto when he wrote his epic in a 'Gothic' rather than a classical form. Although these defenders did not approach other aspects of his rhetoric historically, in sharing his rhetorical tradition, they were better able than the later Romantic critics to appreciate his moral purpose, his allegory, and 'the more minute Beauties of his Epithets, his Figures, and his Similes' (Hughes in Spenser ed 1715, 1: lxxv).

The Romantics exalted the very elements in Spenser that the previous age had dismissed as indecorous and improbable. He became the poet of rest and dream, imagination and wonder, metrical music and pictorial delight, but certainly not of moral persuasion and conscious art (see *Hunt). Readers were advised not to 'meddle with the allegory' (Hazlitt 'On Chaucer and Spenser' in *Lectures on the English Poets* 1818). Spenser's violation of the classical canons of epic was celebrated as the sign of his natural, untutored genius.

The nineteenth century also witnessed the development of philology (see *scholarship, 1579–1932). Impressed by the achievements of the historical and comparative study of languages, critics at the end of the century began examining Spenser's diction, especially in *The Shepheardes Calender*, for archaism, neologism, dialect, foreign borrowings, color words, and figures of speech. They likewise discussed the influence of continental theorists, especially the Pléiade, on Spenser's language. (Their debates, made possible by the completion of the *Concordance* and the *OED*, are summarized in *Var* 7:614–30.) At least one early influence study, Renwick's *Edmund Spenser* (1925), recognized the rhetorical tradition shared by English and continental poets. In the next decade, H.O. White (1935) and Crane (1937) pioneered the study of Elizabethan rhetoric. T.W. Baldwin (1944), Joseph (1947), Howell (1956), Ong (1971), and others have since examined English rhetorical theory, training, and practice in its European context. Thus the linguistic features catalogued by the philologists were finally recognized as products, at least in part, of a rhetorical poetics. While most post-Romantic critics still condemned them as ornamental rather than organic, Rix (1940) and Rubel (1941) conceded that Spenser's skill often made them effective.

The New Criticism of the 1930s and 1940s demanded not only an organic fusion of form and content but also that 'direct sensuous apprehension of thought, or a recreation of thought into feeling' that Eliot and other poets of his generation praised in Donne. The poet of imaginative fancy, of mindless sensuous beauty, as the Romantics had defined Spenser, could not compare with one who wrote not just from the heart but also from 'the cerebral cortex, the nervous system, and the digestive tracts' (Eliot ed 1950:241–50). Spenser's complexity was lost on New Critics because they sought a different kind of difficulty.

Critical reevaluation of Spenser had to await critical reevaluation of Donne. Tuve (1947) provided both in the context of Renaissance rhetoric, arguing that the two poets share criteria for evaluating poetry – 'significancy' and 'rhetorical efficacy' – that differ from those of their twentieth-century critics. Unlike post-Romantic critics, who expect imagery to record sense impressions accurately, Renaissance critics limited their demand for 'sensuous vividness' to a few rhetorical figures, such as *icon*, prosopopoeia, and *descriptio*. Spenser writes in genres requiring these figures more often than Donne, but they agree in expecting images to delight not the senses by their beauty so much as the mind by their intellectual subtlety, not to express the emotions of the poet so much as to move the audience by magnifying the subject. In the Renaissance demand for decorum, Tuve saw a concern for the fusion of form and content.

Tuve's study changed criticism of Spenser in several ways. First, critics modified Romantic notions of his 'pictorialism' in the light of Renaissance rhetorical theory (eg, Dundas 1968). Second, Tuve's argument initiated a New Critical search for the functions of rhetorical figures in Spenser's poetry (eg, Craig 1959, 1967; Vickers 1970). Third, criticism began to consider his rhetoric of argument and organization. Several studies have analyzed the deliberative rhetoric of Despair and Una in *FQ* I (eg, Vickers 1970) and the judicial rhetoric of Mutabilitie and Nature in the *Cantos of Mutabilitie* (eg, Davidson 1982, Grimm 1986). Others have read the whole poem as epideictic in praise of Elizabeth (Cain 1978, Hardison 1962, Wells 1983).

Having seen the similarities between poetry and rhetoric, critics have begun recently to study their differences. The orator strives for clarity. The poet may assume rather a prophetic role, hiding truth behind a 'veil of allegory' (Murrin 1969, 1980). Or, reacting against aristocratic corruption, he may usurp the function of the ideal courtier, using the deceptions of art to teach truth by delighting (Javitch 1978). For these critics, rhetoric fails to explain the 'darke conceit' of *The Faerie Queene*.

The New Critics have been challenged in the past two decades by structuralist and post-structuralist critics who draw their inspiration from twentieth-century linguistics. The concept of a poem as a 'well-wrought urn' preserving in its language a meaning to be discovered by future generations is yielding to critical recognition that communication is a complex interplay of many elements. New Critics focused on the text, labeling as fallacies any interest in the poet's creation of or the reader's response to the text. Insofar as more recent movements turn critical attention to the common assumptions and values of poet and reader, they share the concerns of the traditional rhetorical critic, who recognizes that the Elizabethan considered the poet a moral teacher and judged his rhetorical efficacy by the reader's response. Thus reader-response criticism of Spenser since Alpers 1967b has often called itself rhetorical.

Much remains to be learned about the history of rhetoric and its relationship to Renaissance poetics, but by comparing current expectations of poetry with the Elizabethan, rhetorical critics today can perhaps recognize their own bias and better understand and appreciate the Prince of Poets.

JUDITH RICE HENDERSON

Herbert Ellsworth Cory 1911 'Spenser, Thomson, and Romanticism' *PMLA* 26:51–91; R.M. Cummings 1971; Arnold E. Davidson 1982 'Dame Nature's Shifting Logic in Spenser's *Cantos of Mutabilitie*' *NM* 83:451–6; Judith Dundas 1968 'The Rhetorical Basis of Spenser's Imagery' *SEL* 8:59–75; Rudolf B. Gottfried 1975 'Spenser Recovered: The Poet and Historical Scholarship' in Frushell and Vondersmith 1975:61–78; Nadine G. Grimm 1986 'Mutabilitie's Plea before Dame Nature's Bar' *Comitatus* 17:22–34; Mueller 1959; Michael Murrin 1972–3 'The Varieties of Criticism' *MP* 70:342–56; Tucker 1976–7; Wurtsbaugh 1936.

---

rhyme The articulatory-acoustic relation between stressed syllables that begin with different sounds and end with the same sound, normally from the last stressed vowel to the end of the syllable. 'Perfect' rhyme occurs when syllables are equally stressed, begin with a readily discernible difference, and end identically. The initial difference may be between two consonants (eg, *call/pall*, *FQ* I iv 16) or between a syllable that begins with a vowel and one that begins with a consonant (eg, *all/call*, VI ii 35). A perfect rhyme at the end of a verse line is called single or masculine; if rhyme syllables are followed by the same undifferentiated syllable (eg, *faces/places*, *SC*, *June* 30, 32), the rhyme is said to be double or feminine. This series continues indefinitely to triple, quadruple, quintuple, and so forth, for example, *dedicate/medicate*, *dedicated/medicated*, *dedicatedly/medicatedly*. Most of Spenser's rhymes are perfect and single. A rare, special type of double or other multiple rhyme involves the so-called mosaic or heteromerous effect of one word rhyming with two or more (eg, *encreased/cease it*, *SC*, *March* 99, 102).

Besides the various sorts of perfect rhymes, there are deficient and redundant rhymes. The deficient lack one or more of the requirements of full rhyme. So-called stress promotion gives conventional stress to a normally unstressed syllable at the end of a word of three or more syllables, thereby assimilating that syllable into a rhyme-pattern (eg, *daintily/hye*, *FQ* I vii 32). The promoted syllable is normally the last of a dactyl (eg, *dáintĭlў*), which becomes an amphimacer (*dáintĭlý*). Promotion usually involves also a change of vowel quality, so that, for example, *daintily* gains a final vowel that sounds like *lie* or *lee*. As a rule, in most poets including Spenser, the full-grade form of the rhyme precedes the promoted syllable; otherwise, a reader may not be able to determine how the promoted vowel ought to sound. Although Spenser adheres to this pattern most of the time (eg, *apply/mortality*, VI iii 28), he is capable of reversing the order (eg, *remedy/aby*, 44) or of rhyming two promoted syllables with no full-grade form being involved (eg, *medicine/discipline*, vi 13).

The stress-promotion type of deficient rhyme is a matter of stress and vowel quality; the two other chief forms of deficient rhyme, called assonance and consonance, involve articulatory-acoustic considerations other than stress. In assonance, the vowel component of the rhyme is perfect but the consonant is not (eg, *dreame/leane*, *SC*, *Julye* 62, 64). In consonance, the consonant component is perfect but the vowel is not (eg, *one/grone/Coridon/none*, *FQ* VI ix 10). Most so-called eye rhymes, which look as though they rhyme but do not, are instances of consonance, because vowels are more versatile than consonants and, furthermore, subject to somewhat greater variation of spelling, as can be seen in confusing groups like *blood/food/good*, or *tomb/bomb/comb*; given shifting linguistic practices, we cannot be sure whether a pair like *ground/wound* (VI iii 27) represents an example of consonance wherein the vowels were never the same or one of perfect rhyme in its time that became divergent through history. Spenser's anomalous rhyme of *couet/renew it* (*Colin Clout* 37, 39) may be a perfect heteromerous rhyme (one word with two) or no rhyme at all (the stressed syllables sound not a bit alike if they are pronounced *cov* and *new* – but any reader of Spenser knows about the graphemic labyrinth of *u/v/w* and *i/j/y*).

Redundant rhyme – also called identical, homophone, or *rime riche* – occurs when syllables both begin and end the same but are not the same word. This phenomenon needs to be distinguished from simple repetition (eg, *two/too* creates a redundant rhyme, while *two/two/twenty-two* creates a repetition). Spenser would commonly put such a pair as *do/undo* in a rhyming position. The very first stanza of *The Faerie Queene* contains a redundant rhyme *reeds/areeds*. Within a page or two, we find the simple repetition of *traine/traine* (I i 18). The classification of such pairs as *show/show* (verb/noun) is problematical; but with different parts of speech seeming to be functionally different words, it is probable that they qualify as a proper redundant rhyme that can be distinguished from outright repetition of same sound, same word, same part of speech. Interestingly, the last rhyme in three of Spenser's poems is an identical: *rest/rest* (noun/verb, *CCCHA* 953, 955); *rehearse/hearse* ('Lay of Clorinda' 107, 108); *ornament/moniment* (*Epithalamion* 432, 433). 'Promotion identicals' also occur freely in verse, as in the *b* rhyme of *FQ* I vii 32: *diuersly/iollity/hye/daintily*; of these four, only *hye* is a normally stressed rhyming syllable, the other three being normally unstressed syllables that have been promoted. But, whereas *diuersly/hye* creates a rhyme between a promoted syllable and a normal stressed syllable, and *diuersly/iollity* creates a rhyme between two promoted syllables, *diuersly/daintily* promotes the same unstressed syllable, *-ly*. Multiple promotion identicals are not unknown (eg, Shakespeare's rhyming of *masonry/memory* along with *enmity/posterity* in Sonnet 55, or Spenser's impressive quartet at the beginning of *FQ* II: *history/forgery/memory/Faery*).

Since rhyme emphasizes likeness, the greatest hazard is monotony – a vice displayed by inept poets and avoided by good ones. The pattern of the Spenserian stanza permits striking variety and virtuosity while nicely preventing unwanted patness, and it achieves this range of effects by generally opposing the patterns of sense and syntax (*ab ab bc bcC*) to the acoustic couplings implicit in the *bb* lines (4 and 5), which are normally not a conspicuous semantic or grammatical couplet, as well as in the *cC* couplet (lines 8 and 9), which is never a metrical couplet, the last line being hexameter. Here is a typical stanza (IV ii 22) wherein the punctuation shows the zoning of thought and grammar in opposition to the zoning of acoustic patterns:

First he desir'd their cause of strife to see:
They said, it was for loue of *Florimell*.
Ah gentle knights (quoth he) how may that bee,
And she so farre astray, as none can tell.
Fond Squire, full angry then sayd *Paridell*,
Seest not the Ladie there before thy face?
He looked backe, and her aduizing well,
Weend as he said, by that her outward grace,
That fayrest *Florimell* was present there in place.

Spenser's most consistent reliance on double rhymes, significantly, seems to come in the pentameter couplets that wrap up his adaptation of the English sonnet (*abab bcbc cdcd ee*), as though he were determined to avoid the 'pounce' (as Keats called it) of exact rhyming couplets.

Unlike most other stanzas (rhyme royal, ottava rima, ballade, sonnets of various types), the Spenserian stanza has a known inventor and bears his name. It provides two complementary pleasures: that of constancy and that of variety, and Spenser seems to have enjoyed the challenge of adhering to a consistent pattern of rhythm, meter, and rhyme while varying a number of elements, with an effect of matchless richness. An inventory would reveal that at least half of the stanzas in *The Faerie Queene* satisfy the formal requirements perfectly, but a significant number depart from the pattern, particularly in the sorts of rhyme in the *b* lines (lines 2, 4, 5, and 7). It is here that Spenser most commonly replaces rhyme with repetition, for example, *teares/teares* (I i 52) and *God/God* (X 53); with repetition of a word in different spellings, for example, *bene* and *beene* (V x 25); of identical rhyme between words spelled differently but sounded alike, for example, *knight/night* (passim); of identical rhyme between words spelled and sounded alike and belonging to the same part of speech but qualifying as different words, for example, the noun *well* meaning both 'source of water' and 'weal' (I ii 43), and the noun *rest* meaning both 'remainder' and 'repose'; the usual sort of identical rhyme between different parts of speech, for example, *sent/sent* (participle/noun, i 43). While most of Spenser's rhymes are single, occasionally he uses a double rhyme; in one stanza (VII vi 44) the *a* rhyme is double (*pleasure/measure*) and the *b* rhyme is double with two mosaics (*better/set her/get her/debter*).

Spenser further avoids monotony by exploiting a range of lexical effects related to rhyme – effects that cover a range from rhyme of synonyms, a 'center of indifference,' and rhyme of antonyms. At the former extreme are rhyming words that mean the same thing or belong at any rate in the same category; in *The Faerie Queene*, Spenser rhymes *shake/quake* (I viii 23), *brest/chest* (II i 47), and *betraid/bewraid* (VII vi 51); another favorite rhyme is between forms of *write* and *endite*, such as *writing/endighting* (Harvey Sonnet). At the opposite extreme are the antithetical rhymes of antonyms (which seem inherently more interesting and satisfying than rhyming synonyms): these are rhymes of the sort that join *womb/tomb*, *hire/fire*, *make/break*, and suchlike. *The Faerie Queene* rhymes *stay/stray* several times (eg, I x 35), with the bonus of alliteration as well as rhyme.

The genius and glory of the Spenserian stanza reside largely in the amplitude of its rhyming – three rhyme sounds in nine lines – combined with the plenitude of variety: two *a* rhymes, four *b*, three *c*. Given the limitations on English noun forms, Spenser seems as a rule to reserve the *a* rhymes for the trickier pairs (eg, *length/strength*, I vii 18) and to use the plentiful *b* rhymes for redundancy, extravagance, and experimentation.

The *ababbcbcC* scheme generates a fairly complex set of possibilities, since it projects a large number of possible arrays. With two *a* rhymes, four *b* rhymes, and three *c* rhymes, there turn out to be ten fundamental bilateral relations. Arithmetically, this results from the calculation 1 + 6 + 3. The scheme offers, that is to say, conspicuous relations between ten pairs of sounds: *a1/a2*, *b1/b2*, *b1/b3*, and so forth. Then, since each relation may take any of four basic forms (repetition, perfect rhyme, redundancy, deficiency), there are 40 (4 × 10) fundamental bilateral possibilities, to which we can add the five multilateral possibilities (*b123*, *b124*, *b234*, *c123*, and *b1234*), so that there is a network of 45 (40 + 5) fundamental possibilities. Finally, this range is further enriched by the possibility of variants (eg, feminine rhymes) in all the positions, not to mention the rare anomalies. One exemplary anomaly is the so-called poysonous rhyme in *FQ* III x 59, wherein the *b* rhymes are *poysonous/rancorous/suspitious/vitious*: the expectation generated at first is that the rhyme will be founded on terminal sounds like *-nous* and *-rous* (by conventional stress-promotion), but in *b3* and *b4* the basis of the rhyme shifts to an earlier syllable (written *-pit-* and *vit-*), with a devious – or poysonous – effect quite appropriate to the topic of the stanza. All in all, then, Spenser exploits about fifty possible permutations in his fixed-but-flexible creature. (See also *versification.) WILLIAM HARMON

R.E. Neil Dodge 1916 'An Obsolete Elizabethan Mode of Rhyming' in *Shakespeare Studies by Members of the Department of English of the University of Wisconsin* (Madison) pp 174–200; Fussell 1979; William Harmon 1987 'Rhyme in English Verse: History, Structures, Functions' *SP* 84:365–93; Hollander 1975; Hollander 1981b; C. Hugh Holman and William Harmon 1986 *A Handbook to Literature* 5th ed (New York).

Rich Strond A narrow beach marking the boundary between land and sea, the 'Rich strond' is the location of Britomart's lament and her subsequent combat with Marinell, who guards this 'rocky shore' (*FQ* III iv 7–18). Hearing of her son's fall, the sea nymph Cymoent comes to it and in despair laments his apparent death. Later it is the setting for the three-day 'spousals' of Marinell and Florimell at the Castle of the Strond (V iii, iv 3). As the wedding site for these eroticized images of the land and sea, the Rich Strond again reveals its importance as a boundary, an intermediary or liminal place.

Strond is an older variant of *strand* (Old English, Old Norse *strond* 'border, edge, or coast'; both spellings occur in Spenser). From Middle English on, *strond* or *strand* meant 'the land bordering a sea, lake, or river; in a more restricted sense, that part of a shore which lies between the tide-marks; sometimes used vaguely for coast, shore' (*OED* sv 'strand' sb[1], 1a). All of these senses are evoked in the episodes on the Rich Strond, for Spenser stresses the action of the waves and tide which leave the sea's treasure on the beach. In II vi 19, he also uses *strond* for a sheet of water, Phaedria's Idle Lake. He often emphasizes the intermediary sense of *strond* (neither land nor sea; a rare usage – see *OED* 2) by using the word to refer specifically to the area on a beach washed by the waves (*Amoretti* 75), by describing it with epithets transferred from the sea to the land (see his comment that Florimell leaping into a boat from the beach 'Did thrust the shallop from the floting strand' III vii 27), and, as in the case of the Rich Strond, by using the word to focus on that part of the shore between the tidal marks.

Like much of Spenser's vocabulary, *strond* has an archaic flavor, with specifically Chaucerian overtones, as in the opening of the *Canterbury Tales*, where it refers loosely to a country or a region, especially a foreign country (*OED* 1e): 'Thanne longen folk to goon on pilgrimages, / And palmeres for to seken straunge strondes.' This sense of the exotic and the foreign also pervades Spenser's treatment of the Rich Strond and even influences Shakespeare in his slightly later use of the word in his Henry plays; see, for example, *1 Henry IV* which refers to 'stronds afar remote' (I i 4). In *2 Henry IV*, Shakespeare uses the word in a Spenserian fashion, describing that part of the beach or shore on which the water has left its mark: 'so looks the strond whereon the imperious flood / Hath left a witness'd usurpation' (I i 62–3). There is even a possibility that Spenser may have learned from *Richard III* 'the glamour of jewells concealed in the secret places of the sea'; like the sea's treasure that Marinell hoards on the Rich Strond, the jewels Clarence sees in his dream come from 'a thousand fearful wracks' (*Richard III* I iv 24–33; Treneer in *Var* 3:240; cf *FQ* III iv 23), and foreshadow the transformation of suffering into beauty that Shakespeare would later describe in the 'sea-change' of *The Tempest*.

Spenser's strond is rich because Cymoent persuaded Nereus, her father and a sea god, to give her son 'threasure and rich store, / Bove all the sonnes, that were of earthly wombes ybore' (III iv 21). Under his command, the sea 'voluntary' brings 'The spoyle of all the world' (23) to the Rich Strond. The allusion to the Golden Age in *voluntary*, combined with the lyrical beauty of the passages describing the ocean world and its nymphs, has led some critics to consider this episode as Spenser's version of piscatorial pastoral poetry, following Sannazaro's *Piscatory Eclogues* (Nohrnberg 1976:586–90, Alpers 1967b:382ff). Whether or not the episode can be described in pastoral terms, the jewels which the sea pours forth exceed human wealth and thus come to symbolize a mythical realm of abundance, perhaps the wealth of myth itself, since the sea is the home of Cymoent and her nymphs.

Spenser stresses that this mythical wealth comes from human suffering and loss: Marinell was 'enriched through the overthrow / And wreckes of many wretches' (22). It is a wealth made available to him precisely because he is half man, half god, and it represents the treasure of a mythical realm which the more fully human characters, such as Britomart, do not visit. In contrast to Marinell, Britomart scorns the wealth left on the strand (18) and is therefore sometimes interpreted as resisting the temptation of riches. She may also indicate the distance between mortal experience and the world of the partly mythical or archetypal characters.

As the two perspectives on the jewels suggest, the Rich Strond also marks the boundary between the human and mythical worlds. It is a boundary Britomart does not cross: when she reaches the Rich Strond, she turns and takes her course along this border (18). The difference between the two worlds is summed up comically in Spenser's description of the 'temed fishes' that pull Cymoent's chariot, a passage which draws on Virgil's description of Neptune's chariot in *Aeneid* 5.817–26. These fish stop at the edge of the beach and swim 'Along the margent of the fomy shore, / Least they their finnes should bruze, and surbate sore / Their tender feet upon the stony ground' (34). The other side of this 'margent' is a 'stony ground,' a world of pain which the mythological beings can avoid or cure. Marinell, having a mortal father and an immortal mother, appropriately inhabits this middle space and finally marries Florimell here. They are boundary figures who stand between the two realms, and when they marry do so in a place where land and sea, mortal and mythical, can meet.

The Rich Strond also marks several other borders or boundaries. Here, Britomart addresses the sea which she sees as a figure for her own tempestuous inner life. Through her words, Spenser puts the sea into an allegorical scheme whereby the inner is represented by external images. The strand marks a boundary between the outer world in which she travels and her inner life, troubled but also enriched by her love. Its location also mirrors an aspect of Britomart's character when she invokes the 'God of winds, that raignest in the seas, / That raignest also in the Continent' (10). Her pun reinforces the allegorical sense of *continent* and reminds the readers that though she stands on the land she is emotionally at sea: she has lost the ability to contain herself or her emotions, so she stands neither 'in the Continent' nor in the sea but somewhere in between. The Rich Strond, then, represents as an external landscape Britomart's divided inner condition. It further marks the boundary between a world in which characters are less overtly allegorical and one in which they are more so. Spenserian allegory depends on these middle places to call attention to the devices which shape its meaning.

Elsewhere in Book III, Spenser uses the edge of the sea to represent similar boundaries. Florimell comes to 'the roring shore' (vii 27) before she, like Marinell, is subsumed by the mythical realm. Malbecco loses his human shape at the sea's edge where he is transformed into an allegorical figure: as he stares out of his cave at the billows below, he 'Is woxen so deform'd, that he has quight / Forgot he was a man, and *Gealosie* is hight' (x 60). Here too the sea's edge marks the boundary between mortal and mythic, and between a recognizably human tale and a more allegorical one. (On the land and sea as symbolic places, see Murtaugh 1973).

As Britomart reaches the Rich Strond, the narrative energy of her story subsides, and she turns to a lyric lament, commenting on her position with an allegorical conceit. Spenser does not return to her story for four-and-a-half cantos, continuing it instead on a different level of the allegory. The Rich Strond thus serves as the setting for a shift from one level of the fiction to another. This beach, a strand between land and sea, between inner and outer, between mortal and mythic, like other intermediary places, marks symbolically the place of Spenserian allegory itself, for it brings together inner and outer, mortal and mythic, story and meaning. SUSANNE L. WOFFORD

Alpers 1967b, ch 3, esp pp 382ff; Blissett 1965, esp pp 92–4; Freeman 1970:197–202; Hankins 1971:166–7, 228–30; Nohrnberg 1976:586–92; Roche 1964:71–2, 189–94 (on the emblem *Potentia amoris* and the union of land and sea); Susanne Lindgren Wofford 1987 'Britomart's Petrarchan Lament: Allegory and Narrative in *The Faerie Queene* III, iv' *CL* 39:28–57.

Rich, Barnaby (1542–1617) While a captain in Ireland, Rich wrote *Allarme to England* (1578) and *Riche His Farewell to Militarie Profession* (1581), which includes a prose tale of Apolonius and Silla, the immediate source for Shakespeare's *Twelfth Night*. Spenser could have known Rich at Dublin in 1580 or later, but neither mentions the other. James VI in 1595 was 'not well pleased' by a story in *Farewell* telling how a devil possesses a King of Scots, as in 1596 he protested against Spenser's portrait of Mary, Queen of Scots, as Duessa (Cranfill and Bruce 1953:124–5). Though Rich was in England from 1592 to 1608, he wrote of his 'forty years' observation' of Ireland in *A New Description of Ireland* (1610) and in manuscript works written in 1608, 1612, and 1615. Elizabeth I granted him a pension for life in 1587, and James I gave him £100 in 1616 as 'the eldest Captain of the Kingdom' (Cranfill and Bruce 1953:39, 126).

Rich presented to James in 1615 a manuscript 'Anothomy of Irelande'; but the suggestion that this dialogue 'both in form and in content models itself, in part at any rate,' upon Spenser's *Vewe*, then unpublished (Hinton 1940:81), is not convincing. Spenser proposes reforms in civil government, customs, and religion; Rich puts first of all 'the rootynge out of popery, and the plantynge of the worde of *God*' (Hinton 1940:84), blaming bishops and corrupt officials who tolerate popery for their profit. Unlike Spenser, he had no use for books written by Catholics or in Irish, in which he found nothing but 'lies, fables, and popish fantasies' (*New Description* 1610:33). His opinions 'upon Irish affairs were those of an ardent combatant ... an ultra-Protestant' (Falkiner 1906:126). MARK ECCLES

The standard work is Thomas M. Cranfill and Dorothy Hart Bruce 1953 *Barnaby Rich: A Short Biography* (Austin, Tex). Excerpts from Rich's *New Description* are in James P. Myers, Jr, ed 1983 *Elizabethan Ireland: A Selection of Writings by Elizabethan Writers on Ireland* (Hamden, Conn). Later mss are printed by C. Litton Falkiner 1906 'Barnaby Rich's "Remembrances of the State of Ireland, 1612," with Notices of Other Manuscript Reports, by the Same Writer, on Ireland under James the First' *PRIA* 26(sec C):125–42, and by Edward M. Hinton 1940 'Rych's *Anothomy of Ireland*, with an Account of the Author' *PMLA* 55: 73–101.

rivers Like many poets, Spenser was sensitive to the personal, patriotic, and historical associations of rivers. His verse shows him to have been unusually responsive to their physical beauties and metaphysical suggestions, and this natural disposition was strengthened by literary tradition. He recognized that the local river served certain poets as a *topos* which was personal and at the same time literary, historical, and universal. In English and Irish rivers particularly, he found a motif that allowed him a private voice within a nationalistic setting and a European literary tradition. In cultivating the river motif throughout his career, he made it his own poetic signature, and it became a distinctive feature of Spenserian verse.

In adapting traditional aspects of river poetry from classical and modern literature, Spenser naturalizes the rivers and integrates them into his own work. We can see continuities in the treatment of rivers in nearly all the literary forms from Homer, Hesiod, and Theocritus, to Virgil, Ovid, and Horace, to Statius and Ausonius. For these and many other writers, the river is generally identified with the *genius loci*, the *mens divina*, or with other mysteries of nature, as well as with historical and moral themes conveyed through landscape (see *topographical description). Authors working in the vernacular and experimenting with new forms – such as Sannazaro, Montemayor, Camoens, du Bellay, and Ronsard – not only contributed to the unbroken development of the motif, but helped to define its distinctive generic qualities in a modern European literary tradition. Leland, writing in Latin and influenced by classical and continental authors, was the first to make extensive use of British rivers as a topos set in the national landscape and used as a vehicle for historic and epideictic themes. His *Cygnea cantio* did much to influence the form of river poetry in England and to encourage its development by Spenser, Camden, and their contemporaries. Late in the 1570s, Camden and Spenser worked apparently independently on river poems of remarkably similar form, the one writing in Latin and integrating his verse within *Britannia*, and the other experimenting with English meter and possibly inserting his poem or a version of it into *The Faerie Queene*. Both saw the river as a classical topos in which to locate the ideas of a larger work. As Leland's interpreters, they were largely responsible for the popularity of river literature in England after 1580, although eventually the river poem became associated with Spenser, as shown by his influence on Drayton's *Poly-Olbion*, Phineas Fletcher's *Piscatorie Eclogs*, William Browne's *Britannia's Pastorals*, Milton's *Comus*, John Denham's *Cooper's Hill*, and Marvell's *Upon Appleton House*.

Rivers of essentially two kinds often appear in symbolically strategic places in Spenser's poetry. Those which appear incidentally in his landscapes as rivers, or as fountains or wells (both of which were traditionally the offspring of rivers), usually remain nameless, and are developed in terms of the symbolic attributes of water. Those which command a more prominent place in the poetic landscape are named, and their elemental qualities acquire further significance from their cultural context. Functioning as topoi, they exert a complex influence on both the form and content of an episode; and in them we see Spenser cultivating the conventions of the genre.

The incidental rivers of the first category not only illustrate Spenser's pervasive interest in the motif but also help to define symbolic dimensions which often remain obscure in the more expansive river episodes. From them we learn that all rivers reflect one of two different aspects of human existence: one pagan, emphatically of nature's sphere and associated with fertility; the other divine and associated with redemption, Christian virtues (especially chastity), grace, and spiritual regeneration. The rivers' role in defining these two aspects is conveniently set forth by the Palmer in *FQ* II ii 5–7. The first, rivers associated with nature, is amoral; their fertility works through the cycle of death and birth, and their prototype is the monster-spawning Nile (see I i 21). The second is defined as endowed with supernatural virtue by a 'later grace' and infused with divinity. This grace links these rivers with the redemptive capacity of fallen nature. This is the river of Christian iconography, whose cycle of spiritual death and redemption is analogous to the mythic cycle of the river of natural fertility. The 'streame of Balme' that regenerates the Red Cross Knight in his combat with the Dragon is such a river (I xi 48). It is implicit in Guyon's name, which is also the river of paradise, Gihon, associated with temperance; by extension, the meandering course of his story traces the course by which he fulfills the prophecy of his name and learns temperance.

Both kinds of river identified by the Palmer help to delineate Spenser's moral and natural landscapes, and each corresponds to one of the two principal contrasting concerns of his verse – for the material world of nature, and for the transcendent, spiritual world of ideas and ideal virtue. In developing a topos in which the river is at once a highly artificial literary device and a part of the descriptive natural landscape, he attempts to bring these two dimensions together, to realize the divine in nature. Thus the many highly symbolic rivers which we encounter incidentally in *The Faerie Queene* prepare us for the more complex river episodes and their more intricate relation to the surrounding poetic landscape. For Spenser, this more ambitious river motif is also a point of contact with a long literary and intellectual tradition which he attempts to integrate into the English landscape and into an English poetic.

Spenser's earliest work reveals his interest in the traditional ideas and forms associated with the river. In *The Shepheardes Calender*, rivers are merely a pastoral convention, vague decorative Theocritean echoes by which the poet-shepherd's harmony with nature is revealed in his ability to tune his song 'unto the Waters fall' (*Aprill* 36). Neither the landscape nor its rivers has a distinctive identity beyond the literary allusion.

A more important apprenticeship to conventions of river verse occurs in the paraphrases and translations in *Complaints*, where Spenser learned how to juxtapose river and architectural ruin, or other images of human achievement, in order to locate his ideas about the effects of mutability and time, and about human access to a timeless dimension. The ambiguous image of the tower-capped river figures both greatness and impermanence in human affairs; used frequently by Spenser, it has its *locus classicus* (in a strikingly literal sense of the phrase) in the scene of the Tiber flowing unceasingly past the ruins of Rome (*Rome* 3).

In *Complaints*, Spenser also develops the association between the poet and the river, for the poet's song resists the effects of time and in so doing harmonizes with the river, much as it does in other pastoral forms. The association is often explicit (*Rome* 31–2), although it is sometimes developed metaphorically through the genius loci (*Bellay* 1), the personified river nymph (*Bellay* 10, *Time*), a Muse in her river habitat (*Teares*, *Petrarch* 4), or a swan, itself a figure of the poet (*Bellay* 11). These, however, are essentially variants on the same topos linking poet and river in an image of the transcendence of time's decay, and they derive from the identification of the Muses and the river in antiquity. In each case, the vision takes place from the vantage point of the river: rising either from the river's banks or its waters, the song outlives the poet and his subject matter. Significantly, in Spenser's Renaissance models, Petrarch and du Bellay, the link between poet and river extends also to the theme of poetry and the development of a vernacular tradition, so that, for Spenser, the river Muse whose song transcends time will sing in English on the banks of a local river.

Spenser's interest in the river embraced models other than those reflected in his earliest published verse, and early in his career he formed a clear conception of the potential of the river poem. At that time he decided to explore the possibilities of the English river poem: one year after publication of *The Shepheardes Calender*, in a letter to Harvey, he identified himself and his poetic aims with the form. Here he describes *Epithalamion Thamesis* as nearly ready for publication; although lost, it would seem to have been a poem of epic dimensions in which the theme of the river marriage was entirely naturalized: 'whyche Booke I dare undertake wil be very profitable for the knowledge, and rare for the Invention, and manner of handling. For in setting forth the marriage of the Thames: I shewe his first beginning, and offspring, and all the Countrey, that he passeth thorough, and also describe all the Rivers throughout Englande, whyche came to this Wedding, and their righte names, and right passage, etc' (*Three Letters* 1, *Var Prose* p 17). According to Spenser, his immediate source for his information was Holinshed (properly understood to be Harrison, whose *Description of Britain* prefaced the *Chronicles*); and here we can discern, at the very least, the indirect influence of Leland's *Cygnea cantio*, Ausonius' *Mosella*, and Virgil's *Aeneid* on the form and content of the work.

In writing his *Epithalamion Thamesis*, Spenser seems to have accepted the futility of devoting an entire work exclusively to the river topos and of attempting a comprehensive description of all the rivers of Britain. In the process, he seems also to have learned the limitations of the reformed English meter, and to have recognized that poetic patriotism is not incompatible with rhymed iambic pentameter, for after 1580 all his rivers bear that classical yoke lightly and gracefully, just as the weathered landscape wears its Roman past. Although never published, *Epithalamion Thamesis* was an important landmark in Spenser's career, awaited eagerly by readers, judging from the comments by William Vallans in his *Tale of Two Swannes* (1590; see *Sp All* p 20).

After 1580, Spenser's rivers reveal the generic variety and indefinability that characterizes all of his verse, while also illustrating the method and purposefulness behind his experiments in form. In *Ruines of Time*, for example, he adapts the lessons he learned in his translations of Petrarch and du Bellay by ironically subverting the conventional treatment of the river nymph and genius loci in order to define the thematic and formal unity of a poem that would otherwise fall into two distinct parts. He exploits the potential ambiguity of juxtaposing river and ruin and undermines the river nymph's identity as the poetic spokesman of universal and durable truths. Unlike the nymphs of *Petrarch* and *Bellay*, his Verlame is the voice of confusion and of moral, historical, and geographic disorientation; she is an ambiguous specter from an imperfectly understood past. Her words, even her very identity, are unclear. From the opening lines of the poem, Spenser forces the reader to question and redefine the convention of the river nymph. In so doing, he initiates the central theme of the poem: the importance of the poet in defining society's moral perspective through myth and history. The nymph, a vestige of the past, is incapable of doing this herself and must rely on the help of 'Poets historicall' such as Sidney, Camden, and presumably Spenser himself. The poem, then, is an experiment in the form Spenser learned during his apprenticeship; it uses river conventions to establish its thematic and formal unity in terms of British poetic tradition and the need for a myth of British history set in a national landscape, and in this it looks forward to his subsequent treatments of the motif.

The culmination of Spenser's original conception of the epic river poem is the marriage of Thames and Medway (*FQ* IV xi), although it is only the end of his first phase of experimenting with the topos. It presents Spenser's most expansive view of cultural history within a mythologized landscape. Characteristically, he uses patterns in nature – in this case, the descent of the Thames to the point of its confluence with the Medway – to frame social myth; thus, marriage becomes a manifestation of *concordia discors*. He expands the historical significance of the episode by using the names and associations of the participating rivers to adumbrate cultural evolution. In many respects, the episode is unique in *The Faerie Queene*: though only a wedding procession, it is the closest thing to a wedding in the poem. It is also a rare instance of the intrusion of real geography: here the mythical landscape coalesces into the recognizable, known world, the harmonious cultural center of which is defined by the Thames, whose brow is crowned by the towers of his capital, Troynovant. The naming of the participants in the procession has an epic resonance, resembling similar catalogues in the *Iliad* and the *Aeneid*; and this literary echo elevates the cultural and historical vision embodied in the British landscape.

The pageant itself has fluidity and force, conveyed by the naming of the river guests. This is countered by a stately, even restrained quality suggested by the confluence of the rivers as they arrive at Proteus' hall, by the overriding historical and geographical sequence of their appearance, and by the structure and control of the verse. The cumulative effect supports the theme of *concordia discors*, and implies the existence of an invisible unmoved mover whose shaping hand is manifest in the landscape and whose influence extends into the moral, social, historical, as well as psychological and personal dimensions of Book IV.

The procession (11–52), made up almost entirely of river names and brief historical or geographical epithets, consists of three broad groups whose members are ordered more or less according to related considerations of social precedence (myths of pageantry) and the guests' place in a cosmogonic mythical order. Culminating in the groom and his parents, the first stage in the procession begins with potentates of myth and legend, advancing in descending order from elemental deities (eg, Neptune and Amphitrite) through their descendants – mythic heroes (Phorcys and Palemon), nation founders (Albion), and the great rivers of both the Old and New Worlds (the Nile and 'Oranochy' [Orinoco?]). All are rivers or offspring of rivers and are related to more primitive gods of water. There is a subtle movement from myth, through legend, to history and charted geography, and back to the mythic and elemental. This evolutionary cycle is reinforced by the geographic and hydrologic cycle which links rivers to the sea, and by the familial or biological myth by which rivers are genealogical descendants of the first creative element, water. Thames, Tame, and the Ouse (or Isis) complete this first part of the procession and, by implication, fulfill the cultural evolution that it implies.

Following Thames and making up the second group are the groom's pages and attendants – rivers of Britain (loosely arranged in the geographical order set forth by Harrison and Camden) and Ireland. Then, in the third wave of the pageant, we see the bride, Medway, the last of the Thames' major tributaries before the sea. Her entourage also joins geography and myth. She is accompanied by her riverine handmaids and the offspring of Doris and Nereus, 50 Nereids associated not only with the Muses but with rivers and water generally.

The ordered circularity, moving from myth through history (focusing on Britain) and back to myth – or from ocean to river to ocean – which we see in each of the three groups, also shapes the procession as a whole. It presents a cultural cycle, a vision of historical renewal that has its particular manifestation in Thames, his parents, and his bride. Thus, in characterizing them, Spenser uses the topos of the tower-capped river not to suggest mutability, but re-creative evolution. Ancient Thame, father of Thames, is adorned with the towers of Oxford and described as the 'noursery / Of Arts.' The aged couple are renewed and continued in their son, who wears the symbols of their ancient wisdom, but who 'full fresh and jolly was.' His 'hundred turrets' announce his kinship with his parents, and signify London, an heroic greatness combining strength and wisdom. This myth of renewal expressed in domestic terms is reiterated in the rivers' names: the Isis recalls the Egyptian goddess of rebirth; her own and Thame's continuity is reflected in the name of their son. Perhaps the broadest expression of the mythic and historical vision is found in the contrast between the bride, with her celestial appearance and mythical attendants, and the groom, decked with symbols of human history and accompanied by an entourage of British rivers. Together they suggest the marriage of heaven and earth, the eventual renewal of nature which, in *The Faerie Queene*, is promised in the vision of the New Jerusalem in Troynovant.

The integration of the episode within Book IV is intricate and itself important: like the other river episodes, it helps define the unity of the larger work. The vast image of *concordia discors* in the river marriage is essential to the poem, as its only vision of universal harmony in historical geography. This symbolic significance is enhanced by the peculiarities of the Book of Friendship, in which we see the reconciliation of four pairs of lovers whose eventual union is absorbed into the marriage. Structurally, the episode functions in the book as the narrative surrogate for these couples, and is a framing device for the reconciliation of two symbolic figures, Marinell and Florimell, whose names suggest the fruitful union of opposites, water and earth. The river marriage provides the occasion for Marinell's learning 'lovers paines to rew' (xii 13), and thus brings the natural harmony within a moral context. Marinell personifies fear of and resistance to love and is symbolically immersed in his own element before coming to terms with love; indeed, others (most notably Britomart) make similar journeys to the destructive and re-creative sea (see *Rich Strond), where they are able to understand themselves and their emotions.

In this way, then, the river marriage is literally a *locus communis* within the poem and has an important role in its overall structure. Moreover, in helping to define the idea of love and friendship in terms of natural harmony, it complements the other image of *concordia discors* in Book IV, the Temple of Venus. The abstract and allegorical image of the force of concord presented there has its manifestation in nature in the river marriage. The reader is forced to read the book in terms of these two complementary but stylistically opposite expressions of the same idea, the one abstract, the other concrete and physical in its representation. The reader must reconcile image and idea, must perform an interpretive process that parallels the central problems of *The Faerie Queene*, and of Spenser's art generally.

The epic river poem is not a form one works in more than once; however, Spenser's interest in the topos was not spent. Thereafter, his objective was to use the river to go to the other extreme of the epic: to realize the Renaissance ideal of concision – to contain much in small. The epyllia of *Colin Clout* and the *Cantos of Mutabilitie*, and the resonant brevity of *Prothalamion*'s refrain demonstrate Spenser's formal skill and his clear, consistent understanding of the river topoi. After *The Faerie Queene*, the British rivers no longer need to be legitimized, and Spenser turns his maturer art to the mythological history of river landscape as a way of defining the world of the poem.

In creating his two rustic Irish river nymphs in *Colin Clout* and the *Cantos of Mutabilitie*, Spenser turns away from the epic models which dominate *FQ* IV xi, and adopts the geographical and etiological tales that are part of the georgic tradition represented by Virgil, Ovid, and Boccaccio. The prototype for this tradition is Virgil's fourth *Georgic*: the story of Aristaeus and his mother, the nymph Cyrene, a river goddess and lover of Apollo. Aristaeus, unintentionally responsible for the death of Eurydice, is the victim of the vengeance of Orpheus and Proteus. His mother is privy to the mysteries of nature (an idea commonly associated with rivers), and in her underwater cave, he learns the Apollonian lore which is necessary to heal him and to enable him to subdue Proteus and restore his aviary, a symbol of his mastery over nature.

In this river episode, Virgil concentrates the central idea of the *Georgics*, that 'felix qui potuit rerum cognoscere causas' ('blessed is he who has been able to win knowledge of the causes of things' 2.490). As an epyllion appearing at the end of the *Georgics* and having a narrative coherence of its own, it forces us to analyze its relevance to the larger work, and thus instructs us in the proper reading of the whole. In *FQ* IV xi, Spenser adapts Virgil by having Marinell learn about himself and love while visiting a similar river cave where his mother attends the river marriage. Spenser's use of the Virgilian model is even clearer and closer in his treatment of Molanna and Mulla and their relation to the surrounding narratives. In *Colin Clout*, the stubborn attraction of Bregog and Mulla to each other and their resistance to any obstacle to their union (88–155) provide a succinct example in nature of the force of universal concord described in abstract terms in Colin's hymn to love (795–894). The river epyllion is the natural manifestation of that intellectual ideal. As such, it illustrates the unifying ideas of the poem: it helps us to understand Spenser's vision of human nature, the force of concord in society, the value of the love and friendship of the Irish shepherds, and the discordant and unnatural effects of the English court, which isolates its members and frustrates both poetry and love.

Identical structural and thematic use is made of the tale of the river nymph in *FQ* VII vi 37–55. Molanna's betrayal of Diana and the disfigurement which is her punishment add to our understanding of the allegorical character Mutabilitie. The etiological river myth describes the passing of a golden age when the gods resorted for their recreation to a landscape of ideal natural beauty; Molanna's story shows how nature and Arlo Hill were disfigured, though not ultimately changed from their first estate. Thus it defines the origin and extent of mutability in nature, and thereby provides information necessary for our understanding of Mutabilitie herself. The river tale is a more complex view of the framing allegory, and the reader is forced to revert to it to appreciate Nature's judgment.

Spenser's use of the topos in *Prothalamion* marks a return to the form of the river pageant which historical poets such as Leland, Camden, and Vallans adapted from *Aeneid* and the *Mosella*, and which he used in *FQ* IV xi. While he abandons the epyllion, he retains the other distinctive features he had experimented with during the preceding fifteen years. The use of the river to identify the world of the poem is reflected in the juxtaposition of the Lee and Thames, and the ideal of conciseness is realized in the concentration of the topos in the refrain. In presenting the confluence of the rivers in terms of the journey of the brides (as swans) down the Lee to the Thames and London, Spenser continues to let geographical nature shape his poetic myth. However, instead of describing marital union as the confluence of two rivers, Spenser has the rivers lead up to the union of the wedding couples. The image of concord in nature is, as it were, displaced by its social manifestation, and in this, Spenser's technique here inverts that used in *FQ* IV.

Characteristically, the rivers define Spenser's view of marital concord in terms of opposites: the pastoral *otium* of the wedding is viewed as a hiatus in a more threatening world of history and time, and is identified with the Lee, which brings the brides to the Thames, to London, and to their future husbands. The feminine world of the Lee is described as a *locus amoenus*. The Thames is distinctly masculine, and its sphere of activity is historical and public. The union of these two opposites in the wedding arrests the flow of time and is a product of the influence of concord in nature. Beyond time, it is creative and regenerative, and the poem itself participates in the quality defined by the marriage and the union of the two rivers. Through the refrain, we see that it, too, shares in the process by which time is transcended and nature renewed: 'Sweete *Themmes* runne softly, till I end my Song.' As in *Time*, the poet and the river work in harmony to give meaning to the world of history; here the brides are delivered to the grooms as a gift of the river and the poet (see 170–80).

The river refrain gains resonance and complexity from Spenser's previous use of the motif. Here it is used more traditionally, echoing not only Spenser's own use of the motif, but also the convention as a whole. In its graceful simplicity, it flows back on the convention of the river poem and calls attention to its form, and in this way participates in the timelessness that the refrain describes. It transcends time while speaking of time, and absorbs history into nature and poetic myth, and this is the ideal presented in *Time*. Indeed, here history and literary myth come together, for *Prothalamion* was the last poem published in Spenser's life.

W.H. Herendeen

Berger 1968e; Braden 1975; Fowler 1960b; Wyman H. Herendeen 1981a; Herendeen 1981b; Herendeen 1986; Herendeen 1987 '"Castara's Smiles ... Sabrin's Tears": Nature and Setting in Renaissance River Poems' *CL* 39:289–305; Oruch 1967; C.G. Osgood 1919–20.

romance Any discussion of romance broad enough to suggest the many strains incorporated into *The Faerie Queene* must include not only works traditionally designated as 'romances' but also romance elements within other texts.

kinds: (*a*) biblical and early Christian *The Faerie Queene* begins with the two major quest patterns of the Bible, the model for the Red Cross Knight's quest in Book I. The first of these extends from the loss of Eden (with its Tree and Water of Life) by Adam and Eve, through the fall into the wilderness of wandering or error, to the regaining of Paradise through Christ, a 'second Adam' who reverses the story of the first. Within this quest pattern is the second: the exodus of Israel, led out of Egypt by Moses, wandering in the wilderness, and finally entering a Promised Land guarded, it is rumored, by giant Anakim who turn out to be bogey or threshold symbols like Spenser's Orgoglio, more terrifying in anticipation than in retrospect (see Frye 1957:191). This quest would seem to be completed when Israel enters the Promised Land under Joshua, whose name is Hebrew for Jesus. But even after his victory, the pattern of Israel's wandering from God, oppression by enemies, and deliverance by a redeemer continues. In the New Testament, this redeemer is Christ, who overcomes Satan in the wilderness (an event recalled in Guyon's temptation by Mammon in *FQ* II vii). The new Israel is the Church, itself now wandering in the wilderness, falling into error, beset by oppression, and anticipating triumphant entry into the New Jerusalem at the apocalyptic Second Coming of Christ.

There are also individual biblical stories with romance elements. The Joseph story in Genesis tells of a younger brother's descent into slavery in Egypt through the treachery of his brothers, his trials and triumphs there, and his final reconciliation with his family – a plot of separation and reunion which resembles that of countless other romances. The Song of Solomon provides the figure of a Bride seeking an absent Bridegroom, interpreted by Christian writers as an allegory of the quest for Christ in the period before Apocalypse. The Book of Esther presents the story of Israel in the romantic form of a bride gaining a king's favor for her people.

The most important single model of biblical romance for Spenser is the Book of Revelation (see *Apocalypse, Bennett 1942: 108–23, Hankins 1971:99–127), which presents the final apocalyptic conflict between the forces of evil (the Great Dragon, the False Prophet, the Whore of Babylon, and Satan or Antichrist) and the forces of good (the archangel Michael, the Woman Clothed with the Sun, the New Jerusalem as the Bride of the Lamb, and a knight on a white horse who defeats the Great Dragon and restores Paradise – the source of the chivalric Christ in Langland's *Piers Plowman* and elsewhere). The vision in Revelation of the Church's present oppressors as already overcome is an apocalyptic technique recalled in the Dragon Redcrosse fights, which is simultaneously terrifying and comically reduced. The biblical dragon-killing motif, in which Christ overcomes the Great Dragon associated with the fallen world, saves the old Adam (whose son and successor he becomes), and gains a bride in the rescued Church, explains why in Book I Spenser could combine biblical romance with the structurally analogous medieval legend of St George, who defeats a dragon holding a kingdom in terror and gains the king's daughter, or with echoes of the Grail legend of the old king whose wound is related to the sterility of his land, made fertile again by the knight who asks the right question.

These biblical motifs were extended in apocryphal writings such as the fourth-century *Gospel of Nicodemus*, a Christian romance contemporary with the Greek romances it resembles. It relates the quest of Seth, who is told that his dying father Adam will in time be healed by a redeemer with oil from the Tree of Life, and who brings back from Eden a branch of the tree which will eventually become the Cross (the bleeding tree of the Grail romances and of Spenser's Fradubio, who recalls the fallen Adam). It also relates Christ's Harrowing of Hell, which later medieval iconography portrayed as Christ's leading Adam, Eve, and the Patriarchs out of the jaws of a defeated monster (echoed in *FQ* I xi 12 in the Dragon whose mouth gapes 'like the griesly mouth of hell'). A crucial debt of Spenserian to biblical romance is the conception of evil as a false look-alike of good (eg, Archimago impersonates Redcrosse, as Satan imitates God), making the quest of both Redcrosse and the reader an education in distinguishing between parody doubles. The early Christian romance *Clementine Recognitions* (L tr from Gr c 400) combines the motif of the demonic double (the magician-orator Simon Magus, whose contest with Simon Peter and implantation of his own face on the hero's father provide resonances for the opposition of Archimago and Redcrosse) with the motif of reuniting a family, in what is clearly an allegory of the Last Judgment, the apocalyptic reunion of the members of God's family (Frye 1976:141). The eighth-century Christian romance of Barlaam and Josaphat (one of the most popular stories in the Middle Ages), which tells of how a hermit delivers to the hero a 'jewel' which turns out to be the biblical story, also contains a counterfeit double, an enemy of Christianity who poses as a defender of it.

The Book of Revelation provides the most concentrated instance of biblical typology (the application of Old Testament figures to the events of the New, and of the pattern of oppression and deliverance to the life of both individual and nation), a tradition which enables Spenser to present the quest of Redcrosse as simultaneously the spiritual biography of a second Adam (encountering a serpentine Error, falling into errancy, and finally gaining a vision of the New Jerusalem and the Edenic Water and Tree of Life), the political history of another errant Israel (his series of partial victories and defeats recalling the pattern of Israel's history), the typological repetition of the quest of Christ (his red and white recalling Christ's blood and body and the colors of the flag borne by Christ in representations of the Harrowing of Hell, his description as 'Right faithfull true' recalling the knight 'Faithful and true' of Revelation 19, and his three-day fight with the Dragon repeating Christ's three-day death and resurrection), and the trials of the St George of an England newly freed from the Church of Rome which is identified typologically with Antichrist.

Biblical romance is also important for Spenser because it envisages something ultimately beyond the romance world, just as the New Jerusalem Redcrosse yearns to enter straightway represents something higher than the earthly Cleopolis for which he still toils, a motif of supersession also found in the medieval Grail romances. The echoes of Revelation in Redcrosse's victory over the Dragon and the restoration of Una to Adam and Eve, her parents in Eden, suggest the end of the romance world of error and ambiguous look-alikes. Yet, as Israel's arrival in the Promised Land yields to a new series of errors and wanderings, or as the vision of the end in Revelation is followed by the figure of John still waiting in the wilderness of history (not unlike the speaker at the end of the *Cantos of Mutabilitie*), so too Redcrosse at the end of Book I leaves Eden to return to Fairyland, a regress from apocalypse in which Archimago is again unbound, the harlot Duessa freed to work her enchantments, and Spenser's own enchanting romance allowed to continue. Hebrews 11 presents all of history as a wilderness journey in quest of the Promised Land. Romance in Spenser, where Arthur continues to seek the vanished Fairy Queen and Redcrosse's victory does not remove the realm of questing, is finally, in its biblical context, linked with the threshold time before Apocalypse, with the wilderness of purgatorial wandering and trial in which the End, though promised, is still delayed.

(*b*) **classical Greek and Latin** The second romance tradition important for Spenser, that of Greek romance, begins with Homer's *Odyssey* (eighth century BC), whose narrative of adventures which delay but do not finally prevent Odysseus' homecoming to Ithaca was viewed in the Renaissance as the classical prototype of romance. Though Spenser would not have known it at first hand, his indirect use of it for the sea voyage of Guyon and the Palmer to Acrasia's bower at the close of *FQ* II involves an identification of the end of the romance quest with the overpowering of an enchantress figure which is faithful to the *Odyssey* itself, where the mastering of Circe foreshadows the completion of both quest and poem. The *Odyssey* establishes a connection important for subsequent romance between the charms of the enchantress who delays the hero's arrival at his destination, and the charm of the romance itself, which delays its own ending as effectively as Penelope's weaving and unweaving puts off a parallel moment of truth – a linking of the poem itself with its impediments which enabled Roger Ascham to condemn Spenser's beloved Italian romances as 'the inchantementes of *Circes*' (ed G.G. Smith 1904, I:2). Two traditions crucial for the moralized version of the Odyssean quest in *FQ* II are the long tradition of interpreting Odysseus' voyage as a series of allegorical encounters or pilgrim's progress through life's hardships and enticements, and (given the association of Acrasia with biblical as well as with Homeric enchantresses) the Christian allegorization of Odysseus as a figure both for classical virtues (such as temperance) and for Christ.

The post-Homeric epic cycle, including the *Telegony* (6th century BC; see Huxley 1969:168–9), which provides the apparently concluded *Odyssey* with a sequel of yet more plot turns, and which, with other such poems, fed the accounts of Dares and Dictys through which the Troy story was for centuries known in Western Europe, provides a striking example of the tendency of romance stories to proliferate beyond the boundaries of a single text, expanding to fill out more limited plots with versions of what happened before and after. In this regard, the counterpart of the evasive Odysseus, Homer's 'man of many turns,' is the shape-changing Proteus of *Odyssey* 4, who prophesies only when bound and who evokes the evasiveness and changeability of romance itself. By the Renaissance, Proteus had become ambiguously associated with the curse as well as the delight of mutability, with the poet as controller of shapes and as prophet or *vates* but also with the potential unmanageability of his materials. In *The Faerie Queene*, he appears both indirectly in Archimago, the deceitful shape-changer whose threatened escape at the end of Book I makes the unbinding of both the biblical Satan and the Homeric Proteus implicit models for the slippery multiplicity of Spenser's romance, and directly in the Proteus of Books III and IV, who is significantly absent during the Marriage of Thames and Medway in his own house, replaced perhaps by the poet who in this episode's marvelously controlled fluidity has Proteus, at least temporarily, bound.

The later, Hellenistic romance *Argonautica* by Apollonius of Rhodes (third century BC) tells of the successful voyage of Jason and the Argonauts in quest of the Golden Fleece, and of the revenge of the enchantress Medea when she is deserted by the hero she has helped, a story whose appearance on the ivory gates of the Bower of Bliss (*FQ* II xii 44–5) attaches the traditional association of Circe and Medea to Spenser's Acrasia, and makes Guyon's sea voyage an Argonautica as well as an Odyssey. Shorter but more episodic than the *Odyssey* it both imitates and departs from, in its very un-Homeric narrator's tongue-in-cheek excuses for his digressions and tall tales it anticipates the narrative asides of Ariosto and Spenser. It is filled with fabulous elements: Phrixus' flying on the Golden Ram, armed men springing from serpents' teeth, the Great Snakes guarding the Golden Apples, the Warden of the Fleece (who is made even more engaging in Valerius Flaccus' unfinished Latin *Argonautica* of the first century AD and transformed into a dragon in William Caxton's 1477 English version of the medieval French *Jason*), and the Argo itself, a ship capable of traveling at its own will and providing a survey of the known and mythical worlds – a geographical impulse in romance which emerges again in the Renaissance, with the flight of Ariosto's hippogriff. Neither the Greek nor the Latin *Argonautica* need have been directly known to Spenser, since Argonaut lore was commonplace in the Renaissance, a fact which facilitated detaching its episodes from their context and distributing them over different characters or events; thus, in Book V, Spenser recalls the *Argonautica*'s bronze giant Talos (associated with the Law in Crete) both in the iron man Talus and in the details of the death of the Giant with the scales.

The latest Greek romances date from the early Christian era: the Ninus romance fragments, Chariton's *Chaereas and Callirhoe*, Xenophon of Ephesus' *Ephesiaca*, Longus' *Daphnis and Chloe*, Heliodorus' *Ethiopica*, possibly *Apollonius of Tyre* (assumed to belong here though known only in an influential fifth- or sixth-century translation), and Achilles Tatius' *Clitophon and Leucippe*. Originating on the fringes of the Greek world which were subject to Persian, Egyptian, and Phoenician influences, they feature oriental settings and heroes, and plots of mysterious birth, foster parents, prophetic dreams and oracles (like the one whose predictions the hero and heroine of the *Ephesiaca* try to escape with no more success than Marinell's mother has in averting a prophecy of woe in *FQ* III iv), the separation of lovers by shipwreck or capture by pirates (a recurrent feature, one suspects, of the actual Mediterranean world), hair's-breadth escapes, attempted rape or human sacrifice (Leucippe escaping as narrowly from sacrifice on the robbers' altar as Serena from the cannibals in *FQ* VI viii), confinement in caves (Chariclea's fate in *Ethiopica* I; Pastorella's in *FQ* VI x-xi), burial alive (the *Ephesiaca*'s drugged Anthia escapes only when awakened by grave robbers), and finally the reunion of hero and heroine in a miraculous happy ending.

A major feature of these romances is the delaying of that ending through labyrinthine plot complications, explicitly linked in the *Ethiopica* to the deviations of Proteus and typically involving the continued preservation of the heroine's virginity. The consummately devious Chariclea of the *Ethiopica* manages to guard hers through ten books of the most compromising adventures (a feat as miraculous as the supposedly preserved virginity of Ariosto's much-pursued Angelica); and in Longus, Daphnis and Chloe's consummation of their love is postponed not as in the other Greek romances by a series of mishaps but by their own very slow discovery of sex, a delaying tactic which makes the romance narrative not a 'Who done it?' but a 'When will they do it?'

The Greek romances were scorned by educated Greeks, who like many of their Renaissance counterparts considered them unfit for serious reading. They were only partially rescued by Byzantine allegorizing (eg, of the *Ethiopica* as the soul's search for God) and by the doubtful tradition that Heliodorus and Achilles Tatius were Christian bishops. In the Renaissance, however, they came into their own. Heliodorus' *Ethiopica*, the most dense and complex, was translated in the sixteenth century into Latin, French, German, Spanish, and Italian, and into English in Thomas Underdowne's *Aethiopian History* (1569, rev ed 1587); it was recommended alongside Virgil's *Aeneid* as a narrative model, and used by Rabelais, Tasso, Cervantes, and by Sidney in his *Arcadia* (1590), through which it provided the subplot for Shakespeare's *King Lear*. The Apollonius story, originally translated into English prose in the eleventh century, influenced the plots of Shakespeare's *Comedy of Errors* and *Pericles*, through versions in John Gower's *Confessio Amantis* and Lawrence Twine's *Patterne of Painefull Adventures* (entered 1576). *Clitophon and Leucippe*, translated by William Burton, appeared in 1597.

It is not clear whether Spenser is echoing Greek romance in *FQ* VI directly or through such intermediaries. Pastorella's fate at the hands of the Brigands recalls both an episode in Achilles Tatius, where pirates quarrel over whether the captured heroine should be sold to slavers and slay their commander who has fallen in love with her, and the fight in Heliodorus between a pirate captain and his subordinate over possession of Chariclea, which leads to a battle in which the pirates destroy each other. It may also recall Orlando's rescue of Isabella from a cave where slave traders are arranging to sell her in Ariosto's *Orlando furioso* 12–13. The adventures in *FQ* VI, however, and perhaps those in Books III and IV as well, owe as much in general terms to the complications of the Greek romances as they do to the digressive form of *Amadis of Gaul* or the Italian romances. The revived Greek romances were profoundly influential not only on Renaissance romance but also on the subsequent development of the novel.

The blending of epic and romance, *Iliad* and *Odyssey*, in Virgil's *Aeneid* provides the model for Renaissance epic romances such as Spenser's combining in a single hero the public (Iliadic) and the private or ethical (Odyssean) virtues; the Odyssean wanderings of Aeneas are also echoed along with the *Odyssey* and the *Argonautica* in Guyon's sea voyage in *FQ* II xii. On the model of the *Aeneid*, *The Faerie Queene* uses romance to convert the Odyssean quest into a labor in the service of a greater good (eg, the Herculean labor associated in both Aeneas and Artegall with establishing a government), and a simple homecoming into a quest for a more elusive goal (as when Artegall and Britomart put off present pleasures for the sake of an objective still unachieved at the poem's end). Virgil also provides many potential romance elements which Renaissance authors edged further in a romance direction: the metamorphosed tree of *Aeneid* 3, echoed in Dante's Piero, Ariosto's Astolfo, and Spenser's Fradubio; the phantom Aeneas echoed in Italian romance and in Spenser's false Florimell; Aeneas' Odyssean sojourn with Dido, echoed in Artegall's with Radigund in *FQ* V v-vii; and the incarnation of the characteristic romance strategy of delay in Allecto, the Virgilian discord figure whose complication of the action and consequent postponement of ending is echoed in Ariosto's Discordia and Spenser's Ate, whose disruptions in *FQ* IV effectively postpone the possibility of an ending like the satisfying close of Book III in the original 1590 version.

Virgil's blending of epic and romance also enables Spenser to combine echoes of the *Aeneid* with episodes reminiscent of medieval romance; for example, the latter's characteristic vigils are combined with a recall of Aeneas' underworld descent in Guyon's temptation by Mammon in *FQ* II vii. Likewise, the common pattern of questing for a delayed or far-off goal enables him to combine Virgilian and biblical resonances; Redcrosse's stopping midway with Duessa in *FQ* I vii provides an example of acedia, which Dante in *Purgatorio* 19 illustrates both by the Trojans who stopped short of the promised land of Italy and by the Israelites who did not complete their exodus through the wilderness. This assimilation of Virgilian, biblical, and romance quests was made easier not only by their analogous structures but also by allegorizations of the *Aeneid* such as that of the Florentine Platonist Cristoforo Landino, who interprets the journey from Troy to Italy as the upward progress of the soul to its true home, or Dante's already traditional combination of Aeneas' quest for Rome with the Christian's quest for the Heavenly Jerusalem.

Ovid's *Metamorphoses* is not generically a romance; but with its seemingly endless

Protean generation of story lines, it provided Renaissance romancers with a model of romance dilatoriness as a deliberate deviation from the more single-minded narrative of Virgilian epic. Ovid pointedly transforms the Sibyl's injunction to epic haste (*Aeneid* 6) into a deferral of the forward journey while she tells the long story of her love for Apollo (*Met* 14) – at the same time telescoping the entire *Aeneid* into a mere two books of his own very different poem. This deferral is echoed in *Orlando furioso* 34, for example, when Lidia's much-dilated story of love delays Astolfo's descent into a very Dantesque hell, in the midst of an episode in which Ariosto manages to telescope Dante's authoritative poem into two cantos of his much more digressive romance. In evoking Ovid's catalogue of trees, whose locus in *Metamorphoses* 10 is the story of the poet Orpheus, Spenser suggests at the outset of *The Faerie Queene* the Ovidian affinities of his own romance metamorphoses, both in the Wood of Error as an opening emblem of his poem, and more particularly in the Protean generation of diverse stories in Books III and IV. Furthermore, the medieval tradition of the *Ovide moralisé* offers a model for combining prolific fable and moral meaning, as does Arthur Golding's preface to his translation of the *Metamorphoses* (1567), in which he allies Ovid's narrative of creation, flood, and final prophetic vision with similar patterns, canonical for Renaissance culture, in the Bible.

Latin romance proper appears in the burlesque imitation of Greek romance in Petronius' first-century *Satyricon*, and in Apuleius' second-century *Golden Ass*. The latter tells of the author's accidental metamorphosis into an ass by the servant of an enchantress, his observation of man's follies and vices, and his final restoration to human form through the goddess Isis. In its 1566 translation by William Adlington, the work is a probable source for the identification of Britomart and Artegall with Isis and Osiris in *FQ* V vii, as well as for the allegory of Cupid and Psyche in III vi. Renaissance interpretations of *The Golden Ass* underscore the affinities between romance and allegory: Adlington, in his address to the reader, sees it as an allegory of the potential upward metamorphosis of human life: 'this booke of Lucius is a figure of mans life, and toucheth the nature and manners of mortall men, egging them forward from their Asinall forme, to their humane and perfect shape.'

(*c*) **medieval** Of all romance forms, it is medieval chivalric romance which provides the definitive matrix for Spenser's combination of biblical and classical romance materials within the form of a knight's quest. Since the twelfth century, medieval romance had been divided into three subjects: the Matter of France, the Matter of Rome, and the Matter of Britain. The first (important for the Italian romances known to Spenser) has chiefly to do with Charlemagne, the Christian champion Roland, the traitor Ganelon, and Archbishop Turpin. These figures appear both in the Old French *Chanson de Roland* (twelfth century) and in the *Pseudo-Turpin*, a popular twelfth-century Latin prose chronicle erroneously attributed to Archbishop Turpin, one of the seven Old French translations of which provides the first mention of love and anger in the story of Roland (a recurrent theme in Boiardo and Ariosto) and provides, in a figure called Braidemunde, the ancestress of the Italians' Bradamante and Spenser's Britomart.

The Matter of Rome recasts Greek and Roman legend in a chivalric form, reflecting a mid-twelfth-century shift in French literary taste away from the war interest of the *chansons de geste* to the love interest of romance. It is represented by the *Roman de Thebes*, a romance version of the Thebes story from Statius' *Thebaid*; the *Roman d'Alexandre*, the chief of the romances on Alexander the Great; the anonymous *Roman d'Eneas*, which transforms the *Aeneid* into a romance of knightly deeds and an allegory of the rejection of destructive love (Dido) for true (Lavinia, a minor Virgilian character, expanded to meet the new interest in love); and, most importantly, the *Roman de Troie* of Benoît de Sainte-Maure, which, drawing on Ovid as well as on the influential versions of the Troy story in Dares and Dictys, applies romance codes of chivalry to the Trojan warriors (a blend still at work in Spenser's Paridell and Hellenore) and emphasizes their loves.

The Matter of Britain focuses on Arthur, a sixth-century Welsh battle leader mentioned in Nennius' *Historia Britonnum* (c 800), and transformed by Geoffrey of Monmouth's *Historia regum Britanniae* into a conqueror rivaling Alexander and Charlemagne. Geoffrey developed the story of the treachery of Arthur's nephew Mordred, their final battle, and the bearing of the mortally wounded Arthur to Avalon. His association of legendary British with biblical events fostered the development of the Anglo-biblical parallel still visible in the simultaneously English and biblical *FQ* I. Also crucial for later Arthurian romance in Britain were his development of Merlin (the chief magus of *FQ*, whose prophecy to Britomart in III iii recalls the *Historia*'s interpolated 'Prophecies of Merlin'), of the popular tradition that Arthur, sleeping in Avalon, would one day restore the golden age to a strife-torn Britain (a national counterpart to the biblical Second Coming), and, from Nennius, the idea of British descent from the Trojan Brute (echoed in Spenser's Troynovant and Arthur's reading in *FQ* II x of a history linking him with Troy). The *Historia* was followed by the vernacular *Roman de Brut* of the Norman poet Wace, which extended knowledge of the Trojan-Arthurian lore to the French aristocracy, and by Layamon's *Brut*, the first English Arthurian poem, which expands Wace's story of the Round Table and adds more fairy elements (the elves present at Arthur's birth, the magic origins of his spear, and his transport to Avalon in a magic boat).

Arthurian romance develops out of the Matter of Rome, the new Arthurian lore, and the Breton *lais* of Marie de France (fl late-twelfth century) and other, anonymous authors. Most important, however, are the five Old French romances of Chrétien de Troyes; with the Vulgate cycle in the next century, they establish Arthur's court (like that of Gloriana in Spenser) as the center from which knights go forth in pursuit of adventure or particular quests. They also demonstrate the remarkable flexibility of romance, its capacity to absorb not just a multiplicity of stories interwoven by the technique of *entrelacement* into a pattern very different from the single dominant plot line of epic, but also a variety of divergent perspectives (adulterous love in *Lancelot*, married love in *Erec and Enide* and *Yvain*, Arthur as paragon of kings in *Cligés* but inglorious cuckold in *Lancelot*, the Grail in *Perceval* as figure of something beyond and even in conflict with the court itself), and a cast of often inconsistently drawn individual characters (as Spenser's Proteus can be at different times lecherous old man or awesome deity). Profoundly influential for subsequent Arthurian romance, Chrétien's works bequeath to it such staples as fights with giants and unnamed knights, tournaments, dwarfs, rings of invisibility, protecting lions, the curing of wounds, the conflicting claims of arms and love, the service of a fairy mistress (*Yvain*), the 'translation' of chivalry from Troy to the west (*Cligés*), and the knight's assisting others' quests while (like Spenser's Arthur) pursuing his own.

Chivalric romance was further developed in Middle High German poems based on Chrétien: Hartmann von Aue's *Erec* and *Iwein*; Wolfram von Eschenbach's *Parzival* (a source of Wagner's *Parsifal*), which greatly expands the Percival story in time and space to include not just Britain but the Near and Far East; and Gottfried von Strassburg's unfinished *Tristan und Isolde*, which retells the most popular tragic love story of the Middle Ages, already extant in the twelfth-century Old French *Tristan* of Béroul and the Anglo-Norman version of Thomas. Chrétien's Grail romance was extended in the early thirteenth century not only in Wolfram's *Parzival* but also in Robert de Boron's *Joseph d'Arimathie*, which links the Grail with the cup used by Christ at the Last Supper and by Joseph of Arimathea to catch the blood from Christ's wounds; in the prose *Didot Perceval*; and in *Perlesvaus*, a romance which, though explicitly allegorical (with its Castle of Enquiry, instructor-hermits, Christ-like hero, and presentation of Christian truth in Arthurian form), is not continuously so, but rather moves like *The Faerie Queene* from literal story to allegory and back, giving its characters an intermittent rather than a rigidly consistent allegorical identity.

The early-thirteenth-century linking of disparate Arthurian stories reaches its culmination in the great anonymous Vulgate Cycle of prose romances (1210–30); its opening *Lestoire del Saint Graal* (presenting the early history of the Grail from Joseph to its preservation in Britain until Arthur's time at the Castle of Corbenic) and *Lestoire de Merlin* were both added later to fill in the narrative preliminaries to its popular and often separately published three-book core. *Lancelot* adds to the familiar story of the adulterous Lancelot and Guinevere the role of Galahad as go-between (the source of Francesca's charge in Dante's *Inferno* 5 that romances and their authors are like 'Galeotto,' inciting to lust). It also foregrounds the romance tension between variety and controlling form in its complex *entrelacement* and frequent unrelated digressions, gives us an Arthur belittled and reduced (perhaps because of contemporary French hatred of England), and, in Gawain's uncomprehending observation of the masque and symbols at the enchanted Castle of Corbenic, offers a possible romance antecedent for Britomart's vigil at the house of Busirane (*FQ* III xi-xii).

The *Queste del Saint Graal* takes up without a gap where *Lancelot* leaves off, replacing the bumbling Percival with the impeccable Galahad as the achiever of a Grail now clearly identified with the Eucharist. By making Galahad the son of Lancelot, it suggests a progression from an impure father and an earthly love to a pure, even Christlike, son and to a divine love which reflects the influence of the great twelfth-century mystic St Bernard of Clairvaux. The *Mort Artu* (much of which is familiar to English readers through Malory and Tennyson) narrates the tragic end of Arthur, whose downfall through the agency of woman is echoed in details of Artegall's story in *FQ* V v.

The Vulgate Cycle as a whole incorporates conflicting ideals, widely divergent tones, and different conceptions of individual characters into a continuous Arthurian narrative. Along with the post-Homeric cycles and early Christian romances, it is a striking example of the tendency of romance stories both to proliferate and to attach themselves to others so as to fill out the details of a character or history, as the thirteenth-century prose *Tristan de Leonois* further links the Tristan romance to an Arthurian setting, and the vast fourteenth-century French *Perceforest* gives Arthur a prehistory stretching back to Alexander the Great. (This linking of romance quest and allegory in *Perlesvaus* and the Vulgate *Queste* also takes non-chivalric form, most influentially in the *Romance of the Rose*.)

The thirteenth and early fourteenth centuries also provide a number of non-Arthurian French chivalric romances important for Spenser. The popular thirteenth-century *Huon de Bordeaux* (likely known to Spenser through the expanded prose version of 1454 or the 1534 English translation by Lord Berners) is cited in *FQ* II i 6. The just rule of its Fairy King Oberon (who also appears in Shakespeare's *Midsummer Night's Dream*) may be a precedent for the peacefulness of Spenser's Fairyland in contrast to the relative chaos of English history as presented in *FQ* II x. *Huon* also provides a model for extending Fairyland into the East (Spenser locates it in India as well as America), and for combining the Matter of France with characters from the Matter of Britain, so that Fairyland becomes a space in which characters and episodes from several romances can meet.

The *Melusine* of Jean d'Arras, one possible source of Guyon's name, anticipates Spenser in its defense of Fairyland; and the discovery by Melusine's husband of her mermaid form supplies a romance antecedent for Fradubio's discovery of Duessa's real identity in *FQ* I ii. Another fourteenth-century French romance, *Artus de Bretagne*, translated by Lord Berners as *Arthur of Little Britain* (1555?), contains romance models for Spenser's Acrasia episode, for the Radigund-Artegall story, and (in Arthur's vigil at the enchanted castle of Porte Noire) for Britomart's vigil at the house of Busirane. Even more importantly for Spenser (who both knew and used it), it includes Arthur's vision of a Fairy Queen whom he then seeks through a number of subsidiary adventures. Yet another French romance, known in its English translation by Henry Watson as *Valentine and Orson*, contains the common romance motif of the falsely accused and banished wife, as well as the figure of the child (Orson) carried off at birth by a bear, reared as a wild man, and brought back at maturity to society – a story which may lie behind the Salvage Man and bear baby of *FQ* VI iv-v.

The earliest English romances focus on what is called the Matter of England since the stories are at least in part localized there, although French as well as English versions often exist. The earliest extant English verse romance, *King Horn* (c 1250), continued in the fourteenth-century *Horn Childe*, follows the common romance pattern of related inner and outer cycles of exile and return (as the biblical story of Joseph is found within the larger story of Israel's descent into and exodus out of Egypt): the beautiful banished child Horn is exiled a second time but finally, after a series of trials and victories, reveals his noble birth, gains his bride, and recovers his kingdom.

Havelok the Dane (c 1300), which recalls the earlier period of Viking conquest, is a hearty Lincolnshire romance with homelier settings and audience than courtly French romance. Like the King Horn romances, it contains a hero's exile from and return to his home and kingdom, together with usurping villains, a period of servitude, a mysterious light which reveals the hero's kingly origin, a narrow escape from death, and finally his coronation as King of England. *Bevis of Hampton* and *The Tale of Gamelyn* are romances of the muscular, adventure-story variety. *Bevis* includes the exiled hero's imprisonment, rescue of his bride from the stake, conversion of the giant Asclopard, and single-handed battle against the citizenry of London; *Gamelyn* recalls the story of Robin Hood in its feats of daring rescue or escape and its band of forest outlaws. The popular *Guy of Warwick* details the hero's exploits (before his death as a hermit) in England and the Holy Land, against Saracens and their Soldan, the Danish giant Colbrand, the dun cow of Dunsmore, and a winged dragon in Northumberland.

There are also several non-Arthurian Middle English romances. The lay of *Sir Orfeo* provides another example of the medieval translation of classical subjects into romance terms in its fusion of the story of Orpheus and Eurydice with Celtic fairy elements (Pluto and Proserpine are transformed into the King and Queen of Fairyland). It makes Orpheus into a good English king and furnishes a distinctly unclassical but typically romance happy ending in the couple's successful return from the Underworld. Gower's *Confessio Amantis* 8.271–2008 contains a version of the Apollonius story. *Floris and Blancheflor* (in four versions, from the thirteenth to the fifteenth centuries) is an English adaptation of a popular twelfth-century French romance whose intricate tale of innocent and much-tried young love resembles the ingenious plot twists of Greek romance or the *Arabian Nights*.

Unlike Arthurian romance abroad, Arthurian romance in England is influenced from the beginning by the fact that Arthur was an ancestral British hero, conqueror even of the Pope. Layamon's *Brut* transforms Wace's *Roman de Brut* into the alliterative meter of native English verse and into a heroic story of Britain's warrior king. Of the Middle English Arthurian romances which survive from the period between 1300 and 1500, the most notable are *Ywain and Gawain*, an abridged transformation of Chrétien's *Yvain* into an English tale of marvel and adventure; the stanzaic *Morte Arthur*, a condensation of the French Vulgate *Mort Artu*; the alliterative *Morte Arthure*, which shapes the heroic life of Arthur into a medieval tragedy of rise and fall; and *Sir Gawain and the Green Knight*.

Gawain, the masterpiece of English alliterative romance though not widely known until its first appearance in print in 1839, combines folktale motifs of beheading game, temptation by a hostess, and exchange of winnings into a single plot which blends the courtliness of French romance with a contemporary English court and bleak northern landscape; it suggests meanings beyond the literal which are not, however, easily categorizable (for example, its Green Knight combines aspects of the devil, the genial host, and the miraculously reborn green man of the fertility rituals); and, in its framing reference to Troy as ancestor of Britain, it conveys a sense (not unlike Spenser's) of the fragility and mutability of civilization itself.

Chaucer, Spenser's great English predecessor, inherits and transforms the long traditions of French and English romance in *Troilus and Criseyde* (based on a story originating in Benoît de Sainte-Maure's *Roman de Troie*) and in several of the *Canterbury Tales*: the Knight's tale of friends divided by love for the same lady; the Franklin's (ostensibly a Breton *lai* though taken from Boccaccio's *Filocolo*); the Wife of Bath's of young knight and aged 'loathly lady,' which is set in Fairyland in the days of King Arthur; and the *Tale of Melibee*, a tedious prose translation of a French romance begun when the parody-romance *Sir Thopas* breaks off unfinished. *Thopas* itself suggests in its circularity the potential endlessness of romance; Sir Thopas' dream and quest for a Fairy Queen anticipate the central quest of Spenser's romance, which provides its own burlesque of chivalric romance behavior in Braggadocchio, Trompart, and the false Florimell. The unfinished *Squire's Tale* (which Spenser combines with the friendship story from the *Knight's Tale* and completes, in a tribute to Chaucer in his Legend of Friendship, *FQ* IV) may also have provided for Spenser a model of romance reflecting on itself. The Squire's repeated disclaimers of his ability to complete his tale delay his continuation of a story which finally does remain unfinished, a dramatization of the difficulties of completion or closure in the midst of the characteristic tarrying and evasions of conclusion in romance. Spenser provides a quick ending for Chaucer's tale, but leaves an unfinished romance of his own. Taken together, *Sir Thopas* and the *Squire's Tale* suggest that Spenser did not have to look outside the English romance tradition for an example of a writer self-consciously and ironically exposing the nature of the form he has adopted.

Malory, whose *Morte Darthur* is the medium through which Arthurian romance is chiefly known to English readers, borrows both from the great French prose romances, including the Vulgate *Mort Artu*, and from the English stanzaic and alliterative versions. From the latter, he inherits not just the tale of Arthur and the Emperor Lucius but also a more straightforward narrative ordering (in contrast to the complex French *entrelacement*), a reduced role for the supernatural, and a more heroic and political conception of Arthur and the Round Table in place of the French emphasis on the individual knight in search of adventure. Though Malory's influence emerges at several points in the incidents, characters, and tone of *The Faerie Queene*, Spenser relies on him remarkably little; the later poem is closer to French Arthurian romance in its conception of Arthur as presiding over other knightly quests, its complex interlace of stories, and its deferral of names and identities as part of a gradual discovery of meaning (in contrast to Malory's more direct clarification of identities). Arthurian romance, from Geoffrey of Monmouth through Malory to the Welsh Tudor monarchs' politically motivated revival of the Welsh Arthurian lore, together with the tradition of combining romance with allegory, stretching from intermittent touches in Chrétien to sustained elaboration in such works as Stephen Hawes' *Pastime of Pleasure* (1509), helped to create the climate for Spenser's allegorical romance, written at the height of the English Renaissance but still strikingly medieval in spirit in its celebration of the Tudor Elizabeth as the Fairy Queen sought by a British Arthur.

Two other medieval works important for Spenser's romance are the *Gesta Romanorum* and *Amadis of Gaul*. The *Gesta Romanorum* (first printed 1472) was an extremely popular Latin collection of saints' legends, chivalric romances, and oriental tales. It circulated in fifteenth-century English manuscript versions (one of which was published by Wynkyn de Worde c 1524) and was used by Chaucer, Gower, Shakespeare, and others. To its tales of monsters and magicians, miraculous escapes, and damsels in distress it attached allegorical explanations: for example, a story of a knight's three-day battle to save the daughter of a king from a usurping tyrant is glossed as Christ's victory over the devil, a gloss with clear affinities to *FQ* I.

The vast and loosely structured *Amadis of Gaul* (known through the printed Spanish version of Garcia Rodríguez de Montalvo but presumed to come from earlier originals) combines the staples of medieval romance (enchanted castles, fearful dwarfs, symbolic masques, mysterious inscriptions) with plot complications and exotic settings reminiscent of Greek romance (to which it is compared unfavorably in Underdowne's preface to his English translation of Heliodorus). In the romance tradition of the 'knight in love' (recalled in the service of Spenser's Timias for Belphoebe, and both imitated and parodied in Cervantes' *Don Quixote*), it tells of the feats and trials of the valorous and chaste Amadis for love of the British princess Oriana (associated in at least one sixteenth-century poem with Spenser's Fairy Queen). Its enchanter Arcalaus impersonates the hero by donning his arms, like Archimago in *FQ* I ii; and two of its adventures parallel Britomart's experience in the house of Busirane (*FQ* III xi-xiii), one of which compares the freeing of Amadis and others from the enchanter's castle to Christ's Harrowing of Hell. Widely popular in Spenser's time as a model of chivalrous conduct, *Amadis* is mentioned in Sidney's *Defence of Poetry* as able to move men to courtesy, liberality, and courage in spite of its literary imperfections, which Sidney tries to correct by incorporating it into his own more tightly structured romance *Arcadia*.

***(d)* Italian** Although the Matter of Britain arrived in Italy through twelfth-century minstrels and was well enough known by the early fourteenth to contribute Tristram, Lancelot, and Galahad to Dante's romance figures in *Inferno* 5, it was the Matter of France which took greater hold in Italy – in the early Franco-Venetian *Machario*, the *Rinaldo da Montalbano*, the prose *Storie de Rinaldo*, Zanobi's late-fourteenth-century *Spagna in Rima*, and Andrea da Barberino's *Reali di Francia*, an immensely popular prose work on the Carolingian heroes. Italian use of the Matter of France characteristically transforms it, making the solemn into the burlesque (reducing Charlemagne, for example, to the old and foolish dupe of Ganelon), giving to the heroic Christian warrior Roland (Orlando) his separate loves and adventures in the Orient (eg, in the fourteenth-century *Orlando* fragment, which anticipates the alternation of scenes and plot lines in Boiardo, Ariosto, and Tasso), and (notably in the fourteenth-century Franco-Lombard *Entree d'Espagne*) increasing the role of the buffoon Estout de Langres, a mocker of chivalry who concentrates the new ironic tone, anticipating Boiardo's and Ariosto's Astolfo and Cervantes' Sancho Panza.

The first great Italian chivalric romance is the Florentine Luigi Pulci's *Morgante maggiore* (1483), which anticipates the giants of Rabelais in its comically appealing giant Morgante and outrageously amoral half-giant Margutte, who finally dies laughing. Its high-spirited sendups of familiar romance staples – the conversion of Saracens, repeated digressions, and the claim to be following an authoritative source in the comically named Altamenonne (a forerunner of Ariosto's Turpin and Cervantes' Cid Hamete Benengeli) – anticipate the later spoofing of chivalric romance in *Orlando furioso* and *Don Quixote*. It still presents a Charlemagne for the most part belittled (in spite of a patron's request for an ennobled one), but Morgante's great suffering and the poem's ending with the disaster at Roncesvalles and Charlemagne's death reveal a profound melancholy beneath the comically skeptical surface.

Boiardo's *Orlando innamorato* first makes self-consciously thematic the union of Carolingian and Arthurian, Holy War and love, giving us an Orlando passionately in love with an elusive Angelica (as the object of male desire, a forerunner of Spenser's fleeing Florimell), but much less, except in the case of Astolfo, of the traditional Italian mocking tone. From Virgilian epic come both its dynastic theme and its fabulous elements such as the phantom double (the phantom Aeneas pursued by Turnus recalled in Orlando's similar pursuit, as Spenser's knights pursue a false Florimell).

The poem's overwhelming debt, however, is to the Ovidian and protean metamorphoses of romance: concentrating and compounding its characteristic machinery (Christians and Saracens, enchanted armor, wizards, giants, marvelous gardens, magic rings, and not one enchantress but three), providing in its own repeated detours a sense of indefinitely postponed conclusion (in Orlando's case, the divagations of love putting off his ultimate death at Roncesvalles) and of time itself as a potentially endless series of moments to be seized (as Orlando must seize the proverbial forelock of the Fortune-figure Morgana before he can release those kept in her underwater crystal prison), and abounding in images of endlessness (the fairies and enchanted heroes who can never die, Balisardo's progressive metamorphoses, and the giant who in dying multiplies, a romance theme on which Spenser's story of Priamond, Diamond, and Triamond in *FQ* IV provides one among many variations). Existing in three parts, the first two published in 1483 and the last (written c 1484–94) broken off by war and, finally, by the poet's death, the *Innamorato* remains unfinished, unable either to face mortality and finite time within itself, or to continue in the face of the outside world (anticipating, perhaps, the intrusion of a hostile outside world into the final stanzas of *FQ* VI).

The enchantment of Boiardo's romance

is in the constant Ovidian metamorphosis which keeps its fiction going and (like Scheherazade's storytelling in the *Arabian Nights*) defers the fateful moment of truth or death. In completing Boiardo in *Orlando furioso* (pub in different versions 1516, 1521, and 1532), Ariosto calls attention to the potential endlessness of romance by transforming precisely those elements which in Boiardo work against closure. With the help of a book given him by Logistilla, enemy of enchantments, Ariosto's Astolfo finally terminates the seemingly endless life of Orrilo, whose reassembling of his dissevered parts had repeatedly postponed his attackers' going forward to their own deaths in France. Astolfo also undoes the enchanted palace built by the magician Atlante (a counterforce to the poet himself, like Spenser's Archimago) to postpone the death of Ruggiero, a labyrinth of illusion in which the traditional freedom of the individual questing knight becomes instead an entrapping Wood of Error within which each pursues the phantom object of his own desire. More detached perspective in Ariosto is offered by the marvelous flying hippogriff, to those knights able to master it, and by the narrator whose control over the diverse strands of the plot he weaves (and finally, like the weaver Fates, cuts off) is presented as only a temporary reprieve from the debilitating madness of love. Ariosto gives us an Orlando no longer simply in love (*innamorato*) but mad (*furioso*), in a poem where the chivalric ethos itself is both treated ironically and rendered obsolete by gunpowder, the herald of modern technological war.

Dramatizing the traditionally conflicting demands of love and war as the generic contrast between romance and epic, the *Furioso* is a virtual *reductio ad absurdum* of romance, edging towards parody its characteristic marvels (the flying horse, Astolfo's horn, Atlante's magic shield), exploiting its links between mental and geographical 'error' and 'deviation,' employing Discordia and Fortuna, techniques of narrative complication as transparently under the author's control as that authorial 'Turpin' who demands that he include the bawdy Canto 28. These elements are combined with echoes of the *Aeneid* which increasingly add an epic dimension to the poem, as Orlando is cured, the errant Ruggiero prepared through conversion for his dynastic marriage, and the chronically distractible knights finally marshaled into the single epic action of the Holy War. But Ariosto's epic exercise of closure both on Boiardo's errant *romanzo* and on his own playfully digressive narrative comes only after the revelation (on the Moon in Canto 34) of the mendacity or error of Homer and Virgil themselves, whose own contamination of epic with romance is subtly recalled in Ariosto's alternation between Iliadic scenes of siege in Paris and Odyssean exploits in the East. Romance in Ariosto is not only subjected to a thorough anatomy of its characteristic errancy – the sense that its potentially infinite digression and variety may be resistant to completion or authorial control; it also becomes a means of revealing the fictiveness and errancy of all literary forms, including epic and even Scripture, since Astolfo on the Moon hears the author of Revelation admit his own allegiance to a patron (Christ) who may demand a praise not unlike that required by Augustus or the Este.

In the *Furioso*, the interaction between epic and romance, in which epic is denied an unironically superior place, anticipates the sixteenth-century debate over the highly popular romance form as contrasted with the more aristocratic epic which Antonio Minturno (*Arte poetica* 1563) and others claimed to be superior in its greater truth to history and its apparent conformity to Aristotle's *Poetics* (tr 1536). Later Italian epic-romances influenced by this debate and by the increasingly stringent moral climate of the Counter-Reformation include Trissino's *L'Italia liberata da' Goti* (1547–48), whose Acratia joins Ariosto's Alcina as a model for Spenser's Acrasia; Bernardo Tasso's *Amadigi* (1560), based on *Amadis of Gaul*; and Torquato Tasso's *Gerusalemme liberata* (1581, accompanied by the poet's own separate allegorical commentary), which anticipates Spenser's aim to overgo Ariosto, reining in both its errant knights and Ariosto's errant romance form with its plot based on the First Crusade. Such a subordination of romance errancy to Christian purpose and epic form also characterizes Camoens' *Lusiads* (1572) and anticipates both *The Faerie Queene* and Milton's *Paradise Lost*.

Spenser's debt to Italian romance goes far beyond his borrowing from it the division of his poem into cantos. More deadpan in his humor than Ariosto, echoes of whose poem are subtly distributed throughout *The Faerie Queene*, Spenser literally overgoes him by incorporating the Italian eight-line stanza (ottava rima) into his nine-line stanza and by containing within his own larger romance structure the unmistakably Ariostan digressiveness, pursuit of a fleeing female, and potentially endless deferral of resolution in Books III and IV. He similarly transforms elements from Boiardo (eg, the forelock of Morgana, which is returned to its explicitly allegorical origins in the figure of Occasion in *FQ* II iv), from Trissino (eg, Acratia), and from Tasso (eg, Armida's garden in the *Gerusalemme*, both emulated and significantly altered in his Bower of Bliss). His own, arguably more medieval and traditionally English romance continues the venerable romance tradition of eclectically borrowing from earlier models, as well as the imperialistic epic tendency to swallow and outdo them.

(*e*) **pastoral** Pastoral romance, which usually takes the form of a complicated prose narrative interspersed with verse and peopled with shepherds and shepherdesses, foregrounds not the chivalric romance activity of questing but rather the encircling retreat which shuts out, at least temporarily, this concern for end-directed pursuit, as does Calidore's sojourn with Pastorella in *FQ* VI. Pastoral romance begins with Longus' *Daphnis and Chloe* (adapted into English by Angell Day in 1587), which differs from other extant Greek romances in being placed entirely in the pastoral world, where the exploitation of the potential contrast between the noble origin of its major figures and their rural surroundings made it a valuable model for Robert Greene's *Pandosto* (1588), Sidney's *Arcadia* (1590) and Shakespeare's *Winter's Tale* (1610–11).

Sannazaro's Italian *Arcadia* (1504), the first Renaissance pastoral romance, establishes the form as a mixture of verse and prose. Its plot of unhappy love (the lover's exile from his lady and subsequent wanderings in Arcadia) owes as much to the medieval romances of Tristan and Lancelot as to Greek and Latin pastoral, and indeed creates a new genre by blending the two. This marriage is made easier by several factors: a faraway or exotic setting generally common to both, structural similarities between the interweaving of multiple plots into a single romance and the linking of poems into sets of pastoral eclogues, and the fact that medieval romances and *pastourelles* frequently combine romance and pastoral in the interludes in which the questing knight enjoys a temporary forest or garden retreat. Imitations of Sannazaro's *Arcadia* include Cervantes' *Galatea* (1585) and Montemayor's *Diana* (1559?), whose addition to Sannazaro's form of the plot complications of Greek romance (either directly or from *Amadis of Gaul*), continued in Gaspar Gil Polo's *Diana enamorada* (1564).

The most celebrated English pastoral romance and clearly a model for Calidore's pastoral excursion is Sidney's *Arcadia* (1590), imitated in Greene's *Menaphon* (1589, rpt as *Greene's Arcadia* 1590), in Lodge's *Rosalynde* (1590) (in turn dramatized by Shakespeare in *As You Like It*), and in the subplot of *King Lear*. Influences on Sidney include Sannazaro's *Arcadia*, Montemayor's *Diana*, Gil Polo's *Diana enamorada*, and *Amadis of Gaul* (from which he takes his main plot and several episodes, tightening its looser structure as Gil Polo had that of Montemayor). Other influences include the Greek romances (chiefly Heliodorus and Achilles Tatius) with their labyrinthine plots, miraculous escapes, and prophetic oracles (particularly in Sidney's first version, known as the *Old Arcadia*), and the great medieval Arthurian cycles (including Malory's *Morte Darthur*, whose Isolde probably suggested Sidney's Gynecia) with their interwoven stories and didactic emphasis. More than any other pastoral romance, Sidney's *Arcadia* is filled with the tournaments and other features of knightly romance, but keeps them subordinate to the pastoral plot, thus providing a contrast (very close to that of *FQ* VI) between the active chivalric sphere and the contemplative and amorous pastoral sphere.

A major feature of pastoral romance is this contrast between the outside and pastoral worlds, whereby the pastoral is viewed ambivalently as the locus of both innocent simplicity and rustic rudeness (as in the pairs of ideal and thick-witted shepherds and shepherdesses in Sidney or in Shakespeare's *As You Like It*). By virtue of their own courtly or urban origins, its heroes bring this double perspective into Arcadia where they are always only sojourners. The pastoral retreat is typically, therefore, only a temporary prelude to the renovated hero's return to the world of city and court; and frequently the work itself ends by also moving out of pastoral into a loftier genre such as epic. Sannazaro's *Arcadia*, for example, includes echoes of Virgil's *Aeneid* when its hero returns from his pastoral retreat – a hint of the *rota Virgilii* or movement from pastoral to epic to which Spenser alludes at the beginning of *The Faerie Queene*, as his model for moving from *The Shepheardes Calender*.

This sense of temporariness also takes the form of a sense of the fragility of the pastoral world itself, immune neither to the conflicts nor to the invasions or mortality of the outside world (thus, the pastoral retreat of *FQ* VI is complicated by love-rivalry and finally invaded by slaughtering brigands); this vulnerability reflects ironically on aristocrats who think to enjoy greater happiness simply by donning shepherds' clothes or who enter the retreat in order to escape an experience that they must undergo and that comes upon them through their very attempt to evade it (in Sidney's *Arcadia*, Basilius' attempt to escape an ambiguous oracle by retreating to the country sets in motion the very events which fulfill the oracle).

This sense of the fragility of a pastoral retreat within an heroic romance is particularly strong in two instances important for Spenser. In *Orlando furioso* 19, the Arcadian setting in which Angelica and Medoro carve on trees mementos of their love is a pastoral oasis in the midst of the hostile world of war, and it is finally destroyed by Orlando's raging. In *Gerusalemme liberata* 6–7, Erminia, pursued and fleeing from disappointment in love, sojourns as a shepherdess with the family of an old shepherd who (like Spenser's Meliboe) has returned from court life to his original abode; but as with Paris' sojourn with Oenone within the larger epic story of Troy, the idyll of Dido and Aeneas in *Aeneid* 4, and Dante's pausing in Eden at the top of Mount Purgatory before ascending to the New Jerusalem of *Paradiso*, this retreat is soon left behind.

The temporary character of the pastoral oasis is also reflected in the frequently concentric structure of the setting: an outermost circle of urban sophistication or epic warfare and death, an inner circle which may be Arcady proper, and a supernatural center (the Cave of the Nymphs in *Daphnis and Chloe*, the tomb of Massilia in Sannazaro's *Arcadia*, the valley of cypresses in Cervantes' *Galatea*, or Mount Acidale in *FQ* VI x). The action of pastoral romance is often the hero's progress into the center and out again, renewed and ready to return to the world from which he had first retreated. Such a three-part pattern is common in Shakespeare's comedies, which start with exile from society, then retreat into a pastoral place (eg, the forests of Arden in *As You Like It* and the wood in *Midsummer Night's Dream*), and finally return to a society which is itself often transformed by the retreat.

images and motifs Romance is remarkable for the recurrences of images and motifs in texts which could not have had direct contact with each other. Indeed, the phenomenon of the detachable motif – capable of recurring independently or traveling from romance to romance – seems one of the defining features of the genre. Because of their multiplicity, only a partial and schematic review of characteristic images and motifs is possible here.

The frequently allegorical or magical landscape of romance on land often includes three elements: forests, clearings, and caves. Typical forests or woods are the magic wood of Oberon in *Huon of Bordeaux* (whose delightful variety and sudden storm resemble features of Spenser's opening canto) and the enchanted forest of Ismeno in Tasso's *Gerusalemme*, whose windings (like those of Spenser's Wood of Error) seem to reflect the uncertainties and winding paths of the romance narrative itself. Clearings or open spaces in the woods seem to be related to clearings or luminous moments in the narrative. Caves may variously house magicians or instructor-hermits (like the one in Chrétien's *Perceval* or Spenser's Contemplation), oracles, ogres (Homer's Polyphemus, Virgil's Cacus and his romance descendants, Ariosto's Caligorante, or Spenser's Malengin), or enchantresses (as in the obvious erotic associations of Calypso's grotto in the *Odyssey*); or, conversely, they may be a prison for damsels in distress (Heliodorus' Chariclea, Spenser's Pastorella), a demonic counterpart of the female romance enclosure, the enclosed garden of the Song of Solomon and *Romance of the Rose*, or its already potentially sinister version, the garden in which a young wife is imprisoned by an old and jealous husband (as in Marie de France's *Guigemar* and Chaucer's *Merchant's Tale*).

Often animistic or demonological, romance landscape is frequently strewn with fairy rings, geniuses guarding its groves and fertile places, and magical, crippling, or healing wells, such as the storm-creating fountain of Chrétien's *Yvain* or the Fountains of Love and Hate in Boiardo and Ariosto. Recurrent within it is the marvelous but often ambivalent garden or *locus amoenus*, such as the Gardens of Alcinous (which Odysseus pauses to admire and which seem related to the temptation to suspend his quest in Phaeacia), the clearly erotic Garden of the Joy in Chrétien's *Erec et Enide*, and the dangerous simulacra of Eden in the enchanted gardens of Circe's descendants in Boiardo and Ariosto, Trissino, Tasso, Camoens, and Spenser (both in the Bower of Bliss and the baneful pleasure garden of *Muiopotmos*). Equally frequent in medieval and Renaissance romance are enchanted castles and houses of instruction, such as the Castle of Corbenic (where Gawain, in the Vulgate *Lancelot*, is uncertain how to interpret the signs he sees), the enchanted castle of Ariosto's Atlante (from whose spell not all its prisoners are happy to be released, 4.39), and the Castle of Enquiry in *Perlesvaus*. Though some of these places initiate and others imprison, virtually every spellbound castle in romance is a potential house of instruction, if its temporary residents, even belatedly, are able to recognize its significance.

Often the landscape as well as the plot of romance is labyrinthine, a generic feature Ariosto seems to be emphasizing in his hippogriff which, lifting knights out of the mazes of their earthbound wandering, implicitly recalls Daedalus as both the architect of the original labyrinth and the mythical inventor of flight. Theseus' quest to kill the Minotaur at the center of this labyrinth is recalled in the labyrinthine or spider-web structure of Dante's *Inferno* with its monstrous Satan at the center, and in the traditional romance pun of Spenser's labyrinthine Wood of Error (*error* being Latin for labyrinth as well as for wandering or mistake), with its culminating monster.

The inhabitants of the landscape vary widely in different traditions but are typically multiple, in keeping with the romance tendency to sheer proliferation of characters as well as to *copia* of plot. They include fairy mistresses (in romances from Marie de France's *Lanval* and the anonymous medieval *lai* of *Guingamor*, where the hero, like Rip Van Winkle, is held by a fairy in an otherworld of eternal life for 300 years, to *Arthur of Little Britain*, *Sir Thopas*, and *The Faerie Queene*), magicians and sorcerers (from Merlin in Arthurian romance to the 'subtil clerk' of Chaucer's *Franklin's Tale*), pirates and brigands (from Greek romance to *FQ* VI), dwarfs (from Chrétien's *Erec* to *FQ* I, where the dwarf's reduced size and bag of needments may represent a buried reality principle in romance like that embodied in Cervantes' Sancho Panza or the mocking Astolfo, who though not literally a dwarf begins his career in Ariosto as a much-disillusioned little myrtle tree), and giants, ranging from terrifying (like the biblical Goliath, the Cyclops of the *Odyssey*, the raping and child-devouring giant of St Michael's Mount in the alliterative *Morte Arthur*, or the giant-oppressor L'Orgueilleux in *Huon of Bordeaux*) to the friendly or comic (like Pulci's Morgante and Margutte). These giants often function as threshold symbols guarding the entrance to an adventure (like the biblical Anakim of Deuteronomy, the giants guarding the lower reaches of Dante's *Inferno*, and the giant herdsman who points the way to the magic fountain in Chrétien's *Yvain*).

Romance also typically contains animals ranging from menacing (like the dragon whose defeat in *Huon of Bordeaux* may have provided a model for Spenser) to helpful or protective (like the lions of *Yvain* or *FQ* I iv), from initiators into other realms (like the white hind of medieval romance or the rabbit in *Alice in Wonderland*) to symbolic concentrations of the story's emotional register (like the dead nightingale directly related to the pathos of thwarted love in Marie de France's *Laüstic*).

The atmosphere of awe or wonder in romance is created in part by its characteristic battery of marvels. Miraculous means of transport are part of the wish-fulfillment dream of freedom from or control over time and space, and are western relatives of the Oriental magic carpet: for example, the self-propelled boat (from Jason's Argo to the anticipations of Phaedria's enchanted skiff in the magic boats of Trissino and Tasso), Ariosto's flying hippogriff, the wooden horse which conveys the dwarf of *Valentine and Orson* instantly wherever he wishes, and the brass horse which carries its riders wherever they want in Chaucer's *Squire's Tale*. Magic rings confer invisibility (eg, in Chrétien and Ariosto) or the ability to understand the language of birds (eg, Canacee's ring in the *Squire's Tale*).

Other marvels include magic shields and marvelous or mysterious swords, from Arthur's Excalibur and the flaming lance of Chrétien's *Lancelot* to the sword in the *Squire's Tale* which can heal the wounds it inflicts, like the sword of the Word in Revelation; technological marvels such as the brass men with iron flails in *Huon of Bordeaux* and similar figures in *Arthur of Little Britain*, both possible precursors of Spenser's Talus; and the virgin-detecting gadget from Greek romance to *FQ* IV, a particularly mechanical version of the dialectical impetus in certain forms of romance to separate the true form from its counterfeit. Further marvels include natural prodigies like the green man of *Sir Gawain and the Green Knight* and Orrilo in Boiardo and Ariosto, who continue to move despite their dissevered parts, and magically invulnerable heroes like Talos in the *Argonautica*, who dies only when Medea discovers his Achilles' heel. They easily shade into the Christian miraculous in the Grail romances and romances clearly related to saints' legends (such as the medieval *Amys et Amiloun*); the self-propelled vessels of Breton *lai* and Arthurian romance, for example, easily combine with the ship symbolizing the church in the Vulgate *Queste* and Malory.

The other ubiquitous marvel of romance is the book. Boiardo's *Innamorato* is filled with a series of amazing volumes, from the book Orlando forgets to consult for the riddle of the Sphinx-like monster (1.5.76–8) to the one which reveals the topography of Falerina's mysterious garden (1.24). Ariosto, however, overgoes them all in the book of Logistilla – that true Renaissance marvel, the encyclopedia with an index; it enables Astolfo to undo the series of enchantments which prevent the romance narrative from ending, a process which suggests that the truly remarkable book of romance is the romance itself. In Chrétien, the true inheritor of the progress of chivalry from East to West is the romance of chivalry he himself is creating. This self-reflexive strain emerges in the riddling texts in Shakespeare's comedies and romances, which bear an oblique relation to the plays themselves, and in Spenser's reflections on his own poem in the proem to *FQ* VI.

The form of quest romance is generally sequential, whether that sequence takes the chivalric form of *avanture* or the marine form of the perilous sea voyage (from the *Odyssey* and Greek romance to the medieval *Voyage of St Brendan* and Camoens). Romances are therefore often filled with threshold symbols of transition or initiation, such as gates and doors, or dreams: the *Odyssey*, for example, contains a series of such symbolic thresholds, from the shore on which Odysseus meets Nausicaa to the trancelike sleep in which he is transported to the shores of Ithaca, a linking of sleep or dream with thresholds or transitions which also figure prominently in Dante's *Purgatorio*. Dream-visions crucial to pivotal moments in the plot also appear in Arthurian romances such as the alliterative *Morte Arthur*, which relates Arthur's premonitory dream of Fortune's wheel, and in Chaucer's *Troilus and Criseyde*. The temporal, journeying form of the romance also frequently transforms the daily activity of eating into the ritual form of the feast: in the *Odyssey*, the marvelous feasts offered to the journeying Odysseus and Telemachus have as their negative counterpart the temptation of a premature or forbidden eating (the Oxen of Helios) or a cannibalistic feast (Cyclops, Laestrygonians) in which the guest is not eater but eaten.

Romances are also often filled with objects or episodes which, like dreams or prophetic oracles, seem to function as signs: mysterious processions, symbols like the Bleeding Lance and vessels of the Grail procession. Frequently, wall hangings, tapestries, or paintings reflect or comment on the plot itself, providing a prospect or retrospect on it (as in the Vulgate *Mort Artu*, where Lancelot's paintings betray to Arthur the story of Guinevere's adultery, and in *Orlando furioso* 33, where future history is depicted in the wall paintings at the Castle of Tristan), a story significantly related to it (as in the story of Venus and Adonis in the tapestries at Castle Joyous in *FQ* III i), or a spatial summary of events sequentially presented in the flow of the narrative.

Other romance motifs are clearly linked to the progress of the narrative or the understanding of its events. The motif of the hunt, in which a knight pursues an animal into a forest which then envelops them both, is a masculine erotic motif; its amatory overtones emerge in the English punning on *hart/heart* and *deer/dear*, and in such scenes as the hunt of the sailors in *Lusiads* 9. In the nightmare reversal of this motif of linear pursuit, the hunter becomes the hunted, as in the story of Actaeon, and in *Sir Gawain and the Green Knight* where the hunts of Sir Bercilak have their counterpart in the lady's erotic pursuit of Gawain. But the hunt is also a potentially demonic double of the quest itself, an extreme version of its resolute pursuit of goal or meaning. In the Grail romances, the quest is as much to comprehend the meaning of the Grail as to possess a particular object; and in Wolfram's *Parzival*, the impulse of questing must be tempered by an ability to wait patiently for revelation or guidance, just as in Spenser the relation of temperance to the tempering of an obsessive quest is suggested in Phedon's demonic hunt (II iv). Spenser speaks explicitly in the proem to Book II of the obsessive 'hunt' for meaning, a hunt whose simultaneously mechanical and apocalyptic fervor may be suggested in the figure of Talus threshing out truth in Book V.

In a different relation to the narrative, the motif of the entranced gaze upon the face or symbol of the beloved provides moments of suspension, temporary stability, and reflection in the quest-narrative's sequential procession, as do the similar epiphanies of Venus and Aeneas in *Aeneid* I: Percival's staring at the blood drops in the snow in Chrétien, the Narcissus gaze of the *Romance of the Rose*, Dante's fixing his eyes on Beatrice in *Purgatorio* 31–2, the awe-inducing epiphanies of the normally helmeted Bradamante in Boiardo and Ariosto and of Britomart in Spenser, and Calidore 'rapt with pleasaunce' by the sight of the dance on Mount Acidale. Such moments, however, also threaten to suspend the narrative permanently, or to freeze its forward movement. In romance influenced by the Bible, all lush gardens after Eden are potential false paradises like Sodom (which promises fertility but ends as a sterile Dead Sea – a progression figured spatially by Tasso's placing of Armida's garden on a 'sterile lake' like the dead or idle lake beneath Spenser's Phaedria in *FQ* II). Any epiphany short of the final epiphany risks a suspension of movement, a problem suggested when Radigund (whose face Artegall sees, as he had seen Britomart's) becomes a potentially entrapping Dido to Artegall's Aeneas in *FQ* V.

Another romance motif intimately linked to the narrative progression is the exposure of an enchantress, from the stripping of the biblical harlot, the overcoming of Circe in the *Odyssey*, and the story of the lamia-wife in Philostratus (*Life of Apollonius* 4.25), to the stripping of the Siren in Dante's *Purgatorio* 19, the husband's discovery of his wife's secret nature in *Melusine*, the exposure of Ariosto's Alcina and Trissino's Acratia, and the convergence of these Odyssean, biblical, and romance figures in the overcoming of Acrasia in *FQ* II xii. Since the movement in all these episodes is from veiling to unveiling, from a version of Calypso (whose name in the *Odyssey* is related to 'covering') to apo-calypse (uncovering or revelation), this motif is not surprisingly a recurrent figure for the completion of the romance quest, of the text itself, or of the process of the quester's or reader's comprehension: the biblical Whore of Babylon is finally exposed in a book called Apocalypse, and Ariosto speaks of the uncovering of Alcina as a form of uncovering the veil of her 'pages' (*OF* 7.74). The symbolically female body of the romance text itself thus joins its characteristically female landscape (enclosing forest, mysterious cave, enveloping bower) as a space the knight or reader must quest through and emerge from. The counterpart of the witch-exposure motif might logically be the transformation of the loathly lady into a beautiful bride (as in Chaucer's *Wife of Bath's Tale*), a movement from ugly to beautiful which reverses the deceptively beautiful enchantress' progress in the opposite direction.

The female figures in romance present a curious contradiction. The motif of the passive damsel in distress continues unabated from the classical story of Perseus rescuing Andromeda from the monster, through the medieval stories of St George and the dragon, Percival's rescuing of Blancheflor, and the multiple echoes of Andromeda in Ariosto, to such modern thrillers of imperiled beauty as *King Kong*; while the motif of the helpless fleeing female extends from Ovid's Daphne and Syrinx, who can save themselves only by joining the landscape, to Spenser's Florimell. Yet heroines in romance from Heliodorus to Shakespeare – and versions of the martial maid from Virgil's Camilla to Ariosto's Marfisa and Bradamante and Spenser's Radigund and questing Britomart – are frequently not merely passive objects of others' quests or pursuits but initiators of the plot.

Several other romance motifs combine as figures for the movement of the narrative towards its ending. The proliferation of twins or counterfeit doubles is frequently related to the extension or dilation of the romance itself. For example, as soon as the erring Redcrosse separates himself from Una, he meets his own double in Fradubio, and the poem doubles itself as well, beginning over again with Duessa; but there is a sense here that if Redcrosse recognized his double in Fradubio, Book I might end at this point. The phantom doubles of Aeneas in Virgil and of rival knights in Italian romance also serve to delay further the resolution of the text. Similarly, the disguising of Odysseus' name and identity both in Phaeacia and in Ithaca also seems to correspond to the romance narrative's postponement of recognition and ending, as do the multiple names of the heroes in Sidney's *Arcadia* and the pseudonyms and disguises of the characters in Shakespeare's *Cymbeline* (where the suppression of name and identity through disguise is structurally parallel to the concealed origin and woodland nonage of the king's sons and to the riddling text before its definitive reading, all belonging to the space before the romance's ending).

The structure of deepening complication and ultimate resolution in romance is, finally, related to the motifs of descent and ascent, which may take literal or metaphoric forms. More or less literal versions of the former include descent to the present world from a higher one, or descent to an underworld (eg, into the mouths of subterranean or submarine monsters in the myth of Perseus, the story of Jonah, the Harrowing of Hell, and Dante's *Inferno*; into pits or graves in Greek romance and the biblical stories of Joseph and Daniel; into enchanted places such as the buried silver city of Marie de France's *Yonec*, the underground castle of perpetual light in *Sir Orfeo*, and Morgana's underwater crystal palace in Boiardo). These descents, often connected with dream (as in the descent to the house of Morpheus in *FQ* I i), frequently involve the vanquishing or harnessing of demonic forces, or the discovery of a buried treasure of wisdom or wealth, the reward of the drama of initiation that the descent represents.

Metaphorical descent often includes downward metamorphosis (like that of Lucius to animal form in Apuleius' *Golden Ass*), exile (like the banishment of Adam and Eve from the garden of Eden, and the exile of children set adrift on water, from Moses at the beginning of the Exodus narrative to the heroes of *Amadis* and *King Horn*), and radical change of fortune (as in the motif of the infant exposed on a hillside and adopted by shepherds, explicit in *Daphnis and Chloe* and recalled in New Testament stories of the birth of Christ, a figure of royal descent born into a semipastoral setting and provided with a foster father in Joseph). Related to the motif of the mysterious foundling is the motif of the latency or *enfance* of the eventual hero (as in the figures of Tristram and Satyrane in Spenser, and the king's sons in *Cymbeline*). The common romance figure of the wild man or noble savage might be seen in this context as the conversion of what is simply a stage along the way to civilized or adult life into an independent, separate state, perceived as a comment on a corrupt civilization, but also shading into the figure of the irredeemable wild man, a possibility which contributes to the ambivalence of the figure of Caliban in Shakespeare's *Tempest*.

The motif of ascent, too, can be literal, as in the emergence of Guyon from Mammon's underworld in *FQ* II, its Virgilian model in the emergence of Aeneas from Hades, Odysseus' escape from the cave of Polyphemus, and Dante's spiral ascent through Purgatory. Or it can be metaphorical, as in the disenchanting of Lucius the ass in Apuleius (and Bottom in *Midsummer Night's Dream*), the waking of a sleeping beauty, and a statue's coming to life as at the end of *The Winter's Tale*. If descent is related to the initiation or complication of the romance narrative, the corresponding ascent is frequently associated with the recognition or recovery of identity, the breaking of enchantment, and the resolution of both the romance text and its central mysteries. Generally, such resolution depends upon a sign which enables recognition, like Odysseus' scar or marriage bed, the birth tokens which reveal the noble origin of Daphnis and Chloe, and the ring by which the wife of the dying Guy of Warwick recognizes him as the hermit she has faithfully attended. The conspicuously unfinished *Faerie Queene* hints at such signs of recognition and resolution, but stops short of realizing them. Pastorella is restored 'to the joyous light' and recognized by her birthmark; but the poem's narrator is last seen besieged by the Blatant Beast, and longing for a final revelatory Sabbath's sight. PATRICIA PARKER

D.C. Allen 1970; Alpers 1979; Ariosto ed 1968 intro; Arthos 1956; Auerbach ed 1953; H. Baker 1971; Beer 1970; Cheney 1966; Ronald S. Crane 1919 *The Vogue of Medieval Chivalric Romance during the English Renaissance* (Menasha, Wis); Walter R. Davis 1965 'A Map of Arcadia: Sidney's Romance in Its Tradition' in *Sidney's Arcadia* pp 1–179 (New Haven); A.B. Ferguson 1960; Fletcher 1971; Frye 1957:186–206; Frye 1963:69–87; Frye 1976; Giamatti 1966; Giamatti 1975; Goldberg 1981; Greene 1963; Edwin A. Greenlaw 1929 'Britomart at the House of Busirane' *SP* 26:117–30; A.C. Hamilton 1982 'Elizabethan Romance: The Example of Prose Fiction' *ELH* 49:287–99; Hamilton 1984 'Elizabethan Prose Fiction and Some Trends in Recent Criticism' *RenQ* 37:21–33; Hankins 1971; Hanning 1977; Laura A. Hibbard 1924 *Mediaeval Romance in England* (New York); Hieatt 1975a; Hough 1962; Hughes 1925–6; Hughes 1929; G.L. Huxley 1969 *Greek Epic Poetry from Eumelos to Panyassis* (London); W.P. Ker 1896 *Epic and Romance* (London; rev ed 1908); George M. Logan and Gordon Teskey, eds 1989 *Unfolded Tales: Essays on Renaissance Romance* (Ithaca, NY); Roger Sherman Loomis 1949 *Arthurian Tradition and Chrétien de Troyes* (New York); Loomis 1959; Loomis 1963; Marinelli 1971; Millican 1932; Murrin 1980; Nohrnberg 1976; P.A. Parker 1979; Parker 1987; Peter Parsons 1981 'Ancient Greek Romances' *LRB* (20 Aug–2 Sept):13–14; Lee W. Patterson 1981 '"Rapt with Pleasaunce": Vision and Narration in the Epic' *ELH* 48:455–75; Ben Edwin Perry 1967 *The Ancient Romances* (Berkeley and Los Angeles); David Quint 1979 'The Figure of Atlante: Ariosto and Boiardo's Poem' *MLN* 94:77–91; Quint 1983 *Origin and Originality in Renaissance Literature* (New Haven); W.B. Stanford 1954 *The Ulysses Theme* (London; rev ed 1963); J. Stevens 1973; Tuve 1966; Vinaver 1971; Kathleen Williams 1964 'Romance Tradition in *The Faerie Queene*' *RS* 32:147–60.

Romance of the Rose This major allegorical romance of a courtly (and extramarital) wooing was launched by Guillaume de Lorris around 1230–5 in an incomplete version of 4028 lines and completed by Jean de Meun around 1275 in a total of 21,750 lines (following ed 1965–70). Partly translated from the Old French into fourteenth-century English as *The Romaunt of the Rose* in a version attributed to Chaucer, its images and themes were constantly echoed and developed by later allegorists until Spenser's own time. A best seller of its period, extant in some 300 manuscripts, many splendidly illuminated, it was still a much cited and oft-printed work in sixteenth-century France – fourteen editions were printed before 1528. The English version was available to Spenser in Thynne's editions of Chaucer (1532, 1542).

The Faerie Queene has many echoes of the *Romance*, especially in scenes of courtship or seduction, where Spenser (like earlier allegorists) plays subtle variations on the allegorical landscapes and personifications that the *Romance* popularized as a means of representing the interior life of the lover. The courtly festivities in the beautiful park where a young man learns to become vulnerable to love and passion, the swift sharp assault of Cupid's arrows, the long, drawn-out wooing where brief hectic moments of hope punctuate interminable agonies of rejection, the unremitting attempts to secure the right allies to break into the castle where his mistress' affections lie imprisoned, the endless discussions with personifications alternately representing counsels of friends, threats of enemies, or his own introspections – all these motifs Spenser would have encountered in many medieval allegories but nowhere with more authority than in their original manifestation in the *Romance*.

Spenser's use of this material displays, on occasion, considerable subtlety. In the *Romance*, Oiseuse (Chaucer's Idleness), representing the necessity of leisure before an affair of the heart can develop, appears as the gatekeeper of the Park of the Courtly Life; lacking her favor, no one enters that equivocal paradise. In *The Faerie Queene*, the figure reappears as Ease, not precisely in the role of porter but with similar allegorical force as presenter of the prologue to the masque of Cupid in the house of Busirane (III xii 4), and in inert rather than fully allegorized form in Castle Joyous where the beds are 'dight ... for untimely ease' (i 39). In cantos ix-x, we encounter a more complex appearance of the figure in Paridell, the descendant of Paris who is idle enough to remain in Malbecco's castle to seduce Hellenore after Britomart and Satyrane have ridden away on their knightly quests. Oiseuse's physical setting is echoed in Spenser's Bower of Bliss, the locale of *The Faerie Queene* closest in allegorical intention to the Park of the *Romance*. Instead of Oiseuse, the figure of Genius is its porter, one who 'doth us procure to fall, / Through guilefull semblaunts' (II xii 46–9, doubtless referring to the ambiguous figure of Jean's Genius who expatiates at length on a heavenly garden attainable only through indulgence in unrestrained sexual activity. At the same time, Spenser's alertness to the original formulation of Idleness as the guardian of the garden of courtly love is echoed in Guyon's rebuff of Genius' 'idle curtesie' (49).

Spenser follows the *Romance* most directly, it would seem, in Scudamour's account of winning Amoret from the Temple of Venus (IV x). Scudamour's way to the temple is opposed by Doubt, Delay, and Daunger, whereas in the *Romance* the lover has to cope with Daunger, Fear, Shame, Wicked Tongue, and so forth, in his quest for the Rose. But the contrasts are as notable as the parallels. Scudamour's adversaries put up no more than a token resistance, as opposed to the almost endless delays inflicted on the lover of the *Romance*. This may well reflect Spenser's presentation of Scudamour's suit as a legitimate courtship in contrast to the less honorable intentions of Jean's Amant, who finally has to instigate a protracted siege of the Castle of Jealousy which protects the Rose Bud.

In general, Spenser follows Chaucer in utilizing his allegory to comment on and respond to the *Romance*. While he makes love relationships almost *the* major theme of *The Faerie Queene*, he breaks away from the oppressively narrow world of Jean's erotic garden where the vast range of topics discussed by Amant with his friends is constantly brought back to his all-absorbing erotic plight. Spenser eschews the interminable dialogues of the *Romance* and expresses that obsession directly in the claustrophobic horrors of Busirane's castle. At the same time, he puts it in context of a range of other erotic relationships, notably that of Britomart and Artegall, which frame allegorical solutions to the questions so provocatively unresolved in the *Romance*. The life of eros is thus brought into harmony with the other major principles of human existence. PAUL PIEHLER

A standard edition of the French *Roman* is Guillaume de Lorris and Jean de Meun 1965–70 *Le Roman de la Rose* ed Félix Lecoy, 3 vols (Paris); English translations include ed 1962 and ed 1971. Studies include John V. Fleming 1969 *The 'Roman de la Rose': A Study in Allegory and Iconography* (Princeton); Hankins 1971; Lewis 1936; Piehler 1971; Quilligan 1977; Roche 1964; Tuve 1966; Van Dyke 1985.

romance since Spenser (English) *The Faerie Queene* and Sidney's *Arcadia* (1590) – courtly, learned, exquisite – are the great English exemplars of the long and rich sophisticated-romance tradition parodied by Nashe before *Don Quixote* (1605) cut off its premodern phase and Milton turned elsewhere for a poetic theme. The eighteenth century saw the rise of bourgeois romance to full-length novel status with *Robinson Crusoe* – Trader's Progress – and the triumph of a Pamela less highborn than Sidney's; and Richard Hurd shortly proclaimed that, except for those who still love Spenser, romance in the sense of chivalric tales of wonder had long been thoroughly obsolete: 'what we have gotten ... is a great deal of good sense. What we have lost, is a world of fine fabling' (*Letters on Chivalry and Romance* 1762). A new stage of prose romance commenced with Horace Walpole's 'Gothic Story,' *The Castle of Otranto* (1764), which under the special patronage of Shakespeare enshrines the age's love of sensation in its arts and its romantic appreciation of the past (Preface to 2nd ed). Walpole's effort to unite the naturalness of modern characterization with the 'resources of fancy' available to older writers makes him the progenitor of three kinds of fiction: the historical novel and historical romance, both practiced preeminently by Scott and continued by Fenimore Cooper, and Gothic fiction, whose great practitioners, if we take *Gothic* in its loose modern sense, were Ann Radcliffe and M.G. Lewis in the 1790s, and Mary Shelley, C.L. Maturin, and James Hogg in the decade after Waterloo. Jane Austen made gentle fun of Radcliffe, and still more her readers, in *Northanger Abbey* (written 1797–8); but by the time her book appeared in 1818, the settings, characters, and conflicts of the best romantic fiction had become instruments for the exploration, partly symbolic and partly realistic, of the mysterious worlds of feeling and subrational intimation; and this function continues to the present. Several of the major Gothic novels in portraying the corruption and destruction of their central figure – *The Monk*, *Frankenstein*, *Melmoth the Wanderer*, *Confessions of a Justified Sinner* – pioneer the shift to irony that by our time dominates serious fiction.

Verse romance reappeared in the late 1790s with the work of Southey and Coleridge, continuing in Scott, Byron, Shelley, and Keats, and on through most of the Victorian period with the medieval recreations of Tennyson and William Morris – the latter like Scott also a prose romancer. Romance is represented by Coleridge's major poems in three different ways, to which later nineteenth-century verse romances conveniently conform: the chivalric-Gothic *Christabel* is the most traditional, with its damsel assailed in her father's castle; *The Rime of the Ancient Mariner* transforms the ballad's romance and other materials, as well as its form, recreating them into the most influential model since *The Pilgrim's Progress* of a tale of outward event and inner discovery; and *Kubla Khan* in a complex dream fragment proclaims the near-identity of passion, vision, and poetry. With *Christabel* we can associate Tennyson's 'Lady of Shalott' and Morris' 'Defence of Guenevere'; with the *Ancient Mariner*, such poems of inner worlds and imaginatively heightened experience as Browning's *Childe Roland*, Thomson's (B.V.'s) *City of Dreadful Night*, and Dylan Thomas' two verse narratives; and with *Kubla Khan* a line of symbolic accounts of dream, vision, ecstasy, and their loss extending from Blake's 'Song' ('How sweet I roam'd') via Shelley's 'Alastor' and Keats's 'La Belle Dame Sans Merci' to such lyrics of the Celtic twilight as Yeats's 'Song of Wandering Aengus' (1899). The irony shaping many of these poems gives them immature or inadequate heroes and settings whose engulfing desolation expresses their silence or despair. By the end of the nineteenth century, the long poem had lost both its 'kinds' and its audience, so that while two of our three types survive – those represented by the *Ancient Mariner* and *Kubla Khan*, which radically transformed traditional forms and contents – they do so mainly as lyrics, single or grouped.

The wide and lasting popularity of such swinging Victorian-chivalric ballads, unshadowed by irony, as Tennyson's 'Sir Galahad' and Longfellow's 'Excelsior' combined with the influence of the more highbrow poems mentioned above to keep sentimental medievalism alive until after the onset of World War I (see Fussell 1975); other sources were the German tales of F. de la Motte Fouqué, especially 'Sintram and His Companions' (tr 1820), and Kenelm Henry Digby's *The Broad Stone of Honour* (1822). The same medievalism affected, besides poets, novelists from Charlotte Mary Yonge to Marie of Roumania (*Ilderim* 1925) and Hannah Closs (*Tristan* 1940) and artists in several media, notably Edward Burne-Jones, painter and designer of stained glass and tapestry. Graham Greene's play with Yonge's text and Digby's name in *The Ministry of Fear* (1943) indicates just how hollow the chivalric picture of the Christian gentleman looked during World War II, while V.S. Naipaul depicts a comparable dead end, the commercialization of that chivalry Burke once called 'the unbought grace of life,' in *Mr. Stone and the Knights Companion* (1963).

Victorian popular fiction from Bulwer Lytton to Marie Corelli, to say nothing of that aimed at the barely literate (*Varney the Vampire*, *Ada the Betrayed*, etc; see James 1963), leaned heavily on Scott and the Gothic romancers. These contributed also to the work of Dickens and the Brontës, and of Poe, Hawthorne, and Melville. The influence of Bunyan, too, can be observed from Charlotte Brontë and Hawthorne through to John Buchan. Although Victorian illustrators sometimes made a knight of Christian, his plebeian origins and analogy to such honest apprentices as Dick Whittington and Crusoe recommended him to holders of the Self-Help ethic. More visibly realistic novelists, such as George Eliot, Meredith, Hardy, and James, sharpen the imaginative outlines of their stories – 'liberate' their 'experience,' James might have said – with elements of romance design. Those the late nineteenth century called its 'romancers' were the spinners of tales of adventure and of Empire: Stevenson, Rider Haggard, Conrad, and Kipling. For a generation after Stevenson, most conscious romancers can be identified by their borrowings from the Scottish-cum-biblical heightened prose of *Kidnapped* (1886) or his *Don Quixote*-cum-*Arabian Nights* style of chapter headings.

While the relatively naive tale of adventure has carried on from Buchan to Ian Fleming and beyond, more thoughtful taletellers like G.K. Chesterton, Charles Williams, C.S. Lewis, J.R.R. Tolkien, and Ursula K. LeGuin (the *Earthsea* trilogy) have revived the initiatic quests, the conflicts of cosmic good and evil, and the symbolic landscapes of medieval and Renaissance romance, while others like David Lindsay, Mervyn Peake, and William Golding have made more untraditional use of romance's otherworlds. Lewis was steeped in Spenser and in George MacDonald, and Chesterton, Williams, and Tolkien all knew both in some degree. Lindsay and Golding, like Graham Greene, are more typical of twentieth-century serious writing in that their designs are bitterly ironic, comparable to those of Kafka's *Castle* and *Trial* – not initiatic or penitential but leading to disillusion, betrayal, or death.

The bulk of modern romances are written to mass-production formulas: the 'romance' or 'women's love-story' (such as those by Barbara Cartland or published by Harlequin Books), the nurse book, the Gothic, the western, the occult thriller, science fiction, 'fantasy,' and the conspiratorial thriller, usually about espionage, that at least in North America has largely ousted the detective story. A very few distinguished writers, among them Leonard Cohen and Thomas Pynchon, have redeemed some of this mostly inert stuff by melting it down in their own highly eclectic romances, in a manner perhaps learned from Joyce's *Ulysses*.

principles The traditional romance world has two essential principles, both expansive: extent and variety in space and materials, and an up-and-down dimension of moral and spiritual order. The first is usually supplied by the quest-journey with its contrasting episodes and halting places and stories heard along the way; settings of castle, garden, forest, valley are integral to the actions taking place in them, and the vicissitudes of the hero's career add to the range of variety and contrast spread before the reader. Later romance heroes continue to travel, from Crusoe through Huck and Kim to hitchhikers through the galaxy, and many like the Scarlet Pimpernel or James Bond aim to extend the reader's social as well as geographic range. A different expansive device is simple juxtaposition, as when *The World's Desire* brings Ulysses and Helen separately to Egypt just as Moses is leading the Israelites out of it (Rider Haggard and Andrew Lang 1890). Spenser like the Italians gained further diversity by telling the stories of several heroes; in the most inventive period of English narrative construction before our own, Lewis' *Monk* (1796) tells alternately the tales of Ambrosio and of Raymond and Lorenzo, strongly contrasting but converging to form the story's climax – what his age calls a 'perplexed narrative.' Romance expansiveness helps Lewis to do more than just spin out Ambrosio's brief history: switching between narrative lines allows him to manage timing and maintain suspense, and to bring in episodes and poems of independent interest.

Lewis wrote for an audience whose expectations were different from those of the readers of classic romance: they enjoyed complication leading to a convergence of threads at the end, some psychological complexity, and a strong ironic component. This last is evident in the way Gothic fictions from Walpole on are apt to center on the fall of the sin-stained villain rather than the victory of the relatively passive bright young hero, to sacrifice at least one innocent life to everyone else's happy ending, and to feature among their settings at least one very dominant one that is not expansive but constrictive, like *The Monk*'s complex in narrow scope of church-monastery-cemetery-convent linked by the vaults where Lorenzo discovers Ambrosio in the act of murder. Spenser's house of Pride despite its splendors perched above foul dungeons and its proximity to the realms of Night is too well balanced by the out-of-doors and the variety of the rest of Book I to do more than hint at the claustrophobic atmosphere of such Gothic settings where the great world narrows down into a trap – emphasized in Lewis by the contrast between the expansive Raymond-Lorenzo plot with its travels in Germany and anticipated happy ending and the confined, constricting story of Ambrosio's downfall.

The up-and-down dimension of romance is supplied by a clear-cut social hierarchy from king to churl, a similarly clear-cut moral scheme of virtues and vices and their friends, and the assurance that both these hierarchies reflect the divine order which has selected the hero for his task and will help him to succeed. The world of *The Monk* is polarized in a traditional way between (presumably) heaven and (definitely) hell. More recently, a late descendant of Crusoe, John Buchan's *Prester John* (1910), replacing heaven with the imposed order of Empire and hell with 'savagery,' develops both a topography of dark depths (cellar, lowland, cavern) out of which the hero has to keep scrambling to reach the white-held heights, and a myth much like that of Spenser's Book I of an Eden that must be rescued from the snake of an impending black kingship before it can bloom. Conrad's *Heart of Darkness* (1902), using comparable African materials to a largely opposite purpose, flattens its landscape to the snakelike course of the river drawing Marlow into 'the depths of the land' and of mankind's past – a form of ironic constriction, for all the 'vast country' surrounding it, and affording no sharp distinctions between black and white, servant and master, savagery and civilization, ideal and abomination.

Traditional romance, centered on a quest-adventure that proceeds into yet-untraveled space, throws any suspense it generates forward to the ending. Gothic romance centers instead on mystery: like *Oedipus Rex*, it intensifies suspense and directs it simultaneously towards what happened in the past. Mysteries concerning (usually) the parental generation need to be resolved before the young people who are (often) at least the technical leads can take up their full adult roles. Thus time ceases to be a straightforward continuum that unrolls with the story, and becomes an important new dimension for exploration. Most Gothic novels are in some sense about the grip of the past on the present: the young hero (or heroine) from whom its secrets are hidden is tyrannized by them, and their revelation sets him free, restoring him to his identity and proper place in society, while for the villain it leads to condemnation.

In romance up to, say, *Robinson Crusoe* (1719) and in the romantic romance strain that continues to the present, the invisible links connecting persons or events are providential or at least positive: orphans turn out to be lost heirs; luck changes in the nick of time. From the Gothic on, these links are often negative or even demonic, if the natural causality set rolling by imperfect human nature isn't (as it is in *Frankenstein* 1818) devastating enough. Later romances often replace or combine the social hierarchy with its microcosmic representation in family or household, and links of this kind often work ironically – hence the importance in Gothic fiction of parental tyranny, fratricide, and incest. In *The Monk*, for example, the convent's complex of labyrinthine vaults, which brings most of the main characters together for the denouement, is reflected in the similarly labyrinthine set of family relationships that links the characters, calamitously including the apparently isolated Monk. Providence here has abdicated in favor of a hostile fate, personified in the powers of darkness that encompass Ambrosio. Their activities bring in another kind of infernal machine, apart from the family that abandoned him and on which he then disastrously impinges (compare the history of Frankenstein's Being), namely, the conspiracy that deals in set-ups and illusions, more prominent in present-day romance than the family trap, though sometimes combined with it (eg, Greene *The Ministry of Fear*, Condon *The Manchurian Candidate* 1959).

In serious late romance, where irony has more and more come to dominate, both heroes and villains have lost in grandeur. Settings, too, have diminished: writers (and movie-makers) make much of shabby streets, disused pleasure grounds, and derelict land; the pastoral glimpse shows simple men fishing in dull canals or feeding pigeons. Power is no longer symbolized by colorful tyrants in castles and abbeys but by white-coated technicians in laboratories, computer centers, or psychiatric hospitals, fronting for some disembodied entity often known as the 'company' or 'firm,' though highly uncompanionate and not above infirmity (cf David Ely *Seconds* 1963). Where, in the nineteenth and early twentieth centuries, sinister masterminds might depend on mesmerism or hypnotism, in the later twentieth century from *Brave New World* (1932) to *Gravity's Rainbow* (1973) these are replaced by more irresistible means of thought control whose practitioners may aim less to dominate the world for themselves or their class than to maintain a disconsolating status quo.

In the past, those in high places if not 'ordained of God' could be expected to embody the order and values of society; now because they have power, they are not to be trusted. Being leaders or spokesmen of 'our side' may not keep them from cynically sacrificing their own players for obscure or merely strategic gains or to maintain their own positions (Le Carré *The Looking-Glass War* 1965). Both sides use the same dirty tricks. Only in mythic romances like Tolkien's *Lord of the Rings* (1954–5) or LeGuin's *Earthsea* trilogy (1968–73) is it possible to divest oneself of evil powers, however reluctantly they were at first acquired. If kept, those fables tell us, such powers eat out the humanity of their possessors: in grittier tales, the character who, exasperated with his dupe's role, presses to the center of the web is apt to find there a hollow man, a mere mask of authority, or a mere programmed machine.

The heroes of such narratives, powerless and shrunk to the dimensions of an ironic age, are damaged, unimpressive, or foredoomed, like Greene's Raven, Orwell's Winston Smith, or Le Carré's Leamas. They serve masters and schemes unworthy of an honest man's respect, and what destroys them is apt to be whatever in them we find most human, when not the mere blind chance that rules a flattened cosmos.

further narrative devices In addition to magnifying the importance of setting and of family relationship and shifting their viewpoint towards that of their villains, the practitioners of Gothic developed a whole cellarful of devices to carry them beyond the 'and then-meanwhile' sequence of the traditional form. The imaginative and also formal possibilities opened up already in *The Castle of Otranto* by the exploration of the past soon led to subordination of the original 'Gothic' representations of a (roughly) historical past to a personal past as represented by one's parents and grandparents. Accordingly, representation of the past by castle or family portrait could be reinforced or replaced by an excursion into it via inset tale or document or – most frequently – a villain's confession placed near the end. Or, the narrative structure itself might dramatize by a frame or by a fictional preface like Walpole's the set-back dimension of the past.

Gothic proliferates frames and insets with an exuberance learned from *Don Quixote*, *The Arabian Nights*, and the *Ancient Mariner*. Mary Shelley, Maturin, and Hogg are the masters of this device. Maturin's lengthy *Melmoth the Wanderer* (1820), with the most elaborate of English tale-within-tale designs, makes of the Wanderer's dream on his last night a grand final symbolic synthesis: besides prophesying the future like other Gothic dreams, it draws together symbols from the rest of the book so as to both resume his past and associate him with other damned adventurers, Faust and Don Juan. Hogg gives his *Confessions of a Justified Sinner* (1824) a frame and inset of similar lengths that tell the same story from different viewpoints, each reflecting obliquely on the other, thus preparing the way for the self-reflexiveness of, say, Nabokov's *Pale Fire* (1962).

In nineteenth-century romance developments, the relation between frame and inset tends to be replaced by the central character's (or narrator's) crossing a symbolic threshold – Lockwood's dream or Alice's passing through the looking glass – or coming into possession of a clue object – the scarlet letter or the ancestral potsherd of *She* (Rider Haggard 1887); or, say from Sherlock Holmes on, a visitor gives (or bequeaths) him a mission, as Guyon acquired his from the bloody-handed babe.

Complex and prominent narrative devices, once as definitive a feature of Gothic as its involved architectural settings and their reflection in involved patterns of family relationship, after long disuse have returned in the romances of our own age. They can be quietly handled, as in *Watership Down*'s series of mythic tales coalescing at the end with the story line (Richard Adams 1972). Or they can help large novels aim at large purviews, as in John Fowles' *The Magus* (1965). Or the grandeur rarely allowed nowadays to characters or action may stride back in through the scope of the narrative structure, as – most astonishingly – in Pynchon's *Gravity's Rainbow*, where the viewpoints of a skin cell and a lightbulb join with others to make up about the fullest and most animate universe available since Paracelsus, till the whole of existence together accelerates its mindless trip to The End.

JAY MACPHERSON

Beer 1970; William Patrick Day 1985 *In the Circles of Fear and Desire: A Study of Gothic Fantasy* (Chicago); Paul Fussell 1975 *The Great War and Modern Memory* (New York) esp pp 135–44, 213; Mark Girouard 1981 *The Return to Camelot: Chivalry and the English Gentleman* (New Haven); Martin Green 1979 *Dreams of Adventure, Deeds of Empire* (New York); Ralph Harper 1969 *The World of the Thriller* (Cleveland); Louis James 1963 *Fiction for the Working Man 1830–1850: A Study of the Literature Produced for the Working Classes in Early Victorian Urban England* (London); David Punter 1980 *The Literature of Terror: A History of Gothic Fictions from 1765 to the Present Day* (London); Ioan Williams 1970 *Novel and Romance, 1700–1800: A Documentary Record* (London).

Rome Of all the real or imagined cities Spenser draws upon, it is Rome that he refers to most often, no doubt because of its rich diversity of associations both for the writers of antiquity and for the civic humanists of the Renaissance. From *Complaints*, we can see the extent to which his notion of the city was formed by du Bellay's meditations on its ruins in his *Antiquitez* and *Songe*, works which Spenser both translated and used as models for his own *Ruines* poems and *Visions of the Worlds Vanitie*. Du Bellay's great exemplum of decayed grandeur presented Spenser with a wide variety of attitudes toward the city: awe over its glorious past, pathos for its present dereliction, and somber consideration of the causes of its decline, namely, the overweening pride that went before its fall and the penchant for civil discord which seemed to precipitate it.

But however much the arrogance, luxury, or 'mutinous uprore' (*Rome* 22) of the city against itself may have contributed to its dissolution, time itself is the primary worker of its woe. Rome serves du Bellay as a dramatic witness to mutability's sway over the world, and the poet of *Antiquitez* continually returns to this realization as he ponders the tragic evanescence of a city built to last forever. His sustained meditation reflects some measure of Augustinian scorn for the mortal work which styles itself divine and then dies.

Yet on the whole, Spenser found in du Bellay not so much condemnation of vanity as nostalgia for Rome's past glory mixed with a melancholy awareness that no earthly thing is sure, no civil structure so sturdy but that 'time in time shall ruinate' the work of human hands (*Rome* 7). Against this inexorable tide, du Bellay offers little divine consolation beyond the possibility that the motion of time's scythe may be part of a providential plan (30). The hope he extends more explicitly, however, is that the poet's words can withstand the very forces of mutability before which marble and porphyry crumble. The 'brave writings' of ancient Rome keep the city alive (5), and modern poets like du Bellay himself (says Spenser in his envoy to *Rome*) give her 'eternall dayes.' The city that survives, therefore, is a verbal construct.

The real degree to which Spenser Englished du Bellay is not to be seen in his translations so much as in his own poem, *Ruines of Time*, with its wholesale appropriation of vocabulary, theme, and tone. Here the narrator is the fallen city herself, not Rome but the vanished citadel of Roman Britain, Verulam ('Verlame'). Having been made princess 'of this small Northerne world' (84) by imperial power, she was inevitably vulnerable to the ravages of imperial decay. But Verlame is concerned less with the reverses of politics than with the entropy of history, the 'devouring death' (52) that has turned an entire Anglo-Roman culture into dust, as it had done before in the successive empires of Assyria, Persia, and Greece. By summoning up the ghost of Roman Britain, Spenser discovers a death's head in Albion, the sure sign of a fall in the midst of a burgeoning sixteenth-century civilization. Thus, Britain has already had her own experience of Roman triumph and decline. The lesson to be learned, as Verlame goes on to say, is that the only abiding record of glory in so utterly transitory a world is the glory that finds its way into words. For Verlame, rescue came through Camden, that 'nourice of antiquitie,' whose *Britannia* kept her memory alive (169–75), even as Spenser's *Time* will attempt to immortalize the second subject of this double lament, the late Philip Sidney.

In *The Faerie Queene*, Spenser uses Rome both to conjure up the civic landscape of Fairyland and to explore Rome's significance for Britain's own self-understanding. One might expect in a poem of epic and Virgilian ambitions that Spenser's Rome would be the civic ideal of the *Aeneid*; yet the city's presence in *FQ* I is, in fact, typological and also largely negative. We see first of all the massed 'antique ruines of the *Romaines* fall' on the junkheap of history hidden beneath Lucifera's palace of Pride (v 48–50). Along with the great kings of Babylon and Egypt, one finds 'High *Caesar*, great *Pompey*, and fierce *Antonius*' in the company of Romulus, Tarquin, and Scipio – all wretchedly enthralled by the vain arrogance of power and finally undone by that enthrallment. Spenser seems to have in mind here the Rome of Augustine's *City of God*, overwhelmed by its own lust for domination. Later, in *FQ* I vii-viii, he also draws on the biblical polemic of Revelation 17–18 in his association of the triple-crowned Duessa with the Whore of Babylon, thereby in standard Protestant fashion applying an apocalyptic indictment of pagan Rome to the Roman Catholic Church. A more positive appropriation, however, lies in the role Rome plays in suggesting the ethos of Gloriana's unseen capital, Cleopolis (x 58–9). Its 'towre of glas' (Panthea) may refer to a prominent feature of the idealized classical city described in the *Mirabilia urbis Romae* (a twelfth-century guide for pilgrims), while the constancy of purpose and longing for virtuous fame that impel Gloriana's knights recall the passion for honor that even Augustine commends in the Stoic heroes of republican Rome (*City of God* 5.12–19).

If *FQ* I exploits Rome's typological ambiguity as an exemplum of both evil and good, Spenser's subsequent use of the city in *FQ* II-IV concerns its importance in Britain's own historical myth. Arthur discovers in *Briton moniments* (Spenser's adaptation of Geoffrey of Monmouth's *Historia*) that civilization came to Britain directly from Troy, even as Christianity, in the person of Joseph of Arimathea, arrived directly from Jerusalem, in both cases bypassing entirely the mediation of Rome. The Romans later invaded the island under Julius Caesar, envying Britain's 'blazed fame' and driven on by 'hideous hunger of dominion' (II x 47). But if Britain was thus made tributary to 'ambitious *Rome*,' the chronicle suggests how in time it would become allied to its conqueror through marriage and birth. From the union of Helena of York and the Roman Constantius would come the child Constantine, 'Who afterward was Emperour of *Rome*' and a monumentally important convert to his mother's 'British' faith. In this way, the Christianization of the empire might be said to begin in Britain.

This sense of connection with Rome, rather than domination by it, is even more strongly asserted in *FQ* III ix 33–51, where Britomart and Paridell discuss history as if it were one vast Trojan succession. Although Aeneas' grandson Brutus is said to have replanted the 'antique *Trojan* stocke' in England before the founding of Rome itself, the glory of that culture nevertheless flourished first in Italy. But as Britomart foretells at the end of their discussion, the time shall come when Britain's hour is at hand, so that Troynovant (London) will at last come into its own and 'in all glory and great enterprise, / Both first and second *Troy* shall dare to equalise' (44).

The ascendancy that Britomart anticipates is celebrated as an accomplished fact within the mythic marriage of Thames and Medway. In IV xi 28, Spenser represents the transfer of world civilization from Rome to Britain by describing the groom in terms of Cybele, a goddess whom Virgil uses as a symbol of Rome's identity as the mother of gods and godlike men (*Aeneid* 6.784–7). Cybele's new residence in England and her connection with the Thames suggests the passage of Roman glory to London, the latest avatar of Troy, albeit one which is far from the ancient source, placed as it is in 'the utmost Angle of the world' (III ix 47). Thus, just as the Virgilian opening of *FQ* I proem I announces Spenser's self-conscious imitation of the great epic poet of Rome, so we can also see his allusions to that city in *FQ* II-IV as an attempt to suggest Britain's participation in Roman virtue, greatness, and heroic destiny. PETER S. HAWKINS

M.W. Ferguson 1984; Greene 1982; Hankins 1971:211–13; Manley 1982; Robert S. Miola 1983 *Shakespeare's Rome* (Cambridge) pp 1–17; Ramsey 1982; Rathborne 1937:24–40; Walter Rehm 1960 *Europäische Romdichtung* 2nd ed (Munich) pp 130–4.

Rome, Ruines of. See **Complaints: Ruines of Rome: By Bellay**

Rosalind (Spanish 'lovely rose') Although she never appears directly as a character in Spenser's poetry, Rosalind is named in six eclogues of *The Shepheardes Calender* and in *Colin Clout* (927–51; cf 464–79, and see also *Var* 7:651). E.K. refers to her as a 'countrie lasse' who lives in a 'neighbour towne' (*SC, Jan* Arg, 50). Hers is a 'feigned name, which being wel ordered' may reveal her real name. In glossing Hobbinoll's claim that she is the 'Widdowes daughter of the glenne,' he refers to her as a 'Gentle woman of no meane house' (*Apr* 26, gloss). She may be alluded to as Colin's love in the dance of the Graces on Mount Acidale (*FQ* VI x 16, although any specific identification is denied at 25). In their correspondence of 1580, furthermore, Harvey addresses Spenser/Immerito's mistress as 'mea Domina Immerito, mea bellissima Collina Clouta' and as 'altera Rosalindula' ('a changed [another?] little Rosalind') (*Var Prose* p 476; see also p 466).

Rosalind may represent some actual person such as Spenser's first wife, or Mary Sidney, or even Queen Elizabeth (Banks 1937, Mohl 1949, McLane 1961); but her identity remains elusive despite the remarks by E.K. and Harvey. Within the fiction of the poetry, she has been interpreted as a destructive influence on Colin Clout or as his best inspiration (Cullen 1970, Shore 1976). The name was apparently first used by Spenser, and his characterization of Rosalind may be recalled in the heroine of Lodge's *Rosalynde* (1590) and Shakespeare's *As You Like It* – although with some irony, for the latter is willing to meet her suitor halfway and suffers pangs of lovesickness. Drayton (in *Idea: The Shepheards Garland* 1593) and Phineas Fletcher (in *Piscatorie Eclogs* 1633) pair Colin and Rosalind as ideal lovers (*Sp All* pp 31, 192).

RICHARD MALLETTE

Theodore H. Banks 1937 'Spenser's Rosalind: A Conjecture' *PMLA* 52:335–7; Ruth Mohl 1949 *Studies in Spenser, Milton and the Theory of Monarchy* (New York).

Ruines of Rome. See **Complaints: Ruines of Rome: By Bellay**

Ruines of Time. See **Complaints: The Ruines of Time**

Ruskin, John (1819–1900) In his youth, Ruskin was introduced to Spenser's poetry in the family reading circle; and late in life, in *Fors Clavigera*, he included the poet among those storytellers suitable for children of 'the upper classes' (ed 1903–12, 29:502). In his middle years, in *The Stones of Venice II* and *III* (1853) and *Modern Painters III* (1856), his analysis of Spenser's allegory indicates his high evaluation.

His esteem originates partly in a recognition of Spenser's place in the allegorical tradition. Familiar from an early age with such works as Bunyan's *Pilgrim's Progress* and Quarles' *Emblems*, Ruskin was alert to sustained allegory, and by the 1850s he was able to extend his vision and relate Spenser's personified depictions of vices and virtues to the carvings of Saint Mark's and the Ducal Palace in Venice, the paintings of Orcagna and Giotto, and the poetry of Dante (10:317–21, 380–409; 11:180). In particular, he found in Spenser 'the exactly intermediate type of conception between the mediaeval and the Renaissance.' To illustrate this, he remarks on Spenser's depiction of Cupid (*FQ* III xii 22–3) as 'under the ancient form of a beautiful winged god ... but still no plaything of the Graces, but full of terror' – a depiction that relates Spenser to Dante rather than to those trivial Renaissance renderings of Cupid as 'confused with angels' (10:401). Such references to different artists, different forms of art, and different eras give scope to Ruskin's commentary and a European significance to Spenser.

Ruskin also finds in Spenser's poetry a distinctive combination of imaginative insight and keen analysis. Correspondingly, he presents vivid responses to such personifications as Envy (*FQ* I iv 30–2; 5:132–3) and Maleger (II xi 21–2; 10:383–4) as well as detailed analyses of Spenser's sustained allegory (most remarkably of *FQ* I, in an appendix entitled 'Theology of Spenser' which remains the best available statement of its moral allegory; 11:251–4 and rpt in *Var* 1:422–4). Single personifications and the overall schematic placing of vices and virtues (which is said to be 'extremely complicated') are both of interest to him.

Above all, Ruskin came to value Spenser for 'the use or fancy of tangible signs to set forth an otherwise less expressible truth' (5:132). This comment may be related both to his increasing respect for allegory as a means of imaginative expression and to his persistent emphasis on visual realizations. Consequently, his more rewarding remarks on Spenser often occur in the context of his elucidations of paintings (eg, Turner's *Hesperides*; 7:404–7). According to Ruskin, the poet and the painter are 'essentially the same' – artists who 'concentrated sermons into sights' (12:496).

In a letter of 1841, Ruskin remarks that Spenser's 'finest passages never *can* be fathomed in a minute, or in ten minutes, or exhausted in as many years' (1:443). The care with which he developed his interpretations in the 1850s shows that he held to this recognition. As he remarks in *The Stones of Venice*, *The Faerie Queene* was 'only half estimated, because few persons take the pains to think out its meaning' (10:383n). In his own commentary, Ruskin writes as both a close practical critic alert to Spenser's artistry and an historian of moral philosophy.

JOHN HAYMAN

References in this article are to Ruskin ed 1903–12. See also Louis E. Dollarhide 1967 'The Paradox of Ruskin's Admiration of Renaissance English Writers' *UMSE* 8:7–12; George P. Landow 1971 *The Aesthetic and Critical Theories of John Ruskin* (Princeton).

S

sacraments The term *sacrament* enters the language of the church and hence western theology from the Roman soldier's oath or *sacramentum*, a public assent to membership in a united body. It is the Vulgate Latin for the Greek New Testament *mystērion*, 'a secret.' Alexander Nowell's *Catechism* (1570), which formulates the religious principles of the Church of England, defines sacrament as 'an outward testifying of God's good-will and bountifulness toward us, through Christ by a visible sign representing an invisible and spiritual grace' (ed 1853: 205). The theological significance of the sacraments is to exhibit the principle of the Incarnation or embodiment of God in Jesus' human form, to express the objectivity of God's action on the soul, and to root Christian life in the church as a holy society. The validity of the sacraments depends upon correct administration by the officiating cleric, and their efficacy depends upon faith and repentance of the recipient. The Book of Common Prayer accordingly states of Communion that if 'we spiritually eat the flesh of Christ, and drink his blood, then we dwell in Christ and Christ in us, we be one with Christ, and Christ with us' (*BCP* 'Holy Communion' ed 1976:258).

Spenser accepts the Protestant reduction of the seven sacraments of the medieval Catholic church to the two 'sacraments of the gospel' ordained by Christ: baptism and Holy Communion or the Lord's Supper (Matt 28.19, Luke 22.14–20). Communion in particular forms the core of the reformed English church service formulated by Thomas Cranmer, Archbishop of Canterbury, in the Book of Common Prayer (1549), which was reinstated (following the 1552 version) in the Elizabethan prayer book of 1559. No longer to be counted as sacraments are confirmation, penance, ordination, marriage, and extreme unction, though all of these continue as rites of the Church of England. Other English rites also lack sacramental status: for example, visitation of the sick, burial of the dead, churching (thanksgiving) of women after childbirth, and commination (cursing) of sinners.

Regeneration does not inhere within the sacraments themselves, which function as 'certayne sure witnesses and effectual signes of grace and Gods good wyll towardes us' (Article 25 of the Thirty-nine Articles of Religion [1571]; see Hardwick 1876, app 3). They are only instrumental in the remission of sins and growth in grace. Spenser's 'newborne knight,' Redcrosse (I xi 34), is a good example of the 'regeneration or newe byrth' signified by the water of baptism (Article 27). Similarly, the bread and wine of Communion signify spiritual feeding and the promise of resurrection. The prayer book emphasizes the active participation of the congregation in both sacraments as a means of joining in the reformed Christian community to be created by the new service.

Sacramental imagery pervades the climactic three-day battle in which Redcrosse defeats the Dragon (*FQ* I xi; see Kaske 1969), but it also appears elsewhere (eg, *Heavenly Love* 194–6). Spenser stresses the general impact of the sacraments in the life of the individual Christian rather than allegorizing specific liturgical ritual or theological doctrine. Thus sacramental concerns represent only one of many aspects of the knight's growth in strength through grace. At the end of the first day of battle in Eden, Redcrosse, as a figure for unregenerate man, falls into the baptismal Well of Life. Rising on the second day with the 'baptized hands' of the believing Christian, he falters before the onslaught of the Dragon's 'mortall sting' and falls into the eucharistic 'streame of Balme' trickling from the Tree of Life (I xi 36, 38, 48). Tudor Protestants identified this tree with the 'life everlasting' derived from Christ's sacrifice (Geneva gloss to Rev 2.7). On the third day, as the faithful Christian bearing Christ within, Redcrosse slays the Dragon.

As a sacramental emblem, the bloody cross on the knight's shield of faith symbolizes Christ's sacrifice on the Cross. The symbolic action of his quest parallels the baptism of children with the sign of the cross and the ministerial admonition 'to continue Christ's faithful soldier and servant unto his life's end' (*BCP* 'Public Baptism' ed 1976:275). The dipping of candidates for baptism into water commemorates John the Baptist's immersion of the penitent into the river Jordan as an act of spiritual cleansing. Christ's baptism associated ritual ablution closely with the work of the Holy Spirit, who alone can produce conviction of sin, repentance, and faith (Mark 1.4–11). Arthur's immersion of Maleger – possibly an embodiment of original sin – into 'a standing lake' (II xi 46) may invoke the baptismal symbolism of water to signify divine power to destroy evil (Woodhouse 1949; for a dissenting view, see L.H. Miller 1966). Guyon's inability to cleanse Ruddymane's 'guiltie hands' in a well (II ii 3) may refer to the power of baptism to renew life without eradicating the sin intrinsic even to the nature of the elect Christian (Article 16 'Of Sinne after Baptisme'; see Fowler 1960–1).

The administration of the Eucharist in the English service rejects the Catholic Mass and its doctrine of transubstantiation (the conversion of the elements of bread and wine into the body and blood of Christ). Instead, the new Protestant rite commemorates Christ's sacrifice on the Cross in propitiation for the sins of mankind (Luke 23) through spiritual feeding rather than the repeated sacrifice of the Mass or priestly absolution. The Catholic overtones of the religion of Isis, whose 'Mas' involves a 'daily sacrifize,' may help to explain why her priests refuse to drink wine: 'for wine they say is blood' (v vii 4, 10, 17). At a time when Protestants identified the Whore of Babylon with the Church of Rome (Geneva glosses to Rev 17), the 'golden cup' of the harlot Duessa links the traditional Mass to the superstitious practice of 'magick artes' (I viii 14). Paridell's spilling of wine to declare his illicit love for Hellenore involves a parody of the divine mystery of Communion when she, too, spills the 'guilty cup' as a sign of understanding his 'sacrament prophane in mistery of wine' (III ix 30–1).

Cranmer's substitution of the term 'Communion' for 'Mass' in the prayer book reflects the original meaning of *koinonīa* (fellowship) in the Greek New Testament. He intended the ritual of the Lord's Supper to gather individuals in a communal act of faith based upon a direct spiritual relation between the individual and God rather than through the intermediate agency of priest or sacrament. Christian fellowship though chiefly receptive involves active participation in Christian service or deeds of active charity (see Booty, et al 1981; King 1982, ch 3). Thus, in spite of Redcrosse's desire to withdraw from the world into contemplation following his vision of the Heavenly Jerusalem (I x 63), he must go on to defeat the Dragon in a battle rich with sacramental imagery, prior to the communal celebration of his betrothal to Una, an act that mirrors the union of Christian and Christ in the Communion service (I xi-xii). (See also *Church; *Reformation). John N. King

Salvage Man For such characters in *The Faerie Queene* as Lust, Timias, Artegall, and especially the Salvage Man himself, Spenser draws on the tradition of the wild man in European culture. This legendary figure was familiar in the literature, visual arts, popular festivals, and more sophisticated entertainments of the Middle Ages and Renaissance. He appeared as a hairy creature, naked or girdled with foliage, and usually carried a great club or uprooted sapling as a weapon. Other characteristics were a secluded dwelling place 'Farre in the forrest' (VI iv 13), a simple diet of acorns, berries, and flesh of beasts, lack of coherent speech, and extraordinary physical strength. The terms applied to him – 'wild' or 'savage' man, 'woodwose,' 'wild man of the woods' – reflect his life in the forest and intimacy with natural forces. His significance became enriched as he was used allegorically (Bernheimer 1952:23).

Just as the primitive condition may be considered positively or negatively (see *primitivism), the wild man himself came to bear contrasting interpretations. Usually he was characterized by uncontrolled passion; *wild* itself implies being passionate and subrational (*OED* II 6b, 12), and the woods were associated with the passions (see Hankins 1971:60–73, 123–5). Yet his very simplicity, naturalness, and dynamism tended to associate him with whatever strengths of character or constitution may be attributed to fundamental human nature. The wild man was a popular heraldic emblem and supporter of arms, signifying such qualities as fortitude, strength, and fecundity.

Aside from characters such as Orgoglio and Satyrane, who have some minor affinities with the wild man, Spenser presents various full-blown versions of the figure. In Book IV, a 'wilde and salvage man' personifies lust (vii 4–36). This absurdly grotesque savage mocks the way in which lust involves privation from real human contact. Artegall's appearance as a wild man at Satyrane's tournament has considerably less negative import (iv 39–44). His 'wyld disguize' renders the conventional fur or hair as 'mosse,' much as was done in festivals; his shield bears the motto 'Salvagesse sans finesse' (wildness without art). More positively, however, he displays the fortitude and strength of his wild counterpart. Spenser applies the wild man tradition here to express the potentially raw, retributive energy of justice.

For the maddened Timias, Spenser's use of wild-man motifs is less pejorative still. When Timias combats Lust, he becomes implicated in that passion, causing Belphoebe to reject him. In desperation, he assumes the life of a solitary, purely instinctive wild man, 'All overgrowen with ... haire,' like Lust, and 'mute,' showing 'Ne signe of sence ... ne common wit' (vii 26–47). For him, this wildness is partly penitential. The wild man's state here constitutes a return to first principles from which renewal can spring.

The Salvage Man in Book VI is Spenser's most richly developed and positive exponent of the tradition. Nameless, he is loosely denominated 'A salvage man,' 'wyld man,' or 'the Salvage' (iv 2, 8, 9), and thus readily seen as a type. Though his hair is not mentioned, he has other traits of the wild man, such as nudity (4), a tree 'Rent by the root' borne as a weapon (vii 24), and a highly instinctual, impassioned temperament (eg, iv 5–6). His purely vegetarian diet (14), however, and his instinctive sense of honor and compassion (iv 3; v 1–2, 29) are departures from the paradigm; in these respects, he is much like the ancients' noble savage (Bernheimer 1952:112–3). Thus Spenser mixes elements of the native and classical traditions in a way that is guardedly optimistic about the potentialities of fundamental human nature.

As Book VI deals with courtesy, root of 'civill conversation,' and 'Civility' (i 1, x 23), the basically favorable portrayal of a primitive human state applies allegorically to human capacities for both courtesy and the advancement of civilization. The knight or courtier and the savage become complementary figures (Cheney 1966:195–6, 204–13), and the contributions that the qualities of each can make to courtesy are analyzed through the actions of Calepine and the Salvage Man. With the latter's aid, Calepine becomes a more well-rounded figure capable of heroism (iii 46–iv 22). Yet, for all his indomitable energy, the Salvage is pathetically weak in skills of self-expression and social intercourse (v 4–5, 30). Through meeting exemplars of civility like Serena, Calepine, and Arthur, he encounters qualities that he lacks. Similarly, as Arthur's assistant, he is an emphatic extension, in effect, of his master's fortitude and energy (vi 18–vii 27, viii 28–9). Calidore too has brought the Calepine and Salvage within himself, as it were, into an apt relation, for he is 'mylde' and skilled in the arts of conduct, yet 'full stout and tall, / And well approv'd in batteilous affray' (i 2). Spenser implies that some aspects of the natural world and some lower or subrational human attributes are essential in life but must serve civilized values as the Salvage serves Arthur.

Ultimately, then, the Salvage's significance may be compared to that of Una's lion, her satyrs, and Satyrane: he embodies fundamental human strengths, while also indicating their limits. In one sense, he relates to the passions as basic, motive energies: in their proper place, the passions were considered good, since they were assumed part of human nature as created. However, because the Salvage is dynamic and irascible, he especially relates to the irascible appetite in its capacity for good (Hankins 1971:30, 180); the symbolism is obviously apt, for that appetite constitutes a potential wild man within. When functioning appropriately, it was held to serve the highest, rational human powers in overcoming inner and outer challenges, and the Salvage's service of Arthur is partly explicable in this way.

The Salvage's cultural significance complements his broad psychological role. His humble way of life epitomizes certain values inherent in the simple and energetic kind of primitive life from which civilization began to evolve; 'obaying natures first beheast' (iv 14) and attuned to the natural order, he approaches Edenic or golden-age ideals of existence. In general, then, he refers us to contributions that elemental human qualities can legitimately make, when appropriately disciplined or sublimated, to the well-being of both our culture and our inner selves. However advanced civility and courtesy have become, we find they are rooted in very deep strata of human development from which we should not distance ourselves too much. Kenneth Borris

For a general survey, see Bernheimer 1952; see further Penelope B.R. Doob 1974 *Nebuchadnezzar's Children: Conventions of Madness in Middle English Literature* (New Haven); Timothy Husband 1980 *The Wild Man: Medieval Myth and Symbolism* (New York); Lynn Frier Kaufmann 1984 *The Noble Savage: Satyrs and Satyr Families in Renaissance Art* (Ann Arbor); D.A. Wells 1975 *The Wild Man from the 'Epic of Gilgamesh' to Hartmann von Aue's 'Iwein'* (Belfast); and H. White 1972. On Tudor manifestations, see Robert Hillis Goldsmith 1958 'The Wild Man on the English Stage' *MLR* 53:481–91; and G.M. Pinciss 1982 'The Savage Man in Spenser, Shakespeare, and Renaissance English Drama' in Hibbard 1982:69–89. Herbert Foltinek 1961 'Die wilden Männer in Edmund Spensers *Faerie Queene*' *NS* ns 10:493–512 surveys the narrative but scants its allegorical implications.

Sanglier (Fr 'wild boar'; cf *sang* 'blood') A brutal and disdainful knight in *FQ* v i 13–30, Sanglier is the first to experience Artegall's justice. His heraldic device, 'A broken sword within a bloodie field' (19), recalls the baffling of dishonorable knights.

From a Squire weeping beside the headless corpse of a lady, Artegall learns that Sanglier in a fit of rage had thrust his own lady from him, seized the Squire's in exchange, and, when the first lady protested, beheaded her. At his master's bidding, the iron man Talus finds the knight and leads him back, 'Bound like a beast,' for judgment. When Sanglier turns the Squire's charges back on his accuser, Artegall resorts to a 'sleight' modeled on Solomon's first judgment, which showed that the wisdom of God was in him (1 Kings 3.16–28). First persuading the knight and Squire to accept his verdict on pain of bearing the dead lady's head for a year should they 'dissent,' Artegall proposes that each lady, the living and the dead, be cut in half and shared equally. When Sanglier agrees and the Squire demurs, Artegall judges the former to be the killer; and Talus compels him, 'his pride represt,' to take up his burden of shame.

In Spenser's Legend of Justice, Sanglier represents the more primitive threats to the achievement of civil society. A law unto himself, he exemplifies criminality in the personal sphere, and his trial contrasts with the more public one of Duessa at Mercilla's palace in canto ix. In Aristotelian terms, he has both taken more than his just share, making him subject to distributive justice in yielding the disputed lady to the Squire, and done injury to others, meriting corrective justice in the form of his 'penaunce.' Viewed as a projection of the hero's own internal struggle, Sanglier embodies that imbalance of the rational and irrational parts which is closely related to intemperance. In administering justice to him, Artegall relies on both force and guile, foreshadowing his later difficulties in defining where the justice of a case lies as well as the need for extreme and duplicitous measures in imposing it on the bestiality of men. (At the tournament in iv iv 39–40, 'Sir *Sangliere*' is the first opponent confronted by the disguised Artegall, who bears the motto 'Salvagesse sans finesse.')

These concerns govern Spenser's use of analogues. The episode combines the austere guile of Solomon's judgment of the harlots, the decapitation motif of folklore (on the headless lady as an ancient hieroglyph of justice, see Manning 1984:66–70), and the imposed penance in Malory's account of Sir Bedivere and his lady (*Morte Darthur* 6.17). Another analogue is the story of Hercules and the Erymanthian boar, an episode read by Renaissance mythographers as an allegory of the overcoming of intemperance. Here Artegall shows his Herculean justice against Sanglier, the boar (see Dunseath 1968: 73–6). The close relation between this kind of injustice and intemperance is suggested by Guyon's similar encounter with a bloody victim at the outset of Book ii; and its chivalric and civic connections, by parallels with the opening episode of Book vi, which likewise involves a hero, a squire, and a knight (Crudor) who mistreats his own lady. JOHN D. BERNARD

Sansfoy, Sansjoy, Sansloy These brothers 'all three bred / Of one bad sire' (i ii 25) play important roles in the allegory of *FQ* i ii-vi. Duessa identifies them as Night's 'Nephewes' (ie, 'grandsons,' from L *nepotes*) and Night calls them sons of Aveugle (Blindness; v 22–3). They are Saracens or Paynims, 'car[ing] not for God or man a point' (ii 12). The theological allegory might be inferred from Galatians 5.22–3: 'But the frute of the Spirit is love, joye, peace, long suffring, gentlenes, goodnes, faith, Mekenes, temperancie: against suche there is no Law.' The allegory implies a progression from the state of infidelity or faithlessness (Fr *sans* + *foy* without faith) occurring upon Redcrosse's separation from Una in ii 6, through a condition of lawlessness (*sans* + *loy* without law), to a state of despair or joylessness (*sans* + *joy* without joy). The narrative journey across these realms unfolds slowly and in carefully interlaced episodes. Sansfoy in canto ii and Sansjoy in iv confront Redcrosse, while Sansloy in iii and vi pursues Una. The outcome of their actions, moreover, is highly ambiguous.

In ii 12–19, Sansfoy succumbs quickly to Redcrosse, but neither Sansjoy nor Sansloy falls so easily. The forces of pagan Night from whom they descend threaten and confuse the children of the new Day in attacks that require defense by the Christian virtues. In iv 38, Sansjoy seeks vengeance against Redcrosse for his brother's death. His desire for revenge, an eye for an eye, clearly links him to the Old Law that Redcrosse will replace with the New Law of forgiveness. In that combat, however, Sansjoy disappears in a cloud (v 13). The indecisive outcome leaves Redcrosse beguiled with his own 'gay chevalree' (16), pointing ironically back to the narrator's initial description of him as 'too solemne sad' (i 2) and ahead to his confrontation with Despair (ix 21–54).

Meanwhile, Sansloy hounds Una. His sort of lawlessness suggests an anarchic overflow of uncontrolled power opposing Una's one, true law. Historically he may figure overly zealous religious reformers, like members of the Puritan Anabaptist sects, who sought the lawless overthrow of the established church. When he enters in iii 33, his appearance whose 'looke was sterne, and seemed still to threat / Cruell revenge, which he in hart did hyde' evokes the attributes of choler or irascibility. In 34–44, he attacks Archimago who is falsely dressed as Redcrosse; and he kills Una's defender, the ramping lion, a type of natural strength aptly standing in for the true Redcrosse whom Una has called her 'Lyon' (7). The lion, also a figure of natural law, 'Lord of everie beast in field,' falls to Sansloy, 'He now Lord of the field,' who vilely abuses Una, 'his pride to fill' (iv 43). Later he fights Satyrane (vi 40–7), Una's second defender, himself a tamer of lions (25). Satyrane's battle with Sansloy, however, remains unresolved, possibly because Satyrane represents the conventional wild man who needs to keep his own natural energies continually in lawful check. Sansloy appears finally in the house of Medina (ii ii 18–37), where he is the lover of Medina's immoderately sensual younger sister, Perissa.

In its broadest sense, the allegory concerns discrepancies between signifiers that refer to holiness, the central theme of Book i. Multiple confusions result from faulty relationships between signs and the things that they refer to. Redcrosse confronts Sansfoy, the eldest brother, after Archimago has deceived him with a false vision of 'Una' copulating with a squire, rendering Una and her knight 'divided into double parts' (ii 9). The stanza that narrates his meeting with Sansfoy reveals his identity as 'The true *Saint George*' (12). Still the champion of faith, he now faces the challenge of faithlessness implicit in the name 'writ' on the shield of the 'faithlesse Sarazin.' In the ensuing encounter, however, signifiers and their signifieds become blurred.

One blurring occurs in a confusion of pronoun references. The welter of pronouns in ii 15 effaces any distinction between Redcrosse and Sansfoy. In a simile comparing the combatants to two rams, both rams are 'stird with ambitious pride' (16). Their 'equall puissaunce' (17) implies both that Redcrosse is equal to fight Sansfoy, and that he may share some of his moral qualities. When Redcrosse appropriates Sansfoy's shield as a 'signe' of victory (20), the significance is highly ambiguous. After claiming the shield of faithlessness, Redcrosse abandons his quest to free Una's parents.

Redcrosse's attraction to Fidessa-Duessa complicates this play of signs. Initially revealed as the Scarlet Whore of Babylon (Rev 17.4) in ii 13, and named 'Fidessa' in 26, she is identified explicitly as Duessa in 44. Again a simple faith in the one-to-one correspondence of signifiers to their signifieds deceives Redcrosse. It also deceives Una: with her new companion, the lion, she falls into the hands of Archimago disguised as Redcrosse (iii 26). Ironically, too, the disguise tricks Sansloy. Keen to avenge his brother, he associates the sign of the red cross on Archimago's shield with its conventional signification (34). Archimago's lawless use of false signs deceives the champion of lawlessness himself.

The sign of Sansfoy's shield plays a major role in Sansjoy's encounter with Redcrosse. The setting is the house of Pride (not identified until v 53) where Redcrosse, led by Duessa, estranges himself from 'joyaunce vaine' (iv 37). As if in response to this estrangement, Sansjoy appears in the next stanza. Viewing Sansfoy's shield as the sign of Redcrosse's victory, Sansjoy seeks revenge (39). The next day, the shield is hung upon a tree to remind them of their cause (v 5). A glance at it prompts Sansjoy to address his brother in Styx. Intertextually the action echoes Aeneas' anger at the sight of Pallas' belt during his battle with Turnus in *Aeneid* 12, an allusion that both confirms Sansjoy's heroism and displaces Redcrosse's joyless heroism. Sansjoy's concealment in the cloud and his descent into hell for a cure, however, link him finally with Turnus, who similarly vanished in *Aeneid* 10, signaling his bewildered opponent's victory by default.

Ambiguities cluster finally around Duessa and her role in the action. In iv 47, she lies to Sansjoy for her own duplicitous purposes. Her ambiguous address during his combat with Redcrosse in v 11 – 'Thine the shield, and I, and all' – could apply to either or both of the contestants. Whatever the outcome, she will gain the advantage. Duessa confirms her strategy when she repeats those words to Redcrosse as the apparent victor (14). So distorted is her use of words and signs that even her own powerful ancestor, Night, fails to recognize her when she pleads for Sansjoy's life (27). Her own faithlessness as 'Fidessa' confirms the implications of Sansfoy's name, while her grim lawlessness confirms the implications of his brothers' names. In his attachment to her, Redcrosse courts the vices of Sansfoy, Sansjoy, and Sansloy under a different designation.

William J. Kennedy

Sapience In *Hymne of Heavenly Beautie* (183–301), Sapience appears seated in the bosom of God, clad like a queen with crown and scepter. She rules the house of God, the sky, and all below it; heaven and earth obey her will; all things partake of her fullness and exist through her, who made them and sustains them. Her beauty, 'Sparkled on her from Gods owne glorious face,' exceeds any power to praise it. The man whom God allows to see her enjoys all bliss, for she pours out the riches of her treasury on her beholders; as the 'faire love of mightie heavens king,' she is the one source of true and lasting ecstasy. Sapience is Heavenly Beauty, the culminating figure of the *Fowre Hymnes*; the only true object of man's desire, she is the celestial counterpart of Venus who presides over the *Hymne of Beautie*.

Sapience's structural position in the *Hymnes* was emphasized in the critical view that the woman enthroned in glory, beloved of God, represented the Virgin Mary, thus setting up a mother-son relationship in the 'heavenly' hymns that matched the Venus-Cupid pair in the 'earthly' ones (Winstanley in *FH* ed 1907). This view is now unfashionable; most modern critics fall into two main camps: the allegorical and the Neoplatonic.

Allegorical commentators claim that Sapience represents a quality of the Godhead, which may or may not be identified with one of the persons of the Trinity (see *God). The biblical personifications of Wisdom in Proverbs 8–9 and Wisdom 6–8 show many parallels to Spenser's Sapience (Osgood 1917), and the medieval iconography of Wisdom is very like his description (Tuve 1940). The biblical Wisdom was identified in early Christian times with the Holy Ghost, but in the later West a much stronger tradition associated her with the Logos of John 1.1, the second person of the Trinity (Fletcher 1910–11, Osgood 1917). Some critics have argued that Sapience is not a person of the Trinity, but a personified attribute of the Godhead; Spenser's figure may be seen at the end of a long tradition of mystical contemplative writings, in which the devout soul is encouraged to meditate on God's works in order to rise to a partial understanding of his wisdom (Collins 1940). This approach has led to attempts to trace in the structure of the poem the threefold ascent of the mystics, or the six stages of illumination of the soul described by Bonaventura in his *Itinerarium mentis ad Deum* (DeNeef 1974).

In sharp contrast, Neoplatonic critics insist that Sapience is a real entity in the cosmos, distinct from the Trinity. They seek her origins in the Renaissance Neoplatonism of Ficino, Leone Ebreo, and especially in Benivieni's *Canzona della Amore celeste et divino* with the commentary by Pico (Fletcher 1911). In this vein, Sapience has been identified as a celestial Venus, the divine mind of Neoplatonism, the first creation of God (Bennett 1931c, 1935), or even the Shekhinah of the Cabala, lowest of the ten sephiroth or emanations of the Godhead and sometimes identified with the Old Testament Wisdom (Saurat 1930:222–37). Such ideas may have come through the mediation of Leone Ebreo (Quitslund 1969). Modern interest in gender and excitement with the idea of 'God-as-mother' finds in Sapience a daringly androgynous presentation of the Godhead (Galyon 1977), or develops the idea of God's love for his 'soveraine dearling' to the verge of blasphemy (Quitslund 1969). Conservative opinion holds that Spenser's Sapience is essentially orthodox – the Son-Logos, or a personified divine attribute – superficially adorned with glamorous Neoplatonic terminology (Ellrodt 1960, Welsford 1967).

Wisdom figures in the Renaissance have extremely complex origins – indeed, the whole of the Western tradition could accurately be summed up as the history of wisdom (Rice 1958) – and Spenser is just vague and rhapsodic enough to lay himself open to a great diversity of interpretations. In *Heavenly Beautie*, the Highest is 'farre beyond all telling'; the poet must therefore contemplate his 'essentiall parts' and his works instead of 'The image of such endlesse perfectnesse' (99–112). He is perhaps aware that almost anything one can say about the Trinity is heretical, and traditionally 'in Englysshe ought not rehereed be' (*Court of Sapience* ed 1984, line 2245). His image of God, then, is deliberately metaphorical: God is seated on the throne of truth, scepter of righteousness in hand, thunder and lightning under his feet; his radiance is brighter than the sun, and Sapience is in his bosom. The context here seems to suggest that Sapience is to be read metaphorically or allegorically; such an allegorical figure has many clear precedents in literature. The fifteenth-century *Court of Sapience* (printed in the early sixteenth century) shows her as the guide of man and the counselor of God; Sapientia, invoked to descend from the throne of God, had appeared in a play performed for Queen Elizabeth in 1565 (in *Sapientia Solomonis* 1.2.22–9), and Milton planned to introduce the character Wisdom in an Ur-*Paradise Lost*. The closest parallel of all is Heinrich Suso's *Horologium Sapientiae*, a fourteenth-century Latin text (with several vernacular translations, including English), which was popular throughout the sixteenth century (Welsford 1967). There Aeterna Sapientia, presented and often pictured as a female figure, is the beloved and the instructress of the disciple, but she is equally clearly Christ, 'as he that is spouse and wyfe of every chosen soule' (*Seven Poyntes* fol 64v).

Suso makes the traditional point that although the Trinity is all-wise, and each person in the Trinity is equal in wisdom, yet man may think of the Son as particularly the embodiment of wisdom. Sapientia is either an aspect of God, or the Son of God: since the Godhead is three-in-one, its identities and distinctions are beyond human comprehension. Allegory is the proper way of talking about such matters, for, if Sapience is allegorical, she can be both the Logos and an aspect of God at the same time; after all, allegory does not equate one thing with another: it merely explores the different facets of an idea by means of personified abstractions. In *Heavenly Beautie*, Spenser is saying nothing more complicated theologically than that God is supremely lovable; his difficulty is to express this in terms which make emotional and imaginative sense. If Sapience is the most complicated allegorical figure in Spenser's entire work, it is because she represents something as comprehensive, as simple, and as unknowable as God; Spenser uses a language both modern and traditional in his own day to express the supremacy of her claim to be loved.

E. Ruth Harvey

Bennett 1931c; Bennett 1935; Sixt Birck 1938 *Sapientia Solomonis (1557)* ed Elizabeth Rogers Payne (New Haven); Collins 1940; *Court of Sapience* ed 1984; DeNeef 1974; Ellrodt 1960; Jefferson B. Fletcher 1910–11 'Benivieni's "Ode of Love" and Spenser's "Fowre Hymnes"' *MP* 8:545–60; Fletcher 1911 'A Study in Renaissance Mysticism: Spenser's "Fowre Hymnes"' *PMLA* 26:452–75; Galyon 1977; Osgood 1917; Frederick Morgan Padelford 1914 'Spenser's *Fowre Hymnes*' *JEGP* 13:418–33; Padelford 1932 'Spenser's *Fowre Hymnes*: A Resurvey' *SP* 29:207–32; Quitslund 1969; Eugene F. Rice, Jr 1958 *The Renaissance Idea of Wisdom* (Cambridge, Mass); Antonio V. Romuáldez 1964 'Towards a History of the Renaissance Idea of Wisdom' *SRen* 11:133–50; Saurat 1930:222–37; Spenser ed 1907; Heinrich Suso 1977 *Horologium Sapientiae* ed Pius Künzle (Fribourg, Switzerland), Eng tr as *The Seven Poyntes of True Love and Everlastyng Wisdom Drawen oute of the Boke That Is Clepid Orologium Sapientie* (Columbia Univ Lib Ms Plimpton 256, fols 62–99), also printed in William Caxton, comp 1491 *Book of Divers Ghostly Matters* (Westminster; *STC* 3305); Tuve 1940; Welsford 1967.

satire A notoriously difficult mode to define; the amount to be found in Spenser's works varies with the definition adopted. Its widest definition, as the censure of the world as it is by contrast with the world as it should be, would bring almost everything he wrote within its scope. By its narrowest definition, as the witty censure of contemporary vices expressed through the realistic detail of everyday life and manners, he wrote almost none. Samuel Butler describes satire as 'a kind of knight-errant, that goes upon adventures to relieve the distressed damsel Virtue' (*Miscellaneous Observations* in ed 1973:280). The definition seems to fit Spenser's work admirably, but only occasionally does he allow the poem itself to be such a knight errant or corrective agent.

Although the new fashion for satire among his contemporaries was showing increasing signs of classical influence, Spenser owed little to the classical satirists and wrote no formal satires. His models were predominantly medieval, in such things as the polemical use of pastoral eclogue, the iconography of the sins, and the whole tradition of complaint. Mantuan's Neo-Latin eclogues influenced the satire of *The Shepheardes Calender*. Langland's *Piers Plowman* (listed by Francis Meres among the finest English satires), Skelton's *Colyn Cloute*, and other complaint poems contributed to his idea of satire. Beast fables also had a long tradition of use as moral correctives, and Caxton's popular translation of the beast epic *Reynard the Fox* (although not itself satirical) probably lies behind *Mother Hubberds Tale*. All these works reinforced the rhetorical prescription that satire should be written in the middle or low styles, and Spenser pitches his own satirical work at those levels.

Some of Spenser's fullest expressions of the imperfection of the world cannot be considered satire because they are concerned not with human evil or folly and its correction but with the state of the universe after the Fall. The *Complaints* volume contains many examples. Matters such as the destructive power of time are beyond human amelioration; but even such a theme as mutability can move into satire when Spenser envisages change as specifically for the worse, brought about through human degeneracy. The myth of the passing of the Golden Age, which directly expresses this falling away from perfection, is alluded to in the opening lines of his one consistently satirical poem, *Mother Hubberd*, and made more specific later: 'But this might better be the world of gold: / For without golde now nothing wilbe got' (152–3). In the proem to the Legend of Justice in *The Faerie Queene*, Spenser describes how the present age is not golden but 'stonie,' and men themselves 'transformed into hardest stone' (V proem 2).

A commoner satirical image for degeneracy is the corruption of men into beasts. This can be expressed as narrative metamorphosis, as with Acrasia's victims, whose physical state is reduced to match the intemperate sensuality of their minds (II xii). Grill the hog even 'repines' at being changed back to his human shape; he is left to his 'hoggish mind' with Guyon's observation that 'the mind of beastly man' has 'so soone forgot the excellence / Of his creation' that he will choose 'To be a beast, and lacke intelligence' (86–7). The contrast between beastliness and intelligence is crucial: the Palmer uses his staff of reason to convert the monsters back into human form, and the whole Legend of Temperance is concerned with the governing of animal appetite by rationality. The same degeneration of man into beast is implicit in the procession of the seven deadly sins (I iv), where their association is traditional, and in the choice of the Fox and Ape as protagonists of *Mother Hubberd*. The Fox indeed claims to be even more like man than the Ape, 'for my slie wyles and subtill craftinesse' (1045). Similar implications underlie the presentation of the Fox in the beast fable of *SC, Maye*, and the ecclesiastical imagery of wolves there and in *September*. Ignorance, too, will reduce men to beasts. In *Teares of the Muses*, Urania, the Muse who in the Renaissance definition raises men to divine contemplation through philosophy, laments, 'What difference twixt man and beast is left, / When th'heavenlie light of knowledge is put out?' (487–8); and she claims that men who lack the 'blis' of wisdom are like 'brute beasts' (530–1).

In addition to his satire on the general state of man, Spenser singles out specific abuses for attack. The most prominent are the corruption of the church; the corruption of love; the corruption of the court and (in *Mother Hubberd*) of government; the corruption of language and poetry; and envy, slander, and backbiting. The categories overlap considerably and are frequently linked by Spenser.

The corruption of the church is treated most fully in the ecclesiastical eclogues of *The Shepheardes Calender* (*Maye*, *Julye*, and *Sept*) and in the episode in *Mother Hubberd* where the Fox becomes a priest and the Ape his parish clerk. The three eclogues all depict the traditional contrast between the good shepherd, who cares for his flock, is humble, and is content with little, and the bad shepherd, who prefers the good life to caring for his sheep and is a lover of 'Lordship' (*Maye* 123). The bad shepherds are loosely associated with Roman Catholicism but certainly not limited to it. In *Mother Hubberd*, the shepherd imagery is implicit since the ecclesiastical episode follows the Fox and Ape's employment as literal shepherds; here the prime target is the laziness of priests within the established church. The Priest who recommends the clerical life contrasts the present easy dispensation to the hardship of the old Catholicism with its monastic requirements of frequent services, fasting, asceticism in clothing, and chastity (353–574). Idleness, first of the seven deadly sins in *FQ* I iv, is similarly depicted as a cleric, though this time 'Like to an holy Monck.'

The inversion of values shown in the pursuit of the worldly or beastly in preference to the ideal or divine is satirized in many forms. *Colin Clouts Come Home Againe* censures the corruption of love, as Colin describes how at court love is no more than 'a complement for courting vaine' (790). The central books of *The Faerie Queene* are filled with episodes that demonstrate the difference between false love and true. The most overtly satirical include the Squire of Dames' references to the difficulty of finding a chaste woman (III vii 53–61: his advances are refused by only three women, one of those being a prostitute who refuses on account of his poverty, and another a nun who does not trust his secrecy), and the episode of Florimell's girdle of chastity, which will not stay fastened (IV v 17–18). Malbecco's inability to choose between saving his wife and his money, and to match up to the satyrs in potency, is also satirized (III x 15, 48).

The corruption of the court is dealt with most specifically in *Mother Hubberd*, when the Ape becomes a courtier (581–942); in Colin's indictment of the court in *Colin Clout* (660–792); and in various passages of *The Faerie Queene*, particularly Philotime's court (II vii 43–9). The characteristics that Spenser most condemns are ambition and the 'wrong wayes' that courtiers use to raise themselves and push down others. Colin's comment that 'each mans worth is measured by his weed' (*CCCHA* 711) is given narrative form in *Mother Hubberd*, when the Ape surpasses all other courtiers in the 'newfanglenesse' of his outfit (675); he also revels, conjures, gambles, pimps, and indulges in all kinds of 'costly riotize' (805). Braggadocchio and Trompart are *The Faerie Queene*'s closest equivalent to the Ape and the Fox – Braggadocchio with his 'gallant shew' unsupported by any inward virtue, and Trompart the clever con man (II iii).

The court provides numerous examples of how the corruption of language dissociates words and inner truth. Braggadocchio's boasts are hollow, the Ape advances himself by flattery, and Colin describes the vicious courtier's prime attribute as 'a guilefull hollow hart, / Masked with faire dissembling curtesie, / A filed toung furnisht with tearmes of art' (*CCCHA* 699–701). Love at court also becomes a matter of words alone with no substance behind them (775–90). Further, false language can promote false philosophy: both the Giant with the scales and the Fox argue for equality and equal shares (*FQ* V ii 30–8, *MHT* 124–66); Spenser comments that the Giant was 'admired much of fooles, women, and boys.'

A similar disjunction is seen between true value and the state of contemporary poetry. *Teares of the Muses* is largely devoted to the pervasiveness of ignorance, 'ribaudrie,' and bad style, which is characterized as 'Heapes of huge words uphoorded hideously, / With horrid sound though having little sence' (213, 553–4); furthermore, courtiers devote their wealth to supporting flatterers rather than patronizing true poets (469–72). *SC, October* shares the same themes.

The ultimate corruption of language – and the most insidious of the dangers in Spenser's moral universe – is slander, language used to make virtue appear vicious. Spenser's most extended treatment (in *FQ* VI) is more serious than satire allows, but slander is more overtly satirized in *Teares of the Muses*, *Mother Hubberd*, and *Colin Clout*.

Political and ecclesiastical satire aimed at specific targets was more dangerous and needed more disguise. There is disagreement over how much Spenser's work contains and who his targets were; but the *Complaints* volume ran into serious trouble and was called in, largely on account of *Mother Hubberd*'s attack on misgovernment and corruption at the highest level in the state. The 1611 edition of Spenser's collected works omits *Mother Hubberd*, and its version of *Ruines of Time* softens and generalizes the passage attacking Burghley (447–54). *The Shepheardes Calender* contains a certain amount of topical satire, especially in the ecclesiastical eclogues; but the most transparent allusions are also the least censorious, and the extent and subject of the rest are problematic. Spenser's satire is never limited to the topical, however: he always looks through that to larger patterns of vice and virtue. HELEN COOPER

K.W. Gransden, ed 1970 *Tudor Verse Satire* (London); Alvin Kernan 1959 *The Cankered Muse: Satire of the English Renaissance* (New Haven); Peter 1956.

Satyrane The first of the beast-taming 'salvage' knights of *The Faerie Queene* that show the natural will to virtue (see *Salvage Man). His exploits appear in contexts that contrast natural and supernatural virtue. In I vi, he helps Una escape from the satyrs, and later battles Sansloy while she flees. In III vii, he is able to bind but not destroy the witch's hyena that pursued Florimell and devoured her horse, and fails to save the Squire of Dames from Argante but must be saved himself by Palladine. In III xi, he pursues Ollyphant uselessly into the forest, for the giant embodies aberrant lust which only Palladine or Britomart, female knights of chastity, may vanquish. In his tournament for Florimell (IV iv-v), he fights to good purpose as a knight of Maidenhead until defeated on the third day by Britomart. As a champion of natural virtue, he is a noble and powerful knight, but his success is limited, and twice he displays cynicism toward women (III vii 57, ix 6–7).

A 'well deserved name' (I vi 20) and satyr-emblazoned shield (III vii 30) associate Satyrane 'armd in rugged steele unfilde' with the forest, the domain of lawless desire. As the offspring of a satyr father and a human mother, he is one-fourth beast (the satyrs being half man and half goat). Even his human descent emphasizes bestial potentialities, if we may so interpret the name of his mother Thyamis (Gr 'passion'), of her father Labryde (Gr 'greedy, turbulent'), and of her husband Therion (Gr 'wild beast'). A natural child, begotten by a satyr on a woman captured in the forest, he is not content to remain a mere creature of nature. His behavior shows a tacit rejection, with recognition, of the circumstances of his birth, for since childhood he has been at war with his bestial affinities. In youth, he exercised his prowess in subduing the beasts of the forest (I vi 25–6); and on reaching maturity, he left the forest but returns periodically to his 'native woods' in order 'To see his sire and ofspring auncient' (30). His motive for returning is appropriately the natural virtue of filial piety. His career as a knight is allegorically a continuation of his youthful pastime: the taming of innate bestiality. Having left the forest, he struggles with incomplete success to get the forest out of himself (Evans 1970:45, 55–6). His victories bear the same relation to those of Redcrosse and Arthur that natural virtue bears to supernatural. The one seeks to transcend, the other to transform, fallen nature.

The ambiguity of Satyrane's characterization suits the allegory of Books I, III, and IV, which stresses the affinity of natural virtue for goodness and truth but also its inferiority to and dependence upon supernatural virtue. Nurture cannot finally change nature though it is not, on that account, to be scorned. The 'greatest and most glorious thing on ground / May often need the helpe of weaker hand,' remarks the narrator concerning Arthur's reliance upon his squire in their battle against Maleger's 'unruly rablement' (II xi 30). But neither can the lesser take precedence over the greater. In the tournament for Florimell's girdle, Satyrane's satyr-emblazoned shield is replaced with a 'maiden-headed shield' (IV iv 17), and he fights powerfully in behalf of virginal chastity until overcome by Britomart, a virgin destined for marriage.

RONALD A. HORTON

satyrs Minor deities associated with the countryside in classical mythology, and mentioned in the Bible (Isa 13.21, 34.14), satyrs are 'gods of the wooddes: they were monsters having the head of a man, the body of a goat' (T. Cooper 1565). They are followers of Dionysus, and in representing the natural forces of fertility, they are often licentious (see also *Faunus). Satyrs figure prominently in *FQ* I and III, and are mentioned incidentally in *FQ* VII vi 39, *Daphnaïda* 156, *Visions of Bellay* 12, *Virgils Gnat* 178, and *Teares of the Muses* 268.

The satyrs in *FQ* I vi are naive, benign creatures whose natural religious instincts lead them to worship Una when they see her unveiled, though these same instincts ultimately lead them to the idolatry of worshiping the ass on which she rides and finally to serve old Sylvanus. Although they are only slightly raised above the condition of animals, they are more virtuous than the pagan Sansloy whom they frighten away, and their offspring in Satyrane shows their capacity to improve. They have been associated with the Renaissance idea of the noble savage (Pearce 1945), although Spenser rejects the view that the light of nature is sufficient to save virtuous pagans (Whitaker 1952:163–4). They have also been seen allegorically as the civilizations of ancient Egypt, Greece, and Rome (Kellogg and Steele in *FQ* ed 1965a:29), or (since Upton 1758) as ignorant, primitive Christians (Steadman 1958 claims that their worship of the ass is a symbol of the ignorant clergy). Finally, they have been seen to represent the Jewish nation, an interpretation based upon Renaissance commentaries on biblical history, which saw the Jews as a people who were shown the truth unveiled, rejected it, and returned to their now-superseded ceremonial law and to idolatry (Jordan 1977).

The satyrs in Book III are so primitive and lecherous as to be excluded from the virtue of chastity and even from its abuse: their sexual appetites are so far distanced from the human and the civilized as to be neither good nor evil. This amorality need not extend to Hellenore, the second Helen, a symbol of woman's infidelity who goes dancing with the satyrs garlanded as Queen of the May, kisses each of them, and then is embraced by one satyr nine times during the night (cf Ovid *Amores* 3.7.25–6). These satyrs 'represent perhaps what human life would be like if human beings were as completely adjusted to the "fallen" level of nature as animals and plants are'; they symbolize the sexual world of ordinary human experience, 'the dreaming experience of the night, with its erotic resonance' (Frye 1976:99). Continuously dancing or fornicating, they are much closer to their classical predecessors than those of Book I.

RICHARD D. JORDAN

Jordan 1977; Lotspeich 1932:105–6; Nohrnberg 1976:218–22; Steadman 1958.

scholarship, 1579-1932 The history of Spenser scholarship begins with E.K.'s glosses and notes to the first edition of *The Shepheardes Calender* (1579), and from the beginning exhibits a need to explain and justify Spenser's methods (especially his use of allegory and archaic language) to readers with different tastes and expectations.

Early editors concentrated on assembling the works: the folio *Faerie Queene* of 1609 was the first to include Book VII, and the *Works* of 1611 first brought together almost all of the poetry known to be Spenser's. Sir James Ware published *Vewe of Ireland*, with notes, in 1633. The remaining seventeenth-century editions debased the text, though the third folio (1679) included a glossary, which suggests that some of Spenser's language was inaccessible to readers. (For the later editorial tradition, see critical *bibliography.)

Camden (1605, 1615), Ware, Thomas Fuller (1662), John Aubrey (1669–), Edward Phillips (1675), and William Winstanley (1687) began to collect and publish material on Spenser's life, packing anecdotes around their skimpy facts; John Hughes gathered this material in the 'Life' which headed his edition of Spenser's works (1715). In an edition of *The Faerie Queene* in 1751, Thomas Birch added a good deal of fresh material, and H.J. Todd in the variorum *Works* of 1805 not only assembled but also documented a biography to which subsequent scholars have added only a few important facts.

Retrospective commentary on the poems began with Kenelm Digby's *Observations* (1643). Essays prefixed to Hughes' edition provided a context and a moral interpretation for the allegory, and began to gather sources and analogues (especially classical) and to discuss Spenser's language in order to defend him against a neoclassical bias which found his work shapeless and uncouth. The relatively narrow critical focus of Hughes' work, the tendency to emphasize those parts of the poems that best satisfied the tastes of the time and to ignore the rest, would be typical of most scholarship and criticism until nearly the end of the nineteenth century. Jortin's *Remarks on Spenser's Poems* (1734) and notes in Upton's edition of *The Faerie Queene* (1758) suggested many other classical and Renaissance sources. Upton's notes for the first time made extensive scholarly materials available to readers stanza by stanza.

Upton, and all the other commentators for the next 150 years, drew heavily on Warton's *Observations on the Fairy Queen* (1754, 1762), especially on his extensive knowledge of Spenser's medieval predecessors. His eclectic historical investigation opened the way for readers to see Spenser in his own terms rather than those of their times, and was thus perhaps the single most influential study of the poet. Warton, Todd, and especially Upton also began to work out the details of the historical allegory. With its full glossary and extensive notes, including long extracts from the studies of his principal predecessors, Todd's edition closed out the first phase of the scholarly history.

Spenser scholarship after Todd has the features characteristic of all English and American literary scholarship during the period. Solid information – bibliographical, lexical, historical – continued to mount up as scholars edited texts, glossed words, confirmed or invalidated dates and relationships, and traced sources. Early in the century, the emphasis fell on biography, but later scholars returned to the wider range of concerns inherited from Warton and Upton, especially with the intellectual traditions Spenser drew upon and the social and political context in which he worked. By the end of the century, scholarly activity had been almost wholly transferred from amateurs to professionals, from literary parsons and lawyers to professors, from general-interest magazines to learned journals. Eventually the sheer bulk of the material assembled to help readers may have come to intimidate all but academics.

No single work of the nineteenth century had as much immediate impact or long-range influence as Warton's *Observations*. G.L. Craik's *Spenser and His Poetry* (1845), which is about one-third selected passages of text, one-third paraphrase tying them together, and one-third background material, added little that was new but mingled text and commentary with the genial authority of a first-rate lecturer. Though G.S. Hillard's 'First American Edition' of *The Poetical Works* (1839) made no significant scholarly contributions, the editions of F.J. Child (1855) and J.P. Collier (1862) included much important new lexical and historical material; Child was the first of many American scholars who by the 1920s had moved the center of Spenser studies across the Atlantic. R.W. Church's critical biography in the English Men of Letters series (1879) applied the work of contemporary historians with significant effect, and emphasized Spenser as a religious poet more than any previous study. A.B. Grosart's elaborate edition (1882–4), though published without the notes and glossary originally called for in its prospectus, included important essays by Edward Dowden, Edmund Gosse, Francis Palgrave, George Saintsbury, and Aubrey de Vere.

Early in the century, romantic emphasis on the poetry as the personal expression of an individual writer meant that scholars were especially concerned with biography. Although Todd had given most of the facts, new information filled out knowledge about Spenser's schooling, added greatly to what is known of his career, turned up the early marriage to Machabyas Chylde, and clarified his relationships with Harvey, the Sidney circle, Raleigh, and Bryskett. But for every grain of new fact about Spenser there was a bushel of speculation, especially about the identities of the fair Rosalind and E.K., the poet's connection with Sidney and the Areopagus, his relationship with other Spensers and Spencers, and the circumstances around the sacking of Kilcolman Castle and his death. As might be expected, the resulting image was of a passionate, sensitive man frustrated and tormented by his failure at court and the brutal conditions of his Irish exile, temporarily solaced by doomed relationships with kindred souls, ending his unhappy life amid violence, rejection, and poverty. By the same token, these studies did not have much room for common domesticity, politics, practical religion, or day-to-day morality, nor for awareness of him as a capable civil servant in an important post.

As the century advanced, attention shifted to political and religious issues. An article in the conservative, English-oriented *Dublin University Magazine* (1843) centering on the destruction of Spenser's home by Irish rebels was almost at once answered by one in the nationalist *Dublin Review* praising Spenser as a poet but censuring him as the willing agent of a repressive colonial power – both the historical record and *Vewe*, then as perhaps now, troubled even Spenser's most enthusiastic readers. Collier's biography (in his edition of 1862) printed in full many of the relevant documents and paid much attention to the historical allegory; the poet of romance, vision, and sentiment was replaced by a writer whose first impulse was political. Efforts to solve the historical allegory of *The Faerie Queene* led scholars towards the relationships among the Leicester circle (especially Sidney), Burghley, and the Queen. Church's critical biography of 1879, however, foregrounded theological concerns. A clergyman deeply affected by the religious revival of the mid-century, he based his study on Ephesians 6.11, the arming of the Christian knight (Spenser as well as Redcrosse and Arthur) drawing heavily on the work of the mid-Victorian historians, especially Froude and J.R. Greene, who had so fully documented the interdependence of political, religious, and literary activities in the Tudor period.

Through the century, admirers of Spenser struggled with the allegory. Most studies were stronger on speculation than on fact, and some were positively ludicrous, like Thomas Pennant's, which saw in the Despair episode (first published in 1590), Spenser's reflections on the loss of family and home in Tyrone's rebellion of 1598, or the *Notes and Queries* series of 1864, unsigned but probably by Robert Cartwright, which concludes by an astonishing sequence of logical leaps that Duessa represents *The Shepheardes Calender*, punished by Sidney and the Areopagus for failure to conform to classical standards. But some strove for scholarly rigor. One of the most stimulating treatments, because it viewed the allegory as part of an entire aesthetic, was Ruskin's sympathetic (and deeply romantic) account in *The Stones of Venice* (1853). An important landmark was set in 1889 by the publication of H.E. Greene's 'The Allegory as Employed by Spenser, Bunyan, and Swift,' the first article on Spenser in *PMLA* and a clear sign of the movement of scholarship on Spenser out of the hands of interested amateurs and into those of academics.

Greene's essay directs attention to those scholars, increasingly numerous as the century went on, who continued the work of Warton and Upton by relating Spenser to his literary forerunners and contemporaries. If the Romantics emphasized biography, the Victorians increasingly addressed sources and influences. The eighteenth-century studies had dealt very fully with Spenser's classical predecessors, Homer and Virgil, and with his main English model, Chaucer. Now Greene was followed by A.S. Cook's gathering of possible sources for the house of Sleep (1890), A.E. (Sawtelle) Randall's *Sources of Spenser's Classical Mythology* (1896, the first book-length study of a single topic in Spenser scholarship), and R.E.N. Dodge's long *PMLA* article (1897), 'Spenser's Imitations from Ariosto.'

All this scholarship meant that by the turn of the century Spenser was being presented to grammar-school students with the extensive introductory materials and notes that classical scholars affixed to Homer or Virgil. H.M. Percival's school-text of *FQ* I (1893), even more than G.W. Kitchin's similar edition of *FQ* I and II (1867-8), was able to relate Spenser to several major literary traditions, to a wide variety of religious, political, and social institutions, and to assorted moral and aesthetic points of view. The range of Percival's concerns and sympathies is much wider than that of any previous scholar, even Warton or Church. A similar catholicity appears in K.M. Warren's school edition of the entire poem (1897–1900).

These trends continued into the twentieth century. A few new lines of inquiry were opened up. W.W. Greg's *Pastoral Poetry and*

Pastoral Drama (1906) and C.H. Herford's edition of *The Shepheardes Calender* (1895) initiated study of Spenser's relationship to pastoral. J.J. Jusserand's 'Spenser's "Twelve Private Morall Vertues as Aristotle Hath Devised"' (1905–6) inaugurated a dispute about the sources of the organizational scheme set forth in the Letter to Raleigh that widened into extensive reconsideration of the structure of *The Faerie Queene*, not in terms of some particular classical or medieval model (as Hughes, Warton, and Church had looked at it) but as unique. Major achievements here were W.L. Renwick's *Edmund Spenser: An Essay on Renaissance Poetry* (1925), also notable for its emphasis on Spenser's Italian and French predecessors besides Petrarch, Boiardo, Ariosto, Tasso, and Marot, and Janet Spens' *Spenser's 'Faerie Queene'* (1934). J.S. Harrison's *Platonism in English Poetry of the Sixteenth and Seventeenth Centuries* (1903) was an important early contribution to twentieth-century Spenser scholarship, soon followed by Lilian Winstanley's edition of *Fowre Hymnes* (1907). Collaterally, the *OED* made possible increasingly detailed study of Spenser's words; and the outpouring of editions, reprints, and studies of other medieval and Renaissance English manuscripts and books made his intellectual context accessible as never before.

Most work pursued previously established topics at higher levels of knowledge and sophistication. Thus M.Y. Hughes' *Virgil and Spenser* (1929), D. Bush's *Mythology and the Renaissance Tradition in English Poetry* (1932), and H.G. Lotspeich's *Classical Mythology in the Poetry of Edmund Spenser* (1932) update Hughes and Jortin, while C.S. Lewis in his *Allegory of Love* (1936) became the twentieth-century Warton. A shelf of basic books on Spenser was produced, including Dodge's (1908) or J.C. Smith and Ernest de Sélincourt's (1912) edition of the works, H.E. Cory's *The Critics of Edmund Spenser* (1911), C.H. Whitman's *Subject-Index to the Poems of Edmund Spenser* (1918), F.I. Carpenter's *Reference Guide* (1923), and H.S.V. Jones' *Spenser Handbook* (1930).

Most significant of all was the appearance of what we might call the professional Spenserian, the scholar whose whole career or a large part of it would be centered on Spenser. Thus in 1907 P. Long contributed the first of seventeen items (mostly biographical) listed in Sipple 1984. In 1909, E. Greenlaw (24 items in Sipple) entered the field, followed by F.M. Padelford (21 items) in 1911. Both were among the instigators and editors of the work that climaxes this second, professionalizing phase of the scholarly history as Todd's had climaxed the first. Their monument is the *Variorum Works*, along with A.C. Judson's definitive *Life* (1945) in the same format, published by the Johns Hopkins University Press beginning in 1932. These massive volumes dwarf the work of Hughes, Upton, Warton, even Todd; in their abundance, but also their intimidating size, they are both a glory and a curse, as they testify to the richness of Spenser's work, but also to its linguistic, intellectual, and emotional distance from us.

DAVID EVETT

SURVEYS OF SCHOLARSHIP: Alpers 1969; Atkinson 1937; Carpenter 1923; Herbert Ellsworth Cory 1911 *The Critics of Edmund Spenser UCPMP* 2:81–182; David Evett 1965 'Nineteenth-Century Criticism of Spenser' diss Harvard Univ; McNeir and Provost 1975; Sipple 1984; Wurtsbaugh 1936.

LANDMARK EDITIONS: Birch (*FQ* ed 1751); Child (*Poetical Works* ed 1855); Church (*FQ* ed 1758b); Collier (*Works* ed 1862); Dodge (*Complete Poetical Works* ed 1908); Greenlaw, et al (*Var* 1932–57); Grosart (*Complete Works* ed 1882–4); Hales and Morris (*Complete Works* ed 1869); Herford (*SC* ed 1895); Hillard (*Poetical Works* ed 1839); Hughes (*Works* ed 1715); Kitchin (*FQ* I-II ed 1867–8); Percival (*FQ* I ed 1893); Smith and de Sélincourt (*Poetical Works* ed 1912); Sommer (*SC* ed 1890; facs ed); Todd (*Works* ed 1805); Upton (*FQ* ed 1758a); Ware (*Vewe* ed 1633); Warren (*FQ* ed 1897–1900); Winstanley (*FH* ed 1907).

SOME SIGNIFICANT WORKS OF SCHOLARSHIP: Bush 1963; Church 1879; Cook 1890; Craik 1845; Kenelm Digby 1644 *Observations on the 22. Stanza in the 9th Canto of the 2d. Book of Spencers Faery Queen* (London; rpt in *Var* 2:472–8); R.E. Neil Dodge 1897 'Spenser's Imitations from Ariosto' *PMLA* 12:151–204; Frederick G. Fleay 1877 *A Guide to Chaucer and Spenser* (London); Jefferson B. Fletcher 1899 'Areopagus and Pléiade' *JGP* 2:429–53; Fuller 1662; Herbert Eveleth Greene 1889 'The Allegory as Employed by Spenser, Bunyan, and Swift' *PMLA* 4:145–93; Greenlaw 1909–10; Greenlaw 1932; W.W. Greg 1906 *Pastoral Poetry and Pastoral Drama* (London); Hallam 1837–9; J.S. Harrison 1903; Samuel Hayman 1843 'Spenser's Irish Residence: By a Dreamer' *Dublin University Magazine* 22:538–57; Henley 1928; Hughes 1929; Hurd 1762; H.S.V. Jones 1930; John Jortin 1734 *Remarks on Spenser's Poems* (London; rpt New York 1970); Judson 1945; Jusserand 1905–6; Keightley 1855; Lewis 1936; Lotspeich 1932; G.C. Moore Smith (Harvey ed 1913); Henry Morley 1887–95 *English Writers: An Attempt towards a History of English Literature* II vols (London); Richard Green Moulton 1876–85 Syllabi for lectures for the University Extension Program, variously printed (Harvard Univ Library); Mueller 1959; Padelford 1911; Edward Phillips 1675 *Theatrum Poetarum* (London; rpt Hildesheim and New York 1970); Randall 1896; Renwick 1925; George Saintsbury 1898 *A Short History of English Literature* (London); F.C. Spencer 1842 'Locality of the Family of Edmund Spenser' *Gentleman's Magazine* ns 18:138–43; Spens 1934; de Vere 1887 ch 2; T. Warton 1762 (1st ed 1754); Whitman 1918; J[ames] Ernest Whitney 1888 'The "Continued Allegory" in the First Book of the Fairy Queene' *TAPA* 19:40–69; William Winstanley 1687 *The Lives of the Most Famous English Poets* (London; rpt Gainesville, Fla 1963).

---

science From the fourteenth to the seventeenth centuries, what we call 'science' was called 'natural philosophy'; 'science' usually meant 'knowledge' or 'skill' (as it does in Spenser). Historians of science disagree whether sixteenth-century science (in our sense) was essentially a 'medieval' or a 'Renaissance' phenomenon, whether the occult sciences contributed significantly to its development, and whether humanism stimulated or retarded its growth. Although it is difficult to define and delimit, a scientific revolution took place between 1450 and 1650 (ie, between the humanists' rediscovery and first printing of classical treatises on science and medicine, and the inauguration of the mechanistic view of the world). This revolution is as much a part of the Renaissance – and as complex in its causes and origins – as is the Reformation. Both movements owe much to a conservative drive to recover ancient wisdom – the one of human intellect, the other of divine revelation – and both made changes that helped reshape our view of the world and of ourselves.

If it is true that the 'new science' profited from the humanists' recovery of such 'lost' works as Lucretius' scientific poem *De rerum natura*, the *Geography* of Ptolemy, and the *De medicina* of the first-century medical authority Celsus, along with better texts of ancient authorities already accessible in the Middle Ages (eg, Aristotle, Ptolemy's *Almagest*, and Galen), it is also true that humanistic discoveries included the Neoplatonic, Hermetic, and Cabalistic texts of late antiquity (see *Hermeticism). These materials are relevant here because 'science,' even through the seventeenth century, was rarely free from magic and was frequently combined with a mystical Christianity.

At the same time that these continuities with ancient scientific and magical traditions were being maintained, there were genuine efforts to break with the past and redefine our relationship to nature. Ironically, this impulse was shared by occultists and scientific rationalists alike. Theophrastus Bombastus von Hohenheim (1493–1541) – who called himself Paracelsus to show that he was 'greater than Celsus' – tried to overthrow Aristotle and Galen, the two greatest scientific authorities in medieval and Renaissance universities. He sought to erect not only a new medicine based on observation and his own version of alchemical principles, but also a Christian, Neoplatonic, and Hermetic philosophy that would reveal all of nature's secrets. Francis Bacon, who also attacked the moribund Aristotelianism of the universities, articulated what was to become the rationalist basis of a science grounded in observation and experiment, and devoid of magic, mysticism, or the entanglements of religion. As shown by the theological and alchemical activities of late seventeenth-century scientists like Robert Boyle, Isaac Newton, and the English *virtuosi* (not to mention those of the professed Paracelsians, Neoplatonists, and Hermeticists), such a separation was not easily achieved; nevertheless, the mathematical quantification of matter by Boyle and Newton extended the work of Galileo (1564–1642), Descartes (1596–1650), and others, and helped bring about the very mechanistic world view that the *virtuosi* and Neoplatonists alike resisted.

Even by the turn of the sixteenth century, however, the great advances in astronomy and physics, medicine and physiology, botany and zoology, mathematics and chemistry that we associate with the development of modern science had begun. There was a complex interplay between the old and the new: between the legacy of ancient science, the theory and practice of late medieval science, and fresh observation and empiricism; between a largely Neoplatonic, magical view of the world (with its implicit analogies between microcosm and macrocosm and its assumption that matter was imbued with spirit) and an emerging 'scientific rationalism' – in short, between the acceptance of past authority and the assertion of present self-sufficiency. To a modern reader, the results of these interactions are somewhat paradoxical. Thus Copernicus (1473–1543) himself acknowledged that his heliocentric system was a revival of ancient Pythagorean theories; and while both Kepler (1571–1630) and Galileo helped to validate the Copernican model, Kepler's laws of planetary motion derived largely from his search for mystical universal harmonies in a vitalist universe, and Galileo's belief in circular planetary orbits persisted despite his mathematical formulation of the laws of physical motion and his discovery of the moons of Jupiter. Similarly, John Dee was a leading mathematician of the sixteenth century, but he also pursued numerology and angel magic via Hermetic texts, astrology, and alchemy. Nor was there a contradiction in the mind of the Aristotelian and Galenist William Harvey (1578–1657) between the minute observation and quantitative arguments by which he arrived at his theory of the circulation of the blood, and his calling the heart the 'sun of the microcosm' (ironically, his genuinely scientific discovery was first defended by the Hermeticist and Paracelsian, Robert Fludd [1574–1637]). Again, the exploration of the New World, Asia, and the East Indies led to representations, both verbal and pictorial, of plants and animals before unknown, and schemes of plant classification began in the late sixteenth century; yet even the new herbals did not entirely supplant that of Dioscorides (1st c AD), and even if the seventeenth-century encyclopedias and monographs devoted to animals went beyond the medieval bestiaries and the fabulous stories of Pliny the Elder's ubiquitous *Natural History* (1st c AD), they still made room for the mythical and monstrous. These characteristic examples suggest that syncretism, as in Renaissance moral philosophy, was common in contemporary natural philosophy as well, and that modern scientific attitudes were to develop only slowly.

Spenser died about a decade before the Copernican astronomy was generally accepted by English scientists, and before the theoretical works of Bacon were published. Hence for him, the new philosophy did not call 'all in doubt,' as it did for Donne in his *Anatomy of the World* (1611). Unlike his friend Gabriel Harvey, Spenser did not keep abreast of the latest scientific investigations and theories. He may have observed a lunar eclipse with interest (Meyer 1983), but his knowledge is mainly that of the conservative handbooks and encyclopedias of the mid-sixteenth century (see Spenser's *reference works), and even that is not always accurate (see *cosmogony and Johnson 1937:194).

Spenser's use of the handbooks is traditional in being mainly illustrative, comparative, and moral. Unlike many heroic poets, he does not include substantial 'digressions' on scientific matters, one means by which the poet could inspire 'wonder' and demonstrate the range of his learning (cf du Bartas *Les Sepmaines*, Milton *Paradise Lost* 7, 8). However, Spenser's mythological exploitation of 'scientific' materials – whether in adopting a traditional myth or adapting one to his own purpose – is shown in his treatment of astronomy, Chaos, constellations, and etiological tales. In some small way, he participates in the ancient tradition of the scientific allegoresis of myth, which derived from the Stoics and was celebrated by Reynolds in his *Mythomystes* (1632).

There is evidence, moreover, that Spenser was interested in science, especially in relation to scientific poetry. He was familiar with a number of scientific poets, both ancient (Hesiod, Empedocles, Lucretius, Virgil in the *Georgics*) and modern (Palingenius' *Zodiacus vitae*, du Bartas, perhaps George Buchanan's *De sphaera*, and Giovanni Pontano's *Meteorum liber*). All four of the latter (along with many other scientific poets) are mentioned by Harvey in the same note where he remarks that even though Spenser is 'not completely without knowledge of the sphere and astrolabe,' he is ignorant of 'astronomical laws, tables, and instruments.' He also tells us that Spenser took pleasure in repeating from memory that part of du Bartas' *Les Sepmaines* which deals with astronomy, 'which he esteemes as the proper profession of Urania' (ed 1913:161–3). While Urania had become the 'Christian Muse' of Renaissance poets like du Bartas, she was originally the Muse of astronomy. In *Teares of the Muses*, Spenser bewails, through Urania, man's lack of scientific knowledge, especially of astronomy and cosmology, which through contemplation would lead to a knowledge of God (499–522); this was a fairly conventional justification for scientific study in general (see Schuler 1985).

While Spenser himself was no practitioner of scientific poetry, his account of the human body in Alma's castle (*FQ* II ix) is related to the anatomical sections of encyclopedic and scientific poems like du Bartas' and John Davies of Hereford's *Microcosmus* (1603), and to versified allegories of human physiology like Robert Underwood's *A New Anatomie* (1605) and Phineas Fletcher's *Purple Island* (1633) (see also Barkan 1975).

See also *Aristotle, *birds, *body, *constellations, *elements, *flowers, *medicine, *natural history, *New World, *plants, *psychology, Spenser's *reference works, *zodiac. ROBERT M. SCHULER

Basic reference works on the history of science include *Dictionary of Scientific Biography* 1970–80 ed Charles Coulston Gillispie, et al, 16 vols (New York); *Isis Cumulative Bibliography ... 1913–1984* 1971–6 ed Magda Whitrow, 6 vols and 1980–5 ed John Neu, 2 vols (London); and the current annual bibliography in the journal *Isis*.

Useful surveys of Renaissance science include Allen G. Debus 1978 *Man and Nature in the Renaissance* (Cambridge; a reinterpretation of the importance of the occult and a thorough bibliographical essay on the basic scholarship); and W[illiam] P.D. Wightman 1962 *Science and the Renaissance* 2 vols (Edinburgh). See also Marie Boas Hall 1982 'Problems of the Scientific Renaissance' in André Chastel, et al 1982 *The Renaissance: Essays in Interpretation* (London) pp 273–96 (an excellent survey of recent historical debates); Johnson 1937; Meyer 1983; Robert M. Schuler 1985 'Theory and Criticism of the Scientific Poem in Elizabethan England' *ELR* 15:3–41; Svendsen 1956.

science fiction Many readers who have been drawn to Spenser have also, like the distinguished scholar C.S. Lewis, been interested in science fiction. Moreover, at least one novel that might be called science fiction is partly set in the world of *The Faerie Queene*: L. Sprague de Camp and Fletcher Pratt's *The Incomplete Enchanter* (New York 1941; rpt 1975 in *The Compleat Enchanter*). In this humorous tale based on the idea of parallel universes, a modern psychologist finds a way to visit various literary worlds, among them Spenser's; there he encounters Britomart and Amoret, attends Satyrane's tournament, and falls in love with Belphoebe, whom he brings back to his own universe to marry.

At times, details in *The Faerie Queene* seem to anticipate science fiction. For example, is Talus, the iron man of *FQ* v, an early robot? However tempting such speculation might be, it is important to recognize that science fiction is a specifically modern genre, one that first appears in the nineteenth century and depends both upon a scientific world view and upon the prior existence of the realistic novel. Spenser is not a science-fiction writer, nor has his work had significant influence on the form. But there are genuine affinities between *The Faerie Queene* and science fiction because both are versions of romance.

The characteristic aesthetic effect of romance is wonder, and concern with the marvelous provides a point of contact between Spenser and science fiction. Giants, magic lances, and enchanted castles have their science-fiction equivalents in alien creatures, superlasers, and strange planets. Science-fiction stories often follow a quest pattern that is structurally similar to the pattern of Spenser's romance narratives. Moreover, in science fiction as in Spenser, fully rendered psychological characters are normally beside the point, for characters in romance tend to be representative rather than individualized: the knight versus the evil magician or, in science fiction, the scientist versus the religious fanatic. Romance forms typically emphasize setting. In *The Faerie Queene*, the most memorable passages are often descriptions of crucial allegorical places such as Lucifera's palace. Likewise, in science fiction, the most significant element of the story is often neither character nor plot but the strange new world that the writer imagines. This generic continuity allows readers to move comfortably between the earlier and the later forms of romance, and comparative study of Spenser and science fiction can be illuminating to both.

MARK ROSE

Mark Rose 1981 *Alien Encounters: Anatomy of Science Fiction* (Cambridge, Mass); Robert Scholes and Eric S. Rabkin 1977 *Science Fiction: History, Science, Vision* (New York).

Sclaunder, slander Spenser's generation found the perennial human temptation to slander particularly worrisome, perhaps because several factors converged to give language and its dangers more importance than ever: humanist stress on rhetoric, increased political opportunity for nonaristocratic but articulate men, arguments over Bible translation, the proliferation of printed books, and widespread anxieties about reputation. Writers feared malicious misinterpretation, clergymen exhorted Christians to govern their tongues, the government harshly enforced statutes against maligning the crown, and judges were deluged by cases concerning slander (Carr 1902; Plucknett 1956, ch 5; Sharpe 1980).

Spenser, too, thought slander important; and to judge from the opening of *The Shepheardes Calender* and from his complaints that backbiters attack poetry (*FQ* I iv 32, VI xii 40–1), he took its threats personally. Even some of the language he applies to the slander of persons could apply also to texts: Detraction likes to 'blot' and 'wrest' (V xii 34). Yet Spenser invents one poet, Bonfont, who for libeling Mercilla deserves blotting; his tongue is nailed to a post and his name revised to 'Malfont' (*FQ* V ix). Malfont, who has disobeyed the injunction of Exodus 22.28 not to 'raile upon the Judges' or the ruler, is guilty of *scandalum magnatum* (slander of great persons) for which the penalty, after a trial most likely held before the equity court of Star Chamber, was sometimes mutilation. After seeing his mother allegorized as Duessa, James VI of Scotland asked Elizabeth to prosecute Spenser himself; but luckily the Queen did not consider Spenser a Malfont (see *James I).

(See **Sclaunder** Fig 1.)

The Elizabethan picture of slander had many traditional elements. Classical authors (eg, Ovid, Horace, and Plutarch), the Bible, medieval allegory and exegesis, and Renaissance moralists, artists, mythographers, common proverbs, and pageants provided images of teeth, double or polished tongues, stings, venom, swords, spears, arrows, dogs, snakes, fire, vomit, poisonous breath, deceitfully laid snares, webs or nets, theft, and ambush. The imagery suggests division, separation, illness, entrapment that halts forward motion, and the penetration of society's and the self's perimeters; the vomit and venom parody the good poet's honeyed mouth and Helicon's waters.

Slander's motivating energy is envy, which inspires one 'to put under and to destroy an other man, that he may be chief himselfe there' ([Slander] 1573: sig C1v). Slander therefore appears where people are most competitive, poisoning life for courtiers, lovers, and poets. Yet, to be plausible, slander often consorts with its seeming opposite, flattery; slanderous Duessa pairs off with smooth Blandamour and maligning Turpine with falsely pleasing Blandina (*FQ* IV i, VI vi-vii). Such deception is worse than a social failing: the Greek for calumniator is *diabolos*, from which comes *devil*, the subtle accuser and slanderer who divides man from man, language from truth, identity from reputation, and humanity from God. Gloriana's capital Cleopolis is threatened by slander's theft of good fame, and Una (Truth) must be lost when doubleness seduces or befuddles us.

Spenser's most explicit personification of calumny is the figure of Sclaunder, the hag with whom Arthur, Amoret, and Aemylia pass the night (IV viii). The spelling of her name, although not uncommon, also recalls *scandal*. Her words are poisonous vomit, snakebites, 'noysome breath' (24–6). A thief of good name, she is poor, filthy, ragged, and (like many of her relatives in *The Faerie Queene*) female, for calumny is the weapon of the inferior and is 'unmanly' in its sneakiness. She sits on the ground, a brief reminder of the association of slander with the earth, found also in the famous image of Time welcoming his daughter from the cave of envy and calumny and, less directly, in Psalm 85.11: 'Trueth shal bud out of the earth,' words usually read as referring to Christ (Saxl 1936, D.J. Gordon 1975). As Pastorella is forced into the dark of the Brigands' underground 'hellish dens,' she reenacts the myth of Persephone (VI x 39–xi 51); but she also represents slandered truth that is restored from imprisonment to 'the joyous light' by a knight who will win at least a temporary victory over the Blatant Beast. Furthermore, Spenser strengthens the association of slander with earth's darkness by comparing this defamatory monster of evil tongues to the hellhound Cerberus, interpreted by mythographers as the man-eating grave.

Sclaunder undermines the community that language creates, for her words do not express her 'inward mind' but rather wound our 'inner part' with venom from her 'inward parts.' Although slander is usually public (Detraction likes 'common haunts' V xii 34), its lies isolate the calumniator in a secret on which he must be silent (Sclaunder lives alone), and its goal is ostracism and inner anguish for the victim. Yet good words, too, may be misread as defamation (even if true, they could sometimes be a *scandalum* legally). Thus, as Arthur and his companions leave the still-barking Sclaunder, the narrator laments that some readers will 'misdeeme' the ladies for their evening spent 'conversing' with Arthur and will wrongly imagine a sexual affair (IV viii 29). As a woman, Amoret would have had little legal recourse in the Renaissance against any such misdeeming if publicly expressed as slander, which may be why Spenser chose Arthur, his most inward and mysterious knight, as her protector in Sclaunder's hut.

Sclaunder detests Amoret because detraction hates love. Similarly, a 'Venemous toung' stirs up 'coles of yre' (*Amoretti* 86), and 'false reports' make a lover's life hell (*Hymne of Love* 261–5). Slander is not wholly arbitrary, however, for it exploits appearance, whether of imprudence (like Serena's in *FQ* VI iii) or of an encounter with Lust, however innocent (like Amoret's in IV vii). Anyone who, like Clarion, is 'regardles of ... governaunce' risks entanglement in envy's and slander's web (*Muiopotmos* 384; see Bond 1976). Courts are particularly dangerous: in Apelles' famous painting (long lost but much discussed and imitated), Calumny holds a wrath-kindling torch and is attended by Envy, who drags Innocence before an ass-eared judge (in many versions a king), as Repentance stands sadly by and naked Truth awaits her revelation (Lucian *Slander*, Cast 1981; cf *FQ* II iv 3). Hippolytus, falsely accused to Theseus (I v), Redcrosse slandered by Duessa to Una's father (who wisely waits to hear the truth, just as Arthur listens patiently to the calumniated Britomart in IV ix 35–6), Guyon maligned by Occasion (II iv), Archimago slandering one knight to another (II i, iii), Artegall misreported to Radigund (V v), Malfont and smooth-tongued Malengin outside Mercilla's court (V ix), and ambitious Defetto's jealousy of Timias' 'favour' (VI v 12–13) – all illustrate Spenser's complaints that courts breed defamation, especially in the ambitious and envious (*Mother Hubberd*, *Colin Clout*). Typically, the Fox destroys the old aristocracy with 'fained crimes' (*MHT* 1186). As the Geneva gloss to Psalm 101.5 says, slander is 'moste pernicious in them that are about Kings.'

Slander is dynamic, generating emotional, narrative, and spatial movement; it literally misleads. Spenser exploits slander's nature in *FQ* I and II; but because it operates chiefly to separate characters, he finds it particularly valuable thematically and structurally in Books III-VI. Friendship, justice, and courtesy – public virtues concerned with appearance and community – find defamation especially troublesome. Thus the story in *FQ* IV is propelled by the slanders of Duessa and double-tongued Ate, 'mother of debate' (i 19). Ate's actions closely recall Ecclesiasticus 28.13–16, which says the 'double tongue' has destroyed cities, ruined the great, cast out chaste women, and led to fiery anger and hellish captivity. 'Whoso hearkeneth unto it, shal never finde rest, and never dwell quietly' (see also Ps 12.2 on the double hearted). In psychosexual terms, this is precisely what happens in *FQ* IV, for after Amoret has been slandered by Ate's comments to Scudamour and then held captive by Lust, she visits Sclaunder and later confronts the sexually imprisoning and wrathful Corflambo, father of Poeana. Poeana's name relates her to penitence and penalty, recalling both the dynamics of Apelles' painting and Ecclesiasticus 5.15 on the repentance following slander. Her marriage to pleasant Placidas seems mischievously to associate quelling the painful wrath that comes from slander with the affection even an external courtesy arouses. (Elsewhere, too, Spenser follows scenes of calumny with images or names indicating fire, for he knew that an evil tongue 'setteth on fyre the course of nature' [James 3.6]. For example, after credulous Phedon who, like Apelles' judge, lacks 'warie governaunce,' comes fiery Pyrochles, II iv-v.) Meanwhile Scudamour has listened to slander and, as Ecclesiasticus foretold, spends a restless night in the noisy house of Care.

There is little protection against slander, although the Hermit in *FQ* VI vi recommends caution and self-discipline. Perhaps the conventional wisdom is right: time is the rescuer of last resort even though the chief slanderer, the dragon Satan, will not finally be bound until the end of time. One of Erasmus' *Adages* says 'Frustra Herculi,' meaning that slander is in vain against a complete hero; and indeed Arthur seems immune. Hercules-like Artegall, however, is rewarded for service to Mercilla by meeting Envy and her sister, the poisonous hag Detraction, who uses her distaff to spin 'false tales' that are doubly painful for being cleverly close to the truth (V xii 36).

Like David ignoring his stone-throwing calumniator (2 Sam 16.5–13), Artegall calmly keeps his 'right course' to Gloriana's court (V xii 43); but Spenser himself continues to wander in the 'strange waies' of Fairyland, making up his own tales (VI proem). Slander is an uncomfortable subject for him. The diabolical Archimago lies and feigns; but as an allegorist, Spenser, too, is an arch imagemaker and arch magician, one whose position is all the more delicate because he loves Una. He detests the slander that misuses our power to invent, in part because he knows so well how feigning – fiction – works. ANNE LAKE PRESCOTT

Bond 1976; Frank Carr 1902 *The Law of Defamation* (London); Cast 1981; Chew 1962; Fletcher 1971; D.J. Gordon 1975:220–32; Theodore F.T. Plucknett 1956 *A Concise History of the Common Law* 5th ed (London), ch 5; Fritz Saxl 1936 'Veritas Filia Temporis' in *Philosophy and History: Essays Presented to Ernst Cassirer* ed Raymond Klibansky and H.J. Paton (Oxford) pp 197–222; Joyce H. Sexton 1978 *The Slandered Woman in Shakespeare* ch 1 (Victoria, BC); J.A. Sharpe 1980 *Defamation and Sexual Slander in Early Modern England: The Church Courts at York* Borthwick Papers 58 (York); [Slander] 1573.

Scott, Walter (1771–1832) The facts that Scott absorbed *The Faerie Queene* in early adolescence, that he could quote whole cantos from memory, and that his review of Todd's edition reveals a thorough understanding of the historical allegory, do not in themselves demonstrate the centrality of Spenser in his work. Scott knew Shakespeare even earlier, read Boiardo, Tasso, and Ariosto in Italian and *Don Quixote* in Spanish, and was familiar with the medieval literature of chivalry, so that the presence of Spenser – whose Protestantism and antiquarianism made him in some ways a more congenial figure than the Italian allegorists – is nevertheless often difficult to pin down. That so many of Scott's protagonists are 'errant' (in both senses) assures their kinship not only with the knights of *The Faerie Queene* but with many other heroes of romance. Moreover, despite his own appropriation of its patterns, Scott consistently attributes to chivalric literature a seductive power which can be somewhat sinister: in a Waverley hero, for instance, enthusiasm for Ariosto and Spenser is the sure sign of an idealistic temperament too ready to interpret events in terms of literary stereotypes, too naive to deal with political and social reality.

Scott's own imagination is demonstrably permeated with Spenser: Spenserian details, phrases, and episodes occur frequently in both his poetry and his prose. Yet perhaps because his ambivalence about the poet's appeal is an aspect of that ambivalence about romance and fantasy, and about the heroic and picturesque past, which informs all of Scott's work, the passages which are the most narrowly Spenserian sometimes betray a certain unsureness of purpose. The most thoroughly Spenserian of the longer poems, *The Bridal of Triermain*, an apocryphal Arthurian tale culminating in an allegorical quest, and *The Vision of Don Roderick*, an historical pageant (in Scott's favorite Spenserian stanzas) recalling Merlin's disclosures to Britomart (*FQ* III iii 26–50), are the slightest and least seminal. In the fiction, some episodes with apparently Spenserian inspiration, like the underworld ordeal in *The Monastery* (ch 12), presided over by a fairy White Lady who warns the hero not to trust his human powers, or the vigil and masque in *The Talisman* (chs 4–5) which recall Britomart's experiences in the houses of Busirane and Dolon (*FQ* III xii, V vi 27), seem both improbable and irrelevant to Scott's historical vision. Powerful creations, like Die Vernon in *Rob Roy*, who is a kind of Belphoebe, or the accursed fountain in *The Bride of Lammermoor* (cf *FQ* II i 35–ii 10), may owe as much to other models (to Shakespeare, for example, or to the ballad tradition) as they do to Spenser.

There is, however, one striking charactertype in the fiction which Scott consistently introduces with direct quotation from *The Faerie Queene*: the recluse with weird power. Examples include the Black Dwarf (*The Black Dwarf* ch 15; *FQ* I ix 35) and old Janet (*Waverley* ch 15; *FQ* III vii 6), Burley (*Old Mortality* ch 43; *FQ* I ix 35), blind Alice and Lucky Gourlay (*The Bride of Lammermoor* chs 4, 31; *FQ* III vii 5–6), Wayland Smith (*Kenilworth* ch 10; *FQ* IV v 34), and Norna (*The Pirate* ch 24; *FQ* III iii 18). The Spenserian association in these cases is not only with a mysterious individual (Despair, Florimell's Witch, Mammon, Care, Merlin) but also with a mysterious place. Indeed, Scott's feeling for the fateful encounter with figures hidden in the heart of a romantic (but not fictitious) countryside, so important an element in both the poetry and the fiction, does seem to owe something specific to Spenser, who domesticated the terrain of romance in a way which appealed deeply to Scott's imagination. That Spenser himself can be invoked as a guide to natural beauty in *Rokeby* (2.6) suggests his presence behind the picturesque landscapes in the narrative poems; that so strong an historical figure as Burley can end up, disconcertingly, as a demon in a wild Spenserian lair strikingly illustrates how Scott's reading of *The Faerie Queene* sometimes shaped critical details in his fiction. MARJORIE GARSON

Walter Scott 1829–33 *Waverley Novels* 48 vols (Edinburgh); Scott 1833–4 *Poetical Works* 12 vols (Edinburgh); Scott 1834–44 *Miscellaneous Prose Works* 28 vols (Edinburgh).

David Brown 1979 *Walter Scott and the Historical Imagination* (London); David Daiches 1951–2 'Scott's Achievement as a Novelist' *NCF* 6:80–95, 153–73; Georg Lukács 1962 *The Historical Novel* tr Hannah and Stanley Mitchell (London; first pub 1937) pp 19–63; Jane Millgate 1984 *Walter Scott: The Making of the Novelist* (Toronto); Harry E. Shaw 1983 *The Forms of Historical Fiction: Sir Walter Scott and His Successors* (Ithaca, NY); Alexander Welsh 1963 *The Hero of the Waverley Novels* (New Haven).

Scottish antecedents Between 1560 and 1584, roughly the time of Spenser's apprenticeship, Scottish writing was in a sorry state. No major figure had emerged to replace the great 'makars' of the past, Henryson, Dunbar, and Douglas. Alexander Scott (1520?-1590?) was still composing his intricate love lyrics, ranging from the Petrarchan idealism of 'Thocht I in grit distres' to the open cynicism of 'A Luvaris Complaint'; but his links are with Wyatt, and he does not adopt the poetic forms most regularly associated with Spenser.

During this period, there are a number of poetic complaints (like Spenser's *Complaints*), mainly contained in the *Bannatyne Manuscript* (1568, ed 1928–34, vol 2). They bewail variously mutability, the vicissitudes of fortune, the temptations of youth, and the vices of courtly life. But there is no example of a sustained allegory nor, more surprisingly, of pastoral verse with or without satiric intent. Henryson's 'Robene and Makyne' is included in the *Bannatyne Manuscript*, but no poet followed either that fine example or the later *Egloges* of Alexander Barclay.

This period encompassed the troubled reign of Mary Tudor and its aftermath, when Scottish poets consciously turned to French rather than English sources in an effort to maintain a distinct literary tradition. Religious and political problems dominated, and most of the occasional verse of the day satirized the weakness of government and looked back wistfully to more stable times. The strong Protestant and anti-Marian line in Spenser's verse was anticipated or echoed by many Scottish Protestant poets led by Robert Sempill. In this tradition, Mary is likened variously to Delilah as the betrayer of a God-fearing husband or to Clytemnestra and Semiramis as husband murderer and voluptuary. The approach is, therefore, more direct than Spenser's, scorning allegory and innuendo for techniques drawn from flyting.

This was the situation when James VI for the first time gained true political power in 1584. Lamenting the state of Scottish letters, he published in that year *Ane Schort Treatise, Conteining Some Reulis and Cautelis*. Setting himself up as the Maecenas of a group of court poets called the Castalian Band, and relying heavily on the then 'maister poete' Alexander Montgomerie (1545?-1598), he started a Renaissance based firmly in the Edinburgh court. Although this was specifically to be a Scottish Renaissance distinct from current movements in England, and although later (1596) his fury at the treatment of his mother, Mary, Queen of Scots, in *The Faerie Queene* turned him against Spenser whom he wished to see 'dewly tryed and punished' (Carpenter 1923:41–2), his *Schort Treatise* with its interest in expanding the resources of the language, its advocacy of alliteration, and its emphasis on a wide variety of verse forms did produce some verse which might loosely be called Spenserian.

The major Scottish Spenserians such as Drummond, William Alexander, and Robert Ayton (who composed a number of pastorals) did not produce their best work until after 1603; but among the early Castalians, three developments are of interest within a Spenserian context.

Of these, the most important concerns the sonnet and the interlacing ('Spenserian') rhyme scheme. The *Bannatyne Manuscript* contains one sonnet rhyming *abab bcbc cdcd ee*. In his *Essayes of a Prentise* (1584), James VI composed fourteen sonnets which adopt this rhyme scheme, a form imitated in the five sonnets of dedication. Although Montgomerie had probably used this form earlier, the King's example established it as the norm in Scottish sonneteering, and the evidence would suggest that many of these Scottish sonnets predate Spenser's first use. This rhyme scheme may well have originated from the sixteenth-century Scottish lyric, for over half the verses in the *Bannatyne Manuscript* use it, while every religious work with an eight-line stanza has the rhyme pattern *abab bcbc*. Using this as the octave, it would be easy to derive the Spenserian rhyme scheme from native sources.

Two major works by the early Castalians bring Spenser to mind, though in different ways. The first is *Roland Furious* by John Stewart of Baldynneis (1550?-1605?), an abridgment of Ariosto's *Orlando furioso*. Like Spenser in *The Faerie Queene*, Stewart tries to impose a moral scheme on those parts of the poem which he treats. The Christian implications of the events are highlighted, characters begin to represent set moral positions, and thematic leitmotifs such as the idea of chastity and the conflict between love and honor are stressed. *Roland* was probably composed before 1586, but there is no question of Spenser's indebtedness to it. It is proof, however, that one Scottish poet did embark on a major poem in some ways similar to *The Faerie Queene* and, like Spenser, tried to introduce a more orderly form and a more obviously moral tone than were to be found in his sources.

The other poem is Montgomerie's *The Cherrie and the Slae*, an allegory which first appeared in an unfinished and corrupt form published in 1597. The links between it and *The Faerie Queene* are slight. The poet is faced with a choice between picking the easily accessible sloe or striving up the crag to seize the distant cherry, and in the end he chooses the latter. The major similarity lies in the allegorical method. Like Spenser's poem, it is in most places multivalent. Cherry and sloe are seen sometimes to represent distant and easy loves, at others to set aspiration against humble contentment, grace against gracelessness, Catholicism against Protestantism, and perhaps even the crown of Britain against that of Scotland. Both poems work through loose associations, like a dream, rather than faithfully translating clear conceptual ideas. R.D.S. JACK

The Bannatyne Manuscript Writtin in Tyme of Pest 1568 1928–34 ed W. Tod Ritchie, STS 2nd ser 22, 23, 26, 3rd ser 5 (Edinburgh); James Cranstoun, ed 1891–3 *Satirical Poems of the Time of the Reformation* STS 20, 24, 28, 30 (Edinburgh); James I ed 1955–8; Alexander Montgomerie 1887 *Poems* ed James Cranstoun, STS 9–11 (Edinburgh); Montgomerie 1910 *Poems* supplementary vol, ed George Stevenson, STS 59 (Edinburgh); Alexander Scott 1896 *Poems* ed James Cranstoun, STS 36 (Edinburgh); John Stewart of Baldynneis 1913 *Poems* ed Thomas Crockett, STS 2nd ser 5 (Edinburgh).

R.D.S. Jack 1985 *Alexander Montgomerie* (Edinburgh); Helena Mennie Shire 1969 *Song, Dance and Poetry of the Court of Scotland under King James VI* (Cambridge).

Scudamore family An ancient family of landed gentry, centered in Herefordshire, whose English ancestry can be traced to the eleventh century; the Scudamores of Holme Lacy, their most important Elizabethan branch, were elevated to the peerage in the seventeenth century ('Lucas-Scudamore of Kentchurch' in *Burke's Landed Gentry* 1965–; 'John Scudamore' in *DNB*). The name was variously spelled in the sixteenth century (Skydmore, Skudmore, Scudamour, etc); by the 1570s, however, it was becoming normalized to Scudamore, the spelling most in keeping with the family motto, *scutum amoris divini* (the shield of divine love). Upton found a correspondence between this name and Sir Scudamour in *The Faerie Queene*; and Todd, taking his claim from Upton, asserted that Spenser had 'immortalized ... the noble family of Scudamore' (*Var* 3:290, 2:223).

Spenser's Scudamour probably represents a special compliment to the family's most eminent Elizabethan members, Sir John Scudamore of Holme Lacy (c 1542–1623, knighted 1591) and his second wife, Lady Mary (d 1603). Sir John was a Gentleman Usher to the Queen (as well as a member of Parliament for Herefordshire, 1571–89), but Mary Scudamore's position at court was the more important, for she was the Queen's second cousin and a member of the Boleyn family, which Elizabeth notoriously favored over her father's. Ann, the younger sister of Thomas Boleyn (father of Henry VIII's Queen Anne), married Sir John Shelton. Their oldest child, John, was Mary Scudamore's father (Rye 1891:52, 247). By 1 September 1574, she and Sir John Scudamore were married and she was already a Lady of the Queen's Bedchamber, an honor which she seems to have held until at least 1602 (see, eg, *Report ... on de l'Isle and Dudley* 1925, 2:20–1, 254, 428; Chambers 1923, 4:67). When Spenser calls Belphoebe and Amoret twins who 'twixt them two did share / The heritage of all celestiall grace' (III vi 4), he may intend a reference to the kinship of the Queen and Lady Mary, though he waits nearly 50 stanzas before revealing that Amoret loves 'the noble knight Sir *Scudamore*.' Praise of Amoret and Scudamour not only celebrates the Scudamore family but may also form a part of the encomium that *The Faerie Queene* offers to Elizabeth.

Though no connection seems to have been previously made between Lady Mary Scudamore and Spenser's Amoret, Spenser's Sir Scudamour has been identified both with Sir John and with his son and heir, James (1568–1619; see Cokayne 1910–59, 11:573n; *DNB*; Gibson 1727). Primarily because of his marriage to Mary Shelton, Sir John Scudamore can be named with some confidence as the likelier of these two candidates.

Moreover, by making Amoret and Scudamour married lovers in Book IV, Spenser may mirror historical fact for the purposes of argument. Belphoebe's anger over Timias' care for the wounded Amoret has been widely interpreted as a thinly veiled reference to the Queen's anger over Raleigh's affair with Elizabeth Throckmorton, her maid of honor. At the same time, however, Spenser may be cunningly doubling Raleigh's Elizabeth with Mary Scudamore, whom the Queen beat and cursed in the mid-seventies for marrying Sir John but later completely restored to favor, as evidenced by the munificent gifts that the Queen bestowed on her in the early nineties (see the letter of Eleanor Bridges in *Mss of... Rutland* 1888, 1:107, and W.T. MacCaffrey 1961:116). By hinting at a parallel between the forgiven Scudamores and the unforgiven Raleighs, Spenser might be suggesting to the Queen that, like the Scudamores, the Raleighs were truly virtuous and worthy of her esteem and that their recent transgressions were just as pardonable as the Scudamores' earlier ones. LINDA R. GALYON

Burke's Landed Gentry 1965–, 18th ed, ed K.P. Townend (London); Chambers 1923; G.E. C[okayne] 1910–59 *Complete Peerage* ed Vicary Gibbs, et al, 13 vols (London); Matthew Gibson 1727 *A View of the Ancient and Present State of the Churches of Door, Home-Lacy, and Hempsted* (London); *The Manuscripts of His*

Grace the Duke of Rutland ... Preserved at Belvoir Castle 1888–1905, 4 vols, Great Britain, Historical Manuscripts Commission Series 24 (London); *Report on the Manuscripts of Lord de l'Isle and Dudley Preserved at Penshurst Place* 1925 ed C.L. Kingsford, Historical Manuscripts Commission Series 77 (London); Walter Rye, ed 1891 *The Visitacion of Norffolk Made by William Hervey* Harleian Society 32 (London).

Scudamour Because Spenser revised Scudamour's role between the 1590 and 1596 editions of *The Faerie Queene*, we must account for him in two different contexts. The 1590 edition closes with the ecstatic reunion and embrace of Scudamour and Amoret which Spenser renders in the famous simile of a 'faire *Hermaphrodite* ... of white marble wrought.' The mythic, mystic, and Christian contexts of this figure are complex and evocative and give resonance to the union of bodies and souls that triumphantly concludes the anatomy of love between women and men in Book III (see *androgyne, *hermaphrodite).

These stanzas disappear from the 1596 edition. The continuation of Scudamour's separation from Amoret in Book IV extends their story to the public context of friendship as well as the more private one of chastity. More subtly, the change remedies the uncharacteristic simplification in the 1590 ending of Book III. The earlier conclusion, striking as it is, suggests that the obstacles to chaste love disappear when separation becomes reunion and 'loves bitter fruit' becomes sweet fulfillment. The more complex combination of Books III and IV, however, indicates that the relevant contexts of love include relations among lovers, their friends, and their culture as well as between the lovers themselves. In Book III, we see Scudamour only twice, for twenty stanzas in canto xi and for a few stanzas at the end of canto xii. The 1596 edition enlarges and enriches his story.

Most critics have been inclined to assess Scudamour according to the terms suggested by the great tableaux in Busirane's castle. The disruptions and excesses of sexual love portrayed there represent threats to all lovers, including Scudamour and Amoret, but Scudamour's particular difficulties are better understood in reference to the story that immediately precedes his appearance: the fabliau of Paridell, Hellenore, and Malbecco, with its treatment of greed and jealousy. For Scudamour suffers from willful and self-consuming jealous rage. The opening stanza of III xi apostrophizes the 'hatefull hellish Snake ... Fowle Gealosie, that turnest love divine / To joylesse dread.' Looking back at Malbecco, the narrator also looks ahead to Scudamour, who appears six stanzas later, disarmed and wallowing in anger and grief. Like Malbecco, he is 'woxen ... deform'd.' He has cast away his shield with its emblem of Cupid – from which he gets his name (Ital *scudo* shield + Fr *amour* love). His love has become 'self-consuming smart,' and his martial confidence turns to despair and 'fell woodnesse [madness]' (27) when he cannot follow Britomart through Busirane's flames. To do Scudamour justice, his desperation has cause, for even Britomart is dismayed at the prospect of facing Busirane, a magician of formidable power.

In Book IV, Scudamour continues to figure forth anxieties about love. Although he defeats Paridell in canto i, Blandamour, Duessa, and Ate play on his jealousy and thereby gain 'triumph without victorie' (50). Canto v details the pathetic comedy of a sleepless Scudamour, tormented all night in the house of Care by 'gealous dread' (45). Unhorsed by Britomart in canto vi, he is also finally disabused of his suspicion of Amoret's faithlessness. But he is not yet reunited with Amoret, for she has been carried off once more. In canto ix, he continues to bewail his amorous misfortunes – rather puzzlingly, as Amoret should be present with Arthur, the last of her rescuers. Possible references to her presence are equivocal and, along with Spenser's failure to include a reunion of the two long-separated lovers, may point toward incomplete revision of the end of Book IV.

Scudamour makes his most lengthy appearance, and his last in *The Faerie Queene*, as both narrator and hero of the episode in which he wins Amoret in the Temple of Venus (IV x). As an untested young knight, he ventures to the temple 'To winne me honour by some noble gest' (4). There he defeats twenty defenders of the Shield of Love, and in gaining it achieves, as his name suggests, his identity. The motto engraved below the shield summarizes Scudamour's subsequent triumphs and frustrations: 'Blessed the man that well can use his blis: / Whose ever be the shield, faire Amoret be his.' Though Scudamour wins the shield, he evidently cannot well use his 'blis.' Busirane abducts Amoret on their wedding night, and Scudamour later discards his trophy in despair.

After defeating the twenty knights, Scudamour continues into the temple, passing Doubt and Delay at the first gate and Daunger at the second. He then penetrates the porch of the temple itself, where Concord holds Love and Hate in dynamic equilibrium. Within the temple, he finds a veiled, probably hermaphroditic statue of Venus which recalls the canceled ending of 1590. This 'Idol' is surrounded by Womanhood and her demure group of handmaidens who personify traditional feminine virtues. Amoret's place in the midst of a setting devoted to the conciliating and civilizing aspects of love contrasts sharply with her captivity in Busirane's house of disruptive and unregulated sexual desire. Despite her pleas, Scudamour leads her from the temple. (Spenser presents a slightly different version of their story in his Letter to Raleigh.) Of all Spenser's allegorical places, the Temple of Venus has perhaps been least expressive for modern readers. This may reflect on Scudamour, who as teller sometimes seems uncomprehending of his own tale; or it may reflect the evasiveness of the central symbol, Venus, who in both classical mythology and for the Renaissance has multiple, shifting signification.

That Scudamour can reach Amoret in the Temple of Venus but not in Busirane's castle is important for assessing him. Commentators who regard his intrusion into the temple as excessively bold or as evincing too much 'maisterie' (dominance) tend to regard the later difficulties of the pair as a consequence of their defective courtship. It is possible, however, to infer that Scudamour has enough strength to face love in its relatively restrained and orderly mode, but not to confront its more passionate and chaotic aspect.

It is worth recalling that the actors in Spenser's poetry may be treated as characters only up to a point; they also function as emblematic figures. As a character, Scudamour may be ambiguous; as a figure, he is clearer. He stands as both Amoret's fulfillment and her affliction. The question the narrator asks during Amoret's captivity in Busirane's castle – 'Ah who can love the worker of her smart?' (xii 31) – applies to Scudamour as well. Paradoxically, it applies to all passionate lovers: we must resent as well as adore the person who galvanizes us with such acute, sometimes painful, emotions.

Paired with Timias as Amoret is paired with Belphoebe, Scudamour participates in the exploration of the human psyche that those four lovers express as a group or as a set of allegorical 'characteristics.' The sum of the virtues of Scudamour and Timias approaches a whole and well-proportioned knight, just as the virtues of Amoret and Belphoebe are joined in the loving yet warlike Britomart. Scudamour and Amoret play leading roles in a masque of amorous vulnerability. Neither can fully overcome Busirane without Britomart's help. Neither can accept with mature equanimity what Britomart tells Scudamour, that 'life is wretchednesse' (xi 14); and both suffer, therefore, from a tendency to hysteria. On the other hand, their mutual devotion provides each with the strength to avoid final defeat. If they cannot vanquish Busirane, neither can he – as formidable as he is – vanquish them.

An embodiment of the ambivalence inherent in love, Scudamour serves as an apt explorer of the Temple of Venus, home of love's longing and fulfillment, eagerness and reticence. He constitutes an emblem of love's contradictions: its weakness and its strength, its ability to enrage and frustrate as well as to civilize and resolve. He remains paradoxical because, as Spenser and his contemporaries were acutely aware, love is paradoxical. Scudamour, to borrow a splendid phrase from James Nohrnberg (1976:478), portrays 'Love against Himself.'

Lesley Brill

sea For Spenser, as for other poets dealing with hexaemeral and cosmogonic themes, the sea is associated with the chaos from which all things emanate, and is identified, as in Virgil, with 'Ocean, father of the world'

(*Georgics* 4.382; cf Homer *Iliad* 18.607–8). Generally preferring the English *sea* to the Greco-Latin *ocean*, Spenser invokes 'the seas abundant progeny' (*FQ* IV xii 1), associating mythic creativity and concord with a setting which is also a center of historical and political allegory. For all their protean inconstancy, Spenser's seas are generally brought into a context of moral and social order, as in Colin's hymn to love (*Colin Clout* 857–60), or the paean to Venus and her ability to 'pacifie / The raging seas' (*FQ* IV x 44). Though part of the natural world, they are usually geographically vaguer than those of Homer, Virgil, and his other European models. Except for the procession in *FQ* IV xi, his references to the sea and ocean lack their sense of a world having a Mediterranean center. Even the Irish Sea of *Colin Clout* resembles the Fairyland sea confronted by Britomart, Marinell, and Florimell in being a generic 'world of waters' (197).

The sea enters Spenser's work in various rhetorical guises: as part of the psychic landscape of *The Faerie Queene* (*topothesia*), as part of the natural world being described (*topographia*; see *topographical description) or praised (*encomium*), in the form of allegorical personification (as with Marinell) or of mythical gods and goddesses figuring physical or symbolic aspects of the sea (eg, Proteus), and as a reservoir of Homeric similes and tropes whose obtrusiveness turns the reader's attention to the artist and his role as traveler and maker (*FQ* I xii 42, VI xii 1). Unlike rivers, which are benign and orderly manifestations of the element and give purpose to the sea, the sea itself is threatening, demanding that order be given to the amorphous material of nature and art.

Colin Clout provides a paradigm for Spenser's method. Working from confusion to recognition, the poem begins with an ignorant, inexperienced view of nature. Describing his initial fear in terms of warring elements, Colin presents the sea as a nightmarish mirror to the shepherd's world, with hills, wilderness, floods, and herds terrible to behold (196–211). The poem moves from this naive vision of nature to the inspired one embodied in the hymn to love where Colin reshapes these elements and submits experience to a poetic and mythic order that explains, and thus tames, fearful contrariety.

Colin's education begins when he meets his alter ego, the 'shepheard of the Ocean,' who navigates the world ruled by the goddess-like '*Cynthia* the Ladie of the sea' and her aquatic herdsmen. His encounter with the world of waters unfolds into a political allegory having its intellectual springs in a Neoplatonic cosmography. For Colin, the sea voyage to Cynthia's court is also a poetic journey, and, appropriately, his poem develops a protean quality as it assumes different forms: the historical, political, and physical allegory provide its various meanings; the hymn to love offers a transcendent view of nature and has its complement in the river epyllion; and its pastoral form makes it the first English version of a piscatorial eclogue.

In similar ways, the sea assumes a prominent place in the affective dimension of *The Faerie Queene*. Before Book III, references to the sea are chiefly limited to rhetorical tropes which adumbrate its ominous nature; an exception is Guyon's Odyssean voyage on 'that sea' which leads to Acrasia's bower (II xii 2–37). In Book III, however, the sea emerges from the rhetoric into a psychological landscape traveled by his characters and inhabited by gods and goddesses of the waters; it becomes one of the major meeting places of *The Faerie Queene*. In the sequence from Britomart's arrival at Marinell's strand (III iv 6), to Marinell's defeat and Florimell's abduction (vii 29), to their engagement (IV xii), Fairyland undergoes a sea change in which the watery element becomes the essence of setting, allegory, character, and action. Powerful, dangerous, fickle, and libidinous, a physical reminder of the need for restraint, the sea is an appropriate setting for the Books of Chastity and Temperance.

What were rhetorical tropes for earlier figures in the poem become for Britomart projections of her mind and desires. When she looks over the sea and complains of her sea of sorrows, her fearful seas of emotion are projected onto the Rich Strond itself in the form of Marinell's challenge. While her chastity must restrain her feelings as she looks at the throbbing sea, Marinell represents the other force that threatens to corrupt chastity, a sea-borne frigidity which stands in Aristotelian opposition to extreme concupiscence and manifests itself in his jealously guarding his jewels and, on his mother's advice, avoiding women. Throughout these episodes, the sea provides a context in which external and internal barriers are eroded and replaced by fertile, 'natural' emotional ties.

The domestic portrait of the sea in Book IV enlarges but remains true to other images of the sea in Spenser. Florimell, for example, flees to the 'roring shore' (III vii 27): her undisguised beauty makes her vulnerable to her own sexuality (as Britomart, for example, is not). But the haven of the sea proves a delusion: the aged Fisher becomes lecherous; she is rescued and then courted in turn by Proteus, 'Shepheard of the seas of yore' (viii 23–30). Florimell's perpetual harassment by denizens of the sea underscores the importance of Britomart's masculine disguise.

The psychological torment of Britomart, Florimell, and Marinell is explicitly identified with the sea and its deities, albeit in the mode of domestic comedy. Cymodoce's troubles with her son and Florimell's with her future in-laws show the process by which the sea must be tamed (as Cynthia tames it in *Colin Clout*), Proteus controlled, and the more benign authority of Nereus and Neptune imposed over the sea. The book culminates in the poem's largest image of order: the marriage of Thames and Medway. In the procession, moving as it does from the grand gods of the watery element to the sea gods tamed by space and history, to the powerful river gods, and then to local rivers located in the immediate present, we see a channeling of the sea occasioned by the ordering institution of marriage. It provides the immediate narrative frame for the reconciliation of Marinell and Florimell, who discover their psychological compatibility, and in whose names we again see the two worlds of water and land. Born of the sea (as we are reminded in IV xii 2), and borne on it, love's force in nature is complex and protean, but capable of being brought within the ken of the Orphic poet and his educated reader. W.H. Herendeen

Alexander Falconer 1964 *Shakespeare and the Sea* (New York); Herendeen 1986; Murtaugh 1973; K. Williams 1970–1.

senses, five The five senses supply sense data from which our faculty of judgment constructs an image of the world (see *memory, *psychology), and to that extent they are indispensable. But as inhabitants of a fallen world whose prince is Satan, we are corruptible by the fallacious reports, especially the pleasant ones, which our senses provide, and likely to forget that sensuous delights are transient and delusive. 'First learne your outward sences to refraine / From things, that stirre up fraile affection,' the Hermit advises Timias and Serena, 'For from those outward sences ill affected, / The seede of all this evill first doth spring' (*FQ* VI vi 7–8). Much of what our senses supply neutrally as information is construed inwardly as temptation, resistance to which is always praiseworthy and sometimes heroic. Given our readiness (in Henry Vaughan's words) 'to dispence / A sev'rall sinne to ev'ry sence' ('The Retreate'), indulgence in the senses is spiritual self-abuse.

Mediating between our souls and the world, our senses fall prey to Satan, who sometimes seduces them and sometimes takes them by force. Each possibility results in a different model of the threat. Temptation is imagined accordingly either as a 'banquet of sense' (at which we undergo systematic provocations of our visual, auditory, olfactory, gustatory, and tactile senses) or as a martial assault on our embattled bodies which are placed consequently under siege conditions by Satan's cohorts. Unlike Guyon, Cymochles succumbs intemperately to a typical 'banquet' in the Bower of Bliss when, smelling the 'daintie odours' of roses and eglantine, and listening to the 'chearefull harmonie' of birdsong, he feasts his eyes on 'a flocke of Damzels' who, in provocative *déshabillé*, excite his senses of taste and touch (those instruments of base carnality) with the 'sugred licour' of their kisses (II v 29–33). The alternative model for temptation is found in the house of Alma episode (ix-xi), where the human body is conceived of as a 'castle' in which the soul (Alma) resides, and which has been under 'long siege' from a 'thousand enemies' (ix 12) led by Maleger (xi 23), an emanation of original sin. Each of the five senses constitutes a 'Bulwarke' of the castellated body, and each is under constant attack by 'fowle misshapen wights' (xi 7–8) who resemble creatures associated emblematically with that particular sense. Relief comes only through the intervention of divine grace.

A more positive response to the senses, however, is expressed in *Amoretti-Epithalamion*, where the lover anticipates 'the bowre of blisse' in his lady (*Am* 76) and his enjoyment of 'her paradise of joyes' after their marriage (*Epith* 366). K.K. RUTHVEN

Barkan 1975; Kermode 1971:84–115; Carl Nordenfalk 1985 'The Five Senses in Late Medieval and Renaissance Art' *JWCI* 48:1–22; *Var* 2:456–7.

Serena The narrative of Serena and Calepine occupies much of the middle of *FQ* VI. They first appear when Calidore stumbles upon their secret dalliance (iii 20). While he apologizes for his intrusion, Serena wanders into a flowery field where she is caught and wounded by the Blatant Beast, then rescued by Calidore (21–6). Calepine seeks 'some place of rest' and 'safe assuraunce' (28) where her wounds may heal. When the shameful Turpine not only refuses to help her but also wounds him, both are rescued by the Salvage Man, who succours them and offers temporary haven. Although Calepine is cured, Serena is not. Again separated from him, she sets out with the faithful Salvage 'To seeke some comfort' (v 7) and meets Arthur together with his squire, Timias, also wounded by the Blatant Beast. Arthur takes them to a Hermit; by following his advice, she is cured. She and Timias set out together and encounter Mirabella being punished by Disdain and Scorn. When Timias falls under Disdain's iron club, Serena flees once more 'To seeke for safety, which long time she sought' (vii 50). In canto viii, she falls asleep and is captured by cannibals who strip her naked and prepare to sacrifice her in an elaborate ritual. Amidst their 'divelish ceremonies' (viii 45), Calepine arrives and rescues her again. The narrative concludes with the lovers once more united, although in the darkness he fails to recognize her and she is too ashamed to reveal who she is.

Spenser seems to have been undecided about Serena's name: some copies of the 1596 *Faerie Queene* call her Crispina at VI iii 23, and in all copies she is called Matilda in the argument to canto v. The fair and tranquil (from L *serenus*) virgin who wanders in a flowery field is, like her mythic analogues Proserpina and Eurydice, captured by a subhuman creature, threatened with ravishment and death, and apparently rescued from darkness and despair. As myth, then, the narrative presents the threat of cannibalism as a *sparagmos* or ritual death preparatory to the desired reunion (Frye 1957:192–3).

Spenser's story may derive from Achilles Tatius' *Clitophon and Leucippe*, but it is shaped by the popular sixteenth-century romance motif of the calumniated mistress: an innocent maiden is falsely accused, suffers shame and scorn, is separated from her beloved and undergoes a kind of 'death,' but finally is reunited with him (cf the story of Phedon and Pryene in II iv). Ariosto's story of Ariodante and Ginevra is one version of the type (*Orlando furioso* 5); Shakespeare's *Much Ado about Nothing* is a second. Another possible source is *Ariodante and Genevora*, a play presented before the Queen in 1583 by Spenser's tutor at Merchant Taylors' School, Richard Mulcaster.

Spenser's interest in Serena is both psychological and social. From the first incident in which she is 'abasht' to the last in which she is 'shame[d],' she is an ironically untranquil innocent who needs constant 'gard' and 'comfort.' Although she is seriously threatened only at the beginning and end of her adventure, her story is interlaced with incidents displaying varying degrees of discourtesy: the ambush of Timias by Despetto, Decetto, and Defetto (v); and Mirabella's public humiliation by Disdain and Scorn (vii-viii). In each incident, a private fear of exposure is matched by a fear of public disgrace, and a natural desire to withdraw into a 'covert shade ... To solace ... in delight' (iii 20) is a prelude to embarrassment. Accordingly, Serena's inwardly festering wound represents the psychological effects of this fear of social victimizing.

If Timias is partly a fictionalized portrait of Raleigh and his wife, Elizabeth Throckmorton, whom Raleigh called Serena, the social basis of her discomfort is clear. Always threatened when she moves from cover of any kind into the open, her predicament illustrates the persistent danger of public slander. This may explain part of the Hermit's 'cure': 'Shun secresie, and talke in open sight' (vi 14).

As a vulnerable beauty in need of continual protection, Serena offers positive lessons in social compassion. Calidore, the Salvage Man, Arthur, the Hermit, and Calepine all take turns guarding and comforting her. Such protectiveness seems very close to the heart of Spenser's notion of human courtesy; but insofar as her story is read as a version of the romance motif of 'beauties chace' (III i 19), it also depicts a parody of such courtesy. As the object of this quest, Serena is twice seen as a fleshly morsel to be consumed. From her initial wound by the Blatant Beast's 'wide great mouth' to the cannibals' final threat, her story charts an inversion of the usual sensory ascent in quest of beauty.

Such a corruption of beauty (associated with the highest sense, sight) into physical food (incited by the lower sense, taste) is common to romance and may derive from the Proserpina myth. Analogues in *The Faerie Queene* include the hyena that feeds on woman's flesh (III vii), Lust (IV vii), and Corflambo (IV viii). In the episode with the cannibals, this perversion is carefully staged. These savages begin, much as any would-be lover, reveling in the sight of Serena's shining face (viii 37); but the conventional adoration of beauty quickly degenerates into a debate over whether she will serve for one meal or many. As Serena is stripped naked, Spenser employs an Elizabethan blazon to praise the various parts of the lady's body, only to pervert that blazon by having the cannibals' leers convert 'dainty flesh' to 'common feast' (38).

In effect, Spenser here grotesquely literalizes the feeding imagery by which Elizabethan writers expressed beauty's attraction. To feast our eyes on beauty may well be the object of our quest, Spenser implies, but such language betrays a gluttonous voyeurism that deforms woman into sexual object, spiritual gazing into lascivious leering, and human courtesy into discourtesy. The naked Serena surrounded by shrieking cannibals parodies and perverts not only Una among the savages in *FQ* I vi and Pastorella among the shepherds in VI ix but especially the climactic vision of the dance of the Graces in VI x. The connection is made explicit by Calidore's second intrusion, but other parallels are implicit: the stately pavilion of Acidale, the shepherd's joyful piping, the innocent singing and dancing of the hundred naked maidens, the one that 'Seem'd all the rest in beauty to excell' who stands 'in the midst' to receive their ceremonial flowers (x 10–17) – each detail of the Acidalian vision is both foreshadowed and perverted in the cannibals' obscene rite. Most striking, perhaps, is the contrast between the lovers: Colin's mistress graces him as he in turn 'pype[s] apace' to make a Grace of her, whereas Serena sits in shamed and disgraced silence refusing to respond to her lover even as he is incapable, in the darkness, of recognizing her.

Although Calepine and Serena are together again at the end of canto viii, the discourtesies each has experienced preclude a joyful reunion. Such anticlimax suits Spenser's own narrative purposes, for out of their failure to achieve complete integration he sets the stage, as it were, for the poem's ultimate emblem of joyous harmony and courteous concord in the visionary dance of the Graces on Mount Acidale.

A. LEIGH DENEEF

Cheney 1966; Frye 1957; McNeir 1968; Staton 1966; Tonkin 1972.

sestina A complex verse form invented by the Provençal poet Arnaut Daniel and employed by Dante and Petrarch; it appears in England in the sixteenth century as part of the Petrarchan lyric mode. The form was not often used by English poets, but Sidney experimented with it in his *Old Arcadia* (70, 71, 76 in ed 1962); and his double sestina (71) led Barnabe Barnes to attempt a triple one in *Parthenophil and Parthenophe* (1593; ed 1971:127–30). Puttenham's description (under *seizino*) gives little idea of the form's complexity, though he does warn that the 'restraint to make the dittie sensible will try the makers cunning' (*Arte of English Poesie* 2.10). Such modern poets as Eliot, Pound, and Auden revived the sestina; and Empson called attention to its possibilities when he discussed its use by Sidney (1930:45–50).

The sestina is composed of 39 lines in six strophes (or stanzas) of six unrhymed lines each, plus an envoy or turn (*tornada*) of three lines. The concluding words of the six lines in the first strophe are rearranged for subsequent strophes in an order rigorously determined by the Provençal troubadours. If numbered 1 2 3 4 5 6 for one strophe, the end words of the next strophe form the sequence 6 1 5 2 4 3. Thus, the six strophes successively end 123456, 615243, 364125, 532614, 451362, and 246531. In the concluding three-line envoy or turn, all six end words are repeated medially and finally, usually though not always in the order of their first appearance (as would be dictated for a seventh strophe in the sequence).

Spenser's only example of the form, Colin's lament in *SC, August* 151–89, is an imitation of a poem by Sannazaro, by way of Sidney (see Harrison 1930:715, Ringler in Sidney ed 1962:416). He adheres to the traditional purpose of the sestina in using it as a vehicle for complaint, to which the form is well suited in view of its plangent repetition of the same words in each successive strophe. The poem is innovative, however, in its frequent run-on lines and its use of energetic verbs (*resound, augment*) as end words. The conflict between forces for change and permanence challenges previous notions of what constitutes a sestina. As Webbe remarks, 'Looke uppon the rufull song of *Colin* sung by *Cuddie* in the *Sheepheardes Calender*, where you shall see a singuler rare devise of a dittie framed upon these sixe wordes *Woe, sounde, cryes, part, sleep, augment*, which are most prettilie turned and wounde uppe mutually together, expressing wonderfully the dolefulnesse of the song' (*A Discourse of English Poetrie* 1586; in G.G. Smith 1904, 1:276). Following the precedent of the Spaniard Gutierre de Cetina (1518–54), he breaks with the conventional order of the end words, so that each successive strophe follows the simpler pattern of 6 1 2 3 4 5. (By way of homage, he translates one of Cetina's end words, *quejas* 'cries.')

The tendency of Spenser's sestina toward run-on lines reaches its climax, significantly, in lines 168–9, at the boundary between the third and fourth stanzas, midway through the six stanzas of the sestina proper: 'When I them see so waist, and fynd no part / Of pleasure past. Here will I dwell apart.' The inability to participate in past joys drives the speaker to apartness and grief in the future. The sixth stanza leads him to a new kind of participation and harmony with nature: 'Hence with the Nightingale will I take part' (183).

Traditionally, the sestina has seemed appropriate to the pastoral setting, inasmuch as the patterned, cyclical sequence of its permutations is suggestive of the passage of the seasons and their reflection in the topography of the mind. In this respect, the form could speak directly to Spenser's recurrent concern for the rhythms of the human and natural worlds, and for the echo he sought to make resonate between them, in joy (as with *Epithalamion*) and in Colin's lovelorn state as well, where 'The forest wide is fitter to resound / The hollow Echo of my carefull cryes' (159–60).

Furthermore, earlier practitioners of the sestina had capitalized on the mythological and Christian significances of the numbers six and seven which figure prominently in the form (without and with the envoy, respectively); not only the figure of the poet merging with the landscape (as Petrarch had meditated on that figure in his poems to Laura-as-Daphne, transformed into the laurel branch), but the weekly rhythm of labors and repose could be found by Spenser in the sestina. Frye has called attention to such hexaemeral groupings in the uncompleted *Faerie Queene*: 'There are six books, and Spenser has a curious fondness for mentioning the number six ... In most of these groups there is a crucial seventh, and perhaps the *Mutabilitie Cantos* have that function in the total scheme of the epic ... The poem brings us to the poet's "Sabbath's sight" after his six great efforts of creation, and there is nothing which at any point can be properly described as "unperfite"' (1963:70–1). Although Spenser had at first proposed a 12- or 24-book poem, in accordance with his epic models, he ended by settling for fewer; and in his sixth book, he returned to the figure of Colin Clout and the pastoral setting. In its calendrical symbolism, and its systematic use of interlace to suggest the persistence of pattern triumphing over change, the sestina would have offered him a miniaturized lyric model for the patterns and resolutions of the myths of romance.

MARIANNE SHAPIRO

Empson 1930; Thomas Perrin Harrison, Jr 1930 'The Relations of Sidney and Spenser' *PMLA* 45:712–31; Shapiro 1980; Spanos 1978.

sex *The Faerie Queene* is the most extended and extensive meditation on sex in the history of European poetry. It charts the full range of human erotic experience, constructing a moral great chain of being from matter to spirit, from the coarsest outbreaks of gross lust to the most elevated refinements of chastity and romantic idealism. Its sexual theme is analogous to its political allegory: the psyche, like society, must be disciplined by good government, or 'justice.' Spenser agrees with classical and Christian philosophers on the primacy of reason over the animal appetites. He anticipates the Romantic poets, however, in showing the sexual impulse as potentially daemonic and barbaric, breeding entrancing witches and sorcerers of evil allure. Like the *Odyssey*, *The Faerie Queene* is a heroic epic in which the masculine must evade female entrapments or delays. But there are two millennia between Homer and Spenser, a history of rising and falling urban culture. In its representation of sex, *The Faerie Queene* absorbs and surpasses its classical and continental sources by its attentiveness to moral and political lessons. Spenser ponders how love is affected by worldly manners, how it is embellished or distorted by the artificiality of courts. Hence sex in *The Faerie Queene* reaches extremes of decadent sophistication not present in literature since Roman satire and never in the genre of epic.

The premiere sexual principle of *The Faerie Queene* is marriage, which in the Renaissance supplanted medieval courtly love, or adultery, as a literary motif, an evolution in which Spenser was instrumental. In the Renaissance, the idea of social order or hierarchy had great prestige. Marriage is the social regulation and placement of sexual energies, which for Spenser otherwise tend toward the anarchic. It is sex harnessed for history, which moves gloriously toward British destiny and the Elizabethan monarchy. In *The Faerie Queene*, marriage appears largely as betrothal, the preliminary state of testing, training, and purification – courtship conceived as moral education. As a quest-romance, the poem is concerned with aspiration and expectation, not with completion. Perhaps in his ambitious original plan, Spenser reserved the perfection of marriage for his climax at the court of the Fairy Queen, an apotheosis of multiple nuptials like those ending Shakespeare's comedies.

Sex in Spenser therefore must always have a social goal. Marriage, moreover, is the sanctified link between nature and society. Among the great artists of the Renaissance, Spenser is paralleled only by Leonardo da Vinci in his broodings upon the secrets of nature, which he honors (quite unlike Shakespeare) for its female fertility. Spenser repeatedly imagines the earth as a fruitful mother, the paradigm of human womanliness in marriage. His vision of great Dame Nature, the ancient Magna Mater, in the Temple of Venus (IV x) and Isis Church (V vii) is unique for Renaissance genius, and it ties him once more to Romanticism, to the myths of fertility in Wordsworth and Keats.

In *The Faerie Queene*, the omphalos-spot of earthly fertility is located in the Gardens of Adonis, a womb-world of perpetual inception and growth with overtly sexualized geography, its 'stately Mount' and odorous dripping boughs the mons veneris of procreative nature (III vi 43). Fertility is so dominant an image that it even controls chastity in Spenser, whose personification of that virtue, Britomart, is to be the mother of a whole race of royal progeny, as foretold by Merlin (iii). The abundance and exuberance of wifely fecundity are displayed by Charissa, a daughter of the house of Holiness, with her ever-bare breasts and 'multitude of babes' playing about her (I x 31). She is an antitype of falsely fertile intellectualized Error, who vomits an abortive pregnancy of books, papers, and toads and whose thousand progeny suck up her blood and burst (I i). Similarly, the malign Duessa has 'dried dugs' and deformed genitals (viii 47–8), signifying the sterility of sin.

Spenser's theory of sex is a continuum from normative to aberrant. Chastity and fruitful marriage occupy one pole, after which the modalities of eroticism darken toward the perverse and monstrous. First in blame is what we would call recreational sex, heterosexual impulses hedonistically squandered. A series of indecorously aggressive females is prominent here: Duessa (a version of the biblical Whore of Babylon), Acrasia, Phaedria, Malecasta, and Hellenore. They draw their male victims and paramours away from the pursuit of chivalric honor into 'lewd slouth' (III v 1), a languid indolence and passivity in which spiritual commitment is lost. Such sex is sterile because self-thwarting; heroic energies are literally dissolved and dissipated. Spenser is the anatomist of an economy of sex, of physiological laws of pressure and control, which he embodies in frequent images of binding and loosing. As an epic, predicated on masculine action, *The Faerie Queene* must oppose random sex in order to keep its heroes in a state of wakeful readiness. For Spenser, the martial and moral wills are identical.

The lascivious women of *The Faerie Queene*, manipulative and exploitative, triumph over men in a sexual victory which justice cannot tolerate. Their greatest power is in womblike closed spaces, in dens, caves, and groves like the lush grotto of Homer's Calypso, where the male is captured, seduced, and infantilized. The Bower of Bliss, wrathfully destroyed by Guyon, is the most lavishly depicted of these female zones, which express the invitation and yet archetypal danger of sex. At the gate of the bower, Excess, a 'comely dame' in disordered clothes, crushes scrotal grape clusters (a Dionysian cult symbol) into a vaginal cup of gold, the male squeezed dry for female pleasure (II xii 55–6). At the heart of the humid bower is enthroned the Circean sorceress Acrasia, hungrily hovering over the recumbent Verdant, enervated and depleted, his arms abandoned and defaced. These affronts to the correct hierarchical relation between the sexes reach their height in Artegall's capitulation to the Amazon Radigund, who dresses him in female clothing and makes him do women's work, like Hercules under the sway of Omphale (V v). Female beauty, by which Artegall is suddenly unmanned, blinds and drugs Spenser's unwary knights and leads them into the imprisoning bower, where the directing soul is overcome by sensuality.

There is a sex war for dominance continually going on in *The Faerie Queene*, a pattern of love debased into the will-to-power. Spenser anticipates Blake, Sade, Nietzsche, and Freud in his shrewd analysis of the psychodynamics of eroticism. Lust is the medium by which each sex strives to subjugate the other. It is personified in several forms: as Lechery riding a goat in the procession of vices (I iv 24), as the lawless knight Sansloy (vi), as enemies of Temperance besieging the sense of touch (II xi 13), and as the grotesque predator Lust, all fangs, nose, and pouchy ears, a walking phallic symbol (IV vii). As a state into which any of the virtuous characters may fall, lust is allegorically projected as a series of felons, cads, and sybarites who use deception, force, or magic to have their way. One of the cardinal events of *The Faerie Queene* is rape, which appears in dozens of forms, real or fabricated. The maidens Una, Belphoebe, Florimell, Amoret, Samient, and Serena are attacked once or repeatedly by rapists. Children born of a rape include Merlin, the knights Satyrane and Marinell, and the chivalric triplets Triamond, Priamond, and Diamond. Males too fall victim to rape, kidnapped by the giantess Argante, her brother Ollyphant, and Jove himself (III vii, xi). Even avarice is imagined as rape, the sacrilegious wounding of the 'quiet wombe' of the earth mother for tinselly silver and gold (II vii 17).

The rape cycle of *The Faerie Queene* is one of the most advanced rhetorical structures in Renaissance poetry. The masculine hurls itself at the feminine in an eternal circle of pursuit and flight, a maelstrom of voracity. Lust and his agents, like the hyena monster which the witch-hag sends after Florimell (III vii 22), literally feed on women's flesh. Woman is meat, and the penis, symbolized by the oak clubs brandished by Orgoglio and Lust, is a thing, a weapon. In Spenser's prescient panoramic vision, sex war is a Darwinian spectacle of nature red in tooth and claw, of the eaters and the eaten. The culmination of this theme appears in Book VI, where Serena is stripped and appreciatively manhandled by slavering cannibals and where Pastorella, lusted after by brigands, is embraced and entangled in a heap of corpses, a victory of matter over spirit (viii, xi). Serena's thighs are like 'a triumphall Arch' hung with 'The spoiles of Princes' (viii 42): woman is booty and trophy, the prize of venery, prey of the traditional amorous hunt by which the sexes are kept in antagonistic relation.

The cruelly turbulent nature into which humanity so easily sinks in *The Faerie Queene* is not the maternal nest of the Gardens of Adonis but a hell of violence and insatiable appetite. Here Spenser is closest not to Rousseau and Wordsworth, with their tender naturism, but to the Blake of 'The Mental Traveller' and to Sade and his late Romantic heirs of the French and English Decadence. However, Spenser insists that humanity can and must escape the vicious circle of sexual strife through individual effort, a personal heroism. By internalizing and harmonizing sexual powers, the virtuous characters of *The Faerie Queene* combat fallen nature, in which the female vampire invades and drains maleness and the male rapist attacks and annihilates femaleness. The optimal psychic state is androgynous.

Spenser is drawn to the classical myth of the Hermaphrodite and uses it in many ways. His mother-goddess figures are persistently double-sexed. In her veiled cult image, Venus is shown 'Both male and female,' 'syre and mother,' begetting and conceiving (IV x 41), a point made differently in *Colin Clouts Come Home Againe* (801–2). Likewise, in the *Cantos of Mutabilitie*, great Dame Nature is veiled to disguise her mysterious true gender (VII vii 5). The 'long white sclender wand' of the idol in Isis Church may also be a masculine motif (V vii 7). Venus calls her son Cupid nymphlike, shortly before old Genius, porter of the Gardens of Adonis, is identified as having 'a double nature' (III vi 23, 31). Finally, in the five stanzas concluding the 1590 *Faerie Queene*, later canceled, the embracing Amoret and Scudamour are compared to a Roman statue of 'faire *Hermaphrodite*.' Spenserian eroticism blends the sexes, in a religious symbolism which purposefully conflates pagan and Christian. In moral terms, *The Faerie Queene* posits the hermaphroditic self as most complete. The male, like Artegall, is rescued from brutishness by feminizing or socializing 'courtesie,' civilization in the making. The female, like Belphoebe and Britomart, renouncing dominance in the boudoir and masochistic vulnerability in the field, is endowed with masculine arms of war, by which she defends herself against rape and pursues her own spiritual quest.

Without tempering and redemptive transformation, Spenser suggests, the sexes are swept into the chaos of libido, for which there was ample symbolism available in the long but increasingly stereotyped Petrarchan tradition. The fire, smoke, and whirlwind of the house of Busirane (III xi-xii) signify the self-torturing emotional storms to which the Petrarchan lover surrenders himself. Spenser seizes upon the sado-masochism implicit in Petrarchan love and develops it to extraordinary length. Love as a sickness or wound: Spenser dissects and diagnoses this received idea as itself diseased. The sexual wounds of *The Faerie Queene* are abundant, beginning with the prototypical gored thigh of Adonis, depicted in a tapestry in the ill-famed Castle Joyous, whose mistress Malecasta is seared with the poisonous fire of lust (III i). Here even Britomart, her side grazed by an arrow, sheds blood of a possibly initiatory meaning. The lustful Cymochles is wounded in the thigh by Arthur, as are Timias by the fosters and Artegall by Radigund (II viii, III v, V v). The Blatant Beast makes putrefying wounds of sexual infamy in the bodies of Timias and Serena (VI v-vi). Pastorella is lanced by the death wound of her amorous brigand kidnapper (xi). Claribell, rejecting her father's authority, is pierced by a 'secret wound / Of love' for Bellamour, which leads to imprisonment, fornication, and pregnancy (xii 4–6). The most spectacular of the erotic traumas of *The Faerie Queene* occurs when, with naked sexual symbolism, the sorcerer Busirane slashes open the breast of Amoret and from the 'wide orifice' extracts her living heart, laying it quivering in a silver baṣin (III xii 20–1). Amoret, by her own spiritual limitations, may have brought this morbid scene of martyrdom into being, as an extrapolation or projection of her internal state.

Spenser appears to feel that convention leads lovers to confuse sex with self-immolation and that love is therefore corrupted by what Freud calls the death instinct, pernicious in *The Faerie Queene* because it frustrates the fertility of creative nature. This belief would account for some of the most troublesome details of the poem: passages of lurid sado-masochistic spectacle unparalleled in English literature until the late Romanticism of Swinburne and Emily Dickinson. Prefiguring Amoret in the house of Busirane is the suicide Amavia, found still conscious by Guyon with a knife in her riven 'white alabaster brest'; next to her is the corpse of Mortdant, bloody but smiling and, according to the poem, still sexually irresistible (II i 39, 41). Proud Mirabella, having tortured her admirers and laughed at their sufferings and death, is subsequently punished by being whipped along by Scorn, who laughs at her cries (VI vii 44). Artegall finds a headless lady, murdered by her knight, Sangliere, who is forced to bear her dead head as a penalty (V i). Talus chops off and nails up the gold hands and silver feet of beautiful Munera, or self-worshiping money (ii 26). Even allowing for the exigencies of allegory, such combinations in Spenser of beauty, laughter, sex, torture, mutilation, and death are emotionally startling and ethically problematic.

In its treatment of the vagaries of sexual desire, licit and illicit, *The Faerie Queene* seems motivated by an encyclopedic impulse, like Krafft-Ebing's *Psychopathia Sexualis*. As a catalog of perversions, it follows directly or indirectly from Ovid's *Metamorphoses*, which vastly influenced Renaissance culture.

Incest: the giants Argante and Ollyphant, children of the incestuous connection of the Titan Typhoeus with his mother Earth, have intercourse in the womb and are born coupling (III vii 47–9). Avarice's rape of the earth is also incestuous (II vii 17). In her instruction of Britomart, Glauce mentions the incestuous crimes of Myrrha and Biblis, who 'lov'd their native flesh against all kind' (III ii 41).

Bestiality: Argante's lusts extend to animals (vii 49). Hellenore becomes the common property of priapic satyrs and, to her husband's dismay, likes it (x). Lust hunts and assaults beasts as well as humans (IV vii 5). Glauce cites Pasiphaë as the ancient model of this 'monstrous' sin, and the tapestries of the house of Busirane show Jove, Phoebus, and Neptune in their many randy incarnations as ram, bull, swan, eagle, serpent, lion, stag, falcon, steer, dolphin, and horse (III ii 41, xi 29–43).

Next, homosexuality: Ollyphant is greedily pursuing a boy when Britomart intervenes (xi). The wicked spirit who becomes the false Florimell is a fawning, epicene female impersonator (viii 8). Jove lusts for Ganymede and Phoebus for Hyacinthus (xi 34, 37). In *The Shepheardes Calender*, Hobbinol pays court to Colin Clout, Spenser's alter ego, but pederasty is refuted by the gloss as 'disorderly love' (*Jan*, *Apr*). Sodomy of a heterosexual kind is implied in the nymphomaniac Argante's kidnapping of young men (vii 50). A lesbian piquancy like that of Ingres' steamy *Turkish Bath* is latent in the wrestling of the naked damsels in the fountain of the Bower of Bliss (II xii 63–4). Lesbian overtones, produced by Spenser's curiously connoisseurlike detachment, also perhaps inadvertently occur in scenes where the wanton Malecasta stealthily enters Britomart's bed (III i 60–1), where Glauce embraces and massages the lovelorn Britomart (ii 34, 42), where Britomart is carried away by her male impersonation and compromises the fearful Amoret, and where Claribell bizarrely rips open the bodice of her long-lost daughter Pastorella (IV i 7–8, 15–16, 49; V 20).

Transvestism: the principal transvestite of *The Faerie Queene* is the warrior Britomart, who even undergoes a double sex change in her dream in Isis Church, where she is first priest and then goddess (V vii 13). Several times the poem takes the sexual point of view of deceived observers, referring to Britomart as *he* and *him* (III i 4–6, ix 12–16, IV iv 43–6). In her eruption of archaic Amazonism, Radigund imposes compulsory transvestism on her male victims, notably Artegall, who emasculates himself by casting away his sword (V iv-v). Malbecco's degradation is suggested by his delusion that the 'womanish' Trompart is his Hellenore (III x 21). Venus conjectures Cupid is masquerading as one of Diana's handmaidens (vi 23). Genius, porter of the Bower of Bliss, is ambiguously dressed in half-feminine robes, accentuated by his weak presentation of the phallic staff of office (II xii 46–8). The witch-hag decks a male demon in Florimell's garments (III viii 5–9), and it would be difficult to say, even with our modern terminology of gender, whether the resultant false Florimell is a transvestite or a transsexual. Correspondingly, the sorcerer Archimago alchemizes a male spirit into a lady clad in Una's costume, sending him/her as a wet dream to the sleeping Red Cross Knight and then staging a malicious mummery or sexual fiction which convinces Redcrosse of Una's unchasteness (I i 45–8, ii 3–5). Transsexualism in the poem is therefore alternately daemonic and benign, a theatrical compounding of the fluidities of Spenserian gender.

A recurrent sado-masochistic motif of *The Faerie Queene* is sexual bondage, one of the enduring special tastes of the erotic underground from antiquity to the present. Language of captivity and enslavement, chains and snares is used for the sexual subordination of Thyamis to her satyr rapist (I vi 22–3); of Mortdant, Cymochles, and Verdant to Acrasia (II i 54, v 27, xii 76–82); of the Squire of Dames to Argante (III vii 50–1); of Amoret to Busirane (xi-xii); of Florimell to Proteus (viii 41–2, IV xi 1–4); of Terpine to the Amazons (V iv 22); of Artegall to Radigund (v-vii); and of Pastorella to the brigand captain (VI x 40–4, xi 1–5). Hellenore's sylvan concubinage and Claribell's paternal incarceration are analogous because partly self-induced or preserved. Sexual bondage in *The Faerie Queene* belongs to a group of larger themes of order and anarchy, imprisonment and liberation. Hierarchy and ceremony, radiations of the great chain of being and master principles of Renaissance culture, are criminally distorted when dominance and submission are illegitimately transferred to the sexual realm. Bondage is a daemonic antimasque, the uncontrolled sexual fantasy of morally secessionist authoritarians. Ultimately, all the sexual chains of *The Faerie Queene* are Blake's 'mind-forg'd manacles': the prison cell is the self, and freedom is a matter of right apprehension and choice.

Autoeroticism: another pathological category is flight from sex, manifested as either sexual fear or frigidity, incorporated by Spenser in a theory of narcissism that is psychoanalytically pioneering. Self-withholding becomes autoeroticism, a pool of psychic stagnancy in which the fire of heroic aspiration is quenched. Again, the self is a prison, curtailing epic travel and quest. In the house of Pride, the maiden queen Lucifera presides from a throne while raptly gazing at herself in her hand mirror, 'And in her selfe-lov'd semblance tooke delight' (I iv 10). In her rudderless boat, Phaedria eerily laughs and sings to herself, 'Making sweet solace to her selfe alone' (II vi 3). The reclusive Mammon sits in onanistic obsession, toying with 'a masse of coyne' in his lap, his sole object of 'covetous desire' (vii 4). Marinell is warned by his oversolicitous mother to avoid women and love, since he is fated to die by the hand of a woman (III iv). Symmetrically, he is loved by Florimell, who flees everyone and everything, dashing across the sightlines of the poem in a swoon of hysterical withdrawal. Like Lucifera, Mirabella is guilty of 'stubborne pride' and refuses all suitors because she craves perpetual praise: 'To love my selfe I learned had in schoole' (VI vii 36, viii 21). Similarly, Pastorella, secretly prompted by her princely blood, spurns her shepherd swains, for which she will suffer the indignities of her squalid brigand adventure.

In this poem which values confrontation, conflict, and engagement, cautious self-withholding is penalized for its sterile exclusivity. Even Britomart, because of her hermaphroditic completeness, must beware a complacent self-sufficiency. After seeing her destined husband Artegall in Venus' mirror, an armed knight like her future self, she compares herself to Narcissus gazing into the fountain. But Glauce demurs: 'Nought like (quoth she) for that same wretched boy / Was of himselfe the idle Paramoure; / Both love and lover, without hope of joy' (III ii 17, 18, 45). Narcissism is *idleness*, a big word in Spenser. In self-love there is no energy of duality and therefore no spiritual progression. As a poem of marriage, *The Faerie Queene* is devoted to the fertile conjunction of opposites. Autoeroticism, self-abuse both literally and figuratively, inhibits the enlargement and multiplication of emotion in marriage and therefore the investment of psychic energy in the public structures of history.

Voyeurism or skeptophilia is one of the poem's most characteristic moods. An observer is posted by chance or choice at the perimeter of a voluptuous sexual scene, to which he plays peeping Tom. Voyeuristic elements are present in the episode of Phedon and Philemon, where a credulous squire is made to observe a sexual charade defaming his bride (II iv). They are rampant in the Bower of Bliss, where Cymochles peruses a bevy of half-naked damsels, ogling them through deceptively half-closed lids; where the lady wrestlers expose themselves to the distinctly interested Guyon; and where the flimsily garbed Acrasia fastens 'her false eyes' on the postcoital Verdant, a scene repeated in the tapestry of Venus and Adonis in Castle Joyous (V 32–4, xii 73; III i 34–7). At Malbecco's banquet, Hellenore and Paridell arouse each other by brazen eye-contact and a lewd sexual theater of spilled wine, a voyeurism to resurface in Malbecco's plight as a hidden spectator of the debauchment of his wife, who is mounted by a satyr nine times in a single night (ix, x). The sleeping Serena is inspected by a tribe of cannibals, who seat themselves like an audience and judiciously weigh the merits of each part of her body (VI viii). On Mount Acidale, Calidore stumbles upon the dazzling scene of a hundred naked maidens dancing in a ring, Spenser's supreme symbol for the harmony of nature and art (x). In the *Cantos of Mutabilitie*, Faunus, like Actaeon, is punished for bawdily witnessing the nude Diana at her bath (VII vi 42–55). Cumulatively, these episodes surely inspired the voyeuristic spying of Milton's Satan on Adam and Eve in the Garden of Eden, a motif without biblical precedent.

The voyeurism of *The Faerie Queene*, which endangers the poem itself, arises from the problem of sensuous beauty, which can lead the soul toward good or toward evil. The power of the eye is exceptionally intense in Spenser, who is a pictorialist, unlike his contemporary Shakespeare, a dramaturge little attracted to the *objet d'art*. Spenser compensates for the lesser achievement in the visual arts of the English as opposed to Italian Renaissance by his brilliant aestheticism, his iconic epiphanies, painterly *tableaux vivants*, and cinematic illusions. Allegory, which is thought visualized, draws Spenser into morally ambiguous territory: perception leads to knowledge but not necessarily to virtue. *The Faerie Queene* often becomes what it condemns, nowhere more overtly than in the issue of voyeurism, in which both poet and reader are deeply implicated.

There has been and will continue to be controversy about the nature and status of sex in *The Faerie Queene*. Most criticism assumes that what Spenser says is what he means. But a poet is not always master of his own poem, for imagination can overwhelm moral intention. Some of the poetically strongest and most fully realized material in *The Faerie Queene* is pornographic. Like Blake's Milton, Spenser may be of the devil's party without knowing it. In a paradox cherished by Sade and Baudelaire, the presence of moral law or taboo intensifies the pleasure of sexual transgression and the luxury of evil. A great poet always has profound ambivalences and obscurities of motivation, which criticism has scarcely begun to study in this case. *The Faerie Queene* is didactic but also self-pleasuring. Not despite but because of his complexity of erotic response, Spenser is a sexual psychologist of the first rank, surpassed only by Freud and Shakespeare. His treatment of erotic archetype, of dream, fantasy, obsession, and perversion, of civilization and sacrifice lifts *The Faerie Queene* out of national into world literature. (See also *gender, *psychology, *womanhood; Paglia.)

CAMILLE PAGLIA

Shakespeare, William (1564–1616) Spenser and Shakespeare (younger by about twelve years) are the acknowledged masters of their literary age, sharing many themes and a late Elizabethan, 'Golden' poetic style; yet the understanding that ought to arise from thinking about them together is still confused and rudimentary. Spenser's undoubted influence on Shakespeare is hard to particularize, and there is no evidence to show what feeling – anxiety or any other – Shakespeare entertained about it. His only generally accepted reference to Spenser (to *Teares of the Muses* at *Midsummer Night's Dream* V i 52–5) seems natural, not mocking as has been suggested. Unsurprisingly, Spenser registers no knowledge of Shakespeare. Living mostly in Ireland, he had little opportunity to see plays, and, when he made his last published remarks on fellow poets (in *Colin Clout* 1595), only two of Shakespeare's narrative poems and four of his plays had been published. It is most unlikely that the Aetion in *Colin Clout* 444 represents Shakespeare.

Their origins (as far as our limited knowledge allows us to say) were about halfway down the social scale; both sought support and self-respect from a chief source of such things – patronage of the nobility – and were finally recognized as gentlemen. Yet Spenser's path through university to the status of court poet, government functionary in Ireland, and landowner there, with the equivocal support of various court figures, differs radically from Shakespeare's employment as an actor and dramatist in London, his ownership of a share in a financially successful stage company which finally attained the patronage of James I, his lesser activity as a poet which evidently gained him further attention by the nobility, and his prosperous retirement to his native market town as the most respected dramatist of his age (a new category in England).

So viewed they seem to inhabit separate worlds, but an overlap is visible even in the given terms. They were both Elizabethans, naturally embedded in the same culture. Both were poets, Shakespeare never more so than in his plays. They shared basically similar personal aspirations. Apart from recent claims about their common concern with the theme of time, the demonstrable literary connection between them amounts to Shakespeare's early borrowing of Spenserian passages, the likely relation between *FQ* VI and Shakespeare's romances, and their analogous use of certain traditional narrative materials.

What separates them sharply, on the other hand, is most visible in their treatment of common themes: love, friendship, jealousy, nature and art, slander, evil, the relation of parents and offspring, England and its destiny. Their full-dress appraisals of justice, equity, and mercy in *FQ* V and *Measure for Measure* constitute a suitable example, although these two works are not their most highly regarded. Spenser evokes a mythology of ancient just heroes, describes his knightly protagonist's upbringing by the goddess of justice, and assembles a conspectus of brief, exemplary, parabolically rendered stories of his hero's just actions in various personal and public realms. This protagonist is then reduced to amatory enslavement by his acceptance of a principle of literal-minded justice, but restored to a right amatory balance by his true-love's enforcement of an equitable solution by combat. Coincidentally, and through the same two characters, Spenser gives us a mythic, symbolic, mysterious version of the colliding and concording of justice and equity in Isis Church. The involvement of this latter sequence with the destiny of England then modulates into a full-scale symbolic rendition of contemporary England's political and military confrontations, with epideictic intent, so that justice, equity, and mercy are seen to belong to the English and Protestant causes. On the individual plane, however, the protagonist's final exposure to unjust envy and slander postpones closure beyond Book V.

Almost all of this is far removed from the tension and emotional, human immediacy of the high-stakes game which Shakespeare plays out to full closure in *Measure*. Shakespeare focuses a set of complex interactions, in strict continuity, among no more than eight main characters so as to make those who accept the literal message of the play see the necessity and complementarity of attentive justice and selfless mercy, unanswerably distinguished in the course of the action from egoism, hypocrisy, the untempered letter of the law, and complicitous leniency. Up to the play's resolution, everything is humanly at risk for all but one main character.

This level of compelling immediacy is scarcely available in narrative verse, and is not the first aim of Spenser's kind of poetry. The consecutively unfolding narrative sequences of Book V accrete as subsets to an extensive, satisfyingly systemic whole amounting to much more than the sum of its parts and opening out in turn towards new permutations. Spenser's magically resourceful thesaurus of symbolic transformations, through which a competent reader can imaginatively reconstitute a way of living in the world, contrasts with the intimate directness and dramatic finalities which Shakespeare offers us for the same purpose. The divergent lines along which the two authors aggressively develop their quite separate inherited traditions of narrative poetry and dramatic enactment create a space between them. Temperamental difference makes the lines diverge farther.

Near the beginning of his career, Shakespeare surely read with absorption *The Faerie Queene* 1590 (I-III) and some other works of Spenser current by 1591. The deliberately poetic style of his early histories was hospitable to Spenser's effects, which usually emerge there in elaborate, set speeches of description, often fused with material from other sources: the golden gates of the morning, releasing a sun which signifies 'the prime of youth, / Trimm'd like a younker prancing to his love' (*3 Henry VI* II i 21–4) mirror *FQ* I v 2; succeeding lines seem to reflect other passages in Book I (Cairncross in Shakespeare ed 1964:185). Part of Clarence's dream (*Richard III* I iv 26–33) is heavily indebted to Guyon's visits to the house of Mammon and the Bower of Bliss (Hammond in Shakespeare ed 1981:80, 336–7; Cairncross p xliv note). 'All plum'd like estridges, that with the wind / Bated like eagles having lately bath'd' (*1 Henry IV* IV i 98–9) relates to the description of Redcrosse rising from the Well of Life (*FQ* I xi 34). Other relationships emerge more briefly (*1 Henry VI* I i 124 and *FQ* III i 66, etc) but speak for the 1590 *FQ*'s having colored Shakespeare's early poetic style in ways that we have not yet traced. Brooks (in Shakespeare ed 1979: lxi-lxii) describes the reappearance of *The Shepheardes Calender* and possibly *Amoretti* and *Epithalamion* in Titania's foul-weather speech and the sylvan beauties of *A Midsummer Night's Dream*. Even as late as *Julius Caesar*, the 'leaden mace' of slumber (IV iii 268) is likely to be the leaden mace of Morpheus in *FQ* I iv 44.

No such clear evidence emerges of Shakespeare's having been influenced by the 1596 *FQ*, although he was surely acquainted with it. The morally schematic, tragicomical pastoralism of *FQ* VI is close to the restrained, self-conscious schematism of *The Winter's Tale* (c 1610–11) and *The Tempest* (c 1611), and, more loosely, Shakespeare's other romances. The relationships are complicated by the influences of Sidney's *Arcadia*, earlier prose romances, and Guarini's *Il pastor fido*, but the closest and most worthy English exemplar for the redemptive worlds of young lovers in *The Winter's Tale* and *The Tempest* lies in the formula of *FQ* VI: the nobly descended, goddess-like Pastorella, an emanation of the nature which environs her but one shielded from its boorish and savage components, finds after many trials her destiny in Calidore, bountifully dowered by nature but similarly noble and courtly, who deserts his institutional role to gain her but, having won her, returns to it. The sober, Spenserian pastoralism of these two plays contrasts with the exuberantly un-Spenserian pastoral inversions of city and country in Shakespeare's earlier *As You Like It*.

Shakespeare bases three plots on material which he was acquainted with in *The Faerie Queene* as well as elsewhere, but the summary or parabolic character of Spenser's treatment of these materials decreases the significance of the parallels. The book of *Briton moniments* in *FQ* II x contains the stories of Lear (27–32) and Cymbeline (50–1). An analogue to Shakespeare's *Much Ado about Nothing* is the story of Phedon (*FQ* II iv), illustrating irascible intemperance. The single feature shared uniquely by Spenser's and Shakespeare's versions in this last case is that the villain who arouses the protagonist's suspicion of his innocent beloved is animated by villainy alone, not by a desire for the same woman. A similar, largely unmotivated evil in arousing suspicion of a beloved woman characterizes Shakespeare's Iago in *Othello* and Iachimo in *Cymbeline*. Shakespeare may have related their names to that of Spenser's Archimago, who gratuitously arouses suspicion in the same direction (*FQ* I ii 2–6; see Potts 1958:221). If so, the name of Don John (Iohn), the villain of *Much Ado*, might be added to the list.

Many sides of Renaissance life show a newly urgent concern with time, which in literature is often seen against the backdrop of eternity. For Spenser and Shakespeare as for many others, love, generation, fame, and literary immortality become metaphors for eternity, erecting a defense of continuity against devouring time (Quinones 1972: 243–443; on time in Shakespeare, see Turner 1971). These themes are only one face, however, of the literary expression of anxiety over time's preemptive character, which constantly blights and finally destroys human constancy, human artifacts, and man himself (as preeminently in Shakespeare's *Sonnets* of 1609). An important vehicle of this perception, as in Spenser's *Ruines of Time* and *Ruines of Rome* (1591) and often in *The Faerie Queene*, originates in a more poignant, precise realization of the Renaissance world's sequestration from antiquity by an abyss of time. This interim is made visible in the physical detritus of centuries, and is only perilously bridged by classical literary artifacts, the sole witnesses to the immortality of a yearned-for ancient excellence pertaining especially to Rome, paradigm of cities and empires (see *antique world).

From among the themes of persistence against time, Shakespeare and Spenser particularly honor the generational one of succession within a princely elite who personify or control a people's welfare. More elaborately than any other sixteenth-century heroic poem, *The Faerie Queene* develops the shared motif of a love match between two main characters whose prophesied offspring will bring into the present and future of the author's first readers a national glory equal to the exploit of the protagonist in the fictional present of the poem, although Spenser's poem, being incomplete, never gets as far as that exploit. *FQ* III iii 26–50 prophesies that from the love of Britomart and Artegall, half-brother of Arthur, will spring future British monarchs; and that, after the Saxon, Danish, and Norman interludes, their distant offspring will return in the Welsh-British family of the Tudor dynasty, culminating in Elizabeth I, to rule a united and triumphant land. In *Henry VIII* V iv 17–62, Shakespeare gives us a similar but more restrained prophecy concerning first the infant Elizabeth of his fictional present and then James I (her offspring in the fashion of the phoenix), but his exploitation of the theme is characteristically more personal and immediate. The dubious relationship between Henry IV and his son is resolved and vindicated in renewed English glory in *1* and *2* Henry IV and *Henry V*; the intensification of York's evil by his son Richard, and the consequent intensification of English civil strife until the arrival of the Tudors, is recorded in the *Henry VI* plays and *Richard III*. The relation of royal parent to offspring is a large element in *Hamlet* and *King Lear*, as is the survival and union of the offspring of quarreling rulers in *The Winter's Tale* and *The Tempest*. The seventeen 'procreation sonnets' beginning Shakespeare's *Sonnets* urge the young friend (a member of an elite although not a ruler) to eternize himself in children who will perpetuate his beauty and excellence.

Many sonnets concerned with time in *Sonnets* 1–126 share expressions with Spenser's sonnet sequence *Ruines of Rome* (Hieatt 1983). These shared materials lend credence to the theory that Shakespeare was impressed with Spenser's orchestration of time's role in *Rome* to the point of imputing to the friend in *Sonnets* a reincarnated Roman excellence, exposed like Rome to time's assaults but immortalized by *Sonnets* as Rome had been by its surviving literature. A sense of the connection between the two works is given by such shared base-expressions as 'War upon time,' 'days outworn,' 'injurious time,' 'devouring time,' 'ruinate,' and 'fade ... vade'; by Shakespeare's much more frequent use in *Sonnets* than elsewhere of forms of the characteristic *Rome* word 'antiquity'; and by his resort to images of monumental ruins like those in *Rome*.

The exploit which Spenser had in mind for Arthur in the possible sequel to *The Faerie Queene* which is mentioned in the Letter to Raleigh may be the conquest of Rome in late classical times, as this traditional story is developed in Book 5 of Caxton's version of Malory's *Morte Darthur* (Hieatt 1988). Writing this letter less than two years after the defeat of the Armada, Spenser would no doubt have allegorized this conquest as a Protestant victory in his days over Roman Catholicism and its Spanish supporters. In the literary sphere, such a poem would have answered Tasso's great Catholic epic of the delivery of Jerusalem from the unbelievers, and might also have seemed to Spenser to constitute a daring symbolic bridge over the abyss of time between Roman antiquity and the Northern Renaissance.

In the sphere of actuality, the probable effects of such Protestant activism are all-too-well illustrated by the devastation of the Thirty Years' War, begun nineteen years after Spenser's death. It is a possible but not necessary scenario that the bellicose aspect of Spenser's epic project aroused a hostile reaction in Shakespeare which played a part in his creation of *Cymbeline* during the period of James I's peaceful foreign policy. The modification of the traditional story in this late play amounts to Cymbeline's pacific resumption of the tribute to Rome even after his Britons have defeated the forces of the Roman general Lucius (a name not directly connected with Cymbeline in any of Shakespeare's sources). The emperor defeated by Malory's Arthur is also named Lucius, and Spenser, as Shakespeare may have noticed, is unique in juxtaposing Arthur's later supposed success and Cymbeline's centuries-earlier supposed failure to end Roman rule in Britain (*FQ* II x 49–51). It is this passage which alludes to Arthur's Roman conquest in terms of one of the main motifs (the gory ending of the tribute) in Malory's story and the traditional stories behind it. If Shakespeare had read Malory's Book 5 attentively, he could easily have recognized Spenser's intention, but the theory needs further confirmation.

A. KENT HIEATT

Judith H. Anderson 1987 'The Conspiracy of Realism: Impasse and Vision in *King Lear*' *SP* 84:1–23; A. Kent Hieatt 1983; Hieatt 1988 'The Passing of Arthur in Malory, Spenser, and Shakespeare: The Avoidance of Closure' in *The Passing of Arthur: New Essays in the Arthurian Tradition* ed Christopher Baswell and William Sharpe (New York) pp 173–92; Quinones 1972; William Shakespeare 1964 *King Henry VI, Part III* ed Andrew S. Cairncross (London); Shakespeare ed 1979; Shakespeare 1981 *King Richard III* ed Antony Hammond (London); Frederick Turner 1971 *Shakespeare and the Nature of Time* (Oxford).

FURTHER READING Potts 1958 (demonstrates that many of Spenser's and Shakespeare's ethical problems can be usefully discussed together, but much of the suggested dependence of Shakespeare on Spenser seems fanciful); Watkins 1950 (little on the actual relation of the two figures).

---

shame As the painful or humiliating awareness of the exposure of anything that is or ought to be hidden, shame is represented in *The Faerie Queene* by characters who become painfully aware of their presence to themselves and to others. Always associated with exposure and loss of identity, 'Shame his ugly face [does] hide from living eye' at the gate of hell (II vii 22).

Shame was recognized as one of the chief effects of the Fall (Gen 3.7, 10); fittingly, Duessa is 'the daughter of Deceipt and Shame' (I v 26). Augustine bequeathed to the Renaissance a link between the Fall, sexual passion, and shame at any activity not controlled by the will: 'the soul is ashamed that the body, which by nature is inferior and subject to it, should resist its authority' (*City of God* 14.23; ed 1948, 2:268–9). Renaissance commentators on Genesis 3 echo Augustine: 'And those parts of the body which serve for generation were then, and still are most shamefull: and studiously covered; because sinne is become naturall, and derived by generation' (Ainsworth 1621:64). They usually note the relation between sexuality and the shame that is a chief result of the Fall, and regret the loss of that most striking sign of our prelapsarian innocence, the lack of shame (A. Williams 1948:109). Such regret is shown in Spenser's admiration for lovers joyfully devoid of shame: 'There with ... *Pleasure* they doe play / Their hurtlesse sports, without rebuke or blame, / And in her snowy bosome boldly lay / Their quiet heads, devoyd of guilty shame' (*Hymne of Love* 287–90; cf *FQ* III vi 41, IV x 28).

Within the classical tradition, Cicero makes shame a part of temperance; for him, 'a sense of shame or decency ... secures observance and firm authority for what is honourable' (*De inventione* 2.54.164). Also, according to La Primaudaye (ed 1586:257), 'Honest shame and shamefastnes (saith Quintilian is the mother of all good counsaile, the right Guardian of dutie, the mistresse of innocencie' (see *Institutes* 12.5.2–3). At times the term was used synonymously with *shamefastness* to denote the fear of dishonor. Shame in this classical sense becomes for Renaissance writers a potentially positive quality that keeps one from sin and impropriety; often they adopt Thomas Aquinas' term *verecundia*, the fear of disgraceful action which makes possible the virtue of temperance (*Summa* 2a2ae 144). Hence, at *FQ* II ix 40–3, Guyon meets Shamefastnesse, who externalizes his reluctance to commit shameful acts and who blushes deeply in his presence.

Spenser also develops notions of shame implicit in the romance tradition, where shame is a painful emotional reaction to dishonor (as in Chrétien de Troyes, esp *Lancelot*). In Spenser's romance, this reaction, most frequently expressed by blushing, abashedness, or an averting of the eyes, is directed to exposure not only of dishonor but also of anything that is private or taboo. Hence shame can be, but is not necessarily, linked to guilt. Male characters are vulnerable to shame because they fail to achieve the high ideals of chivalry, eg, when Guyon almost strikes the red cross on the Red Cross Knight's shield, he is aware that he almost 'with reprochfull shame mine honour shent' (*FQ* II i 27). Female characters suffer shame when their chastity is threatened, eg, when Serena is found naked by Calepine, she conceives 'inward shame of her uncomely case ... through care of womanhood' (VI viii 51). Shame is expressed when any character fails to meet expected codes of conduct. When Britomart rescues Artegall from Radigund, upon seeing him dressed 'In womans weedes, that is to manhood shame' (V v 20), she is 'abasht with secrete shame' and turns 'her head aside, as nothing glad, / To have beheld a spectacle so bad' (vii 38).

Spenser expands his treatment of shame to include painful responses to exposure – even to oneself – of hidden, private, or emotional realities. Britomart seems ashamed when she first falls in love (III ii), ashamed chiefly because of the power of her involuntary sexual desire (cf Augustine *City of God* 14) and the sudden intensity of her self-awareness. Like Adam and Eve, she has become aware of her 'nakedness' and her fallen human condition.

Shame is found only sporadically in *FQ* I. It is suggested by Redcrosse's torment on seeing the false Una and Squire 'knit ... in *Venus* shamefull chaine' (ii 4), in his despair at 'The ugly vew of his deformed crimes' (ix 48), and in his desire to hide and to seek oblivion – inevitable aspects of shame in Spenser – in the house of Holiness (x 21, 25).

FQ II offers several episodes of erotic observation which show both the reciprocal pleasures of voyeurism and exhibitionism, and their grounding in the perverse pleasure of revealing the sexual members which the Fall has made objects of shame. The antics of the nymphs in the Bower's fountain to arouse Guyon's lust (xii 63–8) and the striptease presented for Cymochles' delectation combine shamelessness with voyeurism (v 32–5). Braggadocchio's shamelessness (iii) would have suggested to an Elizabethan reader 'a blockish and senseless nature' (La Primaudaye ed 1586:257–8). But his shamelessness makes him more wicked than comic at Florimell's wedding (V iii 37), where he is subjected to the purposeful exposure and shame of baffling, a disgrace necessary for bogus or upstart claimants to virtue, nobility, or power (cf also Turpine, VI vi 33–6).

FQ III contains an intensive treatment of shame as a response to sexual violation and to vulnerability to the gaze of others. In the masque of Cupid, which personifies Amoret's agonies, Shame is the central figure with Reproach and Repentance following Cupid (xii 24). The relationship between erotic drives and shame is adumbrated in the story of Malbecco, driven by the 'privie guilt' of impotence into a doomed desire to escape the shame of his own diminished being (ix-x). In the brief episode of Diana's response at being discovered naked by Venus (vi 18–19), as in its longer analogue in the *Cantos of Mutabilitie* (VII vi 42–55), Spenser appropriates powerful notions of taboo and transgression from his Ovidian sources, and psychologizes them to represent Diana's shame and anger as both a violated goddess and an embarrassed woman. Her punishment of Faunus begins in the comic tone of the earlier portions of the episode; but its excess and ferocity, difficult to reconcile fully with the comedy of the opening, precisely reflect the excess and arbitrariness that can exist in shame.

Amoret's position and behavior in the Temple of Venus, and her response when Scudamour claims her (IV x 50–4, 57), suggest that kind of shame called *pudicitia*, the shamefastness that controls sexual desire through fear of lust. Her ambivalent responses of modest shamefastness and 'witching smyles' match Scudamour's aggression and hesitation (cf his 'shamefast feare' 53). The whole episode again links shame with the violation of boundaries, the exposure of the private, and the aggressive viewing of the hidden.

The poem's most sustained exploration of shame and honor is found in Book VI, in many small emblematic depictions: a knight on horseback attacks a knight on foot (iii 46–51), two knights debate whether to attack the sleeping Arthur (vii 18–23), a knight hides behind a lady to protect himself (iii 46–51, vi 31–2), an armed knight fights an unarmed youth (ii 18–19). Besides these dishonorable, unchivalric, shameful acts, there is the shame that results from exposure of failure (as in Timias, whose 'shame would be hid' viii 5). The Briana episode in canto i is a sustained play on shame. Mirabella is instructed to feel shame when disciplined by Scorn and Disdain (vii 27–38, viii 19–24). Most important, the long nightmare of Serena's adventure with the cannibals (viii 37–51) combines many aspects of Spenser's treatment of shame: painful response to exposure (her 'inward shame' at being shown naked, 51), sexual observation (she is the object of 'loose lascivious sight' 43), the romance motif (here, she is also the *admired* woman) developed to describe dishonor as a psychic event and shame as the involuntary and inescapable quality of the fallen human condition.

THERESA M. KRIER

La Primaudaye ed 1586 contains early definitions 'Of Shame, Shamefastnesse, and of Dishonour'; see also Henry Ainsworth 1621 *Annotations upon ... Genesis* (London), and A. Williams 1948.

Shamefastnesse Two allegorical maidens in *The Faerie Queene* are named Shamefastnesse, one in the castle of Alma (II ix 40–4) and the other in the Temple of Venus (IV x 50). Although they share the name, meaning literally 'held fast by shame,' and show the same signs of embarrassment (downcast eyes, blushes), they stand for two different attributes.

The Shamefastnesse of Alma's castle represents *verecundia*, modesty which fears doing a disgraceful act and which is traditionally, as here, associated with temperance (see Macrobius *Commentary on the Dream of Scipio* 1.8.7). Froward, or withdrawing, *verecundia* resides with the other passions in the heart (the 'goodly Parlour') and must be held in check by the temperate soul (Alma) and by the presence of its forward, or outgoing, opposite, Prays-desire. Thus Elyot, in his *Boke Named the Governour*, identifies shamefastness and the desire for praise as attributes necessary in a gentleman: 'By shamfastnes, as it were with a bridell, they rule as well theyr dedes as their appetites. And desire of prayse addeth to a sharpe spurre to their disposition towarde lernyng and vertue' (1.9; cf Aristotle *Ethics* 3.8; see Hamilton in *FQ* ed 1977). The unnamed bird 'which shonneth vew' (probably a turtledove; see Ripa 1603, sv 'Modesty') and the blue of Shamefastnesse's garment also indicate withdrawal from the world. Guyon blushes self-consciously in recognition that shamefastness is central to his own character. An extreme, it must be governed but not eliminated; the harmful effects of its absence are evident in the intemperate and shameless Braggadocchio.

The Shamefastnesse of Book IV is *pudicitia*, the feminine modesty which controls sexual desire and conduct such as suggestive looks and speech. Associated with chastity, it is a traditional and essential attribute of a good woman (*Womanhood); as such, it moderates and is moderated by its opposite, Cherefulnesse. The absence of *pudicitia* is best illustrated in the lascivious Malecasta. Although not mentioned by name in *Epithalamion*, *pudicitia* is evident in the wedding stanza (lines 223–41). ROBERT A. WHITE

Kerby Neill 1934 'Spenser's *Shamefastnesse, Faerie Queene*, II, ix, 40–44' *MLN* 49:387–91 argues that the figure in Book II is one of excess. See also Robert A. White 1981 'Shamefastnesse as *Verecundia* and as *Pudicitia* in *The Faerie Queene*' *SP* 78:391–408.

Shelley, Percy Bysshe (1792–1822) With the publication of Henry John Todd's eight-volume variorum edition of Spenser in 1805 and a new edition of Thomas Warton's *Observations on the Fairy Queen of Spenser* in 1807, Spenser's claim to classic status was at last placed beyond dispute. Publication of these important works of criticism and scholarship was partly engendered by the intense interest in the recovery of early romances that took place during the first decade of the nineteenth century, and they in turn served to focus attention on Spenser as the greatest, if maybe the last, exemplar of writing in this mode. An intense, serious, and bookish adolescent, Shelley grew up with an avid passion for romances, mostly in prose and all tinged with the Gothic. Before his twentieth birthday he had published two of his own, *Zastrozzi* and *St. Irvyne, or The Rosicrucian*, which are terror-ridden and generally terrible, as well as two volumes of poetry that include titles like 'Ghasta, or The Avenging Demon.' It took several years for Shelley's tastes to mature to the point where Spenser's less histrionic romance would appeal to him; but it was inevitable that it would do so, given the climates of his mind and his culture.

It is unlikely that Shelley had any deep acquaintance with Spenser before 1813, when he acquired an edition, though there are two early poems in what is known as the Esdaile Notebook written in a loosely-conceived Spenserian stanza: 'Henry and Louisa' (1809) and 'Lines on Leaving London for Wales' (1812). References to Shelley's reading in Spenser, however, are spotty before the spring of 1817, when Spenser suddenly became his constant fare. This was no accident, for the poet was then engaged in writing the most ambitious poem ever conceived in the Spenserian stanza after *The Faerie Queene* itself: *Laon and Cythna, or The Revolution of the Golden City: A Vision of the Nineteenth Century* (rev and pub 1818 as *The Revolt of Islam: A Poem, in Twelve Cantos*). Yet critics have been loath to note exact sources in Spenser for characters and events in Shelley's epic-romance. Part of the problem lies in the extent to which Spenser had already influenced Shelley's immediate predecessors and contemporaries. It is probable that Shelley's resolute heroine Cythna is influenced by Britomart, and that his hermit of Cantos 3 and 4 owes something to the similar figure in *FQ* VI, but there are also analogues like Southey's *Joan of Arc* or the hermit who educates Edwin in Beattie's *Minstrel* (another poem in Spenserian stanzas), not to mention numerous other less-famous analogues which may owe their existence to an original in Spenser but are also aspects of the general romance revival in the midst of which Shelley writes. Shelley's saturation in Spenser at this time may indicate less that he was picking over *The Faerie Queene* for details of character and episode than that he was apprenticed to a master both of versification in a difficult form and of inventive allegory. Spenser's greatest influence on Shelley comes later and is felt most directly in his technical facility, in what Harold Bloom has indelibly marked by his simple title, *Shelley's Mythmaking*, and in a pronounced tendency toward complex and polysemous allegory. For Shelley, Spenser resembled Milton in being a teacher whose greatest gift was to liberate his student.

This is largely how Spenser has been conceived by the group of critics who began the recovery of Shelley's reputation a generation ago. Carlos Baker can rely on the assured and detailed learning that came from his writing a doctoral dissertation on Shelley and Spenser; but he is most often content to use Spenser to illuminate Shelley's temperamental affinity, for instance, in the allegorical procession of *The Masque of Anarchy*. Earl Wasserman shows how the structure of Spenser's Garden of Adonis (*FQ* III vi) can inform but at the same time not dictate the allegorical elaboration of *The Sensitive Plant*. Harold Bloom similarly demonstrates how Spenser, particularly in *Muiopotmos*, freed Shelley to indulge in the playful inventiveness of *The Witch of Atlas*. In charting this critical course, the authors not only allow their sense of interpretive delicacy to transcend the older form of tracing echoes, but they are also true to the way Shelley used his learning in, and his veneration for, older literature. His friend Peacock recalled how Shelley characteristically read the encounter of Artegall and the Giant with the scales for rectifying injustice in *FQ* V ii (Shelley ed 1964, 2:71n):

> 'Artegall argues with the Giant; the Giant has the best of the argument; Artegall's iron man knocks him over into the sea and drowns him. This is the usual way in which power deals with opinion.' I said: 'That was not the lesson which Spenser intended to convey.' 'Perhaps not,' he said; 'it is the lesson which he conveys to me. I am of the Giant's faction.'

Peacock was illustrating the most salient reference to Spenser in Shelley's letters, where the poet claims that in *Prometheus Unbound* he was endeavoring to 'cast what weight I can into the right scale of that balance which the Giant (of Arthegall) holds,' that is, in support of democratic equality (Shelley ed 1964, 2:71). In the one poem in which Shelley mentions Spenser, he is equally playful and perverse. The 'Letter to Maria Gisborne' (1820) begins with the poet surveying his study, spinning verse from its contents like a spider its web. Twice he refers to Spenser – the association being the customary one of Spenser's sheer creativity – and the second time thinks of himself, and perhaps by extension Spenser, too, as 'like some weird Archimage ... Plotting dark spells, and devilish enginery' (106–7). Spenser would perhaps not have wanted to see Archimago as an aspect of himself; yet Shelley here and in the nearly contemporary *Witch of Atlas* regards the play of the creative mind, its mythmaking, as frankly amoral and requiring no justification.

Another perspective in Shelley criticism sees Spenser as a source of Platonic ideas in Shelley, from the 'Hymn to Intellectual Beauty' onward. In the last decade or so, as emphasis on the skeptical basis of Shelley's world view has dominated criticism, this view has lost general credibility. It can best be seen, however, in readings of *Adonais*, the poem in which Shelley's homage to Spenser is most explicit. This elegy for

Keats has its progenitor in 'Astrophel,' Spenser's lament for Sidney, and it has been argued that it shares the same Christian and Neoplatonic values (Silverman 1972). To pay tribute to an earlier lament for a poet, however, is by no means to adopt its ideological underpinnings; more likely, Shelley incorporates Spenser's lament into his poem, both to extend his own vision and to secularize Spenser's (Curran 1983).

None of Shelley's references to Spenser suggests sympathy with his political or religious allegiances. In *A Defence of Poetry*, Spenser is classed among poets who 'frequently affected a moral aim, and the effect of their poetry is diminished in exact proportion to the degree in which they compel us to advert to this purpose' (Shelley ed 1977:488). Yet he is also represented as among the greatest writers of the modern world who 'have celebrated the dominion of love, planting as it were trophies in the human mind of that sublimest victory over sensuality and force' (p 497). Even if Spenser were thought of as 'a poet laureate' (a sardonic thrust at Robert Southey, the chief myth-maker among contemporary writers of romance and a politically reactionary laureate), such 'errors have been weighed and found to have been dust in the balance' with genius (p 506).

It seems less likely, then, that Spenser can be judged as influencing the ideas of the skeptical Shelley than that the later poet recognized temperamental affinities with his predecessor and learned much from studying him. Stylistic examination of Shelley's translations has suggested that he automatically reverted to Milton for epic and to Spenser for pastoral and romance subjects (Webb 1976:116–22). Yet he was interested in more than an antique diction. He appears to have read widely in Spenser, and his allusions to poems other than *The Faerie Queene* mark that breadth. His own instinct for symbolic allegory is manifest, as is his love of mythic invention and concern with the nature of the imagination: these are the elements that drew him most closely to Spenser and what he most honored in him.

STUART CURRAN

Percy Bysshe Shelley ed 1964; Shelley 1977 *Shelley's Poetry and Prose* ed Donald H. Reiman and Sharon B. Powers (New York).

Carlos Baker 1948 *Shelley's Major Poetry: The Fabric of a Vision* (Princeton); Bloom 1959; Stuart Curran 1983 '*Adonais* in Context' in *Shelley Revalued: Essays from the Gregynog Conference* ed Kelvin Everest (Leicester) pp 165–82; Frederick L. Jones 1942 'Shelley and Spenser' *SP* 39:662–9; Edwin B. Silverman 1972 *Poetic Synthesis in Shelley's 'Adonais'* (The Hague); Earl R. Wasserman 1959 *The Subtler Language: Critical Readings of Neoclassic and Romantic Poems* (Baltimore); Timothy Webb 1976 *The Violet in the Crucible: Shelley and Translation* (Oxford).

The Shepheardes Calender (See ed 1912: 415–68; see also illustrations below.) Under the date 5 December 1579 in the Stationers' Register, the following entry occurs beside the name Hugh Singleton: 'Lycenced unto him *the Shepperdes Calender conteyninge xii ecloges proportionable to the xii monthes.*' Spenser is not identified here as the author, but the text we know as *The Shepheardes Calender* appeared shortly thereafter, printed in quarto by Singleton, a somewhat disreputable London printer with Protestant affiliations (Byrom 1933). The rights of publication were assigned over from Singleton to John Harrison on 29 October 1580, a notably short time after the first printing, and later separate quartos were issued by Harrison in 1581, 1586, 1591, and 1597 (Johnson 1933:2–8). The work retained its popularity throughout Spenser's lifetime, and eventually was subsumed in the first folio of his collected works (1611). There is no serious difficulty in establishing a sound text.

The Shepheardes Calender is a complex poem comprising many distinct but interrelated parts. There is considerable prefatory material: an eighteen-line verse addressed 'To His Booke' by the author, who signs himself Immeritô; a dedicatory epistle addressed to Gabriel Harvey, signed only by the initials E.K., 'his verie special and singular good frend'; and a short essay entitled 'The generall argument of the whole booke,' presumably also by E.K. The body of the volume consists of twelve eclogues, each made up of several parts: at its head, a prominent woodcut presents a visual image of the subject matter (see *SC, printing and illustration); next comes a brief 'Argument' in prose, presumably by E.K. or perhaps by the poet himself; the verse text of the eclogue follows; the eclogue concludes with one or more verbal emblems (see *SC, mottos), usually one for each of the speakers; and finally there is an extensive gloss on specific passages in the text and on the emblems, presumably again by E.K. At the end of the volume, there is a twelve-line epilogue, untitled and unsigned but presumably by the author.

The model for this typographical layout was Francesco Sansovino's illustrated edition of Sannazaro's *Arcadia* first printed at Venice in 1571 (Heninger 1988). The identity of E.K. has not been established, though Harvey is a strong candidate. It seems likely that Spenser published the *Calender* with the complicity of Harvey in the hope of furthering their careers in the turbulent politics of Elizabethan England.

The *Calender* was Spenser's earliest independent publication, and it shows him to be a serious and very self-conscious poet. Only the few sonnets which he contributed to van der Noot's *Theatre* (1569) had preceded it. By 1579, Spenser was reaching his late twenties and attempting to establish himself in a career of public service. He had completed a seven-year residence at Cambridge, had served for a year in the household of John Young, Bishop of Rochester, and now for several months had been employed by Robert Dudley, Earl of Leicester. The *Calender* was his first appearance in print after coming to London.

The poem draws upon several established literary genres, including classical eclogue, calendar-almanac, beast fable, romance, satire, and Petrarchan lyric (Friedland 1937, DeNeef 1976, Luborsky 1980, B.R. Smith 1980). Most evidently, though, it is a pastoral. Like many Renaissance poets, Spenser followed the example of Virgil and began his poetic career by publishing eclogues. He was much aware of writing in imitation of Theocritus, Bion, Virgil, Mantuan, Sannazaro, Marot, and perhaps others. His poem is located in an anglicized version of Arcadia, with the full bucolic panoply of shepherds and their flocks. The set pieces of pastoral poetry – the amorous complaint, the débat, the panegyric, the singing match, the dirge, the hymn to Pan – all duly appear, each in an appropriate month.

There is, however, no precedent in pastoral for the wide variety of metrical forms that Spenser employs. Unlike earlier pastoralists, he changes the stanza from one eclogue to another, and often introduces more than one stanzaic pattern in a single eclogue. In only two instances are metrical forms repeated. In *December*, Colin sings in the same six-line stanza he had used in *Januarye*, thereby linking the closing and opening eclogues. Also, the satirical eclogues *Februarie*, *Maye*, and *September* are linked by the use in each of rough iambic tetrameter couplets, while *Julye* is related to this group by the use of a similar atavistic meter, the ballad stanza. Evidently Spenser took great pains with the metrics of the *Calender* and considered metrical forms to be an integral element in its structure (Røstvig 1969).

The possessive 'shepheardes' in the title indicates that the genre of the work is pastoral, at that time a relatively untried mode in English attempted previously only by Barclay and Googe. 'Calendar' indicates its form: twelve eclogues corresponding to the twelve months. There had been in print since the beginning of the century a familiar perennial almanac entitled *The Kalender of Sheepehards*, to which E.K. refers in the dedicatory epistle. Like its namesake, *The Shepheardes Calender* purports to be a calendar and uses the shepherd as a prototype for mankind, but otherwise except for the woodcuts there is little connection between that heterogeneous handbook of kitchen astrology and Spenser's sophisticated eclogues.

The dates at which Spenser composed the individual eclogues are indeterminate. Apparently, though, the several eclogues that comprise the *Calender* were put together in a single volume during the latter months of 1579, when the Queen was entertaining a marriage proposal from the Duc d'Anjou, younger brother of the French king and a Catholic (*Var* 7:610–14). The title page conspicuously dedicates it to Philip Sidney, nephew of the Earl of Leicester. An intimate adviser of the Queen, Leicester was also leader of a powerful faction with Puritan leanings. At least on one level, the *Calender* is an occasional poem responding to these contentious issues of the day in both religion and politics (Greenlaw 1911, McLane 1961). Following earlier practice, Spenser found the pastoral mode a ready vehicle for propagandistic comment.

(See ***The Shepheardes Calender*** Fig 1.)

In addition to its topical significance, however, there is a larger meaning in the poem. Spenser the poet – as distinguished from Spenser the polemicist – chose the calendrical form to convey ideas about larger aspects of human experience. This form identifies the *Calender* with a well-known motif popular since the Middle Ages in which each month is represented by a different activity (see Fig 1): for instance, January depicts a two-faced Janus feasting at a table; February, an old man warming himself before a fire; March, a husbandman clearing his land of rocks; April, the husbandman pruning his trees; May, a young man courting his lady. Here the various activities of mankind are interrelated into a single system. Just as the months are integrated into an annual unit of time, a year, so these activities are integrated into a unit, the complete life. At the end of the year, the calendar begins anew as time goes on. The individual person, though, like a single year, is finite. His course goes not in an eternal circle, but in a straight line, with death as its destination. Nevertheless, because his finite course coincides with one complete cycle of nature and reproduces in small the pattern which is the integer of eternity, the individual transcends mere mortality and participates in the Christian scheme of redemption. Presenting this paradoxical relationship between the finite and the infinite, between the actual and the ideal, between a mortal and eternity, is the larger dimension of the *Calender* (Heninger 1962, Rosenberg 1981, M. Brown 1984, Farmer 1986; but see also Bristol 1970).

Recent criticism of the *Calender* has concentrated upon the relationship between Spenser and his fictional character Colin Clout, especially the significance of the poem as an indication of his aspirations. Most readers, under E.K.'s urging, interchange the two, and many have assumed that Colin's longing for Rosalind records an actual affair in which Spenser's love went unrequited. The degree of autobiography in the poem is highly debatable, however, and it raises questions which are fundamental to its interpretation.

Januarye This eclogue is an amorous complaint in the strict pastoral tradition, with Virgil's Eclogue 2 as its most evident model. Colin's sorrow and physical state are documented in detail by comparison with the dreary season, so that the theme is eminently suitable for the month. At the core of the eclogue, the lovesick shepherd addresses in turn the 'barrein ground,' the 'naked trees,' and the 'feeble flocke,' in each case applying their forlorn condition to his own.

The structure of the eclogue is simple and firm. Two stanzas of introduction establish the setting and the mood, then Colin takes over for ten stanzas of amorous complaint, and finally a concluding stanza ends the piece in the traditional way at sunset. The change in poetic voices at the third stanza is noteworthy because despite E.K.'s comments it militates against an easy identification of Spenser with Colin Clout.

The metrical form is a six-line stanza of iambic pentameters rhyming *ababcc*. The lines are smooth and euphonious, as the lines of Colin and Hobbinol always are. The last line of the eclogue is a hexameter, bringing with it the finality of the alexandrine.

The identity of Rosalind has proved an interpretative crux (see McLane 1961). In this eclogue, though, she may be no more than the idealized object of the shepherd-poet's love (cf *Colin Clout* 464–79, 931–51). The identification of Hobbinol as Harvey is readily made, although here too the character may be not so much an historical personage as the stereotypical friend.

This is the most sentimental but also one of the simplest eclogues, uncomplicated by satire. The usual accoutrements of pastoral are here: a lovesick shepherd, his mistress and his rustic companion, a bucolic setting, the regretted trip to the town, the rural deity Pan, rhetorical repetition (eg, 13–14, 29–30, 48, 61–2). Most of all, the eclogue fulfills the obsession of pastoral to idealize beauty and yet show that even Arcadia is subject to time and death. The wistful sadness established here echoes insistently in *June* and *December*, and provides an undersong for the entire work (Moore 1975, S.F. Walker 1979).

Februarie This debate between the elderly shepherd Thenot and Cuddie, a herdsman's boy, is a 'morall and generall' eclogue, as E.K. tells us in the Argument – that is, it demonstrates the difficulties that arise from the disparity between youth and old age. To dramatize the conflict, Thenot recounts a fable about the Oak and the Briar. An eclogue overtly deferential to age is appropriate to February, the last month of the year according to the pagan calendar which ended at the vernal equinox, 'For Age and Winter accord full nie' (27).

Spenser found the name Thenot in Marot, as E.K. discloses in the gloss. It is used also in *Aprill* and *November*. Cuddie, a shortened form of Cuthbert, was especially common in northern England. In *August*, Cuddie sings Colin's sestina, and again in *October* he is Spenser's mouthpiece; but it seems unlikely that the Cuddie of these eclogues is the same heedless clod who appears in *Februarie*.

The fable of the Oak and the Briar, the focal piece of *Februarie*, purportedly comes from 'Tityrus,' an allusion to Chaucer with Virgil behind him. Although Chaucer never wrote such a tale, Spenser chooses this opportunity to praise his revered master in English poetry, who was known in the sixteenth century primarily as a moralist. The fable's gnomic wisdom recalls also Aesop's *Fables*.

There have been several attempts to read topical allusions into the fable and to identify the Oak and Briar as historical personages (*Var* 7:254, 261–2). McLane (1961: ch 5) makes a case for the Earl of Leicester and the Earl of Oxford, with the Queen as the husbandman. Yet perhaps we should honor E.K.'s opening sentence in the Argument and not work too hard at uncovering 'any secrete or particular purpose.' Bond (1981) interprets the eclogue more generally as Spenser's warning to the Queen about the envy and slander that pervaded the court (see also Montrose 1981). Another moralistic conclusion about the folly of youth, divorced from any specific application, is forcefully put by Thenot just before he relates the fable (87–90).

The eclogue is structured to emphasize the fable. In the 101 lines of introductory dialogue, Cuddie complains of cold and discomfort, and Thenot recommends stoic patience. But Cuddie scorns this cautious counsel and flaunts his own vigor. Then in 137 lines Thenot tells the parable against the sin of pride 'as if the thing were set forth in some Picture before our eyes' (Argument), emphasizing its vividness. The eclogue concludes quickly with eight saucy lines given to Cuddie, in which he demonstrates dramatically the heedlessness of youth. The dialogue provides a setting for the fable, and the relationship between Thenot and Cuddie subtly repeats its moral.

The verse paragraphs are made up of rather ragged tetrameter rhyming couplets, similar to those in *Maye* and *September*. The basic foot is iambic, although there is much anapestic substitution, so the meter seems to be old-fashionedly accentual. The metrics are cruder than those in *Januarye*, to accord with the lesser talent of Thenot and Cuddie, and with the unpretentious genre of the fable. Moreover, the vocabulary, especially Thenot's, contains an unusually high number of archaic and dialectal words.

This eclogue has little to do with Colin and his sentiments about love. It takes place not in Arcadia, but in a harsher world where folly and contention and injustice are facts of life. Thenot and Cuddie, with their hard-headedness and blunt speech, anticipate the polemicists who argue religion and politics in the overtly satirical eclogues that follow.

March The banter between Willye and Thomalin, 'two shepheards boyes' (Argument), becomes an analysis of love, and therefore proves timely for the first month of the new year according to the pagan calendar. That love dispels the torpor of winter and quickens the fresh cycle of life in spring is a much repeated commonplace. Spenser's shepherds take a ruder view of love, however, and mythologize it as a rustic Cupid.

E.K. in his gloss cites Theocritus as the analogue for Thomalin's experience with 'the little God' (68), although the actual source is Bion, Idyll 4. Bion's text was available not only in the Greek original, but also in a series of redactions, including a French paraphrase by Ronsard, so Spenser was reworking a familiar hand-me-down (Spitzer 1950, D.C. Allen 1968). In *Februarie*, Spenser devised an Aesopic fable; here, for contrast, he tells an idyllic tale.

Thomalin in *Julye* has been identified as Dr Thomas Cooper, Bishop of Lincoln. If this identification is carried back to *March*, the 'unhappye Ewe' (49) who gets into trouble may refer to a specific scandal. In the Argument, however, E.K. speculates that Thomalin is 'some secrete freend,' an acquaintance involved in adolescent attitudes that hardly fit the learned Bishop of Lincoln. So the identity of Thomalin remains a crux, although fortunately not an important one. The name Willye is so common that it does not invite scrutiny.

The structure of *March* is similar to that of *Februarie*, even if not so strongly marked. The two shepherds carry on a sprightly dialogue enlivened by native wit and bawdy innuendo, culminating in Thomalin's account of shooting at Cupid and being shot in return. Willye attempts to cap Thomalin's performance by recalling another story about Cupid, originally told by his father, and their conversation ends at nightfall.

The basic metrical unit consists of six lines (two of tetrameter and one of trimeter, repeated) rhyming *aabccb*. The meter is iambic, though with much anapestic substitution; and frequent use of feminine rhymes contributes to the free-swinging rhythm. In effect, this is the old romance stanza, jokingly employed by Chaucer in *Sir Thopas*.

The opening dialogue between the love-anxious boys may elicit an indulgent smile and Thomalin's encounter with Cupid is engagingly narrated, but the eclogue is not wholly pleasing in either subject matter or style. The disparity between Arcadian delicacy and English homeliness is not satisfactorily resolved.

Aprill Following the analysis of love in *March*, this eclogue brings again to the foreground the theme of Colin's unrequited love for Rosalind. Hobbinol sadly reports what we saw at the end of *Januarye*: the lovesick lad has broken his pipes. To satisfy Thenot's request for an example of the young poet's excellence, Hobbinol then sings Colin's panegyric of Elisa, queen of the shepherds, with its wide variety of hyperbolic praise. The reference points unmistakably to Queen Elizabeth.

Theocritus had eulogized his monarch (Idyll 17), and Virgil had frequently acclaimed his influential friends (eg, Eclogue 4). The Muses and Graces also contribute to the classical elegance of *Aprill*. But this is an English queen, so local nymphs, ladies of the lake, and shepherds' daughters add a homelier, more spontaneous touch to the joyful proceedings. The catalogue of flowers, given their kitchen-garden names, fittingly climaxes this honest admiration of 'fayre *Elisa*.' Much attention has been given to the eclogue's rhetoric of praise for Elizabeth (Cullen 1969, Cain 1978, J.N. Brown 1980, Montrose 1980).

Despite its double purpose – to recall Colin's despairing love and to flatter the Queen – the eclogue is well unified. The opening dialogue between Thenot and Hobbinol recounts effectively the lovesickness and despondency of Colin, and leads naturally to the lengthy panegyric of Elizabeth. A rather formal exchange between the two shepherds – one stanza given to each – closes the scene with further recognition of Colin's hopeless love. The eclogue unfolds, despite abrupt shifts in mood and tempo, with consummate smoothness and logicality.

The duality of this eclogue is reflected also in its metrics. The dialogue is composed in a simple quatrain of iambic pentameters rhyming *abab*, but the encomium takes the form of a grandiose ode employing an intricate nine-line stanza made up of varying lines. This experiment in plastic verse corresponds to the highly wrought dirge of *November*, and foreruns the extended lyrical stanzas of *Epithalamion* and *Prothalamion*.

In *Aprill*, Colin is shown again as Rosalind's lover and Hobbinol's friend, the triangle that provides a scant narrative sequence in the *Calender*. He also appears in a new role, as poet laureate to a praiseworthy queen. We have further evidence of Colin's poetic skill in *August* and *November*, and we hear more of his problems in *June* and *October*. These hints, of course, correlate closely with Spenser's own attempts at seeking Elizabeth's favor through poetic praise, attempts that culminate in *The Faerie Queene*.

Maye For the first time in the poem, Spenser speaks directly to religious issues, and the shepherd appears primarily in his role as clergyman. Pastoral provides a convenient vehicle for ecclesiastical debate because much religious language comes from country life. In the Argument for *Maye*, E.K. notes the equivalence of pastor and minister. The flock is, of course, the congregation, as in line 49. Pan, despite the identification as Henry VIII in *Aprill* (51 gloss) is commonly 'the shepheards God' – that is, Christ.

Petrarch in his *Bucolicum carmen* had established for the Renaissance this Christian adaptation of pastoral, and Mantuan in his *Adolescentia* had employed it as an instrument for ecclesiastical reform. They had been followed by Marot in France and by Skelton and Googe in England. Spenser was familiar with this adaptation of pastoral for satire – in fact, his persona is Colin Clout, the name assumed by Skelton in his attack on clerical abuses (McLane 1961). Puritans added another equivalence to this metaphorical complex: wolves or foxes represent papists who try to steal away unsuspecting lambs from the Protestant fold. Such wolves, 'ful of fraude and guile,' creep into *Maye* (127).

Spenser is careful to tie in the ecclesiastical debate with the winsomeness of the season. The opening remarks of Palinode call attention to the maypole festivities, and thereby introduce the question of what constitutes the good – and godly – life. Piers manifestly depicts a Protestant clergyman of integrity and insists upon abstinence. His name would bring to mind Langland's Plowman, another Piers in the same tradition. The name may also be a topical allusion to John Piers, the much admired Bishop of Salisbury (McLane 1961:175–87). Palinode probably does not represent an historical personage, but rather suggests a Catholic priest who accepted the Act of Conformity but then recanted; or perhaps he is just a backsliding English minister who has resumed some papist attitudes and practices. He disputes the puritanical asceticism of Piers by arguing that God offers the delights of this world for man's enjoyment, and therefore refusal of earthly pleasure is a denial of God's goodness.

Set in this debate, though hardly a continuation of it, is Piers' fable of the Fox and the credulous Kid. It seeks to expose the guile of the papists who deceitfully gain the confidence of ingenuous Protestants and then snatch them from the safety of Puritan morality. The tale is told with much child-like detail, such as the description of the Fox's disguise and of the baubles in his pack. Spenser follows the conventions in the medieval cycle of stories about Reynard the Fox, quite different from the Aesopic fable of *Februarie*. The former warns against danger, and must be recognizably realistic; the latter exhorts to virtuous behavior, and must be generally applicable.

The structure of *Maye* recalls that of *Februarie*. After considerable converse between the two shepherds, there comes a fable with a pointed moral, and then a brief concluding dialogue. Again, as in *Februarie*, the fable reflects the relationship between the two speakers: Palinode with his seductive invitation to enjoy the delights of Maytime is indeed tempting Piers from the steadfastness of his cloistered virtue. But unlike *Februarie*, where the fable is the focus of interest, *Maye* concentrates upon the relative positions of the two clergymen as their arguments develop in the dialogue, and the fable seems incidental, an afterthought about a peripheral problem.

Just as the structure of *Maye* is similar to that of *Februarie*, so are the metrics. Both consist of free-flowing verse paragraphs in rough tetrameter rhyming couplets. This parallelism in structure and metrics indicates that *Maye* carries on the moral earnestness of the earlier eclogue.

This is by far the longest eclogue, and also the most intellectually demanding. In the Argument, E.K. oversimplifies the matter beyond recognition. *Maye* is not merely antipapist sentiment. Spenser does not pit Catholic against Puritan with a foregone conclusion, but in the dialogue explores painstakingly the pull of the flesh against the timidity and fear of the soul. Even though the argumentative edge lies with Piers (Hume 1969, but see also Waters 1974), the religious and moral issues are honestly dissected. When Milton probed his commitment in *Lycidas*, he also used the same terms of Christian pastoral.

The fable of the Fox and Kid is another matter. There Piers speaks with the strident voice of a propagandist. We shall hear this voice again in *Julye* and *September*, and especially in *Mother Hubberds Tale*, where the poetry is harshly didactic and the allegory crushingly blunt. In the debate between Piers and Palinode, however, Spenser is more problematical and philosophical.

June At this midway point in the calendar, Colin reiterates the hopelessness of his love. Rosalind proves worse than indifferent; she has bestowed her affection elsewhere. Even in the midst of summer when nature is herself joyful and compliant, the shepherd is denied fulfillment in Arcadia. In *Januarye* he was desolate, in keeping with the weather; but since nature now smiles while he is sad, his sorrow is all the more acute. Furthermore, Hobbinol lacks nothing for his happiness and in Colin's view has found Adam's lost Paradise. Compared to his friend's blissful state, Colin feels luckless and displaced. The touchstone here is Virgil's Eclogue 1, where Tityrus pipes comfortably secure beneath the beech tree, while Meliboeus sadly leads away his flock into the harsh nonpastoral world.

If the Colin-Rosalind romance is interpreted autobiographically, Menalcas in this eclogue should stand for some rival to Spenser; but no historical identification has been more than a wild guess. The name itself comes from Virgil, Eclogues 3 and 5. McLane (1961:36–40) reads Menalcas as an anagram of Alençon, the former title of the Duc d'Anjou, and interprets this eclogue in terms of Spenser's despair when the Queen looked favorably upon the French marriage. In another vein, if Rosalind is simply the idealized lady of the young poet's dream, Menalcas is no more than a rival suitor, a conventional obstacle in the course of true love. Hobbinol is still, of course, the confidant, Harvey. His advice to Colin to forsake the hills and move into the pleasurable dales is interpreted by E.K. as a suggestion that the poet leave northern England for the south. This seems a scarcely veiled allusion to Spenser's employment by John Young in Kent.

The stanzas of dialogue are divided equally between Hobbinol and Colin, except for Colin's long six-stanza speech which begins about the middle of the eclogue. At this climax, Colin gives two stanzas each to a falsely modest evaluation of his poetic hopes, a eulogy of Chaucer, and an announcement of Rosalind's discourtesy in ignoring his suit while accepting that of Menalcas. Hobbinol concludes with a single stanza of conventionally sympathetic sentiment.

The metrics of this eclogue are experimental and not wholly successful. The basic unit is an eight-line stanza of polished iambic pentameters rhyming *ababbaba*. It is an academic exercise in the same spirit as Colin's sestina in *August* and exhibits some of the same awkwardness. Yet in large part Spenser manages to overcome the inherent stiffness of eight identical lines and the monotony of four-times repeated rhymes. Not since *Januarye*, Colin's last appearance, have the verses rolled so smoothly.

June is uncomplicated by protest or didacticism, and critics have singled it out as one of the more artful eclogues. Certainly the mood of melancholy and desolate longing is sustained, poignantly reprising the amorous complaint of *Januarye*. Colin is a poet *manqué*, driven out of Arcadia by the desperate knowledge that Rosalind is lost to him.

Julye This eclogue resumes the religious controversy of *Maye* in the same spirit of Mantuan's pastoral of protest (Eclogue 8), and the relative positions of hill and plain represent the clerical stance of pride or humility. The poet's choice clearly tends toward the plain, although the debate in this eclogue is not so acrimonious as E.K. makes out in the Argument. The worst accusations made against the proud clergy are relic worship, the wearing of vestments, and mercenary dealings. Neither of the disputants is persuaded, or even brought seriously to reconsider his point of view, and they part amicably (Anderson 1970a, Shore 1979).

The disguise of the characters in this eclogue is thin indeed. The goatherd 'Morrell' by a simple transposition of syllables is derived from Elmore – John Aylmer, Bishop of London, who was unpopular because of his heavy-handed treatment of the Puritans. The shepherd 'Thomalin' is almost as readily identified as Thomas Cooper, Bishop of Lincoln, a prodigious scholar and preacher. 'Algrind' is obviously Edmund Grindal, from 1576 Archbishop of Canterbury. Thomalin's account of how Algrind was brained by the shellfish dropped by an eagle alludes to the heavy censure inflicted upon Grindal by the Queen in 1577.

The structure of *Julye* is similar to that of *June*. There is no set piece upon which to focus, but rather the dialogue builds to its own climax in the long central speech of Thomalin. Then like an addendum comes the commiserative report of Algrind's mishap, protracting the main argument. This is perhaps the most casual eclogue in its wandering from topic to topic.

The verse paragraphs are composed of four-line units that closely resemble the standard ballad stanza, with the first and third lines also rhyming. There is clear analogy to the rough tetrameters of the other moral eclogues – *Februarie*, *Maye*, and *September*. The vulgar meter and the colloquial vocabulary lend a crude tone to the speech of Thomalin and Morrell.

The style of this eclogue is pedestrian and the subject matter hackneyed, and the theme, largely borrowed from Mantuan, lacks conviction. Morrell's reply to Thomalin's harangue is allowed to stand without refutation. *Julye*, too docile for satire, seems inadequate also as eloquent compromise.

August This singing match between Willye and Perigot adapts one of the traditional set pieces of pastoral poetry. Two shepherds sing in competition for a wager, while a herdsman's boy serves as judge. E.K. in the Argument notes the precedent for this convention in Theocritus (Idylls 5 and 6) and in Virgil (Eclogues 3 and 7), and imitations were rife. Spenser's innovation lies in the song that he assigns to Cuddie, the judge – actually another sort of set piece – a lament, purportedly composed by Colin and sung in his absence. There is no inherent connection between a singing match and August, but Spenser takes pains to notice 'the scortching heate' of this late summer month.

Willye in *March* was a shepherd's boy concerned with love, and so he appears here in perhaps a lighter vein. Perigot, a meaningless name apparently original with Spenser, is a fit companion. Cuddie may be the callow youth who impatiently listened to the fable of the Oak and the Briar in *Februarie*; if so, his critical perceptions have greatly improved, and will improve even more by *October*. This is a recreative eclogue, rather than satirical, and the characters do not likely represent actual personages.

The structure of *August* is its most arresting feature. The various elements within the whole are clearly defined and yet neatly interrelated. In the opening 52 lines of dialogue, the challenge is made by Willye and accepted by Perigot, and the stakes are laid: a carved bowl against a spotted lamb. The contest itself, a lively song in a popular manner, occupies 72 lines. An interlude of 26 lines permits Cuddie to proclaim a tie, and to propose the recitation of a 'doolefull verse' that Colin made about Rosalind. Then comes Colin's 39-line lament. The eclogue is closed with four lines of standard praise by Perigot and two lines of conventional farewell by Cuddie.

The moods of the eclogue are likewise firmly delineated. At the beginning, Willye's insistent gaiety is contrasted with Perigot's reticent love-melancholy. Their song resolves this contrast, however, and turns to falderal. The roundelay describes the suddenness of love and playfully mocks the unsuccessful suitor. But then in absolute contrast comes Colin's 'heavy laye' which reveals the wretchedness of the unrequited lover. Perigot, himself a sympathetic victim of lovesickness, in his concluding criticism seeks a synthesis by praising Colin as 'the shepheards joye,' while at the same time emphasizing the dolefulness of his verse.

The metrics also support the abrupt shifts in mood. The dialogue between Willye and Perigot, and later Cuddie, employs a six-line stanza rhyming *ababcc* made up of rough iambic tetrameters. The lines of any one stanza may be distributed between two speakers. This is a debased form of the *Januarye* stanza, and suggests that Willye and Perigot, though singing conventional pastoral pieces, are inferior poets to Colin and Hobbinol. The next movement, the roundelay of Willye and Perigot, defies scansion and echoes the strong but undisciplined rhythms of folk music. Colin's lament, on the other hand, in the metrical form of the sestina, is a display of academic restraint in rhythm and studied manipulation in rhyme.

The mechanical construction of *August* is salient. For the first 24 lines, the gregarious Willye has four lines of each stanza, which the disconsolate Perigot then completes with a final couplet. Next Willye has two stanzas, followed by Perigot's one, with the 2:1 ratio maintained. And finally a stanza is assigned 2–2–2 between them. This formality by contrast accentuates the rollicking rhythm of the song that follows – which, despite its lyrical freedom, has its own stringently monitored form. The interlude between the roundelay and Colin's sestina returns to the metrics of the opening dialogue, and is just as carefully apportioned. After the studied contrivance of the sestina itself, the eclogue concludes with another stanza divided 4–2 between two speakers, closing with the same arrangement as it opened. This étude in form makes order a foil for virtuousity.

The song composed by Willye and Perigot, supposedly extempore, is little more than a pleasant game. But Colin's sestina describes his lovesickness with a pathetic fallacy reminiscent of *Januarye* and *June*, thereby recalling the Colin-Rosalind narrative thread. The aesthetic purpose of the eclogue, however, is to allow Spenser a full run of poetic skills. Behind the personae of the various characters, he races through the extremes, from a homely English song to an overwrought Italianate exercise. By using a variety of metrics and moods, he audaciously dazzles us with his virtuosity within the rigid limits of convention.

September This eclogue, like *August*, employs one of the most anciently honored motifs in pastoral poetry. Diggon Davie has visited the town, and returns destitute and disillusioned to tell Hobbinol what he has seen. This motif reveals a basic premise of the pastoral mode, which plays the perfect world of Arcadia against the depravity of actual society. September, when 'the Westerne wind bloweth sore,' provides a suitable setting for Diggon's sorry recital.

Lifting much from Mantuan's Eclogue 9, *September* develops further the ecclesiastical satire prominent in *Maye* and *Julye*. Diggon Davie is readily identified as Richard Davies, Bishop of St David's in Wales (Diggon is Welsh dialect for Diccon, or Richard). Hobbinol, as usual, is the mask for Harvey, still sympathetic, though here his solicitations comfort a hard-pressed Puritan rather than a lovesick poet. Their conversation highlights the problems faced by the provincial prelate.

The story of Roffy and his dog Lowder has not been fully explicated. Roffy, a name cleverly taken from Marot, undoubtedly represents John Young, Bishop of Rochester, the Latin for which is Roffensis; and Diggon reports some recent incident in which he uncovered and destroyed a subversive papist. The precise identities of Lowder and of the wolf in sheep's clothing, however, remain hidden.

The structure of *September* recalls *Februarie* and *Maye*. A story overtly moralistic is set as a climax in a sustained dialogue. But here the story itself, a particular scandal, is incidental. It is not an autonomous unit; rather it integrates casually with the dialogue. It is but one more instance in the list of church-related evils.

The metrics also echo *Februarie* and *Maye*. Again verse paragraphs are formed from couplets of uneven iambic tetrameters. This forthrightly simple unit is appropriate to the degraded state of Diggon. Moreover, it provides an agreeable context for the number of dialectal words that locate him as a Welshman and for the number of proverbs that display his wry wisdom.

This eclogue continues the exposé of a degenerate clergy, and it repeats the warning in *Maye* about the guilefulness of papists. The wicked town that Diggon has visited may be Rome or London, perhaps intentionally unspecified. But the protest against clerical greed is strong and clear.

October This half-bitter, half-nostalgic survey of the decayed state of poetry takes its cue from Theocritus' Idyll 16 and Mantuan's Eclogue 5. Assuming the familiar stance of the unappreciated poet, Cuddie frets about the progress of his career and complains that poetry has fallen upon evil days. Piers attempts to counter his pessimism, but Cuddie maintains that the poet is poorly rewarded by the public and that the nobles withhold their patronage. Moreover, the manly deeds of yesteryear have given way to mediocrity, leaving no worthy subject for poetry. Spenser elaborates this theme in *Teares of the Muses*, there speaking very much in the lamenting tone of *October* 61–72. Such a theme of decay is fitting for the month.

Cuddie in this eclogue is 'the perfecte paterne of a Poete,' as E.K. labels him in the Argument, though he is disillusioned about the poet's estate. In his disappointment, he seems to speak for Spenser himself, while Piers voices Spenser's aspirations. Cuddie's career, like Spenser's, has begun with pastorals; but Piers counsels that now he should turn to more rewarding genres. They consider epic and panegyric and romance, with Elizabeth and Leicester as subjects.

Piers not only instigates this discussion but also expresses a point of view not present in Theocritus or Mantuan. He is an optimistic idealist in the philosophical sense, espousing a theory of art set forth most succinctly in Plato's *Ion* and *Phaedrus*. According to this theory, the poet is inspired by a divine force; and in an ecstasy, rising above bodily sensations and his individual personality, he views the eternal world of essences and becomes the mouthpiece for truth. The poet serves as a sacred vessel of holy wisdom, a seer, a *vates*. This theory directly opposes the Horatian premise that poetry is a skill to be learned by the study of rules and by practice. E.K. in the Argument calls into play these aesthetic principles when he declares that poetry is 'no arte, but a divine gift and heavenly instinct not to bee gotten by laboure and learning, but adorned with both: and poured into the witte by a certaine *enthousiasmos* and celestiall inspiration.' Into his mind had come Horace's *Ars poetica*, where *ars* means 'skill' or 'technique,' and he sternly dissociates *October* from this theory of poetry by rote.

As the eclogue proceeds, Piers develops other themes in the Platonic tradition. When Cuddie describes his destitute state, Piers replies that fame – the reward of the poet measured against eternity – is more to be desired than gold. In a Puritan context, the honor of the poet comes from moral instruction of the young, but also operative here is Plato's conclusion in *Republic* 10 that only ethical poets could be tolerated. In this same speech, Piers alludes to the basic tenet of Platonist aesthetics: when the poet sings for his audience, it 'Seemeth thou dost their soule of sence bereave' – he seems to take his listeners along the route of ecstasy until the soul perceives celestial truth, leaving behind the body and its senses. Later when Cuddie grieves that the poet no longer has either patrons or worthy subjects, Piers in an impassioned outburst concludes that poetry must fly back to heaven, whence it came. When Cuddie expresses doubt whether poetry's wings can accomplish such a flight, Piers rejoins that love can lift Colin from the 'loathsome myre' of this world and raise his mind 'above the starry skie.' This ascent using love as the impetus starts with the mistress, the 'immortall mirrhor,' the mundane reflection of all that is heavenly. Spenser elucidates this relationship between beauty and love in *Fowre Hymnes*.

The conclusion of this debate is frank and touching. Piers' argument reaches its high point in the eulogy on the powers of love. But Cuddie rejoins that love is debilitating, since it precludes the sort of repose that a pastoral poet requires. It is an experience of the flesh, and therefore detrimental to the experience of the soul. Instead, Cuddie develops another theme implicit in the *Ion*, and suggests that wine might be more effective than love for lifting the spirit above the body. With the poet in a wine-soaked euphoria, 'The nombers flowe as fast as spring doth ryse.' But this means of inspiration is likewise dismissed, and Cuddie resigns himself to the humble status of a shepherd's life.

The stanza comprises six lines of even iambic pentameters rhyming *abbaba*. This is a self-conscious variation of the *Januarye* stanza, and by its regularity suggests the artistic achievement of the speakers.

In this eclogue, the shepherd appears primarily as poet. The pastoral world with its loveliness and leisure was a natural haven for the dismayed novice; and if he had Platonist leanings, how easy to see the longed-for beauty and goodness and truth in the serenity of Arcadia. *October* is at the same time the most noble and the most personal of the eclogues, an embodiment of Spenser's own dilemma (but see Hardin 1975–6). Through Piers he expresses admiration for the poet's noble calling, while through Cuddie he recognizes the slim chance for worldly gain. The new poet struggles toward a manifesto.

November This eclogue is structured around a dirge, the most persistent of the set pieces in pastoral. Theocritus had lamented the death of Daphnis in sentimental terms (Idyll 1), and Moschus and Bion had composed even more eloquent pastoral elegies. Virgil had appended to the genre an apotheosis of the loved one (Eclogue 5). The immediate model for *November*, as E.K. says in the Argument, was Marot's *Complaincte de Madame Loyse de Savoye*, a lament for the mother of Francis I.

The interlocutors here are Thenot, the venerable shepherd of *Februarie* and *Aprill*, and Colin. As in *Aprill*, Thenot asks his companion to sing a song, and the set piece follows after a gracious exchange of compliments. Colin sings a dirge for Dido, by far the greatest portion of the eclogue, and Thenot concludes with a single stanza of appreciation.

The dirge itself is likewise simple but definite in structure. It follows the conventional movement from invocation of the Muse, through exhortation of the shepherds to mourn and the enumeration of Dido's virtues, to the response of nature, and finally to apotheosis of the loved one. The transformation from earthly maid to divinity is prepared for by a stanza of *contemptus mundi* and is echoed in the change of refrain from 'heavie herse' and 'carefull verse' to 'happye herse' and 'joyfull verse.' The body is mortal, and therefore heavy and full of care; but not the soul, which is happy and full of joy. E.K. suggests that the dirge for Dido is the high point of Colin's achievement (Davies 1981).

The opening dialogue consists of an urbane arrangement of quatrains compatible with the reverend age of Thenot and the disciplined talent of Colin. The lines of dignified iambic pentameter rhyme in contrived fashion *abab*, and the *b* rhyme of one quatrain becomes the *a* rhyme of the next quatrain, which then rhymes *bcbc*, so that an interlacing is achieved through rhyme. Spenser found this arrangement in Marot, and he experimented with it in the dialogue of *Aprill*. The dirge has its own elegant stanza of ten lines, like nothing else in the *Calender* except Colin's encomium of Elizabeth in *Aprill*. The basic foot is iambic, but the length of the line varies. This stanza includes a refrain, and has the unique peculiarity of beginning with an alexandrine. Spenser manages the intricacies both of the interlaced quatrains and of the ten-line stanza with a high degree of fluency. Thenot's concluding comment is couched in the six-line stanza of *Januarye* – which is the metrical unit for *December* as well, so the final stanza of *November* leads naturally into the next eclogue.

The interpretative crux of *November* rests with the identity of Dido. Attempts to determine her identity have proved unconvincing. The question of whether or not she was an actual person, however, has implications for the fictionality of the *Calender* and therefore must be addressed. In any case, an eclogue that bewails the death of a highborn maiden is eminently suitable for dreary November, and it allows Spenser to display again his talent for 'doolefull verse' (*Aug* 140).

E.K. gives no reason for his claim that *November* surpasses all the other eclogues, but probably the dirge for him epitomized the pastoral tradition. The tension between the ideal and reality, between what is longed for and what actually occurs, provides the impetus for pastoral, and the image of death in an idyllic setting presents most concisely this opposition.

December Of all the eclogues, this one generates the strongest mood of languid, graceful melancholy. In both tone and metrical form, it recalls *Januarye*. *December* is similar to *Januarye* also in the simplicity of its structure. One stanza by an unidentified narrator establishes the setting, and then Colin sings uninterruptedly in his own voice. Spenser's intention to link this last eclogue with the first is unmistakable.

In essence, *December* is a hymn to the shepherds' god Pan, closely imitating Marot's *Eglogue au Roy*. After a conventional plea for the god's good will, Colin recounts the course of his life proportioned to the four seasons of the year. Carefree youth in spring, summer hot with love, and the disappointing harvest now give way to winter full of care. This analogy was commonplace, though Spenser follows the immediate precedent of Marot. Functionally, this motif, a truncated calendar, serves as a reprise of the entire work, with the decline of Colin repeated in brief compass for emphasis. The eclogue concludes simultaneously with the end of Colin's song, with his formal leave-taking of all that has been dear to him.

This mournful eclogue, prepared for by the dirge of *November*, completes the narrative of Colin's luckless devotion to Rosalind. His love has been unreturned. At the end he says farewell to his flock, to the woods, to Hobbinol, and to Rosalind. But this eclogue in its turn leads back to *Januarye*. The speaker, the subject matter, the structure, the metrics – all bring us back to the amorous complaint that initiated this calendar. The cycle has been completed, and yet will start anew.

In the epilogue to the *Calender*, Spenser abruptly steps back from the pastoral world of Colin Clout and objectifies it. He speaks in his own voice, precluding the simple identification between himself and his shepherds, and creates the distance that allows authorial comment about the meaning of his fiction. 'Loe I have made a Calender for every yeare,' he claims triumphantly, pointing to both the specificity and the universality of his poem. Although Colin approaches death, the appointed end of every individual, the story of his life will have continuous viability. Each person must die, but the Arcadian values epitomized in the ongoing calendar and preserved in the poem will persist. The perfection of the calendar is played off against the pain of Colin's actual experiences, and the promise of its perpetuation brings hope. This is the vatic message that Spenser proclaims in *The Shepheardes Calender*.

E.K. in the dedicatory epistle designates the author as 'our new Poete,' but this partisan comment is little more than puffery. Although the *Calender* deals with contemporary social and religious issues, it is largely traditional in its poetics. Spenser followed current practice in the use of genres, metrics, and the language arts, as E.K. indicates incessantly in his gloss. Spenser is not nearly so innovative an author as Sidney, for example, or even Gascoigne. Furthermore, except for the twelve-part form, there is little hint of Spenser's greatest work, *The Faerie Queene*.

Nonetheless, the *Calender* was remarkably popular in its own time, and not merely because of its topicality. It enjoyed four subsequent editions before Spenser died in 1599, and it exerted an immediate and lasting influence on the lyric tradition (*Var* 7:641–5, Koller 1940, Alpers 1985). While we may not remember the poem for the power of particular passages, we must admire the sophistication that conceived and executed so intricate an artifact. We must also recognize it as the first poem in English with its own programmatic set of illustrations, thereby blending verbal and visual images. So *The Shepheardes Calender* seems secure in its place as a landmark in our literary landscape. It fascinates by challenging us to reconstruct the circumstances that surrounded its composition. Finally, without minimizing the anguish inherent in the human condition, it reassures us with the optimism of its syncretic vision.

S.K. Heninger, Jr

Scholarship on *SC* during the first half of the twentieth century concentrated upon its sources and analogues, upon the historical identification of characters and events, and upon the archaic diction. Because the text did not submit to the sort of close analysis dictated by the New Criticism, it received scant attention from formalist critics. After publication of the *Variorum*, however, criticism turned to thematic concerns. Since mid-century, a lively debate has developed about the context in which the poem first appeared and about the significance of this context. Readers of quite different persuasions have offered interpretations in the light of literary tradition, of Spenser's own career, and of political and social conditions.

For Hamilton (1956), Spenser sets out to explore the role of the poet-pastor in society. Beginning with what Spenser added to the pastoral form, the calendar, Hamilton emphasizes the synchronization of *SC* with the Nativity and notes its depiction of mankind alternately in both an Edenic state, the 'unreal' world of Arcadia, and a fallen state, the 'real' world of the moral and satiric eclogues. Colin's disconsolate act of hanging up his pipes in *December* becomes Spenser's rejection of the pastoral life of innocence and ease in order to enter upon a dedicated life of politics, which for him meant writing an heroic poem such as *FQ*.

Several later critics have developed themes explicit or implicit in Hamilton's essay, usually by way of taking issue with him. Durr (1957) emphasizes the unity of *SC*, which harmoniously interrelates the topics of love, religion, and poetry into a single theme of *contemptus mundi*. For him, the poem presents the age-old conflict between flesh and spirit, and Colin justly reaps the reward of his sins. His death signals that he is a failed poet as well as a failed lover and pastor. Berger (1969–70), starting from Hamilton's analysis of E.K.'s classification of the eclogues into three categories (plaintive, moral, and recreative), ponders how Spenser fits the diction of his shepherds to varying notions of pastoral, and how he created superior poetry from the integration of the natural speech of the moral pastors with the figured rhetoric of Colin Clout. According to him, Spenser thereby surpasses the convention-bound life of Colin and achieves a broader, more mature perspective. Cullen (1970) similarly distinguishes two types of Renaissance pastoral: the 'Arcadian,' characterized by the *pastor felix* and the soft life of *otium*, and the 'Mantuanesque,' characterized by a moralistic attitude toward those entrusted with Christian duties. Noting how Spenser patterns these different points of view, Cullen offers an ethical analysis of Colin's performance, finding him reprehensible, a failed lover and poet, though not identical with Spenser.

Working largely from the texts themselves, MacCaffrey (1969) attempts to characterize Spenser's distinctive genius. She delineates the proclivities of his powerful imagination, which seized upon the calendar form as a means of displaying discontinuous continuity, multiple reference, and analogical relationships that point simultaneously to likeness and to unlikeness – the formal paradoxes that Spenser developed even further in *FQ*. Alpers (1972), however, objects to the portentousness of this reading at the expense of poetic surface and presence, and seeks to rescue the poem (and the larger tradition for pastoral in the Renaissance) from those who would separate man from nature. In his view, Colin is not a failed poet, but by December is the wise old shepherd revered in Arcadia. Shore (1976) similarly seeks to redeem the incapacitated Colin by reminding us that he is the poet of a world that by literary tradition is informed by love. Mallette (1981), reading *SC* alongside *Colin Clout*, sees both poems as an expression of certain practical problems that Spenser confronted in his own life and concludes that Colin is a failed poet because he is a poor lover. Bernard (1981) refutes Berger's view that Colin is simply a younger, more callow Spenser. Emphasizing the essential simplicity of the pastoral mode, Bernard searches for an underlying form (with *June* as its center) which reveals *SC* to be a guide to the landscape of the mind, the traditional territory of pastoral.

What is new in criticism of the last decade is the transformation of *SC* into a sociopolitical document. Hoffman (1977) continues to obliterate the distinction between Spenser the poet and Colin Clout the persona, though for purposes other than biographical or psychological. In the light of Spenser's historical moment, she considers the political implications of the pastoral mode as manifested in *SC* and finds that the poem offers moral counsel both to the individual Christian and to society at large. Helgerson (1978) returns the focus of criticism to Spenser's progress as a poet, though a poet bound by the system of expectations inflicted upon him by Elizabethan culture. He argues that Spenser was the first Englishman to think of writing as a professional vocation rather than an incidental distraction. Consequently, *SC* conceals the uncertainties of Spenser at the outset of his career, the struggle between the love poet who culpably neglects his duties to proclaim his passion and the vatic poet who inspires his countrymen to heroic deeds. Montrose (1979) argues that in the Petrarchan context of Colin's repeated praise of women – Rosalind, Elisa, Dido – Spenser explores particular modes of poetic power and seeks to transform language into worldly power. Miller (1979b), pointing to the medieval tradition for anonymity among poets, reads *SC* as Spenser's self-conscious effort to produce a classic and to create his own identity as a writer, though he disagrees with Helgerson that Spenser and Colin are one. Readings along these lines continue to proliferate.

D.C. Allen 1956 'Three Poems on Eros' *CL* 8:177–93; Allen 1968:1–19; Paul Alpers 1972 'The Eclogue Tradition and the Nature of Pastoral' *CE* 34:352–71; Alpers 1985 'Pastoral and the Domain of Lyric in Spenser's *Shepheardes Calender*' *Representations* 12:83–100; Anderson 1970a; Berger 1969–70; John D. Bernard 1981 '"June" and the Structure of Spenser's *Shepheardes Calender*' *PQ* 60:305–22; Bond 1981; Bristol 1970; J.N. Brown 1980; Marianne Brown 1984 'Spenserian Technique: *The Shepheardes Calender*' *REALB* 2:55–118; Byrom 1933; Cain 1968; Cain 1978:14–24; Donald Cheney 1989 'The Circular Argument of *The Shepheardes Calender* in Logan and Teskey 1989:137–61; Patrick Cullen 1969 'Imitation and Metamorphosis: The Golden-Age Eclogue in Spenser, Milton, and Marvell' *PMLA* 84:1559–70; Cullen 1970; H. Neville Davies 1981 'Spenser's *Shepheardes Calender*: The Importance of November' *CahiersE* 20(Oct): 35–48; A. Leigh DeNeef 1976 'The Dialectic of Genres in *The Shepheardes Calender*' *RenP 1975* pp 1–10; DeNeef 1982:17–27; Michael F.N. Dixon 1977 'Rhetorical Patterns and Methods of Advocacy in Spenser's *Shepheardes Calender*' *ELR* 7:131–54; Robert Allen Durr 1957 'Spenser's Calendar of Christian Time' *ELH* 24:269–95; Farmer 1986; Friedland 1937; Gilbert 1948; Greenlaw 1910; Greenlaw 1911; Greenlaw 1913; David G. Hale 1980 'Another Source for Spenser's Oak and Briar' *N&Q* 225:301; A.C. Hamilton 1956 'The Argument of Spenser's *Shepheardes Calender*' *ELH* 23:171–82; Hamilton 1982 '"The Grene Path Way to Lyfe": Spenser's *Shepheardes Calender* as Pastoral' in Hibbard 1982:1–21; Richard F. Hardin 1975–6 'The Resolved Debate of Spenser's "October"' *MP* 73:257–63; Helgerson 1978; S.K. Heninger, Jr 1962; Heninger 1988; Nancy Jo Hoffman 1977 *Spenser's Pastorals: 'The Shepheardes Calender' and 'Colin Clout'* (Baltimore); Anthea Hume 1969 'Spenser, Puritanism, and the "Maye" Eclogue' *RES* ns 20:155–67; Johnson 1933:2–8; L. Staley Johnson 1981 'Elizabeth, Bride and Queen: A Study of Spenser's April Eclogue and the Metaphors of English Protestantism' *SSt* 2:75–91; J.M. Kennedy 1980; Kathrine Koller 1940 'Abraham Fraunce and Edmund Spenser' *ELH* 7:108–20; Luborsky 1980; Luborsky 1981; Isabel G. MacCaffrey 1969 'Allegory and Pastoral in *The Shepheardes Calender*' *ELH* 36:88–109; Michael McCanles 1982 '*The Shepheardes Calender* as Document and Monument' *SEL* 22:5–19; McLane 1961; McLane 1973; H. Maclean 1978; Waldo F. McNeir 1977 'The Drama of Spenser's *The Shepheardes Calender*' *Anglia* 95:34–59; Richard Mallette 1981 *Spenser, Milton, and Renaissance Pastoral* (Lewisburg, Pa) pp 19–74; Miller 1979b; Louis Adrian Montrose 1979; Montrose 1980; Montrose 1981 'Interpreting Spenser's February Eclogue: Some Contexts and Implications' *SSt* 2:67–74; Montrose 1983; Moore 1975; Nelson 1963:30–63; Mary Parmenter 1936 'Spenser[’s] *Twelve Aeglogues Proportionable to the Twelve Monethes*' *ELH* 3:190–217; David A. Richardson 1978 'Duality in Spenser's Archaisms' *SLitI* 11.1:81–98; D[onald] M. Rosenberg 1981 *Oaten Reeds and Trumpets: Pastoral and Epic in Virgil, Spenser, and Milton* (Lewisburg, Pa) pp 55–88; Røstvig 1969; David R. Shore 1976; Shore 1979 'Morrell's Earthly Paradise and the Varieties of Pastoral in Spenser's July Eclogue' *ESC* 5:1–15; Shore 1985; Bruce R. Smith 1980 'On Reading *The Shepheardes Calender*' *SSt* 1:69–93; Hallett Smith 1952, esp pp 32–51; Leo Spitzer 1950; Walter F. Staton, Jr 1962 'Spenser's "April" Lay as a Dramatic Chorus' *SP* 59:111–18; S.F. Walker 1979; Waters 1974.

***The Shepheardes Calender*, mottos in** The 'emblemes' of *The Shepheardes Calender* are an intimate part of the poems which they conclude. They are products of the 'curious imaginations' of 'the Courtly maker,' and their 'wittie sentence or secrete conceit' needs to be 'unfolded or explaned by some interpretation.' Their 'use and intent ... is to insinuat some secret, wittie, morall and brave purpose presented to the beholder, either to recreate his eye, or please his phantasie, or examine his judgement, or occupie his braine or to manage his will either by hope or by dread, every of which respectes be of no litle moment to the interest and ornament of the civill life' (Puttenham 'Of the device or embleme' *Arte* 2.11).

The use of the word *embleme* in *The Shepheardes Calender* can cause difficulties for modern readers accustomed to the restriction of this term to the combination of motto, picture, and verses popularized by Alciati, or to the device where the emphasis is on the picture, as in Paradin. Spenser's usage is not unusual: Harvey scoffingly addresses Greene, 'remember thine owne marginal Embleme *Fortuna favet fatuis*' (ed 1922:48), and Florio (1598) equates 'an imprese, a mot, an embleme, a word' in translating *impresa*. However, both sixteenth-century and modern scholars have been concerned to make distinctions. The emblems of *The Shepheardes Calender* belong to that particular family of devices known as the *mot*, a group akin to the *impresa*, in relation to which Paolo Giovio 'enjoys a primacy analogous to that of Alciati for the emblem' (Praz 1933 'Impresa' in *Enciclopedia italiana* 18:938a-40a). In his prefatory letter to Daniel's translation of Giovio, N.W. distinguishes between *imprese* and emblems: '*Impreses* manifest the special purpose of Gentlemen in warlike combats or chamber tornaments. *Emblems* are generall conceiptes rather of moral matters then perticulare deliberations: rather to give credit to the wit, then to reveale the secretes of the minde.' In 'To the Frendly Reader,' Daniel enlarges upon the manner in which such 'devises' declare 'inward pretended purposes and enterprises' and 'discover our secret intentions'; he divides them into four kinds, one of which is the mot. Of mots, 'which truely are of great excellencie if they bee gallantly composed,' he gives the following main characteristics: (1) 'this word *mot* signifieth as much as *Gnome*, a shorte sentence or Posie'; (2) 'the mots which are chiefly used, are either amorus or grave, and they beare a great grace if they be perfectly composed with their circumstances and properties'; (3) they should be short, preferably not exceeding a verse in any tongue, and using only part of a Latin or Greek hexameter; (4) 'better are they esteemed being taken out of some famos autor'; (5) 'above all, if it be possible, let them leave some scruple whereon to meditate, to him who either readeth or heares them'; (6) 'it is lawfull to use them without figures [ie, illustrations], although that *Paulus Jovius* vainly termeth them so used, soules without bodies' (Giovio ed 1585: sigs *6v-7r, A1v-2r, A5r-6r).

The mot is often referred to in English as the 'word' (as in Sidney's descriptions of devices for Phalantus' tournament in *New Arcadia*, ed 1977:162, 164) or, as Daniel says, a 'Posie.' E.K. prefers the latter term, frequently referring to the emblem as the 'Poesye.' The closest similar use of such 'posies' in English before *The Shepheardes Calender* occurs in Gascoigne's *Hundreth Sundrie Flowres* (1573) and is repeated in his volume *The Posies* (1575), but his use does not demonstrate the complexity of relationships achieved by Spenser.

In his use of emblems, Spenser combines rich tradition, current fashion, and startling innovation. It was both familiar and fashionable for a motto to declare an individual's nature or situation, or to sum up the theme of a poem, but the combination of functions (as in Colin's *Januarye* emblem) is fresh. Even more unusual are the counterbalanced poesies reflecting debated positions as in the moral eclogues of *Februarie*, *Maye*, and *Julye*, or the several perspectives of complementary emblems in the recreative eclogues of *March*, *Aprill*, and *August*.

Giovio recommends that the posie 'ought to differ in language from the *Idioma* of him which beareth the *Impresa*.' Spenser's adherence to this advice (even the English emblems of *March* are translations of Latin tags) increases the enigmatic qualities of the device, and certainly for modern readers ensures that the meaning will not be 'so apparant that every rusticke may understand it' (ed 1585: B3v). E.K.'s gloss on each emblem (except the last) is the single most important source of information both for translations of the texts, and for teasing out the 'subtilitie and multiplicitie of sense' (Puttenham 2.11) of each, but it must always be remembered that his commentary is partial, and often deliberately and playfully obscure: Spenser himself notes of E.K.'s commentary on his unpublished *Dreames*, 'Therin be some things excellently, and many things wittily discoursed' (*Three Letters* 1, *Var Prose* p 18).

There are nineteen emblems in *The Shepheardes Calender*, seven in Italian, seven in Latin, two in Greek, two in English, and one in French. To this total may perhaps be added the 'missing' emblem of *December*, an emblem for Piers in *October*, and the signature of 'To His Booke,' 'Immeritô.' The following notes provide translations, sources where known, and possible interpretations. Because of the enigmatic nature of the form, even the translations may be ambiguous, and the applications of the sense are manifold. The interpretation as well as 'the framing of an *Impresa* is the adventure of a readie and phantasticall braine' (Giovio ed 1585: E2v).

'To His Booke' 'Immeritô' (Italian) may be translated 'the unworthy one.' It is used to refer to Spenser by both himself and Harvey throughout their correspondence (1580); in *Two Letters* 1, the Latin poem 'Ad ornatissimum virum,' presenting Immerito as a poor and lowly novice in contrast to the outstanding and established poet Harvey, is akin to his stance here, both suggesting the familiar topos of modesty in the poet. Harvey's jesting on the Italianate name 'Il Magnifico Segnior "Immerito" Benivolo' in a letter concerning the glory accorded to foreign poets and the neglect of English poets (ed 1884:66) draws attention to one of Spenser's aims in his poetic career: to exploit the resources of the English language and establish it as the equal or superior of other modern or ancient tongues. In another letter, Harvey states that his friend at court 'since a certayn chaunce befallen unto him, a secrett not to be revealid, calleth himself Immerito' (p 101); it has been suggested that this secrecy was related to the 'dangerous' political material of the moral eclogues (*Var* 7:235). In conjunction with the final emblem, the word Immerito can be seen as a disclaimer of personal desert or merit in religious terms.

Januarye 'Colins Embleme. / *Anchôra speme*' (Italian) may be translated '[there is] yet hope.' Shifting the emphasis to the first syllable of *anchora* suggests the Latin motto familiar in England as a printer's device (see title page of 1596 *FQ*), 'Anchora spei,' the Christian symbol, 'anchor of hope.' E.K.'s gloss, that 'leaning on hope, he is some what recomforted,' draws attention to the pun, but his interpretation is restricted to the amatory meaning, ignoring the religious connotations: Colin is still hoping for comfort in 'his extreme passion and lucklesse love'; a change of emphasis in the first word would remind him that the 'strong consolation' available to him is that hope which is the 'ancre of the soule, bothe sure and stedfast' (Heb 6.18–19).

Februarie 'Thenots Embleme. / *Iddio perche è vecchio, / Fa suoi al suo essempio*' and 'Cuddies Embleme. / *Niuno vecchio, / Spaventa Iddio*' (Italian) may be translated 'God, because he is old, / Makes his own to his own pattern' and 'No old man / Fears God.' Cuddie's 'byting and bitter proverbe' appears in Florio's collection of proverbs (*Giardino di ricreatione* 1591: sig R2v), but the Latin version quoted by E.K. ('Nemo Senex metuit Jovem') has not been located in Erasmus' *Adages*. E.K.'s lengthy commentary emphasizes the ambiguity of response possible to the eclogue's debate: his strictures fall quite evenhandedly on 'the rashheaded boy' and on 'olde men' for rash 'securitie' and 'fond fooleries' of superstition.

March 'Willyes Embleme. / *To be wise and eke to love, / Is graunted scarce to God above.* / Thomalins Embleme. / *Of Hony and of Gaule in love there is store: / The honye is much, but the Gaule is more.*' The homely English couplets are translations of familiar Latin tags found in many Renaissance schoolbooks, the first by Publilius Syrus ('Amare et sapere vix deo conceditur' *Minor Latin Poets* [Loeb] p 16), and the second by Plautus ('Namque ecastor Amor et melle et felle est fecundissimus; / gustui dat dulce, amarum ad satietatem usque oggerit' *Cistellaria, or The Casket Comedy* 1.69–70 [Loeb]). The first and one verse of the second appear in the popular collection by Georg Major, *Sententiae veterum poetarum* (Paris 1551:82, 85; in this edition *ecastor* 'by Castor' has become *castus* 'chaste,' and the line appears under 'Amor pudicus'; see Renwick in *SC* ed 1930:188–9n; also *FQ* IV x 1 and VI xi 1, Shakespeare *Troilus and Cressida* III ii 156–7, *Three Letters* 3 in *Var Prose* pp 469–70, and Tilley 1950: L 558). The associations of the emblems point to a youthfully superficial understanding of proverbial truths; but E.K.'s gloss, particularly in its reminiscence of Chaucer's 'For bothe I hadde thyng which that I nolde, / And ek I nadde that thyng that I wolde' (*Parliament of Fowls* 90–1), expands the meaning to touch on the growth of experience in love, art, and life, and looks forward to Colin's folly in *Aprill*, where he 'loves the thing, he cannot purchase' (159).

Aprill 'Thenots Embleme. / *O quam te memorem virgo?*' and 'Hobbinols Embleme. / *O dea certe*' (Latin) are from the *Aeneid* (1.327–8), and may be translated 'Oh what shall I call thee, virgin?' and 'Oh goddess surely!' Spenser draws on the same incident, of Aeneas mistaking his mother Venus for Diana, in the first appearance of Belphoebe (*FQ* II iii 21–33). The most obvious application of this famous episode is pointed out by E.K. in the gloss and Argument: the 'similitude of divinitie' is 'purposely intended to the honor and prayse of our most gracious sovereigne, Queene Elizabeth.' E.K.'s reversal of the attribution of the emblems in his gloss may be intended to suggest the complete unanimity of the shepherds in recognizing the Virgin Queen's divinity. The 'mayden Queene,' 'Like *Phoebe* fayre' is also a goddess of love: 'the question is not unjustified whether the worship of Queen Elizabeth as Diana was not also a cult of Venus in disguise' (Wind 1958:75). There are other implications of the episode. Venus appears to Aeneas to help him find the way to pursue his destiny of founding the Roman empire; similarly Elizabeth embodies and fulfills the national destiny of the British descendants of Aeneas. E.K. draws attention to 'the worthynes of Colins song,' adumbrating the destiny of the poet in epic celebration. Venus' last words to Aeneas are 'Only go forward and, where the path leads thee, turn thy steps!' (1.401): the path leads to Dido and a distracting love that must be renounced in favor of heroic fulfillment, a context which provides another perspective for considering the development of the poet, whether Colin, Immerito, or Spenser.

Maye 'Palinodes Embleme. / *Pas men apistos apistei*' and 'Piers his Embleme. / *Tis* *d'ara pistis apistō*' are translated by E.K. from the Greek as 'who doth most mistrust is most false' and 'what fayth then is there in the faythlesse.' Although E.K. claims that the first emblem is from Theognis, it has not been located. There is a comparable phrase in Mantuan's Eclogue 4.15: 'Qui non credit, inops fidei' (who does not believe, is poor in faith). E.K. in the Argument and gloss gives most weight to Piers' position, but the balanced forcefulness of the emblems supports those who see the ambivalence of this debate. Nevertheless, Palinode's experiences in Rome as reported by Thomalin in *Julye* indicate that his trustfulness was misplaced.

June 'Colins Embleme. / *Gia speme spenta*' (Italian) may be translated 'now hope [is] extinguished.' E.K. relates this to 'Colins Poesie' of *Januarye*, and interprets it as a reaction to the rejection of Rosalind. However, his comments are themselves wittily ambiguous, and his provocative conclusions to the Argument and gloss ('And this is the whole Argument of this Aeglogue' and 'Which is all the meaning of thys Embleme') invite speculation beyond the amatory meaning to the religious and poetic themes of the *Calender*. The faithless Rosalind recalls the debate about faith in *Maye*; and the despair which renounces 'all comfort and hope of goodnesse to come' is a denial of the Christian anchor of hope in God's grace and mercy suggested in *Januarye*, indicating that Colin's love for Rosalind is like the kind described in *March* 'wherein wanton youth walloweth' (glosse to emblem), which should be extinguished, so that Colin may leave childish ways and find the 'faith, hope, love [that] abide' (1 Cor 13, RSV). A considerable part of the eclogue, with its strong reminiscences of Virgil and Chaucer, is devoted to Colin as poet, who in lamenting 'I am not, as I wish I were' (105) suggests that at this point his poetic as well as his amatory hopes are damped.

Julye 'Thomalins Embleme. / In medio virtus' and 'Morrells Embleme. / In summo foelicitas' may be translated 'virtue [is found] in the middle' and 'happiness [is found] in the highest.' The balanced authority of each emblem is emphasized by E.K.'s paired statements 'Suorum Christus humillimus' and 'Suorum deus altissimus' (Christ the lowliest of his own; God the highest of his own). The emblems and gloss suggest that both points of view in the debate have validity; however, the description in the Argument of Morrell as a 'proude and ambitious' pastor and the authoritative appeal of 'the meane and lowly state' favor Thomalin's position. We are told to imitate Christ, but wishing to be as God caused our fall; Christian virtue may be humbly sought, but heavenly felicity may not be ambitiously aspired to. The assigning of the first emblem to Palinode in all the Quartos and Folios, while probably an error, does serve to call attention to the importance of Palinode's experience as described by Thomalin, which may have taught him that it is better to seek virtue in the mean, than 'usen ... freely our felicitie' (*Maye* 155).

August 'Perigot his Embleme. / *Vincenti gloria victi*,' 'Willyes Embleme. / *Vinto non vitto*,' and 'Cuddies Embleme. / *Felice chi può*' may be translated 'to the victor is the glory of the vanquished,' 'excelled not vanquished,' and '[he is] happy who can.' The juxtaposing of different languages (Latin for Perigot, Italian for Willye and Cuddie) is unique to this eclogue's emblems. They are, moreover, difficult to translate: *Vinto* and *vitto*, for example, mean the same, and the many English synonyms for each and for the infinitive *vincere* offered in Florio 1598 yield fascinating possibilities for various combinations. Harvey quotes the first emblem in the margin of his copy of Foord's *Synopsis politica* (1582; see Harvey ed 1913:192), and E.K.'s gloss of these 'very ambiguous' mottos is itself wittily enigmatic, even misleading. Perigot does not himself claim the conquest, though at first Cuddie seems inclined to award it to him, and the compromise of the exchange of wagers is happily accepted by both contestants. It is not clear in the eclogue how Cuddie is patron of his own cause, for it is not until *October* that he is seen as a poet himself, rather than crowned in Colin's stead. Cuddie's emblem is broken off and invites completion: happy he who can write poetry? win the contest? give voice to woe? win sympathy? find a patron? E.K.'s variant completions, 'win the beste, or moderate him selfe being best, and leave of with the best,' suggest that some meanings may refer beyond the particular poetic contest to ethical demeanor.

September 'Diggons Embleme. / *Inopem me copia fecit*' is from Ovid *Metamorphoses* 3.466, and is translated by Spenser 'plenty makes me poore' (*Amoretti* 35). The story of the beautiful boy who pined away for frustrated love of his own image reflected in water is primarily concerned with self-knowledge. Tiresias had prophesied that Narcissus would live to old age if he did *not* know himself, an apparent contradiction of the maxim that one's highest duty is to know oneself. The dangers of knowledge, particularly of a superficial or delusory kind, are demonstrated in Diggon, who has lost his vocation and his way through acquisition of a store of experience. E.K. also draws attention to the fascination this 'poesie' exerted over 'the author.' The insatiable desire for the unattainable which makes Narcissus, like Tantalus, a type of avarice is emphasized in *Amoretti* 35 and *FQ* I iv 29; but the sonnet is also concerned with such themes as vainglory, the shadows of the world, and the nature of true beauty. A frequent interpretation of Narcissus' destructive delusion was that it resulted from a failure to distinguish between the idolatrous attraction of corporal beauty and the true beauty of the soul. His confusion of shadow and reality may also be seen as an adolescent difficulty in distinguishing between self and non-self (see, eg, Rhodiginus 1542, 26.21; Edwards 1958:139–65). Colin, like Diggon and Cuddie, must learn to know himself truly and constructively, and to distinguish the true objects of desire in love, in art, in religion.

October 'Cuddies Embleme. / *Agitante calescimus illo etc*' is the second half of the verse in Ovid *Fasti* 6.5. The 'etc' suggests that more verses should be recalled; lines 5 and 6 read 'est deus in nobis; agitante calescimus illo: / impetus hic sacrae semina mentis habet' ('There is a god within us. It is when he stirs us that our bosom warms; it is his impulse that sows the seeds of inspiration'. This definition of poetry is obviously relevant to the eclogue, but its oddly broken presentation perhaps suggests defects in Cuddie or in his understanding. E.K.'s gloss implies that there should also be a summary or acclamatory emblem for Piers in praise of poetic skill. If 'skyll' is to be understood as acquired art distinguished from 'divine instinct,' Piers' motto might have suggested what aspect of Cuddie as poet was not sufficiently developed.

November 'Colins Embleme. / *La mort ny mord*' is translated by E.K. as 'death biteth not.' It was the personal motto of Marot (see *Ladolescence clementine: autrement, Les Oeuvres de Clement Marot* Paris 1532: sig iiv, where it appears following the date at the end of Marot's prefatory epistle); moreover, *November* is modeled on two of Marot's eclogues, and 'Colin' is the French poet's pastoral name. E.K.'s gloss emphasizes the religious message that Christ's death has made mortality the way to eternal life; death has lost its sting, 'For this corruptible must put on incorruption: and this mortal must put on immortalitie' (1 Cor 15.53, 55). Marot's fame as translator of the psalms (in the version completed by Theodore Beza) helps recall Psalm 23, where the good shepherd leads the psalmist through the valley of the shadow of death to dwell in the house of the Lord for ever. Marot was also famous as a court poet, which suggests the poet's relationship with his monarch, thereby reinforcing the connections between *Aprill* and *November* (Elisa and Dido-Elissa). The parallel with Marot is a reminder that the English author aspires to go beyond a pastoral song 'made in honor of her Majestie' (*Aprill* Arg) to the epic heights when he can 'consecrate these his labours to live with the eternitie of her fame' (*FQ* dedication).

December In all early editions, 'Colins Embleme' is lacking, although E.K. glosses its meaning as 'all thinges perish and come to theyr last end, but workes of learned wits and monuments of Poetry abide for ever.' By back translation from the gloss, Hughes in 1715 supplied a line from a poem ascribed to Virgil in Renaissance editions and used also in the first of Wither's *Collection of Emblemes* (1635): 'Vivitur ingenio, caetera mortis erunt' ('Elegiae in Maecenatem' 1.38, Virgil ed 1966). E.K.'s extended translation appears to draw on the preceding line: '†marmora minaei† vincent monumenta libelli.' Hughes' proposal has won general assent, though Renwick argues that 'La mort ny mord' is supposed to serve for *December* as well as *November* (*Var* 7:425–6), and A.H. Gilbert suggests that the final words of the *Calender*, 'Merce non mercede,' are intended as Colin's emblem (1948). E.K.'s quotations from Horace and Ovid also stress the immortal fame and immortalizing power of the poet. His paraphrase of lines from Horace's *Odes* 3.30 may be translated 'I have completed a monument more lasting than bronze, that neither the devouring rain nor north wind etc'; and his slightly altered quotation of Ovid's *Metamorphoses* 15.871–2 may be translated 'I have completed the great work that neither the wrath of Jove nor fire, nor sword nor voracious age will be able to efface.' The opening lines of Spenser's envoy echo both Horace and Ovid, and provide a strong contrast to Colin's elegiac farewell. Colin bids adieu to the delights of youth, the love of Rosalind, and the keeping of sheep; but E.K. and Immerito point to the poetic achievement completed, and suggest the aspirations of the future epic poet.

Epilogue 'Merce non mercede' may be translated 'grace not wages.' Because the Italian words *merce*, *mercé*, and *mercede* share a common root and many of the same meanings, it is difficult to translate this motto (cf 'vinto non vitto' for *August*). The most common interpretation is 'for reward [in the sense of substantial and intelligent response] not for hire [or salary]' (Maclean in Spenser ed 1982:467n). This translation does not embrace the moral and spiritual senses of the words, such as the riches of virtue, or the pity, compassion, mercy, or grace sought from the beloved or from God. Romans, particularly 4.3–5, often cited in support of the doctrine of justification by faith, provides a suitable religious context in setting out the importance of reward received by grace and not earned as wages. The motto affirms that as poet, as lover, and as Christian, one must rely on grace freely bestowed, not on rewards paid to desert. Placed beyond the epilogue, and not assigned to a speaker, the motto may be seen as applying to Immerito, who has reached an understanding of his life that Colin failed to find (see J.M. Kennedy 1980).

JUDITH M. KENNEDY

John Florio *Giardino di ricreatione* in ed 1591; Florio 1598; George Gascoigne 1942 *A Hundreth Sundrie Flowres* (1573) ed C.T. Prouty (Columbia, Mo); Paolo Giovio 1585 *The Worthy Tract of Paulus Jovius* tr Samuel Daniel (London; rpt Delmar, NY 1976); Harvey ed 1884; Harvey ed 1913; Harvey ed 1922; Philip Sidney 1977 *The Countess of Pembroke's Arcadia* ed Maurice Evans (Harmondsworth).

Calvin R. Edwards 1958 'Spenser and the Ovidian Tradition' (diss Yale Univ); Gilbert 1948; J.M. Kennedy 1980; Wind 1958.

***The Shepheardes Calender*, printing and illustration of** To the reader of 1579, the physical presentation of *The Shepheardes Calender* surely looked new. For the first time, original English poetry appeared as the central element in a tripartite unit of verse, scholarly apparatus, and freshly designed woodcuts. It is a unit that continued to so appear, despite changes in printers, in the succeeding four quarto editions and in the 1611 folio.

The following analysis concerns the salient features of the unit, with emphasis on the illustrations. Because the cuts were made by at least three craftsmen, and because the images relate inconsistently to the poem as a whole and to the particular eclogue, the basis for selecting what is salient is complicated. The method was comparison with contemporary practice and deduction of the artistic program, both by looking for consistency in kind of image and in attaching importance to elements that are clearly and carefully drawn.

(See ***SC*** illustrations, below in vol 2.)

Each of the twelve monthly units is composed of the name of the month, a woodcut illustration (60 × 100 mm, height by width), the Latin number of the 'Aegloga,' a prose Argument, the poem, one 'Embleme' or two, and a 'Glosse.' No precedent exists for the entire unit, but a few of its parts would have been familiar to the contemporary reader. The Argument by E.K., for instance, appears where this element is ordinarily printed in many books, including some that he cites in his dedicatory Epistle to Harvey, such as sixteenth-century editions of Virgil and Turbervile's translation of Mantuan. The equivalent to E.K.'s gloss in these books is a commentary; but, unlike the gloss, it is customarily printed between sections of the text or as marginalia. In the edition of Sannazaro's *Arcadia*, printed in Venice by Varisco in 1571, both the Argument and the gloss are printed as in *The Shepheardes Calender*, but the comparison is inexact because the *Arcadia* edition contains one unit not in the *Calender* (a prose paragraph after the *Argomento*) and omits the emblem in the *Calender*. It is only in the contemporary annotated emblem book that a unit appears bearing an inexact but close physical resemblance to the entire *Shepheardes Calender* unit.

The concept of the emblematic unit pertains only partially to the one in the *Calender*. (Spenser's 'embleme' may or may not invite this comparison; the word was used variously at the time.) The elements in the emblematic unit – picture, motto, text – are separate but equal; their combination creates what was called the *significatio*. The *Calender* unit is also composed of three elements – poem, scholarly apparatus, picture – but the poem is central; and the editorial matter and illustrations, which are not emblematic, function in different ways to locate and extend the poetic environment.

The pictures do not consistently illustrate the text in the modern sense of depicting or interpreting events in it; sometimes they do, but sometimes they are disjunctive. Instead, they stress the book's title by enveloping the poem with pervasive calendrical images; and they illustrate consistently only one topic of the poem – poetry. The ways in which this is accomplished are not plays on current illustrative conventions: they are experiments. Ordinarily, one or more general illustrations announcing the kind of book coexisted with particular illustrations relating to the text. In the *Calender*, however, the general is not separated but incorporated into the particular. Thus, the kind of illustration is signaled in each of the cuts by a zodiacal figure in a wreath of clouds, an element that until now had appeared only in some contemporary series of the labors of the months. This method of incorporating an element from familiar illustrations into a new picture means that the reader, without even knowing the title of the book, could have identified the major family to which the illustrations – and by extension, the book – belonged.

(See ***SC*, printing** Fig 1.)

The general calendrical identification is emphasized by particular images appearing throughout the illustrations. For the labors of the months, the image is sometimes a quotation from previous labors. In *June*, for example, where the customary labor of mowing is depicted, the awkward manner of drawing the haystacks is quoted from an English almanac (Fig 1). It is only in *June*, *Julye*, and *August* that the labor of the month is isolated from the central action. In other months, it is incorporated, as in *Februarie* where the stance of Thenot's husbandman engaged in the labor of wood-chopping imitates a traditional posture seen, for example, in 'Février' in *Les Très Riches Heures du Duc de Berry*.

(See ***SC*, printing** Fig 2.)

The wood-chopping vignette exemplifies the several ways calendrical images relate to the poem: the image depicts an event in the eclogue by quoting from older calendrical illustration, and it gives a visual clue to the reason the fable of the Oak and the Briar is placed in this particular eclogue. A story about tree-chopping belongs to a month whose illustrated labor typically includes an image either of the activity of chopping (as in Fig 2) or of its result – a servant carrying in logs for a fire. Analogous connections between the image, the name of the month or a labor associated with it, and a part of the eclogue emerge for *March*, *Aprill*, *November*, and more problematically *Januarye*. In *March*, the illustration depicts what the text describes: Cupid, the god of love, caught in a net – an event that belongs to a month named for Mars, the god who was caught in a net while making love. In *Aprill* – the month when 'all things come to life again' (the Latin text in the *Shepherds' Kalendar* [*STC* 22407–23]), the month whose name derives from *aperio* 'open,' whose traditional labor includes carrying the flowers that grow from the opening earth, and whose eclogue catalogues flowers – the first plant in flower in the illustrations appears above the bottom border of the cut. The main subject of the illustration and the eclogue is the playing of music, a second traditional labor of the month. (For example, a shepherd plays a pipe in 'Avril' in both sets of blocks to the two editions of the *Calendrier historial* [Lyons 1563], and in an illustration for Venus, the patron goddess of the month, in the 1528 edition of the *Shepherds' Kalendar* [*STC* 22411] whose design is an adaptation from yet another calendrical illustration [*Le Grant Kalendrier* (Troyes 1499)], where there is a close resemblance to the Colin figure in *Aprill*.) The main activity in the illustration to *Maye* is the traditional labor of merrymaking, the dance described by Palinode. In *November*, the month when man should prepare for death according to the conventional counsel in the *Shepherds' Kalendar*, the elegy in the text is depicted by a funeral procession.

Within the context of the dominant calendrical environment, many other kinds of images exist. The most important is the depiction of the subject of poetry. Of the three major topics of the poem – love, poetry, and politics – only poetry is consistently illustrated whenever it is a subject. It is shown by images of the poet's ambition and by the conditions under which that ambition is realized or fails. When the poet has an audience and a theme other than himself, he succeeds, the subject of his poetry is represented, and he plays an unbroken instrument, as in *Aprill*, *August*, and *November* – the eclogues containing the lay, the singing match and sestina, and the elegy. When no one listens or he has only a solipsistic subject, he fails, and a broken pipe lies at his feet, as in *Januarye*, *June*, and *December*.

In *November*, the topic of poetry is illustrated in several ways. The prominent right-hand portion shows Thenot crowning Colin; all of Colin's accoutrements are precisely drawn: the wreath of laurel; the shawm (a kind of oboe); the costume of cape, shoes, and hat; the hair and moustache. Much less space and care are given to the subsidiary left-hand part illustrating the subject of Colin's elegy, the funeral cortege. The image may very well allude to a similar one in a translation by Clément Marot (*Le Premier Livre de la Metamorphose d'Ovide* [Paris 1534]), where it appears beneath his standard motto, 'La mort ny mord,' that is adopted as Colin's 'Embleme' in *November*. In *November*, then, the topic of poetry is illustrated by the poet figure, by the subject of his poetry, and by allusion to another poet, Marot; but more space and care are given to the state of the poet than to the subject of his poetry.

The proportions and some of the details are reversed in the companion piece, *Aprill*, where the poet is the small figure on the lower left playing an indistinctly drawn instrument (probably a cornetto) and tuning it 'unto the Waters fall' that touches his feet. The dominant space is occupied by the subject of the poet's lay, and its elements are carefully drawn in detail: the wreath is worn by Queen Elizabeth, not by the poet figure as in *November*; her dress is distinguished from the courtly costume of her eleven attendants; four instruments are clearly shown (from the left: harp, viol, lute, and transverse flute).

Only in *October* is an instrument depicted as unbroken yet unplayed, an image that visually translates Cuddie's lament. He no longer wants to be a pastoral poet, to play his 'Oten reedes' – the precisely drawn panpipe or syrinx. His ambition now is to follow the career of Virgil, the 'Romish *Tityrus*' who had been helped by 'Mecoenas' (55–6) to transcend his role as pastoral poet. This wish is given form by the two or three classical buildings behind him, which are the most carefully drawn architecture in all of the cuts and which, in the context of the poem, represent the 'Princes pallace' of Augustan Rome and the patronage that was Virgil's.

In the cut to *September*, the topic of pastoral poetry is alluded to in another way. The postures of Hobbinol and Diggon Davie resemble the figures in a cut from older English pastoral verse, the *Egloges* of Alexander Barclay.

(See *SC*, **printing** Fig 3.)

In *Januarye* – the illustration with the most important position and designed and made with most care of all the illustrations – the subject of poetry is depicted by the broken bagpipe at Colin's feet. The expected calendrical association, however, is not immediately evident, nor is it clear in what way the cut relates to the text. With his back to his sheep and a rustic shack, Colin in ragged costume stands gazing to his right at the classical buildings (including an apparent colosseum) that are less precisely drawn than those in *October*. Two non-incompatible readings are possible. On the one hand, the buildings may represent the visit to the 'neighbour towne' (50) that Colin rues; but this reading omits any calendrical allusion and seems simplistic compared with the complexity of such references in the other illustrations. On the other hand, since the month takes its name from Janus, the two-faced god who looks before and behind, Colin may be a Janus figure turning his back on the past and looking toward the future: the past is pastoral poetry, figured as the sheep and the shack; the future is epic poetry, figured by the classical buildings associated with the Virgilian career as they are in *October*. If this is so, the buildings may well allude to those above which a Janus head appears in an illustration in a contemporary edition of Alciati's *Emblemata*.

(See *SC* Fig 4.)

The practice of alluding to other illustrations extends to the fabulist genre that is implied by E.K.'s mentioning Aesop in his Epistle to Harvey and represented many times in the text. In the crowded illustration to *Maye*, where the story of the Fox and the Kid is shown in three episodes ringing the central dancing scene, the left-hand vignette follows the traditional way of illustrating Aesop's fable of 'The Wolf and the Kid.'

Some episodes in the eclogues are directly illustrated without reference to any prior rendering. These include, for instance, Cuddie's 'Bullocke' in *Februarie*; in *Julye*, the positions and postures of Thomalin and Morrell, and the orderliness and disorder of their flock; and in *August*, the singing match and prizes.

These precise depictions coexist with disjunctions between image and text. As examples, the flock in *Januarye* is described in the Argument as 'winterbeaten' and in the eclogue as 'feeble,' yet the sheep are obviously the sturdiest of all those depicted. In *December*, Colin's pipe lies broken on the ground, yet according to the text he proposes to hang it 'upon this tree' (141). In addition, a detail may be illustrated in one eclogue and ignored in another (the sun in *Maye* and *Julye*), or the same character depicted differently (Colin, usually clean shaven, is bearded in *November*).

Disjunctions occur often in illustrated books of the time. The most sensible explanation for those in *The Shepheardes Calender* is that the designers were given only partial directions and relied on their stock in trade for the rest, supervision was inconsistent, and the final products were not checked.

These speculations are necessary because so much about the production of the book remains mysterious. Yet when what is known about the printer is combined with current knowledge about how illustrations were paid for and produced at the time, some conclusions seem reasonable. Although it was usually the printer or publisher who commissioned illustrations, gave directions for their design and production, and retained possession of them, the practice was by no means invariable. Sometimes directions for the design came from patron or author; sometimes, as with *The Shepheardes Calender*, the cuts were seen as an integral part of the book and transferred to the next printer(s). Because the first printer of the *Calender*, Hugh Singleton, was impoverished and in jail for part of 1579, and because he had no known previous experience with commissioning illustrations, it is most unlikely that he was responsible for these illustrations. Because designers, if left on their own, would have produced conventional illustrations, it is most unlikely that they decided on the unique features in these illustrations. Only someone who knew the poem intimately could have chosen to create an environment of calendrical images, to quote from previous illustration, and to illustrate consistently the topic of poetry. It seems most probable that these decisions came originally from the author.

Ruth Samson Luborsky

Margery Corbett and Ronald W. Lightbown 1979 *The Comely Frontispiece: The Emblematic Title-page in England 1550–1660* (London); Eugénie Droz 1974 'Le Calendrier Lyonnais' in *Chemins de l'hérésie* 3:1–29 (Geneva); Freeman 1948; Heninger 1988; Richard Krautheimer 1980 *Rome: Profile of a City, 312–1308* (Princeton); Luborsky 1981; Derek Pearsall and Elizabeth Salter 1973 *Landscapes and Seasons of the Medieval World* (London); Lucien Scheler 1966 'La Persistance du motif dans l'illustration flamande des fables d'Esope du seizième au dix-huitième siècle' in *Studia bibliographica in honorem Herman de La Fontaine Verwey* (Amsterdam) pp 350–5; *SC* ed 1930; James Carson Webster 1938 *The Labors of the Months in Antique and Mediaeval Art to the End of the Twelfth Century* (Evanston, Ill); Emanuel Winternitz 1967 *Musical Instruments and Their Symbolism in Western Art* (New Haven).

ship imagery A vehicle for psychological, moral, political, religious, and metaphysical meanings, the traditional figure of a sea-tossed ship is used prominently in *The Shepheardes Calender* (*Feb*, *Sept*), *Time*, *Teares*, *Rome*, *Muiopotmos*, *Vanitie*, *Petrarch*, *Bellay*, *Colin Clout*, *Amoretti*, and above all in *The Faerie Queene*, where it functions as a metaphor connecting the quests of each of the main characters with the narrator's quest for poetic meaning. The connection is most apparent in the heroic similes addressed to Redcrosse (I vi 1), Una (iii 31–2), and Guyon (II vii 1) and applied to the narrator himself at I xii 1, 42 and VI xii 1. But Spenser resorts habitually to the ship simile at crucial moments in each protagonist's quest (eg, III iv 8–10; IV iii 1; V xi 29, xii 18; VI iv 1, ix 19, 31). These figures of speech join with literal images of ships and the sea (Guyon's Odyssean voyages in II, the myths of Marinell and Florimell in III and IV, the international affairs of Artegall and Arthur in V) and with a pervasive nautical diction (eg, *anchor*, *canvas*, *card*, *compass*, *haven*, *helm*, *hulk*, *keel*, *mariner*, *ocean*, *port*, *sea*, *voyage*, and over fifteen varieties of sailing vessel, including *bark*, *cockboat*, *frigate*, *gondola*, *shallop*, and *skippet*) to create a rich symbolic texture dominated by a sense of mutability, deepened perhaps by Spenser's own acquaintance with the sea (*CCHA* 212–27), and evoking a tradition that extends back through Chaucer, Petrarch, and Dante to Quintilian, Ovid, and Virgil (see Curtius ed 1953:128–30).

In *The Faerie Queene*, the ship image is closely aligned to the poem's conflicting impulses toward engagement in or withdrawal from life, joy or despair, freedom of expression or discipline of form. Such conflicts are inherently implicit in a ship's vulnerability to the 'cruell billowes' on which it gains way toward a 'gladsome port' (III iv 8, 10; cf I iii 31, vi 1; II ii 24). The narrator makes them explicit as he 'bend[s]' his poem's 'wearie course' to a 'quiet rode' in order to 'land some ... passengers' and repair 'tackles spent' before 'merry wind and weather' call him 'againe abroad' (I xii 1, 42; cf II proem 2). As the poem progresses, the image increasingly polarizes the 'stormie surges' in which the poem is 'tost' and the 'one certaine cost [coast]' to which it aims (VI xii 1; cf Calidore's desire 'quite ... for to retrate' from his 'stormes of fortune' in ix 19, 27, 31). This change parallels both a growing skepticism about the power of heroic action to embody the highest ideals of virtue and the narrator's search for inner solace from an increasingly wearisome poetic voyage.

JEROME S. DEES

Jerome S. Dees 1975 'The Ship Conceit in *The Faerie Queene*: "Conspicuous Allusion" and Poetic Structure' *SP* 72:208–25; K. Williams 1970–1.

Sidney, Philip (1554–86) Sidney and Spenser were the harbingers of the English literary Renaissance and its twin glories, never surpassed by their successors. They profited from the same classical and continental models and shared an admiration for Chaucer; yet even when they are writing in the same genres and using the same verse forms, their voices are readily distinguishable. Most of their work was written independently, for their personal contact was brief – almost certainly confined to the months from October 1579 through April 1580, when Spenser was at Leicester House. Spenser was pleased to report that Sidney and his friend Edward Dyer had him 'in some use of familiarity' (*Two Letters* 1, *Var Prose* p 6). There were discussions about poetry, and it is hard to believe that these never turned to the eclogues they were composing in conformity with the tradition that pastoral was the appropriate mode for the young beginner. We should not be surprised to find both poets introducing themselves as shepherds – Spenser as Colin Clout, Sidney as Philisides – nor to find them both essaying the usual pastoral forms of elegy, blazon, and singing match.

Among Sidney's great gifts to his contemporaries were his respect for tradition and his willingness to experiment. It is unfortunate, though, that he was preoccupied at this time with quantitative verse in English and so perhaps muted Spenser's reactions to the strange music he created in hexameters (*Old Arcadia* 13) or asclepiads (*OA* 34). He had a better grasp of the sestina than Spenser and ambitiously achieved a double sestina (*OA* 71). When he handled the singing match (*OA* 7), he made it a metrical contest between two shepherds, whereas Spenser was content with a duet and refrain. On the other side, Spenser had almost completed *The Shepheardes Calender* when he joined the Sidney circle, and it is more than likely that the few archaisms in the beast fable Sidney wrote to honor his old tutor, Hubert Languet (*OA* 66) owe something to Spenser's eclogues. Possibly Sidney, who is sparing in his use of unusual words – though credited by Joseph Hall with the introduction of compound epithets – drew a distinction between this flavoring and what he later called 'that same framing of his style to an old rustic language' (ed 1973b:112), which he dared not allow in *The Shepheardes Calender*. Still this was selected among the handful of English works Sidney felt able to praise in *A Defence of Poetry*.

For whatever reason, Spenser did not presume to dedicate *The Shepheardes Calender* to the Earl of Leicester and Sidney became the 'Patron of my young *Muses*' (dedication to *Time*). It was probably at this time that Sidney encouraged Spenser to proceed with *The Faerie Queene*, and he may have helped to get him a post with Lord Grey in Ireland, for Sidney's father was three times Lord Deputy of Ireland. Despite Sidney's Irish interests and some mutual friends, there is no evidence to suggest that the two poets ever met again. When Spenser came, rather tardily, in *Ruines of Time*, *Astrophel*, and *Colin Clouts Come Home Againe*, to add his tributes to some 200 elegies which commemorated Sidney's death, the pastoral mode cloaks the harsh reality, and the poetry seems designed to continue the Sidney myth under the patronage of the Countess of Pembroke, rather than to express personal grief.

Sidney's death at Arnhem, from a wound in his thigh received during a skirmish at Zutphen 26 days earlier, brought him the fame he had never enjoyed in his lifetime. In the *DNB*, he is labeled 'soldier, statesman and poet'; and though he declared that poetry is 'the companion of camps' (ed 1973b:105), that order accurately reflects the importance he attached to his three roles. Despite his birth and long, careful training, he never held high office. He belonged to the party of his uncle, the Earl of Leicester (at whose instigation he wrote a 'Letter to the Queen' against her proposed marriage to the French duc d'Alençon), and of his father-in-law, Sir Francis Walsingham, who wanted to strengthen the alliance of the German Protestant princes and who favored active intervention in the Netherlands, against Burghley's more cautious policies of avoiding conflict with Spain and of furthering negotiations for the French marriage of Elizabeth. *Mother Hubberds Tale* and *FQ* V x suggest that Spenser shared Sidney's outlook, and endorsed the expedition to the Netherlands under Leicester's command which cost Sidney his life. Until his appointment as governor of Flushing in 1585, Sidney led a rather frustrated life, exacerbated by lack of funds; and his begging letters to the Queen contrast with Spenser's adulation. Yet when Leicester entertained Elizabeth at Wanstead in the spring of 1578 or 1579, Sidney composed the *Lady of May*, and he contributed to the splendor of Gloriana's court by devising, and taking part in, tilts such as the *Four Foster Children of Desire*, presented in 1581 for the entertainment of the French commissioners. If he wrote the verses for this show, they are the only poems of his published during his lifetime.

As Sidney put it, he had slipped into the title of poet; and after his death, there was a scramble among the stationers for his manuscripts. An attempt to publish the first version of the *Arcadia*, written for his sister, the Countess of Pembroke, was foiled. All Spenser is likely to have known of this prose romance interspersed with poems and composed in the framework of a five-act tragicomedy was some of the eclogues Sidney placed between the acts and the last three books printed in the edition of 1593. Sidney decided to recast this early work in the form of an epic; by 1584, when he abandoned the project, he had recast Books 1 and 2 and added an entirely new but unfinished Book 3. An edition of this version was published in the same year (1590) by the same stationer (William Ponsonby) as the first three books of *The Faerie Queene*. This *New Arcadia* is the equivalent in Sidney's *oeuvre* to *The Faerie Queene*; both are unfinished heroic poems. Of course, there are striking differences: Spenserian stanzas are replaced by elaborate rhetorical prose in accordance with the contention in *A Defence of Poetry* that 'it is not rhyming and versing that maketh poesy' (ed 1973b:101). Both works are full of 'that delightful teaching which is the end of poesy' (p 116), but Sidney eschews 'allegorie's curious frame' (*Astrophil and Stella* 28) in favor of exemplary characters and action.

Astrophil and Stella is the first and most exciting of the Elizabethan sonnet sequences. It is possible that the placing of the songs at the end of the unauthorized edition of 1591 led to the arrangement of *Amoretti*.

In true Petrarchan fashion, *Astrophil and Stella* tells a story, and a story of unattainable love ending in despair. That it is the story of Sidney's infatuation for Penelope Devereux, recently wedded to Lord Rich, is made abundantly clear by numerous autobiographical details. (Here Spenser is an innovator in addressing his sonnets to his bride-to-be.) Sidney's mastery of the form is revealed in the structure of the sequence and of individual sonnets. He ranges widely in subject matter, mood, and style, moving with ease from blunt speech to highly wrought conceits, and exploiting endlessly the possibilities of the sonnet form, playing off the rhyme schemes of octave and sestet against the syntactical structure. Even when he ends with a couplet, the last line often reverses all that went before, as Astrophil wrestles with his unlawful passion for thirteen lines and then succumbs to desire in the fourteenth. From the sonnets in alexandrines to the songs in various measures, Sidney's scansion is remarkably regular. Perhaps for this reason, his lyrics attracted many more musical settings than did Spenser's. In an early collection, published under the title *Certain Sonnets* with Sidney's other works in 1598, there are several poems written to be sung to extant tunes.

Two editions of *A Defence of Poetry* appeared in 1595. Although the exact date of composition cannot be determined, one can infer from some of its arguments and asides that *Astrophil and Stella* and the *New Arcadia* had been, or were in the process of being, written. Spenser reports that Gosson had dedicated his *Schoole of Abuse* (1579) to Sidney, and that he had been for his labor scorned (*2 Lett* 1, *Var Prose* p 6); but this should not be taken to indicate that Sidney's *Defence* was written to answer Gosson. It is an original argument based on his own arrangement of the ideas of Aristotle, Minturno, Scaliger, and others, colored by Sidney's own religious convictions, and written in a gracious and disarming style which blends earnestness and humor. The *sprezzatura* that prompts Sidney's references to his own works as toys and trifles is a far cry from the puffs of E.K. for 'the new Poete' (*SC* Epistle to Harvey). There is no means of knowing the contents of Spenser's treatise, the *English Poete*, one of the lost works. That he would have endorsed most of Sidney's arguments is evident, save that Sidney does not go so far as to claim divine inspiration for poetry, attributing it rather to the poet's own creative ability – though his *idea* or *fore-conceit* must be borne on the wings of art, imitation, and exercise. Sidney does not presume to discuss divine poetry, but he rests the whole case for poetry on its power to move readers to virtuous action; he had begun to translate du Bartas and Duplessis-Mornay and to compose a version of the Psalms. Both he and Spenser were profoundly Christian writers.

JEAN ROBERTSON

Although the complete works are contained in Sidney ed 1912–26, subsequent authoritative editions with commentaries include ed 1962 (poems); ed 1973a (*Old Arcadia*); ed 1973b (miscellaneous prose, including *A Defence of Poetry*); and ed 1987 (*New Arcadia*); *Correspondence* ed C.S. Levy (Oxford) is forthcoming. The *Apology for Poetry* ed 1965 contains an excellent commentary. The standard life is M.W. Wallace 1915, although Roger Howell 1968 *Sir Philip Sidney: The Shepherd Knight* (London) adds information not available earlier. Hamilton 1977 is a thorough introductory study. Lewis 1954 on 'Sidney and Spenser' has some odd biases, but is still a valuable and entertaining introduction. For a general bibliography, see W.A. Ringler in the *NCBEL* 1:1047–57.

Sidney, Robert (1563–1626) The death of Philip Sidney at Arnhem on 17 October 1586 left his younger brother Robert as head of his family a month before his twenty-third birthday. Robert had gained a knighthood for his conduct on the ill-fated day at Zutphen (22 September) when Philip received what proved his death wound, and the two brothers remained together at Arnhem during the agonizing three-and-a-half weeks that Philip lay there after the battle.

Robert's own poetry probably dates from the 1590s, but his poetic achievement has remained concealed until our own day, for his poems – sonnets intermixed with songs in a sequence whose overall structure is modeled on that of Philip's *Astrophil and Stella* – are preserved only in a single modest notebook which is unsigned though entirely in the poet's own handwriting. Robert avoided public recognition as a poet, influenced perhaps by a wish to avoid invidious comparisons with a brother whose memory had been consecrated by death. It is now possible, however, to recognize echoes of Robert's work in a few other poems by members of the courtly circle in the 1590s, and we may deduce that some at least of his sonnets were allowed to circulate on loose sheets of manuscript among a select few. The contemporary readership for Robert's poems probably consisted of the same circle of 'private friends' as were also reading Shakespeare's 'sugred Sonnets' in manuscript at the same period. Connections both personal and literary suggest that this privileged circle included Fulke Greville and Spenser. Characteristic of the Elizabethan courtly poets is the way they respond to each other's work: it follows that where relationships can be detected between their poems it may not always be possible to determine which is echoing which.

The genre to which Robert Sidney's sequence and Spenser's *Amoretti* both belong exists to show the reader 'what it is to love,' to portray the lover's experience in a sequence of sometimes meditative, sometimes dramatic, monologues. Behind Spenser's and Robert Sidney's sequences lies *Astrophil and Stella*, and all three poets allude to the Neoplatonic philosophy of love whose central textbook was Ficino's commentary on Plato's *Symposium*. Comparison between the three sequences brings each into sharper focus – and what comparison highlights in this case is how three poets who share the same literary and philosophical background can yet differ as individuals in their responses to perennial human experience.

Astrophil and Stella is remarkable for its bold representation of an adulterous passion and for its deliberately planted clues to the identity of the poet's beloved. The little volume containing Spenser's *Amoretti* concludes with his own *Epithalamion* and thus implies that the sonnets themselves are addressed to the lady whom the poet eventually marries: in this way, Spenser's sequence invites us to see it as a counterbalance to the adulterous *Astrophil and Stella*. Robert's sequence is different again, for it portrays two kinds of love: (1) what Ficino terms *simplex amor* where the lover's passion is unrequited, and (2) what Ficino terms *mutuus amor* where each lives in the other. Most of Robert's sequence is occupied with an unattainable love for an ideal beauty, but Song 6 – which is his longest poem, and centrally positioned within the sequence – depicts a wholly reciprocated love for a lady whom covert clues within the poem identify as his own wife Barbara. But Robert's love, whether wholly reciprocated or wholly unreciprocated, remains in both kinds true to the Neoplatonic ideal of a love which transcends the body. The pure idealism which informs the whole of Robert's sequence is brought home when his Song 6 is compared with Spenser's *Epithalamion*, that richly sensual hymn to sexual love glorified and made holy by religious ceremony. By contrast, Robert's particular idealism excludes all dwelling on the sexual aspect of love and – although we cannot doubt that his marriage had in real life its physical side – his celebration of that marriage in Song 6 is in essence akin to Shakespeare's *The Phoenix and Turtle* rather than to Spenser's *Epithalamion*.

Robert Sidney's Sonnet 25 is a witty address to his cruel beloved and is founded on the idea of her as a type or reflection of the deity. He gives a fresh turn to this idea at the start of the sestet, 'O love yowr self: bee yow yowrself yowr care,' which echoes Spenser's line describing how the eternal power begot the universe: 'It lov'd it selfe, because it selfe was faire' (*Heavenly Love* 29). Spenser himself is here directly echoing Ficino's teaching that it was the divine power's wish to propagate its own perfection – a kind of love for itself – which created the universe.

Sonnet 25, which contains the clearest direct echo of Spenser in Robert's verse, nicely illustrates the important truth that Renaissance love poetry will be properly understood only by those aware of its philosophical background. Spenser's epistle (1 Sept 1596) dedicating *Fowre Hymnes* to the 'two honorable sisters' the Countess of Cumberland and the Countess of Warwick indicates that the two 'heavenly' hymns had been recently composed to 'reforme' the former two which 'one of you two most excellent Ladies' had asked him to call in. The intricate network connecting those associated with the Elizabethan court is always worth bearing in mind when considering their poetry, and we may here recall that the Countess of Warwick was the widow of

Robert Sidney's maternal uncle (d 1590) and was herself a staunch supporter of Robert's interests at court during the 1590s.

Philip Sidney's death is reflected in both Spenser's and Robert's work in ways which afford some insight into the complex interactions between the actual and the imagined in Elizabethan poetry. Robert's failure to produce an elegy on his brother's death may be attributed to his being too close to the painful reality. Robert's own surviving poetry was probably composed ten years and more after Philip's death, but it contains one vivid image – of the man whose limbs are infected with gangrene – behind which we can recognize the physical reality of Philip's last illness. Also to be recognized, however, is a passage in the *Old Arcadia* about the constant man who 'for the saving of all his body he will not spare the cutting off a limb' (ed 1973a:296). This imagined speech of Pyrocles in Philip's romance may have seemed to Robert in retrospect ironically to anticipate the reality of Philip's own death, when despite Philip's exhortations the doctors failed to act after the injured leg became infected and amputation might have given him his only chance of life. At all events, Robert has assimilated the image of the man infected with gangrene to the purposes of his own poetry, where it becomes a symbol of the poet's hopeless love.

The fact that Spenser delayed producing his own elegy on Philip Sidney, 'Astrophel,' until 1595 may mean that he was himself too personally grieved by the loss to be able soon to turn the experience into art. Some inside knowledge of the tragedy on Spenser's part may be deduced from his alluding to a circumstance which does not seem to have been widely known – the presence of Philip's nineteen-year-old wife at his bedside through the final days. This is poetically represented in Spenser's pastoral elegy where the shepherds carry the wounded Astrophel to his 'loved lasse' (147) who stays with him lamenting until he departs this life. As it develops, Spenser's elegy merges the two loves of Philip's life – the Stella whom he had celebrated in his poetry, and the girl whom he had married in 1583 when she was still only in her sixteenth year. The elegy which says of Stella 'Her he did love, her he alone did honor, / His thoughts, his rimes, his songs were all upon her' is dedicated 'To the most beautifull and vertuous Ladie, the Countesse of *Essex*' who (as the initiated would realize) was actually Philip's widow, by now remarried.

Spenser and Robert Sidney, in the way their work deals with the tragedy of Philip's death, both remind us that the Elizabethans when they took up the pen became conscious artists: if we fail to understand this we will be equally liable to go astray whether we interpret their poetry as literal biography or ignore the biographical element which the poetry contains. P.J. Croft

Robert Sidney 1984 *Poems* ed P.J. Croft (Oxford); Millicent V. Hay 1984 *The Life of Robert Sidney, Earl of Leicester (1563–1626)* (Washington, D.C.).

Sidney circle Like many other poets, Spenser wrote an elegy, though belatedly, commemorating Philip Sidney's death in 1586 ('Astrophel' 1595); and *Ruines of Time* (1591), dedicated to Sidney's sister Mary Sidney, Countess of Pembroke, laments his death (281–343). *FQ* III vi 45 – '*Amintas* wretched fate, / To whom sweet Poets verse hath given endlesse date' – may also refer to him. Spenser had important connections with other members of the so-called Sidney circle, a loosely linked group of late Elizabethan courtiers, poets, philosophers, divines, and educators who for some twenty years, at Wilton House and elsewhere, were dedicated to Sidney's ideals for the reform of literature (see *Areopagus) and Elizabethan court culture. The group may have included Breton, Daniel, Dyer, Fraunce, Greville, and Philip's brother Robert. Its work, achievements, and limitations reveal both residual and emerging cultural forms, some of which look nostalgically back to medieval chivalric and courtly practices while others struggle to express the values by which a new phase of English culture was taking shape.

While Sidney's complaint in the *Defence of Poetry* that 'England, the mother of excelent minds' should be 'so hard a stepmother to poets' (ed 1973b:110) was a frustrated response to the comparative lack of sophistication in English culture, and his retirement to rural Wilton to write at various times from 1579 to his death may be seen as an attempt to exemplify his literary ideals, nonetheless his withdrawal from the Elizabethan court had more than a literary motivation. His ideals were never totally literary; and he articulated in his writing the political and cultural ideals which in life he found frustratingly unattainable (Hamilton 1977, McCoy 1979). Similarly, after his death, when the Countess took an active part in the work of the Sidney circle, more than merely literary ideals were at stake, though certainly Sidney's hopes for literature were seriously pursued. His early interest in quantitative verse was continued by his sister and Fraunce, and she also encouraged the writing of closet dramas like Greville's *Mustapha* and *Alaham* and her own *Antonie*. More fruitful was her highly successful transference of the rhetorical riches of the Elizabethan lyric tradition into religious verse, while the verses of Greville, Breton, Lok, and Fraunce laid the ground for the tantalizing combination of courtly grace and introspection in Herbert's poetry. Other poetry written by the circle includes Robert Sidney's Petrarchan lyrics, like his brother's *Astrophil and Stella* a rich assemblage of songs and sonnets expressing both a frustrated but compelling love and much pent-up political anxiety in an evocative rhetoric. Important, too, was the Countess' patronage and, in particular, the way in which Wilton became a refuge for Sidney's admirers – a 'little Court' as Breton put it (*Wits Trenchmour* 1597; in ed 1879, 2:19).

What were the distinctive features of the circle – apart from the aura of its founder – and why would Spenser have found it congenial? Probably its peculiar blend of courtliness and piety – of Castiglione and Calvin. Its militant piety undoubtedly attracted him as he saw his own idealized court of Elizabeth crumbling under corruption, betrayal, and all that he represented in the Blatant Beast. The circle's importance for students of Spenser lies therefore in its place within the structures of literary and cultural discourse that were becoming dominant in the last twenty years of Elizabeth's reign. Within the increasingly strained world of the years following Sidney's death with which Spenser clearly felt more and more uneasy, countermovements were developing. As a crucial instance of how a dominant culture was producing a counterculture, one particular aspect of the circle is especially important for the reader of *FQ* VI: the sense in which Wilton became isolated as a 'little Court.' It is significant that among Sidney's last poems was a 'Dispreyse of a Courtly Life,' and that *FQ* VI radically calls into question the very court which the poem set out to idealize. Increasingly, the members of the Sidney circle saw Wilton, like the dead Sidney himself, as a reminder of a lost ideal.

One of the emergent cultural movements of the early seventeenth century was a strong reaction against the court both as an ideal and as the age's dominant political entity. This transition in the 1590s is part of a fundamental change in the cultural life of England, and few writers at the time or in the early 1600s were able to point to the direction in which their world was rapidly moving.

The greatness of a work of art may often lie in its power to let those things be heard, about which it seems uneasy or even tries deliberately to repress. In a period like the 1580s and 1590s, when new values were being experienced but still not expressed because there were as yet no adequate forms for them, one understandable reaction was to take refuge in the past. Sidney and his circle represented such a refuge for a significant number of courtiers and poets of later decades who saw an ideal from which their times had degenerated. In the 1580s when Spenser praised the dead Astrophel, he expressed his own growing unease with the Elizabethan age, and his ambivalence was echoed by many in the next half-century. As aspects of the Stuart court became increasingly unpalatable to those who recalled, or thought they recalled, a more dignified age, the spirit of Sidney as the epitome of that age was almost superstitiously invoked.

The virtue and wholeness which Breton saw epitomized in Wilton remained only in the great country houses like Wilton, Great Tew, or Penshurst. The culture of the early seventeenth century showed a widespread tendency towards social decentralization and dislocation; and interesting parallels can be made with such literary changes as the development of more introspective literary forms, such as the meditative devotional lyric, which replaced the earlier lyric of communal feeling. So while the idealizing of the court and courtly virtues in the *Arcadia* and *The Faerie Queene* may have seemed at the time to celebrate the vital spirit of civilization and human order, from another viewpoint, it can be seen as an attempt to hold back the forces of change. From a further viewpoint – one that subsequent history has revealed more and more clearly – we can see it as contributing (despite itself) to the breakdown of the cultural hegemony of the court and aristocratic culture. The very forces of Reformation piety, sound learning, individual integrity, and moral probity which Spenser clearly admired in the Sidneys and their circle became the forces that in the next century destroyed the cultural hegemony of the court that Spenser, like Sidney, had served and celebrated, yet come to feel so uneasy about. The result was eventually a new society and, with it, a new literature. In the beliefs and the tensions of the members of the Sidney circle, therefore, we can see, better than they themselves knew, the seeds of a brave new world. As such the circle shares in an emergent discourse, literary and social, with Spenser's work, revealing more than they knew about the world towards which their work (in the inimitable way of great art) was pointing.

GARY WALLER

Bennan 1988; Hamilton 1977; Javitch 1978; Lamb 1981; Lamb 1982; Richard C. McCoy 1979 *Sir Philip Sidney: Rebellion in Arcadia* (New Brunswick, NJ); Waller 1979; Waller 1986.

Singleton, Hugh (d 1593) The printer of the first edition of *The Shepheardes Calender* was the son of a currier in London. He was abroad in the early 1540s when he may have been learning his trade in a continental printing house. In 1544, he printed in London his first known book, an octavo religious tract by Thomas Becon, which bore the imprint 'Strasburgh in Elsas at the sign of the golden Bibel.' Trading from the sign of St Augustine in St Paul's Churchyard, Singleton took full advantage of the freedom granted to the press by Protector Somerset during Edward VI's reign and gained a reputation as a printer of radical Protestant propaganda. Many of his books contain the false imprints of 'Rome' or 'Strasburg' but may be recognized by his printer's device, a rebus with his initials and mark and a single tun. He probably stayed in London during Mary's reign and continued to issue Protestant tracts from a secret press.

It is not known how Singleton was chosen as the printer of *The Shepheardes Calender*, which he entered in the Stationers' Register on 5 December 1579. He had gained considerable notoriety earlier in the same year by printing John Stubbs' *Discoverie of a Gaping Gulf*, an attack on the projected marriage of Elizabeth to the Duc d'Alençon. For this act of sedition, Stubbs lost his right hand, and Singleton almost received the same punishment. Spenser may have been attracted by Singleton's strong Protestant sympathies (he printed many works of Foxe) or been put in touch with him by a friend or patron, but no lasting professional relationship developed between them: the *Calender* was assigned on 29 October 1580 to John Harrison the younger, who had the 1581 second edition printed by Thomas East. Although Singleton succeeded John Day as printer to the City of London on 4 August 1584, his business was frequently uncertain and he was not one of that elite group of stationers, such as Ponsonby, Spenser's other printer, who grew rich in their trade. He entered his last book on 31 March 1592. (See Byrom 1933.)

MICHAEL G. BRENNAN

---

sins, seven deadly The seven deadly sins are pride (L *superbia*), envy (*invidia*), wrath (*ira*), avarice (*avaritia*), sloth (*acedia*), gluttony (*gula*), and lechery (*luxuria*). At the house of Pride in *FQ* I iv, the Red Cross Knight sees the sins as six counselors riding animals also representing the sins who in pairs behind each other (as on either side of a wagon tongue) pull the chariot of Lucifera (Pride). The sustained artistry of this pageant surpasses all other literary representations of the sins, rivaled only by the confessing personifications in *Piers Plowman* B Passus 5 where, as in Spenser, the sins shift between being caricatures and characters, and likewise should be interpreted with reference to medieval conventions, immediate context, and relation to the whole poem. (See **sins, seven deadly** Figs 1–7.)

While the Bible includes lists of evils (eg, Rom 1.29–31), the phrase 'seven deadly sins' does not occur nor does the heptad ever appear there as a discrete group, although they were identified with the seven heads of the beast of Revelation 17.3 (cf *FQ* I vii 17; see Tuve 1966:102–3). Bloomfield (1952) traces the concept from primitive lists of sins and ancient Eastern versions of the soul-journey. At first, Christian writers distinguished between the 'deadly sins,' those prohibited in the Ten Commandments, and seven capital or cardinal sins representing chief sinful tendencies. Especially after the thirteenth century, writers used the term 'deadly' to refer to the latter group.

Systematic discussion of the seven sins, such as Cassian's (c 420), though at first directed to monks, reached a wider audience after Gregory the Great (d 604) popularized the scheme in his *Moralia in Job*; here pride is depicted as the root of seven sins, each a captain over other sins. Although the order of the sins varies, the one associated with Gregory (given above) is most frequent. Adapting Prudentius' *Psychomachia* (c 400), Gregory also pictures the sins as an army attacking the Christian soul defended by Christ.

Use of the seven sins as a penitential scheme, which dates from the seventh-century Celtic church, became more widespread after the Fourth Lateran Council (c 1215) established penance as the seventh sacrament, issued decrees on mandatory confession, and named the seven sins as a required annual homiletic subject, along with the Creed, the Ten Commandments, and the Lord's Prayer. This instructional movement generated penitential, homiletic, and catechetical manuals (such as Guilielmus Peraldus' influential *Summa de vitiis* [c 1236]), many of which included long descriptions of the sins' physical causes and effects (diseases), relation to other sins, offspring, psychology, biblical and classical authorities, social history, short narrative exempla, and vivid iconography.

Allegorically, the seven sins were described as engendered from Pride, who was the daughter of Lucifer (*Le Somme le roi* 1279), or from the union of death and sin; Pride then begot other daughter sins (Gower *Mirour de l'omme* 1381). Or they were described as a tree (related to the Tree of Knowledge in Genesis 2–3) springing from the root of pride and divided into seven main branches which had lesser limbs representing sub-sins (*Cursor mundi* 1320, *Kalendrier des bergers* 1493). In the *physiologus* tradition, the sins were portrayed as animals (*Ancrene Riwle* 1225; see chart in Bloomfield 1952:245–9) and were sometimes linked to the seven-headed Beast of the Apocalypse (*Le Somme le roi*). Perhaps most often, the sins appear as grotesque humanoids with typical physiognomy (Wrath has white eyes and hair standing on end; Envy is pale and shakes), diseases (Avarice has dropsy), clothing and possessions (Pride has fur robes, Wrath has daggers, Avarice has money bags, Lechery has a mirror). The seven sins were sometimes divided into two physical sins (gluttony and lechery, the companion 'sins of the tavern') and five spiritual; or, a scheme used by Spenser, into those of the flesh (sloth, gluttony, lechery), the world (avarice), and the devil (envy, wrath, pride).

Popular frameworks for these iconographic motifs in medieval literature include (1) confession (Langland *Piers Plowman* and Gower *Confessio amantis*), (2) attacks on the castle of mankind (see *psychomachia and *The Castle of Perseverance*), and (3) pilgrimage of life including visions of hell or heaven (Dante *Divine Comedy* and Deguileville *Pèlerinage de la vie humaine*).

In *FQ* I iv, Spenser brings together many of the motifs mentioned above. The sins occur during Redcrosse's spiritual pilgrimage to the New Jerusalem; they are associated with a castle (the house of Pride), depicted both as human beings and animals, and related to typical diseases, physiognomy, behavior, and physical accoutrements. Spenser's details have analogues in Renaissance visual arts (see Stephen Bateman *A Christall Glasse of Christian Reformation* 1569 and Chew 1962); obvious literary precedents besides *Piers Plowman* B Passus 5 are Gower's procession of the sins as seven women elaborately geared, who ride on different animals to their marriage with the world (*Mirour de l'omme*), and the procession of the seven sins as Vice's 'captains' who on varied beasts battle against the Virtues in the *Assembly of Gods* (c 1420), attributed to Lydgate.

Unlike these works, however, Spenser's seven sins are not doctrinally instructional. Also, while he carefully balances the number of lines and kind of detail accorded each sin, his pageant is not just a gorgeous set piece, for it dynamically sets in relief Redcrosse's particular problems, as well as signals Spenser's deepest concerns. As in Marlowe's *Doctor Faustus*, the sins provide entertainment which distracts the hero from his real sin – spiritual and physical sloth – which in its extreme form leads to despair and suicide. Political, rather than religious, Spenser's sins focus on right doing in this world. Hence his depiction of the sins as advisors supporting a realm ruled not with 'laws' but with 'policie,' a phrasing reflecting the basic tension throughout the poem between moral order mindful of history and community, and self-serving expediency. That those mired in sin cannot make or sustain right judgment is the one detail common to all Spenser's portraits.

Since the sins were integral to centuries of tradition which analyzed their complexity, they may be seen as types behind many more of Spenser's characters and situations, including Error's monstrous brood (I i 14–26), the seven troops deployed against the gate of Alma's castle (II xi 6), Malecasta and her Castle Joyous (lechery) in III i 31–67, Ate (wrath) in IV, and the Blatant Beast (a compendium of the 'sins of the tongue,' and associated with envy and wrath) in VI.

JOAN HEIGES BLYTHE

Bloomfield 1952; Blythe 1972; Chew 1962; Crossett and Stump 1984; Cullen 1974; Tuve 1966; Siegfried Wenzel 1967 *The Sin of Sloth: Acedia in Medieval Thought and Literature* (Chapel Hill). Oscar Lovell Triggs 1895 gives a comprehensive brief overview of literary examples of the seven deadly sins in 'The Allegory of the Vices and Virtues,' in the introduction to John Lydgate *The Assembly of Gods* (Chicago) pp lxiii-lxxvi.

Skelton, John (c 1460–1529) The literary relationship between Skelton, the Henrician laureate and self-styled *orator regis*, author of the ecclesiastical satire *Colyn Cloute*, and Spenser, the Elizabethan 'new Poete,' is ambivalent, complicated, important, yet incomplete, despite Spenser's assumption of the cognomen Colin Clout.

In the first gloss to *SC, Januarye*, that ambivalence is present. 'COLIN CLOUTE ... a Poesie of M. Skeltons' is mentioned cheek by jowl with a French 'Colin ... used of the French Poete Marot.' By the end of *The Shepheardes Calender*, Marot and his Colin will have insinuated themselves more completely into Spenser's practice and consciousness than Skelton and his Colyn, as *September* begins to suggest, and as the courtly elegy and pastoral reminiscences of *November* and *December* amply illustrate.

Complicated the matter surely is, for Spenser's resort to Skelton's *Colyn Cloute* relies on the integrity of a poem whose author's reputation had exceeded literary proprieties and escaped into the popular imagination. On 20 December 1578, almost four months before the date of the dedicatory Epistle to *The Shepheardes Calender*, 'Master Spensar' loaned four jestbooks to Gabriel Harvey, among them *The Merie Tales ... by Master Skelton* (1567; Stern 1979:49). The sardonic Skelton of popular tradition was already known to Harvey. After the death of his friend Gascoigne in October 1577, Harvey (ed 1884:57) had scrawled out quatrains telling of various eminent countrymen his 'merry' friend might meet in heaven, among them 'Skelton that same madbraynd knave' gnawing 'a deade horse boane' (this last a possible allusion to line 476 in Colyn Cloute's wild prophecy of Wolsey's fall).

Six of the fifteen *Merie Tales* find 'Skelton' quarreling pungently with religious pettifoggers, friars, false priests, and officious bishops; two of them present him in cutting and prophetic repartee with Thomas Wolsey 'cardynall and archbyshop of Yorke.' The loan of the specific volume seems almost a teasing argument for, or a jesting consent to, the inclusion of Skelton, an English poet with popular associations as an outspoken critic of the clergy, into the carefully defined pattern of poetic precedent and predecessors taking shape in the *Calender* (Theocritus, Virgil, and Mantuan; Petrarch, Sannazaro, and Marot; Chaucer, Langland, and now Skelton).

When Spenser decided to include Skelton as one of his poetic forebears, he deliberately assumed the particular cognomen Colin Clout, the name of Skelton's shrewdly observant wandering clerk. In so doing, as E.K. remarks, he 'chose rather to unfold great matter of argument covertly,' and from the 'basenesse of the name' make accord with the commonness of the matter and the homeliness of the manner – after the fashion of the 'best and most auncient Poetes' (Epistle).

Spenser could have learned of Skelton's Colyn Cloute from the text of that poem which had gone into a fourth edition by 1560 or from the version of the poem included in Skelton's *Pithy Pleasaunt and Profitable Workes* edited by John Stow and published in 1568, the year after the *Merie Tales* had appeared. (Stow also edited *Certaine Worthye Manuscript Poems* which he dedicated 'To the worthiest Poet Maister Ed. Spenser.') It is Colyn, the vagabonding clerk, who out of his 'connynge bagge' documents the charges of spiritual dereliction advanced by the laity against the ecclesiastical hierarchy, and, to a lesser extent, those preferred by the clergy against the 'lay fee.' It is Colyn as shielding persona who apologizes for a style 'rude and playne'; it is Colyn who pretends to conduct a dialogue of sorts within his monologue by reporting what men say.

Under this name, 'not greatly used,' so E.K. comments, 'this Poete secretly shadoweth himself' (*Jan* 1 gloss; cf Epistle). Because we find Spenser's Colin wandering in 'the common Labyrinth of Love' (Epistle), unknown to Skelton's Colyn who laments no country lass by the name of Rosalind, we think again of the possible and deliberate confusion or complementarity of the two separate Colins, Skelton's and Marot's. In *September*, however, an eclogue of pastoral care, we are told that the Colin Clout of line 176 – not a lover, not a poet, but a working shepherd's boy, whose shepherd employer must face a wily wolf – 'no man doubteth ... is ever meante the Authour selfe.'

Since our Colin Clout seems to be the personal authentication of some actual event underlying the ecclesiastical satire, we suspect at last that the 'great matter of argument covertly' unfolded rests in the moral eclogues, particularly *Maye*, *Julye*, and *September*. Although Colin himself is not a speaker in any of them, their themes of 'coloured deceipt' and 'dissolute shepheards and pastours' (Gen Arg) constitute familiar topics handled in Skelton's *Colyn Cloute*.

In *Maye*, a debate between two elders, the permissive Palinode and the stringent Piers, prompted by the activities of a 'shole' (20) of young shepherds a-maying, we hear resonances of Skelton's language. Piers' accusation that pluralists and absentee bishops are careless of what befalls their flock so long as they have the fleece and get the gain (40–50) echoes charges reported by Skelton's Colyn that irresponsible clergy 'take no hede / Theyr sely shepe to fede, / But plucke away and pull / Theyr fleces of wull' (*CC* 76–9). Piers' longest accusation (73–131) twice recalls the language of Skelton's poem. His charge that ambitious shepherds 'gape for greedie governaunce' echoes Colyn's accusation that the clergy 'gaspe' and 'gape' to have promotion (*CC* 85–6); his remark that under the pretense of being shepherds, 'Wolves, ful of fraude and guile' have 'devoured their owne sheepe' extends Colyn Cloute's observation that very few bishops are able to keep the wolf from the door and from their 'goostly shepe' (*CC* 147–55).

In *Julye*, Spenser seems to rely less on Skelton's language for precedence and more on his favorite technique of reporting things heard. In his longest assault on proud and ambitious shepherds, Thomalin (*Thom*as Cooper, Bishop of *Lin*coln) subtly provides us proper moral measures by reporting what he has 'heard' old Algrind (Bishop Edmund *Grindal*) say of two uncorrupted shepherds of the past, Abel and Moses (125–40, 157–60). He twice more reports what goes on in 'Rome' (London, Westminster) among the grasping, greedy, and power seeking, 'as some have seene.' By telling his listener what others have told him, Thomalin can cite for us exemplary sources and show us that he has not left his flock for an idle pilgrimage.

By *September*, Spenser has converted to his own use and purpose the practices, characters, and themes of his predecessors, including Virgil, Mantuan, Marot, and Skelton. As noted earlier, Colin Clout is here briefly alluded to as a shepherd's boy, working for wise old Roffy (Spenser was secretary to Dr John Young, Bishop of Rochester, *Episcopus Roffensis*, in 1578). Diggon Davie (Richard *Davies*, Bishop of St David's) tells of his unhappy experiences when he foolishly drove his sheep into a far country. There shepherds made a 'Mart' of their good name: they beguiled, robbed, and even murdered one another, and ignored or misled their flocks. Filled with covetousness and spite, they kindled coals of 'conteck and yre.'

Invited by Hobbinol to clarify his remarks, Diggon does so in 'flatt' English, by rehearsing in Skeltonic manner what people say of these viciously ambitious shepherds. In the space of 32 lines (104–35), Diggon relies six times on such documentation as 'Thus chatten the people' and 'They sayne' or 'Other sayne,' and seasons his speech with proverbial utterance as did Skelton's Colyn. He begins with 'Badde is the best,' works in 'other the fat from their beards doen lick,' and concludes with 'better leave of with a little losse, / Then by much wrestling to leese the grosse.'

Yet even here, in one of the ecclesiastical eclogues most akin to his approach, Skelton is beginning to give way to Marot, and the presence of Colyn Cloute is starting to fade. The hero whom Colin Clout serves is Roffy, the name of the maker of reed pipes in Marot's *Complaincte* (1.42). Ironically for us, E.K. in glossing that name, mistakenly derives it from the name of a 'shepehearde in Marot his Aeglogue of Robin and the Kinge,' an eclogue that Spenser imitates in *December*. Also, Marot and his Colin occupy high and commanding ground in *November*'s dirge, as evidenced in the argument, in the poem proper, and in Colin's emblem which was Marot's own: 'La mort ny mord.'

The selective absorption of Skelton's popular reputation, and of his techniques in *Colyn Cloute* into Spenser's Colin Clout is completed, yet the literary relationship remains incomplete. Completed in that Spenser has been able to imply an authority in ecclesiastical satire without actually invoking Colin Clout as a speaker; and completed also in that a familiar voice has been recreated in a new register, a means of associating the views of the favored Spenserian persona with the voice of the many, of providing a subtle moral measure with which to indict the ambitious and corrupt ecclesiastics.

But incomplete in that Skelton's *Colyn Cloute* could never have filled the two other 'ranckes' or 'formes' of *The Shepheardes Calender*, the recreative and plaintive (Gen Arg); for these, Spenser had to turn to Marot's Colin. Incomplete also in that while Spenser advocated going a 'lowly gate emongste the meaner sorte' (envoy), he nonetheless avoided the rapid clatter of Skeltonic verse as such; indeed never resorted to the 'Skeltoniad' as did some of his contemporaries.

Although Spenser clung to the English authority behind the cognomen Colin Clout, not even in *Colin Clouts Come Home Againe* did he again return to full-fledged satire on ecclesiastical abuses. Skelton's concentrated focus was scarcely adequate for the range of the new poet's experience now that a new persona had been forged, one with the choice of a familiar given name – Colin – repeatable in two accents, as it were, a character variously skilled for the variety of poetic enterprises and concerns found in *The Shepheardes Calender*, one for whom a private as well as a public mode of expression had been found.

ROBERT STARR KINSMAN

John Skelton 1983 *Complete English Poems* ed John Scattergood (New Haven); Spenser *SC* ed 1930. Edwards 1981; Helgerson 1978; Robert S. Kinsman 1979 *John Skelton, Early Tudor Laureate: An Annotated Bibliography, c 1488–1977* (Boston); McLane 1961; McLane 1973; Mallette 1979; Patterson 1986; William A. Ringler, Jr 1956 'John Stow's Editions of Skelton's *Workes* and of *Certaine Worthye Manuscript Poems*' *SB* 8:215–17.

Socrates (c 469–399 BC) Accorded a place of especial honor in the Christian-humanist pantheon, Socrates attained the status of a culture hero. His death for the sake of truth was held to foreshadow Christ's death, and his teaching to prefigure Christ's doctrine (Lewalski 1966:240). Ficino could perceive in Socrates both Christ and Eros; Erasmus enthusiastically canonized him in the colloquy 'Convivium religiosum' with 'Sancte Socrates ora pro nobis' (Saint Socrates, pray for us); the skeptical Montaigne became fascinated with Socrates the man, using him in the *Essais* as both a transfigured alter ego and as an ideal of human conduct.

Given this background, Spenser's references to Socrates are surprisingly few and puzzlingly inaccurate. The allusion to him as 'the wisest thought alive' (*FQ* II ix 48) is conventional, but the only two direct references (both involving Critias, one of the interlocutors in Plato's *Critias*) are oddly askew. The description of 'Wise *Socrates*, who thereof quaffing glad / Pourd out his life, and last Philosophy / To the faire *Critias* his dearest Belamy' (vii 52) either mistakes 'Critias' for 'Crito' (the correct name of Socrates' friend at his death), or, as Upton first suggested, substitutes for Socrates' death that of Theramenes described in Xenophon, Cicero, and Achille Bocchi's *Symbolicarum quaestionum ... libri quinque* (1574). That latter parallel is strengthened by Theramenes' ironic toast to his 'beautiful' young friend and betrayer, Critias; this toast is found in Cicero and in Bocchi's emblem.

If Spenser really translated the pseudo-Platonic dialogue *Axiochus*, its stoic attitude of *contemptus mundi* accords well with the Bocchi emblem illustrating *Contemptio mortis, metu cor liberat* ('Contempt for death frees the heart from fear'). But if the reference to 'Critias' is read as ironic (following the Theramenes story), what is to be made of *FQ* IV proem 3, in which Critias appears as friend, not enemy? Moreover, this later description of a dialogue about love wherein the two characters are 'shaded oft from sunne' alludes to the *Phaedrus*; but the substitution of 'Critias' for 'Phaedrus' is baffling. The charge that the sum of Spenser's references to Socrates demonstrates no more than a confused recollection of Cicero (A.E. Taylor in *Var* 2:264) is baldly inconsistent with the poet's serious Neoplatonism. But it has not yet been substantially disproved.

RAYMOND B. WADDINGTON

Hieatt 1975a app D discusses 'Socrates, Critias, Theramenes.' See also T.M. Gang 1956 'Spenser and the Death of Socrates' *TLS* (3 Aug):463; and A.E. Taylor 1924 'Spenser's Knowledge of Plato' *MLR* 19:208–10. For the image of Socrates, see Lynda Gregorian Christian 1972 'The Figure of Socrates in Erasmus' Works' *SCJ* 3.2:1–10; Barbara Kiefer Lewalski 1966 *Milton's Brief Epic: The Genre, Meaning, and Art of 'Paradise Regained'* (Providence); Raymond Marcel 1951 '"Saint" Socrate patron de l'humanisme' *RIPh* 5:135–43; and Raymond B. Waddington 1980 'Socrates in Montaigne's "Traicté de la phisionomie"' *MLQ* 41:328–45. See also A.H.T. Levi 1970 'The Neoplatonist Calculus' in *Humanism in France at the End of the Middle Ages and in the Early Renaissance* ed A.H.T. Levi (Manchester) pp 229–48.

song In the Renaissance, *song* is both a loose synonym for poetry in general, and the more specific term for verse-with-music (including the air, madrigal, broadside ballad, and other forms). If we take verse-with-music to represent song proper, Spenser wrote none, with the possible exception of three eclogues in *The Shepheardes Calender*. His verse, lyric and otherwise, displays to the reader a textual elaboration that is unsuitable for full conveyance in singing; in this he stands with Donne and the Shakespeare of the sonnets at a watershed of English lyric poetry, which after his time seldom returns to the singable. Air (or lute song) and madrigal collections of the late sixteenth and early seventeenth centuries set to music the verse of many poets of the time, whether they seem to have intended singing (as did most courtly lyric poets) or not; but Spenser is very little represented in these musical settings. Compared with that of his contemporaries, Spenser's verse has seldom been sung. By contrast, song is often represented and sometimes formally imitated in his work, and it figures prominently in the image his poetry gives of itself and its poet.

Spenser's poetry often calls itself 'song' even when it is also describing itself as written: 'Goe little booke ... A shepheards swaine saye did thee sing ... And when his honor has thee redde, / Crave pardon' (*SC* 'To His Booke'). In turning from the 'Oaten reeds' of pastoral to 'sing of Knights and Ladies gentle deeds' – albeit with an 'afflicted stile' or pen as well as 'trumpets sterne' – Spenser models himself on Virgil, who similarly 'sang' of arms and the man. The conventional blurring of any distinction between singing and writing is similarly found in *Orlando furioso* 14 when Ariosto mentions both his pen and (later) his hoarse voice. The convention posits or recalls that poetry and song began as one thing. For the poet in a serious mood, it invokes the spiritually and socially important role of the inspired, inspiring singer; for the maker of love poems, it invokes the possibly magic power of primitive piper or harper. The idea of both serious and amorous poetry as 'song' found sanction as well in the biblical 'excellent song which was Salomons,' and which Spenser may have translated (see lost *works). When a Renaissance poet calls himself a singer, he affirms the ancient dignity of his profession. Some poems claiming this heritage are closer than others to words really intended for music. Spenser's *Fowre Hymnes* belong to a poetic genre, the hymn, that has little in common with musical hymns such as those of George Wither (1623); on the other hand, *Epithalamion* and

Prothalamion are songlike in their use of refrains.

Song heard in the worlds of pastoral or romance provides a poetic image of poetry and the poet: Colin Clout singing is a version of Spenser writing, idealized as powerful, spontaneously creative, acting immediately on his society. In the mirror of pastoral convention, Colin appears as a musician-poet highly admired by his fellows. In *June*, he is careless of fame, reverent to his mentor Tityrus (Chaucer), hopeful that he may bring shame to his unkind Rosalind and infamy to his rival lover. In *August*, two singers vie for a prize and display pride of craft in their festive extemporizing. In *November*, Colin shows the power of song to pay tribute to the dead. In *October*, the weary Cuddie laments the failure to gain patronage for his music, which is variously described as pipe, string, and singing. (The central irony of *The Shepheardes Calender* is that the fiction of Colin's simple pastoral song is set against Spenser's bravura display of the writer's craft.) While the elaborate art of the various verse forms heightens the charm of the simple life, and the picture of simplicity flatters the sophistication of reader and poet, pastoral song defends in its own world the powers and merit of Spenser's verse.

Beyond these allusions to song, three passages in *The Shepheardes Calender* are presented dramatically as song, and these are the likeliest examples of actual songs composed by Spenser. In *August*, the first undersong of the competitive roundelay (in the convention of the *amoebaeum carmen*) is 'hey ho hollidaye,' the burden of a playful song that was noted down (music, however, unreadable) in a surviving commonplace book (BL, Add Ms 4338; see Pattison 1948:174). In *August* and in Colin's *Aprill* and *November* songs, apparent irregularities of meter are consistent with a supposition that Spenser had a tune in mind (Doughtie 1970:21n, citing Jane K. Fenyo).

In *The Faerie Queene*, song is described with surprisingly little approval. Pastoral song is carefree and still blameless: Colin Clout himself appears briefly to play rustic music to which the Graces 'both daunce and sing' (VI x 12), and the fauns and satyrs who sing to Una are unreproved: their song is not so different from that of the joyful birds that often sing in the poem (I vi 13–14). Both human and heavenly epithalamia are sung for Una and Redcrosse (I xii 38–9), and Apollo's 'celestiall song' at the wedding of Peleus and Thetis is recalled as an instance of 'Musicks wondrous might' (VII vii 12). These songs are pictured as innocent and outside the world of heroic activity; but most singing in the poem is courtly dalliance, and Spenser typically describes it with disdain. Lechery is a courtly lover skilled at song and dance (I iv 25), and the flirtatious Phaedria sings light songs in her 'vaine jolliment' (II vi 3). Although social singing in Alma's parlor expresses harmonious joy (II ix 35), consort song, like solo song, is apt to be abused, as when mermaids make treacherous melody to Guyon on his way to Acrasia's bower (II xii 32), and when dallying ladies and 'lascivious boyes' in the bower sing and mix 'their song with light licentious toyes' (72). There is loose Lydian caroling in Malecasta's court that Britomart and Redcrosse hear with scorn (III i 40); the seducer Paridell is accomplished in all the varieties of courtly song (x 8); and in the masque of Cupid, 'wanton Bardes, and Rymers impudent' sing of love's delight (xii 5). With the Graces, Spenser seems to hold out a promise of song as a shared moment of nearly heavenly harmony; but the business of his romance world intrudes, even in the person of his hero. Insofar as song is performed for anyone to hear, and in particular with calculated effect, it is suspect.

Twice in *The Faerie Queene*, stanzas are presented dramatically as the text of a song being sung. Both songs are seductive: Phaedria's perverts 'consider the lilies' (KJV) into 'present pleasures chuse' (II vi 15–17); a voice in Acrasia's bower sings *carpe diem*: 'Gather the Rose of love, whilest yet is time' (xii 74–5). Like the Bower of Bliss itself, these songs exhibit the dangerous charm of art misapplied: in both cases the music displays bad artfulness, a 'morally unwholesome blending of its musical categories' (Hollander 1971:230). Both imitate songs associated with Armida's imprisoning enchantment in Tasso's *Gerusalemme liberata* (14.62–4, 16.14–15). Like Spenser, Tasso is wary of light sophisticated song; his presentation of song differs from Spenser's mainly in his several references to psalms and hymns sung by clerics. Ariosto, on the other hand, is more tolerant of song as courtly pastime, as he is of dalliance in general; for example, love songs are credited to the fallen Olimpio in a battlefield elegy, and later to a whole group of poets including Ariosto's friend Nicolò da Correggio and apparently Ariosto himself (*OF* 16.72, 42.81–95). *The Faerie Queene* has no such tributes, for Spenser's high muse of history frowns on most light song. (See also *music.)

MARK W. BOOTH

Mark W. Booth 1981 *The Experience of Songs* (New Haven); Donker and Muldrow 1982 svv *Epithalamion, Hymn, Lyric, Song*; Edward Doughtie, ed 1970 *Lyrics from English Airs 1596–1622* (Cambridge, Mass); Hollander 1961; Hollander 1971; W.J.W. Koster 1953 *Traité de métrique grecque, suivi d'un précis de métrique latine* 2nd ed (Leiden); Bruce Pattison 1948 *Music and Poetry of the English Renaissance* (London); Whitman 1918:221–2.

sonnet, sonnet sequence The sonnet is a short lyric form which, since its invention in Italy in the thirteenth century, has provided European poets with the most exacting test of their formal prowess. Though the canzone's interwoven rhymes seem more complicated, and the sestina's six recurrent endwords or the haiku's seventeen syllables more restricting, in the sonnet mere stringency of means operates upon a complex dynamic structure to create unexpectedly large poetic resources. It is this interaction to which the form owes its perennial attraction.

The sonnet was invented about 1230, probably by Jacopo da Lentino, an official in the train of Frederick II of Sicily, whose court was then the most brilliant and learned in Europe. The sonnet and sestina were the only fixed forms available to the earliest poets of the Romance languages, for in others, like the canzone and ballata, the poet himself controlled the number and arrangement of his rhymes within the differing structural schemes which marked off one genre from another. In the sonnet, however, the very form of the poem was determined by the restricted number of rhymes and their near-invariable arrangement.

The genesis of the sonnet has been much debated, and it is sometimes thought to have emerged as a hybrid from other forms like the strambotto; but the rhyme scheme shows clearly its kinship with the two-part structure (*abab* / x) nearly universal in early romance lyric: a *frons* composed of two *pedes*, followed by a *sirima* employing different rhymes (see *versification). This is the structure of the sonnet's typical rhyme scheme: *abba abba* (*frons* composed of two *pedes*) and *cde cde* (*sirima*, with three new rhymes which could be arranged in different ways). The genesis of the sonnet will become intelligible only when we understand why this two-part structure, which was developed with so much amplitude and flexibility in the longer stanza of the canzone, should in the case of the sonnet have been endowed with such rigor.

Current investigations into the different ways in which early scribes wrote out sonnets suggest that like modern concrete poetry their appearance on the page embodied a visual scheme related to their theme or purpose. The *frons* was written out in four long lines of 22 syllables each; the *sirima* was sometimes written in the same way, but appeared in at least two other combinations of long and short lines. A marked internal caesura divided the long lines, which were unified by both internal and end rhyme. Wilhelm Pötters (1983) has drawn attention to the particular scribal convention chosen by Petrarch for his *Canzoniere*, where the fourteen 11-syllable lines of the Italian sonnet as we now know it were arranged in seven long lines of 22 syllables each. The visual form of the sonnet thus expressed the fraction 22/7 or *pi*, the formula used by Archimedes to describe the relation between the circumference and diameter of a circle, and the sonnet itself constituted a graphic attempt to square the circle. Such numerological-spatial conceits were important in the sestina as well, a form which Petrarch used expertly, though he did so with the effect of fracturing its ideal fixity (Spanos 1978).

The sonnet thus began as an intensely unified structure, 'an integrative vehicle, one created to regain a lost, or diminished sense of wholeness' (Kleinhenz 1978). But the persistence of *frons*- and *sirima*-like divisions meant that the poem invariably fell into two unequal parts, the first four long lines employing one set of rhymes, the next three a different set. The result was to establish the conditions for that sense of contrariousness, that dialectical principle of expansion and contraction which gives the sonnet its dynamic, and which was to make it – no matter what its rhyme scheme – fundamentally disputatious, pointed, and elegant.

As a fixed form, the sonnet deflected emphasis from the virtuoso display of new rhyme schemes permitted by the canzone stanza towards the content of the poem itself. Thus despite its courtly origin, the form was immediately put to use during its first experimental century on a variety of topics by poets of every class. But its first and most enduring subject was love. The amorous lyrics of Jacopo and other lyricists of the Sicilian court evolved within a thematic tradition already well developed by the troubadours of Provence, in which the poet sang of his devotion to a woman superior to him both in social station and in personal excellence. Guided by her example and rewarded by the creation of the lyric itself, the poet willingly submitted to the torments of a love which could never seek completion. This led to the elaboration of multitudes of standard *topoi* or conceits, many of which go back to Greek and Latin love poetry, and which were eventually to receive their apotheosis in the much exploited and much parodied conventions of Petrarchan lyric. These conventions were deployed with great rhetorical skill, creating an ornate poetic texture in which the contrariousness of the experience of love was expressed in the sharply juxtaposed alternatives typical of an age when formal public debate was an intellectual spectator sport.

The Northern Italian poets of the century after Jacopo – among them Cavalcanti, Dante, and eventually the archetype of all sonneteers, Petrarch – were attracted to the sonnet not only by its concentration of forces, but by its potentially unstable amalgam of rigid form and argumentative matter. In their sonnets, the question of the rightness of love was debated with increasing persistence, casting upon the topoi inherited from classical and Provençal love poetry an ever more problematic perspective. Whether because of this, or for some reason as yet undiscovered, the early visual conceits of the sonnet disappeared. By the end of the fourteenth century, the stanza-like poem we know today had appeared, resolving the same rhymes used by early practitioners into the imbalanced octave and sestet of the 'Italian' sonnet (frequently but inaccurately known as the 'Petrarchan' form). Throughout the sonnet's history, there has always been a conflict between the evident disproportion in its rhyme scheme and the integrity of effect at which the poem aims. Renaissance critics debated whether the quatrains and tercets ought to be complete in themselves, and even whether enjambment from line to line was permissible. Most controversial was the question of the so-called *volta* or 'turn' which later critics perceived between the octave and the sestet. What seems clear is that the sonnet aimed at wholeness but had within it a principle of imbalance which was always available, and that the conflicts of love-debate and the often controverted matter of the 'occasional' sonnet encouraged a pointedness which tended to disrupt the poem's self-sufficiency. The same effect is evident in the epigram, to which Renaissance theorists often compared the sonnet. Thus, from very early in its development, the sonnet contained within itself the sources of its own disruption; and it is their exploitation, whether as a formal 'turn' or as a final reversing couplet, which distinguishes the sonnet from a mere stanza of fourteen lines.

The most influential of all sonnet writers was Petrarch. His *Rerum vulgarium fragmenta*, known also as the *Canzoniere* and as the *Rime sparse*, combines 366 sonnets, canzoni (including sestine), ballate, and madrigals into a unified collection which the poet began in his twenties and was still revising at his death in 1374 at age seventy. The *Canzoniere* consolidated amorous topoi from classical, Provençal, and Sicilian sources for transmission to the poets of the next two centuries, who treated Petrarch's sonnets as exemplary models of style, as well as looking on Petrarch himself as a paradigmatic instance of the love poet's formative experience of sorrow and isolation. In his hands, the powerful but still relatively unpolished sonnet became an exquisitely controlled poetic instrument, joining verbal music and metaphoric complexity in a union new to the vernacular languages.

The idea of an assemblage of shorter lyrics designed as a complete book had first appeared in modern literature with Dante's *Vita nuova* (c 1300), and Petrarch's much larger *Canzoniere* was composed under the influence – often denied but nevertheless pervasive – of his great predecessor. Framed by an opening sonnet in which the poet reflects sorrowfully on his misdirected life and by a final prayerful canzone to the Virgin, the lyrics of the *Canzoniere* compose a prismatic set of meditations on the conflict the poet suffers between his search for fame and the obligations of prophecy, his love of Laura, and the love of God. In his opening sonnet, Petrarch calls his poems *rime sparse* (scattered rhymes); and the separateness of the poems allows him to exploit the classical aesthetic value of *varietas*, according to which poems are arranged to compare and contrast their versions of a subject. In a late letter, Petrarch insists that the 'variety' of the poems is in fact caused by the fragmented state of the sorrowing lover's mind. Attempts have been made to discover a numerological scheme in the *Canzoniere*, but they founder on Petrarch's persistent revision of his collection, a habit which is the compositional equivalent of his fascination with disjunction as a theme.

The ironically contrasted images of scattering and gathering provide a leitmotif of the collection. The poems of the first section of the *Canzoniere* flaunt Petrarch's mastery of classical and Provençal love idioms, those of the last section are in the 'gray-haired style' of superb but grieving old age. Between them lies the divide caused by the poet's mid-life reexamination of himself which is symbolized by the death of his beloved Laura, occurring at precisely this moment of Augustinian revaluation. The *Canzoniere* as a whole is thus governed by the same structural dichotomy as the sonnets which compose so much of its fabric. The passion and virtuosity of the poems *in vita* is contracted, pointed, and turned gravely back on itself in the poems *in morte*.

Though the amorous sonnet as codified by Petrarch has remained the archetypal expression of the form's potential, the sonnet did not remain a love poem. Its courtly origin and stylistic complexity suited it ideally for serious philosophical, religious, and scientific topics, and it was also vigorously exploited as an epistolary medium. Very early, too, the humorous and satirical *sonetto caudato* appeared, with its tail of two-and-a-half lines appended to the traditional fourteen. But the sonnet was essentially a serious genre; Renaissance poets thought of it as a vernacular equivalent of the Latin epigram: brief, formally elegant, and pointed. The sonnet's idealized vision of beauty, and the polished style it required, ensured that it remained a courtly and learned form even when those who practiced it most assiduously belonged to the new class of vernacular humanists – professional teachers and scholars, often of bourgeois origin – who were pressing the claims of the early emergent national languages of Europe to the eloquence and poetic range of Latin and Greek. The very restricted themes and motifs of the love sonnet provided a useful repertoire of topoi for late medieval poets accustomed to think of composition in terms of the amplification of conceits, and for their successors in the Renaissance who sought out sources of rhetorical *copia*. In the sixteenth century, the influential poet and theorist Pietro Bembo treated Petrarch's *Canzoniere* as an ideal model of perfected style. In Italy and later in France, 'Bembism' laid important foundations for neoclassicism, but it also led to many dully imitative sonnets and sonnet collections.

Though the individual sonnet flourished from the time of its invention, the canzoniere or sonnet sequence emerged as an important new genre in Italian poetry only in the fifteenth century. Petrarch's *Canzoniere* became immensely popular among the sonnet writers of Italian vernacular humanism, who regarded it as a modern version of the classical elegiac collections by Propertius and Ovid. The Renaissance sonnet sequence thus evolved as a fusion of Petrarchan and classical example. In their own individual sonnets, these poets imitated Petrarch's style assiduously, but in constructing sequences, they operated with greater freedom, fusing Petrarchan and classical models to produce many different arrangements for their poems. The sonnet's facility in endlessly reduplicating itself, combined with the canzoniere's loose organization, meant that any such lyric collection tended to become an encyclopedia of motifs. In this way, the pure sonnet sequence, devoid of other forms, was engendered. Laid out in books in imitation of the classical elegists, or in numerically rounded groups of 100, or frequently in groups of 33 (or one more, or one less), such sequences lent themselves to the kind of numerological patterning which can be seen in the increasingly Hermetic collections of the late sixteenth century. Throughout the Renaissance, the lyric collections which trace their ancestry to Petrarch are amazingly diverse. In some, there are prose commentaries and headnotes which turn the sequence into a quasi narrative. In others, a collection of sonnets and other short lyrics is joined to a set of longer poems, on the example of Petrarch, whose *Canzoniere* was accompanied in many manuscripts and printed texts by his equally well-known set of *capitoli*, the *Trionfi*. Many true cycles or canzonieri are not in fact composed primarily of sonnets at all: Maurice Scève's *Délie* (1544) and Herbert's religious collection *The Temple* (1633) are notable examples.

In the fifteenth century, both sonnet and sonnet collection tended to be cultivated by elite and essentially courtly groups in Florence, Naples, and the northern Italian courts. With the inception of printing, however, the sonnet gained a large bourgeois audience, which provided a market for the more than 160 editions of Petrarch before 1600, and for the anthologies of single sonnets published by editors like Domenichi in the mid-sixteenth century. What had once been the province of a cultivated few rapidly became a popular poetic industry. It has been estimated (perhaps too cautiously) that over 200,000 sonnets are extant from this period. During the same period and by the same means, the sonnet and sonnet collection were taken up by certain Spanish noblemen, by the French Pléiade, and more tentatively by poets in England. The first English sonnets are by Wyatt, whose journey to Italy in 1527 had introduced him to the sonnets of the currently popular Serafino da Aquila, and to Petrarch in the edition of Vellutello.

For English poets, the sonnet presented acute problems of language and form. The Italian language yields rhymes with facility, unlike English, and the concreteness and large vocabulary of English means that the allusive density which the sonnet possessed in Italian had to be achieved by different means. English poetry in the sixteenth century was still discovering cadences and vocabulary fitting for a language no longer medieval, and the goals of its own vernacular humanists were not at all clear. These problems account in part for the wrenched nature of Wyatt's translations from Petrarch, and they led his younger contemporary Surrey to invent a new kind of 'English' sonnet, sometimes called 'Shakespearean' after its greatest practitioner. It has three quatrains and a couplet, rhymed *abab cdcd efef gg*, a structure which produces a sonnet with a more meditative, slower-developing body than the Italian sonnet but with a much sharper and more conclusive ending, a characteristic we already see in Wyatt. Sidney uses the Italian octave-sestet division but rhymes his sestet to achieve the same sudden termination, which often reverses the argument of what has gone before, and most sonnets in English, whatever their form, show this tendency to sudden closure.

The sonnets of Wyatt and Surrey were published, along with a few by other poets, in *Tottel's Miscellany* (1557); but English lyricists, though they compiled canzoniere-like personal miscellanies made up of other kinds of poems, took little interest in the sonnet or the canzoniere until the 1580s, when Thomas Watson's *Hekatompathia* (1582) was printed, and sequences written under the influence of continental Petrarchism by Sidney, and eventually Daniel and Constable, were compiled. Here, as in Italy a century before, the rise of the sonnet was associated with a self-conscious 'modernism' in poetry. English poets began to practice the form when its idealistic intellectual content and the rhetorical skills it made possible became important to them, and when a courtly, stylistically self-conscious ambience arose which made these values of use. In the 1580s, such interests were still the preserve of a small group communicating by manuscript, though there is evidence that when Sidney composed *Astrophil and Stella* he had read with a sharp eye the Tudor miscellanies, along with Petrarch.

But with the printing of Sidney's sequence in 1591 (the same year in which Spenser issued his *Complaints* with its four groups of original and translated sonnets), an explosion of public interest took place which made the sonnet a popular fashion throughout most of the 1590s; Spenser's *Amoretti* (1595) appeared at the height of the mode. By the early seventeenth century, the sonnet had become *démodé*. Though Shakespeare's own collection was published in 1609, Donne shunned the sonnet in his early poetry. His *Holy Sonnets*, however, mine a rich tradition (English as well as continental) of such religious verse. Milton's 24 sonnets, several of them in Italian, owe more to the broadening range with which della Casa, Tasso, and the Italian *eruditi* endowed the form after Petrarchism had spent its energies than they do to the tradition which culminated in England in the Elizabethan love sonnet.

English poets have continued to use both the Italian and English forms of the sonnet, one endowed with the prestige of Milton, the other that of Shakespeare. Spenser, with his great power of strophic invention, turned away from both of these to yet a third kind of sonnet, one which superimposes the five rhymes of the Italian poem on the quatrain structure of the English. Its scheme is *abab bcbc cdcd ee*, and the linked rhymes of lines 4–5 and 8–9 look back both to the rhyme royal used in the ballade stanza of Chaucer and Wyatt and to the linked quatrains of Marot. This form appears before Spenser in the twenty 'Spenserian' sonnets by James VI of Scotland and others printed in *Essayes of a Prentise* (1584), but no one knows whether or not Spenser had encountered this book. The form may have developed independently in Scotland and England (Markland 1963). Spenser's earliest 'sonnets,' however, are in blank verse; they are the translations of sonnets by Marot and du Bellay published in *Theatre for Worldlings* when he was seventeen. Like Milton in the next century, the young Spenser may have associated the absence of rhyme with classical severity; certainly these poems show how aware he was of the sonnet's status as epigram. By 1586, he had discovered his own form (a sonnet to Harvey bears that date); but in the translations of du Bellay published in *Complaints*, he employs the English rhyme scheme, with occasional rhyme-linked quatrains, reserving his personal form for *Visions of the Worlds Vanitie*, the only original sequence in that book.

The dynamics of the Spenserian sonnet are determined by the cohesion made possible by its internal rhyme links. Dialectical tension is set aside as the poem seeks a coherence of statement reminiscent of that sought by the sonnet's earliest practitioners. The Spenserian sonnet thus rarely presents us with the imbalance or argumentativeness of the Italian sonnet; and though its rhymes preserve the concluding couplet of the English form, Spenser is more likely to make it a triumphant confirmation of the poem's theme than to produce an ironic reversal in the manner of Sidney. His structure is fundamentally aggregative rather than dialectical. If his gifts are at variance with the direction then being taken by the sonnet, it is also true that he knew this, and was bold enough to mold the form anew to his needs.

With four exceptions, Spenser wrote no sonnets outside the frame of the sequence or collection, for even the seventeen dedicatory sonnets to *The Faerie Queene* are interrelated by their virtuoso variations on the theme of praise. Yet only one of his sequences, *Amoretti*, is a true Petrarchan canzoniere, in form at least, though not in substance. Sidney's sonnets, all confrontations with Petrarch on Petrarch's own grounds, are formal attempts to enter the 'singing school' which the discipline of the canzoniere afforded Renaissance lyricists. Spenser, however, approaching the genre through the neoclassical epigram, reflects modes favored in the detached world of the philosophical sonneteers; and even the short original sequence *Vanitie* shows a wider and more meditative understanding of the canzoniere's range than those of many Elizabethan sonnet writers. This understanding he owes to du Bellay, whom he had translated in *Theatre* and whose *Antiquitez de Rome* he returned to translate in *Complaints*.

The four sequences collected in *Complaints* illustrate the technical range and detachment that Spenser the sonnet writer possessed when he began *Amoretti*. The Spenserian sonnet is reserved for original poems, the English for translations. In *Ruines of Rome*, the English sonnet forces a couplet ending on du Bellay's immaculate Italian sonnets, but it preserves the dialectical tendency of the Italian form as Spenser's own rhyme scheme would not have done. *Complaints* also contains three brief sequences unified by dream-vision motifs: *Vanitie*, *Bellay*, and *Petrarch*. If these are the

Dreames mentioned in *Three Letters*, they predate 1580. They tell us three things. First, Spenser's sense of the genre was sufficient to interest him in translating as complete sequences, and as sonnets, poems he had originally done 'to order' in obedience to van der Noot's selections. Second, in *Bellay* and *Petrarch*, Spenser's model (and Marot's and du Bellay's as well) was an early canzone of Petrarch for which dream-vision provides a singleness of perspective at variance with the shifting and allusive texture of the whole *Canzoniere*. The same singleness of vision appears in the tight organization of Spenser's true canzoniere, *Amoretti*, and the great tradition of dream-vision in English makes it a comfortable structural model for a poet seeking usable strengths in his native tradition. It is not surprising that *Vanitie*, Spenser's only original sequence besides *Amoretti*, takes this form as well. A third feature of the *Complaints* volume hints at his awareness of the power of number: the sonnets in du Bellay's *Antiquitez* add up to 32, a number popular among continental sonneteers for reasons never fully examined. Spenser adds an envoy to make it 33, and his own *Visions* balance this by also adding up to 33, a conceit achieved by leaving the climactic seventh vision of *Petrarch* without a number.

If these sequences place Spenser equally among the continental *eruditi* and the English writers of dream-visions, his canzoniere *Amoretti* (1595), with its accompanying *Epithalamion*, is somewhat idiosyncratically in the tradition of Petrarchism. In it, the sober themes of the meditative canzoniere give way to the standard topoi of the continental love canzoniere, and the cohesive structure of dream-vision is replaced by the model of the manuscript book of diverse lyrics accompanied by one or more longer poems. But just as Petrarch's sonnet structure provides a model in small of the dialectical tensions of his whole *Canzoniere*, so Spenser's personally devised sonnet with its aggregative structure prepares us for that happy conclusion to the poet's love-service, a conclusion which seems only temporarily withheld as the reader passes from sonnets to wedding canzone. The absence of true Petrarchan *varietas* in *Amoretti* is symptomatic of Spenser's less Augustinian, more festive view of love. It leaves his sonnets free to achieve that 'glow worm' light which Wordsworth, who understood the obligations of sonnet making very well, so justly and discerningly praised in Spenser.

GERMAINE WARKENTIN

Most of the standard Italian sources on the sonnet are referred to in John Fuller 1972 *The Sonnet* (London); more recent research is listed in Christopher Kleinhenz 1978 'Giacomo da Lentini and Dante: The Early Italian Sonnet Tradition in Perspective' *JMRS* 8:217–34. The list which follows is highly selective and, except for Pötters' important recent article, is confined to studies in English.

Austin 1947; Lois Borland 1913–14 'Montgomerie and the French Poets of the Early Sixteenth Century' *MP* 11:127–34; Walter L. Bullock 1923 'The Genesis of the English Sonnet Form' *PMLA* 38:729–44; van Dorsten 1970; Oliver Farrar Emerson 1917 'Spenser, Lady Carey, and the *Complaints* Volume' *PMLA* 32:306–22; Fowler 1979b; G.K. Hunter 1973; Christopher Kleinhenz 1975 'Petrarch and the Art of the Sonnet' in Scaglione 1975:177–91; Kleinhenz 1976 'Giacomo da Lentini and the Advent of the Sonnet: Divergent Patterns in Early Italian Poetry' *Forum Italicum* 10:218–32; Kostić 1959b; J.W. Lever 1956 *The Elizabethan Love Sonnet* (London; rev ed 1966); Markland 1963; Martz 1961; Nelson 1963; Wilhelm Pötters 1983 'La natura e l'origine del sonetto: Una nuova teoria' in *Miscellanea di studi in di onore Vittorio Branca* 178:71–8, Biblioteca dell' 'Archivum Romanicum' Series 1(Florence); F.T. Prince 1954; Prince 1960 'The Sonnet from Wyatt to Shakespeare' in Brown and Harris 1960:10–29; Reichert 1963; Elias L. Rivers 1958 'Certain Formal Characteristics of the Primitive Love Sonnet' *Spec* 33:42–55; Roche 1974; Aldo Scaglione 1980 'The Structure of the *Canzoniere* and Petrarch's Method of Composition' in *Francesco Petrarca, Citizen of the World* ed Aldo S. Bernardo (Padua and Albany, NY) pp 301–13; Shapiro 1980; Spanos 1978; Norman C. Stageberg 1948–9 'The Aesthetic of the Petrarchan Sonnet' *JAAC* 7:132–7; Stein 1934; Stillman 1984; Germaine Warkentin 1975 '"Love's sweetest part, variety": Petrarch and the Curious Frame of the Renaissance Sonnet Sequence' *Ren&R* 11:14–23; Warkentin 1980 'The Form of Dante's "Libello" and Its Challenge to Petrarch' *Quaderni d'Italianistica* 2:160–70; Hendrik van der Werf 1972 *The Chansons of the Troubadours and Trouvères: A Study of the Melodies and Their Relation to the Poems* (Utrecht); Ernest Hatch Wilkins 1959 *The Invention of the Sonnet and Other Studies in Italian Literature* (Rome) pp 1–39; James Anderson Winn 1981 *Unsuspected Eloquence: A History of the Relations between Poetry and Music* (New Haven).

soul Renaissance thinkers generally agreed with Bartholomaeus Anglicus that the soul is 'a manner of spiritual and reasonable substaunce, that GOD maketh of naught for to give life and perfection to mans body'; it 'maye receyve contraryes' (understanding and forgetting, virtue and vice) without altering its basic substance; and it draws together in hierarchical order all levels of creation, making man a microcosm. Most important, being 'beautified and made fayre with the Image and likenesse of God,' it is immortal, finding its happy end in oneness with the body of Christ, 'spoused in spirit ... assisted with Angells, pertaker of blisse, heyre of salvation' (3.3–4, 1582: sigs 12v-13r).

Traditional images of the soul are manifold, and they abound in Spenser's poetry, though it is necessary in each instance to question whether the soul is being directly or only glancingly alluded to. These images include jewel (diamond, ruby, pearl), beautiful flower (rose, lily), light-giving heavenly body (sun, moon, morning star, constellation), life-giving stream (fountain or river, flowing to and from a springhead or ocean source), winged creature (eagle, phoenix, dove, swan, angel), pilot of a ship, rider of a horse or driver of a chariot, sacrificial victim (lamb, gored ox, fallen flower, bleeding heart), and, most important for Spenser, 'virgin Queene' (*FQ* II xi 2) at the center of a castle or paradisal garden. In Spenser's most explicit portrait of the soul within the castle of the body, the maiden is Alma (ix 18); in the revelation of her heavenly origin, nature, and end as she works within the church, she is Caelia (I x 3); in her earthly garden, enjoying the hard-won pleasures of her spousal with Love, she is Psyche (III vi 50). Revealing other attributes of the soul within its earthly castle or garden are Venus, Astraea, Isis, Mercilla, and the central Grace on Mount Acidale. Evil characters pose as false duplicates for certain 'soul-maidens': especially Duessa, Acrasia, the false Florimell, and Radigund. The soul is regularly feminine but may, as a quasi-divine soul of the world, be represented as androgynous, as are Venus (IV x 40–1) and Nature (VII vii 5).

Spenser's various accounts of the soul's origin and entry into the body show a subordination of natural theology to Christian doctrine. Charron (*Of Wisdome*) lists four 'celebrated opinions' (1.7, p 27). First, the Manichees and others held the rational soul to be not merely superior to the body and to animals, but 'a part or parcell of the substance of God, who inspireth it into the bodie.' Spenser does not fully subscribe to this gnostic view: though he celebrates the 'pouring' of divine light and love into humankind (*FQ* III iii 1; and cf Chrysogone's solar impregnation, III vi 2–7) and the soul's ability to mirror divinity (*HL* 192–6, *HB* 176–210, *HHL* 113–19, *HHB* 113–19), he protests abject humility when approaching the throne of God (*HHB* 113–51, 204–59).

Second, a group headed by Tertullian 'affirmeth that the *Soule* proceedeth and is derived from the soules of our parents with the seed, as the *Soule* of the beast.' Spenser stresses the influence of heredity ('gentle bloud': VI ii 24–7, iii 1–2, v 1, xii 3–22) in engendering nobility of soul, but he allows also the spark of divinity in the human creature, regardless of parentage and environment, as in the bear-child (iv 35–8).

Third, Pythagoreans and Platonists, Origen and some other Christian and Jewish thinkers maintain that all souls were created out of nothing by God's command at the beginning of the world, 'and reserved in heaven, afterwards to be sent into the lower parts, as need should require, and that the bodies of men are formed and disposed to receive them.' Spenser's account of generation in the Garden of Adonis reflects the idea of a 'seminary of souls' (III vi 30); and Platonic metempsychosis, the reduction of human souls into animal or vegetable forms, is pervasive as a moral metaphor in his allegory though not as a literal doctrine. Of considerable interest to him (*HB* 99–126) was the Platonic myth of the soul's gradual descent into the fleshly body and its ability to reascend to the realm of Being – a notion popularized by Macrobius, Boethius, Martianus Capella, and the school of Chartres;

for Spenser this was an equivocal analogue of Christian doctrine.

Fourth, orthodox Christian doctrine held that the souls 'are all created of God, and infused into bodies prepared in such manner that the creation and infusion is done at one and the same instant.' Spenser (*HHL* 99–119) couches this doctrine in the broader context of the unfolding of the Trinity, the creation and fall of the angels, the creation and fall of man, the incarnation and atonement of Christ – all seen as successive stages of the purposeful working of divine love.

With regard to the soul's manner of conjunction with the body, Spenser's allegory reflects several views. In the popular Platonism widespread in Christianity, the soul-body relation is a dualism, *as mover to thing moved*. The soul is an unwilling and encumbered guest of the body, temporarily governing the mortal and mutable parts, like the master of a house, the pilot of a ship, the rider of a horse, or the driver of a chariot (cf *Nosce Teipsum* 145ff, 273–388, 493ff, 1357ff in J. Davies ed 1975; Bartholomaeus 3.3). Such dualistic images of the body-soul relationship, with the soul often being encouraged to govern or even to transcend its fleshly mire, are widespread in Spenser's poetry (esp *FQ* I x, *HHL* 218ff, *HHB* 18ff, 134ff). The Aristotelian-Thomist view is *as form in matter*, stressing the soul's dependence on bodily humors, passions, and senses, and their total coalescence into a unity. Many parts and functions of Alma's castle show the integration of faculty psychology within the idealized frame of the house, yet the arithmological stanza (II ix 22) indicates the castle's essentially Platonic cast. In *Timaeus*, Plato treats the soul not simply as an errant and unwilling tenant but as the sum and perfection of the body, purposely placed therein by a divine creator (see Rohde ed 1925, 2:466, 480). In Christian mystical thought, the soul-body relation is *as light illuminating the human form*, like sunlight dispersing itself throughout the universe while remaining 'indivisible, incorruptible,' and continually reflecting the 'Eternal Light' from which it springs (see Davies, line 372; Bartholomaeus 3.3). The heavenly light reflected from perfectly armed knights, especially Redcrosse and Arthur, and revealed at each unveiling of Una and Britomart, suggests the purity of the soul as an image of God. (For further aspects of the body-soul relationship, see *psychology and Platonic *psychology.)

In depicting the soul's moral struggle, Spenser draws from numerous metaphors of medieval romance, colored by Platonic and Christian allegory and myth: warfare (see *psychomachia); pilgrimage (or voyage, quest); governance of a house (or ship, chariot, horse); assumption of clothing and armor (or veil, girdle, garland, crown); endurance of a descent into caves, forests, houses of fleshly idolatry; and perseverance in moral and intellectual activity, avoiding temptations to idle ease. All such worthy exercises of the resolved soul, though deserving praise in Cleopolis, are insufficient to assure salvation and reward in the heavenly kingdom or to defeat conclusively the enemies of the soul. Only the heroes who are endowed with transcendent powers and weaponry and are sustained by the light and love of divine grace are capable of conclusive victories. ROBERT L. REID

Bartholomaeus Anglicus 1582; Charron (before 1612); J. Davies ed 1975; La Primaudaye ed 1586; Erwin Rohde 1925 *Psyche: The Cult of Souls and Belief in Immortality among the Greeks* tr W.B. Hillis from the 8th ed, (London).

---

space Since Lessing's *Laokoön* (1766), it has been a critical commonplace that poetry articulates sounds in time while painting employs figures and colors in space. From this theoretical distinction, it has been easy to ignore space in literature, seeing it either as marginal, an obvious fictional epiphenomenon, or as nonexistent. Yet ever since Coleridge observed that *The Faerie Queene* 'is in the domains neither of history or geography ... it is truly in land of Faery, that is, of mental space' (ed 1936:36), literary space has concerned literary theorists.

Recent theory especially has begun to reexamine the problem of fictional space in literature. Although its analyses often seem complex, they can be simplified into three areas of investigation. First, fictional works create explicit spatial indices (through deictics and descriptive phrases) which readers interpret as constituting specific places. Thus, a semantic question arises about those explicit indices that allow readers to experience a text as a number of identifiable places. Second, different fictional works create distinct places with different features and properties. Generally, they take distinct attitudes towards the spatial aspects of their stories (eg, the types and range of deictics, scale, distance, plasticity, etc), so it is possible to talk about the 'world' of any particular work. In this sense, a fictional world is the totality of definite features, some of which are spatial, that go into its making. These spatial features, however many or few, work together according to a number of fictional assumptions which may be called 'axioms' or 'rules'; but by whatever name, they express the text-specific conditions that govern the spatial possibilities of the work and allow readers to interpret it as a distinct world. Third, different modes of spatialization in literature may be identified. An idea (a theme or even a character) may be said to have been spatialized when it does not develop, when there is no incremental modification with each subsequent appearance – it seems rather to have been 'unfolded' in all of its logically subordinate aspects – and all of its instances must be grasped together, or perceived in a single interpretative act, in order to be understood. *The Faerie Queene* may be seen to exemplify each of these areas of investigation.

Places in *The Faerie Queene* are always allegorical. They are determined by the conceptual demands of the larger purposes of the book in which they appear and must be interpreted in light of these demands. Although his creation of place is normally vivid (and often intricate), Spenser does not provide his readers with descriptive re-creations of recognizable places in the actual world. The house of Pride (I iv) is reached by a 'broad high way' that has been worn bare by the feet of those who have traveled there; it is built of 'squared bricke' covered by golden foil, its lofty towers are surmounted by a clock, and it is built upon a 'sandie hill, that still did flit, / And fall away' (2–5). These and other precisely indicated features make it imaginable as a definite place that can be experienced; but there is no realistic motivation for these features, only an allegorical one. The house is built upon sand because that alludes to the house of the foolish man in Matthew 7.26 and constitutes a conceptually appropriate foundation for pride. Other places in the poem are constructed by precise conceptual indices with an internal logic of allegorical coherence.

Spenser's places can be experienced in the reader's imagination but neither as, nor in terms of, realistic physical description. Thus the Bower of Bliss, 'A place pickt out by choice of best alive, / That natures worke by art can imitate' (II xii 42), manifests a number of descriptive features which together allow it to be experienced as a definite place, but which are all determined by the conceptual demands of an immensely seductive garden of erotic delights representing the extremities of human sexual intemperance. By focusing upon the figure of lasciviousness (Acrasia) who dominates the place, occupies its center, and represents in a total manner what the various parts indicate separately, the Bower of Bliss is definite, spatially localized, and imaginable.

The larger problem of spatiality (the space of the whole, of all the specific places) concerns assumptions about the fictional world, which, in recent theory, is sometimes posed as a problem of possible worlds, of the fictional creation of heterocosms, or (as in science fiction) of alternative worlds. It is closely related to Renaissance theory about the poet's creation of a second nature or, in Sidney's phrase, a 'golden' world (ed 1973b:78). If, however, one discusses fiction as another nature, one must conclude that such fictional worlds do not necessarily obey extratextual laws. The world of a work of fiction is constituted by all the things that occur within it: by events and by the systematic relationships of existents which include not only things as aspects of the setting but also characters. Thus, to speak of a fictional world implies some reference to the assumptions (the rules or axioms) according to which certain things are possible, certain kinds of relationships are allowed, and distinct permutations or metamorphoses occur. In *The Faerie Queene*, considered as a fictional world, space follows three rules. First, existents appear and disappear according to allegorical demands. Second, both existents and events fill just as much local space as is needed to satisfy their allegorical functions. Third, local places and the distances between them are (like allegorical time) quite plastic in their potential for deformation or metamorphosis.

The first rule may seem obvious to any reader, for existents are motivated only by the demands of allegory. The world of the poem contains many allegorical places and all manner of personifications. The allegorical houses which dominate the books appear and may be visited as the unfolding fortunes of the hero dictate. In every case, the motivation (never dependent upon a requirement to represent the extratextual world) is twofold: conceptual and literary. The various existents are also traditional elements of European literature.

The second rule of spatiality extends the first. Particular places may be as large or small, full or empty, as the allegory requires. Malengin, for example, inhabits a 'hollow cave' (v ix 10) to which he brings the victims whom he (as Guile) has captured in his net. When Artegall and Arthur block its entrance, he climbs the rock to escape and demonstrates his ability to dance 'Like a wyld Gote' upon the slippery heights. The landscape that is appropriate for him is as metamorphic as his body, which undergoes a series of protean transformations in an effort to escape Talus. The house of Mammon includes a number of rooms culminating in the one ruled by Philotime, which is 'large and wide' like 'some Gyeld or solemne Temple' and contains a vast number of people 'Of every sort and nation under skye' (II vii 43–4). The house is not only an open place beneath the ground but also, in its flexible inclusiveness, a self-contained microcosm of human life. Other places in the poem manifest the same significant discrepancy between an apparently ordinary exterior and an extraordinary interior.

The plastic capacities of inner spaces are nowhere clearer than in Spenser's accounts of fabulous animals. These hybrid creatures may possess mouths with any number of teeth or tongues. Their bodies, wings, and tails may be of any size, and they need not manifest a consistent anatomy. The Blatant Beast has a hundred tongues (v xii 41) but later a thousand (VI i 9). Insofar as the assumptions that govern spatial capacity are concerned, it might have both numbers. In allegorical space, the inside of a place may be greater than its outside, as if the interior had folded outwards to include the exterior.

The third rule of spatiality makes possible an indefinite series of transformations in the physical shape of particular places and in the distances between them. Not only do characters arrive at the same places by different routes which incorporate diverse experiences, but the ways to them change radically. The way to the Bower of Bliss, for example, varies with each character's journey. Only Guyon must reach it in a voyage of several days, and only he encounters the vast inventory of sea horrors (II xii 2–25) of which, the narrator observes, there are 'thousand thousands many more, / And more deformed Monsters thousand fold.' By contrast, Atin travels to the Bower virtually instantaneously, and Cymochles on his return from the Bower is delayed only by the interlude with Phaedria. The space which they must cross is empty while that which Guyon crosses is full. *The Faerie Queene* abounds in instances of variable time-schemes and corresponding transformations of space. In Book I, after Redcrosse deserts her, Una is said to have wandered 'from one to other *Ynd*' (vi 2), which indicates the time-lapse and the rigors of her search and also functions to distend (and declarify) the frontiers of Fairyland itself. After Orgoglio imprisons Redcrosse, the dwarf sets out in search of Una 'to tell his great distresse' (vii 19). He encounters her almost at once, but their return trip to rescue Redcrosse takes much longer. This extension of narrative time is paralleled by a corresponding deformation of space: 'Long tost with stormes, and bet with bitter wind, / High over hils, and low adowne the dale, / She wandred many a wood, and measurd many a vale' (28). The space of the return trip, marked by geographical diversity, is full, while that of the dwarf's journey *from* the place of Orgoglio's victory had been empty. The distances between places are, like the local spaces themselves, open to transformation. In *The Faerie Queene*, space is plastic and metamorphic.

Spatialization concerns the nonnarrative, or purely conceptual, dimension of fiction. When an idea has been spatialized, it exists synchronically in the narrative without development. Although spatial form is strikingly a twentieth-century problem, the actual practice was so common to Renaissance notions of allegorical narrative that it did not require a technical designation. In each book of *The Faerie Queene*, the dominating concept is displaced through a large number of partial images (places, characters, and events), and it cannot be completely understood until all the diffused images in which it is fragmentarily embodied are grasped. The concept may be learned through its partial images but not completely understood. Thus in Book III the concept of chastity that governs the whole is scattered through the narrative in an intricate web of allegorical images, each a partial embodiment of the whole, that incorporates in fragments the concept's total significance. Even the antithetical concept, lasciviousness, is fragmented and diffused in a counter, or negative, allegorical web. Neither, however, could be described as becoming more themselves, or as developing through incrementation, since they must always be what they are. The trip from Malecasta's castle to Busirane's house does not involve a growth or development of these two semiotically interlocked concepts but rather a display, or paradigmatic representation (or spatialization), of the complete concept to be grasped in and through its logically subordinate parts.

The Faerie Queene is the 'most deliberate artifact in our language' (Hamilton 1961a:207). Through its intricate construction, its inherent self-containedness, and its projection of its own text-specific assumptions governing occurrence and transformation, it proclaims its careful artifice. The rather minor problem of space lucidly serves to exemplify Spenser's deliberate craft in producing, like a golden world, a narrative heterocosm. (See also *FQ, geography; *labyrinths; *topographical description.)

R. RAWDON WILSON

Joseph Frank 1963 *The Widening Gyre: Crisis and Mastery in Modern Literature* (New Brunswick, NJ) ch 1; Frank 1977 'Spatial Form: An Answer to Critics' *CritI* 4:231–52; Alexander Gelley 1980 'Metonymy, Schematism, and the Space of Literature' *NLH* 11:469–87; Ricardo Gullón 1975 'On Space in the Novel' *CritI* 2:11–28; Hamilton 1961a; Mari Riess Jones 1981 'Only Time Can Tell: On the Topology of Mental Space and Time' *CritI* 7:557–76; J. Hillis Miller 1980 'The Figure in the Carpet' *Poetics Today* 1:107–18; W.J.T. Mitchell 1980 'Spatial Form in Literature: Toward a General Theory' *CritI* 6:539–67; Eric S. Rabkin 1977 'Spatial Form and Plot' *CritI* 4:253–70; Jeffrey R. Smitten 1978 'Approaches to the Spatiality of Narrative' *PLL* 14:296–314; Sharon Spencer 1971 *Space, Time and Structure in the Modern Novel* (New York); Gabriel Zoran 1984 'Towards a Theory of Space in Narrative' *Poetics Today* 5:309–35.

speech As an Elizabethan poet, Spenser was particularly aware of the importance of speech. Speech becomes a central theme in his poetry and is related to the Elizabethans' keen awareness, on both learned and popular levels, of the potency of speech.

Anyone who wrote on the subject of mankind discussed speech as the special gift which God gave Adam and Eve, reflecting their reason and distinguishing them from animals. After the Fall, speech had declined from its original probity; once the first liar had corrupted mankind, the tongue became hopelessly dual, at once our worst and best instrument. If evil, the tongue inflicted an incurable wound and wielded divisive power; if good, it could reform mankind. Many works treat these commonplace ideas, among them Wilson's *Arte of Rhetorique* (1553), Pierre de La Primaudaye's *French Academie* (1586), Stefano Guazzo's *Civile Conversation* (1581–6), especially Jean de Marconville's *Treatise of the Good and Evell Tounge* (c 1592), Simon Goulart's commentary on du Bartas' *Babilon* (tr 1595), Peter Charron's *Of Wisdome* (before 1612), and Godfrey Goodman's *Fall of Man* (1616).

While such books defined the tongue's potential for good and evil, Elizabethans in their daily life were more aware of the evil. News circulated not by a network of media but by word of mouth, and evil tongues could quickly ruin a reputation. Rumor was no pale abstraction but a monstrous reality feared even by the Queen (see *Sclaunder). Elizabethan drama reflected the reality: often slander triggered a plot and Rumor, painted all over with tongues, sometimes walked on the stage. Fulke Greville refers to 'that Curre, Rumor,' that 'runnes in every place' (*Caelica* 38). People badly bitten could be stung into defending themselves in print, as in the anonymous *A Plaine Description of the Auncient Petigree of Dame Slaunder* (1573), John Dee's *Letter* (written 1594, pub 1603), and William Vaughan's *Spirit of Detraction* (1611). Spenser would have known that Dee was accused of being a 'conjuror,' notably in John Foxe's popular *Actes and Monuments* (1563), and his reference to 'most learned wits' attacked by the Blatant Beast (*FQ* VI xii 40) may glance at him. Spenser was familiar enough himself with rumor and envy. A probable reason for his removal to Ireland was that he overplayed his mouth, and biting criticism from Burghley may have kept him there. *The Shepheardes Calender* opens with his complaint that Envy will surely bark at him, and *The Faerie Queene* concludes with the complaint that his poetry has suffered because 'some wicked tongues did it backebite' (VI xii 41).

It is against this background that we should read the theme of speech in Spenser. Some of his minor poems – *SC, Februarie, Mother Hubberd, Colin Clout, Gnat, Amoretti* 86 – refer to slander and the backbiting at court. *The Faerie Queene* is concerned with speech more broadly, and reflects both the learned and popular awareness of the power of the tongue.

A major issue of *FQ* I is how we know, for the 'unweeting' Redcrosse is deceived by the evil tongue. In a book with central reference to the story of the Fall, Archimago, who 'well could file his tongue as smooth as glas' (i 35) and hates Truth 'as the hissing snake' (ii 9), is kin to the old serpent (cf the fiery tongues of the Dragon, viii 6) and first liar, 'Sathan the workmaster of al wyles' (*Petigree of Slaunder* 1573: F8). The wiliest speaker in the whole poem is the 'man of hell,' Despair, and the debate with Despair sounds like two voices in Redcrosse's own mind (ix 38–47). Spenser suggests that the way out of such self-deception is by listening to God speak: whether in the form of Una's speech, Fidelia's, or Contemplation's (ix 53, x 18–20, 57), the Word of God can teach us how to know reality.

The claim that the word of man is 'the only companion, and witnesse of reason' (Goodman 1616:295) could serve as an epigraph for *FQ* II. Guyon and the Palmer bring reason to bear on each situation and then habitually pronounce upon it. As unrestrained speech is enemy to such reasoned utterance, Guyon silences Occasion by locking her tongue (iv 12). His and his Palmer's limitations, though, are betrayed in their reduction of complexities to sententiae.

Books III and IV introduce ideas about speech as an instrument of society. The character of Glauce demonstrates the healing power of speech, and Arthur shows the creative role of speech in society. Wilson had written of Hercules taming men with reason and eloquence, and the defeat of the Hydra was read as loquacious sophistry overcome by true eloquence. These ideas relate to the portrayal of Artegall, just as Mercury's rod (interpreted as 'an eloquent tongue' in Marconville c 1592: sig B7) relates to the triumph of Cambina (IV iii); Concord herself maintains peace by her 'powrefull speach' (x 36). This creative aspect of speech is interlaced with its opposite, the forces of Ate and her lying tongue. Associated with Babylon and Nimrod (i 22), she is a Babel principle, and presumptuous 'Babblers' like Faunus (VII vi 46) and Braggadocchio may be added to her crew. One of the most vicious is Sclaunder (IV viii 23–36); another is the pair Envy and Detraction with their 'cursed tongs' (V xii 41); and one of the most unnerving, uncomfortably close to the Elizabethan writer, is the poet Bonfont, whose tongue is nailed to a post for his 'evill words, and wicked sclaunders' (ix 26).

Book VI is the most explicit on speech, for here the pervasive evil is its abuse, and the arch-evil is the Blatant Beast with its hundred (xii 33) or thousand (i 9) tongues. The questing knight Calidore succeeds chiefly because his 'gracious speach' can 'steale mens hearts away' (i 2); in addition there are his surrogate Calepine with his 'sensefull speach' (iv 37), honey-tongued Meliboe, and Colin Clout. The particular evil of Book VI reflects Spenser's society in which even the most innocent were not safe from evil tongues. The book is also profoundly concerned with how we communicate in the fallen world – with the question, what is civilization? The mode of the poem adjusts accordingly: there is a high proportion of dialogue, direct or reported, and the romance episodes unfold in exchanges of speech. *FQ* VI shows that speech can link society together but also rend it asunder. Of itself, speech does not bring civility – witness the barbarous Turpine and the gentle savage who cannot speak – for the tongue can create or destroy society, depending on how it is used (cf Marconville c 1592: C4v, C6v-C8v). Spenser explores that idea poetically. Thus he evokes a parallel between widely ranging forces like the Brigands and the Blatant Beast careering at random, for both destroy society. The inspired poet, in touch with a prelapsarian world and graced with special powers of speech, can call forth a vision of divine order (canto x), and Calidore, 'gracious speach' persevering in society, can bring the Blatant Beast under control (canto xii). Spenser doubts, however, that such civilizing influences, including his own voice, can be permanently effective in a fallen world. BEVERLEY SHERRY

Berger 1961b, on Spenser's preoccupation with the spiritual evil of slander and with the importance of civilized communication; Freake 1977; I.G. MacCaffrey 1976, esp Part 3.5: 'The Order of Words and Its Limits'; Beverley Sherry 1975 'Speech in *Paradise Lost*' *MiltonS* 8:247–66, on 16th- and 17th-c ideas about speech and the Fall.

Spenser, Edmund (1552?-1599) Although Spenser had a successful career as an important civil servant and was well known in his lifetime as a poet, there are many gaps in our knowledge of his life. While the general pattern and many details are well established, when and where he composed many of his works, his relations with his patrons, the exact nature of his duties in Ireland, and other important aspects of his life that bear on his literary chronology and on the historical allegory of *The Faerie Queene* are only matters of conjecture.

Spenser was born in London, 'my most kyndly Nurse, / That to me gave this Lifes first native sourse' (*Prothalamion* 128–9). The date is not known, for his baptismal record was lost during the Great Fire of 1666. He may have been born in 1552 or 1553 if he was the usual age of sixteen when he matriculated at Cambridge on 20 May 1569. Or he may have been born between 1551 and 1554 if he really was forty years old (and not just writing loosely) in *Amoretti* 60, perhaps written between 1591 and 1594. The year of his birth is traditionally given as 1552; and if this is so, he was born in the reign of Edward VI and was baptized as a Protestant, lived the next years during the reign of Mary, and from the age of six was a subject of Elizabeth, whom he celebrates in his poetry.

The parish of his birth is likewise not known. Early in the eighteenth century, the antiquary William Oldys believed that he was born 'in East Smithfield.' About the same time, another historian, George Vertue, claimed to have read on a perspective view of London engraved by Wenceslaus Hollar in the early seventeenth century the following statement in English and Latin: 'East Smithfield near the Tower: the birth place of Edmund Spencer that Famous Poet, and our Second Chaucer' (Judson 1945:9). Yet surviving copies of the map lack this annotation, leaving the claim unsubstantiated. Moreover, as late as 1586 there were only four buildings on a former nunnery farm in East Smithfield, so that if Spenser was born in the neighborhood, a more likely place would be West Smithfield.

Of his parents, we know for certain only that his mother's name was Elizabeth (*Amoretti* 74). He may have had a sister Elizabeth, and a number of brothers have been suggested (including one named John who matriculated at Pembroke Hall, Cambridge, in 1575). His father may have been John Spenser, a native of Hurstwood, Lancashire, who learned his trade of cloth weaving in Burnsley or Bradford and then moved to London to become a member of the Merchant Taylors' Company. There are records for the Spenser family in Hurstwood from the thirteenth century onwards. It has been suggested that this John Spenser may also have been the one named in Stow's *Survey*: a clothworker who became an alderman in 1583, bought a house that had belonged to the Duke of Gloucester in the neighborhood of Merchant Taylors' Hall, built a large warehouse nearby, and served as Lord Mayor in 1594, for which he received the usual knighthood. Yet there were other Spensers, including two other John Spensers, one a simple journeyman, who were associated with the Company. It is certain, though, that Spenser was not born a gentleman (an important distinction at the time), but became one, without arms, by virtue of having studied at the university; later, by acquiring property in Ireland, he gained the status of a landed gentleman. Even so, he makes much of his connection by name with the ancient family of the Despencers, in *Prothalamion*, for instance, saying, 'from another place I take my name, / An house of auncient fame' (130–1), and in *Colin Clouts Come Home Againe* stressing his relation to three daughters of Sir John and Lady Katherine Spencer of Wormleighton and Althorp: 'Ne lesse praisworthie are the sisters three, / The honor of the noble familie: / Of which I meanest boast my selfe to be, / And most that unto them I am so nie' (536–9). In *Complaints* (1591), he dedicated *Mother Hubberd* to Anne (Lady Compton and Monteagle), *Teares* to Alice (Lady Strange), and *Muiopotmos* to Elizabeth (Lady Carey).

Spenser went to Merchant Taylors' School, a large and recently founded boys' school in London, where Richard Mulcaster, later to become well known as a humanist educator, was headmaster. Spenser may have been among the first group of boys to proceed through all the forms of the school if he began there, as is often claimed, in 1561. Yet the register book of the school does not list his name, and the only record of his attendance is found in his last year, 1569: he was one of six boys from the school who were given, along with a shilling apiece, gowns to wear at the funeral of Robert Nowell, a wealthy lawyer originally from Lancashire and brother of Alexander Nowell, Dean of St Paul's and an examiner at Merchant Taylors'. Yet it is none too clear how poor he was. If his father was the successful John Spenser already mentioned, the family was probably prosperous. Spenser may have been one of the poor boys paying reduced fees at Merchant Taylors' School; yet not much later, Thomas Lodge, son of the Lord Mayor, was registered as paying reduced fees. Evidently the category of 'poor' was flexible. Nonetheless, there is a very strong possibility that the Spensers were poor. We know that in his early years at Cambridge he was supported by several decreasing payments from the Nowell bequest (10*s* on 28 Apr 1569, 6*s* on 7 Nov 1570, 2*s* 6*d* on 24 Apr 1571).

About the time that he went up to the university, Spenser translated for publication the series of 'Epigrams' and 'Sonets' in the English version of Jan van der Noot's *Theatre for Worldlings*, entered by the publisher Henry Bynneman on 22 July 1569 in the Stationers' Register, and published later that year. Although this work is unsigned, he later revised the two series as, respectively, *The Visions of Petrarch, Formerly Translated* and *The Visions of Bellay* at the end of *Complaints*. His involvement in the English *Theatre* is unusual for a boy of sixteen or seventeen years, especially since van der Noot was a major Dutch poet. Perhaps Mulcaster, who had friends in the Dutch community (chiefly through van der Noot's cousin, the merchant and scholar Emanuel van Meteren), steered his pupil towards this early publication.

In the spring of 1569, Spenser matriculated at Pembroke Hall, Cambridge, as a sizar (a poor but not necessarily penniless scholar given servants' duties in exchange for room and board). Although he later referred to 'My mother Cambridge' (*FQ* IV xi 34), he says nothing of his friends, studies, and activities there. In the absence of college records, one may assume that he followed the usual course of studies leading to the degrees of BA (1573, coming eleventh in a list of 120) and MA (1576, fourth from the end in a list of 70). Pembroke was a small college, and he would have known the other members well. Lancelot Andrewes, later a bishop and the most famous sermon writer of his day, followed him from Merchant Taylors' just two years later. One member of the college he got to know very well: Gabriel Harvey, made a fellow in 1570, was his friend and mentor during these years and afterwards, although there is no record of a close friendship after 18 July 1586, the date of a sonnet from Spenser to Harvey, published in Harvey's *Foure Letters* of that year. Harvey was a notable figure at Cambridge – a remarkably well-read and skilled Latinist who was also involved in a number of college and university disputes. By the 1590s, when he became notorious in the pamphlet wars with Nashe, he and Spenser may have drifted apart. Yet the references to Harvey in *The Shepheardes Calender* (1579) and *Letters* (1580), as well as Harvey's to Spenser in his unpublished correspondence, suggest that lively intellectual and emotional bonds kept them friends, as Spenser declares in presenting his sonnet to Harvey: 'Your devoted frend during life.'

With his MA, Spenser had a number of choices of a career. Most of his fellow graduates took positions in the church, which was the usual career of the university-educated and the institution for which their education best suited them. A few remained as college fellows, usually the next stage towards a degree in divinity or other subject, and some became schoolmasters. A very few, usually those with good social connections, chose places in government (often after a year or more of legal training at the inns of court). It is possible that immediately on finishing his second degree Spenser may have gone to Ireland in the retinue of Sir Henry Sidney, perhaps as a secretary. In *Vewe of Ireland*, Irenius, the character based on Spenser, claims to have witnessed the execution of Murrough O'Brien at Limerick (July 1577).

Sometime in the mid-to-late 1570s – if we are to believe E.K.'s commentary to *SC, June* 18 – Spenser 'for his more preferment removing out of the Northparts, came into the South, as Hobbinoll [Harvey] indeede advised him privately.' Either he moved directly from Cambridge to London, or he first made an extended trip to Lancashire to visit relatives. Closely connected with this move is the relationship with the mysterious Rosalind, perhaps just an idealized fictional figure of the poetry and the letters, but perhaps a woman who came from 'the Northparts.' That she may have been Spenser's affianced is suggested by Harvey's reference to 'mea Domina Immerito, mea bellissima Collina Clouta' (my lady Immerito, my most beautiful Colina Clout; *3 Lett* 3).

By 1578, Spenser was secretary to Dr John Young, Bishop of Rochester, who had been master of Pembroke while he was there. Among Harvey's annotated books, there is a copy of Jerome Turler's *The Traveiler* (1575) with the inscription 'Ex dono Edmundi Spenserii, Episcopi Roffensis Secretarii. 1578' (Harvey ed 1913:173). This would have been some time after 1 April, the date of the Bishop's installation. During the second half of 1578 until some time in 1579, Spenser probably lived at Bromley, Kent, ten miles from London, for the Bishop preferred this residence to the episcopal palace in Rochester.

On 20 December 1578, Spenser met Harvey in London where they engaged in a lively exchange. Spenser gave him four books to read before 1 January; otherwise, Harvey was to give him his four-volume Lucian. The conditions are recorded in a copy of Murner's version of Till Eulenspiegel called *A Merye Jest of a Man That Was Called Howleglas* (London c 1528; see Harvey ed 1913:23, Stern 1979:228). The other three books, identified by Harvey as 'Skoggin, Skelton, and Lazarillo,' are probably Andrew Borde's *Jests of Scoggin* (London c 1566?; earliest extant ed 1613), *Merie Tales ... by Master Skelton* (1567), and *The Pleasaunt Historie of Lazarillo de Tormes* (tr D. Rowland c 1569; earliest extant ed 1586). The little contest over these 'foolish books' (so Harvey terms them) accords well with Harvey's mocking image of Spenser as a 'young Italianate signor and French monsieur' (July 1579, in Harvey ed 1884:65), now sporting a mustache and beard.

It was not long before this well-educated would-be sophisticate left the relative quiet of the Bishop's residence to enter the larger world of the court. On 5 October 1579, he wrote Harvey from 'Leycester House' to tell him that he was now in the service of the Earl of Leicester, a notable patron, and that he expected at any time to be sent to France. Just ten days later, he wrote Harvey again, this time from 'Mystresse *Kerkes*' in Westminster, suggesting that he was in 'some use of familiarity' with Sidney and Dyer and had discussed with them a plan to reform English meter (see *Areopagus). In another letter, Harvey implies that they shared a friendship with Daniel Rogers, an important friend of Sidney.

That Spenser was gaining entrance to literary circles seems to be owing to *The Shepheardes Calender*, presumably finished earlier that year, for the prefatory Epistle to Harvey by E.K. (perhaps Edward Kirke, also of Pembroke Hall, although the identification remains uncertain) is dated 10 April. *The Shepheardes Calender* was not his only work, however, for within the notes and preliminaries are references to other works: *Dreames*, *Legendes*, *Court of Cupide*, a translation from Moschus, *Pageaunts*, *Sonetts* (if a title), and a critical treatise called *The English Poete*. By 30 June of 1580, another work was entered for publication, the two series of familiar letters between Harvey and Spenser. These letters contain references to even more works: *My Slomber*,

Dreames (also referred to by E.K.), *The Dying Pellicane, Epithalamion Thamesis, Nine Comoedies*, and *Stemmata Dudleiana* (see also lost *works). As well, there is the first reference to *The Faerie Queene* (one part of which Harvey sees as '*Hobgoblin* runne away with the Garland from *Apollo*' *3* Lett 3).

It is not known if Spenser wrote any of these works, but allusions to them serve to promote him as a prodigiously fertile writer. As well, the whole presentation of *The Shepheardes Calender* with introductions, text, illustrations, and glosses draws attention to an entirely new kind of poet. The publication of a personal correspondence with Harvey is equally attention-getting, if not more so. With these two works, Spenser firmly established himself as 'the new Poete' (*SC* Epistle).

While he gathered confidence in the public sphere, he seems also to have made a decisive move in his private life. On 27 October 1579, one 'Edmounde Spenser' (apparently the poet) married Machabyas Chylde at Westminster. The two children from this match were named (as deduced from later documents in Ireland) Sylvanus and Katherine. (Perhaps coincidentally, his teacher Mulcaster was married to a Katherine, and two of their children were named Sylvanus and Katherine.) If we accept the possibility of correspondence between text and life, his first wife seems to have lived until 1591 or later, for there may be a tribute to her in *Colin Clout*, where Colin (the poet's alter ego) says, 'I do professe to be / Vassall to one, whom all my dayes I serve' (466–7).

Another important change took place in 1580. Spenser, now married and recognized at the court, became private secretary to Arthur, Lord Grey of Wilton, the new lord deputy of Ireland, and moved there, most likely arriving with him on 12 August. Until his death he was to live and work in Ireland, with only occasional visits to England. Until Grey's recall to England in 1582, Spenser worked mainly at Dublin Castle, as a Clerk of the Privy Council at the salary of £10 half-yearly. He was not the only literary figure seeking a fortune in Ireland: Walter Raleigh, Barnaby Rich, Geoffrey Fenton, Lodowick Bryskett, and Barnabe Googe all had military or secretarial positions with the English colony. Like them, he witnessed the violence between the English and the Irish; as an administrator, much of his work was in keeping the peace (with the repressiveness that such work would sometimes entail); as a colonist, he seems to have gathered as much property for himself as he could during the upheavals in that troubled land.

He was probably present at the siege of Smerwick in Munster in November 1580. In March 1581, he succeeded Bryskett as Clerk of the Chancery for Faculties (ie, dispensations and licenses issued by the Archbishop of Dublin), a seven-year appointment. As was standard, Spenser appointed a deputy to do the work and kept the difference in salary, while he remained Grey's secretary. At the same time, he was involved in a number of real estate transactions: in December he leased a castle and manor at Enniscorthy, County Wexford, but evidently forfeited them almost immediately. He leased a dissolved monastery at New Ross, also in Wexford, which he held until 1584. He also leased a house in Dublin and a ruined Franciscan monastery called New Abbey, near Kilcullen, County Kildare, about 25 miles from Dublin. The Abbey was on the river Liffey (see *FQ* IV xi 41) close to the 'fennes of Allan' (II ix 16) and had an orchard, a garden, a burial ground, and eight acres of pasture. The lease was for 21 years at £3 a year, but Spenser forfeited the lease in 1590, apparently having paid the rent only once (in Aug 1583). The probable reason for this neglect is that by 1584 he had moved south. In 1583, he was appointed a Commissioner of Musters for County Kildare for two years, and probably in 1584 he became deputy for Bryskett who was Clerk of the Council of Munster, and therefore, by nature of the position, secretary to Sir John Norris, President of the Council. Spenser kept this position for another three years, but had a deputy to work for him. He succeeded Bryskett as Clerk of the Council in Munster in 1589. In 1585, he had become prebendary of Effin, a benefice attached to the cathedral at Limerick (open to a layman), and which probably required no duties from him (the kind of nonresident living he had earlier attacked in *SC*).

In 1586, Spenser was assigned 3028 acres in Cork, one of the smallest parcels from over half a million acres confiscated by the crown from the Earl of Desmond, the Irish rebel. Sometime around 1588 he took possession of these lands, residing at Kilcolman; and finally, by 1590, he was granted full perpetual lease to the property for £17 17*s* a year. Part of his work as a colonist (Ireland, especially the depopulated Munster, was to be colonized by the English in much the same way as Virginia, with a consequential reform of the 'natives') was to establish on his property a total of 24 households. Kilcolman Castle remained his principal residence until it was sacked by rebels in 1598. Its environs are described in the Faunus and Molanna episode in the *Cantos of Mutabilitie*, and Kilcolman is the scene of a visit by his neighbor, Raleigh (who had 42,000 acres around Lismore Castle 30 miles away), described in *Colin Clout*.

In the 1580s, during a busy career in government, Spenser was also actively writing poetry. The most important work was, of course, *The Faerie Queene*, by 1589 ready to be published in its first three books, for in October, Spenser went to England with Raleigh (see **Colin Clout*) to present it to the Queen, the principal dedicatee. Elizabeth granted Spenser an audience and, taking delight in the poem, 'it desir'd at timely houres to heare' (*CCCHA* 362). In December, Books I-III were entered in the Stationers' Register, and published in January. In 1590, he may have returned to Ireland to deal with litigation brought against him by another landowner, Lord Roche, over the ownership of certain properties. Yet by 1591 he is known to have returned to Ireland to resume his duties as clerk at Munster. He returned somewhat richer, for the Queen in February 1591 honored him more than she did any other poet by granting him an annual pension of £50, considerably more than he had ever made in direct payments for government service (although what he made from the usual trading of favors and perquisites of his office is not known). It may be that his clerkship was an honorific appointment, for we know that he had a deputy working for him. Yet he remained active in public life. In 1594, he served as Queen's Justice for Cork, and before 1598 he wrote the very full report called *A Vewe of the Present State of Ireland*. In 1598, he was named sheriff-designate for County Cork, being praised as a gentleman known 'for his good and commendable parts (being a man endowed with good knowledge in learning and not unskilful or without experience in the service of the wars' (Judson 1945:200); had he attained this office and continued his rise in the government of Ireland, he might well have gained a knighthood.

Evidence of his having arrived in the eyes of the leaders of his community is his marriage to Elizabeth Boyle, kinswoman to Sir Richard Boyle. *Amoretti* contains many allusions to the courtship. The marriage took place on St Barnabas' Day (11 June), most likely in 1594, and is celebrated in Spenser's *Epithalamion*. The only child of this match was Peregrine, born perhaps early in 1595. In 1597, Spenser bought for him the castle and lands of Renny in south Cork, and about the same time, Buttevant Abbey near the Kilcolman property.

By the 1590s, fame had come to Spenser. *The Faerie Queene* was recognized immediately as a masterpiece, the outstanding poetic work of that generation. By 1596, a second installment was ready, and Books I-III were reprinted in a combined edition with Books IV-VI. The same decade also saw published *Complaints* (1591), *Daphnaïda* (1591), *Amoretti* and *Epithalamion* (1595), *Colin Clout* (1595), *Fowre Hymnes* (1596), and *Prothalamion* (1596). Some of these were early works, brought out for a ready audience; others, along with a number of commendatory sonnets, were written as occasional poems. Some of them had been gathered together in Spenser's absence by the printer. For a few, however, he seems to have been present in London to help with their publication (for instance, *Fowre Hymnes*, signed 'Ed. Sp.' from 'Greenwich this first of September. 1596'). *The Faerie Queene* was being read attentively by his contemporaries, and not just in London: on 12 November 1596, James VI of Scotland claimed that his mother Mary had been slandered as Duessa (V ix) and unsuccessfully sought that the poet 'be dewly tryed and punished.'

During the 1590s, Spenser seems to have made several trips to London. As the civil strife in Ireland worsened, and as his involvement in government policy became greater, he was called on to present the positions of the local government to the court in Westminster. In 1598, at the time he was named sheriff-designate for Cork, his property at Kilcolman was attacked and burned by Irish rebels during Tyrone's uprising. He and his family took refuge in Cork. On 9 December of that year, he again left for London bearing dispatches from the governor of Munster to the Privy Council, along with a discussion of the current crisis called *A Brief Note of Ireland*, the last section of which ('Certain pointes to be considered of in the recovery of the Realme of Ireland') summarizes a few of the points from his *Vewe*. This was delivered at Whitehall on Christmas Eve, 1598, and for the delivery he was paid the usual stipend of £8.

Two weeks later, on 13 January 1599, Spenser died in Westminster. His sudden death, due possibly to the exhaustion he felt from the turmoil at Kilcolman and Cork, has provoked much speculation. The traditional view was enforced by Jonson in conversation with William Drummond twenty years later: 'the Irish having robd Spensers goods, and burnt his house and a little child new born, he and his wyfe escaped, and after, he died for lake of bread in King Street' (*Sp All* p 154). The last part of the statement seems quite fanciful: Spenser had just received a stipend, he had a sizable pension that could be borrowed against, and he had friends at court who would certainly have helped him had he been in need. Indeed, what is so curious about Jonson's claim is that he goes on to say that Spenser 'refused 20 pieces sent to him by my Lord of Essex, and said he was sorry he had no time to spend them.'

The funeral, according to Camden's *Annales*, was held in the south transept of Westminster Abbey, 'neere *Chawcer*, at the charges of the Earle of *Essex*, all Poets carrying his body to Church, and casting their dolefull Verses, and Pens too into his grave' (*Sp All* pp 178–9). The Queen's order that a memorial be erected was not carried out. Twenty years later, Anne Clifford, Countess of Dorset (*Fowre Hymnes* was dedicated to her mother and her aunt), had a monument designed by Nicholas Stone set up. The inscription, which had wrong dates for both birth and death, read 'Heare lyes (expecting the Second comminge of our Saviour Christ Jesus) the body of Edmond Spencer, the Prince of Poets in his tyme; whose Divine Spirrit needs noe othir witnesse then the works which he left behinde him. He was borne in London in the yeare 1510. And Died in the yeare 1596' (Judson 1945:207). The monument was restored in 1778.

Spenser was survived by his son Sylvanus (died c 1638) and daughter Katherine (married to William Wiseman), both of the first marriage, and by his widow, Elizabeth Boyle (who later remarried several times), and their son Peregrine (died 1642). Although Katherine Wiseman is not known to have had children, both Sylvanus and Peregrine did, and from them there were many descendants. Sylvanus later successfully sued Elizabeth Boyle (then married to Roger Seckerstone) for possession of Kilcolman.

RUTH MOHL

The standard account is Judson 1945, which includes most of the facts and is based on many years of intense scrutiny of documents. Few new documents have been added to the biography since 1960, by which time Spenser's life was regarded as a 'work' within the context of changing social and literary patterns in Elizabethan England. Greenblatt 1980 and Helgerson 1983, following Bradbrook 1960, reassess Spenser's life and poetry as a consciously shaped creation.

F.I. Carpenter 1923 and Atkinson 1937 have useful chronologies of the major documents. A summary of the life based on a full reading of the sources is the chronology by A.C. Hamilton in Spenser *FQ* ed 1977. The *Variorum* cites a great deal of biographical material.

A treatment of the life and descendants is given by W.H. Welply 1932 'Edmund Spenser: Being an Account of Some Recent Researches into His Life and Lineage, with Some Notice of His Family and Descendants' *N&Q* 162:110–14, 128–32, 146–50, 165–9, 182–7, 202–6, 220–4, 239–42, 256–60. To these may be added Welply 1924; Welply 1933 'More Notes on Edmund Spenser' *N&Q* 165:92–4, 111–16; Welply 1941 'Some Spenser Problems' *N&Q* 180:56–9, 74–6, 92–5, 151, 224, 248, 436–9, 454–9. Welply's work should be read in conjunction with Douglas Hamer 1932 'Edmund Spenser: Some Further Notes' *N&Q* 162:380–4; and Hamer 1941 'Some Spenser Problems' *N&Q* 180:165–7, 183–4, 206–9, 220–4, 238–41, for they differ about the early marriage, the identity of E.K., Spenser in Ireland (Welply saw many documents that were destroyed in 1922), and the descendants of the family.

For Spenser's early years, see also Ray Heffner 1938–9 'Edmund Spenser's Family' *HLQ* 2:79–84; and Percy W. Long 1916a 'Spenser's Birth-date' *MLN* 31:178–80. For his school years, see Alexander B. Grosart 1877 *The Spending of the Money of Robert Nowell* (Manchester). For the connection of Mulcaster and van der Noot, see Forster 1967 and van der *Noot.

For his university years, see the lists in *Cambridge and *Harvey. For the years after university and before Ireland, see Percy W. Long 1917 'Spenser's Visit to the North of England' *MLN* 32:58–9; and Long 1916. For connections with patrons, see *Leicester, *Sidney, and *patronage. On the marriage problem, see Mark Eccles 1931 'Spenser's First Marriage' *TLS* (31 Dec):1053; and Hamer 1931, with discussion also of the marriages of Elizabeth Boyle. Eccles 1944 'Elizabethan Edmund Spensers' *MLQ* 5:413–27 shows there were between seven and twelve Edmund Spensers known to be living in London in 1579, but only one (the poet, he argues) lived in Westminster.

For Ireland, see Frederic Ives Carpenter 1921–2 'Spenser in Ireland' *MP* 19:405–19; Frank F. Covington, Jr 1924 'Spenser's Use of Irish History in the *Veue of the Present State of Ireland*' *TexSE* 4:5–38; Ray Heffner 1931 'Spenser's Acquisition of Kilcolman' *MLN* 46:493–8; Hulbert 1936–7; Jenkins 1932; Jenkins 1937; Jenkins 1938; Judson 1947; and F.P. Wilson 1926 'Spenser and Ireland' *RES* 2:456–7. See also *Boyle family, **Brief Note*, articles on *Ireland, and **Vewe*.

Three articles look at the controversy surrounding his death: Josephine Waters Bennett 1937 'Did Spenser Starve?' *MLN* 52:400–1; Berry and Timings 1960; and Heffner 1933 'Did Spenser Die in Poverty?' *MLN* 48:221–6. See also *Essex. On his remains, see Roderick L. Eagle 1956 'The Search for Spenser's Grave' *N&Q* 201:282–3, reviewing the search on 2–3 November 1938 as reported also in *Baconiana* 23.92 (1939):22–5.

Squire of Dames Introduced in *FQ* III vii 37–61 and last heard from in IV v 18, the Squire of Dames helps link the two central books. More important, like Paridell (whom he always accompanies after his first appearance), he serves as an 'ensample of the bad' to show 'good by paragone / Of evill' (III ix 2). His story, based on Ariosto's host's tale (*Orlando furioso* 28), tells how the chastity of women is tested (vii 53–60). Spenser's Ariostan borrowing was noted early: in 1591 Harington remarked, 'The hosts tale ... is a bad one: *M. Spencers* tale ... is to the like effect, sharpe and well conceyted' (Ariosto ed 1591:373).

Unlike Ariosto, however, Spenser uses the chastity-test motif to ridicule licentiousness and to burlesque unquestioning service of a proud mistress. As the Squire narrates the story of his adventures, 'The which himselfe, then Ladies more defames' (viii 44), he becomes the butt of his own tale of loyal obedience to his lady: ordered by her to serve other ladies, he 'served' (ie, seduced) 300 in a year; then commanded to find an equal number of women he cannot seduce, he is comically trapped, having met but three – of whom only one is chaste – in as many years. Spenser's tone in these Ariostan stanzas is lighter, more mocking than in the earlier stanzas which describe the Squire's rescue by Satyrane from the giantess Argante. The juxtaposition of the two parts of the episode implies an affinity between unnatural depravity and the Squire's philandering.

The Squire of Dames appears three more times. In III ix 3–7, he tells the other knights about Malbecco and Hellenore in terms that reiterate his sexual definition of service. In Book IV, as one of several squires in this continuation of Chaucer's *Squire's Tale*, he makes an uneasy peace, a parody of true concord, between Blandamour and Paridell (ii 20–9), becoming 'their Squire' (iv 2). Finally, after Satyrane's tournament he loudly scorns the ladies unable to wear Venus' girdle (v 18). Conspicuous here is his lack of that courteous speech previously his major grace and sole virtue. LINDA R. GALYON

---

stanza, Spenserian One of the few major verse forms known to have been invented by a major poet, the Spenserian stanza consists of nine iambic lines rhyming *ababbcbcC*, the first eight being pentamenter, the last a hexameter, or alexandrine.

For a poet aspiring to the heroic poem, the choice of verse form was as important as the choice of subject. The only commentary Milton thought necessary for the reading of *Paradise Lost* was a brief 'Note on the Verse' explaining his choice of blank verse over rhyme. Spenser does not supply any record of his devising his stanza, but it is possible to reconstruct hypothetically some reasons for his rejecting its rivals.

We have no difficulty in distinguishing, not only on the page but by ear, the difference between short and long lines. This seems to imply that the pentameter, being of middle length, is the natural vocal unit of impassioned speech in English. English surnames are overwhelmingly trochaic, as are most two-syllable words, and yet iambic movement in verse has always seemed to go with the grain of the language, so that extended poems in trochees (Browning's 'One Word More') must seem strange. Triple meters – anapests, dactyls, amphibrachs – have in English an inherent lightness and rapidity that discourages their use in serious poems.

Spenser could find few instances of non-iambic verse, but he had examples of short and long lines to assay. The Skeltonic rattle is a dimeter, frisky, funny, rowdy, childish, occasionally lyrical and moving – an impossible vehicle for a long narrative. The ballad stanzas (tetrameter quatrains or alternating tetrameter and trimeter, rhyming *abab*), though not so odd as Skeltonics, would preclude any grand or deep-breathed effect, and Spenser restricted them to the argument of each canto.

The possibilities afforded by longer lines may have detained Spenser. Because the meter used by Homer and Virgil is an hexameter, classically trained English poets have often attempted English hexameters, expecially when they are also aware of the twelve-syllable French *alexandrin*. The record is one of failure interspersed with occasional successes, such as the opening sonnet of Sidney's *Astrophil and Stella*: the meter almost always sounds drowsy, and it is difficult to prevent the successive lines from breaking monotonously at the midpoint.

Two other long lines were common in the English Renaissance – poulter's measure and the fourteener. The fourteener is a couplet of seven-stress iambic lines: before Spenser it had been used by Golding in his translation of Ovid's *Metamorphoses* (1567); in it Chapman was soon to 'speak out loud and bold' in his translation of the *Iliad*. Almost equally popular in the sixteenth century, but to later ears deplorable, was poulter's measure (thirteen to the dozen), an alternation of six- and seven-stress rhymed lines, used by Gascoigne.

Once the decision to use iambic pentameter was made, probably the first form considered was the heroic couplet, not blank verse. Blank verse in English was a rare and experimental meter in Spenser's formative years. It had been introduced by Surrey in his translation from the *Aeneid* and used by Sackville and Norton in *Gorboduc*; but the first serviceable blank verse in the theater was Kyd's and the first great poetry in it was Marlowe's; Milton's epic blank verse lay far in the future. The heroic couplet was well established by Chaucer (the metrical regularity of whose Middle English Spenser, we must remember, was unable to recognize), and he used it for narrative on all levels of discourse, including description and dialogue, rapid action and thoughtful comment; and Marlowe was to prove in Spenser's lifetime, in *Hero and Leander*, that it could be similarly used in Elizabethan English. Spenser himself uses rough, vigorous couplets in *The Shepheardes Calender* and *Mother Hubberds Tale*. It seems probable that he rejected it for *The Faerie Queene* because the brilliance of couplet art worked against the visionary waking dream he wished to evoke.

The heroic or elegiac quatrain (*abab*), known to us in Gray's *Elegy*, had not been developed in Spenser's time and probably did not occur to him: it is essentially meditative and unsuited to narrative. There remained three stanza forms of Italian origin: terza rima, ottava rima, and rhyme royal, the meters respectively of Dante, of Ariosto and Tasso, and of Chaucer's *Troilus*. Terza rima (*aba bcb*, etc) had been introduced to English by Wyatt in 'Satire I,' but it had few imitators: the high number of rhymes required must have daunted many, though not Spenser, but its nervous swiftness (shown in Shelley's 'Ode to the West Wind') would work against the digressions and dilations of Spenser's art. Ottava rima (*abababcc*) was the stanza of Italian Renaissance epic (Boiardo, Ariosto, Tasso). Adapted to English, as by Harington in his translation of *Orlando furioso*, it gives the impression of rapid narrative in the alternating lines and of epigrammatic comment in the couplet: Ariosto comes over as lighter and slighter than he is said to be in Italian – more like Byron, whose *Don Juan* is in 'octaves.' Rhyme royal (*ababbcc*) is described by Gascoigne as 'a royall kinde of verse, serving best for grave discourses' (in G.G. Smith 1904, 1:54). This *Troilus* stanza is clearly adapted for ample development of narrative, character, and authorial comment; it must have been a seriously considered choice in Spenser's deliberations. The stanza he invented is closer to rhyme royal than to any other except the unusual stanza (*ababbcbc*) Chaucer employed in his *Monk's Tale*.

The Spenserian stanza includes two quatrains (*abab* and *bcbc*) but has an overlap at the center that allows some of the effect of a couplet, while the presence of *b* rhymes in both quatrains allows the ottava-rima effect of rapid alternation. The final alexandrine, in completing a couplet, gives the effect of closure, but by being unequal in length carries the reader as if on a wave into the next stanza.

Wordsworth's lines – 'Sweet Spenser, moving through his clouded heaven / With the moon's beauty and the moon's soft pace' (*Prelude* 3.281–2) – convey something of the fullness, translucency, and continuity of this stanza. Yeats may well have been thinking of his admired Spenser and his stanza when he wrote in 'The Symbolism of Poetry' (1900) that 'The purpose of rhythm ... is to prolong the moment of contemplation, the moment when we are both asleep and awake, which is the one moment of creation, by hushing us with an alluring monotony, while it holds us waking by variety, to keep us in the state of perhaps real trance, in which the mind liberated from the pressure of the will is unfolded in symbols' (ed 1961:159).

The 'variety' needs more proof than the 'monotony' in a poem of over 3800 stanzas with hardly a metrical irregularity. The reading aloud of stanzas that differ markedly in pace, volume, roughness or smoothness, concentration or sparseness of sound patterning, narrative movement or meditative stasis should supply this proof. Examples may be taken from the opening canto: narration (7), catalogue (8–9), dialogue (12), Archimago's piety darkening into devilry with deepening sound (34–7), a concentration of soporific sound and image (41), the false sprite self-betrayed by false rhetoric and bad syntax (51). Other powers of the stanza are evinced in the slow, inexorable and disorienting arguments of Despair (ix 33–47), the exultation at the death of the Dragon (xi 54), the shallow twitter of Phaedria (II vi 5–7, 15–17), the voice from another world cutting across the meter (viii 3), smooth song in Acrasia's Bower (xii 74–5), and strong lines in the house of Care (IV v 40–5). Some of Spenser's effects, though elaborate, are unsophisticated, such as the childlike delight in a jingle of names (IV ii 42); others take the reader deep into the design of a whole book: contrast the menace and hidden danger in navigating in the Legend of Holiness (I vi 1) with the plain sailing of the skillful navigator in the Legend of Temperance (II ii 24).

Drummond quoted Ben Jonson as saying, 'Spencers stanzaes pleased him not, nor his matter' (*Conversations* 1619, in Jonson ed 1925–52, 1:132); and in 1751 Samuel Johnson (*Rambler* 121) wrote that the stanza is 'at once difficult and unpleasing; tiresome to the ear by its uniformity, to the attention by its length.' In the twentieth century, Virginia Woolf in *The Common Reader* complains that 'the verse becomes for a time a rocking-horse; swaying up and down; a celestial rocking-horse, whose pace is always rhythmical and seemly, but lulling, soporific. It sings us to sleep; it lulls the teeth of the wind' (ed 1966–7, 1:17); and Yvor Winters dismisses the stanza as 'clumsy and tyrannical' (1956:357).

Most of the poets, however, have admired Spenser and his stanza, and imitations have been attempted, often with some success, though few achieve anything like his mastery and variety. One of the earliest is one of the best – Sir Richard Fanshawe's translation of Virgil's *Aeneid* 4 (1648). Pope's few stanzas are a burlesque *jeu-d'esprit*; Thomson in *The Castle of Indolence* catches the lassitude of Spenser, but his knight of Industry has none of the believable energy and derring-do of Spenser's active characters; Shenstone's 'School-Mistress' is a pleasant exercise in diminution and nostalgia; Beattie's *Minstrel*, in unarchaic English, uses the stanza for ballad effects; and Byron's *Childe Harold* is hostile alike to its own verse form and to its progenitor. Only Keats, especially in 'The Eve of St Agnes,' and Shelley in *The Revolt of Islam* and *Adonais* move freely and far in it. Since their time, the Spenserian stanza has hardly been attempted, even by such notably stanzaic poets as Tennyson (except in the narrative section of 'The Lotos-Eaters') and Swinburne. Auden, who tried everything, did not try this. The Spenserian stanza is Spenser's invention; it remains his property. (See *canto, *Tudor poetry, *versification.) WILLIAM BLISSETT

Alpers 1967b, ch 2; Robert Beum 1963 'Some Observations on Spenser's Verse Forms' *NM* 64:180–96; Leicester Bradner 1928 'Forerunners of the Spenserian Stanza' *RES* 4:207–8; P.G. Davies 1973–4; Empson 1930:33–4; Emma Field Pope 1926–7 'The Critical Background of the Spenserian Stanza' *MP* 24:31–53; Yvor Winters 1956 'Problems for the Modern Critic of Literature' *HR* 9:325–86. Fanshawe ed 1964 contains the translation of Virgil's *Aeneid* 4 and Fanshawe's own 'Canto on the *Progresse of Learning*,' also in Spenserian stanzas.

Statius (Publius Papinius Statius, c 45–c 96) Unlike later periods, the Middle Ages and the Renaissance set great store by the works of the Roman poet Statius, ranking him with Homer and Virgil. He appears as a Christian in Dante's *Purgatorio* 21.10, Boccaccio derives the plot of *Teseida* from his *Thebaid*, and Chaucer pays homage to him in *House of Fame* 1460–3.

E.K. refers to Statius as a matter of course in his gloss on *Januarye* 60, and Spenser repeatedly evokes his writings. He may have borrowed details of the stories of Marinell (*FQ* III iv 20–7) and Satyrane (I vi 24–9) from the account of the upbringing of Achilles in the unfinished *Achilleid*. He echoes *Silvae* 5.4 (the famous invocation to Sleep; cf *FQ* I i) and above all 1.2, the 'Epithalamium in Honour of Stella and Violentilla' (see *Var* 8:462–91). Most of his borrowings are from the *Thebaid*, whose twelve books recount the story of the Seven against Thebes. In this work, Statius stands out as a pessimist, brooding on man's lust for self-destruction, his proclivity to anger and bellicosity; and it is only towards the very end, after the sons of Oedipus, Polynices and Eteocles, have killed one another and the reader has been through much bloodshed that victorious *pietas* triumphs in the person of Theseus.

If Statius differs from Spenser in his obsession with human destructiveness, his use of mythological figures to personify ruling passions often seems to approximate similar techniques in *The Faerie Queene*. Also, Spenser would have been impressed by Statius' sympathy for suffering humanity, and Cymoent's lament for Marinell echoes the bereaved Ismenis moaning for her son Crenaeus (III iv 36, *Thebaid* 9.376–7). However, his indebtedness to the *Thebaid* is found chiefly in his reworkings of Statius' justly renowned examples of ecphrasis, elaborate descriptions chiefly of works of art but also of landscapes and buildings. In *FQ* I i, interrelated passages in Ovid, Lucan, Statius, and Tasso link the Wood of Error with the subsequent description of Morpheus' house. The *Thebaid* contexts involved here are 10.84–5 (cf 'Not perceable with power of any starre' *FQ* I i 7), 10.132–6 (Morpheus' unwillingness to wake up, stanza 42), and 4.419–87 (cf *FQ* I i 7 and more specifically Archimago's invocation of Daemogorgon, stanza 37).

Both poets share a taste for emblematic imagery: Spenser's account of the pictures in Ate's dwelling exactly recalls Statius' description of Mars' house (*FQ* IV i 21, *Thebaid* 7.34–63). The serpent's discovery of the attacking Argives is probably the basis for the Dragon's reaction on seeing Redcrosse (*Thebaid* 5.556–8, *FQ* I xi 4). Britomart and Paridell disputing their right to the pigsty in stormy weather recalls the encounter between Polynices and Tydeus in stormy weather at the house of Adrastus (*FQ* III ix 11–16, *Thebaid* 1.401–46). The role of Venus' girdle, the cestus, as a symbol of 'wivehood true' may depend on Statius' qualification of it as 'iugalem / ceston' (*FQ* IV v 3, *Thebaid* 5.62–3; quoted by Boccaccio *Genealogia* 3.22). LARS-HÅKAN SVENSSON

David Vessey 1973 *Statius and the 'Thebaid'* (Cambridge) is a well-informed study. For Statius' importance in the English epic tradition, see Tillyard 1954:99–104. For Spenser, see R.N. Ringler 1963.

stones, precious A lengthy lapidary tradition lies behind the descriptions of precious stones in Spenser's poetry. Belief in magical and medical properties of jewels is present in the earliest human documents, including Assyrian tablets from the Royal Library at Nineveh, Egyptian papyri, and Greek treatises. Pliny's systematic treatment of precious stones in the first century, *Natural History*, was the basis and point of departure for Western lapidary writings of the Middle Ages and the Renaissance. *De materia medica* by Dioscorides, another first-century work listing the medical virtues of precious stones, was considered authoritative in the sixteenth century, as were treatments of gems by Hippocrates and Galen. Foremost among other important lapidaries accessible in sixteenth-century England are Isidore of Seville's *Etymologies*, Marbode's Latin poem *Liber lapidum, seu De gemmis*, Bartholomaeus Anglicus' *De proprietatibus rerum* (especially popular in English versions by John Trevisa [1397] and Stephen Bateman [1582]), Vincent of Beauvais's *Speculum naturale*, and the lapidary in Albertus Magnus' *De mineralibus*. The relationship among these and other lapidary works is complex, and exactly how information passed from earlier authors to later ones is impossible to determine. Despite many errors and discrepancies in transmission, however, lapidary literature was remarkably consistent and provided a fund of lore about the 'secret powers' (Milton *Prolusions* 3) of precious stones.

Spenser would have been introduced to Pliny's work in grammar school and would have studied it as part of the philosophy curriculum at Cambridge. One with his education would have encountered lapidary material in medical treatises, travel accounts, heraldic literature, and also the Bible and commentaries on it, such as Bede's on Revelation. Ficino, Pico della Mirandola, and such popular writers as the anonymous author of Mandeville's *Travels* included redactions of gem lore. In addition, traditional literary meanings associated with gems were available to Spenser and his readers from classical, medieval, and contemporary literature.

Some of Spenser's uses of gem lore are broadly conventional. His use of jewels, for example, repeats standard Petrarchan images. Eyes are sapphires; lips, rubies; teeth, pearls; or, as the speaker claims in *Amoretti* 15, the beloved's attributes are more precious than gems (see also *Am* 9, 81; *Virgils Gnat* 285; *Epithalamion* 171; *FQ* II iii 24). Poets also conventionally bestowed praise by describing the whole person as a jewel, as Spenser does in calling Queen Elizabeth 'The pearle of peerlesse grace and modestie' (*Colin Clout* 471). Likewise, the walls and towers of the heavenly city at *FQ* I x 55 are said to be made of pearl and precious stone because these gems are the material of the Heavenly Jerusalem in Revelation 21.

Other uses reflect the traditional dichotomy in attitudes toward precious stones: they are the earth's most precious things but also material objects of worldly vanity. Thus in *The Faerie Queene*, association with gems emphasizes both true worth (eg, in Britomart's vision predicting her success and marriage, she is dressed in gems and jewels, V vii 13) and worldliness (eg, both Duessa and Lucifera are dressed in precious stones, like the biblical Whore of Babylon, I iv 8, v 21; cf Rev 17.4).

Some of Spenser's gem imagery seems informed by specific material from lapidaries. Arthur's diamond shield, made by Merlin (I vii 36), exhibits the invincibility and magical power lapidaries assigned to diamond. The shield cannot be pierced or broken, it reveals falsity and repels pagan horses and soldiers, and its light overcomes Orgoglio and Duessa (I vii 33, viii 19ff; V viii 37–8, xi 10). Spenser is echoing descriptions of shields in earlier literature (eg, Ariosto *Orlando furioso* 2.55–6 and Tasso *Gerusalemme liberata* 7.82) and the Bible (Eph 6.16). The powers of the shield, however, are inherent in diamond itself, which represents Arthur's indestructible virtue.

Other references to diamond suggest similar attributes. Care's hammer seems strong enough to break a rock of diamond, an impossibility according to the lapidaries (IV v 37); Una remains steadfast like a 'rocke of Diamond' against Sansloy's temptations (I vi 4); the healing liquor which Arthur gives Redcrosse is securely contained in a box of diamond (I ix 19). (Spenser follows the lapidaries in using *adamant* sometimes interchangeably with *diamond*, sometimes for steel or tempered iron.)

The significance given to other jewels in *The Faerie Queene* depends on fairly specific gem lore. Florimell's girdle, cestus, is 'curiously embost / With pearle and precious stone' (IV iv 15) because pearls, symbolic of purity, were believed to ensure chastity (eg, see Camillus Leonardus *Speculum lapidum clarissimi artium* 1502). Diamond (or adamant) and emerald also preserved chastity and would make an unchaste woman leap out of bed or else would break in the presence of the carnal act (eg, see Bartholomaeus 16.8 and Albertus *De mineralibus* 2.2.17). The ruby given by Belphoebe to Timias and later returned to her (IV viii 6ff) is 'of right perfect hew, / Shap'd like a heart, yet bleeding of the wound.' In lapidary writings, red stones are almost always related to blood. The gem here may represent Belphoebe's control of Timias' affections, as rubies were believed to control the flow of blood (eg, see Bartholomaeus 16.25) and to control the amorous affections of the wearer. Here Spenser draws upon literature – Chaucer's Criseyde gives Troilus a brooch set with a ruby in the shape of a heart as a love token (3.1370–2) – and life: Arthur Throckmorton gave Queen Elizabeth a heart-shaped ruby to assuage her displeasure at the disclosure of the marriage of Raleigh and Elizabeth Throckmorton (see Brink 1972). ABBY HANSEN AND MARGARET GRISSOM

Don Cameron Allen 1937 'Arthur's Diamond Shield in *The Faerie Queene*' *JEGP* 36:234–43; Joan Evans 1922 *Magical Jewels of the Middle Ages and the Renaissance* (Oxford); Margaret Sims Grissom 1981 'The Lapidary Tradition and Seventeenth-Century English Poetry' diss Univ of Louisville; Abby Jane Dubman Hansen 1977 'Sermons in Stones: The Symbolism of Gems in English Renaissance Literature' diss Harvard Univ; George Frederick Kunz 1913 *The Curious Lore of Precious Stones* (Philadelphia).

style However one defines poetic style – as a means of expression, as the language and devices suitable for a given subject, or as manipulation of language for its own sake – Spenser is clearly a formidable stylist. The conspicuous variety of his first major work, *The Shepheardes Calender* (1579), shows that it was intended as a virtuoso stylistic performance. Its fundamental stylistic principle is stated in the prefatory Epistle to Harvey, in which E.K. praises the young poet for 'his dewe observing of Decorum everye where.' This is to say that the verse form, the diction, and the rhetorical mode and level of each eclogue are answerable, first, to the general pastoralism of the work as a whole; second, to one of the three general types identified by E.K. in the General Argument (plaintive, recreative, and moral); and finally, to the nature of the specific month to which each poem is assigned. For example, Colin Clout's 'laye / Of fayre *Eliza*' in *Aprill* is exuberantly elaborate in its stanza form, its mythological allusions, and in some of its diction, as befits a poem praising Queen Elizabeth in pastoral guise. But it is also fresh and unaffected in some of its imagery and modes of address, thus reflecting both the season and the fact that it is said to have been composed in Colin's youth, when he was innocent of love. In the eclogues for the winter months, on the other hand, the language and rhetorical tactics reflect the fact that these poems are concerned with death, aging, and the distresses of love.

Decorum could be said to be the stylistic principle of all Spenser's poems – from the narrative and satiric forthrightness of *Mother Hubberds Tale* and the Ovidian prettiness of *Muiopotmos* early in his career, to the ceremonial abundance of *Epithalamion* and the Petrarchan and philosophical vocabularies and stances of *Fowre Hymnes*. Nevertheless, 'dewe observing of Decorum' is not the way Spenser's readers have characteristically expressed admiration of his stylistic prowess. The last of the anonymous *Parnassus* plays (performed 1602) praises him in the following terms:

A sweeter swan than ever sung in Po,
A shriller nightingale than ever blessed
The prouder groves of self-admiring Rome.
Blithe was each valley and each shepherd proud,
While he did chant his rural minstrelsy.
Attentive was full many a dainty ear,
Nay, hearers hung upon his melting tongue,
While sweetly of his Fairy Queen he sung,
While to the waters' fall he tuned her fame,
And in each bark engraved Eliza's name.
(Alpers 1969:52)

These lines are a pastiche from both *The Shepheardes Calender* and *The Faerie Queene*; in emphasizing harmonious sound and decorative loveliness, they provide a general characterization of Spenser's verse that will seem obvious to any reader. This sense that there is a general Spenserian style is also felt by those who express reservations about it. When Jonson complains that 'Spenser, in affecting the ancients, writ no language,' he seems to be referring to *The Faerie Queene*, but his remark equally calls to mind *The Shepheardes Calender*, which Sidney criticized for 'that same framing of his style to an old rustic language' (Alpers 1969:57, 37). When Yvor Winters criticizes Spenser's 'decadent' cultivation of 'the pleasures of rhetoric for its own sake,' he is thinking of qualities of diction and rhythm that seem to pervade all his verse (Alpers 1967a:105–6).

Historically, then, Spenser's style has seemed a single phenomenon, either impressive or problematic. *The Faerie Queene* has dominated accounts of it, partly because of its preeminence, and partly because of its affinities with many of the minor poems. Modern understanding of the Spenserian style derives (often by reaction) from Romantic poets and critics, who in their turn had transformed older notions of poetry's spiritual and psychological reality and value. It was a Romantic critic (Charles Lamb) who called Spenser 'the poet's poet.' The specific force of this epithet is conveyed by Hazlitt's variant, 'of all the poets, he is the most poetical.' Coleridge's praise makes the meaning of such terms clear: *The Faerie Queene*, he says, 'is truly in land of Fairy, that is, of mental space. The poet has placed you in a dream, a charmed sleep.' Hazlitt fills out the way a reader of the Romantic era would construe 'mental space': 'In Spenser, we wander in another world, among ideal beings ... He waves his wand of enchantment – and at once embodies airy beings, and throws a delicious veil over all actual objects.' The stylistic implications of such characterizations appear in Coleridge's praise of 'the indescribable sweetness and fluent projection of [Spenser's] verse' and in Hazlitt's attention to the 'voluptuous pathos and languid brilliancy of fancy' conveyed by the imagery and verse movement of *The Faerie Queene*. Spenser's versification, Hazlitt says, 'is the perfection of melting harmony, dissolving the soul in pleasure, or holding it captive in the chains of suspense. Spenser was the poet of our waking dreams; and he has invented not only a language, but a music of his own for them' (see Alpers 1969:131–8, 141–4).

Esteemed this way, the Spenserian style was an example and a resource for Romantic poets and for some of their Victorian heirs. But a century and a half later, it is difficult to think that such terms represent a central imaginative achievement, and it is not surprising that modern writers, readers, and critics reacted against the Spenserian style, as the Romantics conceived it. One reaction was dismissive and deprecatory. Spenser was an obvious victim of the revolution, in both poetry and criticism, that is associated with the writings of T.S. Eliot. Eliot turned against the Romantic and Victorian separation of the realms of imagination and reality and championed modes of poetry that brought them into contact with each other. He and his followers argued that the stylistic models for English poets should no longer be Spenser and Milton, but Shakespeare, Donne, the 'metaphysical poets,' and the Jacobean tragedians, whose writing, in its irony, wit, dramatic urgency, and sense of physical fact, reflects the mutual pressures of real life and imaginative impulse. To such readers and critics, Spenser's style seemed rhetorical and decorative, both pejorative epithets. A style that is rhetorically conceived inherently simplifies experience (it was felt), for it seeks to impress and manipulate according to predetermined moral and aesthetic purposes. To be decorative was felt to evade the complexities of experience in another way, for a style as prolix and technically elaborate as Spenser's regards words and their intricacies as detached from things, and therefore makes style an overlay or embroidery, rather than a fully engaged dramatic representation, of narrative realities.

Against what it is fair to call this modern orthodoxy, C.S. Lewis mounted a vigorous defense of Spenser's style. He denied that *The Faerie Queene* answers to a debilitated Romantic account of itself; he denied that its merits lie in a sheer voluptuousness and poeticalness. Where its style is voluptuous, he argued, Spenser is involved in a serious analysis of voluptuousness itself. Elsewhere, he said, the style is very different from what the reader has been taught to expect. Spenser offers 'a poetry far more nervous and masculine – a drier flavour and a wine with more body' (1936:319). Lewis codified such observations by claiming that 'Spenser is essentially a narrative poet,' and he distinguished three styles in *The Faerie Queene*. One, disturbingly awkward and prosaic, is the remnant of the 'drab' verse of the mid-sixteenth century. The second, which Lewis calls 'golden,' is characterized by 'unsubtle yet delicious flow, frank alliteration, frequent images, Homeric echoes,' and the like. 'But thirdly, there is Spenser not Golden, not sugared at all (in his manner) but thoroughly good, pressing his tale ... Much of the *Faerie Queene* is ... a "poetry of statement." The typical Spenserian line tells you what somebody did or wore or where he went' (1954:389–91).

Praising Spenser in these terms had a certain shock value and served to alert readers to certain qualities of diction and representation in *The Faerie Queene*. But valuing the poem for its story goes against what Lewis himself emphasized as central to the poem, its ceremonial and hieratic nature. Feeling himself in profound disagreement with much of modern culture, Lewis sought to give a serious social and moral justification to the qualities other critics dismissed as decorative, and he justified the 'lack of tension' in Spenser's verse precisely on the grounds that it 'reflects the lack of tension in his mind' (Lewis 1954:392). Spenser's confidence in Christian revelation, in the world beyond this earth, and in traditional wisdom led him (so Lewis argued) to write verse that meditates on, but does not fully engage and measure itself by, the realities of the secular and historical world.

With all due allowances for differences of attitude and aesthetic interest, this line of argument is probably the mainstream of current understanding of Spenser's style. It amounts to saying that Spenser's style is allegorical: that is, that its purpose is not to represent worldly realities and events, and not (*pace* Lewis) to tell a story, but to represent worldly events in such a way as to body forth their participation in the eternal truths that underlie and direct them. Language that seems decorative or merely repetitive with reference to an earthly event may in fact be the way to represent, or to enable us to see, various aspects of that event when viewed in relation to a larger scheme of things. This is the argument of Martha Craig's important essay, 'The Secret Wit of Spenser's Language,' in which the oldest stylistic problem about Spenser's verse – his use of archaisms – is set in its true light. Craig shows that Spenser's 'artificial' way with language (a term that was honorific in the sixteenth century but suspect in our time) was a means of bringing out the permanent realities of the world and human nature, particularly with reference to their origins.

No one stanza can represent all of *The Faerie Queene*, but an example at this point will be useful. The following stanza is the second describing Arthur's helmet, in the middle of a long description of his armor (I vii 32):

Upon the top of all his loftie crest,
  A bunch of haires discolourd diversly,
  With sprincled pearle, and gold full richly drest,
  Did shake, and seem'd to daunce for jollity,
  Like to an Almond tree ymounted hye
  On top of greene *Selinis* all alone,
  With blossomes brave bedecked daintily;
  Whose tender locks do tremble every one
At every little breath, that under heaven is blowne.

Certain stylistic touches are commonplaces of Spenserian commentary: archaism ('ymounted'), alliteration, diction that seems to imitate the qualities it renders ('bedecked daintily'), and diction suggestive of sensory fullness (line 3, where the general 'full richly drest' is as important to the effect as 'sprincled pearle,' which itself appeals to touch as well as sight). These effects are combined in the phrase, 'Whose tender locks do tremble,' which appears in a climactic position.

Just as the Spenserian stanza is an independent unit, so too is the Spenserian line. Not only does each line have a single grammatical function; though the stanza consists of a single sentence, that sentence can be construed as completed at the end of every line but the first. This characteristically additive procedure explains why Yeats compared Spenser's lines to 'bars of gold thrown ringing one upon another' (Alpers 1969:177) and why Lewis spoke of the verse of *The Faerie Queene* as a 'poetry of statement.' The additive unfolding of the stanza makes us conscious less of a single phenomenon or event, continuously represented, than of individual verbal formulas that call a good deal of attention to themselves. We can thus understand – without endorsing the view – why Spenser's verse has been subject to the charge of being decorative or even decadent. This particular stanza, with its sense of refinement and delicacy, might seem particularly to call for such a limiting judgment.

Nevertheless, this stanza has been one of the most admired in *The Faerie Queene*. Marlowe imitates it in *Tamburlaine* (part 2, IV iii 115–24), and we might suggest, following Eliot's acute observation (1950:102), that Marlowe's 'mighty line' owes as much to the additive, formulaic verse of *The Faerie Queene* as to any earlier blank verse. The eighteenth-century editor, John Upton, calls the simile of the almond tree 'exceeding elegant,' and Coleridge and Hazlitt both use the stanza to illustrate a leading principle of Spenser's verse. To Coleridge, it exemplifies 'the exceeding vividness of Spenser's descriptions,' which 'are composed of a wondrous series of images, as in our dreams' (Alpers 1969:143). Hazlitt quotes it to show how Spenser 'at times ... becomes picturesque from his intense love of beauty,' and he goes on to say that 'the love of beauty ... and not of truth, is the moving principle of his mind' (Alpers 1969:132).

Modern commentary predictably reacts against such views and seeks to align the language of the stanza with the truth as Spenser conceived it. Modern editors thus refer various details of the almond tree simile to Biblical texts and to the *Aeneid*. But what is allegorical in the verse here lies less in allusions and symbols than in the use of personification, which (as Craig points out, comparing this stanza with Marlowe's imitation) 'is so radical and persistent that the language seems continuously symbolic of the hero' (Alpers 1967a:460). This usage is allegorical, because it suggests that human qualities are connected with, and find a place in, a larger world which answers to them. The qualities particularly brought out in this stanza are Arthur's capacity to sympathize (cf 'tremble,' of which the moral suggestions are drawn out by the personification in 'locks') with the abandoned Una, whom he is approaching at this moment, and a sense of confidence in earthly life (cf 'under heaven'), which he instills in her when they meet. In its symbolic or representational aspect, the simile of the almond tree suggests that the hero's grandeur and isolation go along with a certain vulnerability and capacity for connection with the world around him. From a stylistic standpoint, we can add to what we have already said a comment on the strengths of the one line of the simile that Marlowe did not imitate: 'With blossomes brave bedecked daintily.' This is perfectly ordinary Spenserian verse, but it is not, as it has often seemed, otiose. The line brings out elements of glamour and tenderness that are essential to the stanza, and it is securely centered on *brave*, with its several relevant meanings (courageous, finely dressed, splendid) and with a double syntax ('brave blossoms' and 'bravely bedecked') that gives the line much of its firmness.

Although the great achievement of modern Spenserian scholarship and criticism is to make clear the profoundly allegorical nature of *The Faerie Queene* and many of the minor poems, we still do not have a fully elaborated account of the way in which the Spenserian style is an allegorical style. Craig's essay stands somewhat alone among recent studies. Critics of *The Faerie Queene* have been much more concerned with matters of moral interpretation and spiritual attitude; with the structure of the poem and the problem of its coherence; with problems of symbolism and iconography; and, most recently, with its cultural and historical situation. Even studies (like those of Alpers and Hamilton) that specify various verbal devices and pay close attention to verbal detail are usually concerned with matters of allegorical meaning and density, rather than with purely stylistic issues.

Nor is it certain that we are yet in a position to give an adequate account of Spenser's style. It is probably not sufficient to point to the allegorical nature of *The Faerie Queene* and view Spenser's style as an instrument of that allegory. Spenser's poems were written at a time of explosive development in English verse. It is clear that much of his verbal energy does not simply come from the purposes of his poems, but that it has to do with a sense of abundance and possibility in the language itself, and the prospects of English poetry and a national literature. By the same token, those aspects of his style which Lewis calls 'golden' belong not to him alone but to a decisive phase of English verse. All the frank loveliness and the pleasure in set procedures and verbal manipulation show not only that Spenser is Spenser, but also that Spenser is an Elizabethan. Similarly, criticism of and reaction against Spenser's style is not simply a prejudice of modern critics, but a constant and varying fact of English literary history. A full account of Spenser's style, therefore, cannot be based simply on Spenser's works. Spenser developed and bequeathed to English poetry verbal resources of extraordinary range and power: various effects of pictorial representation, sound patterning, sensuous suggestiveness, and artificial diction are as decisively Spenserian as other devices and effects are Shakespearean, Miltonic, Popean, Wordsworthian, Keatsian, or Whitmanesque. To call his style decorative, sensuous, rhetorical, fanciful, imaginative, or allegorical tells us little until we understand what such notions meant for various epochs of English poetry and what they mean to us now. Our understanding of Spenser's style must to some extent await a more adequate stylistic history of English poetry than we currently possess. PAUL ALPERS

Alpers 1967a; Alpers 1967b; Alpers 1969; Craig 1967; Hamilton 1972b; Lewis 1936; Lewis 1954.

style, prose The characteristic syntax, diction, imagery, and rhythms of Spenser's prose are demonstrated in his letters to Harvey and Raleigh and, most fully, in the *Vewe of the Present State of Ireland*. To these may be added two works of disputed authorship, *Axiochus* and *A Brief Note of Ireland*. This is a small inventory if compared to the author's verse; even more than Milton's, Spenser's prose was the work of his left hand, subsidiary to his main effort as a lyric and epic poet. The sample is large enough, however, to define and contrast his style with other prose styles fashionable in the late Elizabethan period.

As a university man and friend of Harvey, a noted lecturer on rhetoric and style, Spenser would have been conversant with a number of emerging models for prose, especially with the opulent Ciceronian style and its opposite, the spare Senecan, Latin styles adapted to English through the influence of English humanism. He would also have known the fashionable Euphuism, an elaborate prose (based on classical models of Isocrates and a modified Cicero) made popular by Lyly's *Euphues: The Anatomy of Wit* (1579). Spenser's prose, however, is allied directly to none of these schools. Although, like any writer's, it is modified by cultural expectations regarding subject, audience, and occasion, it has many characteristics of an earlier Tudor tradition: colloquial vigor, a minimum of formal patterning, and relatively plain diction.

The dominant feature of Spenser's prose is a long, loosely constructed sentence that when compared to Hooker's carefully orchestrated periods or Bacon's terse phrasing often seems ungainly or even formless. The primary effect is one of artlessness, especially against the background of Elizabethan rhetorical exuberance. Spenser's writing is never florid; figures of sound like alliteration and assonance are rare and when present are more accidental than deliberate. The modest parallelism seems functional rather than decorative.

Spenser's prose style can be more exactly defined by reference to individual works. In his letters to Harvey and Raleigh, and the *Brief Note* to Queen Elizabeth (supposing it to be his), audience is a controlling influence. The letters to Harvey, for example, are written in the easy, informal style of personal correspondence (see *letter as genre), even though they were evidently written with publication in mind. In the Letter to Raleigh, his style is more formal and artful, befitting the person to whom the letter is addressed, respectful but avoiding servility or obsequiousness. The Letter has therefore something of the grand manner of the literary dedication, a sub-genre of the period. There are more periodic sentences, more parallelism, and often an epigrammatic neatness that is rarely found elsewhere in Spenser's prose.

Spenser's dialogues, *Axiochus* and *Vewe*, provide the best examples of his prose style. The first has been praised as a 'prose poem of beauty and feeling, rapid, imaginative, and musical' (Padelford in *Var Prose* p 492). This high praise has been disputed by those who have seen traces of Euphuism in the work. But there is nothing peculiar to Euphuism in its style, and its greater elegance seems due to the noble character of Socrates and the somber theme of the dialogue.

The *Vewe* is his most sustained effort in prose. Its loose, informal style following naturally from the dialogue form is expository rather than dramatic, aiming at clarity and cogency of argument. Yet the work is not without passages of graceful expression in which the vernacular substratum of Spenser's style is disciplined by the patterns of formal rhetoric. His description of the horrors of famine resulting from the Munster wars, perhaps the most famous passage, shows his ability to write a prose that is at once simple and eloquent, and create thereby a picture of remarkable vividness. In describing the miserable survivors of battle, he writes:

> Out of everie Corner of the woods and glinnes they Came Crepinge forthe uppon theire handes for theire Leggs Coulde not beare them, they loked like Anotomies of deathe, they spake like ghostes Cryinge out of theire graves, they did eate the dead Carrions, happie wheare they Coulde finde them, Yea and one another sone after, in so muche as the verye carkasses they spared not to scrape out of theire graves. And if they founde a plotte of water Cresses or Shamarocks theare they flocked as to a feaste for the time, yeat not able longe to Continue theare-withall, that in shorte space theare weare non allmoste lefte and a moste populous and plentifull Countrye sodenlye lefte voide of man or beaste, yeat sure in all that warr theare perished not manie by the sworde but all by the extreamitye of famine which they themselves had wroughte. (*Var Prose* p 158)

Characteristically, Spenser prefers coordination over subordination: the ideas are laid side by side, working to a cumulative effect of horror. The long first sentence is in fact composed of several independent clauses of parallel structure ('they Came Crepinge ... they loked ... they spake ... they did eate ... they spared not') with sufficient variation to avoid monotony and the artificiality of rhetorical contrivance. At the same time, the continuing metaphor of death – the survivors are compared to skeletons ('Anotomies'), they cry out like ghosts – gives the passage thematic unity, vividness, and momentum. Some alliteration ('flocked as to a feaste ... populous and plentifull Countrye') shows a sensitive ear. One would not call this style sonorous, but the cumulative swelling of the passage toward the climactic short balanced clause with which it concludes is strengthened by the measured phrases.

Spenser's distinction as a prose writer is in adapting the language of speech to the functional needs of exposition, and steering an independent course between the florid excesses of Euphuism and Ciceronianism and the equally mannered expression of the anti-Ciceronian school. The result was a plain style not without moments of lucidity, grace, and power. LEONARD TOURNEY

T

Tantalus, Pilate Before Guyon emerges from his underground visit to the house of Mammon, he encounters two wretches, Tantalus and Pilate, nearly submerged in stinking water that flows by a black tree with gold apples (*FQ* II vii 57–62). The two make an odd pair, one biblical, the other famous in classical mythology (but not for that reason presumed unhistorical in the Renaissance; see, eg, Alciati ed 1621, Emblem 85 *Avaritia*; Boccaccio *Genealogia* 12.1; Conti *Mythologiae* sv 'Tantalus'; Ovid *Metamorphoses* ed 1589: sig I5, N6v for Sabinus' comments). Yet they share a tragic perversity concerning wealth, divine truth, and sons (that is, the new life, rebirth); and their very differences show how defect and excess can both lead to deadly sin and fruitless suffering.

(See **Tantalus** Fig 1.)

Rich, pleasure-loving, and a son of Jove, King Tantalus of Phrygia was an intimate of the gods until he stole their food for his friends, disclosed their secrets, and at a banquet fed them his son Pelops to test their omniscience. The gods restored Pelops, giving him an ivory shoulder to replace that inadvertently eaten by Ceres, but they condemned their host to torments that Spenser locates in the garden of Ceres' daughter, Proserpina (51–65). Like Horace (*Satires* I.I) and Lucian (*Timon* 18), the Renaissance found Tantalus a symbol of avarice, of anxious and laborious poverty amidst unused plenty. No wonder that in Plato's *Cratylus* (395E) his name is said to be an anagram of *talantatos* 'most wretched.' In a related tradition, found for example in Eusebius, Tantalus helped Jupiter, king of Crete, steal young Ganymede. Ganymede's father, King Tros (some say his son Ilus), then defeated and expelled Tantalus (a battle celebrated, it was said, in a lost epic poem by Phanocles) and thus confirmed his rule over the Trojans, named after him. Tros was the direct ancestor of Brute, so Tantalus is thus an ancestral enemy of Spenser's own dynasty, parallel to the giant Gogmagog or Philip II.

Pontius Pilate, Roman governor of Judea, allowed Jesus to be killed although he thought him guiltless (Acts 3.14–15, Matt 27.11–26). Some Christians later sympathized with him, but others called him the archetypal false judge who yields to fear out of worldly ambition. Pilate washed his hands to show his innocence, says Augustine in a sermon (*PLat* 39:2041; cf Ps 26.6), but he could not wash his infected mind, an irony Spenser notes. According to one widespread tradition, Pilate was proud, avaricious, and impious, an envious murderer who got his post by bribery, put false images in the Temple, and used its treasure to build 'conduytes for Water' to his own house ([*Golden Legend*] tr William Caxton, London 1527: sig c3v; similarly Higden *Polycronicon* ch 7). Eventually he killed himself, some said, and his corpse was thrown into the Tiber and other waters only to be rejected each time by indignant demons until it was buried in an alpine well.

Greedy mismanagers of treasure, self-promoting, and blasphemous, the two fallen potentates share an association with food – purloined nectar and ambrosia, human sacrifice, and the broken Body that Christians eat or remember at Holy Communion – and with water that unlike baptism or God's Word fails to clean, satisfy, or temper. Thus the two sum up and extend the dangers visible in Mammon's house – riches, glory, and impiety – and their sins and punishments touch thematically on washing, nourishment, right use, judgment, and sight (the mythographer Fulgentius claims that *Tantalus* is from the Greek for 'covetous of sight' [ed 1971:131], something Guyon might bear in mind as he feeds his eyes).

The couple's postures and frenetically repeated gestures show the inward significance of grasping or murderous hands and loose or unjust mouths. One seeks with dry lips to drink water named Cocytus, or 'lamentation' (C. Estienne 1596), and to eat inedibly rich fruit (Spenser's own version of the traditional garden of Tantalus, symbol of delusion; see Erasmus *Adages* 2.1.46); the other lies submerged in the element he misused, except for his busy hands smeared with the sin he was once literal-minded enough to suppose he could wash off. The two situations are related but dissimilar, for although each killed a son or Son, Tantalus did so by wicked action and Pilate by equally intemperate inaction; and whereas Tantalus was too curious and talkative about divine matters, Pilate rejected the divine Word standing right before him. Now the excessive monarch blindly curses the gods and the defective judge hates himself forever. Filthy and miserable, the two reveal the angry compulsiveness, sterile desire, and self-preoccupied pain that Mammon offers to us all but especially to those who govern. Condemnation is easy; but in a passage often quoted in Spenser's day, Horace says not to sneer at Tantalus, for change the name and 'de te fabula' – the story is about you (*Satires* I.I.69–70). ANNE LAKE PRESCOTT

Hieatt 1973b; Hieatt 1975a; Kermode 1971; Tonkin 1973. See also Eusebius *Chronicorum liber prior* in Joseph Justus Scaliger 1606 *Thesaurus temporum* 2 vols (Leiden; rpt Osnabrück 1968); Richard Lynche 1601 *An Historical Treatise of the Travels of Noah into Europe* (London; a loose tr of Berosus [Giovanni Nanni]); Diodorus Siculus *Library of History* 4.74; and Arthur Kelton 1546 *A Commendacion of Welshmen* sigs 66–8 (London).

tapestries The production of designs or pictures in cloth by interweaving warp and colored weft threads is an ancient and widely practiced art. The great ages of European tapestry were the Gothic and Renaissance; the most famous centers of production were Flemish and Burgundian cities, notably Arras and Tournai. In the sixteenth century, some of the most sought-after work came from Brussels; by the middle of the century, Italy too had become influential, especially the Medici factory in Florence.

The manufacture and trade in tapestry was of considerable economic importance. Tapestries commanded high prices as coveted trappings of wealth and power. They were prominent among the gifts, ceremonial gestures, and self-advertisement of Renaissance diplomacy and aristocratic competition for prestige and influence. Pope Leo X was reliably reported to have paid 16,000 ducats in 1519 for the ten tapestries of the *Acts of the Apostles* done to cartoons by Raphael; rumor put the total as high as 50,000 (Shearman 1972:13). Because of their cost, real tapestries decorated only the residences of royalty, nobility, higher clergy, and the very wealthy. The middle classes made do with painted cloth hangings or wall paintings. As either status symbol or appropriate display of magnificence, therefore, Spenser briefly mentions tapestry, arras, or cloth-of-gold in *FQ* I iv 6, I viii 35, II ix 33, III xi 51, VII vii 10, *Epithalamion* 304, and *Time* 632 (see *visual arts).

Practicing an art form vital in the sixteenth century, tapestry weavers (or their patrons) responded eagerly to a changing aesthetic in other arts. While religious subjects dominated in earlier periods, classical myth, secular legend, and history became more popular in the Renaissance. Ovid's *Metamorphoses*, which provides much of the matter for all three of Spenser's most significant descriptions of tapestry, was the most important source of nonreligious subjects; Renaissance editions of the *Metamorphoses* were often printed with the designation 'Bible of poets and painters' on the title page (d'Hulst 1967:213). The conventions of Gothic style were rapidly replaced by work in a full-blown Renaissance style as a result of the popularity of Raphael's 'painterly' designs for the often-copied Sistine *Acts of the Apostles*. Master painters of the Renaissance such as Mantegna, Giulio Romano, Bronzino, and Jan Cornelisz Vermeyen provided cartoons for tapestries. Spenser would undoubtedly have seen examples in various styles.

As an important contemporary decorative art, tapestry figures with other forms of mural decoration in many medieval and Renaissance instances of ecphrasis before Spenser. The long history of this *topos* in classical as well as medieval literature comprises the significant context for Spenser's three important extended descriptions of tapestry in *Muiopotmos* 257–352, *FQ* III i 34–8 (the story of Venus and Adonis in Malecasta's Castle Joyous), and *FQ* III xi 28–46 (the metamorphoses and triumphs of Cupid in the house of Busirane).

Malecasta's and Busirane's tapestries have seemed so 'real' or 'pictorial' that some readers have been convinced that Spenser was describing actual hangings, rather than imitating literary models (see *Var* 3:208, 3:392–9, 8:402; Hard 1930). Spenser's ecphrases, however, no matter how vivid, lack sufficient detailed information about spatial relationships, perspective, and design to permit us confidently to identify even the style of the tapestries. Their presentation cannot reliably be said to imitate or evoke any particular master, work, or style in either painting or tapestry. If they are called pictorial at all, it seems safest to use the term only to indicate that they induce in the reader a mental process *like* the experience of 'reading' a visual representation (see *pictorialism). Recent scholarship on Spenser's tapestries has turned from interest in the influence of the visual arts to the study of their literary qualities, and rhetorical analysis has largely superseded the search for literary sources and analogues.

The richness of Spenser's rhetoric in describing tapestries in Book III derives from an extraordinary ability to combine what he had learned from Ovid with the lessons of medieval allegorical ecphrasis. Malecasta's Venus and Adonis objectify the alluring sensuous appeal of love, but they also strongly suggest its fragility as a pastoral escape from the heroic world. Like Ovid's artful descriptions, Busirane's metamorphoses and triumphs of Cupid are stunning in their bewildering variety and detail (eg, *FQ* III xi 41; cf stanza 30 and *Metamorphoses* 6.103–7).

However, Spenser's morally loaded language creates an undercurrent of implication quite unlike Ovid's witty irreverence and preciosity. Diction such as 'straunge disguize,' 'slake his scalding smart,' and 'pervart' reminds the reader that Busirane's luxuriant art celebrates pernicious inversions consequent upon love pursued beyond measure. Jove's roving eye leads him to rove out of his place, and Cupid thrusts into his throne (III xi 30–5).

Stanza 28, which introduces Busirane's tapestries, suggests that Spenser demands to be read in two ways at once. The evocation of surface and appearance is Ovidian; but the charge on certain words subtly refers to a world of moral universals that transcends the particularities of the representations, as in the sinister suggestion of the 'discolourd Snake, whose hidden snares / Through the greene gras his long bright burnisht backe declares.' The detail recalls the medieval insistence that images be read to learn what they *mean*. Yet, like the fineness of work in the tapestries themselves, this moral sense is 'Woven ... so close and nere' that it cannot adequately be considered merely as a referent separated from its sign. Moreover, the *enargeia* of the tapestry descriptions is functionally related to their context. The tapestries in Book III both seduce and intimidate, presenting differing tests for chastity which Britomart meets: she is 'amazed,' but not finally dismayed.

In tapestry, many discrete threads are woven into conventional images of considerable resonance and power – heroes, gods, pleasant gardens, tumultuous fields of the chase or war. A crowded, various scene and a highly wrought, richly textured surface combine in an aesthetic experience that transcends its materials – bits of thread and colored cloth – to delight and teach. It is tempting to see this artistic mode as Spenser's conscious metaphor for his own poetic technique, as he weaves rhythms, words, stanzas, colors of rhetoric, allusion, and narrative incident into a moral and aesthetic world dense with variety and suggestion. His descriptions of these rich, costly, in every sense luxurious art objects, these beguiling and significant fictions, show in brief compass how to read and respond to his own rich, complex, and multileveled art.

MICHAEL L. DONNELLY

E.A.B. Barnard and A.J.B. Wace 1928 *The Sheldon Tapestry Weavers and Their Work* (Oxford); Dubois 1982; Heinrich Göbel 1924 *Tapestries of the Lowlands* tr Robert West (New York); Hard 1930; Hulse 1981, esp ch 6; Roger-A[dolf] d'Hulst 1967 *Flemish Tapestries from the Fifteenth to the Eighteenth Century* tr Frances J. Stillman (New York) esp pp 213–14, 218; Madeleine Jarry 1968 *La Tapisserie des origines à nos jours* (Paris); Lewis 1936, ch 7; John Shearman 1972 *Raphael's Cartoons in the Collection of Her Majesty the Queen and the Tapestries for the Sistine Chapel* (London); C.A. Thompson 1972; William George Thomson 1906 *A History of Tapestry from the Earliest Times until the Present Day* 3rd ed with revisions, 1973 ed F.P. and E.S. Thomson (East Ardsley, Yorks), esp pp 137–63, 165–88, and 239–76 for tapestries in the British Isles; R.R. Wilson 1986.

Tasso, Torquato (1544–95) Among Spenser's contemporary poets, none enjoyed so high a European reputation as Tasso. Upon its first complete publication in 1581, his *Gerusalemme liberata* (*Jerusalem Delivered*) was judged to be the greatest achievement of modern poetry. In England, Samuel Daniel referred to it in 1603 as 'that admirable Poem of *Jerusalem*, comparable to the best of the ancients' (ed 1930:141). Such verdicts would be upheld by literary taste in the two succeeding centuries. Tasso's epic about the conquest of Jerusalem by the knights of the First Crusade became a favorite subject for painters, dramatists, and opera composers; and his heroes and heroines – Rinaldo, Armida, Tancredi, Clorinda – were as familiar to educated readers as the protagonists of classical epics.

In the early 1580s when the *Liberata* became known in England, Spenser would still have been at an early stage of planning *The Faerie Queene*, and Tasso's epic had a notable effect upon his theory and practice in writing it. In the Letter to Raleigh, he names Tasso as one of the 'Poets historicall' whom he intends to follow. He notes that two heroes of the *Liberata*, Goffredo and Rinaldo, embody the virtues of the political and the private man respectively – the dual subject which is also the matter of his own epic, although he combines the virtues in a single hero, Arthur. In form and function, Spenser's Letter appears to be modeled upon the *Allegoria del poema* which Tasso wrote as a guide to the meaning of the *Liberata* and which often appeared in early editions of the poem. Spenser's statement revises Tasso's own explanation that epic is divided in its subject matter between poems of the contemplative and poems of the active man. For Tasso, Aeneas embodies contemplation and action, while for Spenser, he embodies the private and public virtues. These two types of virtue are subsumed in Tasso's category of the active life, the announced subject of his epic; Spenser asserts that, at least in the first twelve books of *The Faerie Queene*, Arthur and the questing knights will illustrate the 'twelve private morall vertues.' The idea that the knight-heroes of the individual books together form a composite picture of the fully virtuous man is similar to Tasso's allegorical conception of the crusader army whose cooperating members constitute 'man disposed into the state of natural justice' (*Prose diverse* ed 1875, 1:301–8).

The experiences of Tasso's two principal heroes are conflated in the visit of Redcrosse to the Mount of Contemplation in *FQ* I x 53–68, a passage which recalls elements in two episodes of the *Gerusalemme liberata*: Rinaldo's penitence on the Mount of Olives (18.12–17), to which Spenser's mountain is compared (54), and Goffredo's heavenly vision (14.4–19). Like Rinaldo, Redcrosse is spiritually purified in preparation for a subsequent battle with demonic forces. Like Goffredo, he wishes to escape from a contemptible earthly existence by a prompt translation to the company of the saints; both are instead confirmed in the divine missions they must fulfill on earth.

The Faerie Queene includes two extended imitations of the *Liberata*. The first takes place in the second half of Book II in the series of adventures leading to the Bower of Bliss. A general progression can be traced in the three books of the 1590 *Faerie Queene* from the teleological narrative of Book I, based on the closed structure of the Christian Bible, to the more open-ended romance narrative of Book III, modeled on Ariosto's *Orlando furioso*. The imitations of the *Liberata* in Book II fit into this progression, for Tasso consciously sought to include romance episodes within his epic. He did so, however, by depicting such episodes as a series of obstacles which must be removed before epic closure can be achieved. He allegorized these obstacles, moreover, as temptations that set the concupiscent and irascible appetites in revolt against the rule of reason. Thus, the return of Tasso's knights from their errantry in the realm of romance and their integration into the crusader army are depicted by the poet as one large drama of temperance. It was logical for Spenser to turn to Tasso's model in order to flesh out his own allegorical treatment of temperance.

Among the knights who must be restored to Tasso's army of crusaders is Rinaldo, captivated by the amorous charms of the pagan Armida in the midst of a pleasure garden which she has created through her magic. Two knights, Carlo and Ubaldo, are dispatched to bring him back to his senses and to the war. It is on their journey to Armida's garden that Spenser bases the voyage of Guyon and the Palmer to Acrasia's Bower. Earlier, Phaedria's boat, which seems to move by pure chance but is actually guided by its owner's desire for temporal evasion and otium (II vi 5–10, xii 14–16), is a vicious double of the boat of a providential Fortune sent to carry Tasso's knights to Armida's enchanted garden (15.6–9). That garden is located on one of the Fortunate Isles (15.37), and Armida herself becomes a figure of Fortune. Tasso's fiction thus offers both positive and negative emblems of the Renaissance idea of fortune: time as opportunity and the source of temporal goods.

By contrast, Spenser's versions of fortune in Book II are all negative, temptations which Guyon must resist: Atin, Mammon, Phaedria, the Quicksand of Unthriftyhed, the Whirlpool of Decay. Phaedria's boat and island also recall the little boat in which Rinaldo crosses to an island in the middle of the river Orontes (14.57–61), and her epicurean lullaby to Cymochles (vi 15–17) imitates the song of the phantom mermaid who sings Rinaldo to sleep (14.62–4). The later siren-song of Spenser's mermaid (xii 32) echoes the speech of Tasso's bathing maiden (15.63), while the song of the rose in the Bower of Bliss (xii 74–5) has its counterpart in the parrot's song in Armida's garden (16.14–15). All these songs urge their hearers to enjoy the good fortune of the moment and to remove themselves from the advancing course of time. The virtue of temperance, however, includes a larger temporal perspective which allows one to know what is appropriate for every moment.

Spenser closely follows Tasso's description of Armida's garden in the scenery of the Bower of Bliss. Armida's animal guardians, dispelled by Ubaldo's magic wand (15.49–52), are amplified by Spenser to include beasts of sea (xii 22–6), air (35–7), and land (39–41) which the Palmer subdues with his staff. Spenser virtually translates Tasso's text about maidens bathing in the fountain of laughter (15.58–66), but his 'naked Damzelles' are somewhat more overt in their sexual advances (xii 63–9). Both Tasso's knights and Guyon are tempted; but Tasso's are checked by their internal faculties of reason, Guyon by the externalized superego figure of the Palmer.

The Lucretian (cf *De rerum natura* 1.33–7) pose of Verdant in Acrasia's lap (xii 76–9) is also modeled on the tableau of Rinaldo and Armida (16.18–20). Yet here Spenser's departure from Tasso becomes evident. Narcissistic and unmanning as it may be, Rinaldo's dalliance with Armida is the excessive indulgence of a natural appetite which nonetheless has its place, though a subordinate one, in the life of the human individual. Moreover, there is an element of mutual love in their relationship. These two factors eventually allow the reconciliation of Rinaldo and Armida in the last canto of Tasso's epic (20.127–36).

In contrast to the ultimately redeemable Armida, Spenser's Acrasia is a witch who belongs to the family of Ariosto's Alcina and Trissino's Acratia. She represents a demonic lust; her capture and bondage, like the binding of Archimago (I xii 35–6), foreshadow the apocalyptic binding of Satan (Rev 20.2). Verdant is unconscious throughout the scene, and Acrasia is seen to 'sucke his spright' (73) – literalizing what had been only an erotic metaphor in Tasso (16.19). The posture of Spenser's couple strongly suggests that Acrasia is a succubus, a demon-witch who causes seminal emissions from sleeping men. Her destruction of Mortdant in II i thus recalls the false Una in Redcrosse's erotic dream in I i and the relationship of that Lilith figure to Duessa, another Circean enchantress who changes Fradubio into a tree. Both Fradubio and Mortdant are types of the fallen Adam; the parallel is characteristic of the way in which Book II recapitulates the allegory of Book I.

Acrasia's demonic cast helps to explain Spenser's revision of the relationship between art and nature in Armida's garden. The art which creates Tasso's garden strives to look like nature, though nature at her most artistic: 'It seems to be an art that belongs to Nature, which for her own delight playfully imitates her own imitator' (16.10). Spenser's translation suggests 'That nature had for wantonesse ensude / Art, and that Art at nature did repine; / So striving each th'other to undermine, / Each did the others worke more beautifie; / So diff'ring both in willes, agreed in fine' (xii 59). Nature, which seemed merely playful in Tasso, is now made to appear wanton by an art which seeks to compete with nature at nature's expense. Armida's art works through nature; Acrasia adds the unnatural to nature. Armida's garden contains grapes in various stages of ripeness on one vine – itself a magical prodigy – which Tasso compares to gold and garnets (16.11). When Spenser imitates the passage, he begins with metaphors but eventually literalizes Tasso's comparison: 'Some deepe empurpled as the *Hyacint*, / Some as the Rubine, laughing sweetly red, / Some like faire Emeraudes, not yet well ripened. / And them amongst, some were of burnisht gold, / So made by art, to beautifie the rest' (54–5). Such unnatural supplements characterize Acrasia's garden and the lust which she embodies.

Belphoebe's first appearance (II iii 21–42) is indebted to the description of Clarice, the heroine in the epic poem of Tasso's youth, *Rinaldo* (1.53–63), by way of Tasso's own source, the appearance of the disguised Venus to Aeneas (*Aeneid* 1.314–34). Spenser also loosely imitates the *Rinaldo* (5.12–61) in the story of Britomart's rescue of Amoret (III xi 7–25). When Britomart, by the power of her chastity, breaches the flames before Busirane's house, her passage is modeled both upon Rinaldo's entrance into the oracle of love, which is reserved for faithful lovers (*Rinaldo* 5.59–61), and upon Tancredi's passage through Ismeno's enchanted fire (*GL* 13.34–6).

FQ VI contains Spenser's other sustained imitation of the *Gerusalemme liberata*. Calidore's sojourn among the shepherds in canto ix draws heavily on Erminia's pastoral interlude in Tasso's poem (7.6–22). Meliboe's narrative of his career at court and his return to the countryside (ix 24–5) is directly lifted from the story which Tasso's aged shepherd tells Erminia (7.12–13). Pastorella, whose noble birth shines through her pastoral dress and demeanor (ix 10–11), recalls Erminia herself, once she has joined the band of shepherds (7.17–18). But whereas Tasso's shepherds are more or less immune to war and the violence of the political world by virtue of their isolation (7.8–9), Meliboe and his fellow shepherds will eventually be killed (xi 18), and their bucolic grove plundered by the Brigands (x 39). Spenser rejects the tradition of pastoral escapism to which Tasso's episode belongs. His own pastoral fictions clothe an aristocratic ideology that defines the relationship between the powerful and the powerless. The natural courtesy of his shepherds is reciprocated by Calidore, the representative of the court society upon which their precarious pastoral contentment depends.

Spenser's adaptation of Tasso's episode within a larger anatomy of the virtue of courtesy suggests, moreover, a major difference between the sensibilities of the two poets. Whatever other thematic resonances it may have in Tasso's poem, Erminia's pastoral sojourn reflects the individual psychology of her character, her almost masochistic desire for captive passivity. The narrative of the *Gerusalemme liberata* is an extension of the inner lives of its protagonists, whose various interactions combine to produce a unified plot. Tasso's Aristotelian concern for epic unity and consistency is happily matched by his genius for penetrating characterization. By contrast, Spenser's episodes are individually governed and collectively linked less by an internally consistent logic of characters and plot than by a strongly articulated program of didactic allegory. To fulfill its particular role in that program, the Spenserian episode acquires an independent life of its own within the loosely organized narrative framework of romance. The contrast with Tasso measures the extent of Spenser's divergence from neoclassical literary norms.

Tasso's lyrical poems, the *Rime* (first ed 1581); contain a collection of Petrarchan love lyrics overlaid with Neoplatonic conceits and motifs. Among them, Spenser found models for sixteen of the *Amoretti* (*Am* 3/*Rime* 35; 5/36; 13/219; 21/80, 218; 43/164–6; 47/88; 49/74; 54/712; 67/388; 72/67; 73/222; 76–7/593; 81/17; 84/120; 89/399). Anacreontics 4 on Cupid and the Bee which ends *Amoretti* is indebted to *Rime* 255. (Numbering of the *Rime* follows ed 1963–5).

The first complete English translation of the *Gerusalemme liberata*, published in 1600 by Edward Fairfax, was highly indebted to Spenser's diction and style in *The Faerie Queene*. These Spenserian influences provide another example in Renaissance letters of how the imitation of an earlier literary work could affect the subsequent history of its translation. DAVID QUINT

Torquato Tasso 1963–5 *Opere* ed Bruno Maier, 5 vols (Milan); Tasso 1875 *Prose diverse* ed Cesare Guasti, 2 vols (Florence). Harold H. Blanchard 1925 'Imitations from Tasso in the *Faerie Queene*' *SP* 22:198–21; C.P. Brand 1965; Brand 1973 'Tasso, Spenser, and the *Orlando Furioso*' in *Petrarch to Pirandello* ed Julius A. Molinaro (Toronto) pp 95–110; Castelli 1936; Durling 1954; Giamatti 1966:179–210, 254–83; Hough 1962:59–81; Chalmers Clifford Huffman 1979 'The Earliest Receptions of Tasso in Elizabethan England' *RLMC* 32:245–61; E. Koeppel 1888 'Edmund Spenser's Verhältniss zu Tasso' *Anglia* 11:341–62; Kostić 1959b; Kostić 1969; Nellist 1963; Nohrnberg 1976:5–67; Janet G. Scott 1927 'The Sources of Spenser's *Amoretti*' *MLR* 22:189–95.

Tasso in England Queen Elizabeth may have encouraged the Elizabethan Tasso to come into being. An Italian company of players that followed her progress of 1574 to Reading entertained her with a pastoral drama, possibly *Aminta*, performed in Ferrara the year before (Chambers 1923, 2:261–2). By 1584, she was sufficiently impressed by *Gerusalemme liberata* to have memorized part of it, declaring the Duke of Ferrara fortunate to be celebrated by so fine a poet (Castelli 1936:11–13). In that year, Scipio Gentili dedicated to her his Latin translation of *GL* 1–2, published in London.

There are several early indications of interest after Harvey noted the brilliance of 'excellent Tasso' in 1572 (ed 1913:162). In 1592, the year Harvey regretted that there was no 'English Tasso,' Lord Strange's men performed the play *Jerusalem* in London. *Godfrey of Bulloigne* (part 2) was staged in 1594 and was followed immediately by *Tasso's Melancholy* – evidence of Elizabethan interest both in Tasso's poem and in the already romanticized version of his life.

After Spenser's memorable imitations of *Gerusalemme liberata* in the 1590 *Faerie Queene* (see *Tasso) and his admiring reference to 'excellente' Tasso in the Letter to Raleigh, the first Elizabethan translation was hardly premature when it appeared in 1594: *Godfrey of Bulloigne, or The Recoverie of Hierusalem* by R[ichard] C[arew], Esquire. Only the first five cantos were published. In 1600, however, there appeared a full and more famous version of the poem by Edward Fairfax. Spenser influenced both translators. Carew honored Spenser as the English Lucan when he proudly catalogued great Elizabethan poets in *The Excellency of the English Tongue* (in G.G. Smith 1904, 2:293). Coleridge considered that Fairfax, when translating Tasso, had Spenser in his memory if not in his eye (Tasso ed 1981:16).

Carew, an educated Cornish landowner and acquaintance of Raleigh, shared Spenser's antiquarian interests in legends, romances, British history, and especially the ancient language. He was a member of the Royal Society of Antiquaries and a friend of Camden and Robert Cotton. His essay on *The Excellency of the English Tongue* has a spirit of aggressive nationalism and is meant to prove that his vernacular is 'macheable, if not preferable, before any other in vogue at this daye' (p 286). His translation is written in a similar spirit, and there can be little doubt that his use of language is influenced by Spenser. He exploits not only the 'Saxon' elements in the language – its brevity and the so-called 'primitive manliness' valued by linguistic nationalists – but also its Latin characteristics. He imitates Spenser's neologisms not only in his foreign borrowings ('crisples' from *crespe*, 'ornes' *orni*, 'meschite' *meschita*, 'adviso' *aviso*, etc) but also in new formations such as 'burgage' from *borgo*, perhaps on the analogy of Spenser's 'fortilage' from *fortalizio*. He uses existing words in new senses, makes new formations, and revives some old words. He avoids Spenser's more unusual archaisms but freely uses words and forms Spenser drew from established poetic diction: *to affray*, *to aread*, *to dight*, *doome*, *stond*, *unneath*, *ybred*, *ycrauld*, etc. Carew also uses a few dialect words and phrases: *halsner* (prediction), *hoyting wanton*, *to slocke*, 'his right hand so wimble was and wight.' In his *Survey of Cornwall* (1602), where he pleads in defense of dialect 'not onely the prescription of antiquitie, but also the title of proprietie, and the benefit of significancy,' he adds that 'as they expresse our meaning more directly, so they want but another Spencer, to make them passable' (fols 56v-57).

Dialect words are found also in the translation of Edward Fairfax. Several Northern words occur in his verse: *bield* (refuge), *cogge* (cockboat), *fornenst* (over against), *lite* (little), *scaldred* (scalded), etc. He too uses Spenserian words and forms and continues the currency of many archaisms that might have gone out of fashion if Spenser had not revived interest in them: *chevisance* (adventure), *embay* (bathe), *flit* (adj: light), *ibore* (born), *icleped* (called), *mister wight*, *needments*, *sdainfull*, *yond* (fierce), *yood* (went), etc. Fairfax also echoes epithets and phrases from Spenser: 'sailing Pine,' 'weeping Firre,' etc (see Tasso ed 1981:53–65).

Both translations are in ottava rima. Fairfax is incomparably more fluent than Carew, whose frequently clumsy syntax makes hard work for the reader. He learned metrical facility from Spenser, perhaps, and with it grace, melody, narrative speed, and sometimes lush sensuality. Some seventeenth-century readers even found Fairfax smoother and more musical than Spenser. His influence on Waller and thus Dryden helped shape the development of the eighteenth-century heroic couplet. His couplets make for effects in versification that are un-Spenserian (and alien to Tasso) as he adds ideas that make for prosodic balance and for sententious, gnomic, and proverbial effects. Carew, however, avoids the models of fluency he had before him in Harington's Ariosto and in *The Faerie Queene*. At his worst, he is sadly harsh, straining meter and syntax, but at his best, he recreates the effects of Tasso's *asprezza* with surprising sensitivity.

Also, Carew's translation is more faithful to the subtleties of characterization in *Gerusalemme liberata* and to its delicate ambiguities and complexities of mood, emotion, and action. He may have learned from Spenser to represent Tasso's women with grace: 'in joyes seemely weede her face she shrinde, / And her bright hew and faire celestiall smile, / Seem'd as a double Sunne, that gleaming shinde, / On thicke and mystie clowds of sorrow sad' (4.91). The finest descriptive moments in the translation not only make Tasso Elizabethan, they must have vividly recalled Spenser's poetry to contemporary readers. Dawn is enchanted by Armida's cheeks, which, bathed in tears, 'Seem'd intermingled roses white and red / If so a dewy cloud do water them ... And morne which them beholds and in them joyes, / Proud with their ornament her lockes accoyes' (4.75). From Spenser he may also have learned the poetry of natural description. There is a Spenserian quality in the diction and in the easy, fluid, varied rhythm of this dawn scene: 'Dawnyng th'Embassadresse was ris'ne from bed, / Tydings to beare, how now grey morne annies [ie, comes nigh], / The whiles she trimmes her selfe, and golden hed, / Beflowres with Roses culd in Paradize' (3.1).

In descriptions of feminine beauty and external nature, Fairfax also recalls the manner of Spenser but more frequently and more fluently than Carew. He decorates such moments more lavishly than Tasso cares to, splashing on colors – purples, saffrons, and golds. This seems to gratify Elizabethan taste: *Englands Parnassus* quotes from his translation abundantly – as often as from Spenser for morning scenes and more often for descriptions of night. It is worth comparing with Spenser his splendid translation of Rinaldo's seduction and enslavement (14.57–71, 16.1–27). The victory over the enchanted forest is finely done (18). A typical lush passage that is worth comparing with Spenser's version is the description of Armida's bower at 15.58–62; compare *FQ* II xii 63–8, Acrasia's Bower.

Although both translators have clearly profited from reading Spenser, Fairfax learned from him, as Carew did not, the secret of a fluid narrative style. As a result, Carew needs readers prepared to search for those felicitous moments when he truly makes Tasso Elizabethan. Fairfax alters Tasso, vulgarizes his most delicate and sophisticated effects, often loses his emotional complexity and characteristic ambiguity, making facile, trite rhythms out of meter that was exquisitely varied. However, he did make available to generations of readers Tasso's characters, reasonably closely represented, and the framework of the fable itself largely true to its original, in easy, often rich, sensuous, and delightful verse.

Traces of Tasso's influence can be found in other works by Elizabethans. Daniel and Drayton both admired Tasso who reinforced their interest in historical subjects and also inspired Drayton's sensuous, erotic, colorful episodes. Elizabethans also copied and translated some of his lyrics and sonnets, although the conventional nature of themes and diction often makes derivation uncertain. Spenser is indebted to him for perhaps a dozen sonnets in *Amoretti*. In Tasso, there is a tension between Neoplatonic reasoning and a lingering, self-indulgent sensuality, a fully savored eroticism. In Spenser, desire is viewed in Protestant moral terms, and courtship has its place in a social framework leading to Christian union. D.N.C. Wood

The text of Carew's translation (London 1594) is rpt with intro by Werner von Koppenfels (Hildesheim 1980); for further discussion see D.N.C. Wood 1977 'Elizabethan English and Richard Carew' *Neophil* 61:304–15, and Wood 1978 '*Gerusalemme liberata* Englished by Richard Carew' *CahiersE* 13:1–13. Fairfax's translation (1600) is edited by Kathleen M. Lea and T.M. Gang (Oxford 1981); numerous other editions are also available. The notes of Lea and Gang show numerous parallels between Fairfax and Spenser. See also Charles G. Bell 1954 'Fairfax's Tasso' *CL* 6:26–52. Still helpful is E. Koeppel 1889–91 'Die englischen Tasso-Ubersetzungen des 16. Jahrhunderts' *Anglia* 11:11–38, 12:103–42, 13:42–71; important general studies of Tasso in England are Brand 1965:205–308 and Castelli 1936.

Teares of the Muses. See ***Complaints: The Teares of the Muses***

temperance *FQ* II draws on various traditions of temperance. Aristotle's *sōphrosynē* is the virtue of moderation in bodily pleasures, chiefly food and sex; temperance in this sense came to stand often for virtue in general, which Aristotle understands as the harmonizing of appetite with reason so as to hit the 'mean' or 'mark' (ie, target) between extremes of excess and defect. The person thus harmonized does not need to exercise self-control; if he must and does do so, he is showing continence (*enkrateia*), which brings Aristotle closer to the Stoic conception of temperance as self-control. Continence also brings Aristotle closer to Plato, for whom temperance is the aspect of virtue by which the spirited element in the soul keeps the appetites under the control of reason, and thus the whole in harmony. Plato is important for the tradition of temperance in other ways as well: he transmits the Pythagorean emphasis on the mathematical or musical character of harmony, which is found explicitly in *FQ* II ix 22 and is implicit when Spenser uses terms like *measure, rule*, and *equal*; there is something more generally Platonic in Spenser's idea of temperance as wisdom, often of a heavenly nature (i 31, 44, 54). Since temperance in this sense was readily adopted by Christianity, it came to be thought of as a virtue of purity and self-denial derived from grace, one of the seven 'gift virtues' set against the seven deadly sins.

Spenser's own idea of temperance can best be approached through his focal emblem for it, a very medieval one. In canto ix, Alma (Ital 'soul') is a feudal lady living in a well-built and well-guarded castle. Her household forms a courteous order dedicated to her service, and she herself behaves with the same courtesy; yet she remains very much a ruler. Other exalted women mentioned in Book II are equally well-ruled and well-ruling: Gloriana (Guyon's own lady), the more private Belphoebe, and the Elizabeth to whom these women allude, primarily a queen in this book and celebrated through her royal ancestry in the British chronicles (x). Guyon too rules himself or – to split him in two – is ruled by his guide, the reasoning Palmer; he can thus rule others, using gracious words where possible and stern force where necessary. His goal in ruling (that of all knights but specially important in this book) is honor: thus the leading emotions of a temperate knight are not only the 'Shamefastnesse' that leads to self-restraint but also desire for praise ('Prays-desire'), a characteristic that belongs primarily to Arthur the aspiring prince but certainly to Guyon as well. The contrary of honor takes various forms: the simple baseness of the first inhabitants of Britain or the rabble outside Alma's castle, the false honor of the huffing Braggadocchio, the subtler false honor offered in Mammon's daughter Philotime (Gr 'love of honor').

What Alma rules is a castle: an upstanding 'goodly frame' (xii 1), parodied in the flimsy stage-sets of Acrasia's pleasure-garden and in Mammon's buried house of Richesse. Allegorically, Alma's castle is the human body as ruled by the soul: even if Spenser also invites us to read the castle as the soul itself, or the whole natural man as ruled by a higher principle, anything so ruled is a kind of body. This body can also be represented as an animal, particularly the spirited horse, which only someone like Guyon can ride: terms from horsemanship like *bridle, handle*, and *menage* (manage) are scattered through the book. Intemperance produces less noble animals or outright monsters, such as those encountered by Guyon on his voyage to the Bower of Bliss.

A body is something unitary, but at the same time a community of members: this is true of Alma's household both as an individual body and as a society or 'body politic.' Temperance lies not only in her rule but in the harmony of such a community, for those who agree to proper rule agree with each other. Guyon himself makes friendships on the basis of common allegiance; so do the four elements, since concord or mixture, in the view of Spenser's day, informs everything from the individual to the universe. The predominance of any one of the elements, in the form of the 'humor' or fluid derived from it, gives a person his particular 'complexion' or 'temper.' Unhealthy excess in a humor produces one of four morbid conditions, represented in Book II by the figures Guyon encounters in its central cantos: the choleric Pyrochles (from Gr 'fire'), the phlegmatic Cymochles (from Gr 'wave'), the melancholy earth-dweller Mammon, and the sanguine Phaedria (from Gr 'shining' or 'mirthful'), an airy figure who skims above the lower elements. (The sanguine temper, in which blood predominates, was linked with the element of air, as is Phaedria in various ways, and was thought to produce mirth.) Just as these four characters work to very different ends, so do the elements in Book II. The pure well of the nymph is fatal to the polluted Mortdant and will not wash the son polluted by Amavia's blood; Pyrochles burns even in the Idle Lake; Tantalus cannot reach the water he craves, Pilate cannot wash his hands; Guyon himself faints when he returns from Mammon's earth-world to the air. A whole world of elements refusing to unite or uniting only in confusion is a chaos, such as Guyon experiences just before he reaches Acrasia's island; when the elements make an order for evil purposes, the result is a parody cosmos.

If Spenser shows us a plurality of elements, these also tend to resolve into a single pair of contraries. Aristotle had paired excess and defect as flanking the mean of virtue, and in Book II we find the sisters Perissa (from Gr 'too much') and Elissa (from Gr 'too little') flanking Medina (from L 'middle'). A basic pairing in the classical tradition was that of pleasure and pain (vi 1). These were commonly understood as the base of the 'concupiscible' and 'irascible' emotions, respectively friendly and hostile to life: joy and sorrow, hope and fear, sometimes love and hate as well. In Book II, the emotions of pleasure are associated most with Phaedria and Acrasia, those of pain with Furor, Pyrochles, and Maleger. The painful emotions include wrath, envy, grief, desire for vengeance, and even love in the painful sense appropriate to Pyrochles (v 16). Equally rooted in pleasure and pain is the distinction between 'forward' and 'froward' (ii 38) emotions, related to that between concupiscible and irascible though not simply the same (a froward character like Prays-desire can represent concupiscence of a healthy kind). 'Loose' or 'light' figures are similarly contrasted with 'grave' ones, and 'careless' (heedless) ones like Phaedria with 'careful' (concerned) ones like Mammon. We can add other pairs of characters here: the careless (though not merely concupiscent) Cymochles and the careful Pyrochles, the hags Impotence and Impatience, and at the very source of Guyon's quest the doomed pair of Amavia ('[she] that loves to live') and Mortdant ('[he] that death does give') (i 55).

To see what such pairs ultimately mean in Book II, we should notice first that, unlike Aristotle's excess and defect, Spenser's contraries are things – elements to be brought into concord; and second, that this concord is not static but a matter of process in time (*tempus* 'time' may be the root of L *temperantia*). In *Fowre Hymnes* a 'tempering' of the jarring elements created the world in the beginning (*HL* 78–91); the individual soul 'tempers' (forms) a body on coming into the world (*HB* 120–6; cf *FQ* III vi 37–8). We also find that gluttony, the type-form of intemperance, comes second in Spenser's pageant of the deadly sins (*FQ* I iv), and that in *The Shepheardes Calender* the second eclogue presents the tempered Thenot, who has been tried by joy and sorrow, summer and winter. The first eclogue is a lament for the lost world of Colin's happiness: in *The Faerie Queene*, similarly, the first virtue of holiness looks to an eternal world 'before' (and 'after') the temporal one. Guyon, however, looks to an earthly rather than a heavenly city. He is neither unholy nor an exemplar of holiness: his special virtue is rather the one that constructs a finite identity for man when he enters time. This identity is the castle or body mentioned earlier, and morally it is the frame of ordinary human integrity. The latter is often symbolized in Book II by sexual intactness: thus most of the virtuous ladies in the book are virgins; Guyon's devotion to Gloriana is chivalrous but not sexual; and even Acrasia is something of a parody virgin in the way she discards her lovers, keeping them only as animals.

Guyon's integrity has often been called in question: he has been seen as failing in temperance, as being intemperately temperate, or as being temperate but sinfully proud of the fact. His actions at times are indeed like those the book treats as intemperate: he takes occasion for adventures, feels curiosity and wrath, and accepts trials that leave him helpless. The temperance that builds an earthly city can in any case be seen as vanity, and its hero as an empty Braggadocchio: if even the holiness of Redcrosse returning from the Mount of Contemplation is vain from a supernatural 'heavenly' perspective (I x 62), it is not surprising to find the castle of Alma associated at one point with the tower of Babel (II ix 21). Yet a legend of temperance, one can argue, must subordinate such a perspective: Book II is primarily what it seems to be, a celebration of temperance and its hero. Nor does it show this hero seriously failing in his virtue, or even having to learn it: Guyon is his temperate self from the outset. What Book II does show repeatedly is Guyon's human frailty.

Frailty is the correlate of passion: either quality can subsume the other, though Spenser also contrasts 'infirmitie' with 'bold furie' (i 57; cf iv 2). As Amavia says (i 52), frailty is inherent in flesh itself, the 'Aegyptian slime' (ix 21) to which the material of Alma's castle is compared. Guyon is far from claiming exemption: in the helpless child Ruddymane he sees the condition of all mankind, including himself (ii 2). There remains the question of guilt, but in this episode it is hard to separate the characters' guilt from their misfortune. The stain on Ruddymane's hands, for instance, indicates hereditary sin – the biblical 'bloudguiltinesse' (ii 4) that echoes through the book – yet he is at the same time an unoffending victim to be protected. So is the Guyon who emerges from Mammon's cave. It is true that he can no longer guard against intemperance, having reached the limit of his natural strength; he is even, like other men, an unmeriting 'foe' of God (viii 1). Yet he also represents an otherwise lost primeval virtue (vii 16), and when he faints he is a martyr, to be helped by an angel against a common enemy. The human helper in this situation is frail like Guyon himself, for Arthur too needs help in his trials, and is so exhausted by his battle with Maleger that he cannot mount his horse afterwards. Arthur and Guyon are temperate because they do their best in spite of their frailty; this is why the latter, refusing Philotime, can speak of his honor and his frailty at the same time (vii 50).

Human integrity, then, is only that of a limited and needy being, made of earth and doomed to fall like all finite structures. Yet we also find in Book II that Guyon is not only supported by grace but called to prove himself on his own. In a larger view this can be said of all the heroes in *The Faerie Queene*, but Book II, and especially its central cantos, is Spenser's great story of initiatory testing. The allusions in the Mammon episode point among other things to the underworld journey of Aeneas and, even more importantly, to Christ's temptation in the wilderness by Satan, another ruler of this world. Guyon is not Christ, but Christ was flesh like Guyon, and Guyon like Christ must be strong by himself in an ordeal where no helper seems present – for in the central cantos Guyon's Palmer is not there, nor is the horse which suggests a lower source of help. This does not mean that Guyon has lost his reason or his strength, but that in the present ordeal he must find them within himself. In doing so, he is equally keeping faith with their divine source: in his final ordeal, he will return to direct alliance with that source, as we can see by following his story.

Near the beginning of each book Spenser presents an epitome of its special virtue in a relatively simple form: in Book II, this gives us the castle of the three sisters in which Medina uses the government of reason to pacify extremes. But Guyon has already been called to his greater quest, for in the deaths of Mortdant and Amavia he has seen something more fatal than the ordinary unruliness of Elissa and Perissa. Several versions of intemperance follow, seemingly digressive though really preparatory. Furor and Occasion, who announce these emblematically, are simple figures, the one sheer rage and the other sheer incitement to it; and the pain they represent, being hostile to order as to life, stands more simply and directly against temperance than does pleasure. But now disorder begins to assume the guise of order. While Pyrochles, the first elemental character, is much like Furor himself, his brother Cymochles is more peaceable (when not provoked); and Phaedria and Mammon have parody worlds of their own – a world of carelessness in the case of Phaedria and of care in that of Mammon. The latter offers the most complete temptation of any elemental character: care as securing pleasure and glory, even the counterpart of an innocent garden hidden within the careful earth. Guyon, now standing alone, has only to renounce the ruder and more strenuous 'antique world' to inherit Mammon's world of gold. He refuses, reaching the limit of his separate strength; now, having proved himself, he once again experiences help from outside, and presently sees the temperate castle of Alma as surrounding him.

The intemperance still to be conquered reflects that of the sequence of elements but is greater than any single one of them. In the ghost Maleger pain becomes the whole world as a body of death, frail yet with its own spectral cohesion and endurance. The witch Acrasia offers pleasure as a whole world of seeming health and temper (xii 51) and thus of harmony: nature and art here may be at strife, but artfully agree 'in fine' (59). Pleasure and pain, carelessness and care, also agree, and now they can be seen plainly as responses to time, the basic condition of the natural world. The song of Acrasia's bower tells man to grasp time – to enjoy the seemingly well-tempered world of nature – and precisely because that world is not well-tempered at all, but frail and short-lived like a flower. Acrasia is thus the same evil as the hag Occasion, and now in its deadliest form: she tempts to the greatest pleasure by arousing fear of the greatest pain, that of death.

To stand against Acrasia's total perversion of nature, humanity must ally itself with a power beyond nature. This power has supported Guyon all along, but in concealed or indirect ways: the angel who came at his faint immediately withdrew, at least in appearance; the Palmer used the strength of Arthur, Arthur used Guyon's own sword; and even when the Palmer's sacred wisdom – indicated by his name – returns to counsel Guyon, it speaks the language of natural reason. But the Palmer's counsel also enables Guyon to remember his supernatural origin and thus overcome Acrasia. Nature here is relying on grace (see *nature and grace), and is in fact most itself in this natural reliance: Guyon in the end is licensed not only to desire the reward of honor but even to engage in 'the tempest of his wrathfulnesse' (xii 83) – to use the very energies that would be intemperate if not allied with something beyond nature.

Temperance as deriving from grace is continuous with holiness; as a sequence, however, *The Faerie Queene* asks us to contrast the two virtues and see temperance as the virtue which gives man his own integrity. Since finite integrity requires the setting of boundaries, Book II may be felt to have a more negative character than its neighbors. With man's natural identity secure, Books III and IV show us the fire of love and the ocean of change as providential forces, leading to a temporal marriage like the eternal one of holiness and truth prepared in Book I. In Book II, on the other hand, love is simply a passion to be ruled like others, and chastity and friendship are only aspects of that rule. The intermediate virtue of temperance thus seems only a disagreeable necessity, neither a heavenly source nor its full incarnation. Yet we can see the matter in an opposite way as well. The book of holiness shows the need to look beyond the world and its vanity; the book of chastity shows the confusion of engaging in the world: it is in the book of temperance that the creation is praised for its excellence, a marriage and incarnation in itself. The 'temp'rament / Of ... complexions' may be only the ephemeral vessel of a beauty from heaven (*HB* 65–7), yet as chosen for that beauty it becomes the body of grace that Guyon is shown in the castle of Alma.

J. CARSCALLEN

Some classical sources are Plato *Republic* 4, and *Gorgias* 503D-8C; Aristotle *Nicomachean Ethics* 3.10–12 and *Rhetoric* 2.1–11; Cicero *De officiis* 1.27–42 and *Tusculan Disputations* 2 and 3; Macrobius *Commentary on the Dream of Scipio* 1.8; Boethius *Consolation of Philosophy* 2.8, 3.12, 4.6. For Renaissance and other contexts or for direct discussion of Spenser, see Bamborough 1952; John C. Bean 1977 'Cosmic Order in *The Faerie Queene*: From Temperance to Chastity' *SEL* 17:67–79; Berger 1957 (for a general discussion of Book II); Carscallen 1967–8; Fowler 1960a; Helen F. North 1973 'Temperance (*SŌPHROSYNĒ*) and the Canon of the Cardinal Virtues' in *DHI* 4:365–78; North 1979 *From Myth to Icon: Reflections of Greek Ethical Doctrine in Literature and Art* (Ithaca, NY); Pollock 1980; Sirluck 1951–2; Leo Spitzer 1963 *Classical and Christian Ideas of World Harmony* (Baltimore).

Tennyson, Alfred, Lord (1809–92) Tennyson's style is often Spenserian; his poetry abounds in Spenserian allusions, and in one Spenserian imitation, 'The Lotos-Eaters,' he carries Spenserianism far beyond Keats's achievement in *The Eve of St Agnes*. In making Arthur an emblem of 'the Ideal Soul of Man coming into contact with the warring elements of the flesh,' Tennyson is doing for his own age what Spenser did for his (ed 1969:1464). Each poet is fulfilling the demand of epic and romance convention by supplementing a *literal* presentation of an external action with an *allegory* of psychological or other inward meanings in which the poet has a more authentic interest. Tennyson's statement (cited but not documented in Pyre 1921:22) that Spenser 'was not much known or admired by him' may have been prompted by his distaste for source hunters. But the statement is not inconsistent with his having absorbed Spenserian qualities, not directly from Spenser but from eighteenth-century imitators like Pope and Thomson, as well as from more immediate Romantic sources like Wordsworth and Keats.

An important feature of Spenser's style that Tennyson shares with Keats is an ability to capture visual effects through sound. Northrop Frye asserts that the most sustained mastery in English of such effects 'of verbal *opsis*' occurs in *The Faerie Queene* (1957:258–62). Like Spenser's line, 'The Eugh obedient to the benders will' (I i 9), where the weak syllables in the middle 'sag out in a bow shape,' Tennyson's alexandrine in 'The Lotos-Eaters' – 'The mild-eyed melancholy Lotos-eaters came' – uses a long Latin word to lighten the rhythm. The weak syllables droop at the center, as if in imitation of the mariners' drooping spirits. This line also illustrates another feature of a Spenserian style: the use of polysyllabic words to span metrical feet instead of being contained inside them. The rising iambic motion of Tennyson's alexandrine is offset by the falling trochaic character of *mild-eyed*, *melancholy*, *Lotos-eaters*, which creates a dying fall characteristic of Spenser and of much of *In Memoriam*. There is also a tendency in Spenser (as opposed to Milton) for stressed syllables to begin with clustered consonants and to end with vowels or weak consonants: 'Whose pleasaunce she him shew'd, and plentifull great store' (*FQ* II vi 11). Because of Tennyson's preference for initial consonants, the language of *In Memoriam* has been found more Spenserian than Miltonic (Sinfield 1971:177–9).

Spenser's influence is most apparent in 'The Lotos-Eaters.' In adapting Spenser's description of the 'trickling streame' and 'ever-drizling raine' that lull Morpheus to sleep (*FQ* I i 41), Tennyson writes like him in an appositional style that defers the principal verbs and makes skillful use of indefinite caesuras. In the even-numbered stanzas of the choric song into which the Spenserian stanzas of the opening dissolve, the mariners draw upon a chorus of seductive Spenserian voices which urge man to renounce the heroic life. The mariners' searching indictment of creation, 'Why should we only toil, the roof and crown of things?' (69), echoes Phaedria's appeal to Cymochles (*FQ* II vi 17). In their culminating resolve to seek rest after 'labour in the deep mid-ocean' (172), we hear an equally enticing echo of the mermaids' appeal to Guyon and the Palmer as they travel to the Bower of Bliss: 'This is the Port of rest from troublous toyle' (II xii 32). In the fourth strophe, the easeful allure of death, which the mariners welcome as 'the end of life' (86), repeats the casuistry of Spenser's Despair: 'Death is the end of woes' (I ix 47). In using both the psychological inwardness and the artifice of Spenser to modernize Homer, 'The Lotos-Eaters' takes a giant step beyond a Spenserian imitation like *The Castle of Indolence* or even a 'perfect' Spenserian artifact like *The Eve of St Agnes*.

In 'The Palace of Art,' as in *The Faerie Queene* where pictures or tapestries are generally found in places Spenser would consider evil, Tennyson uses the overriding artifice of the panels to criticize souls who fail to humanize their paradise. Spenser's influence is even clearer in 'The Lady of Shalott,' which like 'The Palace of Art' and 'The Lotos-Eaters' is a parable about the transition every soul must make if it is to escape the fate of Auden's 'intellectuals without love.' In revising 'The Lady of Shalott,' Tennyson gives greater prominence to its Spenserian elements by moving to the head of the sixth stanza the mirror in which the Lady sees the knight's reflection in another mirror, the river. His source is the magic mirror in which Britomart sees the image of Artegall (*FQ* III ii 17–26).

In the Spenserian alexandrine of the last refrain of Tennyson's song 'The Splendour Falls on Castle Walls,' it may be possible to hear in the echoed word *answer* a fading echo of Spenser's *Epithalamion* refrain (Hollander 1981a:129–30); and it has been observed that the stars are merry in *Maud* (1.629) because Tennyson 'is attended by an unmodern poet, Spenser: "All night therefore attend your merry play"' (*Epith* 368; Ricks 1981:100). But the more Tennyson assimilates into *Maud*'s garden poetry the festivity of celebration in the *Epithalamion*, the more diffused his Spenserianism becomes. We might risk a paradox and say that it is precisely because Tennyson's vision in *Maud* is so authentically Spenserian that it ceases to be consciously modeled on Spenser. As he, like Spenser, achieves the symbolic range of a miniature biblical epic in which Maud is both Eve and Mary, the virgin of the *hortus conclusus* of the Song of Solomon, we sense that these garden lyrics are less a Spenserian imitation than the vision of a lost Eden that all pastoral poetry exists to express.

Tennyson's explanation that Arthur is 'Ideal manhood closed in real man' ('To the Queen' 38) owes more to Tasso's outline of the allegory in *Gerusalemme liberata* than to Spenser's elaboration of his allegory in the Letter to Raleigh. Yet in embracing the drift of epic toward romance and psychology, Tennyson is continuing Spenser's own practice. He even turns Merlin's 'looking glasse' in *FQ* III ii 18 into a psychological metaphor, the 'glass' of Merlin's 'presageful mood' (*Merlin and Vivien* 293). And he makes clear that to be loyal to Arthur is to be loyal to more than the authority of a sovereign. It is to be 'loyal to the royal' in oneself.

Tennyson seems to be a High Church agnostic who admires everything about medieval allegories except their theological content. Gareth's most formidable opponent, the Star of Evening, though curiously resilient like Maleger, is physically decrepit. In Gareth's last antagonist, Tennyson parodies Spenser's sad and serious portrait of Night, the progenitor of Duessa, the mere counterfeit of light (*FQ* I v 20–45). The collapse of Tennyson's pasteboard figure, who as a 'blooming boy' proves to be the least dangerous of Gareth's opponents, makes mock-heroic use of Artegall's misdirected attack on the armed Britomart (IV vi 19). Few passages in Tennyson better illustrate the growing separation of sign and referent in Victorian allegory. Tennyson's Night uses the bare derisive mask of allegory – skeletal and grimacing.

As Tennyson more directly identifies each successive adversary with a psychological reaction in the minds of Gareth and the reader, these parodic Malegers and Britomarts, like other characters in *Idylls of the King*, become familiar and untamed potentialities of every heart and mind. The reader who seeks the comfort of allegorical understanding is made to feel as insecure as Arthur. He lacks the security of any vantage point from which to hammer into certainty Arthur's platitudes about prayer or Merlin's weird prophecies about dying to come again. It is as if Tennyson were continually using allegory to subvert allegory. If he finds he can be most contemporary by being most medieval, most psychological and agnostic by being most Spenserian, it is because few poets have a deeper sense of Spenser's own feeling for the emblems of inwardness and mystery. W. DAVID SHAW

Alfred, Lord Tennyson 1969 *Poems* ed Christopher Ricks (London). William E. Buckler 1980 'Tennyson's *The Lotos-Eaters*: Emblem of a New Poetry' in *The Victorian Imagination: Essays in Aesthetic Exploration* (New York) pp 101–18; J.M. Gray 1980 *Thro' the Vision of the Night: A Study of Source, Evolution and Structure in Tennyson's 'Idylls of the King'* (Montreal); Hollander 1981a; Paul Leveloh 1909 *Tennyson und Spenser* (Marburg); Robert Pattison 1979 *Tennyson and Tradition* (Cambridge, Mass); J.F.A. Pyre 1921 *The Formation of Tennyson's Style* (*UWSLL* 12; Madison, Wis); Christopher Ricks 1981 'Tennyson Inheriting the Earth' in *Studies in Tennyson* ed Hallam Tennyson (London) pp 66–104; Alan Sinfield 1971 *The Language of Tennyson's 'In Memoriam'* (Oxford).

Terpine After resolving the dispute between Bracidas and Amidas, Artegall encounters a 'haplesse' knight about to be hanged by armed women (*FQ* V iv 21–35). Disdaining to attack women himself, he sends Talus to disperse them with his flail. When the knight is freed and brought to him, Artegall recognizes him as Sir Terpine (26; in 1596, Sir Turpine), who explains that the Amazon Radigund captures knights and forces them to dress and work as women; whoever refuses is hanged. Although he has rebuked Terpine for submitting to women – in fact, Terpine is about to be hanged for not submitting to them – and then blaming fate, Artegall himself will submit to Radigund all the more disgracefully; and he will blame the heavens for his delay in fulfilling his quest (xi 41). After leading Artegall to Radigund's city, Terpine is again defeated by her, is recaptured, and, when Artegall is also defeated by her the next day, is finally hanged (v 18).

Terpine's name carries connotations of shame (L *turpis*, though the name Turpine will be reserved for Calepine's opponent in Book vi); he is also 'thrice wretched' in that Artegall offers three possible explanations for his dilemma when he first addresses him (Cheney 1966:203). As Terpine replies, 'Most haplesse well ye may / Me justly terme, that to this shame am brought.' Like the similarly named Terwin in the Despair episode (i ix 27–30), he fails to survive an encounter from which the protagonist is ultimately rescued. Yet despite echoes of the earlier episode (most notably, the halter as a sign of shameful death), Terpine does not succumb to a despairing suicide but chooses death over dishonor; and Artegall is rescued not by any faith in heavenly mercy but by temporizing with Clarinda and her mistress until he is saved by the stronger arm of his own martial maid. The story of Terpine which frames Artegall's fall and redemption illustrates the unhappy conditions under which justice functions in a fallen world: 'Artegall suffers, and Terpine and justice suffer much more' (Nohrnberg 1976:371).

Julia M. Walker

---

tetrads Spenser's narrative and thematic rationale in building relationships of four characters – tetrads – into *FQ* iv seems to have been that he wished to embody the two related virtues of love and friendship in single character-groups. Book iv, of friendship, builds on Book iii, of love, in which the relation (or hoped-for relation) between only two lovers is characteristic. His philosophical rationale, however, seems to have been that tetrads best embody Pythagorean and Platonic thinking about universal, cosmological harmony (see *Platonism, *Pythagoras). This characteristically humanist association of human love and friendship with the cosmological harmonizing of the four warring elements is central to the main allegorical locus of Book iv – the Island of Venus in canto x. An essential feature of virtuous human tetrads, however, unlike those in nonhuman nature, is that the relationship is entered freely, not by necessity.

Before we are told how they convert their strife to concord (iii 49–52), we see the titular heroes of Book iv, Cambell (1) and Triamond (2), riding abreast as protectors of their two loves, Cambina (3) and Canacee (4), who ride side-by-side behind them, completing a square formation (ii 30). 1 and 3 are bound by love; so are 2 and 4. 1 and 2 are bound by friendship; so are 3 and 4. 1 and 4 are bound in a loving and friendly blood-relationship, as siblings; so are 2 and 3. (The meanings or concordant sounds of the names of the members of a tetrad usually reinforce the relationship unless Spenser has other considerations in mind. 'Cambell' fits 'Cambina,' but 'Canacee' necessarily perpetuates Chaucer's name for the character. 'Triamond' is the third member of a triad with 'Priamond' and 'Diamond.')

(See **tetrads** Fig 1.)

The philosophical basis for this kind of relationship seems to be Plato's *Timaeus* 31–2, a passage which the Renaissance considered characteristically Pythagorean. Speaking of the four elements constituting the cosmos, Plato says that the extremes of earth and fire need the two other elements water and air as the twofold mean, or connecting middle terms, to bind them together. A single mean would have bound them insufficiently and unstably. Water is bound to the one extreme, earth, by shared coldness; air is bound to the other extreme, fire, by shared warmth. Then, however, the two mean elements of water and air share 'moisture,' so that the four are tied together in harmony by common features between each pair. Other aspects of the universe and of human society are linked tetradically in this way. Spenser seems to have been thinking of this cosmological idea in creating his tetrads. Friendly love or loving friendship, modulated through various keys, harmonizes the cosmos, the nation, friends, families, and lovers. In terms of rigorously applied tetradic thinking, it is only when Cambina (with her last-minute nepenthe and caduceus of peace) is added as a second mean to Canacee that the strife between the extremes Cambell and Triamond can be ended.

The harmonizing of Love and Hate by Concord (x 32–4) gives Book iv its nuclear allegorical formulation: cosmological harmony, available in sexual love (by nature) and friendship (by veracious human art). It is triadic rather than tetradic, unless Concord's twins Peace and Friendship can be thought of as the two means (Fowler 1964:27). In any case, Book iv contains at least four tetrads. Cambell's true tetrad meets its travesty (ii 30–1): Paridell, Blandamour, Ate, and the false Florimell (who has recently replaced Duessa in this unstable, wretched relationship). Their equivocal, flickering friendship and promiscuous, jealous love are not freely chosen for loving and charitable motives but are in slavery to ulterior, passionate self-aggrandizement. Ate, the cosmological principle of discord opposing Concord in canto x, conveys her quality when she stirs up strife by seconding Duessa's paraphrase and misuse at i 46 of Britomart's first utterance (the Chaucerian lines at iii i 25 stating the need for freedom, not mastery, in love). The false Florimell's quality is suggested by her later reaction to the second of the three repetitions of Britomart's sentiment, at v 25 (the third repetition is Arthur's in ix 37): she freely chooses the worst possible (although fitting) love, Braggadocchio.

A third, very clear tetrad emerges from the story of the two faithful friends Amyas and Placidas, Aemylia (beloved of Amyas, imprisoned by Lust when she is caught in an unchaste situation with Amyas), and Poeana (viii 38–ix 17). (Poeana's father, the lust-provoking Corflambo, had imprisoned Amyas, and she had used her position to force her love on Amyas, Placidas, and others.) Arthur (with the help of Belphoebe's eradication of Lust) situates all four members so that they can freely choose each other. After physically destroying the irredeemable blocking agent Corflambo, he educates Poeana in the art of friendship (she needs no education in love that comes by nature). She and Placidas can then harmonize. Having been released from Corflambo and Lust, Amyas and Aemylia can do the same. The friendship of Amyas and Placidas continues, and that of the two women is taken for granted. The ties are not quite so manifold as in the Cambell tetrad, but the parallel is obvious.

Britomart's and Arthur's achievements in Book iv are often parallel, as, for instance, when in turn they are the protectors of Amoret, but with the difference that Arthur takes no sexual advantage of his protégée because he is virtuous while Britomart takes none because she is female (although she fulfills a male role). Like Arthur she too creates a tetrad; but, unlike him, she participates in hers, occupying two roles in accord with her symbolic androgyny (i 5–15). As a male knight she travels with Amoret, whom she protects but who fears her intentions. They seek lodging at a castle having the custom that no man may be admitted unless he is escorting a woman. A young knight also seeking lodging tries to take Amoret from Britomart so as to satisfy the custom. Britomart defeats him and leaves him without. Once inside, she establishes her right as the male protector of Amoret but then, removing her helmet, reveals her alternative role with a cascade of blond hair. She now offers herself as the companion of the knight outside so that he may gain lodging for the night. Entering, he is bound to her in friendship. At the same time she has shown Amoret that her fear is baseless: the two then sleep as friends in the same bed. (In i 47, Ate, misusing Britomart's definition of the freedom of love, describes this cohabitation to Scudamour, Amoret's lover, exclusively in terms of Britomart's male role.) By charitable manipulation, not force directed at its members as often in the travesty above, Britomart has created another tetrad in which she functions as the twofold mean between the two extremes.

There may be other tetrads in Book iv, such as the pro-tem relationship among Scudamour, Artegall, and Britomart in canto vi, where she again takes a double role with the release of her hair (Hieatt 1975a:82–3); it has also been suggested that this same group consists of four characters: Scudamour (patron of love), Artegall (having scorned love), Britomart (a mean term between them, but insufficient to achieve harmony), and then Glauce, the second mean through which all is 'upknit' (vi 30; Fowler 1964:30–1). Various tetradic scenarios with partly according names suggest themselves for Spenser's planned completion of *The Faerie Queene*: Marinell (over-reluctant in love but finally brought to his senses), Scudamour (wrongly masterful in love), Florimell, and Amoret; or Arthur, Gloriana, Artegall, and Britomart. (See also *number symbolism articles and *topomorphical approach.)

A. Kent Hieatt

Reed Way Dasenbrock 1986 'Escaping the

Squires' Double Bind in Books III and IV of *The Faerie Queene*' *SEL* 26:25–45; Fowler 1964:24–33; Heninger 1974:160–77, 372–3; Hieatt 1975a:75–94; Nohrnberg 1976:621–5, which mistakenly reverses the sibling relationships of Canacee and Cambina.

A Theatre for Worldlings (See ed 1912:605–8 and *Var* 8:1–25.) Discussions of Spenser's poetry usually begin with *The Shepheardes Calender* of 1579, but in fact his first published work appeared ten years earlier as anonymous epigrams and sonnets in the English translation of a work by the Dutchman Jan van der Noot. Commonly referred to by the running title *Theatre for Worldlings*, its full title is *A theatre wherein be represented as wel the miseries and calamities that follow the voluptuous Worldlings, As also the greate joyes and plesures which the faithfull do enjoy. An Argument both profitable and delectable, to all that sincerely love the word of God. Devised by S. John vander Noodt.*

Theatre, entered in the Stationers' Register on 22 July 1569, was published in London by Henry Bynneman in the same year. Spenser's name is not mentioned, but because revisions of most of the *Theatre* poems appear in his 1591 *Complaints*, the poems of 1569 are generally regarded as his earliest published verse. *Theatre* consists of a Latin commendatory poem by the Antwerp poet Melchior van Baerle (born c 1540), a dedication to Queen Elizabeth signed by van der Noot and dated 25 May, a series of illustrated poems (six 'Epigrams' with four concluding lines of verse, followed by fifteen 'Sonets'), and a long prose commentary headed 'A briefe declaration of the Authour upon his visions ... Translated out of French into Englishe by Theodore Roest.'

The original Dutch book, entitled *Het theatre oft Toon-neel*, had also been published in London, but by John Day. It was dedicated on 18 September 1568 to Roger Martin, Lord Mayor of London, who had helped many Protestant refugees from Flanders such as van der Noot. A French edition of the same work, also published by Day, was dedicated to Elizabeth on 28 October of the same year. For this edition, only the prose commentary had to be translated, for the poems (probably with the exception of the last four which van der Noot had written himself) were French originals: seven Petrarch translations by Clément Marot and eleven sonnets from *Songe* in *Antiquitez de Rome* by du Bellay. (It is possible, however, that the French edition was in fact earlier than the Dutch, in spite of the date of its dedication.) Spenser appears to have translated all 22 poems from the French, checking them against an English draft translation from the Dutch.

The poems in the Dutch and French editions are illustrated with etchings executed almost certainly by the Flemish artist Lucas de Heere of Ghent, then resident in England, whose 'Ode' is part of the preliminary matter in the Dutch edition. For the English version, a set of woodcuts was made after the original etchings. Van der Noot liked to have his works illustrated to make the poems more memorable (cf *The Shepheardes Calender*, though there is no reason to call *Theatre* the first English emblem book as some have claimed).

Van der Noot, an Antwerp patrician whose association with Calvinism forced him to leave his home town and seek refuge in England with many other Flemings in 1567, was one of the first Dutch Renaissance poets, and his Dutch *Theatre* is a landmark in Dutch literary history. For it, he translated Marot's poems into Dutch rhymed pentameters (calling them 'Epigrammes') and du Bellay's sonnets into regular rhymed sonnets (some in pentameters, some in alexandrines) and added four sonnets of his own in alexandrines, each on a subject taken from the Book of Revelation. He clearly intended the poetic part of his *Theatre* to culminate in these four apocalyptic visions which, as the prose commentary explains, encourage the reader to see the preceding poems, too, as poetic instances of divine revelation. The consistent emphasis on a combination of descriptive, 'visionary' poems (in English most of them begin with phrases such as 'I saw') with equally 'revealing' pictures indicate that van der Noot, like many of his contemporaries, adopted the role of the prophet-poet who seeks to offer spiritual enlightenment to his readers.

It is not known why the young Spenser, who was only just leaving Merchant Taylors' School, was called upon to translate this unusual, very 'modern' set of poems, nor why he translated them the way he did. Four of the six 'Epigrams' are rendered as rhyming twelve-line poems in iambic pentameter; the other two, unlike the originals, have fourteen lines and the rhyme scheme of a Shakespeare sonnet. The fifteen 'Sonets,' however, are all rendered in blank verse (the eighth with a puzzling fifteenth line). This may reflect an experimental phase in early Elizabethan humanistic poetry; in 1568 one finds another blank verse sonnet next to a fourteen-line Latin epigram in Thomas Jeney's translation of Ronsard's *Discours des misères de ce temps*. But in the absence of other Spenser juvenilia before *The Shepheardes Calender* and comparable work by his associates, one can only guess whether he was attempting to produce unrhymed 'sonnets' as some sort of vernacular equivalent to the then very fashionable Neo-Latin epigram. His translations, much revised, reappeared in the 1591 *Complaints* as *The Visions of Petrarch. formerly translated*, and as *The Visions of Bellay* (with four poems added, but without van der Noot's four apocalyptic sonnets). Although many of the phrases of the 1569 *Theatre* are preserved, each revised poem reads like a typical Elizabethan sonnet without the curious, somewhat prosaic compactness of the earlier versions.

Even if Spenser actually volunteered to translate *Theatre* and even if he subscribed to the religious views expressed in van der Noot's commentary, the book tells us little more about his theological position than that in 1569 he was involved in an anti-Catholic publication. *Theatre* is a Protestant book, but, like Spenser's own work in later years, it is concerned with universal representations of the divine rather than with specific points of Puritan controversy. In many other ways, too, it anticipates some of Spenser's major concerns. More than any other Elizabethan, he continued to be fascinated by the visionary, at times ritual, effects of poetry (see *visions). Also, he remained intrigued by the theme of mutability. Perhaps one should conclude that, quite apart from the fact that he returned to Marot and du Bellay more than once (especially in the *Calender* and *Complaints*), his early encounter with this rather special kind of mid-century Franco-Flemish poetry continued to influence his work. JAN VAN DORSTEN

Van Dorsten 1970; Leonard W. Forster 1967; Forster 1967a *Janus Gruter's English Years: Studies in the Continuity of Dutch Literature in Exile in Elizabethan England* (Leiden); Lewalski 1979; van der Noot ed 1569; van der Noot ed 1953; Prescott 1978; Carl J. Rasmussen 1980 '"Quietnesse of Minde": *A Theatre for Worldlings* as a Protestant Poetics' *SSt* 1:3–27; Satterthwaite 1960; Stein 1934.

Theocritus The last of the great poets of ancient Greece, Theocritus flourished in the first half of the third century BC. As the originator of the pastoral genre, he had a substantial but indirect influence on Spenser. The pastoral mode and motifs and the eclogue form he established and passed on to later European literature via the *Eclogues* of Virgil, were used by Spenser to great effect, notably in *The Shepheardes Calender*, *FQ* VI, and *Colin Clouts Come Home Againe*. Working in a tradition established by Theocritus and continued by Virgil, Spenser was praised by William Webbe, who considered *The Shepheardes Calender* 'in my judgment inferiour to the workes neither of *Theocritus* in Greeke, nor *Virgill* in Latine, whom hee narrowly immitateth' (*Discourse of English Poetrie* 1586; *Sp All* p 7). Later Pope, echoing the traditional association of Spenser with Theocritus in the pastoral, would say 'In the manners, thoughts, and characters, he comes near to *Theocritus* himself' (*Discourse on Pastoral Poetry* 128–9).

The case for any direct influence, however, is weak. Although Vives had recommended reading Theocritus ('Theocritus' pastorals in the Doric dialect are very charming, but the allegory must be explained in order to make them more intelligible' (ed 1913:147), and Ascham's *Scholemaster* (1570) had mentioned him, there is little justification for assuming that Spenser ever read the *Idylls* (the title under which all the extant poems of Theocritus, and poems of doubtful authenticity as well, were passed down from antiquity) or even the seven poems of roughly 50–150 lines each that form the true Theocritean pastoral sequence (Idylls I, 3–7, II). Poets in France and Italy were more familiar with the Theocritean corpus, which had been the object of humanistic commentary ever since Politian made it the topic for his lectures in Florence in 1482–3. The text of Theocritus was published a number of times from the late fifteenth century onwards, and the magnificent volume *Theocriti aliorumque poetarum idyllia* with appendixes listing the numerous Theocritean references in later pastoral poetry was published by Henri Estienne in 1579. Yet nothing in Spenser requires the assumption that he had read Theocritus either in the original Greek or in Latin translation; he neither mentions him nor, *pace* Webbe, does he imitate him directly.

E.K.'s references to Theocritus and to alleged parallels and sources (Epistle to Harvey and *SC* glosses) are thus a problem. One can appreciate his desire to bring the prestige of the name of Theocritus – 'Theocritus in whom is more ground of authoritie, then in Virgile' (Gen Arg) – to Spenser's eclogues, for the name of Theocritus was synonymous with pastoral for the humanists. Nevertheless, one may note a curious disproportion between his citing of Theocritus as a model for Spenser and his quoting from the text of Theocritus only once (*Julye* 85–6 gloss) – and from a minor poem (Epigram I) – even though he quotes Virgil a number of times. One might expect that at least one tag from Theocritus would have found its way into the emblems, where Virgil, Ovid, and even Theognis are quoted. One tends to conclude that E.K. admired Theocritus as the originator of the pastoral genre, but that both he and Spenser were less than familiar with the actual texts.

Several years after the success of *The Shepheardes Calender*, two partial translations or paraphrases of Theocritus into English were published (*Six Idillia* 1588, for Idylls II and 18; and *The Shepherds Starre* 1591, for Idyll 3). Of course, continental vernacular and Neo-Latin imitations of Theocritus abound, and Virgil's *Eclogues* were well known to Spenser's generation as well as to earlier English poets and scholars. Both Virgilian and Renaissance pastoral (beginning with Politian and Sannazaro) were shaped by the conditions and informed by the spirit of Theocritean pastoral, and one imagines that Spenser was at least familiar with the French Pléiade's imitations (eg, Ronsard 1560 'Le Cyclope amoureux,' an imitation of Idyll II). A whole set of pastoral topics and procedures of Theocritean origin were thus available to Spenser, of which the most important were the figure of the herdsman as lover and poet, and the complex thematology concerning erotic passion and poetic achievement. Colin Clout owes much to Theocritus' mythical herdsmen and archpoets Daphnis and Polyphemus, to their 'plaintive' and 'recreative' moods, and not least when he serves as a mask for the poet himself.

STEVEN F. WALKER

The standard modern text with translation and commentary is *Theocritus* ed A.S.F. Gow, 2 vols (Cambridge 1952). Two introductions see the poetry within the tradition of pastoral: Thomas G. Rosenmeyer 1969 *The Green Cabinet: Theocritus and the European Pastoral Lyric* (Berkeley and Los Angeles); and Steven F. Walker 1980 *Theocritus* (Boston). For Theocritus and Spenser, see Merritt Y. Hughes 1923 'Spenser and the Greek Pastoral Triad' *SP* 20:184–215; Robert Thomas Kerlin 1910 *Theocritus in English Literature* (Lynchburg, Va); and S.F. Walker 1979.

Theseus, Hippolytus Theseus was a mythical hero of classical Athens; Hippolytus was his son by an Amazonian queen. Despite Theseus' popularity with medieval and Renaissance writers, Spenser's references to him consist of brief allusions to traditional matter.

(See **Theseus** Figs 1–3.)

In describing the horrors of Avernus, Spenser lists those whose crimes against the gods merited punishment and adds '*Theseus* condemned to endlesse slouth by law' (*FQ* I v 35). Apparently he alludes to *Aeneid* 6.617–18 but may be translating Boccaccio, *Genealogia* I.14: 'Theseum perpetuo damnatum otio' (Lotspeich 1932:111). Later, Theseus' seat of sloth to which his flesh grew is implicitly associated with Mammon's silver stool (II vii 63). The catalogue of male lovers in *FQ* IV includes 'Stout *Theseus*, and *Pirithous* his feare [companion]' (x 27) to illustrate the virtue of friendship.

Allusions to Theseus usually focus on characters accessory to his history. Two involve Hippolytus, who was thrown from his chariot and dismembered after Theseus' wife Phaedra accused her stepson of attempting to rape her and Theseus prayed for his death. Diana persuaded Aesculapius to restore him to life as Viribus, 'twice man.' Spenser tells this story when he describes Duessa's descent into hell in order to persuade Aesculapius to cure the wounded Sansjoy (I v 37–9). (On the relevance of this story to Redcrosse's plight, see Cheney 1966:52, 62, 137 and Nohrnberg 1976:172–3.) Another reference to Hippolytus as 'the cursed sonne of *Theseus*' (V viii 43) ends a passage of mythic layering. The Souldan, dying under the wheels of his chariot, is compared to Hippolytus.

A final reference to Theseus occurs in conjunction with Ariadne's nuptial crown, worn when '*Theseus* her unto his bridale bore, / When the bold *Centaures* made that bloudy fray, / With the fierce *Lapithes*, which did them dismay' (VI x 13). Spenser follows Pausanias and Hyginus in connecting the crown to Theseus' wedding to Ariadne; traditionally, it was Dionysus' gift. The wedding is conflated with that of Pirithous to Hippodamia, at which Theseus joined the Lapiths in rescuing her. The conflated image of crown and battle has been seen as dramatizing 'the impermanence of any human attainment of concord' and anticipating the 'strife which interrupts ... Calidore's own pastoral interlude' (Cheney 1966: 232–3).

D'ORSAY W. PEARSON

D'Orsay W. Pearson 1974 '"Unkinde" Theseus: A Study in Renaissance Mythography' *ELR* 4:276–98.

Thomson, James (1700–48) Though Thomson praises and occasionally echoes Spenser in his *Seasons*, he is significantly influenced only in *The Castle of Indolence: An Allegorical Poem, Written in Imitation of Spenser* (1748). Composition of this poem began casually and lightheartedly, as 'little more than a few detached stanzas, in the way of raillery on himself, and on some of his friends, who would reproach him with indolence' (Patrick Murdoch in Thomson ed 1762, I: xiv). Thomson's preliminary advertisement declares defensively, 'This poem being writ in the Manner of *Spenser*, the obsolete Words, and a Simplicity of Diction in some of the Lines, which borders on the Ludicrous, were necessary to make the Imitation more perfect' (ed 1986:173); but *The Castle of Indolence* does not read like a burlesque. Thomson makes limited and cautious use of Spenser's archaisms, the spellings and meanings of which he takes from the glossary in Hughes' edition (1715): often we find several successive stanzas with no noticeable archaism. He frequently employs such Spenserian metrical devices as alliteration, assonance, internal rhyme, and repetition within the line, but he makes the Spenserian stanza his own: for instance, in the first four stanzas of canto 2, the verse has 'a vigour and an ease, almost one would say a lordly Byronic assumption of careless power, not it is true sustained, but never far away' (Dobrée 1959:498).

The poem consists of 158 Spenserian stanzas arranged in two cantos: the first paints the honeyed delights and some of the hidden dangers in a castle ruled by an 'archimage' or enchanter, Indolence, and the second narrates the destruction of the castle by the Knight of Arts and Industry. Thomson's allegorical castle and surrounding 'Land of Drowsy-hed' are based chiefly upon Castle Joyous, the Bower of Bliss, and Phaedria's island. His knight resists temptation and overthrows the false paradise as does Guyon, but the moral values exemplified in his quest are bourgeois rather than courtly. For instance, the allegory in canto 2 tells how the Knight of Arts and Industry, having brought civilization to Egypt, Greece, and Rome, settles in Britain to develop its agriculture, trade, manufactures, and political institutions; it is a typical eighteenth-century progress piece. At another, equally non-Spenserian, level of allegory, Thomson makes himself a dweller in the Castle of Indolence; his poem becomes an introspective meditation upon neurotic incapacity (Greene 1977).

The poem is primarily concerned, however, with the poet's calling: the struggle between the enchanter and the knight allegorizes what Thomson sees as an inner conflict between poetic roles. The indolence advocated by the enchanter in canto I is a state of creative reverie; the castle is a palace of art which houses a shifting, shadowy pageant of delight, the allurements and gratifications of romantic dream. In canto 2 Thomson ostensibly rejects the world of romantic images, from Arabia to the Hebrides by way of fairyland, which he took from Spenser and Milton and handed on to the nineteenth century (Parker 1973). He aspires to be a socially responsible moralist whose art is based on historic truth, not a self-indulgent, self-absorbed romantic dreamer.

Thomson's social, personal, and literary allegories are bound together by a Protestant belief in the moral value of work. His didactic purpose works against his romantic impulse, rather than through it as in *The Faerie Queene*; but his bourgeois, subjective poem bears witness to the adaptability of Spenser's method of moral allegory.

James Sambrook

James Thomson 1762 *Works* 4 vols (London); Thomson 1961 *The Castle of Indolence and Other Poems* ed Alan Dugald McKillop (Lawrence, Kans); Thomson 1986 *Liberty, The Castle of Indolence, and Other Poems* ed James Sambrook (Oxford). Bonamy Dobrée 1959 *English Literature in the Early Eighteenth Century, 1700–1740* Oxford History of English Literature (Oxford); Donald Greene 1977 'From Accidie to Neurosis: *The Castle of Indolence* Revisited' in Maximilian E. Novak, ed 1977 *English Literature in the Age of Disguise* (Berkeley and Los Angeles) pp 131–56; Patricia A. Parker 1973 'The Progress of Phaedria's Bower: Spenser to Coleridge' *ELH* 40:372–97; Patricia Meyer Spacks 1967 *The Poetry of Vision: Five Eighteenth-Century Poets* (Cambridge, Mass) pp 46–65.

thresholds In *The Faerie Queene*, thresholds are places of passage in a hero's journey, marking the beginning of an initiation. As boundaries where the known and the unknown meet, they are both anatomical and cosmological (as in the house of Alma and Gardens of Adonis respectively), both spatial and symbolic. Movement through specific gates or doors corresponds to continuing transitions in the quest, the crossing of frontiers of identity – social and psychological, sexual and spiritual.

The traditional symbolism of thresholds is ambiguous and paradoxical. Gates in Scripture open to paradise and to death; doors open in hospitality, welcome lovers (Song of Solomon), and anointed with blood close to protect the people of Israel (Exodus 12). They mark boundaries between sacred and profane, but may partake of both. In I Samuel 5, Dagon falls before the stolen ark, head and hands cut off at the threshold (cf Maleffort's death, *FQ* VI i 23). Jacob's pillow marks 'the gate of heaven' in Genesis 28.17. In John 10.9, Jesus is the door of salvation; in Revelation, the door of life is opened by the key of David; Christ knocks at the door; John ascends through the open door of heaven to the holy city of Jerusalem with its twelve gates. In Matthew 7.13–14, the wide gate and easy way lead to destruction (cf *FQ* I iv 2, II vii 21), while the narrow gate and hard way lead to life (cf I x 5, 35).

In classical literature, doors are places of love and death. Lovers complain of their exclusion, or celebrate their entry in marriage hymns. Doors of hospitality may become doors of death: Cassandra enters the palace of Agamemnon, and Oedipus moves toward fatal knowledge past the Sphinx at the gate of Thebes. Doors to caves, huts, houses, palaces, temples, and Hades span the sacred and profane (Haight 1950). Aeneas, guided by the Sibyl, enters Hades through a cave – a first threshold before which sit Grief, Cares, Death, Sleep, a tree of false dreams, and various monsters – and is ferried across Acheron by Charon. His encounters initiate him into new knowledge, but he issues forth, like false dreams, from the gate of ivory (*Aeneid* 6.268–90, 893–8; cf *FQ* I i 31–4, II vii 21–5).

The roles of Hermes or Mercury exhibit the various meanings of thresholds. As messenger between heaven and earth, he is the guide of souls to and from the underworld; he is patron of shepherds, heralds, thieves, scholars, and traders; he is ruler of speech, sleep, and dreams; but above all, he is the 'wayfinder,' as in the *Odyssey* (5.29–115). In Whitney's emblems (1586:2), Mercurius shows the 'perfect pathe' to the 'travaylinge man, uncertaine where to goe' who 'doth tell our wandringe state.'

The Faerie Queene abounds in such questing travelers, uncertain of their 'perillous wandring wayes' (I v 18). Gates, doors, and paths are entrances for the heroes as they wander over an ambiguous geography of forest (see *woods), lake, island, and seashore (see *Rich Strond), guided through instruction and seduction. They cross thresholds of continuing initiation. In Book I, the Red Cross Knight is led by Una, Duessa, and Mercie; he takes 'bywaies ... Where never foot of living wight did tread' (vii 50). In Book II, Guyon is led by the Palmer, Mammon, and Alma; he is met at a threshold by Medina (ii 14), ferried by Phaedria across a 'perilous bourne' or boundary (vi 10), and descends the 'darkesome way' to the house of Mammon (vii 20). In Book III, Arthur and Guyon pursue adventures through 'wastefull wayes' (i 3), and part at crossroads where they are 'doubtfull which to take.'

When Calidore addresses Artegall, his language unites several of these motifs: 'But where ye ended have, now I begin / To tread an endlesse trace, withouten guyde, / Or good direction, how to enter in, / Or how to issue forth in waies untryde, / In perils strange' (VI i 6). Quests often overlap: Scudamour's quest for Amoret at the Temple of Venus – his crossing over bridge and river, through a series of gates with threshold guardians – comments upon Britomart's actions at the house of Busirane. Though accompanied along the way by guides who help or hinder them, heroes often enter initiatory experience alone. Redcrosse and Una go their separate ways in I ii; Guyon continues 'on his way, of none accompanide' toward Mammon (II vii 2); Britomart is separated from Arthur and Guyon before she comes to the gates of Castle Joyous (III i 18–19), and she passes alone into the house of Busirane; Artegall leaves her in IV vi 44, 'Ne wight him to attend, or way to guide'; and Amoret, true to her passive 'quest,' is stolen by Lust as she wanders 'In salvage forrests, and in deserts wide ... Withouten comfort, and withouten guide' (vii 2). As in initiatory myth and ritual, threshold crossings are fraught with danger, uncertainty, ambiguity, and mystery – all qualities of the 'liminality' (L *limen* threshold), a condition of passage from one status (social, psychological, sexual, religious) to another, in which one is 'neither this nor that, and yet is both' (Turner 1967:99). Because fixed categories and identities are blurred, it is a time of uncertainty and wonder. Liminal beings, outsiders such as magicians, hermits, shepherds, salvage men, and beings of combined natures such as centaurs, satyrs, and hermaphrodites, are characterized by doubleness, as are door guardians: guileful Genius at the gate of the Bower of Bliss (II xii 46–9); old Genius, who 'letteth in' and 'letteth out' at the double gates to the Gardens of Adonis (III vi 31–2); Doubt, porter of the bridge at the Temple of Venus, whose 'double face' resembles that of Janus, who 'hath in charge the ingate of the yeare' (IV x 12). Gates themselves are often double, as at the house of Morpheus (ivory and silver, I i 40) and the house of Alma (II ix 23). Veils are similarly ambiguous and liminal: traditionally associated with separation from the profane and incorporation into the sacred (van Gennep 1960:166), they conceal and reveal. Arthur's shield is veiled (I viii 19, V viii 37), as is Una (I i 4), the face of Venus (IV x 41), and Nature (VII vii 5–6).

Doubleness, danger, and doubt are most explicitly associated with Britomart in Books III-V, for her double nature struggles to achieve equilibrium between masculine aspirations and feminine identity, aggression and eroticism. The three main components of initiation into the mysteries are exhibitions (what is shown), actions (what is done), instructions (what is said) – all often performed by masked figures (see Turner 1967:102–8 on *sacra*). They provide a way of viewing not only the thresholds at the house of Busirane and the masque of Cupid, but Britomart's instruction through encounters (with Malecasta, Marinell, and Radigund – all of whom exhibit and act out extreme erotic tendencies within herself), and through revelations (Merlin in III iii, Isis Church in V vii). When Merlin urges, 'let no whit thee dismay / The hard begin, that meets thee in the dore, / And with sharpe fits thy tender hart oppresseth sore' (III iii 21), he anticipates her passage through the entrance to the house of Busirane and her subsequent watching, waiting, acting, and leading Amoret forth – 'More easie issew now, then entrance late' (xii 43). Dominant images of doubt and deception recall her ambivalent visions of love – 'why make ye such Monster of your mind?' asks Glauce (ii 40) – and prefigure her 'misdoubtfull mynde' and 'vaine fancies, working her unrest' (V vi 3, 7). After meeting Talus 'in the dore' (9), she travels to spend the night at Dolon's house in watchfulness, between 'wrath and griefe' (34, 17). To learn that 'lovers heaven must passe by sorrowes hell' (IV vi 32) will require passage over more than one threshold. Rather than arriving transformed at a new state, heroes in *The Faerie Queene* must reperceive and reenter their own ambivalent natures.

Finally, Spenser invites the reader to view his poem as a threshold. The poet 'thrusteth into the middest ... recoursing to the thinges forepaste, and divining of thinges to come' (Letter to Raleigh); he wraps his images in 'covert vele' and 'shadowes light' (II proem 5), becoming himself a traveler through Fairyland, asking the Muses to 'Guyde ... my footing, and conduct me well / In these strange waies, where never foote did use' (VI proem 2–3), so directing his readers beyond the threshold to prospects of rescue, healing, and restoration 'to the joyous light' (VI xi 50). LYNN ANTONIA DE GERENDAY

Brooks-Davies 1977; Marjorie Garber 1987 *Shakespeare's Ghost Writers: Literature as Uncanny Causality* (London); Arnold van Gennep 1960 *The Rites of Passage* tr Monika B. Vizedom and Gabrielle L. Caffee (London); Elizabeth Hazelton Haight 1950 *The Symbolism of the House Door in Classical Poetry* (New York); Louise Carus Mahdi, Steven Foster, and Meredith Little, eds 1987 *Betwixt and Between: Patterns of Masculine and Feminine Initiation* (La Salle, Ill); Victor Turner 1967 *The Forest of Symbols: Aspects of Ndembu Ritual* (New York).

time In Spenser's poetry, time manifests itself in complex ways. It appears, as it commonly does in Renaissance literature, as an obsessive preoccupation, both pervasive and intricate, and may be analyzed from five perspectives: as conventional images; as conventional temporal sequences and measurements (eg, the calendar year, which provides the structural and thematic basis for *SC*); as the interplay of traditional *topoi* concerning time (eg, being linear and/or providential); as developed images, either lyrically or narratively extended, that express one or more temporal concepts; and, especially interesting, as narrative time, particularly in *The Faerie Queene*.

conventional images These include general images of decay and human time-wasting, traditional motifs, and iconographical details associated with the personified figure of Time.

Images of decay abound, for 'All things decay in time, and to their end do draw' (*FQ* III vi 40). *Ruines of Rome* and *Ruines of Time* are extended accounts, imagistically familiar and unmistakable, of the irreversible destruction of human existence and its artifacts by time. The most common images evoke the seasonal cycle, such as the withered flower which symbolizes the radical transitoriness of existence (that 'lyke flowres untymely fade' *Amoretti* 79). Other images specifically exemplify the decay of human achievements. The dungeon beneath the house of Pride (I v 45–51) contains various exempla of the 'antique ruines of the *Romaines* fall,' all of which point to the inevitability of human waste. The house itself is an unstable edifice resting precariously upon shifting foundations (cf the 'statelie Towre' in *Time* 512–14). Cupid's pageant in the house of Busirane includes 'Lewd *Losse of Time*' (*FQ* III xii 25). Such images of decay show the essential correspondence between these unstable labors and the 'fraile mansion of mortality' itself (VI iii 28).

Traditional temporal motifs include such classical topoi as *carpe diem*, *carpe florem*, and *ubi sunt*. The 'lovely lay' which Guyon hears as he enters the Bower of Bliss (II xii 74–6) urging him to pluck the virgin Rose exemplifies the first two topoi. *Ubi sunt* constitutes an implicit construction in Spenser's catalogues of the fallen mighty of the past, such as the empires in *Time* (eg, 'What nowe is of th'*Assyrian* Lyonesse, / Of whome no footing now on earth appeares?' 64–5). The convention that only the power of poetry can defeat the depredations of time recurs persistently, for example in *Amoretti* 75. In *Time*, Spenser varies the motif to include the historian Camden (174–5; cf *FQ* II ix 51–60, IV xi 10).

The iconographical personification of Time, so characteristic of Renaissance art and literature, does not appear frequently in Spenser. In the Garden of Adonis, the figure of Time which has been called an 'activated abstraction' (Alpers 1967b:7) carries the traditional scythe, possesses 'flaggy wings,' and engages in the destructive activity of mowing life (III vi 39). In the *Cantos of Mutabilitie*, Time appears as 'an hory / Old aged Sire, with hower-glasse in hand' (VII vi 8); and in the penultimate stanza, Spenser laments that 'Short *Time* shall soon cut down [life] with his consuming sickle.' Mutabilitie herself is an image of growth and decay, that is, of transience within the impermanence which characterizes the fallen world. *Epithalamion* refers to the 'feathers' of Time (281; cf *Heavenly Love* 24). There are implicit allusions to Time in the 'chamfred browes, / Full of wrinckles and frostie furrowes' in *SC, Februarie* 43–6, which invokes the Time-figure without explicitly naming it. Isolated allusions to the 'rust of age' (*Rome* 174) or 'blacke oblivions rust' (*Time* 98), or even the rust that overgrows Mammon's 'yron coate' (*FQ* II vii 4) belong to the category of images that specify time, or the effects of time, by the use of traditional iconographical detail.

temporal sequences Conventional sequences of time (months, days, and hours) are used by Spenser as thematic and structuring devices. In the *Cantos of Mutabilitie*, Mutabilitie presents a pageant of the 'thousand sorts of *Change*' (VII vii 25) to which humankind is subject. It is called forth by Order acting under Nature's command, begins with the Seasons ('First, lusty *Spring*, all dight in leaves of flowres' 28), proceeds through the Months, Day and Night, and the Hours, and concludes with Life and Death. It demonstrates her claim that '*Time* on all doth pray' (47). As a whole and in each subdivision, it shows that time is the condition both of transience and decay and of growth and renewal. The tension between these concepts creates a rich suggestiveness, for not only do all things decay in time but time is a condition of becoming, as shown in the Garden of Adonis (III vi). The calendrical organization of *The Shepheardes Calender* also shows time as recurring. Both the laments for the passing of time and the reflections upon maturing within time (in particular, Colin's song in *December*) are framed by the structural pattern of seasonal recurrence, and show that human life is lived linearly (historically and providentially), as a pilgrimage, within cyclical natural patterns. Similarly, the daily sequence of hours provides a structure for *Epithalamion* (see **Amoretti, Epithalamion*; also *number symbolism).

traditional topoi The interplay of topoi concerning time constitutes a traditional dimension in Spenser's poetry. Since time is the condition of human existence, every human action and attribute must be seen in terms of transience: everything passes ('in the passing of a day' II xii 75) in terms of prior antecedents, future direction, and an eternal standard. Some of the most important time-concepts that occur in Spenser's poetry are that it is linear (from Creation to Apocalypse), that it is providential, that it can be psychologized (Spenser follows the Augustinian position that subjective time is opposed to the physical concept of time as the measurement of motion), that it can be abstracted into particular images representing timeless (because unchanging and universal) aspects of time, that it parallels eternity as its moving counterpart, that it curves upward towards eternity in a final juncture that defines the purpose of both individual existence and historical collectivity.

In the *Fowre Hymnes*, eternity is expressed in largely Neoplatonic terms: it encompasses a number of timeless patterns which have served as the models for physical existence. The 'great workmaister' cast all things ('such as we now behold') according to the perfect mold of a 'goodly Paterne' (*Hymne of Beautie* 29–32). Whether the patterns or ideas are placed within the workmaster's mind (the Christian view) or allowed to subsist independently (the Platonic view) matters less than that the world is conceived generally as a number of physical existences which owe their essential identity to, and must be judged by, certain timeless standards. Two conclusions follow: all temporal existence depends upon an eternal ideal which it imperfectly reflects, and time itself as a moving image mirrors eternal stasis.

Spenser attributes an eternal purposefulness to human action in time. The divine purpose is providential, and its eternal pattern (corresponding to the perfect molds that accord essences to things) unfolds imperfectly in time, manifested by individual and collective human actions. God's providence may seem obscure, but insofar as it can be known, its direction is twofold: first, that human action should tend toward the perfection of virtue; second, that human action moves inexorably towards divine judgment, either eternal salvation or damnation. Accordingly, in *The Faerie Queene*, the adventures of the separate heroes move in time towards the perfection of the hero's individual virtue.

The Shepheardes Calender embodies an analogous movement towards education and moral development. The temporal scheme of a calendar provides a paradigmatic frame for the development of a moral consciousness: the succession of typical human problems and corresponding reflections leads to Colin's meditative acceptance of, and resignation to, the passage of time in *December*. The bipolarities of time and eternity, considered either as Neoplatonic or as Christian antinomies, pervade Spenser's poetry and appear on every level.

developed images Spenser employs a number of relatively complex images that express one or more concepts relating to time as the ground of existence: as transience, recurrence, the context of moral action, and the condition of development and maturation. Some are lyrical or configurational (ie, they help to create a surface pattern of significance), while others are allegoremic (see Wilson 1974). In the latter case, the extended images are themselves narrative (ie, they are self-enclosed tales or brief allegories) and highly abstract: essential conceptual blocks within the larger allegory of the book in which they appear.

The chief instances of configurational temporal imagery refer to the seasonal cycle (the plant life that grows, withers, and dies within time but is also subject to renewal) or to rivers and the sea. For example, *The Shepheardes Calender* begins with the image of 'Winters wastful spight' (*Jan* 2) while *March* points to the transition between the 'joyous time' of spring and the 'bitter blast' of winter (4–6). *Amoretti* 4 builds upon an image of the two-sided seasonal cycle like that in *March* ('And calling forth out of sad Winters night, / fresh love, that long hath slept in cheerlesse bower'). These images focus on the concept of transience as an aspect of time, recognizing that plant life recurs in time but human life does not. The scattered images of seafaring underscore the voluntary and responsible nature of human actions in time (see *ship imagery).

An allegoreme expresses an aspect of the conceptual substructure of the 'continued Allegory' from which it is inseparable. Such allegorical imagery is common in Spenser's poetry, for example, the image of the 'goodly Cedar' which is destroyed by a 'litle wicked worme, perceiv'd of none' (*Vanitie* 85–98), the 'great Oke drie and dead' (*Rome* 379), and the maturing in time that occurs in the story of Sir Bruin (*FQ* VI iv). Another example of such imagery concerns the education of Artegall by Astraea, who represents an unchanging standard of justice which contrasts with the nature of human life since 'the world with sinne gan to abound' (V i 11). Talus, the iron man whom she seconds to Artegall to perform 'what ever thing he did intend' (12) manifests eternal justice, unmodified by the exigencies of time, attributed to Astraea and hence to the mature Artegall.

narrative time Spenser's treatment of narrative time, which is a remarkable dimension of his art in *The Faerie Queene*, presents three kinds of problems: the general uncertainty concerning the time of Fairyland (when, for how long, and in what sequence do events occur there); the use of narrative anachrony, in particular the intercutting and juxtaposing of separate narrative time-schemes; and the deformation in the sequence of parallel narrative time-schemes.

Fairyland is set in an indefinite past or indefinable present, as in earlier Italian and French romance. The use of archaic diction and spellings reinforces an impression of the historical pastness of the action. The thin line that separates historical from fictional narrative is graphically illustrated by the parallel genealogies that Arthur and Guyon read in the chamber of Eumnestes or good memory in the house of Temperance (II x). Congruence between name, place, and historical text indicates the importance assigned to memory as a precondition of narrative. Past events must be remembered in order to be narrated. The pastness of the narrative does not, of course, mean that it has no present connections. The allegorical import consistently brings narrative pastness to bear upon, and to provide equivalences for, an actual present. The span of narrative time covering the events in Fairyland is problematical. In the Letter to Raleigh, Spenser indicates that the beginning of the story would have been narrated in the unwritten twelfth book devoted to recounting the events of Gloriana's annual twelve-day feast. The stress upon 'Annuall' suggests that Spenser had in mind twelve separate adventures taking place during the span of a single year with narrative lines stretching forwards and backwards as required. However, internal evidence often suggests periods longer than a single year. Also, it is impossible to determine precisely the sequence or chronology of the events narrated. There is overlap, for example, when Braggadocchio reappears during the tournament in Book IV. Neither the duration of the internal time span nor the chronology in Fairyland is given sufficient detail to be clearly determined.

Generally, Spenser's control of narrative time depends upon his awareness that in narrative there are no reasons (other than specific genre-memory or custom) why time cannot be almost boundlessly anachronic. There are, on the order of narrative, neither natural nor necessary temporal sequences, as Spenser notes in the Letter when he observes that the method of 'Poets historicall,' unlike that of historiographers, allows him to thrust into the midst of the action 'even where it most concerneth him.' However, his method involves more than just beginning *in medias res*. It assumes that the chronological order of a story can be modified by intercutting with the distinct time-schemes of embedded narratives, or by doubling and foreshortening. The conceptual distinction between story (what can be told) and narrative (how it is told) is important in understanding Spenser's narrative anachrony.

Analepsis, the device of alluding to a moment in the story prior to the present narrative instant, may include exposition (III ii), background (II x), summary and recapitulation (Guyon's 'pitteous tale' in II ii 45–6 or the dwarf's account of Redcrosse's misadventures in I vii 26–7). *The Faerie Queene* itself is profoundly analeptic in that the festival in Cleopolis, from which the separate adventures were to have begun, would have been narrated only in the twelfth and final book. Spenser's narrative anachrony is further evident in his complex use of embedded narratives each having its own temporal sequence. Phedon's tale (II iv 17–33) and the Squire of Dames' tale (III vii 51–60) are examples of temporally distinct embedded narratives. There are several pseudo-narratives (tales recounted only to deceive), such as the account Duessa gives to Redcrosse of her past (I ii 21–6), but the principle of distinct time-schemes within embedded narratives applies to these as well. Spenser employs ecphrasis throughout *The Faerie Queene*, such as the tapestry depicting 'all *Cupids* warres' (III xi 28–46). These intercut embeddings of temporally distinct narratives help to create the impression of many time-schemes, each subject to variation and modification, coexisting, though distinct and distant from each other, in a condition of narrative interpenetration.

The most emphatic mode of narrative anachrony in *The Faerie Queene* occurs in the careful deformation of specific time-schemes. Spenser recognizes that any story may be doubled by telling it through the focalization of two (or more) characters (eg, VI i 16–20, ii 43). Once a story has been focused through another character (thus doubled), it may be extended or foreshortened as the narrative requires. Stories may be narrated, then, according to a double time-scheme with at least two temporally distinct narratives of the same story embedded in the containing narrative of the book. Or there may be an extended and a foreshortened version, each of which may be appropriate to the focalized character. For example, after Una is deserted by Redcrosse, she pursues him for a long time: 'She wandred had from one to other *Ynd*,' the narrator explains, and stayed a 'long time' with the 'salvage people' after which Satyrane 'kept her goodly company' in order to learn her 'discipline of faith and veritie' (I vi 2, 19, 31). The parallel narrative in which Redcrosse's adventures are recounted creates an impression of speed. His time-scheme is foreshortened while hers is extended. After he is imprisoned in the dungeon, he seems to spend a long time in captivity, as indicated by his physical description and by his explicit statement that he has lain in the dungeon for the duration of three moons (viii 38, 41). Una seems to underscore the point when she laments that Redcrosse 'his better dayes hath wasted all' (28). However, Arthur seems to spend only a short time in rescuing him. Thus the time-scheme of Redcrosse's imprisonment is extended while that of his rescue is foreshortened. Similar doublings of narrative time are found in each of the books: for example, varying amounts of time are required for different characters to reach the Bower of Bliss (II); Timias' separation from Arthur is radically extended for the former but contracted for the latter (III and IV, with the actual reunion occurring at VI v 23–5); Artegall endures Radigund's thralldom for a long time while Britomart appears to require only two days from the moment she hears Talus' account until she rescues him (V v-vii); and when Pastorella is captured by the Brigands, she is said to spend a great deal of time under 'continuall watch and ward,' but Calidore hears of her captivity on the very day of the Brigands' attack and rescues her the same night (VI x-xi). In each of these instances, the story-time is doubled by creating two distinct focalizations. It is appropriate in an allegory for characters to languish in captivity, but also to be rescued swiftly. Spenser's use of deformed time-schemes, like his use of narrative anachrony in general, invariably serves conceptual ends. The deformed time-schemes indicate logical relationships of priority, contingency, and subordination. The time experienced by different characters is, thus, symbolically appropriate. Doubling the narrative time of a story makes explicit the relationship between characters on the level of the abstractions which they embody.

On all levels, then, Spenser's sense of time proves to be intricately complex. It is a measure both of his conceptual grasp and of his narrative control.

R. RAWDON WILSON

Chatman 1978; Goldberg 1981; Kaske 1975; L.C. Knights 1946 *Explorations: Essays in Criticism Mainly on the Literature of the Seventeenth Century* (London); Lewis 1954; Panofsky 1939; P.A. Parker 1979; C.A. Patrides, ed 1976 *Aspects of Time* (Manchester); Georges Poulet 1956–9 *Studies in Human Time* tr Elliott Coleman, 2 vols (Baltimore); Richardo J. Quinones 1972; Quinones 1976 'Time and Historical Values in the Literature of the Renaissance' in Patrides 1976:38–56; Joan Rees 1985 'Past and Present in the Sixteenth Century: Elizabethan Double Vision' *Trivium* 20:97–112; C. Thompson 1985; G. F. Waller 1976 *The Strong Necessity of Time: The Philosophy of Time in Shakespeare and Elizabethan Literature* (The Hague); Waller 1986; Robert Rawdon Wilson 1971–2 'The Deformation of Narrative Time in *The Faerie Queene*' *UTQ* 41:48–62; Wilson 1974.

Time, The Ruines of. See ***Complaints: The Ruines of Time***

Timias The narrative history of Timias offers an unusually clear example of the ways Spenser accommodates the characters and incidents of *The Faerie Queene* to various intertextual and extratextual pressures. As the loyal squire of Books I and II becomes the historical courtier of Books III and IV and again becomes the loyal squire in Book VI, his career charts both the ideal successes and the real dangers of the Renaissance courtier who would be an honorable and virtuous gentleman. This shifting of allegorical emphases also highlights the problems of trying to force Spenser's poem into a rigid allegorical scheme.

Timias first appears as Arthur's unnamed squire in I vii 37. Carrying Arthur's 'heben' spear and a 'horne of bugle small' (viii 3), he assists in the defeat of Duessa and Orgoglio. In Book II, he again carries Arthur's spear and shield (viii 17), blows his magic bugle (ix 11), and assists Arthur in battle – this time against Maleger, Impotence, and Impatience (xi 17–48). In both episodes, he serves to clarify the moral virtue of Arthur, knight of Magnificence and human instrument of divine grace. Like Arthur, Timias is a 'fresh bud of vertue springing fast' (I viii 27) and stands as a 'bulwarke' (12) against the forces of evil. As well, by his bugle – which is analogous to the horn of justice given by Logistilla (Reason) to a good Englishman in *Orlando furioso* 15.14–15, to the horn of Roland, and to the horn of salvation figuring the redemptive power of the Word of God (Rom 10.18, Josh 6.3–20, Rev 8–9) – he somewhat idealistically affirms the power of truth to see through and defeat the forces of deceit. In all three features, Timias helps define the 'righteous man' (I viii 1) through whose efforts God's grace operates in earthly affairs. The only complication of the two incidents occurs when he defends and rescues Arthur and, with 'stedfast hand,' keeps his fainting lord on his horse while leading him back to the castle of Alma (I viii 12; II xi 31, 48). Here Spenser shows that even the instrument of earthly salvation may need help from a 'weaker hand.'

In Books I and II, Timias functions solely as a secondary character, a dutiful squire. In Book III, however, he acquires both an individualizing name and a history. In fact, he receives a double history, for his story is shaped by two distinct extratextual narratives. The first derives from Ariosto's *Orlando furioso*, the second from contemporary relations between the chief persons to whom Spenser addresses *The Faerie Queene*: Elizabeth and Raleigh. In III i 18, as Arthur and Guyon chase Florimell, Timias – here first named – chases the Foster who has been chasing her. Although he manages to defeat him and his two brothers, he is wounded in the thigh and falls into a 'deadly swowne' (v 26). He is discovered by Belphoebe, who is also on a chase for a beast she has wounded. Her heart is pierced with pity, and she treats him with a special, unnamed herb. On awakening from his swoon, Timias is struck by her beauty, believing at first that she is an angel or goddess. After she and her nymphs take him to her forest glade, she cures his wound but wounds his heart. He tries to quell his passion for her, but it soon overwhelms him. The love-chase in which he is initially wounded suggests his susceptibility to lust (see *Foster), but that he will be faithful to the promise of his name (Gr *timios* honored) is suggested by his determination never to love disloyally. He prefers to die rather than 'with dishonorable termes her to entreat.'

The issues broached here are clarified by the literary and historical analogues, chiefly Ariosto's pastoral idyll in *Orlando furioso* 14 in which the beautiful though proud Angelica is chastened by her love for the wounded Medoro, whom she cures with herbs. Spenser may initially have chosen this episode because he saw it as an allegory of honor, as did Harington (Ariosto ed 1972:218). But his other source will not allow any Ariostan resolution, for Belphoebe 'shadows' the Virgin Queen. Spenser must radically rewrite Ariosto's climax, which occurs when Angelica permits Medoro 'to pluck ... the virgin rose' (19.33 in ed 1968). It is this rose that Belphoebe withholds from Timias (51), thereby maintaining her role as Virgin and her identification as the Tudor Rose, the mistress of England in whose person was combined the beauty of Venus and the chastity of Diana. In this episode, the fanciful promise of the literary source confronts and frustrates the reality of the historical one.

The cult of Elizabeth informs and defines the ideal, if problematic, position of the courtier who would participate in such a love-pageant as that of III v. The fictional Timias, like the historical Raleigh, must find the terms by which to respond fully to his lady's double nature – to her femininity *and* to her sovereignty. But the historical identity of Timias is less important to the canto than its depiction of the formal adoration Elizabeth demanded and received from her courtiers. All the conventional terms of such public 'courting' are here: representation of the Queen as both human and divine, as woman and ruler, as grace and chastity. Timias' difficulty in mastering his conflicting emotions, his struggle to achieve an *unspoken* manner by which to offer both passionate wooing *and* chaste service, defines the ways Elizabeth and her courtiers adapted Petrarchan and Platonic love-roles into serious vehicles for expressing personal loyalty to her. Timias represents honor, therefore, as he is honored by Belphoebe: it is in such transfers of 'grace' that we perceive the political morality of the episode. Thus, while Spenser focuses on Timias' internal conflicts, he also sketches the idealized form of Elizabethan courtly and courting conduct. As one of the pageants that love plays (v 1), the Timias-Belphoebe episode offers a political norm of high desert and chaste honor.

In Book IV vii, however, Spenser's fiction suddenly takes account of the pressures of contemporary history, for Raleigh's secret marriage to one of Elizabeth's maids of honor, Elizabeth Throckmorton, was revealed in 1592: she was banished from the court, and Raleigh was not to return to royal favor for five years. Timias' devotion for Belphoebe becomes a dramatic instance of queenly favor lost, of exile from her company, of his dishonor and her 'deepe disdaine, and great indignity' (36).

While hunting with Belphoebe and her wood nymphs, Timias becomes separated from her and encounters Lust carrying off her twin, Amoret. Though unable to defeat him, he does force the monster to drop Amoret. When Belphoebe returns having slain Lust, she discovers her squire with 'that new lovely mate,' kissing her, 'handling soft' her wounds, one of which he has inflicted himself. Outraged, she considers slaying them both but instead asks – with heavy import – 'Is this the faith,' and abruptly forsakes him. So dishonored, Timias retreats to the woods where, overcome by melancholy, he becomes so hirsute that even Arthur cannot recognize him. The canto ends with Arthur departing 'Till time for him should remedy provide, / And him restore to former grace againe.'

As the fiction yields to reality, Spenser

redeploys his Ariostan source. Timias becomes not the favored Medoro but the mad Orlando, pining away for his now unrealizable love. Historically, Raleigh referred to Elizabeth as Belphoebe in lamenting his disgrace (*Ocean to Cynthia* 327–30 in ed 1951). While Amoret is not Timias' wife and cannot therefore represent Throckmorton (but see Oakeshott 1971), it is clear that Spenser subjects the courtship of Book III to increasing psychological analysis. And this, perhaps, is the function of Amoret in the episode, for she makes not only tangible but problematic the doubleness of Belphoebe/Elizabeth. Timias is unable to mediate between sovereignty (Belphoebe) and womanhood (Amoret), and the accommodation he apparently learns in Book III is now torn apart by the conflicting demands of public courtier and private lover. Like the historical Raleigh, he loses both his good name and his position once the Queen refuses to honor him. Spenser moralizes both the fictional and the political lesson at the beginning of canto viii: 'the displeasure of the mighty is / Then death it selfe more dread and desperate' (cf Prov 16.14).

Spenser completes the Timias-Belphoebe story in IV viii 2–18. As Timias consumes himself through sorrow and weeping, he is visited by a turtledove also mourning a lost love. Spenser may have linked this traditional image of steadfast love to the 'milke white Dove' Raleigh calls the Queen in his poem. The dove bears Timias' heart-shaped ruby – a jewel given him by Belphoebe – back to her, and then leads her back to him. For the second time in the poem, she discovers the woeful Timias, pities him, and finally restores him 'to former favours state.' He reassumes the name and 'good accord' of an honored squire.

This little romance vignette is a striking addition to the historical narrative (in which, it is known, Arthur Throckmorton petitioned the Queen with a gift of a heart-shaped ruby for his sister's return to court; see Brink 1972), for Spenser depicts a reconciliation that was not to come about until 1597 – a year after the second installment of *The Faerie Queene* was published. If, therefore, we see his fiction in Book III being revised and rewritten in IV vii in order to accommodate the altered contemporary reality, he now seeks to use the fictional revision to elicit an actual one. By calling for Raleigh's return to favor, he tries directly to affect the ethical action of the court. This is one of the clearest attempts in the poem to move a particular person outside the fiction, to ensure that the 'ending end' of the narrative is not merely *gnosis* (here, perhaps, Elizabeth's knowledge of Raleigh's worthiness), but *praxis* (cf Sidney ed 1973b:83, 91).

Given this historical and practical turn in Book IV, it is surprising to find Timias in Book VI involved in an essentially moral allegory largely independent of the Raleigh affair. His wounding by the Blatant Beast could be seen as a warning that even with queenly favor Raleigh would not be free from court backbiters and slanderers, but there is no need to force the historical allegory. What seems more to Spenser's point is that Timias' trials and troubles in Book VI make him an appropriate example of the risks to personal honor of any public figure. Spenser rewrites the earlier private ambush of three lustful foresters into the more public attack of Despetto, Decetto, and Defetto. Again wounded (that is, his honor tainted), Timias (along with Serena – Raleigh's name for his lady in his poem 'Now Serena bee not coy'; see Oakeshott 1971:220–2) is finally healed by the wise Hermit, who argues that the only way to protect against the bite of the Beast is to avoid the occasion of ill. Such counsel of withdrawal from society – a rustication very different from that in Book IV – may express Spenser's own darkening view of the unrealizable ideal in Book III.

Timias' final appearance in the poem (VI vii) involves Mirabella, the conventional 'cruel fair' of the Petrarchan love tradition. Sentenced by Cupid and scourged by Disdain and Scorn, she expresses one aspect of the cult of queenly adoration: without the sense of honor that Timias represents, such adoration turns destructive when sovereign chastity becomes proud disdain and regal virtue becomes feminine scorn. Mirabella, in short, predicts a very different end for Timias/Raleigh if his beloved Belphoebe/Elizabeth were herself to misread the Petrarchan role her cult encourages. To this extent, the incident brings us back, by a negative instance, to the wholesome courtly ideal presented in the Timias-Belphoebe concord in Book III. A. LEIGH DENEEF

Gilbert 1947; Greenblatt 1973; Oakeshott 1960; and Oakeshott 1971.

Titans In classical mythology, Titans are the giant children of Earth and Sky, first-generation gods led by Saturn, deposed by Saturn's son Jove, and after their rebellion hurled to Tartarus. One Titan, Hyperion, begot the sun, so Titan is also a solar epithet; Spenser uses it this way fairly often (eg, *SC, Julye* 59). Most of Spenser's giants resemble Titans and some are identified as such. Argante, Ollyphant (*FQ* III), Disdain (II, VI), and Mutabilitie (VII) are all Titanic giants of Spenser's own invention; and, since Orgoglio (I) is a 'sib' (VI vii 41) of Disdain, his equal and opposite in sexual pride, he too is one.

Spenser's Titans, however, derive primarily from the sometimes conflicting information in Renaissance mythological handbooks (Starnes and Talbert 1955). These Titans are the sons or brothers of the giant Titan, who gives up his rule to his younger brother Saturn on the condition that the latter sacrifice a dynasty by eating his male offspring (see VII vi 27); the plan fails when through trickery the infant Jove is preserved from his father's maw. The Titans rebel against Saturn and chain him until Jove, having seized power, suppresses his insurgent Titan relatives and liberates his father without (of course) restoring him. Earth begets other giants, who heap up mountains to assault Olympus; like many other writers, Spenser sometimes merges these two wars (eg, III vii 47) and uses *Titan* and *giant* synonymously.

With a few exceptions like Hecate and Bellona (VII vi 3), Titans are archetypal rebels and blasphemers, refusing, like Mutabilitie, to accept Jove's right of conquest and 'Fates decree' (33); but because they misuse power, they are also 'tyrants.' Interestingly, though, Spenser's most political giants are the least explicitly Titanic, perhaps because he knew the myth of the Titans was also read as metaphysics and science. Conti, for example, says that Titan and Saturn together represent the operations of time, the forces of generation and decay working through elements that perpetually move upward only to meet superior energies and bodies that in turn dissolve or repel them (*Mythologiae* 6.20). Titans thus indicate, in frightening and perverted (because inflated) shape, an upsurge of mutability and mortality, of matter that resists or swallows form, of all that is elemental, primordial, and libidinous. Mutabilitie and Argante, Spenser's two female Titans, reinforce this significance, for Titans are closely associated with their mother Earth (not the Olympians' mother the earth goddess Rhea, but old Gaea, 'the very essence of the earth': Fraunce *The Third Part of the Countesse of Pembrokes Yvychurch*).

Uprisings of giants may be resisted on behalf of spirit, order, reason, patriarchy, and right; but the giants themselves cannot be eliminated. Titanic impulses in the individual, commonweal, and cosmos can be deflated like Orgoglio, chased off like Argante and Ollyphant, subdued like Disdain, or restrained like Mutabilitie; but they survive in Fairyland – and England – until the God of Hosts (also, through his chosen people, a queller of giants) establishes his 'stedfast rest.' ANNE LAKE PRESCOTT

---

topographical description To make imagined situations and scenes comprehensible and meaningful, Spenser typically connected them with familiar details of British history and landscape. According to his contemporaries, topography (or chorography), the description of particular places, differed from geography, which used mathematics to show relationships among locations in the whole earth, and from cosmography, which treated the four elements and the circles of the celestial spheres. Physical description of the landscape constituted only one part of topography, to which anything pertaining to local history and customs was appropriate.

Classical and medieval writers had produced topographical description only sporadically or incidentally, leaving the Renaissance few notable models. The *Mosella* and *Ordo nobilium urbium* of Ausonius (4th c) are the most significant early pieces and perhaps led Prudentius, Claudian, Rutilius, and Fortunatus to include some topography in their work. The Renaissance explosion of interest in history, antiquities, and nature encouraged topographical writing, for example, by Petrarch (*Africa* and *Itinerarium Syriacum*), Aeneas Silvius Piccolomini (large parts of *Cosmographia*), Flavio Biondo (*Roma instaurata* and *Italia illustrata*), and Conrad Celtis (*Carmen ad Vistulam fluviam* and the immense, projected *Germania illustrata*).

In sixteenth-century England, the prose topographers John Leland, Humphrey Llwyd, William Lambarde, William Harrison, William Camden, John Norden, John Stow, and others treated cities, counties, regions, and the whole nation with great zeal, describing the air and climate, crops and soil, wild and domestic animals, people and customs, and especially rivers, buildings, monuments, ruins, and the previous names of places. The nationalism, appetite for knowledge, and quest for fame that pervaded Europe prompted them to lavish attention on the smallest features in encyclopedic surveys, the best of which are Harrison's *Description of Britain*, prefixed to Holinshed's *Chronicles* (1577, 1587), and Camden's *Britannia*, a thick quarto of 1586 that grew to a massive folio by the sixth edition in 1607. But from another perspective, handbooks of rhetoric distinguished *topographia*, the description of a real place, from *topothesia*, the description of a fictional one (both listed as figures under *descriptio*). Thus Richard Sherry in *A Treatise of Grammer and Rhetorike* (1555) exemplified *topographia* by citing the presentation of Carthage in *Aeneid* I and *topothesia* by naming More's *Utopia*. For a practicing poet, this distinction might prove arbitrary because the fictive details for invented places could correspond closely to the factual details of real ones.

The youthful Spenser shared the enthusiasm of prose topographers when he wrote to Harvey in 1580 about his plans for a poem called *Epithalamion Thamesis*, 'For in setting forth the marriage of the Thames: I shewe his first beginning, and offspring, and all the Countrey, that he passeth thorough, and also describe all the Rivers throughout Englande, whyche came to this Wedding, and their righte names, and right passage' (*Three Letters* I in *Var Prose* p 17). He expected the composition to be a great labor but planned to draw heavily on Harrison's six chapters on English rivers, which he admired. Spenser is unlikely to have got far with this extravagant poem as originally conceived, apparently having realized that such a huge amount of factual material would be impossible to assimilate without its overwhelming the imaginative features of the work. Later, when he did use topographical description, he did so for metaphors and brief examples; in extended passages, he embellished topography with personification or a mythological narrative structure. That is, he followed the rhetoricians in making topography essentially a figure of speech, in contrast to the antiquarians and historians, who made it a subject unto itself.

Spenser includes short notices or descriptions of actual places, chiefly British, in most of his poems, and topography assumes a significant but still subordinate role in *Ruines of Time*, *Ruines of Rome* (a translation), *Faerie Queene* IV xi and VII, *Colin Clouts Come Home Againe*, and *Prothalamion*. For *Ruines of Time*, which opens the *Complaints*, Spenser personifies the genius of the ancient Roman city Verulam. The speaker meets Verlame on the shore of the Thames and hears her mourn the loss of her glory. Ten stanzas of mingled topography and history (lines 85–154) comprise a closely packed account of Verulam in its prime and subsequent fall, beginning with a catalogue of its once-fine architecture and ending with the lament that the Thames now has deserted Verulam out of grief or repugnance at having blood spilled in it so often; likewise, the lake through which the river ran is gone. Verlame concludes that only Camden bothers to preserve her memory for posterity (169–75). Later Verlame enumerates failed attempts at immortality through monuments such as the pyramids, the Pharos of Alexandria, and Trajan's Danube bridge.

Two Renaissance themes merge in *Ruines of Time*: the continental love of ruins, particularly those of Rome, and the nationalistic devotion to one's native topography, the latter openly acknowledged through Spenser's praise of Camden and his choice of Verulam as subject. The poet's greatest debt is to du Bellay's *Antiquitez* and its appendix, the *Songe*, which he translated for the *Complaints* as *Ruines of Rome*; but he probably knew similar expressions by Petrarch, Boccaccio, Fazio degli Uberti, Poggio, Biondo of Forli, Sannazaro, Petrus Lotichius II, and the Englishman Thomas Churchyard, whose pedestrian topographical poem, the *Worthines of Wales* (1587), elegizes at length King Arthur's city Caerleon.

Spenser centers his later topographical poetry on rivers. In *FQ* IV xi, he returns to the subject of the *Epithalamion Thamesis*, this time with more modest aims: the narrator says he will only selectively enumerate the gods, water spirits, and rivers that attended the wedding of Thames and Medway. He then devotes most of the canto to an impressive catalogue of 18 great foreign rivers and 64 English and Irish ones. Topographical details abound: the origins of names, for example, of the Mole; locations of courses, such as those of the Tamar and Plim; descriptions of the rivers themselves, as in 'The sandy Slane, the stony Aubrian' (xi 41), and the fish they contain – ruffs in the Yar, pike in the Lindus, salmon in the Barrow.

Fortunately, the objective, factual quality of good topographical description was not a constraint Spenser held himself to. He was particularly fond of myths of locality – creation stories in the manner of Hesiod, Ovid, and several Renaissance poets – explaining how a place acquired its name or appearance. For example, he motivates the legendary story of Locrine's drowning of Humber by adding six brother knights of York drowned by Humber (all seven giving their names to rivers) and offers the apparently original account of three Irish rivers born to Rheusa and Blomius.

The Irish countryside near his adopted home of Kilcolman also prompted Spenser to invent (or, possibly, retell) two other place myths. In *Colin Clouts Come Home Againe* (116–55), Colin explains that the river Bregog secretly reached the 'bed' of the nymph Mulla (perhaps Spenser's favorite river) by dividing himself into many small streams and even by flowing underground. Upon discovering the ruse, Mulla's 'father,' the mountain Mole, rolled many huge stones down on Bregog until he was unrecognizable, a river no more. This setting also serves for the location of the trial in *FQ* VII, the narrative of which Spenser interrupts (vi 36–55) to tell how the Arlo Hill region was cursed by Diana when her handmaid Molanna (Mulla's sister) betrayed the goddess' bathing place to Faunus. Diana ordered Molanna overwhelmed with stones, but Faunus kept his promise to unite her with her beloved Fanchin to form one river. Although these myths reflect much accurate topographical observation, few readers would have known it because Ireland was unfamiliar, and Spenser modifies several names for poetic effect.

Epithalamion and *Prothalamion* present a sharp contrast in the way Spenser adapted topography to occasional poems. The setting of the former is the Cork-Kilcolman area, established almost entirely by the mention of Mulla (Spenser's name for the river Awbeg) and the less specific details introduced in the fourth stanza: the fish in the river, the fishless rushy lake, the deer sought by wolves on the mountain nearby. The setting of *Prothalamion*, on the other hand, is specific and prominent. For readers who knew London and the Thames, the poem's images must have been more evocative than those of the Irish myths. Organized by the topography of the rivers Lee and Thames, the narrative moves from the confluence of the two up the Thames to 'mery London,' past the Temple to Essex House. Ten times the lovely refrain sounds, 'Sweete *Themmes* runne softly, till I end my Song.' Whether so much topographical detail is desirable in a 'spousall verse' is open to question, but it provided Spenser with a means of celebrating two betrothals and justification for including encomia (following earlier topographical poets such as Leland, Camden, Churchyard, and William Vallans) of the homes of past and prospective patrons as well as the patrons themselves.

Instead of merely conveying antiquarian information in verse as others had done, Spenser charged his descriptions with imaginative energy and thereby caused a major shift in subsequent English topographical poetry. Examples of his influence include the Neo-Ovidian *E.W. His Thameseidos* (1600); pageants and masques by Munday, Dekker, Daniel, and Jonson; and pastorals by Drayton, Browne, and Phineas Fletcher. Spenser's most zealous imitator was Drayton, who not only included topographical description in pastorals but fashioned a catalogue of English rivers in *Ideas Mirrour* (no 24) and a virtual *Epithalamion Thamesis* in the fifteenth song of his massive topographical poem *Poly-Olbion* (1612, 1622). Finally, Spenser's influence appears in Milton, especially the treatment of topographical details, place myths, and river nymphs in *Comus* (the Sabrina story), *Lycidas*, and *Epitaphium Damonis*. Spenser's influence declined in topographical poetry after Sir John Denham's *Cooper's Hill* (1642) introduced a mingling of picturesque description and didactic moralizing. JACK B. ORUCH

Braden 1975; P.R. Butler 1953 'Rivers of Milton and Spenser' *QR* 291:373–84; Robin Flower 1935 'Laurence Nowell and the Discovery of England in Tudor Times' *PBA* 21:47–73; Gottfried 1937; Herendeen 1981b; J.K. Hyde 1965–6 'Medieval Descriptions of Cities' *BJRL* 48:308–40; Joyce 1878; Kendrick 1950; Oruch 1967; Osgood 1919–20; R.M. Smith 1935a; Gerald Strauss 1959 *Sixteenth-Century Germany: Its Topography and Topographers* (Madison, Wis).

topomorphical approach A term coined to refer to the study of literary texts composed according to a plan which determines the location of *topoi* within the body or form (*morphē*) of the text (Røstvig 1980). The numerical and symmetrical patterns of such a plan are integrated with verbal patterns based on rhetorical schemes such as *chiasmus*, *epanados*, or *epanalepsis*. One applied to the poem as a whole the rhetorical technique of unifying a sentence by repeating identical or similar words so as to join the beginning to the middle, or the middle to the end (epanados), or again the beginning to the end (epanalepsis). Within a whole poem, though, what is repeated will often be a more substantial element than a single word or group of words; parallels and antitheses may establish the linkage between parts which creates the desired form (topomorph), but a parallel may accommodate a striking contrast, while an antithesis may convey an interesting point of similarity. The point of the pattern is to unify, and the study of unifying linkages will often yield important critical insights.

The elements that create the pattern will as a rule be concrete objects, actions, and situations. In *The Faerie Queene*, acts of veiling/unveiling and elevating/debasing are recurring topoi whose function is like that of biblical types which provide insight into truths that constitute major themes. One good example is the crowning with a garland of the false and true Una at *FQ* I i 48 (eighth stanza from the end of the canto) and at I xii 8. The linkage between these balanced stanzas is reinforced by verbal repetitions, including an identical rhyme on *Queene* at the beginning of one and the end of the other.

This approach emphasizes the influence of Augustine, who told artists to imitate the creative procedure of the Deity by arranging parts in symmetrical or graded structures (see tradition of *number symbolism). Poets should incorporate into their own artifacts the structures which inform God's two great works, of creation and re-creation through Christ. The unity established by these structures points to God as their source; order unifies, and the highest beauty is found in unified wholes (Augustine *Confessions* 13.28). This argument was transmitted to the Renaissance by such writers as Cristoforo Landino and Torquato Tasso.

A few basic points of procedure in this new approach may be explained by reference to *FQ* I and II (see Røstvig 1980).

book structures *Simple recessed symmetry* is shown in the following diagram:

The topos of crowning which links *FQ* I i 48 and xii 8 connects with the topos of veiling/unveiling. Una is introduced as veiled (i 4), and she unveils after Redcrosse's victory (xii 8). When canto vi begins, she is unveiled by Sansloy as she resists him, her 'constant hart' being 'As rocke of Diamond stedfast evermore' (4). Towards the end of canto vii, Una meets a knight with a veiled diamond shield who offers assistance (33–6). The veiled Una and the veiled shield are connected by the emblematic diamond. Unveiling ensures mastery over the lion (iii 6), and the removal of the veil from Redcrosse's spiritual vision promises victory in the fight to come (x 55–8). While Duessa is darkness veiled in deceptive light (v 26), the unveiling of the diamond shield (viii 19–20) decides the battle at the end of which Duessa stands unveiled (46–9).

Confinement is another topos whose importance is indicated by its structural function. While Morpheus courts confinement (i 40–4), it is suffered in great pain by Fradubio and Fraelissa, 'enclosd in wooden wals full faste' (ii 42). The promise of redemption (43) points forward to xi 29–30 and 48, while the willing confinement of Morpheus (his sloth) contrasts with the joyous release at xii 3 when the brazen gate is opened wide so that all may issue forth. An additional link between cantos ii and xi is found in Redcrosse's confinement within armor which has become an instrument of torture, like Fradubio's 'wooden wals': his 'fyrie steele now burnt, that earst him arm'd' (xi 27). This is appropriate punishment for a man who once doffed his armor and burned with the fire of concupiscence (vii 1–7).

The topos of trees and a fountain occurs first at ii 28 and 43 when Redcrosse courts Duessa and listens to the tale of Fradubio; it is repeated with even stronger negative connotations at vii 1–7, but elevated to the highest possible spiritual key at xi 29–30 and 46–8. If we see Fradubio and Fraelissa as enacting the primal Fall, this myth of metamorphosis has been given a typological function or dimension which reinforces the connection with biblical exegesis. The typological structures which inform the Bible are reflected in *FQ* I, for topoi in the second half reveal profound spiritual truths, as do the antitypes in the New Testament. Thus the liberation of Una's parents is a release from sin (seen as confinement) through the grace of God freely given.

Houses of holiness – false and true – connect cantos iii and x, and spiritual blindness (iii 12–14) is played off against spiritual vision which induces temporary physical blindness (x 67). Redcrosse's blindness to the blatant display of sin in the house of Pride (iv 6–12, 16–37) leads to his confrontation with sin and death in the cave of Despair, where the deadly sins become a reality within his own breast (ix 33–51). The links between cantos v and viii are mentioned above. Cantos vi and vii are linked by rescues of Una: one from physical attack (vi 3–8) and the other from despair (vii 38–42). Linkages like these that serve to create a desired unified symmetrical pattern reveal the importance of interpolated tales, similes, and descriptions, as is seen even more clearly in the passage which constitutes the center of *FQ* I (see also Baybak, et al 1969).

The *extended center* is found by counting the stanza totals of cantos i-vi and vii-xii (respectively 296 and 320, or 321 in the edition of 1596). The difference is located at vii 1–24/25 (296 stanzas precede and follow). The action is simple: vii 1–7 feature sloth and feebleness, 8–18 the debasement of Redcrosse and the elevation of Duessa, and 19–24/25 Una's weakness as she faints three times. The 1596 text displays perfect symmetry (7–11–7 stanzas), while the advantage of the 1590 text is that stanzas 12–13 are at the center of the segment and hence also of the book as a whole. It is sufficiently plain that Redcrosse is saved from annihilation by 'heavenly grace' (vii 12), but it is less obvious that the simile in vii 13 is an allusion to Mount Sinai – a type of Judgment Day familiar from iconographical representations. This reading (which places Mercy and Judgment at the center) is supported by the description of the encounter between Arthur and Orgoglio at viii 7 and 9, which repeats the simile while making the connection with punitive justice quite explicit. The giant's blow is like that of 'almightie *Jove* in wrathfull mood,' bent on punishing 'mortall sins' so that he 'Hurles forth his thundring dart ... Enrold in flames, and smouldring dreriment, / Through riven cloudes.' This recalls the 'thundring noyse' and 'smouldry cloud of duskish stincking smoke' of vii 13. The connection with the beginning and the end of Book I is also plain. In canto i, Redcrosse beheads the serpent Error ('full of filthie sin') and does so with 'more then manly force,' which means that he is aided by divine grace (24; cf 19.3); later, he tempers his wrath and stays his hand on seeing the false Una (50). In canto xii, heavenly grace undoubtedly graces the betrothal scene (21–3 and 39), while the fate of Archimago is just retribution (35–6).

THE DOUBLE PATTERN The symmetrical structure of Book I coexists with a *graded arrangement* (see tradition of *number symbolism) whereby it divides into eight plus four cantos. It is significant that canto ix begins with a self-contained episode: Arthur tells his story, and he and Redcrosse join hands in friendship and exchange gifts before each leaves to pursue his particular quest (1–19/20). (As stanza 20 is transitional, the addition of one stanza in the 1596 edition makes no difference.) Since 398 stanzas precede and 199 follow, the ratio of the diapason (2:1) prevails even in the stanza totals. The narrative segment at ix 1–19/

20 has a pivotal function, so that the exact division must be intended as a structural tour de force. The topos of the joining of hands occurs again in the betrothal scene at xii 37, while Arthur's encounter with the Fairy Queen contrasts with the false Una in bed with a young squire (ii 3) or posing as the queen of beauty (i 48). Moreover, Arthur's quest is for 'That greatest Glorious Queene of *Faerie* lond' (i 3), and her combined earthly and heavenly glory is reflected in the betrothal scene when heavenly music mingles with that of the minstrels (xii 38–9).

The two pivotal centers are related through antithesis: ix 1–19/20 features strength through loving union (between virtues and between friends), while vii 1–24/25 shows feebleness and the elevation of falsehood. The vision of the Fairy Queen contrasts strongly with that of the scarlet whore; another contrast is between the sacred gifts exchanged (ix 19) and the beast that tramples all 'sacred things' underfoot (vii 18).

The *halfway point* in each sequence (i-viii and ix-xii) presents Redcrosse fired by the show of earthly glory as he fights Sansjoy (v 1–8), and humbly reaffirming his will to serve (x 63–9). (An equal number of stanzas precedes and follows these halfway points.)

canto structures Narrative segments within cantos may reveal *symmetrical patterns*, and so may individual cantos or groups of cantos. *Graded arrangements*, too, can be found, as in Book II ii, where the 46 stanzas on the establishment of temperance in the castle of Medina are divided into a sequence of 30–1–15 by the praise of 'lovely concord' in stanza 31. The halfway point in the first part (15–16) shows how Medina's two sisters violate the golden mean by staging lavish feasts, while the halfway point in the second part (39) describes the temperate feast given by Medina in honor of the establishment of concord ('Thus fairely she attempered her feast'). The pivotal stanza on concord, then, is flanked by stanzas on strife and excess and on temperance.

Canto iii of Book I shows how *events* may reveal a symmetrical pattern, and how the pattern may be supported by verbal repetitions. It shows, too, how a single segment may have a structure of its own.

1-2 2 Una's fate lamented.

3-21 19 Una and the lion spend the night in the house of Corceca and Abessa. The truth revealed by Kirkrapine; his death.

22-3 2 Corceca and Abessa lament his death and curse Una.

24-42 19 Una meets Archimago disguised like Redcrosse; his true identity revealed as he attacks Sansloy. Sansloy kills the lion.

43-4 2 Una's fate lamented.

Two two-stanza laments frame the two stories, a third occurs at the center, and the twofold repetition of 'all the way' in stanza 23 occurs again in the last stanza, thus strengthening the structure. The use of verbal repetitions is best illustrated in the passage on the false house of holiness (rhyme words are italicized):

10 her wandring knight / *pas* / *has*

11 *call* / *hand* / *understand* / *land*

15 *night* / *sleepe* / her deare loved *knight* / *night*

16 deadly sleepe

20 *call* / *hand* / *land* / *night* / *understand*

21 *has* / *pas* / her wandring knight

Cantos i-ii of Book I overlap, and the cycle of events divides the 100 stanzas into three equal parts:

i 1-33 33 *Daytime events*

1-5 5 Introduction

6-28 23 Entry into forest and exit

29-33 5 Hermit's offer accepted

i 34-55 22 *Two moves toward destruction*

34-44 11 The false dream fetched

45-55 11 The first temptation

ii 1-11 11 The second temptation leads to division

ii 12-45 34 *Redcross' two adventures*

12-27 16 Meets Sansfoy and Duessa

28-9 2 Dalliance in the shade

30-45 16 Tale of Fradubio (30-44) and Duessa's faint (45)

The 'harmony' of Archimago's creation is shown in the ratio 2:1 formed by stanzas i 34–55 and ii 1–11, at the same time that the number of transgression is featured in the three groups of 11 stanzas. (11 transgresses by going beyond the just number of the decalogue.) When Archimago assumes the appearance of Redcrosse at ii 11 (both numbers spell sin), this 66th stanza harks back to the first, thus dividing the cycle into 66–33–1 stanzas. However, the division into 33–33–34 is the basic one, and on checking the midpoint in each group we see that an Aristotelian sequence emerges. Redcrosse proceeds from fierceness ('As Lyon fierce' i 17) via temperance ('hasty heat tempring with sufferance wise' i 50) to weariness ('Till weary of their way' ii 28). As the 100–stanza cycle ends, Redcrosse has proceeded from a promising beginning to an ominous conclusion.

The trials of Una in cantos vi-vii similarly require 100 stanzas, as she proceeds from an ominous beginning (the attack by Sansloy) to a promising end as Arthur arrives. In between are her two trials in the forest (those of Redcrosse are within the enclosure of the hermitage): she refuses to permit herself to be worshiped (vi 16–19), and never considers taking Satyrane as her champion (vi 31–2). But the subsequent temptation to despair is so dangerous that she has to be admonished by Arthur: 'Despaire breedes not ... where faith is staid' (vii 41). Una's three faints (vii 20–4) are a kind of passion analogous to Redcrosse's three-day battle. Her near faint in the last stanza (vii 52) contrasts with Duessa's feigned loss of consciousness at the end of canto ii.

non-Spenserian examples The longevity of the constructivist method may be illustrated by one medieval and one Romantic poem. Bonaventura transmitted Augustine's poetics to the Middle Ages, and he applied this method in his own Latin poem in praise of the Cross, 'Laudismus de Sancta Cruce' – a rhymed poem in 39 stanzas, which is the number of the Cross (as in Robert Herrick's two poems on the same subject). An analysis of thematic and verbal structures shows that the stanzas are grouped as follows:

13 – (6 – 1 – 6) – 13

26

Again, recessed symmetry is combined with a graded arrangement, and the many chiastic (crossed) verbal patterns recall the form of the Cross. The thematic movement from joy to compassion, which divides the poem into 26 and 13 stanzas, signifies harmony restored through the Cross. (The number 13 is associated with Christ as head of the twelve apostles.)

In Keats's Spenserian poem, 'The Eve of St Agnes,' the rhyme words *cold/told/old* of stanza 1 recur in the last, 42nd stanza in inverse order. At the textual center (21–2), Porphyro first and then Madeline enter her chamber; but a graded arrangement into 14:28 is suggested when stanza 14 harks back to the first, while stanza 15 repeats the subject rhymes (*told/cold/old*), thus setting up a link with the first and last stanza. Madeline is introduced at the center of stanzas 1–14 (ie, 7–8), while the climactic entry of the lover into his 'paradise,' as he parts the bed curtains and prepares the feast, occupies the center of stanzas 15–42 (ie, 28–9). Spenser's constructivist method apparently appealed to Keats's imagination. The total of stanzas (42) recalls the 3 × 14 generations of Matthew 1. The number reinforces the impression that the story did indeed happen 'ages long ago' (42.1), but it may also suggest that Porphyro is the long-awaited savior who turns death into life.

MAREN-SOFIE RØSTVIG

TOPOMORPHIC READINGS Roy T. Eriksen 1981 '"Un certo amoroso martire": Shakespeare's "The Phoenix and the Turtle" and Giordano Bruno's *De gli heroici furori*' *SSt* 2:193–215; Eriksen 1987 *'The Forme of Faustus Fortunes': A Study of 'The Tragedie of Doctor Faustus' (1616)* (Oslo); Maren-Sofie Røstvig 1979 'A Frame of Words: On the Craftsmanship of Samuel Daniel' *ES* 60:122–37; Røstvig 1980.

topos (Gr 'place') *Topoi*, or commonplaces, are traditional ideas, images, formulae, aphorisms, and situations presented in language that is also traditional to such a degree that readers may distinguish their presence as discrete events within a work. The term is applied to literary materials derived from the rhetorical tradition of Late Latin as it was transmitted through the Middle Ages to the Renaissance. The forms topoi take are various: a compliment, an introductory or closing remark, an apology, a statement of an ideal, a list, a value judgment, a characterization, an analogy, some advice, part of a narrative, a description. What they share is that they are not peculiar to the work in which they are found but are traditional. Their functions depend upon their specificity and their context, but generally they will contribute to a work's allusiveness, in effect, its literariness.

This understanding of topoi defines a present critical usage which has developed from a more restricted meaning originating in classical rhetoric with Aristotle, Cicero, and Quintilian. For Cicero, the topoi were perspectives, points of view from which any subject might be considered productively. Those he lists in *De topica* – including definition, partition, etymology, conjugation, genus, and species – are barren of specific content (18.71). He writes, 'if we wish to track down some argument, we ought to know the places: for that is the name given by Aristotle to the "regions" [L *sedes*], as it were, from which arguments are drawn. Accordingly, we may define a topic as the region of an argument' (2.7). Considering such *loci communes* (commonplaces) would help an orator to think of what might be said about a subject. To Cicero, the *places* were *common* because either side might use them in arguing a legal case.

School exercises, called *progymnasmata*, trained students of rhetoric in the use of topoi which might be used in themes, speeches, and verse. Furthermore, the term came to be applied to content. In the Renaissance, students were encouraged to set down under suitable headings extracts from their reading that might be useful in compositions. These compilations of predigested wisdom were called commonplace books (see Lechner 1962:55–60).

Spenser may well have kept such a commonplace book. Milton did (Mohl 1969), and so did other writers. Harvey speaks with some irony of dependence on it: 'There are some men, not ineloquent in my opinion and exceedingly eloquent in their own, who think that everything depends on their jotting down in a diary proper words, figurative words, synonyms, phrases, epithets, differences, contraries, similes, and a few notable maxims; after gleaning these from everywhere, they compile them into commonplace books' (*Ciceronianus* 1557, ed 1945:91; cf *Hamlet* I v 107–8: 'My tables – meet it is I set it down / That one may smile, and smile, and be a villain!'). With the decline of rhetorical instruction, topoi were less frequently used or at least less consciously used as such.

The term was reintroduced into critical currency by Curtius (1948, tr 1953) in a survey of the transmission of classical culture from the early Middle Ages to the Renaissance. He considered as topoi motifs ranging from such a figure as the *puer senex* (youth with the wisdom of maturity) to the formulaic ending (eg, nightfall as a pretext for closing a poem). Modern discussions, directly indebted to Curtius, use the term topos more loosely than he did, so that any classically derived cliché, or even one lacking classical ancestry, may be given the label.

From the opening to the close of his career, Spenser drew upon topoi of all kinds, structural and conceptual: seven eclogues of *The Shepheardes Calender* end with the topos 'We must stop because night is coming on' (Curtius ed 1953:90–1). *Prothalamion* presents a Thames-side meadow as a *locus amoenus* (pleasant place) with a reference to Thessalian Tempe, which, according to Servius' gloss on Virgil's *Georgics* 2.469–71, is exemplary of any *locus amoenus* (Curtius ed 1953:198–9). A selective list of other prominent commonplaces in Spenser would include the chronographia or astronomical periphrasis as an indication of time (eg, *Mother Hubberd* 1–8), the comparison of poem to voyage (see *ship imagery), *agere et pati* (to do and to suffer: *FQ* I viii 44), *fortitudo et sapientia* (courage and wisdom), the theater of the world (Harvey Sonnet), the catalogue of trees (*FQ* I i 8–9), nature as the maker of the beautiful human being (IV vi 17), the outdoing topos, affected modesty, and a large number of topoi based upon metaphorical books (books of history, fate, nature, redemption, soul, heart, and the beloved's face among them) as well as permutations of this family based upon processes and implements of reading and writing (cf *Amoretti* 1, 3, 10, 43, 85).

A brief glance at one topos, *fortitudo et sapientia*, in some of its Spenserian settings will illustrate how the poet exploits the full range of this traditional element in his art, which is found in Homer, pervasive in Latin and vernacular literatures, and widely current in the Renaissance. At its lower end, Pyrochles claims 'force' for himself and attributes 'guile' to Guyon (*FQ* II v 5); and in Mammon's house, Force and Fraud are personified (vii 25). Atin appeals to Archimago, 'Helpe with thy hand, or with thy counsell sage' (vi 48). Another form of *fortitudo et sapientia* is the topos of arms and studies or pen and sword used at II iii 40, and especially *SC, October* 66–81, where Piers transcends the distinction with the claim that the prince's court is the place most fit for poesy (see Curtius ed 1953:178). In speaking of the Red Cross Knight, Spenser deliberately invokes, and splits, the doublet in the diction of heroic intent: 'He never meant with *words*, but *swords* to plead his right' (*FQ* I iv 42, emphasis added). Britomart and Elizabeth figure emblematically in another disjunctive *fortitudo et sapientia*, one differently shaped and pointed: 'Of warlike puissaunce in ages spent, / Be thou faire *Britomart*, whose prayse I write, / But of all wisedome be thou precedent, / O soveraigne Queene' (III ii 3).

One among many passages in *The Faerie Queene* in which *fortitudo et sapientia* figures demonstrates how topoi helped organize material. Donwallo, ancestor of Arthur, is introduced as 'a man of matchlesse might, / And wondrous wit to menage high affaires' (II x 37). 'Might' and 'wit' then order in turn the details that follow: stanza 38 is devoted to Donwallo's conquests, stanza 39 to his lawgiving. The sketch draws toward a close, observing that, until Donwallo, dominion 'By strength was wielded without pollicie' (39). Another panegyrical topos, that all, even the great, must die, closes the account: '*Donwallo* dyde (for what may live for ay?)' (40). These stanzas are inset in a canto deeply indebted to two other commonplaces, the praise of forebears' deeds and the book of history. Such framing and interlayering of topoi is frequent.

But perhaps most characteristic of Spenser is the topos of affected modesty, the poet's avowal of unworthiness to approach a subject. Six examples appear in the four stanzas of the proem to *FQ* I. To this convention, Spenser could bring a sly, less-modest hand. In *SC, June*, Colin's topos of elaborate modesty counters Hobbinol's topos of outdoing which claims that the Muses put aside 'Luyts and Tamburins' (59) to hear Colin overgo their art. Spenser, author of both topoi, lets his alter ego Colin have it both ways.

This review merely suggests how full, resilient, and productive was Spenser's composition with the topoi his age inherited.

GEORGIA RONAN CRAMPTON

Curtius ed 1953; Ludwig Fischer 1973 'Topik' in *Grundzüge der Literatur- und Sprachwissenschaft* vol I, ed Heinz Ludwig Arnold and Volker Sinemus (Munich) pp 157–64, 518–19; Peter Jehn, ed 1972 *Toposforschung: Eine Dokumentation* (Frankfurt am Main); Sister Joan Marie Lechner 1962 *Renaissance Concepts of the Commonplace* (New York); Ruth Mohl 1969 *John Milton and His Commonplace Book* (New York) pp 11–30; Rix 1940.

tournaments A form of public war game as spectacle that involved heavily armored knights riding one against another in an effort to break lances or to unhorse each other. The tournaments and tilts in *The Faerie Queene* derive some of their significance from contemporary practice and literary tradition. They were essentially the creation of a military aristocracy and flourished, often despite official disapproval, throughout the later Middle Ages. By the fifteenth century, however, they were used to display and assert the honor, the power, and especially the loyalty of the military class to the ruler. In the Burgundian court, whose example powerfully influenced later English practice, these celebrations reached their climax in romantic, almost theatrical tournaments which also, by enhancing the power and independence of the ruling duke, were strongly political. Both Henry VII and Henry VIII followed the Burgundian example, and the tradition was kept alive throughout Elizabeth's reign and into the seventeenth century in court ceremonies such as the chivalric spectacles of the Order of the Garter and in actual tournaments. Rules for them were first promulgated in 1464 by Lord Tiptoft and adapted for Elizabethan court practice in 1562 (see Segar 1590 and Cripps-Day 1918, app 4).

The tournaments of the 1580s were a military anachronism: the skills practiced in them were outmoded, tournament arms and armor were inadequate for modern warfare, and knighthood was no longer an exclusively military office. Yet they served an important symbolic function: they confirmed the military pretensions of the aristocracy through conspicuous display and helped to celebrate Elizabeth as the ultimate, ever-unattainable beauty at the heart of an endless quest. This function is seen most strikingly in the annual Accession Day tilts that celebrated her accession to the throne on 17 November for which there are records from 1581 onwards, though they undoubtedly began earlier. In elaborately organized spectacles, the younger and fitter members of the court would act out romance-based fantasies and stories expressing their relationship with the Queen. Although the combats were closely judged – there are even surviving 'jousting cheques' or score cards – the main point was the ceremony. Each participant entered in striking costume, often accompanied by suitably dressed attendants whose disguise and adopted roles supported the main figure's conceit. Each tilter would take some explicative text to the Queen, conveying the theme of his entry by weaving around his entrance some story, often a mixture of autobiography and allegory. There are scenes in contemporary literature that give the flavor of these English celebrations, for instance the tilts participated in by the Earl of Surrey in Nashe's *Unfortunate Traveller* and the annual jousts at the court of Helen of Corinth in Sidney's *New Arcadia* (2.21). These fictional accounts combine romance narrative and actual practice: indeed Sidney was a participant, having gone against Sir Henry Lee, the Queen's Champion (and sometime master of ceremonies for the tilts) in 1581 in the tilt of the Four Foster Children of Desire, an elaborate allegory that argued against Elizabeth's proposed marriage to Alençon (Yates 1975).

Although Elizabethan authors reflected contemporary events in their depictions of tournaments, they were very familiar with the literary tradition (which was never entirely separate from actual practice, for court entertainments were often replete with literary allusion). The portrayal of martial combat to celebrate social order and to display moral and religious conflict is found in the earliest literature. All the classical epics have battles and even games preparatory to battle (as in the funeral games of *Aeneid* 5). By the late classical period, a battle was allegorized according to the polarizing morality of Christianity, as in the *Psychomachia* of Prudentius where virtues fight vices. The martial conflicts in the Arthurian cycle (as in Malory's redaction, known to Spenser) have strong religious and moral overtones. Even the battles in the Italian romances of Boiardo and Ariosto depend for their effect on the self-conscious mockery of a deeply felt nostalgia for the older tradition of the moral tournament, which survived in popular romance.

Awareness of contemporary sociopolitical context and the extended literary tradition is essential in order to understand the allegorical significance of the tournaments in *The Faerie Queene*. Although there are many conflicts between knights that might be termed jousts (in which two knights ride against each other), there are few tournaments in which combat is formally observed by an audience. In *FQ* I, the Red Cross Knight is challenged to a 'doughtie turnament' by Sansjoy before Lucifera's court at the house of Pride. In some ways, the staging of the event follows practice familiar to the Elizabethan observers, with a few significant differences, for it is more of a personal duel than a tilt, being a mounted combat with swords *à outrance*. After the knights swear oaths 'T'observe sacred lawes of armes,' Lucifera 'is ybrought unto a paled greene,' that is, to the royal box or viewing stand beneath a 'stately canapee' and before a fenced and grassy area. The prizes are displayed publicly (Duessa and Sansjoy's shield), and then the knights begin their battle. That they do not fight on horseback immediately suggests a debased and non-aristocratic tournament; and that they seek to wound each other indicates that the normal rules of the tournament (in which only strikes are counted) have been disregarded. Moreover, the cloud that protects Sansjoy is the result of a charm that violates the 'sacred lawes of armes.' As is consistent with the allegorical context of the house of Pride, this tournament has pretensions to formal majesty yet is marked by baseness (no horses), violence (wounding), and treachery (the cloud). These distortions of normal jousting practices indicate the inherent evil of the house of Pride.

Tournaments provide the opportunity to display the ideal virtues of chivalry, including friendship among knights; and therefore such an event in a chivalric epic is a natural set piece for Spenser's Book of Friendship. Yet Satyrane's tournament in IV iv is not instituted to celebrate chivalric brotherhood but to quell the rising tide of malice concerning his possession of Florimell's girdle. Tellingly, the canto opens with the sordid and unresolved disputes of Paridell and Blandamour; and their arrival with the false Florimell and 'That masked Mock-knight,' Braggadocchio, is a warning of the acrimonious travesty into which the tournament will degenerate.

On the first day, courtly combat degenerates into violence, as often happened in early tournaments. Only the conclusion of the second day's fighting offers a suitable model for friendship in the reciprocal altruism of Cambell and Triamond. On the third day, with the arrival of Artegall, chaos follows. His guise as the Salvage Knight stresses the failure of all participants to make the tournament a civilized event: his motto reads, appropriately, 'Salvagesse sans finesse,' and his ferocity enables him to 'tyrannize ... By his sole manhood' (42–3). Ironically, his costume of leaves and moss is the only one to approximate the tournament garb worn in the Accession Day tilts (see *armor). His behavior, 'Hewing, and slashing shields, and helmets bright, / And beating downe, what ever nigh him came' (41), is in anything but the courtly style of the balletic tournament. Britomart's sudden eruption, charging him down 'in middest of his pryde' (44), seems to restore order; but the subsequent contest for the cestus reveals the superficiality of the apparently harmonious conclusion, dissolving into farce and strife. The superficial beauty of the false and faithless Florimell triumphs, only to choose to ally itself with the bogus chivalry of Braggadocchio.

Marinell's tournament in *FQ* V iii picks up so many of the themes and images of Satyrane's tournament that they are clearly meant to be read in conjunction: for example, each lasts three days, and several actions initiated at Satyrane's tournament are concluded at Marinell's. Also, there are echoes of Elizabethan tournaments: a wedding as the occasion, the many 'devicefull sights,' and knights 'full rich aguiz'd, / As each one had his furnitures deviz'd' (3–4). Unlike the description of Satyrane's tournament, however, little is said about the pageantry or costumes, and the combat of the first two days is allowed no more than two stanzas.

With their reappearance at Marinell's tournament, Braggadocchio and the false Florimell corrupt the practice and rewards of chivalry as they so triumphantly did at the earlier tournament. Braggadocchio's attempt to pass himself off as the knight of true chivalry is startlingly bold as he claims the prize earned by Artegall; and his challenge to true beauty becomes open as the two Florimells are brought side by side. The link between these two challenges is made clearer by Braggadocchio's imitation of Satyrane's behavior: like Satyrane's concealing, then revealing, Florimell's lost girdle as a relic, Braggadocchio presents his snowy maiden with an equally dubious, ritualistic flourish (17). The result is the same: a corrupting doubt concerning the validity of the original, which seduces even Marinell into thinking the imitation 'The more to be true *Florimell*' (18).

Artegall's intervention begins the process of reestablishing the chivalric order challenged in Satyrane's tournament. In repossessing the sun-shield which the boaster had used as the basis of his false claim to victory in the tournament, he asserts the right of true valor to the outward signs of chivalry. Then he demonstrates the superiority of female virtue over the outward show of beauty by restoring the cestus to its just owner and presiding over the disintegration of the false Florimell. The baffling of Braggadocchio, the representative of bogus and faithless knighthood, is completed by Talus.

The tournaments in *The Faerie Queene* operate on several levels, serving as components of the poem's internal allegory and participating in its commentary on Spenser's society. Of course, any clear distinction between these levels is ultimately futile; and the impossibility of disentangling them constitutes the richness of the poem's chivalric metaphor. The tournaments subject chivalric virtues, the chivalric ideal, and Elizabethan chivalry to the most searching scrutiny.

EDITORS

Norman Council 1975–6 '"O Dea Certe": The

Allegory of *The Fortress of Perfect Beauty*' *HLQ* 39:329–42; Francis Henry Cripps-Day 1918 *A History of the Tournament in England and in France* (London); Katherine Duncan-Jones 1968 'Nashe and Sidney: The Tournament in *The Unfortunate Traveller*' *MLR* 63:3–6; Fletcher 1971; Kipling 1977a; Leslie 1983; Schulze 1938; Strong 1977; A. Young 1987.

Tourneur, Cyril (1575?-1626) The first published work of Tourneur, author of *The Revenger's Tragedy* and *The Atheist's Tragedy*, was *The Transformed Metamorphosis* (1600), a bizarrely written satirical elegy that may obscurely commemorate Spenser's death. In a series of visions, the first half of the poem depicts the world's metamorphosis into hell. The second half (from 351) praises the hero Mavortio for slaying a hellish monster and laments that he has been killed by unexplained forces. Images of death and decline are found throughout the poem: as Tourneur declares in his epilogue, 'my subject was a heav'nly tapers death,' referring both to the sun and to his hero, who is 'Knight of the lilly' and 'heavens champion.'

The echoes of Spenser in the poem are distinct. The opening attack on the '*Hydra*-headed vice' of the Church of Rome (60) and the poet's wish to 'see ere long her *Babel* Babelliz'd' (77) recall *Visions of Bellay* 2–4. The reader first encounters Mavortio 'pricking on the plaine' (365; cf *FQ* I i 1). The battle with the beast Hyenna is reminiscent of Calidore's pursuit of the Blatant Beast (*FQ* VI) and, in certain details, of Redcrosse's battle with Error (I i).

For the figure of Mavortio, several identifications have been proposed, the chief of which is the Earl of Essex. Yet the emphasis in the poem is on Mavortio as consort of the Muses, not as champion of Mars (despite his name, from L *Mavor*, a variant of Mars). He is '*Pieria's* darling ... *Boeotia's* pearle ... tongue pure *Castalion*' (491–3). The Spenser allusions in the poem, the emphasis on Mavortio as 'warres melodie' (457), and the fact that the poem appeared a year after Spenser's death, suggest that the poem may be a disguised elegy to Spenser.

SHOHACHI FUKUDA

The text of *The Transformed Metamorphosis* is found in Cyril Tourneur 1929 *Works* ed Allardyce Nicoll (London). For discussion, see A.C. Hamilton 1957 'Spenser and Tourneur's *Transformed Metamorphosis*' *RES* ns 8:127–36; John Peter 1948 'The Identity of Mavortio in Tourneur's *Transformed Metamorphosis*' *N&Q* 193:408–12; Dorothy Pym 1938 'A Theory on the Identification of Cyril Tourneur's "Mavortio"' *N&Q* 174:201–4.

tragedy Although Spenser wrote no tragedies for the stage, he wrote various complaints and lines of plot that he termed tragedies. Most of these follow a tradition established by Boccaccio's *De casibus virorum illustrium* and continued in England in Chaucer's *Monk's Tale*, Lydgate's *Fall of Princes*, the *Mirror for Magistrates*, and various Elizabethan plays. Works in this tradition (broadly termed *de casibus* tragedy) typically sketch the rise and fall of someone famous in order to demonstrate the vanity of worldly ambitions and the greater security of rewards in heaven. In the Renaissance, the form gained popularity by appealing to Stoicism, which stressed the fickleness of the goddess Fortune and the self-discipline needed to avoid entanglements with mutable things, and Christianity, which taught contempt for the world and promised divine judgment upon evil rulers.

Spenser's interest in *de casibus* tragedy is most evident in *Teares of the Muses* (115–73). Melpomene (the Muse of tragedy) begins her lament by calling this 'wretched' world 'the den of wickednesse' and 'the house of heavinesse.' Her chief task is to teach wisdom so that mankind may bear 'this worlds affliction' and 'Fortunes freakes.' For her, the characters proper to the genre are those 'heapt with spoyles of fortune' and thus fearful of worldly loss, and the action encompasses 'all mans life,' which is portrayed as a series of miseries from the womb to the grave.

Elsewhere in the *Complaints*, Spenser presents 'ruines tragicall' in the same tradition (*Vanitie* 163). In *Ruines of Time*, the deaths of Sidney and his kin provide an occasion for moralizing on the vanity of fortune's gifts. Lines 59–75 echo a form of poem related to *de casibus* tragedy: the so-called *ubi sunt*, which inquires after great things carried away by the depredations of time. Likewise, Spenser's lament for the city of Verulam has precedents in the tradition, notably in Sackville's *Induction* to the *Mirror for Magistrates*. Although many of the *Complaints* portray beasts and even inanimate objects as 'tragicke Pageants' (*Time* 490), these, too, seem to be representations of human loss, as in *Ruines of Rome* where the city itself is personified as a tragic figure. In *SC, October*, Cuddie aspires to 'reare the Muse on stately stage, / And teache her tread aloft in bus-kin fine' (112–13), alluding to the tragic cothurnus.

Tragic convention also informs passages in Spenser's heroic poetry. In antiquity, tragedy and epic had been sister genres, with epic providing incidents and techniques of design for the drama. In *Muiopotmos*, Spenser plays upon the relation between genres when he invokes the Muse of tragedy to inspire a mock-heroic poem. In *The Faerie Queene*, he terms the career of the Red Cross Knight a 'wofull Tragedie' (I vii 24) and shapes the action in the rising and falling pattern of *de casibus* narratives. In the first four cantos, the hero rises in worldly accomplishments, enjoying such gifts of fortune as victory and fame. At the same time, however, he is falling into sin, shown in his journey with Duessa to the house of Pride; and his tragedy reaches a turning point when he offers his service to Lucifera. Although the dwarf warns him of the illustrious persons (many well known in the *de casibus* tradition) who lie in misery in her dungeon, the knowledge does the hero little good: he is imprisoned by Orgoglio, and his earthly fortunes reach their nadir in the cave of Despair.

Although Spenser often expresses the contempt for the world common among authors in the *de casibus* tradition, he is more sanguine than most about the possibility of happiness and lasting achievement in this life. In *Time* and *Rome*, for example, he allows an exception to the traditional warning that fame 'Doth as a vapour vanish' (*Time* 56), asserting that poetry can confer immortal glory. In Redcrosse's tragic career, there is no final renunciation of earthly ambitions: Contemplation sends him back to the world for a time, explaining that fame acquired there is 'immortall' and 'well beseemes all knights of noble name' (I x 59). When Redcrosse completes his quest and celebrates his betrothal to Una, the tragedy of Book I turns to comedy (Hamilton 1961a:59–76).

In Book II, Spenser's departures from the *de casibus* tradition are even more pronounced. The stories of Mortdant and Amavia and of Phedon (which the poet explicitly calls tragedies) follow a pattern more like that of classical Greek and Roman tragedy. The lesson is no longer renunciation of the world but right conduct in the world. The plots are unified around a single action, and they turn, not on bad luck or gross sin, but on understandable misjudgments or lapses in temperance. In consequence, the characters are less easily condemned than most in medieval tragedy – a point that Guyon recognizes when he leaves the judgment of Amavia to God. Tragedy of a similar sort befalls other characters in the poem, including Timias, Scudamour, Amoret, and Artegall.

Further evidence of Spenser's interest in tragedy is indicated by his frequent use and reformulation of Aristotle's phrase 'pity and fear' for the emotions aroused by the genre (Herrick 1930:31; see *Time* 579, *FQ* I vi 9, viii 39; II iv 28; III xi 12; V ix 46). It is also indicated by the masque of Cupid in III xii, where Ease appears 'With comely haveour and count'nance sage, / Yclad in costly garments, fit for tragicke Stage' (3).

DONALD V. STUMP

Farnham 1936; Herrick 1930.

trees In Spenser's poetry, trees embody symbolic meanings drawn generally from classical mythology, emblem books, biblical commentary, and contemporary medical literature, though there are a few specific sources (see *plants). In *The Faerie Queene*, trees are used in several ways: in epic catalogues, for their emblematic meanings, for their heraldic significance, as devices to identify poetic landscapes, and for the conventions associated with them.

Catalogues of trees are found in Virgil (*Aeneid* 6.179–82), Ovid (*Metamorphoses* 10.86–105), Statius (*Thebaid* 6.98–106), Claudian (*Rape of Proserpina* 2.107–11), Boccaccio (*Teseida* 11.22–4), and Chaucer (*Parliament of Fowls* 176–82). Spenser's catalogues are pieces of technical bravura within this tradition, but, apart from the list in his translation of the *Culex* (*Virgils Gnat* 190–228), only Chaucer's catalogue is a direct source.

Spenser often selects his trees for their

emblematic meaning in order to make a significant statement about their context. The trees that introduce the labyrinth of Error (*FQ* I i 8–9) are symbols of our passage through life, being emblems of secular activities – shipbuilding, agriculture, love, and warfare – set against reminders of human mortality and weaknesses. The list provides a warning and an eschatological setting for the Red Cross Knight's battle with Error. Similarly, the Garden of Proserpina (II vii 51–6) is introduced by a catalogue of funereal trees (cypress, oak, ebony) in order to express the significance of Guyon's passage through the underworld. By setting the tree of the Hesperides with its golden apples in Proserpina's garden, Spenser enforces the analogue to the fatal tree in Eden, and associates Mammon's power with death. The association of the Fall with the Tree of the Knowledge of Good and Evil in Genesis led to an account of the Fall as a process of arborization. In the Vulgate version of Genesis, Adam hides his sin 'in medio ligni paradisi' (in the middle of the wood of paradise). Trees as woods were identified with the flesh through Servius' commentary on *Aeneid* 1.314 which equates *silva* with Greek *hyle* meaning 'chaos' or 'primary matter' (Nelson 1963:159). When Harington describes 'how men given over to sensualitie leese in the end the verie forme of man (which is reason) and so become beastes or stockes' (Ariosto ed 1972:79), he is describing a descent into the vegetable soul. Accordingly, by submitting to Duessa and then seeking to escape from her, Fradubio is metamorphosed into a tree.

Heraldic trees are popular in Spenser's poetry as records of battle honor, historical prophecy, or motifs in genealogy. Thus the Dodonian tree is hung with trophies which record the history of Rome (*Bellay* 5), and the decayed oak symbolizes Rome's present state (*Rome* 28). Britomart's progeny are described as a tree of Jesse (III iii 22). Battles are often marked by decorated trees: Redcrosse and Sansjoy fight before a tree with Sansfoy's shield hanging on it and Duessa placed by it, 'Both those the lawrell girlonds to the victor dew' (I v 5); Arthur hangs the Souldan's shield and armor on a tree by the tyrant's door as a public monument of his defeat (V viii 45); Book VI contrasts the squire tied hand and foot to a tree (i 11) to Turpine hung by his heels from a tree (vii 27). Spenser alludes to the custom of rewarding worthy citizens with garlands when Una is crowned with the olive of peace (I vi 13) and Calidore with the oak (VI ix 44).

The three kinds of style developed by Donatus in his commentary on Virgil called for distinct landscapes often identified by a particular kind of tree. The pastoral landscape of spring and grassy bank was shaded by beech, poplar, willow, or plane; middle poetry was placed in a setting of fruit trees similar to Alcinous' orchard (*Odyssey* 7.112); and epic action filled nearby forests with pine, ash, or oak. While Spenser does not use trees simply to identify poetic modes, he does stay within their conventions. Accordingly, olive, pear, hawthorn, maple, walnut, bay, and willow are found in *The Shepheardes Calender*, but the oak only when weak in age (*Feb* 102, *Nov* 125). The oak is his favorite simile in epic battle scenes (eg, *FQ* I viii 18, III vii 41, V vi 40).

In *The Faerie Queene*, each tree needs to be interpreted within its particular allegorical context and an extended literary tradition. MARILLENE ALLEN

Triamond In *FQ* IV ii 31–54, Spenser begins the story of Agape and her three sons – Triamond, Diamond, and Priamond – as part of 'The Legend of Cambel and Telamond [ie, Triamond], or of Friendship' (title page). The titular knights first appear as part of a marriage tetrad: Triamond is wed to Canacee, sister to Cambell, who is wed to Cambina, sister to Triamond. To explain the origin of the knights' friendship, Spenser declares that he will complete Chaucer's unfinished *Squire's Tale*.

First he tells how Cambell aims to end the discord among Canacee's suitors by offering her to anyone who can defeat him in battle. Since he is protected by her magic ring, only the sons of Agape 'that hardie chalenge tooke in hand' (iii 3).

Then Spenser explains why three brothers who 'love each other dearely well' (ii 43) fight for one woman. Their mother Agape is a Fay who bore all three at once, 'As if but one soule in them all did dwell.' Since they love adventure, she descends to the Fates to learn their destiny. The Fates reveal that the brothers will die young, but allow a process of 'traduction' (iii 13): when the eldest, Priamond, dies, his life will pass into the next eldest, Diamond, and when he dies, his twofold life will pass into the youngest, Triamond, so that his life 'may so be trebly wext.'

Finally, in canto iii, Spenser presents the battle for Canacee. When Priamond is killed by Cambell, his soul enters Diamond; when Diamond is killed, his double soul enters Triamond. In turn, when Cambell is mortally wounded, his sister's ring enables him to arise like 'Some newborne wight.' Thus the battle hangs in doubtful balance until Cambina arrives and uses her magic cup and wand to change the enemies into friends: 'So all alike did love, and loved were.' In canto iv, the knights display their friendship at Satyrane's tournament (22–45). On the first day, Satyrane defeats Triamond. On the second, Cambell dons Triamond's armor to 'purchase honour in his friends behalve'; when he is overcome, Triamond dons Cambell's armor to free him, so that together they win the second day; each then displays friendship by giving the prize to the other. On the third day, both are defeated by Britomart. In canto v, Triamond rejects the false Florimell for his wife (21).

The story of Cambell and Triamond treats friendship as a social virtue which depends on the equally virtuous minds of the two individuals: 'For vertue is the band, that bindeth harts most sure' (ii 29; see Aristotle *Nicomachean Ethics* 8.3.5–8.8.2, Erskine 1915:847). While occasion may provoke enmity among the virtuous, such enmity ends with the occasion, since it 'of no ill proceeds' (iv 1). But the story extends the idea of friendship beyond a social relation. The names of the characters, the imagery of magic, and the synthesis of Christian, Platonic, and Aristotelian ideas reveal a complex 'metaphysical' allegory (Roche 1964:16) in which friendship is also the condition of psychological concord underlying that relation, and a principle of cosmic harmony from which psychological concord and social peace originate. Spenser thus follows Renaissance Neoplatonism in seeing friendship as a universal principle of love harmonizing the universe (Evans 1961:132).

Agape's name (Gr 'charity, love') identifies her as a figure of Christian love. For St Paul, *agape*, 'the bonde of perfectnes' (Col 3.14), refers to the threefold form of this love: the love of God and Christ for man, man's love in return, and the love among men. In a Christian reading, the three brothers suggest the threefold nature of *agape*, as well as its three agents, the Trinity (Pichaske 1977:83–4). The title page to Book IV could read 'Cambell and the Perfect World' (Telamond from Gr *téleios* 'perfect' + L *mundus* 'world'; see Roche 1964:17): for man, love creates a perfect world.

Yet Spenser does not write a strictly Christian allegory: Agape is a pagan magician who 'had the skill / Of secret things, and all the powres of nature, / Which she by art could use unto her will, / And to her service bind each living creature' (ii 44). In the *Symposium* (203D), Plato portrays love as a magus, while portraits of love by Plotinus (*Enneads* 4.4.40) and Ficino ('Commentary' 6.10) and the portrait of the magus as a divine lover by Pico (*Oration* 32–3) establish a Neoplatonic idea of love as the 'true magic' of the universe. By combining Christian and Platonic material, Spenser creates a cosmogonic myth about the genesis of friendship (Burchmore 1984:53, Pichaske 1977:83).

Thus the names of Priamond, Diamond, and Triamond suggest the first, second, and third worlds that Neoplatonists such as Ficino and Pico found in Plato's *Timaeus* (30B): terrestrial, celestial, and supercelestial (see Roche 1964:16). The birth of Agape's sons, her fear of their early death, and her securing of the traduction show how love creates and (after the Fall) recreates harmony among the three worlds (P. Cheney 1985:148). Spenser uses a metaphysical art, magic, to figure a metaphysical idea in which love is the true magic of the universe because it creates perfect harmony among the three worlds.

The story of Agape and her sons also suggests the scholastic doctrine of the soul, in which during the generation of the individual the two lesser souls, the vegetative and the sensitive, are drawn into the higher soul, the rational, so that man has one perfect soul combining the three (Thomas Aquinas *Summa Theologiae* Ia 118.2, 77.8, 76.3; see Nohrnberg 1976:612–13, Burchmore 1984: 48). The traduction, then, suggests human love of the intellectual soul as it leads to immortality (Nohrnberg 1976:609–10; cf Blair 1941:111). In Virgil, Feronia procures three souls for her son Erulus so that he must be slain three times before he dies (*Aeneid* 8.564–7) – a mystery Servius says symbolizes man's multiplicity of souls (Fowler 1964:28).

Scholastic doctrine further suggests that the three powers of the soul correspond to three kinds of love, named by Aquinas as natural, sensitive, and rational (*ST* 1a2ae 26.1, 17.8; 1a 80.1, 60.1; Aristotle *Ethics* 8.2.4–8.3.4). Spenser identifies these three kinds of love as love of kin, woman, and friend, and says that 'faithfull friendship doth [the other two] suppresse' (IV ix 2). Allegorically, the traduction shows Triamond moving from love of kin (brotherly love) to love of woman (Canacee) to love of friend (Cambell). While Spenser sees friendship as the highest of the three, he shows how it originates from *concordia discors* between the other two: Cambell begins loving a sister, Canacee; Triamond begins loving her as well. The tetrad formed by the marriage of Cambell and Cambina, Triamond and Canacee, shows the harmony among the three kinds of love in permitting each individual to participate in all at once.

Thus the story of Agape and her three sons reveals Spenser's 'habit of analogical thought so characteristic of Renaissance Neoplatonic syncretism' (Burchmore 1984: 46). Cambell's friendship with Triamond suggests man's success in harmonizing his three souls, the three loves, and the three worlds. Cambina's divine magic (her wand is linked with Mercury's caduceus at iii 42 and her nepenthe with 'soverayne grace' at 43) suggests that this harmony is providentially ordained.

Since the traduction mirrors the 'infusion sweete' by which Spenser says Chaucer's spirit survives in him (ii 34), he extends his cosmogonic myth about the genesis of friendship to poetic creation: in the Legend of Cambell and Triamond, he reveals how his 'friendship' with Chaucer creates continuity in a national tradition of heroic poetry. PATRICK CHENEY

Seabury M. Blair 1941 'The Succession of Lives in Spenser's Three Sons of Agape' *MLQ* 2:109–14; Burchmore 1984; P. Cheney 1985; Erskine 1915; Maurice Evans 1961 'Platonic Allegory in *The Faerie Queene*' *RES* ns 12:132–43; Jefferson B. Fletcher 1938 '"The Legend of Cambel and Triamond" in the *Faerie Queene*' *SP* 35:195–201; Fowler 1964; Nohrnberg 1976; David R. Pichaske 1977 '*The Faerie Queene* IV.ii and iii: Spenser on the Genesis of Friendship' *SEL* 17:81–93; Roche 1964.

triplex vita The idea of a threefold life (*contemplativa, activa, voluptuosa*) is founded on Christian ascetic and mystical tradition describing the relation between contemplation and action. The contemplative life was held to be higher; but since contemplation does not endure, those who enjoy it are required to return to the lower, active life of ascetic practice and the cultivation of virtue (Macarius *Institutes of Christian Perfection* 1.18, Gregory the Great *Homilies on Ezekiel* 2.2, Thomas à Kempis *Of the Imitation of Christ* 1.2). Consequently, human experience is at best a blend of action and contemplation, and spiritual writers describe variously the condition mediating between the two extremes.

During the fourteenth century, the term 'mixed life' was applied to those whose perfection in contemplation was held to inform their active life, endowing it with a special graciousness. In Langland's *Piers Plowman*, Dowel, Dobet, and Dobest suggest respectively the active, contemplative, and mixed lives. Other threefold schemes – such as those distinguishing between the purgative, illuminative, and unitive ways, and between beginners, proficients, and the perfected (*Cloud of Unknowing* ch 35; Bonaventura *De triplici via* prologue; William of St Thierry *Golden Epistle* 1.12.41, 1.11.39) – are also intended to clarify the relation between action and contemplation. Especially under the influence of Florentine Neoplatonism, the mediating third state was sometimes held to be heavenly pleasure (*voluptas Urania*). Ficino repeats the well-established idea that contemplation cannot continue without a return to action, and recommends pleasure as the criterion of a right relationship between the two (*De triplici vita et fine triplici*; see also *Pyrochles).

Spenser uses elements of these loosely woven traditions in his poetry. The *Fowre Hymnes* deal with contrasting yet linked claims of earthly and heavenly love and beauty. The flight of the soul heavenward in contemplation is compared to that of an eagle (*HHB* 138), and the vision is said to be beyond the power of Spenser's muse to describe (230–1). Poetry, however, leads us towards the contemplative ideal through pleasure (the mediating principle) and instruction in the virtues (the active life). The eagle in this context symbolizes St John, whose Gospel was often held to be directed at the contemplative life, as distinct from the other evangelists, whose main interest was in the active life.

In the account of the Red Cross Knight's progress in holiness, the same elements occur. Under the guidance of Contemplation, whose spiritual sight is as sharp as an eagle's (*FQ* I x 47), he glimpses the New Jerusalem (55–6). The house of Holiness through which he has passed provides the purgation and illumination preceding vision. Spenser, however, tends to emphasize the trials of spiritual life, rather than the achievement of perfect contemplation through systematic practice of prayer. Redcrosse returns to the active life (68), as do both Artegall after the glimpse of his 'celestiall vision,' Britomart (IV vi 21–4, 42–4), and also Calidore after seeing the Graces (VI x 10–17, 31–2). Although Spenser allows the validity of the conventional active and contemplative vocations – represented, for instance, by Belphoebe (virginity) and Amoret (married love) – he stresses how both alike engage the world and its woes. He tends to emphasize the first two stages of the traditional scheme, namely purgation (Redcrosse in the house of Holiness, I x; Guyon in Mammon's underworld, II vii; Artegall in Radigund's prison, V v; Timias' love-melancholy, IV vii 38–41; and Mirabella's repentance, VI viii 19–24) and illumination by the action of grace (especially through Arthur's role in each book except III).

The Renaissance Neoplatonic interest in pleasure as part of the threefold life entails a sense that the world's strife (represented in mythology by the golden apple of discord, to which Spenser alludes at II vii 55) can be overcome by reconciling the contending principles of Venus and Mars. The proem to *FQ* I invokes the harmony of Mars, Venus, and Cupid. A heavenly pleasure results, such as that expressed in the vision of Mount Acidale in Book VI. Departure from this ideal is presented throughout the poem by lovers who relinquish their active (martial) vigilance by leaving off their armor to indulge in sensual delight: so it is with Redcrosse (I vii 2–7) and Verdant (II xii 80). By contrast, Britomart will not disarm at Castle Joyous or at Dolon's house (III i 42, V vi 23). Before beauty's bait (the attractions of false contemplation), Samson, Hercules, and Antony (V viii 1–2) forgot their (active) duty for the sake of sensual gratification (*voluptas* in the worldly sense). Thus, they turned away from the contemplative ideal represented by the vision of the New Jerusalem, wherein the pleasures of poetry and the active pursuit of holiness alike find fulfillment. PATRICK GRANT

Dom Cuthbert Butler 1922 *Western Mysticism* (London; rev ed 1926); Patrick Grant 1983 *Literature of Mysticism in Western Tradition* (London); Wind 1958.

Trissino, Giangiorgio (1478–1550) Poet, dramatist, grammarian, and literary critic. Although he was a pupil of the famous Greek scholar Demetrius Chalcondyles and an accomplished Latinist, his principal work was in the reform of the Italian language, including orthography. His literary works were part of this program of reform; in them he sought to accommodate Italian letters to the principles he perceived in ancient Greek literature. His popular *Sofonisba* (1515) was the first tragedy in a modern language to follow the norms of Aristotle's *Poetics*, as he indicates in the 1524 dedication to Pope Leo X (Weinberg 1961, 1:369–70). *La poetica* (parts 1–4, 1529; parts 5–6, 1562) introduced linguistic norms and (in parts 5–6) critical rules derived from Aristotle, and was one of the first important critical treatises to appear in Italy in the sixteenth century.

Trissino's most ambitious undertaking was his blank-verse epic *L'Italia liberata dai Goti* (27 books, 1547–8). The poem depicts the early part of the Greco-Gothic War (AD 535–9) in which the Byzantine army led by Justinian and Belisarius liberated Italy from the Goths. It aims at historical accuracy and was meant to be a practical example of how classical authors, especially Homer, should be imitated in a Christian tradition. Despite Trissino's enormous labor of twenty years, his epic proved a failure. Uninspired and with few passages of literary merit, it was not reprinted until the eighteenth century; there is no modern edition. Nevertheless, it is a brave attempt at a heroic poem on a high and serious historical theme, in marked contrast to the romantic epics of Boiardo and Ariosto, and it gave Tasso direction for his *Gerusalemme liberata*.

There is evidence that Spenser read *L'Italia liberata*. Traces of Trissino's influence have been detected mainly in the early books of *The Faerie Queene*, and principally in the treatment of Acrasia in *FQ* II (cf Acratia in *L'Italia liberata* 5). In Trissino's narrative, Acratia is an enchantress (modeled partly on Ariosto's Circean Alcina) who has imprisoned several of the Greek knights in her garden. Their rescuers break through the ivory door of the garden and find the captive Greeks delighting themselves in luxury with other courtiers, both men and women. The soldiers render themselves impervious to Acratia's charms by lifting her skirt and looking beneath it (cf the stripping of Duessa in *FQ* I viii 46–9); they capture her and her fellow enchantress Ligridonia, destroy the power of the corrupting fountain in the middle of the garden, and restore the charmed knights to their senses. They bring Acratia and Ligridonia to Areta (Gr *aretē* virtue), whom they restore to her castle of harmonious proportions.

The whole episode in Trissino is close to the story of Guyon's victory over Acrasia, and to other scenes in *FQ* II such as the castle of Alma (Fowler 1964:264n). Spenser's borrowings indicate that although he did not imitate Trissino as closely and consistently as he did Ariosto, he was clearly attracted to the symbolic narrative he found in *L'Italia liberata*. VESELIN KOSTIĆ

Giamatti 1966:171–9; Kostić 1969:297–302; Lemmi 1928; Weinberg 1961.

Tristram The only character in *The Faerie Queene* derived from Arthurian legend apart from Arthur himself, Tristram is discovered by Calidore fighting on foot, armed only with hunting weapons, against a fully armed knight, while a lady watches 'in foule array' (VI ii 3–39). Before Calidore can intervene, the youth kills the knight. Challenged on the grounds that he has been overbold in slaying his social superior, 'which armes impugneth plaine' (7), Tristram explains that he acted in self-defense, having been assaulted by the knight after rebuking him for his unchivalrous treatment of his lady. The lady confirms the story, and tells of her knight's earlier attack on Aladine and Priscilla.

Tristram goes on to tell Calidore that his mother, Queen Emiline, widow of King Meliogras of Cornwall, had sent him at the age of ten from Lionesse where he had been bred, 'Into the land of *Faerie*' to escape his uncle who had usurped the throne (28–30). He is thus 'a Briton borne / Sonne of a King,' and though living in forced exile for seven years, trained 'In gentle thewes.' His nobility, evident to Calidore even before he hears his story, is manifest in his courteous behavior. He is thus one of many exemplars of courtesy in Book VI, and his 'natural' courtesy and disguised nobility link him with other characters such as the Salvage Man and Pastorella, the Hermit (a retired knight 'of mickle name' V 37), and by inversion, the orphan babe rescued from the bear, who, brought up by a knight and his wife 'in goodly thewes' (iv 38), will become a famous and noble knight.

Spenser's Tristram is not yet a knight or even a squire, just as his Arthur is not yet King of Britain. For source material, Spenser probably relied on Malory's account of Tristram's youth at the beginning of his *Book of Sir Tristram de Lyones*, altering some details and omitting others. In Malory, Tristram's parents are named Elizabeth and Melyodas, and the child's name means 'sorowfull-borne,' an allusion to his mother's death in childbirth; in Spenser it is the father who 'Untimely dyde.' Spenser leaves unnamed the infamous uncle, King Mark of Cornwall. Malory's Tristram is sent to France by his father (his stepmother having tried to poison the boy) and remains there for seven years, learning the skills of harping, hunting, and hawking. He returns to Cornwall (Malory uses 'Lyones' and 'Cornwall' interchangeably), where he remains until he is eighteen when he has his first chivalrous adventure, against the Irish knight Marhalt.

This episode in Spenser's Legend of Courtesy contrasts Tristram with those who are knights but behave unchivalrously: Crudor, Turpine, and the proud discourteous knight whom Tristram slays, for example. He is rewarded for having behaved according to the spirit of chivalry when Calidore makes him a squire, the next step toward fulfilling an avowed ambition to 'beare armes, and learne to use them right' (33). Details of the episode reinforce Calidore's first impression that Tristram, whose identity is not revealed until stanza 28, is 'borne of noble race' (5); he is therefore *naturally* chivalrous.

A pair of tableaux which frame the episode exemplify its theme of false and true chivalry. Tristram tells of being distracted from his hunting when he saw a knight riding while his lady 'On her faire feet by his horse side did pas' (10). The knight, furthermore, was so brutal as to 'thumpe her forward' with his spear when she lagged. As the episode ends, Tristram is seen dressed in the dead knight's armor – he now has the apparel of chivalry as well as the thing itself (but has not yet learned that 'To spoile the dead of weed / Is sacrilege' II viii 16) – helping the lady onto the horse and leading her to safety, as she directs. That this is an example of true chivalry is confirmed in the next canto, when Calepine treats the injured Serena in the same fashion (VI iii 28) – and in his turn is subjected to the taunts of discourteous Turpine. In behaving as he does, Tristram emulates the principal exemplars of courteous chivalry in Book VI – Calepine, Calidore, and Arthur.

CHARLES WALTERS WHITWORTH, JR

triumphs The word *triumph* originally referred to the solemn procession of a victorious general and his army in ancient Rome. There were accurate reenactments of such processions on the continent during the Renaissance, and we find frequent references to classical triumphs in Renaissance literature; for example, Shakespeare's Pompey is being led to prison when he is accosted by Lucio: 'How now, noble Pompey? What, at the wheels of Caesar? Art thou led in triumph?' (*Measure for Measure* III ii 43–4). By extension, a triumph came to refer to any celebration of military victory, as in *FQ* V when Arthur defeats the Souldan – signifying the defeat of the Armada – and is 'With tryumph entertayn'd' (viii 51).

Both these references to military triumphs, like the majority of such references in Renaissance literature, also include a moral dimension (Pompey is morally disgraced; Arthur is morally vindicated) because by Spenser's time the triumph had come to represent not merely military but also moral and spiritual victory – or defeat – due, in large part, to the influence of Dante's *Purgatorio* 29, Petrarch's *Trionfi* (Eng tr by Henry Parker, Lord Morley 1555), and the *Hypnerotomachia Poliphili*. The triumph in *Purgatorio*, for example, is an emphatically Christian procession which, in celebrating the sacrament, includes among its figures the church elders, the four beasts of the Apocalypse, the seven books of the New Testament, the three theological virtues, and the four cardinal virtues, while the triumphs in *Hypnerotomachia*, as seen by Poliphilus the dreamer, serve as a complex representation of the psychological interrelationship between love, sex, and death.

The *Trionfi* were the best-known triumphal series of the Renaissance. They were more popular than the *Canzoniere* in the century after Petrarch's death, judging from the greater number of extant fifteenth-century manuscripts. The *Trionfi* describe, in six poems, six triumphs – those of Love, Chastity, Death, Fame, Time, and Eternity. Victorious Love is defeated by Chastity, who is overcome by Death, who, in turn, is superseded by Fame. Fame is then conquered by Time, who is finally triumphed over by Eternity. The *Trionfi* thus involve a search for the highest, eternal value; and the term *triumph* could refer to any ceremony, including royal entries, tournaments, progress pageants, and masques, that presented allegorically, whether in poetry, drama, or entertainments, higher values struggling to overcome lower. Such a struggle may be seen in the tilt held by Elizabeth's court in 1581. This event, entitled a triumph, presented four knights – one of whom was Sidney – attempting to conquer the Fortress of Perfect Beauty, represented by the Queen's palace of Whitehall, and eventually being overcome by her beauty. In these allegorical shows, the ruler, as triumphator, achieves the final victory by being the ultimate embodiment of all the virtues. James I and Charles I were given a similar role in such masques as *Neptune's Triumph for the Return of Albion* by Jonson and *The Triumph of Peace* by Shirley.

This Petrarchan tradition of the triumph, as a ceremony which celebrates the ruler by depicting the struggle between the vices and virtues, had a lengthy and elaborate history on the continent in the nearly two hundred years between the death of Petrarch and the birth of Spenser. It had a profound effect on the moral function of pageantry in *The Faerie Queene*, as in the crucial episode in Book III where Britomart watches the procession of masquers in the house of Busirane. Already in canto xi, Britomart has seen depicted in a tapestry the 'tryumphant bayes' of conquerors and captains trodden in the dust by cruel love (52). In canto xii, the masquers, who include Desire, Daunger, Fear, and Hope, are to be seen as the allegorical personifications peculiar to a triumph of love in the Petrarchan tradition. The following night, Britomart finds that the triumph is a vanished illusion. As a champion of chastity, she has defeated cruel love.

If the triumph of Britomart's chastity in the masque of Cupid reminds us of the triumph of chastity over love in the Petrarchan *trionfi* tradition, so also the structure of *The Faerie Queene* bears a resemblance to the entire sequence of the Petrarchan *trionfi*. Each book can be seen as one in a series of complex triumphs that involve the victory of a personified virtue over vices, the work as a whole culminating presumably in a celebration of all the virtues embodied in both Arthur and Gloriana.

In the *Cantos of Mutabilitie*, we see the triumph of time – a pageant of temporal emblems presented by Mutabilitie under the marshalship of Nature's sergeant Order – as an image of transience (VII vii). Time asks why, because nothing appears firm and permanent in the universe, she should not rear aloft her 'Trophee, and from all, the triumph beare?' (56). Nature replies that all things rule over change and a time will come when finally they will be 'firmely stayd / Upon the pillours of Eternity' (viii 2). Thus the triumph of Eternity will supersede that of Time as it does at the conclusion of the *Trionfi*. In eternity, everything will rest with 'Him that is the God of Sabbaoth hight.' As in *Purgatorio*, the triumph here also serves to demonstrate the ultimate victory of God, in this instance through the exercise of his justice at the Day of Judgment rather than through Christ's sacrifice as embodied in the sacrament. It functions as an ultimate Christian celebration not only in *The Faerie Queene* but also in *Paradise Lost*, where Christ 'celebrated rode / Triumphant through mid heaven, into the courts / And temple of his mighty Father' after the defeat of Satan (6.888–90). The precise moment of Christ's earlier triumph – 'He in celestial panoply all armed / Of radiant urim, work divinely wrought, / Ascended, at his right hand Victory / Sat, eagle-winged' (6.760–3) – comes at the exact center of Milton's original ten-book epic.

The Faerie Queene works towards a Christian triumph of eternity through a series of preliminary triumphs that are at worst perverted, as in the triumph of cruel love, or at best provisional, as when 'the trumpets Triumph sound on hie' (I v 15) in the house of Pride to proclaim Redcrosse's victory over Sansjoy – the victory of a figure of holiness over one of pride; this triumph is provisional because Redcrosse is prevented by Duessa from slaying his enemy. By contrast, Arthur and Artegall in V viii not only defeat the Souldan, they also kill him and consequently would appear to celebrate a more complete triumph, but at the conclusion of Book V Artegall encounters the Blatant Beast, whom Calidore is unable to subdue permanently in the following book – a reminder that all temporal triumphs are but fleeting. NIGEL BROOKS

Petrarch 1971 *Lord Morley's 'Tryumphes of Fraunces Petrarcke': The First English Translation of the 'Trionfi'* ed D.D. Carnicelli (Cambridge, Mass); Fowler 1970b.

Trompart (Fr *tromper* deceive; Eng *trompant* deceiving) Trompart's name defines his role in *The Faerie Queene*. In his first appearance, he is attacked by Braggadocchio, prostrates himself in 'base humilitee,' and flatters him by cleverly blowing 'the bellowes to his swelling vanity.' His 'cunning sleights and practick knavery' display him as an accomplished deceiver of the witless Braggadocchio, and he is able to deceive even the arch-deceiver Archimago (II iii 6–13). In his role as the trumpet of vanity, he parodies the traditional trumpet of Clio, Muse of history (Brooks-Davies 1977:128), and suggests the hypocrites of Matthew 6.2 who sound a trumpet when giving alms (Nohrnberg 1976:356n).

Trompart is to Braggadocchio as the crafty or sycophantic servant is to the boastful soldier (or *miles gloriosus*) in the tradition of comedy, in every way the antithesis to the Palmer and Guyon. Analogues are the relationships between Shakespeare's Falstaff and Colevile (*2 Henry IV* IV iii) and between Jonson's Captain Bobadill and Matthew (*Every Man in His Humour* I iv). He has also been seen as an allusion to Simier, agent of the vain Duc d'Alençon (Braggadocchio) whose courtship of Elizabeth (Belphoebe) was strongly opposed by Protestants.

Trompart's address to Belphoebe as a goddess echoes Aeneas' to the disguised Venus (*Aeneid* 1.327–8) and shows him taking over the role of a pseudo-Aeneas from his master, who trembles under a bush. When Braggadocchio emerges, Trompart keeps alive his master's false knighthood by describing him as a warrior 'farre renowmd through many bold emprize' (33–5).

In Book III, Trompart orders the hapless Malbecco to appear before 'his soveraine Lord' who is 'the whole worlds commune remedy'; and he later forges the plot to steal Malbecco's treasure (x 23–54).

At Marinell's wedding, it is fitting that Trompart is entrusted with the keeping of the false Florimell, 'Covered from peoples gazement with a vele' (V iii 17), and that this 'guilefull groome' should flee when Braggadocchio is disgraced. It is equally fitting that Trompart not only should be similarly disgraced in the end, but also scourged by Talus (iii 37–8). ELIZABETH J. BELLAMY

Troy Since the Augustinian revision of the value of earthly cities, the genre *de excidio*, 'concerning the destruction' of famous cities, was nearly as widespread as its companion genre *de casibus*, 'concerning the falls' of the famous. Augustine's Rome declined because it was not the City of God; Troy, too, was a mere city, founded on perjury (*City of God* 3.2) and demolished in adultery. The Middle Ages typically took Troy as a figure of human pride and the world-shaking consequences of sin. As Chaucer knew, the word *Troy* seems built into *destroy* (*Troilus* 1.68, 76–7). Since the prize of the judgment of Paris, the cause of the fall of Troy, was associated with the forbidden fruit eaten by Adam and Eve, the fall of cities was associated with the Fall of Man. The brief recapitulation of the Trojan War in *Virgils Gnat* (479–592) emphasizes almost exclusively the themes of violence and fire to make the point that 'all that vaunts in worldly vanitie, / Shall fall through fortunes mutabilitie' (559–60). Elsewhere Spenser lists antique Babylon, fatal Thebes, 'sacred Salem, and sad Ilion, / For memorie of which on high there hong / The golden Apple, cause of all their wrong, / For which the three faire Goddesses did strive' (*FQ* IV i 22). In *The Shepheardes Calender*, he contrasts the proud and lustful Trojan Paris, who left his shepherd's task 'to fetch a lasse' (Helen, his reward for granting the golden apple to Venus), with the virtuous shepherd Moses, who saw 'hys makers face' (*Julye* 145–60).

The medieval vision of Troy, though classical in origin, came mainly from Dares and Dictys, through the great inventor Benoît who wrote the *Roman de Troie* in the twelfth century, Guido delle Colonne, Boccaccio, Raoul Lefèvre, and the English writers Joseph of Exeter, Chaucer, Lydgate, and Caxton. A new vision of Troy emerged in the Renaissance, one which is above all humanist in being self-consciously classicist and antiquarian. It accompanied an increased interest in two other sources, Geoffrey of Monmouth's *Historia regum Britanniae* (see *chronicles) and Homer's *Iliad*. Geoffrey contributed the story, crucial to Spenser, of the founding of Britain by the Trojan Brute, great-grandson of Aeneas, who settled the island with Trojans now called Britons (in modern terms, the Celtic as opposed to the Germanic peoples), whose great hero was Arthur, and whose line culminated in the Welsh-connected Tudor dynasty. Brute founded a city named Trinovantum (Caesar wrote of an actual Celtic tribe, the Trinovantes), that is, Troynovant, Troia Nova, 'New Troy' (the latter names concocted by Geoffrey). When Troia Nova was rebuilt by the British King Lud, both a gate (Ludgate) and the town London took on his name. A proposal much debated in the Renaissance had it that Elizabeth was of Trojan blood.

The Renaissance vision of Troy was antiquarian, conscious of a political renewal of ancient glory, admiring of imperial heroism, and nostalgic over ruins. The Protestant contempt for papal Rome was tempered by consciousness of Aeneas' city as the 'second seat' of Troy, the 'glory of the later world' (*FQ* III ix 44), and by Petrarchan melancholy over the Roman ruins and the memory of that 'brave races greatnes ... That whilome from the *Troyan* blood did flow' (*Bellay* 5).

In *The Faerie Queene*, Book II presents the heroic vision of humanist Troy: Arthur reads in *Briton moniments* of Brute, and of Lud: 'The ruin'd wals he did reaedifye / Of *Troynovant*' (x 46). In III ii, Britomart is relentlessly Trojanized: her vision of Artegall in the mirror shows him wearing Achilles' arms (25), and Merlin explains to her that from her will spring a mighty tree (the same image used for Rome in *Bellay* 5), a 'famous Progenie ... out of the auncient *Trojan* blood, / Which shall revive the sleeping memorie / Of those same antique Peres the heavens brood, / Which *Greeke* and *Asian* rivers stained with their blood' (iii 22). The line will culminate in a 'royall virgin' (49), that is, Elizabeth. In III ix, Britomart encounters one of many shadows of herself, Paridell, whose name recalls his ancestor Paris, even as 'Britomart' recalls 'Brute.' He tells of the bad Troy, the city of lasciviousness and destruction, rape and adultery.

Like Odysseus when he heard the same story in the *Odyssey*, Britomart is moved by Paridell's story because she has heard that 'noble *Britons* sprong from *Trojans* bold, / And *Troynovant* was built of old *Troyes* ashes cold' (ix 38). When she asks him to turn back through history again and tell of Aeneas, he replies with another skewed account, this time defaming Aeneas. Britomart adds that, after the second Troy, Rome, a third will rise which 'Both first and second *Troy* shall dare to equalise' (44). Paridell admits that he has forgotten to tell about the city founded by 'Trojan Brute,' and proceeds to retell (though more delicately) the story that Arthur had read, underrating the British achievement as he had the Roman. Paridell is a kind of shadow Spenser, who can manipulate the various received attitudes toward Troy, the glorious and the fallen, and refashion the past for his own purposes. STEPHEN A. BARNEY

Modern editions of the basic texts include Dares Phrygius *De excidio Troiae historia* ed Ferdinandus Meister (Leipzig 1873) and Dictys of Crete *Ephemeridos belli Troiani* ed Werner Eisenhut (Leipzig 1958), both translated in *The Trojan War* tr R.M. Frazer Jr (Bloomington, Ind 1966); Benoît de Sainte-Maure 1904–12 *Roman de Troie* ed Léopold Constans, 6 vols (Paris); Guido delle Colonne *Historia destructionis Troiae* ed Nathaniel Edward Griffin (Cambridge, Mass 1936), tr Mary Elizabeth Meek (Bloomington 1974); Joseph of Exeter *Frigii Daretis Yliados* ed Ludwig Gompf (Leiden 1970), tr Gildas Roberts as *The 'Iliad' of Dares Phrygius* (Cape Town 1970); Raoul Lefèvre *Le Recueil des histoires de Troyes* 1464, printed by Mansion (Bruges c 1477), tr by Caxton as *Recuyell of the Historyes of Troye* (Bruges c 1473), which was edited by H. Oskar Sommer, 2 vols (London 1894); John Lydgate *Troy Book* ed Henry Bergen, EETS es 97, 103, 106, 126 (London 1906–35).

Studies include G. Gordon 1946; S.K. Heninger, Jr 1962 'The Tudor Myth of Troy-novant' *SAQ* 61:378–87; Kendrick 1950; Parsons 1929; Tatlock 1950.

Tudor poetry At the beginning of the sixteenth century, principles of effective writing and versification in English were imperfectly understood, and few native models were available, for the Tudors could read back through less than two centuries. A few antiquaries, like John Stow or William Camden, consulted old manuscripts, but most readers were limited for their knowledge of older poems to those that appeared in print, and only 6% of the Middle English poems now known were printed in the first half of the century. A handful of these were reprinted during Elizabeth's reign, but the only new printing of Middle English verse at that time, aside from additions to 'Chaucer,' was *Certaine Worthye Manuscript Poems* – three fifteenth-century items edited in 1597 by J[ohn] S[tow] and dedicated 'To the worthiest Poet Maister Ed. Spenser.'

A mere dozen of the 60–odd Middle English metrical romances were printed, but only *Bevis of Hampton*, *Eglamoure*, *Degore*, *Guy of Warwick*, *Isumbras*, *Tryamour*, and *Lamwell* were reprinted in Elizabeth's time. Langland's *Vision of Piers Plowman* was printed in 1550 and 1561 as a Protestant apocalypse; its verse was considered 'but loose meetre' and its 'termes hard and obscure, so as in them is litle pleasure to be taken' (Puttenham *Arte of English Poesie* I.31; Anderson 1976, Hamilton 1961b, King 1982:322–39). Gower's *Confessio Amantis* had its third and last edition in 1554. Two late-fifteenth-century information allegories wrongly attributed to Lydgate, *The Assembly of the Gods* and *The Court of Sapience*, were not reprinted after 1529, when the anonymous *Temple of Glas* (attributed to Lydgate in one ms) had its sixth and last edition. Several of his shorter poems were printed in the first half of the century, and of his translations, *The Fall of Princes* had its fourth edition in 1554 and his *Destruction of Troy* a second edition in 1555; but of his longer poems, only *The Siege of Thebes* survived into the Elizabethan age in editions of Chaucer.

Chaucer was the first English poet to have his works collected in print. Spenser read him in the 1542 or 1561 edition, the latter of which attributed 61 poems to him, 40 of which are not his: he had been effectively deprived of his proper authorship and his works turned into an anthology of Middle English and even later verse. In consequence, Spenser, who looked back to him as a 'well of English undefyled' (*FQ* IV ii 32), borrowed without discrimination words from the spurious as well as from the genuine poems (eg, E.K.'s gloss to *SC, Feb* 149 attributes to Chaucer a phrase that is not his but that appears in the spurious *Plowman's Tale*; see also his misattribution to Chaucer of the statement that death is 'the grene path way to lyfe' gloss to *Nov* emblem). Furthermore, changes in the language and degeneration of the printed texts made his verse difficult to read and impossible to scan. ⟨'Whán that Áprill with his shóures sóote / The dróghte of Márche, hath pérced to the róote'⟩ could be read only as four-stress with an irregular syllable count, which Gascoigne called 'riding rhyme,' and which Spenser thought he imitated in *SC, Februarie*, *Maye*, and *September*.

At the beginning of the century, most writers were satisfied with maintaining a regular pattern of rhymes and neglected a strict syllable count and a fixed pattern of stresses. For example, of the three most important poets of the early part of the century, Hawes composed personification allegories in shapeless rhyme royal with lines of 4–6 stresses and 6–14 syllables. In his *Pastime of Pleasure* (1509), the questing knight Grande Amour chooses the active life, goes through the Trivium and Quadrivium in the Tower of Doctrine, and, clad in St Paul's 'whole armour of God' (Eph 6.11), fights a dragon and marries La Belle Pucelle. This work had five editions by 1555 and then dropped from sight. Somewhat more regular in versification were the translations by Alexander Barclay, whose *Ship of Fooles* (1509), *Certayne Egloges* (c 1515), and *Mirrour of Good Maners* (1523) were reprinted together in 1570.

The third of these early poets, Skelton, remained the best known because his individual poems were often reprinted and his *Workes* collected by Stow in 1568. His earliest verses were in uncertain rhyme royal, but he later avoided the difficulties of the long line by adopting a breathless kind of verse which was named Skeltonic after him, with lines usually of 2 or 3 stresses with varying syllable count, rhyming in leashes of 2–11 lines: 'From Occyan the great se / Unto the Iles of Orchady, / From Tyllbery fery / To the playne of Salysbery' (*Phillip Sparowe* 318–21). He was learned in a medieval rather than in a humanistic way, and used an extensive vocabulary both aureate and colloquial.

Skelton was the first Englishman after Chaucer to construct a persona in his poetry and to advertise his own bibliography, which he did in *The Crowne of Lawrell*, appropriately placed first in his *Workes*. He had immense energy and originality, and he is the only one of his contemporaries whose verses remain alive today. His most successful poem is the delightfully comic *Phillip Sparowe*, the earliest example of stream-of-consciousness narrative, in which a young woman mourns the death of a pet sparrow against a background of phrases from the Latin burial service, and reveals more than she intends of her own amorous fantasizing. Skelton was best known as a satirist, especially for his *Colyn Cloute*, in which he assumes the persona of a spokesman for the discontents of the common people, and attacks the abuses of the clergy. Spenser did not follow in the ways Skelton pointed but did adopt the name Colin Clout rather than Piers Plowman for his own persona.

After its unlovely decrepitude in the earlier sixteenth century, the revival of English poetry was marked by Richard Tottel's publication of *Songes and Sonettes* (1557) by Sir Thomas Wyatt (d 1542), Henry Howard, Earl of Surrey (d 1547), and anonymous poets at the court of Henry VIII who, as Puttenham said, partly following the models of Italian (and French) poets, 'greatly polished our rude and homely maner of vulgar Poesie, from that it had bene before' (*Arte* 1.31). Fifteenth-century verse had employed only a limited number of metrical forms: couplets, quatrains, tail rhyme, rhyme royal, ballade, and carols (Robbins 1952: xlix). Wyatt, however, strove for variety and used 61 different forms, the most notable of his importations being the sonnet (in 7 different rhyme schemes) and terza rima, and the most notable of his inventions the sixain and (unfortunately) poulter's measure (alternately 12- and 14-syllable lines in couplets). He was most successful in his short-lined songs which drew their stanzaic patterns and use of the refrain from traditional carols, but he fumbled the longer line.

The main 'polisher' was Surrey, who produced melodiously varied lines on a solid accentual-syllabic foundation which was to be the norm of English verse for the next three centuries. Isolated earlier poets had produced regular accentual syllabic verse, such as *The Nutbrown Maid* (before 1503) and a few anonymous pieces in BL Ms Add 17492 (transcribed 1532–39), but Surrey was the preeminent polisher. He favored poulter's measure and the sonnet, especially the form consisting of three quatrains and a couplet; his one invention was English blank verse.

The prevailing rhythm at this time was the accentual iambic. A few writers, such as Thomas Tusser in *A Hundreth Good Pointes of Husbandrie* (1557), continued the late fifteenth-century accentual anapestic; and Sidney later introduced the accentual trochaic. In the 1540s, a few poets sought a substitute for 'rude beggerly ryming' (Ascham ed 1904:289) by composing English verses on the quantitative principles used by the Greeks and Romans, as illustrated by Thomas Watson's

> Āll trăvĕl | lērs dō | glādlў rĕ | pōrt grēat
> | prāyse ŏf Ŭ | lȳssēs,
> Fōr thăt hĕ | knēw mănў | mēns mā | nērs,
> ānd | sāw mănў | Cītiēs.
> (in Ascham *Scholemaster* ed 1904:224)

Thomas Drant (d 1568), translator of Horace, drew up a set of rules for English quantities, which Sidney obtained and showed to Spenser, who toyed only briefly with this artificial 'Englishe Versifying' (*Three Letters* 1 in *Var Prose* p 17); Hellenic and Italic duration is not adaptable to Teutonic stress.

Another product of the pre-Elizabethan years was *The Mirror for Magistrates*, a continuation of Lydgate's *Fall of Princes*, containing the tragedies of illustrious English figures from the late fourteenth to the early sixteenth century as if reported by themselves. It had been arranged and partly written by William Baldwin in 1554, but was not published until 1555, after which, revised and added to by others, it reached a seventh edition by 1587. Only the *Induction*, added to the 1563 edition by the youthful Thomas Sackville, is noteworthy. It is in regular and supple rhyme royal, with Chaucerian vocabulary and classical imagery, elaborated according to rhetorical precepts for copiousness (eg, Virgil's 'tristisque senectus' is expanded to 42 lines vividly describing an old man). It opens, 'The wrathfull winter prochinge on a pace, / With blustring blastes had al ybared the treen, / And olde Saturnus with his frosty face / With chilling colde had pearst the tender green.' Spenser admired the 'golden verse' of Sackville's 'learned Muse' (*FQ* Buckhurst Sonnet).

A poet who spanned the reigns was Churchyard (c 1520–1604), who claimed to have learned to write verse from Surrey. He began to publish broadsides at the end of Edward VI's reign, and lived to mourn the passing of Elizabeth, who had awarded him a pension – the only poet other than Spenser whom she so honored (Chester 1935). He published more than 40 broadsides and pamphlets containing amatory and moral verse, journalistic accounts of military engagements, memorials of important personages, and short novella-like narratives, in regular accentual-syllabic lines. He was most proud of 'Shores wife, Edwarde the fowerthes concubine,' a rhetorical exercise in pathos that appeared in the 1563 *Mirror* and which he enlarged and reissued in his *Challenge* (1593). He assumed, probably rightly, that Spenser referred to him as old Palemon 'That sung so long untill quite hoarse he grew' (*Colin Clout* 399; see *Sp All* pp 40, 46).

The most widely disseminated English poems of the sixteenth and seventeenth centuries were those in *The Whole Booke of Psalmes, Collected into Englysh Metre ... with Apt Notes to Synge Them Withal*, by Thomas Sternhold, John Hopkins, and others. The translation, begun under Edward VI, was completed by 1562 and, appended to editions of the Bible and Book of Common Prayer, had more than 150 printings by the end of the century. It was not prescribed, but was 'allowed to be sung in all churches' and was recommended as a substitute for 'all ungodlie songs, and balades, which tend onelie to the nourishing of vice,' in accordance with the injunction of James 5.13, 'If anie be merie, let him sing Psalmes.' Their old-fashioned thumping fourteeners were universally known, and the Old Hundredth is still sung.

Similarly old-fashioned were the collections of verse published in the early part of Elizabeth's reign: Googe's *Eglogs, Epytaphes, and Sonettes* (1563); Turbervile's *Epitaphes, Epigrams, Songs, and Sonets* (1567, 1570); Thomas Howell's *Arbor of Amitie* (1568) and *Pleasant Sonnets and Prettie Pamphlets* (1568); and Breton's *Smale Handfull of Fragrant Flowers* (1575), *A Floorish upon Fancie* (1577, 1582), and *The Workes of a Young Wyt* (1577). These contain short moral and amatory pieces in mechanically regular verse of minimal poetic quality.

Gascoigne (d 1577), whom E.K. calls 'the very chefe of our late rymers' but then adds patronizingly 'he altogyther wanted not learning' (gloss to *SC, Nov* 141), published a collection, *A Hundreth Sundrie Flowres* (1573, rev 1575), and a blank verse satire, *The Steele Glas*, with *The Complaynt of Phylomene*, Ovid's tale elaborated in poulter's measure (1576). Gascoigne was the most prolific writer of sonnets between Wyatt and Sidney, but otherwise favored poulter's measure and the sixain. He knew Italian, from which he tried new forms such as translations of a tragedy in blank verse and a comedy in prose. He wrote competently, with a judicious use of older terms for heightening (Rubel 1941:186–94). He is chiefly noted for 'Certayne Notes of Instruction Concerning the Making of Verse or Ryme in English,' the first treatise on English metrics. He sensibly advised keeping to the same stanza form and having metrical stress fall on naturally accented syllables; but he improperly prescribed a regular succession of unstressed and stressed syllables, with a pause in the same position in every line. He confined English verse in a straitjacket of monotonous regularity until Spenser and Sidney freed it.

In 1579, the year of *The Shepheardes Calender*, the veteran Churchyard published two volumes of pedestrian verse. The new poets of the year were four in number: 'a student in Cambridge,' whose friend I.C. had printed for him *A Poore Knight His Pallace of Private Pleasures*; W.A., 'Artificer,' *A Speciall Remedie against the Furious Force of Lawlesse Love*; and H.C., *The Forrest of Fancy*. The last three purveyors of commonplace amorous and moral complaints were never heard of again; but the fourth, Immerito's *Shepheardes Calender*, went through five editions before the end of the century and ushered in a new era of English poetry.

Despite E.K.'s assertion, the composition of eclogues in English was not new. Barclay had published five c 1515, Googe had published eight in 1563 with a time scheme from March to August, and Turbervile had translated the *Eglogs of Mantuan* (see *Mantuan) in 1567 in a language containing archaisms and dialect words, 'phrase of speach as Countreymen do use' (Rubel 1941:113, 136–43). What was new was the verse and artistry of *The Shepheardes Calender*. Three different kinds of meter are used – accentual-syllabic with a new suppleness, four-stress accentual (riding rhyme), and quantitative (in the gloss to *Maye* 69) – in sixteen different stanza forms, embellished with the varied devices of classical rhetoric which E.K. is at pains to point out in his gloss. The work was daringly experimental and heralded 'our new Poete.'

Sidney, to whom the *Calender* was dedicated, was an equally innovative poet, but he avoided print, and his writings were not published until the 1590s after his death. He had Spenser 'in some use of familiarity' in October 1579 (*Two Letters* 1 in *Var Prose* p 6) and discussed quantitative versifying with him. At this time, Sidney was writing his pastoral romance in prose, the *Arcadia*, which he completed the following year. It contained four sets of eclogues in verse, longer and considerably more varied than those in the *Calender* and with a wider range of technical devices. The *Calender*, however, was all but completed by October 1579; and the only traces of Sidney's example in Spenser at this time are the sestina added to *August*, some English quantitative elegiacs and iambics in *Two Letters* and *Three Letters*, and a Surreyan sonnet which circulated in manuscript in the early 1580s and later was used as *Amoretti* 8. Sidney believed that poetry requires art – that is, a knowledge of aesthetic principles – and the highest craftsmanship; and in his own *Arcadia*, *Defence of Poetry*, and *Astrophil and Stella*, he tried to provide his countrymen with the 'imitative patterns' and 'artificial rules' that he thought they lacked (Sidney ed 1973b:112).

After Spenser went to Ireland in 1580, he probably kept up with what was being printed in England and Scotland, such as James I's *Essayes of a Prentise in the Divine Art of Poesie* (Edinburgh 1584), in which the young king prescribes interlocked rhymes for the sonnet, which Spenser first follows in his 1586 sonnet to Harvey. In the decade, the only poem of even medium length was William Warner's *Albions England*, a patriotic chronicle in septenary couplets enlivened with inset stories. The first four books (from Noah to the Norman Conquest) appeared in 1586, and enlarged to six books (to Henry VII) in 1589. Spenser gave it no attention. He was apparently more attracted to the Latin poetry written by his fellow Englishmen, especially to Watson's *Amyntas* (1585; see *FQ* III vi 45; W.A. Ringler 1954) and *Meliboeus* (1590). He may also have known Richard Willes' *Poematum liber* (1573), who added notes pointing out the technical excellencies of his poems in the manner of E.K.'s glosses; and Camden's *Britannia* (1586), with its verse extracts from 'De connubio Tamae et Isis,' which may have provided hints for the marriage of Thames and Medway in *FQ* IV xi (Oruch 1967).

Except for translations and metrical annals, the only long poems written in English by the Tudors were Hawes' *Pastime*; Henry Bradshaw's *Holy Lyfe and History of Saynt Werburge* (1521), a conventional saint's life; and John Heywood's *Spider and the Flie* (1556), an allegorical debate which contemporaries found unintelligible. Spenser had nothing to learn from Hawes' dragon-slaying knight in Christian armor, nor did he find any other model for his type of long poem among the Tudor poets. What he did get from them was language slightly flavored with 'such good and naturall English words, as have ben long time out of use' (*SC* Epistle), not only from the *Workes* of 'Chaucer,' but also from Sackville, Turbervile, and Gascoigne; and a solid foundation of accentual-syllabic meter on which he could construct new harmonies.

WILLIAM A. RINGLER, JR

Turbervile, George (c 1543–97?) Early Elizabethan poet and translator. Turbervile may be given the credit – or blame – for introducing in his translation of Mantuan's eclogues (1567) the archaic and neologistic diction that Spenser adopted in *The Shepheardes Calender*, but he is less important as an influence on Spenser than as an index to the kinds of poetry and attitudes toward it that were dominant in the England of Spenser's youth (see *Tudor poetry).

Among the most prolific writers of the 1560s and 1570s, Turbervile joined his generation's effort to augment the stock of vernacular literature. He published two collections of rhetorically polished short poems and a series of translations that included, besides Mantuan, versions of Ovid's *Heroides* (1567), Dominicus Mancinus' moral treatise *De quatuor virtutibus* (1568), and a group of *Tragical Tales* (1576?) mostly taken from the *Decameron*. Like Spenser, he was an eager student of foreign and classical models, but only in his experiments with epigrams from the *Greek Anthology* did he show a comparable ability to synthesize borrowed resources and make them his own.

In his 'Discourse of the Friendly Affections of *Tymetes* to *Pyndara* His Ladie' (1567), Turbervile compiled the first narrative sequence of love poems in English and posed the moral problems of love poetry that Spenser would address in *Amoretti*, *Epithalamion*, and *Faerie Queene* III and IV. He excused these exercises in amatory rhetoric as being either warnings against 'poysoned and unlawful love' or polite trifles, mere tokens of good manners in his courtly social set.

By 1579, when the 'new Poete' Spenser was announcing his dedication to a serious career, the bookish courtly amateur Turbervile had already abandoned his poetic avocation and fallen silent. Years later, if Spenser did indeed pay tribute to Turbervile among the poets at court listed in *Colin Clouts Come Home Againe*, it was as 'good *Harpalus*, now woxen aged' (380), a shepherd who had outlived his songs (Hankins 1940:23–4).

WILLIAM E. SHEIDLEY

Dominicus Mancinus 1568 *A Plaine Path to Perfect Vertue* tr George Turbervile (London); Mantuan 1567 *Eglogs* tr George Turbervile (London; rpt New York 1937); Ovid 1567 *The Heroycall Epistles ... with A. Sabinus Aunsweres* tr George Turbervile (London); *Tragical Tales* 1587 tr George Turbervile (orig pub 1576[?]; includes *Epitaphes and Sonnettes*) (London; *STC* 24330); George Turbervile 1567 *Epitaphes, Epigrams, Songs and Sonets, with a Discourse of the Friendly Affections of Tymetes to Pyndara His Ladie* (London; rpt Delmar, NY 1977 incl *Epitaphes and Sonnettes 1576*).

John Erskine Hankins 1940 *The Life and Works of George Turbervile* (Lawrence, Kans); Rubel 1941; William E. Sheidley 1970 'George Turbervile and the Problem of Passion' *JEGP* 69:631–49; Sheidley 1972 'George Turbervile's Epigrams from the Greek Anthology: A Case-study of "Englishing"' *SEL* 12:71–84.

U

Una Although she has a forceful significance as an independent character, Una's main function is to be Redcrosse's companion and to encourage him at moments of extreme moral and spiritual danger; it is she who, through her love and grief when Redcrosse has succumbed to Orgoglio, chances to encounter Arthur and so arranges his redemption from the giant's dark dungeon (*FQ* I vii 29ff). Above all, it is she who saves Redcrosse by snatching the dagger from his hand when he is about to succumb to Despair's temptation to suicide (ix 52); and she ensures his salvation by leading him to Caelia's house of Holiness.

Redcrosse is separated from her by Archimago in I ii and reunited in I viii. While he is paired with her parody, Duessa, the 'faithfull' and 'forsaken' Una is shown wandering in the wilderness. In canto iii, she is protected by the lion-substitute for her faithless knight, until the beast is killed by Sansloy (the noble and reverential creature succumbs to the lawless human cunning of the pagan). In canto vi, Sansloy attacks Una but flees when the 'wyld woodgods' assemble after hearing her cries. After lion, pagan, and wood gods, she encounters Satyrane, the knight of the woods, whom she educates (like Redcrosse) in 'faith and veritie' (vi 31), and who then leads her from the satyrs' woodland haunts.

Una's significance in the allegory of Book I is best understood through explication of her iconographical attributes. The primary meaning of her name, from the Latin, is 'oneness,' though Una is also a recognizably Irish name. She is described at i 4–5 but is not named until stanza 45, after Redcrosse has defeated Error and her numerous brood, and while Archimago is preparing delusive dreams for Redcrosse with the aid of two false sprites. Her name is given at the point when Archimago has manufactured a false Una to complement the false Una/Venus of the first dream and to tempt the knight to 'unwonted lust.' Una's double, in the dream and at his awakening, announces the arrival of Duessa in canto ii. Redcrosse encounters Duessa only after he abandons Una, and the two remain separated until Duessa's falsehood is revealed in canto viii.

The significance of the opposition of unity and duality or multiplicity derives from the Christianized version of Pythagorean-Platonic numerology, in which the monad embodies 'one Lord, one Faith, one Baptism,' and the dyad represents evil, 'the beginning of division, of Multitude, and ... discord' (Agrippa ed 1651, 2.4–5 quoting Eph 4.4–6; see Fowler 1964:3ff). Una is the principle of indivisibility, Truth in its philosophical and religious aspects. Moreover, Una is a cult name for Elizabeth, the one Supreme Governor of the Church of England; Spenser's Una signifies Elizabeth as prince of universal religious reform – hence the emphasis on her 'Royall lynage' of world-ruling kings and queens at i 5. She thus embodies both the theological and the political dimensions of the Elizabethan church (Kermode 1971:14ff, 40ff; Millican 1938–9; Rosinger 1968–9; R.M. Smith 1935b; Yates 1975: 29ff).

(See **Una** Fig 1.)

As she accompanies Redcrosse at the beginning of Book I, Una is the princess of the St George legend, the potential sacrificial victim of a dragon which is terrorizing her parents' realm. This legend figured both in popular entertainment and in propaganda for Protestant religious reform in which George represented England, the princess and her lamb the church, and the dragon the papal Antichrist. Spenser adds precise iconographical details: the white lamb, the white ass on which Una rides, her physical whiteness that is covered by a black stole, and her veiled face and sadness. The whiteness signifies truth and virginity and, at the moment of her betrothal to Redcrosse, identifies her as the bride ready to marry Christ (xii 22; cf Rev 19.7–8) and as the spotless typological church (cf Song of Sol 4.7). Una is thus allegorically the true church awaiting recognition by England and anagogically the heavenly church of the end of time (Rev 21). In contrast to Duessa's barbaric and papal splendor (ii 13), Una's black and white apparel suggests a Puritan simplicity in vestments. Black and white were Elizabeth's personal colors, her assertion of Protestant austerity in monarchical regalia, as in the 'Sieve' portrait in Siena (Strong 1963:21, 68 and pl 10).

(See **Elizabeth, images of** Fig 1.)

Una's lamb, on one level belonging to the St George legend and on another symbolizing Christ, is also the 'lambe ... without blemish' of the Passover (Exod 12.5), and emblematic of truth and innocence. It is 'milke white' to reinforce the theological symbolism by alluding to the 'milke of the worde' (1 Pet 2.2), and to anticipate the assimilation into Una of the nursing Charissa of x 30, emblem of mother church (Gal 4). It also relates to the biblical source for Una's parentage, 'Kings shalbe thy nourcing fathers, and Quenes shalbe thy nources' (Isa 49.23), a text used to support patriarchal aspects of absolutism and interpreted as indicating monarchical 'preservation of the Church' (Geneva gloss). The ass recalls Christ's regal humility (Zech 9.9, Matt 21.5).

That Una is daughter and heir to Adam and Eve (vii 43, xii 26) confirms that English Protestant Truth inherits the primordial religion revealed to Adam. Her sadness (which identifies her fleetingly with Mary Magdalene) is for the Fall of Man with its consequent veiling of truth until its revelation to those who accept Christ as 'grace and trueth' (John 1.14, 17), as symbolized by the killing of the Satanic dragon and the liberation of Adam and Eve. *Eden* means 'pleasure,' so that their liberation announces the virtual end of the joylessness that has permeated Book I. Thus, at xii 21, Una rises unveiled at dawn (cf iii 21 and xi 33) and is identified as 'the morning starre,' at once Christ (Rev 22.16) and truth (*Vewe*, *Var Prose* p 137), but also Venus, the planetary goddess of love and pleasure (cf Tasso *Gerusalemme liberata* 15.60). Sylvanus mistakes Una for Venus at vi 16; she is earlier connected with a wanton Venus *pandemos* at i 48. Through association with Flora, the Roman spring goddess whose festival was celebrated from late April into May (Ovid *Fasti* 5.185; Una is a 'flowre in May' at xii 22), Venus became goddess of gardens, so that Una/Venus is the goddess of the liberated Eden as well as the spring goddess of a golden age restored by Flora/Elizabeth (note her garlands at vi 13 and xii 8, parodied proleptically at i 48 and ii 30). There is the further suggestion that she is the comely black woman who is the 'garden inclosed' of the Song of Solomon (4.12).

Unveiled, Una's face is 'sunshyny' (xii 23, iii 4), associating her with the sun of monarchy and (in conjunction with her wanderings in the wilderness, canto iii) the 'woman clothed with the sunne' (Rev 12.1 – the Protestant church 'compassed about' with Christ, according to the Geneva gloss). The solar symbolism also connects her with solar Arthur and especially with his sun-bright diamond but veiled shield (vii 33–4); at vi 4, Una is steadfast as diamond, solar emblem of faith and immutability. When unveiled, Arthur's shield petrifies and blinds the faithless. It is the aggressive counterpart to Una who, with veils removed, reveals the glory of a loving Christ (2 Cor 3.7ff). This aspect of 'faithfull' Una is made more explicit by her association with sunny-faced and white-robed Fidelia (x 12–13). As the true church in action, Una is faith, just as she is love (yellow-robed and Venerean Charissa).

(See **Una** Fig 2.)

Una's relationship with these theological virtues recalls the frontispiece to the Bishops' Bible which depicts Elizabeth flanked by Faith and Charity (Hind 1952–64, 1:68–9). The cartouche beneath this engraving is supported by the royal lion and dragon who appear as part of the iconographical furniture of *FQ* I via the St George legend and Psalm 91.13 (*Var* 1:477–8). The lion, substitute for Redcrosse and Una's special companion in canto iii, identifies Una as true prince and virgin (*Var* 1:398), as white Albion accompanied by the lion of Brutus (frontispiece to Drayton *Poly-Olbion* 1612 'Upon the *Frontispice*' 9), as Justice (Fowler 1964:68), and as zodiacal Virgo/Astraea, adjacent to Leo (Brooks-Davies 1977:36–7). After the lion is killed by the false lion Sansloy, Una becomes hostage to lawlessness until rescued by the woodfolk (vi 7ff; cf 2 Tim 4.17) who, though in their idolatry culpably like the Old Testament Jews, perceive certain truths about her (Rom 1.23ff). Unlike Sansloy, they recognize her as a queen and crown her with the olive of peace and wisdom. They connect her with civilizing Bacchus (she has wandered the Indies at vi 2) and the earth mother Cybele, on whom civilizations are founded and whose chariot is drawn by lions.

The satyrs take Una for Venus and Diana, thereby introducing into the poem the Venus-virgin topos from *Aeneid* 1.314ff; that they idolatrously worship her ass suggests the Jews as ass-worshipers, at the same time recalling the typological ass of the gospel (via commentaries on Judg 15.16), and the ass that carries the image of Isis. Isis the moon goddess is the veiled and ultimate female deity incorporating Cybele, Venus, and other goddesses. In *FQ* V, she will be an image of Elizabeth. At the center of *FQ* I, she is unveiled for a moment to display Una as Elizabeth, defender of the faith and reminder that 'we speake the wisdome of God in a mysterie' which will be 'reveiled ... unto us by his Spirit' (1 Cor 2.7, 10).

Douglas Brooks-Davies

Margaret J. Allen 1978 'The Harlot and the Mourning Bride' in Campbell and Doyle 1978:13–28; Brooks-Davies 1977; Hind 1952–64; Jordan 1977; Kermode 1971; Millican 1938–9; Lawrence Rosinger 1968–9 'Spenser's Una and Queen Elizabeth' *ELN* 6:12–17; R.M. Smith 1935b; Steadman 1958; Yates 1975.

Una's lamb Apart from any allegorical significance, Una's lamb owes its existence to an iconographical tradition that is primarily though not solely a feature of English versions of the St George story. Italian Renaissance painting and sculpture show no lamb with the princess, not even the delicate miniature that Raphael made for Order of the Garter presentation late in the reign of Henry VII (National Gallery, Washington, D.C.).

Voragine's *Golden Legend* and other medieval authorities on England and the Garter's patron saint report that the dragon's original ration consisted of sheep; only a shortage of these required partial substitution of children chosen by lot. English versions standardize the notion that the rescued princess was leading a lamb on a leash (as in a Garter miniature c 1445 in British Library Ms Royal 15.E.VI, fol 439). Thus the George poem that Lydgate wrote as captions for murals in a London hall describe her as 'quakyng in hir dreed; / Upon hir hande a sheep she did leed' (*Var* 1:387). Like similar murals in English churches, including the Gild Chapel at Stratford-on-Avon, the paintings have not survived. Presumably the lamb appeared in the lost George folk plays, for it survived in the pageant for the coronation of young Edward VI in 1547. (See *visual arts for the suggestion that Spenser owed this detail to a Book of Hours that belonged to Raleigh.)

(See **Una's lamb** Fig 1.)

The most striking example of the English tradition is the large woodcut on the title page of a series of Latin missals of Sarum Use (the common English liturgy) printed in Rouen and Paris between 1500 and 1520 for the English market. Here reproduced from the earliest edition, it seems a perfect illustration for *FQ* I xi, even though Spenser fails to make explicit mention of the lamb after canto i. This woodcut inspired other illustrations, notably the anonymous panel of the family of Henry VII in the royal collection at Windsor, where George's combat serves as backdrop to the family at prayer. The popularity of the image is shown by the fact that although no lamb appears in the text of Mantuan's original Latin nor in Alexander Barclay's verse translation, the title page of *The Life of St George* (1515?) has a woodcut showing the lamb on a string.

Doubtless Spenser knew of a contemporary pictorial allegorization more relevant to *FQ* V than *FQ* I. While a religious refugee in England, the Belgian engraver Marcus Gheeraerts the elder engraved a famous series showing the 1576 procession of the Order of the Garter. In 1577 he produced an exceedingly rare print showing William the Silent as George slaying the dragon of Spanish tyranny while princess and lamb cower prayerfully; the key identifies the princess as Belgium, the lamb as *Ecclesia Christi*.

FRANKLIN B. WILLIAMS, JR

Hind 1952–64, 1:121–2 and plate 51; *Var* 1:379–90; Franklin B. Williams, Jr 1980 'The Iconography of Una's Lamb' *PBSA* 74:301–5.

Upton, John (1707–60) An important critic and editor of Spenser. Educated at Oxford and by vocation an Anglican priest supported by many benefices, he was a classicist by training, like many other eighteenth-century editors of English literature. His publications include the first scholarly edition of Epictetus to approach completeness (1739–41) and *Critical Observations on Shakespeare* (1746, rev and enl 1748). The anonymous *A New Canto of Spencer's Fairy Queen* (1747) and *Remarks on Three Plays of Benjamin Jonson* (1749) have been attributed to him (Radcliffe 1984); but his most noteworthy contributions to Spenser studies are *A Letter concerning a New Edition of Spenser's 'Faerie Queene'* (1751) and the first annotated edition of *The Faerie Queene* (1758).

Upton's *Letter* states the principles on which he intended to edit Spenser's works: 'the last editor should consult every former edition, and ... should faithfully and fairly exhibit all the various readings of even the least authority.' If he is to appreciate Spenser's 'allusions and various beauties,' he must also master the poet's 'learning' (see Wurtsbaugh 1936:75–6). The *Letter* prepares for Warton's influential *Observations on the Faerie Queene* (1754, 2nd ed 1762).

Upton's edition of *The Faerie Queene* appeared in two quarto volumes, and included Sir Kenelm Digby's commentary on *FQ* II ix 22. While it was the most careful edition of the poem to date, the text fails to meet modern scholarly criteria for several reasons: Books I–III are based on the first quarto rather than on the last edition published during the author's lifetime, Upton's account of textual variations is sometimes mistaken, and some conjectural emendations find their way into the text despite the editor's claim to relegate them all to his notes (Wurtsbaugh 1936:76–8). His additions, however, remain of interest. The preface compares the poem to Homer and argues for its comparable greatness and unity of action. It assumes Spenser's conscious artistry, and defends *The Faerie Queene* as an epic and moral poem by appealing to the Letter to Raleigh and the basic tenets of neoclassical theory. The glossary is more elaborate and extensive than any former one, and cites parallel passages so that it may 'serve both for an index and dictionary' (1: xli).

Upton's greatest contribution is his notes, which try to establish and elucidate a correct text, following the critical methods of Richard Bentley, Lewis Theobald, and their successors. They show a rare breadth and quality of erudition, using material from poets, dramatists, critics, scholars, grammarians, theologians, antiquaries, historians, and virtually every branch of knowledge. Textual notes record variant and conjectural readings with reasons for their rejection or selection. Explanatory notes try to remove textual obscurities and explicate Spenser's 'darke conceit.' Upton comments in detail on the historical and moral allegories of the poem, on Spenser's knowledge of older literature and the Bible, on influences and imitations, and on the poet's style, language, and meter. His eighteenth-century taste leads him to complain that he is not 'an admirer of the jingling sound of like endings (as Milton calls rhyme)' (1: xxxiii), and to declare that 'angry' is an 'improper epithet' for Jove because it has no classical precedent (see his commentary for I i 6). Nevertheless, his notes are an exceptional achievement and his *Faerie Queene* has rightly been called 'one of the best of the eighteenth-century editions of any poet' (Jones 1919:243).

JOHN G. RADCLIFFE

Richard Foster Jones 1919 *Lewis Theobald* (New York); Alexander Judson 1952–3 'The Eighteenth-Century Lives of Edmund Spenser' *HLQ* 16:161–81; John G. Radcliffe 1984 '*A New Canto of Spencer's Fairy Queen* (1747)' *N&Q* 229:396–7; Tucker 1976–7; Wurtsbaugh 1936.

ut pictura poesis (as painting, so poetry: Horace *Ars poetica* 361) A conventional summary of the ancient analogy between painting and poetry. Spenser's pictorialism in *The Faerie Queene* reflects the mimetic view of art also to be found in Renaissance literary criticism: 'Poesy therefore is an art of imitation ... that is to say, a representing, counterfeiting, or figuring forth – to speak metaphorically, a speaking picture – with this end, to teach and delight' (Sidney ed 1973b:79–80). Besides echoing Aristotle and Horace in Scaliger's formulation (*Poetice* 1.1), Sidney alludes to the words which Plutarch attributes to Simonides, that poetry is a speaking picture, painting a silent poetry (*Moralia* 346F). According to this view of the sister arts, the skill of both painter and poet can be measured in terms of the degree to which each succeeds in creating the illusion of the rival art. So common was the use of this topos for praising any vivid narration that E.K. uses it to commend the tale of the Oak and the Briar: even though it is only a modest example, he remarks that this fable is told 'so lively and so feelingly, as if the thing were set forth in some Picture before our eyes, more plainly could not appeare' (*SC, Feb* Argument).

As the model of imitative art, painting might be praised for its lifelikeness, or condemned for deceiving the sight with a mere copy of what is real. To counter this charge associated with Plato and his followers, both poet and painter could point to the ideal as their true subject. After all, Aristotle in his *Poetics* (9.1) allowed the poet to show how men should or might behave, not simply how they actually behave; he had also implied that poets are 'makers,' working as nature works to create a second universe (cf 9.9–10). Thus the artist's freedom to exercise his imagination exempted him from the task of making replicas, giving him, potentially at least, the higher calling to follow the dictates of his own vision. Although Horace warns the poet not to be like a painter who incongruously joins the parts of man and beast to produce a monster in blind obedience to his fantasy, it was conceded, even by Horace (9–10), that both enjoy the liberty of the imagination, which is 'not tied to the laws of matter' (Bacon *Advancement of Learning* 2.4). But the all-important principle of decorum, or propriety of style and expression, required that limits be set to the artist's wildest flights of fancy. Only rational control over the imagination could ensure that the poetic or pictorial illusion might occupy a respectable place in a society concerned with humanistic values.

For Sidney, the 'speaking picture' means that through its visual qualities poetry can have the same impact on the reader as a painting has on the viewer. Philosophically and psychologically, the eye, of all the senses, was considered to give quickest access to the soul, so that there were clear advantages to stressing the visual aspect in a defense of the moral value of poetry. At the same time, emphasis on the visual inevitably raised the problem of illusion as posed by Platonists and Puritans: that in deceiving the senses poetry may also delude the mind. Sidney attempts to resolve the problem by means of Aristotle's concept of the artist as not merely imitating nature but improving upon it – becoming, as it were, the imitator of ideas rather than of material reality. Through the image, the poet can fulfill his twofold purpose of teaching and delighting, providing both sensuous appeal and an insight into what would otherwise 'lie dark before the imaginative and judging power' of the mind (Sidney ed 1973b:86). It thus became a Renaissance conviction that poetry *should* resemble painting if it is to prove more successful than the precepts of philosophy in inculcating virtue. That Spenser was fully aware of these issues is evident from the Letter to Raleigh, where he indicates that his moral purpose can better be served by 'an historicall fiction' than by plain precept. In choosing fiction, he commits himself to mimesis and the art of the poet-painter as set forth by Sidney.

For Renaissance painters, the analogy between painting and poetry was equally useful. In their desire to avoid the imputation that they were simply craftsmen, they borrowed from rhetorical treatises the three stages of composition, comparing their invention, design, and colors to the *inventio*, *dispositio*, and *elocutio* of the poets (Lee 1940). But poets were most influential in matters of invention, for from their writings came the subjects of many great paintings. A certain rivalry between poets and painters was manifest the moment they shared the same themes and subject matter. Painters such as Leonardo da Vinci denied that poetry fashions images as well as a painting can, while Spenser speaks of 'Poets wit, that passeth Painter farre / In picturing the parts of beautie daint' (*FQ* III proem 2). In the continuing debate between poet and painter known as the *paragone* (comparison, rivalry), Jonson neatly summarizes the case for the poet: 'Yet of the two, the Pen is more noble, then the Pencill. For that can speake to the Understanding; the other, but to the Sense' (ed 1925–52, 8:610).

Besides the rival claims of poet and painter to be able to move people through visual imagery, both put forward their ability to present higher truths through allegory. Almost by definition, allegory was viewed as a kind of picture language, using feigned images of virtue and vice. When a Renaissance poet such as Spenser wrote allegory, he was not only adhering to the Horatian principle of teaching through delight but was also committing himself to a pictorial style.

One type of allegory which may have helped him with pictorial models for some of his figures was the emblem book. Though emblems, using both picture and poem in complementary fashion, suggest a more literal view of *ut pictura poesis* than that endorsed by Sidney and Spenser, they could have aided Spenser in creating his 'speaking pictures' by their use of identifying attributes for personifications. But Spenser brings his emblems to life by building a story around them. In so doing, he enters into competition with the painter, who similarly aspires to verisimilitude (never a strong point in emblems), to bring a story to life and make it seem like a real experience.

In the latter part of the eighteenth century, when both poetry and painting found new directions, the analogy began to lose some of its force, no longer remaining an unquestioned dictum. The most notable criticism of the *ut pictura* tradition occurs in Lessing's *Laokoön* (1766). He attempted to reassert the importance of medium in the arts, drawing a distinction between poetry as a time art and painting as a space art, and arguing that each is at its best when observing its own limitations. For the Renaissance, such a distinction was hardly necessary, simply because artists of the time took for granted that the analogy between poetry and painting alluded, not to the literal nature of these arts, but to their expressive power. JUDITH DUNDAS

Bender 1972; Judith Dundas 1978–9 'Style and the Mind's Eye' *JAAC* 37:325–34; Dundas 1985; Gent 1981; Hagstrum 1958; Rensselaer W. Lee 1940 '*Ut Pictura Poesis*: The Humanistic Theory of Painting' *ArtB* 22:197–269 (rpt separately New York 1967); Mario Praz 1970 *Mnemosyne: The Parallel between Literature and the Visual Arts* (Princeton); Trimpi 1973.

V

Vanitie, Visions of the Worlds. See ***Complaints: Visions***

veils In Spenser's poetry, veils have both literal and figurative significance. The veil that hides the whiteness of Una's face (*FQ* I i 4, vi 4) and the veil that covers the brightness of Arthur's diamond shield (vii 33, viii 19) hint that what they cover is too bright for mortal eyes. Britomart, enveloped in floor-length tresses 'like a silken veile,' seems 'prodigious' (IV i 13; cf III ix 20); amazed beholders take her for a phantasm or for warlike Bellona. The veils of the androgynous goddesses Venus (IV x 40) and Nature (VII vii 5) conceal a sexual mystery. Paradoxically, the veil may equally ward us off and draw us in: it conceals in order to reveal. The narrator himself cannot say whether Nature is veiled to protect frail men from 'the terror of her uncouth hew' or to accommodate her splendid beauty to their weak eyes (6). If he prefers the latter explanation, it is because Jesus' Transfiguration on Mount Tabor provides the sacred precedent (Matt 17.1–8). In the Bower of Bliss, Acrasia, wearing a 'vele of silke and silver thin,' exploits the divine aura of veils (II xii 77), even as her 'wanton Maidens' arouse lust in Guyon when their naked bodies are seen through the water 'as through a vele' (64, 66).

When an authentic sacred veil is removed, or when in a comparable gesture Britomart raises her visor, a glorious vision shines forth. Spenser's punning use of *veale* and *reveale* (IV v 10) suggests apocalyptic discovery. In an unguarded moment when Una lays by her stole, her 'angels face' reduces a charging lion to fawning obeisance (I iii 4–6); at her betrothal, her unveiled 'glorious light' astounds Redcrosse and disables the narrator's speech (xii 21–3).

As a literary image, the veil is a traditional metaphor for the surface level of allegory, the letter which conceals an inner meaning. According to Clement of Alexandria (*Stromata* 5.9), both pagan philosophers and Scripture use the veil of allegory to heighten the grandeur of spiritual truth. It serves both to keep out the unlearned and to attract the wise. According to Boccaccio, naked Truth becomes more precious when garbed in a veil: she is protected from the cheapening gaze of the vulgar, while the learned, who must labor to see behind the garment, will value her more highly (*Genealogia* 14.7–9, 12). Sidney says much the same in referring to 'the veil of fables': 'there are many mysteries contained in poetry, which of purpose were written darkly, lest by profane wits it should be abused' (ed 1973b:121). Spenser conceives of his own 'darke conceit' (Letter to Raleigh) in similar terms. In one dedicatory sonnet to *The Faerie Queene*, he tells Burghley that if the 'dim vele' which hides the 'fairer parts' of his 'ydle rimes' from common view be laid aside, 'Perhaps not vaine they may appeare to you'; and in another, he urges Oxford to accept his poem because the glory of his ancestry 'Under a shady vele is therein writ.' Again in the proem to Book II, he begs Elizabeth, who had herself adopted the sun shining through a veil of clouds as an icon of her majesty, to forgive him for enfolding her light 'In covert vele': he does so in order that she may be seen. In the proem to Book III, he allows that he shadows the Queen 'in colourd showes' because 'choicest wit / Cannot [her] glorious pourtraict figure plaine.'

In this awareness of the gap between the poetic sign and the ineffable truth to which it points, Spenser readapts traditional imagery. In the Middle Ages, the veil was used to save worldly beauty for Christianity: if the created world is regarded as the outer veil or visible sign of an inner, spiritual referent, it might properly be enjoyed. For the Renaissance, enamored of earthly beauty and less committed to religious idealism. the veil became an independent aesthetic category, more compellingly real than spiritual truth. ANTOINETTE B. DAUBER

John Freccero 1975 'The Fig Tree and the Laurel: Petrarch's Poetics' *Diacritics* 5:34–40 includes a discussion of the veil image from St Paul to Petrarch. See also Giamatti 1971; Murrin 1969; Nohrnberg 1976:90–1n. Guy de Tervarent 1958 (sv 'Voile') examines the veiled Fortune and the veiled Venus.

Venus The goddess of love, beauty, pleasure, and procreation. For Spenser, Venus is 'Queene of love' (*Amoretti* 39, *Prothalamion* 96), 'beauties Queene' (*SC, Aug* 138), and 'Queene of beautie' (*FQ* IV x 29, 44); she delights in 'joyfulnesse' (III vi 22), and is herself 'The joy of Gods and men' (IV x 44), who inspires all living things to generation (46). As Beauty, her characteristic epithet is 'fair,' and as the goddess of creation she is appropriately styled 'great mother *Venus*' (III vi 40, IV x 5; *Hymne of Love* 52).

The Renaissance adopted the view that 'the so-called gods are really natural phenomena [*rerum naturae*], not divine persons at all' (Cicero *De natura deorum* 3.24.63). Accordingly, in Spenser, Venus appears as the planet which 'under skie / Doest fayrest shine' (*FQ* IV x 44) and which pours forth its benign astrological influence upon the earth (*SC, Dec* 84; *Hymne of Beautie* 50–63, 99–119; *FQ* III vi 2, VII vii 51; *Epithalamion* 286–93). Most frequently, however, the goddess represents the vital force that urges all creatures to multiply their kind. 'Venus,' claims Conti, 'is nothing else than that hidden appetite for sexual union which Nature has instilled in all creatures so that they may reproduce' ('Nihil est autem aliud Venus, quam occultum coitus desiderium a natura insitum ad procreandum' *Mythologiae* 4.13). She and her son Cupid were not gods, he explains, but desires and natural appetites ('desideria et impetus naturae'): all things concerning sensual desire ('omnia commoda ad libidinem spectantia').

Spenser's imitation of the opening lines of Lucretius' *De rerum natura* at *FQ* IV x 44–7 hymns the goddess who inspires all creatures to procreation. Spenser does not follow Lucretius exactly, but his departures from the Latin model explicitly interpret the goddess' powers in terms of natural phenomena, as Conti had done. Where Lucretius' birds are 'pierced to the heart by [the goddess'] might' ('volucres ... perculsae corda tua vi'), Spenser's are 'Privily pricked with ... lustfull powres,' where *privily* and *lustfull* indicate that 'occultum desiderium' which Conti attributed to Venus. Lucretius' beasts are captivated by the goddess' charm ('capta lepore'), while Spenser's are drawn 'with desire'; and instead of 'soft love' ('blandum amorem'), Spenser's Venus inspires 'fury' and 'kindly rages,' those natural (ie, 'kindly') desires and lusts which Conti referred to as 'desideria et impetus naturae.' Spenser's hymn reaches its climax when he praises the goddess as the creator and preserver of the world (47). There is no mention of this in Lucretius, but there is in Conti, who bestows upon her her ancient title, 'rerum omnium procreatrix,' the creator of all things.

Spenser's enthusiasm for myths as cosmological allegories is apparent in his handling of the story of the birth of Venus from 'the fomy sea' (IV xii 2). He commends the ingenuity of those 'antique wisards' who 'invented' the myth, because they understood how to impart scientific truth – here the sea's abundant fertility – under the guise of mere fables. The myth derives from Hesiod, *Theogony* 176–201, which describes how the goddess was born from the foam of the sea when the amputated genitals of Coelus were thrown into the ocean. Spenser silently suppresses the gory details, as Plato recommended (*Republic* 378A), and follows the authority of Aristotle in choosing to interpret the myth as an allegory of fertility (*Generation of Animals* 2.2.21–2).

The goddess was believed to have traveled to Cythera, and later to Cyprus, where a temple, mentioned at *FQ* IV x 5, was built in her honor. Spenser therefore calls her the '*Cyprian* goddesse,' 'the Cyprian Queene' (II xii 65, *Hymne of Beautie* 55, *Epith* 103), Cytherea, or, perhaps for metrical reasons, 'Cytheree' (*FQ* III vi 20, *Teares* 397, *Muiopotmos* 98). These titles do not so much distinguish local cults of the deity as reveal specific aspects of her allegorical meaning. The mythographers derived *Cytherea* from Greek *kueō* 'to be with child,' or *kuō* 'to conceive.' It is therefore appropriate that Venus should assume this title at *FQ* III vi, a canto that deals with conception and generation. At II xii 65, however, she is referred to as the '*Cyprian* goddesse,' a title the mythographers derived from Greek *kryptō* 'to hide, conceal.' Giraldi explains that this means that shame or lust should be concealed ('ab occultando turpi, sive cupidine'): Spenser links this reference to Guyon's 'secret pleasaunce.'

Spenser's references to the goddess are not always so recondite. The simple rhetorical trope of metonymy accounts for several of his allusions: '*Venus* shamefull chaine' (I ii 4) refers to illicit sexual congress, or to those whom he in non-mythological idiom describes as 'In chaines of lust and lewd desires ybound' (II i 54); '*Venus* sting' (xii 39) is the 'secret sting of greedy lust' (III viii 25) or the 'sting of lust' (IV ii 5). When Venus appears in the Red Cross Knight's false dream (I i 48), she acts simply as a procuress, the patronness of harlots and harlotry (see Lactantius *Divine Institutes* 1.17). Yet these comparatively straightforward references are exceptional, for Venus is one of Spenser's more complex mythological figures. This complexity stems in part from the fact that Spenser inherited not one but many Venuses from classical tradition: Cicero discovered no less than four (*De natura deorum* 3.23.59); Plato held that there were two: Urania or Coelestis concerned with virtuous love, Pandemos or Vulgaris with carnal appetites (*Symposium* 180D-E); and Giraldi distinguished no less than fifty. Poets, however, approached the gods rather differently than did the philosophers, historians of religion, and antiquarians. 'The poets,' wrote the Renaissance mythographer Haurech, 'often fail to distinguish [these Venuses], and assume there is just one Venus' ('Sed poetae saepe confundunt, unam tantum Venerem ponentes' *De cognominibus deorum* 2.294). Boccaccio usually followed the Ciceronian practice of separating distinct deities who shared the same name, yet he gives it as his own belief that there is only one love and no more ('Credo ego amorem tantum unicum esse'); 'but,' he continues, 'whenever it changes character, or exhibits different emotions, it acquires a new genealogy, and new titles' ('sed hunc totiens et mutare mores et novum cognomen patremque acquiere, quotiens in diversos sese trahi permittit affectus' *Genealogia* 3.22). Spenser appears to agree. He depicts only one Venus, but he recognizes that her nature is inherently composite, containing a multiplicity of often mutually antagonistic qualities. He signals the ascendency of particular powers by giving her appropriate titles, by pairing her with other deities, by associating her with certain localities, and by adopting a precise iconography.

These techniques are most evident when he uses the goddess to exemplify moral subjects. The gods were not only symbols of physical phenomena, but could refer to 'the reforming and institution of folks maners.' Therefore 'the worke of *Venus* is not carnall companie and medling of two bodies ... but rather mirth and solace, affectionate love, mutuall amitie, conversation, and familiarity one with another ... I assure you *Venus* is the work-mistresse of mutual concord, solace and benevolence between men and women, mingling and melting (as it were) together with the bodies their soules also, by meanes of pleasure' (Plutarch ed 1603:337 [*Moralia* 156C-D]). When Spenser depicts this 'work-mistresse of mutual concord,' he locates her on Mount Acidale, gives her the Graces as companions, and assigns her a symbolic attribute, the cestus, 'Dame *Venus* girdle' (*FQ* IV v 3). He embroiders inventively on classical tradition. Acidalia is one of the names of Venus (see Virgil *Aeneid* 1.720). The grammarian Servius, commenting on this line, derives it from Greek *akidēs*: 'she inflicts the pains of love, which the Greeks call *akidēs*' ('quia injicit curas, quas Graeci *akidas* dicunt'), and from the fount Acidalius 'where the Graces, who everyone knows are consecrated to Venus, bathe' ('a fonte Acidalio ... in quo se Gratiae lavant, quas Veneri constat esse sacratas'). Like Servius, Spenser connects Acidale with the pains of love: Calidore finds it only because 'love his heart hath sore engrieved' (VI x 1). And in Spenser it is also the place of resort for Venus and her handmaids, the Graces (IV v 5, VI x 9). Here the similarities end, however, as Spenser develops the Acidalian Venus into a symbol of all the bonds of mutual concord.

At *FQ* IV v 3–6, she is linked with the 'vertue of chast love, / And wivehood true' by the symbol of her 'goodly belt,' the cestus. Homer (*Iliad* 14.214–21) first described this curiously embroidered adornment, but Spenser's treatment owes more to the mythographers than to Homer. He closely follows Boccaccio (3.22) when he says that the function of the cestus is to 'bind lascivious desire, / And loose affections streightly to restraine.' Boccaccio has 'ut aliquali coertione vaga nimis lascivia freneratur' ('in order that excessively promiscuous lust should be curbed by some kind of restraint'), and later in the same chapter, following Lactantius, he says 'we have said that Venus wore this girdle only in her virtuous marital love-making, and hence all her other sexual acts, for which she discarded this cestus, are called *incestuous*' ('Hoc cingulum ... diximus, Venerem non ferre nisi ad honestas nuptias, et ob id omnem alium concubitum, eo quo ad eum ceston delatum non sit, incestum vocari'). Spenser, ignoring the false etymology, expresses the same sentiment more concisely: Venus valued her girdle 'What time she usd to live in wively sort; / But layd aside, when so she usd her looser sport.' He further reinforces the connection of the cestus with 'wivehood true' by inventing the fact that Vulcan made the precious girdle as a wedding gift for her. While others dignified the adultery of Mars and Venus as an allegory of cosmic harmony (Wind rev ed 1967:86–9), Spenser refuses to see it as any more than Venus' 'looser sport,' indulged in when she has left Acidale and 'layd [it] aside.' He disapproves more overtly in *Muiopotmos* 371–3: their 'shamefull sin' exposes them to the 'common mockerie' of all the gods. Similarly in *FQ* IV v, those ladies who cannot keep the girdle firmly tied suffer the jests and scornful laughter of the assembled knights.

While *FQ* IV v associates the Acidalian Venus with the faithful bond of marriage, her rule is extended in VI x to encompass order, harmony, civility, 'friendly offices that bynde, / And all the complements of curtesie' (23), as symbolized by the three Graces. These 'Handmaides of *Venus*' express the qualities to which the goddess lent her name in the Latin word *venustas*: beauty, order, grace, and cheerfulness. Hence Spenser, alluding to the etymology, says that 'all, that *Venus* in her selfe doth vaunt' is borrowed from the Graces (VI x 15). The three damsels share the goddess' characteristic epithets, 'mylde' and 'faire,' while the third Grace, '*Thalia* merry,' expresses the happiness associated with the 'sweete smyling' 'Mother of laughter.' The dance of the Graces is an exemplary vision of human felicity, which requires Spenser to elevate the classical fount Acidalius to the status of *Mount* Acidale: the iconography of Morrell's emblem (*SC, Julye*) requires that 'foelicitas' be placed 'in summo.'

The statue of Venus at IV x 39–42 exhibits a curious iconography: she is veiled, her feet and legs are bound by a snake 'whose head and tail were fast combyned,' and, more mysteriously, the goddess is believed to be hermaphroditic, 'Both male and female.' Pausanias described an image of Venus, the *Venus Morpho*, whose feet were fettered (*Description of Greece* Laconia 15.10–11; see *emblems). It was said to be a symbol of matrimonial fidelity. The Renaissance adopted the veiled and bound image as an emblem of faithfulness and marital concord, which illustrated the fact that chaste modesty, constancy in love, and attendance to household tasks should be the duties of a wife (see Junius 1565 *Emblemata* 12; Valeriano 1602 *Hieroglyphica* 48, 33). But where the iconographers depict Venus tied with stocks and chains, Spenser has her bound 'with a snake.' The serpent biting its own tail was a hieroglyph of eternity (see Horapollo *Hieroglyphica* 1.1), and in late antiquity Macrobius took it as 'a visible image of the universe which feeds on itself and returns to itself again' (*Saturnalia* 1.9.12 in ed 1969). Behind these interpretations, and basic to Spenser's use of the image, lies the sexual significance of the serpent (see Fowler 1964:164). He depicts conjugal loyalty sustained not by physical restraints, as in the *Venus Morpho*, but by generative union, which conquers time and sustains the universe through procreation. The hermaphroditic nature of the statue is a symbol of the sexual union of male and female, and indicates the joining of man and wife in the one flesh of matrimony (Fowler 1964:162–3; Wind rev ed 1967:77, 129, 200, 211–13). Thus the hermaphroditic Venus is said to bring forth the 'pure and spotlesse *Cupid*' (*Colin Clout* 803), sexual desire which is blameless, because marriage is 'a remedy against sin' (*BCP*). The exaltation of Christian marriage implicit in this mystery leads Spenser to assert his statue's superiority over 'All other Idoles, which the heathen adore.'

In preferring the 'shape and beautie' of his 'covered' Venus, Spenser overturns the opinion of antiquity. The image with which 'that wretched Greeke' fell in love was naked, the very first statue of Venus, Pliny tells us, without drapery. Antiquity judged it 'superior to anything ... in the whole world,' not least to its companion piece, a draped Venus, which was purchased by the more strict and modest people of Cos (*Natural History* 36.4.20ff). Although the Neoplatonists identified the naked Venus with the celestial (see Panofsky 1969:114), Spenser favors the veiled goddess, not for reasons of prudery or 'womanish shame,' but because of the high value he places on sex and procreation. But the real reason behind his preference lies in his veneration for the religious mystery embodied by the goddess, which the priests 'From peoples knowledge labour'd to concele.' Upton, in drawing attention to the fact that Spenser borrowed Venus' 'slender veile' from Plutarch's description of Athena at Sais, whose 'veil no mortal yet has uncovered' (*Var* 4:231), leads us to suspect that Spenser also adopted Plutarch's interpretation of this symbolic attribute: religious knowledge should be imparted in an indirect fashion, shrouded in myths and enigmas (*Isis and Osiris* 354).

The mystery that the priests so carefully guarded is explicated in part when Spenser transfers the iconography of Venus to 'great dame *Nature*': like Venus, she is hidden 'with a veile,' so that no one can tell 'Whether she man or woman inly were' (VII vii 5). Her secret is only partly the fact that the goddess is also a god. Spenser openly declares as much when he addresses Venus as 'Great God of men and women' (IV x 47), for which there is ample classical precedent. But his iconography indicates a more profound point: considered as the powerful cosmic force that creates and preserves the world, any distinctions of sex and gender, even her name, cease to matter. She can be called goddess or god, Venus or Nature, the meaning is the same. Seneca understood as much when he advised, 'You may ... address this being who is the author of this world of ours by different names ... his [or her] titles may be as countless as are his benefits' (*De beneficiis* 4.7). On this authority, the erudite Renaissance scholar Beroaldo could claim that 'Nature is called by both male and female names' and that 'all the gods are ... both male and female' (1501:937). Spenser's Venus, when her pagan mysteries are understood aright, is simply another name for God: 'for there is no Nature without God, nor God without Nature' (Seneca 4.8).

FQ III vi provides a compendium of the goddess' powers and functions. At the outset, she is a celestial influence in the natal horoscope of Belphoebe and Amoret. Not unrelated to her astrological character is her subsequent appearance as the mother of Cupid: Boccaccio (II.5) interprets the birth of Cupid from the union of Venus and Jove (cf *FQ* I proem 3) as a planetary allegory. Spenser, however, signals his modulation to a more human level of experience by referring to the goddess' descent from her 'heavenly hous' (III vi 12). In her search for her runaway son and when she fosters Amoret, we glimpse her maternal and nurturing roles. When she encounters Diana, the two goddesses rapidly become the traditional antagonists of moral allegory: Diana as Chastity, Venus as Love and Pleasure. But Venus reconciles their differences through her conciliating charm and grace. The final section of the canto shifts to a more Olympian perspective as Venus' dominion over all aspects of generation is shown in her 'joyous Paradize.' We see her divine pity for earthly mortality and her creative efforts to mitigate the ravages wrought by time within the world. Spenser had portrayed the goddess' love for the mortal Adonis earlier (III i 34–48) as the mythological subject of an erotic tapestry in Malecasta's house. There it served as a poignant reminder of the fleetingness of the joys of love, cut short by 'dest'ny,' and against which there could be 'no helpe.' In the face of the inevitability of death, the tapestry implies, love should be enjoyed. The Garden of Adonis by its very name does not deny the fleetingness of mortal existence, nor does it exclude Pleasure. But whereas Malecasta's tapestry could only commemorate the goddess' 'endlesse mone,' the Garden celebrates the 'joyous company' of the two lovers. The sexual delights of Venus' 'stately Mount' are set within a context of teeming natural fertility in all its diverse aspects. The implication here is that human love, when it is directed towards procreation, fulfills the divinely sanctioned natural order of the universe.

Spenser mentions the contest between the three goddesses Venus, Juno, and Minerva, and Paris' judgment in favor of the 'Queene of beautie' on several occasions (*SC, Julye* 145–52, *Aug* 138; *FQ* II vii 55, IV i 22). It becomes a moral exemplum of strife, or the disastrous consequences of a heedless preference for beauty over wisdom or riches. But Spenser more frequently uses Venus' title for the purposes of psychological or cosmological allegory. He pairs the titles 'queene of Beauty, / Mother of love'

(*HB* 15–16, *FQ* IV x 29) to show that love arises from the perception of beauty, a Platonic doctrine explained at some length in *Hymne of Beautie*. Similarly, in conjunction with the Muse Erato, Venus can inspire love poets with 'Thoughts halfe devine ... With beawtie kindled' (*Teares* 361–4) through celestial or astrological influence. Also Venus impresses beauty in the physical body of each individual. According to Macrobius (*Commentary on the Dream of Scipio* I.II.12–I.12.14), the soul in its journey from heaven to its embodiment in mortal flesh passes through the planetary sphere of Venus, where it receives that light 'which kindleth lovers fire' (*HB* 99–140). On a grander cosmological level, her beauty becomes the Platonic pattern from which the material universe was constructed (*HB* 29–56, *Colin Clout* 839–94). In mythological terms, Venus is said to 'lend ... light' to Love, when he creates the material universe (*HL* 73).

JOHN MANNING

Philippo Beroaldo 1501 *Commentarii in Asinum aureum* (Venice); [Julianus Aurelius Haurech] 1543 *De cognominibus deorum gentilium libri tres* (Basel); Erwin Panofsky 1969 *Problems in Titian, Mostly Iconographic* (New York); Plutarch 1603 *The Philosophie, Commonlie Called, The Morals* tr Philemon Holland (London).

Verdant The young knight freed by Guyon and the Palmer after they find him in the Bower of Bliss, his head in the lap of Acrasia, who has charmed him to sleep (*FQ* II xii 72–84). Verdant's subjection to Acrasia is an exemplum of the consequences of intemperance. Distracted by her erotic pleasures, he has put aside his 'warlike armes,' as the Red Cross Knight took off his 'yron-coted Plate' to rest by the fountain where he was found by Duessa, and as Cymochles cast off his 'warlike weapons,' also for Acrasia (I vii 2, II v 28). The most immediate models for Verdant are Tasso's Rinaldo, discovered by two fellow knights in the garden of Armida with his flower-adorned sword like a useless ornament, unfit for war (*Gerusalemme liberata* 16.30), and, at a further remove, Ariosto's Ruggiero, who lays aside his shield, helmet, and gauntlets when he arrives on the island of Alcina (*Orlando furioso* 6.24). Behind all three are the victims of Circe, who is Acrasia's direct analogue, and the common classical motif of the warrior disarmed by love: Mars and Venus, Hercules and Omphale, Bacchus and Ariadne, Antony and Cleopatra.

Verdant's name suggests the 'green' youthfulness appropriate to one who has yielded to the Bower's sensual appeal (Ital *verde* 'greene ... Also new, yong, fresh, youthfull, in prime' Florio 1611:594), but it also indicates his emblematic status within the poem's allegory. His name recalls by contrast Acrasia's previous victim, the 'death-giving' Mortdant; and in its literal meaning of 'spring-giving' (L *ver* + *dans*), his name also suggests a reversal of the tragic pattern with which Book II begins.

Without Guyon's intervention, however, Verdant's history would exemplify only a sterile cycle (a pattern interestingly suggested by Florio's dictionary entry for *verde*: 'Petrarke hath used the word Vérde for a finall end, when he saith, giónto al vérde, alluding to a Candle, which they were wont to colour greene ... at the big end ... as we would say in English, burning in the socket, decaying, drawing to an end, almost consumed, or beginning to faint' 1611:594). Until his release, Verdant simply repeats the history of Mortdant, who is described as being in his prime 'The gentlest knight, that ever on greene gras / Gay steed with spurs did pricke' (i 49). Verdant's name associates him with the 'greene gras' (see 'verdant gras' at I ix 13, and cf I ii 17, III i 5). Yet when Acrasia is described as 'greedily depasturing delight' as with her kisses she 'through his humid eyes did sucke his spright,' the suggestions of death are unequivocal. To be subject to Acrasia is not only, like Marlowe's Faustus, to lose one's soul; it is also to be shut out of the natural goodness of the generative pattern. Within the sterility of the Bower, life is simply consumed, leaving behind, in Spenser's metaphor, only the exhausted soil of an overgrazed pasture.

Verdant's sexuality is not culpable, only his failure to set it within the larger providential context. After he has been freed from Acrasia's enchantments and the Palmer has given him 'counsell sage,' he nevertheless remains 'sorrowfull and sad' – sorry for his folly, perhaps, or, like so many of the poem's readers, for the loss of the Bower's delights. But only when he is freed from Acrasia is there the possibility of a love that is genuinely life-giving and spring-giving: only then is he named in the narrative (82) and only then does the poem turn to celebrate the capacity for love in Book III. When they are caught in the Palmer's net, Acrasia and Verdant recall Venus and Mars caught in Vulcan's net (cf Ovid *Metamorphoses* 4.173–89). Acrasia, however, is a demonic parody of the Venus who appears at the heart of the Garden of Adonis (III vi); there, the mythic potential of Verdant is fully realized in Adonis, 'the Father of all formes ... that living gives to all,' and from whom Venus 'reape[s] sweet pleasure' (46–7). The triumph of temperance makes possible the triumph of chastity; and the freeing of Verdant from Acrasia anticipates Britomart's freeing of Amoret from Busirane, another enchanter, and the joyous release of sexual love into the Christian context of *The Faerie Queene*.

DAVID R. SHORE

versification Now the more common and comprehensive term for the branch of poetics formerly called prosody. (Prosody refers to the sound patterns of language, usually considered separate from their semantic content, and is a branch of phonology applicable to all registers of a language.) Versification is the art of poetic forms, particularly meters, rhythms, rime schemes and strophic patterns, and other elements of poetic prosody and structure. It includes consideration of those elements of a language (such as English stress patterns) from which are abstracted rules of verse and verse construction; it also includes the nature and application of those rules. In Spenser's time, English versification was a confluence of a native tradition (which was itself a hybrid of Germanic and Romance elements), of French and Italian influences, and of an academic and experimental interest in classical quantitative versification. Spenser was the foremost experimenter and consolidator of English versification between Chaucer and Milton.

In this article, *meter* refers to the formal measure of verse, usually determined by counting the number or kind of syllables in a single line. *Rhythm* refers to the interaction between meter and the various properties of sound and meaning in an actual line of verse. *Accent* describes a syllable highlighted within a line of verse, affecting the rhythm. It may refer either to the change in pitch characteristic of Romance languages, or to emphasis produced by syllabic stress characteristic of Germanic languages. *Stress*, a basic and characteristic phonological feature of English, combines pitch, loudness, duration, vowel tension, and precise articulation (as in the forming of syllable or word boundaries) to form the basis of English verse accents. *Rime* refers to like-sounding syllables (following Sidney's definition, ed 1973b:119), usually at the ends of lines (see *rhyme). It is spelled here in the Romance manner to distinguish it from *rhyme*, a term derived from medieval Latin syllabic or 'rhythmic' verse. Spenser and his contemporaries perceived 'rhyme' as a metrical system in opposition to unrimed classical quantitative verse, which was based on conventions of syllabic length or duration.

the medieval heritage By Spenser's time, versification had only recently emerged from its medieval confusion, and its future direction was uncertain. The unrimed, heavily stressed alliterative verse of Old English had long since faded under the influence of rimed Romance meters, which English borrowed from the precise syllabics of Latin hymnody and French courtly lyrics. As early as 1200, the English lyric imitated French and Latin forms, including the soon-naturalized ballad stanza (*abcb*, usually of alternating 8 and 6 syllables). The lyric's development over the next 300 years was rich and varied, with Romance syllabification and accent patterns readily accommodating English natural stress patterns. In the ballad stanza, for example, alternating patterns of 4 and 3 stressed syllables developed easily from lines of approximately 8 or 6 syllables. In the well-known thirteenth-century *reverdie* (spring song) 'Sumer is icumen in,' the syllable pattern of 7, 5, 7, 6 is loosely based on the 8–6 (or often 9–7) pattern found commonly in French and medieval Latin lyrics. More regular than syllable count in the English meter, however, is the stress count, which is consistently 4–3:

Súmer ís icúmen ín

Lhúde síng cuccú
Gróweth séd and blóweth méd
And spríngeth the wúde nú.

In the fifteenth and early sixteenth centuries, English hymns and popular lyrics were based on a combination of *long meter*, or 4-stress lines, *short meter*, or 3-stress lines, or *common meter*, the alternating 4-3 stress pattern basic to the ballad. These patterns continue to underlie much song writing in English. More sophisticated lyrics, then as now, might incorporate lines of 2 stresses or, rarely, 1 stress.

Spenser's experimentation with lyrics of complex and various line lengths throughout *The Shepheardes Calender* therefore had some precedent in the English lyric tradition. His contribution to English versification rests both on his effective use of a variety of lines and on his domestication and display of the longer decasyllabic or 5-stress (pentameter) line, either by itself or integrated into various stanzaic structures. The pentameter line, indeed any line longer than 8 or 9 syllables (or 4 stresses), had always been elusive and problematic in English poetry.

The medieval difficulty with longer lines was a result of the Germanic-Romance mix in English verse. With short lines, the tension between a Romance meter based primarily on syllable count and a Germanic meter based on the number of stress accents could scarcely be felt. On the contrary, the native tradition of stress count, which tended to dominate, was given grace and precision by the rimed syllabic forms it inherited. Lines longer than 8 or 9 syllables appear to have been more difficult to manage. Since longer lines were the traditional medium for serious narrative poetry (probably on the model of Greek and Latin hexameters), medieval English narrative suffered formal constraints. Until Chaucer's time, the narrative line was based almost exclusively on the French octosyllabic couplet. A thirteenth-century English translation of a French narrative, *King Alisaundre*, for example, is in 4-stress couplets despite the 12-syllable alexandrine lines of its model. Exceptions, such as Layamon's *Brut*, seem to be efforts at new or revived stress meters with little attention to precise syllable count, and are usually in less prestigious dialects than the increasingly important London English of Chaucer.

Chaucer introduced into English the five-stress decasyllabic line borrowed from French and Italian courtly verse, and his poetry reveals its utility for both lyric and narrative. His fifteenth-century English followers, however, allowed themselves so wide a range of deviation from his 10-syllable, 5-stress, mostly iambic verse that the line's gracefulness had to be all but rediscovered by early sixteenth-century poets, notably by Wyatt and Surrey. Despite the line's weakness among English poets, a group of Scottish poets, commonly called the Scottish Chaucerians, wrote graceful decasyllabic verse, both lyric and narrative, in the last quarter of the fifteenth century and the beginning of the sixteenth. One of them, Gavin Douglas, translated Virgil's *Aeneid* into decasyllabic couplets, a version that influenced Surrey's translation of *Aeneid* 2 and 4, the first iambic pentameter blank verse in English.

By the mid-sixteenth century, the English decasyllabic line had taken on the regular pattern of alternating stresses that we call the English iambic pentameter, a line destined to serve as the basis for most serious English poetry over the next 400 years. When Spenser began writing in the late 1560s, however, there was no clear victory for iambic pentameter. Serious verse, including Thomas Phaer's translation of Virgil's *Aeneid* (1558) and Arthur Golding's translation of Ovid's *Metamorphoses* (1567), was more likely to be written in poulter's measure, couplets of alternating 12- and 14-syllable lines, or in fourteeners, couplets of 14-syllable, 7-accent lines. These lines, popularized and perhaps invented by Wyatt, tended toward rigid iambic movement and singsong monotony. Their fashion in the mid-century is hard to understand, but may have come from their balladlike familiarity, their length (with its implied imitation and even overgoing of the classical hexameter), and their iambic smoothness. Despite some effective poems in these meters (notably by Gascoigne, Greville, and Chapman), tedium and inflexibility eventually destroyed their popularity.

The Shepheardes Calender (1579) helped bring an end to poulter's measure and fourteeners as the major English meters. Except for the balladic narrative of *Julye*, Spenser's extraordinarily various work contains no verse suggestive of them. It provides instead an exploration of English 4-stress and decasyllabic meters, both by themselves and in combination with other meters. As such it announces the powerful metrical skills of the new poet and helps to establish the viability of what Spenser's friend Gabriel Harvey called 'the Inglish Pentameter' (marginal gloss to Gascoigne's *Certayne Notes of Instruction concerning the Making of Verse or Ryme in English* 1575).

Spenser's verse forms *The Shepheardes Calender* reflects the unity in complexity typical of Spenser's verse; here, as in his other poems, he uses a variety of materials to form remarkably coherent structures. Including its dedication and envoy, the poem contains 14 different verse forms. Within its 12 eclogues are 16 different units of verse (2 in *Aprill* and *November*, and at least 4 in *August*), with very little overlap in form.

Januarye and *December*, two of Colin Clout's monologue complaints, appropriately reflect each other with the stanza Gascoigne (somewhat mistaking the European tradition) had earlier called *ballade*: 5*ababcc*. (The number indicates the number of stresses in the lines that follow; the letters refer to rime patterns.) The rough-hewn, 4-accent couplets (frequently decasyllabic and approaching 5 stresses) in *Februarie*'s dialogue between Cuddie and Thenot are picked up again by Piers and Palinode in *Maye* and by Hobbinol and Diggon Davie in *September*.

The dialogue section of the complex *August* eclogue is in the ballade stanza of *Januarye* and *December*, though the effect is different, as the lines are variously given to Willye and Perigot. A quatrain between Perigot and Cuddie introduces *August*'s roundelay between Perigot and Willye, which in turn begins:

Perigot. It fell upon a holly eve,
Willye. hey ho hollidaye,
Per. When holly fathers wont to shrieve:
Wil. now gynneth this roundelay.
(53-6)

The subsequent interchange between Cuddie, Willye, and Perigot returns to ballade stanzas, with a pivotal couplet inserted into the middle of the 26-line section, giving it a reflective balance typical of verse structures throughout the *Calender*. (The dialogue between Hobbinol and Colin Clout in *June* is reminiscent of Colin's *Januarye* and *December* stanzas, for example; but, set in the middle of the year, its form mirrors itself, looking back to *Januarye* and forward to *December*: 5*ababbaba*.) *August* continues with Cuddie's recitation of one of Colin's laments for Rosalind, a sestina beginning 'Ye wastefull woodes beare witnesse of my woe' (151), and concludes with Perigot's quatrain and Cuddie's couplet forming a final ballade stanza. It is difficult to assign a precise number of verse forms to *August*, but one might call the quatrain by Perigot and Cuddie before the roundelay and the couplet by Willye in the second dialogue section the two parts of a broken ballade stanza, and leave the count at four (ballade, broken ballade, roundelay, and sestina).

August, the most varied of the eclogues, is indicative of the care and ordered complexity Spenser brings to the structure of the whole *Calender*. His genius for stanzaic construction is evident here and throughout his poetry. In addition to the forms already mentioned, there are the rough accentual stanzas of *March* (4*aa*3*b*4*cc*3*b*, with the last line unrimed); the introductory quatrains of *Aprill* (5*abab*) followed by the high lyric stanzas in praise of 'fayre *Eliza*, Queene of shepheardes all' (5*a*2*b*5*a*2*b*5*cc*2*dd*4*c*); the elegant overlap of couplet and quatrain in *October* (5*abbaba*); the introductory stanzas in *November* (5*ababbcbc*), which have some stanza-connecting rimes, followed by Colin's elegy on Dido (6*a*5*babb*4*cc*2*d*5*b*2*d*) with *herse*/*verse* as the repeated *d* rimes throughout; the tetrameter triplets of 'To His Booke'; and the hexameter couplets of the envoy. In the final analysis, there are twelve different verse forms scattered through the twelve eclogues representing the twelve months, but the arrangement is not simply one form for each month.

In Spenser's other poems, the verse forms include several elegant renderings of received structures. *Ruines of Time* and *Fowre Hymnes* are in rime royal (5*ababbcc*); *Teares of the Muses* and 'Astrophel' are in ballade stanzas (5*ababcc*); *Ruines of Rome*, *Visions* *of Bellay*, and *Visions of Petrarch* are in the English sonnet form invented by Surrey (5*abab cdcd efef gg*); *Mother Hubberds Tale* is in iambic pentameter couplets; and *Virgils Gnat* and *Muiopotmos* are in the Italian epic and epigram stanza, ottava rima (5*ababa-bcc*).

Even more indicative of Spenser's maturing skills of verse construction are his transformations of received forms, often bordering on or becoming outright invention. The sonnet form of *Amoretti*, for example, is an emblem of the coherence that characterizes Spenser's poetry generally, interconnecting its quatrains by its rime scheme: 5*abab bcbc cdcd ee*. Spenser also uses this form in *Visions of the Worlds Vanitie*. In *Daphnaïda* he uses a 7-line stanza, 5*ababcbc*, which also begins *Colin Clouts Come Home Againe*, a poem otherwise in iambic pentameter quatrains arranged in verse paragraphs.

For his two marriage poems, *Epithalamion* and *Prothalamion*, Spenser took the high lyric of the Italian canzone and fused it with the classical marriage song. In the canzone (which he inherited from the Provençal *canso* and French *chanson* by way of Petrarch), stanzas ranged from 7 to 20 lines and were conceived to be constructed in triads: two similar *piedi* and one dissimilar *sirima* (or *cauda*). A concluding *commiato* at the end of the whole poem functioned as an envoy. Stanza lines were predominantly decasyllabic, interspersed with some shorter lines. Although the similarity of the canzone's tripartite structure to the Pindaric ode has led some commentators (including Saintsbury 1906–10) to credit Spenser with England's first such ode in *Epithalamion*, there is little indication that he was following Pindar. His principal classical model is Catullus (especially Catullus 61), but the canzone provides the formal model, inviting as it does both structural coherence and inventiveness. *Epithalamion*'s 24 stanzas, varying from 17 to 18 lines with a concluding 7-line *commiato*, skillfully combine sameness and variety. The lines are mostly iambic pentameter, with the exceptions of concluding alexandrines for the refrain, trimeter verses interspersed through the stanza (typically at lines 6, 11, and 17), and a few tetrameter lines scattered throughout. The first 9 lines of each stanza are the same: 5*ababc*3*c*5*dcd*. This underlying sameness sustains the poem's formal unity and foregrounds its variety, reinforcing the alternating perspectives of personal and formal occasion, and of time and eternity. (See also **Amoretti, Epithalamion*.)

Prothalamion, like *Epithalamion*, is complexly constructed and uses trimeter lines for metrical variety and emphasis, but its stanzas are consistently 18 lines, with trimeter occurring regularly at lines 5, 10, 15, and 16. The rime scheme is similar throughout, with lines 1–5 always *ababa*, some variation in lines 6–10 (*bcbcc* or *cbcbb* or, most often, *cdcdd*), and a consistent pattern in lines 11–18 (*ddedeeff* or *eefeffgg*). The refrain of lines 17–18, with its *long/Song* rime, varies only slightly across the poem's ten stanzas. The greater consistency of this poem as compared to *Epithalamion* probably reflects the different function of the poet for this 'Spousall Verse.' Insofar as the verse structure of *Epithalamion* is felt as irregular or idiosyncratic, it may be understood as the decorous reflection of a tension between the formal detachment of the public poet and the impatience of the bridegroom. *Prothalamion*, however, is all public, and although the poet is personally present in the poem, he is the more traditional servant of his culture and society, rather than the lover singing 'unto my selfe alone' (*Epith* line 18).

The origins of the Spenserian stanza (sometimes called the *Faerie Queene* stanza) are probably several. Its versatility for Spenser's many different purposes confirms his genius as an inventor and transformer of verse structures. The 9-line stanza is in iambic pentameter except for the famous concluding alexandrine, and uses medial and concluding couplet rime for a wide range of effects: 5*ababbcbcC*.

The medial couplet is useful for pivoting focus and point of view, as well as for delineating sections of the stanza. So, for example, III x 60 shifts from story to moral as it concludes Malbecco's transformation from jealous man to jealousy itself:

Yet can he never dye, but dying lives,
And doth himselfe with sorrow new sustaine,
That death and life attonce unto him gives.
And painefull pleasure turnes to pleasing paine.
There dwels he ever, miserable swaine,
Hatefull both to him selfe, and every wight;
Where he through privy griefe, and horrour vaine,
Is woxen so deform'd, that he has quight
Forgot he was a man, and *Gealosie* is hight.

Here the alexandrine in the concluding couplet has the effect of closure. Elsewhere it may effect a continuation of the narrative despite the sense of closure indicated by a final couplet. When Cambell and Satyrane engage in battle in IV iv 28–9, it helps to lead the narrative along. Cambell challenges Satyrane,

Who seeing him come on so furiously,
Met him mid-way with equall hardiment,
That forcibly to ground they both together went.

They up againe them selves can lightly reare,
And to their tryed swords them selves betake.

The alexandrine can be used equally for epigrammatic turn and conclusion or for narrative extension and summary, serving variously Spenser's narrative, descriptive, symbolic, or epigrammatic purposes.

Spenser's important contribution to English verse is therefore his invention, transformation, and multiple uses of verse and stanza forms, constructed with a wide variety of line lengths and rime schemes. A second contribution is his wide-ranging use of many possibilities for line rhythms, particularly across the new iambic pentameter. (See Renwick 1925, appendix, for a catalogue of 'Spenser's Metres.')

Spenser's iambic pentameter English iambic pentameter and its origins have been the subject of considerable debate. Wimsatt and Beardsley (1959) summarize and codify a fairly traditional view of English verse as accentual-syllabic, measured by both number of syllables and number and position of accented syllables. They continue the tradition of borrowing language from classical quantitative meters to describe English meter in terms of accentual (rather than quantitative) feet. Iambic pentameter for them designates an abstractable pattern of stress relationships in English decasyllabic verse. Recognition of this meter provides a 'metrical emblem,' based on a mutual expectation between poet and reader (Hollander 1975:163), with the variation of stress levels within a line of poetry providing variety over sameness and producing the actual rhythm of a given line or series of lines. Morris Halle and Samuel Jay Keyser (1971) follow a tradition of linguists that goes back at least to Otto Jespersen (1900); they see the whole line (not the foot) as the unit of iambic pentameter, and define meter as the patterned relation of 'weak' and 'strong' syllables across the line. Attridge (1982) also finds the concept of the foot cumbersome for English meter, and rejects the Wimsatt-Beardsley distinctions between meter and rhythm.

Spenser's iambic pentameter versification readily illustrates the difficulty of deciding whether a poem's metrical unit is the foot, that is, a group (in iambic poetry, a pair) of syllables, or the whole line. In some of his verse, it is clear that the unit is the line or the half line; in other, especially later, verse, the flow of the poetry is best understood, and the sense of its grace enhanced, if one hears the interaction between a derivable foot-meter, with its binary pattern of unaccented-accented, and a fulfilling language whose stress levels offer complex variations. Trager and Smith (1957) suggest that four levels of stress are discernible in spoken English. Although Attridge and others have rejected the Trager-Smith theory, the tension between four levels and the binary direction of the iambic pentameter metrical emblem nonetheless often provides exquisite effects in Spenser:

x / x / x / x / x /
Strange thing me seemd to see a beast so wyld,
2 1 4 3 3 2 4 1 3 1

x / x / x / x / x /
so goodly wonne with her owne will beguyld.
3 2 4 1 4 3 2 1 3 1

Particularly notable is the 4–3–2–1 progression in the second line. The effect of the meter, in Wimsatt's terms, is to promote *her* and suppress *owne*. Overall, 'her owne will' gets strong rhetorical emphasis; one can also hear, in that progressive emphasis, the wonder in the speaker's voice. Beyond these mimetic effects, the lines are a marvel of sameness (the meter) and variety (the various levels of rhythmic strain against the meter), typical of the beauties Spenser routinely achieves.

The *Januarye* eclogue of *The Shepheardes Calender* shows half-line rhythms, built around a midline pause (or caesura) usually after the fourth syllable. This pause divides the lines into rhythmic sections that underscore schematic balance and parallelism:

Thou barrein ground, || whome winters wrath hath wasted,
Art made a myrrhour, || to behold my plight. (*Jan* 19–20)
I love thilke lasse, || (alas why doe I love?)
And am forlorne, || (alas why am I lorne?)
She deignes not my good will, || but doth reprove,
And of my rurall musick || holdeth scorne. (61–4)

A good sense of the phrasal (rather than binary iambic) rhythms of Spenser's half lines or line sections helps considerably in reading *The Faerie Queene*, where mid-line pauses combine with mostly end-stopped lines to produce a variety of intralinear rhythms. One graceful example, directly imitative of its subject matter, is the lullaby rhythms Despair puts into a dangerously soothing speech inviting the Red Cross Knight to commit suicide: 'Is not short paine well borne, that brings long ease, / And layes the soule to sleepe in quiet grave? / Sleepe after toyle, port after stormie seas, / Ease after warre, death after life does greatly please' (I ix 40).

Although half-line rhythms are dominant, much of the power of these lines also depends on Spenser's ability to exploit iambic movement. He can emphasize disyllabic iambs:

x / x / x / x / x /
And layes the soule to sleepe in quiet grave

He is also able to exploit those tensions that Wimsatt and Beardsley, Hollander, and others have suggested are the particular virtues of perceiving English meter in units smaller than the line. The first line in the passage above will yield an iambic meter, if syllables are tested against each other within each foot. In each case, the second syllable is *relatively* more stressed than the first:

x / x / x / x /
Is not | short paine | well borne, | that brings |
x /
long ease

According to Trager and Smith, the four levels of stress again help illustrate obvious tensions between the meter pattern of the foot and some of the phrasing:

Is not short paine well borne, that brings
4 3 2 1 2 1 4 2
long ease
3 1

As in the sonnet, the iambic pattern remains; in each case the even syllable is more stressed than the odd syllable that precedes it. But patterns such as 4–3–2–1–2–1 create an ascending movement which, Wimsatt and Beardsley would argue, produces a stronger emphasis on the central 'short paine well borne' than if it were read simply as a prose phrase.

However one analyzes it, Spenser is clearly one of the great masters of English iambic pentameter. *Amoretti* alone is a handbook of the line's many possibilities, with certain poems (including sonnet 67, 'Lyke as a huntsman after weary chace') case studies of variety in intralinear pauses and in levels of tension between iambic pentameter and the fulfilling language of a poem. Spenser had both a scholar's appreciation for metrical possibilities and a master poet's magnificent ear for language rhythms. Above all, his verse should be read aloud, and heard.

SUSANNE WOODS

Derek Attridge 1982 *The Rhythms of English Poetry* (London); Morris Halle and Samuel Jay Keyser 1971 *English Stress: Its Form, Its Growth, and Its Role in Verse* (New York); Hollander 1975; Otto Jespersen 1900 'Notes on Metre' rpt in Harvey Gross, ed 1960 *The Structure of Verse: Modern Essays on Prosody* (Greenwich, Conn), pp 111–30; George Saintsbury 1906–10 *A History of English Prosody from the Twelfth Century to the Present Day* 3 vols (London); George L. Trager and Henry Lee Smith, Jr 1957 *An Outline of English Structure* rev ed (Washington, D.C.); W.K. Wimsatt, Jr, and Monroe C. Beardsley 1959 'The Concept of Meter: An Exercise in Abstraction' *PMLA* 74:585–98. For definitions, see Fussell 1979; Hollander 1981b; *Princeton Enc.* For specialized studies, see Renwick's commentary in *Var* 8:593–5, 643–4, 654–8, 674–7; John Thompson 1961 *The Founding of English Metre* (New York); Susanne Woods 1985 *Natural Emphasis: English Versification from Chaucer to Dryden* (San Marino, Calif).

A Vewe of the Present State of Ireland (See *Var Prose* pp 39–231.) Spenser's only sustained piece of prose writing, *Vewe of Ireland* contains his considered opinions about the Ireland he knew so well after sixteen years of living (or exile) there. (See also **Brief Note of Ireland* and articles on *Ireland.) Superficially, it is very like many other projects for the reform of Ireland presented to the Elizabethan government over a long period. It is also written as a contribution towards the solution of a major crisis in English power in Ireland, the rebellion of Hugh O'Neill, Earl of Tyrone. In both these respects, it may be seen as Spenser's attempt to win the attention of English statesmen, perhaps even the Queen, and so reward him, most probably recall to a post in England, or at least some amelioration of his position in Munster, even though he enjoyed income from nearly 4000 acres of land as an undertaker – a landowner holding from the crown – and was also an official in the provincial administration.

Vewe, however, is more complex than most, if not all perhaps, of the many projects of the period. Its complexity arises from Spenser's varied knowledge of Ireland (though he is wholly unfamiliar with the special problems of Ulster for which he prescribes) and also from his deeper concepts of what society might or should be like in general terms. *FQ* v stresses absolute justice to which he hoped the realms ruled by Elizabeth should some day approach. This may provide a key to the wider implications of the argument set out in *Vewe* that some man of power and authority should attempt to establish under the Queen's authority a regime approaching justice as he saw it. This appears to be why Spenser returns so frequently to the aborted plans of Lord Grey of Wilton, his first master in Ireland, for a comprehensive reform of the administration there. By implication (though on account of the political situation he cannot openly say so), this is also why many of Sir John Perrot's plans for Irish reform, thwarted alike by the resistance of the Irish parliament and by English pusillanimity, conform to the plans he puts forward, and why he still looks forward to the emergence of such a master plan and master planner, in the person, perhaps, of the Earl of Essex.

But if Spenser's mind is set on absolutes, he is largely concerned in *Vewe* with the preliminary stages through which such an overall reform could be reached. This explains why he spends so long in its early pages on bringing out what to him are the most glaring faults in the existing system, alike of Gaelic society, of the Old English aristocracy, and of the Dublin administration, so that he can approach the problems of reforming and reshaping Ireland in his fashion in a more fundamental way. What stands out in this preliminary discourse is his close and generally correct description of Irish social customs. His intimate knowledge of them clearly stems from close study, even though we do not know who were his mentors in the details of Gaelic custom and even its literature.

He shows from the first considerable understanding and sympathy for the individual Irishman, with some appreciation of the potential value of Irish literature, combined with the clear resolution that many of the practices of Gaelic life are wholly unsuited to a settled and ordered society and must, therefore, be abolished or drastically curbed. He is prepared, as Camden was in writing on the ancient Britons, to equate Gaelic custom with the practices of the Scythians as depicted in classical literature, and with those of the early inhabitants of the Iberian peninsula. He objected fundamentally to the Brehon Law which substituted compensation for punishment and was in any event controlled by the great lords. He considered that the method of succession, tanistry (the choice of a successor from the immediate family of the existing ruler), was a recipe for contested succession and lawlessness. He saw the Gaelic doctrine of kincogish (collective responsibility) as an obstacle to law enforcement. He saw the Irish pastoral practice of booleying (the removal of cattle from winter to summer pastures, accompanied by the transit of whole communities with them) as disruptive of social order and stability; and in any event, he considered the Irish attachment to cattle as the prime source of wealth, as inimical to settled, agricultural stability implied by growing many more crops. He strongly objected to coyne and livery (the practice of imposing undefined levies by the lords on their people both during peace and, more particularly, during war), which he saw as fostering the traditional summer campaigning and mutual cattle stealing in so many parts of Ireland. He did not condemn these practices solely among the purely Gaelic lordships, but also among the many Old English lordships which had adopted them in part or as a whole – and he was daring enough to name Thomas, Earl of Ormond, Elizabeth's distant cousin and favorite, as one of the greatest offenders. He also criticized the ineffectiveness and corruption of many English officials, which he knew very well both from living in the Pale and in Munster for so many years. Without much more effective discipline, English laws and customs, however much they were already part of the law of the land, must remain ineffective. In particular, he was convinced that English Common Law must be enforced by the judiciary and the local magistracy in a way far different from current practice. Moreover, a common basis for taxation of all localities must be found in order to finance not only an effective civil but also a military administration.

Following on these criticisms, Spenser planned more far-reaching changes. He wished to see the establishment of a Protestant church in Ireland, but he urged great caution in its imposition, stressing that it could be done only by Irish clergy, trained, presumably, in the newly established Trinity College. He was concerned also to clear the Irish roads (such as they were) of all itinerants – craftsmen, bards, gamesters, whores, and simple beggars. This was to be done by martial law so that they could be killed without mercy (Perrot had adopted this policy in Munster in the early 1570s). His first specific territorial plan covered Ulster, where resistance under Hugh O'Neill was rapidly spreading. A military scheme for garrisons which would gradually quell resistance does not show any close knowledge of the situation there, but his final solution is unqualified: 'all the Lands I will geve unto Englishe men whome I will have drawne thither whoe shall have the same with suche estates as shalbe thoughte mete and for suche rente as shall efte sones be rated / Under everye of those Englishe men will I place some of those Irishe to be Tenantes ... whearein this speciall regarde shalbe had that in no place under anie Lanlord theare shalbe manie of them planted togeather' (*Var Prose* p 179). The same policy should be applied to the other main rebellious area in Leinster, south and southeast of Dublin. This first stage in the creation of his 'perfecte establishement and new Common wealthe' (p 176) is entirely unrealistic, but it fits neatly into his theoretical pattern.

From this solution of the Ulster – and the Leinster – question, he turns to the rest of Gaelic Ireland. He recognizes that the Irish cannot be eliminated from their own country but he looks forward to an arrangement by which new English settlers in close association with small, broken-up units of Irish occupiers, would create uniformity over a great part of the rest of the island:

> since Irelande is full of her owne nacion that maye not be roted out and somwhat stored with Englishe allreadye and more to be, I thinke it best by an union of manners and Conformitye of mindes to bringe them to be one people, and to put awaie the dislikefull Conceite bothe of thone and thother which wilbe by no meanes better then by there enterminglinge of them, that neither all the Irishe maye dwell togeather, nor all the Englishe, but by translatinge of them and scatteringe them in smalle nombers amonge the Englishe, not onely to bringe them by dailye Conversacion unto better likinge of eache other but allsoe to make bothe of them lesse hable to hurte. (pp 211–12)

These proposals are as unrealistic as those regarding Ulster and Leinster. They imply dividing into tiny fractions all the remaining Gaelic lordships and so destroying the Irish polity. This does not, however, appear to affect family life, nor language or even literature, even if Spenser hoped in the long run that Irish custom would give way to English. On this framework, an elaborate structure of local institutions and English garrisons, funded by effective local taxation, would be built.

In the context of his underlying approach to the imposition of a just and stable regime in Ireland, Spenser's propositions made sense, even if they might not be practicable. But they did not cover the whole of Ireland. The Old English, both directly under English jurisdiction in the English Pale around Dublin and, more significantly, in the great lordships of the Earls of Ormond, Clanricard, and Kildare, still remained outside the scope of his scheme. He had, therefore, to content himself with imposing, in theory, palliatives on such excesses, such as the adoption of Gaelic customs in dealing with tenants, their arbitrary control of judicial officers in their dealings with tenants who followed English feudal custom and were, in effect, outside the jurisdiction of the government in Dublin. Much of the latter part of *Vewe* is concerned with limiting their power: taxation, the imposition of garrisons, the development of a system of local government officials free from pressure by the lords, and the supersession of feudal and Gaelic custom by the Common and Statute Law to be imposed by impartial judges. If these methods worked, then Ireland, if not wholly brought to the absolute perfection he aimed at, would be within reach of it. He might then satisfy himself that he had constructed a definitive scheme for the reform of Ireland as a whole.

This bald summary of a plan which had clearly no chance whatever of being implemented does not do justice to the richness of the texture of *Vewe*. The device of a prose dialogue between Eudoxus and Irenius enabled Spenser to toss arguments about his specific projects from one to the other and so bring out the various debatable aspects, as he saw them, of each of his propositions, Eudoxus taking the questioning and often moderate part, Irenius the positive and constructive part, the variety of the illustrative detail adds much interest to the argument even if it is, in the end, sad to see a creative intellect taking the view that whole communities could be treated like chessmen and moved on a board, displaying an insensitivity which had little basis in reality. This is not to say that many of his detailed propositions made no sense: many were born from his practical experience in Ireland and might well have been implemented. It was much of his overall plan which was unrealistic. It is significant that Ware, in publishing *Vewe* for the first time in 1633 (the abortive attempt to have it published in 1598 was hopeless from the start as no English official would sanction it) was able to say that many of his recommendations had been implemented in some form or another; but nevertheless he deleted some 50 items as objectionable to men of all groups in Ireland in his time.

Some readers of *Vewe* have tended to take Spenser's favorable and unfavorable remarks about Gaelic practices out of context. It can be argued that he does show some considerable sympathy towards Irishmen as individuals, and some appreciation of their right to cultural differences from the English, but this has to be set against his overriding sense that the survival of what to him was a primitive social order in so many respects was wholly inappropriate to a Renaissance state, where authority must proceed directly from the center and be effective in every part of the Irish dominion of the Queen. All his proposals regarding the Irish are governed by this overriding consideration. It is easy for modern critics to see how his broader proposals could destroy much, if not quite all, that was distinctive about Gaelic society. It is not unlikely that he felt something of this himself and regretted in some degree the potential loss of its picturesqueness and originality. But justice, as he conceived it, came first. The only case where he can be said to have displayed wanton cruelty in his proposals about the Irish is in recommending that the itinerants in Irish society, a much more important constituent than in more settled communities, should be summarily executed. Though there were precedents for this, it cannot be removed from the indictment against him of being irreconcilable to many aspects of the Gaelic order, even if in general he showed sympathy towards others. DAVID B. QUINN

Though *Vewe* was written in 1596 as a piece of practical advice for the English government, there is no evidence that Spenser presented it directly to the Queen. The Huntington Library manuscript (Ellesmere Ms 7041) is probably the result of his presentation of a finished copy to Sir Thomas Ellesmere, then Attorney General. A less-finished version in the Public Record Office may represent an attempt to bring it to the notice of some other official (SP 63/202/iv,58). The text in the Bodleian manuscript (Gough Ms, Ireland 2) is one prepared probably by some of his friends for publication, but though it was received by the Stationers' Company, it was committed for official scrutiny and was never approved.

The standard modern text is that in *Var Prose* pp 39–231, begun by Ray Heffner and completed by Rudolf Gottfried. It is based on the Ellesmere Ms collated with other surviving mss and texts. The edition by Renwick (1934, rev ed 1970) is based on the Bodleian Ms.

Opinions on *Vewe* have varied widely. Some have found it dull and unworthy of Spenser's genius; others have found it more sympathetic to Gaelic Ireland than most of the contemporary English writing on the subject; still others, that it is openly antagonistic to the Irish. Discussions include Brady 1986; Canny 1983; Canny and Brady 1988; Ray Heffner 1942 'Spenser's *View of Ireland*: Some Observations' *MLQ* 3:507–15; MacCarthy-Morrow 1986, passim; Walter J. Ong, SJ 1942 'Spenser's *View* and the Tradition of the "Wild" Irish' *MLQ* 3:561–71; Quinn 1966; Roland M. Smith 1943 'The Irish Background of Spenser's *View*' *JEGP* 42:499–515; Helen Watanabe-O'Kelly 1980 'Edmund Spenser and Ireland: A Defence' *PNR* 6.6:16–19.

Victorian age, influence and reputation in · The Victorians regularly set Spenser beside Chaucer, Shakespeare, and Milton at the summit of the English Parnassus both as a poet and as a national hero, the first great figure in a specifically English literary renaissance. After the accolades, more often than not, came a lament that Spenser was now little read. To make a case for Spenser's poetry, particularly *The Faerie Queene*, the early Victorians had to contend with a contemporary distaste for allegorical poetry that was given memorable expression by Macaulay in the December 1831 *Edinburgh Review*:

> Nay, even Spencer himself, though assuredly one of the greatest poets that ever lived, could not succeed in the attempt to make allegory interesting. It was in vain that he lavished the riches of his mind on the House of Pride, and the House of Temperance. One unpardonable fault, the fault of tediousness, pervades the whole of the Fairy Queen. We become sick of Cardinal Virtues and Deadly Sins, and long for the society of plain men and women. Of the persons who read the first Canto, not one in ten reaches the end of the First Book, and not one in a hundred perseveres to the end of the poem. Very few and very weary are those who are in at the death of the Blatant Beast. (pp 451–2)

In defending Spenser's poetry generally, and *The Faerie Queene* in particular, the early Victorians developed two approaches. The first extended the traditional view, sanctioned by Milton, of 'sage and serious' Spenser, Christian poet and moral teacher, whose fusion of beauty and edification overcame the limitations of allegory. The second was romantic and aesthetic. Although the Romantics generally disparaged allegory, preferring Coleridge's multivalent and imaginative symbol to the mere fancy of allegorical correspondences, they found in Spenser a poet's poet. He is accidentally rather than essentially allegorical – a genius of English meter and creator of the dreamlike fairyland setting for a series of unforgettable verbal portraits. The Spenser of Coleridge and Hazlitt was carried into the later period most notably by Leigh Hunt, who actually assigned selected descriptive passages of *The Faerie Queene* to appropriate painters (*Imagination and Fancy* 1844). This emphasis upon literary pictorialism runs concurrently with Spenser's influence upon Victorian poets. Though largely mediated by Keats, Spenser is a discernible influence on the element of static portraiture in Victorian poetry (Tennyson's embowered maidens and their progeny, the form and atmosphere of 'The Lotos-Eaters') and on Victorian treatments of Arthurian materials, particularly the *Idylls of the King* (see legend of *Arthur since Spenser).

Spenser's principal champions in the 1830s were the traditionalists. After calling for a new edition, a call to be answered many times during the century, John Wilson (*Blackwood's*' 'Christopher North') made a paradigm case for Spenser in two articles based on a brief biography illustrated with 'beautiful specimens,' building toward a pointed defense of religious poetry. He applied the Wordsworthian criterion of sincerity to the minor poems, praising Spenser's elegies and his love poetry, particularly *Epithalamion*, while finding *The Shepheardes Calender* 'cold' and lacking Wordsworth's particularity: 'Nature is starved, and life hungry' (1833:832). *Epithalamion*, on the other hand, demonstrates Spenser's most exquisite sense of the beautiful and his love of woman's life: 'spiritual – yet voluptuous; and desire itself is hallowed' (p 852), an opinion echoed throughout a century concerned with the domestication of romantic longing.

In his second article on *The Faerie Queene* (1834), Wilson assumed that many readers would be unfamiliar with even the first three books, and therefore combined a survey of plot with a defense of Spenser's allegory against those who denigrated it either for aesthetic reasons or because it seemed to toy with sacred mysteries. Anticipating Ruskin, Wilson associated poetic inspiration with the Protestant's unmediated experience of the divine spirit, saying about the Red Cross Knight's vision of the New Jerusalem that Spenser 'borrows the pen of St John – and that the two revelations coincide – or rather that there is but one revelation – at first derived from heaven, and then given again – in poetry' (1834:416). Spenser's poetry as evangel of religion received clerical imprimatur in John Keble's lectures on poetry (1832–41, tr 1912), and Keble's religious verse, though very un-Spenserian in form, alludes to *The Faerie Queene*. Wilson's praise of Spenser's learning and beneficent poetic and moral influence received the prestigious endorsement of Henry Hallam in the second volume of his *Introduction to the Literature of Europe* (1837–9).

To the domestication of the erotic that early Victorians so admired in *Epithalamion*, the medieval revival added a chivalric ideal. Spenser's heroines in particular become models of the feminine in general discussions of ideal womanhood (eg, Ruskin's 'Of Queens' Gardens' 1865, in ed 1903–12, 18) and in articles on the poet. 'The purest and most brilliant qualities of chivalry were found united in him: the chaste and passionate admiration of women; the fidelity and loyalty of knighthood; the hatred of injustice ... the scorn of all that is low, mean, unmanly and overbearing ... purified by an almost evangelic love of religion,' proclaimed the *Athenaeum* in celebrating the generally neglected *FQ* III (18 Jan 1862:73). Contrast between the 'purity' of Book III and the 'licentousness' of Spenser's Italian models became a means of demonstrating the superiority of English Protestantism in 'Religio Spenseri' (*Blackwood's* 99[1866]:200–23).

The romantic and aesthetic Spenser was created by readers for whom the essence of poetry lay less in instruction than in delight. Like Thomas Campbell in his *Specimens of the British Poets* (1819, rev ed 1841), they took *The Pilgrim's Progress* to be the model of allegory; by comparison Spenser was too complex and overly historical. For these readers, Spenser was the Rubens of poetry, a painter whose magic of coloring overcame defects of design (see *illustrators). Indeed, this pictorial Spenser, despite his 'vehement love of allegory,' became a regular source for Victorian painters: 'every year our exhibitions are sure to display one or two Unas, with the well-known lion, or some nymph on the Idle Lake, or some Britomart shedding down her yellow hair, or some Florimel, wobegone in the witche's hut; but ask the first half-dozen people standing by, catalogue in hand, about these pictures, and they will just refer to the quotation as all they know about the subject, and we doubt whether the painters themselves know much more' (Keightley 1855:368). Even a clerical editor of Spenser, George Gilfillan, finds his allegory to be a mighty maze without a plan, a work of imagination on the order of *The Thousand and One Nights* and best appreciated a canto at a time. *The Faerie Queene* 'has a high moral purpose, but it is not steadily pursued: [Spenser] diverges from it in every direction where the picturesque opens up a path, or beauty sheds a bewitching and bewildering smile. His passion for form, colour, the new, the fair, the pictorial, amounts almost to a disease' (Spenser ed 1859, 2: xiii).

As a classic of English poetry whose power to move and even to teach was thought to be experienced best in isolated episodes, *The Faerie Queene* was bound to be anthologized, issued in selected editions, and even rewritten in prose tales conforming to the age's conception of romantic narration (see *scholarship). Such editions of Spenser may account for the otherwise anomalous assumption that certain passages from the great unread poet will be familiar to a general audience. Ruskin and Gilfillan take for granted that their readers will know the description of Despair. In *Mary Barton*, Mrs Gaskell compares her heroine's resolved purpose of right-doing to the lion that accompanies Una through wilderness and danger. Becky Sharp is of Duessa's lineage, and Thackeray connects her by illustration and imagery with the mermaids in *FQ* II xii 30–4. In *The Eustace Diamonds*, Trollope suspends Frank Greystock between a Lucy who is 'truth itself,' and the deceitful Lizzie Eustace. Lizzie at one point resolves to read *The Faerie Queene* from sunrise to sundown and notably fails to do so. Ultimately, though she is outwardly fair, Frank sees her as 'soiled, haggard, dishevelled, and unclean.' (The opposition between the redemptive and deceptive woman is common in Victorian fiction, and Trollope is unusual in alluding specifically to *FQ*.) Markham Sutherland, the protagonist of J.A. Froude's *The Nemesis of Faith* (1849), remembers *The Faerie Queene* as second only to the Bible in his childhood, though his recollection, like that of Sir Walter Scott, is not of the allegory but of Una as a maiden in distress. *The Faerie Queene* is a much stronger presence in Charles Kingsley's historical novel *Westward Ho!* (1855). Not only do the heroes exemplify the traits and trials of friendship and justice, but one named Amyas is engaged like Artegall in saving Ireland from Spain. The book itself is devoted to the depiction of the manful and godly English gentleman, and Spenser himself appears as a character promising to devote a book to the adventures of Frank and Amyas Leigh. But *Westward Ho!* is an exception to the general Victorian practice of turning to *The Pilgrim's Progress* when overtones of allegory are required.

Of the popular abridged editions of Spenser, George L. Craik's *Spenser and His Poetry* (1845, rev ed 1871) was the most elaborate and influential. His three volumes weave biography, summary, commentary, and extensive quotation with the aim of freeing the universal, the indestructible, the 'living substance' of Spenser's poetry, from what time has petrified or made unintelligible. The result, in retrospect, is an extraordinary picture of Victorian understanding and taste. Even Spenser's Victorian champions were occasionally made uncomfortable by an imagination that, as Gilfillan put it, 'luxuriates downwards as well as upwards' (Spenser ed 1859, 2: xiii). Craik quotes most of the description of the fountain by the Bower of Bliss, including the jolly naked boys, but he veils the wanton maidens in prose: 'Guyon is somewhat agitated by the sight, painted by the poet in only too warm and life-like colours, which he chances to see as he passes near this fountain' (ed 1871:250). A similar discretion marks such illustrated adaptations as M.H. Towry's *Spenser for Children* (1878) and Mary Macleod's *Stories from 'The Faerie Queene'* (1897) (see *FQ, children's versions).

It was considered sufficiently important for every Englishman to have at least heard of Spenser that F.D. Maurice lectured on 'Spenser's *Faery Queene*' at the Working Men's College in 1864. The tone of his address, however, tells more about the Victorian view of the worker than the content does about Spenser (*The Friendship of Books and Other Lectures* 1874). The spread of general education created a demand for texts of the English classics to complement those in Greek and Latin, a demand that neither annotated anthologies nor children's editions could satisfy. In 1867, G.W. Kitchin's model school text of *FQ* I appeared from Oxford's Clarendon Press. Like his subsequent edition of Book II, (1868), it contains a general introduction, elaborate notes, and a glossary. These texts were the occasion of some controversy. Thomas Arnold (Matthew's younger brother) challenged not only the propriety of creating 'classbooks in *English* which may replace, so far as possible, the unequalled models furnished by antiquity,' but objected to the anti-Catholic nature of the allegory as explicated in the Introduction and the 'sensual taint' that pervades the verse. 'In all, about three hundred and thirty lines, in a third part only of the model work of this model writer, are necessarily excluded on the score of indecency' (1880:322, 326).

Both traditionalist and romantic readers tied Spenser's poetry to his life. The 1864 index to the popular monthly *Leisure Hour*, for example, lists the article on 'Edmund Spenser as a Sacred Poet' under biography (13:745–51). The notes and glossary of the Kitchin editions, however, connect the study of Spenser to the growing interest in historical causation, to an enthusiasm for philology that was to lead to the *New English Dictionary*, and to the emergence of English literature as a legitimate object of school and university study. These developments are evident in R.W. Church's *Spenser* in the English Men of Letters series (1879), the most complete statement of the Victorian understanding of Spenser. Church ties the poems to the progress of Spenser's life and places them in their historical contexts; he stresses the importance of *The Shepheardes Calender* as a turning point in the history of English poetry; and he entertains the standard objections to *The Faerie Queene* – the faulty or inconsistent construction of the allegory, the archaism, the prolixity – and, without directly disputing them, offers historical explanations. He balances faults with an appreciation of Spenser's imaginary world, the beauty and melody of his verse, and the intrinsic nobleness of his ethics and conception of human life generally. Although he finds insufficient unity in the story, he locates a compensatory consistency in its 'character and its ideal,' especially as it expresses the (particularly Victorian) virtue of 'manliness' (1879:149–51).

The emphasis on character also pervades the Spenser essays of Aubrey de Vere and Edward Dowden. De Vere actually interrupts an essay on 'Spenser as a Philosophic Poet' to attack the claims both of women for civil and political equality and of socialism by invoking the ideal relationship of Artegall to Britomart, who freed him from subjection to the Amazon and restored him to lordship (*Essays, Chiefly on Poetry* 1887). Dowden's essay on 'The Heroines of Spenser' is likewise an appropriation of Spenser's characters for a covert discussion of ideal womanhood. In de Vere's essay on 'Characteristics of Spenser's Poetry,' however, and even more in Dowden's 'Spenser, the Poet and Teacher' (a reply to James Russell Lowell's version of the romantic, picture-gallery Spenser), we find anticipations of the historical essays on Spenser that mark the reaction against nineteenth-century impressionism by the newly established professors of English literature at the beginning of this century (Dowden *Transcripts and Studies* 1888).

In 1897, T.E. Brown was still asking: 'Who now reads Spenser?' (p 393). It is a question to which the Victorians provided at least one answer that still pertains: teachers and their students. (See also Elizabeth Barrett *Browning and Robert *Browning.)

JEFFREY L. SPEAR
AND CHRISTINE KRUEGER

Thomas Arnold 1880 'Spenser as a Textbook' *Dublin Review* 3rd ser 4:321–32; T.E. Brown 1897 'Spenser: A Causerie' *The New Review* 16:393–404; Church 1879; Craik 1845; Dowden 1888; John Keble 1912 *Lectures on Poetry, 1832–1841* tr Edward Kershaw Francis, 2 vols (Oxford); Keightley 1855; Thomas Babington Macaulay 1831 [Review of Southey's edition of *The Pilgrim's Progress*] *Edinburgh Review* 54:450–61; 'Religio Spenseri' 1866 *Blackwood's* 99:200–23; Spenser ed 1859; Spenser ed 1867–87; [unsigned rev of Spenser's *Works* ed J. Payne Collier] 1862 *Athenaeum* 18 Jan: 72–6; de Vere 1887; John Wilson [Christopher North] 1833 'Spenser. No. I' *Blackwood's* 34(Nov):824–56; Wilson 1834 'Spenser. No. II' *Blackwood's* 36(Sept):408–30.

villeins The *OED* provides examples of the medieval term *villein* (also spelled *villain*, *villaine*, and *villen* in Spenser): a serf bound to a feudal overlord, '*spec.* a peasant occupier or cultivator entirely subject to a lord ... or attached to a manor ... a tenant in villeinage ... a bondsman. Hence formerly in general use, a peasant, country labourer, or lowborn rustic.' In Spenser's time, the term might refer to a specimen of this obsolete social category or, more often in a figurative sense, to the base and the cowardly, as throughout *The Faerie Queene*, where base behavior of lowborn 'villeins' reveals the kinship of ignobility and evil.

Although Spenser frequently uses the term in its more common contemporary figurative sense, he also refers explicitly to the archaic feudal institution in developing major concerns such as the social, political, and religious upheavals characterizing Elizabeth's reign and the fear of rebellion (eg, in Ireland). In *The Faerie Queene* especially, he examines these concerns against the backdrop of an imagined feudal past, its aura having been established through (among other devices) technical terms such as *villein* or assumptions about institutions such as villeinage. Yet villeinage as social and legal reality was not entirely extinct. Only ten or twelve years after Spenser's death, the crown was to sell various presumably obsolete feudal rights, among them dues to be assessed 'in lieu of villein works'; still later, landlords exploited these rights to squeeze the tenantry (Stone 1965:322–3). That villeins appear in several major episodes of a poem so suffused with antiquarian feeling is not then surprising.

In *The Faerie Queene*, *villein* frequently refers to the Irish. In Book II, for example, Maleger is a villein and his bondage to the flesh is called 'sinfull vellenage' (xi I, 26, 29, 35). His band, 'A thousand villeins' like 'a swarme of Gnats ... Out of the fennes of Allan' (ix 13, 16), may suggest the Irish peasants of *Vewe of Ireland* ('tenants at will' subjected to a landlord in a state similar to the medieval English condition of villeinage; see Gray in *Var* 2:281–2). Certainly the idea of being in bondage to the flesh exploits the figurative sense of the term as well as the literal. In *FQ* V, 'that Tyrant' Grantorto leads a gang of 'villens' (eg, xi 60, xii 3). As usurper of Irena's properly constituted authority, he and her champion Artegall reenact, in the political allegory, Lord Grey of Wilton's attempts to pacify the Irish who improperly gave fealty to Catholic Spain. Thus the term *villen* refers to this misplaced allegiance and to its base nature at the same time. Similarly in *FQ* VI, 'Those villeins' the cannibals with their shrieking bagpipes and their priest and altar may also resemble Spenser's vision of the wild, uncouth Catholic Irish.

More purely figurative uses of the term usually turn on the hierarchical relationships among characters. Despair is three times called 'villen' or a variant (eg, I ix 28), as well as more obviously disparaging terms such as 'carle' and 'Miscreant.' His opponents are inappropriately knights, his social and feudal superiors. This violation reflects the damage he perpetrates on the moral and spiritual order, as does Orgoglio's 'villeins powre' (I vii 12). Furor in Book II is called a 'villein' (iv 9), as are many enemies of justice in *FQ* V: Malengin, Pollente's groom, Dolon, and Braggadocchio. In *FQ* III-IV, *villein* and its variants frequently refer to enemies of virtuous love (cf *SC*, *June* 104, *Teares* 387). Yet the implications about feudal hierarchy are not completely effaced. When Timias turns the label against himself (III v 45), he defines his relationship to Belphoebe. This quite specific use of the term to indicate service due and social distance from a feudal superior reinforces the Petrarchan conceit of the passage. Similar examples abound in Book VI. JANE W. BROWN

Virgil (70–19 BC) The life of Publius Virgilius Maro spanned the turbulent period of the Triumvirate and the assassination of Julius Caesar as well as the ensuing civil wars and Octavian's ascendancy as Emperor Augustus. It also embraced the full flowering of Roman literary culture. Before Virgil, Latin poetry included only a few attempts at epic by Naevius (3rd century BC) and Ennius (239–169 BC), the didactic *De rerum natura* of Lucretius, and the neoteric lyrics of Catullus. Yet with the publication of the *Aeneid* shortly after Virgil's death, Latin literature reached its zenith. His influence cast its spell over all subsequent writing, indeed over all of Western literature.

For both the antique world and the Renaissance, Virgil's career exemplified the successful union of a poetic talent with a national destiny. After the battle of Philippi (42 BC), Octavian and Antony confiscated his ancestral property and gave it as a reward to their discharged veterans. Virgil's petition against the action brought him to the notice of Maecenas, the closest of Octavian's advisors, who became his patron and principal benefactor. Virgil dramatized these events in the pastoral fiction of his earliest published poetry, ten carefully crafted eclogues composed between 43 and 37 BC.

Maecenas' largesse enabled the poet to live in peaceful retirement, wholly absorbed in study and writing. It also enabled him to celebrate the emerging ideology of *romanitas* in his next publication, four *Georgics* (30 BC) that describe the labor needed to revive a land depleted by constant warfare. The same ideology dominates his posthumously published masterpiece, the *Aeneid*. Uniting myth, history, legendary materials, and allusions to contemporary events, his heroic poem celebrates Rome's national destiny.

Later generations aspired to the timeliness of Virgil's success. Certainly the emerging nationalism of the Renaissance prompted many poets, not least Spenser whom his contemporaries called 'the English Virgil,' to model their careers on Virgil's. This pattern is called the *rota Virgilii* or *cursus Virgilii*, the Virgilian wheel or course, and it is explained in a four-line proemium of unknown authorship appended to Renaissance editions of the *Aeneid*: 'Ille ego, qui quondam gracili modulatus avena / carmen, et egressus silvis vicina coegi / ut quamvis avido parerent arva colono, / gratum opus agricolis, at nunc horrentia Martis' (I am he who, after singing on the shepherd's slender pipe and leaving the woodside for the farmlands, urged the plowed lands ever so much to obey their eager tenant; my work was welcome to the farmers, but now I turn to the sterner stuff of Mars).

Virgil begins with the 'shepherd's slender pipe' (the pastoral *Eclogues*), proceeds to the 'farmlands' (the didactic *Georgics*), and finally arrives at the 'sterner stuff of Mars' (the epic *Aeneid*). Spenser describes his own career in similar terms in *FQ* I proem I: 'Lo I the man, whose Muse whilome did maske, / As time her taught, in lowly Shepheards weeds, / Am now enforst a far unfitter taske, / For trumpets sterne to chaunge mine Oaten reeds.'

The Renaissance received Virgil's *oeuvre* through a gigantic maze of commentary that began in antiquity, developed in the Middle Ages, and became more complicated after the invention of print. Medieval commentators regarded Virgil as divinely inspired, a Christian before Christ, because they construed Eclogue 4 as a prophecy of Christ's birth. Older commentators had focused more narrowly on textual criticism. In this domain, Virgil's first influential critic, Marcus Valerius Probus (fl AD 58–88), established a standard that successors emulated. The corpus of early commentary gradually uncovered and published in the sixteenth century indicates that the ancients found Virgil's style controversial. They criticized as a particular fault his new or rare application of old words in the figure of *cacozelia*, so that Jonson's later remark about Spenser applies equally to Virgil: 'in affecting the Ancients [he] writ no Language' (*Timber, or Discoveries*, ed 1925–52, 8:618). Certainly E.K. attributes *cacozelia* to Spenser in his commentary on *SC*, *October* 96, at one stroke identifying 'this our new Poete' (Epistle to Harvey) with his ancient master.

Other early commentators provided a base that the Renaissance expanded considerably. Foremost was Servius (4th c), who coined the word *polysemus* to designate the many levels of philosophical and historical meaning that radiate from Virgil's poetry. Servius' older contemporary, Aelius Donatus, annotated the text in a more literal manner with valuable insight into its diction, syntax, and rhetorical figures. Printed editions of Virgil's works from the Florentine edition of 1487–8 onwards routinely included these commentaries as aids for the reader. Renaissance editors like Cristoforo Landino (1488), Antonio Mancinello (1490), Badius Ascensius (1500), and Piero Valeriano (1523) hoped to modify the distortions of medieval interpretation and restore to the text something of its ancient sense. Readings of the poetry as Christian allegory nonetheless continued to play a large role well into the Renaissance.

Christian interpretation of the *Aeneid* begins with Fulgentius' *De expositione virgilianae continentia* (5th c). He sees *Aeneid* 1–6 as representing *sub figuralitate* the life of a man from youth (1–3) through maturity (4–5) to old age (6). This pattern governs Bernard Sylvestris' assertions in his *Commentum super sex libros Eneidos Virgilii* (c 1136) that Virgil wrote *sub integumento*, wrapping truth in the veil of fiction. Combining narrative analysis and etymological deconstruction (eg, Ant-andros, the name of Aeneas' first retreat in Book 3, means 'contrarium virilitatis'), Bernard shows how Aeneas passes through important stages in his maturation. The most notable Renaissance commentators, however, subordinated these explicitly Christian meanings to more abstract and universally applicable ones, or else they related the poetic action to historical events in Virgil's lifetime. In his *Quaestiones Camaldulenses* (1470), Landino articulates a Neoplatonic interpretation.

Aeneas' quest represents a pursuit of the highest good, which is true wisdom. The hero's many wanderings educate him in the forces of evil at work in the world. Landino later modified this interpretation in his edition (1488) of Virgil's works with line-by-line annotations that ground the action in its concrete detail, its historical reference, and its rhetorical particularity.

Spenser came to Virgil through such editions and commentaries, though we cannot identify the specific ones he used. Certainly his sense of the Virgilian tradition included poems that we no longer consider part of the canon. For example, his longest sustained debt to the tradition is *Virgils Gnat* (c 1580, pub 1591), an elegant paraphrase of the *Culex*, a minor poem attributed doubtfully to the Latin poet. Later he paraphrased large portions of yet another doubtfully Virgilian poem, *Ciris*. Its outlines help shape the narrative of Britomart's exchange with Glauce after discovering her love for Artegall in *FQ* III ii 30–51.

Spenser's deep knowledge of Virgil's three major poems permeated his entire creative endeavor. Early in his career, he found that the *Eclogues* had much to offer him. Within their lyric frame, they incorporate Homeric myths, epyllionic narratives, epic descriptions, folk-song refrains, witty epigrams, lyric expression, aspects of comic and tragic characterization, and the flow of conversation from Socratic dialogues. The medley of genres, modes, and styles provided the young poet a perfect training ground in all these forms.

Virgil himself achieved this medley by imitating the *Idylls* of Theocritus. The model was ideal because it was itself an allusive amalgam of earlier literary achievements. Composed in the hellenistic age after the great achievements of earlier ages, the *Idylls* reprise the whole history of Greek literature in miniature form. While Virgil adopted most of Theocritus' pastoral conventions, including the dactylic hexameter with its bucolic dieresis or pause after the fourth foot in each verse, he nonetheless transformed his model into an extraordinarily complex composition. On the one hand, he integrated a profusion of social, political, and moral themes. On the other, he incorporated a sequential patterning that links individual poems in subtle and sophisticated ways. To each eclogue, moreover, he imparted a poetic self-consciousness that confirms his own artistic seriousness. The dramatic situations of 3 and 7, for example, depict singing contests (the *amoebaeum carmen*) that sharpen their participants' aesthetic awareness. Others depict a poet's coming of age. In 5, the elder Menalcas summons young Mopsus to sing a lament (*epicedium*) for the dead Daphnis, often identified with Julius Caesar. Mopsus' topic, however, seems less important than the technical skill of his performance. It so impresses the elder poet that he acknowledges the younger poet as his successor.

Spenser sustained a delicate relationship with Virgil's *Eclogues* throughout his career. As a mature poet, he recalled Gallus' lament from Eclogue 10.31–69 in the dying lady's lament of *Daphnaïda* 263–92, and Thyrsis' enthusiasm from Eclogue 7.55–9 in Hobbinol's welcome for Colin in *Colin Clout* 22–31. As a younger poet, he found inspiration for *The Shepheardes Calender* in the general structure of the *Eclogues*. E.K. describes the pastoral mode as plaintive, recreative, and moral (Gen Arg), qualities of the *Eclogues* as well as *The Shepheardes Calender*. While no single eclogue of the *Calender* directly imitates any of Virgil's, the singing contest of *August* parallels those of Eclogues 3 and 7, and the funeral lament of *November* recalls that of Eclogue 5. Somewhat closer imitations include the wooing of the beloved in *Januarye* 55–60 from Virgil's Eclogue 2.54–6 and the description of the *locus amoenus* in *June* 1–16 from Eclogue 1.48–58. More important for Spenser than any direct verbal borrowing was the pattern that the *Eclogues* projected at the beginning of Virgil's career.

Virgil's mid-career achievement, the *Georgics*, combines such myths as those of the Golden Age (1.121–59) and Orpheus (4.314–557) with the implacable givens of history and science. Overtly the text expounds the arts of horticulture, soil conservation, animal husbandry, the cultivation of bees, and a host of other skills as aids for reclaiming the homeland from temporal and human disorders. Covertly it relates this labor not only to nature, but also to a social order that signals Octavian's redemption of the state from its civil wars. Labor itself is cognate with heroic control, both private and public, personal and political, and the fullest use of time occurs in the field of communal action for a new society.

Spenser's relationship with the *Georgics* seems more tenuous than his relationship with Virgil's other works. In *The Shepheardes Calender*, he acknowledges Virgil's purpose 'to yield the timely eare' (*Oct* 58) by prescribing a course of action, a purpose congenial with Spenser's own efforts in *The Faerie Queene* to fashion a courtesy book for the aristocracy of a new empire. His direct imitations from the *Georgics* are less overt: in *FQ* II x 3, the fall of the giants echoes *Georgics* 1.278–83; in IV x 44–7, part of the hymn to Venus echoes *Georgics* 2.323–31; and in *Daphnaïda* 463–539, the lament for the beloved recalls the tale of Orpheus in *Georgics* 4.453–527. Like the *Eclogues*, however, the *Georgics* most influenced as a general model. It is a sequence of didactic poems depicting varied endeavors as *The Shepheardes Calender* would do on a pastoral scale and as *The Faerie Queene* would do on an epic scale.

With their pious reverence for Roman life, the *Georgics* provide an important introduction to the *Aeneid*. Virgil's epic narrates three conflicts: a cosmic one between fate and free will, a private one between Aeneas and his own impulses, and a public one between Aeneas and others who become obstacles to him. The dramatic confrontations of cosmic, private, and public typify the norms of Renaissance epic. Aeneas is preeminently the type of character who searches for the best public role to implement his own destiny and his private sense of what is right for him. As the whole man in all his parts, he provides a model for imitation. As Spenser observes in his Letter to Raleigh, Homer 'ensampled' in Agamemnon 'a good governour' and in Ulysses 'a vertuous man,' but Virgil combined both states 'in the person of Aeneas.'

In Virgil's epic, however, the main character does not appear from the outset as such a hero. His heroism develops only in the course of the poem, both in its first six books or 'Odyssean' half narrating his wanderings, and in its last six books or 'Iliadic' half narrating the wars in Italy. One important element of the *Aeneid*'s epic style qualifies this structure. It is the intrusion of the speaker's own subjective voice into the poem's action. On occasion, the speaker directly addresses the fictional characters, as in the apostrophes to Dido (4.408), Palinurus (5.840), and Camilla (11.665). In these cases, the narrator is a wholly sympathetic observer whose point of view is a private, human, dramatic one, concerned with the happiness of individuals, their personal choices, and their personal preferences. On other occasions, however, he is a detached observer concerned with the political destiny of Rome, her proud and sometimes bloody past, her havoc-ridden present, her hoped-for future. The prophecies of imperial destiny that recur throughout the poem (1.257–96, 6.756–888, 8.608–728, 10.1–117) stretch the tension between private and public points of view to the limit. Virgil, of course, hopes for all the joy that the Augustan victory promised, above all the *pax Romana* that eventually became a fact of history (though he himself could not know it); but his speaker is too subtle, too sophisticated, too aware of the ironic pitfalls in human nature and human history to give a univocal voice to the triumph.

Virgil's pathos provided a model for every Renaissance epic poet. Spenser appropriates it for *The Faerie Queene* in a complex manner. His vision, generally more optimistic than Virgil's, nonetheless blurs at the edges in the dynastic narratives and prophetic encomia of I ix where Arthur tells of his lineage, of II x where the speaker recounts the genealogy of British kings and Elfin emperors, of III iii where Britomart learns that competing families will unite in marriage, of IV xi where a nation of mighty rivers results from the union of many tributaries, and of V vii where Britomart at Isis Church dreams that clemency (Isis) and justice (the crocodile) produce a mighty lion. In each case, Spenser appropriates the melancholy of his Virgilian analogue where historical reality emerges as a compromise between individual freedom and collective necessity.

Spenser alludes to the *Aeneid* everywhere in his own work, in his shorter poems as well as *The Faerie Queene*. Among the former, for example, the felling of an oak in *SC*, *Februarie* 215–21 recalls a simile in *Aeneid* 2.628–31, the evocation of the Elysian fields in *Time* 332–42 summons their description in *Aeneid* 6.637–78, and Jove's commission of Mercury in *Mother Hubberd* 1225–99 replicates the same action in *Aeneid* 1.223–301. In *FQ* I ii, the tale of Fradubio evokes the fate of Polydorus in *Aeneid* 3; in I v, Night's dwelling recalls the underground of *Aeneid* 6, as do the house of Mammon in II vii and Ate's house in IV i 19–25; in II iii 21–31, the appearance of Belphoebe echoes the appearance of Venus in *Aeneid* 1.314–29; in III iii 22–5, Merlin's prophecy suggests the Sibyl's prophecy in *Aeneid* 6.83–97; the account of the Trojan War in III ix 40–3 parodies *Aeneid* 2; Arthur's slaying of the Souldan in V viii 30–43 follows Aeneas' slaying of Mezentius in *Aeneid* 11; and in V x 9–10, Geryon reflects his counterpart in *Aeneid* 7.659–63. References to other texts, both classical and Renaissance, mediate many of these allusions. The tale of Fradubio, for example, follows an episode in *Orlando furioso* 6 that Ariosto in turn appropriated from *Inferno* 13 where Dante evoked *Aeneid* 3. Spenser shaped his poetry with a full knowledge of the Virgilian origin of all these texts.

Spenser received a many-sided Virgil, and he reflects this complexity in the variety of his own appropriations. Some paraphrase Virgil closely; others follow only the broadest structural patterns; most combine with allusions to many different authors. On the whole, they reflect the growing secularization of Virgilian interpretation in Spenser's age, though they strike an easy accommodation with Spenser's own Christian allegory. They fully exemplify the enduring value and permanent relevance of Virgil's art.

WILLIAM J. KENNEDY

A standard modern edition of Virgil is the *Opera* ed R.A.B. Mynors (Oxford 1969); see also *Appendix Vergiliana* ed W.V. Clausen, et al (Oxford 1966). There are recent translations of the *Aeneid* by Robert Fitzgerald (New York 1983), the *Georgics* by L.P. Wilkinson (Harmondsworth 1982), and *Eclogues* by Guy Lee (rev ed Harmondsworth 1984). There is also the Loeb Classical Library edition by H. Rushton Fairclough. One of the great, and often reprinted, early translations of the three works is by Dryden (1697). Earlier translations, some perhaps known to Spenser, include the various *Aeneids* (in whole or part) of Caxton (1490), Douglas (1513, including Book 13 by Mapheus Vegius; see Virgil ed 1957–64 for a modern ed), Surrey (c 1555, though written earlier, a translation of Book 4), Phaer and Twyne (1583, the 13 books, an expansion of Phaer's earlier English version of 1558–62), and Stanyhurst (1582, Books 1–4). Fleming (1575, 1589) translated the *Eclogues* and the *Georgics*.

Giuliano Mambelli 1954 *Gli annali delle edizioni virgiliane* (Florence) lists and describes principal editions and translations (before 1600, there are some 275 European editions of the collected works in Latin and many more of the individual works in Latin or in translation). Still a valuable history of the reception of the text and life is Comparetti ed 1895, though the allegorical tradition of interpretation is dealt with in greater detail in D.C. Allen 1970 and Murrin 1980. Few of the early commentaries are translated, though they are essential to an understanding of the Virgilian tradition: Tiberius Claudius Donatus 1905–6 *Interpretationes vergilianae* ed Henricus Georgius, 2 vols (Leipzig; rpt Stuttgart 1969); Servius ed 1878–87; Bernard Sylvestris ed 1977 and ed 1979. These early commentaries are often combined with those of Cristoforo Landino (1488), Antonio Mancinello (1490), Badius Ascensius (1500), and Piero Valeriano (1523) in Renaissance editions of Virgil.

Useful introductions to the life and works include W.F. Jackson Knight 1944 *Roman Virgil* (London) and R[obert] D[eryck] Williams 1967 *Virgil* Greece and Rome: New Surveys in the Classics No 1 (Oxford). Among the many modern commentaries, see, for instance, W.R. Johnson 1976 *Darkness Visible: A Study of Vergil's 'Aeneid'* (Berkeley and Los Angeles); Otis 1963; Viktor Pöschl 1962 *The Art of Virgil* (Ann Arbor); and Kenneth Quinn 1968 *Virgil's 'Aeneid': A Critical Description* (London).

For Virgil and Spenser, see Hughes 1929, with many parallels; Bush 1963, esp pp 98–102, who sees more of a difference than a similarity between the two; William Stanford Webb 1937 'Vergil in Spenser's Epic Theory' *ELH* 4:62–84; O'Connell 1977, on the historical themes; and Fichter 1982, on the tradition of the dynastic epic.

See also the reading lists for *Dido, *georgic, *heroic poem before Spenser, *pastoral.

Virgils Gnat. See **Complaints: *Virgils Gnat***

Virgin Mary, imagery of Camden's observation that Elizabeth had been born on the eve of the Nativity of the Virgin Mary, and died on the eve of the Annunciation, summarized the life of the Virgin Queen in terms of a providential imagery that pious Elizabethans would have recognized and felt to be appropriate. One of the essential beliefs of the early Protestants was the predestinate nature of the Reformation. When Elizabeth acceded to the throne, she was greeted as a godly prince providentially appointed to deliver a chosen people from the Antichrist. As it became apparent that she would never marry, her virginity began to assume an apocalyptic meaning. It was as if she had by providential design attained a symbolic kinship with the Virgin Mary and could therefore without impropriety be venerated by Protestant patriots in terms and images formerly reserved for the Queen of Heaven.

For an Elizabethan poet undertaking to vindicate his prince's claim to be the predestined ruler of an elect nation, identification of the Queen with the Virgin Mary provided a vehicle of praise well suited to his purpose. From the early years of her reign, Elizabeth was regularly compared with such Old Testament national heroines as Judith and Esther, who had traditionally been regarded as prefigurations of the Virgin Mary in their roles as conqueror of the devil and savior of the chosen people. The classical figure of the lunar goddess Diana provided a pagan image of virginity expressive of Elizabeth's control over the seas that were bringing new wealth to her people. Furthermore, Astraea, the virgin queen of justice invoked in Virgil's fourth eclogue as returning to usher in a period of universal peace, had long been identified with the Virgin Mary. For Elizabethan poets, their Queen's virginity could be taken as emblematic of her kinship with all these virgins at once, in her roles as temporal and spiritual ruler of her people.

PETER McCLURE AND ROBIN HEADLAM WELLS

On the iconography of the Virgin Mary, see Mirella Levi d'Ancona 1957 *The Iconography of the Immaculate Conception in the Middle Ages and Early Renaissance* ([New York]); Michael P. Carroll 1986 *The Cult of the Virgin Mary: Psychological Origins* (Princeton); Stanley Stewart 1966 *The Enclosed Garden: The Tradition and the Image in Seventeenth-Century Poetry* (Madison, Wis); Marina Warner 1976 *Alone of All Her Sex: The Myth and the Cult of the Virgin Mary* (London); Arthur Watson 1934 *The Early Iconography of the Tree of Jesse* (Oxford). On the Elizabethan adaptation of Marian imagery, see Cain 1978; Wells 1983:14–21; E.C. Wilson 1939:167–229; Yates 1975:29–87.

virtues To Renaissance philosophers and poets, the traditional virtues were not barren abstractions but vital entities, and their relations to one another and to the vices were important areas of reality to be explored. Theories of the virtues underlay legal treatises and shaped the education of the ruling classes. Consequently they had implications for the safety and prosperity of the state. In conceiving an heroic poem expounding the virtues, Spenser was undertaking a practical work in the public interest as well as participating in intellectual discussion that engaged the best minds of the age.

Elizabethan poet-moralists such as Spenser tended to think in categories established by a long tradition of philosophical exegesis, ancient and medieval, pagan and Christian. Knowledge of the virtues, like other knowledge, tended to be formulaic, and their interrelations were often diagrammatically expressed. The resulting schemata were models of reality just as valid to serious thinkers then as are molecular models to modern physicists. They were practical as well as speculative, serving as guides to conduct in a world of baffling possibilities. In particular, they clarified the frontiers of the continuing conflict between good and evil, a savage struggle whose stakes were nothing less than the present happiness and eternal destiny of man.

Earthly happiness rather than eternal destiny was increasingly the focus of Renaissance moral philosophy. Moralists sided with Cicero against Gregory and Thomas Aquinas in preferring the active to the contemplative life and in exalting duty over felicity. Both learned treatises and popular poetry stressed the claims of public good on private virtue, reflected in Sidney's conviction that 'the ending end of all earthly learning [is] virtuous action' (ed 1973b:83). Educational treatises such as Elyot's *Boke Named the Governour* and Bryskett's *Discourse of Civill Life* typically founded their moral ideal on the four cardinal, or axial, virtues: prudence, temperance, fortitude, and justice. This tetrad, expounded in

Plato's *Republic* 4 as the core of right conduct, was transmitted through the Stoics and Cicero to the medieval church. Ambrose, Augustine, and ultimately Aquinas Christianized the cardinal virtues and made them subservient or instrumental to the three 'theological' virtues – faith, hope, and charity – derived from I Corinthians 13:13. Thus pagan and Christian ethics, the teachings of Plato and Paul, united to form a perfect series of seven, the greatest or root virtue being charity. In *The Faerie Queene*, the three theological virtues appear in Fidelia, Speranza, and Charissa of I x and the four cardinal supply the framework of the poem.

This framework is not disclosed in the Letter to Raleigh that accompanied the 1590 edition of *The Faerie Queene*; instead Spenser explains that his poem will treat 'the twelve private morall vertues, as Aristotle hath devised,' reserving the 'polliticke vertues' to a sequel. This division between the private and political hemispheres of moral conduct was standard in his time, deriving from Aristotle's *Ethics* and *Politics*, and it constitutes almost all of Aristotle's contribution to the general organization of the poem. Attempts to reconcile Spenser's virtues with Aristotle's in the *Ethics*, or even to draw from Aristotle a total of twelve, have been unfruitful (*Var* 1:342–3; see entries above on chastity, courtesy, holiness, justice and equity, temperance). More successful have been the efforts of Josephine Bennett and especially Rosemond Tuve to associate Spenser's virtues with the medieval tradition of the cardinal virtues and their branches (Bennett 1942:229–30). Tuve, citing the phrase 'Aristotle and the rest' in the Letter, cautions against ignoring the contribution of 'the rest,' singling out in particular the influential treatises of Cicero (*De inventione*), Macrobius (*Commentary on the Dream of Scipio*), and Martin of Braga (the pseudo-Senecan *Formula honestae vitae*). In the writings of these and their successors, each cardinal virtue appears in the company of other virtues related to it as aspects or manifestations in particular situations (Tuve 1966, ch 2). Thus Bryskett remarks that 'there are then by the generall consent of all men foure principall vertues appertaining to civill life, which are Fortitude, Temperance, Justice, and Prudence; from which foure are also derived (as branches from their trees) sundry others to make up the number of twelve' (*Discourse* 1606:214).

Macrobius' scheme of the cardinal virtues and their branches – simply a list without definitions or analysis – was widely used as a ground plan by medieval moral theorists, who added virtues from other sources. It is not surprising, therefore, that Macrobius' and Spenser's schemes show correspondences. Among the virtues associated by Macrobius with temperance are *pudicitia* (purity; ed 1952:122) and *castitas* (chastity), corresponding to the titular virtues of *FQ* I and III. Among those associated with justice are *amicitia* (friendship) and *concordia*, the concerns of Book IV, and *humanitas*, for which Thomas Cooper's *Thesaurus* (1565) includes among its meanings 'gentilnesse: curteisie: gentill behavuour: civilitie: pleasantnesse in maners,' the concerns of Book VI. In the six books completed by Spenser, then, the cardinal virtues of temperance and justice appear between their branches as depicted in the most influential medieval scheme of the virtues.

The nineteenth-century critic Thomas Keightley suggested that Spenser may have intended to use the other two cardinal virtues, fortitude and prudence, as the subjects of Books VIII and XI, the cores of his remaining three-book groupings (*Fraser's Magazine* 60[1859]:410–22). The attribution of the *Cantos of Mutabilitie* to a Book VII on constancy by Spenser's 1609 editor supports this suggestion, for *constantia* is regarded by Macrobius as a branch of fortitude. This hypothesis is attractive in that the resulting scheme would have the advantage of reserving to the second half of the poem the virtues regarded since ancient times as composing the heroic ideal (Curtius ed 1953:173–9, Steadman 1967:9–12). Though all four cardinal virtues were basic to the education of the ruler (Harris 1965:145–52), fortitude and prudence had a special status, as Machiavelli recognized in his similes, drawn from Cicero, of the prince as both lion and fox (*The Prince* 18, *De officiis* 1.13.41). Furthermore, each without the other was a travesty of itself, as Shakespeare made clear in the rashness of Hotspur (fortitude without prudence) and the 'discretion' of Falstaff (prudence without fortitude). Arthur's proficiency in this pair of virtues, like Prince Hal's, would signify his worthiness to rule. The distribution of the cardinal virtues in the plan of *The Faerie Queene* permits the heroic ideal to be expounded climactically and allows for the same progression from private to public virtue within the twelve books treating the 'private morall vertues' that was to appear in the private-political dichotomy of the 24-book plan.

This progression from private to public virtue appears also in the smaller structural dichotomies of the poem. The virtues of the first three books – holiness, temperance, and chastity – when considered together are less public in scope than are those of the second three – friendship, justice, and courtesy – whose domains are mainly social. Cicero declares that one who conceives of good apart from social duty can 'value neither friendship nor justice nor generosity' (*De officiis* 1.2.5). On the even more fundamental level of pairs of books, holiness and temperance are intrapersonal in their moral concerns, and their domains are those of revealed religion and natural ethics respectively in the quest for personal moral integrity. Chastity and friendship are interpersonal, and their domains are the sexual and asexual kinds of attraction between persons in the quest for enduring relationships. Justice and courtesy are social, and their domains are those of law and manners (the sphere of moral obligation unenforceable by law) in the pursuit of social stability and harmony.

Furthermore, within each pair of books, there is a movement from a virtue that is a spiritual absolute to one that is an empirical norm. The virtues of the odd-numbered books – holiness, chastity, and justice – are, as treated by Spenser, derived from heaven and bestowed upon their champions (human knights) by supernatural agency. Those of the even-numbered books – temperance, friendship, and courtesy – are experiential in nature and are lodged in their champions (fairy knights) from birth. The first set, consisting of rectitude to an intuited standard, are such as Aquinas would call infused virtues; the second, ethical habits or skills, are such as he would designate acquired virtues, those 'by which man behaves well in relation to human affairs' (*Summa theologica* 1a2ae 63.4, in ed 1964–76, 23:163). In each pairing there appears, therefore, a progression from a virtue whose moral reference is vertical and whose essential concern is conformity to a divine absolute to a virtue whose moral reference is horizontal and whose essential concern is with earthly harmony. Within each structural dichotomy, we may discern a progression from supernatural to natural, invisible to visible, private to public, supporting the general movement of the poem toward its goal of earthly moral perfection (Horton 1978:124–37).

This goal Spenser represents geographically in Cleopolis, 'historically' in Arthur, and abstractly in the virtue of magnificence. As described in the Letter to Raleigh, magnificence is a crowning virtue – 'the perfection of all the rest' – and a subsuming virtue – one that 'conteineth in it them all.' Spenser's magnificence is not Aristotle's, nor is it a mistake for magnanimity, which, however, occupies a somewhat similar position in Aristotle's series (*Ethics* 4.3.14–16) and has to do with the seeking and claiming of honor (4.3.17–22, 38; 4.4.1–6). It is descended instead from Cicero through medieval treatises as a branch of fortitude with the twofold signification of high aspiration and perseverance: 'the contemplation and execution of great and sublime projects with a certain grandeur and magnificence of imagination' (Cicero *De inventione* 2.54.163; Tuve 1966:59). When we read of Redcrosse that 'Upon a great adventure he was bond' I i 3), we are to understand that magnificence is for him, as for Arthur, a motivating and sustaining virtue, just as it is for all the knights their ultimate moral destination. In his aspiration 'to all high desert and honour' and in his unrelenting 'poursuit' of his goal (III v 1–2), Arthur is the paragon of magnificence. Since the pursuit of ideal love as well as magnificence is characterized by high desire and perseverance, Arthur's quest for Gloriana may easily serve to symbolize his and the reader's moral growth. The moral significance of the quest is in keeping with the teaching of Augustine, according to whom all the virtues, including the cardinal, are forms of love (Curtius ed 1953:523).

Magnificence as perseverance implies struggle; and in the moral-allegorical mode of *The Faerie Queene*, the virtues battle with the vices. Their allegorical conflict for possession of the soul is conspicuous in medieval devotional treatises (in which frequently the seven 'spiritual virtues' of Isaiah II.2 combat the seven deadly sins) and in the morality plays of the fifteenth century, and it continued to fascinate readers well into the seventeenth (see, eg, Bunyan's *Holy War* 1682). This abiding interest in moral allegory was not limited to the unlearned. The intellectual circle of Thomas More probably took seriously his account of an after-dinner game of the Utopians 'in which the vices fight a pitched battle with the virtues' (ed 1963–, 4:129). In his *Discourse*, Bryskett has Spenser excuse himself from participating in a discussion of the virtues on the grounds that he has undertaken a heroic poem treating the virtues and their corresponding vices. In the poem, each virtue is to be given a knightly champion 'in whose actions and feates of armes and chivalry, the operations of that vertue, whereof he is the protector, are to be expressed, and the vices and unruly appetites that oppose themselves against the same, to be beaten downe and overcome' (ed 1970:22).

The prototype of the allegorical battle of the virtues and vices is Prudentius' *Psychomachia*, contemporary with which was the late-classical tendency to read moral-allegorical conflict into the Homeric and Virgilian epics. The military metaphor is prominent in the New Testament (eg, 1 Tim 1.18, 6.12; 2 Tim 2.4), the *locus classicus* being Paul's description of the Christian armor in Ephesians 6, cited by Spenser in the Letter to Raleigh.

According to Bryskett, Spenser intended the allegorical conflict in *The Faerie Queene* to serve the purposes not only of moral motivation but also of moral definition. Cicero distinguishes two ways in which vices are related to virtues: on the one hand are the vices that are the direct opposites of the virtues, and on the other are 'those qualities which seem akin and close to these but are really far removed from them.' For example, 'diffidence is the opposite of confidence, and is therefore a vice; temerity is not opposite to courage, but borders on it and is akin to it, and yet is a vice. In a similar way each virtue will be found to have a vice bordering upon it, either one to which a definite name has become attached, as temerity which borders on courage, or stubbornness which borders on perseverance, or superstition which is akin to religion; or one without any definite name' (*De inventione* 2.54.165). Cicero's example of religion and superstition as apparent neighbors calls to mind *FQ* I iii in which true religion meets its 'bordering vice' in Corceca as spurious faith and its 'opposite,' its overt and avowed enemy, in Sansloy as rebellious irreligion. Thus the clash of virtue and vice yields distinctions necessary to an accurate understanding of the desired moral qualities.

These qualities, according to a tradition of biblical interpretation descending from Philo Judaeus in the first century AD, are planted and nurtured in the garden of the mind. Commenting on Genesis, he remarks, 'God plants in the soul as it were a garden of virtues and of the modes of conduct corresponding to each of them, a garden that brings the soul to perfect happiness' (*Noah's Work as a Planter* 2.36–8 [Loeb ed 3:231]). Prominent among the trees of this garden, according to Ambrose, are the four cardinal virtues (*De paradiso* 12–14). The notion of a paradise within the mind potentially equal to or greater than that forfeited by Adam is one of the most frequently encountered *topoi* of medieval literature, and reflections of it appear throughout *The Faerie Queene*, vying with the image of the fully accoutred and accomplished knight as an emblem of moral maturity. In a parallel tradition, paradise was regarded as a place of instruction. The garden setting of Plato's Academy, together with the experience reported by Paul in 2 Corinthians 12.2–4 and interpreted by Origen in *De principiis* 2.1.6, encouraged the notion of the garden as an ideal environment for moral and spiritual tutelage. There is thus a firm basis in the classical and Christian exegetical traditions, as well as in Spenser's own references to the flowers of chastity and courtesy and their bower (III v 52, VI proem), for regarding *The Faerie Queene* itself as both the pattern of the reader's moral education and its setting. The positioning of the cardinal virtues between their branches in each three-book grouping enables the garden of virtue to be shadowed in the very frame of the poem, creating a great Renaissance image of a medieval commonplace and symbolizing the effect of the poem upon the reader's mind.

Whether this effect – what Edward Dowden called the 'grand self-culture' it proposes (quoted in Mueller 1959:125) – can be squared with the Protestant doctrine of human depravity and justification by faith, in which Spenser evidently believed (I x I), is a question worth raising. In the light of 2 Peter 1.5–7 ('joyne moreover vertue with your faith'), we should note the anterior positioning of holiness in Spenser's scheme and its dependence upon faith and divine grace. Redcrosse is insufficient in himself to defeat his enemies; he must be saved by Arthur from Orgoglio and by Una from Despair. We should note also the homage paid by Guyon and his Palmer to Redcrosse in II i 26–31. In a theological context, Spenser assigns temperance in particular and pagan ethics in general to the process of sanctification, distinguishing their province from that of justification and regeneration, which are the work of faith. In Pauline and Petrine theology, the office of temperance and the other virtues is posterior to that of faith (Eph 2.8–10, 2 Pet 1:5–7). The entire moral action of *The Faerie Queene* is posterior to that moment, described in the Letter to Raleigh and assumed in the poem, in which Redcrosse first put on the Christian armor and appeared in a splendor unimagined before.

Spenser's scheme of the virtues is wholly conventional, being deeply rooted in tradition. It is also extraordinarily inventive – an intricate, dynamic structure marvelously suited to the didactic and aesthetic intentions of the poem. As an organizing structure, it is so contrived that the successive stages of the poem – Books I, I-II, I-III, I-VI – may approximate rounded units while supporting (with only slight revision of the ending of I-III and perhaps ultimately of I-VI) the symmetry of the unfolding pattern. The addition of the *Cantos of Mutabilitie* crowned the six-book fragment with something very like thematic wholeness. One may be grateful for the unity of the poem as it exists while believing it compensates only partly for the noncompletion of the grand design. RONALD A. HORTON

vision The prominence of vision in Spenser's poetry is readily apparent. His earliest works are the translated visionary sonnets in *Theatre for Worldlings*, and most of the *Complaints* also present themselves as visions. From beginning to end, seeing something in *The Faerie Queene* causes or marks crucial narrative turns; the poem draws upon a tradition, as old as Plato, of figuring acts of cognition and understanding with visual metaphors (Robinson 1972). Spenser's heroes must learn to see properly in an allegory that works largely by visualizing moral, spiritual, or intellectual issues. The prominence of vision has helped to animate discussions of the rhetorical or mimetic nature of his narrative, as well as of his pictorialism. Above all, it has encouraged a Romantic and post-Romantic tendency to read Spenser as a prophetic poet who modeled both his rhetoric and his fictions on biblical apocalyptic.

The importance of Apocalypse for Spenser can hardly be overestimated; but it is essential to recognize how cautiously he indulged his prophetic impulse, and how rigorously he distinguished visionary poetics from any arrogation of prophetic authority. Characters within *The Faerie Queene* see visions, but the narrative voice (unlike Dante's) reports no visions of its own to warrant the poem's truth. Instead, Spenser cites 'antique rolles' laid up in the Muses' 'everlasting scryne' (I proem 2), alleging prior texts as authorities rather than prophetically attesting to his own experience. Similarly, even in the most visionary of the shorter poems, he relies on the mediation of written or spoken language – that is, on authority – as against the immediacy of vision.

In the *Theatre* sonnets, for example, the apocalyptic refrain 'I saw' elevates everyday perception of the world's decay into emblematic revelation; it also presents Spenser's youthful translations from Petrarch, du Bellay, and St John as if they were firsthand experience. Van der Noot provided woodcuts for his *Theatre* on the model of Apocalypse so that his readers could join in the visionary refrain (Wittreich 1979:19–26). The sonnets thus initially appear to subsume within the same visionary rhetoric both emblem and revelation, both literature and Scripture, both poetry and prophecy. But a subtle change marks the turn in sonnet 15 from the world's vanity to the consolations of faith. Everyone sees the world's vanity, but not everyone sees the last things; that vision must be accepted on authority. Therefore, although the last sonnet preserves the visionary chant 'I saw,' it has now become the quoted speech of an identified seer: 'I saw new Earth, new Heaven, *sayde Saint John*. / And loe, the sea (*quod he*) is now no more' (italics added). This shift from experience to authority, from seeing to hearing, also occurs in Spenser's other vision poems in accordance with biblical formulas for both faith and false prophecy.

False prophets steal the Lord's words from one another; they 'have sene nothing,' but 'speake the vision of their owne heart and not out of the mouth of the Lord' (Jer 23.16, 30; Ezek 13.3). True prophets, on the contrary, see visions incongruously 'out of the mouth of the Lord.' Their experience of God's will transcends all authorities and traditions; therefore they see rather than hear God's word (eg, Isa 2.1, Hab 2.1, Amos 1.1, Rev 1.12). Although we come after prophecy has ceased and too late to share the apostles' immediate experience, we still have access to revelation, but only at second hand, only by hearing the testimony of others. Faith, therefore, 'is by hearing'; it is 'the evidence of things which are not sene' (Rom 10.17, Heb 11.1).

Spenser's vision poems deploy vision and hearing to accord with these biblical formulas. *Visions of the Worlds Vanitie*, for example, begins with a disclaimer. Unlike a false prophet, Spenser announces that he speaks these visions from his own mind. Even more telling are *Visions of Bellay* and *Visions of Petrarch*, which rework the *Theatre* sonnets to avoid the prophetic pretensions of the earlier poems. The four sonnets adapted from Apocalypse are omitted, so that the visionary chant no longer covers the gap between poetry and revelation. The new titles – *Bellay* and *Petrarch* – cite the poet's precedents, his *auctores*, where the earlier versions had claimed immediate experience. The poet is no longer presented as a seer, but as a translator or redactor. Moreover, the later version includes a poem from du Bellay's *Songe* (one omitted from *Theatre*), which describes a vision of 'a Citie like unto that same, / Which saw the messenger of tidings glad' (*Bellay* 184–5). The messenger was St John; but du Bellay's city crumbles, proving that the likeness between poetic and scriptural visions is illusory. Finally, Spenser comments on the visions of *Petrarch* in his own brief envoy. He has seen enough of the trustless state of the world to wish that his 'free spirite might not anie moe / Be vext with sights, that doo her peace molest' (91–2). He claims no visionary experience here; he has seen enough without it. If there is a biblical model for this humble seeing, it is not in prophecy or apocalyptic, but in the most earthbound writer in the Bible, Ecclesiastes, whom Spenser is said to have translated (see lost *works), and who said repeatedly, 'I have seen all the works that are done under the sun; and, behold, all is vanity and vexation of spirit' (1.14, KJV).

Spenser's vision poems are all 'complaints and meditations of the worlds vanitie' (*Complaints* 'Printer'), urging contempt of the world, but never envisioning the answering promises of Christianity. At most, they gesture toward the consolations of faith: 'all is vanitie and griefe of minde, / Ne other comfort in this world can be, / But hope of heaven, and heart to God inclinde' (*Time* 583–6). These lines are spoken by a voice that calls to the poet after the last vision of *Time*, so that (as in the *Theatre* sonnets) hearing replaces vision at the moment that exposure of the world's vanity gives way to the consolations of faith. 'Hope that is sene, is not hope'; 'faith is by hearing' (Rom 8.24, 10.17).

Seeing and hearing apportion the varying claims of experience and authority in *FQ* VII, too. Canto vi begins by matching the experience of anyone who 'sees the ever-whirling wheele / Of *Change*' to the humble authority of the tale that Spenser says he 'whylome ... heard say.' Canto vii, by contrast, begins by invoking the Muse and then claims prophetic experience when the poet speaks as if he had *seen* Nature's garments that day on Arlo and compares his own bewilderment at the sight to that of the apostles at the Transfiguration (vii 7). Mutabilitie's pageant continues the claims of seeing and hearing, re-creating Spenser's earlier visions of the world's vanity, now with the plural refrain, 'we see.' For her, seeing is believing. Jove's verbal claim to authority counts for nothing because Mutabilitie's case rests on de facto experience: 'what we see not, who shall us perswade?' (49). Nature's terse verdict leaves the poet considering his own fiction, not as something seen or experienced, but as 'that speech whyleare, / Of *Mutability*' and 'that which Nature sayd' (viii 1–2). His tale is again only a verbal authority; and his closing prayer for the 'Sabaoths sight' shows how far it falls short of the prophetic union of seeing and hearing, personal experience and transcendent authority.

Throughout *The Faerie Queene*, Spenser links seeing and hearing in ways that circumscribe his visionary poetics. He likens Parnassus to biblical mountains of revelation, but he does not claim to have shared Redcrosse's vision, which he concedes is 'Too high a ditty for my simple song' (I x 53–5). Moreover, Redcrosse arrives at the Mount of Contemplation only after authoritative (and largely verbal) instruction in the house of Holiness. Hearing has begotten seeing, as is the normal pattern for those who are not prophets. Britomart's vision in *FQ* III ii must be supplemented by the words of Merlin's prophetic history in III iii, but the poet does not see what Merlin sees; he records only what Merlin says.

Finally, though the epic voice seems to share the vision of the Graces in *FQ* VI x ('Looke how the Crowne, which *Ariadne* wore') and can mingle voices with Colin Clout (13, 28), the episode works to distinguish vision from narration, Colin from the voice of the epic narrator. The two figures represent impulses of Spenser's imagination, various possibilities or resources of his art. They are parts of a whole, just as are Alma's counselors in Book II, who with their chambers represent the faculties of the mind (ix 50–8). Spenser's poems show obvious reliance on the visible images painted on the walls of Phantastes. They do not, however, base their claim to truth on visual or visionary experience, but rather on verbal authority – on the 'immortall scrine,' the 'rolles, / And old records from auncient times deriv'd' that hang about the chamber of Eumnestes (II ix 56–7), on the Muses' 'everlasting scryne' (I proem 2), and on the hearing that replaces seeing in even the most visionary shorter poems. To avoid the prophet's claim to vision – the only kind of experience that overrides all prior authority – Spenser subsumes his visionary poetics within the imagery of received authority and presents even *The Faerie Queene*, with all its visions and visionaries, as 'matter of just memory' (II proem 1). Like Doubting Thomas, Spenser cannot believe what he has only heard. At the end of the poem, he still waits to see and hear firsthand.

THOMAS HYDE

Alpers 1977; Dallett 1960; David O. Frantz 1985 'The Union of Florimell and Marinell: The Triumph of Hearing' *SSt* 6:115–27; Hyde 1983; Forrest G. Robinson 1972 *The Shape of Things Known: Sidney's 'Apology' in Its Philosophical Tradition* Cambridge, Mass; Kathleen Williams 1969; Williams 1974 'Spenser and the Metaphor of Sight' *RUS* 60.2:153–69.

---

visions Wordsworth inaugurated the nineteenth-century view that Spenser is the finest of visionary poets: 'the grand storehouses of enthusiastic and meditative Imagination, of poetical ... Imagination, are the prophetic and lyrical parts of the Holy Scriptures, and the works of Milton; to which I cannot forbear to add those of Spenser' (ed 1940–9, 2:439). Of Spenser's poems, *The Faerie Queene* contributes most substantially to forming and authenticating a distinctively English tradition of visionary art.

The term 'visions' is applied by the *Variorum* editors to the epigrams, sonnets, and four visions from the Apocalypse in *Theatre*, together with various poems in *Complaints* which Spenser entitled visions (especially *Visions of Bellay*, *Visions of Petrarch*), and even to *Visions of the Worlds Vanitie*. All these poems may be related to the lost *Dreames*; they may even be those poems printed under separate titles (see *Var* 8:511–12). More important than this conjecture, however, is the possibility that in their original form, *Dreames* (like the poems in *Theatre* and the individual eclogues in *The Shepheardes Calender*) were accompanied by emblems, which claim indebtedness to a visionary tradition of literature whose premier authority and text were St John and his Apocalypse (cf *Three Letters* 3, *Var Prose* p 471).

Spenser's vision poems all reflect upon the nature of visionary art. The fourth vision of *Ruines of Rome* is so laced with memories of the concluding chapters of Revelation that it may be said to point to the 'allegoric and subtly apocalyptic intention' of all these poems which, though experimental, 'are experiments of the greatest moment for the poet's maturer art' (Friedland in *Var* 8:304, 625). *The Faerie Queene* is a visionary poem of the first order, as is signaled by the mountaintop visions in Books I and VI; it is also a summa of all that the Renaissance comprehended within a visionary poetic.

Describing a chamber in the castle of Alma filled with flies that 'encombred all mens eares and eyes,' Spenser represents his age's distrust of visions: 'All those were idle thoughts and fantasies, / Devices, dreames, opinions unsound, / Shewes, visions ... And all that fained is, as leasings, tales, and lies' (II ix 51). Already the Red Cross Knight had been 'subtilly betrayd' through visions wrought by an enchantress (I iii 3). Yet *The Faerie Queene* also testifies to the power of visions, both joyful and sorrowful: they can steady individuals in their course, impose reality and embody truth, even alter the course of human affairs. Merlin reports that Cadwallader 'Shalbe by vision staid from his intent' (III iii 41). The poem includes 'dreadfull visions' that fill men with fear, weary their spirits, and deprive them of rest and happiness (IV 57); but there are also new ideals of law, government, and justice 'reveald in vision' (II x 39). Scudamour encounters Britomart as if she were 'some celestiall vision' (IV vi 24), and Britomart herself sees a strange vision in Isis Church: 'A wondrous vision, which did close implie / The course of all her fortune and posteritie' (V vii 12). That vision recalls Geoffrey of Monmouth's story of Brutus' vision in the temple when Diana foretells his success; in like manner, 'Britomart has a vision figuring the future glory of Britain' (Upton in *Var* 5:220). The realm of vision or imaginative reality available to Arthur (though not to Guyon) becomes available to all readers when vision and commentary are complexly interwoven throughout *The Faerie Queene*.

Spenser's poetry harbors two interrelated, positive conceptions of vision: it is both an instrument for perceiving reality and a way of expanding upon it. Like Calvin, Spenser stresses the important connection between vision and the seeing eye: 'Between *visions* and *revelations*,' says Calvin, 'there is this distinction – that a *revelation* is often made either in a dream, or by an oracle, without any thing being presented to the eye' (ed 1848–9, 2:366). 'I saw,' the formulaic opening of several poems in *Theatre for Worldlings* – even the emendation of the last Revelation design to show St John looking upon not the angel but the Heavenly Jerusalem (*Var* 8:627) – points to Spenser's own insistence on the importance of seeing, and also indicates his own conception of his enterprise as involving the textualization of vision. Such features mark *The Faerie Queene* emphatically, as if in response to Gabriel Harvey's admonition, 'They that have Eyes and Tongues, let them see, and reade' (*3 Lett* 2, *Var Prose* p 457).

Significantly, the initial commendatory verses in *The Faerie Queene* are visions upon Spenser's own vision, upon a poem whose first proem contains a petition for divine light from a poet with 'feeble eyne' (4). This visionary poem is delivered not to a golden but to a stony age in which the sun is going out – an age marked, and marred, by the loss of vision and withdrawal of revelation (V proem 2, 7). The poem delivers the fundamental paradox of visionary art: that a world of fallen vision will be redeemed by vision. Such an art is given its surest definition by William Blake when he proclaims that the poet's visions are not 'a cloudy vapour or a nothing: they are organized and minutely articulated ... [They are] infinitely more perfect and more minutely organized than any thing seen by his mortal eye' (*Descriptive Catalogue* 4 in ed 1966:576–7). *The Faerie Queene* is a poem of tremendous visionary imagination – as a hybrid genre and literary microcosm, and in its literary pictorialism, multiperspectivism, prophetic obscurity, multifarious allusiveness, antilinear narrative, and continual veiling and unveiling, it accords in every detail with the salient features of Renaissance visionary poetics (see Wittreich 1979). Indeed, it fully pursues the objectives of that poetic, which are to liberate the senses through a new optical system and to produce an apocalypse of the mind by expanding its circumference of awareness. (See also *oracles, *prophecies.)

JOSEPH WITTREICH

Blake ed 1966; John Calvin 1848–9 *Commentary on the Epistles ... to the Corinthians* tr John Pringle, 2 vols (Edinburgh); W. Wordsworth ed 1940–9.

Visions of Bellay. See ***Complaints: Visions***

Visions of Petrarch. See ***Complaints: Visions***

Visions of the Worlds Vanities. See ***Complaints: Visions***

---

visual arts Pope thought that Joseph Spence's mother said very right when she called *The Faerie Queene* 'a collection of pictures' (Spence ed 1966, no 419), and most of Spenser's readers would agree (see *pictorialism). But recognition of the vivid pictorial quality of his imagination cannot imply that he had a wide knowledge of actual paintings. Indeed, after he went out to Ireland as a young man in 1580 he would have had opportunities of seeing important collections only during his few visits to England. The first would have been too late for any effect on *FQ* I–III and the second too late for the rest. He probably knew the collections of the Earl of Leicester before he left for Ireland, but when he returned Leicester was dead. He would have seen something of the Royal collections during his visit in 1589–91, and possibly before 1580, though this seems unlikely; and in 1595–6 he would have seen the collections of the Earl of Essex, which included many items from those of Leicester. References to paintings which he had seen are therefore not likely to be discovered in Spenser's poetry.

The earliest probable reference to any work of art is in *The Shepheardes Calender*, where the prize pledged by Willye for the song contest is 'A mazer ywrought of the Maple warre' (*Aug* 26). This description may recall the Mary Valence mazer which was in Spenser's day, and still is in ours, one of the treasures of his Cambridge college, Pembroke (Tuve 1937). It would be like him to give actuality to his description of a cup 'made in imitation' of Theocritus' first idyll (Arg) by recalling one which he had recently seen in Cambridge, just as, in the same eclogue, he uses the English roundelay to give actuality to his imitation of Theocritus' use of folk song. However much he relies on literary tradition, he always makes of it something uniquely his own.

For Spenser, then, the visual arts must not be thought to imply primarily paintings (especially since most paintings in collections in his day were portraits, including miniatures) but must include engravings and book illustrations, such as he included in *The Shepheardes Calender* and *FQ* I, wall paintings, maps – Leicester had many in his collection – which were normally adorned with illustrations, and, perhaps most important of all, tapestries. These were widely used as wall coverings (to protect against drafts) and usually represented classical or biblical themes: at *FQ* II ix 33, Spenser notes as strange the absence of any representations from the arras in the house of Alma. The most extensive account of tapestries describes those that adorn the house of Busirane (III xi 28–46). Here Spenser writes as if he had in mind tapestries which he had actually seen, of Europa and the Bull, of Danae and the Golden Shower, and especially of Leda and the Swan. In these tapestries, the mythological scene is surrounded, as was usual, with a decorative border. Henry VIII had tapestries of 'The History of Jupiter' and of other subjects described by Spenser in this passage, which he might have seen or heard tell of; but it was certainly not beyond his power to give verisimilitude to his description; and one cannot attempt to define the treatment in a tapestry of a theme listed under a short title as 'Vulcanus, Mars, and Venus' or 'Venus and Cupido' (both in Henry VIII's possession). One can say no more than that the subjects of tapestries in the house of Busirane are such as were treated in contemporary tapestries. But the principal source for both was Ovid's *Metamorphoses*, and Spenser was as capable as a designer of tapestry of designing a representation of classical myths. In Castle Joyous, the story of Venus and Adonis is portrayed in tapestry (III i 34–8) as it was in a Fountainebleau series which Spenser could not have seen, but the myth was obviously a suitable subject.

Biblical subjects such as 'The Stories of Abraham, of Melchizedek, and of Tobias' at Hampton Court were among the tapestries which Spenser might have seen, but it is hardly possible to claim that he was thinking of any particular piece. A fine Sheldon 'tapestry' (really a tablecloth) now at Sudeley Castle near Winchcombe, Gloucestershire, once belonged to Leicester, in whose possession Spenser could have seen it. The central medallion shows the Expulsion from Paradise, and to either side are three roundels, those on the left showing the theological virtues of Faith, Hope, and Charity, those on the right showing three of the complementary cardinal virtues, Temperance, Prudence, and Justice. But these representations, with such details as an anchor and a ship at sea for Hope, are so frequent and so well established that it would be as absurd as unnecessary to derive Spenser's description of Fidelia, Speranza, and Charissa in *FQ* I x from them. He would have seen many other such images in books and engravings. Some such source may have suggested Speranza and the opposing vice, Despair; but no visual image could have suggested the elaborate account of Despair and his cave (I ix 33–6).

Spenser is a poet of ideas which he embodies through the method of allegory in vigorous narrative. 'Hence the development of allegory, to supply the subjective element in literature' (Lewis 1936:113). Of the great painters of that age, Botticelli is closest to Spenser, though Spenser could never have seen any of his work. His depiction of the three Graces in *FQ* VI x 24 derives, as does Botticelli's in the *Primavera*, from Servius' commentary on the *Aeneid*. E.K. quotes Boccaccio on paintings of the Graces: 'they be painted naked ... the one having her backe toward us, and her face fromwarde, as proceeding from us: the other two toward us, noting double thanke to be due to us for the benefit, we have done' (*Aprill* 109 gloss). Illustrations were innumerable, so it is impossible to suggest which Spenser might have had in mind.

Similarly, with figures which had no classical source, such as Occasion in *FQ* II iv 4–5, which was often represented in emblem books: Whitney's *A Choice of Emblemes* (1586), dedicated to Leicester, has an engraving of Occasion which Spenser probably knew, though he omits the whirling wheel on which she is there shown. Emblem books also provide some details in the description of the seven deadly sins in *FQ* I iv: Gluttony, whose neck 'like a Crane ... was long and fyne' (21), is so represented by Alciati; but the image derives ultimately from Aristotle, where Spenser is as likely to have found it.

Here and elsewhere, Spenser may have had in mind pageants and ceremonies which were much employed in the sixteenth century, often for political propaganda, but of which no visual record remains. In describing encounters between Christian knights and Paynim foes, he is recalling jousts, such as those which took place in Whitehall on the Queen's Accession Day; to his contemporaries, these accounts would have had the interest of reports of sporting events. The procession of the Seasons and Months in *FQ* VII vii suggests a pageant, no less than that of the seven deadly sins, but here again the source is ultimately Ovid's *Fasti* and *Metamorphoses*, which were as well known to painters and designers of tapestry as to poets. Ruskin's comparison of Spenser's Months with sculptures in St Mark's in Venice and with descriptions in Books of Hours may be relevant since, though Spenser never visited Venice, many Englishmen of his time, including Sidney, did so, and probably described what they had seen; and Spenser certainly knew one Book of Hours which belonged to Raleigh, in whose possession he presumably saw it. There the story of St George and the Dragon is portrayed, with the threatened Princess standing in the background, but there is the additional, and unusual detail of a lamb. Spenser's recollection of this illumination no doubt led him to add this detail to his description of Una: 'And by her in a line a milke white lambe she lad' (I i 4). Since no further reference is made to the lamb, its inclusion is purely pictorial, and therefore likely to derive from a visual image. This is one of the very few passages where he seems to have been recalling an image which he had seen.

Spenser often gives clear visual images in similes, which may derive from observation of daily life as in bear-baiting (I xii 35, II xi 33), bull-baiting (II viii 42), or a swarm of gnats out of the fens of Allen (ix 16); but they also may derive from paintings or tapestries, as in the simile of the lion 'which hath long time saught / His robbed whelpes, and at the last them fond / Emongst the shepheard swaynes' (viii 40). The image of Maleger – with 'many arrowes under his right side, / All deadly daungerous, all cruell keene, / Headed with flint, and feathers bloudie dide, / Such as the *Indians* in their quivers hide' (xi 21) – may recall a drawing by John White of an American Indian, or perhaps Raleigh's recollection of such a drawing, or a decoration in a map of the New World. Some such origin in a map may have suggested the description of the Rock of Reproach (xii 7–8) and especially of the sea monsters (23–4).

(See **visual arts** Fig 1.)

Throughout any examination of Spenser's knowledge of the visual arts, all must remain uncertain. We know the titles of tapestries which he could have seen, but now that they have perished, we cannot judge whether the treatment of the subject affected him. We know of some paintings which he could have seen – *Venus and Adonis*, painted by Titian for Philip II and sent to London for his marriage to Queen Mary, or Hans Eworth's *Judgment of Paris*, now at Hampton Court, in which Queen Elizabeth is shown in the role of Paris – but there is no proof that he had these paintings in mind when he recounts these myths. Spenser, like the rest of us, would have had the power to visualize myths which he knew from Ovid's *Metamorphoses* without the intermediary influence of tapestries or paintings; he would have been able to picture in his imagination representations of which he had been told but which he had not himself seen. He lived at a time when visual images, often allegorical or emblematic, abounded, and his imagination was as apt to create as to recall them. In a very few instances, we may think it probable that he had a particular image in mind, but certainty eludes us throughout. Even when, as in Britomart's vision of Artegall who on his shield 'bore a crowned litle Ermilin, / That deckt the azure field with her faire pouldred skin' (III ii 25) we are reminded of the Ermine portrait of the Queen at Hatfield House, there can be no certainty that Spenser was thinking of it. The portrait was painted in 1585, after he had gone to Ireland, and he must have completed Book III before returning to England. Probably he derived the image, as did the painter, from Petrarch's *Trionfo della Castità*.

Spenser's references to architecture are often fantastic, as was much contemporary architecture. Burghley is condemned in *Mother Hubberds Tale* because 'his owne treasure he encreased more / And lifted up his loftie towres thereby, / That they began to threat the neighbour sky' (1172–41). There is no hint of praise of Theobalds or Burghley House, and, though political antagonism may have motivated Spenser here, he nowhere shows any interest in the houses of his patrons at Penshurst, Wilton, or Kenilworth, though one would expect Penshurst to be more to his taste than Burghley House. Even 'that bright towre all built of christall cleene' (*FQ* I x 58) in which the Fairy Queen dwells cannot be identified with any of Elizabeth's palaces. The one place where Spenser may have had a contemporary house in mind is in his description of the house of Alma at II ix 22. He may have heard of Sir Thomas Gorges' plans for the Longford Castle (which was being built near Salisbury in the 1580s) through Raleigh, who was related to the Gorges family. But he could not have seen Longford Castle until after the publication of *FQ* I-III. The description of the bridge to the Temple of Venus, built 'On stately pillours, fram'd after the Doricke guize' (IV x 6), provides an unexpected detail. There is no such detail in the description of Isis Church (V vii 5). But here as elsewhere, Spenser notes as worthy of praise 'the workemans passing skill.' A poet of sophisticated technical mastery was likely to admire comparable qualities in the practitioners of the other arts. But it is to be noted that the temples and churches which he describes bear no resemblance to churches which he had seen in England, and though he must have visited Westminster Abbey, no allusion to it or to its tombs can be found in his poetry. No doubt he knew the Gates of Honour and of Virtue at Caius College, Cambridge, but only once, in his description of the gate to the Bower of Bliss (II xii 44), does he indicate sculptured decoration.

Spenser was a member of a society which delighted in the visual arts, and his patrons included patrons of painters and architects; but he lived most of his maturity away from that society, where he had little opportunity of seeing notable architecture, sculpture, or painting. His vivid, pictorial imagination apparently sufficed to supply him with an endless succession of images without specific reference to the visual arts.

JOHN BUXTON

Hagstrum 1958 is a useful introduction to the relation between poetry and other arts, with ch 3 on 'The Renaissance' and some discussion of Spenser. General background is given in Buxton 1963. Farmer 1984 has chapters on individual writers, most notably Sidney, and valuable notes. A list of one collection perhaps known to Spenser is William J. Thoms 1862 'Pictures of the Great Earl of Leicester' *N&Q* 3rd ser 2:201–2, 224–6. Katherine Duncan-Jones 1980 'Sidney and Titian' in *English Renaissance Studies Presented to Dame Helen Gardner* ed John Carey (Oxford) pp 1–11 shows the kind of relation between an English poet and a great Italian painter that cannot be established for Spenser. A more fruitful line of research is found in Rosemond Tuve 1937 'Spenser and Mediaeval Mazers; with a Note on Jason in Ivory' *SP* 34:138–47. E.K.'s comments on 'disorderly order' in landscape painting (*SC*, Epistle to Harvey), along with later parallels, are discussed in Frederick Hard 1940 'E.K.'s Reference to Painting: Some Seventeenth Century Adaptations' *ELH* 7:121–9. See also Gent 1981.

Wales In the world of Spenser's imagination, Wales occupied the same region as in that of his contemporaries: it was the home of the Tudor dynasty, whose accession to the English throne with the victory of Henry VII at Bosworth Field was believed to fulfill ancient Welsh prophecies (*FQ* III iii 48); and it was also the home of the British people. Early in the sixteenth century, *Britain*, which had long been used only in an historical context, acquired contemporary political connotation, which was no doubt emphasized by the Act of Union of England and Wales in 1536, and *British* came into fashion (as *Anglo-Saxon* would 300 years later) to promote one element in the national character. The term *The British Empire* was coined by the Welsh geographer John Dee; and such terms as *the Cambro-Britons* for the Welsh, and *North Britain* (on which James I especially insisted) for Scotland became accepted. In the Act of Uniformity of 1662, *British* was taken to be synonymous with *Welsh*, and throughout *The Faerie Queene*, the *Britons* are identified with the Welsh.

Only the mischance of the early death of a Prince of Wales born at Winchester (which Malory took to be Camelot) prevented the succession to Henry VII of a King Arthur. The Arthurian cycle of stories was, to the disgust of Roger Ascham (who considered that 'the whole pleasure' of the *Morte Darthur* 'standeth in ... open mans slaughter, and bold bawdrye' *Scholemaster* ed 1904:231), favorite reading in the sixteenth century, principally in Malory's recension. William Caxton had published this work at Westminster in 1485, three weeks before the defeat of Richard III by the man whom he had recently dismissed as 'an unknown Welshman.' Spenser made constant and skillful use of his readers' familiarity with the Arthurian legends in order to involve them more closely in his poem. Thus, when he first introduces his principal hero at I vii 29, he calls him simply 'A goodly knight, faire marching by the way'; only after he has invited the reader to identify him, by disclosing that his warlike shield and sword had been made by Merlin, does he refer to him as 'Prince' (36). (With characteristic humor, he adds that Prince Arthur's armor may still be seen 'if sought' in Fairyland.) Further, it is Una who first names him (ix 6). The description of Arthur's helmet, which Marlowe knew before the publication of *The Faerie Queene* (2 *Tamburlaine* 4.3.116–24), is taken from Geoffrey of Monmouth, who claimed that he drew on Welsh sources and who first established Arthur as a hero of romance. The Welsh associations of Arthur, whatever their historical validity, cannot be denied.

In the 'chronicle of Briton kings' in II x, which is largely dependent on Geoffrey, Spenser breaks off abruptly in stanza 68 with the accession of Uther Pendragon: it was time to end a history in which he did not believe before associating Prince Arthur with his legendary father, and 'th'Authour selfe could not at least attend / To finish it.' For Spenser was a serious antiquary who was skeptical of the historical truth of the Arthurian stories, but he recognized in Irish legends 'relickes of the trewe Antiquitye thoughe disguised, which a well eyde man maye happelye discover and finde out' (*Vewe* in *Var Prose* p 86). His response to the Arthurian cycle was similar: this was not history, but it might preserve 'relickes of the trewe Antiquitye.'

In a poem addressed to Queen Elizabeth in 1565, Ronsard suggested an English epic to honor Arthur as the foundation of England's glory. About the same time, Tasso, in his *Discorsi dell'arte poetica* (the earlier version of *Discorsi del poema eroico*) argued in favor of an historical subject for an heroic poem, which should be drawn from a Christian rather than from a pagan society and therefore not from the sources of classical epic. The three periods which he suggested as providing the most suitable material were the time of Charlemagne (which Ariosto had used), the Crusades (which he himself chose), and the Matter of Britain. For Spenser, with a patriotic motive similar to Virgil's, the choice was inevitable; and the Matter of Britain – the phrase had been current since the twelfth century – brought with it Welsh associations which were conformable with Tudor propaganda.

There is no reason to suppose that Spenser understood Welsh, in spite of the presence of two Welsh phrases, *Scuith guiridh* and *y Scuith gogh*, at II x 24. These caused trouble to the compositor, who left a blank in most surviving copies; where the Welsh words appear, *Scuith* is wrongly printed *Seuith* in all except one copy, but corrected in the 'Faults Escaped.' Spenser would have had no difficulty in finding someone, perhaps a client of the Earl of Pembroke, to tell him the Welsh for 'green shield' and 'red shield.' The fine Welsh poet Lewis Glyn Cothi (who addressed a congratulatory poem to Henry VII after his victory at Bosworth Field) had celebrated the achievements of the Herbert family during three generations; and the second Earl (who later married Mary Sidney) was addressed in Welsh poems on the death of his second wife, Catherine (Talbot). His kinsman Lord Herbert of Cherbury was to complain in his autobiography a generation later of having had to learn Welsh as a young man. William Middleton, who wrote a *marwnad* (elegy) on the second Lady Pembroke, translated the whole book of Psalms into classical Welsh *cynghanedd* (alliterative measures); one of the Queen's equerries, Richard Hughes (Dic Huws), wrote Welsh poems; and a gentleman of the Queen's Guard named Lewis Edwards (Lewis ap Edwart) composed a series of bawdy *englynion* or *englyns* to excuse himself from keeping an engagement to dine with some of his friends. In Ireland, Spenser had Irish poems translated to him (*Vewe* p 127); but Welsh was much more widely known, and some at least of the descendants of those who came in with Henry VII retained their knowledge of the language. Sidney notes that its poetry was respected: 'In Wales, the true remnant of the ancient Britons ... yet do their poets even to this day last' (ed 1973b:76). Spenser refers to Welsh bards at I v 3 and again at III iii 54, where he alludes to their tradition of praising warlike deeds. As Aubrey records, William Camden 'much studied the Welch language, and kept a Welsh servant to improve him in that language, for the better understanding of our Antiquities' (*Brief Lives* I.145–6). There can be little doubt that Welsh was more widely understood in England in Spenser's day than it is now. The new interest in Wales and the Welsh finds frequent literary record, in such works as Churchyard's *Worthines of Wales* (1587) and in the fourth, fifth, and sixth songs of Drayton's *Poly-Olbion* (1612). Shakespeare could assume that a London audience would be familiar with the Welsh intonation of English speech in *Henry V*. Caradoc of Llancarfan's *Historie of Cambria, Now Called Wales* was translated into English by H. Lhoyd in 1584 and dedicated to Sidney, through whom Spenser probably knew it.

Britomart says that her 'native soyle' is the 'greater *Britaine*' (III ii 7), that is, Wales (the lesser Britain was Brittany). The Red Cross Knight springs 'from ancient race / Of *Saxon* kings' who conquered Britain (I x 65), but Britomart is to be the ancestor of a famous progeny by Artegall which will resume the crown of Britain 800 years after the death of Cadwallader c 690, that is, through the accession of the Tudor prince as Henry VII. By a nice touch, Spenser gives to Redcrosse the task of describing Artegall to

Britomart, in token of the reconciliation under the Tudors of English and British.

Spenser probably never visited Wales, and the topographical confusion in III iii 8, where he places the river Barry instead of the Towy 'Emongst the woodie hilles of *Dynevowre*,' certainly suggests that he had never been in '*Deheubarth* that now South-wales is hight' (ii 18). It is the countryside of Ireland, not of Wales nor even of England, that leaves most impress on his poetry.

JOHN BUXTON

Examples of Welsh verse include Lewys Glyn Cothi ed *Poetical Works* 1837–9, 2 vols (Oxford) and William Middleton 1603 *Psalmae* (London). More on the literary traditions may be found in Thomas Parry 1955 *A History of Welsh Literature* tr H. Idris Bell (Oxford); and Gwyn Williams 1953 *An Introduction to Welsh Poetry from the Beginnings to the Sixteenth Century* (London). The Elizabethan antiquarian interest in Wales is discussed in Kendrick 1950 and Millican 1932. For historical background, see G. Dyfnallt Owen 1962 *Elizabethan Wales: The Social Scene* (Cardiff). See also Donald Williams Bruce 1985 'Spenser's Welsh' *N&Q* 230:465–7.

Waller, Edmund (1606–87) Although the influence of Spenser on Waller was considerable, the Spenser we find in Waller's poems is not the one with which twentieth-century readers will be most familiar. Waller, a Member of Parliament for many years, enjoyed a reputation as a wit and a graceful speaker; in his poetry, he specialized in elegant, personalized heroic praise. Though he never wrote an epic, he found exemplars for his practice within the heroic tradition – in particular, Virgil, Spenser, and Edward Fairfax, the translator of Tasso. Dryden's comments on Waller frequently associate him with Spenser and Virgil in terms of explicit discipleship and imitation, and their dedication to 'numerous ... various, and ... harmonious' verse: 'For Spenser and Fairfax both flourished in the reign of Queen Elizabeth; great masters in our language, and who saw much further into the beauties of our numbers than those who immediately followed them. Milton was the poetical son of Spenser, and Mr. Waller of Fairfax' (Dryden ed 1962, 2:84, 270).

Though this last passage distinguishes between Spenser and Fairfax, for Waller the influences of the two poets were essentially one: heroic poetry was a species of panegyric, and he tended overwhelmingly to emphasize its ethical and topical dimensions. The extensive 'Observations on Some of Mr. Waller's Poems' in Elijah Fenton's edition of the *Works* (London 1729) see Waller in precisely the way Waller saw Spenser: 'it was his principal intention to recommend with all the ornaments of poetry the brightest examples of his own age to the imitation of all that should succeed' (iii). Epic poetry is thus seen, rather simply, as the praise of heroic virtue; and even if such praise is seen as a prescriptive teaching by delight, the emphasis on the 'brightest examples' can lead in Waller's poems to a certain monotony of tone, courtly and deferential, though not without a degree of sly irony.

Various stylistic similarities have been found in Spenser and Waller – a 'ceremonial manner,' rich in epithets, working 'by harmonies rather than dissonances' (Miles 1948:81–2). The several passages in Waller directly allusive to Spenser (*Sp All* pp 217–18) are less significant than the overall discipleship to the tradition of heroic romance, by which Waller consistently treats the events of everyday life in a manner appropriate to epic poetry; in Fenton's words, 'our Author illustrates a plain historical fact with all the graces of poetical fiction' (iv).

WARREN L. CHERNAIK

Warren L. Chernaik 1968 *The Poetry of Limitation: A Study of Edmund Waller* (New Haven); Dryden ed 1962; Josephine Miles 1948 *The Primary Language of Poetry in the 1640's* (Berkeley).

warfare Conflicting intellectual traditions made war a thorny issue not only for Spenser but for the entire Renaissance. Refined by Catholic theologians like Vitoria, Bellarmine, and Suarez, the Thomistic doctrine of the just war mediated between the Augustinian doctrine of war as punishment for sin and Aristotelian acceptance of war for the public good. While Thomas Aquinas extolled peace as the goal of just war, Protestant sects like the Anabaptists espoused antiwar doctrines closer to the pacifism of the New Testament. From its classical background, humanism derived a heroi-centric ethos. But though a few Christian humanists like Zwingli were sufficiently martial to die sword in hand, more were inclined to a pacifism of which Erasmus was the leading spokesman. Like Erasmus, Luther saw war as incompatible with the Gospel spirit and denounced soldier clerics like Zwingli, but his respect for the state's legitimate temporal authority made him regard military service as among those things to be rendered unto Caesar. Though Christians should not fight Turks to convert them, at the Emperor's behest they may well fight them for political reasons. The theocratic Calvin went further in linking the state to religion, sanctioning not merely just wars but holy wars.

Spenser synthesized such conflicting ideals less logically but more wholeheartedly than either Shakespeare, who was apparently skeptical of pacifism, or Milton, who plainly distrusted martial heroism. In *SC, October*, Piers' heroic ethos makes him lament the spectacle of armor rusting ingloriously during the long Elizabethan peace. But throughout *The Faerie Queene*, the militancy of Spenser's patriotism is offset by his delight in recalling the Golden Age when 'No warre was knowne, no dreadfull trompets sound, / Peace universall rayn'd mongst men and beasts' (*FQ* V proem 9). As an heroic poet, he promises that 'Fierce warres and faithfull loves shall moralize my song' (I proem 1). But these ideals are contradictory. He seems to 'sing of Knights and Ladies gentle deeds' most vibrantly when those deeds are gentle in every sense and thus unwarlike. Battling for his faith against Paynim and Catholic like a Puritan crusader, the Red Cross Knight is a holy warrior who must renounce the 'guilt of bloudy field,' for 'wars but sorrowes yield' (I x 60).

Though Spenser routinely celebrates the prowess of his knights, in scenes like the combat between Cambell and Triamond an almost Virgilian abhorrence of warfare tempers his admiration for warriors. When Guyon encounters Huddibras and Sansloy locked in mortal combat, he first tries to pacify them; but he is immediately drawn into the duel, which becomes a melee where 'Wondrous great prowesse and heroick worth / He shewd that day' (II ii 25). The entire episode dramatizes the tension between ideals requiring knights to be both conquerors and peacemakers. So does the encounter with Phaedria, who counsels Guyon to make love, not war. Her speech mollifies his ire but leaves the reader uncertain whether to interpret this response as sensual self-indulgence or 'courteous clemencie' (vi 36). Likewise, the historical account of 'The land, which warlike Britons now possesse' (x 5) lacks any consistent standard by which the merits of its kings may be judged. A panegyric on the second Brute for successfully invading France is followed by equally approving accounts of his less bellicose heirs, who, though not increasing the realm, 'Enjoyd an heritage of lasting peace' and 'taught the land from wearie warres to cease' (25). Merlin's patriotic prophecy is a typically contradictory expression of Spenser's enthusiasms (III iii 49):

Thenceforth eternall union shall be made
  Betweene the nations different afore,
  And sacred Peace shall lovingly perswade
  The warlike minds, to learne her goodly lore,
  And civile armes to exercise no more:
  Then shall a royall virgin raine, which shall
  Stretch her white rod over the *Belgicke* shore,
  And the great Castle smite so sore with all,
That it shall make him shake, and shortly learne to fall.

Spenser describes the Belgian campaigns at length in *FQ* V x-xi. No book in the poem deals more literally with the minutiae of warfare (an episode in canto ii even urges the wisdom of making swimming drill part of basic military training). Arthur's exploits obviously idealize Leicester's activity in the Lowlands as head of Elizabeth's expeditionary forces from 1585 to 1587, perhaps telescoping his incompletely successful campaigns with those of his successor, Sir Francis Vere. Yet Arthur resembles the poem's other heroes in being a lone knight-errant. He implausibly defeats massed enemies by prowess rather than generalship. Artegall may be the closest Spenser comes to representing an ideal of military leadership like Tasso's Goffredo. His iron companion Talus suggests that the virtue of justice depends on an army for enforcement.

Elsewhere in *The Faerie Queene* troops seldom appear except for a few episodes like the siege of the castle of Alma. Single combat is the norm, its model the tournament or joust. Like many Reformation theologians for whom war was a fertile trope, Spenser spiritualized armed conflict by treating it mainly as a metaphor for the struggles of the aspiring Christian's individual soul. Whereas infantry dominated cavalry on sixteenth-century battlefields, chivalric allegory discouraged realistic treatment of Renaissance warfare in the poem. Yet Spenser's nostalgia for chivalry may reflect the backwardness of Elizabethan armies, which were penuriously underfinanced and among the last in Europe to abandon the lance.

Improving English military performance in Ireland is a central concern of the *Vewe of Ireland.* Spenser wants to curb the guerilla warfare of the native Irish by enforcing apparel laws against the mantle and quilted leather jacket, since the former converts readily to bedding for field use while the latter 'is fittest to be under his shirte for anie occasion of sodaine service' (*Var Prose* p 120). He advocates numerous army reforms and, like his employer Lord Grey, urges war *à outrance*. At one point he cites Machiavelli's *Discorsi*, and there are parallels between his doctrine of warfare and Machiavelli's in *The Prince*. But Machiavelli scarcely inspired Spenser's conviction that success in war 'usethe Comonlie to be acordinge to the Justnes of the Cause' (*Var Prose* p 169). His military philosophy probably owes more to French theorists like Jean Bodin. His hawkish policy has been often criticized as discordant with the Christian humanism of *The Faerie Queene*, but it was this harsh strategy carried out by generals like Mountjoy, Strafford, and Cromwell that finally subjugated Ireland – at least for three centuries more.

The extent of Spenser's firsthand acquaintance with warfare has been debated inconclusively. It has been argued that he was a Dublin bureaucrat unfamiliar with Connaught or Ulster. However, he may have gone into the field to witness nearby battles like Glenmalure, for he mentions 'balefull Oure, late staind with English blood' (*FQ* IV xi 44). At one point in the *Vewe*, Irenius – normally his spokesman – disclaims detailed personal knowledge of garrison tactics, saying 'I am noe marshall man' (*Var Prose* p 173). When the rising of 1598 burned Spenser's castle at Kilcolman and forced him to flee, the privy council had just nominated him to be sheriff of Cork. They described him perhaps without exaggeration as 'a man endowed with good knowledge in learning and not unskilful or without experience in the service of the wars' (cited in Judson 1945:200).

MICHAEL WEST

Cyril Falls 1950 *Elizabeth's Irish Wars* (London); James A. Freeman 1980 *Milton and the Martial Muse: 'Paradise Lost' and European Traditions of War* (Princeton); Paul A. Jorgensen 1956 *Shakespeare's Military World* (Berkeley and Los Angeles); Leslie 1983; Charles Oman 1937 *A History of the Art of War in the Sixteenth Century* (London); Eugene Vance 1966 'Warfare as Metaphor in Spenser's *Faerie Queene*' diss Cornell Univ; Henry J. Webb 1965 *Elizabethan Military Science: The Books and the Practice* (Madison, Wis); Michael West 1988 'Spenser's Art of War: Chivalric Allegory, Military Technology, and the Elizabethan Mock-Heroic Sensibility' *RenQ* 41:654–704.

Warton, Thomas, the younger (1728–90) Fellow of Trinity College, Oxford, Poet Laureate (1785), and literary historian. Warton's *Observations on the Faerie Queene of Spenser* (1754, enlarged to 2 vols 1762) is a young scholar's labor of love, the product of his intensive reading in medieval and Elizabethan literature in the Oxford libraries. Combining the taste of a poet with an antiquarian's eye for detail, he explores in *The Faerie Queene* the romance motifs, fairy legends, ancient traditions, Arthurian and chivalric tales – those many fictions that so stirred Spenser's imagination (and his own).

Warton's aim is to encourage in eighteenth-century readers an historical and imaginative sympathy, and to free criticism from the patronizing and constricting attitude of 'we who live in the days of writing by rule' (1:15) – in other words, to move English criticism away from an imported French model toward a native historical tradition with roots in the English Middle Ages. To this end, he accumulates a wealth of detail, glosses obscurities, examines analogues, and places Spenser within a tradition extending from Chaucer and the romances to Shakespeare and Milton.

Part of the book's significance for English literary history is its espousal of the historical method of criticism. Warton explains, 'I have considered the customs and genius of his age; I have searched his cotemporary writers, and examined the books on which the peculiarities of his style, taste, and composition, are confessedly founded' (2:264). For him, Spenser is a consummation of the older 'allegorical' poetry, 'a Romantic poet' who wrote with great rapidity 'hurried away by the impetuosity of imagination' (2:3, 88, 112), drawing upon his romance reading and the popular pageants that he witnessed; such public spectacles with their personifications of vices and virtues influenced his allegorizing even more than did the fictions of Ariosto, and led him to paint his figures 'in so distinct and animated a style' (2:92).

Warton's annotated copy of the 1617 folio, given him by his grandfather in 1744, is now in the British Library. From his marginal notes, it is clear that he began preparing an edition of Spenser. Although he never finished it, his preparations resulted in the capacious, digressive *Observations*. He planned a companion volume discussing *The Shepheardes Calender* and other poems, to be prefaced by an 'Account of the Progress of Pastoral'; but his annotations show that he did not admire Spenser's work in this genre: 'No Merit in the Pastorals – as Hughes asserts – no new rural Imagery – The best Images in those he has translated from Marot.'

Spenserianism is rare in Warton's poetry: his 'Pastoral in the Manner of Spenser' is a paraphrase of Theocritus' Idyll 20 in the stanza of *Januarye* and *December*, a feeble tissue of Spenserian allusions and vocabulary. But his poetry has many allusions to Spenser himself, all asserting the poet's power to rouse the imagination (eg, 1787 Birthday Ode 17–32; and 'Pleasures of Melancholy' 153–65: 'In magic Spenser's wildly-warbled song / I see deserted Una wander wide / Thro' wasteful solitudes'). For Warton, the world of *The Faerie Queene* held enchantment and fancy; it was a fairyland which the eighteenth-century poet might enter as a refuge from an age of correctness and judgment. His ode 'Sent to Mr Upton, on His Edition of the *Faerie Queene*' describes how he used Spenser to enter an imaginary world: 'As oft, reclined on Cherwell's shelving shore, / I trac'd romantic Spenser's moral page, / And sooth'd my sorrows with the dulcet lore / Which Fancy fabled in her elfin age; / Much would I grieve, that envious Time so soon / O'er the loved strain had cast his dim disguise; / As lowering clouds, in April's brightest noon, / Mar the pure splendors of the purple skies' (1–8). This lament for Spenser's inaccessibility points to a paradox: Warton wanted to make Spenser's poetry available to a modern age while recognizing that for him its very remoteness was its charm.

DAVID FAIRER

General studies on Warton include David Fairer 1981 'The Origins of Warton's *History of English Poetry*' *RES* 32:37–63; Frances Schouler Miller 1938 'The Historic Sense of Thomas Warton, Junior' *ELH* 5:71–92; Joan Pittock 1973 *The Ascendancy of Taste: The Achievement of Joseph and Thomas Warton* (London); and John A. Vance 1983 *Joseph and Thomas Warton: An Annotated Bibliography* (New York). For background, see Johnston 1964; Lawrence Lipking 1970 *The Ordering of the Arts in Eighteenth-Century England* (Princeton) pp 352–404; Earl R. Wasserman 1937; Wasserman 1947 *Elizabethan Poetry in the Eighteenth Century* (*ISLL* 32.2–3; Urbana, Ill); Wellek 1941; and Wurtsbaugh 1936. For Hurd and Warton, see Edwine Montague 1941 'Bishop Hurd's Association with Thomas Warton' in *Stanford Studies in Language and Literature* ed Hardin Craig (Stanford) pp 233–56.

Watson, Thomas (1556?–1592) The first English poet to publish a sonnet sequence, Watson was born in London, studied at Winchester and Oxford, and for seven years lived in Italy and France, where he knew Sir Francis and Thomas Walsingham in Paris. Spenser may have met him in 1579, when both were living at Westminster and were friends of Camden; but Watson's closer friends included Lyly, Peele, Greene, and Marlowe (Eccles 1934, 1982).

Spenser's allusion to 'sweet Poets verse' that 'hath given endlesse date' to Amintas (*FQ* III vi 45) is a complimentary reference to Watson's Latin poem *Amyntas* (1585) and to its English paraphrase by Fraunce, in which Amyntas, having died through grief for Phillis, is transformed into the amaranthus (Ringler 1954). Watson was the first to praise *The Faerie Queene* in print, writing in *Meliboeus*, translated as *An Eglogue* on the death of Sir Francis Walsingham (1590), that he would leave praise of the Queen to Spenser, 'Whose neverstooping quill can best set forth / such things of state, as passe my Muse, and me. / Thou *Spencer* art the alderliefest swaine, / or haply if that word be all to base, / Thou art *Apollo* whose sweet hunnie vaine / amongst the Muses hath a chiefest place' (*Sp All* pp 20–1). He urges Spenser to console the Queen after Walsingham's death, 'for well shee likes thy vaine.' Spenser wrote the next year that Walsingham was fortunate to have a poet 'To sing his living praises being dead' (*Time* 435–7). Similarities have been noted between *Amoretti* 30 and Watson's *Hekatompathia* 43 (ice and fire) and between 'Upon a day,' the fourth of the anacreontics that follow *Amoretti*, and *Hekatompathia* 53 (bee-stung Cupid). Nashe wrote in 1589 that 'Watson's *Amintas*, and translated *Antigone*, may march in equippage of honour with any of our ancient Poets' (Nashe ed 1904–10, 3:320). Watson was not the 'T.W.' who in *The Tears of Fancie* (1593) borrowed five lines from *FQ* II vi 13 (Alpers 1967b).

MARK ECCLES

Thomas Watson 1870 *Poems* ed Edward Arber (London); Watson ed 1967. Alpers 1967b; Mark Eccles 1934 *Christopher Marlowe in London* (Cambridge, Mass); Eccles 1982; W.A. Ringler 1954.

wells Fountains and wells are not sharply distinguished in Spenser, since when he speaks of the former he generally refers to natural springs or sources. Thus, the spring of the Chaste Nymph in Book II is interchangeably a 'fountaine' and a 'well' (i 40, 55; ii 3, 7). Spenser seems to use *well* to indicate bounty or subterranean vitality, but without reference to the merely mutable, delusive, or treacherous play of water. Hence, Duessa's bubbling 'fountaine' (I vii 2–4); but Chaucer the 'well of English undefyled' (IV ii 32), Helicon the 'learned well' (*SC, Aprill* 42, *Julye* 48), the Well of Life (*FQ* I xi 29). The latter must be visualized as having some considerable depth (Scripture has 'fountaine of living waters' Jer 2.13, which becomes a river in Rev 22.1; cf John 4.10), since the baptismal symbolism of the episode requires that Redcrosse be submerged, not merely rinsed off.

TERRY COMITO

Wilson, Thomas (1525?-81) A foremost English humanist, educator, lawyer, statesman, controversialist, and Latinist, Wilson was also (not always typical of humanists) a Hellenist and a militant Protestant. His chief contributions to discursive theory in the Elizabethan age were his two works on the art of disputation: *The Rule of Reason, Conteinying the Arte of Logique* (1551) and *The Arte of Rhetorique* (1553). These were, respectively, the first English logic and the first English rhetoric. The latter work, perhaps because it was thoroughly Ciceronian and was written in a clear and engaging manner, was the English rhetoric most reprinted (eight times) in the sixteenth century. It illuminates the ways of literary argument as understood by Spenser and his contemporaries. Too, it helped bring English style into its own, as Barnaby Barnes noted: 'Wilson's discretion did redresse / Our English Barbarisme.'

The Rule of Reason, issued six times before Wilson's death, restates Aristotle's and Cicero's works on argumentative reasoning, though the book itself is structured like the theory of the Dutch humanist Agricola. Called 'logic' in the Renaissance, the subject is actually dialectic, the procedures of argumentation among experts. Rhetoric, for Wilson as for most humanists, was aimed at particular and more varied audiences. His *Rhetorique* was the first to encompass in English all five of the Ciceronian compositional procedures for reaching those audiences: invention, arrangement, style, delivery, and memory. But the book's most important lesson is shown rather than talked about: Wilson gives practical demonstrations, in English, of Cicero's personalism, the great orator's emphasis on moral character in communication. Whether offering contemporary examples or discussing theory, the *Rhetorique* continually brings its reader into the presence of one speaking. Thus, in a sense, the entire book is a rhetorical act, an essay in ethos. It reveals the humanist mind in action, as a natural if only implicit consequence of discussing how to write for various audiences.

The overt aim of each book is mainly to teach one how to think controversially, like a lawyer. But a difference between 'logic' and rhetoric is (to use a metaphor Wilson borrows from Zeno) that between the clenched fist (the almost exclusive emphasis on the forms of reasoning in 'logic') and the open hand (the need to accommodate reasoning to the capacities of a mixed audience). The difference between the two is not, thus, the difference between 'truth' and 'persuasion.' For humanists, truth was a function of language and the result of effective communication. Humanist truth was therefore to be pursued through the forms of reasoning in 'logic'; through the varied embodiments of thought and emotion in rhetoric; and, as Wilson's *Rhetorique* preeminently shows, beyond all formal matters, through the speaking style and action of an adroit, genial, almost defiantly nonsystematic and learned man faced with the often intractable particularities of speaking to people in concrete situations.

THOMAS O. SLOANE

Modern editions of *The Arte of Rhetorique* include those by G.H. Mair (Oxford 1909; based on the 1585 ed collated with 1560 and 1567 eds), Robert Hood Bowers (Gainesville, Fla 1962), and Thomas J. Derrick (New York 1982); there is a facs rpt of the 1553 ed (Amsterdam 1969). *The Rule of Reason* is available in ed 1972.

Clark 1948; Howell 1956; Raymond F. Howes, ed 1961 *Historical Studies of Rhetoric and Rhetoricians* (Ithaca, NY).

winds Allusions to the winds in Spenser match traditional meteorological lore, based on Aristotle and Pliny, which saw them as dry exhalations drawn up by the sun from components of the earth's crust into the region of the lower air. Such exhalations, arising in caverns, might be trapped and thus cause earthquakes ('Master Hs ... Judgement of Earthquakes' *3 Letters* 2, in *Var Prose* pp 453–8). Spenser's interest in the subject is non-technical and literary in derivation: the north wind or Boreas is 'bitter bleake' (*FQ* I ii 33), the west wind or Zephyr is 'Sweete breathing' (*Prothalamion* 2), and the south wind is 'watry' (*FQ* III iv 13). Such general ideas could be found in classical epic, and it is likely that Spenser knew du Bartas' account in *La Sepmaine*.

Spenser's references to winds are usually negative, conveying overtones of instability, chance, or destructive force in accord with biblical and classical precedents and the proverbial experience of a sea-going age (Ovid *Metamorphoses* 1.262). Occasionally, 'gentle warbling wind' reveals beneficent nature (*FQ* II xii 71; *Gnat* 236; *SC, June* 4) and 'happie winde' indicates favorable opportunity (*Gnat* 563; *Mother Hubberd* 80; *FQ* I xii 1, II xii 87). But most frequently the wind is 'wrathfull,' 'wreckfull,' or 'troublous' (IV xi 52, VI viii 36; *Muiopotmos* 48), and it appears with these negative qualities throughout Spenser's poetry.

Most references to specific winds are to the north wind (*Daphnaïda* 396; *FQ* II ix 16, III v 51), which in one case serves as the chariot of Archimago (II iii 19). The wind's proverbial instability symbolizes court intrigue in *Mother Hubberd* 722–3, and it conveys the moral irresponsibility of Phaedria as well as Blandamour's drifting fancy (II vi 10, 23; IV ii 5). It is thus a fitting instrument of Mutabilitie (VII vii 20), stripping leaves from trees and blowing down fruit (*SC, Sept* 49; *Daphnaïda* 244). In an alternative application, the plan of the Giant with the scales to weigh the elements (*FQ* V ii 31) fails to allow for 'or wind, or wether'; in this episode, closely modeled on 2 Esdras 5–9, the wind would seem to figure those imponderable or contingent features of creation which baffle human reason and the best-laid plans. As a metaphor of destruction, wind inflates speech (*Colin Clout* 716–17; *FQ* IV v 27, VI vi 42) or adds to the cold blast of Sclaunder and Detraction (IV viii 26, V xii 33).

Spenser also repeatedly associates winds with physical threat (eg, *Muiopotmos* 419, *FQ* III viii 21) or disordered passions. For example, wrathful Paridell is described as a boistrous, earth-shaking wind (III ix 15); and in a prelude to the masque of Cupid, Britomart experiences a whirlwind which parodies the wind of Pentecost and thus suggests the moral disorder of Busirane's house (xii 2–3). These destructive winds are often associated with Aeolus.

According to Greek mythology, Aeolus was appointed by Zeus as ruler of the winds, which he kept confined in a cave on the island of Aeolia, north of Sicily. Occasionally Aeolus or others loosed them, with dire results (*Odyssey* 10.1–79, *Aeneid* 1.52–86). Spenser's most extended allusion to Aeolus compares a raging tempest of the four winds' 'rude unruliment' to the implacable enmity of four representatives of disordered loves (*FQ* IV ix 21–34). (Here, Spenser follows Ovid *Metamorphoses* 11.430 in assimilating Aeolus, keeper of the winds, to his grandfather Aeolus, King of Magnesia in Thessaly and father of Arne. The younger Aeolus was the son of Arne and Neptune, whose union is recalled in Busirane's tapestry at III xi 42.) Spenser excludes '*Aeolus* sharp blast' from the creatively fertile Garden of Adonis (III vi 44), whereas in Orgoglio's monstrous conception which parodies the creation of Adam, the 'emptie wind' of 'blustring *Aeolus*' is appropriately the 'stormie yre' which inseminates the womb of earth (I vii 9). Britomart's prayer in *FQ* III iv 8–10 again associates winds and stormy oceans with disordered passion; she fittingly addresses her prayer to Aeolus, who, because he was keeper of the winds, was sometimes identified with reason, controller of the passions (eg, Conti *Mythologiae* 8.10). In all of these cases, physical tempest in the macrocosm figures moral turmoil in the microcosm. DOMINIC BAKER-SMITH

Heninger 1959; Heninger 1960.

witches In the sixteenth century, witchcraft was viewed as idolatry in which false gods were worshiped to achieve aims not granted by God or brought about by the working of natural laws. It involved the aid of demons and, by extension, vain ceremonies. A witch, according to Jean Bodin, is 'one who wittingly works by diabolical means to cause something to happen' (*Daemonomanie* 1593: 361).

Emphasis on 'diabolical means' blurred a distinction made since classical times between the learned occultist or magus and the common witch who practiced sympathetic and imitative magic. In Spenser's time, witchcraft included both, for orthodox writers denied the existence of good spirits who could be controlled for some purpose. Protestant theologians, evaluating what they saw as actual practices of witchcraft, frequently discussed them as violations of the first commandment, as did Bishop John Hooper (*A Declaration of the Ten Commandments* 1548, ed 1843:308). Because vain ceremonies and objects were believed to be the basis of witchcraft rituals, Luther, in his *Lectures on Galatians* (1535), extended the definition: 'Paul applies the bewitchment of the senses to the bewitchment of the spirit. But with this spiritual witchcraft that ancient serpent (Rev. 12:9) captures, not men's senses but their minds, and deceives them with false and wicked opinions; those who are bewitched in this way suppose that these opinions are true and godly' (ed 1958–75, 26:192). Luther and other Protestant writers applied this definition of 'spiritual witchcraft' to beliefs, images, ceremonies, and sacraments of the Roman Catholic Church. More narrowly, witchcraft served as metaphor for the Roman Mass (Waters 1970).

Belief in and prosecution of witches were more widespread during this period than at any other time in history, especially in Europe. England largely escaped 'witch mania,' but not entirely. Pamphlets publicized the more sensational trials; English treatises multiplied after 1590 but were influenced by three earlier works: Lambert Daneau's *Les Sorciers* translated as *A Dialogue of Witches* (1575), Reginald Scot's *Discoverie of Witchcraft* (1584), and George Gifford's *Discourse of the Subtill Practises of Devilles* (1587). English witchcraft during Spenser's lifetime was little affected by the supposedly empirical treatises of continental writers. The English continued to resort to the 'cunning' or 'wise' man or woman for charms, herbal potions, recovery of lost or stolen goods, and countercharms against spells and curses cast by evil witches. Witches frequently were said to work by means of a 'familiar': a toad, cat, or dog believed to be a demon in disguise.

Sixteenth-century writers could draw upon numerous references to witchcraft in classical literature. They also inherited a number of literary archetypes of the witch: the black witch such as Lucan's Erichtho and Euripides' and Seneca's Medea, and the beautiful enchantress Circe of Homer's *Odyssey*. But these were believed to be more than literary. Bodin and Agrippa held that witches could transform men; others denied any actual metamorphosis and claimed that the devil deluded men. With the Renaissance failure to distinguish types of evidence, the 'reality' described in treatises gave literary figures contemporary verisimilitude. Such literary precedents and learned and popular ideologies help to account for the characterization and significance of Spenser's witches.

Four of the witch figures in *The Faerie Queene* are identified frequently by pejorative epithets and images: Archimago, Duessa, Acrasia, and the 'Hag' of III vii-viii. The fifth, Glauce, is closely related to the 'cunning woman' of history.

Archimago's name suggests that he is the arch-magus, Satan himself. When he turns to his 'Magick bookes and artes of sundry kindes' (I i 36) to frame his invocation to Proserpina (whom Conti equates with Lucifera-Hecate, goddess of witchcraft, *Mythologiae* 3.15–16), the poet labels him 'A bold bad man, that dar'd to call by name / Great *Gorgon*, Prince of darknesse and dead night, / At which *Cocytus* quakes, and *Styx* is put to flight' (37). The spirits he conjures flutter about 'his ever damned hed' (38). He creates a succubus, a demon in female form, to help corrupt Redcrosse (45); when 'she' and the lying dream of the first demon fail, the 'wicked maister' creates an incubus, a demon in male form, and separates knight and lady (ii 2–4). Imagery and action make Archimato a type of the evil learned magician whose ancestry includes Simon Magus and Zoroaster.

Duessa with her golden cup 'replete with magick artes' (viii 14) has biblical and Circean connotations. Like Archimago, she is identified by pejorative epithets: as a witch, she is 'cruel,' 'wicked,' and 'false' (ii 33, 38, 39). Her seduction of Fradubio and Redcrosse, and her ability to metamorphose the former, connect her with her Circean archetype and associate her with Luther's 'spiritual witchcraft' (Waters 1967, Shroeder 1962). She employs 'wicked herbes and ointments,' 'secret poyson ... charmes and some enchauntments' (ii 42, viii 14), practices of both literary and contemporary witches. When she is stripped of her ceremonial trappings, she appears more demonic than human (viii 48): her animal characteristics and hybrid shape of loathly human and beastly parts reflect fifteenth- and sixteenth-century artistic depictions of demons.

(See **witches** Figs 1–2.)

While Duessa's witchcraft, representing institutionalized vanity and idolatry, is insidiously dangerous and damnable, Acrasia's is equally so, representing sins of the flesh which become sins of the spirit. She is called 'witch' and 'wicked witch' (II i 54, xii 26), but chiefly 'enchaunteresse' (i 51, 55; v 27; xii 81, 85).

The third malefic witch is the 'Hag' in III vii-viii. So closely does she resemble the typical black witch of the period, a social outcast with the power to 'hurt far off unknowne, whom ever she envide' (vii 6), that she has been called 'the most complete witch in the regular English tradition' (Briggs 1962:75). She and her loutish, lustful son have been viewed as prototypes of similar pairs in English Renaissance literature, such as Sycorax and Caliban in Shakespeare's *The Tempest*. She uses herbs and charms (vii 21), and the 'hideous beast' of lust which she can call up at will (22–3) is her familiar. Yet the 'Sprights' that she conjures as 'maisters of her art' (viii 4) are not a usual feature of vulgar witchcraft. She summons them to help her create the false Florimell: 'and in the stead / Of life, she put a Spright to rule the carkasse dead' (7). Her ability to shape and animate a lifeless form by calling up a demon has its nearest analogue in Archimago's creation of an incubus and succubus by thickening the air (I i 45, ii 3), a means of demonic manifestation cited by demonologists. In the Hermetic *Asclepius*, magi are said to have power to create a god and call up a daemon to give it speech and motion (Yates 1964:39–40).

Although Glauce appears to depict the Renaissance 'blessing witch' or 'cunning woman,' her rituals have their analogues in classical literature (*Var* 3:221–2). Her name may suggest Minerva's clear-sighted owl or Diana's mother (see Fowler 1964:126n) and therefore may associate her with the demonic, for Diana as Lucifera-Hecate-Proserpina was the goddess of witchcraft. Her herbal charm, her turning Britomart widdershins, and her verse incantations were practiced by sixteenth-century men and women whom the learned saw as more dangerous than malefic witches because they appeared undiabolic. 'Cunning' witches seemingly thrived in country and town (Thomas 1971:233–4). Her 'idle' incantations and charms suggest superstition (ii 48, 51); and that they do not change Britomart's love reflects the belief that magic could affect only ephemeral physical passion.

In *The Shepheardes Calender*, witchcraft may symbolize the Roman Mass (Waters 1974). In *September*, the spiritual witchcraft of Luther's broader definition is suggested when Diggon claims that 'I wote ne Hobbin how I was bewitcht / With vayne desyre, and hope to be enricht' (74–5), and then lists ecclesiastical errors and abuses he discovered when he drove his sheep into a far country. In *June*, Rosalind appears as a metaphorical Circe who enervates Colin's poetic power. Hobbinol urges him, 'Forsake the soyle, that so doth the bewitch: / Leave me those hilles, where harbrough nis to see, / Nor holybush, nor brere, nor winding witche' (18–20). It is not the 'soyle' but Rosalind, the 'winding witche,' who bewitches Colin.

It is not surprising then, that in his *Epithalamion* Spenser resorts to the magic of words to compose a house charm (334–52), and that among the other evils which he seeks to ward off are 'evill sprights' and 'mischivous witches with theyr charmes.'

D'ORSAY W. PEARSON

Jean Bodin ed 1593 *Daemonomanie* (Paris); Hooper ed 1843; James VI ed 1597; Luther ed 1958–75; Scot 1584.

Sydney Anglo, ed 1977 *The Damned Art: Essays in the Literature of Witchcraft* (London); Julio Caro Baroja 1964 *The World of the Witches* tr O.N.V. Glendinning (Chicago); Briggs 1962; Christina Hole 1945 *Witchcraft in England* (London); Richard Kieckhefer 1976 *European Witch Trials: Their Foundations in Popular and Learned Culture, 1300–1500* (Berkeley and Los Angeles); Christina Larner 1984 *Witchcraft and Religion: The Politics of Popular Belief* (Oxford); E. William Monter 1980 'French and Italian Witchcraft' *History Today* 30(Nov): 31–5; David Nicholls 1980 'The Devil in Renaissance France' *History Today* 30(Nov): 25–30; Rossell Hope Robbins 1959 *The Encyclopedia of Witchcraft and Demonology* (New York); Thomas 1971; Thorndike 1923–58; D.P. Walker 1958; D. Douglas Waters 1967 'Duessa and Orgoglio: Red Crosse's Spiritual Fornication' *RenQ* 20:211–20; Waters 1970; Waters 1974; Yates 1964.

Womanhood A personified Womanhood appears in the Temple of Venus (*FQ* IV x), in Scudamour's story of how he first won Amoret by penetrating the Temple (as does the lover in the *Romance of the Rose*) and circumventing such conventional courtly-love barriers as Daunger and Delay to arrive at its inmost recesses. Here, however, instead of a sexual consummation rendered in bawdy allegory, Spenser offers an allegorical tableau unlike the *Romance* or similar allegories of chivalry and eroticism: Scudamour encounters an androgynous Venus and the figure of Womanhood, attended by six virtues and holding Amoret in her lap. Over the objections of Womanhood and of Amoret herself but encouraged by Venus, he takes Amoret from the Temple, despite some uncertainty over the rightness of this course: 'For sacrilege me seem'd the Church to rob, / And folly seem'd to leave the thing undonne' (53); his uncertainty is shared by many readers.

Womanhood is *prima inter pares* of the virtues of Shamefastnesse, Cherefulnesse, Modestie, Curtesie, Silence, and Obedience. These do not exhaust the virtues and qualities Spenser associates with women: in other contexts he introduces chastity, beauty, grace, wisdom, bounty, gravity, compassion, and valor (see, eg, *FQ* II ii 15; III iii 54, V 54–5, vii 10; *Colin Clout* 186–91; *Daphnaïda* 211–17). Formal defenses of women, like Robert Vaughan's *A Dyalogue Defensyve for Women* (1542) or Daniel Tuvil's *Asylum Veneris* (1616), often attributed to women beauty, chastity, cleanliness, constancy, courage, eloquence, fortitude, helpfulness, homekeeping, humility, learning, liberality, magnanimity, mercy, modesty, nurturing of mankind, obedience, patience, piety, reason, silence, temperence, tenderheartedness, thrift, and wisdom. Since each of these qualities characterizes one or more of Spenser's female characters, one wonders how he arrived at the highly circumscribed group attending Womanhood.

The number itself may be significant: Amoret's hand is being won for marriage, and the number six was known as a Pythagorean marriage number (Fowler 1964:48). Six womanly virtues also appear in another marital context, in a central passage of *Epithalamion* (185–222) displaying many verbal and imagistic similarities to the Womanhood passage in Book IV: the bride at the 'temple,' the 'heavenly guifts' (cf IV x 51 'gifts of God'), garlands for saints, and an anthem. *Epithalamion*, however, offers a different list: love, chastity, faith, womanhood, honor, and modesty. Where Womanhood presides over the personifications in *FQ* IV, 'vertue raynes' in *Epithalamion*. The incompleteness of both lists, and the fact that they differ, suggests that the number six is itself more important here than a complete representation of womanhood or wifehood.

The possibility that number symbolism restricted Spenser to six virtues does not account, however, for apparent redundancies. Shamefastnesse and Modestie are virtually identical, to judge from other contexts in which Spenser applies those terms to female behavior, and Curtesie and Cherefulnesse are closely related. Further, in carefully specifying their seating arrangement, Spenser indicates their relationships (as he does not in *Epith*). It appears that superimposed upon this group of six figures led by a seventh is a scheme fitting into the system of tetrads by which Spenser organizes Book IV (Hieatt 1975a). The seating arrangement may be variously diagrammed to display a central group of four virtues, Shamefastnesse, Curtesie, Modestie, and Cherefulnesse. (The first diagram appears in *FQ* ed 1977:505. Spenser's specifying that the virtues are seated 'a round' does not preclude a square – one speaks of sitting 'around' a square table, for example.)

Spenser's insistence on who is sitting opposite whom creates two complementary sets: Shamefastnesse complements Chere-

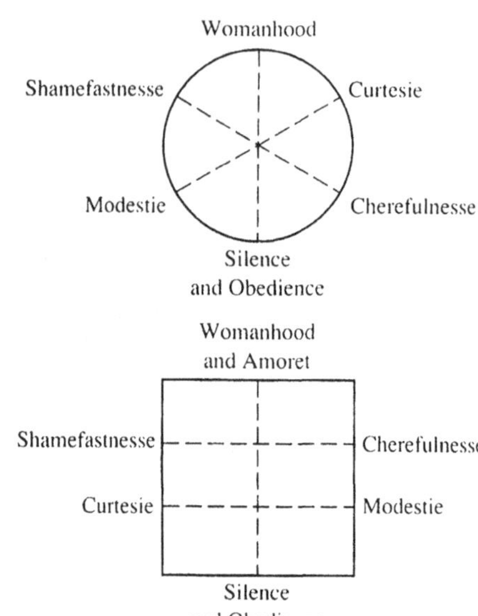

fulnesse, and Modestie complements Curtesie, a complementarity reinforced by the forms of the words, the first set being Anglo-Saxon words with *-nesse* suffixes, the second set Latinate words with *-ie* suffixes. The introduction of the first set suggests through eye imagery that these virtues may tend to extremes, between which Womanhood must steer: Shamefastnesse stares at the ground, in danger of becoming too withdrawn ('Ne ever durst her eyes from ground upreare, / Ne ever once did looke up from her desse [dais]'); Cherefulnesse, 'Whose eyes like twinkling stars in evening cleare, / Were deckt with smyles, that all sad humors chaced, / And darted forth delights,' is charming but risks being regarded as a lady of easy virtue, like Phaedria, whose jesting passes 'the bonds of modest merimake' (II vi 21). Womanhood's achievement of a mean between these extremes is expressed in her gazing straight ahead: 'stedfast still her eyes did fixed rest, / Ne rov'd at randon after gazers guyse, / Whose luring baytes oftimes doe heedlesse harts entyse.'

The danger women face when their innocent friendliness is misconstrued as sexual forwardness is a common Renaissance theme: 'Kindnesse, is tearmed Lightnesse, in our sex' (line 33 in John Cooke *Greenes Tu Quoque* 1614). The golden mean here is similar to the mean Medina seeks in Book II ii, between Elissa and Perissa, the former (like Shamefastnesse) too withdrawn from human company, the latter (like Cherefulnesse) too forward in company. As Spenser augmented his commentary on moderation in that earlier context through the immoderate suitors of Elissa and Perissa, creating a foursome of extremists, so in the Womanhood passage he doubles the pair of 'extremist' virtues, adding a similar pair: Modestie, like Shamefastnesse, must be kept from degenerating into extreme introversion, while Curtesie, like Cherefulnesse, must be tempered with its contrary virtue, Modestie, lest it overstep its outgoing nature to become social or sexual forwardness. Thus a tetrad is created, which like other tetrads in Book IV (Cambell, Triamond, Canacee, Cambina;

Love, Hate, Peace, Friendship; Amyas, Placidas, Aemylia, Poeana; Druon, Claribell, Blandamour, Paridell) possesses two nearly identical terms, Shamefastnesse and Modestie (Fowler 1964:27, 168). Like the other tetrads, this one achieves concord by yoking together potentially discordant qualities, just as the four elements are kept from war by the powers of concord in the universe.

The remaining two figures, 'Soft *Silence*, and submisse *Obedience*,' are carefully set apart from the tetrad by being described as 'gifts of God not gotten but from thence, / Both girlonds of his Saints against their foes offence.' These two are qualitatively different from the first four: where the tetrad comprises traits of character or personality, silence and obedience are more nearly duties; where shamefastness, modesty, courtesy, and cheerfulness have a virginal quality appropriate to the maiden, silence and obedience are among the duties so relentlessly recommended to wives by preachers on marriage like William Whately, Robert Cleaver, and William Gouge. Indeed, although Amoret displays a becoming mixture of courtesy, modesty, shamefastness, and cheerfulness when attempting to resist Scudamour's leading her from the Temple, she shows no tendency towards either silence or obedience: she is not yet a wife.

Silence and Obedience are the twins in the episode, 'Both linckt together never to dispart'; and this, too, sets them apart from the tetrad of single virtues seated individually. We will miss observing a second tetrad only if we forget that seated in Womanhood's lap is Amoret, Love personified. (As love is one of the six womanly qualities in *Epithalamion*, Amoret can be regarded here in the same light as the other personifications.) Two sets of twinned figures, then, face each other across the tetrad: Womanhood with Amoret, Silence with Obedience. The result is a double tetrad, like that in IV ix when Druon, Claribell, Blandamour, and Paridell are joined by Britomart and Scudamour, Arthur and (apparently) Amoret; the product of such convergences, in this Legend of Concord, is harmony. Like tetrads, twins were a common Renaissance emblem of harmony, and Book IV offers many twinnings – Peace and Friendship the twin daughters of Concord, the twins Amoret and Belphoebe, the indistinguishable Florimell and false Florimell, Amyas and Placidas. It is significant, therefore, that Spenser closely pairs the members of his second Womanhood tetrad, with Silence inseparably linked to Obedience and Amoret in Womanhood's lap.

It is possible that the first tetrad comprises virtues of maidenhood, while the second is associated with marriage. Womanhood and Amoret have been linked from birth, with Amoret intended by Venus for a life of sexual fulfillment, 'upbrought in goodly womanhed'; womanhood is here defined as the opposite of the virginal life, a contrast with Belphoebe, 'upbrought in perfect Maydenhed' (III vi 28; cf 51). Concord is achieved in the individual female life when the double tetrad exists: when the woman is perfect maiden and goodly wife successively.

In other Spenserian contexts, shamefastness and modesty are virtues usually associated with women, while cheerfulness and courtesy are attributed to both sexes. The allegory suggests that Womanhood must achieve concord by mediating between, or combining, 'feminine' virtues with 'hermaphroditic' ones. This vision of bisexual concord recalls the opening to Book IV, where riding together are found the very 'feminine' Amoret and the distinctly hermaphroditic Britomart whose radiant feminine beauty is concealed by her masculine armor. This pair reminds us of a number of Shakespearean duos who achieve the concord of comedy: Rosalind and Celia, Julia and Sylvia, Viola and Olivia – all juxtapositions of the beautiful woman in masculine attire with the more conventionally feminine heroine: hermaphrodite counterpoised against woman. In Spenser, as in Shakespeare, the combination that produces concord is female with hermaphrodite as often as female with male: witness the two presiding figures of the Temple of Venus, the female Womanhood and the hermaphroditic Venus. Such combinations are weighted in the direction of the female, and indeed Spenser associates Concord with the female principle in Book IV: in our culture peace has traditionally been associated with women, war with men. Male figures receive short shrift in Book IV: Britomart defeats an embarrassing number of them in armed combat; two of them waste away from feeling rejected by women; and there are no fathers in the book, in contrast to numerous important mothers – Agape, Concord, Cymodoce, Venus herself. One reason for the prominence of women in Book IV – and for the emphatic position of the Womanhood episode – may be that Concord was traditionally female when personified in emblem books or civic pageants, owing probably to the feminine grammatical gender of the Latin noun *concordia*. (The feminine gender of the virtues may have contributed to the prominence of female allegorical figures in *The Faerie Queene* as a whole, and it is interesting that Renaissance defenses of women often adduced the grammatical femininity of the virtues in Latin as proof of the worthiness of womankind.) But Discordia is feminine, too, as are major figures of discord in Book IV such as Duessa, Ate, false Florimell; it is probable that not only grammatical gender but also the deep Western ambivalence towards women contributed to the fact that in Book IV the major figures of evil as of good are female.

Readers have disagreed profoundly on how we are to regard Scudamour's removal of Amoret from the lap of Womanhood and the Temple of Venus (see Evans 1970; Hamilton 1961a; Hieatt 1962, 1975a; Roche 1964). Many who have defended Scudamour's 'rape' as the happy ending conventional to the erotic allegory have ignored the significant difference between the impediments to sexual consummation (Fear, Shame, Resistance, Mal Bouche) who oppose the hero in the *Romance of the Rose*, and the innermost circle of allegorical figures who resist Scudamour. Neither Womanhood nor any of her attendant virtues is ultimately an impediment to sexual consummation, and two of them (Silence, Obedience) were thought necessary to marriage. What are the implications of Amoret's being removed from the company of Womanhood, of Silence and Obedience, of Modestie, Curtesie, Shamefastnesse, Cherefulnesse? To divorce such qualities from Love would certainly be considered dangerous in the Renaissance; and the sinister implications are compounded both by the fact that removing Amoret unbalances the double tetrad, thus courting disharmony, and by the episode's ambiguous ending, where Scudamour compares himself to Orpheus leading his love out of Hadean captivity – the reader must recall Orpheus' disastrous failure. Still, Venus smiles on the enterprise, and this is not Venus in her carnal aspect but a hermaphroditic Venus symbolizing wholeness and concord. It is possible that Scudamour is abducting Amoret not from Womanhood but from an overly self-sufficient Womanhood, towards the domestic hermaphroditism or *enosis* that is marriage, that union of male and female which is prefigured in the *Venus biformis* and is an important Renaissance symbol of universal concord (Woodbridge 1984). These two interpretations of Scudamour's 'capture' of Amoret seem mutually exclusive, and the matter remains unresolved: the Womanhood tableau, like the Temple of Venus episode in which it is embedded, is highly ambiguous in meaning, and awaits further exploration. LINDA WOODBRIDGE

women, defense of In the proem to *FQ* III, Spenser announces his intention to praise Elizabeth's rule as well as her chastity. With this statement, he enters a lively contemporary controversy in which the proposition that women were as intellectually, morally, and even physically capable as men was defended and attacked in court circles and the popular press. Although some apologies for women may be merely rhetorical exercises (eg, C. Pyrrye c 1569 *The Praise and Dispraise of Women*) and others use attacks on men as their main defense of women (Jane Anger 1589 *Jane Anger, Her Protection for Women*, Edward More 1560 *A Lytle and Bryefe Treatyse, Called The Defence of Women*), many are serious examinations of woman's role in society that use all evidence, even the most extreme, to refute charges of women's moral and intellectual weakness.

Extremely popular in Italy, where the new notions about women had their origin, and on the continent, the defense of women had two special practical applications in England. Protestants exploring the potential of Christian marriage drew on arguments in defense of women to demonstrate that wives were fit spiritual companions for their husbands (eg, Henry Smith 1591 *A Preparative to Mariage*), and defenders of the Queen's right to rule the nation and the church gathered their evidence from the popular defenses and from compilations of biographies of famous women.

Fundamental to the defense of women was proof that chastity came naturally to them. Evidence for instinctive chastity (such as the 'fact' that women are naturally more modest than men because they float face downward when they drown whereas men float face up) reinforced society's expectation that women be chaste; and those arguing that girls should be given a humanist education or that women ought to be allowed to act in traditionally male social spheres first had to establish that ignorance was not a precondition for chastity (eg, Richard Hyrde 1526?, preface to Erasmus *A Devout Treatise upon the Pater Noster* tr Margaret More Roper [*STC* 10477]; T. More, Letter to William Gonell, no 63 in ed 1947; Richard Mulcaster 1581 *Positions*).

Those who defended women's ability and right to act in male fields argued that famous women of the past who excelled in arts, sciences, writing, law, and arms proved that women are as able as men (Thomas Elyot 1545 *The Defence of Good Women*), and that the limited record of women's deeds is due to men's envious repression of the facts (Anthony Gibson tr 1599 *A Womans Woorth*). Some writers suggested that modern women's achievements were beginning to equal those of ancient women (Robert Vaughan or Burdet? 1542 *A Dyalogue Defensyve for Women*).

The main locus of the serious defense of women was in responses to John Knox's condemnation of government by women (*The First Blast of the Trumpet against the Monstruous Regiment of Women* 1558). Written to attack Catholic Mary Tudor, the book was perceived as an attack on Elizabeth, and other Protestants came to the defense of the new queen's right to rule. Calvin formulated the most conservative defense; he praises the Queen as a heaven-sent exception to the natural law of male rule. She, like Deborah, is a savior of her nation; but her abilities establish no precedent for other women (Calvin ed 1845). Although in her personal conduct Elizabeth frequently presented herself as raised above the natural limitations of her sex by her role as Queen (speech at Tilbury), she did not favor this position among her supporters. All defenses that received official approval argue that female rule is natural. John Aylmer (*An Harborowe for Faithfull and Trewe Subjectes* 1559), George Whetstone (*The English Myrror* 1586), and John Bridges (*A Defence of the Government* 1587) cite Elizabeth's genealogy as proof of her natural claim to the throne, but stress the historical precedent of successful queens and female generals from biblical and secular history: Artemisia, Tomyris, Penthesilea, Joanna of Naples, among many more. The arts, sciences, and crafts invented by such women as Ceres, the Muses, and Athena as well as by historical women show the general excellence of the sex. These authors assert that authority and accomplishments need not hinder a woman's obedience to her husband and that power does not necessarily corrupt women's sexual morals. In answer to the claim that women's inferior social position is evidence of God's intention, they allege that in the ancient past sexual roles were equal or even reversed – witness the Amazons. The modern age is seen as a corrupt period in which men have forcibly suppressed women, and male writers throughout the ages are accused of having deliberately ignored women's accomplishments.

Spenser treats chastity and female rule separately, although the topics are linked through Britomart and Elizabeth, whose chastity and activity in the male sphere suggest that activity does not lead to promiscuity. Spenser clearly regards women as naturally capable of chastity (as far, that is, as any fallen human being is capable of virtue). Questions about this ability are raised only once, by the Squire of Dames (III vii 57–60); and extreme praise of the virtue in terms borrowed from the debate occurs only twice, in the encomium of Florimell when she rejects Proteus (viii) and in the disclaimer of malice before the story of Hellenore (ix). All three of these passages are based on *Orlando furioso* (28 and 29) and involve Spenser in a dialogue with Ariosto more than with his English contemporaries. In each case, he modifies the passage to remove the antifeminist edge. Ariosto's equivalent to the Squire of Dames finds no chaste women at all; the Squire finds an honest country maid. Ariosto's narrator praises his heroine as extraordinary because chastity is an almost unknown virtue; Spenser's narrator praises Florimell as a model for the conduct of 'honourable Dame[s]' (viii 43), his contemporaries. Ariosto's narrator's disclaimer of sympathy with antifeminism is so extreme that it seems insincere; Spenser's convincingly suggests the native goodness of women. With these three passages, Spenser overgoes Ariosto, the primary literary player in the game of the defense of women, as he wittily demonstrates women's moral capacity.

One episode seems to cross the boundary between the topics of women's sexuality and their social rights. In order to gain entry for herself, Amoret, and a knight at a castle at which only couples are given lodging (IV i), Britomart uses her outwardly male appearance to form a couple with Amoret and then reveals her sex to claim the young knight as her companion. Although the action suggests very mildly that women ought to be allowed to play whatever social role their skills fit them for, Britomart does not make the argument nor does the narrator. Britomart's ambiguous sexuality, not women's rights, is the subject of the episode. Spenser's suppression of the profeminist material is clear in comparison with *Orlando furioso* 32, where Bradamante speaks about women's right to be judged on what they can do and enforces her rhetoric with physical threats.

On the topic of rule by women, Spenser engages directly in the contemporary debate, using the social and historical arguments made in favor of female regiment to praise the Queen, but not endorsing the official position that her rule has a basis in nature as well as in the divine will. He does not use his good queens – Gloriana, Mercilla – to justify or condemn rule by women. Mercilla and Gloriana are types of Elizabeth: they mirror her, but they do not link her to historical precedents for her rule. Through them, Spenser celebrates Elizabeth's reign for qualities and acts peculiar to her.

In two encomiums of Britomart and the Queen, Spenser isolates Elizabeth from other queens (III ii 1–3, iv 1–3). He treats her as extraordinary in a manner related to but not identical with Calvin's. These encomiums are derived from *Orlando furioso* 20.1–3; but unlike the passages in praise of chastity which go beyond Ariosto in their appreciation of women, they fall far short of the extreme profeminist stance of the Italian. They have been taken as defenses of the general right of women to rule (Durling 1965:217; Berger 1969b:236), but comparing them with Aylmer, Bridges, Whetstone, and other English defenders of female regiment shows that Spenser subverts the officially sanctioned position. He uses the defenders' arguments about the greatness of ancient women and their political repression by men only to create a sense of the greatness of Elizabeth, who has triumphed over the odds.

In III ii, the poet opens with a profeminist gambit. He assumes that military prowess and wisdom are natural to women and suggests that male historians have deliberately downplayed the importance of women. He invokes an age of female authority and blames its decline on male envy, but he does not advocate the rewriting of history or celebrate modern times as a return to ancient appreciation of women. Instead, he suggests that women's freedom to exercise political skill, the modern equivalent of ancient prowess, is now being threatened by male envy. He does not protest this new repression; rather he celebrates Elizabeth as, alone among contemporary women, able to withstand modern repression because she has no need of men to praise her: her greatness is known through her own efforts. This encomium cleverly weds appreciation of women's abilities with a Calvinist sense of a sexual hierarchy created by God. Women are capable of rule but have not been assigned it as a normal role. Elizabeth is an exception to the natural order. The second encomium (III iv 1–3) asserts that ancient women like Penthesilea, Deborah, and Britomart were as successful in war as men and laments the lack of great women in modern times. By insisting on the failure of modern women and offering no excuse or remedy, the poet creates no hope for a return to excellence and power. In this context, Elizabeth stands out as extraordinary.

These two encomiums of Elizabeth's rule frame Spenser's celebration of her genealogy in which he stresses God's guiding hand behind her accession. Instead of proving that any woman could accede given the proper family relationships, the genealogy shows that she is chosen by God. Together with the encomiums, it establishes that the Queen is to be admired because she is exceptional. She has natural abilities beyond the scope of contemporary women, and the justification for her power is beyond the scope of human law.

In the Radigund episode (V v-vii), Spenser states directly the Calvinist attitude toward woman rule that is veiled in Book III (Phillips 1941–2b:233–4); his narrator cites Radigund's Amazonian government as proof of the danger of woman rule and rejects rule by all women except those elevated to it by God. That Britomart should depose her and restore male rule instead of assuming the rule herself reaffirms the principle that personal merit alone does not give women the right to govern.

PAMELA JOSEPH BENSON

Pamela Joseph Benson 1985 'Rule, Virginia: Protestant Theories of Female Regiment in *The Faerie Queene*' *ELR* 15:277–92; Diane Bornstein ed 1980 *The Feminist Controversy of the Renaissance* (Delmar, NY); John Calvin 1845 Letter to William Cecil, no 15 in *Zurich Letters* Second Series, tr Hastings Robinson, Parker Society (Cambridge); Hull 1982; Constance Jordan 1986 'Feminism and the Humanists: The Case of Sir Thomas Elyot's *Defence of Good Women*' in Ferguson, et al 1986:242–58, 376–83; Joan Kelly 1984 'Early Feminist Theory and the *Querelle des Femmes*, 1400–1789' in *Women, History, and Theory* (Chicago) pp 65–109; Kelso 1956; Knox 1558 rpt in ed 1927; I. Maclean 1980; Thomas More 1947 *Correspondence* ed Elizabeth Frances Rogers (Princeton); Kerby Neill 1937 'Spenser on the Regiment of Women: A Note on the *Faerie Queene* V, v, 25' *SP* 34:134–7; James Emerson Phillips, Jr 1941–2a 'The Background of Spenser's Attitude toward Women Rulers' *HLQ* 5:5–32; Phillips 1941–2b 'The Woman Ruler in Spenser's *Faerie Queene*' *HLQ* 5:211–34; Paula Louise Scalingi 1978–9 'The Scepter or the Distaff: The Question of Female Sovereignty, 1516–1607' *Historian* 41:59–75; Woodbridge 1984; Susanne Woods 1985 'Spenser and the Problem of Women's Rule' *HLQ* 48:140–58.

woods In the complex inner geography of *The Faerie Queene*, the predominant landscape is the forest. All adventures take place if not in the actual woods then in places, whether lofty castles, seductive bowers, awesome temples, or humbler cottages, which are felt as little more than breaks in the forest continuum. Although the English countryside known to Spenser was already suffering extensive deforestation, the Irish landscape was forested to a degree that corresponds remarkably well with the imaginative geography of *The Faerie Queene* (see also **FQ*, geography of). Nor, according to contemporary accounts, were the Irish woods much less perilous in historical reality than in Spenser's imagination (Wilson 1984:43).

Contemporary experience apart, the heroic and allegorical literary traditions with which Spenser and his audience were acquainted were rich in accounts of heroic quests, allegorical or otherwise, in woods and forests, as far back as the earliest recorded myths. Moreover, the hero's forest exploits can be seen to fall into certain patterns which persist, with constant adaptation to circumstances of time and place, through millennia of evolution. These patterns pertain in the first place to the challenge of the monstrous, the half-real, half-nightmare beings which manifest and give sinister form to the terrors engendered by the hostility of a featureless terrain where the rational mind finds no familiar external structures to answer its need to order and interpret its environment.

But once the woodland terrors have been mastered, the hero comes to realize that the absence of the normal structures and institutions of civilization also means absence of restraints, most particularly those irksome sexual restraints that were often but superficially accepted in his native society. Thus the next challenge is that of the enchantress who threatens to overthrow the hero's nascent maturity and self-control through seduction rather than terror. The third and culminating trial normally involves a descent into the underworld where the hero has both to accept and transcend the limitations of his mortal existence.

This threefold pattern of heroic testing is remarkably widespread in the literature of the western world, extending as far back as the Sumerian *Gilgamesh* epic, and occurring frequently in literature with which Spenser was well acquainted (see J. Campbell 1949). Occasionally, as in the *Odyssey*, we find such adventures taking place in environments, such as oceans or deserts, other than the forest, but we find in all cases the absence of institutional structures to supply external correlation and support of the inward psychological and moral principles of conduct on which the hero's civilization is based. Thus the testing of the hero essentially verifies whether his adherence to the principles of his society is independent of such external support.

Spenser's most immediate source and inspiration for the traditional threefold forest testing was probably Hawes' *Example of Virtue*, particularly for its structural scheme. He would also have been aware of its deeper implications from Virgil's *Aeneid* with its commentaries, as well as Ariosto's *Orlando furioso* and Tasso's *Gerusalemme liberata* with their commentaries. Hawes' hero, personified at the beginning as Youth, first encounters the beasts of the 'wyldernes' (which, at this stage of the evolution of the motifs, cause him little trouble). Then he is given the severer test of resisting the lures of Ladies Sensuality and Pride and fights a culminating battle with a dragon representing the world, the flesh, and the devil before receiving the reward of his chosen Lady Cleanness in marriage.

In *FQ* I, Spenser varies, extends, and deepens such forest imagery without ever quite departing from it; and his entire poem plays incessant and brilliant variations on the themes of monster and enchantress, the underworld journey being reserved chiefly for Book II. In the woods of *The Faerie Queene*, then, take place the multifarious unpredictable encounters with the personified or mythic beings of Fairyland; within the woods, equally, lies the extraordinary range of allegorical places which represent the permanent states of mind of the inner life which it was Spenser's avocation to explore.

Each age, each mental type will make its own interpretations of these woods. For Jungians they might represent the generalized subconscious mind, out of which the particular states constantly take form. Spenser would be familiar with ancient philosophical theories of surprisingly similar import. Servius, the fourth-century commentator on the *Aeneid*, associates Latin *silva* 'forest' with Greek *hyle*, also 'forest,' but interpreted philosophically as 'the chaotic mass of elements out of which all things are created' (gloss on *Aeneid* 1.314). Nor should this 'chaotic mass' be necessarily thought of as merely physical for Servius, or indeed for medieval or Renaissance interpreters. Servius himself, for instance, in his gloss on *Aeneid* 6.131, equates the *silva* with places where animal nature and the passions dominate. It was Spenser's achievement to take the analysis of this fundamental poetic image to both a point of intricacy and a depth surpassing all previous explorations.

Yet, at the same time, with an acute sense of the temporal limitations of this traditional system of allegory and symbolism, he uttered, in the *Cantos of Mutabilitie*, a prophetic lament for its passing. Diana, goddess of the woods, outraged by the corruption of her nymph by the lustful and voyeuristic Faunus, bids a final and bitter farewell to her forest haunts (VII vi 54–5). The new age of commercial and industrial development regarded the forests as raw material for exploitation, and had already reduced them to the point where industry was turning to coal for fuel. With such a shift in the attitude towards the natural world, it was inevitable that the ancient forest symbolism would lose its imaginative force, and indeed, after Milton's profound and brilliant use of it in *Comus*, the forest appears to lose its symbolic attraction for British writers. In Bunyan it hardly appears.

PAUL PIEHLER

Bernard Sylvestris ed 1973; Bernheimer 1952; J. Campbell 1949; Cirlot 1962; Hankins 1971; Nelson 1963; Piehler 1971; Sehrt 1968; Whitman 1918; Charles Wilson 1984 *England's Apprenticeship, 1603–1763* 2nd ed (London).

Woolf, Virginia (1882–1941) Although Virginia Woolf makes only a few allusions to Spenser in her fiction, she read him with appreciation and understanding. A copy of *The Faerie Queene* is found both in Jacob's room at Cambridge (*Jacob's Room* 1922, ed 1976:37) and in the library at Pointz Hall (*Between the Acts* 1941, ed 1969:26). The phrase 'sea-shoulding Whales' (*FQ* II xii 23, quoted in Woolf's reading notes) is alluded to in an early draft of *Between the Acts*. One of the characters is seen 'shouldering his way – as William called it, applying instinctively the romantic word "shouldering" – the word that was used of whales "shouldering" the sea' (*Pointz Hall* ed 1983:118). In Woolf's fanciful biography *Orlando*, her heroine, a contemporary of Spenser, recalls that she once 'held in her hands the rough brown sheets on which Spenser had written in his little crabbed hand' (1928, ed 1970:255).

It is in Virginia Woolf's reading notes and essays, however, that we find detailed evidence of her perceptive response to Spenser's poetry. Her notes show that she read *The Shepheardes Calender* in 1924, when she was preparing to write an essay on Elizabethan literature for *The Common Reader* (1925). 'Where has this shepherd world come from?' she wonders. 'Not in Chaucer ... A sweetness and smoothness before unknown.' However, it seems not to have been until 1935, when she first read *The Faerie Queene*, that she gave sustained attention to Spenser's poetry. In January of that year, she wrote in her diary, 'I am reading the Faery Queen – with delight. I shall write about it' (ed 1977–84, 4:275). She read steadily until March and completed the first four books (in her father, Leslie Stephen's, copy of John Payne Collier's large 1862 edition, now in the Washington State University Library). Feeling the need for something 'particular,' she put *The Faerie Queene* aside until June, when she resolved to finish it. The fruits of her reading are found in eighteen pages of reading notes (now at the University of Sussex), in her essay '*The Faery Queen*,' which was published posthumously in *The Moment and Other Essays* (1947; rpt *Collected Essays* ed 1966–7, vol I), and in 'Anon,' the history of English literature that she was writing at the time of her death.

In her first essay, Woolf shaped the notes which were a running account of her response to *The Faerie Queene* into an exploration of the process of reading the poem. 'Reading poetry is a complex art,' she writes at the beginning of her essay. 'The mind has many layers, and the greater the poem the more of these are roused and brought into action.' While reading *The Faerie Queene*, she finds her mind 'perpetually enlarged by the power of suggestion,' 'uncabined,' and allowed to move about freely in a 'great bubble blown from the poet's brain.' She may not always know exactly what the poet means, she admits, but she is moved by the words themselves which have 'that meaning which comes from their being parts of a whole design' (ed 1966–7, I:14–18).

Woolf anticipates her reader's dislike of allegory and compares the conventions Spenser uses to those of the novelist. The novelist makes his characters think; Spenser 'impersonated his psychology. Thus if the novelist now wished to convey his hero's gloom, he would tell us his thoughts; Spenser creates a figure called Despair ... who shall say that [Spenser's method] is the less natural, the less realistic?' (I:16).

Woolf also compares Spenser's method to that of the dramatist. In her notes, she observed that 'Shakespeare and [the] dramatists make the person speak[,] have the advantage of the stage, which is to sum up, to make people say what they would say in fact.' In Spenser's poem, 'All these undramatic characters are much more closely allied to the writer.' The scene between Britomart and her nurse (*FQ* III ii) drew from Woolf the observation, 'Spenser's old nurse not a patch on Juliet's; but the stanza wrong for dialogue.' She develops this contrast further in her essay when she says that Spenser's characters 'lack the final embodiment which is forced so drastically upon the playwright. They sink back into the poet's mind and thus lack definition' (I:17).

Although she felt that Spenser's characters 'lack definition' when compared to men and women on a stage, her notes show that many scenes in *The Faerie Queene* struck her as both moving and realistic. She singled out several for praise: the description of the old man in the castle (Ignaro) who 'could not tell' (I viii 30–4), which reminded her of Wordsworth and Scott, though Spenser 'does not moralise so severely,' she added; the episode of Phaedria in her 'Gondelay' (II vi), which prompted her to write, 'Here is some adumbration of the difficulty of life: temptations, passion. All great books are the story of the souls adventures – nothing else – a perpetual odyssey and divine comedy'; the Mammon episode (II vii); Acrasia in the Bower of Bliss (II xii); the 'Chorle' (Braggadocchio) and the lady (III viii); the lovemaking of the Satyrs (III x 44–8), which she thought 'very realistic'; Care (IV v 33–45), about whom she noted, 'Blessing to find reality ... the internal mood externalised'; and Belphoebe's reproof of Timias (IV vii 36), which she found 'rather tense and effective.'

In both her notes and her essay, Woolf's reflections on Spenser's allegory are linked to her thoughts about his belief in the world he creates. In her essay, she cites the lines from the proem to Book II in which Spenser says he knows *The Faerie Queene* will be called by some 'th'aboundance of an idle braine' as evidence that he believed in this world only 'sufficiently to make it serviceable.' He is not asking his readers to believe in it, she says, but only to 'think poetically.' To do this, the modern reader must make some adjustments, but 'there is nothing false in what is to be done; it is easier to read Spenser,' she adds, 'than to read William Morris' (I:17).

Woolf was deeply impressed by the way Spenser mixes 'the high-flown and the vernacular' in his language. She praises 'the spray of fresh hard words, little colloquialisms, tart green words that might have been spoken at dinner, joining in easily with the more stately tribe' (I:17). Early in her notes, she expresses her delight in Spenser's 'beautiful free stepping measure'; but in her essay, she reflects her later reservations about its effect on the reader. The pace of the verse is 'always rhythmical and seemly,' she says, but it can become 'lulling, soporific. It sings us to sleep' (I:17). Her notes suggest in more detail than her essay that it was the content as much as the style of *The Faerie Queene* that had at times a sleep-inducing effect on Woolf. 'The history of Britain is merely perfunctory: also there are too many fights, one the same as the other,' she complained when halfway through Book II. While reading Book III, she noted, 'More chronicle history – not his strong point.' She felt sleep overcoming her while reading Book IV. 'Why? Because these figures dont have the weight of the book behind them. They taper off. Also the repetition of battles, loves becomes monotonous. The old metaphors in poetry too high flown ... And it may be,' she added, 'that the mind is saturated with too much poetry.' She assumed her lapses of attention to be caused as much by the 'cycle' of her taste as by the quality of Spenser's poem. 'It may be that the first books of the *FQ* are in fact the best,' she wrote on 11 March, when she had finished Book IV and had decided to stop reading the poem for a while. 'But I think the ebb and flow of my feeling is also at the back of it.'

Woolf did not have room in her essay to explore all of the ideas that occurred to her as she read Spenser. She remarked, for example, that it was 'odd that Christianity should rule in faery land. The knight has the Testament.' She anticipated later critical discussions when she noted 'Spenser as a feminist,' a comment prompted by her reading of the opening stanzas of Book III ii and iv. Under this heading, she quoted the lines in which the poet castigates 'envious' and 'boastfull men' for being jealous of the achievements of women. Unfortunately, she did not elaborate further.

Woolf returned to Spenser in 'Anon' (edited by Silver 1979) to explore his role as the first poet to emerge from the anonymity of the minstrel and the chronicler. 'He is aware of his art,' she writes, as Chaucer, Langland, and Malory were not. 'His is no longer a wandering voice, but the voice of a man practising an art, asking for recognition, and bitterly conscious of his relation [to] the world, of the worlds scorn.' One feels Woolf's deep sympathy with Spenser in this remark and in her description of his concern with the decay and corruption of language since Chaucer, who gave Spenser, she says, 'the standard by which to measure his own words.' Perhaps Spenser used 'the crabbed old words,' she writes, 'not as we now might revert to them to rub sharp what much use has worn smooth; but to restrain what was to come.' She again praises Spenser's way of presenting his figures 'pictorially; grouped, like the figures in a fresco.' Woolf concludes by seeing Spenser pictorially, as she imagines him standing on the threshold of Sidney's Penshurst 'half in shadow, half in light.' He is a transitional figure emerging from the shadows of anonymity into the light of modern self-consciousness (pp 390–1).

Although Woolf seems to have taken her own advice to 'put off [reading *The Faerie Queene*] as long as possible' (ed 1966–7, I:14), when she did turn to Spenser's poem late in her career, she found much in it to praise. Spenser may not have moved her as profoundly as some other writers did, but she clearly found in him a poet whose sense of language and whose concern with the expectations of his audience in many ways mirrored her own. SUSAN DICK

Virginia Woolf ed 1966–7; Woolf 1969 *Between the Acts* (London); Woolf 1970 *Orlando* (London); Woolf 1976 *Jacob's Room* (London); Woolf 1977–84 *Diary* ed Anne Olivier Bell, 5 vols (New York); Woolf 1983 *Pointz Hall: The Earlier and Later Typescripts of 'Between the Acts'* ed Mitchell A. Leaska (New York). Unpublished manuscript material: Virginia Woolf's Reading Notebook, Berg Collection, New York Public Library; Virginia Woolf's Reading Notebooks, Monk's House Papers B.2c and B.2m, University of Sussex.

Alice Fox 1983 '"What right have I, a woman?": Virginia Woolf's Reading Notes on Sidney and Spenser' in *Virginia Woolf: Centennial Essays* ed Elaine K. Ginsberg and Laura Moss Gottlieb (New York) pp 249–56; Beverly Ann Schlack 1979 *Continuing Presences: Virginia Woolf's Use of Literary Allusion* (University Park, Pa); Brenda R. Silver, ed 1979 '"Anon" and "The Reader": Virginia Woolf's Last Essays' *TCL* 25:356–441; Silver 1983 *Virginia Woolf's 'Reading Notebooks'* (Princeton).

Permission to quote from Virginia Woolf's reading notebooks has been granted by Quentin Bell and Angelica Garnett, administrators of the Author's Literary Estate, by the University of Sussex Library, and by the Henry W. and Albert A. Berg Collection, The New York Public Library, Astor, Lenox and Tilden Foundations.

Wordsworth, William (1770–1850) According to his nephew and biographer, Wordsworth was acquainted with Spenser as a boy: 'the Poet's father set him very early to learn portions of the works of the best English poets by heart, so that at an early age he could repeat large portions of Shakespeare, Milton, and Spenser' (C. Wordsworth 1851, 1:34). Since his father died in December 1783, Wordsworth presumably undertook this task before he reached his teens.

Dorothy Wordsworth's Journal records his later reading: he read Spenser in November 1801; she put him to sleep by reading Spenser to him in March 1802; they read *Prothalamion* together in April 1802; she read the first canto of *The Faerie Queene* to him in June 1802; and he read Spenser himself in July 1802 (ed 1971:59, 62, 102, 116, 137, 144). Likewise in the correspondence: in November 1802, Wordsworth advised his brother John to buy an edition containing the *Vewe of Ireland*; in November 1805, he was 'sadly disappointed with Todd's [1805 edition of] Spencer'; the Life is adequate, 'but three parts of four of the Notes are absolute trash.' In May 1809, he proposed to insert *FQ* III xii 36 into *The Convention of Cintra*, but the insertion was not in fact made. He was reading *The Faerie Queene* in February 1815. 'Chaucer and Spenser are apt to be overlooked' among the great English poets (Nov 1824). Though he admires the Scottish poets, he does not wish to be separated 'from the Country of Chaucer, Spencer, Shakespeare, and Milton' (Nov 1825). 'The Poetic Genius of England with the exception of Chaucer, Spenser, Milton, Dryden, Pope, and a very few more, is to be sought in her Drama' (Apr 1830) (*Letters* ed 1967:378, 641; ed 1969–70, 1:301, 2:204; ed 1978–88, 1:284, 402, 2:234).

Direct references to Spenser himself occur in *The Prelude* 3.279–83 (as a Cambridge man), and 6.104–9 (as a poet of 'visions' and of 'human forms and superhuman powers' which could not, however, match the fairy-like quality of an ash tree in winter on the Cambridge Backs). In 8.191–203, Spenser is used as the type of the English pastoral poet, perhaps actually in contact with rustic life; words and phrases are taken over from *SC, Maye*. The 'moral and imaginative genius of our divine Spenser' and a 'false Gloriana' (false Florimell?) are mentioned in the *Reply to 'Mathetes'* (1809; ed 1974, 2:20). He is grouped with 'all the Men of Genius of his Age' who 'tenderly bemoaned' the death of Sidney, presumably in the elegies headed by 'Astrophel' (*Essays upon Epitaphs* II [1810]; ed 1974, 2:72). 'Spenser's fairy themes' appear in *Artegal and Elidure* (1815) 49, but the narrative is based on Milton's *History of Britain*, with only occasional reference (lines 16, 33–40) to the chronicle matter of *FQ* II x. More significant references occur in the Preface and Essay, Supplementary to the Preface of 1815: Spenser shares with parts of the Bible, and with Milton, 'enthusiastic and meditative Imagination ... poetical, as contradistinguished from human and dramatic Imagination'; his 'allegorical spirit at one time incit[es] him to create persons out of abstractions; and, at another, by a superior effort of genius, to give the universality and permanence of abstractions to his human beings, by means of attributes and emblems that belong to the highest moral truths and the purest sensations, of which his character of Una is a glorious example' (ed 1974, 3:34–5). Spenser, 'whose genius is of a higher order than even that of Ariosto,' was 'a great power, and bears a high name: the laurel [cf *FQ* I i 9] has been awarded to him'; yet in his day 'the Fairy Queen faded before' du Bartas' 'Creation.' George Hakewill (Wordsworth records) cites Spenser (and Ariosto, Tasso, and du Bartas) 'as instances that poetic genius had not degenerated' in modern times (3:67–8). Johnson (characteristically, according to Wordsworth) omitted Spenser from his *Lives* (3:79). The sonnet-form ('Scorn Not the Sonnet' pub 1827) 'cheered mild Spenser, called from Faery-land / To struggle through dark ways': seemingly a reference to the Petrarchan statements of lover's woes in the *Amoretti*.

A few nineteenth-century reports of Wordsworth's conversations contain references to Spenser. According to John Payne Collier's Diary for 20 October 1811,

> Tasso's 'Jerusalem Delivered' and Spenser's obligations to Tasso were discussed, and Wordsworth pronounced the Twelfth Canto of the Second Book of the 'Fairy Queen' unrivalled in our own, or perhaps in any language, in spite of some pieces of description imitated from the great Italian poets. The allegory, he said, was miraculous and miraculously maintained, yet with the preservation of the liveliest interest in the impersonations of Sir Guyon and the Palmer, as the representatives of virtue and prudence. I collected, however, that Spenser was not in all respects a great favourite with Wordsworth, dealing, as he does so much, in description, and comparatively little in reflection.

On the same day, Wordsworth commented on the alexandrine in the Spenserian stanza and instanced his own use of it (Coleridge ed 1856: xxxii, xxxv-xxxvi).

About 1827 Wordsworth told Christopher Wordsworth, Jr, that 'Spenser's "Marriage"' (*Epithalamion*? *Prothalamion*?) showed that good poetry can be written on contemporary events; he observed also that 'Ariosto is not always sincere; Spenser always so' (ed 1876, 3:461, 465). In 1841 he told Lady Richardson that he ranked Homer and Shakespeare above all others as impersonal poets: 'At the head of the second class, those whom you can trace individually in all they write, I would place Spenser and Milton. In all that Spenser writes you can trace the gentle affectionate spirit of the man' (3:435). He repeated this ranking to Crabb Robinson in 1843 (Robinson ed 1938, 2:627); both observations were intended to disparage Goethe.

References to Spenser's works rather than to the man can probably be seen in nonspecific statements about, and motifs from, chivalric romance: a topic proposed for a substantial poem in *The Prelude* 1.181–4, a passage considerably expanded in late revision of the poem, and more precisely tied to Spenser by brief quotations from *The Faerie Queene* and elsewhere (see Wordsworth ed 1985:32, 373, 1170–3). In 9.456–63 we have jousting knights, satyrs, and a captive maiden, suggesting *FQ* I ii 15–19 *et alibi*, vi 7–19; III x 36–51; VI viii 31–51, x 39–xi 23. Wordsworth found *FQ* VI 'exceedingly delightful,' according to a marginal note written in a copy of Anderson's *British Poets* in the Folger Library (Coleridge ed 1936:454; see also *Reply to 'Mathetes,'* cited above).

Direct quotations intended to be recognized as such, and distinct from adaptations and allusions, are rather rare in Wordsworth. The sonnet 'The World Is Too Much with Us' (1802–4?) quotes more or less verbatim from *Colin Clouts Come Home Again* 283 and 245. The sonnet 'Pelion and Ossa' (1802–4?) adapts *Virgils Gnat* 21–4, and quotes the lines in a manuscript note intended for the *Poems* of 1807 but not printed there. The phrase 'bold bad man' (*FQ* I i 37) appears in *The Prelude* 7.322, and (in the plural) in *The Convention of Cintra* (ed 1974, 1:256) and 'To the Lady Fleming' (1823) 81 – in each case marked as a quotation. The *Guide to the Lakes* (1810–35, in various editions) quotes *FQ* III v 39–40, from 'the divine Spenser,' to illustrate the art of building inoffensively in natural surroundings (ed 1974, 2:212). The Dedication to *The White Doe* (1807–8, pub 1815) 23 quotes *FQ* I viii 33. The sonnet 'Occasioned by the Battle of Waterloo' (1816) 9 quotes *FQ* VI v 37, with an acknowledging note; another, 'Blest Statesman He' (1838) 14 adapts, and in one version quotes, *FQ* V ii 36, with an acknowledging note.

Adaptations and obvious or disguised allusions to Spenser are more numerous. The earliest is perhaps the fragmentary *Vale of Esthwaite* (1787?) 554–9, where the poet complains that he must resign Fancy 'To delve in Mammon's joyless mine' (cf *FQ* II vii passim; and for *delve*, cf II vii argument, viii 4). A little later, in *An Evening Walk* (1788?, pub 1793) occurs a reference to Una (text of 1793, 333), and a footnote cites *FQ* I iii 4. Thereafter Una becomes the most frequently cited Spenserian character in Wordsworth: she is mentioned (with her lamb) in the quartet of sonnets entitled 'Personal Talk' (pub 1807) 42; in the Dedication to *The White Doe* stanzas 1–2; in the Preface of 1815 as a successful poetic symbol (ed 1974, 3:35, cited above); in *Ecclesiastical Sonnets* 1.25 (1821) 7–9, along with the Red Cross Knight. More important than these direct references, however, is the role of Una as a model for Emily, the heroine of *The White Doe*, as a noble, long-suffering, and deserted woman, who is associated with gentle beasts and who eventually achieves spiritual repose. The relation between the two characters, and between the two poems in general, is exhaustively treated in Comparetti's edition (1940), and needs no elaboration here. Una's enemy Archimago makes a solitary appearance in 'Epistle to Sir George Howland Beaumont, Bart.' (1811) 152–3, where a decaying dog is likened to 'a gaunt shaggy Porter forced to wait / In days of old romance at Archimago's gate.' Archimago's hermitage in *FQ* I i 34 has no porter; perhaps Wordsworth has in mind Ignaro, who acts as an incompetent porter at the castle of Orgoglio (I viii).

Allusions to Spenser occur in *The Prelude* as well as the more direct references cited above. The description of the arras in the house of Busirane (*FQ* III xi 28) is the basis for Wordsworth's treatment of the 'artificial life / And manners' of Cambridge (3.590–4). Spenser's pastoralism and the use of the *Maye* eclogue in 8.191–203 are mentioned above; *Epithalamion* 207–8 may have contributed to the same passage. *Muiopotmos* 209–11 is used for the phrasing of a semisarcastic passage on Wordsworth's hopes for the Revolution (10.836–9); from the same stanza (213), Wordsworth took 'weeds of glorious feature' for his description of the woman, never seen by him, in 'Beggars' (1802) 18.

Wordsworth's interest in the *Vewe of Ireland*, indicated by his advice to his brother to secure a text (noted above), and confirmed by unsuccessful efforts by Charles Lamb to secure a copy for Wordsworth himself, is puzzling. His use of it in a long and carefully prepared letter of 1829 to Charles James Blomfield, Bishop of London (ed 1978–88, 2:36–46), mainly on the Catholic Relief Bill but secondarily on the perpetual troubles of British rule in Ireland, is convincingly demonstrated by Marjarum (1940): Wordsworth follows Spenser in lamenting that firmer measures to dominate the native and Catholic Irish were not taken in Elizabeth's reign. No explanation emerges, however, for his interest in the *Vewe* in 1802, when his opinions were probably more liberal than in 1829, and when danger from Ireland such as appeared in 1798 with the entry of Humbert's force was long over, as, indeed, was the war with France for the time being.

Considering his interest in Spenser and in eighteenth-century Spenserian poems such as Thomson's *Castle of Indolence*, Beattie's *Minstrel*, and Shenstone's *School-Mistress*, Wordsworth's use of the Spenserian stanza is not very frequent. It appears most extensively in *Guilt and Sorrow* (pub 1842) and its unpublished precursors *Salisbury Plain* (1793) and *Adventures on Salisbury Plain* (1798?), and the extract *The Female Vagrant* (pub 1798). The most successful of these as a Spenserian imitation, in verse form, language, and imagery, is probably *Salisbury Plain*. Here the atmosphere of the gloomier parts of *The Faerie Queene* is better caught than in the somewhat prosier later versions, and the language is more obviously based on Spenser; Gill notes most of the verbal borrowings in Wordsworth ed 1975. Some of these are transferred to the sequence on Salisbury Plain in *The Prelude* 12.312–53.

The stanza is used also in 'Stanzas Written in My Pocket-Copy of Thomson's "Castle of Indolence"' (1802, pub 1815), where the model is, obviously, Thomson rather than Spenser. It appears again in two of the poems in *Memorials of a Tour on the Continent, 1820* (1822): 'Processions' and 'Desultory Stanzas,' neither a very Spenserian poem in versification (the number of run-on lines is excessive), matter, or style. The purpose of 'Desultory Stanzas,' an afterthought and envoy to the volume of 1822, faintly recalls the envoy to the *Calender*, though the wording ('Go forth, my little Book!') is closer to Chaucer's *Troilus* (5.1786) than to Spenser.

Two early and unpublished fragments use a modified Spenserian stanza rhyming *ababcbcdD*, the last line an alexandrine: 'Fragment of a Gothic Tale' and 'No Spade for Leagues' (ed 1940–9, 1:287, 293; for the first see also *The Borderers* in ed 1982:21–4, 746–809). Both pieces, the 'Fragment' more especially, have occasional touches of Spenserian gloom. A rhymed pentameter and alexandrine, and what appears to be a Spenserian stanza lacking its first line, survive in manuscript from the lost *Somersetshire Tragedy* (see *TLS* [21 July 1966]:642). The stanza of 'Resolution and Independence' (1802, pub 1807), rhyming *ababbcC*, the last line an alexandrine, is sometimes considered a version of the Spenserian, but since its obvious and appropriate source is Chatterton's *Excellent Ballade of Charitie*, no Spenserian model need be sought.

Several comments on the stanza appear in correspondence and elsewhere. In 1814, Collier told Wordsworth that he was 'extremely fond of the Spenserian stanza ... and [Wordsworth] admitted that it was the best form of stanza in our language; but he seemed to think any set form comparatively bad, and that nothing, especially for a poem of any continuance, was equal to blank verse' (Coleridge ed 1856: li-lii). In February 1815, Wordsworth was reading *The Faerie Queene*, as noted above; consequently, perhaps, he wrote to Southey in the same year that 'Spenser's stanza is infinitely finer than the *ottava rima* [of Tasso], but even Spenser's will not allow the epic movement as exhibited by Homer, Virgil, and Milton' (*Letters* ed 1969–70, 2:268). The following year, he made similar remarks to Southey on the unsuitability of a stanzaic form for a long poem: 'if [the stanza] be long, it will be as apt to generate diffuseness as to check it. Of this we have innumerable instances in Spenser and the Italian poets. The sense required cannot be included in one given stanza, so that another whole stanza is added ... for the sake of matter which would naturally include itself in a very few lines' (2:324–5). In 1829 he advised Catherine Grace Godwin,

> The Spenserian stanza is a fine structure of verse; but that is also almost insurmountably difficult. You have succeeded in the broken and more impassioned movement – of which Lord Byron has given good instances ... If you write more in this stanza, leave Lord Byron for Spenser. In him the stanza is seen in its perfection ... Spenser never gives way to violent and conflicting passion, and ... his narrative is bare of circumstances, slow in movement, and (for modern relish) too much clogged with description ... One great objection to [the stanza in circumstantial narrative] is the poverty of our language in rhymes. (ed 1978–88, 2:58–9)

Except where the intention to imitate Spenser is obvious, as in the Salisbury Plain poems and *The White Doe*, Spenser's style seems not to have influenced Wordsworth to any great degree; even the famous reference to him and his 'clouded heaven' in *The Prelude* (3.279–83) draws its vocabulary from Milton rather than from Spenser. A stray instance of brief but intensive borrowing can be seen in the sonnet to Sleep ('A Flock of Sheep'), where the rain, bees, fall of rivers, and winds, are obviously derived from *FQ* I i 41. Similar examples can no doubt be found elsewhere. That Wordsworth was aware of a Spenserian style, and the possibility of using (or avoiding) it, is, however, clear from a comment on a draft of 'A Farewell': '"Primrose vest" cannot stand. I should never have thought of such an expression but in a Spenserian poem, Spenser having many such expressions' (ed 1967:365). The line criticized evidently once read '[c]lad in its primrose vest,' of a rock (see ed 1983:589). The poem is not very Spenserian in its published form; it uses the eight-line stanza commonly called Chaucerian (*ababbcbc*), perhaps the source of Spenser's. A more general view of Spenser's aesthetics as understood by Wordsworth can be extracted from a letter of 1799: Spenser might have contributed ideas towards constructing an impressive waterfall (in the river Ure): 'with something of vastness or grandeur it is at once formal and wild' (ed 1967:277–8).

Scholarly discussions of Wordsworth's relation to Spenser have been few over the last half-century. Potts (1932) makes a strained attempt to connect the Immortality Ode, and especially its rhyme scheme, with *Prothalamion*. Marjarum (1940) on Wordsworth's use of *Vewe*, and Comparetti (in Wordsworth ed 1940) on *The White Doe*, are mentioned above. Mounts (1944) claims *Peter Bell* as an anti-Coleridgean, anti-supernaturalist, and therefore anti-Spenserian poem: for instance, the hermit Archimago and his hermitage (*FQ* I i 34) are to be recalled by the absent hermit and missing cottage of *Peter Bell* 376–80, and the matter-of-factness of Wordsworth's story is to be emphasized by the absence of fairy-tale apparatus. Gillcrist (1969), similarly, proposes that the 'mace of Reason' as a weapon against oppression and 'foul Error's monstrous race' (*Salisbury Plain* 544–5; cf *FQ* I i 13–26) is a Godwinian, anti-Spenserian substitute for Talus and his flail as the destroyer of the communistic giant of *FQ* V ii 30–50. Maxwell (1970) finds a borrowing from *SC, Februarie* 35–6 in *The White Doe* 11–13. Schulman (1981–2) traces the development of 'Resolution and Independence' from 'The Leech-Gatherer' in terms of the destruction of a Bower of Bliss (Wordsworth's morally over-comfortable situation in Grasmere in 1802), with reference to the destruction of the hazel bower in Wordsworth's own 'Nutting,' of the falsely comfortable castle in Thomson, and of the bower in *FQ* II xii (a canto admired by Wordsworth, according to Collier, Coleridge ed 1856: xxxii); and the substitution of a morally sterner attitude in the poet. Schulman (1981) revives the attempt of Potts (1932) to connect the Immortality Ode with *Prothalamion*, and, more convincingly, compares the pastoral situation of Wordsworth in the Ode with that of Palinode and Piers in *SC, Maye*, used (as Schulman fails to note) in *The Prelude* 8.191–203, as recorded above. Schulman (1985) traces the increased use of Spenserian logic in narrative and character-drawing in the revision of *Salisbury Plain* towards *Adventures on Salisbury Plain*, and, in particular, instances the use of a quasi-Spenserian episode in *Adventures* 604–66 where, as in *FQ* II i 35–7, travelers come upon a tragic situation from which they draw moral profit. W.J.B. OWEN

For the poems, see *Poetical Works* ed Ernest de Selincourt and Helen Darbishire, 5 vols (Oxford 1940–9); *'Poems, in Two Volumes' and Other Poems, 1800–1807* ed Jared Curtis (Ithaca, NY 1983); editions of individual works include *The Borderers* ed Robert Osborn (Ithaca, NY 1982); *The Fourteen-Book 'Prelude'* ed W.J.B. Owen (Ithaca, NY 1985); *The Prelude* ed Ernest de Selincourt, rev Helen Darbishire (Oxford 1959; the text of 1805 is cited except where otherwise noted); *The Salisbury Plain Poems* ed Stephen Gill (Ithaca, NY 1975); *The White Doe of Rylstone* ed Alice Pattee Comparetti (Ithaca, NY 1940), ed Kristine Dugas (Ithaca, NY 1988). For the prose, see *Prose Works* ed Alexander B. Grosart, 3 vols (London 1876); *Prose Works* ed W.J.B. Owen and Jane Worthington Smyser, 3 vols (Oxford 1974). For the correspondence, *Letters of William and Dorothy Wordsworth* ed Ernest de Selincourt, has been revised in three editions: *Early Years, 1787–1805* rev Chester L. Shaver (Oxford 1967); *Middle Years, 1806–1820* rev Mary Moorman and Alan G. Hill, 2 vols (Oxford 1969–70); *Later Years, 1821–1853* rev Alan G. Hill, 4 vols (Oxford 1978–88).

Samuel Taylor Coleridge 1856 *Seven Lectures on Shakespeare and Milton* ed John Payne Collier (London); Coleridge ed 1936; T.J. Gillcrist 1969 'Spenser and Reason in the Conclusion of "Salisbury Plain"' *ELN* 7:11–18; E. Wayne Marjarum 1940 'Wordsworth's View of the State of Ireland' *PMLA* 55:608–11; J.C. Maxwell 1970 'An Echo of Spenser in *The White Doe of Rylstone*' *N&Q* 215:380; Charles E. Mounts 1944 'The Place of Chaucer and Spenser in the Genesis of *Peter Bell*' *PQ* 23:108–15; Abbie Findlay Potts 1932 'The Spenserian and Miltonic Influence in Wordsworth's *Ode* and *Rainbow*' *SP* 29:607–16; Henry Crabb Robinson 1938 *Henry Crabb Robinson on Books and Their Writers* ed Edith J. Morley, 3 vols (London); Samuel E. Schulman 1981 'The Spenser of the Intimations Ode' *WC* 12:31–5; Schulman 1981–2 'The Spenserian Enchantments of Wordsworth's "Resolution and Independence"' *MP* 79:24–44; Schulman 1985 'Wordsworth's Salisbury Plain Poems and Their Spenserian Motives' *JEGP* 84:221–42; Christopher Wordsworth 1851 *Memoirs of William Wordsworth, Poet Laureate* ed Henry Reed, 2 vols (Boston); Dorothy Wordsworth 1971 *Journals* ed Mary Moorman (London).

works, lost A substantial part of Spenser's writing, over 30 works, may have been lost. Only the titles or descriptions survive together with two lines of a sonnet and one line of another poem. We know of their possible existence from comments by Spenser himself, those closely connected with him, and others of the period.

In *The Shepheardes Calender*, E.K. mentions seven items as if they were finished. In the prefatory Epistle to Harvey, he expresses the hope that the poet will 'put forth divers other excellent works of his, which slepe in silence, as his Dreames, his Legendes, his Court of Cupide, and sondry others.' In glossing *March* 79–80, he suggests that those interested in 'Cupids colours and furniture' read the 'Idyllion of wandring love' by Moschus, translated into Latin by Politian, and adds, 'whych worke I have seene amongst other of thys Poets doings, very wel translated also into Englishe Rymes.' In describing the Graces, he notes that 'thys same Poete in his Pageaunts sayth: "An hundred Graces on her eyeledde satte"' (*June* 25 gloss), an imitation of a line in Musaeus. In the Argument to *October*, he remarks that poets write by divine inspiration and adds, 'as the Author hereof els where at large discourseth, in his booke called the English Poete, which booke being lately come to my hands, I mynde also by Gods grace upon further advisement to publish.' It sounds much like Sidney's *Defence of Poetry*. In glossing *October* 90, he quotes two lines from a sonnet that does not survive: 'The silver swanne doth sing before her dying day / As shee that feeles the deepe delight that is in death.' Finally, he remarks (*Nov* 195 gloss) that he has written a 'Commentarye upon the dreames of the same Authour.'

Certain lost works are mentioned in the Spenser-Harvey correspondence. Spenser refers to 'entituling [ie, dedicating] *My Slomber*, and the other Pamphlets' to Sidney or to Dyer (*Two Letters* 1, *Var Prose* p 6). In praising Harvey's efforts at writing iambics, he offers him some of his own: 'And nowe requite I you with the like, not with the verye beste, but with the verye shortest' (p 7), which suggests that he may have written others.

Spenser's second letter reveals his plans for *Epithalamium Thamesis*, 'whyche Booke I dare undertake wil be very profitable for the knowledge, and rare for the Invention, and manner of handling. For in setting forth the marriage of the Thames: I shewe his first beginning, and offspring, and all the Countrey, that he passeth thorough, and also describe all the Rivers throughout Englande, whyche came to this Wedding, and their righte names, and right passage, etc' (*Three Letters* 1, *Var Prose* p 17; see *rivers, *topographical description). He notes that his *Dreames* and *Dying Pellicane* (probably on the death of Christ) are 'fully finished' and soon to be printed. In a postscript, he confides that he prefers to publish his *Dreames* separately since, with E.K.'s excellent and witty glosses 'running continually in maner of a Paraphrase,' the book is 'full as great as my *Calendar*.' Michelangelo could not improve the best of its pictures nor blame the worst, and Spenser is sure Harvey will like them. Regarding his *Stemmata Dudleiana*, however, and especially its apostrophes 'addressed you knowe to whome,' Spenser says he must consider longer whether to send them out, although, in his own fancy, he 'never dyd better' (pp 17–18).

Responding to these remarks, Harvey tells Spenser he will no longer dream of the *Dying Pellicane* and *Dreames* until he sees them. He imagines that 'your *Magnificenza* [*Faerie Queene*?], will holde us in suspense as long for your nine Englishe *Commoedies*, and your Latine *Stemmata Dudleiana*,' the latter two of which Harvey expects to be successful – if only Spenser would spend a week polishing and trimming each (*3 Lett* 2, *Var Prose* pp 459–60). Mocking Spenser in the fifth letter, Harvey says Colin Clout 'may happely live by *dying Pellicanes*, and purchase great landes, and Lordshippes, with the money, which his *Calendar* and *Dreames* have, and will affourde him.' Claiming to put joking aside, he praises the *Dreames* as in the manner of the 'delicate, and fine conceited' Greeks and Italians who write in 'lively Hyperbolicall Amplifications,' above the comprehension of a common scholar. Spenser would be well satisfied if his *Dreames* were esteemed in England as Petrarch's *Visions* are in Italy (*3 Lett* 3, *Var*

Prose p 471). Finally, Harvey reports that he is returning *The Faerie Queene* and adds that Spenser's *Nine Comoedies*, named for the nine Muses in imitation of Herodotus, may come closer 'eyther for the finenesse of plausible Elocution, or the rarenesse of Poetical Invention, than that *Elvish Queene* doth to his *Orlando Furioso*.' All of the best wits, especially the Italians, advance themselves by writing comedies, and Harvey chides that Hobgoblin will 'runne away with the Garland from *Apollo*' (pp 471–2).

Introducing *Complaints* eleven years later, William Ponsonby declares that he is attempting to locate and publish items he understands Spenser has written: '*Ecclesiastes*, and *Canticum canticorum* [Song of Solomon] translated, *A senights slumber* [the same as *Dreames* and *My Slomber* noted above?], *The hell of lovers, his Purgatorie* [one work or two?], being all dedicated to Ladies.' He seeks other 'Pamphlets' by the 'new Poet': '*The dying Pellican, The howers of the Lord, The sacrifice of a sinner, The seven Psalmes*, etc.' Apparently he was not successful.

Contrasting with Ponsonby's focus on mainly religious titles, Spenser confesses that as a youth he wrote 'Many lewd layes (ah woe is me the more) / In praise of that mad fit, which fooles call love' (*Heavenly Love* 8–9). More specific internal references in *Vewe of Ireland* point to plans for a prose *Antiquities of Ireland* (*Var Prose* pp 81–2, 230–1), perhaps much like Camden's *Britannia*.

The final and most tantalizing mystery of the lost works is the possibility that Spenser wrote more of *The Faerie Queene* than has survived. He vows in *Amoretti* 80 to write six more books after resting from the first six. The printing in 1609 of *Two Cantos of Mutabilitie* may suggest that more of *The Faerie Queene* existed; its title page says the fragments 'appeare to be parcell of some following Booke of the *Faerie Queene*, under the legend of *Constancie*.'

Four men less close to Spenser than Harvey, E.K., and Ponsonby mentioned several lost works with varying degrees of implied or claimed knowledge. William Webbe, pleading for more publications by the poet of *The Shepheardes Calender*, named four titles from those given by E.K., called the poet 'Master *Sp*.' to keep the name secret, and said he knew that the poet's friends held many pieces in 'close custodie' (1586; see *Sp All* pp 7–8). John Stradling composed a cryptic epigram on the occasion of some of Spenser's manuscripts being burned by Irish rebels (*Epigrammatum libri quatuor* 1607:100; see *Sp All* p 116). About 1600, John Ramsey included in his commonplace book *Legendes* and *Court of Cupide*, along with *The Faerie Queene*, as poems he wanted; and since his stationer was Ponsonby, he may have known that the missing items existed (Strathmann 1931). Much later, in the Preface to the first edition of Spenser's *Vewe of Ireland*, Sir James Ware declared that in Cork Spenser finished *The Faerie Queene*, 'which was soone after unfortunately lost by the disorder and abuse of his servant, whom he had sent before him into *England*' (see *Var Prose* p 531).

What is to be made of this remarkable story of loss upon loss? For each item several possibilities exist: accidental disappearance, theft, deliberate suppression, incorporation into another work by a new title, or Spenser's failure to write what he and others spoke of as planned, in progress, or completed. That poems circulated among friends is likely, but that this led to so many losses is not – at least a few would have been preserved, and Spenser would have kept the originals. Most scholarship on the subject tries to identify lost works among surviving ones, for example seeing *Stemmata Dudleiana* translated and subsumed into *Ruines of Rome*; *Legendes*, *Pageaunts*, and *Court of Cupide* woven into *The Faerie Queene* (eg, the third appearing in VI vii 32–7); *The Hell of Lovers, His Purgatory* retitled *Hymne of Love* in *Fowre Hymnes* (see *Var* 8:510–20).

Two explanations may account for the loss of most of these works. Possibly more than most writers, Spenser frequently put poems aside, planning to revise them with better inspiration or to issue them at a propitious time that never arrived. Yet it seems equally possible that few of the 'lost' works ever existed except as ideas. The discussions of them in 1579–80 may have been intended as part of a campaign to promote 'the new Poete' (E.K.'s phrase echoed by Ponsonby) as a prolific, virtuoso writer in all genres, one who could supply much fine work to patron and public if only he were properly encouraged and rewarded. In such a scheme, E.K. and Harvey would praise the poet's unpublished work extravagantly, coaxing him to issue it, and Spenser would present himself as reluctant to risk publication yet divulge information about it. Among the many titles thus bandied about, only part of *The Faerie Queene* reached print – and that in installments, long after. Ponsonby could have been a late conspirator in this endeavor or its pawn. Nor would Spenser be the only beneficiary: E.K. praises and encourages Harvey (*SC* Epistle) and names five Latin poems by him now lost (*Sept* 176 gloss), while Spenser praises Harvey's work in his published letters. Harvey's zeal for preferment is well known. Or the campaign might have been a private joke, a hoax, with clues for the cognoscenti such as the bizarre idea of a comedy named for the Muse of tragedy.

Judging by the titles and what E.K., Spenser, and Harvey say, the lost works would fall into several groups: poetry of love, mainly Petrarchan and pastoral (*Court of Cupide*; *Pageaunts*; sonnets; many 'lewd lays' praising love; *The Hell of Lovers, His Purgatory*; the translation from Moschus; and the *Dreames* or *A Senights Slumber*); epic and antiquarian (*Epithalamion Thamesis*, *Stemmata Dudleiana*, and the remainder of *FQ*); religious (*The Howers of the Lord, The Sacrifice of a Sinner, The Seven Psalms*, Ecclesiastes, *Canticum canticorum*, and *The Dying Pellicane*); drama (nine comedies); prose (*Antiquities of Ireland* and *The English Poete*); and what cannot be classified by the evidence we have, *Legendes* and some English poems in classical meters. The range is almost that of Spenser's age with the most notable omissions being tragedy and prose fiction. The most surprising item is the nine comedies, for no drama by Spenser exists. Most of the others are close in subject and form to what survives.

Works by other Renaissance writers also disappeared, including plays by many authors that we know were performed; but Ben Jonson alone suffered a loss comparable to Spenser's (assuming again that his lost works once existed). Like Spenser, he was concerned to shape his literary career.

JACK B. ORUCH

Bradbrook 1960; Carpenter 1923; Helgerson 1978; Helgerson 1979; *Var* 8:270, 510–20; Strathmann 1931.

Y

Yeats, William Butler (1865–1939) Except for Shelley and Blake, Spenser influenced Yeats perhaps more than did any other English predecessor. His impact extended from Yeats's early verse of the 1880s through the Rose poems of the 1890s and his edition of Spenser in 1906, to culminate in some of the great mature lyrics on Lady Gregory and her son Robert. Yeats sought at first simply to imitate Spenser, then to project onto him conflicts in his own thought, and finally to adapt Spenser's stance toward aristocratic patrons for his own uses.

The period of emulation began with a long, unpublished narrative poem in Spenserian stanzas on the adventures of a medieval knight. Shortly thereafter came *The Island of Statues*, Yeats's first major published work. In his later autobiography, he described it as 'an Arcadian play in imitation of Edmund Spenser.' Imitative elements include characters like the Enchantress and the singing shepherds Thernot and Colin, pastoral settings like Arcadia and the enchanted island, and the rich mellifluence of the verse. This early but still superficial emulation deepened in the 1890s when Yeats came to appreciate the Neoplatonic elements in *Fowre Hymnes*. He devised numerous lyrics around the Rose as a symbol of intellectual beauty, and in a prose note explicitly linked them to 'the Intellectual Beauty of Shelley and of Spenser,' even while claiming originality for having such beauty share in human suffering.

Yeats's edition of *Poems of Spenser* (1906) for the Golden Poets series marks the middle phase of his interest. He eschewed representativeness as a principle of selection and instead chose 'only those passages from Spenser that I want to remember and carry about with me.' The extracts thus offer a fair map of the parts of Spenser that mattered most to Yeats; the texts themselves and some of the notes derive from J. Payne Collier's five-volume *Poetical Works of Edmund Spenser* (1862). Yeats began with *Hymne of Heavenly Beautie*, included *Epithalamion* and extracts from *Teares of the Muses*, *Ruines of Time*, and *The Shepheardes Calender*, and cited a few other passages on love or shepherds. From *The Faerie Queene*, he excerpted his favorite sections, including those on the islands of Phaedria and Acrasia, the Garden of Adonis, and Scudamour's conquest of Amoret. His manuscript notes indicate Romantic parallels and show the tension between his own preference for long passages and the publisher's demand for a compact selection. The accompanying introduction, an important critical statement in Yeats's canon, displays his characteristic fondness for antinomies. He saw Spenser as divided between a positive, poetically symbolic, aristocratic, and Anglo-Norman delight in the senses and a negative, prosaically allegorical, middle-class, and Anglo-Saxon allegiance to the emerging State. These antitheses allowed him to admire the Romantic and poetic side of Spenser even while recognizing the harshness of *Vewe of Ireland*, which troubled his nationalist sympathies. The essay teems with memorable phrases, as when Yeats calls Spenser 'a poet of the delighted senses' or describes his lines as 'like bars of gold thrown ringing one upon another.' Yet the resultant portrait owes as much to the problems of Yeats's own career as to Spenser's, particularly in its stress on 'that conflict between the aesthetic and moral interests that was to run through well nigh all his works.'

The last phase of Yeats's interest centered on Spenser's poetic relation to the aristocracy. Much influenced by Castiglione's concept of the courtier, he drew upon Spenser to enrich his own expressions of allegiance to the Gregory family, particularly in the elegiac mode. Spenser's laments for Sidney in 'Astrophel' and for the Earl of Leicester in *Ruines of Time* lie behind Yeats's own commemorative efforts. In a letter to Lady Gregory (22 February 1918), he described his first elegy for her son Robert, *Shepherd and Goatherd*, as 'in manner like one that Spenser wrote for Sir Philip Sidney.' The subsequent and more powerful *In Memory of Major Robert Gregory* differs in design but still refers to Robert as 'our Sidney and our perfect man.' Finally, in the very late *Municipal Gallery Revisited* (1937), Yeats laments the demise of Coole Park in an explicit recollection of *Time* 216–17: 'And now that end has come I have not wept; / No fox can foul the lair the badger swept – / (An image out of Spenser and the common tongue).' Yet even that explicit echo revises Spenser's image of an unworthy successor as a fox creeping into the badger's hole by proscribing the fox from defiling its heritage. Here as elsewhere, Yeats's Spenser belongs less to literary scholarship than to the artifice of eternity.

GEORGE BORNSTEIN

Spenser ed 1906; Yeats 1954 *Letters* ed Allan Wade (London); Yeats 1955 *Autobiographies* (London); Yeats 1957 *The Variorum Edition of the Poems* ed Peter Allt and Russell K. Alspach (New York); Yeats ed 1961 (includes rpt with slight changes of intro to Spenser ed 1906).

George Bornstein 1984 'The Making of Yeats's Spenser' in *Yeats: An Annual of Critical and Textual Studies* ed Richard Finneran (Ithaca, NY) 2:21–9; T. McAlindon 1967 'Yeats and the English Renaissance' *PMLA* 82:157–69; C.A. Patrides 1979–80 'The Achievement of Edmund Spenser' *YR* ns 69:427–43; A.G. Stock 1965 'Yeats on Spenser' in *In Excited Reverie: A Centenary Tribute to William Butler Yeats 1865–1939* ed A. Norman Jeffares and K.G.W. Cross (New York) pp 93–101.

Young, John, Bishop of Rochester (1534–1605) During Spenser's residence at Cambridge, Young served as vice-chancellor in 1569 and as master of Pembroke Hall from 1567 to 1578. Early in his career, he held several benefices in London and was appointed chaplain to Archbishop Grindal, who presided over his consecration in 1578 as Bishop of Rochester, in Kent. A note in Gabriel Harvey's copy of Jerome Turler's *Traveiler* (1575) reveals that Young selected Spenser to be his secretary: 'Ex dono Edmundi Spenserii, Episcopi Roffensis Secretarii. 1578' (A gift of Edmund Spenser, secretary of the Bishop of Rochester; *Sp All* p 4). *Roffensis*, Latin for 'Rochester,' is apparently behind the 'Roffynn' or 'Roffy' of *SC, September*, who has been identified with Young. Hobbinol (Harvey's allegorical double) praises Roffynn for being a 'meeke, wise, and merciable' shepherd, adding that Colin Clout is 'his selfe boye' (*Sept* 174–6). Diggon Davie then narrates the fable of Roffy and a wolf in sheep's clothing (180–225), a possible allusion to Young's vigilance in refuting the heretical Family of Love (McLane 1961:163–7). Hobbinol also mentions Spenser's living in Kent when he refers to the poet as 'the Southerne shepheardes boye' (*Aprill* 21); E.K.'s gloss here refers to the 'Kentish downes,' and his gloss on *June* 21 reiterates that the poet 'nowe abydeth' in the 'Southpartes.' These statements and a network of allusions to Kent in seven of the twelve eclogues may suggest that Spenser wrote most of *The Shepheardes Calender* while serving as Young's secretary; this would account in part for the poem's elaborate treatment of current ecclesiastical affairs. Spenser had vacated this position by the summer of 1579, since Harvey, in a letter written on 10 July, describes him as currently immersed in the social life of London, far from the more sedate environs of Young's residence at Bromley, Kent (Judson 1934). JAMES P. BEDNARZ

Z

zodiac (Gr *zōidiakos kyklos* circle of carved figures) The cycle of twelve constellations (as distinct from signs) through which the sun traditionally passes in the course of a year. Spenser's principal treatment of the zodiac occurs in the illustrations to the twelve months of *The Shepheardes Calender*, where each woodcut contains two representations of the appropriate zodiacal sign: a picture of the creature or object giving the sign its name, and the conventional glyph of the sign. The fact that these images are separated from the rest of the woodcut by a border of cloud suggests a degree of celestial supervision over the activities depicted. This effect ultimately derives from depictions of the labors of the months, which in almanacs, books of hours, and cathedral sculpture are usually presided over by the signs (see **SC*, printing and illustration). Since the labors appropriate to each month are determined by the position of the sun in the zodiac, they are ideally suited for demonstrating the integration of human life into the cosmic order. Moreover, Spenser's calendrical framework provides a sense of cyclical unity in the poem's variety (Heninger 1962). It has also been argued that Spenser's handling of character, situation, and theme throughout the *Calender* corresponds to the traditional significations of the planetary and zodiacal governors of the twelve eclogues. For example, Colin Clout's misfortune, melancholy, and assumption of the attributes of old age in *Januarye* and *December* correspond closely to the effects astrologers had long associated with Saturn and its signs, Aquarius and Capricorn (Richardson 1983).

(See **zodiac** Fig 1.)

Spenser also invokes the zodiac in the proem to Book v of *The Faerie Queene*, positing a causal relationship between physical, moral, and political degeneration on earth and various alleged symptoms of progressive physical disorder in the heavens. One of these is the 'wandering' of the zodiacal figures: the Ram has shouldered the Bull, which has butted the Twins, who have crushed the Crab and driven it into the abode of the Lion. Today we attribute this apparent movement to the precession of the equinoxes, but the explanation likely to be familiar to Spenser is the more complex one of trepidation devised for the late thirteenth-century Latin version of the Alphonsine Tables and still appearing in sixteenth-century works like Blundeville's *Exercises* (1594; see Dreyer 1953:276–7).

The zodiac makes its final major appearance in Mutabilitie's pageant, in which each month is represented by a human figure who rides on, or is otherwise associated with, a zodiacal sign (VII vii 31–43). That the pageant's zodiacal figures (many of which also symbolize vices or are dangerous creatures) are under the control of the human figures of the months may suggest that Spenser's 'real concern is to disable the astrological notion of the stars as fate' by implying that the stars influence mundane matters only as agents of a higher power (Hawkins 1961:98). Many astrologers, however, stopped short of claiming that human destiny is indelibly written in the stars, and argued that because astral influence affects the mental faculties not directly but through the four bodily humors which in turn help determine character, individuals can, by exercising free will and self-discipline, resist the effects of the stars and planets just as they can resist the passions caused by the humors. Spenser may be in agreement with this more moderate, and humanistic, astrological recognition that one need not be a passive victim of celestial forces.

J.M. RICHARDSON

J.L.E. Dreyer 1953 *A History of Astronomy from Thales to Kepler* rev W.H. Stahl (New York; first pub Cambridge 1906 as *A History of the Planetary Systems from Thales to Kepler*); J.M. Richardson 1989 *Astrogical Symbolism in Spenser's 'Shepheardes Calender'* (Lewiston, NY).

NOTE

The following illustrations have been made available through the generosity of many individuals and institutions. We have made every effort to obtain permission from all copyright owners, where we could identify them, and apologize to any we may have overlooked. Illustrations reproduced from volumes in the collections of The Thomas Fisher Rare Book Library in the University of Toronto are designated (Fisher).

In receptatores sicariorum.
EMBLEMA LII.

LATRONVM, furumq́ manus tibi, Scæua, per vrben
It comes, & diris cincta cohors gladijs:
Atque ita te mentis generosum, prodige, censes,
Quòd tua complures allicit olla malos.
En nouus Actæon, qui postquàm cornua sumpsit,
In prædam canibus se dedit ipse suis.

Actaeon Fig 1

Aesculapius Fig 1

Actaeon Fig 1: *In receptatores sicariorum* in Alciati ed 1577: no 52 (Fisher)

Adicia Fig 1: *Impresa* of Philip II, in Girolamo Ruscelli ed 1580 *Imprese illustri* (Venice) p 190 (Fisher)

Aesculapius Fig 1: *Aesculapius* in Whitney 1586:212 (Courtesy of the Stirling Maxwell Collection, Glasgow Univ Library)

Alciati Fig 1: Title page of Alciati ed 1621 (Fisher)

Adicia Fig 1

ANDREÆ ALCIATI

EMBLEMATA

CVM COMMENTARIIS

CLAVDII MINOIS I.C. FRANCISCI SANCTII BROCENSIS,

& Notis

LAVRENTII PIGNORII PATAVINI.

Nouißima hac editione in continuam vnius Commentarij seriem congestis, in certas quasdam quasi Classes dispositis, & plusquam dimidia parte auctis.

OPERA ET VIGILIIS

IOANNIS THVILII MARIAEMONTANI TIROL.

Phil. & Med. D. atq; olim in Archiduc. Friburg. Brisgoiæ Vniuersitate Human. liter. Professoris ordinarij.

Opus copiosa Sententiarum, Apophthegmatum, Adagiorum, Fabularum, Mythologiarum, Hieroglyphicorum, Nummorum, Picturarum & Linguarum varietate instructum & exornatum: Proinde omnibus Antiquitatis & bonarum literarum studiosis cùm primis vtile.

Accesserunt in fine Federici Morelli Professoris Regij Corollaria & Monita, ad eadem Emblemata.

CVM INDICE TRIPLICI.

Patauij apud Petrum Paulum Tozzium,

Sub Signo SS. Nominis IESV. 1621.

Alciati Fig 1

Archimago Fig 1

Archimago Fig 2

Archimago Fig 3

Archimago Fig 1: *Zoraster* in Maso Finiguerra 1898 *A Florentine Picture-Chronicle* ed Sidney Colvin 1970 (London) pl 14 detail (Figs 1 and 2 by permission of the British Library)

Archimago Fig 2: *Mage Hostanes* in Finiguerra 1898: pl 50
Archimago Fig 3: *Hippocrisia* from Cesare Ripa 1625 *Della novissima iconologia* (Padua) p 291

Archimago Fig 4

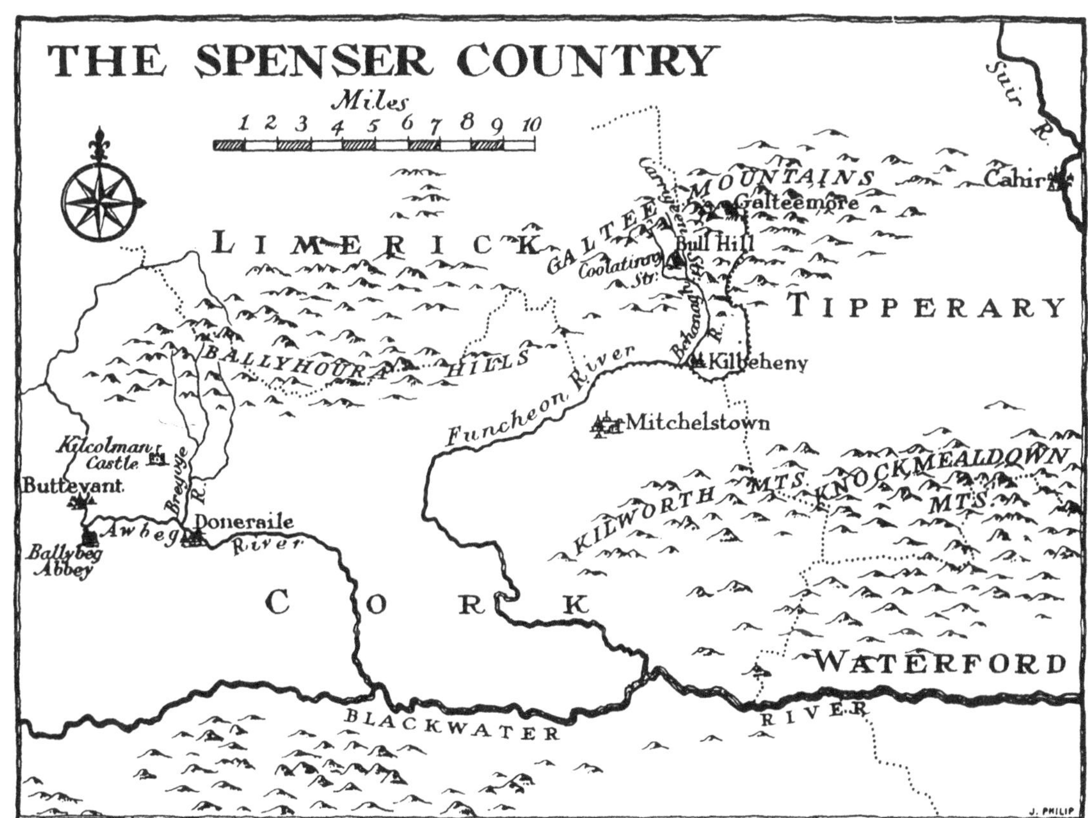

Arlo Hill Fig 1

Archimago Fig 4: Edward Kelley, in Meric Casaubon 1659 *A True and Faithful Relation ... Dr. John Dee* (London) frontispiece, detail (Courtesy of the Van Pelt Library, Univ of Pennsylvania)

Arlo Hill Fig. 1: 'The Spenser Country' in Judson 1933:59

Blake Fig 1

Blake Fig 2

Blake Fig 1: Blake's *Head of Spenser* (Butlin, cat 343, 9) (Courtesy of the City of Manchester Art Galleries)
Blake Fig 2: Blake's *Characters in Spenser's 'Faerie Queene'* (Courtesy of the Egremont Collection/The National Trust Photographic Library)

Burbon Fig 1

The Author being caried by his horse Will to the palace of disordered liuers, seeing then the abuse of all vertues, and the maintenance of filthy luxuria, remembreth his promise made to Age, looketh in the glasse of reformation, straight taketh his iorney, forsaking vtterly those abuses.

The Author seeing Abusion of all ordered vertues, so deckt like a foole, suspecteth that all the rest inhabiters, are no fit companions, concerning his promise to Age, leaueth all and departeth with Memorie. G.i.

Burgundy Fig 1

The trauailed Pilgrime

The Author and Memorie walking on foote, beholdeth the auncient showe and Funerals, of mightie Conquerours past.

Whereupon the Author beholding the same, desireth Memorie to show him the meaning thereof, as earst to fore she had begonne.

Burgundy Fig 2

Burbon Fig 1: *Henri IV tenant la France par la main* in Antoine, Duc de Lévis-Mirepois 1971 *Henri IV* (Paris) between pp 378–9 (Courtesy of the Bibliothèque Nationale, Paris)

Burgundy Fig 1: *The Author being carried by his horse Will to the palace of disordered livers* in Stephen Bateman 1569 *The Travayled Pylgrime* (London, *STC* 1585) fol G1r (Figs 1 and 2 Courtesy of The Huntington Library, San Marino, Calif)

Burgundy Fig 2: *The Author and Memorie walking on foote, beholdeth the auncient showe and Funerals, of mightie Conquerours past* in Bateman 1569: fol L3r

Circe Fig 1: *Circe* attributed to Dürer, in *Nuremberg Chronicle* 1493 (Nuremberg) fol 41r (By kind permission of the Dean and Chapter of Exeter Cathedral). See also the reproduction in Walter L. Strauss 1980 *Albrecht Dürer: Woodcuts and Woodblocks* (New York) p 36

cosmogony Fig 1: Aristotle 1519 *Libri de caelo. IIII* (Augsburg) fol 29v (Courtesy of Special Collections, Rare Book Room, Duke Univ Library)

cosmogony Fig 2: Frontispiece to Franchino Gafurius 1496 *Practica musicae* (Milan) (Courtesy of The Huntington Library, San Marino, Calif)

Circe Fig 1

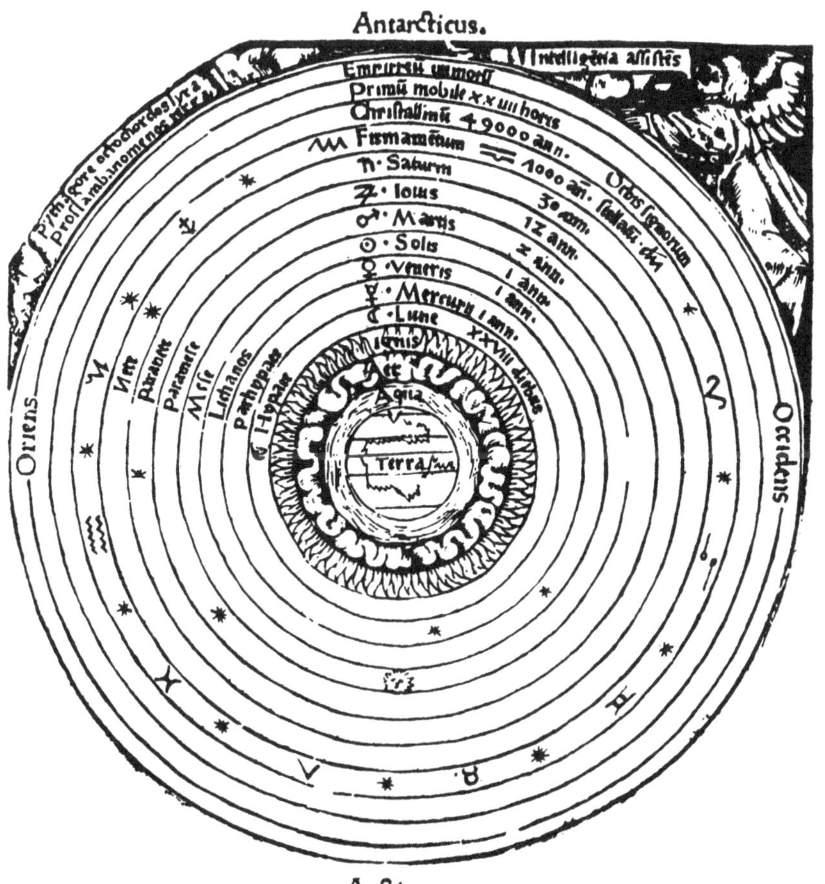

cosmogony Fig 1

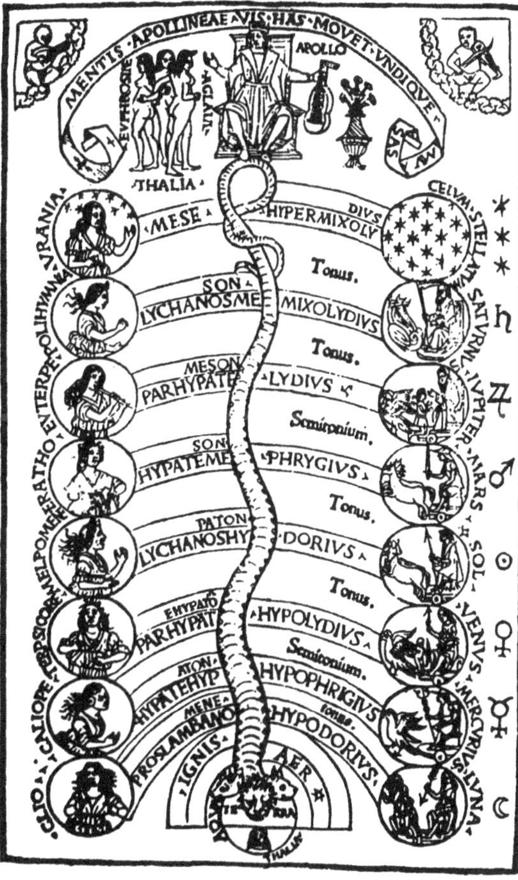

cosmogony Fig 2

46 ANDREAE ALCIATI

Custo d as uirgines.

Vera hæc effigies innuptæ est Palladis, eius
Hic Draco, qui dominæ constitit ante pedes.
Cur diuæ comes hoc animal? custodia rerum
Huic data, sic lucos sacraq; templa colit.
Innuptas opus est cura asseruare puellas
Peruigili, laqueos undiq; tendit amor.

dragon, Cupid's, Fig 1

Impudentia.

EMBLEMA LXVIII.

P*VBE tenus mulier, succincta latrantibus infra*
Monstrorum catulis, Scylla biformis erat.
Monstra putantur auarities, audacia, raptus:
At Scylla est, nullus cui sit in ore pudor.

dragons Fig 1

dragon, Cupid's, Fig 1: *Custodienda virgines* in Alciati 1544 *Emblematum libellus* (Leiden) p 46 (Fisher)
dragons Fig 1: *Impudentia* in Alciati ed 1621: no 68 (Fisher)

Elizabeth I, images, Fig 1

Elizabeth I, images, Fig 1: Attributed to Cornelius Ketel c 1580–3 *The 'Sieve' Portrait* (Pinacoteca Nazionale, Siena; courtesy of Alinari-Anderson, Florence/Art Resource, New York)

Elizabeth I, images, Fig 2

Elizabeth I, images, Fig 2: Attributed to William Segar 1585 *The 'Ermine' Portrait* (Hatfield House; courtesy of the Courtauld Institute of Art, London)

Elizabeth I, images, Fig 3

Elizabeth I, images, Fig 3: George Gower *The 'Armada' Portrait* (Bedford Estates; courtesy of SNARK/Art Resource, New York)

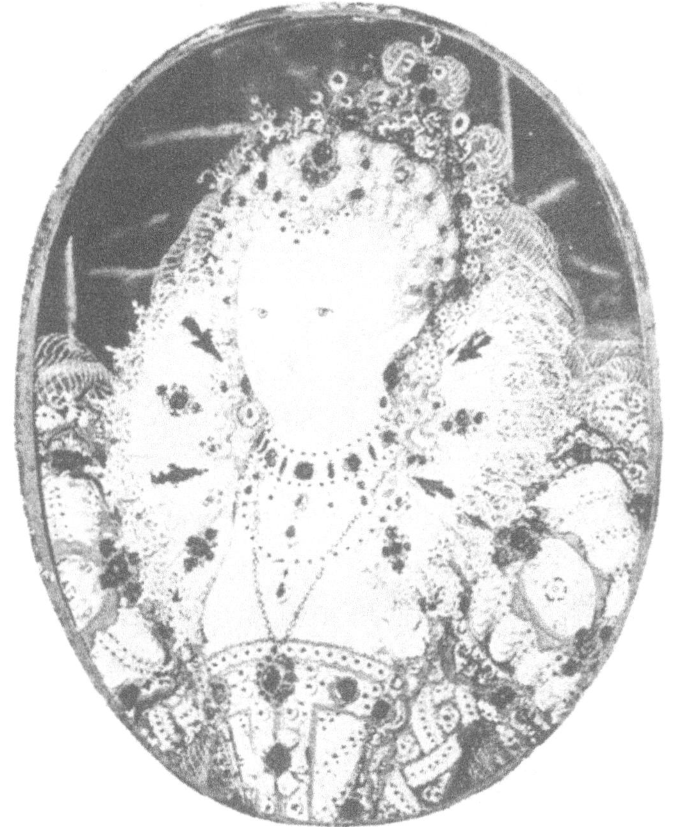

Elizabeth I, images, Fig 4

Elizabeth I, images, Fig 5

Elizabeth I, images, Fig 4: Nicholas Hilliard c 1595–1600 miniature of Queen Elizabeth (Private collection; courtesy of Bridgeman Art Library/Art Resource, New York)

Elizabeth I, images, Fig 5: Nicholas Hilliard c 1572 miniature of Queen Elizabeth (Victoria and Albert Museum; courtesy of Bridgeman Art Library/Art Resource, New York)

Elizabeth I, images, Fig 6

Elizabeth I, images, Fig 6: Attributed to Marcus Gheeraerts *The 'Rainbow' Portrait* (Hatfield House; courtesy of the Courtauld Institute of Art, London)

LXXIX. 80

NOXA NOCENTI.

Improbitas ſolet eſſe ſibi juſtiſſima merces,
Auctor es interitus ſic Baſiliſce tibi.

emblematics Fig 1

IN OCCASIONEM

emblematics Fig 3

emblematics Fig 1: *Noxa nocenti* in Joachim Camerarius 1590–1604 *Symbola et emblemata* (Nuremberg) 4: no 79 (Figs 1–4, 7 courtesy of the Stirling Maxwell Collection, Glasgow Univ Library)

emblematics Fig 2: *Incerta pro certis amplecti stultum* in Nicolas Reusner 1581 *Emblemata* (Frankfurt) 2: no 23

emblematics Fig 3: *In occasionem* in Alciati 1531 *Emblematum liber* (Augsburg) fol A8

emblematics Fig 4: *Gratiae* in Alciati 1546 *Emblemata* (Venice) fol 5v

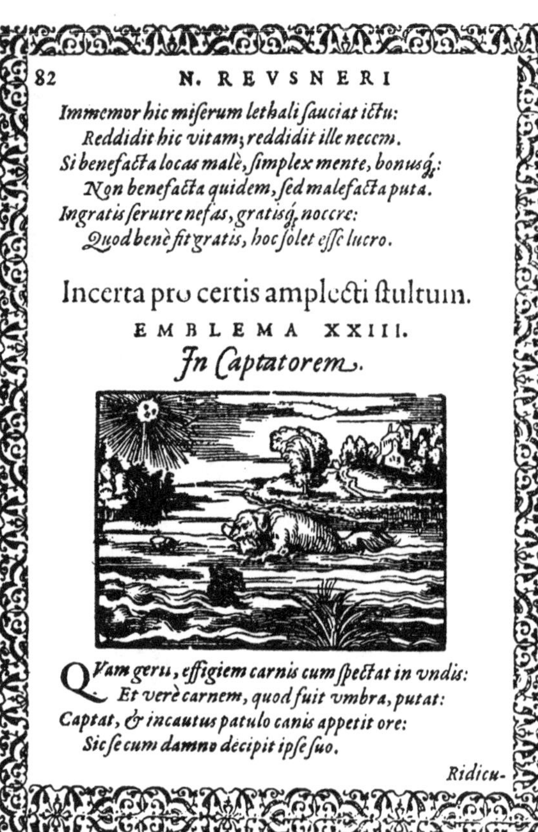

82 N. REVSNERI

Immemor hic miſerum lethali ſauciat ictu:
Reddidit hic vitam; reddidit ille necem.
Si benefacta locas malè, ſimplex mente, bonusq;:
Non benefacta quidem, ſed malefacta puta.
Ingratis ſeruire nefas, gratisq; nocere:
Quod benè fit gratis, hoc ſolet eſſe lucro.

Incerta pro certis amplecti ſtultum.

EMBLEMA XXIII.

In Captatorem.

QVam geris, effigiem carnis cum ſpectat in vndis:
Et verè carnem, quod fuit vmbra, putat:
Captat, & incautus patulo canis appetit ore:
Sic ſe cum damno decipit ipſe ſuo.

Ridicu-

emblematics Fig 2

ANDREAE ALCIATI

Gratiæ.

Tres Charites Veneri aſſiſtunt, dominamq; ſequuntur.
Hincq; uoluptates, atque alimenta parant.
Lætitiam Euphroſyne, ſpecioſum Aglaia nitorem,
Suadela eſt Pithus, blandus & ore lepos.
Cur nudæ? mentis quoniam candore uenuſtas
Conſtat., & eximia ſimplicitate placet.
An quia nil referunt ingrati atque arcula inanis,
Eſt charitum? qui dat munera, nudus eget.
Addita cur nuper pedibus talaria? bis dat
Qui cito dat, minimi gratia tarda pretij eſt.
Implicitis ulnis cur uertitur altera? gratus
Fœnerat, huic remanent una abeunte duæ.
Iuppiter ijs genitor, cœli de ſemine diuas
Omnibus acceptas edidit Eurynome.

emblematics Fig 4

Gratiæ.

EMBLEMA CLIII.

TRES Charites Veneri assistunt, dominamq́ sequuntur,
Hincq́ voluptates, atque alimenta parant.
Lætitiam Euphrosyne, speciosum Aglaia nitorem,
Suadela est Pithus, blandus & ore lepos.
Cur nuda? Mentis quoniam candore venustas
Constat, & eximia simplicitate placet.
An quia nil referunt ingrati, atque arcula inanis
Est Charitum? qui dat munera, nudus eget.
Addita cur nuper pedibus talaria? Bis dat,
Qui citò dat: minimi gratia tarda preti est.
Implicitis vlnis cur vertitur altera? Gratus
Fœnerat: huic remanent vna abeunte duæ.
Iuppiter ijs genitor, cœli de semine diuas
Omnibus acceptas edidit Eurynome.

emblematics Fig 5

Au simulacre de trois Graces Aglaia, Euphrosiné & Thalia.

D'ou vient cela qu'Aglaïa la sage
Et ses deux seurs en vertus tant ornées,
O sent aller par ce beau paysage,
Nues d'habitz & si mal atournées,
C'est le pourtrait des seurs à plaisirs nées,
Qui à bienfaitz n'ont ny fin ny mesure,
Et en presentz sont tant desordonées
Jusqu'à donner leur habit & vesture.

emblematics Fig 6

DE BENEFICIIS.

19

emblematics Fig 7

emblematics Fig 5: *Gratiae* in Alciati ed 1621: no 53 (Fisher)
emblematics Fig 6: *Au simulacre de trois Graces* in Costalius 1560:350 (Fisher)
emblematics Fig 7: *De beneficiis* in Laurens van Haecht Goidtsenhoven 1592 *Mikrocosmos parvus mundus* (Antwerp) no 19

envy Fig 2

envy Fig 2: Giotto c 1308 *La Carità* and *L'Invidia* (Capella degli Scrovegni, Padua; courtesy of Alinari-Anderson, Florence/Art Resource, New York)

envy Fig 1

fables Fig 1

envy Fig 1: *Invidia descriptio* in Whitney 1586:94 (originally in Alciati ed 1577: no 71) (Courtesy of the Stirling Maxwell Collection, Glasgow Univ Library)

fables Fig 1: *Esopus* in William Caxton 1484 *The Subtyl Historyes and Fables of Esope* (Westminster) fol 1v (By permission of the British Library)

THE FAERIE QVEENE.

Diſpoſed into twelue bookes,

Faſhioning

XII. Morall vertues.

LONDON

Printed for VVilliam Ponſonbie.

1596.

Faerie Queene **Fig 1**

Faerie Queene **Fig 1:** Title page of the 1596 edition (Courtesy of the Folger Shakespeare Library)

TO
THE MOST HIGH,
MIGHTIE
And
MAGNIFICENT
EMPRESSE RENOVV-
MED FOR PIETIE, VER-
TVE, AND ALL GRATIOVS
GOVERNMENT ELIZABETH BY
THE GRACE OF GOD QVEENE
OF ENGLAND FRAVNCE AND
IRELAND AND OF VIRGI-
NIA, DEFENDOVR OF THE
FAITH, &c. HER MOST
HVMBLE SERVAVNT
EDMVND SPENSER
DOTH IN ALL HV-
MILITIE DEDI-
CATE, PRE-
SENT
AND CONSECRATE THESE
HIS LABOVRS TO LIVE
VVITH THE ETERNI-
TIE OF HER
FAME.

Faerie Queene Fig 2

Faerie Queene Fig 2: Dedication of the 1596 edition (Courtesy of T. Hoffman and Scolar Press)

***Faerie Queene*, children's versions, Fig 1**

***Faerie Queene*, children's versions, Fig 2**

***Faerie Queene*, children's versions, Fig 3**

***Faerie Queene*, children's versions, Fig 1:** *In the Cave of Despair* by H.J. Ford, in Andrew Lang 1905 *The Red Romance Book* (London) p 121 (Figs 1–3 courtesy of the Osborne Collection of Early Children's Books, Toronto Public Library)

***Faerie Queene*, children's versions, Fig 2:** *Arthur Fights the Seven-Headed Serpent* by H.J. Ford, in Lang 1905:113

***Faerie Queene*, children's versions, Fig 3:** *Una and the Lion* by H.J. Ford, in Lang 1905:113

gardens Fig 1

gardens Fig 1: Jan Soens *Rinaldo and Armida in the Enchanted Garden* (Courtesy of the Walters Art Gallery, Baltimore)

George, St, Fig 1

Grill Fig 1

giants Fig 1

Isis Church Fig 1

George, St, Fig 1: *St George and the Dragon* in Spenser ed 1596, 1:184 (Courtesy of T. Hoffman and Scolar Press)
giants Fig 1: *Typhon* in Cartari ed 1580:440 (Fisher)
Grill Fig 1: *Grillus* in Costalius 1560:224 (Fisher)
Isis Church Fig 1: *Isis* in Cartari ed 1580:120 (Fisher)

handwriting Fig 1

handwriting Fig 2

handwriting Fig 3

handwriting Fig 1: Conclusion of letter from Thomas Meagh, 17 May 1582 (*A7, B40*), in Spenser's *secretary* hand with his *italic* signature of attestation (Figs 1–3 courtesy of the Public Record Office, London)

handwriting Fig 2: Opening of Spenser's answer to Articles, May 1589 (*A9, B55*), in his *secretary* hand with *italic* signature

handwriting Fig 3: Marginalia from John Nugent's confession, 5 February 1582 (*B22*), in Spenser's *mixed italic* hand

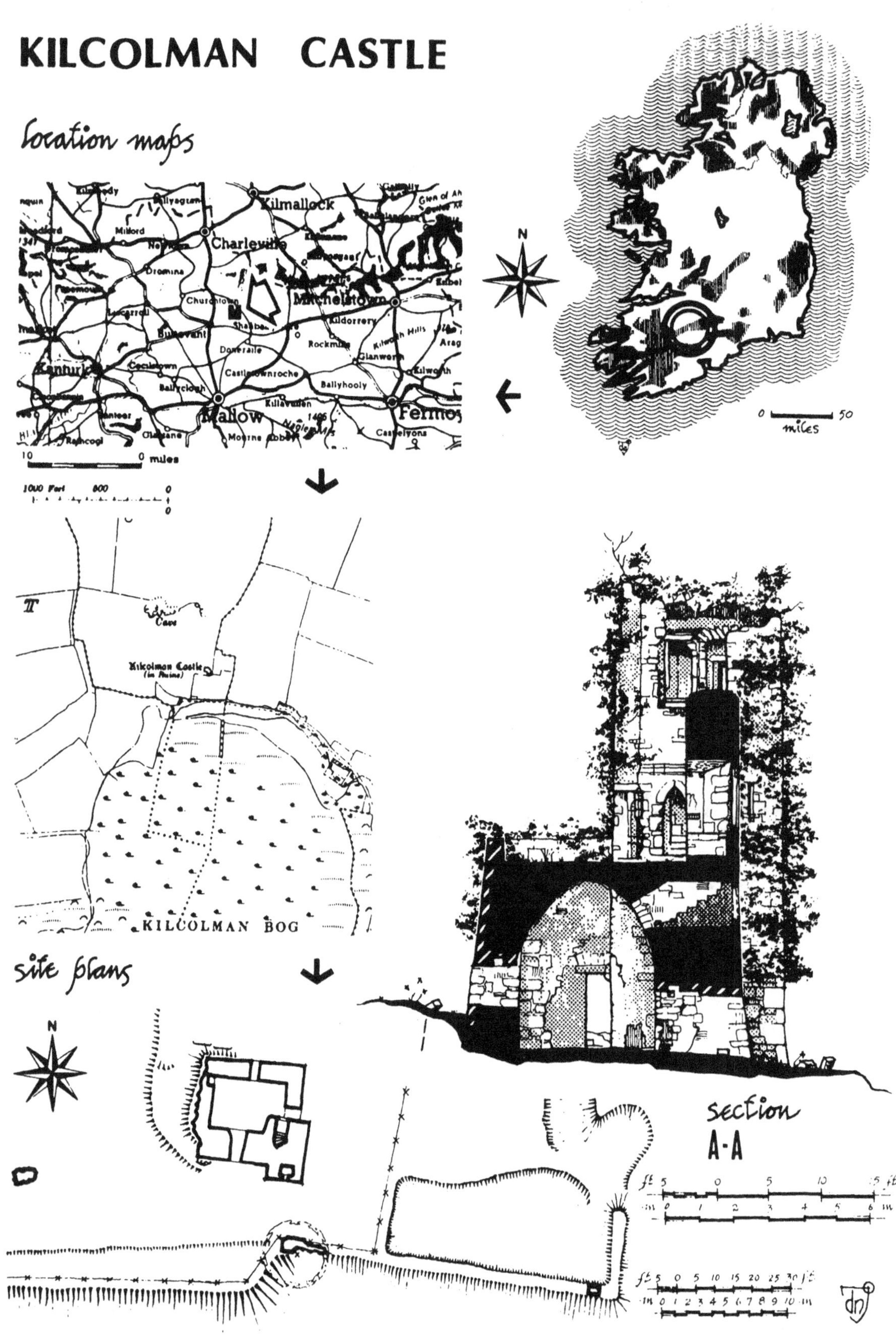

Kilcolman Castle Fig 1

Kilcolman Castle Fig 1: Location maps 1985. Site plans and cross-section through the castle measured and drawn by the author. Based on the 1937 1:10,000 Ordnance Survey (By permission of the Government of Ireland, Permit No 4906)

KILCOLMAN CASTLE

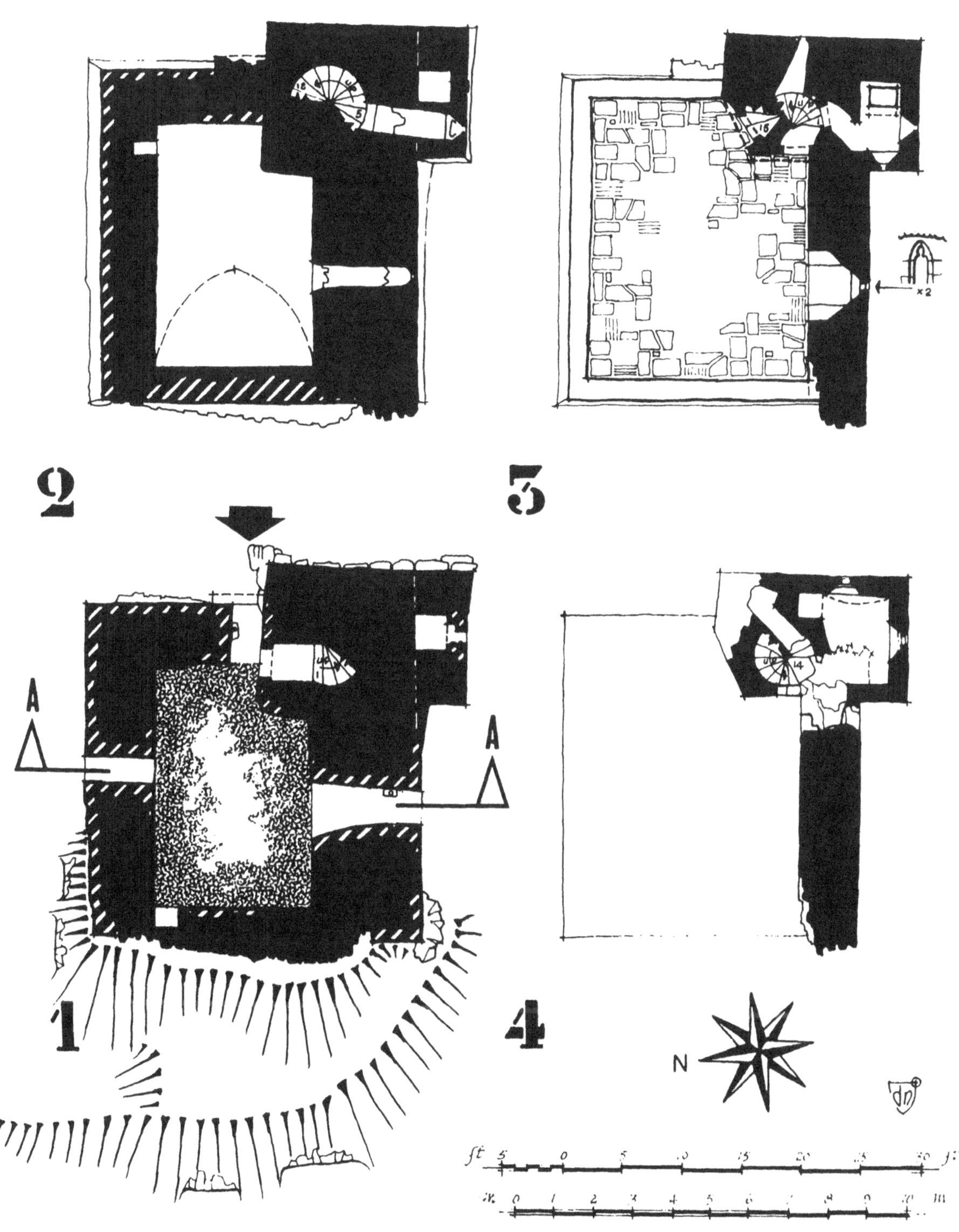

Kilcolman Castle Fig 2

Kilcolman Castle Fig 2: Floor plans 1985. Measured and drawn by the author

Kilcolman Castle Fig 3

Kilcolman Castle Fig 4

Kilcolman Castle Fig 3: William Sadler c 1820, oil painting (Private collection; courtesy of Damian McGarry, 196 Rathfarnham Road, Dublin 14)

Kilcolman Castle Fig 4: Engraving after T. Crofton Croker in Mr and Mrs S.C. Hall 1841–3 *Ireland: Its Scenery, Characters, etc* 3 vols (London) 1:93

Kilcolman Castle Fig 5

Kilcolman Castle Fig 6

Kilcolman Castle Fig 7

Kilcolman Castle Fig 5: Engraving after W.H. Bartlett, in W.H. Bartlett 1842 *The Scenery and Antiquities of Ireland* 2 vols (London) opposite p 80

Kilcolman Castle Fig 6: John Windele 1850, ink sketch in Royal Irish Academy Mss No 12 I 10: p 181 (By permission of the Royal Irish Academy)

Kilcolman Castle Fig 7: Richard Lovett 1888 *Irish Pictures Drawn with Pen and Pencil* (London) p 99

Kilcolman Castle Fig 8

Kilcolman Castle Fig 9

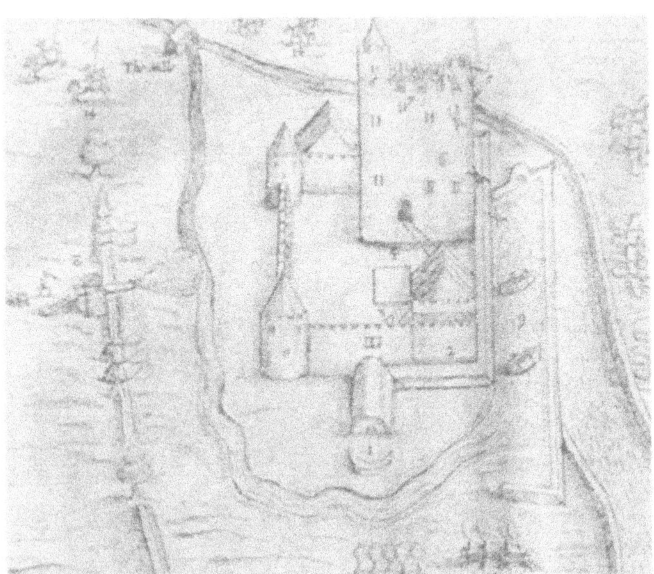

Kilcolman Castle Fig 10

Kilcolman Castle Fig 8: Kilcolman Castle from the north 1985. Photograph by the author

Kilcolman Castle Fig 9: South wall 1985, cusped lancet window of early 15th-century type with window seats. Photograph by the author

Kilcolman Castle Fig 10: *The Castle of the Glin, in County Limerick* in Thomas Stafford 1633 *Pacata Hibernia, Ireland Appeased and Reduced* (London) map 5, between pp 62–3 (Courtesy of Special Collections, Cleveland Public Library)

Kilcolman Castle Fig 11: Simplified section through Blarney Castle, County Cork, by the author, after H.G. Leask 1941 *Irish Castles and Castellated Houses* (Dundalk) Figs 78, 115, with corrections

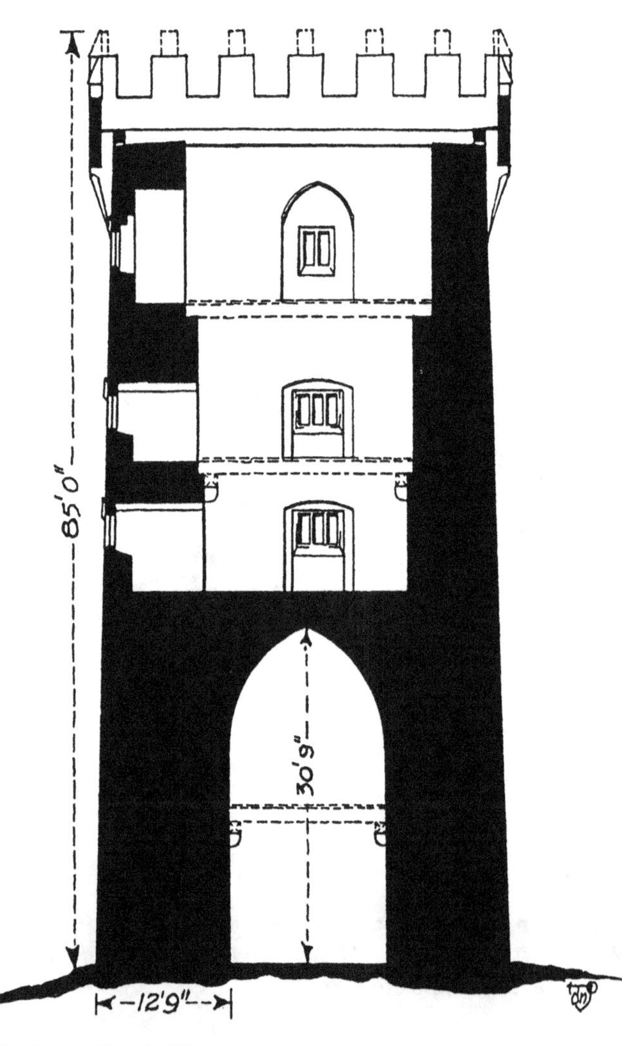

Kilcolman Castle Fig 11

In Thesaurum Thomæ Cooperi Magdalenensis, hexastichon Richardi Stephani.

Vilescat rutila dives Pactôlus arena,
Hermus, & auriferi nobilis unda Tagi.
Vilescant Crœsi gemmæ, Midæq; talenta:
Maior apud Britones eruta gaza patet.
Hoc Wainfletæ suo gens Anglica debet alumno,
Qui vigili nobis tanta labore dedit.

Impressum Londini.
1578.

Leicester, Robert, Fig 1

London Fig 1

London Fig 2

Leicester, Robert, Fig 1: Leicester's device from title page of Thomas Cooper 1578 *Thesaurus linguae romanae et britannicae* (London) (Fisher)
London Fig 1: *Augusta Londinum* in William Camden 1610 *Britannia* tr P. Holland (London) pp 418–19 (Figs 1–3 Courtesy of The Beinecke Rare Book and Manuscript Library, Yale Univ)
London Fig 2: *Westminster* and *London* in Michael Drayton 1613 *Poly-Olbion* (London) between pp 256–7

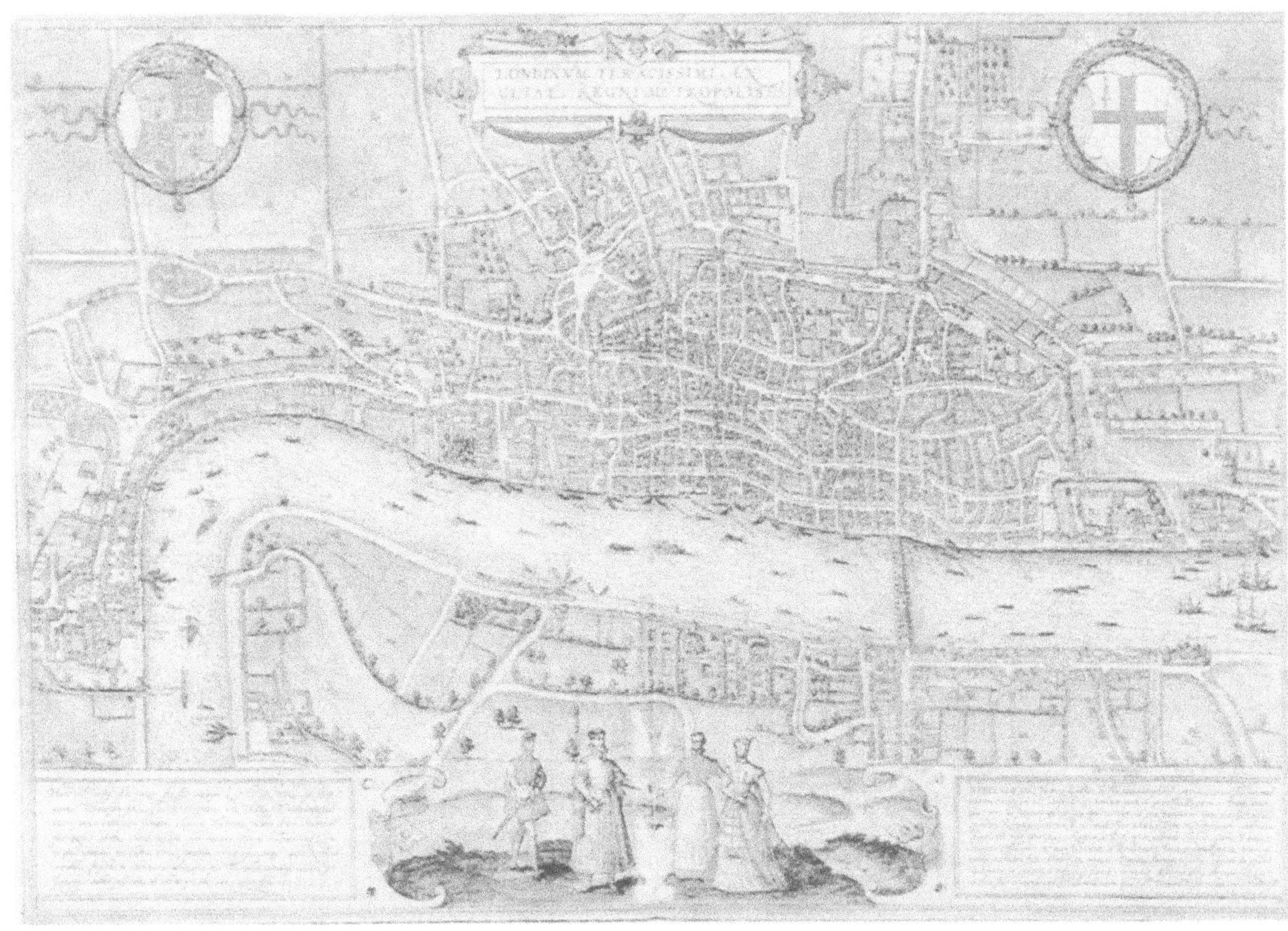

London Fig 3

London Fig 3: Georg Braun 1572 *Londinum feracissimi angliae regni metropolis* in *Civitates orbis terrarum* (London) fols Av–A2

magic, amatory, Fig 1

magic, amatory, Fig 2

Malengin Fig 1:

magic, amatory, Fig 1: *Hyena odorata* in Petrus Castellus 1638 *Hyaena Odorifera* (Messina) p 20 (Figs 1–2 Courtesy of the British Library: BL 975.d.25)

magic, amatory, Fig 2: *Hyaena odorifera* in Castellus 1638:13. A: genitale, B: vas zibethi, C: testes, D: anus

Malengin Fig 1: *Inganno* in Cesare Ripa 1613 *Iconologia* (Siena) p 372 (Fisher)

Mercury Fig 1

Mercury Fig 2

Mercury Fig 3

Mercury Fig 4

Mercury Fig 1: *Hermes Psychopompos raising a soul from the shades by the virtue of his wand* in C[harles] W[illiam] King 1872 *Antique Gems and Rings* 2 vols (London) 2: pl xxi, no 5
Mercury Fig 2: *Alchemical Mercury* in Basilius Valentinus 1656 *Twelve Keys,* in *Musaeum hermeticum* 1678 (Frankfurt). Reproduced from *The Hermetic Museum* 1893 (London) 1:327 (Courtesy of The John Rylands Univ Library, Manchester)

Mercury Fig 3: *Silentio deum cole* in Achille Bocchi 1574 *Symbolicae quaestiones* (Bologna) p 138 (Fisher)
Mercury Fig 4: *Mercury and Ceres* in Cartari 1580:311 (Fisher)

miniatures Fig 1

miniatures Fig 2

miniatures Fig 3

miniatures Fig 1: Nicholas Hilliard *Unknown Lady* c 1585–90 (1¾ × 1½ inches) (Figs 1–3 Courtesy of the Victoria and Albert Museum, London)
miniatures Fig 2: Nicholas Hilliard *Young Man among Roses* c 1587–8 (5⅜ × 2¾ inches)
miniatures Fig 3: Nicholas Hilliard *Man against a Background of Flames* c 1595 (2⅝ × 2⅛ inches)

natural history Fig 1

natural history Fig 1: *Zifius* and *Rosmarus* in Conrad Gesner 1604 *Historiae animalium* (Frankfurt) 4:210 (Fisher)

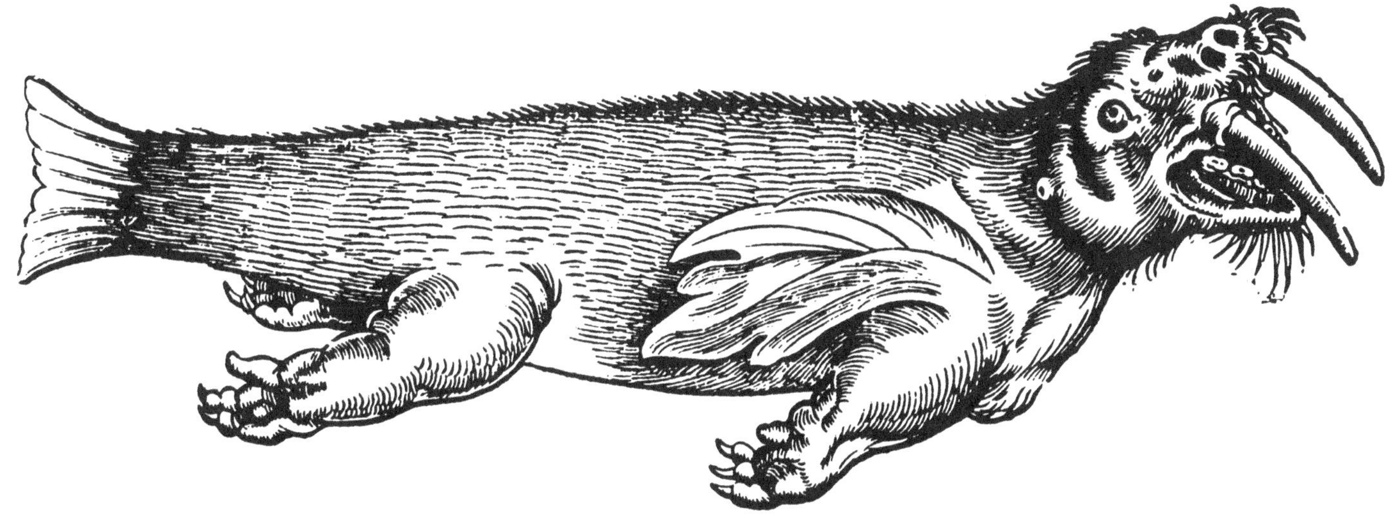

natural history Fig 2

natural history Fig 3

natural history Fig 2: *Morsz* in Gesner ed 1604, 4:211 (Fisher)

natural history Fig 3: *Moneceros* in Gesner ed 1604, 4:208 (Fisher)

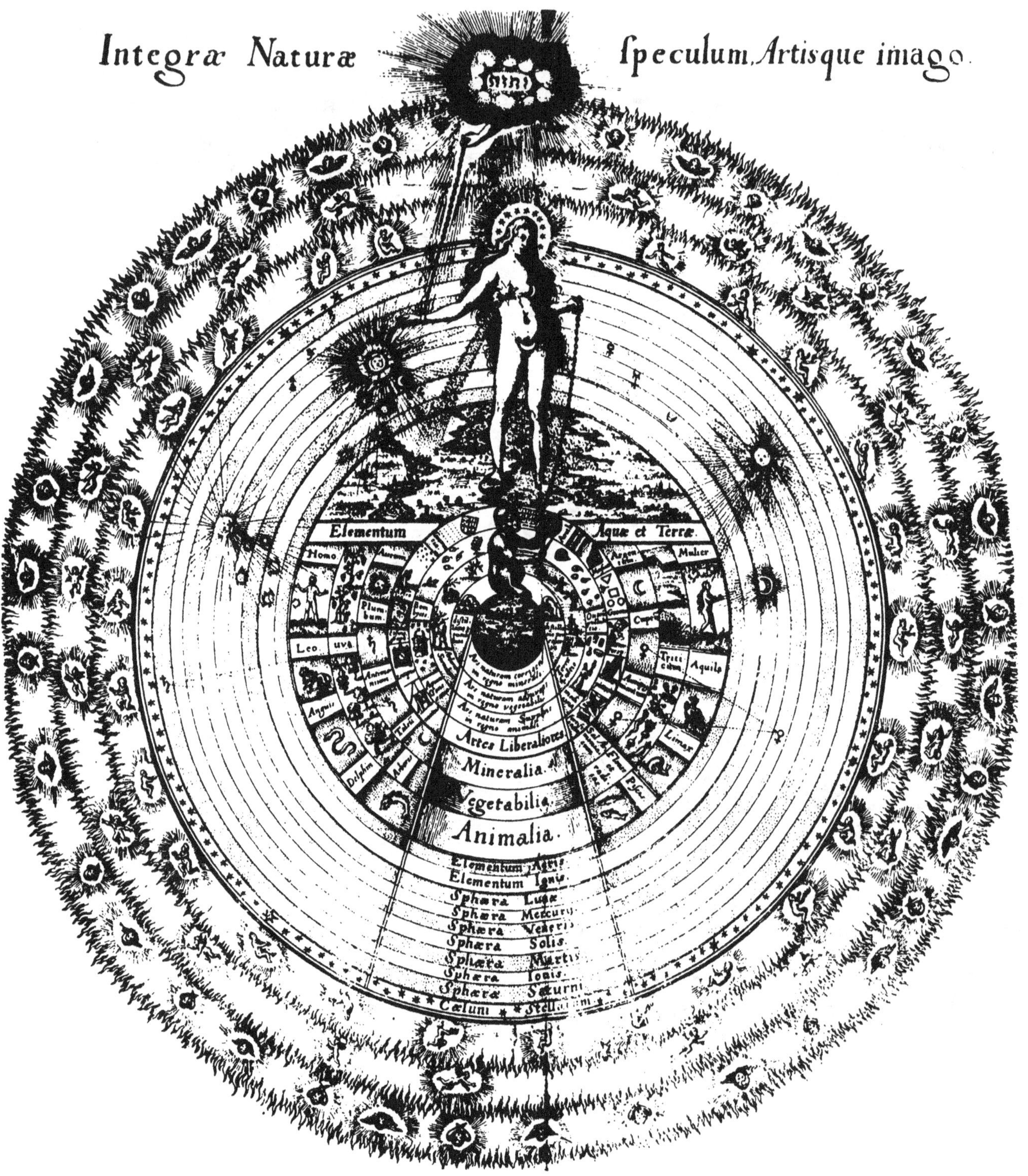

nature and art Fig 1

nature and art Fig 1: *Integrae Naturae speculum Artisque imago (The mirror of prime Nature and the image of Art)* in Robert Fludd 1617–21 *Utriusque cosmi maioris scilicet et minoris metaphysica, physica atque technica historia* (Oppenheim) pp 4–5 (Fisher)

Occasion Fig 1: *In occasionem* in Whitney 1586:181 (Courtesy of the Stirling Maxwell Collection, Glasgow Univ Library)

Peacham Fig 1: *Nulla penetrabilis* from Peacham 1612:182. Line 7 is taken from *FQ* I i 7: 'Not perceable with power of any starre' (Courtesy of the Stirling Maxwell Collection, Glasgow Univ Library)

Phaethon Fig 1: *In temerarios* in Alciati ed 1621: no 56 (Fisher)

Sclaunder Fig 1: *Veritas temporis filia* in Whitney 1586:4 (By permission of the Houghton Library, Harvard Univ)

To my Kinsman M. GEFFREY WHITNEY.

WHAT creature thou? *Occasion I doe showe.*
On whirling wheele declare why doste thou stande?
Bicause, I still am tossed too, and froe.
Why doest thou houlde a rasor in thy hande?
That men maie knowe I cut on euerie side,
And when I come, I armies can deuide.

Horat. lib. 1 Ep. 11. ad Bullatium. *Tu quamcumque Deus tibi fortunauerit horā, Grata sume manu: nec dulcia differ in annum.*

But wherefore hast thou winges vppon thy feete?
To showe, how lighte I flie with little winde.
What meanes longe lockes before? *that suche as meete,*
Maye houlde at firste, when they occasion finde.
Thy head behinde all balde, what telles it more?
That none shoulde houlde, that let me slippe before.

Why doest thou stande within an open place?
That I maye warne all people not to staye,
But at the firste, occasion to imbrace,
And when shee comes, to meete her by the waye.
Lysippus so did thinke it best to bee,
Who did deuise mine image, as you see.

Occasion Fig 1

A SHADIE Wood, pourtraicted to the sight,
With vncouth pathes, and hidden waies vnknowne:
Resembling *CHAOS*, or the hideous night,
Or those sad Groues, by banke of *ACHERON*
With banefull *Ewe*, and *Ebon* overgrowne:
Whose thickest boughes, and inmost entries are
Not peirceable, to power of any starre.

Thy Imprese *SILVIVS*, late I did devise,
To warne the what (if not) thou oughtst to be,
Thus inward close, vnsearch'd with outward eies,
With thousand angles, light should never see:
For fooles that most are open-hearted free,
Vnto the world, their weakenes doe bewray,
And to the net, the first themselues betray.

Peacham Fig 1

In temerarios.

EMBLEMA LVI.

ASPICIS aurigam currus Phaethonta paterni,
Ignivomos ausum flectere Solis equos:
Maxima qui postquàm terris incendia sparsit,
Est temerè insesso lapsus ab axe miser.
Sic plerique rotis fortuna ad sidera Reges
Evecti, ambitio quos iuuenilis agit;
Post magnam humani generis clademq; suamq;,
Cunctorum pœnas denique dant scelerum.

Phaethon Fig 1

Veritas temporis filia.

THREE furies fell, which turne the worlde to ruthe,
Both Enuie, Strife, and Slaunder, heare appeare,
In dungeon darke they longe inclosed truthe,
But Time at lengthe, did loose his daughter deare,
And setts alofte, that sacred ladie brighte,
Whoe things longe hidd, reueales, and bringes to lighte.

Thoughe strife make fier, thoughe Enuie eate hir harte,
The innocent though Slaunder rente, and spoile:
Yet Time will comme, and take this ladies parte,
And breake her bandes, and bring her foes to foile.
Dispaire not then, thoughe truthe be hidden ofte,
Bycause at lengthe, shee shall bee sett alofte.

Sclaunder Fig 1

The Sheepheardes Kalender.

Shepheardes Calender **Fig 1**

THE
Shepheardes Calender
Conteyning twelue Æglogues proportionable
to the twelue monethes.

Entitled
TO THE NOBLE AND VERTV-
ous Gentleman most worthy of all titles
both of learning and cheualrie M.
Philip Sidney.

AT LONDON.
Printed by Hugh Singleton, dwelling in
Creede Lane neere vnto Ludgate at the
signe of the gylden Tunne, and
are there to be solde.
1579.

Shepheardes Calender **Fig 2**

***Shepheardes Calender* Fig 1:** *The Kalender of Sheepehards (c. 1585)* ed S.K. Heninger, Jr (Delmar, NY 1979) p 141 (Courtesy of the Bodleian Library, Oxford)

***Shepheardes Calender* Fig 2:** Title and twelve woodcuts (continued on following page) from *The Shepheardes Calender* 1579 (Courtesy of the Harry Ranson Humanities Research Center, Univ of Texas at Austin)

Januarye.

Ægloga prima.

Februarie.

Ægloga Secunda.

March.

Ægloga Tertia.

Aprill.

Ægloga Quarta.

Maye.

Ægloga Quinta

June.

Ægloga ſexta.

Iulye. *fol.26*

Ægloga ſeptima.

Auguſt. *fol.31*

Ægloga octaua.

September. *fol.[illegible]*

Ægloga Nona.

October.

Ægloga decima.

Nouember.

Ægloga vndecima.

December.

Ægloga Duodecima.

Shepheardes Calender **Fig 2**

¶Of Iuly.

Shepheardes Calender, printing and illustration, Fig 1

Shepheardes Calender, printing and illustration, Fig 2

***Shepheardes Calender*, printing and illustration, Fig 1:** 'Of July' in Joachim Hubrigh 1569 *An Almanack and Prognostication for 1569* (London) (Courtesy of the British Library)

***Shepheardes Calender*, printing and illustration, Fig 2:** 'Février' in *Les très riches heures du Duc de Berry* p 3 (Musée Condé, Chantilly; courtesy of Giraudon/Art Resource, New York)

¶Thus endeth the fyrst Egloge of the myseryes of the Courters compyled and drawen by Alexander Barclay.

Shepheardes Calender, **printing and illustration, Fig 3**

Prudentes.

PROBLEMA.

XVIII.

IANE *bifrons, qui iam transacta futuraq; calles,*
Quiq; retro sannas, sicut & antè, vides:
Te tot cur oculis, cur fingunt vultibus? an quòd
Circumspectum hominem forma fuisse docet?

Shepheardes Calender, **printing and illustration, Fig 4**

***Shepheardes Calender*, printing and illustration, Fig 3:** Alexander Barclay c 1530 *Egloges* (Southwark, printed by P. Treveris; *STC* 1384) (Courtesy of The Huntington Library, San Marino, Calif)

***Shepheardes Calender*, printing and illustration, Fig 4:** *Prudentes* in Alciati 1577 *Emblemata* (Antwerp) no 18 (Fisher)

sins, seven deadly, Fig 1

sins, seven deadly, Fig 2

sins, seven deadly, Fig 3

sins, seven deadly, Fig 4

sins, seven deadly, Fig 1: *Covetousnes* in Stephen Bateman 1569 *A Cristall Glasse of Christian Reformation* (London; *STC* 1581) sig Biiii (Figs 1–7 Courtesy of the Beinecke Rare Book and Manuscript Library, Yale Univ)

sins, seven deadly, Fig 2: *Wrath* in Bateman 1569: sig Ciiv

sins, seven deadly, Fig 3: *Lechery* in Bateman 1569: sig Diiv

sins, seven deadly, Fig 4: *Gluttony* in Bateman 1569: sig Fii

sins, seven deadly, Fig 5

sins, seven deadly, Fig 6

sins, seven deadly, Fig 7

74 *Auaritia.*

Ouid. Metam. lib. 4.

HEARE TANTALVS, as Poëttes doe deuine,
This guerdon hathe, for his offence in hell:
The pleaſante fruite, dothe to his lippe decline,
A riuer faire vnto his chinne doth ſwell:
Yet, twixt theſe two, for foode the wretche dothe ſterue,
For bothe doe flee, when they his neede ſhoulde ſerue.

The couetons man, this fable reprehendes,
For chaunge his name, and TANTALVS hee is,
Hee dothe abounde, yet ſterues and nothing ſpendes,
But keepes his goulde, as if it weare not his:
With ſlender fare, he doth his hunger feede,
And dare not touche his ſtore, when hee doth neede.

Horat. ſerm. 1. Sat. 1.

Tantalus à labris ſitiens fugientia captat
Flumina, quid rides? mutato nomine de te
Fabula narratur, congeſtis vndique ſaccis
Indormis inhians: & tanquam parcere ſacris
Congeris &c. —— ——

O vita,

Tantalus Fig 1

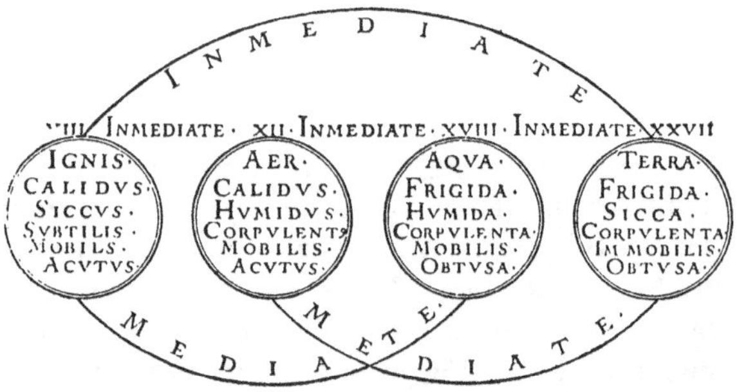

tetrads Fig 1

sins, seven deadly, Fig 5: *Sloth* in Bateman 1569: sig Gii

sins, seven deadly, Fig 6: *Envie* in Bateman 1569: sig Hii

sins, seven deadly, Fig 7: *Pride* in Bateman 1569: sig Iii

Tantalus Fig 1: *Avaritia* in Whitney ed 1586:74 (By permission of the Houghton Library, Harvard Univ)

tetrads Fig 1: *De natura rerum* in Bede 1563 *Opera* (Basel) 2:5 (Courtesy of the Van Pelt Library, Univ of Pennsylvania)

Theseus Fig 1

Theseus Fig 2

Theseus Fig 1: *Theseus before the Labyrinth* in Maso Finiguerra 1898 *A Florentine Picture-Chronicle* ed Sidney Colvin 1970 (London) pls xlvi–vii (Figs 1–2 by permission of the British Library)

Theseus Fig 2: *Theseus and Ariadne* attributed to Baccio Baldini c 1460–70, engraving British Museum A II 10; see Arthur M. Hind 1938 *Early Italian Engraving* (London) 1:69 no 16, 2: pl 101

Una Fig 1

Una Fig 2

Una's Lamb Fig 1

visual arts Fig 1

Una Fig 1: Paolo Ucello *Saint George and the Dragon* (Musée Jacquemart-André, Paris; courtesy of Giraudon/Art Resource, New York)
Una Fig 2: Title page of the Bishops' Bible 1568 (London) (Fisher)
Una's lamb Fig 1: *The Princess and Her Lamb* title page of Sarum Missal c 1500 (*STC* 16170) (By permission of the Houghton Library, Harvard Univ)

visual arts Fig 1: *Indian with Body Paint* from *The Drawings of John White, 1577–1590* ed Paul Hulton and David Beers Quinn (Chapel Hill 1964) 1: no 52, pl 47. Published by the University of North Carolina Press 1964. © 1964 British Library (Used with permission of the publisher and the British Library)

witches Fig 1

witches Fig 2

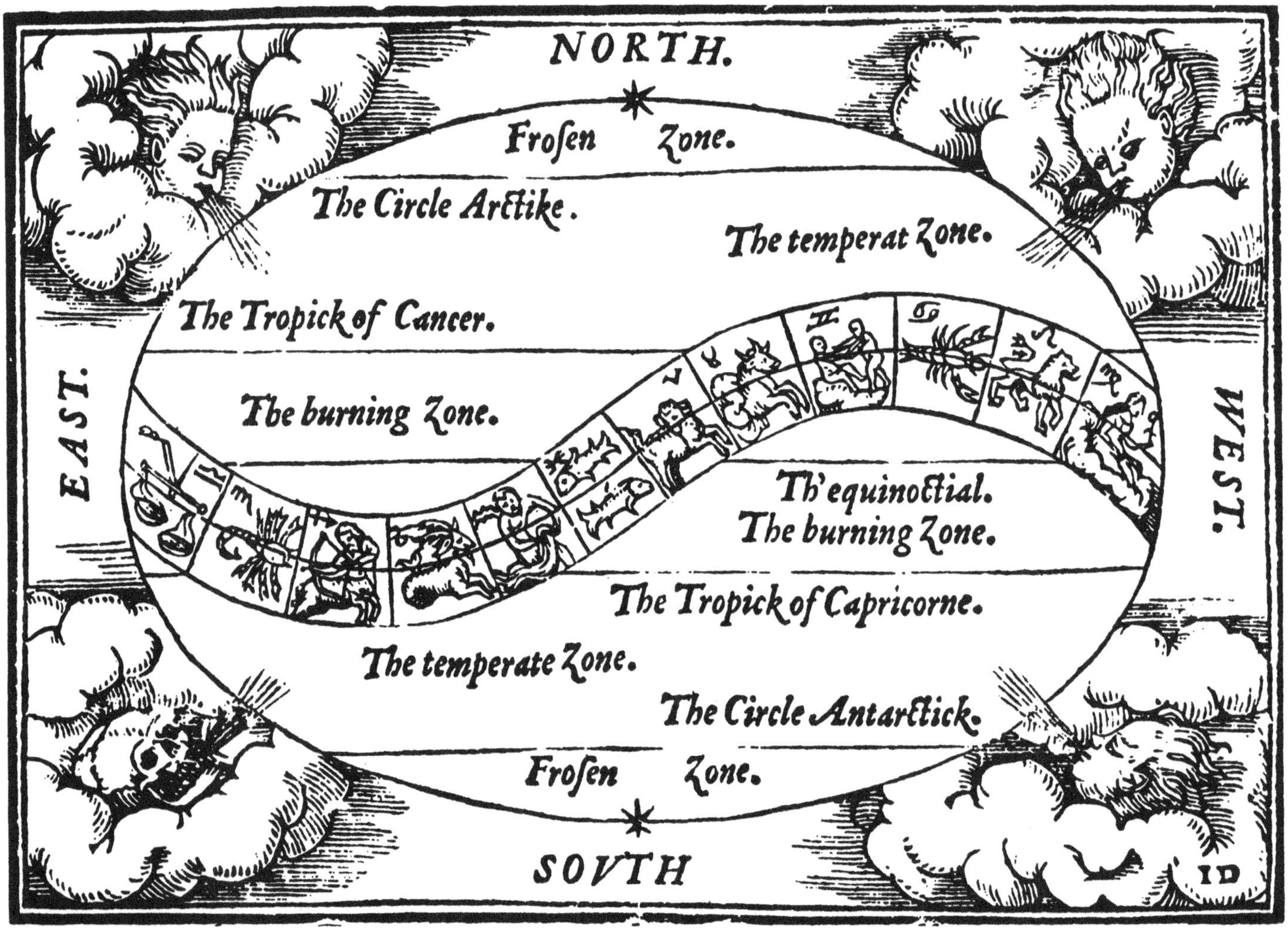

zodiac Fig 1

witches Fig 1: *Baptizing a Witch* in Francesco-Maria Guazzo 1610 *Compendium maleficarum* (Milan) p 14
witches Fig 2: *The infamous kiss* in Guazzo 1610:40

zodiac Fig 1: The climatic zones plus the zodiac according to William Cuningham 1559 *The Cosmographical Glasse* (London) p 64 (Courtesy of The Huntington Library, San Marino, Calif)

General Bibliography

Works cited more than once in *The Spenser Encyclopedia* are listed below. Works cited only once are given full bibliographical listings in the reading list at the end of the article in which they appear. Unless otherwise indicated, texts and translations of classical writers are taken from the Loeb Classical Library. Spenser's poetry is cited from *Poetical Works* ed 1912, his prose from the *Variorum Prose* volume (i/j and u/v normalized).

Abbreviations

Am America, -n
Assoc Association
Bib Bibliography, -ical
Brit British
Bul Bulletin
Can Canada, -ian
Chron Chronicle
Class Classics, -ical
Coll College
Comp Comparative
Diss Dissertation
Eng English
Hist History Histoire
Inst Institute(s)
J Journal
Lang Language(s)
Lib Library, -ies
Lit Literature(s)
Mag Magazine
Mod Modern /-es
Phil Philology, -ical /-ie /-us, -ische/-ica
Proc Proceedings
Psych Psychology, -ical
Pub Publication(s)
Q Quarterly
Ren Renaissance
Rev Review Revue
Soc Society
Trans Transactions
Univ University, -ies

Citations of periodicals and series use the following short titles or acronymns:

ABR *Am Benedictine Rev*
AEB *Analytical and Enumerative Bib*
AJPh *Am J of Phil*
AL *Am Lit*
AN&Q *Am Notes and Queries*
AnM *Annuale mediaevale*
AnnSci *Annals of Science* (London)
AR *Architectural Rev*
ArchitHist *Architectural Hist*
Archiv *Archiv für das Studium der neueren Sprachen und Literaturen*
ARG *Archiv für Reformationsgeschichte*
ArtB *Art Bul*
ATQ *Am Transcendental Q*
ATR *Anglican Theological Rev*
AUMLA *J of the Australasian Univ Lang and Lit Assoc*

Botany See *GC* (*Gardeners' Chron*)
BB *Bul of Bib*
BHR *Bibliothèque d'humanisme et ren*
BIS *Browning Inst Studies*
BJRL *Bul of the John Rylands Lib*
BL *Brit Lib*
Blackwood's *Blackwood's Mag*
BNYPL *Bul of the NY Public Lib*
BQR *Brit Q Rev*
BSRS *Bul of the Soc for Ren Studies*
BuR *Bucknell Rev*

C&L *Christianity and Lit*
CahiersE *Cahiers elisabéthains*
CamJ *Cambridge J*
CCR *Claflin Coll Rev*
CE *Coll Eng*
CFMA *Classiques Français du Moyen Age*
CL *Comp Lit*
CLAJ *Coll Lang Assoc J*
ClassP *Class Phil*
CLS *Comp Lit Studies*
CM *Classica et mediaevalia*
CML *Class and Mod Lit*
CRCL *Can Rev of Comp Lit*
CritI *Critical Inquiry*
CritQ *Critical Q*
CS *Cahiers du sud*
CW *Class World*

DA *Diss Abstracts*
DAI *Diss Abstracts International*
DR *Dalhousie Rev*
DUJ *Durham Univ J*
DUM *Dublin Univ Mag*
DVLG *Deutsche Vierteljahrsschrift für Literaturwissenschaft und Geistesgeschichte*

E&S *Essays and Studies*
ECent *The Eighteenth Century* (formerly *Studies in Burke and His Time*)
ECS *Eighteenth-Century Studies*
ECW *Essays on Can Writing*
EDAM *EDAM Newsletter*
EETS Early Eng Text Soc
EHR *Eng Historical Rev*
EIC *Essays in Criticism*
EIE *Eng Inst Essays*
Eigse *Eigse: A J of Irish Studies*
Eire *Eire-Ireland: A Journal of Irish Studies*
ELH formerly ELH: *J of Eng Literary Hist*
ELN *Eng Lang Notes*
ELR *Eng Literary Ren*
ELWIU *Essays in Lit* (Macomb, Ill)
EM *Eng Miscellany*
ErasmusR *Erasmus Rev*
ES *Eng Studies*
ESC *Eng Studies in Can*
ESQ *ESQ: J of the Am Ren* (formerly *Emerson Soc Q*)
Expl *Explicator*

FCEMN *Fourteenth Century Eng Mystics Newsletter*
Fraser's *Fraser's Mag*
FS *French Studies*

GC *Gardeners' Chron*
GentM *Gentleman's Mag*

HAR *Humanities Assoc Rev* (formerly HAB: *Humanities Assoc Bul*)
HES *Harvard Eng Studies*
HistRel *Hist of Religions*
HLB *Harvard Lib Bul*
HLF *Hist Littéraire de la France*
HLQ *Huntington Lib Q*
HR *Hudson Rev*
HRB *Hopkins Research Bul*
HSE *Hungarian Studies in Eng*
HSL *Univ of Hartford Studies in Lit*
HSNPL *Harvard Studies and Notes in Phil and Lit*
HTR *Harvard Theological Rev*
HumLov *Humanistica Lovaniensia*

IHS *Irish Historical Studies*
IllQuart *Illinois Q*
IrishS *Irish Sword: The J of the Military Hist Soc of Ireland*
ISLL *Illinois Studies in Lang and Lit*

JAAC *J of Aesthetics and Art Criticism*
JAE *J of Aesthetic Education*
JAF *J of Am Folklore*
JAS *J of Am Studies*
JCHAS *J of the Cork Historical and Archaeological Soc*
JDJ *John Donne J*
JEGP *J of Eng and Germanic Phil*
JGP *J of Germanic Phil*
JHI *J of the Hist of Ideas*
JJQ *James Joyce Q*
JMRS *J of Medieval and Ren Studies*
JNT *J of Narrative Technique*
JRSAI *J of the Royal Soc of Antiquaries of Ireland*
JWCI *J of the Warburg and Courtauld Inst*

KR *Kenyon Rev*
KRQ *Kentucky Romance Q* (now *Romance Q*)
KSJ *Keats-Shelley J*

L&H *Lit and Hist*
L&P *Lit and Psych*
LJHum *Lamar J of the Humanities*
LRB *London Rev of Books*

M&H *Medievalia et humanistica*
MedRen *Mediaeval and Ren Studies*
MethQR *Methodist Q Rev*
MiltonS *Milton Studies*
MLN (formerly) *Mod Lang Notes*
MLQ *Mod Lang Q*
MLQ (London) *Mod Lang Q* (London)
MLR *Mod Lang Rev*
MLS *Mod Lang Studies*
MP *Mod Phil*
MQ *Milton Q*
MS *Mediaeval Studies*
MSE *Massachusetts Studies in Eng*
MSEx *Melville Soc Extracts*

NA *Nuova Antologia*
N&Q *Notes and Queries*
NAR *North Am Rev*
NCF *Nineteenth-Century Fiction* (now *Nineteenth-Century Literature*)
Neophil *Neophil* (Groningen)
NEQ *New England Q*
NLH *New Literary Hist*

NM *Neuphil Mitteilungen*
NS *Die Neueren Sprachen*
NUSH *Northwestern Univ Studies in the Humanities*

PBA *Proc of the Brit Academy*
PBSA *Papers of the Bib Soc of Am*
PLL *Papers on Lang and Lit*
PMLA *Pub of the Mod Lang Assoc of Am*
PNR *PN Rev*
P&P *Past and Present*
PQ *Phil Q*
PRIA *Proc of the Royal Irish Academy*
PULC *Princeton Univ Lib Chron*

QQ *Queen's Q*
QR *Q Rev*

RBPH *Rev belge de phil et d'hist*
REAL *Yearbook of Research in Eng and Am Lit*
REL *A Rev of Eng Lit*
RELV *Rev de l'enseignement des langues vivantes*
Ren&R *Ren and Reformation/Ren et Réforme*
RenD *Ren Drama*
RenP *Ren Papers*
RenQ *Ren Q* (formerly *Ren News*)
RES *Rev of Eng Studies*
RIPh *Rev internationale de philosophie*
RLC *Rev de littérature comparée*
RLM *Rev des lettres mod*
RLMC *Rivista di letterature mod e comparate*
RMS *Ren and Mod Studies*
RMSt *Reading Medieval Studies*
RN *Ren News* (now *Ren Q*)
Ro *Romania*
RomN *Romance Notes*
RORD *Research Opportunities in Ren Drama*
RPh *Romance Phil*
RPLit *Res publica litterarum*
RQ *Riverside Q*
RS *Research Studies*
RSL *Royal Soc of Lit*
RTP *Rev de théologie et de philosophie*
RUS *Rice Univ Studies*

SAB *South Atlantic Bul* (now *South Atlantic Rev*)
SAC *Studies in the Age of Chaucer*
SAQ *South Atlantic Q*
SAR *Studies in the Am Ren*
SB *Studies in Bib*
SCB *South Central Bul*
SCJ *Sixteenth Century J*
SCSML *Smith Coll Studies in Mod Lang*
SEL *SEL: Studies in Eng Lit, 1500–1900*
SFQ *Southern Folklore Q*
ShAB *Shakespeare Assoc Bul*
SHR *Southern Humanities Rev*
ShS *Shakespeare Survey*
ShakS *Shakespeare Studies*
SIcon *Studies in Iconography*
SJ *Silliman J*
SLitI *Studies in the Literary Imagination*
SMed *Studi medievali*
SN *Studia neophil*
SNovel *Studies in the Novel*
SoQ *Southern Q*
SORA *Southern Rev* (Australia)
SP *Studies in Phil*
Spec *Speculum*
SpKal *Spenser at Kalamazoo* (proc)
SpMon *Speech Monographs*
SpN *Spenser Newsletter*
Spring *Spring: An Annual of Archetypal Psych and Jungian Thought*
SQ *Shakespeare Q*
SR *Sewanee Rev*
SRen *Studies in the Ren*
SSL *Studies in Scottish Lit*
SSt *Spenser Studies*
STS Scottish Text Soc
SzEP *Studien zur englischen Phil*

TAPA *Trans of the Am Phil Assoc*
TCAAS *Trans of the Connecticut Academy of the Arts and Sciences*
TCL *Twentieth Century Lit*
TCLC *Travaux de cercle linguistique de Copenhague*
TexSE *Texas Studies in Eng*
TLS *Times Literary Supplement*
TPS *Trans of the Phil Soc*
TRHS *Trans of the Royal Historical Soc*
TSE *Tulane Studies in Eng*
TSL *Tennessee Studies in Lit*
TSLL *Texas Studies in Lit and Lang*
TWA *Trans of the Wisconsin Academy of Sciences, Arts, and Letters*

UCAT *Univ of Chicago Abstracts of Theses, Humanistic Series*
UCC *Univ of California Chron*
UCPMP *Univ of California Pub in Mod Phil*
UCSCP *Univ of Chicago Studies in Class Phil*
UMoS *Univ of Missouri Studies*
UNCSRLL *Univ of North Carolina Studies in the Romance Lang and Lit*
UNSH *Univ of Nebraska Studies in the Humanities*
UTQ *Univ of Toronto Q*
UVS *Univ of Virginia Studies*
UWSLL *Univ of Wisconsin Studies in Lang and Lit*

VN *Victorian Newsletter*

WC *Wordsworth Circle*
WF *Western Folklore*
WMQ *William and Mary Q*

YCS *Yale Classical Studies*
YES *Yearbook of Eng Studies*
YFS *Yale French Studies*
YIS *Yearbook of Italian Studies*
YR *Yale Rev*
YSE Yale Studies in Eng
YWES *Year's Work in Eng Studies*

Aesop ed 1952 Aesop 1952 *Aesopica* ... vol 1: *Greek and Latin Texts* ed Ben Edwin Perry. Urbana

Agrippa [c 1600] Agrippa, Henry Cornelius [Heinricus Cornelius of Nettesheim] [c 1600] *Opera* 2 vols. Lyons, rpt ed Richard H. Popkin. Hildesheim 1970

Agrippa ed 1651 —— 1651 *Three Books of Occult Philosophy* tr J.F. London

Alanus ed 1980 Alanus de Insulis [Alain de Lille] 1980 *The Plaint of Nature* tr and ed James J. Sheridan. Toronto

Alciati 1531 Alciati, Andrea 1531 *Emblematum liber* Augsburg. Holbein Society, rpt Manchester and London 1870

Alciati ed 1577 —— 1577 *Emblemata* ed Claudius Minos [Claude Mignault]. Antwerp

Alciati ed 1581 —— 1581 *Emblemata* Antwerp

Alciati ed 1621 —— 1621 *Emblemata cum commentariis* Padua, rpt New York and London 1976, rpt in part with translation in Alciati 1985 *Index Emblematicus* ed Peter M. Daly, et al. Toronto

D.C. Allen 1958 Allen, Don Cameron, ed 1958 *Studies in Honor of T.W. Baldwin* Urbana

D.C. Allen 1968 —— 1968 *Image and Meaning: Metaphoric Traditions in Renaissance Poetry* Rev ed. Baltimore

D.C. Allen 1970 —— 1970 *Mysteriously Meant: The Rediscovery of Pagan Symbolism and Allegorical Interpretation in the Renaissance* Baltimore

M.J.B. Allen 1984 Allen, M.J.B. 1984 *The Platonism of Marsilio Ficino: A Study of His 'Phaedrus' Commentary, Its Sources and Genesis* Berkeley and Los Angeles

Alpers 1962 Alpers, Paul J. 1962 'Narrative and Rhetoric in *The Faerie Queene*' *SEL* 2:27–46

Alpers 1967a —— ed 1967a *Elizabethan Poetry: Modern Essays in Criticism* New York

Alpers 1967b —— 1967b *The Poetry of 'The Faerie Queene'* Princeton

Alpers 1968 —— 1968 '[Review Article:] How to Read *The Faerie Queene*' *EIC* 18:429–43

Alpers 1969 —— ed 1969 *Edmund Spenser: A Critical Anthology* Harmondsworth

Alpers 1977 —— 1977 'Narration in *The Faerie Queene*' *ELH* 44:19–39

Alpers 1979 —— 1979 *The Singer of the 'Eclogues': A Study of Virgilian Pastoral* Berkeley and Los Angeles

Anacreontea. See headnote

Anderson 1969 Anderson, Judith H. 1969 'Redcrosse and the Descent into Hell' *ELH* 36:470–92

Anderson 1970a —— 1970a 'The July Eclogue and the House of Holiness: Perspective in Spenser' *SEL* 10:17–32

Anderson 1970b —— 1970b 'The Knight and the Palmer in *The Faerie Queene*, Book II' *MLQ* 31:160–78

Anderson 1970c —— 1970c '"Nor Man It Is": The Knight of Justice in Book V of Spenser's *Faerie Queene*' *PMLA* 85:65–77

Anderson 1971a —— 1971a '"Nat worth a boterflye": *Muiopotmos* and *The Nun's Priest's Tale*' *JMRS* 1:89–106

Anderson 1971b —— 1971b 'Whatever Happened to Amoret?: The Poet's Role in Book IV of "The Faerie Queene"' *Criticism* 13:180–200

Anderson 1972 —— 1972 '"Come, Let's Away to Prison": Fortune and Freedom in *The Faerie Queene*, Book VI' *JNT* 2:133–7

Anderson 1976 —— 1976 *The Growth of a Personal Voice: 'Piers Plowman' and 'The Faerie Queene'* New Haven

Anderson 1982 —— 1982 '"In liuing colours and right hew": The Queen of Spenser's Central Books' In Maynard Mack and George deForest Lord, eds *Poetic Traditions of the English Renaissance* pp 47–66. New Haven

Anderson 1985 —— 1985 '"A Gentle Knight was pricking on the plaine": The Chaucerian Connection' *ELR* 15:166–74

Anglo 1969 Anglo, Sydney 1969 *Spectacle, Pageantry, and Early Tudor Policy* Oxford

Apollonius Rhodius. See headnote

Aptekar 1969 Aptekar, Jane 1969 *Icons of Justice: Iconography and Thematic Imagery in Book V of 'The Faerie Queene'* New York

Apuleius ed 1975 Apuleius 1975 *The Isis-Book (Metamorphoses, Book XI)* tr and ed J. Gwyn Griffiths. Leiden

Apuleius. See also headnote

Aquinas ed 1964–81 Aquinas, St Thomas 1964–81 *Summa theologiae* tr and ed Thomas Gilby, et al. 61 vols. London

A. Arber 1912 Arber, Agnes 1912 *Herbals: Their Origin and Evolution ... 1470–1670* Cambridge. Rev ed 1938

A. Arber 1931 —— 1931 'Edmund Spenser and Lyte's "Nievve Herball"' *N&Q* 160:345–7

E. Arber 1875–94 Arber, Edward, ed 1875–94 *A Transcript of the Registers of the Company of Stationers of London 1554–1640* 5 vols. London

Ariosto ed 1591 Ariosto, Ludovico 1591 *Orlando Furioso in English Heroical Verse* tr John Harington. London, rpt Amsterdam and New York 1970; ed Robert McNulty, Oxford 1972

Ariosto ed 1968 —— 1968 *Orlando Furioso* tr William Stewart Rose, ed Stewart A. Baker and A. Bartlett Giamatti. Indianapolis

Aristotle ed 1984 Aristotle 1984 *Complete Works* ed Jonathan Barnes. 2 vols. Princeton

Arthos 1956 Arthos, John 1956 *On the Poetry of Spenser and the Form of Romances* London

Articles of Religion / Thirty-nine Articles See Hardwick 1876

Ascham ed 1904 Ascham, Roger 1904 *English Works* ed William Aldis Wright. Cambridge

Ashton 1957 Ashton, John W. 1957 'Folklore in the Literature of Elizabethan England' *JAF* 70:10–15, 23–4

Atchity 1973 Atchity, Kenneth John 1973 'Spenser's *Mother Hubberds Tale*: Three Themes of Order' *PQ* 52:161–72

Atkinson 1937 Atkinson, Dorothy F. 1937 *Edmund Spenser: A Bibliographical Supplement* Baltimore

Aubrey ed 1949 Aubrey, John 1949 *Brief Lives* ed Oliver Lawson Dick. London

Auerbach ed 1953 Auerbach, Erich 1953 *Mimesis: The Representation of Reality in Western Literature* tr Willard Trask. Princeton

Auerbach ed 1959 —— 1959 *Scenes from the Drama of European Literature* tr Ralph Manheim and Catherine Garvin. New York

Auerbach ed 1965 —— *1965 Literary Language and Its Public in Late Latin Antiquity and in the Middle Ages* tr Ralph Manheim. Princeton

Augustine ed 1610 Augustine, St 1610 *Of the Citie of God, with the Learned Comments of Jo. Ludovicus Vives* tr J[ohn] H[ealey]. London

Augustine ed 1948 —— 1948 *Basic Writings* ed Whitney J. Oates. 2 vols. New York

Austin 1947 Austin, Warren B. 1947 'Spenser's Sonnet to Harvey' *MLN* 62:20–3

Babb 1951 Babb, Lawrence 1951 *The Elizabethan Malady: A Study of Melancholia in English Literature from 1580 to 1642* East Lansing, Mich

Bacon ed 1857–74 Bacon, Francis 1857–74 *Works* (incl *Life*) ed James Spedding, et al. 14 vols. London

H. Baker 1947 Baker, Herschel 1947 *The Dignity of Man* Cambridge, Mass, rpt New York 1952 as *The Image of Man*

H. Baker 1971 —— ed 1971 *Four Essays on Romance* Cambridge, Mass

J.H. Baker 1971 Baker, J.H. 1971 *An Introduction to English Legal History* London, rev ed 1979

Bald 1970 Bald, R.C. 1970 *John Donne: A Life* Oxford

T.W. Baldwin 1944 Baldwin, T.W. 1944 *William Shakspere's Small Latine and Lesse Greeke* 2 vols. Urbana

W. Baldwin 1547 Baldwin, William 1547 *A Treatise of Morall Phylosophie* London; rev ed 1557

Bamborough 1952 Bamborough, J[ohn] B. 1952 *The Little World of Man* London

Barclay ed 1955 Barclay, Alexander 1955 *The Life of St. George* (c 1515) ed William Nelson. EETS os 230. London

Barkan 1975 Barkan, Leonard 1975 *Nature's Work of Art: The Human Body as Image of the World* New Haven

Barkan 1980 —— 1980 'Diana and Actaeon: The Myth as Synthesis' *ELR* 10:317–59

Barkan 1986 —— 1986 *The Gods Made Flesh: Metamorphosis and the Pursuit of Paganism* New Haven

Barnes ed 1971 Barnes, Barnabe 1971 *Parthenophil and Parthenophe* ed Victor A. Doyno. Carbondale, Ill

Barney 1979 Barney, Stephen A. 1979 *Allegories of History, Allegories of Love* Hamden, Conn

du Bartas ed 1979 du Bartas, Guillaume de Saluste 1979 *The Divine Weeks and Works* tr Joshua Sylvester, ed Susan Snyder. 2 vols. Oxford

Bartholomaeus Anglicus 1582 Bartholomaeus Anglicus 1582 *Batman uppon Bartholome His Booke 'De proprietatibus rerum'* tr Stephen Bateman. London, rpt Hildesheim 1976

Baskervill 1920–1 Baskervill, C.R. 1920–1 'The Genesis of Spenser's Queen of Faerie' *MP* 18:49–54

Bauckham 1978 Bauckham, Richard 1978 *Tudor Apocalypse* Abingdon, Oxf

Baybak, et al 1969 Baybak, Michael, et al 1969 'Placement "In the Middest" in *The Faerie Queene*' *PLL* 5:227–34

BCP See Church of England

Beal 1980 Beal, Peter 1980 *Index of English Literary Manuscripts* vol I, *1450–1625* 2 pts. London

Becon ed 1844 Becon, Thomas 1844 *Prayers and Other Pieces* ed John Ayre. Parker Society. Cambridge

Bednarz 1983 Bednarz, James P. 1983 'Ralegh in Spenser's Historical Allegory' *SSt* 4:49–70

Beer 1970 Beer, Gillian 1970 *The Romance* London

du Bellay ed 1948 du Bellay, Joachim 1948 *La Deffence et illustration de la langue françoyse* ed Henri Chamard. Rev ed. Paris; first pub 1904

Belson 1964 Belson, Joel Jay 1964 'The Names in *The Faerie Queene*' Diss Columbia Univ

Bender 1972 Bender, John B. 1972 *Spenser and Literary Pictorialism* Princeton

Bennett 1931a Bennett, Josephine Waters 1931a 'Spenser and Gabriel Harvey's *Letter-Book*' *MP* 29:163–86

Bennett 1931b —— 1931b 'Spenser's Hesiod' *AJPh* 52:176–81

Bennett 1931c —— 1931c 'The Theme of Spenser's *Fowre Hymnes*' *SP* 28:18–57

Bennett 1932 —— 1932 'Spenser's Garden of Adonis' *PMLA* 47:46–80
Bennett 1935 —— 1935 'Spenser's *Fowre Hymnes*: Addenda' *SP* 32:131–57
Bennett 1942 —— 1942 *The Evolution of 'The Faerie Queene'* Chicago
van den Berg, Kent. See Van den Berg 1978
Berger 1957 Berger, Harry, Jr 1957 *The Allegorical Temper: Vision and Reality in Book II of Spenser's 'Faerie Queene'* New Haven
Berger 1960–1 —— 1960–1 'Spenser's Gardens of Adonis: Force and Form in the Renaissance Imagination' *UTQ* 30:128–49 rpt in Berger 1988:131–53
Berger 1961a —— 1961a 'The Prospect of Imagination: Spenser and the Limits of Poetry' *SEL* 1:93–120
Berger 1961b —— 1961b 'A Secret Discipline: *The Faerie Queene* Book VI' In Nelson 1961:35–75, 171–4, and in Berger 1988:215–42
Berger 1968a —— 1968a 'Archaism, Immortality, and the Muse in Spenser's Poetry' *YR* ns 58:214–31, rpt in Berger 1988:36–50
Berger 1968b —— 1968b 'The *Mutabilitie Cantos*: Archaism and Evolution in Retrospect' In Berger 1968c:146–76, rpt in Berger 1988:243–73
Berger 1968c —— ed 1968c *Spenser: A Collection of Critical Essays* Englewood Cliffs, NJ
Berger 1968d —— 1968d 'The Spenserian Dynamics' *SEL* 8:1–18 rpt in Berger 1988:19–35
Berger 1968e —— 1968e 'Two Spenserian Retrospects: The Antique Temple of Venus and the Primitive Marriage of Rivers' *TSLL* 10:5–25, rpt in Berger 1988:195–214
Berger 1969a —— 1969a 'The Discarding of Malbecco: Conspicuous Allusion and Cultural Exhaustion in *The Faerie Queene* III. ix-x' *SP* 66:135–54, rpt in Berger 1988:154–71
Berger 1969b —— 1969b '*Faerie Queene* Book III: A General Description' *Criticism* 11:234–61, rpt in Berger 1988:89–117
Berger 1969–70 —— 1969–70 'Mode and Diction in *The Shepheardes Calender*' *MP* 67:140–9
Berger 1971 —— 1971 'Busirane and the War Between the Sexes: An Interpretation of *The Faerie Queene* III, xi-xii' *ELR* 1:99–121, rpt in Berger 1988:172–94
Berger 1988 —— *Revisionary Play: Studies in the Spenserian Dynamics* Berkeley and Los Angeles
Bergeron 1971 Bergeron, David M. 1971 *English Civic Pageantry, 1558–1642* London
Berleth 1973 Berleth, Richard J. 1973 'Heavens Favorable and Free: Belphoebe's Nativity in *The Faerie Queene*' *ELH* 40:479–500
Berman 1983 Berman, Ruth 1983 'Blazonings in *The Faerie Queene*' *CahiersE* 23:1–14
Bernard Sylvestris ed 1973 Bernard Sylvestris 1973 *The Cosmographia* tr Winthrop Wetherbee. New York
Bernard Sylvestris ed 1977 —— 1977 *Commentary on the First Six Books of the 'Aeneid' of Vergil* ed Julian Ward Jones and Elizabeth Frances Jones. Lincoln, Nebr
Bernard Sylvestris ed 1979 —— 1979 *Commentary on the First Six Books of Virgil's 'Aeneid'* tr Earl G. Schreiber and Thomas E. Maresca. Lincoln, Nebr
Bernheimer 1952 Bernheimer, Richard 1952 *Wild Men in the Middle Ages: A Study in Art, Sentiment, and Demonology* Cambridge, Mass
Berry 1961 Berry, Lloyd E. 1961 'Five Latin Poems by Giles Fletcher, the Elder' *Anglia* 79:338–77
Berry and Timings 1960 Berry Herbert, and E.K. Timings 1960 'Spenser's Pension' *RES* ns 11:254–9
Bersuire 1509 Bersuire, Pierre 1509 *Metamorphosis ovidiana moraliter ... explanata* Paris, rpt London and New York 1979
Bible, Geneva Bible, Geneva 1560 *The Geneva Bible: A Facsimile of the 1560 Edition* ed Lloyd E. Berry 1969. Madison
Bieman 1968 Bieman, Elizabeth 1968 'Britomart in Book v of *The Faerie Queene*' *UTQ* 37:156–74
Bieman 1983 —— 1983 '"Sometimes I ... mask in myrth lyke to a Comedy": Spenser's *Amoretti*' *SSt* 4:131–41
Bindoff, et al 1961 Bindoff, S.T., et al, eds 1961 *Elizabethan Government and Society* London
Bjorvand 1973 Bjorvand, Einar 1973 *A Concordance to Spenser's 'Fowre Hymnes'* Oslo
Bjorvand 1975 —— 1975 'Spenser's Defence of Poetry: Some Structural Aspects of the *Fowre Hymnes*' In Røstvig 1975:13–53, 203–6
Blackburn 1980 Blackburn, William 1980 'Spenser's Merlin' *Ren&R* ns 4:179–98
Blake ed 1966 Blake, William 1966 *Complete Writings* ed Geoffrey Keynes. London
Blanchard 1925 Blanchard, Harold H. 1925 'Spenser and Boiardo' *PMLA* 40:828–51
Blissett 1964 Blissett, William 1964 'Spenser's Mutabilitie' In MacLure and Watt 1964:26–42
Blissett 1965 —— 1965 'Florimell and Marinell' *SEL* 5:87–104
Blissett 1989 —— 1989 'Caves, Labyrinths, and *The Faerie Queene*' In Logan and Teskey 1989:281–311
Blitch 1973 Blitch, Alice Fox 1973 'Proserpina Preserved: Book VI of the *Faerie Queene*' *SEL* 13:15–30
Blondel 1976 Blondel, Jacques 1976 'Allégorie, éros et religion dans *The Fowre Hymnes*' In *Imaginaire et croyance: Etudes de poésie anglaise* pp 49–56. Grenoble
Bloom 1959 Bloom, Harold 1959 *Shelley's Mythmaking* New Haven
Bloomfield 1952 Bloomfield, Morton W. 1952 *The Seven Deadly Sins* East Lansing, Mich
Blythe 1972 Blythe, Joan Heiges 1972 'Spenser and the Seven Deadly Sins: Book I Cantos iv and v' *ELH* 39:342–52
Boccaccio ed 1494 Boccaccio, Giovanni 1494 *Genealogiae* Venice, rpt New York and London 1976
Boccaccio ed 1930 —— 1930 *Boccaccio on Poetry: Being the Preface and the Fourteenth and Fifteenth Books of Boccaccio's 'Genealogia deorum gentilium'* tr Charles G. Osgood. Princeton
Boccaccio ed 1951 —— 1951 *Genealogie deorum gentilium libri* ed Vincenzo Romano. 2 vols. Bari
Boethius ed 1962 Boethius 1962 *The Consolation of Philosophy* tr Richard Green. Indianapolis
Boethius. See also headnote
Bolgar 1954 Bolgar, R.R. 1954 *The Classical Heritage and Its Beneficiaries* Cambridge
Bolgar 1955 —— 1955 'Classical Reading in Renaissance Schools' *Durham Research Rev* 2.6:18–26
Bolgar 1975 —— 1975 'Hero or Anti-Hero?: The Genesis and Development of the *Miles Christianus*' In Burns and Reagan 1975:120–46
Bolgar 1976 —— ed 1976 *Classical Influences on European Culture A.D. 1500–1700* Cambridge
Bolzani. See Valeriano 1602
Bond 1976 Bond, Ronald B. 1976 '*Invidia* and the Allegory of Spenser's *Muiopotmos*' *ESC* 2:144–55
Bond 1981 —— 1981 'Supplantation in the Elizabethan Court: The Theme of Spenser's February Eclogue' *SSt* 2:55–65
Book of Common Prayer See Church of England
Booty, et al 1981 Booty, John E., et al 1981 *The Godly Kingdom of Tudor England: Great Books of the English Reformation* Wilton, Conn
Bornstein 1975 Bornstein, Diane 1975 *Mirrors of Courtesy* Hamden, Conn
Boswell ed 1934–50 Boswell, James 1934–50 *Life of Johnson* ed George Birkbeck Hill, rev L.F. Powell. 6 vols. Oxford
Bowra 1945 Bowra, C.M. 1945 *From Virgil to Milton* London
Bradbrook 1936 Bradbrook, M[uriel] C. 1936 *The School of Night: A Study in the Literary Relationships of Sir Walter Ralegh* Cambridge
Bradbrook 1960 —— 1960 'No Room at the Top: Spenser's Pursuit of Fame' In Brown and Harris 1960:91–109
Braden 1975 Braden, Gordon 1975 'riverrun: An Epic Catalogue in *The Faerie Queene*' *ELR* 5:25–48
Bradner 1935–6 Bradner, Leicester 1935–6 'The Latin Translations of Spenser's *Shepheardes Calender*' *MP* 33:21–6
Bradshaw 1987 Bradshaw, Brendan 1987 'Edmund Spenser on

Justice and Mercy' In *The Writer as Witness* pp 76–89. Historical Studies 16 ed Tom Dunne. Cork

Brady 1986 Brady, Ciaran 1986 'Spenser's Irish Crisis: Humanism and Experience in the 1590s' *P&P* 111(May):17–49

Brand 1965 Brand, C.P. 1965 *Torquato Tasso: A Study of the Poet and of His Contribution to English Literature* Cambridge

Brennan 1988 Brennan, Michael G. 1988 *Literary Patronage in the English Renaissance: The Pembroke Family* London

Breton ed 1879 Breton, Nicholas 1879 *Works in Verse and Prose* ed Alexander B. Grosart. 2 vols. Edinburgh

Briggs 1962 Briggs, K[atharine] M. 1962 *Pale Hecate's Team: An Examination of the Beliefs on Witchcraft and Magic among Shakespeare's Contemporaries and His Immediate Successors* London

Brill 1971 Brill, Lesley W. 1971 'Chastity as Ideal Sexuality in the Third Book of *The Faerie Queene*' *SEL* 11:15–26

Brink 1972 Brink, J.R. 1972 'The Masque of the Nine Muses: Sir John Davies's Unpublished "Epithalamion" and the "Belphoebe-Ruby" Episode in *The Faerie Queene*' *RES* ns 23:445–7

Brinkley 1981 Brinkley, Robert A. 1981 'Spenser's *Muiopotmos* and the Politics of Metamorphosis' *ELH* 48:668–76

Bristol 1970 Bristol, Michael D. 1970 'Structural Patterns in Two Elizabethan Pastorals' *SEL* 10:33–48

Brooks-Davies 1977 Brooks-Davies, Douglas 1977 *Spenser's 'Faerie Queene': A Critical Commentary on Books I and II* Manchester

Brooks-Davies 1983 —— 1983 *The Mercurian Monarch: Magical Politics from Spenser to Pope* Manchester

Brown 1973 Brown, James Neil 1973 '"Lyke Phoebe": Lunar Numerical and Calendrical Patterns in Spenser's *Amoretti*' *The Gypsy Scholar* 1:5–15

Brown 1980 —— 1980 'A Note on Symbolic Numbers in Spenser's "Aprill"' *N&Q* 225:301–4

Brown and Harris 1960 Brown, John Russell, and Bernard Harris, eds 1960 *Elizabethan Poetry* London

Browning 1842 [Browning, Elizabeth Barrett] 1842 'Review of *The Book of the Poets*' *Athenaeum* 11 June:520–3

Bruno ed 1964a Bruno, Giordano 1964a *The Expulsion of the Triumphant Beast* tr Arthur D. Imerti. New Brunswick, NJ

Bruno ed 1964b —— 1964b *Giordano Bruno's 'The Heroic Frenzies'* tr Paul Eugene Memmo, Jr. Chapel Hill

Bryskett 1606 Bryskett, Lodowick 1606 *A Discourse of Civill Life* London, rpt Amsterdam and New York 1971, ed Thomas E. Wright, Northridge, Calif 1970; rpt also in Bryskett ed 1972

Bryskett ed 1972 —— 1972 *Literary Works* ed J.H.P. Pafford. Farnsborough, Eng

Bullough 1957–75 Bullough, Geoffrey, ed 1957–75 *Narrative and Dramatic Sources of Shakespeare* 8 vols. London

Burchmore 1977 Burchmore, David W. 1977 'The Image of the Centre in *Colin Clouts Come Home Againe*' *RES* ns 28:393–406

Burchmore 1981 —— 1981 'The Medieval Sources of Spenser's Occasion Episode' *SSt* 2:93–120

Burchmore 1984 —— 1984 'Triamond, Agape, and the Fates: Neoplatonic Cosmology in Spenser's Legend of Friendship' *SSt* 5:45–64

Burckhardt ed 1945 Burckhardt, Jacob 1945 *The Civilization of the Renaissance in Italy* tr S.G.C. Middlemore. Oxford; first pub 1860

Burke 1950 Burke, Kenneth 1950 *A Rhetoric of Motives* New York

Burns and Reagan 1975 Burns, Norman T., and Christopher J. Reagan, eds 1975 *Concepts of the Hero in the Middle Ages and the Renaissance* Albany, NY

Burton ed 1893 Burton, Robert 1893 *The Anatomy of Melancholy* ed A.R. Shilleto. 3 vols. London

Bush 1939 Bush, Douglas 1939 *The Renaissance and English Humanism* Toronto

Bush 1952 —— 1952 *Classical Influences in Renaissance Literature* Cambridge, Mass

Bush 1963 —— 1963 *Mythology and the Renaissance Tradition in English Poetry* Rev ed. New York; first pub 1932

Bush 1968 —— 1968 *Pagan Myth and Christian Tradition in English Poetry* Philadelphia

C. Butler 1970a Butler, Christopher 1970a *Number Symbolism* London

C. Butler 1970b —— 1970b 'Numerological Thought' In Fowler 1970a:1–31

Butler ed 1973 Butler, Samuel 1973 *'Hudibras' Parts I and II and Selected Other Writings* ed John Wilders and Hugh de Quehen. Oxford

Buxton 1963 Buxton, John 1963 *Elizabethan Taste* London

Byrom 1933 Byrom, H.J. 1933 'Edmund Spenser's First Printer, Hugh Singleton' *Library* ser 4, 14:121–56

Cain 1968 Cain, Thomas H. 1968 'The Strategy of Praise in Spenser's "Aprill"' *SEL* 8:45–58

Cain 1978 —— 1978 *Praise in 'The Faerie Queene'* Lincoln, Nebr

Calvin ed 1561 Calvin, John 1561 *The Institution of Christian Religion* tr Thomas Norton. London

Calvin ed 1960 —— 1960 *Institutes of the Christian Religion* tr Ford Lewis Battles, ed John T. McNeill. Vols 20–1 in *Library CC*

Cambridge History of Classical Literature (CHCL) 1982. Vol 2: *Latin Literature* ed E.J. Kenney with W.V. Clausen. Cambridge

Camden ed 1970 Camden, William 1970 *'The History of the Most Renowned and Victorious Princess Elizabeth Late Queen of England,' Selected Chapters* ed Wallace T. MacCaffrey. Chicago

Camden ed 1985 —— 1985 *Remains Concerning Britain* ed R.D. Dunn. Toronto

Camoens ed 1952 Camoens, Luis Vaz de 1952 *The Lusiads* tr William C. Atkinson. Harmondsworth

J. Campbell 1949 Campbell, Joseph 1949 *The Hero with a Thousand Faces* New York, 2nd ed Princeton 1968

J. Campbell 1955 —— ed 1955 *The Mysteries: Papers from the Eranos Yearbooks* tr Ralph Manheim and R.F.C. Hull. Vol 2. New York

L.B. Campbell 1959 Campbell, Lily B. 1959 *Divine Poetry and Drama in Sixteenth-Century England* Cambridge

Campbell and Doyle 1978 Campbell, Jane, and James Doyle, eds 1978 *The Practical Vision: Essays in English Literature in Honour of Flora Roy* Waterloo, Ont

Canny 1976 Canny, Nicholas P. 1976 *The Elizabethan Conquest of Ireland: A Pattern Established 1565–76* Hassocks, Sussex

Canny 1983 —— 1983 'Edmund Spenser and the Development of an Anglo-Irish Identity' *YES* 13:1–19

Canny and Brady 1988 ——, and Ciaran Brady 1988 'Debate: Spenser's Irish Crisis: Humanism and Experience in the 1590s' *P&P* 120(August):201–15

Carley 1984 Carley, James P. 1984 'Polydore Vergil and John Leland on King Arthur: The Battle of the Books' *Interpretations* (Memphis) 15.2:86–100

Carpenter 1923 Carpenter, Frederic Ives 1923 *A Reference Guide to Edmund Spenser* Chicago

Carroll 1954 Carroll, William Meredith 1954 *Animal Conventions in English Renaissance Non-Religious Prose (1550–1600)* New York

Carscallen 1967–8 Carscallen, James 1967–8 'The Goodly Frame of Temperance: The Metaphor of Cosmos in *The Faerie Queene*, Book II' *UTQ* 37:136–55

Cartari 1571 Cartari, Vincenzo 1571 *Le Imagini con la spositione de i dei de gli antichi* Venice, rpt Venice 1580, New York and London 1976

Cartari ed 1599 —— 1599 *The Fountaine of Ancient Fiction* tr Richard Lynche. London, rpt New York and London 1976

Cassirer ed 1963 Cassirer, Ernst 1963 *The Individual and the Cosmos in Renaissance Philosophy* tr Mario Domandi. New York

Cast 1981 Cast, David 1981 *The Calumny of Apelles: A Study in the Humanist Tradition* New Haven

Castelli 1936 Castelli, Alberto 1936 *'La Gerusalemme liberata' nella Inghilterra di Spenser* Milan

Castiglione ed 1928 Castiglione, Baldassare 1928 *The Book of the Courtier* (1561) tr Sir Thomas Hoby. London

Castiglione ed 1959 —— 1959 *The Book of the Courtier* tr Charles S. Singleton. Garden City, NY
Chambers 1903 Chambers, E. K. 1903 *The Mediaeval Stage* 2 vols. Oxford
Chambers 1923 —— 1923 *The Elizabethan Stage* 4 vols. Oxford
Chapman, George. See Homer ed 1967
Charron (before 1612) Charron, Pierre (before 1612) *Of Wisdome* tr S[amson] Lennard. London, rpt Amsterdam and New York 1971
Chatman 1978 Chatman, Seymour 1978 *Story and Discourse: Narrative Structure in Fiction and Film* Ithaca, NY
Chaucer ed 1894–7 Chaucer, Geoffrey 1894–7 *Complete Works* ed Walter W. Skeat. 7 vols. Oxford, rev ed 1899–1900
Chaucer ed 1933 —— 1933 *Works* ed F.N. Robinson. Boston, rev ed 1957; 3rd ed, as *The Riverside Chaucer* gen ed Larry D. Benson 1987
Chaucer ed 1969 —— 1969 *The Works 1532* facs with intro by D.S. Brewer. Menston, Yorks
CHCL. See *Cambridge History of Classical Literature*
Cheney 1966 Cheney, Donald 1966 *Spenser's Image of Nature: Wild Man and Shepherd in 'The Faerie Queene'* New Haven
Cheney 1972 —— 1972 'Spenser's Hermaphrodite and the 1590 *Faerie Queene*' *PMLA* 87:192–200
Cheney 1983 —— 1983 'Spenser's Fortieth Birthday and Related Fictions' *SSt* 4:3–31
P. Cheney 1985 Cheney, Patrick 1985 'Spenser's Completion of *The Squire's Tale*: Love, Magic, and Heroic Action in the Legend of Cambell and Triamond' *JMRS* 15:135–55
Chester 1935 Chester, Allan Griffith 1935 'Thomas Churchyard's Pension' *PMLA* 50:902
Chesterton 1950 Chesterton, G.K. 1950 *The Common Man* London
Chew 1962 Chew, Samuel C. 1962 *The Pilgrimage of Life* New Haven
Chiappelli 1976 Chiappelli, Fredi, ed 1976 *First Images of America: The Impact of the New World on the Old* 2 vols. Berkeley and Los Angeles
Church 1879 Church, R.W. 1879 *Spenser* London
Homilies ed 1623 Church of England 1623 *Certaine Sermons or Homilies* London, rpt Gainesville, Fla 1968
BCP ed 1976 —— *The Book of Common Prayer, 1559: The Elizabethan Prayer Book* 1976 ed John E. Booty. Charlottesville
Articles of Religion / Thirty-Nine Articles See Hardwick 1876
Cicero. See headnote
Cirlot 1962 Cirlot, J[uan] E. 1962 *A Dictionary of Symbols* tr Jack Sage. London, rev ed 1971
Clark 1948 Clark, Donald Lemen 1948 *John Milton at St. Paul's School: A Study of Ancient Rhetoric in English Renaissance Education* New York
Claudian. See headnote
Clemen 1968 Clemen, Wolfgang 1968 'The Uniqueness of Spenser's *Epithalamion*' In *The Poetic Tradition* ed Don Cameron Allen and Henry T. Rowell, pp 81–98. Baltimore
Coeffeteau ed 1621 Coeffeteau, Nicolas 1621 *A Table of Humane Passions* tr E. Grimeston. London
Coleridge ed 1835–6 Coleridge, Samuel Taylor 1835–6 *Specimens of the Table Talk* ed Henry Nelson Coleridge. 2 vols. London
Coleridge ed 1936 —— 1936 *Coleridge's Miscellaneous Criticism* ed Thomas Middleton Raysor. London
Colie 1966 Colie, Rosalie L. 1966 *Paradoxia Epidemica: The Renaissance Tradition of Paradox* Princeton
Colie 1973 —— 1973 *The Resources of Kind: Genre-Theory in the Renaissance* ed Barbara K. Lewalski. Berkeley and Los Angeles
Collins 1940 Collins, Joseph B. 1940 *Christian Mysticism in the Elizabethan Age* Baltimore
Collins, William. See Lonsdale 1969
Collinson 1967 Collinson, Patrick 1967 *The Elizabethan Puritan Movement* London
Collinson 1979 —— 1979 *Archbishop Grindal, 1519–1583: The Struggle for a Reformed Church* London
Collinson 1982 —— 1982 *The Religion of Protestants: The Church in English Society, 1559–1625* Oxford
Comes, Natalis. See Conti, Natale
Comito 1978 Comito, Terry 1978 *The Idea of the Garden in the Renaissance* New Brunswick, NJ
Comparetti ed 1895 Comparetti, Domenico 1895 *Vergil in the Middle Ages* tr E.F.M. Benecke. London
Conti 1567 Conti, Natale [Natalis Comes] 1567 *Mythologiae sive explicationum fabularum libri decem* Venice, rpt New York and London 1976
Cook 1890 Cook, Albert S. 1890 'The House of Sleep: A Study in Comparative Literature' *MLN* 5:9–21
H. Cooper 1977 Cooper, Helen 1977 *Pastoral: Mediaeval into Renaissance* Ipswich
T. Cooper 1565 Cooper, Thomas 1565 *Thesaurus linguae Romanae et Britannicae* London, rpt Menston, Yorks 1969
Cornelius 1930 Cornelius, Roberta D. 1930 'The Figurative Castle' Diss Bryn Mawr
Corrozet 1540 Corrozet, Gilles 1540 *Hecatomgraphie* Paris, rpt Ilkley, Yorks and London 1974
Costalius ed 1555 Costalius, Petrus ed 1555 *Pegma, cum narrationibus philosophicis* Leiden (Pierre Coustau *Le pegme* Lyons 1540, 1555, 1560)
Couliano 1987 Couliano, Ioan P. 1987 *Eros and Magic in the Renaissance* tr Margaret Cook. Chicago
Court of Sapience ed 1984 *The Court of Sapience* (c 1483) 1984 ed E. Ruth Harvey. Toronto
Cowley ed 1906 Cowley, Abraham 1906 *Essays, Plays, Sundry Verses* ed A.R. Waller. Cambridge
Cox ed 1899 Cox, Leonard 1899 *The Arte or Crafte of Rhethoryke* (1530?) ed Frederic Ives Carpenter. Chicago
Craig 1959 Craig, Martha Alden 1959 'Language and Concept in *The Faerie Queene*' Diss Yale Univ
Craig 1967 —— 1967 'The Secret Wit of Spenser's Language' In Alpers 1967a:447–72
Craik 1845 Craik, George L. 1845 *Spenser and His Poetry* 3 vols. London, rev ed 1871
Crampton 1974 Crampton, Georgia Ronan 1974 *The Condition of Creatures: Suffering and Action in Chaucer and Spenser* New Haven
Crane 1937 Crane, William G. 1937 *Wit and Rhetoric in the Renaissance: The Formal Basis of Elizabethan Prose Style* New York
Crinò 1968 Crinò, Anna Maria 1968 'La Relazione Barducci-Ubaldini sull'impresa d'Irlanda 1579–1581' *EM* 19:339–67
Crossett and Stump 1984 Crossett, John M., and Donald V. Stump 1984 'Spenser's Inferno: The Order of the Seven Deadly Sins at the Palace of Pride' *JMRS* 14:203–18
Crowley ed 1872 Crowley, Robert 1872 *Select Works* ed J.M. Cowper. EETS, es 15. London
Cullen 1970 Cullen, Patrick 1970 *Spenser, Marvell, and Renaissance Pastoral* Cambridge, Mass
Cullen 1974 —— 1974 *Infernal Triad: The Flesh, the World, and the Devil in Spenser and Milton* Princeton
Culp 1971 Culp, Dorothy Woodward 1971 'Courtesy and Moral Virtue' *SEL* 11:37–51
L. Cummings 1964 Cummings, L. 1964 'Spenser's *Amoretti* VIII: New Manuscript Versions' *SEL* 4:125–35
R.M. Cummings 1970 Cummings, R.M. 1970 'An Iconographical Puzzle: Spenser's Cupid at *Faerie Queene*, II, viii' *JWCI* 33:317–21
R.M. Cummings 1971 —— ed 1971 *Spenser: The Critical Heritage* London
Curtius ed 1953 Curtius, Ernst Robert 1953 *European Literature and the Latin Middle Ages* tr Willard R. Trask. New York

Dallett 1960 Dallett, Joseph B. 1960 'Ideas of Sight in *The Faerie Queene*' *ELH* 27:87–121
Daly 1979 Daly, Peter M. 1979 *Literature in the Light of the Emblem: Structural Parallels between the Emblem and Literature in the Sixteenth and Seventeenth Centuries* Toronto
Daniel ed 1885–96 Daniel, Samuel 1885–96 *Complete Works in Verse and Prose* ed Alexander B. Grosart. 5 vols. London
Daniel ed 1930 —— 1930 *'Poems' and 'A Defence of Ryme'* ed Arthur Colby Sprague. Cambridge, Mass

Dante ed 1966 Dante Alighieri 1966 *Dantis Alagherii Epistolae: The Letters of Dante* tr and ed Paget Toynbee. 2nd ed. Oxford
H. Davies 1961–70 Davies, Horton 1961–70 *Worship and Theology in England from Cranmer to Hooker, 1534–1603* 5 vols. Princeton
J. Davies ed 1975 Davies, Sir John 1975 *Poems* ed Robert Krueger. Oxford
P.G. Davies 1973–4 Davies, Phillips G. 1973–4 'A Check List of Poems, 1595–1833, Entirely or Partly Written in the Spenserian Stanza' *BNYPL* 77:314–28
S. Davies 1986 Davies, Stevie 1986 *The Idea of Woman in Renaissance Literature: The Feminine Reclaimed* Brighton, Sussex
W.R. Davis 1981 Davis, Walter R. 1981 'The Houses of Mortality in Book II of *The Faerie Queene*' *SSt* 2:121–40
W.V. Davis 1969 Davis, William V. 1969 'Edmund Spenser's "Epithalamion"' *AN&Q* 7:84–5
Dees 1970–1 Dees, Jerome S. 1970–1 'The Narrator of *The Faerie Queene*: Patterns of Response' *TSLL* 12:537–68
Deguileville ed 1893 Deguileville, Guillaume de 1893 *Le Pèlerinage de la vie humaine* ed J[akob] J. Stürzinger. Roxburghe Club. London
Deguileville ed 1899–1904 —— 1899–1904 *The Pilgrimage of the Life of Man* tr John Lydgate, ed F.J. Furnivall. EETS es 77, 83, 92. London
de Lorris, Guillaume. See Lorris and de Meun
de Meun, Jean. See Lorris and de Meun
DeMolen 1978 DeMolen, Richard L., ed 1978 *Essays on the Works of Erasmus* New Haven
DeMoss 1918–19 DeMoss, William Fenn 1918–19 'Spenser's Twelve Moral Virtues "According to Aristotle"' *MP* 16:23–38, 245–70
DeNeef 1974 DeNeef, A. Leigh 1974 'Spenserian Meditation: The *Hymne of Heavenly Beautie*' *ABR* 25:317–34
DeNeef 1979 —— 1979 'Spenser's *Amor Fuggitivo* and the Transfixed Heart' *ELH* 46:1–20
DeNeef 1982 —— 1982 *Spenser and the Motives of Metaphor* Durham, NC
de Vere, Aubrey. See Vere, Aubrey de
Dickens 1964 Dickens, A.G. 1964 *The English Reformation* London
Dictionary of the History of Ideas (*DHI*) 1973–4 ed Philip P. Wiener, et al. 5 vols. New York
The Dictionary of National Biography (*DNB*) 1885–1900 ed Leslie Stephen and Sidney Lee. 63 vols. London
Diodorus Siculus. See headnote
Dixon, John. See Hough 1964
Dodoens ed 1578 Dodoens, Rembert 1578 *A Niewe Herball, or Historie of Plantes* tr Henry Lyte. Antwerp
Donker and Muldrow 1982 Donker, Marjorie, and George M. Muldrow 1982 *Dictionary of Literary-Rhetorical Conventions of the English Renaissance* Westport, Conn
Donne ed 1953–62 Donne, John 1953–62 *Sermons* ed George R. Potter and Evelyn M. Simpson. 10 vols. Berkeley and Los Angeles
Donne ed 1980 —— 1980 *Paradoxes and Problems* ed Helen Peters. Oxford
Donno 1974 Donno, Elizabeth Story 1974 'The Triumph of Cupid: Spenser's Legend of Chastity' *YES* 4:37–48
Doran 1954 Doran, Madeleine 1954 *Endeavors of Art: A Study of Form in Elizabethan Drama* Madison
Dorangeon 1974 Dorangeon, Simone 1974 *L'Eglogue anglaise de Spenser à Milton* Paris
van Dorsten 1962 van Dorsten, J[an] A. 1962 *Poets, Patrons, and Professors: Sir Philip Sidney, Daniel Rogers, and the Leiden Humanists* Leiden
van Dorsten 1970 —— 1970 *The Radical Arts: First Decade of an Elizabethan Renaissance* Leiden
Dowden 1888 Dowden, Edward 1888 *Transcripts and Studies* London
Doyle 1973 Doyle, Charles Clay 1973 '*Daphnis and Chloe* and the Faunus Episode in Spenser's *Mutability*' *NM* 74:163–8
F.W.M. Draper 1962 Draper, F.W.M. 1962 *Four Centuries of Merchant Taylors' School, 1561–1961* London
J.W. Draper 1932 Draper, John W. 1932 'Classical Coinage in the *Faerie Queene*' *PMLA* 47:97–108
Drayton ed 1931–41 Drayton, Michael 1931–41 *Works* ed J. William Hebel, et al. 5 vols. Oxford; corr ed 1961
Dryden ed 1956– Dryden, John 1956– *Works* ed Edward Niles Hooker, et al. Berkeley and Los Angeles
Dryden ed 1962 —— 1962 *Of Dramatic Poesy and Other Critical Essays* ed George Watson. 2 vols. London
du Bartas. See Bartas, Guillaume de Saluste
du Bellay. See Bellay, Joachim du
Dubois 1982 Dubois, Page 1982 *History, Rhetorical Description and the Epic: From Homer to Spenser* Cambridge
Dudley and Novak 1972 Dudley, Edward, and Maximillian E. Novak, eds 1972 *The Wild Man Within: An Image in Western Thought from the Renaissance to Romanticism* Pittsburgh
Dundas 1965 Dundas, Judith 1965 'Elizabethan Architecture and *The Faerie Queene*: Some Structural Analogies' *DR* 45:470–8
Dundas 1985 —— 1985 *The Spider and the Bee: The Artistry of Spenser's 'Faerie Queene'* Urbana
Dunlop 1969 Dunlop, Alexander 1969 'Calendar Symbolism in the "Amoretti"' *N&Q* 214:24–6
Dunlop 1970 —— 1970 'The Unity of Spenser's *Amoretti*' In Fowler 1970a:153–69
Dunlop 1980 —— 1980 'The Drama of *Amoretti*' *SSt* 1:107–20
Dunseath 1968 Dunseath, T[homas] K. 1968 *Spenser's Allegory of Justice in Book Five of 'The Faerie Queene'* Princeton
Durling 1954 Durling, Robert M. 1954 'The Bower of Bliss and Armida's Palace' *CL* 6:335–47
Durling 1965 —— 1965 *The Figure of the Poet in Renaissance Epic* Cambridge, Mass

Eade 1972 Eade, J.C. 1972 'The Pattern in the Astronomy of Spenser's *Epithalamion*' *RES* ns 23:173–8
Eccles 1982 Eccles, Mark 1982 *Brief Lives: Tudor and Stuart Authors*, *SP* Texts and Studies 79
Edwards 1981 Edwards, A[nthony] S.G., ed 1981 *Skelton: The Critical Heritage* London
Eighteenth-Century Short-Title Catalogue: The British Library Collection (ESTC) 1983 ed R.C. Alston. London. Microfiche
Elias 1978 Elias, Norbert 1978 *The History of Manners* vol I of *The Civilizing Process* tr Edmund Jephcott. Oxford
Eliot ed 1950 Eliot, T.S. 1950 *Selected Essays* Rev ed. New York
Ellrodt 1960 Ellrodt, Robert 1960 *Neoplatonism in the Poetry of Spenser* Geneva
Elton 1960 Elton, G.R., ed 1960 *The Tudor Constitution: Documents and Commentary* Cambridge, rev ed 1982
Elyot 1538 Elyot, Thomas 1538 *Dictionary* London, rpt Menston, Yorks 1970
Elyot ed 1883 —— 1883 *The Boke Named The Governour* (1531) ed Henry Herbert Stephen Croft. 2 vols. London
Empson 1930 Empson, William 1930 *Seven Types of Ambiguity* London. Rev ed New York 1947
Erasmus ed 1703–6 Erasmus, Desiderius 1703–6 *Opera omnia* ed Jean LeClerc. 10 vols in 11. Leiden
Erasmus ed 1906–58 —— 1906–58 'Letter to Sigismund I (2034)' In vol 7 (1928) of *Opus Epistolarum* ed P.S. Allen, et al. 12 vols. Oxford
Erasmus ed 1965 —— 1965 *Colloquies* tr and ed Craig R. Thompson. Chicago
Erasmus ed 1974– —— 1974– *Collected Works* Toronto
Erskine 1915 Erskine, John 1915 'The Virtue of Friendship in the *Faerie Queene*' *PMLA* 30:831–50
Essex, Earl of. See Oxford and Essex ed 1980
ESTC See *Eighteenth-Century Short-Title Catalogue*
C. Estienne 1561 Estienne, Charles [Carolus Stephanus] 1561 *Dictionarium historicum ac poeticum* Paris; ed 1596 rpt New York and London 1976
R. Estienne 1573 Estienne, Robert [Robertus Stephanus] 1573 *Thesaurus linguae Latinae* Lyons
Ettin 1982 Ettin, Andrew V. 1982 'The Georgics in *The Faerie Queene*' *SSt* 3:57–71
Evans 1970 Evans, Maurice 1970 *Spenser's Anatomy of Heroism: A Commentary on 'The Faerie Queene'* Cambridge

The Faerie Queene See Spenser eds
Fanshawe ed 1964 Fanshawe, Richard 1964 *Shorter Poems and Translations* ed N.W. Bawcutt. Liverpool
Farmer 1984 Farmer, Norman K., Jr 1984 *Poets and the Visual Arts in Renaissance England* Austin
Farmer 1986 —— 1986 'Spenser's Homage to Ronsard: Cosmic Design in *The Shepheardes Calender*' *Studi di letteratura francese* 12:249–63
Farnham 1936 Farnham, Willard 1936 *The Medieval Heritage of Elizabethan Tragedy* Berkeley
Favyn ed 1623 Favyn, André 1623 *The Theater of Honour and Knight-hood* tr W.J. (A. Munday?). London
Feinstein 1968 Feinstein, Blossom 1968 '*The Faerie Queene* and Cosmogonies of the Near East' *JHI* 29:531–50
A.B. Ferguson 1960 Ferguson, Arthur B. 1960 *The Indian Summer of English Chivalry* Durham, NC
M.W. Ferguson 1984 Ferguson, Margaret W. 1984 '"The Afflatus of Ruin": Meditations on Rome by Du Bellay, Spenser, and Stevens' In Patterson 1984:23–50
Ferguson, et al 1986 Ferguson, Margaret W., et al, eds 1986 *Rewriting the Renaissance: The Discourses of Sexual Difference in Early Modern Europe* Chicago
W.K. Ferguson 1948 Ferguson, Wallace K. 1948 *The Renaissance in Historical Thought: Five Centuries of Interpretation* Cambridge, Mass
Fichter 1982 Fichter, Andrew 1982 *Poets Historical: Dynastic Epic in the Renaissance* New Haven
Ficino ed 1964–70 Ficino, Marsilio 1964–70 *Théologie platonicienne de l'immortalité des âmes* tr and ed Raymond Marcel. 3 vols. Paris
Ficino ed 1981 —— 1981 *Marsilio Ficino and the Phaedran Charioteer* tr and ed Michael J.B. Allen. Berkeley and Los Angeles
Ficino ed 1985 —— 1985 *Commentary on Plato's 'Symposium' on Love* tr Sears Reynolds Jayne. Dallas
Firth 1979 Firth, Katharine R. 1979 *The Apocalyptic Tradition in Reformation Britain 1530–1645* Oxford
Fitzgeffrey 1601 Fitzgeffrey, Charles 1601 *Affaniae, sive Epigrammatum libri tres, eiusdem cenotaphia* Oxford
Fletcher 1964 Fletcher, Angus 1964 *Allegory: The Theory of a Symbolic Mode* Ithaca, NY
Fletcher 1971 —— 1971 *The Prophetic Moment: An Essay on Spenser* Chicago
Fletcher and Fletcher ed 1908–9 Fletcher, Giles, and Phineas Fletcher 1908–9 *Poetical Works* ed Frederick S. Boas. 2 vols. Cambridge
Flinker 1980 Flinker, Noam 1980 'Father-Daughter Incest in *Paradise Lost*' *MQ* 14:116–22
Florio 1591 Florio, John 1591 *Florios Second Frutes* and *Giardino di recreatione* London, rpt Amsterdam and New York 1969
Florio 1598 —— 1598 *A Worlde of Wordes, or Most Copious, and Exact Dictionarie in Italian and English* London, rpt Hildesheim and New York 1972
Florio 1611 —— 1611 *Queen Anna's New World of Words* London, rpt Menston, Yorks 1968
Floris ed 1927 *Floris and Blancheflour* 1927 ed A.B. Taylor. Oxford
Forster 1967 Forster, Leonard 1967 'The Translator of the "Theatre for Worldlings"' *ES* 48:27–34
Forster 1969 —— 1969 *The Icy Fire: Five Studies in European Petrarchism* Cambridge
Fowler 1959 Fowler, Alastair [A.D.S.] 1959 'Six Knights at Castle Joyous' *SP* 56:583–99
Fowler 1960a —— 1960a 'Emblems of Temperance in *The Faerie Queene*, Book II' *RES* ns 11:143–9
Fowler 1960b —— 1960b 'The River Guyon' *MLN* 75:289–92
Fowler 1960–1 —— 1960–1 'The Image of Mortality: *The Faerie Queene*, II, i-ii' *HLQ* 24:91–110
Fowler 1964 —— 1964 *Spenser and the Numbers of Time* London
Fowler 1970a —— ed 1970a *Silent Poetry: Essays in Numerological Analysis* London
Fowler 1970b —— 1970b *Triumphal Forms: Structural Patterns in Elizabethan Poetry* Cambridge
Fowler 1973 —— 1973 'Emanations of Glory: Neoplatonic Order in Spenser's *Faerie Queen*' In Kennedy and Reither 1973:53–82
Fowler 1975 —— 1975 *Conceitful Thought: The Interpretation of English Renaissance Poems* Edinburgh
Fowler 1982 —— 1982 *Kinds of Literature: An Introduction to the Theory of Genres and Modes* Cambridge, Mass
Fowler and Leslie 1981 —— and Michael Leslie 1981 'Drummond's Copy of *The Faerie Queene*' *TLS* (17 July): 821–2
E.B. Fowler 1921 Fowler, Earle Broadus 1921 *Spenser and the Courts of Love* Menasha, Wis, rpt as *Spenser and the System of Courtly Love* Louisville 1935
Foxe 1563 Foxe, John 1563 *Actes and Monuments* London
Foxe ed 1843–9 —— 1843–9 *Acts and Monuments* ed George Townsend. 8 vols. London
Fraser 1969 Fraser, Antonia 1969 *Mary, Queen of Scots* London
Fraunce 1588 Fraunce, Abraham 1588 *Insignium, armorum, emblematum, hieroglyphicorum, et symbolorum ... explicatio* London, rpt New York and London 1979
Fraunce ed 1975 —— 1975 *The Third Part of the Countesse of Pembrokes Yuychurch, Entitled 'Amintas Dale'* (1592) ed Gerald Snare. Northridge, Calif
Freake 1977 Freake, Douglas 1977 'Speech in *The Faerie Queene*: "Faire Feeling Words"' Diss Univ of Toronto
Freeman 1948 Freeman, Rosemary 1948 *English Emblem Books* London
Freeman 1970 —— 1970 *'The Faerie Queene': A Companion for Readers* London
Freud ed 1953–74 Freud, Sigmund 1953–74 *Standard Edition* tr and ed James Strachey, et al. 24 vols. London
Friedland 1937 Friedland, Louis S. 1937 'Spenser as a Fabulist' *ShAB* 12:85–108, 133–54, 197–207
Friedmann 1966 Friedmann, Anthony E. 1966 'The Diana-Acteon Episode in Ovid's *Metamorphoses* and *The Faerie Queene*' *CL* 18:289–99
Frushell and Vondersmith 1975 Frushell, Richard C., and Bernard J. Vondersmith, eds 1975 *Contemporary Thought on Edmund Spenser* Carbondale, Ill
Frye 1957 Frye, Northrop 1957 *Anatomy of Criticism* Princeton
Frye 1963 —— 1963 *Fables of Identity: Studies in Poetic Mythology* New York
Frye 1965 —— 1965 'Allegory' In *Princeton Enc*
Frye 1970 —— 1970 *The Stubborn Structure: Essays on Criticism and Society* Ithaca, NY
Frye 1976 —— 1976 *The Secular Scripture: A Study of the Structure of Romance* Cambridge, Mass
Frye 1982 —— 1982 *The Great Code: The Bible and Literature* Toronto
Fulgentius ed 1971 Fulgentius 1971 *Fulgentius the Mythographer* tr Leslie George Whitbread. Columbus, Ohio
Fuller 1662 Fuller, Thomas 1662 *The History of the Worthies of England* London
Fussell 1979 Fussell, Paul, Jr 1979 *Poetic Meter and Poetic Form* rev ed New York

Galen. See headnote
Galinsky 1972 Galinsky, G. Karl 1972 *The Herakles Theme: The Adaptations of the Hero in Literature from Homer to the Twentieth Century* Oxford
Galyon 1977 Galyon, Linda R. 1977 'Sapience in Spenser's "Hymne of Heavenly Beavtie"' *FCEMN* 3.3:9–12
Gang 1959 Gang, Theodor 1959 'Nature and Grace in *The Faerie Queene*: The Problem Reviewed' *ELH* 26:1–22
Gans 1978–9 Gans, Nathan A. 1978–9 'Archaism and Neologism in Spenser's Diction' *MP* 76:377–9
Garin 1965 Garin, Eugenio 1965 *Italian Humanism: Philosophy and Civic Life in the Renaissance* tr Peter Munz. Oxford
Garin 1969 —— 1969 *Science and Civic Life in the Italian Renaissance* tr Peter Munz. Garden City, NY
Gascoigne ed 1907–10 Gascoigne, George 1907–10 *The Complete Works* ed John W. Cunliffe. 2 vols. Cambridge
Gaskell 1972 Gaskell, Philip 1972 *A New Introduction to Bibliography* Oxford

Gasquet 1974 Gasquet, Emile 1974 *Le Courant machiavélien dans la pensée et la littérature anglaises du XVIe siècle* Paris
Geller 1972 Geller, Lila 1972 'The Acidalian Vision: Spenser's Graces in Book VI of *The Faerie Queene*' *RES* 23:267–77
Geller 1976 —— 1976 'Venus and the Three Graces: A Neoplatonic Paradigm for Book III of *The Faerie Queene*' *JEGP* 75:56–74
Geneva Bible. See Bible, Geneva
Gent 1981 Gent, Lucy 1981 *Picture and Poetry 1560–1620* Leamington Spa, Eng
George and George 1961 George, Charles H., and Katherine George 1961 *The Protestant Mind of the English Reformation 1570–1640* Princeton
Gesner 1551–8 Gesner, Conrad 1551–8 *Historiae animalium* 5 vols. Zurich
Giamatti 1966 Giamatti, A. Bartlett 1966 *The Earthly Paradise and the Renaissance Epic* Princeton
Giamatti 1968 —— 1968 'Proteus Unbound: Some Versions of the Sea God in the Renaissance' In *The Disciplines of Criticism: Esssays in Literary Theory, Interpretation, and History* ed Peter Demetz, et al, pp 437–75. New Haven, rpt in Giamatti 1984: 115–50, 161–7
Giamatti 1971 —— 1971 'Spenser: From Magic to Miracle' in H. Baker 1971:15–31, 76–80, rpt in Giamatti 1984:76–88, 155–8
Giamatti 1975 —— 1975 *Play of Double Senses: Spenser's 'Faerie Queene'* Englewood Cliffs, NJ
Giamatti 1976 —— 1976 'Primitivism and the Process of Civility in Spenser's *Faerie Queene*' In Chiappelli 1976, 1:71–82, rpt in Giamatti 1984:89–100, 158–61
Giamatti 1984 —— 1984 *Exile and Change in Renaissance Literature* New Haven
Gil 1619 Gil, Alexander 1619 *Logonomia Anglica* London, rpt Stockholm 1972, rev ed 1621 rpt Menston, Yorks 1969
Gilbert 1940 Gilbert, Allan H. 1940 *Literary Criticism: Plato to Dryden* New York
Gilbert 1941 —— 1941 'The Ladder of Lechery, *The Faerie Queene*, III, i, 45' *MLN* 56:594–7
Gilbert 1947 —— 1947 'Belphoebe's Misdeeming of Timias' *PMLA* 62:622–43
Gilbert 1948 —— 1948 'The Embleme for December in the *Shepheardes Calender*' *MLN* 63:181–2
Gimson 1962 Gimson, A[lfred] C. 1962 *An Introduction to the Pronunciation of English* London
Giraldi 1548 Giraldi, Lilio Gregorio 1548 *De deis gentium* Basel, rpt New York and London 1976
Girouard 1981 Girouard, Mark 1981 *The Return to Camelot: Chivalry and the English Gentleman* New Haven
Girouard ed 1983 —— 1983 *Robert Smythson and the Elizabethan Country House* rev ed. New Haven; first pub 1966 as *Robert Smythson and the Architecture of the Elizabethan Era*
Goldberg 1975–6 Goldberg, Jonathan 1975–6 'The Mothers in Book III of *The Faerie Queene*' *TSLL* 17:5–26
Goldberg 1981 —— 1981 *Endlesse Worke: Spenser and the Structures of Discourse* Baltimore
Goldberg 1983 —— 1983 *James I and the Politics of Literature: Jonson, Shakespeare, Donne, and Their Contemporaries* Baltimore
Golden Legend. See Voragine, Jacobus de
D.J. Gordon 1975 Gordon, D.J. 1975 '*Veritas Filia Temporis*: Hadrianus Junius and Geoffrey Whitney' In *The Renaissance Imagination* ed Stephen Orgel, pp 220–32. Berkeley and Los Angeles
G. Gordon 1946 Gordon, George 1946 'The Trojans in Britain' In *The Discipline of Letters* pp 35–58. Oxford
Gottfried 1937 Gottfried, Rudolf B. 1937 'Spenser and the Italian Myth of Locality' *SP* 34:107–25
Gray and Stanley 1983 Gray, Douglas, and E.G. Stanley, eds 1983 *Middle English Studies Presented to Norman Davis* Oxford
Gray, Thomas. See Lonsdale 1969
Graziani 1964a Graziani, René 1964a 'Elizabeth at Isis Church' *PMLA* 79:376–89
Graziani 1964b —— 1964b 'Philip II's *Impresa* and Spenser's Souldan' *JWCI* 27:322–4
Greaves 1964 Greaves, Margaret 1964 *The Blazon of Honour: A Study in Renaissance Magnanimity* London
Greenblatt 1973 Greenblatt, Stephen J. 1973 *Sir Walter Ralegh: The Renaissance Man and His Roles* New Haven
Greenblatt 1980 —— 1980 *Renaissance Self-Fashioning: From More to Shakespeare* Chicago
R. Greene ed 1881–6 Greene, Robert 1881–6 *Life and Complete Works* ed Alexander B. Grosart. 15 vols. London
R. Greene ed 1905 —— 1905 *Plays and Poems* ed J. Churton Collins. 2 vols. Oxford
Greene 1957 Greene, Thomas M. 1957 'Spenser and the Epithalamic Convention' *CL* 9:215–28
Greene 1963 —— 1963 *The Descent from Heaven: A Study in Epic Continuity* New Haven
Greene 1982 —— 1982 *The Light in Troy: Imitation and Discovery in Renaissance Poetry* New Haven
Greenfield 1981 Greenfield, Concetta Carestia 1981 *Humanist and Scholastic Poetics, 1250–1500* Lewisburg, Pa
Greenlaw 1909–10 Greenlaw, Edwin A. 1909–10 'The Influence of Machiavelli on Spenser' *MP* 7:187–202
Greenlaw 1910 —— 1910 'Spenser and the Earl of Leicester' *PMLA* 25:535–61
Greenlaw 1911 —— 1911 '*The Shepheards Calender*' *PMLA* 26:419–51
Greenlaw 1913 —— 1913 '*The Shepheards Calender*, II' *SP* 11:3–25
Greenlaw 1918 —— 1918 'Spenser's Fairy Mythology' *SP* 15:105–22
Greenlaw 1920 —— 1920 'Spenser and Lucretius' *SP* 17:439–64
Greenlaw 1932 —— 1932 *Studies in Spenser's Historical Allegory* Baltimore
Grennan 1982 Grennan, Eamon 1982 'Language and Politics: A Note on Some Metaphors in Spenser's *A View of the Present State of Ireland*' *SSt* 3:99–110
Greville ed 1939 Greville, Fulke 1939 *Poems and Dramas* ed Geoffrey Bullough. 2 vols. Edinburgh
Greville ed 1986 —— 1986 *Prose Works* ed John Gouws. Oxford
Grindal ed 1843 Grindal, Edmund 1843 *Remains* ed William Nicholson. Parker Society. Cambridge
Gross 1985 Gross, Kenneth 1985 *Spenserian Poetics: Idolatry, Iconoclasm, and Magic* Ithaca, NY
Grundy 1969 Grundy, Joan 1969 *The Spenserian Poets: A Study in Elizabethan and Jacobean Poetry* London
Guazzo ed 1925 Guazzo, Stefano 1925 *The Civile Conversation of M. Steeven Guazzo* (1581) tr George Pettie and Barth[olomew] Young, ed Edward Sullivan. 2 vols. London
Guillory 1983 Guillory, John 1983 *Poetic Authority: Spenser, Milton, and Literary History* New York

Hagstrum 1958 Hagstrum, Jean H. 1958 *The Sister Arts: The Tradition of Literary Pictorialism and English Poetry from Dryden to Gray* Chicago
Hakluyt 1589 Hakluyt, Richard 1589 *The Principall Navigations, Voiages and Discoveries of the English Nation* London
Hall 1550 Hall, Edward 1550 *The Union of the Two Noble and Illustre Famelies of Lancastre and Yorke* London, rpt Menston, Yorks 1970; ed 1809 London, rpt New York 1965
Hallam 1837–9 Hallam, Henry 1837–9 *Introduction to the Literature of Europe* 4 vols. London; rev ed in 2 vols, New York 1882
Hamer 1931 Hamer, Douglas 1931 'Spenser's Marriage' *RES* 7:271–90
Hamilton 1958a Hamilton, A.C. 1958a '"Like Race to Runne": The Parallel Structure of *The Faerie Queene*, Books I and II' *PMLA* 73:327–34
Hamilton 1958b —— 1958b 'A Theological Reading of *The Faerie Queene* Book II' *ELH* 25:155–62
Hamilton 1961a —— 1961a *The Structure of Allegory in 'The Faerie Queene'* Oxford
Hamilton 1961b —— 1961b 'The Visions of *Piers Plowman* and *The Faerie Queene*' In Nelson 1961:1–34, 169–70
Hamilton 1972a —— ed 1972a *Essential Articles for the Study of Edmund Spenser* Hamden, Conn
Hamilton 1972b —— 1972b 'Our New Poet: Spenser, "Well of

English Undefyld"' In Hamilton 1972a:488–506, rpt in Kennedy and Reither 1973:101–23
Hamilton 1977 —— 1977 *Sir Philip Sidney: A Study of His Life and Works* Cambridge
—— See also Spenser *FQ* ed 1977
Hankins 1945 Hankins, John Erskine 1945 'Spenser and the Revelation of St. John' *PMLA* 60:364–81
Hankins 1971 —— 1971 *Source and Meaning in Spenser's Allegory: A Study of 'The Faerie Queene'* Oxford
Hanning 1966 Hanning, Robert W. 1966 *The Vision of History in Early Britain: From Gildas to Geoffrey of Monmouth* New York
Hanning 1977 —— 1977 *The Individual in Twelfth-Century Romance* New Haven
Hard 1930 Hard, Frederick 1930 'Spenser's "Clothes of Arras and of Toure"' *SP* 27:162–85
Hard 1934 —— 1934 '"Princelie Pallaces": Spenser and Elizabethan Architecture' *SR* 42:293–310
Hardison 1962 Hardison, O.B., Jr 1962 *The Enduring Monument: A Study of the Idea of Praise in Renaissance Literary Theory and Practice* Chapel Hill
Hardison 1972 —— 1972 '*Amoretti* and the *Dolce Stil N[u]ovo*' *ELR* 2:208–16
Hardwick 1876 Hardwick, Charles 1876 *A History of the Articles of Religion* 3rd ed. London
Harper 1910 Harper, Carrie Anna 1910 *The Sources of the British Chronicle History in Spenser's 'Faerie Queene'* Philadelphia
Harris and Steffen 1978 Harris, Duncan, and Nancy L. Steffen 1978 'The Other Side of the Garden: An Interpretive Comparison of Chaucer's *Book of the Duchess* and Spenser's *Daphnaida*' *JMRS* 8:17–36
Harris 1965 Harris, William O. 1965 *Skelton's 'Magnyfycence' and the Cardinal Virtue Tradition* Chapel Hill
J.S. Harrison 1903 Harrison, John Smith 1903 *Platonism in English Poetry of the Sixteenth and Seventeenth Centuries* New York
T.P. Harrison 1930 Harrison, Thomas Perrin, Jr 1930 '*The Faerie Queene* and the *Diana*' *PQ* 9:51–6
Harvey 1592 Harvey, Gabriel 1592 *Foure Letters* and *Certaine Sonnets* London, rpt Menston, Yorks 1969; ed G.B. Harrison, London 1922
Harvey 1593 —— 1593 *Pierces Supererogation* London, rpt Menston, Yorks 1970
Harvey ed 1884 —— 1884 *Letter-Book A.D. 1573–1580* ed Edward John Long Scott. Camden Society. London
Harvey ed 1913 —— 1913 *Marginalia* ed G.C. Moore Smith. Stratford-upon-Avon
Harvey ed 1945 —— 1945 *Ciceronianus* tr Clarence A. Forbes, ed Harold S. Wilson. Lincoln, Nebr
Hawes ed 1928 Hawes, Stephen 1928 *The Pastime of Pleasure* ed William Edward Mead. EETS os 173. London
Hawkins 1961 Hawkins, Sherman 1961 'Mutabilitie and the Cycle of the Months' In Nelson 1961:76–102, 174–8
Hazlitt ed 1930–4 Hazlitt, William 1930–4 *Complete Works* ed P.P. Howe. 21 vols. London
Heffner 1933 Heffner, Ray 1933 'Did Spenser Die in Poverty?' *MLN* 48:221–6
Helgerson 1976 Helgerson, Richard 1976 *The Elizabethan Prodigals* Berkeley and Los Angeles
Helgerson 1978 —— 1978 'The New Poet Presents Himself: Spenser and the Idea of a Literary Career' *PMLA* 93:893–911
Helgerson 1979 —— 1979 'The Elizabethan Laureate: Self-Presentation and the Literary System' *ELH* 46:193–220
Helgerson 1983 —— 1983 *Self-Crowned Laureates: Spenser, Jonson, Milton, and the Literary System* Berkeley and Los Angeles
Heninger 1959 Heninger, S.K., Jr 1959 'The Orgoglio Episode in *The Faerie Queene*' *ELH* 26:171–87
Heninger 1960 —— 1960 *A Handbook of Renaissance Meteorology* Durham, NC
Heninger 1961 —— 1961 'Some Renaissance Versions of the Pythagorean Tetrad' *SRen* 8:7–35
Heninger 1962 —— 1962 'The Implications of Form for *The Shepheardes Calender*' *SRen* 9:309–21
Heninger 1974 —— 1974 *Touches of Sweet Harmony: Pythagorean Cosmology and Renaissance Poetics* San Marino, Calif
Heninger 1977 —— 1977 *The Cosmographical Glass: Renaissance Diagrams of the Universe* San Marino, Calif
Heninger 1988 —— 1988 'The Typographical Layout of Spenser's *Shepheardes Calender*' In *Word and Visual Imagination* ed Karl Josef Höltgen, et al., pp 33–71 Erlangen
Henkel and Schöne 1967 Henkel, Arthur, and Albrecht Schöne 1967 *Emblemata: Handbuch zur Sinnbildkunst des XVI. und XVII. Jahrhunderts* Supplement 1976. Stuttgart
Henley 1928 Henley, Pauline 1928 *Spenser in Ireland* Cork
Henryson ed 1981 Henryson, Robert 1981 *Poems* ed Denton Fox. Oxford
Herbert ed 1977 Herbert, Mary, Countess of Pembroke 1977 *'The Triumph of Death' and Other Unpublished and Uncollected Poems by Mary Sidney, Countess of Pembroke, 1561–1621* ed G[ary] F. Waller. Salzburg
Herendeen 1981a Herendeen, Wyman H. 1981a 'The Rhetoric of Rivers: The River and the Pursuit of Knowledge' *SP* 78:107–27
Herendeen 1981b —— 1981b 'Spenserian Specifics: Spenser's Appropriation of a Renaissance *Topos*' *M&H* ns 10:159–88
Herendeen 1986 —— 1986 *From Landscape to Literature: The River and the Myth of Geography* Pittsburgh
Hermes Trismegistus ed 1924–36 Hermes Trismegistus 1924–36 *Hermetica* tr and ed Walter Scott. 4 vols. Oxford
Herrick 1930 Herrick, Marvin Theodore 1930 *The 'Poetics' of Aristotle in England* New Haven
Hesiod ed 1966 Hesiod 1966 *Theogony* ed M.L. West. Oxford
Hesiod. For *The Homeric Hymns* and *Homerica*, see headnote
Hibbard 1982 Hibbard, G.R., ed 1982 *The Elizabethan Theatre* VIII Port Credit, Ont
Hieatt 1960 Hieatt, A. Kent 1960 *Short Time's Endless Monument: The Symbolism of the Numbers in Edmund Spenser's 'Epithalamion'* New York
Hieatt 1961 —— 1961 'The Daughters of Horus: Order in the Stanzas of *Epithalamion*' In Nelson 1961:103–21, 178–9
Hieatt 1962 —— 1962 'Scudamour's Practice of *Maistrye* upon Amoret' *PMLA* 77:509–10
Hieatt 1973a —— 1973a 'A Numerical Key for Spenser's *Amoretti* and Guyon in the House of Mammon' *YES* 3:14–27
Hieatt 1973b —— 1973b 'Three Fearful Symmetries and the Meaning of *Faerie Queene* II' In Kennedy and Reither 1973:19–52
Hieatt 1975a —— 1975a *Chaucer, Spenser, Milton: Mythopoeic Continuities and Transformations* Montreal and London
Hieatt 1975b —— 1975b 'A Spenser to Structure Our Myths (Medina, Phaedria, Proserpina, Acrasia, Venus, Isis)' In Frushell and Vondersmith 1975:99–120, 228–30
Hieatt 1983 —— 1983 'The Genesis of Shakespeare's *Sonnets*: Spenser's *Ruines of Rome: by Bellay*' *PMLA* 98:800–14
Hind 1952–64 Hind, Arthur M. 1952–64 *Engraving in England in the Sixteenth and Seventeenth Centuries: A Descriptive Catalogue with Introductions* 3 vols. Cambridge
Hinks 1939 Hinks, Roger 1939 *Myth and Allegory in Ancient Art* London
Holahan 1976 Holahan, Michael 1976 '*Iamque opus exegi*: Ovid's Changes and Spenser's Brief Epic of Mutability' *ELR* 6:244–70
Holinshed ed 1807–8 Holinshed, Raphael 1807–8 *Chronicles* [ed Henry Ellis, et al]. 6 vols. London
Hollander 1961 Hollander, John 1961 *The Untuning of the Sky: Ideas of Music in English Poetry, 1500–1700* Princeton
Hollander 1971 —— 1971 'Spenser and the Mingled Measure' *ELR* 1:226–38
Hollander 1975 —— 1975 *Vision and Resonance: Two Senses of Poetic Form* New York. 2nd ed 1985
Hollander 1981a —— 1981a *The Figure of Echo: A Mode of Allusion in Milton and After* Berkeley and Los Angeles
Hollander 1981b —— 1981b *Rhyme's Reason: A Guide to English Verse* New Haven
Homer ed 1967 Homer 1967 *Chapman's Homer* ed Allardyce Nicoll. Rev ed. 2 vols. Princeton

Homer. See also headnote

Homilies See Church of England

Honig 1959 Honig, Edwin 1959 *Dark Conceit: The Making of Allegory* Evanston

Hooker ed 1888 Hooker, Richard 1888 *Works* ed John Keble. 7th ed, rev R.W. Church and F. Paget. 3 vols. Oxford

Hooker ed 1977– —— 1977– *Works* ed W. Speed Hill, et al. Cambridge, Mass and Binghamton, NY

Hooper ed 1843 Hooper, John 1843 *Early Writings* ed Samuel Carr. Parker Society. Cambridge

Hoopes 1954 Hoopes, Robert 1954 '"God Guide Thee, *Guyon*": Nature and Grace Reconciled in *The Faerie Queene*, Book II' *RES* ns 5:14–24

Hopper 1938 Hopper, Vincent Foster 1938 *Medieval Number Symbolism: Its Sources, Meaning, and Influence on Thought and Expression* New York

Hopper 1940 —— 1940 'Spenser's "House of Temperance"' *PMLA* 55:958–67

Horace. See headnote

Horapollo ed 1950 Horapollo 1950 *Hieroglyphics* tr George Boas. New York

Horton 1978 Horton, Ronald Arthur 1978 *The Unity of 'The Faerie Queene'* Athens, Ga

Hough 1962 Hough, Graham 1962 *A Preface to 'The Faerie Queene'* London

Hough 1964 —— 1964 *The First Commentary on 'The Faerie Queene'* (by John Dixon) Privately pub

Howell 1956 Howell, Wilbur Samuel 1956 *Logic and Rhetoric in England, 1500–1700* Princeton

Hoy 1980 Hoy, Cyrus, ed 1980 *Introductions, Notes, and Commentaries to Texts in 'The Dramatic Works of Thomas Dekker' ed by Fredson Bowers*. 4 vols. Cambridge

Hudson 1935 Hudson, Hoyt H. 1935 'Penelope Devereux as Sidney's Stella' *Huntington Lib Bul* 7:89–129

Hughes 1925–6 Hughes, Merritt Y. 1925–6 'Spenser's Debt to the Greek Romances' *MP* 23:67–76

Hughes 1926 —— 1926 'Burton on Spenser' *PMLA* 41:545–67

Hughes 1929 —— 1929 *Virgil and Spenser* Berkeley

Hughes 1943 —— 1943 'Spenser's Acrasia and the Circe of the Renaissance' *JHI* 4:381–99

Hughes, et al 1970– —— et al, eds 1970– *A Variorum Commentary on the Poems of John Milton* New York

Huizinga ed 1924 Huizinga, J[ohan] 1924 *The Waning of the Middle Ages* tr F. Hopman. London

Hulbert 1936–7 Hulbert, Viola Blackburn 1936–7 'Spenser's Relation to Certain Documents on Ireland' *MP* 34:345–53

Hull 1982 Hull, Suzanne W. 1982 *Chaste, Silent, and Obedient: English Books for Women 1475–1640* San Marino, Calif

Hulse 1981 Hulse, Clark 1981 *Metamorphic Verse: The Elizabethan Minor Epic* Princeton

Hume 1984 Hume, Anthea 1984 *Edmund Spenser: Protestant Poet* Cambridge

Hunt 1844 Hunt, Leigh 1844 *Imagination and Fancy, or Selections from the English Poets* London

G.K. Hunter 1962 Hunter, G.K. 1962 *John Lyly: The Humanist as Courtier* London

G.K. Hunter 1973 —— 1973 'Spenser's *Amoretti* and the English Sonnet Tradition' In Kennedy and Reither 1973:124–44

G.K. Hunter 1975 —— 1975 '"Unity" and Numbers in Spenser's *Amoretti*' *YES* 5:39–45

W.B. Hunter 1946 Hunter, William B., Jr 1946 'Eve's Demonic Dream' *ELH* 13:255–65

Hurd 1762 Hurd, Richard 1762 *Letters on Chivalry and Romance* London, rpt New York 1971; ed Hoyt Trowbridge, Los Angeles 1963

Hyde 1983 Hyde, Thomas 1983 'Vision, Poetry, and Authority in Spenser' *ELR* 13:127–45

Hyde 1986 —— 1986 *The Poetic Theology of Love: Cupid in Renaissance Literature* Newark, Del

IJsewijn 1977 IJsewijn, Jozef 1977 *Companion to Neo-Latin Studies* Amsterdam

Ingham 1970–1 Ingham, Patricia 1970–1 'Spenser's Use of Dialect' *ELN* 8:164–8

Iredale 1966 Iredale, Roger O. 1966 'Giants and Tyrants in Book Five of *The Faerie Queene*' *RES* ns 17:373–81

Jackson 1964 Jackson, W.T.H. 1964 'Allegory and Allegorization' *RS* 32:161–75

Jacobus de Voragine. See Voragine, Jacobus de

James I ed 1955–8 James I of England 1955–8 *Poems* ed James Craigie. STS 3rd ser 22, 26. Edinburgh

James VI ed 1597 James VI of Scotland 1597 *Daemonologie* Edinburgh, rpt New York and Amsterdam 1969; ed G.B. Harrison, Edinburgh 1966

James 1905 James, Montague Rhodes 1905 *A Descriptive Catalogue of the Manuscripts in the Library of Pembroke College, Cambridge* Cambridge

Jardine 1974a Jardine, Lisa 1974a *Francis Bacon: Discovery and the Art of Discourse* Cambridge

Jardine 1974b —— 1974b 'The Place of Dialectic Teaching in Sixteenth-Century Cambridge' *SRen* 21:31–62

Javitch 1978 Javitch, Daniel 1978 *Poetry and Courtliness in Renaissance England* Princeton

Jayne 1952 Jayne, Sears 1952 'Ficino and the Platonism of the English Renaissance' *CL* 4:214–38

Jenkins 1932 Jenkins, Raymond 1932 'Spenser and the Clerkship in Munster' *PMLA* 47:109–21

Jenkins 1937 —— 1937 'Spenser with Lord Grey in Ireland' *PMLA* 52:338–53

Jenkins 1938 —— 1938 'Spenser: The Uncertain Years 1584–1589' *PMLA* 53:350–62

Jewel ed 1963 Jewel, John 1963 *An Apology of the Church of England* ed J.E. Booty. Ithaca, NY

Johnson 1933 Johnson, Francis R. 1933 *A Critical Bibliography of the Works of Edmund Spenser Printed before 1700* Baltimore

Johnson 1937 —— 1937 *Astronomical Thought in Renaissance England: A Study of the English Scientific Writings from 1500 to 1645* Baltimore

P. Johnson 1972 Johnson, Paula 1972 *Form and Transformation in Music and Poetry of the English Renaissance* New Haven

W.C. Johnson 1974 Johnson, William C. 1974 'Spenser's *Amoretti* and the Art of the Liturgy' *SEL* 14:47–61

W.C. Johnson 1976 —— 1976 '"Sacred Rites" and Prayer-Book Echoes in Spenser's *Epithalamion*' *Ren&R* 12:49–54

Johnston 1964 Johnston, Arthur 1964 *Enchanted Ground: The Study of Medieval Romance in the Eighteenth Century* London

Jones, et al 1978 Jones, Cheslyn, et al, eds 1978 *The Study of Liturgy* London

H.S.V. Jones 1919 Jones, H.S.V. 1919 *Spenser's Defense of Lord Grey* (*ISLL* 5.3) Urbana

H.S.V. Jones 1926 —— 1926 'The *Faerie Queene* and the Mediaeval Aristotelian Tradition' *JEGP* 25:283–98

H.S.V. Jones 1930 —— 1930 *A Spenser Handbook* New York

R.F. Jones 1953 Jones, Richard Foster 1953 *The Triumph of the English Language* Stanford

Jonson ed 1925–52 Jonson, Ben 1925–52 *Ben Jonson [Works]* ed C.H. Herford, Percy Simpson, and Evelyn Simpson. 11 vols. Oxford

Jordan 1977 Jordan, Richard Douglas 1977 'Una among the Satyrs: *The Faerie Queene*, 1.6' *MLQ* 38:123–31

Jordan 1980 —— 1980 '*The Faerie Queene* II ix 22: The Missing Link' *RES* ns 31:436–40

Joseph 1947 Joseph, Sister Miriam 1947 *Shakespeare's Use of the Arts of Language* New York, rpt as *Rhetoric in Shakespeare's Time* New York 1962

Joyce 1878 Joyce, P[atrick] W. 1878 'Spenser's Irish Rivers' *Fraser's* ns 17:315–33, rpt in *The Wonders of Ireland and Other Papers on Irish Subjects* London 1911

Judson 1932 Judson, Alexander Corbin 1932 'Spenser's Theory of Courtesy' *PMLA* 47:122–36

Judson 1933 —— 1933 *Spenser in Southern Ireland* Bloomington

Judson 1934 —— 1934 *A Biographical Sketch of John Young, Bishop of Rochester, with Emphasis on His Relations with Edmund Spenser* Bloomington

Judson 1945 —— 1945 *The Life of Edmund Spenser* Baltimore

Judson 1947 —— 1947 'Spenser and the Munster Officials' *SP* 44:157–73

Jung 1953–79 Jung, Carl G. 1953–79 *Collected Works* tr R.F.C. Hull, et al, ed Herbert Read, et al. 17 vols. Princeton

Junius 1565 Junius, Hadrianus 1565 *Emblemata* Antwerp, rpt Menston, Yorks 1972

Jusserand 1905–6 Jusserand, J.J. 1905–6 'Spenser's "Twelve Private Morall Vertues as Aristotle Hath Devised"' *MP* 3:373–83

Kahin 1941 Kahin, Helen Andrews 1941 'Spenser and the School of Alanus' *ELH* 8:257–72

Kalender ed 1892 *The Kalender of Shepherdes* (1506) 1892 ed H. Oskar Sommer. London

Kane 1983 Kane, Sean 1983 'Spenserian Ecology' *ELH* 50:461–83

Kane 1989 —— 1989 *Spenser's Moral Allegory* Toronto

Kantorowicz 1957 Kantorowicz, Ernst H. 1957 *The King's Two Bodies: A Study in Mediaeval Political Theology* Princeton

Kaske 1969 Kaske, Carol V. 1969 'The Dragon's Spark and Sting and the Structure of Red Cross's Dragon-Fight: *The Faerie Queene*, I xi-xii' *SP* 66:609–38

Kaske 1975 —— 1975 'Spenser's Pluralistic Universe: The View from the Mount of Contemplation (F.Q. I. x)' In Frushell and Vondersmith 1975:121–49, 230–3

Kaske 1976 —— 1976 'The Bacchus Who Wouldn't Wash: *Faerie Queene* II i-ii' *RenQ* 29:195–209

Kaske 1977 —— 1977 'Another Liturgical Dimension of "Amoretti" 68' *N&Q* 222:518–19

Kaske 1978 —— 1978 'Spenser's *Amoretti and Epithalamion* of 1595: Structure, Genre, and Numerology' *ELR* 8:271–95

Kaske 1979 —— 1979 '"Religious Reuerence Doth Buriall Teene": Christian and Pagan in *The Faerie Queene*, II. i-ii' *RES* ns 30:129–43

Keats ed 1978 Keats, John 1978 *Complete Poems* ed Jack Stillinger. Cambridge, Mass; rev ed 1982

Keightley 1855 Keightley, Thomas attrib [=Hannah Lawrance] 1855 'Edmund Spenser, His Life and Poetry' *BQR* 22:368–412

Kelly 1970 Kelly, Henry Ansgar 1970 *Divine Providence in the England of Shakespeare's Histories* Cambridge, Mass

Kelso 1929 Kelso, Ruth 1929 *The Doctrine of the English Gentleman in the Sixteenth Century* Urbana

Kelso 1956 —— 1956 *Doctrine for the Lady of the Renaissance* Urbana, 2nd ed 1978

Kendrick 1950 Kendrick, T[homas] D. 1950 *British Antiquity* London

G.A. Kennedy 1980 Kennedy, George A. 1980 *Classical Rhetoric and Its Christian and Secular Tradition from Ancient to Modern Times* Chapel Hill

J.M. Kennedy 1980 Kennedy, Judith M. 1980 'The Final Emblem of *The Shepheardes Calender*' *SSt* 1:95–106

Kennedy and Reither 1973 Kennedy, Judith M., and James A. Reither, eds 1973 *A Theatre for Spenserians* Toronto

W.J. Kennedy 1973 Kennedy, William J. 1973 'Rhetoric, Allegory, and Dramatic Modality in Spenser's Fradubio Episode' *ELR* 3:351–68

W.J. Kennedy 1978 —— 1978 *Rhetorical Norms in Renaissance Literature* New Haven

Kermode 1960 Kermode, Frank 1960 'The Cave of Mammon' In Brown and Harris 1960:151–73, rpt in Kermode 1971:60–83

Kermode 1964–5 —— 1964–5 '*The Faerie Queene*, I and V' *BJRL* 47:123–50, rpt in Kermode 1971:33–59

Kermode 1971 —— 1971 *Shakespeare, Spenser, Donne: Renaissance Essays* London

King 1982 King, John N. 1982 *English Reformation Literature: The Tudor Origins of the Protestant Tradition* Princeton

King 1985 —— 1985 'Was Spenser a Puritan?' *SSt* 6:1–31

King 1986 —— 1986 'Spenser's *Shepheardes Calender* and Protestant Pastoral Satire' In Lewalski 1986:369–98

Kipling 1977a Kipling, Gordon 1977a *The Triumph of Honour: Burgundian Origins of the Elizabethan Renaissance* The Hague

Kipling 1977b —— 1977b 'Triumphal Drama: Form in English Civic Pageantry' *RenD* ns 8:37–56

Klein 1973 Klein, Joan Larsen 1973 'The Anatomy of Fortune in Spenser's *Faerie Queene*' *AnM* 14:74–95

Kleinbaum 1983 Kleinbaum, Abby Wettan 1983 *The War against the Amazons* New York

Knight 1970 Knight, W. Nicholas 1970 'The Narrative Unity of Book V of *The Faerie Queene*: "That Part of Justice Which Is Equity"' *RES* ns 21:267–94

Knox ed 1927 Knox, John 1927 'The First Blast of the Trumpet against the Monstrous Regiment of Women' (1558) In *A Miscellany of Tracts and Pamphlets* ed A.C. Ward, pp 30–88. Oxford

Kocher 1953 Kocher, Paul H. 1953 *Science and Religion in Elizabethan England* San Marino, Calif

Kostić 1959a Kostić, Veselin 1959a 'Spenser and the Bembian Linguistic Theory' *EM* 10:43–60

Kostić 1959b —— 1959b 'Spenser's *Amoretti* and Tasso's Lyrical Poetry' *RMS* 3:51–77

Kostić 1969 —— 1969 *Spenser's Sources in Italian Poetry* Belgrade

Kouwenhoven 1983 Kouwenhoven, Jan Karel 1983 *Apparent Narrative as Thematic Metaphor: The Organization of 'The Faerie Queene'* Oxford

Krieg 1985 Krieg, Joann Peck 1985 'The Transmogrification of Faerie Land into Prairie Land' *JAS* 19:199–223

Kristeller 1943 Kristeller, Paul Oskar 1943 *The Philosophy of Marsilio Ficino* tr Virginia Conant. New York

Kristeller 1955 —— 1955 *Renaissance Thought: The Classic, Scholastic, and Humanist Strains* New York

Kristeller 1956 —— 1956 'Humanism and Scholasticism in the Italian Renaissance' In *Studies in Renaissance Thought and Letters* pp 553–83. Rome

Kristeller 1964 —— 1964 *Eight Philosophers of the Italian Renaissance* Stanford

Kristeller 1974 —— 1974 'Thomism and the Italian Thought of the Renaissance' In *Medieval Aspects of Renaissance Learning* tr and ed Edward P. Mahoney, pp 29–91. Durham, NC

Kristeller 1979 —— 1979 *Renaissance Thought and Its Sources* ed Michael Mooney. New York

Kristeller, et al 1948 —— et al, eds 1948 *The Renaissance Philosophy of Man* Chicago

La Perrière 1539 La Perrière, Guillaume de 1539 *Le Theatre des bons engins* Paris, rpt Gainesville, Fla 1964, Menston, Yorks 1973

La Primaudaye ed 1586 La Primaudaye, Pierre de 1586 *The French Academie* tr Thomas Bowes. London

Lake 1982 Lake, Peter 1982 *Moderate Puritans and the Elizabethan Church* Cambridge

Lamb and Lamb ed 1935 Lamb, Charles, and Mary Lamb 1935 *Letters* ed E.V. Lucas. 3 vols. London

Lamb 1981 Lamb, Mary Ellen 1981 'The Myth of the Countess of Pembroke: The Dramatic Circle' *YES* 11:194–202

Lamb 1982 —— 1982 'The Countess of Pembroke's Patronage' *ELR* 12:162–79

Langland ed 1975 Langland, William 1975 *Piers Plowman: The B Version* ed George Kane and E. Talbot Donaldson. London

Lanham 1968 Lanham, Richard A. 1968 *A Handlist of Rhetorical Terms* Berkeley and Los Angeles

Lapide 1614–45 Lapide, Cornelius a (van den Steen) 1614–45 *Commentaria in scripturam sacram* Antwerp

Latham 1930 Latham, Minor White 1930 *The Elizabethan Fairies: The Fairies of Folklore, and the Fairies of Shakespeare* New York

Latimer ed 1844–5 Latimer, Hugh 1844–5 *Works* ed George Elwes Corrie. 2 vols. Parker Society. Cambridge

Lawlor 1966 Lawlor, John, ed 1966 *Patterns of Love and Courtesy* London

Leland ed 1907–10 Leland, John 1907–10 *The Itinerary ... 1535–1543* ed Lucy Toulmin Smith. 5 vols. London

Lemmi 1928 Lemmi, Charles W. 1928 'The Influence of Trissino on *The Faerie Queene*' *PQ* 7:220–3

Lemmi 1929 —— 1929 'The Symbolism of the Classical Episodes in *The Faerie Queene*' *PQ* 8:270–87

Lerner 1979 Lerner, Laurence 1979 *Love and Marriage: Literature and Its Social Context* New York

Leslie 1983 Leslie, Michael 1983 *Spenser's 'Fierce Warres and Faithfull Loves': Martial and Chivalric Symbolism in 'The Faerie Queene'* Cambridge
Levin 1969 Levin, Harry 1969 *The Myth of the Golden Age in the Renaissance* Bloomington
Levy 1967 Levy, F.J. 1967 *Tudor Historical Thought* San Marino, Calif
Lewalski 1979 Lewalski, Barbara Kiefer 1979 *Protestant Poetics and the Seventeenth-Century Religious Lyric* Princeton
Lewalski 1986 —— ed 1986 *Renaissance Genres: Essays on Theory, History, and Interpretation* Cambridge, Mass
Lewis 1936 Lewis, C.S. 1936 *The Allegory of Love: A Study in Medieval Tradition* London
Lewis 1954 —— 1954 *English Literature in the Sixteenth Century, Excluding Drama* Oxford History of English Literature. Oxford
Lewis 1964 —— 1964 *The Discarded Image: An Introduction to Medieval and Renaissance Literature* Cambridge
Lewis 1966 —— 1966 *Studies in Medieval and Renaissance Literature* Cambridge
Lewis 1967 —— 1967 *Spenser's Images of Life* ed Alastair Fowler. Cambridge
Library CC *Library of Christian Classics* 1954–69. 25 vols. Philadelphia
Lodge ed 1883 Lodge, Thomas 1883 *Complete Works* ed Edmund W. Gosse. 4 vols. Glasgow
Loeb Classical Library. See headnote
Loewenstein 1984 Loewenstein, Joseph 1984 *Responsive Readings: Versions of Echo in Pastoral, Epic, and the Jonsonian Masque* New Haven
Loewenstein 1986 —— 1986 'Echo's Ring: Orpheus and Spenser's Career' *ELR* 16:287–302
Logan and Teskey 1989 Logan, George M., and Gordon Teskey, eds 1989 *Unfolded Tales: Essays on Renaissance Romance* Ithaca, NY
Long 1916 Long, Percy W. 1916 'Spenser and the Bishop of Rochester' *PMLA* 31:713–35
Lonsdale 1969 Lonsdale, Roger, ed 1969 *The Poems of Thomas Gray, William Collins, Oliver Goldsmith* London
Loomis 1959 Loomis, Roger Sherman, ed 1959 *Arthurian Literature in the Middle Ages: A Collaborative History* Oxford
Loomis 1963 —— 1963 *The Development of Arthurian Romance* London
de Lorris and de Meun ed 1962 de Lorris, Guillaume, and Jean de Meun 1962 *The Romance of the Rose* tr Harry W. Robbins. New York
de Lorris and de Meun ed 1965–70 —— 1965–70 *Le Roman de la Rose* ed Félix Lecoy. 3 vols. Paris
de Lorris and de Meun ed 1971 —— 1971 *The Romance of the Rose* tr Charles Dahlberg. Princeton
Lotspeich 1932 Lotspeich, Henry Gibbons 1932 *Classical Mythology in the Poetry of Edmund Spenser* Princeton
Lotspeich 1935 —— 1935 'Spenser's *Virgil's Gnat* and Its Latin Original' *ELH* 2:235–41
Lovejoy and Boas 1935 Lovejoy, Arthur O., and George Boas 1935 *A Documentary History of Primitivism and Related Ideas in Antiquity* Vol 1: *Primitivism and Related Ideas in Antiquity* Baltimore
Lubac 1959–64 Lubac, Henri de 1959–64 *Exégèse médiévale: Les Quatre Sens de l'Ecriture* 3 vols. Paris
Luborsky 1980 Luborsky, Ruth Samson 1980 'The Allusive Presentation of *The Shepheardes Calender*' *SSt* 1:29–67
Luborsky 1981 —— 1981 'The Illustrations to *The Shepheardes Calender*' *SSt* 2:3–53
Lucian. See headnote
Lucretius. See headnote
Luther ed 1883–1987 Luther, Martin 1883–1987 *Werke* 60 vols. 3 suppl. Weimar
Luther ed 1958–75 —— 1958–75 *Works* ed Jaroslav Pelikan, et al. 56 vols. St Louis
Lyte, Henry. See Dodoens ed 1578
Lytle and Orgel 1981 Lytle, Guy Fitch, and Stephen Orgel, eds 1981 *Patronage in the Renaissance* Princeton
I.G. MacCaffrey 1976 MacCaffrey, Isabel G. 1976 *Spenser's Allegory: The Anatomy of Imagination* Princeton
W.T. MacCaffrey 1961 MacCaffrey, Wallace T. 1961 'Place and Patronage in Elizabethan Politics' In Bindoff, et al 1961:95–126
W.T. MacCaffrey 1981 —— 1981 *Queen Elizabeth and the Making of Policy, 1572–1588* Princeton
MacCarthy-Morrogh 1986 MacCarthy-Morrogh, Michael 1986 *The Munster Plantation: English Migration to Southern Ireland 1583–1641* Oxford
McConica 1965 McConica, James Kelsey 1965 *English Humanists and Reformation Politics under Henry VIII and Edward VI* Oxford
McElderry 1932 McElderry, B.R., Jr 1932 'Archaism and Innovation in Spenser's Poetic Diction' *PMLA* 47:144–70
MacIntyre 1966 MacIntyre, Jean 1966 'Spenser's Herculean Heroes' *HAB* 17.1:5–12
McKerrow 1927 McKerrow, Ronald B. 1927 *An Introduction to Bibliography for Literary Students* Oxford
McKisack 1971 McKisack, May 1971 *Medieval History in the Tudor Age* Oxford
MacLachlan 1980 MacLachlan, Hugh 1980 'The "carelesse heauens": A Study of Revenge and Atonement in *The Faerie Queene*' *SSt* 1:135–61
MacLachlan 1983 —— 1983 'The Death of Guyon and the *Elizabethan Book of Homilies*' *SSt* 4:93–114
McLane 1961 McLane, Paul E. 1961 *Spenser's 'Shepheardes Calender': A Study in Elizabethan Allegory* Notre Dame, Ind
McLane 1973 —— 1973 'Skelton's *Colyn Cloute* and Spenser's *Shepheardes Calender*' *SP* 70:141–59
H. Maclean 1978 Maclean, Hugh 1978 '"Restlesse anguish and unquiet paine": Spenser and the Complaint, 1579–1590' In Campbell and Doyle 1978:29–47
I. Maclean 1980 Maclean, Ian 1980 *The Renaissance Notion of Woman: A Study in the Fortunes of Scholasticism and Medical Science in European Intellectual Life* Cambridge
MacLure 1961 MacLure, Millar 1961 'Nature and Art in *The Faerie Queene*' *ELH* 28:1–20
MacLure 1970 —— 1970 'Spenser' In Ricks 1970:60–81
MacLure 1973 —— 1973 'Spenser and the Ruins of Time' In Kennedy and Reither 1973:3–18
MacLure and Watt 1964 MacLure, Millar, and F.W. Watt, eds 1964 *Essays* in *English Literature from the Renaissance to the Victorian Age Presented to A.S.P. Woodhouse* Toronto
McManaway 1934 McManaway, James G. 1934 '"Occasion," *Faerie Queene* II. iv. 4–5' *MLN* 49:391–3
McNamee 1960 McNamee, Maurice B. 1960 *Honor and the Epic Hero: A Study of the Shifting Concept of Magnanimity in Philosophy and Epic Poetry* New York
McNeir 1968 McNeir, Waldo F. 1968 'The Sacrifice of Serena: *The Faerie Queene*, VI. viii. 31–51' In *Festschrift für Edgar Mertner* ed Bernhard Fabian and Ulrich Suerbaum, pp 117–56. Munich
McNeir and Provost 1975 McNeir, Waldo F., and Foster Provost, eds 1975 *Edmund Spenser: An Annotated Bibliography 1937–1972* Pittsburgh; first pub 1962 (for 1937–60)
McPeek 1936 McPeek, James A.S. 1936 'The Major Sources of Spenser's *Epithalamion*' *JEGP* 35:183–213
McPeek 1939 —— 1939 *Catullus in Strange and Distant Britain* Cambridge, Mass
MacQueen 1970 MacQueen, John 1970 *Allegory* London
Macrobius ed 1952 Macrobius 1952 *Commentary on the Dream of Scipio* tr William Harris Stahl. New York
Macrobius ed 1969 —— 1969 *Saturnalia* tr Percival Vaughan Davies. New York
Magill 1970 Magill, A.J. 1970 'Spenser's Guyon and the Mediocrity of the Elizabethan Settlement' *SP* 67:167–77
Mallette 1979 Mallette, Richard 1979 'Spenser's Portrait of the Artist in *The Shepheardes Calender* and *Colin Clouts Come Home Againe*' *SEL* 19:19–41
Malory ed 1947 Malory, Sir Thomas 1947 *Works* ed Eugène Vinaver. 3 vols. Oxford, rev ed 1967

Malory ed 1983 —— 1983 *Caxton's Malory* ed James W. Spisak. 2 vols. Berkeley and Los Angeles

Manley 1982 Manley, Lawrence 1982 'Spenser and the City: The Minor Poems' *MLQ* 43:203–27

Manley 1986 —— ed 1986 *London in the Age of Shakespeare: An Anthology* London

Manning 1984 Manning, R.J. 1984 '"Deuicefull Sights": Spenser's Emblematic Practice in *The Faerie Queene*, V. 1–3' *SSt* 5:65–89

Manning and Fowler 1976 Manning, R. John, and Alastair Fowler 1976 'The Iconography of Spenser's Occasion' *JWCI* 39:263–6

Maplet 1567 Maplet, John 1567 *A Greene Forest, or A Naturall Historie* London, rpt London 1930, Amsterdam 1970

Maresca 1979 Maresca, Thomas E. 1979 *Three English Epics: Studies of 'Troilus and Criseyde', 'The Faerie Queene', and 'Paradise Lost'* Lincoln, Nebr

Marinelli 1971 Marinelli, Peter V. 1971 *Pastoral* London

Marinelli 1987 —— 1987 *Ariosto and Boiardo: The Origins of 'Orlando Furioso'* Columbia, Mo

Markland 1963 Markland, Murray F. 1963 'A Note on Spenser and the Scottish Sonneteers' *SSL* 1:136–40

Marlowe ed 1973 Marlowe, Christopher 1973 *Complete Works* ed Fredson Bowers. 2 vols. Cambridge, rev ed 1981

Marshall 1959 Marshall, William H. 1959 'Calvin, Spenser, and the Major Sacraments' *MLN* 74:97–101

Martyr, Peter. See Vermigli, Peter Martyr ed 1583

Martz 1961 Martz, Louis L. 1961 'The *Amoretti*: "Most Goodly Temperature"' In Nelson 1961:146–68, 180

Mason 1935 Mason, John E. 1935 *Gentlefolk in the Making: Studies in the History of English Courtesy Literature and Related Topics from 1531 to 1774* Philadelphia

May 1972–3 May, Steven 1972–3 'Spenser's "Amyntas": Three Poems by Ferdinando Stanley, Lord Strange, Fifth Earl of Derby' *MP* 70:49–52

Mazzeo 1965 Mazzeo, Joseph Anthony 1965 'Castiglione's *Courtier*: The Self as a Work of Art' In *Renaissance and Revolution: Backgrounds to Seventeenth-Century English Literature* pp 131–60. New York

MED See Stratmann 1891

Melville 1850 Melville, Herman 1850 'Hawthorne and His Mosses' in *The Literary World* 17 Aug:125–7

Melville ed 1967 —— 1967 *Moby-Dick, or The Whale* ed Harrison Hayford and Hershel Parker. New York

Mercer 1962 Mercer, Eric 1962 *English Art 1553–1625* Oxford

Merriman 1973 Merriman, James Douglas 1973 *The Flower of Kings: A Study of the Arthurian Legend in England between 1485 and 1835* Lawrence, Kans

de Meun, Jean. See Lorris and de Meun

Meyer 1983 Meyer, Russell J. 1983 '"Fixt in heauens hight": Spenser, Astronomy, and the Date of the *Cantos of Mutabilitie*' *SSt* 4:115–29

A Middle-English Dictionary See Stratmann 1891

Miller 1979a Miller, David Lee 1979a 'Abandoning the Quest' *ELH* 46:173–92

Miller 1979b —— 1979b 'Authorship, Anonymity, and *The Shepheardes Calender*' *MLQ* 40:219–36

Miller 1983 —— 1983 'Spenser's Vocation, Spenser's Career' *ELH* 50:197–231

Miller 1988 —— 1988 *The Poem's Two Bodies: The Poetics of the 1590 'Faerie Queene'* Princeton

L.H. Miller 1966 Miller, Lewis H., Jr 1966 'A Secular Reading of *The Faerie Queene*, Book II' *ELH* 33:154–69

Millican 1932 Millican, Charles Bowie 1932 *Spenser and the Table Round: A Study in the Contemporaneous Background for Spenser's Use of the Arthurian Legend* Cambridge, Mass

Millican 1938–9 —— 1938–9 'Spenser's and Drant's Poetic Names for Elizabeth: Tanaquil, Gloriana, and Una' *HLQ* 2:251–63

Mills 1973 Mills, Jerry Leath 1973 'Spenser, Lodowick Bryskett, and the Mortalist Controversy: *The Faerie Queene*, II.ix.22' *PQ* 52:173–86

Mills 1976 —— 1976 'Spenser and the Numbers of History: A Note on the British and Elfin Chronicles in *The Faerie Queene*' *PQ* 55:281–7

Mills 1978 —— 1978 'Prudence, History, and the Prince in *The Faerie Queene*, Book II' *HLQ* 41:83–101

Milne 1973 Milne, Fred L. 1973 'The Doctrine of Act and Potency: A Metaphysical Ground for Interpretation of Spenser's Garden of Adonis Passages' *SP* 70:279–87

Milton ed 1953–82 Milton, John 1953–82 *Complete Prose Works* ed Don M. Wolfe, et al. 8 vols. New Haven

Milton ed 1968 —— 1968 *Poems* ed John Carey and Alastair Fowler. London

Milton Enc *A Milton Encyclopedia* 1978–83 ed William B. Hunter, Jr, et al. 9 vols. Lewisburg, Pa

Milward 1977 Milward, Peter, SJ 1977 *Religious Controversies of the Elizabethan Age: A Survey of Printed Sources* Lincoln, Nebr

Miola 1980 Miola, Robert S. 1980 'Spenser's Anacreontics: A Mythological Metaphor' *SP* 77:50–66

Mirror ed 1938 *The Mirror for Magistrates* 1938 ed Lily B. Campbell. Cambridge

Miskimin 1975 Miskimin, Alice S. 1975 *The Renaissance Chaucer* New Haven

Miskimin 1978 —— 1978 'Britomart's Crocodile and the Legends of Chastity' *JEGP* 77:17–36

Moloney 1953 Moloney, Michael F. 1953 'St. Thomas and Spenser's Virtue of Magnificence' *JEGP* 52:58–62

Montrose 1979 Montrose, Louis Adrian 1979 '"The perfecte paterne of a Poete": The Poetics of Courtship in *The Shepheardes Calender*' *TSLL* 21:34–67

Montrose 1980 —— 1980 '"Eliza, Queene of shepheardes," and the Pastoral of Power' *ELR* 10:153–82

Montrose 1983 —— 1983 'Of Gentlemen and Shepherds: The Politics of Elizabethan Pastoral Form' *ELH* 50:415–59

Moody, et al 1976 Moody, T.W., et al, eds 1976 *A New History of Ireland* vol 3: *Early Modern Ireland, 1534–1691* Oxford

Moore 1975 Moore, John W., Jr 1975 'Colin Breaks His Pipe: A Reading of the "January" Eclogue' *ELR* 5:3–24

Moorman 1967 Moorman, Charles 1967 *A Knyght There Was: The Evolution of the Knight in Literature* Lexington, Ky

More ed 1963– More, St Thomas 1963– *Complete Works* New Haven

Morris 1963 Morris, Harry 1963 *Richard Barnfield, Colin's Child* Tallahassee, Fla

'MS Notes' ed 1957 'MS Notes to Spenser's "Faerie Queene"' ed 1957 *N&Q* 202:509–15

Mueller 1959 Mueller, William R. 1959 *Spenser's Critics: Changing Currents in Literary Taste* Syracuse, NY

Mulcaster 1581 Mulcaster, Richard 1581 *Positions* London, rpt New York and Amsterdam 1971

Mulcaster 1582 —— 1582 *The First Part of the Elementarie* London, rpt Menston, Yorks 1970

Mulryan 1971 Mulryan, John 1971 'Spenser as Mythologist: A Study of the Nativities of Cupid and Christ in the *Fowre Hymnes*' *MLS* 1:13–16

Mulryan 1972 —— 1972 'The Occult Tradition and English Renaissance Literature' *BuR* 20.3:53–72

Mulryan 1974 —— 1974 'Venus, Cupid and the Italian Mythographers' *HumLov* 23:31–41

Murphy 1983 Murphy, James J., ed 1983 *Renaissance Eloquence: Studies in the Theory and Practice of Renaissance Rhetoric* Berkeley and Los Angeles

Murrin 1969 Murrin, Michael 1969 *The Veil of Allegory: Some Notes Toward a Theory of Allegorical Rhetoric in the English Renaissance* Chicago

Murrin 1980 —— 1980 *The Allegorical Epic: Essays in Its Rise and Decline* Chicago

Murtaugh 1973 Murtaugh, Daniel M. 1973 'The Garden and the Sea: The Topography of *The Faerie Queene*, III' *ELH* 40:325–38

Mustard 1914 Mustard, W.P. 1914 'Lodowick Brysket and Bernardo Tasso' *AJPh* 35:192–9

Nashe ed 1904–10 Nashe, Thomas 1904–10 *Works* ed Ronald B. McKerrow. 5 vols. London; rev ed F.P. Wilson, Oxford 1958

NCBEL See *The New Cambridge Bib of Eng Lit*

Neale 1934 Neale, J[ohn] E. 1934 *Queen Elizabeth* London

Neff 1934 Neff, Merlin L. 1934 'Spenser's Allegory of the Toll Bridge' *PQ* 13:159–67

Nellist 1963 Nellist, B. 1963 'The Allegory of Guyon's Voyage: An Interpretation' *ELH* 30:89–106

Nelson 1953 Nelson, William 1953 'A Source for Spenser's Malbecco' *MLN* 68:226–9

Nelson 1961 —— ed 1961 *Form and Convention in the Poetry of Edmund Spenser* New York

Nelson 1963 —— 1963 *The Poetry of Edmund Spenser* New York

Nelson 1973 —— 1973 'Spenser *ludens*' In Kennedy and Reither 1973:83–100

Nestrick 1975 Nestrick, William V. 1975 'Spenser and the Renaissance Mythology of Love' *Literary Monographs* 6:35–70, 161–6

Neuse 1968 Neuse, Richard 1968 'Book VI as Conclusion to *The Faerie Queene*' *ELH* 35:329–53

The New Cambridge Bibliography of English Literature (*NCBEL*) 1974–7 ed George Watson. 5 vols. Cambridge

F.J. Nichols 1979 Nichols, Fred J. 1979 *An Anthology of Neo-Latin Poetry* New Haven

J. Nichols 1823 Nichols, John 1823 *The Progresses and Public Processions of Queen Elizabeth* 3 vols. London

Nohrnberg 1976 Nohrnberg, James 1976 *The Analogy of 'The Faerie Queene'* Princeton

van der Noot ed 1569 van der Noot, Jan 1569 *A Theatre [for] Voluptuous Worldlings* London, rpt New York 1939 and Delmar, NY 1977

van der Noot ed 1953 —— 1953 *Het Bosken en Het Theatre* ed W.A.P. Smit and W. Vermeer. Amsterdam

Norbrook 1984 Norbrook, David 1984 *Poetry and Politics in the English Renaissance* London

Northrop 1968–9 Northrop, Douglas A. 1968–9 'Spenser's Defence of Elizabeth' *UTQ* 38:277–94

Northrop 1972–3 —— 1972–3 'Mercilla's Court as Parliament' *HLQ* 36:153–8

Novarr 1956 Novarr, David 1956 'Donne's "Epithalamion Made at Lincoln's Inn": Context and Date' *RES* ns 7:250–63

Nowell ed 1853 Nowell, Alexander 1853 *A Catechism* tr Thomas Norton (1570) ed G[eorge] E[lwes] Corrie. Parker Society. Cambridge

Oakeshott 1960 Oakeshott, Walter 1960 *The Queen and the Poet* London

Oakeshott 1971 —— 1971 'Carew Ralegh's Copy of Spenser' *Library* 5th ser 26:1–21

Oates 1983 Oates, Mary I. 1983 '*Fowre Hymnes*: Spenser's Retractations of Paradise' *SSt* 4:143–69

OCD See *Oxford Classical Dictionary*

O'Connell 1971 O'Connell, Michael 1971 '*Astrophel*: Spenser's Double Elegy' *SEL* 11:27–35

O'Connell 1977 —— 1977 *Mirror and Veil: The Historical Dimension of Spenser's 'Faerie Queene'* Chapel Hill

ODEP See *Oxford Dictionary of English Proverbs*

OED See *Oxford English Dictionary*

Olin 1965 Olin, John C., ed 1965 *Christian Humanism and the Reformation: Selected Writings of Erasmus* New York

Olsen 1973 Olsen, V. Norskov 1973 *John Foxe and the Elizabethan Church* Berkeley and Los Angeles

Olson 1982 Olson, Glending 1982 *Literature as Recreation in the Later Middle Ages* Ithaca, NY

Ong 1971 Ong, Walter J., SJ 1971 *Rhetoric, Romance, and Technology* Ithaca, NY

Oram 1981 Oram, William A. 1981 '*Daphnaida* and Spenser's Later Poetry' *SSt* 2:141–58

Oruch 1967 Oruch, Jack B. 1967 'Spenser, Camden, and the Poetic Marriages of Rivers' *SP* 64:606–24

Osgood 1915 Osgood, Charles Grosvenor, ed 1915 *A Concordance to the Poems of Edmund Spenser* Washington

Osgood 1917 —— 1917 'Spenser's Sapience' *SP* 14:167–77

Osgood 1919–20 —— 1919–20 'Spenser's English Rivers' *TCAAS* 23:65–108

Otis 1963 Otis, Brooks 1963 *Virgil: A Study in Civilized Poetry* Oxford

Otten 1985 Otten, Charlotte F. 1985 *Environ'd with Eternity: God, Poems, and Plants in Sixteenth and Seventeenth Century England* Lawrence, Kans

Ousby 1976 Ousby, Heather Dubrow 1976 'Donne's "Epithalamion made at Lincolnes Inne": An Alternative Interpretation' *SEL* 16:131–43

Ovid ed 1904 Ovid 1904 *Shakespeare's Ovid, Being Arthur Golding's Translation of the 'Metamorphoses'* (1567) ed W.H.D. Rouse. London, rpt London 1961

Ovid. See also headnote

Ovide moralisé *Ovide moralisé* 1915–38 ed C[ornelius] de Boer et al *Verhandelingen der Koninklijke Akademie van Wetenschappen (Afdeeling Letterkunde)* 5 vols. Nieuwe Reeks 15; 21; 30.3; 37; 43. All rpt Wiesbaden 1966–8

Oxford and Essex ed 1980 Oxford, Edward de Vere, Seventeenth Earl of, and Robert Devereaux, Second Earl of Essex 1980 *Poems* ed Steven W. May. *SP* Texts and Studies 77

The Oxford Classical Dictionary (*OCD*) 1970 ed N.G.L. Hammond and H.H. Scullard. 2nd ed. Oxford

The Oxford Dictionary of English Proverbs (*ODEP*) 1970, 3rd ed, rev F.P. Wilson. Oxford

The Oxford English Dictionary (*OED*) 1933 ed James A.H. Murray, et al. 12 vols and Supplement. Oxford. [First pub as 10 vols, 1884–1928.] Cumulative supplements, 4 vols, 1972–86. 2nd ed 1989

Ozment 1980 Ozment, Steven 1980 *The Age of Reform (1250–1550): An Intellectual and Religious History of Late Medieval and Reformation Europe* New Haven

Padelford 1913–14 Padelford, Frederick Morgan 1913–14 'Spenser and the Puritan Propaganda' *MP* 11:85–106

Padelford and O'Connor 1926 —— and Matthew O'Connor 1926 'Spenser's Use of the St. George Legend' *SP* 23:142–56

Paglia 1979 Paglia, Camille A. 1979 'The Apollonian Androgyne and the *Faerie Queene*' *ELR* 9:42–63

Paglia 1990 —— 1990 *Sexual Personae: Art and Decadence from Nefertiti to Emily Dickinson*, New Haven

Panofsky 1930 Panofsky, Erwin 1930 *Hercules am Scheidewege und andere antike Bildstoffe in der neueren Kunst* Leipzig

Panofsky 1939 —— 1939 *Studies in Iconology: Humanistic Themes in the Art of the Renaissance* Oxford

Panofsky 1955 —— 1955 *Meaning in the Visual Arts* Garden City, NY

M.P. Parker 1963 Parker, M. Pauline [M. Paolina] 1963 'Spenser and Dante' *EM* 14:27–44

P.A. Parker 1979 Parker, Patricia A. 1979 *Inescapable Romance: Studies in the Poetics of a Mode* Princeton

P.A. Parker 1987 —— 1987 'Suspended Instruments: Lyric and Power in the Bower of Bliss' In *Literary Fat Ladies: Rhetoric, Gender, Property* pp 54–66. London

Parsons 1929 Parsons, A.E. 1929 'The Trojan Legend in England: Some Instance[s] of Its Application to the Politics of the Times' *MLR* 24:253–64, 394–408

Partridge 1971 Partridge, A.C. 1971 *The Language of Renaissance Poetry: Spenser, Shakespeare, Donne, Milton* London

Patch 1950 Patch, Howard Rollin 1950 *The Other World According to Descriptions in Medieval Literature* Cambridge, Mass

Patrides 1966 Patrides, C.A. 1966 *Milton and the Christian Tradition* Oxford

Patrides and Wittreich 1984 —— and Joseph Wittreich, eds 1984 *The Apocalypse in English Renaissance Thought and Literature* Ithaca, NY

Patrologiae cursus completus, series Graeca (*PGr*) 1857–66 ed Jacques Paul Migne. 161 vols. Paris

Patrologiae cursus completus, series Latina (*PLat*) 1844–64 ed Jacques Paul Migne. 221 vols. Paris

Patterson 1984 Patterson, Annabel, ed 1984 *Roman Images* (*EIE* 1982) Baltimore

Patterson 1986 —— 1986 'Re-opening the Green Cabinet: Clément Marot and Edmund Spenser' *ELR* 16:44–70

Pattison 1948 Pattison, Bruce 1948 *Music and Poetry of the English Renaissance* London

Pausanias. See headnote

Peacham 1612 Peacham, Henry (the Younger) 1612 *Minerva Bri-*

tanna, or A Garden of Heroical Devises London, rpt Menston, Yorks 1969
Pearce 1945 Pearce, Roy Harvey 1945 'Primitivistic Ideas in the *Faerie Queene*' *JEGP* 44:139–51
Pearcy 1980–1 Pearcy, Lee T. 1980–1 'A Case of Allusion: Stanza 18 of Spenser's *Epithalamion* and Catullus 5' *CML* 1:243–54
Peele ed 1888 Peele, George 1888 *Works* ed A.H. Bullen. 2 vols. London
Peele ed 1952–70 —— 1952–70 *Life and Works* ed Charles Tyler Prouty, et al. 3 vols. New Haven
Pépin 1958 Pépin, Jean 1958 *Mythe et allégorie: Les Origines grecques et les contestations judéo-chrétiennes* Paris, rev ed 1976
Peter 1956 Peter, John 1956 *Complaint and Satire in Early English Literature* Oxford
Petigree of Slaunder 1573. See [Slander] 1573
PGr See *Patrologiae cursus completus, series Graecae*
Phillips 1964 Phillips, James Emerson, Jr 1964 *Images of a Queen: Mary Stuart in Sixteenth-Century Literature* Berkeley and Los Angeles
Phillips 1965 —— 1965 'Daniel Rogers: A Neo-Latin Link between the Pléiade and Sidney's *Areopagus*' In James Emerson Phillips, Jr, and Don Cameron Allen *Neo-Latin Poetry of the Sixteenth and Seventeenth Centuries* pp 5–28. Los Angeles
Phillips 1969–70 —— 1969–70 'Renaissance Concepts of Justice and the Structure of *The Faerie Queene*, Book v' *HLQ* 33:103–20
M.M. Phillips 1964 Phillips, Margaret Mann 1964 *The 'Adages' of Erasmus: A Study with Translations* Cambridge
Philo Judaeus. See headnote
Phoenix Nest ed 1931 *The Phoenix Nest (1593)* 1931 ed Hyder Edward Rollins. Cambridge, Mass
Pico ed 1572–3 Pico della Mirandola, Giovanni 1572–3 *Opera omnia* 2 vols. Basel, rpt Turin 1971
Pico ed 1948 —— 1948 *Oration on the Dignity of Man* In Kristeller, et al 1948:223–54
Pico ed 1965 —— 1965 *On the Dignity of Man* tr Charles Glenn Wallis, *On Being and the One* tr Paul J.W. Miller, *Heptaplus* tr Douglas Carmichael. Indianapolis
Piehler 1971 Piehler, Paul 1971 *The Visionary Landscape: A Study in Medieval Allegory* London
Pigman 1982 Pigman, G.W., III 1982 'Du Bellay's Ambivalence towards Rome in the *Antiquitez*' In Ramsey 1982:321–32
Pigman 1985 —— 1985 *Grief and English Renaissance Elegy* Cambridge
A Plaine Description of Slaunder See [Slander] 1573
PLat See *Patrologiae cursus completus, series Latina*
Plato ed 1961 Plato 1961 *Collected Dialogues* ed Edith Hamilton and Huntington Cairns. Princeton
Pliny. See headnote
Plotinus. See headnote
Plutarch ed 1970 Plutarch 1970 *De Iside et Osiride* tr and ed J. Gwyn Griffiths [Cardiff]
Plutarch. See also headnote
Poe 1836 Poe, Edgar Allan 1836 'Pinakidia 67' *Southern Literary Messenger* (August)
Poggioli 1975 Poggioli, Renato 1975 *The Oaten Flute: Essays on Pastoral Poetry and the Pastoral Ideal* Cambridge, Mass
Pollock 1980 Pollock, Zailig 1980 'Concupiscence and Intemperance in the Bower of Bliss' *SEL* 20:43–58
Pope 1926 Pope, Emma Field 1926 'Renaissance Criticism and the Diction of *The Faerie Queene*' *PMLA* 41:575–619
Porter 1958 Porter, H.C. 1958 *Reformation and Reaction in Tudor Cambridge* Cambridge
Potts 1958 Potts, Abbie Findlay 1958 *Shakespeare and 'The Faerie Queene'* Ithaca, NY
Praz 1964 Praz, Mario 1964 *Studies in Seventeenth-Century Imagery* 2nd ed. Rome
Prescott 1978 Prescott, Anne Lake 1978 *French Poets and the English Renaissance: Studies in Fame and Transformation* New Haven
Prescott 1985 —— 1985 'The Thirsty Deer and the Lord of Life: Some Contexts for *Amoretti* 67–70' *SSt* 6:33–76
Prince 1954 Prince, F.T. 1954 *The Italian Element in Milton's Verse* Oxford
Princeton Enc *Princeton Encyclopedia of Poetry and Poetics* 1974 ed Alex Preminger, et al. Enl ed. Princeton
Prudentius. See headnote
Puttenham 1589 Puttenham, George 1589 *The Arte of English Poesie* London, rpt Menston, Yorks 1968 and Amsterdam 1971; ed Gladys Doidge Willcock and Alice Walker, Cambridge 1936

Quilligan 1977 Quilligan, Maureen 1977 'Words and Sex: The Language of Allegory in the *De planctu naturae*, the *Roman de la Rose*, and Book III of *The Faerie Queene*' *Allegorica* 2:195–216
Quilligan 1979 —— 1979 *The Language of Allegory: Defining the Genre* Ithaca, NY
Quilligan 1983 —— 1983 *Milton's Spenser: The Politics of Reading* Ithaca, NY
Quinn 1966 Quinn, David Beers 1966 *The Elizabethans and the Irish* Ithaca, NY
Quinones 1972 Quinones, Ricardo J. 1972 *The Renaissance Discovery of Time* Cambridge, Mass
Quitslund 1969 Quitslund, Jon A. 1969 'Spenser's Image of Sapience' *SRen* 16:181–213

Rainolde 1563 Rainolde, Richard 1563 *A Booke Called the Foundacion of Rhetorike* London, rpt Amsterdam and New York 1969, Menston, Yorks 1972
Raleigh ed 1829 Raleigh, Sir Walter 1829 *Works* ed William Oldys and Thomas Birch. 8 vols. Oxford
Raleigh ed 1951 —— 1951 *Poems* ed Agnes M.C. Latham. London
Ramsey 1982 Ramsey, P[aul] A., ed 1982 *Rome in the Renaissance: The City and the Myth* Binghamton, NY
Randall 1896 Randall, Alice Elizabeth (Sawtelle) 1896 *The Sources of Spenser's Classical Mythology* New York
Rasmussen 1981 Rasmussen, Carl J. 1981 '"How Weak Be the Passions of Woefulness": Spenser's *Ruines of Time*' *SSt* 2:159–81
Rathborne 1937 Rathborne, Isabel E. 1937 *The Meaning of Spenser's Fairyland* New York
Real-Encyclopädie 1894– *Real-Encyclopädie der classischen Altertumswissenschaft* 1894–, ed A.F. von Pauly, rev Georg Wissowa. Stuttgart
Rebhorn 1980 Rebhorn, Wayne A. 1980 'Du Bellay's Imperial Mistress: *Les Antiquitez de Rome* as Petrarchist Sonnet Sequence' *RenQ* 33:609–22
Rees 1971 Rees, Christine 1971 'The Metamorphosis of Daphne in Sixteenth- and Seventeenth-Century English Poetry' *MLR* 66:251–63
Reichert 1963 Reichert, John F. 1963 'Formal Logic and English Renaissance Poetry' Diss Stanford Univ
Reid 1981a Reid, Robert L. 1981a 'Alma's Castle and the Symbolization of Reason in *The Faerie Queene*' *JEGP* 80:512–27
Reid 1981b —— 1981b 'Man, Woman, Child or Servant: Family Hierarchy as a Figure of Tripartite Psychology in *The Faerie Queene*' *SP* 78:370–90
Reid 1981–2 —— 1981–2 'Spenserian Psychology and the Structure of Allegory in Books 1 and 2 of *The Faerie Queene*' *MP* 79:359–75
Reiss, et al (forthcoming) Reiss, Edmund, Louise Horner Reiss, and Beverly Taylor (forthcoming) *Arthurian Legend and Literature: An Annotated Bibliography*
Remains of Old Latin See headnote
Renwick 1922a Renwick, W.L. 1922a 'The Critical Origins of Spenser's Diction' *MLR* 17:1–16
Renwick 1922b —— 1922b 'Mulcaster and Du Bellay' *MLR* 17:282–7
Renwick 1925 —— 1925 *Edmund Spenser: An Essay on Renaissance Poetry* London
Reusner 1581 Reusner, Nicolaus 1581 *Emblemata* Frankfurt am Main
R[eynolds] 1632 R[eynolds], H[enry] 1632 *Mythomystes* London, rpt Menston, Yorks 1972 with intro by Arthur F. Kinney

Reynolds, Richard. See Rainolde, Richard
Rhodiginus 1542 Rhodiginus, L. Caelius 1542 *Lectionum antiquarum libri xxx* Basel
Ricks 1970 Ricks, Christopher, ed 1970 *English Poetry and Prose, 1540–1674* London
Riedner 1908 Riedner, Wilhelm 1908 'Spensers Belesenheit: I Teil: Die Bibel und das klassische Altertum' *Münchener Beiträge zur romanischen und englischen Philologie* 38:vii-x, 1–131
R.N. Ringler 1963 Ringler, Richard N. 1963 'Spenser and the *Achilleid*' *SP* 60:174–82
R.N. Ringler 1965–6 —— 1965–6 'The Faunus Episode' *MP* 63:12–19
W.A. Ringler 1954 Ringler, William A., Jr 1954 'Spenser and Thomas Watson' *MLN* 69:484–7
Ripa 1603 Ripa, Cesare 1603 *Iconologia* Rome, rpt Hildesheim and New York 1970
Rix 1940 Rix, Herbert David 1940 *Rhetoric in Spenser's Poetry* State College, Pa
Robbins 1952 Robbins, Rossell Hope, ed 1952 *Secular Lyrics of the XIVth and XVth Centuries* Oxford
Roberts 1978 Roberts, Gareth 1978 'Three Notes on Uses of Circe by Spenser, Marlowe and Milton' *N&Q* 223:433–5
Robin 1932 Robin, P[ercy] Ansell 1932 *Animal Lore in English Literature* London
Roche 1964 Roche, Thomas P., Jr 1964 *The Kindly Flame: A Study of the Third and Fourth Books of Spenser's 'Faerie Queene'* Princeton
Roche 1974 —— 1974 'The Calendrical Structure of Petrarch's *Canzoniere*' *SP* 71:152–72
Rollinson 1971 Rollinson, Philip B. 1971 'A Generic View of Spenser's *Four Hymns*' *SP* 68:292–304
Romance of the Rose See Lorris and de Meun
Rose 1968 Rose, Mark 1968 *Heroic Love: Studies in Sidney and Spenser* Cambridge, Mass
Rose 1975 —— 1975 *Spenser's Art: A Companion to Book One of 'The Faerie Queene'* Cambridge, Mass
Rosenberg 1955 Rosenberg, Eleanor 1955 *Leicester: Patron of Letters* New York
Rossky 1958 Rossky, William 1958 'Imagination in the English Renaissance: Psychology and Poetic' *SRen* 5:49–73
Røstvig 1963 Røstvig, Maren-Sofie 1963 'The Hidden Sense: Milton and the Neoplatonic Method of Numerical Composition' in Maren-Sofie Røstvig, et al *The Hidden Sense and Other Essays* pp 1–112. Oslo
Røstvig 1969 —— 1969 '*The Shepheardes Calender*: A Structural Analysis' *RMS* 13:49–75
Røstvig 1975 —— ed 1975 *Fair Forms: Essays in English Literature from Spenser to Jane Austen* Cambridge
Røstvig 1980 —— 1980 'Canto Structure in Tasso and Spenser' *SSt* 1:177–200
Rowse 1971 Rowse, A.L. 1971 *The Elizabethan Renaissance: The Life of the Society* London
Rubel 1941 Rubel, Veré L. 1941 *Poetic Diction in the English Renaissance: From Skelton through Spenser* New York
Ruskin ed 1903–12 Ruskin, John 1903–12 *Works* ed E.T. Cook and Alexander Wedderburn. 39 vols. London

Sale 1968 Sale, Roger 1968 *Reading Spenser: An Introduction to 'The Faerie Queene'* New York
Sambucus 1564 Sambucus, Joannes 1564 *Emblemata* Antwerp, rpt Budapest 1982
Sandler 1984 Sandler, Florence 1984 '*The Faerie Queene*: An Elizabethan Apocalypse' In Patrides and Wittreich 1984:148–74
Sandys ed 1970 Sandys, George 1970 *Ovid's 'Metamorphosis' Englished, Mythologized, and Represented in Figures* (1632) ed Karl K. Hulley and Stanley T. Vandersall. Lincoln, Nebr
Sargent 1935 Sargent, Ralph M. 1935 *At the Court of Queen Elizabeth: The Life and Lyrics of Sir Edward Dyer* London, rpt as *The Life and Lyrics of Sir Edward Dyer* London 1968
Satterthwaite 1960 Satterthwaite, Alfred W. 1960 *Spenser, Ronsard, and Du Bellay: A Renaissance Comparison* Princeton
Saurat 1930 Saurat, Denis 1930 'Spenser's Ideas' and 'Spenser and the Cabala' In *Literature and Occult Tradition* tr Dorothy Bolton, pp 163–221 and 222–37. London
Sawtelle, Alice Elizabeth. See Randall 1896
Scaglione 1975 Scaglione, Aldo, ed 1975 *Francis Petrarch, Six Centuries Later: A Symposium* Chapel Hill
Schmitt 1983a Schmitt, Charles B. 1983a *Aristotle and the Renaissance* Cambridge, Mass
Schmitt 1983b —— 1983b *John Case and Aristotelianism in Renaissance England* Kingston and Montreal
Schulze 1931 Schulze, Ivan L. 1931 'Spenser's Belge Episode and the Pageants for Leicester in the Low Countries, 1585–86' *SP* 28:235–40
Schulze 1935 —— 1935 'Elizabethan Chivalry and the Faerie Queene's Annual Feast' *MLN* 50:158–61
Schulze 1938 —— 1938 'Reflections of Elizabethan Tournaments in *The Faerie Queene*, 4.4 and 5.3' *ELH* 5:278–84
Scot 1584 Scot, Reginald 1584 *The Discoverie of Witchcraft* London, rpt Carbondale, Ill 1964, rpt Amsterdam and New York 1971
Segar 1590 Segar, William 1590 *The Booke of Honor and Armes* London, rpt Delmar, NY 1975
Sehrt 1968 Sehrt, Ernst Th. 1968 'Der Wald des Irrtums: Zur allegorischen Funktion von Spensers *Faerie Queene* I [i] 7–9' *Anglia* 86:463–91
Seigel 1968 Seigel, Jerrold E. 1968 *Rhetoric and Philosophy in Renaissance Humanism: The Union of Eloquence and Wisdom, Petrarch to Valla* Princeton
Seneca, Lucius. See headnote
Servius ed 1878–87 Servius, Honoratus Maurus [Grammaticus] 1878–87 *Servii grammatici qui feruntur in Vergilii carmina commentarii* ed Georgius Thilo and Hermannus Hagen. 3 vols. Leipzig, rpt Hildesheim 1961
Seznec ed 1953 Seznec, Jean 1953 *The Survival of the Pagan Gods: The Mythological Tradition and Its Place in Renaissance Humanism and Art* tr Barbara F. Sessions. New York; first pub 1940
Shaheen 1976 Shaheen, Naseeb 1976 *Biblical References in 'The Faerie Queene'* Memphis, Tenn
Shakespeare ed 1974 Shakespeare, William 1974 *The Riverside Shakespeare* ed G. Blakemore Evans, et al. Boston
Shakespeare ed 1979 —— 1979 *A Midsummer Night's Dream* ed Harold F. Brooks. London
Shakespeare's England *Shakespeare's England: An Account of the Life and Manners of His Age* [by various authors]. 2 vols. Oxford 1916
Shapiro 1980 Shapiro, Marianne 1980 *Hieroglyph of Time: The Petrarchan Sestina* Minneapolis
Sheehan 1982 Sheehan, Anthony J. 1982 'The Overthrow of the Plantation of Munster in October 1598' *IrishS* 15:11–22
Sheidley 1981 Sheidley, William E. 1981 *Barnabe Googe* Boston
Shelley ed 1964 Shelley, Percy Bysshe 1964 *Letters* ed Frederick L. Jones. 2 vols. Oxford
Shepherd's Kalendar See *Kalender* ed 1892
Shore 1976 Shore, David R. 1976 'Colin and Rosalind: Love and Poetry in the *Shepheardes Calender*' *SP* 73:176–88
Shore 1985 —— 1985 *Spenser and the Poetics of Pastoral: A Study of the World of Colin Clout* Kingston and Montreal
Short-Title Catalogue ... 1475–1640 (STC) 1976– ed A.W. Pollard and G.R. Redgrave in 1926, rev and enl W.A. Jackson, F.S. Ferguson, and Katharine F. Pantzer. London
Short-Title Catalogue ... 1641–1700 See Wing ed 1972–88 and *Eighteenth-Century Short-Title Catalogue*
Shroeder 1962 Shroeder, John W. 1962 'Spenser's Erotic Drama: The Orgoglio Episode' *ELH* 29:140–59
Shumaker 1972 Shumaker, Wayne 1972 *The Occult Sciences in the Renaissance: A Study in Intellectual Patterns* Berkeley and Los Angeles
Sidney ed 1912–26 Sidney, Philip 1912–26 *Complete Works* ed Albert Feuillerat. 4 vols. Cambridge
Sidney ed 1962 —— 1962 *Poems* ed William A. Ringler, Jr. Oxford
Sidney ed 1965 —— 1965 *'An Apology for Poetry' or 'The Defence of Poesy'* ed Geoffrey Shepherd. London

Sidney ed 1973a —— 1973a *The Countess of Pembroke's Arcadia (The Old Arcadia)* ed Jean Robertson. Oxford

Sidney ed 1973b —— 1973b *Miscellaneous Prose* ed Katherine Duncan-Jones and Jan van Dorsten. Oxford

Sidney ed 1987 —— 1987 *The Countess of Pembroke's Arcadia (The New Arcadia)* ed Victor Skretkowicz. Oxford

Silberman 1986 Silberman, Lauren 1986 'Singing Unsung Heroines: Androgynous Discourse in Book 3 of *The Faerie Queene*' In Ferguson, et al 1986:259–71

Silvestris, Bernardus. See Bernard Sylvestris

Sinfield 1983 Sinfield, Alan 1983 *Literature in Protestant England 1560–1660* London

Sipple 1984 Sipple, William L. 1984 *Edmund Spenser, 1900–1936: A Reference Guide* Boston

Sirluck 1951–2 Sirluck, Ernest 1951–2 'The *Faerie Queene*, Book II, and the *Nicomachean Ethics*' *MP* 49:73–100

Skulsky 1980–1 Skulsky, Harold 1980–1 'Spenser's Despair Episode and the Theology of Doubt' *MP* 78:227–42

Skulsky 1981 —— 1981 *Metamorphosis: The Mind in Exile* Cambridge, Mass

[Slander] 1573 [Slander] 1573 *A Plaine Description of the Auncient Petigree of Dame Slaunder* London (*STC* 22630)

C.G. Smith 1970 Smith, Charles G. 1970 *Spenser's Proverb Lore: With Special Reference to His Use of the 'Sententiae' of Leonard Culman and Publilius Syrus* Cambridge, Mass

G.G. Smith 1904 Smith, G. Gregory, ed 1904 *Elizabethan Critical Essays* 2 vols. Oxford

Hallett Smith 1952 Smith, Hallett 1952 *Elizabethan Poetry: A Study in Conventions, Meaning, and Expression* Cambridge, Mass

Hallett Smith 1961 —— 1961 'The Use of Conventions in Spenser's Minor Poems' In Nelson 1961:122–45, 179–80

Henry Smith ed 1593 Smith, Henry 1593 *Sermons* London

R.M. Smith 1935a Smith, Roland M. 1935a 'Spenser's Irish River Stories' *PMLA* 50:1047–56

R.M. Smith 1935b —— 1935b 'Una and Duessa' *PMLA* 50:917–19

R.M. Smith 1958 —— 1958 'Spenser's Scholarly Script and "Right Writing"' In D.C. Allen 1958:66–111

Snare 1969 Snare, Gerald 1969 'The Muses on Poetry: Spenser's *The Teares of the Muses*' *TSE* 17:31–52

Snare 1970 —— 1970 'Satire, Logic, and Rhetoric in Harvey's Earthquake Letter to Spenser' *TSE* 18:17–33

Snyder 1961 Snyder, Susan 1961 'Guyon the Wrestler' *RN* 14:249–52

Sonnino 1968 Sonnino, Lee A. 1968 *A Handbook to Sixteenth-Century Rhetoric* London

Spanos 1978 Spanos, Margaret 1978 'The Sestina: An Exploration of the Dynamics of Poetic Structure' *Spec* 53:545–57

Spence ed 1966 Spence, Joseph 1966 *Observations, Anecdotes, and Characters of Books and Men* (1820) ed James M. Osborn. 2 vols. Oxford

Spens 1934 Spens, Janet 1934 *Spenser's 'Faerie Queene': An Interpretation* London

Spenser 1579 Spenser, Edmund 1579 *The Shepheardes Calender* London

Spenser 1590 —— 1590 *The Faerie Queene* London

Spenser ed 1596 —— 1596 *The Faerie Queene* 2 vols. London

Spenser ed 1609 —— 1609 *The Faerie Queen* incl 'Two Cantos of Mutabilitie.' London

Spenser ed 1611 —— 1611 *The Faerie Queen: The Shepheards Calendar: Together with the Other Works of England's Arch-Poet, Edm. Spenser* London

Vewe ed 1633 —— 1633 *A Vewe of the Present State of Ireland* in *The Historie of Ireland* ed James Ware. Dublin, rpt Amsterdam and New York 1971

Spenser ed 1715 —— 1715 *Works* ed John Hughes. 6 vols. London

FQ ed 1751 —— 1751 *The Faerie Queene* ed Thomas Birch. 3 vols. London

FQ ed 1758a —— 1758a *Spenser's 'Faerie Queene': A New Edition with a Glossary, and Notes Explanatory and Critical* by John Upton. 2 vols. London

FQ ed 1758b —— 1758b *The Faerie Queene* ed Ralph Church. 4 vols. London

Spenser ed 1805 —— 1805 *Works* ed Henry John Todd. 8 vols. London

Spenser ed 1839 —— 1839 *Poetical Works* ed George S. Hillard. 5 vols. Boston

Spenser ed 1840 —— 1840 *Works* with 'Observations on His Life and Writings' by J.C. London

Spenser ed 1855 —— 1855 *Poetical Works* ed Francis J. Child. 5 vols. Boston

Spenser ed 1862 —— 1862 *Works* ed J. Payne Collier. 5 vols. London

FQ ed 1867–8 —— 1867–8 *The Faerie Queene, Books* I–II ed G[eorge] W. Kitchin. 2 vols. Oxford

Spenser ed 1869 —— 1869 *Complete Works* ed Richard W. Morris and J.W. Hales. London

Spenser ed 1882–4 —— 1882–4 *Complete Works* ed Alexander B. Grosart. 9 vols. London

SC ed 1890 —— 1890 *The Shepheardes Calender* (1579) ed H. Oskar Sommer. London

FQ ed 1893 —— 1893 *The Faerie Queene, Book* I ed H.M. Percival. London

SC ed 1895 —— 1895 *The Shepheardes Calender* ed C.H. Herford. London

FQ ed 1897–1900 —— 1897–1900 *The Faerie Queene* ed Kate M. Warren. 6 vols. London

Spenser ed 1906 —— 1906 *Poems* ed W.B. Yeats. Edinburgh

FH ed 1907 —— 1907 *The Fowre Hymnes* ed Lilian Winstanley. Cambridge

Spenser ed 1908 —— 1908 *Complete Poetical Works* ed R.E. Neil Dodge. Boston

FQ ed 1909 —— 1909 *Spenser's 'Faerie Queene'* ed J.C. Smith. 2 vols. Oxford

Spenser ed 1910 —— 1910 *Spenser's Minor Poems* ed Ernest de Sélincourt. Oxford

Spenser ed 1912 —— 1912 *Poetical Works* ed J.C. Smith and Ernest de Selincourt. Oxford

FQ ed 1914 —— 1914 *The Faerie Queene, Book* II ed Lilian Winstanley. Cambridge, rev ed 1919

FQ ed 1918 —— 1918 *The Faerie Queene, Book* V ed Alfred B. Gough. Oxford

Complaints ed 1928 —— 1928 *Complaints* ed W.L. Renwick. London

Spenser ed 1929 —— 1929 *Daphnaïda and Other Poems* ed W.L. Renwick. London

SC ed 1930 —— 1930 *The Shepherd's Calendar* ed W.L. Renwick. London

Var —— 1932–57 *The Works of Edmund Spenser, A Variorum Edition* ed Edwin Greenlaw, et al. 11 vols. Baltimore

Vewe ed 1934 —— 1934 *A View of the Present State of Ireland* ed W.L. Renwick. London, rev ed Oxford 1970

CCCHA ed 1956 —— 1956 *Colin Clouts Come Home Againe* ed Anna Maria Crinò. Rome

FQ ed 1965a —— 1965a *Books I and II of 'The Faerie Queene,' The Mutability Cantos and Selections from the Minor Poetry* ed Robert Kellogg and Oliver Steele. New York

Spenser ed 1965b —— 1965b *Selections from the Minor Poems and 'The Faerie Queene'* ed Frank Kermode. London

Spenser ed 1968 —— 1968 *The Mutabilitie Cantos* ed S.P. Zitner. London

Spenser ed 1970 —— 1970 *Selections from the Poetical Works* ed S.K. Heninger, Jr. Boston

FQ ed 1977 —— 1977 *The Faerie Queene* ed A.C. Hamilton. London

FQ ed 1978 —— 1978 *The Faerie Queene* ed Thomas P. Roche, Jr. Harmondsworth

Spenser ed 1982 —— 1982 *Edmund Spenser's Poetry* ed Hugh Maclean. Rev ed. New York; first pub 1968

Spenser ed 1989 —— 1989 *Shorter Poems* ed William A. Oram, et al. New Haven

Sp All *Spenser Allusions in the Sixteenth and Seventeenth Centuries* 1971–2 ed William Wells. *SP* Texts and Studies 68–9

Spingarn 1908 Spingarn, J.E. 1908 *A History of Literary Criticism in the Renaissance* Rev ed. New York; new intro by Bernard Weinberg 1963

Sprenger and Krämer 1580 Sprenger, Jacob, and Heinrich Kramer 1580 *Malleus maleficarum* Frankfurt, rpt London 1948 and New York 1970; ed Montague Summers, London 1928

Spurgeon 1925 Spurgeon, Caroline F.E. 1925 *Five Hundred Years of Chaucer Criticism and Allusion, 1357–1900* 3 vols. Cambridge

Stambler 1977 Stambler, Peter D. 1977 'The Development of Guyon's Christian Temperance' *ELR* 7:51–89

Starnes 1942 Starnes, DeWitt T. 1942 'Spenser and the Muses' *TexSE* 22:31–58

Starnes and Talbert 1955 —— and Ernest William Talbert 1955 *Classical Myth and Legend in Renaissance Dictionaries* Chapel Hill

Stationers' Register See E. Arber 1875–94

Statius. See headnote

Staton 1966 Staton, Walter F., Jr 1966 'Italian Pastorals and the Conclusion of the Serena Story' *SEL* 6:35–42

STC See *Short-Title Catalogue ... 1475–1640*; see also Wing ed 1972–88 and *Eighteenth-Century Short-Title Catalogue*

Steadman 1958 Steadman, John M. 1958 'Una and the Clergy: The Ass Symbol in *The Faerie Queene*' *JWCI* 21:134–7

Steadman 1960 —— 1960 'Acrasia in *The Tablet of Cebes*' *N&Q* 205:48–9

Steadman 1967 —— 1967 *Milton and the Renaissance Hero* Oxford

Steadman 1974 —— 1974 *The Lamb and the Elephant: Ideal Imitation and the Context of Renaissance Allegory* San Marino, Calif

Steadman 1979 —— 1979 *Nature into Myth: Medieval and Renaissance Moral Symbols* Pittsburgh

Stein 1934 Stein, Harold 1934 *Studies in Spenser's 'Complaints'* New York

Stephanus, Carolus. See Estienne, Charles

Stephanus, Robertus. See Estienne, Robert

Stern 1979 Stern, Virginia F. 1979 *Gabriel Harvey: His Life, Marginalia and Library* Oxford

J. Stevens 1973 Stevens, John 1973 *Medieval Romance: Themes and Approaches* London

W. Stevens 1951 Stevens, Wallace 1951 *The Necessary Angel: Essays on Reality and the Imagination* New York

Stillman 1984 Stillman, Carol A. 1984 'Politics, Precedence, and the Order of the Dedicatory Sonnets in *The Faerie Queene*' *SSt* 5:143–8

Stocker 1986 Stocker, Margarita 1986 *Apocalyptic Marvell: The Second Coming in Seventeenth Century Poetry* Brighton, Sussex

Stone 1965 Stone, Lawrence 1965 *The Crisis of the Aristocracy 1558–1641* Oxford

Stow ed 1908 Stow, John 1908 *A Survey of London* (1603) ed C.L. Kingsford. 2 vols. Oxford

Strathmann 1931 Strathmann, Ernest A. 1931 'Spenser's *Legends* and *Court of Cupid*' *MLN* 46:498–501

Stratmann 1891 Stratmann, Francis Henry 1891 *A Middle-English Dictionary* rev Henry Bradley. London

Strong 1963 Strong, Roy C. 1963 *Portraits of Queen Elizabeth I* Oxford

Strong 1977 —— 1977 *The Cult of Elizabeth: Elizabethan Portraiture and Pageantry* London

Strong 1979 —— 1979 *The Renaissance Garden in England* London

Strong and van Dorsten 1964 —— and J[an] A. van Dorsten 1964 *Leicester's Triumph* London

Stump 1982 Stump, Donald V. 1982 'Isis Versus Mercilla: The Allegorical Shrines in Spenser's Legend of Justice' *SSt* 3:87–98

Sugden 1936 Sugden, Herbert W. 1936 *The Grammar of Spenser's 'Faerie Queene'* Philadelphia

Summerson 1953 Summerson, John 1953 *Architecture in Britain, 1530 to 1830* Harmondsworth, 4th ed 1963

Svendsen 1956 Svendsen, Kester 1956 *Milton and Science* Cambridge, Mass

Svensson 1980 Svensson, Lars-Håkan 1980 *Silent Art: Rhetorical and Thematic Patterns in Samuel Daniel's 'Delia'* Lund

Szőnyi 1984 Szőnyi, György E. 1984 '"O worke diuine": The Iconography and Intellectual Background of Alma's House in *The Faerie Queene*' In *Shakespeare and the Emblem: Studies in Renaissance Iconography and Iconology* ed Tibor Fabiny, pp 353–94. Szeged, Hungary

Tasso ed 1581 Tasso, Torquato 1581 *Gerusalemme liberata ... con l'allegoria dello stesso autore* ed Febo Bonà. Ferrara

Tasso ed 1600 —— 1600 *Jerusalem Delivered* (1600) tr Edward Fairfax; ed Roberto Weiss, 1962; ed John Charles Nelson, London 1963

Tasso ed 1973 —— 1973 *Discourses on the Heroic Poem* tr Mariella Cavalchini and Irene Samuel. Oxford

Tatlock 1950 Tatlock, J[ohn] S.P. 1950 *The Legendary History of Britain: Geoffrey of Monmouth's 'Historia Regum Britanniae' and Its Early Vernacular Versions* Berkeley and Los Angeles

Tayler 1964 Tayler, Edward William 1964 *Nature and Art in Renaissance Literature* New York

Temkin 1973 Temkin, Owsei 1973 *Galenism: Rise and Decline of a Medical Philosophy* Ithaca, NY

de Tervarent 1958 de Tervarent, Guy 1958 *Attributs et symboles dans l'art profane, 1450–1600: Dictionnaire d'un langage perdu* Geneva; *Supplément et Index* 1964

Teskey 1986 Teskey, Gordon 1986 'From Allegory to Dialectic: Imagining Error in Spenser and Milton' *PMLA* 101:9–23

Thirty-nine Articles / Articles of Religion See Hardwick 1876

Thomas Aquinas, St. See Aquinas, St Thomas

Thomas 1971 Thomas, Keith 1971 *Religion and the Decline of Magic* London

A. Thompson 1978 Thompson, Ann 1978 *Shakespeare's Chaucer: A Study in Literary Origins* Liverpool

C. Thompson 1985 Thompson, Charlotte 1985 'Love in an Orderly Universe: A Unification of Spenser's *Amoretti*, "Anacreontics," and *Epithalamion*' *Viator* 16:277–335

C.A. Thompson 1972 Thompson, Claud A. 1972 'Spenser's "Many Faire Pourtraicts, And Many a Faire Feate"' *SEL* 12:21–32

S. Thompson 1955–8 Thompson, Stith 1955–8 *Motif-Index of Folk-Literature* rev ed. 6 vols. Bloomington

Thorndike 1923–58 Thorndike, Lynn 1923–58 *A History of Magic and Experimental Science* 8 vols. New York

Tilley 1950 Tilley, Morris Palmer 1950 *A Dictionary of the Proverbs in England in the Sixteenth and Seventeenth Centuries* Ann Arbor

Tillyard 1954 Tillyard, E.M.W. 1954 *The English Epic and Its Background* London

Tonkin 1972 Tonkin, Humphrey 1972 *Spenser's Courteous Pastoral: Book Six of 'The Faerie Queene'* Oxford

Tonkin 1973 —— 1973 'Discussing Spenser's Cave of Mammon' *SEL* 13:1–13

Topsell 1607 Topsell, Edward 1607 *The Historie of Four-Footed Beastes* London, rpt Amsterdam and New York 1973

Torczon 1961 Torczon, Vern[on] 1961 'Spenser's Orgoglio and Despaire' *TSLL* 3:123–8

Trimpi 1973 Trimpi, Wesley 1973 'The Meaning of Horace's *Ut pictura poesis*' *JWCI* 36:1–34

Trinkaus 1970 Trinkaus, Charles 1970 *In Our Image and Likeness: Humanity and Divinity in Italian Humanist Thought* 2 vols. Chicago

Tucker 1976–7 Tucker, Herbert F., Jr 1976–7 'Spenser's Eighteenth-Century Readers and the Question of Unity in *The Faerie Queene*' *UTQ* 46:322–41

Tufte 1970 Tufte, Virginia 1970 *The Poetry of Marriage: The Epithalamium in Europe and Its Development in England* Los Angeles

Tung 1972 Tung, Mason 1972 'Spenser's Graces and Costalius' "Pegma"' *EM* 23:9–14

Tung 1984 —— 1984 'Spenser's "Emblematic" Imagery: A Study of Emblematics' *SSt* 5:185–207

Turner 1551–62 Turner, William 1551–62 *A New Herball* 2 parts. London

Tuve 1935 Tuve, Rosemond 1935 'Spenser and the *Zodiake of Life*' *JEGP* 34:1–19

Tuve 1940 —— 1940 'Spenser and Some Pictorial Conventions' *SP* 37:149–76

Tuve 1947 —— 1947 *Elizabethan and Metaphysical Imagery: Renaissance Poetic and Twentieth-Century Critics* Chicago
Tuve 1964 —— 1964 'Spenserus' In MacLure and Watt 1964:3–25
Tuve 1966 —— 1966 *Allegorical Imagery: Some Mediaeval Books and Their Posterity* Princeton
Tuve 1970 —— 1970 *Essays by Rosemond Tuve: Spenser, Herbert, Milton* ed Thomas P. Roche, Jr. Princeton

Valeriano 1602 Valeriano Bolzani, G. P[ierio] 1602 *Hieroglyphica, seu De sacris Aegyptiorum aliarumque gentium literis commentarii* Lyons, rpt New York and London 1976
Van den Berg 1978 Van den Berg, Kent T. 1978 '"The Counterfeit in Personation": Spenser's *Prosopopoia, or Mother Hubberds Tale*' In *The Author in His Work*, ed Louis L. Martz and Aubrey Williams, pp 85–102. New Haven
Van der Noot, Jan. See Noot, Jan van der
Van Dorsten, J.A. See Dorsten, J.A. van
Van Dyke 1985 Van Dyke, Carolynn 1985 *The Fiction of Truth: Structures of Meaning in Narrative and Dramatic Allegory* Ithaca, NY
Variorum See Spenser *Var* ed 1932–57
Variorum Commentary on ... Milton See Hughes, et al 1970–
Vaughan 1542 Vaughan, Robert [= R. Burdet?] 1542 *A Dyalogue Defensyve for Women* London
de Vere 1887 de Vere, Aubrey 1887 *Essays, Chiefly on Poetry* 2 vols. London
Vergil. See Virgil
Vermigli ed 1583 Vermigli, Peter Martyr 1583 *The Common Places* tr Anthony Marten. London
Vickers 1970 Vickers, Brian 1970 *Classical Rhetoric in English Poetry* London
Vickers 1984a —— 1984a 'Introduction' and 'Analogy versus Identity: The Rejection of Occult Symbolism, 1580–1680' In Vickers 1984b:1–55, 95–163
Vickers 1984b —— ed 1984b *Occult and Scientific Mentalities in the Renaissance* Cambridge
Vickers 1988 —— 1988 *In Defence of Rhetoric* Oxford
Vida ed 1976 Vida, Marco Girolamo 1976 *The 'De Arte Poetica' of Marco Girolamo Vida* (1517, 1527) tr and ed Ralph G. Williams. New York
Vinaver 1971 Vinaver, Eugène 1971 *The Rise of Romance* Oxford
Virgil ed 1957–64 Virgil 1957–64 *Virgil's 'Aeneid' Translated into Scottish Verse by Gavin Douglas* ed David F.C. Coldwell. 4 vols. STS 3rd ser 25, 27, 28, 30. Edinburgh
Virgil ed 1966 —— 1966 *Appendix Vergiliana* ed W.V. Clausen, et al. Oxford
- See also headnote
Vives ed 1913 Vives, Juan Luis 1913 *On Education: A Translation of the 'De tradendis disciplinis'* (1531) Foster Watson. Cambridge
Voragine ed 1900 Voragine, Jacobus de 1900 *The Golden Legend, or Lives of the Saints* tr William Caxton, ed F[rederick] S. Ellis. 7 vols. London

Waith 1962 Waith, Eugene M. 1962 *The Herculean Hero in Marlowe, Chapman, Shakespeare and Dryden* London
D.P. Walker 1958 Walker, D.P. 1958 *Spiritual and Demonic Magic from Ficino to Campanella* London
S.F. Walker 1979 Walker, Steven F. 1979 '"Poetry is/is not a cure for love": The Conflict of Theocritean and Petrarchan *Topoi* in the *Shepheardes Calender*' *SP* 76:353–65
Wall 1976 Wall, John N., Jr 1976 'The "Book of Homilies" of 1547 and the Continuity of English Humanism in the Sixteenth Century' *ATR* 58:75–87
Wall 1983 —— 1983 'The English Reformation and the Recovery of Christian Community in Spenser's *The Faerie Queene*' *SP* 80:142–62
Wall 1988 —— 1988 *Transformations of the Word: Spenser, Herbert, Vaughan* Athens, Ga
D.D. Wallace 1982 Wallace, Dewey D., Jr 1982 *Puritans and Predestination: Grace in English Protestant Theology, 1525–1695* Chapel Hill
M.W. Wallace 1915 Wallace, Malcolm William 1915 *The Life of Sir Philip Sidney* Cambridge
Waller 1979 Waller, Gary F. 1979 *Mary Sidney, Countess of Pembroke: A Critical Study of Her Writings and Literary Milieu* Salzburg
Waller 1986 —— 1986 *English Poetry of the Sixteenth Century* London
Ware, James. See Spenser *Vewe* ed 1633
J. Warton ed 1806 Warton, Joseph 1806 *An Essay on the Genius and Writings of Pope* 2 vols. 5th ed. London; first pub 1756, 1782
T. Warton ed 1762 Warton, Thomas 1762 *Observations on the Fairy Queen of Spenser* 2nd ed. 2 vols. London, rpt Westmead, Hants 1969; first pub 1754
Wasserman 1937 Wasserman, Earl Reeves 1937 'The Scholarly Origin of the Elizabethan Revival' *ELH* 4:213–43
Waters 1970 Waters, D. Douglas 1970 *Duessa as Theological Satire* Columbia, Mo
Waters 1974 —— 1974 'Spenser and Symbolic Witchcraft in *The Shepheardes Calender*' *SEL* 14:3–15
Watkins 1950 Watkins, W.B.C. 1950 *Shakespeare and Spenser* Princeton
Watson ed 1967 Watson, Thomas 1967 *Thomas Watson's Latin 'Amyntas' (1585)* ed Walter F. Staton, Jr, and *Abraham Fraunce's Translation: 'The Lamentations of Amyntas' (1587)* ed Franklin M. Dickey. Chicago
Weatherby 1982 Weatherby, Harold L. 1982 '"Pourd out in Loosnesse"' *SSt* 3:73–85
Weatherby 1984 —— 1984 'The Old Theology: Spenser's Dame Nature and the Transfiguration' *SSt* 5:113–42
Weatherby 1987a —— 1987a 'The True Saint George' *ELR* 17:119–41
Weatherby 1987b —— 1987b 'What Spenser Meant by Holinesse: Baptism in Book One of *The Faerie Queene*' *SP* 84:286–307
Weinberg 1961 Weinberg, Bernard 1961 *A History of Literary Criticism in the Italian Renaissance* 2 vols. Chicago
Weiss 1941 Weiss, R[oberto] 1941 *Humanism in England during the Fifteenth Century* Oxford
Wellek 1941 Wellek, René 1941 *The Rise of English Literary History* Chapel Hill
Wells 1983 Wells, Robin Headlam 1983 *Spenser's 'Faerie Queene' and the Cult of Elizabeth* London
Welply 1924 Welply, W.H. 1924 'Edmund Spenser: Some New Discoveries and the Correction of Some Old Errors' *N&Q* 146:445–7, 147:35
Welsford 1967 Welsford, Enid 1967 *Spenser: 'Fowre Hymnes,' 'Epithalamion': A Study of Edmund Spenser's Doctrine of Love* Oxford
Whetstone 1586 Whetstone, George 1586 *The English Myrror* London, rpt Amsterdam and New York 1973
Whigham 1981 Whigham, Frank 1981 'The Rhetoric of Elizabethan Suitors' Letters' *PMLA* 96:864–82
Whigham 1984 —— 1984 *Ambition and Privilege: The Social Tropes of Elizabethan Courtesy Theory* Berkeley and Los Angeles
Whitaker 1950 Whitaker, Virgil K. 1950 *The Religious Basis of Spenser's Thought* Stanford
Whitaker 1952 —— 1952 'The Theological Structure of *The Faerie Queene*, Book I' *ELH* 19:151–64
H.O. White 1935 White, Harold Ogden 1935 *Plagiarism and Imitation during the English Renaissance* Cambridge, Mass
H. White 1972 White, Hayden 1972 'The Forms of Wildness: Archaeology of an Idea' In Dudley and Novak 1972:3–38
T.H. White 1954 White, T.H., tr and ed 1954 *The Book of Beasts* (from a Latin bestiary of the twelfth century) London
Whiting 1968 Whiting, Bartlett Jere, with Helen Wescott Whiting 1968 *Proverbs, Sentences, and Proverbial Phrases from English Writings Mainly before 1500* Cambridge, Mass
Whitman 1918 Whitman, Charles Huntington 1918 *A Subject-Index to the Poems of Edmund Spenser* New Haven
Whitman ed 1902 Whitman, Walt 1902 *Complete Writings* ed Richard Maurice Bucke, et al. 10 vols. New York
Whitney 1586 Whitney, Geoffrey 1586 *A Choice of Emblemes and*

Other Devises Leiden, rpt Amsterdam and New York 1967, Menston, Yorks 1969

Wickert 1968 Wickert, Max A. 1968 'Structure and Ceremony in Spenser's *Epithalamion*' *ELH* 35:135–57

Wilkie 1965 Wilkie, Brian 1965 *Romantic Poets and Epic Tradition* Madison

A. Williams 1948 Williams, Arnold 1948 *The Common Expositor: An Account of the Commentaries on Genesis, 1527–1633* Chapel Hill

A. Williams 1967 —— 1967 *Flower on a Lowly Stalk: The Sixth Book of the 'Faerie Queene'* East Lansing, Mich

F.B. Williams 1962 Williams, Franklin B., Jr 1962 *Index of Dedications and Commendatory Verses in English Books before 1641* London

K. Williams 1952 Williams, Kathleen 1952 '"Eterne in Mutabilitie": The Unified World of *The Faerie Queene*' *ELH* 19:115–30

K. Williams 1961 —— 1961 'Venus and Diana: Some Uses of Myth in *The Faerie Queene*' *ELH* 28:101–20

K. Williams 1966 —— 1966 *Spenser's World of Glass: A Reading of 'The Faerie Queene'* Berkeley and Los Angeles

K. Williams 1969 —— 1969 'Vision and Rhetoric: The Poet's Voice in *The Faerie Queene*' *ELH* 36:131–44

K. Williams 1970–1 —— 1970–1 'Spenser: Some Uses of the Sea and the Storm-tossed Ship' *RORD* 13–14:135–42

E.C. Wilson 1939 Wilson, Elkin Calhoun 1939 *England's Eliza* Cambridge, Mass

H.B. Wilson 1812–14 Wilson, H[arry] B[ristow] 1812–14 *The History of Merchant Taylors' School from Its Foundation to the Present Time* London

R.R. Wilson 1973 Wilson, R[obert] Rawdon 1973 'Spenser's Reputation in Italy and France' *HAR* 24:105–9

R.R. Wilson 1974 —— 1974 'Images and "Allegoremes" of Time in the Poetry of Spenser' *ELR* 4:56–82

R.R. Wilson 1986 —— 1986 'Narrative Allusiveness: The Interplay of Stories in Two Renaissance Writers, Spenser and Cervantes' *ESC* 12:138–62

T. Wilson 1560 Wilson, Thomas 1560 *Arte of Rhetorique* London, rpt ed G.H. Mair, Oxford 1909; ed Thomas J. Derrick, New York 1982

T. Wilson ed 1972 —— 1972 *The Rule of Reason Conteinyng the Arte of Logique* 1551 ed Richard S. Sprague. Northridge, Calif

Wind 1958 Wind, Edgar 1958 *Pagan Mysteries in the Renaissance* London, rev ed Harmondsworth 1967

Wing ed 1972–88 Wing, Donald G., ed 1972–88 *Short-Title Catalogue ... 1641–1700* (Wing). 3 vols. New York; first pub 1945–51

Wittreich 1975 Wittreich, Joseph Anthony, Jr, ed 1975 *Milton and the Line of Vision* Madison

Wittreich 1979 —— 1979 *Visionary Poetics: Milton's Tradition and His Legacy* San Marino, Calif

Woodbridge 1984 Woodbridge, Linda 1984 *Women and the English Renaissance: Literature and the Nature of Womankind, 1540–1620* Urbana

Woodhouse 1949 Woodhouse, A.S.P. 1949 'Nature and Grace in *The Faerie Queene*' *ELH* 16:194–228

Woodhouse 1960 —— 1960 'Spenser, Nature and Grace: Mr. Gang's Mode of Argument Reviewed' *ELH* 27:1–15

J.R. Woodhouse 1978 Woodhouse, J.R. 1978 *Baldesar Castiglione: A Reassessment of 'The Courtier'* Edinburgh

Woods 1977 Woods, Susanne 1977 'Closure in *The Faerie Queene*' *JEGP* 76:195–216

Woolf ed 1966–7 Woolf, Virginia 1966–7 *Collected Essays* 4 vols. London

Wordsworth ed 1940–9 Wordsworth, William 1940–9 *Poetical Works* ed E[rnest] de Selincourt and Helen Darbishire. 5 vols. Oxford

Wordsworth ed 1959 —— 1959 *The Prelude* ed Ernest de Selincourt, rev Helen Darbishire. Oxford

Wordsworth and Wordsworth ed 1967 Wordsworth, William, and Dorothy Wordsworth 1967 *Letters: Early Years, 1787–1805* ed Ernest de Selincourt, rev Chester L. Shaver. Oxford

Wrenn 1943 Wrenn, C.L. 1943 'On Re-reading Spenser's *Shepheardes Calender*' *E&S* 29:30–49

Wurtsbaugh 1936 Wurtsbaugh, Jewel 1936 *Two Centuries of Spenserian Scholarship (1609–1805)* Baltimore

Yates 1964 Yates, Frances A. 1964 *Giordano Bruno and the Hermetic Tradition* London

Yates 1975 —— 1975 *Astraea: The Imperial Theme in the Sixteenth Century* London

Yates 1979 —— 1979 *The Occult Philosophy in the Elizabethan Age* London

Yeats ed 1961 Yeats, W.B. 1961 *Essays and Introductions* New York

A. Young 1987 Young, Alan 1987 *Tudor and Jacobean Tournaments* London

F.B. Young 1973–4 Young, Frank B. 1973–4 'Medusa and the *Epithalamion*: A Problem in Spenserian Imagery' *ELN* 11:21–9

Index

This index provides an alphabetical list of topics in *The Spenser Encyclopedia* and entries in which those topics are treated. A heading in boldface refers to an article title and the main discussion of that topic. For synonyms and variant titles, consult the parenthetical references to other headings.

In the entries listed under any heading will be found a full discussion of the topic, an important fact or example, a key definition, or other noteworthy information. The resulting list thus gives a conceptual context for any topic rather than a list of page numbers. For some broad subjects, the list is representative rather than complete. (D.A.R.)

For Product Safety Concerns and Information please contact our EU
representative GPSR@taylorandfrancis.com
Taylor & Francis Verlag GmbH, Kaufingerstraße 24, 80331 München, Germany

www.ingramcontent.com/pod-product-compliance
Lightning Source LLC
Chambersburg PA
CBHW081426090726
47908CB00009B/2633

* 9 7 8 0 4 1 5 7 5 5 6 1 0 *